® RAND McNALLY

GOODE'S
W O R L D   A T L A S

19TH EDITION

Edward B. Espenshade, Jr.
EDITOR

John C. Hudson
ASSOCIATE EDITOR

Joel L. Morrison
SENIOR CONSULTANT

® RAND McNALLY

CONTENTS

Goode's World Atlas
Copyright © 1995 by Rand McNally & Company
Copyright © 1922, 1923, 1932, 1933, 1937, 1939, 1943, 1946, 1949, 1954, 1957, 1960, 1964, 1970, 1974, 1978, 1982, 1986, 1990 by Rand McNally & Company
Formerly *Goode's School Atlas*
Made in U.S.A.

Library of Congress Catalog Card Number 94-68645

CONTENTS, *continued*

Major Cities Maps *Scale 1:300,000* [226–244]

Geographical Tables and Indexes [245–372]

ACKNOWLEDGMENTS

This is the nineteenth edition of the Rand McNally *Goode's World Atlas*, which was first published more than seventy years ago. The name of Dr. J. Paul Goode, the original editor and distinguished cartographer who designed the early editions, has been retained to affirm the high standards that all those who have participated in the preparation of the atlas during these years have sought to attain.

Through the years, general-reference map coverage has been expanded; the number of thematic maps has been increased and their subject range broadened; and systematic improvements in symbolism, cartographic presentation, and map production and printing have been incorporated.

The nineteenth edition continues this tradition, and includes five new thematic maps. World maps have been added on ecoregions, conflicts, refugees and tectonics. A new map of the United States and Southern Canada depicts federal lands and the interstate highway system. New reference maps for the Caucasus and parts of central Asia have been added. Finally, a new design for the maps of the Indian and Atlantic Oceans replaces the former ones.

Thematic maps, statistics, graphs and various tables have been revised to incorporate the latest available data. The list of source materials and an index to thematic topics (subject index) have been revised. These additions and other revisions reflect the editors' and publisher's commitment to increasing the usefulness and quality of each edition of the Rand McNally *Goode's World Atlas*, thus maintaining it as a standard among world atlases.

Sources

Every effort was made to assemble the latest and most authentic source materials to use in this edition. In the general physical-political maps, data from national and state surveys, recent military maps, and hydrographic charts were utilized. Source materials for the specialized maps were even more varied (see the partial list of sources at the end of the atlas). They included both published and unpublished items in the form of maps, descriptions in articles and books, statistics, and correspondence with geographers and others. To the various agencies and organizations, official and unofficial, that cooperated, appreciation and thanks are expressed. Noteworthy among these organizations and agencies were: The United Nations (for demographic and trade statistics); the Food and Agriculture Organization of The United Nations (for production statistics on livestock, crops, and forest products and for statistics on world trade); the Population Reference Bureau (for population data); the Office of the Geographer, Department of State (for the map "Surface Transport Facilities" and other items); the office of Foreign Agricultural Relations, Department of Agriculture (for information on crop and livestock production and distribution); the Bureau of Mines, Department of the Interior (for information on mineral production); various branches of the national military establishment and the Weather Bureau, Department of Commerce (for information on temperature, wind, pressure, and ocean currents); the Maritime Commission and the Department of Commerce (for statistics on ocean trade); the American Geographical Society (for use of its library and permission to use the Miller cylindrical projection); the University of Chicago Press, (for permission to use Goode's Homolosine equal-area projection); the McGraw-Hill Book Company (for cooperation in permitting the use of Glenn Trewartha's map of climatic regions and Petterssen's diagram of zones of precipitation); the Association of American Geographers (for permission to use Richard Murphy's map of landforms); and publications of the World Bank (for nutrition, health, and economic information).

Some additional sources of specific data and information are as follows: World Oil (for oil and gas data); International Labor Organization (for labor statistics); and the International Road Federation (for transportation data). The United Nations High Commissioner for refugees (UNHCR) and the Bureau for Refugee Programs, U.S. Department of State provided data for the refugees map.

Other Acknowledgments

The variety and complexity of the problems involved in the preparation of a world atlas make the participation of specialists highly desirable. In preparation of this new edition, the editors have been ably assisted by several such experts. They express their deep appreciation and thanks to each of them.

They are particularly indebted to the following experts who have cooperated over the years. A. W. Kuchler, Department of Geography, University of Kansas; Richard E. Murphy, late professor of geography, University of New Mexico; Erwin Raisz, late cartographer, Cambridge, Massachusetts; Glenn T. Trewartha, late professor of geography, University of Wisconsin; Derwent Whittlesey, late professor of geography, Harvard University; and Bogdan Zaborski, professor emeritus of geography, University of Ottawa.

The editors thank the entire Cartographic and Design staff of Rand McNally & Company for their continued outstanding contributions. We particularly appreciate the help and dedication of the following staff members: Pat Healy and Jon Leverenz for many years of valuable input, along with Jill M. Stift, Susan Hudson, Winifred Farbman, Dara Thompson, Patty Porter and Audrey Curry. Joel L. Morrison has continued to act as a consultant.

Edward B. Espenshade, Jr.
John C. Hudson

INTRODUCTION

Geography and Maps

The study of geography is the study of the location, description, and interrelations of the earth's features—its people, landforms, climate, and natural resources. In fact, anything on the earth is fair game for geographic inquiry, and mapping. Helping to answer the questions of *where* something is, and *why* it is there, is fundamental to any geographic study.

Maps, photographs, and images based on radar and the electromagnetic spectrum increase one's ability to study the earth. They enable geographers and other earth scientists to record information about the earth through time and to examine and study areas of the earth's surface far too large to view firsthand.

Geographic Education

There are five fundamental themes of geography that help people organize and understand information about the earth. The maps in *Goode's World Atlas* present information that is essential for applying these themes. The themes are as follows:

Theme 1. **Location: Absolute and Relative.** Maps show where places are located in absolute terms, such as latitude and longitude, and where they are in relation to other places—their relative location. By locating and graphically portraying places and things, maps reveal the patterns of the earth's diverse landscape.

Theme 2. **Place: Physical and Human Characteristics.** Maps provide useful information about the physical and human characteristics of places. Landform maps show the surface features of the earth. Climate and natural vegetation maps may be compared to reveal how vegetation responds to climate conditions. Human characteristics include those effects people have on places. Population maps show the density and distribution of people, while maps of language and religion provide information about cultural characteristics.

Theme 3. **Human/Environment Interaction.** People interact with the natural environment, and the extent to which they alter the environment can be studied by viewing maps. The maps in the atlas provide information about current and past conditions of the environment and are useful in making informed decisions about the future effects of people on the land.

Theme 4. **Movement: Interactions Between Places.** The movement of people and products between places results in networks that span the earth. The dynamics of global interdependence are illustrated by maps that show the movement of commodities from places of production to places of consumption. Maps in the atlas depict highways, air traffic corridors, and shipping lanes that use the world's rivers, lakes, and oceans.

Theme 5. **Regions: How They Form and Change.** A *region* is a part of the earth's surface that displays similar characteristics in terms of selected criteria. Climates, nations, economies, languages, religions, diets, and urban areas are only a few of the topics that can be shown regionally on maps. The region is the basic unit of geographic study. It makes the complex world more readily understandable by organizing the earth according to selected criteria, allowing the similarities and differences from place to place to be studied and understood more fully.

Organization of the Atlas

The maps in *Goode's World Atlas* are grouped into four parts, beginning with *World Thematic Maps*, portraying the distribution of climatic regions, raw materials, landforms, and other major worldwide features. The second part is the *Regional Maps* section and main body of the atlas. It provides detailed reference maps for all inhabited land areas on a continent-by-continent basis. Thematic maps of the continents are also contained in this part. The third part is devoted to *Ocean Maps*. In the fourth part, *Major Cities Maps*, the focus is on individual cities and their environs, all mapped at a consistent scale.

Geographical tables, an index of places, a subject index, and a list of sources complete the atlas. The tables provide comparative data, a glossary of foreign geographical terms, and the index of places—a universal place-name pronouncing index for use with the reference maps.

Cartographic Communication

To communicate information through a map, cartographers must assemble the geographic data, use their personal perception of the world to select the relevant information, and apply graphic techniques to produce the map. Readers must then be able to interpret the mapped data and relate it to their own experience and need for information. Thus, the success of any map depends on both the cartographer's and the map reader's knowledge and perception of the world and on their common understanding of a map's purpose and limitations.

The ability to understand maps and related imagery depends first on the reader's skill at recognizing how a curved, three-dimensional world is symbolized on a flat, two-dimensional map. Normally, we view the world horizontally (that is, our line of vision parallels the horizon), at the eye level about five and one-half to six feet above ground. Images appear directly in front and to either side of us, with our eyes encompassing all details as nonselectively as a camera. Less frequently, when we are atop a high platform or in an airplane, we view the world obliquely, as shown in *Figure 1*, in which both vertical and horizontal facets of objects can be seen. And only those persons at very high altitudes will view the world at a vertical angle (*Figure 2*). Yet maps are based on our ability to visualize the world from an overhead, or vertical, perspective.

A map differs from a purely vertical photograph in two important respects. First, in contrast to the single focal point of a photograph, a map is created as if the viewer were directly overhead at all points (See *Figure 3*). Second, just as our brains select from the myriad items in our field of vision those objects of interest or importance to us, so each map presents only those details necessary for a particular purpose—a map is not an inventory of all that is visible. Selectivity is one of a map's most important and useful characteristics.

Skill in reading maps is basically a matter of practice, but a fundamental grasp of cartographic principles and the symbols, scales, and projections commonly employed in creating maps is essential to comprehensive map use.

Map Data

When creating a map, the cartographer must select the objects to be shown, evaluate their relative importance, and find some way to simplify their form. The combined process is called *cartographic generalization*. In attempting to generalize data, the cartographer is limited by the purpose of the map, its scale, the methods used to produce it, and the accuracy of the data.

Figure 1. Oblique aerial photograph of New York City.

Figure 2. High-altitude vertical photograph of New York City area.

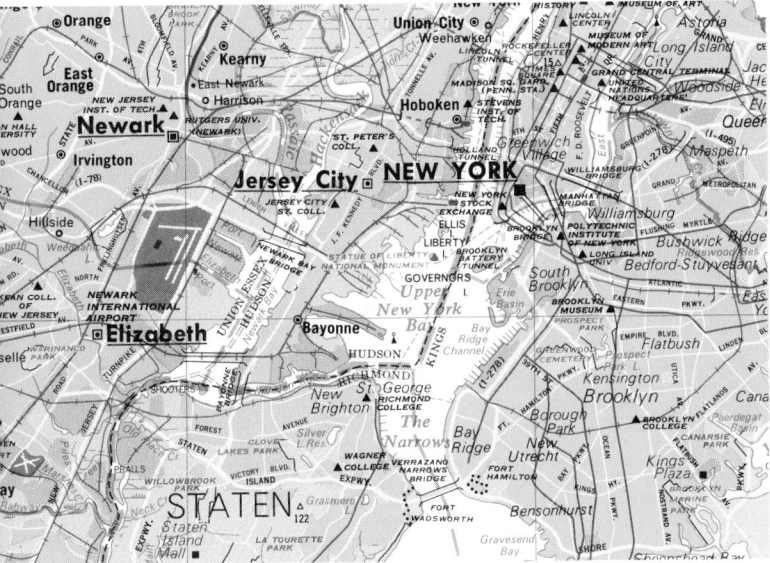

Figure 3. Map of New York City and environs.

Cartographic generalization consists of simplification, classification, symbolization, and induction.

Simplification involves omitting details that will clutter the map and confuse the reader. The degree of simplification depends on the purpose and scale of the map. If the cartographer is creating a detailed map of Canada and merely wants to show the location of the United States, he or she can draw a simplified outline of the country. However, if the map requires a precise identification of the states in New England and the Great Lakes region, the mapmaker will have to draw a more detailed outline, still being careful not to distract the reader from the main features of the Canadian map.

Classification of data is a way of reducing the information to a form that can be easily presented on a map. For example, portraying precise urban populations in the United States would require using as many different symbols as there are cities. Instead, the cartographer groups cities into population categories and assigns a distinct symbol to each one. With the help of a legend, the reader can easily decode the classifications.

Symbolization of information depends largely on the nature of the original data. Information can be *nominal* (showing differences in kind, such as land versus water, grassland versus forest); or *ordinal* (showing relative differences in quantities as well as kind, such as *major* versus *minor* ore deposits); or *interval* (degrees of temperature, inches of rainfall) or *ratio* (population densities), both expressing quantitative details about the data being mapped.

Cartographers use various shapes, colors, or patterns to symbolize these categories of data, and the particular nature of the information being communicated often determines how it is symbolized. Population density, for example, can be shown by the use of small dots or different intensities of color. However, if nominal data is being portrayed—for instance, the desert and fertile areas of Egypt—the mapmaker may want to use a different method of symbolizing the data, perhaps pattern symbols. The color, size, and style of type used for the different elements on a map are also important to symbolization.

Induction is the term cartographers use to describe the process whereby more information is represented on a map than is actually supplied by the original data. For instance, in creating a rainfall map, a cartographer may start with precise rainfall records for relatively few points on the map. After deciding the interval categories into which the data will be divided (e.g., thirty inches or more, fifteen to thirty inches, under fifteen inches), the mapmaker infers from the particular data points that nearby places receive the same or nearly the same amount of rainfall and draws the lines that distinguish the various rainfall regions accordingly. Obviously, generalizations arrived at through induction can never be as precise as the real-world patterns they represent. The map will only tell the reader that all the cities in a given area received about the same amount of rainfall; it will not tell exactly how much rain fell in any particular city in any particular time period.

Cartographers must also be aware of the map reader's perceptual limitations and preferences. During the past two decades, numerous experiments have helped determine how much information readers actually glean from a map and how symbols, colors, and shapes are recognized and interpreted. As a result, cartographers now have a better idea of what kind of rectangle to use; what type of layout or lettering suggests qualities such as power, stability, movement; and what colors are most appropriate.

Map Scale

Since part or all of the earth's surface may be portrayed on a single page of an atlas, the reader's first question should be: What is the relation of map size to the area represented? This proportional relationship is known as the *scale* of a map.

Scale is expressed as a ratio between the distance or area on the map and the same distance or area on the earth. The map scale is commonly represented in three ways: (1) as a simple fraction or ratio called the representative fraction, or RF; (2) as a written statement of map distance in relation to earth distance; and (3) as a graphic representation or a bar scale. All three forms of scale for distances are expressed on Maps A–D.

The RF is usually written as 1:62,500 (as in Map A), where 1 always refers to a unit of distance on the map. The ratio means that 1 centimeter or 1 millimeter or 1 foot on the map represents 62,500 centimeters or millimeters or feet on the earth's surface. The units of measure on both sides of the ratio must always be the same.

Maps may also include a *written statement* expressing distances in terms more familiar to the reader. In Map A the scale 1:62,500 is expressed as being (approximately) 1 inch to 1 mile; that is, 1 inch on the map represents roughly 1 mile on the earth's surface.

The *graphic scale* for distances is usually a bar scale, as shown in Maps A–D. A bar scale is normally subdivided, enabling the reader to measure distance directly on the map.

An *area scale* can also be used, in which one unit of area (square inches, square centimeters) is proportional to the same square units on the earth. The scale may be expressed as either $1:62,500^2$ or 1 to the square of 62,500. Area scales are used when the transformation of the globe to the flat map has been made so that areas are represented in true relation to their respective area on the earth.

When comparing map scales, it is helpful to remember that the *larger* the scale (see Map A) the smaller the area represented and the greater the amount of detail that a map can include. The *smaller* the scale (see Maps B, C, D) the larger the area covered and the less detail that can be presented.

Large-scale maps are useful when readers need such detailed information as the location of roadways, major buildings, city plans, and the like. On a smaller scale, the reader is able to place cities in relation to one another and recognize other prominent features of the region. At the smallest scale, the reader can get a broad view of several states and an idea of the total area. Finer details cannot be shown.

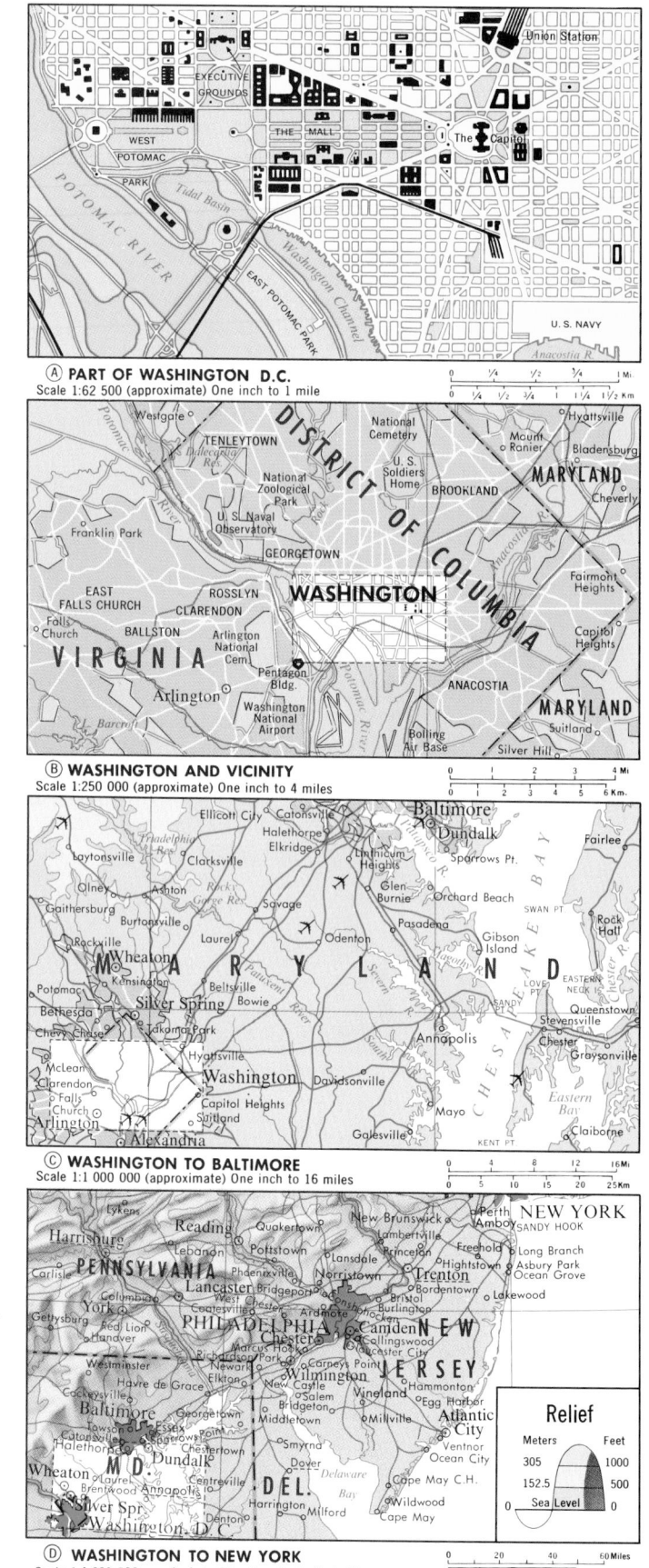

Ⓐ **PART OF WASHINGTON D.C.**
Scale 1:62 500 (approximate) One inch to 1 mile

Ⓑ **WASHINGTON AND VICINITY**
Scale 1:250 000 (approximate) One inch to 4 miles

Ⓒ **WASHINGTON TO BALTIMORE**
Scale 1:1 000 000 (approximate) One inch to 16 miles

Ⓓ **WASHINGTON TO NEW YORK**
Scale 1:4 000 000 one inch to 64 miles. Conic Projection

Map Projections

Every cartographer is faced with the problem of transforming the curved surface of the earth onto a flat plane with a minimum of distortion. The systematic transformation of locations on the earth (spherical surface) to locations on a map (flat surface) is called projection.

It is not possible to represent on a flat map the spatial relationships of angle, distance, direction, and area that only a globe can show faithfully. As a result, projection systems inevitably involve some distortion. On large-scale maps representing a few square miles, the distortion is generally negligible. But on maps depicting large countries, continents, or the entire world, the amount of distortion can be significant. Some maps of the Western Hemisphere, because of their projection, incorrectly portray Canada and Alaska as larger than the United States and Mexico, while South America looks considerably smaller than its northern neighbors.

One of the more practical ways map readers can become aware of projection distortions and learn how to make allowances for them is to compare the projection grid of a flat map with the grid of a globe. Some important characteristics of the globe grid are found listed on page xi.

There are an infinite number of possible map projections, all of which distort one or more of the characteristics of the globe in varying degrees. The projection system that a cartographer chooses depends on the size and location of the area being projected and the purpose of the map. In this atlas, most of the maps are drawn on projections that give a consistent area scale; good land and ocean shape; parallels that are parallel; and as consistent a linear scale as possible throughout the projection.

The transformation process is actually a mathematical one, but to aid in visualizing this process, it is helpful to consider the earth reduced to the scale of the intended map and then projected onto a simple geometric shape—a cylinder, cone, or plane. These geometric forms are then flattened to two dimensions to produce cylindrical, conic, and plane projections (see Figures 4, 5, and 6). Some of the projection systems used in this atlas are described on the following pages. By comparing these systems with the characteristics of a globe grid, readers can gain a clearer understanding of map distortion.

Mercator: This transformation—bearing the name of a famous sixteenth century cartographer—is conformal; that is, land masses are represented in their true shapes. Thus, for every point on the map, the angles shown are correct in every direction within a limited area. To achieve this, the projection increases latitudinal and longitudinal distances away from the equator. As a result, land *shapes* are correct, but their *areas* are distorted. The farther away from the equator, the greater the area distortion. For example, on a Mercator map, Alaska appears far larger than Mexico, whereas in fact Mexico's land area is greater. The Mercator projection is used in nautical navigation, because a line connecting any two points gives the compass direction between them. (See Figure 4.)

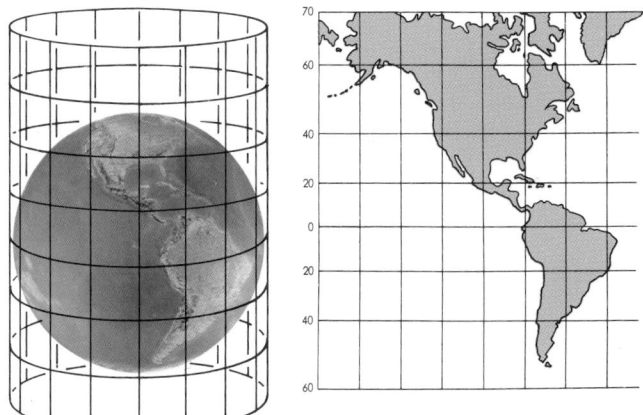

Figure 4. Mercator Projection (right), based upon the projection of the globe onto a cylinder.

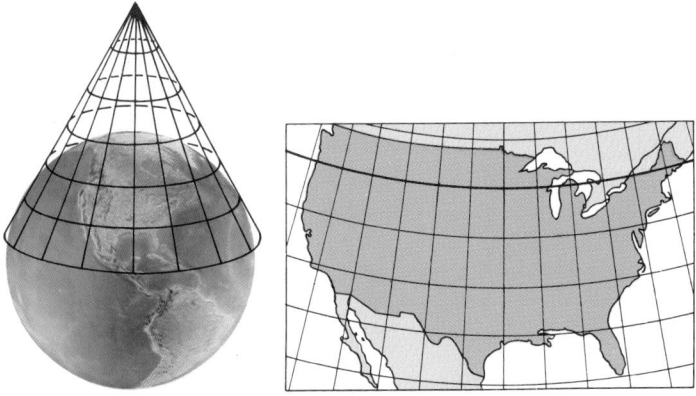

Figure 5. Projection of the globe onto a cone and a resultant Conic Projection.

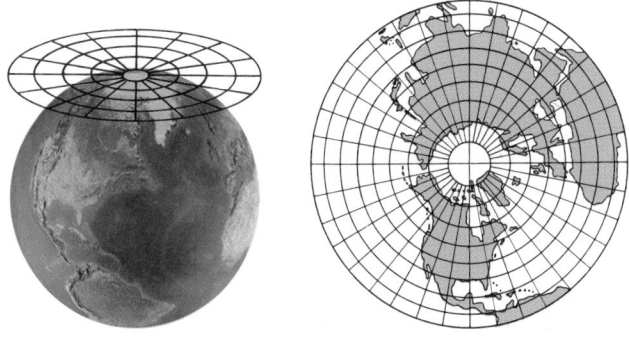

Figure 6. Lambert Equal-Area Projection (right), which assumes the projection of the globe onto a plane surface.

ix

Conic: In this transformation—a globe projected onto a tangent cone—meridians of longitude appear as straight lines, and lines of latitude appear as parallel arcs. The parallel of tangency (that is, where the cone is presumed to touch the globe) is called a standard parallel. In this projection, distortion increases in bands away from the standard parallel. Conic projections are helpful in depicting middle-latitude areas of east-west extension. (See Figure 5.)

Lambert Equal Area *(polar case):* This projection assumes a plane touching the globe at a single point. It shows true distances close to the center (the tangent point) but increasingly distorted ones away from it. The equal-area quality (showing land areas in their correct proportion) is maintained throughout; but in regions away from the center, distortion of shape increases. (See Figure 6.)

Miller Cylindrical: O. M. Miller suggested a modification to the Mercator projection to lessen the severe area distortion in the higher latitudes. The Miller projection is neither conformal nor equal-area. Thus, while shapes are less accurate than on the Mercator, the exaggeration of *size* of areas has been somewhat decreased. The Miller cylindrical is useful for showing the entire world in a rectangular format. (See Figure 7.)

Mollweide Homolographic: The Mollweide is an equal-area projection; the least distorted areas are ovals centered just above and below the center of the projection. Distance distortions increase toward the edges of the map. The Mollweide is used for world-distribution maps where a pleasing oval look is desired along with the equal-area quality. It is one of the bases used in the Goode's Interrupted Homolosine projection. (See Figure 8.)

Sinusoidal, or Sanson-Flamsteed: In this equal-area projection the scale is the same along all parallels and the central meridian. Distortion of shapes is less along the two main axes of the projection but increases markedly toward the edges. Maps depicting areas such as South America or Africa can make good use of the Sinusoidal's favorable characteristics by situating the land masses along the central meridian, where the shapes will be virtually undistorted. The Sinusoidal is also one of the bases used in the Goode's Interrupted Homolosine. (See Figure 9.)

Goode's Interrupted Homolosine: An equal-area projection, Goode's is composed of the Sinusoidal grid from the equator to about 40° N and 40° S latitudes; beyond these latitudes, the Mollweide is used. This grid is interrupted so that land masses can be projected with a minimum of shape distortion by positioning each section on a separate central meridian. Thus, the shapes as well as the sizes of land masses are represented with a high degree of fidelity. Oceans can also be positioned in this manner. (See Figure 10.)

Robinson: This projection was designed for Rand MçNally to present an uninterrupted and visually correct map of the earth. It maintains overall shape and area relationships without extreme distortion and is widely used in classrooms and textbooks. (See Figure 11.)

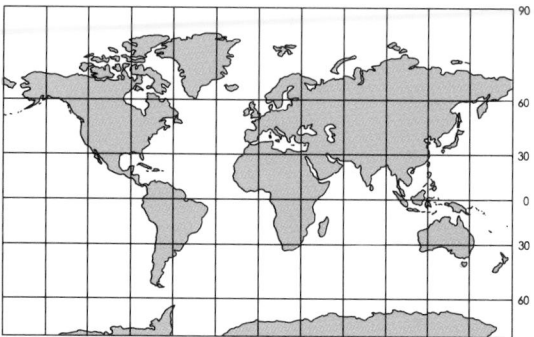

Figure 7. Miller Cylindrical Projection.

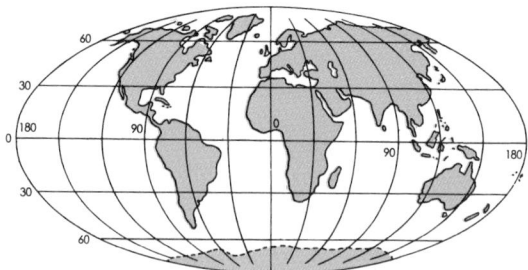

Figure 8. Mollweide Homolographic Projection.

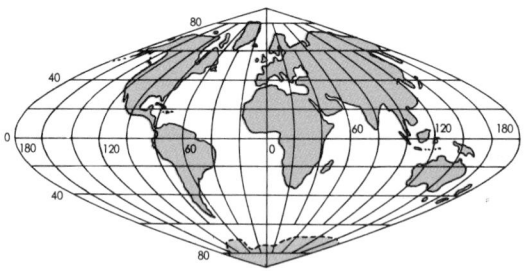

Figure 9. Sinusoidal Projection.

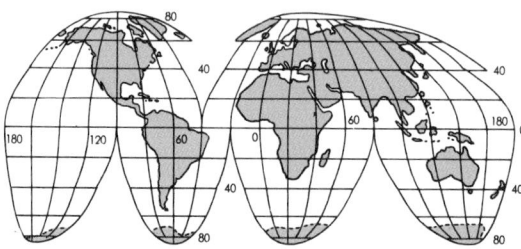

Figure 10. Goode's Interrupted Homolosine Projection.

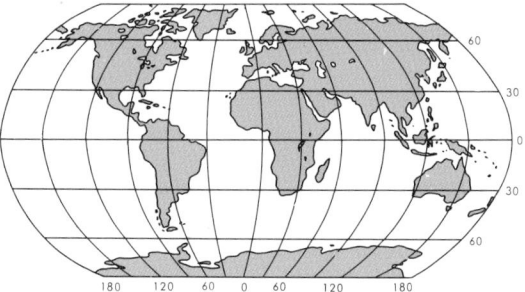

Figure 11. Robinson Projection.

Bonne: This equal-area transformation is mathematically related to the Sinusoidal. Distances are true along all parallels and the central meridian. Farther out from the central meridian, however, the increasing obliqueness of the grid's angles distorts shape and distance. This limits the area that can be usefully projected. Bonne projections, like conics, are best employed for relatively small areas in middle latitudes. (See Figure 12.)

Conic with Two Standard Parallels: The linear scale of this projection is consistent along two standard parallels instead of only one as in the simple conic. Since the spacing of the other parallels is reduced somewhat between the standard parallels and progressively enlarged beyond them, the projection does not exhibit the equal-area property. Careful selection of the standard parallels, however, provides good representation of limited areas. Like the Bonne projection, this system is widely used for areas in middle latitudes. (See Figure 13.)

Polyconic: In this system, the globe is projected onto a series of strips taken from tangent cones. Parallels are nonconcentric circles, and each is divided equally by the meridians, as on the globe. While distances along the straight central meridian are true, they are increasingly exaggerated along the curving meridians. Likewise, general representation of areas and shapes is good near the central meridian but progressively distorted away from it. Polyconic projections are used for middle-latitude areas to minimize all distortions and were employed for large-scale topographic maps. (See Figure 14.)

Lambert Conformal Conic: This conformal transformation system usually employs two standard parallels. Distortion increases away from the standard parallels, being greatest at the edges of the map. It is useful for projecting elongated east-west areas in the middle latitudes and is ideal for depicting the forty-eight contiguous states. It is also widely used for aeronautical and meteorological charts. (See Figure 15.)

Lambert Equal Area *(oblique and polar cases):* This equal-area projection can be centered at any point on the earth's surface, perpendicular to a line drawn through the globe. It maintains correct angles to all points on the map from its center (point of tangency), but distances become progressively distorted toward the edges. It is most useful for roughly circular areas or areas whose dimensions are nearly equal in two perpendicular directions.

The two most common forms of the Lambert projection are the oblique and the polar, shown in Figures 6 and 16. Although the meridians and parallels for the forms are different, the distortion characteristics are the same.

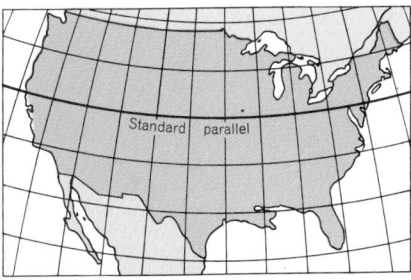

Figure 12.
Bonne Projection.

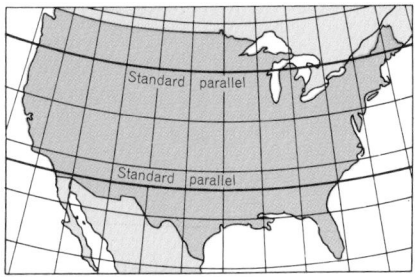

Figure 13.
Conic Projection with Two Standard Parallels.

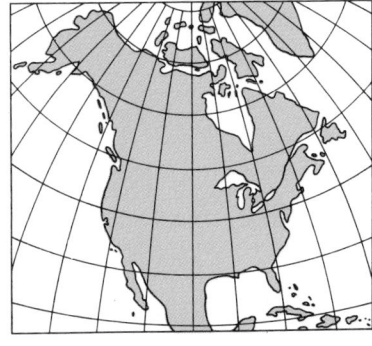

Figure 14.
Polyconic Projection.

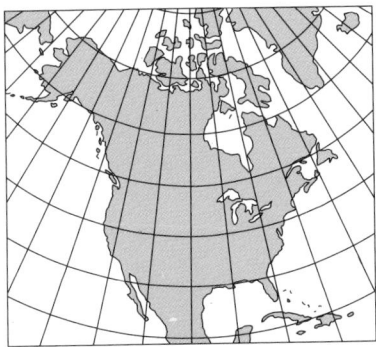

Figure 15.
Lambert Conformal Conic Projection.

Figure 16.
Lambert Equal-Area Projection (oblique case).

Important characteristics of the globe grid

1. All meridians of longitude are equal in length and meet at the Poles.
2. All lines of latitude are parallel and equally spaced on meridians.
3. The length, or circumference, of the parallels of latitude decreases as one moves from the equator to the Poles. For instance, the circumference of the parallel at 60° latitude is one-half the circumference of the equator.
4. Meridians of longitude are equally spaced on each parallel, but the distance between them decreases toward the Poles.
5. All parallels and meridians meet at right angles.

EDWARD B. ESPENSHADE, JR.
JOHN C. HUDSON

xi

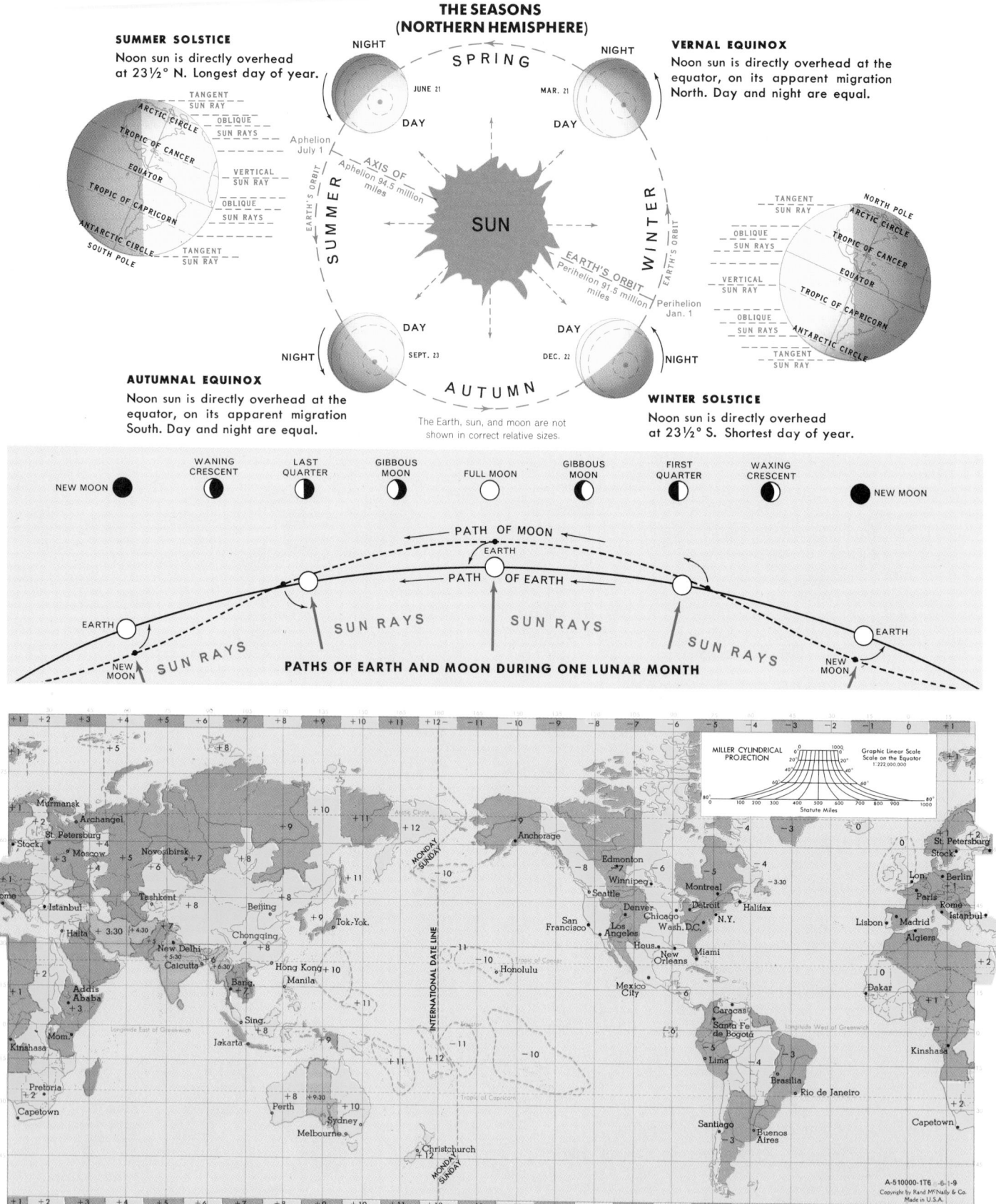

THE SEASONS
(NORTHERN HEMISPHERE)

SUMMER SOLSTICE
Noon sun is directly overhead at 23½° N. Longest day of year.

VERNAL EQUINOX
Noon sun is directly overhead at the equator, on its apparent migration North. Day and night are equal.

AUTUMNAL EQUINOX
Noon sun is directly overhead at the equator, on its apparent migration South. Day and night are equal.

WINTER SOLSTICE
Noon sun is directly overhead at 23½° S. Shortest day of year.

The Earth, sun, and moon are not shown in correct relative sizes.

PATHS OF EARTH AND MOON DURING ONE LUNAR MONTH

Time Zones

The surface of the earth is divided into 24 time zones. Each zone represents 15° of longitude or one hour of time. The time of the initial, or zero, zone is based on the central meridian of Greenwich and is adopted eastward and westward for a distance of 7½° of longitude. Each of the zones in turn is designated by a number representing the hours (+ or −) by which its standard time differs from Greenwich mean time. These standard time zones are indicated by bands of orange and yellow. Areas which have a fractional deviation from standard time are shown in an intermediate color. The irregularities in the zones and the fractional deviations are due to political and economic factors.
(After U.S. Defense Mapping Agency)

WORLD THEMATIC MAPS

This section of the atlas consists of more than sixty thematic maps presenting world patterns and distributions. Together with accompanying graphs, these maps communicate basic information on mineral resources, agricultural products, trade, transportation, and other selected aspects of the natural and cultural geographical environment.

A thematic map uses symbols to show certain characteristics of, generally, one class of geographical information. This "theme" of a thematic map is presented upon a background of basic locational information—coastline, country boundaries, major drainage, etc. The map's primary concern is to communicate visually basic impressions of the distribution of the theme. For instance, on page 43 the distribution of cattle shown by point symbols impresses the reader with relative densities—the distribution of cattle is much more uniform throughout the United States than it is in China, and cattle are more numerous in the United States than in China.

Although it is possible to use a thematic map to obtain exact values of a quantity or commodity, it is not the purpose intended, any more than a thematic map is intended to be used to give precise distances from New York to Moscow. If one seeks precise statistics for each country, he may consult the bar graph on the map or a statistical table.

The map on this page is an example of a special class of thematic maps called cartograms. The cartogram assigns to a named earth region an area based on some value other than land surface area. In the cartogram below the areas assigned are proportional to their countries' populations and tinted according to their rate of natural increase. The result of mapping on this base is a meaningful way of portraying this distribution since natural increase is causally related to existing size of population. On the other hand, natural increase is not causally related to earth area. In the other thematic maps in this atlas, relative earth sizes have been considered when presenting the distributions.

Real and hypothetical geographical distributions of interest to man are practically limitless but can be classed into point, line, area, or volume information relative to a specific location or area in the world. The thematic map, in communicating these fundamental classes of information, utilizes point, line, and area symbols. The symbols may be employed to show *qualitative* differences (differences in *kind*) of a certain category of information and may also show *quantitative* differences in the information (differences in *amount*). For example, the natural-vegetation map (page 18) was based upon information gathered by many observations over a period of time. It utilizes area symbols (color and pattern) to show the difference in the *kind* of vegetation as well as the extent. Quantitative factual information was shown on the annual-precipitation map, page 16, by means of isohyets (lines connecting points of equal rainfall). Also, area symbols were employed to show the intervals between the lines. In each of these thematic maps, there is one primary theme, or subject; the map communicates the information far better than volumes of words and tables could.

One of the most important aspects of the thematic-map section is use of the different maps to show comparisons and relationships among the distributions of various types of geographical information. For example, the relationship of dense population (page 24) to areas of intensive subsistence agriculture (page 34) and to manufacturing and commerce (page 32) is an important geographic concept.

The statistics communicated by the maps and graphs in this section are intended to give an idea of the relative importance of countries in the distributions mapped. The maps are not intended to take the place of statistical reference works. No single year affords a realistic base for production, trade, and certain economic and demographic statistics. Therefore, averages of data for three or four years have been used. Together with the maps, the averages and percentages provide the student with a realistic idea of the importance of specific areas.

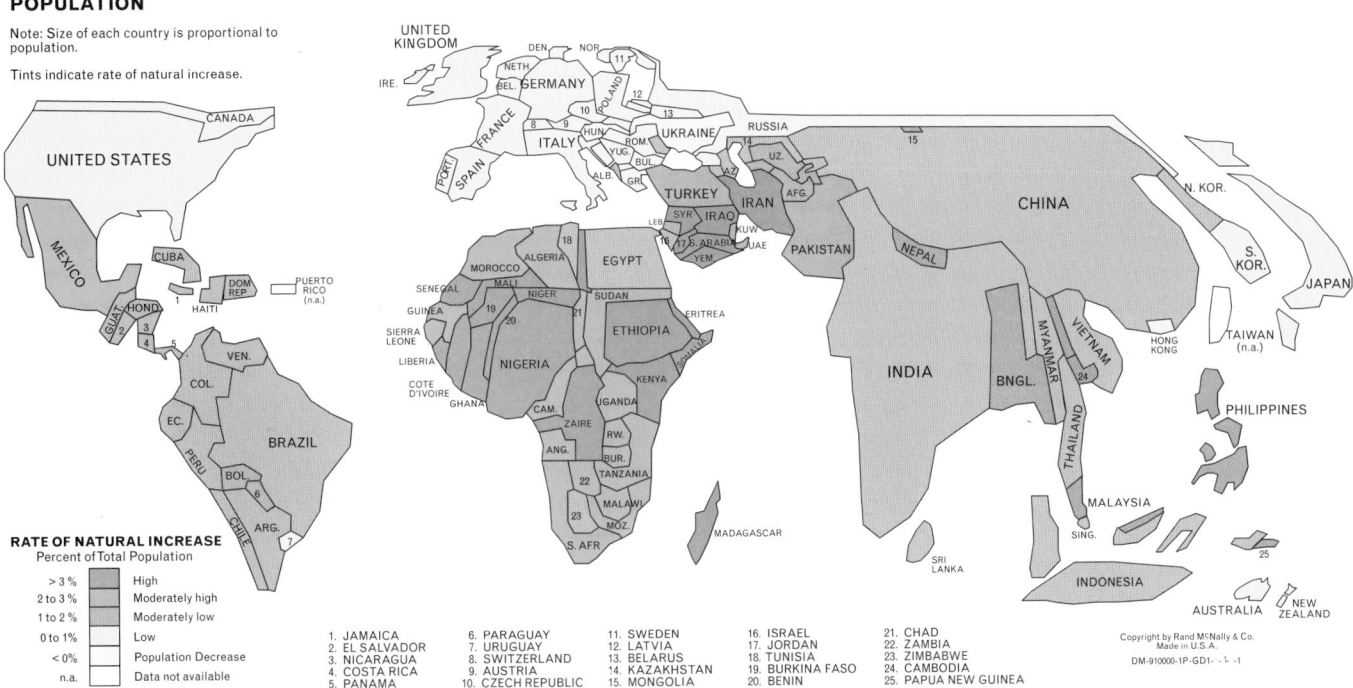

POPULATION

Note: Size of each country is proportional to population.

Tints indicate rate of natural increase.

RATE OF NATURAL INCREASE
Percent of Total Population

>3 %	High
2 to 3 %	Moderately high
1 to 2 %	Moderately low
0 to 1%	Low
< 0%	Population Decrease
n.a.	Data not available

1. JAMAICA
2. EL SALVADOR
3. NICARAGUA
4. COSTA RICA
5. PANAMA
6. PARAGUAY
7. URUGUAY
8. SWITZERLAND
9. AUSTRIA
10. CZECH REPUBLIC
11. SWEDEN
12. LATVIA
13. BELARUS
14. KAZAKHSTAN
15. MONGOLIA
16. ISRAEL
17. JORDAN
18. TUNISIA
19. BURKINA FASO
20. BENIN
21. CHAD
22. ZAMBIA
23. ZIMBABWE
24. CAMBODIA
25. PAPUA NEW GUINEA

Copyright by Rand McNally & Co.
Made in U.S.A.
DM-910000-1P-GD1- -L -1

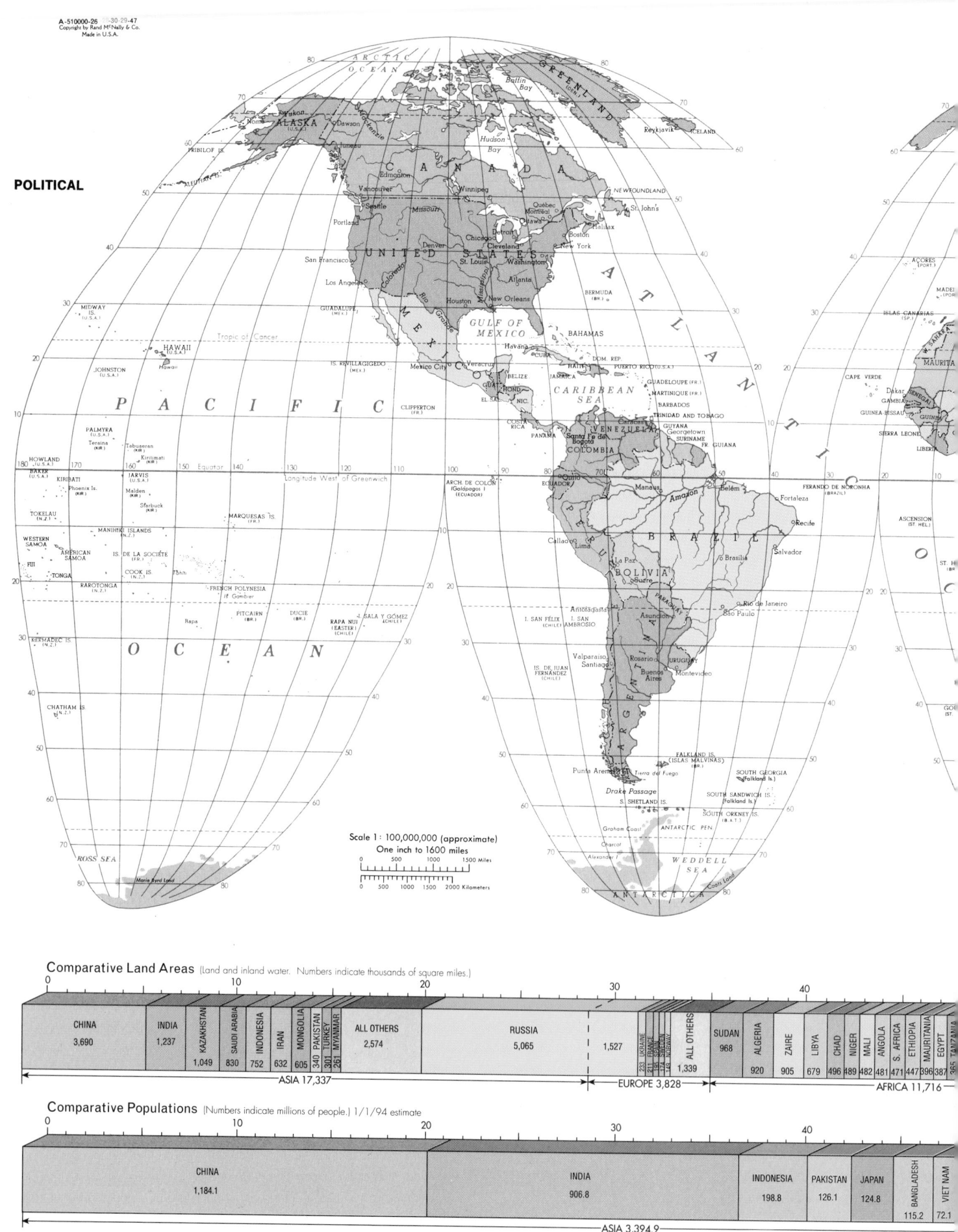

A-510000-26 30-29-47
Copyright by Rand McNally & Co.
Made in U.S.A.

POLITICAL

Scale 1 : 100,000,000 (approximate)
One inch to 1600 miles

0 500 1000 1500 Miles

0 500 1000 1500 2000 Kilometers

Comparative Land Areas (land and inland water. Numbers indicate thousands of square miles.)

| CHINA 3,690 | INDIA 1,237 | KAZAKHSTAN 1,049 | SAUDI ARABIA 830 | INDONESIA 752 | IRAN 632 | MONGOLIA 605 | PAKISTAN 340 | TURKEY 301 | MYANMAR 261 | ALL OTHERS 2,574 | RUSSIA 5,065 | 1,527 | UKRAINE 233 | FRANCE 211 | SPAIN 195 | SWEDEN 174 | NORWAY 149 | ALL OTHERS 1,339 | SUDAN 968 | ALGERIA 920 | ZAIRE 905 | LIBYA 679 | CHAD 496 | NIGER 489 | MALI 482 | ANGOLA 481 | S. AFRICA 471 | ETHIOPIA 447 | MAURITANIA 396 | EGYPT 387 | TANZANIA 365 |

ASIA 17,337 — EUROPE 3,828 — AFRICA 11,716

Comparative Populations (Numbers indicate millions of people.) 1/1/94 estimate

| CHINA 1,184.1 | INDIA 906.8 | INDONESIA 198.8 | PAKISTAN 126.1 | JAPAN 124.8 | BANGLADESH 115.2 | VIET NAM 72.1 |

ASIA 3,394.9

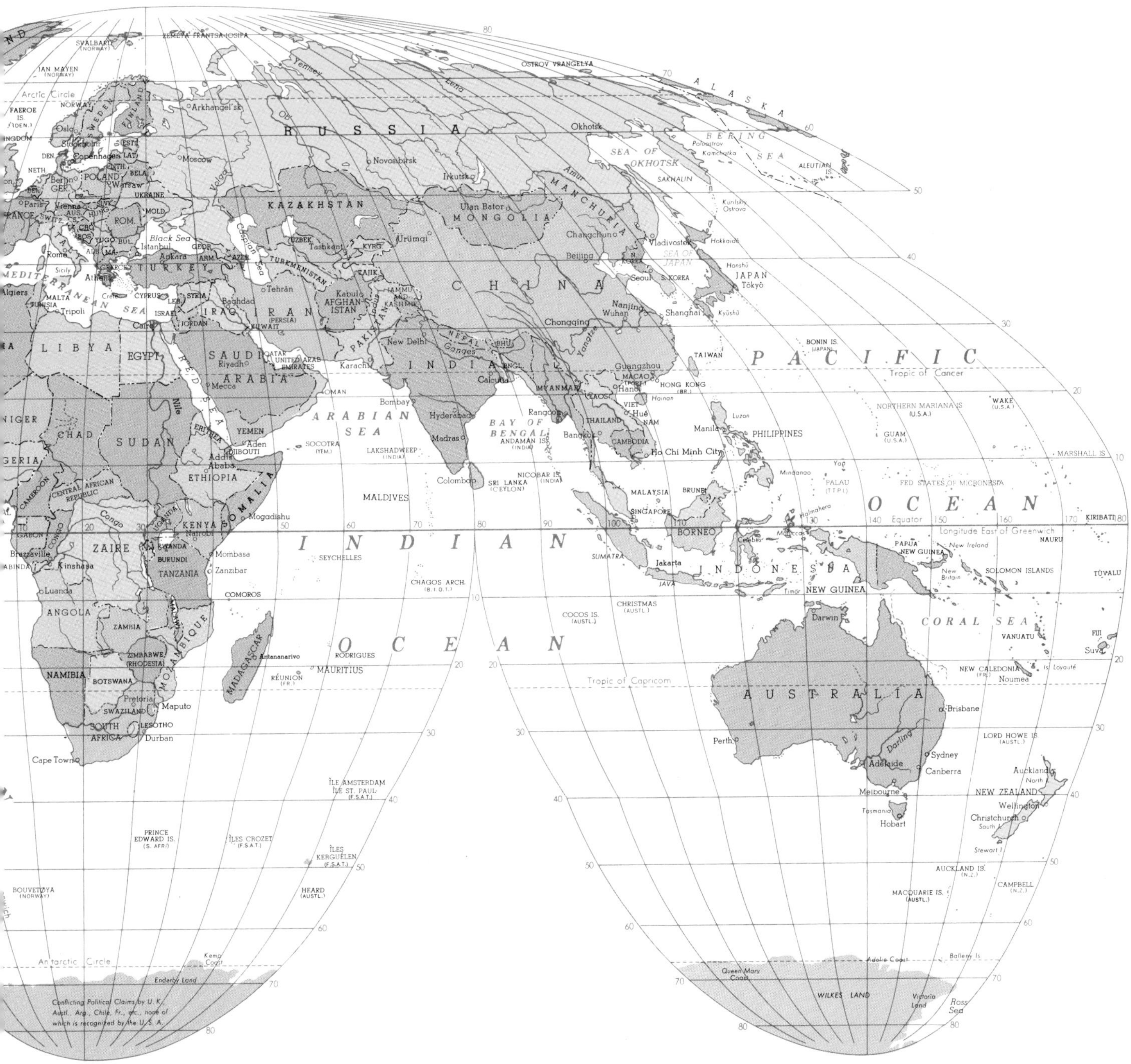

Goode's Homolosine Equal Area Projection

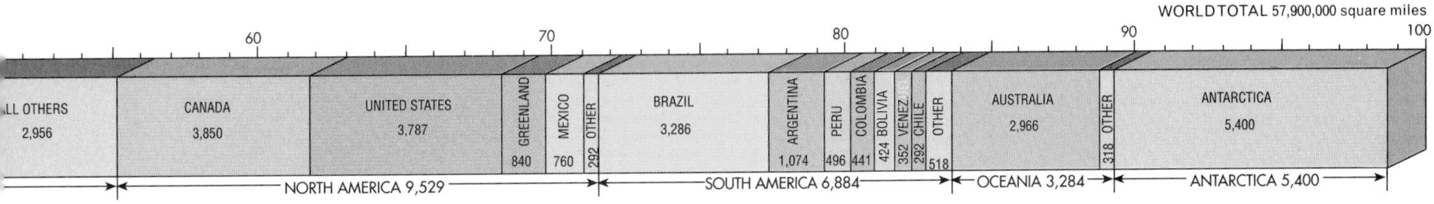

Arctic Circle

RUSSIA　ALASKA　SEA OF OKHOTSK　BERING SEA　ALEUTIAN IS.

KAZAKHSTAN　MONGOLIA　MANCHURIA　SEA OF JAPAN　JAPAN　Tōkyō

CHINA　PACIFIC OCEAN

TURKEY　IRAN　AFGHANISTAN　PAKISTAN　INDIA　Chongqing　Wuhan　Shanghai　TAIWAN　Tropic of Cancer

SAUDI ARABIA　EGYPT　LIBYA　YEMEN　BONIN IS. (JAPAN)　NORTHERN MARIANA IS. (U.S.A.)　WAKE (U.S.A.)

CHAD　SUDAN　ETHIOPIA　SOMALIA　ARABIAN SEA　BAY OF BENGAL　MYANMAR　THAILAND　VIET NAM　CAMBODIA　PHILIPPINES　GUAM (U.S.A.)　MARSHALL IS.

ZAIRE　KENYA　TANZANIA　MALDIVES　SRI LANKA (CEYLON)　MALAYSIA　SINGAPORE　BRUNEI　PALAU (T.T.P.I.)　FED. STATES OF MICRONESIA

ANGOLA　ZAMBIA　ZIMBABWE (RHODESIA)　MADAGASCAR　SEYCHELLES　INDIAN OCEAN　SUMATRA　BORNEO　INDONESIA　NEW GUINEA　PAPUA NEW GUINEA　SOLOMON ISLANDS　TUVALU

NAMIBIA　BOTSWANA　SOUTH AFRICA　MAURITIUS　RÉUNION (FR.)　Tropic of Capricorn　AUSTRALIA　CORAL SEA　VANUATU　FIJI　NEW CALEDONIA (FR.)

Cape Town　Durban　ÎLE AMSTERDAM ÎLE ST. PAUL (F.S.A.T.)　Perth　Adelaide　Sydney　Canberra　NEW ZEALAND　Wellington　Christchurch

PRINCE EDWARD IS. (S. AFR.)　ÎLES CROZET (F.S.A.T.)　ÎLES KERGUÉLEN (F.S.A.T.)　Melbourne　Hobart　AUCKLAND IS. (N.Z.)

BOUVETØYA (NORWAY)　HEARD (AUSTL.)　MACQUARIE IS. (AUSTL.)　CAMPBELL (N.Z.)

Antarctic Circle

Conflicting Political Claims by U. K., Austl., Arg., Chile, Fr., etc., none of which is recognized by the U. S. A.

WILKES LAND　Ross Sea

WORLD TOTAL 57,900,000 square miles

| ALL OTHERS 2,956 | CANADA 3,850 | UNITED STATES 3,787 | GREENLAND 840 | MEXICO 760 | OTHER 292 | BRAZIL 3,286 | ARGENTINA 1,074 | PERU 496 | COLOMBIA 441 | BOLIVIA 424 | VENEZ. 352 | CHILE 292 | OTHER 518 | AUSTRALIA 2,966 | OTHER 318 | ANTARCTICA 5,400 |

NORTH AMERICA 9,529　SOUTH AMERICA 6,884　OCEANIA 3,284　ANTARCTICA 5,400

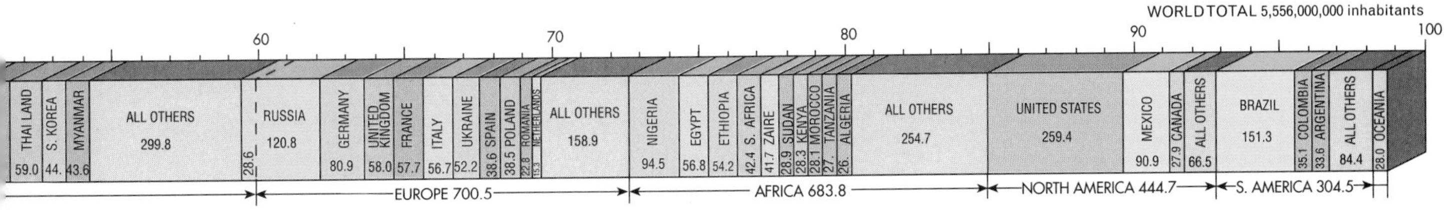

WORLD TOTAL 5,556,000,000 inhabitants

| THAILAND 59.0 | S. KOREA 44.3 | MYANMAR 43.6 | ALL OTHERS 299.8 | RUSSIA 120.8 | GERMANY 80.9 | UNITED KINGDOM 58.0 | FRANCE 57.7 | ITALY 56.7 | UKRAINE 52.2 | SPAIN 38.6 | POLAND 38.5 | ROMANIA 22.8 | NETHERLANDS 15.3 | ALL OTHERS 158.9 | NIGERIA 94.5 | EGYPT 56.8 | ETHIOPIA 54.2 | S. AFRICA 42.4 | ZAIRE 41.7 | SUDAN 28.9 | KENYA 28.1 | MOROCCO 27 | TANZANIA 27 | ALGERIA 26 | ALL OTHERS 254.7 | UNITED STATES 259.4 | MEXICO 90.9 | CANADA 27.9 | ALL OTHERS 66.5 | BRAZIL 151.3 | COLOMBIA 35.1 | ARGENTINA 33.6 | ALL OTHERS 84.4 | OCEANIA 28.0 |

EUROPE 700.5　AFRICA 683.8　NORTH AMERICA 444.7　S. AMERICA 304.5

4

PHYSICAL

North Pole

ARCTIC OCEAN

ASIA

PT. BARROW
Beaufort Sea
BANKS I.
Victoria Island
Great Bear L.
BAFFIN ISLAND
Baffin Bay
GREENLAND
N. Magnetic Pole
KAP FARVEL
Denmark Str.
Hekla 4 747
ICELAND
KAP FARVEL

BERING SEA
PRIBILOF IS.
Nunivak I.
Mt. McKinley 20 320
Mt. Logan 19 551
Alaska Pen.
Gulf of Alaska
Great Slave L.
HUDSON BAY
Belcher
NORTHERN LOWLAND
LABRADOR PENINSULA AND PLATEAU
Str. of Belle Isle
NEWFOUNDLAND

ALEUTIAN ISLANDS
ALEUTIAN TRENCH
VANCOUVER I.
Mt. Rainier 14 410
L. Winnipeg
Great

NORTH AMERICA

C. Mendocino
GREAT BASIN
Mt. Whitney 14 494
Pikes Peak 14 110
Mt. Mitchell 6 684
C. SABLE
C. COD
C. HATTERAS

San Francisco Bay
PENINSULA DE BAJA CALIFORNIA
Guadalupe
C. SAN LUCAS
GULF OF MEXICO
C. Sable
FLORIDA PEN.
BAHAMA ISLANDS
BERMUDA
NORTH AMERICAN BASIN

MIDWAY IS.
HAWAIIAN ISLANDS
Mauna Kea (Vol.) 13 796
Hawaii
IS. REVILLAGIGEDO
Pico de Orizaba 18 406
ISTMO DE TEHUANTEPEC
Pen. de Yucatán
Cuba
WEST INDIES
GREATER ANTILLES
Hispaniola
Jamaica
Puerto Rico
CARIBBEAN SEA
Guadeloupe
Martinique
LESSER ANTILLES
WINDWARD ISLANDS
Barbados
Trinidad

Johnston
Clipperton
Irazú (Vol.) 11 260
ISTMO DE PANAMA
G. de
Pta. de Gallinas

ATLANTIC

AÇORES (AZ.)
IS. CANARIAS
Jebel
C. VERT
ARQUIPELAGO DE CABO VERDE

PACIFIC OCEAN

Palmyra
Teraina
Tabuaeran
Kiritimati
Howland
Baker
Jarvis
Malden
Starbuck
PHOENIX ISLANDS
MANIHIKI IS.
MARQUESAS IS.

ARCH. DE COLÓN (GALÁPAGOS IS.)
G. de Guayaquil
PTA. PARIÑAS
Chimborazo 20 702
SELVAS
SOUTH AMERICA
GUIANA HIGHLANDS
MARAJÓ I.
Fernando de Noronha
CABO DE SÃO ROQUE

ASCENSION

TOKELAU IS.
WESTERN SAMOA
Tutuila
FIJI IS.
TONGA IS.
TONGA
SOCIETY IS.
Tahiti
ÎLES AUSTRALES
TUAMOTU
Is. Gambier
Rapa
Pitcairn
Ducie
I. Sala y Gómez
Rapa Nui (Easter)

CAMPOS
LLANOS
L. Titicaca
ATACAMA TRENCH
PLATEAU OF MATO GROSSO
Pico da Bandeira 9 482
C. FRIO
CENTRAL LOWLAND

KERMADEC IS.
KERMADEC TRENCH
CHATHAM IS.

I. San Félix
I. San Ambrosio
Aconcagua (Vol.) 22 831
IS. DE JUAN FERNANDEZ
PAMPA
Río de la Plata

TRISTAN CUNH.

ROSS SEA
Marie Byrd Land

ARCH. DE LOS CHONOS
PATAGONIA
G. San Matías
G. San Jorge
G. de Peñas
Estr. de Magallanes
FALKLAND IS.
Tierra del Fuego
CABO DE HORNOS
Drake Passage
SOUTH SHETLAND IS.
SHAG ROCKS
SOUTH GEORGIA
SOUTH SANDWICH IS.
SOUTH ORKNEY IS.
ANTARCTIC PENINSULA
Graham Coast
Alexander I.
WEDDELL SEA
Coats Land

South Pole

Scale 1:100,000,000 (approximate)
One inch to 1600 miles

0   500   1000   1500 Miles
0 500 1000 1500 2000 Kilometers

Meters		Feet
3 050		10 000
1 525		5 000
610		2 000
305		1 000
SEA L.	0	SEA L.
152.5		BELOW SEA LEVEL 500
3 050		10 000
6 100		20 000

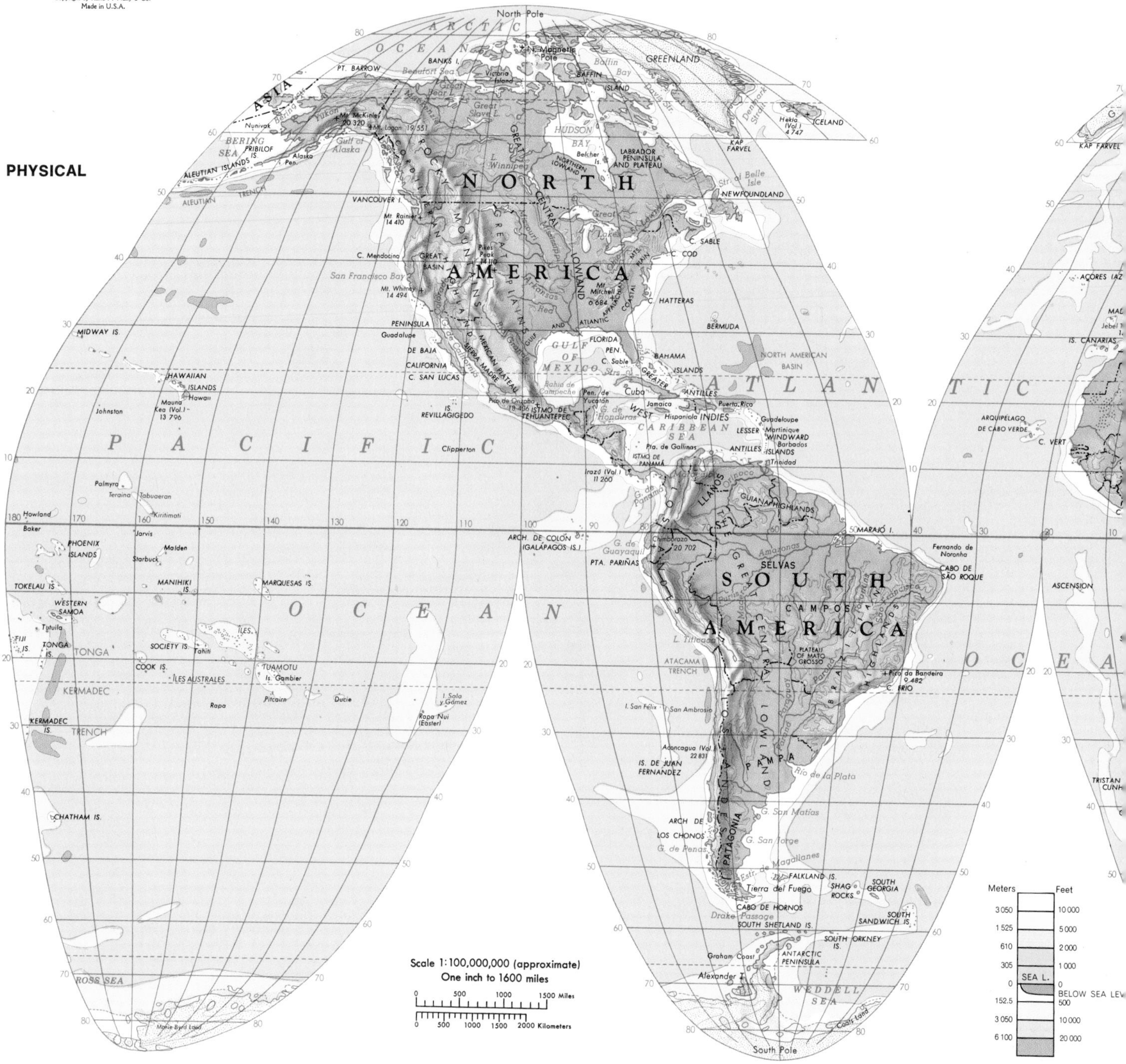

Land Elevations in Profile

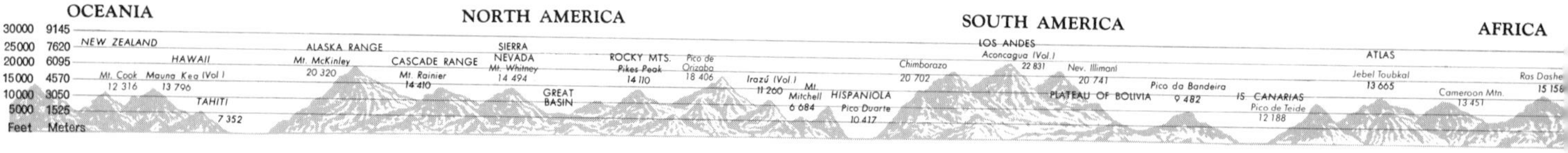

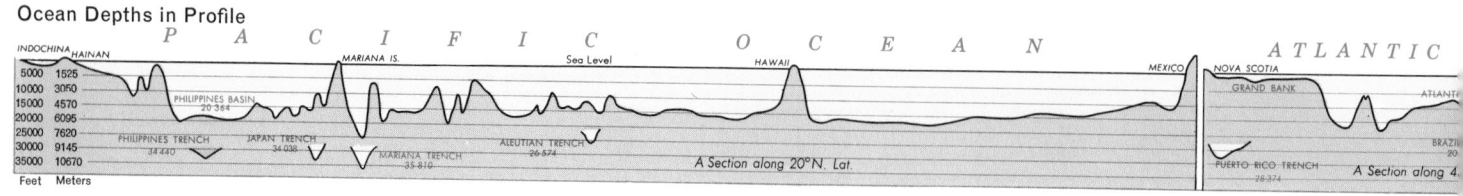

OCEANIA | NORTH AMERICA | SOUTH AMERICA | AFRICA

NEW ZEALAND
HAWAII
Mt. Cook 12 316
Mauna Kea (Vol.) 13 796
TAHITI 7 352
ALASKA RANGE
Mt. McKinley 20 320
CASCADE RANGE
Mt. Rainier 14 410
SIERRA NEVADA
Mt. Whitney 14 494
ROCKY MTS.
Pikes Peak 14 110
Pico de Orizaba 18 406
Irazú (Vol.) 11 260
Mt. Mitchell 6 684
GREAT BASIN
HISPANIOLA
Pico Duarte 10 417
LOS ANDES
Chimborazo 20 702
Aconcagua (Vol.) 22 831
Nev. Illimani 20 741
Pico da Bandeira 9 482
PLATEAU OF BOLIVIA
IS. CANARIAS
Pico de Teide 12 188
ATLAS
Jebel Toubkal 13 665
Cameroon Mtn. 13 451
Ras Dashen 15 158

30000 9145
25000 7620
20000 6095
15000 4570
10000 3050
5000 1525
Feet Meters

Ocean Depths in Profile

PACIFIC OCEAN | ATLANTIC

INDOCHINA
HAINAN
PHILIPPINES BASIN 20 364
PHILIPPINES TRENCH 34 440
JAPAN TRENCH 34 038
MARIANA IS.
MARIANA TRENCH 35 810
Sea Level
ALEUTIAN TRENCH 26 574
HAWAII
MEXICO
A Section along 20° N. Lat.
NOVA SCOTIA
GRAND BANK
ATLANTIC
PUERTO RICO TRENCH 28 374
BRAZIL
A Section along 4.

5000 1525
10000 3050
15000 4570
20000 6095
25000 7620
30000 9145
35000 10670
Feet Meters

Elevations and depr

For Glossary of Foreign Geographical Terms see page 252

Goode's Homolosine Equal Area Projection

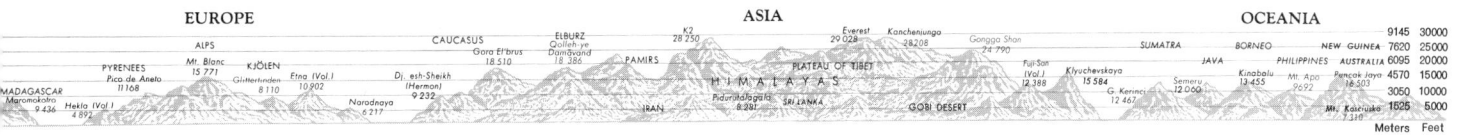

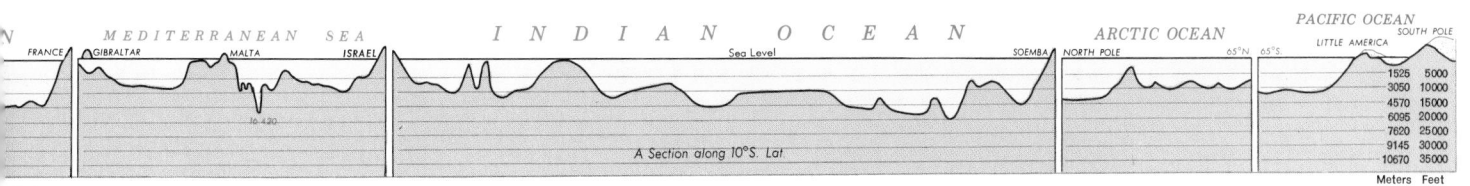

A Section along 10°S. Lat

6

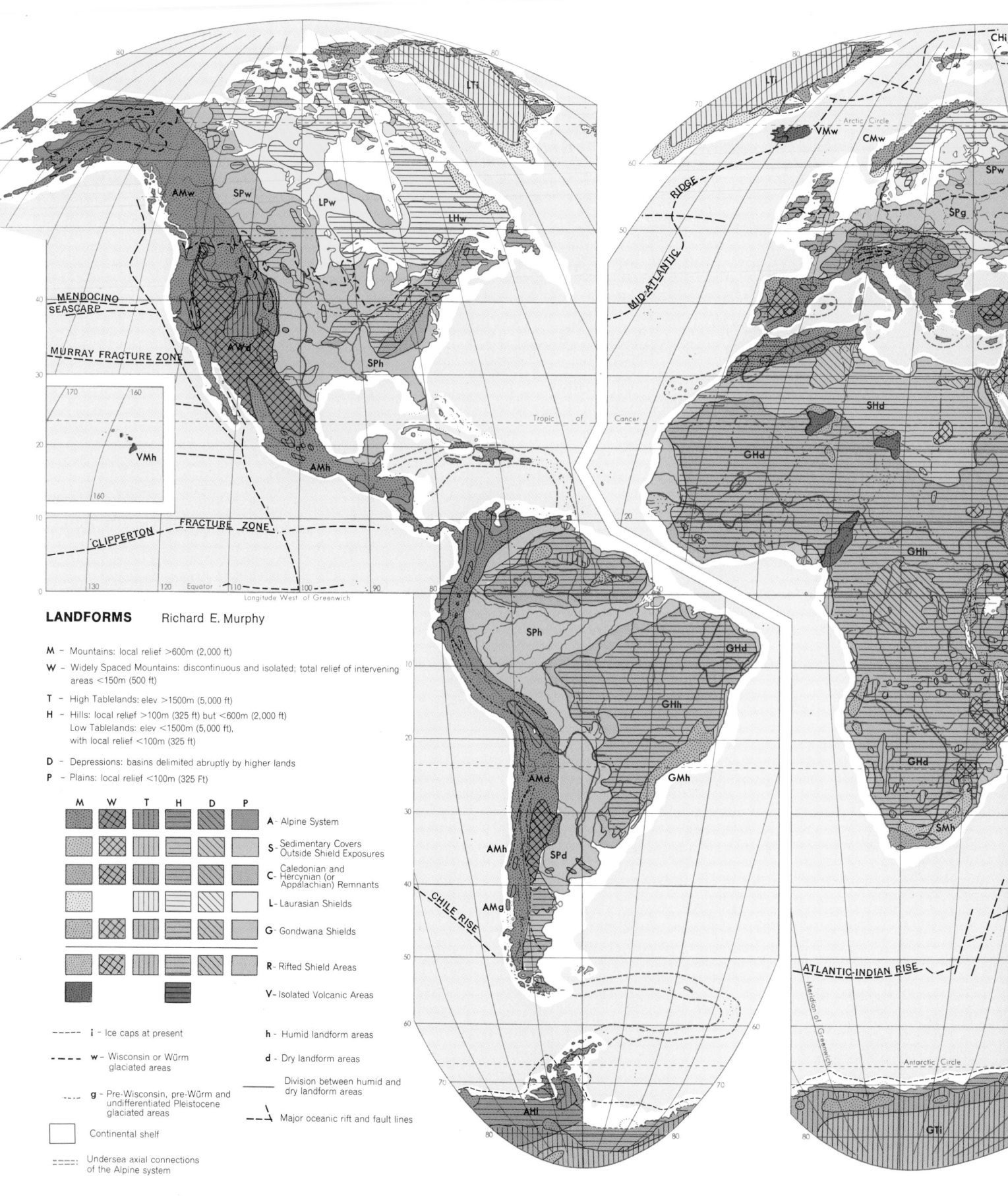

LANDFORMS   Richard E. Murphy

M – Mountains: local relief >600m (2,000 ft)

W – Widely Spaced Mountains: discontinuous and isolated; total relief of intervening areas <150m (500 ft)

T – High Tablelands: elev >1500m (5,000 ft)

H – Hills: local relief >100m (325 ft) but <600m (2,000 ft)
Low Tablelands: elev <1500m (5,000 ft), with local relief <100m (325 ft)

D – Depressions: basins delimited abruptly by higher lands

P – Plains: local relief <100m (325 Ft)

M	W	T	H	D	P	
						A- Alpine System
						S- Sedimentary Covers Outside Shield Exposures
						C- Caledonian and Hercynian (or Appalachian) Remnants
						L- Laurasian Shields
						G- Gondwana Shields
						R- Rifted Shield Areas
						V- Isolated Volcanic Areas

----- **i** - Ice caps at present

- - - **w** - Wisconsin or Würm glaciated areas

-·-·- **g** - Pre-Wisconsin, pre-Würm and undifferentiated Pleistocene glaciated areas

☐ Continental shelf

===== Undersea axial connections of the Alpine system

h - Humid landform areas

d - Dry landform areas

—— Division between humid and dry landform areas

-·-·\ Major oceanic rift and fault lines

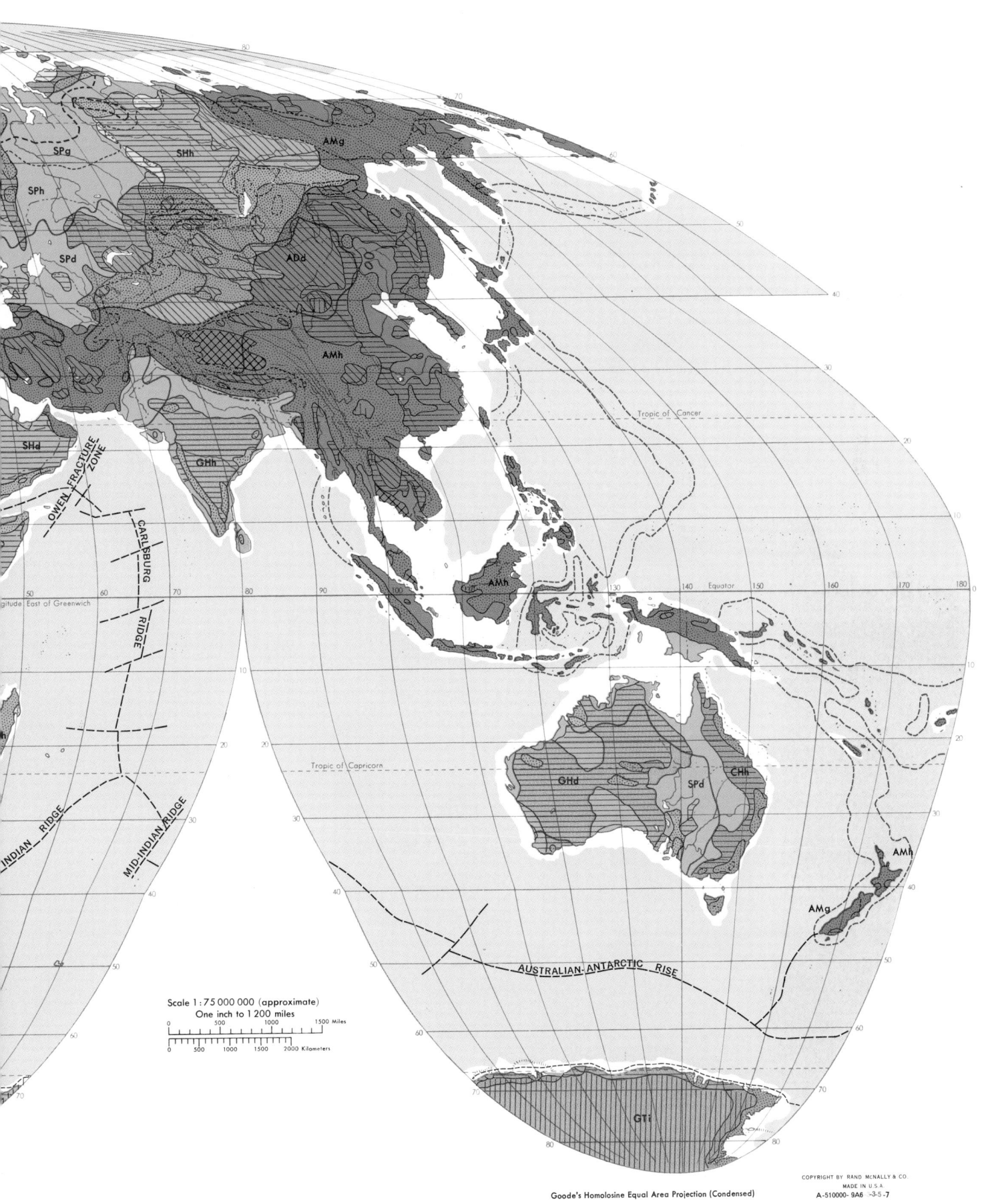

SPg

SHh

AMg

SPh

SPd

ADd

AMh

SHd

OWEN FRACTURE ZONE

CARLSBURG RIDGE

GHh

AMh

Tropic of Cancer

Equator

gitude East of Greenwich

INDIAN RIDGE

MID-INDIAN RIDGE

Tropic of Capricorn

GHd

SPd

CHh

AMh

AMg

AUSTRALIAN-ANTARCTIC RISE

Scale 1 : 75 000 000 (approximate)
One inch to 1 200 miles

0   500   1000   1500 Miles

0   500   1000   1500   2000 Kilometers

GTi

Goode's Homolosine Equal Area Projection (Condensed)   A-510000- 9A6 -3-5 -7

CONTINENTAL DRIFT

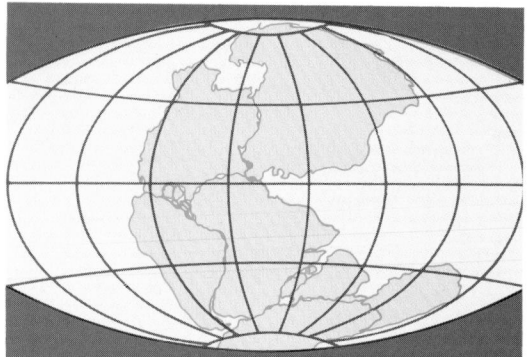

225 million years ago the supercontinent of Pangaea exists and Panthalassa forms the ancestral ocean. Tethys Sea separates Eurasia and Africa.

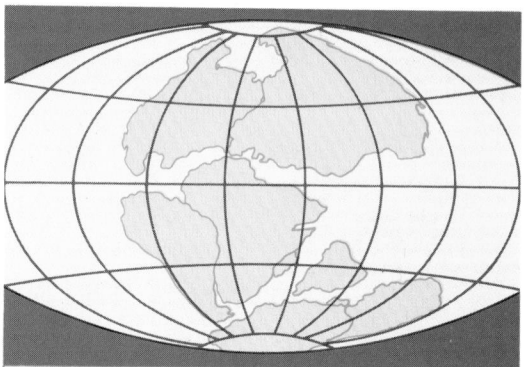

180 million years ago Pangaea splits, Laurasia drifts north. Gondwanaland breaks into South America/Africa, India, and Australia/Antarctica.

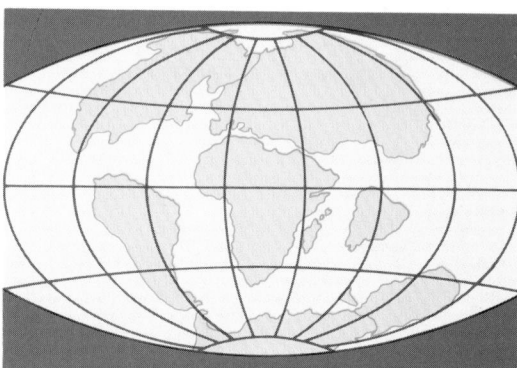

65 million years ago ocean basins take shape as South America and India move from Africa and the Tethys Sea closes to form the Mediterranean Sea.

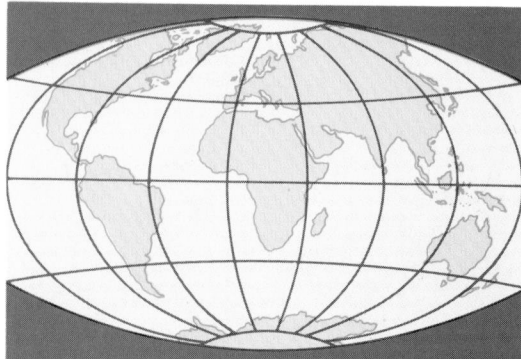

The present day: India has merged with Asia, Australia is free of Antarctica, and North America is free of Eurasia.

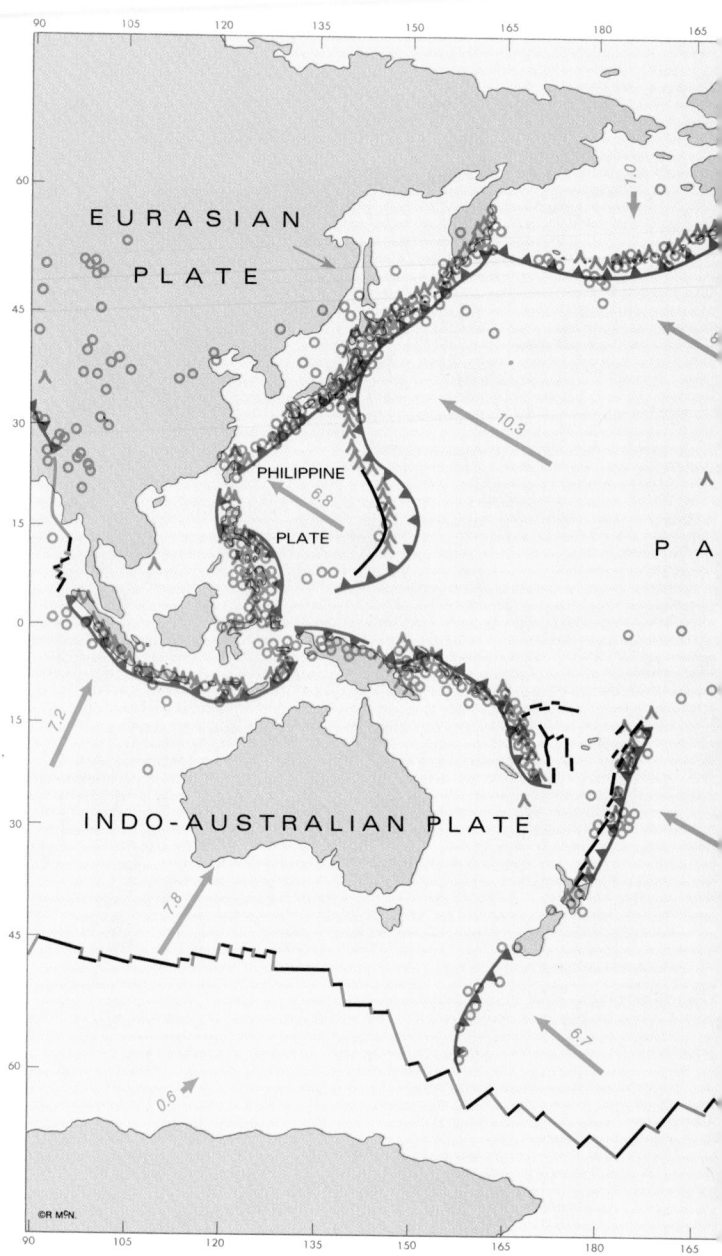

PLATE TECTONICS

Types of plate boundaries

────── **Divergent:** magma emerges from the earth's mantle at the mid-ocean ridges forming new crust and forcing the plates to spread apart at the ridges.

▲▲▲▲ **Convergent:** plates collide at subduction zones where the denser plate is forced back into the earth's mantle forming deep ocean trenches.

────── **Transform:** plates slide past one another producing faults and fracture zones.

Other map symbols

→ Direction of plate movement

6.7 → Length of arrow is proportional to the amount of plate movement (number indicates centimeters of movement per year)

○ Earthquake of magnitude 7.5 and above (from 10 A.D. to the present)

∧ Volcano (eruption since 1900)

✳ Selected hot spots

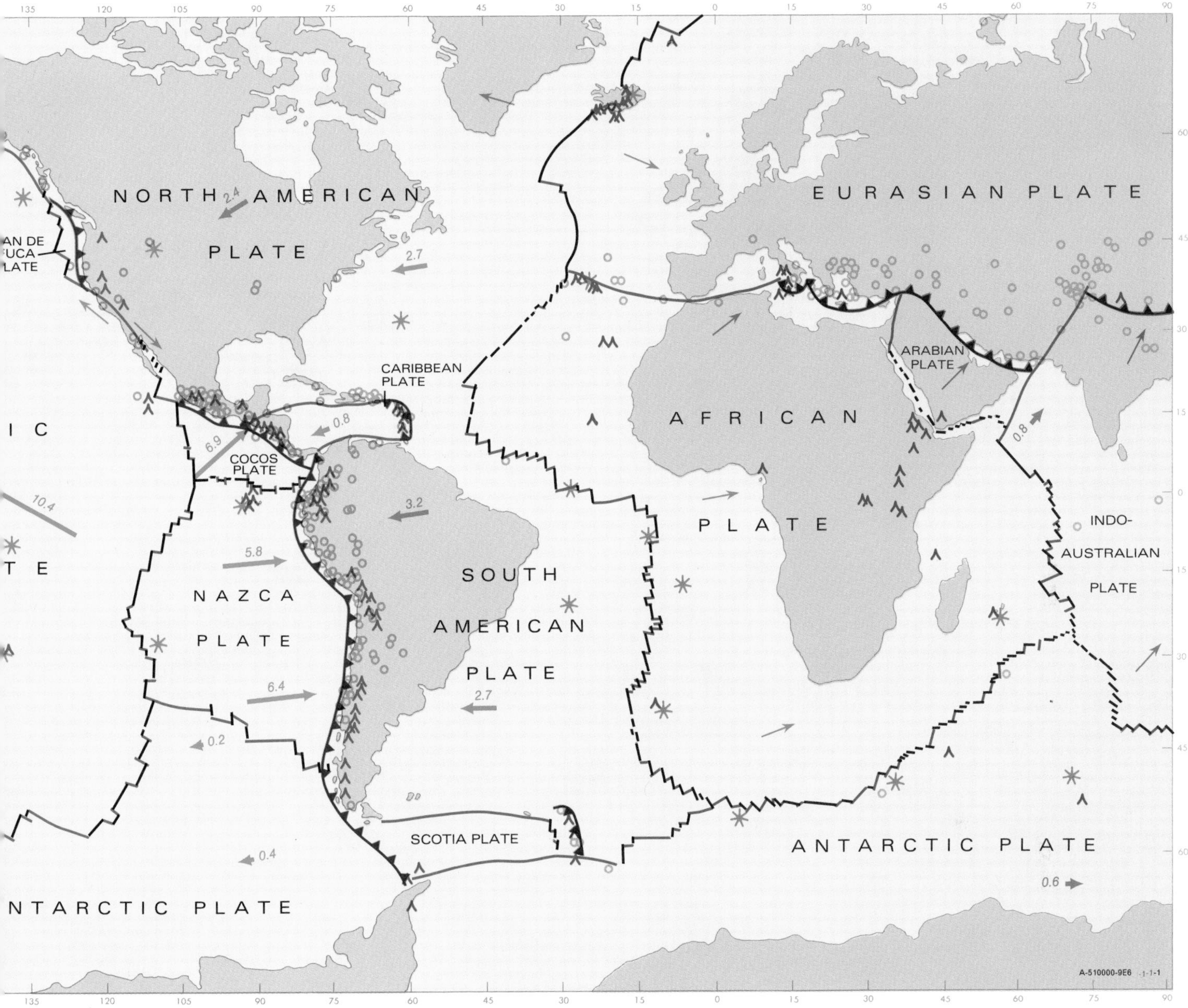

NORTH AMERICAN

PLATE

AN DE
UCA
LATE

CARIBBEAN
PLATE

COCOS
PLATE

NAZCA

PLATE

SOUTH

AMERICAN

PLATE

SCOTIA PLATE

NTARCTIC PLATE

EURASIAN PLATE

ARABIAN
PLATE

AFRICAN

PLATE

INDO-
AUSTRALIAN

PLATE

ANTARCTIC PLATE

A-510000-9E6

The plate tectonic theory describes the movement of the earth's surface and subsurface and explains why surface features are where they are.

Stated concisely, the theory presumes the lithosphere - the outside crust and uppermost mantle of the earth - is divided into about a dozen major rigid plates and several smaller platelets that move relative to one another. The position and names of the plates are shown on the map above.

The motor that drives the plates is found deep in the mantle. The theory states that because of temperature differences in the mantle, slow convection currents circulate there. Where two molten currents converge and move upward, they separate, causing the crustal plates to bulge and move apart in mid-ocean regions. Transverse fractures disrupt these broad regions. Lava wells up at these points to cause volcanic activity and to form ridges. The plates grow larger by accretion along these mid-ocean ridges, cause vast regions of the crust to move apart, and force the plates to collide with one another. As the plates do so, they are destroyed at subduction zones, where the plates are consumed downward, back into the earth's mantle, forming deep ocean trenches. The diagrams to the right illustrate the processes.

Most of the earth's volcanic and seismic activities

occur where plates slide past each other at transform boundaries or collide along subduction zones. The friction and heat caused by the grinding motion of the subducted plates causes rock to liquify and rise to the surface as volcanoes and eventually form vast mountain ranges. Strong and deep earthquakes are common here.

Volcanoes and earthquakes also occur at random locations around the earth known as "hot spots". Hot rock from deep in the mantle rises to the surface creating some of the earth's tallest mountains. As the lithospheric plates move slowly over these stationary plumes of magma, island chains (such as the Hawaiian Islands) are formed.

The overall result of tectonic movement is that the crustal plates move slowly and inexorably as relatively rigid entities, carrying the continents along with them. The history of this continental drifting is illustrated in the four maps to the left. It began with a single landmass called the supercontinent of Pangaea and the ancestral sea, the Panthalassa Ocean. Pangaea first split into a northern landmass called Laurasia and a southern block called Gondwanaland and subsequently into the continents we map today. The map of the future will be significantly different as the continents continue to drift.

Subduction
Zone

Ocean Ridge
Zone

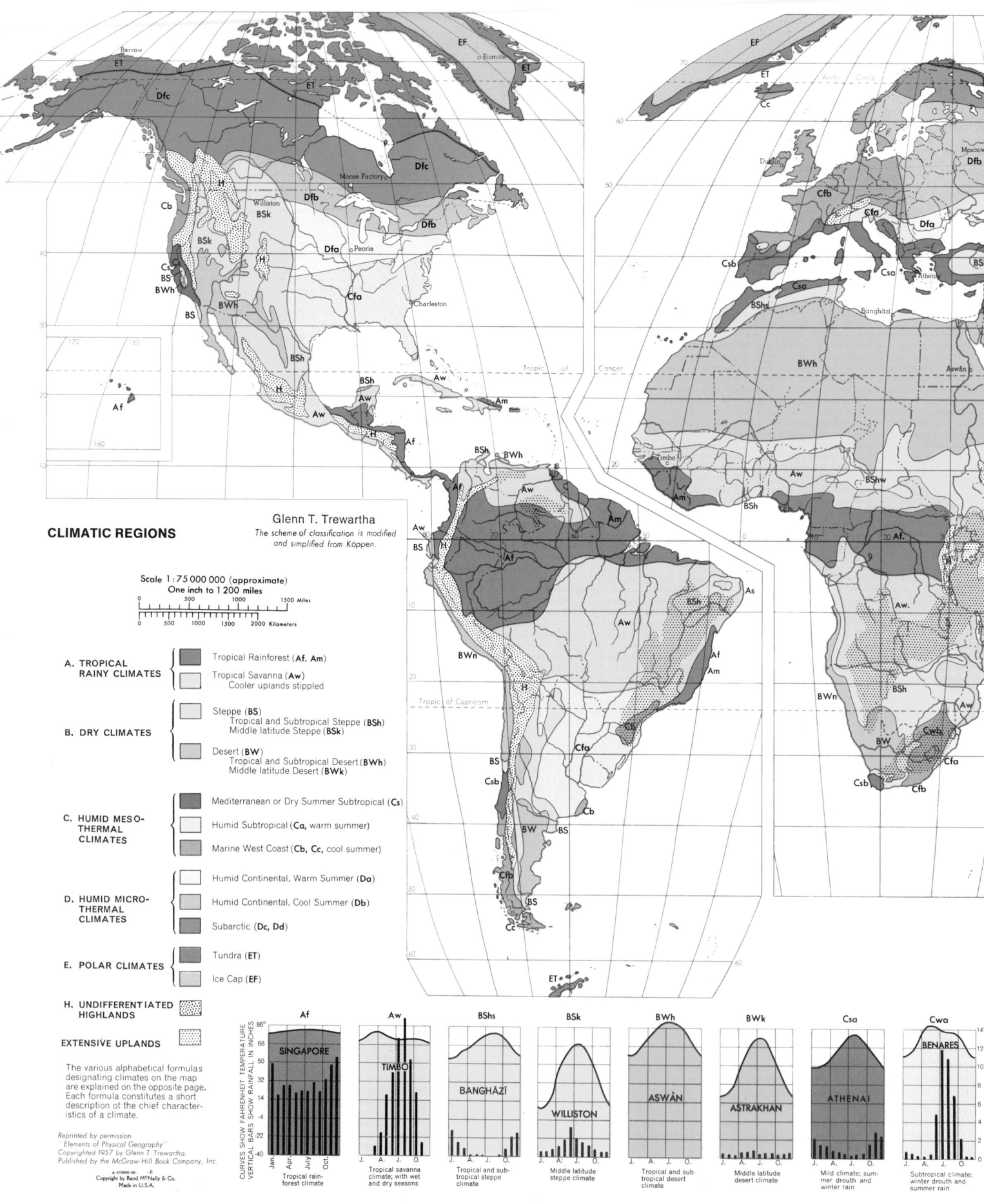

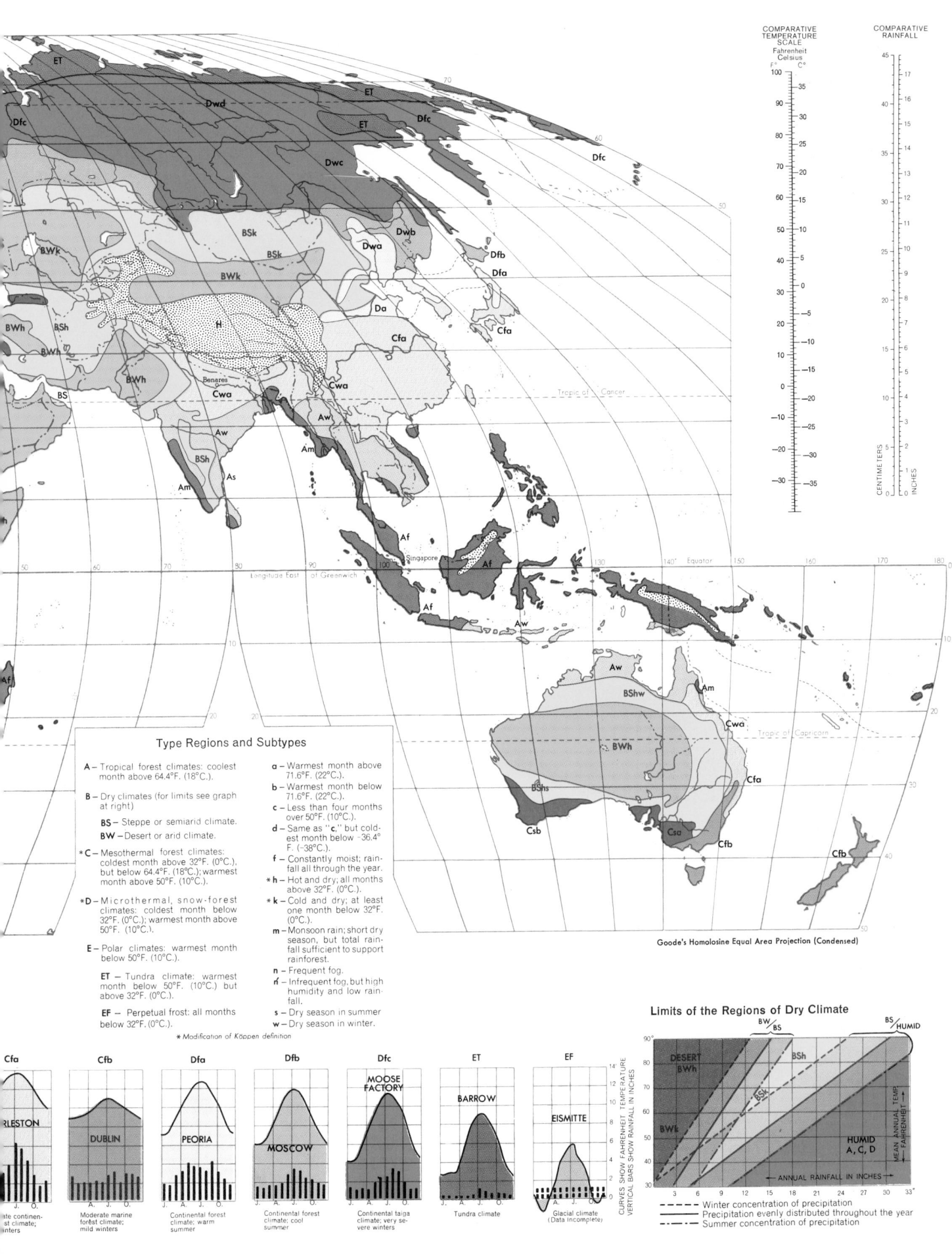

COMPARATIVE
TEMPERATURE
SCALE
Fahrenheit
Celsius
F° C°

COMPARATIVE
RAINFALL

Goode's Homolosine Equal Area Projection (Condensed)

Type Regions and Subtypes

A – Tropical forest climates: coolest
month above 64.4°F. (18°C.).

B – Dry climates (for limits see graph
at right)

　BS – Steppe or semiarid climate.

　BW – Desert or arid climate.

*C – Mesothermal forest climates:
coldest month above 32°F. (0°C.),
but below 64.4°F. (18°C.); warmest
month above 50°F. (10°C.).

*D – Microthermal, snow-forest
climates: coldest month below
32°F. (0°C.); warmest month above
50°F. (10°C.).

E – Polar climates: warmest month
below 50°F. (10°C.).

　ET – Tundra climate: warmest
month below 50°F. (10°C.) but
above 32°F. (0°C.).

　EF – Perpetual frost: all months
below 32°F. (0°C.).

a – Warmest month above
71.6°F. (22°C.).

b – Warmest month below
71.6°F. (22°C.).

c – Less than four months
over 50°F. (10°C.).

d – Same as "c," but coldest month below -36.4°
F. (-38°C.).

f – Constantly moist; rainfall all through the year.

*h – Hot and dry; all months
above 32°F. (0°C.).

*k – Cold and dry; at least
one month below 32°F.
(0°C.).

m – Monsoon rain; short dry
season, but total rain-
fall sufficient to support
rainforest.

n – Frequent fog.

n′ – Infrequent fog, but high
humidity and low rain-
fall.

s – Dry season in summer.

w – Dry season in winter.

* Modification of Köppen definition

Limits of the Regions of Dry Climate

- - - - Winter concentration of precipitation
——— Precipitation evenly distributed throughout the year
-·-·- Summer concentration of precipitation

DESERT
BWh

BWk

BSh

BSk

HUMID
A, C, D

ANNUAL RAINFALL IN INCHES

MEAN ANNUAL TEMP.
FAHRENHEIT

Cfa	Cfb	Dfa	Dfb	Dfc	ET	EF

CHARLESTON

DUBLIN

PEORIA

MOSCOW

MOOSE
FACTORY

BARROW

EISMITTE

CURVES SHOW FAHRENHEIT TEMPERATURE
VERTICAL BARS SHOW RAINFALL IN INCHES

Late continen-
tal climate;
winters

Moderate marine
forest climate;
mild winters

Continental forest
climate; warm
summer

Continental forest
climate; cool
summer

Continental taiga
climate; very se-
vere winters

Tundra climate

Glacial climate
(Data incomplete)

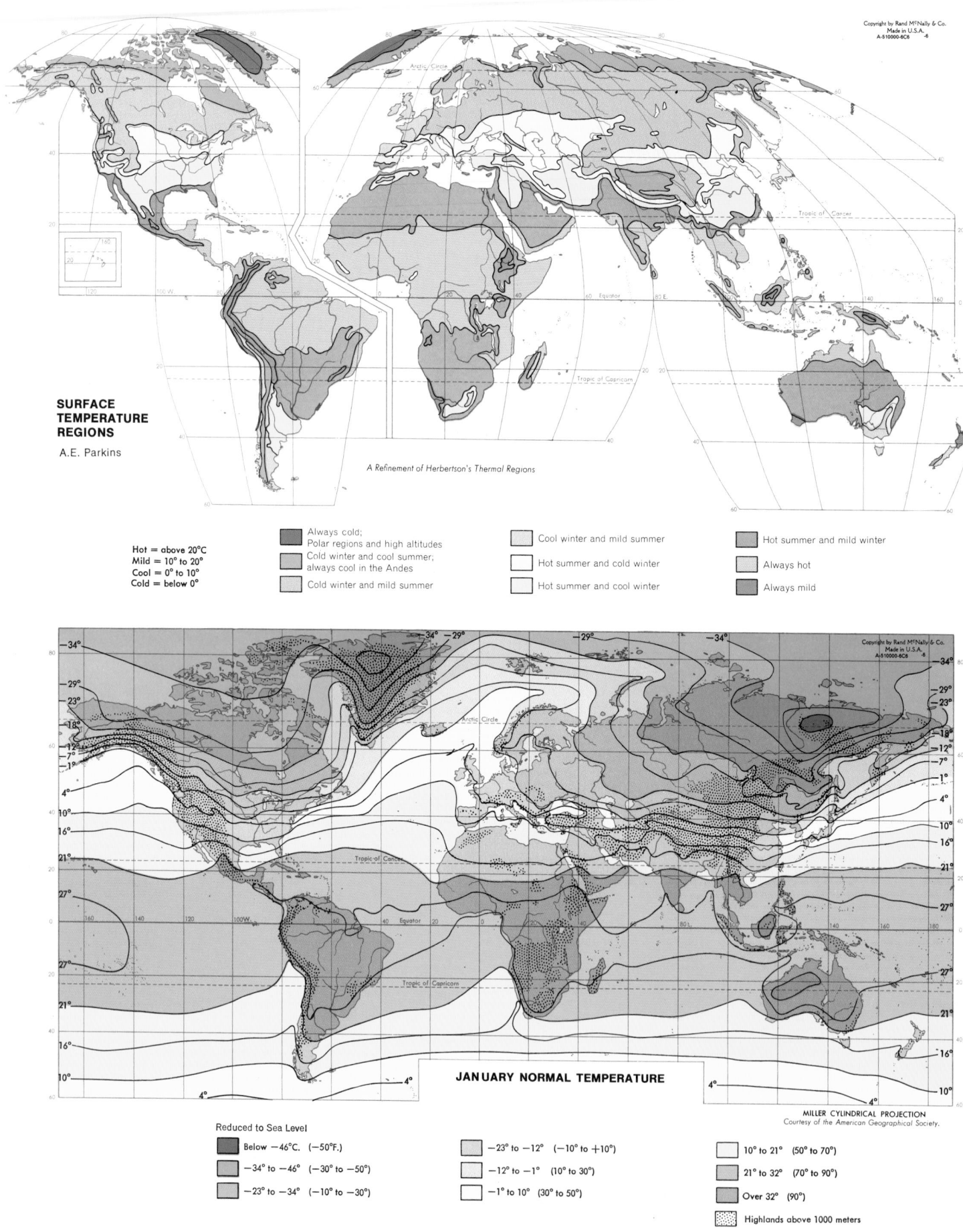

**SURFACE
TEMPERATURE
REGIONS**

A.E. Parkins

A Refinement of Herbertson's Thermal Regions

Hot = above 20°C
Mild = 10° to 20°
Cool = 0° to 10°
Cold = below 0°

Always cold;
Polar regions and high altitudes

Cold winter and cool summer;
always cool in the Andes

Cold winter and mild summer

Cool winter and mild summer

Hot summer and cold winter

Hot summer and cool winter

Hot summer and mild winter

Always hot

Always mild

JANUARY NORMAL TEMPERATURE

MILLER CYLINDRICAL PROJECTION
Courtesy of the American Geographical Society.

Reduced to Sea Level

Below −46°C. (−50°F.)

−34° to −46° (−30° to −50°)

−23° to −34° (−10° to −30°)

−23° to −12° (−10° to +10°)

−12° to −1° (10° to 30°)

−1° to 10° (30° to 50°)

10° to 21° (50° to 70°)

21° to 32° (70° to 90°)

Over 32° (90°)

Highlands above 1000 meters

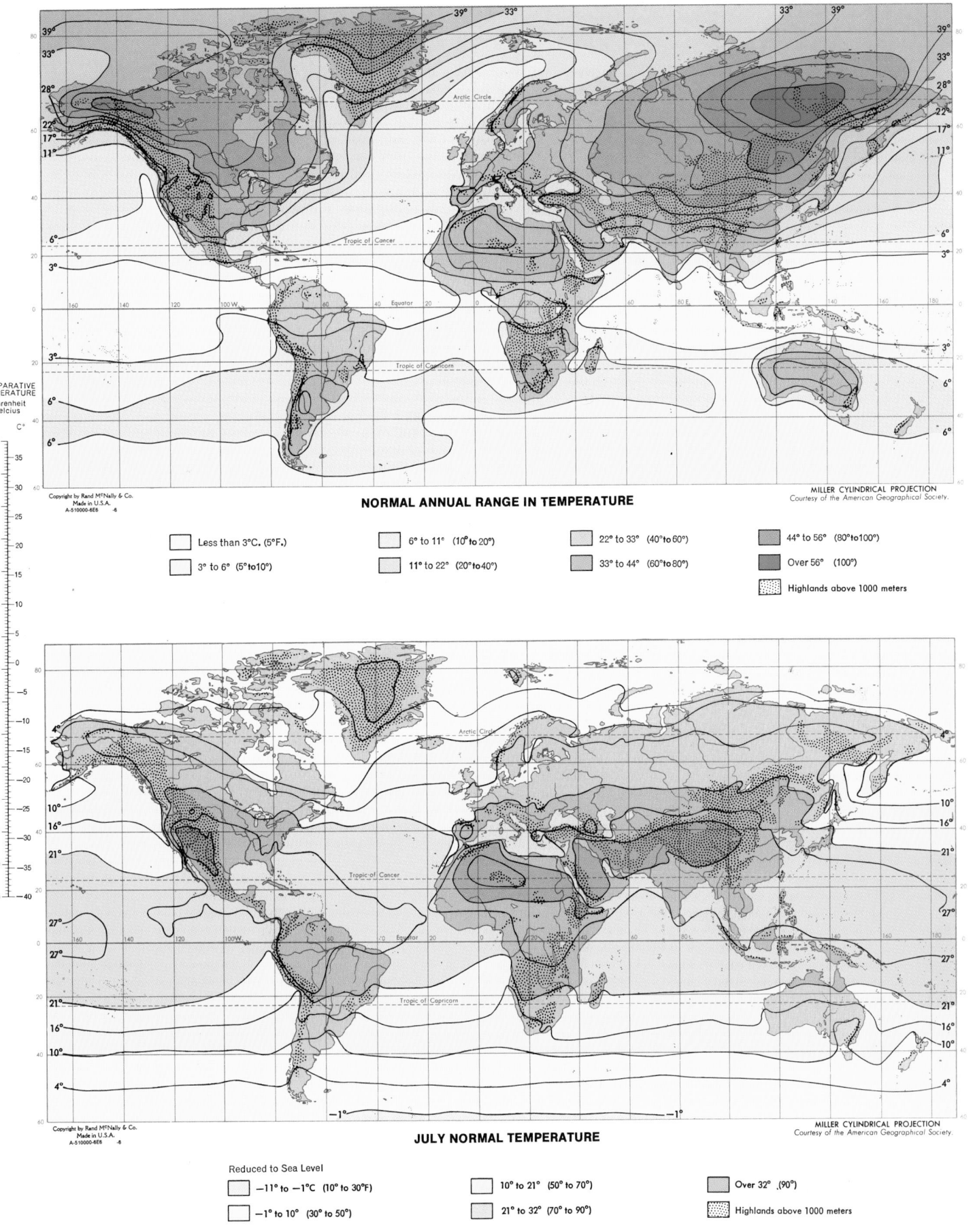

MILLER CYLINDRICAL PROJECTION
Courtesy of the American Geographical Society.

NORMAL ANNUAL RANGE IN TEMPERATURE

Less than 3°C. (5°F.)	6° to 11° (10° to 20°)	22° to 33° (40° to 60°)	44° to 56° (80° to 100°)
3° to 6° (5° to 10°)	11° to 22° (20° to 40°)	33° to 44° (60° to 80°)	Over 56° (100°)
			Highlands above 1000 meters

MILLER CYLINDRICAL PROJECTION
Courtesy of the American Geographical Society.

JULY NORMAL TEMPERATURE

Reduced to Sea Level

−11° to −1°C (10° to 30°F)	10° to 21° (50° to 70°)	Over 32° (90°)
−1° to 10° (30° to 50°)	21° to 32° (70° to 90°)	Highlands above 1000 meters

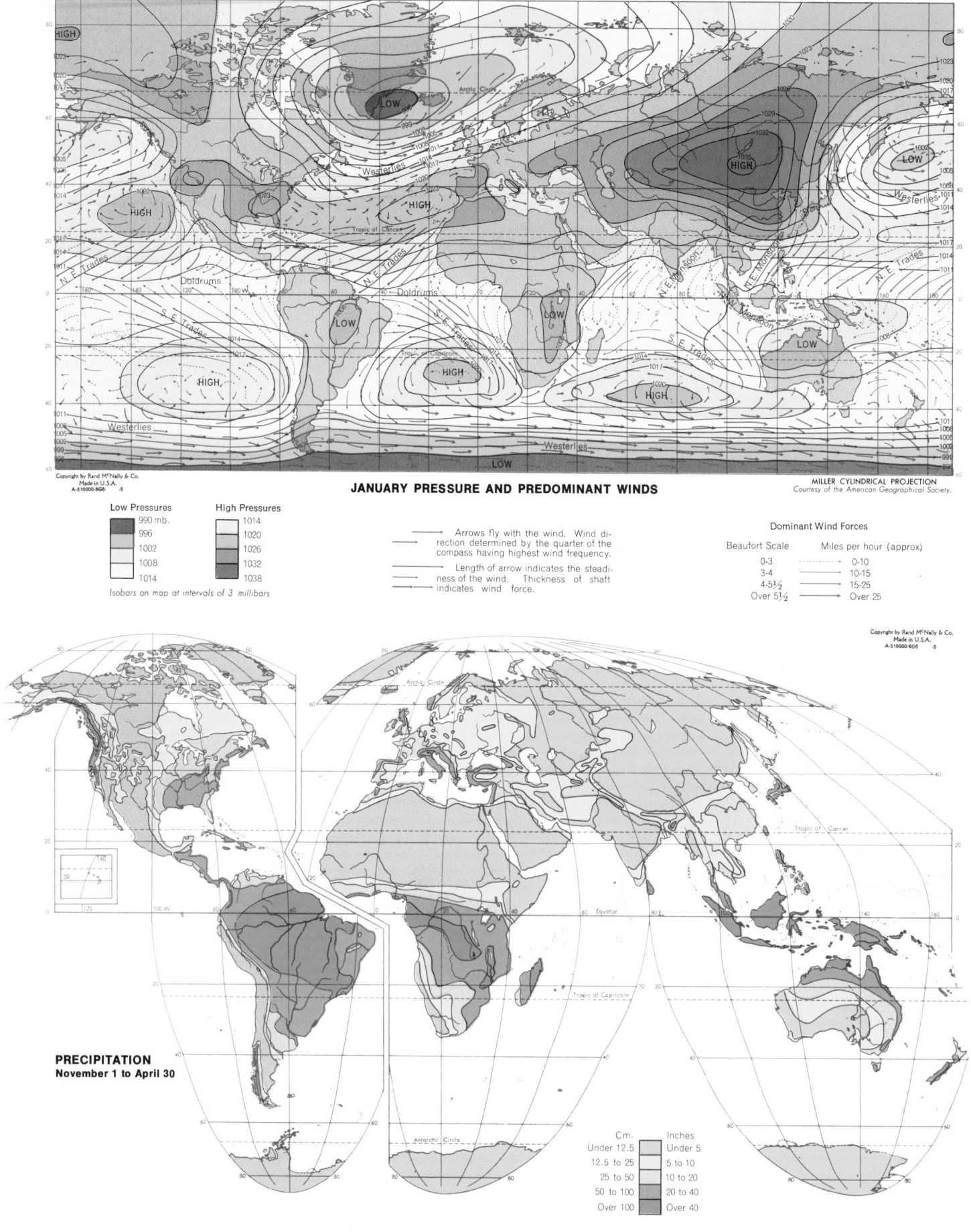

JANUARY PRESSURE AND PREDOMINANT WINDS

MILLER CYLINDRICAL PROJECTION
Courtesy of the American Geographical Society.

Low Pressures	High Pressures
990 mb.	1014
996	1020
1002	1026
1008	1032
1014	1038

Isobars on map at intervals of 3 millibars

Arrows fly with the wind. Wind direction determined by the quarter of the compass having highest wind frequency.

Length of arrow indicates the steadiness of the wind. Thickness of shaft indicates wind force.

Dominant Wind Forces

Beaufort Scale	Miles per hour (approx)
0-3	0-10
3-4	10-15
4-5½	15-25
Over 5½	Over 25

PRECIPITATION
November 1 to April 30

Cm.	Inches
Under 12.5	Under 5
12.5 to 25	5 to 10
25 to 50	10 to 20
50 to 100	20 to 40
Over 100	Over 40

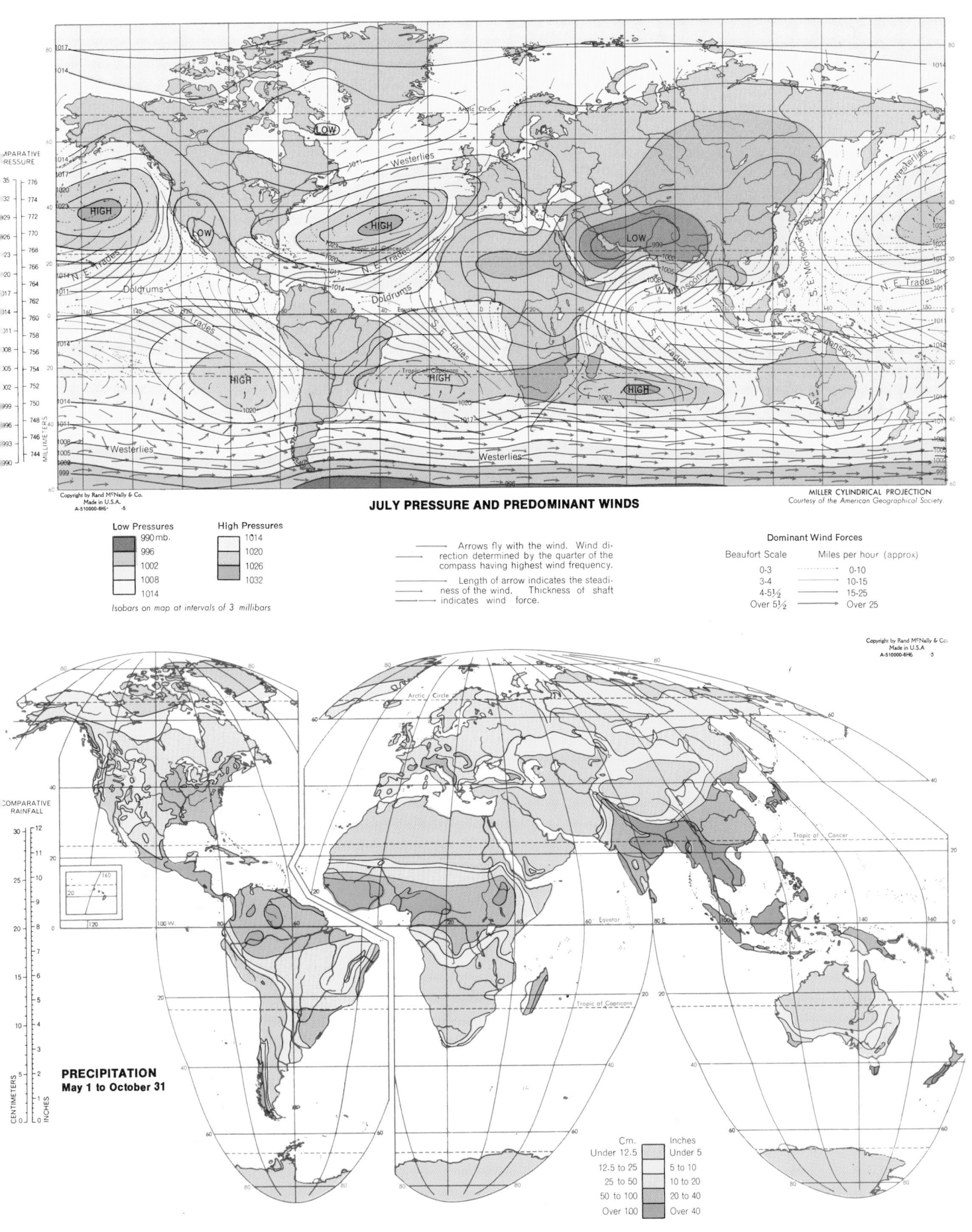

JULY PRESSURE AND PREDOMINANT WINDS

MILLER CYLINDRICAL PROJECTION
Courtesy of the American Geographical Society.

Low Pressures
990 mb.
996
1002
1008
1014

High Pressures
1014
1020
1026
1032

Isobars on map at intervals of 3 millibars

Arrows fly with the wind. Wind direction determined by the quarter of the compass having highest wind frequency.
Length of arrow indicates the steadiness of the wind. Thickness of shaft indicates wind force.

Dominant Wind Forces

Beaufort Scale	Miles per hour (approx)
0-3	0-10
3-4	10-15
4-5½	15-25
Over 5½	Over 25

PRECIPITATION
May 1 to October 31

Cm.	Inches
Under 12.5	Under 5
12.5 to 25	5 to 10
25 to 50	10 to 20
50 to 100	20 to 40
Over 100	Over 40

**ANNUAL
PRECIPITATION
AND OCEAN
CURRENTS**

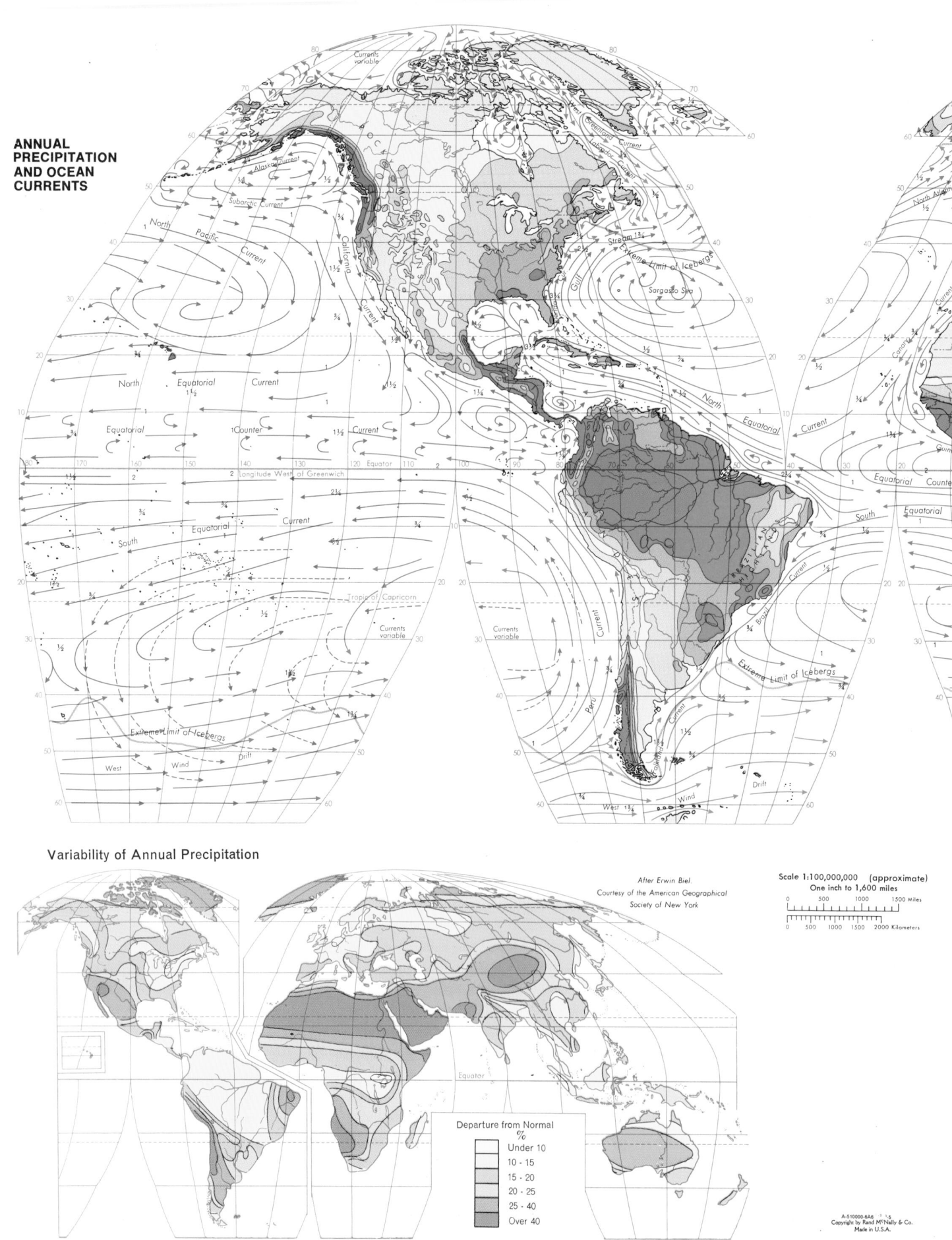

Variability of Annual Precipitation

After Erwin Biel.
Courtesy of the American Geographical
Society of New York

Scale 1:100,000,000   (approximate)
One inch to 1,600 miles

0   500   1000   1500 Miles

0   500   1000   1500   2000 Kilometers

Departure from Normal
%
Under 10
10 - 15
15 - 20
20 - 25
25 - 40
Over 40

A-510000-6A8
Copyright by Rand McNally & Co.
Made in U.S.A.

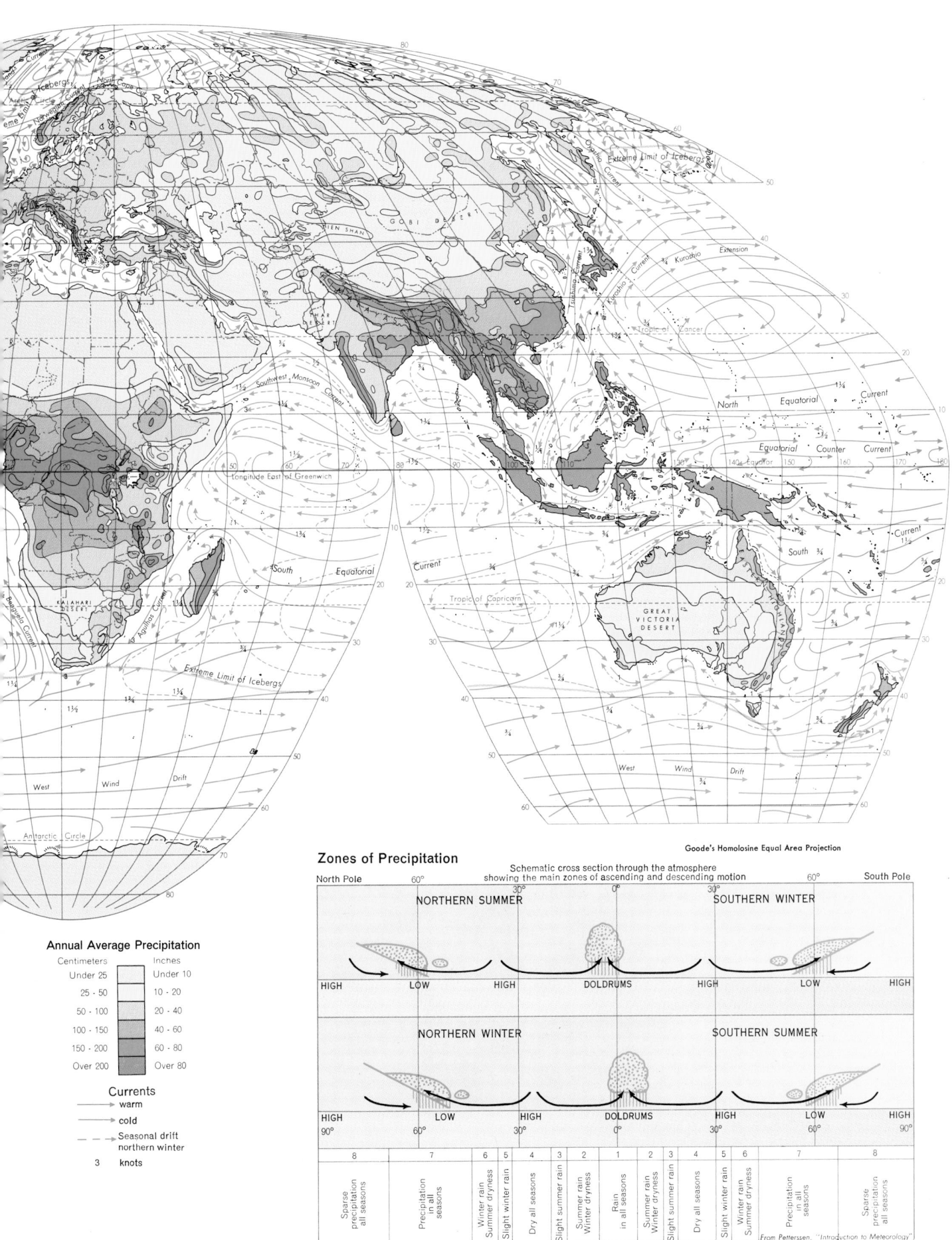

Goode's Homolosine Equal Area Projection

Zones of Precipitation

Annual Average Precipitation

Centimeters	Inches
Under 25	Under 10
25 - 50	10 - 20
50 - 100	20 - 40
100 - 150	40 - 60
150 - 200	60 - 80
Over 200	Over 80

Currents

→ warm

→ cold

- - → Seasonal drift
northern winter

3   knots

Schematic cross section through the atmosphere
showing the main zones of ascending and descending motion

North Pole   60°   30°   0°   30°   60°   South Pole

NORTHERN SUMMER   SOUTHERN WINTER

HIGH   LOW   HIGH   DOLDRUMS   HIGH   LOW   HIGH

NORTHERN WINTER   SOUTHERN SUMMER

HIGH		LOW		HIGH		DOLDRUMS		HIGH		LOW		HIGH		
90°		60°		30°		0°		30°		60°		90°		

8	7	6	5	4	3	2	1	2	3	4	5	6	7	8
Sparse precipitation all seasons	Precipitation in all seasons	Winter rain Summer dryness	Slight winter rain	Dry all seasons	Slight summer rain	Summer rain Winter dryness	Rain in all seasons	Summer rain Winter dryness	Slight summer rain	Dry all seasons	Slight winter rain	Winter rain Summer dryness	Precipitation in all seasons	Sparse precipitation all seasons

From Petterssen, "Introduction to Meteorology"

18

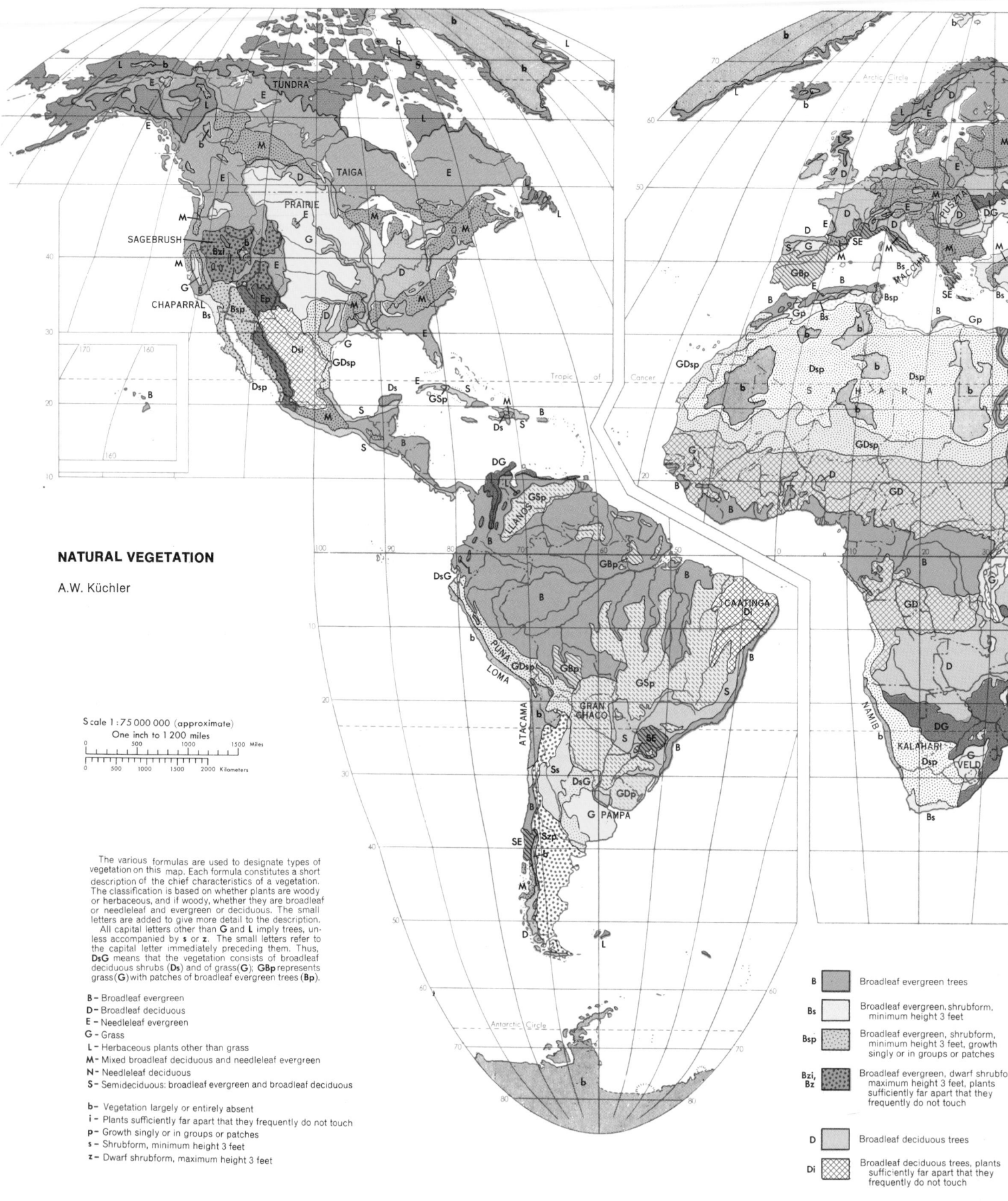

NATURAL VEGETATION

A.W. Küchler

Scale 1:75 000 000 (approximate)
One inch to 1 200 miles

0   500   1000   1500 Miles

0 500 1000 1500 2000 Kilometers

The various formulas are used to designate types of
vegetation on this map. Each formula constitutes a short
description of the chief characteristics of a vegetation.
The classification is based on whether plants are woody
or herbaceous, and if woody, whether they are broadleaf
or needleleaf and evergreen or deciduous. The small
letters are added to give more detail to the description.
All capital letters other than **G** and **L** imply trees, unless accompanied by **s** or **z**. The small letters refer to
the capital letter immediately preceding them. Thus,
DsG means that the vegetation consists of broadleaf
deciduous shrubs (**Ds**) and of grass(**G**); **GBp** represents
grass(**G**)with patches of broadleaf evergreen trees (**Bp**).

B – Broadleaf evergreen
D – Broadleaf deciduous
E – Needleleaf evergreen
G – Grass
L – Herbaceous plants other than grass
M – Mixed broadleaf deciduous and needleleaf evergreen
N – Needleleaf deciduous
S – Semideciduous: broadleaf evergreen and broadleaf deciduous

b – Vegetation largely or entirely absent
i – Plants sufficiently far apart that they frequently do not touch
p – Growth singly or in groups or patches
s – Shrubform, minimum height 3 feet
z – Dwarf shrubform, maximum height 3 feet

B	Broadleaf evergreen trees
Bs	Broadleaf evergreen, shrubform, minimum height 3 feet
Bsp	Broadleaf evergreen, shrubform, minimum height 3 feet, growth singly or in groups or patches
Bzi, Bz	Needleleaf evergreen, dwarf shrubform maximum height 3 feet, plants sufficiently far apart that they frequently do not touch
D	Broadleaf deciduous trees
Di	Broadleaf deciduous trees, plants sufficiently far apart that they frequently do not touch

TUNDRA

TAIGA

GOBI

TAKLA MAKAN

TERAI

MALLEE

Tropic of Cancer

Equator

Tropic of Capricorn

Longitude East of Greenwich

Goode's Homolosine
Equal Area Projection
(Condensed)

	Broadleaf deciduous, shrubform, minimum height 3 feet
	Broadleaf deciduous, shrubform, minimum height 3 feet, plants sufficiently far apart that they frequently do not touch
	Broadleaf deciduous, shrubform, minimum height 3 feet, growth singly or in groups or patches
	Broadleaf deciduous, dwarf shrubform, maximum height 3 feet, growth singly or in groups or patches
	Broadleaf deciduous, shrubform, minimum height 3 feet / Grass and other herbaceous plants
	Broadleaf deciduous trees / Grass and other herbaceous plants
	Broadleaf deciduous trees / Broadleaf evergreen, shrubform, minimum height 3 feet

E		Needleleaf evergreen trees
Ep		Needleleaf evergreen trees, growth singly or in groups or patches
G		Grass and other herbaceous plants
Gp		Grass and other herbaceous plants, growth singly or in groups or patches
GBp		Grass and other herbaceous plants / Broadleaf evergreen trees, growth singly or in groups or patches
GD		Grass and other herbaceous plants / Broadleaf deciduous trees
GDp		Grass and other herbaceous plants / Broadleaf deciduous trees, growth singly or in groups or patches

GDsp		Grass and other herbaceous plants / Broadleaf deciduous, shrubform, minimum height 3 feet, growth singly or in groups or patches
GSp		Grass and other herbaceous plants / Semideciduous: broadleaf evergreen and broadleaf deciduous trees, growth singly or in groups or patches
L		Herbaceous plants other than grass
M		Mixed: broadleaf deciduous and needleleaf evergreen trees
N		Needleleaf deciduous trees
ND		Needleleaf deciduous trees / Broadleaf deciduous trees

S		Semideciduous: broadleaf evergreen and broadleaf deciduous trees
Ss		Semideciduous: broadleaf evergreen and broadleaf deciduous, shrubform, minimum height 3 feet
SsG		Semideciduous: broadleaf evergreen and broadleaf deciduous, shrubform, minimum height 3 feet / Grass and other herbaceous plants
Szp		Semideciduous: broadleaf evergreen and broadleaf deciduous, dwarf shrubform, maximum height 3 feet, growth singly or in groups or patches
SE		Semideciduous: broadleaf evergreen and broadleaf deciduous trees / Needleleaf evergreen trees
b		Vegetation largely or entirely absent

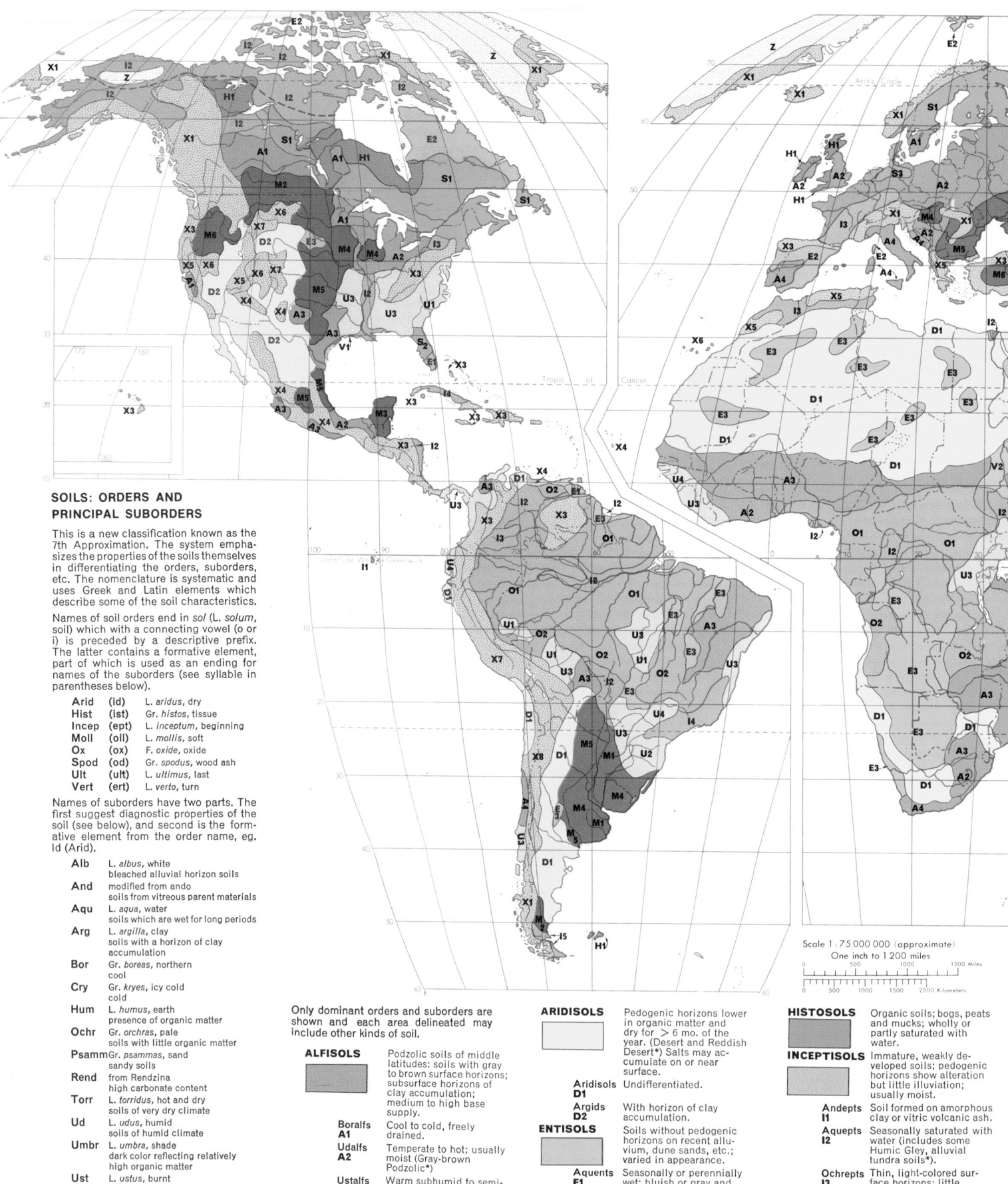

SOILS: ORDERS AND PRINCIPAL SUBORDERS

This is a new classification known as the 7th Approximation. The system emphasizes the properties of the soils themselves in differentiating the orders, suborders, etc. The nomenclature is systematic and uses Greek and Latin elements which describe some of the soil characteristics.

Names of soil orders end in *sol* (L. *solum*, soil) which with a connecting vowel (o or i) is preceded by a descriptive prefix. The latter contains a formative element, part of which is used as an ending for names of the suborders (see syllable in parentheses below).

Arid	(id)	L. *aridus*, dry
Hist	(ist)	Gr. *histos*, tissue
Incep	(ept)	L. *inceptum*, beginning
Moll	(oll)	L. *mollis*, soft
Ox	(ox)	F. *oxide*, oxide
Spod	(od)	Gr. *spodus*, wood ash
Ult	(ult)	L. *ultimus*, last
Vert	(ert)	L. *verto*, turn

Names of suborders have two parts. The first suggest diagnostic properties of the soil (see below), and second is the formative element from the order name, eg. Id (Arid).

Alb	L. *albus*, white bleached alluvial horizon soils
And	modified from ando soils from vitreous parent materials
Aqu	L. *aqua*, water soils which are wet for long periods
Arg	L. *argilla*, clay soils with a horizon of clay accumulation
Bor	Gr. *boreas*, northern cool
Cry	Gr. *kryes*, icy cold cold
Hum	L. *humus*, earth presence of organic matter
Ochr	Gr. *orchras*, pale soils with little organic matter
Psamm	Gr. *psammas*, sand sandy soils
Rend	from Rendzina high carbonate content
Torr	L. *torridus*, hot and dry soils of very dry climate
Ud	L. *udus*, humid soils of humid climate
Umbr	L. *umbra*, shade dark color reflecting relatively high organic matter
Ust	L. *ustus*, burnt soils of dry climates with summer rains
Xer	Gr. *xeros*, dry soils of dry climates with winter rains

Only dominant orders and suborders are shown and each area delineated may include other kinds of soil.

ALFISOLS

Podzolic soils of middle latitudes: soils with gray to brown surface horizons; subsurface horizons of clay accumulation; medium to high base supply.

Boralfs **A1**	Cool to cold, freely drained.
Udalfs **A2**	Temperate to hot; usually moist (Gray-brown Podzolic*)
Ustalfs **A3**	Warm subhumid to semi-arid; dry > 90 days (some Reddish Chestnut and Red & Yellow Podzolic soils*)
Xeralfs **A4**	Warm, dry in summer; moist in winter.

ARIDISOLS

Pedogenic horizons lower in organic matter and dry for > 6 mo. of the year. (Desert and Reddish Desert*) Salts may accumulate on or near surface.

Aridisols **D1**	Undifferentiated.
Argids **D2**	With horizon of clay accumulation.

ENTISOLS

Soils without pedogenic horizons on recent alluvium, dune sands, etc.; varied in appearance.

Aquents **E1**	Seasonally or perennially wet; bluish or gray and mottled.
Orthents **E2**	Shallow; or recent erosional surfaces (Lithosols*). A few on recent loams.
Psamments **E3**	Sandy soils on shifting and stabilized sands.

HISTOSOLS

Organic soils; bogs, peats and mucks; wholly or partly saturated with water.

INCEPTISOLS

Immature, weakly developed soils; pedogenic horizons show alteration but little illuviation; usually moist.

Andepts **I1**	Soil formed on amorphous clay or vitric volcanic ash.
Aquepts **I2**	Seasonally saturated with water (includes some Humic Gley, alluvial tundra soils*).
Ochrepts **I3**	Thin, light-colored surface horizons; little organic matter.
Tropepts **I4**	Continuously warm to hot; brownish to reddish.
Umbrepts **I5**	Dark colored surface horizons; rich in organic matter; medium to low base supply.

Scale 1:75 000 000 (approximate)
One inch to 1 200 miles

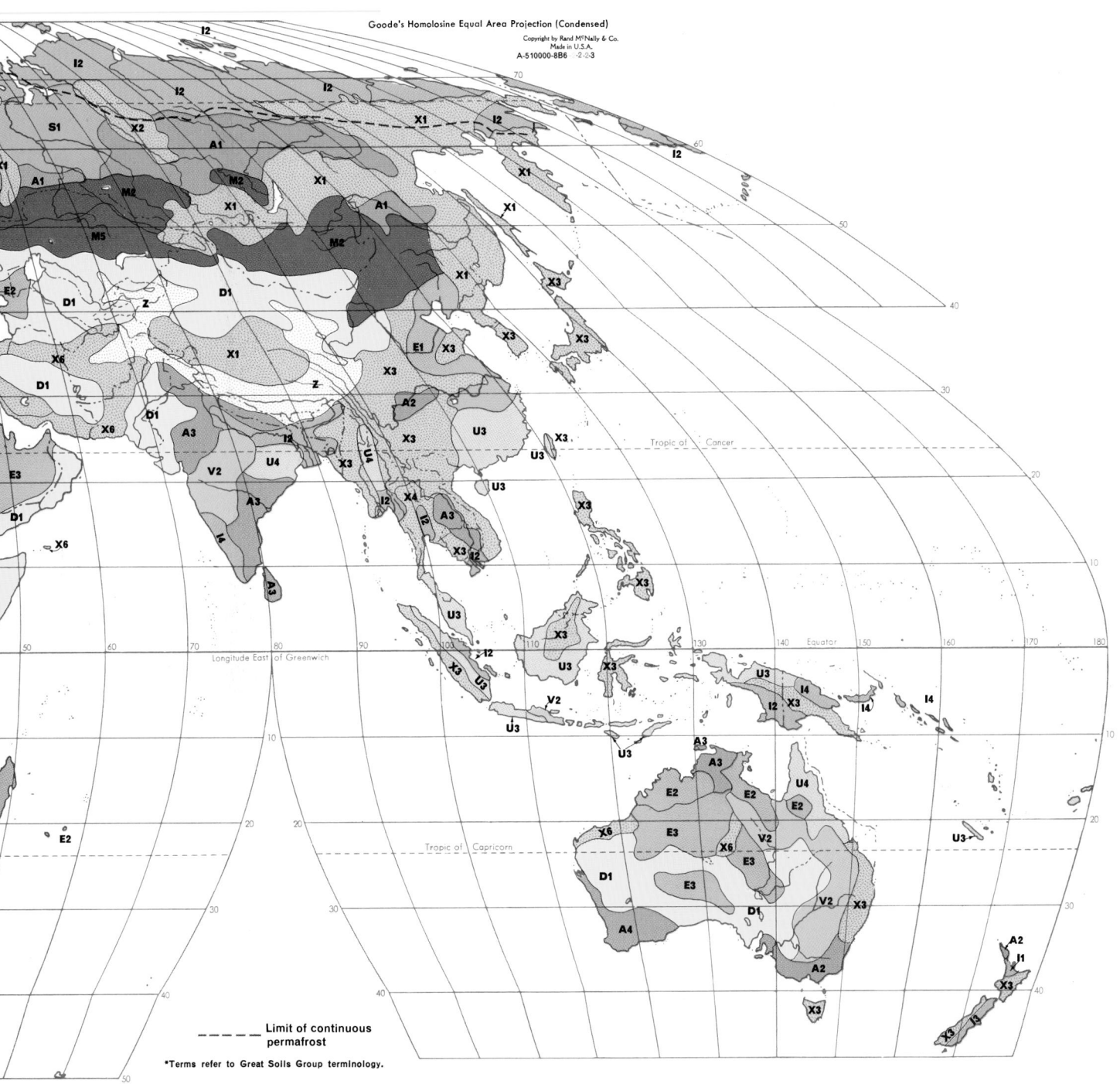

Goode's Homolosine Equal Area Projection (Condensed)
Copyright by Rand McNally & Co.
Made in U.S.A.
A-510000-8B6 -2-4-3

- - - - - Limit of continuous
permafrost

*Terms refer to Great Soils Group terminology.

MOLLISOLS	Soils of the steppe (incl. Chernozem and Chestnut soils*). Thick, black organic rich surface horizons and high base supply.
Albolls **M1**	Seasonally saturated with water; light gray subsurface horizon.
Borolls **M2**	Cool or cold (incl. some Chernozem, Chestnut and Brown soils*).
Rendolls **M3**	Formed on highly calcareous parent materials (Rendzina*).
Udolls **M4**	Temperate to warm; usually moist (Prairie soils*).
Ustolls **M5**	Temperate to hot; dry for > 90 days (incl. some Chestnut and Brown soils*).
Xerolls **M6**	Cool to warm; dry in summer; moist in winter.

OXISOLS	Deeply weathered tropical and subtropical soils (Laterites*); rich in sesquioxides of iron and aluminum; low in nutrients; limited productivity without fertilizer.
Orthox **O1**	Hot and nearly always moist.
Ustox **O2**	Warm or hot; dry for long periods but moist > 90 consecutive days.

SPODOSOLS	Soils with a subsurface accumulation of amorphous materials overlaid by a light colored, leached sandy horizon.
Spodosols **S1**	Undifferentiated (mostly high latitudes).
Aquods **S2**	Seasonally saturated with water; sandy parent materials.
Humods **S3**	Considerable accumulations of organic matter in subsurface horizon.
Orthods **S4**	With subsurface accumulations of iron, aluminum and organic matter (Podzols*).

ULTISOLS	Soils with some subsurface clay accumulation; low base supply; usually moist and low inorganic matter and low in organic matter; can be productive with fertilization.
Aquults **U1**	Seasonally saturated with water; subsurface gray or mottled horizon.
Humults **U2**	High in organic matter; dark colored; moist, warm to temperate all year.
Udults **U3**	Low in organic matter; moist, temperate to hot (Red-Yellow Podzolic; some Reddish-Brown Lateritic soils*).
Ustults **U4**	Warm to hot; dry > 90 days.

VERTISOLS	Soils with high content of swelling clays; deep, wide cracks in dry periods dark colored.
Uderts **V1**	Usually moist; cracks open < 90 days.
Usterts **V2**	Cracks open > 90 days; difficult to till (Black tropical soils*).

MOUNTAIN SOILS	Soils with various moisture and temperature regimes; steep slopes and variable relief and elevation; soils vary greatly within short distance.
X1	Cryic great groups of Entisols, Inceptisols and Spodosols.
X2	Boralfs and Cryic groups of Entisols and Inceptisols.
X3	Udic great groups of Alfisols, Entisols and Ultisols; Inceptisols.
X4	Ustic great groups of Alfisols, Entisols, Inceptisols, Mollisols and Ultisols.
X5	Xeric great groups of Alfisols, Entisols, Inceptisols, Mollisols and Ultisols.
X6	Torric great groups of Entisols; Aridisols.
X7	Ustic and cryic great groups of Alfisols, Entisols; Inceptisols and Mollisols; ustic great groups of Ultisols; cryic great groups of Spodosols.
X8	Aridisols; torric and cryic great groups of Entisols, and cryic great groups of Spodosols and Inceptisols.

| **Z** | Areas with little or no soil; icefields, and rugged mountain. |

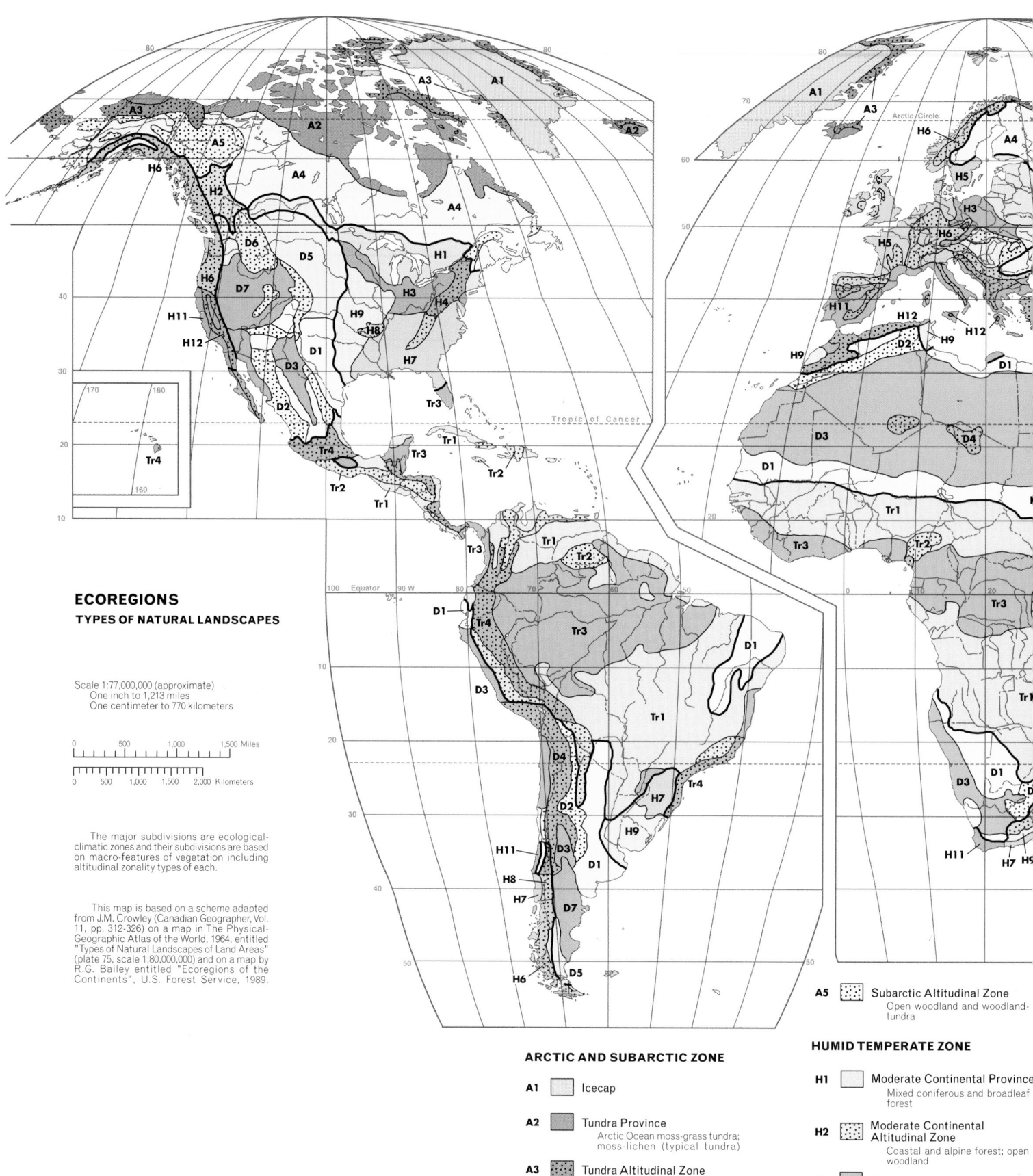

ECOREGIONS

TYPES OF NATURAL LANDSCAPES

Scale 1:77,000,000 (approximate)
One inch to 1,213 miles
One centimeter to 770 kilometers

0   500   1,000   1,500 Miles

0   500   1,000   1,500   2,000 Kilometers

The major subdivisions are ecological-climatic zones and their subdivisions are based on macro-features of vegetation including altitudinal zonality types of each.

This map is based on a scheme adapted from J.M. Crowley (Canadian Geographer, Vol. 11, pp. 312-326) on a map in The Physical-Geographic Atlas of the World, 1964, entitled "Types of Natural Landscapes of Land Areas" (plate 75, scale 1:80,000,000) and on a map by R.G. Bailey entitled "Ecoregions of the Continents", U.S. Forest Service, 1989.

A5 Subarctic Altitudinal Zone
Open woodland and woodland-tundra

ARCTIC AND SUBARCTIC ZONE

A1 Icecap

A2 Tundra Province
Arctic Ocean moss-grass tundra; moss-lichen (typical tundra)

A3 Tundra Altitudinal Zone
Polar desert

A4 Subarctic Province
Dark evergreen forest; needleleaf taiga; mixed coniferous and small-leafed forest

HUMID TEMPERATE ZONE

H1 Moderate Continental Province
Mixed coniferous and broadleaf forest

H2 Moderate Continental Altitudinal Zone
Coastal and alpine forest; open woodland

H3 Warm Continental Province
Broadleaf deciduous forest

H4 Warm Continental Altitudinal Zone
Upland broadleaf and alpine needleleaf forest

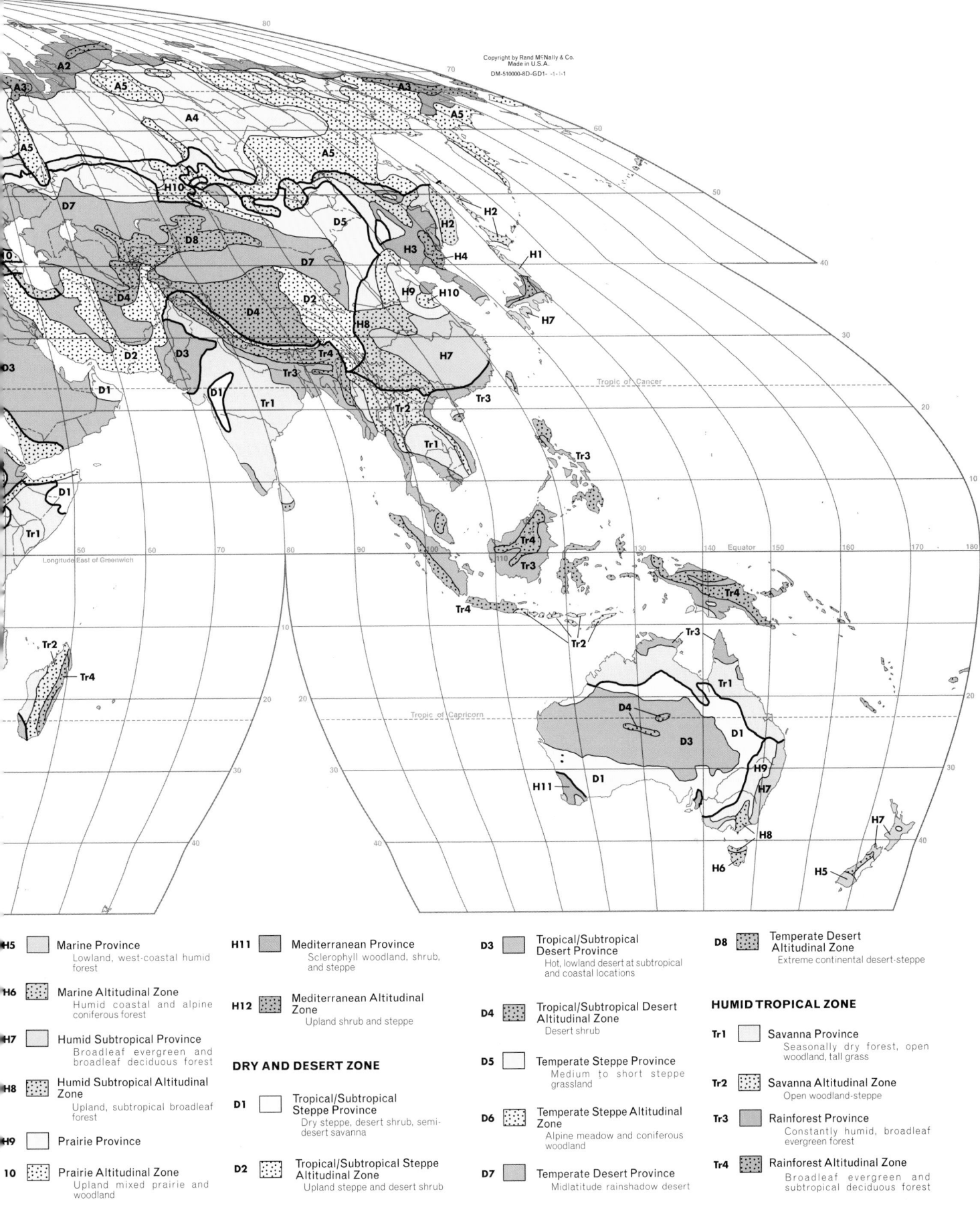

Copyright by Rand McNally & Co.
Made in U.S.A.
DM-510000-8D-GD1- -1-1-1

H5	Marine Province	Lowland, west-coastal humid forest
H6	Marine Altitudinal Zone	Humid coastal and alpine coniferous forest
H7	Humid Subtropical Province	Broadleaf evergreen and broadleaf deciduous forest
H8	Humid Subtropical Altitudinal Zone	Upland, subtropical broadleaf forest
H9	Prairie Province	
10	Prairie Altitudinal Zone	Upland mixed prairie and woodland

H11	Mediterranean Province	Sclerophyll woodland, shrub, and steppe
H12	Mediterranean Altitudinal Zone	Upland shrub and steppe

DRY AND DESERT ZONE

D1	Tropical/Subtropical Steppe Province	Dry steppe, desert shrub, semi-desert savanna
D2	Tropical/Subtropical Steppe Altitudinal Zone	Upland steppe and desert shrub

D3	Tropical/Subtropical Desert Province	Hot, lowland desert at subtropical and coastal locations
D4	Tropical/Subtropical Desert Altitudinal Zone	Desert shrub
D5	Temperate Steppe Province	Medium to short steppe grassland
D6	Temperate Steppe Altitudinal Zone	Alpine meadow and coniferous woodland
D7	Temperate Desert Province	Midlatitude rainshadow desert

D8	Temperate Desert Altitudinal Zone	Extreme continental desert-steppe

HUMID TROPICAL ZONE

Tr1	Savanna Province	Seasonally dry forest, open woodland, tall grass
Tr2	Savanna Altitudinal Zone	Open woodland-steppe
Tr3	Rainforest Province	Constantly humid, broadleaf evergreen forest
Tr4	Rainforest Altitudinal Zone	Broadleaf evergreen and subtropical deciduous forest

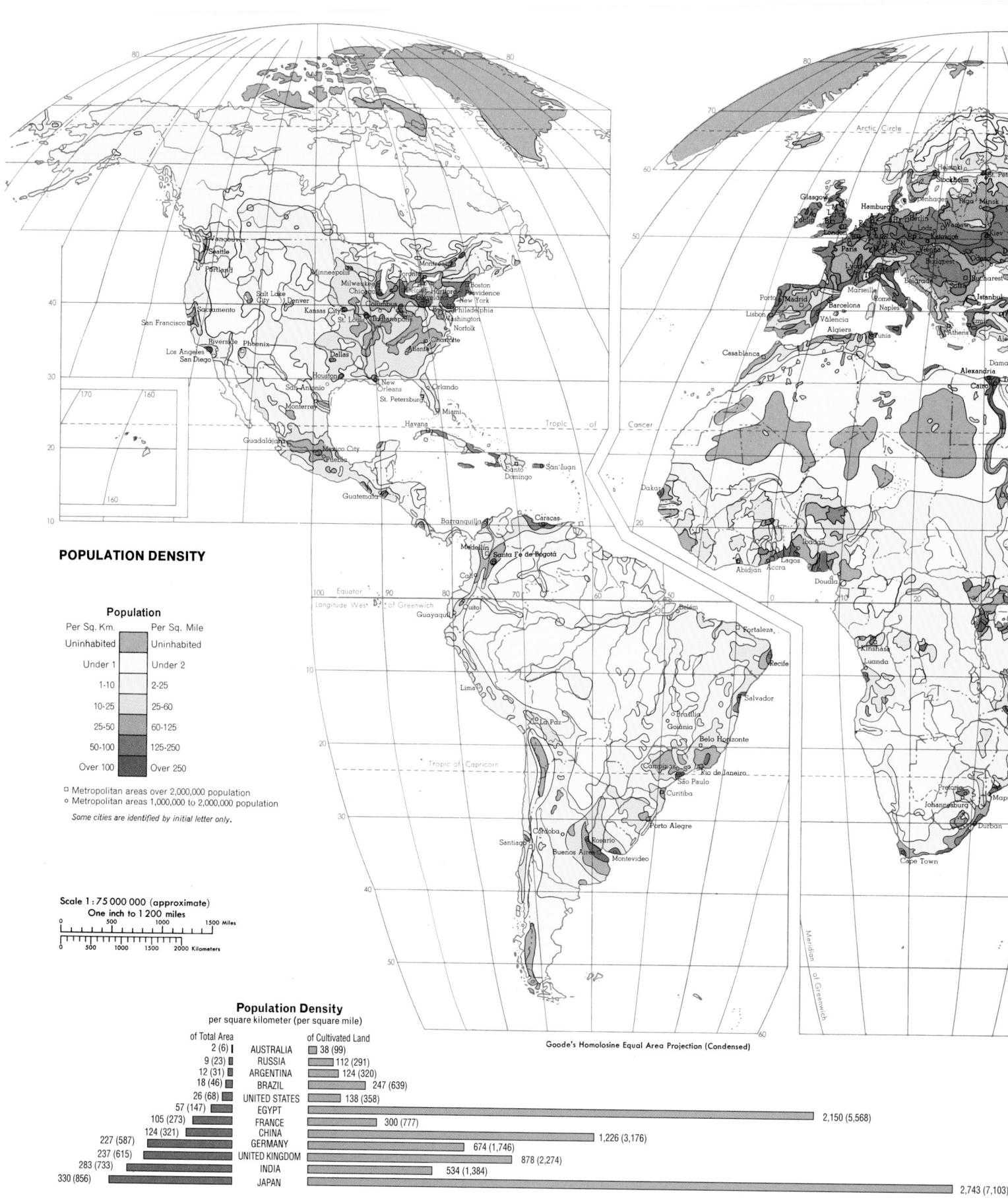

POPULATION DENSITY

Population

Per Sq. Km.	Per Sq. Mile
Uninhabited	Uninhabited
Under 1	Under 2
1-10	2-25
10-25	25-60
25-50	60-125
50-100	125-250
Over 100	Over 250

□ Metropolitan areas over 2,000,000 population
○ Metropolitan areas 1,000,000 to 2,000,000 population

Some cities are identified by initial letter only.

Scale 1 : 75 000 000 (approximate)
One inch to 1 200 miles

Goode's Homolosine Equal Area Projection (Condensed)

Population Density
per square kilometer (per square mile)

	of Total Area		of Cultivated Land
AUSTRALIA	2 (6)		38 (99)
RUSSIA	9 (23)		112 (291)
ARGENTINA	12 (31)		124 (320)
BRAZIL	18 (46)		247 (639)
UNITED STATES	26 (68)		138 (358)
EGYPT	57 (147)		2,150 (5,568)
FRANCE	105 (273)		300 (777)
CHINA	124 (321)		1,226 (3,176)
GERMANY	227 (587)		674 (1,746)
UNITED KINGDOM	237 (615)		878 (2,274)
INDIA	283 (733)		534 (1,384)
JAPAN	330 (856)		2,743 (7,103)

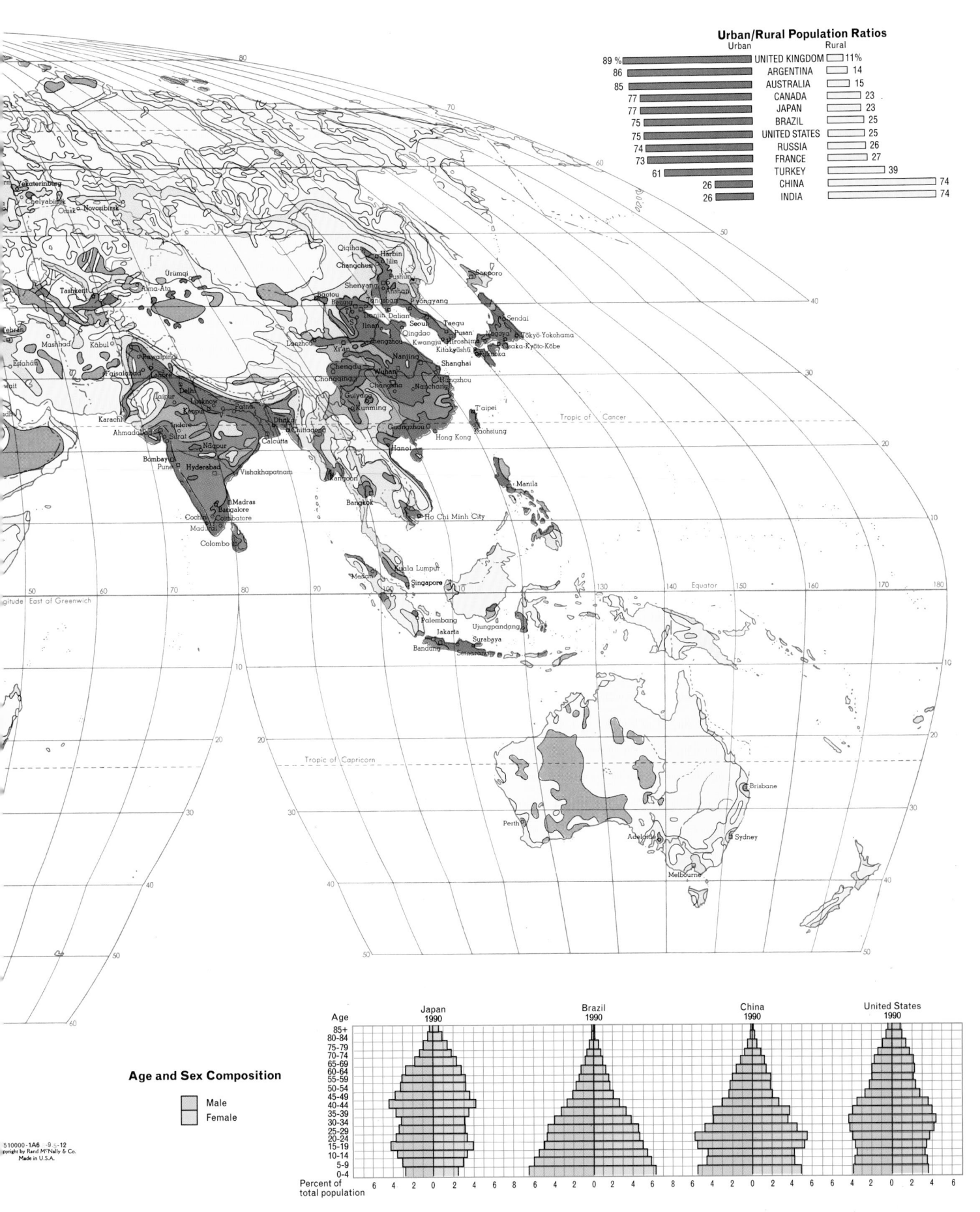

Urban/Rural Population Ratios

	Urban		Rural
UNITED KINGDOM	89 %		11%
ARGENTINA	86		14
AUSTRALIA	85		15
CANADA	77		23
JAPAN	77		23
BRAZIL	75		25
UNITED STATES	75		25
RUSSIA	74		26
FRANCE	73		27
TURKEY	61		39
CHINA	26		74
INDIA	26		74

Age and Sex Composition

Male
Female

Age
85+ 80-84 75-79 70-74 65-69 60-64 55-59 50-54 45-49 40-44 35-39 30-34 25-29 20-24 15-19 10-14 5-9 0-4

Japan 1990 · Brazil 1990 · China 1990 · United States 1990

Percent of total population

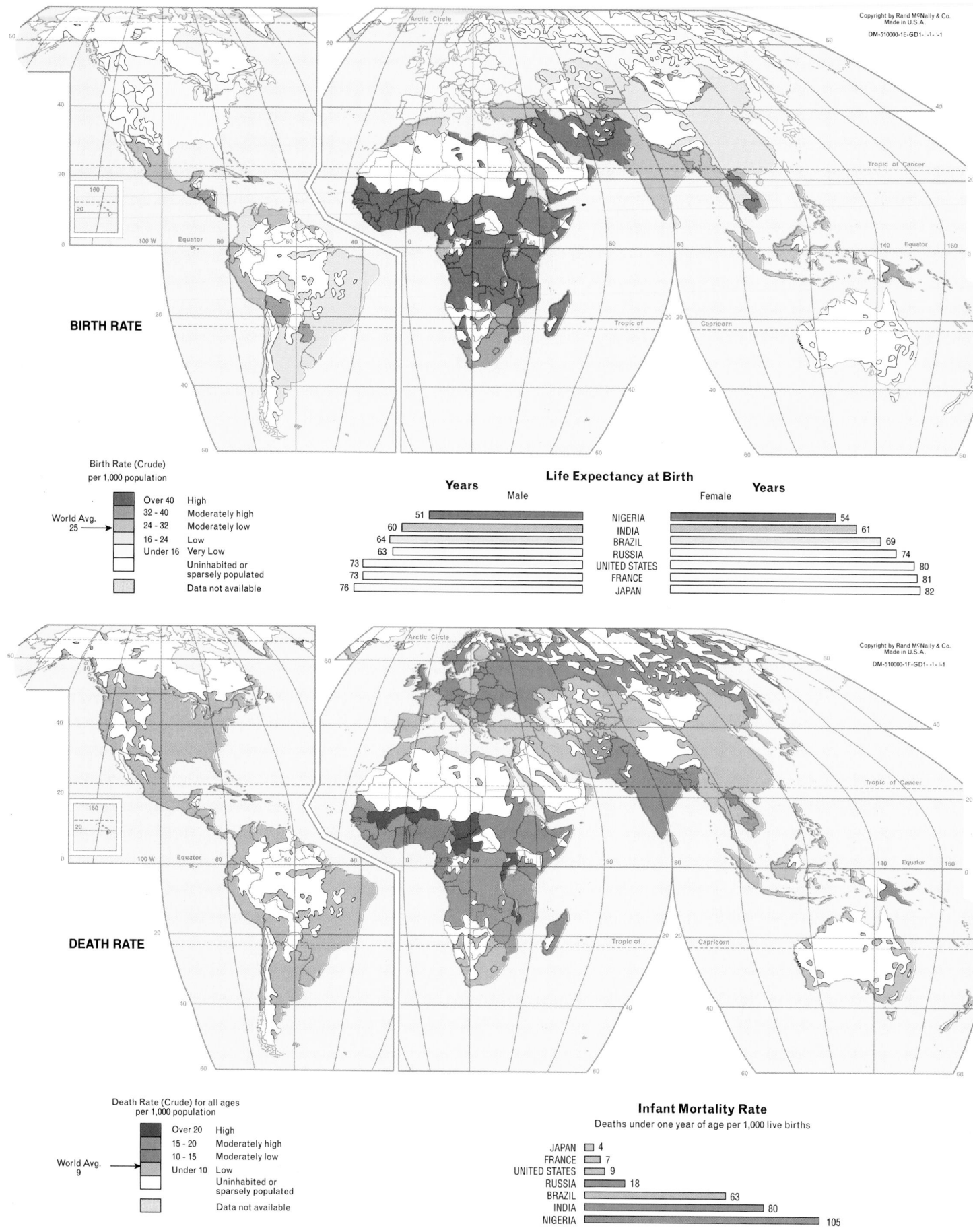

BIRTH RATE

Birth Rate (Crude)
per 1,000 population

	Over 40	High
	32 - 40	Moderately high
	24 - 32	Moderately low
	16 - 24	Low
	Under 16	Very Low
		Uninhabited or sparsely populated
		Data not available

World Avg.
25 →

Life Expectancy at Birth

Years				Years
	Male		Female	
51		NIGERIA		54
60		INDIA		61
64		BRAZIL		69
63		RUSSIA		74
73		UNITED STATES		80
73		FRANCE		81
76		JAPAN		82

DEATH RATE

Death Rate (Crude) for all ages
per 1,000 population

	Over 20	High
	15 - 20	Moderately high
	10 - 15	Moderately low
	Under 10	Low
		Uninhabited or sparsely populated
		Data not available

World Avg.
9 →

Infant Mortality Rate

Deaths under one year of age per 1,000 live births

JAPAN	4
FRANCE	7
UNITED STATES	9
RUSSIA	18
BRAZIL	63
INDIA	80
NIGERIA	105

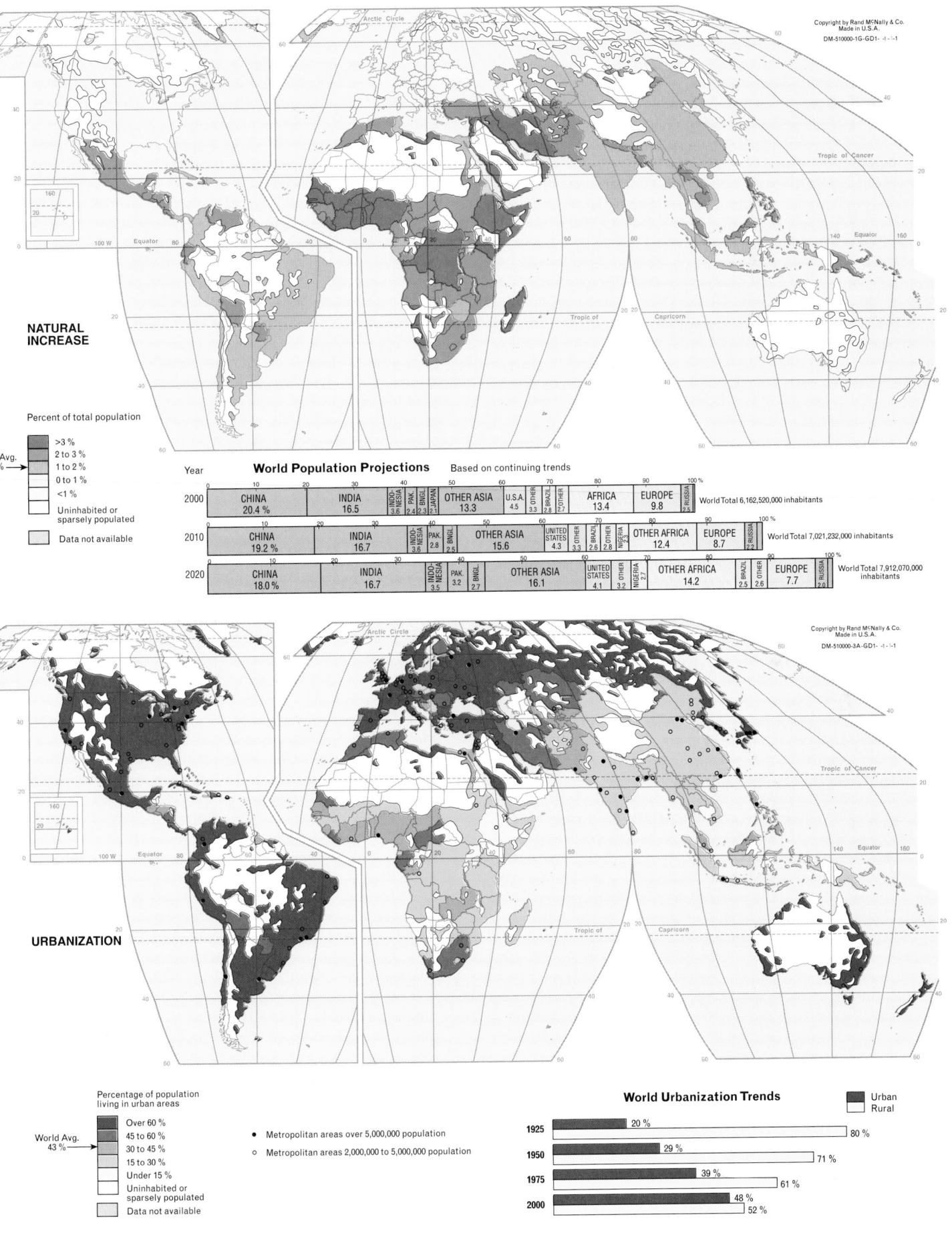

NATURAL INCREASE

Percent of total population

Avg. % →
- >3 %
- 2 to 3 %
- 1 to 2 %
- 0 to 1 %
- <1 %
- Uninhabited or sparsely populated
- Data not available

World Population Projections   Based on continuing trends

Year															
2000	CHINA 20.4 %	INDIA 16.5	INDO-NESIA 3.6	PAK. 2.4	BNGL. 2	JAPAN 1	OTHER ASIA 13.3	U.S.A. 4.5	OTHER 3.3	BRAZIL 2.7	AFRICA 13.4	EUROPE 9.8	RUSSIA 2.5	World Total 6,162,520,000 inhabitants	
2010	CHINA 19.2 %	INDIA 16.7	INDO-NESIA 3.6	PAK. 2.8	BNGL. 2.5	OTHER ASIA 15.6	UNITED STATES 4.3	OTHER 3.3	BRAZIL 2.6	NIGERIA 2.3	OTHER AFRICA 12.4	EUROPE 8.7	RUSSIA 2.2	World Total 7,021,232,000 inhabitants	
2020	CHINA 18.0 %	INDIA 16.7	INDO-NESIA 3.5	PAK. 3.2	BNGL. 2.7	OTHER ASIA 16.1	UNITED STATES 4.1	OTHER 3.2	NIGERIA 2.7	OTHER AFRICA 14.2	BRAZIL 2.5	OTHER 2.6	EUROPE 7.7	RUSSIA 2.0	World Total 7,912,070,000 inhabitants

URBANIZATION

Percentage of population living in urban areas

World Avg. 43 % →
- Over 60 %
- 45 to 60 %
- 30 to 45 %
- 15 to 30 %
- Under 15 %
- Uninhabited or sparsely populated
- Data not available

● Metropolitan areas over 5,000,000 population
○ Metropolitan areas 2,000,000 to 5,000,000 population

World Urbanization Trends   ■ Urban □ Rural

Year	Urban	Rural
1925	20 %	80 %
1950	29 %	71 %
1975	39 %	61 %
2000	48 %	52 %

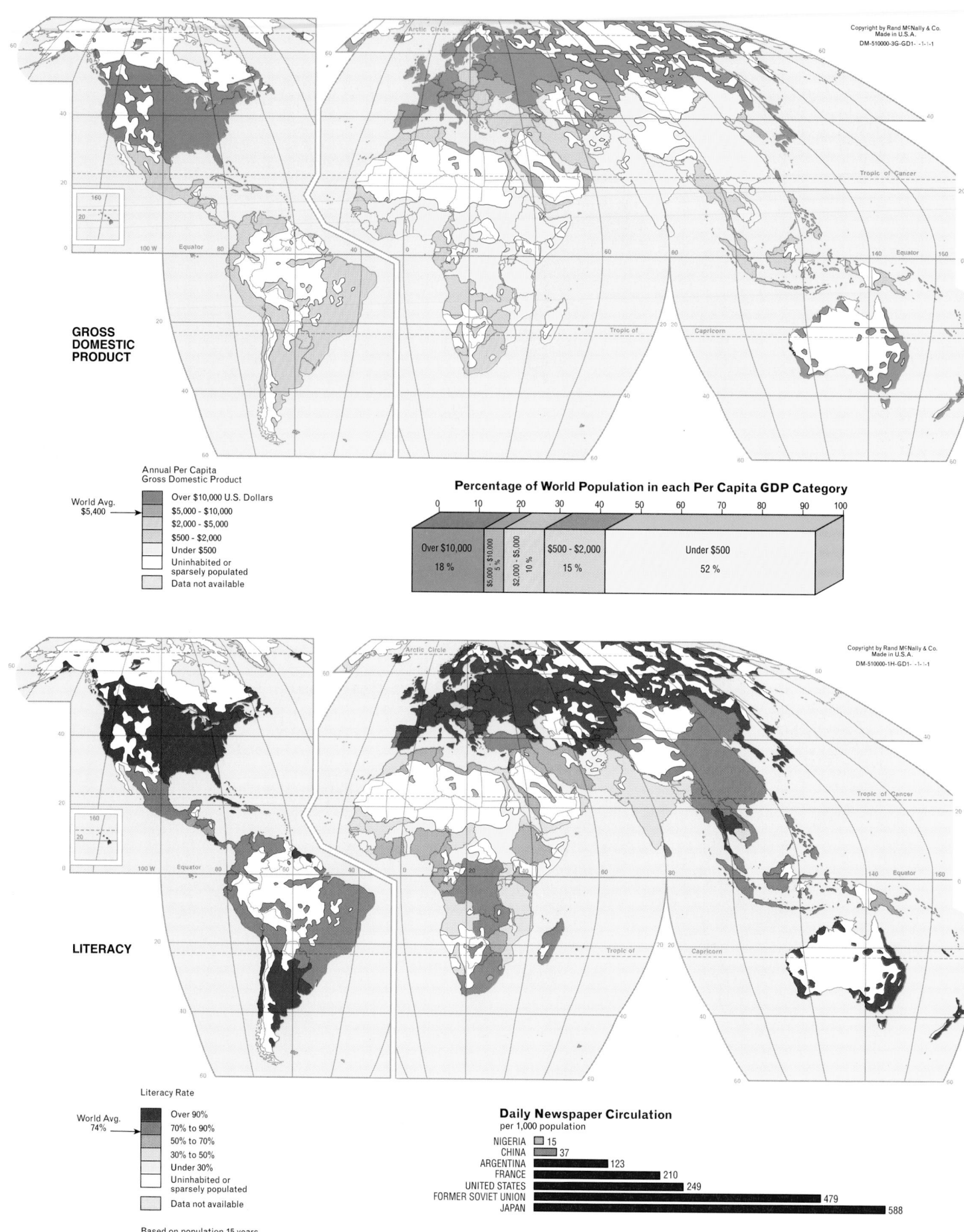

GROSS DOMESTIC PRODUCT

Annual Per Capita
Gross Domestic Product

World Avg. $5,400

- Over $10,000 U.S. Dollars
- $5,000 - $10,000
- $2,000 - $5,000
- $500 - $2,000
- Under $500
- Uninhabited or sparsely populated
- Data not available

Percentage of World Population in each Per Capita GDP Category

Over $10,000 18 %	$5,000 - $10,000 5 %	$2,000 - $5,000 10 %	$500 - $2,000 15 %	Under $500 52 %

LITERACY

Literacy Rate

World Avg. 74%

- Over 90%
- 70% to 90%
- 50% to 70%
- 30% to 50%
- Under 30%
- Uninhabited or sparsely populated
- Data not available

Based on population 15 years and over who can read and write.

Daily Newspaper Circulation
per 1,000 population

- NIGERIA 15
- CHINA 37
- ARGENTINA 123
- FRANCE 210
- UNITED STATES 249
- FORMER SOVIET UNION 479
- JAPAN 588

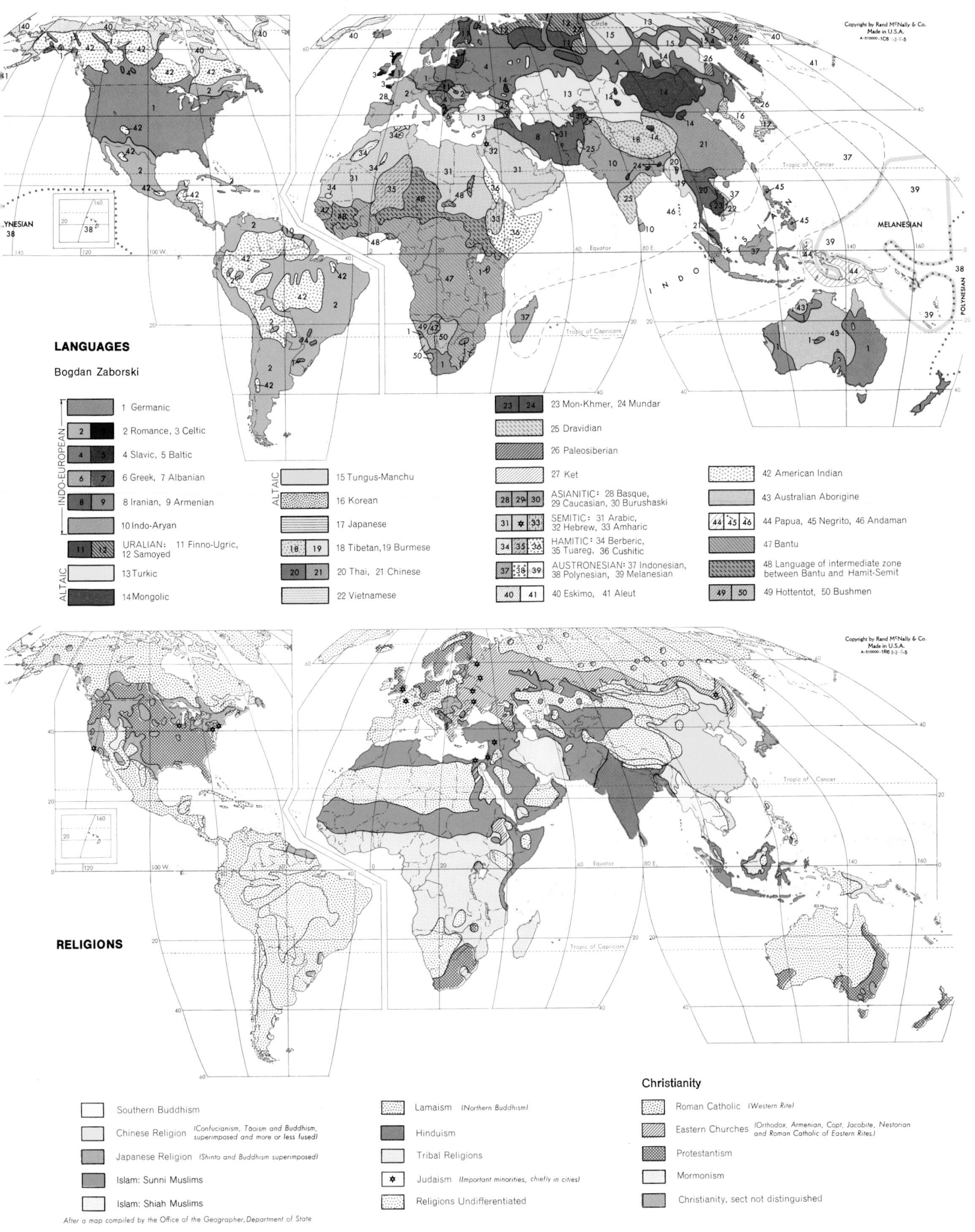

Copyright by Rand McNally & Co.
Made in U.S.A.
A-510000-1C6 -3-2-5

POLYNESIAN 38

MELANESIAN

POLYNESIAN 38

LANGUAGES

Bogdan Zaborski

INDO-EUROPEAN
- 1 Germanic
- 2 Romance, 3 Celtic
- 4 Slavic, 5 Baltic
- 6 Greek, 7 Albanian
- 8 Iranian, 9 Armenian
- 10 Indo-Aryan

URALIAN: 11 Finno-Ugric, 12 Samoyed

ALTAIC
- 13 Turkic
- 14 Mongolic
- 15 Tungus-Manchu
- 16 Korean
- 17 Japanese
- 18 Tibetan, 19 Burmese
- 20 Thai, 21 Chinese
- 22 Vietnamese

- 23 Mon-Khmer, 24 Mundar
- 25 Dravidian
- 26 Paleosiberian
- 27 Ket
- **ASIANITIC:** 28 Basque, 29 Caucasian, 30 Burushaski
- **SEMITIC:** 31 Arabic, 32 Hebrew, 33 Amharic
- **HAMITIC:** 34 Berberic, 35 Tuareg, 36 Cushitic
- **AUSTRONESIAN:** 37 Indonesian, 38 Polynesian, 39 Melanesian
- 40 Eskimo, 41 Aleut

- 42 American Indian
- 43 Australian Aborigine
- 44 Papua, 45 Negrito, 46 Andaman
- 47 Bantu
- 48 Language of intermediate zone between Bantu and Hamit-Semit
- 49 Hottentot, 50 Bushmen

Copyright by Rand McNally & Co.
Made in U.S.A.
A-510000-1R6 3-3-7-5

RELIGIONS

- Southern Buddhism
- Chinese Religion (Confucianism, Taoism and Buddhism, superimposed and more or less fused)
- Japanese Religion (Shinto and Buddhism superimposed)
- Islam: Sunni Muslims
- Islam: Shiah Muslims

- Lamaism (Northern Buddhism)
- Hinduism
- Tribal Religions
- Judaism (Important minorities, chiefly in cities)
- Religions Undifferentiated

Christianity
- Roman Catholic (Western Rite)
- Eastern Churches (Orthodox, Armenian, Copt, Jacobite, Nestorian and Roman Catholic of Eastern Rites.)
- Protestantism
- Mormonism
- Christianity, sect not distinguished

After a map compiled by the Office of the Geographer, Department of State

CALORIE SUPPLY

Note: Size of each country is proportional to population.

Calorie supply per capita
(percentage of requirements*)

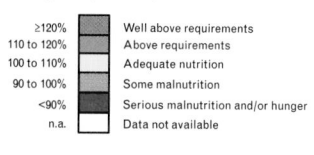

≥120%	Well above requirements
110 to 120%	Above requirements
100 to 110%	Adequate nutrition
90 to 100%	Some malnutrition
<90%	Serious malnutrition and/or hunger
n.a.	Data not available

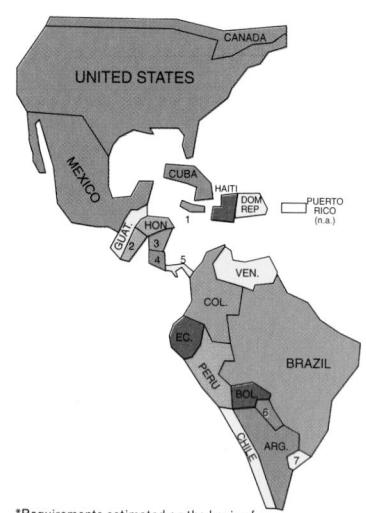

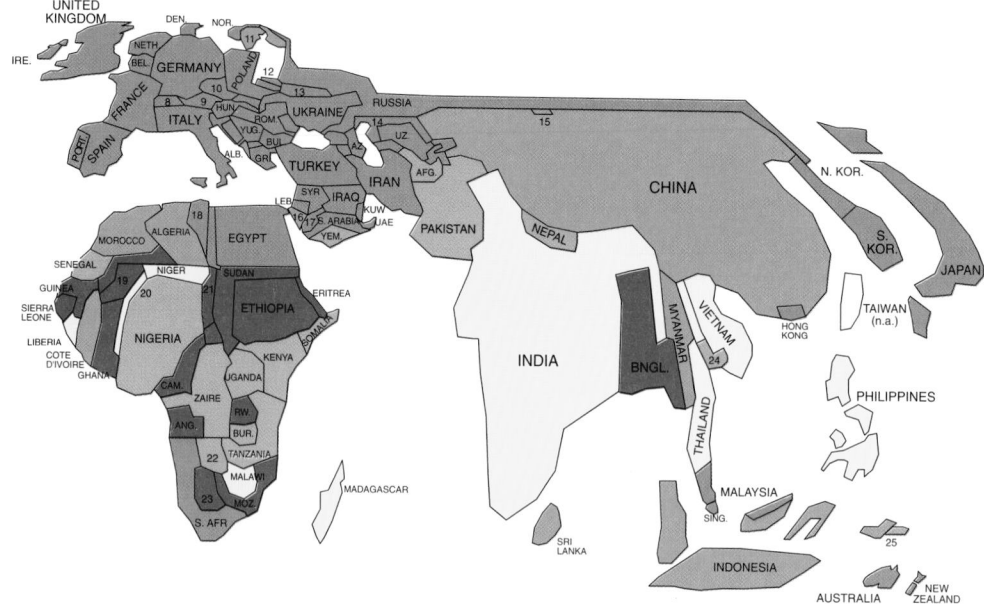

*Requirements estimated on the basis of physiological needs for normal activity with consideration of environmental temperature, body weight, and age and sex distribution of the population in various countries. Estimates are for 1990.

Copyright by Rand McNally & Co.
Made in U.S.A.
DM-910000-1V-GD1- - -:- -1

1. JAMAICA	6. PARAGUAY	11. SWEDEN	16. ISRAEL	21. CHAD
2. EL SALVADOR	7. URUGUAY	12. LATVIA	17. JORDAN	22. ZAMBIA
3. NICARAGUA	8. SWITZERLAND	13. BELARUS	18. TUNISIA	23. ZIMBABWE
4. COSTA RICA	9. AUSTRIA	14. KAZAKHSTAN	19. BURKINA FASO	24. CAMBODIA
5. PANAMA	10. CZECH REPUBLIC	15. MONGOLIA	20. BENIN	25. PAPUA NEW GUINEA

PROTEIN CONSUMPTION

Note: Size of each country is proportional to population.

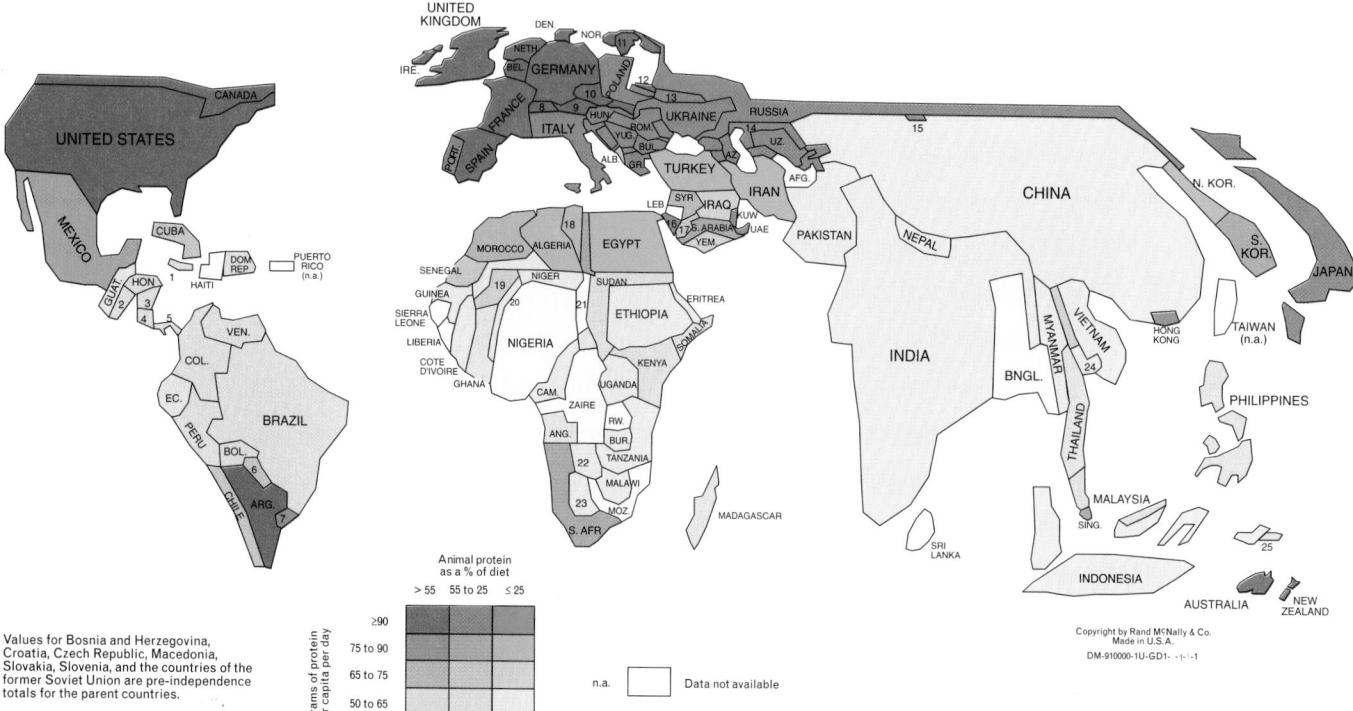

Values for Bosnia and Herzegovina, Croatia, Czech Republic, Macedonia, Slovakia, Slovenia, and the countries of the former Soviet Union are pre-independence totals for the parent countries.

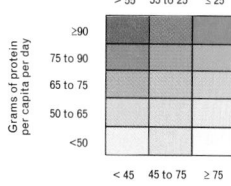

Animal protein
as a % of diet

> 55   55 to 25   ≤ 25

Grams of protein per capita per day

≥90
75 to 90
65 to 75
50 to 65
<50

< 45   45 to 75   ≥ 75

Vegetable protein
as a % of diet

n.a. | Data not available

Copyright by Rand McNally & Co.
Made in U.S.A.
DM-910000-1U-GD1- - -:- -1

PHYSICIANS

Note: Size of each country is proportional to population.

Population per Physician

- Less than 1,000
- 1,000 to 6,000
- 6,000 to 18,000
- Greater than 18,000

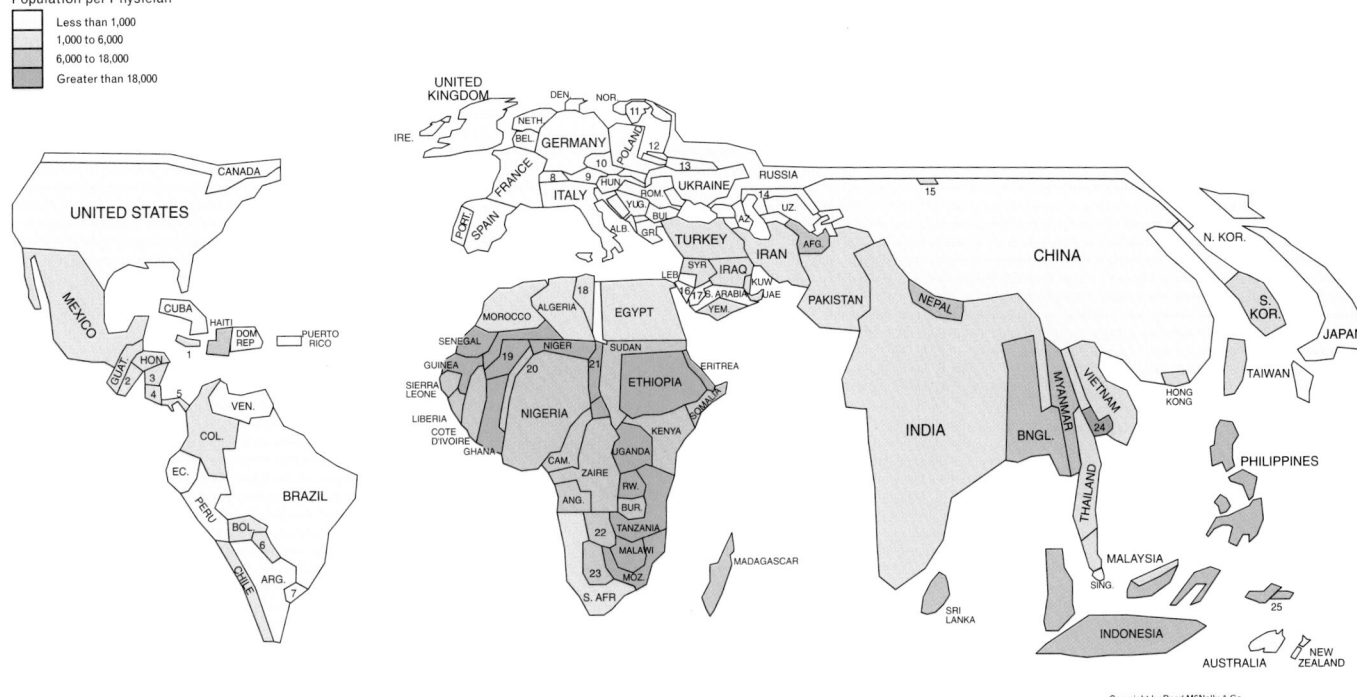

Copyright by Rand McNally & Co.
Made in U.S.A.
DM-910000-1L-GD1- - -:-1

1. JAMAICA	6. PARAGUAY	11. SWEDEN	16. ISRAEL	21. CHAD
2. EL SALVADOR	7. URUGUAY	12. LATVIA	17. JORDAN	22. ZAMBIA
3. NICARAGUA	8. SWITZERLAND	13. BELARUS	18. TUNISIA	23. ZIMBABWE
4. COSTA RICA	9. AUSTRIA	14. KAZAKHSTAN	19. BURKINA FASO	24. CAMBODIA
5. PANAMA	10. CZECH REPUBLIC	15. MONGOLIA	20. BENIN	25. PAPUA NEW GUINEA

LIFE EXPECTANCY

Note: Size of each country is proportional to population.

Life Expectancy at Birth

- Greater than 70 years
- 60 to 70
- 50 to 60
- Less than 50
- Data not available

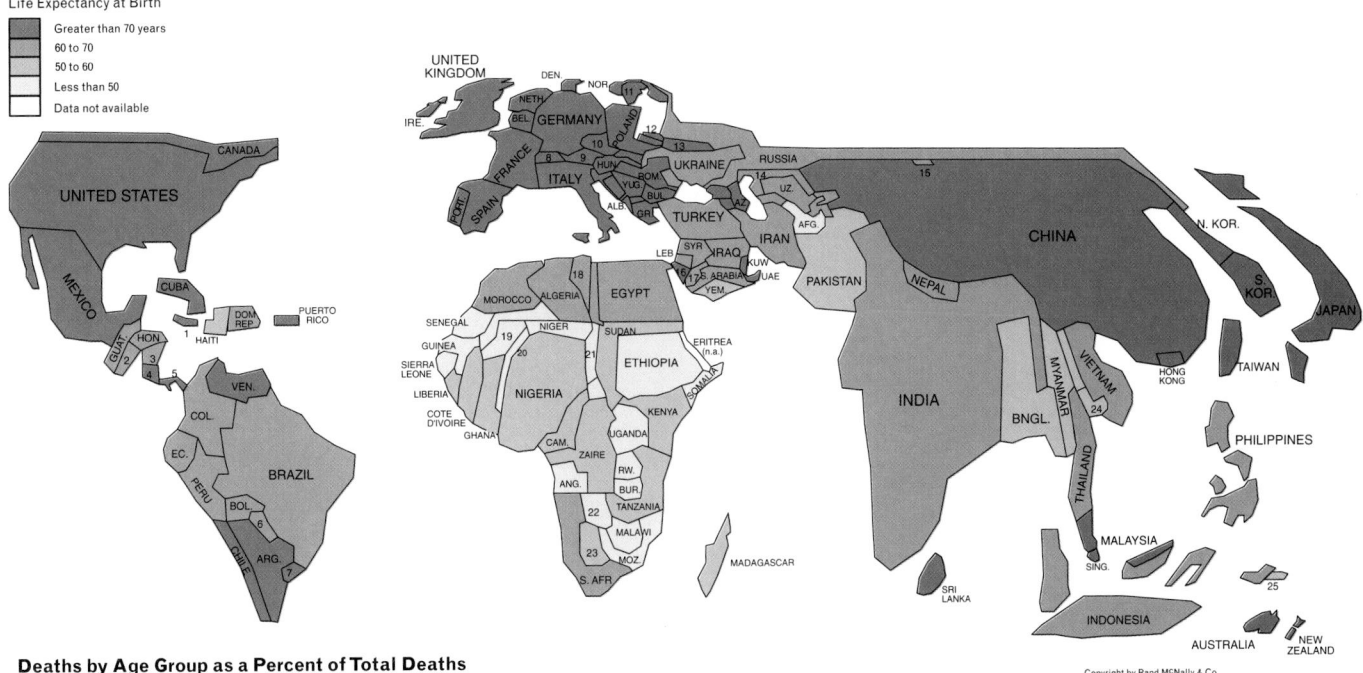

Copyright by Rand McNally & Co.
Made in U.S.A.
DM-910000-1M-GD1- - -:-1

Deaths by Age Group as a Percent of Total Deaths

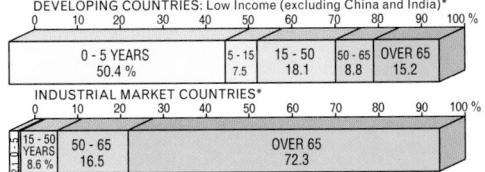

DEVELOPING COUNTRIES: Low Income (excluding China and India)*

0 - 5 YEARS 50.4 %	5 - 15 7.5	15 - 50 18.1	50 - 65 8.8	OVER 65 15.2

INDUSTRIAL MARKET COUNTRIES*

15 - 50 YEARS 8.6 %	50 - 65 16.5	OVER 65 72.3

Life Expectancy at Birth

LOW INCOME*	62 years
LOWER-MIDDLE INCOME*	67
UPPER-MIDDLE INCOME*	69
HIGH INCOME*	77

*as defined by the World Bank

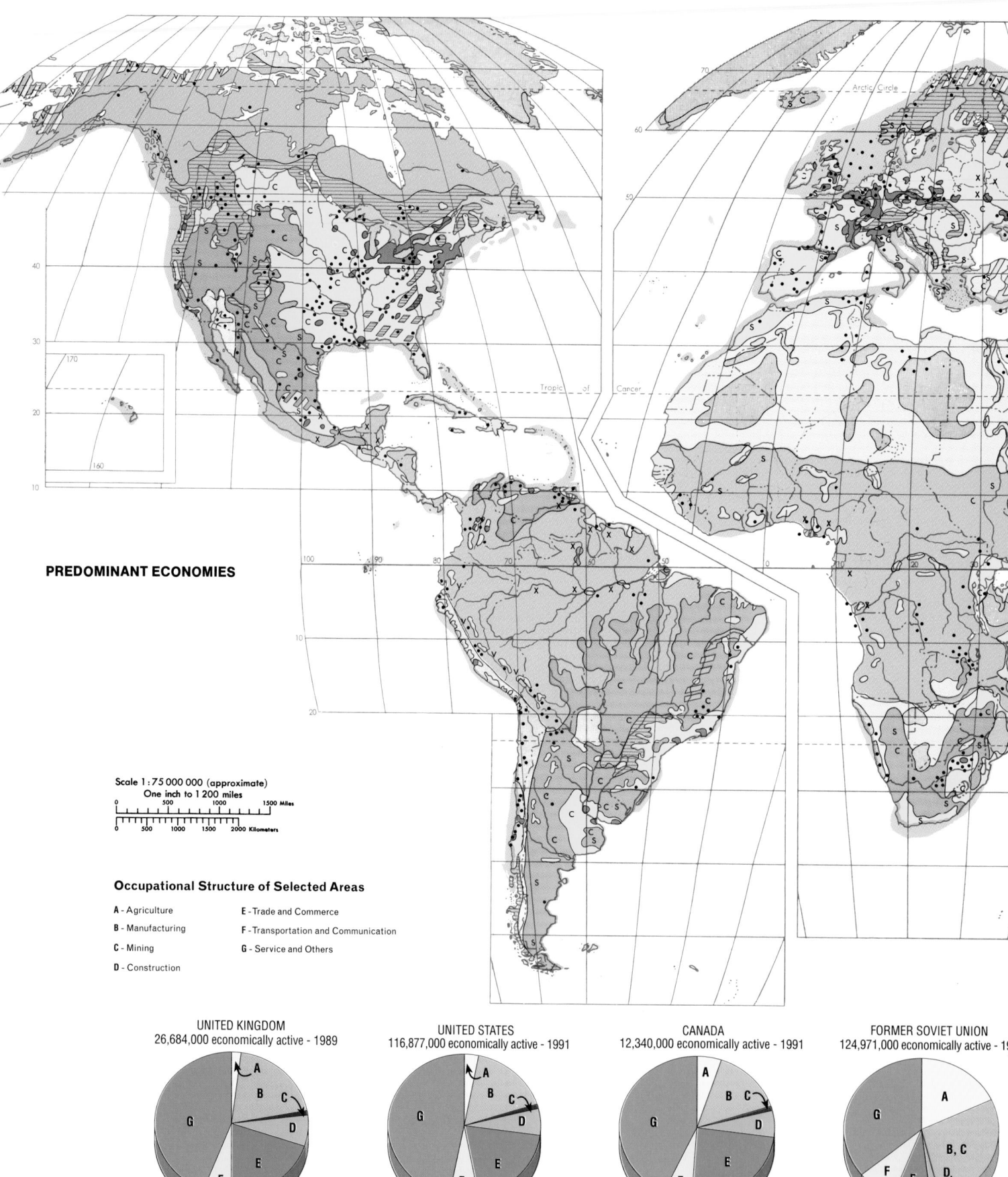

PREDOMINANT ECONOMIES

Scale 1 : 75 000 000 (approximate)
One inch to 1 200 miles

Occupational Structure of Selected Areas

A - Agriculture **E** - Trade and Commerce

B - Manufacturing **F** - Transportation and Communication

C - Mining **G** - Service and Others

D - Construction

UNITED KINGDOM
26,684,000 economically active - 1989

UNITED STATES
116,877,000 economically active - 1991

CANADA
12,340,000 economically active - 1991

FORMER SOVIET UNION
124,971,000 economically active - 19

A-510000-36-7-7-6-7
Copyright by Rand M⁀Nally & Co.
Made in U.S.A.

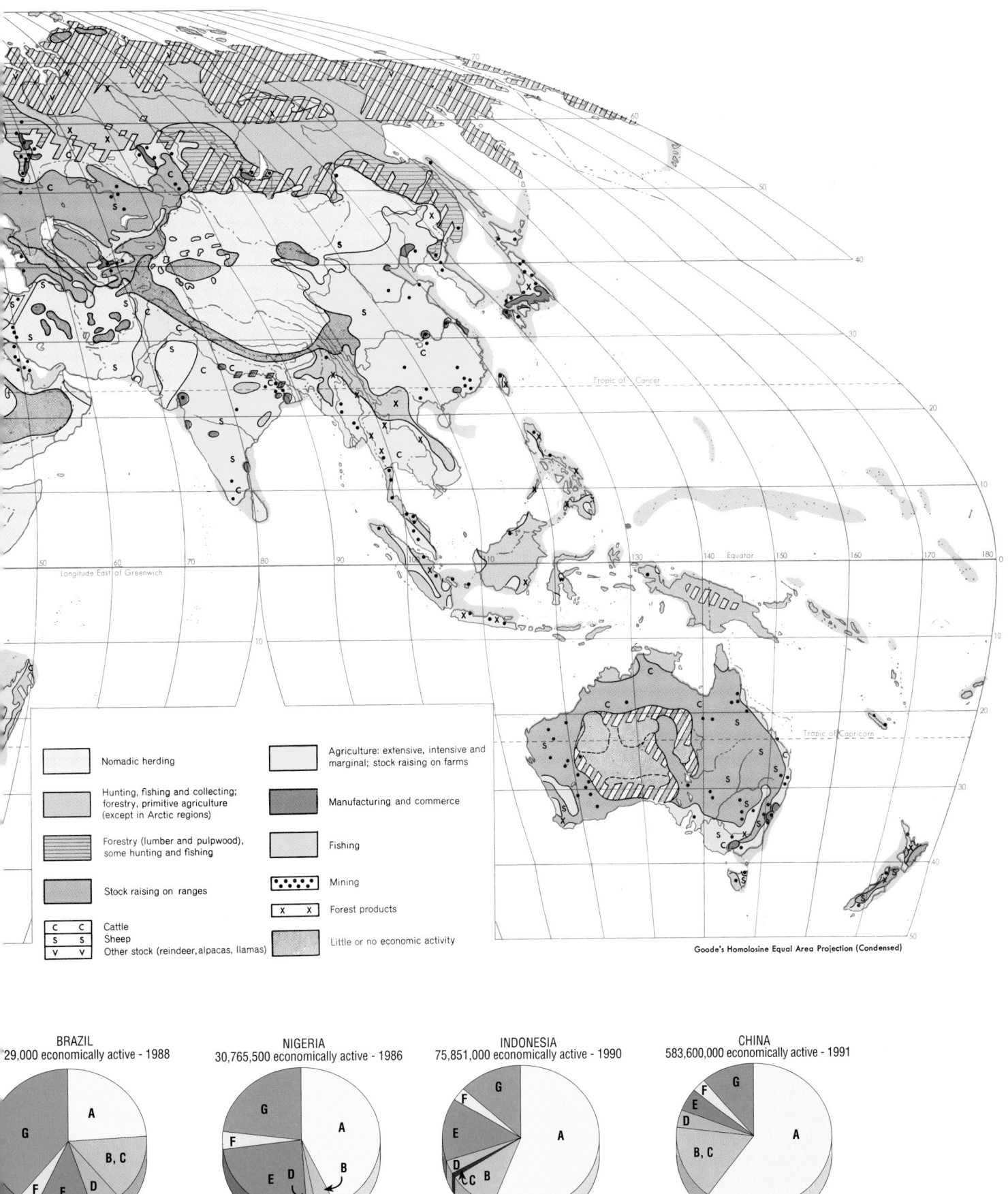

Legend:

- Nomadic herding
- Hunting, fishing and collecting; forestry, primitive agriculture (except in Arctic regions)
- Forestry (lumber and pulpwood), some hunting and fishing
- Stock raising on ranges

C C	Cattle
S S	Sheep
V V	Other stock (reindeer, alpacas, llamas)

- Agriculture: extensive, intensive and marginal; stock raising on farms
- Manufacturing and commerce
- Fishing
- Mining
- Forest products (X X)
- Little or no economic activity

Goode's Homolosine Equal Area Projection (Condensed)

BRAZIL
'29,000 economically active - 1988

NIGERIA
30,765,500 economically active - 1986

INDONESIA
75,851,000 economically active - 1990

CHINA
583,600,000 economically active - 1991

34

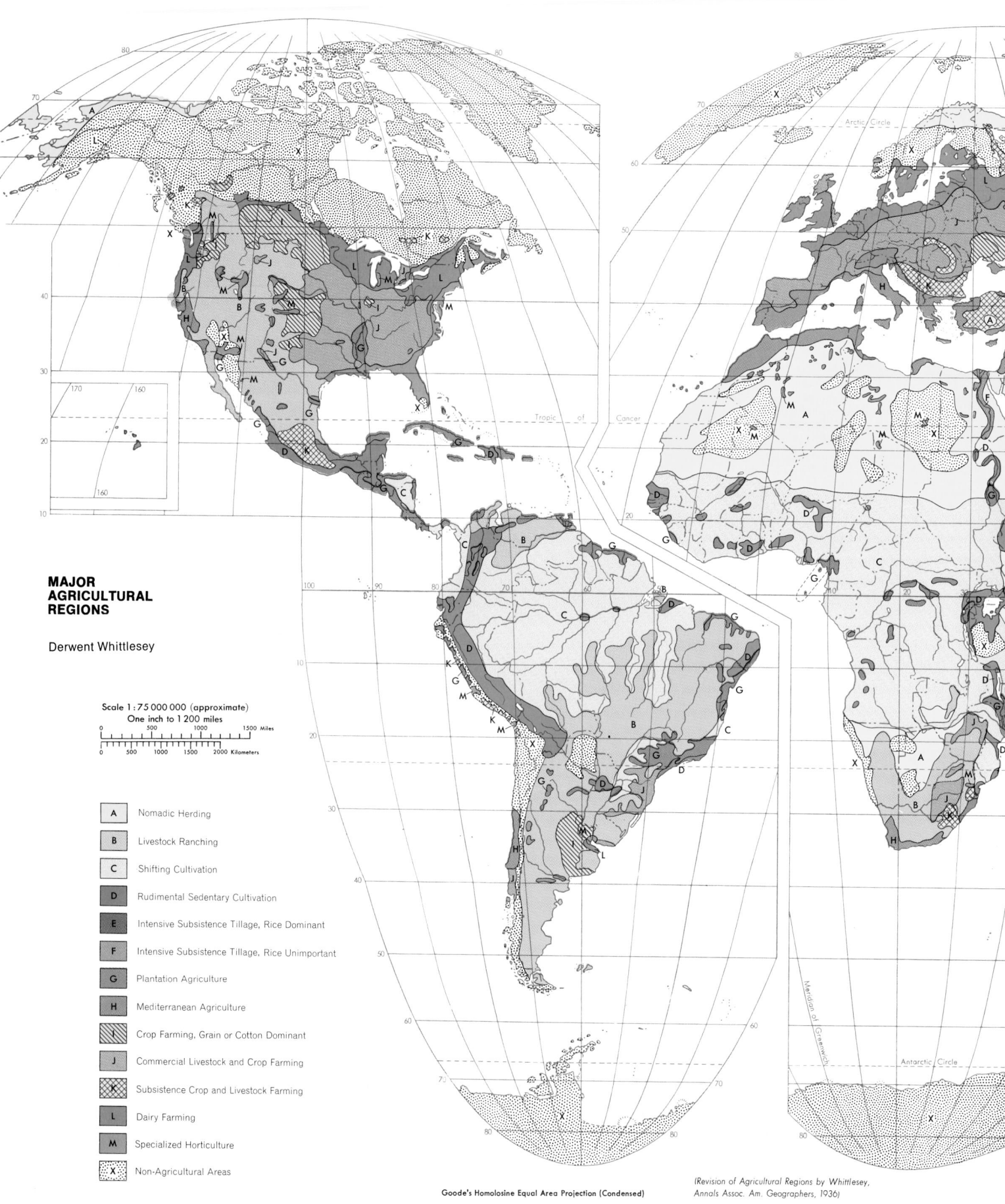

MAJOR
AGRICULTURAL
REGIONS

Derwent Whittlesey

Scale 1 : 75 000 000 (approximate)
One inch to 1 200 miles

A	Nomadic Herding
B	Livestock Ranching
C	Shifting Cultivation
D	Rudimental Sedentary Cultivation
E	Intensive Subsistence Tillage, Rice Dominant
F	Intensive Subsistence Tillage, Rice Unimportant
G	Plantation Agriculture
H	Mediterranean Agriculture
I	Crop Farming, Grain or Cotton Dominant
J	Commercial Livestock and Crop Farming
K	Subsistence Crop and Livestock Farming
L	Dairy Farming
M	Specialized Horticulture
X	Non-Agricultural Areas

Goode's Homolosine Equal Area Projection (Condensed)

*(Revision of Agricultural Regions by Whittlesey,
Annals Assoc. Am. Geographers, 1936)*

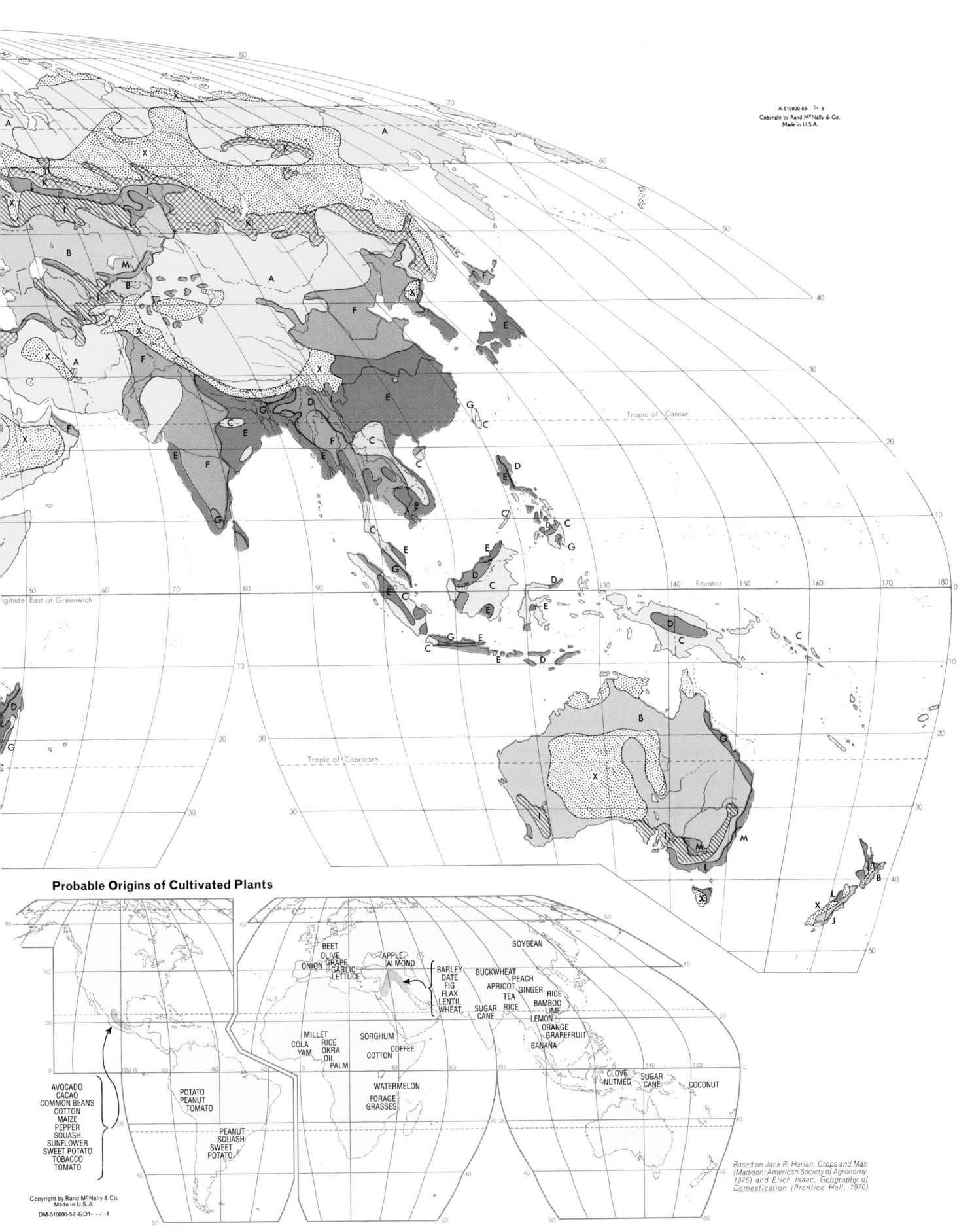

A-510000-56- 24 -5
Copyright by Rand McNally & Co.
Made in U.S.A.

Probable Origins of Cultivated Plants

SOYBEAN

BEET
OLIVE
GRAPE
ONION
GARLIC
LETTUCE

APPLE
ALMOND

BARLEY
DATE
FIG
FLAX
LENTIL
WHEAT

BUCKWHEAT
PEACH
APRICOT
TEA   GINGER
SUGAR   RICE
CANE   RICE BAMBOO
             LIME
             LEMON
             ORANGE
             GRAPEFRUIT
             BANANA

MILLET
COLA   RICE
YAM   OKRA
        OIL
        PALM

SORGHUM

COTTON   COFFEE

CLOVE
NUTMEG   SUGAR
          CANE   COCONUT

AVOCADO
CACAO
COMMON BEANS
COTTON
MAIZE
PEPPER
SQUASH
SUNFLOWER
SWEET POTATO
TOBACCO
TOMATO

POTATO
PEANUT
TOMATO

WATERMELON

FORAGE
GRASSES

PEANUT
SQUASH
SWEET
POTATO

Based on Jack R. Harlan, *Crops and Man*
(Madison: American Society of Agronomy,
1975) and Erich Isaac, *Geography of
Domestication* (Prentice Hall, 1970)

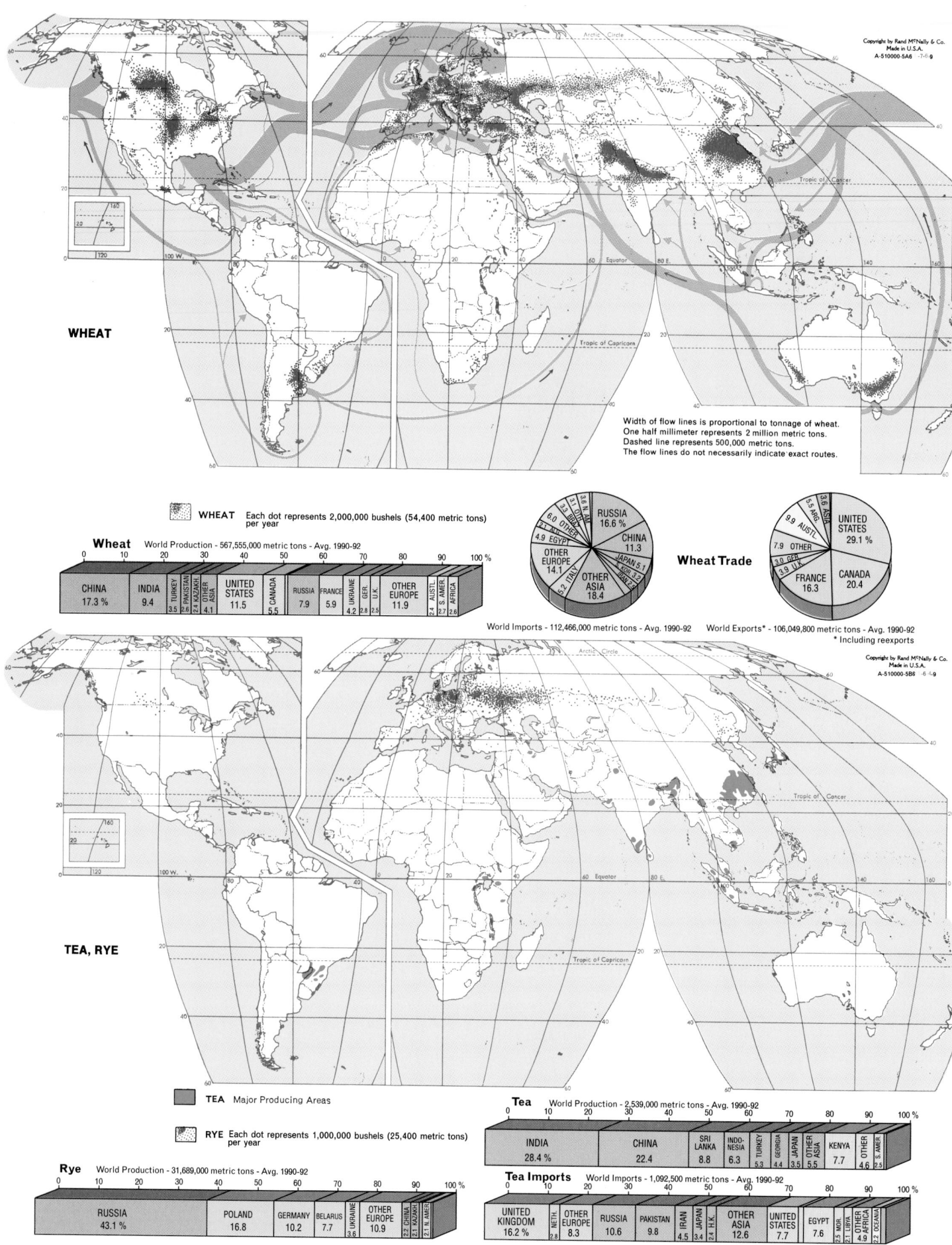

WHEAT

Width of flow lines is proportional to tonnage of wheat.
One half millimeter represents 2 million metric tons.
Dashed line represents 500,000 metric tons.
The flow lines do not necessarily indicate exact routes.

WHEAT Each dot represents 2,000,000 bushels (54,400 metric tons) per year

Wheat World Production - 567,555,000 metric tons - Avg. 1990-92

0	10	20	30	40	50	60	70	80	90	100 %

| CHINA 17.3 % | INDIA 9.4 | TURKEY 3.5 | PAKISTAN 2.6 | OTHER ASIA 4.1 | UNITED STATES 11.5 | CANADA 5.5 | RUSSIA 7.9 | FRANCE 5.9 | UKRAINE 4.2 | GER 2.8 | U.K. 2.5 | OTHER EUROPE 11.9 | AUSTL. 2.4 | S. AMER. 2.7 | AFRICA 2.6 |

Wheat Trade

World Imports - 112,466,000 metric tons - Avg. 1990-92

Pie: RUSSIA 16.6 %, CHINA 11.3, JAPAN 5.1, KOR 3.2, OTHER ASIA 18.4, ITALY 5.2, OTHER EUROPE 14.1, EGYPT 4.9, OTHER 6.0, 3.3 OTH, 2.1 OTH, 3.6 N. AM.

World Exports* - 106,049,800 metric tons - Avg. 1990-92
* Including reexports

Pie: UNITED STATES 29.1 %, CANADA 20.4, FRANCE 16.3, U.K. 3.9, GER 3.0, OTHER 7.9, AUSTL. 9.9, ASIA 5.5, 3.6

TEA, RYE

TEA Major Producing Areas

RYE Each dot represents 1,000,000 bushels (25,400 metric tons) per year

Rye World Production - 31,689,000 metric tons - Avg. 1990-92

0	10	20	30	40	50	60	70	80	90	100 %

| RUSSIA 43.1 % | POLAND 16.8 | GERMANY 10.2 | BELARUS 7.7 | UKRAINE 3.6 | OTHER EUROPE 10.9 | CHINA 2.2 | KAZAKH 2.1 | N. AMER. 2.1 |

Tea World Production - 2,539,000 metric tons - Avg. 1990-92

0	10	20	30	40	50	60	70	80	90	100 %

| INDIA 28.4 % | CHINA 22.4 | SRI LANKA 8.8 | INDO-NESIA 6.3 | TURKEY 5.3 | GEORGIA 4.4 | JAPAN 3.5 | OTHER ASIA 5.5 | KENYA 7.7 | OTHER 4.6 | S. AMER. 2.5 |

Tea Imports World Imports - 1,092,500 metric tons - Avg. 1990-92

0	10	20	30	40	50	60	70	80	90	100 %

| UNITED KINGDOM 16.2 % | NETH. 2.8 | OTHER EUROPE 8.3 | RUSSIA 10.6 | PAKISTAN 9.8 | IRAN 4.5 | JAPAN 3.4 | H.K. 2.4 | OTHER ASIA 12.6 | UNITED STATES 7.7 | EGYPT 7.6 | MOR 2.5 | LIBYA 2.1 | OTHER AFRICA 4.9 | OCEANIA 2.2 |

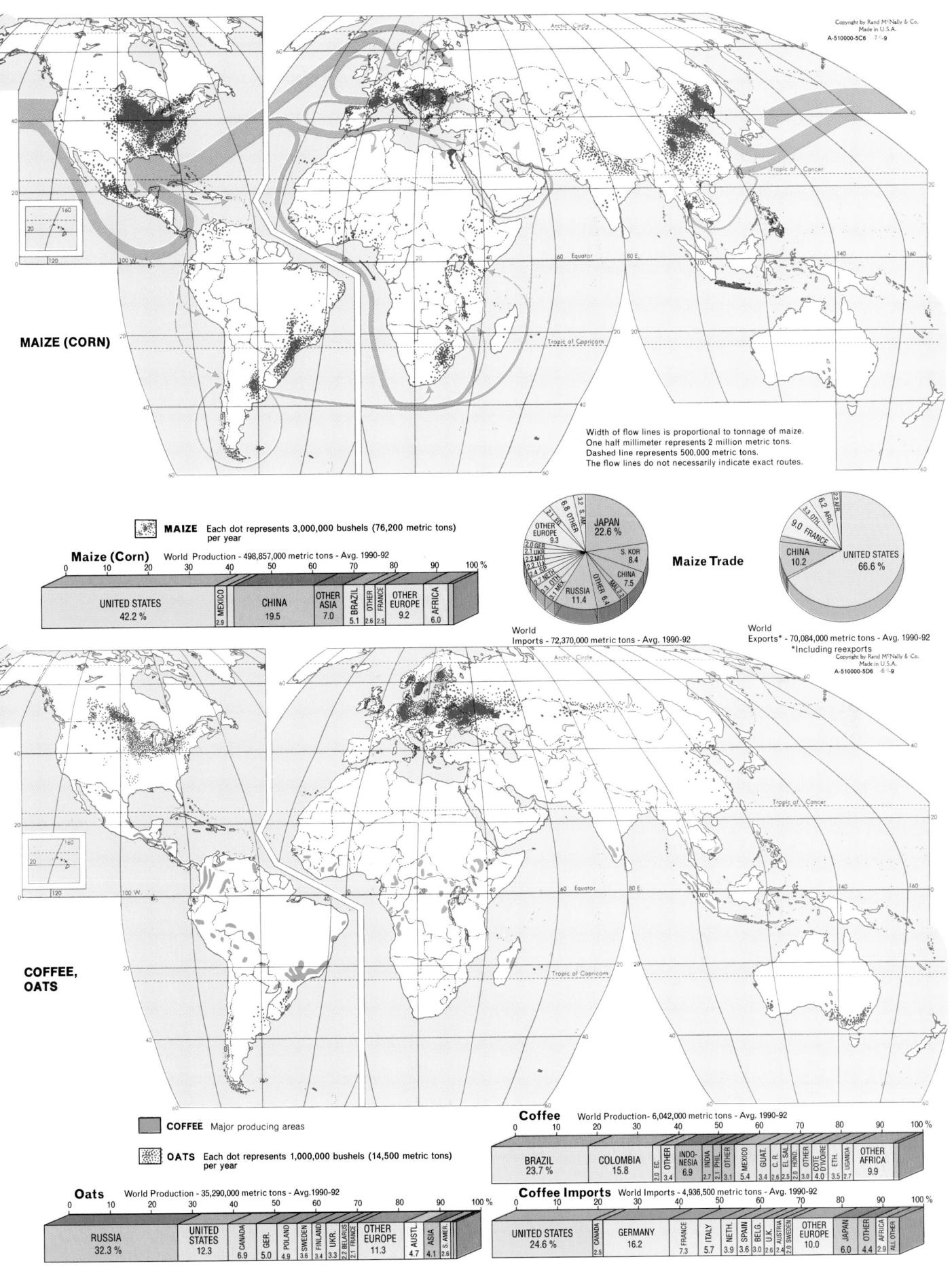

MAIZE (CORN)

Width of flow lines is proportional to tonnage of maize.
One half millimeter represents 2 million metric tons.
Dashed line represents 500,000 metric tons.
The flow lines do not necessarily indicate exact routes.

MAIZE Each dot represents 3,000,000 bushels (76,200 metric tons) per year

Maize (Corn) World Production - 498,857,000 metric tons - Avg. 1990-92

0	10	20	30	40	50	60	70	80	90	100 %

UNITED STATES 42.2 %	MEXICO 2.9	CHINA 19.5	OTHER ASIA 7.0	BRAZIL 5.1	OTHER 2.5	FRANCE 2.5	OTHER EUROPE 9.2	AFRICA 6.0

Maize Trade

World Imports - 72,370,000 metric tons - Avg. 1990-92

JAPAN 22.6 %
S. KOR 8.4
CHINA 7.5
OTHER EUROPE 9.3
RUSSIA 11.4
MID 2.1
OTHER 6.4
6.8 OTHER
3.2 S. AM.
2.7 ME.
2.0 GER.
2.1 UKR.
2.2 ULK.
2.4 SP.
2.1 NETH.
9.3 OTH.
3.1 MEX.

World Exports* - 70,084,000 metric tons - Avg. 1990-92
*Including reexports

UNITED STATES 66.6 %
CHINA 10.2
9.0 FRANCE
3.3 OTH.
6.2 ARG.
2.2 AFR.

COFFEE, OATS

COFFEE Major producing areas

OATS Each dot represents 1,000,000 bushels (14,500 metric tons) per year

Coffee World Production- 6,042,000 metric tons - Avg. 1990-92

0	10	20	30	40	50	60	70	80	90	100 %

BRAZIL 23.7 %	COLOMBIA 15.8	OTHER 2.0	EC.	INDO-NESIA 6.9	INDIA 3.4	PHIL. 2.1	OTHER 3.1	MEXICO 5.4	GUAT. 3.4	C.R. 2.6	EL SAL 2.5	HOND. 2.0	COTE D'IVOIRE 4.0	ETH. 3.5	UGANDA 2.7	OTHER AFRICA 9.9

Oats World Production - 35,290,000 metric tons - Avg.1990-92

0	10	20	30	40	50	60	70	80	90	100 %

RUSSIA 32.3 %	UNITED STATES 12.3	CANADA 6.9	GER. 5.0	POLAND 4.9	SWEDEN 3.6	FINLAND 3.4	UKR. 3.3	BELARUS 2.2	FRANCE 2.1	OTHER EUROPE 11.3	AUSTL. 4.7	ASIA 4.1	S. AMER. 2.6

Coffee Imports World Imports - 4,936,500 metric tons - Avg. 1990-92

0	10	20	30	40	50	60	70	80	90	100 %

UNITED STATES 24.6 %	CANADA 2.5	GERMANY 16.2	FRANCE 7.3	ITALY 5.7	NETH. 3.9	SPAIN 3.6	BELG. 3.0	U.K. 2.6	AUSTRIA 2.4	SWEDEN 2.0	OTHER EUROPE 10.0	JAPAN 6.0	OTHER 4.4	AFRICA 2.9	ALL OTHER

BARLEY,
COCOA
BEANS

BARLEY Each dot represents 3,000,000 bushels (65,400 metric tons) per year

COCOA
BEANS   Major Producing Areas

Barley World Production - 168,598,000 metric tons - Avg. 1990-92

0	10	20	30	40	50	60	70	80	90	100 %

| RUSSIA 14.8 % | GER. 8.0 | FRANCE 6.2 | UKR. 5.4 | SPAIN 4.9 | U.K. 4.5 | DEN. 2.6 | FMR. CZ. POLAND 2.2 | OTHER EUROPE 12.8 | CAN. 7.1 | UNITED STATES 5.8 | TURKEY 4.3 | KAZAKH. 3.9 | IRAN 2.0 | OTHER ASIA 5.5 | AUSTL. 2.8 | AFRICA 3.3 |

Cocoa Beans World Production - 2,409,000 metric tons - Avg. 1990-92

0	10	20	30	40	50	60	70	80	90	100 %

| CÔTE D'IVOIRE 31.6 % | GHANA 11.2 | NIGERIA 5.4 | CAMER. 4.4 | OTHER 2.4 | BRAZIL 14.1 | ECUADOR 3.8 | COL 2.4 | MALAYSIA 9.6 | INDON. 6.7 | N. AMER. 4.5 |

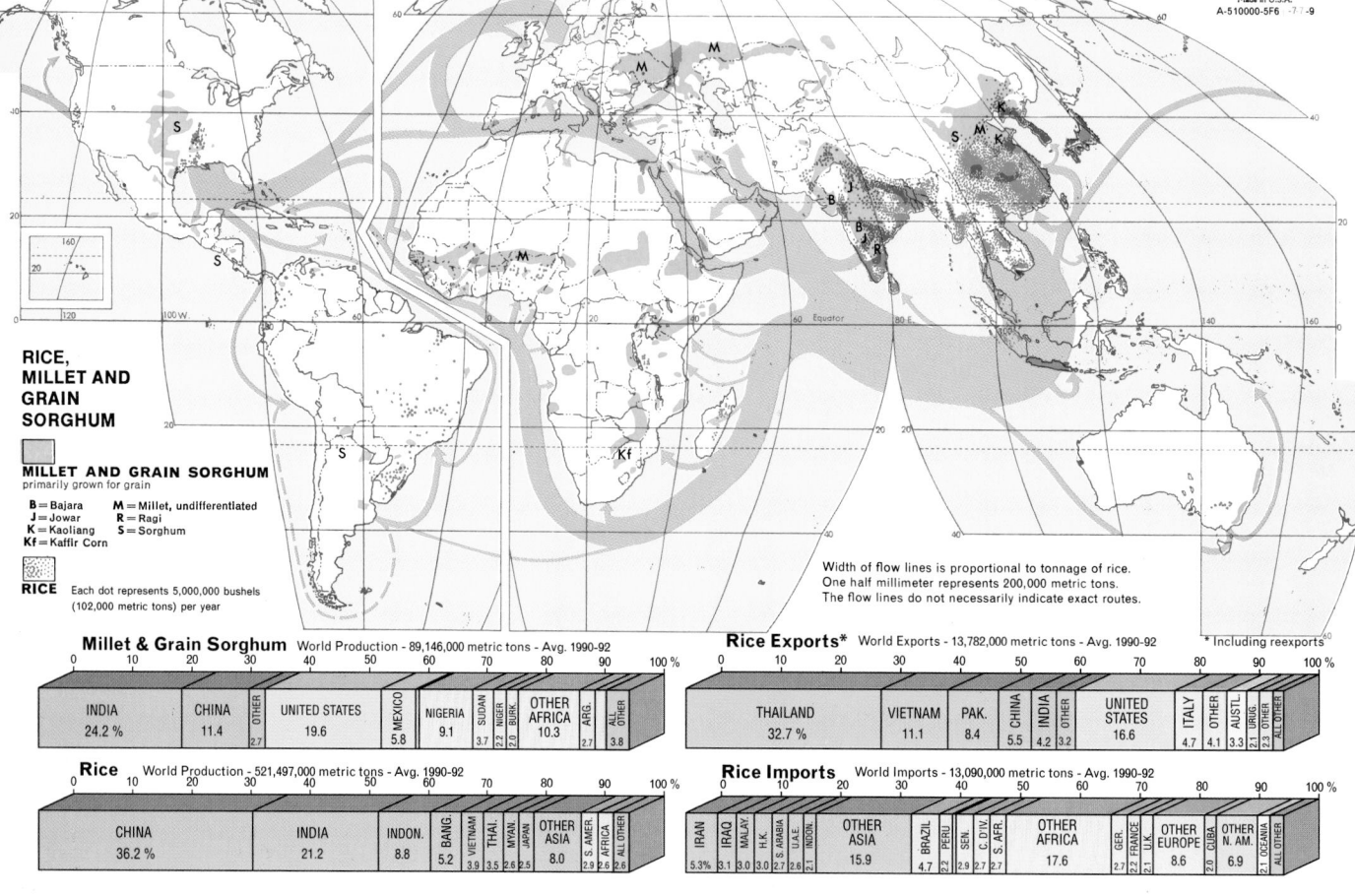

RICE,
MILLET AND
GRAIN
SORGHUM

MILLET AND GRAIN SORGHUM
primarily grown for grain

B = Bajara   M = Millet, undifferentiated
J = Jowar   R = Ragi
K = Kaoliang   S = Sorghum
Kf = Kaffir Corn

RICE Each dot represents 5,000,000 bushels
(102,000 metric tons) per year

Width of flow lines is proportional to tonnage of rice.
One half millimeter represents 200,000 metric tons.
The flow lines do not necessarily indicate exact routes.

Millet & Grain Sorghum World Production - 89,146,000 metric tons - Avg. 1990-92   * Including reexports

0	10	20	30	40	50	60	70	80	90	100 %

| INDIA 24.2 % | CHINA 11.4 | OTHER 2.7 | UNITED STATES 19.6 | MEXICO 5.8 | NIGERIA 9.1 | SUDAN 3.7 | NIGER 2.2 | BURK 2.0 | OTHER AFRICA 10.3 | ARG 2.7 | ALL OTHER 3.8 |

Rice Exports* World Exports - 13,782,000 metric tons - Avg. 1990-92

0	10	20	30	40	50	60	70	80	90	100 %

| THAILAND 32.7 % | VIETNAM 11.1 | PAK. 8.4 | CHINA 5.5 | INDIA 4.2 | OTHER 3.2 | UNITED STATES 16.6 | ITALY 4.7 | OTHER 4.1 | AUSTL. 3.3 | URUG. 2.3 | ALL OTHER |

Rice World Production - 521,497,000 metric tons - Avg. 1990-92

0	10	20	30	40	50	60	70	80	90	100 %

| CHINA 36.2 % | INDIA 21.2 | INDON. 8.8 | BANG. 5.2 | VIETNAM 3.9 | THAI. 3.5 | MYAN 2.6 | JAPAN 2.5 | OTHER ASIA 8.0 | S. AMER. 2.9 | AFRICA 2.6 | ALL OTHER |

Rice Imports World Imports - 13,090,000 metric tons - Avg. 1990-92

0	10	20	30	40	50	60	70	80	90	100 %

| IRAN 5.3% | IRAQ 3.1 | MALAY. 3.0 | H.K. 2.7 | S. ARABIA 2.1 | UAE 2.1 | INDON. | OTHER ASIA 15.9 | BRAZIL 4.7 | PERU 2.2 | SEN. 2.9 | C. D'IV. 2.7 | S. AFR. | OTHER AFRICA 17.6 | GER. 2.2 | FRANCE 2.1 | U.K. | OTHER EUROPE 8.6 | CUBA 2.1 | OTHER N. AM. 6.9 | OCEANIA 2.0 | ALL OTHER |

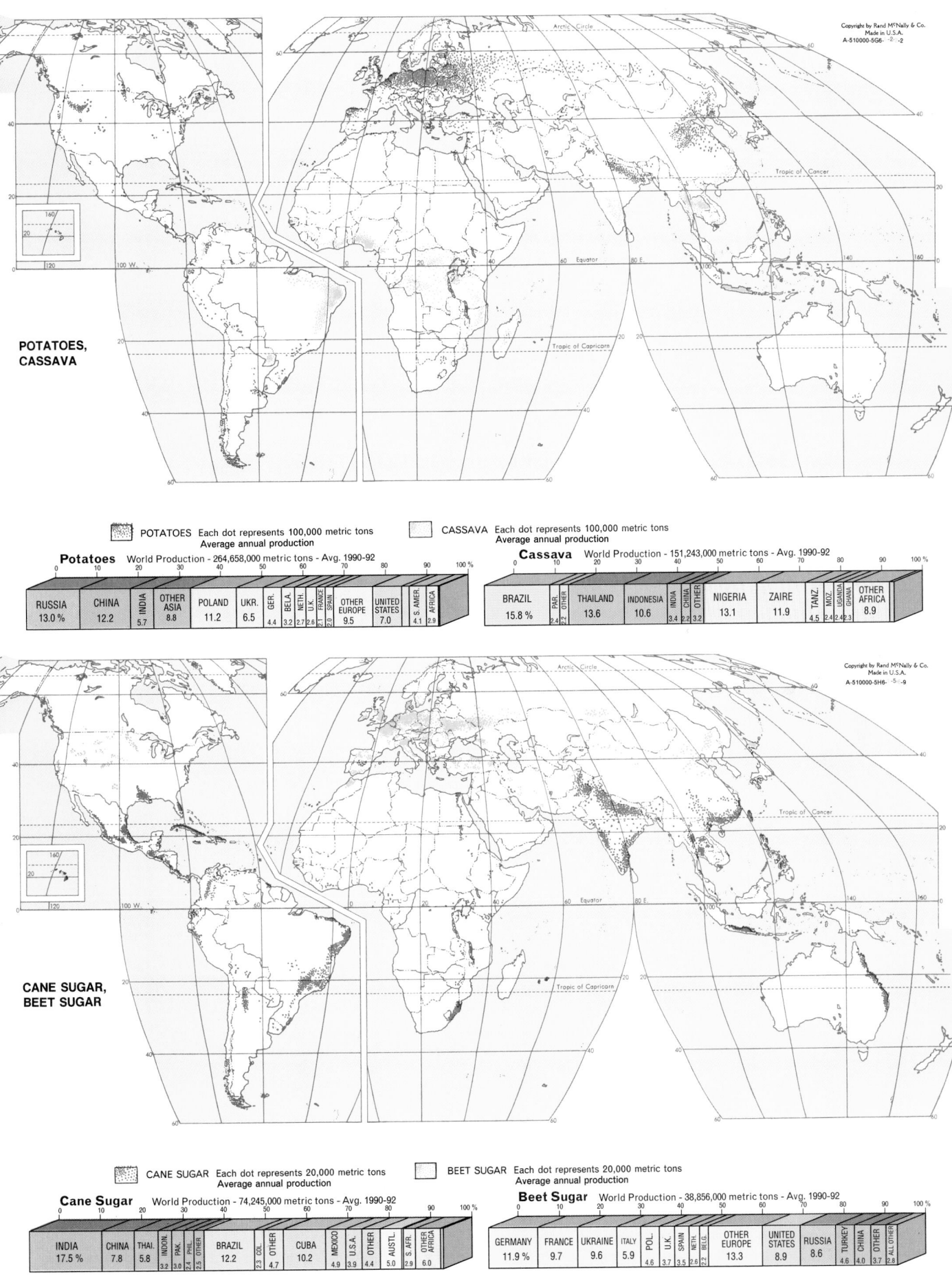

Copyright by Rand McNally & Co.
Made in U.S.A.
A-510000-5G6- -2- -2

POTATOES, CASSAVA

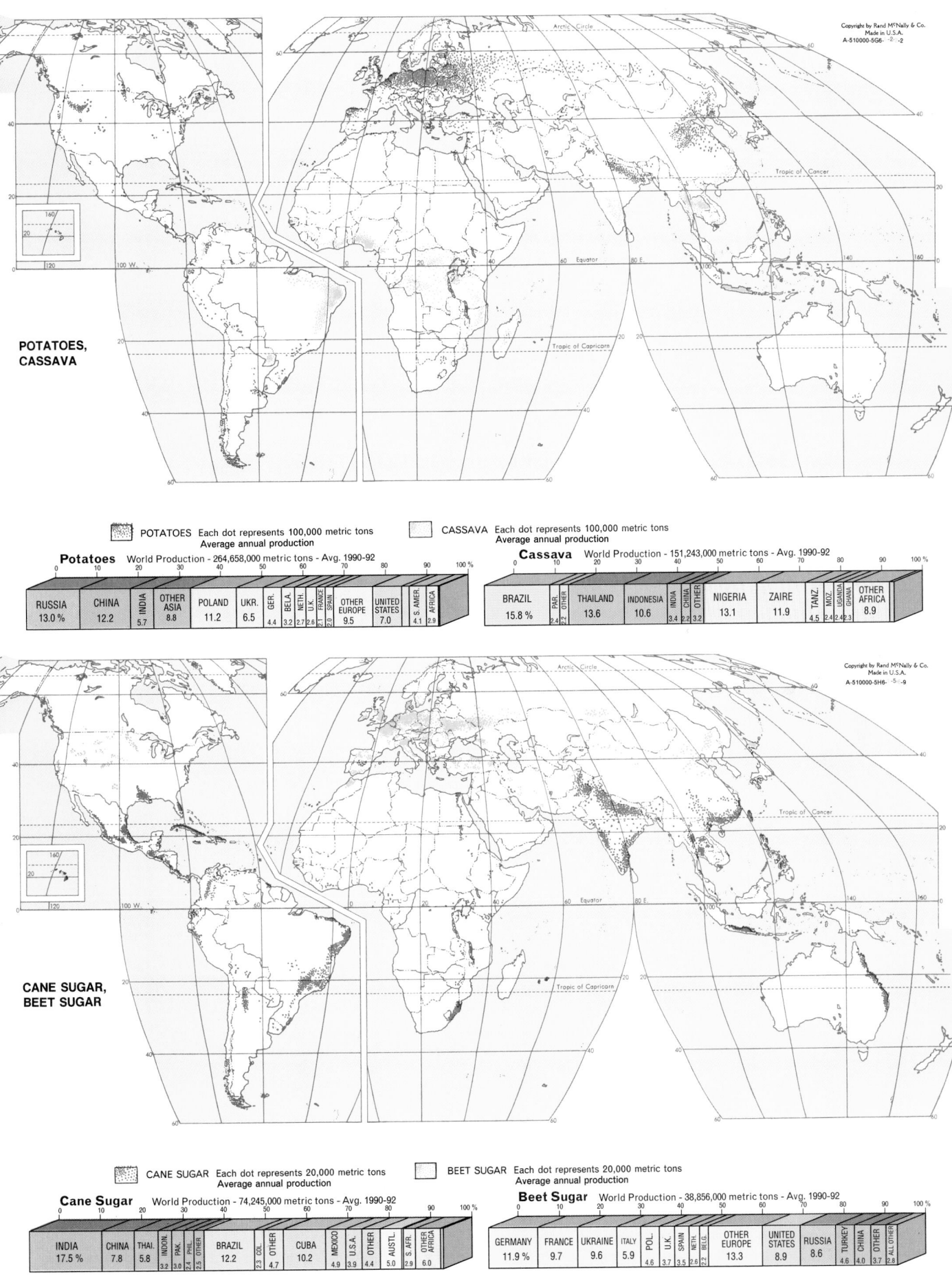

POTATOES	Each dot represents 100,000 metric tons
	Average annual production

CASSAVA	Each dot represents 100,000 metric tons
	Average annual production

Potatoes World Production - 264,658,000 metric tons - Avg. 1990-92

| 0 | 10 | 20 | 30 | 40 | 50 | 60 | 70 | 80 | 90 | 100 % |

| RUSSIA 13.0 % | CHINA 12.2 | INDIA 5.7 | OTHER ASIA 8.8 | POLAND 11.2 | UKR. 6.5 | GER. 4.4 | BELA. 3.2 | NETH. 2.7 | U.K. 2.6 | FRANCE 2.1 | SPAIN 2.0 | OTHER EUROPE 9.5 | UNITED STATES 7.0 | S. AMER. 4.1 | AFRICA 2.9 |

Cassava World Production - 151,243,000 metric tons - Avg. 1990-92

| 0 | 10 | 20 | 30 | 40 | 50 | 60 | 70 | 80 | 90 | 100 % |

| BRAZIL 15.8 % | PAR. 2.4 | OTHER 2.2 | THAILAND 13.6 | INDONESIA 10.6 | INDIA 3.4 | CHINA 2.2 | OTHER 3.2 | NIGERIA 13.1 | ZAIRE 11.9 | TANZ. 4.5 | MOZ. 2.4 | UGANDA 2.4 | GHANA 2.3 | OTHER AFRICA 8.9 |

Copyright by Rand McNally & Co.
Made in U.S.A.
A-510000-5H6- -5- -9

CANE SUGAR, BEET SUGAR

CANE SUGAR	Each dot represents 20,000 metric tons
	Average annual production

BEET SUGAR	Each dot represents 20,000 metric tons
	Average annual production

Cane Sugar World Production - 74,245,000 metric tons - Avg. 1990-92

| 0 | 10 | 20 | 30 | 40 | 50 | 60 | 70 | 80 | 90 | 100 % |

| INDIA 17.5 % | CHINA 7.8 | THAI. 5.8 | INDON. 3.2 | PAK. 3.0 | PHIL. 2.4 | OTHER | BRAZIL 12.2 | COL. 2.3 | OTHER 4.7 | CUBA 10.2 | MEXICO 4.9 | U.S.A. 3.9 | OTHER 4.4 | AUSTL 5.0 | S. AFR. 2.9 | OTHER AFRICA 6.0 |

Beet Sugar World Production - 38,856,000 metric tons - Avg. 1990-92

| 0 | 10 | 20 | 30 | 40 | 50 | 60 | 70 | 80 | 90 | 100 % |

| GERMANY 11.9 % | FRANCE 9.7 | UKRAINE 9.6 | ITALY 5.9 | POL. 4.6 | U.K. 3.7 | SPAIN 3.5 | NETH. 2.6 | BELG. 2.2 | OTHER EUROPE 13.3 | UNITED STATES 8.9 | RUSSIA 8.6 | TURKEY 4.6 | CHINA 4.0 | OTHER 3.7 | ALL OTHER 2.8 |

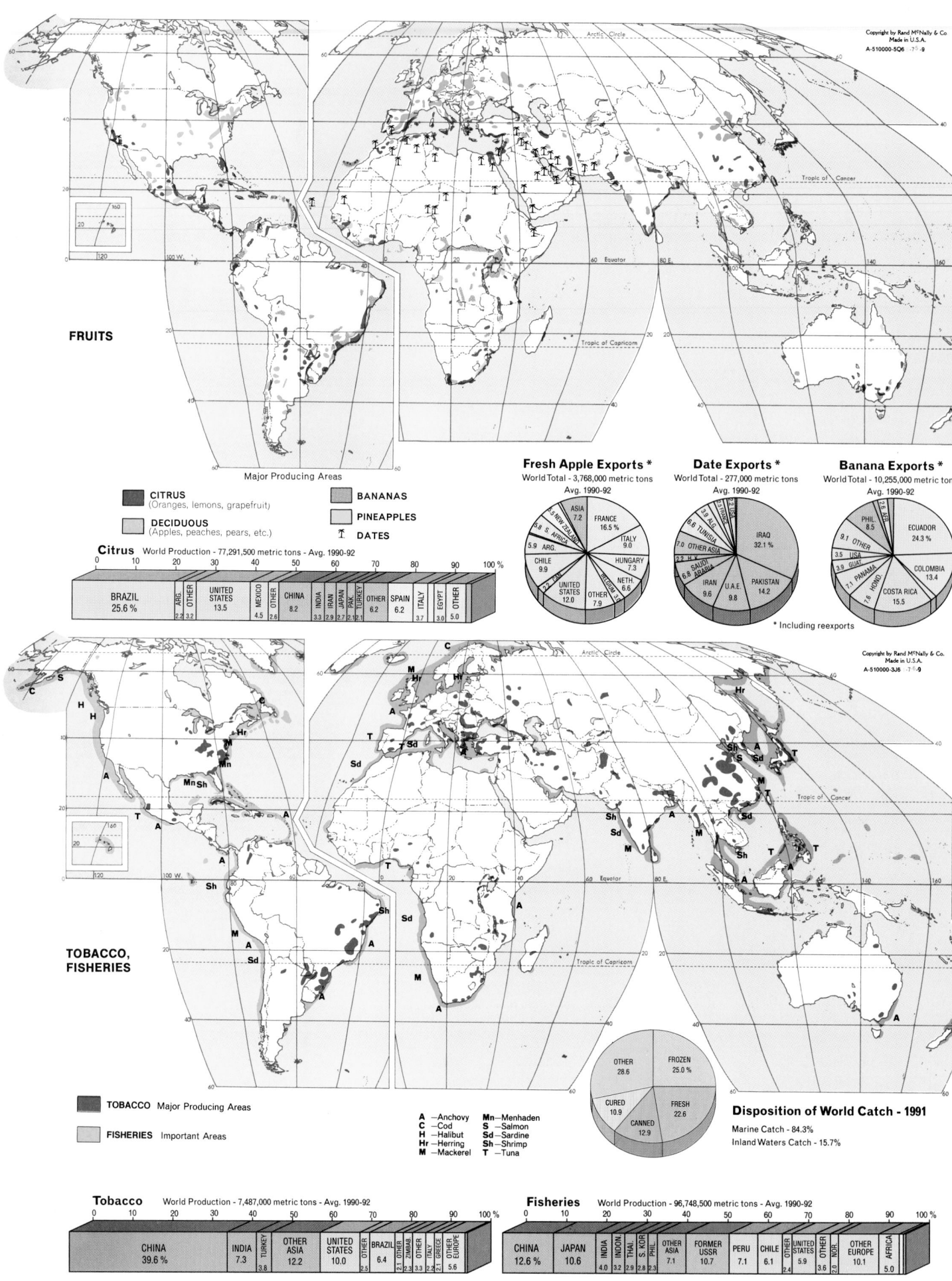

Copyright by Rand McNally & Co.
Made in U.S.A.
A-510000-5Q6 -7⁰-9

FRUITS

Major Producing Areas

CITRUS
(Oranges, lemons, grapefruit)

DECIDUOUS
(Apples, peaches, pears, etc.)

⬥ **DATES**

BANANAS

PINEAPPLES

Citrus World Production - 77,291,500 metric tons - Avg. 1990-92

0	10	20	30	40	50	60	70	80	90	100 %

BRAZIL 25.6 % | ARG. 2.2 | OTHER 3.2 | UNITED STATES 13.5 | MEXICO 4.5 | OTHER 2.6 | CHINA 8.2 | INDIA 3.3 | IRAN 2.9 | JAPAN 2.7 | PAK. 2.1 | TURKEY 2.1 | OTHER 6.2 | SPAIN 6.2 | ITALY 3.7 | EGYPT 3.0 | OTHER 5.0

Fresh Apple Exports *
World Total - 3,768,000 metric tons
Avg. 1990-92

ASIA 7.2 | FRANCE 16.5 % | ITALY 9.0 | S. AFRICA 5.8 | NEW ZEALAND | ARG. 5.9 | CHILE 9.9 | HUNGARY 7.3 | NETH. | UNITED STATES 12.0 | BELGIUM 3. | OTHER 7.9

Date Exports *
World Total - 277,000 metric tons
Avg. 1990-92

ALG. | TUNISIA 6.6 | OTHER ASIA 7.0 | IRAQ 32.1 % | H K | SAUDI ARABIA 6.8 | IRAN 9.6 | U.A.E. 9.8 | PAKISTAN 14.2

Banana Exports *
World Total - 10,255,000 metric tons
Avg. 1990-92

PHIL. 8.5 | OTHER 9.1 | ECUADOR 24.3 % | USA 3.5 | GUAT. 3.9 | PANAMA 7.1 | HOND. | COSTA RICA 15.5 | COLOMBIA 13.4

* Including reexports

Copyright by Rand McNally & Co.
Made in U.S.A.
A-510000-3J6 -7⁰-9

TOBACCO, FISHERIES

TOBACCO Major Producing Areas

FISHERIES Important Areas

A —Anchovy	Mn—Menhaden
C —Cod	S —Salmon
H —Halibut	Sd—Sardine
Hr —Herring	Sh—Shrimp
M —Mackerel	T —Tuna

OTHER 28.6 | FROZEN 25.0 % | CURED 10.9 | FRESH 22.6 | CANNED 12.9

Disposition of World Catch - 1991

Marine Catch - 84.3%
Inland Waters Catch - 15.7%

Tobacco World Production - 7,487,000 metric tons - Avg. 1990-92

0	10	20	30	40	50	60	70	80	90	100 %

CHINA 39.6 % | INDIA 7.3 | TURKEY 3.8 | OTHER ASIA 12.2 | UNITED STATES 10.0 | OTHER 2.5 | BRAZIL 6.4 | ZIMBAB 2.1 | ITALY 3.3 | GREECE 2.1 | OTHER EUROPE 5.6

Fisheries World Production - 96,748,500 metric tons - Avg. 1990-92

0	10	20	30	40	50	60	70	80	90	100 %

CHINA 12.6 % | JAPAN 10.6 | INDIA 4.0 | INDON. 3.2 | THAI. 2.9 | S. KOR 2.8 | PHIL 2.3 | OTHER ASIA 7.1 | FORMER USSR 10.7 | PERU 7.1 | CHILE 6.1 | OTHER 2.3 | UNITED STATES 5.9 | OTHER 3.6 | NOR. 2.0 | OTHER EUROPE 10.1 | AFRICA 5.0

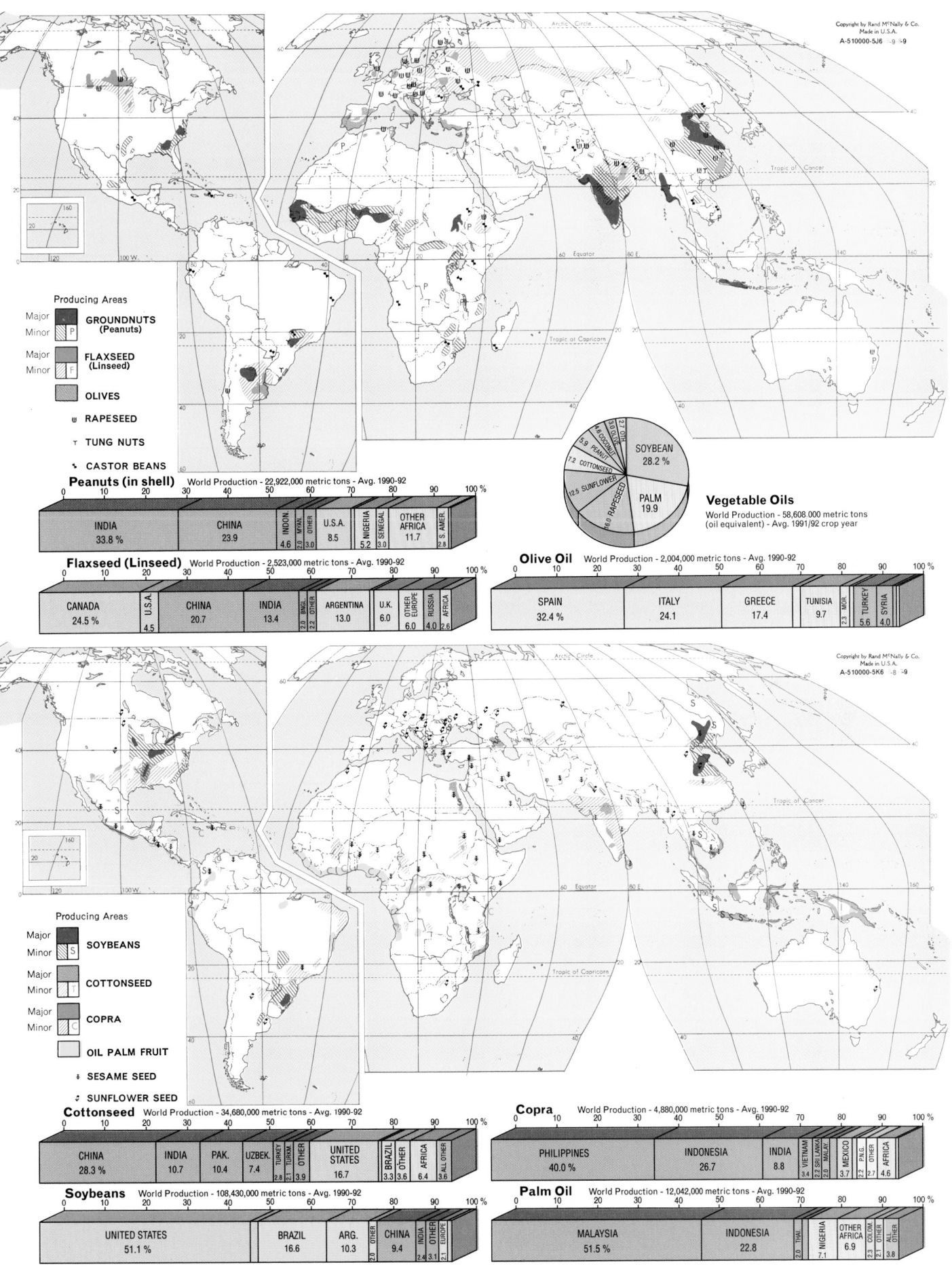

Producing Areas

Major / Minor **GROUNDNUTS** (Peanuts) P

Major / Minor **FLAXSEED** (Linseed) F

OLIVES

ɯ **RAPESEED**

⊤ **TUNG NUTS**

✦ **CASTOR BEANS**

Peanuts (in shell) — World Production - 22,922,000 metric tons - Avg. 1990-92

| INDIA 33.8% | CHINA 23.9 | INDON. 4.6 | MYAN. 2.0 | OTHER 3.0 | U.S.A. 8.5 | NIGERIA 5.2 | SENEGAL 3.0 | OTHER AFRICA 11.7 | S. AMER. 2.8 |

Flaxseed (Linseed) — World Production - 2,523,000 metric tons - Avg. 1990-92

| CANADA 24.5% | U.S.A. 4.5 | CHINA 20.7 | INDIA 13.4 | BNGL 2.0 | OTHER 2.2 | ARGENTINA 13.0 | U.K. 6.0 | OTHER EUROPE 6.0 | RUSSIA 4.0 | AFRICA 2.6 |

Vegetable Oils
World Production - 58,608,000 metric tons
(oil equivalent) - Avg. 1991/92 crop year

Pie chart: SOYBEAN 28.2%, PALM 19.9, RAPESEED 16.0, SUNFLOWER 12.5, COTTONSEED 7.2, PEANUT 5.9, COCONUT 4.6, OLIVE 3.0, OTH. 2.7

Olive Oil — World Production - 2,004,000 metric tons - Avg. 1990-92

| SPAIN 32.4% | ITALY 24.1 | GREECE 17.4 | TUNISIA 9.7 | MOR. 2.3 | TURKEY 5.6 | SYRIA 4.0 |

Producing Areas

Major / Minor **SOYBEANS** S

Major / Minor **COTTONSEED** T

Major / Minor **COPRA** C

OIL PALM FRUIT

≬ **SESAME SEED**

↻ **SUNFLOWER SEED**

Cottonseed — World Production - 34,680,000 metric tons - Avg. 1990-92

| CHINA 28.3% | INDIA 10.7 | PAK. 10.4 | UZBEK. 7.4 | TURKEY 2.8 | TURKM 2.1 | OTHER 3.9 | UNITED STATES 16.7 | BRAZIL 3.3 | OTHER 3.6 | AFRICA 6.4 | ALL OTHER 3.6 |

Copra — World Production - 4,880,000 metric tons - Avg. 1990-92

| PHILIPPINES 40.0% | INDONESIA 26.7 | INDIA 8.8 | VIETNAM 3.4 | SRI LANKA 2.0 | MALAY 2.0 | MEXICO 3.7 | P.N.G. 2.2 | OTHER 2.7 | AFRICA 4.6 |

Soybeans — World Production - 108,430,000 metric tons - Avg. 1990-92

| UNITED STATES 51.1% | BRAZIL 16.6 | ARG. 10.3 | CHINA 9.4 | INDIA 2.0 | OTHER 2.4 | EUROPE 3.1 |

Palm Oil — World Production - 12,042,000 metric tons - Avg. 1990-92

| MALAYSIA 51.5% | INDONESIA 22.8 | THAI. 2.0 | NIGERIA 7.1 | OTHER AFRICA 6.9 | COLOM. 2.3 | ALL OTHER 3.8 |

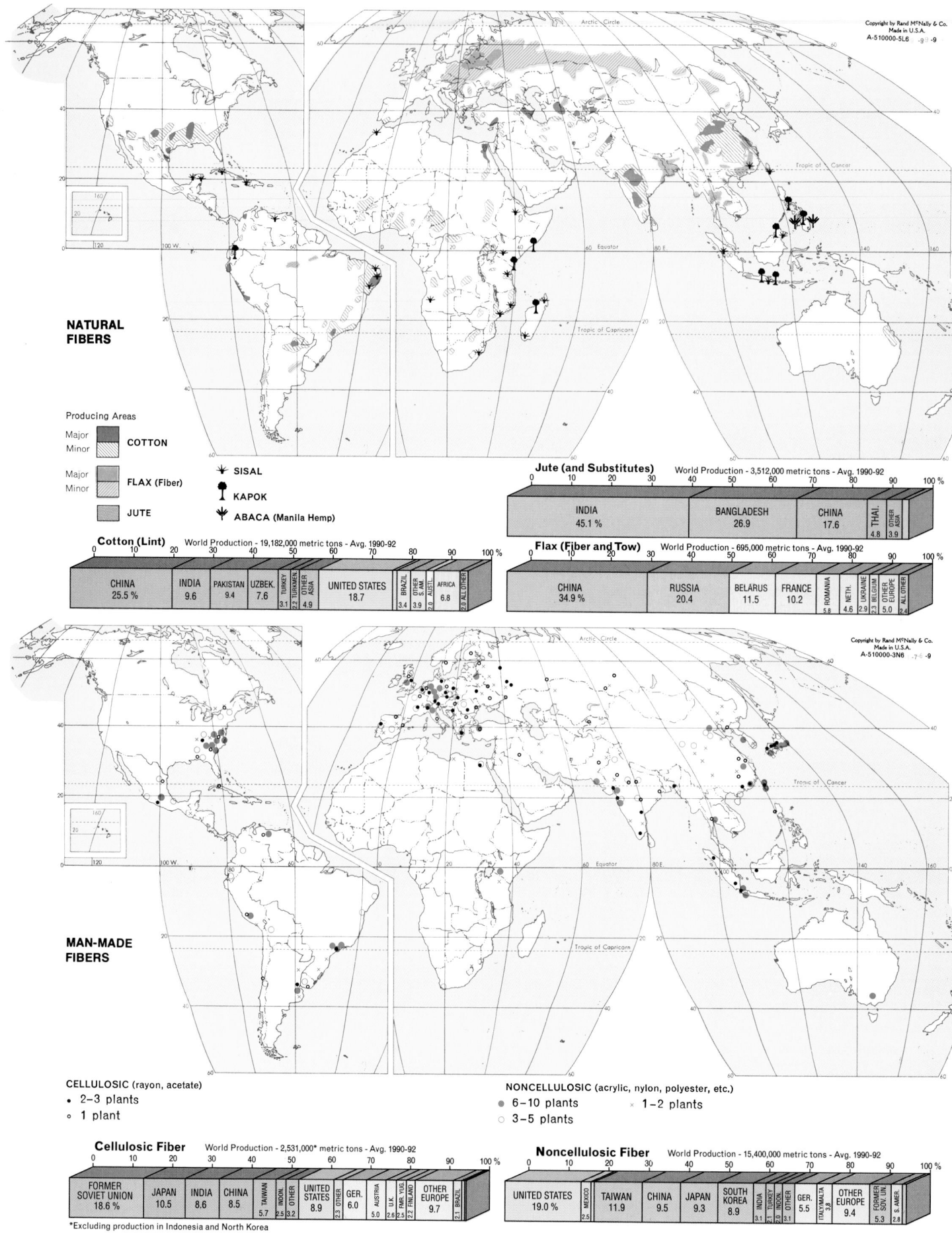

NATURAL FIBERS

Producing Areas

Major	**COTTON**
Minor	

Major	**FLAX (Fiber)**
Minor	

JUTE

✹ SISAL

🌿 KAPOK

✹ ABACA (Manila Hemp)

Jute (and Substitutes)
World Production - 3,512,000 metric tons - Avg. 1990-92

INDIA 45.1 %	BANGLADESH 26.9	CHINA 17.6	THAI. 4.8	OTHER ASIA 3.9

Flax (Fiber and Tow)
World Production - 695,000 metric tons - Avg. 1990-92

CHINA 34.9 %	RUSSIA 20.4	BELARUS 11.5	FRANCE 10.2	ROMANIA 5.8	NETH. 4.6	UKRAINE 2.9	BELGIUM 5.0 OTHER EUROPE	ALL OTHER 2.4

Cotton (Lint)
World Production - 19,182,000 metric tons - Avg. 1990-92

CHINA 25.5 %	INDIA 9.6	PAKISTAN 9.4	UZBEK. 7.6	TURKEY 3.1	TURKMEN. 2.5	OTHER ASIA 4.9	UNITED STATES 18.7	BRAZIL 3.4	OTHER S. AM. 3.9	AUSTL. 2.0	AFRICA 6.8	ALL OTHER 2.0

MAN-MADE FIBERS

CELLULOSIC (rayon, acetate)
- • 2–3 plants
- ○ 1 plant

NONCELLULOSIC (acrylic, nylon, polyester, etc.)
- ● 6–10 plants   × 1–2 plants
- ○ 3–5 plants

Cellulosic Fiber
World Production - 2,531,000* metric tons - Avg. 1990-92

FORMER SOVIET UNION 18.6 %	JAPAN 10.5	INDIA 8.6	CHINA 8.5	TAIWAN 5.7	INDON. 3.2	OTHER	UNITED STATES 8.9	OTHER 2.3	GER. 6.0	AUSTRIA 5.0	U.K. 2.6	FMR. YUG. 2.2	FINLAND	OTHER EUROPE 9.7	BRAZIL 2.5

*Excluding production in Indonesia and North Korea

Noncellulosic Fiber
World Production - 15,400,000 metric tons - Avg. 1990-92

UNITED STATES 19.0 %	MEXICO 2.5	TAIWAN 11.9	CHINA 9.5	JAPAN 9.3	SOUTH KOREA 8.9	INDIA 3.1	TURKEY 2.0	OTHER	GER. 5.5	ITALY 3.8 MALTA	OTHER EUROPE 9.4	FORMER SOV. UN. 5.3	S. AMER. 2.8

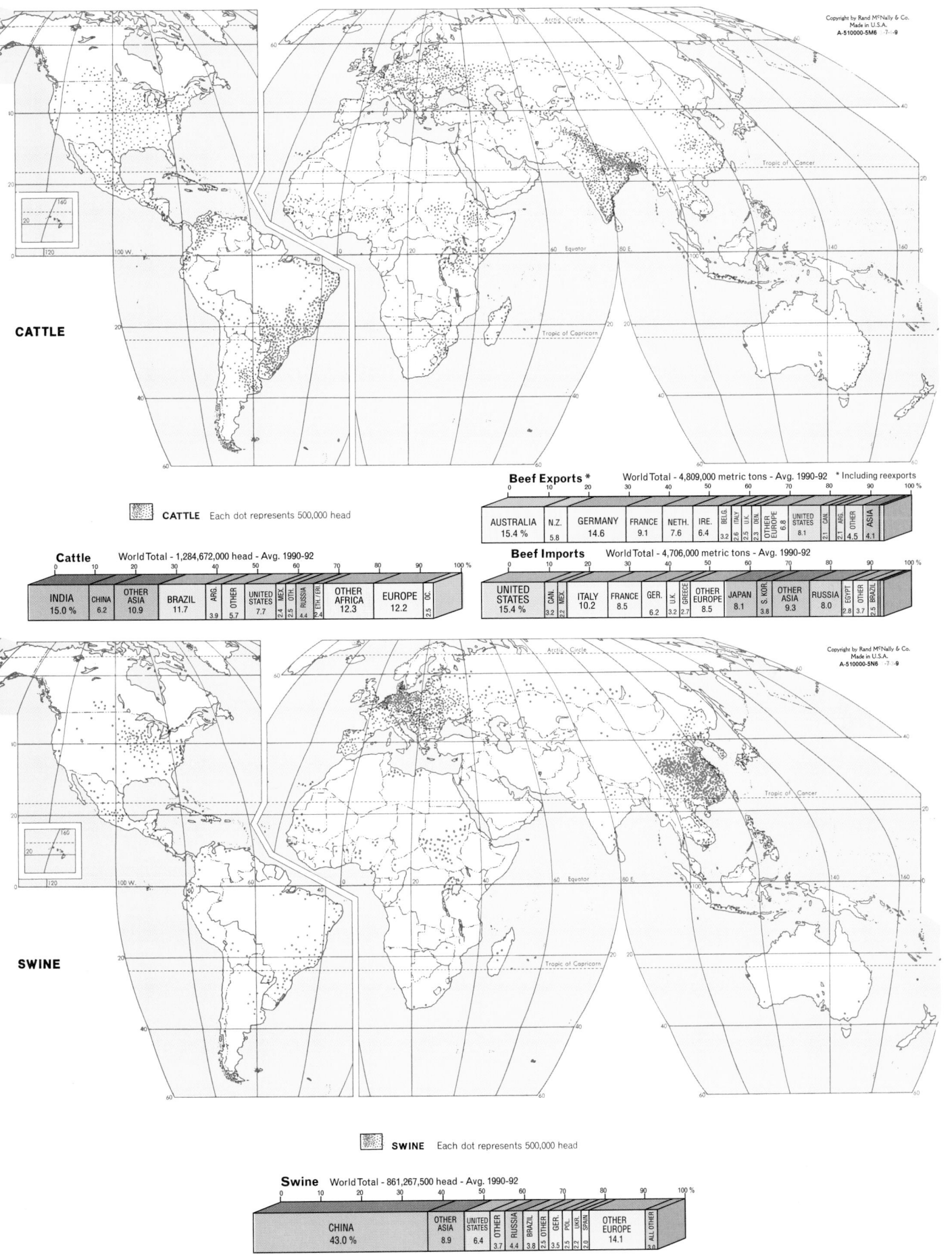

CATTLE

CATTLE Each dot represents 500,000 head

Cattle World Total - 1,284,672,000 head - Avg. 1990-92

| INDIA 15.0 % | CHINA 6.2 | OTHER ASIA 10.9 | BRAZIL 11.7 | ARG. 3.9 | OTHER 5.7 | UNITED STATES 7.7 | MEX. 2.4 | OTH. 2.5 | RUSSIA 4.4 | ETH./ERI. 2.4 | OTHER AFRICA 12.3 | EUROPE 12.2 | OC. 2.5 |

Beef Exports * World Total - 4,809,000 metric tons - Avg. 1990-92 * Including reexports

| AUSTRALIA 15.4 % | N.Z. 5.8 | GERMANY 14.6 | FRANCE 9.1 | NETH. 7.6 | IRE. 6.4 | BELG. 3.2 | ITALY 2.6 | U.K. 2.5 | DEN. 2.3 | OTHER EUROPE 6.8 | UNITED STATES 8.1 | CAN. 2.1 | ARG. 2.1 | OTHER 4.5 | ASIA 4.1 |

Beef Imports World Total - 4,706,000 metric tons - Avg. 1990-92

| UNITED STATES 15.4 % | CAN. 3.2 | MEX. 2.2 | ITALY 10.2 | FRANCE 8.5 | GER. 6.2 | U.K. 3.2 | GREECE 2.7 | OTHER EUROPE 8.5 | JAPAN 8.1 | S. KOR. 3.8 | OTHER ASIA 9.3 | RUSSIA 8.0 | EGYPT 2.8 | OTHER 3.7 | BRAZIL 2.5 |

SWINE

SWINE Each dot represents 500,000 head

Swine World Total - 861,267,500 head - Avg. 1990-92

| CHINA 43.0 % | OTHER ASIA 8.9 | UNITED STATES 6.4 | OTHER 3.7 | RUSSIA 4.4 | BRAZIL 3.8 | OTHER 2.5 | GER. 3.5 | POL. 2.5 | SPAIN 2.0 | OTHER EUROPE 14.1 | ALL OTHER 3.0 |

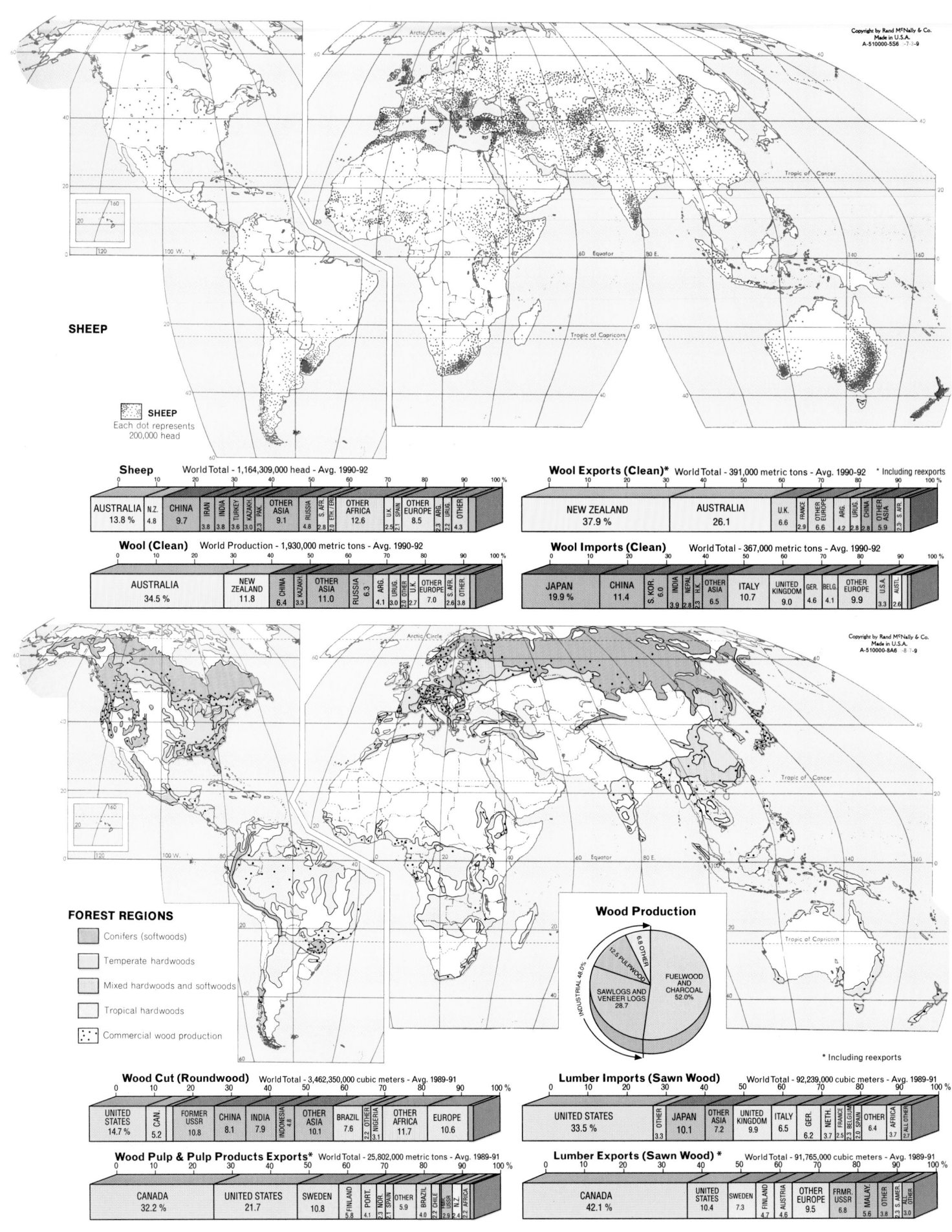

Copyright by Rand McNally & Co.
Made in U.S.A.
A-510000-5S6 -7-9 -9

SHEEP

SHEEP
Each dot represents
200,000 head

Sheep   World Total - 1,164,309,000 head - Avg. 1990-92

0	10	20	30	40	50	60	70	80	90	100 %

| AUSTRALIA 13.8 % | N.Z. 4.8 | CHINA 9.7 | IRAN 3.8 | INDIA 3.8 | TURKEY 3.6 | KAZAKH. 3.0 | PAK. 2.3 | OTHER ASIA 9.1 | RUSSIA 4.8 | S. AFR. 2.0 | ETH./ERI. 2.5 | OTHER AFRICA 12.6 | U.K. 2.1 | SPAIN | OTHER EUROPE 8.5 | ARG. 2.3 | URUG. 2.2 | OTHER 4.3 |

Wool Exports (Clean)*   World Total - 391,000 metric tons - Avg. 1990-92   * Including reexports

0	10	20	30	40	50	60	70	80	90	100 %

| NEW ZEALAND 37.9 % | AUSTRALIA 26.1 | U.K. 6.6 | FRANCE 2.9 | OTHER EUROPE 6.6 | ARG. 4.2 | URUG. 2.8 | CHINA 2.8 | OTHER ASIA 5.9 | S. AFR. 2.3 |

Wool (Clean)   World Production - 1,930,000 metric tons - Avg. 1990-92

0	10	20	30	40	50	60	70	80	90	100 %

| AUSTRALIA 34.5 % | NEW ZEALAND 11.8 | CHINA 6.4 | KAZAKH. 3.3 | OTHER ASIA 11.0 | RUSSIA 6.3 | ARG. 4.1 | URUG. 3.0 | U.K. 2.7 | OTHER EUROPE 7.0 | S. AFR. 2.6 | OTHER 3.8 |

Wool Imports (Clean)   World Total - 367,000 metric tons - Avg. 1990-92

0	10	20	30	40	50	60	70	80	90	100 %

| JAPAN 19.9 % | CHINA 11.4 | S. KOR. 6.0 | INDIA 3.9 | NEPAL 2.8 | H.K. 2.3 | OTHER ASIA 6.5 | ITALY 10.7 | UNITED KINGDOM 9.0 | GER. 4.6 | BELG. 4.1 | OTHER EUROPE 9.9 | U.S.A. 3.3 | AUSTL. 2.6 |

Copyright by Rand McNally & Co.
Made in U.S.A.
A-510000-8A6 -8-7-9

FOREST REGIONS

■ Conifers (softwoods)
□ Temperate hardwoods
▨ Mixed hardwoods and softwoods
□ Tropical hardwoods
⋯ Commercial wood production

Wood Production

INDUSTRIAL 48.0%
6.8 OTHER
12.5 PULPWOOD
SAWLOGS AND VENEER LOGS 28.7
FUELWOOD AND CHARCOAL 52.0%

* Including reexports

Wood Cut (Roundwood)   World Total - 3,462,350,000 cubic meters - Avg. 1989-91

0	10	20	30	40	50	60	70	80	90	100 %

| UNITED STATES 14.7 % | CAN. 5.2 | FORMER USSR 10.8 | CHINA 8.1 | INDIA 7.9 | INDONESIA 4.8 | OTHER ASIA 10.1 | BRAZIL 7.6 | OTHER 2.2 | NIGERIA 3.1 | OTHER AFRICA 11.7 | EUROPE 10.6 |

Lumber Imports (Sawn Wood)   World Total - 92,239,000 cubic meters - Avg. 1989-91

0	10	20	30	40	50	60	70	80	90	100 %

| UNITED STATES 33.5 % | OTHER 3.3 | JAPAN 10.1 | OTHER ASIA 7.2 | UNITED KINGDOM 9.9 | ITALY 6.5 | GER. 6.2 | NETH. 3.7 | FRANCE 2.5 | BELGIUM 2.3 | OTHER 6.4 | AFRICA 3.7 | ALL OTHER |

Wood Pulp & Pulp Products Exports*   World Total - 25,802,000 metric tons - Avg. 1989-91

0	10	20	30	40	50	60	70	80	90	100 %

| CANADA 32.2 % | UNITED STATES 21.7 | SWEDEN 10.8 | FINLAND 5.8 | PORT. 4.1 | NOR. 2.3 | SPAIN 2.1 | OTHER 5.9 | BRAZIL 4.0 | CHILE 2.2 | FRMR. USSR 2.9 | S. AFR. 2.4 | AFRICA |

Lumber Exports (Sawn Wood) *   World Total - 91,765,000 cubic meters - Avg. 1989-91

0	10	20	30	40	50	60	70	80	90	100 %

| CANADA 42.1 % | UNITED STATES 10.4 | SWEDEN 7.3 | FINLAND 4.7 | AUSTRIA 4.6 | OTHER EUROPE 9.5 | FRMR. USSR 6.8 | MALAY. 3.8 | OTHER 3.7 | S. AMER. 2.6 | N.Z. 3.0 | ALL OTHER |

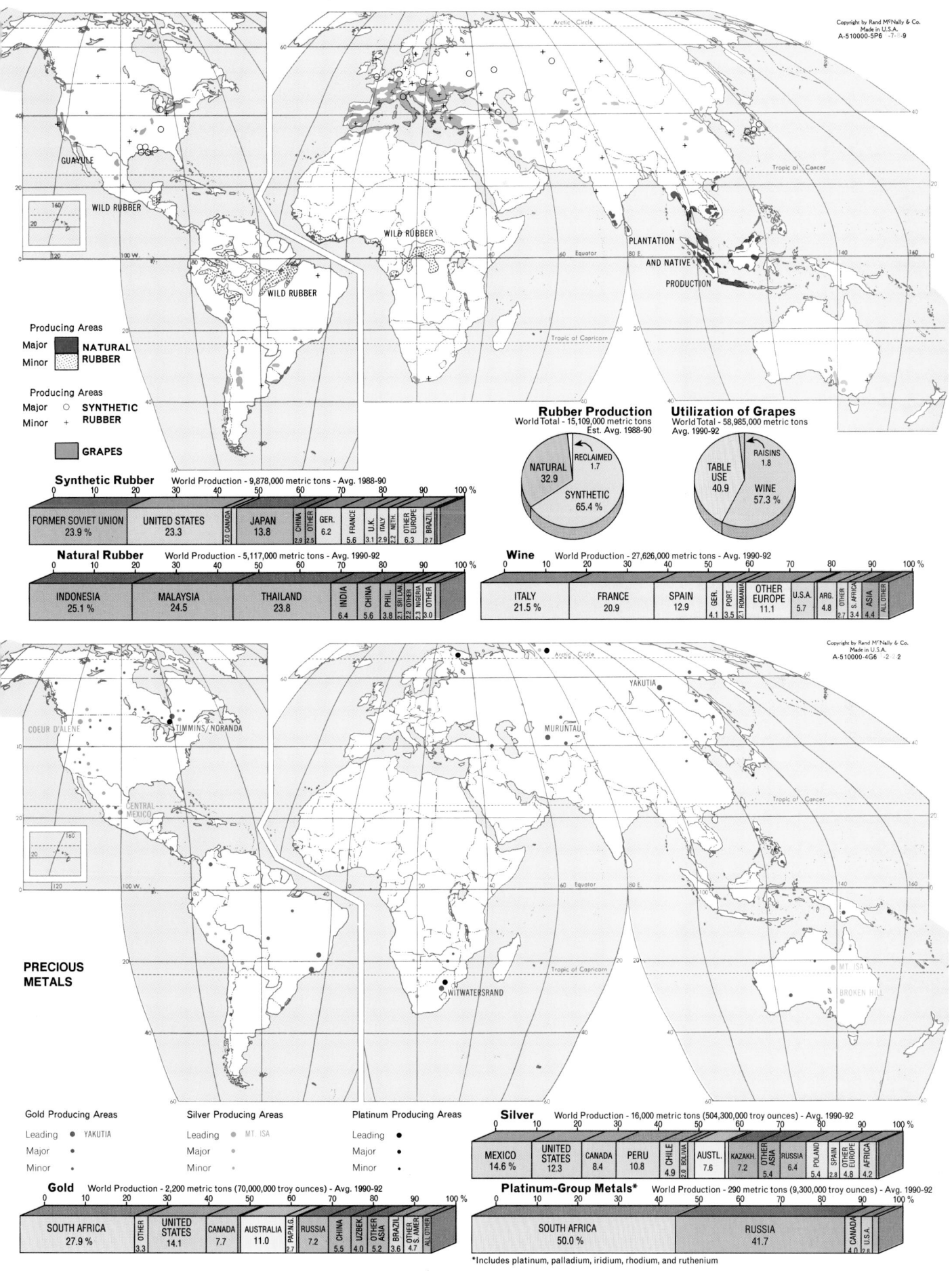

GUAYULE

WILD RUBBER

WILD RUBBER

WILD RUBBER

PLANTATION AND NATIVE PRODUCTION

Producing Areas
Major / Minor NATURAL RUBBER

Producing Areas
Major ○ / Minor + SYNTHETIC RUBBER

GRAPES

Rubber Production
World Total - 15,109,000 metric tons
Est. Avg. 1988-90

NATURAL 32.9 / RECLAIMED 1.7 / SYNTHETIC 65.4 %

Utilization of Grapes
World Total - 58,985,000 metric tons
Avg. 1990-92

TABLE USE 40.9 / RAISINS 1.8 / WINE 57.3 %

Synthetic Rubber
World Production - 9,878,000 metric tons - Avg. 1988-90

| FORMER SOVIET UNION 23.9 % | UNITED STATES 23.3 | CANADA 2.0 | JAPAN 13.8 | CHINA 2.9 | OTHER 2.5 | GER. 6.2 | FRANCE 5.6 | U.K. 3.1 | ITALY 2.2 | NETH. | OTHER EUROPE 6.3 | BRAZIL 2.7 |

Natural Rubber
World Production - 5,117,000 metric tons - Avg. 1990-92

| INDONESIA 25.1 % | MALAYSIA 24.5 | THAILAND 23.8 | INDIA 6.4 | CHINA 5.6 | PHIL. 3.8 | SRI LAN. 2.1 | OTHER 2.2 | NIGERIA | OTHER 3.0 |

Wine
World Production - 27,626,000 metric tons - Avg. 1990-92

| ITALY 21.5 % | FRANCE 20.9 | SPAIN 12.9 | GER. 4.1 | PORT. 3.5 | ROMANIA 2.1 | OTHER EUROPE 11.1 | U.S.A. 5.7 | ARG. 4.8 | OTHER 2.7 | S. AFRICA 3.4 | ASIA 4.4 | ALL OTHER |

YAKUTIA

MURUNTAU

COEUR D'ALENE

TIMMINS / NORANDA

CENTRAL MEXICO

WITWATERSRAND

MT. ISA

BROKEN HILL

PRECIOUS METALS

Gold Producing Areas
Leading ● YAKUTIA
Major ●
Minor ●

Silver Producing Areas
Leading ● MT. ISA
Major ●
Minor ●

Platinum Producing Areas
Leading ●
Major ●
Minor ●

Silver
World Production - 16,000 metric tons (504,300,000 troy ounces) - Avg. 1990-92

| MEXICO 14.6 % | UNITED STATES 12.3 | CANADA 8.4 | PERU 10.8 | CHILE 4.9 | BOLIVIA 2.0 | AUSTL. 7.6 | KAZAKH. 7.2 | OTHER ASIA 5.4 | RUSSIA 6.4 | POLAND 5.4 | SPAIN 2.9 | OTHER EUROPE 4.8 | AFRICA 4.2 |

Gold
World Production - 2,200 metric tons (70,000,000 troy ounces) - Avg. 1990-92

| SOUTH AFRICA 27.9 % | OTHER 3.3 | UNITED STATES 14.1 | CANADA 7.7 | AUSTRALIA 11.0 | PAP'N.G. 2.7 | RUSSIA 7.2 | CHINA 5.5 | UZBEK. 4.0 | OTHER ASIA 3.2 | BRAZIL 3.6 | OTHER S. AMER. 4.7 | ALL OTHER |

Platinum-Group Metals*
World Production - 290 metric tons (9,300,000 troy ounces) - Avg. 1990-92

| SOUTH AFRICA 50.0 % | RUSSIA 41.7 | CANADA 4.0 | U.S.A. 2.8 |

*Includes platinum, palladium, iridium, rhodium, and ruthenium

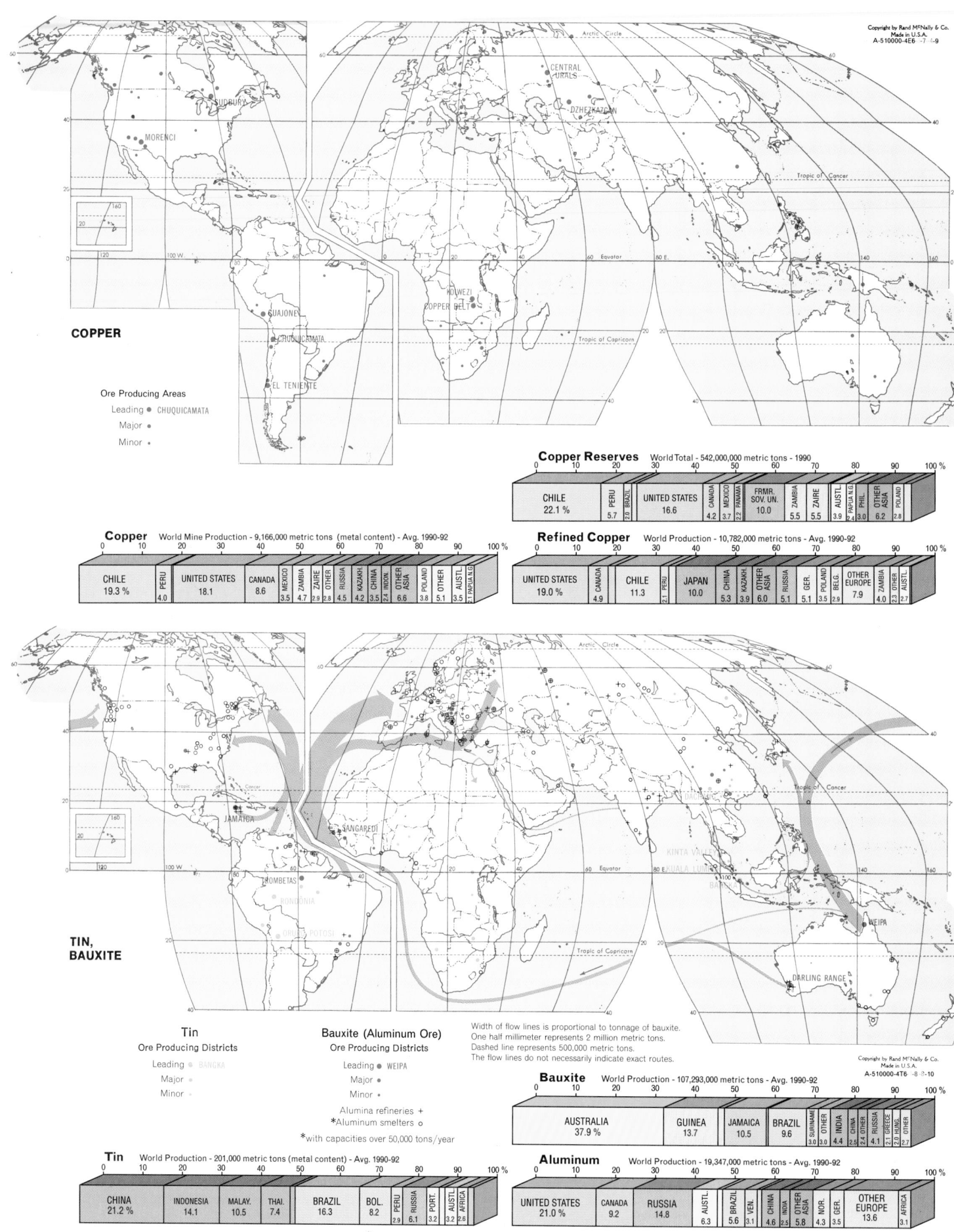

COPPER

Ore Producing Areas

Leading ● CHUQUICAMATA

Major ●

Minor ●

Copper Reserves World Total - 542,000,000 metric tons - 1990

| CHILE 22.1 % | PERU 5.7 | BRAZIL 2.0 | UNITED STATES 16.6 | CANADA 4.2 | MEXICO 3.7 | PANAMA 2.2 | FRMR. SOV. UN. 10.0 | ZAMBIA 5.5 | ZAIRE 5.5 | AUSTL 3.9 | PAPUA N.G. 3.0 | PHIL. | OTHER ASIA 6.2 | POLAND 2.8 |

Copper World Mine Production - 9,166,000 metric tons (metal content) - Avg. 1990-92

| CHILE 19.3 % | PERU 4.0 | UNITED STATES 18.1 | CANADA 8.6 | MEXICO 3.5 | ZAMBIA 4.7 | ZAIRE 2.9 | OTHER 2.8 | RUSSIA 4.5 | KAZAKH. 4.2 | CHINA 3.5 | INDON. 2.4 | OTHER ASIA 6.6 | POLAND 3.8 | OTHER 5.1 | AUSTL 3.5 | PAPUA N.G. 2.1 |

Refined Copper World Production - 10,782,000 metric tons - Avg. 1990-92

| UNITED STATES 19.0 % | CANADA 4.9 | CHILE 11.3 | PERU 2.1 | JAPAN 10.0 | CHINA 5.3 | KAZAKH. 3.9 | OTHER ASIA 6.0 | RUSSIA 5.1 | GER. 5.1 | POLAND 3.5 | BELG. 2.9 | OTHER EUROPE 7.9 | ZAMBIA 4.0 | AUSTL. 2.3 |

TIN, BAUXITE

Tin
Ore Producing Districts

Leading ● BANGKA

Major ●

Minor ●

Bauxite (Aluminum Ore)
Ore Producing Districts

Leading ● WEIPA

Major ●

Minor ●

Alumina refineries +
*Aluminum smelters o

*with capacities over 50,000 tons/year

Width of flow lines is proportional to tonnage of bauxite.
One half millimeter represents 2 million metric tons.
Dashed line represents 500,000 metric tons.
The flow lines do not necessarily indicate exact routes.

Bauxite World Production - 107,293,000 metric tons - Avg. 1990-92

| AUSTRALIA 37.9 % | GUINEA 13.7 | JAMAICA 10.5 | BRAZIL 9.6 | SURINAME 3.0 | OTHER 3.0 | INDIA 4.4 | CHINA 2.5 | OTHER 4.0 | RUSSIA 4.1 | GREECE 2.1 | HUNG. 2.0 | OTHER 2.7 |

Tin World Production - 201,000 metric tons (metal content) - Avg. 1990-92

| CHINA 21.2 % | INDONESIA 14.1 | MALAY. 10.5 | THAI. 7.4 | BRAZIL 16.3 | BOL. 8.2 | PERU 2.9 | RUSSIA 6.1 | PORT. 3.2 | AUSTL. 3.2 | AFRICA 2.6 |

Aluminum World Production - 19,347,000 metric tons - Avg. 1990-92

| UNITED STATES 21.0 % | CANADA 9.2 | RUSSIA 14.8 | AUSTL. 6.3 | BRAZIL 5.6 | VEN. 3.1 | CHINA 4.6 | INDIA 2.5 | OTHER ASIA 5.8 | NOR. 4.3 | GER. 3.5 | OTHER EUROPE 13.6 | AFRICA |

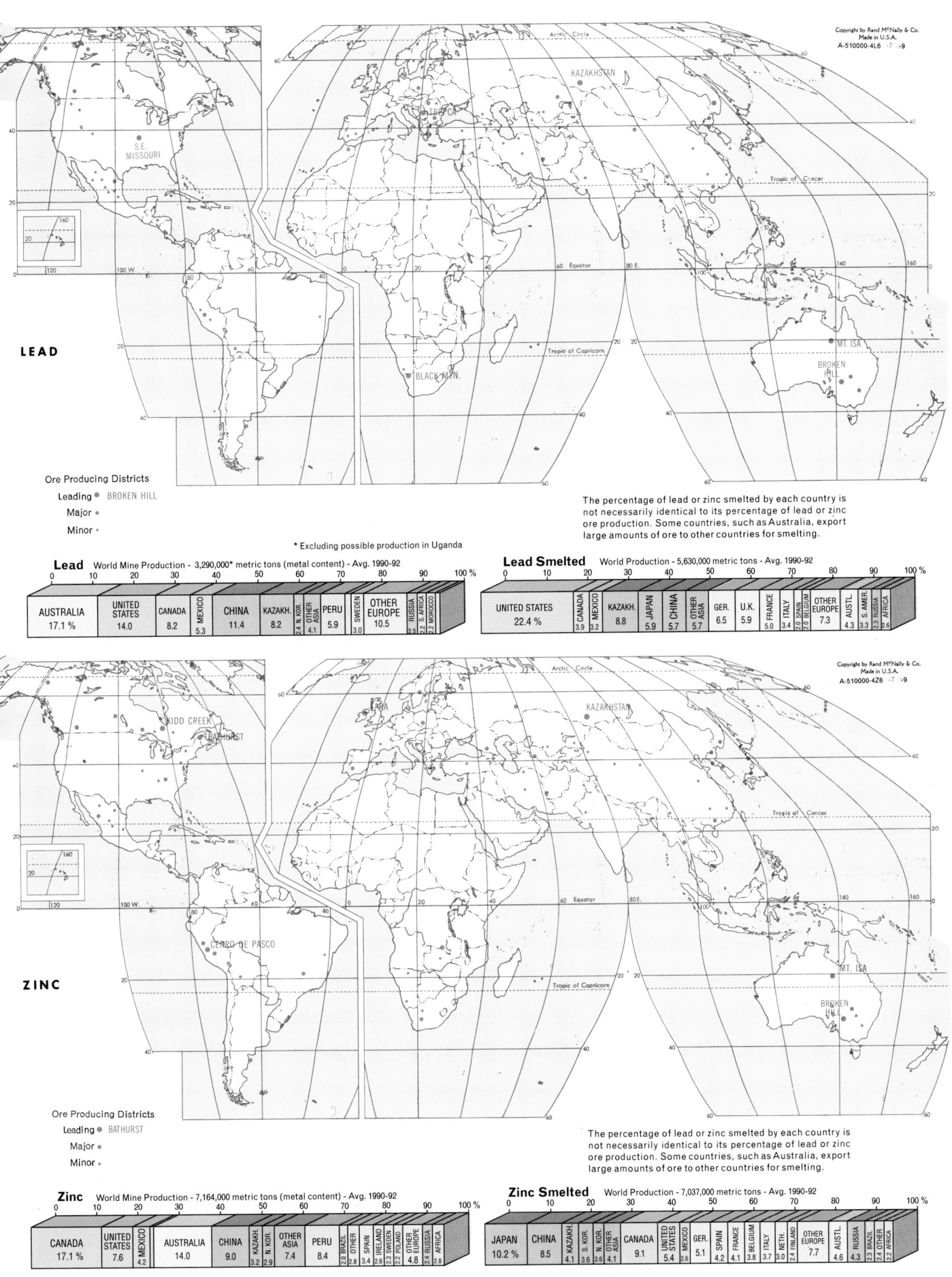

LEAD

Ore Producing Districts

Leading ● BROKEN HILL

Major ●

Minor ·

The percentage of lead or zinc smelted by each country is not necessarily identical to its percentage of lead or zinc ore production. Some countries, such as Australia, export large amounts of ore to other countries for smelting.

* Excluding possible production in Uganda

Lead World Mine Production - 3,290,000* metric tons (metal content) - Avg. 1990-92

0	10	20	30	40	50	60	70	80	90	100 %

AUSTRALIA 17.1 % | UNITED STATES 14.0 | CANADA 8.2 | MEXICO 5.3 | CHINA 11.4 | KAZAKH. 8.2 | N. KOR. 2.4 | OTHER ASIA 4.1 | PERU 5.9 | SWEDEN 3.0 | OTHER EUROPE 10.5 | RUSSIA 2.5 | S. AFRICA 2.2 | MOROCCO 2.2

Lead Smelted World Production - 5,630,000 metric tons - Avg. 1990-92

0	10	20	30	40	50	60	70	80	90	100 %

UNITED STATES 22.4 % | CANADA 3.9 | MEXICO 3.2 | KAZAKH. 8.8 | JAPAN 5.9 | CHINA 5.7 | OTHER ASIA 5.7 | GER. 6.5 | U.K. 5.9 | FRANCE 5.0 | ITALY 3.4 | SPAIN 2.0 | BELGIUM | OTHER EUROPE 7.3 | AUSTL. 4.3 | S. AMER. 3.3 | RUSSIA 2.3 | AFRICA 2.6

ZINC

Ore Producing Districts

Leading ● BATHURST

Major ●

Minor ·

The percentage of lead or zinc smelted by each country is not necessarily identical to its percentage of lead or zinc ore production. Some countries, such as Australia, export large amounts of ore to other countries for smelting.

Zinc World Mine Production - 7,164,000 metric tons (metal content) - Avg. 1990-92

0	10	20	30	40	50	60	70	80	90	100 %

CANADA 17.1 % | UNITED STATES 7.6 | MEXICO 4.2 | AUSTRALIA 14.0 | CHINA 9.0 | KAZAKH. 3.2 | N. KOR. 2.9 | OTHER ASIA 7.4 | PERU 8.4 | BRAZIL 2.0 | OTHER 2.8 | SPAIN 3.4 | IRELAND 2.3 | POLAND 2.8 | OTHER EUROPE 4.8 | AFRICA 2.8

Zinc Smelted World Production - 7,037,000 metric tons - Avg. 1990-92

0	10	20	30	40	50	60	70	80	90	100 %

JAPAN 10.2 % | CHINA 8.5 | KAZAKH. 4.1 | S. KOR. 3.6 | N. KOR. 4.1 | OTHER ASIA | CANADA 9.1 | UNITED STATES 5.4 | MEXICO 2.6 | GER. 5.1 | SPAIN 4.2 | FRANCE 4.1 | BELGIUM 3.8 | ITALY 3.7 | NETH. 3.0 | FINLAND 2.4 | OTHER EUROPE 7.7 | AUSTL. 4.6 | RUSSIA 4.3 | BRAZIL 2.4 | OTHER 2.2 | AFRICA 2.2

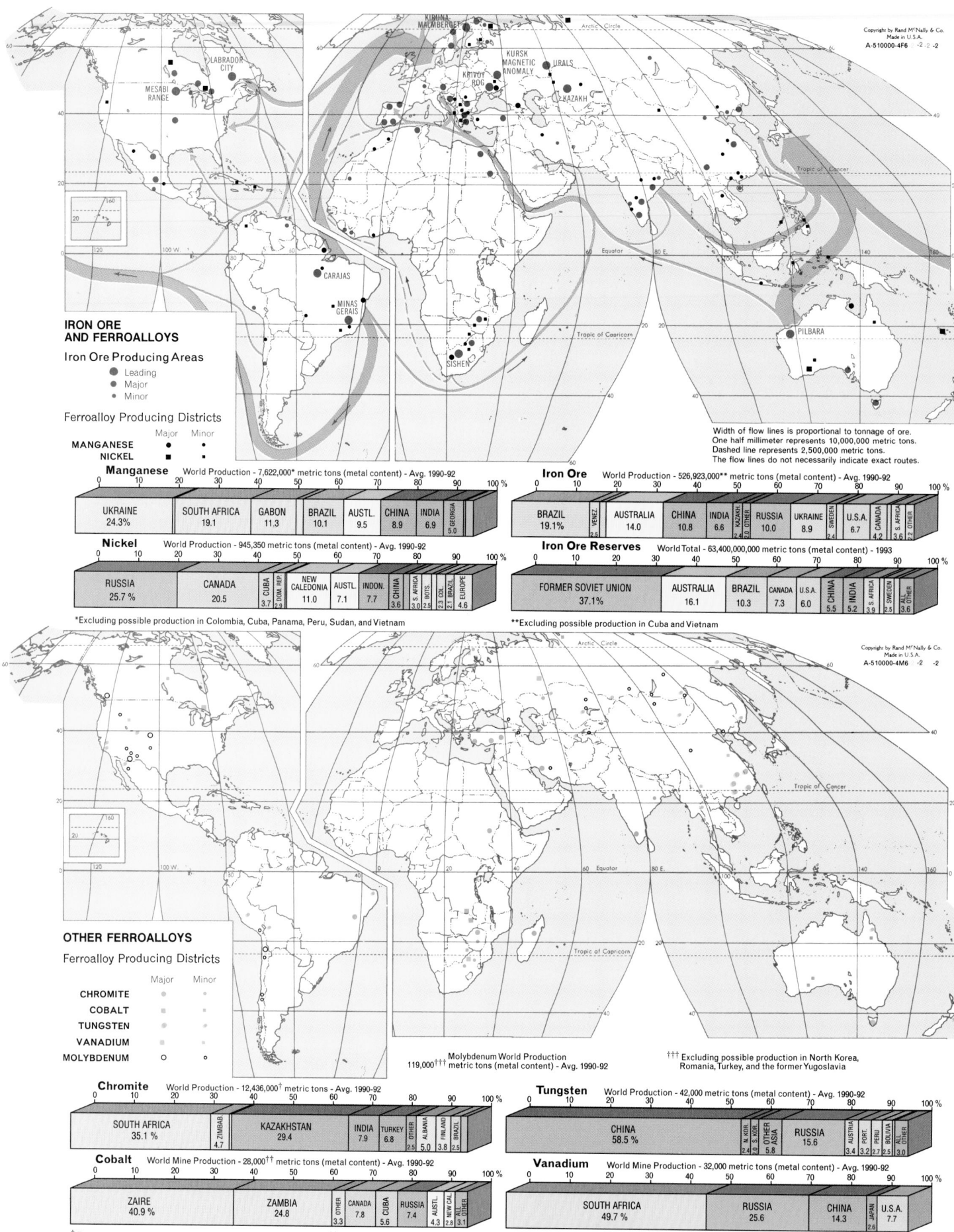

IRON ORE
AND FERROALLOYS

Iron Ore Producing Areas
- ● Leading
- ● Major
- ● Minor

Ferroalloy Producing Districts

	Major	Minor
MANGANESE	●	●
NICKEL	■	■

Width of flow lines is proportional to tonnage of ore.
One half millimeter represents 10,000,000 metric tons.
Dashed line represents 2,500,000 metric tons.
The flow lines do not necessarily indicate exact routes.

Manganese World Production - 7,622,000* metric tons (metal content) - Avg. 1990-92

UKRAINE 24.3%	SOUTH AFRICA 19.1	GABON 11.3	BRAZIL 10.1	AUSTL. 9.5	CHINA 8.9	INDIA 6.9	GEORGIA 5.0

Nickel World Production - 945,350 metric tons (metal content) - Avg. 1990-92

RUSSIA 25.7%	CANADA 20.5	CUBA 3.7	DOM. REP 2.9	NEW CALEDONIA 11.0	AUSTL. 7.1	INDON. 7.7	CHINA 3.6	S. AFRICA 3.0	BOTS. 2.5	COL. 2.3	BRAZIL 2.2	EUROPE 4.6

*Excluding possible production in Colombia, Cuba, Panama, Peru, Sudan, and Vietnam

Iron Ore World Production - 526,923,000** metric tons (metal content) - Avg. 1990-92

BRAZIL 19.1%	VENEZ. 2.5	AUSTRALIA 14.0	CHINA 10.8	INDIA 6.6	KAZAKH 2.4	OTHER 2.0	RUSSIA 10.0	UKRAINE 8.9	SWEDEN 4.7	U.S.A. 6.7	CANADA 4.2	S. AFRICA 2.2	OTHER

Iron Ore Reserves World Total - 63,400,000,000 metric tons (metal content) - 1993

FORMER SOVIET UNION 37.1%	AUSTRALIA 16.1	BRAZIL 10.3	CANADA 7.3	U.S.A. 6.0	CHINA 5.5	INDIA 5.2	S. AFRICA 3.9	SWEDEN 2.5	ALL OTHER 3.6

**Excluding possible production in Cuba and Vietnam

OTHER FERROALLOYS

Ferroalloy Producing Districts

	Major	Minor
CHROMITE	●	●
COBALT	■	■
TUNGSTEN	●	●
VANADIUM	●	●
MOLYBDENUM	○	○

Molybdenum World Production
119,000††† metric tons (metal content) - Avg. 1990-92

††† Excluding possible production in North Korea,
Romania, Turkey, and the former Yugoslavia

Chromite World Production - 12,436,000† metric tons - Avg. 1990-92

SOUTH AFRICA 35.1%	ZIMBAB. 4.7	KAZAKHSTAN 29.4	INDIA 7.9	TURKEY 6.8	OTHER ASIA 5.0	ALBANIA 3.8	FINLAND	BRAZIL 2.5

Cobalt World Mine Production - 28,000†† metric tons (metal content) - Avg. 1990-92

ZAIRE 40.9%	ZAMBIA 24.8	OTHER 3.3	CANADA 7.8	CUBA 5.6	RUSSIA 7.4	AUSTL 4.3	NEW CAL 2.8	OTHER 3.1

Tungsten World Production - 42,000 metric tons (metal content) - Avg. 1990-92

CHINA 58.5%	N. KOR 2.5	S. KOR	OTHER ASIA 5.8	RUSSIA 15.6	AUSTRIA 3.4	PORT. 3.2	PERU 2.7	BOLIVIA	ALL OTHER

Vanadium World Mine Production - 32,000 metric tons (metal content) - Avg. 1990-92

SOUTH AFRICA 49.7%	RUSSIA 25.6	CHINA 14.3	JAPAN	U.S.A. 7.7

† Excluding possible production in Bulgaria and North Korea   †† Excluding possible production in Bulgaria, China, Germany, Indonesia, and Poland

Copyright by Rand McNally & Co.
Made in U.S.A.
A-510000-4F6 -2 -2 -2

Copyright by Rand McNally & Co.
Made in U.S.A.
A-510000-4M6 -2 -2

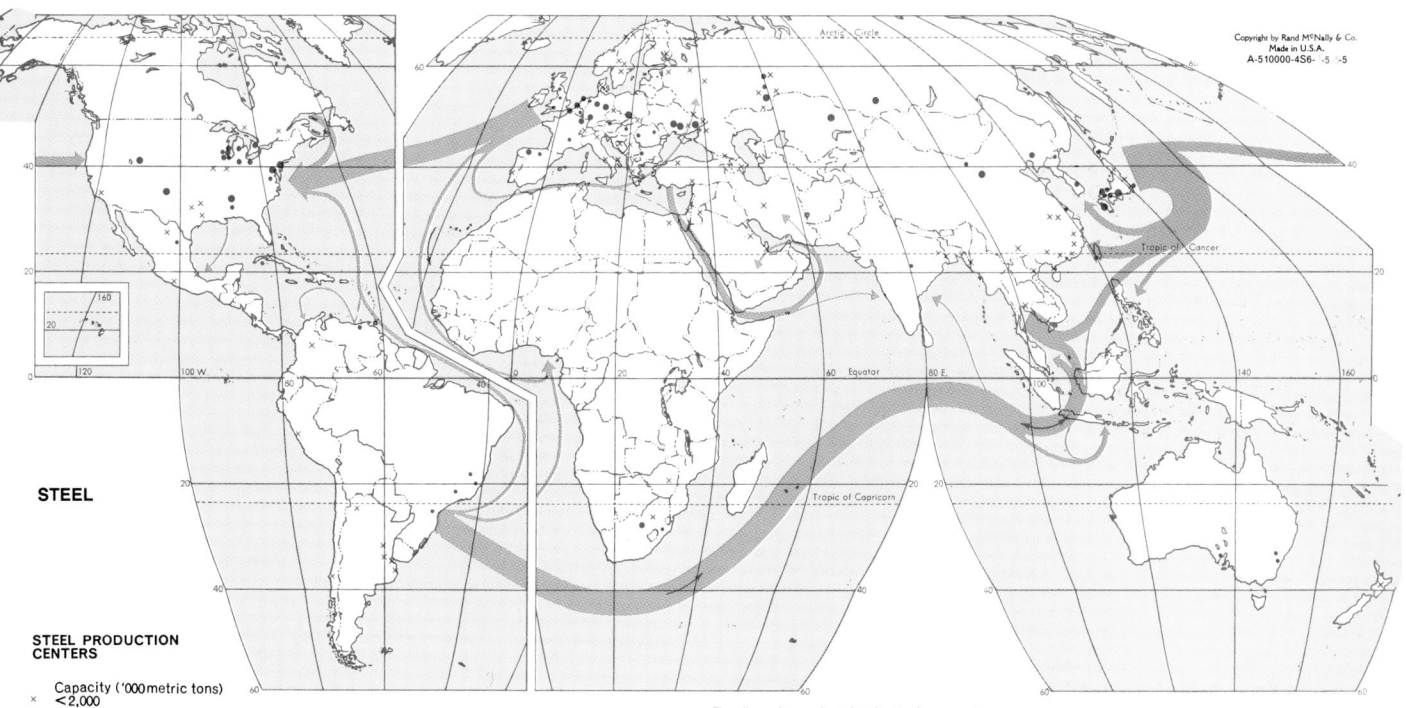

STEEL

STEEL PRODUCTION CENTERS

Capacity ('000 metric tons)
- ×   <2,000
- ✳   2,000–5,000
- ◦   5,000–10,000
- ●   >10,000

Flow lines show selected major steel movements
(forms, shapes, plates, etc.) among Market Economy Countries
Internal movement within Europe not shown.
Width of flow lines is proportional to tonnage of steel.
One half millimeter represents 1,000,000 metric tons.
Dashed line represents 250,000 metric tons.
The flow lines do not necessarily indicate exact routes.

Crude Steel   World Production - 742,831,000 metric tons - Avg. 1990-92

JAPAN 14.3 %	CHINA 9.7	S. KOREA 3.5	INDIA 2.2	OTHER ASIA 6.4	UNITED STATES 11.4	OTHER 3.0	RUSSIA 10.4	UKRAINE 6.5	GERMANY 5.7	ITALY 3.4	FRANCE 2.3	U.K.	OTHER EUROPE 11.6	BRAZIL 3.0	ALL OTHER 3.1

Pig Iron   World Production - 531,392,000* metric tons - Avg. 1990-92

JAPAN 14.6 %	CHINA 12.7	S. KOREA 3.3	INDIA 2.8	OTHER ASIA 5.3	RUSSIA 9.6	UNITED STATES 8.9	OTHER 2.9	UKRAINE 7.5	GERMANY 5.8	FRANCE 2.2	U.K. 2.1	ITALY	OTHER EUROPE 10.2	BRAZIL 4.2	AFRICA 2.2

*Excluding possible production in Vietnam

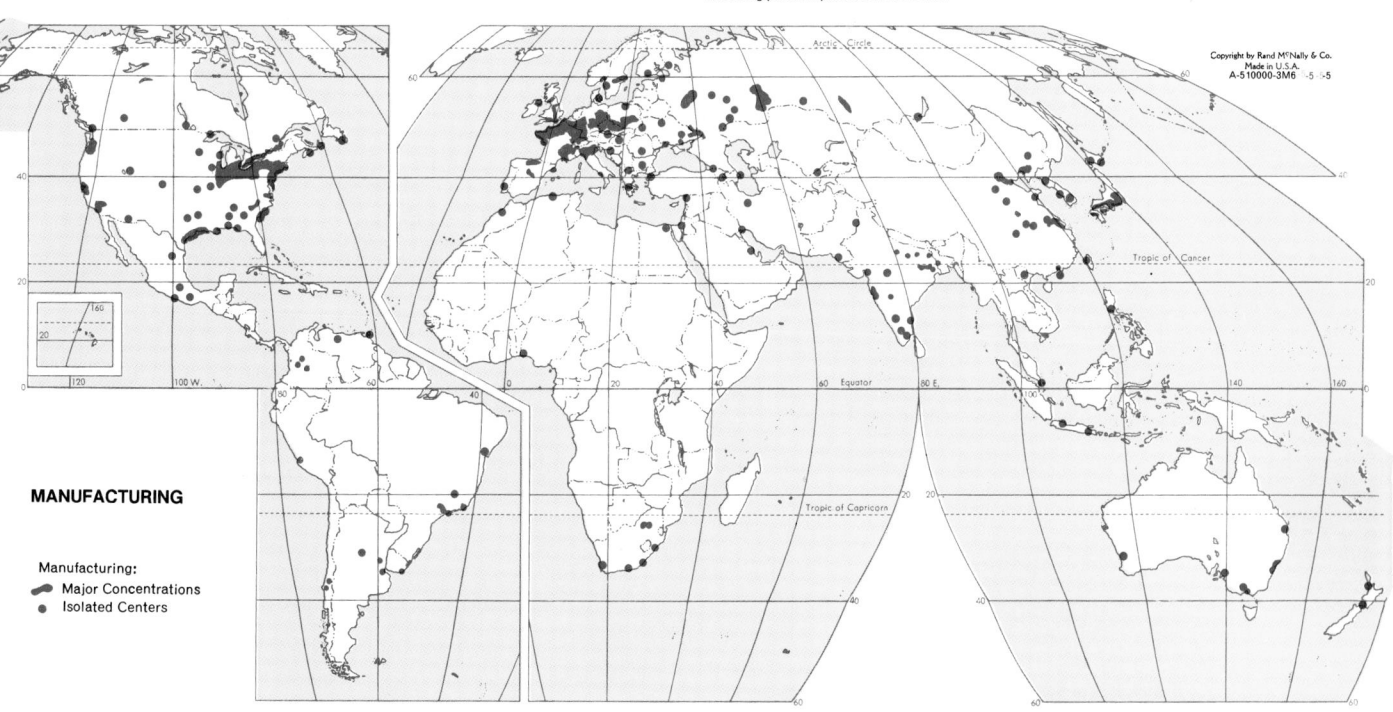

MANUFACTURING

Manufacturing:
- ⌇   Major Concentrations
- ●   Isolated Centers

Manufacturing: Value Added by Country   World Total - $2,800 billion (U.S. dollars)

UNITED STATES 29.4 %	CANADA 2.1	WESTERN EUROPE 24.1	E. EUROPE 4.2	JAPAN 14.4	CHINA 3.5	OTHER ASIA 4.9	FORMER SOV. UN. 10.5	S. AMER. 3.7

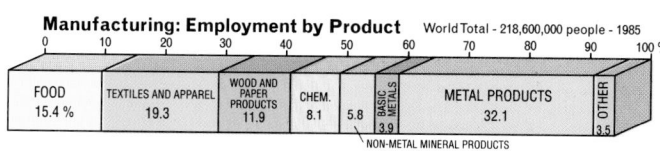

Manufacturing: Employment by Product   World Total - 218,600,000 people - 1985

FOOD 15.4 %	TEXTILES AND APPAREL 19.3	WOOD AND PAPER PRODUCTS 11.9	CHEM. 8.1	NON-METAL MINERAL PRODUCTS 5.8	BASIC METALS 3.9	METAL PRODUCTS 32.1	OTHER 3.5

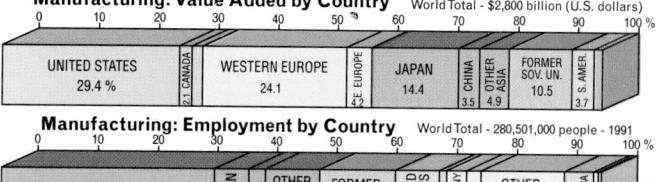

Manufacturing: Employment by Country   World Total - 280,501,000 people - 1991

CHINA 35.4 %	JAPAN 5.7	INDON. 2.8	OTHER ASIA 9.2	FORMER SOV. UN. 12.6	UNITED STATES 7.3	GERMANY 3.3	U.K. 2.4	OTHER EUROPE 13.9	SOUTH AMERICA 4.9

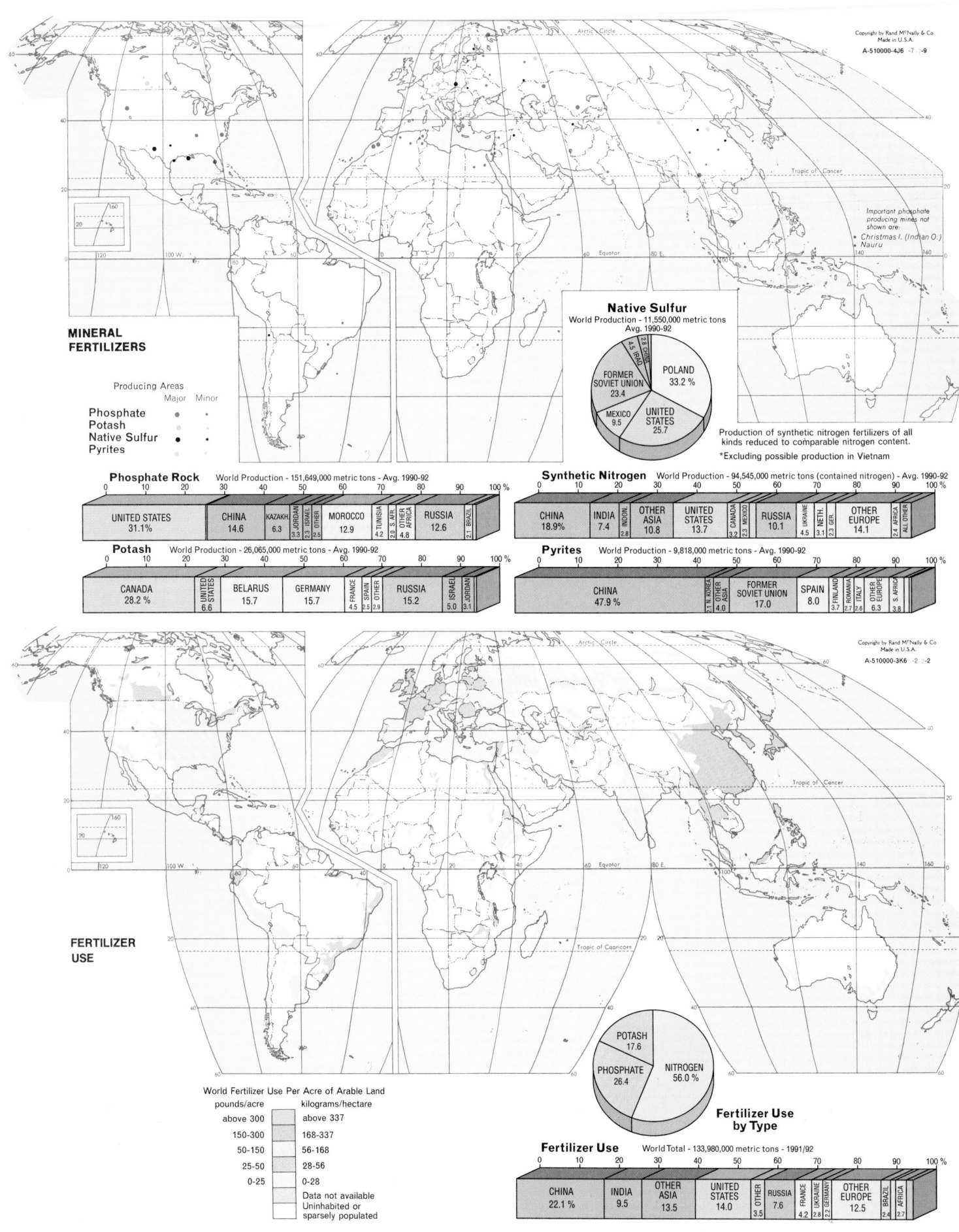

MINERAL FERTILIZERS

Producing Areas

	Major	Minor
Phosphate		
Potash		
Native Sulfur		
Pyrites		

Copyright by Rand McNally & Co.
Made in U.S.A.
A-510000-4J6 -7 -9

Important phosphate producing mines not shown are:
Christmas I. (Indian O.)
Nauru

Native Sulfur
World Production - 11,550,000 metric tons
Avg. 1990-92

- POLAND 33.2 %
- FORMER SOVIET UNION 23.4
- UNITED STATES 25.7
- MEXICO 9.5
- IRAQ 4.5
- CHINA 2.2

Production of synthetic nitrogen fertilizers of all kinds reduced to comparable nitrogen content.
*Excluding possible production in Vietnam

Phosphate Rock   World Production - 151,649,000 metric tons - Avg. 1990-92

0	10	20	30	40	50	60	70	80	90	100 %

| UNITED STATES 31.1% | CHINA 14.6 | KAZAKH. 6.3 | JORDAN 3.3 | ISRAEL 2.3 | OTHER 2.5 | MOROCCO 12.9 | TUNISIA 4.2 | S. AFR. 2.0 | OTHER AFRICA 4.8 | RUSSIA 12.6 | BRAZIL 2.1 |

Potash   World Production - 26,065,000 metric tons - Avg. 1990-92

0	10	20	30	40	50	60	70	80	90	100 %

| CANADA 28.2 % | UNITED STATES 6.6 | BELARUS 15.7 | GERMANY 15.7 | FRANCE 4.5 | SPAIN 2.5 | OTHER 2.9 | RUSSIA 15.2 | ISRAEL 5.0 | JORDAN 3.1 |

Synthetic Nitrogen   World Production - 94,545,000 metric tons (contained nitrogen) - Avg. 1990-92

0	10	20	30	40	50	60	70	80	90	100 %

| CHINA 18.9% | INDIA 7.4 | INDON. 2.8 | OTHER ASIA 10.8 | UNITED STATES 13.7 | CANADA 3.2 | MEXICO 2.3 | RUSSIA 10.1 | UKRAINE 4.5 | NETH. 3.1 | GER. 2.3 | OTHER EUROPE 14.1 | AFRICA 2.4 | ALL OTHER |

Pyrites   World Production - 9,818,000 metric tons - Avg. 1990-92

0	10	20	30	40	50	60	70	80	90	100 %

| CHINA 47.9 % | N. KOREA 2.1 | OTHER ASIA 4.0 | FORMER SOVIET UNION 17.0 | SPAIN 8.0 | FINLAND 3.7 | ROMANIA 2.7 | ITALY 2.6 | OTHER EUROPE 6.3 | S. AFRICA 3.8 |

FERTILIZER USE

Copyright by Rand McNally & Co.
Made in U.S.A.
A-510000-3K6 -2 -2

World Fertilizer Use Per Acre of Arable Land

pounds/acre	kilograms/hectare
above 300	above 337
150-300	168-337
50-150	56-168
25-50	28-56
0-25	0-28
	Data not available
	Uninhabited or sparsely populated

Fertilizer Use by Type

- NITROGEN 56.0 %
- PHOSPHATE 26.4
- POTASH 17.6

Fertilizer Use   World Total - 133,980,000 metric tons - 1991/92

0	10	20	30	40	50	60	70	80	90	100 %

| CHINA 22.1 % | INDIA 9.5 | OTHER ASIA 13.5 | UNITED STATES 14.0 | OTHER 3.5 | RUSSIA 7.6 | FRANCE 4.2 | UKRAINE | OTHER EUROPE 12.5 | BRAZIL 2.4 | AFRICA 2.7 |

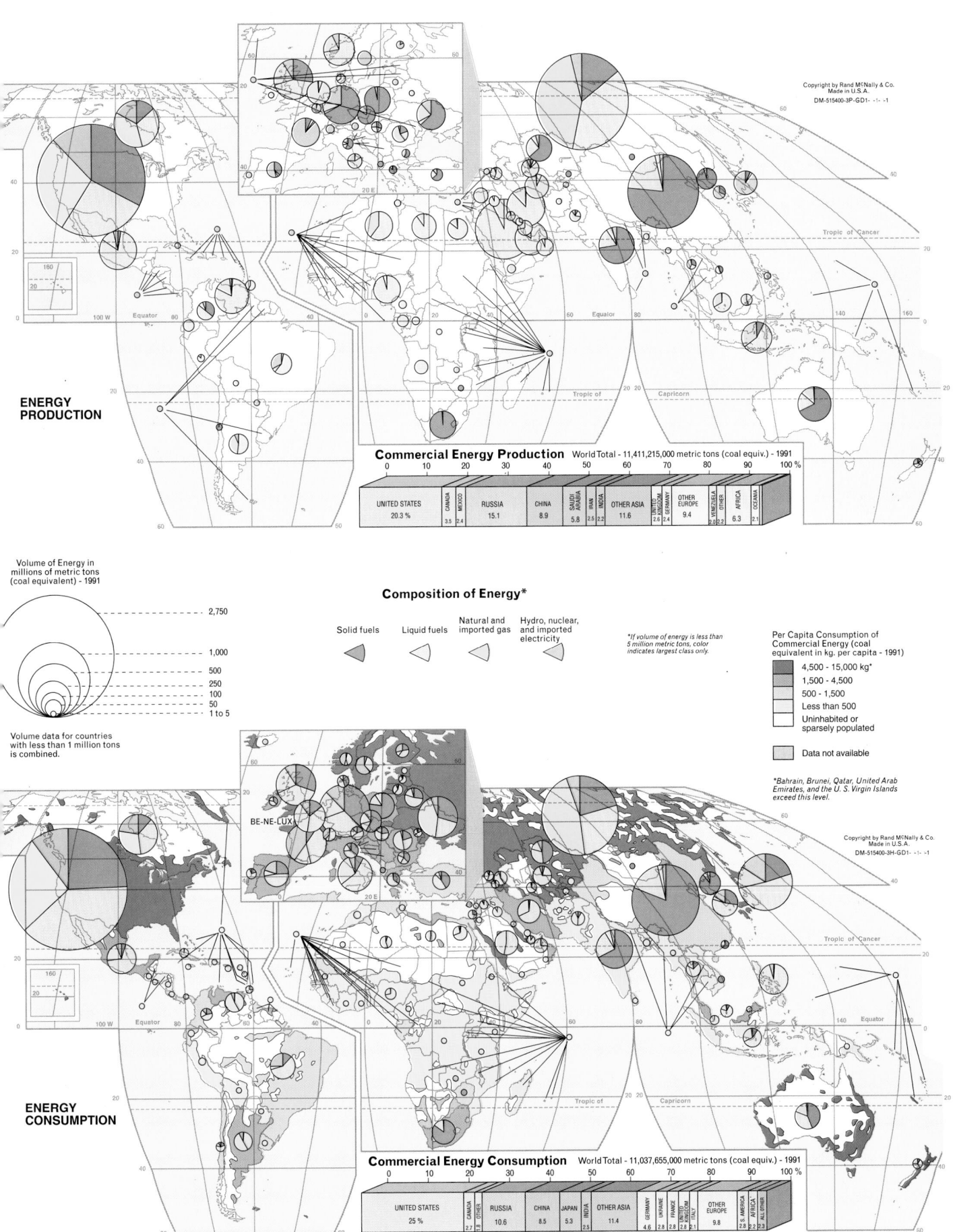

ENERGY PRODUCTION

Copyright by Rand McNally & Co.
Made in U.S.A.
DM-515400-3P-GD1- -!- -1

Commercial Energy Production World Total - 11,411,215,000 metric tons (coal equiv.) - 1991

	0	10	20	30	40	50	60	70	80	90	100 %

| UNITED STATES 20.3 % | CANADA 3.5 | MEXICO 2.4 | RUSSIA 15.1 | CHINA 8.9 | SAUDI ARABIA 5.8 | IRAN 2.5 | INDIA 2.2 | OTHER ASIA 11.6 | UNITED KINGDOM 2.6 | GERMANY 2.2 | OTHER EUROPE 9.4 | VENEZUELA 2.0 | OTHER 2.2 | AFRICA 6.3 | OCEANIA 2.1 |

Volume of Energy in
millions of metric tons
(coal equivalent) - 1991

2,750
1,000
500
250
100
50
1 to 5
160
20

Volume data for countries
with less than 1 million tons
is combined.

Composition of Energy*

Solid fuels   Liquid fuels   Natural and imported gas   Hydro, nuclear, and imported electricity

*If volume of energy is less than 5 million metric tons, color indicates largest class only.

Per Capita Consumption of
Commercial Energy (coal
equivalent in kg. per capita - 1991)

4,500 - 15,000 kg*
1,500 - 4,500
500 - 1,500
Less than 500
Uninhabited or
sparsely populated

Data not available

*Bahrain, Brunei, Qatar, United Arab
Emirates, and the U. S. Virgin Islands
exceed this level.

Copyright by Rand McNally & Co.
Made in U.S.A.
DM-515400-3H-GD1- -!- -1

BE-NE-LUX

ENERGY CONSUMPTION

Commercial Energy Consumption World Total - 11,037,655,000 metric tons (coal equiv.) - 1991

	0	10	20	30	40	50	60	70	80	90	100 %

| UNITED STATES 25 % | CANADA 2.7 | OTHER 1.8 | RUSSIA 10.6 | CHINA 8.5 | JAPAN 5.3 | INDIA 2.5 | OTHER ASIA 11.4 | GERMANY 4.6 | UKRAINE 2.8 | FRANCE 2.8 | UNITED KINGDOM 2.8 | ITALY 2.1 | OTHER EUROPE 9.8 | S. AMERICA 2.4 | AFRICA 2.2 | ALL OTHER 2.3 |

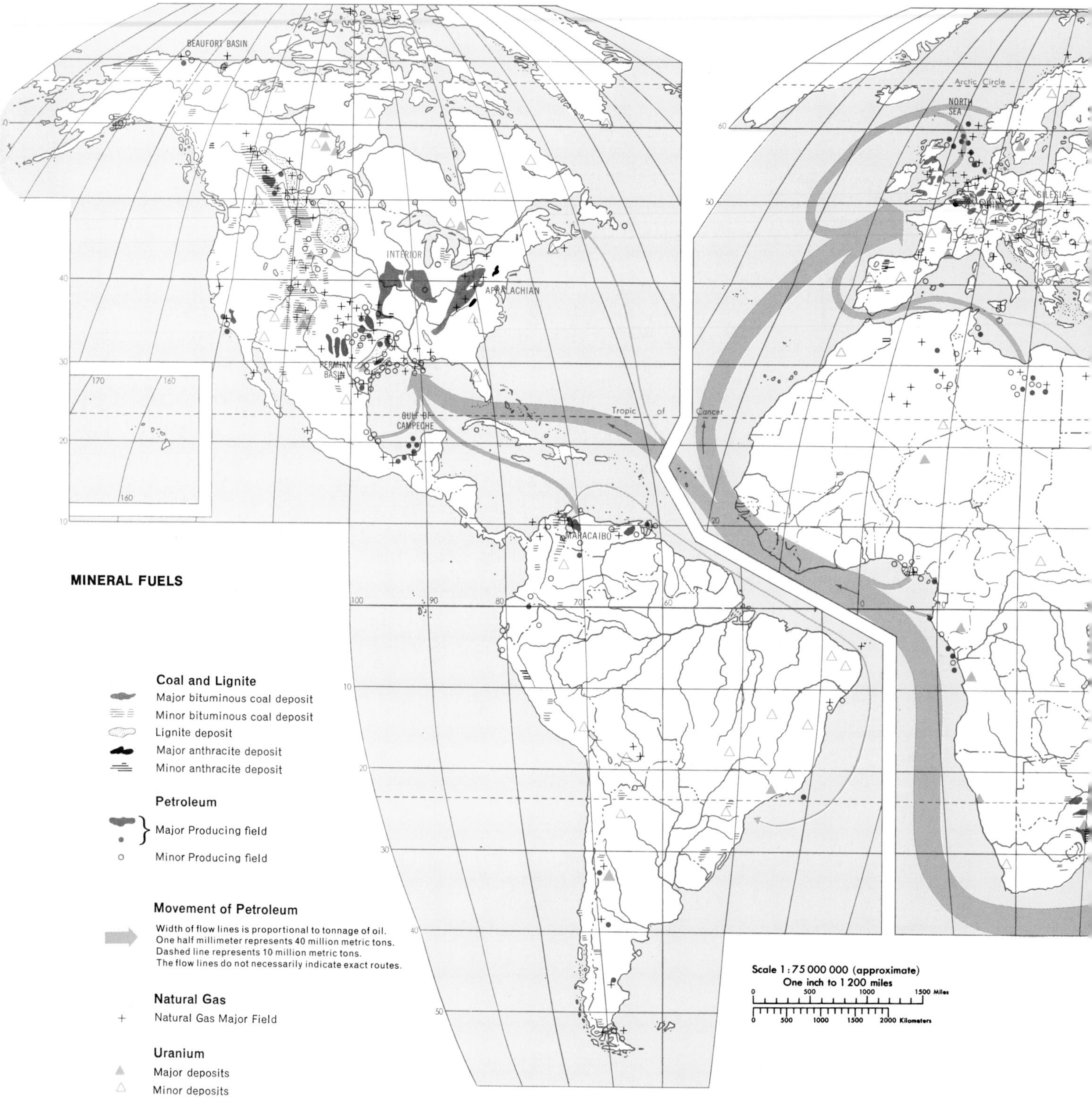

52

MINERAL FUELS

BEAUFORT BASIN

Arctic Circle

NORTH SEA

SILESIA

INTERIOR

APPALACHIAN

PERMIAN BASIN

GULF OF CAMPECHE

Tropic of Cancer

MARACAIBO

Coal and Lignite

— Major bituminous coal deposit
— Minor bituminous coal deposit
— Lignite deposit
— Major anthracite deposit
— Minor anthracite deposit

Petroleum

} Major Producing field

o   Minor Producing field

Movement of Petroleum

Width of flow lines is proportional to tonnage of oil.
One half millimeter represents 40 million metric tons.
Dashed line represents 10 million metric tons.
The flow lines do not necessarily indicate exact routes.

Natural Gas

+   Natural Gas Major Field

Uranium

▲   Major deposits
△   Minor deposits

Scale 1:75 000 000 (approximate)
One inch to 1 200 miles

0   500   1000   1500 Miles
0   500   1000   1500   2000 Kilometers

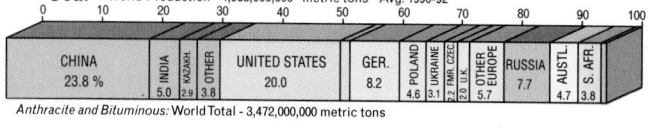

Coal   World Production - 4,568,000,000* metric tons - Avg. 1990-92

0	10	20	30	40	50	60	70	80	90	100 %

| CHINA 23.8 % | INDIA 5.0 | KAZAKH 2.9 | OTHER 3.8 | UNITED STATES 20.0 | GER. 8.2 | POLAND 4.6 | UKRAINE 3.1 | FMR. CZEC. 2.0 | U.K. | OTHER EUROPE 5.7 | RUSSIA 7.7 | AUSTL. 4.7 | S. AFR. 3.8 |

Anthracite and Bituminous: World Total - 3,472,000,000 metric tons

Coal Reserves   World Total - 1,038,462,000,000* metric tons - 1992

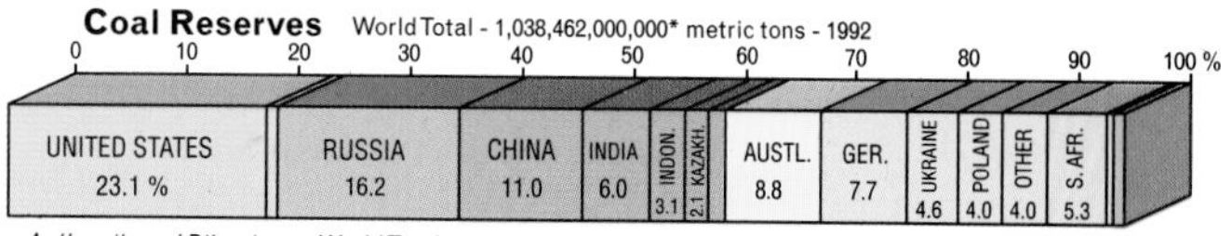

0	10	20	30	40	50	60	70	80	90	100 %

| UNITED STATES 23.1 % | RUSSIA 16.2 | CHINA 11.0 | INDIA 6.0 | INDON. 3.1 | KAZAKH 2.1 | AUSTL. 8.8 | GER. 7.7 | UKRAINE 4.6 | POLAND 4.0 | OTHER 4.0 | S. AFR. 5.3 |

Anthracite and Bituminous: World Total - 519,231,000,000 metric tons
* Includes anthracite, subanthracite, bituminous, subbituminous, lignite, and brown coal

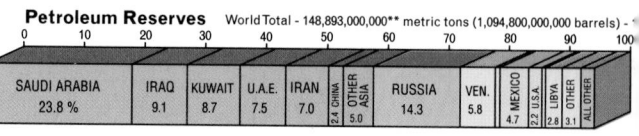

Petroleum   World Production - 2,949,000,000** metric tons (21,685,000,000 barrels) - Avg. 1990-92

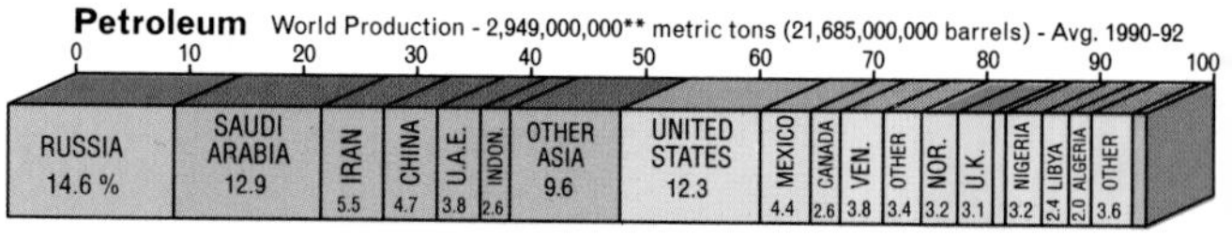

0	10	20	30	40	50	60	70	80	90	100

| RUSSIA 14.6 % | SAUDI ARABIA 12.9 | IRAN 5.5 | CHINA 4.7 | U.A.E. 3.8 | INDON. 2.6 | OTHER ASIA 9.6 | UNITED STATES 12.3 | MEXICO 4.4 | CANADA 2.6 | VEN. 3.8 | OTHER 3.4 | NOR. 3.2 | U.K. 3.1 | NIGERIA 3.2 | ALGERIA 2.0 | LIBYA | OTHER 3.6 |

Petroleum Reserves   World Total - 148,893,000,000** metric tons (1,094,800,000 barrels) -

0	10	20	30	40	50	60	70	80	90	100

| SAUDI ARABIA 23.8 % | IRAQ 9.1 | KUWAIT 8.7 | U.A.E. 7.5 | IRAN 7.0 | CHINA 2.4 | OTHER ASIA 5.0 | RUSSIA 14.3 | VEN. 5.8 | MEXICO 4.7 | U.S.A. 2.2 | LIBYA 2.8 | ALGERIA 3.1 | ALL OTHER |

** Crude Petroleum

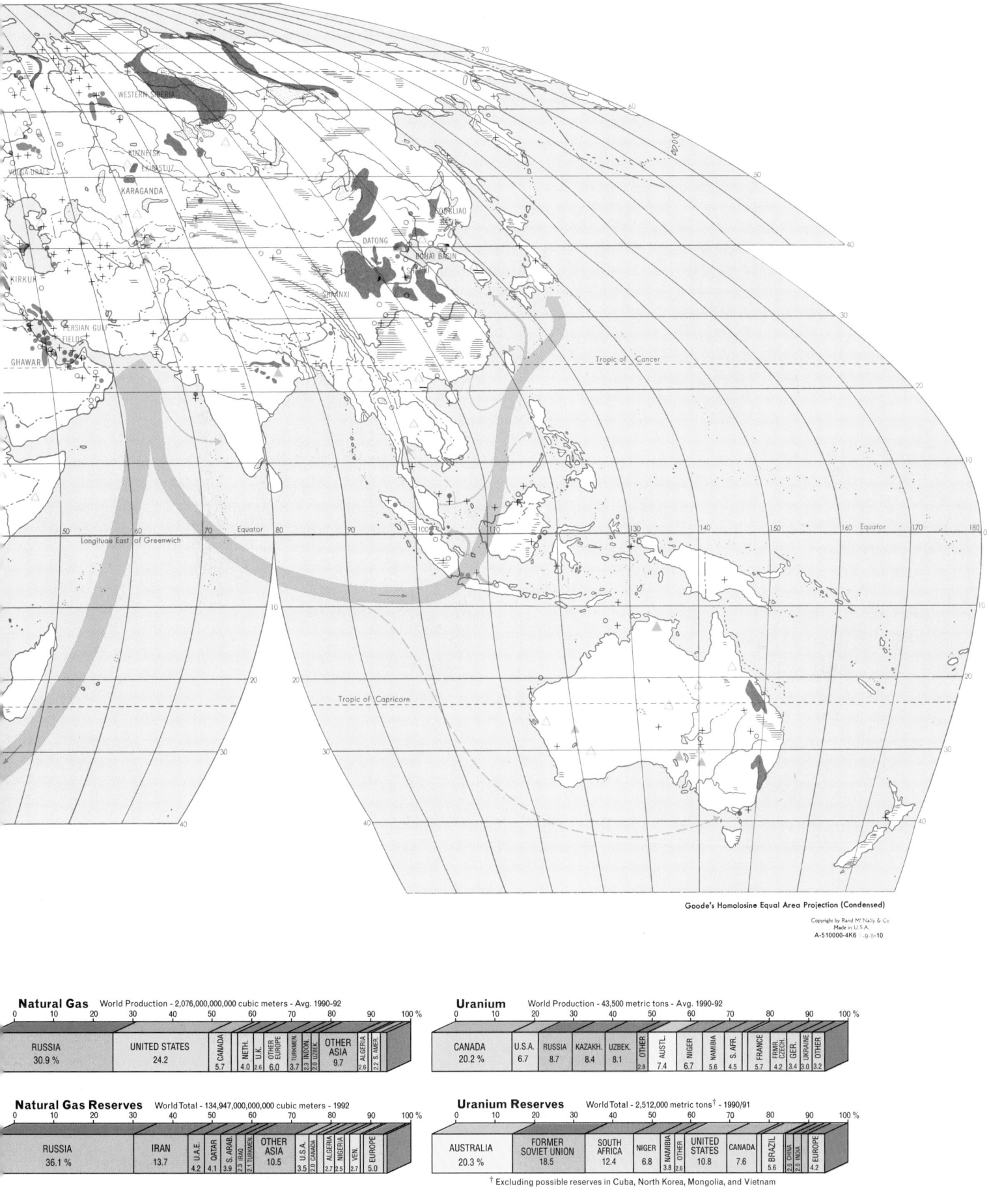

WESTERN SIBERIA
KUZNETSK
EKIBASTUZ
VOLGA-URALS
KARAGANDA
KIRKUK
PERSIAN GULF
FIELDS
GHAWAR
DATONG
DONGLIAO
BOHAI BASIN
SHANXI

Tropic of Cancer
Equator
Longitude East of Greenwich
Tropic of Capricorn

Goode's Homolosine Equal Area Projection (Condensed)

Copyright by Rand McNally & Co.
Made in U.S.A.
A-510000-4K6 9-8-10

Natural Gas   World Production - 2,076,000,000,000 cubic meters - Avg. 1990-92

| | 0 | 10 | 20 | 30 | 40 | 50 | 60 | 70 | 80 | 90 | 100 % |

| RUSSIA 30.9 % | UNITED STATES 24.2 | CANADA 5.7 | NETH. 4.0 | U.K. 2.6 | OTHER EUROPE 6.0 | TURKMEN. 3.7 | UZBEK. 2.3 | INDON. 2.0 | OTHER ASIA 9.7 | ALGERIA 2.6 | S. AMER. 2.2 |

Natural Gas Reserves   World Total - 134,947,000,000,000 cubic meters - 1992

| | 0 | 10 | 20 | 30 | 40 | 50 | 60 | 70 | 80 | 90 | 100 % |

| RUSSIA 36.1 % | IRAN 13.7 | U.A.E. 4.2 | QATAR 4.1 | S. ARAB. 3.9 | IRAQ 2.3 | OTHER ASIA 10.5 | U.S.A. 3.5 | CANADA 2.0 | ALGERIA 2.7 | NIGERIA 2.5 | VEN. 2.7 | EUROPE 5.0 |

Uranium   World Production - 43,500 metric tons - Avg. 1990-92

| | 0 | 10 | 20 | 30 | 40 | 50 | 60 | 70 | 80 | 90 | 100 % |

| CANADA 20.2 % | U.S.A. 6.7 | RUSSIA 8.7 | KAZAKH. 8.4 | UZBEK. 8.1 | OTHER 2.8 | AUSTL. 7.4 | NIGER 6.7 | NAMIBIA 5.6 | S. AFR. 4.5 | FRANCE 5.7 | FMR. CZECH 4.2 | GER. 3.4 | UKRAINE 3.0 | OTHER 3.2 |

Uranium Reserves   World Total - 2,512,000 metric tons† - 1990/91

| | 0 | 10 | 20 | 30 | 40 | 50 | 60 | 70 | 80 | 90 | 100 % |

| AUSTRALIA 20.3 % | FORMER SOVIET UNION 18.5 | SOUTH AFRICA 12.4 | NIGER 6.8 | NAMIBIA 3.8 | OTHER 2.6 | UNITED STATES 10.8 | CANADA 7.6 | BRAZIL 5.6 | CHINA 2.0 | INDIA | EUROPE 4.2 |

† Excluding possible reserves in Cuba, North Korea, Mongolia, and Vietnam

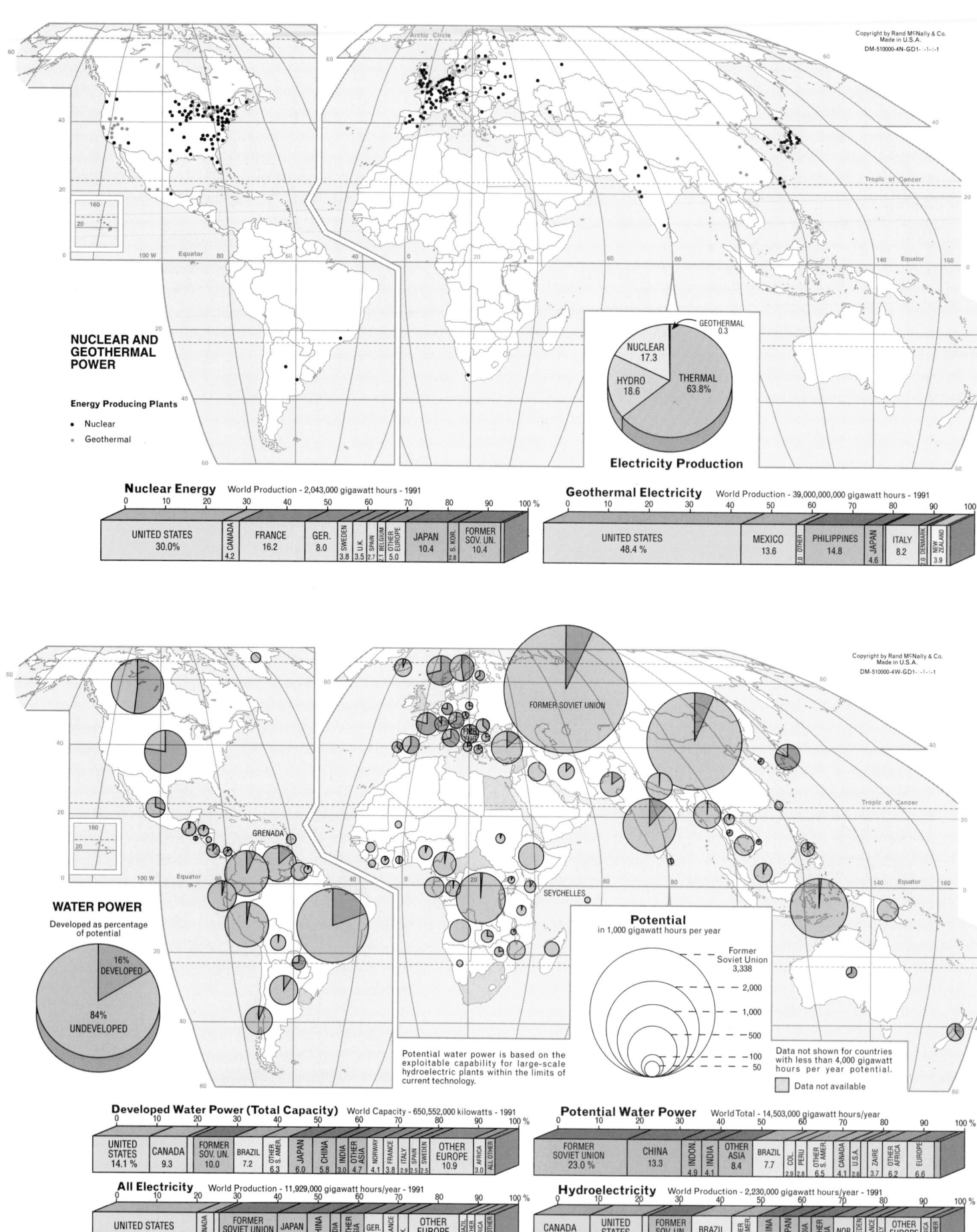

NUCLEAR AND GEOTHERMAL POWER

Energy Producing Plants

- Nuclear
- Geothermal

Electricity Production

GEOTHERMAL 0.3
NUCLEAR 17.3
HYDRO 18.6
THERMAL 63.8%

Nuclear Energy
World Production - 2,043,000 gigawatt hours - 1991

UNITED STATES 30.0%	CANADA 4.2	FRANCE 16.2	GER. 8.0	SWEDEN 3.8	U.K. 3.5	SPAIN 2.7	BELGIUM	OTHER EUROPE 5.0	JAPAN 10.4	S. KOR. 2.8	FORMER SOV. UN. 10.4

Geothermal Electricity
World Production - 39,000,000,000 gigawatt hours - 1991

UNITED STATES 48.4 %	MEXICO 13.6	OTHER 2.0	PHILIPPINES 14.8	JAPAN 4.6	ITALY 8.2	DENMARK	NEW ZEALAND 3.9

WATER POWER

Developed as percentage of potential

16% DEVELOPED
84% UNDEVELOPED

FORMER SOVIET UNION

GRENADA

SEYCHELLES

Potential water power is based on the exploitable capability for large-scale hydroelectric plants within the limits of current technology.

Potential
in 1,000 gigawatt hours per year

Former Soviet Union 3,338
— 2,000
— 1,000
— 500
— 100
— 50

Data not shown for countries with less than 4,000 gigawatt hours per year potential.

Data not available

Developed Water Power (Total Capacity)
World Capacity - 650,552,000 kilowatts - 1991

UNITED STATES 14.1 %	CANADA 9.3	FORMER SOV. UN. 10.0	BRAZIL 7.2	OTHER S. AMER. 6.3	JAPAN 6.0	CHINA 5.8	INDIA 4.7	OTHER ASIA 4.1	NORWAY 3.8	FRANCE	ITALY 2.9	SPAIN 2.5	SWEDEN 2.5	OTHER EUROPE 10.9	AFRICA 3.0	ALL OTHER

Potential Water Power
World Total - 14,503,000 gigawatt hours/year

FORMER SOVIET UNION 23.0 %	CHINA 13.3	INDON. 4.9	INDIA 4.1	OTHER ASIA 8.4	BRAZIL 7.7	COL. 2.9	PERU 2.8	OTHER S. AMER. 6.5	CANADA 4.1	U.S.A. 2.6	ZAIRE 3.7	OTHER AFRICA 6.2	EUROPE 6.6

All Electricity
World Production - 11,929,000 gigawatt hours/year - 1991

UNITED STATES 25.8 %	CANADA 4.3	FORMER SOVIET UNION 14.4	JAPAN 7.4	CHINA 5.7	INDIA 2.6	OTHER ASIA 5.8	GER. 4.8	FRANCE 3.8	U.K.	OTHER EUROPE 12.5	BRAZIL 2.0	OTHER AFRICA 2.7	ALL OTHER

Hydroelectricity
World Production - 2,230,000 gigawatt hours/year - 1991

CANADA 13.8 %	UNITED STATES 12.9	FORMER SOV. UN. 10.5	BRAZIL 9.8	OTHER S. AMER. 6.3	CHINA 5.6	JAPAN 4.7	INDIA 5.5	OTHER ASIA	NOR. 5.0	SWEDEN	FRANCE 2.0	ITALY	OTHER EUROPE 8.9	AFRICA 2.4	ALL OTHER

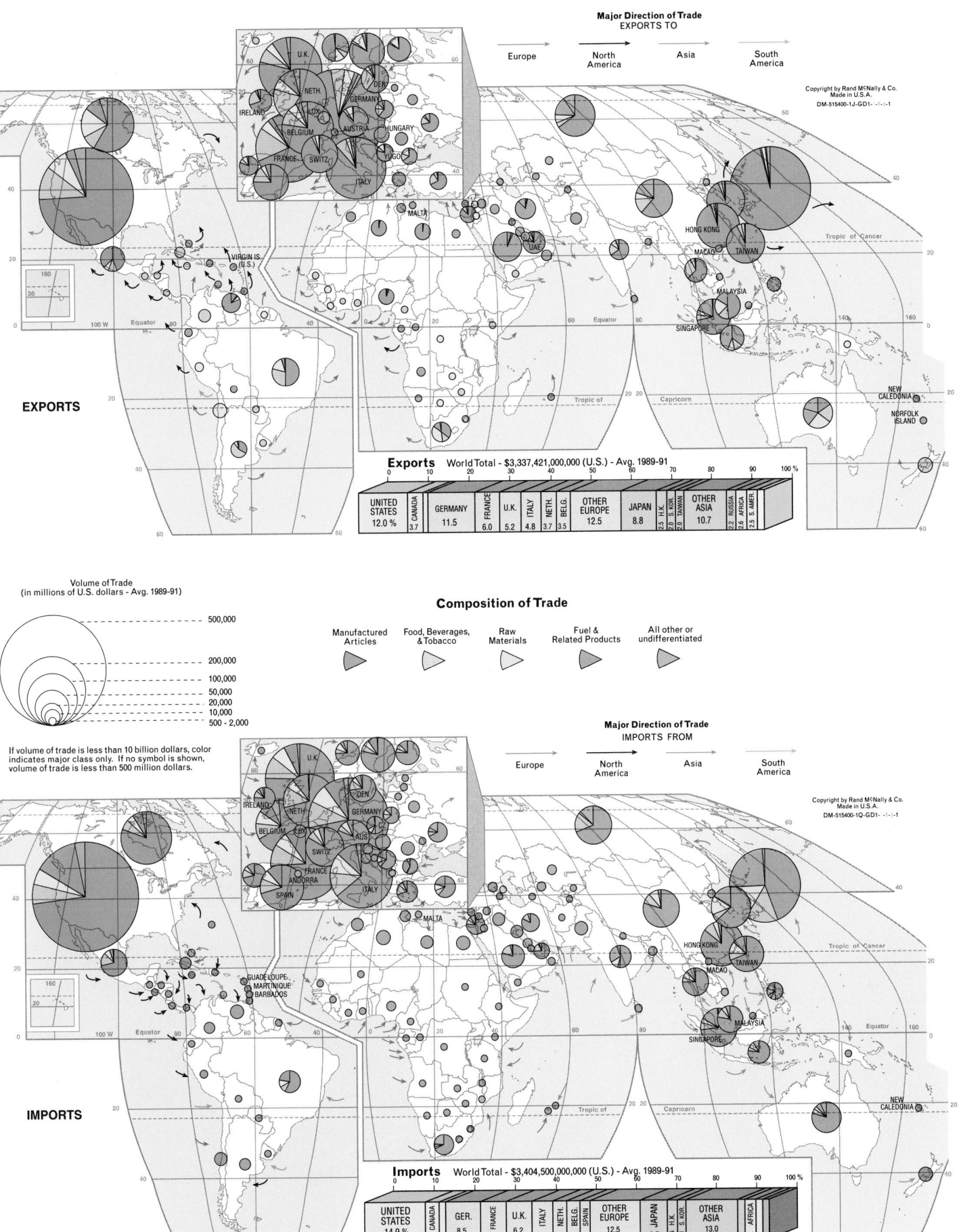

Major Direction of Trade
EXPORTS TO

Europe North America Asia South America

EXPORTS

Exports World Total - $3,337,421,000,000 (U.S.) - Avg. 1989-91

UNITED STATES 12.0 %	CANADA 3.7	GERMANY 11.5	FRANCE 6.0	U.K. 5.2	ITALY 4.8	NETH. 3.7	BELG. 3.5	OTHER EUROPE 12.5	JAPAN 8.8	H.K. 2.5	S. KOR. 2.0	TAIWAN 2.0	OTHER ASIA 10.7	RUSSIA 2.2	AFRICA 2.6	S. AMER. 2.5

Volume of Trade
(in millions of U.S. dollars - Avg. 1989-91)

500,000
200,000
100,000
50,000
20,000
10,000
500 - 2,000

If volume of trade is less than 10 billion dollars, color indicates major class only. If no symbol is shown, volume of trade is less than 500 million dollars.

Composition of Trade

Manufactured Articles   Food, Beverages, & Tobacco   Raw Materials   Fuel & Related Products   All other or undifferentiated

Major Direction of Trade
IMPORTS FROM

Europe North America Asia South America

IMPORTS

Imports World Total - $3,404,500,000,000 (U.S.) - Avg. 1989-91

UNITED STATES 14.9 %	CANADA 3.4	GER. 8.5	FRANCE 6.4	U.K. 6.2	ITALY 5.1	NETH. 3.5	BELG. 3.3	SPAIN 2.5	OTHER EUROPE 12.5	JAPAN 6.7	H.K. 2.5	S. KOR. 2.1	OTHER ASIA 13.0	AFRICA 2.6

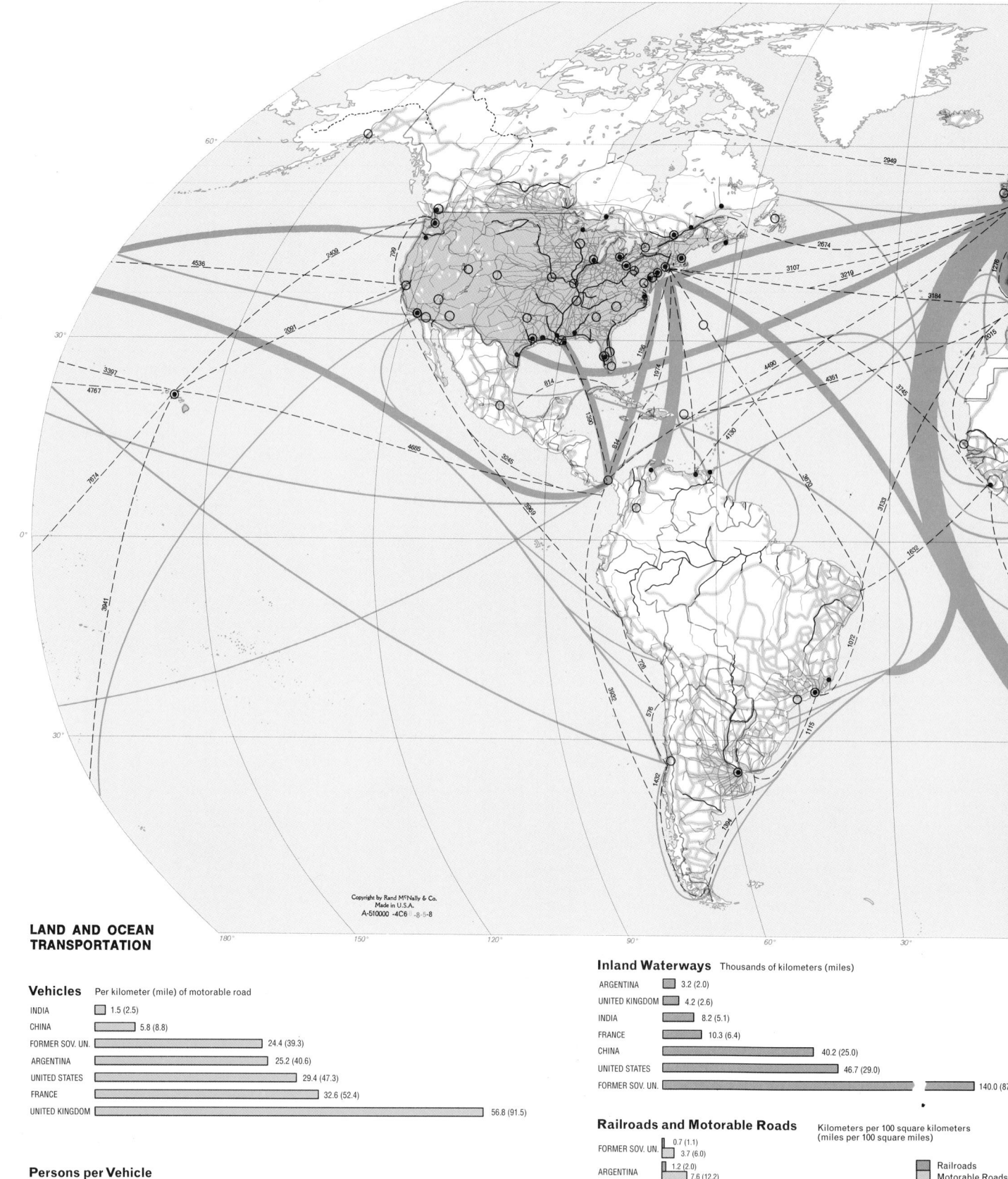

Copyright by Rand McNally & Co.
Made in U.S.A.
A-510000 -4C6 -8-5-8

LAND AND OCEAN TRANSPORTATION

Vehicles Per kilometer (mile) of motorable road

INDIA	1.5 (2.5)
CHINA	5.8 (8.8)
FORMER SOV. UN.	24.4 (39.3)
ARGENTINA	25.2 (40.6)
UNITED STATES	29.4 (47.3)
FRANCE	32.6 (52.4)
UNITED KINGDOM	56.8 (91.5)

Persons per Vehicle

UNITED STATES	1.3
FRANCE	2.0
UNITED KINGDOM	2.2
ARGENTINA	5.6
FORMER SOV. UN.	11.9
INDIA	179.1
CHINA	186.7

Inland Waterways Thousands of kilometers (miles)

ARGENTINA	3.2 (2.0)
UNITED KINGDOM	4.2 (2.6)
INDIA	8.2 (5.1)
FRANCE	10.3 (6.4)
CHINA	40.2 (25.0)
UNITED STATES	46.7 (29.0)
FORMER SOV. UN.	140.0 (87

Railroads and Motorable Roads Kilometers per 100 square kilometers (miles per 100 square miles)

Railroads
Motorable Roads
(excluding city st

FORMER SOV. UN.	0.7 (1.1)
	3.7 (6.0)
ARGENTINA	1.2 (2.0)
	7.6 (12.2)
CHINA	0.5 (0.9)
	10.1 (16.2)
INDIA	1.9 (3.1)
	54.8 (88.3)
UNITED STATES	2.1 (3.4)
	63.5 (102.2)
UNITED KINGDOM	6.8 (11.0)
	143.6 (23
FRANCE	6.3 (10.2)
	147.

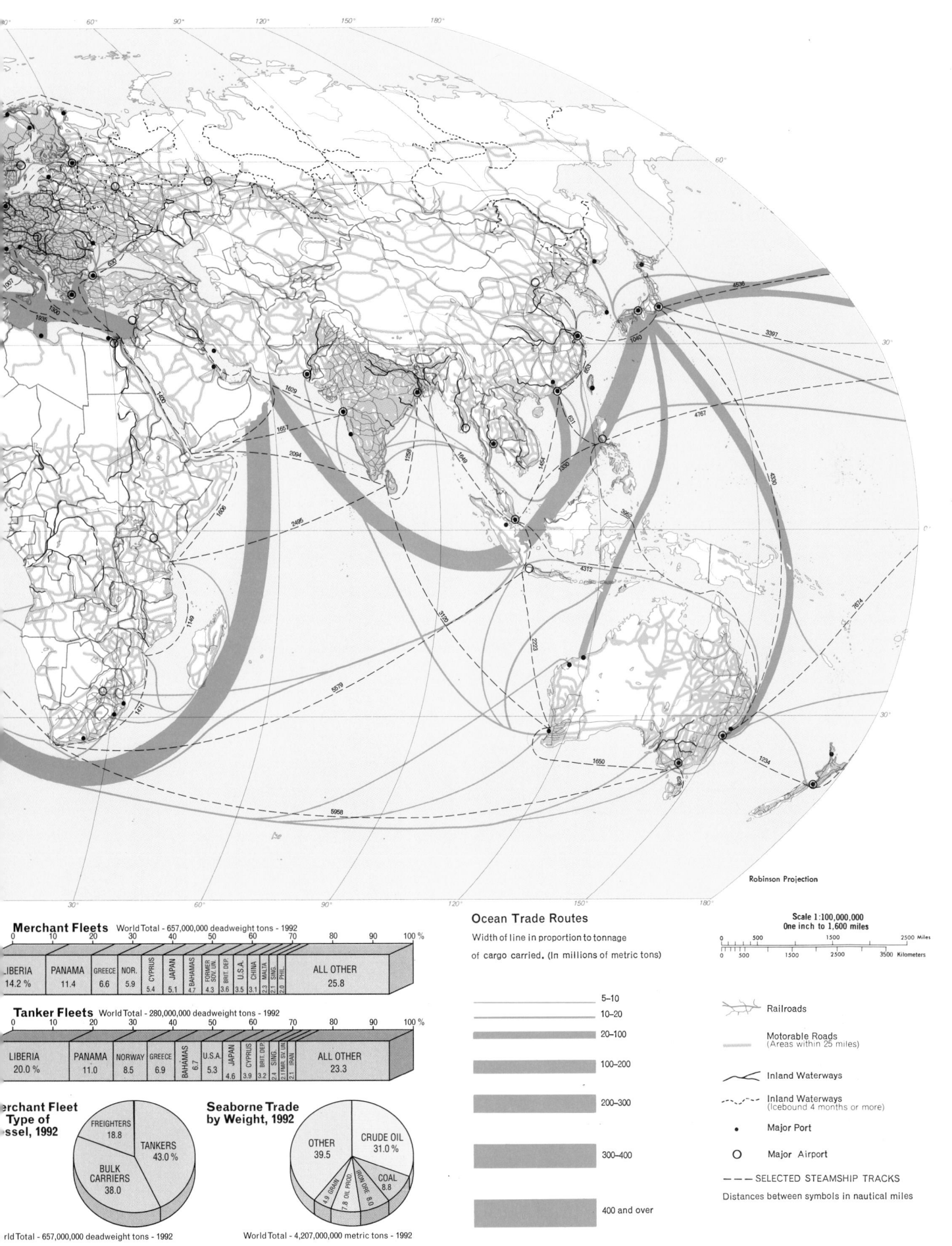

Robinson Projection

Merchant Fleets   World Total - 657,000,000 deadweight tons - 1992

LIBERIA 14.2 %	PANAMA 11.4	GREECE 6.6	NOR. 5.9	CYPRUS 5.4	JAPAN 5.1	BAHAMAS 4.7	FORMER SOV. UN. 4.3	BRIT. DEP. 3.6	U.S.A. 3.5	CHINA 2.3	MALTA 2.3	SING. 2.1	PHIL. 2.0	ALL OTHER 25.8

0 10 20 30 40 50 60 70 80 90 100 %

Tanker Fleets   World Total - 280,000,000 deadweight tons - 1992

LIBERIA 20.0 %	PANAMA 11.0	NORWAY 8.5	GREECE 6.9	BAHAMAS 6.7	U.S.A. 5.3	JAPAN 4.6	CYPRUS 3.9	BRIT. DEP. 3.2	SING. 2.4	FMR. SV. UN. 2.1	IRAN 2.1	ALL OTHER 23.3

0 10 20 30 40 50 60 70 80 90 100 %

Merchant Fleet by Type of Vessel, 1992

FREIGHTERS 18.8
TANKERS 43.0 %
BULK CARRIERS 38.0

World Total - 657,000,000 deadweight tons - 1992

Seaborne Trade by Weight, 1992

OTHER 39.5
CRUDE OIL 31.0 %
COAL 8.8
IRON ORE 8.0
OIL PROD. 7.8
GRAIN 4.9

World Total - 4,207,000,000 metric tons - 1992

Ocean Trade Routes

Width of line in proportion to tonnage
of cargo carried. (In millions of metric tons)

5–10
10–20
20–100
100–200
200–300
300–400
400 and over

Scale 1:100,000,000
One inch to 1,600 miles

0   500   1500   2500 Miles
0   500   1500   2500   3500 Kilometers

Railroads

Motorable Roads
(Areas within 25 miles)

Inland Waterways

Inland Waterways
(Icebound 4 months or more)

• Major Port

O Major Airport

– – – SELECTED STEAMSHIP TRACKS

Distances between symbols in nautical miles

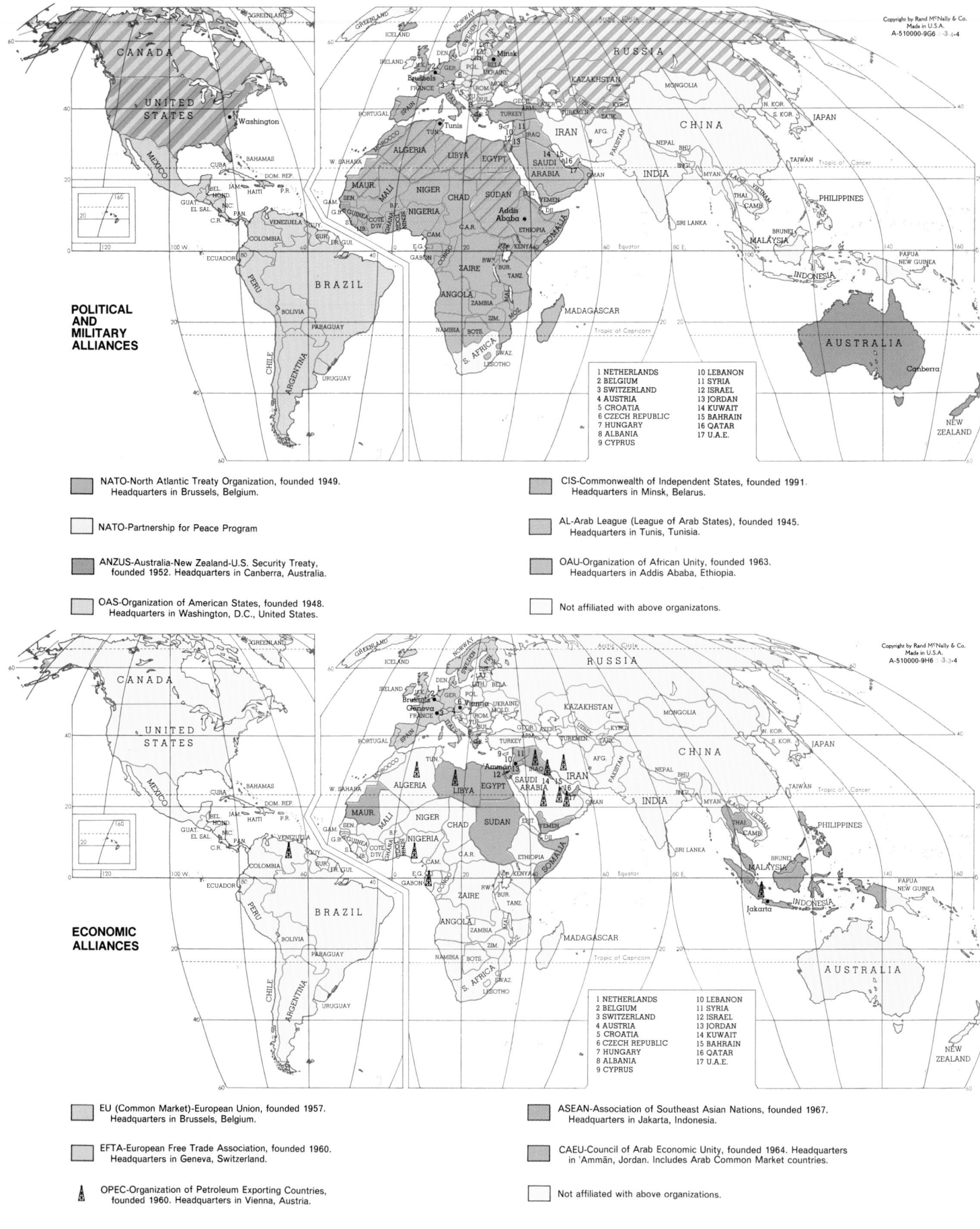

POLITICAL AND MILITARY ALLIANCES

1 NETHERLANDS	10 LEBANON
2 BELGIUM	11 SYRIA
3 SWITZERLAND	12 ISRAEL
4 AUSTRIA	13 JORDAN
5 CROATIA	14 KUWAIT
6 CZECH REPUBLIC	15 BAHRAIN
7 HUNGARY	16 QATAR
8 ALBANIA	17 U.A.E.
9 CYPRUS	

NATO-North Atlantic Treaty Organization, founded 1949. Headquarters in Brussels, Belgium.

NATO-Partnership for Peace Program

ANZUS-Australia-New Zealand-U.S. Security Treaty, founded 1952. Headquarters in Canberra, Australia.

OAS-Organization of American States, founded 1948. Headquarters in Washington, D.C., United States.

CIS-Commonwealth of Independent States, founded 1991. Headquarters in Minsk, Belarus.

AL-Arab League (League of Arab States), founded 1945. Headquarters in Tunis, Tunisia.

OAU-Organization of African Unity, founded 1963. Headquarters in Addis Ababa, Ethiopia.

Not affiliated with above organizatons.

ECONOMIC ALLIANCES

1 NETHERLANDS	10 LEBANON
2 BELGIUM	11 SYRIA
3 SWITZERLAND	12 ISRAEL
4 AUSTRIA	13 JORDAN
5 CROATIA	14 KUWAIT
6 CZECH REPUBLIC	15 BAHRAIN
7 HUNGARY	16 QATAR
8 ALBANIA	17 U.A.E.
9 CYPRUS	

EU (Common Market)-European Union, founded 1957. Headquarters in Brussels, Belgium.

EFTA-European Free Trade Association, founded 1960. Headquarters in Geneva, Switzerland.

OPEC-Organization of Petroleum Exporting Countries, founded 1960. Headquarters in Vienna, Austria.

ASEAN-Association of Southeast Asian Nations, founded 1967. Headquarters in Jakarta, Indonesia.

CAEU-Council of Arab Economic Unity, founded 1964. Headquarters in 'Ammān, Jordan. Includes Arab Common Market countries.

Not affiliated with above organizations.

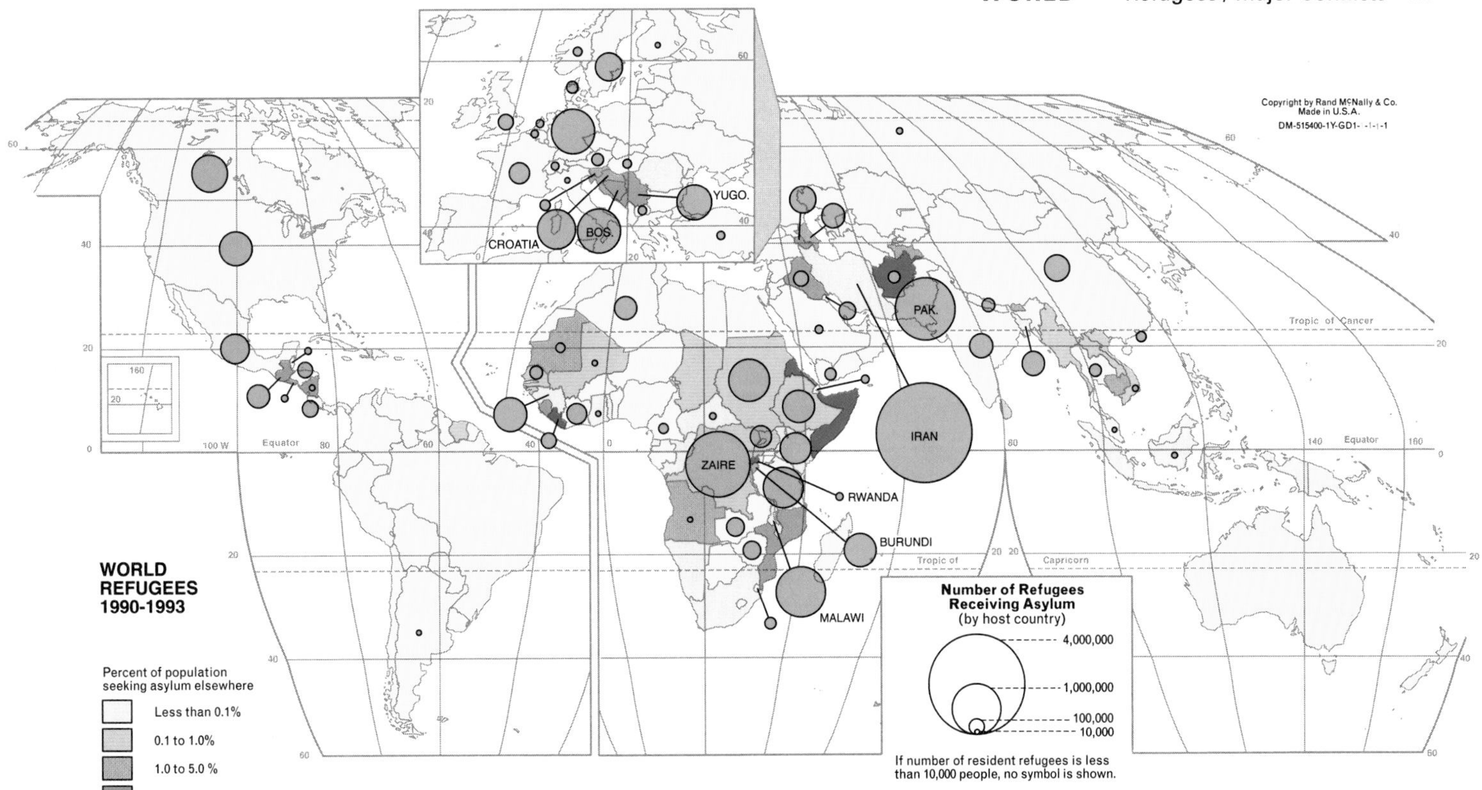
WORLD
REFUGEES
1990-1993
Percent of population seeking asylum elsewhere
Less than 0.1%
0.1 to 1.0%
1.0 to 5.0 %
5.0 to 10.0%
Greater than 10.0%
Number of Refugees Receiving Asylum
(by host country)
4,000,000
1,000,000
100,000
10,000
If number of resident refugees is less than 10,000 people, no symbol is shown.
YUGO.
CROATIA
BOS.
PAK.
IRAN
ZAIRE
RWANDA
BURUNDI
MALAWI
Tropic of Cancer
Equator
Tropic of Capricorn
Copyright by Rand McNally & Co. Made in U.S.A. DM-515400-1Y-GD1- -1-1-1
Map data for Rwanda, Tanzania, and Zaire revised 07/20/94

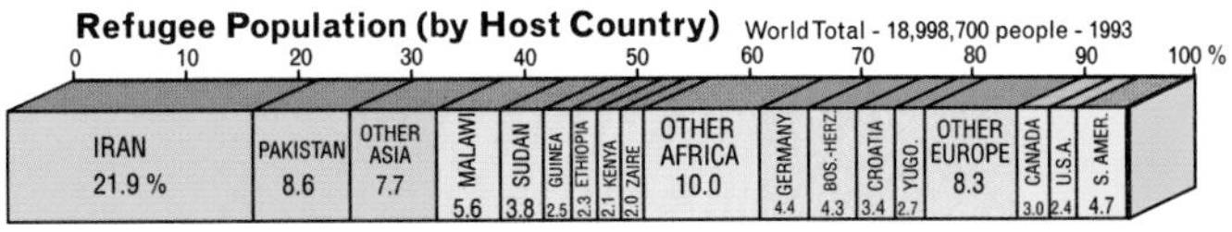
Refugee Population (by Host Country)
World Total - 18,998,700 people - 1993
0
10
20
30
40
50
60
70
80
90
100 %
IRAN 21.9 %
PAKISTAN 8.6
OTHER ASIA 7.7
MALAWI 5.6
SUDAN 3.8
GUINEA 2.5
ETHIOPIA 2.3
KENYA 2.1
ZAIRE 2.0
OTHER AFRICA 10.0
GERMANY 4.4
BOS.-HERZ. 4.3
CROATIA 3.4
YUGO. 2.7
OTHER EUROPE 8.3
CANADA 3.0
U.S.A. 2.4
S. AMER. 4.7

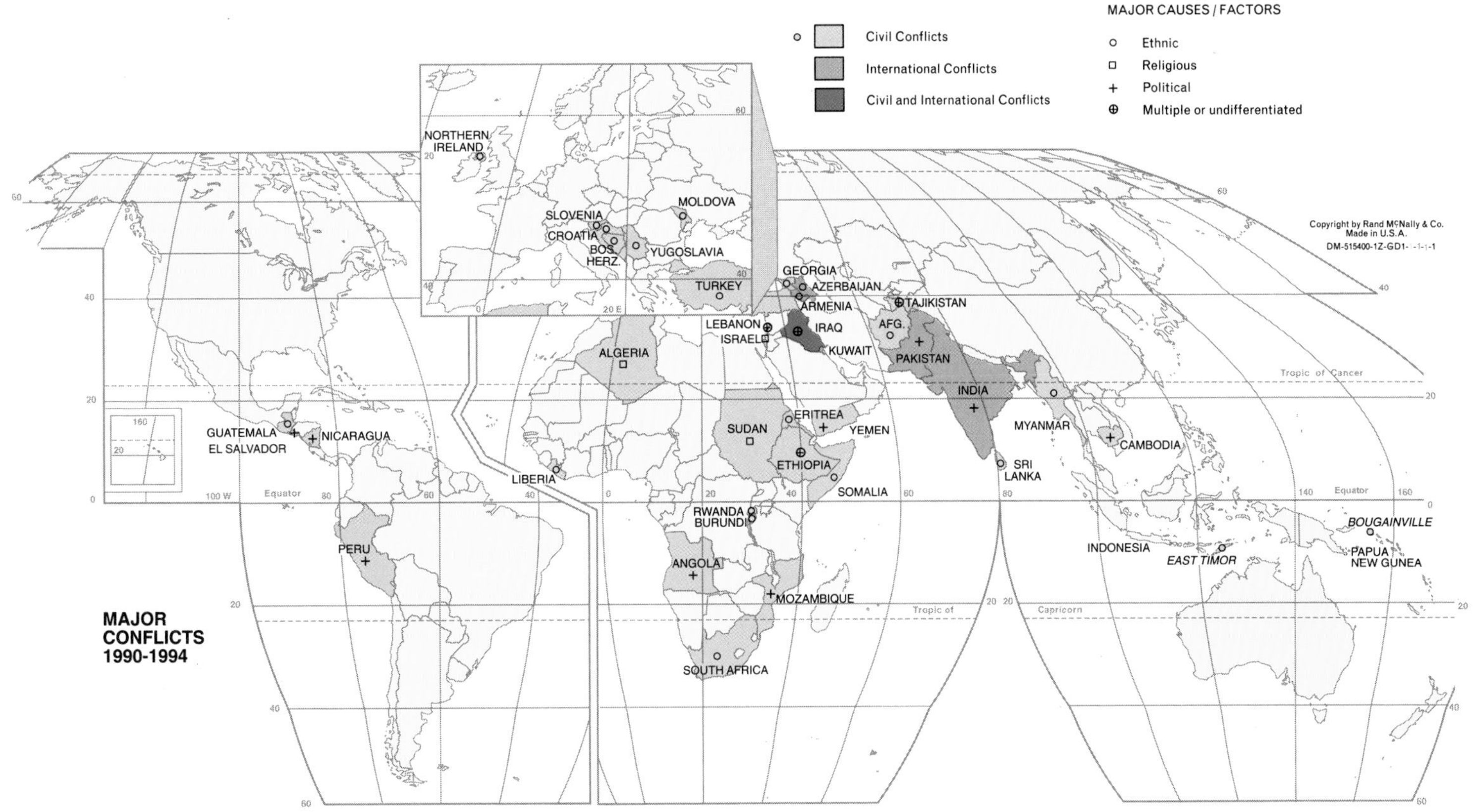
Civil Conflicts
International Conflicts
Civil and International Conflicts
MAJOR CAUSES / FACTORS
Ethnic
Religious
Political
Multiple or undifferentiated
MAJOR
CONFLICTS
1990-1994
NORTHERN IRELAND
SLOVENIA
CROATIA
BOS. HERZ.
YUGOSLAVIA
MOLDOVA
TURKEY
GEORGIA
AZERBAIJAN
ARMENIA
TAJIKISTAN
LEBANON
ISRAEL
IRAQ
KUWAIT
AFG.
PAKISTAN
INDIA
ALGERIA
SUDAN
ERITREA
YEMEN
ETHIOPIA
SOMALIA
MYANMAR
CAMBODIA
SRI LANKA
GUATEMALA
NICARAGUA
EL SALVADOR
LIBERIA
RWANDA
BURUNDI
ANGOLA
MOZAMBIQUE
SOUTH AFRICA
PERU
INDONESIA
EAST TIMOR
BOUGAINVILLE
PAPUA NEW GUNEA
Tropic of Cancer
Equator
Tropic of Capricorn
Copyright by Rand McNally & Co. Made in U.S.A. DM-515400-1Z-GD1- -1-1-1

REGIONAL MAPS

Basic continental and regional coverage of the world's land areas is provided by the following section of physical-political reference maps. The section falls into a continental arrangement: North America, South America, Europe, Asia, Australia, and Africa. (Introducing each regional reference-map section are basic thematic maps and the environment maps.)

To aid the student in acquiring concepts of the relative sizes of continents and of some of the countries and regions, uniform scales for comparable areas were used so far as possible. Continental maps are at a uniform scale of 1:40,000,000. In addition, most of the world is covered by a series of regional maps at scales of 1:16,000,000 and 1:12,000,000.

Maps at 1:10,000,000 provide even greater detail for parts of Europe, Africa, and Southeast Asia. The United States, parts of Canada, and much of Europe are mapped at 1:4,000,000. Seventy-six urbanized areas are shown at 1:1,000,000. The new, separate metropolitan-area section contains larger-scale maps of selected urban areas.

Many of the symbols used are self-explanatory. A complete legend below provides a key to the symbols on the reference maps in this atlas.

General elevation above sea level is shown by layer tints for altitudinal zones, each of which has a different hue and is defined by a generalized contour line. A legend is given on each map, reflecting this color gradation.

The surface configuration is represented by hill-shading, which gives the three-dimensional impression of landforms. This terrain representation is superimposed on the layer tints to convey a realistic and readily visualized impression of the surface. The combination of altitudinal tints and hill-shading best shows elevation, relief, steepness of slope, and ruggedness of terrain.

If the world used one alphabet and one language, no particular difficulty would arise in understanding place-names. However, some of the people of the world, the Chinese and the Japanese, for example, use nonalphabetic languages. Their symbols are transliterated into the Roman alphabet. In this atlas a "local-name" policy generally was used for naming cities and towns and all local topographic and water features. However, for a few major cities the Anglicized name was preferred and the local name given in parentheses, for instance, Moscow *(Moskva)*, Vienna *(Wien)*, Cologne *(Köln)*. In countries where more than one official language is used, a name is in the dominant local language. The generic parts of local names for topographic and water features are self-explanatory in many cases because of the associated map symbols or type styles. A complete list of foreign generic names is given in the Glossary.

Place-names on the reference maps are listed in the Pronouncing Index, which is a distinctive feature of *Goode's World Atlas*.

Physical-Political Reference Map Legend

Cultural Features

Political Boundaries

International (over water) (Demarcated, Undemarcated, and Administrative)

Disputed de facto

Claim Boundary

Indefinite or Undefined

Secondary, State, Provincial, etc. (over water)

Parks, Indian Reservations

City Limits   Urbanized Areas

Neighborhoods, Sections of City

Populated Places

⊙ 1,000,000 and over

◎ 250,000 to 1,000,000

⊙ 100,000 to 250,000

• 25,000 to 100,000

○ 0 to 25,000

TŌKYŌ National Capitals

Boise Secondary Capitals

Note: On maps at 1:20,000,000 and smaller the town symbols do not follow the specific population classification shown above. On all maps, type size indicates the relative importance of the city.

Transportation

Railroads

Railroads On 1:1,000,000 scale maps

Railroad Ferries

Roads

Major On 1:1,000,000 scale maps
Other

Major On 1:4,000,000 scale maps
Other

On other scale maps

Caravan Routes

✈ Airports

Other Cultural Features

Dams

Pipelines

▲ Points of Interest

∴ Ruins

Land Features

△ Peaks, Spot Heights

= Passes

Sand

Contours

Water Features

Lakes and Reservoirs

Fresh Water

Fresh Water: Intermittent

Salt Water

Salt Water: Intermittent

Other Water Features

Salt Basins, Flats

Swamps

Ice Caps and Glaciers

Rivers

Intermittent Rivers

Aqueducts and Canals

Ship Channels

Falls

Rapids

Springs

Water Depths

Fishing Banks

Sand Bars

Reefs

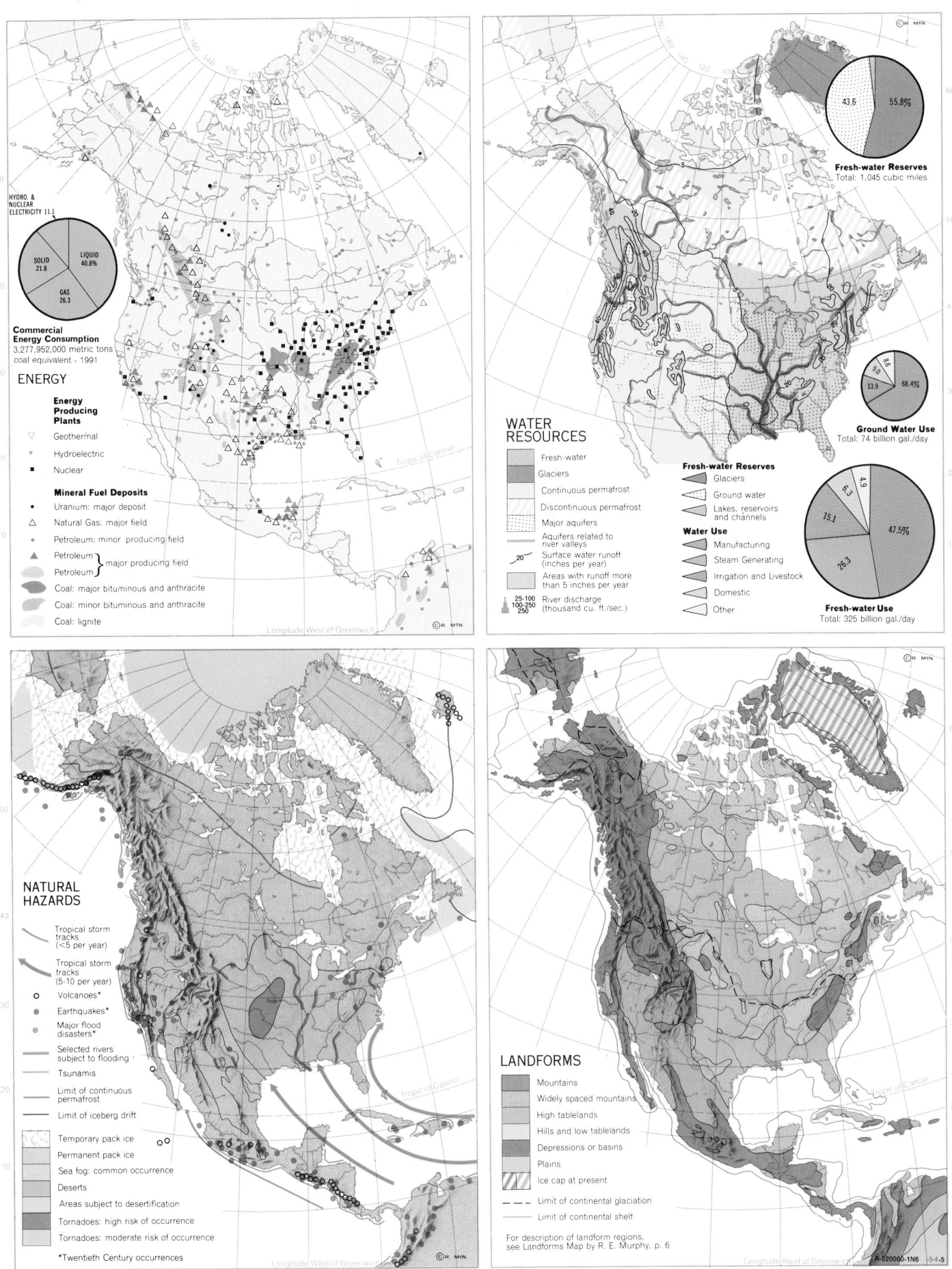

ENERGY

HYDRO. & NUCLEAR ELECTRICITY 11.1

SOLID 21.8
LIQUID 40.8%
GAS 26.3

Commercial Energy Consumption
3,277,952,000 metric tons coal equivalent - 1991

Energy Producing Plants
▽ Geothermal
• Hydroelectric
■ Nuclear

Mineral Fuel Deposits
• Uranium: major deposit
△ Natural Gas: major field
• Petroleum: minor producing field
▲ Petroleum } major producing field
Petroleum }
Coal: major bituminous and anthracite
Coal: minor bituminous and anthracite
Coal: lignite

WATER RESOURCES

Fresh-water
Glaciers
Continuous permafrost
Discontinuous permafrost
Major aquifers
Aquifers related to river valleys
—20— Surface water runoff (inches per year)
Areas with runoff more than 5 inches per year
River discharge (thousand cu. ft./sec.)
25-100
100-250
250

Fresh-water Reserves
Total: 1,045 cubic miles
43.6   55.8%

Fresh-water Reserves
◁ Glaciers
◁ Ground water
◁ Lakes, reservoirs and channels

Ground Water Use
Total: 74 billion gal./day
8.6 9.0
13.9   68.4%

Water Use
◁ Manufacturing
◁ Steam Generating
◁ Irrigation and Livestock
◁ Domestic
◁ Other

Fresh-water Use
Total: 325 billion gal./day
4.9
6.3
15.1   47.5%
26.3

NATURAL HAZARDS

Tropical storm tracks (<5 per year)
Tropical storm tracks (5-10 per year)
○ Volcanoes*
● Earthquakes*
● Major flood disasters*
Selected rivers subject to flooding
Tsunamis
Limit of continuous permafrost
Limit of iceberg drift
Temporary pack ice
Permanent pack ice
Sea fog: common occurrence
Deserts
Areas subject to desertification
Tornadoes: high risk of occurrence
Tornadoes: moderate risk of occurrence

*Twentieth Century occurrences

LANDFORMS

Mountains
Widely spaced mountains
High tablelands
Hills and low tablelands
Depressions or basins
Plains
Ice cap at present
─ ─ ─ Limit of continental glaciation
─── Limit of continental shelf

For description of landform regions, see Landforms Map by R. E. Murphy, p. 6

A-520000-1N6   -5-4-5

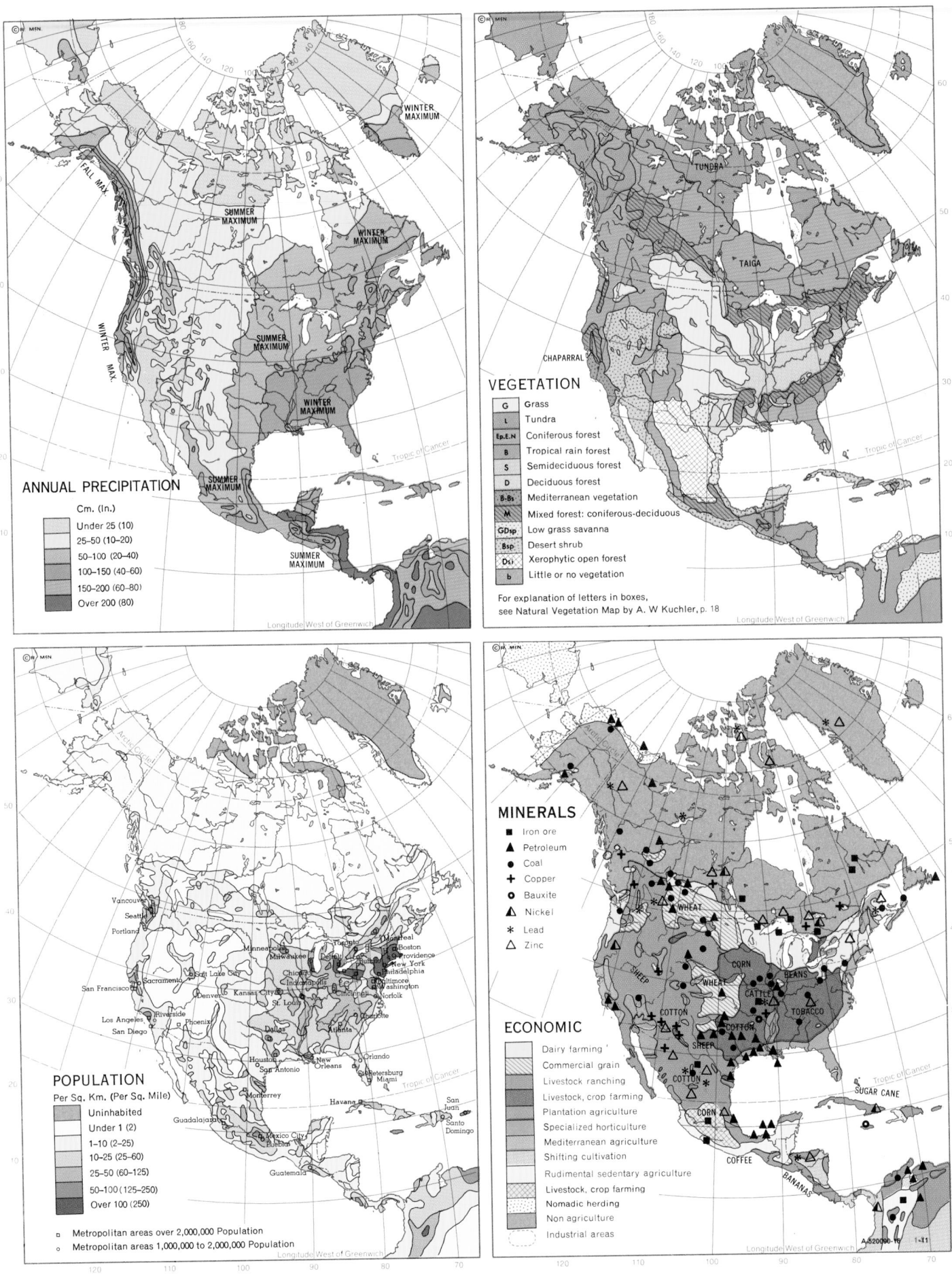

ANNUAL PRECIPITATION

Cm. (In.)

	Under 25 (10)
	25–50 (10–20)
	50–100 (20–40)
	100–150 (40–60)
	150–200 (60–80)
	Over 200 (80)

WINTER MAXIMUM
FALL MAX.
SUMMER MAXIMUM
WINTER MAXIMUM
WINTER MAX.
SUMMER MAXIMUM
WINTER MAXIMUM
SUMMER MAXIMUM
SUMMER MAXIMUM
Tropic of Cancer
Longitude West of Greenwich

VEGETATION

G	Grass
L	Tundra
Ep.E.N	Coniferous forest
B	Tropical rain forest
S	Semideciduous forest
D	Deciduous forest
B-Bs	Mediterranean vegetation
M	Mixed forest: coniferous-deciduous
GDsp	Low grass savanna
Bsp	Desert shrub
Dxi	Xerophytic open forest
b	Little or no vegetation

For explanation of letters in boxes,
see Natural Vegetation Map by A. W Kuchler, p. 18

TUNDRA
TAIGA
CHAPARRAL
Tropic of Cancer
Longitude West of Greenwich

POPULATION

Per Sq. Km. (Per Sq. Mile)

	Uninhabited
	Under 1 (2)
	1–10 (2–25)
	10–25 (25–60)
	25–50 (60–125)
	50–100 (125–250)
	Over 100 (250)

▫ Metropolitan areas over 2,000,000 Population

○ Metropolitan areas 1,000,000 to 2,000,000 Population

Vancouver
Seattle
Portland
Minneapolis
Milwaukee
Detroit
Toronto
Montreal
Boston
Providence
New York
San Francisco
Sacramento
Salt Lake City
Denver
Kansas City
Chicago
Indianapolis
Cincinnati
Cleveland
Pittsburgh
Baltimore
Philadelphia
Washington
St. Louis
Norfolk
Los Angeles
Riverside
Phoenix
San Diego
Dallas
Charlotte
Atlanta
Houston
San Antonio
New Orleans
Orlando
Tampa
St. Petersburg
Miami
Monterrey
Havana
San Juan
Santo Domingo
Guadalajara
Mexico City
Puebla
Guatemala
Tropic of Cancer
Longitude West of Greenwich

MINERALS

■	Iron ore
▲	Petroleum
●	Coal
+	Copper
○	Bauxite
△	Nickel
✳	Lead
△	Zinc

ECONOMIC

	Dairy farming
	Commercial grain
	Livestock ranching
	Livestock, crop farming
	Plantation agriculture
	Specialized horticulture
	Mediterranean agriculture
	Shifting cultivation
	Rudimental sedentary agriculture
	Livestock, crop farming
	Nomadic herding
	Non agriculture
	Industrial areas

WHEAT
WHEAT
CORN
BEANS
SHEEP
CATTLE
TOBACCO
COTTON
COTTON
COTTON
SHEEP
CORN
COFFEE
SUGAR CANE
BANANAS
Tropic of Cancer
Longitude West of Greenwich
A 520000-16   1-71

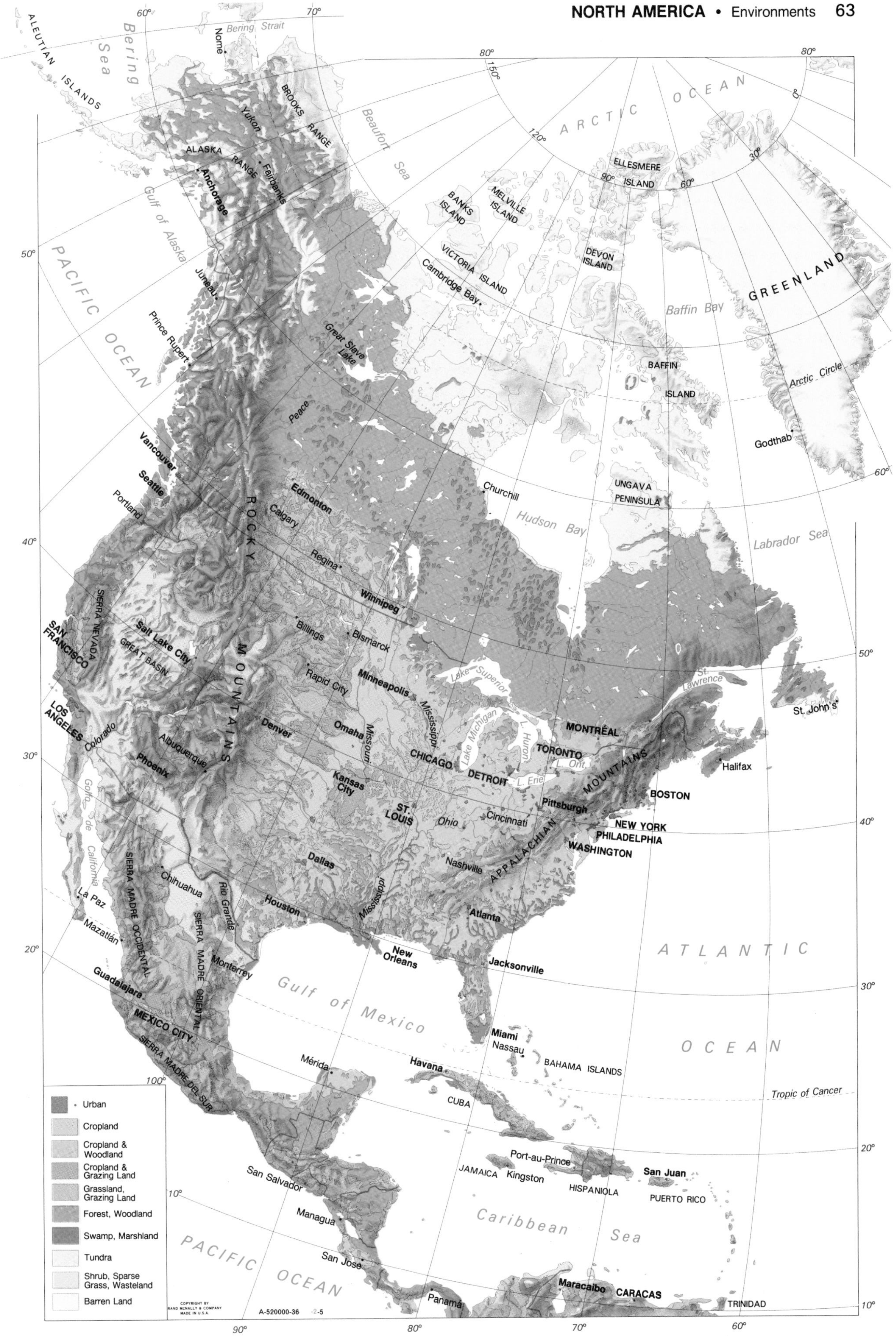

ALEUTIAN ISLANDS

Bering Strait
Nome
Bering Sea

ARCTIC OCEAN

BROOKS RANGE
Yukon
ALASKA RANGE
Fairbanks
ALASKA
Anchorage
Beaufort Sea

ELLESMERE ISLAND

BANKS ISLAND
MELVILLE ISLAND

VICTORIA ISLAND
Cambridge Bay

DEVON ISLAND

GREENLAND

Baffin Bay

Gulf of Alaska
Juneau

PACIFIC OCEAN

Prince Rupert

Great Slave Lake

BAFFIN ISLAND

Arctic Circle

Godthab

Churchill

UNGAVA PENINSULA

Vancouver
Seattle
Portland

ROCKY

Edmonton
Calgary

Peace

Hudson Bay

Labrador Sea

San Francisco

SIERRA NEVADA

Salt Lake City
GREAT BASIN

Regina

Winnipeg

MOUNTAINS

St. Lawrence

St. John's

Los Angeles
Colorado

Billings
Bismarck

Rapid City

Minneapolis
Mississippi

Lake Superior

Lake Michigan
Lake Huron

MONTRÉAL
TORONTO
L. Ont.

Halifax

Phoenix
Albuquerque

Denver

Omaha
Missouri

CHICAGO

DETROIT
L. Erie

BOSTON

Pittsburgh
Cincinnati

NEW YORK
PHILADELPHIA
WASHINGTON

Kansas City

ST. LOUIS
Ohio

Nashville

APPALACHIAN MOUNTAINS

Chihuahua
Rio Grande

Dallas

Atlanta

SIERRA MADRE OCCIDENTAL
La Paz

Golfo de California

Houston
Mississippi

New Orleans

Jacksonville

ATLANTIC OCEAN

Mazatlán

Monterrey

SIERRA MADRE ORIENTAL

Gulf of Mexico

Guadalajara

MEXICO CITY

SIERRA MADRE DEL SUR

Mérida

Miami
Nassau
BAHAMA ISLANDS

Tropic of Cancer

Havana

CUBA

San Salvador

San José

Managua

Panamá

San Juan

Port-au-Prince
JAMAICA Kingston
HISPANIOLA

PUERTO RICO

Caribbean Sea

Maracaibo CARACAS

TRINIDAD

PACIFIC OCEAN

Legend:
- Urban
- Cropland
- Cropland & Woodland
- Cropland & Grazing Land
- Grassland, Grazing Land
- Forest, Woodland
- Swamp, Marshland
- Tundra
- Shrub, Sparse Grass, Wasteland
- Barren Land

COPYRIGHT BY RAND McNALLY & COMPANY MADE IN U.S.A.
A-520000-36 -2-5

Scale 1:36,000,000; one inch to 570 miles. Lambert Azimuthal Equal-Area Projection

0 100 200 400 600 800 Miles
0 150 300 600 900 1200 Kilometers

64

PACIFIC

OCEAN

PACIFIC

OCEAN

Vancouver

Seattle

Spokane

Portland

Columbia

CASCADE   RANGE

Medford

Boise

Reno

GREAT   BASIN

Great Salt
Lake

Salt Lake City

SIERRA

NEVADA

Fresno

SAN
FRANCISCO

Las Vegas

LOS ANGELES

San Diego

Colorado

Phoenix

Albuquerque

El Paso

Odessa

Hermosillo

Gulf   of   California

SIERRA

MADRE

OCCIDENTAL

Chihuahua

Rio Grande

Torreón

SIERRA

MADRE

ORIENTAL

Monterrey

Rio Grande

San Antonio

Red

Wichita

Amarillo

Denver

Casper

Rapid City

Missouri

Bismarck

Billings

Calgary

Regina

Lake Winnipeg

ROCKY   MOUNTAINS

ROCKY   MOUNTAINS

50°

45°

40°

35°

30°

25°

125°

120°

115°

110°

105°

100°

125°

120°

115°

Scale 1:12,000,000; one inch to 190 miles.
Albers Conical Equal Area Projection

0	50	100	200	300	400 Miles
0	75	150	300	450	600 Kilometers

Legend:
- Urban
- Cropland
- Cropland & Woodland
- Cropland & Grazing Land
- Grassland, Grazing Land
- Forest, Woodland
- Swamp, Marshland
- Shrub, Sparse Grass, Wasteland
- Barren Land

66

PHYSIOGRAPHIC DIVISIONS

1 Pacific Mountain System
2 Intermontane Plateaus
3 Rocky Mountain System
4 Interior Plains
5 Ozark-Ouachita Highlands
6 Gulf-Atlantic Plain
7 Appalachian Highlands
8 Laurentian Upland (Canadian Shield)
9 Hudson Bay Lowland

Scale 1: 12 000 000; One inch to 190 miles.   POLYCONIC PROJECTION

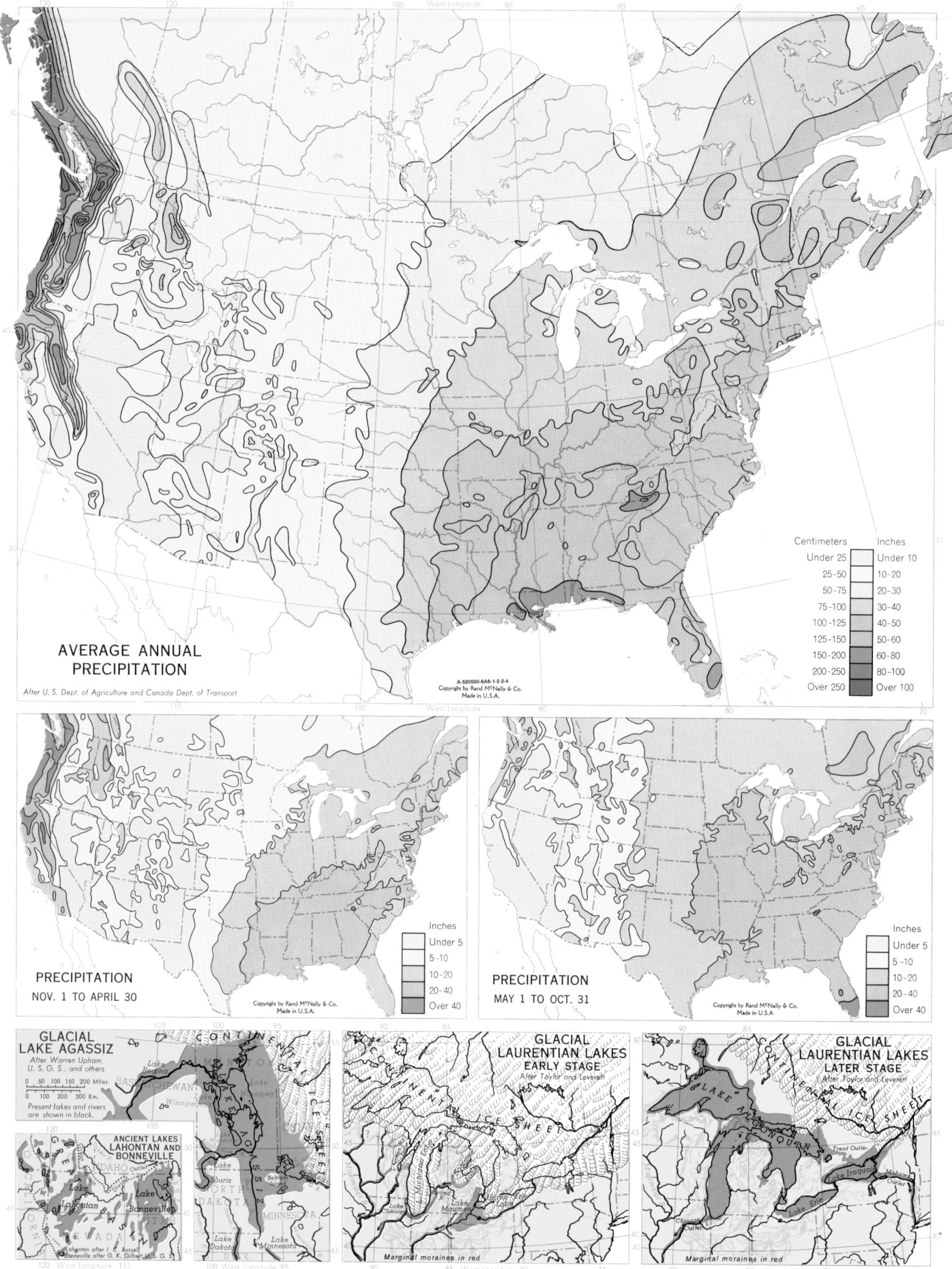

AVERAGE ANNUAL PRECIPITATION

After U. S. Dept. of Agriculture and Canada Dept. of Transport

A-520500-6A6-1-2-2-4
Copyright by Rand McNally & Co.
Made in U.S.A.

Centimeters	Inches
Under 25	Under 10
25-50	10-20
50-75	20-30
75-100	30-40
100-125	40-50
125-150	50-60
150-200	60-80
200-250	80-100
Over 250	Over 100

PRECIPITATION
NOV. 1 TO APRIL 30

Copyright by Rand McNally & Co.
Made in U.S.A.

Inches
Under 5
5-10
10-20
20-40
Over 40

PRECIPITATION
MAY 1 TO OCT. 31

Copyright by Rand McNally & Co.
Made in U.S.A.

Inches
Under 5
5-10
10-20
20-40
Over 40

GLACIAL LAKE AGASSIZ
*After Warren Upham,
U. S. G. S., and others*

0 50 100 150 200 Miles
0 100 200 300 Km.

*Present lakes and rivers
are shown in black.*

ANCIENT LAKES LAHONTAN AND BONNEVILLE

*Lahontan after I. C. Russell
Bonneville after G. K. Gilbert U.S.G.S.*

GLACIAL LAURENTIAN LAKES
EARLY STAGE
After Taylor and Leverett

Marginal moraines in red

GLACIAL LAURENTIAN LAKES
LATER STAGE
After Taylor and Leverett

Marginal moraines in red

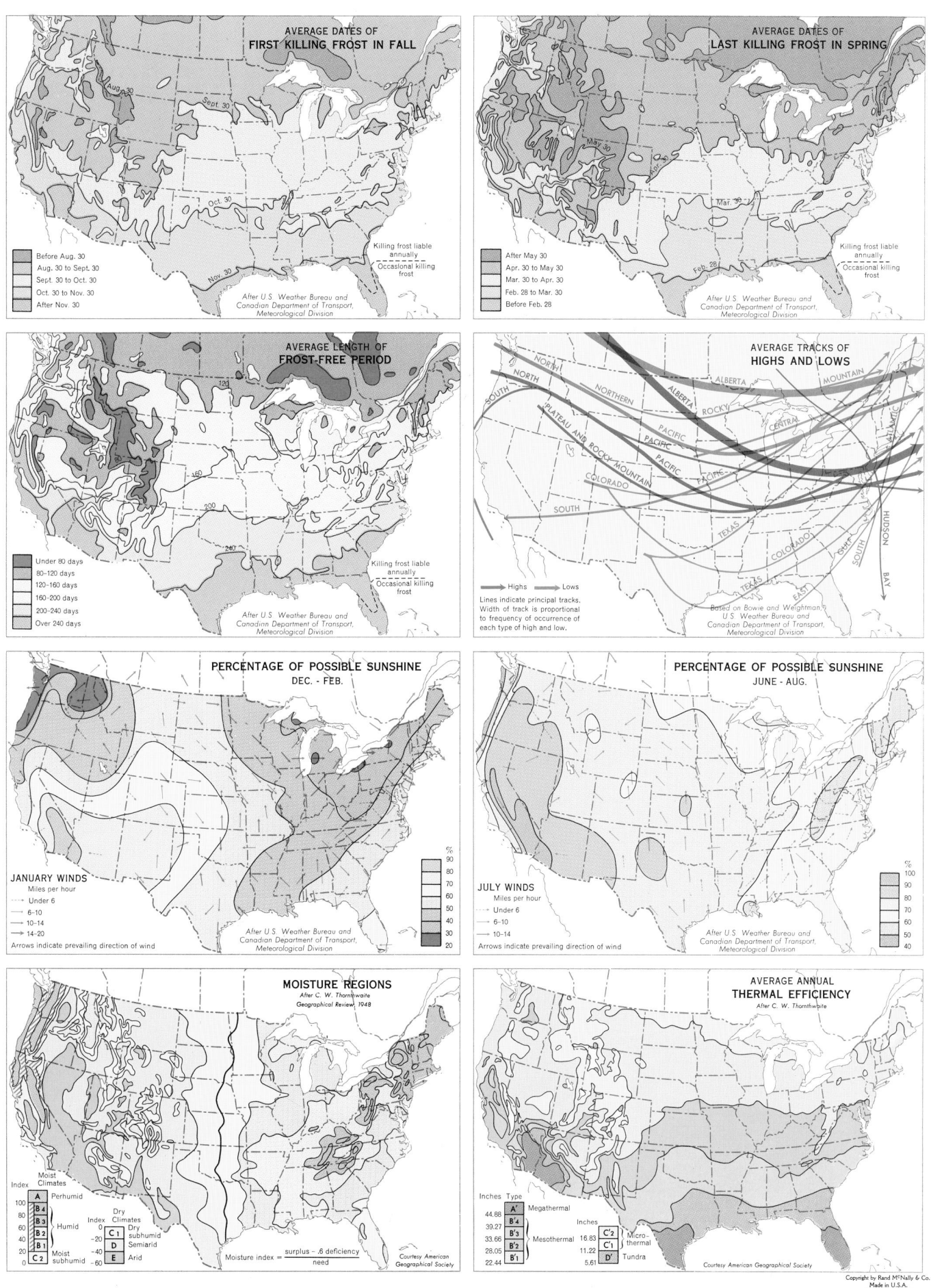

AVERAGE DATES OF
FIRST KILLING FROST IN FALL

Before Aug. 30
Aug. 30 to Sept. 30
Sept. 30 to Oct. 30
Oct. 30 to Nov. 30
After Nov. 30

Killing frost liable annually
Occasional killing frost

After U.S. Weather Bureau and Canadian Department of Transport, Meteorological Division

AVERAGE DATES OF
LAST KILLING FROST IN SPRING

After May 30
Apr. 30 to May 30
Mar. 30 to Apr. 30
Feb. 28 to Mar. 30
Before Feb. 28

Killing frost liable annually
Occasional killing frost

After U.S. Weather Bureau and Canadian Department of Transport, Meteorological Division

AVERAGE LENGTH OF
FROST-FREE PERIOD

Under 80 days
80–120 days
120–160 days
160–200 days
200–240 days
Over 240 days

Killing frost liable annually
Occasional killing frost

After U.S. Weather Bureau and Canadian Department of Transport, Meteorological Division

AVERAGE TRACKS OF
HIGHS AND LOWS

→ Highs   → Lows
Lines indicate principal tracks.
Width of track is proportional to frequency of occurrence of each type of high and low.

Based on Bowie and Weightman, U.S. Weather Bureau and Canadian Department of Transport, Meteorological Division

PERCENTAGE OF POSSIBLE SUNSHINE
DEC. - FEB.

JANUARY WINDS
Miles per hour
---- Under 6
→ 6–10
→ 10–14
→ 14–20
Arrows indicate prevailing direction of wind

%
90
80
70
60
50
40
30
20

After U.S. Weather Bureau and Canadian Department of Transport, Meteorological Division

PERCENTAGE OF POSSIBLE SUNSHINE
JUNE - AUG.

JULY WINDS
Miles per hour
---- Under 6
→ 6–10
→ 10–14
Arrows indicate prevailing direction of wind

%
100
90
80
70
60
50
40

After U.S. Weather Bureau and Canadian Department of Transport, Meteorological Division

MOISTURE REGIONS
*After C. W. Thornthwaite
Geographical Review, 1948*

Index | Moist Climates
100 | A — Perhumid
80 | B4
60 | B3 — Humid
40 | B2
20 | B1 — Moist subhumid
0 | C2

Index | Dry Climates
0 | C1 — Dry subhumid
-20 | D — Semiarid
-40 | E — Arid
-60

$$\text{Moisture index} = \frac{\text{surplus} - .6 \text{ deficiency}}{\text{need}}$$

Courtesy American Geographical Society

AVERAGE ANNUAL
THERMAL EFFICIENCY
After C. W. Thornthwaite

Inches | Type
44.88 | A′ — Megathermal
39.27 | B′4
33.66 | B′3 — Mesothermal
28.05 | B′2
22.44 | B′1

Inches
16.83 | C′2 — Microthermal
11.22 | C′1
5.61 | D′ — Tundra

Courtesy American Geographical Society

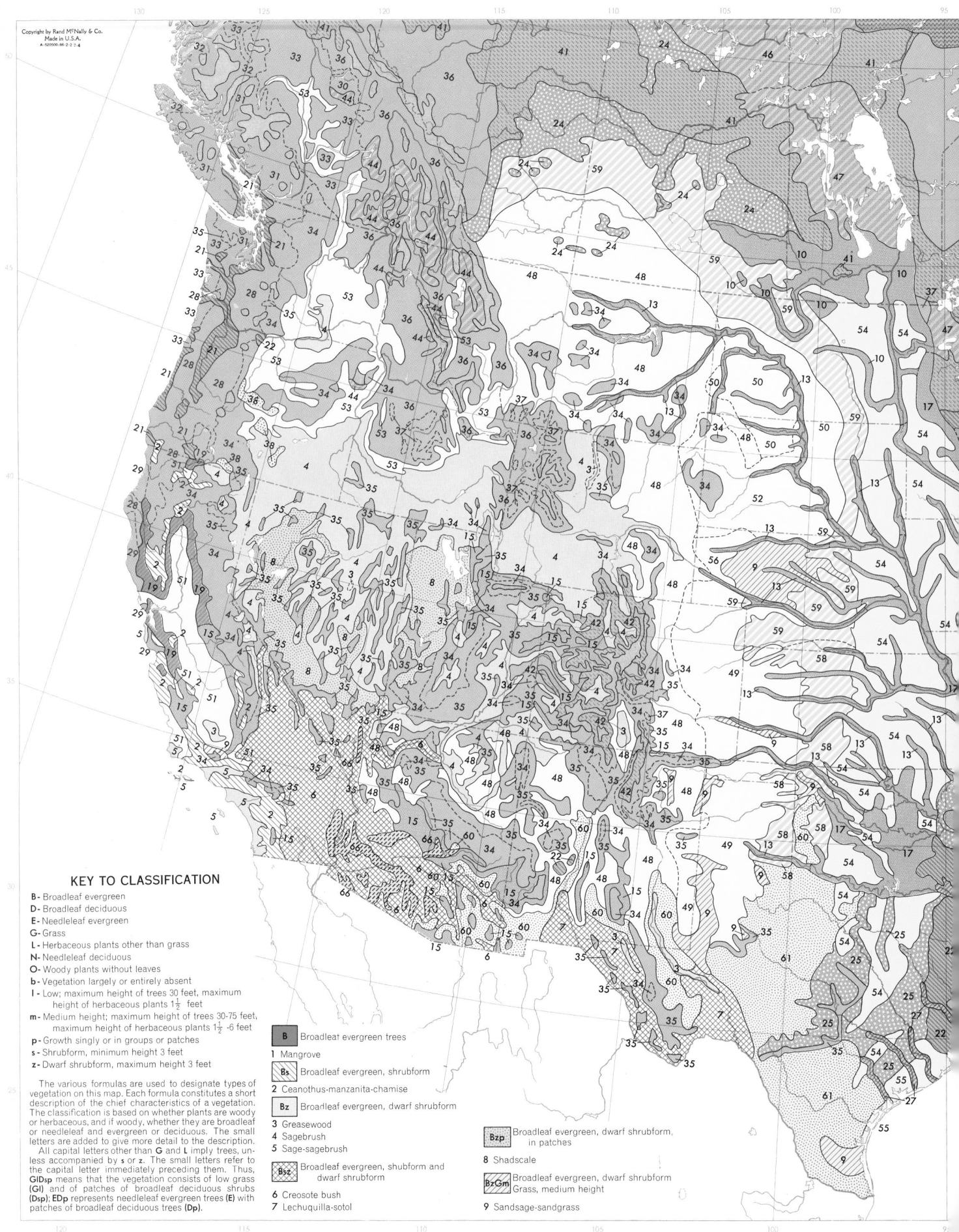

Copyright by Rand McNally & Co.
Made in U.S.A.
A-520500-86-2-2 2-4

KEY TO CLASSIFICATION

B - Broadleaf evergreen
D - Broadleaf deciduous
E - Needleleaf evergreen
G - Grass
L - Herbaceous plants other than grass
N - Needleleaf deciduous
O - Woody plants without leaves
b - Vegetation largely or entirely absent
l - Low; maximum height of trees 30 feet, maximum height of herbaceous plants 1½ feet
m - Medium height; maximum height of trees 30-75 feet, maximum height of herbaceous plants 1½ -6 feet
p - Growth singly or in groups or patches
s - Shrubform, minimum height 3 feet
z - Dwarf shrubform, maximum height 3 feet

The various formulas are used to designate types of vegetation on this map. Each formula constitutes a short description of the chief characteristics of a vegetation. The classification is based on whether plants are woody or herbaceous, and if woody, whether they are broadleaf or needleleaf and evergreen or deciduous. The small letters are added to give more detail to the description.

All capital letters other than **G** and **L** imply trees, unless accompanied by **s** or **z**. The small letters refer to the capital letter immediately preceding them. Thus, **GlDsp** means that the vegetation consists of low grass (**Gl**) and of patches of broadleaf deciduous shrubs (**Dsp**); **EDp** represents needleleaf evergreen trees (**E**) with patches of broadleaf deciduous trees (**Dp**).

B Broadleaf evergreen trees

1 Mangrove

Bs Broadleaf evergreen, shrubform

2 Ceanothus-manzanita-chamise

Bz Broadleaf evergreen, dwarf shrubform

3 Greasewood
4 Sagebrush
5 Sage-sagebrush

Bsz Broadleaf evergreen, shubform and dwarf shrubform

6 Creosote bush
7 Lechuquilla-sotol

Bzp Broadleaf evergreen, dwarf shrubform, in patches

8 Shadscale

BzGm Broadleaf evergreen, dwarf shrubform Grass, medium height

9 Sandsage-sandgrass

0 25 50 75 100   200   300   400   500 Miles

0 50 100   200   400   600   800 Kilometers

Scale 1:14 000 000;   One inch to 22

NATURAL VEGETATION

BY A. W. KÜCHLER

Based on "A Physiognomic Classification of Vegetation"
Annals of the Assoc. of American Geographers, Vol. 39, September, 1949

D Broadleaf deciduous trees

10 Aspen-oak
11 Beech-maple
12 Beech-tulip tree-maple-basswood
13 Cottonwood-willow
14 Maple-basswood
15 Oak
16 Oak-ash-maple
17 Oak-hickory
18 Oak-tulip tree

DB Broadleaf deciduous trees
Broadleaf evergreen trees

19 Oak-madrone

DE Broadleaf deciduous trees
Needleleaf evergreen trees

20 Maple-yellow birch-hemlock-pine
21 Oak-Douglas fir
22 Oak-pine
23 Maple-beech-hemlock

D / Gm Broadleaf deciduous trees
Grass, medium height, in patches

24 Aspen-needle grass-wheat grass
25 Oak-hickory-bluestem

DN Broadleaf deciduous trees
Needleleaf deciduous trees

26 Bay trees-bald cypress
27 Tupelo-gum-bald cypress

E Needleleaf evergreen trees

28 Douglas fir
29 Douglas fir-redwood
30 Hemlock-arbor vitae
31 Hemlock-arbor vitae-Douglas fir
32 Hemlock-arbor vitae-fir
33 Hemlock-spruce
34 Pine
35 Pine-juniper
36 Pine-spruce
37 Spruce-fir

Esp Needleleaf evergreen, shrubform,
in patches

38 Juniper

EDp Needleleaf evergreen trees
Broadleaf deciduous trees, in patches

39 Douglas fir-pine-aspen
40 Pine-spruce-birch
41 Spruce-aspen
42 Spruce-fir-aspen
43 Spruce-poplar-birch

EN Needleleaf evergreen trees
Needleleaf deciduous trees

44 Hemlock-arbor vitae-Douglas fir-larch
45 Pine-bald cypress
46 Pine-spruce-larch
47 Spruce-larch

Gl Grass, low

48 Grama grass
49 Grama grass-buffalo grass
50 Grama grass-needle grass
51 Needle grass-blue grass
52 Wheat grass
53 Wheat grass-blue grass

Gm Grass, medium height

54 Bluestem
55 Broom grass-water grass
56 Marsh grass
57 Saw grass

Gml Grass, medium and low height

58 Bluestem-bunch grass
59 Needle grass-wheat grass

Gl / Dsp Grass, low
Broadleaf deciduous, shrubform, in patches

60 Bunch grass-oak

Gm / Dsp Grass, medium height
Broadleaf deciduous, shrubform, in patches

61 Mesquite grass-mesquite

L Herbaceous plants other than grass

62 Lichens, etc.

LEp Herbaceous plants other than grass
Needleleaf evergreen trees, in patches

63 Lichens-spruce

LEp / Np Herbaceous plants other than grass
Needleleaf evergreen trees, in patches
Needleleaf deciduous trees, in patches

64 Lichens-spruce-larch

N Needleleaf deciduous trees

65 Bald cypress

Op Woody plants without leaves, in patches

66 Palo verde-cacti-ocotillo

b Vegetation largely or entirely absent

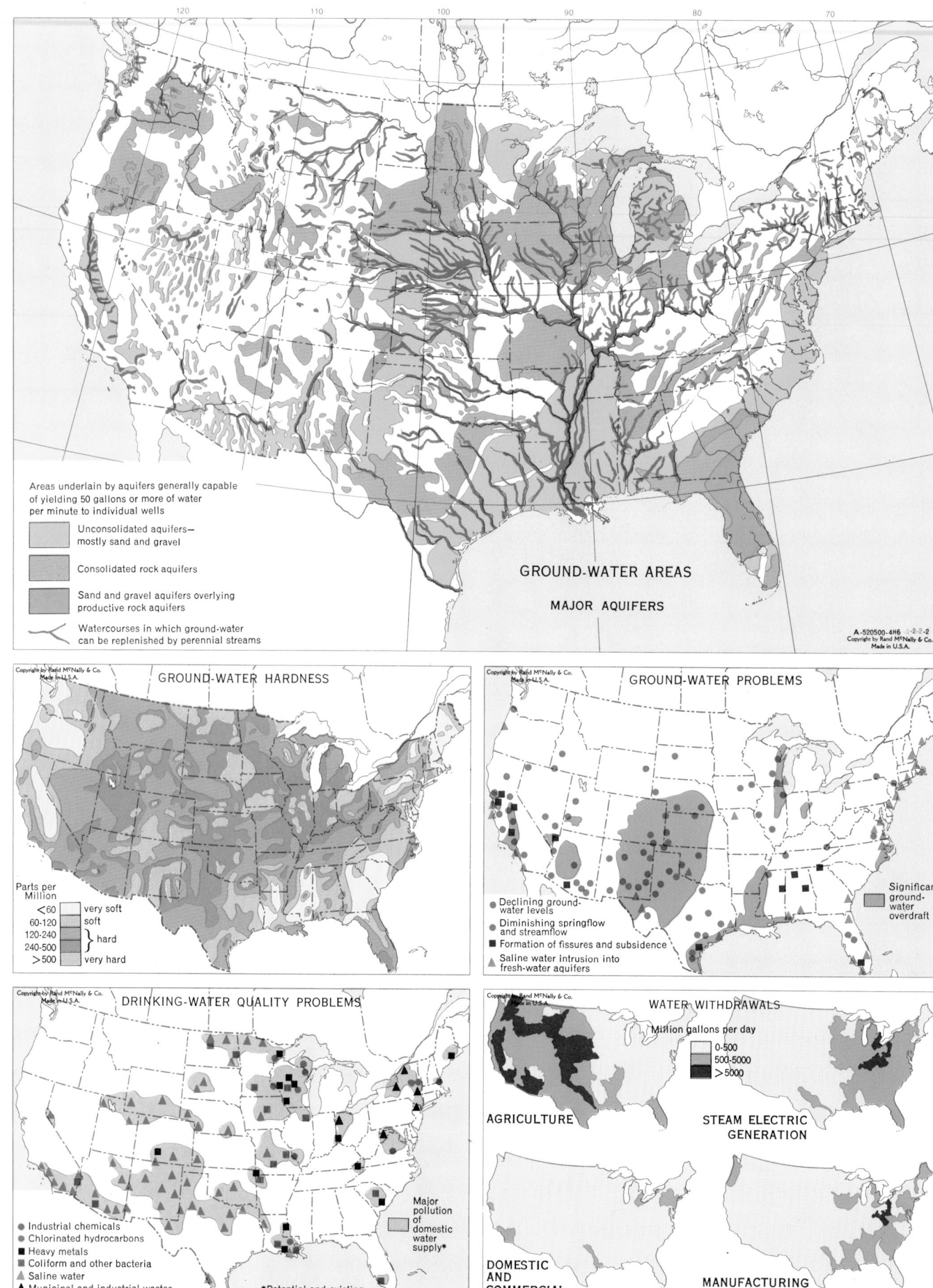

Areas underlain by aquifers generally capable
of yielding 50 gallons or more of water
per minute to individual wells

Unconsolidated aquifers—
mostly sand and gravel

Consolidated rock aquifers

Sand and gravel aquifers overlying
productive rock aquifers

Watercourses in which ground-water
can be replenished by perennial streams

GROUND-WATER AREAS

MAJOR AQUIFERS

A-520500-4H6
Copyright by Rand McNally & Co.
Made in U.S.A.

GROUND-WATER HARDNESS

Copyright by Rand McNally & Co.
Made in U.S.A.

Parts per
Million
<60   very soft
60-120   soft
120-240   } hard
240-500
>500   very hard

GROUND-WATER PROBLEMS

Copyright by Rand McNally & Co.
Made in U.S.A.

● Declining ground-
   water levels
● Diminishing springflow
   and streamflow
■ Formation of fissures and subsidence
▲ Saline water intrusion into
   fresh-water aquifers

Significant
ground-
water
overdraft

DRINKING-WATER QUALITY PROBLEMS

Copyright by Rand McNally & Co.
Made in U.S.A.

● Industrial chemicals
● Chlorinated hydrocarbons
■ Heavy metals
■ Coliform and other bacteria
▲ Saline water
▲ Municipal and industrial wastes

Major
pollution
of
domestic
water
supply*

*Potential and existing

WATER WITHDRAWALS

Copyright by Rand McNally & Co.
Made in U.S.A.

Million gallons per day
0-500
500-5000
>5000

AGRICULTURE

**STEAM ELECTRIC
GENERATION**

**DOMESTIC
AND
COMMERCIAL**

MANUFACTURING

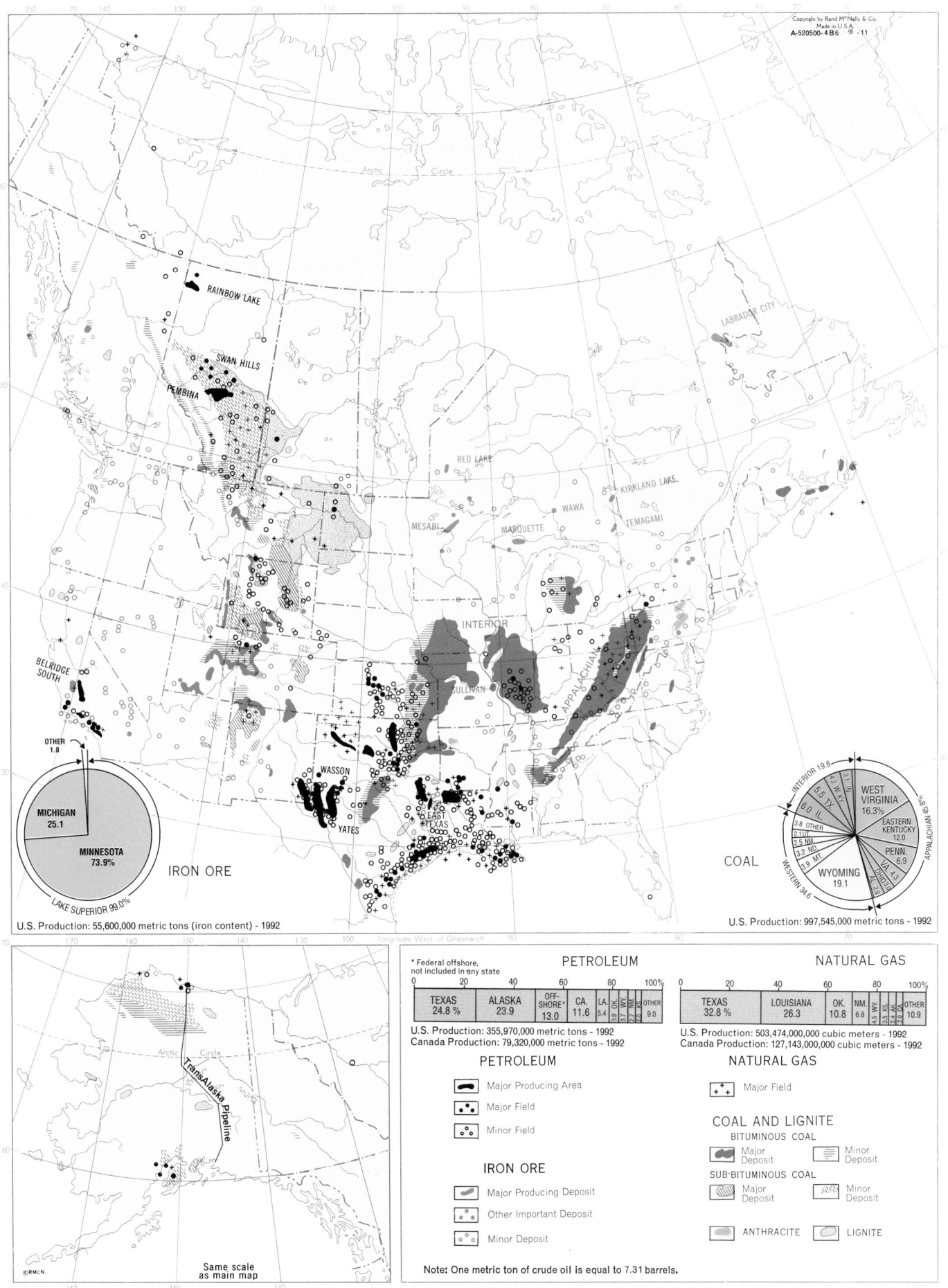

Copyright by Rand McNally & Co.
Made in U.S.A.
A-520500-4 B 6   98 -11

RAINBOW LAKE

LABRADOR CITY

SWAN HILLS

PEMBINA

RED LAKE

KIRKLAND LAKE

MESABI

MARQUETTE   WAWA

TEMAGAMI

BELRIDGE
SOUTH

INTERIOR

SULLIVAN

APPALACHIAN

OTHER
1.0

MICHIGAN
25.1

MINNESOTA
73.9%

IRON ORE

WASSON

EAST
TEXAS

YATES

LAKE SUPERIOR 99.0%

U.S. Production: 55,600,000 metric tons (iron content) - 1992

COAL

INTERIOR 19.6
5.5 TX.
4.2 KY.
3.1 IL.
6.0 IL.
3.8 OTHER
2.7 UT.
2.5 NM.
3.9 ND.
3.2 MT.
WESTERN 34.6

WEST
VIRGINIA
16.3%

APPALACHIAN 45.6%

EASTERN
KENTUCKY
12.0

PENN.
6.9

VA. 4.3
AL. 2.1

WYOMING
19.1

U.S. Production: 997,545,000 metric tons - 1992

TransAlaska Pipeline

Arctic Circle

Same scale
as main map

©RMcN.

PETROLEUM

* Federal offshore,
not included in any state

0	20	40	60	80	100%

TEXAS 24.8 %	ALASKA 23.9	OFF-SHORE* 13.0	CA. 11.6	LA. 5.4	OK. 3.9	WY. 3.7	KS. 2.2	OTHER 9.0

U.S. Production: 355,970,000 metric tons - 1992
Canada Production: 79,320,000 metric tons - 1992

NATURAL GAS

0	20	40	60	80	100%

TEXAS 32.8 %	LOUISIANA 26.3	OK. 10.8	NM. 6.8	WY. 4.5	KS. 3.5	AK. 2.4	LA. 2.0	OTHER 10.9

U.S. Production: 503,474,000,000 cubic meters - 1992
Canada Production: 127,143,000,000 cubic meters - 1992

PETROLEUM

- Major Producing Area
- Major Field
- Minor Field

IRON ORE

- Major Producing Deposit
- Other Important Deposit
- Minor Deposit

NATURAL GAS

- Major Field

COAL AND LIGNITE

BITUMINOUS COAL
- Major Deposit
- Minor Deposit

SUB-BITUMINOUS COAL
- Major Deposit
- Minor Deposit

- ANTHRACITE
- LIGNITE

Note: One metric ton of crude oil is equal to 7.31 barrels.

Scale 1: 32 000 000; One inch to 500 miles.   LAMBERT CONFORMAL CONIC PROJECTION

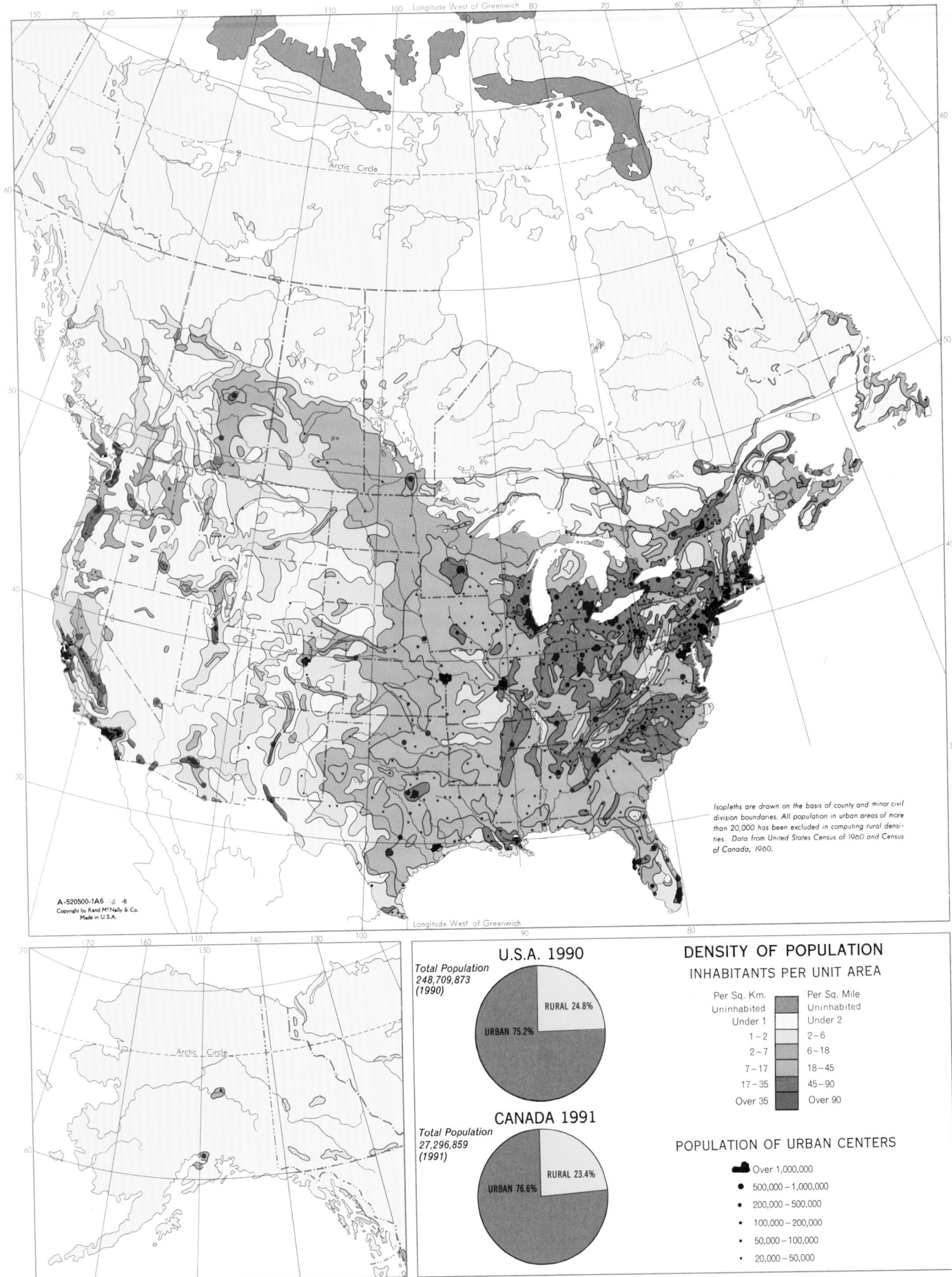

Isopleths are drawn on the basis of county and minor civil division boundaries. All population in urban areas of more than 20,000 has been excluded in computing rural densities. Data from United States Census of 1960 and Census of Canada, 1960.

A-520500-1A6 -S -6
Copyright by Rand McNally & Co.
Made in U.S.A.

U.S.A. 1990

Total Population
248,709,873
(1990)

RURAL 24.8%

URBAN 75.2%

CANADA 1991

Total Population
27,296,859
(1991)

RURAL 23.4%

URBAN 76.6%

DENSITY OF POPULATION
INHABITANTS PER UNIT AREA

Per Sq. Km.	Per Sq. Mile
Uninhabited	Uninhabited
Under 1	Under 2
1–2	2–6
2–7	6–18
7–17	18–45
17–35	45–90
Over 35	Over 90

POPULATION OF URBAN CENTERS

Over 1,000,000
500,000 – 1,000,000
200,000 – 500,000
100,000 – 200,000
50,000 – 100,000
20,000 – 50,000

Scale 1: 32 000 000; One inch to 500 miles. LAMBERT CONFORMAL CONIC PROJECTION

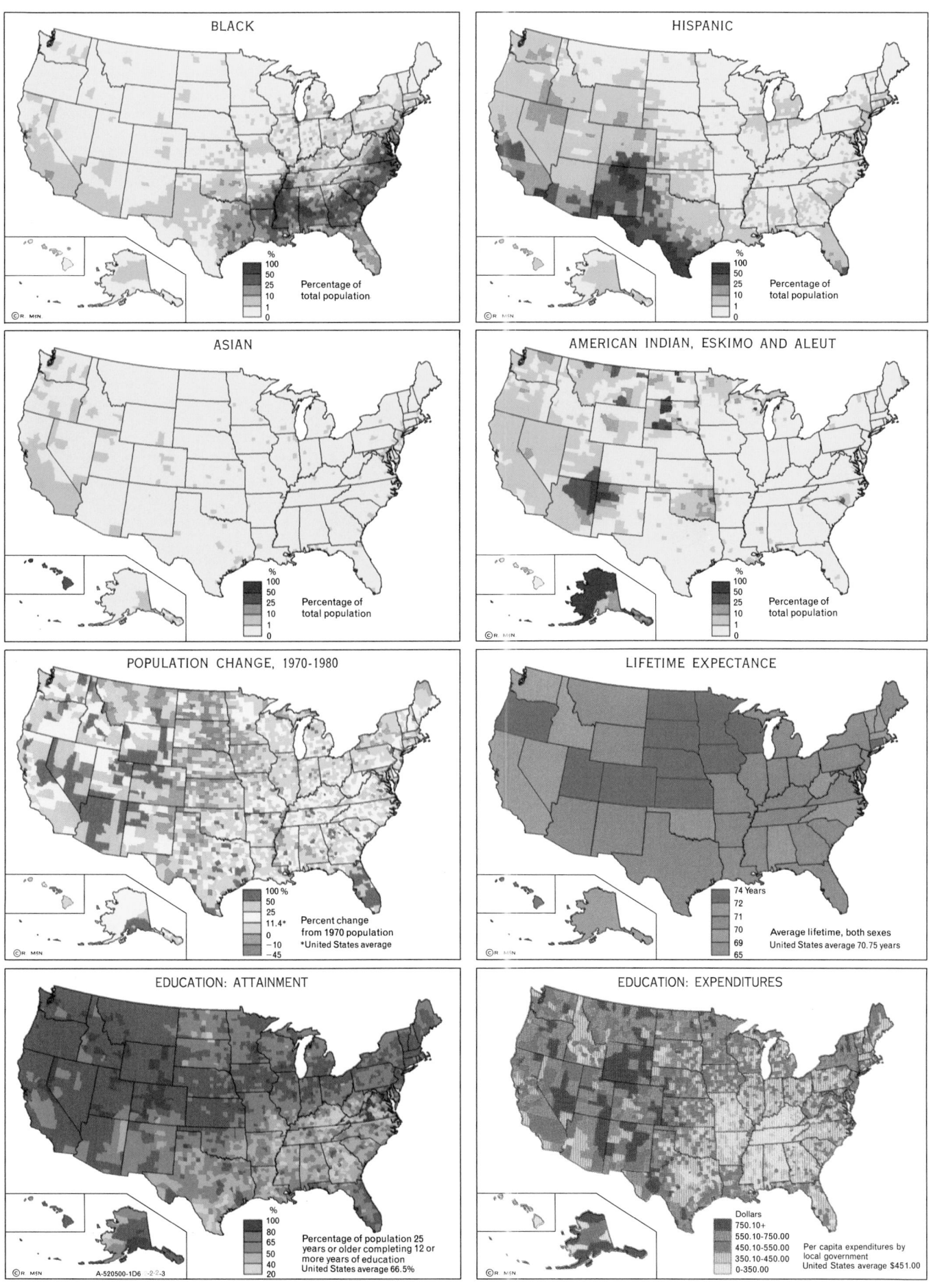

BLACK

%
100
50
25
10
1
0
Percentage of
total population

HISPANIC

%
100
50
25
10
1
0
Percentage of
total population

ASIAN

%
100
50
25
10
1
0
Percentage of
total population

AMERICAN INDIAN, ESKIMO AND ALEUT

%
100
50
25
10
1
0
Percentage of
total population

POPULATION CHANGE, 1970-1980

100 %
50
25
11.4*
0
−10
−45
Percent change
from 1970 population
*United States average

LIFETIME EXPECTANCE

74 Years
72
71
70
69
65
Average lifetime, both sexes
United States average 70.75 years

EDUCATION: ATTAINMENT

%
100
80
65
50
40
20
Percentage of population 25
years or older completing 12 or
more years of education
United States average 66.5%

A-520500-1D6

EDUCATION: EXPENDITURES

Dollars
750.10+
550.10-750.00
450.10-550.00
350.10-450.00
0-350.00
Per capita expenditures by
local government
United States average $451.00

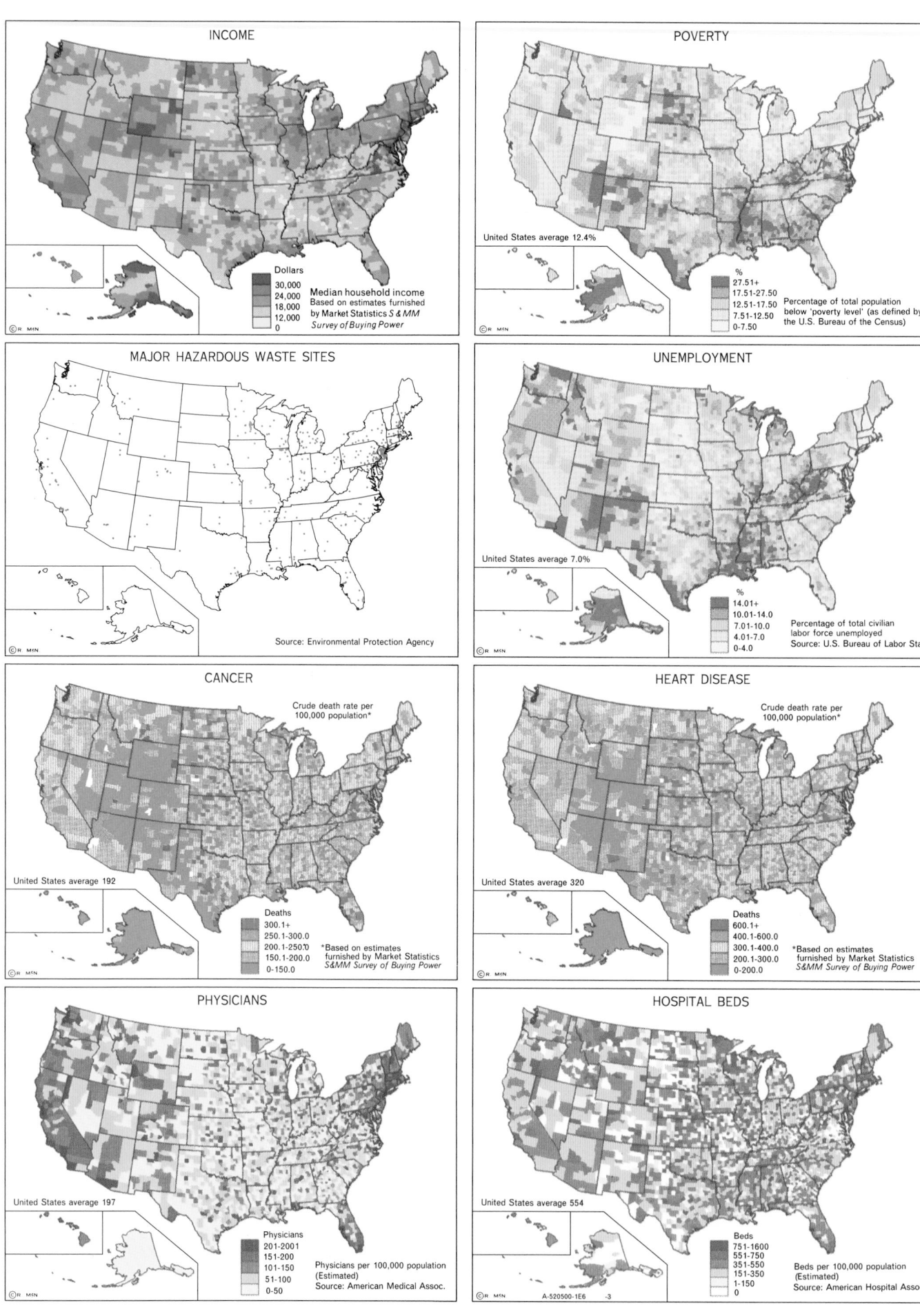

INCOME

Dollars
30,000
24,000
18,000
12,000
0

Median household income
Based on estimates furnished
by Market Statistics S & MM
Survey of Buying Power

POVERTY

United States average 12.4%

%
27.51+
17.51-27.50
12.51-17.50
7.51-12.50
0-7.50

Percentage of total population
below 'poverty level' (as defined by
the U.S. Bureau of the Census)

MAJOR HAZARDOUS WASTE SITES

Source: Environmental Protection Agency

UNEMPLOYMENT

United States average 7.0%

%
14.01+
10.01-14.0
7.01-10.0
4.01-7.0
0-4.0

Percentage of total civilian
labor force unemployed
Source: U.S. Bureau of Labor Stat.

CANCER

Crude death rate per
100,000 population*

United States average 192

Deaths
300.1+
250.1-300.0
200.1-250.0
150.1-200.0
0-150.0

*Based on estimates
furnished by Market Statistics
S&MM Survey of Buying Power

HEART DISEASE

Crude death rate per
100,000 population*

United States average 320

Deaths
600.1+
400.1-600.0
300.1-400.0
200.1-300.0
0-200.0

*Based on estimates
furnished by Market Statistics
S&MM Survey of Buying Power

PHYSICIANS

United States average 197

Physicians
201-2001
151-200
101-150
51-100
0-50

Physicians per 100,000 population
(Estimated)
Source: American Medical Assoc.

HOSPITAL BEDS

United States average 554

Beds
751-1600
551-750
351-550
151-350
1-150
0

Beds per 100,000 population
(Estimated)
Source: American Hospital Assoc.

A-520500-1E6   -3

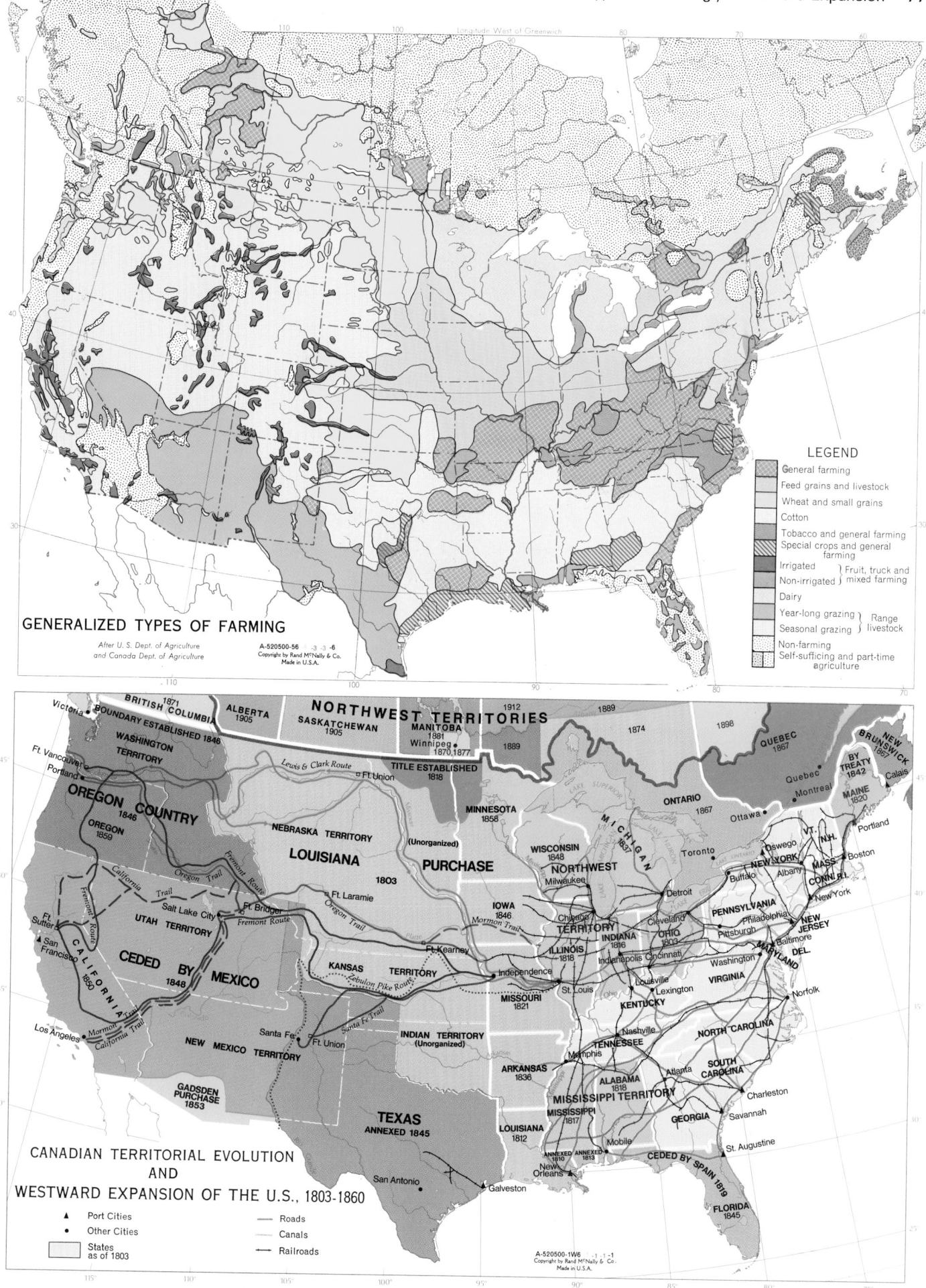

GENERALIZED TYPES OF FARMING

After U. S. Dept. of Agriculture
and Canada Dept. of Agriculture

A-520500-56   -3 -3 -6
Copyright by Rand McNally & Co.
Made in U.S.A.

LEGEND

General farming
Feed grains and livestock
Wheat and small grains
Cotton
Tobacco and general farming
Special crops and general farming
Irrigated }
Non-irrigated } Fruit, truck and mixed farming
Dairy
Year-long grazing } Range livestock
Seasonal grazing }
Non-farming
Self-sufficing and part-time agriculture

CANADIAN TERRITORIAL EVOLUTION
AND
WESTWARD EXPANSION OF THE U.S., 1803-1860

▲ Port Cities
● Other Cities
▢ States as of 1803

━━ Roads
━━ Canals
━━ Railroads

A-520500-1W6   -1 -1 -1
Copyright by Rand McNally & Co.
Made in U.S.A.

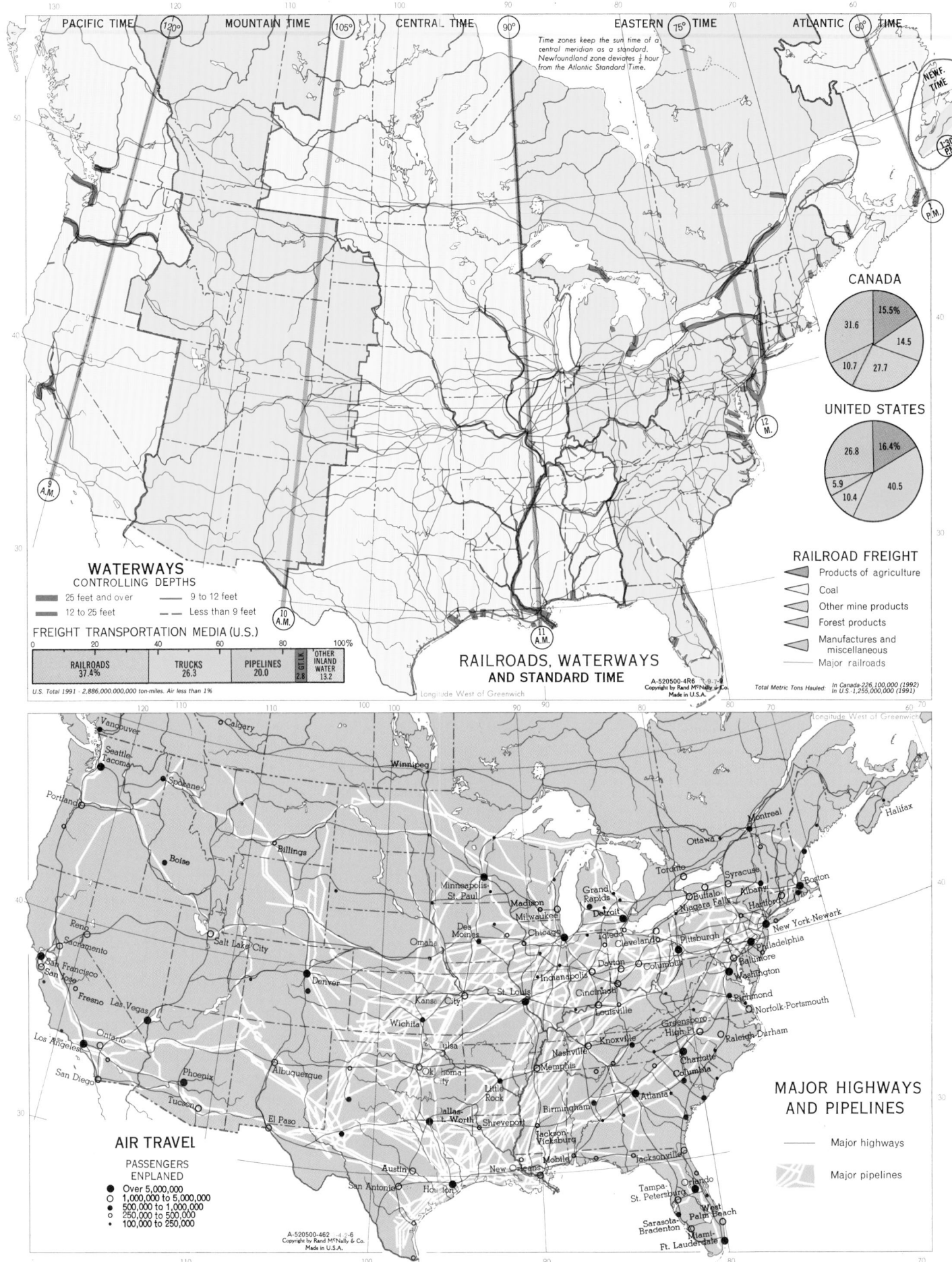

Time zones keep the sun time of a central meridian as a standard. Newfoundland zone deviates ½ hour from the Atlantic Standard Time.

NEWF. TIME

1:30 P.M.

1 P.M.

CANADA
15.5%
31.6
14.5
10.7
27.7

UNITED STATES
26.8
16.4%
5.9
40.5
10.4

12 M.

9 A.M.

WATERWAYS
CONTROLLING DEPTHS
━━━ 25 feet and over   ━━━ 9 to 12 feet
━━━ 12 to 25 feet   ----- Less than 9 feet

FREIGHT TRANSPORTATION MEDIA (U.S.)
0   20   40   60   80   100%

| RAILROADS 37.4% | TRUCKS 26.3 | PIPELINES 20.0 | GT.LK 2.8 | OTHER INLAND WATER 13.2 |

U.S. Total 1991 - 2,886,000,000,000 ton-miles. Air less than 1%

10 A.M.

11 A.M.

RAILROAD FREIGHT
◁ Products of agriculture
◁ Coal
◁ Other mine products
◁ Forest products
◁ Manufactures and miscellaneous
── Major railroads

RAILROADS, WATERWAYS
AND STANDARD TIME

A-520500-4R6
Copyright by Rand McNally & Co.
Made in U.S.A.

Total Metric Tons Hauled: In Canada-226,100,000 (1992)
In U.S.-1,255,000,000 (1991)

Longitude West of Greenwich

AIR TRAVEL
PASSENGERS ENPLANED
● Over 5,000,000
○ 1,000,000 to 5,000,000
○ 500,000 to 1,000,000
○ 250,000 to 500,000
· 100,000 to 250,000

MAJOR HIGHWAYS
AND PIPELINES
── Major highways
▨ Major pipelines

A-520500-462
Copyright by Rand McNally & Co.
Made in U.S.A.

Scale 1:28 000 000; One inch to 440 miles.   LAMBERT CONFORMAL CONIC PROJECTION

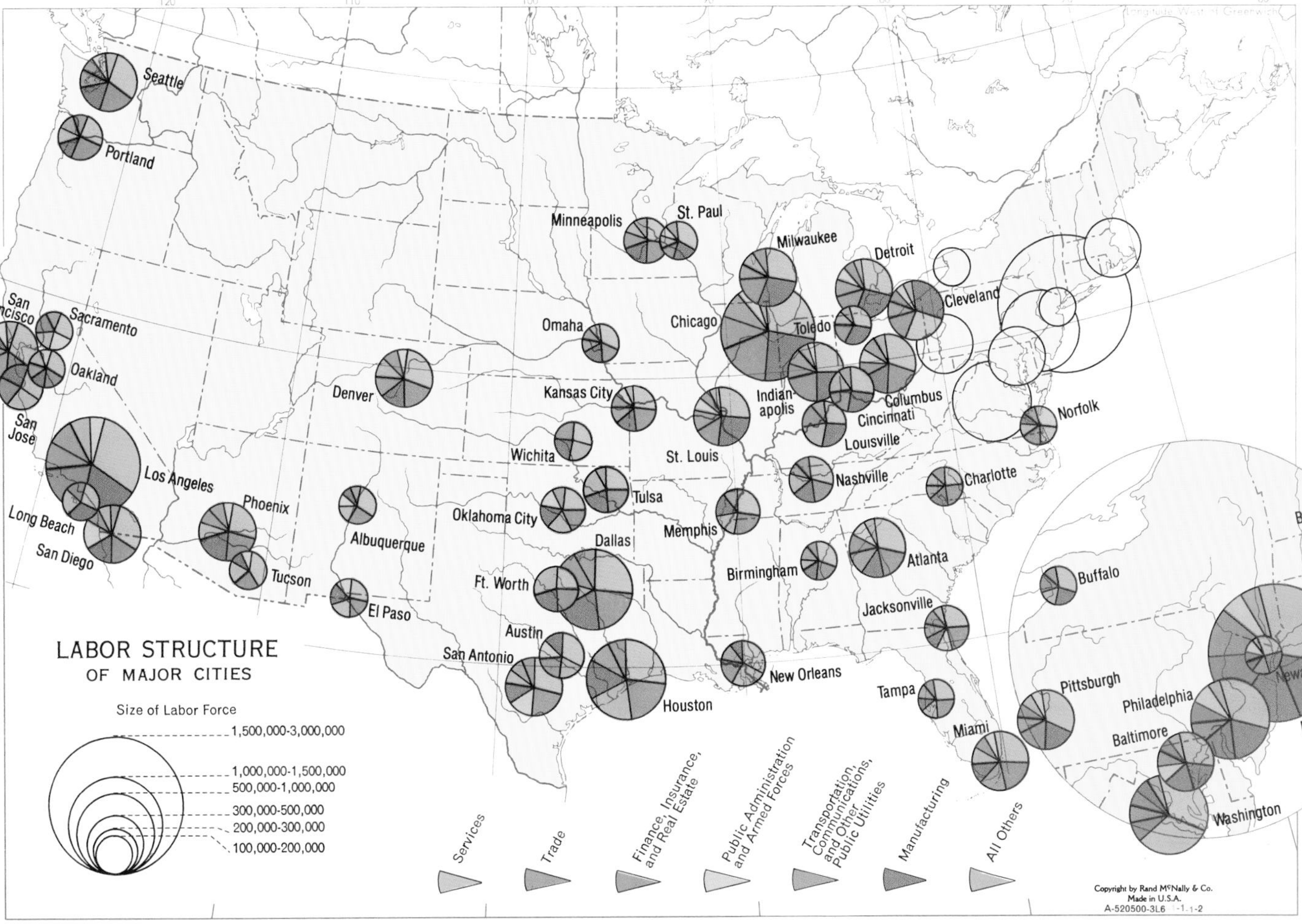

LABOR STRUCTURE
OF MAJOR CITIES

Size of Labor Force

- 1,500,000–3,000,000
- 1,000,000–1,500,000
- 500,000–1,000,000
- 300,000–500,000
- 200,000–300,000
- 100,000–200,000

Services

Trade

Finance, Insurance, and Real Estate

Public Administration and Armed Forces

Transportation, Communications, and Other Public Utilities

Manufacturing

All Others

Seattle
Portland
San Francisco
Sacramento
Oakland
San Jose
Los Angeles
Long Beach
San Diego
Phoenix
Tucson
El Paso
Albuquerque
Denver
Minneapolis
St. Paul
Omaha
Kansas City
Wichita
Oklahoma City
Tulsa
Dallas
Ft. Worth
Austin
San Antonio
Houston
Chicago
Milwaukee
Detroit
Cleveland
Toledo
Indianapolis
Cincinnati
Columbus
Louisville
St. Louis
Memphis
Nashville
Birmingham
New Orleans
Atlanta
Charlotte
Jacksonville
Tampa
Miami
Norfolk
Buffalo
Pittsburgh
Philadelphia
Baltimore
Washington
New York
Newark
Boston

Copyright by Rand McNally & Co.
Made in U.S.A.
A-520500-3L6

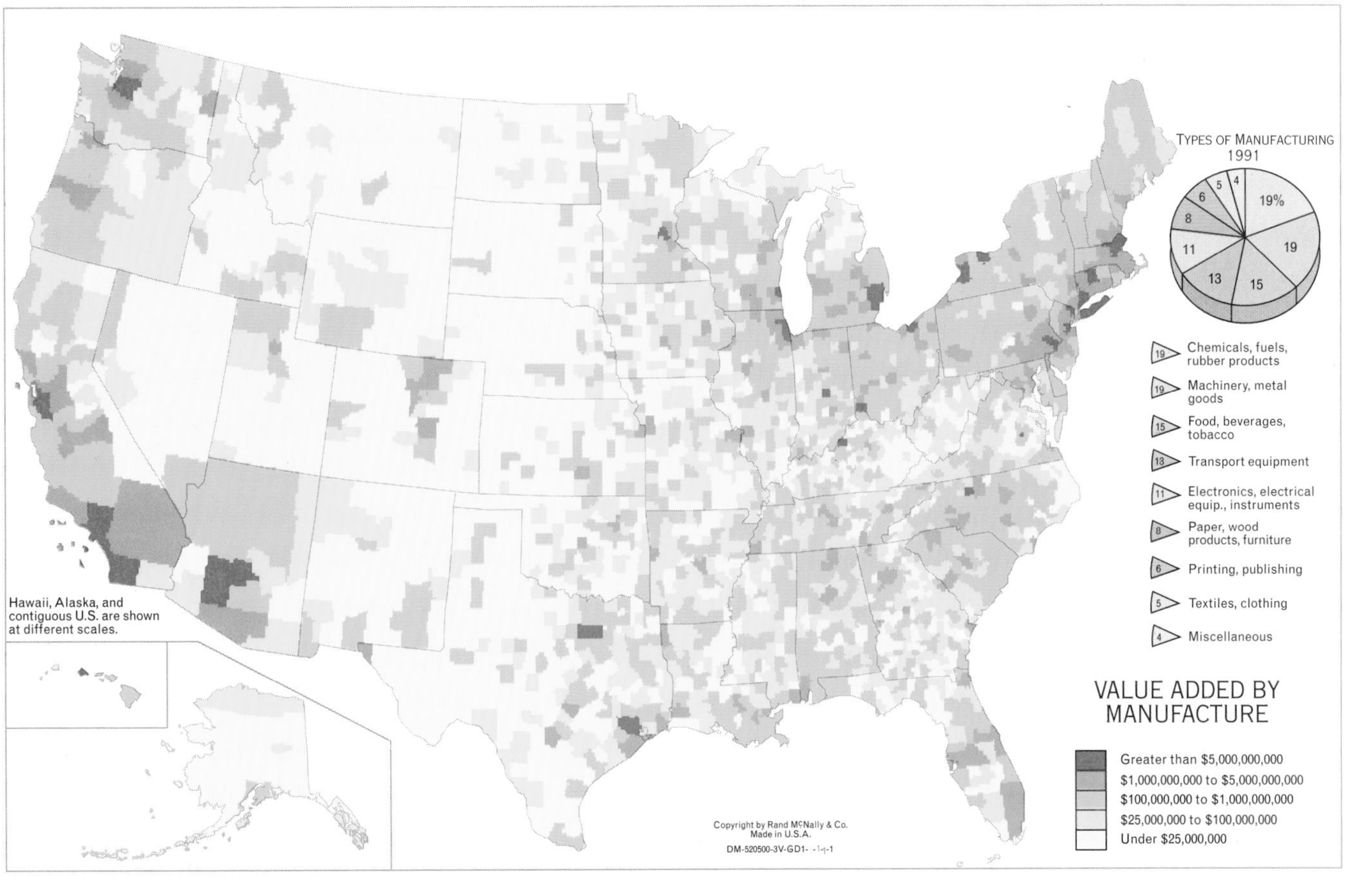

TYPES OF MANUFACTURING
1991

19%
19
15
13
11
8
6
5
4

- 19 Chemicals, fuels, rubber products
- 19 Machinery, metal goods
- 15 Food, beverages, tobacco
- 13 Transport equipment
- 11 Electronics, electrical equip., instruments
- 8 Paper, wood products, furniture
- 6 Printing, publishing
- 5 Textiles, clothing
- 4 Miscellaneous

VALUE ADDED BY MANUFACTURE

- Greater than $5,000,000,000
- $1,000,000,000 to $5,000,000,000
- $100,000,000 to $1,000,000,000
- $25,000,000 to $100,000,000
- Under $25,000,000

Hawaii, Alaska, and contiguous U.S. are shown at different scales.

Copyright by Rand McNally & Co.
Made in U.S.A.
DM-520500-3V-GD1

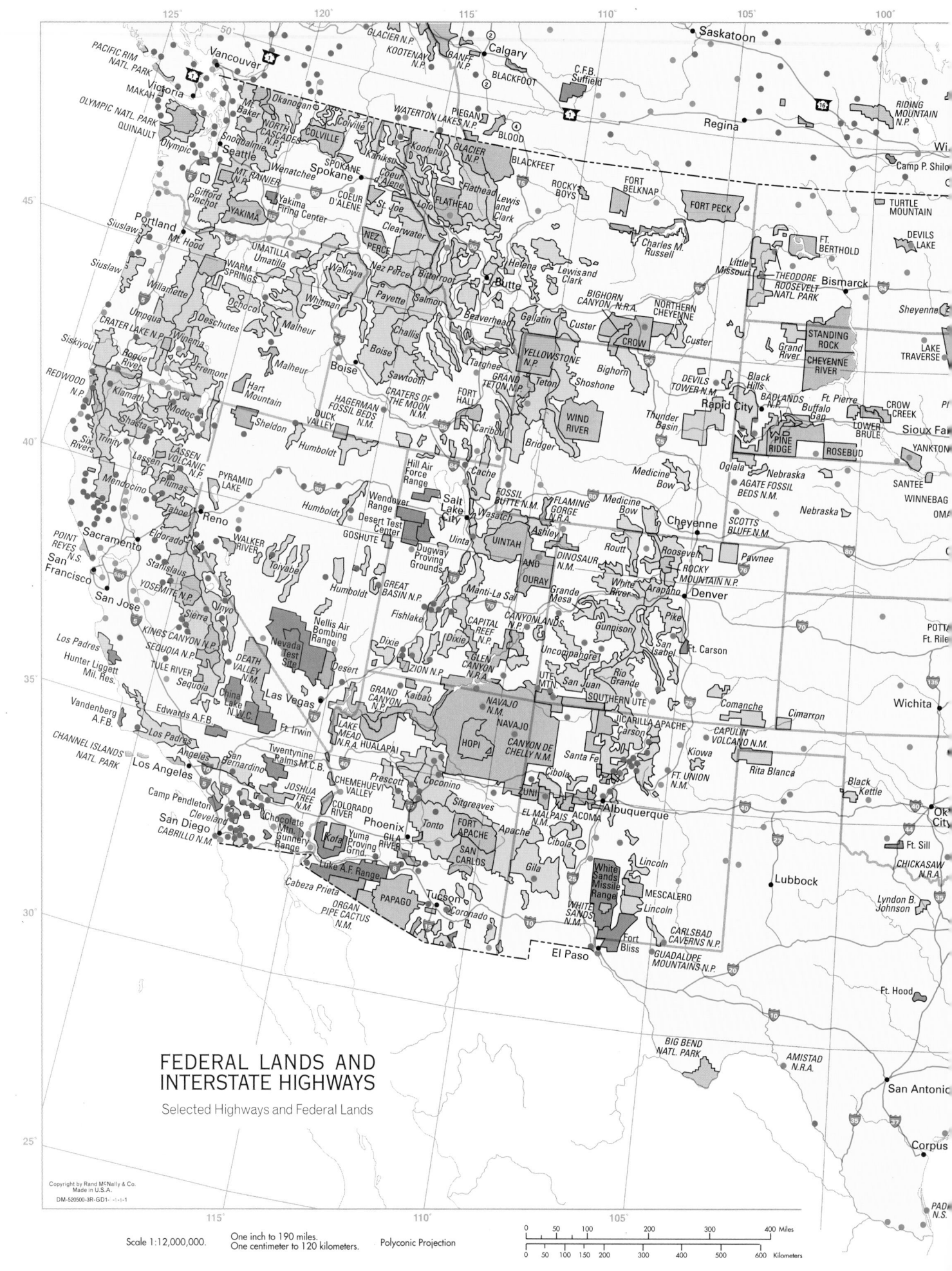

80

FEDERAL LANDS AND
INTERSTATE HIGHWAYS

Selected Highways and Federal Lands

Copyright by Rand M&Nally & Co.
Made in U.S.A.
DM-520500-3R-GD1- -|-|-1

Scale 1:12,000,000.   One inch to 190 miles.   Polyconic Projection
                        One centimeter to 120 kilometers.

0   50 100   200   300   400 Miles

0 50 100 150 200   300   400   500   600 Kilometers

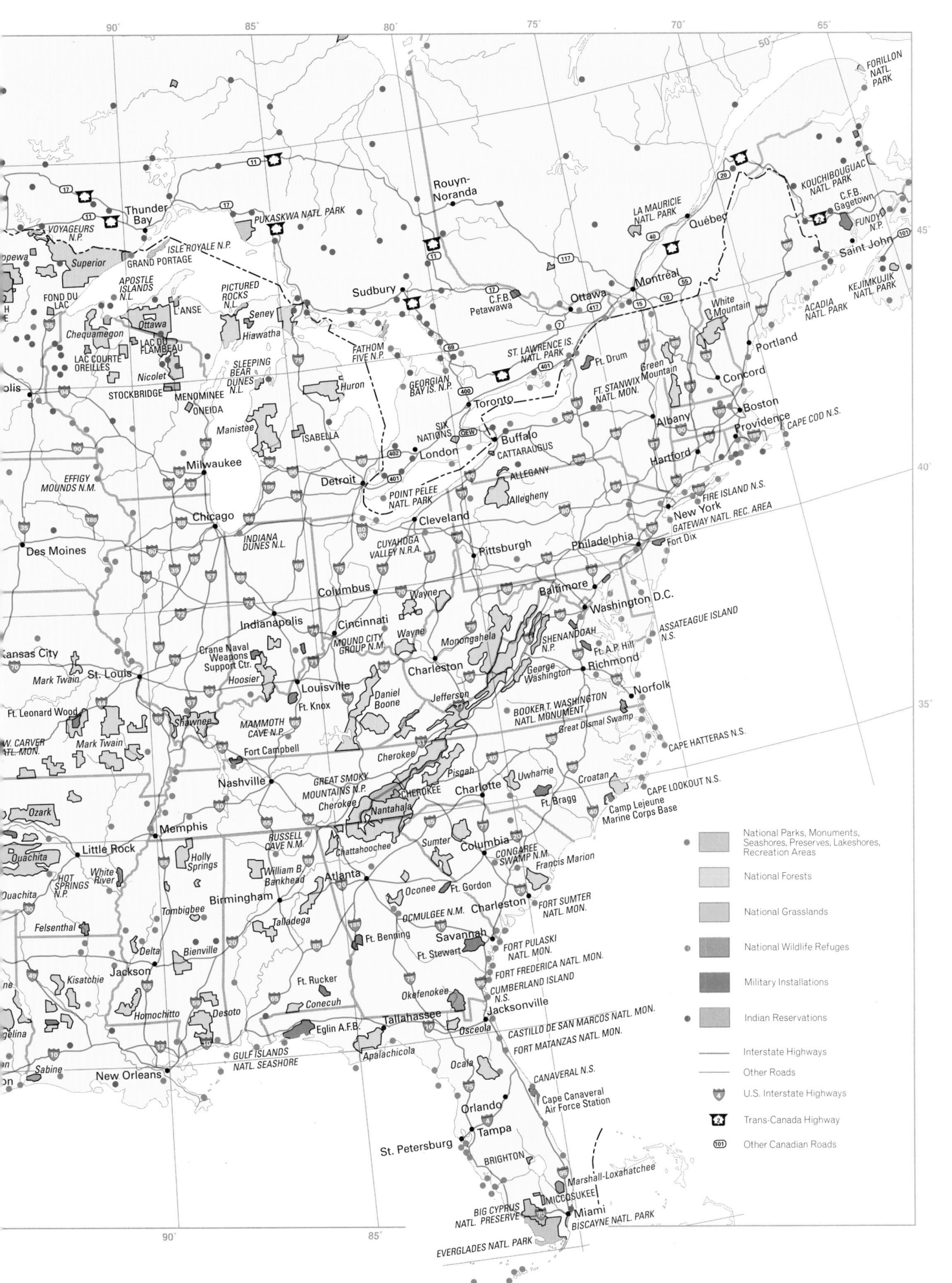

National Parks, Monuments, Seashores, Preserves, Lakeshores, Recreation Areas

National Forests

National Grasslands

National Wildlife Refuges

Military Installations

Indian Reservations

Interstate Highways

Other Roads

U.S. Interstate Highways

Trans-Canada Highway

Other Canadian Roads

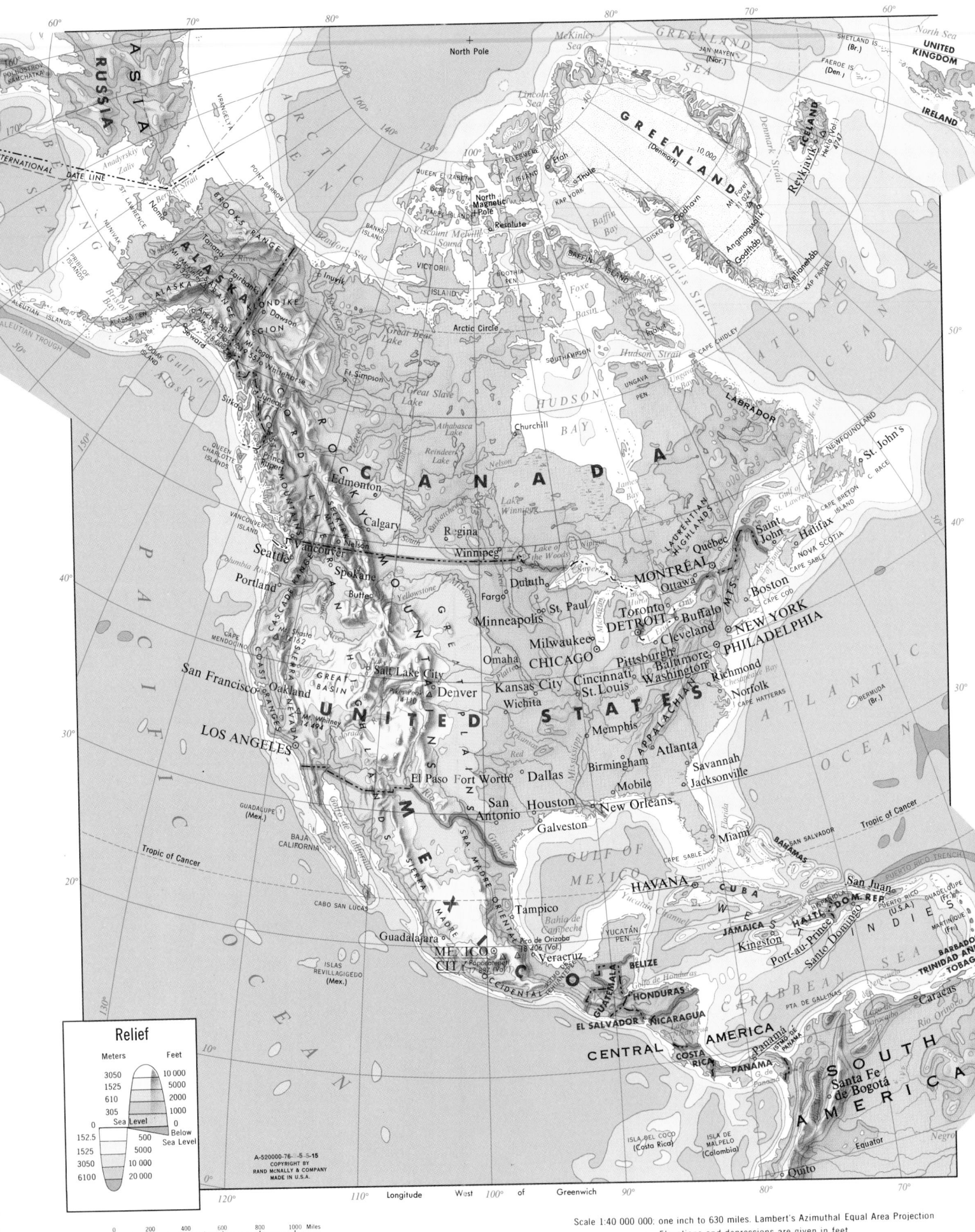

ASIA
RUSSIA
POLNOSTROV KAMCHATKA
Anadyrskiy Zaliv
INTERNATIONAL DATE LINE
BERING SEA
Bristol Bay
ALEUTIAN ISLANDS
ALEUTIAN TROUGH
PRIBILOF ISLANDS
Nome
Nunivak
KODIAK ISLAND
Gulf of Alaska

North Pole
McKinley Sea
GREENLAND SEA
JAN MAYEN (Nor.)
SHETLAND IS. (Br.)
UNITED KINGDOM
IRELAND
North Sea
Lincoln Sea
ICELAND
Reykjavík
Hella (Vol.) 4744
Denmark Strait
GREENLAND (Denmark)
10,000
Mt. Forel
Godthaab
Godhavn
DISKO
Angmagssalik
Julianehåb
KAP FARVEL

POINT BARROW
Beaufort Sea
BROOKS RANGE
ALASKA
Fairbanks
Tanana
ALASKA RANGE
Mt. McKinley 20,320
Mt. Logan 19,550
Whitehorse
KLONDIKE REGION
Dawson
ST. LAWRENCE I.
BANKS ISLAND
Inuvik
Ft. Simpson
VICTORIA ISLAND
Great Bear Lake
QUEEN ELIZABETH ISLANDS
ELLESMERE ISLAND
Etah
North Magnetic Pole
Resolute
PARRY ISLANDS
Viscount Melville Sound
BOOTHIA PEN.
KAP YORK
Thule
Baffin Bay
BAFFIN ISLAND
Davis Strait

ARCTIC OCEAN
Arctic Circle
Great Slave Lake
Athabasca Lake
Reindeer Lake
CANADA
Edmonton
Calgary
Churchill
HUDSON BAY
SOUTHAMPTON
Hudson Strait
FOXE BASIN
UNGAVA PEN.
UNGAVA BAY
CAPE CHIDLEY
LABRADOR
Nelson R.
Lake Winnipeg
Regina
Saskatchewan R.
South R.
Winnipeg
Lake of the Woods
JAMES BAY
Lake Nipigon
NEWFOUNDLAND
St. John's
C. RACE

PACIFIC OCEAN
QUEEN CHARLOTTE ISLANDS
Prince Rupert
VANCOUVER ISLAND
Vancouver
Seattle
Spokane
Portland
CAPE MENDOCINO
COAST RANGES
San Francisco
Oakland
Sitka
Juneau
Nelson
Butte
Yellowstone
CASCADE RANGE
Mt. Shasta 14,162
SIERRA NEVADA
Mt. Whitney 14,494
LOS ANGELES
GUADALUPE (Mex.)
BAJA CALIFORNIA
CABO SAN LUCAS
ISLAS REVILLAGIGEDO (Mex.)
Tropic of Cancer

ROCKY MOUNTAINS
GREAT PLAINS
GREAT BASIN
Salt Lake City
Pikes Peak 14,110
Denver
Fargo
Minneapolis
St. Paul
Omaha
Platte R.
Missouri R.
Colorado R.
Columbia River
UNITED STATES
Kansas City
Wichita
Memphis
Red R.
El Paso
Fort Worth
Dallas
San Antonio
Houston
Galveston
Rio Grande
MEXICO
SIERRA MADRE OCCIDENTAL
SIERRA MADRE ORIENTAL
Guadalajara
MEXICO CITY
Popocatepetl 17,887 (Vol.)
Pico de Orizaba 18,406 (Vol.)
Tampico
Bahía de Campeche
Veracruz
YUCATÁN PEN.
Yucatan Channel

Duluth
LAKE SUPERIOR
Milwaukee
CHICAGO
LAKE MICHIGAN
LAKE HURON
Toronto
DETROIT
Cleveland
Buffalo
Pittsburgh
Cincinnati
St. Louis
MONTRÉAL
Ottawa
Québec
LAURENTIAN HIGHLANDS
Saint John
Halifax
NOVA SCOTIA
CAPE BRETON ISLAND
CAPE SABLE
Boston
CAPE COD
NEW YORK
PHILADELPHIA
Baltimore
Washington
APPALACHIAN MTS.
Richmond
Norfolk
Chesapeake Bay
CAPE HATTERAS
Birmingham
Atlanta
Savannah
Jacksonville
Mobile
New Orleans
Miami
BERMUDA (Br.)
ATLANTIC OCEAN
Tropic of Cancer

GULF OF MEXICO
HAVANA
CUBA
CAPE SABLE
BAHAMAS
SAN SALVADOR
San Juan
PUERTO RICO (U.S.A.)
GUADELOUPE (Fr.)
MARTINIQUE (Fr.)
HAITI
DOM. REP.
JAMAICA
Port-au-Prince
Santo Domingo
Kingston
WEST INDIES
BARBADOS
TRINIDAD AND TOBAGO
CARIBBEAN SEA
PTA. DE GALLINAS
Caracas
Rio Orinoco
BELIZE
GUATEMALA
HONDURAS
Golfo de Honduras
EL SALVADOR
NICARAGUA
COSTA RICA
PANAMA
Panamá
ISTMO DE PANAMÁ
CENTRAL AMERICA
ISLA DEL COCO (Costa Rica)
ISLA DE MALPELO (Colombia)
SOUTH AMERICA
Santa Fe de Bogotá
Quito
Equator
Negro

Relief

Meters		Feet
3050		10 000
1525		5000
610		2000
305		1000
0	Sea Level	0
152.5		500 Below Sea Level
1525		5000
3050		10 000
6100		20 000

A-520000-76   -5-5-15
COPYRIGHT BY
RAND McNALLY & COMPANY
MADE IN U.S.A.

Longitude   West   of   Greenwich

Scale 1:40 000 000; one inch to 630 miles. Lambert's Azimuthal Equal Area Projection
Elevations and depressions are given in feet

0   200   400   600   1000 Miles
0   400   800   1600 Kilometers

RELIEF

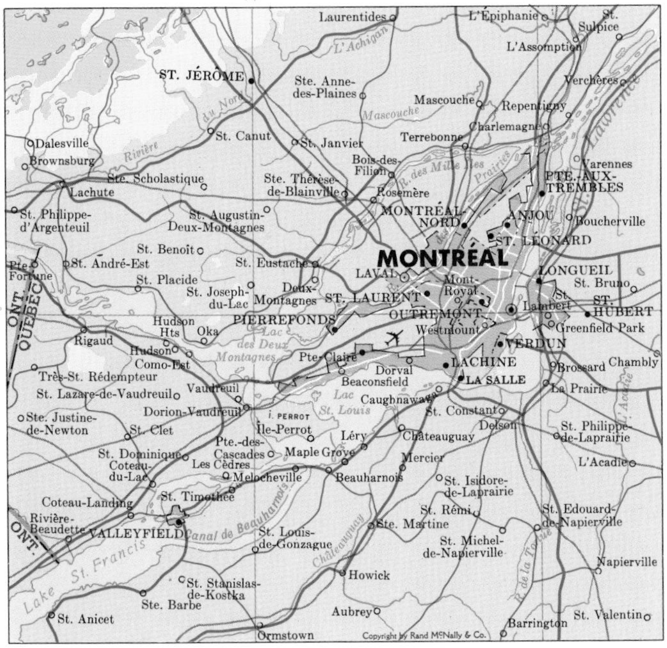

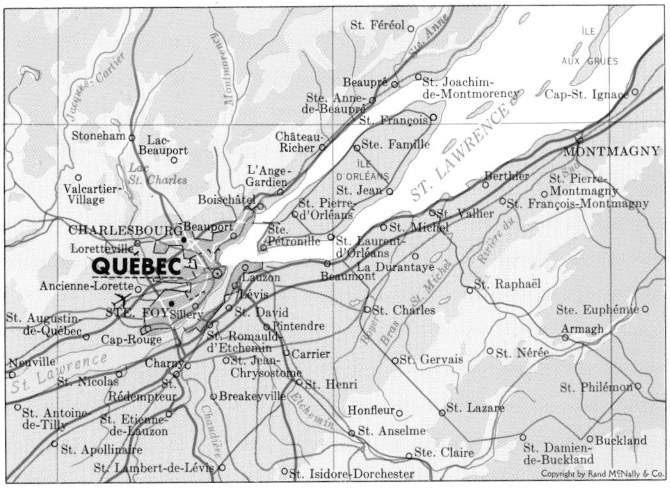

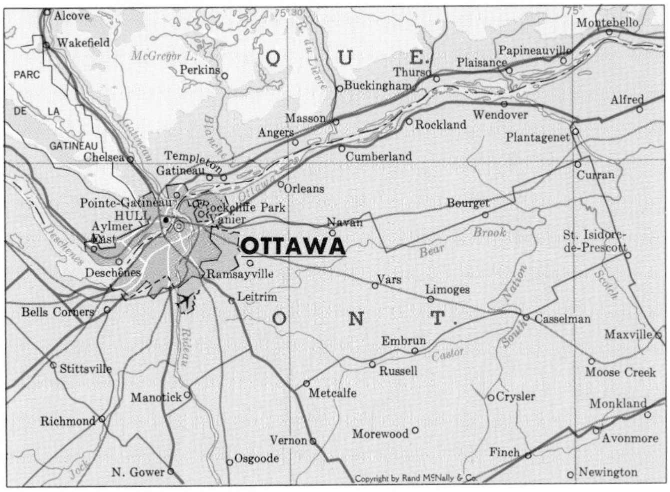

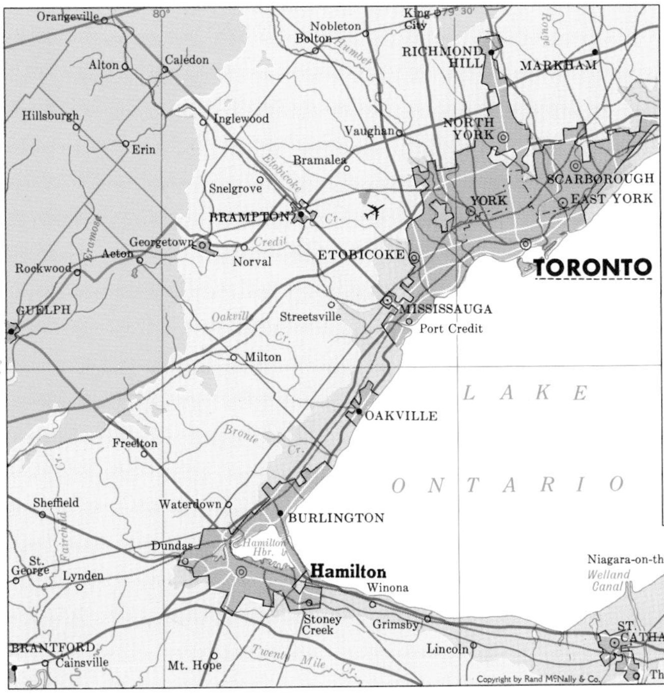

Meters		Feet
3 050		10 000
1 525		5 000
610		2 000
305		1 000
152.5		500
0	Sea Level	0
152.5		500

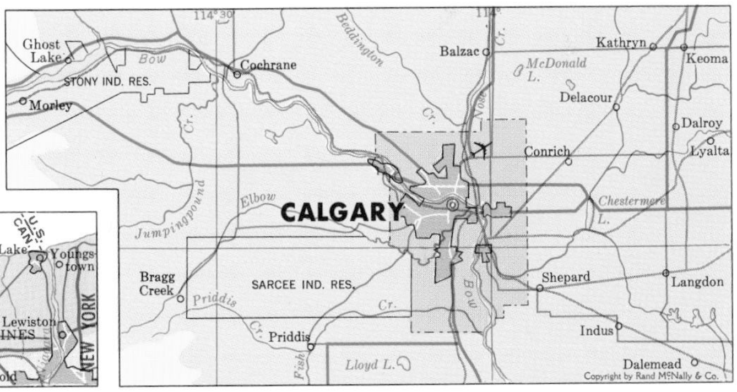

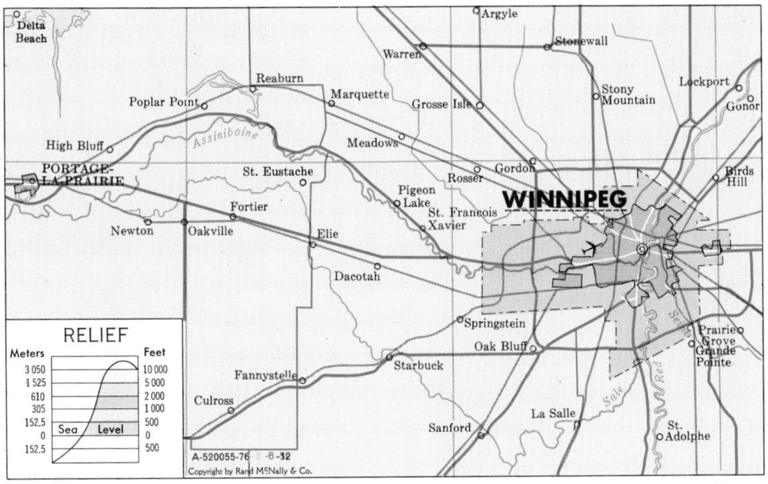

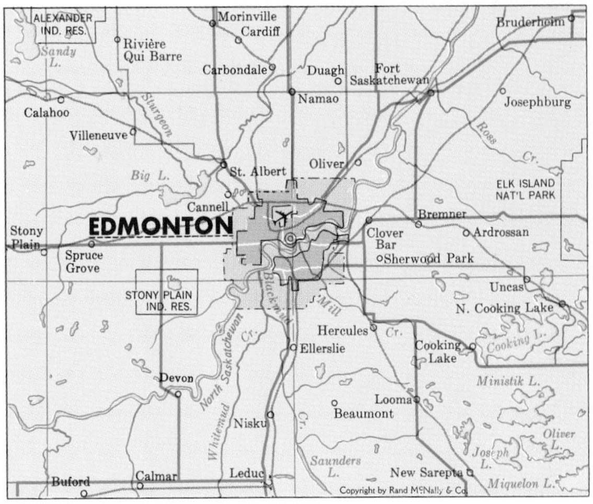

Scale 1:1 000 000; One inch to 16 miles.
Elevations and depressions are given in feet.

A-520055-76 6-32

Copyright by Rand McNally & Co.

Miles
Kilometers

For larger scale coverage of Montréal and Toronto see page 227.

84

CAPE BATHURST

MELVILLE HILLS

VICTORIA ISLAND

BOOTHIA PENINSULA

A L A S K A

KLONDIKE REGION

OGILVIE MTS.

RICHARDSON MTS.

Old Crow

Inuvik

Tuktoyaktuk

Amundsen Gulf

C. BARING

PRINCE ALBERT SOUND

WOLLASTON PEN.

KING WILLIAM I.

Y U K O N

Fr. McPherson

Fr. Good Hope

Arctic Circle

Coppermine

Cambridge Bay

Dease Strait

KENT PEN.

Dolphin and Union Str.

Coronation Gulf

Queen Maud Gulf

Chantrey Inlet

MACKENZIE MTS.

Norman Wells

Great Bear Lake

Contwoyto

PEACOCK HILLS

Pelly

Garry

Baker Lake

N O R T H W E S T   T E R R I T O

Back

Bathurst Inlet

Chesterfield

COAST

STIKINE RANGES

PELLY MTS.

Whitehorse

Carcross

NAHANNI NAT'L PARK

Watson Lake

HORN PLATEAU

Fr. Simpson

Yellowknife

MacKay

Aylmer

Lac la Marte

Clinton-Colden

Dubawnt

Rankin

Yathkyed

Telegraph Creek

Churchill Peak

Fr. Liard

Fr. Providence

Great Slave Lake

Nonacho

Thelon

Fr. Nelson

CAMERON HILLS

Hay River

Fr. Resolution

Trout

Thanne

M O U N T A I N S

B R I T I S H

R O C K Y

ALASKA HIGHWAY

Fr. St. John

Dawson Creek

WOOD BUFFALO NAT'L PARK

CARIBOU MTS.

Fr. Smith

Fr. Fitzgerald

Uranium City

Selwyn

Slave

Nuelti

CLEAR HILLS

Fr. Vermilion

BUFFALO HEAD HILLS

BIRCH MTS.

Fort McMurray

Fr. Chipewyan

Claire

Athabasca

Wollaston

Reindeer

Southern Indian

Granville

Chu

C O L U M B I A

Peace River

McLennan

Grouard Mission

CHEECHAM HILLS

Cree

Frobisher

Peter Pond Lake

Lynn Lake

Thompson

Sipiwesk

SWAN HILLS

High Prairie

Lesser Slave Lake

Smith

Churchill

Lac la Ronge

M A N I T

CARIBOO MTS.

Quesnel

Wells

McBride

Whitecourt

Athabasca

Barrhead

A L B E R T A

Beaver

Lac La Biche

St. Paul

Meadow Lake

S A S K A T C H E W A N

PRINCE ALBERT NAT'L PARK

Flin Flon

Cross

The Pas

Norway House

Edmonton

Fr. Saskatchewan

Edson

JASPER NAT'L PARK

ELK ISLAND NAT'L PARK

Wetaskiwin

Vegreville

St. Walburg

Big River

Prince Albert

Nipawin

Melfort

Tisdale

Canora

Swan River

Gypsumville

Winnipegosis

M O U N T A I N S

Jasper

Mountain Park

Ponoka

Lacombe

Red Deer

Camrose

Wainwright

Lloydminster

North Battleford

Humboldt

Wynyard

DUCK MTN.

Winnipegosis

GLACIER NAT'L PARK

MT. REVELSTOKE NAT'L PARK

Blue River

BANFF NAT'L PARK

Innisfail

Olds

Stettler

Wilkie

Saskatoon

Biggar

Lanigan

Big Quill

Yorkton

RIDING MOUNTAIN NAT'L PARK

Manitoba

Lake Winnipeg

Berens

Wells Gray

SELKIRK MTS.

Banff

Drumheller

Hanna

Kindersley

Rosetown

Watrous

Melville

Russell

Minnedosa

Neepawa

Selkirk

Kamloops

Calgary

Bassano

Red Deer

Diefenbaker

East

Canora

Dauphin

Merritt

High River

Claresholm

Redcliff

Swift Current

Moose Jaw

Regina

Yirden

Brandon

Winnipeg

Vernon

Kelowna

Last Mountain

Qu'Appelle

Indian Head

Portage la Prairie

Carman

VANCOUVER ISLAND

Port Alice

Campbell River

Courtenay

Powell River

Penticton

Oliver

Nelson

Kimberley

Cranbrook

Creston

Fernie

Macleod

Taber

South Saskatchewan

Maple Creek

Gravelbourg

Assiniboia

Weyburn

Boissevain

Mordena

Nanaimo

Vancouver

North Vancouver

Burnaby

Chilliwack

Grand Forks

Rossland

Trail

WATERTON-GLACIER INT. PEACE PARK

Lethbridge

Magrath

Stavely

Milk

Govenlock

CANADA

U.S.A.

Estevan

Victoria

CAPE FLATTERY

Str. of Juan de Fuca

SEATTLE

Tacoma

Olympia

Spokane

MT. ADAMS 12,276

W A S H I N G T O N

Moscow

Missouri

Williston

Minot

Great Falls

Grand Forks

N O R T H   D A K O T A

Vancouver

Portland

Salem

Eugene

Yakima

Walla Walla

Pendleton

Baker

O R E G O N

C A S C A D E   R A N G E

Salmon

Helena

Butte

M O N T A N A

LITTLE BELT MTS.

BIG BELT MTS.

Yellowstone

Billings

Granite Peak 12,799

Bismarck

Fargo

Valley City

BITTERROOT RANGE

I D A H O

W Y O

S O U T H   D A K O T A

PACIFIC OCEAN

VANCOUVER ISLAND

Prince Rupert

QUEEN CHARLOTTE ISLANDS

GRAHAM I.

MORESBY I.

Hecate Strait

Dixon Entrance

DALL I.

PRINCE OF WALES I.

Ketchikan

Masset

Kitimat

Kimsquit

Ocean Falls

Bella Coola

CALVERT I.

Queen Charlotte Str.

CAPE SCOTT

Alert Bay

BARANOF

SITKA

CHICHAGOF

Skagway

Haines

WHITE PASS

Carcross

Dawson

Mayo

Stewart

Yukon

Pelly

YUKON

Continued on pages 96-97

Longitude West of Greenwich

Scale 1: 12 000 000; one inch to 190 miles. Conic Projection

Elevations and depressions are given in feet

Longitude West of Greenwich

Same scale as main map

QUEBEC

CAPE BAULD

Gulf of
St. Lawrence

LONG RANGE MTS.

GROS MORNE
NAT'L PARK
Deer Lake

C. ST. JOHN

Twillingate

Botwood

Corner Brook
Stephenville

Windsor
Gander

Grand Falls

TERRA NOVA
NAT'L PARK

Bonavista

C. ST. GEORGE

St.
George's

NEWFOUNDLAND

Trinity

Channel-Port-aux-Basques

CAPE RAY

St. John's

CAPE NORTH

Grand Bank
Burin

CAPE BRETON
ISLAND

ST. PIERRE AND MIQUELON (Fr.)

ATLANTIC OCEAN

©RMCN

a

Foxe
Basin

MELVILLE
PENINSULA

BAFFIN ISLAND
NAT'L PARK

Igloolik

Pangnirtung

BAFFIN

ISLAND

PRINCE
CHARLES
ISLAND

Nettilling

CUMBERLAND
PEN.

Arctic Circle

Cumberland Sound

C. MERCY

Iqaluit

Lake Harbour

HALL
PEN.

Frobisher Bay

EVERETT
MTS.

RESOLUTION

Foxe
Channel

FOXE
PEN.

SOUTHAMPTON
ISLAND

C. LOW

Roes Welcome Sound

Fisher Strait

COATS

MANSEL

NOTTINGHAM
ISLAND

SALISBURY

Hudson

C. DE
NOUVELLE-
FRANCE

Strait

C. HOPES
ADVANCE

AKPATOK

KILLINIQ I.

Ungava
Bay

TORNGAT
MTS.

Nain

Hebron

NEW

Hopedale

Makkovik

Rigolet

Hamilton Inlet

Cartwright

Battle Harbour

LONG RANGE MTS.

St. Anthony

Povungnituk

OTTAWA
ISLANDS

PENINSULE
D'UNGAVA

Payne

aux
Feuilles

Kuujjuaq

MEALY MTS.

Mushuau

Happy
Valley-
Goose Bay

FOUN

GROS MORNE
NAT'L PARK

Corner Brook

Stephenville
St. George

HUDSON

BAY

All islands within bays and straits
lie within Northwest Territories.

Minto

Ft. Severn

C. HENRIETTA MARIA

BELCHER
ISLANDS

Lac
Bienville

Grande de la Baleine

Caniapiscau

Nichicun

Schefferville

LABRADOR

Churchill Falls

Little Mecatina

Natashquan

DLAND

PTE. LOUIS-XIV

La Grande

Easemain

Eastmain

MTS.
OTISH

Lac
Manicouagan

ILE D'ANTICOSTI

James
Bay

Chisasibi

AKIMISKI

Ft. Albany

Moosonee

Opinaca

Mistassini

Nottaway

Lac
Mistassini

Chibougamau

R. aux Outardes

Clarke City

Sept-Îles

Gulf of
St. Lawrence

ONTARIO

St.
Joseph

Winisk

Missinaibi

Albany

Caral Rapids
Fraserdale

QUEBEC

Mont-Joli
Rimouski
Rivière-du-Loup

Matane
Cap-Chat

MTS.
CHIC-CHOCS

Gaspé

New Carlisle

PEN. DE GASPÉ

Chandler

Caraquet

P.E.I.
PRINCE EDWARD
ISLAND

Summerside

Charlottetown

CANADA
NATL PARK

Lac
Seul

Armstrong Sta.

Nakina

Hearst

La Sarre

Amos
Senneterre

Parent

Réservoir Gouin

St. Félicien
Roberval
Chambord

Dolbeau
Alma

Kenogami
Jonquière
Chicoutimi

Baie-
St. Paul

La Malbaie

Riv. Croche

NEW
BRUNSWICK

Bathurst

Newcastle

Chatham
Richibucto

Moncton

NOVA SCOTIA

Springhill
Amherst
Truro

New Glasgow

Sydney Mines
Sydney

x Lookout

Nipigon

Geraldton
Longlac

Oba

Kapuskasing

Cochrane
Iroquois Falls

Timmins

Rouyn
Malartic
Val-d'Or

La Tuque

Shawinigan

Trois-
Rivières

Victoriaville

Grand
Mère

Joliette
St.
Jacinthe

Drummondville

Granby

Sherbrooke

MAINE

Edmundston

Woodstock

Fredericton

FUNDY
NAT'L PARK

St. Andrews
St. Stephen

Saint John

Kentville

Digby

Lunenburg
Bridgewater

Halifax
Dartmouth

Shelburne

Liverpool

Dryden

Nipigon

Marathon

PUKASKWA
NAT'L PARK

MICHIPICOTEN I.

Chapleau

Cobalt
Ville-Marie

Témiscaming

Kirkland Lake

Augusta

Portland

VERMONT
NEW HAMPSHIRE

Concord

BOSTON

MASS.

Hartford
CONN.

R.I. Providence

CAPE COD

ATLANTIC

OCEAN

Thunder Bay

Lake of
the Woods

Rainy

Thunder Bay

Lake Superior

Sault Ste. Marie

Thessalon

Blind River

Sudbury

North
Bay

Sturgeon Falls

Espanola

MANITOULIN

Mattawa

Pembroke

Renfrew

Huntsville

Bancroft

Parry Sound

Smiths Falls
Brockville

Kingston

Alexandria
Bay

Ottawa

Hull

MONTREAL

Laval

Valleyfield

Ogdensburg

NEW
YORK

Albany

Duluth

Superior

Marquette

Escanaba

Sault Ste. Marie

Kincardine

Wiarton

Owen Sound

Georgian
Bay

Midland

Barrie

Orillia

Lindsay

Peterborough

Trenton

Cobourg

Whitby
Oshawa

Lake Ontario

Rochester

Relief

MINNESOTA

St. Paul

NEAPOLIS

Green Bay

WISCONSIN

Madison

MILWAUKEE

ILLS.
CHICAGO

Lake Michigan

MICHIGAN

Lake Huron

Saginaw

Flint
Lansing

DETROIT

Grand
Rapids

Windsor

Leamington

Chatham

Lake Erie

Sarnia

Port
Huron

London

St. Thomas

Kitchener

TORONTO

Hamilton

St.
Catharines

BUFFALO

Niagara
Falls

NEW YORK

PENNSYLVANIA

Scranton

N.J.

Toledo

OHIO

A-520200-76   9-8-20
COPYRIGHT BY
RAND McNALLY & COMPANY
MADE IN U.S.A.

Relief		
Meters		Feet
3050		10 000
1525		5000
610		2000
305		1000
152.5		500
Sea Level		0
152.5		500
1525		5000
3050		10 000

0 25 50 75 100   200   300   400   500 Miles

0   100   200   400   600   800 Kilometers

134° 132° 130° 128° 126° 124°

PRINCE OF WALES ISLAND
Klawock
Hydaburg
Copper Mtn. 3916 △
LONG ISLAND
DALL ISLAND
Ketchikan
Metlakatla
ANNETTE ISLAND
MT. Reid 4592 △
REVILLAGIGEDO ISLAND
Revillagigedo Channel

Alice Arm
Hazelton
SKEENA MOUNTAINS
Shedin Pk. 8750 △
Mt. Thomlinson 8050 △

OMINECA MOUNTAINS
Williston Lake
Umineca
Takla Lake
Tchentlo Lake
McLe

UNITED STATES
CANADA

Dixon Entrance
DUNDAS ISLAND

Nass
Terrace
Smithers
BULKLEY MOUNTAINS
Hawson Pk. 9050 △
BULKLEY RANGES

Babine Lake
Stuart Lake
Fort St. James
NECHAKO

CAPE KNOX
Masset
PORCHER ISLAND
Prince Rupert
Skeena
Kitimat
Morice Lake
Burns Lake
Morice Lake
Endako
Vanderhoof

QUEEN CHARLOTTE ISLANDS
GRAHAM ISLAND
Masset
Hecate Strait
PITT ISLAND
KITIMAT
COAST
BANKS ISLAND
Kitimat

Ootsa Lake
Michel Pk. 7396 △
Nechako Reservoir
KENNEY DAM
PLATEAU
Nechako
NECHAKO RANGE

Skidegate Inlet
Hartley Bay
ESTEVAN GROUP
PRINCESS ROYAL ISLAND
RANGES
Whitesail Lake
Eutsuk Lake
Tetachuck Lake
West Road

MORESBY ISLAND
Mount Kermode 3550 △
ARISTAZABAL ISLAND
Mt. Parry 3450 △
RODERICK ISLAND
GOLD ISLAND
SWINDLE ISLAND
BRITISH
MOUNTAINS
FRA

CAPE ST. JAMES
Ocean Falls
Bella Coola
Charlotte Lake
Redstone

Bella Bella
COLU
Monarch Mtn. 11590 △
PACIFIC

Queen
Namu
Razorback Mtn. 10432 △
Silverthrone Mtn. 9700 △
Mt. Tatlow 10058 △
Chiko Lake
PL

Charlotte
Rivers Inlet
CALVERT ISLAND
Mt. Waddington 13163 △
Mt. Queen Bess 10791 △
Good Hope Mtn. 10515 △
Tsusko

Sound
CAPE CAUTION
Monmouth 10480 △
Mt. Gilbert 3109 △

Queen Charlotte Strait
Bull Harbour
CAPE SCOTT
Port Hardy
Simood Sound
RANGES

PACIFIC
CAPE COOK
Quatsino Sound
Port Alice
Kelsey Bay
Powell River
Mt. Ga

OCEAN
VANCOUVER ISLAND
Nootka Sound
Victoria Pk. 7095 △
Bloedel
Golden Hinde 7219 △
Courtenay
Comox
Vananda
TEXADA ISLAND
Squamish

Tofino
PACIFIC RIM NATIONAL PARK
Port Alberni
Nanaimo
North Vancouver
Vancouver
Burn
New West

Barkley Sound
CAPE BEALE
Mt. Whymper 5656 △
Eddyston
Lake Cowichan
Duncan

Strait of Juan de Fuca
CAPE FLATTERY
Esquimalt
Vic
OLYMPIC NATIONAL PARK
Port Angeles
OLYMPIC NATIONAL PARK

Relief

Meters		Feet
3050		10 000
1525		5000
610		2000
305		1000
152.5		500
0	Sea Level	0
152.5		500
1525		5000

A-520220-76   6-68
COPYRIGHT BY
RAND MCNALLY & COMPANY
MADE IN U.S.A.

Continued on pages 104-105   Longitude West of Greenwich

Scale 1:4 000 000; one inch to 64 miles. Conic Projection
Elevations and depressions are given in feet.

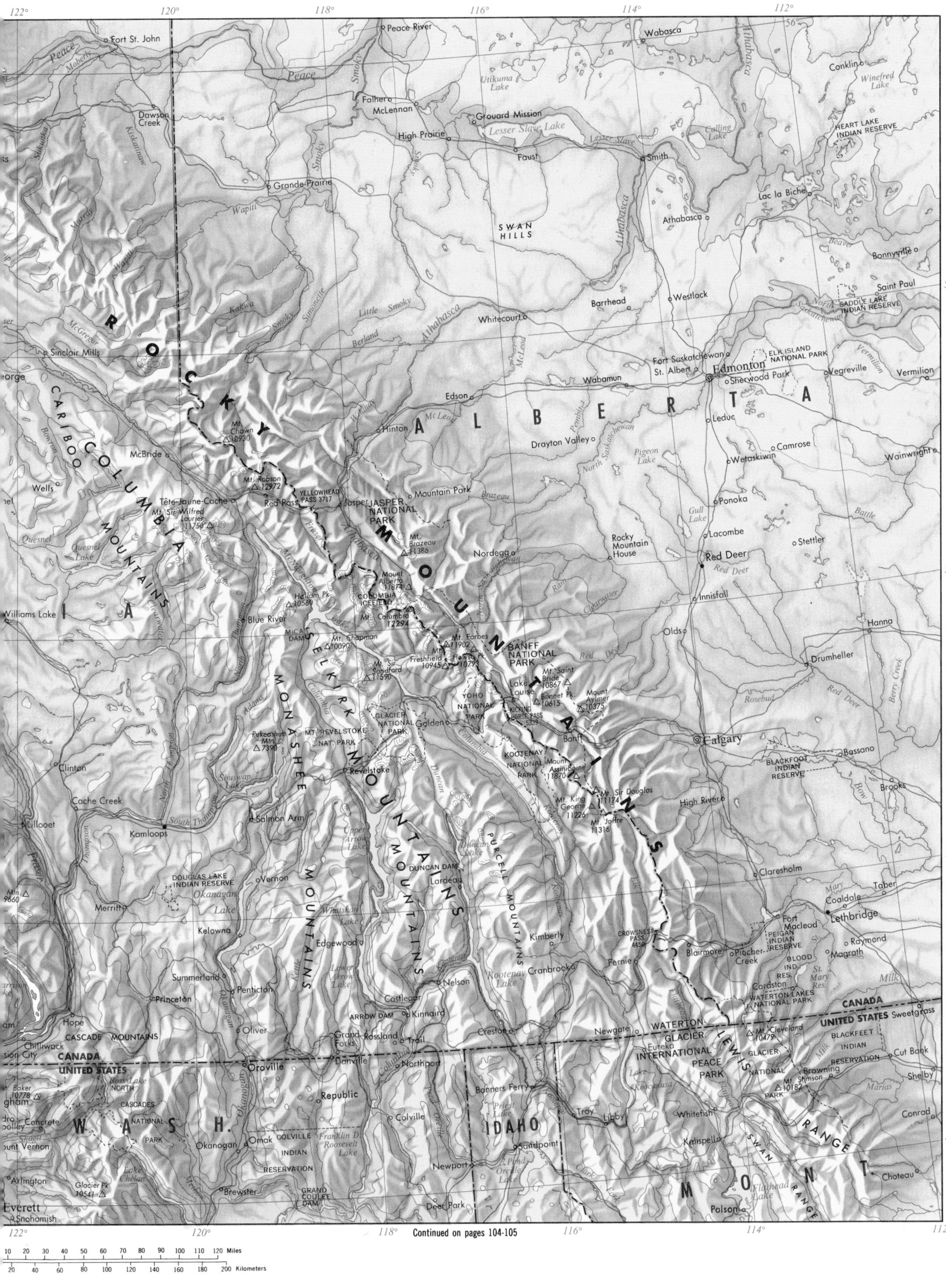

Fort St. John
Peace River
Wabasca
Conklin
Dawson Creek
Falher
McLennan
Grouard Mission
Winefred Lake
High Prairie
Lesser Slave Lake
HEART LAKE INDIAN RESERVE
Grande Prairie
Faust
Smith
Wapiti
SWAN HILLS
Lac la Biche
Athabasca
Bonnyville
Saint Paul
SADDLE LAKE INDIAN RESERVE
Barrhead
Westlock
ROCKY
Sinclair Mills
Fort Saskatchewan
St. Albert
ELK ISLAND NATIONAL PARK
Vegreville
Vermilion
Whitecourt
Edmonton
Sherwood Park
McBride
Edson
Hinton
McLeod
Leduc
Camrose
Wainwright
Mt. Chown 10930
ALBERTA
Drayton Valley
Wetaskiwin
Wells
COLUMBIA
Mt. Robson 12972
YELLOWHEAD PASS 3717
Red Pass
Jasper
JASPER NATIONAL PARK
Mountain Park
Brazeau
Nordegg
Pigeon Lake
Ponoka
Tête-Jaune-Cache
Mt. Sir Wilfred Laurier 11750
Mt. Brazeau 11386
Rocky Mountain House
Gull Lake
Lacombe
Quesnel Lake
Quesnel
Williams Lake
Hallam Pk. 10580
Mount Alberta 11870
COLUMBIA (ICEFIELD)
Mt. Columbia 12294
Innisfall
Red Deer
Stettler
Battle
Blue River
Mt. Forbes 11902
BANFF NATIONAL PARK
Hanna
MICA DAM
Mt. Chapman 10090
Mt. Sir Sandford 11590
Freshfield 10945
Mt. Lyell Pk. 11079
Mt. Saint Bride 10867
Mount Aylmer 10375
Olds
Drumheller
Red Deer
Rosebud
YOHO NATIONAL PARK
Lake Louise
Bonnet Pk. 10615
KICKING HORSE PASS 5339
Pukeashun Mtn. 7390
GLACIER NATIONAL PARK
Golden
Banff
MT. REVELSTOKE NAT. PARK
Berry Creek
Revelstoke
KOOTENAY NATIONAL PARK
Mount Assiniboine 11870
Calgary
BLACKFOOT INDIAN RESERVE
Bassano
Brooks
Mt. King George 11226
Mt. Sir Douglas 11174
Mt. Joffre 11316
Clinton
High River
Clearwater
Cache Creek
Lillooet
Kamloops
DOUGLAS LAKE INDIAN RESERVE
Okanagan Lake
Vernon
DUNCAN DAM
Lardeau
Claresholm
Mtn. 9660
Merritt
Kelowna
Edgewood
Kimberly
Mary
Coaldale
Taber
Lethbridge
Summerland
Penticton
Nelson
Cranbrook
Kootenay Lake
CROWSNEST PASS 4450
Blairmore
Pincher Creek
PEIGAN INDIAN RESERVE
Raymond
Magrath
Princeton
Castlegar
Fernie
BLOOD IND. RES.
St. Mary Res.
Cardston
WATERTON LAKES NATIONAL PARK
Hope
ARROW DAM
Kinnaird
Creston
Newgate
CANADA
UNITED STATES
Sweetgrass
Chilliwack
CASCADE MOUNTAINS
Rossland
Trail
WATERTON GLACIER INTERNATIONAL PEACE PARK
Mt. Cleveland 10479
BLACKFEET INDIAN RESERVATION
Cut Bank
CANADA
UNITED STATES
Oroville
Danville
Northport
Eureka
GLACIER NATIONAL PARK
Browning
Shelby
Mt. Baker 10778
Bellingham
Ross Lake
CASCADES NATIONAL PARK
Republic
Colville
Bonners Ferry
IDAHO
Troy
Libby
Whitefish
Mt. Stimson 10142
Conrad
Concrete
Sedro Woolley
Mount Vernon
Okanogan
Omak
COLVILLE INDIAN RESERVATION
Franklin D. Roosevelt Lake
Colville
Priest Lake
Sandpoint
Kalispell
SWAN RANGE
Arlington
Glacier Pk. 10541
WASH.
Brewster
GRAND COULEE DAM
Coulee Dam
Newport
Pend Oreille Lake
Deer Park
MONT.
Flathead Lake
Choteau
Everett
Snohomish
Polson

Continued on pages 88-89
Continued on pages 104-105

10 20 30 40 50 60 70 80 90 100 110 120 Miles
20 40 60 80 100 120 140 160 180 200 Kilometers

116°　114°　112°　110°　108°　106°　104°

A-520218-76
COPYRIGHT
RAND MCNALLY & COMPANY
MADE IN U.S.A.

56°

MacKay

Fort
McMurray
Clearwater

Utikuma
Lake
Wabasca

CHEECHAM
HILLS

Frobisher L.
Churchill L.

Decenton L.

Lesser Slave Lake

Faust

Peter Pond L.

Niska L.

Wathaman L.

Smith
Calling
Lake

Athabasca

Winefred L.

Île-à-la-Crosse

Nemeiben L.

Lesser Slave

Lac
la Ronge
LaRonge

HEART LAKE
INDIAN
RESERVE

Canoe L.

Lac la Plonge

Wapawekka L.

Barrhead　Westlock

Athabasca

Lac la Biche

Primrose
L.

Doré L.

WAPAWEKKA
HILLS
Deschambault
Lake

54°

Beaver

MOSTOOS HILLS

Montreal
Lake

CUB HILLS

Wabamun

St. Albert

Moose L.

Cold
Lake

THUNDER
HILLS

Pembina

Edmonton

North
Saskatchewan

Bonnyville

SADDLE LAKE
INDIAN RESERVE

St. Paul

Meadow
Lake

Lac Voisn

PRINCE

ALBERT

Fort
Saskatchewan

ELK ISLAND
NATIONAL
PARK

NATIONAL

Sherwood Park

Vegreville

Leduc

Vermilion

St. Walburg

Big River

PARK

Pigeon
Lake

Wetaskiwin

Camrose

Lloydminster

Prince Albert

Saskatchewan

Nipawi

Ponoka

Shellbrook

Gull
Lake

Wainwright

Battle

Duck
Lake

Melfort

Tisdale

Lacombe

Sweet Grass
Indian Reserve

Rosthern

Carrot

Red Deer

Red Deer

Stettler

Manito L.

North Battleford

52°

Innisfail

NEUTRAL HILLS

Unity

Wilkie

SASKATCHEW

Humboldt

Olds

ALBERTA

Hanna

Kerrobert

Biggar

Saskatoon

Lanigan

Big
Quill
L.

Wynyard

Drumheller

Sounding

Creek

Kindersley

Rosetown

Watrous

TOUCHWOOD HIL

Rosebud

Calgary

BLACKFOOT
INDIAN RESERVE

Berry

Creek

Eston

Outlook

GARDINER
DAM

THE
COTEAU

Diefenbaker

Last
Mountain
Lake

High River

Bassano

Red Deer

South
Saskatchewan

Leader

Lake

QU'APPELLE
DAM

Brooks

Bow

VERMILION
HILLS

Fort Qu'Appelle

50°

Claresholm

GREAT SAND

HILLS

Swift Current

South Saskatchewan

Moose Jaw

Regina

Fort
Macleod

Redcliff
Medicine
Hat

Gull Lake

Indian Head

ASSINIBOINE
INDIAN
RESERVE

Coaldale
Taber

Lethbridge

Maple Creek

Old Wives
L.

Weybur

Raymond

CYPRESS HILLS

Shaunavon

Gravelbourg

Assiniboia

Cypress L.

Notukeu

Milk

Pinto Butte
3350 △

Wood Mountain
3350 △

Sweetgrass

Govenlock

Frenchman

Whitemud

CANADA
UNITED STATES

Cut Bank

M O N T.

Hogeland

Opheim

112°　110°　108°　106°　104°

Continued on pages 104-105

Longitude West of Greenwich

Scale 1:4 000 000; one inch to 64 miles. Conic Projection
Elevations and depressions are given in feet.

Relief

Meters	Feet
1525	5000
610	2000
305	1000
152.5	500
0	Sea Level	0

Continued on pages 86-87

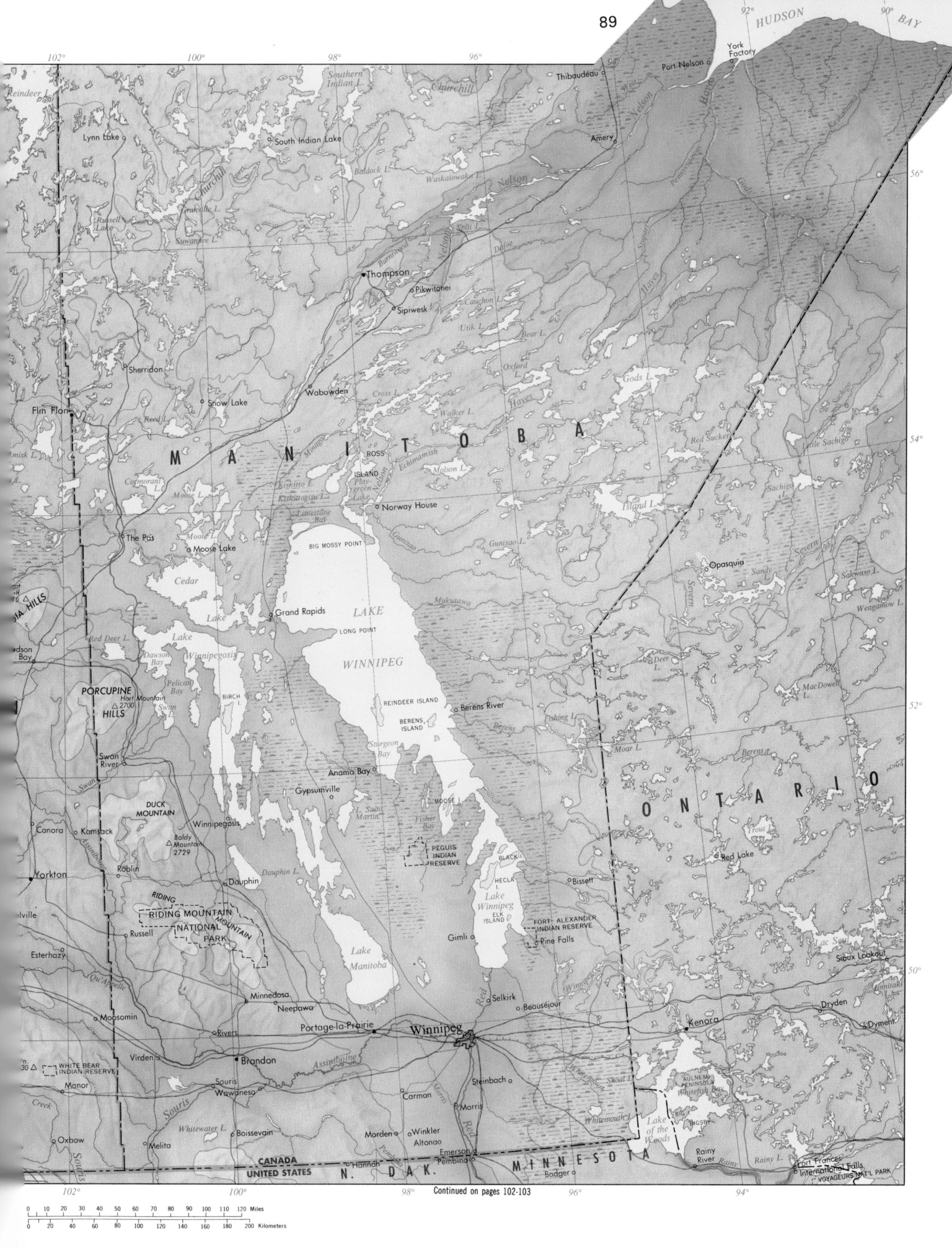

HUDSON
92°
90°
BAY

York
Factory

Port Nelson

Thibaudeau

Amery

56°

Southern
Indian L.

Churchill

South Indian Lake

Lynn Lake

Reindeer L.

Baldock L.

Waskaiowaka L.

Nelson

Russell
Lake

Granville L.

Siowance L.

Split L.

Pennsueogan

Thompson

Pikwitonei

Sipiwesk

Cauchon L.

Bear L.

Utik L.

Sherridon

Oxford L.

Gods L.

54°

Flin Flon

Snow Lake

Reed L.

Wabowden

Cross L.

Walker L.

Echimamish

Hayes

Red Sucker L.

Little Sachigo

M A N I T O B A

Cormorant

Moose L.

Kiskitto L.

Kiskittogisu L.

ROSS
ISLAND
Pigeon
Lake

Molson L.

Island L.

Sachigo

The Pas

S. Moose L.

Moose Lake

Limestone
Bay

Norway House

Gunisao

Gunisao L.

Opasquia

Sandy

Sakswaso L.

Cedar

BIG MOSSY POINT

Mukutawa

Weagamiow L.

Grand Rapids

LAKE

LONG POINT

Severn

Red Deer L.

Lake

WINNIPEG

Dawson
Bay

Winnipegosis

Pelican
Bay

BIRCH

Deer
L.

MacDowell
L.

PORCUPINE
Hart Mountain
△ 2700
HILLS

Swan
Mountain

REINDEER ISLAND

BERENS
ISLAND

Berens River

Berens

Fishing L.

Berens L.

Moar L.

52°

Swan
River

Sturgeon
Bay

O N T A R I O

Canora

Kamsack

DUCK
MOUNTAIN

Winnipegosis

Anama Bay

Gypsumville

L. Saint
Martin

MOOSE I.

Fisher
Bay

Trout

Roblin

Baldy
Mountain
2729

Dauphin L.

PEGUIS
INDIAN
RESERVE

BLACK I.

Red Lake

Yorkton

Dauphin

HECLA
I.

Lac Seul

RIDING

Lake
Winnipeg

ELK
ISLAND

Bissett

English

Sioux Lookout

lville

RIDING MOUNTAIN

MOUNTAIN

NATIONAL
PARK

Russell

Gimli

FORT ALEXANDER
INDIAN RESERVE

Pine Falls

50°

Esterhazy

Lake
Manitoba

Minnedosa

Neepawa

Selkirk

Beausejour

Kenora

Dryden

Dyment

Moosomin

Rivers

Portage-la-Prairie

Winnipeg

Qu'Appelle

Assiniboine

30 △
WHITE BEAR
INDIAN RESERVE

Virden

Brandon

Steinbach

AULNEAU
PENINSULA
Whitefish Bay

Manor

Souris

Wawanesa

Carman

Morris

Shoal L.

BIGSBY

Lake
of the
Woods

Oxbow

Whitewater L.

Boissevain

Morden

Winkler
Altona

Whitemouth L.

Rainy
River

Melita

Souris

Creek

CANADA
UNITED STATES

Hannah

Pembina

Emerson

N. DAK.

Badger

MINNESOTA

Fort Frances
International Falls
VOYAGEURS NAT'L PARK

102°   100°   98°   96°   94°

Continued on pages 102-103

0 10 20 30 40 50 60 70 80 90 100 110 120 Miles

0   20   40   60   80   100   120   140   160   180   200 Kilometers

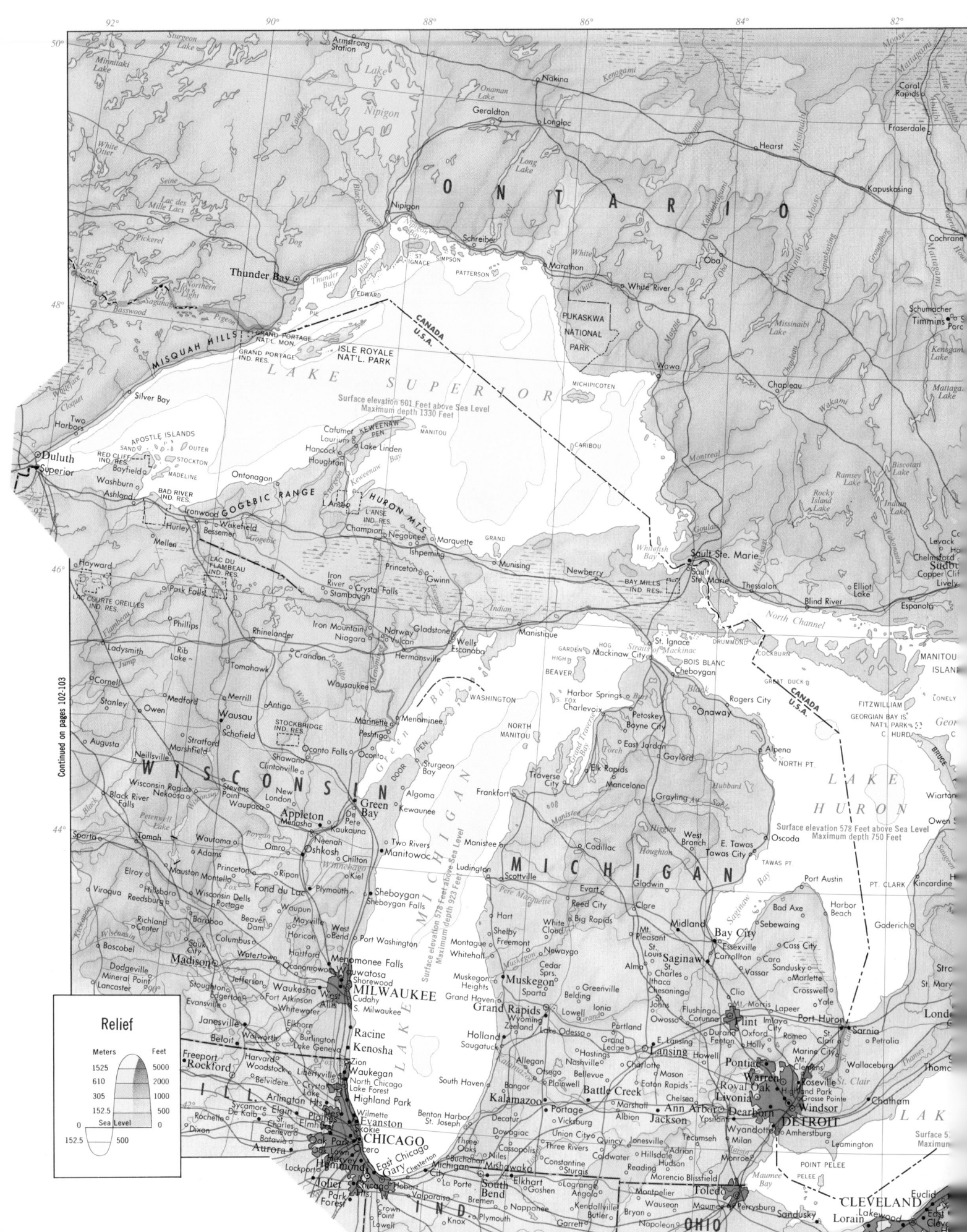

Continued on pages 102-103

Relief

Meters	Feet
1525	5000
610	2000
305	1000
152.5	500
Sea Level	0
152.5	500

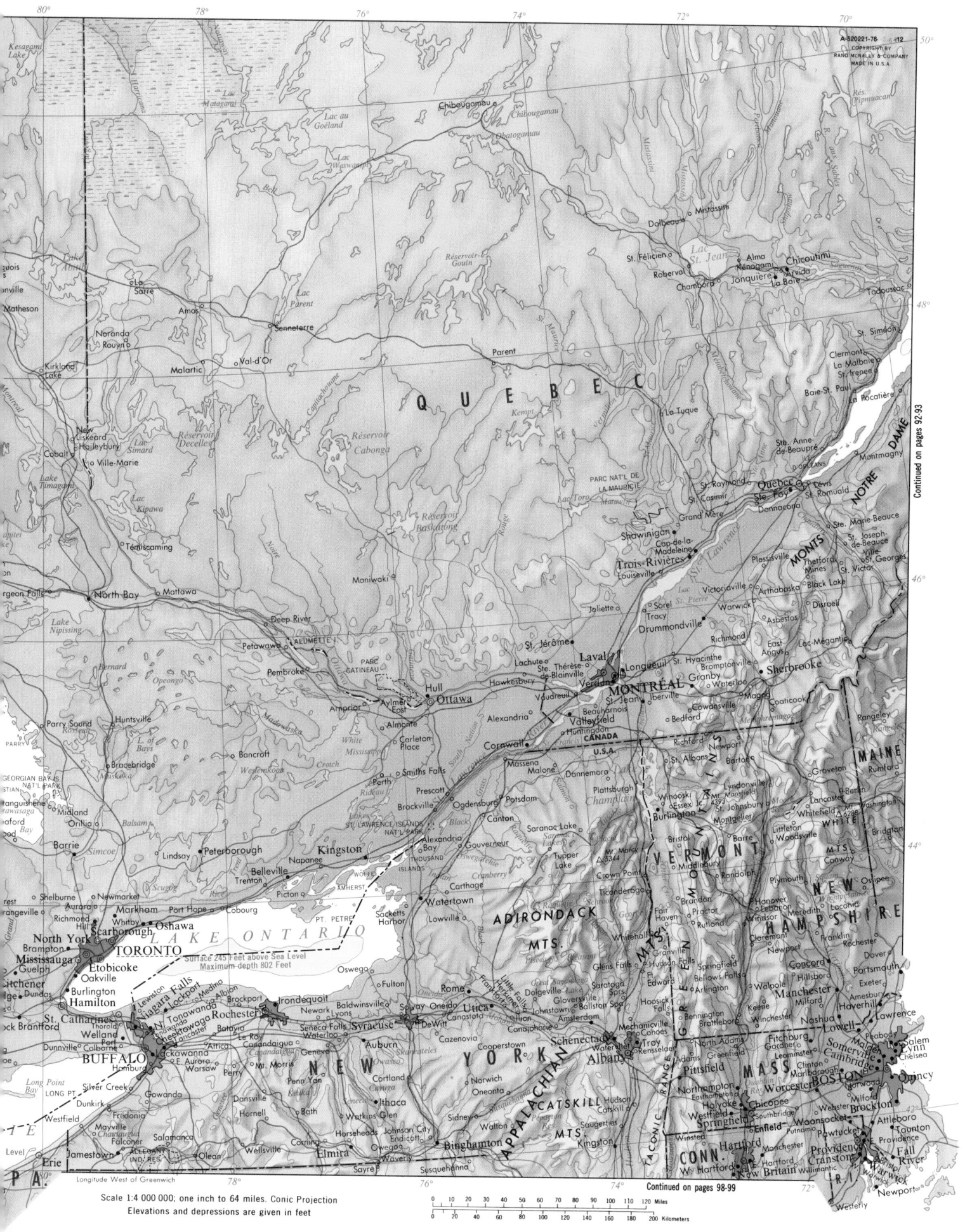

A-520221-76
COPYRIGHT BY
RAND MCNALLY & COMPANY
MADE IN U.S.A.

Continued on pages 92-93

Continued on pages 98-99

Scale 1:4 000 000; one inch to 64 miles. Conic Projection
Elevations and depressions are given in feet

Longitude West of Greenwich

| 0 | 10 | 20 | 30 | 40 | 50 | 60 | 70 | 80 | 90 | 100 | 110 | 120 | Miles |

| 0 | 20 | 40 | 60 | 80 | 100 | 120 | 140 | 160 | 180 | 200 | Kilometers |

Scale 1:4 000 000; one inch to 64 miles. Conic Proje

Elevations and depressions are given in feet.

Continued on pages 90-91

Continued on pages 98-99

For larger scale coverage
of Boston see page 227.

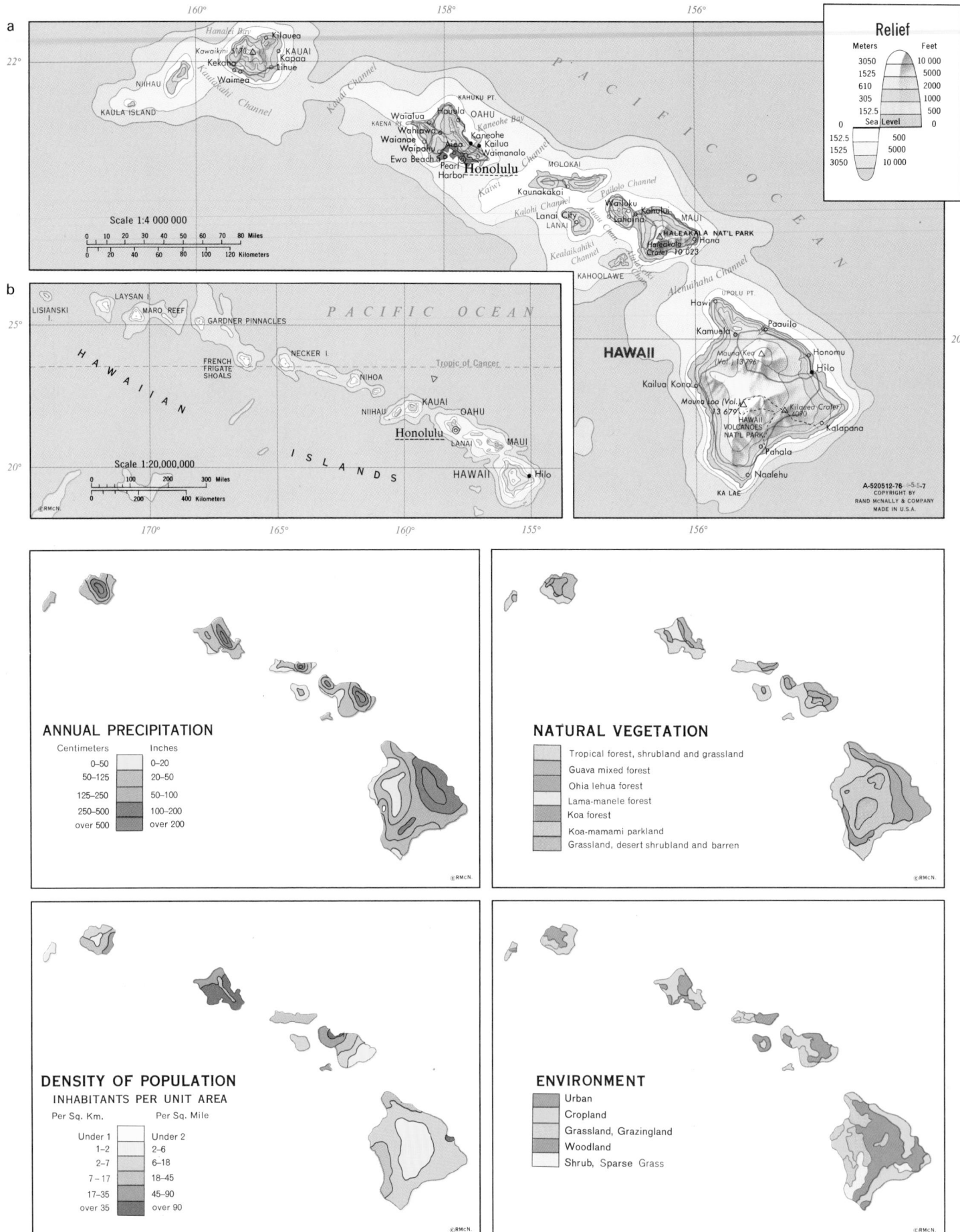

a

160°   158°   156°

22°

Hanalei Bay
Kilauea
Kawaikini 5170 △   ○ **KAUAI**
Kekaha ○   Kapaa
Lihue
NIIHAU
Waimea

KAULA ISLAND

Kauai Channel

Kaieie Channel

KAHUKU PT.
Waialua   Hauula   **OAHU**
KAENA PT.   Wahiawa   *Kaneohe Bay*
Waianae   Kaneohe
Waipahu   Aiea   ○ Kailua
Ewa Beach   Waimanalo
Pearl   **Honolulu**
Harbor

Kaiwi Channel

MOLOKAI

Kaunakakai

Kalohi Channel

Lanai City
LANAI

Pailolo Channel

Wailuku   Kahului
Lahaina   **MAUI**

▲ HALEAKALA NAT'L PARK
○ Hana
Haleakala
Crater 10,023

Kealaikahiki Channel

KAHOOLAWE

Alenuihaha Channel

Relief

Meters	Feet
3050	10 000
1525	5000
610	2000
305	1000
152.5	500
0	Sea Level 0
152.5	500
1525	5000
3050	10 000

PACIFIC OCEAN

Scale 1:4 000 000

0 10 20 30 40 50 60 70 80 Miles
0 20 40 60 80 100 120 Kilometers

U'POLU PT.
Hawi
Kamuela   Paauilo
HAWAII
Mauna Kea △   Honomu
(Vol.) 13,796   ● Hilo
Kailua Kona ○
Mauna Loa (Vol.) △   △ Kilauea Crater 4090
13 679   HAWAII   ○ Kalapana
VOLCANOES
NAT'L PARK
○ Pahala
○ Naalehu
KA LAE

A-520512-76 5-5-7
COPYRIGHT BY
RAND MCNALLY & COMPANY
MADE IN U.S.A.

b

LISIANSKI I.   LAYSAN I.
MARO REEF
○ GARDNER PINNACLES

PACIFIC OCEAN

25°

H A W A I I A N

FRENCH
FRIGATE
SHOALS

NECKER I.
NIHOA

Tropic of Cancer

NIIHAU   **KAUAI**
OAHU
Honolulu
LANAI   **MAUI**

I S L A N D S

20°

HAWAII
● Hilo

Scale 1:20,000,000
0 100 200 300 Miles
0 200 400 Kilometers
©RMcN.

170°   165°   160°   155°   156°

ANNUAL PRECIPITATION

Centimeters	Inches
0–50	0–20
50–125	20–50
125–250	50–100
250–500	100–200
over 500	over 200

©RMcN.

NATURAL VEGETATION

- Tropical forest, shrubland and grassland
- Guava mixed forest
- Ohia lehua forest
- Lama-manele forest
- Koa forest
- Koa-mamami parkland
- Grassland, desert shrubland and barren

©RMcN.

DENSITY OF POPULATION
INHABITANTS PER UNIT AREA

Per Sq. Km.	Per Sq. Mile
Under 1	Under 2
1–2	2–6
2–7	6–18
7–17	18–45
17–35	45–90
over 35	over 90

©RMcN.

ENVIRONMENT

- Urban
- Cropland
- Grassland, Grazingland
- Woodland
- Shrub, Sparse Grass

©RMcN.

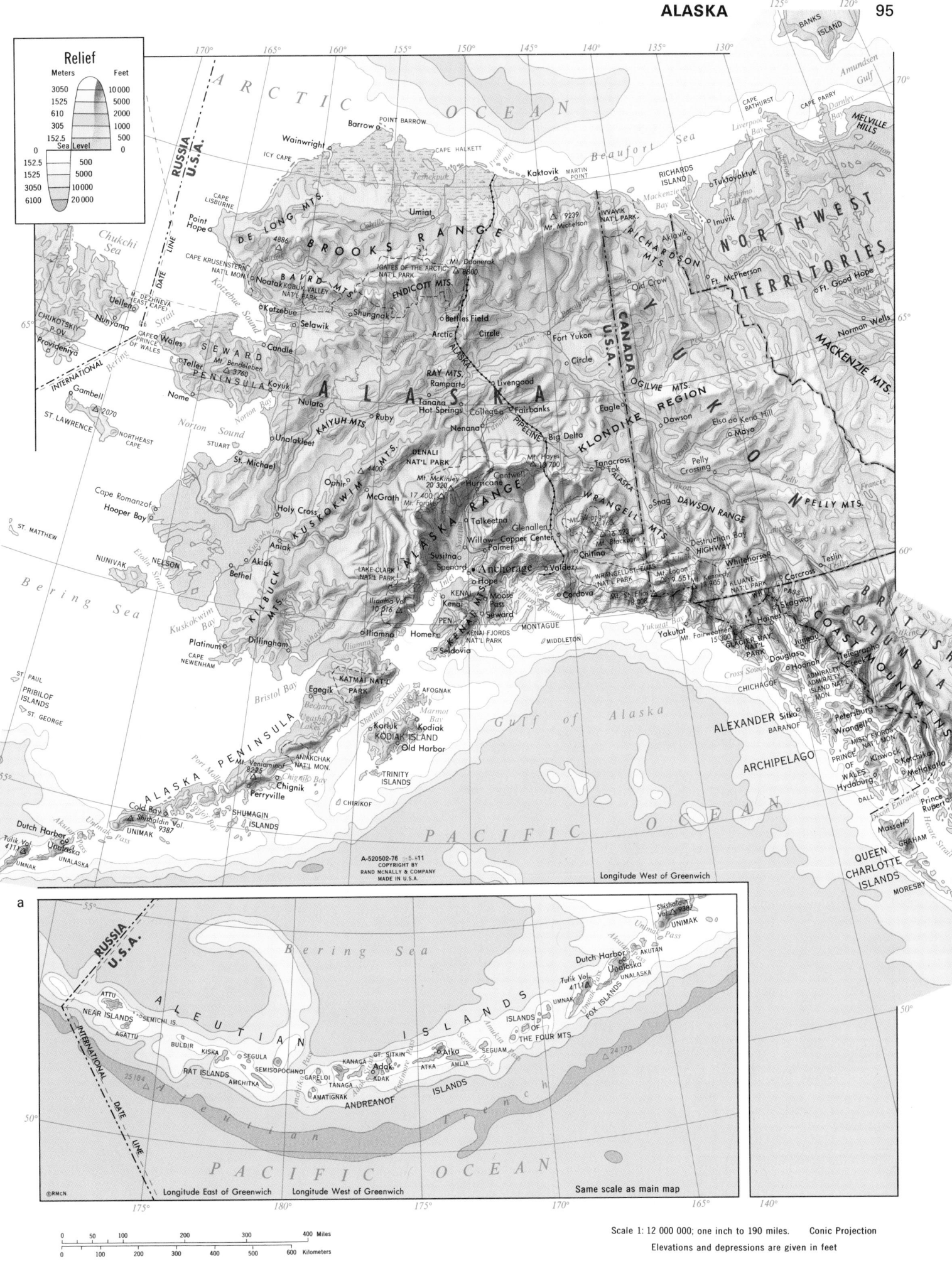

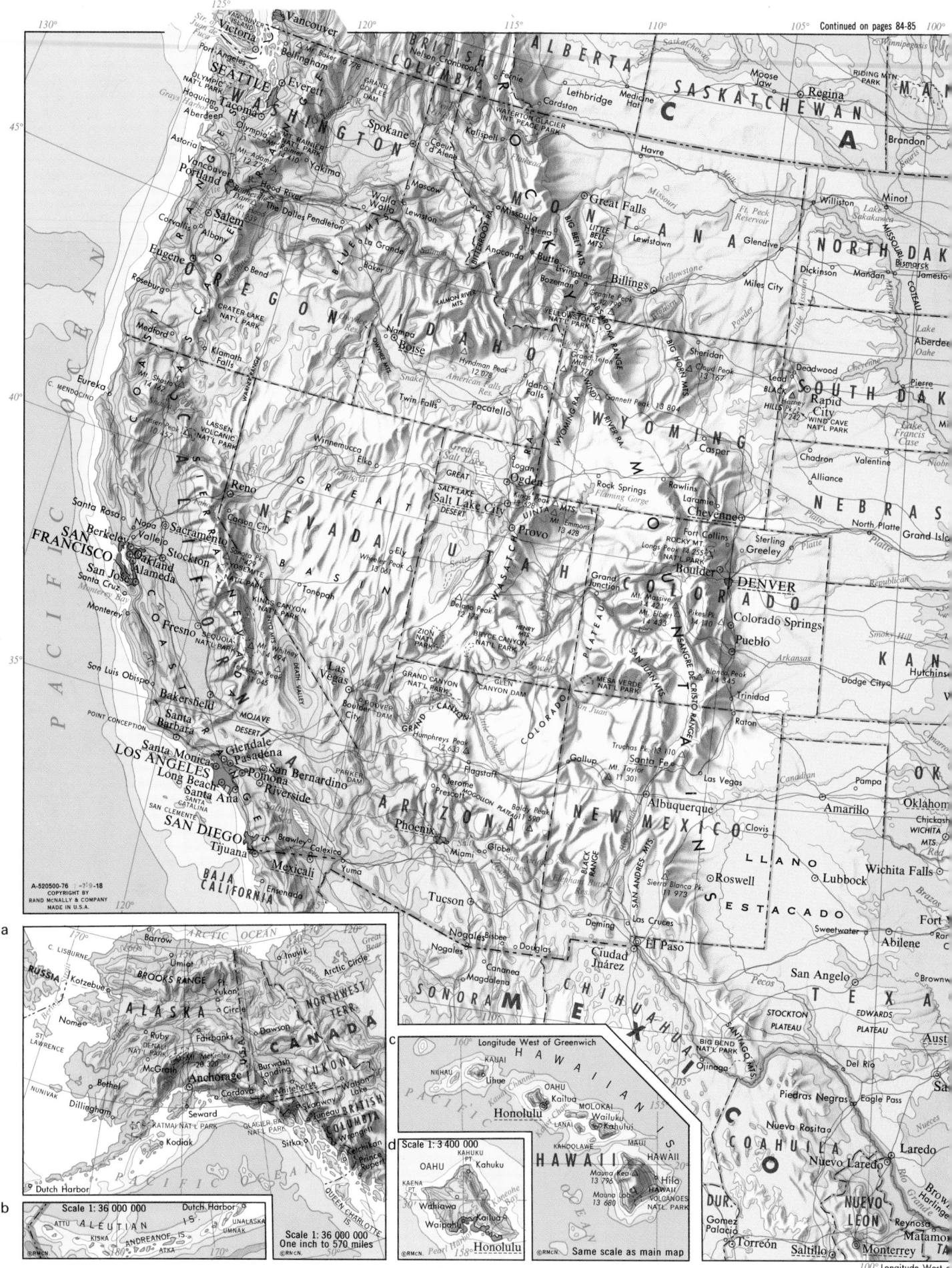

Relief

Meters	Feet
3050	10 000
1525	5000
610	2000
305	1000
152.5	500
Sea Level	0
	Below
152.5	500 Sea Level
1525	5 000
3050	10 000
6100	20 000

Cities and Towns

| 0 to 50,000 | • | 500,000 to 1,000,000 | ◉ |
| 50,000 to 500,000 | ⊙ | 1,000,000 and over | ▣ |

0 50 75 100   200   300   400   500 Miles

100   200   400   600   800 Kilometers

Continued on pages 114-115

Cities
and
Towns

0 to 50,000

50,000 to 500,000

500,000 to 1,000,000

1,000,000 and over

Longitude West of Greenwich

Scale 1:4 000 000; one inch to 64 miles. Conic Projection
Elevations and depressions are given in feet

Continued on pages 90-91

Relief

Meters		Feet
1525		5000
610		2000
305		1000
152.5		500
0	Sea Level	0
152.5		500
1525		5000
3050		10 000

A-520596-76 -5512
COPYRIGHT BY
RAND MCNALLY & COMPANY
MADE IN U.S.A.

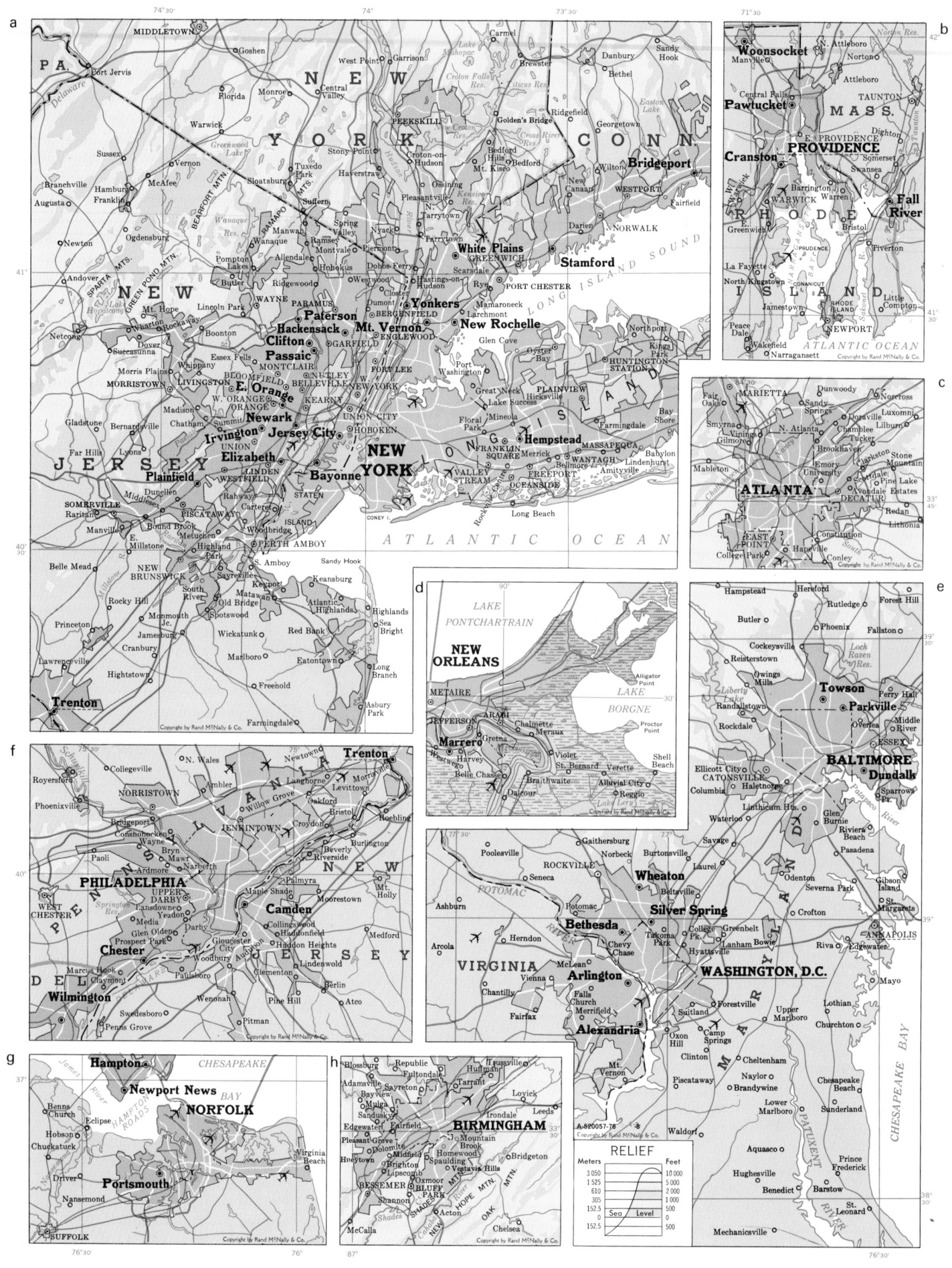

Scale 1:1 000 000; One inch to 16 miles.
Elevations and depressions are given in feet.

For larger scale coverage of New York, Baltimore,
Washington, D.C. and Philadelphia see pages 228 and 229.

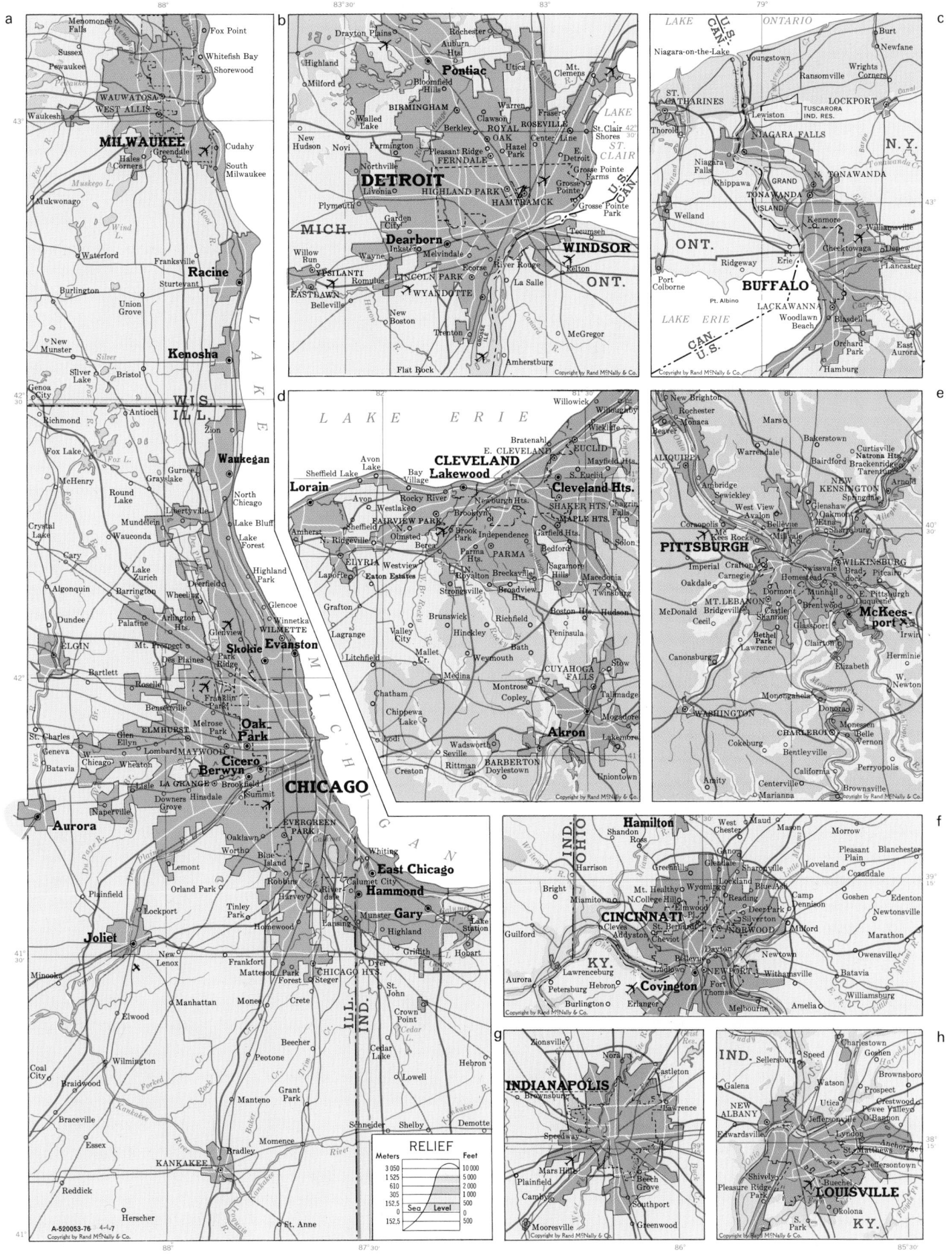

RELIEF

Meters	Feet
3 050	10 000
1 525	5 000
610	2 000
305	1 000
152.5	500
Sea Level	
152.5	500

Scale 1:1 000 000; One inch to 16 miles.
Elevations and depressions are given in feet.

For larger scale coverage of Cleveland, Buffalo, Pittsburgh, Detroit and Chicago see pages 229-231.

Copyright by Rand McNally & Co.

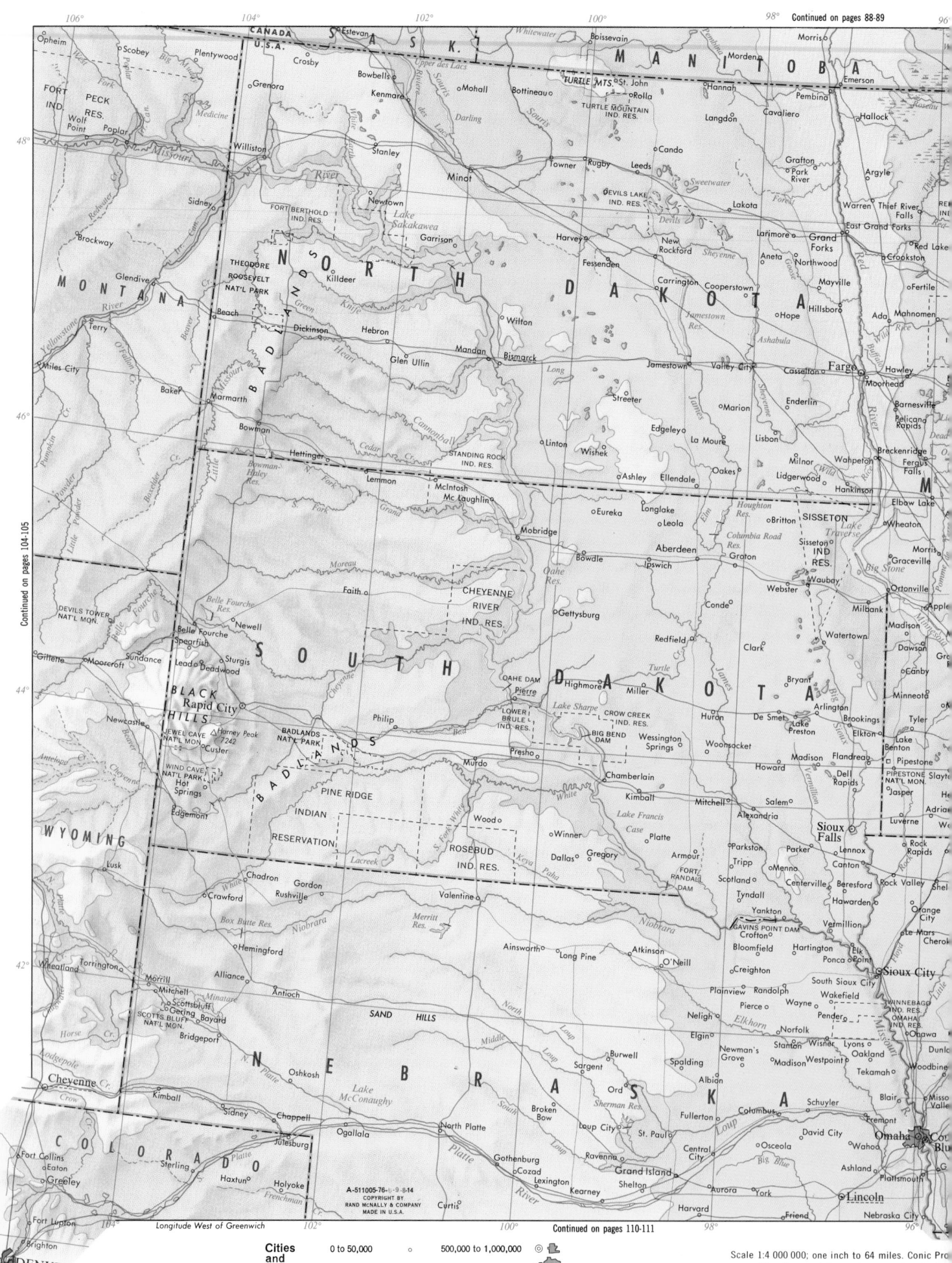

Continued on pages 88-89

Continued on pages 104-105

Continued on pages 110-111

CANADA
U.S.A.

106° 104° 102° 100° 98° 96°

S A S K. MANITOBA

Opheim Scobey Plentywood
FORT Crosby Estevan Whitewater Boissevain Morris
PECK Grenora Bowbells Upper des Lacs Mohall Bottineau TURTLE MTS. St. John Morden Emerson
RES. Kenmare Souris Rolla Hannah Cavalier Pembina
Wolf Point Poplar Williston Stanley Minot TURTLE MOUNTAIN IND. RES. Langdon Hallock

48° NORTH Towner Rugby Leeds DEVILS LAKE IND. RES. Lakota Grafton Park River Argyle East Grand Forks
Sidney Newtown Lake Sakakawea Garrison Harvey New Rockford Fessenden Carrington Cooperstown Larimore Northwood Grand Forks Crookston
Brockway FORT BERTHOLD IND. RES. Killdeer Aneta Mayville Fertile

MONTANA Glendive THEODORE ROOSEVELT NAT'L PARK Beach DAKOTA Wilton Carrington Hope Hillsboro Ada Mahnomen
Terry Dickinson Hebron Mandan Bismarck Jamestown Valley City Casselton Fargo Hawley Moorhead
Miles City Baker Marmarth Glen Ullin Long Jamestown Res. Ashtabula Barnesville
46° Bowman Heart Streeter Marion Enderlin Lisbon Pelican Rapids Fergus Falls Breckenridge
Hettinger Cannonball Linton Edgeley La Moure Oakes Milnor Lidgerwood Hankinson Wahpeton Elbow Lake
Bowman-Haley Res. Lemmon STANDING ROCK IND. RES. Wishek Ashley Ellendale SISSETON IND. RES. Wheaton
McIntosh Eureka Longlake Leola Columbia Road Res. Sisseton Graceville
Mc Laughlin Mobridge Bowdle Aberdeen Groton Webster Waubay Ortonville
Faith Belle Fourche Res. CHEYENNE Gettysburg Ipswich Conde Clark Milbank Madison
SOUTH RIVER Redfield Watertown Dawson Canby
DEVILS TOWER NAT'L MON. Newell IND. RES. Oahe Res. Bryant Minneota
Gillette Moorcroft Belle Fourche Spearfish OAHE DAM Highmore Miller Huron De Smet Arlington Brookings Tyler
44° Sundance Lead Deadwood Sturgis Pierre LOWER BRULE IND. RES. CROW CREEK IND. RES. Lake Preston Elkton Lake Benton
BLACK Rapid City Philip Lake Sharpe BIG BEND DAM Wessington Springs Madison Flandreau Pipestone
HILLS JEWEL CAVE NAT'L MON. Harney Peak 7242 Bad Presho Big Bend Howard Dell Rapids PIPESTONE NAT'L MON. Jasper Slayte
Newcastle Custer BADLANDS NAT'L PARK Murdo Kimball Mitchell Salem Adria
WIND CAVE NAT'L PARK Chamberlain Alexandria Sioux
Hot Springs BADLANDS PINE RIDGE Wood Winner Lake Francis Case Howard Parkston Parker Lennox Falls Rock Rapids
Edgemont INDIAN Dallas Gregory Platte Tripp Menno Canton Rock Valley She
WYOMING RESERVATION ROSEBUD FORT RANDALL DAM Scotland Centerville Beresford Rock Valley
Lusk Chadron Gordon IND. RES. Valentine Tyndall Hawarden Orange City
Crawford Rushville Lacreek Keya Paha Armour Yankton Vermillion Le Mars Cherok

42° Wheatland Torrington Merritt Res. Niobrara GAVINS POINT DAM Crofton Elk Point Sioux City
Morrill Alliance Ainsworth Long Pine Atkinson O'Neill Bloomfield Hartington Ponca South Sioux City
Mitchell Antioch Creighton Plainview Randolph Wakefield WINNEBAGO IND. RES.
Scottsbluff Bayard SAND HILLS Nebling Wayne Pierce Pender OMAHA IND. RES. Onawa
SCOTTS BLUFF NAT'L MON. Bridgeport Norfolk Elgin Stanton Wisner Lyons Oakland
Geering NEBRASKA Burwell Newman's Grove Madison Westpoint Tekamah Woodbine
Horse Cr. Oshkosh Sargent Albian Woodbine
Lodgepole Cheyenne Cr. Kimball Lake McConaughy Loup City Ord Spalding Columbus Schuyler Blair Misso
Sidney Chappell Broken Bow St. Paul Fullerton David City Fremont Valle
COLORADO Ogallala North Platte Gothenburg Ravenna Central City Wahoo Omaha
Fort Collins Julesburg Platte Cozad Lexington Shelton Grand Island Aurora Osceola Ashland Plattsmouth
Eaton Sterling Kearney York Lincoln Nebraska City Bluf
Greeley Holyoke Harvard Friend
Fort Lupton Haxtun Frenchman Curtis
40° Brighton A-511005-76-6-9-8-14 COPYRIGHT BY RAND McNALLY & COMPANY MADE IN U.S.A. Longitude West of Greenwich

DENVER

Cities and Towns

0 to 50,000 ○ 500,000 to 1,000,000 ◎
50,000 to 500,000 ⊙ 1,000,000 and over

Scale 1:4 000 000; one inch to 64 miles. Conic Pro
Elevations and depressions are given in fee

Continued on pages 98-99

Continued on pages 110-111

Continued on pages 86-87

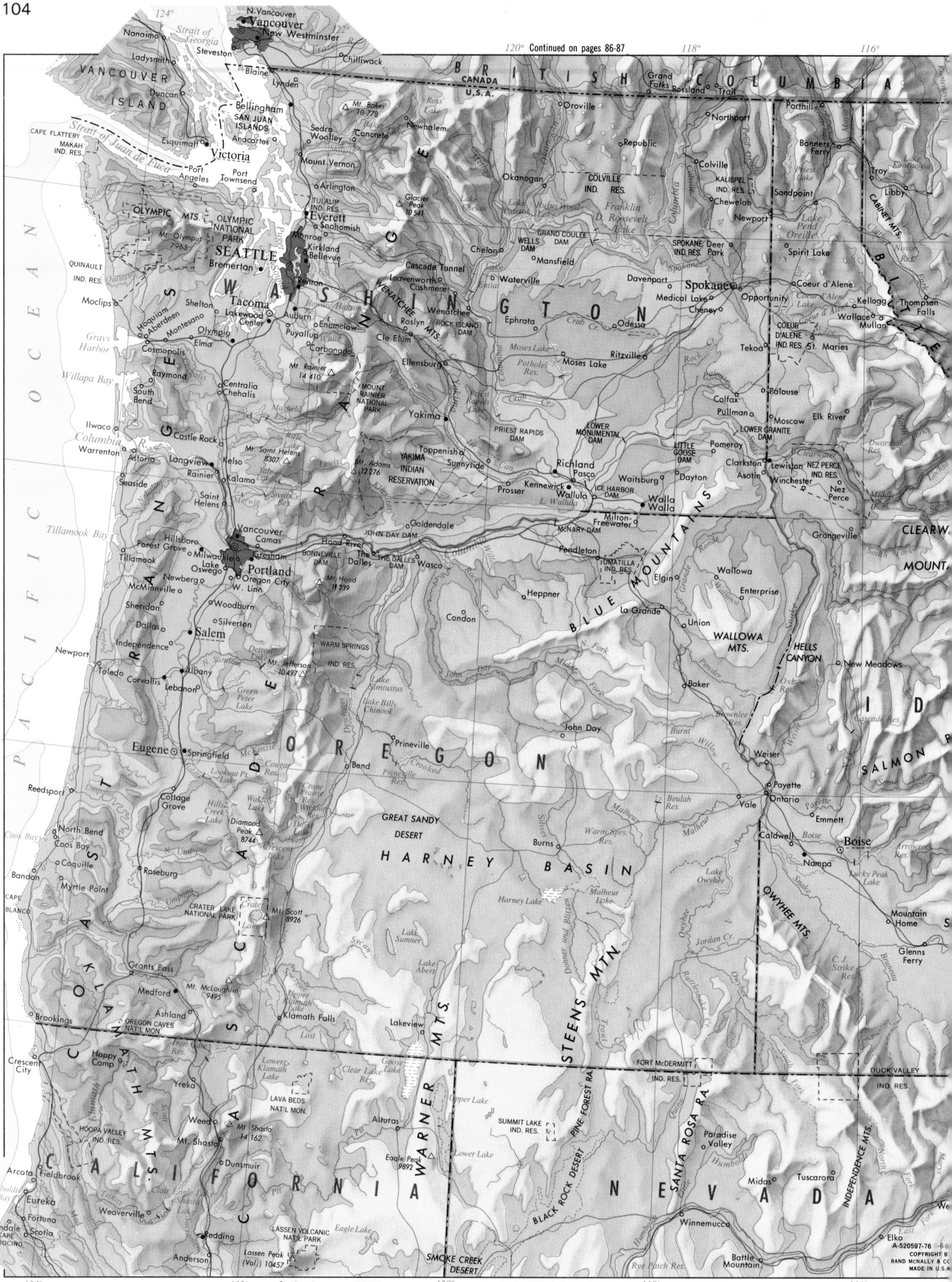

124° 120° 118° 116°

BRITISH COLUMBIA
CANADA
U.S.A.

N. Vancouver
Vancouver
New Westminster
Nanaimo
Ladysmith
Steveston
Blaine
Lynden
Chilliwack

VANCOUVER ISLAND

Duncan
Esquimalt
Victoria
Port Angeles
Port Townsend

Strait of Georgia
Strait of Juan de Fuca

CAPE FLATTERY
MAKAH IND. RES.

Bellingham
SAN JUAN ISLANDS
Anacortes
Sedro Woolley
Concrete
Mt. Baker 10,778
Newhalem
Ross Lake

Oroville
Grand Forks
Rossland
Trail
Northport
Porthill
Bonners Ferry
Troy
Libby

Mount Vernon
Arlington
Glacier Peak 10,541
Okanogan
COLVILLE IND. RES.
Republic
Colville
KALISPEL IND. RES.
Sandpoint
Lake Pend Oreille

48°

OLYMPIC MTS.
OLYMPIC NATIONAL PARK
Mt. Olympus 7965
QUINAULT IND. RES.
Moclips

Everett
Snohomish
Monroe
Kirkland
Bellevue
SEATTLE
Bremerton
TULALIP IND. RES.

Cascade Tunnel
Leavenworth
Cashmere
Wenatchee
Chelan
Lake Chelan
WELLS DAM
GRAND COULEE DAM
Mansfield
Waterville
Davenport
Spokane
Medical Lake
Cheney
Opportunity
Deer Park
SPOKANE IND. RES.
Newport
Spirit Lake
Coeur d'Alene
Kellogg
Wallace
Mullan
Thompson Falls

WASHINGTON

Shelton
Hoquiam
Aberdeen
Lakewood Center
Tacoma
Olympia
Montesano
Elma
Cosmopolis
Raymond
South Bend
Grays Harbor
Willapa Bay

Auburn
Puyallup
Enumclaw
Carbonado
Renton
Roslyn
Cle Elum
WENATCHEE MTS.
ROCK ISLAND DAM
Ellensburg
Ephrata
Moses Lake
Ritzville
Odessa
Colfax
Palouse
Pullman
Moscow
Elk River
LOWER GRANITE DAM

Mt. Rainier 14,410
MOUNT RAINIER NATIONAL PARK
Yakima
Toppenish
PRIEST RAPIDS DAM
LOWER MONUMENTAL DAM
Pomeroy
Dworshak Res.

46°

Centralia
Chehalis
Castle Rock
Astoria
Warrenton
Columbia R.
Longview
Kelso
Rainier
Kalama
Mt. Saint Helens 8307
Saint Helens

Mt. Adams 12,276
YAKIMA INDIAN RESERVATION
Sunnyside
Prosser
Richland
Pasco
Kennewick
Wallula
ICE HARBOR DAM
Walla Walla
Waitsburg
Dayton
Clarkston
Lewiston
NEZ PERCE IND. RES.
Asotin
Winchester
Nez Perce

Seaside
Goldendale
JOHN DAY DAM
Vancouver
Camas
Hood River
BONNEVILLE DAM
THE DALLES DAM
The Dalles
Wasco
McNARY DAM
Milton-Freewater
Pendleton
UMATILLA IND. RES.
Elgin
Grangeville
CLEARWATER MOUNT

Hillsboro
Forest Grove
Milwaukie
Gresham
Portland
Lake Oswego
Oregon City
W. Linn
Tillamook
Newberg
McMinnville
Sheridan
Dallas
Woodburn
Silverton
Independence
Salem
Mt. Hood 11,239
Heppner
Condon
Wallowa
Enterprise
La Grande
Union
WALLOWA MTS.
HELLS CANYON
Baker
New Meadows

Tillamook Bay

Newport
Toledo
Corvallis
Albany
Lebanon
Detroit Lake
Mt. Jefferson 10,497
WARM SPRINGS IND. RES.
Lake Simtustus
Lake Billy Chinook
John Day
Weiser
SALMON R.

44°

Eugene
Springfield
Bend
Prineville
Crooked R.
Prineville Res.
Payette
Ontario
Emmett
Boise
IDAHO

Reedsport
Cottage Grove
Diamond Peak 8744
Crescent Lake
Vale
Beulah Res.
Nampa
Caldwell

Coos Bay
North Bend
Coquille
Roseburg
Myrtle Point
Bandon
CAPE BLANCO

CRATER LAKE NATIONAL PARK
Crater Lake
Mt. Scott 8926
Lake Sumner
Lake Abert

GREAT SANDY DESERT
HARNEY BASIN
Burns
Harney Lake
Malheur Lake
WARM SPRS. RES.
Lake Owyhee
OWYHEE MTS.
Mountain Home
Glenns Ferry
C J Strike Res.

Grants Pass
Medford
Ashland
OREGON CAVES NAT'L MON.
Mt. McLoughlin 9495
Upper Klamath Lake
Klamath Falls
Lakeview
STEENS MTN.

42°

Brookings
Crescent City
Happy Camp
Yreka
Weed
Mt. Shasta 14,162
Dunsmuir
HOOPA VALLEY IND. RES.
KLAMATH MTS.
Lower Klamath Lake
Clear Lake Res.
Goose Lake
Alturas
Lower Lake
Upper Lake
WARNER MTS.
FORT McDERMITT IND. RES.
SUMMIT LAKE IND. RES.
PINE FOREST RA.
SANTA ROSA RA.
Paradise Valley
DUCK VALLEY IND. RES.
INDEPENDENCE MTS.

Arcata
Fieldbrook
Eureka
Fortuna
Scotia
Ferndale
CAPE MENDOCINO
Humboldt Bay
Weaverville
Redding
Anderson
LASSEN VOLCANIC NAT'L PARK
Lassen Peak (Vol.) 10,457
LAVA BEDS NAT'L MON.
Eagle Peak 9892
Eagle Lake

CALIFORNIA
NEVADA
BLACK ROCK DESERT
SMOKE CREEK DESERT
Rye Patch Res.
Winnemucca
Battle Mountain
Midas
Tuscarora
Elko

CASCADE RANGE
COAST RANGE
BLUE MOUNTAINS

OREGON

124° 122° 120° 118° 116°

Continued on pages 108-109

Longitude West of Greenwich

Scale 1: 4,000 000; one inch to 64 miles. Conic Projection
Elevations and depressions are given in feet

A-520597-76
COPYRIGHT B
RAND McNALLY & CO.
MADE IN U.S.A.

Continued on pages 88-89

Continued on pages 102-103

Continued on pages 108-109

Relief

Meters		Feet
3050		10000
1525		5000
610		2000
305		1000
152.5		500
0	Sea Level	0
1525		500

20 40 60 80 100 120 Miles
40 60 80 100 120 140 160 180 200 Kilometers

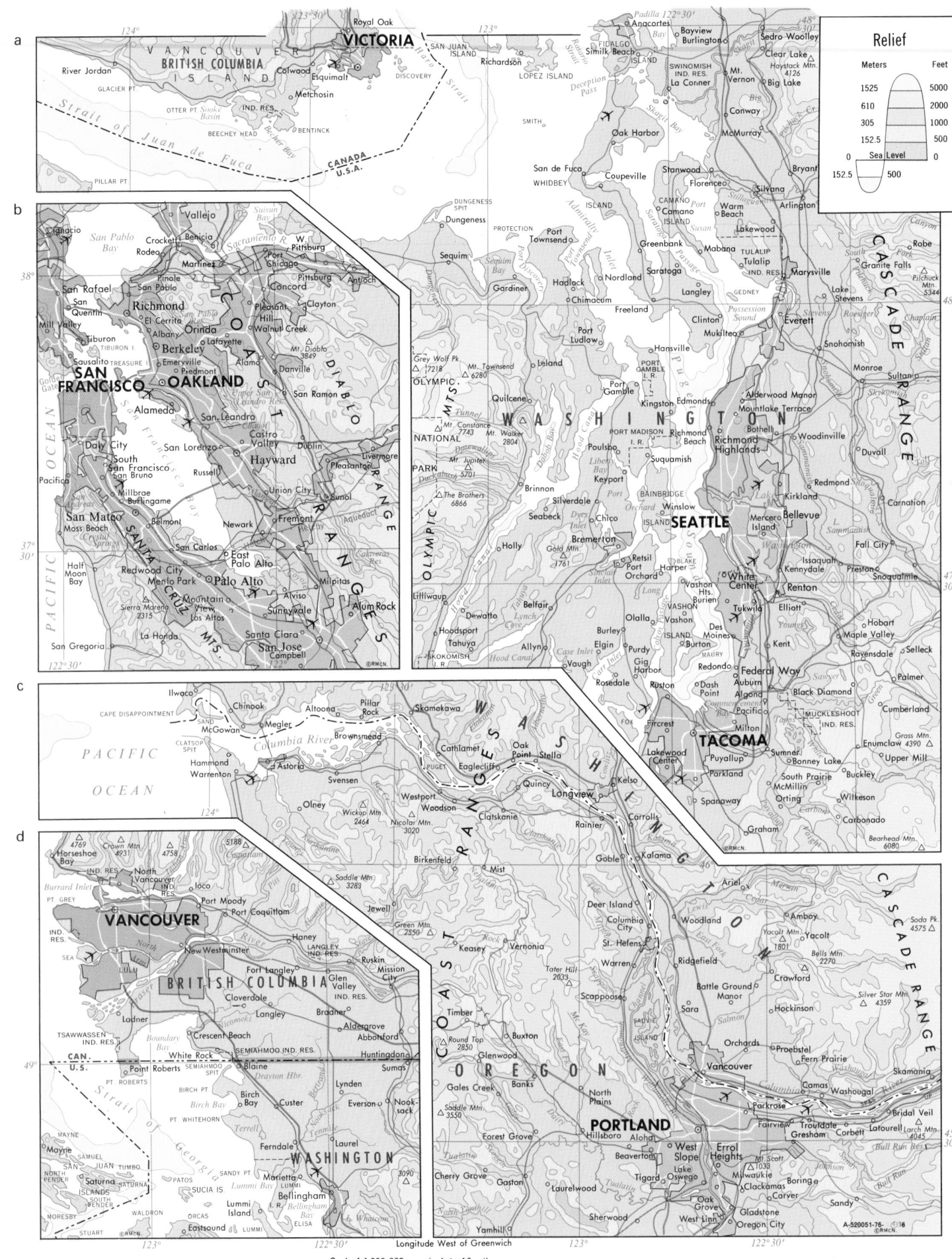

Scale 1:1 000 000; one inch to 16 miles.
Elevations and depressions are given in feet.

For larger scale coverage of San Francisco see page 231.

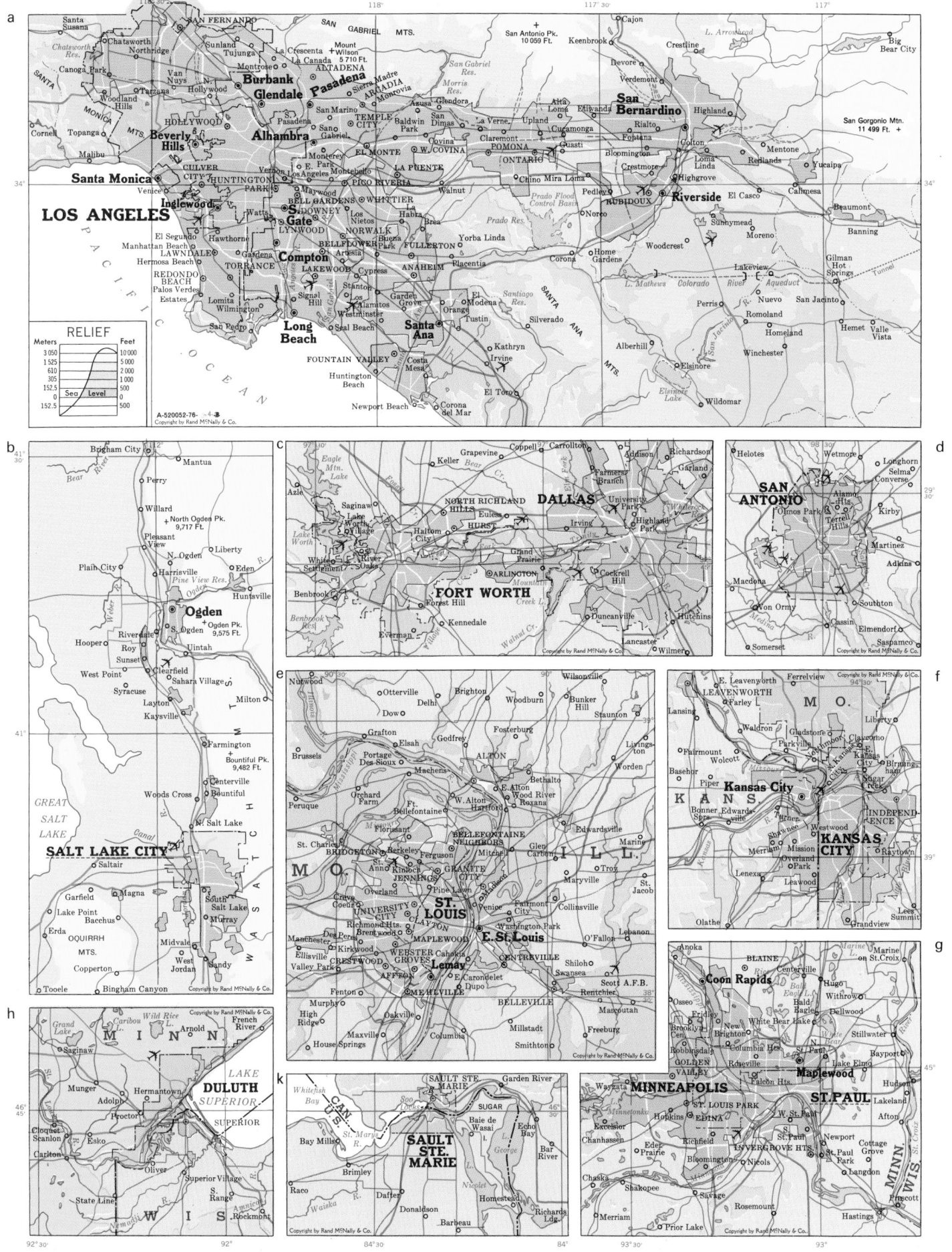

Scale 1:1 000 000; One inch to 16 miles.
Elevations and depressions are given in feet.

For larger scale coverage
of Los Angeles see page 232.

Continued on pages 104-105

SISKIYOU MTS.

Anderson
Miranda
Red Bluff
Leggett
Lassen Peak (Vol.) 10 457
LASSEN VOLCANIC NATL. PARK
Westwood
Susanville
SMOKE CREEK DESERT
Battle Mountain

Fort Bragg
Redwood Valley
Mendocino
Ukiah
Anthony Peak 6 954
Black Butte Lake
Chico
Willows
Honey Lake
PYRAMID LAKE
Pyramid Lake
Winnemucca
Lovelock
Humboldt
HUMBOLDT RA.
RUBY MTS.
Ruby

COAST RANGES
Cloverdale
Healdsburg
Lakeport
Colusa
Gridley
Oroville
Lake Oroville
Downieville
INDIAN RESERVATION
Sparks
Wadsworth
Humboldt Sink
Carson Sink
STILLWATER RA.
Humboldt Salt Marsh
Austin
Eureka

POINT ARENA
Sebastopol
Santa Rosa
Napa
Petaluma
Woodland
Lincoln
Auburn
Placerville
Marysville
Yuba City
Nevada City
Grass Valley
Roseville
Folsom
Reno
Virginia City
Truckee
Carson City
Yerington
Fallon
NEVADA
TOIYABE RA.
Arc Dome 11 773
Duckwater Pk. 11 493

POINT REYES
MUIR WOODS NATL. MON.
San Rafael
Richmond
Berkeley
Oakland
Alameda
Vallejo
Benicia
Pittsburg
Sacramento
Jackson
San Andreas
Angels Camp
Sonora Pk. 11 459
Hawthorne
WALKER RIVER IND. RES.
Walker Lake
WASSUK RANGE

San Francisco
Daly City
Sausalito
Burlingame
San Mateo
Redwood City
Palo Alto
Santa Clara
San Jose
Los Gatos
Stockton
Oakdale
Lodi
Tracy
Livermore
Modesto
Turlock
Merced
YOSEMITE NATIONAL PARK
Mt. Dana 13 053
Mt. Lyell 13 114
DEVILS POSTPILE N.M.
Mono Lake
Boundary Pk. 13 140
Benton
White Mtn. Peak 14 246
Goldfield
Tonopah

Santa Cruz
Watsonville
Gilroy
Hollister
San Juan Bautista
PINNACLES NATL. MON.
Madera
Mariposa
Fresno
Sanger
Reedley
Dinuba
Visalia
Exeter
Tulare
Hanford
KINGS CANYON NATL. PARK
SEQUOIA NATL. PARK
Mt. Whitney 14 494
Lone Pine
Bishop
Owens Lake
INYO MTS.
PANAMINT RA.
DEATH VALLEY
282 Ft. below sea level
Beatty
FRENCHMAN FLAT

Pacific Grove
Monterey
Salinas
King City
Coalinga
Selma
Porterville
Delano
Tronoa
TULE RIVER IND. RES.
Telescope Peak 11 045
Death Valley
DEATH VALLEY NATL. MON.
SPRING MTS.
Henderson

Paso Robles
Atascadero
Estero Bay
San Luis Obispo
San Luis Obispo Bay
Twitchell Res.
Buena Vista Lake Bed
Tulare Lake Bed
Taft
Bakersfield
Inyokern
Searles Lake
Cadiz

COAST RANGES
Santa Maria
Lompoc
POINT ARGUELLO
POINT CONCEPTION
Cuyama
Mojave
TEHACHAPI MTS.
MOJAVE DESERT
Barstow
Daggett
Soda Lake

Santa Barbara
Ventura
Oxnard
Santa Paula
Santa Clara
SAN MIGUEL
SANTA ROSA
SANTA CRUZ
Santa Barbara Channel
Burbank
Glendale
Pasadena
Monrovia
LOS ANGELES
San Bernardino
SAN BERNARDINO MTS.
JOSHUA TREE NATL. MON.

Santa Monica
Inglewood
Redondo Beach
Alhambra
Pomona
Compton
Huntington Park
San Pedro
Long Beach
Orange
Santa Ana
Newport Beach
Huntington Beach
Riverside
Redlands
Palm Springs
Lake Elsinore
AGUA CALIENTE IND. RES.
Eagle Mtn.
Colorado River

CHANNEL ISLANDS
SANTA BARBARA
CHANNEL ISLANDS NATIONAL PARK
SANTA CATALINA
Avalon
SAN NICOLAS
SAN CLEMENTE
Gulf of Santa Catalina
Oceanside
Escondido
Salton Sea
Bottom 235 Ft. below sea level
Calipatria
Brawley
IMPERIAL VALLEY
Holtville

PACIFIC OCEAN
SAN DIEGO
Coronado
National City
Chula Vista
Tijuana
BAJA CALIFORNIA
El Centro
Calexico
Mexicali
Laguna Salada

Longitude West of Greenwich

Scale 1:4 000 000; one inch to 64 miles. Conic Projection
Elevations and depressions are given in feet

0 20 40 60 80 100 120 Miles
0 20 40 60 80 100 120 140 160 180 200 Kilometers

a

PACIFIC OCEAN
Del Mar
La Jolla
CALIFORNIA
Lakeside
Santee
El Cajon
La Mesa
Spring Valley
Lemon Grove
SAN DIEGO
CABRILLO NATL. MON.
National City
Chula Vista
Coronado
Sweetwater Reservoir
Lower Otay Lake
Otay
Imperial Beach
Tijuana
USA
MEXICO
BAJA CALIFORNIA

Scale 1:1 000 000
0 5 10 Miles
0 4 8 12 16 Kilometers
®RMCN.

Relief

Meters		Feet
3050		10000
1525		5000
610		2000
305		1000
152.5		500
0	Sea Level	0
152.5		Below 500 Sea Level
1525		5000
3050		10000

Continued on pages 110-111

Continued on pages 112-113

Continued on pages 102-103

106°   104°   102°   100°

Continued on pages 108-109

WYO   Cheyenne   Lodgepole Cr   Oshkosh   Lake McConaughy   Ord
Kimball   Sidney   Chappell   North Platte   Broken Bow   Middle Loop   Sherman Res   St. Paul   Loup City

40°   FRONT RANGE   Fort Collins   Windsor   Eaton   Sterling   Haxtun   Ogallala   Julesburg   North Platte   Gothenburg   Cozad   Lexington   Grand Island   Kearney   Shelton
Loveland   Greeley   Brush   Fort Morgan   Akron   Yuma   Holyoke   Wray   Benkelman   Swanson Res   Hugh Butler Lake   Cambridge   Holdrege   Minden   Hastings
Boulder   Fort Lupton   Brighton   Curtis   Harry Strunk Lake   Mc Cook   Beaver City   Alma   Red Cloud   Franklin   NEBRA

ROCKY   Golden   DENVER   Aurora   Limon   Burlington   Goodland   Colby   Atwood   Beaver   Oberlin   Norton   Phillipsburg   Smith Center
Lakewood   Engelwood   Littleton   Kit Carson   Cheyenne Wells   Sharon Springs   Hill City   Stockton   Osborne   Down
38°   Pueblo   Ordway   Sugar City   Wiley   Lamar   Syracuse   Garden City   Dodge City   Greensburg   Pratt   K A N

TEX

Aurora
CHICAGO
Joliet

Continued on pages 102-103

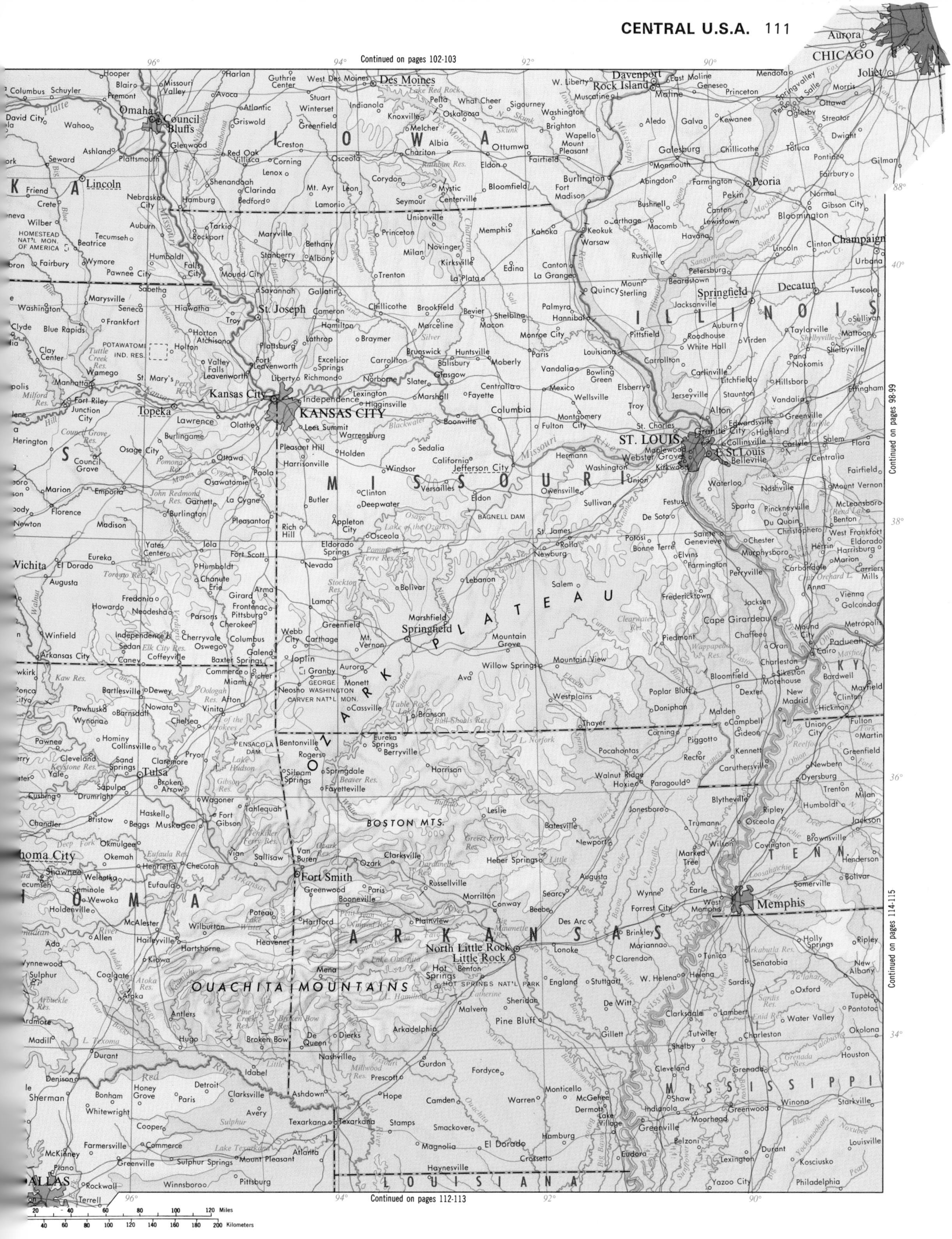

96° 94° 92° 90° 88°

Hooper Harlan West Des Moines Des Moines W. Liberty Davenport Mendota
Columbus Schuyler Blairo Guthrie Center Muscatine Rock Island Geneseo Princeton Morris Springvalley
David City Fremont Stuart East Moline Kewanee Ottawa La Salle Oglesby Streator Dwight
Omaha Avoca Atlantic Winterset Indianola Pella What Cheer Sigourney Washington Matine Galva Aledo Princeton Peru Gilman
Council Bluffs Griswold Creston Greenfield Knoxville Melcher Oskaloosa Brighton Wapello Galesburg Monmouth Chillicothe Toluca Pontiac Fairbury
Ashland Glenwood Red Oak Villsca Corning Osceola Chariton Albia Ottumwa Mount Pleasant Burlington Abingdon Farmington Peoria Normal Bloomington
Lincoln Plattsmouth Shenandoah Clarinda Lenox Leon Corydon Centerville Bloomfield Fort Madison Pekin Canton Lewistown Gibson City Champaign
Seward Nebraska City Hamburg Bedford Mt. Ayr Lamoni Seymour Mystic Keokuk Warsaw Bushnell Macomb Havana Lincoln Clinton Urbana
Crete Auburn Tarkio Maryville Bethany Princeton Milan Kirksville Memphis Kahoka Quincy Rushville Beardstown Decatur Tuscola
Wilber Tecumseh Rockport Stanberry Albany Trenton La Plata Edina Canton La Grange Mount Sterling Springfield Jacksonville Sullivan
Fairbury Wymore Falls City Savannah Gallatin Chillicothe Brookfield Bevier Shelbina Monroe City Hannibal Palmyra Louisiana Roodhouse White Hall Auburn Taylorville Mattoon
Pawnee City Humboldt St. Joseph Cameron Hamilton Marceline Silver Macon Pittsfield Carrollton Virden Pana Nokomis Shelbyville
Washington Marysville Hiawatha Troy Plattsburg Braymer Brunswick Huntsville Paris Vandalia Carlinville Litchfield Hillsboro
Seneca Horton Atchison Lathrop Salisbury Moberly Bowling Green Elsberry Jerseyville Staunton Greenville Vandalia
Frankfort Holton Fort Leavenworth Excelsior Springs Carrollton Glasgow Centralia Mexico Wellsville Troy Alton Edwardsville Effingham
Blue Rapids Valley Falls Leavenworth Liberty Richmond Norborne Slater Fayette Columbia Fulton Montgomery City St. Charles Granite City Highland Salem
Clay Center Manhattan St. Mary's Kansas City Independence Lexington Higginsville Marshall Boonville Washington St. Louis Collinsville Carlyle Flora
Milford Res. Fort Riley Junction City Topeka Lawrence Olathe Lees Summit Warrensburg Sedalia Jefferson City Hermann ST. LOUIS Maplewood Webster Groves Kirkwood Belleville Fairfield
Herington Burlingame Osage City Pleasant Hill Holden Windsor California Versailles Eldon Owensville Sullivan Union Waterloo Mount Vernon
Council Grove Ottawa Paola Harrisonville Clinton Deepwater BAGNELL DAM St. James Rolla Potosi Bonne Terre Festus Nashville Pinckneyville
Marion Emporia Garnett La Cygne Butler Appleton City Osceola Newburg Elvins De Soto Sparta McLeansboro
Florence Madison Burlington Pleasanton Rich Hill Lake of the Ozarks Farmington Sainte Genevieve Du Quoin Benton
Newton Yates Center Iola Fort Scott Eldorado Springs Pomme de Terre Res. Bolivar Lebanon Salem Fredericktown Chester Murphysboro Herrin West Frankfort
Eureka Humboldt Nevada Lamar Marshfield Springfield PLATEAU Mountain Grove Piedmont Perryville Carbondale Marion Harrisburg
El Dorado Chanute Erie Armo Greenfield Mt. Vernon Jackson Anna Vienna Eldorado Carriers Mills
Augusta Fredonia Girard Frontenac Pittsburg Webb City Carthage Joplin Aurora Willow Springs Mountain View Cape Girardeau Chaffee Oran Golconda Metropolis
Winfield Neodesha Parsons Cherokee Ava Westplains Bloomfield Sikeston Morehouse Charleston Paducah
Independence Cherryvale Columbus Galena Granby Monett Cassville Poplar Bluff Dexter New Madrid Cairo
Arkansas City Sedan Caney Coffeyville Commerce Picher Neosho GEORGE WASHINGTON CARVER NAT'L MON. Branson Bull Shoals Res. Thayer Doniphan Malden Campbell Gideon Union City Fulton Mayfield
Bartlesville Dewey Miami Table Rock Lake Corning Piggotto Kennett Hickman Clinton
Pawhuska Barnsdall Nowata Afton Vinita Eureka Springs Berryville Harrison Pocahontas Rector Caruthersville Dyersburg
Wynona Hominy Collinsville Chelsea PENSACOLA DAM Bentonville Rogers Siloam Springs Springdale Walnut Ridge Hoxie Paragould Trenton Milan
Cleveland Sand Springs Claremore Pryor Lake Hudson Fayetteville Beaver Lake L. Norfork Jonesboro Blytheville Ripley Humboldt Jackson
Tulsa Broken Arrow Gibson Res. Tahlequah Wagoner Fort Gibson BOSTON MTS. Leslie Batesville Newport Trumann Osceola Brownsville Henderson
Sapulpa Drumright Haskell Muskogee Vian Sallisaw Van Buren Ozark Clarksville Heber Springs Augusta Wilson Covington Bolivar
Cushing Bristow Beggs Checotah Fort Smith Ozark Russellville Searcy Wynne Earle Somerville
Chandler Okmulgee Henryetta Eufaula Greenwood Paris Booneville Morrilton Conway Beebe Des Arc Forrest City West Memphis Memphis
Shawnee Weleetka Seminole Wewoka McAlester Wilburton Hartford Plainview TENN.
Holdenville Hartshorne Poteau Plainview North Little Rock Little Rock Lonoke Clarendon Brinkley Marianna Holly Springs Ripley
Ada Allen Kiowa Heavener Mena Hot Springs Benton England Stuttgart W. Helena Helena New Albany
Sulphur Coalgate Atoka Res. Hartshorne HOT SPRINGS NAT'L PARK Malvern Sheridan De Witt Sardis Oxford Pontotoc
Arbuckle Res. OUACHITA MOUNTAINS Hot Springs Arkadelphia Pine Bluff Gillett Clarksdale Lambert Water Valley Tupelo
Madill Antlers De Queen Dierks Nashville Gurdon Fordyce Monticello McGehee Shaw Greenwood Winona Starkville
Denison Durant Hugo Broken Bow De Queen Millwood Res. Prescott Hope Camden Warren Dermott Indianola Moorhead Okolona
Sherman Bonham Honey Grove Paris Clarksville Ashdown Smackover El Dorado Crossett Eudora Lexington Louisville
Whitewright Idabel Avery Texarkana Stamps Magnolia Belzoni Durant Yazoo City Philadelphia
DALLAS McKinney Plano Rockwall Terrell Winnsboro Pittsburg Atlanta Haynesville LOUISIANA Kosciusko

Continued on pages 112-113
Continued on pages 98-99
Continued on pages 114-115

IOWA MISSOURI ILLINOIS ARKANSAS OUACHITA MOUNTAINS OZARK PLATEAU BOSTON MTS. OKLAHOMA KANSAS NEBRASKA TENN. KY. MISSISSIPPI

20 40 60 80 100 120 Miles
40 60 80 100 120 140 160 180 200 Kilometers

112

Continued on pages 110-111

NEW MEXICO

Alamogordo
Alamo Pk.
7820
WHITE SANDS
NAT'L MON.
Penasco
Artesia
McMillan
Dayton

Carlsbad
CARLSBAD
CAVERNS
NAT'L PARK

Seagraves
O'Donnell
Haskell
Newcastle
Graham

Seminole
Lamesa
Rotan
Hamlin
Stamford
Hamlin

Wind Mtn.
7278
Hobbs
Snyder
Anson
Albany
Breckenridge
Strawn

Red Bluff Res.
Roscoe
Sweetwater
Baird
Cisco
Eastland
Desdemona

N. Franklin Mtn.
7176
Guadalupe Pk.
8749
Colorado
City
Merkel
Abilene
Ranger
Thurber
Steph

El Paso
Ysleta
Ciudad Juárez
Fabens
Midland
Stanton
Winters
Gorman
De Leon
Dublin

Guadalupe
Wink
Odessa
Sterling City
Ballinger
Coleman
Comanche

Villa
Ahumada
Sierra
Blanca
Van Horn
Pecos
North
Concho
Santa Anna
Brownwood
Hamil

Toyah
Pecos
Middle
Concho
San Angelo
Eden
Brady
San Saba
Lampa

Eagle Pk.
7496
DAVIS MTS.
Baldy Peak
8382
McCamey
Sonora
Menard
Mason
Llano
Buchanan

Marfa
Alpine
Fort Stockton
STOCKTON PLATEAU
Sanderson
Rocksprings
Junction
Fredericksburg

Chinati Pk.
7730
Cathedral Mt.
6860
SANTIAGO MTS.
Big Canyon
U.S.A.
MEXICO
SERRANÍAS DEL BURRO
Del Rio
Camp Wood
Kerrville
Boerne
New Braunfels

Coyame
Ojinaga
Presidio
BIG BEND
NAT'L PARK
Emory Pk.
7835
Villa Acuña
Brackettville
Uvalde
San Antonio
Honda
Floresville

Cuchillo Parado
Aldama
Jiménez
Piedras Negras
Fuente
Eagle Pass
Crystal City
Sabinal
Poteet
Pearsall
Pleasant

CHIHUAHUA
Zaragoza
Morelos
Nava
Allende
Guerrero
Carrizo Springs
Asherton
Cotulla
Fowlerton
Georg
Wes

Meoqui
SIERRA
Rosales
Muzquiz
San Juan de Sabinas
Encinal
Corpus

Naica
Gigantes
COAHUILA
MADRE
Hidalgo
Dolores
San Diego

Ciudad Camargo
(Santa Rosalía)
Jaco
BOLSÓN
Sierra Mojada
Laguna de la Leche
ORIENTAL
Progreso
Presa de Martin
Nuevo Laredo
Laredo
Mirando City
Premor

Jimenez
Villa Lopez
DE
Abasolo
Nadadores
Lampazos
Guerrero
Zapata
Hebbronville
Falfurria

Hidalgo del Parral
Santa Barbara
Rey
Palomas
MAPIMI
Sacramento
Cuatro Ciénegas
San Buenaventura
Nadadores
Monclova
Bustamante
Villaldama
Sabinas Hidalgo
Mier
Riogrande
Camargo
Mission

Rosario
Villa Coronado
Escalón
MEXICO
Agualeguas
Cerralvo
Falcon Res.

Villa Ocampo
Indé
Santa Cruz
Rio de la Parida
Mapimí
San Pedro de las Colonias
Laguna de Mayran
Paredón
Salinas Victoria
General Zuazua
Los Herreras
Reynosa

San Luis del Cordero
Gómez Palacio
Torreón
Lerdo
Matamoros
Laguna de Viesca
García
NUEVO
Santa Catarina
Monterrey
Cadereyta Jiménez
China

Rodeo
Nazas
Parras
Ramos Arizpe
General Cepeda
Arteaga
Saltillo
Villa de Allende
Montemorelos
LEON

DURANGO
Cuencamé
San Pedro de las Colonias
Sacramento
Viesca
Gomez Farias
Linares
Burgos
San Fernando

Laguna de Santiaguillo
San Juan del Rio
Cuencamé
San Bartolo
San Juan de Guadalupe
Mazapil
Concepción del Oro
Galeana
TAMAUL

Canatlán
Pánuco de Coronado
Santa Clara
Juan Aldama
ZACATECAS
San Carlos
Villagran
Cruillas

Durango

Continued on pages 118-119

Longitude West of Greenwich

Relief

Meters	Feet
1525	5000
610	2000
305	1000
152.5	500
0	Sea Level	0
152.5	5000
1525	5000
3050	10000

Scale 1:4 000 000; one inch to 64 miles. Conic Proj
Elevations and depressions are given in feet

Continued on pages 110-111

Continued on pages 114-115

96°   94°   92°   90°

ARK.

Denton
McKinney Farmersville Greenville Sulphur Springs Mount Pleasant Atlanta Haynesville Lake Lake Providence Yazoo City Canton
Garza-Little Plano Lancaster Lake Pittsburg Vivian Homer d'Arbonne Bastrop Ross Barnette Forest
Elm Lk. Fort DALLAS Rockwall Winnsboro Jefferson Bayou Minden Arcadia Monroe Rayville Delhi Vicksburg Res.
Worth Terrell Lake Tawakoni Marshall Bossier City Rustona Pearl
Arlington Kaufman Wills Point Longview Shreveport Eros Aito Tallulah Jackson Pelahatchie
Waxahachie Mabank Kilgore Winnsboro Port Gibson
Ennis Mineola Carthage Mansfield Coushatta Jonesboro Winnsboro Vidalia Natchez Crystal Springs Hazlehurst
Italy Cedar Creek Tyler Henderson Winnfield Ferriday
Navarro Mills Res. Athens Res. Natchitoches Colfax Jonesville Fayette Brookhaven Sumrall
Hillsboro Corsicana Jacksonville Timpson Toledo Bend MISSISSIPPI Collins
Hubbard Rusk Fisher Pineville Marksville Norfield McComb Columbia
Waco Palestine Nacogdoches Peason Alexandria Woodville Magnolia Tylertown Lumberton
McGregor Wortham San Augustine Leesville Lecompte Jackson Kentwood Poplarville
Moody Mexia Teague Elkhart Hemphill Fullerton McNary Bunkie Amite Franklinton Bogalusa
Temple Groesbeck Oakwood Ratcliff Wiergate Glenmora Ville Platte Melville New Roads Hammond Picayune
S Calvert Buffalo Crockett Jasper De Ridder Oakdale Covington
Bartlett Marquez Madisonville Groveton Newton Merryville Longville Eunice Opelousas Baton Rouge Madisonville Bay St. Louis
Cameron Hearne Trinity Woodville Kirbyville De Quincy Kinder Crowley Plaquemine White Castle Lutcher Kenner Slidell
Rockdale Bryan Huntsville Saratoga Silsbee Vinton Lake Jennings Rayne Lafayette Donaldsonville Metairie New Orleans Gretna
Taylor Caldwell Willis Conroe Cleveland Orange Charles Lake Arthur Abbeville St. Martinville Napoleonville
Elgin Somerville Brenham Hempstead Dayton Beaumont Ged New Iberia Thibodaux Houma
Bastrop Giddings Port Neches Jeanerette Franklin Morgan Port Sulphur
Smithville HOUSTON Humble Liberty Port Arthur Sabine Gueydan Patterson City
Lagrange Bellville Richmond Baytown Grand L. Caillou

GULF OF MEXICO

Scale 1:1 000 000
0 5 10 Miles
0 4 8 12 16 Kilometers

A-511007-76- 5 5-7
COPYRIGHT BY
RAND McNALLY & COMPANY
MADE IN U.S.A.

a

HOUSTON

Crosby
Sheldon Hankamer
Highlands Wallisville
Mont Belvieu
Jacinto City Channelview Anahuac
West University Place Galena Pk. Baytown Turtle Bay
Bellaire Pasadena
Missouri City South Houston La Porte
Genoa
Pearland Seabrook Smith Point GALVESTON High Island
Kemah BAY EAST BAY
Areola Friendswood League City
Manvel Dickinson
Alvin Algoa BOLIVAR PENINSULA
Sandy Point Alta Loma Texas City
Hitchcock La Marque Port Bolivar
Liverpool
Galveston GULF
OF MEXICO
Danbury GALVESTON
ISLAND
Angleton Bastrop

Cities
and 0 to 50,000   500,000 to 1,000,000
Towns 50,000 to 500,000   1,000,000 and over

20 40 60 80 100 120 Miles
20 40 60 80 100 120 140 160 180 200 Kilometers

114

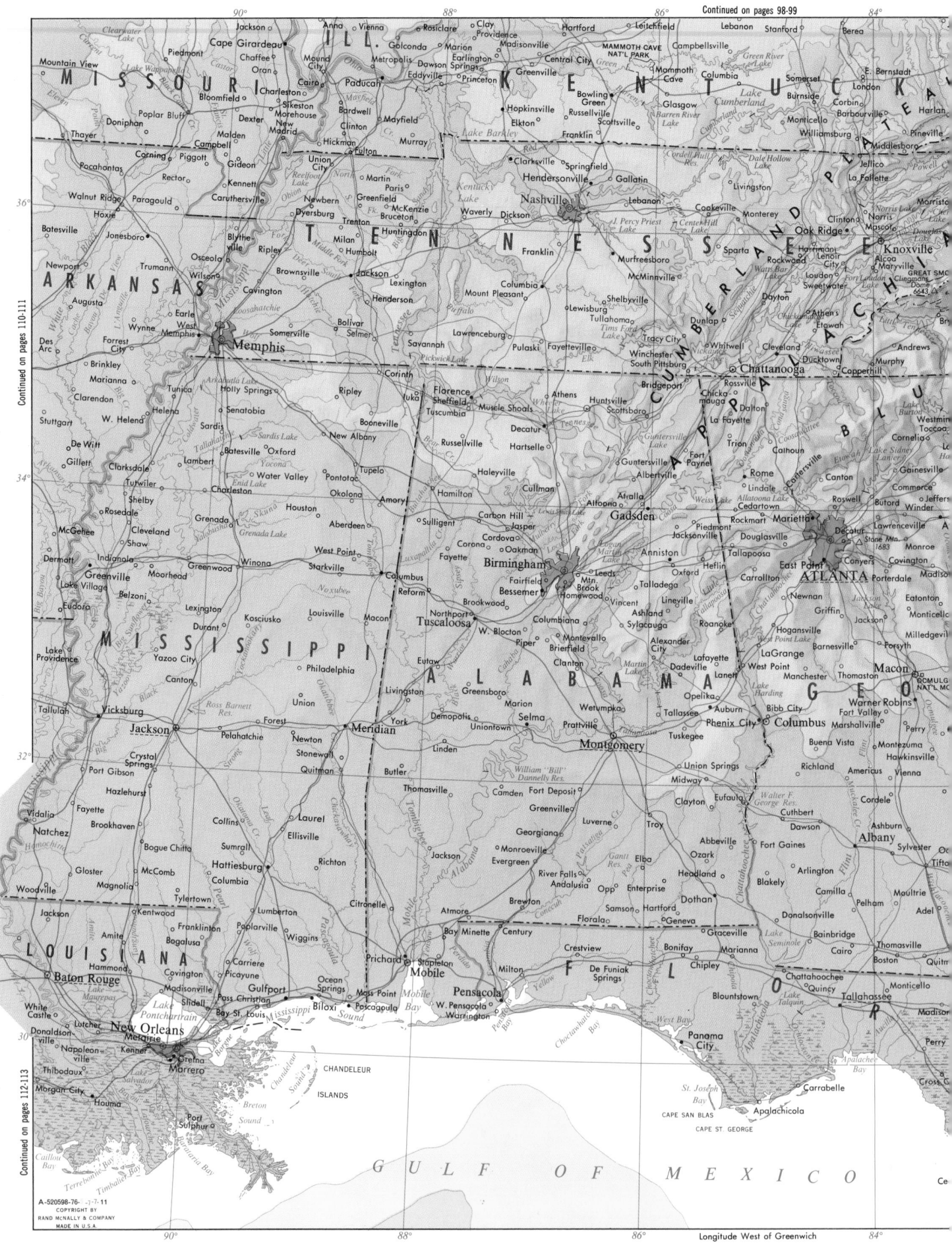

Continued on pages 98-99
Continued on pages 110-111
Continued on pages 112-113

90°   88°   86°   84°

36°

34°

32°

30°

MISSOURI

ILL.

KENTUCKY

TENNESSEE

ARKANSAS

APPALACHIAN

CUMBERLAND PLATEAU

BLUE

MISSISSIPPI

ALABAMA

GEO

LOUISIANA

FLOR

Mountain View
Piedmont
Cape Girardeau
Chaffee
Oran
Charleston
Sikeston
Morehouse
New Madrid
Poplar Bluff
Dexter
Bloomfield

Jackson
Anna
Vienna
Mound City
Metropolis
Cairo
Paducah
Bardwell
Mayfield
Clinton
Murray

Rosiclare
Golconda
Marion
Dawson Springs
Eddyville
Princeton

Clay
Providence
Madisonville
Earlington
Greenville

Hartford
Central City
Mammoth Cave
MAMMOTH CAVE NAT'L PARK

Leitchfield
Campbellsville
Columbia
Somerset
Russell Springs

Lebanon
Stanford
Mammoth Cave
Green River Lake

Berea
E. Bernstadt
London
Corbin
Barbourville

Doniphan
Thayer
Campbell
Corning
Piggott
Pocahontas
Rector
Walnut Ridge
Paragould
Hoxie
Batesville
Jonesboro
Newport
Trumann
Augusta
Des Arc
Wynne
West Memphis
Forrest City
Brinkley
Marianna
Clarendon
Stuttgart
De Witt
Gillett
Helena
W. Helena

Hickman
Fulton
Union City
Martin
Paris
Dyersburg
Trenton
Newbern
Greenfield
McKenzie
Bruceton
Humboldt
Milan
Huntingdon
Jackson
Lexington
Henderson

Clarksville
Springfield
Hendersonville
Gallatin
Waverly
Dickson
Nashville
Franklin
Murfreesboro
Columbia
Mount Pleasant
Shelbyville
Lewisburg
Tullahoma

Hopkinsville
Elkton
Russellville
Scottsville
Franklin
Bowling Green
Glasgow

Scottsville
Livingston
Cookeville
Monterey
Sparta
McMinnville

Williamsburg
Pineville
Middlesboro
La Follette
Clinton
Oak Ridge

Morris
Norris Lake
Mascot
Knoxville
Alcoa
Maryville
GREAT SMC
Clingmans Dome 6643

Memphis
Covington
Somerville
Selmer
Bolivar
Savannah
Lawrenceburg
Pulaski
Fayetteville
Winchester
South Pittsburg

Corinth
Iuka
Florence
Sheffield
Tuscumbia
Muscle Shoals
Athens
Decatur

Harriman
Rockwood
Dayton
Dunlap
Whitwell
Tracy City

Lenoir City
Loudon
Sweetwater
Athens
Etowah
Cleveland
Ducktown
Copperhill

Andrews
Murphy

Holly Springs
Ripley
Booneville
New Albany
Tupelo
Pontotoc
Okolona
Aberdeen

Russellville
Hartselle
Haleyville
Cullman

Huntsville
Scottsboro
Guntersville
Albertville
Fort Payne

Bridgeport
Rossville
Chickamauga
La Fayette
Trion
Calhoun

Chattanooga
Dalton

Rome
Lindale
Cartersville

Rockmart
Cedartown

Canton
Gainesville
Commerce
Jefferson
Winder

Cornelia
Toccoa
Lake Sidney Lanier

Batesville
Oxford
Water Valley
Charleston
Sardis Lake
Enid Lake

Houston
Pontotoc

Hamilton
Carbon Hill
Jasper
Corona
Cordova
Oakman
Fayette

Altoona
Gadsden
Attalla

Jacksonville
Anniston
Oxford
Heflin

Tallapoosa
Douglasville
Marietta
Atlanta
East Point
Decatur

Roswell
Buford
Lawrenceville
Conyers
Porterdale

Stone Mtn. 1683
Monroe
Covington
Madison

Tutwiler
Clarksdale
Shelby
Cleveland
Shaw
Indianola
Moorhead
Greenwood
Winona

Grenada
Grenada Lake

West Point
Starkville
Columbus
Reform
Northport
Tuscaloosa
W. Blocton

Birmingham
Fairfield
Bessemer
Brookwood
Leeds
Homewood
Mtn. Brook
Vincent

Columbiana
Montevallo
Brierfield
Clanton
Ashland
Sylacauga
Talladega
Lineville
Alexander City

Lafayette
Dadeville
Lanett
West Point

Roanoke
Hogansville
Barnesville
Griffin
Jackson
Forsyth
Eatonton
Monticello
Milledgeville

LaGrange
Manchester
Thomaston
Macon

Belzoni
Lake Village
Greenville
Eudora
Lake Providence
Tallulah
Vicksburg

Lexington
Durant
Kosciusko
Louisville
Macon

Philadelphia
Union
Forest

Livingston
Eutaw
Greensboro
Demopolis
Uniontown
Marion
Selma

Wetumpka
Prattville
Montgomery

Tallassee
Auburn
Opelika
Tuskegee

Phenix City
Bibb City
Columbus
Marshallville
Perry
Fort Valley

Warner Robins
Buena Vista
Montezuma
Hawkinsville

Yazoo City
Canton
Jackson
Crystal Springs
Port Gibson
Hazlehurst

Pelahatchie
Newton
Stonewall
Quitman

Meridian
Butler
Thomasville
Linden
Camden
Fort Deposit
Greenville

Midway
Union Springs
Clayton
Eufaula
Troy

Richland
Americus
Cordele
Ashburn
Sylvester
Albany
Dawson
Cuthbert
Fort Gaines

Vidalia
Natchez
Brookhaven
Bogue Chitta
McComb
Magnolia
Woodville

Fayette
Collins
Laurel
Ellisville
Sumrall
Richton
Columbia
Jackson

Georgiana
Luverne
Monroeville
Evergreen
River Falls
Andalusia
Opp
Enterprise
Elba
Samson
Hartford
Geneva

Abbeville
Ozark
Headland
Dothan
Donalsonville

Arlington
Camilla
Pelham
Moultrie
Adel
Tifton

Jackson
Kentwood
Tylertown
Lumberton
Poplarville
Wiggins

Bay Minette
Century
Atmore
Brewton
Florala

Crestview
Milton
De Funiak Springs

Graceville
Bonifay
Chipley
Marianna
Cairo
Thomasville
Boston
Quitm

Amite
Bogalusa
Franklinton
Carriere
Picayune

Prichard
Stapleton
Mobile
Pensacola
W. Pensacola
Warrington

Bountstown
Chattahoochee
Quincy
Tallahassee
Madison

Baton Rouge
Hammond
Covington
Madisonville
Slidell
Gulfport
Pass Christian
Bay St. Louis
Biloxi
Ocean Springs
Pascagoula
Moss Point
Mobile Bay

Panama City
Apalachicola
Carrabelle
Apalachee Bay
Cross S

White Castle
Donaldsonville
Napoleonville
Thibodaux
Morgan City
Houma

New Orleans
Metairie
Kenner
Gretna
Marrero
Lake Pontchartrain
Mississippi R.

CHANDELEUR ISLANDS

Breton Sound
Port Sulphur
Caillou Bay
Terrebonne Bay
Timbalier Bay
Barataria Bay

St. Joseph Bay
CAPE SAN BLAS
CAPE ST. GEORGE
West Bay

GULF OF MEXICO

90°   88°   86°   84°

Longitude West of Greenwich

Scale 1:4 000 000; one inch to 64 miles. Conic P
Elevations and depressions are given in fe

Relief

Meters		Feet
1525		5000
610		2000
305		1000
152.5		500
0	Sea Level	0
152.5		500
1525		5000

a

Same scale as main map

a

Scale 1:1 000 000

PANAMA

Caribbean Sea

Bahía de Panamá

Scale 1:16 000 000; one inch to 250 miles. Polyconic Pro

Elevations and depressions are given in feet

A-530000-76-9 8-25
COPYRIGHT BY
RAND MCNALLY & COMPANY
MADE IN U.S.A.

Continued on pages 130-131

Continued on pages 112-113

106°   104°   102°   100°

S I E R R A

N U E V O

Ascensión
Hidalgo

Jiménez

Abaso
Padilla

San Dimas
Durango

Miguel Auza
Juan Aldama

Z A C A T E C A S

Gruñidora

Aramberri
Zaragoza

Ciudad Victoria

Soto la Marín

El Salto
Nombre de Dios
Nieves
Río Grande

Vanegas
Cedral
La Paz
Matehuala

Peña Nevada
13 300

T A M A U L I P A

Pánuco
Mezquital
Chalchihuites
Sain Alto
Cañitas

Doctor Arroyo
Miquihuana

Llera

Siqueros
Concordia
Villa Unión

10 100
Sombrerete

Catorce

Mier y
Noriega

Jaumave

Xicotencati

Ciudad Mante

S I N A L O A
Santa María
de Ocotán
C. Pimal
11 700

Fresnillo

Calera
Víctor Rosales
Morelos

Charcas

S A N   L U I S

Venado
Moctezuma

Villa de
Guadalupe

Ocampo

Magiscatzin
Gonza

Rosario
Escuinapa

Valparaíso
Huejuquilla el Alto
Ciudad
García
Zacatecas

Ramos

Bocas
Peotillos

Guadalcázar

Ciudad del Maíz

El Ebano
Pan

N A Y A R I T
Mezquitic
Huejúcar
Villanueva

Ojocaliente
Salinas

11 000

P O T O S I

Cerritos

Soledad Díez Gutiérrez
Pozos
Zaragoza

Ciudad del Maíz

Tamuín
Cárdenas

San Felipe
Rosamorada
Ruiz
Tuxpan

Monte
Escobedo
Sta. María de
los Angeles
Rincón
de Romos
Tepezalá

Villa García

San Luis
Potosí

Gogorrón

Ojo Caliente
Sta. María del Río

Ciudad de Valles

Laguna
de Agua Brava

Acaponeta
Tecuala
San Blas
Jalisco

Colotlán

A G U A S C A L I E N T E S

Calvillo
Aguascalientes

Fernández
Ríoverde

Villa de
Reyes
Villa Pedro
Montoya

Lagunillas
Arroyo Seco

General Pedro
Antonio Santos

San Felipe

San Diego
de la Unión

San Luis
de la Paz

Xilitla
San Martín
Chalchi
Tamazunchale

Tepic
Pochotitán
Chimaltitán

Bolaños
(Tlaltenango)
Sánchez Román

Tabasco
M E X I C A N A
Villa
Hidalgo

Encarnación
de Díaz

Dolores Hidalgo

10 469

Huitzitzilingo
Jaltocan
Huaut
Jala

Sta. María
del Oro
San Pedro
Lagunillas

Jaipa

Teocaltiche

Lagos de
Moreno

Jalpan
Jacala
Calnalí

Compostela
Jala

Jiménez del Teul
Juchipila

San Juan
de los Lagos

León

G U A N A J U A T O

La Luz

San Luis
de la Paz

Tolimán
Zimapán
Zacualtipan
Ixt

PUNTA
DE MITA

SIERRA
DE VALLEJO
O C C I D E N T A L

Nochistlán
Mexticacán

Yahualica
Jalostotlán

Guanajuato
Silao
Romita

San Miguel
de Allende

Colón

Metztitlán

Bahía de
Banderas

Puerto Vallarta

Amatlán de Cañas
Ahualulco

García de la Cadena
Moyahua

Cuquío

San Miguel
el Alto
Tepatitlán de Morelos

San Francisco
del Rincón

Comonfort

Cadereyta
Tasquillo
Ixmiquilpan

CABO
CORRIENTES

Talpa de Allende
Mascota

Etzatlán

J A L I S C O

Arandas

Ciudad Manuel
Doblado

Irapuato

Juventino
Rosas

Querétaro
Cayetano Rubio

Apasa

Huichapan
Mixquiahuala

Actopan

Atotonilco e
Huai

S A. D E L C U A L E

Tenamaxtlán
Ayutla

Cocula
Tecolotlán

Zapopan
Guadalajara
Tlaquepaque
Tonalá
Zapotlanejo

Atotonilco el Alto
Ayo
el Chico

Ciudad Manuel
Doblado

Salamanca

Cortazar

Juventino
Rosas

Celaya

Valle de
Santiago

Tequisquiapan

San Juan
del Río

Tecozautla

Q U E R É T A R O

Tula

Tezontepec de Aldama

H I D A L G O

Mineral del
Chico

Atotonilco e
Mineral del
Monte

Pachuca
Tulancingo

Cuautep

Tala

Jocotepec
Chapala

Ocotlán
Jamay
La Barca

Pénjamo

La Piedad
Cabadas
Angamacutiro

Jaral del Progreso
Salvatierra

Acámbaro

Amealco

Teloloapan
Maravatío

El Oro

Huatamo de Núñez

Tepeji
del Río

Toltayuca
Atotonilco e
Huejutla

Tezontepec
Teoloyucan

Tula
Apan

Tepeapulco
Tulancingo

Otumba

Juchitlán

Unión
de Tula

Venustiano
Carranza

Sayula

Tamazula
de Gordiano

Jiquilpan
de Juárez

Chavinda

Zamora

Purépero
Chilchota

Cotija
de la Paz

Tinguindin
Los Reyes

Villa Morelos

Zacapú
Cherán

Coeneo de la Libertad
Zinapécuaro

Quiroga
Morelia

Ciudad
Hidalgo
Anganguéo

Ixtlahuaca
de Rayón

C. G. A.
MADERO
Atzcapotzalco

MEXICO
CITY

Coyoacán

Temascaltepec
Texmelucan
Sta.

Purificación
El Grullo

Tomatlán

Ciudad Guzmán
Zapotiltic
Tuxpan
Tecalitlán

Pátzcuaro

Uruapan
Paracho

Zitácuaro

Capulhuac

Toluca

Tlatlaya

Metepec
Tlalpan

Almoloya
DISTRITO FEDERAL
Tenango

Amecameca
Volcán
Cholula

17 159

Calpula
Apizac

Nevado de Colima
13 911
de Colima
12 620
Comala

Minatitlán

Tuxpan
Tecalitlán

Cerro
de Tancítaro
12 660
9 186

Tacámbaro de Codallos

Acuitzio del Canje
Tacámbaro

Turicato

Valle de Bravo

Nevado de Toluca
14 409

Tenancingo
Tenango

Tejupilco
de Hidalgo

Tecaltitlán
Malinalco
Zacualpan

Pop.catépetl
930

Temcat

Volcán 17 930
Iztaccíhuatl

Atlí

PTA. FARALLÓN

C O L I M A
Cihuatlán

Colima
Villa de Álvarez
Tepalcatepec
Tancítaro

Coalcomán de Matamoros

Carácuaro de Morelos

Miacatlán

C U E R N A V A C A

M O R E L O S

Huaquechula

Bahía de
Manzanillo

Manzanillo

Cuyutlán

Tecomán

Apatzingán
de la Constitución

M I C H O A C Á N

Coatetelco

Tetecala

Tlaltizapán

Cuautla
Jojutla

Tepalcingo

Axochiapan
Tehuitzingo

Jiguro de
Trujano

Ac

Tumbiscatío

Coalcomán de Matamoros
Aguililla

S I E R R A   D E

Coalcomán

V. de Toruño
4 330

Churumuco
Huetamo de Núñez

Zirándaro
de Pinzón
Ciudad Altamirano
Coahuayutla
Coyuca de Catalán

Tlapehuala

Ajuchitlán del Progreso

Zacualpan

Cuetzalá
del Progreso

Río Balsas

Acapulco
Taxco
de Alarcón

Iguala
Huitzuco

Apipilulco

Tepecoacuilco
de Trujano

Tlacotepec

Tulcingo

Xochih

PUNTA TEJUPAN

Coahuayutla

Tlacotepec

Apango

Zitlala

Olinalá
Huamuxtlán

La Unión

S I E R R A

Petatlán

G U E R R E R O
Chilpancingo
de los Bravo

Tixtla de Guerrero

Atliaca

Tecpan
de Galeana

M A D R E

Chilapa

Mochitlán

Hueycatepango

Tlapa
Sile

Zapotitlán

San Jerónimo
de Juárez

Atoyac de Álvarez

Coyuca de Benítez

San Marcos

Malinalte

Ayutla

Cozoye
Ometep

P A C I F I C   O C E A N

Acapulco
Cuautepec

Tecoanapa

Azóyu

Santa C.

PTA. MALDONADO

Puer

A-531695-76   6 14
COPYRIGHT BY
RAND McNALLY & COMPANY
MADE IN U.S.A.

Longitude West of Greenwich

104°   102°   100°

Cities and Towns

0 to 50,000 ○   500,000 to 1,000,000 ◉

50,000 to 500,000 ⊙   1,000,000 and over

Scale 1:4 000 000; one inch to 64 miles. Conic Pro
Elevations and depressions are given in feet

24°   22°   20°   18°   16°

a

Morelos
Cuautitlán
Tecamac
Teotihuacán
Otumba
HIDALGO

Nicolás
Romero
Coacalco
Acolman
Chiconautla
Tepexpan
Pyramids of Teotihuacán
Calpulalpan

Cahuacán
Tutitlán
TLAXCALA

San Bartolo
Atizapán
Tlalnepantla
Tulpetlac
Tepetlaoxtoc
San Jerónimo
Nanacamilpa

Ixtlahuaca
Mazatla
Texcoco

Jiquipilco
Cerro
La Catedral
13 000
Atzcapotzalco
Naucalpan
de Juárez
Gustavo A. Madero
Lago de
Texcoco
(Dry Lake)
San Jerónimo

Temoaya
Mimiapan
Chimalpa
**MEXICO
CITY**
Coatlinchán

Huixquilucan
Cuajimalpa
Ixtacalco
Nezahualcóyotl
Chicoloapan

Toluca
Lerma
Villa Obregón
Contreras
Ixtapalapa
Los Reyes
Río Frío

Capultitlán
Metepec
Mexicalcingo
San Andrés
Tláhuac
Tlalpan
Xochimilco
Coyoacán
Ayotla
Ixtapaluca
INTER - AMERICAN
Texmelucan
PUEBLA

Cerro Muneco
12 655
Ajusco
Topilejo
Tecómitl
Milpa
Alta
Tlalmanalco
Iztaccíhuatl
17 343

Almoloya
Cerro
Ajusco
12 850
Oxtotepec
Tenango
Amecameca

Nevado de Toluca
14 409
Coatepec
DISTRITO
FEDERAL

Tenango
Tres Cumbres
Ozumba
Volcán
Popocatépetl
17 887

Scale 1:1 000 000
Huitzilac
Tepoztlán
Tlalnepantla

0   10 Miles
0 4 8 12 16 Kilometers
©RMcN
MORELOS
Tlayacapan

Cuernavaca

96° 99°30' 99° 98°30'
24°
19°30'
22°
19°

GULF OF MEXICO

94° 92° 90°

BAHÍA DE CAMPECHE

YUCATÁN
Sisal
Hunucmá
Maxcanú
Halachó
Calkini
Dzitbalché
Hecelchakán

Lerma
Campeche
Seybaplaya
Champotón
Pustunich
CAMPECHE
Chicbul
Mamantel

ISLA DEL
CARMEN
Laguna
de Términos
Arroyo Caribe

San Pedro
PUNTA FONTERA
Ciudad
del Carmen
Sabancuy

Paraíso
Frontera
Palizada

Allende
Comalcalco
Jalpa
Cárdenas
Cunduacán
Jonuta
TABASCO
Balancán
MEXICO
GUATEMALA

Villahermosa
San Carlos
Emiliano Zapata

Huimanguillo
Tacotalpa
Teapa
Patenque
Palenque
Tenosique

Pichucalco
MESETA
DE AGUA
ESCONDIDA

Chapultenango
Yajalón

Tecpatán
Pantepec
Simojovel
Bachajón
Ocosingo

Compainalá
Jitotol

Cancuc
Oxchuc
Tuxtla
Gutiérrez
9400
Ocozocautla
Chiapa de Corzo
Bohóm
San Cristóbal de las Casas

Berriozabal
Acala
Suchiapa
Amatenango
Teopisca
Las Rosas

Cintalapa
Las Cruces
Chiapa
CHIAPAS
Venustiano Carranza
Socoltenango
Comitán

8202
Villa Flores
La Concordia
Trinitaria

Arriaga
SA. CUCHUMATANES
GUATEMALA

Tonalá
La Concordia

SIERRA
MADRE
Cuauhtémoc
Jacaltenango

CORD. DE CHIAPAS
Pijijiapan

Mapastepec

18°
20°
16°

Tropic of Cancer

CABO ROJO
BARRECIFE BLANQUILLA
ISLA DE LOBOS

Tamiahua
ARRECIFE TANQUIJO
ARRECIFE TÚXPAN

Poza Rica
Tecolutla
Gutiérrez Zamora
Furbero
Nautla

Coxquihui
Vega de Alatorre

Cuetzalan
Tlapacoyan
Misantla

Atempan
Jalacingo
Altotonga
Naolinco
PUNTA ZEMPOALA

Perote
Las Vigas
Xalapa
Antigua Veracruz

14 048
Coatepec
Teocelo
Veracruz
ARRECIFE CABEZA

Huatusco
Cascomatepec
Medellin
Tlatixcoyan
Jamapa

Ciudad
Serdán
Pico de Orizaba (Vol.)
18 406
Orizaba
Córdoba
Omealca
Cotaxtla

Maltrata
Heroico
Nogales
Alvarado

Tehuacan
Zoquitlán
Tierra Blanca
San Martín (Vol.)
6000
Santiago
Tuxtla
PTA ZAPOTILÁN

Gabriel
Ajalpan
Huatla
de Jiménez
San Andrés Tuxtla
Catemaco

Chilac
Zinacatepec
Ojitlán
(S. Lucas)
Cosamaloápan
Chacaltianguis
Pajapán
Coatzacoalcos
(Puerto México)

S. Miguel
Teotitlán
del Camino
Jalapa
de Díaz
(San Felipe)
Tesecheacan
Soteapan
Acayucan
Minatitlán

Tepelmeme
Coixtlahuaca
Cuicatlán
Tuxtepec
Jaltipan
Texistepec
Sayula

Tejúpan (Santiago)
Playa Vicente
San Juan
Evangelista
Jesús Carranza
Cosoleacaque

Nochixtlán
(Asunción)
San Pablo
Ixtlán de Juárez
Talea de Castro
(San Miguel)
Villa Alta (San Ildefonso)
Puebla Viejo

María Asunción
Hidalgo
Yalalag
Zempoaltépetl
11 142
Zacatepec (Santiago)
ISTMO
DE
TEHUANTEPEC

Chalcatongo
San Mateo
(Etlatongo)
Oaxaca
Zaachila
Tlacolula de
Matamoros
Mazatlán
(San Juan)
Guichicovi
(San Juan)

Sta. Catarina
Zimatlán
de Alvarez
Ocotlán
de Morelos
Ixtepec
Ixtaltepec
(Asunción)
Unión Hidalgo
Berriozabal

Cruz
Sola de Vega
(S. Miguel)
Tavíche
Ejutla de Crespo
INTER
AMERICAN
HY
Jalapa del
Marqués
Ixtepec
Juchitán de Zaragoza
Tapanatepec

Sta. María
Miahuatlán
Las Vacas
Tehuantepec
Sto. Domingo
Ixhuatán (San Francisco)
Arriaga

SIERRA DE OAXACA
OAXACA
SUR
Laguna
Superior
Laguna
Inferior
Mar Muerto

Loxicha (Sta. Catarina)
Salina Cruz
Golfo de Tehuantepec

Pluma Hidalgo
Pochutla (San Pedro)
Puerto Ángel

CORDOBA
VERACRUZ

Laguna
del Carmen
Laguna
Rosario
Laguna
Matillas
Usumacinta

96° 94° 92°

20 40 60 80 100 120 Miles
40 80 120 140 160 180 200 Kilometers

For larger scale coverage
of Mexico City see page 233.

Continued on pages 120-121

Continued on pages 118-119
Continued in inset below

92° 90° 88° 86°

MEXICO

Comitán
Trinitaria
(Zapaluta)
16°
Cuauhtémoc
Jacaltenango
La Libertad
Huehuetenango
Tacaná (Vol.)
13 417
Tajumulco (Vol.)
13 845
S. Marcos
S. María (Vol.)
12 363
Tapachula
Quezaltenango
Ayutla
Coatepeque
Retalhuleu
Cuyotenango
Ocós
Champerico
Concepción
del Mar
San José
14°

Santa Cruz Barillas
S. Cristóbal
Cobán
Panzós
Quiché
Momostenango
Totonicapán
Sololá
Comalapa Chimaltenango
Patzicía
Patzún
Mazatenango
Fuego (Vol.)
12 582
Agua (Vol.)
12 307

GUATEMALA

SA. DE LOS CUCHUMATANES
SA. DE CHAMA
SA. DE LAS MINAS
SA. DE MERENDÓN

BELIZE
Monkey River
Punta Gorda
Barranco
Bahía de
Amatique
Livingston
Puerto Barrios
Morales
Golfo Dulce
Izabal
L. Izabal
Gualán
Zacapa
Copán
(Ruins)
Santa Rosa
Chiquimula
Quezaltepeque
Jalapa
San Luis
Jilotepeque
Salama
Sanarate
Palencia
Guatemala
Antigua
Amatitlán
Palín
Escuintla
Santa Rosa
Cuilapa
Jutiapa
Asunción
Mita
Moyuta
Ahuachapán
Ahuizaya
Chalchuapa
Santa Ana
Chalatenango
Suchitoto
Ilobasco
Sensuntepeque
San Pedro
Quezaltepeque
Ojutepeque
San Vicente
San Francisco
Gotera
Chinameca
Coatepeque
Nahuizalco Izalco
Sonsonate
Armenia
Acajutla
Nueva S. Salvador
(Santa Tecla)
San Salvador
La Libertad
Usulután
Zacatecoluca
Jiquilisco
El Triunfo
S. Miguel (Vol.)
6994
San Miguel
Sirama
La Unión
Juquapa
Golfo de Fonseca
Cosiguina (Vol.)
2 776

ROATAN
Roatán
UTILA
Puerto Castilla
Limón
Nueva
Armenia
Balfate
Puerto
Cortés
Omoa
Bahía de
Tela
Progreso
San Pedro
Sula
Macuelizo
Villanueva
Potrerillos
Santa Bárbara
Yoro
Minas de Oro
Salamá
Cedros
Tela
Salado
La Ceiba
Trujillo
Tocoa
San Esteban
Catacamas
Juticalpa
Comayagua
Talanga
La Paz
Marcala
La Esperanza
Siguatepeque
Tegucigalpa
Yuscarán
Sabanagrande
Gascorán
San Lorenzo
Choluteca
Amapala
El Triunfo
Nacaome
San Marcos
de Colón
Danlí
El Paraíso
Ocotal
Somoto
El Espino
Condega
Estelí
Jinotega
Matagalpa
Sébaco
Ciudad Darío

HONDURAS

CORDILLERA DE AGAL

SIERRA DE OPALACA
CORDILLERA DE MONTECILLOS

CORD. DE
CORDILLERA

NICAR

El Viejo (Vol.)
5839
Santa Clara (Vol.)
4512
Telica (Vol.)
3409
Chinandega
El Viejo
Corinto
León
Las Pilas (Vol.)
3515
Guisisil (Vol.)
3900
Surface
elev.
120 ft.
Tipitapa
Momotombo
Nagarote
Managua
Masaya
Masatepe
Granada
Diriamba
Jinotepe
Surface elev.
105 ft.
above sea level
ISLA
ZAPATERA
Concepción (Vol.)
5106
ISLA DE
Mad 4960

Boaco

Lago

PACIFIC   OCEAN

San Juan del Sur
La Cruz
Orosí (Vol.)
Liberia
Filadelfia
Santa
Cruz
PEN.
DE NICOYA

CORD.
CORD.
C
Nicoya

Inset map (a)

GULF OF MEXICO

Lagartos
El Cuyo
ISLA
HOLBOX
Holbox
Progreso
Dzilam
González
Dzidzantún
Panabá
Isla Mujeres
Cancún
Sisal
Chicxulub
Motul
Cansahcab
Temax
Tizimín
Kantunilkín
Mérida
Hunucmá
Tixkokob
Izamal
Espita
Calotmul
Celestún
Kanasín
Seyé
Hoctún
Acancéh
Dzitás
Chichimilá
Umán

YUCATAN

Chichén Itzá
(Ruins)
Valladolid
Maxcanú
Halachó
Muna
Tekit
Sotuta
Cozumel
Becal
Ticul
Teabo
ISLA DE
COZUMEL
Calkiní
Uxmal
(Ruins)
Oxkutzcab
Coba (Ruins)
Dzitbalché
Tekax de
Álvaro Obregón
Peto
Tulum
(Ruins)
Hecelchakán
Pomuch
Tzucacab
Nunkiní
Bolonchenticul
20°
Tenabó

YUCATAN

PENINSULA

PUNTA
NICCHEHABIN

Campeche
Hopelchén
Iturbide
Lago de
Chichancanab
Felipe Carrillo Puerto
Bahía de la
Ascensión

QUINTANA

Hool
Dzibalchén
L. Ocom
ROO

CAMPECHE
Pedro Antonio Santos
(Sta. Cruz Chico)
PUNTA
HERRERO
Aguada
Carolina
Laguna de
Bácalar
Espíritu Santo

MEXICO

BANCO
CHINCHORRO
O L. Misteriosa
10°
Ciudad Chetumal
(Payo Obispo)
Corozal
18°
Xcalak
Orange Walk
AMBERGRIS
CAY
MEX.

CARIBBEAN SEA

BELIZE
Belize
City
TURNEFFE
Tikal
(Ruins)
(Ruins)
(Ruins)
Belmopan
San
Ignacio
Mullins River
Benque Viejo
(Ruins)
Stann Creek
All Pines
Laguna de Petén
(S. Andrés)
Flores
GUATEMALA
La Libertad
(Ruins)
MONTAÑAS
MAYAS
Victoria
Peak 3681
(Ruins)
R. San Pedro
La Pasión
(Ruins)
Monkey River

Same scale as main map

Longitude West of Greenwich

90° 88° 86°

Cities and Towns

0 to 50,000	○	500,000 to 1,000,000 ◎
50,000 to 500,000 ⊙		1,000,000 and over

Scale 1:4 000 000; one inch to 64 miles. Sinusoidal P
Elevations and depressions are given in feet

Longitude West of Greenwich

ANGUILLA (Br.)
ST. MARTIN (Neth. and Fr.)
ST. BARTHÉLEMY (Fr.)

SABA (Neth.)
ST. EUSTATIUS (Neth.)
Mt. Misery 3792
Basseterre
ST. KITTS
ST. KITTS AND NEVIS
Charlestown Nevis Peak 3596
NEVIS

Codrington   BARBUDA

St. Johns
ANTIGUA AND BARBUDA
Boggy Peak 1319
REDONDA

MONTSERRAT (Br.)
Plymouth   Chances Pk. 3000

Relief

Meters	Feet
3050	10 000
1525	5000
610	2000
305	1000
152.5	500
Sea Level	
152.5	500
1525	5000
3050	10 000

b

POINTE DE LA GRANDE VIGIE
GRANDE TERRE
Ste. Rose   Le Moule   DESIRADE (Fr.)
Pointe-à-Pitre   Ste. Anne   PETITE TERRE (Fr.)
BASSE TERRE
Soufrière 4813
Basse Terre   Capesterre (Fr.)   GUADELOUPE
LES SAINTES IS.   MARIE GALANTE
Grand Bourg

L E E W A R D

Guadeloupe Passage

Portsmouth   Morne Diablotins 4747
St. Joseph   **DOMINICA**
Roseau

Dominica Channel

Mt. Pelée (Vol.) 4583
St. Pierre   Trinité
Pitons du Carbet 3960
Fort-de-France   Le François
Le Marin   **MARTINIQUE (Fr.)**
POINTE D'ENFER

St. Lucia Channel

Castries
Morne Gimie 3117   **ST. LUCIA**
Soufrière

I S.

C A R I B B E A N   S E A

W I N D W A R D

St. Vincent Passage

Soufrière 4048
ST. VINCENT AND THE GRENADINES
Kingstown
BEQUIA
MUSTIQUE
CANOUAN

THE GRENADINES

CARRIACOU

Mt. St. Catherine 2757
St. George's   Grenville
GRENADA

NORTH POINT
BARBADOS
Mt. Hillaby 1115   Bathsheba
Bridgetown
SOUTH POINT

A T L A N T I C   O C E A N

©RMcN.

Same scale as main map

PUNTA PATUCA

Cabo Gracias a Dios

Coco (Segovia)

CAYOS MISKITO

C A R I B B E A N

Lone Star
Laguna Carata
Puerto Cabezas

M O S Q U I T O S

Laguna Caratasca

Prinzapolca
Huaunta
Prinzapolca
Laguna Huaunta

Laguna las Perlas

ISLA DE PROVIDENCIA (Colombia)

S E A

LITTLE CORN
GREAT CORN
SAN ANDRÉS (Colombia)
CAYOS DE ESE
CAYOS DE ALBUQUERQUE (Colombia)

Rama
Bluefields
ISLA DE LA CIERVO

Escondido

Punta Mico

Rio Punta Gorda

Bahía de San Juan del Norte

San Juan del Norte (Greytown)

Carlos

C O S T A

PUNTA QUEPOS

Alajuela Heredia Cairo Matina
San José 11 260
Cartago Paraíso Irazú (Vol.) Turrialba
Limón

R I C A

Parrita
Quepos

PUNTA CAHUITA

Cerro Chirripó 12 530

Bahía de Coronada

Puerto Cortés

Cerro Kámuk 11 696
Cerro Echandi 10 394
Boquete
Volcán Barú 11 401

ISLA DE CAÑO
PENÍNSULA DE OSA
Puerto Jiménez
Golfito

CABO MATAPALO

Golfo Dulce
Puerto Armuelles

PUNTA BURICA

C O R D I L L E R A   D E   T A L A M A N C A

Buenos Aires

Guabito
Bocas del Toro
Bahía de Almirante
Almirante

PUNTA CHIRIQUI

Laguna de Chiriquí
Chiriquí Grande

Golfo de los Mosquitos

ESCUDO DE VERAGUAS

La Cuesta
Concepción
David
Horconcitos

Bahía Charco de Azul

C. de Santa Catalina
SERRANÍA DE TABASARÁ 5249
C. Negro 4429

Remedios
Las Palmas
Soná
Santiago

PENÍNSULA DE AZUERO

ISLA COIBA

ISLA CEBACO

Bahía Montijo

Río de Jesús Chitré Los Santos
Las Tablas

PUNTA MALA

ISLA JICARÓN

PUNTA MARIATO

Punta Manzanillo Nombre de Dios El Porvenir PUNTA SAN BLAS
Portobelo Mandinga Golfo de San Blas
Colón Gatún Silver City
C. Brewster 3018   CORD. DE SAN BLAS

ISTMO DE PANAMÁ

Lago Gatún
North Gamboa
Balboa Heights
Balboa Panamá Chepo

P A N A M Á

Chorrera Bahía de Panamá

PUNTA CHAME

Bejuco
Penonomé
Antón
Natá
Aguadulce
Río Hato

Golfo de Parita

ARCHIPIÉLAGO DE LAS PERLAS

San Miguel
ISLA DEL REY

ISLA DE SAN JOSE
Bahía San Miguel

La Palma

Garachiné
PUNTA GARACHINE

Golfo de Panamá

El Real

CABO TIBURON

S E R R A N Í A   D E L   D A R I E N

C O L O M B I A

| 20 | 40 | 60 | 80 | 100 | 120 Miles |
| 40 | 80 | 120 | 160 | 200 Kilometers |

122

FLORIDA

SANIBEL

Naples
Big Cypress
Swamp
SEMINOLE
IND. RES.
Delray Beach

Fort Lauderdale
Dania

GULF

CAPE ROMANO
TEN THOUSAND
ISLANDS
Everglades
EVERGLADES
MIAMI
Miami Beach
Biscayne
Bay

OF
EVERGLADES
NATIONAL PARK
Homestead
Whitewater
Bay
KEY
LARGO

GREAT ISAAC
LITTLE ISAAC
BROTHERS

NORTH BIMINI
SOUTH BIMINI
Barnett Harbor
N. CAT CAY

Dollar Harbor

RIDING
ROCKS

ORANGE CAY

LITTLE BAHAMA
BANK
GREAT SALE
CAY
LITTLE
ABACO

SETTLEMENT PT.
West
End
Freeport GRAND BAHAMA
PINDER POINT

GREAT
ABACO

MORES
GORDA CAY

Northwest Providence Channel

GREAT STIRRUP
CAY
SOUTHWEST
PT.
BERRY

ISLANDS
BONDS CAY
WHALE CAY

FRAZIERS HOG CAY

JOULTER'S CAYS

Nicolls Town
Nassau Paradise
SIMMS PT.
NEW PROVIDENCE
Staniard Creek
Ship Channel Cay
HIGHBORNE CAY

26°

Marsh
Harbour
ELBOW

Cherokee
Sound

Cornwall

ROYAL

MEXICO

DRY TORTUGAS

MARQUESAS
KEYS

PINE IS.
Key
West
FLORIDA
KEYS

Florida Bay

Straits of Florida

Santaren
Bank

NORTH ELBOW CAYS

CAY SAL
BANK

CAY SAL

DOG ROCKS
DAMAS
CAYS

ANGUILLA
CAYS

HURRICANE FLATS

Nicholas Channel

WILLIAMS

ANDROS ISLAND

Turner Sound
North Bight
Middle Bight
South Bight

GREEN CAY

BOOBY R

SALVADOR PT.

SNAP PT.
CURLY CUT CAYS

SHROUD

24°

Tropic of Cancer

HAVANA
CIUDAD DE
LA HABANA
Marianao
Regla
Guanabacoa

Guangay
San Antonio de los Baños
Artemisa
Güira de Melena
Matanzas
Bejucal
Güines
Jovellanos
Alacranes

Bahía Honda

ARCHIPIELAGO DE
LOS COLORADOS

Pan de Guajaibón
2532

Candelaria

LOS PALACIOS

Consolación del Sur

SIERRA
VUELTA

Pinar del Río

Guane
San Juan y Martínez

PINAR
DEL RÍO

HABANA

Batabanó

Unión de Reyes

MATANZAS

Colón

Pedro Betancourt

Jagüey Grande

Santo Domingo

Corralillo

Martí

Quemado de Güines
Sagua la Grande

VILLA CLARA

Santa Clara

Esperanza
Cruces
Lajas
Rodas

CIENFUEGOS

Cienfuegos
Palmira

Remedios
Caibarién
Camajuaní
Zulueta

Yaguajay

Placetas

Florida

SANCTI
SPIRITUS

Jatibonico

Sancti Spiritus

CAYO BLANCOS

Bahía Matanzas
Bahía de Santa Clara
ARCHIPIELAGO DE SABANA
Cárdenas

Bahía de Cárdenas

CAYO

FRAGOSO

CAYO SANTA MARÍA

CAYO COCO

Bahía Buena
Vista

CAYO LOBOS

Old Bahama Channel

TURIGUANO

Morón
Laguna de
la Leche

CIEGO DE
ÁVILA

Ciego de Ávila

Júcaro

CAYO
CRUZ

CAYO GUAJABA

CAYO SABINAL

22°

84°

82°

80°

78°

Santa Lucía

ARCHIPIELAGO
DE LOS CANARREOS

Nueva Gerona
Santa Fé

ISLA DE LA
JUVENTUD

PTA. FRANCES

CABO FRANCES
CAYOS DE SAN FELIPE
CAYOS DE LOS INDIOS

CABO CORRIENTES

PEN.
DE GUANAHACABIBES

CABO PEPE

Bahía de
Guadiana

Ensenada de Cortés

GOLFO DE BATABANÓ

PUNTA GORDA

ISLAS DE MANGLES
CAYOS LAGUNA

CAYO DE DIOS

CAYOS DE
JUAN LUIS

PENÍNSULA DE ZAPATA

Ensenada
de la Broa

CAYO ROSARIO

CAYO CANTILES

CAYO LARGO

BANCO JARDINES

BANCO
XAGUA

Ensenada de la Siguanea

Laberinto de los Canarreos

Golfo de Cazones

Bahía de Cochinos

Pico San Juan
3792
Trinidad
SIERRA DE TRINIDAD
Casilda
Tunas de Zaza

CAYOS CINCO BALAS

CAYOS
ANA MARÍA

CAYOS
DE LAS DOCE LEGUAS

Canal de Caballones

LABERINTO DE LAS
DOCE LEGUAS

Fomento

CAMAGÜEY

Minas
Camagüey
Santa Lucía

Guayabal

Santa Cruz
del Sur

Nuevitas

Bahía de
Nuevitas

Puerto
Principe

LAS
TUNAS

Victoria de
las Tunas

GOLFO DE
GUACANAYABO

Campechuela

Niquero

Pico Ojo del Toro
1748

Manzan

GRA
SIERR

20°

CARIBBEAN

LITTLE CAYMAN
CAYMAN BRAC
(Br.)

CAYMAN ISLANDS

George Town
GRAND CAYMAN

CABO CRUZ

Montego Bay
Falmouth
St. Ann's B
Lucea
JAMAICA
Mt. Denham
3236
Bull Head
2728
SOUTH NEGRIL PT.
Savanna la Mar
May Pen
Black River
GT. PEDRO BLUFF
PORTLAND PT.

Annott

Port

18°

Relief

Meters   Feet
3050   10000
1525   5000
610   2000
305   1000
152.5   500
0 Sea Level 0
152.5   500
1525   5000
3050   10000
6100   20000

A-533200-76 6-40
COPYRIGHT BY
RAND McNALLY & COMPANY
MADE IN U.S.A.

84°

82°

80°

78°

Longitude West of Greenwich

**Cities
and
Towns**

0 to 50,000

50,000 to 500,000

500,000 to 1,000,000

1,000,000 and over

Scale 1:4 000 000; one inch to 64 miles. Conic Pr

Elevations and depressions are given in fee

For larger scale coverage
of Havana see page 233.

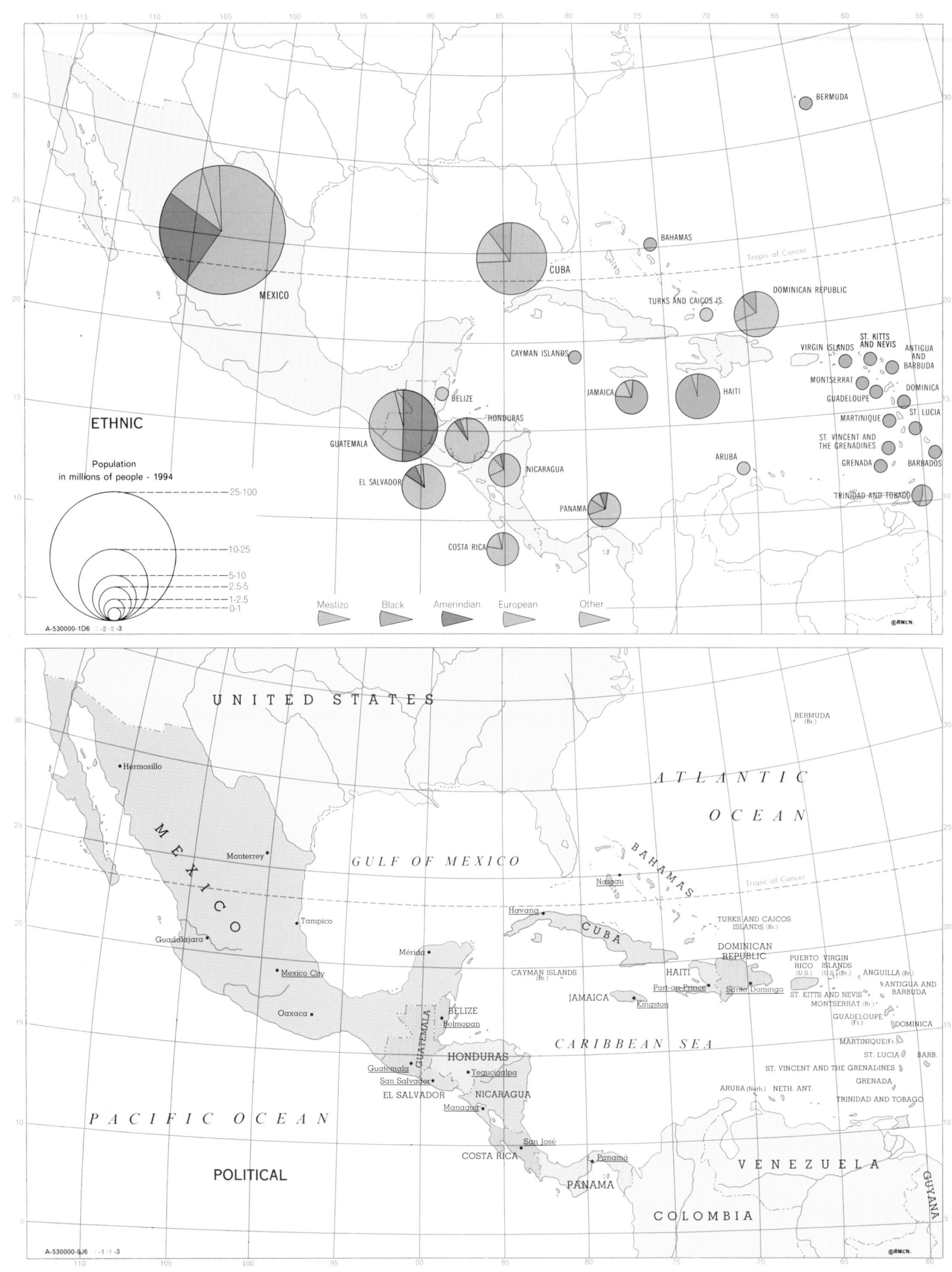

ETHNIC

Population
in millions of people - 1994

25-100

10-25

5-10
2.5-5
1-2.5
0-1

Mestizo   Black   Amerindian   European   Other

A-530000-1D6

BERMUDA

MEXICO

CUBA

BAHAMAS

TURKS AND CAICOS IS.

DOMINICAN REPUBLIC

CAYMAN ISLANDS

VIRGIN ISLANDS

ST. KITTS AND NEVIS

ANTIGUA AND BARBUDA

MONTSERRAT

DOMINICA

GUADELOUPE

ST. LUCIA

MARTINIQUE

ST. VINCENT AND THE GRENADINES

GRENADA

BARBADOS

BELIZE

HONDURAS

GUATEMALA

JAMAICA

HAITI

EL SALVADOR

NICARAGUA

ARUBA

COSTA RICA

PANAMA

TRINIDAD AND TOBAGO

Tropic of Cancer

©RMCN.

POLITICAL

UNITED STATES

• Hermosillo

M E X I C O

• Monterrey

GULF OF MEXICO

• Tampico

Guadalajara •

• Mexico City

Mérida •

• Oaxaca

ATLANTIC

OCEAN

BERMUDA (Br.)

BAHAMAS

Nassau •

Tropic of Cancer

Havana •

CUBA

CAYMAN ISLANDS (Br.)

TURKS AND CAICOS ISLANDS (Br.)

DOMINICAN REPUBLIC

HAITI

Port-au-Prince •

JAMAICA

Kingston •

Santo Domingo •

PUERTO RICO (U.S.)

VIRGIN ISLANDS (U.S.)(Br.)

ANGUILLA (Br.)

ST. KITTS AND NEVIS

ANTIGUA AND BARBUDA

MONTSERRAT (Br.)

GUADELOUPE (Fr.)

DOMINICA

MARTINIQUE (Fr.)

ST. LUCIA

CARIBBEAN SEA

BARB.

ST. VINCENT AND THE GRENADINES

GRENADA

ARUBA (Neth.)

NETH. ANT.

TRINIDAD AND TOBAGO

BELIZE

Belmopan •

GUATEMALA

HONDURAS

Guatemala •

• Tegucigalpa

San Salvador •

EL SALVADOR

NICARAGUA

Managua •

PACIFIC OCEAN

• San José

COSTA RICA

• Panama

PANAMA

VENEZUELA

COLOMBIA

GUYANA

A-530000-9J6

©RMCN.

ENERGY

Energy Producing Plants

·   Hydroelectric

■   Nuclear

Mineral Fuel Deposits

•   Uranium: major deposit

△   Natural Gas: major field

·   Petroleum: minor producing field

▲   Petroleum } major producing field

Petroleum

  Coal: major bituminous

  Coal: minor bituminous

  Coal: lignite

HYDRO. & NUCLEAR ELECTRICITY 14.7

SOLID 7.9

GAS 25.6

LIQUID 51.8%

Commercial Energy Consumption
323,900,000 metric tons coal equivalent - 1991

© RMcN

PEOPLES

Predominant Racial Groups

  European

  Andean Indian

  Other Indian

  Mixed European and Indian

  Mixed with large African proportion

Names on map represent significant language/culture groups

Map after
Preston E. James

© RMcN

NATURAL HAZARDS

○   Volcanoes*

●   Earthquakes*

●   Major flood disasters *

  Tsunamis

  Limit of iceberg drift

  Deserts

  Areas subject to desertification

*Twentieth Century occurrences

© RMcN

LANDFORMS

  Mountains

  Widely spaced mountains

  High tablelands

  Hills and low tablelands

  Depressions or basins

  Plains

  Limit of continental shelf

For description of landform regions,
see Landforms Map by R. E. Murphy, p. 6

A-540000-1S6-   -5-3-5

© RMcN

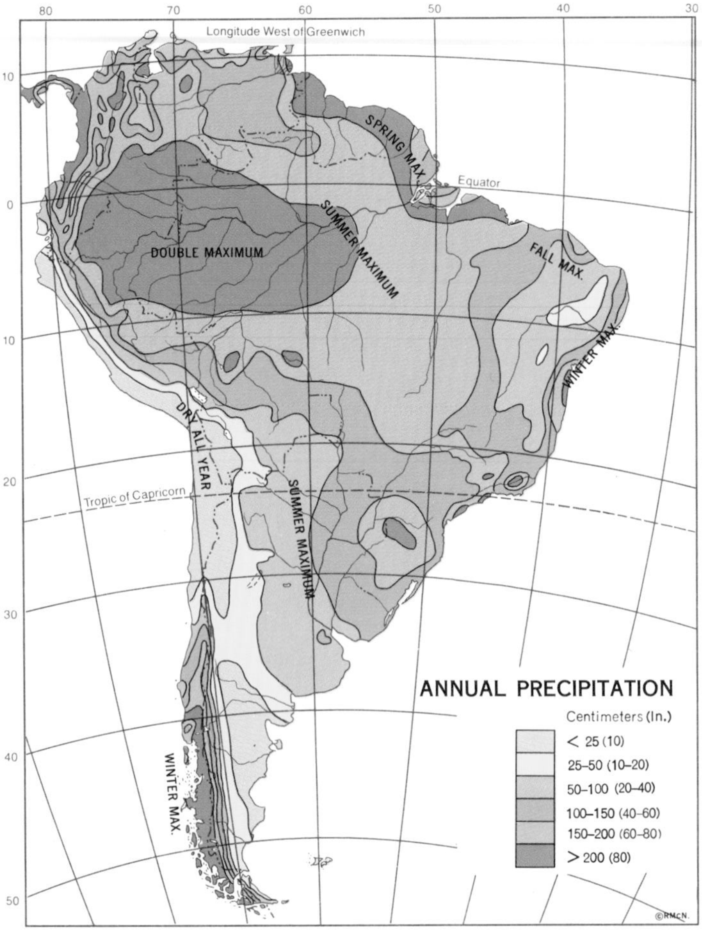

ANNUAL PRECIPITATION

Longitude West of Greenwich

Equator

Tropic of Capricorn

SPRING MAX.

SUMMER MAXIMUM

DOUBLE MAXIMUM

FALL MAX.

WINTER MAX.

DRY ALL YEAR

SUMMER MAXIMUM

WINTER MAX.

ANNUAL PRECIPITATION

Centimeters (In.)

- < 25 (10)
- 25–50 (10–20)
- 50–100 (20–40)
- 100–150 (40–60)
- 150–200 (60–80)
- > 200 (80)

©RMCN.

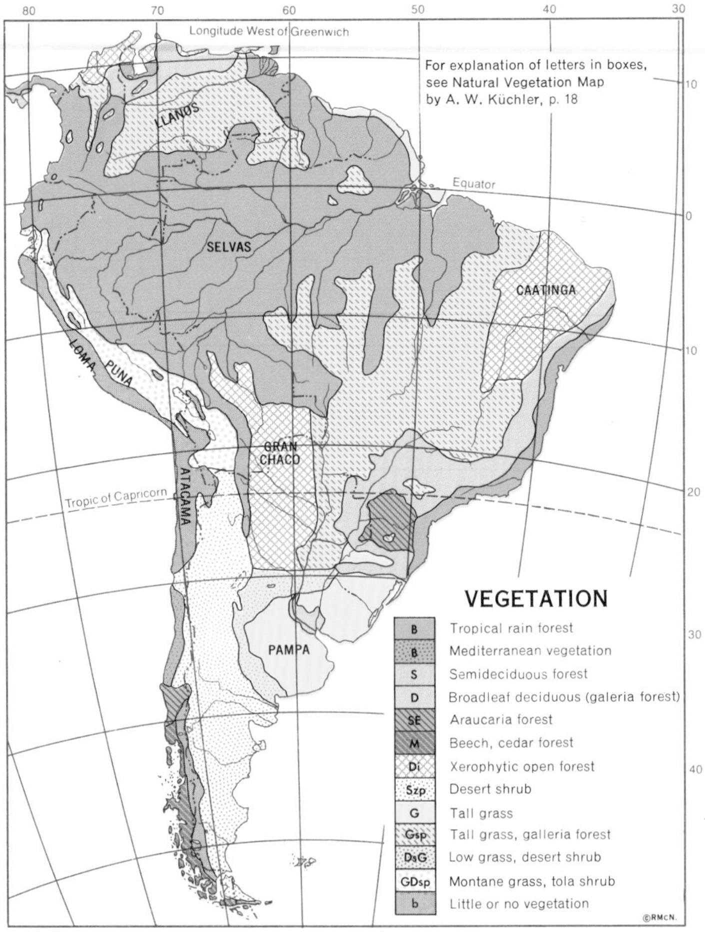

VEGETATION MAP

For explanation of letters in boxes, see Natural Vegetation Map by A. W. Küchler, p. 18

Longitude West of Greenwich

Equator

Tropic of Capricorn

LLANOS

SELVAS

CAATINGA

LOMA

PUNA

ATACAMA

GRAN CHACO

PAMPA

VEGETATION

B	Tropical rain forest
B	Mediterranean vegetation
S	Semideciduous forest
D	Broadleaf deciduous (galeria forest)
SE	Araucaria forest
M	Beech, cedar forest
Di	Xerophytic open forest
Szp	Desert shrub
G	Tall grass
Gsp	Tall grass, galleria forest
DsG	Low grass, desert shrub
GDsp	Montane grass, tola shrub
b	Little or no vegetation

©RMCN.

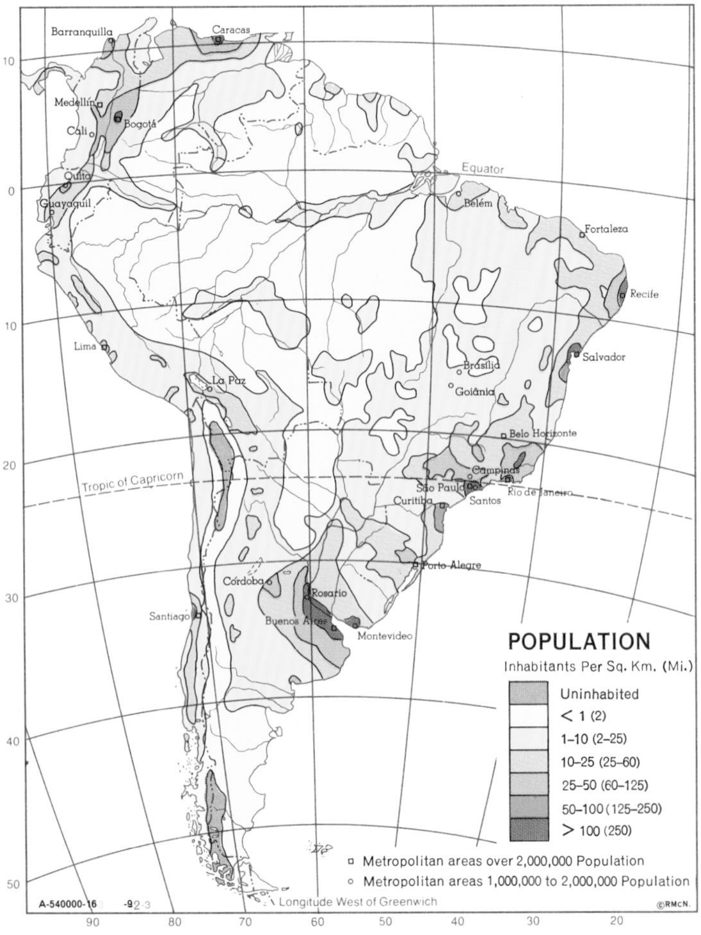

POPULATION

Barranquilla

Caracas

Medellín

Cali

Bogotá

Quito

Guayaquil

Belém

Fortaleza

Recife

Lima

La Paz

Brasília

Salvador

Goiânia

Belo Horizonte

Campinas

São Paulo

Rio de Janeiro

Curitiba

Santos

Córdoba

Rosario

Porto Alegre

Santiago

Buenos Aires

Montevideo

Equator

Tropic of Capricorn

POPULATION

Inhabitants Per Sq. Km. (Mi.)

- Uninhabited
- < 1 (2)
- 1–10 (2–25)
- 10–25 (25–60)
- 25–50 (60–125)
- 50–100 (125–250)
- > 100 (250)

□ Metropolitan areas over 2,000,000 Population
○ Metropolitan areas 1,000,000 to 2,000,000 Population

A-540000-16 -92-3

Longitude West of Greenwich

©RMCN.

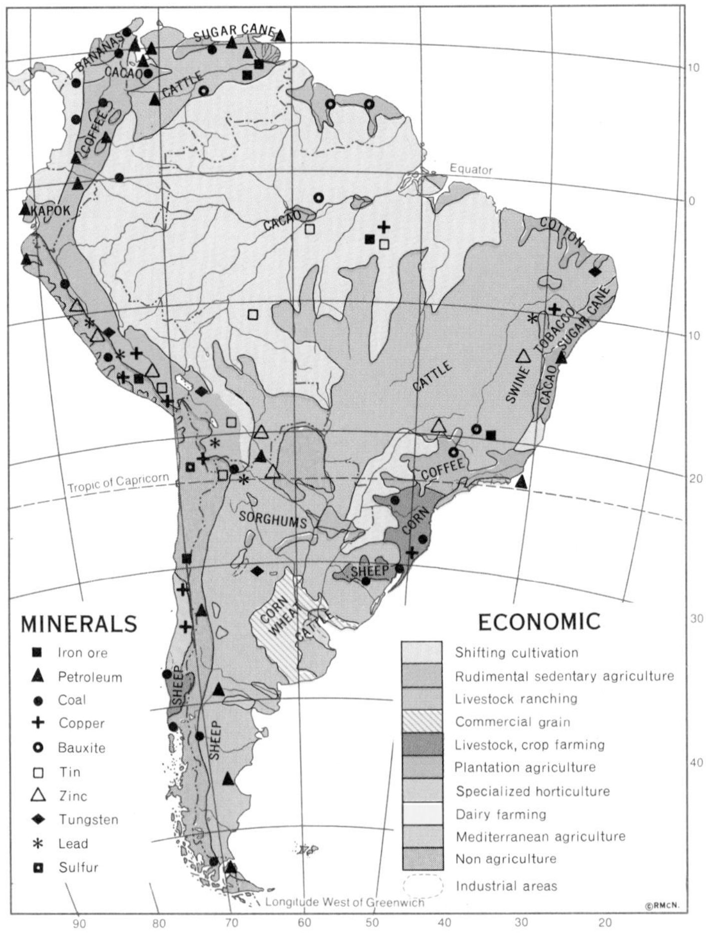

MINERALS / ECONOMIC

BANANAS

SUGAR CANE

CACAO

CATTLE

COFFEE

KAPOK

CACAO

COTTON

TOBACCO

SWINE

CACAO

SUGAR CANE

CATTLE

COFFEE

SORGHUMS

CORN

SHEEP

CORN

WHEAT

CATTLE

SHEEP

SHEEP

Equator

Tropic of Capricorn

MINERALS

- ■ Iron ore
- ▲ Petroleum
- ● Coal
- ✛ Copper
- ◎ Bauxite
- ☐ Tin
- △ Zinc
- ◆ Tungsten
- ✳ Lead
- ▣ Sulfur

ECONOMIC

- Shifting cultivation
- Rudimental sedentary agriculture
- Livestock ranching
- Commercial grain
- Livestock, crop farming
- Plantation agriculture
- Specialized horticulture
- Dairy farming
- Mediterranean agriculture
- Non agriculture
- Industrial areas

Longitude West of Greenwich

©RMCN.

CUBA
JAMAICA
Kingston
HISPANIOLA
San Juan
PUERTO RICO

Caribbean Sea

ATLANTIC

OCEAN

Barranquilla
Maracaibo
CARACAS
Port of Spain
TRINIDAD

Panamá

Orinoco

Georgetown

LLANOS

SANTA FE
DE BOGOTÁ

Quito

Negro

Equator

Belém

Fortaleza

Iquitos

Amazon

Manaus

S E L V A S

A
N
D
E
S

Rio Branco

São Francisco

Recife

LIMA

Salvador

La Paz

Cuiabá

M A T O

Brasília

GROSSO

Iquique

Belo Horizonte

A
N
D
E
S

G
R
A
N

C
H
A
C
O

Paraná

SÃO
PAULO

RIO DE JANEIRO

Tropic of Capricorn

Asunción

San Miguel
de Tucumán

Porto Alegre

Córdoba

Montevideo

SANTIAGO

BUENOS AIRES

PACIFIC

P A M P A

ATLANTIC

OCEAN

Bahía Blanca

OCEAN

P
A
T
A
G
O
N
I
A

Puerto Montt

FALKLAND
ISLANDS

Punta Arénas

TIERRA
DEL FUEGO

SOUTH
GEORGIA

Drake   Passage

A-540000-36 -2-6
COPYRIGHT BY
RAND McNALLY & COMPANY
MADE IN U.S.A.

	Urban
	Cropland
	Cropland & Woodland
	Cropland & Grazing Land
	Grassland, Grazing Land
	Forest, Woodland
	Swamp, Marshland
	Shrub, Sparse Grass, Wasteland
	Barren Land

Scale 1:36,000,000; one inch to 570 miles   Lambert Azimuthal Equal-Area Projection

0   100   200   400   600   800 Miles

0   150   300   600   900   1200 Kilometers

Relief

Meters		Feet
3050		10 000
1525		5000
610		2000
305		1000
	Sea Level	0
152.5		500
1525		5000
3050		10 000
6100		20 000

Scale 1:40 000 000; one inch to 630 miles. Lambert's Azimuthal, Equal Area Projection
Elevations and depressions are given in feet

A-540000-76 3-5- -14
COPYRIGHT BY
RAND MCNALLY & COMPANY
MADE IN U.S.A.

Longitude West of Greenwich

0 200 400 600 800 1000 Miles
0 400 800 1200 1600 Kilometers

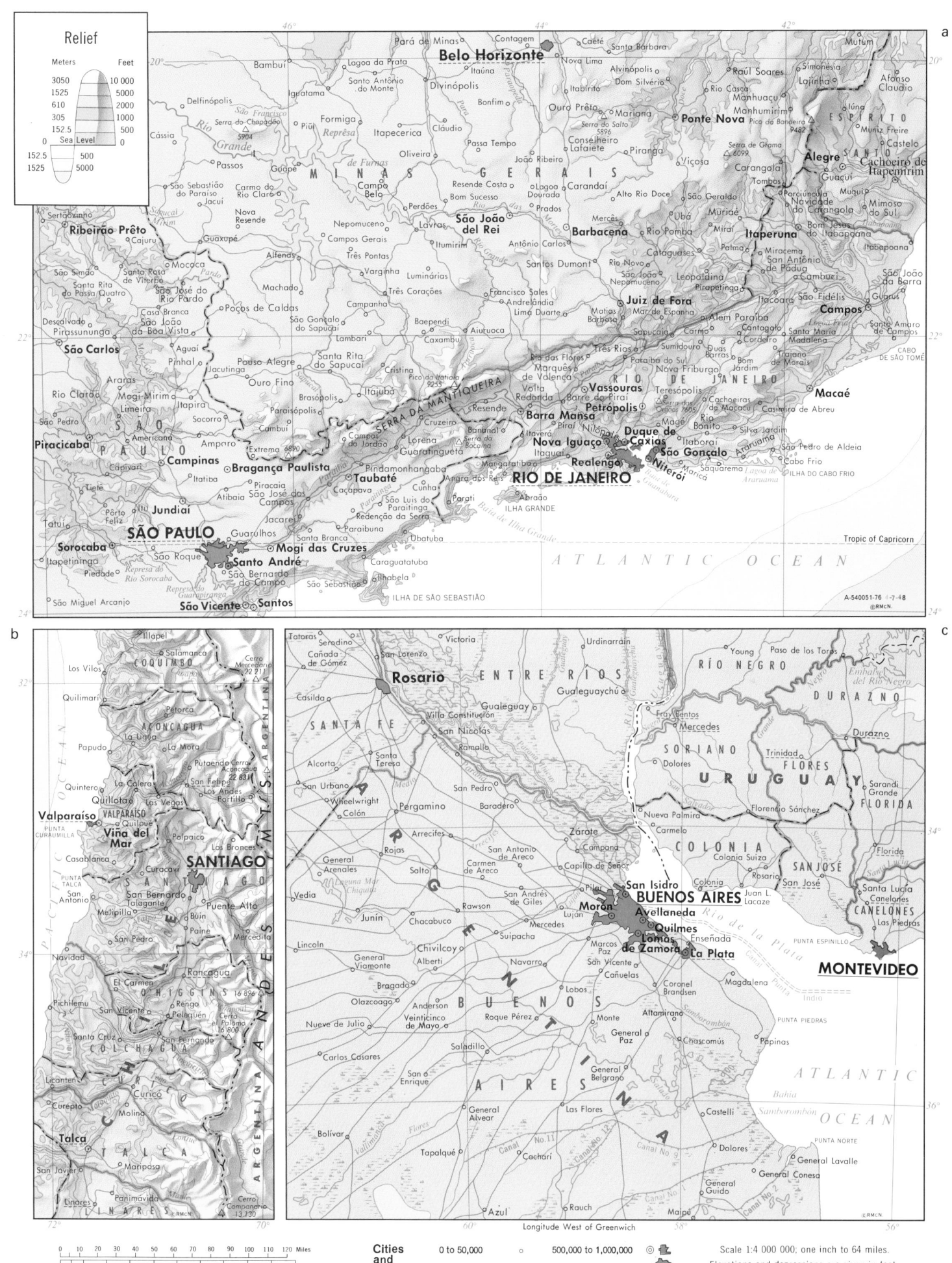

a

Relief

Meters	Feet
3050	10 000
1525	5000
610	2000
305	1000
152.5	500
0	Sea Level	0
152.5	500
1525	5000

Pará de Minas — Contagem — *Caeté* — Santa Bárbara — Mutum

Belo Horizonte — Nova Lima — Alvinópolis — Simonésia — Lajinha

Bambuí — Lagoa da Prata — Itaúna — Itabirito — Dom Silvério — Raúl Soares — Afonso Cláudio

Delfinópolis — Santo Antônio do Monte — Divinópolis — Bonfim — Ouro Prêto — Mariana — Rio Casca — Manhuaçu — Muni Freire — **ESPÍRITO**

Formiga — Cláudio — **Ponte Nova** — Pico da Bandeira 9482 — Iúna — ESPÍRITO

Cássia — Piuí — Itapecerica — Passa Tempo — Serra do Salto 5896 — Manhumirim — Castelo

Serra do Chapadão 5904 — Oliveira — Conselheiro Lafaiete — Piranga — **Alegre** — SANTO — Cachoeiro de Itapemirim

Passos — Guapé — João Ribeiro — Resende Costa — Alto Rio Doce — São Geraldo — Porciúncula — Navidade do Carangola — Guaçuí — Muqui

São Sebastião do Paraíso — Carmo do Rio Claro — Campo Belo — **São João del Rei** — Antônio Carlos — Carandaí — Alvarenga — Mercês — Ubá — Muriaé — Bom Jesus do Itabapoana — Itabapoana

MINAS GERAIS — Lavras — Campos Gerais — Itumirim — Lagoa Dourada — Prados — São João Nepomuceno — Leopoldina — Palma — Miracema — San Antônio de Pádua — São João da Barra

Sertãozinho — Nova Resende — Machado — Alfenas — Perdões — Bom Sucesso — Santos Dumont — Cambuci — São Fidélis — Guarus

Ribeirão Prêto — Cajuru — Guaxupé — Três Pontas — Varginha — Rio Novo — Pirapetinga — Itacoara — **Campos**

São Simão — Santa Rosa de Viterbo — Mococa — Luminárias — Campanha — Francisco Sales — Andrelândia — Matias Barbosa — Mar de Espanha — Alem Paraíba — Cordeiro — Santa Maria Madalena — Santo Amaro de Campos

São José do Rio Pardo — Poços de Caldas — Três Corações — Lambari — Baependi — Lima Duarte — **Juiz de Fora** — Sapucaia — Carmo — Cantagalo — CABO DE SÃO TOMÉ

Descalvado — Casa Branca — São João da Boa Vista — Santa Rita do Sapucaí — Aiuruoca — Sumidouro — Duas Barras — Bom Jardim — Traíano de Morais

São Carlos — Pirassununga — Aguaí — Pouso Alegre — Caxambu — Cristina — Três Rios — **RIO DE JANEIRO** — Nova Friburgo — Trajano de Morais

Pinhal — Santa Rita do Sapucaí — Pico do Itatiaia 9255 — Rio das Flores — Marquês de Valença — Teresópolis — Cachoeiras de Macacu — **Macaé**

Rio Claro — Araras — Mogi-Mirim — Ouro Fino — Itajubá — Resende — Volta Redonda — Barra do Piraí — Paraíba do Sul — Serra dos Orgãos 7605 — Casimiro de Abreu

São Paulo — Limeira — Amparo — Brasópolis — Cruzeiro — Barra Mansa — **Vassouras** — Magé — Rio Bonito

Piracicaba — Capivari — Socorro — Paraisópolis — Serra da Bocaína — Lorena — **Barra Mansa** — **Petrópolis** — Silva Jardim — São Pedro de Aldeia

São Pedro — Itatiba — **Bragança Paulista** — Extrema 6890 — Campos do Jordão — Guaratinguetá — Pirai — Nilópolis — Itaboraí — Araruama — Cabo Frio

Campinas — Pindamonhangaba — **Nova Iguaçu** — **Duque de Caxias** — Saquarema — Lagoa de Araruama

Piracicaba — Tietê — **Taubaté** — Angra dos Reis — **Realengo** — **São Gonçalo** — ILHA DO CABO FRIO

Tatuí — Pôrto Feliz — Itu — Jacareí — Cunha — Parati — **RIO DE JANEIRO** — Niterói — Maricá

Sorocaba — **Jundiaí** — Guarulhos — São José dos Campos — São Luís do Paraitinga — Abraão — Baía de Guanabara

SÃO PAULO — São Roque — Santa Branca — Redenção da Serra — ILHA GRANDE — Tropic of Capricorn

Mogi das Cruzes — Paraibuna — Ubatuba

Itapetininga — Piedade — Represa do Rio Sorocaba — **Santo André** — **Santo** — Caraguatatuba — **ATLANTIC OCEAN**

São Miguel Arcanjo — **São Vicente** — São Bernardo do Campo — São Sebastião — Ilhabela — ILHA DE SÃO SEBASTIÃO

Represa de Guarapiranga — **Santos** — A-540051-76 4-7-48 ©RMcN

---

b

Illapel — COQUIMBO — RÍO NEGRO — Tatoras — Serodino — Victoria — Urdinarrain — Young — Paso de los Toros — c

Los Vilos — Salamanca — Cerro Mercedario 22 211 — Cañada de Gómez — San Lorenzo — Gualeguaychú — Fray Bentos — DURAZNO

Quilimarí — Petorca — **Rosario** — **ENTRE RÍOS** — Mercedes — Durazno

Quillaimarí — ACONCAGUA — Cerro Aconcagua 22 831 — Casilda — Villa Constitución — SORIANO — Trinidad — FLORES

Papudo — La Ligua — La Mora — Putaendo — San Felipe — Los Andes Portillo — **SANTA FE** — San Nicolás — Ramallo — Dolores — **URUGUAY** — Sarandí Grande

Quintero — La Calera — Las Vegas — Santa Teresa — San Pedro — Florencio Sánchez — FLORIDA

Quillota — Alcorta — Baradero — Nueva Palmira — Colonia Suiza — Rosario — San José — **Florida**

Valparaíso — **VALPARAÍSO** — San Urbano — Wheelwright — Zárate — Campana — Carmelo — **COLONIA** — Colonia — San José — Santa Lucía

Viña del Mar — Casablanca — Curacaví — **SANTIAGO** — Colón — Arrecifes — Rojas — San Antonio de Areco — Capilla de Señor — Colonia — Juan L. Lacaze — CANELONES — Las Piedras

San Antonio — Melipilla — Talagante — Puente Alto — General Arenales — Salto — Carmen de Areco — Luján — Pilar — **San Isidro** — **BUENOS AIRES** — Río de la Plata

San Bernardo — Buín — Vedia — Junín — Chacabuco — San Andrés de Giles — Mercedes — **Morón** — **Avellaneda** — PUNTA ESPINILLO

San Pedro — Paine — Lincoln — Rawson — Suipacha — Marcos Paz — **Quilmes** — **Lomas de Zamora** — **La Plata** — Ensenada

Navidad — Rancagua — General Viamonte — Alberti — San Vicente — **MONTEVIDEO**

O'HIGGINS 16 896 — Chivilcoy — Navarro — Lobos — Cañuelas — Coronel Brandsen — Magdalena — PUNTA PIEDRAS

El Carmen — Cerro el Palomo 16 800 — Bragado — Olazcoago — Roque Pérez — Monte — General Paz — Attamirano — Samborombón

Pichilemu — Renго — Peleguén — Nueve de Julio — Veinticinco de Mayo — Saladillo — General Alvear — Las Flores — Chascomús — PUNTA NORTE

COLCHAGUA — San Fernando — Carlos Casares — **BUENOS** — Castelli — **ATLANTIC OCEAN**

Santa Cruz — San Enrique — General Belgrano — General Paz — Bahía Samborombón

Licanten — Curepto — Molina — Bolívar — General Alvear — **AIRES** — Coronel Conesa — Dolores — General Lavalle

Talca — TALCA — Mariposa — Tapalqué — Azul — Rauch — General Guido — Maipú

San Javier — Linares — Panimávida — Cerro Companario 13 730 — LINARES — Cacharí — PUNTA NORTE

Longitude West of Greenwich

Cities and Towns

0 to 50,000 ○ — 500,000 to 1,000,000 ◉

50,000 to 500,000 ⊙ — 1,000,000 and over

Scale 1:4 000 000; one inch to 64 miles.
Elevations and depressions are given in feet.

0 10 20 30 40 50 60 70 80 90 100 110 120 Miles
0 20 40 60 80 100 120 140 160 180 200 Kilometers

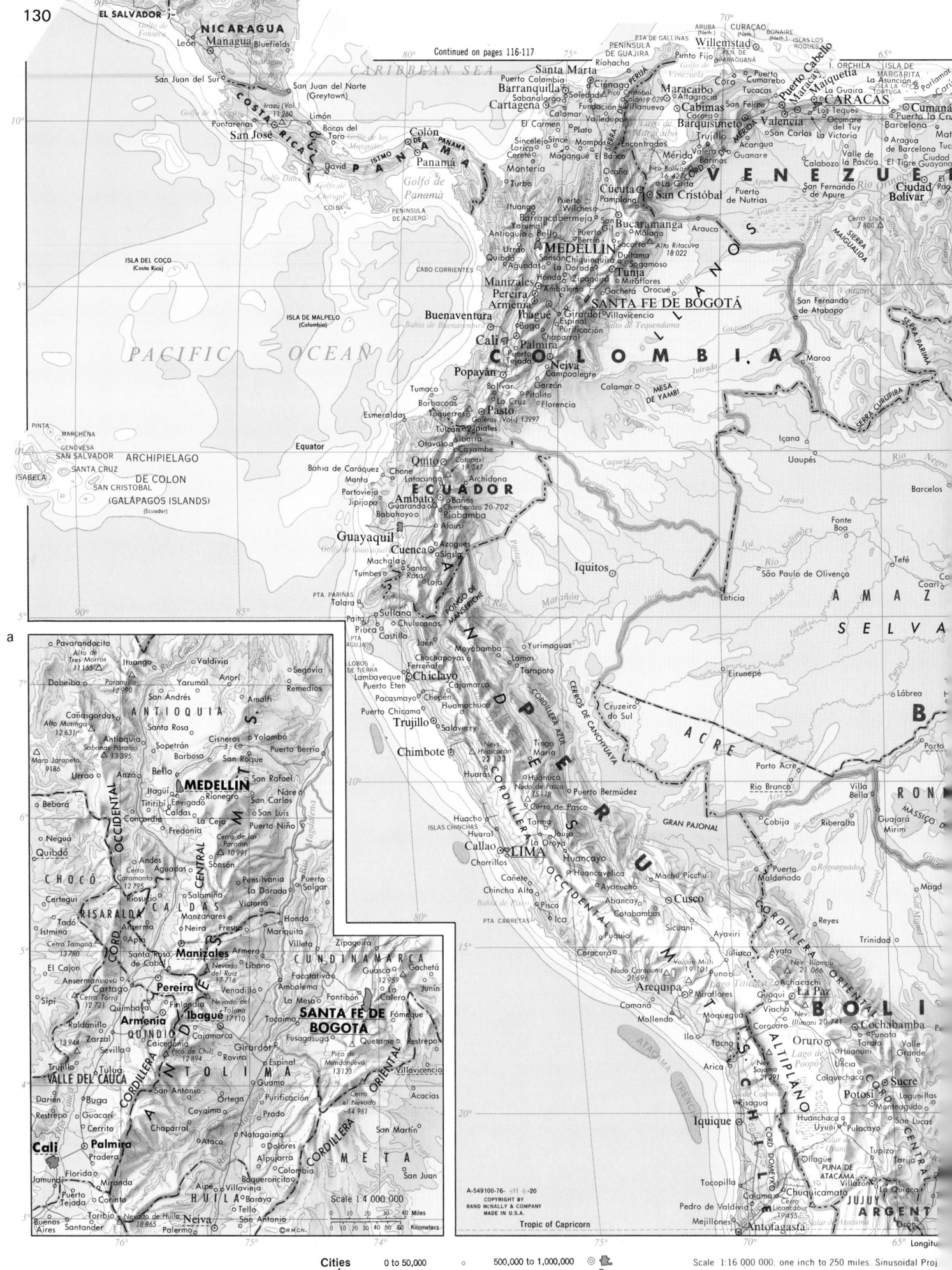

NICARAGUA

EL SALVADOR

Golfo de
Fonseca

León

Managua

Bluefields

CARIBBEAN SEA

ARUBA (Neth.)

CURAÇAO (Neth.)

BONAIRE (Neth.)

ISLAS LOS ROQUES

Continued on pages 116-117

PTA. DE GALLINAS

PENÍNSULA DE GUAJIRA

Willemstad

ISLA DE MARGARITA

La Asunción

San Juan del Sur

San Juan del Norte (Greytown)

Santa Marta

Ríohacha

PEN. DE PARAGUANÁ

La Guaira

Porlamar

I. ORCHILA

Puerto Colombia

Ciénaga

Golfo de Venezuela

Coro

Puerto Cabello

Maiquetía

Cumarebo

COSTA RICA

Irazú (Vol.) 11,260

Limón

Puerto Colombia

Barranquilla

Sabanalarga

Soledad

Cartagena

El Carmen

Plato

Calamar

Valledupar

Cumarebo

CARACAS

Los Teques

Ocumare del Tuy

Puerto la Cruz

Barcelona

San José

Puntarenas

Bocas del Toro

Golfo de los Mosquitos

Colón

Panamá

Sincelejo

Sincé

Mompós

El Banco

Ocaña

Cúcuta

Pamplona

San Cristóbal

Mérida

Valera

Valencia

San Carlos

La Victoria

Aragua de Barcelona

Matu

David

Golfo de Chiriquí

COIBA

PENÍNSULA DE AZUERO

Golfo de Panamá

Montería

Cereté

Magangué

Turbo

Puerto Wilches

Barrancabermeja

Puerto Berrío

Bucaramanga

Arauca

San Fernando de Apure

El Tigre

Ciudad Guayana

Ciudad Bolívar

El Pao

CABO CORRIENTES

ISLA DEL COCO (Costa Rica)

Ituango

Yarumal

Antioquia

Bello

MEDELLÍN

Sonsón

Chiquinquirá

Duitama

Sogamoso

Alto Ritacuva 18,022

CORDILLERA

Río Meta

Puerto de Nutrias

VENEZUELA

ISLA DE MALPELO (Colombia)

Quibdó

Aguadas

La Dorada

Honda

Zipaquirá

Gachetá

Miraflores

Orocué

SIERRA MAIGUALIDA 7,800

Manizales

Pereira

Armenia

Ibagué

Ambalema

Girardot

Villavicencio

SANTA FE DE BOGOTÁ

San Fernando de Atabapo

Buenaventura

Cali

Buga

Palmira

Espinal

Purificación

Salto de Tequendama

Gachetá

Guaviare

COLOMBIA

Maroa

Bahía de Buenaventura

Puerto Tejada

Neiva

Campoalegre

Inírida

SIERRA PARIMA

PACIFIC OCEAN

Popayán

Bolívar

Garzón

Pitalito

Calamar

MESA DE YAMBI

Tumaco

La Cruz

Florencia

Vaupés

SIERRA CURUPIRA

Barbacoas

Pasto

Esmeraldas

Tuquerres

Ipiales

Galeras (Vol.) 13,997

Içana

Uaupés

Río Negro

PINTA

MARCHENA

GENOVESA

San Salvador

SANTA CRUZ

ISABELA

Tulcán

Otavalo

Ibarra

Cayambe

Equator

Caquetá

Archidona

Japurá

Barcelos

ARCHIPIELAGO DE COLON (GALÁPAGOS ISLANDS) (Ecuador)

Quito

Cotopaxi 19,347

Latacunga

Bahía de Caráquez

Chone

ECUADOR

Tigre

Rio Içá

Fonte Boa

Tefé

Bahía de Caráquez

Manta

Portoviejo

Jipijapa

Babahoyo

Ambato

Baños

Guaranda

Riobamba

Chimborazo 20,702

Alausí

Iquitos

São Paulo de Olivença

Coari

Guayaquil

Cuenca

Azogues

Sígsig

Marañón

Leticia

AMAZ

SELVA

PTA. PARIÑAS

Talara

Machala

Santa Rosa

Tumbes

Loja

PONGO DE MANSERICHE

Javari

Eirunepé

Juruá

Lábrea

Paita

Piura

Castilla

Chulucanas

Sullana

Jaén

Chachapoyas

Moyobamba

Yurimaguas

Lamas

Tarapoto

Cruzeiro do Sul

ACRE

B

Porto

LOBOS DE TIERRA

Lambayeque

Ferreñafe

Puerto Eten

Chiclayo

Cajamarca

Huamachuco

Tingo María

Pucallpa

Purus

Porto Acre

RON

MASSICO

Pacasmayo

Chepén

Puerto Chicama

Salaverry

Trujillo

PERU

Cerro de Pasco

Río Branco

Cobija

Villa Bella

Guajará Mirim

Chimbote

Huaraz

Nev. Huascarán 22,133

Nudo de Pasco 15,118

Puerto Bermúdez

GRAN PAJONAL

Riberalta

ISLAS CHINCHAS

Huacho

Huaral

Callao

LIMA

Chorrillos

Cañete

Chincha Alta

Pisco

Huánuco

Tarma

La Oroya

Jauja

Huancayo

Huancavelica

Ayacucho

Machu Picchu

Cusco

Abancay

Cotabambas

CORDILLERA ORIENTAL

Puerto Maldonado

Reyes

Trinidad

Magd

BOLI

Rogoaguado

PTA. CARRETAS

Bahía de Pisco

Ica

Coracora

Puquio

Sicuani

Ayaviri

Juliaca

Puno

Lago Titicaca

Viacha

La Paz

Cochabamba

Punata

Tarata

Valle Grande

Nev. Illampu 21,066

Achacachi

Arequipa

Miraflores

Camaná

Mollendo

Moquegua

Ilo

Nudo Coropuna 21,696

Volcán Misti 19,101

ALTIPLANO

Oruro

Coroico

Nev. Illimani 20,741

Guaqui

CORD. REAL

Camana

Tacna

Arica

Nev. Sajama 21,391

Uncía

Uyuni

Colquechaca

Sucre

Potosí

Lagunillas

Monteagudo

San Lucas

ATACAMA TRENCH

de Coipasa

Lago de Poopó

Pisagua

Iquique

Pulacayo

Salar de Uyuni

PUNA DE ATACAMA

Tupiza

CORD. CENTRAL

Tocopilla

Calama

Chuquicamata

Cerro Licancábur 19,455

La Quiaca

JUJUY

ARGENT

Pedro de Valdivia

Mejillones

Antofagasta

Tropic of Capricorn

Inset map (a):

Pavarandócito

Alto de Tres Morros 11,155

Ituango

Valdivia

Segovia

Dabeiba

Paramillo 12,990

San Andrés

Yarumal

Anorí

Remedios

ANTIOQUIA

Santa Rosa

Amalfi

Cañasgordas

Alto Musinga 12,631

Antioquia

Sopetrán

Yolombó

Puerto Berrío

Mapa Jarapeto 9,186

Cerro 13,395

Bello

Cisneros

Barbosa

San Roque

Lábrea

Urrao

Anzá

Itagüí

MEDELLÍN

Rionegro

San Rafael

San Carlos

OCCIDENTAL

Bebará

CORDILLERA

Envigado

Titiribí

Caldas

La Ceja

San Luis

Neguá

Quibdó

Andes

Aguadas

Fredonia

Cerro de las Paradas 10,991

Sonsón

CHOCÓ

Cerro Caramanta 12,795

CENTRAL

Pensilvania

La Dorada

Certegui

Tadó

Ríosucio

Salamina

Manzanares

Fresno

Puerto Salgar

Istmina

Anserma

Apía

CALDAS

Victoria

RISARALDA

Cerro Tamaná 13,780

Santa Rosa de Cabal

Marquita

Villeta

Honda

Zipaquirá

CUNDINAMARCA

Guasca

Gachetá

El Cajón

MTS.

Manizales

Líbano

Facatativá

Ambalema

Fontibón

Junín

Ansermanuevo

Cartago

PEREIRA

Nevado del Ruiz 17,716

Armero

La Mesa

Tocaima

SANTA FE DE BOGOTÁ

La Calera

Cerro Torrá 12,721

Quimbaya

Finlandia

Cajamarca

Caicedonia

Nevado del Tolima 17,110

Fusagasugá

Quetame

Restrepo

Sipí

Roldanillo

ANDES

QUINDÍO

ARMENIA

IBAGUÉ

Girardot

Rovira

Espinal

Villavicencio

13,944

Zarzal

Sevilla

TOLIMA

Pico de Chili 12,894

Pico de Mundanueva 13,123

Acacías

ORIENTAL

VALLE DEL CAUCA

Tuluá

San Antonio

Ortega

Coyaima

Guamo

Prado

San Martín

Darién

Buga

Guacarí

CORDILLERA

Chaparral

Atáco

Natagaima

Dolores

Colombia

META

CALI

Pradera

Cerro el Nevado de Huila 14,961

Aipe

Villavieja

San Juan

PALMIRA

Miranda

Florida

Puerto Tejada

Baraya

Tello

Jamundí

Buenos Aires

Toribío

Santander

Nevado de Huila 18,865

Neiva

San Antonio

Palermo

R.McN.

Scale 1:4 000 000

0   10   20   40 Miles
0   10 20 30 40 50 60 Kilometers

CORDILLERA

Continued on page 132

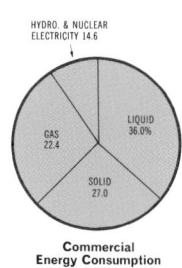

HYDRO. & NUCLEAR
ELECTRICITY 14.6

GAS
22.4

LIQUID
36.0%

SOLID
27.0

**Commercial
Energy Consumption**
2,768,953,000 metric tons
coal equivalent - 1991

ENERGY

Energy Producing Plants

▽ Geothermal
· Hydroelectric
■ Nuclear

Mineral Fuel Deposits

· Uranium: major deposit
△ Natural Gas: major field
· Petroleum: minor producing field
▲ Petroleum } major producing field
   Petroleum }
   Coal: major bituminous and anthracite
   Coal: minor bituminous and anthracite
   Coal: lignite

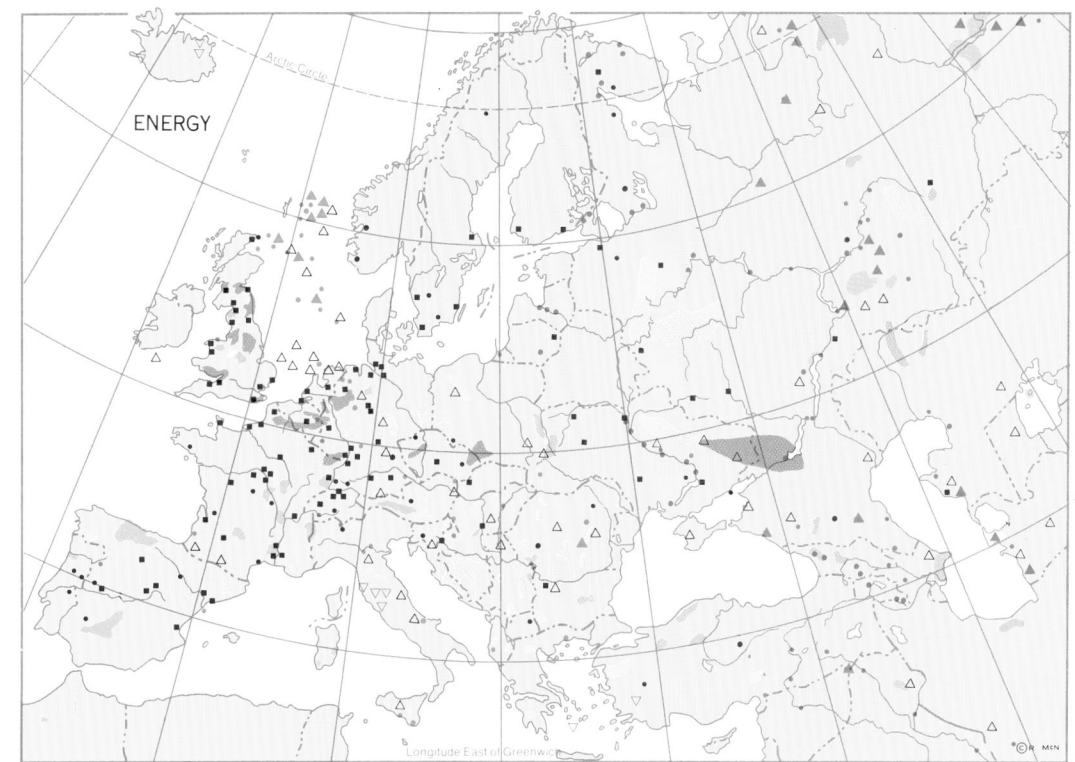

ENERGY

NATURAL HAZARDS

○ Volcanoes*
● Earthquakes*
● Major flood disasters*
── Tsunamis
── Limit of iceberg drift
   Temporary pack ice
   Areas subject to desertification

*Twentieth Century occurrences

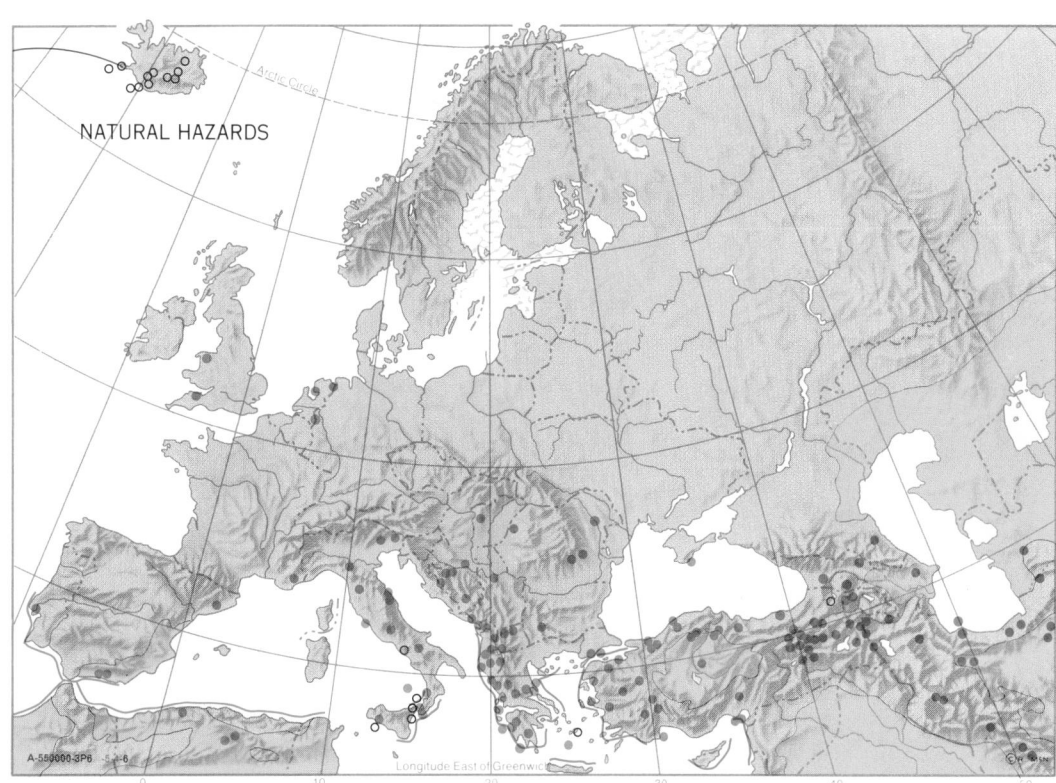

NATURAL HAZARDS

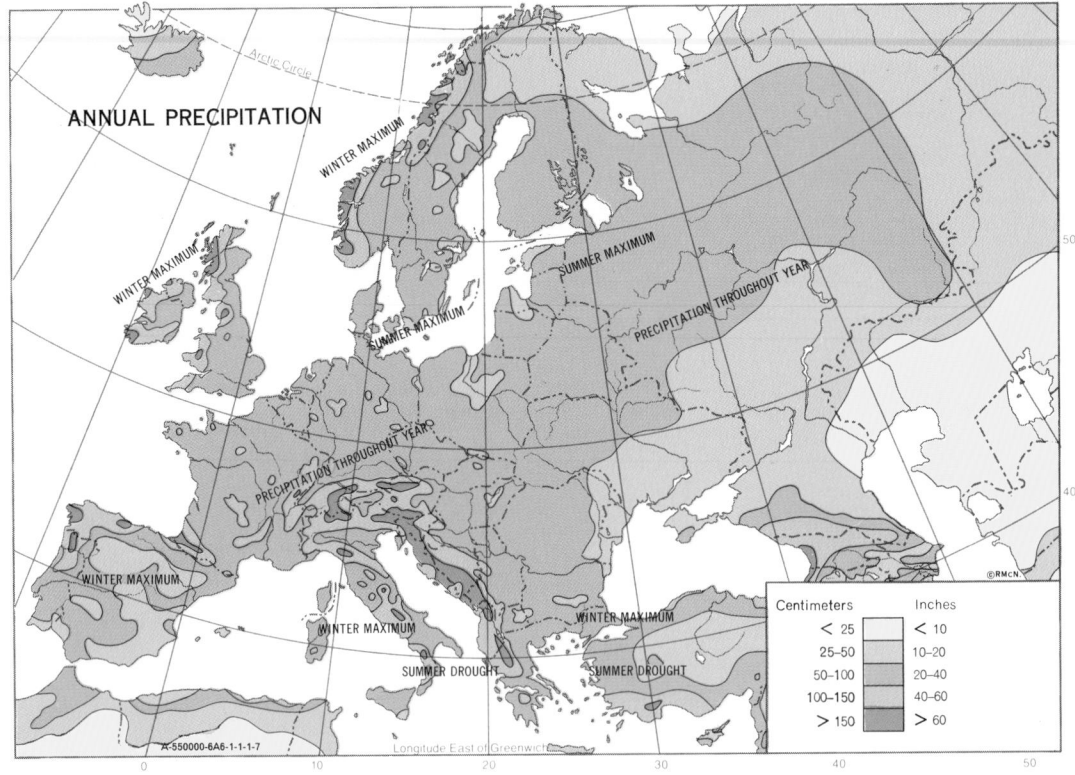

ANNUAL PRECIPITATION

Centimeters	Inches
< 25	< 10
25–50	10–20
50–100	20–40
100–150	40–60
> 150	> 60

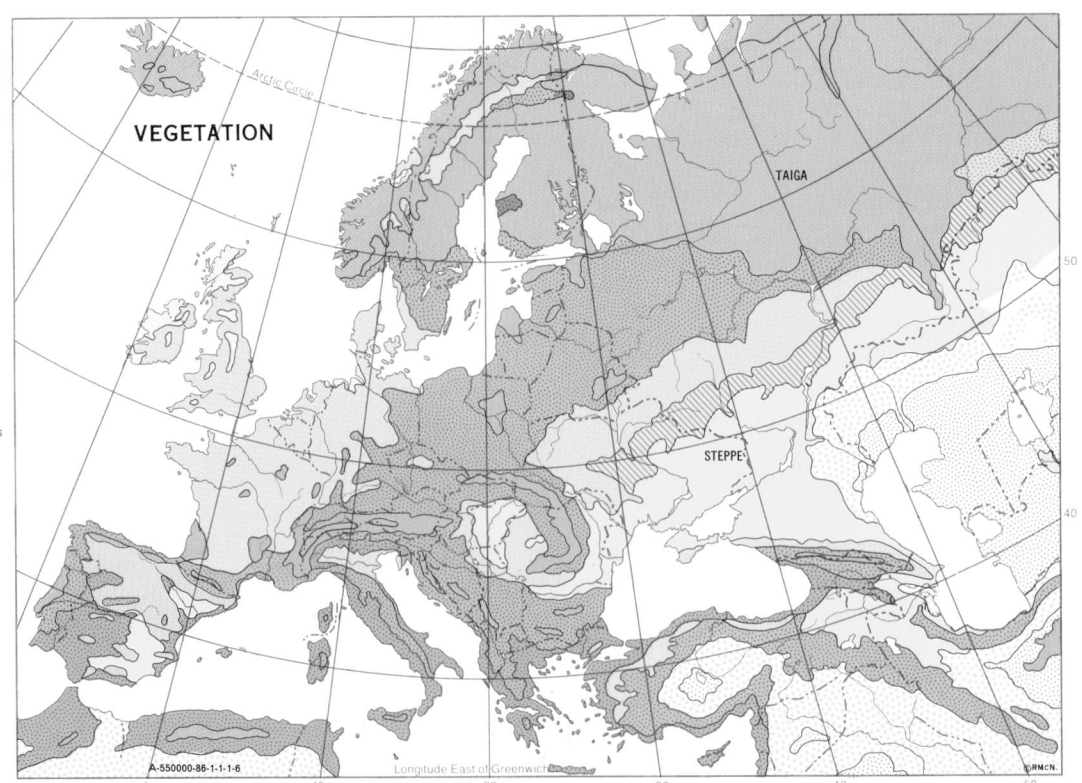

VEGETATION

VEGETATION

E	Coniferous forest
B,Bs	Mediterranean vegetation
M	Mixed forest: coniferous-deciduous
S	Semi-deciduous forest
D	Deciduous forest
DG	Wooded steppe
G	Grass (steppe)
Gp	Short grass
Dsp	Desert shrub
L	Heath and moor
L	Alpine vegetation, tundra
b	Little or no vegetation

For explanation of letters in boxes,
see Natural Vegetation Map
by A. W. Kuchler, p. 18

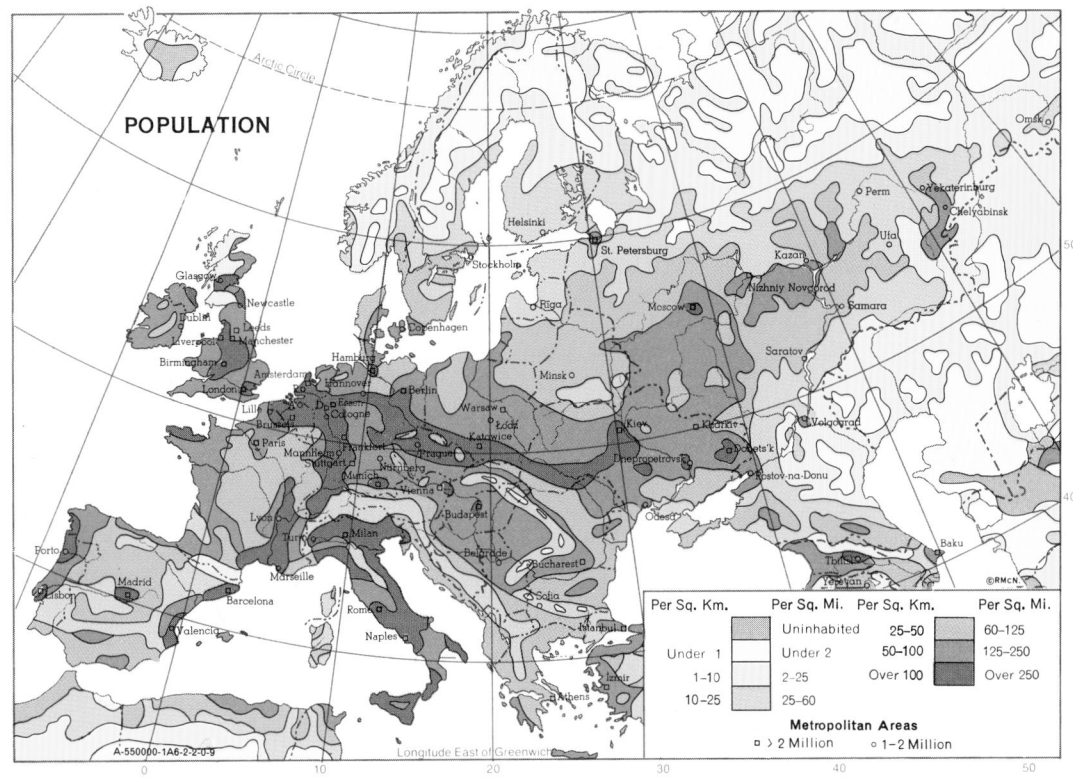

POPULATION

Per Sq. Km.	Per Sq. Mi.	Per Sq. Km.	Per Sq. Mi.
	Uninhabited	25–50	60–125
Under 1	Under 2	50–100	125–250
1–10	2–25	Over 100	Over 250
10–25	25–60		

Metropolitan Areas
□ > 2 Million   ○ 1–2 Million

A-550000-1A6-2-2-0-9

Longitude East of Greenwich

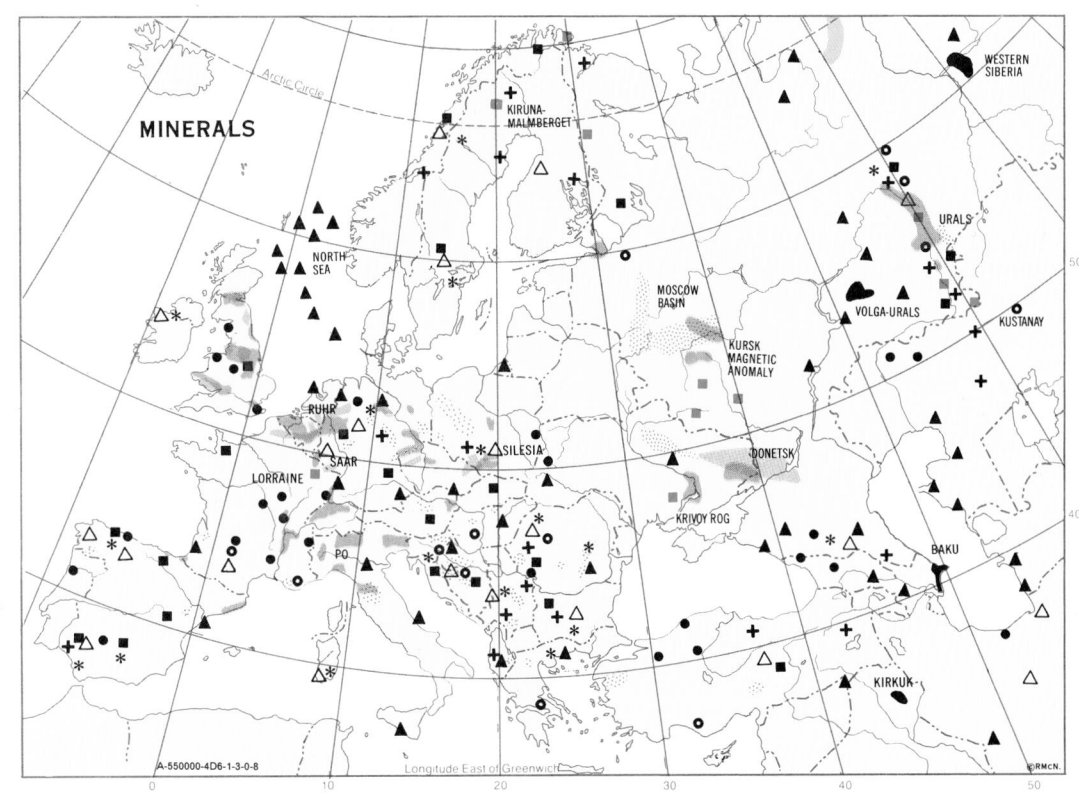

MINERALS

MINERALS

Industrial areas
Major coal deposits
Major petroleum deposits
Lignite deposits
▲ Minor petroleum deposits
● Minor coal deposits
■ Major iron ore
■ Minor iron ore
✳ Lead
◉ Bauxite
△ Zinc
✛ Copper

A-550000-4D6-1-3-0-8

Longitude East of Greenwich

Urban

Cropland

Cropland & Woodland

Cropland & Grazing Land

Grassland, Grazing Land

Forest, Woodland

Swamp, Marshland

Tundra

Shrub, Sparse Grass,
Wasteland (pattern)

Barren Land

• Oasis

ATLANTIC

OCEAN

North
Sea

Reykjavik

Narvik
Murman
Ume
Trondheim
Bergen
Oslo
Helsinki
ST. PETERSBURG
Tallinn
Stockholm
Göteborg
Copenhagen
Baltic Sea
Gulf of Bothnia
Rīga
Kaliningrad
Vilnius
Minsk

Glasgow
Belfast
MANCHESTER
Dublin
LONDON
Amsterdam
Hamburg
BERLIN
Antwerp
Essen
Leipzig
Oder
Warsaw
Pripy
Frankfurt
Elbe
Brest
PARIS
Seine
Strasbourg
Prague
Kraków
L'viv
Loire
Rhine
Munich
Danube
VIENNA
CARPATHIANS
Zürich
Lyon
ALPS
MILAN
BUDAPEST
Tisza
Bay of Biscay
Bordeaux
Garonne
Rhône
Venice
Zagreb
Sava
La Coruña
Bilbao
PYRENEES
Genoa
Belgrade
Bucharest
Douro
Ebro
MADRID
Marseille
Danube
Lisbon
BARCELONA
CORSICA
ROME
Sofia
Sevilla
SARDINIA
Naples
Tirane
ISLAS BALEARES
Tyrrhenian Sea
Adriatic Sea
Tanger
Algiers
Mediterranean
Palermo
Aegean Sea
Casablanca
Oran
ATLAS
MOUNTAINS
Tunis
SICILY
Athens
MALTA
Sea
CRETE

Longitude West of Greenwich 0° Longitude East of Greenwich

Scale 1: 16,000,000; one inch to 250 miles. Conic Projection

0	50	100	200	300	400	500 Miles

0	100	200	400	600	800 Kilometers

White Sea

Nar'yan-Mar

Pechora

Ob'

Irtysh

Novosibirsk

Ob'

Omsk

Archangelsk

URALS

YEKATERINBURG

Perm'

Qaraghandy

Kirov

Vologda

Kama

Ufa

Balqash

Volga

Magnitogorsk

Nizhniy Novgorod

Kazan'

MOSCOW

Samara

Orsk

Tula

Volga

Qyzylorda

Syr Darya

Saratov

Ural

PESKI KYZYLKUM

DEPRESSION

Aral Sea

Don

Kharkiv

VOLGOGRAD

CASPIAN

Amu Dar'ya

Volga

Kiev

Dnipropetrovs'k

Donets'k

Astrakhan'

MANYCH   DEPRESSION

PESKI KARAKUMY

Dnieper

Odesa

Krasnodar

Ashkhabad

CAUCASUS

Caspian   Sea

BAKU

Black   Sea

TBILISI

Yerevan

ELBURZ MTS.

DASHT-E-KAVIR

ISTANBUL

TEHRAN

Ankara

Kerman

TOROS

AĞRI

Tigris

ZAGROS

Nicosia

CYPRUS

Euphrates

Baghdad

MOUNTAINS

Beirut

Abadan

40° 50° 60° 70° 60° 80°

50°

40°

30°

30° 40° 50°

Scale 1:16 000 000; one inch to 250 miles. Conic Projection
Elevations and depressions are given in feet.

EUROPE LANGUAGES
BY
BOGDAN ZABORSKI

Scale 1:16,500,000; one inch to 260 miles Conic Projection

B-550000-1C8-1-1-1-3
COPYRIGHT BY
RAND McNALLY & COMPANY
MADE IN U.S.A.

| 0 | 100 | 200 | 300 | 400 | 500 | 600 Miles |

| 0 | 200 | 400 | 600 | 800 | 1000 Kilometers |

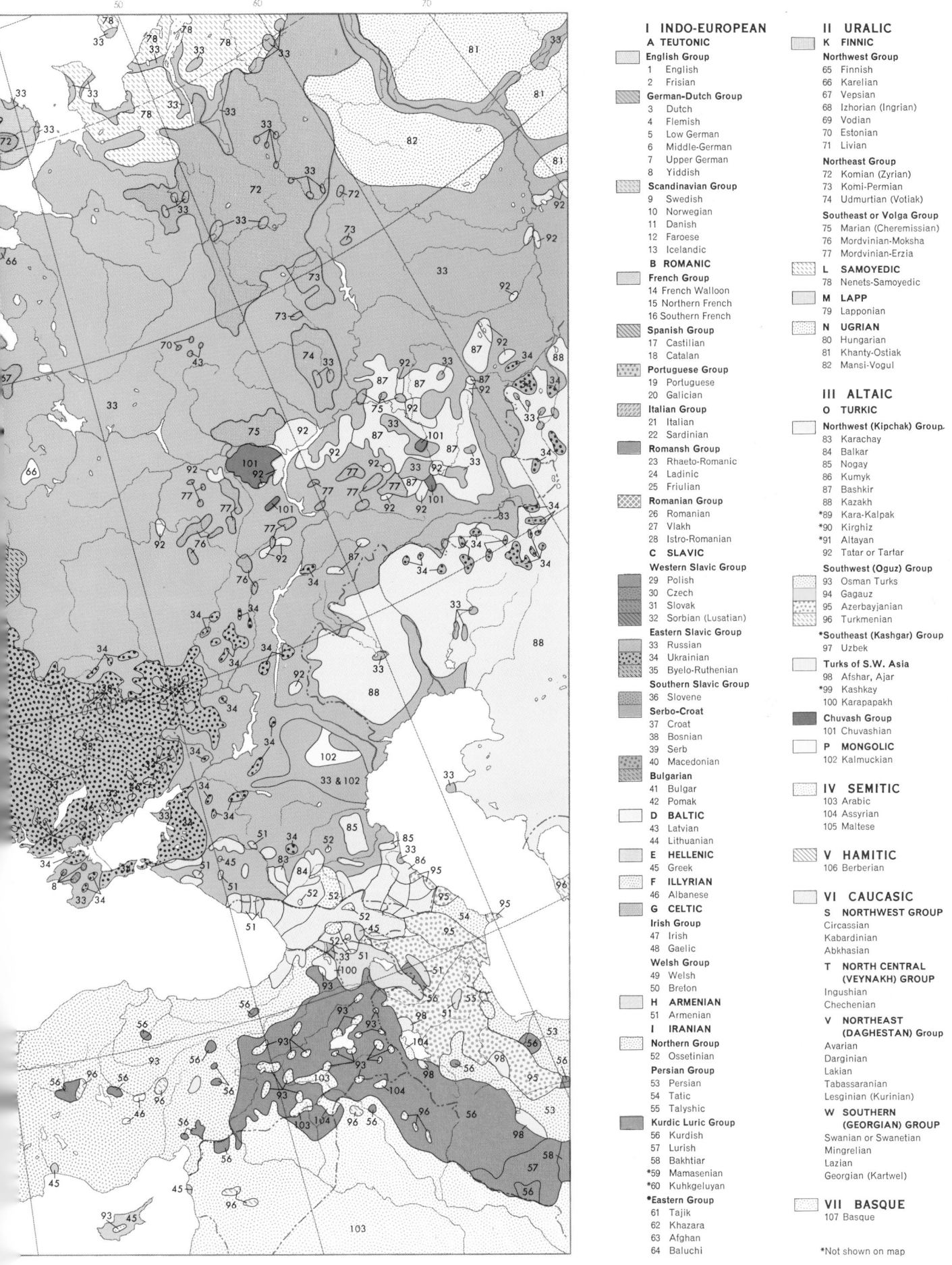

I **INDO-EUROPEAN**
A **TEUTONIC**
English Group
1 English
2 Frisian
German-Dutch Group
3 Dutch
4 Flemish
5 Low German
6 Middle-German
7 Upper German
8 Yiddish
Scandinavian Group
9 Swedish
10 Norwegian
11 Danish
12 Faroese
13 Icelandic
B **ROMANIC**
French Group
14 French Walloon
15 Northern French
16 Southern French
Spanish Group
17 Castilian
18 Catalan
Portuguese Group
19 Portuguese
20 Galician
Italian Group
21 Italian
22 Sardinian
Romansh Group
23 Rhaeto-Romanic
24 Ladinic
25 Friulian
Romanian Group
26 Romanian
27 Vlakh
28 Istro-Romanian
C **SLAVIC**
Western Slavic Group
29 Polish
30 Czech
31 Slovak
32 Sorbian (Lusatian)
Eastern Slavic Group
33 Russian
34 Ukrainian
35 Byelo-Ruthenian
Southern Slavic Group
36 Slovene
Serbo-Croat
37 Croat
38 Bosnian
39 Serb
40 Macedonian
Bulgarian
41 Bulgar
42 Pomak
D **BALTIC**
43 Latvian
44 Lithuanian
E **HELLENIC**
45 Greek
F **ILLYRIAN**
46 Albanese
G **CELTIC**
Irish Group
47 Irish
48 Gaelic
Welsh Group
49 Welsh
50 Breton
H **ARMENIAN**
51 Armenian
I **IRANIAN**
Northern Group
52 Ossetinian
Persian Group
53 Persian
54 Tatic
55 Talyshic
Kurdic Luric Group
56 Kurdish
57 Lurish
58 Bakhtiar
*59 Mamasenian
*60 Kuhgeluyan
***Eastern Group**
61 Tajik
62 Khazara
63 Afghan
64 Baluchi

II **URALIC**
K **FINNIC**
Northwest Group
65 Finnish
66 Karelian
67 Vepsian
68 Izhorian (Ingrian)
69 Vodian
70 Estonian
71 Livian
Northeast Group
72 Komian (Zyrian)
73 Komi-Permian
74 Udmurtian (Votiak)
Southeast or Volga Group
75 Marian (Cheremissian)
76 Mordvinian-Moksha
77 Mordvinian-Erzia
L **SAMOYEDIC**
78 Nenets-Samoyedic
M **LAPP**
79 Lapponian
N **UGRIAN**
80 Hungarian
81 Khanty-Ostiak
82 Mansi-Vogul

III **ALTAIC**
O **TURKIC**
Northwest (Kipchak) Group
83 Karachay
84 Balkar
85 Nogay
86 Kumyk
87 Bashkir
88 Kazakh
*89 Kara-Kalpak
*90 Kirghiz
*91 Altayan
92 Tatar or Tartar
Southwest (Oguz) Group
93 Osman Turks
94 Gagauz
95 Azerbayjanian
96 Turkmenian
***Southeast (Kashgar) Group**
97 Uzbek
Turks of S.W. Asia
98 Afshar, Ajar
*99 Kashkay
100 Karapapakh
Chuvash Group
101 Chuvashian
P **MONGOLIC**
102 Kalmuckian

IV **SEMITIC**
103 Arabic
104 Assyrian
105 Maltese

V **HAMITIC**
106 Berberian

VI **CAUCASIC**
S **NORTHWEST GROUP**
Circassian
Kabardinian
Abkhasian
T **NORTH CENTRAL
(VEYNAKH) GROUP**
Ingushian
Chechenian
V **NORTHEAST
(DAGHESTAN) Group**
Avarian
Darginian
Lakian
Tabassaranian
Lesginian (Kurinian)
W **SOUTHERN
(GEORGIAN) GROUP**
Swanian or Swanetian
Mingrelian
Lazian
Georgian (Kartwel)

VII **BASQUE**
107 Basque

*Not shown on map

Relief

Meters		Feet
3050		10 000
1525		5000
610		2000
305		1000
152.5		500
0	Sea Level	0
		Below
152.5		Sea Level
1525		5000
3050		10 000

Continued on pages 210-211

Scale 1: 16 000 000; one inch to 250 miles. Conic Projection
Elevations and depressions are given in feet

| 0 | 50 | 100 | 200 | 300 | 400 | 500 Miles |
| 0 | 100 | 200 | 400 | 600 | 800 Kilometers |

Longitude West of Greenwich   Longitude East of Greenwich

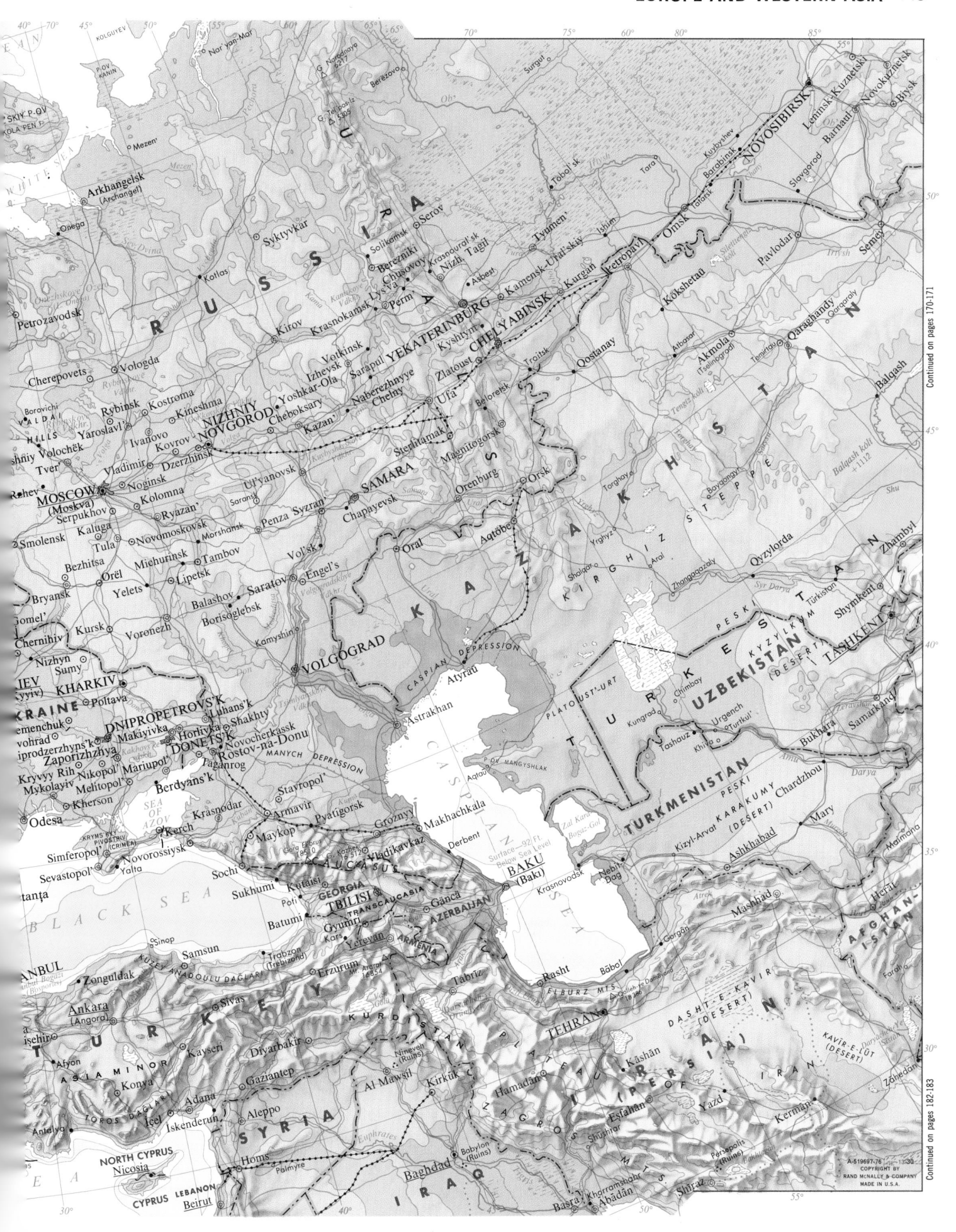

Continued on pages 170-171

Continued on pages 182-183

A-519697-76
AK-13:30
COPYRIGHT BY
RAND McNALLY & COMPANY
MADE IN U.S.A.

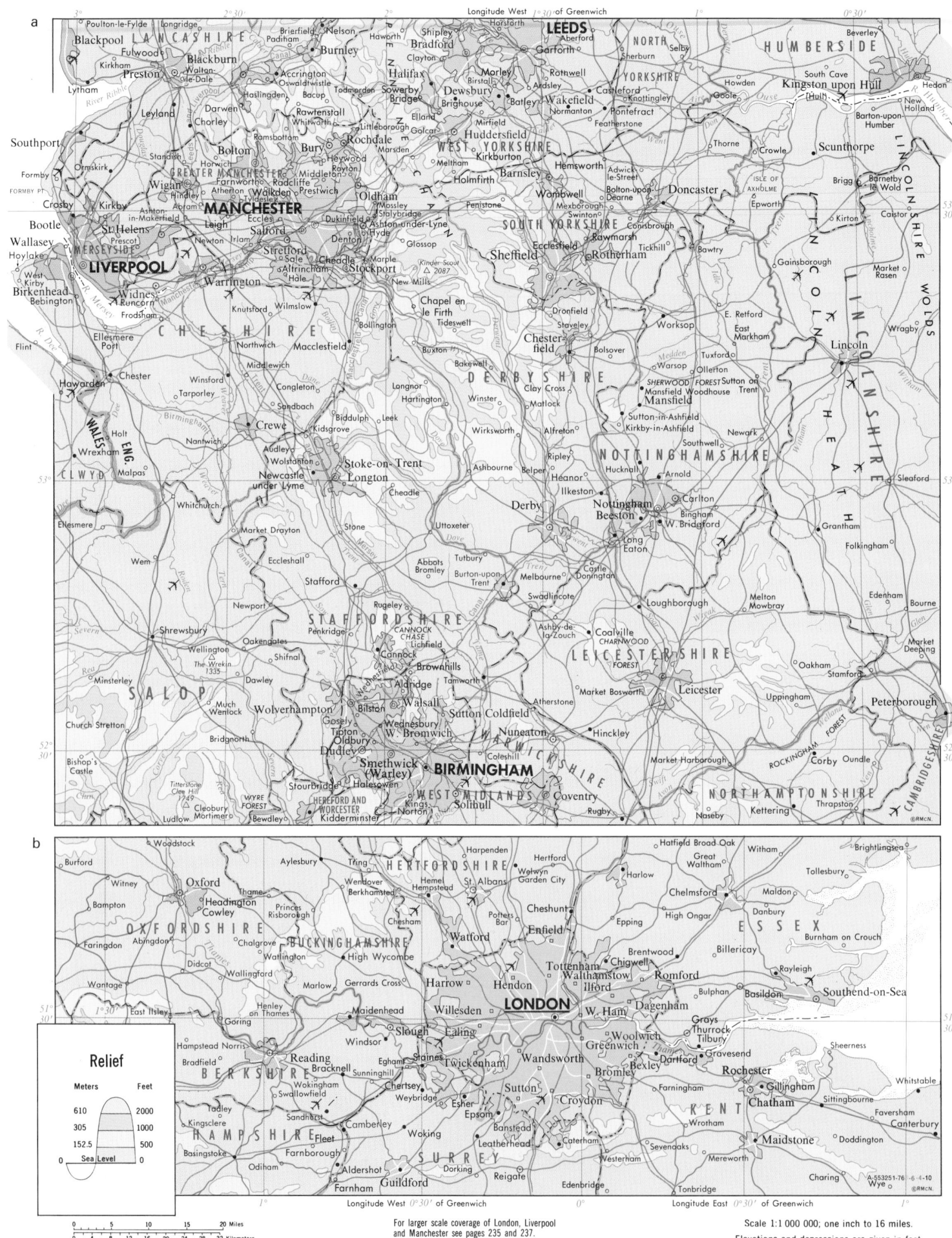

a

Longitude West 1°30' of Greenwich

Blackpool LANCASHIRE
Poulton-le-Fylde Longridge
Fulwood Brierfield Nelson
Kirkham Padiham
Lytham Preston Walton-le-Dale Accrington Oswaldtwistle
Southport River Ribble Blackburn Haslingden Bacup
Leyland Darwen Rawtenstall Whitworth
Formby Ormskirk Chorley Ramsbottom
FORMBY PT Standish Horwich Bury Heywood Rochdale
Crosby Kirkby Wigan Bolton Radcliffe Middleton Royton
Bootle St Helens Leigh Farnworth Atherton Walkden Prestwich
Wallasey Hindley Tyldesley Eccles
Hoylake MERSEYSIDE Newton Irlam Salford MANCHESTER
West Kirby Prescot Stretford
Birkenhead LIVERPOOL Warrington Sale Altrincham Stockport
Bebington Widnes Runcorn CHESHIRE Hale Cheadle
Flint Frodsham
Ellesmere Port Northwich
Hawarden Chester Middlewich Knutsford Wilmslow
WALES Tarporley Winsford Congleton Macclesfield
ENG. Holt Sandbach
CLWYD Wrexham Nantwich Crewe Kidsgrove Leek
Malpas Audley Biddulph
Whitchurch Wolstanton Newcastle under Lyme Stoke-on-Trent Longton
Ellesmere Wem Market Drayton Stone
Minsterley Eccleshall Stafford
SALOP Shrewsbury Newport Rugeley
Wellington Oakengates STAFFORDSHIRE
The Wrekin 1335 Shifnal CANNOCK CHASE Cannock Lichfield
Dawley Penkridge Brownhills
Church Stretton Much Wenlock Wolverhampton Aldridge Tamworth
Bridgnorth Bilston Walsall
Bishop's Castle Dudley W. Bromwich Sutton Coldfield
Tittterstone Clee Hill Stourbridge Smethwick (Warley) BIRMINGHAM Nuneaton Hinckley
Cleobury Mortimer WYRE FOREST Halesowen Coleshill WARWICKSHIRE
Ludlow HEREFORD AND WORCESTER Kings Norton WEST MIDLANDS Solihull Coventry Rugby
Bewdley Kidderminster

LEEDS
Horsforth Aberford
Shipley Bradford Garforth
Haworth Clayton NORTH Sherburn Selby
Nelson Morley Rottwell Aldsley YORKSHIRE Howden
Halifax Sowerby Bridge Dewsbury Batley Wakefield Castleford Knottingley Goole
Todmorden Brighouse Mirfield Normanton Pontefract Thorne Crowle
Littleborough Elland Golcar Huddersfield WEST YORKSHIRE Featherstone
Marsden Kirkburton Meltham Hemsworth Adwick-le-Street Epworth
Holmfirth Barnsley Wombwell Bolton-upon-Dearne Doncaster ISLE OF AXHOLME
Penistone Mexborough Swinton Conisbrough
Glossop SOUTH YORKSHIRE Rawmarsh Bawtry
Kinder Scout 2087 Sheffield Ecclesfield Rotherham Tickhill E. Retford
New Mills Dronfield East Markham
Chapel en le Firth Tideswell Staveley Worksop Tuxford
Buxton Chesterfield Bolsover Warsop SHERWOOD FOREST Sutton on Trent
Bakewell Clay Cross Mansfield Woodhouse Mansfield
DERBYSHIRE Winster Matlock Sutton-in-Ashfield Ollerton
Wirksworth Alfreton Kirkby-in-Ashfield Newark
Ashbourne Belper Ripley Heanor NOTTINGHAMSHIRE Southwell
Hucknall Arnold
Ilkeston Nottingham Carlton
Derby Beeston W. Bridgford Bingham
Long Eaton Castle Donington
Tutbury Melbourne Swadlincote
Abbots Bromley Burton-upon-Trent Loughborough
Uttoxeter Ashby-de-la-Zouch Coalville CHARNWOOD Melton Mowbray
Cheadle Market Bosworth LEICESTERSHIRE FOREST
CANNOCK CHASE Atherstone Leicester Oakham Uppingham
Market Harborough ROCKINGHAM FOREST Corby Oundle
NORTHAMPTONSHIRE
Naseby Kettering Thrapston

HUMBERSIDE
Beverley
South Cave Kingston upon Hull [Hull] Hedon
New Holland Barton-upon-Humber
Brigg Barnetby le Wold
Scunthorpe Caistor LINCOLNSHIRE WOLDS
Kirton Market Rasen Wragby
Gainsborough Lincoln
LINCOLN HEATH
Sleaford
Grantham Folkingham
Edenham Bourne
Stamford Market Deeping
Peterborough CAMBRIDGESHIRE

53° 30'
53°
52° 30'

b

OXFORDSHIRE
Woodstock
Burford Witney Oxford
Bampton Headington Cowley
Faringdon Abingdon Thame
Didcot Chalgrove
BUCKINGHAMSHIRE
Wantage Wallingford Watlington High Wycombe
East Ilsley Goring
Hampstead Norris BERKSHIRE Henley on Thames Marlow Gerrards Cross
Bradfield Reading Maidenhead
Bracknell Windsor Slough
Aylesbury Tring Harpenden HERTFORDSHIRE Hertford
Wendover Berkhamsted Hemel Hempstead Welwyn Garden City St Albans
Princes Risborough Chesham Potters Bar Cheshunt Enfield
Amersham Watford
Harrow Hendon Tottenham Walthamstow Ilford
Willesden LONDON W. Ham
Ealing
Staines Twickenham Wandsworth
Egham Bromley
Sunninghill Chertsey Sutton Croydon
Wokingham Weybridge Esher Epsom Banstead
Swallowfield Woking Leatherhead Caterham
Camberley Sevenoaks
Sandhurst Farnborough SURREY
Fleet Aldershot Dorking Reigate
Basingstoke Farnham Guildford Edenbridge
HAMPSHIRE Odiham Kingsclere Tadley
Hatfield Broad Oak Great Waltham Witham Brightlingsea
Harlow Chelmsford Maldon Tollesbury
Epping ESSEX Danbury
High Ongar Billericay Burnham on Crouch
Brentwood Rayleigh
Chigwell Romford Basildon Southend-on-Sea
Bulphan
Dagenham Grays Thurrock Tilbury Sheerness
Woolwich Greenwich Gravesend
Bexley Dartford Rochester Whitstable
Farningham KENT Gillingham
Wrotham Chatham Sittingbourne Faversham Canterbury
Westerham Maidstone Doddington
Mereworth Charing Wye
Tonbridge

51° 30'
51°

Longitude West 1° 0°30' of Greenwich 0° Longitude East 0°30' 1° of Greenwich

Relief

Meters		Feet
610		2000
305		1000
152.5		500
0	Sea Level	0

0 5 10 15 20 Miles
0 4 8 12 16 20 24 28 32 Kilometers

For larger scale coverage of London, Liverpool and Manchester see pages 235 and 237.

Scale 1:1 000 000; one inch to 16 miles.
Elevations and depressions are given in feet.

A-553251-76 · 6-4-10
®RMcN

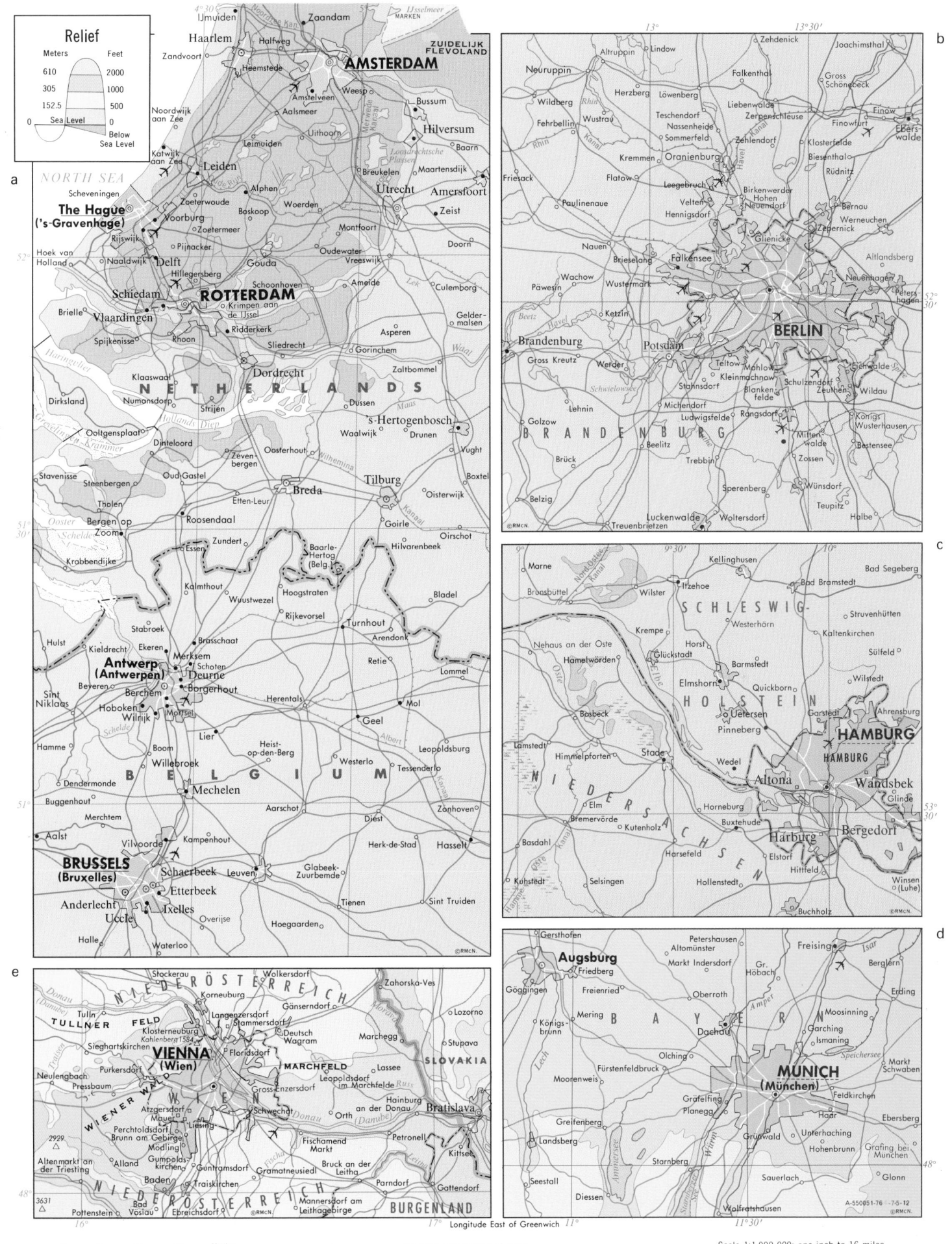

BELARUS

Continued on pages 166-167

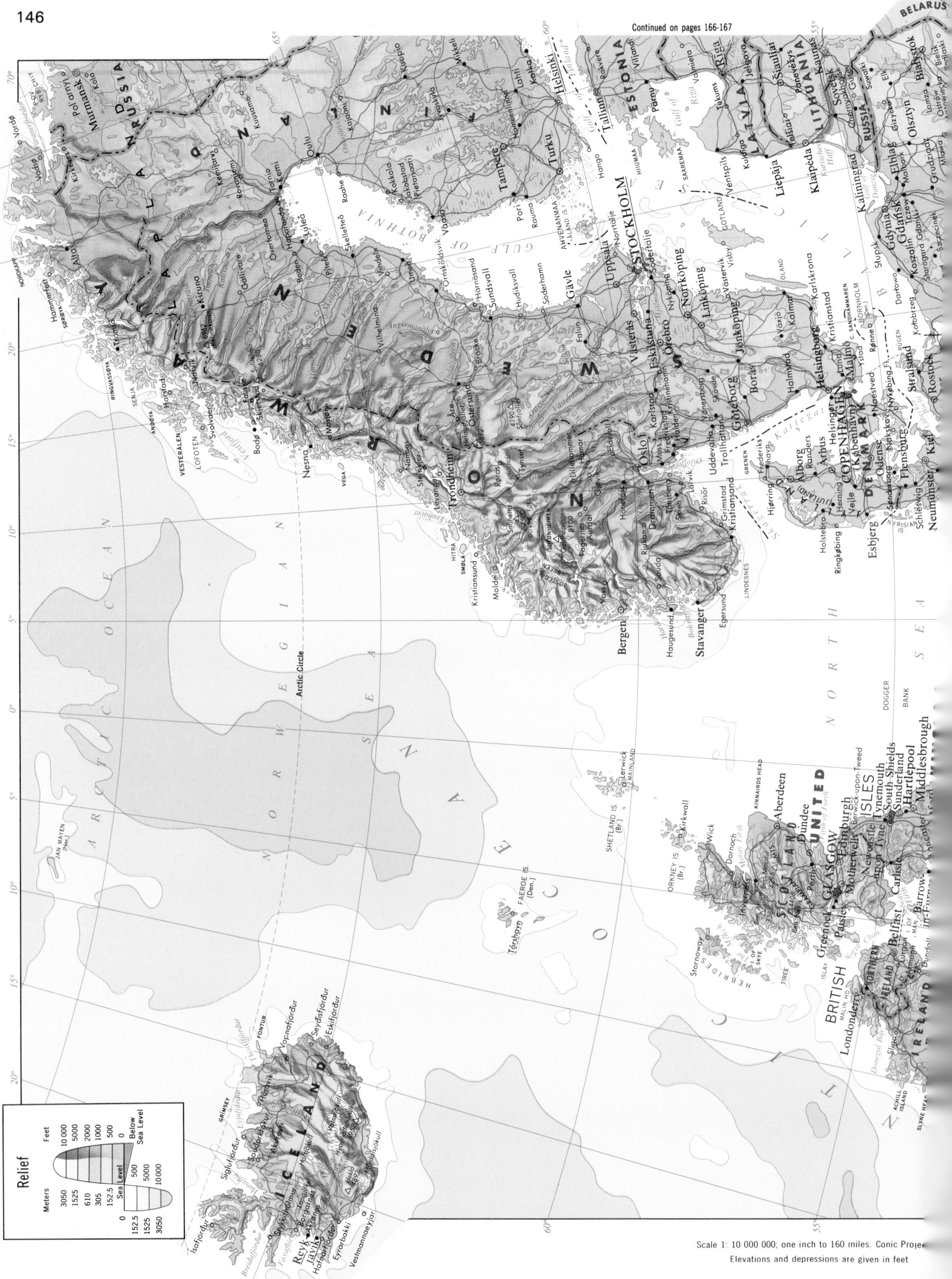

RUSSIA

FINLAND

ESTONIA

LATVIA

LITHUANIA

Helsinki

Tallinn

Riga

Murmansk

S W E D E N

N O R W A Y

LAPLAND

STOCKHOLM

Uppsala

Oslo

Göteborg

Bergen

Stavanger

Trondheim

COPENHAGEN

DENMARK

Tampere

Turku

GULF OF BOTHNIA

Kiruna

Gällivare

Luleå

Umeå

Sundsvall

Gävle

Örebro

Norrköping

Linköping

Jönköping

Borås

Halmstad

Helsingborg

Malmö

Kristianstad

Kalmar

GOTLAND

ÖLAND

Karlskrona

Kaliningrad

Gdańsk

Gdynia

Klaipėda

Liepāja

Ventspils

A R C T I C   O C E A N

N O R W E G I A N   S E A

N O R T H   S E A

Arctic Circle

JAN MAYEN (Nor.)

FAEROE IS. (Den.)

Tórshavn

SHETLAND IS. (Br.)

Lerwick

ORKNEY IS. (Br.)

Kirkwall

I C E L A N D

Reykjavík

DOGGER BANK

UNITED

BRITISH ISLES

SCOTLAND

Aberdeen

Dundee

Edinburgh

GLASGOW

Newcastle

Sunderland

Middlesbrough

Hartlepool

Carlisle

Barrow

Belfast

NORTHERN IRELAND

Londonderry

HEBRIDES

IRELAND

Stornoway

ISLE OF SKYE

TIREE

ISLAY

Inverness

Perth

Paisley

Greenock

Esbjerg

Odense

Århus

Ålborg

JUTLAND

Kiel

Neumünster

Rostock

Stralsund

Szczecin

Koszalin

Słupsk

Kołobrzeg

Olsztyn

Białystok

Suwałki

Grudziądz

Elbląg

Sovetsk

Kaunas

Šiauliai

Panevėžys

Rostov

Pärnu

Villandi

Pori

Rauma

Oulu

Kemi

Tornio

Boden

Piteå

Skellefteå

Vaasa

Kokkola

Mikkeli

Kuopio

Joensuu

Lahti

Kotka

VESTERÅLEN

LOFOTEN

Narvik

Bodø

Mo

Nesna

Hammerfest

Vardø

Vadsø

Kirkenes

NORDKAPP

Tromsø

Harstad

Alta

SENJA

ANDØYA

RINGVASSØYA

SØRØYA

MAGERØYA

SMØLA

HITRA

VEGA

FRØYA

Molde

Kristiansund

Ålesund

Lillehammer

Hamar

Drammen

Skien

Larvik

Kristiansand

Egersund

Haugesund

Stavanger

LINDESNES

JOSTEDAL

KATTEGAT

SKAGERRAK

Frederikshavn

Randers

Holstebro

Herning

Ringkøbing

Vejle

Kolding

Flensburg

Schleswig

Scale 1: 10 000 000; one inch to 160 miles. Conic Projection

Elevations and depressions are given in feet

Relief

Meters	Feet
3050	10 000
1525	5000
610	2000
305	1000
152.5	500
0	Sea Level

Below Sea Level

152.5	500
1525	5000
3050	10000

A-559400-76-'73-22
COPYRIGHT BY
RAND M°NALLY & COMPANY
MADE IN U.S.A.

148

Continued on pages 146-147

ATLANTIC OCEAN

BAY OF BISCAY

FRANCE

SPAIN

PORTUGAL

LISBON

MADRID

BARCELONA

MEDITERRANEAN SEA

MOROCCO

ALGERIA

TUNISIA

Algiers

ATLAS MOUNTAINS

SAHARAN ATLAS

GRAND ERG OCCIDENTAL

GRAND ERG ORIENTAL

TARABULUS (TRIPOLITANIA)

Relief

Meters	Feet
3050	10000
1525	5000
610	2000
305	1000
152.5	500
0 Sea Level	0
	Below Sea Level
152.5	500
1525	5000
3050	10000

A-558300-76   '78-12-33
COPYRIGHT BY
RAND McNALLY & COMPANY
MADE IN U.S.A.

Longitude West of Greenwich   0°   Longitude East of Greenwich

Scale 1:10 000 000; one inch to 160 miles. Bonne's Project
Elevations and depressions are given in feet

a

Same scale as main map

ATLANTIC

SHETLAND

YELL

St. Magnus Bay

ISLANDS
(Br.)

MAINLAND

Lerwick

FOULA

OCEAN

FAIR
ISLAND

WESTRAY

N. RONALDSAY

ROUSAY

SANDAY

STRONSAY

Kirkwall

ORKNEY

HOY

MAINLAND
(Br.)

S. RONALDSAY

ISLANDS

Thurso

Pentland
Firth

DUNCANSBY HD.

©RMcN.

SCOTLAND

ATLANTIC

OCEAN

Relief

Meters   Feet
610   2000
305   1000
152.5   500
0 Sea Level   0
152.5   500 Below
1525   5000 Sea Level

A-559700-76 'g...'15
COPYRIGHT BY
RAND McNALLY & COMPANY
MADE IN U.S.A

ISLES OF SCILLY

Longitude West of Greenwich

Scale 1: 4 000 000; one inch to 64 miles. Conic Pro
Elevations and depressions are given in fee

Continued on pages 152-153

Continued on pages 154-155

Continued on pages 156-157

Longitude East of Greenwich

20 30 40 50 60 70 80 90 100 110 120 Miles
40   60   80   100   120   140   160   180   200 Kilometers

152

NORWEGIAN SEA

NORWAY

SWEDEN

DENMARK

NORTH SEA

GERMANY

POLAND

Oslo

Bergen

Stavanger

Trondheim

Göteborg

COPENHAGEN (København)

Malmö

Helsingborg

Uppsala

Gävle

Sundsvall

Östersund

Örebro

Linköping

Jönköping

Kalmar

GOTLAND

ÖLAND

BORNHOLM (Den.)

Skagerrak

Kattegat

BALTIC SEA

Relief

Meters		Feet
1525		5000
610		2000
305		1000
152.5		500
0	Sea Level	0
152.5	Below Sea Level	500

A-559195-76
COPYRIGHT BY
RAND McNALLY & COMPANY
MADE IN U.S.A.

Longitude East of Greenwich

Continued on pages 162-163

Continued on pages 154-155

Scale 1:4 000 000; one inch to 64 miles. Conic Projection
Elevations and depressions are given in feet.

0 10 20 30 40 50 60 70 80 90 100 110 120 Miles

0 20 40 60 80 100 120 140 160 180 200 Kilometers

Continued on pages 152-153

NORTH SEA

DENMARK

Svendborg
Langeland
Tønder
Flensburg
Sønderborg
Rudkøbing
Nakskov
MØN
Maribo
Nykøbing
FALSTER
Gedser

SCHLESWIG
Husum
Schleswig
Eckernförde
Kiel
Rendsburg
Heide
Tönning
HOLSTEIN
Neustadt in Holstein
Lübecker Bucht
Kiel Bay

BALTIC

Sassnitz
RÜGEN
Bergen
Barth
Stralsund

FRISIAN ISLANDS
Norderney
Helgoland
Wangerooge
Borkum
Cuxhaven
Stade
Bad Oldesloe
Elmshorn
HAMBURG
Lübeck
Wismar
Schwerin
Rostock
Warnemünde
Greifswald
Wolgast
Anklam
Koszalin

Swinoujscie
Kamien Pomorski
Trzebiatów
Gryfice
POMERANIA
Szczecin (Stettin)
Goleniów
Stargard Szczeciński
Białogard
Świdwin
Drawsko Pomorskie
Piła

TEXEL
Vlieland
Terschelling
Ameland
Schiermonnikoog
Den Helder
Alkmaar
Leeuwarden
Groningen
Delfzijl
Emden
Wilhelmshaven
Bremerhaven

NETHERLANDS
AMSTERDAM
Zwolle
Almelo
Enschede
Nordhorn
Oldenburg
Delmenhorst
Bremen
Verden
NIEDERSACHSEN
LÜNEBURGER HEIDE
Lüneburg
Soltau
Uelzen
Wittenberge
Salzwedel
Stendal
Neu Ruppin
Oranienburg
Eberswalde
Bad Freienwalde

Apeldoorn
Deventer
Utrecht
Arnhem
Nijmegen
s-Hertogenbosch
Kleve
Hengelo
Enschede
Rheine
Osnabrück
Minden
Nienburg
Celle
Wolfsburg
Hannover
Braunschweig
Hildesheim
Helmstedt
Magdeburg
Schönebeck
Zerbst
Brandenburg
Potsdam
BERLIN
Fürstenwalde
Frankfurt an der Oder
Świebodzin

MECKLENBURG
Güstrow
Teterow
Friedland
Pasewalk
Ueckermünde
Demmin
Neubrandenburg
Waren
Müritz
Parchim
Ludwigslust
Pritzwalk
Perleberg
Templin
Zehdenick
Angermünde
Schwedt
Prenzlau
Gryfino

Międzyrzecz
Poznań
Grodzisk
Gorzów Wlkp.
Świerzyna
Kostrzyn
Warta
Notec
Debno
Świebodzin
Eisenhüttenstadt
Zielona Góra
Nowa Sól

Tilburg
Eindhoven
Tegelen
Duisburg
DÜSSELDORF
Mönchengladbach
Heerlen
Maastricht
COLOGNE (Köln)
Aachen
Liège
Verviers
Eupen
Malmédy
NORDRHEIN
Bonn
Siegburg
Gummersbach
Siegen
WESTFALEN
Bielefeld
Herford
Gütersloh
Detmold
Paderborn
Lippstadt
Soest
Hamm
Dortmund
Bochum
Essen
Gelsenkirchen
Gladbeck
Bottrop
Wuppertal
Solingen
Remscheid
Hagen
Münster
Ahlen
Minden
Hamelin
Goslar
Göttingen
Northeim
Nordhausen
Eisleben
Halberstadt
Quedlinburg
Bernburg
Aschersleben
Dessau
Wittenberg
Bitterfeld
Delitzsch
Lübben
Guben
Cottbus
Spremberg
Forst
Żary
Żagań
Głogów
Nowa Sól
Lubin
Bolesławiec
Zielona Góra
Szprotawa

GERMANY

HARZ
Stassfurt
Sangerhausen
Merseburg
Halle
Leipzig
Eilenburg
Wurzen
Grimma
Riesa
Meissen
DRESDEN
Bautzen
Görlitz
Luban
Zgorzelec
Jawor
Legnica
Świdnica
Wałbrzych

THÜRINGEN
Heiligenstadt
Mühlhausen
Eisenach
Gotha
Erfurt
Weimar
Jena
Gera
Altenburg
Zwickau
Chemnitz
Freiberg
Pirna
Sebnitz
Zittau
Liberec
Jablonec nad Nisou
Trutnov
Broumov
Náchod
Jelenia Góra
SUDETEN

WESTERWALD
RHEIN
Koblenz
Neuwied
Andernach
Mayen
Limburg an der Lahn
Wetzlar
Giessen
Marburg an der Lahn
HESSEN
Bad Hersfeld
Fulda
Schmalkalden
Zella-Mehlis
Suhl
Meiningen
Hildburghausen
Saalfeld
Sonneberg
Coburg
Kronach
Hof
Plauen
Oelsnitz
Reichenbach
Greiz
Crimmitschau
Glauchau
Meerane
Aue
Annaberg
ERZGEBIRGE
Chomutov
Most
Teplice
Ústí nad Labem
Děčín
Mělník
Česká Lípa
Litoměřice
Mladá Boleslav
Turnov
Jičín
Dvůr Králové
Hradec Králové

EIFEL
RHEINLAND
Wittlich
Echternach
LUXEMBOURG
Luxembourg
Trier
Kirn
Idar-Oberstein
HUNSRÜCK
Bingen
Mainz
WIESBADEN
FRANKFURT AM MAIN
Hanau
Offenbach
Aschaffenburg
Bad Kissingen
Schweinfurt
Würzburg
Bamberg
Bayreuth
Marktredwitz
Cheb
Karlovy Vary
Mariánské Lázně
Plzeň
Rakovník
Kladno
PRAGUE (Praha)
Beroun
Nymburk
Kolín
Pardubice
Vysoké Mýto
Litomyšl
CZECH REPUBLIC

Thionville
Metz
Sarreguemines
Saarbrücken
Zweibrücken
Neustadt
Pirmasens
Kaiserslautern
SAARLAND
PFALZ
Bad Kreuznach
Worms
Ludwigshafen
MANNHEIM
Speyer
Heidelberg
Darmstadt
Bensheim
ODENWALD
Mosbach
Bad Mergentheim
Rothenburg
Ansbach
Nürnberg
Fürth
Schwabach
Erlangen
Forchheim
Weiden
Amberg
Schwandorf
BAYERN (BAVARIA)
Regensburg
Domažlice
Klatovy
Nýřany
Rokycany
Příbram
Benešov
Tábor
Jihlava
Třebíč
Brno
VYSOČINA
ČESKOMORAVSKÁ VYSOČINA
Havlíčkův Brod
Humpolec
Pelhřimov

Nancy
Lunéville
Sarrebourg
Saverne
Strasbourg
Haguenau
Wissembourg
Karlsruhe
Bruchsal
Rastatt
Baden-Baden
Pforzheim
Ludwigsburg
STUTTGART
Esslingen
Schwäbisch Gmünd
Aalen
Ellwangen
Nördlingen
Weissenburg
Eichstätt
Ingolstadt
Neuburg
Landshut
Straubing
Deggendorf
Passau
BOHEMIAN FOREST
ŠUMAVA
Sušice
Vimperk
Strakonice
Písek
Prachatice
České Budějovice
Třeboň
Jindřichův Hradec
Znojmo
Laa
Hollabrunn
Krems

Épinal
Remiremont
Mirecourt
St. Dié
Colmar
Guebwiller
Mulhouse
Belfort
Montbéliard
Freiburg
FRANCE
ELSASS
Offenburg
Lahr
Villingen-Schwenningen
SCHWARZWALD
BADEN-WÜRTTEMBERG
Tübingen
Reutlingen
Rottweil
Heilbronn
Heidenheim
Ulm
Neu Ulm
Günzburg
Augsburg
Memmingen
Landsberg
Dachau
MUNICH (München)
Freising
Mühldorf
Braunau
Ried
Wels
Linz
St. Pölten
Amstetten
VIENNA (Wien)
OBERÖSTERREICH
Steyr
Waidhofen

Vesoul
Montbéliard
Basel
Lörrach
Schaffhausen
Winterthur
Zürich
Baden
Aarau
Konstanz
Friedrichshafen
Ravensburg
Lindau
Bregenz
Dornbirn
Kempten
Kaufbeuren
Weilheim
Bad Tölz
Garmisch-Partenkirchen
Rosenheim
Traunstein
Bad Reichenhall
Salzburg
Bad Ischl
Gmunden
Kufstein
Schwaz
Innsbruck
VORARLBERG
Feldkirch
Bludenz
Arlberg Tunnel
Brenner Pass
HOHE TAUERN
NIEDERE TAUERN
SALZBURG
STEIERMARK
Leoben
Bruck
Kapfenberg
Mürzzuschlag
SEMMERING
Wiener Neustadt
Neunkirchen
Baden
Berndorf

La Chaux-de-Fonds
Le Locle
Neuchâtel
Biel
Bern
Burgdorf
Langnau
Thun
Fribourg
Lausanne
Montreux
Geneva (Genève)
Thonon
JURA
Solothurn
Olten
SWITZERLAND
Luzern
Schwyz
Glarus
Chur
Davos
St. Moritz
LIECHTENSTEIN
Wildspitze 12,382
BERNER ALPEN
GOTTHARD PASS
PENNINE ALPS
Mont Blanc
Locarno
Lugano
Bellinzona
Bolzano
Merano
Bressanone
Pieve di Cadore
Belluno
CARNIC ALPS
Lienz
Spittal
KÄRNTEN
St. Veit
Villach
KARAWANKEN
Klagenfurt
Maribor
SLOVENIA
Celje
Kranj
Škofja Loka
Tolmin
CROATIA

ITALY
Aosta
Chiasso
Lecco
Como
Sondrio
Trento
Udine
Adige

Continued on pages 156-157

Continued on pages 160-161

Longitude East of Greenwich

COPYRIGHT BY
RAND McNALLY & COMPANY
MADE IN U.S.A.

Scale 1:4 000 000; one inch to 64 miles. Conic Projection
Elevations and depressions are given in feet.

Continued on pages 152-153
Continued on pages 162-163

Relief

Meters	Feet
3050	10 000
1525	5000
610	2000
305	1000
152.5	500
0 Sea Level	0
Below Sea Level	

Countries/Regions: RUSSIA, LITHUANIA, BELARUS, POLAND, UKRAINE, SLOVAKIA, HUNGARY, ROMANIA, MOLDOVA, YUGO.

Physical features: MASURIA, GALICIA, CARPATHIAN, BESKIDY, HIGH TATRA MTS., NÍZKE TATRY, RUTHENIA, BUKOVINA, MOLDAVIA, TRANSYLVANIA, ROMANIAN MOUNTAINS, MUNTII RODNEI, MUNTII HARGHITA, MUNTII ZARAND, MUNTII GILLAU, Gulf of Danzig, SEA

Cities and towns:

Kaliningrad (Königsberg), Sovetsk (Tilsit), Ragnit, Jurbarkas, Kybartai, Šakiai, Vilkija, Kaunas (Kovno), Kudirkos Naumiestis, Vilkaviškis, Prienai, Trakai, Vilnius, Slobodka, Vileyka, Molodechno, Oshmyany, Volozhin

Wejherowo, Puck, Hel, Gdynia, Sopot, Gdańsk (Danzig), Baltiysk, Tczew, Elbląg, Braniewo, Pravdinsk, Znamensk, Gusev, Nesterov, Virbalis, Marijampolé, Kalvarija, Alytus, Varéna, Merkiné, Jašiūnai, Voronovo, Lida, Mir, Novogrudok, Nesvizh, Dzerzhinsk, Minsk

Lebork, Kościerzyna, Starogard Gdański, Czersk, Malbork, Lidzbark, Orneta, Bartoszyce, Kętrzyn, Gizycko, Wegorzewo, Goldap, Trakiszki, Suwalki, Augustów, Grodno, Volkovysk, Baranovichi, Kletsk, Slutsk

Olsztyn, Mrągowo, Szczytno, Elk, Grajewo, Grodno, Sokółka, Krynki, Ruzhany, Slonim, Nesvizh

Grudziądz, Kwidzyn, Iława, Ostróda, Nidzica, Mława, Przasnysz, Kolno, Szczuczyn, Łomża, Knyszyn, Wasilków, Białystok, Semionówka, Bereza, Ruzhany, Shereshevo

Toruń, Chelmno, Brodnica, Rypin, Sierpc, Ciechanów, Nasielsk, Ostrołęka, Zambrów, Ostrów Mazowiecki, Bielsk Podlaski, Wysokie Mazowieckie, Hajnówka, Pinsk, Stolin, David-Gorodok, Luninets, Petrikov, Korosten

Bydgoszcz, Aleksandrów Kujawski, Inowrocław, Lipno, Włocławek, Płock, Gostynin, Nowy Dwór Mazowiecki, Wyszków, Siemiatycze, Brańsk, Sokołów Podlaski, Węgrów, Sarny

Września, Konin, Koło, Kutno, Łowicz, WARSAW (Warszawa), Wołomin, Mińsk Mazowiecki, Siedlce, Biała Podlaska, Brest, Kobrin, Drogichin

Łódź, Zgierz, Pabianice, Ursus, Pruszków, Grodzisk, Żyrardów, Skierniewice, Rawa Mazowiecka, Grójec, Otwock, Garwolin, Żelechów, Łuków, Radzyń Podlaski, Parczew, Włodawa, Tomashevka

Kalisz, Ostrów Wlkp., Sieradz, Zduńska Wola, Złoczew, Wieluń, Tomaszów Mazowiecki, Opoczno, Kozienice, Puławy, Dęblin, Lubartów, Ostrów Lubelski, Chelm, Kovel, Volodymyr-Volyns'kyy, Luts'k

Piotrków Trybunalski, Radom, Szydłowiec, Opole Lubelskie, Lublin, Krasnystaw, Rivne, Zdolbuniv, Korets', Novohrad-Volyns'kyy

Oleśnica, Kępno, Kluczbork, Opole, Radomsko, Przedbórz, Końskie, Ostrowiec Świętokrzyski, Kielce, Włoszczowa, Chmielnik, Sandomierz, Krasnik, Janów Lubelski, Zamość, Hrubieszów, Szczebrzeszyn, Tomaszów Lubelski, Dubno, UKRAINE, Ostroh, Slavuta, Shepetivka, Polonne, Lyubar

Częstochowa, Jędrzejów, Pińczów, Staszów, Nisko, Stalowa Wola, Biłgoraj, Rava-Rus'ka, Sokal', Brody, Kremenets, Zbarazh, Starokostyantyniv, Khmil'nyk

Strzelce Opolskie, Zawiercie, Działoszyce, Mielec, Leżajsk, Lubaczów, Zhovkva, L'viv, Bus'k, Zolochiv, Pidvolochys'k, Medzhybizh

Prudnik, Kozle, Bytom, Gliwice, Zabrze, KATOWICE, Sosnowiec, Jaworzno, Chrzanów, Kraków, Bochnia, Tarnów, Rzeszów, Błażowa, Jarosław, Yavoriv, Horodok, Komarno, Ternopil', Berezhany, Terebovlya, Kopychyntsi, Khmel'nyts'kyy, Letychiv

Racibórz, Rybnik, Oświęcim, Wadowice, Kęty, Sucha, Nowy Sącz, Stary Sącz, Gorlice, Jasło, Krosno, Sanok, Przemyśl, Sambir, Drohobych, Boryslav, Turka, Skole, Stryy, Kalush, Rohatyn, Bibrka, Chortkiv, Borshchiv, Bar, Zhmerynka

Opava, Karvina, Ostrava, Český Těšín, Cieszyn, Żywiec, Zakopane, Nowy Targ, Kežmarok, Bardejov, Duklá Pass, Uzhhorod, Ivano-Frankivs'k, Nadvirna, Tlumach, Horodenka, Kam'yanets-Podil's'kyy, Mohyliv-Podil's'kyy

Olomouc, Přerov, Hranice, Nový Jičín, Vsetín, Kroměříž, Žilina, Vrutky, Martin, Gerlachovsky štit 8199, 8711, Levoča, Spišská Nová Ves, Prešov, Michalovce, Mukacheve, Berehove, Chust, Rakhiv, Velykyy Bychkiv, Chernivtsi, MOLDOVA

Trenčín, Nové Mesto nad Váhom, Banská Bystrica, Dobšiná, Rožňava, Košice, Trebišov, Sátoraljaújhely, Sárospatak, Tyachiv, Sighetu Marmatiei, Solotvyno, Kolomyya, Kuty, Storozhynets, Zastavna, Khotyn, Darabani, Dorohoi, Bălţi

Piešťany, Topol'čany, Zvolen, Rimavská Sobota, Kazincbarcika, Tokaj, Rakamaz, Nyíregyháza, Satu Mare, Vârfu Pietrosu 7562, Botoşani, Siret, Rădăuţi, Fălești

Bratislava, Sered', Nitra, Levice, Lučenec, Salgótarján, Miskolc, Eger, Polgár, Hajdúnánás, Baia Mare, Câmpulung Moldovenesc, Suceava, Fălticeni, Iaşi

Nové Zámky, Komárno, Vác, Gyöngyös, Mezőkövesd, Hajdúböszörmény, Hajdúhadház, Carei, Baia de Criş, Vatra Dornei, Târgu-Neamţ, Paşcani, Vaslui

Győr, Tatabánya, Esztergom, Szentendre, BUDAPEST, Jászberény, Jászapáti, Balmazújváros, Debrecen, Hajdúszoboszló, Oradea, Gherla, Bistriţa, Reghin, Piatra-Neamţ, Roman, Bârlad

Pápa, Mór, Bicske, Cegléd, Szolnok, Karcag, Berettyóújfalu, Simleu Silvaniei, Zalău, Dej, Gheorgheni, Târgu Ocna, Bacău, Adjud

Székesfehérvár, Veszprém, Dunaújváros, Sárbogárd, Nagykőrös, Kecskemét, Mezőtúr, Szarvas, Békés, Vésztő, Mezőberény, Salonta, Cluj-Napoca, Turda, Aiud, Târgu Mureş, Sighişoara, Mediaş, Miercurea-Ciuc, Odorhei, Târgu Secuiesc, Odobeşti, Focşani

Dombóvár, Szekszárd, Dunaföldvár, Paks, Kalocsa, Kiskunfélegyháza, Kiskunhalas, Csongrád, Szentes, Hódmezővásárhely, Orosháza, Gyula, Békéscsaba, Sebeş, Alba Iulia, Făgăraş, Sibiu, Braşov, Ocna Sibiului, Sfântu Gheorghe, Tecuci

Szigetvár, Pécs, Mohács, Baja, Bácsalmás, Subotica, Senta, Ada, Bačka Topola, Kanjiza, Makó, Nădlac, Jimbolia, Timişoara, Arad, Târnăveni, Blaj, Sighişoara

Siklós, YUGO., Sombor, Bačko, Melykut, Bačko Topola, Arad, Lipova, Kikinda

Lakes: Balaton

Scale:
0 10 20 30 40 50 60 70 80 90 100 110 120 Miles
0 20 40 60 80 100 120 140 160 180 200 Kilometers

Continued on pages 150-151

Relief

Meters		Feet
3050		10 000
1525		5000
610		2000
305		1000
152.5		500
0	Sea Level	0
152.5		500
1525		5000

ENGLISH

CHANNEL

UNITED KINGDOM

Folkestone   Dover   Dunkerque   Roeselare   Gent   Aalst   Mechelen
Honiton   Hove   Lewes   Hastings   Str. of Dover   Calais   Ieper   Kortrijk   Leuven   Anderlecht   BRUSSELS
Exeter   Southampton   Worthing   Bexhill   Eastbourne   Boulogne-sur-Mer   Armentières   Tourcoing   Roubaix   BELGIU
Dorchester   Poole   Portsmouth   Chichester   Brighton   St. Omer   Lille   Valenciennes   Mons   Charleroi   Namur
Launceston   Cowes   Newport   ISLE OF WIGHT   Étaples   Béthune   Bruay-en-Artois   Douai   Denain   Maubeuge   Dinant
Torquay (Torbay)   Weymouth   Bournemouth   Berck   Arras   Hautmont   Cambrai   Givet
Plymouth   Dartmouth   PICARDIE   Crécy-en-Ponthieu   Albert   Guise   Hirson   Nouzonvi
START POINT   St. Valéry-sur-Somme   Abbeville   en-Vermandois   Fourmies   Revin   Sedan
Le Tréport   Péronne   St. Quentin   Charleville-Mézières   ARGONNE
C. DE LA HAGUE   Dieppe   Amiens   Corbie   Chauny   Laon   Rethel
ALDERNEY   Fécamp   Neufchâtel-en-Bray   Roye   Soissons   Vouziers
GUERNSEY   Cherbourg   Bolbec   Yvetot   Montdidier   Compiègne   Oise   Reims   Châlons-sur-Marne
St. Peter Port   SARK   Baie de la Seine   Le Havre   Creil   Aisne
CHANNEL ISLANDS (Br.)   Valognes   Honfleur   Pont-Audemer   Rouen   Beauvais   Méru   Château-Thierry   Épernay   CHAMPAGNE
JERSEY   St. Helier   Carentan   Bayeux   Trouville   Elbeuf   Louviers   Gisors   Pontoise   Meaux   Bar-
Saint-Lô   Caen   Lisieux   Évreux   St. Germain-en-Laye   Argenteuil   St-Denis   Marne   le-Duc
Condé   Vernon   Mantes-la-Jolie   Versailles   Clichy   PARIS   Vitry-le-François   Arcis-sur-Aube   Joinville
Golfe de St. Malo   NORMANDIE   L'Aigle   Dreux   Boulogne-Billancourt   Melun   Romilly-sur-Seine   Aube
St. Pol-de-Léon   Granville   Flers   Argentan   Rambouillet   Corbeil-Essonnes   Troyes
Morlaix   St. Malo   Avranches   COLLINES DE NORMANDIE   Chartres   Étampes   Montereau-faut-Yonne
I. D'OUESSANT   Landerneau   Guingamp   St. Brieuc   Dinard   COLLINES DU PERCHE   Nogent-le-Rotrou   Fontainebleau   Sens   Joigny
Brest   MTS. D'ARRÉE   Carhaix-Plouguer   Dinan   Lamballe   Fougères   Vitré   Alençon   Nemours   Auxerre   Montbard
Douarnenez   Lannion   Pontivy   Montfort   Laval   Le Mans   Châteaudun   Pithiviers   Montargis   CÔTE D'OR   Dijon
Quimper   BRETAGNE   Rennes   Orléans   MORVAN
PTE. DU RAZ   Audierne   Ploërmel   Sablé-sur-Sarthe   Vendôme   Gien   Briare   Clamecy   Avallon
Pont-l'Abbé   Concarneau   Hennebont   Vannes   Redon   Château-Gontier   La Flèche   Blois   SOLOGNE   Cosne-sur-Loire   Autun   Le Creuso
ÎLES DE GLÉNAN   Lorient   Château-Renault   Romorantin-Lanthenay   Nevers   Chalon-sur-Saône
ÎLE DE GROIX   Quiberon   Angers   Trélazé   Tours   Amboise   Loire   Bourges   Digoin   Montceau   Paray-le-Monial   Cluny
St. Nazaire   Saumur   Chinon   Loches   Vierzon   Mehun-sur-Yèvre   St. Florent-sur-Cher
BELLE-ÎLE   Nantes   FRANCE   Cher   St. Amand-Mont Rond   Moulins
ÎLE DE NOIRMOUTIER   Pornic   Chemillé   Thouars   Loudun   Vienne   Issoudun   Châteauroux   Roanne   Villefranche
Cholet   HAUTEURS DE GÂTINE   Châtellerault   Creuse   Argenton-sur-Creuse   Vichy   MTS. DU FOREZ   Tarare
ÎLE D'YEU   Bressuire   Parthenay   Poitiers   Le Blanc   Montmorillon   Thiers   Villeurban
La Roche-sur-Yon   Fontenay-le-Comte   Montmorillon   Riom   Clermont-Ferrand
Les Sables-d'Olonne   Luçon   Guéret   Aubusson   Ambert   Outlins
Pertuis Breton   ÎLE DE RÉ   La Rochelle   Ruffec   Confolens   Ussel   Issoire   Brioude   Firminy   St. Étienn
BAY OF BISCAY   Surgères   Rochefort   St. Junien   PLATEAUX DU LIMOUSIN   Puy de Sancy 6185   St. Chamond   Annonay   Yssingeaux   Romans
ÎLE D'OLÉRON   St. Jean-d'Angely   Limoges   Aubusson   AUVERGNE   Montbrison   Rive-de-Gier
Marennes   Saintes   Charente   Angoulême   LIMOUSIN   Bort-les-Orgues   MASSIF   Le Puy   Valen
La Tremblade   Cognac   St. Yrieix-la-Perche   Brive-la-Gaillarde   Tulle   Argentat   Murat   St. Flour   Mt. Mézenc 5751   Privas
Royan   Barbezieux   Périgueux   Plomb du Cantal 6076   CENTRAL   Aubenas   Le Tei
Gironde   Jonzac   Coutras   Salat-la-Caneda   Aurillac   Langogne   Bessèges
Blaye-et-Ste. Luce   Libourne   Dordogne   Bergerac   Figeac   Mende   Bagnols-sur-Cèze
Étang de Carcans   Blanquefort   Mérignac   Pessac   Bordeaux   La Réole   Entraygues   La Grand Combe   Alès
Bassin d'Arcachon   Bègles   Marmande   Lot   Decazeville   Rodez   CÉVENNES
Arcachon   La Teste-de-Buch   Langon   Tonneins   Cahors   Aubin   Millau   VIGAN
Étang de Cazaux   Villeneuve-sur-Lot   Villefranche-de-Rouergue   Aveyron   Nîmes
LANDES   Labouheyre   Agen   Moissac   Carmaux   Lodève   Avignon
Étang de Biscaros   Nérac   Condom   Castelsarrasin   Montauban   Albi   St. Affrique   Béziers
Mont-de-Marsan   Verdun   Gaillac   Castres   Bédarieux   Montpellier   Lunel
Dax   Aire-sur-l'Adour   GASCOGNE   Auch   Toulouse   Baziège   Pézenas   Sète   Golfe du
Biarritz   Bayonne   Orthez   Salies-de-Béarn   Muret   Castelnaudary   Carcassonne   Limoux   Narbonne   Agde
Irún   St. Jean-de-Luz   Pau   Tarbes   St. Gaudens   Pamiers   Sigean
Oloron-Ste. Marie   Lourdes   Bagnères-de-Bigorre   St. Girons   Foix   Tarascon   Quillan   Rivesaltes   Perpignan
Roncesvalles   PYRÉNÉES   Bagnères-de-Luchon   Ax-les-Thermes   Prades   Port Vendres
Pamplona   Mt. Perdido 11168   Pico de Aneto 11007   ANDORRA   Céret   C. DE CREUS
Tafalla   Jaca   SPAIN   Andorra
Boltaña

A-550900-76 1.76-12
COPYRIGHT BY
RAND McNALLY & COMPANY
MADE IN U.S.A.

Longitude West of Greenwich   Longitude East of Greenwich

Scale 1:4 000 000; one inch to 64 miles. Conic Proje
Elevations and depressions are given in feet

a

Miramas   Équilles   Aix-en-Provence
St. Chamas   Istres   Rognac   Gardanne   Simiane
Berre-l'Étang   Étang de Berre   Marignane   St. Victoret
Port-de-Bouc   Martigues   Châteauneuf   L'Estaque   Allauch
Lavéra   La Couronne   Carry-le-Rouet   Carro   Sausset-les-Pins   La Penne-sur-Huveaune   MARSEILLE
Mazargues   Golfe du Lion   La Madrague   CÔTE DE LA GINESTE 1075
MEDITERRANEAN SEA

Scale 1:1 000 000
0   4   8   12   16 Kilometers
0   10 Miles

©RMCN.

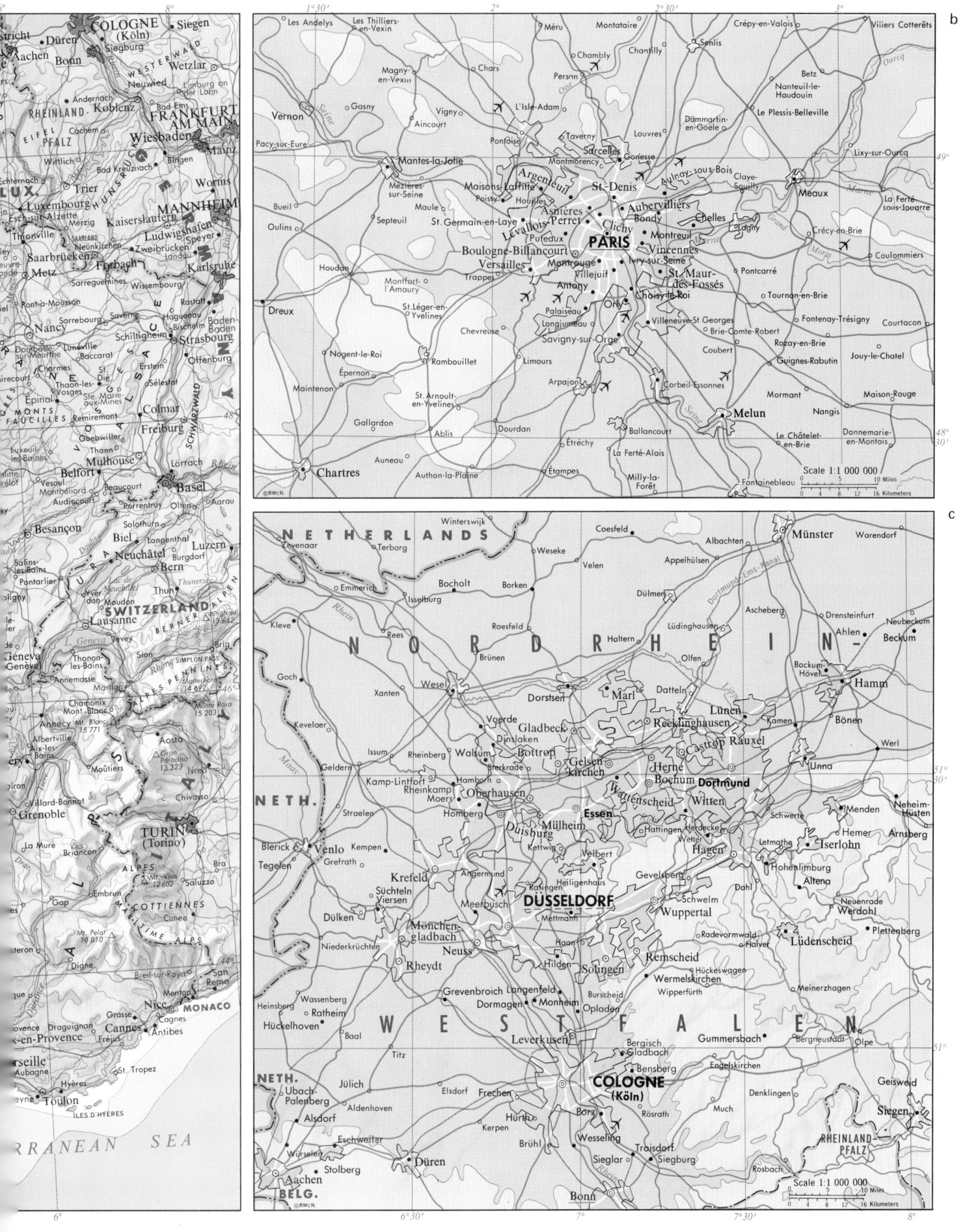

b

Les Andelys Les Thilliers-en-Vexin Méru Montataire Crépy-en-Valois Villers Cotterêts

Magny-en-Vexin Chars Chambly Chantilly Senlis Betz Nanteuil-le-Haudouin Le Plessis-Belleville Ourcq

Vernon Gasny Vigny Aincourt Persan Dammartin-en-Goële Lixy-sur-Ourcq

Pacy-sur-Eure L'Isle-Adam Taverny Louvres 49°

Mantes-la-Jolie Pontoise Montmorency Sarcelles Gonesse Claye-Souilly Meaux La Ferté-sous-Jouarre

Mézières-sur-Seine Poissy Argenteuil St-Denis Aulnay-sous-Bois Marne

Buel Maule Maisons-Laffitte Houilles Aubervilliers Bondy Chelles Lagny Crécy-en-Brie

Oulins St. Germain-en-Laye Asnières-Perret Clichy Montreuil Coulommiers

Septeuil Levallois-Perret Puteaux **PARIS** Vincennes

Houdan Boulogne-Billancourt Montrouge Ivry-sur-Seine St. Maur-des-Fossés Pontcarré

Montfort-l'Amaury Versailles Villejuif Tournan-en-Brie

Dreux Trappes Antony Orly Choisy-le-Roi Villeneuve-St Georges Fontenay-Trésigny Courtacon

St.Léger-en-Yvelines Palaiseau Longjumeau Brie-Comte-Robert Rozay-en-Brie Jouy-le-Chatel

Chevreuse Savigny-sur-Orge Arpajon Coubert Guignes-Rabutin

Nogent-le-Roi Rambouillet Limours Corbeil-Essonnes Maison-Rouge

Épernon Mormant Nangis

Maintenon St. Arnoult-en-Yvelines Ballancourt **Melun** Donnemarie-en-Montois 48°30'

Gallardon Dourdan Étrechy Le Châtelet-en-Brie 48°30'

Ablis Auneau La Ferté-Alais Scale 1:1 000 000

Chartres Authon-la-Plaine Étampes Milly-la-Forêt Fontainebleau

c

NETHERLANDS Winterswijk Coesfeld Albachten Münster Warendorf

Zevenaar Terborg Weseke Velen Appelhülsen Dortmund-Ems-Kanal

Emmerich Bocholt Borken Dülmen Ascheberg Drensteinfurt Neubeckum

Kleve Isselburg Raesfeld Haltern Lüdinghausen Ahlen Beckum

Goch Rees N O R D R H E I N -

Xanten Wesel Brünen Olfen Bockum-Hövel Hamm

Kevelaer Dorstsen Datteln Lünen Kamen Bönen Werl

Voerde Marl Recklinghausen

Issum Gladbeck Castrop Rauxel Unna

Rheinberg Dinslaken Bottrop Gelsenkirchen Herne

Geldern Walsum Steckrade Bochum **Dortmund**

Kamp-Lintfort Hamborn Oberhausen Wattenscheid Witten

NETH. Moers Homberg **Essen** Herdecke Schwerte Menden

Straelen Mülheim Hattingen Wetter Hagen Letmathe Hemer Arnsberg

Blerick Duisburg Kettwig Velbert Iserlohn

Venlo Kempen Angermund Heiligenhaus Gevelsberg Hohenlimburg Altena

Tegelen Grefrath Ratingen Dahl Neuenrade Werdohl

Krefeld Schwelm Lüdenscheid Plettenberg

Dülken Viersen Meerbusch Mettmann **DÜSSELDORF** Wuppertal

Niederkrüchten Mönchen-gladbach Haan Radevormwald Halver Meinerzhagen

Rheydt Neuss Hilden Remscheid Hückeswagen

Grevenbroich Langenfeld Solingen Wermelskirchen Wipperfürth

Heinsberg Wassenberg Dormagen Monheim Burscheid 51°30'

Ratheim Opladen Neunenrade

Hückelhoven Baal W E S T F A L E N Leverkusen Bergisch-Gladbach Gummersbach Bergneustadt Olpe

NETH. Titz Bensberg Engelskirchen 51°

Ubach-Palenberg Jülich Elsdorf Frechen **COLOGNE (Köln)** Denklingen

Aldenhoven Kerpen Rösrath Much Geisweid

Alsdorf Hürth Bors Siegen

Wurselen Kerpen Wesseling **RHEINLAND-PFALZ**

Eschweiler Brühl Sieglar Troisdorf Siegburg

Düren Rosbach

Aachen Stolberg Bonn Scale 1:1 000 000

BELG.

For larger scale coverage of Dusseldorf and Paris see pages 236 and 237.

[Left panel:]

COLOGNE (Köln) Siegen Maastricht Düren Aachen Bonn Siegburg

WESTERWALD Wetzlar

Andernach Neuwied Limburg an der Lahn

RHEINLAND- Koblenz Bad Ems FRANKFURT AM MAIN

EIFEL PFALZ Cochem Wiesbaden Mainz

Echternach Wittlich Bad Kreuznach Bingen

LUX. Trier Worms

Luxembourg Esch-sur-Alzette Merzig MANNHEIM

Thionville SAARLAND Kaiserslautern Ludwigshafen Speyer

Neunkirchen Zweibrücken Landau Karlsruhe

Saarbrücken Forbach

Metz Sarreguemines Wissembourg

Pont-à-Mousson Saverne Rastatt Baden-Baden

Nancy Sarrebourg Haguenau Bischeim Offenburg

Lunéville Saverne Erstein Strasbourg

Baccarat Schiltigheim Sélestat

Charmes St. Dié Ste.Marie-aux-Mines Colmar

Épinal Thaon-les-Vosges Remiremont Freiburg SCHWARZWALD 48°

MONTS FAUCILLES Goebwiller Thann 47°

Luxeuil-les-Bains Mulhouse Lörrach Rhein

Belfort Beaucourt Porrentruy Olten Aarau

Montbéliard Audincourt Basel

Vesoul Solothurn

Besançon Biel Langenthal Luzern

Neuchâtel Burgdorf

Salins-les-Bains Lac de Neuchâtel Bern Thunersee

Pontarlier Meudon Thun Brig

SWITZERLAND Jungfrau 13 642

Lausanne Vevey BERNER ALPEN

Geneva Thonon-les-Bains Sion Matterhorn 14 692 Monte Rosa 15 203

Genève Annemasse SIMPLON PASS PENNINES

Martigny 46°

Annecy Mt. Blanc 15 771 Aosta Gran Paradiso 13 323 Ivrea

Albertville Moûtiers Chivasso

Villard-Bonnot ALPES Mt. Visa 12 602 Saluzzo

Grenoble Briançon COTTIENNES Cuneo Bra

La Mure Embrun Gap

Mt. Pelat 10 010 44°

Digne MARITIME ALPS Breil-sur-Roya San Remo

Draguignan Grasse Menton Nice **MONACO**

Provence Fréjus Cagnes Antibes

Cannes

Marseille Aubagne St. Tropez Hyères

Toulon ILES D'HYÈRES

MEDITERRANEAN SEA

20 30 40 50 60 70 80 90 100 110 120 Miles

40 60 80 100 120 140 160 180 200 Kilometers

158

Continued on pages 156-157

For larger scale coverage of Lisbon, Madrid and Rome see pages 238 and 239.

Continued on pages 154-155

Continued on pages 156-157

Scale 1:4 000 000; one inch to 64 miles. Conic Projection
Elevations and depressions are given in feet

a

AEGEAN SEA

Same scale
as main map

MEDITERRANEAN SEA

Relief

	Feet
	5000
	2000
	1000
	500
	0
	Sea Level
	500

Meters	
1525	
610	
305	
152.5	
0	
152.5	

Cities and Towns

0 to 50,000	o
50,000 to 500,000	⊙
500,000 to 1,000,000	⊚
1,000,000 and over	

Continued on pages 152-153

Scale 1:4 000 000; one inch to 64 miles. Conic Proj

Elevations and depressions are given in feet

Scale 1:20 000 000; one inch to 315 m
Lambert's Azimuthal, Equal Area Proje
Elevations and depressions are given

Relief

Meters		Feet
3050		10 000
1525		5000
610		2000
305		1000
152.5		500
	Sea Level	
0		0
152.5		500
1525		5000
3050		10 000

Below Sea Level

ARCTIC OCEAN

SEVERNAYA ZEMLYA
(NORTHERN LAND)

M. CHELYUSKIN

TAYMYR
BYRRANGA
GORY

P-OV
GORY

Nordvik
Khatangskiy Zaliv
Taymyr

BOL'SHOY BEGICHEV

LAPTEV
SEA

Ust'-Olenek

Tiksi

DE LONGA

NOVAYA SIBIR
FADDEYA

NOVOSIBIRSKIYE O-VA
(NEW SIBERIAN ISLANDS)

KOTEL'NYY
MALYY LYAKHOVSKIY
LYAKHOVSKIY

M. SVYATOY NOS

M. BUOR-KHAYA

Ust'-Olenek

Balun

Zhigansk

Kazach'ye

Abyy

Verkhoyansk

Alleykha

EAST SIBERIAN SEA

M. SHELAGSKIY

AYON

M. MEDVEZH'I

MEDVEZH'I

Nizhne-Kolymsk

Srednie-Kolymsk

Zyryanka

Yamsk

Markovo

Penzhino

Anadyr'

CHUKOTSKIY P-OV

Arctic Circle

CHUKOTSKOYE NAGOR'YE

Anabar

Amberchik

KHREBET GYDAN (KOLYMSKIY)

Gizhiga

Magadan

Ol'a

Okhotsk

M. TAYGONOS

Zaliv Shelikhova

Tilichiki

KORYAKSKIY KHREBET

KARAGIN

Palana

M. OL'UTORSKIY

Ust'-Kamchatsk

KAMCHATKA

Verkhne-Kamchatsk

Klyuchevskaya Sopka 4750

Petropavlovsk-Kamchatskiy

Ust'-Bol'sheretsk

Noril'sk

GORY PUTORANA

ukhansk

Yartsevo

G. Polkan 3543

eniseysk

G. Piramida 10801

K Krasnoyarsk

Kansk

Tayshet

Bratsk

Nizhneudinsk

Tulun

Balakhna

ski

Minusinsk

Abakan

AYAN

SAYAN

KHREBET

Cheremkhovo

Angarsk

Munku Sardyk 11457

Kyzyl

TANNU-OLA

Uvs Nuur

Ubsu Nuur

Har Us Nuur

Hövd

HANGAYN NURUU KHANGAI MTS.

Uliastay

Taast Bogd 13419

MONGOLIA

Hami

GOBI OR SHAMO
(DESERT)

Sayr Usa

Khatanga

Tura

Nizhnyaya Tunguska

Baykit

Podkamennaya Tunguska

Olenek

Zhigansk

VERKHOYANSKIY KHREBET

Vilyuy

Vilyuysk

Suntar

Yakutsk

Olëkminsk

Lena

Aldan

Amga

Tommot

Aldan

Ust'-Maya

Nel'kan

Ayan

DZHUGDZHUR KHREBET

Chumikan

Uil'skaya Guba

SHANTAR

Nikolayevsk-na-Amure

M. VELIZAVETY

Okha

SAKHALIN

Aleksandrovsk

Poronaysk

M. TERPENIYA

Uglegorsk

Tatar Strait

Kholmsk

Yuzhno-Sakhalinsk

Korsakov

Sôya Kaikyô

Wakkanai

HOKKAIDO

Otaru

Sapporo

Asahi

Mukutya

Peleduy

Vitim

G. Golets Purpula 5377

PATOM PLATEAU

Bodaybo

Golets Skalistyy 9186

STANOVOY KHREBET

Tyndinskiy

Zeya

Skovorodino

Belogorsk

Ust'-Tygda

Bureya

Svobodnyy

Nikolayevsk-na-Amure

KHREBET BUREINSKIY

Komsomol'sk-na-Amure

Sovetskaya Gavan'

Malmyzh

Khabarovsk

Bikin

Dal'nerechensk

Spassk-Dal'niy

Arsen'yev

Artëm

Nakhodka

Partizansk

Vladivostok

Chita

Kirensk

Ilimsk

Nizhne-Angarsk

Zhigalovo

Kachugo

Oz. Baykal (Lake Baikal)
Surface elev 1535 Ft. above sea level

Barguzin

Ust'-Kut

Irkutsk

Ulan-Ude

Petrovsk-Zabaykal'skiy

Gorodok

Kyakhta

BAYKAL'SKIY KHREBET

YABLONOVYY

VITIM KHREBET

Aginskoye

Chita

Sretensk

Nerchinsk

Nerchinskiy Zavod

NERCHINSKIY KHREBET

Borzya

Aksha

Onon

Kutulik

Syren

Hövsgöl Nuur

Selenge

Ulan Bator
(Ulaanbaatar)

Ondörhaan

Kerulen

Wenquan

Tao'an

Jarud Qi

CHANGCHUN

Shuangliao

GREATER KHINGAN RANGE

LESSER KHINGAN RANGE

Nenjiang

Goukou

Hailun

Suihua

Qiqihar

Fuyu

HARBIN

MANCHURIA

Jilin

Mudanjiang

Dunhua

Boli

Suifen

Hunchun

USSURIYSK

SIKHOTE ALIN'

KHREBET SIKHOTE ALIN'

Ol'ga

Najin

Chŏngjin

NORTH KOREA

P'yŏngyang

Kaesong

SEOUL

SOUTH KOREA

Andong

Taegu

PUSAN

Kwangju

Korea Bay

Chifeng

Chengde

Weichang

SHENYANG

FUSHUN

CHINA

Zhangjiakou

Fengzhen

BEIJING

TIANJIN

Baoding

Lüshun

Dalian

Bo Hai

SHANDONG BANDAO

YELLOW SEA

Korea Strait

Matsue

Tottori

Hiroshima

Okayama

KOBE

OSAKA

KYOTO

Kanazawa

Kôchi

HONSHU

SEA OF JAPAN

J A P A N

SEA OF OKHOTSK

70°

60°

50°

40°

80°

90°

100°

110°

120°

130°

140°

150°

160°

170°

180°

100 200 300 400 500 600 Miles

200 400 600 800 1000 Kilometers

A-570000-78 -1514-34
COPYRIGHT BY
RAND McNALLY & COMPANY
MADE IN U.S.A.

Cities and Towns

Symbol	Population
○	0 to 50,000
⊙	50,000 to 500,000
◎	500,000 to 1,000,000
(large)	1,000,000 and over

Relief

Meters	Feet
3050	10000
1525	5000
610	2000
305	1000
152.5	500
0	Sea Level
152.5	500
1525	5000
3050	10000

Below Sea Level

Scale:
0 50 100 150 200 250 300 Miles
0 100 200 300 400 500 Kilometers

RUSSIA

BASHKORTOSTAN
TATARSTAN
UDMURTIA
MARI EL
CHUVASHIA
MORDVINIA
YEKATERINBURG
NIZHNIY NOVGOROD
MOSCOW (Moskva)
ST. PETERSBURG (Sankt-Peterburg) (Leningrad)

U R A L

WESTERN SIBERIAN LOWLAND
YAMAL
NENETS
PECHORA BASIN
KHREBET PAY-KHOY

KARA SEA
BARENTS SEA
Obskaya Guba
NOVAYA ZEMLYA
KOLGUYEV
ARCTIC OCEAN
WHITE SEA
Arkhangelsk (Arkhangel)
KOL'SKIY P-OV (KOLA PEN.)
Murmansk
Kirovsk

KARELIA
FINLAND
SWEDEN
NORWAY
NORD KAPP
MAGERØYA
SØRØYA

Petrozavodsk
Helsinki
Tampere
Turku
Oulu

BALTIC SEA
GULF OF FINLAND
GULF OF BOTHNIA

ESTONIA
Tallinn
LATVIA
Riga
LITHUANIA
Vilnius
Kaunas
Klaipeda
Minsk

Arctic Circle

Continued on pages 146-147

Scale 1:10 000 000; one inch to 160 miles. Conic Projection

Elevations and depressions are given in feet.

Continued on pages 148-149

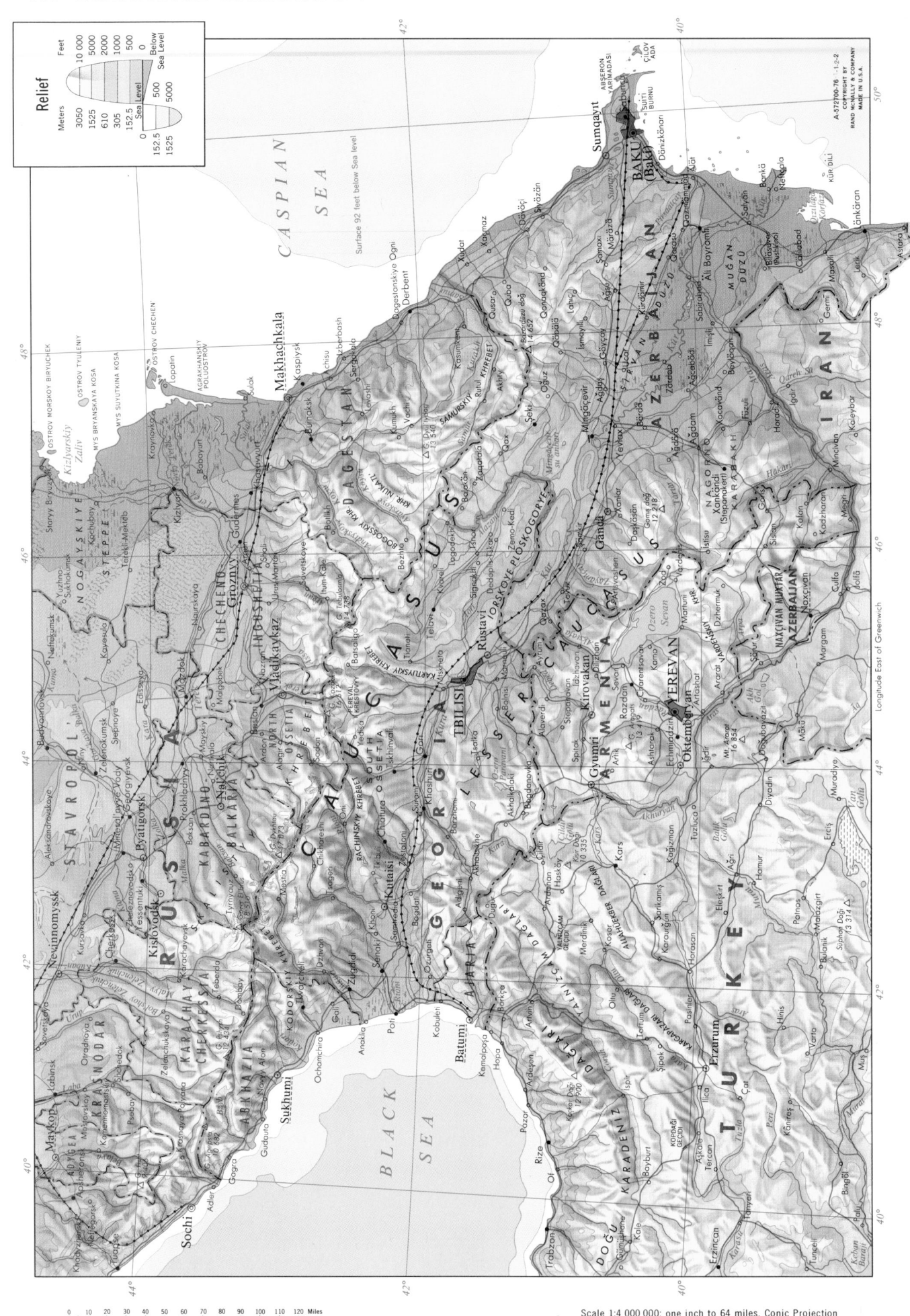

Relief

Meters	Feet
3050	10 000
1525	5000
610	2000
305	1000
152.5	500
0	Sea Level
152.5	500
1525	5000

Below Sea Level

CASPIAN SEA

Surface 92 feet below sea level

BLACK SEA

Scale 1:4 000 000; one inch to 64 miles. Conic Projection
Elevations and depressions are given in feet

0 10 20 30 40 50 60 70 80 90 100 110 120 Miles
0 20 40 60 80 100 120 140 160 180 200 Kilometers

A-572100-76 -1-2-2
COPYRIGHT BY
RAND McNALLY & COMPANY
MADE IN U.S.A.

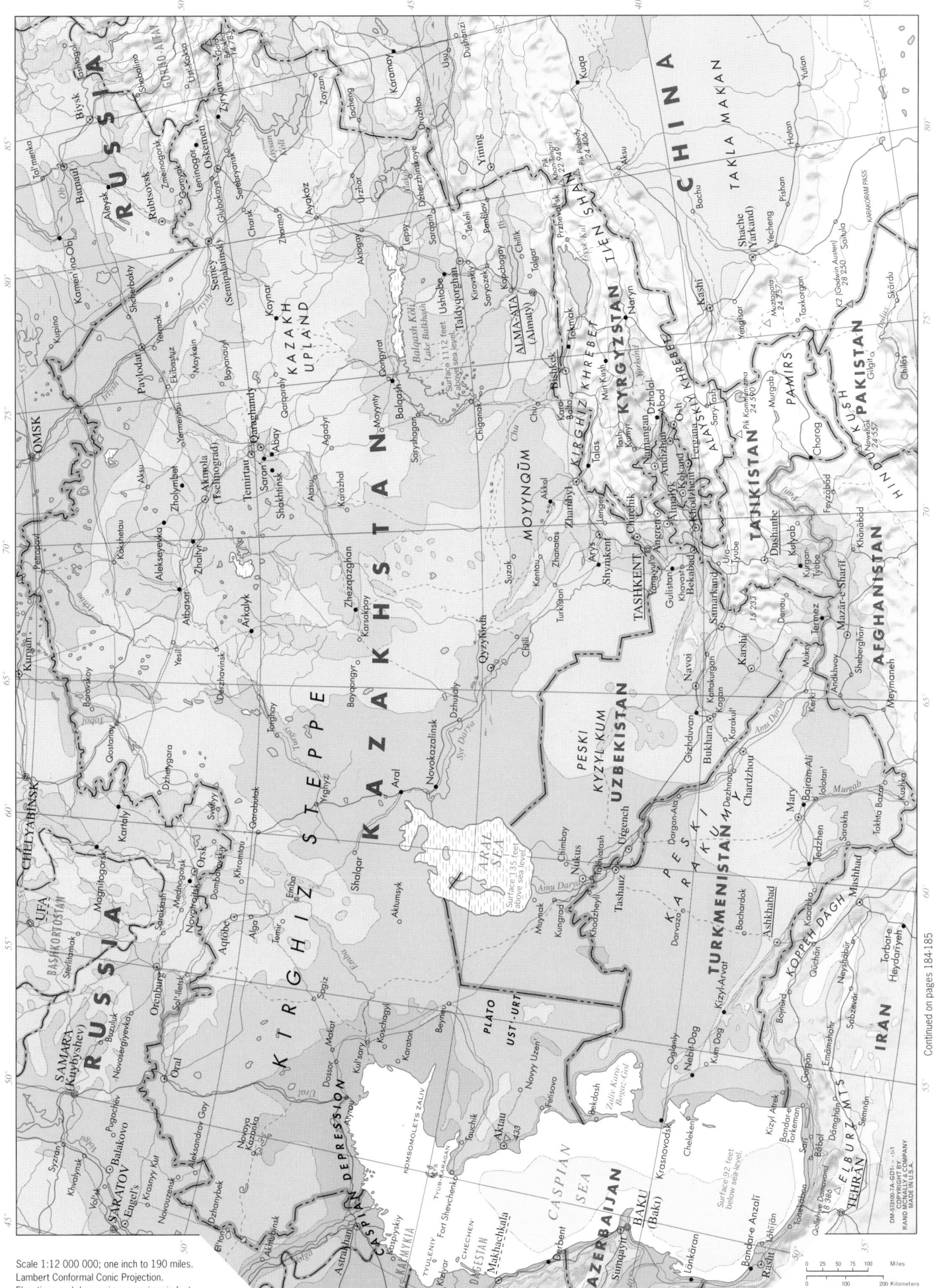

Continued on pages 184-185

Scale 1:12 000 000; one inch to 190 miles.
Lambert Conformal Conic Projection.
Elevations and depressions are given in feet.

RUSSIA

GORNO·ALTAY

CHINA

TAKLA MAKAN

KYRGYZSTAN

TIEN SHAN

KIRGHIZ KHREBET

ALAYSKIY KHREBET

PA·MIRS

HINDU KUSH

PAKISTAN

AFGHANISTAN

TAJIKISTAN

KAZAKHSTAN

KAZAKH UPLAND

MOYYNQŪM

KIRGHIZ STEPPE

PESKI KYZYL KUM

UZBEKISTAN

ARAL SEA

PLATO UST·URT

TURKMENISTAN

PESKI KARA·KUM

KOPPEH DAGH

IRAN

ELBURZ MTS

CASPIAN SEA

AZERBAIJAN

RUSSIA

SAMARA (Kuybyshev)

BASHKORTOSTAN

KALMYKIA

CASPIAN DEPRESSION

OMSK

CHELYABINSK

UFA

TASHKENT

ALMA·ATA (Almaty)

KARAKORAM PASS

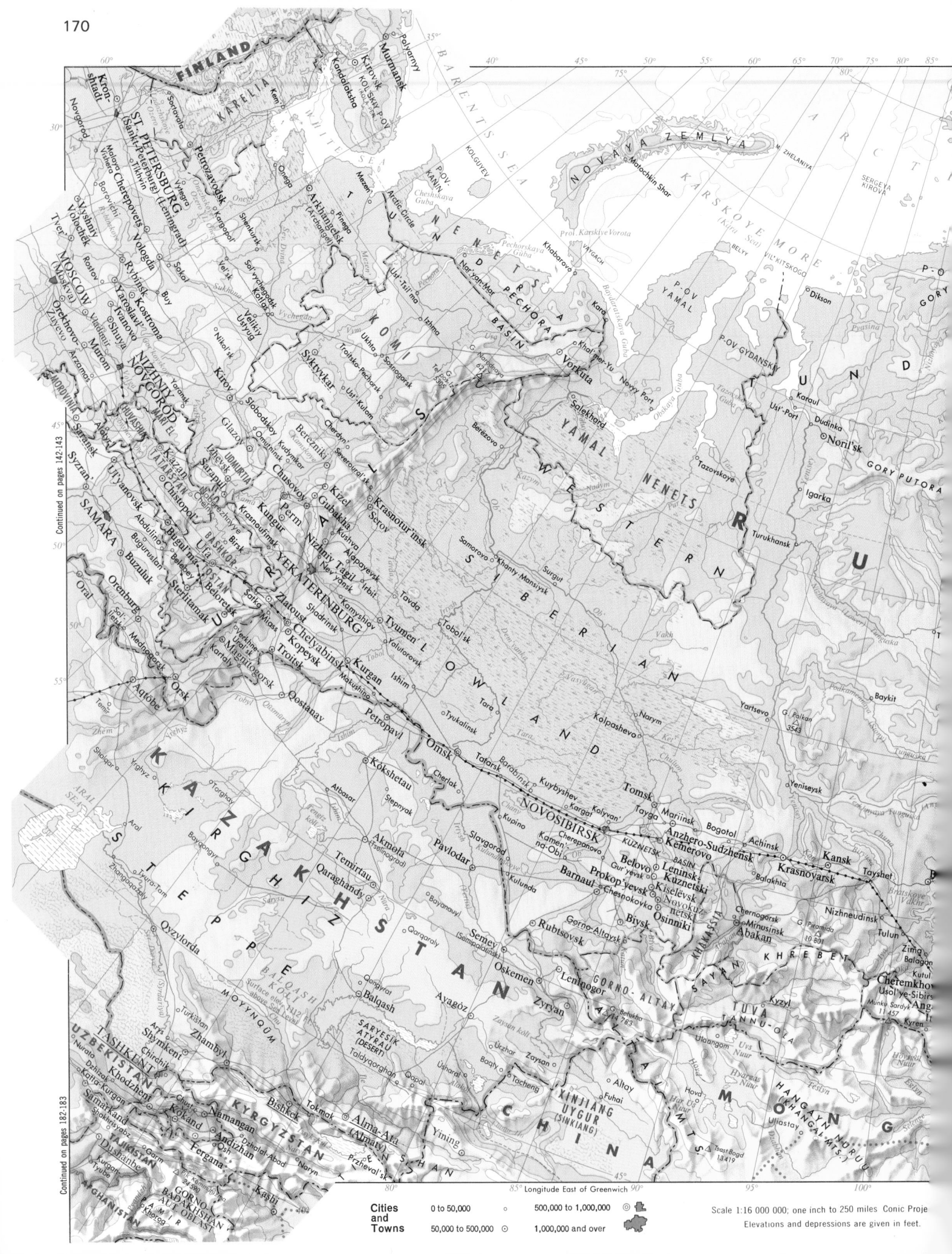

Continued on pages 142-143

Continued on pages 182-183

FINLAND

KATELIA

BARENTS SEA

NOVAYA ZEMLYA

KARSKOYE MORE (Kara Sea)

SERGEYA KIROVA

Kron-shtadt

ST. PETERSBURG (Sankt-Peterburg) (Leningrad)

MOSCOW (Moskva)

NIZHNIY NOVGOROD

MORDVINIA

CHUVASH EL

TATARSTAN

UDMURTIA

BASHKOR-TOSTAN

YEKATERINBURG

KOMI

NENETS

PECHORA BASIN

YAMAL

NENETS

P-OV YAMAL

P-OV GYDANSKIY

GORY PUTORA

WESTERN SIBERIAN LOWLAND

SAMARA

U R A L

R U S S I A

Murmansk

KOLSKIY POV

WHITE SEA

Arkhangelsk

Vorkuta

Salekhard

Noril'sk

Dikson

Karaul

Ust'-Port

Dudinka

Igarka

Turukhansk

Yeniseysk

Baykit

Yartsevo

KAZAKHSTAN

KIRGIZ STEPPE

ARAL SEA

UZBEKISTAN

TASHKENT

KYRGYZSTAN

TAJIKISTAN

GORNO-BADAKHSHAN AUT OBLAST'

AFGHANISTAN

TIEN SHAN

XINJIANG UYGUR (SINKIANG)

C H I N A

M O N G O L I A

ALTAI MTS

SAYAN KHREBET

TUVA TANNU-OLA

HANGAYN (KHANGAI) NURU

GORNO-ALTAY

KHAKASSIA

NOVOSIBIRSK

KUZNETSK BASIN

Omsk

Tomsk

Kemerovo

Krasnoyarsk

Kansk

Tayshet

Abakan

Tulun

Cheremkhovo

Usol'ye-Sibirs

Nizhneudinsk

BALQASH KÖLI

SARYESIK ATYRAU (DESERT)

MOYYNQUM

Bishkek

Alma-Ata (Almaty)

Dushanbe

Samarkand

Bering Strait

CHUKOTSKIY P-OV

VRANGELYA (WRANGEL I.)

M SHELAGSKIY

ANADYRSKIY ZALIV

Anadyr'

CHUKOTSKOYE NAGORYE

Markovo

Penzhino

KORYAKSKIY KHREBET

O C E A N

SEVERNAYA ZEMLYA (NORTHERN LAND)

MALYY TAYMYR

M CHELYUSKIN

NOVOSIBIRSKIYE O-VA (NEW SIBERIAN ISLANDS)

FADDEYA

NOVAYA SIBIR'

DE LONGA

BEL'KOVSKIY

KOTEL'NYY

MALYY LYAKHOVSKIYE

LYAKHOVSKIYE

STOLBOVOY

M SVYATOY NOS

EAST SIBERIAN SEA

Ambarchik

AYON

MEDVEZH'I

Nizhne-Kolymsk

Arctic Circle

Srednne-Kolymsk

Ust'-Penzhino

Gizhiga

KHREBET GYDAN (KOLYMSKIY)

M OLYUTORSKIY

Tilichiki

ZALIV SHELEKHOVA

KABAGIN

BYRRANGA TAYMYR

Nordvik

Ust'-Olenëk

Tiksi

Kazach'ye

Allaykha

Zashiversk

Zyryanka

Kolyma

Palana

POLUOSTROV

LAPTEV SEA

BOL'SHOY BEGICHEV

G. SELLYA KHSKAYA

M BIOR KHAYA

GUBA BUOR KHAYA

Bulun

KHREBET KULAR

Abyy

Oymyakon

VERKHOYANSKIY KHREBET

KHREBET CHERSKOGO

Gora Chen 10,171

Palana

Verkhne-Kamchatsk

KAMCHATKA

Klyuchevskaya (Vg) △ 4,864

Ust'-Kamchatsk

hatanga

Olenëk

Zhigansk

Verkhoyansk

Lena

Markha

S

I

B

I

R

Magadan

Yamsk

M ALEVINA

Okhotsk

SEA OF OKHOTSK

Petropavlovsk-Kamchatskiy

SAKHA (YAKUTIA)

Vilyuysk

Yakutsk

Aldanskaya

Ust'-Bol sheretsk

Ozero Olenëk

Suntar

Vilyuy

Amga

Ust'-Maya

M YELIZAVETY

Mukhtuya

Olëkminsk

Tommot

ALDAN PLATEAU

Nel'kan

DZHUGDZHUR KHREBET

Ayan

Peleduy

Vitim

PATOM 5377 G. Golets Purpula PLATEAU

Aldan

UDSKAYA G.

SHANTAR

Okha

SAKHALIN (Russia)

Kirensk

Bodaybo

Golets Skalistyy 9186

STANOVOY KHREBET

Chumikan

Ude

Nikolayevsk-na-Amure

Aleksandrovsk

M TERPENIYA

KURIL ISLANDS

Nizhne-Angarsk

Tyndinskiy

Zeya

Poronaysk

Uglegorsk

BURYATIA

Barguzin

Ozero Baykal (Lake Baikal) Surface elev 1535 Ft above Sea Level

Skovorodino

Beketovo

Zeya

KHREBET BUREINSKIY

Komsomol'sk-na-Amure

Malmyzh

Dalinsk

Yuzhno-Sakhalinsk

TATAR STRAIT

Ulan-Ude

Chita

Sretensk

Nerchinsk

Nerchinskiy Zavod

LESSER KHINGAN RANGE

Svobodnyy

Belogorsk

Ust'-Tyrma

Sovetskaya Gavan'

Kholmsk

Korsakov

Petrovsk

Zabaykal'skiy

Baley

Aginskoye

NERCHINSKIY KHREBET

MANCHURIA RANGE

Zavitinsk

Bureya

Raychikinsk

Birobidzhan

Khabarovsk

Sôya Kaik

HOKKAIDO

Kyakhta

Aksha

Borzya

Onon

NEI MONGGOL

Blagoveshchensk

Aihun

GREATER KHINGAN RANGE

Longzhen

LESSER KHINGAN RANGE

Dalnerechensk

SIKHOTE ALIN'

JAPAN

Manzhouli

Hailar

Goukou

CHINA HEILUNGKIANG

Yilan

Spassk-Dal'niy

Ol'ga

Ulan Bator (Ulaanbaatar)

Öndörhaan

Qiqihar

Hulan HARBIN

Sifenhe

Ussuriysk

KHREBET SIKHOTE ALIN'

Artëm

Arsen'yevo

Ning'an

Suchan

SEA OF JAPAN

Nakhodka

Vladivostok

A-579300-76 COPYRIGHT BY RAND McNALLY & COMPANY MADE IN U.S.A.

Relief

Meters	Feet
3050	10 000
1525	5000
610	2000
305	1000
152.5	500
0	Sea Level 0
152.5	500
1525	5000
3050	10 000

Continued on pages 188-189

50 100 200 300 400 500 Miles

100 200 400 600 800 Kilometers

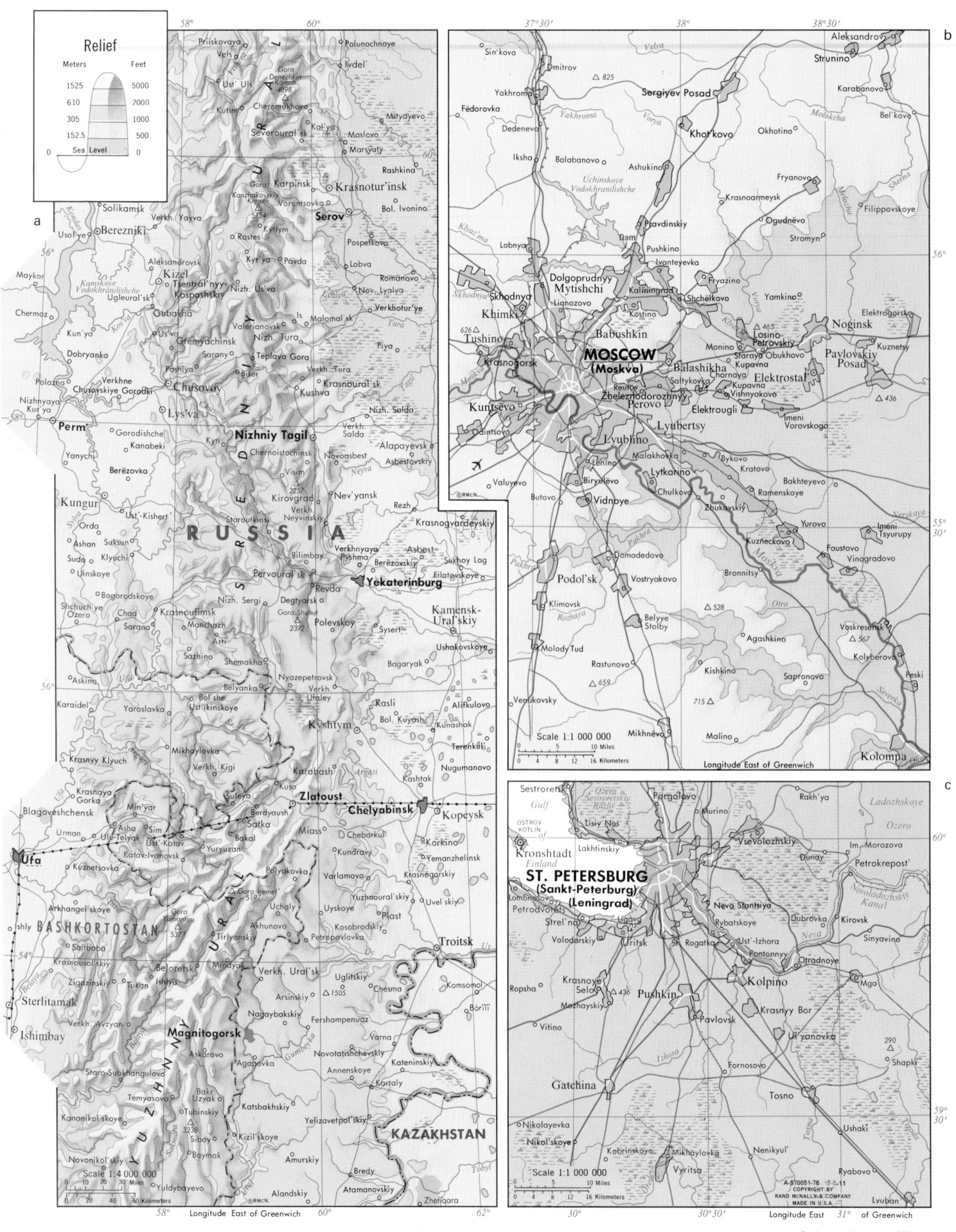

Relief

Meters	Feet
1525	5000
610	2000
305	1000
152.5	500
Sea Level	0

a

b

c

Scale 1:1 000 000

Longitude East of Greenwich

Scale 1:4 000 000

Longitude East of Greenwich

Scale 1:1 000 000

Longitude East of Greenwich

A-570051-76   7-5-11
COPYRIGHT BY
RAND McNALLY & COMPANY
MADE IN U.S.A.

Cities and Towns

0 to 50,000	500,000 to 1,000,000
50,000 to 500,000	1,000,000 and over

For larger scale coverage of Moscow
and St. Petersburg see page 239.

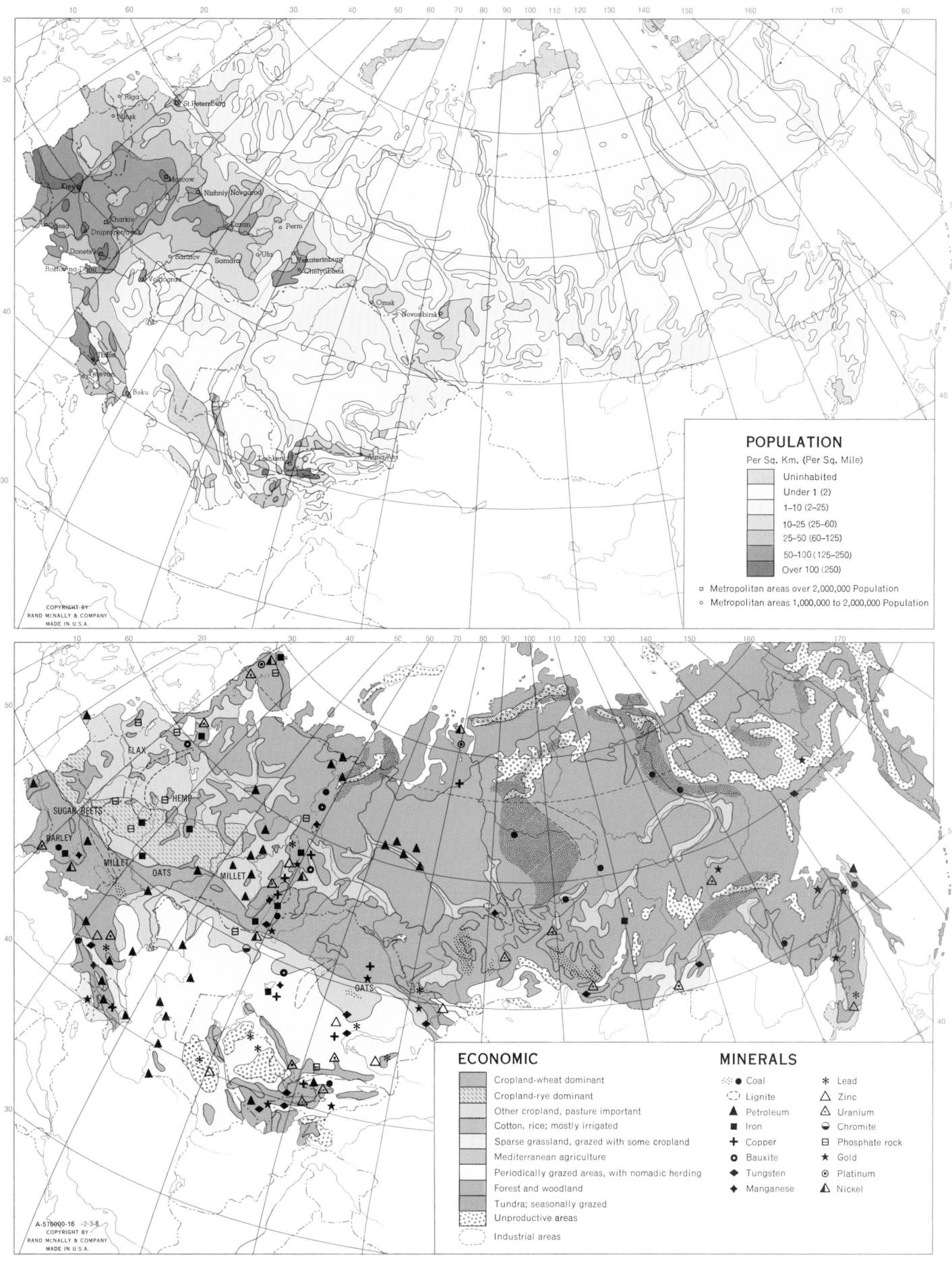

POPULATION

Per Sq. Km. (Per Sq. Mile)

	Uninhabited
	Under 1 (2)
	1–10 (2–25)
	10–25 (25–60)
	25–50 (60–125)
	50–100 (125–250)
	Over 100 (250)

□ Metropolitan areas over 2,000,000 Population
○ Metropolitan areas 1,000,000 to 2,000,000 Population

ECONOMIC

- Cropland-wheat dominant
- Cropland-rye dominant
- Other cropland, pasture important
- Cotton, rice; mostly irrigated
- Sparse grassland, grazed with some cropland
- Mediterranean agriculture
- Periodically grazed areas, with nomadic herding
- Forest and woodland
- Tundra; seasonally grazed
- Unproductive areas
- Industrial areas

MINERALS

●	Coal	✳	Lead
◌	Lignite	△	Zinc
▲	Petroleum	△	Uranium
■	Iron	⌔	Chromite
✛	Copper	⊟	Phosphate rock
◉	Bauxite	★	Gold
◆	Tungsten	⊙	Platinum
◆	Manganese	◮	Nickel

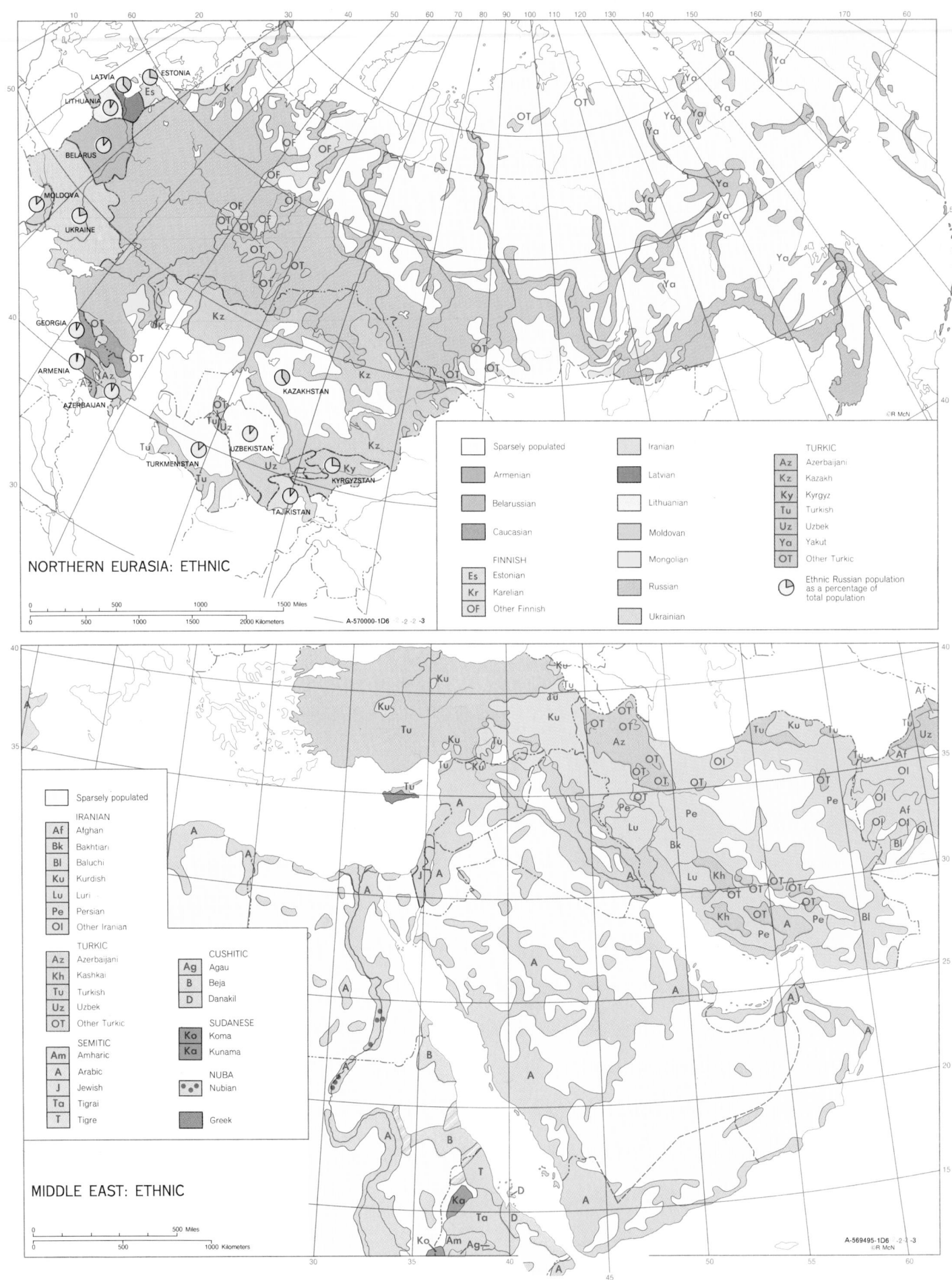

NORTHERN EURASIA: ETHNIC

☐ Sparsely populated		☐ Iranian		**TURKIC**	
☐ Armenian		☐ Latvian		Az	Azerbaijani
☐ Belarussian		☐ Lithuanian		Kz	Kazakh
☐ Caucasian		☐ Moldovan		Ky	Kyrgyz
FINNISH		☐ Mongolian		Tu	Turkish
Es	Estonian	☐ Russian		Uz	Uzbek
Kr	Karelian	☐ Ukrainian		Ya	Yakut
OF	Other Finnish			OT	Other Turkic

Ethnic Russian population
as a percentage of
total population

MIDDLE EAST: ETHNIC

☐ Sparsely populated				
IRANIAN		**CUSHITIC**		
Af	Afghan	Ag	Agau	
Bk	Bakhtiari	B	Beja	
Bl	Baluchi	D	Danakil	
Ku	Kurdish			
Lu	Luri	**SUDANESE**		
Pe	Persian	Ko	Koma	
OI	Other Iranian	Ka	Kunama	
TURKIC		**NUBA**		
Az	Azerbaijani	Nubian		
Kh	Kashkai			
Tu	Turkish	Greek		
Uz	Uzbek			
OT	Other Turkic			
SEMITIC				
Am	Amharic			
A	Arabic			
J	Jewish			
Ta	Tigrai			
T	Tigre			

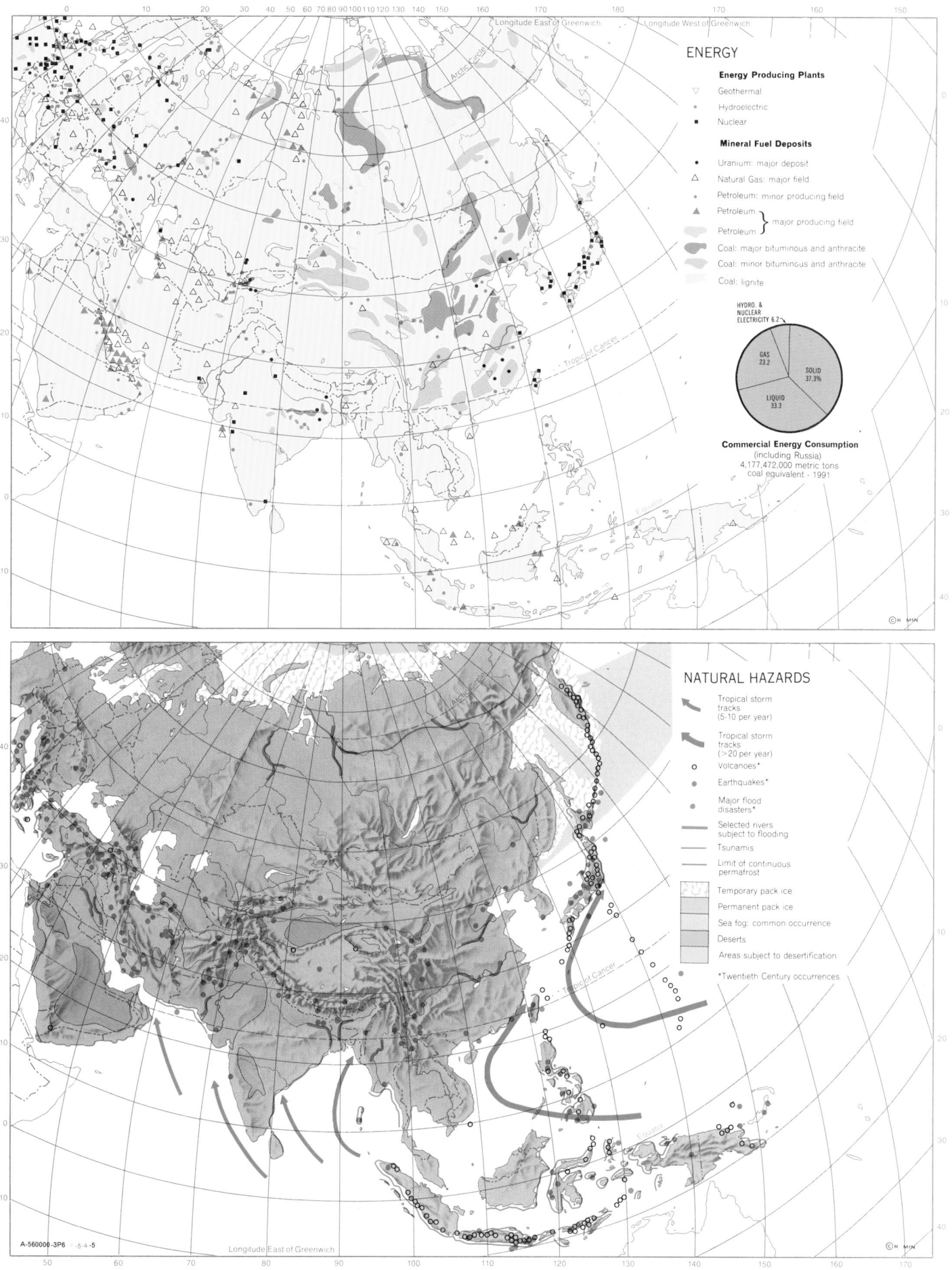

ENERGY

Energy Producing Plants

▽ Geothermal

• Hydroelectric

■ Nuclear

Mineral Fuel Deposits

• Uranium: major deposit

△ Natural Gas: major field

• Petroleum: minor producing field

▲ Petroleum }

Petroleum } major producing field

Coal: major bituminous and anthracite

Coal: minor bituminous and anthracite

Coal: lignite

HYDRO. & NUCLEAR ELECTRICITY 6.2

GAS 23.2

SOLID 37.3%

LIQUID 33.3

Commercial Energy Consumption
(including Russia)
4,177,472,000 metric tons
coal equivalent · 1991

NATURAL HAZARDS

Tropical storm tracks (5-10 per year)

Tropical storm tracks (>20 per year)

○ Volcanoes*

• Earthquakes*

• Major flood disasters*

Selected rivers subject to flooding

Tsunamis

Limit of continuous permafrost

Temporary pack ice

Permanent pack ice

Sea fog: common occurrence

Deserts

Areas subject to desertification

*Twentieth Century occurrences

A-560000-3P6   -5-4-5

Longitude East of Greenwich

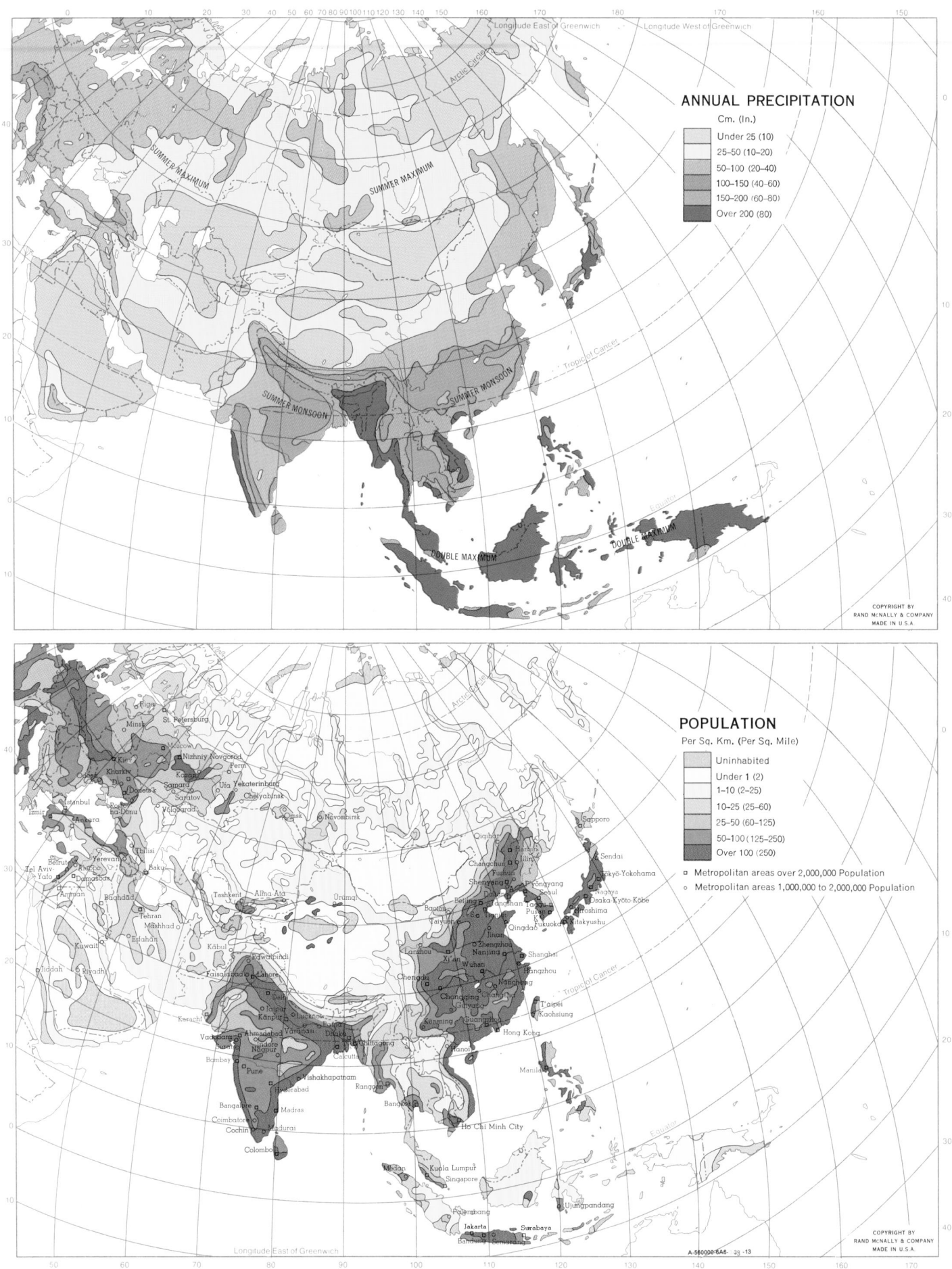

ANNUAL PRECIPITATION

Cm. (In.)

- Under 25 (10)
- 25–50 (10–20)
- 50–100 (20–40)
- 100–150 (40–60)
- 150–200 (60–80)
- Over 200 (80)

SUMMER MAXIMUM

SUMMER MAXIMUM

SUMMER MONSOON

SUMMER MONSOON

DOUBLE MAXIMUM

DOUBLE MAXIMUM

POPULATION

Per Sq. Km. (Per Sq. Mile)

- Uninhabited
- Under 1 (2)
- 1–10 (2–25)
- 10–25 (25–60)
- 25–50 (60–125)
- 50–100 (125–250)
- Over 100 (250)

□ Metropolitan areas over 2,000,000 Population
○ Metropolitan areas 1,000,000 to 2,000,000 Population

A-560000-6A6- 33 -13

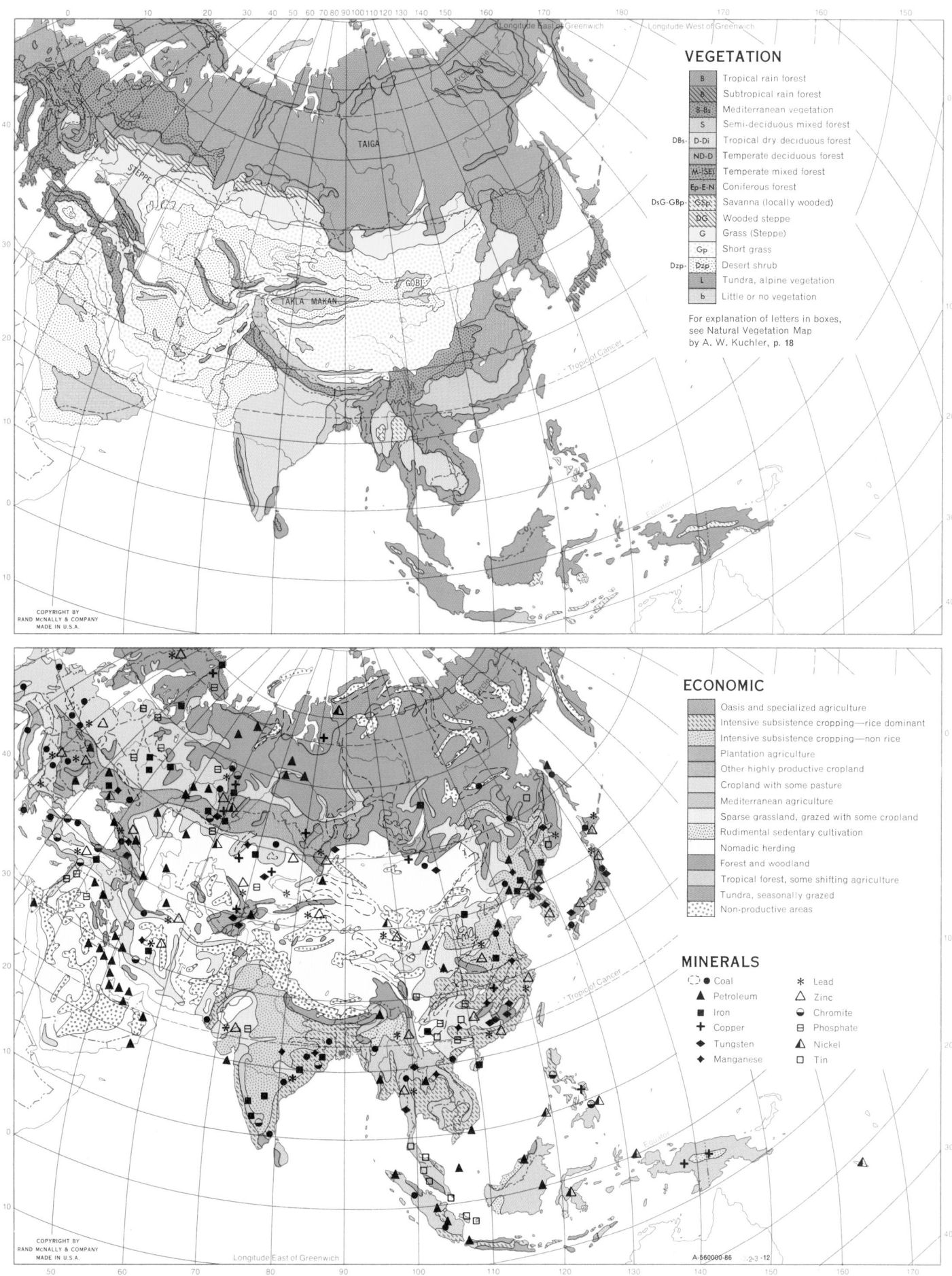

VEGETATION

B	Tropical rain forest
B	Subtropical rain forest
B-Bs	Mediterranean vegetation
S	Semi-deciduous mixed forest
D-Di	Tropical dry deciduous forest
ND-D	Temperate deciduous forest
M-ISE	Temperate mixed forest
Ep-E-N	Coniferous forest
GSp	Savanna (locally wooded)
DG	Wooded steppe
G	Grass (Steppe)
Gp	Short grass
Dzp	Desert shrub
L	Tundra, alpine vegetation
b	Little or no vegetation

For explanation of letters in boxes,
see Natural Vegetation Map
by A. W. Kuchler, p. **18**

ECONOMIC

- Oasis and specialized agriculture
- Intensive subsistence cropping—rice dominant
- Intensive subsistence cropping—non rice
- Plantation agriculture
- Other highly productive cropland
- Cropland with some pasture
- Mediterranean agriculture
- Sparse grassland, grazed with some cropland
- Rudimental sedentary cultivation
- Nomadic herding
- Forest and woodland
- Tropical forest, some shifting agriculture
- Tundra, seasonally grazed
- Non-productive areas

MINERALS

●	Coal	＊	Lead
▲	Petroleum	△	Zinc
■	Iron	◖	Chromite
✛	Copper	⊟	Phosphate
◆	Tungsten	▲	Nickel
◆	Manganese	☐	Tin

A-560000-86

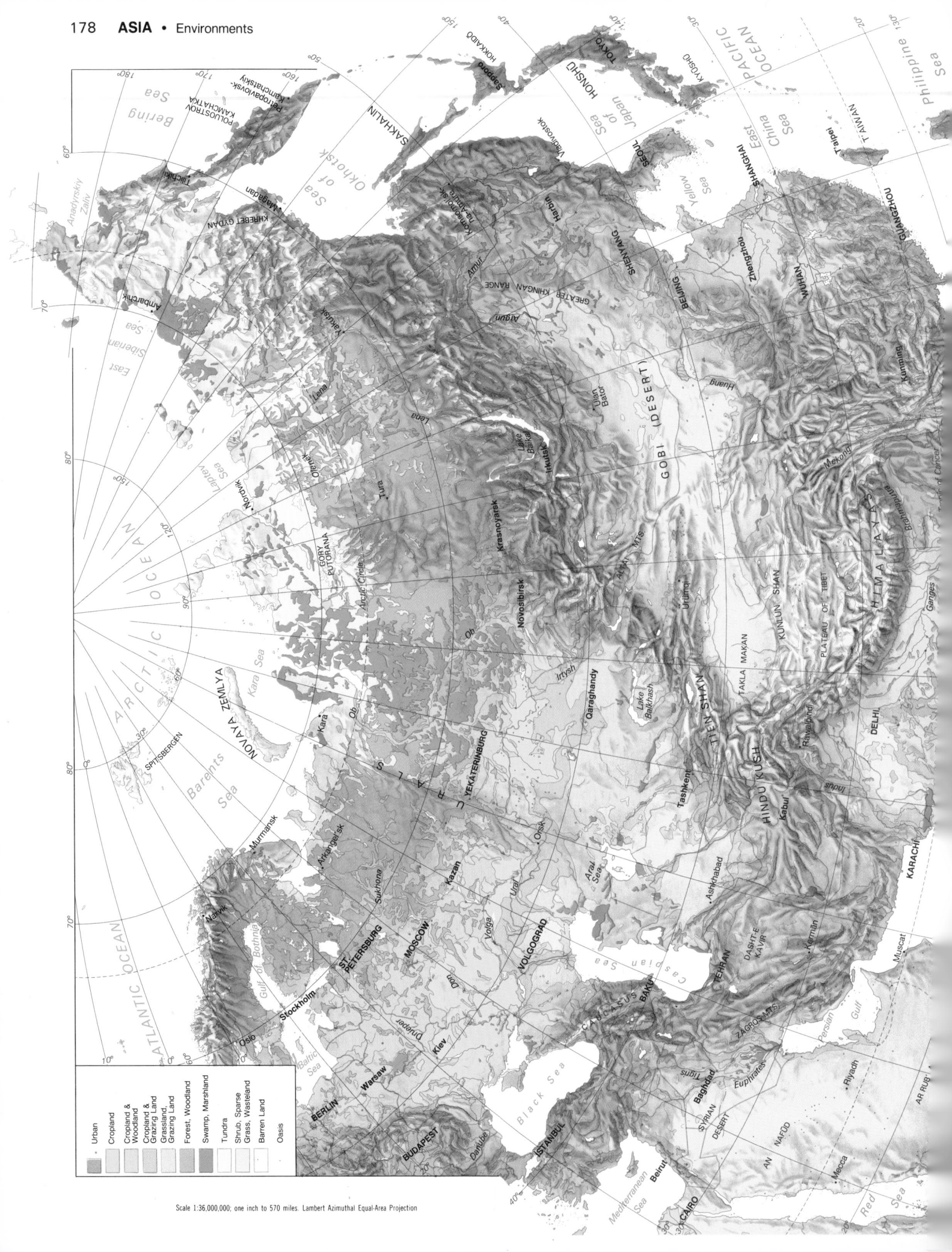

Scale 1:36,000,000; one inch to 570 miles. Lambert Azimuthal Equal-Area Projection

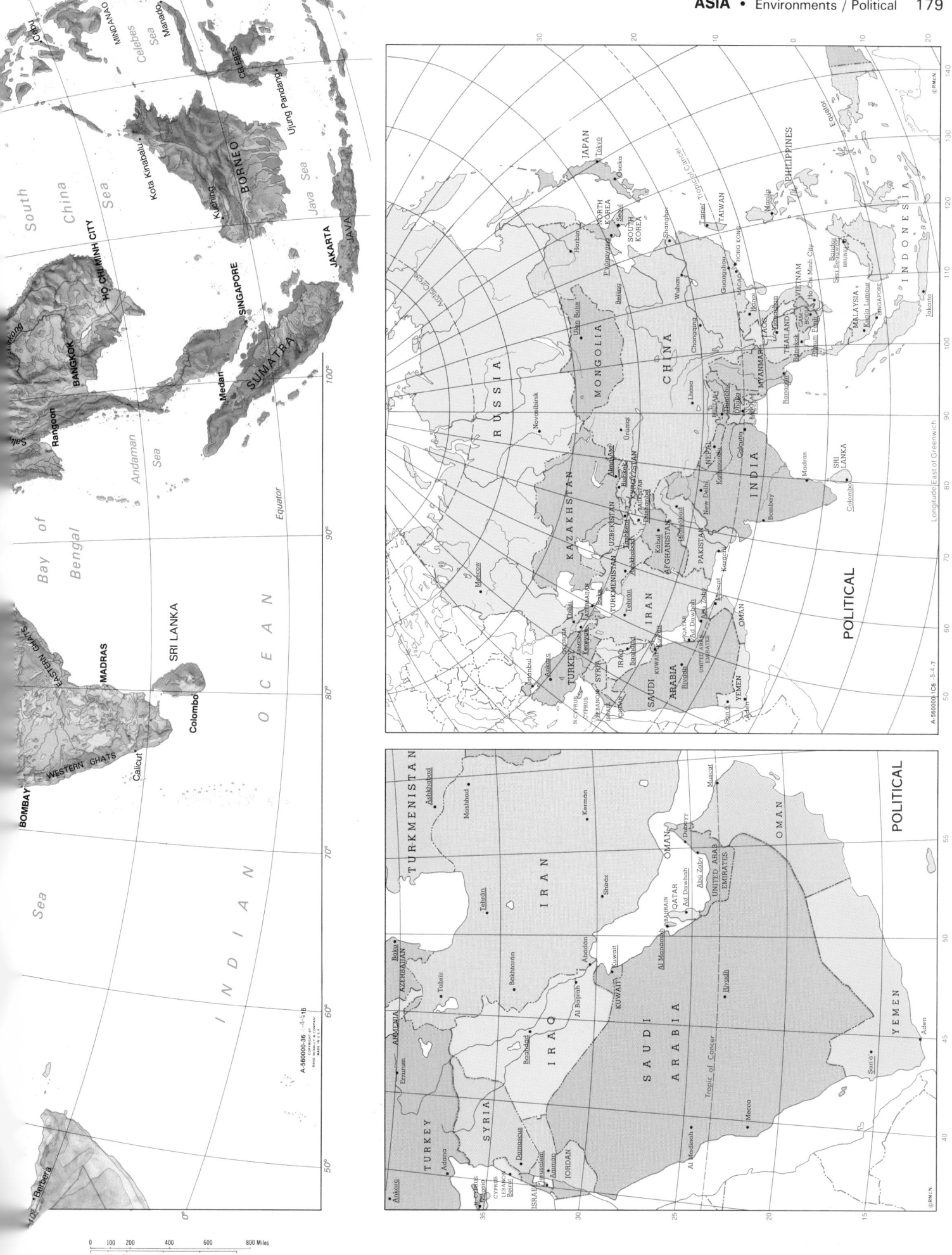

MINDANAO

Cebu

Celebes Sea

Manado

CELEBES

Ujung Pandang

BORNEO

Kota Kinabalu

Kuching

South China Sea

HO CHI MINH CITY

JAKARTA

JAVA

Java Sea

SINGAPORE

Medan

SUMATRA

BANGKOK

Rangoon

Mekong

Andaman Sea

Bay of Bengal

Equator

EASTERN GHATS

SRI LANKA

MADRAS

Colombo

Calicut

WESTERN GHATS

BOMBAY

INDIAN OCEAN

Arabian Sea

Berbera

A-560000-36 -4-5-6

0 100 200 400 600 800 Miles
0 150 300 600 900 1200 Kilometers

POLITICAL

JAPAN
Tokyo
Osaka

NORTH KOREA
Pyongyang
Harbin
SOUTH KOREA
Seoul
Shanghai

RUSSIA

Novosibirsk

MONGOLIA
Ulan Bator

Beijing

CHINA

Wuhan

Chongqing

Lhasa

Urumqi

KAZAKHSTAN

Moscow

UZBEKISTAN
KYRGYZSTAN
TURKMENISTAN
TAJIKISTAN
AFGHANISTAN
Kabul

NEPAL
Kathmandu
New Delhi

INDIA

Calcutta

Madras

SRI LANKA
Colombo

MYANMAR

Hanoi
LAOS
THAILAND
Bangkok
VIETNAM
Ho Chi Minh City
CAMBODIA
Phnom Penh

MALAYSIA
Kuala Lumpur
SINGAPORE

Bandar Seri Begawan
BRUNEI

PHILIPPINES
Manila

HONG KONG
MACAO
Guangzhou

TAIWAN
Taipei

INDONESIA

Jakarta

Equator

GEORGIA
ARMENIA
AZERBAIJAN
Baku
Yerevan
Tbilisi
Istanbul
Ankara
TURKEY
N. CYPRUS
CYPRUS
LEBANON
ISRAEL
SYRIA
Baghdad
IRAQ
KUWAIT
Kuwait
Tehran
IRAN
QATAR
BAHRAIN
Ad Dawhah
Abu Dhabi
UNITED ARAB EMIRATES
Muscat
OMAN
SAUDI ARABIA
Riyadh
YEMEN
Aden
Sanʿa

POLITICAL

Longitude East of Greenwich

A-560000-1C6 5-4-7

POLITICAL

TURKMENISTAN
Ashkhabad
Moshhad

IRAN
Kermān
Shiraz
Tehran

ARMENIA
AZERBAIJAN
Baku
Tabriz
Bakhtaran

IRAQ
Baghdad
Al Başrah
Abadan
KUWAIT
Kuwait

Al Manāmah
BAHRAIN
QATAR
Ad Dawhah
Dubayy
Abū Ẓaby
UNITED ARAB EMIRATES

Muscat
OMAN

SAUDI ARABIA
Riyadh

YEMEN
Aden
Sanʿa

Mecca

Al Madinah

Tropic of Cancer

TURKEY
Erzurum
Adana

SYRIA
Damascus

LEBANON
Beirut
ISRAEL
Jerusalem
Amman
JORDAN

CYPRUS
Nicosia
Ankara

Continued on page 209

Relief

Meters		Feet
3050		10 000
1525		5000
610		2000
305		1000
0	Sea Level	0
		Below Sea Level
152.5		500
1525		5000
3050		10 000
6100		20 000

A-519695-76   -1918-37
COPYRIGHT BY
RAND McNALLY & COMPANY
MADE IN U.S.A.

Scale 1:40 000 000; one inch to 630 miles. Lambert's Azimuthal, Equal Area Projecti
Elevations and depressions are given in feet

a

ÓIimbos 33° Lárnax Kólpas 34°
6401 △ PIDÁLION
Néa Páfos Lemesós Lárnakos Longitude 35° East of Greenwich 36°

Episkopi Lemesós
CYPRUS
AKR. GÁTAS
AKR. PIDÁLION

Ṭarābulus Halba Al Qusayr
(Tripoli) Al Hirmil
Al Batrūn Zgharta
Amyūn 1073 8625
Jubayl (Byblos) Jūniyah Ba'labakk 34°
Beirut
(Bayrūt) Zaḥlah
Ad Dāmūr Az Zabdānī
Ṣaydā **Damascus** Dūmā
(Sidon) (Dimashq)
Rāshayyā Al Kiswah
SYRIA
Ṣūr Marj 'Uyūn
(Tyre) Qiryat Shemona
Tibnīn Al Qunayṭirah
Nahariyya Zefat As Sanamayn
Hora A
Meron 3964
'Akko Ṭaveṛya
Haifa Dar'ā
(Ḥefa) Nazerat As Suwaydā
'Afula
Bet She'an Irbid
Hadera Jenin Jarash Al Mafraq
Netanya Ṭūlkarm Shechem
Herzliyya (Ruins)
Petaḥ Tiqwa Nābulus
Tel Aviv-Yafo B As Salṭ Az Zarqā'
Rishon leẒiyyon Arīḥā
Reḥovot (Jericho) **Ammān**
Ashdod **Jerusalem** Mā'dabā
Ashqelon Qiryat Zuwayzā
Gat Bayt Laḥm
(Bethlehem) Dhībān
Gaza Al Khalīl
(Ghazzah) (Hebron)
Khān Yūnus Be'er Sheva'
Rafah C 'Arad Al Mazra'ah
Al Karak
Port Said (Būr Sa'īd) Dimona Al Mazar
Sedom Maḥaṭṭat
Sabkhat al Aṭ Ṭafīlah ad Qaṭrānah
Khalīj aṭ Bardawil
Ṭīnah Horvot Shivta
(Ruins) Maḥaṭṭat Jurf
Al 'Arīsh Qezi'ot Ash Shawbak ad Dārāwīsh
Rummānah 5383
Al Qantarah Jabal al 'Arā'itah Petra
Daphnae Al Qusaymah (Ruins)
(Ruins) Ismailia Wādī Mūsā Ma'ān
(Al Ismā'īlīyah) **NEGEV** QA' AL JAFR
Ra's Abū Qurūn JABAL
3578 △ YU 'ALLIQ
Great Bitter
Fā'id Lake Ra's an Naqb
△ 4136 Al Kuntillah
EGYPT JABAL Elat Al 'Aqabah Maḥaṭṭat
Ṣuez JALĀLAH An Nakhl 5755 ar Ramlah
(As Suways) AL BAHRĪYAH Jabal Ramm Al Mudawwarah
Bi'r Za'farānah Ath Thamad △ 3513
△ 4838 △ 3789 Al Maḥraḥ
JABAL AL JALĀLAT Ra's al Junaynah **SAUDI ARABIA**
AL QIBLĪYAH SINAI PEN Nuwaybi' al JABAL MAZHAFAH Scale 1:4 000 000
Abū Zanimah (SHIBH JAZĪRAT SĪNĀ') Muzayyinah △ 6232 0 10 20 30 40 50 Miles
©RMcN. 0 20 40 60 80 Kilometers

Ⓐ Golan Heights area. Occupied by Israel since 1967.
Unilaterally annexed by Israel, 1981.

Ⓑ West Bank area. Unilaterally annexed by
Jordan, 1950. Occupied by Israel since 1967.
Status to be determined.

Ⓒ Gaza Strip. Occupied by Israel since 1967.
Status to be determined.

MEDITERRANEAN SEA

---

b

Kuala Lumpur Scale 1:4 000 000
Kelang 0 10 20 30 40 50 Miles
SELANGOR Kajang Kuala Klawang 0 20 40 60 80 Kilometers
Gunong Telapa **PAHANG**
Telok Datok 3915 △ Burok TIOMAN
NEGERI SEMBILAN Bahau △ Gunong Kajang
Sepang Rantau Seremban Rompin 3444
Port Dickson Rembau Gemas Padang Endau PEMANGGIL
Tampin Segamat △ Gunong Besar
CAPE RACHADO Alor Gajah Jasin 3403 Labis Mersing AUR
Mr. Ophir **MALAYSIA** △ 2002
Melaka △ 4187 Paloh SOUTH
(Malacca) Panchor **JOHOR** TINGGI
MELAKA Bandar △ 3312 Keluang
Maharani Rengam Gunong Blumut **MALAY** CHINA
Jumrah TANJONG Ayer Layang Layang **PENINSULA** Jason Bay
RUPAT TOHOR Batu Hitam SEA
Teluklecak Pahat Kota Tinggi
Batupanjang Johor
Dumai TANJONG Baharu TANJONG
Bengkalis PIAI RAMUNIA
BENGKALIS Pontian Kechil
Bukitbatu SINGAPORE
Kudap **SINGAPORE** TANJUNG
SUMATRA 341 △ Telesung BERAKIT
Pinggir KARIMUN Singapore Strait
BESAR BATAM Tanjungpinang 1181 △
INDONESIA 1837 △ Tanjungbatu KEPULAUAN RIAU BINTAN
RIAU PADANG RANGSANG Sekanak
Siaksriinderapura TEBINGTINGGI Serangbung
Buatan KUNDUR Baranpauh
©RMcN. 102° 103° Longitude East of Greenwich 104°

North America
Bering Str.
NORTH AMERICA 60° 50°
M. DEZHNEVA
EAST CAPE
Arctic Circle
PRIBILOF IS
(U.S.A.)
VRANGELYA
(WRANGEL) IS
Chukotskiy
Pol.
70° 170°
SIBERIAN SEA
Kólpas Penzhinskaya
Gulf
West Longitude
East Longitude
ALEUTIAN ISLANDS (U.S.A.)
KOMANDORSKIYE OSTROVA (Sov. Union)
ALEUTIAN TRENCH
Yakutsk
Okhotsk
Petropavlovsk-Kamchatskiy
M. LOPATKA
SEA OF OKHOTSK
KAMCHATKA
KHREBET GYDAN
KORYAKSKIY KHREBET
STANOVOY
Kolyma
Indigirka
Aldan
Lena
DZHUGDZHUR
KHREBET
OYANSKIY
KHREBET
STANOVOY KHREBET
Blagoveshchensk
Sovetskaya Gavan
Khabarovsk
Komsomolsk
SIKHOTE ALIN
SAKHALIN (Sov. Union)
KURIL ISLANDS (Sov. Union)
KURIL TRENCH
Tatar Strait
Amur
MANCHURIA
HARBIN
CHANGCHUN
Vladivostok
Jilin
Pyongyang
NORTH KOREA
SEOUL
SOUTH
SHENYANG
Zhangjiakou
Dalian
Bo Hai
TIANJIN
Jinan
QINGDAO
TAIYUAN
JING
NANJING
SHANGHAI
WUHAN
HAINAN DAO
Soya Strait
Hokkaido
Hakodate
HOKKAIDO TRENCH
JAPAN
SEA OF JAPAN
Sendai
HONSHU
TOKYO
YOKOHAMA
KYOTO
KOBE OSAKA
SHIKOKU
KITAKYUSHU
KYUSHU
Nagasaki
NANSEI SHOTO
EAST CHINA SEA
Tropic of Cancer
T'AIPEI
TAIWAN (FORMOSA)
Taiwan Strait
Fuzhou
Xiamen
Shantou
GUANGZHOU
HONG KONG
Macao (Port.)
BABUYAN IS
LUZON
PHILIPPINE SEA
PHILIPPINES
Quezon City
MANILA
MINDORO
SAMAR
LEYTE
PANAY
NEGROS
PALAWAN
MINDANAO
PHILIPPINE TRENCH
Penh
10 CHI NH CITY (Saigon)
SOUTH CHINA SEA
Kota Kinabalu
Sandakan
BRUNEI
MALAYSIA
Kuching
BORNEO
CELEBES
CELEBES SEA
SULU SEA
SULU IS
NEW GUINEA
HALMAHERA
Equator
SHENYANG
ZHANGJIAKOU
PACIFIC OCEAN
0 200 400 600 800 1000 Miles
0 400 800 1200 1600 Kilometers
120° 130° 140° 150° 160° 170°

BLACK SEA

İstanbul Boğazı (Bosporus)
İstanbul
Troy (Ruins)
Mihhara
Marmara Denizi
İzmir
Bergama
Kütahya
Eskişehir
Afyon
Aydın
Muğla
Isparta
TURKEY
Ankara
Kırşehir
Kütahya
Konya
Karamanmaraş
TOROS DAĞLARI
Antalya
İçel
Adana
Tarsus
İskenderun
Hatay
Gaziantep
Şanlıurfa
Diyarbakır
Siverek
Malatya
Elâzığ
Mardin
Cizre
Erzurum
Kayseri
Sivas
Erzincan
Tokat
Çorum
Yozgat
Amasya
Merzifon
Samsun
Giresun
Trabzon
Zonguldak
Kastamonu
Çankırı
Sinop
Bursa
Batumi
Poti
CAUCASUS
RUSSIA
Groznyy
Vladikavkaz
Makhachkala
Fort Shevchenko
KAZA
ARAL SEA
MANGYSHLAK
Aqtaū
Kutaisi
GEORGIA
Tbilisi
Gyumri
Kars
ARMENIA
Yerevan
AZERBAIJAN
Gänca
BAKU (Bakı)
Derbent
PLATO UST-URT
Kungrad
Chimbay
Nukus
UZBEKISTAN
Khiva
Turtkul
PESKI KYZYLK (DESERT)
TURKESTAN
PESKI KARAKUMY (DESERT)
Krasnovodsk
Nebit-Dag
Chardzhou
Bukha
Ashkhabad
Mary
KOPPET DAGH
TURKMENISTAN
Bojnūrd
Mashhad

CYPRUS
NORTH CYPRUS
Nicosia
RÓDHOS
MEDITERRANEAN SEA
Areas occupied by Israel since 1967
Rashīd
Damietta
Port Said (Būr Saʿīd)
ALEXANDRIA (Al Iskandarīyah)
CAIRO (Al Qāhirah)
Suez (As Suways)
Būr Safājah
Al Qusayr
EGYPT
SUDAN
Bur Sūdān
Sawākin
Tawkar
ADMINISTR. BDY.
Continued on pages 210-211

LEBANON
Tarābulus (Tripoli)
Beirut
Ṣaydā (Sidon)
ISRAEL
Tel Aviv-Yafo
Jerusalem
Gaza
Haifa
Ladhiqiyah (Latakia)
Aleppo
Ḥimṣ
Ḥamāh
SYRIA
Damascus (Dimashq)
As Suwaydā
Amman
JORDAN
Al Mawṣil
Palmyra (Ruins)
Abū Kamāl
Dayr az Zawr
Ar Raqqah
Tikrīt
Ar Ramādī
BAGHDAD
Karbalā
An Najaf
Babylon (Ruins)
IRAQ
SYRIAN DESERT
Al Ţurayf
Badanah
Rutbah
Maʿān
Al ʿAqabah
Jabal Shār
Jabal Ramm
PEN EL at
SINAI
Elat
Al Jawf
Sakākah
Rafḥā
An Nafūd
Taymā
Tabūk
Al Wajh
Khaybar
Jabal Radwah
Al Madīnah (Medina)
Yanbu
Jiddah
Mecca (Makkah)
Al Khurmah
Aṭ Ṭāʾif
Jabal Ibrāhīm
Al Līdām
Qalʿat Bīshah
Al Qunfudhah
Abhā
Najrān
HIJAZ
RED SEA

Kirkūk
Sulaymānīyah
Irbīl
KURDISTAN
Van
Bitlis
Siirt
Rawanduz
Nineveh
Ararat 16,854
Khvoy
Ardabīl
Tabrīz
Urūmiyeh
Miāneh
Orūmīyeh
Rasht
Bandar-e Anzalī
Bandar-e Torkeman
Gorgān
ELBURZ MTS
Qalleh-ye
TEHRAN
Sanandaj
Zanjān
Qazvīn
Karaj
Bābol
Āmol
Dāmghān
Emāmshahr
Neyshābūr
Sarī
CASPIAN SEA Surface 92 feet below sea level
Zal Kara-Bogaz-Gol

Kangāvar
Hamadān
Bakhtaran
Arāk
Borūjerd
Qom
Kāshān
DASHT-E KAVIR DESERT
Qayen
Birjand
Farāh
AFGH
HERĀT
PAR

Deẕfūl
Shūshtar
Ahvāz
Masjed Soleymān
Qomsheh
Eṣfahān
Yazd
PLATEAU OF IRAN
DASHT-E LŪT (DESERT)
Bājestān
Ferdows

Khorramshahr
Ābādān
Al Baṣrah
An Nāṣirīyah
Bandar-e Khomeynī
KUWAIT
Kuwait (Al Kuwayt)
Al Qayṣūmah
Ḥāʾil
JABAL SHAMMAR
SAUDI
Buraydah
ʿUnayzah
Sudayr
Ash Shaqrā
NAJD
Riyadh (Ar Riyāḍ)
AL AFLAJ
Ad Dilam
AD DAHNĀ
AL HASĀ
Al Qaṭīf
Az Zahrān (Dhahran)
Ad Dammām
BAHRAIN
Al Manāmah
Al Hufūf
QATAR
Ad Dawḥah
ARABIA
AD DAWĀSIR
NAFŪD
Mubarraz
JABAL TUWAYQ
AR RUBʿ AL KHĀLĪ
UNITED ARAB EMIRATES
Abū Ẕaby
Al Buraymī
JABAL AL AKHDAR
Jabal ash Shām 9957
OMAN

Zāgros
Shīrāz
Kāzerūn
Borāzjān
Persepolis (Ruins)
Daryācheh-ye Bakhtegān
Jahrom
Lār
Furgun 10,760
Kermān
Bandar-e Būshehr
Bandar-e Bandar-e Abbās
tengeh
Rafsanjān
Bāft
Rīgān
Zāhedān
Khāsh
Bampūr
CHAGA
Qeshm
QESHM
PERSIAN GULF
Strait of Hormuz
RAʾS AL HADD
RAʾS AT TANNŪRAH
Al Jubayl
Jāsk
GULF OF OMAN
Bandar Beheshtī
Gwādar
Dubayy
Ajman
Matrah
Al Khābūrah
Muscat
Sūr

Tropic of Cancer
Sawākin
Tawkar
Kassalā
Sebderat
ERITREA
Keren
Asmera
Akordat
Barentu
Ethiopia
Adi Ugri
Marsa Fatma
ABYSSINIAN
Mitsiwa (Massawa)
DAHLAK ARCH
Bārangī
Jabal Remān 10,729
Jāza ir Farasan
Qīzān
Abū ʿArīsh
Ṣaʿdah
Al Luḥayyah
Al Ḥudaydah
Al Mukhā (Mocha)
KAMARĀN
San'ā
Hajar Shuʿayb 3,008
Dhamār
RAMLAT AS SABʿATAYN
Shibām
Tarīm
Say'ūn
Al Ḥawṭah
YEMEN
Madīnat ash Sha'b
HADRAMAWT
Mirbāṭ
Shabwah
Aden (ʿAdan)
Ash Shiḥr
Al Mukallā
Sayhūt
RAʾS FARTAK
RAʾS AL MADRAKAH
RAʾS AL HADD
ARA
AS

OMAN
Al Maṣīrah
KHŪRYĀN-MŪRYĀN (Oman)

Tadjoura
DENAKIL
DJIBOUTI
Djibouti
Aysha
Dese
Beylul
GULF OF ADEN
SUQUTRA (SOCOTRA) (Yemen)
Hadibū
Caluula
GEES GWARDAFUY
Berbera
Lass Qoray
SOMALIA

A-569400-76 -21 -37
COPYRIGHT BY
RAND McNALLY & COMPANY
MADE IN U.S.A.

Longitude East of Greer

Scale 1:16 000 000; one inch to 250 miles. Polyconic Project
Elevations and depressions are given in feet

Relief		
Meters		Feet
3050		10 000
1525		5000
610		2000
305		1000
152.5		500
0	Sea Level	0
152.5		500 Below
1525		5000 Sea Level
3050		10 000

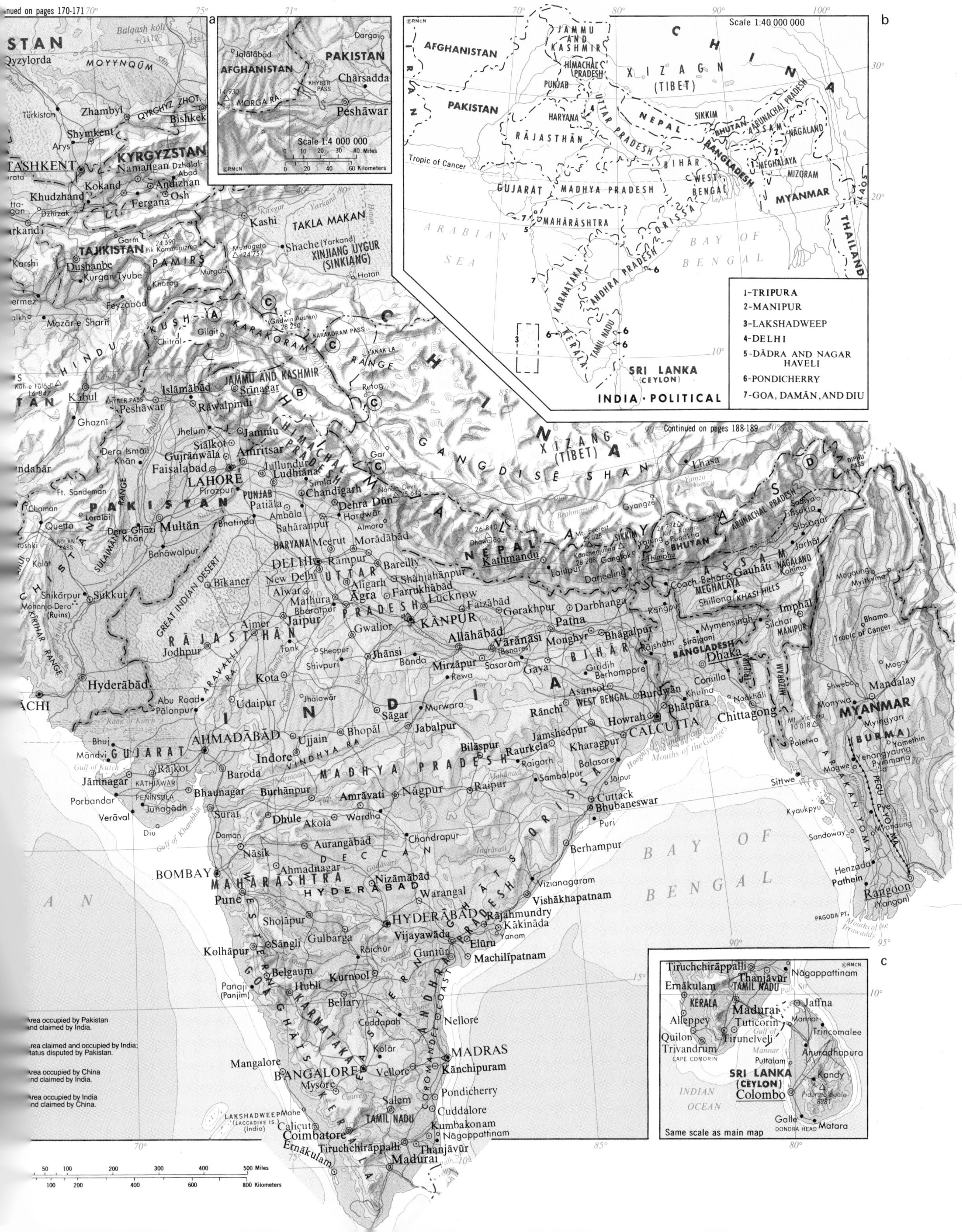

Inset a — Afghanistan / Pakistan
AFGHANISTAN
Jalālābād • Dargai
KHYBER PASS
△930 MORGA RA.
PAKISTAN
Chārsadda
Peshāwar
Scale 1:4 000 000
0 10 20 30 40 Miles
0 20 40 60 Kilometers

Inset b — India · Political
Scale 1:40 000 000
AFGHANISTAN
PAKISTAN
JAMMU AND KASHMIR
HIMACHAL PRADESH
PUNJAB
CHINA
XIZANG (TIBET)
HARYANA
UTTAR PRADESH
NEPAL
SIKKIM
BHUTAN
ARUNACHAL PRADESH
RĀJASTHĀN
ASSAM
NĀGALAND
Tropic of Cancer
BIHAR
MEGHALAYA
MIZORAM
GUJARAT
MADHYA PRADESH
WEST BENGAL
ORISSA
BANGLADESH
MYANMAR
MAHĀRĀSHTRA
ARABIAN SEA
KARNATAKA
ANDHRA PRADESH
BAY OF BENGAL
THAILAND
KERALA
TAMIL NADU
SRI LANKA (CEYLON)
INDIA · POLITICAL

1 - TRIPURA
2 - MANIPUR
3 - LAKSHADWEEP
4 - DELHI
5 - DĀDRA AND NAGAR HAVELI
6 - PONDICHERRY
7 - GOA, DAMĀN, AND DIU

Main Map

KYRGYZSTAN
TAJIKISTAN
PAMIRS
HINDU KUSH
KARAKORAM RANGE
TAKLA MAKAN
XINJIANG UYGUR (SINKIANG)
Kashi
Shache (Yarkand)
Islāmābād
Srīnagar
JAMMU AND KASHMIR
Peshāwar
Rāwalpindi
HIMĀLAYA
CHINA
PAKISTAN
Lahore
Amritsar
Jammu
HIMACHAL PRADESH
Multān
Chandigarh
Dehra Dūn
PUNJAB
HARYANA
Meerut
DELHI
New Delhi
UTTAR PRADESH
Bīkaner
Jaipur
Āgra
Lucknow
RĀJASTHĀN
GREAT INDIAN DESERT
ARAVALLI RA.
Jodhpur
KĀNPUR
Allāhābād
Vārānasi
NEPAL
Kathmandu
XIZANG (TIBET)
GANGDISE SHAN
Lhasa
Mt. Everest
SIKKIM
BHUTAN
ARUNACHAL PRADESH
Darjeeling
Gauhāti
ASSAM
NĀGALAND
MEGHALAYA
Shillong
KHASI HILLS
Imphāl
MANIPUR
Patna
BIHĀR
Dhaka
BANGLADESH
MYANMAR (BURMA)
Mandalay
Chittagong
MIZORAM
Hyderābād
Ahmadābād
GUJARAT
INDIA
MADHYA PRADESH
Bhopāl
Indore
Nāgpur
ORISSA
CALCUTTA
Howrah
WEST BENGAL
Ranchi
Jamshedpur
Bhubaneswar
Cuttack
BAY OF BENGAL
BOMBAY
MAHĀRĀSHTRA
DECCAN
Pune
HYDERĀBĀD
ANDHRA PRADESH
Vishākhapatnam
Vijayawāda
WESTERN GHĀTS
EASTERN GHĀTS
KARNATAKA
BANGALORE
Mysore
MADRAS
Pondicherry
TAMIL NADU
KERALA
Calicut
Coimbatore
Madurai
ARABIAN SEA
INDIAN OCEAN
RANGOON (Yangon)
ARAKAN YOMA

Area occupied by Pakistan and claimed by India.
Area claimed and occupied by India; status disputed by Pakistan.
Area occupied by China and claimed by India.
Area occupied by India and claimed by China.

Inset c — Sri Lanka
Tiruchchirāppalli
Thanjāvūr
Nāgappattinam
Ernākulam
TAMIL NADU
KERALA
Madurai
Jaffna
Alleppey
Tuticorin
Trincomalee
Quilon
Tirunelveli
Anurādhapura
Trivandrum
CAPE COMORIN
Puttalam
Kandy
SRI LANKA (CEYLON)
Colombo
Galle
Matara
DONDRA HEAD
INDIAN OCEAN
Same scale as main map

50 100 200 300 400 500 Miles
100 200 400 600 800 Kilometers

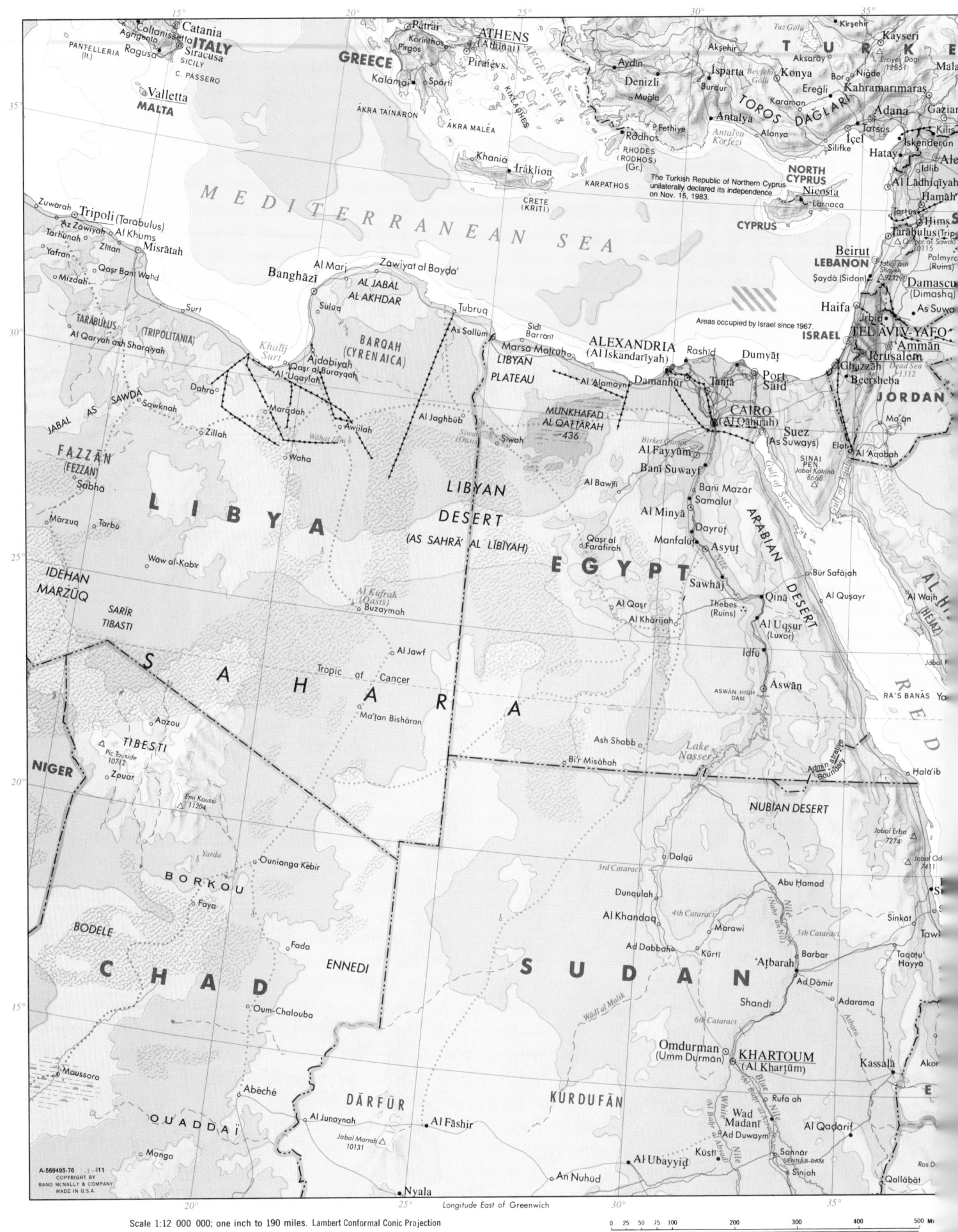

184

MEDITERRANEAN SEA

TURKE

GREECE
ATHENS
(Athínai)

Catania
ITALY
Siracusa
SICILY
C. PASSERO
Agrigento
Caltanissetta
Ragusa
PANTELLERIA
(It.)

Valletta
MALTA

Pátrai
Korinthos
Piraiévs
Spárti
Kalámai
ÁKRA TAÍNARON
ÁKRA MALÉA
KIKLÁDHES
AEGEAN SEA

Khaniá
Iráklion
CRETE
(KRITI)
KARPATHOS

RHODES
(RODHOS)
(Gr.)

Ródhos

Aydın
Denizli
Muğla
Fethiye
Antalya
Antalya
Körfezi
Alanya

Akşehir
Isparta
Beyşehir
Gölü
Burdur
Karaman
Silifke
İçel
Tarsus

Aksaray
Konya
Ereğli
Bor Niğde

Kırşehir

Kayseri
Erciyes Daği
12851

The Turkish Republic of Northern Cyprus
unilaterally declared its independence
on Nov. 15, 1983.

NORTH
CYPRUS
Nicosia
Larnaca

CYPRUS

Adana
Kahramanmaraş
Gazian
Kilis

Hatay
İskenderun
İdlib
Ale

Al Ladhiqiyah
Hamāh
Tartūs
Tarābulus (Trip)

Beirut
LEBANON
Şaydā (Sidan)

Damascu
(Dimashq)
As Suwa

Haifa
Areas occupied by Israel since 1967.

TEL AVIV–YAFO
Amman
Jerusalem
Dead Sea
1312
Beersheba

ISRAEL

JORDAN

Ma'ān

Zuwārah Tripoli (Tarābulus)
Az Zawiyah Al Khums
Tarhūnah Zlitan Misrātah
Yafran
Qaşr Banī Walīd
Mizdah

Banghāzī
Al Marj
Zawiyat al Baydā'
Sulūq
Tubruq
Sīdī
Barrāni
As Sallūm

ALEXANDRIA
(Al Iskandarīyah)
Marsa Matrūh

Rashid
Dumyāţ
Damanhūr Tanta Port
Said

Gulf of Suez

Ghazzah
Suez
(As Suways)
Elat Al 'Aqabah

AL JABAL
AL AKHDAR

BARQAH
(CYRENAICA)

LIBYAN
PLATEAU
Al 'Alamayn

CAIRO
(Al Qāhirah)
Al Fayyūm
Banī Suwayf

SINAI
PEN.
Jabal Katrina
8668

TARĀBULUS
(TRIPOLITANIA)
Al Qaryah ash Sharqīyah

Surt

Khalīj
Surt

Ajdabiyah
Qaşr al Burayqah
Al 'Uqaylah

Dahra
Sawknah
Zillah
Marādah
Awjilah

Al Jaghbūb

Siwah
(Oasis)
Sīwah

MUNKHAFAD
AL QATTĀRAH
−436

Birket Qārūn
Al Bawiti

Al Minya
Samalūt
Bani Mazār
Dayrūt
Manfalūt
Asyūţ

ARABIAN

JABAL
AS SAWDĀ

FAZZĀN
(FEZZAN)
Sabha

Waha
Wāhat Jālū &

Sawhāj
Al Qaşr

LIBYAN
DESERT
(AS SAHRĀ AL LĪBĪYAH)

Qaşr al
Farāfirah

EGYPT

Qinā

Thebes
(Ruins)
Al Uqşur
(Luxor)

Būr Safājah
Al Quşayr

Al Wajh
HEJAZ

Mārzuq Tarbū

Waw al-Kabīr

IDEHAN
MARZŪQ
SARĪR
TIBASTI

Al Kufrah
(Oasis)
Buzaymah

Al Khārijah

Idfū

Aswān

Aswān HIGH
DAM

RA'S BANĀS Ya

NIGER

TIBESTI
Pic Toussidé
10712
Aozou
Zouar

Emi Koussi
11204

SAHARA

Al Jawf

Tropic of Cancer

Ma'tan Bishāran

Ash Shabb
Bi'r Misāhah

Lake
Nasser

NUBIAN DESERT

Admin strative
Boundary

Halā'ib

Jabal Erba
7274

Jabal Od
7411

RED

BORKOU
BODELE

Faya

Yarda
Ouniangà Kébir

Dalqū

3rd Cataract

Dunqulah
Abu Hamad

Kūrti
Marawi

5th Cataract

Sinkāt

SEA

Jabal Erba

CHAD

Fada

ENNEDI

SUDAN

Al Khandaq
4th Cataract

Ad Dabbah

Barbar

Taqātu
Hayya

Tawi

Maussoro

Oum-Chalouba

'Aţbarah
Ad Dāmir

Adarama

OUADDAÏ

Abéché

DĀRFŪR

Al Junaynah Al Fāshir

Jabal Marrah
10131

KURDUFĀN

Shandī

6th Cataract

Wādī al Malik

Omdurman
(Umm Durmān)

Wādī al Malik

KHARTOUM
(Al Kharţūm)

Kassalā

Akor

Mongo

Nyala

Al Ubayyid

An Nuhūd

Kūstī

White Nile
(Al Bahr al Abyaḍ)
Blue Nile
(Al Bahr al Azraq)

Wad
Madanī
Ad Duwaym

Sannār
SANNĀR DAM

Rufa ah

Al Qadārif

Ras
Sinjah

Qallābāt

E

A-569495-76 7-411
COPYRIGHT BY
RAND McNALLY & COMPANY
MADE IN U.S.A.

20°

Longitude East of Greenwich

25°

30°

35°

Scale 1:12 000 000; one inch to 190 miles. Lambert Conformal Conic Projection

Elevations and depressions are given in feet

0 25 50 75 100   200   300   400   500 Mi

0   100   200   400   600   800 Kil

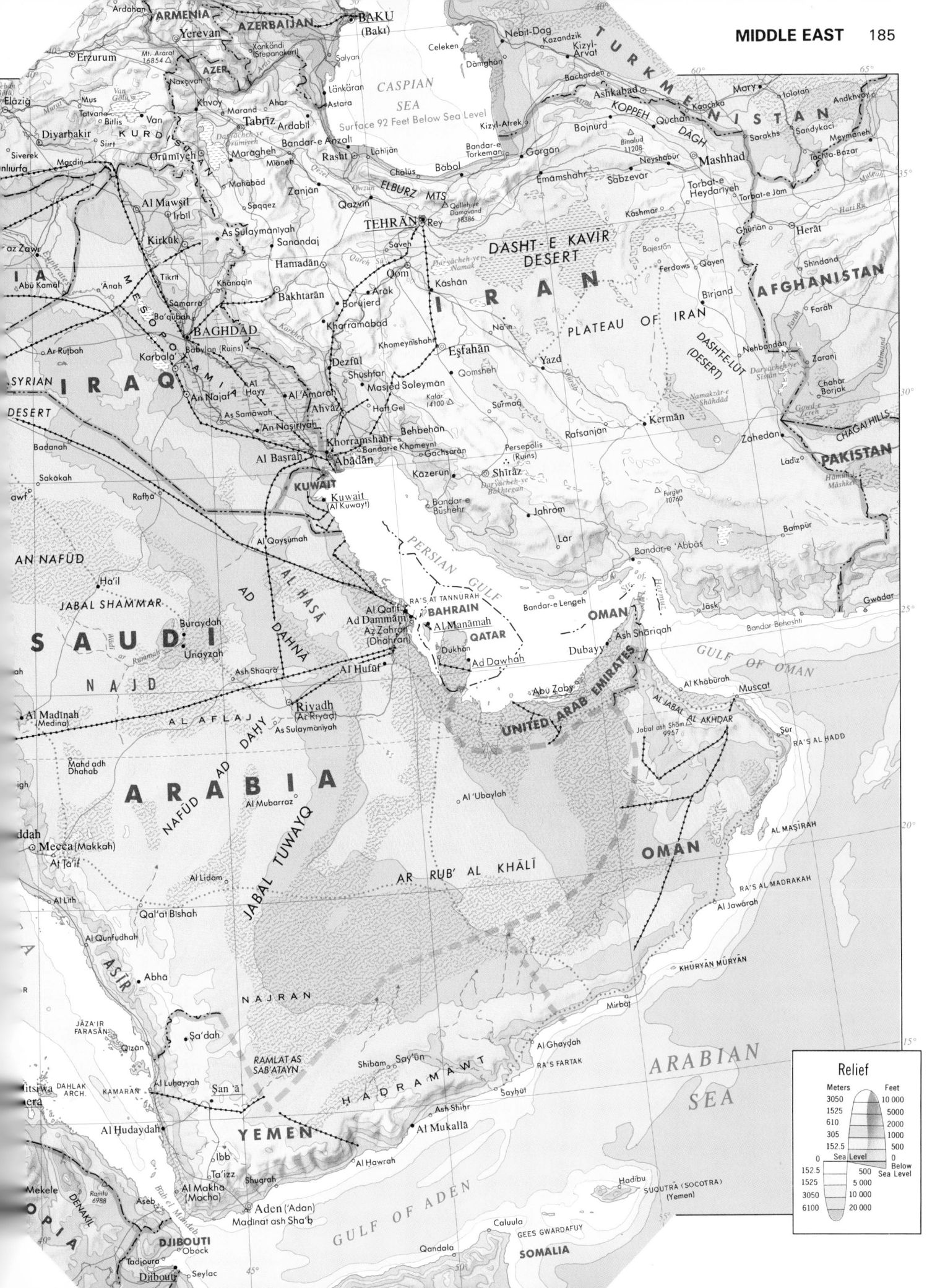

ARMENIA
AZERBAIJAN
Ardahan
Yerevan
BAKU
(Bakı)
Celeken
Nebit-Dag
Kazandzik
Kızyl-
Arvat
TURKMENISTAN
AZER.
Xankändi
(Stepanakert)
Salyan
Damghän
Bacharden
Ashkabad
Kaachka
Mary
Iolotan
Andkhvoy
Erzurum
Mt. Ararat
16854
Naxçivan
Khvoy
Astara
Kizyl-Afrek
Bojnürd
KOPPEH
Quchan
DÄGH
Sarakhs
Sandykaci
Meymaneh
Elâzig
Mus
Tatvan
Van Gölü
Marand
Ahar
Länkäran
Bandar-e
Torkeman
Gorgan
Binalud
11208
Neyshäbür
Mashhad
Tächta-Bazar
Diyarbakir
Bitlis
Van
KURDISTAN
Tabrîz
Ardabil
Bandar-e Anzali
Rasht
Lähijän
Chälüs
Babol
Emämshahr
Sabzevär
Torbat-e
Heydariyeh
Torbat-e Jäm
Siverek
Mardin
Orümiyeh
Marägheh
Mianeh
Qazvin
ELBURZ MTS
Ghürian
Herät
nlurfa
Al Mawsil
Irbil
Mahabad
Saqqez
Zanjän
TEHRÄN
Rey
Qolleh-ye
Damävand
18386
Kashmar
DASHT-E KAVIR
DESERT
AFGHANISTAN
az Zawr
Kirkük
As Sulaymaniyah
Sanandaj
Hamadän
Qom
Saveh
Bajestän
Ferdows
Qäyen
Abü Kamäl
'Anah
Tikrit
Khänaqin
Arak
Na'in
Birjand
Nehbandän
Samarra
Bakhtärän
Borüjerd
Kashan
IRAN
Yazd
DASHT-E-LUT
(DESERT)
Zaranj
Ba'qübah
Kharramabad
PLATEAU OF IRAN
Faräh
Ar Rutbah
BAGHDAD
Babylon (Ruins)
Dezfül
Shüshtar
Khomeynishahr
Esfahän
Qomsheh
Chahar
Borjak
Gowd-e
Zereh
SYRIAN
Karbala
An Najaf
Al Hayy
Masjed Soleymän
Kalar
14100
Behbehän
Gachsärän
Persepolis
(Ruins)
Rafsanjän
Kermän
Zähedän
Lädiz
PAKISTAN
DESERT
IRAQ
As Samäwah
Al 'Amärah
Ahväz
Haft Gel
Sürmaq
Hämün-i
Mäshkel
Badanah
An Näsiriyah
Khorramshahr
Bandar-e Khomeyni
Behbehän
Shiräz
Daryächeh-ye
Bakhtegan
Kazerün
Furgun
10760
Bampür
Sakäkah
Al Basrah
Abädän
Gachsärän
Bandar-e
Büshehr
Jahrom
Bandar-e 'Abbäs
Jäsk
Gwadar
awf
Rafha
KUWAIT
Kuwait
(Al Kuwayt)
Lar
Bandar-e Lengeh
Bandar Beheshti
AN NAFÜD
Ha'il
JABAL SHAMMAR
Buraydah
Al Qaysümah
AL HASA
PERSIAN GULF
RA'S AT TANNÜRAH
BAHRAIN
Al Manämah
OMAN
Ash Shäriqah
Unayzah
AD DAHNÄ
Al Qatif
Ad Dammäm
Az Zahrän
(Dhahran)
QATAR
Dukhän
Ad Dawhah
Dubayy
Al Khäbürah
Muscat
SAUDI
Ash Shaqra
Al Hufüf
Abü Zaby
UNITED ARAB EMIRATES
AL JABAL
AL AKHDAR
Sür
RA'S AL HADD
NAJD
Al Madinah
(Medina)
AL AFLAJ
Riyadh
(Ar Riyäd)
As Sulaymaniyah
Jabal ash Sham
9957
Mahd adh
Dhahab
AD DAHY
Al Mubarraz
Al 'Ubaylah
AL MASIRAH
igh
ARABIA
NAFÜD
Al Lidäm
JABAL TUWAYQ
AR RUB' AL KHÄLI
OMAN
RA'S AL MADRAKAH
ddah
Mecca (Makkah)
At Ta'if
Al Lith
Qal'at Bishah
Al Jawärah
Al Qunfudhah
ASÎR
Abha
NAJRAN
Mirbät
KHÜRYÄN MÜRYÄN
JÄZA'IR
FARASÄN
Sa'dah
Qizan
RAMLAT AS
SAB'ATAYN
Shibäm
Say'ün
Al Ghaydah
RA'S FARTAK
ARABIAN
SEA
tsiwa
DAHLAK
ARCH.
era
KAMARAN
Al Luhayyah
San'a'
HADRAMAWT
Ash Shihr
Sayhüt
Hadibu
SUQUTRÄ (SOCOTRA)
(Yemen)
Al Hudaydah
YEMEN
Ibb
Al Hawrah
Al Mukalla
Mekele
Ramlu
6988
Ta'izz
Shuqrah
OPIA
DENAKIL
Al Makha
(Mocha)
BAB EL MANDEB
Aden ('Adan)
Madinat ash Sha'b
GULF OF ADEN
Caluula
GEES GWARDAFUY
DJIBOUTI
Obock
Qandala
SOMALIA
Tadjoura
Djibout
Seylac

CASPIAN
SEA
Surface 92 Feet Below Sea Level

GULF OF OMAN

Relief		
Meters		Feet
3050		10 000
1525		5000
610		2000
305		1000
152.5		500
0	Sea Level	0
152.5		Below Sea Level
		500
1525		5 000
3050		10 000
6100		20 000

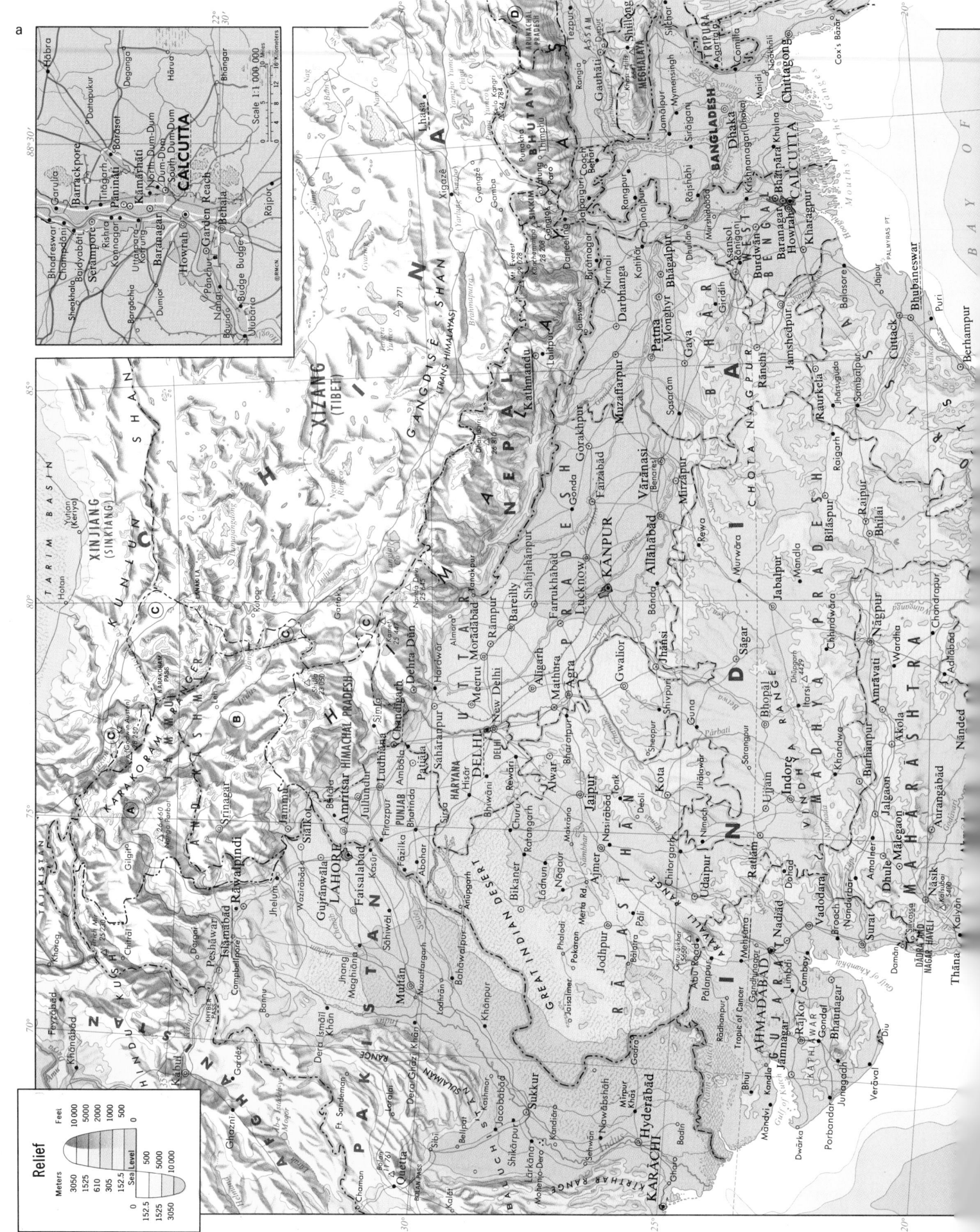

186

a

CALCUTTA

Scale 1:1 000 000

Hābra
Degangā
Bhāngar
Dattapukur
Bārāsat
Hārud
Barrackpore
Garulia
Bhadreswar
Chamdaṇ̄i
Bäidyabāti
Serampore
Rishra
Konnagar
Kāmārhāti
North-Dum-Dum
South Dum-Dum
Dum-Dum
Garden Reach
Howrah
Pānchur
Behala
Rājpur
Budge Budge
Baranagar
Nangi
Bāruipāra
Bargāchia
Dumjor
Uluberia
Sheakhala

Scale 1:10 000 000; one inch to 160 miles. Lambert Conformal Conic Projectio
Elevations and depressions are given in feet

Relief

Feet
10 000
5000
2000
1000
500

Meters
3050
1525
610
305
152.5
0
Sea Level
500
5000
10 000
152.5
1525
3050

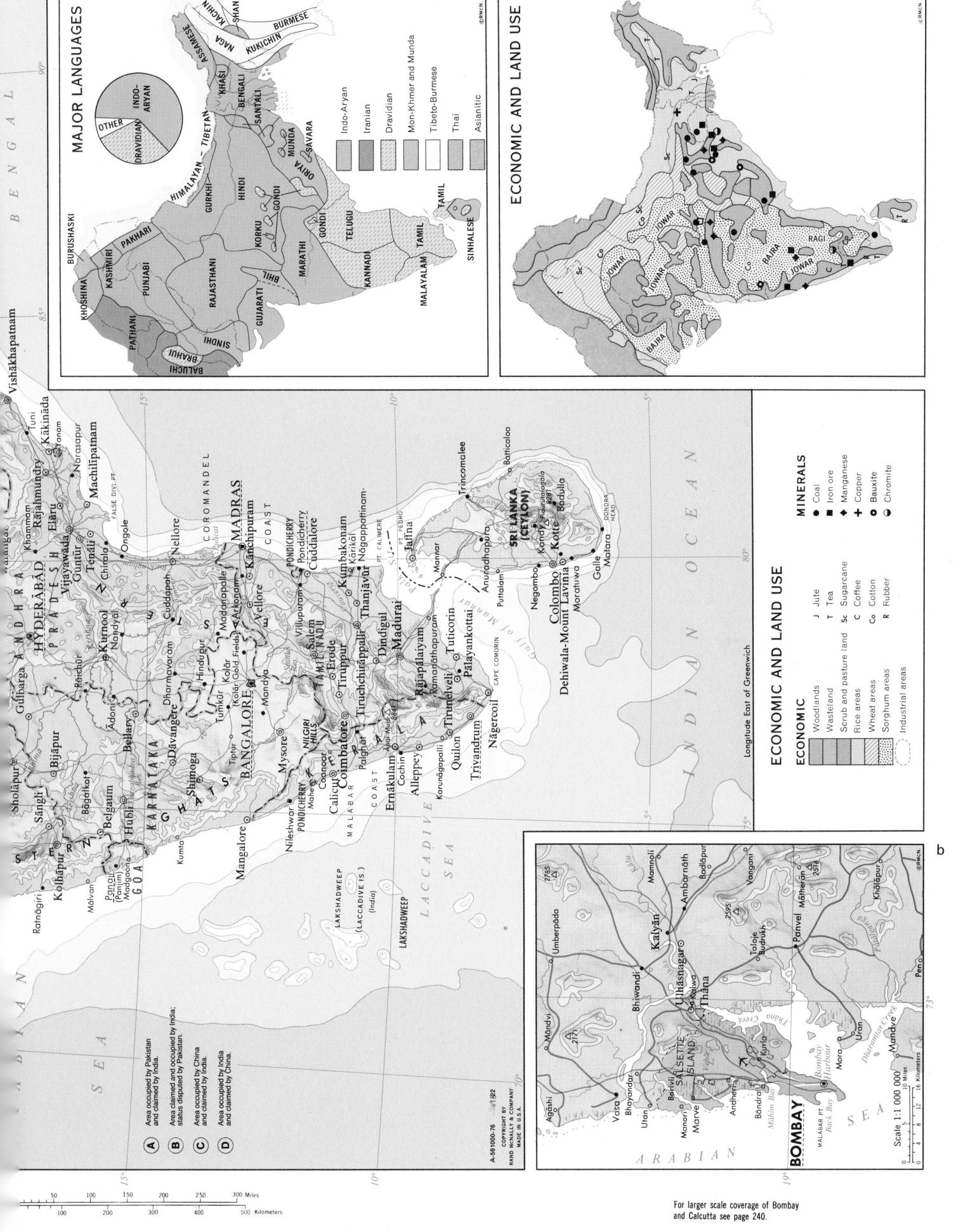

For larger scale coverage of Bombay and Calcutta see page 240.

Continued on pages 170-171

Continued on pages 182-183

Scale 1:16 000 000; one inch to 250 miles. Polyconic Projection
Elevations and depressions are given in feet

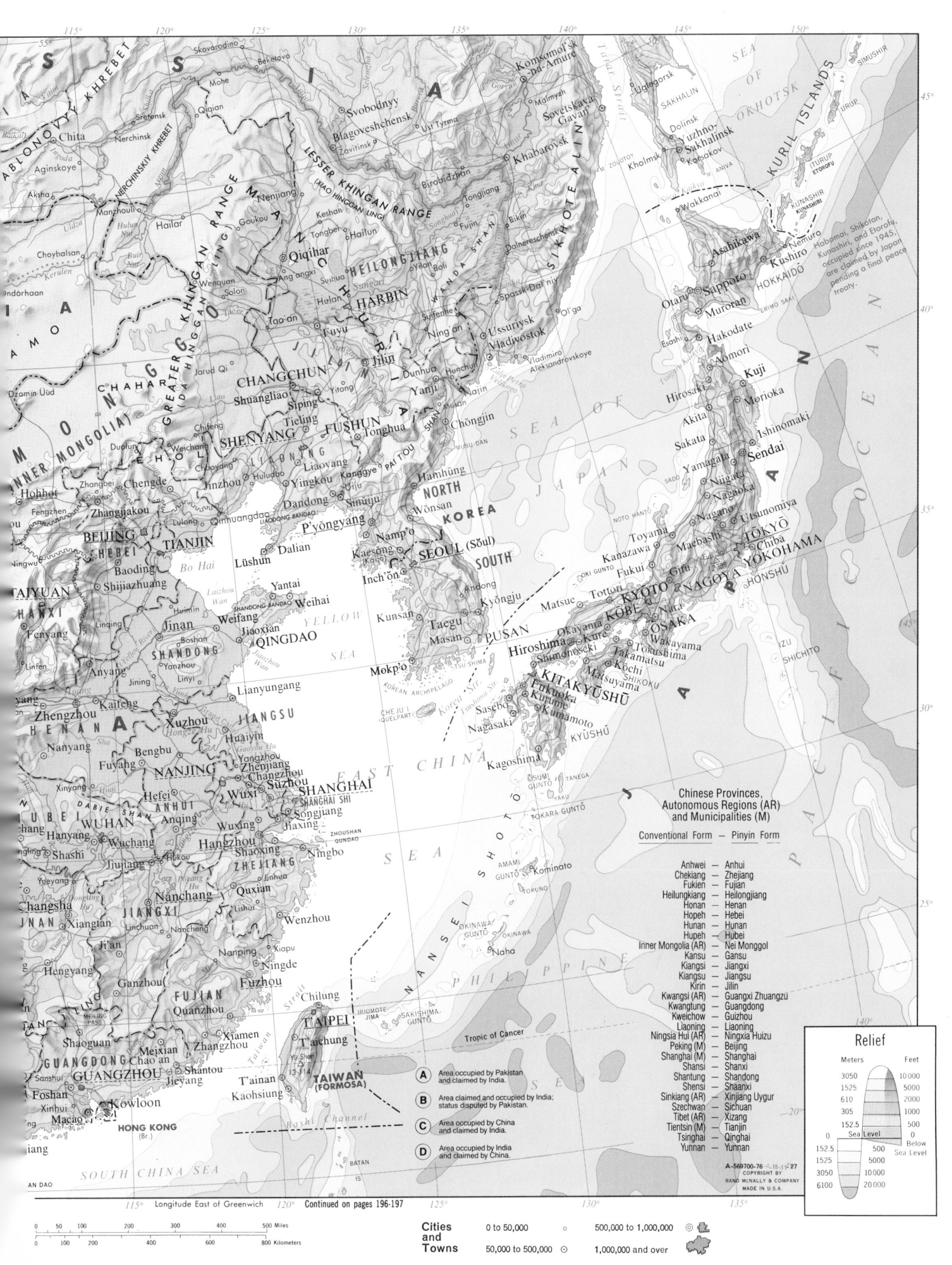

Continued on pages 196-197

Chinese Provinces,
Autonomous Regions (AR)
and Municipalities (M)

Conventional Form — Pinyin Form

Conventional Form		Pinyin Form
Anhwei	—	Anhui
Chekiang	—	Zhejiang
Fukien	—	Fujian
Heilungkiang	—	Heilongjiang
Honan	—	Henan
Hopeh	—	Hebei
Hunan	—	Hunan
Hupeh	—	Hubei
Inner Mongolia (AR)	—	Nei Monggol
Kansu	—	Gansu
Kiangsi	—	Jiangxi
Kiangsu	—	Jiangsu
Kirin	—	Jilin
Kwangsi (AR)	—	Guangxi Zhuangzu
Kwangtung	—	Guangdong
Kweichow	—	Guizhou
Liaoning	—	Liaoning
Ningsia Hui (AR)	—	Ningxia Huizu
Peking (M)	—	Beijing
Shanghai (M)	—	Shanghai
Shansi	—	Shanxi
Shantung	—	Shandong
Shensi	—	Shaanxi
Sinkiang (AR)	—	Xinjiang Uygur
Szechwan	—	Sichuan
Tibet (AR)	—	Xizang
Tientsin (M)	—	Tianjin
Tsinghai	—	Qinghai
Yunnan	—	Yunnan

(A) Area occupied by Pakistan and claimed by India.
(B) Area claimed and occupied by India; status disputed by Pakistan.
(C) Area occupied by China and claimed by India.
(D) Area occupied by India and claimed by China.

A-569700-76   15-1-27
COPYRIGHT BY
RAND MCNALLY & COMPANY
MADE IN U.S.A.

Relief

Meters		Feet
3050		10 000
1525		5000
610		2000
305		1000
152.5		500
0	Sea Level	0
152.5		Below Sea Level
1525		5000
3050		10 000
6100		20 000

0   50   100   200   300   400   500 Miles
0   100   200   400   600   800 Kilometers

Cities and Towns

| 0 to 50,000 | ○ | 500,000 to 1,000,000 | ⊙ |
| 50,000 to 500,000 | ⊙ | 1,000,000 and over | |

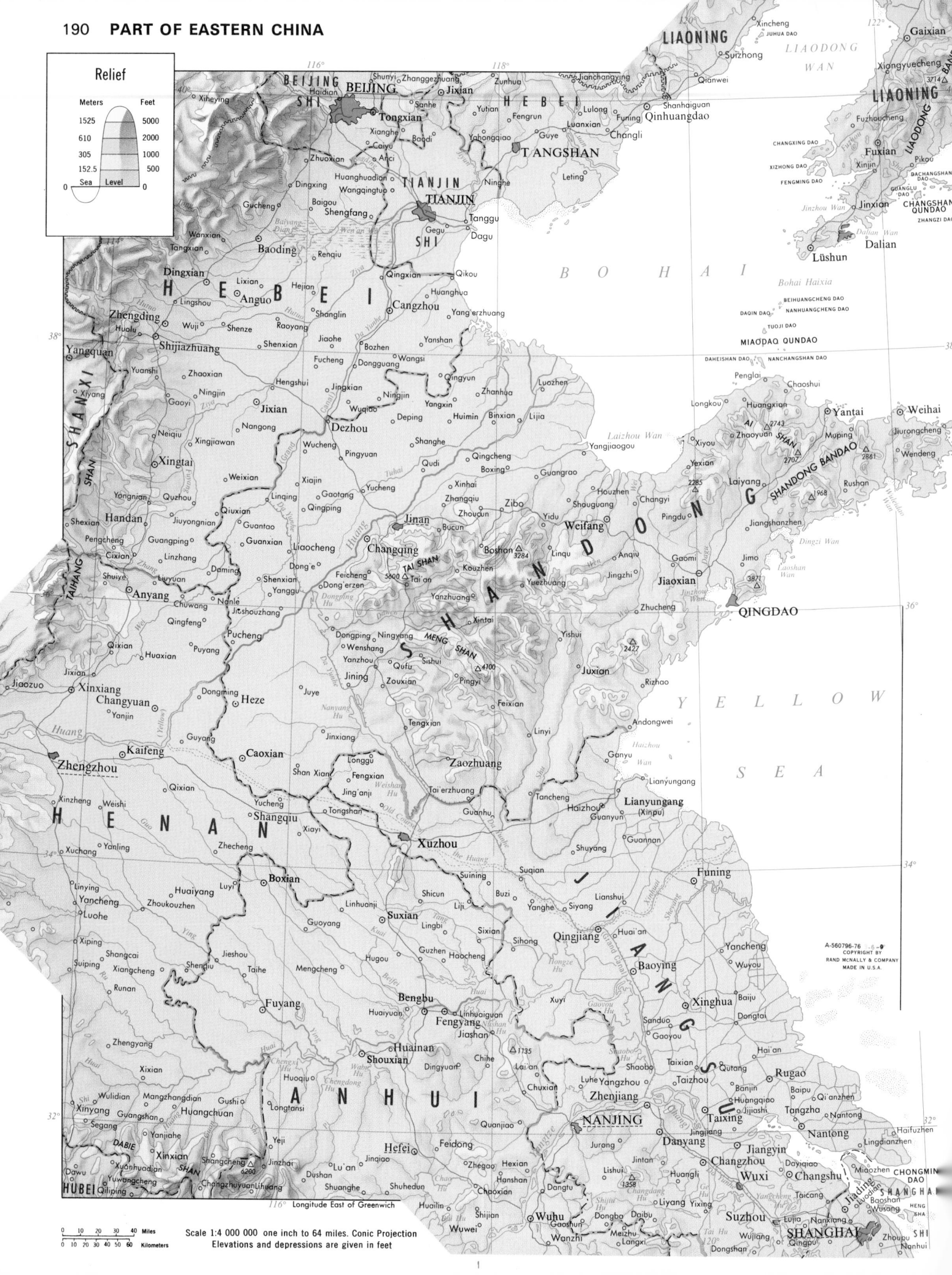

Relief

Meters	Feet
1525	5000
610	2000
305	1000
152.5	500
0 Sea Level 0	

LIAONING
Xincheng
Juhua Dao
Gaixian
LIAODONG
WAN
Suizhong
Qianwei
Xiongyuecheng
3714
Qinhuang

LIAONING
Fuzhoucheng
CHANGXING DAO
XIZHONG DAO
FENGMING DAO
Fuxian
Xinjin
Pikou
DACHANGSHAN
DAO
GUANGLU
DAO
CHANGSHAN
QUNDAO
ZHANGZI DAO

BEIJING
SHI
Shunyi
Zhanggezhuang
Zunhua
HEBEI
Jianchangying
Haidian
BEIJING
Jixian
Sanhe
Yutian
Fengrun
Lulong
Funing
Qinhuangdao
Tongxian
Xianghe
Baodi
Yahongqiao
Guye
Luanxian
Changli
Zhuoxian
Caiyu
Anci
Ninghe
TANGSHAN
Dingxing
Huanghuadian
Wangqingtuo
TIANJIN
Leting
Gucheng
Baigou
Shengfang
TIANJIN
Gegu
Tanggu
Wanxian
SHI
Dagu
Tangxian
Baoding
Renqiu
Qikou
BOHAI

Dingxian
Lixian
Hejian
Qingxian
Huanghua
Yang'erzhuang
Bohai Haixia
Anguo
Shanglin
Cangzhou
Zhengding
Wuji
Shenze
Raoyang
Jiaohe
Yanshan
BEIHUANGCHENG DAO
Hualu
Lingshou
Shenxian
Bozhen
Wangsi
NANHUANGCHENG DAO
Shijiazhuang
Hengshui
Jingxian
Qingyun
Zhanhua
Luozhen
DAQIN DAO
TUOJI DAO
MIAODAO QUNDAO
Xiyang
Zhaoxian
Ningjin
Wuqiao
Ningjin
Yangxin
Penglai
Chaoshui
DAHEISHAN DAO
NANCHANGSHAN DAO
Yuanshi
Gaoyi
Fucheng
Longkou
Huangxian
Yantai
Weihai
Neiqiu
Xingjiawan
Deping
Huimin
Binxian
Lijia
Laizhou Wan
Xiyou
Zhaoyuan
Muping
Xingtai
Weixian
Xiajin
Gaotang
Shanghe
Yexian
2861
Jiurongcheng
Nangong
Dezhou
Pingyuan
Qingcheng
Boxing
Yangjiaogou
AI 2743 SHAN
Wendeng
Yongnian
Quzhou
Qingping
Xinhai
Zhangqiu
Zibo
Shouguang
Guangrao
Houzhen
Changyi
2707
Laiyang
1968
Rushan
Handan
Guantao
Jinan
Zhoucun
Yidu
Weifang
SHANDONG BANDAO
Shexian
Pengcheng
Guangping
Jiuyongnian
Liaocheng
Changqing
Bucun
Boshan
3284
Linqu
Anqiu
Gaomi
Pingdu
Jimo
3871
Linzhang
Daming
Dong'e
TAI SHAN
Kouzhen
Tai'an
Yuezhuang
Jingzhi
Jiaoxian
Dingzi Wan
Cixian
Shuiye
Liyuan
Shenxian
Yanggu
Feicheng
5600
Dong'erzhuang
Yanzhuang
Xintai
Zhucheng
Laoshan Wan
Anyang
Chuwang
Nanle
Jieshouzhang
Dongping Hu
QINGDAO
Qingfeng
Pucheng
Dongping
Ningyang
MENG SHAN
Yishui
2427
Qixian
Huaxian
Wenshang
Yanzhou
Sishui
4100
Jiaozuo
Xinxiang
Puyang
Guyang
Dongming
Heze
Juye
Jining
Zouxian
Qufu
Pingyi
Feixian
Juxian
YELLOW
Changyuan
Yanjin
Jinxiang
Tengxian
Linyi
Rizhao
Kaifeng
Caoxian
Zhengzhou
Qixian
Yucheng
Longgu
Shan Xian
Fengxian
Weishan Hu
Tai'erzhuang
Tancheng
Andongwei
Xinzheng
Weishi
Jing'anji
Zaozhuang
Haizhou Wan
SEA
Xuchang
Yanling
Zhecheng
Tongshan
Guanhu
Haizhou
Lianyungang
HENAN
Xiayi
Xuzhou
Shuyang
Guanyun
(Xinpu)
Linying
Shangqiu
Suining
Suqian
Guannan
Yancheng
Boxian
Shicun
Buzi
Funing
Luohe
Huaiyang
Luyi
Linhuaiji
Liji
Yanghe
Siyang
Lianshui
JIANGSU
Zhoukouzhen
Guoyang
Sixian
Sihong
Xiping
Guyang
Suixian
Lingbi
Huai'an
Shangcai
Jieshou
Taihe
Mengcheng
Guzhen
Haocheng
Qingjiang
Yancheng
Suiping
Xiangcheng
Shenqiu
Hugou
ANHUI
Baoying
Wuyou
Runan
Fuyang
Huai
Xuyi
Gaoyou
Xinghua
Zhengyang
Bengbu
Huaiyuan
Sanduo
Dongtai
Xixian
Shouxian
Chihu
1135
Gaoyou Hu
Baiju
Huoqiu
Dingyuan
Lai'an
Taixian
Hai'an
Shaobo Hu
Wulidian
Manzhangdian
Gushi
Longtansi
Chengdong Hu
Huainan
Fengyang
Jiashan
Luhe
Yangzhou
Taizhou
Qutang
Rugao
Xinyang
Guangshan
Huangchuan
Yeji
Chuxian
Zhenjiang
Banjin
Baipu
Qi'anzhen
Segang
Yanjiahe
Quanjiao
Jurong
Huangqiao
Jijiashi
Tangzha
DABIE
Xinxian
Shangcheng
Jinzhai
Lu'an
Jinqiao
Zhegao
Hexian
Dangtu
Huangli
Jintan
Tangzha
Nantong
Haifuzhen
Dawu
Xuanhuadian
Yuwangcheng
Lihuang
Changzhuyuan
Dushan
Shanghe
Shuhedun
Hanshan
Chaoxian
Zhenjiang
Liyang
Yixing
Changzhou
Wuxi
Dayiqiao
Miaozhen
Lingdianzhen
HUBEI
Qiliping
NANJING
Lishui
Jintan
Changshu
CHONGMING
DAO
Hefei
Feidong
Shijian
Daibu
Jiading
SHANGHAI
SHI
Wuhu
Dongba
Tai Hu
Jiangyin
Taicang
Wujiang
Baoshan
Wusong
Wuwei
Wanzhi
Meizhu
Langxi
Suzhou
Lujia
Nanxiang
HENG
SHA
Zhoushan
SHANGHAI
Dongshan
Qingpu
Nanhui
Zhoupu

0 10 20 30 40 Miles
0 10 20 30 40 50 60 Kilometers
Scale 1:4 000 000 one inch to 64 miles. Conic Projection
Elevations and depressions are given in feet
Longitude East of Greenwich

A-560796-76
COPYRIGHT BY
RAND MCNALLY & COMPANY
MADE IN U.S.A.

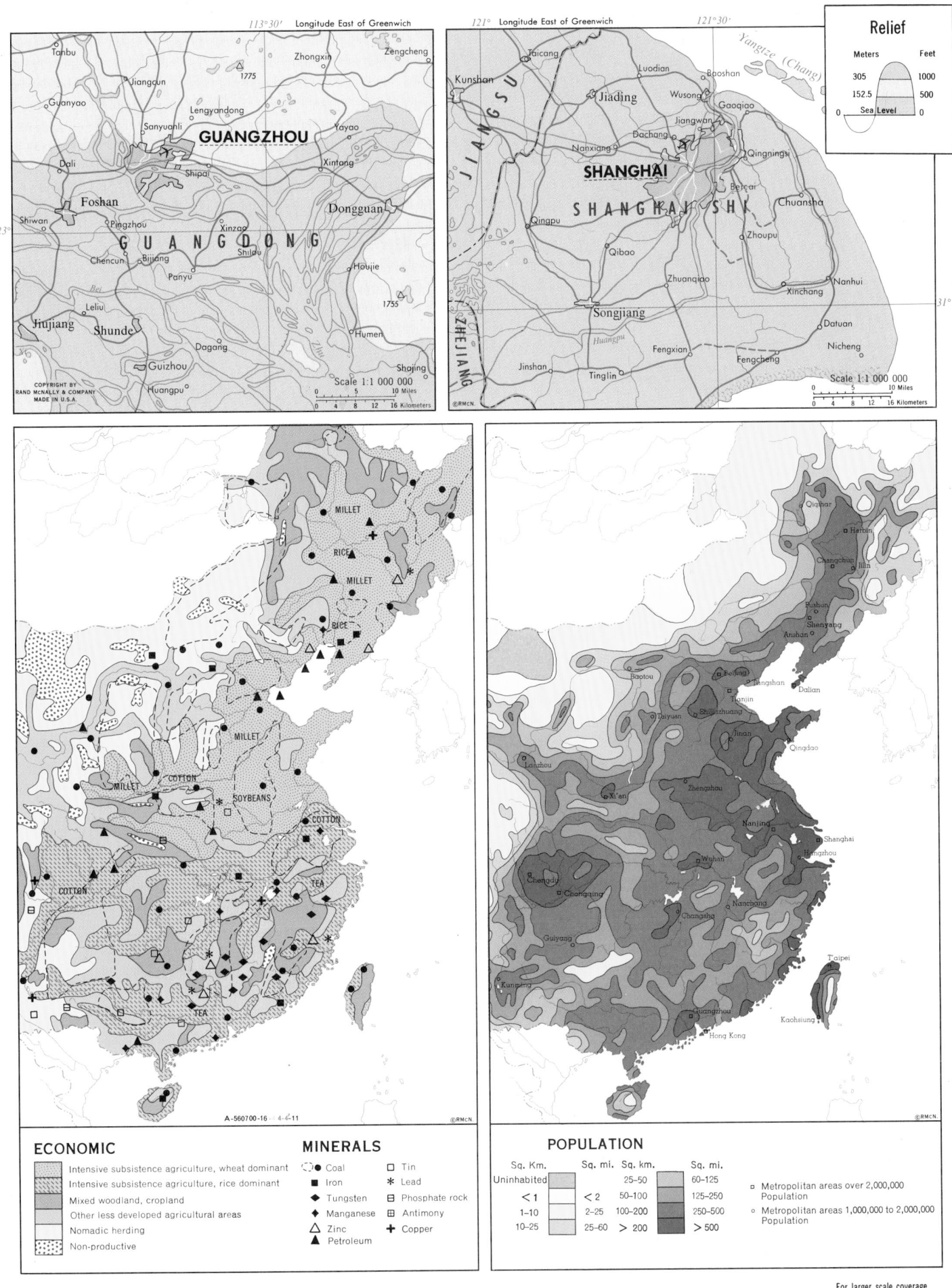

Relief

Meters	Feet
305	1000
152.5	500
0 Sea Level	0

Scale 1:1 000 000

Scale 1:1 000 000

ECONOMIC

- Intensive subsistence agriculture, wheat dominant
- Intensive subsistence agriculture, rice dominant
- Mixed woodland, cropland
- Other less developed agricultural areas
- Nomadic herding
- Non-productive

MINERALS

- ◖ Coal
- ◆ Iron
- ● Tungsten
- ◆ Manganese
- △ Zinc
- ▲ Petroleum
- ☐ Tin
- ✳ Lead
- ⊞ Phosphate rock
- ⊞ Antimony
- ✛ Copper

POPULATION

Sq. Km.	Sq. mi.	Sq. km.	Sq. mi.
Uninhabited		25–50	60–125
<1	< 2	50–100	125–250
1–10	2–25	100–200	250–500
10–25	25–60	> 200	> 500

- ☐ Metropolitan areas over 2,000,000 Population
- ○ Metropolitan areas 1,000,000 to 2,000,000 Population

A-560700-16 4-4-11

COPYRIGHT BY
RAND McNALLY & COMPANY
MADE IN U.S.A.

For larger scale coverage
of Shanghai see page 241.

Continued on page 194

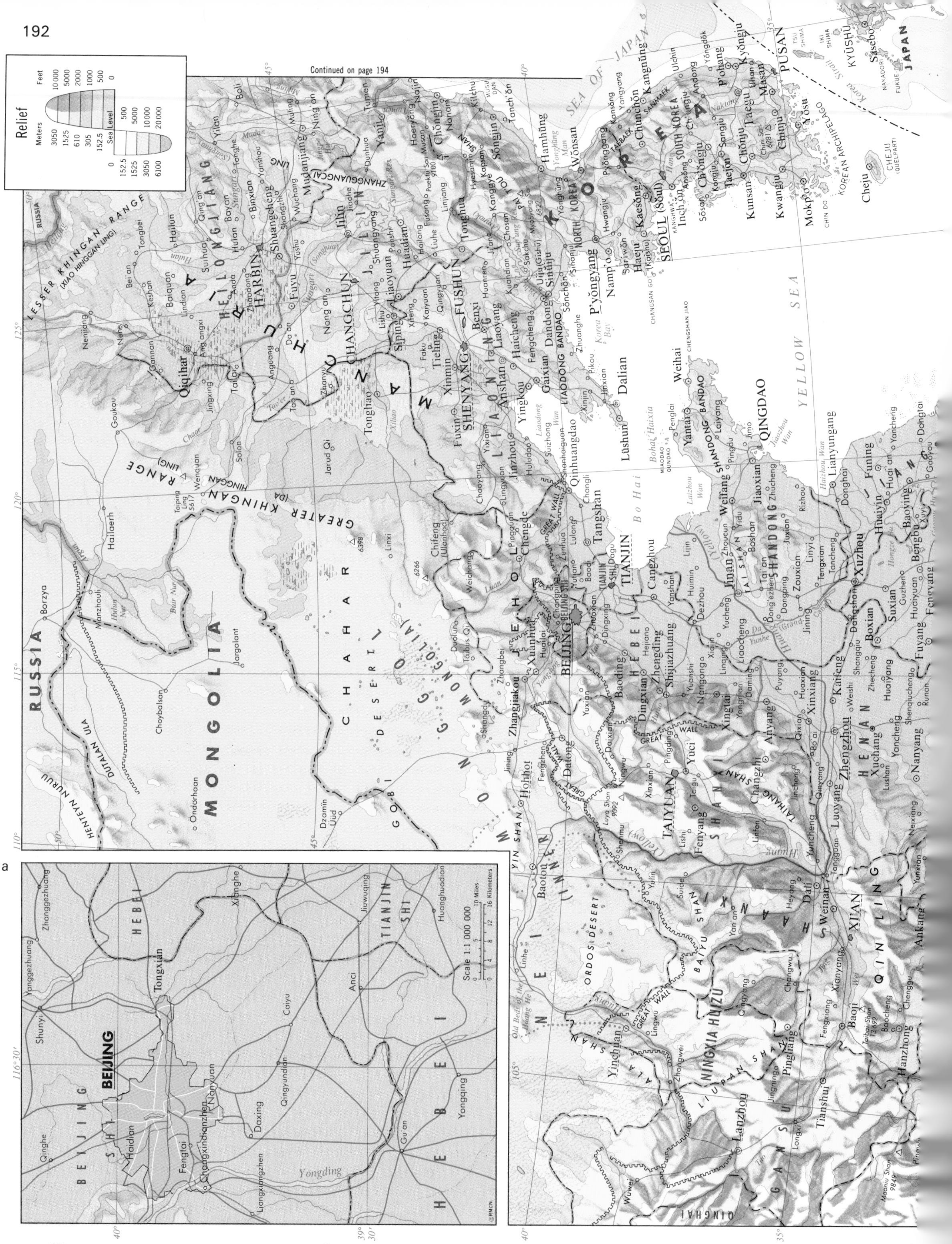

Relief

Feet
10 000
5000
2000
1000
500
0

Meters
3050
1525
610
305
152.5
Sea Level

152.5
1525
3050
6100

500
5000
10 000
20 000

Major labels

RUSSIA

MONGOLIA

HEILONGJIANG

JILIN

LIAONING

HEBEI

SHANXI

SHANDONG

HENAN

SHAANXI

GANSU

NINGXIA HUIZU

NEI MONGOL

CHAHAR

JEHOL

QINGHAI

NORTH KOREA

SOUTH KOREA

JAPAN

SEA OF JAPAN

YELLOW SEA

Bo Hai

Korea Bay

GOBI DESERT

ORDOS DESERT

LESSER KHINGAN RANGE (XIAO HINGGAN LING)

GREATER KHINGAN RANGE (DA HINGGAN LING)

HENTIYEN NURUU

DUTAYAYAN ULA

ZHANGGUANGCAI SHAN

TAIHANG SHAN

QIN LING

YIN SHAN

ALA SHAN

LIUPAN SHAN

BAYU SHAN

Cities (selected)

HARBIN, Qiqihar, CHANGCHUN, SHENYANG, FUSHUN, BENXI, Anshan, Dalian, Lüshun, TIANJIN, BEIJING, Baoding, Shijiazhuang, TAIYUAN, Datong, Hohhot, Baotou, Yinchuan, Lanzhou, XI'AN, Baoji, Tianshui, QINGDAO, Jinan, Xuzhou, Kaifeng, Zhengzhou, Luoyang, Nanyang, Xuchang, Ankang, Hanzhong

Harbin, Jiamusi, Mudanjiang, Jilin, Siping, Tonghua, Dandong, Pyŏngyang, SEOUL (Sŏul), Inch'ŏn, Taejŏn, Taegu, Kwangju, Pusan, Mokp'o, Cheju, Hamhŭng, Wŏnsan, Weihai, Yantai, Weifang, Zibo, Linyi, Lianyungang

GREAT WALL

SHANDONG BANDAO

LIAODONG BANDAO

KOREAN ARCHIPELAGO

CHEJU (QUELPART)

Huang He (Yellow)

Yongding

Inset (a) — Beijing area

BEIJING SHI

BEIJING

HEBEI

TIANJIN SHI

Haidian, Fengtai, Tongxian, Daxing, Qinghe, Shunyi, Yangezhuang, Zhanggezhuang, Xinghe, Changxindianzhen, Nanyuan, Qingyundian, Anci, Caiyu, Jiuwangqing, Huangcun, Huangbaodian, Qingqing, Gu'an, Yongqing

Yongding

Scale 1:1 000 000

10 Miles

16 Kilometers

Cities and Towns

0 to 50,000 · | 500,000 to 1,000,000 ◎

50,000 to 500,000 ○ | 1,000,000 and over

For larger scale coverage of Beijing see page 240.

Scale 1:10 000 000; one inch to 160 miles. Lambert Conformal Conic Project
Elevations and depressions are given in feet

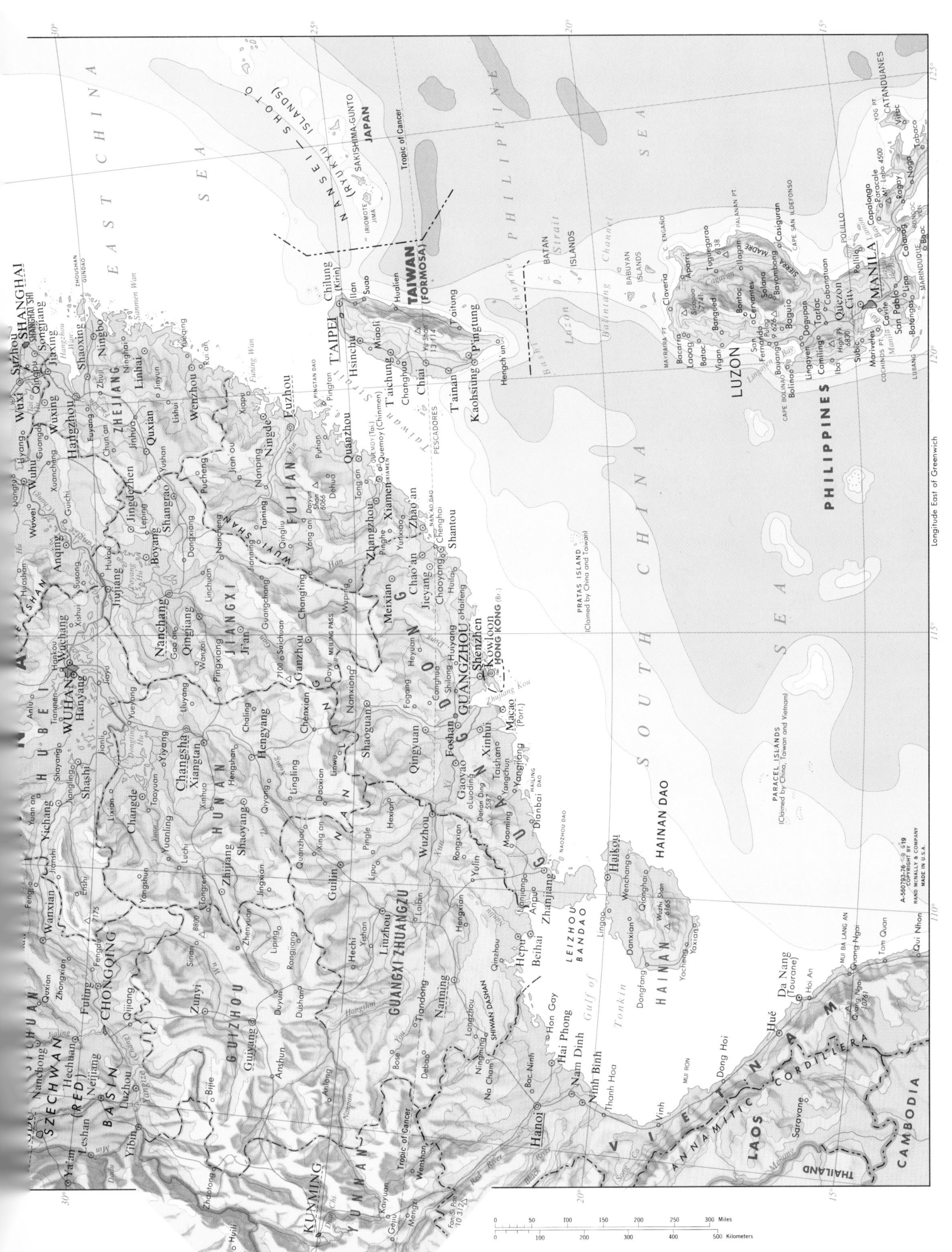

SHANGHAI
SUZHOU
WUXI
Liyang
Wuhu
Wuxing
Xuancheng
Hangzhou
Guangde
Huzhou
Fuyang
Jiaxing
Jiaxing
Songjiang
SHANGHAI SHI
Qingpu
Ningbo
Shaoxing
ZHEJIANG
Linhai
Xiuning
Quxian
Wenzhou
Lishui
Jinhua
Ningde
Fuzhou
Nanping
Putian
Quanzhou
Xiamen
Zhangzhou
Shantou
FUJIAN
Chenghai
Chao'an
Jieyang
Meixian
JIANGXI
Nanchang
Qingjiang
Ganzhou
Nanxiong
Shaoguan
Heyuan
Huizhou
Shenzhen
Kowloon
HONG KONG
GUANGZHOU
Foshan
Xinhui
Macao
Taishan
Yangjiang
GUANGDONG
HUNAN
Changsha
Xiangtan
Hengyang
Shaoyang
Lingling
Guilin
GUANGXI ZHUANGZU
Liuzhou
Nanning
Wuzhou
Zhanjiang
HAINAN DAO
Haikou
LEIZHOU BANDAO
HAINAN
HUBEI
WUHAN
Wuchang
Hanyang
Changde
CHONGQING
GUIZHOU
Guiyang
Zunyi
SICHUAN
SZECHWAN
CHUAN
BASIN (RED)
Chongqing
Leshan
YUNNAN
KUNMING

EAST CHINA SEA
PHILIPPINE SEA
SOUTH CHINA SEA
Gulf of Tonkin
TAIWAN (FORMOSA)
T'AIPEI
Chilung
Kaohsiung
Tainan
Taichung
PESCADORES
JAPAN
RYUKYU ISLANDS
NANSEI-SHOTO
SAKISHIMA-GUNTO
Tropic of Cancer

PHILIPPINES
LUZON
MANILA
Quezon City
Baguio
Batan Islands
Babuyan Islands
CATANDUANES
MARINDUQUE

VIETNAM
Hanoi
Hai Phong
Da Nang
Hué
LAOS
THAILAND
CAMBODIA
ANNAMITIC CORDILLERA

PRATAS ISLAND
(Claimed by China and Taiwan)

PARACEL ISLANDS
(Claimed by China, Taiwan and Vietnam)

Longitude East of Greenwich

| 0 | 50 | 100 | 150 | 200 | 250 | 300 Miles |
| 0 | 100 | 200 | 300 | 400 | 500 Kilometers |

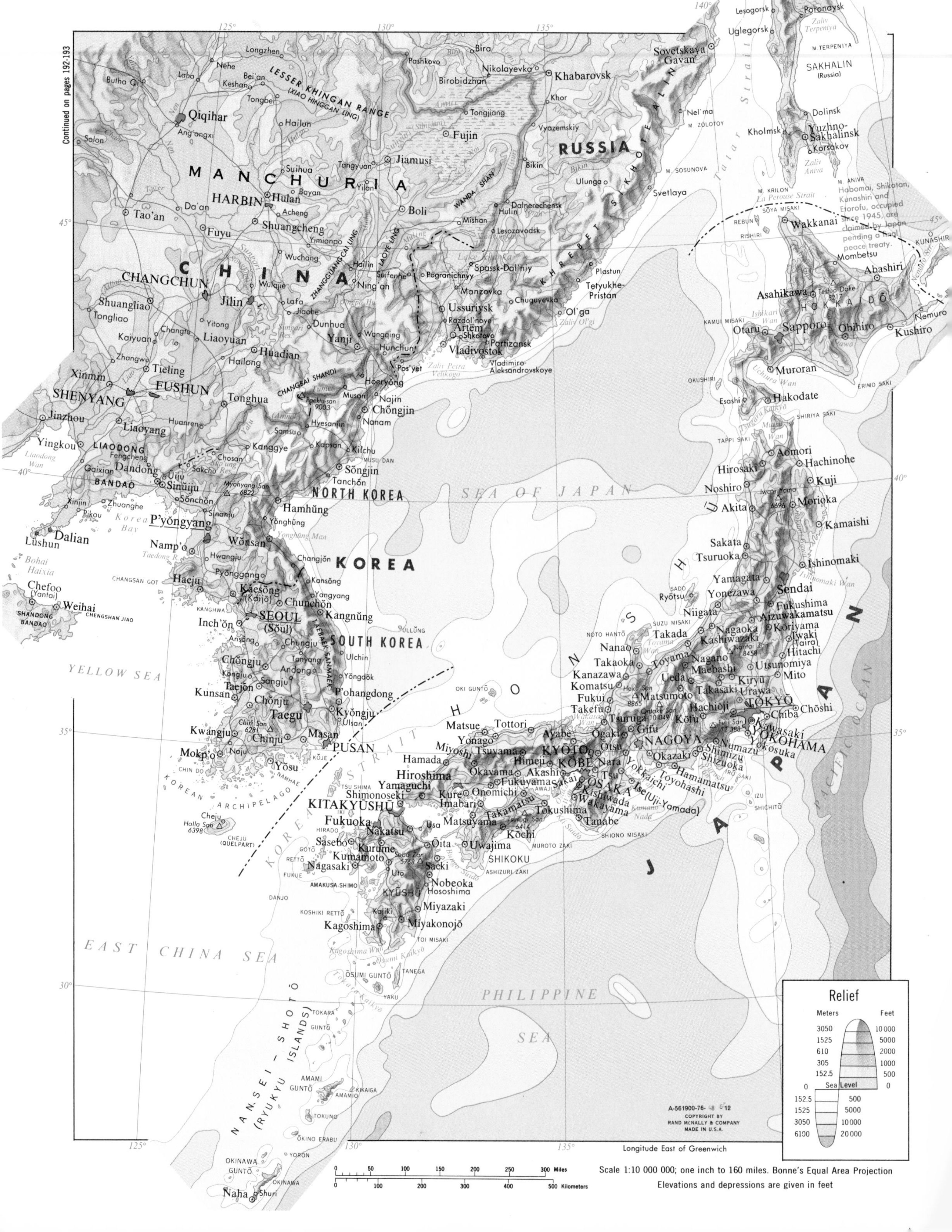

Continued on pages 192-193

RUSSIA

MANCHURIA

CHINA

HARBIN

SHENYANG

FUSHUN

LIAODONG

BANDAO

NORTH KOREA

KOREA

SOUTH KOREA

SEOUL (Sŏul)

PUSAN

KITAKYŪSHŪ

YELLOW SEA

SEA OF JAPAN

HOKKAIDŌ

HONSHU

SHIKOKU

KYŪSHŪ

TŌKYŌ

YOKOHAMA

KYŌTO

KŌBE

ŌSAKA

NAGOYA

JAPAN

PACIFIC OCEAN

EAST CHINA SEA

PHILIPPINE SEA

NAN-SEI-SHOTŌ (RYUKYU ISLANDS)

KOREAN ARCHIPELAGO

KOREA STRAIT

SAKHALIN (Russia)

Relief

Meters		Feet
3050		10 000
1525		5000
610		2000
305		1000
152.5		500
0	Sea Level	0
152.5		500
1525		5000
3050		10 000
6100		20 000

A-561900-76- 48 12
COPYRIGHT BY
RAND McNALLY & COMPANY
MADE IN U.S.A.

Longitude East of Greenwich

Scale 1:10 000 000; one inch to 160 miles. Bonne's Equal Area Projection
Elevations and depressions are given in feet

| Miles | 0 | 50 | 100 | 150 | 200 | 250 | 300 |
| Kilometers | 0 | 100 | 200 | 300 | 400 | 500 |

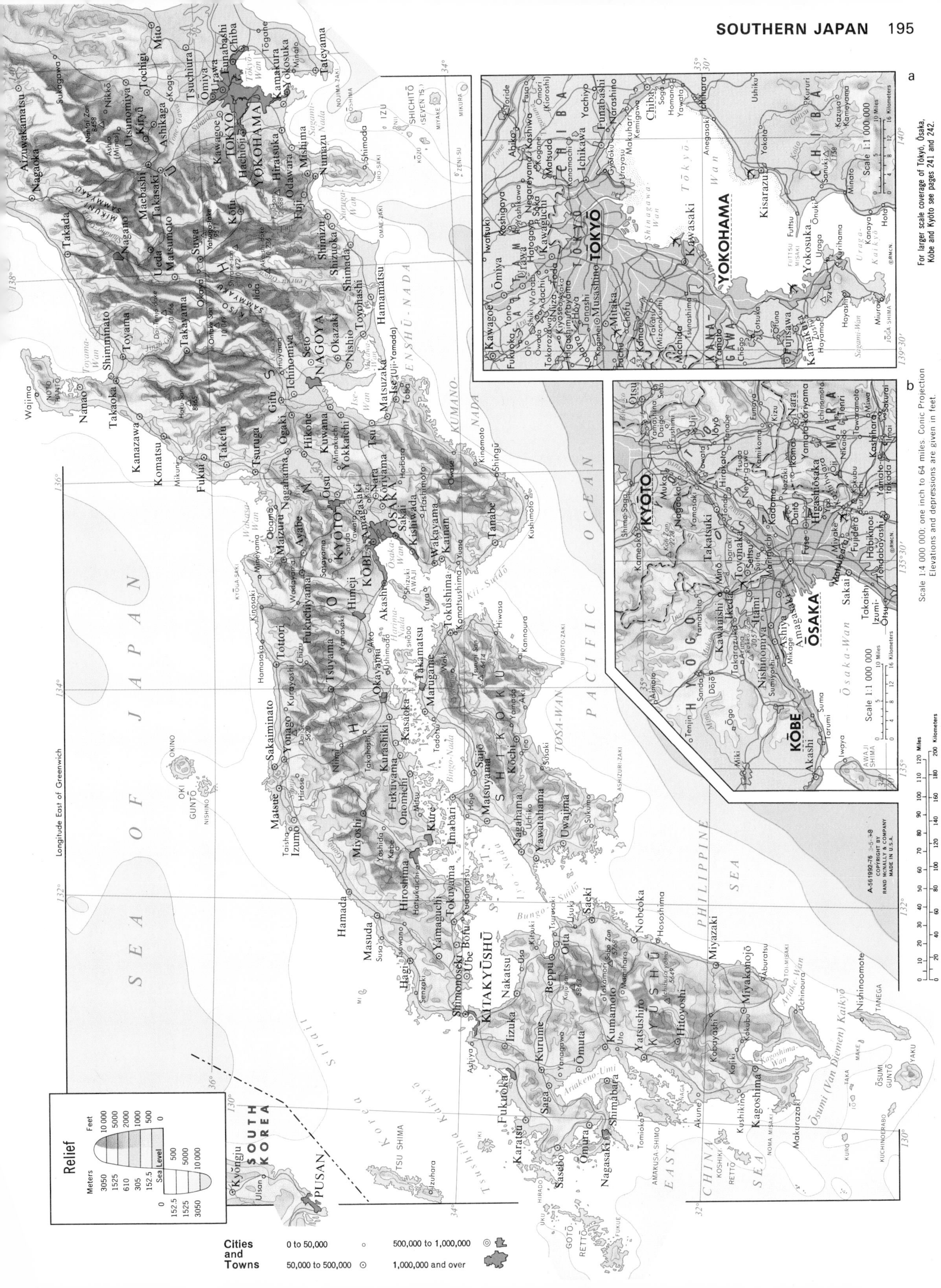

a

For larger scale coverage of Tōkyō, Ōsaka, Kōbe and Kyōto see pages 241 and 242.

Scale 1:1 000 000

TŌKYŌ
YOKOHAMA
KANAGAWA
CHIBA

b

Scale 1:4 000 000; one inch to 64 miles. Conic Projection
Elevations and depressions are given in feet.

KYŌTO
NARA
HYŌGO
ŌSAKA
KŌBE
Ōsaka-Wan

Scale 1:1 000 000

SEA OF JAPAN

PACIFIC OCEAN

PHILIPPINE SEA

EAST CHINA SEA

TOKYO
YOKOHAMA
NAGOYA
KYŌTO
ŌSAKA
KŌBE
HIROSHIMA
SHIKOKU
KYŪSHŪ
KITAKYŪSHŪ

SOUTH KOREA
PUSAN
Kyŏngju
Ulsan

Longitude East of Greenwich

ENSHŪ-NADA
KUMANO-NADA
TOSA-WAN
BINGO-NADA
HARIMA-NADA
Kii-Suidō
Bungo-Suidō

A-561992-76 —3-5-49
COPYRIGHT BY
RAND McNALLY & COMPANY
MADE IN U.S.A.

Relief

Meters	Feet
3050	10 000
1525	5000
610	2000
305	1000
152.5	500
0	Sea Level
152.5	500
1525	5000
3050	10 000

Cities and Towns

0 to 50,000 ○
50,000 to 500,000 ⊙
500,000 to 1,000,000 ◉
1,000,000 and over

196

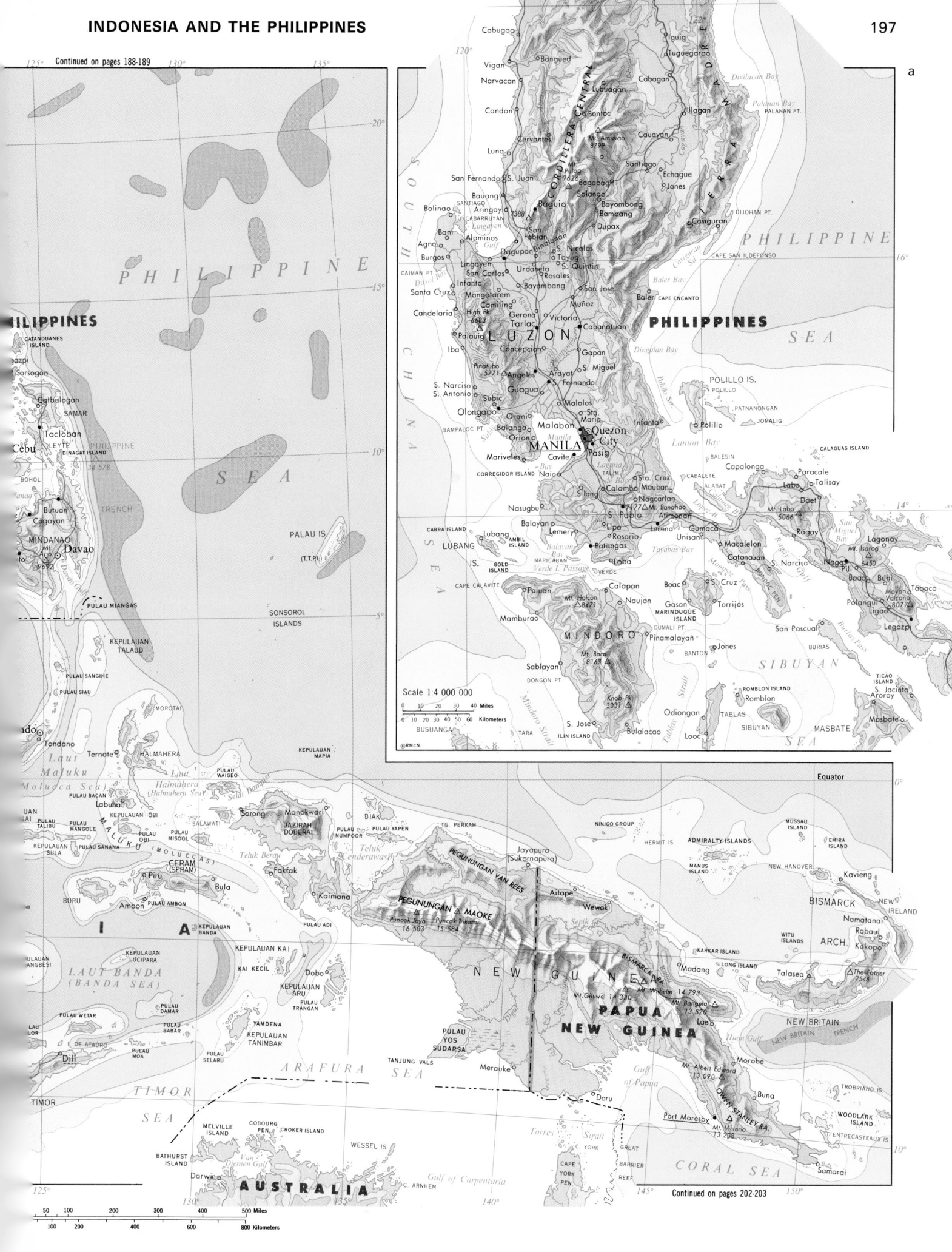

Continued on pages 188-189

PHILIPPINE

SEA

SOUTH

CHINA

SEA

CORDILLERA CENTRAL

SIERRA MADRE

PHILIPPINES

LUZON

MANILA
Quezon City

MINDORO

SIBUYAN SEA

Scale 1:4 000 000

0 10 20 30   40 Miles

0 10 20 30 40 50 60 Kilometers

©RMCN.

PHILIPPINES

Cebu

SAMAR

LEYTE

PHILIPPINE SEA

MINDANAO
Davao

PALAU IS.
(T.T.PI.)

SONSOROL
ISLANDS

KEPULAUAN
TALAUD

KEPULAUAN
MAPIA

MOROTAI

HALMAHERA

MALUKU
(MOLUCCAS)

Laut Maluku
(Molucca Sea)

Laut
Halmahera
(Halmahera Sea)

CERAM
(SERAM)

BURU

Ambon

INDONESIA

LAUT BANDA
(BANDA SEA)

Dili

TIMOR

TIMOR
SEA

NEW GUINEA

PEGUNUNGAN VAN REES

PEGUNUNGAN MAOKE

Jayapura
(Sukarnapura)

PAPUA
NEW GUINEA

ARAFURA SEA

Merauke

Daru

Port Moresby

OWEN STANLEY RA.

Gulf
of Papua

CORAL SEA

Equator

BISMARCK
ARCH.

NEW
IRELAND

Rabaul

NEW BRITAIN

NEW BRITAIN
TRENCH

ADMIRALTY ISLANDS

AUSTRALIA

Darwin

Gulf of Carpentaria

Continued on pages 202-203

50 100   200   300   400 500 Miles

100   200   400   600   800 Kilometers

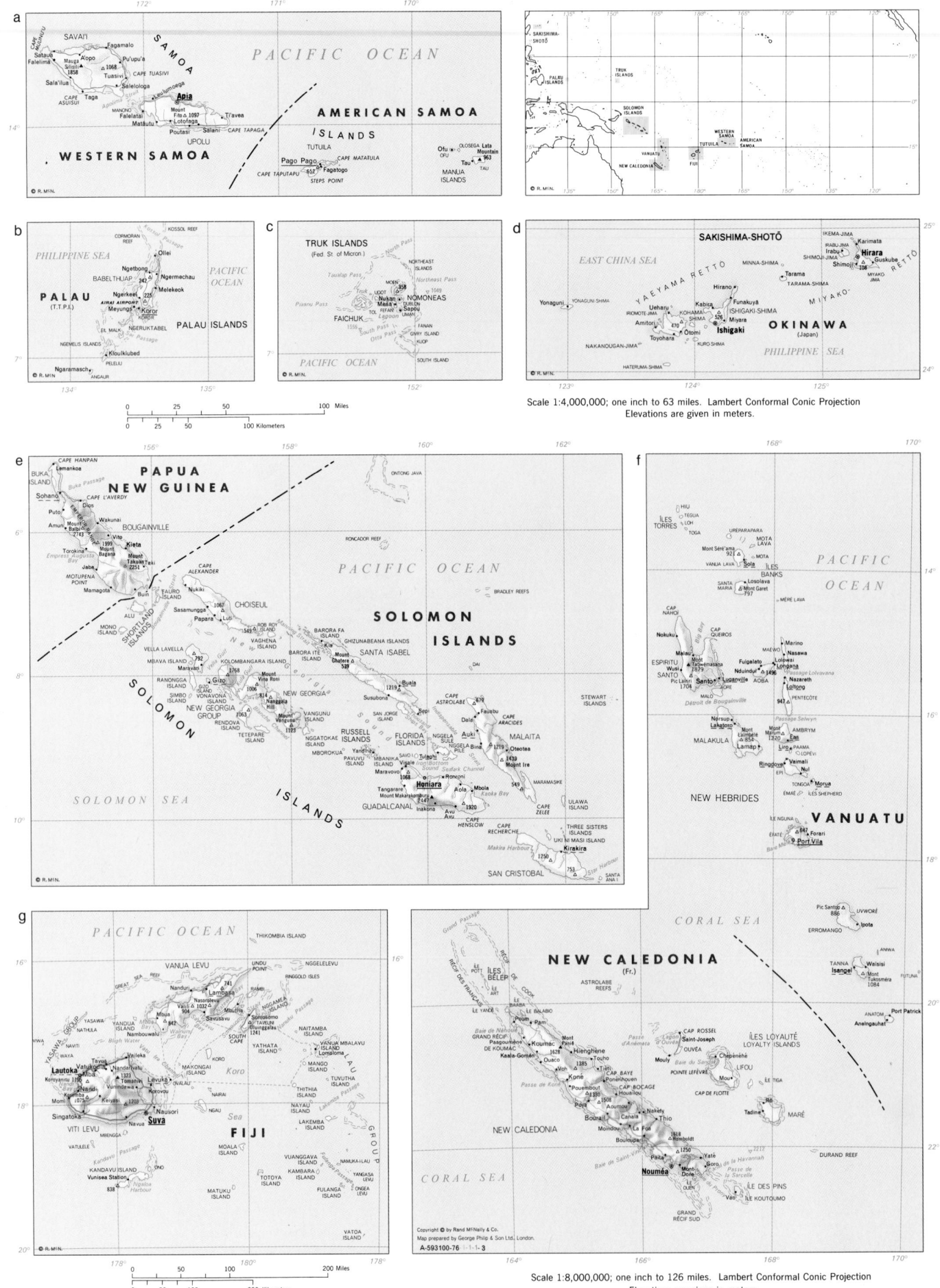

Scale 1:4,000,000; one inch to 63 miles. Lambert Conformal Conic Projection
Elevations are given in meters.

Scale 1:8,000,000; one inch to 126 miles. Lambert Conformal Conic Projection
Elevations are given in meters.

Copyright © by Rand McNally & Co.
Map prepared by George Philip & Son Ltd., London.
A-593100-76

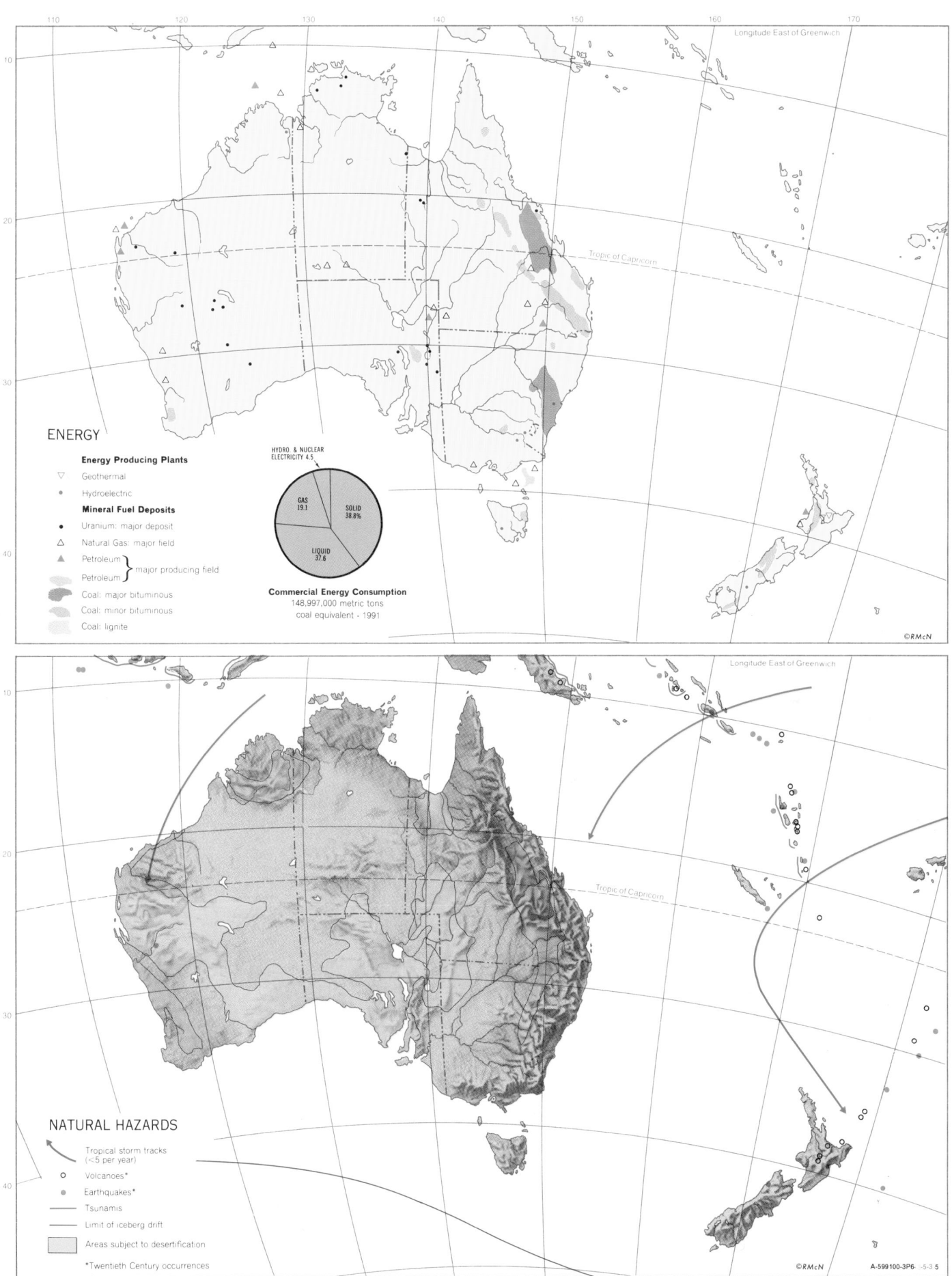

ENERGY

Energy Producing Plants

▽ Geothermal

• Hydroelectric

Mineral Fuel Deposits

• Uranium: major deposit

△ Natural Gas: major field

▲ Petroleum

Petroleum } major producing field

Coal: major bituminous

Coal: minor bituminous

Coal: lignite

HYDRO. & NUCLEAR
ELECTRICITY 4.5

GAS
19.1

SOLID
38.8%

LIQUID
37.6

Commercial Energy Consumption
148,997,000 metric tons
coal equivalent · 1991

©RMcN

NATURAL HAZARDS

↰ Tropical storm tracks
    (<5 per year)

○ Volcanoes*

• Earthquakes*

—— Tsunamis

—— Limit of iceberg drift

▨ Areas subject to desertification

*Twentieth Century occurrences

©RMcN   A-599100-3P6· -5-3 5

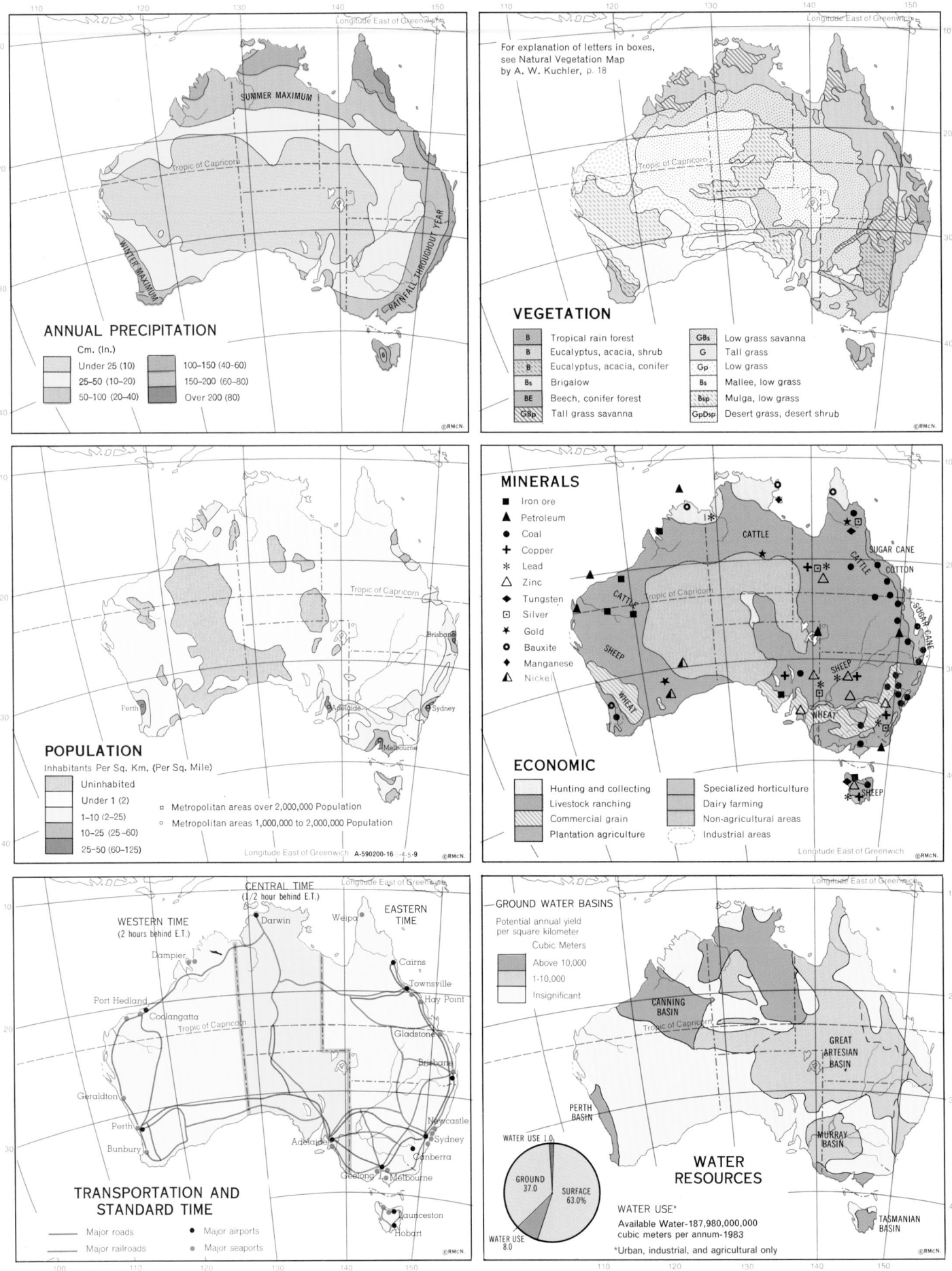

ANNUAL PRECIPITATION

SUMMER MAXIMUM

WINTER MAXIMUM

RAINFALL THROUGHOUT YEAR

Tropic of Capricorn

Cm. (In.)

- Under 25 (10)
- 25–50 (10–20)
- 50–100 (20–40)
- 100–150 (40–60)
- 150–200 (60–80)
- Over 200 (80)

VEGETATION

For explanation of letters in boxes,
see Natural Vegetation Map
by A. W. Kuchler, p. 18

B	Tropical rain forest	GBs	Low grass savanna
B	Eucalyptus, acacia, shrub	G	Tall grass
B	Eucalyptus, acacia, conifer	Gp	Low grass
Bs	Brigalow	Bs	Mallee, low grass
BE	Beech, conifer forest	Bsp	Mulga, low grass
GBp	Tall grass savanna	GpDsp	Desert grass, desert shrub

POPULATION

Brisbane
Perth
Adelaide
Sydney
Melbourne

Inhabitants Per Sq. Km. (Per Sq. Mile)

- Uninhabited
- Under 1 (2)
- 1–10 (2–25)
- 10–25 (25–60)
- 25–50 (60–125)

□ Metropolitan areas over 2,000,000 Population
○ Metropolitan areas 1,000,000 to 2,000,000 Population

A-590200-16

MINERALS

- ■ Iron ore
- ▲ Petroleum
- ● Coal
- + Copper
- ✱ Lead
- △ Zinc
- ◆ Tungsten
- ▣ Silver
- ✶ Gold
- ◎ Bauxite
- ◆ Manganese
- ▲ Nickel

CATTLE
SUGAR CANE
COTTON
CATTLE
CATTLE
SHEEP
SHEEP
WHEAT
WHEAT
SHEEP

Tropic of Capricorn

ECONOMIC

- Hunting and collecting
- Livestock ranching
- Commercial grain
- Plantation agriculture
- Specialized horticulture
- Dairy farming
- Non-agricultural areas
- Industrial areas

TRANSPORTATION AND STANDARD TIME

CENTRAL TIME
(1/2 hour behind E.T.)

WESTERN TIME
(2 hours behind E.T.)

EASTERN TIME

Darwin
Weipa
Dampier
Cairns
Townsville
Hay Point
Port Hedland
Coolangatta
Tropic of Capricorn
Gladstone
Brisbane
Geraldton
Newcastle
Perth
Sydney
Bunbury
Adelaide
Canberra
Geelong
Melbourne
Launceston
Hobart

- —— Major roads
- —— Major railroads
- ● Major airports
- ● Major seaports

WATER RESOURCES

GROUND WATER BASINS

Potential annual yield
per square kilometer

Cubic Meters

- Above 10,000
- 1–10,000
- Insignificant

CANNING BASIN
GREAT ARTESIAN BASIN
PERTH BASIN
MURRAY BASIN
TASMANIAN BASIN

Tropic of Capricorn

WATER USE 1.0
GROUND 37.0
SURFACE 63.0%
WATER USE 8.0

WATER USE*

Available Water–187,980,000,000
cubic meters per annum–1983

*Urban, industrial, and agricultural only

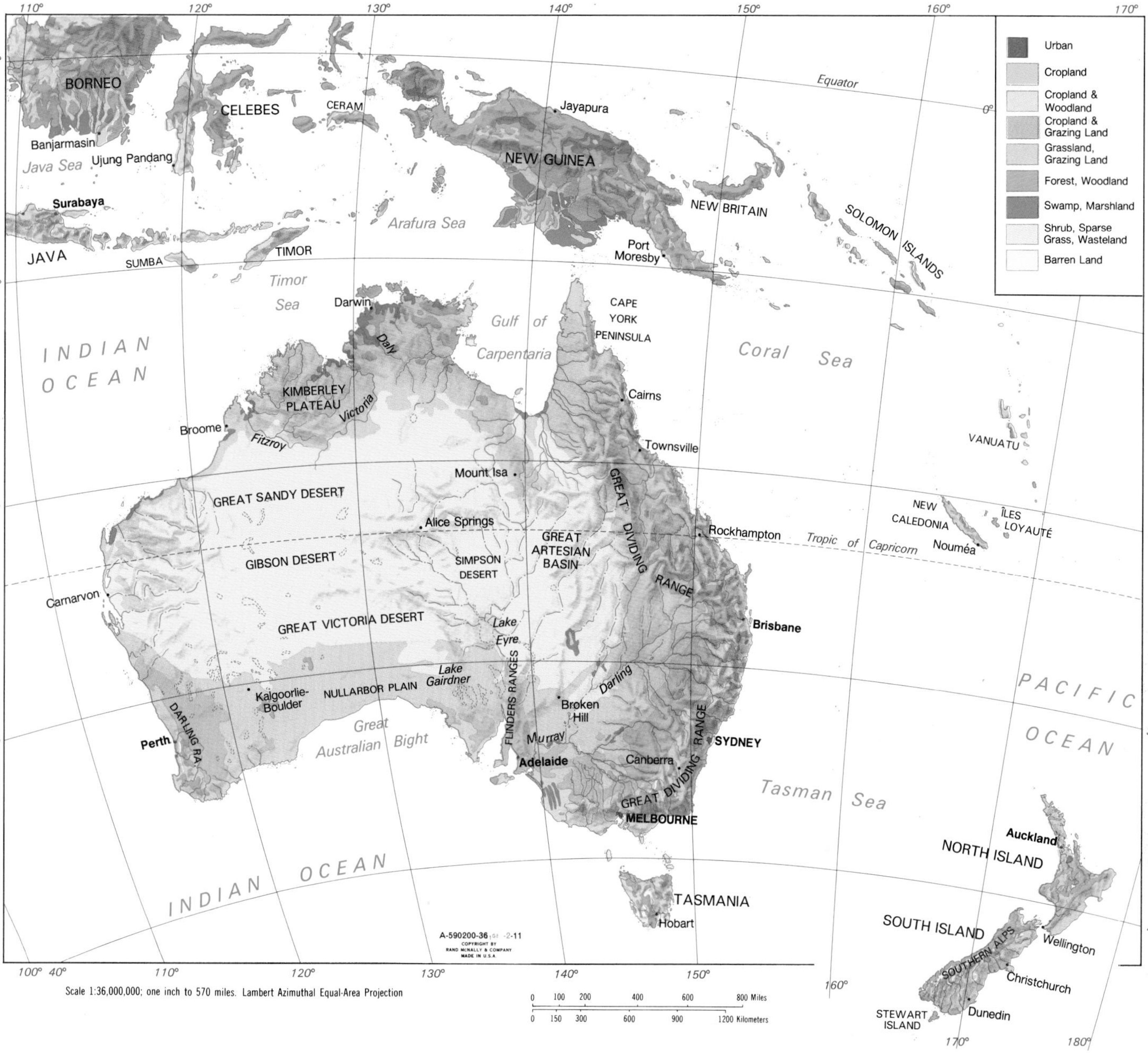

Legend:
- Urban
- Cropland
- Cropland & Woodland
- Cropland & Grazing Land
- Grassland, Grazing Land
- Forest, Woodland
- Swamp, Marshland
- Shrub, Sparse Grass, Wasteland
- Barren Land

BORNEO
Banjarmasin
Java Sea
Ujung Pandang
Surabaya
JAVA
SUMBA
CELEBES
CERAM
TIMOR
Timor Sea
INDIAN OCEAN

New Guinea
Jayapura
NEW BRITAIN
Port Moresby
SOLOMON ISLANDS
Arafura Sea
Equator
Coral Sea

Darwin
Daly
CAPE YORK PENINSULA
Gulf of Carpentaria
KIMBERLEY PLATEAU
Victoria
Broome
Fitzroy
Cairns
Townsville
GREAT SANDY DESERT
Mount Isa
Alice Springs
GREAT DIVIDING RANGE
GIBSON DESERT
SIMPSON DESERT
GREAT ARTESIAN BASIN
Rockhampton
Tropic of Capricorn
Carnarvon
GREAT VICTORIA DESERT
Lake Eyre
Brisbane
Lake Gairdner
Darling
Kaigoorlie-Boulder
NULLARBOR PLAIN
Broken Hill
SYDNEY
Perth
DARLING RA.
Great Australian Bight
FLINDERS RANGES
Murray
Canberra
GREAT DIVIDING RANGE
Adelaide
MELBOURNE

VANUATU
NEW CALEDONIA
Nouméa
ÎLES LOYAUTÉ
PACIFIC OCEAN
Tasman Sea

TASMANIA
Hobart

Auckland
NORTH ISLAND
SOUTH ISLAND
SOUTHERN ALPS
Wellington
Christchurch
STEWART ISLAND
Dunedin

A-590200-36 -2-11
COPYRIGHT BY
RAND McNALLY & COMPANY
MADE IN U.S.A.

Scale 1:36,000,000; one inch to 570 miles. Lambert Azimuthal Equal-Area Projection

0 100 200 400 600 800 Miles
0 150 300 600 900 1200 Kilometers

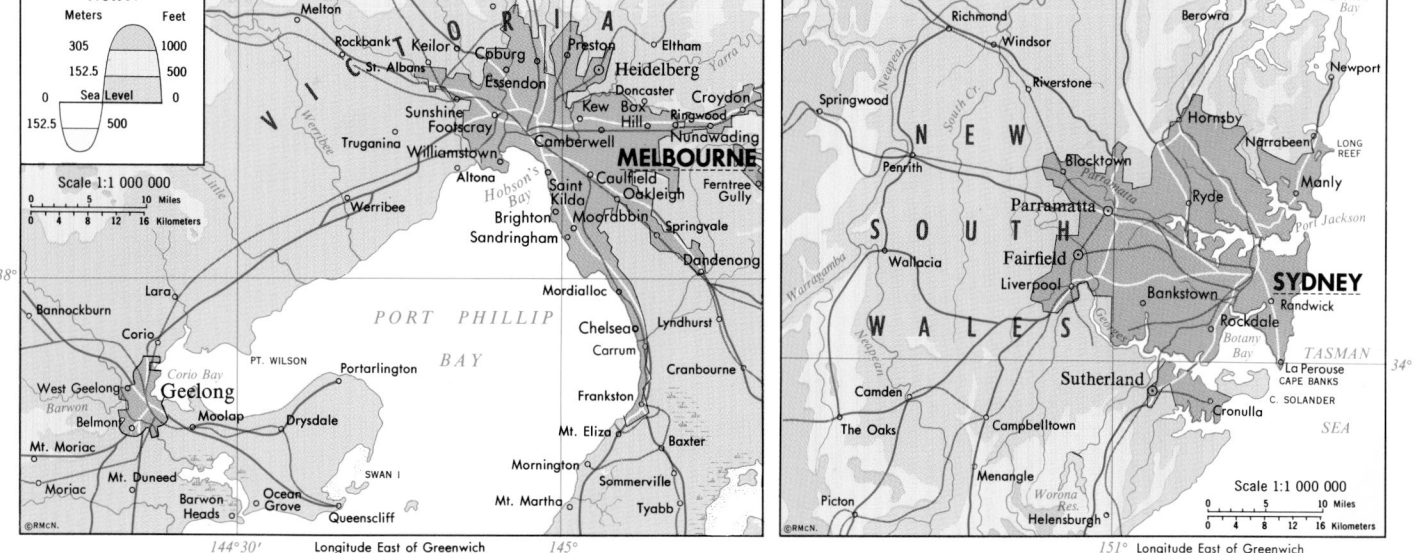

a — Melbourne inset map, Scale 1:1 000 000
b — Sydney inset map, Scale 1:1 000 000

For larger scale coverage of Melbourne and Sydney see page 243.

202

Continued on pages 196-197

INDONESIA

Pasuruan
J A V A △10,932
G. Mohameru △ Rinjani
12,060 △ 1225
Singaraja Bali Lombok Selat
BALI Lombok Sumbawa Rapua
LOMBOK Besar
SUMBAWA
Sumba Waingapu
SAWU
SUMBA ROTI
Kupang

SAVU SEA
FLORES
LOMBLEN PANTAR
TIMOR
Dili
ALOR

SELARU
TANJUNG VALS

ARAFURA SEA

S U N D A

I S L A N D S

SUNDA TRENCH

TIMOR SEA

INDIAN

I N D I A N

O C E A N

C. VAN DIEMEN
CROKER
COBURG PEN.
BATHURST
MELVILLE
Van Diemen
Gulf
Clarence Str.
Darwin
Anson Bay

WESSEL IS.
CAPE ARNHEM

Blue Mud Bay

GROOTE
EYLANDT

GULF O

CAPE
LONDONDERRY
Joseph
Bonaparte Gulf
Dundas Str.

ARNHEM LAND
Pine Creek
Katherine

Limmen
Bight
Roper

CARPENTAR

SIR EDWARD PELLEW
GROUP
WELLESLE

Collier Bay
Sunday ARCH.
BUCCANEER ARCH.
CAPE LEVEQUE
King Sd.
DAMPIER LAND
Broome
BROOME LAND
Derby
Roebuck Bay
LaGrange
Fitzroy
LARREY POINT
EIGHTY MILE BEACH

Wyndham
Mt. Hann
2800
KING LEOPOLD RANGES
GEIKIE RANGE
Fitzroy
Crossing
Halls Creek
Stuart Cr.

NORTHERN

Victoria River
Downs
Daly Waters

Newcastle Waters

Woods B.
Victoria

Barkly TABLELAND

Burketown
Leichha

Tanami

TERRITORY

Alexandria
Dobb
Camooweal
Mount Isa
Mc

RIPON
Dampier Port Hedland
DeGrey
ARCH.
MONTE BELLO IS.
BARROW
NORTH WEST CAPE
Roebourne
Millstream
Onslow
HAMERSLEY RANGE
Mt. Bruce
4052
POINT CLOATES

Marble Bar
Nullagine
GREAT SANDY DESERT
Mackay
Macdonald

Tennant Creek
Barrow Creek

Mt. Ziel
4955
MACDONNELL RANGES
Arltunga
Alice Springs
JAMES RANGE
SIMPSON

Dajar
Q

Tropic of Capricorn
CAPE FARQUHAR
Geographe Chan.
BERNIER I.
DORRE I.
Shark Bay
DIRK HARTOG
STEEP POINT

Carnarvon
Gascoyne
Jiggalong
Disappointment
WESTERN
GIBSON DESERT
Peak Hill
Nabberu
Carnegie
Gillen
Wells
Yeo

Ayers Rock △
2844
MUSGRAVE RANGES
Mt. Woodroffe
4724
EVERARD RANGES
Amadeus
Finke
Charlotte
Waters
The Alberga

DESERT

Birdsville

Oodnadatta

Eyre
39

Gascoyne
Meekatharra
Nannine
Cue
Mount
Magnet
Sandstone
Austin
Wiluna
AUSTRALIA
Carey
Ballard

Laverton

GREAT VICTORIA DESERT
SOUTH AUSTRALIA

STUART RANGE
William Creek
Martee
Farina

Ajana
Northampton
HOUTMAN ROCKS
Geraldton
Dongara
Mingenew
Moore
Pithara
Miling
Moora
Lake Brown
Barlee
Southern Cross
Cowan
Menzies
Coolgardie
Kalgoorlie-Boulder
Lefroy
Goddards Soak
Norseman
Dundas
Salmon Gums
Rawlinna
Eucla
Hughes
Ooldea Station
NULLARBOR PLAIN
Penong
Point Fowler
Eyre
Ceduna

Waomera
Pimbo
Everard
FLI
Port Aug

DARLING RANGE
SWANLAND
Perth
Fremantle
Northam
York
Narrogin
Collie
Bunbury
Busselton
CAPE NATURALISTE
CAPE LEEUWIN
Nornalup
Albany
PT. D'ENTRECASTEAUX
WEST CAPE HOWE
King George Sd.
Geographe Bay
Ravensthorpe
Hopetoun
ARCHIPELAGO
OF THE RECHERCHE
Esperance

GREAT AUSTRALIAN BIGHT

Port Lincoln

Whyalla
Port Pirie

EYRE
PENINSULA

Moonta
Wallaroo
Port W
Pe
Glads

Port
GA
A

KANGAROO
KANGAROO
Ki
CAPE J
M

I N D I A N   O C E A N

Longitude 115°   East of Greenwich

Scale 1:16 000 000; one inch to 250 miles. Lambert's Azimuthal, Equal Area Pro
Elevations and depressions are given in feet

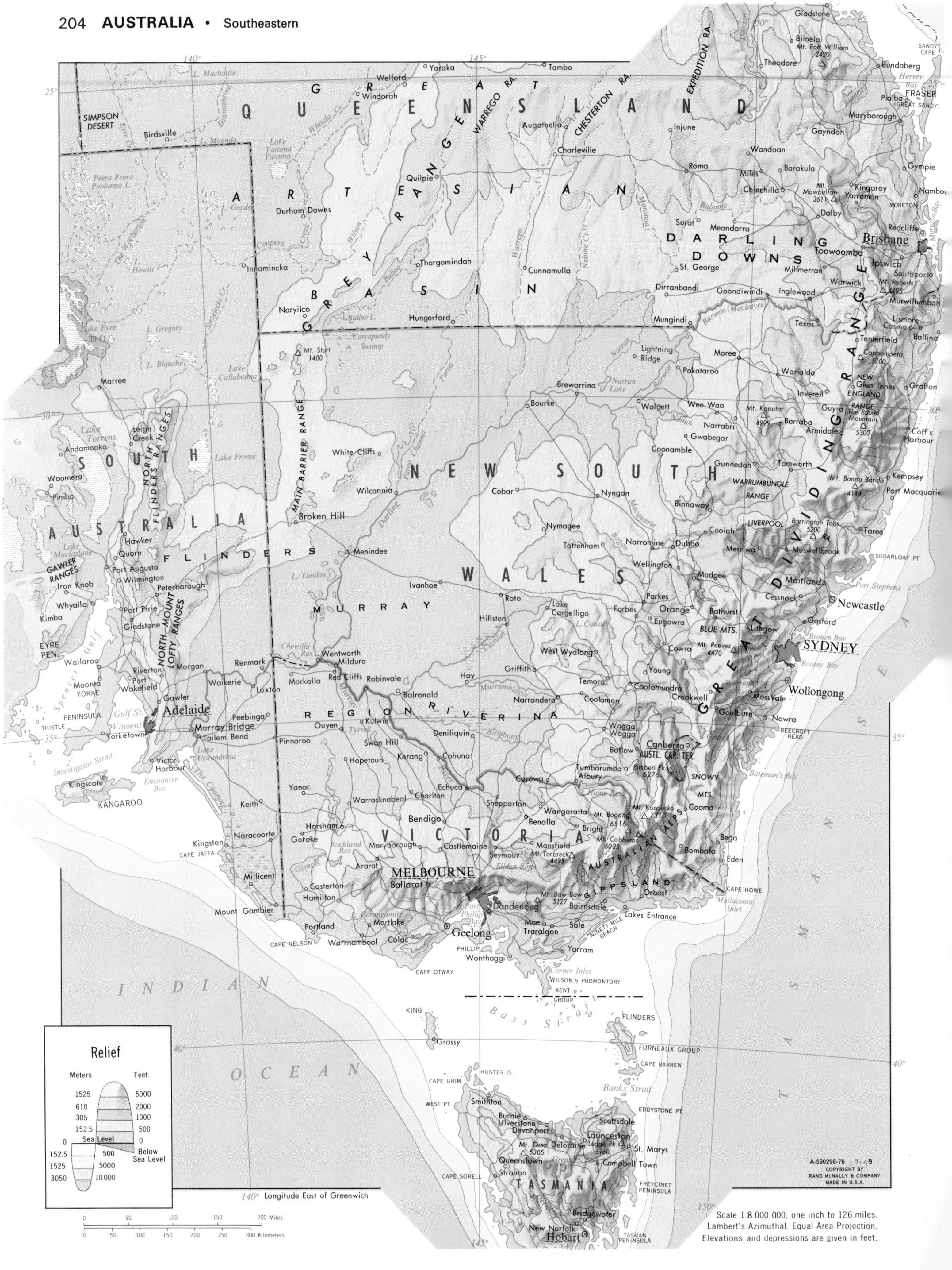

QUEENSLAND

SIMPSON DESERT

Birdsville

L. Machattie

L. Moonda

Lake Yamma Yamma

Durham Downs

Welford

Windorah

Yataka

Tambo

GREAT

WARREGO RA.

CHESTERTON RA.

EXPEDITION RA.

Gladstone

Biloela

Mt. Fort William 2420

Theodore

Bundaberg

Hervey Bay

FRASER

SANDY CAPE

Augathella

Charleville

Injune

Roma

Miles

Wandoan

Barakula

Chinchilla

Maryborough

Gayndah

Pialba

Gympie

Nambour

MORETO

Quilpie

Cunnamulla

Surat

Meandarra

Dalby

Kingaroy

Yarraman

Mt. Mowbullan 3615

ARTESIAN

GREY

RANGES

BASIN

Thargomindah

St. George

Millmerran

Toowoomba

DARLING

DOWNS

Redcliffe

Brisbane

Ipswich

Southport

Naryilco

Bulloo L.

Hungerford

Dirranbandi

Goondiwindi

Inglewood

Warwick

Mt. Roberts 4495

Murwillumbah

Lismore

Casino

Ballina

Texas

Tenterfield

Cappompeta 5100

Mungindi

Barwon (Macintyre)

NEW ENGLAND

Caryapundy Swamp

Mt. Sturt 1400

Moree

Lightning Ridge

Pokataroo

Warialda

Inverell

Guyra

RANGE

The Round Mountain 5300

Grafton

Coff's Harbour

Marree

L. Gregory

L. Blanche

Lake Callabonna

Strzelecki Cr.

Innamincka

Coopers

Cr.

Brewarrina

Narran Lake

Bourke

Walgett

Wee Waa

Narrabri

Mt. Kaputar 4999

Barraba

Armidale

Mt. Banda Banda 4144

Kempsey

Port Macquarie

SOUTH

AUSTRALIA

Lake Torrens

Leigh Creek

Andamooka

Woomera

Pimba

Hawker

Quorn

Wilmington

NORTH FLINDERS RANGES

Lake Frome

White Cliffs

MAIN BARRIER RANGE

Wilcannia

Cobar

Nymagee

Tottenham

Nyngan

Macquarie

Coonamble

Narromine

Dubbo

Binnaway

Gunnedah

Tamworth

WARRUMBUNGLE RANGE

Mt. Banda Banda

Coolah

LIVERPOOL

Barrington Tops 5200

Taree

NEW SOUTH WALES

GAWLER RANGES

Iron Knob

Whyalla

Kimba

Port Augusta

Port Pirie

Gladstone

FLINDERS

RANGES

NORTH MOUNT LOFTY RANGES

Broken Hill

Menindee

Darling

L. Tandou

MURRAY

Ivanhoe

Roto

Hillston

Lake Cargelligo

Forbes

West Wyalong

Griffith

Parkes

Orange

Bathurst

Eugowra

Cowra

Young

Mudgee

Wellington

Merriwa

Muswellbrook

Maitland

Cessnock

Newcastle

Port Stephens

SUGARLOAF PT.

BLUE MTS.

Lithgow

Mt. Reeves 4470

Broken Bay

SYDNEY

Botany Bay

EYRE PEN.

Wallaroo

Moonta

YORKE

Kadina

Port Wakefield

Riverton

Morgan

Waikerie

Loxton

Renmark

Mildura

Wentworth

Chowilla Res.

Morkalla

Red Cliffs

Robinvale

Balranald

Hay

Murrumbidgee

Narrandera

Coolamon

Temora

Cootamundra

Crookwell

Goulburn

Moss Vale

Nowra

Wollongong

BEECROFT HEAD

Adelaide

Gawler

Peebinga

REGION

Ouyen

Kulwin

Swan Hill

Deniliquin

Lachlan

RIVERINA

Wagga Wagga

Albury

Batlow

Canberra

AUSTL. CAP. TER.

Bimberi Pk. 6276

SNOWY

Cooma

Bateman's Bay

Murray Bridge

Tailem Bend

Pinnaroo

Lameroo

Tyrrell

Karang

Cohuna

Corowa

Tumbarumba

Mt. Kosciusko 7310

Bombala

Bega

Eden

Victor Harbour

Kingscote

KANGAROO

Yanac

Warracknabeal

Charlton

Echuca

Shepparton

Benalla

Wangaratta

Bright

Mt. Bogong 6516

Mt. Cobberas 6025

AUSTRALIAN ALPS

Orbost

GIPPSLAND

CAPE HOWE

Keith

Naracoorte

Horsham

Gotoke

VICTORIA

Bendigo

Castlemaine

Maryborough

Seymour

Eildon Res.

Mt. Torbreck 4495

Mansfield

Kingston

CAPE JAFFA

Millicent

Ararat

Casterton

Hamilton

Glenelg

Ballarat

MELBOURNE

Dandenong

Mt. Baw Baw 5127

Bairnsdale

Sale

Lakes Entrance

NINETY MILE BEACH

Mallacoota Inlet

Mount Gambier

Portland

Warrnambool

Colac

Corangamite

Mortlake

Geelong

Port Phillip Bay

Moe

Traralgon

Yarram

Wonthaggi

PHILLIP

CAPE OTWAY

CAPE NELSON

Corner Inlet

WILSON'S PROMONTORY

KENT GROUP

INDIAN OCEAN

KING

Grassy

Bass Strait

FLINDERS

FURNEAUX GROUP

CAPE BARREN

HUNTER IS.

CAPE GRIM

WEST PT.

Smithton

Burnie

Ulverstone

Devonport

Mt. Ossa 5305

Deloraine

Launceston

Legas Pk. 5160

St. Marys

Scottsdale

Banks Strait

EDDYSTONE PT.

TASMANIA

Queenstown

Strahan

Campbell Town

CAPE SOREL

FREYCINET PENINSULA

New Norfolk

Bridgewater

Hobart

TASMAN PENINSULA

A-590298-76 5-6-9
COPYRIGHT BY
RAND McNALLY & COMPANY
MADE IN U.S.A.

Scale 1:8 000 000; one inch to 126 miles.
Lambert's Azimuthal, Equal Area Projection.
Elevations and depressions are given in feet.

Relief

Meters	Feet
1525	5000
610	2000
305	1000
152.5	500
0 Sea Level	Sea Level
152.5	500
1525	5000
3050	10 000

Below Sea Level

140° Longitude East of Greenwich

0 50 100 150 200 Miles

0 50 100 150 200 250 300 Kilometers

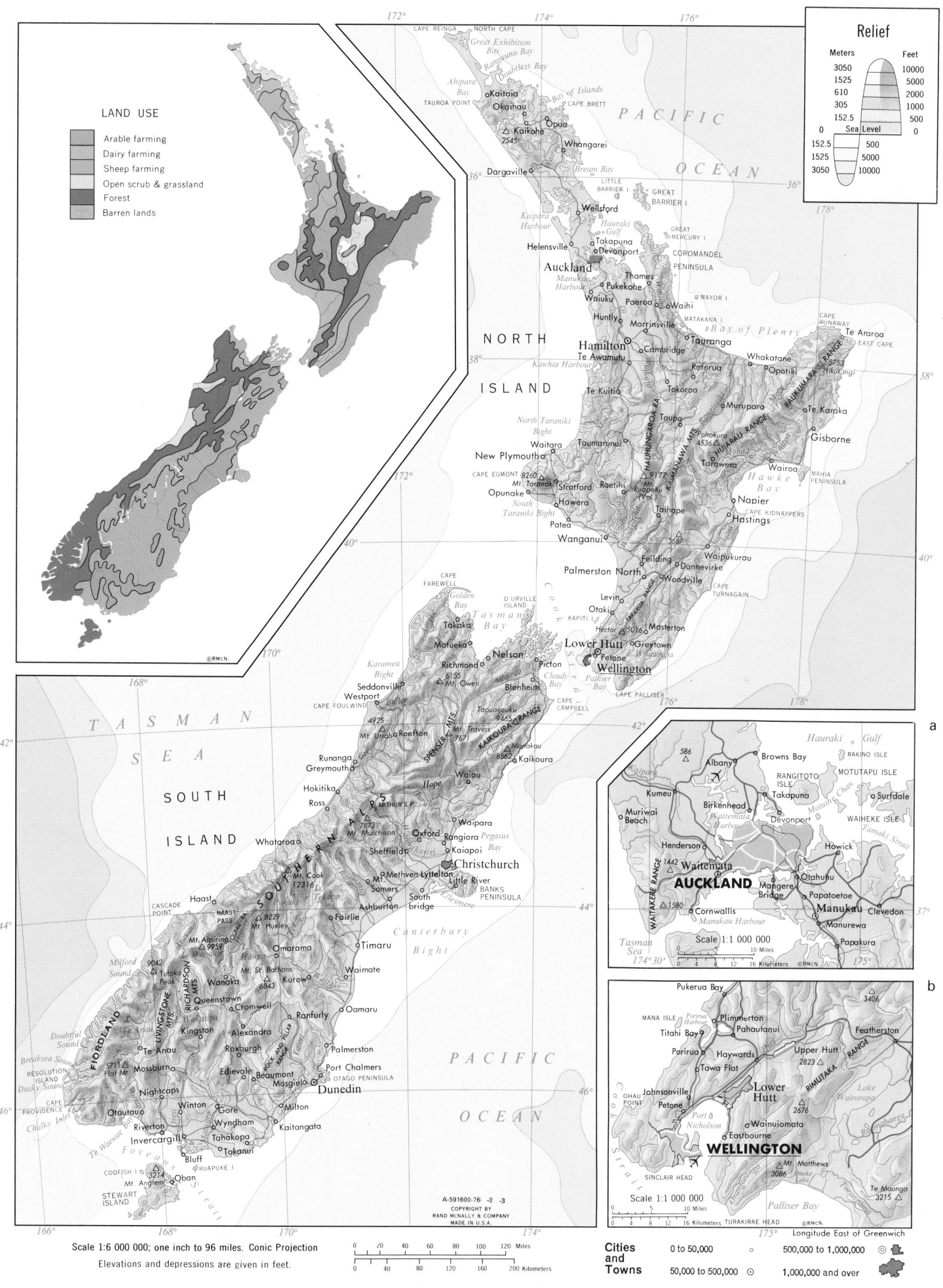

Relief

Meters		Feet
3050		10000
1525		5000
610		2000
305		1000
152.5		500
0	Sea Level	0
152.5		500
1525		5000
3050		10000

LAND USE

- Arable farming
- Dairy farming
- Sheep farming
- Open scrub & grassland
- Forest
- Barren lands

PACIFIC OCEAN

NORTH ISLAND

TASMAN SEA

SOUTH ISLAND

SOUTHERN ALPS

PACIFIC OCEAN

a
Scale 1:1 000 000

b
Scale 1:1 000 000

Longitude East of Greenwich

Scale 1:6 000 000; one inch to 96 miles. Conic Projection
Elevations and depressions are given in feet.

A-591600-76 -2 -3
COPYRIGHT BY
RAND McNALLY & COMPANY
MADE IN U.S.A.

Cities and Towns

0 to 50,000 o	500,000 to 1,000,000 ⊚
50,000 to 500,000 ⊙	1,000,000 and over

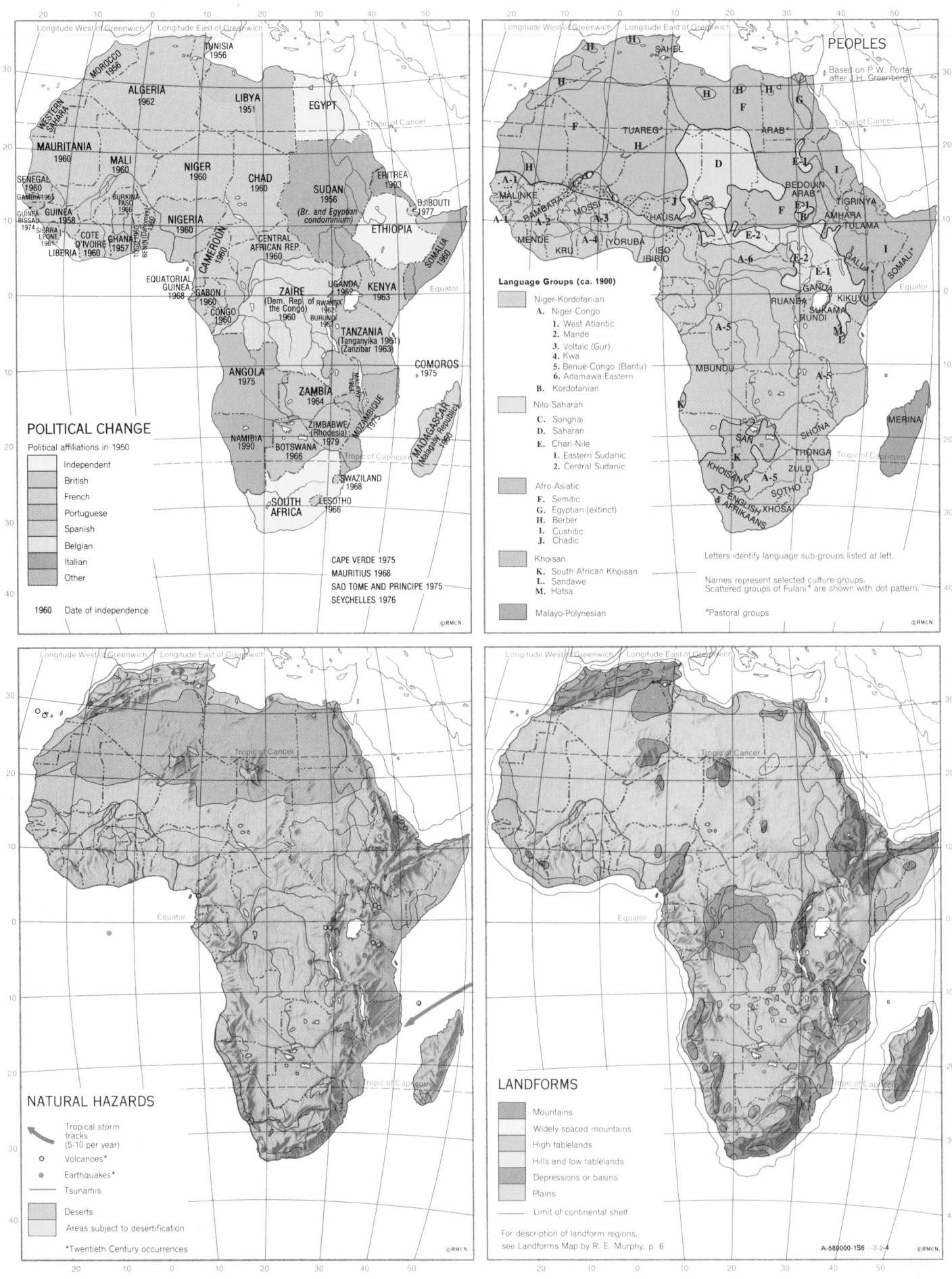

POLITICAL CHANGE

Political affiliations in 1950

- Independent
- British
- French
- Portuguese
- Spanish
- Belgian
- Italian
- Other

1960   Date of independence

MOROCCO 1956
TUNISIA 1956
ALGERIA 1962
LIBYA 1951
EGYPT
WESTERN SAHARA
MAURITANIA 1960
MALI 1960
NIGER 1960
CHAD 1960
SUDAN 1956 (Br. and Egyptian condominium)
ERITREA 1993
DJIBOUTI 1977
SENEGAL 1960
GAMBIA 1965
GUINEA-BISSAU 1974
GUINEA 1958
SIERRA LEONE 1961
LIBERIA
COTE D'IVOIRE 1960
BURKINA FASO 1960
GHANA 1957
TOGO 1960
BENIN (Dahomey) 1960
NIGERIA 1960
CAMEROON 1960
CENTRAL AFRICAN REP. 1960
ETHIOPIA
SOMALIA 1960
EQUATORIAL GUINEA 1968
GABON 1960
CONGO 1960
ZAIRE (Dem. Rep. of the Congo) 1960
RWANDA 1962
BURUNDI 1962
UGANDA 1962
KENYA 1963
TANZANIA (Tanganyika 1961) (Zanzibar 1963)
ANGOLA 1975
ZAMBIA 1964
MALAWI
MOZAMBIQUE 1975
ZIMBABWE (Rhodesia) 1979
MADAGASCAR (Malagasy Republic) 1960
NAMIBIA 1990
BOTSWANA 1966
SWAZILAND 1968
SOUTH AFRICA
LESOTHO 1966
COMOROS 1975

CAPE VERDE 1975
MAURITIUS 1968
SAO TOME AND PRINCIPE 1975
SEYCHELLES 1976

©RMcN.

PEOPLES

Based on P. W. Porter after J. H. Greenberg

Language Groups (ca. 1900)

Niger-Kordofanian
- A. Niger-Congo
  1. West Atlantic
  2. Mande
  3. Voltaic (Gur)
  4. Kwa
  5. Benue-Congo (Bantu)
  6. Adamawa-Eastern
- B. Kordofanian

Nilo-Saharan
- C. Songhai
- D. Saharan
- E. Chari-Nile
  1. Eastern Sudanic
  2. Central Sudanic

Afro-Asiatic
- F. Semitic
- G. Egyptian (extinct)
- H. Berber
- I. Cushitic
- J. Chadic

Khoisan
- K. South African Khoisan
- L. Sandawe
- M. Hatsa

Malayo-Polynesian

Letters identify language sub-groups listed at left.

Names represent selected culture groups.
Scattered groups of Fulani* are shown with dot pattern.

*Pastoral groups

©RMcN.

NATURAL HAZARDS

- → Tropical storm tracks (5-10 per year)
- ○ Volcanoes*
- • Earthquakes*
- — Tsunamis
- Deserts
- Areas subject to desertification

*Twentieth Century occurrences

©RMcN.

LANDFORMS

- Mountains
- Widely spaced mountains
- High tablelands
- Hills and low tablelands
- Depressions or basins
- Plains
- — Limit of continental shelf

For description of landform regions, see Landforms Map by R. E. Murphy, p. 6

A-580000-1S6 -3-2-4
©RMcN.

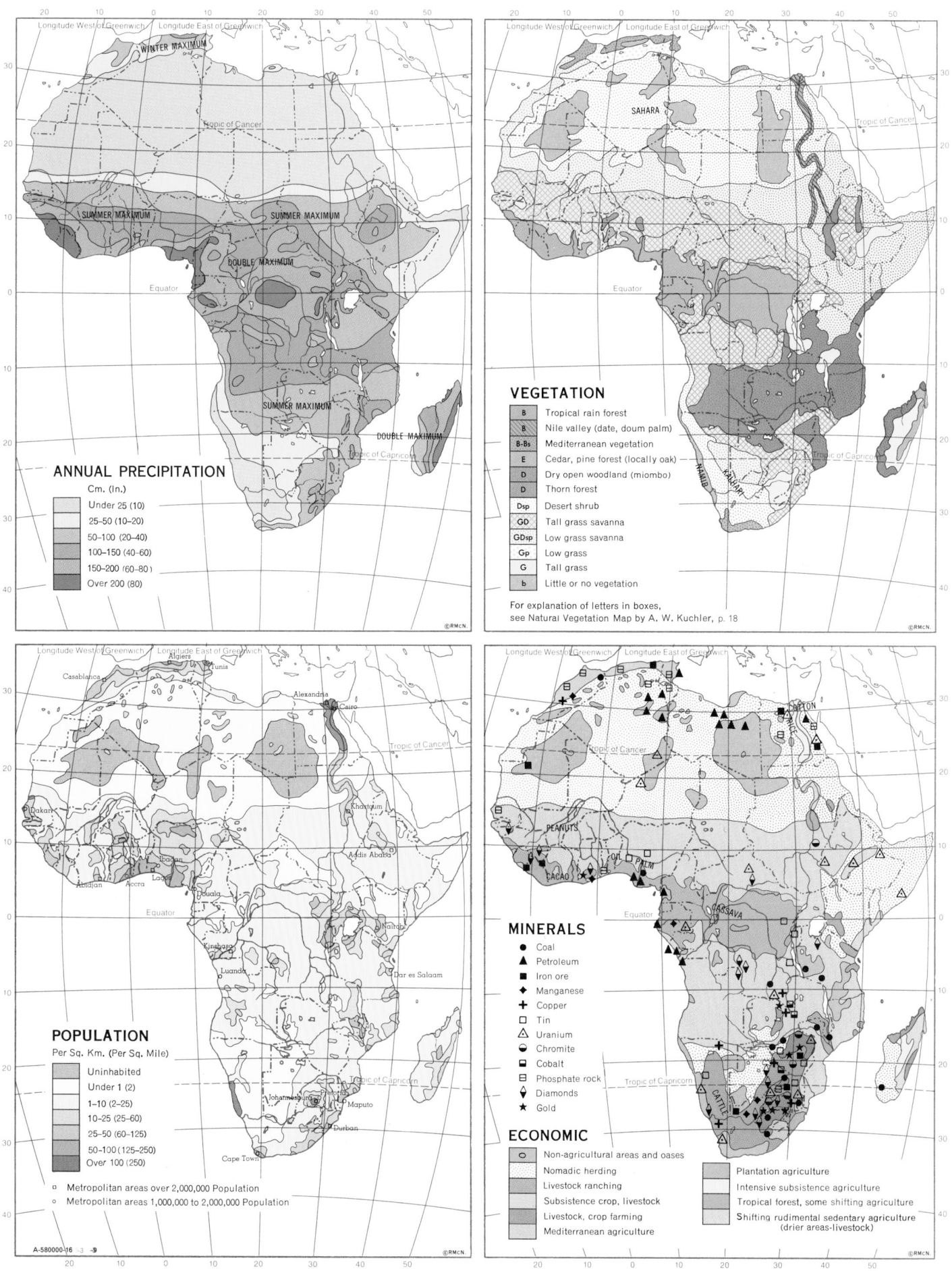

ANNUAL PRECIPITATION

Cm. (In.)

- Under 25 (10)
- 25–50 (10–20)
- 50–100 (20–40)
- 100–150 (40–60)
- 150–200 (60–80)
- Over 200 (80)

VEGETATION

B	Tropical rain forest
B	Nile valley (date, doum palm)
B–Bs	Mediterranean vegetation
E	Cedar, pine forest (locally oak)
D	Dry open woodland (miombo)
D	Thorn forest
Dsp	Desert shrub
GD	Tall grass savanna
GDsp	Low grass savanna
Gp	Low grass
G	Tall grass
b	Little or no vegetation

For explanation of letters in boxes,
see Natural Vegetation Map by A. W. Kuchler, p. 18

POPULATION

Per Sq. Km. (Per Sq. Mile)

- Uninhabited
- Under 1 (2)
- 1–10 (2–25)
- 10–25 (25–60)
- 25–50 (60–125)
- 50–100 (125–250)
- Over 100 (250)

□ Metropolitan areas over 2,000,000 Population
○ Metropolitan areas 1,000,000 to 2,000,000 Population

A-580000-16 -3 -9

MINERALS

- ● Coal
- ▲ Petroleum
- ■ Iron ore
- ◆ Manganese
- ✛ Copper
- □ Tin
- △ Uranium
- ◓ Chromite
- ⬓ Cobalt
- ⊟ Phosphate rock
- ⬦ Diamonds
- ★ Gold

ECONOMIC

- ⬭ Non-agricultural areas and oases
- Nomadic herding
- Livestock ranching
- Subsistence crop, livestock
- Livestock, crop farming
- Mediterranean agriculture
- Plantation agriculture
- Intensive subsistence agriculture
- Tropical forest, some shifting agriculture
- Shifting rudimental sedentary agriculture (drier areas–livestock)

ATLANTIC OCEAN

MADRID
CORSICA
ROME
SARDINIA
ISTANBUL
BAKU
Black Sea
Caspian Sea

Mediterranean Sea

SICILY
Athens
TEHRĀN

Algiers
Tunis
MALTA
CRETE
CYPRUS
Beirut
Baghdad

Casablanca

Tripoli
Banghāzī
Alexandria
SYRIAN DESERT
Euphrates
Tigris

CANARY ISLANDS
CAIRO
AN NAFŪD

El Aaíun
ATLAS MOUNTAINS
LIBYAN DESERT
ARABIAN DESERT
Riyadh

Tropic of Cancer
GRAND ERG OCCIDENTAL
GRAND ERG ORIENTAL
Lake Nasser
Red Sea
Mecca

S A H A R A
AHAGGAR
TIBESTI
NUBIAN DESERT
Nile

Tamenghest
ADRAR DES ÍFÔGHAS
ENNEDI
Khartoum
Asmera
Aden
Gulf of Aden

Tombouctou
EL DJOUF
S U D A N
Al-Fāshir
White Nile
DANAKIL
Berbera

Dakar
Niger
Lake Chad
Blue Nile
Addis Ababa

Bamako
Kano
N'Djamena
Mountain Nile

Freetown
Niger
Lake Volta
Lagos
Mogadishu

Abidjan
Yaoundé
Bangui
Uele
Nairobi

Gulf of Guinea
Ubangi
Congo (Zaire)
Kisangani
Lake Victoria

Equator
Kasai
Lake Tanganyika
INDIAN OCEAN

Congo (Zaire)
Kinshasa

Luanda
Dar es Salaam

ATLANTIC OCEAN
Lubumbashi
Lake Nyasa
COMORO ISLANDS

Lusaka
Blantyre
Moçambique

Zambezi
Harare
Mozambique Channel
Antananarivo

NAMIB DESERT
KALAHARI DESERT
Limpopo
MADAGASCAR

Tropic of Capricorn
Windhoek

Johannesburg
Orange

Orange
Durban

Cape Town
INDIAN OCEAN

Legend:
- Urban
- Cropland
- Cropland & Woodland
- Cropland & Grazing Land
- Grassland, Grazing Land
- Forest, Woodland
- Swamp, Marshland
- Shrub, Sparse Grass, Wasteland
- Barren Land
- • Oasis

A-580000-36--2 3-9
COPYRIGHT BY
RAND McNALLY & COMPANY
MADE IN U.S.A.

Scale 1:36,000,000; one inch to 570 miles.   Lambert Azimuthal Equal-Area Projection

0 100 200   400   600   800 Miles
0 150 300   600   900   1200 Kilometers

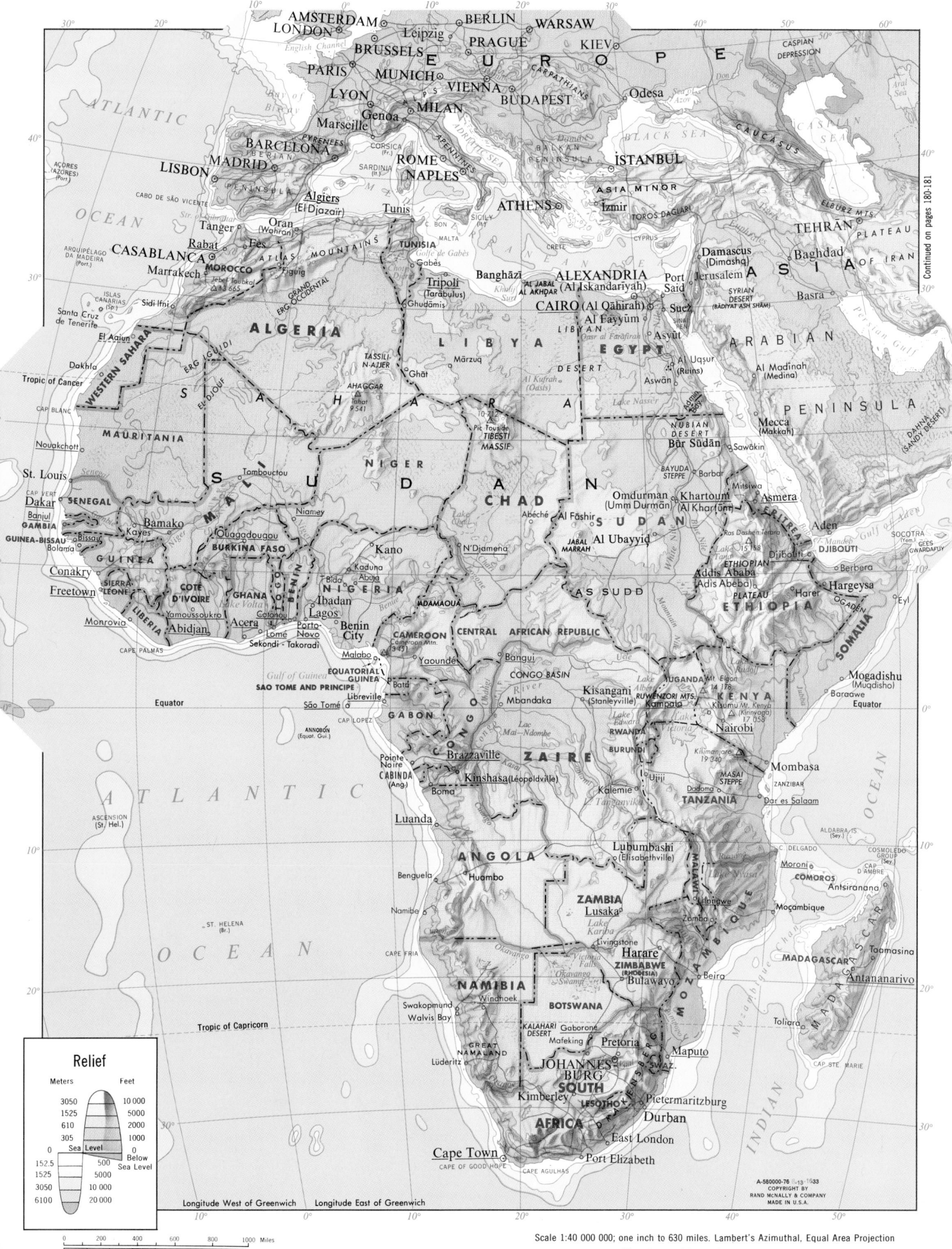

Continued on pages 180-181

Relief

Meters		Feet
3050		10 000
1525		5000
610		2000
305		1000
0	Sea Level	0
		Below
152.5		500 Sea Level
1525		5000
3050		10 000
6100		20 000

Longitude West of Greenwich   Longitude East of Greenwich

0   200   400   600   800   1000 Miles

0   400   800   1200   1600 Kilometers

Scale 1:40 000 000; one inch to 630 miles. Lambert's Azimuthal, Equal Area Projection

Elevations and depressions are given in feet.

A-580000-76   -13-1533
COPYRIGHT BY
RAND McNALLY & COMPANY
MADE IN U.S.A.

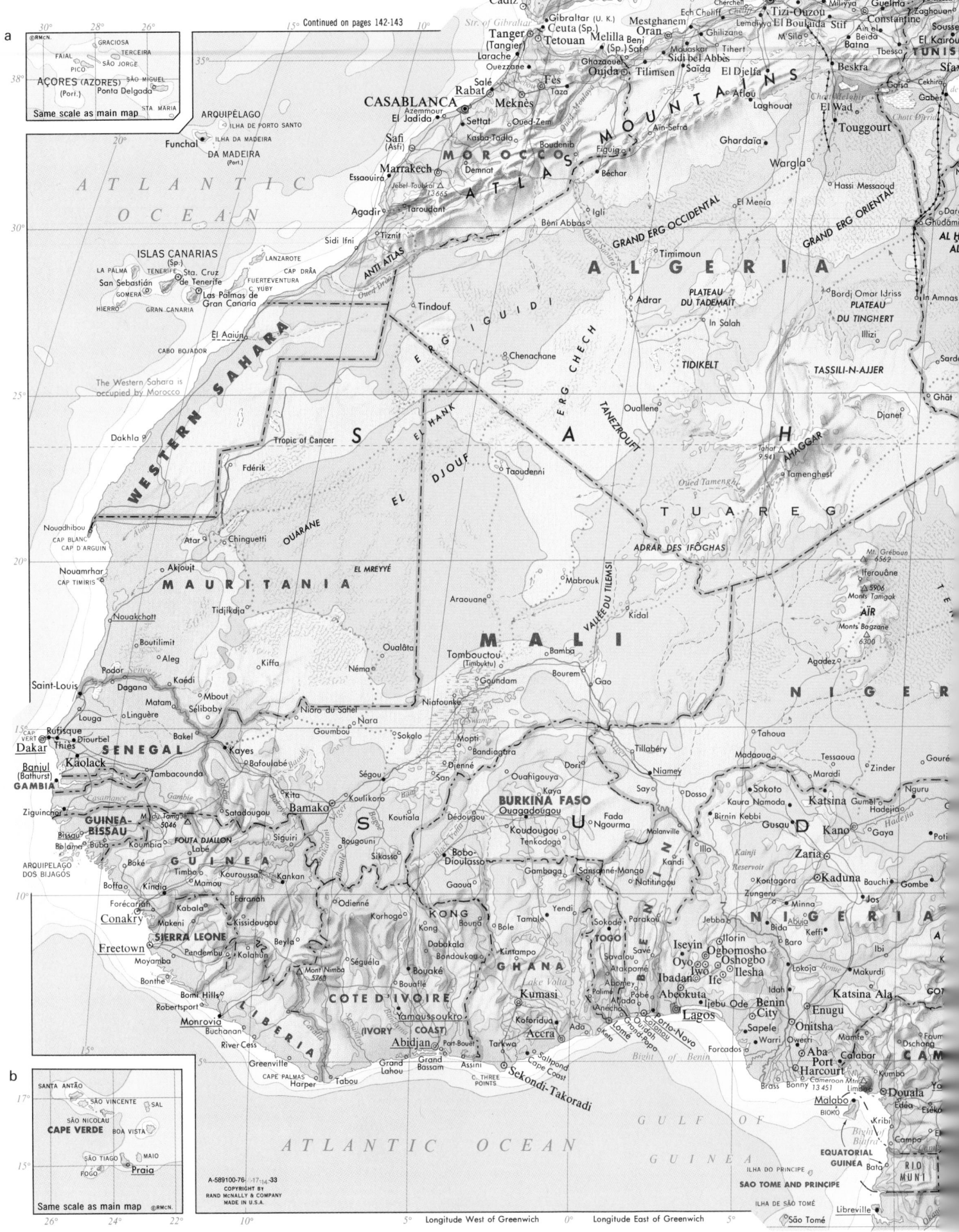

210

a

AÇORES (AZORES) (Port.)

GRACIOSA
TERCEIRA
SÃO JORGE
FAIAL PICO
SÃO MIGUEL
STA. MARIA
Ponta Delgada

Same scale as main map

Continued on pages 142-143

SPAIN

Cádiz

Str. of Gibraltar
Gibraltar (U.K.)
Ceuta (Sp.)
Tanger (Tangier)
Tetouan
Larache
Ouezzane

Algiers (El Djazair)
Delles Bejaïa (Bougie) El Skikda Annaba (Bône) Bizerte
Cherchell Tizi-Ouzou Mila Guelma Tunis
Ech Cheliff Lemdiyya El Boulaïda Stif Beida TUNISIA
Mestghanem Ghilizane M'Sila Batna Constantine
Oran Sidi bel Abbès Saïda Beskra El Kairoua
Tilimsen El Djelfa Laghouat Tbessa Zaghouan
Ain-Sefra Aflou Sfax

CASABLANCA
Rabat Salé Fès Taza
Meknès
Azemmour
El Jadida Settat Oued-Zem
Safi (Asfi) Kasba-Tadla
Marrakech Demnat Boudenib Figuig Ghardaïa Wargla
Essaouira Jebel Toubkal 13 665 Taroudant
Agadir Igli

MOROCCO
ATLAS MOUNTAINS
Béchar Chatt Melrhir
El Wad
Touggourt

Sidi Ifni Tiznit ANTI ATLAS
Ghudamis
AL H AL

CAP DRÂA
C. YUBY
El Aaiún

Béni Abbas GRAND ERG OCCIDENTAL
Timimoun GRAND ERG ORIENTAL
Hassi Messaoud
Adrar PLATEAU DU TADEMAÏT
In Salah Bordj Omar Idriss
In Amnas
PLATEAU DU TINGHERT
Illizi

A L G E R I A

TIDIKELT
TASSILI-N-AJJER

FUNCHAL ILHA DE PORTO SANTO
DA MADEIRA (Port.)
ILHA DE MADEIRA (Port.)

ISLAS CANARIAS (Sp.)
LA PALMA TENERIFE Sta. Cruz de Tenerife
San Sebastián LANZAROTE
GOMERA GRAN CANARIA CAP DRÂA
HIERRO Las Palmas de Gran Canaria
FUERTEVENTURA

CABO BOJADOR

ATLANTIC OCEAN

Dakhla

The Western Sahara is occupied by Morocco

WESTERN SAHARA

Tindouf

Tropic of Cancer
Fdérik

Chenachane
Ouallene
Djanet Ghât

S A H A R A
ERG IGUIDI
ERG CHECH
TANEZROUFT
EL HANK
EL DJOUF
Taoudenni

TAHAT 9 541 AHAGGAR
Tamenghest
Oued Tamenghe

TUAREG
ADRAR DES IFÔGHAS

Mt. Grébown 4562
Iferouâne 5906
Monts Tamgak
AÏR
Monts Bagzane 6300

Nouadhibou
CAP BLANC
CAP D'ARGUIN
Nouamrhar
CAP TIMIRIS

Atar Chinguetti
OUARANE
EL MREYYÉ
Araouane
Mabrouk
VALLÉE DU TILEMSI
Kidal

M A U R I T A N I A

Akjoujt
Nouakchott Tidjíkdja
Boutilimit Kiffa
Aleg Néma Oualâta

M A L I

Tombouctou (Timbuktu) Bamba
Gao
Bourem
Agadez

N I G E R

Saint-Louis Dagana
Podor Kaédi Mbout
Matam Sélibaby
Louga Linguère
Nioro du Sahel
Nara Niafounké
Goundam

Tahoua
Tessaoua Gouré

Dakar CAP VERT
Rufisque Thiès
Diourbel
Kaolack
Bakel
Kayes
Goumbou Sokolo
Mopti Bandiagara
Ségou San Djenné
Dori
Ouahigouya
Tillabéry
Niamey Say Dosso
Madaoua Maradi Zinder Nguru

SENEGAL
Banjul (Bathurst)
GAMBIA

Tambacounda
Bafoulabé
Kita
BURKINA FASO
Kaya
Ouagadougou
Birnin Kebbi
Sokoto Katsina Gumel Hadejia
Gusau Gaya Poti

Ziguinchor
GUINEA-BISSAU
Bissau Bolama
ARQUIPÉLAGO DOS BIJAGÓS

Koumbia Satadougou
FOUTA DJALLON
M. du Tamgué 5046
Labé
Koulikoro
Bamako
Ségou
Koutiala
Dédougou
Fada N'Gourma
Malanville
Kandi

S U D A N
N I G E R I A

Boké Timbo
Buba
Boffa
GUINEA
Kindia
Forécariah
Conakry
Makeni
SIERRA LEONE
Freetown
Moyamba
Bonthe

Siguiri
Kouroussa
Kankan
Faranah
Kissidougou
Beyla

Bougouni
Sikasso
Bobo-Dioulasso
Gaoua
Koudougou
Tenkodogo
Gambaga
Natitingou
Sansanné-Mango

Zaria
Kaduna
Zungeru
Kontagora
Bauchi Gombe
Minna
Jos
Ibi

Kabala
Kolahun
Pandembu
Odienné
Korhogo
KONG
Kong Bouna
Bole

Séguéla
Bondoukou
Kintampo
Savalou
Atakpamé
Sokodé
Yendi
Tamale
Parakou

ABUJA
Keffi
NIGERIA

Bomi Hills
Robertsport
LIBERIA
Monrovia
Buchanan
River Cess

Mont Nimba 5760
Dabakala
Bouaké
Bouaflé
GHANA
Kumasi
Koforidua

TOGO
Savé
Oyo Iseyin Ilorin Ogbomosho Jebba Baro
Abomey Ife Oshogbo Oyo Iwo Ilesha Lokoja
Palimé Abeokuta Ibadan
Porto-Novo Ijebu Ode Benin City
Anecho Lomé Lagos Sapele Onitsha
Warri Owerri

Bida Minna
Idah
Makurdi

Yamoussoukro
CÔTE D'IVOIRE (IVORY COAST)
Abidjan
Greenville
CAPE PALMAS
Harper
Tabou

Grand Lahou
Grand Bassam
Assini
Tarkwa
Accra
Sekondi-Takoradi
Cape Coast
C. THREE POINTS
Saltpond

Koko
Forcados

Benin City
Enugu
Aba Port Harcourt
Brass Bonny
Calabar
Kumbo
Cameroon Mtn. 13 451
Limbe
Mamfe
Dschang
CAM

MALABO BIOKO
EQUATORIAL GUINEA Bata
SÃO TOMÉ AND PRINCIPE
ILHA DO PRINCIPE
ILHA DE SÃO TOMÉ
São Tomé
Douala
Edéa Eséka
Kribi Campo
Libreville
RIO MUNI

GULF OF GUINEA

Bight of Benin
Bight of Biafra

ATLANTIC OCEAN

b

SANTA ANTÃO
SÃO VICENTE SAL
SÃO NICOLAU BOA VISTA
CAPE VERDE
SÃO TIAGO MAIO
FOGO Praia

Same scale as main map

A-589100-76 17-14-33
COPYRIGHT BY
RAND McNALLY & COMPANY
MADE IN U.S.A.

Longitude West of Greenwich | Longitude East of Greenwich

Scale 1:16 000 000; one inch to 250 miles. Sinusoidal Project
Elevations and depressions are given in feet

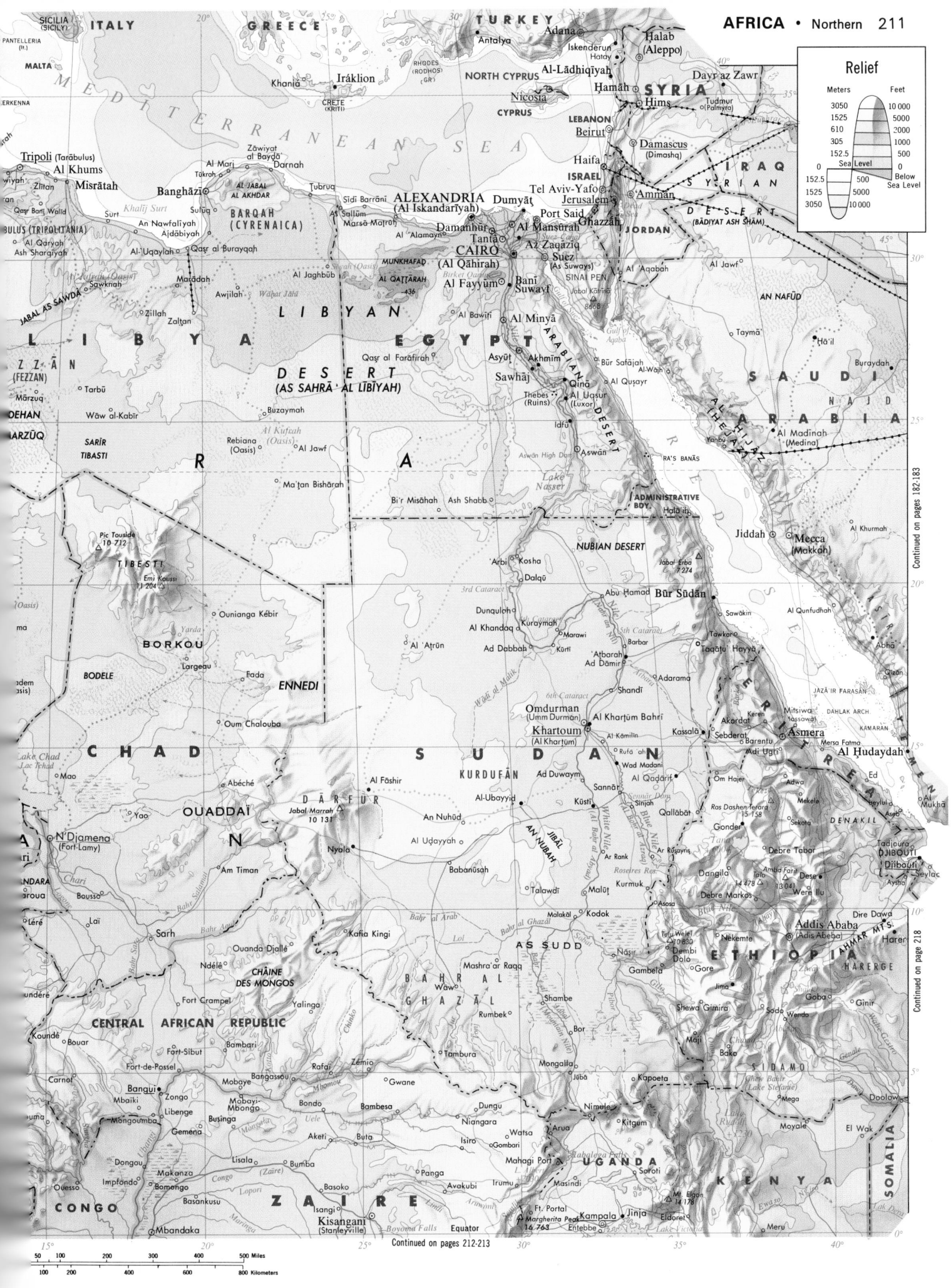

212

GABON
CONGO
Libreville
Kango
Ndjolé
Lambaréné
Lastoursville
Franceville
Port Gentil
Equator
Sette Cama
Tchibanga
Mbigou
Moanda
Mayumba
Sibiti
CABINDA
Pointe-Noire
(Léopoldville)
CABINDA (Angola)
Cabinda
Landana
Tshela
Boma
Matadi
N'zeto
Noqui
M'banza
Cango
Bembe
Soyo
Maquela
do Zombo
Uíge
Damba

CONGO
Brazzaville
Kinshasa
Mbanza-Ngungu
Popokabaka

Owando
Irébou
Mbandaka
Bikoro
Boende
Ubundu
Lukolela
Lac Mai-Ndombe
(Lake Leopold II)
1076
Itoko
Monkoto
Lomela

UGANDA
Ripon Falls Jinja
Entebbe Kampala
Rutshuru
Giseny
Kigali
RWANDA
Bukavu
Astrida
BURUNDI
Gitega
Bujumbura
Uvira
Kigoma
Ujiji

ZAIRE
Lusanga
Kikwit
Bulungu
Bandundu
Mushie
Djokupunda
Luebo
Kananga
(Luluabourg)
Ilebo
Bena Dibele
Lusambo
Kasongo
Kabambare
Kabinda
Kanda Kanda
Ankoro
Mutombo Mukulu
Kongolo
Kabalo
Kamina
KATANGA
Bukama
Kiambi
Moba
Karema
Kasanga
Tukuyu

Luanda
Golungo Alto
Caxito
Cafete
Dondo
Kalandula
Malanje

ANGOLA
Porto Amboim
Sumbe
Waku Kundo
Luena
Munhango
Chinguar
Kuito
Huambo
Caconda
Cangumbe
Dongo
Cuchi

Lobito
Benguela
Namibe
Tombua
SERRA DA CHELA
Cassinga
Cahama
Humbe
Xangongo

PENÍNSULA DOS TIGRES
CAPE FRIA

NAMIBIA
OWAMBO
Ruacana Falls
Namutoni
Tsumeb
Otavi
Grootfontein
Outjo
Otjiwarongo
Brandberg 8550
Omaruru
Karibib
Okahandja
Usakos
Swakopmund
Walvis Bay
Windhoek
Rehoboth
DAMARALAND
Gobabis

Tropic of Capricorn

ZAMBIA
BAROTSELAND
Mongu
Mumbwa
Lusaka
Kafue
Mazabuka
Kalomo
Livingstone
Pemba

Kolwezi
Tenke
Kambove
Likasi
Lubumbashi
(Elisabethville)
Chingola
Ndola
Kasempa
Kabwe

Dilolo
Cazombo
Mansa
Serenje
Mchinji
Chipata

ZIMBABWE
Victoria Falls
Hwange
Kwekwe
Gweru
Shurugwi
Kadoma
Chegutu
Harare (Salisbury)
Chinhoyi
Chitungwiza
Marondera
Mutare (Umtali)
(RHODESIA)
Bulawayo
Zvishavane
Masvingo

BOTSWANA
KALAHARI
DESERT
Ghanzi
Maun
Ntwetwe Pan
Lake Xau
Francistown
Old Tate
Serowe
Palapye
Tuli
Messina

CAPRIVI STRIP
Okavango Swamp
Ngami

KWAZULU
Ladysmith

A-589200-76
COPYRIGHT BY
RAND McNALLY & COMPANY
MADE IN U.S.A.

SOUTH AFRICA
Gibeon
GREAT NAMALAND
Maltahöhe
Bethanien
Keetmanshoop
Lüderitz
Aroab
Oranjemund
Port Nolloth
Springbok
BUSHMANLAND
Calvinia
Saldanha
Malmesbury
Worcester
Paarl
Cape Town
CAPE OF GOOD HOPE
CAPE AGULHAS
Bredasdorp

Tshabong
Mmabatho
Mafeking
Vryburg
Taung
Kuruman
Warmbad
Augrabies
Upington
Kimberley
Prieska
Hopetown
Springfontein
Carnarvon
Victoria West
Beaufort West
Willowmore
Oudtshoorn
GREAT KARROO
LITTLE KARROO
Mosselbaai
Humansdorp

Mochudi
Molepolole
Gaborone
Lobatse
Nylstroom
Potgietersrus
Pietersburg
Thohoyandou
KRUGER NATL
Lydenburg
Barberton
Carolina
Pretoria
Krugersdorp
JOHANNESBURG
Benoni
Germiston
Potchefstroom
Kroonstad
Welkom
Bethlehem
Bloemfontein
Maseru
LESOTHO
Wepener
De Aar
Middelburg
Cradock
Graaff Reinet
Bisho
East London
Port Alfred (Kowie)
Port Elizabeth
Uitenhage

Komatipoort
Maputo
(Lourenço Marques)
Mbabane
SWAZILAND
Piet Retief
Vryheid
Ubombo
Wakkerstroom
Standerton
Harrismith
DRAKENSBERG
Mt aux Sources 10 822
Cathkin 10 438
Pietermaritzburg
Durban
Harding
Scottburgh
Port Shepstone
Umtata
Maclear
Port St. Johns

MOZAMBIQUE
Beira
Dondo
Vila de Manica
Tete
Vilanculos
Inhambane
Xai-Xai
Magude
Manjacaze

TANZANIA
Tabora
Dodoma
Kilimatinde
Kipembawe
Mwaya
Livingstonia
Karonga
Mzimba
Chinteche
Nkhota K

Lake Tanganyika
+2534
Lake Mweru
Lake Bangweulu
3764
Cabora Bassa Res.
Zumbo
Lake Kariba

Inset map:

CAPE TOWN
MOUILLE PT
ROBBENEILAND
Bloubergstrand
Durbanville
Kommetjie 1502
Milnerton
Table Bay
Parow
Bellville
Camps Bay
Table Mt. 3567
Goodwood
Pinelands
Kuilsrivier
Nuweland
Wynberg
Ottery
CAPE FLATS
Houtbaai 3048
Muizenberg
Vishoek
Chapman's Bay
Grootkop 1286
Simonstad
Swartkop 2229
SMITSWINKEL VLAKTE
KAAPPUNT
SEAL ISLAND
Valsbaai
(False Bay)
St. Helenabaai
KAAPPUNT
CAPE OF GOOD HOPE

Scale 1:1 000 000
Miles
0   5   10
Kilometers
0 4 8 12 16

Scale 1:16 000 000; one inch to 250 miles. Sinusoidal Projection
Elevations and depressions are given in feet

Continued on pages 210-211

15° Longitude East of Greenwich 20°

18°30'

Mt. Kenya
(Kirinyaga)
17,058
Ft. Hall
Nairobi
SOMALIA
Buur Gaabo
Equator
Kismaayo
Witu
Lamu
Kilimanjaro
19,340
Malindi
Takaungu
Lushoto
Vanga
Tanga
Mombasa
Pangani
PEMBA ISLAND
ZANZIBAR
Zanzibar
Bagamoyo
Morogoro
Dar es Salaam
Kisaki
MAFIA
Utete
Kilwa Kivinje
Lindi
Mikindani
Masasi
CABO DELGADO
Mocímboa da Praia
Ibo
Pemba
Lúrio
Memba
Nacala
Moçambique
Angoche
ILHA ANGOCHE
INDIAN

ALDABRA IS. (Sey.)
COSMOLEDO GROUP (Sey.)
ÎLES GLORIEUSES (Fr.)
Moroni
COMOROS
NJAZIDJA
MWALI
NZWANI
Dzaoudzi
MAYOTTE (Fr.)
CAP D'AMBRE
Antsiranana
NOSY BE
Iharana
Maromokotra 9436
Maroantsetra
Mahajanga
Mandritsara
CAP SAINT ANDRÉ
Helodrano Antongila
NOSY BORAHA
Besalampy
Ambatondrazaka
Fenoarivo Atsinanana
ÎLE JUAN DE NOVA (Fr.)
Alaotra
Toamasina
NOSY BARREN
Maintirano
Moramanga
Antananarivo
Vatomandry
Tsiafajavona 8671
Antsirabe
Mahanoro
MADAGASCAR
Morondava
Ambositra
Mananjary
BASSAS DA INDIA (Fr.)
Fianarantsoa
EUROPA (Fr.)
Manakara
Morombe
Ivohibé
Betroka
Toliara
Trafonomby 4417
Mahaly
Farafangana
CAP STE. MARIE

ZAMBEZI
MOZAMBIQUE CHANNEL
Ligonha

Arlington
Paul Roux
Bethlehem
Senekal
ORANGE FREE STATE
Fouriesburg
Clarens
Clocolan
Ficksburg
Teyateyaneng
Butha Buthe
Leribe
Pitseng
Machache 9464
Mohale's Hoek
Roma
LESOTHO
Mokhotlong
Thabana Ntlenyana 11425
Harrismith
Kestell
Royal Natal Nat'l. Pk.
10,822 Mt. aux Sources
Bergville
Cathedral Pk. 9850
Winterton
Cathkin Pk. 10438
Mooirivier
Mt. Gilboa 5803
Dannhauser
Glencoe
Wasbank
Ladysmith
Colenso
Weenen
Estcourt
New Hanover
Nqutu
Pomeroy
Nkandla
Babanango
Tugela Ferry
Kranskop
Greytown
Wartburg
Ntshoni 5851
Camperdown
Pinetown
Durban
Isipingo
Mahlabatini
Melmoth
Eshowe
Mapumulo
Stanger
Howick
Dalton
Pietermaritzburg
Verulam
Richmond
Donnybrook
Mid Illovo
Umkomaas

Dundee
White
Underberg
Bulwer
Impendle
Creighton
Ixopo
Swartberg 7619
Qacha's Nek
Franklin
Kokstad
Harding
Scottburgh
Park Rynie
Sezela
Umtentweni
Port Shepstone
Uvongo Beach
Margate
Port Edward

Zastron
Mohale's Hoek
The Twins 8820
Matatiele
Cedarville
Mt. Currie 7297
7426
EASTERN CAPE
Bizana
Tabankulu
Flagstaff
Lusikisiki
Libode
Port St. Johns
RAME HEAD

Quthing
Witberg 2853
Herschel
Lady Grey
Ben Macdhui 9846
Rhodes
Mount Fletcher
Maclear
Mount Frere
Qumbu
Tsolo
Umtata
Ngqeleni
Elliotdale
Mqanduli
Willowvale
Kentani
Butterworth
Idutywa
Tsomo
Ngamakwe
Komga
Macleantown
Kei Mouth
Morgan's Bay
Gonubie

Jamestown
Rossouw
8430
Elliot
Ugie
Barkly East
Dordrecht
Indwe
Cala
Engcobo
Sterkstroom
Cofimvaba

EASTERN CAPE
Molteno
STORMBERG
Waverly
Tarkastad
Cradock
Whittlesea
Tylden
Queenstown
Lady Frere
SOUTH
Carthcart
Stutterheim
Frankfort
Seymour
Keiskammahoek
Adelaide
Bisho
Berlin
Breidbach
King William's Town
East London
Kidd's Beach
Hamburg

BANKBERG
6606
WINTERBERGE
7778
Pearston
Bedford
Fort Beaufort
Fort Alice
Somerset East
SUURBERGE
Alicedale
Riebeek-Oos
Grahamstown
Peddie
Kirkwood
Salem
Addo
Bathurst
Alexandria
Port Alfred (Kowie)
Uitenhage
SAINT CROIX ISLAND
BIRD ISLAND
Port Elizabeth
KAAP RECIFE

SOUTH AFRICA
DRAKENSBERG
NATAL
MALOTI MTS.
Orange River

INDIAN
OCEAN

Scale 1:4 000 000
0 10 20 30 40 Miles
0 10 20 30 40 50 60 Kilometers

Longitude East of Greenwich

40° 45° 50°
5°
10°
15°
20°
25°
30°
32°
34°
35°
45° 26° 28° 30°

For larger scale coverage of Johannesburg see page 244.

©RMcN
Wolhuterskop
Jacksonstuin
Kosmos
Hartbeespoort
Swartspruit
Pretoria North
Pretoria
Cullinan
MAGALIESBERG
Skeerpoort
4549
Hennopsrivier
Voortrekkerhoogte
Valhalla
Sesmyl
Silverton
Rayton
4426
Tierport
Magalies
Foothills
Olievenhoutpoort
4602
Irene
Lyttelton
Riefeldrum
WITWATERSBERG
Krokodil
Hennop
Halfway House
Bapsfontein
Tarlton
Krugersdorp
Modderfontein
Kaalfontein
Kempton Park
Putfontein
Randfontein
JOHANNESBURG
Alexandra
Roodepoort
Discovery
Edenvale
5557
Florida
Primrose
Maraisburg
Boksburg
Benoni
5725
Orlando
Turffontein
Rosettenville
Germiston
Brakpan
Pimville
Alberton
Springs
WITWATERSRAND

Scale 1:1 000 000
0   5   10 Miles
0 4 8 12 16 Kilometers

28° 28°30'
26°

b

c

Relief

Meters		Feet
3050		10 000
1525		5000
610		2000
305		1000
152.5		500
Sea Level		0
152.5		500
1525		5000
3050		10 000

©RMcN

214

Scale 1:10,000,000; one inch to 160 miles. Lambert Azimuthal Equal Area Proje
Elevations and depressions are given in feet.

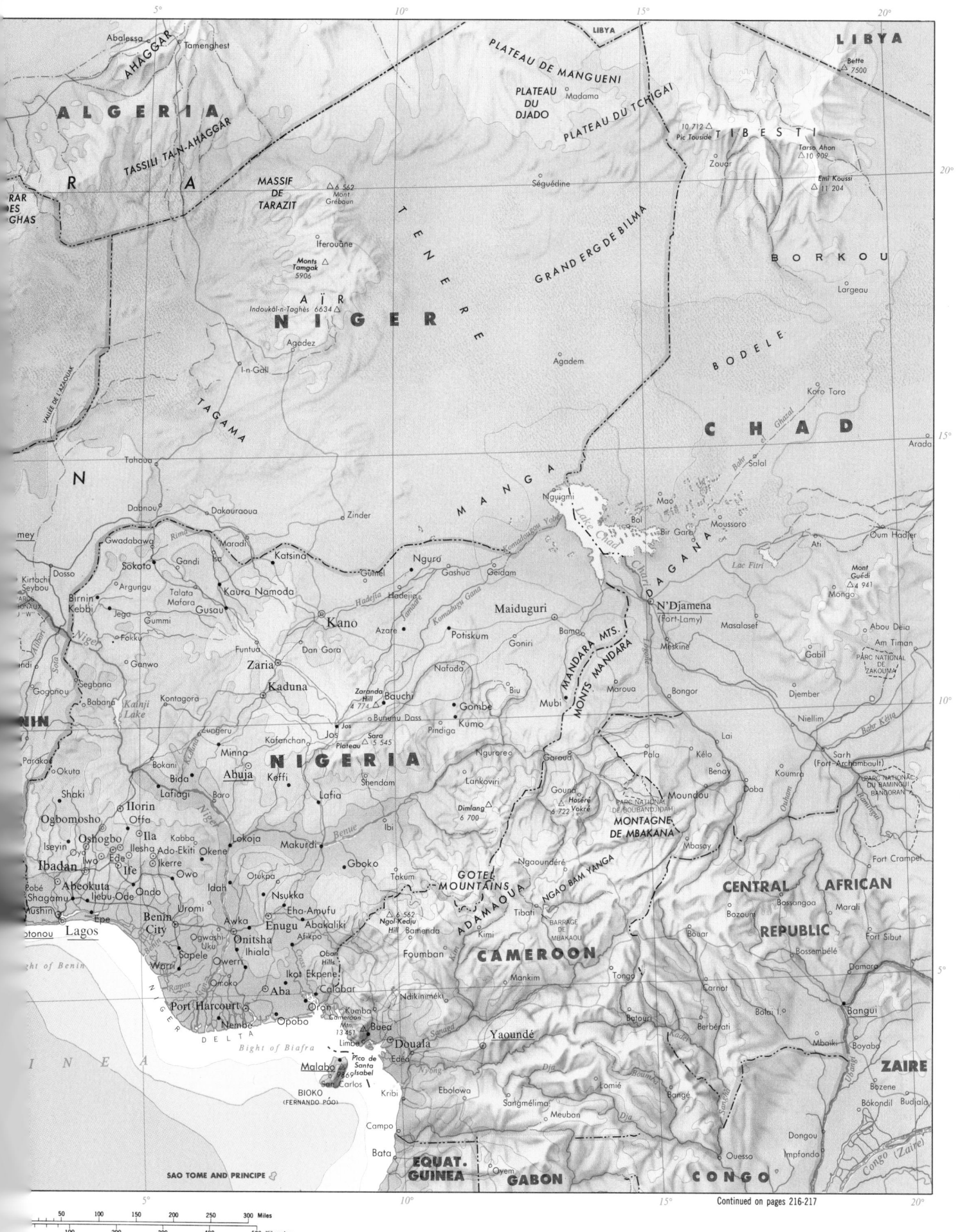

ALGERIA

Abalessa   Tamenghest

AHAGGAR

TASSILI TA-N-AHAGGAR

RAR
ES
GHAS

MASSIF
DE
TARAZIT   △ 6 562
Mont
Grébaun

Iferouâne

Monts
Tamgak
5906 △

AÏR
Indoukâl-n-Taghès 6634 △

NIGER

Agadez

I-n-Gall

TAGAMA

N

Tahoua

Dabnou   Dakouraoua   Zinder

mey   Gwadabawa
Rima   Maradi
Dosso   Gandi
Sokoto   Isa   Katsina
Argungu
Birnin   Talata   Kaura Namoda
Kebbi   Mafara
Jega   Gummi   Gusau
Fokku   Funtua
Ganwo   Dan Gora
Segbana   Babana   Kontagora   Zaria
Goganou   Kaduna
Kalnji
Lake   Zungeru
Parako   Bokani   Minna
Okuta   Bida
Shaki   Lafiagi
Ogbomosho   Ilorin   Baro
Offa
Iseyin   Oshogbo   Ila   Kabba
Oyo   Ilesha   Ado-Ekiti   Okene
Ibadan   Ede   Ikerre   Owo
Ife
Pobé   Abeokuta   Ondo   Idah
Ijebu-Ode   Uromi
Mushin   Ogwashi   Awka
Shagamu   Uku   Onitsha
otonou   Lagos   Epe   Benin   Ihiala
City
Warri   Sapele   Owerri
Oroko   Aba
ght of Benin   Ikot Ekpene
Port Harcourt   Oron
Nembe   Opobo
DELTA

Dabnou

NIGERIA

Abuja   Keffi

Kafanchan   Jos
Jos
Sara
Plateau   5 545
Zaranda
Hill   Bauchi
4 771   Bununu Dass
Pindiga
Kumo
Gombe
Biu

Lafia

Shendam

Ngurore

Lankoviri

Dimlang
6 700

Takúm

GOTEL
MOUNTAINS   Tibati
Ngol Kedju   Bamenda
6 562   Hill
Oban
Hills   Kimi
Foumban
CAMEROON
Mankim

Ndikiniméki

Buea
Douala

Malabo   Pico de
Santa
San Carlos   Isabel
3869   Edea

BIOKO
(FERNANDO PÓO)   Kribi

Campo

Bata

SAO TOME AND PRINCIPE

EQUAT.
GUINEA   Oyem

GABON

Gusau   Kano   Azare

Gummel   Gashua   Geidam
Nguru

Potiskum   Goniri
Nafada
Biu

Maiduguri

Bama

Mubi

MANDARA MTS.
MONTS MANDARA

Maroua

Garoua

Pala

Hosere
Yokré
6 722

Gouna
Moundou

PARC NATIONAL
DE BOUBAND DAH

Ngaoundéré   MONTAGNE
DE MBAKANA

ADAMAOUA   NGAO BAM YANGA

Mbsayi

BARRAGE
DE
MBAKAOU

Yaoundé

Ebolowa

Sangmélima   Dja

Meuban   Dja

TENERE

GRAND ERG DE BILMA

Séguédine

Agadem

BODELE

Koro Toro

CHAD

MANGA   Nguigmi
Komadougou Yobé
Lake Chad
Bol
DAGANA   Bir Gara
Lac Fitri
N'Djamena
(Fort-Lamy)
Meskine

Bongor

Niellim

Lai

Kélo   Benoy

Doba

Koumra

Kimi   Bozoum

Bouar

Batouri
Tongo

Carnot

Bangé

Lomié

PLATEAU DE MANGUENI

PLATEAU
DU
DJADO   Madama

PLATEAU DU TCHIGAI

10 712 △   TIBESTI
Pic Tousidé   Tarso Ahon
Zouar   △10 909
Emi Koussi
△ 11 204

LIBYA

Bette
7500

LIBYA

BORKOU

Largeau

Salal

Moussoro   Ati   Oum Hadjer

Mao   Bahr
Ghazal

Mont
Guédi
△4 941
Mongo

Masalasef

Abou Deia

Am Timan

Gabil   PARC NATIONAL
DE
ZAKOUMA

Djember

Bahr Keïta

Sarh
(Fort-Archambault)

PARC NATIONAL
DU RAMINGUI
BANGORAN

Fort Crampel

CENTRAL   AFRICAN

REPUBLIC   Fort Sibut

Bossangoa   Marali

Bossembélé

Damara

Bolai I.   Bangui

Berbérati   Mbaïki   Boyaba

ZAIRE

Bozene
Bókondji   Budjala

Dongou

Ouesso   Impfondo

CONGO

Congo (Zaïre)

Arada

Benue

Sanaga

Nyong

Niger

Benin

GINEA   Bight of Biafra

Continued on pages 216-217

50   100   150   200   250   300 Miles
100   200   300   400   500 Kilometers

Continued on pages 214–215

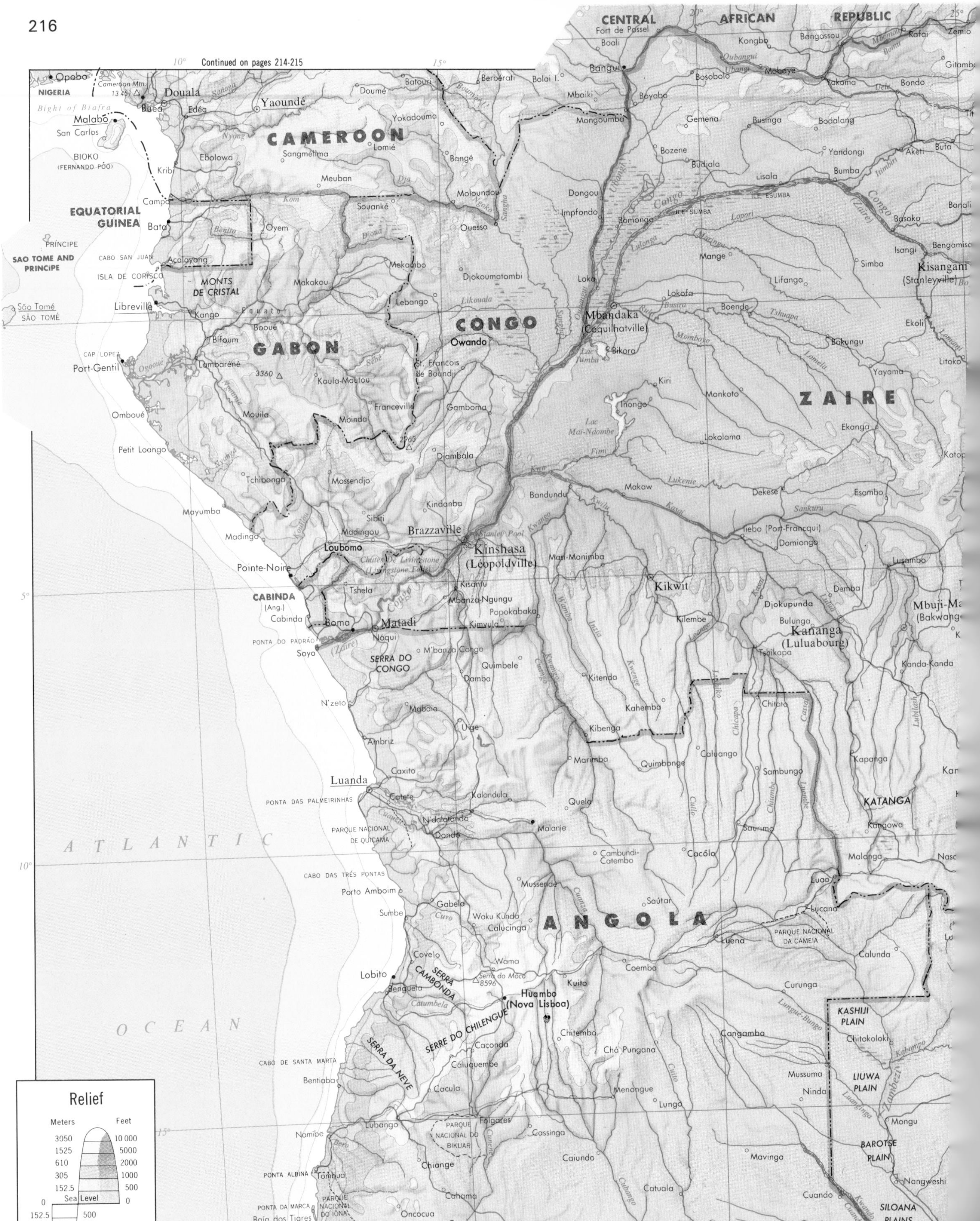

CENTRAL AFRICAN REPUBLIC

Fort de Possel
Boali
Bangui
Kongbo
Bangassou
Zemio
Mobaye
Yakoma
Bondo
Mbaiki
Boyabo
Bosobolo
Takoma
Uele
Gitamba
Batouri
Berberati
Bolai
Mongoumba
Gemena
Bustinga
Bodalang
Akoti
Buta
Doumé
Yokadouma
Bozene
Budjala
Yandongi
Bumba
Banali

NIGERIA
Opobo
Malabo
San Carlos
BIOKO (FERNANDO PÓO)
Cameroon Mtn. 13 451
Buéa
Douala
Edéa
Yaoundé
Sangmélima
Ebolowa
Lomié
Bangé
Molundou
Moloko
Mbandaka (Coquilhatville)
Lisala
Isangi
Bengamisa
Simba
Kisangani (Stanleyville)
Lifanga
Mange
Bumba

Bight of Biafra

EQUATORIAL GUINEA
Bata
Campo
Oyem
Souanké
Ouesso
Djoumatombi
Loka
Lakafa
Boende
Tshuapa
Ekoli
Litoko

PRÍNCIPE
SAO TOME AND PRINCIPE
CABO SAN JUAN
ISLA DE CORISCO

São Tomé
SÃO TOMÉ
Libreville
Acalayong
MONTS DE CRISTAL
Makokou
Mekambo
Lebango
Likouala
CONGO
Owando
Bikoro
Lac Tumba
Bokungu
Yayama
Litoko

GABON
Kango
Booué
Bifoum
3360
Koula-Moutou
Franceville
St. François de Boundji
Gamboma
Kiri
Inongo
Monkoto
Lokolama
Ekanga
ZAIRE

Port-Gentil
Omboué
Lambaréné
Mouila
Mbinda
3230
Djambala
Lac Mai-Ndombe
Fimi
Dekese
Esombo
Katot

Petit Loango
Tchibango
Mossendjo
Kindanba
Bandundu
Makaw
Lukenie
Tiebo (Port-Francqui)
Domiongo
Sankuru

Mayumba
Sibiti
Madingou
Madinga
Brazzaville
Stanley Pool
Kwango
Masi-Manimba
Kikwit
Kilembe
Demba
Lusambo
Loubomo
Chutes de Livingstone (Livingstone Falls)
Kinshasa (Léopoldville)
Djokupunda
Bulunga
Kananga (Luluabourg)
Pointe-Noire
Kisantu
Kana-Kanda
Mbuji-Ma (Bakwanga)

CABINDA (Ang.)
Cabinda
Boma
Tshela
Mbanza-Ngungu
Popokabaka
Kimvula
Kitenda
Kwenge
Tshikapa
PONTA DO PADRÃO
Matadi
Nóqui
Soyo
M'banza Congo
Quimbele
Kahemba
Chitata
Cassai
SERRA DO CONGO
Damba
Kibenga
Caluango
Kapanga
KATANGA

N'zeto
Mabaia
Uíge
Marimba
Quimbonge
Sambungo
Kangowa
Ambriz
Caxito
Malanga
Nasc
Luanda
PONTA DAS PALMEIRINHAS
Catete
Kalandula
Quela
Cacôlo
Luao
Lucano
PARQUE NACIONAL DE QUIÇAMA
N'dalatando
Dondo
Malanje
Cambundi-Catembo
Luena
PARQUE NACIONAL DA CAMEIA
Calunda

CABO DAS TRÊS PONTAS
Porto Amboim
Gabela
Waku Kundo
Calucinga
Musserde
Saútar
Coemba
Curunga
Cangamba

Sumbe
Covelo
SERRA CAMBONDA
Wama
Kuito
ANGOLA
KASHIJI PLAIN
Chitokoloki

Lobito
Benguela
SERRA DO CHILENGUE
Serra do Moco 8596
Huambo (Nova Lisboa)
Chitembo
Chá Pungana
Mussuma
LIUWA PLAIN
Ninda

SERRA DA NEVE
Caconda
Caluquembe
Chibia
Menongue
Lunga
Mongu
BAROTSE PLAIN
Nangweshi

CABO DE SANTA MARTA
Bentiaba
Cacula
Folgares
PARQUE NACIONAL DO BIKUAR
Cassinga
Caiundo
Mavinga
SILOANA PLAINS

Namibe
Lubango
Chiange
Cahama
Oncocua
Cuamato
Melunga
Cuangar
CAPRIVI STRIP

PONTA ALBINA
Tombua
PARQUE NACIONAL DO IÔNA
Ruacana Falls
NAMIBIA
BOTS.
CHOBE N

PONTA DA MARCA
Baía dos Tigres
Foz do Cunene
Cunene

ATLANTIC OCEAN

Relief

Meters	Feet
3050	10 000
1525	5000
610	2000
305	1000
152.5	500
0 Sea Level	0
152.5	500
1525	5000
3050	10 000

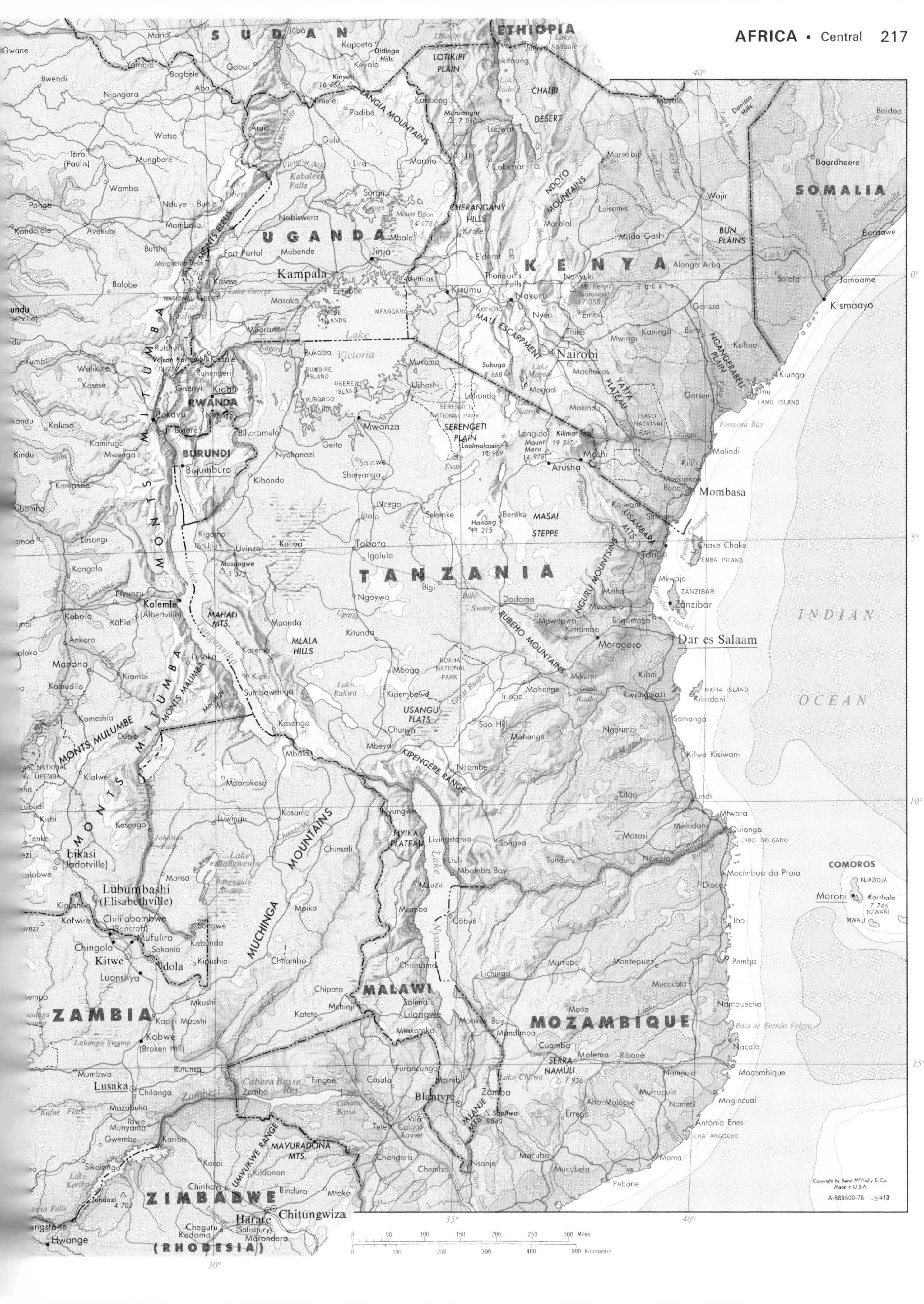

SUDAN
ETHIOPIA
SOMALIA
UGANDA
KENYA
RWANDA
BURUNDI
TANZANIA
ZAMBIA
MALAWI
MOZAMBIQUE
ZIMBABWE
(RHODESIA)
COMOROS

INDIAN OCEAN

Maridi
Yambio
Bagbele
Aba
Gobur
Juba
Kapoeta
Didinga Hills
Keyala
Nimule
Kinyeti 10 456
LOTIKIPI PLAIN
Lokitaung
Jinen
Lake Stefanie
Lokichar
CHALBI DESERT
Baidoa
Bwindi
Niangara
Watsa
Mungbere
Istro (Paulis)
Wamba
Panga
Arua
Gulu
Padibe
Lira
Moroto 9 118
Lodwar
NDOTO MOUNTAINS
Marsabit
Mado Gashi
Baardheere
Kondolole
Avakubi
Mambasa
Butsha
Fort Portal
Mubende
Nabiswera
Mbale
Mount Elgon 14 178
CHERANGANY HILLS
Kitale
Eldoret
Laisamis
Wajir
BUN PLAINS
Baraawe
MONTS BLEUS
Kasese
MONTS MITUMBA
Kampala
Entebbe
Masaka
Jinja
Mumias
Kisumu
Thomson's Falls
Nakuru
Nanyuki
Mt. Kenya (Kirinyaga) 17 058
Alanga Arba
Garissa
Balobe
Kabalega Falls
Lake Albert
PARC NATIONAL ALBERT
Lake Edward
Lake George
SESSE ISLANDS
MFANGANO
Kericho
Nyeri
Embu
Thika
Mwingi
Kaningo
Bura
Kolbio
Solata
Jamaame
Kismaayo
Rutshuru
Volcan Karisimbi
Kabale
Ruhengeri
Kigali
Biharamulo
Bukoba
Lake Victoria
Musoma
Subugo 8 668
Lake Magadi
Nairobi
Machakos
YATA PLATEAU
Garsen
Lamu
LAMU ISLAND
Formosa Bay
Giseny
Kibungo
Butare
Nyanza
UKEREWE ISLAND
RUBONDO
Ushashi
SERENGETI NATIONAL PARK
Loliondo
Lake Natron
Longido
Kilimanjaro 19 340
Mount Meru 14 978
Makindu
TSAVO NATIONAL PARK
Malindi
Bukavu
Kamituga
Mwenga
Bujumbura
Nyakanazi
Geita
Mwanza
SERENGETI PLAIN
Loolmalassin 11 969
Moshi
Arusha
Kilifi
Mombasa
Kindu
Kalima
Elila
Kampene
Kasongo
Kibondo
Nzega
Shinyanga
Salawe
Ipala
Sekenke
Bereku
Hanang 11 215
MASAI STEPPE
Kisiwani
USAMBARA MTS.
Shirati
Tanga
Lukuga
Nyunzu
Kongolo
Lusangi
Uvinza
Kigoma
Ujiji
Kaliua
Tabora
Igalula
Itigi
Ngoywa
Dodoma
Bahi Swamp
Mvomero
Bagamoyo
PEMBA ISLAND
Chake Chake
Mkwaja
ZANZIBAR
Zanzibar
Zanzibar Channel
Kalemie (Albertville)
MAHALI MTS.
Masangwe 5 373
Mpanda
MLALA HILLS
Kitunda
Mbogo
RUAHA NATIONAL PARK
Mpwapwa
Kimamba
Morogoro
Kibiti
MAFIA ISLAND
Kilindoni
Dar es Salaam
Kabalo
Kahia
Karema
Kipili
Sumbawanga
Molwo
Lake Rukwa
Kipembawe
Great Ruaha
Iringa
Mahenge
NGURU MOUNTAINS
RUBEHO MOUNTAINS
Mikumi
Kwandwazi
Ankoro
Kamudilo
Maporo
Kiambi
Komeshia
Dubie
MONTS MITUMBA
MONTS MALUMBA
MONTS MULUMBE
Kasanga
USANGU FLATS
Chunya
Sao Hill
Mbeya
Ngorimbi
Somanga
Kilwa Kisiwani
Kiswani
PARC NATIONAL DE L'UPEMBA
Kialwe
Mporokoso
KIPENGERE RANGE
Njombe
Mbala
Lindi
Kishi
Tenke
Kasenga
Luwingu
Kasama
Chinsali
Mwimba
NYIKA PLATEAU
Livingstonia
Songea
Masasi
Newala
Mtwara
Mikindani
Quionga
CABO DELGADO
Likasi (Jadotville)
Mansa
Lake Bangweulu
Bangweulu Swamp
Mpika
Chitambo
Mzuzu
Liuli
Mbamba Bay
Tunduru
Diaca
Mocimboa da Praia
Ibo
COMOROS
NJAZIDJA
Moroni
Karthala 7 746
NZWANI
MWALI
Lubumbashi (Elisabethville)
Kipushi
Chililabombwe (Bancroft)
Mufulira
Sakania
Kabunda
Kipushia
MUCHINGA MOUNTAINS
Mzimba
Cóbuè
Lichinga
Maúa
Montepuez
Pemba
Chingola
Kitwe
Ndola
Songwe
Chitambo
Mkushi
Chipata
Katete
Mchinji
MALAWI
Salima
Lilongwe
Ntakataka
Monkey Bay
Mandimba
Cuamba
Malema
Ribaué
MOZAMBIQUE
Mucacata
Nampuecha
Luanshya
Kapiri Mposhi
Kabwe (Broken Hill)
Rutunsa
SERRA NAMÚLI 7 936
Nametil
Mumbwa
ZAMBIA
Lusaka
Chilanga
Cabora Bassa Res.
Zumbo
Fíngoe
Casula
Furancungo
Mpimb
Lake Chilwa
Blantyre
Zomba
Alto Molócuè
Errego
Nampula
Moçambique
António Enes
ILHA ANGOCHE
Mazabuka
Lukanga Swamp
Kafue Flats
Zambezi
Cahora Bassa
Tete
Vila Caldas Xavier
MLANJE MTS.
Sapitwa 9849
Murrupula
Mogincual
Mumbwa
Gwembe
Kariba
MAVURADONA MTS.
UMVUKWE RANGE
Kildonan
Changara
Chemba
Nsanje
Mocuba
Mucubela
Moma
Pebane
Baia de Fernão Veloso
Nacala
Sikalongo
Lake Kariba
Chinhoyi (Salisbury)
Bindura
Mtoko
ZIMBABWE
(RHODESIA)
Harare (Salisbury)
Chitungwiza
Chegutu
Kadoma
Marondera
Hwange
Karoi

Copyright by Rand McNally & Co.
Made in U.S.A.
A-589500-76   -3-413

0   50   100   150   200   250   300 Miles
0   100   200   300   400   500 Kilometers

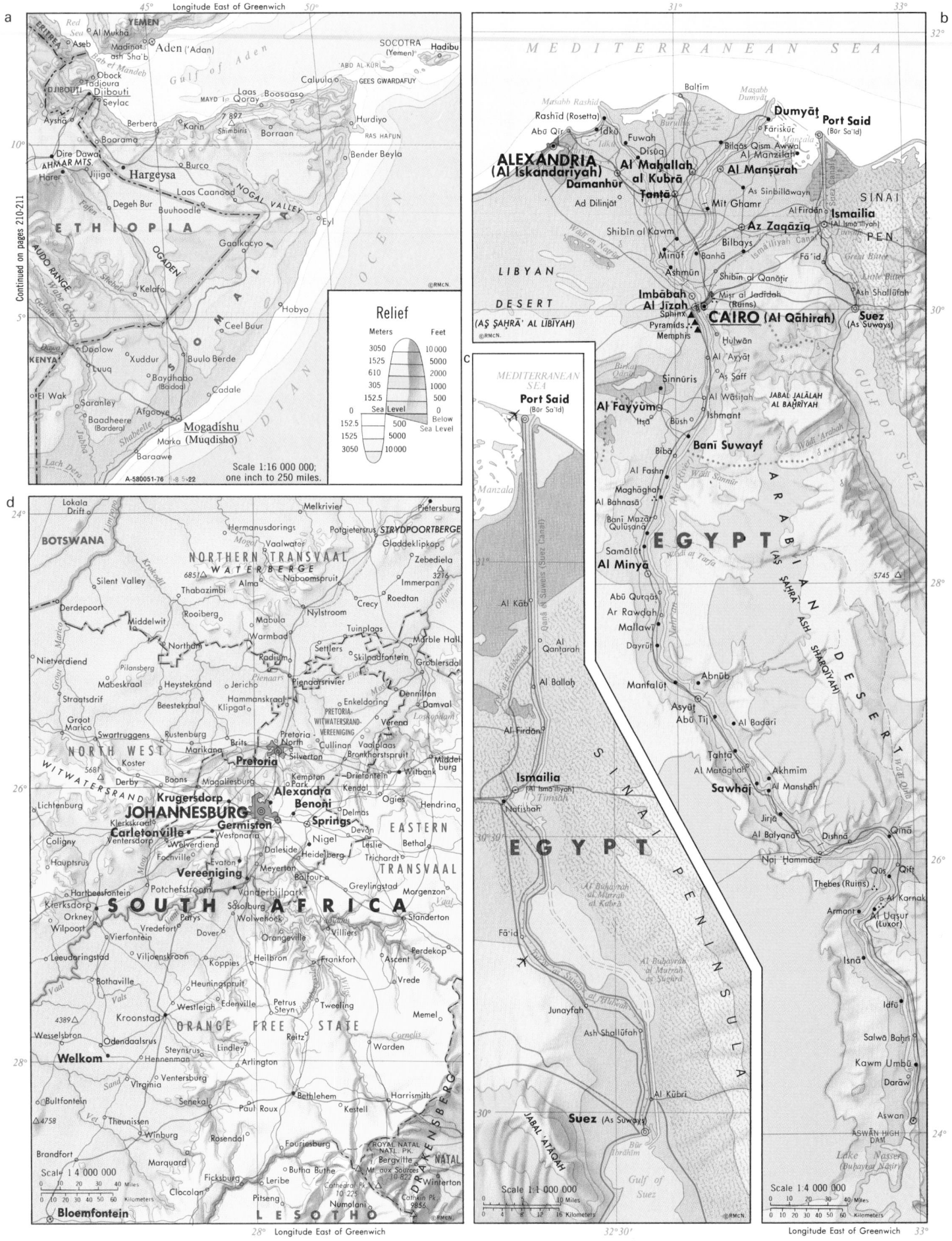

a

Longitude East of Greenwich

Continued on pages 210-211

Red Sea

YEMEN

Al Mukha

Aden ('Adan)

SOCOTRA (Yemen) Hadibu

ERITREA

Aseb

Gulf of Aden

ABD AL-KURI

GEES GWARDAFUY

Obock

Tadjoura

DJIBOUTI Djibouti

Seylac

MAYD 1

Laas Qoray

Boosaaso

Caluula

RAS HAFUN

Aysha

Berbera

Karin

Shimbiris

Hurdiyo

7 897

Dire Dawa

Jijiga

Burco

Borraan

Bender Beyla

AHMAR MTS.

Harer

Hargeysa

Laas Caanood

Degeh Bur

Buuhoodle

NOGAL VALLEY

Eyl

ETHIOPIA

OGADEN

Gaalkacyo

Kelafo

AUDO RANGE

Doolow

Ceel Buur

KENYA

Luuq

Xuddur

Hobyo

El Wak

Saranley

Baydhabo (Baidoa)

Buulo Berde

Baardheere (Bardera)

Cadale

Afgooye

Marka

Mogadishu (Muqdisho)

Baraawe

INDIAN OCEAN

S O M A L I A

Relief

Meters		Feet
3050		10 000
1525		5000
610		2000
305		1000
152.5		500
0	Sea Level	0
152.5		500
1525		5000
3050		10 000
		Below Sea Level

Scale 1:16 000 000; one inch to 250 miles.

A-580051-76 -8 5-22

b

MEDITERRANEAN SEA

Masabb Rashid

Maşabb Dumyat

Rashid (Rosetta)

Baltim

Abu Qir

Idku

Fuwah

Disuq

Faraskur

Dumyat

Port Said (Bur Sa'id)

Bilqas Qism Awwal

Al Manzilah

ALEXANDRIA (Al Iskandariyah)

Al Mahallah al Kubra

Damanhur

Ad Dilinjat

Tanta

Mit Ghamr

Al Mansurah

As Sinbillawayn

SINAI

Shibin al Kawm

Az Zaqaziq

Al Firdan

Ismailia (Al Isma'iliyah)

PEN.

Minuf

Banha

Bilbays

Fa'id

LIBYAN

Ashmun

Shibin al Qanatir

Ismailiyah Canal

Great Bitter

Little Bitter

DESERT

Imbabah

Misr al Jadidah

Ash Shallufah

(AS SAHRA' AL LIBIYAH)

Al Jizah

(Ruins)

Sphinx

CAIRO (Al Qahirah)

Suez (As Suways)

Pyramids

Memphis

Hulwan

Al 'Ayyat

As Saff

Sinnuris

Al Wasitah

JABAL JALALAH AL BAHRIYAH

Al Fayyum

Itsa

Bush

Ishmant

Bani Suwayf

Biba

Al Fashn

Wadi Sannur

A R A B I A N

Maghaghah

Al Bahnasa

EGYPT

Bani Mazar

Qulusana

Samalut

Al Minya

Abu Qurqas

Ar Rawdah

AS SAHRA ASH SHARQIYAH

5745

Mallawi

Dayrut

DESERT

Abnub

Manfalut

Asyut

Abu Tij

Al Badari

Tahta

Al Maraghah

Akhmim

Sawhaj

Al Manshah

Jirja

Al Balyana

Dishna

Qina

Naj' Hammadi

Thebes (Ruins)

Qus

Qift

Al Karnak

Armant

Al Uqsur (Luxor)

Isna

Idfu

Salwa Bahri

Kawm Umbu

Daraw

ASWAN HIGH DAM

Aswan

Lake Nasser (Buhayrat Nasir)

Longitude East of Greenwich

Scale 1:4 000 000

c

MEDITERRANEAN SEA

Port Said (Bur Sa'id)

Manzala

Qana el Suweis (Suez Canal)

Al Kab

Al Qantarah

Al Ballah

Al Firdan

Al Qantarah

SINAI

Nafishah

Ismailia (Al Isma'iliyah)

Timsah

EGYPT

PENINSULA

Fa'id

Al Buhayrah al Murrah al Kubra

Al Buhayrah al Murrah as Sughra

Junayfah

Ash Shallufah

Al Kubri

Suez (As Suways)

JABAL ATAQAH

Bur Ibrahim

Gulf of Suez

Scale 1:1 000 000

d

Lokala Drift

Melkrivier

Pietersburg

BOTSWANA

Hermanusdorings

Potgietersrus

STRYDPOORTBERGE

Silent Valley

NORTHERN TRANSVAAL

Vaalwater

Gladdeklipkop

Zebediela

Thabazimbi

WATERBERGE

Alma

Naboomspruit

Immerpan

6851

3216

Derdepoort

Rooiberg

Nylstroom

Crecy

Roedtan

Middelwit

Mabula

Tuinplaas

Northam

Warmbad

Settlers

Skilpadfontein

Marble Hall

Pilansberg

Radium

Groblersdal

Nietverdiend

Heystekrand

Jericho

Pienaars

Piendaarsrivier

Elo

Mabeskraal

Hammanskraal

Klipgat

Dennilton

Damval

Straatsdrif

Beestekraal

Enkeldoring

Verena

Groot Marico

Swartruggens

Rustenburg

Brits

PRETORIA-WITWATERSRAND-VEREENIGING

Loskopdam

Middelburg

Coligny

NORTH WEST

Koster

Marikana

Pretoria North

Cullinan

Bronkhorstspruit

Witbank

Derby

5681

Magaliesburg

Pretoria

Silverton

Kendal

Ogies

Hendrina

WITWATERSRAND

Boons

Kempton Park

Driefontein

Lichtenburg

Krugersdorp

Alexandra

Delmas

JOHANNESBURG

Benoni

Germiston

Springs

Nigel

Devon

Leslie

EASTERN

Carletonville

Westonaria

Bethal

Coligny

Fochville

Welverdiend

Daleside

Heidelberg

Trichardt

TRANSVAAL

Hauptrus

Vereeniging

Evaton

Meyerton

Klerksdorp

Vanderbijlpark

Greylingstad

Morgenzon

Hartbeesfontein

Sasolburg

Wolwehoek

Standerton

Orkney

SOUTH AFRICA

Patys

Villiers

Perdekop

Wilpoort

Vierfontein

Dover

Ascent

Leeudoringstad

Viljoenskroon

Koppies

Orangeville

Frankfort

Vrede

Memel

Bothaville

Heilbron

ORANGE

Westleigh

Edenville

Vredefort

Tweeling

Kroonstad

Petrus Steyn

4389

Lindley

Reitz

FREE

STATE

Wesselsbron

Odendaalsrus

Warden

Welkom

Steynsrus

Arlington

Hennenman

Cornelis

Virginia

Ventersburg

Harrismith

Bultfontein

Senekal

Bethlehem

4758

Theunissen

Paul Roux

Kestell

NATAL

Brandfort

Winburg

Rosendal

Fouriesburg

DRAKENSBERG

ROYAL NATAL NATL. PK.

Marquard

Ficksburg

Leribe

Bergville

Cathedral Pk.

Winterton

10 225

9856

Clocolan

Butha Buthe

Pitseng

Mt. aux Sources 10 822

Bloemfontein

LESOTHO

Longitude East of Greenwich

Scale 1:4 000 000

©RMcN

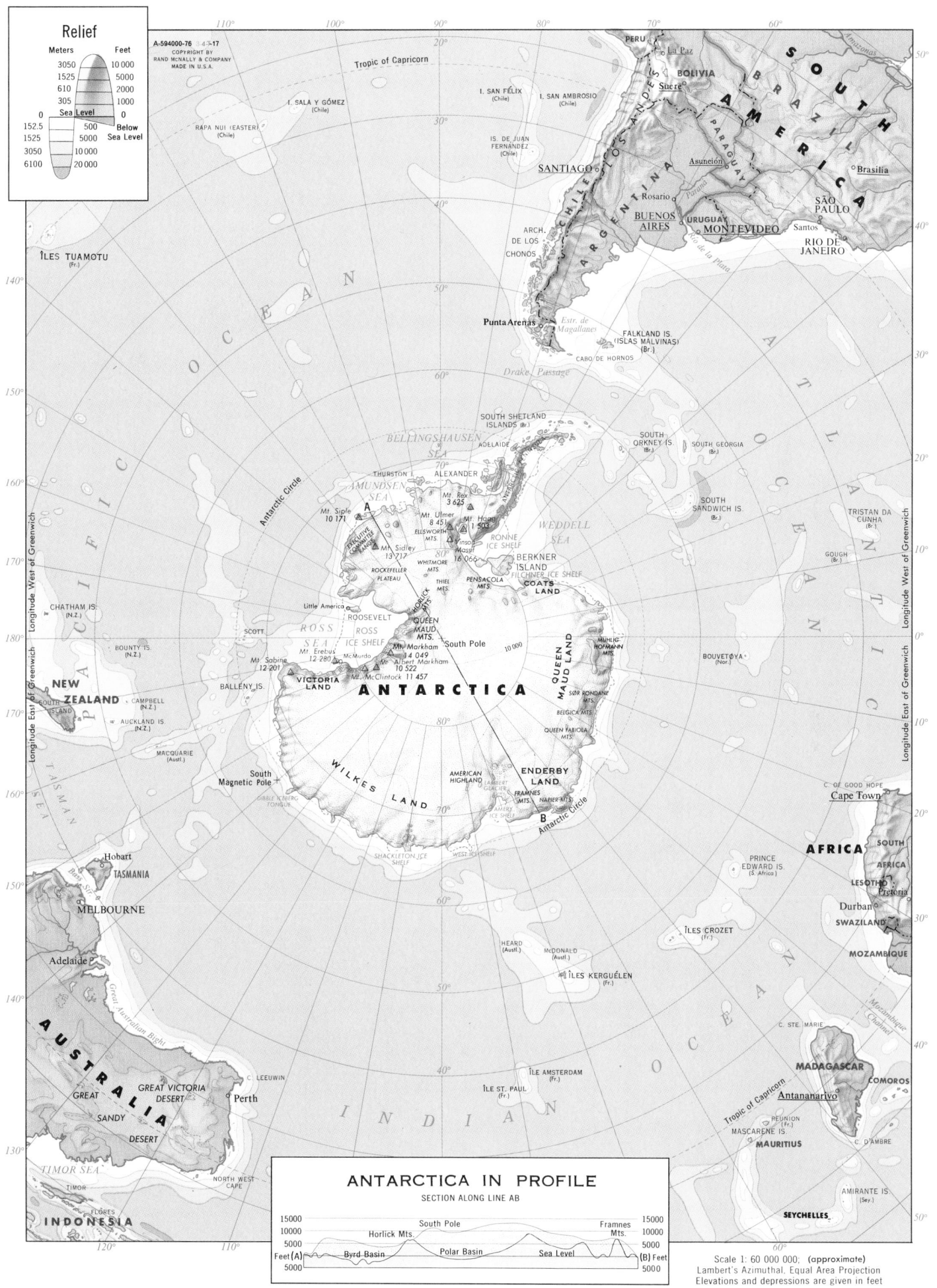

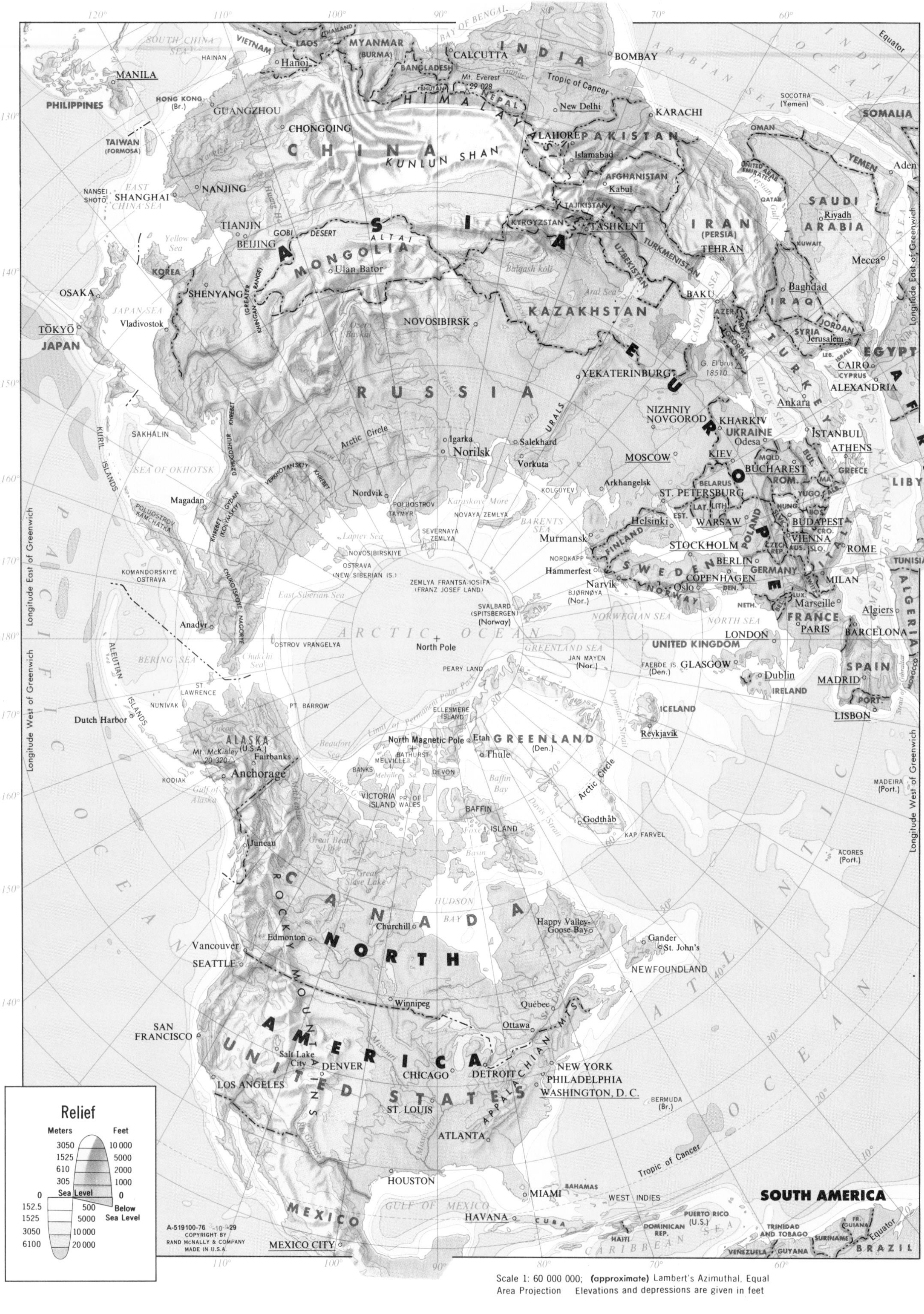

SOUTH CHINA SEA
VIETNAM
LAOS
MYANMAR (BURMA)
THAILAND
BAY OF BENGAL
INDIA
BOMBAY
ARABIAN SEA
SOCOTRA (Yemen)
SOMALIA
HAINAN
MANILA
PHILIPPINES
HONG KONG (Br.)
GUANGZHOU
CHONGQING
HANOI
CALCUTTA
BANGLADESH
Mt. Everest 29 028
NEPAL
BHUTAN
HIMALAYA
Ganges
New Delhi
Tropic of Cancer
KARACHI
LAHORE
PAKISTAN
Islamabad
OMAN
YEMEN
Aden
UNITED ARAB EMIRATES
QATAR
Gulf
TAIWAN (FORMOSA)
NANSEI SHOTŌ
SHANGHAI
EAST CHINA SEA
CHINA
KUNLUN SHAN
AFGHANISTAN
Kabul
TAJIKISTAN
KYRGYZSTAN
TASHKENT
UZBEKISTAN
TURKMENISTAN
IRAN (PERSIA)
TEHRĀN
SAUDI ARABIA
Riyadh
Mecca
KUWAIT
Longitude East of Greenwich
NANJING
TIANJIN
GOBI DESERT
ALTAI
MONGOLIA
Ulan Bator
GREATER KHINGAN RANGE
BEIJING
KOREA
OSAKA
SHENYANG
Vladivostok
Balqash köli
Aral Sea
KAZAKHSTAN
CASPIAN SEA
BAKU
AZER.
IRAQ
Baghdad
JORDAN
SYRIA
Jerusalem
LEB.
EGYPT
CAIRO
ALEXANDRIA
CYPRUS
TURKEY
Ankara
RED SEA
AFRICA
TŌKYŌ
JAPAN
JAPAN SEA
YEKATERINBURG
G. El'brus 18510
GEORGIA
BLACK SEA
ISTANBUL
ATHENS
GREECE
LIBYA
RUSSIA
Yenisey
Ob
URALS
NIZHNIY NOVGOROD
KHARKIV
UKRAINE
Odesa
BUCHAREST
ROM.
BULG.
MED.
SAKHALIN
KURIL ISLANDS
SEA OF OKHOTSK
Lake Baykal
Angara
Lena
Igarka
Salekhard
Norilsk
Vorkuta
MOSCOW
KIEV
BELARUS
LAT. LITH.
EST.
YUGO.
MILAN
ALGERIA
TUNISIA
Magadan
POLUOSTROV KAMCHATKA
KOMANDORSKIYE OSTROVA
KHREBET DZHUGDZHUR
VERKHOYANSKIY KHREBET
KOLYMA
Nordvik
POLUOSTROV TAYMYR
NOVAYA ZEMLYA
Arkhangelsk
KOLGUYEV
BARENTS SEA
Murmansk
ST. PETERSBURG
WARSAW
POLAND
FINLAND
Helsinki
CZECH REP.
HUNG.
VIENNA
AUS.
SLO.
CRO.
BUDAPEST
ROME
Anadyr
OSTROV VRANGELYA
Chukchi Sea
East Siberian Sea
Laptev Sea
Karskoye More
SEVERNAYA ZEMLYA
NOVOSIBIRSKIYE OSTROVA (NEW SIBERIAN IS.)
ZEMLYA FRANTSA-IOSIFA (FRANZ JOSEF LAND)
SVALBARD (SPITSBERGEN) (Norway)
Narvik
Hammerfest
NORDKAPP
BJØRNØYA (Nor.)
NORWEGIAN SEA
STOCKHOLM
SWEDEN
NORWAY
Oslo
COPENHAGEN
DEN.
BERLIN
GERMANY
NORTH SEA
NETH.
BELG.
LUX.
Marseille
FRANCE
PARIS
Algiers
BARCELONA
SPAIN
MADRID
PORT.
LISBON
MOROCCO
Strait of Gibraltar
ARCTIC OCEAN
North Pole
North Magnetic Pole
Limit of Permanent Polar Pack
GREENLAND SEA
JAN MAYEN (Nor.)
FAERØE IS. (Den.)
GLASGOW
UNITED KINGDOM
LONDON
Dublin
IRELAND
ICELAND
Reykjavík
MADEIRA (Port.)
Denmark Strait
Etah
Thule
GREENLAND (Den.)
BATHURST
MELVILLE
DEVON
ELLESMERE ISLAND
PEARY LAND
BERING SEA
ALEUTIAN ISLANDS
Dutch Harbor
ST. LAWRENCE
NUNIVAK
KODIAK
Gulf of Alaska
ALASKA (U.S.A.)
Mt. McKinley 20 320
Fairbanks
Anchorage
Yukon
PT. BARROW
Beaufort Sea
BANKS
VICTORIA ISLAND
PR. OF WALES
Amundsen
MELVILLE PEN.
Baffin Bay
BAFFIN ISLAND
Davis Strait
Godthåb
KAP FARVEL
ACORES (Port.)
Longitude West of Greenwich
PACIFIC OCEAN
Juneau
Vancouver
SEATTLE
ROCKY MOUNTAINS
CANADA
NORTH AMERICA
Great Bear Lake
Great Slave Lake
HUDSON BAY
Churchill
Edmonton
Happy Valley-Goose Bay
Gander
St. John's
NEWFOUNDLAND
ATLANTIC OCEAN
SAN FRANCISCO
Salt Lake City
DENVER
Winnipeg
Missouri
CHICAGO
ST. LOUIS
DETROIT
Québec
Ottawa
St. Lawrence
APPALACHIAN MTS.
NEW YORK
PHILADELPHIA
WASHINGTON, D.C.
BERMUDA (Br.)
LOS ANGELES
UNITED STATES
ATLANTA
HOUSTON
MIAMI
BAHAMAS
WEST INDIES
SOUTH AMERICA
MEXICO
GULF OF MEXICO
HAVANA
CUBA
HAITI
DOMINICAN REP.
PUERTO RICO (U.S.)
CARIBBEAN SEA
TRINIDAD AND TOBAGO
FR. GUIANA
VENEZUELA
GUYANA
SURINAME
BRAZIL
MEXICO CITY
Tropic of Cancer
Arctic Circle
Equator

Relief
Meters		Feet
3050		10 000
1525		5000
610		2000
305		1000
152.5	Sea Level	500
1525		5000
3050		10 000
6100	Below Sea Level	20 000

A-519100-76 -10-29
COPYRIGHT BY
RAND McNALLY & COMPANY
MADE IN U.S.A.

Scale 1: 60 000 000; (approximate) Lambert's Azimuthal, Equal Area Projection Elevations and depressions are given in feet

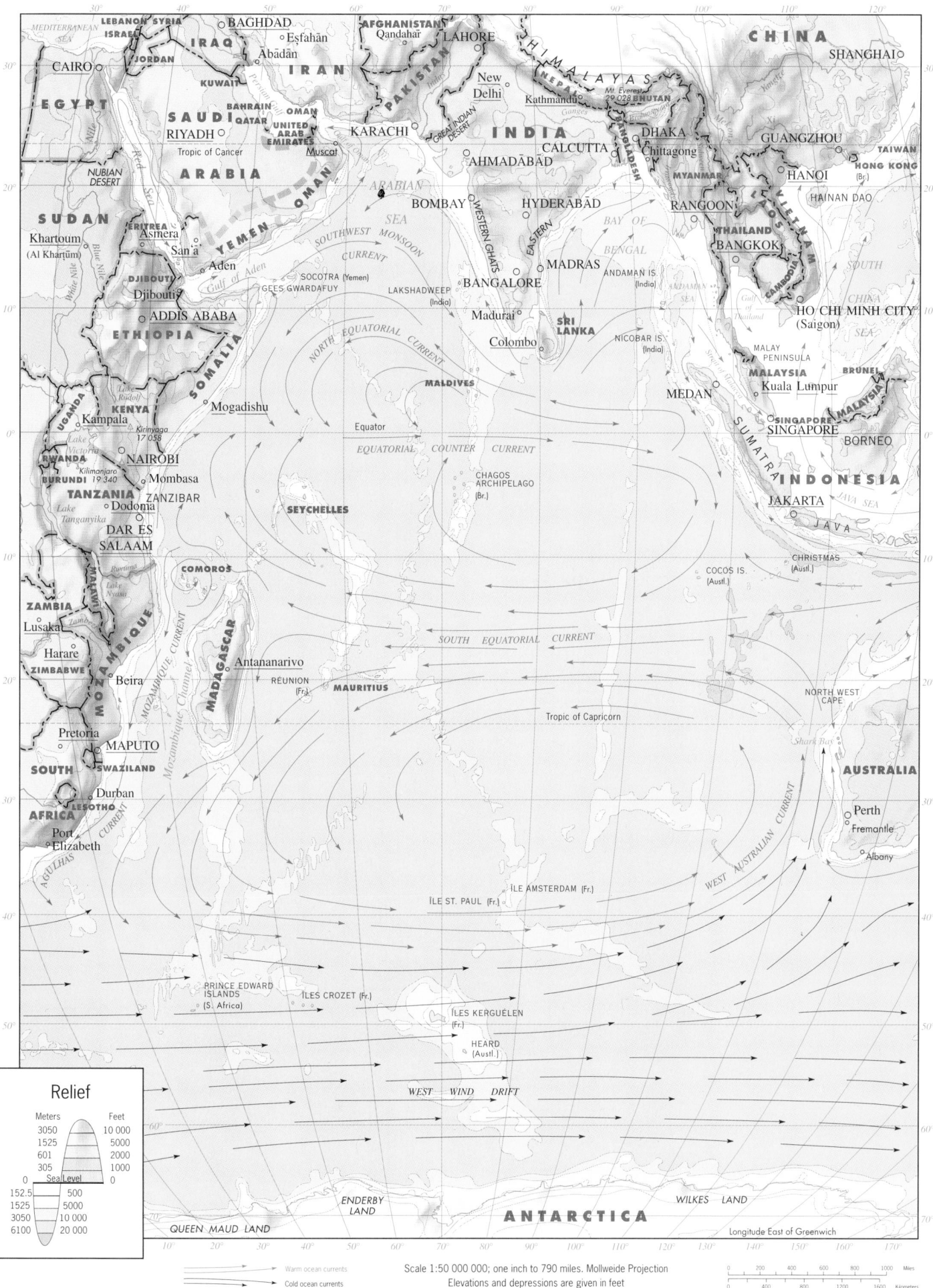

MEDITERRANEAN SEA
LEBANON SYRIA
ISRAEL
JORDAN
IRAQ
BAGHDAD
Esfahān
Abādān
IRAN
AFGHANISTAN
Qandahār
LAHORE
CHINA
SHANGHAI
CAIRO
KUWAIT
BAHRAIN
QATAR
OMAN
UNITED
ARAB
EMIRATES
PAKISTAN
HIMALAYAS
Mt. Everest 29,028
NEPAL
BHUTAN
Kathmandu
GUANGZHOU
TAIWAN
HONG KONG
(Br.)
EGYPT
SAUDI
RIYADH
ARABIA
Tropic of Cancer
Muscat
New Delhi
KARACHI
GREAT INDIAN DESERT
INDIA
CALCUTTA
BANGLADESH
DHAKA
Chittagong
HANOI
HAINAN DAO
SUDAN
Khartoum
(Al Khartūm)
NUBIAN DESERT
Red Sea
ERITREA
Asmera
San'a
YEMEN
OMAN
Aden
Gulf of Aden
ARABIAN SEA
AHMADĀBĀD
BOMBAY
WESTERN GHATS
HYDERABAD
EASTERN GHATS
MADRAS
BAY OF BENGAL
ANDAMAN IS.
(India)
MYANMAR
RANGOON
THAILAND
BANGKOK
LAOS
VIETNAM
CAMBODIA
SOUTH CHINA SEA
DJIBOUTI
Djibouti
SOCOTRA (Yemen)
GEES GWARDAFUY
SOUTHWEST MONSOON CURRENT
LAKSHADWEEP
(India)
BANGALORE
Madurai
SRI LANKA
Colombo
NICOBAR IS.
(India)
ANDAMAN SEA
Gulf of Thailand
HO CHI MINH CITY
(Saigon)
ADDIS ABABA
ETHIOPIA
SOMALIA
NORTH EQUATORIAL CURRENT
MALDIVES
MALAY PENINSULA
MALAYSIA
Kuala Lumpur
BRUNEI
MALAYSIA
UGANDA
Kampala
KENYA
Kirinyaga 17,058
NAIROBI
Mombasa
Lake Rudolf
Lake Victoria
Kilimanjaro 19,340
Mogadishu
Equator
EQUATORIAL COUNTER CURRENT
CHAGOS ARCHIPELAGO
(Br.)
MEDAN
SINGAPORE
SINGAPORE
BORNEO
INDONESIA
RWANDA
BURUNDI
TANZANIA
Dodoma
ZANZIBAR
DAR ES SALAAM
Lake Tanganyika
SEYCHELLES
JAKARTA
JAVA
JAVA SEA
MALAWI
Lake Nyasa
COMOROS
MADAGASCAR
Ruvuma
ZAMBIA
Lusaka
Zambezi
MOZAMBIQUE
MOZAMBIQUE CURRENT
MOZAMBIQUE CHANNEL
Antananarivo
RÉUNION
(Fr.)
MAURITIUS
SOUTH EQUATORIAL CURRENT
COCOS IS.
(Austl.)
CHRISTMAS
(Austl.)
NORTH WEST CAPE
Harare
ZIMBABWE
Beira
Tropic of Capricorn
Shark Bay
SOUTH AFRICA
Pretoria
MAPUTO
SWAZILAND
LESOTHO
Durban
Port Elizabeth
AGULHAS CURRENT
AUSTRALIA
Perth
Fremantle
Albany
WEST AUSTRALIAN CURRENT
ÎLE AMSTERDAM (Fr.)
ÎLE ST. PAUL (Fr.)
PRINCE EDWARD ISLANDS
(S. Africa)
ÎLES CROZET (Fr.)
ÎLES KERGUÉLEN
(Fr.)
HEARD
(Austl.)
WEST WIND DRIFT
ENDERBY LAND
QUEEN MAUD LAND
WILKES LAND
ANTARCTICA
Longitude East of Greenwich

Relief

Meters	Feet
3050	10 000
1525	5000
601	2000
305	1000
0	Sea Level 0
152.5	500
1525	5000
3050	10 000
6100	20 000

Warm ocean currents
Cold ocean currents

Scale 1:50 000 000; one inch to 790 miles. Mollweide Projection
Elevations and depressions are given in feet

Miles 0 200 400 600 800 1000
Kilometers 0 400 800 1200 1600

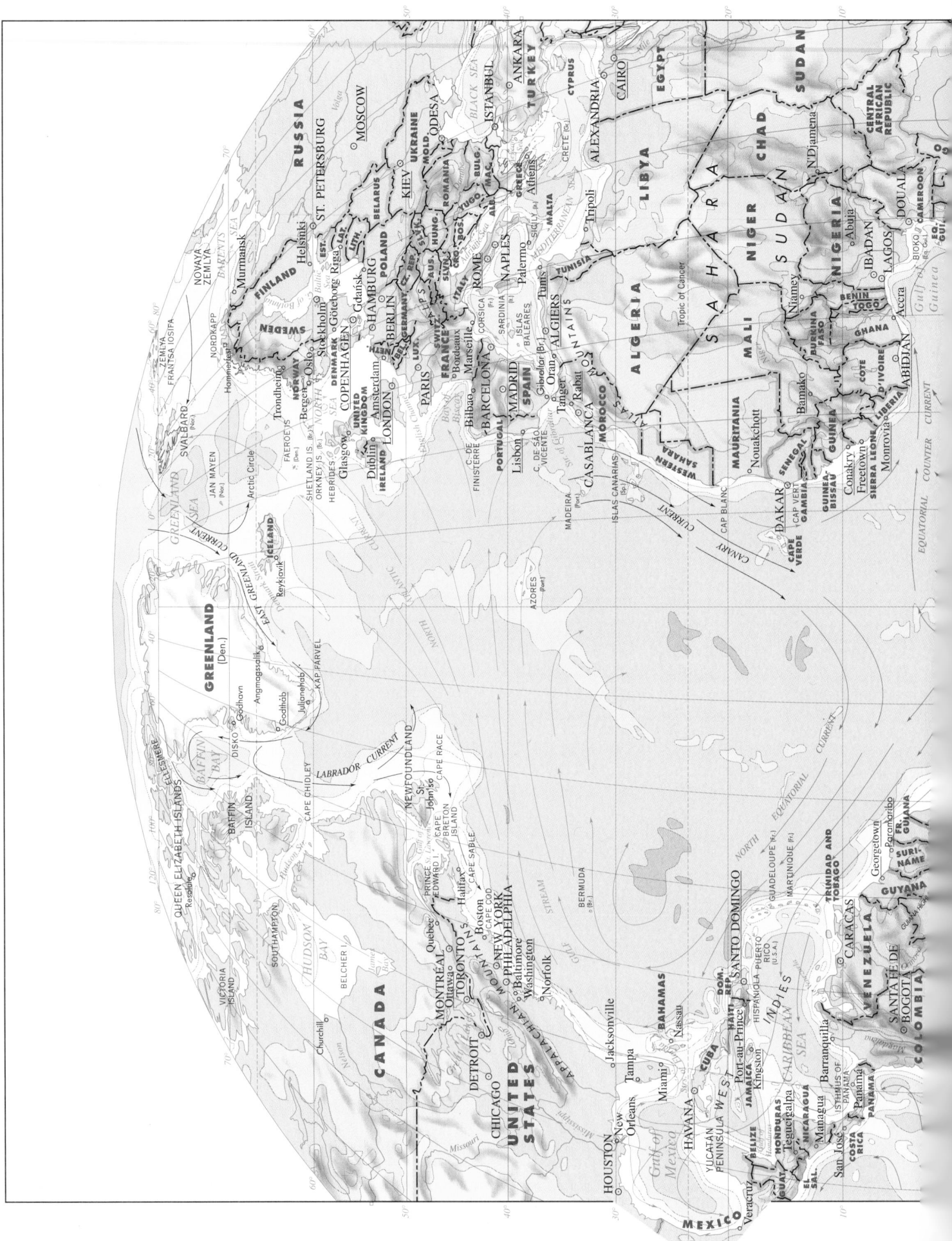

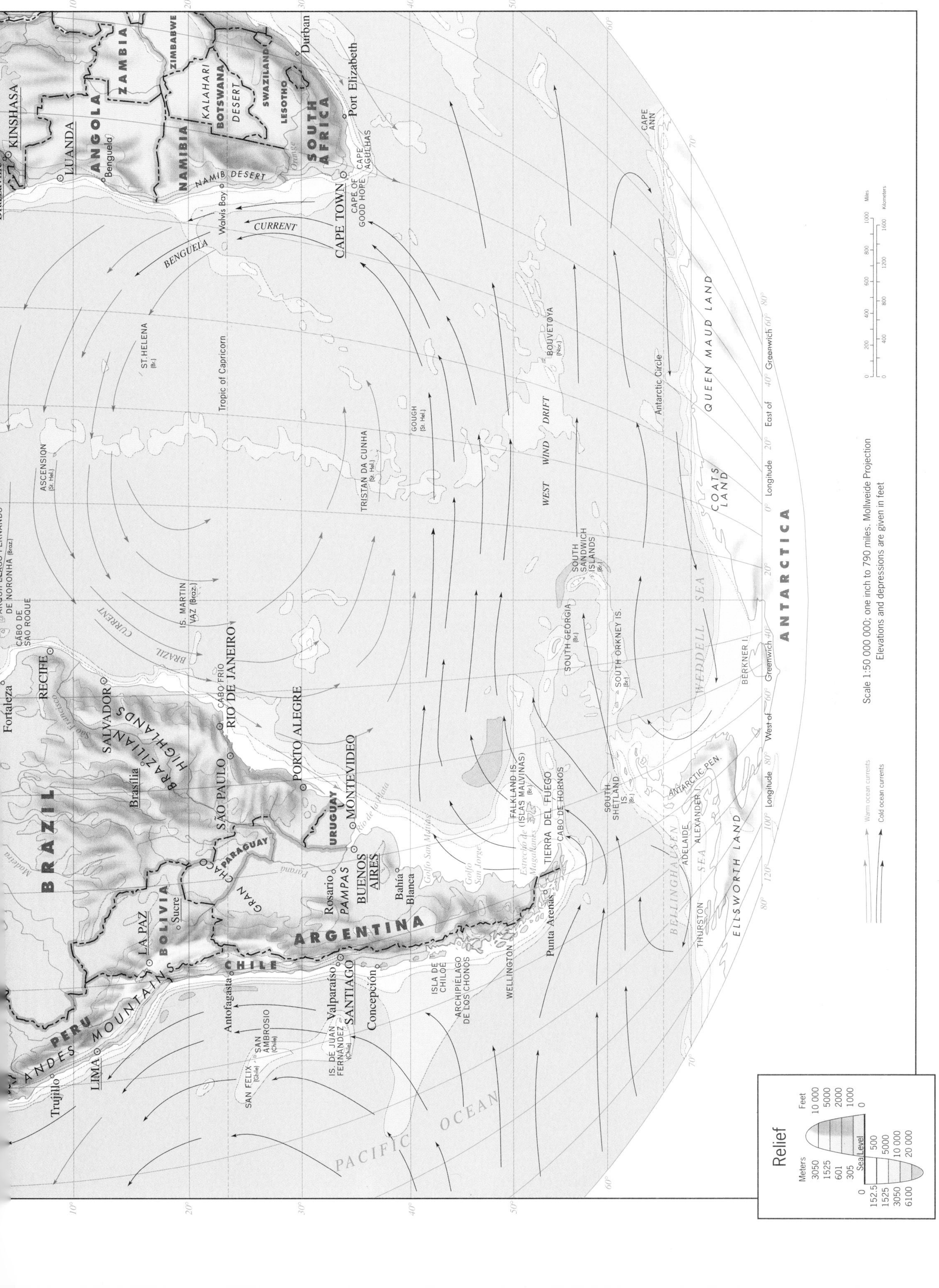

ZAIRE

KINSHASA

Brazzaville

ANGOLA

LUANDA

Benguela

ZAMBIA

ZIMBABWE

KALAHARI DESERT

BOTSWANA

NAMIBIA

SWAZILAND

LESOTHO

SOUTH AFRICA

Durban

Port Elizabeth

CAPE TOWN

CAPE OF GOOD HOPE

CAPE AGULHAS

Walvis Bay

NAMIB DESERT

Orange

CAPE ANN

QUEEN MAUD LAND

COATS LAND

CURRENT

BENGUELA

ST. HELENA
(Br.)

Tropic of Capricorn

BOUVETØYA
(Nor.)

Antarctic Circle

East of   40° Greenwich   60°   80°

20°   0°   Longitude   20°

ASCENSION
(St. Hel.)

GOUGH
(St. Hel.)

WEST   WIND   DRIFT

WEDDELL   SEA

ANTARCTICA

TRISTAN DA CUNHA
(St. Hel.)

ARQUIPELAGO FERNANDO DE NORONHA (Braz.)

CABO DE SAO ROQUE

Fortaleza

RECIFE

IS. MARTIN VAZ (Braz.)

SOUTH SANDWICH ISLANDS
(Br.)

SOUTH GEORGIA
(Br.)

SOUTH ORKNEY IS.
(Br.)

BERKNER I.

West of   60°   Greenwich

BRAZIL

SALVADOR

BRAZILIAN HIGHLANDS

Brasília

SÃO PAULO

RIO DE JANEIRO

CABO FRIO

BRAZIL   CURRENT

PORTO ALEGRE

São Francisco

Madeira

PERU

LIMA

Trujillo

BOLIVIA

LA PAZ

Sucre

PARAGUAY

GRAN CHACO

Paraná

URUGUAY

MONTEVIDEO

Rio de la Plata

BUENOS AIRES

Rosario

PAMPAS

Bahía Blanca

ARGENTINA

Golfo San Matías

Golfo San Jorge

Estrecho de Magallanes

FALKLAND IS.
(ISLAS MALVINAS)
(Br.)

TIERRA DEL FUEGO

CABO DE HORNOS

Punta Arenas

SOUTH SHETLAND IS.
(Br.)

ANTARCTIC PEN.

ADELAIDE

Alexander I.

BELLINGHAUSEN   SEA

THURSTON

ELLSWORTH LAND

100°   120°

CHILE

Antofagasta

SAN AMBROSIO
(Chile)

SAN FÉLIX
(Chile)

IS. DE JUAN FERNÁNDEZ
(Chile)

Valparaíso

SANTIAGO

Concepción

ISLA DE CHILOÉ

ARCHIPIELAGO DE LOS CHONOS

WELLINGTON

ANDES   MOUNTAINS

PACIFIC   OCEAN

Scale 1:50 000 000; one inch to 790 miles. Mollweide Projection

Elevations and depressions are given in feet

Miles
Kilometers

0   200   400   600   800   1000

0   400   800   1200   1600

Warm ocean currents

Cold ocean currents

Relief

Meters		Feet
3050		10 000
1525		5000
601		2000
305		1000
Sea Level		Sea Level
152.5		500
1525		5000
3050		10 000
6100		20 000

10°   20°   30°   40°   50°

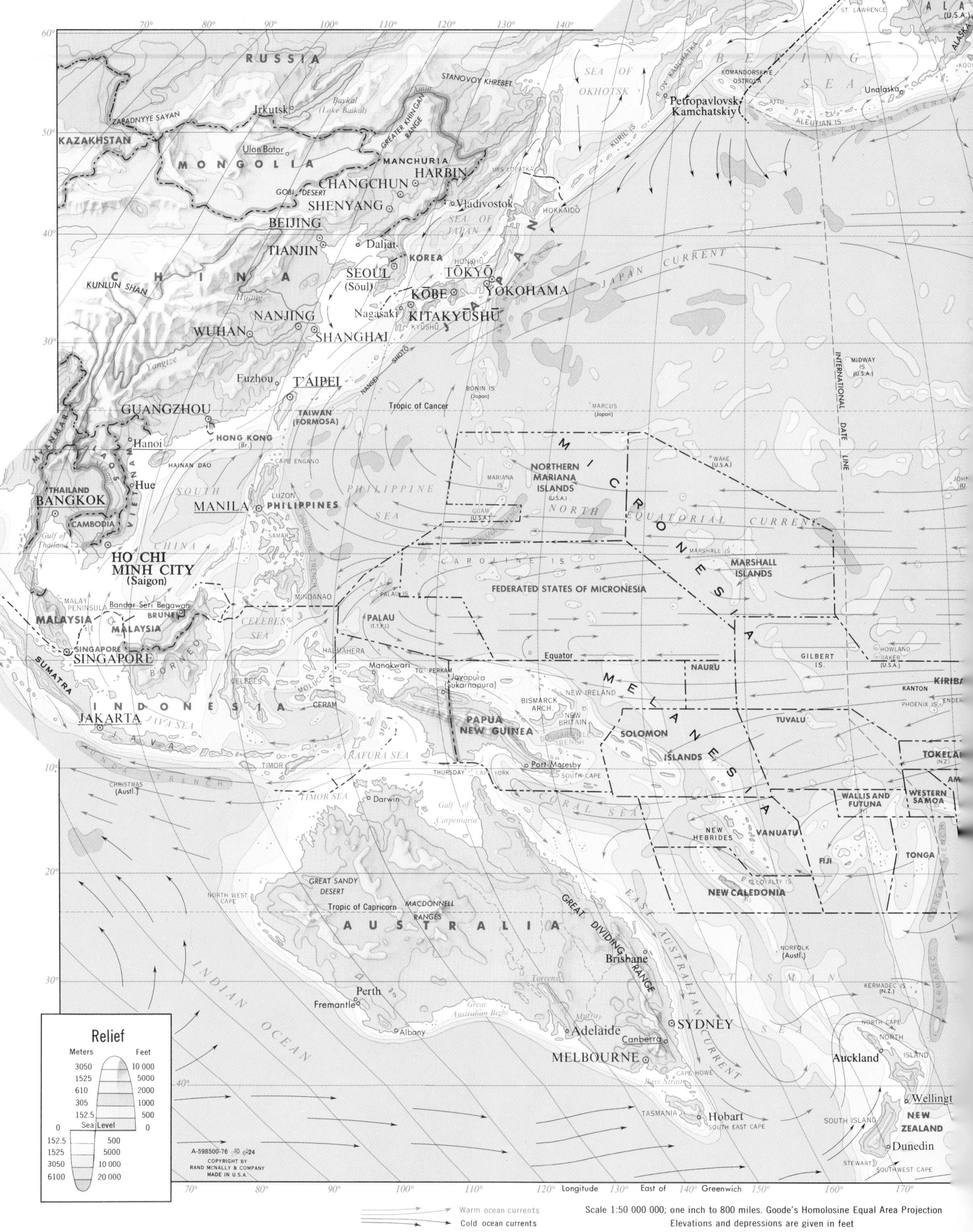

Relief

Meters	Feet
3050	10 000
1525	5000
610	2000
305	1000
152.5	500
0	Sea Level 0
152.5	500
1525	5000
3050	10 000
6100	20 000

A-598500-76 40 p-24
COPYRIGHT BY
RAND McNALLY & COMPANY
MADE IN U.S.A.

Longitude East of Greenwich

Warm ocean currents
Cold ocean currents

Scale 1:50 000 000; one inch to 800 miles. Goode's Homolosine Equal Area Projection
Elevations and depressions are given in feet

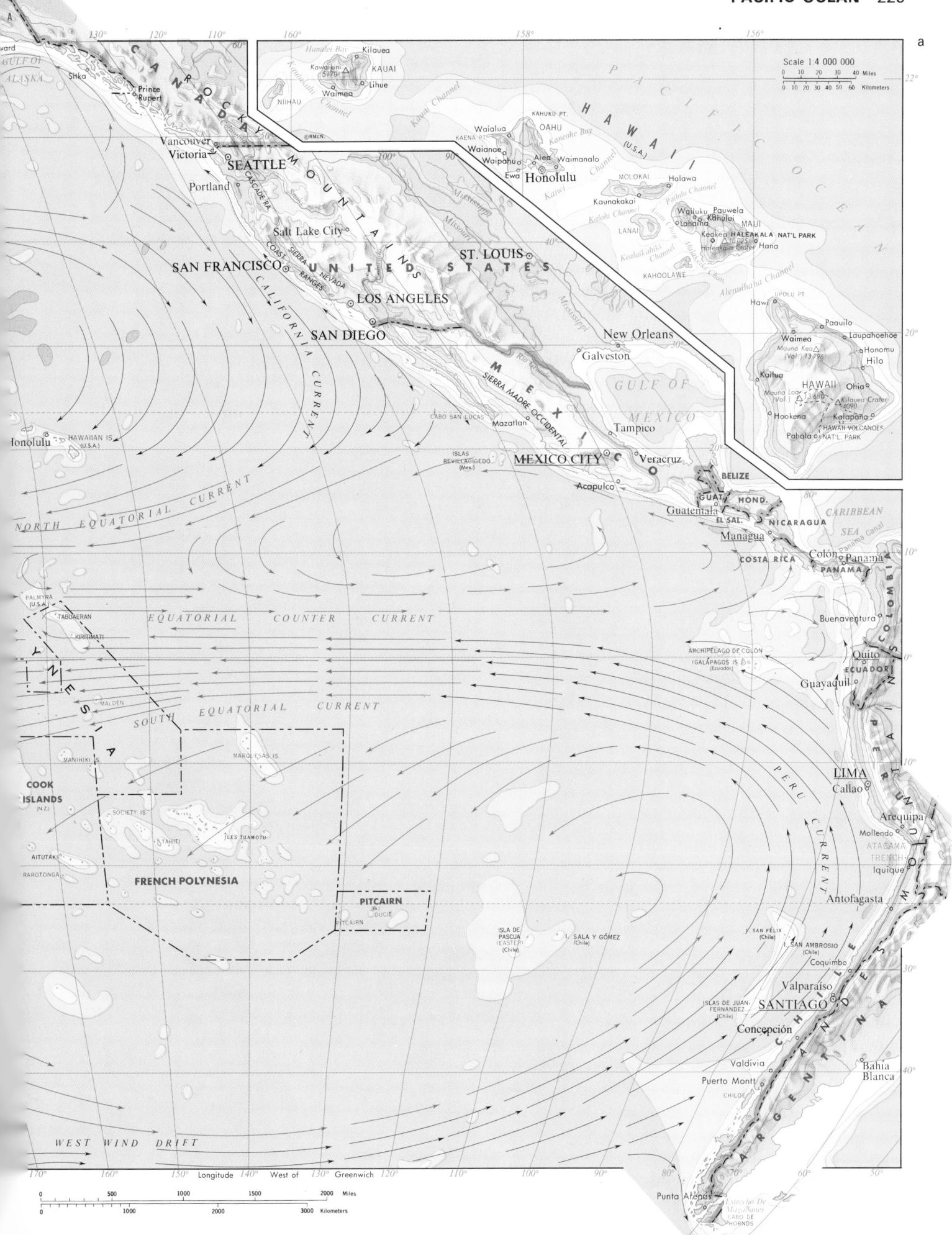

a

Scale 1:4 000 000
0   10   20   30   40 Miles
0 10 20 30 40 50   60 Kilometers

PACIFIC

OCEAN

HAWAII
(U.S.A.)

Handlei Bay   Kilauea
Kawaikini 5170△   KAUAI
Lihue
NIIHAU   Waimea   KAHUKU PT.
Kaunakahi Channel   OAHU
©RMCN.   Waialua   KAENA PT.   Kaneohe Bay
Waianae   Waipahu   Alea   Waimanalo
Ewa   Honolulu   MOLOKAI
Kaunakakai   Halawa
Paibio Channel
Kaloni Channel   Wailuku   Pauwela
LANAI   Lahaina   Kohului   MAUI
Kealaikahiki Channel   Keokea HALEAKALA NAT'L PARK
△4090 Haleakala Crater   Hana
KAHOOLAWE   Alenuihaha Channel
UPOLU PT.
Hawi   Paauilo
Waimea   Laupahoehoe
Mauna Kea△   Honomu
(Vol.) 13 796   Hilo
Kailua   HAWAII   Ohia
Mauna Loa   Kilauea Crater
(Vol.) △13 680   4090
Hookena   HAWAII VOLCANOES
Pahala   NAT'L PARK

CANADA

GULF OF ALASKA

Sitka

Prince Rupert

Vancouver
Victoria
SEATTLE
Portland

CASCADE RA.

R O C K Y   M O U N T A I N S

Salt Lake City

SIERRA NEVADA

COAST RANGES

SAN FRANCISCO

CALIFORNIA CURRENT

LOS ANGELES

SAN DIEGO

U N I T E D   S T A T E S

ST. LOUIS

Missouri

Mississippi

Rio Grande

SIERRA MADRE OCCIDENTAL

M E X I C O

CABO SAN LUCAS
Mazatlan

ISLAS REVILLAGIGEDO
(Mex.)

MEXICO CITY

Acapulco

New Orleans
Galveston

GULF OF MEXICO

Tampico

Veracruz

BELIZE
GUAT.   HOND.
Guatemala
EL SAL.   NICARAGUA
Managua
COSTA RICA   Colón   Panama
PANAMA   Panama Canal

CARIBBEAN SEA

Honolulu
HAWAIIAN IS.
(U.S.A.)

N O R T H   E Q U A T O R I A L   C U R R E N T

PALMYRA
(U.S.A.)
TABUAERAN

KIRITIMATI

E Q U A T O R I A L   C O U N T E R   C U R R E N T

P O L Y N E S I A

MALDEN

S O U T H   E Q U A T O R I A L   C U R R E N T

MANIHIKI IS.

COOK ISLANDS
(N.Z.)

SOCIETY IS.

MARQUESAS IS.

ÎLES TUAMOTU

TAHITI

AITUTAKI

RAROTONGA

FRENCH POLYNESIA

PITCAIRN
(Br.)   DUCIE
PITCAIRN

ISLA DE PASCUA
(EASTER)
(Chile)

I. SALA Y GÓMEZ
(Chile)

SAN FÉLIX
(Chile)
I. SAN AMBROSIO
(Chile)

ARCHIPÉLAGO DE COLÓN
(GALÁPAGOS IS.)
(Ecuador)

Buenaventura

COLOMBIA

Quito
ECUADOR
Guayaquil

LIMA
Callao

Arequipa
Mollendo
ATACAMA TRENCH
Iquique

PERU CURRENT

Antofagasta

Coquimbo

Valparaíso

ISLAS DE JUAN FERNÁNDEZ
(Chile)
SANTIAGO

Concepción

Valdivia

Puerto Montt

CHILOE

C H I L E

A N D E S

ARGENTINA

Bahía Blanca

W E S T   W I N D   D R I F T

Punta Arenas
Estrecho De Magallanes
CABO DE HORNOS

Longitude   West of   Greenwich

170° 160° 150° 140° 130° 120° 110° 100° 90° 80° 70° 60° 50°

0   500   1000   1500   2000 Miles
0   1000   2000   3000 Kilometers

MAJOR CITIES MAPS

This section consists of 62 maps of the world's most populous metropolitan areas. In order to make comparison easier, all the metropolitan areas are shown at the same scale, 1:300,000.

Detailed urban maps are an important reference requirement for a world atlas. The names of many large settlements, towns, suburbs, and neighborhoods can be located on these large-scale maps. From a thematic standpoint the maps show generalized land-use patterns. Included were the total urban extent, major industrial areas, parks, public land, wooded areas, airports, shopping centers, streets, and railroads. A special effort was made to portray the various metropolitan areas in a manner as standard and comparable as possible. (For the symbols used, see the legend below.)

Notable differences occur in the forms of cities. In most of North America these forms were conditioned by a rectangular pattern of streets; land-use zones (residential, commercial, industrial) are well defined. The basic structure of most European cities is noticeably different and more complex; street patterns are irregular and zones are less well defined. In Asia, Africa, and South America the form tends to be even more irregular and complex. Widespread dispersion of craft and trade activities has lessened zonation, there may be cities with no identifiable city centers, and sometimes there may be dual centers (old and modern). Higher population densities result in more limited, compact urban places in these areas of the world.

Inhabited Localities

The symbol represents the number of inhabitants within the locality

- ·   0—10,000
- ○   10,000—25,000
- ⊙   25,000—100,000
- ⊡   100,000—250,000
- ▣   250,000—1,000,000
- ■   >1,000,000

The size of type indicates the relative economic and political importance of the locality

Écommoy	
Trouville	**St.-Denis**
Lisieux	**PARIS**

Hollywood	Section of a City,
Westminster	Neighborhood
Northland ■	
Center	Major Shopping Center

    Urban Area (area of continuous industrial, commercial, and residential development)

    Major Industrial Area

    Wooded Area

Political Boundaries

International (First-order political unit)

— · — · — Demarcated, Undemarcated, and Administrative

— — — — Demarcation Line

Internal

    State, Province, etc. (Second-order political unit)

    County, Oblast, etc. (Third-order political unit)

    Okrug, Kreis, etc. (Fourth-order political unit)

- - - - - - - City or Municipality (may appear in combination with another boundary symbol)

Capitals of Political Units

BUDAPEST	Independent Nation
Recife	State, Province, etc.
White Plains	County, Oblast, etc.
Iserlohn	Okrug, Kreis, etc.

Transportation

Road

PASSAIC EXPWY. (I-80)	Primary
BERLINER RING	Secondary
	Tertiary

Railway

CANADIAN NATIONAL	Primary
	Secondary
	Rapid Transit

Airport

    LONDON (HEATHROW) AIRPORT

Rail or Air Terminal

■ SÜD BAHNHOF

REICHS-BRÜCKE	Bridge
	Tunnel
GREAT ST. BERNARD TUNNEL	
Houston Ship Channel	Shipping Channel
Canal du Midi	Navigable Canal
TO MALMÖ	Ferry

Hydrographic Features

	Shoreline
	Undefined or Fluctuating Shoreline
Amur	River, Stream
	Intermittent Stream
SALTO ÁNGEL	Rapids, Falls
Canal du Midi	Navigable Canal
	Irrigation or Drainage Canal
Los Angeles Aqueduct	Aqueduct
	Pier, Breakwater
GREAT BARRIER REEF	Reef
L. Victoria	Lake, Reservoir
	Intermittent Lake
The Everglades	Swamp

Miscellaneous Cultural Features

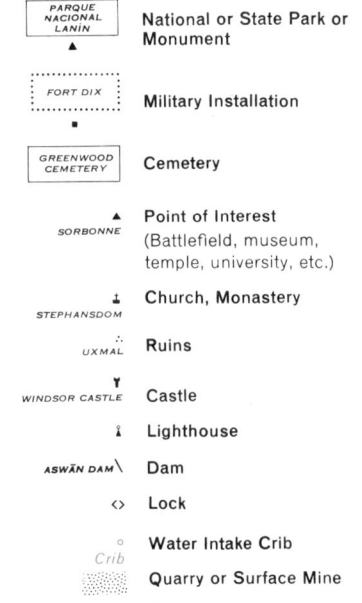

PARQUE NACIONAL LANÍN ▲	National or State Park or Monument
FORT DIX ▪	Military Installation
GREENWOOD CEMETERY	Cemetery
▲ SORBONNE	Point of Interest (Battlefield, museum, temple, university, etc.)
⚓ STEPHANSDOM	Church, Monastery
∴ UXMAL	Ruins
⚲ WINDSOR CASTLE	Castle
⚑	Lighthouse
ASWĀN DAM \	Dam
<>	Lock
○ Crib	Water Intake Crib
▨	Quarry or Surface Mine
⊶	Subsurface Mine

Topographic Features

| Mt. Kenya 5199 △ | Elevation Above Sea Level |

Elevations are given in meters

⋆	Rock
A N D E S KUNLUNSHANMAI	Mountain Range, Plateau, Valley, etc.
BAFFIN ISLAND	Island
POLUOSTROV KAMČATKA *CABO DE HORNOS*	Peninsula, Cape, Point, etc.

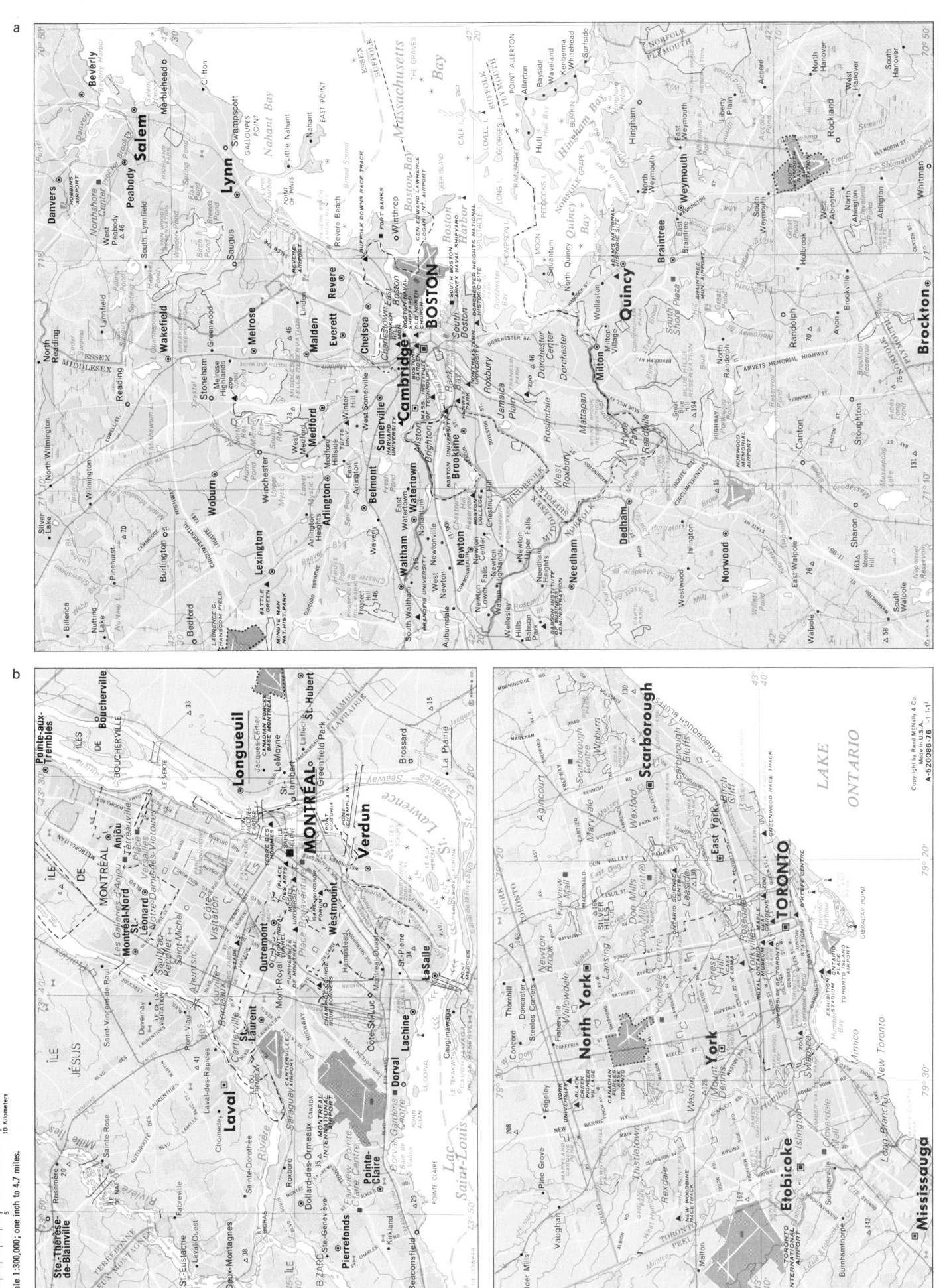

a

b

c

Scale 1:300,000; one inch to 4.7 miles.

10 Miles

10 Kilometers

ATLANTIC OCEAN

LONG ISLAND

Long Island Sound

CONN.
NEW YORK

NEW JERSEY

STATEN ISLAND

NEW YORK

Jersey City

Newark

Paterson

Passaic

Paramus

Hackensack

Yonkers

Mount Vernon

New Rochelle

Glen Cove

Hempstead

Plainview

Hicksville

Massapequa

Merrick

East Meadow

Levittown

Bethpage

Garden City

New Hyde Park

Franklin Square

West Hempstead

Valley Stream

Lynbrook

Rockville Centre

Baldwin

Freeport

Oceanside

Long Beach

Elmont

Elizabeth

Rahway

Linden

Wayne

Ridgewood

Fair Lawn

Clifton

Nutley

Belleville

Kearny

Bloomfield

Montclair

West Orange

East Orange

Orange

Union

Irvington

Hudson River

Passaic River

Hackensack River

Copyright by Rand McNally & Co.
Made in U.S.A.
A-520060-76

Scale 1:300,000; one inch to 4.7 miles.

10 Miles

10 Kilometers

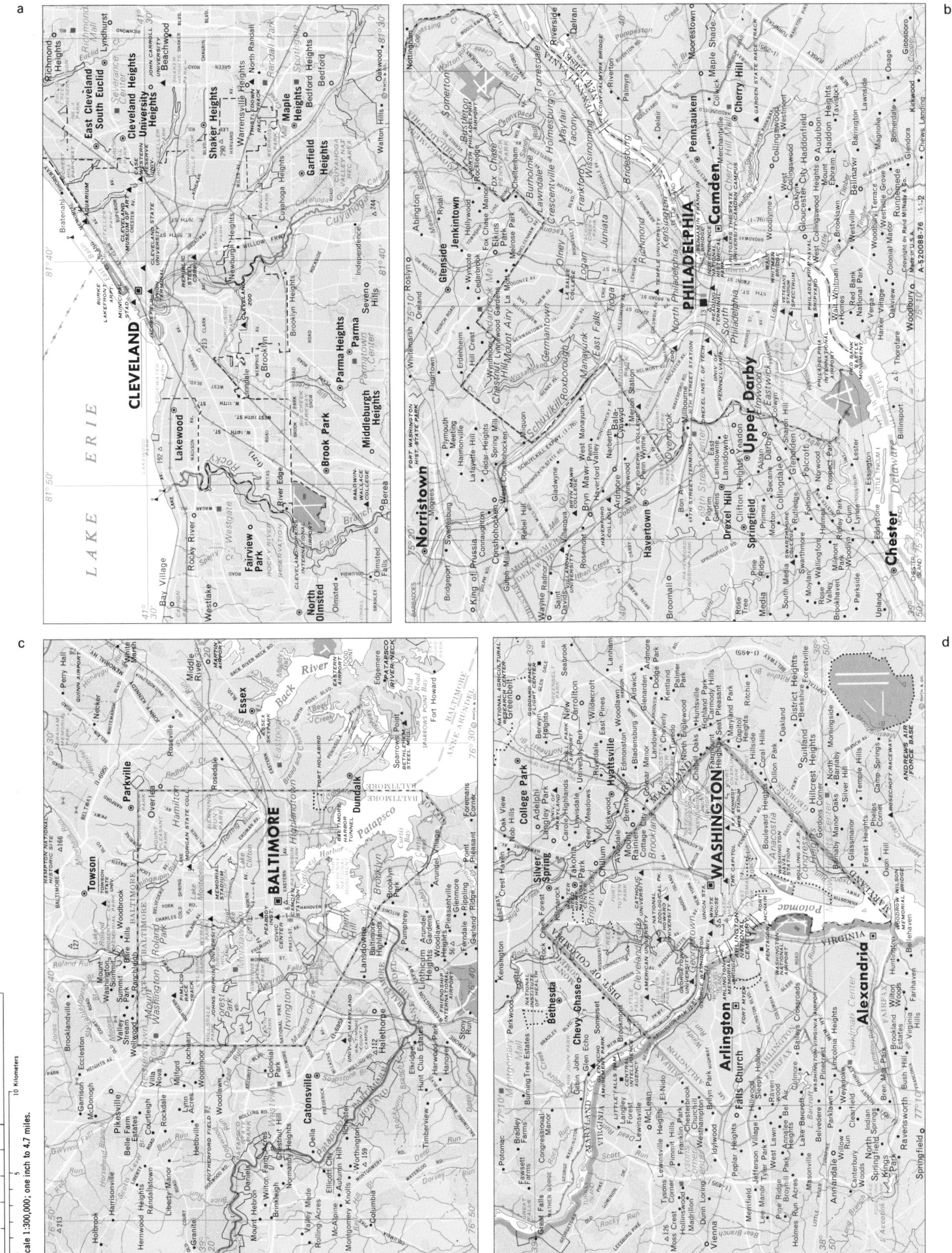

a

b

c

d

Scale 1:300,000; one inch to 4.7 miles.

10 Miles

10 Kilometers

a

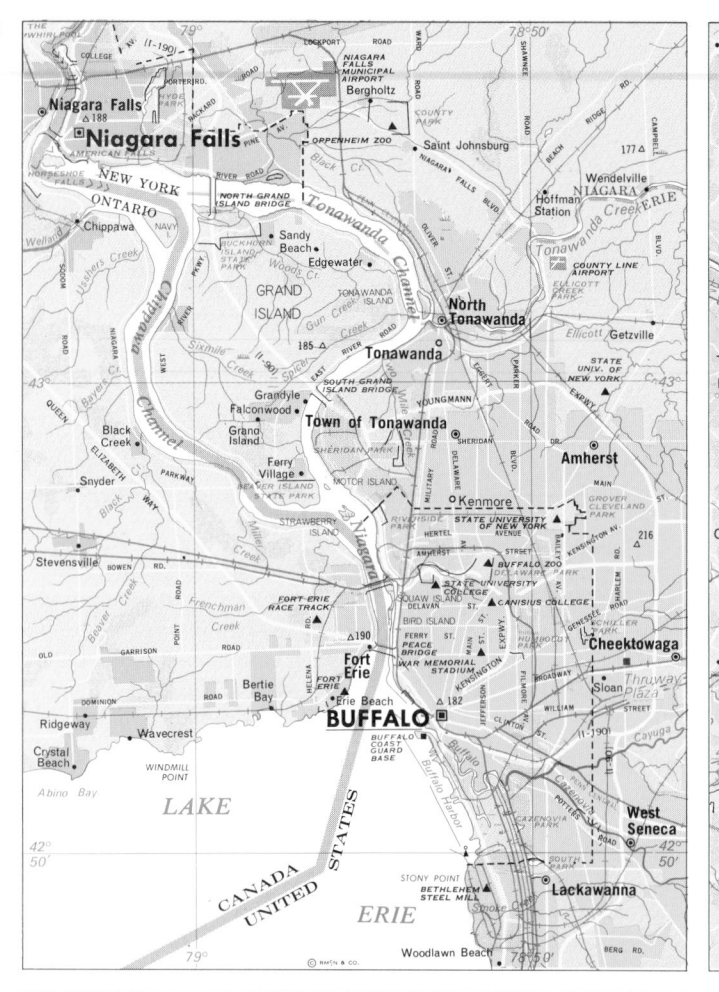

b

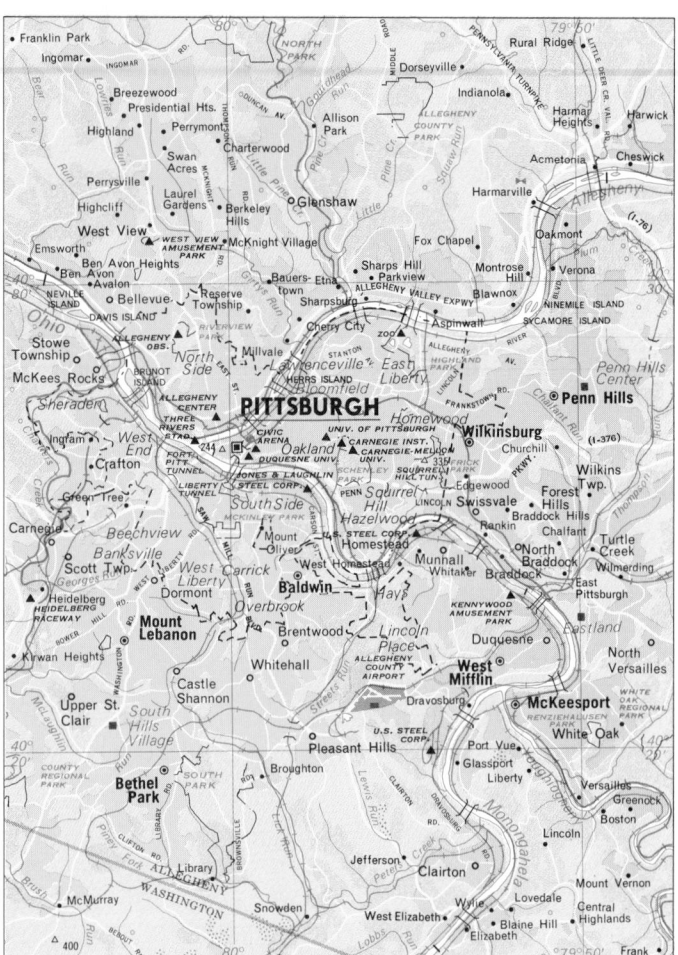

c

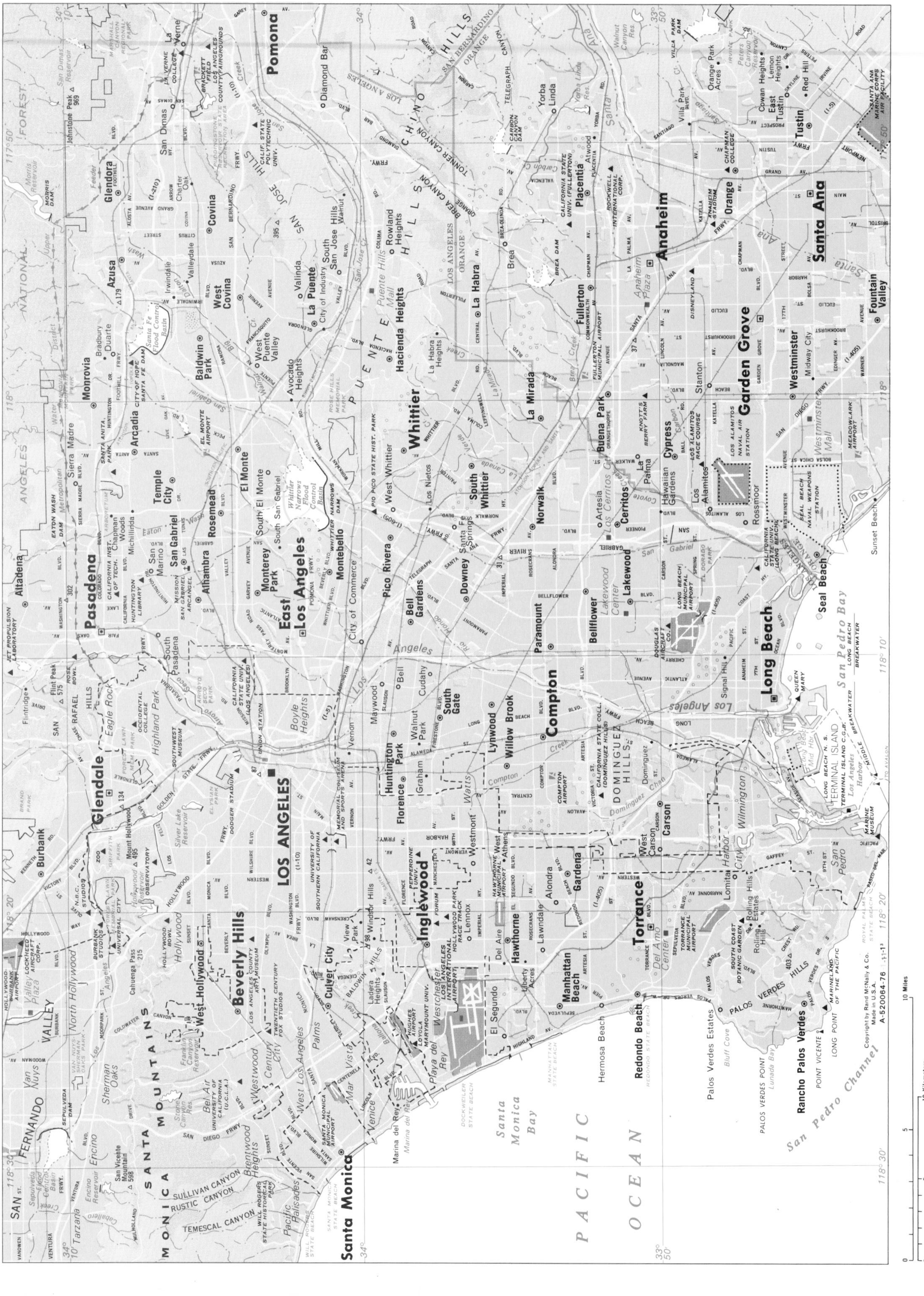

LOS ANGELES

Pomona

Santa Ana

Anaheim

Garden Grove

Westminster

Fountain Valley

Tustin

Orange

Placentia

Fullerton

La Habra

Brea

Yorba Linda

Glendora

Covina

West Covina

Azusa

Monrovia

Duarte

Arcadia

Pasadena

Altadena

Sierra Madre

Temple City

El Monte

South El Monte

Rosemead

San Gabriel

Alhambra

Monterey Park

East Los Angeles

Montebello

Whittier

West Whittier

South Whittier

La Mirada

Norwalk

Downey

Pico Rivera

Santa Fe Springs

Cerritos

Artesia

La Palma

Cypress

Buena Park

Hawaiian Gardens

Los Alamitos

Rossmoor

Seal Beach

Long Beach

Lakewood

Bellflower

Paramount

Compton

South Gate

Lynwood

Willow Brook

Bell Gardens

Bell

Cudahy

Maywood

Huntington Park

Walnut Park

Florence

Watts

Westmont

Carson

West Carson

Gardena

Hawthorne

Lawndale

Inglewood

Torrance

Manhattan Beach

Hermosa Beach

Redondo Beach

Rancho Palos Verdes

Palos Verdes Estates

Rolling Hills

El Segundo

Playa del Rey

Marina del Rey

Venice

Santa Monica

West Los Angeles

Westwood

Culver City

Beverly Hills

West Hollywood

Hollywood

Los Angeles

Glendale

Burbank

North Hollywood

Sherman Oaks

Encino

Tarzana

Van Nuys

San Fernando Valley

Santa Monica Mountains

San Dimas

La Verne

Diamond Bar

Walnut

Rowland Heights

Hacienda Heights

La Puente

Valinda

West Puente Valley

Avocado Heights

Baldwin Park

Irwindale

Charter Oak

Lemon Heights

Cowan Heights

Red Hill

East Tustin

Villa Park

Orange Park Acres

Wilmington

San Pedro

Terminal Island

PACIFIC OCEAN

Santa Monica Bay

San Pedro Bay

San Pedro Channel

SANTA MONICA MOUNTAINS

SAN JOSE HILLS

CHINO HILLS

PUENTE HILLS

DOMINGUEZ HILLS

ANGELES NATIONAL FOREST

Copyright by Rand McNally & Co.
Made in U.S.A.
A-520064-76

Scale 1:200,000, one inch to 17 miles.

10 Miles

10 Kilometers

a

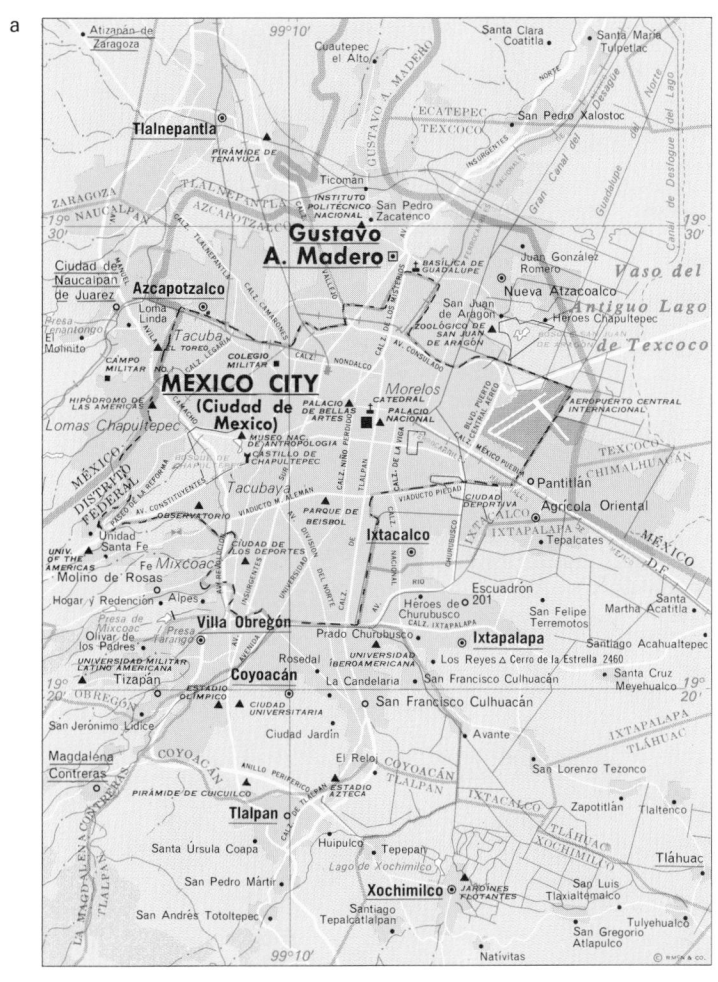

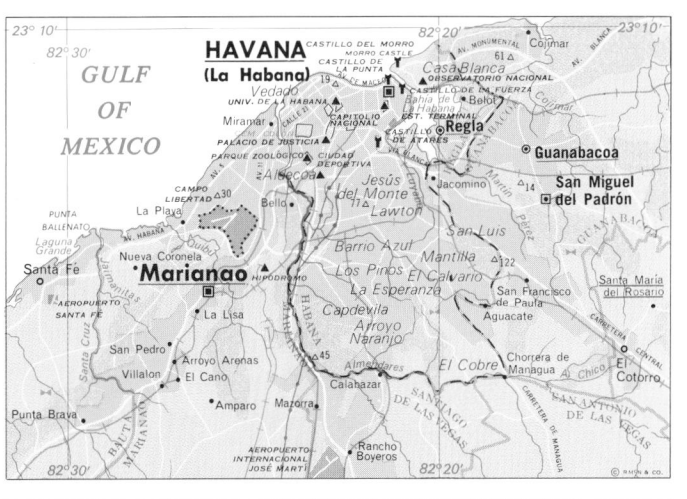

b

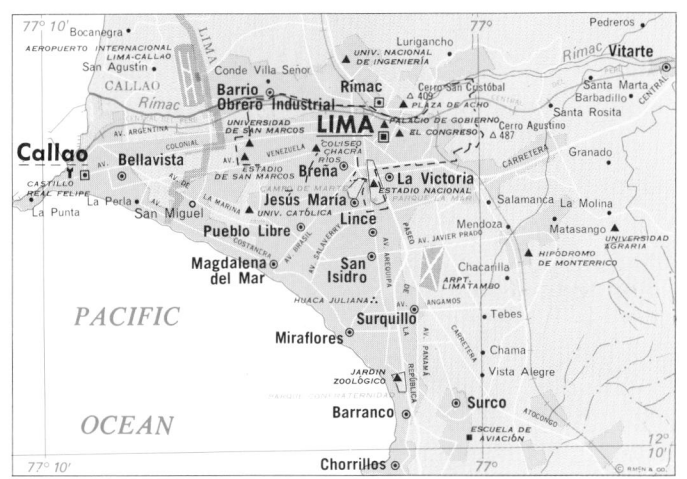

c

d

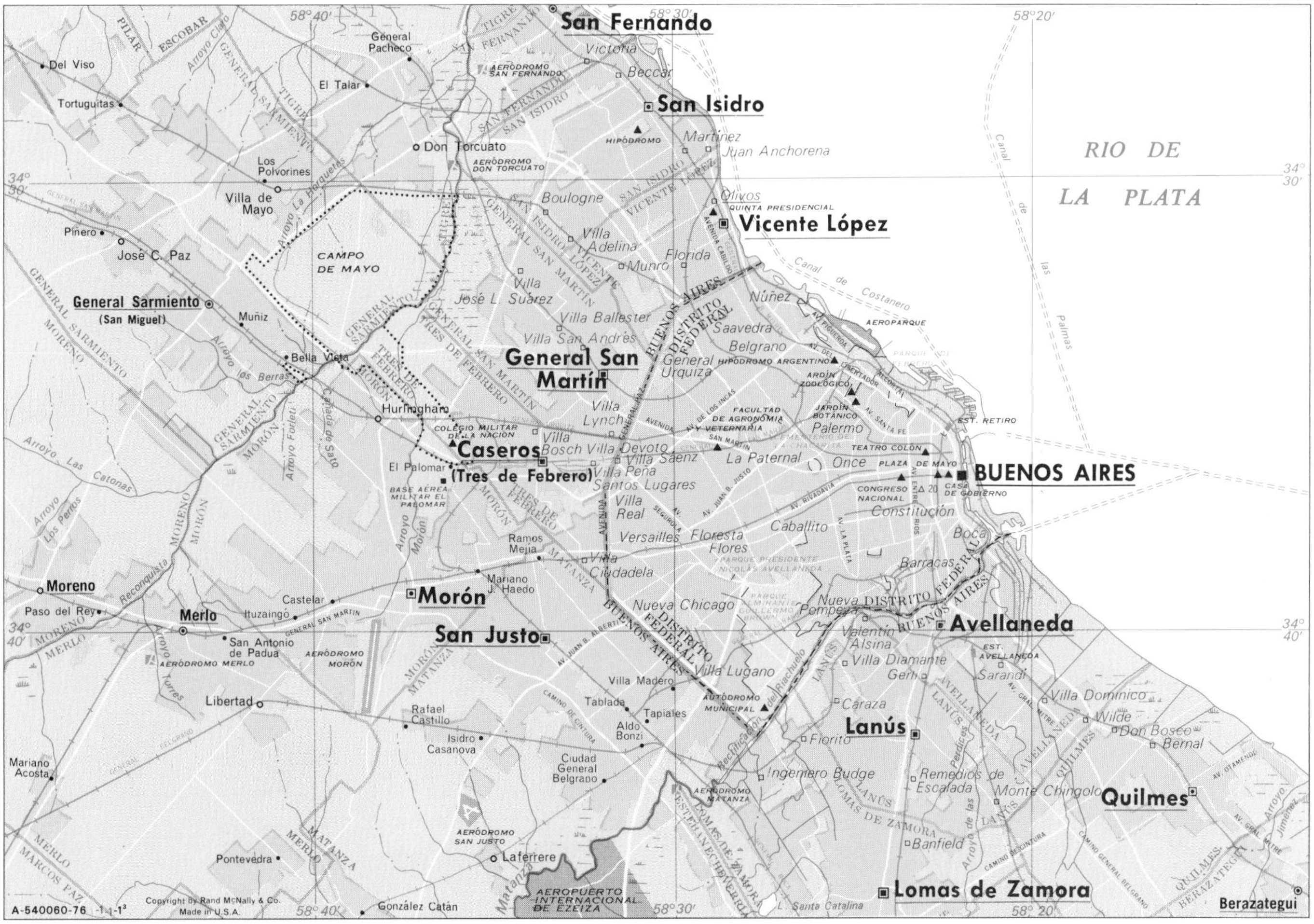

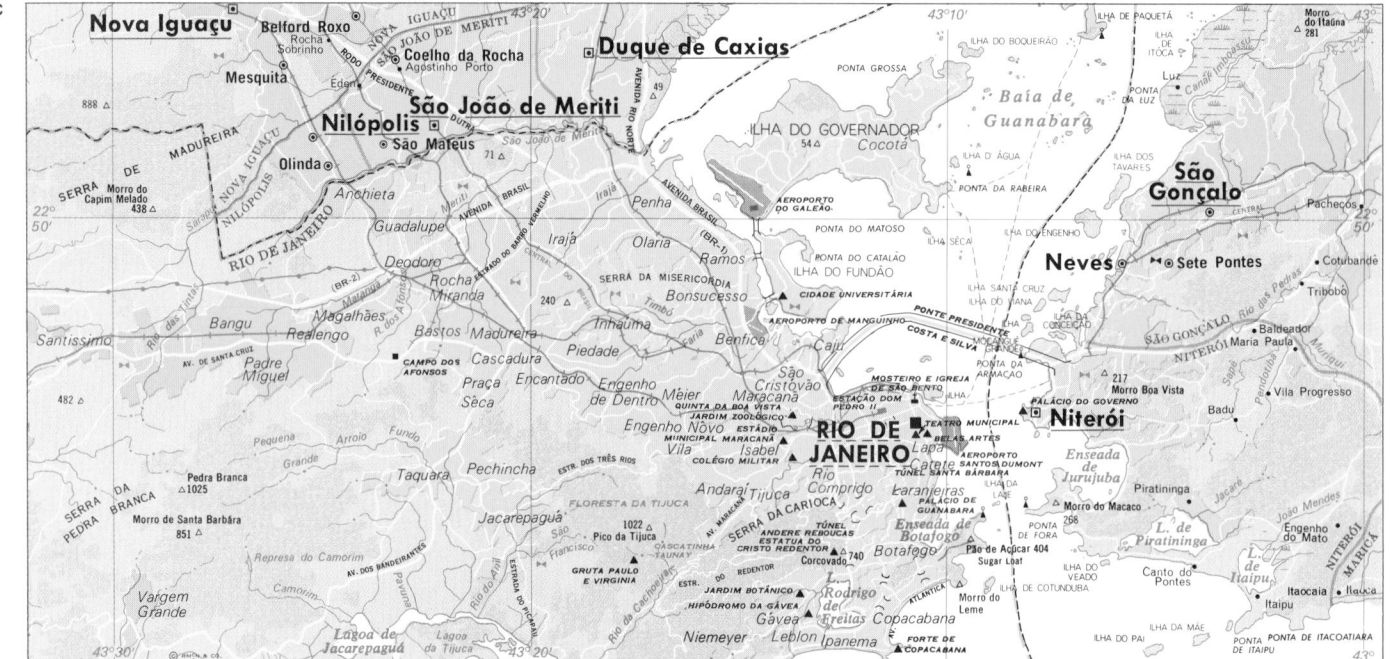

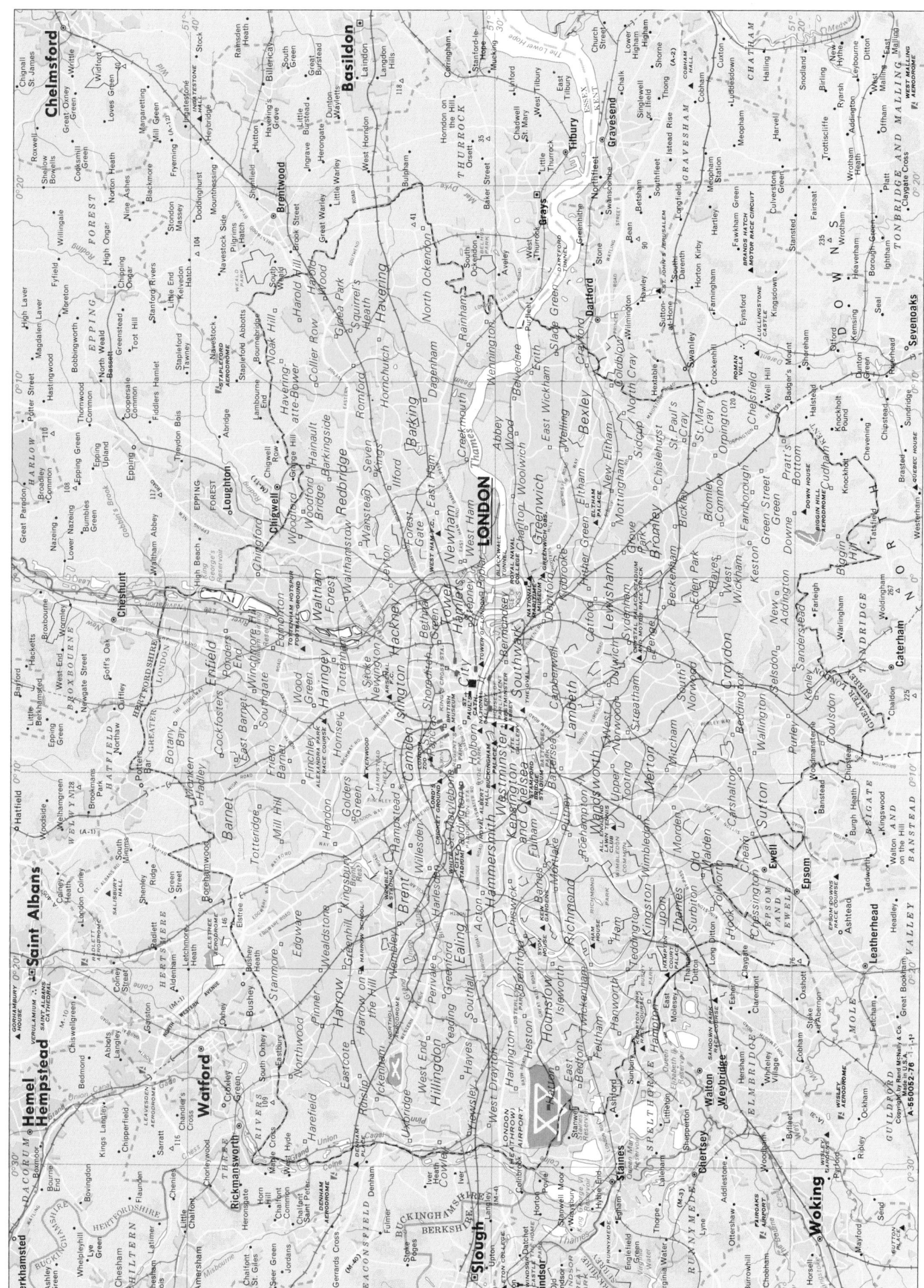

Scale 1:300,000; one inch to 4.7 miles.

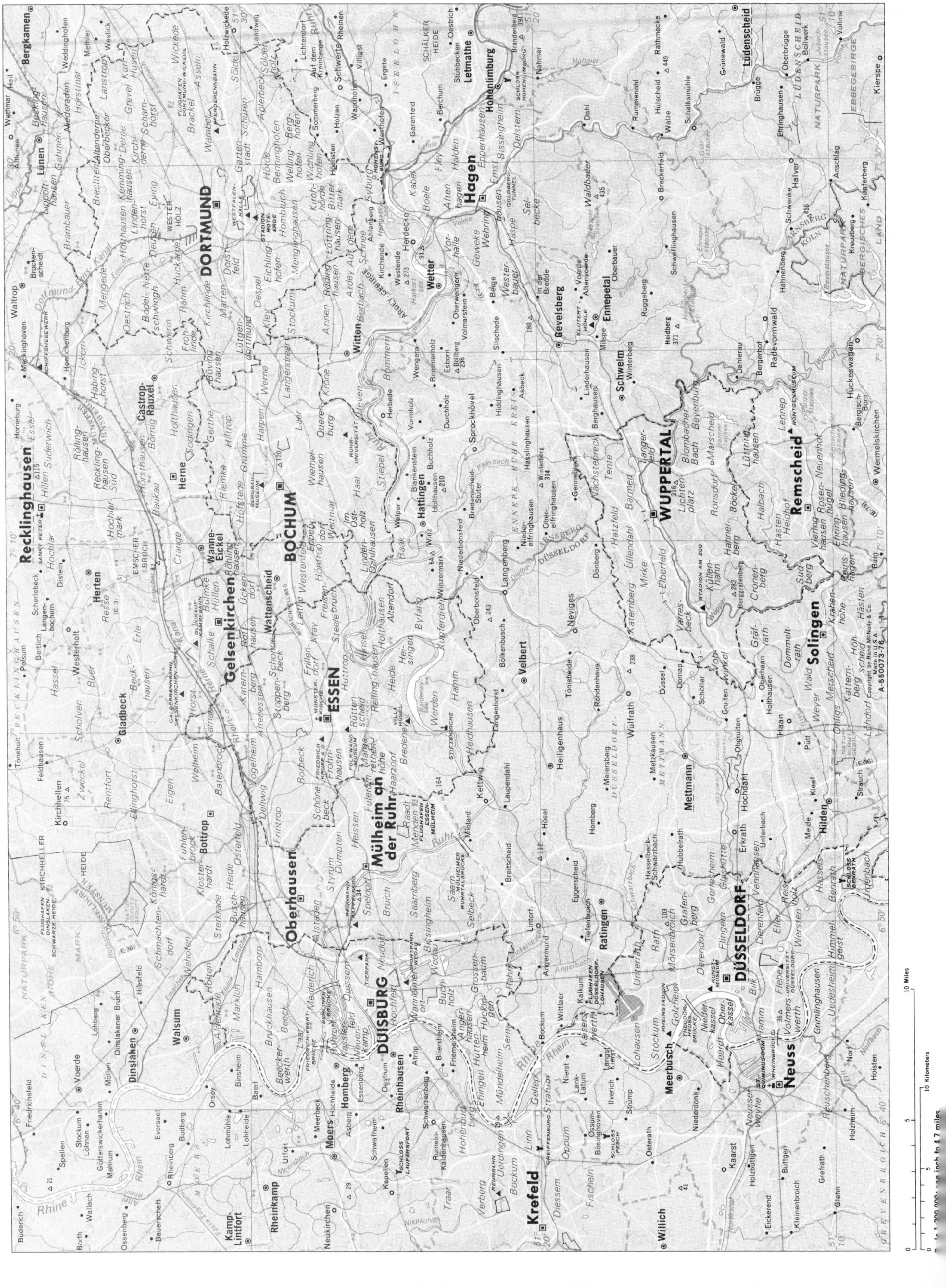
Recklinghausen
Bergkamen
Lünen
Waltrop
Castrop-Rauxel
Herne
Herten
Gelsenkirchen
Wanne-Eickel
Wattenscheid
Gladbeck
Bottrop
Dorsten
Dinslaken
Walsum
Oberhausen
Mülheim an der Ruhr
ESSEN
BOCHUM
DORTMUND
Witten
Wetter
Hagen
Herdecke
Hohenlimburg
Letmathe
Lüdenscheid
Gevelsberg
Ennepetal
Schwelm
WUPPERTAL
Remscheid
Solingen
Velbert
Hattingen
Sprockhövel
Heiligenhaus
Ratingen
Mettmann
Hilden
DÜSSELDORF
DUISBURG
Rheinhausen
Homberg
Moers
Kamp-Lintfort
Rheinkamp
Krefeld
Meerbusch
Willich
Neuss
Kaarst
Rhine
Ruhr
Wupper
Emscher
Lippe
Rhein-Herne-Kanal
Dortmund-Ems-Kanal
RECKLINGHAUSEN
ENNEPE-RUHR-KREIS
METTMANN
DÜSSELDORF
ARNSBERG
MÜNSTER
KÖLN
Copyright by Rand McNally & Co.
Made in U.S.A.
A-550073-76
0 5 10 Miles
0 5 10 Kilometers

a

WEST LANCASHIRE

WOODVALE AIRFIELD
Freshfield
Formby
FORMBY POINT
FORMBY HILLS
TO BELFAST
TO DOUGLAS
TO DUBLIN
Hightown
Haskayne
Great Altcar
Lunt
Maghull
Aughton Park
Lydiate
Aughton
Melling
Ince Blundell
Thornton
Great Crosby
Netherton
Sefton
Crosby
Waterloo
Seaforth
Litherland
Aintree
AINTREE RACE COURSE
Kirkby
New Brighton
Bootle
Wallasey
Seacombe
LIVERPOOL
EVERTON FOOTBALL GROUND
LIVERPOOL FOOTBALL GROUND
STANLEY PARK
EXCHANGE STATION
MERSEY TUNNEL
LIME STREET STATION
UNIV. OF LIVERPOOL
Everton
West Derby
Bidston
Moreton
Birkenhead
BIRKENHEAD PARK
Upton
Greasby
Tranmere
Rock Ferry
New Ferry
Port Sunlight
Dingle
Edge Hill
Mossley Hill
Knotty Ash
Roby
Huyton
Olive Mount
Gateacre
Woolton
Aigburth
Grassendale
Garston
Allerton
Halewood
Hunt's Cross
Frankby
Irby
WIRRAL
Pensby
Barnston
Storeton
Bebington
Heswall
Geyton
Thornton Hough
Raby
Parkgate
Neston
Ness
Burton
Ledsham
Capenhurst
Little Sutton
Great Sutton
Whitby
Childer Thornton
Ince
Stanlow
Hooton
Willaston
Eastham
Bromborough
Ellesmere Port
Frodsham
Helsby
Helsby Hill 141
Elton
Thornton-le-Moors
Hapsford
Alvanley
Little Stanney
Puddington
Flint
Flint Castle
ENGLAND
WALES
CLWYD
CHESHIRE
Dee
MERSEYSIDE
CHESHIRE
LANCASHIRE ROAD
LANCASHIRE
(M-57)
(M-62)
SEFTON
Ormskirk
Westhead
Scarth Hill
Skelmersdale
Dalton
Ashurst's Beacon 170
Digmoor
Up Holland
Simmonswood
SIMMONSWOOD MOSS
Bickerstaffe
Rainford
Crank
Moss Bank
KNOWSLEY
Saint Helens
Eccleston
Knowsley
KNOWSLEY PARK
CROXTETH PARK
KNOWSLEY HALL
Thatto Heath
Prescot
Whiston
Rainhill
Tarbock Green
Cronton
Hough Green
Rainhill Stoops
Farnworth
Widnes
Hale
HALE HEAD
Runcorn
Weston
HALTON
Mersey
Liverpool (Speke) Airport
SPEKE HALL
Speke
Hale
(M-56)
Manchester Ship Canal
Liverpool Bay

b

Chapeltown
Edgworth
Wayoh Reservoir
Ramsbottom
Wardle
Littleborough
Hollingworth Lake
Summerseat
Norden
Firgrove
Milnrow
LANCASHIRE
GREATER MANCHESTER
Smallbridge
Greenbooth Reservoir
Ashworth Moor Res.
Rochdale
Astley Bridge
Bradshaw
Tottington
Greenmount
Walmersley
Limefield
Lower Place
New Hey
Denshaw
Toppings
Bolton
HALL-I'-TH'-WOOD
Harwood
Ainsworth
Bury
Heywood
Castleton
Shaw
Moorside
Fishpool
Radcliffe
Birch
Top of Hebers
Royton
Little Lever
Whitefield
Middleton
Chadderton
Oldham
Lees
Kearsley
Farnworth
Little Hulton
Walkden
Prestwich
Rhodes
Failsworth
Mossley
Swinton
Cheetham Hill
Harpurhey
Boothstown
Worsley
Pendlebury
Higher Broughton
Blackley
TAMESIDE
Leigh
Eccles
Ellesmere Park
Lower Broughton
MANCHESTER RACE COURSE
BELLE VUE ZOOLOGICAL GARDENS
MANCHESTER
VICTORIA STATION
MANCHESTER CATHEDRAL
PICCADILLY STATION
Ashton-under-Lyne
Droylsden
Audenshaw
Dukinfield
Irlam
Barton Aerodrome
BARTON WATER SWING BRIDGE
SALFORD
Salford
MANCHESTER DOCKS
VICTORIA UNIV. OF MANCHESTER
OLD TRAFFORD CRICKET GROUND
MANCHESTER UNITED FOOTBALL GROUND
MANCHESTER CITY FOOTBALL GROUND
Stretford
Urmston
Davyhulme
Ashton upon Mersey
Chorlton-cum-Hardy
Withington
Rusholme
Levenshulme
Gorton
Denton
Haughton Green
Hyde
Gee Cross
Cadishead
Carrington
CARRINGTON MOSS
Partington
Sale
PLATT HALL
Didsbury
FLETCHER MOSS MUSEUM
Heaton Moor
Burnage
Reddish
Romiley
Marple
TRAFFORD
Broadheath
WYTHENSHAWE HALL
Timperley
Gatley
Heaviley
Stockport
Dunham Town
Altrincham
Wythenshawe
Cheadle
Cheadle Hulme
BRAMALL HALL
Hazel Grove
DISLEY TUNNEL
DUNHAM PARK
Bowdon
Hale
Heald Green
Bramhall
Poynton
LYME PARK
Bollington
Halebarns
GREATER MANCHESTER
CHESHIRE
MANCHESTER (RINGWAY) AIRPORT
Handforth
Woodford
WOODFORD AERODROME
ADLINGTON HALL
PEAK DISTRICT NATIONAL PARK
Rostherne Mere
TATTON PARK
The Mere
TATTON HALL
Mere
Rostherne
Morley Green
Styal
Dean Row
MACCLESFIELD
Wilmslow

c

Jouy-le-Moutier
Neuville-sur-Oise
L'Hautil
Chennevières
Ecouen
Goussainville
Le Mesnil-Amelot
Thieux
Juilly
Saint-Prix
Villiers-le-Bel
CHÂTEAU D'ÉCOUEN
Beauchamp
Le Plessis-Bouchard
Saint-Brice-sous-Forêt
Montlignon
AÉROPORT CHARLES DE GAULLE
Nantouillet
Compans
Maurecourt
Herblay
Montigny-lès-Cormeilles
Eaubonne
Montmorency
Roissy-en-France
Tremblay-en-France
Mitry-Mory
Saint-Mesmes
Conflans-Sainte-Honorine
Andrésy
Franconville
Cormeilles-en-Parisis
La Frette-sur-Seine
Soisy-sous-Montmorency
Groslay
Montmagny
Vaudherland
Gonesse
AÉROPORT DE PARIS-LE BOURGET
Messy
Gressy
Chanteloup-les-Vignes
Triel-sur-Seine
FORÊT
Sannois
Enghien-les-Bains
Deuil-la-Barre
Sarcelles
Villepinte
Mitry-Neuf
Denouval
Carrières-sous-Poissy
Les Gressillons
Achères
Pierrefitte-sur-Seine
Stains
Gargès-lès-Gonesse
Dugny
Villeparisis
Annet-sur-Marne
Médan
SAINT-GERMAIN
Carrières-sous-Bois
Le Mesnil-le-Roi
Maisons-Laffitte
CHÂTEAU
Épinay-sur-Seine
Villeneuve-la-Garenne
Saint-Denis
BASILIQUE SAINT-DENIS
Le Blanc-Mesnil
SEINE-ST-DENIS
Le Bourget
Sevran
Aulnay-sous-Bois
Vaujours
Courtry
Montjay-la-Tour
Poissy
Houilles
Sartrouville
Bezons
Argenteuil
Gennevilliers
Colombes
Drancy
Bondy
Les Pavillons-sous-Bois
Le Pin
Tressancourt
TERRASSE
Montesson
Carrières-sur-Seine
Bois-Colombes
La Garenne-Colombes
Asnières
La Courneuve
Aubervilliers
Bobigny
Clichy-sous-Bois
Le Raincy
Montfermeil
AÉRODROME DE CHELLES-LE-PIN
Carnetin
CHÂTEAU DE SAINT-GERMAIN-EN-LAYE
Chambourcy
Le Pecq
Chatou
FACULTÉ DES LETTRES
Courbevoie
Clichy
Levallois-Perret
Saint-Ouen
Pantin
Le Pré-Saint-Gervais
Romainville
Noisy-le-Sec
Villemomble
Gagny
FORÊT DE BONDY
Chelles
Thorigny-sur-Marne
Pomponne
Saint-Germain-en-Laye
Fourqueux
Mareil-Marly
Le Vésinet
Croissy-sur-Seine
Nanterre
MONTMARTRE
SACRÉ-COEUR
NORD EST
Les Lilas
Bagnolet
Rosny-sous-Bois
Le Perreux-sur-Marne
Neuilly-sur-Marne
Gournay-sur-Marne
Vaires-sur-Marne
Lagny
Feucherolles
Saint-Nom-la-Bretèche
L'Étang-la-Ville
Marly-le-Roi
Louveciennes
LA MALMAISON
Puteaux
Suresnes
Rueil-Malmaison
162 M1 Valérien
ARC DE TRIOMPHE
SAINT-LAZARE
Neuilly-sur-Seine
LOUVRE
SEINE-ST-DENIS
CIMETIÈRE DU PÈRE-LACHAISE
Montreuil
Vincennes
Fontenay-sous-Bois
Neuilly-Plaisance
Noisy-le-Grand
Champs-sur-Marne
Noisiel
Torcy
Guermantes
Chavenay
Noisy-le-Roi
Garches
HIPPODROME DE LONGCHAMP
Passy
TOUR EIFFEL
NOTRE DAME
JARDIN DU LUXEMBOURG
PARIS
Lyon
AUSTERLITZ
SORBONNE
SEINE
CHÂTEAU DE VINCENNES
BOIS DE VINCENNES
HIPPODROME DE VINCENNES
Saint-Mandé
Nogent-sur-Marne
Le Perreux-sur-Marne
Saint-Thibault-des-Vignes
Villepreux
Rocquencourt
Ville-d'Avray
Sèvres
Saint-Cloud
HAUTS-DE-SEINE
Issy-les-Moulineaux
Malakoff
Vanves
Montrouge
Gentilly
Arcueil
Cachan
CITÉ UNIVERSITAIRE
Charenton-le-Pont
Saint-Maurice
Alfortville
Joinville-le-Pont
Maisons-Alfort
Saint-Maur-des-Fossés
La Queue-en-Brie
Combault
Les Clayes-sous-Bois
Fontenay-le-Fleury
Le Chesnay
AÉRODROME DE SAINT-CYR
L'ÉCOLE
ÉCOLE MILITAIRE
CHÂTEAU DE VERSAILLES
Versailles
Viroflay
Chaville
Meudon
Clamart
Bagneux
Bourg-la-Reine
La Hay-les-Roses
Ivry-sur-Seine
Villejuif
Vitry-sur-Seine
Créteil
Le Plessis-Trévise
Croissy-Beaubourg
Ferrières
Emerainville
AÉRODROME DE LOGNES-ÉMERAINVILLE
Bois-d'Arcy
YVELINES
HAUTS-DE-SEINE
AÉRODROME DE VILLACOUBLAY
Fontenay-aux-Roses
Sceaux
Châtenay-Malabry
PARC DE SCEAUX
Antony
Fresnes
Rungis
MARCHÉ DE RUNGIS-HALLES
Thiais
Chevilly-Larue
Choisy-le-Roi
Valenton
Bonneuil-sur-Marne
CARREFOUR POMPADOUR
VAL-DE-MARNE
Sucy-en-Brie
Noiseau
Ozoir-la-Ferrière
BOIS NOTRE DAME
Montigny-le-Bretonneux
Guyancourt
CAMP DE SATORY
Buc
LOUIS-BLÉRIOT
166
AÉROPORT DE GUYANCOURT
Saint-Cyr-l'École
ARPT. DE BUC
Jouy-en-Josas
Bièvres
Les Loges-en-Josas
MEUDON
LE PETIT CLAMART
VERRIÈRES
Verrières-le-Buisson
Igny
Bièvre
Villeneuve-le-Roi
Orly
AÉROPORT DE PARIS-ORLY
Athis-Mons
PARC DU TREMBLAY
Champigny-sur-Marne
Chennevières-sur-Marne
Ormesson-sur-Marne
La Queue-en-Brie
Trappes
Montigny-le-Bretonneux
ABBAYE DE PORT-ROYAL-DES-CHAMPS
Voisins-le-Bretonneux
Toussus-le-Noble
AÉROPORT DE TOUSSUS-LE-NOBLE
Les Loges-en-Josas
Le Val-d'Albian
Bièvres
Wissous
AÉROPORT DE PARIS-ORLY
Morangis
Rhodon
Chevreuse
Courcelle
Milon-la-Chapelle
Magny-les-Hameaux
Saint-Lambert
Étang de Saclay
Saclay
Vauhallan
Igny
Massy
Palaiseau
Champlan
Chilly-Mazarin
Longjumeau
Epinay-sur-Orge
Savigny-sur-Orge
Juvisy-sur-Orge
Draveil
Villeneuve-Saint-Georges
Crosne
116
Yerres
Montgeron
Brunoy
Marolles-en-Brie
Santeny
Villecresnes
Mandres-les-Roses
Servon
Chevry-Cossigny
Brie-Comte-Robert
CHÂTEAU DE DAMPIERRE
Milon-la-Chapelle
Cernay-la-Ville
Saint-Rémy-lès-Chevreuse
Choisel
ESSONNE
Gif-sur-Yvette
Orsay
Villebon-sur-Yvette
Bures-sur-Yvette
UNIVERSITÉ
123

Scale 1:300,000; one inch to 4.7 miles.
10 Kilometers
5
0
10 Miles
5
0

Copyright by Rand McNally & Co.
Made in U.S.A.
A-550078-76

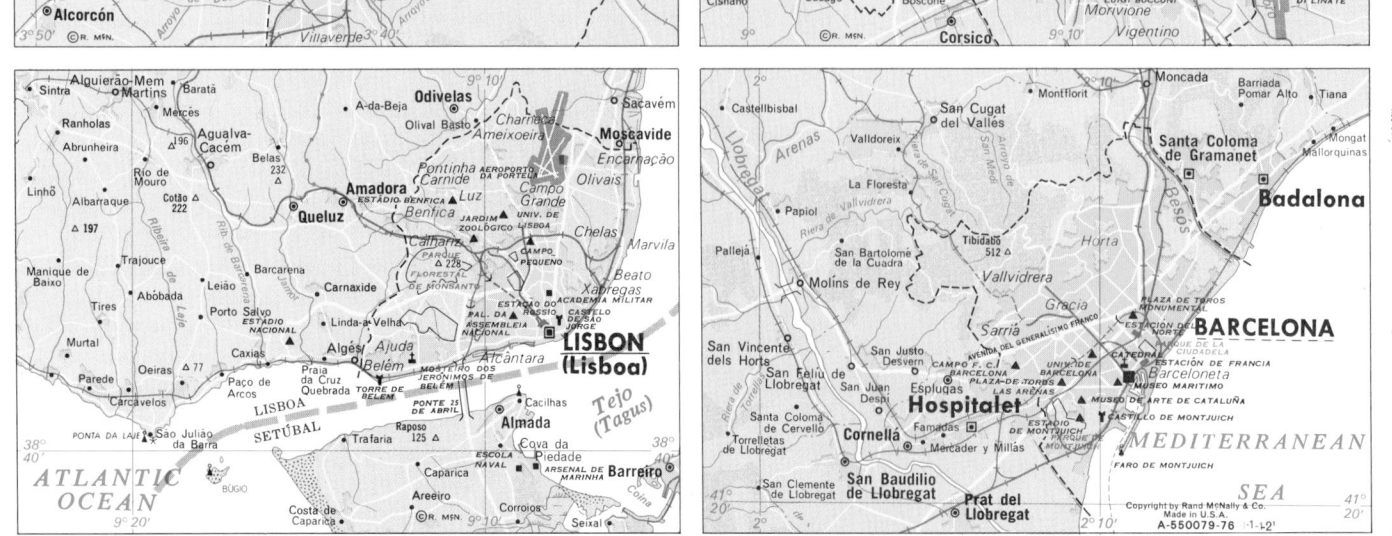

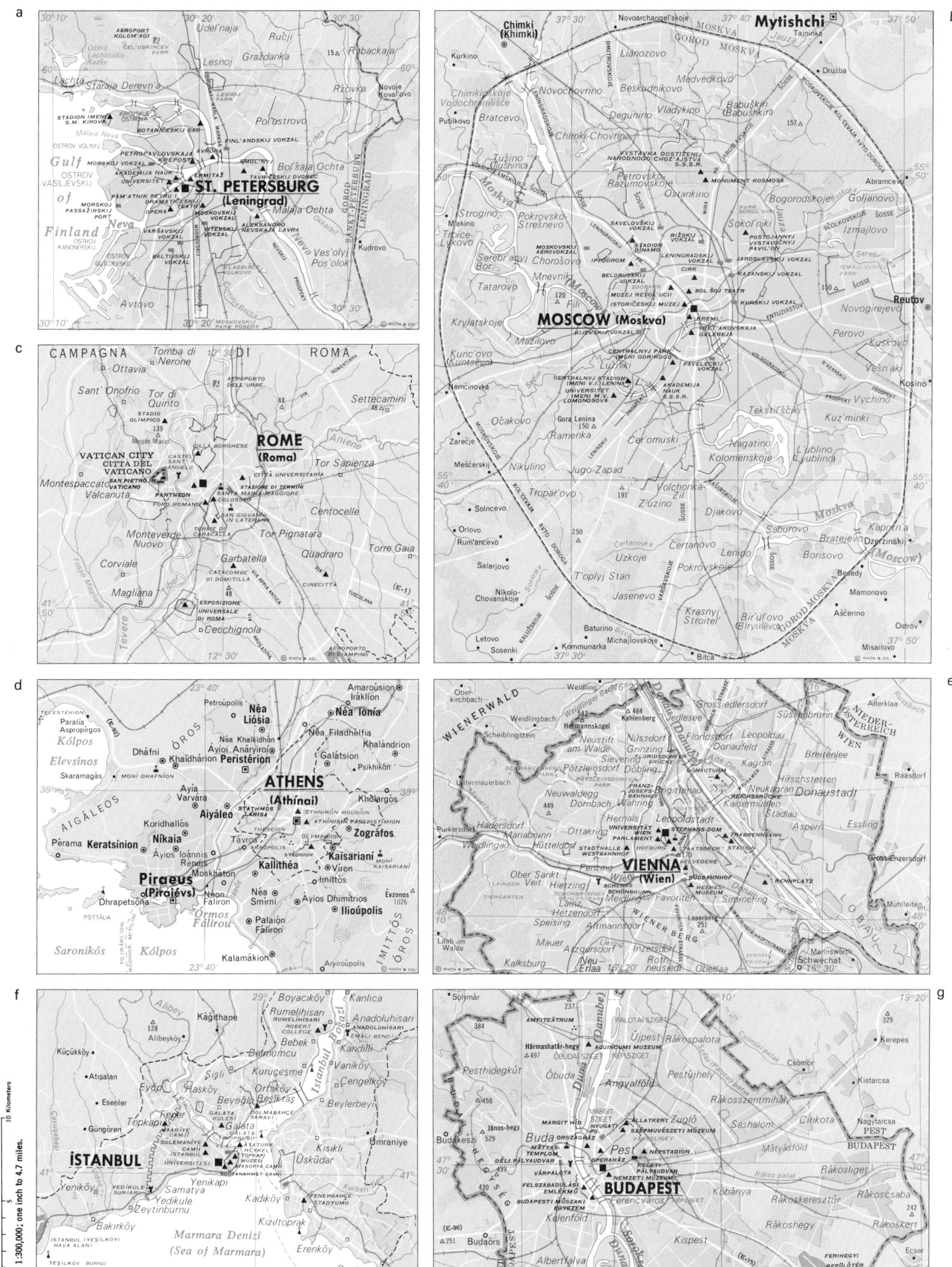

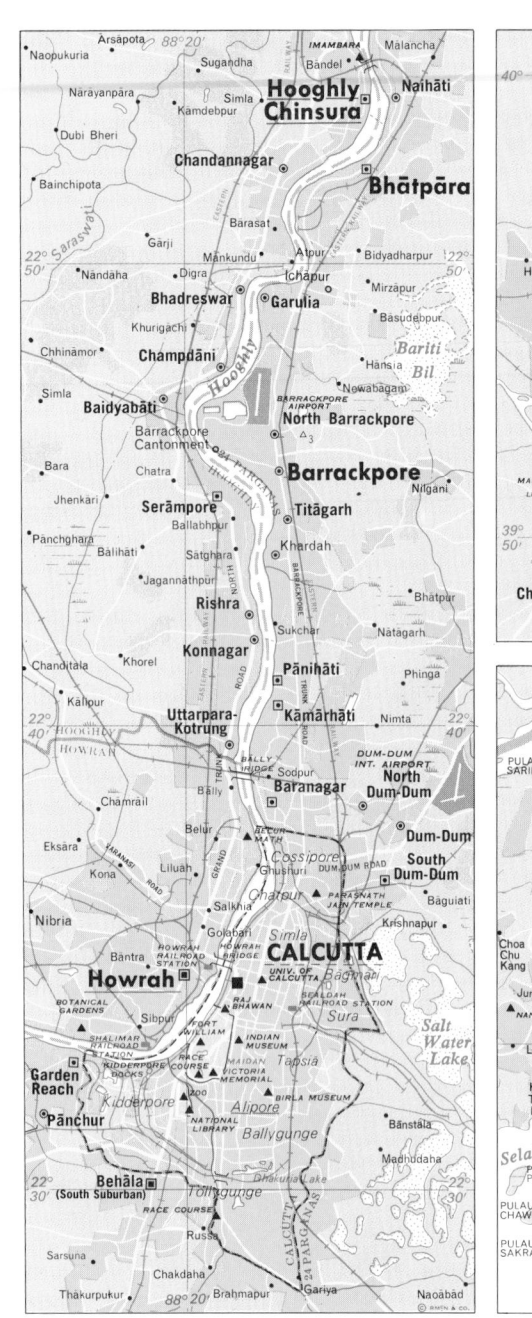

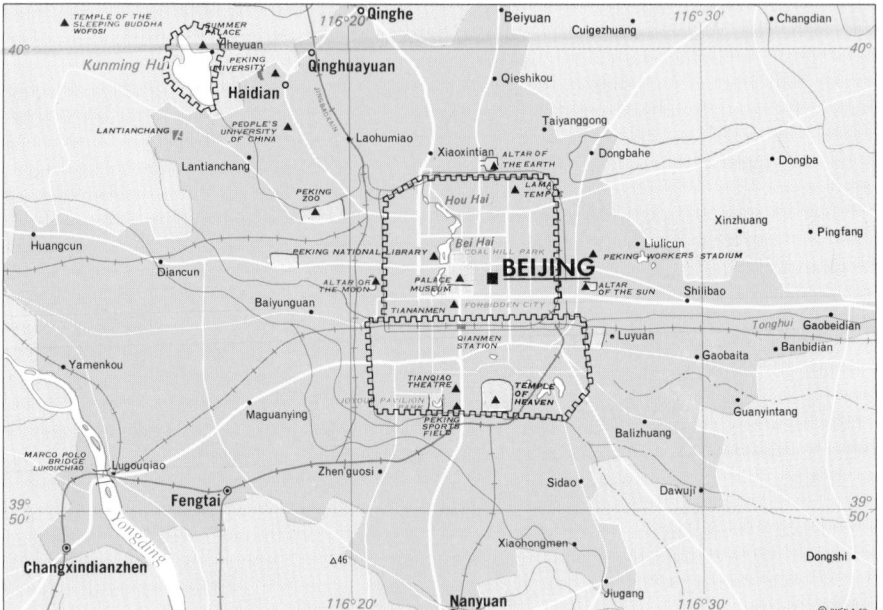

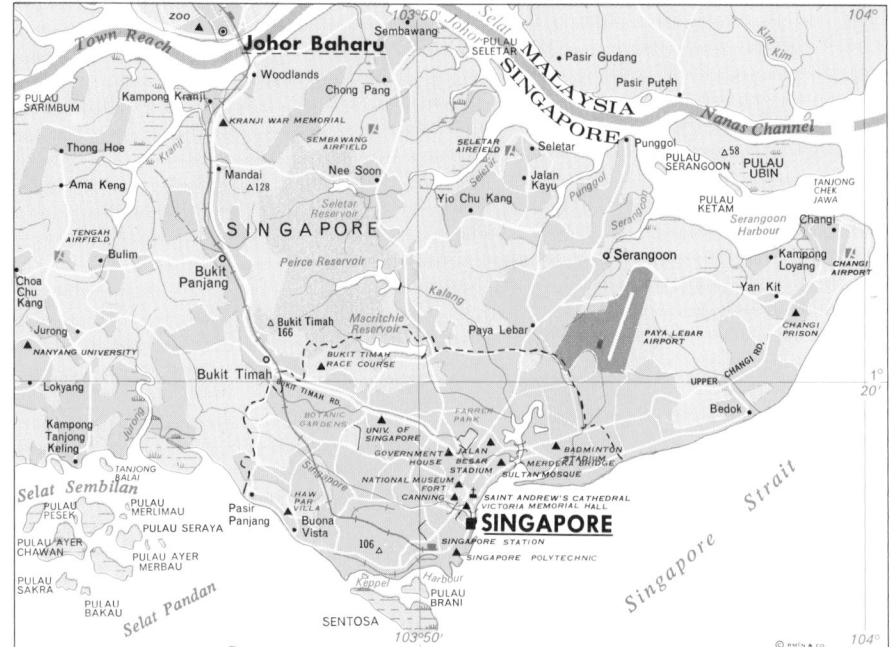

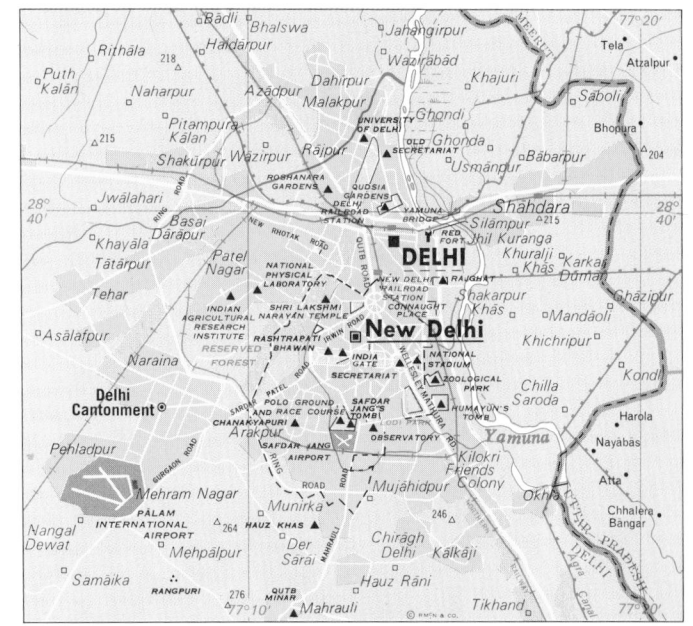

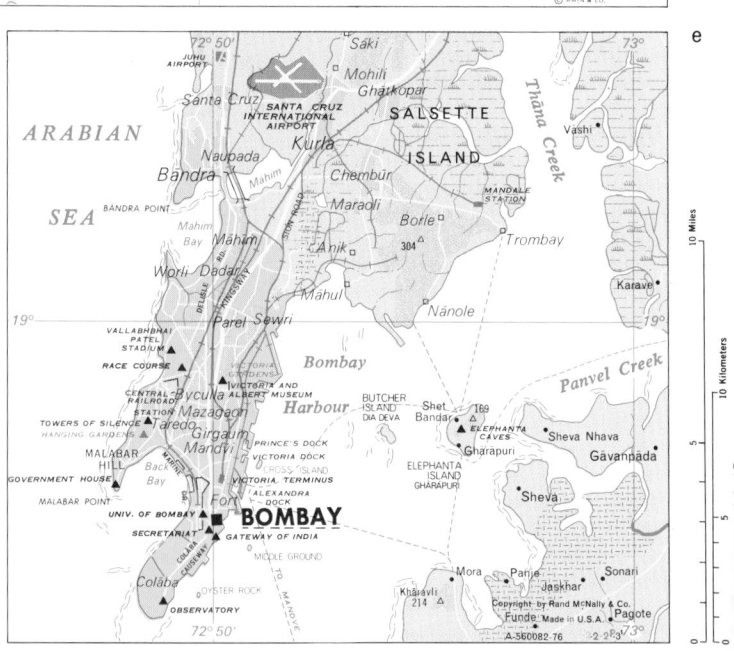

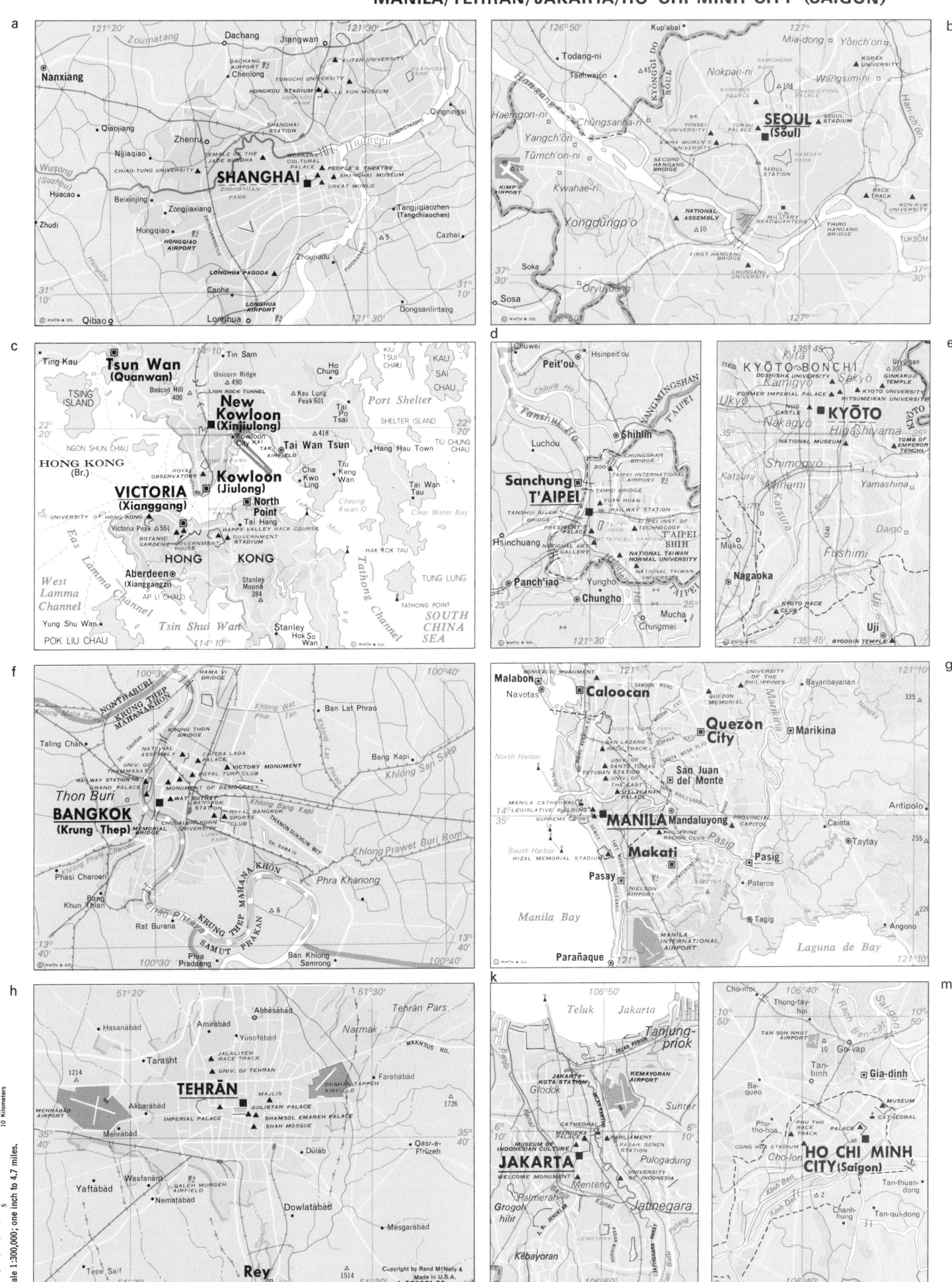

a

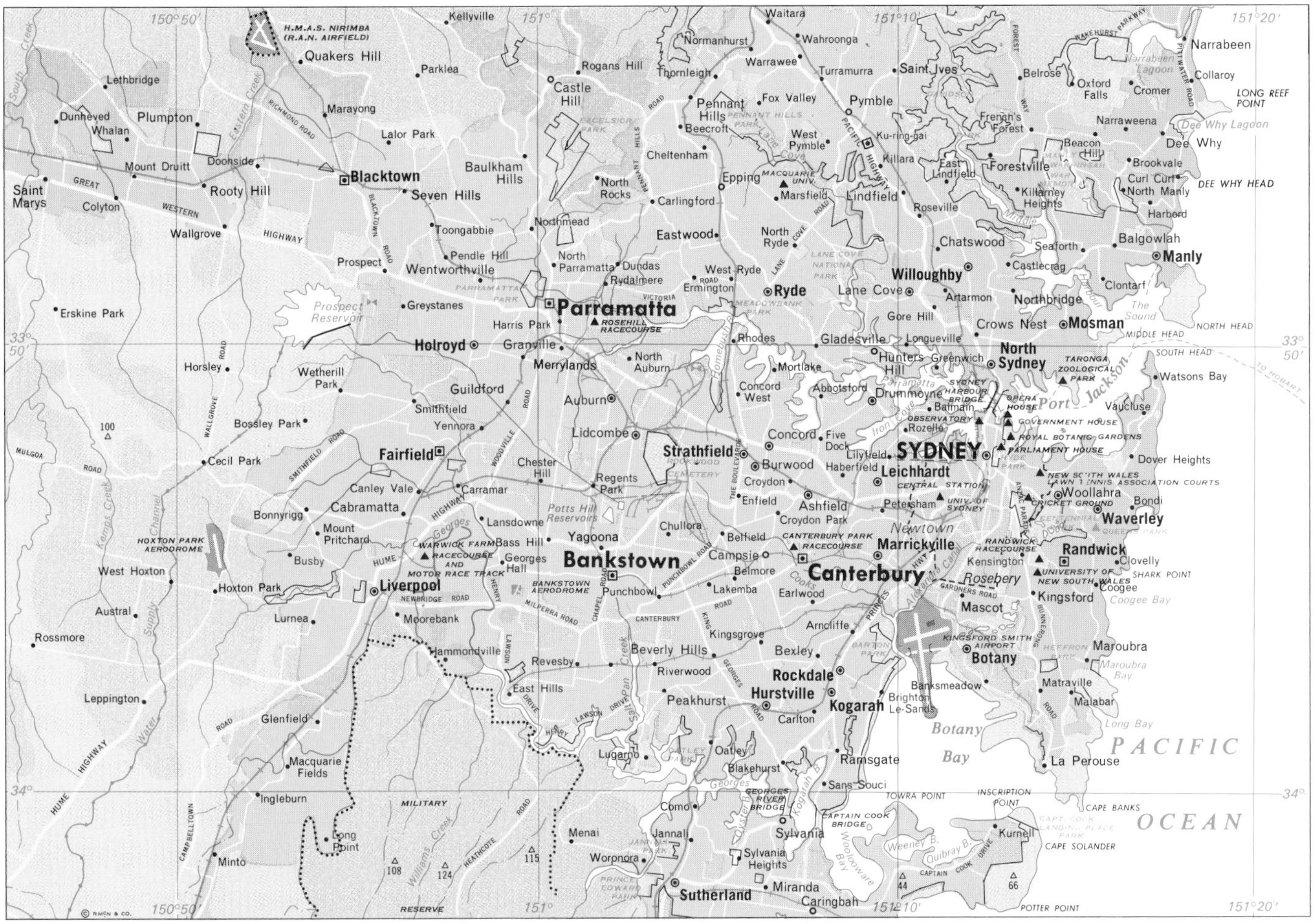

Map a (Sydney)

150°50' · 151° · 151°10' · 151°20' · 33°50' · 34°

H.M.A.S. NIRIMBA (R.A.N. AIRFIELD) · Kellyville · Waitara · Normanhurst · Wahroonga · Saint Ives · Belrose · Oxford Falls · Cromer · Narrabeen · Collaroy · LONG REEF POINT

Quakers Hill · Parklea · Rogans Hill · Castle Hill · Thornleigh · Warrawee · Turramurra · French's Forest · Beacon Hill · Narraweena · Dee Why · DEE WHY LAGOON

Lethbridge · Dunheved · Whalan · Plumpton · Marayong · Pennant Hills · Beecroft · West Pymble · Ku-ring-gai · Killara · East Lindfield · Roseville · Killarney Heights · Brookvale · Curl Curl · North Manly · DEE WHY HEAD

Mount Druitt · Doonside · Rooty Hill · Baulkham Hills · Seven Hills · North Rocks · Carlingford · Epping · Marsfield · Lindfield · Chatswood · Seaforth · Harbord · Balgowlah · Manly

Saint Marys · Colyton · Blacktown · Toongabbie · Northmead · Eastwood · North Ryde · West Ryde · Ermington · Lane Cove · Willoughby · Northbridge · Clontarf · The Sound · NORTH HEAD

Wallgrove · WESTERN HIGHWAY · Pendle Hill · Wentworthville · North Parramatta · Dundas · Rydalmere · Ryde · Gore Hill · Crows Nest · Mosman · MIDDLE HEAD

Erskine Park · Prospect · Greystanes · Harris Park · Parramatta · ROSEHILL RACECOURSE · Rhodes · Gladesville · Hunters Hill · Greenwich · North Sydney · TARONGA ZOOLOGICAL PARK · Watsons Bay · SOUTH HEAD

Horsley · Wetherill Park · Holroyd · Granville · Merrylands · North Auburn · Mortlake · Abbotsford · Drummoyne · Balmain · SYDNEY HARBOUR BRIDGE · OPERA HOUSE · GOVERNMENT HOUSE · ROYAL BOTANIC GARDENS · PARLIAMENT HOUSE · Vaucluse

Bossley Park · Smithfield · Yennora · Auburn · Lidcombe · Concord West · Concord · Five Dock · Lilyfield · Rozelle · SYDNEY · Dover Heights

Cecil Park · Fairfield · Canley Vale · Carramar · Regents Park · Chester Hill · Croydon · Burwood · Strathfield · Haberfield · Leichhardt · NEW SOUTH WALES LAWN TENNIS ASSOCIATION COURTS · UNIV. OF SYDNEY · CENTRAL STATION · Woollahra · Bondi

Bonnyrigg · Cabramatta · Mount Pritchard · Lansdowne · Bass Hill · Yagoona · Chullora · Enfield · Ashfield · Croydon Park · Petersham · Newtown · SYDNEY CRICKET GROUND · Waverley

West Hoxton · Busby · WARWICK FARM RACECOURSE AND MOTOR RACE TRACK · Georges Hall · Belfield · Campsie · Marrickville · Kensington · Randwick · RANDWICK RACECOURSE · Clovelly · SHARK POINT

HOXTON PARK AERODROME · Hoxton Park · Liverpool · Moorebank · BANKSTOWN AERODROME · Bankstown · Punchbowl · Lakemba · Belmore · Canterbury · CANTERBURY PARK RACECOURSE · Roseberry · UNIVERSITY OF NEW SOUTH WALES · Kingsford · Coogee · Coogee Bay

Austral · Lurnea · East Hills · Revesby · Kingsgrove · Earlwood · Arncliffe · Mascot · KINGSFORD SMITH AIRPORT · Botany · Maroubra · Maroubra Bay

Rossmore · Hammondville · Beverly Hills · Riverwood · Bexley · Rockdale · Banksmeadow · Matraville · Malabar · Long Bay

Leppington · Glenfield · Peakhurst · Hurstville · Carlton · Kogarah · Brighton Le-Sands · La Perouse · PACIFIC OCEAN

Macquarie Fields · Lugarno · Oatley · Blakehurst · Ramsgate · Sans Souci · Botany Bay · CAPE BANKS · CAPE SOLANDER

Ingleburn · MILITARY RESERVE · Como · Menai · GEORGES RIVER BRIDGE · Sylvania · Kurnell · CAPTAIN COOK LANDING PLACE PARK · CAPE SOLANDER

Minto · Long Point · Jannali · Worpnora · Sylvania Heights · CAPTAIN COOK BRIDGE · TOWRA POINT · INSCRIPTION POINT · POTTER POINT

PRINCE EDWARD PARK · Sutherland · Miranda · Caringbah · Woolooware · Cronulla

© RMN & CO. · 150°50' · 151° · 151°10' · 151°20'

b

Map b (Melbourne)

144°50' · 145° · 145°10' · 145°20' · 37°50' · 38°

Broadmeadows · TULLAMARINE INTERNATIONAL AIRPORT · Tullamarine · Campbellfield · Thomastown · Diamond Creek · Kangaroo Ground · Little Sugarloaf · 271

Sydenham · Jacana · Glenroy · Keon Park · Bundoora · Greensborough · Research · Mount Lofty · 237

Keilor · Oak Park · Hadfield · Fawkner · Reservoir · Watsonia · Mont Park · Macleod · Montmorency · Eltham

Saint Albans · Airport West · Merlynston · Pascoe Vale · Coburg · Preston · Thornbury · West Heidelberg · Rosanna · Lower Plenty · Wonga Park

North Essendon · ESSENDON AIRPORT · Brunswick · Northcote · Heidelberg · Ivanhoe · ELTHAM LOWER PARK · VICTORIA STATE CAR CLUB RACE CIRCUIT · Warrandyte

Essendon · Avondale Heights · Maribyrnong · MOONEE VALLEY RACECOURSE · North Fitzroy · Templestowe · Warrandyte South · Black Springs · Lilydale · 205 · Black Springs Hill

Albion · Braybrook · FLEMINGTON RACECOURSE · ZOO · Fitzroy · UNIV. OF MELBOURNE · CARLTON GARDENS · Collingwood · Kew · Doncaster · Park Orchards

Deer Park · Sunshine · Maidstone · Footscray · STATE PARLIAMENT HOUSE · MELBOURNE · Richmond · Hawthorn · Doncaster East · Ringwood North · Mooroolbark · Croydon

Kingsville · MELBOURNE CRICKET GROUND · GOVERNMENT HOUSE · ROYAL BOTANIC GARDENS · Camberwell · Canterbury · North Balwyn · Balwyn · Blackburn · Mitcham · Ringwood · Kilsyth · Montrose

Yarraville · Spotswood · South Melbourne · Port Melbourne · Prahran · VICTORIAN LAWN TENNIS ASSOCIATION COURTS · Kooyong · Burwood · Box Hill · Nunawading · Heathmont · Bayswater North · Mount Dandenong · 633

Altona North · Newport · Paisley · Williamstown · Hobsons Bay · Toorak · Malvern · Ashburton · Bennettswood · East Burwood · Forest Hill · Vermont · Wantirna · Bayswater · The Basin · Olinda

Galvin · Seaholme · ALBERT PARK · PRINCES HIGHWAY · Saint Kilda · Caulfield · Mount Waverley · Wantirna South · Boronia · One Tree Hill · Sassafras

Laverton · Altona · POINT GELLIBRAND · Elwood · CAULFIELD RACE COURSE · Chadstone · Holmesglen · Syndal · Glen Waverley · Scoresby · Knox · 502 · Ferny Creek

Oakleigh · Glenhuntly · Notting Hill · Wheelers Hill · Upper Ferntree Gully · Upwey · Belgrave

Point Cook · POINT COOK ROYAL AUSTRALIAN AIR FORCE STATION · Brighton · Bentleigh · Ormond · Clayton · MONASH UNIVERSITY · Mulgrave · Rowville · Lysterfield · Mount Morton · 276

Moorabbin · Hampton · Oakleigh South · SANDOWN PARK RACECOURSE · Harrisfield · 225 · Lysterfield Hills · Sugarloaf Hill · 184

Sandringham · Highett · Heatherton · Springvale · Noble Park · LYSTERFIELD RESERVOIR · CHURCHILL NATIONAL PARK

Black Rock · Cheltenham · MOORABBIN AIRPORT · Dingley · Springvale South · Dandenong · Narre Warren North

Beaumaris · Braeside · Keysborough · Hallam · Doveton · Harkaway

RICKETTS POINT · Half Moon Bay · Mentone · Mordialloc · BEAUMARIS BAY · Port Phillip Bay

144°50' · 145° · 145°10' · 145°20'

Scale 1:300,000; one inch to 4.7 miles.

10 Kilometers · 5 · 0

10 miles · 5 · 0 · 11

a

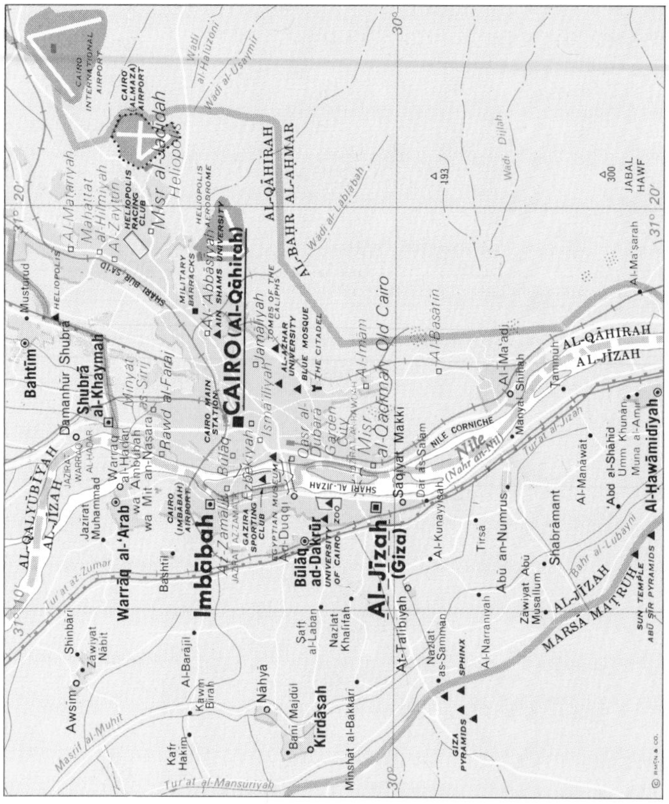

CAIRO (Al-Qāhirah)
Cairo International Airport
Cairo (Almaza) Airport
Heliopolis Racing Club
Heliopolis
Military Barracks
Ain Shams University
Al-ʿAbbāsīyah
Al-Qāhirah
Al-Bahr Al-Ahmar
Blue Mosque
The Citadel
Tombs of the Mamluks
Al-Qāhirah Old Cairo
Al-Jīzah
Bahtim
Shubrā al-Khaymah
Danmanhur Shubrā
Al-Qalyūbīyah
Al-Jīzah
Warrāq al-ʿArab
Imbābah
Būlāq ad-Dakrūr
Al-Jīzah (Giza)
Egyptian Museum
Cairo (Imbābah) Airport
Gazira Sporting Club
University of Cairo
Al-Hawāmidīyah
Kirdāsah
MARSĀ MATRŪH
Giza Pyramids
Sphinx
Sun Temple

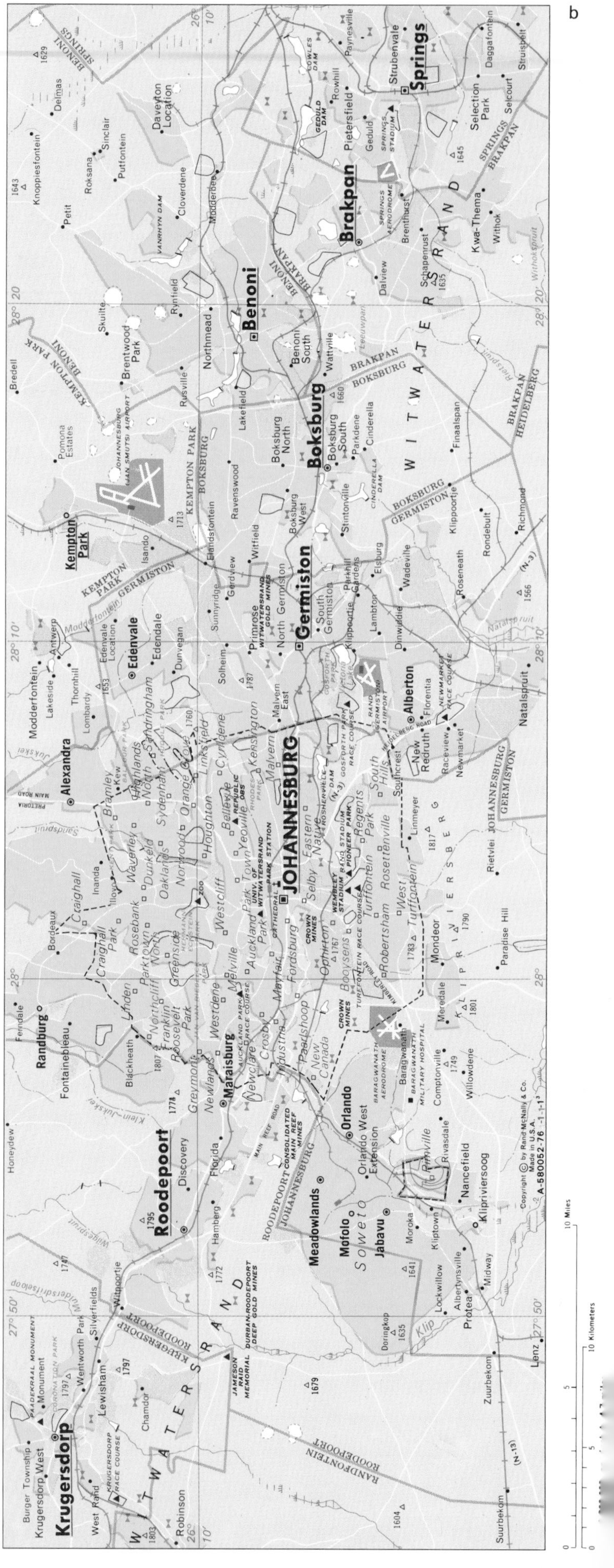

b

Springs
Brakpan
Benoni
Boksburg
Germiston
Kempton Park
Edenvale
Alexandra
JOHANNESBURG
Alberton
Randburg
Maraisburg
Roodepoort
Meadowlands
Mofolo
Jabavu
Orlando
Krugersdorp
WITWATERSRAND
WITWATERSBERG

c

BRAZZAVILLE (Congo)
CONGO
ZAIRE
ÎLE MBAMOU
KINSHASA (Leopoldville)
Baudouin Stadium
Kinshasa (Ndolo) Airport
Camp Leopold
Government Palace
Military Base
Brazzaville (Maya Maya) Airport
Zoo
Government House
St. Anne of the Congo
Military Base
Cathedral of Kinshasa St. Anne
Hydro-Electric Station

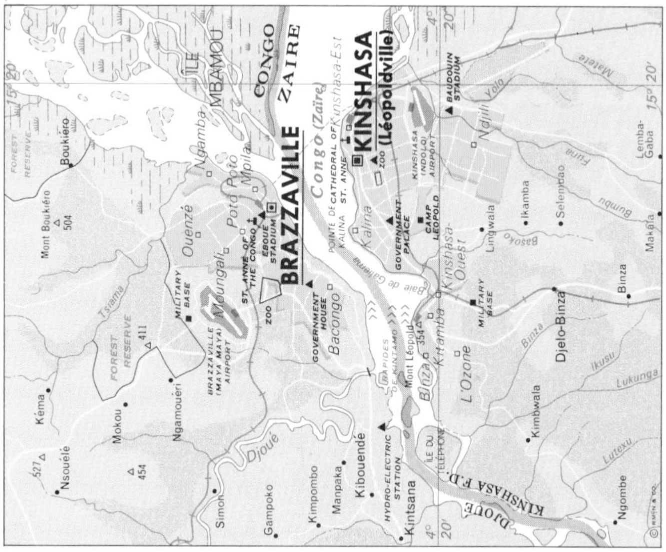

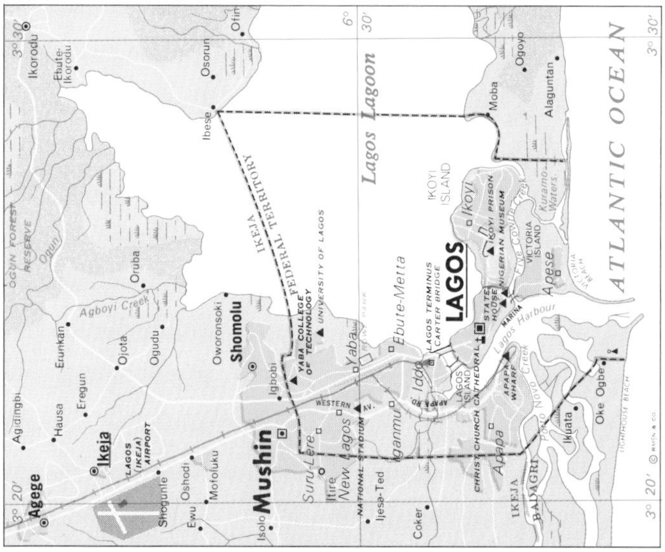

d

ATLANTIC OCEAN
Lagos Lagoon
IKEJA FEDERAL TERRITORY
IKOYI ISLAND
LAGOS
VICTORIA ISLAND
Ikeja
Agege
Mushin
Shomolu
Ikeja (Lagos) Airport
Yaba College of Technology
University of Lagos
Nigerian Museum
Christ Church Cathedral

10 Miles
10 Kilometers

WORLD POLITICAL INFORMATION TABLE

This table gives the area, population, population density, political status, capital, and predominant languages for every country in the world. The political units listed are categorized by political status in the form of government column of the table, as follows: A—independent countries; B—internally independent political entities which are under the protection of another country in matters of defense and foreign affairs; C—colonies and other dependent political units; and D—the major administrative subdivisions of Australia, Canada, China, the United Kingdom, and the United States. For comparison, the table also includes the continents and the world. A key to abbreviations of country names appears on page 249. All footnotes to this table appear on page 245.

The populations are estimates for January 1, 1994, made by Rand McNally on the basis of official data, United Nations estimates, and other available information. Area figures include inland water.

REGION OR POLITICAL DIVISION	Area Sq. Mi.	Est. Pop. 1/1/94	Pop. Per. Sq. Mi.	Form of Government and Ruling Power		Capital	Predominant Languages
Afars and Issas see Djibouti							
† Afghanistan	251,826	16,595,000	66	Islamic republic	A	Kābul	Dari, Pashto, Uzbek, Turkmen
Africa	11,700,000	683,700,000	58				
Alabama	52,423	4,202,000	80	State (U.S.)	D	Montgomery	English
Alaska	656,424	597,000	0.9	State (U.S.)	D	Juneau	English, indigenous
† Albania	11,100	3,424,000	308	Republic	A	Tiranë	Albanian, Greek
Alberta	255,287	2,599,000	10	Province (Canada)	D	Edmonton	English
† Algeria	919,595	26,780,000	29	Provisional military government	A	Algiers (El Djazaïr)	Arabic, Berber dialects, French
American Samoa	77	53,000	688	Unincorporated territory (U.S.)	C	Pago Pago	Samoan, English
† Andorra	175	58,000	331	Parliamentary co-principality (Spanish and French)	B	Andorra	Catalan, Spanish (Castilian), French
† Angola	481,354	11,040,000	23	Republic	A	Luanda	Portuguese, indigenous
Anguilla	35	7,000	200	Dependent territory (U.K. protection)	B	The Valley	English
Anhui	53,668	58,850,000	1,097	Province (China)	D	Hefei	Chinese (Mandarin)
Antarctica	5,400,000	(¹)					
† Antigua and Barbuda	171	64,000	374	Parliamentary state	A	St. John's	English, local dialects
† Argentina	1,073,519	33,635,000	31	Republic	A	Buenos Aires and Viedma (⁴)	Spanish, English, Italian, German, French
Arizona	114,006	3,943,000	35	State (U.S.)	D	Phoenix	English
Arkansas	53,182	2,438,000	46	State (U.S.)	D	Little Rock	English
† Armenia	11,506	3,743,000	325	Republic	A	Yerevan	Armenian, Russian
Aruba	75	68,000	907	Self-governing territory (Netherlands protection)	B	Oranjestad	Dutch, Papiamento, English, Spanish
Ascension	34	1,000	29	Dependency (St. Helena)	C	Georgetown	English
Asia	17,300,000	3,385,900,000	196				
† Australia	2,966,155	17,950,000	6.1	Federal parliamentary state	A	Canberra	English, indigenous
Australian Capital Territory	927	303,000	327	Territory (Australia)	D	Canberra	English
† Austria	32,377	7,913,000	244	Federal republic	A	Vienna (Wien)	German
† Azerbaijan	33,436	7,481,000	224	Republic	A	Baku (Bakı)	Azeri, Russian, Armenian
† Bahamas	5,382	270,000	50	Parliamentary state	A	Nassau	English, Creole
† Bahrain	267	572,000	2,142	Monarchy	A	Al Manāmah	Arabic, English, Farsi, Urdu
† Bangladesh	55,598	115,240,000	2,073	Republic	A	Dhaka	Bangla, English
† Barbados	166	260,000	1,566	Parliamentary state	A	Bridgetown	English
Beijing (Peking)	6,487	11,365,000	1,752	Autonomous city (China)	D	Beijing (Peking)	Chinese (Mandarin)
† Belarus	80,155	10,380,000	129	Republic	A	Minsk	Belarussian, Russian
Belau see Palau							
† Belgium	11,783	10,050,000	853	Constitutional monarchy	A	Brussels (Bruxelles)	Dutch (Flemish), French, German
† Belize	8,866	205,000	23	Parliamentary state	A	Belmopan	English, Spanish, Mayan, Garifuna
† Benin	43,475	5,292,000	122	Republic	A	Porto-Novo and Cotonou	French, Fon, Yoruba, indigenous
Bermuda	21	76,000	3,619	Dependent territory (U.K.)	C	Hamilton	English
† Bhutan	17,954	1,707,000	95	Monarchy (Indian protection)	B	Thimphu	Dzongkha, Tibetan and Nepalese dialects
† Bolivia	424,165	7,582,000	18	Republic	A	La Paz and Sucre	Aymara, Quechua, Spanish
† Bosnia and Herzegovina	19,741	4,442,000	225	Republic	A	Sarajevo	Serbo-Croatian
† Botswana	224,711	1,424,000	6.3	Republic	A	Gaborone	English, Tswana
† Brazil	3,286,500	151,310,000	46	Federal republic	A	Brasília	Portuguese, Spanish, English, French
British Columbia	365,948	3,354,000	9.2	Province (Canada)	D	Victoria	English
British Indian Ocean Territory	23	(¹)		Dependent territory (U.K.)	C		English
British Virgin Islands	59	13,000	220	Dependent territory (U.K.)	C	Road Town	English
† Brunei	2,226	279,000	125	Monarchy	A	Bandar Seri Begawan	Malay, English, Chinese
† Bulgaria	42,855	8,813,000	206	Republic	A	Sofia (Sofiya)	Bulgarian, Turkish
† Burkina Faso	105,869	9,922,000	94	Republic	A	Ouagadougou	French, indigenous
Burma see Myanmar							
† Burundi	10,745	6,015,000	560	Republic	A	Bujumbura	French, Kirundi, Swahili
California	163,707	31,905,000	195	State (U.S.)	D	Sacramento	English
† Cambodia	69,898	10,010,000	143	Transitional government	A	Phnum Pénh (Phnom Penh)	Khmer, French
† Cameroon	183,568	12,845,000	70	Republic	A	Yaoundé	English, French, indigenous
† Canada	3,849,674	27,950,000	7.3	Federal parliamentary state	A	Ottawa	English, French
† Cape Verde	1,557	414,000	266	Republic	A	Praia	Portuguese, Crioulo
Cayman Islands	100	32,000	320	Dependent territory (U.K.)	C	George Town	English
† Central African Republic	240,535	3,089,000	13	Republic	A	Bangui	French, Sango, Arabic, indigenous
Ceylon see Sri Lanka							
† Chad	495,755	6,149,000	12	Republic	A	N'Djamena	Arabic, French, indigenous
Channel Islands	75	149,000	1,987	Dependent territory (U.K.)	B		English, French
† Chile	292,135	13,795,000	47	Republic	A	Santiago	Spanish
† China (excl. Taiwan)	3,689,631	1,184,060,000	321	Socialist republic	A	Beijing (Peking)	Chinese dialects
Christmas Island	52	1,300	25	External territory (Australia)	C	The Settlement	English, Chinese, Malay
Cocos (Keeling) Islands	5.4	600	111	Territory (Australia)	C	West Island	English, Cocos-Malay, Malay
† Colombia	440,831	35,085,000	80	Republic	A	Santa Fe de Bogotá	Spanish
Colorado	104,100	3,528,000	34	State (U.S.)	D	Denver	English
† Comoros (excl. Mayotte)	863	508,000	589	Federal Islamic republic	A	Moroni	Arabic, French, Comoran
† Congo	132,047	2,403,000	18	Republic	A	Brazzaville	French, Lingala, Kikongo, indigenous
Connecticut	5,544	3,272,000	590	State (U.S.)	D	Hartford	English
Cook Islands	91	19,000	209	Self-governing territory (New Zealand protection)	B	Avarua	English, Maori
† Costa Rica	19,730	3,285,000	166	Republic	A	San José	Spanish
† Cote d'Ivoire	124,518	13,930,000	112	Republic	A	Abidjan and Yamoussoukro (⁴)	French, Dioula and other indigenous
† Croatia	21,829	4,796,000	220	Republic	A	Zagreb	Sebo-Croatian
† Cuba	42,804	11,015,000	257	Socialist republic	A	Havana (La Habana)	Spanish
† Cyprus	2,276	574,000	252	Republic	A	Nicosia (Levkosía)	Greek, English

REGION OR POLITICAL DIVISION	Area Sq. Mi.	Est. Pop. 1/1/94	Pop. Per. Sq. Mi.	Form of Government and Ruling Power	Capital	Predominant Languages
Cyprus, North (2)	1,295	193,000	149	Republic . . . . A	Nicosia (Lefkoşa)	Turkish
† Czech Republic	30,450	10,400,000	342	Republic . . . . A	Prague (Praha)	Czech, Slovak
Delaware	2,489	700,000	281	State (U.S.) . . . . D	Dover	English
† Denmark	16,639	5,181,000	311	Constitutional monarchy . . . . A	Copenhagen (København)	Danish
District of Columbia	68	576,000	8,471	Federal district (U.S.) . . . . D	Washington	English
† Djibouti	8,958	579,000	65	Republic . . . . A	Djibouti	French, Arabic, Somali, Afar
† Dominica	305	87,000	285	Republic . . . . A	Roseau	English, French
† Dominican Republic	18,704	7,715,000	412	Republic . . . . A	Santo Domingo	Spanish
† Ecuador	105,037	10,515,000	100	Republic . . . . A	Quito	Spanish, Quechua, indigenous
† Egypt	386,662	56,820,000	147	Socialist republic . . . . A	Cairo (Al Qāhirah)	Arabic
Ellice Islands see Tuvalu						
† El Salvador	8,124	5,179,000	637	Republic . . . . A	San Salvador	Spanish, Nahua
England	50,352	48,320,000	960	Administrative division (U.K.) . . . . . D	London	English
† Equatorial Guinea	10,831	379,000	35	Republic . . . . A	Malabo	Spanish, indigenous, English
† Eritrea	36,170	3,540,000	98	Republic . . . . A	Asmera	Tigre, Kunama, Cushitic dialects, Nora Bana, Arabic
† Estonia	17,413	1,608,000	92	Republic . . . . A	Tallinn	Estonian, Latvian, Lithuanian, Russian
† Ethiopia	446,953	54,170,000	121	Provisional military government . . . . A	Addis Ababa	Amharic, Tigrinya, Orominga, Guaraginga, Somali, Arabic
Europe	3,800,000	709,300,000	187			
Faeroe Islands	540	48,000	89	Self-governing territory (Danish protection) B	Tórshavn	Danish, Faroese
Falkland Islands (3)	4,700	2,200	0.5	Dependent territory (U.K.) C	Stanley	English
† Fiji	7,056	759,000	108	Republic . . . . A	Suva	English, Fijian, Hindustani
† Finland	130,559	5,056,000	39	Republic . . . . A	Helsinki (Helsingfors)	Finnish, Swedish, Lapp, Russian
Florida	65,758	13,855,000	211	State (U.S.) . . . . D	Tallahassee	English
† France (excl. Overseas Departments)	211,208	57,680,000	273	Republic . . . . A	Paris	French
French Guiana	35,135	134,000	3.8	Overseas department (France) C	Cayenne	French
French Polynesia	1,359	211,000	155	Overseas territory (France) C	Papeete	French, Tahitian
Fujian	46,332	31,375,000	677	Province (China) . . . . D	Fuzhou	Chinese dialects
† Gabon	103,347	1,127,000	11	Republic . . . . A	Libreville	French, Fang, indigenous
† Gambia	4,127	919,000	223	Republic . . . . A	Banjul	English, Malinke, Wolof, Fula, indigenous
Gansu	173,746	23,445,000	135	Province (China) . . . . D	Lanzhou	Chinese (Mandarin), Mongolian, Tibetan dialects
Gaza Strip	146	745,000	5,103	Israeli territory with limited self-government		Arabic
Georgia	59,441	6,875,000	116	State (U.S.) . . . . D	Atlanta	English
† Georgia	26,911	5,646,000	210	Republic . . . . A	Tbilisi	Georgian, Russian, Armenian, Azeri
† Germany	137,822	80,930,000	587	Federal republic . . . . A	Berlin and Bonn	German
† Ghana	92,098	16,595,000	180	Republic . . . . A	Accra	English, Akan and other indigenous
Gibraltar	2.3	32,000	13,913	Dependent territory (U.K.) C	Gibraltar	English, Spanish, Italian, Portuguese, Russian
Gilbert Islands see Kiribati						
Golan Heights	454	29,000	64	Occupied by Israel		Arabic, Hebrew
Great Britain see United Kingdom						
† Greece	50,949	10,500,000	206	Republic . . . . A	Athens (Athínai)	Greek, English, French
Greenland	840,004	57,000	0.1	Self-governing territory (Danish protection) B	Godthåb	Danish, Greenlandic, Inuit dialects
† Grenada	133	91,000	684	Parliamentary state . . . . A	St. George's	English, French
Guadeloupe (incl. Dependencies)	687	424,000	617	Overseas department (France) C	Basse-Terre	French, Creole
Guam	209	147,000	703	Unincorporated territory (U.S.) C	Agana	English, Chamorro, Japanese
Guangdong	68,726	65,830,000	958	Province (China) . . . . D	Guangzhou (Canton)	Chinese dialects, Miao-Yao
Guangxi Zhuangzu	91,236	44,285,000	485	Autonomous region (China) . . . . . . D	Nanning	Chinese dialects, Thai, Miao-Yao
† Guatemala	42,042	10,510,000	250	Republic . . . . A	Guatemala	Spanish, Amerindian
Guernsey (incl. Dependencies)	30	63,000	2,100	Crown dependency (U.K. protection) . . . . B	St. Peter Port	English, French
† Guinea	94,926	6,274,000	66	Provisional military government . . . . A	Conakry	French, indigenous
† Guinea-Bissau	13,948	1,078,000	77	Republic . . . . A	Bissau	Portuguese, Crioulo, indigenous
Guizhou	65,637	33,985,000	518	Province (China) . . . . D	Guiyang	Chinese (Mandarin), Thai, Miao-Yao
† Guyana	83,000	732,000	8.8	Republic . . . . A	Georgetown	English, indigenous
Hainan	13,127	6,867,000	523	Province (China) . . . . D	Haikou	Chinese, Min, Tai
† Haiti	10,714	6,411,000	598	Provisional military government . . . . A	Port-au-Prince	Creole, French
Hawaii	10,932	1,167,000	107	State (U.S.) . . . . D	Honolulu	English, Hawaiian, Japanese
Hebei	73,359	63,940,000	872	Province (China) . . . . D	Shijiazhuang	Chinese (Mandarin)
Heilongjiang	181,082	36,945,000	204	Province (China) . . . . D	Harbin	Chinese dialects, Mongolian, Tungus
Henan	64,479	89,520,000	1,388	Province (China) . . . . D	Zhengzhou	Chinese (Mandarin)
Holland see Netherlands						
† Honduras	43,277	5,206,000	120	Republic . . . . A	Tegucigalpa	Spanish, indigenous
Hong Kong	414	5,890,000	14,227	Chinese territory under British administration C	Victoria (Hong Kong)	Chinese (Cantonese), English, Putonghua
Hubei	72,356	56,480,000	781	Province (China) . . . . D	Wuhan	Chinese dialects
Hunan	81,081	63,580,000	784	Province (China) . . . . D	Changsha	Chinese dialects, Miao-Yao
† Hungary	35,919	10,295,000	287	Republic . . . . A	Budapest	Hungarian
† Iceland	39,769	262,000	6.6	Republic . . . . A	Reykjavík	Icelandic
Idaho	83,574	1,089,000	13	State (U.S.) . . . . D	Boise	English
Illinois	57,918	11,750,000	203	State (U.S.) . . . . D	Springfield	English
† India (incl. part of Jammu and Kashmir)	1,237,062	906,770,000	733	Federal republic . . . . A	New Delhi	English, Hindi, Telugu, Bengali, indigenous
Indiana	36,420	5,733,000	157	State (U.S.) . . . . D	Indianapolis	English
† Indonesia	752,410	198,810,000	264	Republic . . . . A	Jakarta	Bahasa Indonesia (Malay), English, Dutch, indigenous
Iowa	56,276	2,827,000	50	State (U.S.) . . . . D	Des Moines	English
† Iran	632,457	63,940,000	101	Islamic republic . . . . A	Tehrān	Farsi, Turkish dialects, Kurdish
† Iraq	169,235	19,335,000	114	Republic . . . . A	Baghdād	Arabic, Kurdish, Assyrian, Armenian
† Ireland	27,137	3,563,000	131	Republic . . . . A	Dublin (Baile Átha Cliath)	English, Irish Gaelic
Isle of Man	221	72,000	326	Crown dependency (U.K. protection) . . . . B	Douglas	English, Manx Gaelic
† Israel (excl. Occupied Areas)	8,019	4,950,000	617	Republic . . . . A	Jerusalem (Yerushalayim)	Hebrew, Arabic
† Italy	116,324	56,670,000	487	Republic . . . . A	Rome (Roma)	Italian, German, French, Slovene
Ivory Coast see Cote d'Ivoire						
† Jamaica	4,244	2,538,000	598	Parliamentary state . . . . A	Kingston	English, Creole
† Japan	145,870	124,840,000	856	Constitutional monarchy . . . . A	Tōkyō	Japanese
Jersey	45	86,000	1,911	Crown dependency (U.K. protection) . . . . B	St. Helier	English, French
Jiangsu	39,614	70,210,000	1,772	Province (China) . . . . D	Nanjing (Nanking)	Chinese dialects
Jiangxi	64,325	39,550,000	615	Province (China) . . . . D	Nanchang	Chinese dialects
Jilin	72,201	25,815,000	358	Province (China) . . . . D	Changchun	Chinese (Mandarin), Mongolian, Korean
† Jordan	35,135	3,858,000	110	Constitutional monarchy . . . . A	'Ammān	Arabic
Kansas	82,282	2,568,000	31	State (U.S.) . . . . D	Topeka	English
† Kazakhstan	1,049,156	17,190,000	16	Republic . . . . A	Alma-Ata (Almaty) and Akmola (4)	Kazakh, Russian
Kentucky	40,411	3,813,000	94	State (U.S.) . . . . D	Frankfort	English
† Kenya	224,961	28,280,000	126	Republic . . . . A	Nairobi	English, Swahili, indigenous

REGION OR POLITICAL DIVISION	Area Sq. Mi.	Est. Pop. 1/1/94	Pop. Per. Sq. Mi.	Form of Government and Ruling Power		Capital	Predominant Languages
Kiribati	313	77,000	246	Republic	A	Bairiki	English, Gilbertese
† Korea, North	46,540	22,735,000	489	Socialist republic	A	Pyŏngyang	Korean
† Korea, South	38,230	44,250,000	1,157	Republic	A	Seoul (Sŏul)	Korean
† Kuwait	6,880	1,734,000	252	Constitutional monarchy	A	Kuwait	Arabic, English
† Kyrgyzstan	76,641	4,645,000	61	Republic	A	Bishkek	Kirghiz, Russian
† Laos	91,429	4,601,000	50	Socialist republic	A	Viangchan (Vientiane)	Lao, French, English
† Latvia	24,595	2,556,000	104	Republic	A	Rīga	Latvian, Russian, Lithuanian
† Lebanon	4,015	3,566,000	888	Republic	A	Beirut (Bayrūt)	Arabic, French, Armenian, English
† Lesotho	11,720	1,907,000	163	Constitutional monarchy under military rule	A	Maseru	English, Sesotho, Zulu, Xhosa
Liaoning	56,255	41,325,000	735	Province (China)	D	Shenyang	Chinese (Mandarin), Mongolian
† Liberia	38,250	2,901,000	76	Republic	A	Monrovia	English, indigenous
† Libya	679,362	4,917,000	7.2	Socialist republic	A	Tripoli (Ṭarābulus)	Arabic
† Liechtenstein	62	30,000	484	Constitutional monarchy	A	Vaduz	German
† Lithuania	25,212	3,777,000	150	Republic	A	Vilnius	Lithuanian, Polish, Russian
Louisiana	51,843	4,332,000	84	State (U.S.)	D	Baton Rouge	English
† Luxembourg	998	401,000	402	Constitutional monarchy	A	Luxembourg	French, Luxembourgish, German
Macao	6.6	380,000	57,576	Chinese territory under Portuguese administration	C	Macao	Portuguese, Chinese (Cantonese)
† Macedonia	9,928	2,198,000	221	Republic	A	Skopje	Macedonian, Albanian
† Madagascar	226,658	13,110,000	58	Republic	A	Antananarivo	Malagasy, French
Maine	35,387	1,245,000	35	State (U.S.)	D	Augusta	English
† Malawi	45,747	8,942,000	195	Republic	A	Lilongwe	Chichewa, English
† Malaysia	127,320	19,060,000	150	Federal constitutional monarchy	A	Kuala Lumpur	Malay, Chinese dialects, English, Tamil
† Maldives	115	246,000	2,139	Republic	A	Male	Divehi
† Mali	482,077	8,922,000	19	Republic	A	Bamako	French, Bambara, indigenous
† Malta	122	365,000	2,992	Republic	A	Valletta	English, Maltese
Manitoba	250,947	1,118,000	4.5	Province (Canada)	D	Winnipeg	English
† Marshall Islands	70	52,000	743	Republic (U.S. protection)	A	Majuro (island)	English, indigenous, Japanese
Martinique	425	377,000	887	Overseas department (France)	C	Fort-de-France	French, Creole
Maryland	12,407	5,006,000	403	State (U.S.)	D	Annapolis	English
Massachusetts	10,555	6,106,000	578	State (U.S.)	D	Boston	English
† Mauritania	395,956	2,142,000	5.4	Republic	A	Nouakchott	Arabic, Pular, Soninke, Wolof
† Mauritius (incl. Dependencies)	788	1,110,000	1,409	Republic	A	Port Louis	English, Creole, Bhojpuri, French, Hindi, Tamil, others
Mayotte (5)	144	91,000	632	Territorial collectivity (France)	C	Dzaoudzi and Mamoudzou (4)	French, Swahili (Mahorian)
† Mexico	759,534	90,870,000	120	Federal republic	A	Mexico City (Ciudad de México)	Spanish, indigenous
Michigan	96,810	9,550,000	99	State (U.S.)	D	Lansing	English
† Micronesia, Federated States of	271	119,000	439	Republic (U.S. protection)	A	Kolonia and Paliker (4)	English, indigenous
Midway Islands	2.0	500	250	Unincorporated territory (U.S.)	C	.....	English
Minnesota	86,943	4,539,000	52	State (U.S.)	D	St. Paul	English
Mississippi	48,434	2,646,000	55	State (U.S.)	D	Jackson	English
Missouri	69,709	5,266,000	76	State (U.S.)	D	Jefferson City	English
† Moldova	13,012	4,425,000	340	Republic	A	Chişinău (Kishinev)	Romanian (Moldovan), Russian
† Monaco	0.7	31,000	44,286	Constitutional monarchy	A	Monaco	French, English, Italian, Monegasque
† Mongolia	604,829	2,314,000	3.8	Republic	A	Ulan Bator (Ulaanbaatar)	Khalkha Mongol, Turkish dialects, Russian, Chinese
Montana	147,046	830,000	5.6	State (U.S.)	D	Helena	English
Montserrat	39	13,000	333	Dependent territory (U.K.)	C	Plymouth	English
† Morocco (excl. Western Sahara)	172,414	28,095,000	163	Constitutional monarchy	A	Rabat	Arabic, Berber dialects, French
† Mozambique	308,642	16,585,000	54	Republic	A	Maputo	Portuguese, indigenous
† Myanmar (Burma)	261,228	43,630,000	167	Provisional military government	A	Rangoon (Yangon)	Burmese, indigenous
† Namibia	318,253	1,555,000	4.9	Republic	A	Windhoek	English, Afrikaans, German, indigenous
Nauru	8.1	10,000	1,235	Republic	A	Yaren District	Nauruan, English
Nebraska	77,358	1,635,000	21	State (U.S.)	D	Lincoln	English
Nei Monggol (Inner Mongolia)	456,759	22,495,000	49	Autonomous region (China)	D	Hohhot	Mongolian
† Nepal	56,827	20,660,000	364	Constitutional monarchy	A	Kathmandu	Nepali, Maithali, Bhojpuri, other indigenous
† Netherlands	16,164	15,320,000	948	Constitutional monarchy	A	Amsterdam and The Hague ('s-Gravenhage)	Dutch
Netherlands Antilles	309	192,000	621	Self-governing territory (Netherlands protection)	B	Willemstad	Dutch, Papiamento, English
Nevada	110,567	1,375,000	12	State (U.S.)	D	Carson City	English
New Brunswick	28,355	755,000	27	Province (Canada)	D	Fredericton	English, French
New Caledonia	7,358	179,000	24	Overseas territory (France)	C	Nouméa	French, indigenous
Newfoundland	156,649	587,000	3.7	Province (Canada)	D	St. John's	English
New Hampshire	9,351	1,167,000	125	State (U.S.)	D	Concord	English
New Hebrides see Vanuatu	.....						
New Jersey	8,722	7,915,000	907	State (U.S.)	D	Trenton	English
New Mexico	121,598	1,608,000	13	State (U.S.)	D	Santa Fe	English, Spanish
New South Wales	309,500	6,117,000	20	State (Australia)	D	Sydney	English
New York	54,475	18,375,000	337	State (U.S.)	D	Albany	English
† New Zealand	104,454	3,486,000	33	Parliamentary state	A	Wellington	English, Maori
† Nicaragua	50,054	4,267,000	85	Republic	A	Managua	Spanish, English, indigenous
† Niger	489,191	8,754,000	18	Provisional military government	A	Niamey	French, Hausa, Djerma, indigenous
† Nigeria	356,669	94,550,000	265	Provisional military government	A	Lagos and Abuja	English, Hausa, Fulani, Yorbua, Ibo, indigenous
Ningxia Huizu	25,637	4,855,000	189	Autonomous region (China)	D	Yinchuan	Chinese (Mandarin)
Niue	100	1,900	19	Self-governing territory (New Zealand protection)	B	Alofi	English, indigenous
Norfolk Island	14	2,700	193	External territory (Australia)	C	Kingston	English, Norfolk
North America	9,500,000	444,600,000	47	.....		.....	.....
North Carolina	53,821	6,955,000	129	State (U.S.)	D	Raleigh	English
North Dakota	70,704	632,000	8.9	State (U.S.)	D	Bismarck	English
Northern Ireland	5,461	1,605,000	294	Administrative division (U.K.)	D	Belfast	English
Northern Mariana Islands	184	49,000	266	Commonwealth (U.S. protection)	B	Saipan (island)	English, Chamorro, Carolinian
Northern Territory	519,771	172,000	0.3	Territory (Australia)	D	Darwin	English, indigenous
Northwest Territories	1,322,910	56,000	0.1	Territory (Canada)	D	Yellowknife	English, indigenous
† Norway (incl. Svalbard and Jan Mayen)	149,412	4,301,000	29	Constitutional monarchy	A	Oslo	Norwegian, Lapp, Finnish
Nova Scotia	21,425	922,000	43	Province (Canada)	D	Halifax	English
Oceania (incl. Australia)	3,300,000	28,000,000	8.5	.....		.....	.....
Ohio	44,828	11,155,000	249	State (U.S.)	D	Columbus	English
Oklahoma	69,903	3,242,000	46	State (U.S.)	D	Oklahoma City	English
† Oman	82,030	1,659,000	20	Monarchy	A	Muscat	Arabic, English, Baluchi, Urdu, Indian dialects
Ontario	412,581	10,315,000	25	Province (Canada)	D	Toronto	English
Oregon	98,386	3,009,000	31	State (U.S.)	D	Salem	English

REGION OR POLITICAL DIVISION	Area Sq. Mi.	Est. Pop. 1/1/94	Pop. Per. Sq. Mi.	Form of Government and Ruling Power		Capital	Predominant Languages
† Pakistan (incl. part of Jammu and Kashmir)	339,732	126,090,000	371	Federal Islamic republic	A	Islāmābād	English, Urdu, Punjabi, Sindhi, Pashto
Palau (Belau)	196	16,000	82	Republic	A	Koror and Melekeok (4)	Angaur, English, Japanese, Palauan, Sonsorolese, Tobi
† Panama	29,157	2,592,000	89	Republic	A	Panamá	Spanish, English
† Papua New Guinea	178,704	3,989,000	22	Parliamentary state	A	Port Moresby	English, Motu, Pidgin, indigenous
† Paraguay	157,048	4,297,000	27	Republic	A	Asunción	Spanish, Guarani
Pennsylvania	46,058	12,145,000	264	State (U.S.)	D	Harrisburg	English
† Peru	496,225	23,305,000	47	Republic	A	Lima	Quechua, Spanish, Aymara
† Philippines	115,831	66,190,000	571	Republic	A	Manila	English, Pilipino, Tagalog
Pitcairn (incl. Dependencies)	19	100	5.3	Dependent territory (U.K.)	C	Adamstown	English, Tahitian
† Poland	121,196	38,540,000	318	Republic	A	Warsaw (Warszawa)	Polish
† Portugal	35,516	9,961,000	280	Republic	A	Lisbon (Lisboa)	Portuguese
Prince Edward Island	2,185	140,000	64	Province (Canada)	D	Charlottetown	English
Puerto Rico	3,515	3,801,000	1,081	Commonwealth (U.S. protection)	B	San Juan	Spanish, English
† Qatar	4,412	502,000	114	Monarchy	A	Doha	Arabic, English
Qinghai	277,994	4,618,000	17	Province (China)	D	Xining	Tibetan dialects, Mongolian, Turkish dialects, Chinese (Mandarin)
Quebec	594,860	7,070,000	12	Province (Canada)	D	Québec	French, English
Queensland	666,876	3,111,000	4.7	State (Australia)	D	Brisbane	English
Reunion	969	643,000	664	Overseas department (France)	C	Saint-Denis	French, Creole
Rhode Island	1,545	1,012,000	655	State (U.S.)	D	Providence	English
Rhodesia see Zimbabwe							
† Romania	91,699	22,770,000	248	Republic	A	Bucharest (Bucureşti)	Romanian, Hungarian, German
† Russia	6,592,849	150,500,000	23	Federal republic	A	Moscow (Moskva)	Russian, Tatar, Ukrainian
† Rwanda	10,169	8,196,000	806	Republic	A	Kigali	French, Kinyarwanda, Kiswahili
St. Helena (incl. Dependencies)	121	7,000	58	Dependent territory (U.K.)	C	Jamestown	English
† St. Kitts and Nevis	104	45,000	433	Parliamentary state	A	Basseterre	English
† St. Lucia	238	151,000	634	Parliamentary state	A	Castries	English, French
St. Pierre and Miquelon	93	7,000	75	Territorial collectivity (France)	C	Saint-Pierre	French
† St. Vincent and the Grenadines	150	115,000	767	Parliamentary state	A	Kingstown	English, French
† San Marino	24	24,000	1,000	Republic	A	San Marino	Italian
† Sao Tome and Principe	372	125,000	336	Republic	A	São Tomé	Portuguese, Fang
Saskatchewan	251,866	1,006,000	4.0	Province (Canada)	D	Regina	English
† Saudi Arabia	830,000	16,585,000	20	Monarchy	A	Riyadh (Ar Riyāḍ)	Arabic
Scotland	30,421	5,130,000	169	Administrative division (U.K.)	D	Edinburgh	English, Scots Gaelic
† Senegal	75,951	8,522,000	112	Republic	A	Dakar	French, Wolof, Fulani, Serer, indigenous
† Seychelles	175	72,000	411	Republic	A	Victoria	English, French, Creole
Shaanxi	79,151	34,455,000	435	Province (China)	D	Xi'an (Sian)	Chinese (Mandarin)
Shandong	59,074	88,450,000	1,497	Province (China)	D	Jinan	Chinese (Mandarin)
Shanghai	2,394	13,970,000	5,835	Autonomous city (China)	D	Shanghai	Chinese (Wu)
Shanxi	60,232	30,075,000	499	Province (China)	D	Taiyuan	Chinese (Mandarin)
Sichuan	220,078	112,250,000	510	Province (China)	D	Chengdu	Chinese (Mandarin), Tibetan dialects, Miao-Yao
† Sierra Leone	27,925	4,538,000	163	Transitional military government	A	Freetown	English, Krio, Mende, Temne, indigenous
† Singapore	246	2,834,000	11,520	Republic	A	Singapore	Chinese (Mandarin), English, Malay, Tamil
† Slovakia	18,933	5,342,000	282	Republic	A	Bratislava	Slovak, Hungarian
† Slovenia	7,820	1,986,000	254	Republic	A	Ljubljana	Slovenian, Serbo-Croatian
† Solomon Islands	10,954	376,000	34	Parliamentary state	A	Honiara	English, indigenous
† Somalia	246,201	6,541,000	27	None	A	Mogadishu (Muqdisho)	Arabic, Somali, English, Italian
† South Africa	471,010	42,320,000	90	Republic	A	Pretoria, Cape Town, and Bloemfontein	Afrikaans, English, Xhosa, Zulu, other indigenous
South America	6,900,000	304,500,000	44				
South Australia	379,925	1,495,000	3.9	State (Australia)	D	Adelaide	English
South Carolina	32,007	3,657,000	114	State (U.S.)	D	Columbia	English
South Dakota	77,121	726,000	9.4	State (U.S.)	D	Pierre	English
South Georgia (incl. Dependencies)	1,450	(1)		Dependent territory (U.K.)	C	Grytviken Harbour	English
South West Africa see Namibia							
† Spain	194,885	38,640,000	198	Constitutional monarchy	A	Madrid	Spanish (Castilian), Catalan, Galician, Basque
Spanish North Africa (6)	12	142,000	11,833	Five possessions (Spain)	C		Spanish, Arabic, Berber dialects
Spanish Sahara see Western Sahara							
† Sri Lanka	24,962	17,970,000	720	Socialist republic	A	Colombo and Sri Jayawardenapura	English, Sinhala, Tamil
† Sudan	967,500	28,900,000	30	Provisional military government	A	Khartoum (Al Kharṭūm)	Arabic, Nubian and other indigenous, English
† Suriname	63,251	418,000	6.6	Republic	A	Paramaribo	Dutch, Sranan Tongo, English, Hindustani, Javanese
† Swaziland	6,704	854,000	127	Monarchy	A	Mbabane and Lobamba	English, siSwati
† Sweden	173,732	8,747,000	50	Constitutional monarchy	A	Stockholm	Swedish, Lapp, Finnish
Switzerland	15,943	7,001,000	439	Federal republic	A	Bern (Berne)	German, French, Italian, Romansch
† Syria	71,498	13,695,000	192	Socialist republic	A	Damascus (Dimashq)	Arabic, Kurdish, Armenian, Aramaic, Circassian
Taiwan	13,900	20,945,000	1,507	Republic	A	T'aipei	Chinese (Mandarin), Taiwanese (Min), Hakka
† Tajikistan	55,251	5,720,000	104	Republic	A	Dushanbe	Tajik, Uzbek, Russian
† Tanzania	364,900	27,450,000	75	Republic	A	Dar es Salaam and Dodoma	English, Swahili, indigenous
Tasmania	26,178	483,000	18	State (Australia)	D	Hobart	English
Tennessee	42,146	5,058,000	120	State (U.S.)	D	Nashville	English
Texas	268,601	17,925,000	67	State (U.S.)	D	Austin	English, Spanish
† Thailand	198,115	58,960,000	298	Constitutional monarchy	A	Bangkok (Krung Thep)	Thai, indigenous
Tianjin (Tientsin)	4,363	9,235,000	2,117	Autonomous city (China)	D	Tianjin (Tientsin)	Chinese (Mandarin)
† Togo	21,925	4,142,000	189	Provisional military government	A	Lomé	French, Ewe, Mina, Kabye, Dagomba
Tokelau	4.6	1,500	326	Island territory (New Zealand)	C		English, Tokelauan
Tonga	288	104,000	361	Constitutional monarchy	A	Nuku'alofa	Tongan, English
† Trinidad and Tobago	1,980	1,288,000	651	Republic	A	Port of Spain	English, Hindi, French, Spanish
Tristan da Cunha	40	300	7.5	Dependency (St. Helena)	C	Edinburgh	English
† Tunisia	63,170	8,605,000	136	Republic	A	Tunis	Arabic, French
† Turkey	300,948	61,540,000	204	Republic	A	Ankara	Turkish, Kurdish, Arabic
† Turkmenistan	188,456	3,935,000	21	Republic	A	Ashkhabad	Turkmen, Russian, Uzbek
Turks and Caicos Islands	193	13,000	67	Dependent territory (U.K.)	C	Grand Turk	English
Tuvalu	10	10,000	1,000	Parliamentary state	A	Funafuti	Tuvaluan, English
† Uganda	93,104	18,425,000	198	Republic	A	Kampala	English, Luganda, Swahili, indigenous
† Ukraine	233,090	52,240,000	224	Republic	A	Kiev (Kyyiv)	Ukrainian, Russian, Romanian, Polish
† United Arab Emirates	32,278	2,692,000	83	Federation of monarchs	A	Abū Ẓaby (Abu Dhabi)	Arabic, Farsi, English, Hindi, Urdu
† United Kingdom	94,249	57,960,000	615	Parliamentary monarchy	A	London	English, Welsh, Scots Gaelic

REGION OR POLITICAL DIVISION	Area Sq. Mi.	Est. Pop. 1/1/94	Pop. Per. Sq. Mi.	Form of Government and Ruling Power		Capital	Predominant Languages
† United States	3,787,425	259,390,000	68	Federal republic	A	Washington	English, Spanish
Upper Volta see Burkina Faso	. . . . . .	. . . . . .	. . . .				
† Uruguay	68,500	3,181,000	46	Republic	A	Montevideo	Spanish
Utah	84,904	1,842,000	22	State (U.S.)	D	Salt Lake City	English
† Uzbekistan	172,742	22,240,000	129	Republic	A	Tashkent	Uzbek, Russian
† Vanuatu	4,707	160,000	34	Republic	A	Port-Vila	Bislama, English, French
Vatican City	0.2	900	4,500	Monarchical-sacerdotal state	A	Vatican City	Italian, Latin, other
† Venezuela	352,145	20,460,000	58	Federal republic	A	Caracas	Spanish, Amerindian
Vermont	9,615	585,000	61	State (U.S.)	D	Montpelier	English
Victoria	87,877	4,566,000	52	State (Australia)	D	Melbourne	English
† Vietnam	127,428	72,080,000	566	Socialist republic	A	Hanoi	Vietnamese, French, Chinese, English, Khmer, indigenous
Virginia	42,769	6,485,000	152	State (U.S.)	D	Richmond	English
Virgin Islands (U.S.)	133	97,000	729	Unincorporated territory (U.S.)	C	Charlotte Amalie	English, Spanish, Creole
Wake Island	3.0	300	100	Unincorporated territory (U.S.)	C	. . . .	English
Wales	8,015	2,905,000	362	Administrative division (U.K.)	D	Cardiff	English, Welsh Gaelic
Wallis and Futuna	98	14,000	143	Overseas territory (France)	C	Mata-Utu	French, Wallisian
Washington	71,303	5,188,000	73	State (U.S.)	D	Olympia	English
West Bank (incl. Jericho and East Jerusalem)	2,347	1,460,000	622	Israeli territory with limited self-government			Arabic, Hebrew
Western Australia	975,101	1,703,000	1.7	State (Australia)	D	Perth	English
Western Sahara	102,703	208,000	2.0	Occupied by Morocco	C	. . . .	Arabic
† Western Samoa	1,093	168,000	154	Constitutional monarchy	A	Apia	English, Samoan
West Virginia	24,231	1,816,000	75	State (U.S.)	D	Charleston	English
Wisconsin	65,503	5,058,000	77	State (U.S.)	D	Madison	English
Wyoming	97,818	467,000	4.8	State (U.S.)	D	Cheyenne	English
Xinjiang Uygur (Sinkiang)	617,764	15,865,000	26	Autonomous region (China)	D	Ürümqi	Turkish dialects, Mongolian, Tungus, English
Xizang (Tibet)	471,045	2,250,000	4.8	Autonomous region (China)	D	Lhasa	Tibetan dialects
† Yemen	203,850	10,840,000	53	Republic	A	Şan'ā'	Arabic
Yugoslavia	39,449	10,730,000	272	Republic	A	Belgrade (Beograd)	Serbo-Croatian 95%, Albanian 5%
Yukon Territory	186,661	28,000	0.2	Territory (Canada)	D	Whitehorse	English, Inuktitut, indigenous
Yunnan	152,124	38,720,000	255	Province (China)	D	Kunming	Chinese (Mandarin), Tibetan dialects, Khmer, Miao-Yao
† Zaire	905,446	41,675,000	46	Republic	A	Kinshasa	French, Kikongo, Lingala, Swahili, Tshiluba, Kingwana
† Zambia	290,586	8,625,000	30	Republic	A	Lusaka	English, Tonga, Lozi, other indigenous
Zhejiang	39,305	43,455,000	1,106	Province (China)	D	Hangzhou	Chinese dialects
† Zimbabwe	150,873	10,605,000	70	Republic	A	Harare (Salisbury)	English, Shona, Sindebele
WORLD	57,900,000	5,556,000,000	96	. . . .		. . . .	. . . .

† Member of the United Nations (1994).
. . . None, or not applicable.
(1) No permanent population.
(2) North Cyprus unilaterally declared its independence from Cyprus in 1983.
(3) Claimed by Argentina.
(4) Future capital.
(5) Claimed by Comoros.
(6) Comprises Ceuta, Melilla, and several small islands.

WORLD COMPARISONS

General Information

Equatorial diameter of the earth, 7,926.38 miles.
Polar diameter of the earth, 7,899.80 miles.
Mean diameter of the earth, 7,917.52 miles.
Equatorial circumference of the earth, 24,901.46 miles.
Polar circumference of the earth, 24,855.34 miles.
Mean distance from the earth to the sun, 93,020,000 miles.
Mean distance from the earth to the moon, 238,857 miles.
Total area of the earth, 197,000,000 square miles.

Highest elevation on the earth's surface, Mt. Everest, Asia, 29,028 feet.
Lowest elevation on the earth's land surface, shores of the Dead Sea, Asia, 1,312 feet below sea level.
Greatest known depth of the ocean, southwest of Guam, Pacific Ocean, 35,810 feet.
Total land area of the earth (incl. inland water and Antarctica), 57,900,000 square miles.

Area of Africa, 11,700,000 square miles.
Area of Antarctica, 5,400,000 square miles.
Area of Asia, 17,300,000 square miles.
Area of Europe, 3,800,000 square miles.
Area of North America, 9,500,000 square miles.
Area of Oceania (incl. Australia) 3,300,000 square miles.
Area of South America, 6,900,000 square miles.
Population of the earth (est. 1/1/94), 5,556,000,000.

Principal Islands and Their Areas

ISLAND	Area (Sq. Mi.)
Baffin I., Canada	195,928
Banks I., Canada	27,038
Borneo (Kalimantan), Asia	287,300
Bougainville, Papua New Guinea	3,600
Cape Breton I., Canada	3,981
Celebes (Sulawesi), Indonesia	73,057
Ceram (Seram), Indonesia	7,191
Corsica, France	3,367
Crete, Greece	3,190
Cuba, N. America	42,804
Cyprus, Asia	3,572
Devon I., Canada	21,331
Ellesmere I., Canada	75,767
Flores, Indonesia	5,502
Great Britain, U.K.	88,816
Greenland, N. America	840,004
Guadalcanal, Solomon Is.	2,060
Hainan Dao, China	13,200
Hawaii, U.S.	4,021
Hispaniola, N. America	29,300
Hokkaidō, Japan	32,245
Honshū, Japan	89,176
Iceland, Europe	39,769
Ireland, Europe	32,600
Jamaica, N. America	4,244
Java (Jawa), Indonesia	51,038
Kodiak I., U.S.	3,670
Kyūshū, Japan	17,129
Leyte, Philippines	2,785
Long Island, U.S.	1,401
Luzon, Philippines	40,420
Madagascar, Africa	226,658
Melville I., Canada	16,274
Mindanao, Philippines	36,537
Mindoro, Philippines	3,759
Negros, Philippines	4,907
New Britain, Papua New Guinea	14,093
New Caledonia, Oceania	6,467
Newfoundland, Canada	42,031
New Guinea, Asia-Oceania	309,000
New Ireland, Papua New Guinea	3,500
North East Land, Norway	6,350
North I., New Zealand	44,702
Novaya Zemlya, Russia	31,892
Palawan, Philippines	4,550
Panay, Philippines	4,446
Prince of Wales I., Canada	12,872
Puerto Rico, N. America	3,500
Sakhalin, Russia	29,498
Samar, Philippines	5,100
Sardinia, Italy	9,301
Shikoku, Japan	7,258
Sicily, Italy	9,927
Somerset I., Canada	9,570
Southampton I., Canada	15,913
South I., New Zealand	58,384
Spitsbergen, Norway	15,260
Sri Lanka, Asia	24,962
Sumatra (Sumatera), Indonesia	182,860
Taiwan, Asia	13,900
Tasmania, Australia	26,200
Tierra del Fuego, S. America	18,600
Timor, Indonesia	5,743
Vancouver I., Canada	12,079
Victoria I., Canada	83,897
Vrangelya (Wrangel), Russia	2,819

Principal Lakes, Oceans, Seas, and Their Areas

LAKE Country	Area (Sq. Mi.)
Arabian Sea	1,492,000
Aral Sea, Kazakhstan-Uzbekistan	14,900
Arctic Ocean	5,400,000
Athabasca, L., Canada	3,064
Atlantic Ocean	31,800,000
Balqash kölī, (L. Balkhash) Kazakhstan	7,066
Baltic Sea, Europe	163,000
Baykal, Ozero, (L. Baikal) Russia	12,162
Bering Sea, Asia-N.A.	876,000
Black Sea, Europe-Asia	178,000
Caribbean Sea, N.A.-S.A.	1,063,000
Caspian Sea, Asia-Europe	143,244
Chad, L., Cameroon-Chad-Nigeria	6,300
Erie, L., Canada-U.S.	9,910
Eyre, L., Australia	3,700
Gairdner, L., Australia	1,660
Great Bear Lake, Canada	12,096
Great Salt Lake, U.S.	1,680
Great Slave Lake, Canada	11,030
Hudson Bay, Canada	475,000
Huron, L., Canada-U.S.	23,000
Indian Ocean	28,900,000
Japan, Sea of, Asia	389,000
Koko Nor, (Qinghai Hu) China	1,770
Ladozhskoye Ozero, (L. Ladoga) Russia	6,834
Manitoba, L., Canada	1,785
Mediterranean Sea, Europe-Africa-Asia	967,000
Mexico, Gulf of, N. America	596,000
Michigan, L., U.S.	22,300
Nicaragua, Lago de, Nicaragua	3,150
North Sea, Europe	222,000
Nyasa, L., Malawi-Mozambique-Tanzania	11,150
Onezhskoye Ozero, (L. Onega) Russia	3,753
Ontario, L., Canada-U.S.	7,540
Pacific Ocean	63,800,000
Red Sea, Africa-Asia	169,000
Rudolf, L., Ethiopia-Kenya	2,473
Superior, L., Canada-U.S.	31,700
Tanganyika, L., Africa	12,350
Titicaca, Lago, Bolivia-Peru	3,200
Torrens, L., Australia	2,280
Vänern, (L.) Sweden	2,156
Van Gölü, (L.) Turkey	1,434
Victoria, L., Kenya-Tanzania-Uganda	26,820
Winnipeg, L., Canada	9,416
Winnipegosis, L., Canada	2,075
Yellow Sea, China-Korea	480,000

Principal Mountains and Their Heights

MOUNTAIN Country	Elev. (Ft.)
Aconcagua, Cerro, Argentina	22,831
Annapurna, Nepal	26,504
Api, Nepal	23,399
Apo, Philippines	9,692
Ararat, Mt., Turkey	16,854
Ayers Rock, Australia	2,844
Barú, Volcán, Panama	11,491
Bangueta, Mt., Papua New Guinea	13,520
Belukha, Gora, Kazakhstan-Russia	14,783
Bia, Phu, Laos	9,249
Blanc, Mont, (Monte Bianco) France-Italy	15,771
Blanca Pk., Colorado, U.S.	14,345
Bolívar, Venezuela	16,427
Bonete, Cerro, Argentina	22,546
Borah Pk., Idaho, U.S.	12,662
Boundary Pk., Nevada, U.S.	13,140
Cameroon Mtn., Cameroon	13,451
Carrauntoohil, Ireland	3,406
Chaltel, Cerro, (Monte Fitzroy) Argentina-Chile	10,958
Chimborazo, Ecuador	20,702
Chirripó, Cerro, Costa Rica	12,530
Colima, Nevado de, Mexico	13,911
Cook, Mt., New Zealand	12,316
Cotopaxi, Ecuador	19,347
Cristóbal Colón, Pico, Colombia	19,029
Damāvand, Qolleh-ye, Iran	18,386
Dhawalāgiri, Nepal	26,810
Duarte, Pico, Dominican Rep.	10,417
Dufourspitze, (Monte Rosa) Italy-Switzerland	15,203
Elbert, Mt., Colorado, U.S.	14,433
El'brus, Gora, Russia	18,510
Elgon, Mt., Kenya-Uganda	14,178
Erciyeş Dağı, Turkey	12,848
Etna, Mt., Italy	10,902
Everest, Mt., China-Nepal	29,028
Fairweather, Mt., Alaska-Canada	15,300
Foraker, Mt., Alaska, U.S.	17,400
Fuji-san, Japan	12,388
Fūlādī, Kūh-e, Afghanistan	16,872
Galdhøpiggen, Norway	8,100
Gannett Pk., Wyoming, U.S.	13,785
Gasherbrum, China-Pakistan	26,470
Gerlachovský Stit, Slovakia	8,710
Giluwe, Mt., Papua New Guinea	14,331
Gongga Shan, China	24,790
Grand Teton Mtn., Wyoming, U.S.	13,770
Grossglockner, Austria	12,461
Hadūr Shu'ayb, Yemen	12,336
Haleakala Crater, Hawaii, U.S.	10,023
Hekla, Iceland	4,892
Hood, Mt., Oregon, U.S.	11,239
Hsinkao Shan, Taiwan	13,113
Huascarán, Nevado, Peru	22,205
Huila, Nevado de, Colombia	18,865
Hvannadalshnúkur, Iceland	6,952
Illampu, Nevado, Bolivia	21,066
Illimani, Nevado, Bolivia	20,741
Iztaccíhuatl, Mexico	17,930
Jaya, Puncak, Indonesia	16,503
Jungfrau, Switzerland	13,642
K2, (Godwin Austen) China-Pakistan	28,250
Kāmet, China-India	25,447
Kānchenjunga, India-Nepal	28,208
Kātrīnā, Jabal, Egypt	8,668
Kebnekaise, Sweden	6,962
Kenya, Mt., (Kirinyaga) Kenya	17,058
Kerinci, Gunung, Indonesia	12,467
Kilimanjaro, Tanzania	19,340
Kinabalu, Gunong, Malaysia	13,455
Klyuchevskaya, Sopka, Russia	15,584
Kommunizma, Pik, Tajikistan	24,590
Kosciusko, Mt., Australia	7,310
Koussi, Emi, Chad	11,204
Kula Kangri, Bhutan	24,784
La Selle, Massif de, Haiti	8,793
Lassen Pk., California, U.S.	10,457
Llullaillaco, Volcán, Argentina-Chile	22,110
Logan, Mt., Canada	19,551
Longs Pk., Colorado, U.S.	14,255
Makālu, China-Nepal	27,825
Margherita Peak, Zaire-Uganda	16,763
Markham, Mt., Antarctica	14,049
Maromokotro, Madagascar	9,436
Massive, Mt., Colorado, U.S.	14,421
Matterhorn, Italy-Switzerland	14,692
Mauna Kea, Hawaii, U.S.	13,796
Mauna Loa, Hawaii, U.S.	13,679
Mayon Volcano, Philippines	7,943
McKinley, Mt., Alaska, U.S.	20,320
Meron, Hare, Israel	3,693
Meru, Mt., Tanzania	14,978
Misti, Volcán, Peru	19,101
Mitchell, Mt., North Carolina, U.S.	6,684
Môco, Serra do, Angola	8,596
Moldoveanu, Romania	8,343
Mulhacén, Spain (continental)	11,424
Musala, Bulgaria	9,596
Muztag, China	25,338
Muztagata, China	24,757
Namjagbarwa Feng, China	25,446
Nanda Devi, India	25,645
Nānga Parbat, Pakistan	26,650
Narodnaya, Gora, Russia	6,217
Nevis, Ben, United Kingdom	4,406
Ojos del Salado, Nevado, Argentina-Chile	22,615
Ólimbos, Cyprus	6,401
Ólimbos, Greece	9,570
Olympus, Mt., Washington, U.S.	7,965
Orizaba, Pico de, Mexico	18,406
Paektu San, North Korea-China	9,003
Paricutín, Mexico	9,186
Parnassós, Greece	8,061
Pelée, Montagne, Martinique	4,800
Pidurutalagala, Sri Lanka	8,281
Pikes Pk., Colorado, U.S.	14,110
Pobedy, pik, China-Kyrgyzstan	24,406
Popocatépetl, Volcán, Mexico	17,930
Pulog, Mt., Philippines	9,606
Rainier, Mt., Washington, U.S.	14,410
Ramm, Jabal, Jordan	5,755
Ras Dashen Terara, Ethiopia	15,158
Rinjani, Gunung, Indonesia	12,224
Robson, Mt., Canada	12,972
Roraima, Mt., Brazil-Guyana-Venezuela	9,452
Ruapehu, Mt., New Zealand	9,177
St. Elias, Mt., Alaska, U.S.-Canada	18,008
Sajama, Nevado, Bolivia	21,391
Semeru, Gunung, Indonesia	12,060
Shām, Jabal ash, Oman	9,957
Shasta, Mt., California, U.S.	14,162
Snowdon, Wales, U.K.	3,560
Tahat, Algeria	9,541
Tajumulco (Vol.), Guatemala	13,845
Taranaki, Mt., New Zealand	8,260
Tirich Mīr, Pakistan	25,230
Tomanivi (Victoria), (Victoria) Fiji	4,341
Toubkal, Jebel, Morocco	13,665
Triglav, Slovenia	9,396
Trikora, Puncak, Indonesia	15,584
Tupungato, Cerro, Argentina-Chile	21,555
Turquino, Pico, Cuba	6,470
Uncompahgre Pk., Colorado, U.S.	14,301
Vesuvio, (Vesuvius) Italy	4,190
Victoria, Mt., Papua New Guinea	13,238
Vinson Massif, Antarctica	16,066
Waddington, Mt., Canada	13,163
Washington, Mt., New Hampshire, U.S.	6,288
Whitney, Mt., California, U.S.	14,494
Wilhelm, Mt., Papua New Guinea	14,793
Wrangell, Mt., Alaska, U.S.	14,163
Xixabangma Feng (Gosainthan), (Gosainthan) China	26,286
Zugspitze, Austria-Germany	9,72

Principal Rivers and Their Lengths

RIVER Continent	Length (Mi.)
Albany, N. America	610
Aldan, Asia	1,412
Amazonas-Ucayali, S. America	4,000
Amu Darya, Asia	1,578
Amur, Asia	2,744
Amur-Argun, Asia	2,761
Araguaia, S. America	1,400
Arkansas, N. America	1,459
Athabasca, N. America	765
Brahmaputra, Asia	1,770
Branco, S. America	580
Brazos, N. America	870
Canadian, N. America	906
Churchill, N. America	1,000
Colorado, N. America (U.S.-Mexico)	1,450
Columbia, N. America	1,243
Congo, (Zaïre) Africa	2,880
Cumberland, N. America	720
Danube, Europe	1,776
Darling, Australia	864
Dnepr, (Dnieper) Europe	1,367
Dniester, Europe	840
Don, Europe	1,162
Elbe, Europe	724
Euphrates, Asia	1,510
Fraser, N. America	851
Ganges, Asia	1,560
Gila, N. America	630
Godāvari, Asia	930
Green, N. America	730
Huang, (Yellow) Asia	3,395
Indus, Asia	1,800
Irrawaddy, Asia	1,300
Juruá, S. America	1,250
Kama, Europe	1,122
Kasai, Africa	1,338
Kolyma, Asia	1,323
Lena, Asia	2,734
Limpopo, Africa	1,100
Loire, Europe	634
Mackenzie, N. America	2,635
Madeira, S. America	2,013
Magdalena, S. America	950
Marañón, S. America	1,000
Mekong, Asia	2,600
Meuse, Europe	590
Mississippi, N. America	2,348
Mississippi-Missouri, N. America	3,740
Missouri, N. America	2,315
Murray, Australia	1,566
Negro, S. America	1,300
Neman, Europe	582
Niger, Africa	2,600
Nile, Africa	4,145
North Platte, N. America	618
Ob'-Irtysh, Asia	3,362
Oder, Europe	567
Ohio, N. America	981
Oka, Europe	900
Orange, Africa	1,398
Orinoco, S. America	1,600
Ottawa, N. America	790
Paraguay, S. America	1,610
Paraná, S. America	2,800
Parnaíba, S. America	850
Peace, N. America	1,195
Pechora, Europe	1,124
Pecos, N. America	735
Pilcomayo, S. America	1,550
Plata-Paraná, S. America	3,030
Purús, S. America	1,860
Red, N. America	1,270
Rhine, Europe	820
Rhône, Europe	505
Rio Grande, N. America	1,885
Roosevelt, S. America	950
St. Lawrence, N. America	800
Salado, S. America	900
Salween, (Nu) Asia	1,750
São Francisco, S. America	1,988
Saskatchewan-Bow, N. America	1,205
Sava, Europe	584
Snake, N. America	1,038
Sungari, (Songhua) Asia	1,140
Syr Darya, Asia	1,370
Tagus, Europe	625
Tarim, Asia	1,328
Tennessee, N. America	65
Tigris, Asia	1,18
Tisa, Europe	60
Tobol, Asia	98
Tocantins, S. America	1,64
Ucayali, S. America	1,22
Ural, Asia	1,50
Uruguay, S. America	1,02
Verkhnyaya Tunguska, (Angara) Asia	1,1
Vilyuy, Asia	1,6
Volga, Europe	2,1
White, N. America (Ark.-Mo.)	7
Wisła (Vistula), Europe	6
Xiang, Asia	9
Xingú, S. America	1,2
Yangtze, (Chang) Asia	3,9
Yellowstone, N. America	6
Yenisey, Asia	2,5
Yukon, N. America	1,9
Zambezi, Africa	1,7

Abidjan, Cote d'Ivoire ... 1,929,079
Accra, Ghana (1,390,000) ... 949,113
Addis Ababa, Ethiopia (1,990,000) ... 1,912,500
Adelaide, Australia (1,023,597) ... 14,843
Ahmadābād, India (3,312,216) ... 2,876,710
Aleppo (Halab), Syria (1,335,000) ... 1,261,000
Alexandria (Al Iskandarīyah), Egypt (3,350,000) ... 2,926,859
Algiers (El Djazaïr), Algeria (2,547,983) ... 1,507,241
Alma-Ata (Almaty), Kazakhstan (1,190,000) ... 1,156,200
'Ammān, Jordan (1,625,000) ... 936,300
Amsterdam, Netherlands (1,875,000) ... 713,407
Ankara (Angora), Turkey (2,650,000) ... 2,559,471
Antananarivo, Madagascar ... 1,250,000
Antwerp (Antwerpen), Belgium (1,100,000) ... 479,748
Asmera, Eritrea ... 358,100
Asunción, Paraguay (700,000) ... 502,426
Athens (Athínai), Greece (3,096,775) ... 748,110
Atlanta, Georgia, U.S. (2,833,511) ... 394,017
Auckland, New Zealand (855,571) ... 315,668
Baghdād, Iraq ... 3,841,268
Baku (Bakı), Azerbaijan (2,020,000) ... 1,080,500
Baltimore, Maryland, U.S. (2,382,172) ... 736,014
Bamako, Mali ... 658,275
Bandung, Indonesia (2,220,000) ... 2,058,122
Bangalore, India (4,130,288) ... 2,660,088
Bangkok (Krung Thep), Thailand (7,060,000) ... 5,620,591
Barcelona, Spain (4,040,000) ... 1,714,355
Beijing (Peking), China (7,320,000) ... 6,710,000
Beirut, Lebanon (1,675,000) ... 509,000
Belém, Brazil (1,355,000) ... 765,476
Belfast, N. Ireland, U.K. (685,000) ... 295,100
Belgrade (Beograd), Yugoslavia (1,554,826) ... 1,136,786
Belo Horizonte, Brazil (3,340,000) ... 1,529,566
Berlin, Germany (4,150,000) ... 3,433,695
Birmingham, England, U.K. (2,675,000) ... 1,013,995
Bishkek, Kyrgyzstan ... 631,300
Bombay, India (12,596,243) ... 9,925,891
Bonn, Germany (575,000) ... 292,234
Boston, Massachusetts, U.S. (4,171,643) ... 574,283
Brasília, Brazil ... 1,513,470
Bratislava, Slovakia ... 441,453
Brazzaville, Congo ... 693,712
Bremen, Germany (790,000) ... 551,219
Brisbane, Australia (1,334,017) ... 751,115
Brussels (Bruxelles), Belgium (2,385,000) ... 136,920
Bucharest (București), Romania (2,300,000) ... 2,064,474
Budapest, Hungary (2,515,000) ... 2,016,774
Buenos Aires, Argentina (11,000,000) ... 2,960,976
Cairo (Al Qāhirah), Egypt (9,300,000) ... 6,068,695
Calcutta, India (11,021,918) ... 4,399,819
Cali, Colombia (1,400,000) ... 1,350,565
Canberra, Australia (303,846) ... 276,162
Cape Town, South Africa (1,900,000) ... 854,616
Caracas, Venezuela (4,000,000) ... 1,822,465
Casablanca, Morocco (2,475,000) ... 2,139,204
Changchun, China (2,000,000†) ... 1,822,000
Chelyabinsk, Russia (1,325,000) ... 1,148,300
Chengdu, China (2,960,000†) ... 1,884,000
Chicago, Illinois, U.S. (8,065,633) ... 2,783,726
Chișinău (Kishinev), Moldova ... 676,700
Chittagong, Bangladesh (2,342,662) ... 1,566,070
Chongqing (Chungking), China (2,890,000†) ... 2,502,000
Cincinnati, Ohio, U.S. (1,744,124) ... 364,040
Cleveland, Ohio, U.S. (2,759,823) ... 505,616
Cologne (Köln), Germany (1,810,000) ... 953,551
Colombo, Sri Lanka (2,050,000) ... 612,000
Columbus, Ohio, U.S. (1,377,419) ... 632,910
Conakry, Guinea ... 800,000
Copenhagen (København), Denmark (1,670,000) ... 464,566
Cordoba, Argentina (1,260,000) ... 1,148,305
Curitiba, Brazil (1,815,000) ... 841,882
Dakar, Senegal ... 1,490,450
Dalian (Lüda), China ... 2,280,000
Dallas, Texas, U.S. (3,885,415) ... 1,006,877
Damascus (Dimashq), Syria (2,000,000) ... 1,326,000
Dar es Salaam, Tanzania ... 1,096,000
Delhi, India (8,419,084) ... 7,206,704
Denver, Colorado, U.S. (1,848,319) ... 467,610
Detroit, Michigan, U.S. (4,665,236) ... 1,027,974
Dhaka (Dacca), Bangladesh (6,537,308) ... 3,637,892
Dnipropetrovs'k, Ukraine (1,600,000) ... 1,189,300
Donets'k, Ukraine (2,125,000) ... 1,121,300
Dresden, Germany (870,000) ... 490,571
Dublin (Baile Átha Cliath), Ireland (1,140,000) ... 502,749
Durban, South Africa (1,740,000) ... 715,669
Düsseldorf, Germany (1,225,000) ... 575,794
Edinburgh, Scotland, U.K. (630,000) ... 434,520
Essen, Germany (5,050,000) ... 626,973
Faisalabad, Pakistan ... 1,104,209
Florence (Firenze), Italy (640,000) ... 402,316
Fortaleza, Brazil (2,040,000) ... 743,335
Frankfurt am Main, Germany (1,935,000) ... 644,865
Fukuoka, Japan (1,750,000) ... 1,237,067
Gdańsk (Danzig), Poland (909,000) ... 465,100
Geneva (Génève), Switzerland (470,000) ... 171,042
Genoa (Genova), Italy (805,000) ... 675,639
Glasgow, Scotland, U.K. (1,800,000) ... 689,210
Goiânia, Brazil (1,130,000) ... 912,136
Guadalajara, Mexico (2,430,000) ... 1,650,042
Guangzhou (Canton), China (3,420,000†) ... 3,100,000
Guatemala, Guatemala (1,400,000) ... 1,057,210
Guayaquil, Ecuador ... 1,508,444
Hamburg, Germany (2,385,000) ... 1,652,363
Hannover, Germany (1,000,000) ... 513,010
Hanoi, Vietnam (1,275,000) ... 905,939
Harare, Zimbabwe (890,000) ... 681,000
Harbin, China ... 2,710,000
Havana (La Habana), Cuba (2,210,000) ... 2,119,059
Helsinki, Finland (1,040,000) ... 497,542
Hiroshima, Japan (1,575,000) ... 1,085,705
Ho Chi Minh City (Saigon), Vietnam (3,300,000) ... 2,796,229
Hong Kong, Hong Kong (4,770,000) ... 1,250,993
Honolulu, Hawaii, U.S. (836,231) ... 365,272
Houston, Texas, U.S. (3,711,043) ... 1,630,553
Hyderābād, India (4,344,437) ... 3,058,093
Ibadan, Nigeria ... 1,144,000
Indianapolis, Indiana, U.S. (1,249,822) ... 731,327
İstanbul, Turkey (7,550,000) ... 6,620,241
İzmir, Turkey (1,900,000) ... 1,757,414
Jakarta, Indonesia (10,200,000) ... 8,227,746
Jerusalem, Israel (560,000) ... 524,500
Jiddah, Saudi Arabia ... 1,300,000
Jinan, China (2,140,000†) ... 1,546,000
Johannesburg, South Africa (4,000,000) ... 712,507
Kābul, Afghanistan ... 1,424,400
Kampala, Uganda ... 773,463
Kānpur, India (2,029,889) ... 1,874,409
Kansas City, Missouri, U.S. (1,566,280) ... 435,146
Kaohsiung, Taiwan (1,900,000) ... 1,401,239
Karāchi, Pakistan (5,300,000) ... 4,901,627
Katowice, Poland (2,778,000) ... 366,800
Kazan', Russia (1,165,000) ... 1,107,300
Kharkiv, Ukraine (2,050,000) ... 1,622,800
Khartoum (Al Kharṭūm), Sudan (1,450,000) ... 473,597
Kiev (Kyyiv), Ukraine (3,250,000) ... 2,635,000
Kingston, Jamaica (820,000) ... 661,600
Kinshasa, Zaire ... 3,000,000
Kitakyūshū, Japan (1,525,000) ... 1,026,455
Kōbe, Japan (*Ōsaka) ... 1,477,410
Kuala Lumpur, Malaysia (1,475,000) ... 919,610
Kunming, China (1,550,000†) ... 1,310,000
Kuwait (Al Kuwayt), Kuwait (1,375,000) ... 44,335
Kyōto, Japan (*Ōsaka) ... 1,461,103
Lagos, Nigeria (3,800,000) ... 1,213,000
Lahore, Pakistan (3,025,000) ... 2,707,215
La Paz, Bolivia ... 1,125,600
Leeds, England, U.K. (1,540,000) ... 445,242
Liège, Belgium (750,000) ... 200,891
Lille, France (1,050,000) ... 172,142
Lima, Peru (4,608,010) ... 371,122
Lisbon (Lisboa), Portugal (2,250,000) ... 807,167
Liverpool, England, U.K. (1,525,000) ... 538,809
London, England, U.K. (11,100,000) ... 6,574,009
Los Angeles, California, U.S. (14,531,529) ... 3,485,398
Luanda, Angola ... 1,459,900
Lucknow, India (1,669,204) ... 1,619,115
Lusaka, Zambia ... 982,362
Lyon, France (1,335,000) ... 415,487
Madras, India (5,421,985) ... 3,841,396
Madrid, Spain (4,650,000) ... 3,102,846
Managua, Nicaragua ... 682,000
Manaus, Brazil ... 1,005,634
Manchester, England, U.K. (2,775,000) ... 437,612
Manila, Philippines (9,650,000) ... 1,598,918
Mannheim, Germany (1,525,000) ... 310,411
Maputo, Mozambique ... 1,069,727
Maracaibo, Venezuela ... 1,249,670
Marseille, France (1,225,000) ... 800,550
Mashhad, Iran ... 1,463,508
Mecca (Makkah), Saudi Arabia ... 550,000
Medan, Indonesia ... 1,730,052
Medellín, Colombia (2,095,000) ... 1,468,089
Melbourne, Australia (3,022,439) ... 60,475
Memphis, Tennessee, U.S. (981,747) ... 610,337
Mexico City, Mexico (14,100,000) ... 8,235,744
Miami, Florida, U.S. (3,192,582) ... 358,548
Milan (Milano), Italy (3,750,000) ... 1,371,008
Milwaukee, Wisconsin, U.S. (1,607,183) ... 628,088
Minneapolis, Minnesota, U.S. (2,464,124) ... 368,383
Minsk, Belarus (1,694,000) ... 1,633,600
Mogadishu, Somalia ... 600,000
Monterrey, Mexico (2,015,000) ... 1,068,996
Montevideo, Uruguay (1,550,000) ... 1,251,647
Montréal, Canada (3,127,242) ... 1,017,666
Moscow (Moskva), Russia (13,150,000) ... 8,801,500
Munich (München), Germany (1,900,000) ... 1,229,026
Nagoya, Japan (4,800,000) ... 2,154,793
Nāgpur, India (1,664,006) ... 1,624,752
Nairobi, Kenya ... 1,505,000
Nanjing, China ... 2,390,000
Naples (Napoli), Italy (2,875,000) ... 1,204,601
Nashville, Tennessee, U.S. (985,026) ... 487,969
New Delhi, India (*Delhi) ... 301,297
New Kowloon, Hong Kong (*Hong Kong) ... 1,526,910
New Orleans, Louisiana, U.S. (1,238,816) ... 496,938
New York, New York, U.S. (18,087,251) ... 7,322,564
Nizhniy Novgorod, Russia (2,025,000) ... 1,445,000
Novosibirsk, Russia (1,600,000) ... 1,446,300
Nürnberg, Germany (1,065,000) ... 493,692
Odesa, Ukraine (1,185,000) ... 1,100,700
Oklahoma City, Oklahoma, U.S. (958,839) ... 444,719
Omsk, Russia (1,190,000) ... 1,166,800
Ōsaka, Japan (16,900,000) ... 2,623,801
Oslo, Norway (720,000) ... 452,415
Ottawa, Canada (920,857) ... 313,987
Panamá, Panama (770,000) ... 411,549
Paris, France (10,275,000) ... 2,152,423
Perm', Russia (1,180,000) ... 1,110,400
Perth, Australia (1,143,249) ... 80,517
Philadelphia, Pennsylvania, U.S. (5,899,345) ... 1,585,577
Phnum Pénh (Phnom Penh), Cambodia ... 620,000
Phoenix, Arizona, U.S. (2,122,101) ... 983,403
Pittsburgh, Pennsylvania, U.S. (2,242,798) ... 369,879
Port-au-Prince, Haiti (880,000) ... 797,000
Portland, Oregon, U.S. (1,477,895) ... 437,319
Porto Alegre, Brazil (2,850,000) ... 1,247,352
Prague (Praha), Czech Republic (1,328,000) ... 1,212,010
Pretoria, South Africa (1,100,000) ... 525,583
Providence, Rhode Island, U.S. (1,141,510) ... 160,728
Puebla, Mexico (1,200,000) ... 1,007,170
Pune, India (2,493,987) ... 1,566,651
Pusan, South Korea (3,800,000) ... 3,797,566
P'yŏngyang, North Korea ... 2,355,000
Qingdao, China ... 1,300,000
Québec, Canada (645,550) ... 167,517
Quezon City, Philippines (*Manila) ... 1,666,766
Quito, Ecuador (1,300,000) ... 1,100,847
Rabat, Morocco (980,000) ... 518,616
Rangoon (Yangon), Myanmar (2,800,000) ... 2,705,039
Recife, Brazil (2,880,000) ... 1,296,995
Rīga, Latvia (1,005,000) ... 910,200
Rio de Janerio, Brazil (11,050,000) ... 5,473,909
Riyadh, Saudi Arabia ... 1,250,000
Rome (Roma), Italy (3,175,000) ... 2,693,383
Rosario, Argentina (1,190,000) ... 894,645
Rostov-na-Donu, Russia (1,165,000) ... 1,027,600
Rotterdam, Netherlands (1,120,000) ... 589,707
St. Louis, Missouri, U.S. (2,444,099) ... 396,685
St. Petersburg (Leningrad), Russia (5,525,000) ... 4,466,800
Salt Lake City, Utah, U.S. (1,072,227) ... 159,936
Salvador, Brazil (2,340,000) ... 2,070,296
Samara, Russia (1,505,000) ... 1,257,300
San Antonio, Texas, U.S. (1,302,099) ... 935,933
San Diego, California, U.S. (2,949,000) ... 1,110,549
San Francisco, California, U.S. (6,253,311) ... 723,959
San José, Costa Rica (1,355,000) ... 278,600
San Juan, Puerto Rico (1,877,000) ... 426,832
San Salvador, El Salvador (920,000) ... 462,652
Santa Fe de Bogotá, Colombia (4,260,000) ... 3,982,941
Santiago, Chile (4,100,000) ... 232,667
Santo Domingo, Dominican Rep. ... 2,411,900
Santos, Brazil (1,165,000) ... 415,554
São Paulo, Brazil (16,925,000) ... 9,393,753
Sapporo, Japan (1,900,000) ... 1,671,742
Sarajevo, Bosnia and Herzegovina (479,688†) ... 341,200
Saratov, Russia (1,155,000) ... 911,100
Seattle, Washington, U.S. (2,559,164) ... 516,259
Seoul (Sŏul), South Korea (15,850,000) ... 10,627,790
Shanghai, China (9,300,000) ... 7,220,000
Shenyang (Mukden), China (4,370,000†) ... 3,910,000
Singapore, Singapore (3,025,000) ... 2,690,100
Skopje, Macedonia (547,214†) ... 444,900
Sofia (Sofiya), Bulgaria (1,205,000) ... 1,136,875
Stockholm, Sweden (1,491,726) ... 674,452
Stuttgart, Germany (2,005,000) ... 579,988
Surabaya, Indonesia ... 2,473,272
Sydney, Australia (3,538,749) ... 13,501
Taegu, South Korea ... 2,228,834
T'aipei, Taiwan (6,200,000) ... 2,706,453
Taiyuan, China (1,980,000†) ... 1,700,000
Tampa, Florida, U.S. (2,067,959) ... 280,015
Tashkent, Uzbekistan (2,325,000) ... 2,113,300
Tbilisi, Georgia (1,460,000) ... 1,279,000
•Tegucigalpa, Honduras ... 576,661
Tehrān, Iran (7,500,000) ... 6,042,584
Tel Aviv-Yafo, Israel (1,735,000) ... 339,400
The Hague ('s-Gravenhage), Netherlands (773,000) ... 445,287
Tianjin (Tientsin), China (5,540,000†) ... 4,950,000
Tiranë, Albania ... 238,100
Tōkyō, Japan (30,300,000) ... 8,163,573
Toronto, Canada (3,893,046) ... 635,395
Tripoli (Tarābulus), Libya ... 591,062
Tunis, Tunisia (1,225,000) ... 596,654
Turin (Torino), Italy (1,550,000) ... 961,916
Ufa, Russia (1,118,000) ... 1,097,000
Ulan Bator, Mongolia ... 548,400
Valencia, Spain (1,270,000) ... 743,933
Vancouver, Canada (1,602,502) ... 471,844
Venice (Venezia), Italy (420,000) ... 85,100
Vienna (Wien), Austria (1,900,000) ... 1,539,848
Vilnius, Lithuania ... 596,900
Vladivostok, Russia ... 648,000
Volgograd (Stalingrad), Russia (1,360,000) ... 1,007,300
Warsaw (Warszawa), Poland (2,323,000) ... 1,655,700
Washington, D.C., U.S. (3,923,574) ... 606,900
Wellington, New Zealand (375,000) ... 150,301
Winnipeg, Canada (652,354) ... 616,790
Wuhan, China ... 3,570,000
Xi'an, China (2,580,000†) ... 2,210,000
Yekaterinburg, Russia (1,620,000) ... 1,375,400
Yerevan, Armenia (1,315,000) ... 1,199,000
Yokohama, Japan (*Tōkyō) ... 3,220,331
Zagreb, Croatia ... 697,925
Zurich, Switzerland (870,000) ... 365,043

Metropolitan area populations are shown in parentheses.
*City is located within the metropolitan area of another city; for example, Kyōto, Japan is located in the Ōsaka metropolitan area.
†Population of entire municipality or district, including rural area.

GLOSSARY OF FOREIGN GEOGRAPHICAL TERMS

Annam	Annamese
Arab	Arabic
Bantu	Bantu
Bur	Burmese
Camb	Cambodian
Celt	Celtic
Chn	Chinese
Czech	Czech
Dan	Danish
Du	Dutch
Fin	Finnish
Fr	French
Ger	German
Gr	Greek
Hung	Hungarian
Ice	Icelandic
India	India
Indian	American Indian
Indon	Indonesian
It	Italian
Jap	Japanese
Kor	Korean
Mal	Malayan
Mong	Mongolian
Nor	Norwegian
Per	Persian
Pol	Polish
Port	Portuguese
Rom	Romanian
Rus	Russian
Siam	Siamese
So. Slav	Southern Slavonic
Sp	Spanish
Swe	Swedish
Tib	Tibetan
Tur	Turkish
Yugo	Yugoslav

å, Nor., Swe	brook, river
aa, Dan., Nor	brook
aas, Dan., Nor	ridge
āb, Per	water, river
abad, India, Per	town, city
ada, Tur	island
adrar, Berber	mountain
air, Indon	stream
akrotírion, Gr	cape
älf, Swe	river
alp, Ger	mountain
altipiano, It	plateau
alto, Sp	height
archipel, Fr	archipelago
archipiélago, Sp	archipelago
arquipélago, Port	archipelago
arroyo, Sp	brook, stream
ås, Nor., Swe	ridge
austral, Sp	southern
baai, Du	bay
bab, Arab	gate, port
bach, Ger	brook, stream
backe, Swe	hill
bad, Ger	bath, spa
bahía, Sp	bay, gulf
bahr, Arab	river, sea, lake
baia, It	bay, gulf
baía, Port	bay
baie, Fr	bay, gulf
bajo, Sp	depression
bak, Indon	stream
bakke, Dan., Nor	hill
balkan, Tur	mountain range
bana, Jap	point, cape
banco, Sp	bank
bandar, Mal., Per.	town, port, harbor
bang, Siam	village
bassin, Fr	basin
batang, Indon., Mal	river
ben, Celt	mountain, summit
bender, Arab	harbor, port
bereg, Rus	coast, shore
berg, Du., Ger., Nor., Swe.	mountain, hill
bir, Arab	well
birkat, Arab	lake, pond, pool
bit, Arab	house
bjaerg, Dan., Nor	mountain
bocche, It	mouth
boğazı, Tur	strait
bois, Fr	forest, wood
boloto, Rus	marsh
bolsón, Sp.	flat-floored desert valley
boreal, Sp	northern
borg, Dan., Nor., Swe	castle, town
borgo, It	town, suburb
bosch, Du	forest, wood
bouche, Fr	river mouth
bourg, Fr	town, borough
bro, Dan., Nor., Swe	bridge
brücke, Ger	bridge
bucht, Ger	bay, bight
bugt, Dan., Nor., Swe	bay, gulf
bulu, Indon	mountain
burg, Du., Ger	castle, town
buri, Siam	town
burun, burnu, Tur	cape
by, Dan., Nor., Swe	village
caatinga, Port. (Brazil)	open brushland
cabezo, Sp	summit
cabo, Port., Sp	cape
campo, It., Port., Sp	plain, field
campos, Port. (Brazil)	plains
cañón, Sp	canyon
cap, Fr	cape
capo, It	cape
casa, It., Port., Sp	house
castello, It., Port	castle, fort
castillo, Sp	castle
càte, Fr	hill
çay, Tur	stream, river
cayo, Sp	rock, shoal, islet
cerro, Sp	mountain, hill
champ, Fr	field
chang, Chn	village, middle
château, Fr	castle
chen, Chn	market town
chiang, Chn	river
chott, Arab	salt lake
chou, Chn.	capital of district; island
chu, Tib	water, stream
cidade, Port	town, city
cima, Sp	summit, peak
città, It	town, city
ciudad, Sp	town, city
cochilha, Port	ridge
col, Fr	pass
colina, Sp	hill
cordillera, Sp	mountain chain
costa, It., Port., Sp	coast
côte, Fr	coast
cuchilla, Sp	mountain ridge
dağ, Tur	mountain(s)
dake, Jap	peak, summit
dal, Dan., Du., Nor., Swe	valley
dan, Kor	point, cape
danau, Indon	lake
dar, Arab	house, abode, country
darya, Per	river, sea
dasht, Per	plain, desert
deniz, Tur	sea
désert, Fr	desert
deserto, It	desert
desierto, Sp	desert
détroit, Fr	strait
dijk, Du	dam, dike
djebel, Arab	mountain
do, Kor	island
dorf, Ger	village
dorp, Du	village
duin, Du	dune
dzong, Tib.	fort, administrative capital
eau, Fr	water
ecuador, Sp	equator
eiland, Du	island
elv, Dan., Nor	river, stream
embalse, Sp	reservoir
erg, Arab	dune, sandy desert
est, Fr., It	east
estado, Sp	state
este, Port., Sp	east
estrecho, Sp	strait
étang, Fr	pond, lake
état, Fr	state
eyjar, Ice	islands
feld, Ger	field, plain
festung, Ger	fortress
fiume, It	river
fjäll, Swe	mountain
fjärd, Swe	bay, inlet
fjeld, Nor	mountain, hill
fjord, Dan., Nor	fiord, inlet
fjördur, Ice	fiord, inlet
fleuve, Fr	river
flod, Dan., Swe	river
flói, Ice	bay, marshland
fluss, Ger	river
foce, It	river mouth
fontein, Du	a spring
forêt, Fr	forest
fors, Swe	waterfall
forst, Ger	forest
fos, Dan., Nor	waterfall
fu, Chn	town, residence
fuente, Sp	spring, fountain
fuerte, Sp	fort
furt, Ger	ford
gang, Kor	stream, river
gangri, Tib	mountain
gat, Dan., Nor	channel
gàve, Fr	stream
gawa, Jap	river
gebergte, Du	mountain range
gebiet, Ger	district, territory
gebirge, Ger	mountains
ghat, India	pass, mountain range
gobi, Mong	desert
gol, Mong	river
göl, gölü, Tur	lake
golf, Du., Ger	gulf, bay
golfe, Fr	gulf, bay
golfo, It., Port., Sp	gulf, bay
gomba, gompa, Tib	monastery
gora, Rus., So. Slav	mountain
góra, Pol	mountain
gorod, Rus	town
grad, Rus., So. Slav	town
guba, Rus	bay, gulf
gundung, Indon	mountain
guntō, Jap	archipelago
gunung, Mal	mountain
haf, Swe	sea, ocean
hafen, Ger	port, harbor
haff, Ger	gulf, inland sea
hai, Chn	sea, lake
hama, Jap	beach, shore
hamada, Arab	rocky plateau
hamn, Swe	harbor
hāmūn, Per	swampy lake, plain
hantō, Jap	peninsula
hassi, Arab	well, spring
haus, Ger	house
haut, Fr	summit, top
hav, Dan., Nor	sea, ocean
havn, Dan., Nor	harbor, port
havre, Fr	harbor, port
háza, Hung	house, dwelling of
heim, Ger	hamlet, home
hem, Swe	hamlet, home
higashi, Jap	east
hisar, Tur	fortress
hissar, Arab	fort
ho, Chn	river
hoek, Du	cape
hof, Ger	court, farmhouse
höfn, Ice	harbor
hoku, Jap	north
holm, Dan., Nor., Swe	island
hora, Czech	mountain
horn, Ger	peak
hoved, Dan., Nor	cape
hsien, Chn	district, district capital
hu, Chn	lake
hügel, Ger	hill
huk, Dan., Swe	point
hus, Dan., Nor., Swe	house
île, Fr	island
ilha, Port	island
indsö, Dan., Nor	lake
insel, Ger	island
insjö, Swe	lake
irmak, irmagi, Tur	river
isla, Sp	island
isola, It	island
istmo, It., Sp	isthmus
järvi, jaur, Fin	lake
jebel, Arab	mountain
jima, Jap	island
jökel, Nor	glacier
joki, Fin	river
jökull, Ice	glacier
kaap, Du	cape
kai, Jap	bay, gulf, sea
kaikyō, Jap	channel, strait
kalat, Per	castle, fortress
kale, Tur	fort
kali, Mal	creek, river
kand, Per	village
kang, Chn	mountain ridge; village
kap, Dan., Ger	cape
kapp, Nor., Swe	cape
kasr, Arab	fort, castle
kawa, Jap	river
kefr, Arab	village
kei, Jap	creek, river
ken, Jap	prefecture
khor, Arab	bay, inlet
khrebet, Rus	mountain range
kiang, Chn	large river
king, Chn	capital city, town
kita, Jap	north
ko, Jap	lake
köbstad, Dan	market-town
kol, Mong	lake
kólpos, Gr	gulf
kong, Chn	river
kopf, Ger	head, summit, peak
köpstad, Swe	market-town
körfezi, Tur	gulf
kosa, Rus	spit
kou, Chn	river mouth
köy, Tur	village
kraal, Du. (Africa)	native village
ksar, Arab	fortified village
kuala, Mal	bay, river mouth
kuh, Per	mountain
kum, Tur	sand
kuppe, Ger	summit
küste, Ger	coast
kyo, Jap	town, capital
la, Tib	mountain pass
labuan, Mal	anchorage, port
lac, Fr	lake
lago, It., Port., Sp	lake
lagoa, Port	lake, marsh
laguna, It., Port., Sp	lagoon, lake
lahti, Fin	bay, gulf
län, Swe	county
landsby, Dan., Nor	village
liehtao, Chn	archipelago
liman, Tur	bay, port
ling, Chn	pass, ridge, mountain
llanos, Sp	plains
loch, Celt. (Scotland)	lake, bay
loma, Sp	long, low hill
lough, Celt. (Ireland)	lake, bay
machi, Jap	town
man, Kor	bay
mar, Port., Sp	sea
mare, It., Rom	sea
marisma, Sp	marsh, swamp
mark, Ger	boundary, limit
massif, Fr	block of mountains
mato, Port	forest, thicket
me, Siam	river
meer, Du., Ger	lake, sea
mer, Fr	sea
mesa, Sp	flat-topped mountain
meseta, Sp	plateau
mina, Port., Sp	mine
minami, Jap	south
minato, Jap	harbor, haven
misaki, Jap	cape, headland
mont, Fr	mount, mountain
montagna, It	mountain
montagne, Fr	mountain
montaña, Sp	mountain
monte, It., Port., Sp.	mount, mountain
more, Rus., So. Slav	sea
morro, Port., Sp	hill, bluff
mühle, Ger	mill
mund, Ger	mouth, opening
mündung, Ger	river mouth
mura, Jap	township
myit, Bur	river
mys, Rus	cape
nada, Jap	sea
nadi, India	river, creek
naes, Dan., Nor	cape
nafud, Arab	desert of sand dunes
nagar, India	town, city
nahr, Arab	river
nam, Siam	river, water
nan, Chn., Jap	south
näs, Nor., Swe	cape
nez, Fr	point, cape
nishi, nisi, Jap	west
njarga, Fin	peninsula
nong, Siam	marsh
noord, Du	north
nor, Mong	lake
nord, Dan., Fr., Ger., It., Nor., Swe	north
norte, Port., Sp	north
nos, Rus	cape
nyasa, Bantu	lake
ö, Dan., Nor., Swe	island
occidental, Sp	western
ocna, Rom	salt mine
odde, Dan., Nor	point, cape
oeste, Port., Sp	west
oka, Jap	hill
oost, Du	east
oriental, Sp	eastern
óros, Gr	mountain
ost, Ger., Swe	east
öster, Dan., Nor., Swe	eastern
ostrov, Rus	island
oued, Arab	river, stream
ouest, Fr	west
ozero, Rus	lake
pää, Fin	mountain
padang, Mal	plain, field
pampas, Sp. (Argentina)	grassy plains
pará, Indian (Brazil)	river
pas, Fr	channel, passage
paso, Sp	mountain pass, passage
passo, It., Port.	mountain pass, passage, strait
patam, India	city, town
pei, Chn	north
pélagos, Gr	open sea
pegunungan, Indon	mountains
peña, Sp	rock
peresheyek, Rus	isthmus
pertuis, Fr	strait
peski, Rus	desert
pic, Fr	mountain peak
pico, Port., Sp	mountain peak
piedra, Sp	stone, rock
ping, Chn	plain, flat
planalto, Port	plateau
planina, Yugo	mountains
playa, Sp	shore, beach
pnom, Camb	mountain
pointe, Fr	point
polder, Du., Ger	reclaimed marsh
polje, So. Slav	plain, field
poluostrov, Rus	peninsula
pont, Fr	bridge
ponta, Port	point, headland
ponte, It., Port	bridge
pore, India	city, town
porthmós, Gr	strait
porto, It., Port	port, harbor
potamós, Gr	river
p'ov, Rus	peninsula
prado, Sp	field, meadow
presqu'île, Fr	peninsula
proliv, Rus	strait
pu, Chn	commercial village
pueblo, Sp	town, village
puerto, Sp	port, harbor
pulau, Indon	island
punkt, Ger	point
punt, Du	point
punta, It., Sp	point
pur, India	city, town
puy, Fr	peak
qal'a, qal'at, Arab	fort, village
qasr, Arab	fort, castle
rann, India	wasteland
ra's, Arab	cape, head
reka, Rus., So. Slav	river
represa, Port	reservoir
rettō, Jap	island chain
ría, Sp	estuary
ribeira, Port	stream
riberão, Port	river
rio, It., Port	stream, river
río, Sp	river
rivière, Fr	river
roca, Sp	rock
rt, Yugo	cape
rūd, Per	river
saari, Fin	island
sable, Fr	sand
sahara, Arab	desert, plain
saki, Jap	cape
sal, Sp	salt
salar, Sp	salt flat, salt lake
salto, Sp	waterfall
san, Jap., Kor	mountain, hill
sat, satul, Rom	village
schloss, Ger	castle
sebkha, Arab	salt marsh
see, Ger	lake, sea
şehir, Tur	town, city
selat, Indon	stream
selvas, Port. (Brazil)	tropical rain forests
seno, Sp	bay
serra, Port	mountain chain
serranía, Sp	mountain ridge
seto, Jap	strait
severnaya, Rus	northern
shahr, Per	town, city
shan, Chn	mountain, hill, island
shatt, Arab	river
shi, Jap	city
shima, Jap	island
shōtō, Jap	archipelago
si, Chn	west, western
sierra, Sp	mountain range
sjö, Nor., Swe	lake, sea
sö, Dan., Nor	lake, sea
söder, södra, Swe	south
song, Annam	river
sopka, Rus	peak, volcano
source, Fr	a spring
spitze, Ger	summit, point
staat, Ger	state
stad, Dan., Du., Nor., Swe.	city, town
stadt, Ger	city, town
stato, It	state
step', Rus	treeless plain, steppe
straat, Du	strait
strand, Dan., Du., Ger., Nor., Swe	shore, beach
stretto, It	strait
strom, Ger	river, stream
ström, Dan., Nor., Swe.	stream, river
stroom, Du	stream, river
su, suyu, Tur	water, river
sud, Fr., Sp	south
süd, Ger	south
suidō, Jap	channel
sul, Port	south
sund, Dan., Nor., Swe	sound
sungai, sungei, Indon., Mal	river
sur, Sp	south
syd, Dan., Nor., Swe	south
tafelland, Ger	plateau
take, Jap	peak, summit
tal, Ger	valley
tanjung, tanjong, Mal	cape
tao, Chn	island
târg, târgul, Rom	market, town
tell, Arab	hill
teluk, Indon	bay, gulf
terra, It	land
terre, Fr	earth, land
thal, Ger	valley
tierra, Sp	earth, land
tō, Jap	east; island
tonle, Camb	river, lake
top, Du	peak
torp, Swe	hamlet, cottage
tsangpo, Tib	river
tsi, Chn	village, borough
tso, Tib	lake
tsu, Jap	harbor, port
tundra, Rus	treeless arctic plains
tung, Chn	east
tuz, Tur	salt
udde, Swe	cape
ufer, Ger	shore, riverbank
ujung, Indon	point, cape
umi, Jap	sea, gulf
ura, Jap	bay, coast, creek
ust'ye, Rus	river mouth
valle, It., Port., Sp	valley
vallée, Fr	valley
valli, It	lake
vár, Hung	fortress
város, Hung	town
varoš, So. Slav	town
veld, Du	open plain, field
verkh, Rus	top, summit
ves, Czech	village
vest, Dan., Nor., Swe	west
vik, Swe	cove, bay
vila, Port	town
villa, Sp	town
villar, Sp	village, hamlet
ville, Fr	town, city
vostok, Rus	east
wad, wādī, Arab.	intermittent stream
wald, Ger	forest, woodland
wan, Chn., Jap	bay, gulf
weiler, Ger	hamlet, village
westersch, Du	western
wüste, Ger	desert
yama, Jap	mountain
yarimada, Tur	peninsula
yug, Rus	south
zaki, Jap	cape
zaliv, Rus	bay, gulf
zapad, Rus	west
zee, Du	sea
zemlya, Rus	land
zuid, Du	south

Afg.	Afghanistan
Afr.	Africa
Ak., U.S.	Alaska, U.S.
Al., U.S.	Alabama, U.S.
Alb.	Albania
Alg.	Algeria
Am. Sam.	American Samoa
And.	Andorra
Ang.	Angola
Ant.	Antarctica
Antig.	Antigua and Barbuda
aq.	Aqueduct
Ar., U.S.	Arkansas, U.S.
Arg.	Argentina
Arm.	Armenia
arpt.	Airport
Aus.	Austria
Austl.	Australia
Az., U.S.	Arizona, U.S.
Azer.	Azerbaijan
b.	Bay, Gulf, Inlet, Lagoon
Bah.	Bahamas
Bahr.	Bahrain
Barb.	Barbados
B.A.T.	British Antarctic Territory
Bdi.	Burundi
Bel.	Belgium
Bela.	Belarus
Bhu.	Bhutan
bk.	Undersea Bank
bldg.	Building
Bngl.	Bangladesh
Bol.	Bolivia
Boph.	Bophuthatswana
Bos.	Bosnia and Hercegovina
Bots.	Botswana
Braz.	Brazil
Bru.	Brunei
bt.	Bight
Bul.	Bulgaria
Burkina	Burkina Faso
c.	Cape, Point
Ca., U.S.	California, U.S.
Cam.	Cameroon
Camb.	Cambodia
can.	Canal
Can.	Canada
Cay. Is.	Cayman Islands
Cen. Afr. Rep.	Central African Republic
C. Iv.	Cote d'Ivoire
clf.	Cliff, Escarpment
co.	County, Parish
Co., U.S.	Colorado, U.S.
Col.	Colombia
Com.	Comoros
cont.	Continent
Cook Is.	Cook Islands
C.R.	Costa Rica
Cro	Croatia
cst.	Coast, Beach
Ct., U.S.	Connecticut, U.S.
C.V.	Cape Verde
Cyp.	Cyprus
Czech Rep.	Czech Republic
d.	Delta
D.C., U.S.	District of Columbia, U.S.
De., U.S.	Delaware, U.S.
Den.	Denmark
dep.	Dependency, Colony
depr.	Depression
dept.	Department, District
des.	Desert
Dji.	Djibouti
Dom.	Dominica
Dom. Rep.	Dominican Republic
Ec.	Ecuador
educ.	Educational Facility
El Sal.	El Salvador
Eng., U.K.	England, U.K.
Eq. Gui.	Equatorial Guinea
Erit.	Eritrea
Est.	Estonia
est.	Estuary
Eth.	Ethiopia
Eur.	Europe
Faer. Is.	Faeroe Islands
Falk. Is.	Falkland Islands
Fin.	Finland
fj.	Fjord
Fl., U.S.	Florida, U.S.
for.	Forest, Moor
Fr.	France
Fr. Gu.	French Guiana
Fr. Poly.	French Polynesia
F.S.A.T.	French Southern and Antarctic Territory
Ga., U.S.	Georgia, U.S.
Gam.	Gambia
Geor.	Georgia
Ger.	Germany
Grc.	Greece
Gren.	Grenada
Grnld.	Greenland
Guad.	Guadeloupe
Guat.	Guatemala
Gui.	Guinea
Gui.-B.	Guinea-Bissau

Guy.	Guyana
Hi., U.S.	Hawaii, U.S.
hist.	Historic Site, Ruins
hist. reg.	Historic Region
H.K.	Hong Kong
Hond.	Honduras
Hung.	Hungary
i.	Island
Ia., U.S.	Iowa, U.S.
ice	Ice Feature, Glacier
Ice.	Iceland
Id., U.S.	Idaho, U.S.
Il., U.S.	Illinois, U.S.
In., U.S.	Indiana, U.S.
Indon.	Indonesia
I. of Man	Isle of Man
I.R.	Indian Reservation
Ire.	Ireland
is.	Islands
Isr.	Israel
Isr. Occ.	Israeli Occupied Areas
isth.	Isthmus
Jam.	Jamaica
Jord.	Jordan
Kaz.	Kazakhstan
Kir.	Kiribati
Ks., U.S.	Kansas, U.S.
Kuw.	Kuwait
Ky., U.S.	Kentucky, U.S.
Kyrg.	Kyrgyzstan
l.	Lake, Pond
La., U.S.	Louisiana, U.S.
Lat.	Latvia
Leb.	Lebanon
Leso.	Lesotho
Lib.	Liberia
Liech.	Liechtenstein
Lith.	Lithuania
Lux.	Luxembourg
Ma., U.S.	Massachusetts, U.S.
Mac.	Macedonia
Madag.	Madagascar
Malay.	Malaysia
Marsh. Is.	Marshall Islands
Mart.	Martinique
Maur.	Mauritania
May.	Mayotte
Md., U.S.	Maryland, U.S.
Me., U.S.	Maine, U.S.
Mex.	Mexico
Mi., U.S.	Michigan, U.S.
Micron.	Micronesia, Federated States of
Mn., U.S.	Minnesota, U.S.
Mo., U.S.	Missouri, U.S.
Mol.	Moldova
Mong.	Mongolia
Monts.	Montserrat
Mor.	Morocco
Moz.	Mozambique
Ms., U.S.	Mississippi, U.S.
Mt., U.S.	Montana, U.S.
mth.	River Mouth or Channel
mtn.	Mountain
mts.	Mountains
Mwi.	Malawi
N.A.	North America
N.C., U.S.	North Carolina, U.S.
N. Cal.	New Caledonia
N. Cyp.	North Cyprus
N.D., U.S.	North Dakota, U.S.
Ne., U.S.	Nebraska, U.S.
neigh.	Neighborhood
Neth.	Netherlands
Neth. Ant.	Netherlands Antilles
N.H., U.S.	New Hampshire, U.S.
Nic.	Nicaragua
Nig.	Nigeria
N. Ire., U.K.	Northern Ireland, U.K.
N.J., U.S.	New Jersey, U.S.
N. Kor.	North Korea
N.M., U.S.	New Mexico, U.S.
N. Mar. Is.	Northern Mariana Islands
Nmb.	Namibia
Nor.	Norway
Nv., U.S.	Nevada, U.S.
N.Y., U.S.	New York, U.S.
N.Z.	New Zealand
o.	Ocean
Oc.	Oceania
Oh., U.S.	Ohio, U.S.
Ok., U.S.	Oklahoma, U.S.
Or., U.S.	Oregon, U.S.
p.	Pass
Pa., U.S.	Pennsylvania, U.S.
Pac. Is.	Pacific Islands, Trust Territory of the
Pak.	Pakistan
Pan.	Panama
Pap. N. Gui.	Papua New Guinea
Para.	Paraguay
pen.	Peninsula
Phil.	Philippines
Pit.	Pitcairn

pl.	Plain, Flat
plat.	Plateau, Highland
Pol.	Poland
Port.	Portugal
P.R.	Puerto Rico
prov.	Province, Region
pt. of i.	Point of Interest
r.	River, Creek
Reu.	Reunion
rec.	Recreational Site, Park
reg.	Physical Region
rel.	Religious Institution
res.	Reservoir
rf.	Reef, Shoal
R.I., U.S.	Rhode Island, U.S.
Rom.	Romania
Rw.	Rwanda
S.A.	South America
S. Afr.	South Africa
Sau. Ar.	Saudi Arabia
S.C., U.S.	South Carolina, U.S.
sci.	Scientific Station
Scot., U.K.	Scotland, U.K.
S.D., U.S.	South Dakota, U.S.
Sen.	Senegal
sea feat.	Undersea Feature
Sey.	Seychelles
S. Ga.	South Georgia
Sing.	Singapore
S. Kor.	South Korea
S.L.	Sierra Leone
Slvk.	Slovakia
Slvn.	Slovenia
S. Mar.	San Marino
Sol. Is.	Solomon Islands
Som.	Somalia
Sp. N. Afr.	Spanish North Africa
Sri L.	Sri Lanka
St. Hel.	St. Helena
St. K./N.	St. Kitts and Nevis
St. Luc.	St. Lucia
St. P./M.	St. Pierre and Miquelon
strt.	Strait, Channel, Sound
S. Tom./P.	Sao Tome and Principe
St. Vin.	St. Vincent and the Grenadines
Sur.	Suriname
Sval.	Svalbard
sw.	Swamp, Marsh
Swaz.	Swaziland
Swe.	Sweden
Switz.	Switzerland
Tai.	Taiwan
Taj.	Tajikistan
Tan.	Tanzania
T./C. Is.	Turks and Caicos Islands
ter.	Territory
Thai.	Thailand
Tn., U.S.	Tennessee, U.S.
trans.	Transportation Facility
Trin.	Trinidad and Tobago
Tun.	Tunisia
Tur.	Turkey
Turk.	Turkmenistan
Tx., U.S.	Texas, U.S.
U.A.E.	United Arab Emirates
Ug.	Uganda
U.K.	United Kingdom
Ukr.	Ukraine
Ur.	Uruguay
U.S.	United States
Ut., U.S.	Utah, U.S.
Uzb.	Uzbekistan
Va., U.S.	Virginia, U.S.
val.	Valley, Watercourse
Vat.	Vatican City
Ven.	Venezuela
V.I., Br.	Virgin Islands, British
Viet.	Vietnam
V.I.U.S.	Virgin Islands (U.S.)
vol.	Volcano
Vt., U.S.	Vermont, U.S.
Wa., U.S.	Washington, U.S.
Wi., U.S.	Wisconsin, U.S.
W. Sah.	Western Sahara
W. Sam.	Western Samoa
wtfl.	Waterfall
W.V., U.S.	West Virginia, U.S.
Wy., U.S.	Wyoming, U.S.
Yugo.	Yugoslavia
Zam.	Zambia
Zimb.	Zimbabwe
Zam.	Zambia

Key to the Sound Values of Letters and Symbols Used in the Index to Indicate Pronunciation

ă-ăt; băttle
ă-fināl; ăppeal
ā-rāte; elāte
â-senâte; inanimâte
ä-ärm; cälm
à-àsk; bàth
a̍-sofa̍; ma̍rine (short neutral or indeterminate sound)
â-fâre; prepâre
ch-choose; church
dh-as th in other; either
ē-bē; ēve
ė-ėvent; crėate
ĕ-bĕt; ĕnd
ĕ-recĕnt (short neutral or indeterminate sound)
ẽ-cratẽr; cindẽr
g-gō; gāme
gh-guttural g
ĭ-bĭt; wĭll
ĭ-(short neutral or indeterminate sound)
ī-rīde; bīte
ĸ-guttural k as ch in German ich
ng-sing
ŋ-baŋk; liŋger
N-indicates nasalized
ŏ-nŏd; ŏdd
ŏ-cŏmmit; cŏnnect
ō-ōld; bōld
ô-ôbey; hôtel
ô-ôrder; nôrth
oi-boil
o͞o-fo͞od; ro͞ot
o̍-as oo in foot; wood
ou-out; thou
s-soft; so; sane
sh-dish; finish
th-thin; thick
ū-pūre; cūre
ů-ůnite; ůsůrp
û-ûrn; fûr
ŭ-stŭd; ŭp
ŭ-circŭs; sŭbmit
ü-as in French tu
zh-as z in azure
'-indeterminate vowel sound

In many cases the spelling of foreign geographic names does not even remotely indicate the pronunciation to an American, i.e., Słupsk in Poland is pronounced swȯpsk; Jujuy in Argentina is pronounced ho͞ohwē'; La Spezia in Italy is lä-spē'zyä.

This condition is hardly surprising, however, when we consider that in our own language Worcester, Massachusetts, is pronounced wȯs'tẽr; Sioux City, Iowa, so͞o si'ti; Schuylkill Haven, Pennsylvania, sko͞ol'kĭl hä-vĕn; Poughkeepsie, New York, pŏ-kĭp'sĕ.

The indication of pronunciation of geographic names presents several peculiar problems:

1. Many foreign tongues use sounds that are not present in the English language and which an American cannot normally articulate. Thus, though the nearest English equivalent sound has been indicated, only approximate results are possible.

2. There are several dialects in each foreign tongue which cause variation in the local pronunciation of names. This also occurs in identical names in the various divisions of a great language group, as the Slavic or the Latin.

3. Within the United States there are marked differences in pronunciation, not only of local geographic names, but also of common words, indicating that the sound and tone values for letters as well as the placing of the emphasis vary considerably from one part of the country to another.

4. A number of different letters and diacritical combinations could be used to indicate essentially the same or approximate pronunciations.

Some variation in pronunciation other than that indicated in this index may be encountered, but such a difference does not necessarily indicate that either is in error, and in many cases it is a matter of individual choice as to which is preferred. In fact, an exact indication of pronunciation of many foreign names using English letters and diacritical marks is extremely difficult and sometimes impossible.

PRONOUNCING INDEX

This universal index includes in a single alphabetical list approximately 34,000 names of features that appear on the reference maps. Each name is followed by a page reference and geographical coordinates.

Abbreviation and Capitalization Abbreviations of names on the maps have been standardized as much as possible. Names that are abbreviated on the maps are generally spelled out in full in the index. Periods are used after all abbreviations regardless of local practice. The abbreviation "St." is used only for "Saint". "Sankt" and other forms of this term are spelled out.

Most initial letters of names are capitalized, except for a few Dutch names, such as "'s-Gravenhage". Capitalization of noninitial words in a name generally follows local practice.

Alphabetization Names are alphabetized in the order of the letters of the English alphabet. Spanish *ll* and *ch*, for example, are not treated as distinct letters. Furthermore, diacritical marks are disregarded in alphabetization — German or Scandinavian *ä* or *ö* are treated as *a* or *o*.

The names of physical features may appear inverted, since they are always alphabetized under the proper, not the generic, part of the name, thus: "Gibraltar, Strait of". Otherwise every entry, whether consisting of one word or more, is alphabetized as a single continuous entity. "Lakeland," for example, appears after "La Crosse" and before "La Salle." Names beginning with articles (Le Havre, Den Helder, Al Manāmah, Ad Dawhah) are not inverted. Names beginning "St.", "Ste." and "Sainte" are alphabetized as though spelled "Saint."

In the case of identical names, towns are listed first, then political divisions, then physical features.

Generic Terms Except for cities, the names of all features are followed by terms that represent broad classes of features, for example, Mississippi, r. or Alabama, state. A list of all abbreviations used in the index is on page 249.

Country names and names of features that extend beyond the boundaries of one country are followed by the name of the continent in which each is located. Country designations follow the names of all other places in the index. The locations of places in the United States and the United Kingdom are further defined by abbreviations that indicate the state or political division in which each is located.

Pronunciations Pronunciations are included for most names listed. An explanation of the pronunciation system used appears on page 249.

Page References and Geographical Coordinates The geographical coordinates and page references are found in the last columns of each entry.

If a page contains several maps or insets, a lowercase letter identifies the specific map or inset.

Latitude and longitude coordinates for point features, such as cities and mountain peaks, indicate the locations of the symbols. For extensive areal features, such as countries or mountain ranges, or linear features, such as canals and rivers, locations are given for the position of the type as it appears on the map.

PLACE (Pronunciation)	PAGE	Lat. °ʹ	Long. °ʹ
A			
Aachen, Ger. (ä′kĕn)	147	50.46N	6.07E
Aalen, Ger. (ä′lĕn)	154	48.49N	10.08E
Aalsmeer, Neth.	145a	52.16N	4.44E
Aalst, Bel.	151	50.58N	4.00E
Aarau, Switz. (är′ou)	147	47.22N	8.03E
Aarschot, Bel.	145a	50.59N	4.51E
Aba, Nig.	210	5.06N	7.21E
Aba, Zaire	217	3.52N	30.14E
Ābādān, Iran (ä-bŭ-dän′)	182	30.15N	48.30E
Abaetetuba, Braz. (ä′bá̤ĕ-tĕ-tōō′bá)	131	1.44S	48.45W
Abajo Peak, mtn., Ut., U.S. (ä-bá′hō)	109	37.51N	109.28W
Abakaliki, Nig.	215	6.21N	8.06E
Abakan, Russia (ŭ-bá-kän′)	165	53.43N	91.28E
Abakan, r., Russia (u-bá-kän′)	170	53.00N	91.06E
Abancay, Peru (ä-bän-kä′ē)	130	13.44S	72.46W
Abashiri, Japan (ä-bä-shē′rē)	194	44.00N	144.13E
Abasolo, Mex. (ä-bä-sō′lŏ)	112	27.13N	101.25W
Abasolo, Mex. (ä-bä-sō′lŏ)	118	24.05N	98.24W
Abaya, Lake, l., Eth. (ä-bä′yá)	211	6.24N	38.22E
'Abbāsābād, Iran	241h	35.44N	51.25E
'Abbāsah, Tur'at al, can., Egypt	218c	30.45N	32.15E
Abbeville, Fr. (ȧb-vēl′)	147	50.08N	1.49E
Abbeville, Al., U.S. (ȧb′ē-vĭl)	114	31.35N	85.15W
Abbeville, Ga., U.S. (ȧb′ē-vĭl)	114	31.53N	83.23W
Abbeville, La., U.S.	113	29.59N	92.07W
Abbeville, S.C., U.S.	115	34.09N	82.25W
Abbey Wood, neigh., Eng., U.K.	235	51.29N	0.08E
Abbiategrasso, Italy (ȧb-byä′tä-gräs′sō)	160	45.23N	8.52E
Abbots Bromley, Eng., U.K. (ȧb′ŭts brŭm′lē)	144a	52.49N	1.52W
Abbotsford, Can. (ȧb′ŭts-fērd)	106d	49.03N	122.17W
Abbots Langley, Eng., U.K.	235	51.43N	0.25W
'Abd al Kūrī, i., Yemen (ȧbd-ĕl-kŏ′rē)	218a	12.12N	51.00E
'Abd al-Shāhīd, Egypt	244a	29.55N	31.13E
Abdulino, Russia (ȧb-dȯ-lē′nŏ)	166	53.42N	53.40E
Abengourou, C. Iv.	214	6.44N	3.29W
Abeokuta, Nig. (ä-bā-ȯ-kōō′tä)	210	7.10N	3.26E
Abercorn see Mbala, Zam.	212	8.50S	31.22E
Aberdare, Wales, U.K. (ȧb-ēr-dâr′)	150	51.45N	3.35W
Aberdeen, Scot., U.K. (ȧb-ēr-dēn′)	142	57.10N	2.05W
Aberdeen, Ms., U.S. (ȧb-ēr-dēn′)	114	33.49N	88.33W
Aberdeen, S.D., U.S. (ȧb-ēr-dēn′)	96	45.28N	98.29W
Aberdeen, Wa., U.S. (ȧb-ēr-dēn′)	96	47.00N	123.48W
Aberford, Eng., U.K. (ȧb′ēr-fērd)	144a	53.49N	1.21W
Abergavenny, Wales, U.K. (ȧb′ēr-gȧ-vĕn′ĭ)	150	51.45N	3.05W
Abert, Lake, l., Or., U.S. (ä′bērt)	104	42.39N	120.24W
Aberystwyth, Wales, U.K. (ä-bĕr-ĭst′wĭth)	150	52.25N	4.04W
Abidjan, C. Iv. (ä-bēd-zhän′)	210	5.19N	4.02W
Abiko, Japan (ä-bē-kō)	195a	35.53N	140.01E
Abilene, Ks., U.S. (ȧb′ĭ-lēn)	111	38.54N	97.12W
Abilene, Tx., U.S.	96	32.25N	99.45W
Abingdon, Eng., U.K.	144b	51.38N	1.17W
Abingdon, Il., U.S. (ȧb′ĭng-dŭn)	103	40.48N	90.21W
Abingdon, Va., U.S.	115	36.42N	81.57W
Abington, Ma., U.S. (ȧb′ĭng-tŭn)	93a	42.07N	70.57W
Abington, Pa., U.S.	229b	40.07N	75.08W
Abiquiu Reservoir, res., N.M., U.S.	109	36.26N	106.42W
Abitibi, l., Can. (ȧb-ĭ-tĭb′ĭ)	85	48.27N	80.20W
Abitibi, r., Can.	85	49.30N	81.10W
Abkhazia, , Geor.	167	43.10N	40.45E
Ablis, Fr. (ȧ-blē′)	157b	48.31N	1.50E
Ablon-sur-Seine, Fr.	237c	48.43N	2.25E
Abnūb, Egypt (ȧb-nōōb′)	218b	27.18N	31.11E
Abo see Turku, Fin.	142	60.28N	22.12E
Abóbada, Port.	238d	38.43N	9.20W
Abohar, India	186	30.12N	74.13E
Aboisso, C. Iv.	214	5.28N	3.12W
Abomey, Benin (ȧb-ȯ-mā′)	210	7.11N	1.59E
Abony, Hung. (ȯ′bō-ny′)	155	47.12N	20.00E
Abou Deïa, Chad	215	11.27N	19.17E
Abra, r., Phil. (ä′brä)	197a	17.16N	120.38E
Abraão, Braz. (äbrä-ou′n)	129a	23.10S	44.10W
Abraham's Bay, b., Bah.	123	22.20N	73.50W
Abram, Eng., U.K. (ä′brăm)	144a	53.31N	2.36W
Abramcevo, Russia	239b	55.50N	37.50E
Abrantes, Port. (á-brän′tĕs)	158	39.28N	8.13W
Abridge, Eng., U.K.	235	51.39N	0.07E
Abrolhos, Arquipélago dos, is., Braz.	131	17.58S	38.40W
Abruka, i., Est. (ä-brō′ká)	153	58.09N	22.30E
Abrunheira, Port.	238d	38.46N	9.21W
Abruzzi e Molise, hist. reg., Italy	160	42.10N	13.55E
Absaroka Range, mts., U.S. (ȧb-sä-rō-kä)	96	44.50N	109.47W
Abşeron Yarımadası, pen., Azer.	167	40.20N	50.30E
Abū an-Numrus, Egypt	244a	29.57N	31.12E
Abū Arīsh, Sau. Ar. (ä-bōō á-rēsh′)	182	16.48N	43.00E
Abu Dhabi see Abū Ẓaby, U.A.E.	182	24.15N	54.28E
Abū Ḥamad, Sudan (ä′bōō hä′-mĕd)	211	19.37N	33.21E
Abuja, Nig.	210	9.12N	7.11E
Abū Kamāl, Syria	182	34.45N	40.46E
Abunã, r., S.A. (á-bōō-nä′)	130	10.25S	67.00W
Abū Qīr, Egypt (ä′bōō kēr′)	218b	31.18N	30.06E
Abū Qurūn, Ra's, mtn., Egypt	181a	30.22N	33.32E
Aburatsu, Japan (ä′bȯ-rät′sōō)	195	31.33N	131.20E
Abu Road, India (ä′bōō)	183	24.38N	72.45E
Abū Şīr Pyramids, hist., Egypt	244a	29.54N	31.12E
Abū Tīj, Egypt	218b	27.03N	31.19E
Abū Ẓaby, U.A.E.	182	24.15N	54.28E
Abū Ẓanīmah, Egypt	181a	29.03N	33.08E
Abyy, Russia	165	68.24N	134.00E
Acacias, Col. (á-ká′sēäs)	130a	3.59N	73.44W
Acadia National Park, rec., Me., U.S. (ä-kä′dǐ-á)	97	44.19N	68.01W
Acajutla, El Sal. (ä-kä-hōōt′lä)	120	13.37N	89.50W
Acala, Mex. (ä-kä′lä)	119	16.38N	92.49W
Acalayong, Eq. Gui.	216	1.05N	9.40E
Acámbaro, Mex. (ä-käm′bä-rō)	118	20.03N	100.42W
Acancéh, Mex. (ä-kän-sě′)	120a	20.50N	89.27W
Acapetlahuaya, Mex. (ä-kä-pĕt′lä-hwä′yä)	118	18.24N	100.04W
Acaponeta, Mex. (ä-kä-pō-nä′tä)	118	22.31N	105.25W
Acaponeta, r., Mex. (ä-kä-pō-nä′tä)	118	22.47N	105.23W
Acapulco, Mex. (ä-kä-pōōl′kō)	116	16.49N	99.57W
Acaraí Mountains, mts., S.A.	131	1.30N	57.40W
Acarigua, Ven. (äkä-rē′gwä)	130	9.29N	69.11W
Acatlán de Osorio, Mex. (ä-kät-län′dä ō-sō′rē-ō)	118	18.11N	98.04W
Acatzingo de Hidalgo, Mex.	119	18.58N	97.47W
Acayucan, Mex. (ä-kä-yōō′kän)	119	17.56N	94.55W
Accord, Ma., U.S.	227a	42.10N	70.53W
Accoville, W.V., U.S. (äk′kȯ-vĭl)	98	37.45N	81.50W
Accra, Ghana (ä′krä)	210	5.33N	0.13W
Accrington, Eng., U.K. (äk′rĭng-tŭn)	144a	53.45N	2.22W
Acerra, Italy (ä-chě′r-rä)	159c	40.42N	14.22E
Achacachi, Bol. (ä-chä-kä′chē)	130	16.11S	68.32W
Achill Island, i., Ire. (ä-chǐl′)	146	53.55N	10.05W
Achinsk, Russia (ä-chěnsk′)	170	56.13N	90.32E
Acireale, Italy (ä-chē-rä-ä′lä)	160	37.37N	15.12E
Acklins, i., Bah. (äk′lĭns)	117	22.30N	73.55W
Acklins, The Bight of, bt., Bah. (äk′lĭns)	123	22.35N	74.20W
Acolman, Mex. (ä-kōl-má′n)	119a	19.38N	98.56W
Acoma Indian Reservation, I.R., N.M., U.S.	109	34.52N	107.40W
Aconcagua, prov., Chile (ä-kŏn-kä′gwä)	129b	32.20S	71.00W
Aconcagua, r., Chile (ä-kŏn-kä′gwä)	129b	32.43S	70.53W
Aconcagua, Cerro, mtn., Arg. (ä-kŏn-kä′gwä)	132	32.38S	70.00W
Açores (Azores), is., Port.	209	37.44N	29.25W
Acoyapa, Nic. (ä-kȯ-yä′pä)	120	11.54N	85.11W
Acqui, Italy (äk′kwē)	160	44.41N	8.22W
Acre, state, Braz. (ä′krä)	130	8.40S	70.45W
Acre, r., S.A.	130	10.33S	68.34W
Acton, Can. (äk′tŭn)	83d	43.38N	80.02W
Acton, Al., U.S. (äk′tŭn)	100h	33.21N	86.49W
Acton, Ma., U.S. (äk′tŭn)	93a	42.29N	71.26W
Acton, neigh., Eng., U.K. (äk′tŭn)	235	51.30N	0.16W
Actopan, Mex. (äk-tȯ-pän′)	118	20.16N	98.57W
Actópan, r., Mex. (äk-tȯ′pän)	119	19.25N	96.31W

ăt; finăl; rāte; senăte; ärm; ȧsk; sofȧ; fâre; ch-choose; dh-as th in other; bē; ĕvent; bĕt; recĕnt; cratēr; g-gō; gh-guttural g; bǐt; ĭ-short neutral; rīde; ᴋ-guttural k as ch in German ich;

PRONOUNCING INDEX

Acuitzio del Canje–Alaska 255

PLACE (Pronunciation)	PAGE	Lat. °′	Long. °′
Acuitzio del Canje, Mex. (ä-kwē̆t′zē-ō dĕl kän′hå)	118	19.28N	101.21W
Acul, Baie de l', b., Haiti (ä-kōōl′)	123	19.55N	72.20W
Ada, Mn., U.S. (ā′dŭ)	102	47.17N	96.32W
Ada, Oh., U.S. (ā′dŭ)	98	40.45N	83.45W
Ada, Ok., U.S. (ā′dŭ)	111	34.45N	96.43W
Ada, Yugo. (ä′dä)	161	45.48N	20.06E
Adachi, Japan	195a	35.50N	39.36E
Adachi, neigh., Japan	242a	35.45N	139.48E
Adak, Ak., U.S. (ă-dăk′)	95a	56.50N	176.48W
Adak, i., Ak., U.S. (ă-dăk′)	95a	51.40N	176.28W
Adak Strait, strt., Ak., U.S. (ă-dăk′)	95a	51.42N	177.16W
Adamaoua, mts., Afr.	210	6.30N	11.50E
Adams, Ma., U.S. (ăd′ămz)	99	42.35N	73.10W
Adams, Wi., U.S. (ăd′ămz)	103	43.55N	89.48W
Adams, r., Can. (ăd′ămz)	87	51.30N	119.20W
Adams, Mount, mtn., Wa., U.S. (ăd′ămz)	96	46.15N	121.19W
Adamsville, Al., U.S. (ăd′ămz-vĭl)	100h	33.36N	86.57W
Adana, Tur. (ä′dä-nä)	182	37.05N	35.20E
Adapazari, Tur. (ä-dä-pä-zä′rē)	149	40.45N	30.20E
Adarama, Sudan (ä-dä-rä′mä)	211	17.11N	34.56E
Adda, r., Italy (äd′dä)	160	45.43N	9.31E
Ad Dabbah, Sudan	211	18.04N	30.58E
Ad Dahnā, des., Sau. Ar.	182	26.05N	47.15E
Ad-Dāmir, Sudan (ad-dä′mĕr)	211	17.38N	33.57E
Ad Dammām, Sau. Ar.	182	26.27N	49.59E
Ad Dāmūr, Leb.	181a	33.44N	35.27E
Ad Dawhah, Qatar	182	25.02N	51.28E
Ad Dilam, Sau. Ar.	182	23.47N	47.03E
Ad Dilinjāt, Egypt	218b	30.48N	30.32E
Addington, Eng., U.K.	235	51.18N	0.23E
Addis Ababa, Eth.	211	9.00N	38.44E
Addison, Tx., U.S. (ă′dĭ-sŭn)	107c	32.58N	96.50W
Addlestone, Eng., U.K.	235	51.22N	0.30W
Addo, S. Afr. (ădō)	213c	33.33S	25.43E
Ad Duwaym, Sudan (ad-dō-ām′)	211	13.56N	32.22E
Addyston, Oh., U.S. (ăd′ē-stŭn)	101f	39.09N	84.42W
Adel, Ga., U.S. (ā-dĕl′)	114	31.08N	83.55W
Adelaide, Austl. (ăd′ē-lād)	202	34.46S	139.08E
Adelaide, S. Afr. (ăd-ĕl′ăd)	213c	32.41S	26.07E
Adelaide Island, i., Ant. (ăd′ē-lād)	219	67.15S	68.40W
Adelphi, Md., U.S.	229d	39.00N	76.58W
Aden ('Adan), Yemen (ä′dĕn)	182	12.48N	45.00E
Aden, Gulf of, b.	182	11.45N	45.45E
Aderklaa, Aus.	239e	48.17N	16.32E
Adi, Pulau, i., Indon. (ä′dē)	197	4.25S	133.52E
Adige, r., Italy (ä′dē-jä)	148	46.38N	10.43E
Adigrat, Eth.	185	14.17N	39.28E
Adilābād, India (ŭ-dĭl-ä-băd′)	186	19.47N	78.30E
Adirondack Mountains, mts., N.Y., U.S. (ăd-ĭ-rŏn′dăk)	97	43.45N	74.40W
Adis Abeba *see* Addis Ababa, Eth.	211	9.00N	38.44E
Adi Ugri, Erit. (ä-dē ōō′grē)	211	14.54N	38.52E
Adjud, Rom. (ăd′zhŏd)	155	46.05N	27.12E
Adkins, Tx., U.S.	107d	29.22N	98.18W
Adlershof, neigh., Ger.	238a	52.26N	13.33E
Admiralty, i., Ak., U.S. (ăd′mĭr*a*l-tē)	95	57.50N	133.50W
Admiralty Inlet, Wa., U.S. (ăd′mĭr*a*l-tē)	106a	48.10N	122.45W
Admiralty Island National Monument, rec., Ak., U.S. (ăd′mĭr*a*l-tē)	95	57.50N	137.30W
Admiralty Islands, is., Pap. N. Gui. (ăd′mĭr*a*l-tē)	197	1.40S	146.45E
Ado-Ekiti, Nig.	215	7.38N	5.12E
Adolph, Mn., U.S. (ā′dolf)	107h	46.47N	92.17W
Ādoni, India	187	15.42N	77.18E
Adour, r., Fr. (ā-dōōr′)	147	43.43N	0.38W
Adra, Spain (ä′drä)	158	36.45N	3.02W
Adrano, Italy (ä-drä′nō)	160	37.42N	14.52E
Adrar, Alg.	210	27.53N	0.15W
Adria, Italy (ä′drē-ä)	160	45.03N	12.01E
Adrian, Mi., U.S. (ā′drĭ-*ă*n)	98	41.55N	84.00W
Adrian, Mn., U.S. (ā′drĭ-*ă*n)	102	43.39N	95.56W
Adrianople *see* Edirne, Tur.	142	41.41N	26.35E
Adriatic Sea, sea, Eur.	142	43.30N	14.27E
Adwa, Eth.	211	14.02N	38.58E
Adwick-le-Street, Eng., U.K. (ăd′wĭk-lē-strēt′)	144a	53.35N	1.11W
Adycha, r., Russia (ä′dĭ-chá)	171	66.11N	136.45E
Adygea, state, Russia	166	45.00N	40.00E
Adzhamka, Ukr. (ád-zhäm′kå)	163	48.33N	32.28E
Adz'va, r., Russia (ädz′vá)	166	67.00N	59.20E
Aegean Sea, sea (ē-jē′ăn)	142	39.04N	24.56E
Affton, Mo., U.S.	107e	38.33N	90.20W
Afghanistan, nation, Asia (ăf-găn-ĭ-stăn′)	182	33.00N	63.00E
Afgooye, Som. (äf-gô′ĭ)	218a	2.08N	45.08E
Afikpo, Nig.	215	5.53N	7.56E
Aflou, Alg. (ä-flōō′)	210	33.59N	2.04E
Afognak, i., Ak., U.S. (ä-fŏg-nák′)	95	58.28N	151.35W
Afonso Claudio, Braz. (äl-fôn′sō-klou′dēō)	129a	20.05S	41.05W
Afragola, Italy (ä-frá′gō-lä)	159c	40.40N	14.19E
Africa, cont.	209	10.00N	22.00E
Afton, Mn., U.S. (ăf′tŭn)	107g	44.54N	92.47W
Afton, Ok., U.S. (ăf′tŭn)	111	36.42N	94.56W
Afton, Wy., U.S. (ăf′tŭn)	105	42.42N	110.52W
'Afula, Isr. (ä-fō′lå)	181a	32.36N	35.17E
Afyon, Tur. (ä-fē-ōn)	182	38.45N	30.20E
Agadem, Niger (ä′gá-dĕm)	211	16.50N	13.17E
Agadez, Niger (ä′g*á*-dĕs)	210	16.58N	7.59E
Agadir, Mor. (ä-g*á*-dēr)	210	30.30N	9.37W
Agalta, Cordillera de, mts., Hond. (kôr-dēl-yĕ′rä-dĕ-ä-gä′l-tä)	120	15.15N	85.42W
Agapovka, Russia (ä-gä-pôv′kä)	172a	53.18N	59.10E
Agartala, India	186	23.53N	91.22E
Agāshi, India	187b	19.28N	72.46E
Agashkino, Russia (å-gäsh′kĭ-nô)	172b	55.18N	38.13E

PLACE (Pronunciation)	PAGE	Lat. °′	Long. °′
Agattu, i., Ak., U.S. (à′gä-tōō)	95a	52.14N	173.40E
Agboville, C. Iv.	214	5.56N	4.13W
Ağdam, Azer. (äg′dăm)	167	40.00N	47.00E
Agde, Fr. (ägd)	156	43.19N	3.30E
Agege, Nig.	244d	6.37N	3.20E
Agen, Fr. (å-zhäN′)	147	44.13N	0.31E
Agincourt, neigh., Can.	227c	43.48N	79.17W
Aginskoye, Russia (ä-hĭn′skô-yĕ)	165	51.15N	113.15E
Agno, Phil. (äg′nō)	197a	16.07N	119.49E
Agno, r., Phil.	197a	15.42N	120.28E
Agnone, Italy (än-yō′nā)	160	41.49N	14.23E
Agogo, Ghana	214	6.47N	1.04W
Agostinho Pôrto, Braz.	234c	22.47S	43.23W
Agra, India (ä′grä)	183	27.18N	78.00E
Ağri, Tur.	167	39.50N	43.10E
Agri, r., Italy (ä′grē)	160	40.15N	16.21E
Agrícola Oriental, Mex.	233a	19.24N	99.05W
Agrínion, Grc. (å-grē′nyôn)	149	38.38N	21.06E
Agua, vol., Guat. (ä′gwä)	120	14.28N	90.43W
Agua Blanca, Río, r., Mex. (rē′ō-ä-gwä-blä′n-kä)	118	21.46N	102.54W
Agua Brava, Laguna de, l., Mex.	118	22.04N	105.40W
Agua Caliente Indian Reservation, I.R., Ca., U.S. (ä′gwä kal-yĕn′tä)	108	33.50N	116.24W
Aguada, Cuba (ä-gwä′d*ä*)	122	22.25N	80.50W
Aguada, l., Mex. (ä-gwä′d*ä*)	120a	18.46N	89.40W
Aguadas, Col. (ä-gwä′dås)	130	5.37N	75.27W
Aguadilla, P.R. (ä-gwä-dēl′yä)	117b	18.27N	67.10W
Aguadulce, Pan. (ä-gwä-dōōl′sä)	121	8.15N	80.33W
Agua Escondida, Meseta de, plat., Mex.	119	16.54N	91.35W
Agua Fria, r., Az., U.S. (ä′gwä frē-ä)	109	33.43N	112.22W
Aguai, Braz. (ägwä-ē′)	129a	22.04S	46.57W
Agualeguas, Mex. (ä-gwä-lä′gwäs)	112	26.19N	99.33W
Agualva-Cacém, Port.	238d	38.46N	9.18W
Aguán, r., Hond. (ä-gwà′n)	120	15.22N	87.00W
Aguanaval, r., Mex. (ä-guä-nä-väl′)	112	25.12N	103.28W
Aguanus, r., Can. (ä-gwä′nŭs)	93	50.45N	62.03W
Aguascalientes, Mex. (ä′gwäs-käl-yĕn′tās)	116	21.52N	102.17W
Aguascalientes, state, Mex. (ä′gwäs-käl-yĕn′tās)	118	22.00N	102.18W
Águeda, Port. (ä-gwā′d*ä*)	158	40.36N	8.26W
Agueda, r., Eur. (ä-gē-dä)	158	40.50N	6.44W
Aguelhok, Mali	214	19.28N	0.52E
Aguilar, Spain	158	37.32N	4.39W
Aguilar, Co., U.S. (ä-gē-lär′)	110	37.24N	104.38W
Aguilas, Spain (ä-gē-läs)	148	37.26N	1.35W
Aguililla, Mex. (ä-gē-lēl-yä)	118	18.44N	102.44W
Aguililla, r., Mex. (ä-gē-lēl-yä)	118	18.30N	102.48W
Aguja, Punta, c., Peru (pŭn′tä á-gōō′ hä)	130	6.00S	81.15W
Agulhas, Cape, c., S. Afr. (ä-gōōl′yäs)	212	34.47S	20.00E
Agusan, r., Phil. (ä-gōō′sän)	197	8.12N	126.07E
Ahaggar, mts., Alg. (á-há-gär′)	210	23.14N	6.00E
Ahar, Iran	185	38.28N	47.04E
Ahlen, Ger. (ä′lĕn)	154	51.45N	7.52E
Ahlenberg, Ger.	236	51.25N	7.28E
Ahmadābād, India (ŭ-mĕd-ä-băd′)	183	23.04N	72.38E
Ahmadnagar, India (ä′mŭd-nŭ-gûr)	183	19.09N	74.45E
Ahmar Mountains, mts., Eth.	211	9.22N	42.00E
Ahoskie, N.C., U.S. (ā-hŏs′kē)	115	36.15N	77.00W
Ahrensburg, Ger. (ä′rĕns-bŏrg)	145c	53.40N	10.14E
Ahrensfelde, Ger.	238a	52.35N	13.35E
Ahrweiler, Ger. (är′vī-lĕr)	154	50.34N	7.05E
Ähtärinjärvi, l., Fin.	153	62.46N	24.25E
Ahuacatlán, Mex. (ä-wä-kät-län′)	118	21.05N	104.28W
Ahuachapán, El Sal. (ä-wä-chä-pän′)	120	13.57N	89.53W
Ahualulco, Mex. (ä-wä-lōōl′kō)	118	20.43N	103.57W
Ahuatempan, Mex. (ä-wä-tĕm-pän)	118	18.11N	98.02W
Ahuntsic, neigh., Can.	227b	45.33N	73.39W
Åhus, Swe. (ô′hòs)	152	55.56N	14.19E
Ahvāz, Iran	182	31.15N	48.54E
Ahvenanmaa (Åland), is., Fin. (ä′vĕ-nán-mô) (ô′lănd)	146	60.36N	19.55E
Aiea, Hi., U.S.	94a	21.18N	157.52W
Aigburth, neigh., Eng., U.K.	237a	53.22N	2.55W
Aiken, S.C., U.S. (ā′kĕn)	115	33.32N	81.43W
Aimorès, Serra dos, mts., Braz. (sĕ′r-rä-dôs-ī-mō-rĕ′s)	131	17.40S	42.38W
Aimoto, Japan (ī-mō-tō)	195b	34.59N	135.09E
Aincourt, Fr. (äN-kōō′r)	157b	49.04N	1.47E
Aïn el Beïda, Alg.	210	35.57N	7.25E
Ainsworth, Eng., U.K.	237b	53.35N	2.22W
Ainsworth, Ne., U.S. (ānz′wûrth)	102	42.32N	99.51W
Aïn Témouchent, Alg. (ä′ēntĕ-mōō-shaN′)	148	35.20N	1.23W
Aintree, Eng., U.K.	237a	53.29N	2.56W
Aïn Wessara, Alg. (ĕn ōō-sä-rá)	159	35.25N	2.50E
Aipe, Col. (ī′pĕ)	130a	3.13N	75.15W
Aïr, mts., Niger	210	18.00N	8.30E
Aire, r., Eng., U.K.	144a	53.42N	1.00W
Aire-sur-l'Adour, Fr. (âr)	156	43.42N	0.17W
Airhitam, Selat, strt., Indon.	181b	0.58N	102.38E
Airport West, Austl.	243b	37.44S	144.53E
Ai Shan, mts., China (äī′shän)	190	37.27N	120.35E
Aisne, r., Fr. (ĕn)	147	49.28N	3.32E
Aitape, Pap. N. Gui. (ä-ē-tä′pá)	197	3.00S	142.10E
Aitkin, Mn., U.S. (āt′kĭn)	103	46.32N	93.43W
Aitolikón, Grc. (å-tō′lĭ-kón)	161	38.27N	21.21E
Aitos, Bul. (ä-ē′tōs)	161	42.42N	27.17E
Aitutaki, i., Cook Is. (ī-tōō-tä′kē)	225	19.00S	162.00W
Aiud, Rom. (ä′ē-ōd)	149	46.19N	23.40E
Aiuruoca, Braz. (āē′ōō-rōōō′-kā)	129a	21.57S	44.36W
Aiuruoca, r., Braz.	129a	22.11S	44.35W
Aix-en-Provence, Fr. (ĕks-prô-vȧNs)	147	43.32N	5.27E
Aix-les-Bains, Fr. (ĕks′-lā-băN′)	157	45.42N	5.56E
Aiyáleo, Grc.	239d	37.59N	23.41E
Aíyina, Grc.	161	37.43N	23.35E
Aíyina, i., Grc.	161	37.43N	23.35E

PLACE (Pronunciation)	PAGE	Lat. °′	Long. °′
Aíyion, Grc.	161	38.13N	22.04E
Aizpute, Lat. (ä′ēz-pōō-tĕ)	153	56.44N	21.37E
Aizuwakamatsu, Japan	194	37.27N	139.51E
Ajaccio, Fr. (ä-yät′chō)	142	41.55N	8.42E
Ajalpan, Mex. (ä-häl′pän)	119	18.21N	97.14W
Ajana, Austl. (ăj-ăn′ĕr)	202	28.00S	114.45E
Ajaria, state, Geor.	168	41.40N	42.00E
Ajdābiyah, Libya	211	30.56N	20.16E
Ajjer, Tassili-n-, plat., Alg.	210	25.40N	6.57E
Ajmah, Jabal al, mts., Egypt	181a	29.12N	34.03E
Ajman, U.A.E.	182	25.15N	54.30E
Ajmer, India (ŭj-mēr′)	183	26.26N	74.42E
Ajo, Az., U.S. (ä′hô)	109	32.20N	112.55W
Ajuchitlán del Progreso, Mex. (ä-hōō-chet-lån′)	118	18.11N	100.32W
Ajuda, neigh., Port.	238d	38.43N	9.12W
Ajusco, Mex. (ä-hōō′s-kō)	119a	19.13N	99.12W
Ajusco, Cerro, mtn., Mex. (sĕ′r-rō-ä-hōō′s-kō)	119a	19.12N	99.16W
Akaishi-dake, mtn., Japan (ä-kī-shē dä′kä)	195	35.30N	138.00E
Akashi, Japan (ä′kä-shē)	194	34.38N	134.59E
Akbarābād, Iran	241h	35.41N	51.21E
Aketi, Zaire (ä-kå-tē)	211	2.44N	23.46E
Akhaltsikhe, Geor. (äkä′l-tsĭ-kĕ)	167	41.40N	42.50E
Akhdar, Al Jabal al, mts., Libya	211	32.00N	22.00E
Akhdar, Al Jabal al, mts., Oman	182	23.30N	56.43W
Akhelóös, r., Grc. (ä-hĕ′lō-ōs)	161	38.45N	21.26E
Akhisar, Tur. (äk-hĭs-sär′)	149	38.58N	27.58E
Akhtarskaya, Bukhta, b., Russia (bōōk′tä äk-tär′skå-yå)	163	45.53N	38.22E
Akhtopol, Bul. (äk′tô-pōl)	161	42.08N	27.54E
Akhunovo, Russia (ä-kû′nô-vô)	172a	54.13N	59.36E
Aki, Japan (ä′kē)	195	33.31N	133.51E
Akiak, Ak., U.S. (äk′yák)	95	61.00N	161.02W
Akimiski, i., Can. (ä-kĭ-mĭ′skĭ)	85	52.54N	80.22W
Akishima, Japan	242a	35.41N	139.22E
Akita, Japan (ä′kē-tä)	189	39.40N	140.12E
Akjoujt, Maur.	210	19.45N	14.23W
'Akko, Isr.	181a	32.56N	35.05E
Aklavik, Can. (äk′lä-vĭk)	84	68.28N	135.26W
'Aklé'Âouâna, dunes, Afr.	214	18.07N	6.00W
Akmola (Tselinograd), Kaz.	169	51.10N	71.43E
Ako, Japan (ä′kō)	195	34.44N	134.22E
Akola, India (á-kō′lä)	183	20.47N	77.00E
Akordat, Erit.	211	15.34N	37.54E
Akpatok, i., Can. (äk′pá-tŏk)	85	60.30N	67.10W
Akranes, Ice.	146	64.18N	21.40W
Akron, Co., U.S. (ăk′rŭn)	110	40.09N	103.14W
Akron, Oh., U.S. (ăk′rŭn)	97	41.05N	81.30W
Akropolis, pt. of i., Grc.	239d	37.58N	23.43E
Aksaray, Tur. (äk-sá-rī′)	149	38.30N	34.05E
Akşehir, Tur. (äk′shå-hĕr)	149	38.20N	31.20E
Akşehir Gölü, l., Tur. (äk′shå-hĕr)	182	38.40N	31.30E
Aksha, Russia (äk′shà)	165	50.28N	113.00E
Aksu, China (ä-kŭ-sōō)	188	41.29N	80.15E
Akune, Japan (ä′kŏ-nā)	195	32.03N	130.16E
Akureyri, Ice. (ä-kō-rå′rē)	146	65.39N	18.01W
Akutan, i., Ak., U.S. (ä-kōō-tän′)	95a	53.58N	169.54W
Akwatia, Ghana	214	6.04N	0.49W
Alabama, state, U.S. (ăl-*á*-băm′*á*)	97	32.50N	87.30W
Alabama, r., Al., U.S. (ăl-*á*-băm′*á*)	97	31.20N	87.39W
Alabat, i., Phil. (ä-lä-bät′)	197a	14.14N	122.05E
Alacam, Tur. (ä-lä-chăm′)	167	41.30N	35.40E
Alacranes, Cuba (ä-lä-krä′nås)	122	22.45N	81.35W
Al Aflaj, des., Sau. Ar.	182	24.00N	44.47E
Alagôas, state, Braz. (ä-lä-gō′ăzh)	131	9.50S	36.33W
Alagoinhas, Braz. (ä-lä-gō-ēn′yäzh)	131	12.13S	38.12W
Alagón, Spain (ä-lä-gōn′)	158	41.46N	1.07W
Alagón, r., Spain (ä-lä-gōn′)	158	39.53N	6.42W
Alaguntan, Nig.	244d	6.26N	3.30E
Alahuatán, r., Mex. (ä-lä-wä-tà′n)	118	18.30N	100.00W
Alajuela, C.R. (ä-lä-hwa′lä)	121	10.01N	84.14W
Alajuela, Lago, l., Pan. (ä-lä-hwa′lä)	116a	9.15N	79.34W
Alakol, l., Kaz.	169	45.45N	81.13E
Alalakeiki Channel, strt., Hi., U.S. (ä-lä-lä-kä′kē)	94a	20.40N	156.30W
Al 'Alamayn, Egypt	211	30.53N	28.52E
Al 'Amārah, Iraq	185	31.50N	47.09E
Alameda, Ca., U.S. (ăl-*á*-mā′d*á*)	96	37.46N	122.15W
Alameda, r., Ca., U.S. (ăl-*á*-mā′d*á*)	106b	37.36N	122.02W
Alaminos, Phil. (ä-lä-mē′nôs)	197a	16.09N	119.58E
Al 'Amirīyah, Egypt	149	31.01N	29.52E
Alamo, Mex. (ä′lä-mô)	119	20.55N	97.41W
Alamo, Ca., U.S. (ă′l*á*-mō)	106b	37.51N	122.02W
Alamo, Nv., U.S. (ă′l*á*-mō)	108	37.22N	115.10W
Alamo, r., Mex. (ä′lä-mô)	112	26.33N	99.35W
Alamogordo, N.M., U.S. (ăl-*á*-mō-gôr′dō)	109	32.55N	106.00W
Alamo Heights, Tx., U.S. (ă′l*á*-mō)	107d	29.28N	98.27W
Alamo Indian Reservation, I.R., N.M., U.S.	109	34.30N	107.30W
Alamo Peak, mtn., N.M., U.S. (ă′l*á*-mō pēk)	112	32.50N	105.55W
Alamosa, Co., U.S. (ăl-*á*-mō′s*á*)	109	37.25N	105.50W
Åland *see* Ahvenanmaa, is., Fin.	146	60.36N	19.55E
Alandskiy, Russia (ä-länt′skĭ)	172a	52.14N	59.48E
Alanga Arba, Kenya	217	0.07N	40.25E
Alanya, Tur.	149	36.40N	32.10E
Alaotra, l., Madag. (ä-lä-ō′tr*á*)	213	17.15S	48.17E
Alapayevsk, Russia (ä-lä-pä′yĕfsk)	164	57.50N	61.35E
Al 'Aqabah, Jord.	182	29.32N	35.00E
Alaquines, Mex. (ä-lä-kē′nås)	118	22.07N	99.35W
Al 'Arīsh, Egypt (ăl-a-rēsh′)	181a	31.08N	33.48E
Alaska, state, U.S. (á-lăs′k*á*)	96a	64.00N	150.00W
Alaska, Gulf of, b., Ak., U.S. (á-lăs′k*á*)	95	57.42N	147.40W

256 Alaska Highway-Al-Manāwāt

PLACE (Pronunciation)	PAGE	Lat. °′	Long. °′
Alaska Highway, trans., Ak., U.S. (á-lăs′kȧ)	95	63.00N	142.00W
Alaska Peninsula, pen., Ak., U.S. (á-lăs′kȧ)	95	55.50N	162.10W
Alaska Range, mts., Ak., U.S. (á-lăs′kȧ)	95	62.00N	152.18W
Al 'Atrūn, Sudan	211	18.13N	26.44E
Alatyr', Russia (ä′lä-tür)	164	54.55N	46.30E
Alazani, r., Asia	168	41.05N	46.40E
Alba, Italy (äl′bä)	160	44.41N	8.02E
Albacete, Spain (äl-bä-thā′tä)	148	39.00N	1.49W
Albachten, Ger. (äl-bä′ĸ-tĕn)	157c	51.55N	7.31E
Alba de Tormes, Spain (äl-bä dā tôr′mās)	158	40.48N	5.28W
Alba Iulia, Rom. (äl-bä yōō′lyá)	149	46.05N	23.32E
Albani, Colli, hills, Italy	159d	41.46N	12.45E
Albania, nation, Eur. (ăl-bā′nĭ-ȧ)	142	41.45N	20.00E
Albano, Lago, l., Italy (lä′-gō äl-bä′nō)	159d	41.45N	12.44E
Albano Laziale, Italy (äl-bä′nō lät-zē-ä′lā)	160	41.44N	12.43E
Albany, Austl. (ôl′bȧ-nĭ)	202	35.00S	118.00E
Albany, Ca., U.S. (ôl′bȧ-nĭ)	106b	37.54N	122.18W
Albany, Ga., U.S. (ôl′bȧ-nĭ)	97	31.35N	84.10W
Albany, Mo., U.S. (ôl′bȧ-nĭ)	111	40.14N	94.18W
Albany, N.Y., U.S. (ôl′bȧ-nĭ)	97	42.40N	73.50W
Albany, Or., U.S. (ôl′bȧ-nĭ)	96	44.38N	123.06W
Albany, r., Can. (ôl′bȧ-nĭ)	85	51.45N	83.30W
Albany Park, neigh., Il., U.S. (ôl′bȧ-nĭ)	231a	41.58N	87.43W
Al-Barājīl, Egypt	244a	30.04N	31.09E
Al Başrah, Iraq	182	30.35N	47.59E
Al Batrūn, Leb. (äl-bä-trōōn′)	181a	34.16N	35.39E
Albemarle, N.C., U.S. (ăl′bē-märl)	115	35.24N	80.36W
Albemarle Sound, strt., N.C., U.S. (ăl′bē-märl)	97	36.00N	76.17W
Albenga, Italy (äl-bĕŋ′gä)	160	44.04N	8.13E
Alberche, r., Spain (äl-bĕr′chå)	158	40.08N	4.19W
Alberga, The, r., Austl. (ăl-bŭr′gȧ)	202	27.15S	135.00E
Albergaria-a-Velha, Port.	158	40.47N	8.31W
Alberhill, Ca., U.S. (ăl′bẽr-hĭl)	107a	33.43N	117.23W
Albert, Fr. (ál-bâr′)	156	50.00N	2.49E
Albert, l., Afr. (ăl′bẽrt) (ál-bâr′)	211	1.50N	30.40E
Albert, Parc National, rec., Zaire	217	0.05N	29.30E
Alberta, prov., Can. (ăl-bûr′tȧ)	84	54.33N	117.10W
Alberta, Mount, mtn., Can. (ăl-bûr′tȧ)	87	52.18N	117.28W
Albert Edward, Mount, mtn., Pap. N. Gui. (ăl′bẽrt ĕd′wẽrd)	197	8.25S	147.25E
Albertfalva, neigh., Hung.	239g	47.27N	19.02E
Alberti, Arg. (ál-bĕ′r-tē)	129c	35.01S	60.16W
Albert Kanaal, can., Bel.	145a	51.07N	5.07E
Albert Lea, Mn., U.S. (ăl′bẽrt lē′)	103	43.38N	93.24W
Albert Nile, r., Ug.	217	3.25N	31.35E
Alberton, Can. (ăl′bẽr-tŭn)	92	46.49N	64.04W
Alberton, S. Afr.	213b	26.16S	28.08E
Albertson, N.Y., U.S.	228	40.46N	73.39W
Albertville, Fr. (ál-bêr-vēl′)	157	45.42N	6.25E
Albertville, Al., U.S. (ăl′bẽrt-vĭl)	114	34.15N	86.10W
Albertville *see* Kalemie, Zaire	212	5.56S	29.12E
Albi, Fr. (äl-bē′)	147	43.54N	2.07E
Albia, Ia., U.S. (ăl-bĭ-ȧ)	103	41.01N	92.44W
Albina, Sur. (äl-bē′nä)	131	5.30N	54.33W
Albina, Ponta, c., Ang.	216	15.51S	11.44E
Albino, Point, c., Can. (äl-bē′nō)	101c	42.50N	79.05W
Albion, Austl. (ăl′bĭ-ŭn)	243b	37.47S	144.49E
Albion, Mi., U.S. (ăl′bĭ-ŭn)	98	42.15N	84.50W
Albion, Ne., U.S. (ăl′bĭ-ŭn)	102	41.42N	98.00W
Albion, N.Y., U.S. (ăl′bĭ-ŭn)	99	43.15N	78.10W
Alboran, Isla del, i., Spain (ē′s-lä-dĕl-äl-bō-rä′n)	142	35.58N	3.02W
Ålborg, Den. (ôl′bôr)	142	57.02N	9.55E
Albuquerque, N.M., U.S. (ăl-bú-kûr′kē)	96	35.05N	106.40W
Albuquerque, Cayos de, is., Col.	121	12.12N	81.24W
Alburquerque, Spain (äl-bōōr-kĕr′kā)	158	39.13N	6.58W
Albury, Austl. (ôl′bẽr-ē)	203	36.00S	147.00E
Alcabideche, Port. (äl-kà-bē-dā′chå)	159b	38.43N	9.24W
Alcácer do Sal, Port. (äb′ĭ-lĕn)	158	38.24N	8.33W
Alcalá de Henares, Spain (äl-kä-lä′ dā ā-na′räs)	159a	40.29N	3.22W
Alcalá la Real, Spain (äl-kä-lä′lä rā-äl′)	158	37.27N	3.57W
Alcamo, Italy (äl′kȧ-mō)	160	37.58N	13.03E
Alcanadre, r., Spain (äl-kä-nä′drå)	159	41.41N	0.18W
Alcanar, Spain (äl-kä-när′)	159	40.35N	0.27E
Alcañiz, Spain (äl-kän-yēth′)	148	41.03N	0.08W
Alcântara, Braz. (äl-kän′tȧ-rȧ)	131	2.17S	44.29W
Alcântara, neigh., Port. (äl-kän′tȧ-ra)	238d	38.42N	9.10W
Alcaraz, Spain (äl-kä-räth′)	158	38.39N	2.28W
Alcaudete, Spain (äb′ĭng-dŭn)	158	37.38N	4.05W
Alcázar de San Juan, Spain (äl-kä′thär dā sän hwän′)	148	39.22N	3.12W
Alcira, Spain (ä-thē′rä)	159	39.09N	0.26W
Alcoa, Tn., U.S. (ăl-kō′ȧ)	114	35.45N	84.00W
Alcobendas, Spain (äl-kō-bĕn′dás)	159a	40.32N	3.39W
Alcochete, Port. (äl-kō-chā′ta)	159b	38.45N	8.58W
Alcorcón, Spain	159a	40.22N	3.50W
Alcorta, Arg. (äl-kôr′tä)	129c	33.32S	61.08W
Alcova Reservoir, res., Wy., U.S. (ăl-kō′vȧ)	105	42.31N	106.33W
Alcove, Can. (ăl-kōv′)	83c	45.41N	75.55W
Alcoy, Spain (äl-koi′)	148	38.42N	0.30W
Alcudia, Bahía de, b., Spain (bä-ē′ä-dĕ-äl-kōō-dhē′á)	159	39.48N	3.20E
Aldabra Islands, is., Sey. (äl-dä′brä)	213	9.16S	46.17E
Aldama, Mex. (äl-dä′mä)	112	28.50N	105.54W
Aldama, Mex. (äl-dä′mä)	118	22.54N	98.04W
Aldan, Russia	165	58.46N	125.19E
Aldan, r., Russia	165	63.00N	134.00E
Aldan Plateau, plat., Russia	171	57.42N	130.28E
Aldanskaya, Russia	165	61.52N	135.29E
Aldeia, Braz.	234d	23.30S	46.51E
Aldenham, Eng., U.K.	235	51.40N	0.21W
Aldenhoven, Ger. (ál′dĕn-hō′vĕn)	157c	50.54N	6.18E
Aldenrade, neigh., Ger.	236	51.31N	6.44E
Aldergrove, Can. (ôl′dẽr-grōv)	106d	49.03N	122.28W
Alderney, i., Guernsey (ôl′dẽr-nĭ)	156	49.43N	2.11W
Aldershot, Eng., U.K. (ôl′dẽr-shŏt)	150	51.14N	0.46W
Alderson, W.V., U.S. (ôl-dẽr-sŭn)	98	37.40N	80.40W
Alderwood Manor, Wa., U.S. (ôl′dẽr-wŏd măn′ŏr)	106a	47.49N	122.18W
Aldridge-Brownhills, Eng., U.K.	144a	52.38N	1.55W
Aledo, Il., U.S. (ȧ-le′dō)	111	41.12N	90.47W
Aleg, Maur.	210	17.03N	13.55W
Alegre, Braz. (álĕ′grĕ)	129a	20.41S	41.32W
Alegre, r., Braz. (álĕ′grĕ)	132b	22.22S	43.34W
Alegrete, Braz. (ä-lå-grā′tä)	132	29.46S	55.44W
Aleksandrov, Russia (ä-lyĕk-sän′ drôf)	166	56.24N	38.45E
Aleksandrovsk, Russia (ä-lyĕk-sän′drôfsk)	165	51.02N	142.21E
Aleksandrovsk, Russia (ä-lyĕk-sän′drôfsk)	172a	59.11N	57.36E
Aleksandrów Kujawski, Pol. (ä-lĕk-säh′drōōv kōō-yav′skē)	155	52.54N	18.45E
Alekseyevka, Russia (ä-lyĕk-sā-yĕf′kȧ)	163	50.39N	38.40E
Aleksin, Russia (äb′ĭng-tŭn)	162	54.31N	37.07E
Aleksinac, Yugo. (à-lyĕk-sē-nák′)	161	43.33N	21.42E
Alemán, Presa, res., Mex. (prä′sä-lĕ-má′n)	119	18.20N	96.35W
Alem Paraíba, Braz. (ä-lĕ′m-pá-räē′bá)	129a	21.54S	42.40W
Alençon, Fr. (à-läɴ-sôɴ′)	147	48.26N	0.08E
Alenquer, Braz. (ä-lĕŋ-kĕr′)	131	1.58S	54.44W
Alenquer, Port. (ä-lĕŋ-kĕr′)	158	39.04N	9.01W
Alentejo, hist. reg., Port. (ä-lĕŋ-tā′zhō)	158	38.05N	7.45W
Alenuihaha Channel, strt., Hi., U.S. (ä′lä-nōō-ē-hä′hä)	94a	20.20N	156.05W
Aleppo, Syria (ȧ-lĕp-ō)	182	36.10N	37.18E
Alès, Fr. (ä-lĕs′)	147	44.07N	4.06E
Alessandria, Italy (ä-lĕs-sän′drē-ä)	148	44.53N	8.35E
Ålesund, Nor. (ô′lĕ-sŏn)	152	62.28N	6.14E
Aleutian Islands, is., Ak., U.S. (ȧ-lu′shăn)	96b	52.40N	177.30W
Aleutian Trench, deep	95a	50.40N	177.10E
Alevina, Mys, c., Russia	165	58.49N	151.44E
Alexander Archipelago, is., Ak., U.S. (ăl-ĕg-zăn′dẽr)	95	57.05N	138.10W
Alexander City, Al., U.S.	114	32.55N	85.55W
Alexander Indian Reserve, I.R., Can.	83g	53.47N	114.00W
Alexander Island, i., Ant.	219	71.00S	71.00W
Alexandra, S. Afr. (ál-ex-än′drȧ)	218d	26.07S	28.07E
Alexandria, Austl. (ăl-ĕg-zăn′drĭ-ȧ)	202	19.00S	136.56E
Alexandria, Can. (ăl-ĕg-zăn′drĭ-ȧ)	91	45.50N	74.35W
Alexandria, Egypt (ăl-ĕg-zăn′drĭ-ȧ)	211	31.12N	29.58E
Alexandria, Rom. (ăl-ĕg-zăn′drĭ-ȧ)	161	43.55N	25.21E
Alexandria, S. Afr. (ăl-ĕx-än-drĭ-ȧ)	213c	33.40S	26.26E
Alexandria, In., U.S. (ăl-ĕg-zăn′drĭ-ȧ)	98	40.20N	85.20W
Alexandria, La., U.S. (ăl-ĕg-zăn′drĭ-ȧ)	97	31.18N	92.28W
Alexandria, Mn., U.S. (ăl-ĕg-zăn′drĭ-ȧ)	102	45.53N	95.23W
Alexandria, S.D., U.S. (ăl-ĕg-zăn′drĭ-ȧ)	102	43.39N	97.45W
Alexandria, Va., U.S. (ăl-ĕg-zăn′drĭ-ȧ)	97	38.50N	77.05W
Alexandria Bay, N.Y., U.S. (ăl-ĕg-zăn′drĭ-ȧ)	99	44.20N	75.55W
Alexandroúpolis, Grc. (äb-ĭ-tĭb′ĭ)	149	40.41N	25.51E
Alfaro, Spain (äl-fä′rō)	158	42.08N	1.43W
Al-Fāshir, Sudan (äl-fä′shēr)	211	13.38N	25.21E
Al Fashn, Egypt	218b	28.47N	30.53E
Al Fayyūm, Egypt	211	29.14N	30.48E
Alfenas, Braz. (äl-fĕ′nás)	129a	21.26S	45.55W
Alfiós, r., Grc.	161	37.33N	21.50E
Al Firdān, Egypt (äl-fer-dän′)	218b	30.43N	32.20E
Alfortville, Fr.	237c	48.49N	2.25E
Alfred, Can. (ăl′frĕd)	83c	45.34N	74.52W
Alfreton, Eng., U.K. (ăl′fẽr-tŭn)	144a	53.06N	1.23W
Algarve, hist. reg., Port. (äl-gär′vĕ)	158	37.15N	8.12W
Algeciras, Spain (äl-hä-thē′räs)	158	36.08N	5.25W
Algeria, nation, Afr. (ăl-gē′rĭ-ȧ)	210	28.45N	1.00E
Algés, Port.	238d	38.42N	9.13W
Algete, Spain (äl-hā′tä)	159a	40.36N	3.30W
Al Ghaydah, Yemen	185	16.12N	52.15E
Alghero, Italy (äl-gâ′rō)	148	40.32N	8.22E
Algiers, Alg. (ăl-jērs)	210	36.51N	2.56E
Algoa, Tx., U.S. (ăl-gō′ȧ)	113a	29.24N	95.11W
Algoma, Wa., U.S.	106a	47.17N	122.15W
Algoma, Wi., U.S.	103	44.38N	87.29W
Algona, Ia., U.S.	103	43.04N	94.11W
Algonac, Mi., U.S. (ăl′gô-năk)	98	42.35N	82.30W
Algonquin, Il., U.S. (ăl-gŏŋ′kwĭn)	101a	42.10N	88.17W
Algonquin Provincial Park, rec., Can.	97	45.50N	78.20W
Alhama de Granada, Spain (äl-hä′mä-dĕ-grä-nä′dä)	158	37.00N	3.59W
Alhama de Murcia, Spain	158	37.50N	1.24W
Alhambra, Ca., U.S. (ăl-hăm′brȧ)	107a	34.05N	118.08W
Al Ḩammān, Egypt	149	30.46N	29.42E
Alhandra, Port. (äl-yän′drȧ)	159b	38.55N	9.01W
Alhaurín, Spain (ä-lou-rēn′)	158	36.40N	4.40W
Al Ḩawāmidīyah, Egypt	244a	29.54N	31.15E
Al Ḩawrah, Yemen	185	13.49N	47.37E
Al Ḩawţah, Yemen	182	15.58N	48.26E
Al Ḩayy, Iraq	185	32.10N	46.03E
Al Ḩijāz, reg., Sau. Ar.	182	23.45N	39.08E
Al Hirmil, Leb.	181a	34.23N	36.22E
Alhos Vedros, Port. (äl′yōs′vā′drōs)	159b	38.39N	9.02W
Alhucemas, Baie d', b., Afr.	158	35.18N	3.50W
Al Ḩudaydah, Yemen	182	14.43N	43.03E
Al Hufūf, Sau. Ar.	182	25.15N	49.43E
Al Ḩulwān, Egypt (äl-hĕl′wän)	218b	29.51N	31.20E
Aliákmon, r., Grc. (äl-ē-äk′mōn)	149	40.26N	22.17E
Äli Bayramlı, Azer.	168	39.56N	48.56E
Alibori, r., Benin	215	11.40N	2.55E
Alicante, Spain (ä-lē-kän′tä)	148	38.20N	0.30W
Alice, S. Afr. (ăl-ĭs)	213c	32.47S	26.51E
Alice, Tx., U.S. (ăl′ĭs)	112	27.45N	98.04W
Alice, Punta, c., Italy (ä-lē′chĕ)	161	39.23N	17.10E
Alice Arm, Can.	86	55.29N	129.29W
Alicedale, S. Afr. (ăl′ĭs-dāl)	213c	33.18S	26.04E
Alice Springs, Austl. (ăl′ĭs)	202	23.38S	133.56E
Alicudi, i., Italy (ä-lē-kōō′dē)	160	38.34N	14.21E
Alifkulovo, Russia (ä-lĭf-kû′lô-vô)	172a	55.57N	62.06E
Alīgarh, India (ä-lē-gŭr′)	183	27.58N	78.08E
Al-Imām, neigh., Egypt	244a	30.01N	31.15E
Alingsås, Swe. (ä′lĭŋ-sôs)	152	57.57N	12.30E
Alipore, neigh., India	240a	22.31N	88.18E
Aliquippa, Pa., U.S. (ăl-ĭ-kwĭp′ȧ)	101e	40.37N	80.15W
Al Iskandarīyah *see* Alexandria, Egypt	218b	31.12N	29.58E
Aliwal North, S. Afr. (ä-lē-wäl′)	212	31.09S	28.26E
Al Jafr, Qa'al, pl., Jord.	181a	30.15N	36.24E
Al Jaghbūb, Libya	211	29.46N	24.32E
Al Jawārah, Oman	185	18.55N	57.17E
Al Jawf, Libya	211	24.14N	23.15E
Al Jawf, Sau. Ar.	182	29.45N	39.30E
Aljezur, Port. (äl-zhä-zōōr′)	158	37.18N	8.52W
Al Jīzah, Egypt	218b	30.01N	31.12E
Al Jubayl, Sau. Ar.	182	27.01N	49.40E
Al Jufrah, oasis, Libya	211	29.30N	15.16E
Al Junaynah, Sudan	184	13.27N	22.27E
Aljustrel, Port. (äl-zhōō-strĕl′)	158	37.44N	8.23W
Al Kāb, Egypt	218c	30.56N	32.19E
Al Kāmilīn, Sudan (käm-lĕn′)	211	15.09N	33.06E
Al Karak, Jord. (kĕ-räk′)	181a	31.11N	35.42E
Al Karnak, Egypt (kär′nak)	218b	25.42N	32.43E
Al Khābūrah, Oman	182	23.45N	57.30E
Al Khalīl, W. Bank	181a	31.31N	35.07E
Al Khandaq, Sudan (kän-däk′)	211	18.38N	30.29E
Al Khārijah, Egypt	184	25.26N	30.33E
Al Khums, Libya	211	32.35N	14.10E
Al Khurmah, Sau. Ar.	182	21.37N	41.44E
Al Kiswah, Syria	181a	33.31N	36.13E
Alkmaar, Neth. (älk-mär′)	151	52.39N	4.42E
Al Kufrah, oasis, Libya	211	24.45N	22.45E
Al-Kunayyisah, Egypt	244a	29.59N	31.11E
Al Kuntillah, Egypt	181a	29.59N	34.42E
Al Kuwayt, Kuw. (äl-kōō-wit)	182	29.04N	47.59E
Al Lādhiqīyah, Syria	182	35.32N	35.51E
Allagash, r., Me., U.S. (ăl′ȧ-găsh)	92	46.50N	69.24W
Allāhābād, India (ŭl-ŭ-hä-bäd′)	183	25.32N	81.53E
All American Canal, can., Ca., U.S. (âl á-mĕr′ĭ-kăn)	108	32.43N	115.12W
Alland, Aus.	145e	48.04N	16.05E
Allariz, Spain (äl-yä-rēth′)	148	42.10N	7.48W
Allatoona Lake, res., Ga., U.S. (ăl′ȧ-tōōn′ȧ)	114	34.05N	84.57W
Allauch, Fr. (ä-lē′ō)	156a	43.21N	5.30E
Allaykha, Russia (ä-lī′ĸá)	165	70.32N	148.53E
Allegan, Mi., U.S. (ăl′ē-găn)	98	42.30N	85.55W
Allegany Indian Reservation, I.R., N.Y., U.S. (ăl-ē-gā′nĭ)	99	42.05N	78.55W
Allegheny, r., Pa., U.S. (ăl-ē-gā′nĭ)	99	41.10N	79.20W
Allegheny Front, mtn., U.S. (ăl-ē-gā′nĭ)	98	38.12N	80.03W
Allegheny Mountains, mts., U.S. (ăl-ē-gā′nĭ)	97	37.35N	81.55W
Allegheny Plateau, plat., U.S. (ăl-ē-gā′nĭ)	98	39.00N	81.15W
Allegheny Reservoir, res., U.S. (ăl-ē-gā′nĭ)	99	41.50N	78.55W
Allen, Ok., U.S. (ăl′ĕn)	111	34.51N	96.26W
Allen, Lough, l., Ire. (lŏk ăl′ĕn)	150	54.07N	8.09W
Allendale, N.J., U.S. (ăl′ĕn-dāl)	100a	41.02N	74.08W
Allendale, S.C., U.S. (ăl′ĕn-dāl)	115	33.00N	81.19W
Allende, Mex.	112	28.20N	100.50W
Allende, Mex. (äl-yĕn′då)	119	18.23N	92.49W
Allen Park, Mi., U.S.	230c	42.15N	83.13W
Allentown, Pa., U.S. (ălĕn-toun)	97	40.35N	75.30W
Alleppey, India (ȧ-lĕp′ē)	183b	9.33N	76.22E
Aller, r., Ger. (äl′ẽr)	154	52.43N	9.50E
Allerton, Ma., U.S.	227a	42.18N	70.53W
Allerton, neigh., Eng., U.K.	237a	53.22N	2.53W
Alliance, Ne., U.S. (ȧ-lī′ăns)	96	42.06N	102.53W
Alliance, Oh., U.S. (ȧ-lī′ăns)	98	40.55N	81.10W
Al Lidām, Sau. Ar.	182	20.45N	44.12E
Allier, r., Fr. (á-lyā′)	156	46.43N	3.03E
Alligator Point, c., La., U.S. (al′ĭ-gā-tẽr)	100d	30.57N	89.41W
Allinge, Den. (äl′ĭŋ-ĕ)	152	55.16N	14.48E
Allison Park, Pa., U.S.	230b	40.34N	79.57W
Al Līth, Sau. Ar.	185	20.09N	40.16E
All Pines, Belize (ôl pīnz)	120a	16.55N	88.15W
Allston, neigh., Ma., U.S.	227a	42.22N	71.08W
Al Luḩayyah, Yemen	182	15.58N	42.48E
Alluvial City, La., U.S.	100d	29.51N	89.42W
Allyn, Wa., U.S. (ăl′ĭn)	106a	47.23N	122.51W
Alma, Can.	85	48.29N	71.42W
Alma, Can. (ăl′mȧ)	92	45.36N	64.59W
Alma, S. Afr.	218d	24.30S	28.05E
Alma, Ga., U.S.	115	31.33N	82.31W
Alma, Mi., U.S.	98	43.25N	84.40W
Alma, Ne., U.S.	110	40.08N	99.21W
Alma, Wi., U.S.	103	44.21N	91.57W
Alma-Ata (Almaty), Kaz.	169	43.19N	77.08E
Al Mabrak, val., Sau. Ar.	181a	29.16N	35.12E
Almada, Port. (äl-mä′dä)	159b	38.40N	9.09W
Almadén, Spain (äl-má-dhän′)	158	38.47N	4.50W
Al Madīnah, Sau. Ar.	182	24.26N	39.42E
Al Mafraq, Jord.	181a	32.21N	36.13E
Almagre, Laguna, l., Mex. (lä-gô′nä-äl-mä′grĕ)	119	23.48N	97.45W
Almagro, Spain (äl-mä′grō)	158	38.52N	3.41W
Al Maḩallah al Kubrā, Egypt	218b	30.58N	31.10E
Al Manāmah, Bahr.	182	26.01N	50.33E
Al-Manāwāt, Egypt	244a	29.55N	31.14E

ăt; finăl; rāte; senâte; ärm; ȧsk; sofȧ; fâre; ch-choose; dh-as th in other; bē; ēvent; bĕt; recĕnt; cratẽr; g-gō; gh-guttural g; bĭt; ĭ-short neutral; rīde; ĸ-guttural k as ch in German ich;

PRONOUNCING INDEX

Almanor–Andaman Sea 257

PLACE (Pronunciation)	PAGE	Lat. °'	Long. °'
Almanor, Lake, l., Ca., U.S. (ăl-măn'ôr)	108	40.11N	121.20W
Almansa, Spain (äl-män'sä)	158	38.52N	1.09W
Al Manshāh, Egypt	218b	26.31N	31.46E
Almansor, r., Port. (äl-män-sôr)	158	38.41N	8.27W
Al Manşūrah, Egypt	211	31.02N	31.25E
Al Manzilah, Egypt (män'za-la)	218b	31.09N	32.05E
Almanzora, r., Spain (äl-män-thō'rä)	158	37.20N	2.25W
Al Marāghah, Egypt	218b	26.41N	31.35E
Almargem do Bispo, Port. (äl-mär-zhĕN)	159b	38.51N	9.16W
Al-Marj, Libya	211	32.44N	21.08E
Al Maşīrah, i., Oman	182	20.43N	58.58E
Al Mawşil, Iraq	182	36.00N	42.53E
Almazán, Spain (äl-mä-thän')	158	41.30N	2.33W
Al Mazār, Jord.	181a	31.04N	35.41E
Al Mazra'ah, Jord.	181a	31.17N	35.33E
Almeirim, Port. (äl-māĭ-rēN')	158	39.13N	8.31W
Almelo, Neth. (äl'mē-lō)	151	52.20N	6.42E
Almendra, Embalse de, res., Spain	158	41.15N	6.10W
Almendralejo, Spain (äl-män-drä-lā'hō)	158	38.43N	6.24W
Almería, Spain (äl-mā-rē'ä)	142	36.52N	2.28W
Almería, Golfo de, b., Spain (gôl-fô-dĕ-äl-māĭ-reN')	158	36.45N	2.26W
Älmhult, Swe. (älm'hōōlt)	152	56.35N	14.08E
Almina, Punta, c., Mor. (äl-mē'nä)	158	35.58N	5.17W
Al Minyā, Egypt	211	28.06N	30.45E
Almirante, Pan. (äl-mē-rän'tā)	121	9.18N	82.24W
Almirante, Bahía de, b., Pan.	121	9.22N	82.07W
Almirós, Grc.	161	39.13N	22.47E
Almodóvar del Campo, Spain (äl-mō-dhō'vär)	158	38.43N	4.10W
Almoloya, Mex. (äl-mō-lō'yä)	118	19.32N	99.44W
Almoloya, Mex. (äl-mō-lō'yä)	119a	19.11N	99.28W
Almonte, Can. (äl-mŏn'tė)	91	45.15N	76.15W
Almonte, Spain (äl-mōn'tā)	158	37.16N	6.32W
Almonte, r., Spain (äl-mōn'tā)	158	39.35N	5.50W
Almora, India	183	29.20N	79.40E
Al Mubarraz, Sau. Ar.	182	22.31N	46.27E
Al Mudawwarah, Jord.	181a	29.20N	36.01E
Al Mukhā (Mocha), Yemen	182	13.11N	43.20E
Almuñécar, Spain (äl-mōōn-yā'kär)	158	36.44N	3.43W
Alnön, i., Swe.	152	62.20N	17.39E
Aloha, Or., U.S. (ä'lō-hā)	106c	45.29N	122.52W
Alondra, Ca., U.S.	232	33.54N	118.19W
Alor, Pulau, i., Indon. (ä'lôr)	197	8.07S	125.00E
Álora, Spain (ä'lō-rä)	158	36.49N	4.42W
Alor Gajah, Malay.	181b	2.23N	102.13E
Alor Setar, Malay. (ä'lôr stär)	196	6.10N	100.16E
Alouette, r., Can. (ä-lōō-ĕt')	106d	49.16N	122.32W
Alpena, Mi., U.S. (ăl-pē'nȧ)	97	45.05N	83.30W
Alpes Cotiennes, mts., Eur.	157	44.46N	7.02E
Alphen, Neth.	145a	52.07N	4.38E
Alpiarça, Port. (äl-pyär'sȧ)	158	39.38N	8.37W
Alpine, N.J., U.S. (ăl'pīn)	228	40.56N	73.56W
Alpine, Tx., U.S. (ăl'pīn)	112	30.21N	103.41W
Alps, mts., Eur. (ălps)	142	46.18N	8.42E
Alpujarra, Col. (ȧl-pōō-ĸȧ'rȧ)	130a	3.23N	74.56W
Al Qaḑārif, Sudan	211	14.03N	35.11E
Al Qāhirah see Cairo, Egypt	211	30.00N	31.17E
Al Qanţarah, Egypt	218c	30.51N	32.20E
Al Qaryah Ash Sharqīyah, Libya	211	30.36N	13.13E
Al Qaşr, Egypt	184	25.42N	28.53E
Al Qaţīf, Sau. Ar.	182	26.30N	50.00E
Al Qayşūmah, Sau. Ar.	182	28.15N	46.20E
Al Qunaytirah, Syria	181a	33.09N	35.49E
Al Qunfudhah, Sau. Ar.	182	19.08N	41.05E
Al Quşaymah, Egypt	181a	30.40N	34.23E
Al Quşayr, Egypt	211	26.14N	34.11E
Al Qusayr, Syria	181a	34.32N	36.33E
Als, i., Den. (äls)	152	55.06N	9.40E
Alsace, hist. reg., Fr. (ȧl-sȧ's)	157	48.25N	7.24E
Alsip, Il., U.S.	231a	41.40N	87.44W
Altadena, Ca., U.S. (ăl-tă-dē'nä)	107a	34.12N	118.08W
Alta Gracia, Arg. (äl'tä grä'sē-a)	132	31.41S	64.19W
Altagracia, Ven.	130	10.42N	71.34W
Altagracia de Orituco, Ven.	131b	9.53N	66.22W
Altai Mountains, mts., Asia (äl'tī')	188	49.11N	87.15E
Alta Loma, Ca., U.S. (ăl'tă lō'mä)	107a	34.07N	117.35W
Alta Loma, Tx., U.S. (ăl'tȧ lō-mȧ)	113a	29.22N	95.05W
Altamaha, r., Ga., U.S. (ôl-tá-má-hô')	115	31.50N	82.00W
Altamira, Braz. (äl-tä-mē'rä)	131	3.13S	52.14W
Altamira, Mex.	119	22.25N	97.55W
Altamirano, Arg. (äl-tä-mē-rä'nō)	132	35.26S	58.12W
Altamura, Italy (äl-tä-mōō'rä)	149	40.40N	16.35E
Altar of Heaven, pt. of i., China	240b	39.53N	116.25E
Altar of the Earth, rel., China	240b	39.57N	116.24E
Altar of the Moon, rel., China	240b	39.55N	116.20E
Altar of the Sun, rel., China	240b	39.54N	116.27E
Altavista, Va., U.S. (ăl-tä-vĭs'tȧ)	115	37.08N	79.14W
Altay, China (äl-tä)	188	47.52N	86.50E
Altenburg, Ger. (äl-tĕn-bōōrgh)	154	50.59N	12.27E
Altenderne Oberbecker, neigh., Ger.	236	51.35N	7.33E
Altenessen, neigh., Ger.	236	51.29N	7.00E
Altenhagen, neigh., Ger.	236	51.22N	7.28E
Altenmarkt an der Triesting, Aus.	145e	48.02N	16.00E
Altenvoerde, Ger.	236	51.18N	7.22E
Alter do Chão, Port. (äl-tĕr'dō shäN'ōN)	158	39.13N	7.38W
Altiplano, pl., Bol. (äl-tē-plá'nō)	130	18.38S	68.20W
Altlandsberg, Ger. (ält länts'bĕrgh)	145b	52.34N	13.44E
Altlünen, Ger.	236	51.38N	7.31E
Altmannsdorf, neigh., Aus.	239e	48.10N	16.20E
Alto, La., U.S. (ăl'tō)	113	32.21N	91.52W
Alto da Moóca, neigh., Braz.	234d	23.34S	46.35W
Alto Marañón, Río, r., Peru (rē'ō-ȧl'tō-mä-rän-yō'n)	130	8.18S	77.13W
Altomünster, Ger. (äl'tō-mün'stĕr)	145d	48.24N	11.16E
Alton, Can. (ôl'tŭn)	83d	43.52N	80.05W
Alton, Il., U.S. (ôl'tŭn)	97	38.53N	90.11W

PLACE (Pronunciation)	PAGE	Lat. °'	Long. °'
Altona, Austl.	201a	37.52S	144.50E
Altona, Can.	89	49.06N	97.33W
Altona, Ger. (äl'tō-nȧ)	145c	53.33N	9.54E
Altona North, Austl.	243b	37.50S	144.51E
Altoona, Al., U.S. (ăl-tōō'nȧ)	114	34.01N	86.15W
Altoona, Pa., U.S. (ăl-tōō'nȧ)	97	40.25N	78.25W
Altoona, Wa., U.S. (ăl-tōō'nȧ)	106c	46.16N	123.39W
Alto Rio Doce, Braz. (äl'tō-rē'ō-dō'sĕ)	129a	21.02S	43.23W
Alto Songo, Cuba (äl-fō-sôŋ'gō)	123	20.10N	75.45W
Altotonga, Mex. (ȧl-tō-tôŋ'gä)	119	19.44N	97.13W
Alto Velo, i., Dom. Rep. (äl-tō-vĕ'lō)	123	17.30N	71.35W
Altrincham, Eng., U.K. (ôl'trĭng-ăm)	144a	53.18N	2.21W
Altruppin, Ger. (ält rōō'ppēn)	145b	52.56N	12.50E
Altun Shan, mts., China (äl-tòn shän)	188	36.58N	85.09E
Alturas, Ca., U.S. (ăl-tōō'răs)	104	41.29N	120.33W
Altus, Ok., U.S. (ăl'tŭs)	110	34.38N	99.20W
Al 'Ubaylah, Sau. Ar.	185	21.59N	50.57E
Al-Uḑayyah, Sudan	211	12.06N	28.16E
Alūksne, Lat. (ä'lòks-nĕ)	166	57.24N	27.04E
Alumette Island, i., Can. (ȧ-lü-mĕt')	91	45.50N	77.00W
Alum Rock, Ca., U.S.	106b	37.23N	121.50W
Al 'Uqaylah, Libya	211	30.15N	19.07E
Al Uqşur, Egypt	211	25.38N	32.59E
Alushta, Ukr. (ä'lshò-tȧ)	163	44.39N	34.23E
Alva, Ok., U.S. (ăl'vȧ)	110	36.46N	98.41W
Alvanley, Eng., U.K.	237a	53.16N	2.45W
Alvarado, Mex. (äl-vä-rä'dhō)	119	18.48N	95.45W
Alvarado, Luguna de, l., Mex. (lä-gò'nä-dĕ-äl-vä-rä'dō)	119	18.44N	95.45W
Älvdalen, Swe. (ĕlv'dä-lĕn)	152	61.14N	14.04E
Alverca, Port. (al-vĕr'kȧ)	159b	38.53N	9.02W
Alvesta, Swe. (äl-vĕs'tä)	152	56.55N	14.29E
Alvin, Tx., U.S. (ăl'vĭn)	113a	29.25N	95.14W
Alvinópolis, Braz. (äl-vēnō'pō-lēs)	129a	20.07S	43.03W
Alviso, Ca., U.S. (ăl-vī'sō)	106b	37.26N	121.59W
Al Wajh, Sau. Ar.	182	26.15N	36.32E
Alwar, India (ŭl'wŭr)	183	27.39N	76.39E
Al Wāsiţah, Egypt	218b	29.21N	31.15E
Alytus, Lith. (ä'lē-tòs)	153	54.25N	24.05E
Amacuzac, r., Mex. (ä-mä-kōō-zák)	118	18.00N	99.03W
Amadeus, l., Austl. (ăm-ȧ-dē'ŭs)	202	24.30S	131.25E
Amadjuak, l., Can. (ä-mädj'wäk)	85	64.50N	69.20W
Amadora, Port.	159b	38.45N	9.14W
Amagasaki, Japan (ä'mä-gä-sä'kė)	195	34.43N	135.25E
Ama Keng, Sing.	240c	1.24N	103.42E
Amakusa-Shimo, i., Japan (ämä-kōō'sä shē-mō)	194	32.24N	129.35E
Åmål, Swe. (ô'môl)	152	59.05N	12.40E
Amalfi, Col. (ä'mȧ'l-fē)	130a	6.55N	75.04W
Amalfi, Italy (ä-mä'l-fē)	159c	40.23N	14.36E
Amaliás, Grc. (ȧ-mäl'yȧs)	161	37.48N	21.23E
Amalner, India	186	21.07N	75.06E
Amambai, Serra de, mts., S.A.	131	20.06S	57.08W
Amami, i., Japan	189	28.10N	129.55E
Amapala, Hond. (ä-mä-pä'lä)	120	13.16N	87.39W
Amarante, Braz. (ä-mä-rän'tā)	131	6.17S	42.43W
Amargosa, r., Ca., U.S. (ȧ'mär-gō'sȧ)	108	35.55N	116.45W
Amarillo, Tx., U.S. (ăm-ȧ-rĭl'ō)	96	35.14N	101.49W
Amaro, Mount, mtn., Italy (ä-mä'rō)	148	42.07N	14.07E
Amaroúsion, Grc.	239d	38.03N	23.49E
Amasya, Tur. (ä-mä'sē-ȧ)	149	40.40N	35.50E
Amatenango, Mex. (ä-mä-tā-naŋ'gō)	119	16.30N	92.29W
Amatignak, i., Ak., U.S. (ä-mȧ'tē-näk)	95a	51.12N	178.30W
Amatique, Bahía de, b., N.A. (bä-ē'ä-dē-ä-mä-tē'kä)	120	15.58N	88.50W
Amatitlán, Guat. (ä-mä-tē-tlän')	120	14.27N	90.39W
Amatlán de Cañas, Mex. (ä-mät-län'dā kän-yäs)	118	20.50N	104.22W
Amazonas, state, Braz. (ä-mä-thō'näs)	130	4.15S	64.30W
Amazonas, Rio (Amazon), r., S.A. (rē'ō-ä-mä-thō'näs)	131	2.03S	53.18W
Ambāla, India (ŭm-bä'lŭ)	183	30.31N	76.48E
Ambalema, Col. (äm-bä-lā'mä)	130	4.47N	74.45W
Ambarchik, Russia (ŭm-bär'chĭk)	165	69.39N	162.18E
Ambarnāth, India	187b	19.12N	73.10E
Ambato, Ec. (äm-bä'tō)	130	1.15S	78.30W
Ambatondrazaka, Madag.	213	17.58S	48.43E
Amberg, Ger. (äm'bĕrgh)	154	49.26N	11.51E
Ambergris Cay, i., Belize (ăm'bĕr-grēs kāz)	120a	18.04N	87.43W
Ambergris Cays, is., T./C. Is.	123	21.20N	71.40W
Ambérieu-en-Bugey, Fr. (äN-bā-rē-u')	157	45.57N	5.21E
Ambert, Fr. (äN-bĕr')	156	45.32N	3.41E
Ambil Island, i., Phil. (äm'bēl)	197a	13.51N	120.25E
Ambler, Pa., U.S. (ăm'blĕr)	100f	40.09N	75.13W
Amboise, Fr. (äN-bwäz')	156	47.25N	0.56E
Ambon, Indon.	197	3.45S	128.17E
Ambon, Pulau, i., Indon.	197	4.50S	128.45E
Ambositra, Madag. (äN-bō-sē'trä)	213	20.31S	47.28E
Amboy, Il., U.S. (ăm'boi)	98	41.41N	89.15W
Amboy, Wa., U.S. (ăm'boi)	106c	45.55N	122.27W
Ambre, Cap d', c., Madag.	213	12.06S	49.15E
Ambridge, Pa., U.S. (ăm'brĭdj)	101e	40.36N	80.13W
Ambrim, i., Vanuatu	203	16.25S	168.15E
Ambriz, Ang.	212	7.50S	13.06E
Amchitka, i., Ak., U.S. (ăm-chĭt'kȧ)	95a	51.25N	178.10E
Amchitka Passage, strt., Ak., U.S. (ăm-chĭt'kȧ)	95a	51.30N	179.36W
Amealco, Mex. (ä-mä-äl'kō)	118	20.12N	100.08W
Ameca, Mex. (ä-mē'kä)	116	20.34N	104.02W
Amecameca, Mex. (ä-mȧ-kä-mä'kä)	118	19.06N	98.46W
Ameide, Neth.	145a	51.57N	4.57E
Ameixoera, neigh., Port.	238d	38.47N	9.10W
Ameland, i., Neth.	151	53.29N	5.54E
Amelia, Oh., U.S. (ȧ-mēl'yȧ)	101f	39.01N	84.12W
American, South Fork, r., Ca., U.S. (ȧ-mĕr'ĭ-kăn)	108	38.43N	120.45W

PLACE (Pronunciation)	PAGE	Lat. °'	Long. °'
Americana, Braz. (ä-mē-rē-kȧ'nȧ)	129a	22.46S	47.19W
American Falls, Id., U.S. (ȧ-mĕr'ĭ-kăn-fôls')	105	42.45N	112.53W
American Falls Reservoir, res., Id., U.S. (ȧ-mĕr'ĭ-kăn-fôls')	96	42.56N	113.18W
American Fork, Ut., U.S.	109	40.20N	111.50W
American Highland, plat., Ant.	219	72.00S	79.00E
American Samoa, dep., Oc.	2	14.20S	170.00W
Americus, Ga., U.S. (ȧ-mĕr'ĭ-kŭs)	97	32.04N	84.15W
Amersfoort, Neth. (ä'mĕrz-fōrt)	145a	52.08N	5.23E
Amersham, Eng., U.K.	235	51.40N	0.38W
Amery, Can. (ā'mĕr-ė)	85	56.34N	94.03W
Amery, Wi., U.S.	103	45.19N	92.24W
Ames, Ia., U.S. (āmz)	103	42.00N	93.36W
Amesbury, Ma., U.S. (āmz'bĕr-ė)	93a	42.51N	70.56W
Amfissa, Grc. (ȧm-fī'sȧ)	161	38.32N	22.26E
Amga, Russia (ŭm-gä')	165	61.08N	132.09E
Amga, r., Russia	171	61.41N	133.11E
Amgun', r., Russia	171	52.30N	138.00E
Amherst, Can. (ăm'hĕrst)	85	45.49N	64.14W
Amherst, N.Y., U.S.	230a	42.58N	78.48W
Amherst, Oh., U.S.	101d	41.24N	82.13W
Amherst, i., Can. (ăm'hĕrst)	91	44.08N	76.45W
Amiens, Fr. (ȧ-myăN')	147	49.54N	2.18E
Amirante Islands, is., Sey.	5	6.02S	52.30E
Amisk Lake, l., Can.	89	54.35N	102.13W
Amistad Reservoir, res., N.A.	112	29.20N	101.00W
Amite, La., U.S. (ȧ-mēt')	113	30.43N	90.32W
Amite, r., La., U.S.	113	30.45N	90.48W
Amity, Pa., U.S. (ăm'ĭ-tĭ)	101e	40.02N	80.11W
Amityville, N.Y., U.S. (ăm'ĭ-tĭ-vĭl)	100a	40.41N	73.24W
Amlia, i., Ak., U.S. (ȧ'mlēȧ)	95a	52.00N	173.28W
'Ammān, Jord. (ăm'mán)	182	31.57N	35.57E
Ammersee, l., Ger. (äm'mĕr)	145d	48.00N	11.08E
Amnicon, r., Wi., U.S. (ăm'nė-kŏn)	107h	46.35N	91.56W
Amorgós, i., Grc. (ä-môr'gōs)	149	36.47N	25.47E
Amory, Ms., U.S. (āmō-rė)	114	33.58N	88.27W
Amos, Can. (ā'mŭs)	85	48.31N	78.04W
Amoy see Xiamen, China	189	24.30N	118.10E
Amparo, Braz. (äm-pá'-rō)	129a	22.43S	46.44W
Amper, r., Ger. (äm'pĕr)	145d	48.18N	11.32E
Amposta, Spain (äm-pōs'tä)	159	40.42N	0.34E
Amqui, Can.	92	48.28N	67.28W
Amrāvati, India	183	20.58N	77.47E
Amritsar, India (ŭm-rĭt'sŭr)	183	31.43N	74.52E
Amstelveen, Neth.	145a	52.18N	4.51E
Amsterdam, Neth. (äm-stĕr-däm')	142	52.21N	4.52E
Amsterdam, N.Y., U.S. (ăm'stĕr-dăm)	99	42.55N	74.10W
Amsterdam, Île, i., Afr.	219	37.52S	77.32E
Amstetten, Aus. (äm'stĕt-ĕn)	154	48.09N	14.53E
Am Timan, Chad (äm'tė-män')	211	11.18N	20.30E
Amu Darya, r., Asia (ä-mò-dä'rēä)	164	38.30N	64.00E
Amukta Passage, strt., Ak., U.S. (ä-mōōk'tȧ)	95a	52.30N	172.00W
Amundsen Gulf, b., Can. (ä'mŭn-sĕn-gŭlf')	84	70.17N	123.28W
Amundsen Sea, sea, Ant. (ä'mŭn-sĕn-sē')	219	72.00S	110.00W
Amungen, l., Swe.	152	61.07N	16.00E
Amur, r., Asia	165	49.00N	136.00E
Amurskiy, Russia (ä-mûr'skĭ)	172a	52.35N	59.36E
Amurskiy, Zaliv, b., Russia (zä'lĭf ä-mòr'skĭ)	194	43.20N	131.40E
Amusgos, Mex.	118	16.39N	98.09W
Amuyao, Mount, mtn., Phil. (ä-mōō-yä'ō)	197a	17.04N	121.09E
Amvrakikos Kólpos, b., Grc.	161	39.00N	21.00E
Amyun, Leb.	181a	34.18N	35.48E
Anabar, r., Russia (ăn-ȧ-bär')	171	71.15N	113.00E
Anaco, Ven. (ä-nä'kô)	131b	9.29N	64.27W
Anaconda, Mt., U.S. (ăn-ȧ-kŏn'dȧ)	96	46.07N	112.55W
Anacortes, Wa., U.S. (ăn-ȧ-kôr'tĕz)	106a	48.30N	122.37W
Anacostia, neigh., D.C., U.S.	229d	38.52N	76.59W
Anadarko, Ok., U.S. (ăn-ȧ-där'kō)	110	35.05N	98.14W
Anadyr', Russia (ŭ-nȧ-dĭr')	165	64.47N	177.01E
Anadyr, r., Russia	171	65.30N	172.45E
Anadyrskiy Zaliv, b., Russia	164	64.10N	178.00W
'Ānah, Iraq	185	34.28N	41.56E
Anaheim, Ca., U.S. (ăn'ȧ-hīm)	107a	33.50N	117.55W
Anahuac, Tx., U.S. (ä-nä'wäk)	113a	29.46N	94.41W
Ānai Mudi, mtn., India	187	10.10N	77.00E
Anama Bay, Can.	89	51.56N	98.05W
Ana María, Cayos, is., Cuba	122	21.25N	78.50W
Anambas, Kepulauan, is., Indon. (ä-näm-bäs)	196	2.41N	106.38E
Anamosa, Ia., U.S. (ăn-ȧ-mō'sȧ)	103	42.06N	91.18W
Anan'yiv, Ukr.	167	47.43N	29.59E
Anapa, Russia (ȧ-nä'pä)	167	44.54N	37.19E
Anápolis, Braz. (ä-nä'pō-lēs)	131	16.17S	48.47W
Añatuya, Arg. (ȧ-nyȧ-tōō'yȧ)	132	28.22S	62.45W
Anchieta, Braz. (äN-chyĕ'tȧ)	132b	22.49S	43.24W
Ancholme, r., Eng., U.K. (ăn'chŭm)	144a	53.28N	0.27W
Anchorage, Ak., U.S. (ăŋ'kĕr-āj)	96a	61.12N	149.48W
Anchorage, Ky., U.S.	101h	38.16N	85.32W
Anci, China (än-tsŭ)	190	39.31N	116.41E
Ancienne-Lorette, Can. (äN-syĕn' lō-rĕt')	83b	46.48N	71.21W
Ancon, Pan. (ăŋ-kōn')	116a	8.55N	79.32W
Ancona, Italy (än-kō'nä)	142	43.37N	13.32E
Ancud, Chile (äŋ-kōōdh')	132	41.52S	73.45W
Ancud, Golfo de, b., Chile (gôl-fô-dĕ-äŋ-kōōdh')	132	41.15S	73.00W
Anda, China	192	46.20N	125.20E
Åndalsnes, Nor.	152	62.33N	7.46E
Andalucia, hist. reg., Spain (än-dä-lōō-sē'ä)	158	37.35N	5.40W
Andalusia, Al., U.S. (ăn-dȧ-lōō'zhĭȧ)	114	31.19N	86.19W
Andaman Islands, is., India (ăn-dȧ-măn')	196	11.38N	92.17E
Andaman Sea, sea, Asia	196	12.44N	95.45E

PLACE (Pronunciation)	PAGE	Lat. °′	Long. °′
Andarax, r., Spain	158	37.00N	2.40W
Anderlecht, Bel. (än′dĕr-lĕkt)	145a	50.49N	4.16E
Andernach, Ger. (än′dĕr-näk)	154	50.25N	7.23E
Anderson, Arg. (á′n-dĕr-sōn)	129c	35.15S	60.15W
Anderson, Ca., U.S. (ăn′dĕr-sŭn)	104	40.28N	122.19W
Anderson, In., U.S. (ăn′dĕr-sŭn)	98	40.05N	85.50W
Anderson, S.C., U.S. (ăn′dĕr-sŭn)	97	34.30N	82.40W
Anderson, r., Can. (ăn′dĕr-sŭn)	84	68.32N	125.12W
Andes Mountains, mts., S.A. (ăn′dēz) (än′dās)	128	13.00S	75.00W
Andheri, neigh., India	187b	19.08N	72.50E
Andhra Pradesh, state, India	183	16.00N	79.00E
Andikíthira, i., Grc.	149	35.50N	23.20E
Andizhan, Uzb. (än-dē-zhän′)	169	40.45N	72.22E
Andong, S. Kor. (än′dŭng′)	189	36.31N	128.42E
Andongwei, China (än-dôŋ-wā)	190	35.08N	119.19E
Andorra, And. (än-dôr′rä)	159	42.38N	1.30E
Andorra, nation, Eur. (än-dôr′rä)	142	42.30N	2.00E
Andover, Ma., U.S. (ăn′dō-vẽr)	93a	42.39N	71.08W
Andover, N.J., U.S. (ăn′dō-vẽr)	100a	40.59N	74.45W
Andøya, i., Nor. (änd-ûē)	146	69.12N	14.58E
Andreanof Islands, is., Ak., U.S. (än-drä-ä′nôf-ĭ′ăndz)	96b	51.10N	177.00W
Andrelândia, Braz. (än-drĕ-lá′n-dyá)	129a	21.45S	44.18W
Andrésy, Fr.	237c	48.59N	2.04E
Andrew Johnson National Historic Site, rec., Tn., U.S. (ăn′drōō jŏn′sŭn)	115	36.15N	82.55W
Andrews, N.C., U.S. (ăn′drōōz)	114	35.12N	83.48W
Andrews, S.C., U.S. (ăn′drōōz)	115	33.25N	79.32W
Andrews Air Force Base, pt. of i., Md., U.S.	229d	38.48N	76.52W
Andria, Italy (än′drē-ä)	149	41.17N	15.55E
Andros, Grc. (án′dhrôs)	161	37.50N	24.54E
Ándros, i., Grc. (án′drôs)	149	37.59N	24.55E
Androscoggin, r., Me., U.S. (ăn-drŭs-kŏg′ĭn)	92	44.25N	70.45W
Andros Island, i., Bah. (ăn′drŏs)	117	24.30N	78.00W
Anefis i-n-Darane, Mali	214	18.03N	0.36E
Anegasaki, Japan (ä′nà-gä-sä′kē)	195a	35.29N	140.02E
Aneityum, i., Vanuatu (ä-nà-ē′tē-ŭm)	203	20.15S	169.49E
Aneta, N.D., U.S. (ă-nē′tȧ)	102	47.41N	97.57W
Aneto, Pico de, mtn., Spain (pē′kō-dĕ-ä-nĕ′tô)	142	42.35N	0.38E
Angamacutiro, Mex. (äŋ′gä-mä-kōō-tē′rô)	118	20.08N	101.44W
Angangueo, Mex. (än-gäŋ′gwá-ō)	118	19.36N	100.18W
Ang'angxi, China (äŋ-äŋ-shyē)	189	47.05N	123.58E
Angarsk, Russia	165	52.48N	104.15E
Ånge, Swe. (ông′ā)	152	62.31N	15.39E
Angel, Salto, wtfl., Ven. (säl′tō-á′n-hĕl)	130	5.44N	62.27W
Ángel de la Guarda, i., Mex. (á′n-hĕl-dĕ-lä-gwä′r-dä)	116	29.30N	113.00W
Angeles, Phil. (än′hå-lās)	197a	15.09N	120.35E
Ängelholm, Swe. (ĕng′ĕl-hôlm)	152	56.14N	12.50E
Angelina, r., Tx., U.S. (ăn-jē lē′nȧ)	113	31.30N	94.53W
Angels Camp, Ca., U.S. (ān′jĕls kămp′)	108	38.03N	120.33W
Angerhausen, neigh., Ger.	236	51.23N	6.44E
Ångermanälven, r., Swe.	146	64.10N	17.30E
Angermund, Ger. (án′ngĕr-mŭnd)	157c	51.20N	6.47E
Angermünde, Ger. (äng′ẽr-mûn-dĕ)	154	53.02N	14.00E
Angers, Can. (äɴ-zhā′)	83c	45.31N	75.29W
Angers, Fr.	156	47.29N	0.36W
Angkor, hist., Camb. (äng′kôr)	196	13.52N	103.50E
Anglesey, i., Wales, U.K. (ăŋ′g'l-sė)	150	53.35N	4.28W
Angleton, Tx., U.S. (aŋ′g'l-tŭn)	113a	29.10N	95.25W
Angmagssalik, Grnld. (àŋ-má′sà-lĭk)	82	65.40N	37.40W
Angoche, Ilha, i., Moz. (ė′lä-ăn-gō′chå)	213	16.20S	40.00E
Angol, Chile (aŋ-gōl′)	132	37.47S	72.43W
Angola, In., U.S. (ăŋ-gō′lȧ)	98	41.35S	85.00W
Angola, nation, Afr. (ăŋ-gō′lȧ)	212	14.15S	16.00E
Angono, Phil.	241g	14.31N	121.08E
Angora *see* Ankara, Tur.	182	39.55N	32.50E
Angoulême, Fr. (äŋ′gōō-lâm′)	156	45.40N	0.09E
Angra dos Reis, Braz. (aŋ′grä dōs rā′ės)	129a	23.01S	44.17W
Angri, Italy (ä′n-grė)	159c	40.30N	14.35E
Anguang, China (än-gůäŋ)	192	45.28N	123.42E
Anguilla, dep., N.A.	117	18.15N	62.54W
Anguilla Cays, is., Bah. (ăŋ-gwĭl′ȧ)	122	23.30N	79.35W
Anguille, Cape, c., Can. (kāp′-äŋ-gē′yē)	93	47.55N	59.25W
Anguo, China (än-gwô)	190	38.27N	115.19E
Angyalföld, neigh., Hung.	239g	47.33N	19.05E
Anholt, i., Den. (än′hôlt)	152	56.43N	11.34E
Anhui, prov., China (än-hwā)	189	31.30N	117.15E
Aniak, Ak., U.S. (ä-nyà′k)	95	61.32N	159.35W
Aniakchak National Monument, rec., Ak., U.S.	95	56.50N	157.50W
Anik, neigh., India	240e	19.02N	72.53E
Animas, r., Co., U.S. (ä′nē-más)	109	37.03N	107.50W
Anina, Rom. (ä-nē′nä)	161	45.03N	21.50E
Anita, Pa., U.S. (á-nē′ȧ)	99	41.05N	79.00W
Aniva, Mys, c., Russia (mĭs á-nē′vá)	194	46.08N	143.13E
Aniva, Zaliv, b., Russia (zä′lĭf á-nē′vá)	194	46.30N	143.00E
Anjou, Can.	83a	45.37N	73.33W
Ankang, China (än-käŋ)	188	32.38N	109.10E
Ankara, Tur. (än′kȧ-rȧ)	182	39.55N	32.50E
Anklam, Ger. (än′kläm)	154	53.52N	13.43E
Ankoro, Zaire (ăŋ-kō′rō)	212	6.45S	26.57E
Anloga, Ghana	214	5.47N	0.50E
Anlong, China (än-loŋ)	193	25.01N	105.32E
Anlu, China (än′lōō′)	193	31.18N	113.40E
Ann, Cape, c., Ma., U.S. (kăp′ăn′)	99	42.40N	70.40W
Anna, Russia (än′ä)	163	51.31N	40.27E
Anna, Il., U.S. (ăn′ȧ)	111	37.28N	89.15W
Annaba, Alg.	210	36.57N	7.39E
Annaberg-Bucholz, Ger. (än′ä-bĕrgh)	154	50.35N	13.02E
An Nafūd, des., Sau. Ar.	182	28.30N	40.30E
An Najaf, Iraq (än nä-jäf′)	182	32.00N	44.25E
An Nakhl, Egypt	181a	29.55N	33.45E
Annamese Cordillera, mts., Asia	196	17.34N	105.38E
Annandale, Va., U.S.	229d	38.50N	77.12W
Annapolis, Md., U.S. (ă-năp′ô-lĭs)	97	39.00N	76.25W
Annapolis Royal, Can.	92	44.45N	65.31W
Ann Arbor, Mi., U.S. (ăn är′bẽr)	97	42.15N	83.45W
An-Narrānīyah, Egypt	244a	29.58N	31.10E
An Nāṣirīyah, Iraq	182	31.08N	46.15E
An Nawfalīyah, Libya	211	30.57N	17.38E
Annecy, Fr. (án sē′)	157	45.54N	6.07E
Annemasse, Fr. (än′mäs′)	157	46.09N	6.13E
Annen, neigh., Ger.	236	51.27N	7.22E
Annenskoye, Kaz. (ä-nĕn′skô-yĕ)	169	53.09N	60.25E
Annet-sur-Marne, Fr.	237c	48.56N	2.43E
Annette Island, i., Ak., U.S.	86	55.13N	131.30W
An Nhon, Viet.	196	13.55N	109.00E
Annieopsquotch Mountains, mts., Can.	93	48.37N	57.17W
Anniston, Al., U.S. (ăn′ĭs-tŭn)	97	33.39N	85.47W
Annobón, i., Eq. Gui.	209	2.00S	3.30E
Annonay, Fr. (ȧn′ĭs-tsiŭn)	156	45.16N	4.36E
Annotto Bay, Jam. (än-nō′tō)	122	18.15N	76.45W
An Nuhūd, Sudan	211	12.39N	28.18E
Anoka, Mn., U.S. (ȧ-nō′kȧ)	107g	45.12N	93.24W
Anori, Col. (á-nō′rė)	130a	7.01N	75.09W
Áno Viánnos, Grc.	160a	35.02N	25.26E
Anpu, China (än-pōō)	188	21.28N	110.00E
Anqiu, China (än-chyô)	190	36.26N	119.12E
Ansbach, Ger. (äns′bäk)	154	49.18N	10.35E
Anschlag, Ger.	236	51.10N	7.29E
Anse à Veau, Haiti (äɴs′ ä-vō′)	123	18.30N	73.25W
Anse d'Hainault, Haiti (äɴs′dĕnō)	123	18.30N	74.25W
Anserma, Col. (á′n-sĕ′r-má)	130a	5.13N	75.47W
Ansermanuevo, Col. (á′n-sĕ′r-má-nwĕ′vō)	130a	4.47N	75.59W
Anshan, China	192	41.00N	123.00E
Anshun, China (än-shōōn′)	188	26.12N	105.50E
Anson, Tx., U.S. (ăn′sŭn)	112	32.45N	99.52W
Anson Bay, b., Austl.	202	13.10S	130.00E
Ansŏng, S. Kor. (än′sŭng′)	194	37.00N	127.12E
Ansongo, Mali	214	15.40N	0.30E
Ansonia, Ct., U.S. (ăn-sō nĭ-ȧ)	99	41.20N	73.05W
Antalya, Tur. (än-tä′lē-ä) (ä-dä′lē-ä)	149	37.00N	30.50E
Antalya Körfezi, b., Tur.	149	36.40N	31.20E
Antananarivo, Madag.	213	18.51S	47.40E
Antarctica, cont.	219	80.15S	127.00E
Antarctic Peninsula, pen., Ant.	219	70.00S	65.00W
Antelope Creek, r., Wy., U.S. (ăn′tē-lōp)	105	43.29N	105.42W
Antequera, Spain (än-tĕ-kĕ′rä)	148	37.01N	4.34W
Anthony, Ks., U.S. (ăn′thô-nē)	110	37.08N	98.01W
Anthony Peak, mtn., Ca., U.S.	108	39.51N	122.58W
Anti Atlas, mts., Mor.	210	28.45N	9.30W
Antibes, Fr. (äɴ-tēb′)	157	43.36N	7.12E
Anticosti, Île d', i., Can. (ăn-tĭ-kŏs′tē)	85	49.30N	62.00W
Antigo, Wi., U.S. (ăn′tĭ-gō)	103	45.09N	89.11W
Antigonish, Can. (ăn-tĭ-gô-nēsh′)	93	45.35N	61.55W
Antigua, Guat. (än-tē′gwä)	116	14.32N	90.43W
Antigua, r., Mex.	119	19.16N	96.36W
Antigua and Barbuda, nation, N.A.	117	17.15N	61.15W
Antigua Veracruz, Mex. (än-tē′gwä vä-rä-krōōz′)	119	19.18N	96.17W
Antilla, Cuba (än-tē′lyä)	123	20.50N	75.50W
Antímano, neigh., Ven.	234a	10.28N	66.59W
Antioch, Ca., U.S. (ăn′tĭ-ŏk)	106b	38.00N	121.48W
Antioch, Il., U.S.	101a	42.29N	88.06W
Antioch, Ne., U.S.	102	42.05N	102.36W
Antioquia, Col. (än-tē-ō′kėä)	130	6.34N	75.49W
Antioquia, dept., Col.	130a	6.48N	75.42W
Antlers, Ok., U.S. (ănt′lẽrz)	111	34.14N	95.38W
Antofagasta, Chile (än-tô-fä-gäs′tä)	132	23.32S	70.21W
Antofalla, Salar de, pl., Arg. (sá-lár′de án′tô-fä′lä)	132	26.00S	67.52W
Antón, Pan. (än-tōn′)	117	8.24N	80.15W
Antongila, Helodrano, b., Madag.	213	16.15S	50.15E
Antônio Carlos, Braz. (än-tō′nėō-kà′r-lôs)	129a	21.19S	43.45W
António Enes, Moz. (ăn-to′nyō ĕn′ēs)	213	16.14S	39.58E
Antonito, Co., U.S. (ăn-tô-nē′tō)	110	37.04N	106.01W
Antonopole, Lat. (än′tô-nô-pō lyĕ)	153	56.19N	27.11E
Antony, Fr.	157b	48.45N	2.18E
Antsirabe, Madag. (änt-sē-rä′bā)	213	19.49S	47.16E
Antsiranana, Madag.	213	12.18S	49.16E
Antsla, Est. (änt′slȧ)	153	57.49N	26.29E
Antuco, vol., S.A. (än-tōō′kō)	132	37.30S	72.30W
Antwerp, Bel.	142	51.13N	4.24E
Antwerp, S. Afr.	244b	26.06S	28.10E
Antwerpen *see* Antwerp, Bel.	142	51.13N	4.24E
Anūpgarh, India (ŭ-nôp′gŭr)	186	29.22N	73.20E
Anuradhapura, Sri L. (ŭ-nōō′rä-dŭ-pōō′rŭ)	183b	8.24N	80.25E
Anxi, China (än-shyē)	188	40.36N	95.49E
Anyang, China (än′yäng)	189	36.05N	114.22E
Anykščiai, Lith. (anīksh-chá′ė)	153	55.34N	25.04E
Anzhero-Sudzhensk, Russia (än′zhâ-rô-sōd′zhĕnsk)	164	56.08N	86.08E
Anzio, Italy (änt′zē-ō)	160	41.28N	12.39E
Anzoátegui, dept., Ven. (án-zôá′tĕ-gē)	131b	9.38N	64.45W
Aoba, i., Vanuatu	198f	15.25S	167.50E
Aomori, Japan (äô-mō′rē)	189	40.45N	140.52E
Aosta, Italy (ä-ôs′tä)	160	45.45N	7.20E
Aouk, Bahr, r., Afr. (ä-ōk′)	211	9.30N	20.45E
Aoukâr, reg., Maur.	214	18.00N	9.40W
Apalachicola, Fl., U.S. (ăp-ȧ-lăch-ĭ-kō′lȧ)	114	29.43N	84.59W
Apan, Mex. (ä-pä′n)	118	19.43N	98.27W
Apango, Mex. (ä-päŋ′gō)	118	17.41N	99.22W
Apaporis, r., S.A. (ä-pä-pō′rĭs)	130	0.48N	72.32W
Aparri, Phil. (ä-pär′rē)	196	18.15N	121.40E
Apasco, Mex. (ä-pá′s-kō)	118	20.33N	100.43W
Apatin, Yugo. (ŏ′pō-tĭn)	161	45.40N	19.00E
Apatzingán de la Constitución, Mex.	118	19.07N	102.21W
Apeldoorn, Neth. (ä′pĕl-dōōrn)	147	52.14N	5.55E
Apennines *see* Appennino, mts., Italy	142	43.48N	11.06E
Apese, neigh., Nig.	244d	6.25N	3.25E
Apía, Col. (á-pē′ä)	130a	5.07N	75.58W
Apia, W. Sam.	198a	13.50S	171.44W
Apipilulco, Mex. (ä-pĭ-pĭ-lōōl′kō)	118	18.09N	99.40W
Apishapa, r., Co., U.S. (ăp-ĭ-shä′pȧ)	110	37.40N	104.08W
Apizaco, Mex. (ä-pė-zä′kō)	118	19.18N	98.11W
Aplerbeck, neigh., Ger.	236	51.29N	7.33E
Apo, Mount, mtn., Phil. (ä′pō)	197	6.56N	125.05E
Apopka, Fl., U.S. (ȧ-pŏp′kȧ)	115a	28.37N	81.30W
Apopka, Lake, l., Fl., U.S.	115a	28.38N	81.50W
Apoquindo, Chile	234b	33.24S	70.32W
Apostle Islands, is., Wi., U.S. (ȧ-pŏs′l)	103	47.05N	90.55W
Appalachia, Va., U.S. (ăpȧ-lăch′ĭ-ȧ)	115	36.54N	82.49W
Appalachian Mountains, mts., N.A. (ăp-ȧ-lăch′ĭ-ȧn)	97	37.20N	82.00W
Appalachicola, r., Fl., U.S. (ăpȧ-lăch′ĭ-cōlä)	97	30.11N	85.00W
Äppelbo, Swe. (ĕp-ĕl-bōō)	152	60.30N	14.02E
Appelhülsen, Ger. (ä′pĕl-hül′sĕn)	157c	51.55N	7.26E
Appennino, mts., Italy (äp-pĕn-nė′nô)	142	43.48N	11.06E
Appleton, Mn., U.S. (ăp′l-tŭn)	102	45.10N	96.01W
Appleton, Wi., U.S.	97	44.14N	88.27W
Appleton City, Mo., U.S.	111	38.10N	94.02W
Appomattox, r., Va., U.S. (ăp-ô-măt′ŭks)	115	37.22N	78.09W
Aprilia, Italy (ȧ-prē′lyȧ)	160	41.36N	12.40E
Apsheronsk, Russia	168	44.28N	39.44E
Apt, Fr. (äpt)	157	43.54N	5.19E
Apure, r., Ven. (ä-pōō′rä)	130	8.08N	68.46W
Apurimac, r., Peru (ä-pōō-rė-mäk′)	130	11.39S	73.48W
Aqaba, Gulf of, b. (ä′kȧ-bȧ)	182	28.30N	34.40E
Aqabah, Wādī al, r., Egypt	181a	29.48N	34.05E
Aqtaū, Kaz.	169	43.35N	51.05E
Aqtöbe, Kaz.	169	50.20N	57.00E
Aquasco, Md., U.S. (ȧ′gwă′scô)	100e	38.35N	76.44W
Aquidauana, Braz. (ä-kē-däwä′nä)	131	20.24S	55.46W
Aquin, Haiti (ä-kăn′)	123	18.20N	73.25W
Ara, r., Japan (ä-rä)	195a	35.40N	139.52E
Arab, Bahr al, r., Sudan	211	9.46N	26.52E
'Arabah, Wādī, val., Egypt	218b	29.02N	32.10E
Arabatskaya Strelka (Tongue of Arabat), spit, Ukr.	163	45.50N	35.05E
Arabi, La., U.S.	100d	29.58N	90.01W
Arabian Desert, des., Egypt (ȧ-rā′bĭ-ăn)	211	27.06N	32.49E
Arabian Sea, sea (ȧ-rā′bĭ-ăn)	180	16.00N	65.15E
Aracaju, Braz. (ä-rä′kä-zhōō′)	131	11.00S	37.01W
Aracati, Braz. (ä-rä′kä-tē′)	131	4.31S	37.41W
Araçatuba, Braz. (ä-rä-sá-tōō′bä)	131	21.14S	50.19W
Aracena, Spain	158	37.53N	6.34W
Aracruz, Braz. (ä-rä-krōō′s)	131	19.58S	40.11W
'Arad, Isr.	181a	31.20N	35.15E
Arad, Rom. (ŏ′rŏd)	149	46.10N	21.18E
Arafura Sea, sea (ä-rä-fōō′rä)	197	8.40S	130.00E
Aragats, Gora, mtn., Arm.	168	40.32N	44.14E
Aragon, hist. reg., Spain (ä-rä-gōn′)	159	40.55N	0.45W
Aragón, r., Spain	158	42.35N	1.10W
Aragua, dept., Ven. (ä-rä′gwä)	131b	10.00N	67.05W
Aragua de Barcelona, Ven.	130	9.29N	64.48W
Araguaía, r., Braz. (ä-rä-gwä′yä)	131	8.37S	49.43W
Araguari, Braz. (ä-rä-gwä′rė)	131	18.43S	48.03W
Araguatins, Braz. (ä-rä-gwä-tēns)	131	5.41S	48.04W
Aragüita, Ven. (ärä-gwė′tá)	131b	10.13N	66.28W
Araj, oasis, Egypt (ä-räj′)	149	29.05N	26.51E
Arāk, Iran	182	34.08N	49.57E
Arakan Yoma, mts., Myanmar (ŭ-rŭ-kŭn′yō′má)	183	19.51N	94.13E
Arakawa, neigh., Japan	242a	35.47N	139.44E
Arakhthos, r., Grc. (är′äĸ-thôs)	161	39.10N	21.05E
Arakpur, neigh., India	240d	28.35N	77.10E
Aral, Kaz.	169	46.47N	62.00E
Aral Sea, sea, Asia	164	45.17N	60.02E
Aralsor, l., Kaz. (á-räl′sôr′)	170	49.00N	48.20E
Aramberri, Mex. (ä-rám-bĕr-rē′)	118	24.05N	99.47W
Arana, Sierra, mts., Spain	158	37.17N	3.28W
Aranda de Duero, Spain (ä-rän′dä dā dwā′rō)	158	41.43N	3.45W
Arandas, Mex. (ä-rän′däs)	118	20.43N	102.18W
Aran Island, i., Ire. (ăr′ăn)	150	54.58N	8.33W
Aran Islands, is., Ire.	146	53.04N	9.59W
Aranjuez, Spain (ä-rän-hwāth′)	148	40.02N	3.24W
Aransas Pass, Tx., U.S. (ȧ-răn′sȧs pȧs)	113	27.55N	97.09W
Araouane, Mali	210	18.54N	3.33W
Arapkir, Tur. (ä-räp-kēr′)	149	39.00N	38.10E
Araraquara, Braz. (ä-rä-rä-kwä′rä)	131	21.47S	48.08W
Araras, Braz. (ä-rá′räs)	129a	22.21S	47.22W
Araras, Serra das, mts., Braz. (sĕ′r-rä-däs-ä-rá′räs)	131	18.03S	53.23W
Araras, Serra das, mts., Braz. (sĕ′r-rä-däs-ä-rá′räs)	132	23.30S	53.00W
Araras, Serra das, mts., Braz.	132b	22.24S	43.15W
Ararat, Austl. (ăr′ȧrăt)	203	37.17S	142.56E
Ararat, Mount, mtn., Tur.	182	39.50N	44.20E
Arari, l., Braz. (ä-rá′rē)	131	0.30S	48.50W
Araripe, Chapada do, hills, Braz. (shä-pä′dä-dô-ä-rä-rē′pĕ)	131	5.55S	40.42W
Araruama, Braz. (ä-rä-rōō-á′mä)	129a	22.53S	42.19W
Araruama, Lagoa de, l., Braz.	129a	23.00S	42.15W
Aras, r., Asia (ä-räs)	182	39.15N	47.10E
Aratuípe, Braz. (ä-rä-tōō-ē′pĕ)	131	13.12S	38.58W
Arauca, Col. (ä-rou′kä)	130	6.56N	70.45W
Arauca, r., S.A.	130	7.13N	68.43W
Aravaca, neigh., Spain	238b	40.28N	3.46W
Aravalli Range, mts., India (ä-rä′vŭ-lė)	183	24.15N	72.40E

ăt; finȧl; rāte; senåte; ärm; åsk; sofȧ; fâre; ch-choose; dh-as th in other; bē; ēvent; bĕt; recĕnt; cratẽr; g-gō; gh-guttural g; bĭt; ĭ-short neutral; rīde; ĸ-guttural k as ch in German ich;

PRONOUNCING INDEX

Araya–Assiniboine 259

PLACE (Pronunciation)	PAGE	Lat. °′	Long. °′
Araya, Punta de, c., Ven. (pün'tä-dĕ-ä-rä'yȧ)	131b	10.40N	64.15W
Arayat, Phil. (ä-rä'yät)	197a	15.10N	120.44E
'Arbi, Sudan	211	20.36N	29.57E
Arboga, Swe. (är-bō'gä)	152	59.26N	15.50E
Arborea, Italy (är-bō-rē'ä)	160	39.50N	8.36E
Arbroath, Scot., U.K. (är-brōth')	150	56.36N	2.25W
Arcachon, Fr. (är-kä-shôN')	147	44.39N	1.12W
Arcachon, Bassin d', Fr. (bä-sĕn' där-kä-shôn')	156	44.42N	1.50W
Arcadia, Ca., U.S. (är-kā'dĭ-ȧ)	107a	34.08N	118.02W
Arcadia, Fl., U.S.	115a	27.12N	81.51W
Arcadia, La., U.S.	113	32.33N	92.56W
Arcadia, Wi., U.S.	103	44.15N	91.30W
Arcata, Ca., U.S. (är-kȧ'tȧ)	104	40.54N	124.05W
Arc de Triomphe, pt. of i., Fr.	237c	48.53N	2.17E
Arc Dome Mountain, mtn., Nv., U.S. (ärk dōm)	108	38.51N	117.21W
Arcelia, Mex. (är-sā'lē-ä)	118	18.19N	100.14W
Archbald, Pa., U.S. (ärch'bôld)	99	41.30N	75.35W
Arches National Park, Ut., U.S. (är'ches)	109	38.45N	109.35W
Archidona, Ec. (är-chē-do'nä)	130	1.01S	77.49W
Archidona, Spain (är-chē-dō'nä)	158	37.08N	4.24W
Arcis-sur-Aube, Fr. (är-sēs'sûr-ōb')	156	48.31N	4.04E
Arco, Id., U.S. (är'kō)	105	43.39N	113.15W
Arcola, Tx., U.S.	113a	29.30N	95.28W
Arcola, Va., U.S. (ăr'cōlă)	100e	38.57N	77.32W
Arcos de la Frontera, Spain (är'kōs-dĕ-lä-frôn-tĕ'rä)	158	36.44N	5.48W
Arctic Ocean, o.	220	85.00N	170.00E
Arcueil, Fr. (ärk'tīk)	237c	48.48N	2.20E
Arda, r., Bul. (är'dä)	161	41.36N	25.18E
Ardabīl, Iran	182	38.15N	48.00E
Ardahan, Tur. (är-dȧ-hän')	167	41.10N	42.40E
Ardatov, Russia (är-dȧ-tôf')	166	54.58N	46.10E
Ardennes, mts., Eur. (ȧr-dĕn')	147	50.01N	5.12E
Ardey, neigh., Ger.	236	51.26N	7.23E
Ardila, r., Eur. (är-dē'lȧ)	158	38.10N	7.15W
Ardmore, Md., U.S.	229d	38.56N	76.52W
Ardmore, Ok., U.S. (ärd'mōr)	96	34.10N	97.08W
Ardmore, Pa., U.S.	100f	40.01N	75.18W
Ardrossan, Can. (är-dros'ȧn)	83g	53.33N	113.08W
Ardsley, Eng., U.K. (ärdz'lē)	144a	53.43N	1.33W
Åre, Swe.	146	63.12N	13.12E
Arecibo, P.R. (ä-rā-sē'bō)	117b	18.28N	66.45W
Areeiro, Port.	238d	38.39N	9.12W
Areia Branca, Braz. (ä-rě'yä-brȧ'n-kă)	131	4.58S	37.02W
Arena, Point, c., Ca., U.S. (ä-rā'nȧ)	108	38.57N	123.40W
Arenas, Punta, c., Ven. (pòn'tä-rĕ'näs)	131b	10.57N	64.24W
Arenas de San Pedro, Spain	158	40.12N	5.04W
Arendal, Nor. (ä'rĕn-däl)	152	58.29N	8.44E
Arendonk, Bel.	145a	51.19N	5.07E
Arequipa, Peru (ä-rā-kē'pä)	130	16.27S	71.30W
Arezzo, Italy (ä-rĕt'sō)	148	43.28N	11.54E
Arga, r., Spain (är'gä)	158	42.35N	1.55W
Arganda, Spain (är-gän'dä)	159a	40.18N	3.27W
Argazi, l., Russia (är'gä-zĭ)	172a	55.24N	60.37E
Argazi, r., Russia	172a	55.33N	57.30E
Argentan, Fr. (ȧr-zhäN-täN')	156	48.45N	0.01W
Argentat, Fr. (ȧr-zhäN-tä')	156	45.07N	1.57E
Argenteuil, Fr. (är-zhäN-tû'y')	156	48.56N	2.15E
Argentina, nation, S.A. (är-jĕn-tē'nȧ)	132	35.30S	67.00W
Argentino, l., Arg. (är-kĕn-tē'nō)	132	50.15S	72.45W
Argenton-sur-Creuse, Fr. (är-zhäN'tôN-sür-krôs)	156	46.34N	1.28E
Argolikos Kólpos, b., Grc.	161	37.20N	23.00E
Argonne, mts., Fr. (ä'r-gôn)	157	49.21N	5.54E
Argos, Grc. (är'gŏs)	161	37.38N	22.45E
Argostólion, Grc. (är-gŏs-tô'lē-ŏn)	161	38.10N	20.30E
Arguello, Point, c., Ca., U.S. (är-gwāl'yō)	108	34.35N	120.40W
Arguin, Cap d', c., Maur.	210	20.28N	17.46W
Argun', r., Asia (ȧr-gōōn')	165	50.00N	119.00E
Argungu, Nig.	215	12.45N	4.31E
Argyle, Can. (är'gīl)	83f	50.11N	97.27W
Argyle, Mn., U.S.	102	48.21N	96.48W
Århus, Den. (ôr'hōōs)	146	56.09N	10.10E
Ariakeno-Umi, b., Japan (ä-rē'ä-kä-nō ōō'nē)	195	33.03N	130.18E
Ariake-Wan, b., Japan (ä'rē-ä'kȧ wän)	195	31.19N	131.15E
Ariano, Italy (ä-rē-ä'nō)	160	41.09N	15.11E
Ariari, r., Col. (ä-ryà'rē)	130a	3.34N	73.42W
Aribinda, Burkina	214	14.14N	0.52W
Arica, Chile (ä-rē'kä)	130	18.34S	70.14W
Arichat, Can. (ä-rĭ-shät')	93	45.31N	61.01W
Ariège, r., Fr. (ȧ-rē-ĕzh')	156	43.26N	1.29E
Ariel, Wa., U.S. (ā'rĭ-ĕl)	106c	45.57N	122.34W
Arieș, r., Rom.	155	46.25N	23.15E
Ariguanabo, Lago de, l., Cuba (lä'gô-dĕ-ä-rē-gwä-nä'bô)	123a	22.52N	82.33W
Arikaree, r., Co., U.S. (ä-rĭ-kȧ-rē')	110	39.51N	102.18W
Arima, Japan (ä'rē-mä')	195b	34.48N	135.16E
Aringay, Phil. (ä-rĭŋ-gä'ē)	197a	16.25N	120.20E
Arino, neigh., Japan	242b	34.50N	135.14E
Arinos, r., Braz. (ä-rē'nōzh)	131	12.09S	56.49W
Aripuanã, r., Braz. (ȧ-rē-pwän'yȧ)	131	7.06S	60.29W
'Arīsh, Wādī al, r., Egypt (ȧ-rēsh')	181a	30.36N	34.07E
Aristazabal Island, i., Can.	86	52.30N	129.20W
Arizona, state, U.S. (ăr-ĭ-zō'nȧ)	96	34.00N	113.00W
Arjona, Spain (är-hō'nä)	158	37.58N	4.03W
Arka, r., Russia	171	60.45N	142.30E
Arkabutla Lake, res., Ms., U.S. (är-kȧ-bŭt'lā)	114	34.48N	90.00W
Arkadelphia, Ar., U.S. (är-kȧ-dĕl'fĭ-ȧ)	111	34.06N	93.05W
Arkansas, state, U.S. (är'kăn-sô) (är-kăn'sȧs)	97	34.50N	93.40W
Arkansas, r., U.S.	96	37.30N	97.00W
Arkansas City, Ks., U.S.	111	37.04N	97.02W
Arkhangelsk (Archangel), Russia (ȧr-käN'gĕlsk)	164	64.30N	40.25E
Arkhangel'skiy, Kaz. (är-kän-gĕl'skĭ)	169	52.52N	61.53E
Arkhangel'skoye, Russia (är-kän-gĕl'skô-yĕ)	172a	54.25N	56.48E
Arklow, Ire. (ärk'lō)	150	52.47N	6.10W
Arkonam, India (är-kō-nām')	187	13.05N	79.43E
Arlanza, r., Spain (är-län-thä')	158	42.08N	3.45W
Arlanzón, r., Spain (är-län-thōn')	158	42.12N	3.58W
Arlberg Tunnel, trans., Aus. (ärl'bĕrgh)	154	47.05N	10.15E
Arles, Fr. (ärl)	156	43.42N	4.38E
Arlington, S. Afr.	218d	28.02S	27.52E
Arlington, Ga., U.S. (är'lĭng-tun')	114	31.25N	84.42W
Arlington, Ma., U.S.	93a	42.26N	71.13W
Arlington, S.D., U.S. (är'lĕng-tŭn)	102	44.23N	97.09W
Arlington, Tx., U.S. (ȧr'lĭng-tŭn)	107c	32.44N	97.07W
Arlington, Vt., U.S.	99	43.05N	73.05W
Arlington, Va., U.S.	100e	38.55N	77.10W
Arlington, Wa., U.S.	106a	48.11N	122.08W
Arlington Heights, Il., U.S. (är'lĕng-tŭn-hī'ts)	101a	42.05N	87.59W
Arlington National Cemetery, pt. of i., Va., U.S.	229d	38.53N	77.04W
Arltunga, Austl. (ärl-tôŋ'gȧ)	202	23.19S	134.45E
Arma, Ks., U.S. (är'mȧ)	111	37.34N	94.43W
Armagh, Can. (är-mä') (är-mäK')	83b	46.45N	70.36W
Armagh, N. Ire., U.K.	146	54.21N	6.25W
Armant, Egypt (är-mänt')	218b	25.37N	32.32E
Armaro, Col. (är-mà'rō)	130a	4.58N	74.54W
Armavir, Russia (ȧr-mȧ-vĭr')	164	45.00N	41.00E
Armenia, Col. (ȧr-mē'nē-ȧ)	130	4.33N	75.40W
Armenia, El Sal. (är-mā'nē-ä)	120	13.44N	89.31W
Armenia, nation, Asia	164	41.00N	44.39E
Armentières, Fr. (ȧr-mäN-tyâr')	156	50.43N	2.53E
Armeria, Río de, r., Mex. (rē'ō-dĕ-är-mȧ-rē'ä)	118	19.36N	104.10W
Armherstburg, Can. (ärm'hĕrst-bōōrgh)	90	42.06N	83.06W
Armidale, Austl. (är'mĭ-dāl)	203	30.27S	151.50E
Armour, S.D., U.S. (är'mẽr)	102	43.18N	98.21W
Armstrong Station, Can. (ärm'strŏng)	85	50.21N	89.00W
Armyans'k, Ukr.	163	46.06N	33.42E
Arnedo, Spain (är-nā'dō)	158	42.12N	2.03W
Arnhem, Neth. (ärn'hĕm)	147	51.58N	5.56E
Arnhem, Cape, c., Austl.	202	12.15S	137.00E
Arnhem Land, reg., Austl. (ärn'hĕm-lănd)	202	13.15S	133.00E
Arno, r., Italy (ä'r-nō)	148	43.30N	11.00E
Arnold, Eng., U.K. (är'nŭld)	144a	53.00N	1.08W
Arnold, Mn., U.S. (ȧr'nŭld)	107h	46.53N	92.06W
Arnold, Pa., U.S.	101e	40.35N	79.45W
Arnprior, Can. (ärn-prī'ẽr)	91	45.25N	76.20W
Arnsberg, Ger. (ärns'bĕrgh)	157c	51.25N	8.02E
Arnstadt, Ger. (ärn'shtät)	154	50.51N	10.57E
Aroab, Nmb. (är'ō-ȧb)	212	25.40S	19.45E
Aroostook, r., Me., U.S. (ȧ-rōs'tŏŏk)	92	46.44N	68.15W
Aroroy, Phil. (ä-rō-rō'ē)	197a	12.30N	123.24E
Arpajon, Fr. (är-pä-jō'n)	157b	48.35N	2.15E
Arpoador, Ponta do, c., Braz. (pô'n-tä-dō-är'pōȧ-dō'r)	132b	22.59S	43.11W
Arraiolos, Port. (är-rī-ō'lōzh)	158	38.47N	7.59W
Arran, Island of, Scot., U.K. (ă'răn)	150	55.25N	5.25W
Ar Rank, Sudan	211	11.45N	32.53E
Arras, Fr. (ȧ-räs')	147	50.21N	2.40E
Ar Rawdah, Egypt	218b	27.47N	30.52E
Arrecifes, Arg. (är-rā-sē'fās)	129c	34.03S	60.05W
Arrecifes, r., Arg.	129c	34.07S	59.50W
Arrée, Monts d', mts., Fr. (är-rā')	156	48.27N	4.00W
Arriaga, Mex. (är-rēä'gä)	119	16.15N	93.54W
Arrone, r., Italy	159d	41.57N	12.17E
Arrow Creek, r., Mt., U.S. (ăr'ō)	105	47.29N	109.53W
Arrowhead, Lake, l., Ca., U.S. (lăk ăr'ōhĕd)	107a	34.17N	117.13W
Arrowrock Reservoir, res., Id., U.S. (ăr'ō-rŏk)	104	43.40N	115.30W
Arroya Arena, Cuba (är-rō'yä-rĕ'nä)	123a	23.01N	82.30W
Arroyo de la Luz, Spain (är-rō'yō-dĕ-lä-lōō'z)	158	39.39N	6.46W
Arroyo Seco, Mex. (är-rō'yō sä'kō)	118	21.31N	99.44W
Ar Rub' al Khālī, des., Asia	182	20.00N	51.00E
Ar Rutbah, Iraq	185	33.02N	40.17E
Arsen'yev, Russia	165	44.13N	133.32E
Arsinskiy, Russia (är-sĭn'skĭ)	172a	53.46N	59.54E
Árta, Grc. (är'tä)	149	39.08N	21.02E
Artarmon, Austl.	243a	33.49S	151.11E
Arteaga, Mex. (är-tä-ä'gä)	112	25.28N	100.50W
Artëm, Russia (ȧr-tyôm')	165	43.28N	132.29E
Artemisa, Cuba (är-tȧ-mē'sä)	122	22.50N	82.45W
Artemivs'k, Ukr.	167	48.37N	38.00E
Arteria, Ca., U.S.	232	33.52N	118.05W
Artesia, N.M., U.S. (är-tē'sĭ-ȧ)	110	32.44N	104.23W
Arthabaska, Can.	91	46.03N	71.54W
Arthur's Town, Bah.	123	24.40N	75.40W
Arti, Russia (är'tĭ)	172a	56.20N	58.38E
Artibonite, r., N.A. (är-tē-bō-nē'tä)	123	19.00N	72.25W
Artigas, neigh., Ven.	234a	10.30N	66.56W
Aru, Kepulauan, is., Indon.	197	6.20S	133.00E
Arua, Ug. (ä'rōō-ä)	211	3.01N	30.55E
Aruba, i., Aruba (ä-rōō'bȧ)	117	12.29N	70.00W
Arunachal Pradesh, state, India	183	27.35N	92.56E
Arundel Gardens, Md., U.S.	229c	39.13N	76.37W
Arundel Village, Md., U.S.	229c	39.13N	76.36W
Arusha, Tan. (ȧ-rōō'shä)	212	3.22S	36.41E
Arvida, Can.	85	48.26N	71.11W
Arvika, Swe. (är-vē'kȧ)	152	59.41N	12.35E
Arzamas, Russia (är-zä-mäs')	166	55.20N	43.52E
Arziw, Alg.	148	35.50N	0.20W
Arzua, Spain (är-thōō'ä)	158	42.54N	8.19W
Aš, Czech Rep. (äsh')	154	50.12N	12.13E
Asahi-Gawa, r., Japan (ä-sä'hē-gä'wä)	195	35.01N	133.40E
Asahikawa, Japan	189	43.50N	142.09E
Asaka, Japan (ä-sä'kä)	195a	35.47N	139.36E
Asālafpur, neigh., India	240d	28.38N	77.05E
Asansol, India	183	23.45N	86.58E
Asbest, Russia (äs-bĕst')	166	57.02N	61.28E
Asbestos, Can. (ăs-bĕs'tŏs)	91	45.49N	71.52W
Asbestovskiy, Russia	172a	57.46N	61.23E
Asbury Park, N.J., U.S. (ăz'bĕr-ĭ)	100a	40.13N	74.01W
Ascención, Bahía de la, b., Mex.	120a	19.39N	87.30W
Ascensión, Mex. (äs-sĕn-sē-ōn')	118	24.21N	99.54W
Ascension, i., St. Hel. (ȧ-sĕn'shŭn)	209	8.00S	13.00W
Ascent, S. Afr. (ăs-ĕnt')	218d	27.14S	29.06E
Aschaffenburg, Ger. (ä-shäf'ĕn-bōrgh)	154	49.58N	9.12E
Ascheberg, Ger. (ä'shĕ-bĕrg)	157c	51.47N	7.38E
Aschersleben, Ger. (äsh'ĕrs-lā-bĕn)	154	51.46N	11.28E
Ascoli Piceno, Italy (äs'kō-lēpē-chā'nō)	160	42.50N	13.55E
Aseb, Erit.	211	12.52N	43.39E
Asenovgrad, Bul.	161	42.00N	24.49E
Aseri, Est. (ȧ'sĕ-rĭ)	153	59.26N	26.58E
Asha, Russia (ä'shä)	172a	55.01N	57.17E
Ashabula, l., N.D., U.S. (ăsh'ȧ-bū-lä)	102	47.07N	97.51W
Ashan, Russia (ä'shän)	172a	57.08N	56.25E
Ashbourne, Eng., U.K. (ăsh'bŭrn)	144a	53.01N	1.44W
Ashburn, Ga., U.S. (ăsh'bŭrn)	114	31.42N	83.42W
Ashburn, Va., U.S.	100e	39.02N	77.30W
Ashburton, r., Austl. (ăsh'bûr-tŭn)	202	22.30S	115.30E
Ashby-de-la-Zouch, Eng., U.K. (ăsh'bĭ-dē-lȧ zōōsh')	144a	52.44N	1.23W
Ashdod, Isr.	181a	31.46N	34.39E
Ashdown, Ar., U.S. (ăsh'doun)	111	33.41N	94.07W
Asheboro, N.C., U.S. (ăsh'bŭr-ô)	115	35.41N	79.50W
Asherton, Tx., U.S. (ăsh'ẽr-tŭn)	112	28.26N	99.45W
Asheville, N.C., U.S. (ăsh'vĭl)	97	35.35N	82.35W
Ashfield, Austl.	243a	33.53S	151.08E
Ashford, Eng., U.K.	235	51.26N	0.27W
Ash Fork, Az., U.S.	109	35.13N	112.29W
Ashikaga, Japan (ä'shē-kä'gȧ)	195	36.22N	139.26E
Ashiya, Japan (ä'shē-yä')	195	33.54N	130.40E
Ashiya, Japan	195b	34.44N	135.18E
Ashizuri-Zaki, c., Japan (ä-shē-zō-rē zä-kē)	194	32.43N	133.04E
Ashkhabad, Turk. (ŭsh-kä-bät')	169	37.57N	58.23E
Ashland, Al., U.S. (ăsh'lȧnd)	114	33.15N	85.50W
Ashland, Ks., U.S.	110	37.11N	99.46W
Ashland, Ky., U.S.	98	38.25N	82.40W
Ashland, Me., U.S.	92	46.37N	68.26W
Ashland, Ma., U.S.	93a	42.16N	71.28W
Ashland, Ne., U.S.	102	41.02N	96.23W
Ashland, Oh., U.S.	98	40.50N	82.15W
Ashland, Or., U.S.	104	42.12N	122.42W
Ashland, Pa., U.S.	99	40.45N	76.20W
Ashland, Wi., U.S.	97	46.34N	90.55W
Ashley, N.D., U.S. (ăsh'lē)	102	46.03N	99.23W
Ashley, Pa., U.S.	99	41.15N	75.55W
Ashley Green, Eng., U.K.	235	51.44N	0.35W
Ashmūn, Egypt (ȧsh-mōōn')	218b	30.19N	30.57E
Ashqelon, Isr. (äsh'kĕ-lōn)	181a	31.40N	34.36E
Ash Shabb, Egypt (shĕb)	211	22.34N	29.52E
Ash Shallūfah, Egypt (shäl'lō-fȧ)	218b	30.09N	32.33E
Ash Shaqrā', Sau. Ar.	182	25.10N	45.08E
Ash Shāriqah, U.A.E.	185	25.22N	55.23E
Ash Shawbak, Jord.	181a	30.31N	35.35E
Ash Shihr, Yemen	182	14.45N	49.32E
Ashtabula, Oh., U.S. (ăsh-tȧ-bū'lȧ)	97	41.55N	80.50W
Ashtead, Eng., U.K.	235	51.19N	0.18W
Ashton, Id., U.S. (ăsh'tŭn)	105	44.04N	111.28W
Ashton-in-Makerfield, Eng., U.K. (ăsh'tŭn-ĭn-māk'ẽr-fēld)	144a	53.29N	2.39W
Ashton-under-Lyne, Eng., U.K. (ăsh'tŭn-ŭn-dẽr-līn')	144a	53.29N	2.04W
Ashuanipi, l., Can. (ăsh-wȧ-nĭp'ĭ)	85	52.40N	67.42W
Ashukino, Russia (ȧ-shōō'kĭnô)	172b	56.10N	37.57E
Asia, cont.	180	50.00N	100.00E
Asia Minor, reg., Tur. (ā'zhȧ)	143	38.18N	31.18E
Asientos, Mex. (ä-sē-ĕn'tōs)	118	22.13N	102.05W
Asilah, Mor.	158	35.30N	6.05W
Asinara, i., Italy	160	41.02N	8.22E
Asinara, Golfo dell', b., Italy (gôl'fô-dĕl-ä-sē-nä'rä)	160	40.58N	8.28E
Asīr, reg., Sau. Ar. (ä-sēr')	182	19.30N	42.00E
Askarovo, Russia (äs-kä-rô'vô)	172a	53.21N	58.32E
Askersund, Swe. (äs'kĕr-sōnd)	152	58.43N	14.53E
Askino, Russia (äs'kĭ-nô)	172a	56.06N	56.29E
Asmara *see* Asmera, Erit.	210	15.17N	38.56E
Asmera, Erit. (äs-mä'rä)	211	15.17N	38.56E
Asnieres, Fr. (ä-nyâr')	157b	48.55N	2.18E
Asosa, Eth.	211	10.13N	34.28E
Asotin, Wa., U.S. (ȧ-sō'tĭn)	104	46.19N	117.01W
Aspen, Co., U.S. (ăs'pĕn)	109	39.15N	106.55W
Asperen, Neth.	145a	51.52N	5.07E
Aspern, neigh., Aus.	239e	48.13N	16.29E
Aspinwall, Pa., U.S.	230b	40.30N	79.55W
Aspy Bay, b., Can. (ăs'pē)	93	46.55N	60.25W
Aş Şaff, Egypt	218b	29.33N	31.23E
As Sallūm, Egypt	211	31.35N	25.05E
As Salt, Jord.	181a	32.02N	35.44E
Assam, state, India (ăs-săm')	183	26.00N	91.00E
As Samāwah, Iraq	185	31.18N	45.17E
Asseln, neigh., Ger.	236	51.32N	7.35E
Assens, Den. (äs'sĕns)	152	55.16N	9.54E
As Sinbillāwayn, Egypt	218b	30.53N	31.37E
Assini, C. Iv. (ȧ-sē-nē')	210	4.52N	3.16W
Assiniboia, Can.	84	49.38N	105.59W
Assiniboine, r., Can. (ă-sĭn'ĭ-boin)	89	50.03N	97.57W
Assiniboine, Mount, mtn., Can.	87	50.52N	115.39W

ng-sing; ŋ-baŋk; N-nasalized n; nŏd; cŏmmit; ōld; ôbey; ôrder; oi-boil; fōōd; ŏ-as oo in foot; ou-out; s-soft; sh-dish; th-thin; pūre; ûnite; ûrn; stŭd; circŭs; ü-as in French tu; '-indeterminate vowel.

260 Assis–Az̧ Z̧ahrān (Dhahran)

PLACE (Pronunciation)	PAGE	Lat. °′	Long. °′
Assis, Braz. (ä-sē's)	131	22.39S	50.21W
Assisi, Italy	148	43.04N	12.37E
As-Sudd, reg., Sudan	211	8.45N	30.45E
As Sulaymānīyah, Iraq	182	35.47N	45.23E
As Sulaymānīyah, Sau. Ar.	185	24.09N	46.19E
As Suwaydā', Syria	182	32.41N	36.41E
Astakós, Grc. (äs'tä-kôs)	161	38.42N	21.00E
Astara, Azer.	167	38.30N	48.50E
Asti, Italy (äs'tē)	148	44.54N	8.12E
Astipálaia, i., Grc.	149	36.31N	26.19E
Astley Bridge, Eng., U.K.	237b	53.36N	2.26W
Astorga, Spain (äs-tôr'gä)	158	42.28N	6.03W
Astoria, Or., U.S. (ăs-tō'rĭ-á)	96	46.11N	123.51W
Astoria, neigh., N.Y., U.S.	228	40.46N	73.55W
Astrakhan', Russia (äs-trá-kän')	164	46.15N	48.00E
Astrida, Rw. (äs-trē'dá)	212	2.37S	29.48E
Asturias, hist. reg., Spain (äs-tōō'ryäs)	158	43.21N	6.00W
Asunción see Nochistlán, Mex.	118	21.23N	102.52W
Asunción see Ixtaltepec, Mex.	119	16.33N	95.04W
Asunción, Para. (ä-sōōn-syōn')	132	25.25S	57.30W
Asunción Mita, Guat. (ä-sōōn-syō'n-mē'tä)	120	14.19N	89.43W
Aswān, Egypt (ä-swän')	211	24.05N	32.57E
Aswān High Dam, dam, Egypt	211	23.58N	32.53E
Atacama, Desierto de, des., Chile (dĕ-syĕ'r-tô-dĕ-ä-tä-kà'mä)	128	23.50S	69.00W
Atacama, Puna de, plat., Bol. (pōō'nä-dĕ-ä-tä-kà'mä)	130	21.35S	66.58W
Atacama, Puna de, reg., Chile (pōō'nä-dĕ-átä-kà'mä)	132	23.15S	68.45W
Atacama, Salar de, l., Chile (sà-lär'dĕ-átä-kà'mä)	132	23.38S	68.15W
Atacama Trench, deep	128	25.00S	71.30W
Ataco, Col. (ä-tà'kō)	130a	3.36N	75.22W
Atacora, Chaîne de l', mts., Benin	214	10.15N	1.15E
Atā 'itah, Jabal al, mtn., Jord.	181a	30.48N	35.19E
Atamanovskiy, Russia (ä-tä-mä'nôv-skĭ)	172a	52.15N	60.47E
'Atāqah, Jabal, mts., Egypt	218c	29.59N	32.20E
Atar, Maur. (ä-tär')	210	20.45N	13.16W
Atascadero, Ca., U.S. (ăt-ăs-ká-dâ'rō)	108	35.29N	120.40W
Atascosa, r., Tx., U.S. (ăt-ăs-kō'sá)	112	28.50N	98.17W
Atauro, Ilha de, i., Indon. (dĕ-ä-tä'ōō-rô)	197	8.20S	126.15E
Atbara, r., Afr.	211	17.14N	34.27E
'Aṭbarah, Sudan (ät'bá-rä)	211	17.45N	33.15E
Atbasar, Kaz. (ät'bä-sär')	169	51.42N	68.28E
Atchafalaya, r., La., U.S.	113	30.53N	91.51W
Atchafalaya Bay, b., La., U.S. (ăch-á-fá-lī'á)	113	29.25N	91.30W
Atchison, Ks., U.S. (ăch'ĭ-sŭn)	97	39.33N	95.08W
Atco, N.J., U.S. (ăt'kō)	100f	39.46N	74.53W
Atempan, Mex. (ä-tĕm-pá'n)	119	19.49N	97.25W
Atenguillo, r., Mex. (ä-tĕn-gē'l-yô)	118	20.18N	104.35W
Athabasca, Can. (ăth-á-băs'ká)	84	54.43N	113.17W
Athabasca, l., Can.	84	59.04N	109.10W
Athabasca, r., Can.	84	57.30N	112.00W
Athens (Athínai), Grc.	161	38.00N	23.38E
Athens, Al., U.S. (ăth'ĕnz)	114	34.47N	86.58W
Athens, Ga., U.S.	97	33.55N	83.24W
Athens, Oh., U.S.	98	39.20N	82.10W
Athens, Pa., U.S.	99	42.00N	76.30W
Athens, Tn., U.S.	114	35.26N	84.36W
Athens, Tx., U.S.	113	32.13N	95.51W
Atherstone, Eng., U.K. (ăth'ēr-stŭn)	144a	52.34N	1.33W
Atherton, Eng., U.K. (ăth'ēr-tŭn)	144a	53.32N	2.29W
Atherton Plateau, plat., Austl. (ădh-ēr-tŏn)	203	17.00S	144.30E
Athi, r., Kenya (ä'tē)	213	2.43S	38.30E
Athínai see Athens, Grc.	142	38.00N	23.38E
Athis-Mons, Fr.	237c	48.43N	2.24E
Athlone, Ire. (ăth-lōn')	146	53.24N	7.30W
Athos, mtn., Grc. (ăth'ŏs)	161	40.10N	24.15E
Ath Thamad, Egypt	181a	29.41N	34.17E
Athy, Ire. (á-thī)	150	52.59N	7.08W
Ati, Chad	215	13.13N	18.20E
Atibaia, Braz. (ä-tē-bà'yá)	129a	23.08S	46.32W
Atikonak, l., Can.	85	52.34N	63.49W
Atimonan, Phil. (ä-tē-mō'nän)	197a	13.59N	121.56E
Atiquizaya, El Sal. (ä'tē-kē-zä'yä)	120	14.00N	89.42W
Atitlan, vol., Guat. (ä-tē-tlän')	120	14.35N	91.11W
Atitlan, Lago, l., Guat. (ä-tē-tlän')	120	14.38N	91.23W
Atizapán, Mex. (ä'tē-zá-pän')	119a	19.33N	99.16W
Atka, Ak., U.S. (ăt'ká)	95a	52.18N	174.18W
Atka, i., Ak., U.S.	96b	51.58N	174.30W
Atkarsk, Russia (åt-kärsk')	167	51.50N	45.00E
Atkinson, Ne., U.S. (ăt'kĭn-sŭn)	102	42.32N	98.58W
Atlanta, Ga., U.S. (ăt-lăn'tá)	97	33.45N	84.23W
Atlanta, Tx., U.S.	111	33.09N	94.09W
Atlantic, Ia., U.S. (ăt-lăn'tĭk)	103	41.23N	94.58W
Atlantic, N.C., U.S.	115	34.54N	76.20W
Atlantic Beach, N.Y., U.S.	228	40.35N	73.44W
Atlantic City, N.J., U.S.	97	39.20N	74.30W
Atlantic Highlands, N.J., U.S.	100a	40.25N	74.04W
Atlantic Ocean, o.	4	5.00S	25.00W
Atlas Mountains, mts., Afr. (ăt'lăs)	210	31.22N	4.57W
Atliaca, Mex. (ät-lē-ä'kä)	118	17.38N	99.24W
Atlin, l., Can. (ăt'lĭn)	84	59.34N	133.20W
Atlixco, Mex. (ät-lēz'kō)	118	18.52N	98.27W
Atmore, Al., U.S. (ăt'mōr)	114	31.01N	87.31W
Atoka, Ok., U.S. (á-tō'ká)	111	34.23N	96.07W
Atoka Reservoir, res., Ok., U.S.	111	34.30N	96.05W
Atotonilco el Alto, Mex.	118	20.35N	102.32W
Atotonilco el Grande, Mex.	118	20.17N	98.41W
Atoui, r., Afr. (á-tōō-ē')	210	21.00N	15.32W
Atoyac, Mex. (ä-tō-yäk')	118	20.01N	103.28W
Atoyac, r., Mex.	118	18.35N	98.16W
Atoyac, r., Mex.	119	16.27N	97.28W
Atoyac de Alvarez, Mex. (ä-tō-yäk'dā äl'vä-räz)	118	17.13N	100.29W
Atoyatempan, Mex. (ä-tō'yá-tĕm-pän')	119	18.47N	97.54W
Atrak, r., Asia	182	37.45N	56.30E
Ätran, r., Swe.	152	57.02N	12.43E
Atrato, Río, r., Col. (rē'ō-ä-trä'tō)	130	7.15N	77.18W
Atsugi, Japan	242a	35.27N	139.22E
Atta, India	240d	28.34N	77.20E
Aṭ Ṭafīlah, Jord. (tä-fē'la)	181a	30.50N	35.36E
Aṭ Ṭā'if, Sau. Ar.	182	21.03N	41.00E
At-Ṭalibīyah, Egypt	244a	30.00N	31.11E
Attalla, Al., U.S. (á-tál'yá)	114	34.01N	86.05W
Attawapiskat, r., Can. (ăt'á-wá-pĭs'kăt)	85	52.31N	86.22W
Attersee, l., Aus.	154	47.57N	13.25E
Attica, N.Y., U.S. (ăt'ĭ-ká)	99	42.55N	78.15W
Attleboro, Ma., U.S. (ăt''l-bŭr-ô)	100b	41.56N	71.15W
Attow, Ben, mtn., Scot., U.K. (bĕn ăt'ô)	150	57.15N	5.25W
Attoyac Bay, Tx., U.S. (ă-toi'yăk)	113	31.45N	94.23W
Attu, i., Ak., U.S. (ăt-tōō')	96b	53.08N	173.18E
Aṭ Ṭūr, Egypt	149	28.09N	33.47E
Aṭ Ṭurayf, Sau. Ar.	182	31.32N	38.30E
Åtvidaberg, Swe. (ôt-vē'dá-bĕrgh)	152	58.12N	15.55E
Atwood, Ks., U.S. (ăt'wŏŏd)	110	39.48N	101.06W
Atyraū, Kaz.	169	47.10N	51.50E
Atzalpur, India	240d	28.43N	77.21E
Atzcapotzalco, Mex. (ät'zkä-pô-tzäl'kō)	118	19.29N	99.11W
Atzgersdorf, Aus.	145e	48.10N	16.17E
Auau Channel, strt., Hi., U.S. (ä'ó-ä'ó)	94a	20.55N	156.50W
Aubagne, Fr. (ō-bän'y')	157	43.18N	5.34E
Aube, r., Fr. (ōb)	156	48.42N	3.49E
Aubenas, Fr. (ōb-nä')	156	44.37N	4.22E
Aubervilliers, Fr. (ō-bĕr-vē-yā')	157b	48.54N	2.23E
Aubin, Fr. (ō-băn')	156	44.29N	2.12E
Aubrey, Can. (ô-brē')	83a	45.08N	73.47W
Auburn, Austl.	243a	33.51S	151.02E
Auburn, Al., U.S. (ô'bûrn)	114	32.35N	85.26W
Auburn, Ca., U.S.	108	38.52N	121.05W
Auburn, Il., U.S.	111	39.36N	89.46W
Auburn, In., U.S.	98	41.20N	85.05W
Auburn, Me., U.S.	97	44.04N	70.24W
Auburn, Ma., U.S.	93a	42.11N	71.51W
Auburn, Ne., U.S.	111	40.23N	95.50W
Auburn, N.Y., U.S.	99	42.55N	76.35W
Auburn, Wa., U.S.	106a	47.18N	122.14W
Auburndale, Ma., U.S.	227a	42.21N	71.22W
Auburn Heights, Mi., U.S.	101b	42.37N	83.13W
Aubusson, Fr. (ō-bü-sôn')	156	45.57N	2.10E
Auch, Fr. (ōsh)	147	43.38N	0.35E
Aucilla, r., Fl., U.S. (ô-sĭl'á)	114	30.15N	83.55W
Auckland, N.Z. (ôk'lănd)	203a	36.53S	174.45E
Auckland Islands, is., N.Z.	3	50.30S	166.30E
Auckland Park, neigh., S. Afr.	244b	26.11S	28.00E
Aude, r., Fr. (ōd)	156	42.55N	2.08E
Audenshaw, Eng., U.K.	237b	53.28N	2.08W
Audierne, Fr. (ō-dyĕrn')	156	48.02N	4.31W
Audincourt, Fr. (ō-dăn-kōōr')	157	47.30N	6.49E
Audley, Eng., U.K. (ôd'lĭ)	144a	53.03N	2.18W
Audo Range, mts., Eth.	218a	6.58N	41.18E
Audubon, Ia., U.S. (ô'dŏŏ-bŏn)	103	41.43N	94.57W
Audubon, N.J., U.S.	100f	39.54N	75.04W
Aue, Ger. (ou'ē)	154	50.35N	12.44E
Auf dem Schnee, neigh., Ger.	236	51.26N	7.25E
Augathella, Austl. (ôr'gá'thĕ-lá)	204	25.49S	146.40E
Aughton, Eng., U.K.	237a	53.32N	2.56W
Augrabiesvalle, wtfl., S. Afr.	212	28.30S	20.00E
Augsburg, Ger. (ouks'bŏŏrgh)	147	48.23N	10.55E
Augusta, Ar., U.S. (ô-gŭs'tá)	111	35.16N	91.21W
Augusta, Ga., U.S.	97	33.26N	82.00W
Augusta, Ks., U.S.	111	37.41N	96.58W
Augusta, Ky., U.S.	98	38.45N	84.00W
Augusta, Me., U.S.	97	44.19N	69.42W
Augusta, N.J., U.S.	100a	41.07N	74.44W
Augusta, Wi., U.S.	103	44.40N	91.09W
Augustow, Pol. (ou-gŏŏs'tŏf)	155	53.52N	23.00E
Auki, Sol.Is.	198e	8.46S	160.42E
Aulnay-sous-Bois, Fr. (ō-nĕ'sōō-bwä')	157b	48.56N	2.30E
Aulne, r., Fr. (ōn)	156	48.08N	3.53W
Auneau, Fr. (ō-nō')	157b	48.28N	1.45E
Auob, r., Afr. (ä'wŏb)	212	25.00S	19.00E
Aur, i., Malay.	181b	2.27N	104.51E
Aura, Fin.	153	60.38N	22.32E
Aurangābād, India (ou-rŭŋ-gä-bäd')	183	19.56N	75.19E
Aurdal, Nor. (äür-däl)	146	60.54N	9.24E
Aurès, Massif de l', mts., Alg.	148	35.16N	5.53E
Aurillac, Fr. (ō-rē-yák')	147	44.57N	2.27E
Aurora, Can.	91	43.59N	79.25W
Aurora, Co., U.S.	110	39.44N	104.50W
Aurora, Il., U.S. (ô-rō'rá)	97	41.45N	88.18W
Aurora, In., U.S.	101f	39.04N	84.55W
Aurora, Mn., U.S.	103	47.31N	92.17W
Aurora, Mo., U.S.	111	36.58N	93.42W
Aurora, Ne., U.S.	110	40.54N	98.01W
Aursunden, l., Nor. (äûr-sûndĕn)	152	62.42N	11.10E
Au Sable, r., Mi., U.S. (ô-sā'b'l)	98	44.40N	84.25W
Ausable, r., N.Y., U.S.	99	44.25N	73.50W
Austerlitz, trans., Fr.	237c	48.50N	2.22E
Austin, Mn., U.S. (ôs'tĭn)	103	43.40N	92.58W
Austin, Nv., U.S.	108	39.30N	117.05W
Austin, Tx., U.S.	96	30.15N	97.42W
Austin, neigh., Il., U.S.	231a	41.54N	87.45W
Austin, l., Austl.	202	27.45S	117.30E
Austin Bayou, Tx., U.S. (ôs'tĭn bī-ōō')	113a	29.17N	95.21W
Austral, Austl.	243a	33.56S	150.48E
Australia, nation, Oc.	202	25.00S	135.00E
Australian Alps, mts., Austl.	204	37.10S	147.55E
Australian Capital Territory, , Austl. (ôs-trā'lĭ-ăn)	203	35.30S	148.40E
Austria, nation, Eur. (ôs'trĭ-á)	142	47.15N	11.53E
Authon-la-Plaine, Fr. (ō-tô'n-lä-plĕ'n)	157b	48.27N	1.58E
Autlán, Mex. (ä-ōōt-län')	116	19.47N	104.24W
Autun, Fr. (ō-tŭn')	156	46.58N	4.14E
Auvergne, mts., Fr. (ō-vĕrn'y')	156	45.12N	2.31E
Auxerre, Fr. (ō-sâr')	147	47.48N	3.32E
Ava, Mo., U.S. (ā'vá)	111	36.56N	92.40W
Avakubi, Zaire (ä-vá-kōō'bē)	211	1.20N	27.34E
Avallon, Fr. (á-vá-lôn')	156	47.30N	3.58E
Avalon, Ca., U.S.	108	33.21N	118.22W
Avalon, Pa., U.S. (ăv'á-lŏn)	101e	40.31N	80.05W
Aveiro, Port. (ä-vä'rō)	148	40.38N	8.38W
Avelar, Braz. (ä'vĕ-lá'r)	132b	22.20S	43.25W
Aveley, Eng., U.K.	235	51.30N	0.16E
Avellaneda, Arg. (ä-vĕl-yä-nä'dhä)	132	34.40S	58.23W
Avellino, Italy (ä-vĕl-lē'nō)	160	40.40N	14.46E
Avenel, N.J., U.S.	228	40.35N	74.17W
Averøya, i., Nor. (ävĕr-ûê)	152	63.40N	7.16E
Aversa, Italy (ä-vĕr'sä)	160	40.58N	14.13E
Avery, Tx., U.S. (ā'vĕr-ĭ)	111	33.34N	94.46W
Avesta, Swe. (ä-vĕs'tä)	152	60.16N	16.09E
Aveyron, r., Fr. (ä-vâ-rôn)	156	44.07N	1.45E
Avezzano, Italy (ä-våt-sä'nō)	160	42.03N	13.27E
Avigliano, Italy (ä-vēl-yä'nō)	160	40.45N	15.44E
Avignon, Fr. (á-vē-nyôn')	147	43.55N	4.50E
Ávila, Spain (ä-vē-lä)	158	40.39N	4.42W
Avilés, Spain (ä-vē-lās')	148	43.33N	5.55W
Avoca, Ia., U.S. (á-vō'ká)	111	41.29N	95.16W
Avocado Heights, Ca., U.S.	232	34.03N	118.00W
Avon, Ct., U.S. (ā'vŏn)	99	41.40N	72.50W
Avon, Ma., U.S. (ā'vŏn)	93a	42.08N	71.03W
Avon, Oh., U.S.	101d	41.27N	82.02W
Avon, r., Eng., U.K. (ā'vŭn)	150	52.05N	1.55W
Avondale, Ga., U.S.	100c	33.47N	84.16W
Avondale Heights, Austl.	243b	37.46S	144.51E
Avon Lake, Oh., U.S.	101d	41.31N	82.01W
Avonmore, Can. (ă'vōn-mōr)	83c	45.11N	74.58W
Avon Park, Fl., U.S. (ā'vŏn pärk')	115a	27.35N	81.29W
Avranches, Fr. (á-vräNsh')	156	48.43N	1.34W
Awaji-Shima, i., Japan	194	34.32N	135.02E
Awe, Loch, l., Scot., U.K. (lŏk ôr)	150	56.22N	5.04W
Awjilah, Libya	211	29.07N	21.21E
Awsīm, Egypt	244a	30.07N	31.08E
Ax-les-Thermes, Fr. (äks'lā tĕrm')	156	42.43N	1.50E
Axochiapan, Mex. (äks-ō-chyä'pän)	118	18.29N	98.49W
Ay, r., Russia	166	55.55N	57.55E
Ayabe, Japan (ä'yä-bĕ)	194	35.16N	135.17E
Ayachi, Arin', mtn., Mor.	148	32.29N	4.57W
Ayacucho, Arg. (ä-yä-kōō'chō)	132	37.05S	58.30W
Ayacucho, Peru	130	13.12S	74.03W
Ayakōz, Kaz.	169	48.00N	80.12E
Ayamonte, Spain (ä-yä-mô'n-tĕ)	148	37.14N	7.28W
Ayan, Russia (á-yän')	165	56.26N	138.18E
Ayase, Japan	242a	35.26N	139.26E
Ayata, Bol. (ä-yä'tä)	130	15.17S	68.43W
Ayaviri, Peru (ä-yä-vē'rē)	130	14.46S	70.38W
Aydar, r., Eur. (ī-där')	163	49.15N	38.48E
Ayden, N.C., U.S. (ā'dĕn)	115	35.27N	77.25W
Aydın, Tur. (āĭy-dĕn)	182	37.40N	27.40E
Ayer, Ma., U.S. (âr)	93a	42.33N	71.36W
Ayer Hitam, Malay.	181b	1.55N	103.11E
Ayers Rock, mtn., Austl.	202	25.23S	131.05E
Ayiassos, Grc.	161	39.06N	26.25E
Ayía Varvára, Grc.	239d	37.59N	23.39E
Áyion Óros (Mount Athos), hist. reg., Grc.	161	40.20N	24.15E
Áyios Evstrátios, i., Grc.	149	39.30N	24.58E
Ayíou Orous, Kólpos, b., Grc.	161	40.15N	24.00E
Aylesbury, Eng., U.K. (ālz'bĕr-ĭ)	150	51.47N	0.49W
Aylmer, l., Can. (āl'mēr)	84	64.27N	108.22W
Aylmer, Mount, mtn., Can.	87	51.19N	115.26W
Aylmer East, Can. (āl'mēr)	91	45.24N	75.50W
Ayo el Chico, Mex. (ä'yō el chē'kō)	118	20.31N	102.21W
Ayon, i., Russia (ī-ôn')	165	69.50N	168.40E
Ayorou, Niger	214	14.44N	0.55E
Ayotla, Mex. (ä-yōt'lä)	119a	19.18N	98.55W
Ayoun el Atrous, Maur.	214	16.40N	9.37W
Ayr, Scot., U.K. (âr)	150	55.27N	4.40W
Aysha, Eth.	211	10.48N	42.32E
Ayutla, Guat. (á-yōōt'lä)	120	14.44N	92.11W
Ayutla, Mex.	118	16.50N	99.16W
Ayutla, Mex.	118	20.09N	104.20W
Ayvalik, Tur. (āĭy-wă-lĭk)	149	39.19N	26.40E
Azādpur, neigh., India	240d	28.43N	77.11E
Azaouad, reg., Mali	214	18.00N	3.20W
Azaouak, Vallée de l', val., Afr.	215	15.50N	3.10E
Azare, Nig.	215	11.40N	10.11E
Azemmour, Mor. (á-zē-mōōr')	210	33.20N	8.21W
Azerbaijan, nation, Asia	164	40.30N	47.30E
Azle, Tx., U.S. (áz'lē)	107c	35.54N	97.33W
Azogues, Ec. (ä-sō'gās)	130	2.47S	78.45W
Azores see Açores, is., Port.	209	37.44N	29.25W
Azov, Russia (á-zôf') (ä-zôf)	167	47.07N	39.19E
Azov, Sea of, sea, Eur.	164	46.00N	36.20E
Aztec, N.M., U.S. (ăz'tĕk)	109	36.40N	108.00W
Aztec Ruins National Monument, rec., N.M., U.S.	109	36.50N	108.00W
Azua, Dom. Rep. (ä'swä)	123	18.30N	70.45W
Azuaga, Spain (ä-thwä'gä)	158	38.15N	5.42W
Azucar, Presa de, res., Mex.	112	26.06N	98.44W
Azuero, Península de, pen., Pan.	117	7.30N	80.34W
Azufre, Cerro (Copiapó), mtn., Chile	132	27.10S	69.00W
Azul, Arg. (ä-sōōl')	132	36.46S	59.51W
Azul, Cordillera, mts., Peru	130	7.15S	75.30W
Azul, Sierra, mts., Mex.	118	23.20N	98.28W
Azusa, Ca., U.S. (á-zōō'sá)	107a	34.08N	117.55W
Az̧ Z̧ahrān (Dhahran), Sau. Ar.	182	26.13N	50.00E

ăt; finăl; rāte; senāte; ärm; åsk; sofá; fâre; ch-choose; dh-as th in other; bē; ēvent; bĕt; recĕnt; cratēr; g-gō; gh-guttural g; bĭt; ĭ-short neutral; rīde; K-guttural k as ch in German ich;

PRONOUNCING INDEX Az-Zamālik – Banās 261

PLACE (Pronunciation)	PAGE	Lat. °′	Long. °′
Az-Zamālik, neigh., Egypt	244a	30.04N	31.13E
Az Zaqāzīq, Egypt	211	30.36N	31.36E
Az Zarqā', Jord.	181a	32.03N	36.07E
Az Zāwiyah, Libya	210	32.28N	11.55E

B

PLACE (Pronunciation)	PAGE	Lat. °′	Long. °′
Baadheere (Bardera), Som.	218a	2.13N	42.24E
Baak, Ger.	236	51.25N	7.10E
Baal, Ger. (bäl)	157c	51.02N	6.17E
Baao, Phil. (bä'ō)	197a	13.27N	123.22E
Baarle-Hertog, Bel.	145a	51.26N	4.57E
Baarn, Neth.	145a	52.12N	5.18E
Babaeski, Tur. (bä'bä-ĕs'kĭ)	161	41.25N	27.05E
Babahoyo, Ec. (bä-bä-ō'yō)	130	1.56S	79.24W
Babana, Nig.	215	10.36N	3.50E
Babanango, S. Afr.	213c	28.24S	31.11E
Babanūsah, Sudan	211	11.30N	27.55E
Babar, Pulau, i., Indon. (bä'bär)	197	7.50S	129.15E
Bābarpur, neigh., India	240d	28.41N	77.17E
Bab-el-Mandeb see Mandeb, Bab-el-, strt.	182	13.17N	42.49E
Babelsberg, neigh., Ger.	238a	52.24N	13.05E
Babelthuap, i., Palau	198b	7.30N	134.36E
Babia, Arroyo de la, r., Mex.	112	28.26N	101.50W
Babine, r., Can.	86	55.10N	127.00W
Babine Lake, l., Can. (băb'ēn)	84	54.45N	126.00W
Bābol, Iran	182	36.30N	52.48E
Babson Park, Ma., U.S.	227a	42.18N	71.23W
Babushkin, Russia	162	55.52N	37.42E
Babushkin, Russia (bä'bŏsh-kĭn)	170	51.47N	106.08W
Babuyan Islands, is., Phil. (bä-bōō-yän')	196	19.30N	122.38E
Babyak, Bul. (bäb'zhák)	161	41.59N	23.42E
Babylon, N.Y., U.S. (băb'ĭ-lŏn)	100a	40.42N	73.19W
Babylon, hist., Iraq	182	32.15N	45.23E
Bacalar, Laguna de, l., Mex. (lä-gōō-nä-dĕ-bä-kä-lär')	120a	18.50N	88.31W
Bacan, Pulau, i., Indon.	197	0.30S	127.00E
Bacarra, Phil. (bä-kär'rä)	193	18.22N	120.40E
Bacău, Rom.	149	46.34N	27.00E
Baccarat, Fr. (bȧ-kȧ-rȧ')	157	48.29N	6.42E
Bacchus, Ut., U.S. (băk'ŭs)	107b	40.40N	112.06W
Bachajón, Mex. (bä-chä-hōn')	119	17.08N	92.18W
Bachu, China (bä-chōō)	188	39.50N	78.23E
Back, r., Can.	84	65.30N	104.15W
Bačka Palanka, Yugo. (bäch'kä pälän-kä)	161	45.14N	19.24E
Bačka Topola, Yugo. (bäch'kä tô'pô-lä')	161	45.48N	19.38E
Back Bay, India (băk)	187b	18.55N	72.45E
Back Bay, neigh., Ma., U.S.	227a	42.21N	71.05W
Backstairs Passage, strt., Austl. (băk-stârs')	202	35.50S	138.15E
Bac Lieu, Viet.	196	9.45N	105.50E
Bac Ninh, Viet. (bäk'nēn'')	193	21.10N	106.02E
Baco, Mount, mtn., Phil. (bä'kō)	197a	12.50N	121.11E
Bacoli, Italy (bä-kō-lē')	159c	40.33N	14.05E
Bacolod, Phil. (bä-kō'lōd)	197	10.42N	123.03E
Bacongo, neigh., Congo	244c	4.18S	15.16E
Bácsalmás, Hung. (bäch'ôl-mäs)	155	46.07N	19.18E
Bacup, Eng., U.K. (băk'ŭp)	144a	53.42N	2.12W
Bad, r., S.D., U.S. (băd)	102	44.04N	100.58W
Badajoz, Spain (bȧ-dhä-hōth')	148	38.52N	6.56W
Badalona, Spain (bä-dhä-lō'nä)	159	41.27N	2.15E
Badanah, Sau. Ar.	182	30.49N	40.45E
Bad Axe, Mi., U.S. (băd' ăks)	98	43.50N	82.55W
Bad Bramstedt, Ger. (bät bräm'shtĕt)	145c	53.55N	9.53E
Baden, Aus. (bä'dĕn)	154	48.00N	16.14E
Baden, Switz.	154	47.28N	8.17E
Baden-Baden, Ger. (bä'dĕn-bä'dĕn)	147	48.46N	8.11E
Baden-Württemberg, hist. reg., Ger. (bä'dĕn vür'tĕm-bĕrgh)	154	48.38N	9.00E
Bad Freienwalde, Ger. (bät frī'ĕn-väl'dĕ)	154	52.47N	14.00E
Badger's Mount, Eng., U.K.	235	51.20N	0.09E
Bad Hersfeld, Ger. (bät hĕrsh'fĕlt)	154	50.53N	9.43E
Badīn, Pak.	186	24.47N	69.51E
Bad Ischl, Aus. (bät ĭsh''l)	154	47.46N	13.37E
Bad Kissingen, Ger. (bät kĭs'ĭng-ĕn)	154	50.12N	10.05E
Bad Kreuznach, Ger. (bät kroits'näk)	154	49.52N	7.53E
Badlands, reg., N.D., U.S. (băd' lănds)	102	46.43N	103.22W
Badlands, reg., S.D., U.S.	102	43.43N	102.36W
Badlands National Park, S.D., U.S.	102	43.56N	102.37W
Badlāpur, India	187b	19.12N	73.12E
Bādli, India	240d	28.45N	77.09E
Badogo, Mali	214	11.02N	8.13W
Bad Oldesloe, Ger. (bät ōl'dĕs-lōē)	154	53.48N	10.21E
Bad Reichenhall, Ger. (bät rī'kĕn-häl)	154	47.43N	12.53E
Bad River Indian Reservation, I.R., Wi., U.S. (băd)	103	46.41N	90.36W
Bad Segeberg, Ger. (bät sĕ'gĕ-bōōrgh)	145c	53.56N	10.18E
Bad Tölz, Ger. (bät tûltz)	154	47.46N	11.35E
Badulla, Sri L.	187	6.55N	81.07E
Bad Vöslau, Aus.	145e	47.58N	16.13E
Badwater Creek, r., Wy., U.S. (băd'wô-tẽr)	105	43.13N	107.55W
Baena, Spain (bä-ā'nä)	148	37.38N	4.20W
Baependi, Braz. (bä-å-pĕn'dĭ)	129a	21.57S	44.51W
Baerl, Ger.	236	51.29N	6.41E
Baffin Bay, b., N.A. (băf'ĭn)	82	72.00N	65.00W
Baffin Bay, b., Tx., U.S.	113	27.11N	97.35W
Baffin Island, i., Can.	82	67.20N	71.00W
Bāfq, Iran (bäfk)	182	31.48N	55.23E
Bafra, Tur. (bäf'rä)	149	41.30N	35.50E
Bagabag, Phil. (bä-gä-bäg')	197a	16.38N	121.16E
Bāgalkot, India	187	16.14N	75.40E
Bagamoyo, Tan. (bä-gä-mō'yō)	213	6.26S	38.54E
Bagaryak, Russia (bȧ-gȧr-yăk')	172a	56.13N	61.32E
Bagbele, Zaire	217	4.21N	29.17E
Bagdad see Baghdād, Iraq	182	33.14N	44.22E
Baghdād, Iraq (bȧgh-dȧd') (băg'dăd)	182	33.14N	44.22E
Bagheria, Italy (bä-gȧ-rē'ä)	160	38.03N	13.32E
Bagley, Mn., U.S. (băg'lē)	102	47.31N	95.24W
Bagnara, Italy (bän-yä'rä)	160	38.17N	15.52E
Bagnell Dam, Mo., U.S. (băg'nĕl)	111	38.13N	92.40W
Bagnères-de-Luchon, Fr. (bän-yâr' dĕ-lu chôn')	156	42.46N	0.36E
Bagneux, Fr.	237c	48.48N	2.18E
Bagnolet, Fr.	237c	48.52N	2.25E
Bagnols-sur-Ceze, Fr. (bä-nyôl')	156	44.09N	4.37E
Bago, Myanmar	196	17.17N	96.29E
Bagoé, r., Mali (bȧ-gō'ȧ)	210	12.22N	6.34W
Baguio, Phil. (bä-gē-ō')	196	16.24N	120.36E
Bagzane, Monts, mtn., Niger	210	18.40N	8.40E
Bahamas, nation, N.A. (bȧ-hä'mȧs)	117	26.15N	76.00W
Bahau, Malay.	181b	2.48N	102.25E
Bahāwalpur, Pak. (bŭ-hä'wŭl-pōōr)	183	29.29N	71.41E
Bahia, state, Braz.	131	11.05S	43.00W
Bahía, Islas de la, i., Hond. (ē's-läs-dĕ-lä-bä-ē'ä)	116	16.15N	86.30W
Bahía Blanca, Arg. (bä-ē'ä bläŋ'kä)	132	38.45S	62.07W
Bahía de Caráquez, Ec. (bä-ē'ä dä kä-rä'kĕz)	130	0.45S	80.29W
Bahía Negra, Para. (bä-ē'ä nā'grä)	131	20.11S	58.05W
Bahi Swamp, sw., Tan.	217	6.05S	35.10E
Bahoruco, Sierra de, mts., Dom. Rep. (sē-ĕ'r-rä-dĕ-bä-ō-rōō'kō)	123	18.10N	71.25W
Bahrain, nation, Asia (bä-rān')	182	26.15N	51.17E
Bahr al Ghazāl, hist. reg., Sudan (bär ĕl ghä-zäl')	211	7.56N	27.15E
Bahrīyah, oasis, Egypt (bȧ-hȧ-rē'yä)	149	28.34N	29.01E
Bahtīm, Egypt	244a	30.08N	31.17E
Baía dos Tigres, Ang.	216	16.36S	11.43E
Baia Mare, Rom. (bä'yä mä'rä)	149	47.40N	23.35E
Baidyabāti, India	186a	22.47N	88.21E
Baie-Comeau, Can.	92	49.13N	68.10W
Baie de Wasai, Mi., U.S. (bā dē wä-sä'ē)	107k	46.27N	84.15W
Baie-Saint Paul, Can. (bā'sănt-pôl')	85	47.27N	70.30W
Baigou, China (bī-gō)	190	39.08N	116.02E
Baihe, China (bī-hŭ)	192	32.30N	110.15E
Bai Hu, l., China (bī-hōō)	190	31.22N	117.38E
Baiju, China (bī-jyōō)	190	33.04N	120.17E
Baikal, Lake see Baykal, Lake, l., Russia	165	53.00N	109.28E
Bailén, Spain (bä-ē-lān')	158	38.05N	3.48W
Băileşti, Rom. (bă-ĭ-lĕsh'tē)	161	44.01N	23.21E
Baileys Crossroads, Va., U.S.	229d	38.51N	77.08W
Bainbridge, Ga., U.S. (bān'brĭj)	114	30.52N	84.35W
Bainbridge Island, i., Wa., U.S.	106a	47.39N	122.32W
Bainchipota, India	240a	22.52N	88.16E
Baipu, China (bī-pōō)	190	32.15N	120.47E
Baiquan, China (bī-chyuäŋ)	192	47.22N	126.00E
Baird, Tx., U.S. (bârd)	112	32.22N	99.28W
Bairdford, Pa., U.S. (bârd'fōrd)	101e	40.37N	79.53W
Baird Mountains, mts., Ak., U.S.	95	67.35N	160.10W
Bairnsdale, Austl. (bârnz'dāl)	203	37.50S	147.39E
Baïse, r., Fr. (bä-ēz')	156	43.52N	0.23E
Baiyang Dian, l., China (bī-yäŋ-dĭĕn)	190	39.00N	115.45E
Baiyunguan, China	240b	39.54N	116.19E
Baiyu Shan, mts., China (bī-yōō shän)	192	37.02N	108.30E
Baja, Hung. (bŏ'yŏ)	155	46.11N	18.55E
Baja California, state, Mex. (bä-hä)	116	30.15N	117.25W
Baja California, pen., Mex.	82	28.00N	113.30W
Baja California Sur, state, Mex.	116	26.00N	113.30W
Bajo, Canal, can., Spain	159a	40.36N	3.41W
Bakal, Russia (bä'kăl)	172a	54.57N	58.50E
Baker, Mt., U.S. (bā'kẽr)	105	46.21N	104.12W
Baker, Or., U.S.	96	44.46N	117.52W
Baker, i., Oc.	2	1.00N	176.00W
Baker, l., Can.	84	63.51N	96.10W
Baker, Mount, mtn., Wa., U.S.	96	48.46N	121.52W
Baker Creek, r., Il., U.S.	101a	41.13N	87.47W
Bakersfield, Ca., U.S. (bā'kẽrz-fēld)	96	35.23N	119.00W
Bakerstown, Pa., U.S. (bā'kerz-toun)	101e	40.39N	79.56W
Baker Street, Eng., U.K.	235	51.30N	0.21E
Bakewell, Eng., U.K. (băk'wĕl)	144a	53.12N	1.40W
Bakhchysaray, Ukr.	163	44.46N	33.54E
Bakhmach, Ukr. (bȧk-mäch')	163	51.09N	32.47E
Bakhtarān, Iran	182	34.01N	47.00E
Bakhtegan, Daryācheh-ye, l., Iran	182	29.29N	54.31E
Bakhteyevo, Russia	172b	55.35N	38.32E
Bakırköy, neigh., Tur.	239f	40.59N	28.52E
Bako, Eth. (bä'kō)	211	5.47N	36.39E
Bakony, mts., Hung. (bȧ-kōn'y')	155	46.57N	17.30E
Bakoye, r., Afr. (bȧ-kō'ē)	210	12.47N	9.35W
Bakr Uzyak, Russia (bȧkr ōōz'yȧk)	172a	52.59N	58.43E
Baku (Bakı), Azer. (bȧ-kōō')	164	40.28N	49.45E
Bakwanga see Mbuji-Mayi, Zaire	216	6.09S	23.28E
Balabac Island, i., Phil. (bä'lä-bäk)	196	8.00N	116.28E
Balabac Strait, strt., Asia	196	7.23N	116.30E
Ba'labakk, Leb.	181a	34.00N	36.13E
Balabanovo, Russia (bȧ-lȧ-bä'nô-vô)	172b	56.10N	37.44E
Bala-Cynwyd, Pa., U.S.	229b	40.00N	75.14W
Balagansk, Russia (bä-lä-gänsk')	170	53.58N	103.09E
Balaguer, Spain (bä-lä-gĕr')	159	41.48N	0.50E
Balakhta, Russia (bȧ'lȧk-tȧ')	165	55.22N	91.43E
Balakliya, Ukr.	163	49.28N	36.51E
Balakovo, Russia (bȧ'lȧ-kô'vô)	167	52.00N	47.40E
Balancán, Mex. (bä-läŋ-kän')	119	17.47N	91.32W
Balanga, Phil. (bä-läŋ'gä)	197a	14.41N	120.31E
Ba Lang An, Mui, c., Viet.	193	15.18N	109.10E
Balashikha, Russia (bȧ-lä'shĭ-kȧ)	172b	55.48N	37.58E
Balashov, Russia (bȧ'lȧ-shôf)	167	51.30N	43.00E
Balasore, India (bä-lȧ-sōr')	183	21.38N	86.59E
Balassagyarmat, Hung. (bô'lôsh-shô-dyôr'môt)	155	48.04N	19.19E
Balaton Lake, l., Hung. (bô'lô-tôn)	149	46.47N	17.55E
Balayan, Phil. (bä-lä-yän')	197a	13.56N	120.44E
Balayan Bay, b., Phil.	197a	13.46N	120.46E
Balboa Heights, Pan. (bäl-bô'ä)	121	8.59N	79.33W
Balboa Mountain, mtn., Pan.	116a	9.05N	79.44W
Balcarce, Arg. (bäl-kär'sä)	132	37.49S	58.17W
Balchik, Bul.	161	43.24N	28.13E
Bald Eagle, Mn., U.S. (bôld ē'g'l)	107g	45.06N	93.01W
Bald Eagle Lake, l., Mn., U.S.	107g	45.08N	93.03W
Baldock Lake, l., Can.	89	56.33N	97.57W
Baldwin, N.Y., U.S.	228	40.39N	73.37W
Baldwin, Pa., U.S.	230b	40.23N	79.58W
Baldwin Park, Ca., U.S. (bôld'wĭn)	107a	34.05N	117.58W
Baldwinsville, N.Y., U.S. (bôld'wĭns-vĭl)	99	43.10N	76.20W
Baldy Mountain, mtn., Can.	89	51.28N	100.44W
Baldy Peak, mtn., Az., U.S. (bôl'dē)	96	33.55N	109.35W
Baldy Peak, mtn., Tx., U.S. (bôl'dē pēk)	112	30.38N	104.11W
Baleares, Islas, is., Spain (ē's-läs bä-lĕ-ä'rĕs)	142	39.25N	1.28E
Balearic Islands see Baleares, Islas, is., Spain	142	39.25N	1.28E
Balearic Sea, sea, Spain (băl-ē-ăr'ĭk)	159	39.40N	1.05E
Baleine, Grande Rivière de la, r., Can.	85	55.00N	75.30W
Baler, Phil. (bä-lar')	197a	15.46N	121.33E
Baler Bay, b., Phil.	197a	15.51N	121.40E
Balesin, i., Phil.	197a	14.28N	122.10E
Baley, Russia (bȧl-yä')	171	51.29N	116.12E
Balfate, Hond. (bäl-fä'tĕ)	120	15.48N	86.24W
Balfour, S. Afr. (băl'fŏr)	218d	26.41S	28.37E
Balgowlah, Austl.	243a	33.48S	151.16E
Bali, i., Indon. (bä'lē)	196	8.00S	115.22E
Bālihāti, India	240a	22.44N	88.19E
Balıkeşir, Tur. (balĭk'ĭysĭr)	167	39.40N	27.50E
Balikpapan, Indon. (bä'lĕk-pä'pän)	196	1.13S	116.52E
Balintang Channel, strt., Phil. (bä-lĭn-täng')	196	19.50N	121.08E
Balizhuang, China	240b	39.52N	116.28E
Balkan Mountains see Stara Planina, mts., Bul.	142	42.50N	24.45E
Balkh, Afg. (bälk)	183	36.48N	66.50E
Balkhash, Lake see Balqash köli	169	45.58N	72.15E
Ballabhpur, India	240a	22.44N	88.21E
Ballancourt, Fr. (bä-än-kôr')	157b	48.31N	2.23E
Ballarat, Austl. (băl'ȧ-răt)	203	37.37S	144.00E
Ballard, l., Austl. (băl'ȧrd)	202	29.15S	120.45E
Ballater, Scot., U.K. (băl'ȧ-tẽr)	150	57.05N	3.06W
Ballenato, Punta, c., Cuba	233b	23.06N	82.30W
Balleny Islands, is., Ant. (băl'ĕ nē)	219	67.00S	164.00E
Ballina, Austl. (băl-ĭ-nä')	204	28.50S	153.35E
Ballina, Ire.	150	54.06N	9.05W
Ballinasloe, Ire. (băl'ĭ-nȧ-slō')	150	53.20N	8.09W
Ballinger, Tx., U.S. (băl'ĭn-jẽr)	112	31.45N	99.58W
Ballston Spa, N.Y., U.S. (bôls'tŭn spä')	99	43.05N	73.50W
Ballygunge, neigh., India	240a	22.31N	88.21E
Balmain, Austl.	243a	33.51S	151.11E
Balmazújváros, Hung. (bŏl'mŏz-ōō'y'vä'rŏsh)	155	47.35N	21.23E
Balobe, Zaire	217	0.05N	28.00E
Balonne, r., Austl. (băl-ōn')	203	27.00S	149.10E
Bālotra, India	186	25.56N	72.12E
Balqash, Kaz.	169	46.58N	75.00E
Balqash köli, l., Kaz.	169	45.58N	72.15E
Balranald, Austl. (băl'-rȧn-ăld)	204	34.42S	143.30E
Balsam, l., Can. (bôl'sȧm)	91	44.30N	78.50W
Balsas, Braz. (bäl'säs)	131	7.09S	46.04W
Balsas, r., Mex.	116	18.00N	101.00W
Balta, Ukr. (bäl'tȧ)	167	47.57N	29.38E
Bălţi, Mol.	167	47.47N	27.57E
Baltic Sea, sea, Eur. (bôl'tĭk)	142	55.20N	16.50E
Baltīm, Egypt (bäl-tēm')	218b	31.33N	31.04E
Baltimore, Md., U.S. (bôl'tĭ-mōr)	97	39.20N	76.38W
Baltiysk, Russia (bäl-tēysk')	153	54.40N	19.55E
Baluarte, Río del, Mex. (rē'ō-dĕl-bä-lōō'r-tĕ)	118	23.09N	105.42W
Baluchistān, hist. reg., Asia (bȧ-lōō-chĭ-stän')	183	27.30N	65.30E
Balwyn, Austl.	243b	37.49S	145.05E
Balzac, Can. (bôl'zăk)	83e	51.10N	114.01W
Bama, Nig.	215	11.30N	13.41E
Bamako, Mali (bä-mä-kō')	210	12.39N	8.00W
Bambang, Phil. (bäm-bäng')	197a	16.24N	121.08E
Bambari, Cen. Afr. Rep. (bäm-bȧ-rē)	211	5.44N	20.40E
Bamberg, Ger. (bäm'bĕrgh)	147	49.53N	10.52E
Bamberg, S.C., U.S. (băm'bûrg)	115	33.17N	81.04W
Bamenda, Cam.	215	5.56N	10.10E
Bamingui, r., Cen. Afr. Rep.	215	7.35N	19.45E
Bampton, Eng., U.K. (băm'tŭn)	144b	51.42N	1.33W
Bampūr, Iran (bŭm-pōōr')	182	27.15N	60.22E
Bam Yanga, Ngao, mts., Cam.	215	8.20N	14.40E
Banahao, Mount, mtn., Phil. (bä-nä-hä'ō)	197a	14.04N	121.45E
Banalia, Zaire	217	1.33N	25.20E
Banamba, Mali	214	13.33N	7.27W
Bananal, Braz. (bä-nä-näl')	129a	22.42S	44.17W
Bananal, Ilha do, i., Braz. (ē'lä-dō-bä-nä-näl')	131	12.09S	50.27W
Banās, r., India (bän-äs')	183	25.20N	75.20E
Banās, Ra's, c., Egypt	211	23.48N	36.39E

ng-sing; ŋ-baŋk; N-nasalized n; nŏd; cŏmmit; ōld; ôbey; ôrder; oi-boil; fōōd; ŏ-as oo in foot; ou-out; s-soft; sh-dish; th-thin; pūre; ůnite; ûrn; stŭd; circŭs; ü-as in French tu; '-indeterminate vowel.

PLACE (Pronunciation)	PAGE	Lat. °′	Long. °′
Banat, reg., Rom. (bä-nät')	161	45.35N	21.05E
Banbidian, China	240b	39.54N	116.32E
Bancroft, Can. (băn'krŏft)	85	45.05N	77.55W
Bancroft see Chililabombwe, Zam.	217	12.18S	27.43E
Bānda, India (bän'dä)	183	25.36N	80.21E
Banda, Kepulauan, is., Indon.	197	4.40S	129.56E
Banda, Laut (Banda Sea), sea, Indon.	197	6.05S	127.28E
Banda Aceh, Indon.	196	5.10N	95.10E
Banda Banda, Mount, mtn., Austl. (băn'dȧ băn'dȧ)	204	31.09S	152.15E
Bandama Blanc, r., C. Iv. (bän-dä'mä)	214	6.15N	5.00W
Bandar Beheshtī, Iran	182	25.18N	60.45E
Bandar-e 'Abbās, Iran (bän-där' ȧb-bäs')	182	27.04N	56.22E
Bandar-e Būshehr, Iran	182	28.48N	50.53E
Bandar-e Lengeh, Iran	182	26.44N	54.47E
Bandar-e Torkeman, Iran	182	37.05N	54.08E
Bandar Maharani, Malay. (bän-där' mä-hä-rä'nė)	181b	2.02N	102.34E
Bandar Seri Begawan, Bru.	196	5.00N	114.59E
Bande, Spain	158	42.02N	7.58W
Bandeira, Pico da, mtn., Braz. (pē'kō dä bän dā'rä)	131	20.27S	41.47W
Bāndel, India	240a	22.56N	88.22E
Bandelier National Monument, rec., N.M., U.S. (băn-dē-lēr')	109	35.50N	106.45W
Banderas, Bahía de, b., Mex. (bä-ē'ä dě bän-dě'räs)	118	20.38N	105.35W
Bandirma, Tur. (bän-dĭr'mȧ)	149	40.25N	27.50E
Bandon, Or., U.S. (băn'dŭn)	104	43.06N	124.25W
Bāndra, India	187b	19.04N	72.49E
Bandundu, Zaire	212	3.18S	17.20E
Bandung, Indon.	196	7.00S	107.22E
Banes, Cuba (bä'nās)	123	21.00N	75.45W
Banff, Can. (bănf)	84	51.10N	115.34W
Banff, Scot., U.K.	150	57.39N	2.37W
Banff National Park, rec., Can.	84	51.38N	116.22W
Bánfield, Arg. (bȧ'n-fyě'ld)	132a	34.44S	58.24W
Banfora, Burkina	214	10.38N	4.46W
Bangalore, India (băŋ'gȧ'lôr)	183	13.03N	77.39E
Bangassou, Cen. Afr. Rep. (bäɴ-gȧ-sōō')	211	4.47N	22.49E
Bangeta, Mount, mtn., Pap. N. Gui.	197	6.20S	147.00E
Banggai, Kepulauan, is., Indon. (bäng-gī')	197	1.05S	123.45E
Banggi, Pulau, i., Malay.	196	7.12N	117.10E
Banghāzī, Libya	211	32.07N	20.04E
Bangka, i., Indon. (bäŋ'kȧ)	196	2.24S	106.55E
Bangkalan, Indon. (bäng-kȧ-län')	196	6.07S	112.50E
Bang Khun Thian, Thai.	241f	13.42N	100.28E
Bangkok, Thai.	196	13.50N	100.29E
Bangladesh, nation, Asia	183	24.15N	90.00E
Bangong Co, l., Asia (bäŋ-gôŋ tswo)	186	33.40N	79.30E
Bangor, Wales, U.K. (băŋ'ŏr)	150	53.13N	4.05W
Bangor, Me., U.S. (băn'gēr)	97	44.47N	68.47W
Bangor, Mi., U.S.	98	42.20N	86.05W
Bangor, Pa., U.S.	99	40.55N	75.10W
Bangs, Mount, mtn., Az., U.S. (băngs)	109	36.45N	113.50W
Bangu, neigh., Braz.	234c	22.52S	43.27W
Bangued, Phil. (bän-gād')	197a	17.36N	120.38E
Bangui, Cen. Afr. Rep. (bäɴ-gē')	211	4.22N	18.35E
Bangweulu, Lake, l., Zam. (băng-wė-ōō'lōō)	212	10.55S	30.10E
Bangweulu Swamp, sw., Zam.	217	11.25S	30.10E
Bani, Dom. Rep. (bä'-nė)	123	18.15N	70.25W
Bani, Phil. (bä'nē)	197a	16.11N	119.51E
Bani, r., Mali	210	13.00N	5.30W
Bánica, Dom. Rep. (bä'-nē-kä)	123	19.00N	71.35W
Banī Majdūl, Egypt	244a	30.02N	31.07E
Banī Mazār, Egypt	184	28.29N	30.48E
Banister, r., Va., U.S. (băn'ĭs-tēr)	115	36.45N	79.17W
Banī Suwayf, Egypt	211	29.05N	31.06E
Banja Luka, Bos. (bän-yä-lōō'kȧ)	149	44.45N	17.11E
Banjarmasin, Indon. (bän-jēr-mä'sėn)	196	3.18S	114.32E
Banjin, China (bän-jyĭn)	190	32.23N	120.14E
Banjul, Gam.	210	13.28N	16.39W
Bankberg, mts., S. Afr. (bäŋk'bûrg)	213c	32.18S	25.15E
Banks, Or., U.S. (bănks)	106c	45.37N	123.07W
Banks, i., Austl.	203	10.10S	143.08E
Banks, Cape, c., Austl.	201b	34.01S	151.17E
Banks Island, i., Can.	82	73.00N	123.00W
Banks Island, i., Can.	86	53.25N	130.10W
Banks Islands, is., Vanuatu	203	13.38S	168.23E
Banksmeadow, Austl.	243a	33.58S	151.13E
Banks Peninsula, pen., N.Z.	205	43.45S	172.20E
Banks Strait, strt., Austl.	204	40.45S	148.00E
Bankstown, Austl.	201b	33.55S	151.02E
Ban Lat Phrao, Thai.	241f	13.47N	100.36E
Bann, r., N. Ire., U.K. (băn)	150	54.50N	6.29W
Banning, Ca., U.S. (băn'ĭng)	107a	33.56N	116.53W
Bannockburn, Austl.	201a	38.03S	144.11E
Bannu, Pak.	186	33.03N	70.39E
Baños, Ec. (bä'-nyỏs)	130	1.30S	78.22W
Banská Bystrica, Slvk. (bän'skä bė'strė-tzä)	147	48.46N	19.10E
Bansko, Bul. (bän'skō)	161	41.51N	23.33E
Banstala, India	240a	22.32N	88.25E
Banstead, Eng., U.K. (băn'stěd)	144b	51.18N	0.09W
Banton, i., Phil. (bän-tōn')	197a	12.54N	121.55E
Bantry, Ire. (băn'trĭ)	150	51.39N	9.30W
Bantry Bay, b., Ire.	150	51.25N	10.09W
Banyak, Kepulauan, is., Indon.	196	2.08N	97.15E
Banyuwangi, Indon. (bän-jỏ-wäŋ'gė)	196	8.15S	114.15E
Baocheng, China (bou-chŭŋ)	192	33.15N	106.58E
Baodi, China (bou-dē)	192	39.44N	117.19E
Baoding, China (bou-dĭŋ)	189	38.52N	115.31E
Baoji, China (bou-jyē)	192	34.10N	106.58E
Baoshan, China (bou-shän)	188	25.14N	99.03E
Baoshan, China	190	31.25N	121.29E

PLACE (Pronunciation)	PAGE	Lat. °′	Long. °′
Baotou, China (bou-tō)	189	40.28N	110.10E
Baoying, China (bou-yĭŋ)	192	33.14N	119.20E
Bapsfontein, S. Afr. (băps-fŏn-tān')	213b	26.01S	28.26E
Ba 'qūbah, Iraq	185	33.45N	44.38E
Ba-queo, Viet.	241j	10.48N	106.38E
Baqueroncito, Col. (bä-kě-rỏ'n-sē-tỏ)	130a	3.18N	74.40W
Bara, India	240a	22.46N	88.17E
Baraawe, Som.	218a	1.20N	44.00E
Barabinsk, Russia (bá'rȧ-bĭnsk)	170	55.18N	78.00E
Baraboo, Wi., U.S. (bâr'ȧ-bōō)	103	43.29N	89.44W
Baracoa, Cuba (bä-rä-kō'ä)	123	20.20N	74.25W
Baracoa, Cuba	123a	23.03N	82.34W
Baradères, Baie des, b., Haiti (bä-rä-dâr')	123	18.35N	73.35W
Baradero, Arg. (bä-rä-dě'ŏ)	129c	33.50S	59.30W
Baragwanath, S. Afr.	244b	26.16S	27.59E
Barahona, Dom. Rep. (bä-rä-ô'nä)	123	18.15N	71.10W
Barajas de Madrid, Spain (bä-rá'häs dä mä-drēdh')	159a	40.28N	3.35W
Baranagar, India	186	22.38N	88.25E
Baranco, Belize (bä-räŋ'kō)	120	16.01N	88.55W
Baranof, i., Ak., U.S. (bä-rä'nôf)	95	56.48N	136.08W
Baranovichi, Bela. (bä'rä-nỏ-vē'chė)	164	53.08N	25.59E
Baranpauh, Indon.	181b	0.40N	103.28E
Barão de Melgaço, Braz. (bä-rouɴ-dě-měl-gä'sỏ)	131	16.12S	55.48W
Bārāsat, India	186a	22.42N	88.29E
Bārasat, India	240a	22.51N	88.22E
Barataria Bay, b., La., U.S.	113	29.13N	89.50W
Baraya, Col. (bä-rá'yä)	130a	3.10N	75.04W
Barbacena, Braz. (bär-bä-sā'nȧ)	131	21.15S	43.46W
Barbacoas, Col. (bär-bä-kō'äs)	130	1.39N	78.12W
Barbacoas, Ven. (bä-bä-kô'ás)	131b	9.30N	66.58W
Barbados, nation, N.A. (bär-bā'dōz)	117	13.30N	59.00W
Barbar, Sudan	211	18.11N	34.00E
Barbastro, Spain (bär-bäs'trō)	159	42.05N	0.05E
Barbeau, Mi., U.S. (bȧr-bō')	107k	46.17N	84.16W
Barberton, S. Afr.	212	25.48S	31.04E
Barberton, Oh., U.S. (bär'bēr-tŭn)	101d	41.01N	81.37W
Barbezieux, Fr. (bärb'zyû')	156	45.30N	0.11W
Barbosa, Col. (bär-bō'-sȧ)	130a	6.26N	75.19W
Barboursville, W.V., U.S. (bär'bērs-vĭl)	98	38.20N	82.20W
Barbourville, Ky., U.S.	114	36.52N	83.58W
Barbuda, i., Antig. (bär-bōō'dȧ)	117	17.45N	61.15W
Barcaldine, Austl. (bär'kôl-dīn)	203	23.33S	145.17E
Barcarrota, Spain (bär-kär-rō'tä)	158	38.31N	6.50W
Barcellona, Italy (bä-chěl-lō'nä)	160	38.07N	15.15E
Barcelona, Spain (bär-thå-lō'nä)	142	41.25N	2.08E
Barcelona, Ven. (bär-sȧ-lō'nä)	130	10.09N	64.41W
Barcelos, Braz. (bär-sě'lỏs)	130	1.04S	63.00W
Barcelos, Port. (bär-thå'lōs)	158	41.34N	8.39W
Barcroft, Lake, res., Va., U.S.	229d	38.51N	77.09W
Bardawīl, Sabkhat al, b., Egypt	181a	31.20N	33.24E
Bardejov, Czech Rep. (bär'dyě-yôf)	155	49.18N	21.18E
Bardsey Island, i., Wales, U.K. (bärd'sė)	150	52.45N	4.50W
Bardstown, Ky., U.S. (bärds'toun)	98	37.50N	85.30W
Bardwell, Ky., U.S. (bärd'wěl)	114	36.51N	88.57W
Bare Hills, Md., U.S.	229c	39.23N	76.40W
Bareilly, India	183	28.21N	79.25E
Barents Sea, sea, Eur. (bä'rěnts)	164	72.14N	37.28E
Barentu, Erit. (bä-rěn'tōō)	211	15.06N	37.39E
Barfleur, Pointe de, c., Fr. (bȧr-flûr')	156	49.43N	1.17W
Barguzin, Russia (bär'gōō-zĭn)	165	53.44N	109.28E
Bar Harbor, Me., U.S. (bär här'bēr)	92	44.22N	68.13W
Bari, Italy (bä'rē)	142	41.08N	16.53E
Barinas, Ven. (bä-rē'näs)	130	8.36N	70.14W
Baring, Cape, c., Can. (bâr'ĭng)	84	70.07N	119.48W
Barisan, Pegunungan, mts., Indon. (bä-rė-sän')	196	2.38S	101.45E
Bariti Bil, l., India	240a	22.48N	88.26E
Barito, r., Indon. (bä-rē'tō)	196	2.10S	114.38E
Barka, r., Afr.	211	16.44N	37.34E
Barking, neigh., Eng., U.K.	235	51.33N	0.06E
Barkingside, neigh., Eng., U.K.	235	51.36N	0.05E
Barkley Sound, strt., Can.	86	48.53N	125.20W
Barkly East, S. Afr. (bärk'lē ēst)	213c	30.58S	27.37E
Barkly Tableland, plat., Austl. (bär'klė)	202	18.15S	137.05E
Barkol, China (bär-kůl)	188	43.43N	92.50E
Bârlad, Rom.	149	46.15N	27.43E
Bar-le-Duc, Fr. (bär-lē-dük')	157	48.47N	5.05E
Barlee, l., Austl. (bär-lē')	202	29.45S	119.00E
Barletta, Italy (bär-lět'tä)	149	41.19N	16.20E
Barmen, neigh., Ger.	236	51.17N	7.13E
Barmstedt, Ger. (bärm'shtět)	145c	53.47N	9.46E
Barnaul, Russia (bär-nä-ỏl')	164	53.18N	83.23E
Barnes, neigh., Eng., U.K.	235	51.28N	0.15W
Barnesboro, Pa., U.S. (bärnz'bēr-ỏ)	99	40.45N	78.50W
Barnesville, Ga., U.S. (bärnz'vĭl)	114	33.03N	84.10W
Barnesville, Mn., U.S.	102	46.38N	96.25W
Barnesville, Oh., U.S.	98	39.55N	81.10W
Barnet, Vt., U.S. (bär'nět)	99	44.20N	72.00W
Barnetby le Wold, Eng., U.K. (bär'nět-bī)	144a	53.34N	0.26W
Barnett Harbor, b., Bah.	122	25.40N	79.20W
Barnsdall, Ok., U.S. (bärnz'dôl)	111	36.38N	96.14W
Barnsley, Eng., U.K. (bärnz'lĭ)	144a	53.33N	1.29W
Barnstaple, Eng., U.K. (bärn'stā-p'l)	150	51.06N	4.05W
Barnston, Eng., U.K.	237a	53.21N	3.05W
Barnum Island, N.Y., U.S.	228	40.36N	73.39W
Barnwell, S.C., U.S. (bärn'wěl)	115	33.14N	81.23W
Baro, Nig. (bä'rỏ)	210	8.37N	6.25E
Baroda, India (bär-rō'dä)	183	22.21N	73.12E
Barotse Plain, pl., Zam.	216	15.50S	22.55E
Barqah (Cyrenaica), hist. reg., Libya	211	31.09N	21.45E
Barquisimeto, Ven. (bär-kė-sė-mā'tō)	130	10.04N	69.16W
Barra, Braz. (bär'rä)	131	11.04S	43.11W
Barraba, Austl.	204	30.22S	150.36E
Barracas, neigh., Arg.	233d	34.38S	58.22W

PLACE (Pronunciation)	PAGE	Lat. °′	Long. °′
Barrackpore, India	186a	22.46N	88.21E
Barra do Corda, Braz. (bär'rä dỏ cōr-dä)	131	5.33S	45.13W
Barra Funda, neigh., Braz.	234d	23.31S	46.39W
Barra Mansa, Braz. (bär'rä män'sä)	129a	22.35S	44.09W
Barrancabermeja, Col. (bär-räŋ'kä-bēr-mā'hä)	130	7.06N	73.49W
Barrancas, Chile	234b	33.27S	70.46W
Barranco, Peru	233c	12.09S	77.02W
Barranquilla, Col. (bär-rän-kēl'yä)	130	10.57N	75.00W
Barras, Braz. (bá'r-räs)	131	4.13S	42.14W
Barre, Vt., U.S. (băr'ė)	99	44.15N	72.30W
Barreiras, Braz. (bär-rā'räs)	131	12.13S	44.59W
Barreiro, Port. (bär-rě'ė-rỏ)	148	38.39N	9.05W
Barren, r., Ky., U.S.	114	37.00N	86.20W
Barren, Cape, c., Austl. (băr'ěn)	203	40.20S	149.00E
Barren, Nosy, is., Madag.	213	18.18S	43.57E
Barren River Lake, res., Ky., U.S.	114	36.45N	86.02W
Barretos, Braz. (bär-rā'tỏs)	131	20.40S	48.36W
Barrhead, Can. (băr'ĭd)	84	54.08N	114.24W
Barriada Pomar Alto, Spain	238e	41.29N	2.14E
Barrie, Can. (băr'ĭ)	85	44.25N	79.45W
Barrington, Can. (bă-rêng-tŏn)	83a	45.07N	73.35W
Barrington, Il., U.S.	101a	42.09N	88.08W
Barrington, N.J., U.S.	229b	39.52N	75.04W
Barrington, R.I., U.S.	100b	41.44N	71.16W
Barrington Tops, mtn., Austl.	204	32.00S	151.25E
Barrio Obrero Industrial, prov., Peru	233c	12.04S	77.04W
Bar River, Can. (bär)	107k	46.27N	84.02W
Barron, Wi., U.S. (băr'ŭn)	103	45.24N	91.51W
Barrow, Ak., U.S. (băr'ō)	96a	71.20N	156.00W
Barrow, i., Austl.	202	20.50S	115.00E
Barrow, r., Ire. (bá-rå)	150	52.35N	7.05W
Barrow, Point, c., Ak., U.S.	95	71.20N	156.00W
Barrow Creek, Austl.	202	21.23S	133.55E
Barrow-in-Furness, Eng., U.K.	146	54.10N	3.15W
Barstow, Ca., U.S. (bär'stō)	108	34.53N	117.03W
Barstow, Md., U.S.	100e	38.32N	76.37W
Barth, Ger. (bärt)	154	54.20N	12.43E
Bartholomew Bayou, r., U.S. (bär-thŏl'ō-mū bī-ōō')	111	33.53N	91.45W
Barthurst, Can. (bär-thŭrst')	85	47.38N	65.40W
Bartica, Guy. (bär'tĭ-kȧ)	131	6.23N	58.32W
Bartin, Tur. (bär'tĭn)	149	41.35N	32.12E
Bartle Frere, Mount, mtn., Austl. (bärt''l frēr')	203	17.30S	145.46E
Bartlesville, Ok., U.S. (bär'tlz-vĭl)	111	36.44N	95.58W
Bartlett, Il., U.S. (bärt'lět)	101a	41.59N	88.11W
Bartlett, Tx., U.S.	113	30.48N	97.25W
Barton, Vt., U.S. (bär'tŭn)	99	44.45N	72.05W
Barton-upon-Humber, Eng., U.K. (bär'tŭn-ŭp'ŏn-hŭm'bēr)	144a	53.41N	0.26W
Bartoszyce, Pol. (bär-tỏ-shĭ'tsȧ)	155	54.15N	20.50E
Bartow, Fl., U.S. (bär'tō)	115a	27.51N	81.50W
Baruta, Ven.	234a	10.26N	66.53W
Barvinkove, Ukr.	163	48.55N	36.59E
Barwon, r., Austl. (bär'wŭn)	203	30.00S	147.30E
Barwon Heads, Austl.	201a	38.17S	144.29E
Barycz, r., Pol. (bä'rĭch)	154	51.30N	16.38E
Basai Dārāpur, neigh., India	240d	28.40N	77.08E
Basankusu, Zaire (bä-sän-kōō'sōō)	211	1.14N	19.45E
Basbeck, Ger. (bäs'běk)	145c	53.40N	9.11E
Basdahl, Ger. (bäs'däl)	145c	53.27N	9.00E
Basehor, Ks., U.S. (bās'hôr)	107f	39.08N	94.55W
Basel, Switz. (bä'z'l)	147	47.32N	7.35E
Bashee, r., S. Afr. (bă-shē')	213c	31.47S	28.25E
Bashi Channel, strt., Asia (bäsh'ė)	189	21.20N	120.22E
Bashkortostan, state, Russia	166	54.12N	57.15E
Bashtanka, Ukr. (bȧsh-tän'kȧ)	163	47.32N	32.31E
Bashtīl, Egypt	244a	30.05N	31.11E
Basilan Island, i., Phil.	196	6.37N	122.07E
Basildon, Eng., U.K.	151	51.35N	0.25E
Basilicata, hist. reg., Italy (bä-zē-lē-kä'tä)	160	40.30N	15.55E
Basin, Wy., U.S. (bā'sĭn)	105	44.22N	108.02W
Basingstoke, Eng., U.K. (bā'zĭng-stōk)	144b	51.14N	1.06W
Baška, Cro. (bäsh'ka)	160	44.58N	14.44E
Baskale, Tur. (bäsh-kä'lě)	167	38.10N	44.00E
Baskatong, Réservoir, res., Can.	91	46.50N	75.50W
Baskunchak, l., Russia	167	48.20N	46.40E
Basoko, Zaire (bȧ-sō'kō)	211	0.52N	23.50E
Basque Lands see Vascongadas, hist. reg., Spain	158	43.00N	2.46W
Basra see Al Başrah, Iraq	182	30.35N	47.59E
Bassano, Can. (băs-săn'ō)	84	50.47N	112.28W
Bassano del Grappa, Italy	160	45.46N	11.44E
Bassari, Togo	214	9.15N	0.47E
Bassas da India, i., Reu. (bäs'säs dä ēn'dē-ȧ)	213	21.23S	39.42E
Basse Terre, Guad. (bás' târ')	117	16.00N	61.43W
Basseterre, St. K./N.	121b	17.20N	62.42W
Basse Terre, i., Guad.	121b	16.10N	62.14W
Bassett, Va., U.S. (băs'sět)	115	36.45N	81.58W
Bass Hill, Austl.	243a	33.54S	151.00E
Bass Islands, is., Oh., U.S. (băs)	98	41.40N	82.50W
Bass Strait, strt., Austl.	203	39.40S	145.40E
Basswood, l., N.A. (băs'wỏd)	103	48.10N	91.36W
Båstad, Swe. (bỏ'stät)	152	56.26N	12.46E
Bastia, Fr. (bäs'tē-ä)	147	42.43N	9.27E
Bastogne, Bel. (băs-tôn'y')	151	50.02N	5.45E
Bastrop, La., U.S. (băs'trŭp)	113	32.47N	91.55W
Bastrop, Tx., U.S.	113	30.08N	97.18W
Bastrop Bayou, Tx., U.S.	113a	29.07N	95.22W
Bāsudebpur, India	240a	22.49N	88.25E
Bata, Eq. Gui. (bä'tä)	210	1.51N	9.45E
Batabano, Golfo de, b., Cuba (gỏl-fỏ-dě-bä-tä-bä'nỏ)	122	22.10N	83.05W
Batāla, India	186	31.54N	75.18E
Bataly, Kaz. (bȧ-tä'lĭ)	169	52.51N	62.03E

ăt; finȧl; rāte; senȧte; ärm; ȧsk; sofȧ; fâre; ch-choose; dh-as th in other; bē; ėvent; bět; recěnt; cratēr; g-gō; gh-guttural g; bĭt; ĭ-short neutral; rīde; ĸ-guttural k as ch in German ich;

PRONOUNCING INDEX Batam – Bellary 263

PLACE (Pronunciation)	PAGE	Lat. °′	Long. °′
Batam, i., Indon. (bä-täm′)	181b	1.03N	104.00E
Batang, China (bä-täŋ)	188	30.08N	99.00E
Batangas, Phil. (bä-tän′gäs)	196	13.45N	121.04E
Batan Islands, is., Phil. (bä-tän′)	196	20.58N	122.20E
Bátaszék, Hung. (bä′tá-sěk)	155	46.07N	18.40E
Batavia, Il., U.S. (bá-tā′vĭ-á)	101a	41.51N	88.18W
Batavia, N.Y., U.S.	99	43.00N	78.15W
Batavia, Oh., U.S.	101f	39.05N	84.10W
Bataysk, Russia (bá-tīsk′)	167	47.08N	39.44E
Bătdâmbâng, Camb. (bát-tám-bäng′)	196	13.14N	103.15E
Batenbrock, neigh., Ger.	236	51.31N	6.57E
Batesburg, S.C., U.S. (bāts′bûrg)	115	33.53N	81.34W
Batesville, Ar., U.S. (bāts′vĭl)	111	35.46N	91.39W
Batesville, In., U.S.	98	39.15N	85.15W
Batesville, Ms., U.S.	114	34.17N	89.55W
Batetska, Russia (bá-tě′tská)	162	58.36N	30.21E
Bath, Can. (bȧth)	92	46.31N	67.36W
Bath, Eng., U.K.	147	51.24N	2.20W
Bath, Me., U.S.	92	43.54N	69.50W
Bath, N.Y., U.S.	99	42.25N	77.20W
Bath, Oh., U.S.	101d	41.11N	81.38W
Bathsheba, Barb.	121b	13.13N	60.30W
Bathurst, Austl. (bȧth′ŭrst)	203	33.28S	149.30E
Bathurst see Banjul, Gam.	210	13.28N	16.39W
Bathurst, S. Afr. (băt-hûrst)	213c	33.26S	26.53E
Bathurst, i., Austl.	202	11.19S	130.13E
Bathurst, Cape, c., Can. (bath′-ŭrst)	84	70.33N	127.55W
Bathurst Inlet, b., Can.	84	68.10N	108.00W
Batia, Benin	214	10.54N	1.29E
Batley, Eng., U.K. (băt′lĭ)	144a	53.43N	1.37W
Batna, Alg. (bät′nä)	210	35.41N	6.12E
Baton Rouge, La., U.S. (băt′ŭn ro͞ozh′)	97	30.28N	91.10W
Battersea, neigh., Eng., U.K.	235	51.28N	0.10W
Batticaloa, Sri L.	187	7.40N	81.10E
Battle, r., Can.	88	52.20N	111.59W
Battle Creek, Mi., U.S. (băt′′l krēk′)	97	42.20N	85.15W
Battle Ground, Wa., U.S. (băt′′l ground)	106c	45.47N	122.32W
Battle Harbour, Can. (băt′′l här′bẽr)	85	52.17N	55.33W
Battle Mountain, Nv., U.S.	104	40.40N	116.56W
Battonya, Hung. (bät-tô′nyä)	155	46.17N	21.00E
Batu, Kepulauan, is., Indon. (bä′to͞o)	196	0.10S	98.00E
Batumi, Geor. (bŭ-to͞o′mē)	164	41.40N	41.30E
Batu Pahat, Malay.	196	1.51N	102.56E
Batupanjang, Indon.	181b	1.42N	101.35E
Bauang, Phil. (bä′wäng)	197a	16.31N	120.19E
Bauchi, Nig. (bá-o͞o′chē)	210	10.19N	9.50E
Bauerschaft, Ger.	236	51.34N	6.33E
Bauerstown, Pa., U.S.	230b	40.30N	79.59W
Baukau, neigh., Ger.	236	51.33N	7.12E
Bauld, Cape, c., Can.	85a	51.38N	55.25W
Baulkham Hills, Austl.	243a	33.46S	151.00E
Baumschulenweg, neigh., Ger.	238a	52.28N	13.29E
Bāuria, India	186a	22.29N	88.08E
Bauru, Braz. (bou-ro͞o′)	131	22.21S	48.57W
Bauska, Lat. (bou′ská)	153	56.24N	24.12E
Bauta, Cuba (bá′o͞o-tä)	123a	22.59N	82.33W
Bautzen, Ger. (bout′sĕn)	147	51.11N	14.27E
Bavaria see Bayern, state, Ger.	154	49.00N	11.16E
Baw Baw, Mount, mtn., Austl.	204	37.50S	146.17E
Bawean, Pulau, i., Indon. (bá′vē-än)	196	5.50S	112.40E
Bawtry, Eng., U.K. (bôtrĭ)	144a	53.26N	1.01W
Baxley, Ga., U.S. (băks′lĭ)	115	31.47N	82.22W
Baxter, Austl.	201a	38.12S	145.10E
Baxter Springs, Ks., U.S. (băks′tẽr sprĭngs′)	111	37.01N	94.44W
Bay, Laguna de, l., Phil. (lä-go͞o′nä dā bä′ē)	197a	14.24N	121.13E
Bayaguana, Dom. Rep. (bä-yä-gwä′nä)	123	18.45N	69.40W
Bay al Kabīr, Wadi, val., Libya	148	29.52N	14.28E
Bayambang, Phil. (bä-yäm-bäng′)	197a	15.50N	120.26E
Bayamo, Cuba (bä-yä′mō)	122	20.25N	76.35W
Bayamón, P.R.	117b	18.27N	66.13W
Bayan, China (bä-yän)	192	46.00N	127.20E
Bayanauyl, Kaz.	169	50.43N	75.37E
Bayard, Ne., U.S. (bā′ẽrd)	102	41.45N	103.20W
Bayard, N.M., U.S.	109	32.45N	108.07W
Bayard, W.V., U.S.	99	39.15N	79.20W
Bayburt, Tur. (bä′ĭ-bòrt)	167	40.15N	40.10E
Bay City, Mi., U.S. (bā)	97	43.35N	83.55W
Bay City, Tx., U.S.	113	28.59N	95.58W
Baydaratskaya Guba, b., Russia	166	69.20N	66.10E
Bay de Verde, Can.	93	48.05N	52.54W
Baydhabo (Baidoa), Som.	218a	3.19N	44.20E
Baydrag, r., Mong.	188	46.09N	98.52E
Bayern (Bavaria), hist. reg., Ger. (bī′ẽrn) (bá-vâ-rĭ-á)	154	49.00N	11.16E
Bayeux, Fr. (bá-yû′)	147	49.19N	0.41W
Bayfield, Wi., U.S. (bā′fēld)	103	46.48N	90.51W
Bayford, Eng., U.K.	235	51.46N	0.06W
Baykal, Ozero (Lake Baikal), l., Russia	165	53.00N	109.28E
Baykal′skiy Khrebet, mts., Russia	165	53.30N	107.30E
Baykit, Russia (bī-kēt′)	165	61.43N	96.39E
Baymak, Russia (bȧy′mäk)	172a	52.35N	58.21E
Bay Mills, Mi., U.S. (bā mĭlls)	107k	46.27N	84.36W
Bay Mills Indian Reservation, I.R., Mi., U.S.	103	46.19N	85.03W
Bay Minette, Al., U.S. (bā′mĭn-ĕt′)	114	30.52N	87.44W
Bayombong, Phil. (bä-yôm-bōng′)	197a	16.28N	121.09E
Bayonne, Fr. (bá-yôn′)	142	43.28N	1.30W
Bayonne, N.J., U.S. (bā-yōn′)	100a	40.40N	74.07W
Bayou Bodcau Reservoir, res., La., U.S. (bī′yo͞o bŏd′kō)	97	32.49N	93.22W
Bay Park, N.Y., U.S.	228	40.38N	73.40W
Bayport, Mn., U.S. (bā′pōrt)	107g	45.02N	92.46W
Bayqongyr, Kaz.	169	47.46N	66.11E
Bayramiç, Tur.	161	39.48N	26.35E
Bayreuth, Ger. (bī-roit′)	154	49.56N	11.35E
Bay Ridge, neigh., N.Y., U.S.	228	40.37N	74.02W
Bay Roberts, Can. (bā rŏb′ẽrts)	93	47.36N	53.16W
Bays, Lake of, l., Can. (bās)	91	45.15N	79.00W
Bay Saint Louis, Ms., U.S. (bā′ sȧnt lo͞o′ĭs)	114	30.19N	89.20W
Bay Shore, N.Y., U.S. (bā′ shôr)	100a	40.44N	73.15W
Bayside, Ma., U.S.	227a	42.18N	70.53W
Bayside, neigh., N.Y., U.S.	228	40.46N	73.46W
Bayswater, Austl.	243b	37.51S	145.16E
Bayswater North, Austl.	243b	37.49S	145.17E
Bayt Lahm, W. Bank (běth′lė-hěm)	181a	31.42N	35.13E
Baytown, Tx., U.S. (bā′town)	113a	29.44N	95.01W
Bayview, Al., U.S. (bā′vū)	100h	33.34N	86.59W
Bayview, Wa., U.S.	106a	48.29N	122.28W
Bayview, neigh., Ca., U.S.	231b	37.44N	122.23W
Bay Village, Oh., U.S. (bā)	101d	41.29N	81.56W
Bayville, N.Y., U.S.	228	40.54N	73.33W
Baza, Spain (bä′thä)	148	37.29N	2.46W
Baza, Sierra de, mts., Spain	158	37.19N	2.48W
Bazar-Dyuzi, mtn., Azer. (bä′zär-dyo͞oz′ē)	167	41.20N	47.40E
Bazaruto, Ilha do, i., Moz. (bá-zá-ro͞o′tō)	212	21.42S	36.10E
Baziège, Fr.	156	43.25N	1.41E
Be, Nosy, i., Madag.	213	13.14S	47.28E
Beach, N.D., U.S. (bēch)	102	46.55N	104.00W
Beachwood, Oh., U.S.	229a	41.29N	81.30W
Beachy Head, c., Eng., U.K. (bēchē hĕd)	151	50.40N	0.25E
Beacon, N.Y., U.S. (bē′kŭn)	99	41.30N	73.55W
Beacon Hill, Austl.	243a	33.45S	151.15E
Beacon Hill, hill, China	241c	22.21N	114.09E
Beaconsfield, Can. (bē′kŭnz-fēld)	83a	45.26N	73.51W
Beals Creek, r., Tx., U.S. (bēls)	112	32.10N	101.14W
Bean, Eng., U.K.	235	51.25N	0.17E
Bear, r., U.S.	105	42.17N	111.42W
Bear, r., Ut., U.S.	107b	41.28N	112.10W
Bear Brook, r., Can.	83c	45.24N	75.15W
Bear Creek, Mt., U.S. (bâr krēk)	105	45.11N	109.07W
Bear Creek, r., Al., U.S. (bâr)	114	34.27N	88.00W
Bear Creek, r., Tx., U.S.	107c	32.56N	97.09W
Beardstown, Il., U.S. (bērds′toun)	111	40.01N	90.26W
Bearfort Mountain, mtn., N.J., U.S. (bē′fōrt)	100a	41.08N	74.23W
Bearhead Mountain, mtn., Wa., U.S. (bâr′hĕd)	106a	47.01N	121.49W
Bear Lake, l., Can.	89	55.08N	96.00W
Bear Lake, l., Id., U.S.	105	41.56N	111.10W
Bear River Range, mts., U.S.	105	41.50N	111.30W
Beas de Segura, Spain (bā′äs dā sä-go͞o′rä)	158	38.16N	2.53W
Beata, i., Dom. Rep. (bě-ä′tä)	123	17.40N	71.40W
Beata, Cabo, c., Dom. Rep. (ká′bô-bě-ä′tä)	123	17.40N	71.20W
Beato, neigh., Port.	238d	38.44N	9.06W
Beatrice, Ne., U.S. (bē′á-trĭs)	96	40.16N	96.45W
Beatty, Nv., U.S. (bēt′ē)	108	36.58N	116.48W
Beattyville, Ky., U.S. (bēt′ē-vĭl)	98	37.35N	83.40W
Beaucaire, Fr. (bō-kâr′)	156	43.49N	4.37E
Beaucourt, Fr. (bō-ko͞or′)	157	47.30N	6.54E
Beaufort, N.C., U.S. (bō′frt)	115	34.43N	76.40W
Beaufort, S.C., U.S.	115	32.25N	80.40W
Beaufort Sea, sea, N.A.	95	70.30N	138.40W
Beaufort West, S. Afr.	212	32.20S	22.45E
Beauharnois, Can. (bō-är-nwä′)	91	45.23N	73.52W
Beaumont, Can.	83b	46.50N	71.01W
Beaumont, Can.	83g	53.22N	113.18W
Beaumont, Ca., U.S. (bō′mŏnt)	107a	33.57N	116.57W
Beaumont, Tx., U.S.	97	30.05N	94.06W
Beaune, Fr. (bōn)	156	47.02N	4.49E
Beauport, Can. (bō-pôr′)	83b	46.52N	71.11W
Beauséjour, Can.	84	50.04N	96.33W
Beauvais, Fr. (bō-vě′)	156	49.25N	2.05E
Beaver, Ok., U.S. (bē′vẽr)	110	36.46N	100.31W
Beaver, Pa., U.S.	101e	40.42N	80.18W
Beaver, Ut., U.S.	109	38.15N	112.40W
Beaver, i., Mi., U.S.	98	45.40N	85.30W
Beaver, r., Can.	84	54.20N	111.10W
Beaver City, Ne., U.S.	110	40.08N	99.52W
Beaver Creek, r., Co., U.S.	110	39.42N	103.37W
Beaver Creek, r., Ks., U.S.	110	39.44N	101.05W
Beaver Creek, r., Mt., U.S.	102	46.45N	104.18W
Beaver Creek, r., Wy., U.S.	102	43.46N	104.25W
Beaver Dam, Wi., U.S.	103	43.29N	88.50W
Beaverhead, r., Mt., U.S.	105	45.25N	112.35W
Beaverhead Mountains, mts., Mt., U.S. (bē′vẽr-hĕd)	105	44.33N	112.59W
Beaver Indian Reservation, I.R., Mi., U.S.	98	45.40N	85.30W
Beaverton, Or., U.S. (bē′vẽr-tŭn)	106c	45.29N	122.49W
Bebek, neigh., Tur.	239f	41.04N	29.02E
Bebington, Eng., U.K. (bē′bĭng-tŭn)	144a	53.20N	2.59W
Beccar, neigh., Arg.	233d	34.28S	58.31W
Bečej, Yugo. (bě′chā)	161	45.36N	20.03E
Béchar, Alg.	210	31.39N	2.14W
Becharof, l., Ak., U.S. (běk-á-rôf)	95	57.58N	156.58W
Becher Bay, b., Can. (bēch′ẽr)	106a	48.18N	123.37W
Beckenham, neigh., Eng., U.K.	235	51.24N	0.02W
Beckley, W.V., U.S. (běk′lĭ)	98	37.40N	81.15W
Bédarieux, Fr. (bā-dá-ryû′)	156	43.36N	3.11E
Beddington, neigh., Eng., U.K.	235	51.22N	0.08W
Beddington Creek, r., Can. (běd′ĕng tŭn)	83e	51.14N	114.13W
Bedford, Can. (běd′fẽrd)	91	45.10N	73.00W
Bedford, S. Afr.	213c	32.43S	26.19E
Bedford, Eng., U.K.	147	52.10N	0.25W
Bedford, In., U.S.	98	38.50N	86.30W
Bedford, Ia., U.S.	103	40.40N	94.41W
Bedford, Ma., U.S.	93a	42.30N	71.17W
Bedford, N.Y., U.S.	100a	41.12N	73.38W
Bedford, Oh., U.S.	101d	41.23N	81.32W
Bedford, Pa., U.S.	99	40.05N	78.20W
Bedford, Va., U.S.	115	37.19N	79.27W
Bedford Heights, Oh., U.S.	229a	41.22N	81.30W
Bedford Hills, N.Y., U.S.	100a	41.14N	73.41W
Bedford Park, Il., U.S.	231a	41.46N	87.49W
Bedford Park, neigh., N.Y., U.S.	228	40.52N	73.53W
Bedford-Stuyvesant, neigh., N.Y., U.S.	228	40.41N	73.55W
Bedmond, Eng., U.K.	235	51.43N	0.25W
Bedok, Sing.	240c	1.19N	103.57E
Beebe, Ar., U.S. (bē′bē)	111	35.04N	91.54W
Beecher, Il., U.S. (bē′chŭr)	101a	41.20N	87.38W
Beechey Head, c., Can. (bē′chĭ hĕd)	106a	48.19N	123.40W
Beech Grove, In., U.S. (bēch grōv)	101g	39.43N	86.05W
Beechview, neigh., Pa., U.S.	230b	40.25N	80.02W
Beeck, neigh., Ger.	236	51.29N	6.44E
Beeckerwerth, neigh., Ger.	236	51.29N	6.41E
Beecroft Head, c., Austl. (bē′krûft)	204	35.03S	151.15E
Beelitz, Ger. (bě′lētz)	145b	52.14N	12.59E
Be'er Sheva', Isr. (bēr-shē′bá)	181a	31.15N	34.48E
Be'er Sheva', r., Isr.	181a	31.23N	34.30E
Beestekraal, S. Afr.	218d	25.22S	27.34E
Beeston, Eng., U.K. (bēs′t′n)	144a	52.55N	1.11W
Beetz, r., Ger. (bětz)	145b	52.28N	12.37E
Beeville, Tx., U.S. (bē′vĭl)	113	28.24N	97.44W
Bega, Austl. (bā′gá)	203	36.50S	149.49E
Beggs, Ok., U.S. (běgz)	111	35.46N	96.06W
Bègles, Fr. (bě′gl′)	156	44.47N	0.34W
Begoro, Ghana	214	6.23N	0.23W
Behala, India	186a	22.31N	88.19E
Behbehān, Iran	185	30.35N	50.14E
Behm Canal, can., Ak., U.S.	86	55.41N	131.35W
Bei, r., China (bā)	191a	22.54N	113.08E
Bei'an, China (bā-än)	192	48.05N	126.26E
Beicai, China (bā-tsī)	191b	31.12N	121.33E
Beifei, r., China (bā-fā)	190	33.14N	117.03E
Beihai, China (bā-hī)	188	21.30N	109.10E
Beihuangcheng Dao, i., China (bā-hůäŋ-chŭŋ dou)	190	38.23N	120.55E
Beijing, China	189	39.55N	116.23E
Beijing Shi, China (bā-jyĭŋ shr)	192	40.07N	116.00E
Beira, Moz. (bā′rá)	212	19.45N	34.58E
Beira, hist. reg., Port. (bě′y-rä)	158	40.38N	8.00W
Beirut, Leb. (bā-ro͞ot′)	182	33.53N	35.30E
Beiyuan, China	240b	40.01N	116.24E
Beja, Port. (bä′zhä)	148	38.03N	7.53W
Béja, Tun.	148	36.52N	9.20E
Bejaïa (Bougie), Alg.	210	36.46N	5.00E
Bejar, Spain	158	40.25N	5.43W
Bejestān, Iran	182	34.30N	58.22E
Bejucal, Cuba (bā-ho͞o-käl′)	122	22.56N	82.23W
Bejuco, Pan. (bě-ko͞o′kō)	121	8.37N	79.54W
Békés, Hung. (bā′kāsh)	155	46.45N	21.08E
Békéscsaba, Hung. (bā′kāsh-chô′bô)	149	46.39N	21.06E
Beketova, Russia (běkě-to′vá)	171	53.23N	125.21E
Bela Crkva, Yugo. (bě′lä tsěrk′vä)	161	44.53N	21.25E
Bel Air, Va., U.S.	229d	38.52N	77.10W
Bel Air, neigh., Ca., U.S.	232	34.05N	118.27W
Belalcázar, Spain (bāl-á-kä′thär)	158	38.35N	5.12W
Belarus, nation, Eur.	164	53.30N	25.33E
Belas, Port.	238d	38.47N	9.16W
Belau see Palau, dep., Oc.	2	7.15N	134.30W
Bela Vista, neigh., Braz.	234d	23.33S	46.38W
Bela Vista de Goiás, Braz.	131	16.57S	48.47W
Belawan, Indon. (bá-lä′wän)	196	3.43N	98.43E
Belaya, r., Russia (byě′lĭ-yá)	167	52.30N	56.15E
Belcher Islands, is., Can. (běl′chẽr)	85	56.20N	80.40W
Belding, Mi., U.S. (běl′dĭng)	98	43.05N	85.25W
Belebey, Russia (byě′lě-bā′ĭ)	166	54.00N	54.10E
Belém, Braz. (bå-lěN′)	131	1.18S	48.27W
Belém, neigh., Port.	238d	38.42N	9.12W
Belén, Para. (bā-lān′)	132	23.30S	57.09W
Belen, N.M., U.S. (bě-lån′)	109	34.40N	106.45W
Belènzinho, neigh., Braz.	234d	23.32S	46.35W
Bélep, Îles, is., N. Cal.	203	19.30S	164.00E
Belëv, Russia (byěl′yěf)	166	53.49N	36.06E
Belfair, Wa., U.S. (běl′far)	106a	47.27N	122.50W
Belfast, N. Ire., U.K.	142	54.36N	5.45W
Belfast, Me., U.S. (běl′fást)	92	44.25N	69.01W
Belfast, Lough, b., N. Ire., U.K. (lŏk běl′fást)	150	54.45N	6.00W
Belford Roxo, Braz.	132b	22.46S	43.24W
Belfort, Fr. (bā-fôr′)	147	47.40N	7.50E
Belgaum, India	183	15.57N	74.32E
Belgium, nation, Eur. (běl′jĭ-ŭm)	142	51.00N	2.52E
Belgorod, Russia (byěl′gŭ-rŭt)	167	50.36N	36.32E
Belgorod, prov., Russia	163	50.40N	36.42E
Belgrade (Beograd), Yugo.	142	44.48N	20.32E
Belgrano, neigh., Arg.	233d	34.34S	58.28W
Belgrave, Austl.	243b	37.55S	145.21E
Belhaven, N.C., U.S. (běl′hā-vĕn)	115	35.33N	76.37W
Belington, W.V., U.S. (běl′ĭng-tŭn)	99	39.00N	79.55W
Belitung, i., Indon.	196	3.30S	107.30E
Belize, nation, N.A.	116	17.00N	88.40W
Belize, r., Belize	120a	17.16N	88.56W
Belize City, Belize (bě-lēz′)	116	17.31N	88.10W
Bel'kovo, Russia (byěl′kô-vô)	172b	56.15N	38.49E
Bel'kovskiy, i., Russia (byěl-kôf′skĭ)	171	75.45N	137.00E
Bell, Ca., U.S.	232	33.58N	118.11W
Bell, i., Can. (běl)	93	50.45N	55.35W
Bell, r., Can.	91	49.25N	77.15W
Bella Bella, Can.	86	52.10N	128.07W
Bella Coola, Can.	86	52.22N	126.46W
Bellaire, Oh., U.S. (běl-âr′)	98	40.00N	80.45W
Bellaire, Tx., U.S.	113a	29.43N	95.28W
Bellary, India (běl-lä′rē)	183	15.15N	76.56E

264 Bella Union–Betsiamites

PLACE (Pronunciation)	PAGE	Lat. °′	Long. °′
Bella Union, Ur. (bĕ'l-yä-ōō-nyô'n)	132	30.18S	57.26W
Bella Vista, Arg.	132	28.35S	58.53W
Bella Vista, Arg. (bä'lyä vēs'tä)	132	27.07S	65.14W
Bella Vista, Arg.	132a	34.35S	58.41W
Bellavista, Chile	234b	33.31S	70.37W
Bella Vista, Para.	131	22.16S	56.14W
Bellavista, Peru	233c	12.04S	77.08W
Belle-Anse, Haiti	123	18.15N	72.00W
Belle Bay, b., Can. (bĕl)	93	47.35N	55.15W
Belle Chasse, La., U.S. (bĕl shäs')	100d	29.52N	90.00W
Belle Farm Estates, Md., U.S.	229c	39.23N	76.45W
Bellefontaine, Oh., U.S. (bel-fŏn'tån)	98	40.25N	83.50W
Bellefontaine Neighbors, Mo., U.S.	107e	38.46N	90.13W
Belle Fourche, S.D., U.S. (bĕl' fōōrsh')	102	44.28N	103.50W
Belle Fourche, r., Wy., U.S.	102	44.29N	104.40W
Belle Fourche Reservoir, res., S.D., U.S.	102	44.51N	103.44W
Bellegarde, Fr. (bĕl-gärd')	157	46.06N	5.50E
Belle Glade, Fl., U.S. (bĕl glād)	115a	26.39N	80.37W
Bellehaven, Va., U.S.	229d	38.47N	77.04W
Belle-Île, i., Fr. (bĕlēl')	147	47.15N	3.30W
Belle Isle, Strait of, strt., Can.	85	51.35N	56.30W
Belle Mead, N.J., U.S. (bĕl mēd)	100a	40.28N	74.40W
Belleoram, Can.	93	47.31N	55.25W
Belle Plaine, Ia., U.S. (bĕl plān')	103	41.52N	92.19W
Bellerose, N.Y., U.S.	228	40.44N	73.43W
Belle Vernon, Pa., U.S. (bĕl vûr'nŭn)	101e	40.08N	79.52W
Belleville, Can. (bĕl'vĭl)	91	44.15N	77.25W
Belleville, Il., U.S.	107e	38.31N	89.59W
Belleville, Ks., U.S.	111	39.49N	97.37W
Belleville, Mi., U.S.	101b	42.12N	83.29W
Belleville, N.J., U.S.	100a	40.47N	74.09W
Bellevue, Ia., U.S. (bĕl'vū)	103	42.14N	90.26W
Bellevue, Ky., U.S.	101f	39.06N	84.29W
Bellevue, Mi., U.S.	98	42.30N	85.00W
Bellevue, Oh., U.S.	98	41.15N	82.45W
Bellevue, Pa., U.S.	101e	40.30N	80.04W
Bellevue, Wa., U.S.	106a	47.37N	122.12W
Belley, Fr. (bĕ-lē')	157	45.46N	5.41E
Bellflower, Ca., U.S. (bĕl-flou'ẽr)	107a	33.53N	118.08W
Bell Gardens, Ca., U.S.	107a	33.59N	118.11W
Bellingham, Ma., U.S. (bĕl'ĭng-hăm)	93a	42.05N	71.28W
Bellingham, Wa., U.S.	96	48.46N	122.29W
Bellingham Bay, b., Wa., U.S.	106d	48.44N	122.34W
Bellingshausen Sea, sea, Ant. (bĕl'ĭngz houz'n)	219	72.00S	80.30W
Bellinzona, Switz. (bĕl-ĭn-tsō'nä)	154	46.10N	9.09E
Bellmawr, N.J., U.S.	229b	39.51N	75.06W
Bellmore, N.Y., U.S. (bĕl-mōr)	100a	40.40N	73.31W
Bello, Col. (bĕ'l-yô)	130	6.20N	75.33W
Bello, Cuba	233b	23.07N	82.24W
Bellow Falls, Vt., U.S. (bĕl'ōz fôls)	99	43.10N	72.30W
Bellpat, Pak.	186	29.08N	68.00E
Bell Peninsula, pen., Can.	85	63.50N	81.16W
Bells Corners, Can.	83c	45.20N	75.49W
Bells Mountain, mtn., Wa., U.S. (bĕls)	106c	45.50N	122.21W
Belluno, Italy (bĕl-lōō'nō)	160	46.08N	12.14E
Bell Ville, Arg. (bĕl vēl')	132	32.33S	62.36W
Bellville, S. Afr.	212a	33.54S	18.38E
Bellville, Tx., U.S. (bĕl'vĭl)	113	29.57N	96.15W
Bellwood, Il., U.S.	231a	41.53N	87.52W
Bélmez, Spain (bĕl'mĕth)	158	38.17N	5.17W
Belmond, Ia., U.S. (bĕl'mŏnd)	103	42.49N	93.37W
Belmont, Ca., U.S.	106b	37.34N	122.18W
Belmont, Ma., U.S.	227a	42.24N	71.10W
Belmonte, Braz. (bĕl-mōn'tä)	131	15.58S	38.47W
Belmopan, Belize	116	17.15N	88.47W
Belmore, Austl.	243a	33.55S	151.05E
Belogorsk, Russia	165	51.09N	128.32E
Belo Horizonte, Braz. (bĕ'lôre-sô'n-tĕ)	131	19.54S	43.56W
Beloit, Ks., U.S. (bē-loit')	110	39.26N	98.06W
Beloit, Wi., U.S.	97	42.31N	89.04W
Belomorsk, Russia (byĕl-ō-môrsk')	166	64.30N	34.42E
Beloretsk, Russia (byĕ'lō-rĕtsk)	166	53.58N	58.25E
Belosarayskaya, Kosa, c., Ukr.	163	46.43N	37.18E
Belot, Cuba	233b	23.08N	82.19W
Belovo, Russia (byĕ'lŭ-vû)	170	54.25N	86.18E
Beloye, l., Russia	166	60.10N	38.05E
Belozersk, Russia (byĕ-lŭ-zyôrsk')	166	60.00N	38.00E
Belper, Eng., U.K. (bĕl'pẽr)	144a	53.01N	1.28W
Belt, Mt., U.S. (bĕlt)	105	47.11N	110.58W
Belt Creek, r., Mt., U.S.	105	47.19N	110.58W
Belton, Tx., U.S. (bĕl'tŭn)	113	31.04N	97.27W
Belton Lake, l., Tx., U.S.	113	31.15N	97.35W
Beltsville, Md., U.S. (belts-vĭl)	100e	39.03N	76.56W
Belukha, Gora, mtn., Asia	164	49.47N	86.23E
Belvedere, Ca., U.S.	231b	37.52N	122.28W
Belvedere, Va., U.S.	229d	38.50N	77.10W
Belvedere, neigh., Eng., U.K.	235	51.29N	0.09E
Belvedere, pt. of i., Aus.	239e	48.11N	16.23E
Belvidere, Il., U.S. (bĕl-vē-dēr')	103	42.14N	88.52W
Belvidere, N.J., U.S.	99	40.50N	75.05W
Belyando, r., Austl. (bĕl-yän'dō)	203	22.09S	146.48E
Belyanka, Russia (byĕl'yan-kȧ)	172a	56.04N	59.16E
Belynichi, Bela. (byĕl-ĭ-nĭ'chĭ)	162	54.02N	29.42E
Belyy, Russia (byĕ'lē)	166	55.52N	32.58E
Belyy, i., Russia	164	73.19N	72.00E
Belyye Stolby, Russia (byĕ'lĭ-ye stôl'bĭ)	172b	55.20N	37.52E
Belzig, Ger. (bĕl'tsēg)	145b	52.08N	12.35E
Belzoni, Ms., U.S. (bĕl-zō'nē)	114	33.09N	90.30W
Bembe, Ang. (bĕn'bĕ)	212	7.00S	14.20E
Bembézar, r., Spain (bĕm-bā-thär')	158	38.00N	5.18W
Bemidji, Mn., U.S. (bē-mĭj'ĭ)	103	47.28N	94.54W
Bena Dibele, Zaire (bĕn'á dē-bĕ'lē)	212	4.00S	22.49E
Benalla, Austl. (bĕn-ăl'á)	203	36.30S	146.00E
Benares see Vārānasi, India	183	25.25N	83.00E
Benavente, Spain (bā-nä-vĕn'tä)	148	42.01N	5.43W
Ben Avon, Pa., U.S.	230b	40.31N	80.05W
Benbrook, Tx., U.S. (bĕn'brōōk)	107c	32.41N	97.27W
Benbrook Reservoir, res., Tx., U.S.	107c	32.35N	97.30W
Bend, Or., U.S. (bĕnd)	96	44.04N	121.17W
Bendeleben, Mount, mtn., Ak., U.S. (bĕn-dĕl-bĕn)	95	65.18N	163.45W
Bender Beyla, Som.	218a	9.40N	50.45E
Bendigo, Austl. (bĕn'dĭ-gō)	203	36.39S	144.20E
Benedict, Md., U.S. (bĕnĕ'dĭct)	100e	38.31N	76.41W
Benešov, Czech Rep. (bĕn'ĕ-shôf)	154	49.48N	14.40E
Benevento, Italy (bā-nā-vĕn'tō)	148	41.08N	14.46E
Benfica, neigh., Braz.	234c	22.53S	43.15W
Benfica, neigh., Port.	238d	38.45N	9.12W
Bengal, Bay of, b., Asia (bĕn-gôl')	180	17.30N	87.00E
Bengamisa, Zaire	217	0.57N	25.10E
Bengbu, China (bŭŋ-bōō)	189	32.52N	117.22E
Benghazi see Banghāzī, Libya	210	32.07N	20.04E
Bengkalis, Indon. (bĕng-kä'lĭs)	196	1.29N	102.06E
Bengkulu, Indon.	196	3.46S	102.18E
Benguela, Ang. (bĕn-gĕl'ȧ)	212	12.35S	13.25E
Beni, r., Bol. (bā'nē)	130	13.41S	67.30W
Béni-Abbas, Alg. (bā'nē ă-bĕs')	210	30.11N	2.13W
Benicia, Ca., U.S. (bē-nĭsh'ĭ-ȧ)	106b	38.03N	122.09W
Benin, nation, Afr.	210	8.00N	2.00E
Benin, r., Nig. (bĕn-ēn')	215	5.55N	5.15E
Benin, Bight of, bt., Afr.	210	5.30N	3.00E
Benin City, Nig.	210	6.19N	5.41E
Beni Saf, Alg. (bā'nē säf')	210	35.23N	1.20W
Benito, r., Eq. Gui.	216	1.35N	10.45E
Benkelman, Ne., U.S. (bĕn-kĕl-mȧn)	110	40.05N	101.35W
Benkovac, Cro. (bĕn'kō-vȧts)	160	44.02N	15.41E
Bennettsville, S.C., U.S. (bĕn'ĕts vĭl)	115	34.35N	79.41W
Bennettswood, Austl.	243b	37.51S	145.07E
Benninghofen, neigh., Ger.	236	51.29N	7.31E
Bennington, Vt., U.S. (bĕn'ĭng-tŭn)	99	42.55N	73.15W
Benns Church, Va., U.S. (bĕnz' chûrch')	100g	36.47N	76.35W
Benoni, S. Afr. (bĕ-nō'nĭ)	212	26.11S	28.19E
Benoni South, S. Afr.	244b	26.13S	28.18E
Benoy, Chad	215	8.59N	16.19E
Benque Viejo, Belize (bĕn-kĕ biĕ'hō)	120a	17.07N	89.07W
Benrath, neigh., Ger.	236	51.10N	6.52E
Bensberg, Ger.	157c	50.58N	7.09E
Bensenville, Il., U.S. (bĕn'sĕn-vĭl)	101a	41.57N	87.56W
Bensheim, Ger. (bĕns-hīm)	154	49.42N	8.38E
Benson, Az., U.S. (bĕn-sŭn)	109	32.00N	110.20W
Benson, Mn., U.S.	102	45.18N	95.36W
Bentiaba, Ang.	216	14.15S	12.21E
Bentleigh, Austl.	243b	37.55S	145.02E
Bentleyville, Pa., U.S. (bent'lē vĭl)	101e	40.07N	80.01W
Benton, Can.	92	45.59N	67.36W
Benton, Ar., U.S. (bĕn'tŭn)	111	34.34N	92.34W
Benton, Ca., U.S.	108	37.44N	118.22W
Benton, Il., U.S.	98	38.00N	88.55W
Benton Harbor, Mi., U.S. (bĕn'tŭn här'bẽr)	98	42.05N	86.30W
Bentonville, Ar., U.S. (bĕn'tŭn-vĭl)	111	36.22N	94.11W
Benue, r., Afr. (bā'nōō-ā)	210	8.00N	8.00E
Benut, r., Malay.	181b	1.43N	103.20E
Benwood, W.V., U.S. (bĕn-wŏd)	98	39.55N	80.45W
Benxi, China (bŭn-shyē)	192	41.25N	123.50E
Beograd see Belgrade, Yugo.	142	44.48N	20.32E
Beppu, Japan (bĕ'pōō)	195	33.16N	131.30E
Bequia Island, i., St. Vin. (bĕk-ē'ä)	121b	13.00N	61.08W
Berakit, Tanjung, c., Indon.	181b	1.16N	104.44E
Berat, Alb. (bĕ-rät')	161	40.43N	19.59E
Berau, Teluk, b., Indon.	197	2.22S	131.40E
Berazategui, Arg. (bĕ-rä-zá'tē-gē)	132a	34.46S	58.14W
Berbera, Som. (bûr'bûr-ȧ)	218a	10.25N	45.05E
Berbérati, Cen. Afr. Rep.	215	4.16N	15.47E
Berchum, Ger.	236	51.23N	7.32E
Berck, Fr. (bĕrk)	156	50.26N	1.36E
Berdyans'k, Ukr.	167	46.45N	36.47E
Berdyans'ka kosa, c., Ukr.	163	46.38N	36.42E
Berdyaush, Russia (bĕr'dyàûsh)	172a	55.10N	59.12E
Berdychiv, Ukr.	164	49.53N	28.32E
Berea, Ky., U.S. (bē-rē'ȧ)	114	37.30N	84.19W
Berea, Oh., U.S.	101d	41.22N	81.51W
Berehove, Ukr.	155	48.13N	22.40E
Bereku, Tan.	217	4.27S	35.44E
Berens, r., Can. (bĕr'ĕnz)	89	52.15N	96.30W
Berens Island, i., Can.	89	52.18N	97.40W
Berens River, Can.	84	52.22N	97.02W
Beresford, S.D., U.S. (bĕr'ĕs-fẽrd)	102	43.05N	96.46W
Berettyóújfalu, Hung. (bĕ'rĕt-tyō-ōō'y'fō-lōō)	155	47.14N	21.33E
Berëza, Bela. (bĕ-rä'zȧ)	155	52.29N	24.59E
Berezhany, Ukr. (bĕr-yĕ'zhä-nĕ)	155	49.25N	24.58E
Berezina, r., Bela. (bĕr-yĕ'zē-nȧ)	162	53.20N	29.05E
Berezino, Bela. (bĕr-yä'zē-nô)	162	53.51N	28.54E
Berezivka, Ukr.	163	47.12N	30.56E
Berezna, Ukr. (bĕr-yôz'nȧ)	163	51.32N	31.47E
Bereznehuvate, Ukr.	163	47.19N	32.58E
Berezniki, Russia (bĕr-yôz'nyē-kē)	166	59.25N	56.46E
Berëzovka, Russia	172a	57.35N	57.19E
Berëzovo, Russia (bĭr-yô'zē-vû)	164	64.10N	65.10E
Berëzovskiy, Russia (bĕr-yô'zôf-skĭ)	172a	56.54N	60.47E
Berga, Spain (bĕr'gä)	159	42.05N	1.52E
Bergama, Tur. (bĕr'gä-mä)	182	39.08N	27.09E
Bergamo, Italy (bĕr'gä-mō)	148	45.43N	9.41E
Bergantin, Ven. (bĕr-gän-tē'n)	131b	10.04N	64.23W
Bergedorf, Ger. (bĕr'gĕ-dôrf)	145c	53.29N	10.12E
Bergen, Ger. (bĕr'gĕn)	154	54.26N	13.26E
Bergen, Nor.	142	60.24N	5.20E
Bergenfield, N.J., U.S.	100a	40.55N	73.59W
Bergen op Zoom, Neth.	151	51.29N	4.16E
Bergerac, Fr. (bĕr-zhĕ-rák')	147	44.49N	0.28E
Bergfelde, Ger.	238a	52.40N	13.19E
Berghausen, Ger.	236	51.18N	7.17E
Bergholtz, N.Y., U.S.	230a	43.06N	78.53W
Bergisch-Born, Ger.	236	51.09N	7.15E
Bergisch Gladbach, Ger. (bĕrg'ĭsh-glät'bäk)	157c	50.59N	7.08E
Bergkamen, Ger.	236	51.38N	7.38E
Berglern, Ger. (bĕrgh'lĕrn)	145d	48.24N	11.55E
Bergneustadt, Ger.	157c	51.01N	7.39E
Bergville, S. Afr. (bĕrg'vĭl)	213c	28.46S	29.22E
Berhampur, India	183	19.19N	84.48E
Bering Sea, sea (bē'rĭng)	224	58.00N	175.00W
Bering Strait, strt.	96a	64.50N	169.50W
Berja, Spain (bĕr'hä)	158	36.50N	2.56W
Berkeley, Ca., U.S. (bûrk'lĭ)	96	37.52N	122.17W
Berkeley, Il., U.S.	231a	41.53N	87.55W
Berkeley, Mo., U.S.	107e	38.45N	90.20W
Berkeley Hills, Pa., U.S.	230b	40.32N	80.00W
Berkeley Springs, W.V., U.S. (bûrk'lĭ springz)	99	39.40N	78.10W
Berkhamsted, Eng., U.K. (bĕk'hȧm'stĕd)	144b	51.44N	0.34W
Berkhamsted, Eng., U.K.	235	51.46N	0.35W
Berkley, Mi., U.S. (bûrk'lĭ)	101b	42.30N	83.10W
Berkovitsa, Bul. (bĕ-kō'vē-tsȧ)	161	43.14N	23.08E
Berkshire, co., Eng., U.K.	144b	51.23N	1.07W
Berland, r., Can.	87	54.00N	117.10W
Berlenga, is., Port. (bĕr-lĕn'gäzh)	158	39.25N	9.33W
Berlin, Ger. (bĕr-lēn')	142	52.31N	13.28E
Berlin, S. Afr. (bĕr-lĭn)	213c	32.53S	27.36E
Berlin, N.H., U.S. (bûr-lĭn)	99	44.25N	71.10W
Berlin, N.J., U.S.	100f	39.47N	74.56W
Berlin, Wi., U.S. (bûr-lĭn')	103	43.58N	88.58W
Berlin-Tempelhof, Zentral Flughafen, arpt., Ger.	238a	52.29N	13.25E
Bermejo, r., S.A. (bĕr-mā'hō)	132	25.05S	61.00W
Bermeo, Spain (bĕr-mā'yō)	158	43.23N	2.43W
Bermuda, dep., N.A.	117	32.20N	65.45W
Bern, Switz. (bĕrn)	142	46.55N	7.25E
Bernal, Arg. (bĕr-näl')	132a	34.43S	58.17W
Bernalillo, N.M., U.S. (bĕr-nä-lē'yō)	109	35.20N	106.30W
Bernard, l., Can. (bĕr-närd')	99	45.45N	79.25W
Bernardsville, N.J., U.S. (bûr nārds'vĭl)	100a	40.43N	74.34W
Bernau, Ger. (bĕr'nou)	154	52.40N	13.35E
Bernburg, Ger. (bĕrn'bŏrgh)	154	51.48N	11.43E
Berndorf, Aus. (bĕrn'dôrf)	154	47.57N	16.05E
Berne, In., U.S. (bûrn)	98	40.40N	84.55W
Berner Alpen, mts., Switz.	154	46.29N	7.30E
Bernier, i., Austl. (bĕr-nēr')	202	24.58S	113.15E
Bernina, Pizzo, mtn., Eur.	154	46.23N	9.58E
Bero, r., Ang.	216	15.10S	12.20E
Beroun, Czech Rep. (bā'rōn)	154	49.57N	14.03E
Berounka, r., Czech Rep. (bĕ-rōn'kȧ)	154	49.53N	13.40E
Berowra, Austl.	201b	33.36S	151.10E
Berre, Étang de, l., Fr. (ā-tôɴ' dĕ bâr')	156a	43.27N	5.07E
Berre-l'Étang, Fr. (bâr'lā-tôɴ')	156a	43.28N	5.11E
Berriozabal, Mex. (bā'rēō-zä-bäl')	119	16.47N	93.16W
Berriyyane, Alg.	148	32.50N	3.49E
Berry Creek, r., Can.	88	51.15N	111.40W
Berryessa, r., Ca., U.S. (bĕ'rĭ ĕs'ȧ)	108	38.35N	122.33W
Berry Islands, is., Bah.	122	25.40N	77.50W
Berryville, Ar., U.S. (bĕr'ē-vĭl)	111	36.21N	93.34W
Bershad', Ukr. (byĕr'shät)	163	48.22N	29.31E
Berthier, Can.	83b	46.56N	70.44W
Bertlich, Ger.	236	51.37N	7.04E
Bertrand, r., Wa., U.S. (bûr'trȧnd)	106d	48.58N	122.31W
Berwick, Pa., U.S. (bûr'wĭk)	99	41.05N	76.10W
Berwick-upon-Tweed, Eng., U.K. (bûr'ĭk)	146	55.45N	2.01W
Berwyn, Il., U.S. (bûr'wĭn)	101a	41.49N	87.47W
Berwyn Heights, Md., U.S.	229d	38.59N	76.54W
Beryslav, Ukr.	163	46.49N	33.24E
Besalampy, Madag. (bĕz-á-lám-pē')	213	16.48S	44.40E
Besançon, Fr. (bĕ-säɴ-sôn)	147	47.14N	6.02E
Besar, Gunong, mtn., Malay.	181b	2.31N	103.09E
Besed', r., Eur. (byĕ'syĕt)	162	52.58N	31.36E
Besedy, Russia	239b	55.37N	37.47E
Beshenkovichi, Bela. (byĕ'shĕn-kōvē'chĭ)	162	55.04N	29.29E
Beskid Mountains, mts., Eur.	155	49.23N	19.00E
Beskra, Alg.	210	34.52N	5.39E
Beskudnikovo, neigh., Russia	239b	55.52N	37.34E
Beslan, Russia	168	43.12N	44.33E
Besós, r., Spain	238e	41.25N	2.12E
Bessarabia, hist. reg., Mol.	163	47.00N	28.30E
Bességes, Fr. (bĕ-sĕzh')	156	44.20N	4.07E
Bessemer, Al., U.S. (bĕs'ē-mẽr)	100h	33.24N	86.58W
Bessemer, Mi., U.S.	103	46.29N	90.04W
Bessemer City, N.C., U.S.	115	35.16N	81.17W
Bestensee, Ger. (bĕs'tĕn-zā)	145b	52.15N	13.39E
Betanzos, Spain (bĕ-tän'thōs)	158	43.18N	8.14W
Betatakin Ruin, Az., U.S. (bĕt-ȧ-tăk'ĭn)	109	36.40N	110.29W
Bethal, S. Afr. (bĕth'ăl)	218d	26.27S	29.28E
Bethalto, Il., U.S. (bȧ-thăl'tō)	107e	38.54N	90.03W
Bethanien, Nmb.	212	26.20S	16.10E
Bethany, Mo., U.S.	111	40.15N	94.04W
Bethel, Ak., U.S. (bĕth'ĕl)	96a	60.50N	161.50W
Bethel, Ct., U.S.	100a	41.22N	73.24W
Bethel, Vt., U.S.	99	43.50N	72.40W
Bethel Park, Pa., U.S.	101e	40.19N	80.02W
Bethesda, Md., U.S. (bĕ-thĕs'dȧ)	100e	39.00N	77.10W
Bethlehem, S. Afr.	212	28.14S	28.18E
Bethlehem, Pa., U.S. (bĕth'lē-hĕm)	99	40.40N	75.25W
Bethlehem see Bayt Lahm, W. Bank	181a	31.42N	35.13E
Bethnal Green, neigh., Eng., U.K.	235	51.32N	0.03W
Bethpage, N.Y., U.S.	228	40.45N	73.29W
Béthune, Fr. (bā-tün')	156	50.32N	2.37E
Betroka, Madag. (bĕ-trŏk'ȧ)	213	23.13S	46.17E
Betsham, Eng., U.K.	235	51.25N	0.19E
Bet She'an, Isr.	181a	32.30N	35.30E
Betsiamites, Can.	85	48.57N	68.36W
Betsiamites, r., Can.	92	49.11N	69.20W

ăt; finăl; rāte; senāte; ärm; ȧsk; sofȧ; fâre; ch-choose; dh-as th in other; bē; ēvent; bĕt; recĕnt; cratẽr; g-gō; gh-guttural g; bĭt; ĭ-short neutral; rīde; ĸ-guttural k as ch in German ich;

PRONOUNCING INDEX Betsiboka–Black Volta (Volta Noire) 265

PLACE (Pronunciation)	PAGE	Lat. °′	Long. °′
Betsiboka, r., Madag. (bĕt-sĭ-bō'kȧ)	213	16.47S	46.45E
Bettles Field, Ak., U.S. (bĕt'tŭls)	95	66.58N	151.48W
Betwa, r., India (bĕt'wȧ)	183	25.00N	78.00E
Betz, Fr. (bĕ)	157b	49.09N	2.58E
Beveren, Bel.	145a	51.13N	4.14E
B. Everett Jordan Lake, res., N.C., U.S.	115	35.45N	79.00W
Beverly, Ma., U.S.	93a	42.34N	70.53W
Beverly, N.J., U.S.	100f	40.03N	74.56W
Beverly Hills, Austl.	243a	33.57S	151.05E
Beverly Hills, Ca., U.S.	107a	34.05N	118.24W
Beverly Hills, Mi., U.S.	230c	42.32N	83.15W
Bevier, Mo., U.S. (bė-vēr')	111	39.44N	92.36W
Bewdley, Eng., U.K. (būd'lĭ)	144a	52.22N	2.19W
Bexhill, Eng., U.K. (bĕks'hĭl)	151	50.49N	0.25E
Bexley, Austl.	243a	33.57S	151.08E
Bexley, Eng., U.K. (bĕks'ly)	144b	51.26N	0.09E
Beyenburg, neigh., Ger.	236	51.15N	7.18E
Beyla, Gui. (bā'lȧ)	210	8.41N	8.37W
Beylerbeyi, neigh., Tur.	239f	41.03N	29.03E
Beylul, Erit.	211	13.15N	42.21E
Beyoğlu, neigh., Tur.	239f	41.02N	28.59E
Beypazari, Tur. (bā-pȧ-zä'rĭ)	149	40.10N	31.40E
Beyşehir, Tur.	167	38.00N	31.45E
Beysugskiy, Liman, b., Russia (lĭ-män' bĕy-so͞og'skĭ)	163	46.07N	38.35E
Bezhetsk, Russia (byĕ-zhĕtsk')	166	57.46N	36.40E
Bezhitsa, Russia (byĕ-zhĭ'tsȧ)	166	53.19N	34.18E
Béziers, Fr. (bā-zyā')	147	43.21N	3.12E
Bezons, Fr.	237c	48.56N	2.13E
Bhadreswar, India	186a	22.49N	88.22E
Bhāgalpur, India (bä'gŭl-pȯr)	183	25.15N	86.59E
Bhalswa, neigh., India	240d	28.44N	77.10E
Bhamo, Myanmar (bŭ-mō')	183	24.00N	96.15E
Bhāngar, India	186a	22.30N	88.36E
Bharatpur, India (bērt'pȯr)	183	27.21N	77.33E
Bhatinda, India (bŭ-tĭn-dȧ)	183	30.19N	74.56E
Bhātpāra, India	183	22.52N	88.24E
Bhaunagar, India (bäv-nŭg'ŭr)	183	21.45N	72.58E
Bhayandar, India	187b	19.20N	72.50E
Bhilai, India	186	21.14N	81.23E
Bhīma, r., India (bē'mȧ)	183	18.00N	74.45E
Bhiwandi, India	187b	19.18N	73.03E
Bhiwāni, India	186	28.53N	76.08E
Bhopāl, India (bō-päl)	183	23.20N	77.25E
Bhopura, India	240d	28.42N	77.20E
Bhubaneswar, India (bȯ-bû-nāsh'vûr)	183	20.21N	85.53E
Bhuj, India (bo͞oj)	183	23.22N	69.39E
Bhutan, nation, Asia (bo͞o-tän')	183	27.15N	90.30E
Biafra, Bight of, bt., Afr.	210	4.05N	7.10E
Biak, i., Indon. (bē'äk)	197	1.00S	136.00E
Biała Podlaska, Pol. (byä'wä pōd-läs'kä)	155	52.01N	23.08E
Białogard, Pol.	154	54.00N	16.01E
Bialystok, Pol. (byä-wĭs'tōk)	142	53.08N	23.12E
Biankouma, C. Iv.	214	7.44N	7.37W
Biarritz, Fr. (byä-rēts')	147	43.27N	1.39W
Bibb City, Ga., U.S. (bĭb' sĭ'tė)	114	32.31N	84.56W
Biberach, Ger. (bē'bēräk)	154	48.06N	9.49E
Bibiani, Ghana	214	6.28N	2.20W
Bic, Can. (bĭk)	92	48.22N	68.42W
Bickerstaffe, Eng., U.K.	237a	53.32N	2.50W
Bickley, neigh., Eng., U.K.	235	51.24N	0.03E
Bicknell, In., U.S. (bĭk'nĕl)	98	38.45N	87.20W
Bicske, Hung. (bĭsh'kė)	155	47.29N	18.38E
Bida, Nig. (bē'dä)	210	9.05N	6.01E
Biddeford, Me., U.S. (bĭd'ė-fērd)	92	43.29N	70.29W
Biddulph, Eng., U.K. (bĭd'ŭlf)	144a	53.07N	2.10W
Bidston, Eng., U.K.	237a	53.24N	3.05W
Biebrza, r., Pol. (byĕb'zhȧ)	155	53.18N	22.25E
Biel, Switz. (bēl)	154	47.09N	7.12E
Bielefeld, Ger. (bē'lĕ-fĕlt)	147	52.01N	8.35E
Biella, Italy (byĕl'lä)	160	45.34N	8.05E
Bielsk Podlaski, Pol. (byĕlsk pŭd-lä'skĭ)	147	52.47N	23.14E
Bien Hoa, Viet.	196	10.59N	106.49E
Bienville, Lac, l., Can.	85	55.32N	72.45W
Biesenthal, Ger. (bē'sĕn-täl)	145b	52.46N	13.38E
Bièvres, Fr.	237c	48.45N	2.13E
Biferno, r., Italy (bē-fĕr'nō)	160	41.49N	14.46E
Bifoum, Gabon	216	0.22S	10.23E
Biga, Tur. (bē'ghȧ)	161	40.13N	27.14E
Big Bay de Noc, Mi., U.S. (bĭg bā dė nok')	103	45.48N	86.41W
Big Bayou, Ar., U.S. (bĭg'bī'yo͞o)	111	33.04N	91.28W
Big Bear City, Ca., U.S. (bĭg bâr)	107a	34.16N	116.51W
Big Belt Mountains, mts., Mt., U.S. (bĭg bĕlt)	96	46.53N	111.43W
Big Bend Dam, S.D., U.S. (bĭg bĕnd)	102	44.11N	99.33W
Big Bend National Park, rec., Tx., U.S.	96	29.15N	103.15W
Big Black, r., Ms., U.S. (bĭg blăk)	114	32.05N	90.49W
Big Blue, r., Ne., U.S. (bĭg blo͞o)	111	40.53N	97.00W
Big Canyon, Tx., U.S. (bĭg kăn'yŭn)	112	30.27N	102.19W
Big Creek, r., Oh., U.S.	229a	41.27N	81.41W
Big Cypress Indian Reservation, I.R., Fl., U.S.	115a	26.19N	81.11W
Big Cypress Swamp, sw., Fl., U.S. (bĭg sī'prĕs)	115a	26.02N	81.20W
Big Delta, Ak., U.S. (bĭg dĕl'tȧ)	95	64.08N	145.48W
Big Fork, r., Mn., U.S. (bĭg fôrk)	103	48.08N	93.47W
Biggar, Can.	84	52.04N	108.00W
Biggin Hill, neigh., Eng., U.K.	235	51.18N	0.04E
Big Hole, r., Mt., U.S. (bĭg hōl)	105	45.53N	113.15W
Big Hole National Battlefield, Mt., U.S. (bĭg hōl băt''l-fēld)	105	45.44N	113.35W
Bighorn, r., U.S.	96	45.30N	108.00W
Bighorn Lake, res., Mt., U.S.	105	45.00N	108.10W
Bighorn Mountains, mts., U.S. (bĭg hôrn)	96	44.47N	107.40W
Big Island, i., Can.	89	49.10N	94.40W
Big Lake, Wa., U.S. (bĭg lāk)	106a	48.24N	122.14W
Big Lake, l., Can.	83g	53.35N	113.47W
Big Lake, l., Wa., U.S.	106a	48.24N	122.14W
Big Lost, r., Id., U.S. (lŏst)	105	43.56N	113.38W
Big Mossy Point, c., Can.	89	53.45N	97.50W
Big Muddy, r., Il., U.S.	98	37.50N	89.00W
Big Muddy Creek, r., Mt., U.S. (bĭg mud'ĭ)	105	48.53N	105.02W
Bignona, Sen.	214	12.49N	16.14W
Big Porcupine Creek, r., Mt., U.S. (pôr'kû-pīn)	105	46.38N	107.04W
Big Quill Lake, l., Can.	84	51.55N	104.22W
Big Rapids, Mi., U.S. (bĭg răp'ĭdz)	98	43.40N	85.30W
Big River, Can.	84	53.50N	107.01W
Big Sandy, r., Az., U.S. (bĭg sănd'ė)	109	34.59N	113.36W
Big Sandy, r., Ky., U.S.	98	38.15N	82.35W
Big Sandy, r., Wy., U.S.	105	42.08N	109.35W
Big Sandy Creek, r., Co., U.S.	110	39.08N	103.36W
Big Sandy Creek, r., Mt., U.S.	105	48.20N	110.08W
Bigsby Island, i., Can.	89	49.04N	94.35W
Big Sioux, r., U.S. (bĭg so͞o)	102	44.34N	97.00W
Big Spring, Tx., U.S. (bĭg sprĭng)	112	32.15N	101.28W
Big Stone, l., Mn., U.S. (bĭg stōn)	102	45.29N	96.40W
Big Stone Gap, Va., U.S.	115	36.50N	82.50W
Big Sunflower, r., Ms., U.S. (sŭn-flou'ēr)	114	32.57N	90.40W
Big Timber, Mt., U.S. (bĭg'tĭm-bēr)	105	45.50N	109.57W
Big Wood, r., Id., U.S. (bĭg wȯd)	105	43.02N	114.30W
Bihār, state, India (bė-här')	186	23.48N	84.57E
Biharamulo, Tan. (bė-hä-rä-mo͞o'lō)	212	2.38S	31.20E
Bihorului, Munții, mts., Rom.	155	46.37N	22.37E
Bijagós, Arquipélago dos, is., Gui.-B.	210	11.20N	17.10W
Bijāpur, India	187	16.53N	75.42E
Bijeljina, Bos.	161	44.44N	19.15E
Bijelo Polje, Yugo. (bē'yĕ-lō pō'lyĕ)	161	43.02N	19.48E
Bijiang, China (bē-jyän)	191a	22.57N	113.15E
Bijie, China (bē-jyĕ)	193	27.20N	105.18E
Bijou Creek, r., Co., U.S. (bē'zho͞o)	110	39.41N	104.13W
Bīkaner, India (bĭ-kă'nûr)	183	28.07N	73.19E
Bikin, Russia (bė-kēn')	194	46.41N	134.29E
Bikin, r., Russia	194	46.37N	135.55E
Bikoro, Zaire (bė-kō'rō)	212	0.45S	18.07E
Bikuar, Parque Nacional do, rec., Ang.	216	15.07S	14.40E
Bilāspur, India (bė-läs'po͞or)	183	22.08N	82.12E
Bila Tserkva, Ukr.	167	49.48N	30.09E
Bilauktaung, mts., Asia	196	14.40N	98.50E
Bilbao, Spain (bĭl-bä'ō)	142	43.12N	2.48W
Bilbays, Egypt	218b	30.26N	31.37E
Bileća, Bos. (bē'lĕ-chä)	161	42.52N	18.26E
Bilecik, Tur. (bē-lĕd-zhĕk')	149	40.10N	29.58E
Bilé Karpaty, mts., Eur.	155	48.53N	17.35E
Biłgoraj, Pol. (bēw-gō'rī)	155	50.31N	22.43E
Bilhorod-Dnistrovs'kyy, Ukr.	167	46.09N	30.19E
Bilimbay, Russia (bē'lĭm-bȧy)	172a	56.59N	59.53E
Billabong, r., Austl. (bĭl'ă-bŏng)	203	35.15S	145.20E
Billerica, Ma., U.S. (bĭl'rĭk-ȧ)	93a	42.33N	71.16W
Billericay, Eng., U.K.	144b	51.38N	0.25E
Billings, Mt., U.S. (bĭl'ĭngz)	96	45.47N	108.29W
Billingsport, N.J., U.S.	229b	39.51N	75.14W
Bill Williams, r., Az., U.S. (bĭl-wĭl'yumz)	109	34.10N	113.50W
Bilma, Niger (bēl'mä)	211	18.41N	13.20E
Bilopillya, Ukr.	167	51.10N	34.19E
Bilovods'k, Ukr.	163	49.12N	39.36E
Biloxi, Ms., U.S. (bĭ-lŏk'sĭ)	97	30.24N	88.50W
Bilqās Qism Awwal, Egypt	218b	31.14N	31.25E
Bimberi Peak, mtn., Austl. (bĭm'bērĭ)	204	35.45S	148.50E
Binalonan, Phil. (bē-nä-lô'nän)	197a	16.03N	120.35E
Bingen, Ger. (bĭn'gĕn)	154	49.57N	7.54E
Bingham, Eng., U.K. (bĭng'ăm)	144a	52.57N	0.57W
Bingham, Me., U.S.	92	45.03N	69.51W
Bingham Canyon, Ut., U.S.	107b	40.33N	112.09W
Bingham Farms, Mi., U.S.	230c	42.32N	83.16W
Binghamton, N.Y., U.S. (bĭng'ăm-tŭn)	97	42.05N	75.55W
Bingo-Nada, b., Japan (bĭn'gō nä-dä)	195	34.06N	133.14E
Binjai, Indon.	196	3.59N	108.00E
Binnaway, Austl. (bĭn'ă-wā)	204	31.42S	149.22E
Binsheim, Ger.	236	51.31N	6.42E
Bintan, i., Indon. (bĭn'tän)	181b	1.09N	104.43E
Bintimani, mtn., S.L.	214	9.13N	11.07W
Bintulu, Malay. (bēn'to͞o-lo͞o)	196	3.07N	113.06E
Binxian, China (bĭn-shyän)	190	37.27N	117.58E
Binxian, China	192	45.40N	127.20E
Bio Gorge, val., Ghana	214	8.30N	2.05W
Bioko (Fernando Póo), i., Eq. Gui.	210	3.35N	7.45E
Bira, Russia (bē'rȧ)	194	49.00N	133.18E
Bira, r., Russia	194	48.55N	132.25E
Birātnagar, Nepal (bĭ-rät'nŭ-gŭr)	186	26.35N	87.18E
Birbka, Ukr.	155	49.36N	24.18E
Birch, Eng., U.K.	237b	53.34N	2.13W
Birch Bay, Wa., U.S. (bûrch)	106d	48.55N	122.45W
Birch Bay, b., Wa., U.S.	106d	48.55N	122.52W
Birch Island, i., Can.	89	52.25N	99.55W
Birch Mountains, mts., Can.	84	57.36N	113.10W
Birch Point, c., Wa., U.S.	106d	48.57N	122.50W
Bird Island, i., S. Afr. (bĕrd)	213c	33.51S	26.21E
Bird Rock, i., Bah. (bûrd)	123	22.50N	74.20W
Birds Hill, Can. (bûrds)	83f	49.58N	97.00W
Birdsville, Austl. (bûrdz'vĭl)	202	25.50S	139.31E
Birdum, Austl. (bûrd'ŭm)	202	15.45S	133.25E
Birecik, Tur. (bē-rĕd-zhĕk')	149	37.10N	37.50E
Bir Gara, Chad	215	13.11N	15.58E
Bīrjand, Iran (bēr'jänd)	182	33.07N	59.16E
Birkenfeld, Or., U.S.	106c	45.59N	123.20W
Birkenhead, Eng., U.K. (bûr'kĕn-hĕd)	150	53.23N	3.02W
Birkenwerder, Ger. (bēr'kĕn-vĕr-dĕr)	145b	52.41N	13.22E
Birkholz, Ger.	238a	52.38N	13.34E
Birling, Eng., U.K.	235	51.19N	0.25E
Birmingham, Eng., U.K.	142	52.29N	1.53W
Birmingham, Al., U.S. (bûr'mĭng-hăm)	97	33.31N	86.49W
Birmingham, Mi., U.S.	101b	42.32N	83.13W
Birmingham, Mo., U.S.	107f	39.10N	94.22W
Birmingham Canal, can., Eng., U.K.	144a	53.07N	2.40W
Bi'r Misāhah, Egypt	211	22.16N	28.04E
Birnin Kebbi, Nig.	210	12.32N	4.12E
Birobidzhan, Russia (bē'rō-bė-jän')	165	48.42N	133.28E
Birsk, Russia (bĭrsk)	164	55.25N	55.30E
Birstall, Eng., U.K. (bûr'stôl)	144a	53.44N	1.39W
Biryulëvo, Russia (bĕr-yo͞ol'yô-vô)	172b	55.35N	37.39E
Biryusa, r., Russia (bēr-yo͞o'sä)	170	56.43N	97.30E
Bi'r Za'farānah, Egypt	181a	29.07N	32.38E
Biržai, Lith. (bėr-zhä'ė)	153	56.11N	24.45E
Bisbee, Az., U.S. (bĭz'bē)	96	31.30N	109.55W
Biscay, Bay of, b., Eur. (bĭs'kā')	142	45.19N	3.51W
Biscayne Bay, b., Fl., U.S. (bĭs-kān')	115a	25.22N	80.15W
Bischeim, Fr. (bĭsh'hīm)	157	48.40N	7.48E
Biscotasi Lake, l., Can.	90	47.20N	81.55W
Biser, Russia (bē'sĕr)	172a	58.24N	58.54E
Biševo, is., Yugo. (bē'shĕ-vō)	160	42.58N	15.50E
Bishkek, Kyrg.	169	42.49N	74.42E
Bisho, S. Afr.	212	32.50S	27.20E
Bishop, Ca., U.S. (bĭsh'ŭp)	108	37.22N	118.25W
Bishop, Tx., U.S.	113	27.35N	97.46W
Bishop's Castle, Eng., U.K. (bĭsh'ŏps käs'l)	144a	52.29N	2.57W
Bishopville, S.C., U.S. (bĭsh'ŭp-vĭl)	115	34.11N	80.13W
Bismarck, N.D., U.S. (bĭz'märk)	96	46.48N	100.46W
Bismarck Archipelago, is., Pap. N. Gui.	197	3.15S	150.45E
Bismarck Range, mts., Pap. N. Gui.	197	5.15S	144.15E
Bissau, Gui.-B. (bė-sa'o͞o)	214	11.51N	15.35W
Bissett, Can.	89	51.01N	95.45W
Bissingheim, neigh., Ger.	236	51.24N	6.49E
Bistineau, l., La., U.S. (bĭs-tĭ-nō')	113	32.19N	93.45W
Bistrita, Rom. (bĭs-trĭt-sä)	149	47.09N	24.29E
Bistrita, r., Rom.	155	47.08N	25.47E
Bitlis, Tur. (bĭt-lēs')	182	38.30N	42.00E
Bitola, Mac. (bė'tō-lä) (mō'nä-stĕr)	160	41.02N	21.22E
Bitonto, Italy (bė-tôn'tō)	160	41.08N	16.42E
Bitter Creek, r., Wy., U.S. (bĭt'ēr)	105	41.36N	108.29W
Bitterfeld, Ger. (bĭt'ēr-fĕlt)	154	51.39N	12.19E
Bittermark, neigh., Ger.	236	51.27N	7.28E
Bitterroot, r., Mt., U.S.	105	46.28N	114.10W
Bitterroot Range, mts., U.S. (bĭt'ēr-o͞ot)	96	47.15N	115.13W
Bityug, r., Russia (bĭt'yo͞og)	163	51.23N	40.33E
Biu, Nig.	215	10.35N	12.13E
Biwabik, Mn., U.S. (bē-wä'bĭk)	103	47.32N	92.24W
Biwa-ko, l., Japan (bė-wä'kō)	195	35.03N	135.51E
Biya, r., Russia (bĭ'yȧ)	170	52.22N	87.28E
Biysk, Russia (bēsk)	164	52.32N	85.28E
Bizana, S. Afr. (bĭz-änä)	213c	30.51S	29.54E
Bizerte, Tun. (bė-zĕrt')	210	37.23N	9.52E
Bjelovar, Cro. (byĕ-lō'vär)	160	45.54N	16.53E
Bjørnafjorden, fj., Nor.	152	60.11N	5.26E
Bla, Mali	214	12.57N	5.46W
Black, l., Mi., U.S. (blăk)	98	45.25N	84.15W
Black, l., N.Y., U.S.	99	44.30N	75.35W
Black, r., Asia	196	21.00N	103.30E
Black, r., Can.	90	49.20N	81.15W
Black, r., U.S.	111	35.47N	91.22W
Black, r., Az., U.S.	109	33.35N	109.35W
Black, r., N.Y., U.S.	99	43.45N	75.20W
Black, r., S.C., U.S.	115	33.55N	80.10W
Black, r., Wi., U.S.	103	44.07N	90.56W
Blackall, Austl. (blăk'ŭl)	203	24.23S	145.37E
Black Bay, b., Can. (blăk)	90	48.36N	88.32W
Blackburn, Austl.	243b	37.49S	145.09E
Blackburn, Eng., U.K. (blăk'bûrn)	150	53.45N	2.28W
Blackburn Mount, mtn., Ak., U.S.	95	61.50N	143.12W
Black Butte Lake, res., Ca., U.S.	108	39.45N	122.20W
Black Creek Pioneer Village, bldg., Can.	227c	43.47N	79.32W
Black Diamond, Wa., U.S. (dī'mŭnd)	106a	47.19N	122.00W
Black Down Hills, hills, Eng., U.K. (blăk'doun)	150	50.58N	3.19W
Blackduck, Mn., U.S. (blăk'dŭk)	103	47.41N	94.33W
Blackfeet Indian Reservation, I.R., Mt., U.S.	105	48.40N	113.00W
Blackfoot, Id., U.S. (blăk'fȯt)	105	43.11N	112.23W
Blackfoot, r., Mt., U.S.	105	46.53N	113.33W
Blackfoot Indian Reservation, I.R., Mt., U.S.	105	48.49N	112.53W
Blackfoot Indian Reserve, I.R., Can.	87	50.45N	113.00W
Blackfoot Reservoir, res., Id., U.S.	105	42.53N	111.23W
Black Forest see Schwarzwald, for., Ger.	154	47.54N	7.57E
Black Hills, mts., U.S.	96	44.08N	103.47W
Black Island, i., Can.	89	51.10N	96.30W
Black Lake, Can.	91	46.02N	71.24W
Blackley, neigh., Eng., U.K.	237b	53.31N	2.13W
Black Mesa, Az., U.S. (blăk māsȧ)	109	36.33N	110.40W
Blackmore, Eng., U.K.	235	51.41N	0.19E
Blackmud Creek, r., Can. (blăk'mŭd)	83g	53.28N	113.34W
Blackpool, Eng., U.K. (blăk'po͞ol)	150	53.49N	3.02W
Black Range, mts., N.M., U.S.	96	33.15N	107.55W
Black River, Jam. (blăk')	122	18.00N	77.50W
Black River Falls, Wi., U.S.	103	44.18N	90.51W
Black Rock, Austl.	243b	37.59S	145.01E
Black Rock Desert, des., Nv., U.S. (rŏk)	104	40.55N	119.00W
Blacksburg, S.C., U.S. (blăks'bûrg)	115	35.09N	81.30W
Black Sea, sea	143	43.01N	32.16E
Blackshear, Ga., U.S. (blăk'shĭr)	115	31.20N	82.15W
Black Springs, Austl.	243b	37.46S	145.19E
Blackstone, Va., U.S. (blăk'stōn)	115	37.04N	78.00W
Black Sturgeon, r., Can. (stû'jŭn)	90	49.12N	88.41W
Blacktown, Austl. (blăk'toun)	201b	33.47S	150.55E
Blackville, Can. (blăk'vĭl)	92	46.44N	65.50W
Blackville, S.C., U.S.	115	33.21N	81.19W
Black Volta (Volta Noire), r., Afr.	210	11.30N	4.00W

266 Black Warrior–Bonthain

PLACE (Pronunciation)	PAGE	Lat. °′	Long. °′
Black Warrior, r., Al., U.S. (blăk wŏr'ĭ-ẽr)	114	32.37N	87.42W
Blackwater, r., Ire. (blăk-wô'tẽr)	150	52.05N	9.02W
Blackwater, r., Mo., U.S.	111	38.53N	93.22W
Blackwater, r., Va., U.S.	115	37.07N	77.10W
Blackwell, Ok., U.S. (blăk'wĕl)	111	36.47N	97.19W
Bladel, Neth.	145a	51.22N	5.15E
Bladensburg, Md., U.S.	229d	38.56N	76.55W
Blagodarnoye, Russia (blä'gô-där-nō'yĕ)	167	45.00N	43.30E
Blagoevgrad, Bul.	161	42.01N	23.06E
Blagoveshchensk, Russia (blă'gŏ-vyĕsh'chĕnsk)	165	50.16N	127.47E
Blagoveshchensk, Russia	172a	55.03N	56.00E
Blaine, Mn., U.S. (blān)	107g	45.11N	93.14W
Blaine, Wa., U.S.	106d	48.59N	122.49W
Blaine, W.V., U.S.	99	39.25N	79.10W
Blaine Hill, Pa., U.S.	230b	40.16N	79.53W
Blair, Ne., U.S. (blâr)	102	41.33N	96.09W
Blairmore, Can.	87	49.38N	114.25W
Blairsville, Pa., U.S. (blârs'vĭl)	99	40.30N	79.40W
Blake, i., Wa., U.S. (blāk)	106a	47.37N	122.28W
Blakehurst, Austl.	243a	33.59S	151.07E
Blakely, Ga., U.S. (blāk'lē)	114	31.22N	84.55W
Blanc, Cap, c., Afr.	210	20.39N	18.08W
Blanc, Mont, mtn., Eur. (môn blän)	142	45.50N	6.53E
Blanca, Bahía, b., Arg. (bä-ē'ä-blàn'kä)	132	39.30S	61.00W
Blanca Peak, mtn., Co., U.S. (blăŋ'kȧ)	96	37.36N	105.22W
Blanche, r., Can.	83c	45.34N	75.38W
Blanche, Lake, l., Austl. (blănch)	204	29.20S	139.12E
Blanchester, Oh., U.S. (blăn'chĕs-tẽr)	101f	39.18N	83.58W
Blanco, r., Mex.	118	24.05N	99.21W
Blanco, r., Mex.	119	18.42N	96.03W
Blanco, Cabo, c., Arg. (bläŋ'kō)	132	47.08S	65.47W
Blanco, Cabo, c., C.R. (kȧ'bō-bläŋ'kō)	120	9.29N	85.15W
Blanco, Cape, c., Or., U.S. (blăn'kō)	104	42.53N	124.38W
Blancos, Cayo, i., Cuba (kä'yō-bläŋ'kōs)	122	23.15N	80.55W
Blanding, Ut., U.S.	109	37.40N	109.31W
Blankenburg, neigh., Ger.	238a	52.35N	13.28E
Blankenfelde, Ger. (blän'kĕn-fĕl-dĕ)	145b	52.20N	13.24E
Blankenfelde, neigh., Ger.	238a	52.37N	13.23E
Blankenstein, Ger.	236	51.24N	7.14E
Blanquefort, Fr.	156	44.53N	0.38W
Blanquilla, Arrecife, i., Mex. (är-rĕ-sē'fē-blän-kē'l-yä)	119	21.32N	97.14W
Blantyre, Mwi. (blăn-tīyr)	212	15.47S	35.00E
Blasdell, N.Y., U.S. (blāz'dĕl)	101c	42.48N	78.51W
Blato, Cro. (blä'tō)	160	42.55N	16.47E
Blawnox, Pa., U.S.	230b	40.29N	79.52W
Blaye-et-Sainte Luce, Fr. (blā'ā-sănt-lüs')	156	45.08N	0.40W
Błażowa, Pol. (bwä-zhō'vȧ)	155	49.51N	22.05E
Bleus, Monts, mts., Zaire	217	1.10N	30.10E
Bliersheim, Ger.	236	51.23N	6.43E
Blind River, Can. (blīnd)	85	46.10N	83.09W
Blissfield, Mi., U.S. (blĭs-fēld)	98	41.50N	83.50W
Blithe, r., Eng., U.K. (blĭth)	144a	52.22N	1.49W
Blitta, Togo	214	8.19N	0.59E
Block, i., R.I., U.S. (blŏk)	99	41.05N	71.35W
Bloedel, Can.	86	50.07N	125.23W
Bloemfontein, S. Afr. (bloom'fŏn-tān)	212	29.09S	26.16E
Blois, Fr. (blwä)	147	47.36N	1.21E
Blombacher Bach, neigh., Ger.	236	51.15N	7.14E
Blood Indian Reserve, I.R., Can.	87	49.30N	113.10W
Bloomer, Wi., U.S. (bloom'ẽr)	103	45.07N	91.30W
Bloomfield, In., U.S. (bloom'fēld)	98	39.00N	86.55W
Bloomfield, Ia., U.S.	103	40.44N	92.21W
Bloomfield, Mo., U.S.	111	36.54N	89.55W
Bloomfield, Ne., U.S.	102	42.36N	97.40W
Bloomfield, N.J., U.S.	100a	40.48N	74.12W
Bloomfield Hills, Mi., U.S.	101b	42.35N	83.15W
Bloomfield Village, Mi., U.S.	230c	42.33N	83.15W
Blooming Prairie, Mn., U.S. (bloom'ĭng prā'rĭ)	103	43.52N	93.04W
Bloomington, Ca., U.S. (bloom'ĭng-tŭn)	107a	34.04N	117.24W
Bloomington, Il., U.S.	97	40.30N	89.00W
Bloomington, In., U.S.	98	39.10N	86.35W
Bloomington, Mn., U.S.	107g	44.50N	93.18W
Bloomsburg, Pa., U.S. (bloomz'bûrg)	99	41.00N	76.25W
Blossburg, Al., U.S. (blŏs'bûrg)	100h	33.38N	86.57W
Blossburg, Pa., U.S.	99	41.45N	77.00W
Bloubergstrand, S. Afr.	212a	33.48S	18.28E
Blountstown, Fl., U.S. (blŭnts'tun)	114	30.24N	85.02W
Bludenz, Aus. (bloo-dĕnts')	154	47.09N	9.50E
Blue Ash, Oh., U.S. (bloo ăsh)	101f	39.14N	84.23W
Blue Earth, Mn., U.S. (bloo ûrth)	103	43.38N	94.05W
Blue Earth, r., Mn., U.S.	103	43.55N	94.16W
Bluefield, W.V., U.S. (bloo'fēld)	115	37.15N	81.11W
Bluefields, Nic. (bloo'fēldz)	117	12.03N	83.45W
Blue Island, Il., U.S.	101a	41.39N	87.41W
Blue Mesa Reservoir, res., Co., U.S.	109	38.25N	107.00W
Blue Mosque, rel., Egypt	244a	30.02N	31.15E
Blue Mountain, mtn., Can.	93	50.28N	57.11W
Blue Mountains, mts., Austl.	203	33.35S	149.00E
Blue Mountains, mts., Jam.	122	18.05N	76.35W
Blue Mountains, mts., U.S.	96	45.15N	118.50W
Blue Mud Bay, b., Austl. (boo mŭd)	202	13.20S	136.45E
Blue Nile, r., Afr.	211	12.30N	34.00E
Blue Rapids, Ks., U.S. (bloo răp'ĭdz)	111	39.40N	96.41W
Blue Ridge, mtn., U.S. (bloo rĭj)	97	35.30N	82.50W
Blue River, Can.	84	52.05N	119.17W
Blue River, r., Mo., U.S.	107f	38.55N	94.33W
Bluff, Ut., U.S.	109	37.18N	109.34W
Bluff Park, Al., U.S.	100h	33.24N	86.52W
Bluffton, In., U.S. (blŭf-tŭn)	98	40.40N	85.15W
Bluffton, Oh., U.S.	98	40.50N	83.55W
Blumenau, Braz. (bloo'mĕn-ou)	132	26.53S	48.58W
Blumut, Gunong, mtn., Malay.	181b	2.03N	103.34E
Blyth, Eng., U.K. (blĭth)	150	55.03N	1.34W

PLACE (Pronunciation)	PAGE	Lat. °′	Long. °′
Blythe, Ca., U.S.	109	33.37N	114.37W
Blytheville, Ar., U.S. (blīth'vĭl)	111	35.55N	89.51W
Bo, S.L.	214	7.56N	11.21W
Boac, Phil.	197a	13.26N	121.50E
Boaco, Nic. (bō-ä'kō)	120	12.24N	85.41W
Bo'ai, China (bwo-ī)	192	35.10N	113.08E
Boa Vista, i., C.V. (bō-ä-vēsh'tȧ)	210b	16.01N	23.52W
Boa Vista do Rio Branco, Braz.	131	2.46N	60.45W
Bobbingworth, Eng., U.K.	235	51.44N	0.13E
Bobigny, Fr.	237c	48.54N	2.27E
Bobo Dioulasso, Burkina (bō'bō-dyoo-lȧs-sō')	210	11.12N	4.18W
Bobr, Bela. (bô'b'r)	162	54.19N	29.11E
Bóbr, r., Pol. (bŭ'br)	154	51.44N	15.13E
Bobrov, Russia (bŭb-rôf')	167	51.07N	40.01E
Bobrovytsya, Ukr. (bŭb-rô'vē-tsȧ)	163	50.43N	31.27E
Bobruysk, Bela. (bŏ-broo'ĭsk)	166	53.07N	29.13E
Bobrynets', Ukr.	163	48.04N	32.10E
Boca, neigh., Arg.	233d	34.38S	58.21W
Boca del Pozo, Ven. (bô-kä-dĕl-pô'zō)	131b	11.00N	64.21W
Boca de Uchire, Ven. (bô-kä-dĕ-oo-chē'rĕ)	131b	10.09N	65.27W
Bocaina, Serra da, mtn., Braz. (sĕ'r-rä-dȧ-bō-kä'ē-nä)	129a	22.47S	44.39W
Bocanegra, Peru	233c	12.01S	77.07W
Bocas, Mex. (bō'käs)	118	22.29N	101.03W
Bocas del Toro, Pan. (bō'käs dĕl tō'rō)	121	9.24N	82.15W
Bochnia, Pol. (bôk'nyä)	155	49.58N	20.28E
Bocholt, Ger. (bō'kôlt)	157c	51.50N	6.37E
Bochum, Ger.	154	51.29N	7.13E
Böckel, neigh., Ger.	236	51.13N	7.12E
Bockum, Ger.	236	51.20N	6.44E
Bockum, neigh., Ger.	236	51.21N	6.38E
Bockum-Hövel, Ger. (bō'kom-hû'fĕl)	157c	51.41N	7.45E
Bodalang, Zaire	216	3.14N	22.14E
Bodaybo, Russia (bō-dī'bō)	165	57.12N	114.46E
Bodele, depr., Chad (bō-dȧ-lā')	211	16.45N	17.05E
Bodelschwingh, neigh., Ger.	236	51.33N	7.22E
Boden, Swe.	146	65.51N	21.29E
Bodensee, l., Eur. (bō'dĕn zā)	142	47.48N	9.22E
Bodmin, Eng., U.K. (bŏd'mĭn)	150	50.29N	4.45W
Bodmin Moor, Eng., U.K. (bŏd'mĭn mòr)	150	50.36N	4.43W
Bodrum, Tur.	167	37.10N	27.07E
Boende, Zaire (bô-ĕn'dȧ)	212	0.13S	20.52E
Boerne, Tx., U.S. (bō'ẽrn)	112	29.49N	98.44W
Boesmans, r., S. Afr.	213c	33.29S	26.09E
Boeuf, r., U.S. (bĕf)	113	32.23N	91.57W
Boffa, Gui. (bôf'ȧ)	210	10.10N	14.02W
Bōfu, Japan (bō'foo)	195	34.03N	131.35E
Bogalusa, La., U.S. (bō-gȧ-loo'sȧ)	113	30.48N	89.52W
Bogan, r., Austl. (bō'gĕn)	204	32.10S	147.40E
Bogense, Den. (bô'gĕn-sĕ)	152	55.34N	10.09E
Boggy Peak, mtn., Antig. (bŏg'ĭ-pēk)	121b	17.03N	61.50W
Bogong, Mount, mtn., Austl.	204	36.50S	147.15E
Bogor, Indon.	196	6.45S	106.45E
Bogoroditsk, Russia (bŏ-gŏ'rô-dĭtsk)	162	53.48N	38.06E
Bogorodsk, Russia	166	56.02N	43.40E
Bogorodskoje, neigh., Russia	239b	55.49N	37.44E
Bogorodskoye, Russia (bô-gô-rôd'skô-yĕ)	172a	56.43N	56.53E
Bogotá see Santa Fe de Bogotá, Col.	130	4.36N	74.05W
Bogota, N.J., U.S.	228	40.53N	74.02W
Bogotol, Russia (bŏ'gŏ-tŏl)	165	56.15N	89.45E
Boguchar, Russia (bō'gŏ-chär)	167	49.40N	41.00E
Bogue Chitto, Ms., U.S. (nôr'fēld)	114	31.26N	90.25W
Boguete, Pan. (bō-gĕ'tĕ)	121	8.54N	82.29W
Bo Hai, b., China	189	38.30N	120.00E
Bohai Haixia, strt., China (bwo-hī hī-shyä)	192	38.05N	121.40E
Bohain-en-Vermandois, Fr. (bō-ăn-ŏn-vĕr-män-dwä')	156	49.58N	3.22E
Bohemia see Čechy, hist. reg., Czech Rep.	154	49.51N	13.55E
Bohemian Forest, mts., Eur. (bō-hē'mĭ-ăn)	142	49.35N	12.27E
Böhnsdorf, neigh., Ger.	238a	52.24N	13.33E
Bohodukhiv, Ukr.	167	50.10N	35.31E
Bohol, i., Phil. (bō-hōl')	197	9.28N	124.35E
Bohom, Mex. (bō-ō'm)	119	16.47N	92.42W
Bohuslav, Ukr.	163	49.34N	30.51W
Boiestown, Can. (boiz'toun)	92	46.27N	66.25W
Bois Blanc, i., Mi., U.S. (boi' blăŋk)	98	45.45N	84.30W
Boischâtel, Can. (bwä-shä-tĕl')	83b	46.54N	71.08W
Bois-Colombes, Fr.	237c	48.55N	2.16E
Bois-des-Filion, Can. (boo-ä'dĕ-fē-yŏn')	83a	45.40N	73.46W
Boise, Id., U.S. (boi'zē)	96	43.38N	116.12W
Boise, r., Id., U.S.	104	43.43N	116.30W
Boise City, Ok., U.S.	110	36.42N	102.30W
Boissevain, Can. (bois'vān)	84	49.14N	100.03W
Boissy-Saint-Léger, Fr.	237c	48.45N	2.31E
Bojador, Cabo, c., W. Sah.	210	26.21N	16.08W
Bojnūrd, Iran	182	37.29N	57.13E
Bokani, Nig.	215	9.26N	5.13E
Boknafjorden, fj., Nor.	146	59.12N	5.37E
Boksburg, S. Afr. (bŏks'bûrgh)	213b	26.13N	28.15E
Boksburg North, S. Afr.	244b	26.12S	28.15E
Boksburg South, S. Afr.	244b	26.14S	28.15E
Boksburg West, S. Afr.	244b	26.13S	28.14E
Bokungu, Zaire	216	0.41S	22.19E
Bol, Chad	215	13.28N	14.43E
Bolai I, Cen. Afr. Rep.	215	4.20N	17.21E
Bolama, Gui.-B. (bō-lä'mä)	210	11.34S	15.41W
Bolan, mtn., Pak. (bō-län')	186	30.13N	67.09E
Bolaños, Mex. (bō-län'yōs)	118	21.40N	103.48W
Bolaños, r., Mex.	118	21.26N	103.54W
Bolan Pass, p., Pak.	183	29.50N	67.10E
Bolbec, Fr. (bôl-bĕk')	156	49.37N	0.26E

PLACE (Pronunciation)	PAGE	Lat. °′	Long. °′
Bole, Ghana (bō'lȧ)	210	9.02N	2.29W
Bolesławiec, Pol. (bō-lĕ-slä'vyĕts)	154	51.15N	15.35E
Bolgatanga, Ghana	214	10.46N	0.52W
Bolhrad, Ukr.	167	45.41N	28.38E
Boli, China (bwo-lē)	189	45.40N	130.38E
Bolinao, Phil. (bō-lē-nä'ō)	197a	16.24N	119.53E
Bolívar, Arg. (bō-lē'vär)	132	36.15S	61.05W
Bolívar, Col.	130	1.46N	76.58W
Bolivar, Mo., U.S. (bŏl'ĭ-vȧr)	111	37.37N	93.22W
Bolivar, Tn., U.S.	114	35.14N	88.56W
Bolívar, Pico, mtn., Ven.	130	8.44N	70.54W
Bolivar Peninsula, pen., Tx., U.S. (bŏl'ĭ-vȧr)	113a	29.25N	94.40W
Bolivia, nation, S.A. (bō-lĭv'ĭ-ȧ)	130	17.00S	64.00W
Bölkenbusch, Ger.	236	51.21N	7.06E
Bolkhov, Russia (bŏl-kôf')	166	53.27N	35.59E
Bollate, Italy	238c	45.33N	9.07E
Bollensdorf, Ger.	238a	52.31N	13.43E
Bollin, r., Eng., U.K. (bŏl'ĭn)	144a	53.18N	2.11W
Bollington, Eng., U.K. (bŏl'ĭng-tŭn)	144a	53.18N	2.06W
Bollington, Eng., U.K.	237b	53.22N	2.25W
Bollnäs, Swe. (bôl'nĕs)	152	61.22N	16.20E
Bollwerk, Ger.	236	51.10N	7.35E
Bolmen, l., Swe. (bôl'mĕn)	152	56.58N	13.25E
Bolobo, Zaire (bō'lō-bō)	212	2.14S	16.18E
Bologna, Italy (bō-lōn'yä)	142	44.30N	11.18E
Bologoye, Russia (bō-lō-gō'yĕ)	166	57.52N	34.02E
Bolonchenticul, Mex. (bō-lōn-chĕn-tē-koo'l)	120a	20.03N	89.47W
Bolondrón, Cuba (bō-lŏn-drōn')	122	22.45N	81.25W
Bol'šaja Ochta, neigh., Russia	239a	59.57N	30.25E
Bolseno, Lago di, l., Italy (lä'gō-dē-bōl-sā'nō)	160	42.35N	11.40E
Bol'shaya Anyuy, r., Russia	171	67.58N	161.15E
Bol'shaya Chuya, r., Russia	171	58.15N	111.40E
Bol'shaya Kinel', r., Russia	166	53.20N	52.40E
Bol'she Ust'ikinskoye, Russia (bôl'she ŏs-tyĭ-kĕn'skô-yĕ)	172a	55.58N	58.18E
Bol'shoy Begichëv, i., Russia	165	74.30N	114.40E
Bol'shoye Ivonino, Russia (ĭ-vŏ'nĭ-nō)	172a	59.41N	61.12E
Bol'shoy Kuyash, Russia (bŏl'-shôy koo'yȧsh)	172a	55.52N	61.07E
Bol'šoj Teatr, bldg., Russia	239b	55.46N	37.37E
Bolsover, Eng., U.K. (bōl'zō-vẽr)	144a	53.14N	1.17W
Boltaña, Spain (bōl-tä'nä)	159	42.28N	0.03E
Bolton, Can. (bōl'tŭn)	83d	43.53N	79.44W
Bolton, Eng., U.K.	150	53.35N	2.26W
Bolton-upon-Dearne, Eng., U.K. (bōl'tŭn-ŭp'ŏn-dûrn)	144a	53.31N	1.19W
Bolu, Tur. (bō'lō)	149	40.45N	31.45E
Bolva, r., Russia (bôl'vä)	162	53.30N	34.30E
Bolvadin, Tur. (bōl-vä-dēn')	149	38.50N	30.50E
Bolzano, Italy (bōl-tsä'nō)	148	46.31N	11.22E
Boma, Zaire (bō'mä)	212	5.51S	13.03E
Bombala, Austl. (bŭm-bä'lȧ)	203	36.55S	149.07E
Bombay, India (bŏm-bā')	183	18.58N	72.50E
Bombay Harbour, b., India	187b	18.55N	72.52E
Bomi Hills, Lib.	210	7.00N	11.00W
Bom Jardim, Braz. (bôn zhär-dēn')	129a	22.10S	42.25W
Bom Jesus do Itabapoana, Braz.	129a	21.08S	41.51W
Bømlo, i., Nor. (bûmlô)	152	59.47N	4.57E
Bommerholz, Ger.	236	51.23N	7.18E
Bommern, neigh., Ger.	236	51.25N	7.20E
Bomongo, Zaire	211	1.22N	18.21E
Bom Retiro, neigh., Braz.	234d	23.32S	46.38W
Bom Sucesso, Braz. (bôn-soo-sĕ'sō)	129a	21.02S	44.44W
Bomu see Mbomou, r., Afr.	211	4.50N	24.00E
Bon, Cap, c., Tun. (bôn)	148	37.04N	11.13E
Bon Air, Pa., U.S.	229b	39.58N	75.19W
Bonaire, i., Neth. Ant. (bō-nâr')	130	12.10N	68.15W
Bonavista, Can. (bō-nȧ-vĭs'tȧ)	85a	48.39N	53.07W
Bonavista Bay, b., Can.	85a	48.45N	53.20W
Bond, Co., U.S. (bŏnd)	110	39.53N	106.40W
Bondi, Austl.	243a	33.53S	151.17E
Bondo, Zaire (bôn'dō)	170	3.49N	23.40E
Bondoc Peninsula, pen., Phil. (bŏn-dŏk')	197a	13.24N	122.30E
Bondoukou, C. Iv. (bŏn-doo'koo)	210	8.02N	2.48W
Bonds Cay, i., Bah. (bŏnds kē)	122	25.30N	77.45W
Bondy, Fr.	157b	48.54N	2.28E
Bône see Annaba, Alg.	210	36.57N	7.39E
Bone, Teluk, b., Indon.	196	4.09S	121.00E
Bonete, Cerro, mtn., Arg. (bô'nĕtĕh çĕrrô)	132	27.50S	68.35W
Bonfim, Braz. (bôn-fē'n)	129a	20.20S	44.15W
Bongor, Chad	215	10.17N	15.22E
Bonham, Tx., U.S. (bŏn'ăm)	111	33.35N	96.09W
Bonhomme, Pic, mtn., Haiti	123	19.10N	72.20W
Bonifacio, Fr. (bō-nē-fä'chō)	160	41.23N	9.10E
Bonifacio, Strait of, strt., Eur.	148	41.14N	9.02E
Bonifay, Fl., U.S. (bŏn-ĭ-fā')	114	30.46N	85.40W
Bonin Islands, is., Japan (bō'nĭn)	225	26.30N	141.00E
Bonn, Ger. (bōn)	142	50.44N	7.06E
Bonne Bay, b., Can. (bŏn)	93	49.33N	57.55W
Bonners Ferry, Id., U.S. (bonẽrz fẽr'ĭ)	104	48.41N	116.19W
Bonner Springs, Ks., U.S. (bŏn'ẽr sprĭngz)	107f	39.04N	94.52W
Bonne Terre, Mo., U.S. (bŏn târ')	111	37.55N	90.32W
Bonnet Peak, mtn., Can. (bŏn'ĭt)	87	51.26N	115.53W
Bonneuil-sur-Marne, Fr.	237c	48.46N	2.29E
Bonneville Dam, dam, U.S. (bŏn'ē-vĭl)	104	45.37N	121.57W
Bonny, Nig. (bŏn'ē)	210	4.29N	7.13E
Bonny Lake, Wa., U.S. (bŏn'ē lăk)	106a	47.11N	122.11W
Bonnyrigg, Austl.	243a	33.54S	150.54E
Bonnyville, Can. (bŏnē-vĭl)	87	54.16N	110.44W
Bonorva, Italy (bō-nôr'vä)	160	40.26N	8.46E
Bonsúcesso, neigh., Braz.	234c	22.52S	43.15W
Bonthain, Indon. (bōn-tīn')	196	5.30S	119.52E

ăt; finăl; rāte; senāte; ärm; ȧsk; sofȧ; fâre; ch-choose; dh-as th in other; bē; ēvent; bĕt; recĕnt; cratẽr; g-gō; gh-guttural g; bĭt; ĭ-short neutral; rīde; ᴋ-guttural k as ch in German ich;

PLACE (Pronunciation)	PAGE	Lat. °'	Long. °'
Bonthe, S.L.	210	7.32N	12.30W
Bontoc, Phil. (bŏn-tŏk')	197a	17.10N	121.01E
Booby Rocks, is., Bah. (bo͞o'bĭ rŏks)	122	23.55N	77.00W
Booker T. Washington National Monument, rec., Va., U.S. (bo͝ok'ẽr tē wŏsh'ĭng-tŭn)	115	37.07N	79.45W
Boom, Bel.	145a	51.05N	4.22E
Boone, Ia., U.S. (bo͞on)	103	42.04N	93.51W
Booneville, Ar., U.S. (bo͞on'vĭl)	111	35.09N	93.54W
Booneville, Ky., U.S.	98	37.25N	83.40W
Booneville, Ms., U.S.	114	34.37N	88.35W
Boons, S. Afr.	218d	25.59S	27.15E
Boonton, N.J., U.S. (bo͞on'tŭn)	100a	40.54N	74.24W
Boonville, In., U.S.	98	38.00N	87.15W
Boonville, Mo., U.S.	111	38.57N	92.44W
Boorama, Som.	218a	10.05N	43.08E
Boosaaso, Som.	218a	11.19N	49.10E
Boothbay Harbor, Me., U.S. (bo͞oth'bā här'bẽr)	92	43.51N	69.39W
Boothia, Gulf of, b., Can. (bo͞o'thĭ-ȧ)	85	69.04N	86.04W
Boothia Peninsula, pen., Can.	82	73.30N	95.00W
Boothstown, Eng., U.K.	237b	53.30N	2.25W
Bootle, Eng., U.K. (bo͞ot'l)	144a	53.29N	3.02W
Booysens, neigh., S. Afr.	244b	26.14S	28.01E
Bor, Sudan (bôr)	211	6.13N	31.35E
Bor, Tur. (bōr)	167	37.50N	34.40E
Boraha, Nosy, i., Madag.	213	16.58S	50.15E
Borah Peak, mtn., Id., U.S. (bō'rä)	105	44.12N	113.47W
Borås, Swe. (bo͝o'rōs)	146	57.43N	12.55E
Borāzjān, Iran (bō-räz-jän')	182	29.13N	51.13E
Borba, Braz. (bôr'bä)	131	4.23S	59.31W
Borbeck, neigh., Ger.	236	51.29N	6.57E
Borborema, Planalto da, plat., Braz. (plä-nàl'tô-dä-bôr-bō-rĕ'mä)	131	7.35S	36.40W
Bordeaux, Fr. (bôr-dō')	142	44.50N	0.37W
Bordeaux, S. Afr.	244b	26.06S	28.01E
Bordentown, N.J., U.S. (bôr'dĕn-toun)	99	40.05N	74.40W
Bordj-bou-Arréridj, Alg. (bôrj-bo͞o-á-rā-rēj')	148	36.03N	4.48E
Bordj Omar Idriss, Alg.	210	28.06N	6.34E
Borehamwood, Eng., U.K.	235	51.40N	0.16W
Borgarnes, Ice.	146	64.31N	21.40W
Borger, Tx., U.S. (bôr'gẽr)	110	35.40N	101.23W
Borgholm, Swe. (bôrg-hŏlm')	152	56.52N	16.40E
Borgne, l., La., U.S. (bôrn'y')	113	30.03N	89.36W
Borgomanero, Italy (bôr'gō-mä-nâ'rō)	160	45.40N	8.28E
Borgo Val di Taro, Italy (bô'r-zhō-väl-dē-tá'rō)	160	44.29N	9.44E
Borili, Kaz.	169	53.36N	61.55E
Boring, Or., U.S. (bōring)	106c	45.26N	122.22W
Borisoglebsk, Russia (bŏ-rē sŏ-glyĕpsk')	164	51.20N	42.00E
Borisov, Bela. (bŏ-rē'sôf)	166	54.16N	28.33E
Borisovka, Russia (bŏ-rē-sôf'kå)	167	50.38N	36.00E
Borivli, India	187b	19.15N	72.48E
Borja, Spain (bôr'hä)	158	41.50N	1.33W
Borjas Blancas, Spain (bô'r-ĸäs-blä'n-käs)	159	41.29N	0.53E
Borken, Ger. (bōr'kĕn)	157c	51.50N	6.51E
Borkou, reg., Chad (bôr-ko͞o')	211	18.11N	18.28E
Borkum, i., Ger. (bōr'ko͞om)	154	53.31N	6.50E
Borlänge, Swe. (bôr-lĕŋ'gĕ)	152	60.30N	15.24E
Borle, neigh., India	240e	19.02N	72.55E
Borneo, i., Asia	196	0.25N	112.39E
Bornholm, i., Den. (bôrn-hôlm)	142	55.16N	15.15E
Bornim, neigh., Ger.	238a	52.26N	13.00E
Bornstedt, neigh., Ger.	238a	52.25N	13.02E
Borodayivka, Ukr.	163	48.44N	34.09E
Boromlya, Ukr. (bŏ-rôm'-l-yä)	163	50.36N	34.58E
Boromo, Burkina	214	11.45N	2.56W
Borough Green, Eng., U.K.	235	51.17N	0.19E
Borough Park, neigh., N.Y., U.S.	228	40.38N	74.00W
Borovan, Bul. (bŏ-rŏ-vän')	161	43.24N	23.47E
Borovichi, Russia (bŏ-rô-vē'chē)	164	58.22N	33.56E
Borovsk, Russia (bô'rŏvsk)	162	55.13N	36.26E
Borraan, Som.	218a	10.38N	48.30E
Borracha, Isla la, i., Ven. (ē's-lä-lá-bôr-rá'chä)	131b	10.18N	64.44W
Borroloola, Austl. (bŏr-rŏ-lo͞o'lȧ)	202	16.15S	136.19E
Borshchiv, Ukr.	155	48.47N	26.04E
Borth, Ger.	236	51.36N	6.33E
Bort-les-Orgues, Fr. (bôr-lā-zôrg)	156	45.26N	2.26E
Borūjerd, Iran	182	33.45N	48.53E
Boryslav, Ukr.	155	49.17N	23.24E
Boryspil', Ukr.	163	50.17N	30.54E
Borzna, Ukr. (bôrz'ná)	167	51.15N	32.26E
Borzya, Russia (bôrz'yá)	165	50.37N	116.53E
Bosa, Italy (bō'sä)	160	40.18N	8.34E
Bosanska Dubica, Bos. (bō'sän-skä do͞o'bĭt-sä)	160	45.10N	16.49E
Bosanska Gradiška, Bos. (bō'sän-skä grä-dĭsh'kä)	161	45.08N	17.15E
Bosanski Novi, Bos. (bō's sän-skĭ nō'vē)	160	45.00N	16.22E
Bosanski Petrovac, Bos. (bō'sän-skĭ pĕt'rō-väts)	160	44.33N	16.23E
Bosanski Šamac, Bos. (bō'sän-skĭ shä'máts)	161	45.03N	18.30E
Boscobel, Wi., U.S. (bŏs'kō-bĕl)	103	43.08N	90.44W
Bose, China (bwo-sŭ)	193	24.00N	106.38E
Boshan, China (bwo-shan)	189	36.32N	117.51E
Boskol', Kaz. (bås-kôl')	169	53.45N	61.17E
Boskoop, Neth.	145a	52.04N	4.39E
Boskovice, Czech Rep. (bŏs'kō-vē-tsĕ)	154	49.26N	16.37E
Bosna, r., Yugo.	161	44.19N	17.54E
Bosnia and Herzegovina, nation, Eur.	161	44.15N	17.30E
Bosobolo, Zaire	216	4.11N	19.54E
Bosporus see İstanbul Boğazi, strt., Tur.	182	41.10N	29.10E

PLACE (Pronunciation)	PAGE	Lat. °'	Long. °'
Bossangoa, Cen. Afr. Rep.	215	6.29N	17.27E
Bossier City, La., U.S. (bŏsh'ẽr)	113	32.31N	93.42W
Bossley Park, Austl.	243a	33.52S	150.54E
Bostanci, neigh., Tur.	239f	40.57N	29.05E
Bosten Hu, l., China (bwo-stŭn ho͞o)	188	42.06N	88.01E
Boston, Ga., U.S. (bôs'tŭn)	114	30.47N	83.47W
Boston, Ma., U.S.	97	42.15N	71.07W
Boston, Pa., U.S.	230b	40.18N	79.49W
Boston Bay, b., Ma., U.S.	227a	42.22N	70.54W
Boston Garden, pt. of i., Ma., U.S.	227a	42.22N	71.04W
Boston Harbor, b., Ma., U.S.	227a	42.20N	70.58W
Boston Heights, Oh., U.S.	101d	41.15N	81.30W
Boston Mountains, mts., Ar., U.S.	97	35.46N	93.32W
Botafogo, neigh., Braz.	234c	22.57S	43.11W
Botafogo, Enseada de, b., Braz.	234c	22.57S	43.10W
Botany, Austl.	243a	33.57S	151.12E
Botany Bay, neigh., Eng., U.K.	235	51.41N	0.07W
Botany Bay, b., Austl. (bŏt'ȧ-nĭ)	203	33.58S	151.11E
Botevgrad, Bul.	161	42.54N	23.41E
Bothaville, S. Afr. (bō'tä-vĭl)	218d	27.24S	26.38E
Bothell, Wa., U.S. (bŏth'ĕl)	106a	47.46N	122.12W
Bothnia, Gulf of, b., Eur. (bŏth'nĭ-á)	142	63.40N	21.30E
Botoşani, Rom. (bō-tō-shän'ĭ)	155	47.46N	26.40E
Botswana, nation, Afr. (bŏtswănă)	212	22.10S	23.13E
Bottineau, N.D., U.S. (bŏt-ĭ-nō')	102	48.48N	100.28W
Bottrop, Ger. (bŏt'trōp)	154	51.31N	6.56E
Botwood, Can. (bŏt'wŏŏd)	85a	49.08N	55.21W
Bötzow, Ger.	238a	52.39N	13.08E
Bouafle, C. Iv. (bŏ-á-flā')	210	6.59N	5.45W
Bouar, Cen. Afr. Rep. (bo͞o-är)	211	5.57N	15.36E
Bou Areg, Sebkha, Mor.	158	35.09N	3.02W
Boubandjidah, Parc National de, rec., Cam.	215	8.20N	14.40E
Boucherville, Can. (bo͞o-shä-vēl')	83a	45.37N	73.27W
Boucherville, Îles de, is., Can.	227b	45.37N	73.28W
Boudenib, Mor. (bo͞o-dĕ-nēb')	210	32.14N	3.04W
Boudette, Mn., U.S. (bo͞o-dĕt)	103	48.42N	94.34W
Boudouaou, Alg.	159	36.44N	3.25E
Boufarik, Alg. (bo͞o-fä-rēk')	159	36.35N	2.55E
Bougainville, i., Pap. N. Gui.	198e	6.00S	155.00E
Bougainville Trench, deep (bo͞o-găɴ-vēl')	225	7.00S	152.00E
Bougie see Bejaïa, Alg.	210	36.46N	5.00E
Bougouni, Mali (bo͞o-go͞o-nē')	210	11.27N	7.30W
Bouïra, Alg. (boo-ē'rá)	148	36.25N	3.55E
Bouïra-Sahary, Alg. (bwē-rá sá'ä-rē)	159	35.16N	3.23E
Bouka, r., Gui.	214	11.05N	10.40W
Boukiéro, Congo	244c	4.12S	15.18E
Boulder, Co., U.S.	96	40.02N	105.19W
Boulder, r., Mt., U.S.	105	46.10N	112.07W
Boulder City, Nv., U.S.	96	35.57N	114.50W
Boulder Peak, mtn., Id., U.S.	105	43.53N	114.33W
Boulogne, neigh., Arg.	233d	34.31S	58.34W
Boulogne-Billancourt, Fr. (bo͞o-lôn'y'-bē-yäɴ-ko͞or')	156	48.50N	2.14E
Boulogne-sur-Mer, Fr. (bo͞o-lôn'y-sür-mâr')	147	50.44N	1.37E
Boumba, r., Cam.	215	3.20N	14.40E
Bouna, C. Iv. (bo͞o-nä')	210	9.16N	3.00W
Bouna, Parc National de, rec., C. Iv.	214	9.20N	3.35W
Boundary Bay, b., N.A. (boun'dȧ-rĭ)	106d	49.03N	122.59W
Boundary Peak, mtn., Nv., U.S.	108	37.52N	118.20W
Bound Brook, N.J., U.S. (bound brŏŏk)	100a	40.34N	74.32W
Bountiful, Ut., U.S. (boun'tĭ-fŏŏl)	107b	40.55N	111.53W
Bountiful Peak, mtn., Ut., U.S. (boun'tĭ-fŏŏl)	107b	40.58N	111.49W
Bounty Islands, is., N.Z.	5	47.42S	179.05E
Bourail, N. Cal.	198f	21.34S	165.30E
Bourem, Mali (bo͞o-rĕm')	210	16.43N	0.15W
Bourg-en-Bresse, Fr. (bo͞or-gĕɴ-brĕs')	147	46.12N	5.13E
Bourges, Fr. (bo͞orzh)	147	47.06N	2.22E
Bourget, Can. (bo͞or-zhĕ')	83c	45.26N	75.09W
Bourg-la-Reine, Fr.	237c	48.47N	2.19E
Bourgoin, Fr. (bo͞or-gwăɴ')	157	45.46N	5.17E
Bourke, Austl. (bŭrk)	203	30.10S	146.00E
Bourne, Eng., U.K. (bōrn)	144a	52.46N	0.22W
Bournebridge, Eng., U.K.	235	51.38N	0.11E
Bourne End, Eng., U.K.	235	51.45N	0.32W
Bournemouth, Eng., U.K. (bôrn'mŭth)	150	50.44N	1.55W
Bou Saâda, Alg. (bo͞o-sä'dä)	148	35.13N	4.17E
Bousso, Chad (bo͞o-sô')	211	10.33N	16.45E
Boutilimit, Maur.	210	17.30N	14.54W
Bouvetøya, i., Ant.	3	55.00S	3.00E
Bövinghausen, neigh., Ger.	236	51.31N	7.19E
Bow, r., Can. (bō)	84	50.35N	112.15W
Bowbells, N.D., U.S. (bō'bĕls)	102	48.50N	102.16W
Bowdle, S.D., U.S. (bōd''l)	102	45.28N	99.42W
Bowdon, Eng., U.K.	237b	53.23N	2.22W
Bowen, Austl. (bō'ĕn)	203	20.02S	148.14E
Bowie, Md., U.S. (bo͞o'ĭ) (bō'ē)	100e	38.59N	76.47W
Bowie, Tx., U.S.	111	33.34N	97.50W
Bowling Green, Ky., U.S. (bōlĭng grēn)	97	37.00N	86.26W
Bowling Green, Mo., U.S.	111	39.19N	91.09W
Bowling Green, Oh., U.S.	98	41.25N	83.40W
Bowman, N.D., U.S. (bō'mȧn)	102	46.11N	103.23W
Bowron, r., Can. (bō'rŭn)	87	53.20N	121.10W
Boxelder Creek, r., Mt., U.S. (bŏks'ĕl-dẽr)	102	45.35N	104.28W
Box Elder Creek, r., Mt., U.S.	105	47.17N	108.37W
Box Hill, Austl.	201a	37.49S	145.08E
Boxian, China (bwo shyĕn)	192	33.52N	115.47E
Boxing, China (bwo-shyĭŋ)	190	37.09N	118.08E
Boxmoor, Eng., U.K.	235	51.45N	0.29W
Boxtel, Neth.	145a	51.40N	5.21E
Boyabo, Zaire	216	3.43N	18.46E
Boyacıköy, neigh., Tur.	239f	41.06N	29.02E
Boyang, China (bwo-yäŋ)	193	29.00N	116.42E
Boyer, r., Can. (boi'ẽr)	83b	46.45N	70.56W

PLACE (Pronunciation)	PAGE	Lat. °'	Long. °'
Boyer, r., Ia., U.S.	102	41.45N	95.36W
Boyle, Ire. (boil)	150	53.59N	8.15W
Boyne, r., Ire. (boin)	150	53.40N	6.40W
Boyne City, Mi., U.S.	98	45.15N	85.05W
Boyoma Falls, wtfl., Zaire	211	0.30N	25.12E
Boysen Reservoir, res., Wy., U.S.	105	43.19N	108.11W
Bozcaada, Tur. (bōz-cä'dä)	161	39.50N	26.05E
Bozca Ada, i., Tur.	161	39.50N	26.00E
Bozeman, Mt., U.S. (bōz'mȧn)	96	45.41N	111.00W
Bozene, Zaire	216	2.56N	19.12E
Bozhen, China (bwo-jŭn)	190	38.05N	116.35E
Bozoum, Cen. Afr. Rep.	215	6.19N	16.23E
Bra, Italy (brä)	160	44.41N	7.52E
Bracciano, Lago di, l., Italy (lä'gō-dē-brä-chä'nō)	160	42.05N	12.00E
Bracebridge, Can. (brās'brĭj)	91	45.05N	79.20W
Braceville, Il., U.S. (brās'vĭl)	101a	41.13N	88.16W
Bräcke, Swe. (brĕk'kĕ)	146	62.44N	15.28E
Brackenridge, Pa., U.S. (brăk'ĕn-rĭj)	101e	40.37N	79.44W
Brackettville, Tx., U.S. (brăk'ĕt-vĭl)	112	29.19N	100.24W
Braço Maior, mth., Braz.	131	11.00S	51.00W
Braço Menor, mth., Braz. (brä'zō-mē-nō'r)	131	11.38S	50.00W
Bradano, r., Italy (brä-dä'nō)	160	40.43N	16.22E
Braddock, Pa., U.S. (brăd'ŭk)	101e	40.24N	79.52W
Braddock Hills, Pa., U.S.	230b	40.25N	79.51W
Bradenburger Tor, pt. of i., Ger.	238a	52.31N	13.23E
Bradenton, Fl., U.S. (brā'dĕn-tŭn)	115a	27.28N	82.35W
Bradfield, Eng., U.K. (brăd'fēld)	144b	51.25N	1.08W
Bradford, Eng., U.K. (brăd'fẽrd)	146	53.47N	1.44W
Bradford, Oh., U.S.	98	40.10N	84.30W
Bradford, Pa., U.S.	99	42.00N	78.40W
Bradley, Il., U.S. (brăd'lĭ)	101a	41.09N	87.52W
Bradner, Can. (brăd'nẽr)	106d	49.05N	122.26W
Bradshaw, Eng., U.K.	237b	53.36N	2.24W
Brady, Tx., U.S. (brā'dĭ)	112	31.09N	99.21W
Braga, Port. (brä'gä)	148	41.20N	8.25W
Bragado, Arg. (brä-gä'dō)	132	35.07S	60.28W
Bragança, Braz. (brä-gän'sä)	131	1.02S	46.50W
Bragança, Port.	158	41.48N	6.46W
Bragança Paulista, Braz. (brä-gän'sä-pä'o͞o-lē's-tá)	132	22.58S	46.31W
Bragg Creek, Can. (brăg)	83e	50.57N	114.35W
Brahmaputra, r., Asia (brä'mȧ-po͞o'trȧ)	183	26.45N	92.45E
Brāhui, mts., Pak.	183	28.32N	66.15E
Braidwood, Il., U.S. (brăd'wŏŏd)	101a	41.16N	88.13W
Brăila, Rom. (brē'ēlá)	142	45.15N	27.58E
Brainerd, Mn., U.S. (brān'ẽrd)	103	46.20N	94.09W
Braintree, Ma., U.S. (brān'trē)	93a	42.14N	71.00W
Braithwaite, La., U.S. (brīth'wīt)	100d	29.52N	89.57W
Brakpan, S. Afr. (brăk'păn)	213b	26.15S	28.22E
Bralorne, Can. (brā'lôrn)	87	50.47N	122.49W
Bramalea, Can.	83d	43.48N	79.41W
Bramhall, Eng., U.K.	237b	53.22N	2.10W
Brampton, Can. (brămp'tŭn)	91	43.41N	79.46W
Branca, Pedra, mtn., Braz. (pĕ'drä-brä'ɴ-kä)	132b	22.55S	43.28W
Branchville, N.J., U.S. (brȧnch'vĭl)	100a	41.09S	74.44W
Branchville, S.C., U.S.	115	33.17N	80.48W
Branco, r., Braz. (bräŋ'kō)	131	2.21N	60.38W
Brandberg, mtn., Nmb.	212	21.15S	14.15E
Brandenburg, Ger. (brän'dĕn-bŏŏrgh)	147	52.25N	12.33E
Brandenburg, hist. reg., Ger.	154	52.12N	13.31E
Brandfort, S. Afr. (brăn'd-fôrt)	218d	28.42S	26.29E
Brandon, Can. (brăn'dŭn)	84	49.50N	99.57W
Brandon, Vt., U.S.	99	43.45N	73.05W
Brandon Mountain, mtn., Ire. (brăn-dŏn)	150	52.15N	10.12W
Brandywine, Md., U.S. (brăndĭ'wīn)	100e	38.42N	76.51W
Branford, Ct., U.S. (brăn'fẽrd)	99	41.15N	72.50W
Braniewo, Pol. (brä-nyĕ'vŏ)	155	54.23N	19.50E
Brańsk, Pol. (brän' sk)	155	52.44N	22.51E
Branson, Mo., U.S.	111	36.39N	93.13W
Brantford, Can. (brănt'fẽrd)	91	43.09N	80.17W
Bras d'Or Lake, l., Can. (brä-dôr')	93	45.52N	60.50W
Brasília, Braz. (brä-sē'lvä)	131	15.49S	47.39W
Brasilia Legal, Braz.	131	3.45S	55.46W
Brasópolis, Braz. (brä-sô'pô-lēs)	129a	22.30S	45.36W
Braşov, Rom.	149	45.39N	25.35E
Brass, Nig. (brăs)	210	4.28N	6.28E
Brasschaat, Bel. (bräs'ĸät)	145a	51.19N	4.30E
Bratcevo, neigh., Russia	239b	55.51N	37.24E
Bratenahl, Oh., U.S. (bră'tĕn-ôl)	101d	41.34N	81.36W
Bratislava, Slvk. (brä'tĭs-lä-vä)	142	48.09N	17.07E
Bratsk, Russia (brätsk)	165	56.10N	102.04E
Bratskoye Vodokhranilishche, res., Russia	165	56.10N	102.05E
Bratslav, Ukr. (brät'slåf)	163	48.48N	28.59E
Brattleboro, Vt., U.S. (brăt''l-bŭr-ô)	99	42.50N	72.35W
Braunau, Aus. (brou'nou)	154	48.15N	13.05E
Braunschweig, Ger. (broun'shvīgh)	147	52.16N	10.32E
Bråviken, r., Swe.	152	58.40N	16.40E
Brawley, Ca., U.S. (brô'lĭ)	96	32.59N	115.32W
Bray, Ire. (brā)	150	53.10N	6.05W
Braybrook, Austl.	243b	37.47S	144.51E
Braymer, Mo., U.S. (brā'mẽr)	111	39.34N	93.47W
Brays Bay, Tx., U.S. (brās'bĭ'yo͞o)	113a	29.41N	95.33W
Brazeau, r., Can.	87	52.55N	116.10W
Brazeau, Mount, mtn., Can. (brä-zō')	87	52.33N	117.21W
Brazil, In., U.S. (brȧ-zĭl')	98	39.30N	87.00W
Brazil, nation, S.A.	131	9.00S	53.00W
Brazilian Highlands, mts., Braz. (brȧ zĭl yȧn hī-lȧndz)	128	14.00S	48.00W
Brazos, r., Tx., U.S. (brä'zōs)	96	33.10N	98.50W
Brazos, Clear Fork, r., Tx., U.S.	112	32.56N	99.14W
Brazos, Double Mountain Fork, r., Tx., U.S.	110	33.23N	101.21W

ng-sing; ŋ-baŋk; ɴ-nasalized n; nŏd; cŏmmit; ōld; ôbey; ôrder; oi-boil; fo͞od; ŏŏ-as oo in foot; ou-out; s-soft; sh-dish; th-thin; pūre; ûnite; ûrn; stŭd; circŭs; ü-as in French tu; '-indeterminate vowel.

268 Brazos-Buckhorn Island State Park

PLACE (Pronunciation)	PAGE	Lat. °′	Long. °′
Brazos, Salt Fork, r., Tx., U.S. (sôlt fôrk)	110	33.20N	101.57W
Brazzaville, Congo (brá-zá-vēl′)	212	4.16S	15.17E
Brčko, Bos. (běrch′kô)	161	44.54N	18.46E
Brda, r., Pol. (běr-dä)	155	53.18N	17.55E
Brea, Ca., U.S. (brē′à)	107a	33.55N	117.54W
Breakeyville, Can.	83b	46.40N	71.13W
Brechten, neigh., Ger.	236	51.35N	7.28E
Breckenridge, Mn., U.S. (brěk′ěn-rĭj)	102	46.17N	96.35W
Breckenridge, Tx., U.S.	112	32.46N	98.53W
Breckerfeld, Ger.	236	51.16N	7.28E
Brecksville, Oh., U.S. (brěks′vĭl)	101d	41.19N	81.38W
Břeclav, Czech Rep. (brzhěl′läf)	154	48.46N	16.54E
Breda, Neth. (brā-dä′)	151	51.35N	4.47E
Bredasdorp, S. Afr. (brā′das-dôrp)	212	34.15S	20.00E
Bredbury, Eng., U.K.	237b	53.25N	2.06W
Bredell, S. Afr.	244b	26.05S	28.17E
Bredeney, neigh., Ger.	236	51.24N	6.59E
Bredenscheid-Stüter, Ger.	236	51.22N	7.11E
Bredy, Russia (brě′dĭ)	172a	52.25N	60.23E
Breezewood, Pa., U.S.	230b	40.34N	80.03W
Bregenz, Aus. (brā′gěnts)	154	47.30N	9.46E
Bregovo, Bul. (brě′gô-vô)	161	44.07N	22.45E
Breidafjördur, b., Ice.	146	65.15N	22.50W
Breidbach, S. Afr. (brēd′băk)	213c	32.54S	27.26E
Breil-sur-Roya, Fr. (brě′y′)	157	43.57N	7.36E
Breitscheid, Ger.	236	51.22N	6.52E
Brejo, Braz. (brå′zhò)	131	3.33S	42.46W
Bremangerlandet, i., Nor.	152	61.51N	4.25E
Bremen, Ger. (brā-měn)	142	53.05N	8.50E
Bremen, In., U.S. (brē′měn)	98	41.25N	86.05W
Bremerhaven, Ger. (brām-ĕr-hä′fĕn)	146	53.33N	8.38E
Bremerton, Wa., U.S. (brěm′ẽr-tŭn)	104	47.34N	122.38W
Bremervörde, Ger. (brě′měr-fûr-dě)	145c	53.29N	9.09E
Bremner, Can. (brěm′nẽr)	83g	53.34N	113.14W
Bremond, Tx., U.S. (brěm′ŭnd)	113	31.11N	96.40W
Breña, Peru	233c	12.04S	77.04W
Brenham, Tx., U.S. (brěn′ăm)	113	30.10N	96.24W
Bren Mar Park, Md., U.S.	229d	38.48N	77.09W
Brenner Pass, p., Eur. (brěn′ẽr)	147	47.00N	11.30E
Brentford, neigh., Eng., U.K.	235	51.29N	0.18W
Brenthurst, S. Afr.	244b	26.16S	28.23E
Brentwood, Eng., U.K. (brěnt′wòd)	151	51.37N	0.18E
Brentwood, Md., U.S.	99	39.00N	76.55W
Brentwood, Mo., U.S.	107e	38.37N	90.21W
Brentwood, Pa., U.S.	101e	40.22N	79.59W
Brentwood Heights, neigh., Ca., U.S.	232	34.04N	118.30W
Brentwood Park, S. Afr.	244b	26.08S	28.18E
Brescia, Italy (brā′shä)	148	45.33N	10.15E
Bressanone, Italy (brěs-sä-nō′nā)	160	46.42N	11.40E
Bresso, Italy	238c	45.32N	9.11E
Bressuire, Fr. (grĕ-swēr′)	156	46.49N	0.14W
Brest, Bela.	164	52.06N	23.43E
Brest, Fr. (brěst)	142	48.24N	4.30W
Brest, prov., Bela.	162	52.30N	26.50E
Bretagne, hist. reg., Fr. (brĕ-tän′yĕ)	156	48.00N	3.00W
Breton, Pertuis, strt., Fr. (pâr-twĕ′brĕ-tôn′)	156	46.18N	1.43W
Breton Sound, strt., La., U.S. (brĕt′ŭn)	114	29.38N	89.15W
Breukelen, Neth.	145a	52.09N	5.00E
Brevard, N.C., U.S. (brē-värd′)	115	35.14N	82.45W
Breves, Braz. (brā′vězh)	131	1.32S	50.13W
Brevik, Nor. (brě′věk)	152	59.04N	9.39E
Brewarrina, Austl. (brōō-ēr-rē′nà)	203	29.54S	146.50E
Brewer, Me., U.S. (brōō′ēr)	92	44.46N	68.46W
Brewerville, Lib.	214	6.26N	10.47W
Brewster, N.Y., U.S. (brōō′stẽr)	100a	41.23N	73.38W
Brewster, Cerro, mtn., Pan. (sĕ′r-rô-brōō′stẽr)	121	9.19N	79.15W
Brewton, Al., U.S. (brōō′tŭn)	114	31.06N	87.04W
Brežice, Slvn. (brě′zhē-tsě)	160	45.55N	15.37E
Breznik, Bul. (brěs′něk)	161	42.44N	22.55E
Briancon, Fr. (brē-än-sôn′)	157	44.54N	6.39E
Briare, Fr. (brē-är′)	156	47.40N	2.46E
Bridal Veil, Or., U.S. (brīd′ál vāl)	106c	45.33N	122.10W
Bridge Point, c., Bah. (brĭj)	122	25.35N	76.40W
Bridgeport, Al., U.S. (brĭj′pôrt)	114	34.55N	85.42W
Bridgeport, Ct., U.S.	97	41.12N	73.12W
Bridgeport, Il., U.S.	98	38.40N	87.45W
Bridgeport, Ne., U.S.	102	41.40N	103.06W
Bridgeport, Oh., U.S.	98	40.00N	80.45W
Bridgeport, Pa., U.S.	100f	40.06N	75.21W
Bridgeport, Tx., U.S.	111	33.13N	97.46W
Bridgeport, neigh., Il., U.S.	231a	41.51N	87.39W
Bridgeton, Al., U.S. (brĭj′tŭn)	100h	33.27N	86.39W
Bridgeton, Mo., U.S.	107e	38.45N	90.23W
Bridgeton, N.J., U.S.	99	39.30N	75.15W
Bridgetown, Barb. (brĭj′ toun)	117	13.08N	59.37W
Bridgetown, Can.	92	44.51N	65.18W
Bridgeview, Il., U.S.	231a	41.45N	87.48W
Bridgeville, Pa., U.S. (brĭj′vĭl)	101e	40.22N	80.07W
Bridgewater, Austl. (brĭj′wô-tẽr)	204	42.50S	147.28E
Bridgewater, Can.	85	44.23N	64.31W
Bridgnorth, Eng., U.K. (brĭj′nôrth)	144a	52.32N	2.25W
Bridgton, Me., U.S. (brĭj′tŭn)	92	44.04N	70.45W
Bridlington, Eng., U.K. (brĭd′lĭng-tŭn)	150	54.06N	0.10W
Brie-Comte-Robert, Fr. (brē-kônt-ĕ-rō-bâr′)	157b	48.42N	2.37E
Brielle, Neth.	145a	51.54N	4.08E
Brierfield, Eng., U.K. (brī′ẽr fēld)	144a	53.49N	2.14W
Brierfield, Al., U.S. (brī′ẽr-fēld)	114	33.01N	86.55W
Brier Island, i., Can. (brī′ẽr)	92	44.16N	66.24W
Brieselang, Ger. (brē′zĕ-läng)	145b	52.36N	12.59E
Briey, Fr. (brē-ĕ′)	157	49.15N	5.57E
Brig, Switz. (brēg)	147	46.17N	7.59E
Brigg, Eng., U.K. (brĭg)	144a	53.33N	0.29W
Brigham City, Ut., U.S. (brĭg′ăm)	107b	41.31N	112.01W
Brighouse, Eng., U.K. (brĭg′hous)	144a	53.42N	1.47W
Bright, Austl. (brīt)	204	36.43S	147.00E
Bright, In., U.S. (brīt)	101f	39.13N	84.51W
Brightlingsea, Eng., U.K. (brī′t-lĭng-sē)	144b	51.50N	1.00E
Brightmoor, neigh., Mi., U.S.	230c	42.24N	83.14W
Brighton, Austl.	201a	37.55S	145.00E
Brighton, Eng., U.K.	147	50.47N	0.07W
Brighton, Al., U.S. (brī′tŭn)	100h	33.27N	86.56W
Brighton, Co., U.S.	110	39.58N	104.49W
Brighton, Il., U.S.	107e	39.03N	90.08W
Brighton, Ia., U.S.	103	41.11N	91.47W
Brighton, neigh., Ma., U.S.	227a	42.21N	71.08W
Brighton Indian Reservation, I.R., Fl., U.S.	115a	27.05N	81.25W
Brighton Le-Sands, Austl.	243a	33.58S	151.09E
Brightwood, neigh., D.C., U.S.	229d	38.58N	77.02W
Brigittenau, neigh., Aus.	239e	48.14N	16.22E
Brihuega, Spain (brē-wā′gä)	158	40.32N	2.52W
Brilyn Park, Va., U.S.	229d	38.54N	77.10W
Brimley, Mi., U.S. (brĭm′lē)	107k	46.24N	84.34W
Brindisi, Italy (brēn′dē-zē)	142	40.38N	17.57E
Brinje, Cro. (brēn′yĕ)	160	45.00N	15.08E
Brinkleigh, Md., U.S.	229c	39.18N	76.50W
Brinkley, Ar., U.S. (brĭŋk′lĭ)	111	34.52N	91.12W
Brinnon, Wa., U.S. (brĭn′ŭn)	106a	47.41N	122.54W
Brion, i., Can. (brē-ôn′)	93	47.47N	61.29W
Brioude, Fr. (brē-ōōd′)	156	45.18N	3.22E
Brisbane, Austl. (brĭz′bån)	204	27.30S	153.10E
Brisbane, Ca., U.S.	231b	37.41N	122.24W
Bristol, Eng., U.K.	147	51.29N	2.39W
Bristol, Ct., U.S. (brĭs′tŭl)	99	41.40N	72.55W
Bristol, Pa., U.S.	100f	40.06N	74.51W
Bristol, R.I., U.S.	100b	41.41N	71.14W
Bristol, Tn., U.S.	97	36.35N	82.10W
Bristol, Vt., U.S.	99	44.10N	73.00W
Bristol, Va., U.S.	97	36.36N	82.00W
Bristol, Wi., U.S.	101a	42.32N	88.04W
Bristol Bay, b., Ak., U.S.	95	58.05N	158.54W
Bristol Channel, strt., Eng., U.K.	147	51.20N	3.47W
Bristow, Ok., U.S. (brĭs′tō)	111	35.50N	96.25W
British Columbia, prov., Can. (brĭt′ĭsh kŏl′ŭm-bĭ-à)	84	56.00N	124.53W
British Indian Ocean Territory, dep., Afr.	2	7.00S	72.00E
British Isles, is., Eur.	142	54.00N	4.00W
Brits, S. Afr.	218d	25.39S	27.47E
Britstown, S. Afr. (brĭts′toun)	212	30.30S	23.40E
Britt, Ia., U.S. (brĭt)	103	43.05N	93.47W
Brittany *see* Bretagne, hist. reg., Fr.	156	48.00N	3.00W
Britton, S.D., U.S. (brĭt′ŭn)	102	45.47N	97.44W
Brive-la-Gaillarde, Fr. (brēv-lä-gī-yärd′ĕ)	147	45.10N	1.31E
Briviesca, Spain (brē-vyās′kä)	158	42.34N	3.21W
Brno, Czech Rep. (b′r′nô)	142	49.18N	16.37E
Broa, Ensenada de la, b., Cuba	122	22.30N	82.00W
Broach, India	186	21.47N	72.58E
Broad, r., Ga., U.S. (brôd)	114	34.15N	83.14W
Broad, r., N.C., U.S.	115	35.38N	82.40W
Broadheath, Eng., U.K.	237b	53.24N	2.21W
Broadley Common, Eng., U.K.	235	51.45N	0.04E
Broadmeadows, Austl. (brôd′měd-ōz)	201a	37.40S	144.53E
Broadmeadows, Austl.	243b	37.40S	144.54E
Broadmoor, Ca., U.S.	231b	37.41N	122.29W
Broadview Heights, Oh., U.S. (brôd′vū)	101d	41.18N	81.41W
Brockenscheidt, Ger.	236	51.38N	7.25E
Brockport, N.Y., U.S. (brŏk′pōrt)	99	43.15N	77.55W
Brockton, Ma., U.S. (brŏk′tŭn)	93a	42.04N	71.01W
Brockville, Can. (brŏk′vĭl)	85	44.35N	75.40W
Brockway, Mt., U.S. (brŏk′wā)	105	47.24N	105.41W
Brodnica, Pol. (brôd′nĭt-så)	155	53.16N	19.26E
Brody, Ukr. (brô′dĭ)	167	50.05N	25.10E
Broich, neigh., Ger.	236	51.25N	6.51E
Broken Arrow, Ok., U.S. (brō′kĕn ăr′ō)	111	36.03N	95.48W
Broken Bay, b., Austl.	204	33.34S	151.20E
Broken Bow, Ne., U.S. (brō′kĕn bō)	102	41.24N	99.37W
Broken Bow, Ok., U.S.	111	34.02N	94.43W
Broken Hill, Austl. (brōk′ĕn)	203	31.55S	141.35E
Broken Hill *see* Kabwe, Zam.	212	14.27S	28.27E
Bromall, Pa., U.S.	229b	39.59N	75.22W
Bromborough, Eng., U.K.	237a	53.19N	2.59W
Bromley, Eng., U.K. (brŭm′lĭ)	144b	51.23N	0.01E
Bromley Common, neigh., Eng., U.K.	235	51.22N	0.03E
Bromptonville, Can. (brŭmp′tŭn-vĭl)	91	45.30N	72.00W
Brønderslev, Den. (brûn′dẽr-slěv)	152	57.15N	9.56E
Bronkhorstspruit, S. Afr.	218d	25.50S	28.48E
Bronnitsy, Russia (brô-nyĭ′tsĭ)	162	55.26N	38.16E
Bronson, Mi., U.S. (brŏn′sŭn)	98	41.55N	85.15W
Bronte Creek, r., Can.	83d	43.25N	79.53W
Bronx, neigh., N.Y., U.S.	228	40.49N	73.56W
Bronxville, N.Y., U.S.	228	40.56N	73.50W
Brood, r., S.C., U.S. (brōōd)	115	34.46N	81.25W
Brookfield, Il., U.S. (bròk′fēld)	101a	41.49N	87.51W
Brookfield, Mo., U.S.	111	39.45N	93.04W
Brookhaven, Ga., U.S. (bròk′hāv′n)	100c	33.52N	84.21W
Brookhaven, Ms., U.S.	114	31.35N	90.26W
Brookhaven, Pa., U.S.	229b	39.52N	75.23W
Brookings, Or., U.S. (bròk′ĭngs)	104	42.04N	124.16W
Brookings, S.D., U.S.	102	44.18N	96.47W
Brookland, neigh., D.C., U.S.	229d	38.56N	76.59W
Brooklandville, Md., U.S.	229c	39.26N	76.41W
Brooklawn, N.J., U.S.	229b	39.53N	75.08W
Brookline, Ma., U.S. (bròk′lĭn)	93a	42.20N	71.08W
Brookline, N.H., U.S.	93a	42.44N	71.37W
Brooklyn, Oh., U.S. (bròk′lĭn)	101d	41.26N	81.44W
Brooklyn, neigh., Md., U.S.	229c	39.14N	76.36W
Brooklyn Center, Mn., U.S.	107g	45.05N	93.21W
Brooklyn Heights, Oh., U.S.	229a	41.24N	81.40W
Brooklyn Park, Md., U.S.	229c	39.14N	76.36W
Brookmans Park, Eng., U.K.	235	51.43N	0.12W
Brookmont, Md., U.S.	229d	38.57N	77.07W
Brook Park, Oh., U.S. (bròk)	101d	41.24N	81.50W
Brooks, Can.	87	50.35N	111.53W
Brooks Range, mts., Ak., U.S. (bròks)	96a	68.20N	159.00W
Brook Street, Eng., U.K.	235	51.37N	0.17E
Brooksville, Fl., U.S. (bròks′vĭl)	115a	28.32N	82.28W
Brookvale, Austl.	243a	33.46S	151.17E
Brookville, In., U.S. (bròk′vĭl)	98	39.20N	85.00W
Brookville, Ma., U.S.	227a	42.08N	71.01W
Brookville, N.Y., U.S.	228	40.49N	73.35W
Brookville, Pa., U.S.	99	41.10N	79.00W
Brookwood, Al., U.S. (bròk′wòd)	114	33.15N	87.17W
Broome, Austl. (brōōm)	202	18.00S	122.15E
Brossard, Can.	83a	45.26N	73.28W
Brothers, is., Bah. (brŭd′hẽrs)	122	26.05N	79.00W
Broughton, Pa., U.S.	230b	40.21N	79.59W
Broumov, Czech Rep. (brōō′môf)	154	50.33N	15.55E
Brou-sur-Chantereine, Fr.	237c	48.53N	2.38E
Brown Bank, bk.	123	21.30N	74.35W
Brownfield, Tx., U.S. (broun′fēld)	110	33.11N	102.16W
Browning, Mt., U.S. (broun′ĭng)	105	48.37N	113.05W
Brownsboro, Ky., U.S. (brounz′bô-rò)	101h	38.22N	85.30W
Brownsburg, Can. (brouns′bûrg)	83a	45.40N	74.24W
Brownsburg, In., U.S.	101g	39.51N	86.23W
Brownsmead, Or., U.S. (brounz′-mēd)	106c	46.13N	123.33W
Brownstown, In., U.S. (brounz′toun)	98	38.50N	86.00W
Brownsville, Pa., U.S. (brounz′vĭl)	101e	40.01N	79.53W
Brownsville, Tn., U.S.	114	35.35N	89.15W
Brownsville, Tx., U.S.	96	25.55N	97.30W
Brownville Junction, Me., U.S. (broun′vĭl)	92	45.20N	69.04W
Brownwood, Tx., U.S. (broun′wòd)	96	31.44N	98.58W
Brownwood, l., Tx., U.S.	112	31.55N	99.15W
Broxbourne, Eng., U.K.	235	51.45N	0.01W
Brozas, Spain (brō′thäs)	158	39.37N	6.44W
Bruce, Mount, mtn., Austl. (brōōs)	202	22.35S	118.15E
Bruce Peninsula, pen., Can.	90	44.50N	81.20W
Bruceton, Tn., U.S. (brōōs′tŭn)	114	36.02N	88.14W
Bruchmühle, Ger.	238a	52.33N	13.47E
Bruchsal, Ger. (bròk′zäl)	154	49.08N	8.34E
Bruck, Aus. (bròk)	154	47.25N	15.14E
Bruck, Aus.	154	48.01N	16.47E
Brück, Ger. (brük)	145b	52.12N	12.45E
Bruckhausen, neigh., Ger.	236	51.29N	6.44E
Bruderheim, Can. (brōō′dẽr-hīm)	83g	53.47N	112.56W
Brugge, Bel.	147	51.13N	3.05E
Brügge, Ger.	236	51.13N	7.34E
Brugherio, Italy	238c	45.33N	9.18E
Brühl, Ger. (brül)	157c	50.49N	6.54E
Bruneau, r., Id., U.S. (brōō-nō′)	104	42.47N	115.43W
Brunei, nation, Asia (brò-nī′)	196	4.52N	113.38E
Brünen, Ger. (brü′něn)	157c	51.43N	6.41E
Brunete, Spain (brōō-nā′tå)	159a	40.24N	4.00W
Brunette, i., Can. (brò-nět′)	93	47.16N	55.54W
Brunn am Gebirge, Aus. (brōōn′äm gě-bĭr′gě)	145e	48.07N	16.18E
Brunoy, Fr.	237c	48.42N	2.30E
Brunsbüttel, Ger. (bròns′büt-těl)	145c	53.58N	9.10E
Brunswick, Austl.	243b	37.46S	144.58E
Brunswick, Ga., U.S. (brŭnz′wĭk)	97	31.08N	81.30W
Brunswick, Me., U.S.	92	43.54N	69.57W
Brunswick, Md., U.S.	99	39.20N	77.35W
Brunswick, Mo., U.S.	111	39.25N	93.07W
Brunswick, Oh., U.S.	101d	41.14N	81.50W
Brunswick, Península de, pen., Chile	132	53.25S	71.15W
Bruny, i., Austl. (brōō′nē)	203	43.30S	147.50E
Brush, Co., U.S. (brŭsh)	110	40.14N	103.40W
Brusque, Braz. (brōō′s-kōōĕ)	132	27.15S	48.45W
Brussels, Bel.	142	50.51N	4.21E
Brussels, Il., U.S. (brŭs′ĕls)	107e	38.57N	90.36W
Bruxelles *see* Brussels, Bel.	142	50.51N	4.21E
Bryan, Oh., U.S. (brī′ăn)	98	41.25N	84.30W
Bryan, Tx., U.S.	113	30.40N	96.22W
Bryansk, Russia	164	53.15N	34.22E
Bryansk, prov., Russia	162	52.43N	32.25E
Bryant, S.D., U.S. (brī′ănt)	102	44.35N	97.29W
Bryant, Wa., U.S.	106a	48.14N	122.10W
Bryce Canyon National Park, rec., Ut., U.S. (brīs)	96	37.35N	112.15W
Bryn Mawr, Pa., U.S. (brĭn mår′)	100f	40.02N	75.20W
Bryson City, N.C., U.S. (brīs′ŭn)	114	35.25N	83.25W
Bryukhovetskaya, Russia (b′ryŭk′ô-vyĕt-skä′yä)	163	45.56N	38.58E
Buala, Sol.Is.	198e	8.08S	159.35E
Buatan, Indon.	181b	0.45N	101.49E
Buba, Gui.-B. (bōō′bà)	210	11.39N	14.58W
Buc, Fr.	237c	48.46N	2.08E
Bucaramanga, Col. (bōō-kä′rä-mäŋ′gä)	130	7.12N	73.14W
Buccaneer Archipelago, is., Austl. (bŭk-à-nēr′)	202	16.05S	122.00E
Buch, neigh., Ger.	238a	52.38N	13.30E
Buchach, Ukr. (bò′chàch)	155	49.04N	25.25E
Buchanan, Lib. (bů-kăn′ăn)	210	5.57N	10.02W
Buchanan, Mi., U.S.	98	41.50N	86.25W
Buchanan, l., Austl. (bû-kân′nŏn)	203	21.40S	145.00E
Buchanan, l., Tx., U.S. (bû-kăn′ăn)	112	30.55N	98.40W
Buchans, Can.	93	48.49N	56.52W
Bucharest, Rom.	142	44.23N	26.10E
Buchholz, Ger. (bōōk′hôltz)	145c	53.19N	9.53E
Buchholz, Ger.	238a	52.35N	13.47E
Buchholz, neigh., Ger.	236	51.23N	6.46E
Buchholz, neigh., Ger.	238a	52.36N	13.26E
Buck Creek, r., In., U.S. (bŭk)	101g	39.43N	85.58W
Buckhannon, W.V., U.S. (bŭk-hăn′ŭn)	98	39.00N	80.10W
Buckhaven, Scot., U.K. (bŭk-hā′v′n)	150	56.10N	3.10W
Buckhorn Island State Park, pt. of i., N.Y., U.S.	230a	43.03N	78.59W

ăt; finăl; rāte; senâte; ärm; åsk; sofà; fâre; ch-choose; dh-as th in other; bē; ēvent; bět; recěnt; cratẽr; g-gō; gh-guttural g; bĭt; ĭ-short neutral; rīde; k-guttural k as ch in German ich;

PLACE (Pronunciation)	PAGE	Lat. °′	Long. °′
Buckie, Scot., U.K. (bŭk′ĭ)	150	57.40N	2.50W
Buckingham, Can. (bŭk′ĭng-ăm)	83c	45.35N	75.25W
Buckingham, can., India (bŭk′ĭng-ăm)	187	15.18N	79.50E
Buckingham Palace, pt. of i., Eng., U.K.	235	51.30N	0.08W
Buckinghamshire, co., Eng., U.K.	144b	51.45N	0.48W
Buckland, Can. (bŭk′lănd)	83b	46.37N	70.33W
Buckland Tableland, reg., Austl.	203	24.31S	148.00E
Buckley, Wa., U.S. (buk′lē)	106a	47.10N	122.02W
Buckow, neigh., Ger.	238a	52.25N	13.26E
Bucksport, Me., U.S. (bŭks′pôrt)	92	44.35N	68.47W
Buctouche, Can. (bük-to͞osh′)	92	46.28N	64.43W
Bucun, China (bo͞o-tsòn)	190	36.38N	117.26E
București see Bucharest, Rom.	142	44.23N	26.10E
Bucyrus, Oh., U.S. (bū-sī′rŭs)	98	40.50N	82.55W
Buda, neigh., Hung.	239g	47.30N	19.02E
Budakeszi, Hung.	239g	47.31N	18.56E
Budaörs, Hung.	239g	47.27N	18.58E
Budapest, Hung. (bo͞o′dá-pĕsht′)	142	47.30N	19.05E
Budberg, Ger.	236	51.32N	6.38E
Büderich, Ger.	236	51.37N	6.34E
Budge Budge, India	186a	22.28N	88.08E
Budjala, Zaire	216	2.39N	19.42E
Budyonnovsk, Russia	168	44.46N	44.09E
Buea, Cam.	215	4.09N	9.14E
Buechel, Ky., U.S. (bē-chûl′)	101h	38.12N	85.38W
Bueil, Fr. (bwā′)	157b	48.55N	1.27E
Buena Park, Ca., U.S. (bwā′ná pärk)	107a	33.52N	118.00W
Buenaventura, Col. (bwā′nä-vĕn-to͞o′rá)	130	3.46N	77.09W
Buenaventura, Cuba	123a	22.53N	82.22W
Buenaventura, Bahía de, b., Col.	130	3.45N	79.23W
Buena Vista, Co., U.S. (bū′ná vĭs′tá)	110	38.51N	106.07W
Buena Vista, Ga., U.S.	114	32.15N	84.30W
Buena Vista, Va., U.S.	99	37.45N	79.20W
Buena Vista, Bahía, b., Cuba (bä-ē′ä-bwĕ-nä-vē′s-tä)	122	22.30N	79.10W
Buena Vista Lake Bed, l., Ca., U.S. (bū′ná vĭs′tá)	108	35.14N	119.17W
Buendia, Embalse de, res., Spain	158	40.30N	2.45W
Buenos Aires, Arg. (bwā′nōs ī′rās)	132	34.20S	58.30W
Buenos Aires, Col.	130a	3.01N	76.34W
Buenos Aires, C.R.	121	9.10N	83.21W
Buenos Aires, prov., Arg.	132	36.15S	61.45W
Buenos Aires, l., S.A.	132	46.30S	72.15W
Buer, neigh., Ger.	236	51.36N	7.03E
Buffalo, Mn., U.S. (buf′á lō)	103	45.10N	93.50W
Buffalo, N.Y., U.S.	97	42.54N	78.51W
Buffalo, Tx., U.S.	113	31.28N	96.04W
Buffalo, Wy., U.S.	105	44.19N	106.42W
Buffalo, r., S. Afr.	213c	28.35S	30.27E
Buffalo, r., Ar., U.S.	111	35.56N	92.58W
Buffalo, r., Tn., U.S.	114	35.24N	87.10W
Buffalo Bayou, Tx., U.S.	113a	29.46N	95.32W
Buffalo Creek, r., Mn., U.S.	103	44.46N	94.28W
Buffalo Harbor, b., N.Y., U.S.	230a	42.51N	78.52W
Buffalo Head Hills, hills, Can.	84	57.16N	116.18W
Buford, Can. (bū′fûrd)	83g	53.15N	113.55W
Buford, Ga., U.S. (bū′fẽrd)	114	34.05N	84.00W
Bug (Zakhidnyy Buh), r., Eur.	155	52.29N	21.20E
Buga, Col. (bo͞o′gä)	130	3.54N	76.17W
Buggenhout, Bel.	145a	51.01N	4.10E
Buglandsfjorden, l., Nor.	152	58.53N	7.55E
Bugojno, Bos. (bò-gō ĭ nò)	161	44.03N	17.28E
Bugul′ma, Russia (bò-gòl′má)	164	54.40N	52.40E
Buguruslan, Russia (bò-gò-ròs-làn′)	164	53.30N	52.32E
Buhi, Phil. (bo͞o′ê)	197a	13.26N	123.31E
Buhl, Id., U.S. (būl)	105	42.36N	114.45W
Buhl, Mn., U.S.	103	47.28N	92.49W
Buin, Chile (bò-ēn′)	129b	33.44S	70.44W
Buinaksk, Russia (bò′ê-näksk)	167	42.40N	47.20E
Buir Nur, l., Asia (bo͞o-ēr no͞or)	189	47.50N	117.00E
Bujalance, Spain (bo͞o-hä-län′thā)	158	37.54N	4.22W
Bujumbura, Bdi.	217	3.23S	29.22E
Buka Island, i., Pap. N. Gui.	198e	5.15S	154.35E
Bukama, Zaire (bo͞o-kä′mä)	212	9.08S	26.00E
Bukavu, Zaire	212	2.30S	28.52E
Bukhara, Uzb. (bò-kä′rä)	169	39.31N	64.22E
Bukitbatu, Indon.	181b	1.25N	101.58E
Bukit Panjang, Sing.	240c	1.23N	103.46E
Bukit Timah, Sing.	240c	1.20N	103.47E
Bukittinggi, Indon.	196	0.25S	100.28E
Bukoba, Tan.	212	1.20S	31.49E
Bukovina, hist. reg., Eur. (bò-kô′vĭ-ná)	155	48.06N	25.20E
Bula, Indon. (bo͞o′lä)	197	3.00S	130.30E
Bulalacao, Phil. (bo͞o-lä-lä′kä-ô)	197a	12.30N	121.20E
Bulawayo, Zimb. (bo͞o-lá-wä′yō)	212	20.12S	28.43E
Buldir, i., Ak., U.S. (bŭl dĭr)	95a	52.22N	175.50E
Bulgaria, nation, Eur. (bòl-gā′rĭ-ă)	142	42.12N	24.13E
Bulim, Sing.	240c	1.23N	103.43E
Bulkley Ranges, mts., Can. (bŭlk′lē)	86	54.30N	127.30W
Bullaque, r., Spain (bò-lä′kå)	158	39.15N	4.13W
Bullas, Spain (bo͞ol′yäs)	158	38.07N	1.48W
Bullfrog Creek, r., Ut., U.S.	109	37.45N	110.55W
Bull Harbour, Can. (hăr′bẽr)	86	50.45N	127.55W
Bull Head, mtn., Jam.	122	18.10N	77.15W
Bull Run, r., Or., U.S. (bòl)	106c	45.26N	122.11W
Bull Run Reservoir, res., Or., U.S.	106c	45.29N	122.11W
Bull Shoals Reservoir, res., U.S. (bòl shōlz)	97	36.35N	92.57W
Bulmke-Hüllen, neigh., Ger.	236	51.31N	7.06E
Bulpham, Eng., U.K. (bo͞ol′făn)	144b	51.33N	0.21E
Bultfontein, S. Afr. (bòlt′fŏn-tān′)	218d	28.18S	26.10E
Bulun, Russia (bo͞o-lòn′)	165	70.48N	127.27E
Bulungu, Zaire (bo͞o-lòŋ′go͞o)	216	6.04S	21.54E
Bulwer, S. Afr. (bòl-wẽr)	213c	29.49S	29.48E
Bumba, Zaire (bòm′bá)	211	2.11N	22.28E
Bumbire Island, i., Tan.	217	1.40S	32.05E
Bumbles Green, Eng., U.K.	235	51.44N	0.02E
Buna, Pap. N. Gui. (bo͞o′ná)	197	8.58S	148.38E
Bunbury, Austl. (bŭn′bŭrĭ)	202	33.25S	115.45E
Bundaberg, Austl. (bŭn′dá-bûrg)	203	24.45S	152.18E
Bundoora, Austl. (Chan.)	243b	37.42S	145.04E
Bunguran Utara, Kepulauan, is., Indon.	196	3.22N	108.00E
Bunia, Zaire	217	1.34N	30.15E
Bunker Hill, Il., U.S. (bŭnk′ẽr hĭl)	107e	39.03N	89.57W
Bunker Hill Monument, pt. of i., Ma., U.S.	227a	42.22N	71.04W
Bunkie, La., U.S. (bŭŋ′kĭ)	113	30.55N	92.10W
Bun Plains, pl., Kenya	217	0.55N	40.35E
Bununu Dass, Nig.	215	10.00N	9.31E
Buona Vista, Sing.	240c	1.16N	103.47E
Buor-Khaya, Guba, b., Russia	171	71.45N	131.00E
Buor Khaya, Mys, c., Russia	165	71.47N	133.22E
Bura, Kenya	217	1.06S	39.57E
Buraydah, Sau. Ar.	182	26.23N	44.14E
Burbank, Ca., U.S. (bûr′bănk)	107a	34.11N	118.19W
Burco, Som.	218a	9.20N	45.45E
Burdekin, r., Austl. (bûr′dē-kĭn)	203	19.22S	145.07E
Burdur, Tur. (bo͞or-dòr′)	149	37.50N	30.15E
Burdwān, India (bòd-wän′)	183	23.29N	87.53E
Bureinskiy, Khrebet, mts., Russia	165	51.15N	133.30E
Bures-sur-Yvette, Fr.	237c	48.42N	2.10E
Bureya, Russia (bòrā′á)	165	49.55N	130.00E
Bureya, r., Russia (bò-rā′yä)	171	51.00N	131.15E
Burford, Eng., U.K. (bûr-fẽrd)	144b	51.46N	1.38W
Burg, Ger.	236	51.08N	7.09E
Burgas, Bul. (bòr-gäs′)	149	42.29N	27.30E
Burgas, Gulf of, b., Bul.	149	42.30N	27.40E
Burgaw, N.C., U.S. (bûr′gô)	115	34.31N	77.56W
Burgdorf, Switz. (bòrg′dôrf)	154	47.04N	7.37E
Burgenland, prov., Aus.	145e	47.58N	16.57E
Burgeo, Can.	93	47.36N	57.34W
Burger Township, S. Afr.	244b	26.05S	27.46E
Burgess, Va., U.S.	99	37.53N	76.21W
Burgh Heath, Eng., U.K.	235	51.18N	0.13W
Burgos, Mex. (bòr′gōs)	112	24.57N	98.47W
Burgos, Phil.	197a	16.03N	119.52E
Burgos, Spain (bo͞o′r-gôs)	148	42.20N	3.44W
Burgsvik, Swe. (bòrgs′vĭk)	152	57.04N	18.18E
Burhānpur, India (bòr′hän-po͞or)	183	21.26N	76.08E
Burholme, neigh., Pa., U.S.	229b	40.03N	75.05W
Burias Island, i., Phil. (bo͞o′rē-äs)	197a	12.56N	122.56E
Burias Pass, strt., Phil. (bo͞o′rē-äs)	197a	13.04N	123.11E
Burica, Punta, c., N.A. (po͞o′n-tä-bo͞o′rē-kä)	121	8.02N	83.12W
Burien, Wa., U.S. (bū′rĭ-ĕn)	106a	47.28N	122.20W
Burin, Can. (bûr′ĭn)	85a	47.02N	55.10W
Burin Peninsula, pen., Can.	93	47.00N	55.40W
Burkburnett, Tx., U.S. (bûrk-bûr′nĕt)	110	34.04N	98.35W
Burke, Vt., U.S. (bûrk)	99	44.40N	72.00W
Burke Channel, strt., Can.	86	52.07N	127.38W
Burketown, Austl. (bûrk′toun)	202	17.50S	139.30E
Burkina Faso, nation, Afr.	210	13.00N	2.00W
Burley, Id., U.S. (bûr′lĭ)	105	42.31N	113.48W
Burley, Wa., U.S.	106a	47.25N	122.38W
Burlingame, Ca., U.S. (bûr′lĭn-găm)	106b	37.35N	122.22W
Burlingame, Ks., U.S.	111	38.45N	95.49W
Burlington, Can. (bûr′lĭng-tŭn)	91	43.19N	79.48W
Burlington, Co., U.S.	110	39.17N	102.26W
Burlington, Ia., U.S.	97	40.48N	91.05W
Burlington, Ks., U.S.	111	38.10N	95.46W
Burlington, Ky., U.S.	101f	39.01N	84.44W
Burlington, Ma., U.S.	93a	42.31N	71.13W
Burlington, N.J., U.S.	100f	40.04N	74.52W
Burlington, N.C., U.S.	115	36.05N	79.26W
Burlington, Vt., U.S.	97	44.30N	73.15W
Burlington, Wa., U.S.	106a	48.28N	122.20W
Burlington, Wi., U.S.	101a	42.41N	88.16W
Burma see Myanmar, nation, Asia	180	21.00N	95.15E
Burnaby, Can.	84	49.14N	122.58W
Burnage, Eng., U.K.	237b	53.26N	2.12W
Burnet, Tx., U.S. (bûrn′ĕt)	112	30.46N	98.14W
Burnham, Il., U.S.	231a	41.39N	87.34W
Burnham on Crouch, Eng., U.K. (bûrn′ăm-ŏn-krouch)	144b	51.38N	0.48E
Burnhamthorpe, Can.	227c	43.37N	79.36W
Burnie, Austl. (bûr′nē)	203	41.15S	146.05E
Burning Tree Estates, Md., U.S.	229d	39.01N	77.12W
Burnley, Eng., U.K. (bûrn′lē)	150	53.47N	2.19W
Burns, Or., U.S. (bûrnz)	104	43.35N	119.05W
Burnside, Ky., U.S. (bûrn′sīd)	114	36.57N	84.33W
Burns Lake, Can. (bûrnz lăk)	84	54.14N	125.46W
Burnsville, Can. (bûrnz′vĭl)	92	47.44N	65.07W
Burnt, r., Or., U.S. (bûrnt)	104	44.26N	117.53W
Burntwood, r., Can.	89	55.53N	97.30W
Burrard Inlet, b., Can. (bûr′árd)	106d	49.19N	123.15W
Burr Gaabo, Som.	213	1.14N	51.47E
Burriana, Spain (bo͞or-rē-ä′nä)	148	39.53N	0.05W
Burro, Serranías del, mts., Mex. (sĕr-rä-nē′äs dĕl bo͞o′r-rô)	112	29.39N	102.07W
Burrowhill, Eng., U.K.	235	51.21N	0.36W
Burr Ridge, Il., U.S.	231a	41.46N	87.55W
Bursa, Tur. (bo͞or′sá)	182	40.10N	28.10E
Būr Safājah, Egypt	211	26.57N	33.56E
Burscheid, Ger. (bo͞or′shīd)	157c	51.05N	7.07E
Būr Sūdān, Sudan (so͞o-dän′)	211	19.30N	37.10E
Burt, N.Y., U.S. (bŭrt)	101c	43.19N	78.45W
Burt, l., Mi., U.S. (bŭrt)	98	45.25N	84.45W
Burton, Eng., U.K.	237a	53.16N	3.01W
Burton, Wa., U.S. (bûr′tŭn)	106a	47.24N	122.28W
Burton, Lake, res., Ga., U.S.	114	34.46N	83.40W
Burtonsville, Md., U.S. (bûrtŏns-vil)	100e	39.07N	76.57W
Burton-upon-Trent, Eng., U.K. (bŭr′tŭn-ŭp′-ŏn-trĕnt)	150	52.48N	1.37W
Buru, i., Indon.	197	3.30S	126.30E
Burullus, l., Egypt	218b	31.20N	30.58E
Burundi, nation, Afr.	212	3.00S	29.30E
Burwell, Ne., U.S. (bûr′wĕl)	102	41.46N	99.08W
Burwood, Austl.	243b	37.51S	145.06E
Bury, Eng., U.K. (bĕr′ĭ)	144a	53.36N	2.17W
Buryatia, state, Russia	171	55.15N	112.00E
Bury Saint Edmunds, Eng., U.K. (bĕr′ĭ-sānt ĕd′mŭndz)	151	52.14N	0.44E
Burzaco, Arg. (bo͞or-zá′kô)	132a	34.50S	58.23W
Busanga Swamp, sw., Zam.	217	14.10S	25.50E
Busby, Austl.	243a	33.54S	150.53E
Buschhausen, neigh., Ger.	236	51.30N	6.51E
Būsh, Egypt (bo͞osh)	218b	29.13N	31.08E
Bushey, Eng., U.K.	235	51.39N	0.22W
Bushey Heath, Eng., U.K.	235	51.38N	0.20W
Bush Hill, Va., U.S.	229d	38.48N	77.07W
Bushmanland, hist. reg., S. Afr. (bòsh-măn lănd)	212	29.15S	18.45E
Bushnell, Il., U.S. (bòsh′nĕl)	111	40.33N	90.28W
Bushwick, neigh., N.Y., U.S.	228	40.42N	73.55W
Businga, Zaire (bò-sĭŋ′gá)	211	3.20N	20.53E
Busira, r., Zaire	216	0.05S	19.20E
Bus′k, Ukr.	155	49.58N	24.39E
Busselton, Austl. (bûs′l-tŭn)	202	33.40S	115.30E
Bussum, Neth.	145a	52.16N	5.10E
Bustamante, Mex. (bo͞os-tá-män′tá)	112	26.34N	100.30W
Bustleton, neigh., Pa., U.S.	229b	40.05N	75.02W
Busto Arsizio, Italy (bo͞os′tō är-sēd′zē-ō)	160	45.47N	8.51E
Busuanga, i., Phil. (bo͞o-swäŋ′gä)	197a	12.20N	119.43E
Buta, Zaire (bo͞o′tá)	211	2.48N	24.44E
Butha Buthe, Leso. (bo͞o-thá-bo͞o′thā)	213c	28.49S	28.16E
Butler, Al., U.S. (bŭt′lẽr)	114	32.05N	88.10W
Butler, In., U.S.	98	41.25N	84.50W
Butler, Md., U.S.	100e	39.32N	76.46W
Butler, N.J., U.S.	100a	41.00N	74.20W
Butler, Pa., U.S.	99	40.50N	79.55W
Butovo, Russia (bò-tô′vô)	172b	55.33N	37.36E
Butsha, Zaire	217	0.57N	29.13E
Buttahatchee, r., Al., U.S. (bŭt-á-hăch′ê)	114	34.02N	88.05W
Butte, Mt., U.S. (būt)	96	46.00N	112.31W
Butterworth, S. Afr. (bŭ tẽr′wûrth)	213c	32.20S	28.09E
Büttgen, Ger.	236	51.12N	6.36E
Butt of Lewis, c., Scot., U.K. (bŭt ŏv lū′ĭs)	150	58.34N	6.15W
Butuan, Phil. (bo͞o-to͞o′än)	197	8.40N	125.33E
Buturlinovka, Russia (bo͞o-to͞o′lē-nôf′ka)	167	50.47N	40.35E
Buuhoodle, Som.	218a	8.15N	46.20E
Buulo Berde, Som.	218a	3.53N	45.30E
Buxtehude, Ger.	145c	53.29N	9.42E
Buxton, Eng., U.K. (bŭks′t′n)	144a	53.15N	1.55W
Buxton, Or., U.S.	106c	45.41N	123.11W
Buy, Russia (bwē)	164	58.30N	41.48E
Büyükmenderes, r., Tur.	182	37.50N	28.20E
Buzău, Rom. (bo͞o-zĕ′ò)	161	45.09N	26.51E
Buzău, r., Rom.	163	45.17N	27.22E
Buzaymah, Libya	211	25.14N	22.13E
Buzi, China (bo͞o-dz)	190	33.48N	118.13E
Buzuluk, Russia (bò-zò-lòk′)	164	52.50N	52.10E
Bwendi, Zaire	217	4.01N	26.41E
Byala, Bul.	161	43.26N	25.44E
Byala Slatina, Bul. (byä′la slä′tēnä)	161	43.26N	23.56E
Byblos see Jubayl, Leb.	181a	34.07N	35.38E
Byculla, neigh., India	240e	18.58N	72.49E
Bydgoszcz, Pol. (bĭd′gôshch)	146	53.07N	18.00E
Byelorussia see Belarus, nation, Eur.	164	53.30N	25.33E
Byesville, Oh., U.S. (bīz-vĭl)	98	39.55N	81.35W
Byfang, neigh., Ger.	236	51.24N	7.06E
Byfleet, Eng., U.K.	235	51.20N	0.29W
Bygdin, l., Nor. (bügh-dēn′)	152	61.24N	8.31E
Byglandsfjord, Nor. (bügh′länds-fyôr)	152	58.40N	7.49E
Bykhovo, Bela.	162	53.32N	30.15E
Bykovo, Russia (bĭ-kô′vô)	172b	55.38N	38.05E
Byrranga, Gory, mts., Russia	170	74.15N	94.28E
Bytantay, r., Russia (byän′täy)	171	68.15N	132.15E
Bytom, Pol. (bĭ′tŭm)	147	50.21N	18.55E
Bytosh′, Russia (bĭ-tôsh′)	162	53.48N	34.06E
Bytow, Pol. (bĭ′tŭf)	155	54.10N	17.30E

C

PLACE (Pronunciation)	PAGE	Lat. °′	Long. °′
Cabagan, Phil. (kä-bä-gän′)	197a	17.27N	121.50E
Cabalete, i., Phil. (kä-bä-lā′tá)	197a	14.19N	122.00E
Caballito, neigh., Arg.	233d	34.37S	58.27W
Caballones, Canal de, strt., Cuba (kä-nä′l-dē-kä-bäl-yō′nĕs)	122	20.45N	79.20W
Caballo Reservoir, res., N.M., U.S. (kä-bä-lyō′)	109	33.00N	107.20W
Cabanatuan, Phil. (kä-bä-nä-twän′)	197a	15.30N	120.56E
Cabano, Can. (kä-bä-nō′)	92	47.41N	68.54W
Cabarruyan, i., Phil. (kä-bä-ro͞o′yän)	197a	16.21N	120.10E
Cabedelo, Braz. (kä-bē-dā′lò)	131	6.58S	34.49W
Cabeza, Arrecife, i., Mex.	119	19.07N	95.52W
Cabeza del Buey, Spain (kä-bā′thä dĕl bwā′)	158	38.43N	5.18W
Cabimas, Ven. (kä-bē′mäs)	130	10.21N	71.27W
Cabinda, Ang. (kä-bĭn′dá)	212	5.33S	12.12E
Cabinda, hist. reg., Ang. (kä-bĭn′dá)	212	5.10S	10.00E

270 Cabinet Mountains–Canadian

PLACE (Pronunciation)	PAGE	Lat. °′	Long. °′
Cabinet Mountains, mts., Mt., U.S. (kăb′ĭ-nĕt)	104	48.13N	115.52W
Cabin John, Md., U.S.	229d	38.58N	77.09W
Cabo Frio, Braz. (kä′bô-frē′ô)	129a	22.53S	42.02W
Cabo Frio, Ilha do, Braz. (ē′lä-dô-kä′bô frē′ô)	129a	23.01S	42.00W
Cabo Gracias a Dios, Hond. (kȧ′bô-grä-syäs-ä-dyô′s)	121	15.00N	83.13W
Cabonga, Réservoir, res., Can.	91	47.25N	76.35W
Cabora Bassa Reservoir, res., Moz.	212	15.45S	32.00E
Cabot Head, c., Can. (kăb′ŭt)	90	45.15N	81.20W
Cabot Strait, strt., Can. (kăb′ŭt)	85a	47.35N	60.00W
Cabra, Spain (käb′rä)	158	37.28N	4.29W
Cabra, i., Phil.	197a	13.55N	119.55E
Cabramatta, Austl.	243a	33.54S	150.56E
Cabrera, i., Spain (kä-brā′rä)	159	39.08N	2.57E
Cabrera, Sierra de la, mts., Spain	158	42.15N	6.45W
Cabriel, r., Spain (kä-brē-ĕl′)	158	39.25N	1.20W
Cabrillo National Monument, rec., Ca., U.S. (kä-brēl′yō)	108a	32.41N	117.03W
Cabuçu, r., Braz. (kä-bo͞o′-so͞o)	132b	22.57S	43.36W
Çabugao, Phil. (kä-bo͞o′gä-ô)	197a	17.48N	120.28E
Čačak, Yugo. (chä′chȧk)	161	43.51N	20.22E
Caçapava, Braz. (kä′sä-pȧ′vä)	129a	23.05S	45.52W
Cáceres, Braz. (kȧ′sĕ-rĕs)	131	16.11S	57.32W
Cáceres, Spain (kȧ′thȧ-rās)	148	39.28N	6.20W
Cachan, Fr.	237c	48.48N	2.20E
Cachapoal, r., Chile (kä-chä-pô-ȧ′l)	129b	34.23S	70.19W
Cache, r., Ar., U.S. (kȧsh)	111	35.24N	91.12W
Cache Creek, Can.	87	50.48N	121.19W
Cache Creek, r., Ca., U.S. (kăsh)	108	38.53N	122.24W
Cache la Poudre, r., Co., U.S. (kȧsh lȧ po͞od′r′)	110	40.43N	105.39W
Cachi, Nevados de, mtn., Arg. (nĕ-vȧ′dôs-dĕ-kȧ′chē)	132	25.05S	66.40W
Cachinal, Chile (kä-chē-näl′)	132	24.57S	69.33W
Cachoeira, Braz. (kä-shô-ā′rä)	131	12.32S	38.47W
Cachoeirá do Sul, Braz. (kä-shô-ā′rä-dô-so͞o′l)	132	30.02S	52.49W
Cachoeiras de Macacu, Braz. (kä-shô-ā′räs-dĕ-mä-kȧ′ko͞o)	129a	22.28S	42.39W
Cachoeiro de Itapemirim, Braz.	131	20.51S	41.06W
Cacilhas, Port.	238d	38.41N	9.09W
Cacólo, Ang.	216	10.07S	19.17E
Caconda, Ang. (kä-kōn′dä)	212	13.43S	15.06E
Cacouna, Can.	92	47.54N	69.31W
Cacula, Ang.	216	14.29S	14.10E
Cadale, Som.	218a	2.45N	46.15E
Caddo, l., La., U.S. (kăd′ō)	113	32.37N	94.15W
Cadereyta, Mex. (kä-dȧ-rā′tä)	118	20.42N	99.47W
Cadereyta Jimenez, Mex. (kä-dä-rā′tä hē-mā′nāz)	112	25.36N	99.59W
Cadi, Sierra de, mts., Spain (sē-ĕ′r-rä-dĕ-kä′dē)	159	42.17N	1.34E
Cadillac, Mi., U.S. (kăd′ĭ-lăk)	98	44.15N	85.25W
Cadishead, Eng., U.K.	237b	53.25N	2.26W
Cádiz, Spain (kȧ′dēz)	142	36.34N	6.20W
Cadiz, Ca., U.S. (kā′dĭz)	108	34.33N	115.30W
Cadiz, Oh., U.S.	98	40.15N	81.00W
Cádiz, Golfo de, b., Spain (gôl-fô-dĕ-kȧ′dēz)	148	36.50N	7.00W
Caen, Fr. (käɴ)	147	49.13N	0.22W
Caernarfon, Wales, U.K.	146	53.08N	4.17W
Caernarfon Bay, b., Wales, U.K.	150	53.09N	4.56W
Cagayan, Phil. (kä-gä-yän′)	197	8.13N	124.30E
Cagayan, r., Phil.	196	16.45N	121.55E
Cagayan Islands, is., Phil.	196	9.40N	120.30E
Cagayan Sulu, i., Phil. (kä-gä-yän so͞o′lo͞o)	196	7.00N	118.30E
Cagli, Italy (käl′yē)	160	43.35N	12.40E
Cagliari, Italy (käl′yä-rē)	142	39.16N	9.08E
Cagliari, Golfo di, b., Italy (gôl-fô-dē-käl′yä-rē)	148	39.08N	9.12E
Cagnes, Fr. (kän′y′)	157	43.40N	7.14E
Cagua, Ven. (kä′gwä)	131b	10.12N	67.27W
Caguas, P.R. (kä′gwäs)	117b	18.12N	66.01W
Cahaba, r., Al., U.S. (kȧ hä-bä)	114	32.50N	87.15W
Cahama, Ang. (kä-ȧ′mä)	212	16.17S	14.19E
Cahokia, Il., U.S. (kȧ-hō′kĭ-ȧ)	107e	38.34N	90.11W
Cahora-Bassa, wtfl., Moz.	217	15.40S	32.50E
Cahors, Fr. (kȧ-ôr′)	147	44.27N	1.27E
Cahuacán, Mex. (kä-wä-kä′n)	119a	19.38N	99.25W
Cahuita, Punta, c., C.R. (po͞o′n-tä-kä-wē′tȧ)	121	9.47N	82.41W
Cahul, Mol.	163	45.49N	28.17E
Caibarién, Cuba (kī-bä-rē-ĕn′)	122	22.35N	79.30W
Caicedonia, Col. (kī-sĕ-dô-nēä)	130a	4.21N	75.48W
Caicos Bank, bk. (kī′kōs)	123	21.35N	72.00W
Caicos Islands, is., T./C. Is.	117	21.45N	71.50W
Caicos Passage, strt., N.A.	123	21.55N	72.45W
Caillou Bay, b., La., U.S. (kȧ-yo͞o′)	113	29.07N	91.00W
Caimanera, Cuba (kī-mä-nā′rä)	123	20.00N	75.10W
Caiman Point, c., Phil. (kī′mȧn)	197a	15.56N	119.33E
Caimito, r., Pan. (kä-ē-mē′tô)	116a	8.50N	79.45W
Caimito del Guayabal, Cuba (kä-ē-mē′tō-dĕl-gwä-yä-bä′l)	123a	22.57N	82.36W
Cairns, Austl. (kârnz)	203	17.02S	145.49E
Cairo, C.R. (kī′rô)	121	10.06N	83.47W
Cairo, Egypt	211	30.00N	31.17E
Cairo, Ga., U.S. (kā′rō)	114	30.48N	84.12W
Cairo, Il., U.S.	97	36.59N	89.11W
Caistor, Eng., U.K. (kâs′tẽr)	144a	53.30N	0.20W
Caiundo, Ang.	216	15.46S	17.28E
Caiyu, China (tsī-yo͞o)	190	39.39N	116.36E
Cajamarca, Col. (kä-ĸä-mȧ′r-kä)	130a	4.25N	75.25W
Çajamarca, Peru (kä-hä-mär′kä)	130	7.16S	78.30W
Čajniče, Bos. (chī′nĭ-chĕ)	161	43.32N	19.04E
Cajon, Ca., U.S. (kȧ-hōn′)	107a	34.18N	117.28W
Çajuru, Braz. (kȧ-zho͞o′ro͞o)	129a	21.17S	47.17W
Čakovec, Cro. (chȧ′kō-vĕts)	160	46.23N	16.27E
Cala, S. Afr. (cä-lȧ)	213c	31.33S	27.41E
Calabar, Nig. (kăl-ȧ-bär′)	210	4.57N	8.19E
Calabazar, Cuba (kä-lä-bä-zä′r)	123a	23.02N	82.25W
Calabozo, Ven. (kä-lä-bō′zō)	130	8.48N	67.27W
Calabria, hist. reg., Italy (kä-lä′brē-ä)	160	39.26N	16.23E
Calafat, Rom. (kȧ-lȧ-fät′)	161	43.59N	22.56E
Calaguas Islands, is., Phil. (kä-läg′wäs)	197a	14.30N	123.06E
Calahoo, Can. (kă-lȧ-ho͞o′)	83g	53.42N	113.58W
Calahorra, Spain (kä-lä-ôr′rä)	148	42.18N	1.58W
Calais, Fr. (kȧ-lĕ′)	142	50.56N	1.51E
Calais, Me., U.S.	97	45.11N	67.15W
Calama, Chile (kä-lä′mä)	132	22.17S	68.58W
Calamar, Col. (kä-lä-mär′)	130	10.24N	75.00W
Calamar, Col.	130	1.55N	72.33W
Calamba, Phil. (kä-läm′bä)	197a	14.12N	121.10E
Calamian Group, is., Phil. (kä-lä-myän′)	196	12.14N	118.38E
Calañas, Spain (kä-län′yäs)	158	37.41N	6.52W
Calanda, Spain	159	40.53N	0.20W
Calapan, Phil. (kä-lä-pän′)	197a	13.25N	121.11E
Călăraşi, Rom. (kŭ-lŭ-rȧsh′ĭ)	149	44.09N	27.20E
Calatayud, Spain (kä-lä-tä-yo͞odh′)	148	41.23N	1.37W
Calauag Bay, b., Phil.	197a	14.07N	122.10E
Calaveras Reservoir, res., Ca., U.S. (kăl-ȧ-vẽr′ăs)	106b	37.29N	121.47W
Calavite, Cape, c., Phil. (kä-lä-vē′tä)	197a	13.29N	120.00E
Calcasieu, r., La., U.S. (kăl′kȧ-shū)	113	30.22N	93.08W
Calcasieu Lake, l., La., U.S.	113	29.58N	93.08W
Calcutta, India (kăl-kŭt′ȧ)	183	22.32N	88.22E
Caldas, Col. (kȧ′l-däs)	130a	6.06N	75.38W
Caldas, dept., Col.	130a	5.20N	75.38W
Caldas da Rainha, Port. (käl′däs dä rīn′yă)	158	39.25N	9.08W
Calder, r., Eng., U.K. (kôl′dẽr)	144a	53.39N	1.30W
Caldera, Chile (käl-dā′rä)	132	27.02S	70.53W
Calder Canal, can., Eng., U.K.	144a	53.48N	2.25W
Caldwell, Id., U.S. (kôld′wĕl)	104	43.40N	116.43W
Caldwell, Ks., U.S.	111	37.04N	97.36W
Caldwell, N.J., U.S.	228	40.51N	74.17W
Caldwell, Oh., U.S.	98	39.40N	81.30W
Caldwell, Tx., U.S.	113	30.30N	96.40W
Caledon, Can. (kăl′ē-dŏn)	83d	43.52N	79.59W
Caledonia, Mn., U.S. (kăl-ē-dō′nĭ-ȧ)	103	43.38N	91.31W
Calella, Spain (kä-lĕl′yä)	159	41.37N	2.39E
Calera Victor Rosales, Mex. (kä-lā′rä-vē′k-tôr-rô-sȧ′lĕs)	118	22.57N	102.42W
Calexico, Ca., U.S. (kȧ-lĕk′sĭ-kō)	96	32.41N	115.30W
Calgary, Can. (kăl′gȧ-rĭ)	84	51.03N	114.05W
Calhariz, neigh., Port.	238d	38.44N	9.12W
Calhoun, Ga., U.S. (kăl-ho͞on′)	114	34.30N	84.56W
Cali, Col. (kä′lē)	130	3.26N	76.30W
Calicut, India (kăl′ĭ-kŭt)	183	11.19N	75.49E
Caliente, Nv., U.S. (käl-yĕn′tä)	109	37.38N	114.30W
California, Mo., U.S. (kăl-ĭ-fôr′nĭ-ȧ)	111	38.38N	92.38W
California, Pa., U.S.	101e	40.03N	79.53W
California, state, U.S.	96	38.10N	121.20W
California, Golfo de, b., Mex. (gôl-fô-dĕ-kä-lē-fôr-nyä)	116	30.30N	113.45W
California Aqueduct, aq., Ca., U.S.	108	37.10N	121.10W
California-Los Angeles, University of (U.C.L.A.), educ., Ca., U.S.	232	34.04N	118.26W
Călimani, Munţii, mts., Rom.	155	47.05N	24.47E
Calimere, Point, c., India	187	10.20N	80.20E
Calimesa, Ca., U.S. (kă-lĭ-mā′sȧ)	107a	34.00N	117.04W
Calipatria, Ca., U.S. (kăl-ĭ-pȧt′rĭ-ȧ)	108	33.03N	115.30W
Calkini, Mex. (käl-kē-nē′)	119	20.21N	90.06W
Callabonna, Lake, l., Austl. (călă′bŏnȧ)	204	29.35S	140.28E
Callao, Peru (käl-yä′ô)	130	12.02S	77.07W
Calling, l., Can. (kôl′ĭng)	87	55.15N	113.12W
Calmar, Can. (kăl′mär)	83g	53.16N	113.49W
Calmar, Ia., U.S.	103	43.12N	91.54W
Caloocan, Phil.	241g	14.39N	120.59E
Caloosahatchee, r., Fl., U.S. (kȧ-loo-sȧ-hăch′ē)	115a	26.45N	81.41W
Calotmul, Mex. (kä-lôt-mo͞ol)	120a	20.58N	88.11W
Calpulalpan, Mex. (käl-po͞o-läl′pän)	118	19.35N	98.33W
Caltagirone, Italy (käl-tä-jē-rō′nȧ)	148	37.14N	14.32E
Caltanissetta, Italy (käl-tä-nē-sĕt′tä)	148	37.30N	14.02E
Caluango, Ang.	216	8.21S	19.40E
Calucinga, Ang.	216	11.18S	16.12E
Calumet, Mi., U.S. (kă-lū-mĕt′)	103	47.15N	88.29W
Calumet, Lake, l., Il., U.S.	101a	41.43N	87.36W
Calumet City, Il., U.S.	101a	41.37N	87.33W
Calumet Park, Il., U.S.	231a	41.44N	87.33W
Calumet Sag Channel, can., Il., U.S.	231a	41.42N	87.57W
Calunda, Ang.	216	12.06S	23.23E
Caluquembe, Ang.	216	13.47S	14.44E
Caluula, Som.	218a	11.53N	50.40E
Calvert, Tx., U.S. (kăl′vẽrt)	113	30.59N	96.41W
Calvert Island, i., Can.	84	51.35N	128.00W
Calvi, Fr. (käl′vē)	160	42.33N	8.35E
Calvillo, Mex. (käl-vēl′yō)	119	21.51N	102.44E
Calvinia, S. Afr. (kăl-vĭn′ĭ-ȧ)	212	31.20S	19.50E
Cam, r., Eng., U.K. (kăm)	151	52.15N	0.05E
Camagüey, Cuba (kä-mä-gwā′)	117	21.25N	78.00W
Camagüey, prov., Cuba	122	21.30N	78.10W
Camajuani, Cuba (kä-mä-hwä′nē)	122	22.25N	79.50W
Camano, Wa., U.S. (kä-mä′no)	106a	48.10N	122.32W
Camano Island, i., Wa., U.S.	106a	48.11N	122.29W
Camargo, Mex. (kä-mär gō)	112	26.19N	98.49W
Camarón, Cabo, c., Hond. (kȧ′bô-kä-mä-rōn′)	120	16.06N	85.05W
Camas, Wa., U.S. (kăm′ȧs)	106c	45.36N	122.24W
Camas Creek, r., Id., U.S.	105	44.10N	112.09W
Camatagua, Ven. (kä-mä-tȧ′gwä)	131b	9.49N	66.55W
Ca Mau, Mui, c., Viet.	196	8.36N	104.43E
Cambay, India (kăm-bā′)	186	22.22N	72.39E
Camberwell, Austl.	243b	37.50S	145.04E
Cambodia, nation, Asia	196	12.15N	104.00E
Cambonda, Serra, mts., Ang.	216	12.10S	14.15E
Camborne, Eng., U.K. (kăm′bôrn)	150	50.15N	5.28W
Cambrai, Fr. (käɴ-brĕ′)	147	50.10N	3.15E
Cambrian Mountains, mts., Wales, U.K. (kăm′brĭ-ăn)	150	52.05N	4.05W
Cambridge, Can.	91	43.22N	80.19W
Cambridge, Eng., U.K. (kām′brĭj)	147	52.12N	0.11E
Cambridge, Md., U.S.	99	38.35N	76.10W
Cambridge, Ma., U.S.	93a	42.23N	71.07W
Cambridge, Mn., U.S.	103	45.35N	93.14W
Cambridge, Ne., U.S.	110	40.17N	100.10W
Cambridge, Oh., U.S.	98	40.00N	81.35W
Cambridge Bay, Can.	84	69.15N	105.00W
Cambridge City, In., U.S.	98	39.45N	85.15W
Cambridgeshire, co., Eng., U.K.	144a	52.26N	0.19W
Cambuci, Braz. (käm-bo͞o′sē)	129a	21.35S	41.54W
Cambuci, neigh., Braz.	234d	23.34S	46.37W
Cambundi-Catembo, Ang.	216	10.09S	17.31E
Camby, In., U.S. (kăm′bē)	101g	39.40N	86.19W
Camden, Austl.	201b	34.03S	150.42E
Camden, Al., U.S. (kăm′dĕn)	114	31.58N	87.15W
Camden, Ar., U.S.	111	33.36N	92.49W
Camden, Me., U.S.	92	44.11N	69.05W
Camden, N.J., U.S.	97	39.56N	75.06W
Camden, S.C., U.S.	115	34.14N	80.37W
Camden, neigh., Eng., U.K.	235	51.33N	0.10W
Cameia, Parque Nacional da, rec., Ang.	216	11.40S	21.20E
Camenca, Mol.	163	48.02N	28.43E
Cameron, Mo., U.S. (kăm′ẽr-ŭn)	111	39.44N	94.14W
Cameron, Tx., U.S.	113	30.52N	96.57W
Cameron, W.V., U.S.	98	39.40N	80.35W
Cameron Hills, hills, Can.	84	60.13N	120.20W
Cameroon, nation, Afr.	210	5.48N	11.00E
Cameroon Mountain, mtn., Cam.	210	4.12N	9.11E
Camiling, Phil. (kä-mē-lĭng′)	197a	15.42N	120.24E
Camilla, Ga., U.S. (kȧ-mĭl′ȧ)	114	31.13N	84.12W
Caminha, Port. (kä-mĭn′yȧ)	158	41.52N	8.44W
Camoçim, Braz. (kä-mô-sēɴ′)	131	2.56S	40.55W
Camooweal, Austl.	202	20.00S	138.13E
Campana, Arg. (käm-pä′nä)	129c	34.10S	58.58W
Campana, i., Chile (käm-pän′yä)	132	48.20S	75.15W
Campanario, Spain (kä-pä-nä′rē-ō)	158	38.51N	5.36W
Campanella, Punta, c., Italy (pô′n-tä-käm-pä-nĕ′lä)	159c	40.20N	14.21E
Campanha, Braz. (käm-pän-yäɴ′)	129a	21.51S	45.24W
Campania, hist. reg., Italy (käm-pän′yä)	160	41.00N	14.40E
Campbell, Ca., U.S. (kăm′bĕl)	106b	37.17N	121.57W
Campbell, Mo., U.S.	111	36.29N	90.04W
Campbell, is., N.Z.	3	52.30S	169.00E
Campbellfield, Austl.	243b	37.41S	144.57E
Campbellpore, Pak.	186	33.49N	72.24E
Campbell River, Can.	84	50.01N	125.15W
Campbellsville, Ky., U.S. (kăm′bĕlz-vĭl)	114	37.19N	85.20W
Campbellton, Can. (kăm′bĕl-tŭn)	85	48.00N	66.40W
Campbelltown, Austl. (kăm′bĕl-toun)	201b	34.04S	150.49E
Campbelltown, Scot., U.K. (kăm′b′l-toun)	150	55.25N	5.50W
Camp Dennison, Oh., U.S. (dĕ′nĭ-sŏn)	101f	39.12N	84.17W
Campeche, Mex. (käm-pā′chȧ)	116	19.51N	90.32W
Campeche, state, Mex.	116	18.55N	90.20W
Campeche, Bahía de, b., Mex. (bä-ē′ä-dĕ-käm-pā′chā)	116	19.30N	93.40W
Campechuela, Cuba (käm-pȧ-chwā′lä)	122	20.15N	77.15W
Camperdown, S. Afr. (kăm′pẽr-doun)	213c	29.44S	30.33E
Câmpina, Rom.	161	45.08N	25.47E
Campina Grande, Braz. (käm-pē′nä grän′dē)	131	7.15S	35.49W
Campinas, Braz. (käm-pē′năzh)	131	22.53S	47.03W
Camp Indian Reservation, I.R., Ca., U.S. (kămp)	108	32.39N	116.26W
Campo, Cam. (käm′pō)	210	2.22N	9.49E
Campoalegre, Col. (kä′m-pô-ȧlĕ′grĕ)	130	2.34N	75.20W
Campobasso, Italy (käm′pô-bäs′sō)	160	41.35N	14.39E
Campo Belo, Braz.	129a	20.52S	45.15W
Campo de Criptana, Spain (käm′pō dā krēp-tä′nä)	158	39.24N	3.09W
Campo Florido, Cuba (kä′m-pō flô-rē′dō)	123a	23.07N	82.07W
Campo Grande, Braz. (käm-pô grän′dĕ)	131	20.28S	54.32W
Campo Grande, Braz.	132b	22.54S	43.33W
Campo Grande, neigh., Port.	238d	38.45N	9.09W
Campo Maior, Braz. (käm-pô mä-yôr′)	131	4.48S	42.12W
Campo Maior, Port.	158	39.03N	7.06W
Campo Real, Spain (käm′pô rȧ-äl′)	159a	40.21N	3.23W
Campos, Braz. (kä′m-pôs)	131	21.46S	41.19W
Campos do Jordão, Braz. (kä′m-pôs-dô-zhôr-dou′ɴ)	129a	22.45S	45.35W
Campos Gerais, Braz. (kä′m-pôs-zhĕ-rȧēs)	129a	21.17S	45.43W
Camps Bay, S. Afr. (kămps)	212a	33.57S	18.22E
Campsie, Austl.	243a	33.55S	151.06E
Camp Springs, Md., U.S. (cămp sprĭngz)	100e	38.48N	76.55W
Camp Springs, Md., U.S.	229d	38.48N	76.55W
Câmpulung, Rom.	149	45.15N	25.03E
Câmpulung Moldovenesc, Rom.	155	47.31N	25.36E
Camp Wood, Tx., U.S. (kămp wŏŏd)	112	29.39N	100.02W
Camrose, Can. (kăm-rōz)	84	53.01N	112.50W
Camu, r., Dom. Rep. (kä′mo͞o)	123	19.05N	70.15W
Canada, nation, N.A. (kăn′ȧ-dȧ)	84	50.00N	100.00W
Canada Bay, b., Can.	93	50.43N	56.10W
Cañada de Gómez, Arg. (kä-nyä′dä-dĕ-gô′mĕz)	132	32.49S	61.24W
Canadian, Tx., U.S. (kȧ-nā′dĭ-ăn)	110	35.54N	100.24W

ăt; finăl; rāte; senåte; ärm; ȧsk; sofȧ; fâre; ch-choose; dh-as th in other; bē; ėvent; bĕt; recĕnt; cratẽr; g-gō; gh-guttural g; bĭt; ĭ-short neutral; rīde; ĸ-guttural k as ch in German ich;

PRONOUNCING INDEX | Canadian-Carrington 271

PLACE (Pronunciation)	PAGE	Lat. °′	Long. °′
Canadian, r., U.S.	96	35.30N	102.30W
Canajoharie, N.Y., U.S. (kăn-ȧ-jô-hăr′ė)	99	42.55N	74.35W
Çanakkale, Tur. (chä-näk-kä′lĕ)	149	40.10N	26.26E
Çanakkale Boğazi (Dardanelles), strt., Tur.	149	40.05N	25.50E
Canandaigua, N.Y., U.S. (kăn-ăn-dā′gwȧ)	99	42.55N	77.20W
Canandaigua, l., N.Y., U.S.	99	42.45N	77.20W
Cananea, Mex. (kä-nä-nĕ′ä)	116	31.00N	110.20W
Canarias, Islas (Canary Is.), is., Spain (ė′s-läs-kä-nä′ryäs)	209	29.15N	16.30W
Canarreos, Archipiélago de los, is., Cuba	122	21.35N	82.20W
Canarsie, neigh., N.Y., U.S.	228	40.38N	73.53W
Canary Islands see Canarias, Islas, is., Spain	209	29.15N	16.30W
Cañas, C.R. (kä′-nyäs)	120	10.26N	85.06W
Cañas, r., C.R.	120	10.20N	85.21W
Cañasgordas, Col. (kä′nyäs-gô′r-däs)	130a	6.44N	76.01W
Canastota, N.Y., U.S. (kăn-ăs-tō′tȧ)	99	43.05N	75.45W
Canastra, Serra de, mts., Braz. (sĕ′r-rä-dĕ-kä-nä′s-trä)	131	19.53S	46.57W
Canatlán, Mex. (kä-nät-län′)	112	24.30N	104.45W
Canaveral, Cape, c., Fl., U.S.	97	28.30N	80.23W
Canavieiras, Braz. (kä-nȧ-vē-ā′räs)	131	15.40S	38.49W
Canberra, Austl. (kăn′bĕr-ȧ)	203	35.21S	149.10E
Canby, Mn., U.S. (kăn′bĭ)	102	44.43N	96.15W
Canchyuaya, Cerros de, mts., Peru (sĕ′r-rôs-dĕ-kän-cho͞o-á′īä)	130	7.30S	74.30W
Cancuc, Mex. (kän-ko͝ok)	119	16.58N	92.17W
Cancún, Mex.	120a	21.25N	86.50W
Candelaria, Cuba (kän-dĕ-lä′ryä)	122	22.45N	82.55W
Candelaria, Phil. (kän-dȧ-lä′rē-ä)	197a	15.39N	119.55E
Candelaria, r., Mex. (kän-dĕ-lä-ryä)	119	18.25N	91.21W
Candeleda, Spain (kän-dhå-lā′dhä)	158	40.09N	5.18W
Candia see Iráklion, Grc.	142	35.20N	25.10E
Candle, Ak., U.S. (kăn′d′l)	95	65.00N	162.04W
Cando, N.D., U.S. (kăn′dō)	102	48.27N	99.13W
Candon, Phil. (kän-dōn′)	197a	17.13N	120.26E
Canelones, Ur. (kä-nĕ-lô-nĕs)	129c	34.32S	56.19W
Canelones, dept., Ur.	129c	34.34S	56.15W
Cañete, Peru (kän-yā′tå)	130	13.06S	76.17W
Caney, Cuba (kä-nā′) (kā′nĭ)	123	20.05N	75.45W
Caney, Ks., U.S. (kā′nĭ)	111	37.00N	95.57W
Caney Fork, r., Tn., U.S.	114	36.10N	85.50W
Cangamba, Ang.	212	13.40S	19.54E
Cangas, Spain (kän′gäs)	158	42.15N	8.43W
Cangas de Narcea, Spain (kä′n-gäs-dĕ-när-sĕ-ä)	158	43.08N	6.36W
Cangzhou, China (tsäŋ-jō)	192	38.21N	116.53E
Caniapiscau, l., Can.	85	54.10N	71.13E
Caniapiscau, r., Can.	85	57.00N	68.45W
Canicatti, Italy (kä-nė-kät′tē)	160	37.18N	13.58E
Canillas, neigh., Spain	238b	40.28N	3.38W
Canillejas, neigh., Spain	238b	40.27N	3.37W
Cañitas, Mex. (kän-yē′täs)	118	23.38N	102.44W
Cannell, Can.	83g	53.35N	113.38W
Cannelton, In., U.S. (kăn′ĕl-tŭn)	98	37.55N	86.45W
Cannes, Fr. (kȧn)	147	43.34N	7.05E
Canning, Can. (kăn′ĭng)	92	45.09N	64.25W
Cannock, Eng., U.K. (kăn′ŭk)	144a	52.41N	2.02W
Cannock Chase, reg., Eng., U.K. (kăn′ŭk chās)	144a	52.43N	1.54W
Cannon, r., Mn., U.S. (kăn′ŭn)	103	44.18N	93.24W
Cannonball, r., N.D., U.S. (kăn′ŭn-bâl)	102	46.17N	101.35W
Caño, Isla de, i., C.R. (ė′s-lä-dĕ-kä′nō)	121	8.38N	84.00W
Canoga Park, Ca., U.S. (kä-nō′gȧ)	107a	34.07N	118.36W
Canoncito Indian Reservation, I.R., N.M., U.S.	109	35.00N	107.05W
Canon City, Co., U.S. (kăn′yŭn)	110	38.27N	105.16W
Canonsburg, Pa., U.S. (kăn′ŭnz-bûrg)	101e	40.16N	80.11W
Canoochee, r., Ga., U.S. (kȧ-no͞o′chē)	115	32.25N	82.11W
Canora, Can. (kȧ-nōrȧ)	84	51.37N	102.26W
Canosa, Italy (kä-nō′sä)	160	41.14N	16.03E
Canouan, i., St. Vin.	121b	12.44N	61.10W
Cansahcab, Mex.	120a	21.11N	89.05W
Canso, Can. (kăn′sō)	93	45.20N	61.00W
Canso, Cape, c., Can.	93	45.21N	60.46W
Canso, Strait of, strt., Can.	93	45.37N	61.25W
Cantabrica, Cordillera, mts., Spain	142	43.05N	6.05W
Cantagalo, Braz. (kän-tä-gá′lo)	129a	21.59S	42.22W
Cantanhede, Port. (kän-tän-yā′då)	158	40.22N	8.35W
Canterbury, Austl.	243a	33.55S	151.07E
Canterbury, Austl.	243b	37.49S	145.05E
Canterbury, Eng., U.K. (kăn′tĕr-bĕr-ė)	151	51.17N	1.06E
Canterbury Bight, bt., N.Z.	203a	44.15S	172.08E
Canterbury Woods, Va., U.S.	229d	38.49N	77.15W
Cantiles, Cayo, i., Cuba (ky-ō-kän-tē′lås)	122	21.40N	82.00W
Canto do Pontes, Braz.	234c	22.58S	43.04W
Canton see Guangzhou, China	189	23.07N	113.15E
Canton, Ga., U.S.	114	34.13N	84.29W
Canton, Il., U.S.	111	40.34N	90.02W
Canton, Ma., U.S.	93a	42.09N	71.09W
Canton, Ms., U.S.	114	32.36N	90.01W
Canton, Mo., U.S.	111	40.08N	91.33W
Canton, N.C., U.S.	115	35.32N	82.50W
Canton, Oh., U.S.	97	40.50N	81.25W
Canton, Pa., U.S.	99	41.50N	76.45W
Canton, S.D., U.S.	102	43.17N	96.37W
Cantu, Italy (kän-tō′)	160	45.43N	9.09E
Cañuelas, Arg. (kä-nyòĕ′-läs)	129c	35.03S	58.45W
Canyon, Ca., U.S.	231b	37.49N	122.09W
Canyon, Tx., U.S. (kăn′yŭn)	110	34.59N	101.57W
Canyon, r., Wa., U.S.	106a	48.09N	121.48W
Canyon de Chelly National Monument, rec., Az., U.S.	109	36.14N	110.00W
Canyon Ferry Lake, res., Mt., U.S.	105	46.33N	111.37W
Canyonlands National Park, Ut., U.S.	109	38.10N	110.00W
Caoxian, China (tsou shyĕn)	190	34.48N	115.33E
Capalonga, Phil. (kä-pä-lôŋ′gä)	197a	14.20N	122.30E
Capannori, Italy (kä-pän′nō-rē)	160	43.50N	10.30E
Capão Redondo, neigh., Braz.	234d	23.40S	46.46W
Caparica, Port.	238d	38.40N	9.12W
Capaya, r., Ven. (kä-pä-īä)	131b	10.28N	66.15W
Cap-Chat, Can. (kȧp-shä′)	85	48.02N	65.20W
Cap-de-la-Madeleine, Can. (kȧp dē lȧ mȧ-d′lĕn′)	91	46.23N	72.30W
Cape Breton, i., Can. (kāp brĕt′ŭn)	93	45.48N	59.50W
Cape Breton Highlands National Park, Can.	85	46.45N	60.45W
Cape Charles, Va., U.S. (kāp chärlz)	115	37.13N	76.02W
Cape Coast, Ghana	210	5.05N	1.15W
Cape Fear, r., N.C., U.S. (kāp fēr)	97	35.00N	79.00W
Cape Flats, pl., S. Afr. (kāp flăts)	212a	34.01S	18.37E
Cape Girardeau, Mo., U.S. (jē-rär-dō′)	97	37.17N	89.32W
Cape Krusenstern National Monument, rec., Ak., U.S.	95	67.30N	163.40W
Cape May, N.J., U.S. (kāp mā)	99	38.55N	74.50W
Cape May Court House, N.J., U.S.	99	39.05N	75.00W
Capenhurst, Eng., U.K.	237a	53.15N	2.57W
Cape Romanzof, Ak., U.S. (rō′ män zôf)	95	61.50N	165.45W
Capesterre, Guad.	121b	16.02N	61.37W
Cape Tormentine, Can.	92	46.08N	63.47W
Cape Town, S. Afr. (kāp toun)	212	33.48S	18.28E
Cape Verde, nation, Afr.	210b	15.48N	26.02W
Cape York Peninsula, pen., Austl. (kāp yôrk)	203	12.30S	142.35E
Cap-Haïtien, Haiti (kȧp ȧ-ē-syăn′)	117	19.45N	72.15W
Capilla de Señor, Arg. (kä-pēl′yä dä sān-yôr′)	129c	34.18S	59.07W
Capitachouane, r., Can.	91	47.50N	76.45W
Capitol Heights, Md., U.S.	229d	38.53N	76.55W
Capitol Reef National Park, Ut., U.S. (kăp′ĭ-tŏl)	109	38.15N	111.10W
Capitol View, Md., U.S.	229d	39.01N	77.04W
Capivari, Braz. (kä-pē-vá′rė)	129a	22.59S	47.29W
Capivari, r., Braz.	132b	22.39S	43.19W
Capoompeta, mtn., Austl. (kȧ-po͞om-pē′tȧ)	203	29.15S	152.12E
Capraia, i., Italy (kä-prä′yä)	148	43.02N	9.51E
Caprara Point, c., Italy (kä-prä′rä)	160	41.08N	8.20E
Capreol, Can.	91	46.43N	80.56W
Caprera, i., Italy (kä-prā′rä)	160	41.12N	9.28E
Capri, Italy	159c	40.18N	14.16E
Capri, Isola di, i., Italy (ė′-sō-lä-dē-kä′prē)	159c	40.19N	14.10E
Capricorn Channel, strt., Austl. (kăp′rĭ-kôrn)	203	22.27S	151.24E
Caprivi Strip, hist. reg., Nmb.	212	18.00S	22.00E
Cap-Rouge, Can. (kȧp ro͞ozh′)	83b	46.45N	71.21W
Cap-Saint Ignace, Can. (kĭp săn-tē-nyás′)	83b	47.02N	70.27W
Captain Cook Bridge, pt. of i., Austl.	243a	34.00S	151.08E
Capua, Italy (kä′pwä)	148	41.07N	14.14E
Capuáva, Braz.	234d	23.39S	46.29W
Capulhuac, Mex. (kä-pōl-hwäk′)	118	19.33N	99.43W
Capulin Mountain National Monument, rec., N.M., U.S. (kȧ-pū′lĭn)	110	36.15N	103.58W
Capultitlán, Mex. (kä-pò′l-tē-tlá′n)	119a	19.15N	99.40W
Caputh, Ger.	238a	52.21N	13.00E
Caquetá (Japurá), r., S.A.	130	0.20S	73.00W
Caraballeda, Ven.	234a	10.37N	66.50W
Carabaña, Spain (kä-rä-bän′yä)	159a	40.16N	3.15W
Carabanchel Alto, neigh., Spain	238b	40.22N	3.45W
Carabanchel Bajo, neigh., Spain	238b	40.23N	3.47W
Carabelle, Fl., U.S. (kăr′á-bĕl)	114	29.50N	84.40W
Carabobo, dept., Ven. (kä-rä-bô′-bô)	131b	10.07N	68.06W
Caracal, Rom. (kȧ-rȧ-kȧl′)	161	44.06N	24.22E
Caracas, Ven. (kä-rä′käs)	130	10.30N	66.58W
Carácuaro de Morelos, Mex. (kä-rä′kwä-rō-dĕ-mō-rĕ-lôs)	118	18.44N	101.04W
Caraguatatuba, Braz. (kä-rä-gwä-tȧ-to͞o′bä)	129a	23.37S	45.26W
Carajás, Serra dos, mts., Braz. (sĕ′r-rä-dôs-kä-rä-zhá′s)	131	5.58S	51.45W
Caramanta, Cerro, mtn., Col. (sĕ′r-rô-kä-rä-mà′n-tä)	130a	5.29N	76.01W
Carangola, Braz. (kä-rän′gō′lä)	129a	20.46S	42.02W
Carapicuíba, Braz.	234d	23.31S	46.50W
Caraquet, Can. (kä-rȧ-kĕt′)	85	47.48N	64.57W
Carata, Laguna, l., Nic. (lä-gò′nä-kä-rä′tä)	121	13.59N	83.41W
Caratasca, Laguna, l., Hond. (lä-gò′nä-kä-rä-täs′kä)	121	15.20N	83.45W
Caravaca, Spain (kä-rä-vä′kä)	158	38.05N	1.51W
Caravelas, Braz. (kȧ-rä-vĕl′äzh)	131	17.46S	39.06W
Carayaca, Ven. (kȧ-rä-īá′kä)	131b	10.32N	67.07W
Caràzinho, Braz. (kä-rä′zē-nyō)	132	28.22S	52.33W
Carballino, Spain (kär-bäl-yē′nō)	148	42.26N	8.04W
Carballo, Spain (kär-bäl′yō)	158	43.13N	8.40W
Carbet, Pitons du, mtn., Mart.	121b	14.40N	61.05W
Carbon, r., Wa., U.S. (kär′bŏn)	106a	47.06N	122.08W
Carbonado, Wa., U.S. (kär-bō-nā′dō)	106a	47.05N	122.03W
Carbonara, Cape, c., Italy (kär-bō-nä′rä)	148	39.08N	9.33E
Carbondale, Can. (kär′bŏn-dāl)	83g	53.45N	113.32W
Carbondale, Il., U.S.	98	37.42N	89.12W
Carbondale, Pa., U.S.	99	41.35N	75.30W
Carbonear, Can. (kär-bō-nēr′)	93	47.45N	53.14W
Carbon Hill, Al., U.S. (kär′bŏn hĭl)	114	33.53N	87.34W
Carcagente, Spain (kär-kä-hĕn′tä)	159	39.09N	0.29W
Carcans, Étang de, l., Fr. (ā-taN-dĕ-kär-käN)	156	45.12N	1.00W
Carcassonne, Fr. (kȧr-kȧ-sôn′)	147	43.12N	2.23E
Carcross, Can. (kär′krôs)	84	60.18N	134.54W
Cárdenas, Cuba (kär′då-näs)	117	23.00N	81.10W
Cárdenas, Mex.	118	22.01N	99.38W
Cárdenas, Mex. (ká′r-dĕ-näs)	119	17.59N	93.23W
Cárdenas, Bahía de, b., Cuba (bä-ē′ä-dĕ-kär′då-näs)	122	23.10N	81.10W
Cardiff, Can. (kär′dĭf)	83g	53.46N	113.36W
Cardiff, Wales, U.K.	147	51.30N	3.18W
Cardigan, Wales, U.K. (kär′dĭ-găn)	147	52.05N	4.40W
Cardigan Bay, b., Wales, U.K.	147	52.35N	4.40W
Cardston, Can. (kärds′tŭn)	84	49.12N	113.18W
Carei, Rom. (kä-rĕ′)	155	47.42N	22.28E
Carentan, Fr. (kä-rôN-täN′)	156	49.19N	1.14W
Carey, Oh., U.S. (kā′rė)	98	40.55N	83.25W
Carey, l., Austl. (kâr′ē)	202	29.20S	123.35E
Carhaix-Plouguer, Fr. (kär-ĕ′)	156	48.17N	3.37W
Caribbean Sea, sea (kăr-ĭ-bē′ăn)	117	14.30N	75.30W
Caribe, Arroyo, r., Mex. (är-ro′ī-kä-rē′bĕ)	119	18.18N	90.38W
Cariboo Mountains, mts., Can. (kă′rĭ-bo͞o)	84	53.00N	121.00W
Caribou, Me., U.S.	92	46.51N	68.01W
Caribou, i., Can.	90	47.22N	85.42W
Caribou Lake, l., Mn., U.S.	107h	46.54N	92.16W
Caribou Mountains, mts., Can.	84	59.20N	115.30W
Caringbah, Austl.	243a	34.03S	151.08E
Carinhanha, Braz. (kä-rĭ-nyän′yä)	131	14.14S	43.44W
Carini, Italy (kä-rē′nē)	160	38.09N	13.10E
Carinthia see Kärnten, prov., Aus.	154	46.55N	13.42E
Carleton Place, Can. (kärl′tŭn)	91	45.15N	76.10W
Carletonville, S. Afr.	218d	26.20S	27.23E
Carlingford, Austl.	243a	33.47S	151.03E
Carlinville, Il., U.S. (kär′lĭn-vĭl)	111	39.16N	89.52W
Carlisle, Eng., U.K. (kär-līl′)	142	54.54N	3.03W
Carlisle, Ky., U.S.	98	38.20N	84.00W
Carlisle, Pa., U.S.	99	40.10N	77.15W
Carloforte, Italy (kär′lō-fôr-tå)	160	39.11N	8.28E
Carlos Casares, Arg. (kär-lôs-kä-sá′rĕs)	132	35.38S	61.17W
Carlow, Ire. (kär′lō)	150	52.50N	7.00W
Carlsbad, N.M., U.S. (kärlz′băd)	112	32.24N	104.12W
Carlsbad Caverns National Park, rec., N.M., U.S.	112	32.08N	104.30W
Carlstadt, N.J., U.S.	228	40.50N	74.06W
Carlton, Eng., U.K. (kärl′tŭn)	144a	52.58N	1.05W
Carlton, Mn., U.S.	107h	46.40N	92.26W
Carlton Center, Mi., U.S. (kärl′tŭn sĕn′tĕr)	98	42.45N	85.20W
Carlyle, Il., U.S. (kärlīl′)	111	38.37N	89.23W
Carmagnolo, Italy (kär-mä-nyô′lä)	160	44.52N	7.48E
Carman, Can. (kär′mȧn)	84	49.32N	98.00W
Carmarthen, Wales, U.K. (kär-mär′thĕn)	150	51.50N	4.20W
Carmaux, Fr. (kȧr-mō′)	156	44.05N	2.09E
Carmel, N.Y., U.S. (kär′mĕl)	100a	41.25N	73.42W
Carmelo, Ur. (kär-mĕ′lo)	129c	33.59S	58.15W
Carmen, Isla del, i., Mex. (ė′s-lä-dĕl-kà′r-mĕn)	119	18.43N	91.40W
Carmen, Laguna del, l., Mex. (lä-gò′nä-dĕl-kà′r-mĕn)	119	18.15N	93.26W
Carmen de Areco, Arg. (kär′mĕn′ dā ä-rā′kō)	129c	34.21S	59.50W
Carmen de Patagones, Arg. (kà′r-mĕn-dĕ-pä-tä-gô′nĕs)	132	41.00S	63.00W
Carmi, Il., U.S. (kär′mī)	98	38.05N	88.10W
Carmo, Braz. (kà′r-mô)	129a	21.57S	42.45W
Carmo do Rio Clara, Braz. (kà′r-mô-dô-rē′ō-klä′rä)	129a	20.57S	46.04W
Carmona, Spain	158	37.28N	5.38W
Carnarvon, Austl. (kär-när′vŭn)	202	24.45S	113.45E
Carnarvon, S. Afr.	212	31.00S	22.15E
Carnation, Wa., U.S. (kär-nā′shŭn)	106a	47.39N	121.55W
Carnaxide, Port. (kär-nä-shē′dĕ)	159b	38.44N	9.15W
Carndonagh, Ire. (kärn-dō-nä′)	150	55.15N	7.15W
Carnegie, Ok., U.S. (kär-nĕg′ĭ)	110	35.06N	98.38W
Carnegie, Pa., U.S.	101e	40.24N	80.06W
Carnegie Institute, pt. of i., Pa., U.S.	230b	40.27N	79.57W
Carnetin, Fr.	237c	48.54N	2.42E
Carneys Point, N.J., U.S. (kär′nės)	99	39.45N	75.25W
Carnic Alps, mts., Eur.	147	46.43N	12.38E
Carnide, neigh., Port.	238d	38.46N	9.11W
Carnot, Alg. (kär nō′)	159	36.15N	1.40E
Carnot, Cen. Afr. Rep.	211	5.00N	15.52E
Carnsore Point, c., Ire. (kärn′sôr)	150	52.10N	6.16W
Caro, Mi., U.S. (kâ′rō)	98	43.30N	83.25W
Carolina, Braz. (kä-rō-lē′nä)	131	7.26S	47.16W
Carolina, S. Afr. (kär-ō-lī′nȧ)	212	26.07S	30.09E
Carolina, l., Mex. (kä-rō-lē′nä)	120a	18.41N	89.40W
Caroline Islands, is., Oc.	5	8.00N	140.00E
Caroni, r., Ven. (kä-rō′nē)	130	5.49N	62.57W
Carora, Ven. (kä-rō′rä)	130	10.09N	70.12W
Carpathians, mts., Eur. (kär-pā′thĭ-ăn)	142	49.23N	20.14E
Carpații Meridionali (Transylvanian Alps), mts., Rom.	142	45.30N	23.30E
Carpentaria, Gulf of, b., Austl. (kär-pĕn-târ′ĭȧ)	202	14.45S	138.50E
Carpentras, Fr. (kär-päN-träs′)	157	44.04N	5.01E
Carpi, Italy	160	44.48N	10.54E
Carrara, Italy (kä-rä′rä)	148	44.05N	10.05E
Carrauntoohil, Ire. (kă-răn-to͞o′ĭl)	150	52.01N	9.48W
Carretas, Punta, c., Peru (po͞o′n-tä-kär-rĕ′tĕ′rås)	130	14.15S	76.25W
Carriacou, i., Gren.	121b	12.28N	61.20W
Carrick-on-Sur, Ire. (kăr′-ĭk)	150	52.20N	7.35W
Carrier, Can. (kăr′ĭ-ĕr)	83b	46.43N	71.05W
Carriere, Ms., U.S. (kä-rēr′)	114	30.37N	89.37W
Carrières-sous-Bois, Fr.	237c	48.57N	2.07E
Carrières-sous-Poissy, Fr.	237c	48.57N	2.03E
Carrières-sur-Seine, Fr.	237c	48.55N	2.11E
Carriers Mills, Il., U.S. (kăr′ĭ-ĕrs)	98	37.40N	88.40W
Carrington, Eng., U.K.	237b	53.26N	2.24W

272 Carrington–Central America

PLACE (Pronunciation)	PAGE	Lat. °′	Long. °′
Carrington, N.D., U.S. (kăr'ĭng-tŭn)	102	47.26N	99.06W
Carr Inlet, Wa., U.S. (kăr ĭn'lĕt)	106a	47.20N	122.42W
Carrion Crow Harbor, b., Bah. (kăr'ĭŭn krō)	122	26.35N	77.55W
Carrión de los Condes, Spain (kär-rē-ōn' dā lōs kōn'dås)	158	42.20N	4.35W
Carrizo Creek, r., N.M., U.S. (kär-rē'zō)	110	36.22N	103.39W
Carrizo Springs, Tx., U.S.	112	28.32N	99.51W
Carrizozo, N.M., U.S. (kär-rē-zō'zō)	109	33.40N	105.55W
Carroll, Ia., U.S. (kăr'ŭl)	103	42.03N	94.51W
Carrollton, Ga., U.S. (kăr-ŭl-tŭn)	114	33.35N	85.05W
Carrollton, Il., U.S.	111	39.18N	90.22W
Carrollton, Ky., U.S.	98	38.45N	85.15W
Carrollton, Mi., U.S.	98	43.30N	83.55W
Carrollton, Mo., U.S.	111	39.21N	93.29W
Carrollton, Oh., U.S.	98	40.35N	81.10W
Carrollton, Tx., U.S.	107c	32.58N	96.53W
Carrols, Wa., U.S. (kăr'ŭlz)	106c	46.05N	122.51W
Carrot, r., Can.	88	53.12N	103.50W
Carry-le-Rouet, Fr. (kä-rē'lĕ-rō-ā')	156a	43.20N	5.10E
Carsamba, Tur. (chär-shäm'bä)	149	41.05N	36.40E
Carshalton, neigh., Eng., U.K.	235	51.22N	0.10W
Carson, Ca., U.S.	232	33.50N	118.16W
Carson, r., Nv., U.S. (kär'sŭn)	108	39.15N	119.25W
Carson City, Nv., U.S.	96	39.10N	119.45W
Carsondale, Md., U.S.	229d	38.57N	76.50W
Carson Sink, Nv., U.S.	108	39.51N	118.25W
Cartagena, Col. (kär-tä-hä'nä)	130	10.30N	75.40W
Cartagena, Spain (kär-tä-kē'nä)	142	37.46N	1.00W
Cartago, Col. (kär-tä'gō)	130a	4.44N	75.54W
Cartago, C.R.	117	9.52N	83.56W
Cartaxo, Port. (kär-tä'shō)	158	39.10N	8.48W
Carteret, N.J., U.S. (kär'tē-ret)	100a	40.35N	74.13W
Cartersville, Ga., U.S. (kär'tērs-vĭl)	114	34.09N	84.47W
Carthage, Tun.	210	37.04N	10.18E
Carthage, Il., U.S. (kär'thåj)	111	40.27N	91.09W
Carthage, Mo., U.S.	111	37.10N	94.18W
Carthage, N.Y., U.S.	99	44.00N	75.45W
Carthage, N.C., U.S.	115	35.22N	79.25W
Carthage, Tx., U.S.	113	32.09N	94.20W
Carthcart, S. Afr. (cärth-că't)	213c	32.18S	27.11E
Cartwright, Can. (kärt'rīt)	85	53.36N	57.00W
Caruaru, Braz. (kä-rò-ä-rōō')	131	8.19S	35.52W
Carúpano, Ven. (kä-rōō'pä-nō)	130	10.45N	63.21W
Caruthersville, Mo., U.S. (kȧ-rŭdh'ērz-vĭl)	111	36.09N	89.41W
Carver, Or., U.S. (kärv'ēr)	106c	45.24N	122.30W
Carvoeiro, Cabo, c., Port. (ká'bō-kär-vó-ĕ'y-rō)	158	39.22N	9.24W
Cary, Il., U.S. (kă'rē)	101a	42.13N	88.14W
Casablanca, Chile (kä-sä-blăŋ'kä)	129b	33.19S	71.24W
Casablanca, Mor.	210	33.32N	7.41W
Casa Branca, Braz. (ká'sä-brá'n-kä)	129a	21.47S	47.04W
Casa Grande, Az., U.S. (kä'sä grän'dā)	109	32.50N	111.45W
Casa Grande National Monument, rec., Az., U.S.	109	33.00N	111.33W
Casale Monferrato, Italy (kä-sä'lā)	160	45.08N	8.26E
Casalmaggiore, Italy (kä-säl-mäd-jō'rā)	160	45.00N	10.24E
Casa Loma, pt. of i., Can.	227c	43.41N	79.25W
Casamance, r., Sen. (kä-sä-mäns')	210	12.30N	15.00W
Cascade Mountains, mts., N.A.	87	49.10N	121.00W
Cascade Point, c., N.Z. (kăs-kād')	203a	43.59S	168.23E
Cascade Range, mts., N.A.	96	42.50N	122.20W
Cascade Tunnel, trans., Wa., U.S.	104	47.41N	120.53W
Cascais, Port. (käs-kȧ-ēzh)	158	38.42N	9.25W
Case Inlet, Wa., U.S. (kās)	106a	47.22N	122.47W
Caseros, Arg. (kä-sā'rōs)	132a	34.35S	58.34W
Caserta, Italy (kä-zĕr'tä)	160	41.04N	14.21E
Casey, Il., U.S. (kā'sĭ)	98	39.20N	88.00W
Cashmere, Wa., U.S. (kăsh'mĭr)	104	47.30N	120.28W
Casiguran, Phil. (käs-sē-gōō'rän)	197a	16.15N	122.10E
Casiguran Sound, strt., Phil.	197a	16.02N	121.51E
Casilda, Arg. (kä-sē'l-dä)	132	33.02S	61.11W
Casilda, Cuba	122	21.50N	80.00W
Casimiro de Abreu, Braz. (kä'sē-mē'ro-dē-á-brē'ōō)	129a	22.30S	42.11W
Casino, Austl. (kȧ-sē'nō)	204	28.35S	153.10E
Casiquiare, r., Ven. (kä-sē-kyä'rä)	130	2.11N	66.15W
Caspe, Spain (käs'på)	159	41.18N	0.02W
Casper, Wy., U.S. (kăs'pēr)	96	42.51N	106.18W
Caspian Depression, depr. (kăs'pĭ-ăn)	164	47.40N	52.35E
Caspian Sea, sea	164	40.00N	52.00E
Cass, W.V., U.S. (kăs)	99	38.25N	79.55W
Cass, l., Mn., U.S.	103	47.23N	94.28W
Cassai (Kasai), r., Afr. (kä-sä'ē)	212	11.30S	21.00E
Cass City, Mi., U.S. (kăs)	98	43.35N	83.10W
Casselman, Can. (kăs''l-mån)	83c	45.18N	75.05W
Casselton, N.D., U.S. (kăs''l-tŭn)	102	46.53N	97.14W
Cássia, Braz. (ká'syä)	129a	20.36S	46.53W
Cassin, Tx., U.S. (kăs'ĭn)	107d	29.16N	98.29W
Cassinga, Ang.	212	15.05S	16.15E
Cassino, Italy (käs-sē'nō)	148	41.30N	13.50E
Cass Lake, Mn., U.S. (kăs)	103	47.23N	94.37W
Cassopolis, Mi., U.S. (kăs-ŏ'pō-lĭs)	98	41.55N	86.00W
Cassville, Mo., U.S. (kăs'vĭl)	111	36.41N	93.52W
Castanheira de Pêra, Port. (käs-tän-yā'rä-dē-pē'rä)	158	40.00N	8.07W
Castellammare di Stabia, Italy	159c	40.26N	14.29E
Castellbisbal, Spain	238e	41.29N	1.59E
Castelli, Arg. (kás-tĕ'zhē)	129c	36.07S	57.48W
Castellón de la Plana, Spain (käs-tĕl-yō'n-dĕ-lä-plä'nä)	148	39.59N	0.05W
Castelnaudary, Fr. (kás'tĕl-nō-dá-rē')	156	43.20N	1.57E
Castelo, Braz. (käs-tĕ'lō)	129a	20.37S	41.13W
Castelo Branco, Port. (käs-tä'lò bräŋ'kò)	148	39.48N	7.37W
Castelo de Vide, Port. (käs-tä'lò dĭ vē'dĭ)	158	39.25N	7.25W
Castelsarrasin, Fr. (kás'tĕl-sá-rá-zăn')	156	44.03N	1.05E
Castelvetrano, Italy (käs'tĕl-vē-trä'nō)	160	37.43N	12.50E
Castilla, Peru (kás-tē'l-yä)	130	5.18S	80.40W
Castilla La Nueva, hist. reg., Spain (käs-tē'lyä lä nwā'vä)	158	39.15N	3.55W
Castilla La Vieja, hist. reg., Spain (käs-tēl'yä lä vyā'hä)	158	40.48N	4.24W
Castillo de San Marcos National Monument, rec., Fl., U.S. (käs-tē'lyä de-sän mär-kōs)	115	29.55N	81.25W
Castle, i., Bah. (kås''l)	123	22.05N	74.20W
Castlebar, Ire. (kås''l-bär)	150	53.55N	9.15W
Castlecrag, Austl.	243a	33.48S	151.13E
Castle Dale, Ut., U.S. (kås'l dāl)	109	39.15N	111.00W
Castle Donington, Eng., U.K. (dŏn'ĭng-tŭn)	144a	52.50N	1.21W
Castleford, Eng., U.K. (kås'l-fērd)	144a	53.43N	1.21W
Castlegar, Can. (kås''l-gär)	87	49.19N	117.40W
Castle Hill, Austl.	243a	33.44S	151.00E
Castlemaine, Austl. (kăs''l-mān)	204	37.05S	144.10E
Castle Peak, mtn., Co., U.S.	109	39.00N	106.50W
Castle Rock, Wa., U.S. (kås''l-rŏk)	104	46.17N	122.53W
Castle Rock Flowage, res., Wi., U.S.	103	44.03N	89.48W
Castle Shannon, Pa., U.S. (shăn'ŭn)	101e	40.22N	80.02W
Castleton, Eng., U.K.	237b	53.35N	2.11W
Castleton, In., U.S. (kås''l-tŏn)	101g	39.54N	86.03W
Castor, r., Can. (kăs'tôr)	83c	45.16N	75.14W
Castor, r., Mo., U.S.	111	36.59N	89.53W
Castres, Fr. (kás'tr')	156	43.36N	2.13E
Castries, St. Luc. (kás-trē')	121b	14.01N	61.00W
Castro, Braz. (käs'trò)	131	24.56S	50.00W
Castro, Chile (käs'tro)	132	42.27S	73.48W
Castro Daire, Port. (käs'trò dīr'ĭ)	158	40.56N	7.57W
Castro del Río, Spain (käs-trô-dĕl rē'ō)	158	37.42N	4.28W
Castrop Rauxel, Ger. (käs'trōp rou'ksĕl)	157c	51.33N	7.19E
Castro Urdiales, Spain (käs'trō ör-dyä'lås)	148	43.23N	3.11W
Castro Valley, Ca., U.S.	106b	37.42N	122.05W
Castro Verde, Port. (käs-trō vĕr'dĕ)	158	37.43N	8.05W
Castrovillari, Italy (käs'trō-vēl-lyä'rē)	160	39.48N	16.11E
Castuera, Spain (käs-tò-ā'rä)	158	38.43N	5.33W
Casula, Moz.	217	15.25S	33.40E
Cat, i., Bah.	123	24.30N	75.30W
Catacamas, Hond. (kä-tä-ká'mäs)	120	14.52N	85.55W
Cataguases, Braz. (kä-tä-gwá'sĕs)	129a	21.23S	42.42W
Catahoula, l., La., U.S. (kăt-ȧ-hò'lȧ)	113	31.35N	92.20W
Catalão, Braz. (kä-tä-loun')	131	18.09S	47.42W
Catalina, i., Dom. Rep. (kä-tä-lē'nä)	123	18.20N	69.00W
Cataluña, hist. reg., Spain	159	41.23N	0.50E
Cataluña, Museo de Arte de, bldg., Spain	238e	41.23N	2.09E
Catamarca, Arg. (kä-tä-mä'r-kä)	132	28.29S	65.45W
Catamarca, prov., Arg. (kä-tä-mär'kä)	132	27.15S	67.15W
Catanaun, Phil. (kä-tä-nä'wän)	197a	13.36N	122.20E
Catanduanes Island, i., Phil. (kä-tän-dwä'nĕs)	197	13.55N	125.00E
Catanduva, Braz. (kä-tán-dōō'vä)	131	21.12S	48.47W
Catania, Italy (kä-tä'nyä)	142	37.30N	15.09E
Catania, Golfo di, b., Italy (gòl-fō-dē-kä-tä'nyä)	160	37.24N	15.28E
Catanzaro, Italy (kä-tän-dzä'rō)	149	38.53N	16.34E
Catarroja, Spain (kä-tär-rō'hä)	159	39.24N	0.25W
Catawba, r., N.C., U.S. (kȧ-tô'bȧ)	115	35.25N	80.55W
Catbalogan, Phil. (kät-bä-lō'gän)	197	11.45N	124.52E
Catemaco, Mex. (kä-tä-mä'kō)	119	18.26N	95.06W
Catemaco, Lago, l., Mex. (lä'gô-kä-tä-mä'kō)	119	18.23N	95.04W
Caterham, Eng., U.K. (kā'tēr-ŭm)	144b	51.16N	0.04W
Catete, Ang. (kä-tĕ'tĕ)	212	9.06S	13.43E
Catete, neigh., Braz.	234c	22.55S	43.10W
Catford, neigh., Eng., U.K.	235	51.27N	0.01W
Cathedral Mountain, mtn., Tx., U.S. (kȧ-thē'drăl)	112	30.09N	103.46W
Cathedral Peak, mtn., Afr. (kă-thē'drăl)	213c	28.53S	29.04E
Catherine, Lake, l., Ar., U.S. (kă-thēr-ĭn)	111	34.26N	92.47W
Cathkin Peak, mtn., Afr. (kăth'kĭn)	212	29.08S	29.22E
Cathlamet, Wa., U.S. (kăth-lăm'ĕt)	106c	46.12N	123.22W
Catia, neigh., Ven.	234a	10.31N	66.57W
Catlettsburg, Ky., U.S. (kăt'lĕts-bûrg)	98	38.20N	82.35W
Catoche, Cabo, c., Mex. (kä-tō'chĕ)	116	21.30N	87.15W
Catonsville, Md., U.S. (kā'tŭnz-vĭl)	100e	39.16N	76.45W
Catorce, Mex. (kä-tôr'sä)	118	23.41N	100.51W
Catskill, N.Y., U.S. (kăts'kĭl)	99	42.15N	73.50W
Catskill Mountains, mts., N.Y., U.S.	97	42.20N	74.35W
Cattaraugus Indian Reservation, I.R., N.Y., U.S. (kăt'tä-rȧ-gŭs)	99	42.30N	79.05W
Catu, Braz. (kȧ-tōō)	131	12.26S	38.12W
Catuala, Ang.	216	16.29S	19.03E
Catumbela, r., Ang. (kä'tŏm-bĕl'ȧ)	216	12.40S	14.10E
Cauayan, Phil. (kou-ä'yän)	197a	16.56N	121.46E
Cauca, r., Col. (kou'kä)	130	7.30N	75.26W
Caucagua, Ven. (käò-kȧ'gwä)	131b	10.17N	66.22W
Caucasus, mts.	164	43.20N	42.00E
Cauchon Lake, l., Can. (kô-shōn')	89	55.25N	96.30W
Caughnawaga, Can.	83a	45.24N	73.41W
Caulfield, Austl.	201a	37.53S	145.03E
Caulonia, Italy (kou-lō'nyä)	160	38.24N	16.22E
Cauquenes, Chile (kou-kā'nās)	132	35.54S	72.14W
Caura, r., Ven. (kou'rä)	130	6.48N	64.40W
Causapscal, Can.	92	48.22N	67.14W
Caution, Cape, c., Can. (kô'shŭn)	86	51.10N	127.47W
Cauto, r., Cuba (kou'tō)	122	20.33N	76.20W
Cauvery, r., India	183	12.00N	77.00E
Cava, Braz. (ká'vä)	132b	22.41S	43.26W
Cava de' Tirreni, Italy (kä'vä-dĕ-tēr-rĕ'nĕ)	159c	40.27N	14.43E
Cávado, r., Port. (kä-vä'dō)	158	41.43N	8.08W
Cavalcante, Braz. (kä-väl-kän'tä)	131	13.45S	47.33W
Cavalier, N.D., U.S. (kăv-ȧ-lēr')	102	48.45N	97.39W
Cavally, r., Afr.	214	4.40N	7.30W
Cavan, Ire. (kăv'ăn)	150	54.01N	7.00W
Cavarzere, Italy (kä-vär'dzå-rā)	160	45.08N	12.06E
Cavendish, Vt., U.S. (kăv'ĕn-dĭsh)	99	43.25N	72.35W
Caviana, Ilha, i., Braz. (kä-vyä'nä)	131	0.45N	49.33W
Cavite, Phil. (kä-vē'tä)	197a	14.30N	120.54E
Caxambu, Braz. (kä-shá'm-bōō)	131	22.00S	44.45W
Caxias, Braz. (kä'shē-äzh)	131	4.48S	43.16W
Caxias, Port.	238d	38.42N	9.16W
Caxias do Sul, Braz. (kä'shē-äzh-dò-sōō'l)	132	29.13S	51.03W
Caxito, Ang. (kä-shē'tò)	212	8.33S	13.36E
Cayambe, Ec. (kä-īä'm-bĕ)	130	0.03N	79.09W
Cayenne, Fr. Gu. (kā-ĕn')	131	4.56N	52.18W
Cayetano Rubio, Mex. (kä-yĕ-tä-nô-rōō'byô)	118	20.37N	100.21W
Cayey, P.R.	117b	18.05N	66.12W
Cayman Brac, i., Cay. Is. (kī-män' brák)	122	19.45N	79.50W
Cayman Islands, dep., N.A.	122	19.30N	80.30W
Cay Sal Bank, bk. (kē-säl)	122	23.55N	80.20W
Cayuga, l., N.Y., U.S. (kä-yōō'gȧ)	99	42.35N	76.35W
Cazalla de la Sierra, Spain	158	37.55N	5.48W
Cazaux, Étang de, l., Fr. (ā-tän' dĕ kä-zō')	156	44.32N	0.59W
Cazenovia, N.Y., U.S. (kăz-ē-nō'vĭ-ȧ)	99	42.55N	75.50W
Cazenovia Creek, r., N.Y., U.S.	101c	42.49N	78.45W
Čazma, Cro. (chäz'mä)	160	45.44N	16.39E
Cazombo, Ang. (kä-zô'm-bŏ)	212	11.54S	22.52E
Cazones, r., Mex. (kä-zô'nĕs)	119	20.37N	97.28W
Cazones, Ensenada de, b., Cuba (ĕn-sĕ-nä-dä-dĕ-kä-zō'nås)	122	22.05N	81.30W
Cazones, Golfo de, b., Cuba (gôl-fô-dĕ-kä-zō'nås)	122	21.55N	81.15W
Cazorla, Spain (kä-thôr'lå)	158	37.55N	2.58W
Cea, r., Spain (thā'ä)	158	42.18N	5.10W
Ceará-Mirim, Braz. (sā-ä-rä'mē-rē'n)	131	6.00S	35.13W
Cebaco, Isla, i., Pan. (ĕ's-lä-sä-bä'kō)	121	7.27N	81.08W
Cebolla Creek, r., Co., U.S. (sē-bōl'yä)	109	38.15N	107.10W
Cebreros, Spain (sē-brĕ'rôs)	158	40.28N	4.28W
Cebu, Phil. (sā-bōō')	197	10.22N	123.49E
Čecchignola, neigh., Italy	239c	41.49N	12.29E
Čechy (Bohemia), hist. reg., Czech Rep.	154	49.51N	13.55E
Cecil, Pa., U.S. (sē'sĭl)	101e	40.20N	80.10W
Cecil Park, Austl.	243a	33.52S	150.51E
Cedar, r., Ia., U.S.	103	42.23N	92.07W
Cedar, r., Wa., U.S.	106c	45.56N	122.32W
Cedar, West Fork, r., Ia., U.S.	103	42.49N	93.10W
Cedar Bayou, Tx., U.S.	113a	29.54N	94.58W
Cedar Breaks National Monument, rec., Ut., U.S.	109	37.35N	112.55W
Cedarbrook, Pa., U.S.	229b	40.05N	75.10W
Cedarburg, Wi., U.S. (sē'dēr bûrg)	103	43.23N	88.00W
Cedar City, Ut., U.S.	109	37.40N	113.10W
Cedar Creek, r., N.D., U.S.	102	46.05N	102.10W
Cedar Falls, Ia., U.S.	103	42.31N	92.29W
Cedar Grove, N.J., U.S.	228	40.51N	74.14W
Cedar Heights, Pa., U.S.	229b	40.05N	75.17W
Cedarhurst, N.Y., U.S.	228	40.38N	73.44W
Cedar Keys, Fl., U.S.	114	29.06N	83.03W
Cedar Lake, In., U.S.	101a	41.22N	87.27W
Cedar Lake, l., In., U.S.	101a	41.23N	87.25W
Cedar Lake, res., Can.	84	53.10N	100.00W
Cedar Rapids, Ia., U.S.	97	42.00N	91.43W
Cedar Springs, Mi., U.S.	98	43.15N	85.40W
Cedartown, Ga., U.S. (sē'dēr-toun)	114	34.00N	85.15W
Cedarville, S. Afr. (cĕdăr'vĭl)	213c	30.23S	29.04E
Cedral, Mex. (sā-dräl')	118	23.47N	100.42W
Cedros, Hond. (sā'drōs)	120	14.36N	87.07W
Cedros, i., Mex.	116	28.10N	115.10W
Ceduna, Austl. (sē-dò'nȧ)	202	32.15S	133.55E
Ceel Buur, Som.	218a	4.35N	46.40E
Cega, r., Spain (thā'gä)	158	41.25N	4.27W
Cegléd, Hung. (tsā'glād)	155	47.10N	19.49E
Ceglie, Italy (chĕ'lyĕ)	161	40.39N	17.32E
Cehegín, Spain (thā-ä-hēn')	158	38.05N	1.48W
Ceiba del Agua, Cuba (sā'bä-dĕl-á'gwä)	123a	22.53N	82.38W
Cekhira, Tun.	210	34.17N	10.00E
Celaya, Mex. (sā-lä'yä)	118	20.33N	100.49W
Celebes (Sulawesi), i., Indon.	196	2.15S	120.30E
Celebes Sea, sea, Asia	196	3.45N	121.52E
Celestún, Mex. (sĕ-lĕs-tōō'n)	120a	20.57N	90.18W
Celina, Oh., U.S. (sĕlī'na)	98	40.30N	84.35W
Celje, Slvn. (tsĕl'yĕ)	160	46.13N	15.17E
Celle, Ger. (tsĕl'ē)	147	52.37N	10.05E
Cement, Ok., U.S. (sē-mĕnt')	110	34.56N	98.07W
Cenderawasih, Teluk, b., Indon.	197	2.20S	135.30E
Ceniza, Pico, mtn., Ven. (pē'kō-sē-nē'zä)	131b	10.24N	67.26W
Center, Tx., U.S. (sĕn'tēr)	113	31.50N	94.10W
Center Hill Lake, res., Tn., U.S. (sĕn'tēr-hĭl)	114	36.02N	86.00W
Center Line, Mi., U.S. (sĕn'tēr līn)	101b	42.29N	83.01W
Centerville, Ia., U.S. (sĕn'tēr-vĭl)	103	40.44N	92.48W
Centerville, Mn., U.S.	107g	45.10N	93.03W
Centerville, Pa., U.S.	101e	40.02N	79.58W
Centerville, S.D., U.S.	102	43.07N	96.56W
Centerville, Ut., U.S.	107b	40.55N	111.53W
Centocelle, neigh., Italy	239c	41.53N	12.34E
Central, Cordillera, mts., Bol. (kôr-dĕl-yĕ'rä-sĕn-trä'l)	130	19.18S	65.29W
Central, Cordillera, mts., Col.	130a	3.58N	75.55W
Central, Cordillera, mts., Dom. Rep.	123	19.05N	71.30W
Central, Cordillera, mts., Phil. (kôr-dĕl-yĕ'rä-sĕn'träl)	197a	17.05N	120.55E
Central African Republic, nation, Afr.	211	7.50N	21.00E
Central America, reg., N.A. (ä-mĕr'ĭ-kȧ)	116	10.45N	87.15W

ăt; finăl; rāte; senåte; ärm; ȧsk; sofȧ; fâre; ch-choose; dh-as th in other; bē; ėvent; bĕt; recĕnt; cratẽr; g-gō; gh-guttural g; bĭt; ĭ-short neutral; rīde; ᴋ-guttural k as ch in German ich;

PRONOUNCING INDEX

Central City-Chaville 273

PLACE (Pronunciation)	PAGE	Lat. °′	Long. °′
Central City, Ky., U.S. (sĕn'trăl)	114	37.15N	87.09W
Central City, Ne., U.S. (sĕn'trăl sĭ'tĭ)	102	41.07N	98.00W
Central Falls, R.I., U.S. (sĕn'trăl fôlz)	100b	41.54N	71.23W
Central Highlands, Pa., U.S.	230b	40.16N	79.50W
Centralia, Il., U.S. (sĕn-trā'lĭ-ă)	98	38.35N	89.05W
Centralia, Mo., U.S.	111	39.11N	92.07W
Centralia, Wa., U.S.	104	46.42N	122.58W
Central Intelligence Agency, pt. of i., Va., U.S.	229d	38.57N	77.09W
Central Park, pt. of i., N.Y., U.S.	228	40.47N	73.58W
Central Plateau, plat., Russia	166	55.00N	33.30E
Central Valley, N.Y., U.S.	100a	41.19N	74.07W
Centre Island, N.Y., U.S.	228	40.54N	73.32W
Centreville, Il., U.S. (sĕn'tẽr-vĭl)	107e	38.33N	90.06W
Centreville, Md., U.S.	99	39.05N	76.05W
Centro Simón Bolívar, pt. of i., Ven.	234a	10.30N	66.55W
Century, Fl., U.S. (sĕn'tů-rĭ)	114	30.57N	87.15W
Century City, neigh., Ca., U.S.	232	34.03N	118.26W
Ceram (Seram), i., Indon.	197	2.45S	129.30E
Céret, Fr.	156	42.29N	2.47E
Cerignola, Italy (chā-rē-nyô'lä)	160	41.16N	15.55E
Cerknica, Slvn. (tsĕr'knē-tsá)	160	45.48N	14.21E
Čern'achovsk, Russia (chĕr-nyä'kôfsk)	166	54.38N	21.49E
Čer'omuski, neigh., Russia	239b	55.41N	37.35E
Cerralvo, Mex. (sĕr-räl'vō)	112	26.05N	99.37W
Cerralvo, i., Mex.	116	24.00N	109.59W
Cerrito, Col. (sĕr-rē'-tô)	130a	3.41N	76.17W
Cerritos, Mex. (sĕr-rē'tôs)	118	22.26N	100.16W
Cerro de Pasco, Peru (sĕr'rō dā päs'kō)	130	10.45S	76.14W
Cerro Gordo, Arroyo de, r., Mex. (är-rô-yô-dĕ-sĕ'r-rô-gôr-dô)	112	26.12N	104.06W
Čertanovo, neigh., Russia	239b	55.38N	37.37E
Certegui, Col. (sĕr-tĕ'gē)	130a	5.21N	76.35W
Cervantes, Phil. (sĕr-văn'tās)	197a	16.59N	120.42E
Cervera del Río Alhama, Spain	158	42.02N	1.55W
Cerveteri, Italy (chĕr-vĕ'tĕ-rē)	159d	42.00N	12.06E
Cesano Boscone, Italy	238c	45.27N	9.06E
Cesena, Italy (chĕ'sĕ-nä)	160	44.08N	12.16E
Cēsis, Lat. (sā'sĭs)	153	57.19N	25.17E
Česká Lípa, Czech Rep. (chĕs'kä lē'pa)	154	50.41N	14.31E
České Budějovice, Czech Rep. (chĕs'kä bōō'dyĕ-yô-vĕt-sĕ)	147	49.00N	14.30E
Českomoravská Vysočina, hills, Czech Rep.	154	49.21N	15.40E
Český Těšín, Czech Rep.	155	49.43N	18.22E
Çeşme, Tur. (chĕsh'mĕ)	161	38.20N	26.20E
Cessnock, Austl.	203	32.58S	151.15E
Cestos, r., Lib.	214	5.40N	9.25W
Cetinje, Yugo. (tsĕt'in-yĕ)	142	42.23N	18.55E
Ceuta, Sp. N. Afr. (thā-ōō'tä)	210	36.04N	5.36W
Cévennes, reg., Fr. (sā-vĕn')	147	44.20N	3.48E
Ceylon see Sri Lanka, nation, Asia	183b	8.45N	82.30E
Chabot, Lake, l., Ca., U.S. (sha'bŏt)	106b	37.44N	122.06W
Chacabuco, Arg. (chä-kä-bōō'kō)	129c	34.37S	60.27W
Chacaltianguis, Mex. (chä-käl-tē-äŋ'gwēs)	119	18.18N	95.50W
Chacao, Ven.	234a	10.30N	66.51W
Chachapoyas, Peru (chä-chä-poi'yäs)	130	6.16S	77.48W
Chaco, prov., Arg. (chä'kō)	132	26.00S	60.45W
Chaco Culture National Historic Park, rec., N.M., U.S. (chä'kô)	109	36.05N	108.00W
Chad, Russia (chäd)	172a	56.33N	57.11E
Chad, nation, Afr.	211	17.48N	19.00E
Chad, Lake, l., Afr.	211	13.55N	13.40E
Chadbourn, N.C., U.S. (chăd'bŭrn)	115	34.19N	78.55W
Chadderton, Eng., U.K.	237b	53.33N	2.08W
Chadron, Ne., U.S. (chăd'rŭn)	96	42.50N	103.10W
Chadstone, Austl.	243b	37.53S	145.05E
Chadwell Saint Mary, Eng., U.K.	235	51.29N	0.22E
Chafarinas, Islas, is., Sp. N. Afr.	158	35.08N	2.20W
Chaffee, Mo., U.S. (chăf'ē)	111	37.10N	89.39W
Chāgal Hills, hills, Afg.	182	29.15N	63.28E
Chagodoshcha, r., Russia (chä-gō-dôsh-chä)	162	59.08N	35.13E
Chagres, r., Pan. (chä'grĕs)	121	9.18N	79.22W
Chagrin, r., Oh., U.S. (shă'grĭn)	101d	41.34N	81.24W
Chagrin Falls, Oh., U.S. (shă'grĭn fôls)	101d	41.26N	81.23W
Chahar, hist. reg., China (chä-här)	189	44.25N	115.00E
Chahār Borjak, Afg.	185	30.17N	62.03E
Chakdaha, India	240a	22.28N	88.20E
Chake Chake, Tan.	217	5.15S	39.46E
Chalatenango, El Sal. (chäl-ä-tĕ-näŋ'gō)	120	14.04N	88.54W
Chalbi Desert, des., Kenya	217	3.40N	36.50E
Chalcatongo, Mex. (chäl-kä-tôŋ'gō)	119	17.04N	97.41W
Chalchihuites, Mex. (chäl-chē-wē'tås)	118	23.28N	103.57W
Chalchuapa, El Sal. (chäl-chwä'pä)	120	14.01N	89.39W
Chalco, Mex. (chäl-kō)	119a	19.15N	98.54W
Chaldon, Eng., U.K.	235	51.17N	0.07W
Chaleur Bay, b., Can. (shá-lûr')	85	47.58N	65.33W
Chalfant, Pa., U.S.	230b	40.25N	79.52W
Chalfont Common, Eng., U.K.	235	51.38N	0.33W
Chalfont Saint Giles, Eng., U.K.	235	51.38N	0.34W
Chalfont Saint Peter, Eng., U.K.	235	51.37N	0.33W
Chalgrove, Eng., U.K. (chăl'grôv)	144b	51.38N	1.05W
Chaling, China (chä'lĭng)	193	27.00N	113.31E
Chalk, Eng., U.K.	235	51.26N	0.25E
Chalmette, La., U.S. (shăl-mĕt')	100d	29.57N	89.57W
Châlons-sur-Marne, Fr. (shá-lôɴ'sür-märn)	147	48.57N	4.23E
Chalon-sur-Saône, Fr.	147	46.47N	4.54E
Chaltel, Cerro (Monte Fitzroy), mtn., S.A. (sĕ'r-rô-chäl'tĕl)	132	48.10S	73.18W
Chālūs, Iran	185	36.38N	51.26E
Chama, Rio, r., N.M., U.S. (chä'mä)	109	36.19N	106.31W
Chama, Sierra de, mts., Guat. (sē-ĕ'r-rä-dĕ-chä-mä)	120	15.48N	90.20W
Chamama, Mwi.	217	12.55S	33.43E
Chaman, Pak. (chŭm-än')	183	30.58N	66.21E
Chambal, r., India (chŭm-bäl')	183	24.30N	75.30E
Chamberlain, S.D., U.S. (chām'bĕr-lĭn)	102	43.48N	99.21W
Chamberlain, l., Me., U.S.	92	46.15N	69.10W
Chambersburg, Pa., U.S. (chām'bẽrz-bûrg)	99	40.00N	77.40W
Chambéry, Fr. (shäm-bā-rē')	147	45.35N	5.54E
Chambeshi, r., Zam.	217	10.35S	31.20E
Chamblee, Ga., U.S. (chăm-blē')	100c	33.55N	84.18W
Chambly, Can. (shäɴ-blē')	83a	45.27N	73.17W
Chambly, Fr.	157b	49.11N	2.14E
Chambord, Can.	85	48.22N	72.01W
Chambourcy, Fr.	237c	48.54N	2.03E
Chame, Punta, c., Pan. (pô'n-tä-chä'må)	121	8.41N	79.27W
Chamelecón, r., Hond. (chä-mĕ-lĕ-kô'n)	120	15.09N	88.42W
Chamo, l., Eth.	211	5.58N	37.00E
Chamonix-Mont-Blanc, Fr. (shá-mô-nē')	157	45.55N	6.50E
Champagne, reg., Fr. (shäm-pän'yĕ)	156	48.53N	4.48E
Champaign, Il., U.S. (shăm-pān')	97	40.10N	88.15W
Champdāni, India	186a	22.48N	88.21E
Champerico, Guat. (chăm-pā-rē'kō)	120	14.18N	91.55W
Champigny-sur-Marne, Fr.	237c	48.49N	2.31E
Champion, Mi., U.S. (chăm'pĭ-ŭn)	103	46.30N	87.59W
Champlain, Lake, l., N.A. (shăm-plān')	97	44.45N	73.20W
Champlan, Fr.	237c	48.43N	2.16E
Champlitte-et-le-Prálot, Fr. (shäɴ-plēt')	157	47.38N	5.28E
Champotón, Mex. (chäm-pō-tōn')	119	19.21N	90.43W
Champotón, r., Mex.	119	19.19N	90.15W
Champs-sur-Marne, Fr.	237c	48.51N	2.36E
Chāmrāil, India	240a	22.38N	88.18E
Chañaral, Chile (chän-yä-räl')	132	26.20S	70.46W
Chances Peak, vol., Monts.	121b	16.43N	62.10W
Chandannagar, India	240a	22.51N	88.21E
Chandeleur Islands, is., La., U.S. (shăn-dĕ-lōōr')	114	29.53N	88.35W
Chandeleur Sound, strt., La., U.S.	114	29.47N	89.08W
Chandīgarh, India	183	30.51N	77.13E
Chandler, Can. (chăn'dlẽr)	85	48.21N	64.41W
Chandler, Ok., U.S.	111	35.42N	96.52W
Chandler's Cross, Eng., U.K.	235	51.40N	0.27W
Chandrapur, India	183	19.58N	79.21E
Chang see Yangtze, r., China	189	30.30N	117.25E
Changane, r., Moz.	212	22.42S	32.46E
Changara, Moz.	217	16.54S	33.14E
Changchun, China (chäŋ-chòn)	189	43.55N	125.25E
Changdang Hu, l., China (chäŋ-däŋ hōō)	190	31.37N	119.29E
Changde, China (chäŋ-dŭ)	189	29.00N	111.38E
Changdian, China	240b	40.01N	116.32E
Changhua, Tai. (chäng'hwä')	193	24.02N	120.32E
Changi, Sing.	240c	1.23N	103.59E
Changjŏn, N. Kor. (chäng'jŭn')	194	38.40N	128.05E
Changli, China (chäŋ-lē)	192	39.46N	119.10E
Changning, China (chäŋ-nĭŋ)	188	24.34N	99.49E
Changping, China (chäŋ-pĭŋ)	192	40.12N	116.10E
Changqing, China (chäŋ-chyĭŋ)	190	36.33N	116.42E
Changsan Got, c., N. Kor.	194	38.06N	124.50E
Changsha, China (chäŋ-shä)	189	28.20N	113.00E
Changshan Qundao, is., China (chäŋ-shän chyòn-dou)	190	39.08N	122.26E
Changshu, China (chäŋ-shōō)	190	31.40N	120.45E
Changting, China	193	25.50N	116.18E
Changwu, China (chäng'wōō')	192	35.12N	107.45E
Changxindianzhen, China (chäŋ-shyĭn-dĭĕn-jŭn)	192a	39.49N	116.12E
Changxing Dao, i., China (chäŋ-shyĭŋ dou)	190	39.38N	121.10E
Changyi, China (chäŋ-yē)	190	36.51N	119.23E
Changyuan, China (chyäŋ-yuän)	190	35.10N	114.41E
Changzhi, China (chäŋ-jr)	192	35.58N	112.58E
Changzhou, China (chäŋ-jō)	189	31.47N	119.56E
Changzhuyuan, China (chäŋ-jōō-yuän)	190	31.33N	115.17E
Chanhassen, Mn., U.S. (shăn'hăs-sĕn)	107g	44.52N	93.32W
Chanh-hung, Viet.	241j	10.43N	106.41E
Channel Islands, is., Eur. (chăn'ĕl)	142	49.15N	3.30W
Channel Islands, is., Ca., U.S.	108	33.30N	119.15W
Channel-Port-aux-Basques, Can.	85	47.35N	59.11W
Channelview, Tx., U.S. (chănêlvū)	113a	29.46N	95.07W
Chantada, Spain (chän-tä'dä)	158	42.38N	7.36W
Chanteloup-les-Vignes, Fr.	237c	48.59N	2.02E
Chanthaburi, Thai.	196	12.37N	102.04E
Chantilly, Fr. (shäɴ-tē-yē')	157b	49.12N	2.30E
Chantilly, Va., U.S. (shăn'tĭlē)	100e	38.53N	77.26W
Chantrey Inlet, b., Can. (chăn-trē)	84	67.49N	95.00W
Chanute, Ks., U.S. (shă-nōōt')	97	37.41N	95.27W
Chany, l., Russia (chä'nē)	164	54.15N	77.31E
Chao'an, China (chou-än)	189	23.48N	116.35E
Chao Hu, l., China	193	31.45N	116.59E
Chao Phraya, r., Thai.	196	16.13N	99.33E
Chaor, r., China (chou-r)	192	47.20N	121.40E
Chaoshui, China (chou-shwā)	190	37.43N	120.56E
Chaoxian, China (chou shyĕn)	190	31.37N	117.50E
Chaoyang, China	189	41.32N	120.20E
Chaoyang, China (chou-yäŋ)	193	23.18N	116.32E
Chapada, Serra da, mts., Braz. (sĕ'r-rä-dä-shä-pä'dä)	131	14.57S	54.34W
Chapadão, Serra do, mtn., Braz. (sĕ'r-rä-dô-shä-pá-dou'ɴ)	129a	20.31S	46.20W
Chapala, Mex. (chä-pä'lä)	118	20.18N	103.10W
Chapala, Lago de, l., Mex. (lä'gô-dĕ-chä-pä'lä)	116	20.14N	103.02W
Chapalagana, r., Mex. (chä-pä-lä-gá'nä)	118	22.11N	104.09W
Chaparral, Col. (chä-pär-rá'l)	130	3.44N	75.28W
Chapayevsk, Russia (châ-pī'ĕfsk)	166	53.00N	49.30E
Chapel Hill, N.C., U.S. (chăp''l hĭl)	115	35.55N	79.05W
Chapel Oaks, Md., U.S.	229d	38.54N	76.55W
Chapeltown, Eng., U.K.	237b	53.38N	2.24W
Chaplain, l., Wa., U.S. (chăp'lĭn)	106a	47.58N	121.50W
Chapleau, Can. (chăp-lō')	85	47.43N	83.28W
Chapman, Mount, mtn., Can. (chăp'măn)	87	51.50N	118.20W
Chapman's Bay, b., S. Afr. (chăp'măns bā)	212a	34.06S	18.17E
Chapman Woods, Ca., U.S.	232	34.08N	118.05W
Chappell, Ne., U.S. (chă-pĕl')	102	41.06N	102.29W
Chapultenango, Mex. (chä-pòl-tĕ-näŋ'gō)	119	17.19N	93.08W
Chapultepec, Castillo de, hist., Mex.	233a	19.25N	99.11W
Chá Pungana, Ang.	216	13.44S	18.39E
Charcas, Mex. (chär'käs)	118	23.09N	101.09W
Charco de Azul, Bahía, b., Pan.	121	8.14N	82.45W
Chardzhou, Turk. (chĕr-jô'ò)	169	38.52N	63.37E
Charente, r., Fr. (shá-räɴt')	156	45.48N	0.28W
Charenton-le-Pont, Fr.	237c	48.49N	2.25E
Chari, r., Afr. (shä-rē')	215	12.45N	14.55E
Charing, Eng., U.K. (chă'rĭng)	144b	51.13N	0.49E
Chariton, Ia., U.S. (châr'ĭ-tŭn)	103	41.02N	93.16W
Chariton, r., Mo., U.S.	111	40.24N	92.38W
Charlemagne, Can. (shärl-mäny')	83a	45.43N	73.29W
Charleroi, Bel. (shár-lē-rwä')	147	50.25N	4.35E
Charleroi, Pa., U.S. (shär'lē-roi)	101e	40.08N79.54	W
Charles, Cape, c., Va., U.S. (chärlz)	99	37.05N	75.48W
Charlesbourg, Can. (shárl-bōōr')	83b	46.51N	71.16W
Charles City, Ia., U.S. (chärlz)	103	43.03N	92.40W
Charles de Gaulle, Aéroport, arpt., Fr.	237c	49.00N	2.34E
Charleston, Il., U.S. (chärlz'tŭn)	98	39.30N	88.10W
Charleston, Ms., U.S.	114	34.00N	90.02W
Charleston, Mo., U.S.	111	36.53N	89.20W
Charleston, S.C., U.S.	97	32.47N	79.56W
Charleston, W.V., U.S.	97	38.20N	81.35W
Charlestown, St. K./N.	121b	17.10N	62.32W
Charlestown, In., U.S. (chärlz'toun)	101h	38.46N	85.39W
Charleville, Austl. (chär'lē-vĭl)	203	26.16S	146.28E
Charleville Mézières, Fr. (shärl-vĕl')	156	49.48N	4.41E
Charlevoix, Mi., U.S. (shär'lē-voi)	98	45.20N	85.15W
Charlevoix, Lake, l., Mi., U.S.	103	45.17N	85.43W
Charlotte, Mi., U.S. (shär'lŏt)	98	42.35N	84.50W
Charlotte, N.C., U.S.	97	35.15N	80.50W
Charlotte Amalie, V.I.U.S. (shär-lŏt'ĕ ä-mä'lĭ-å)	117	18.21N	64.54W
Charlotte Harbor, b., Fl., U.S.	115a	26.49N	82.00W
Charlotte Lake, l., Can.	86	52.07N	125.30W
Charlottenberg, Swe. (shär-lŭt'ĕn-bĕrg)	152	59.53N	12.17E
Charlottenburg, neigh., Ger.	238a	52.31N	13.16E
Charlottenburg, Schloss, hist., Ger.	238a	52.31N	13.14E
Charlottesville, Va., U.S. (shär'lŏtz-vĭl)	97	38.00N	78.25W
Charlottetown, Can. (shär'lŏt-toun)	85	46.14N	63.08W
Charlotte Waters, Austl. (shär'lŏt)	202	26.00S	134.50E
Charlton, neigh., Eng., U.K.	235	51.29N	0.02E
Charmes, Fr. (shärm)	157	48.23N	6.19E
Charneca, neigh., Port.	238d	38.47N	9.08W
Charnwood Forest, for., Eng., U.K. (chärn'wòd)	144a	52.42N	1.15W
Charny, Can. (shär-nē')	83b	46.43N	71.16W
Chars, Fr. (shär)	157b	49.09N	1.57E
Chārsadda, Pak. (chŭr-sä'dä)	183a	34.17N	71.43E
Charters Towers, Austl. (chär'tẽrz)	203	20.03S	146.20E
Charterwood, Pa., U.S.	230b	40.33N	80.00W
Chartres, Fr. (shärt'r')	147	48.26N	1.29E
Chascomús, Arg. (chäs-kō-mōōs')	132	35.32S	58.01W
Chase City, Va., U.S. (chās)	115	36.45N	78.27W
Chashniki, Bela. (chäsh'nyē-kē)	162	54.51N	29.08E
Chaska, Mn., U.S. (chăs'ká)	107g	44.48N	93.36W
Châteaudun, Fr. (shä-tō-däɴ')	156	48.04N	1.23E
Châteaufort, Fr.	237c	48.44N	2.06E
Château-Gontier, Fr. (chá-tō'gôɴ'tyā')	156	47.48N	0.43W
Châteauguay, Can. (chá-tō-gā)	83a	45.22N	73.45W
Châteauguay, r., N.A.	83a	45.13N	73.51W
Châteauneaut, Fr.	156a	43.23N	5.11E
Château-Renault, Fr. (shá-tō-rĕ-nō')	156	47.36N	0.57E
Château-Richer, Can. (shá-tō'rē-shā')	83b	47.00N	71.01W
Châteauroux, Fr. (shá-tō-rōō')	147	46.47N	1.39E
Château-Thierry, Fr. (shá-tō'ty-ĕr-rē')	156	49.03N	3.22E
Châtellerault, Fr. (shä-tĕl-rō')	147	46.48N	0.31E
Châtenay-Malabry, Fr.	237c	48.46N	2.17E
Chatfield, Mn., U.S. (chăt'fēld)	103	43.50N	92.10W
Chatham, Can.	85	47.02N	65.28W
Chatham, Can. (chăt'ăm)	85	42.25N	82.10W
Chatham, Eng., U.K. (chăt'ŭm)	151	51.23N	0.32E
Chatham, N.J., U.S. (chăt'ăm)	100a	40.44N	74.23W
Chatham, Oh., U.S.	101d	41.06N	82.01W
Chatham Islands, is., N.Z.	2	44.00S	178.00W
Chatham Sound, strt., Can.	86	54.32N	130.35W
Chatham Strait, strt., Ak., U.S.	95	57.00N	134.40W
Châtillon, Fr.	237c	48.48N	2.17E
Chatou, Fr.	237c	48.54N	2.09E
Chatpur, neigh., India	240a	22.36N	88.23E
Chatswood, Austl.	243a	33.48S	151.12E
Chatsworth, Ca., U.S. (chătz'wûrth)	107a	34.16N	118.36W
Chatsworth Reservoir, res., Ca., U.S.	107a	34.15N	118.41W
Chattahoochee, Fl., U.S. (chăt-tá-hōō' chēē)	114	30.42N	84.47W
Chattahoochee, r., U.S.	97	32.00N	85.10W
Chattanooga, Tn., U.S. (chăt-ă-nōō'gă)	97	35.01N	85.15W
Chattooga, r., Ga., U.S. (chă-tōō'gă)	114	34.47N	83.13W
Chaudière, r., Can. (shō-dyĕr')	91	46.26N	71.10W
Chaumont, Fr. (shō-môɴ')	147	48.08N	5.07E
Chaunskaya Guba, b., Russia	171	69.15N	170.00E
Chauny, Fr. (shō-nē')	156	49.40N	3.09E
Chau-phu, Viet.	196	10.49N	104.57E
Chausy, Bela. (chou'sĭ)	162	53.57N	30.58E
Chautauqua, l., N.Y., U.S. (shă-tô'kwă)	99	42.10N	79.25W
Chavaniga, Russia	166	66.02N	37.50E
Chavenay, Fr.	237c	48.51N	1.59E
Chaves, Port. (chä'vĕzh)	158	41.44N	7.30W
Chaville, Fr.	237c	48.48N	2.10E

ŋ-sing; ŋ-baŋk; ɴ-nasalized n; nŏd; cŏmmit; ōld; ôbey; ôrder; oi-boil; fōōd; ò-as oo in foot; ou-out; s-soft; sh-dish; th-thin; pūre; ůnite; ûrn; stŭd; circŭs; ü-as in French tu; '-indeterminate vowel.

PLACE (Pronunciation)	PAGE	Lat. °′	Long. °′
Chavinda, Mex. (chä-vē'n-dä)	118	20.01N	102.27W
Chazumba, Mex. (chä-zōm'bä)	119	18.11N	97.41W
Cheadle, Eng., U.K. (chē'd'l)	144a	52.59N	1.59W
Cheadle Hulme, Eng., U.K.	237b	53.22N	2.12W
Cheam, neigh., Eng., U.K.	235	51.21N	0.13W
Cheat, W.V., U.S. (chēt)	99	39.35N	79.40W
Cheb, Czech Rep. (κĕb)	154	50.05N	12.23E
Chebarkul', Russia (chĕ-bár-kûl')	172a	54.59N	60.22E
Cheboksary, Russia (chyĕ-bôk-sä'rė)	166	56.00N	47.20E
Cheboygan, Mi., U.S. (shė-boi'găn)	98	45.40N	84.30W
Chech, Erg, des., Alg.	210	24.45N	2.07W
Chechen', i., Russia (chyĕch'ĕn)	167	44.00N	48.10E
Checheno-Ingushetia, state, Russia	168	43.15N	45.40E
Checotah, Ok., U.S. (chė-kō'tȧ)	111	35.27N	95.32W
Chedabucto Bay, b., Can. (chĕd-ȧ-bŭk-tō)	93	45.23N	61.10W
Cheduba Island, i., Myanmar	196	18.45N	93.01E
Cheecham Hills, hills, Can. (chēē'hăm)	88	56.20N	111.10W
Cheektowaga, N.Y., U.S. (chēk-tō-wä'gȧ)	101c	42.54N	78.46W
Cheetham Hill, neigh., Eng., U.K.	237b	53.31N	2.15W
Chefoo *see* Yantai, China	189	37.32N	121.22E
Chegutu, Zimb.	212	18.18S	30.10E
Chehalis, Wa., U.S. (chė-hā'lĭs)	104	46.39N	122.58W
Chehalis, r., Wa., U.S.	104	46.47N	123.17W
Cheju, S. Kor. (chĕ'jōō')	194	33.29N	126.40E
Cheju (Quelpart), i., S. Kor.	194	33.20N	126.25E
Chekalin, Russia (chĕ-kä'lĭn)	162	54.05N	36.13E
Chela, Serra da, mts., Ang. (sĕr'rȧ dä shä'lȧ)	212	15.30S	13.30E
Chelan, Wa., U.S. (chė-lăn')	104	47.51N	119.59W
Chelan, Lake, l., Wa., U.S.	104	48.09N	120.20W
Chelas, neigh., Port.	238d	38.45N	9.07W
Cheleiros, Port. (shĕ-la'rōzh)	159b	38.54N	9.19W
Chéliff, r., Alg. (shā-lēf)	210	36.00N	2.00E
Chelles, Fr.	157b	48.53N	2.36E
Chełm, Pol. (κĕlm)	147	51.08N	23.30E
Chełmno, Pol. (κĕlm'nō)	155	53.20N	18.25E
Chelmsford, Can.	90	46.35N	81.12W
Chelmsford, Eng., U.K. (chĕlm's-fērd)	151	51.44N	0.28E
Chelmsford, Ma., U.S.	93a	42.36N	71.21W
Chelsea, Austl.	201a	38.05S	145.08E
Chelsea, Can.	83c	45.30N	75.46W
Chelsea, Al., U.S. (chĕl'sė)	100h	33.20N	86.38W
Chelsea, Ma., U.S.	93a	42.23N	71.02W
Chelsea, Mi., U.S.	98	42.20N	84.00W
Chelsea, Ok., U.S.	111	36.32N	95.23W
Cheltenham, Eng., U.K. (chĕlt'nŭm)	150	51.57N	2.06W
Cheltenham, Md., U.S. (chĕltĕn-hăm)	100e	38.45N	76.50W
Chelva, Spain (chĕl'vä)	158	39.43N	1.00W
Chelyabinsk, Russia (chĕl-yä-bėnsk')	164	55.10N	61.25E
Chelyuskin, Mys, c., Russia (chĕl-yōs'-kĭn)	165	77.45N	104.45E
Chemba, Moz.	217	17.08S	34.52E
Chembūr, neigh., India	240e	19.04N	72.54E
Chemnitz, Ger.	147	50.48N	12.53E
Chemung, r., N.Y., U.S. (shė-mŭng)	99	42.20N	77.25W
Chĕn, Gora, mtn., Russia	165	65.13N	142.12E
Chenāb, r., Asia (chė-näb)	183	30.30N	71.30E
Chenachane, Alg. (shĕ-ná-shän')	210	26.14N	4.14W
Chencun, China (chŭn-tsòn)	191a	22.58N	113.14E
Cheney, Wa., U.S. (chē'nȧ)	104	47.29N	117.34W
Chengde, China (chŭŋ-dŭ)	189	40.50N	117.50E
Chengdong Hu, l., China (chŭŋ-dôŋ hōō)	190	32.22N	116.32E
Chengdu, China (chŭŋ-dōō)	188	30.30N	104.10E
Chenggu, China (chŭŋ-gōō)	192	33.05N	107.25E
Chenghai, China (chŭŋ-hī)	193	23.22N	116.40E
Chengshan Jiao, c., China (jyou chŭŋ-shän)	192	37.28N	122.40E
Chengxi Hu, l., China (chŭŋ-shyē hōō)	190	32.31N	116.04E
Chenies, Eng., U.K.	235	51.41N	0.32W
Chennevières, Fr.	237c	49.00N	2.07E
Chenxian, China (chŭn-shyĕn)	193	25.40N	113.00E
Chepén, Peru (chĕ-pĕ'n)	130	7.17S	79.24W
Chepo, Pan. (chā'pō)	121	9.12N	79.06W
Chepo, r., Pan.	121	9.10N	78.36W
Cher, r., Fr. (shâr)	147	47.14N	1.34E
Cherán, Mex. (chā-rän')	118	19.41N	101.54W
Cherangany Hills, hills, Kenya	217	1.25N	35.20E
Cheraw, S.C., U.S. (chē'rô)	115	34.40N	79.52W
Cherbourg, Fr. (shär-bōōr')	142	49.39N	1.43W
Cherdyn', Russia (chĕr-dyēn')	164	60.25N	56.32E
Cheremkhovo, Russia (chĕr'yĕm-kô-vō)	165	52.58N	103.18E
Cherëmukhovo, Russia (chĕr-yĕ-mû-kô-vô)	172a	60.20N	60.00E
Cherepanovo, Russia (chĕr'yĕ pä-nō'vō)	164	54.13N	83.22E
Cherepovets, Russia (chĕr-yĕ-pô'vyĕtz)	164	59.08N	37.59E
Chereya, Bela. (chĕr-ā'yä)	162	54.38N	29.16E
Chergui, i., Tun.	148	34.50N	11.40E
Chergui, Chott ech, l., Alg. (chĕr gē)	148	34.12N	0.10W
Cherikov, Bela. (chĕ'rē-kôf)	162	53.34N	31.22E
Cherkasy, Ukr.	163	49.26N	32.03E
Cherkasy, prov., Ukr.	163	48.58N	30.55E
Cherkessk, Russia	168	44.14N	42.04E
Cherlak, Russia (chĭr-läk')	164	54.04N	74.28E
Chermoz, Russia (chĕr-môz')	166	58.47N	56.08E
Chern', Russia (chĕrn)	162	53.28N	36.49E
Chërnaya Kalitva, r., Russia (chôr'nȧ yȧ ká-lēt'vȧ)	163	50.15N	39.16E
Chernihiv, Ukr.	167	51.23N	31.15E
Chernihiv, prov., Ukr.	163	51.28N	31.18E
Chernihivka, Ukr.	163	47.08N	36.20E
Chernivtsi, Ukr.	164	48.18N	25.56E
Chernobyl' (Chornobyl'), Ukr. (chĕr-nō-bĭl')	163	51.17N	30.14E
Chernogorsk, Russia (chĕr-nŏ-gôrsk')	170	54.01N	91.07E
Chernoistochinsk, Russia (chĕr-nôy-stô'chĭnsk)	172a	57.44N	59.55E
Chernyanka, Russia (chĕrn-yäŋ'kä)	163	50.56N	37.48E
Cherokee, Ia., U.S. (chĕr-ô-kē')	102	42.43N	95.33W
Cherokee, Ks., U.S.	111	37.21N	94.50W
Cherokee, Ok., U.S.	110	36.44N	98.22W
Cherokee Lake, res., Tn., U.S.	114	36.22N	83.22W
Cherokees, Lake of the, res., Ok., U.S. (chĕr-ô-kēz')	97	36.32N	95.14W
Cherokee Sound, Bah.	122	26.15N	76.55W
Cherry City, Pa., U.S.	230b	40.29N	79.58W
Cherryfield, Me., U.S. (chĕr'ĭ-fēld)	92	44.37N	67.56W
Cherry Grove, Or., U.S.	106c	45.27N	123.15W
Cherry Hill, N.J., U.S.	229b	39.55N	75.01W
Cherry Hill, neigh., Md., U.S.	229c	39.15N	76.38W
Cherryvale, Ks., U.S.	111	37.16N	95.33W
Cherryville, N.C., U.S. (chĕr'ĭ-vĭl)	115	35.32N	81.22W
Cherskogo, Khrebet, mts., Russia	165	67.15N	140.00E
Chertsey, Eng., U.K.	144b	51.24N	0.30W
Cherven', Bela. (chĕr'vyĕn)	162	53.43N	28.26E
Chervonoye, l., Bela. (chĕr-vô'nō-yĕ)	162	52.24N	28.12E
Chesaning, Mi., U.S. (chĕs'ȧ-nĭng)	98	43.10N	84.10W
Chesapeake, Va., U.S. (chĕs'ȧ-pēk)	100g	36.48N	76.16W
Chesapeake Bay, b., U.S.	97	38.20N	76.15W
Chesapeake Beach, Md., U.S.	100e	38.42N	76.33W
Chesham, Eng., U.K. (chĕsh'ŭm)	144b	51.41N	0.37W
Chesham Bois, Eng., U.K.	235	51.41N	0.37W
Cheshire, Mi., U.S. (chĕsh'ĭr)	98	42.25N	86.00W
Cheshire, co., Eng., U.K.	144a	53.16N	2.30W
Chëshskaya Guba, b., Russia	164	67.25N	46.00E
Cheshunt, Eng., U.K.	144b	51.43N	0.02W
Chesma, Russia (chĕs'mȧ)	172a	53.50N	60.42E
Chesnokovka, Russia (chĕs-nŏ-kôf'kȧ)	164	53.28N	83.41E
Chessington, neigh., Eng., U.K.	235	51.21N	0.18W
Chester, Eng., U.K. (chĕs'tēr)	150	53.12N	2.53W
Chester, Il., U.S.	111	37.54N	89.48W
Chester, Pa., U.S.	100f	39.51N	75.22W
Chester, Pa., U.S.	229b	39.51N	75.21W
Chester, S.C., U.S.	115	34.42N	81.11W
Chester, Va., U.S.	115	37.20N	77.24W
Chester, W.V., U.S.	98	40.35N	80.30W
Chesterbrook, Va., U.S.	229d	38.55N	77.09W
Chesterfield, Eng., U.K. (chĕs'tēr-fēld)	150	53.14N	1.26W
Chesterfield, Îles, is., N. Cal.	203	19.38S	160.08E
Chesterfield Inlet, Can.	85	63.19N	91.11W
Chesterfield Inlet, b., Can.	85	63.59N	92.09W
Chestermere Lake, l., Can. (chĕs'tē-mēr)	83e	51.03N	113.45W
Chesterton, In., U.S. (chĕs'tēr-tŭn)	98	41.35N	87.05W
Chestertown, Md., U.S. (chĕs'tēr-toun)	99	39.15N	76.05W
Chestnut Hill, Md., U.S.	229c	39.17N	76.47W
Chestnut Hill, Ma., U.S.	227a	42.20N	71.10W
Chesuncook, l., Me., U.S. (chĕs'ŭn-kŏŏk)	92	46.03N	69.40W
Cheswick, Pa., U.S.	230b	40.32N	79.47W
Chetek, Wi., U.S. (chĕ'tĕk)	103	45.18N	91.41W
Chetumal, Bahía de, b., N.A. (bä-ē'ä dĕ chĕt-ōō-mäl')	116	18.07N	88.05W
Chevelon Creek, r., Az., U.S. (shĕv'ȧ-lŏn)	109	34.35N	111.00W
Chevening, Eng., U.K.	235	51.18N	0.08E
Cheverly, Md., U.S.	229d	38.55N	76.55W
Chevilly-Larue, Fr.	237c	48.46N	2.21E
Cheviot, Oh., U.S. (shĕv'ĭ-ŭt)	101f	39.10N	84.37W
Chevreuse, Fr. (shĕ-vrûz')	157b	48.42N	2.02E
Chevy Chase, Md., U.S. (shĕvĭ chās)	100e	38.58N	77.06W
Chevy Chase View, Md., U.S.	229d	39.01N	77.05W
Chew Bahir, Afr. (stĕf-a-nē)	211	4.46N	37.31E
Chewelah, Wa., U.S. (chē-wē'lä)	104	48.17N	117.42W
Cheyenne, Wy., U.S. (shī-ĕn')	96	41.10N	104.49W
Cheyenne, r., U.S.	96	44.20N	102.15W
Cheyenne River Indian Reservation, I.R., S.D., U.S.	102	45.07N	100.46W
Cheyenne Wells, Co., U.S.	110	38.46N	102.21W
Chhalera Bāngar, India	240d	28.33N	77.20E
Chhināmor, India	240a	22.48N	88.18E
Chhindwāra, India	186	22.08N	78.57E
Chiai, Tai. (chī'ī')	193	23.28N	120.28E
Chiange, Ang.	216	15.45S	13.48E
Chiang Mai, Thai.	196	18.38N	98.44E
Chiang Rai, Thai.	196	19.53N	99.48E
Chiapa, Río de, r., Mex.	120	16.00N	92.20W
Chiapa de Corzo, Mex. (chė-ä'pä dä kôr'zō)	119	16.44N	93.01W
Chiapas, state, Mex. (chė-ä'päs)	116	17.10N	93.00W
Chiapas, Cordilla de, mts., Mex. (kôr-dēl-yĕ'rä-dĕ-chyä'räs)	119	15.55N	93.15W
Chiari, Italy (kyä'rē)	160	45.31N	9.57E
Chiasso, Switz.	154	45.50N	8.57E
Chiatura, Geor.	168	42.17N	43.17E
Chiautla, Mex. (chyä-ōōt'lȧ)	118	18.16N	98.37W
Chiavari, Italy (kyä-vä'rē)	160	44.18N	9.21E
Chiba, Japan (chē'bȧ)	189	35.37N	140.08E
Chiba, dept., Japan	195a	35.47N	140.02E
Chibougamau, Can. (chē-bōō'gä-mou)	85	49.57N	74.23W
Chibougamau, l., Can.	91	49.53N	74.21W
Chicago, Il., U.S. (shĭ-kô-gō) (chĭ-kä'gō)	97	41.49N	87.37W
Chicago, North Branch, r., Il., U.S.	231a	41.53N	87.38W
Chicago Heights, Il., U.S.	101a	41.30N	87.38W
Chicago Lawn, neigh., Il., U.S.	231a	41.47N	87.41W
Chicago-O'Hare International Airport, arpt., Il., U.S.	231a	41.59N	87.54W
Chicago Ridge, Il., U.S.	231a	41.42N	87.47W
Chicago Sanitary and Ship Canal, can., Il., U.S.	231a	41.42N	87.58W
Chicapa, r., Afr. (chē-kä'pä)	212	7.45S	20.25E
Chicbul, Mex. (chēk-bōō'l)	119	18.45N	90.56W
Chic-Chocs, Monts, mts., Can.	85	48.38N	66.37W
Chichagof, i., Ak., U.S. (chĕ-chä'gôf)	95	57.50N	137.00W
Chichancanab, Lago de, l., Mex. (lä'gô-dĕ-chē-chän-kä-nä'b)	120a	19.50N	88.28W
Chichén Itzá, hist., Mex.	120a	20.40N	88.35W
Chichester, Eng., U.K. (chĭch'ĕs-tēr)	150	50.50N	0.55W
Chichimilá, Mex. (chē-chē-mē'lä)	120a	20.36N	88.14W
Chichiriviche, Ven. (chē-chē-rē-vē-chĕ)	131b	10.56N	68.17W
Chickamauga, Ga., U.S. (chĭk-ȧ-mô'gȧ)	114	34.50N	85.15W
Chickamauga Lake, res., Tn., U.S.	114	35.18N	85.22W
Chickasawhay, r., Ms., U.S. (chĭk-ȧ-sô'wā)	114	31.45N	88.45W
Chickasha, Ok., U.S. (chĭk'ȧ-shā)	96	35.04N	97.56W
Chiclana de la Frontera, Spain (chē-klä'nä)	158	36.25N	6.09W
Chiclayo, Peru (chē-klä'yō)	130	6.46S	79.50W
Chico, Ca., U.S. (chē'kō)	108	39.43N	121.51W
Chico, Wa., U.S.	106a	47.37N	122.43W
Chico, r., Arg.	132	44.30S	66.00W
Chico, r., Arg.	132	49.15S	69.30W
Chico, r., Phil.	197a	17.33N	121.24E
Chicoloapan, Mex. (chė-kō-lwä'pän)	119a	19.24N	98.54W
Chiconautla, Mex.	119a	19.39N	99.01W
Chicontepec, Mex. (chė-kōn'tē-pĕk')	118	20.58N	98.08W
Chicopee, Ma., U.S. (chĭk'ō-pē)	99	42.10N	72.35W
Chicoutimi, Can. (shē-kōō'tē-mē')	85	48.26N	71.04W
Chicxulub, Mex. (chēk-sōō-lōō'b)	120a	21.10N	89.30W
Chiefland, Fl., U.S. (chēf'lănd)	115	29.30N	82.50W
Chiemsee, l., Ger. (κēm zā)	154	47.58N	12.20E
Chieri, Italy (kyâ'rē)	160	45.03N	7.48E
Chieti, Italy (kyĕ'tē)	148	42.22N	14.22E
Chifeng, China (chr-fŭŋ)	189	42.18N	118.52E
Chignall Saint James, Eng., U.K.	235	51.46N	0.25E
Chignanuapan, Mex. (chē'g-ŋä-nwä-pä'n)	118	19.49N	98.02W
Chignecto Bay, b., Can. (shĭg-nĕk'tō)	92	45.33N	64.50W
Chignik, Ak., U.S. (chĭg'nĭk)	95	56.14N	158.12W
Chignik Bay, b., Ak., U.S.	95	56.18N	157.22W
Chigu Co, l., China (chr-gōō tswo)	186	28.55N	91.47E
Chigwell, Eng., U.K.	144b	51.38N	0.05E
Chigwell Row, Eng., U.K.	235	51.37N	0.07E
Chihe, China (chr-hŭ)	190	32.32N	117.57E
Chihuahua, Mex. (chē-wä'wä)	116	28.37N	106.06W
Chihuahua, state, Mex.	116	29.00N	107.30W
Chikishlyar, Turk. (chė-kēsh-lyär')	170	37.40N	53.50E
Chilanga, Zam.	217	15.34S	28.17E
Chilapa, Mex. (chē-lä'pä)	118	17.34N	99.14W
Chilchota, Mex. (chēl-chō'tä)	118	19.40N	102.04W
Chilcotin, r., Can. (chĭl-kō'tĭn)	86	52.20N	124.15W
Childer Thornton, Eng., U.K.	237a	53.17N	2.57W
Childress, Tx., U.S. (chīld'rĕs)	110	34.26N	100.11W
Chile, nation, S.A. (chē'lā)	132	35.00S	72.00W
Chilecito, Arg. (chē-lā-sē'tō)	132	29.06S	67.25W
Chilengue, Serra do, mts., Ang.	216	13.20S	15.00E
Chilibre, Pan. (chē-lē'brĕ)	116a	9.09N	79.37W
Chililabombwe, Zam.	217	12.18S	27.43E
Chilka, l., India	186	19.26N	85.42E
Chilko, r., Can. (chĭl'kō)	86	51.53N	123.53W
Chilko Lake, l., Can.	86	51.20N	124.05W
Chillán, Chile (chēl-yän')	132	36.44S	72.06W
Chillicothe, Il., U.S. (chĭl-ĭ-kŏth'ė)	98	41.55N	89.30W
Chillicothe, Mo., U.S.	111	39.46N	93.32W
Chillicothe, Oh., U.S.	98	39.20N	83.00W
Chilliwack, Can. (chĭl'ĭ-wăk)	84	49.10N	121.57W
Chillum, Md., U.S.	229d	38.58N	76.59W
Chilly-Mazarin, Fr.	237c	48.42N	2.19E
Chiloé, Isla de, i., Chile	132	42.30S	73.55W
Chilpancingo de los Bravo, Mex.	116	17.32N	99.30W
Chilton, Wi., U.S. (chĭl'tŭn)	103	44.00N	88.12W
Chilung, Tai. (chĭ'lung)	189	25.02N	121.48E
Chilwa, Lake, l., Afr.	212	15.12S	36.30E
Chimacum, Wa., U.S. (chĭm'ȧ-kŭm)	106a	48.01N	122.47W
Chimalpa, Mex. (chē-mäl'pä)	119a	19.26N	99.22W
Chimaltenango, Guat. (chė-mäl-tā-näŋ'gō)	120	14.39N	90.48W
Chimaltitan, Mex. (chėmäl-tē-tän')	118	21.36N	103.50W
Chimbay, Uzb. (chĭm-bī')	169	43.00N	59.44E
Chimborazo, mtn., Ec. (chėm-bō-rä'zō)	130	1.35S	78.45W
Chimbote, Peru (chėm-bō'tā)	130	9.02S	78.33W
Chimki-Chovrino, neigh., Russia	239b	55.51N	37.30E
China, Mex. (chē'nä)	112	25.43N	99.13W
China, nation, Asia (chī'nȧ)	188	36.45N	93.00E
Chinameca, El Sal. (Chē-nä-mä'kä)	120	13.31N	88.18W
Chinandega, Nic. (chē-nän-dä'gä)	120	12.38N	87.08W
Chinati Peak, mtn., Tx., U.S. (chĭ-nä'tē)	112	29.56N	104.29W
Chinatown, neigh., Ca., U.S.	231b	37.48N	122.26W
Chincha Alta, Peru (chĭn'chä äl'tä)	130	13.24S	76.04W
Chinchas, Islas, is., Peru (ē's-läs-chē'n-chäs)	130	11.27S	79.05W
Chinchilla, Austl. (chĭn-chĭl'ȧ)	204	26.44S	150.36E
Chinchorro, Banco, bk., Mex. (bä'n-kō-chĕn-chō'r-rō)	120a	18.43N	87.25W
Chincilla de Monte Aragon, Spain	158	38.54N	1.43W
Chinde, Moz. (shĕn'dĕ)	212	17.39S	36.34E
Chin Do, i., S. Kor.	194	34.30N	125.43E
Chindwin, r., Myanmar (chĭn-dwĭn)	183	23.30N	94.34E
Chingford, neigh., Eng., U.K.	235	51.38N	0.01E
Chingmei, Tai.	241d	24.59N	121.32E
Chingola, Zam. (chĭng-gōlä)	212	12.32S	27.52E
Chinguar, Ang. (chĭng-gär)	212	12.35S	16.15E
Chinguetti, Maur. (chĕŋ-gĕt'ė)	210	20.34N	12.34W
Chinhoyi, Zimb.	212	17.22S	30.12E
Chinju, S. Kor. (chĭn'jōō)	194	35.13N	128.10E
Chinko, r., Cen. Afr. Rep. (shĭn'kō)	211	4.50N	24.31E
Chinmen *see* Quemoy, Tai.	193	24.30N	118.20E
Chino, Ca., U.S. (chē'nō)	107a	34.01N	117.42W
Chinon, Fr. (shē-nôn')	156	47.09N	0.13E
Chinook, Mt., U.S. (shĭn-ŏk')	105	48.35N	109.15W
Chinsali, Zam.	217	10.34S	32.03E
Chinteche, Mwi. (chĭn-tĕ'chĕ)	212	11.48S	34.14E

PLACE (Pronunciation)	PAGE	Lat. °′	Long. °′
Chioggia, Italy (kyôd'jä)	160	45.12N	12.17E
Chipata, Zam.	212	13.39S	32.40E
Chipera, Moz. (zhė-pě'rä)	212	15.16S	32.30E
Chipley, Fl., U.S. (chĭp'lĭ)	114	30.45N	85.33W
Chipman, Can. (chĭp'măn)	92	46.11N	65.53W
Chipola, r., Fl., U.S. (chĭ-pō'lȧ)	114	30.40N	85.14W
Chippawa, Can. (chĭp'ė-wä)	101c	43.03N	79.03W
Chipperfield, Eng., U.K.	235	51.42N	0.29W
Chippewa, r., Mn., U.S. (chĭp'ė-wä)	102	45.07N	95.41W
Chippewa, r., Wi., U.S.	103	45.07N	91.19W
Chippewa Falls, Wi., U.S.	103	44.55N	91.26W
Chippewa Lake, Oh., U.S.	101d	41.04N	81.54W
Chipping Ongar, Eng., U.K.	235	51.43N	0.15E
Chipstead, Eng., U.K.	235	51.17N	0.09E
Chipstead, Eng., U.K.	235	51.18N	0.10W
Chiputneticook Lakes, l., N.A. (chĭ-pŏt-nĕt'ĭ-kŏŏk)	92	45.47N	67.45W
Chiquimula, Guat. (chē-kė-mōō'lä)	120	14.47N	89.31W
Chiquimulilla, Guat. (chē-kē-mōō-lē'l-yä)	120	14.08N	90.23W
Chiquinquira, Col. (chė-kēŋ'kė-rä')	130	5.33N	73.49W
Chirāgh Delhi, neigh., India	240d	28.32N	77.14E
Chirala, India	187	15.52N	80.22E
Chirchik, Uzb. (chĭr-chĕk')	169	41.28N	69.18E
Chire (Shire), r., Afr.	217	17.15S	35.25E
Chiricahua National Monument, rec., Az., U.S. (chĭ-rä-cä'hwä)	109	32.02N	109.18W
Chirikof, i., Ak., U.S. (chĭ'rĭ-kôf)	95	55.50N	155.35W
Chiriquí, Punta, c., Pan. (pŏŏ'n-tä-chē-rė-kē')	121	9.13N	81.39W
Chiriquí Grande, Pan. (chē-rė-kē' grän'dä)	121	8.57N	82.08W
Chiri San, mtn., S. Kor. (chĭ'rĭ-sän')	194	35.20N	127.39E
Chiromo, Mwi.	212	16.34S	35.13E
Chirpan, Bul.	149	42.12N	25.19E
Chirripó, Río, r., C.R.	121	9.50N	83.20W
Chisasibi, Can.	85	53.40N	78.58W
Chisholm, Mn., U.S. (chĭz'ŭm)	103	47.28N	92.53W
Chişinău, Mol.	164	47.02N	28.52E
Chislehurst, neigh., Eng., U.K.	235	51.25N	0.04E
Chistopol', Russia (chĭs-tô'pôl-y')	164	55.21N	50.37E
Chiswellgreen, Eng., U.K.	235	51.44N	0.22W
Chiswick, neigh., Eng., U.K.	235	51.29N	0.16W
Chita, Russia (chė-tá')	165	52.09N	113.39E
Chitambo, Zam.	217	12.55S	30.39E
Chitato, Ang.	216	7.20S	20.47E
Chitembo, Ang.	216	13.34S	16.40E
Chitina, Ak., U.S. (chĭ-tē'ná)	95	61.28N	144.35W
Chitokoloki, Zam.	216	13.50S	23.13E
Chitorgarh, India	186	24.59N	74.42E
Chitrāl, Pak. (chē-träl')	183	35.58N	71.48E
Chittagong, Bngl. (chĭt-á-gông')	183	22.26N	90.51E
Chitungwiza, Zimb.	212	17.51S	31.05E
Chiumbe, r., Afr. (chė-ŏm'bȧ)	212	9.45S	21.00E
Chivasso, Italy (kė-väs'sō)	160	45.13N	7.52E
Chivhu, Zimb.	212	18.59S	30.58E
Chivilcoy, Arg. (chē-vēl-koi')	132	34.51S	60.03W
Chixoy, r., Guat. (chē-koi')	120	15.40N	90.35W
Chizu, Japan (chė-zōō')	195	35.16N	134.15E
Chloride, Az., U.S. (klō'rīd)	109	35.25N	114.15W
Chmielnik, Pol. (kmyĕl'nēk)	155	50.36N	20.46E
Choa Chu Kang, Sing.	240c	1.22N	103.41E
Choapa, r., Chile (chỏ-á'pä)	129b	31.56S	70.48W
Chobham, Eng., U.K.	235	51.21N	0.36W
Choctawhatchee, r., Fl., U.S.	114	30.37N	85.56W
Choctawhatchee Bay, b., Fl., U.S. (chôk-tô-hăch'ē)	114	30.15N	86.32W
Chodziez, Pol. (kōj'yĕsh)	154	52.59N	16.55E
Choele Choel, Arg. (chỏ-ĕ'lĕ-chỏĕ'l)	132	39.14S	65.46W
Chōfu, Japan (chō'fōō')	195a	35.39N	139.33E
Chōgo, Japan (chō-gō)	195a	35.25N	139.28E
Choisel, Fr.	237c	48.41N	2.01E
Choiseul, i., Sol.Is. (shwä-zûl')	203	7.30S	157.30E
Choisy-le-Roi, Fr.	157b	48.46N	2.25E
Chojnice, Pol. (kōī-nē-tsĕ)	155	53.41N	17.34E
Cholet, Fr. (shỏ-lĕ')	147	47.06N	0.54W
Cho-lon, neigh., Viet.	241j	10.46N	106.40E
Cholula, Mex. (chō-lōō'lä)	118	19.04N	98.19W
Choluteca, Hond. (chō-lōō-tā'kä)	120	13.18N	87.12W
Choluteco, r., Hond.	120	13.34N	86.59W
Cho-moi, Viet.	241j	10.51N	106.38E
Chomutov, Czech Rep. (kō'mỏ-tôf)	154	50.27N	13.23E
Chona, r., Russia (chō'nä)	171	60.45N	109.15E
Chone, Ec. (chô'nĕ)	130	0.48S	80.06W
Chŏngjin, N. Kor. (chŭng-jĭn')	189	41.48N	129.46E
Chŏngju, S. Kor. (chŭng-jōō')	194	36.35N	127.30E
Chongming Dao, i., China (chôŋ-mĭŋ dou)	193	31.40N	122.30E
Chong Pang, Sing.	240c	1.26N	103.50E
Chongqing, China (chôŋ-chyĭŋ)	188	29.38N	107.30E
Chŏnju, S. Kor. (chŭn-jōō')	194	35.48N	127.08E
Chonos, Archipiélago de los, is., Chile	132	44.35N	76.15W
Chorley, Eng., U.K. (chôr'lĭ)	144a	53.40N	2.38W
Chorleywood, Eng., U.K.	235	51.39N	0.31W
Chorlton-cum-Hardy, Eng., U.K.	237b	53.27N	2.17W
Chornaya, neigh., Russia	172b	55.45N	38.04E
Chornobay, Ukr. (chĕr-nō-bī')	163	49.41N	32.24E
Chornomors'ke, Ukr.	167	45.29N	32.43E
Chorošovo, neigh., Russia	239b	55.47N	37.28E
Chorrera de Managua, Cuba	233b	23.02N	82.19E
Chorrillos, Peru (chôr-rē'l-yōs)	130	12.17S	76.55W
Chortkiv, Ukr.	155	49.01N	25.48E
Chosan, N. Kor. (chō-sän')	194	40.44N	125.48E
Chosen, Fl., U.S. (chō'z'n)	115a	26.41N	80.41W
Chōshi, Japan (chō'shē)	194	35.40N	140.55E
Choszczno, Pol. (chỏsh'chnỏ)	154	53.10N	15.25E
Chota Nagpur, plat., India	186	23.40N	82.50E
Choteau, Mt., U.S. (shō'tō)	105	47.51N	112.10W
Chowan, r., N.C., U.S. (chỏ-wän')	115	36.13N	76.46W
Chowilla Reservoir, res., Austl.	204	34.05S	141.20E
Chown, Mount, mtn., Can. (choun)	87	53.24N	119.22W
Choybalsan, Mong.	189	47.50N	114.15E
Christchurch, N.Z. (krīst'chûrch)	203a	43.30S	172.38E
Christian, i., Can. (krĭs'chăn)	91	44.50N	80.00W
Christiansburg, Va., U.S. (krĭs'chănz-bûrg)	115	37.08N	80.25W
Christiansted, V.I.U.S.	117b	17.45N	64.44W
Christmas Island, dep., Oc.	196	10.35S	105.40E
Christopher, Il., U.S. (krĭs'tỏ-fẽr)	111	37.58N	89.04W
Chrudim, Czech Rep. (krōō'dyĕm)	154	49.57N	15.46E
Chrzanów, Pol. (kzhä'nỏf)	155	50.08N	19.24E
Chuansha, China (chůän-shä)	191b	31.12N	121.41E
Chubut, prov., Arg. (chỏ-bōōt')	132	44.00S	69.15W
Chubut, r., Arg. (chỏ-bōōt')	132	43.05S	69.00W
Chuckatuck, Va., U.S. (chŭck á-tŭck)	100g	36.51N	76.35W
Chucunaque, r., Pan. (chōō-kōō-nä'kȧ)	121	8.36N	77.48W
Chudovo, Russia (chỏ'dỏ-vỏ)	162	59.03N	31.56E
Chudskoye Ozero, l., Eur. (chỏt'skỏ-yĕ)	166	58.43N	26.45E
Chuguchak, hist. reg., China (chōō'gōō-chäk')	188	46.09N	83.58E
Chuguyevka, Russia (chỏ-gōō'yĕf-kȧ)	194	43.58N	133.49E
Chugwater Creek, r., Wy., U.S. (chŭg'wô-tẽr)	102	41.43N	104.54W
Chuhuyiv, Ukr.	167	49.52N	36.40E
Chukot National Okrug, , Russia	171	68.15N	170.00E
Chukotskiy Poluostrov, pen., Russia	164	66.12N	175.00W
Chukotskoye Nagor'ye, mts., Russia	165	66.00N	166.00E
Chula Vista, Ca., U.S. (chōō'lȧ vĭs'tȧ)	108a	32.38N	117.05W
Chulkovo, Russia (chōōl-kô vô)	172b	55.33N	38.04E
Chulucanas, Peru	130	5.13S	80.13W
Chulum, r., Russia	170	57.52N	84.45E
Chumikan, Russia (chōō-mē-kän')	165	54.47N	135.09E
Chun'an, China (chỏn-än)	193	29.38N	119.00E
Chunchŏn, S. Kor. (chỏn-chŭn')	194	37.51N	127.46E
Chungju, S. Kor. (chŭng'jōō')	194	37.00N	128.19E
Chungking see Chongqing, China	188	29.38N	107.30E
Chŭngsanha-ri, neigh., S. Kor.	241b	37.35N	126.54E
Chunya, Tan.	217	8.32S	33.25E
Chunya, r., Russia (chỏn'yä')	170	61.45N	101.28E
Chuquicamata, Chile (chōō-kė-kä-mä'tä)	132	22.08S	68.57W
Chur, Switz. (kōōr)	147	46.51N	9.32E
Churchill, Can. (chûrch'ĭl)	85	58.50N	94.10W
Churchill, Pa., U.S.	230b	40.27N	79.51W
Churchill, Va., U.S.	229d	38.54N	77.10W
Churchill, r., Can.	84	58.00N	95.00W
Churchill, Cape, c., Can.	85	59.07N	93.50W
Churchill Falls, wtfl., Can.	85	53.35N	64.27W
Churchill Lake, l., Can.	88	56.12N	108.40W
Churchill Peak, mtn., Can.	84	58.10N	125.14W
Church Street, Eng., U.K.	235	51.26N	0.28E
Church Stretton, Eng., U.K. (chûrch strĕt'ŭn)	144a	52.32N	2.49W
Churchton, Md., U.S.	100e	38.49N	76.33W
Churu, India	186	28.22N	75.00E
Churumuco, Mex. (chōō-rōō-mōō'kō)	118	18.39N	101.40W
Chuska Mountains, mts., Az., U.S. (chŭs-kȧ)	109	36.21N	109.11W
Chusovaya, r., Russia (chōō-sỏ-vä'yȧ)	166	58.08N	58.35E
Chusovoy, Russia (chōō-sỏ-vỏy')	164	58.18N	57.50E
Chust, Uzb. (chỏst)	169	41.05N	71.28E
Chuvashia, state, Russia	166	55.45N	46.00E
Chuviscar, r., Mex. (chōō-vēs-kär')	112	28.34N	105.36W
Chuwang, China (chōō-wäŋ)	190	36.08N	114.53E
Chuxian, China (chōō shyĕn)	192	32.19N	118.19E
Chuxiong, China (chōō-shyỏŋ)	188	25.19N	101.34E
Chyhyryn, Ukr.	163	49.02N	32.39E
Cicero, Il., U.S. (sĭs'ẽr-ō)	101a	41.50N	87.46W
Cide, Tur. (jē'dĕ)	149	41.50N	33.00E
Ciechanów, Pol. (tsyĕ-kä'nỏf)	155	52.52N	20.39E
Ciego de Avila, Cuba (syā'gō dā ä'vē-lä)	117	21.50N	78.45W
Ciego de Avila, prov., Cuba	122	22.00N	78.40W
Ciempozuelos, Spain (thyĕm-pỏ-thwā'lōs)	158	40.09N	3.36W
Ciénaga, Col. (syā'nä-gä)	130	11.01N	74.15W
Cienfuegos, Cuba (syĕn-fwā'gōs)	117	22.10N	80.30W
Cienfuegos, prov., Cuba	122	22.15N	80.40W
Cienfuegos, Bahía, b., Cuba (bä-ē'ä-syĕn-fwā'gōs)	122	22.00N	80.35W
Ciervo, Isla de la, i., Nic. (ē's-lä-dĕ-lä-syĕ'r-vō)	121	11.56N	83.20W
Cieszyn, Pol. (tsyĕ'shĕn)	155	49.47N	18.45E
Cieza, Spain (thyā'thä)	158	38.13N	1.25W
Cigüela, r., Spain	158	39.53N	2.54W
Cihuatlán, Mex. (sē-wä-tlá'n)	118	19.13N	104.36W
Cihuatlán, r., Mex.	118	19.11N	104.30W
Cijara, Embalse de, res., Spain	158	39.25N	5.00W
Cilician Gates, p., Tur.	167	37.30N	35.30E
Cimarron, r., U.S. (sĭm-ȧ-rōn')	96	36.26N	98.27W
Cimarron, r., Co., U.S.	110	37.13N	102.30W
Cinca, r., Spain (thēŋ'kä)	159	42.09N	0.08E
Cincinnati, Oh., U.S. (sĭn-sĭ-nát'ĭ)	97	39.08N	84.30W
Cinco Balas, Cayos, is., Cuba (kä'yōs-thēŋ'kō bä'läs)	122	21.05N	79.25W
Cinderella, S. Afr.	244b	26.15S	28.16E
Cinisello Balsamo, Italy	238c	45.33N	9.13E
Cinkota, neigh., Hung.	239g	47.31N	19.14E
Cintalapa, Mex. (sēn-tä-lä'pä)	119	16.41N	93.44W
Cinto, Monte, mtn., Fr. (chēn'tō)	147	42.24N	8.54E
Circle, Ak., U.S. (sûr'k'l)	96a	65.49N	144.22W
Circleville, Oh., U.S. (sûr'k'lvĭl)	98	39.35N	83.00W
Cirebon, Indon.	196	6.50S	108.33E
Ciri Grande, r., Pan. (sē'rē-grá'n-dĕ)	116a	8.55N	80.04W
Cisco, Tx., U.S. (sĭs'kō)	112	32.23N	98.57W
Cisliano, Italy	238c	45.27N	8.59E
Cisneros, Col. (sēs-nĕ'rỏs)	130a	6.33N	75.05W
Cisterna di Latina, Italy (chēs-tĕ'r-nä-dē-lä-tē'nä)	159d	41.36N	12.53E
Cistierna, Spain (thės-tyĕr'nä)	158	42.48N	5.08W
Citronelle, Al., U.S. (cĭt-rō'nĕl)	114	31.05N	88.15W
Cittadella, Italy (chēt-tä-dĕl'lä)	160	45.39N	11.51E
Città di Castello, Italy (chēt-tä'dē käs-tĕl'lō)	160	43.27N	12.17E
City College of New York, pt. of i., N.Y., U.S.	228	40.49N	73.57W
City Island, neigh., N.Y., U.S.	228	40.51N	73.47W
City of Baltimore, Md., U.S.	229d	39.18N	76.37W
City of Commerce, Ca., U.S.	232	33.59N	118.08W
City of Industry, Ca., U.S.	232	34.01N	117.57W
City of London, neigh., Eng., U.K.	235	51.31N	0.05W
City of Westminster, neigh., Eng., U.K.	235	51.30N	0.09W
Ciudad Altamirano, Mex. (syōō-dä'd-äl-tä-mē-rä'nỏ)	118	18.24N	100.38W
Ciudad Bolívar, Ven. (syōō-dhädh' bỏ-lē'vär)	130	8.07N	63.41W
Ciudad Camargo, Mex.	116	27.42N	105.10W
Ciudad Chetumal, Mex.	116	18.30N	88.17W
Ciudad Darío, Nic. (syōō-dhädh'dä'rė-ō)	120	12.44N	86.08W
Ciudad de la Habana, prov., Cuba	122	23.20N	82.10W
Ciudad del Carmen, Mex. (syōō-dä'd-dĕl-kà'r-mĕn)	116	18.39N	91.49W
Ciudad del Maíz, Mex. (syōō-dhädh'del mä-ēz')	118	22.24N	99.37W
Ciudad Deportive, rec., Mex.	233a	19.24N	99.06W
Ciudadela, Spain (thyōō-dhä-dhä'lä)	159	40.00N	3.52E
Ciudad Fernández, Mex. (syōō-dhädh'fĕr-nän'dĕz)	118	21.56N	100.03W
Ciudad García, Mex. (syōō-dhädh'gär-sē'ä)	116	22.39N	103.02W
Ciudad General Belgrano, Arg.	233d	34.44S	58.32W
Ciudad Guayana, Ven.	130	8.30N	62.45W
Ciudad Guzmán, Mex. (syōō-dhädh'gòz-män)	116	19.40N	103.29W
Ciudad Hidalgo, Mex. (syōō-dä'd-ē-dä'l-gō)	118	19.41N	100.35W
Ciudad Juárez, Mex. (syōō-dhädh hwä'räz)	116	31.44N	106.28W
Ciudad Madero, Mex. (syōō-dä'd-mä-dĕ'rō)	119	22.16N	97.52W
Ciudad Mante, Mex. (syōō-dä'd-màn'tĕ)	116	22.34N	98.58W
Ciudad Manuel Doblado, Mex. (syōō-dä'd-män-wāl'dō-blä'dō)	118	20.43N	101.57W
Ciudad Obregón, Mex. (syōō-dhädh-ô-brē-gō'n)	116	27.40N	109.58W
Ciudad Real, Spain (thyōō-dhädh'rā-äl')	158	38.59N	3.55W
Ciudad Rodrigo, Spain (thyōō-dhädh'rỏ-drē'gō)	148	40.38N	6.34W
Ciudad Serdán, Mex. (syōō-dä'd-sĕr-dá'n)	119	18.58N	97.26W
Ciudad Universitaria, educ., Spain	238b	40.27N	3.44W
Ciudad Victoria, Mex. (syōō-dhädh'vĕk-tō'rē-ä)	116	23.43N	99.09W
Civitavecchia, Italy (chē'vē-tä-vĕk'kyä)	160	42.06N	11.49E
Cixian, China (tsē shyĕn)	190	36.22N	114.23E
Clackamas, Or., U.S. (klăc-kȧ'măs)	106c	45.25N	122.34W
Claire, l., Can. (klâr)	84	58.33N	113.16W
Clair Engle Lake, l., Ca., U.S.	104	40.51N	122.41W
Clairton, Pa., U.S. (klârtŭn)	101e	40.17N	79.53W
Clamart, Fr.	237c	48.48N	2.16E
Clanton, Al., U.S. (klăn'tŭn)	114	32.50N	86.38W
Clare, Mi., U.S. (klâr)	98	43.50N	84.45W
Clare Island, i., Ire.	150	53.46N	10.00W
Claremont, Eng., U.K.	235	51.21N	0.22W
Claremont, Ca., U.S. (klâr'mŏnt)	107a	34.06N	117.43W
Claremont, N.H., U.S. (klâr'mŏnt)	99	43.20N	72.20W
Claremont, W.V., U.S.	98	37.55N	81.00W
Claremore, Ok., U.S. (klâr'mōr)	111	36.16N	95.37W
Claremorris, Ire. (klâr-mŏr'ĭs)	150	53.46N	9.05W
Clarence Strait, strt., Austl. (klăr'ĕns)	202	12.15S	130.05E
Clarence Strait, strt., Ak., U.S.	86	55.25N	132.00W
Clarence Town, Bah.	123	23.05N	75.00W
Clarendon, Ar., U.S. (klâr'ĕn-dŭn)	111	34.42N	91.17W
Clarendon, Tx., U.S.	110	34.55N	100.52W
Clarens, S. Afr. (clâ-rĕns)	213c	28.34S	28.26E
Claresholm, Can. (klâr'ĕs-hōlm)	84	50.02N	113.35W
Clarinda, Ia., U.S. (klȧ-rĭn'dȧ)	102	40.42N	95.00W
Clarines, Ven. (klä-rē'nĕs)	131b	9.57N	65.10W
Clarion, Ia., U.S. (klăr'ĭ-ŭn)	103	42.43N	93.45W
Clarion, Pa., U.S.	99	41.10N	79.25W
Clark, N.J., U.S.	228	40.38N	74.19W
Clark, S.D., U.S. (klärk)	102	44.52N	97.45W
Clark, Point, c., Can.	90	44.05N	81.50W
Clarkdale, Az., U.S. (klärk-dāl)	109	34.45N	112.05W
Clarke City, Can.	85	50.12N	66.38W
Clarke Range, mts., Austl.	203	20.30S	148.00E
Clark Fork, r., Mt., U.S.	104	47.50N	115.35W
Clarksburg, W.V., U.S. (klärkz'bûrg)	97	39.15N	80.20W
Clarksdale, Ms., U.S. (klärks-dāl)	114	34.10N	90.31W
Clark's Harbour, Can. (klärks)	92	43.26N	65.38W
Clarks Hill Lake, res., U.S. (klärk-hĭl)	97	33.50N	82.35W
Clarkston, Ga., U.S. (klärks'tŭn)	100c	33.49N	84.15W
Clarkston, Wa., U.S.	104	46.24N	117.01W
Clarksville, Ar., U.S. (klärks-vĭl)	111	35.28N	93.26W
Clarksville, Tn., U.S.	114	36.30N	87.23W
Clarksville, Tx., U.S.	111	33.37N	95.02W
Clatskanie, Or., U.S.	106c	46.04N	123.11W
Clatskanie, r., Or., U.S. (klăt-skā'nė)	106c	46.06N	123.11W
Clatsop Spit, Or., U.S. (klăt-sŏp)	106c	46.13N	124.04W
Cláudio, Braz. (klou'-dēō)	129a	20.26S	44.44W
Claveria, Phil. (klä-vȧ-rē'ä)	193	18.38N	121.08E
Clawson, Mi., U.S. (klô's'n)	101b	42.32N	83.09W
Claxton, Ga., U.S. (kläks'tŭn)	115	32.07N	81.54W
Clay, Ky., U.S. (klā)	114	37.28N	87.50W

ŋ-sing; ŋ-baŋk; ɴ-nasalized n; nŏd; cŏmmit; ōld; ôbey; ôrder; oi-boil; fōōd; ŏŏ-as oo in foot; ou-out; s-soft; sh-dish; th-thin; pūre; ůnite; ûrn; stŭd; circŭs; ü-as in French tu; '-indeterminate vowel.

276 Clay Center – Colotepec

PLACE (Pronunciation)	PAGE	Lat. °'	Long. °'
Clay Center, Ks., U.S. (klā sĕn'tēr)	111	39.23N	97.08W
Clay City, Ky., U.S. (klā sĭ'tĭ)	98	37.50N	83.55W
Claycomo, Mo., U.S. (kla-kō'mo)	107f	39.12N	94.30W
Clay Cross, Eng., U.K. (klā krŏs)	144a	53.10N	1.25W
Claye-Souilly, Fr. (klĕ-sōō-yē')	157b	48.56N	2.43E
Claygate, Eng., U.K.	235	51.22N	0.20W
Claygate Cross, Eng., U.K.	235	51.16N	0.19E
Claymont, De., U.S. (klā-mōnt)	100f	39.48N	75.28W
Clayton, Eng., U.K.	144a	53.47N	1.49W
Clayton, Al., U.S. (klā'tŭn)	114	31.52N	85.25W
Clayton, Ca., U.S.	106b	37.56N	121.56W
Clayton, Mo., U.S.	107e	38.39N	90.20W
Clayton, N.M., U.S.	110	36.26N	103.12W
Clayton, N.C., U.S.	115	35.40N	78.27W
Clear, l., Ca., U.S.	108	39.05N	122.50W
Clear Boggy Creek, r., Ok., U.S. (klēr bŏg'ĭ krēk)	111	34.21N	96.22W
Clear Creek, r., Az., U.S.	109	34.40N	111.05W
Clear Creek, r., Tx., U.S.	113a	29.34N	95.13W
Clear Creek, r., Wy., U.S.	105	44.35N	106.20W
Clearfield, Pa., U.S. (klēr-fēld)	99	41.00N	78.25W
Clearfield, Ut., U.S.	107b	41.07N	112.01W
Clear Hills, Can.	84	57.11N	119.20W
Clearing, neigh., Il., U.S.	231a	41.47N	87.47W
Clear Lake, Ia., U.S.	103	43.09N	93.23W
Clear Lake, Wa., U.S.	106a	48.27N	122.14W
Clear Lake Reservoir, res., Ca., U.S.	104	41.53N	121.00W
Clearwater, Fl., U.S. (klēr-wô'tēr)	115a	27.43N	82.45W
Clearwater, r., Can.	87	52.00N	114.50W
Clearwater, r., Can.	87	52.00N	120.10W
Clearwater, r., Can.	88	56.10N	110.40W
Clearwater, r., Id., U.S.	104	46.27N	116.33W
Clearwater, Middle Fork, r., Id., U.S.	104	46.10N	115.48W
Clearwater, North Fork, r., Id., U.S.	104	46.34N	116.08W
Clearwater, South Fork, r., Id., U.S.	104	45.46N	115.53W
Clearwater Mountains, mts., Id., U.S.	104	45.56N	115.15W
Cleburne, Tx., U.S. (klē'bŭrn)	96	32.21N	97.23W
Cle Elum, Wa., U.S. (klē ĕl'ŭm)	104	47.12N	120.55W
Clementon, N.J., U.S. (klē'mĕn-tŭn)	100f	39.49N	75.00W
Cleobury Mortimer, Eng., U.K. (klēō-bēr'ĭ môr'tĭ-mēr)	144a	52.22N	2.29W
Clermont, Austl. (klēr'mŏnt)	203	23.02S	147.46E
Clermont, Can.	91	47.45N	70.20W
Clermont-Ferrand, Fr. (klĕr-môn'fĕr-rän')	142	45.47N	3.03E
Cleveland, Ms., U.S. (klēv'lănd)	114	33.45N	90.42W
Cleveland, Oh., U.S.	97	41.30N	81.42W
Cleveland, Ok., U.S.	111	36.18N	96.28W
Cleveland, Tn., U.S.	114	35.09N	84.52W
Cleveland, Tx., U.S.	113	30.18N	95.05W
Cleveland Heights, Oh., U.S.	101d	41.30N	81.35W
Cleveland Museum of Art, pt. of i., Oh., U.S.	229a	41.31N	81.37W
Cleveland Park, neigh., D.C., U.S.	229d	38.56N	77.04W
Cleveland Peninsula, pen., Ak., U.S.	86	55.45N	132.00W
Cleves, Oh., U.S. (klē'vĕs)	101f	39.10N	84.45W
Clew Bay, b., Ire. (klōō)	150	53.47N	9.45W
Clewiston, Fl., U.S. (klē'wis-tŭn)	115a	26.44N	80.55W
Clichy, Fr. (klē-shē)	156	48.54N	2.18E
Clichy-sous-Bois, Fr.	237c	48.55N	2.33E
Clifden, Ire. (klĭf'dĕn)	150	53.31N	10.04W
Cliffside Park, N.J., U.S.	228	40.49N	73.59W
Clifton, Az., U.S. (klĭf'tŭn)	109	33.05N	109.20W
Clifton, Ma., U.S.	227a	42.29N	70.53W
Clifton, N.J., U.S.	100a	40.52N	74.09W
Clifton, S.C., U.S.	115	35.00N	81.47W
Clifton, Tx., U.S.	113	31.45N	97.31W
Clifton Forge, Va., U.S.	99	37.50N	79.50W
Clifton Heights, Pa., U.S.	229b	39.56N	75.18W
Clinch, r., Tn., U.S. (klĭnch)	114	36.30N	83.19W
Clingmans Dome, mtn., U.S. (klĭng'măns dōm)	114	35.37N	83.26W
Clinton, Can. (klĭn-'tŭn)	84	51.05N	121.35W
Clinton, Il., U.S.	98	40.10N	88.55W
Clinton, In., U.S.	98	39.40N	87.25W
Clinton, Ia., U.S.	103	41.50N	90.13W
Clinton, Ky., U.S.	114	36.39N	88.56W
Clinton, Md., U.S.	100e	38.46N	76.54W
Clinton, Ma., U.S.	93a	42.25N	71.41W
Clinton, Mo., U.S.	111	38.23N	93.46W
Clinton, N.C., U.S.	115	34.58N	78.20W
Clinton, Ok., U.S.	110	35.31N	98.56W
Clinton, S.C., U.S.	115	34.27N	81.53W
Clinton, Tn., U.S.	114	36.05N	84.08W
Clinton, Wa., U.S.	106a	47.59N	122.22W
Clinton, r., Mi., U.S.	101b	42.36N	83.00W
Clinton-Colden, l., Can.	84	63.58N	106.34W
Clintonville, Wi., U.S. (klĭn'tŭn-vĭl)	103	44.37N	88.46W
Clio, Mi., U.S. (klē'ō)	98	43.10N	83.45W
Cloates, Point, c., Austl. (klōts)	202	22.47S	113.45E
Clocolan, S. Afr.	218d	28.56S	27.35E
Clonakilty Bay, b., Ire. (klŏn-ă-kĭltē)	150	51.30N	8.50W
Cloncurry, Austl. (klŏn-kŭr'ē)	202	20.58S	140.42E
Clonmel, Ire. (klŏn-mĕl)	150	52.21N	7.45W
Clontarf, Austl.	243a	33.48S	151.16E
Cloquet, Mn., U.S. (klō-kā')	107h	46.42N	92.28W
Closter, N.J., U.S. (klōs'tēr)	100a	40.58N	73.57W
Cloud Peak, mtn., Wy., U.S. (kloud)	96	44.23N	107.11W
Clover, S.C., U.S. (klō'vēr)	115	35.08N	81.08W
Clover Bar, Can. (klō'vēr bär)	83g	53.34N	113.20W
Cloverdale, Can.	106d	49.06N	122.44W
Cloverdale, Ca., U.S. (klō'vēr-dāl)	108	38.47N	123.03W
Cloverdene, S. Afr.	244b	26.09S	28.22E
Cloverport, Ky., U.S. (klō'vēr pōrt)	98	37.50N	86.35W
Clovis, N.M., U.S. (klō'vĭs)	96	34.24N	103.11W
Cluj-Napoca, Rom.	142	46.46N	23.34E
Clun, r., Eng., U.K. (klŭn)	144a	52.25N	2.56W
Cluny, Fr. (klü-nē')	156	46.27N	4.40E

PLACE (Pronunciation)	PAGE	Lat. °'	Long. °'
Clutha, r., N.Z. (klōō'thȧ)	203a	45.52S	169.30E
Clwyd, co., Wales, U.K.	144a	53.01N	2.59W
Clyde, Ks., U.S.	111	39.34N	97.23W
Clyde, Oh., U.S.	98	41.15N	83.00W
Clyde, r., Scot., U.K.	150	55.35N	3.50W
Clyde, Firth of, b., Scot., U.K. (fûrth ŏv klīd)	150	55.28N	5.01W
Côa, r., Port. (kô'ä)	158	40.28N	6.55W
Coacalco, Mex. (kō-ä-käl'kō)	119a	19.37N	99.06W
Coachella, Canal, can., Ca., U.S. (kō'chĕl-lȧ)	108	33.15N	115.25W
Coahuayana, Río de, r., Mex. (rē'ō-dĕ-kô-ä-wä-yä'nä)	118	19.00N	103.33W
Coahuayutla, Mex. (kō'ä-wī-yōōt'lä)	118	18.19N	101.44W
Coahuila, state, Mex. (kō-ä-wē'lä)	116	27.30N	103.00W
Coal City, Il., U.S. (kōl sĭ'tĭ)	101a	41.17N	88.17W
Coalcomán, Río de, r., Mex. (rē'ō-dĕ-kō-äl-kō-män')	118	18.45N	103.15W
Coalcomán, Sierra de, mts., Mex.	118	18.30N	102.45W
Coalcomán de Matamoros, Mex.	118	18.46N	103.10W
Coaldale, Can. (kōl'dāl)	87	49.43N	112.37W
Coalgate, Ok., U.S. (kōl'gāt)	111	34.44N	96.13W
Coal Grove, Oh., U.S. (kōl grōv)	98	38.20N	82.40W
Coal Hill Park, rec., China	240b	39.56N	116.23E
Coalinga, Ca., U.S. (kō-ă-lĭŋ'gă)	108	36.09N	120.23W
Coalville, Eng., U.K. (kōl'vĭl)	144a	52.43N	1.21W
Coamo, P.R. (kō-ä'mō)	117b	18.05N	66.21W
Coari, Braz. (kō-är'ē)	130	4.06S	63.10W
Coast Mountains, mts., N.A. (kōst)	84	54.10N	128.00W
Coast Ranges, mts., U.S.	96	41.28N	123.30W
Coatepec, Mex. (kō-ä-tä-pĕk)	118	19.23N	98.44W
Coatepec, Mex.	119	19.26N	96.56W
Coatepec, Mex.	119a	19.08N	99.25W
Coatepeque, El Sal.	120	13.56N	89.30W
Coatepeque, Guat. (kō-ä-tä-pä'kå)	120	14.40N	91.52W
Coatesville, Pa., U.S. (kōts'vĭl)	99	40.00N	75.50W
Coatetelco, Mex. (kō-ä-tå-tĕl'kō)	118	18.43N	99.17W
Coaticook, Can. (kō'tĭ-ko͝ok)	91	45.10N	71.55W
Coatlinchán, Mex. (kô-ä-tlē'n-chä'n)	119a	19.26N	98.52W
Coats, i., Can. (kōts)	85	62.23N	82.11W
Coats Land, reg., Ant.	219	74.00S	30.00W
Coatzacoalcos, Mex.	116	18.09N	94.26W
Coatzacoalcos, r., Mex.	119	17.40N	94.41W
Coba, hist., Mex. (kô'bä)	120a	20.23N	87.23W
Cobalt, Can. (kō'bôlt)	85	47.21N	79.40W
Cobán, Guat. (kō-bän')	116	15.28N	90.19W
Cobar, Austl.	203	31.28S	145.50E
Cobberas, Mount, mtn., Austl. (cŏ-bēr-ăs)	204	36.45S	148.15E
Cobequid Mountains, mts., Can.	92	45.35N	64.10W
Cobh, Ire. (kôv)	142	51.52N	8.09W
Cobham, Eng., U.K.	235	51.23N	0.24E
Cobija, Bol. (kō-bē'hä)	130	11.12S	68.49W
Cobourg, Can. (kō'bôrgh)	85	43.55N	78.05W
Cobre, r., Jam. (kō'brā)	122	18.05N	77.00W
Coburg, Austl.	201a	37.45S	144.58E
Coburg, Ger. (kō'bōōrg)	154	50.16N	10.57E
Cocentaina, Spain (kō-thån-tä-ē'nȧ)	159	38.44N	0.27W
Cochabamba, Bol.	130	17.24S	66.09W
Cochin, India (kō-chĭn')	187	9.58N	76.19E
Cochinos, Bahía, b., Cuba (bä-ē'ä-kō-chē'nōs)	122	22.05N	81.10W
Cochinos Banks, bk.	122	22.20N	76.15W
Cochiti Indian Reservation, I.R., N.M., U.S.	109	35.37N	106.20W
Cochran, Ga., U.S. (kŏk'răn)	114	32.23N	83.23W
Cochrane, Can.	83e	51.11N	114.28W
Cochrane, Can. (kŏk'răn)	85	49.01N	81.06W
Cockburn, i., Can. (kŏk-bûrn)	90	45.55N	83.25W
Cockeysville, Md., U.S. (kŏk'ĭz-vĭl)	100e	39.30N	76.40W
Cockfosters, neigh., Eng., U.K.	235	51.39N	0.09W
Cockrell Hill, Tx., U.S. (kŏk'rĕl)	107c	32.44N	96.53W
Coco, r., N.A.	117	14.55N	83.45W
Coco, Cayo, i., Cuba (kä'-yō-kô'kô)	122	22.30N	78.30W
Coco, Isla del, i., C.R. (ē's-lä-dĕl-kô-kô)	116	5.33N	87.02W
Cocoa, Fl., U.S. (kō'kō)	115a	28.21N	80.44W
Cocoa Beach, Fl., U.S.	115a	28.20N	80.35W
Cocoli, Pan. (kŏ-kô'lē)	116a	8.58N	79.36W
Coconino, Plateau, plat., Az., U.S. (kō kō nē'nō)	109	35.45N	112.28W
Cocos (Keeling) Islands, is., Oc. (kō'kōs) (kē'lĭng)	3	11.50S	90.50E
Coco Solito, Pan. (kô-kô-sō-lē'tō)	116a	9.21N	79.53W
Cocotá, neigh., Braz.	234c	22.49S	43.11W
Cocula, Mex. (kō-kōō'lä)	118	20.23N	103.47W
Cocula, r., Mex.	118	18.17N	99.45W
Cod, Cape, pen., Ma., U.S.	97	41.42N	70.15W
Codajás, Braz. (kō-dä-hăzh')	130	3.44S	62.09W
Codera, Cabo, c., Ven. (kă'bô-kō-dĕ'rä)	131b	10.35N	66.06W
Codogno, Italy (kō-dō'nyō)	160	45.08N	9.43E
Codrington, Antig. (kŏd'rĭng-tŭn)	121b	17.39N	61.49W
Cody, Wy., U.S. (kō'dĭ)	105	44.31N	109.02W
Coelho da Rocha, Braz.	132b	22.47S	43.23W
Coemba, Ang.	216	12.08S	18.05E
Coesfeld, Ger. (kûs'fĕld)	157c	51.56N	7.10E
Coeur d'Alene, Id., U.S. (kûr dȧ-lān')	96	47.43N	116.35W
Coeur d'Alene, r., Id., U.S.	104	47.26N	116.35W
Coeur d'Alene Indian Reservation, I.R., Id., U.S.	104	47.18N	116.45W
Coeur d'Alene Lake, l., Id., U.S.	104	47.32N	116.39W
Coffeyville, Ks., U.S. (kŏf'ĭ-vĭl)	97	37.01N	95.38W
Coff's Harbour, Austl.	204	30.20S	153.10E
Cofimvaba, S. Afr. (căfĭm'vä-bȧ)	213c	32.01S	27.37E
Coghinas, r., Italy (kō'gē-näs)	160	40.31N	9.00E
Cognac, Fr. (kōn-yak')	147	45.41N	0.22W
Cohasset, Ma., U.S. (kō-hăs'ĕt)	93a	42.14N	70.48W
Cohoes, N.Y., U.S. (kō-hōz')	99	42.50N	73.40W

PLACE (Pronunciation)	PAGE	Lat. °'	Long. °'
Coig, r., Arg. (kô'ĕk)	132	51.15N	71.00W
Coimbatore, India (kô-ĕm-bȧ-tôr')	183	11.03N	76.56E
Coimbra, Port. (kô-ēm'brä)	142	40.14N	8.23W
Coín, Spain (kô-ēn')	158	36.40N	4.45W
Coina, Port. (kô-ē'nȧ)	159b	38.35N	9.03W
Coina, r., Port. (kô'y-nä)	159b	38.35N	9.02W
Coipasa, Salar de, pl., Bol. (sä-lä'r-dĕ-koi-pä'-sä)	130	19.12S	69.13W
Coixtlahuaca, Mex. (kō-ēks'tlä-wä'kä)	119	17.42N	97.17W
Cojedes, dept., Ven. (kô-kĕ'dĕs)	131b	9.50N	68.21W
Cojimar, Cuba (kō-hē-mär')	123a	23.10N	82.19W
Cojutepeque, El Sal. (kô-hô-tĕ-pā'kå)	120	13.45N	88.50W
Cokato, Mn., U.S. (kō-kā'tō)	103	45.03N	94.11W
Cokeburg, Pa., U.S. (kōk bŭgh)	101e	40.06N	80.03W
Coker, Nig.	244d	6.29N	3.20E
Colāba, neigh., India	240e	18.54N	72.48E
Colac, Austl. (kŏ'lăc)	204	38.25S	143.40E
Colares, Port. (kō-lä'rĕs)	159b	38.47N	9.27W
Colatina, Braz. (kō-lä-tē'nä)	131	19.33S	40.42W
Colby, Ks., U.S. (kōl'bĭ)	110	39.23N	101.04W
Colchagua, prov., Chile (kôl-chä'gwä)	129b	34.42S	71.24W
Colchester, Eng., U.K. (kōl'chĕs-tēr)	151	51.52N	0.50E
Coldblow, neigh., Eng., U.K.	235	51.26N	0.10E
Cold Lake, l., Can. (kōld)	88	54.33N	110.05W
Coldwater, Ks., U.S. (kōld'wô-tēr)	110	37.14N	99.21W
Coldwater, Mi., U.S.	98	41.55N	85.00W
Coldwater, r., Ms., U.S.	114	34.25N	90.12W
Coldwater Creek, r., Tx., U.S.	110	36.10N	101.45W
Coleman, Tx., U.S. (kōl'măn)	112	31.50N	99.25W
Colenso, S. Afr. (kŏ-lĕnz'ō)	213c	28.48S	29.49E
Coleraine, N. Ire., U.K.	150	55.08N	6.40W
Coleraine, Mn., U.S. (kōl-rān')	103	47.16N	93.29W
Coleshill, Eng., U.K. (kōlz'hĭl)	144a	52.30N	1.42W
Colfax, Ia., U.S. (kōl'făks)	103	41.40N	93.13W
Colfax, La., U.S.	113	31.31N	92.42W
Colfax, Wa., U.S.	104	46.53N	117.21W
Colhué Huapi, l., Arg. (kôl-wā'óá'pê)	132	45.30S	68.45W
Coligny, S. Afr.	218d	26.20S	26.18E
Colima, Mex. (kōlē'mä)	116	19.13N	103.45W
Colima, state, Mex.	118	19.10N	104.00W
Colima, Nevado de, mtn., Mex. (nĕ-vä'dô-dĕ-kô-lē'mä)	116	19.30N	103.38W
Coll, i., Scot., U.K. (kŏl)	150	56.42N	6.23W
College, Ak., U.S.	95	64.43N	147.50W
College Park, Ga., U.S. (kŏl'ĕj)	100c	33.39N	84.27W
College Park, Md., U.S.	100e	38.59N	76.58W
College Point, neigh., N.Y., U.S.	228	40.47N	73.51W
Collegeville, Pa., U.S. (kŏl'ĕj-vĭl)	100f	40.11N	75.27W
Collie, Austl. (kŏl'ē)	202	33.20S	116.20E
Collier Bay, b., Austl. (kŏl-yēr)	202	15.30S	123.30E
Collier Row, neigh., Eng., U.K.	235	51.36N	0.10E
Collingdale, Pa., U.S.	229b	39.55N	75.17W
Collingswood, N.J., U.S. (kŏl'ĭngz-wŏŏd)	100f	39.54N	75.04W
Collingwood, Austl.	243b	37.48S	145.00E
Collingwood, Can.	91	44.30N	80.20W
Collins, Ms., U.S. (kŏl'ĭns)	114	31.40N	89.34W
Collinsville, Il., U.S. (kŏl'ĭnz-vĭl)	107e	38.41N	89.59W
Collinsville, Ok., U.S.	111	36.21N	95.50W
Colmar, Fr. (kôl'mär)	147	48.03N	7.25E
Colmenar de Oreja, Spain (kôl-mä-när'dāōrā'hä)	158	40.06N	3.25W
Colmenar Viejo, Spain (kôl-mä-när'vyā'hō)	158	40.40N	3.46W
Colnbrook, Eng., U.K.	235	51.29N	0.31W
Colney Heath, Eng., U.K.	235	51.44N	0.15W
Colney Street, Eng., U.K.	235	51.42N	0.20W
Cologne, Ger.	142	50.56N	6.57E
Cologno Monzese, Italy	238c	45.32N	9.17E
Colombes, Fr.	237c	48.55N	2.15E
Colombia, Col. (kō-lôm'bē-ä)	130a	3.23N	74.48W
Colombia, nation, S.A.	130	3.30N	72.30W
Colombo, Sri L. (kô-lôm'bō)	183b	6.58N	79.52W
Colón, Arg. (kō-lōn')	129c	33.55S	61.08W
Colón, Cuba (kō-lō'n)	122	22.45N	80.55W
Colón, Mex. (kō-lōn')	118	20.46N	100.02W
Colón, Pan. (kō-lô'n)	117	9.22N	79.54W
Colón, Archipiélago de, is., Ec.	130	0.10S	87.45W
Colón, Montañas de, mts., Hond. (môn-tä'n-yäs-dĕ-kō-lô'n)	121	14.58N	84.39W
Colonail Park, Md., U.S.	229c	39.19N	76.45W
Colonia, N.J., U.S.	228	40.35N	74.18W
Colonia, Ur. (kō-lō'nē-ä)	132	34.27S	57.50W
Colonia, dept., Ur.	129c	34.08S	57.50W
Colonial Manor, N.J., U.S.	229b	39.51N	75.09W
Colonia Suiza, Ur. (kô-lō'nēä-sōē'zä)	129c	34.17S	57.15W
Colonna, Capo, c., Italy	161	39.02N	17.15E
Colonsay, i., Scot., U.K. (kŏl-ŏn-sā')	151	56.08N	6.08E
Coloradas, Lomas, Arg. (lō'mäs-kō-lō-rä'däs)	132	43.30S	68.00W
Colorado, state, U.S.	96	39.30N	106.55W
Colorado, r., N.A.	96	36.00N	113.30W
Colorado, r., Tx., U.S.	96	30.08N	97.33W
Colorado, Río, r., Arg.	132	38.30S	66.00W
Colorado City, Tx., U.S. (kŏl-ô-rä'dō sĭ'tĭ)	112	32.24N	100.50W
Colorado National Monument, rec., Co., U.S.	109	39.00N	108.40W
Colorado Plateau, plat., U.S.	96	36.20N	109.25W
Colorado River Aqueduct, aq., Ca., U.S.	108	33.38N	115.43W
Colorado River Indian Reservation, I.R., Az., U.S.	109	34.03N	114.02W
Colorados, Archipiélago de los, is., Cuba	122	22.25N	84.25W
Colorado Springs, Co., U.S. (kŏl-ô-rä'dō)	96	38.49N	104.48W
Colosseo, hist., Italy	239c	41.54N	12.29E
Colotepec, r., Mex. (kô-lô'tĕ-pĕk)	119	15.56N	96.57W

ăt; finăl; rāte; senâte; ärm; åsk; sofȧ; fâre; ch-choose; dh-as th in other; bē; ėvent; bĕt; recĕnt; cratēr; g-gō; gh-guttural g; bĭt; ĭ-short neutral; rīde; ĸ-guttural k as ch in German ich;

PRONOUNCING INDEX Colotlán–Coronel Oviedo 277

PLACE (Pronunciation)	PAGE	Lat. °′	Long. °′
Colotlán, Mex. (kô-lô-tlän′)	118	22.06N	103.14W
Colotlán, r., Mex.	118	22.09N	103.17W
Colquechaca, Bol. (kôl-kä-chä′kä)	130	18.47S	66.02W
Colstrip, Mt., U.S. (kōl′strip)	105	45.54N	106.38W
Colton, Ca., U.S. (kōl′tŭn)	107a	34.04N	117.20W
Columbia, Il., U.S. (kô-lŭm′bĭ-ȧ)	107e	38.26N	90.12W
Columbia, Ky., U.S.	114	37.06N	85.15W
Columbia, Md., U.S.	100e	39.15N	76.51W
Columbia, Ms., U.S.	114	31.15N	89.49W
Columbia, Mo., U.S.	97	38.55N	92.19W
Columbia, Pa., U.S.	99	40.00N	76.25W
Columbia, S.C., U.S.	97	34.00N	81.00W
Columbia, Tn., U.S.	114	35.36N	87.02W
Columbia, r., N.A.	84	46.00N	120.00W
Columbia, Mount, mtn., Can.	87	52.09N	117.25W
Columbia City, In., U.S.	98	41.10N	85.30W
Columbia City, Or., U.S.	106c	45.53N	112.49W
Columbia Heights, Mn., U.S.	107g	45.03N	93.15W
Columbia Icefield, ice., Can.	87	52.08N	117.26W
Columbia Mountains, mts., N.A.	87	51.30N	118.30W
Columbiana, Al., U.S. (kô-ŭm-bĭ-ă′nȧ)	114	33.10N	86.35W
Columbia University, pt. of i., N.Y., U.S.	228	40.48N	73.58W
Columbretes, is., Spain (kô-lōōm-brĕ′tĕs)	159	39.54N	0.54E
Columbus, Ga., U.S. (kô-lŭm′bŭs)	97	32.29N	84.56W
Columbus, In., U.S.	98	39.15N	85.55W
Columbus, Ks., U.S.	111	37.10N	94.50W
Columbus, Ms., U.S.	114	33.30N	88.25W
Columbus, Mt., U.S.	105	45.39N	109.15W
Columbus, Ne., U.S.	102	41.25N	97.25W
Columbus, N.M., U.S.	109	31.50N	107.40W
Columbus, Oh., U.S.	97	40.00N	83.00W
Columbus, Tx., U.S.	113	29.44N	96.34W
Columbus, Wi., U.S.	103	43.20N	89.01W
Columbus Bank, bk. (kô-lŭm′bŭs)	123	22.05N	75.30W
Columbus Grove, Oh., U.S.	98	40.55N	84.05W
Columbus Point, c., Bah.	123	24.10N	75.15W
Colusa, Ca., U.S. (kô-lū′sȧ)	108	39.12N	122.01W
Colville, Wa., U.S. (kōl′vĭl)	104	48.33N	117.53W
Colville, r., Ak., U.S.	95	69.00N	156.25W
Colville Indian Reservation, I.R., Wa., U.S.	104	48.15N	119.00W
Colville R, Wa., U.S.	104	48.25N	117.58W
Colvos Passage, strt., Wa., U.S. (kōl′vōs)	106a	47.24N	122.32W
Colwood, Can. (kŏl′wŏod)	106a	48.26N	123.30W
Colwyn, Pa., U.S.	229b	39.55N	75.15W
Comacchio, Italy (kô-mäk′kyô)	160	44.42N	12.12E
Comala, Mex. (kō-mä-lä′)	118	19.22N	103.47W
Comalapa, Guat. (kō-mä-lä′-pä)	120	14.43N	90.56W
Comalcalco, Mex. (kō-mäl-käl′kō)	119	18.16N	93.13W
Comanche, Ok., U.S. (kô-măn′chê)	111	34.20N	97.58W
Comanche, Tx., U.S.	112	31.54N	98.37W
Comanche Creek, r., Tx., U.S.	112	31.02N	102.47W
Comayagua, Hond. (kō-mä-yä′gwä)	116	14.24N	87.36W
Combahee, r., S.C., U.S. (kŏm-bȧ-hē′)	115	32.42N	80.40W
Comer, Ga., U.S. (kŭm′ẽr)	114	34.02N	83.07W
Comete, Cape, c., T./C. Is. (kô-mä′tȧ)	123	21.45N	71.25W
Comilla, Bngl. (kô-mĭl′ä)	183	23.33N	91.17E
Comino, Cape, c., Italy (kô-mē′nō)	160	40.30N	9.48E
Comitán, Mex. (kô-mē-tän′)	116	16.16N	92.09W
Commencement Bay, b., Wa., U.S. (kŏ-mĕns′mĕnt bā)	106a	47.17N	122.21W
Commentry, Fr. (kô-mäN-trē′)	156	46.16N	2.44E
Commerce, Ga., U.S. (kŏm′ẽrs)	114	34.10N	83.27W
Commerce, Ok., U.S.	111	36.57N	94.54W
Commerce, Tx., U.S.	111	33.15N	95.52W
Como, Austl.	243a	34.00S	151.04E
Como, Italy (kō′mō)	148	45.48N	9.03E
Como, Lago di, l., Italy (lä′gō-dē-kō′mō)	148	46.00N	9.30E
Comodoro Rivadavia, Arg.	132	45.47S	67.31W
Como-Est, Can.	83a	45.27N	74.08W
Comonfort, Mex. (kô-mōn-fô′rt)	118	20.43N	100.47W
Comorin, Cape, c., India (kō′mô-rĭn)	183b	8.05N	78.05E
Comoros, nation, Afr.	213	12.30S	42.45E
Comox, Can. (kō′mŏks)	86	49.40N	124.55W
Companario, Cerro, mtn., S.A. (sĕ′r-rô-kôm-pä-nä′ryô)	129b	35.54S	70.23W
Compans, Fr.	237c	49.00N	2.40E
Compiègne, Fr. (kôN-pyĕn′y′)	147	49.25N	2.49E
Comporta, Port. (kôm-pôr′tȧ)	159b	38.24N	8.48W
Compostela, Mex. (kōm-pô-stä′lä)	118	21.14N	104.54W
Compton, Ca., U.S. (kŏmpt′tŭn)	107a	33.54N	118.14W
Comrat, Mol. (kôm-rät′)	167	46.17N	28.38E
Conakry, Gui. (kô-nȧ-krē′)	210	9.31N	13.43W
Conanicut, i., R.I., U.S. (kŏn′ȧ-nĭ-kŭt)	100b	41.34N	71.20W
Conasauga, r., Ga., U.S. (kô-nȧ)	114	34.40N	84.51W
Concarneau, Fr. (kôN-kär-nō′)	156	47.54N	3.52W
Concepción, Bol. (kôn-sĕp′syōn′)	131	15.47S	61.08W
Concepción, Chile	132	36.51S	72.59W
Concepción, Pan.	121	8.31N	82.38W
Concepción, Para.	132	23.29S	57.18W
Concepcion, Phil.	197a	15.19N	120.40E
Concepción, vol., Nic.	120	11.36N	85.43W
Concepción, r., Mex.	116	30.25N	112.20W
Concepción del Mar, Guat. (kôn-sĕp-syōn′dĕl mär′)	120	14.07N	91.23W
Concepción del Oro, Mex. (kôn-sĕp-syōn′ dĕl ō′rō)	116	24.39N	101.24W
Concepción del Uruguay, Arg. (kôn-sĕp-syô′n-dĕl-ōō-rōō-gwī′)	132	32.31S	58.10W
Conception, i., Bah.	123	23.50N	75.05W
Conception, Point, c., Ca., U.S.	96	34.27N	120.28W
Conception Bay, b., Can. (kŏn-sĕp′shŭn)	93	47.50N	52.50W
Conchalí, Chile	234b	33.24S	70.39W
Concho, r., Tx., U.S. (kŏn′chō)	112	31.34N	100.00W
Conchos, r., Mex. (kōn′chōs)	112	25.03N	99.00W
Conchos, r., Mex.	116	29.30N	105.00W
Concord, Austl.	243a	33.52S	151.06E
Concord, Can.	227c	43.48N	79.29W
Concord, Ca., U.S. (kŏŋ′kŏrd)	106b	37.58N	122.02W
Concord, Ma., U.S.	93a	42.28N	71.21W
Concord, N.H., U.S.	97	43.10N	71.30W
Concord, N.C., U.S.	115	35.23N	80.11W
Concordia, Arg. (kŏn-kôr′dĭ-ȧ)	132	31.18S	57.59W
Concordia, Col.	130a	6.04N	75.54W
Concordia, Mex. (kôn-kô′r-dyä)	118	23.17N	106.06W
Concordia, Ks., U.S.	111	39.32N	97.39W
Concord West, Austl.	243a	33.51S	151.05E
Concrete, Wa., U.S. (kŏn-′krēt)	104	48.33N	121.44W
Conde, Fr.	156	48.50N	0.36W
Conde, S.D., U.S. (kŏn-dē′)	102	45.10N	98.06W
Condega, Nic. (kŏn-dĕ′gä)	120	13.20N	86.27W
Condeúba, Braz. (kōn-dā-ōō′bä)	131	14.47S	41.44W
Condom, Fr.	156	43.58N	0.22E
Condon, Or., U.S. (kŏn′dŭn)	104	45.14N	120.10W
Conecun, r., Al., U.S. (kô-nē′kŭ)	114	31.05N	86.52W
Conegliano, Italy (kō-nāl-yä′nō)	160	45.59N	12.17E
Conejos, r., Co., U.S. (kô-nā′hōs)	109	37.07N	106.19W
Conemaugh, Pa., U.S. (kŏn′ē-mô)	99	40.25N	78.50W
Coney Island, neigh., N.Y., U.S.	228	40.34N	74.00W
Coney Island, i., N.Y., U.S. (kō′nĭ)	100a	40.34N	73.27W
Conflans-Sainte-Honorine, Fr.	237c	48.59N	2.06E
Confolens, Fr. (kôN-fä-läN′)	156	46.01N	0.41E
Congaree, r., S.C., U.S. (kŏŋ-gȧ-rē′)	115	33.53N	80.55W
Conghua, China (tsôŋ-hwä)	193	23.30N	113.40E
Congleton, Eng., U.K. (kŏŋ′g′l-tŭn)	144a	53.10N	2.13W
Congo, nation, Afr. (kŏŋ′gō)	212	3.00S	13.48E
Congo (Zaire), r., Afr. (kŏŋ′gō)	209	2.00S	17.00E
Congo, Serra do, mts., Ang.	216	6.25S	13.30E
Congo, The *see* Zaire, nation, Afr.	212	1.00S	22.15E
Congo Basin, basin, Zaire	209	2.47N	20.58E
Congress Heights, neigh., D.C., U.S.	229d	38.51N	77.00W
Conisbrough, Eng., U.K. (kŏn′ĭs-bŭr-ô)	144a	53.29N	1.13W
Coniston, Can.	91	46.29N	80.51W
Conklin, Can. (kŏŋk′lĭn)	87	55.38N	111.05W
Conley, Ga., U.S. (kŏn′lĭ)	100c	33.38N	84.19W
Conn, Lough, l., Ire. (lŏk kŏn)	150	53.56N	9.25W
Connacht, hist. reg., Ire. (cŏn′ât)	150	53.50N	8.45W
Connaughton, Pa., U.S.	229b	40.05N	75.19W
Conneaut, Oh., U.S. (kŏn-ē-ôt′)	98	41.55N	80.35W
Connecticut, state, U.S. (kŏ-nĕt′ĭ-kŭt)	97	41.40N	73.10W
Connecticut, r., U.S.	97	43.55N	72.15W
Connellsville, Pa., U.S. (kŏn′nĕlz-vĭl)	99	40.00N	79.40W
Connemara, mts., Ire. (kŏn-nê-mȧ′rȧ)	150	53.30N	9.54W
Connersville, In., U.S. (kŏn′ẽrz-vĭl)	98	39.35N	85.10W
Connors Range, mts., Austl. (kŏn′nŏrs)	203	22.15S	149.00E
Conrad, Mt., U.S. (kŏn′răd)	105	48.11N	111.56W
Conrich, Can. (kŏn′rĭch)	83e	51.06N	113.51W
Conroe, Tx., U.S. (kŏn′rō)	113	30.18N	95.23W
Conselheiro Lafaiete, Braz.	131	20.40S	43.46W
Conshohocken, Pa., U.S. (kŏn-shô-hŏk′ĕn)	100f	40.04N	75.18W
Consolação, neigh., Braz.	234d	23.33S	46.39W
Consolación del Sur, Cuba (kŏn-sô-lä-syōn′)	122	22.30N	83.55W
Consolidated Main Reef Mines, quarry, S. Afr.	244b	26.11S	27.56E
Con Son, is., Viet.	196	8.30N	106.28E
Constance, Mount, mtn., Wa., U.S. (kŏn′stăns)	106a	47.46N	123.08W
Constanţa, Rom. (kōn-stan′tsȧ)	142	44.12N	28.36E
Constantina, Spain (kŏn-stän-tē′nä)	158	37.52N	5.39W
Constantine, Alg. (kôN-stäN-tēn′)	210	36.28N	6.38E
Constantine, Mi., U.S. (kŏn′stăn-tēn)	98	41.50N	85.40W
Constitución, Chile (kōn′stĭ-tōō-syōn′)	132	35.24S	72.25W
Constitución, neigh., Arg.	233d	34.37S	58.23W
Constitution, Ga., U.S. (kŏn-stĭ-tū′shŭn)	100c	33.41N	84.20W
Contagem, Braz. (kōn-tá′zhĕm)	129a	19.54S	44.05W
Contepec, Mex. (kōn-tĕ-pĕk′)	118	20.04N	100.07W
Contreras, Mex. (kôn-trĕ′räs)	119a	19.18N	99.14W
Contwoyto, l., Can.	84	65.42N	110.50W
Converse, Tx., U.S. (kŏn′vĕrs)	107d	29.31N	98.17W
Conway, Ar., U.S. (kŏn′wā)	111	35.06N	92.27W
Conway, N.H., U.S.	99	44.00N	71.10W
Conway, S.C., U.S.	115	33.49N	79.01W
Conway, Wa., U.S.	106a	48.20N	122.20W
Conyers, Ga., U.S. (kŏn′yŏrz)	114	33.41N	84.01W
Cooch Behār, India (kōōch bē-hār′)	183	26.25N	89.34E
Coogee, Austl.	243a	33.55S	151.16E
Cook, Cape, c., Can. (kŏŏk)	86	50.08N	127.55W
Cook, Mount, mtn., N.Z.	203a	43.27S	170.13E
Cook, Point, c., Austl.	243b	37.55S	144.48E
Cookeville, Tn., U.S. (kŏŏk′vĭl)	114	36.07N	85.30W
Cooking Lake, Can. (kōōk′ĭng)	83g	53.25N	113.08W
Cooking Lake, l., Can.	83g	53.25N	113.02W
Cook Inlet, b., Ak., U.S.	95	60.50N	151.38W
Cook Islands, dep., Oc.	2	20.00S	158.00W
Cooksmill Green, Eng., U.K.	235	51.44N	0.22E
Cook Strait, strt., N.Z.	203a	40.37S	174.15E
Cooktown, Austl. (kŏŏk′toun)	203	15.40S	145.20E
Cooleemee, N.C., U.S. (kōō-lē′mē)	115	35.50N	80.32W
Coolgardie, Austl. (kōōl-gär′dē)	202	31.00S	121.25E
Cooma, Austl. (kōō′mȧ)	203	36.22S	149.10E
Coonamble, Austl. (kōō-năm′b′l)	203	31.00S	148.30E
Coonoor, India	187	10.22N	76.15E
Coon Rapids, Mn., U.S. (kōōn)	107g	45.09N	93.17W
Cooper, Tx., U.S. (kōōp′ẽr)	111	33.23N	95.40W
Cooper Center, Ak., U.S.	95	61.54N	15.30W
Coopersale Common, Eng., U.K.	235	51.42N	0.08E
Coopers Creek, r., Austl. (kōō′pẽrz)	203	27.32N	141.19E
Cooperstown, N.Y., U.S. (kōōp′ẽrs-toun)	99	42.45N	74.55W
Cooperstown, N.D., U.S.	102	47.26N	98.07W
Coosa, Al., U.S. (kōō′sȧ)	114	32.43N	86.25W
Coosa, r., U.S.	97	34.00N	86.00W
Coosawattee, r., Ga., U.S.	114	34.37N	84.45W
Coos Bay, Or., U.S. (kōōs)	104	43.21N	124.12W
Coos Bay, b., Or., U.S.	104	43.19N	124.40W
Cootamundra, Austl. (kŏŏtȧ-mŭnd′rȧ)	204	34.25S	148.00E
Copacabana, Braz. (kō′pä-kȧ-bȧ′nä)	132b	22.57S	43.11W
Copalita, r., Mex. (kô-pä-lē′tä)	119	15.55N	96.06W
Copán, hist., Hond. (kō-pän′)	120	14.50N	89.10W
Copano Bay, b., Tx., U.S. (kō-pän′ō)	113	28.08N	97.25W
Copenhagen (København), Den.	142	55.43N	12.27E
Copiapó, Chile (kō-pyä-pō′)	132	27.16S	70.28W
Copley, Oh., U.S. (kŏp′lê)	101d	41.06N	81.38W
Copparo, Italy (kôp-pä′rō)	160	44.53N	11.50E
Coppell, Tx., U.S. (kŏp′pĕl)	107c	32.57N	97.00W
Copper, r., Ak., U.S. (kŏp′ẽr)	95	62.38N	145.00W
Copper Cliff, Can.	90	46.28N	81.04W
Copper Harbor, Mi., U.S.	103	47.27N	87.53W
Copperhill, Tn., U.S. (kŏp′ẽr hĭl)	114	35.00N	84.22W
Coppermine, Can. (kŏp′ẽr-mīn)	84	67.46N	115.19W
Coppermine, r., Can.	84	66.48N	114.59W
Copper Mountain, mtn., Ak., U.S.	86	55.14N	132.36W
Copperton, Ut., U.S. (kŏp′ẽr-tŭn)	107b	40.34N	112.06W
Coquilee, Or., U.S. (kô-kēl′)	104	43.11N	124.11W
Coquilhatville *see* Mbandaka, Zaire	212	0.04N	18.16E
Coquimbo, Chile (kô-kēm′bō)	132	29.58S	71.31W
Coquimbo, prov., Chile	129b	31.50S	71.05W
Coquitlam Lake, l., Can. (kō-kwĭt-lȧm)	106d	49.23N	122.44W
Corabia, Rom. (kô-rä′bĭ-ȧ)	149	43.45N	24.29E
Coracora, Peru (kō′rä-kō′rä)	130	15.12S	73.42W
Coral Gables, Fl., U.S.	115a	25.43N	80.14W
Coral Rapids, Can. (kŏr′ăl)	85	50.18N	81.49W
Coral Sea, sea, Oc. (kŏr′ăl)	203	13.30S	150.00E
Coralville Reservoir, res., Ia., U.S.	103	41.45N	91.50W
Corangamite, Lake, l., Austl. (cŏr-ăŋ′gȧ-mĭt)	204	38.05S	142.55E
Coraopolis, Pa., U.S. (kō-rä-ŏp′ô-lĭs)	101e	40.30N	80.09W
Corato, Italy (kô′rä-tô)	160	41.08N	16.28E
Corbeil-Essonnes, Fr. (kôr-bă′yĕ-sŏn′)	156	48.31N	2.29E
Corbett, Or., U.S. (kôr′bĕt)	106c	45.31N	122.17W
Corbie, Fr. (kôr-bē′)	156	49.55N	2.27E
Corbin, Ky., U.S. (kôr′bĭn)	114	36.55N	84.06W
Corby, Eng., U.K. (kôr′bĭ)	144a	52.29N	0.38W
Corcovado, mtn., Braz. (kôr-kô-vä′dô)	132b	22.57S	43.13W
Corcovado, Golfo, b., Chile (kôr-kô-vä′dhō)	132	43.40S	75.00W
Cordeiro, Braz. (kôr-dā′rō)	129a	22.03S	42.22W
Cordele, Ga., U.S. (kôr-dēl′)	114	31.55N	83.50W
Cordell, Ok., U.S. (kôr-dĕl′)	110	35.19N	98.58W
Córdoba, Arg. (kôr′dô-vä)	132	30.20S	64.03W
Córdoba, Mex. (kô′r-dô-bä)	116	18.53N	96.54W
Córdoba, Spain (kô′r-dô-bä)	158	37.55N	4.45W
Córdoba, prov., Arg. (kôr′dô-vä)	132	32.00S	64.00W
Córdoba, Sierra de, mts., Arg.	132	31.15S	64.30W
Cordova, Al., U.S. (kôr′dô-ȧ)	114	33.45N	86.22W
Cordova, Ak., U.S. (kôr′dô-vä)	96a	60.34N	145.38W
Cordova Bay, b., Ak., U.S.	86	54.55N	132.35W
Corfu *see* Kérkira, i., Grc.	142	39.33N	19.36E
Corigliano, Italy (kō-rē-lyä′nō)	160	39.35N	16.30E
Corinth *see* Kórinthos, Grc.	142	37.56N	22.54E
Corinth, Ms., U.S. (kŏr′ĭnth)	114	34.55N	88.30W
Corinto, Braz. (kô-rē′n-tō)	131	18.20S	44.16W
Corinto, Col.	130a	3.09N	76.12W
Corinto, Nic. (kŏr-ĭn′to)	120	12.30N	87.12W
Corio, Austl.	201a	38.05S	144.22E
Corio Bay, b., Austl.	201a	38.07S	144.25E
Corisco, Isla de, i., Eq. Gui.	216	0.50N	8.40E
Cork, Ire. (kôrk)	142	51.54N	8.25W
Cork Harbour, b., Ire.	150	51.44N	8.15W
Corleone, Italy (kôr-lâ-ō′nā)	160	37.48N	13.18E
Cormano, Italy	238c	45.33N	9.10E
Cormeilles-en-Parisis, Fr.	237c	48.59N	2.12E
Cormorant Lake, l., Can.	89	54.13N	100.47W
Cornelia, Ga., U.S. (kôr-nē′lyȧ)	114	34.31N	83.30W
Cornelis, r., S. Afr. (kôr-nē′lĭs)	218d	27.48S	29.15E
Cornell, Ca., U.S. (kôr-nĕl′)	107a	34.06N	118.46W
Cornell, Wi., U.S.	103	45.10N	91.10W
Cornellá, Spain	238e	41.21N	2.05E
Corner Brook, Can. (kôr′nẽr)	85	48.57N	57.57W
Corner Inlet, b., Austl.	204	38.55S	146.45E
Corning, Ar., U.S. (kôr′nĭng)	111	36.26N	90.35W
Corning, Ia., U.S.	103	40.58N	94.40W
Corning, N.Y., U.S.	99	42.10N	77.05W
Corno, Monte, mtn., Italy (kôr′nō)	148	42.28N	13.37E
Cornwall, Bah.	122	25.55N	77.15W
Cornwall, Can. (kôrn′wôl)	91	45.05N	74.35W
Coro, Ven. (kō′rō)	130	11.22N	69.43W
Corocoro, Bol. (kō-rō-kō′rō)	130	17.15S	68.21W
Coromandel Coast, cst., India (kŏr-ô-man′dĕl)	183	13.30N	80.30E
Coromandel Peninsula, pen., N.Z.	205	36.50S	176.00E
Corona, Al., U.S. (kô-rō′nȧ)	114	33.42N	87.28W
Corona, Ca., U.S.	107a	33.52N	117.34W
Coronada, Bahía de, b., C.R. (bä-ē′ä-dĕ-kô-rô-nä′dō)	121	8.47N	84.04W
Corona del Mar, Ca., U.S. (kô-rō′nȧ dĕl mär)	107a	33.36N	117.53W
Coronado, Ca., U.S. (kŏr-ô-nä′dō)	108a	32.42N	117.12W
Coronation Gulf, b., Can. (kŏr-ô-nā′shŭn)	84	68.07N	112.50W
Coronel, Chile (kō-rō-nĕl′)	132	37.00S	73.10W
Coronel Brandsen, Arg. (kŏ-rō-nĕl-brä′nd-sĕn)	129c	35.09S	58.15W
Coronel Dorrego, Arg. (kŏ-rō-nĕl-dôr-rē′gô)	132	38.43S	61.16W
Coronel Oviedo, Para. (kŏ-rō-nĕl-ô-vē′dô)	132	25.28S	56.22W

ng-sing; ŋ-baŋk; N-nasalized n; nŏd; cŏmmit; ōld; ôbey; ôrder; oi-boil; fōōd; ŏŏ-as oo in foot; ou-out; s-soft; sh-dish; th-thin; pūre; ůnite; ûrn; stŭd; circŭs; ü-as in French tu; ′-indeterminate vowel.

PLACE (Pronunciation)	PAGE	Lat. °′	Long. °′
Coronel Pringles, Arg. (kō-rō-nĕl-prēn′glĕs)	132	37.54S	61.22W
Coronel Suárez, Arg. (kō-rō-nĕl-swä′rās)	132	37.27S	61.49W
Corowa, Austl. (cŏr-ŏwă)	204	36.02S	146.23E
Corozal, Belize (cŏr-ŏth-äl′)	120a	18.25N	88.23W
Corpus Christi, Tx., U.S. (kôr′pŭs krĭstē)	96	27.48N	97.24W
Corpus Christi Bay, b., Tx., U.S.	113	27.47N	97.14W
Corpus Christi Lake, l., Tx., U.S.	112	28.08N	98.20W
Corral, Chile (kō-räl′)	132	39.57S	73.15W
Corral de Almaguer, Spain (kō-räl′dā äl-mä-gâr′)	158	39.45N	3.10W
Corralillo, Cuba (kō-rä-lē-yō)	122	23.00N	80.40W
Corregidor Island, i., Phil. (kō-rā-hē-dōr′)	197a	14.21N	120.25E
Correntina, Braz. (kō-rĕn-tē-nă)	131	13.18S	44.33W
Corrib, Lough, l., Ire. (lŏk kŏr′ĭb)	150	53.25N	9.19W
Corrientes, Arg. (kō-ryĕn′tās)	132	27.25S	58.39W
Corrientes, prov., Arg.	132	28.45S	58.00W
Corrientes, Cabo, c., Col. (ká′bō-kō-ryĕn′tās)	130	5.34N	77.35W
Corrientes, Cabo, c., Cuba (ká′bō-kôr-rē-ĕn′tĕs)	122	21.50N	84.25W
Corrientes, Cabo, c., Mex.	116	20.25N	105.41W
Corringham, Eng., U.K.	235	51.31N	0.28E
Corroios, Port.	238d	38.38N	9.09W
Corry, Pa., U.S. (kŏr′ĭ)	99	41.55N	79.40W
Corse, Cap, c., Fr. (kôrs)	147	42.59N	9.19E
Corsica, i., Fr. (kŏ′r-sē-kă)	142	42.10N	8.55E
Corsicana, Tx., U.S. (kôr-sĭ-kăn′ă)	96	32.06N	96.28W
Corsico, Italy	238c	45.26N	9.07E
Cortazar, Mex. (kôr-tä-zär)	118	20.30N	100.57W
Corte, Fr. (kôr′tā)	160	42.18N	9.10E
Cortegana, Spain (kôr-tâ-gä′nä)	158	37.54N	6.48W
Corte Madera, Ca., U.S.	231b	37.55N	122.31W
Cortes, bldg., Spain	238b	40.25N	3.41W
Cortés, Ensendada de, b., Cuba (ĕn-sĕ-nä-dä-dĕ-kôr-tās′)	122	22.05N	83.45W
Cortez, Co., U.S.	109	37.21N	108.35W
Cortland, N.Y., U.S. (kôrt′lănd)	99	42.35N	76.10W
Cortona, Italy (kôr-tō′nä)	160	43.16N	12.00E
Corubal, r., Gui.-B.	214	11.43N	14.40W
Coruche, Port. (kō-rōō′she)	158	38.58N	8.34W
Çoruh, r., Asia (chō-rōōk′)	167	40.30N	41.10E
Çorum, Tur. (chō-rōōm′)	182	40.34N	34.45E
Corunna, Mi., U.S. (kō-rŭn′ă)	98	43.00N	84.05W
Coruripe, Braz. (kō-rō-rē′pĭ)	131	10.09S	36.13W
Corvallis, Or., U.S. (kŏr-văl′ĭs)	96	44.34N	123.17W
Corve, r., Eng., U.K. (kôr′vē)	144a	52.28N	2.43W
Corviale, neigh., Italy	239c	41.52N	12.25E
Corydon, In., U.S. (kŏr′ĭ-dŭn)	98	38.10N	86.05W
Corydon, Ia., U.S.	103	40.45N	93.20W
Corydon, Ky., U.S.	98	37.45N	87.40W
Cosamaloápan, Mex. (kō-sä-mä-lwä′pän)	119	18.21N	95.48W
Coscomatepec, Mex. (kôs′kōmä-tē-pĕk′)	119	19.04N	97.03W
Cosenza, Italy (kō-zĕnt′sä)	149	39.18N	16.15E
Cosfanero, Canal de, strt., Arg.	233d	34.34S	58.22W
Coshocton, Oh., U.S. (kō-shŏk′tŭn)	98	40.15N	81.55W
Cosigüina, vol., Nic.	120	12.59N	87.35W
Cosmoledo Group, is., Sey. (kŏs-mō-lā′dō)	213	9.42S	47.45E
Cosmopolis, Wa., U.S. (kŏz-mŏp′ō-lĭs)	104	46.58N	123.47W
Cosne-sur-Loire, Fr. (kōn-sür-lwär′)	156	47.25N	2.57E
Cosoleacaque, Mex. (kō sō lä-ä-kä′kē)	119	18.01N	94.38W
Costa de Caparica, Port.	159b	38.40N	9.12W
Costa Mesa, Ca., U.S. (kŏs′tă mā′să)	107a	33.39N	118.54W
Costa Rica, nation, N.A. (kŏs′tă rē′kă)	117	10.30N	84.30W
Cosumnes, r., Ca., U.S. (kō-sŭm′nĕz)	108	38.21N	121.17W
Cotabambas, Peru (kō-tä-bám′bäs)	130	13.49S	72.17W
Cotabato, Phil. (kō-tä-bä′tō)	197	7.06N	124.13E
Cotaxtla, Mex. (kō-täs′tlä)	119	18.49N	96.22W
Cotaxtla, r., Mex.	119	18.54N	96.21W
Coteau-du-Lac, Can. (cō-tō′dü-läk)	83a	45.17N	74.11W
Coteau-Landing, Can.	83a	45.15N	74.13W
Coteaux, Haiti	123	18.15N	74.05W
Cote d'Ivoire (Ivory Coast), nation, Afr.	210	7.43N	6.30W
Côte d'Or, reg., Fr.	156	47.02N	4.35E
Côte-Saint-Luc, Can.	227b	45.28N	73.40W
Côte Visitation, neigh., Can.	227b	45.33N	73.36W
Cotija de la Paz, Mex. (kō-tē′-ĸä-dĕ-lä-pá′z)	118	19.46N	102.43W
Cotonou, Benin (kō-tō-nōō′)	210	6.21N	2.26E
Cotopaxi, mtn., Ec. (kō-tō-păk′sē)	130	0.40S	78.26W
Cotorro, Cuba (kō-tôr-rō)	123a	23.03N	82.17W
Cotswold Hills, hills, Eng., U.K. (kŭtz′wōld)	150	51.35N	2.16W
Cottage City, Md., U.S.	229d	38.56N	76.57W
Cottage Grove, Mn., U.S. (kŏt′áj grōv)	107g	44.50N	92.52W
Cottage Grove, Or., U.S.	104	43.48N	123.04W
Cottbus, Ger. (kŏtt′bōōs)	147	51.47N	14.20E
Cottonwood, r., Mn., U.S. (kŏt′ŭn-wŏd)	102	44.25N	95.35W
Cotulla, Tx., U.S. (kō-tŭl′lă)	112	28.26N	99.14W
Coubert, Fr. (kōō-bâr′)	157b	48.40N	2.43E
Coudersport, Pa., U.S. (koŭ′dērz-port)	99	41.45N	78.00W
Coudres, Île aux, i., Can.	92	47.17N	70.12W
Coulommiers, Fr. (kōō-lō-myā′)	157b	48.49N	3.05E
Coulsdon, neigh., Eng., U.K.	235	51.19N	0.08W
Coulto, Serra do, mts., Braz. (sĕ′r-rä-dō-kō-ó′tō)	132b	22.33S	43.27W
Council Bluffs, Ia., U.S. (koun′sĭl blŭf)	97	41.16N	95.53W
Council Grove, Ks., U.S. (koun′sĭl grōv)	111	38.39N	96.30W
Coupeville, Wa., U.S. (kōōp′vĭl)	106a	48.13N	122.41W
Courantyne, r., S.A. (kôr′ăntĭn)	131	4.28N	57.42W
Courbevoie, Fr.	237c	48.54N	2.15E
Courcelle, Fr.	237c	48.42N	2.06E
Courtenay, Can. (cōōrt-nā′)	84	49.41N	125.00W
Courtleigh, Md., U.S.	229c	39.22N	76.46W
Courtry, Fr.	237c	48.55N	2.36E
Coushatta, La., U.S. (kou-shăt′ă)	113	32.02N	93.21W

PLACE (Pronunciation)	PAGE	Lat. °′	Long. °′
Coutras, Fr. (kōō-trá′)	156	45.02N	0.07W
Cova da Piedade, Port.	238d	38.40N	9.10W
Covelo, Ang.	216	12.06S	13.55E
Cove Neck, N.Y., U.S.	228	40.53N	73.31W
Coventry, Eng., U.K. (kŭv′ĕn-trĭ)	150	52.25N	1.29W
Covina, Ca., U.S. (kō-vē′nă)	107a	34.06N	117.54W
Covington, Ga., U.S. (kŭv′ĭng-tŭn)	114	33.36N	83.50W
Covington, In., U.S.	98	40.10N	87.15W
Covington, Ky., U.S.	97	39.05N	84.31W
Covington, La., U.S.	113	30.30N	90.06W
Covington, Oh., U.S.	98	40.10N	84.20W
Covington, Ok., U.S.	111	36.18N	97.32W
Covington, Tn., U.S.	114	35.33N	89.40W
Covington, Va., U.S.	98	37.50N	80.00W
Cowal, Lake, l., Austl. (kou′ăl)	204	33.30S	147.10E
Cowan, l., Austl. (kou′ăn)	202	32.00S	122.30E
Cowan Heights, Ca., U.S.	232	33.47N	117.47W
Cowansville, Can.	91	45.13N	72.47W
Cow Creek, r., Or., U.S. (kou)	104	42.45N	123.35W
Cowes, Eng., U.K. (kouz)	150	50.43N	1.25W
Cowichan Lake, l., Can.	86	48.54N	124.20W
Cowley, neigh., Eng., U.K.	235	51.32N	0.29W
Cowlitz, r., Wa., U.S. (kou′lĭts)	104	46.30N	122.45W
Cowra, Austl. (kou′ră)	204	33.50S	148.33E
Coxim, Braz. (kō-shēn′)	131	18.32S	54.43W
Coxquihui, Mex. (kōz-kē-wē′)	119	20.10N	97.34W
Cox's Bāzār, Bngl.	186	21.32N	92.00E
Coyaima, Col. (kō-yáē′mä)	130a	3.48N	75.11W
Coyame, Mex. (kō-yä′mä)	112	29.26N	105.05W
Coyanosa Draw, Tx., U.S. (kō yá-nō′sä)	112	30.55N	103.07W
Coyoacán, Mex. (kō-yō-á-kän′)	118	19.21N	99.10W
Coyote, r., Ca., U.S. (kī′ōt)	106b	37.37N	121.57W
Coyuca de Benítez, Mex. (kō-yōō′kä dā bā-nē′tāz)	118	17.04N	100.06W
Coyuca de Catalán, Mex. (kō-yōō′kä dā kä-tä-län′)	118	18.19N	100.41W
Coyutla, Mex. (kō-yōō′tlä)	119	20.13N	97.40W
Cozad, Ne., U.S. (kō′zăd)	110	40.53N	99.59W
Cozaddale, Oh., U.S. (kō-zăd-dăl)	101f	39.16N	84.09W
Cozoyoapan, Mex. (kō-zō-yō-ä-pá′n)	118	16.45N	98.17W
Cozumel, Mex. (kŏ-zōō-mĕ′l)	120a	20.31N	86.55W
Cozumel, Isla de, i., Mex. (ē′s-lä-dĕ-kŏ-zōō-mĕ′l)	116	20.26N	87.10W
Crab Creek, r., Wa., U.S. (krăb)	104	46.47N	119.43W
Crab Creek, r., Wa., U.S.	104	47.21N	119.09W
Cradock, S. Afr. (kră′dŭk)	212	32.12S	25.38E
Crafton, Pa., U.S. (krăf′tŭn)	101e	40.26N	80.04W
Craig, Co., U.S. (krāg)	105	40.32N	107.31W
Craighall Park, neigh., S. Afr.	244b	26.08S	28.01E
Craiova, Rom. (krá-yō′vá)	149	44.18N	23.50E
Cranberry, l., N.Y., U.S. (krăn′bĕr-ĭ)	99	44.10N	74.50W
Cranbourne, Austl.	201a	38.07S	145.16E
Cranbrook, Can. (krăn′brŏk)	84	49.31N	115.46W
Cranbury, N.J., U.S. (krăn′bē-rĭ)	100a	40.19N	74.31W
Crandon, Wi., U.S. (krăn′dŭn)	103	45.35N	88.55W
Crane Prairie Reservoir, res., Or., U.S.	104	43.50N	121.55W
Cranford, N.J., U.S.	228	40.39N	74.19W
Crank, Eng., U.K.	237a	53.29N	2.45W
Cranston, R.I., U.S. (krăns′tŭn)	100b	41.46N	71.25W
Crater Lake, l., Or., U.S. (krā′tĕr)	104	43.00N	122.08W
Crater Lake National Park, rec., Or., U.S.	104	42.58N	122.40W
Craters of the Moon National Monument, rec., Id., U.S. (krā′tĕr)	105	43.28N	113.15W
Crateús, Braz. (krä-tā-ōōzh′)	131	5.09S	40.35W
Crato, Braz. (krä′tō)	131	7.19S	39.13W
Crawford, Ne., U.S. (krô′fērd)	102	42.41N	103.25W
Crawford, Wa., U.S.	106c	45.49N	122.24W
Crawfordsville, In., U.S. (krô′fērdz-vĭl)	98	40.00N	86.55W
Crazy Mountains, mts., Mt., U.S. (krā′zĭ)	105	46.11N	110.25W
Crazy Woman Creek, r., Wy., U.S.	105	44.08N	106.40W
Crecy, S. Afr. (krē-sē)	218d	24.38S	28.52E
Crécy-en-Brie, Fr. (krā-sē′-ĕɴ-brē′)	157b	48.52N	2.55E
Crécy-en-Ponthieu, Fr.	156	50.13N	1.48E
Credit, r., Can.	83d	43.41N	79.55W
Cree, l., Can. (krē)	84	57.35N	107.52W
Creekmouth, neigh., Eng., U.K.	235	51.31N	0.06E
Creighton, S. Afr. (cre-tŏn)	213c	30.02S	29.52E
Creighton, Ne., U.S. (krā′tŭn)	102	42.27N	97.54W
Creil, Fr. (krĕ′y′)	156	49.18N	2.28E
Crema, Italy (krā′mä)	160	45.21N	9.53E
Cremona, Italy (krā-mō′nä)	148	45.09N	10.02E
Crépy-en-Valois, Fr. (krā-pē′ĕɴ-vä-lwä′)	157b	49.14N	2.53E
Cres, Cro. (tsrĕs)	160	44.58N	14.21E
Cres, i., Yugo.	160	44.50N	14.31E
Crescent Beach, Can.	106d	49.03N	122.58W
Crescent City, Ca., U.S. (krĕs′ĕnt)	104	41.46N	124.13W
Crescent City, Fl., U.S.	115	29.26N	81.35W
Crescent Lake, l., Fl., U.S. (krĕs′ĕnt)	115	29.33N	81.30W
Crescent Lake, l., Or., U.S.	104	43.25N	121.58W
Crescentville, neigh., Pa., U.S.	229b	40.02N	75.05W
Cresco, Ia., U.S. (krĕs′kō)	103	43.23N	92.07W
Cresskill, N.J., U.S.	228	40.57N	73.57W
Crested Butte, Co., U.S. (krĕst′ĕd būt)	109	38.50N	107.00W
Crest Haven, Md., U.S.	229d	39.02N	76.59W
Crestline, Ca., U.S. (krĕst-līn)	107a	34.15N	117.17W
Crestline, Oh., U.S.	98	40.50N	82.40W
Crestmore, Ca., U.S. (krĕst′môr)	107a	34.02N	117.23W
Creston, Can. (krĕs′tŭn)	84	49.06N	116.31W
Creston, Ia., U.S.	103	41.04N	94.22W
Creston, Oh., U.S.	101d	40.59N	81.54W
Crestview, Fl., U.S. (krĕst′vū)	114	30.44N	86.35W
Crestwood, Il., U.S.	231a	41.39N	87.44W
Crestwood, Ky., U.S. (krĕst′wŏd)	101h	38.20N	85.28W
Crestwood, Mo., U.S.	107e	38.33N	90.23W
Crete, Il., U.S. (krēt)	101a	41.26N	87.38W
Crete, Ne., U.S.	111	40.38N	96.56W

PLACE (Pronunciation)	PAGE	Lat. °′	Long. °′
Crete, i., Grc.	142	35.15N	24.30E
Créteil, Fr.	237c	48.48N	2.28E
Creus, Cabo de, c., Spain (kā′-bō-dĕ-krĕ-ōōs)	159	42.16N	3.18E
Creuse, r., Fr. (krûz)	156	46.51N	0.49E
Creve Coeur, Mo., U.S. (krēv kŏr)	107e	38.40N	90.27W
Crevillente, Spain (krâ-vē-lyĕn′tâ)	159	38.12N	0.48W
Crewe, Eng., U.K. (krōō)	150	53.06N	2.27W
Crewe, Va., U.S.	115	37.09N	78.08W
Crimean Peninsula *see* Kryms'kyy pivostriv, pen., Ukr.	167	45.18N	33.30E
Crimmitschau, Ger. (krĭm′ĭt-shou)	154	50.49N	12.22E
Cripple Creek, Co., U.S. (krĭp′′l)	110	38.44N	105.12W
Crisfield, Md., U.S. (krĭs-fēld)	99	38.00N	75.50W
Cristal, Monts de, mts., Gabon	216	0.50N	10.30E
Cristina, Braz. (krēs-tē′-nä)	129a	22.13S	45.15W
Cristóbal Colón, Pico, mtn., Col. (pē′kō-krēs-tô′bäl-kō-lôn′)	130	11.00N	74.00W
Cristo Redentor, Estatua do, hist., Braz.	234c	22.57S	43.13W
Crişul Alb, r., Rom. (krē′shōōl älb)	155	46.20N	22.15E
Crna, r., Yugo. (ts′r′nà)	161	41.03N	21.46E
Crna Gora (Montenegro), hist. reg., Yugo.	161	42.55N	18.52E
Črnomelj, Slvn. (ch′r′nō-māl′)	160	45.35N	15.11E
Croatia, nation, Eur.	160	45.24N	15.18E
Crockenhill, Eng., U.K.	235	51.23N	0.10E
Crockett, Ca., U.S. (krŏk′ĕt)	106b	38.03N	122.14W
Crockett, Tx., U.S.	113	31.19N	95.28W
Crofton, Md., U.S.	100e	39.01N	76.43W
Crofton, Ne., U.S.	102	42.44N	97.32W
Croissy-Beaubourg, Fr.	237c	48.50N	2.40E
Croissy-sur-Seine, Fr.	237c	48.53N	2.09E
Croix, Lac la, l., N.A. (läk lä krōō-ä′)	103	48.19N	91.53W
Croker, i., Austl. (krō′kă)	202	10.45S	132.25E
Cromer, Austl.	243a	33.44S	151.17E
Cronenberg, neigh., Ger.	236	51.12N	7.08E
Cronton, Eng., U.K.	237a	53.23N	2.46W
Cronulla, Austl. (krō-nŭl′ă)	201b	34.03S	151.09E
Crooked, i., Bah.	123	22.45N	74.10W
Crooked, l., Can.	93	48.25N	56.05W
Crooked, r., Can.	87	54.30N	122.55W
Crooked, r., Or., U.S.	104	44.07N	120.30W
Crooked Creek, r., Il., U.S. (krōōk′ĕd)	111	40.21N	90.49W
Crooked Island Passage, strt., Bah.	123	22.40N	74.50W
Crookston, Mn., U.S. (krŏŏks′tŭn)	102	47.44N	96.35W
Crooksville, Oh., U.S. (krŏŏks′vĭl)	98	39.45N	82.05W
Crosby, Eng., U.K.	144a	53.30N	3.02W
Crosby, Mn., U.S. (krôz′bĭ)	103	46.29N	93.58W
Crosby, N.D., U.S.	102	48.55N	103.18W
Crosby, Tx., U.S.	113a	29.55N	95.04W
Crosby, neigh., S. Afr.	244b	26.12N	27.59E
Crosne, Fr.	237c	48.43N	2.28E
Cross, l., La., U.S.	113	32.33N	93.58W
Cross, r., Nig.	215	5.35N	8.05E
Cross City, Fl., U.S.	114	29.55N	83.25W
Crossett, Ar., U.S. (krôs′ĕt)	111	33.08N	92.00W
Cross Lake, l., Can.	84	54.45N	97.30W
Cross River Reservoir, res., N.Y., U.S. (krôs)	100a	41.14N	73.34W
Cross Sound, strt., Ak., U.S. (krŏs)	95	58.12N	137.20W
Crosswell, Mi., U.S. (krŏz′wĕl)	98	43.15N	82.35W
Crotch, l., Can.	91	44.55N	76.55W
Crotone, Italy (krō-tō′nĕ)	161	39.05N	17.08E
Croton Falls Reservoir, res., N.Y., U.S. (krōtŭn)	100a	41.22N	73.44W
Croton-on-Hudson, N.Y., U.S. (krō′tŭn-ŏn hŭd′sŭn)	100a	41.12N	73.53W
Crouse Run, r., Pa., U.S.	230b	40.35N	79.58W
Crow, l., Can.	103	49.13N	93.29W
Crow Agency, Mt., U.S.	105	45.36N	107.27W
Crow Creek, r., Co., U.S.	110	41.08N	104.25W
Crow Creek Indian Reservation, I.R., S.D., U.S.	102	44.17N	99.17W
Crow Indian Reservation, I.R., Mt., U.S. (krō)	105	45.26N	108.12W
Crowle, Eng., U.K. (kroul)	144a	53.36N	0.49W
Crowley, La., U.S. (krou′lē)	113	30.13N	92.22W
Crown Mountain, mtn., Can. (kroun)	106d	49.24N	123.05W
Crown Mountain, mtn., V.I.U.S.	117c	18.22N	64.58W
Crown Point, In., U.S. (kroun point′)	101a	41.25N	87.22W
Crown Point, N.Y., U.S.	99	44.00N	73.25W
Crows Nest, Austl.	243a	33.50S	151.12E
Crowsnest Pass, p., Can.	87	49.39N	114.45W
Crow Wing, r., Mn., U.S.	103	46.42N	94.48W
Crow Wing, r., Mn., U.S. (krō)	103	44.50N	94.01W
Crow Wing, North Fork, r., Mn., U.S.	103	45.16N	94.28W
Crow Wing, South Fork, r., Mn., U.S.	103	44.59N	94.42W
Croxley Green, Eng., U.K.	235	51.39N	0.27W
Croydon, Austl.	201a	37.48S	145.17E
Croydon, Austl. (kroi′dŭn)	203	18.15S	142.15E
Croydon, Eng., U.K.	147	51.22N	0.06W
Croydon, Pa., U.S.	100f	40.05N	74.55W
Crozet, Îles, is., Afr. (krō-zĕ′)	3	46.20S	51.30E
Cruces, Cuba (krōō′sås)	122	22.20N	80.20W
Cruces, Arroyo de, r., Mex. (är-rŏ′yô-dĕ-krōō′sĕs)	112	26.17N	104.32W
Cruillas, Mex. (krōō-ēl′yäs)	112	24.45N	98.31W
Crum Lynne, Pa., U.S.	229b	39.52N	75.20W
Cruz, Cabo, c., Cuba (kå′-bō-krōōz)	117	19.50N	77.45W
Cruz, Cayo, i., Cuba (kä′yō-krōōz)	122	22.15N	77.50W
Cruz Alta, Braz. (krōōz äl′tä)	132	28.41S	54.02W
Cruz del Eje, Arg. (krōō′s-dĕl-ĕ-kĕ)	132	30.46S	64.45W
Cruzeiro, Braz. (krōō-zā′rō)	129a	22.36S	44.57W
Cruzeiro do Sul, Braz. (krōō-zā′rō dō sōōl)	130	7.34S	72.40W
Crysler, Can.	83c	45.13N	75.09
Crystal Beach, Can.	230a	42.52N	79.04

ăt; finăl; rāte; senâte; ärm; ásk; sofă; fâre; ch-choose; dh-as th in other; bē; ėvent; bĕt; recĕnt; cratĕr; g-gō; gh-guttural g; bĭt; ĭ-short neutral; rīde; ĸ-guttural k as ch in German ich;

PRONOUNCING INDEX

Crystal City–Dania 279

PLACE (Pronunciation)	PAGE	Lat. °'	Long. °'
Crystal City, Tx., U.S. (krĭs'tăl sĭ'tĭ)	112	28.40N	99.50W
Crystal Falls, Mi., U.S. (krĭs'tăl fôls)	103	46.06N	88.21W
Crystal Lake, Il., U.S. (krĭs'tăl lăk)	101a	42.15N	88.18W
Crystal Springs, Ms., U.S. (krĭs'tăl sprĭngz)	114	31.58N	90.20W
Crystal Springs, oasis, Ca., U.S.	106b	37.31N	122.26W
Csömör, Hung.	239g	47.33N	19.14E
Csongrád, Hung. (chôn'gräd)	155	46.42N	20.09E
Csorna, Hung. (chôr'nä)	155	47.39N	17.11E
Cúa, Ven. (kōō'ä)	131b	10.10N	66.54W
Cuajimalpa, Mex. (kwä-hē-mäl'pä)	119a	19.21N	99.18W
Cuale, Sierra del, mts., Mex. (sē-ĕ'r-rä-dĕl-kwá'lĕ)	118	20.20N	104.58W
Cuamato, Ang. (kwä-mä'tō)	216	17.05S	15.09E
Cuamba, Moz.	217	14.49S	36.33E
Cuando, Ang. (kwän'dō)	216	16.32S	22.07E
Cuando, r., Afr.	212	14.30S	20.00E
Cuangar, Ang.	216	17.36S	18.39E
Cuango, r., Afr.	212	9.00S	18.00E
Cuanza, r., Ang. (kwän'zä)	212	9.45S	15.00E
Cuarto, r., Arg.	132	33.00S	63.25W
Cuatro Caminos, Cuba (kwä'trō-kä-mē'nōs)	123a	23.01N	82.13W
Cuatro Ciénegas, Mex. (kwä'trō syā'nä-gäs)	112	26.59N	102.03W
Cuauhtemoc, Mex. (kwä-ōō-tē-mŏk')	119	15.43N	91.57W
Cuautepec, Mex. (kwä-ōō-tĕ-pĕk)	118	16.41N	99.04W
Cuautepec, Mex.	118	20.01N	98.19W
Cuautepec el Alto, Mex.	233a	19.34N	99.08W
Cuautitlán, Mex. (kwä-ōō-tĕt-län')	119a	19.40N	99.12W
Cuautla, Mex. (kwä-ōō'tlä)	118	18.47N	98.57W
Cuba, Port. (kōō'bȧ)	158	38.10N	7.55W
Cuba, nation, N.A. (kū'bȧ)	117	22.00N	79.00W
Cubagua, Isla, i., Ven. (ē's-lä-kōō-bä'gwä)	131b	10.48N	64.10W
Cubango (Okavango), r., Afr. (kōō-bäŋ'gō)	212	17.10S	18.20E
Cub Hills, hills, Can. (kŭb)	88	54.20N	104.30W
Cucamonga, Ca., U.S. (kōō-kȧ-mŏŋ'gȧ)	107a	34.05N	117.35W
Cuchi, Ang.	212	14.40S	16.50E
Cuchillo Parado, Mex. (kōō-chē'lyō pä-rä'dō)	112	29.26N	104.52W
Cuchumatanes, Sierra de los, mts., Guat.	120	15.35N	91.10W
Cúcuta, Col. (kōō'kōō-tä)	130	7.56N	72.30W
Cudahy, Wi., U.S. (kŭd'ȧ-hī)	101a	42.57N	87.52W
Cuddalore, India (kŭd ȧ-lōr')	183	11.49N	79.46E
Cuddapah, India (kŭd'ȧ-pä)	183	14.31N	78.52E
Cudham, neigh., Eng., U.K.	235	51.19N	0.05E
Cue, Austl. (kū)	202	27.30S	118.10E
Cuéllar, Spain (kwā'lyär')	158	41.24N	4.15W
Cuenca, Ec. (kwĕn'kä)	130	2.52S	78.54W
Cuenca, Spain	148	40.05N	2.07W
Cuenca, Sierra de, mts., Spain (sē-ĕ'r-rä-dĕ-kwĕ'n-kä)	158	40.02N	1.50W
Cuencame, Mex. (kwĕn-kä-mä')	112	24.52N	103.42W
Cuerámaro, Mex. (kwā-rä'mä-rō)	118	20.39N	101.44W
Cuernavaca, Mex. (kwĕr-nä-vä'kä)	116	18.55N	99.15W
Cuero, Tx., U.S. (kwā'rō)	113	29.05N	97.16W
Cuetzalá del Progreso, Mex. (kwĕt-zä-lä dĕl prō-grā'sō)	118	18.07N	99.51W
Cuetzalan del Progreso, Mex.	119	20.02N	97.33W
Cuevas del Almanzora, Spain (kwĕ'väs-dĕl-äl-män-zō-rä)	148	37.19N	1.54W
Cuffley, Eng., U.K.	235	51.42N	0.07W
Cuglieri, Italy (kōō-lyā'rē)	160	40.11N	8.37E
Cuicatlán, Mex. (kwē-kä-tlän')	119	17.46N	96.57W
Cuigezhuang, China	240b	40.01N	116.28E
Cuilapa, Guat. (kō-ē-lä'pä)	120	14.16N	90.20W
Cuilo (Kwilu), r., Afr.	216	9.15S	19.30E
Cuito, r., Ang. (kōō-ē'tō)	212	14.45S	19.00E
Cuitzeo, Mex. (kwēt'zä-ō)	118	19.57N	101.11W
Cuitzeo, Laguna de, l., Mex. (lä-ō'nä-dĕ-kwēt'zä-ō)	118	19.58N	101.05W
Cul de Sac, pl., Haiti (kōō'l-dĕ-sä'k)	123	18.35N	72.05W
Culebra, i., P.R. (kōō-lā'brä)	117b	18.19N	65.32W
Culebra, Sierra de la, mts., Spain (sē-ĕ'r-rä-dĕ-lä-kōō-lĕ-brä)	158	41.52N	6.21W
Culemborg, Neth.	145a	51.57N	5.14E
Culfa, Azer.	168	38.58N	45.38E
Culgoa, r., Austl. (kŭl-gō'ȧ)	203	29.21S	147.00E
Culiacán, Mex. (kōō-lyä-kä'n)	116	24.45N	107.30W
Culion, Phil. (kōō-lē-ōn')	196	11.43N	119.58E
Cúllar de Baza, Spain (kōō'l-yär-dĕ-bä'zä)	158	37.36N	2.35W
Cullera, Spain (kōō-lyā'rä)	148	39.12N	0.15W
Cullinan, S. Afr. (kŏ'lĭ-năn)	218d	25.41S	28.32E
Cullman, Al., U.S. (kŭl'mȧn)	114	34.10N	86.50W
Culmore, Va., U.S.	229d	38.51N	77.08W
Culpeper, Va., U.S. (kŭl'pĕp-ĕr)	99	38.30N	77.55W
Culross, Can. (kŭl'rôs)	83f	49.43N	97.54W
Culver, In., U.S. (kŭl'vĕr)	98	41.15N	86.25W
Culver City, Ca., U.S.	107a	34.00N	118.23W
Culverstone Green, Eng., U.K.	235	51.20N	0.21E
Cumaná, Ven.	130	10.28N	64.10W
Cumberland, Can. (kŭm'bĕr-lȧnd)	83c	45.31N	75.25W
Cumberland, Md., U.S.	97	39.40N	78.40W
Cumberland, Wa., U.S.	106a	47.17N	121.55W
Cumberland, Wi., U.S.	103	45.31N	92.01W
Cumberland, r., U.S.	114	36.45N	85.33W
Cumberland, Lake, res., Ky., U.S.	97	36.55N	85.20W
Cumberland Islands, is., Austl.	203	20.20S	149.46E
Cumberland Peninsula, pen., Can.	85	65.59N	64.05W
Cumberland Plateau, plat., U.S.	114	35.25N	85.30W
Cumberland Sound, strt., Can.	85	65.27N	65.44W
Cundinamarca, dept., Col. (kōōn-dē-nä-mä'r-kä)	130a	4.57N	74.27W
Cunduacán, Mex. (kōn-dōō-ȧ-kän')	119	18.04N	93.23W
Cunene (Kunene), r., Afr.	212	17.05S	12.35E
Cuneo, Italy (kōō'nā-ō)	160	44.24N	7.31E
Cunha, Braz. (kōō'nyȧ)	129a	23.05S	44.56W
Cunnamulla, Austl. (kŭn-ȧ-mŭl-ȧ)	203	28.00S	145.55E
Cupula, Pico, mtn., Mex. (pē'kō-kōō'pōō-lä)	116	24.45N	111.10W
Cuquío, Mex. (kōō-kē'ō)	118	20.55N	103.03W
Curaçao, i., Neth. Ant. (kōō-rä-sä'ō)	130	12.12N	68.58W
Curacautín, Chile (kä-rä-käōō-tē'n)	132	38.25S	71.53W
Curaumilla, Punta, c., Chile (kōō-rou-mē'lyä)	129b	33.05S	71.44W
Curepto, Chile (kōō-rĕp-tō)	129b	35.06S	72.02W
Curitiba, Braz. (kōō-rē-tē'bȧ)	131	25.20S	49.15W
Curly Cut Cays, is., Bah.	122	23.40N	77.40W
Currais Novos, Braz. (kōōr-rä'ēs nō-vōs)	131	6.02S	36.39W
Curran, Can. (kü-räN')	83c	45.30N	74.59W
Current, i., Bah. (kŭ-rĕnt)	122	25.20N	76.50W
Current, r., Mo., U.S. (kûr'ĕnt)	111	37.18N	91.21W
Currie, Mount, mtn., S. Afr. (kŭ-rē)	213c	30.28S	29.23E
Currituck Sound, strt., N.C., U.S. (kûr'ĭ-tŭk)	115	36.27N	75.42W
Curtis, Ne., U.S. (kûr'tĭs)	110	40.36N	100.29W
Curtis, i., Austl.	203	23.38S	151.43E
Curtis B, Md., U.S.	229c	39.13N	76.35W
Curtisville, Pa., U.S. (kûr'tĭs-vĭl)	101e	40.38N	79.50W
Ćurug, Yugo. (chōō'rōg)	161	45.27N	20.03E
Curunga, Ang.	216	12.51S	21.12E
Curupira, Serra, mts., S.A. (sĕr'rȧ kōō-rōō-pē'rȧ)	130	1.00N	65.30W
Cururupu, Braz. (kōō-rō-rō-pōō')	131	1.40S	44.56W
Curvelo, Braz. (kōr-vĕl'ō)	131	18.47S	44.14W
Cusano Milanino, Italy	238c	45.33N	9.11E
Cusco, Peru	130	13.36S	71.52W
Cushing, Ok., U.S. (kŭsh'ĭng)	111	35.58N	96.46W
Custer, S.D., U.S. (kŭs'tĕr)	102	43.46N	103.36W
Custer, Wa., U.S.	106d	48.55N	122.39W
Custer Battlefield National Monument, rec., Mt., U.S. (kŭs'tĕr băt'’l-fēld)	105	45.44N	107.15W
Cut Bank, Mt., U.S. (kŭt bănk)	105	48.38N	112.19W
Cuthbert, Ga., U.S. (kŭth'bĕrt)	114	31.47N	84.48W
Cuttack, India (kŭ-täk')	183	20.38N	85.53E
Cutzamala, r., Mex. (kōō-tzä-mä-lä')	118	18.57N	100.41W
Cutzamalá de Pinzón, Mex. (kōō-tzä-mä-lä'dĕ-pēn-zō'n)	118	18.28N	100.36W
Cuvo, r., Ang. (kōō'vō)	212	11.00S	14.30E
Cuxhaven, Ger. (kōks'hä-fĕn)	146	53.51N	8.43E
Cuxton, Eng., U.K.	235	51.22N	0.27E
Cuyahoga, r., Oh., U.S. (kī-ȧ-hō'gȧ)	101d	41.22N	81.38W
Cuyahoga Falls, Oh., U.S.	101d	41.08N	81.29W
Cuyahoga Heights, Oh., U.S.	229a	41.26N	81.39W
Cuyapaire Indian Reservation, I.R., Ca., U.S. (kū-yȧ-pâr)	108	32.46N	116.20W
Cuyo Islands, is., Phil. (kōō'yō)	196	10.54N	120.08E
Cuyotenango, Guat. (kōō-yō-tĕ-näŋ'gō)	120	14.30N	91.35W
Cuyuni, r., S.A. (kōō-yōō'nē)	131	6.40N	60.44W
Cuyutlán, Mex. (kōō-yōō-tlän')	118	18.54N	104.04W
Cyclades see Kikládhes, is., Grc.	142	37.30N	24.45E
Cynthiana, Ky., U.S. (sĭn-thĭ-ăn'ȧ)	98	38.20N	84.20W
Cypress, Ca., U.S. (sī'prĕs)	107a	33.50N	118.03W
Cypress Hills, hills, Can.	88	49.40N	110.20W
Cypress Lake, l., Can.	88	49.28N	109.43W
Cyprus, nation, Asia (sī'prŭs)	182	35.00N	31.00E
Cyprus, North, nation, Asia	182	35.15N	33.40E
Cyrenaica see Barqah, hist. reg., Libya	211	31.09N	21.45E
Cyrildene, neigh., S. Afr.	244b	26.11S	28.06E
Czech Republic, nation, Eur.	142	50.00N	15.00E
Czersk, Pol. (chĕrsk)	155	53.47N	17.58E
Częstochowa, Pol. (chăN-stô kô'vá)	147	50.49N	19.10E

D

PLACE (Pronunciation)	PAGE	Lat. °'	Long. °'
Da'an, China (dä-än)	192	45.25N	124.22E
Dabakala, C. Iv. (dä-bä-kä'lä)	210	8.16N	4.36W
Daba Shan, mts., China (dä-bä shän)	188	32.25N	108.20E
Dabeiba, Col. (dä-bā'bä)	130a	7.01N	76.16W
Dabie Shan, mts., China (dä-bĭē shän)	189	31.40N	114.50E
Dabnou, Niger	215	14.09N	5.22E
Dabob Bay, b., Wa., U.S. (dā'bŏb)	106a	47.50N	122.50W
Dabola, Gui.	214	10.45N	11.07W
Dąbrowa Białostocka, Pol.	155	53.37N	23.18E
Dacca see Dhaka, Bngl.	182	23.45N	90.29E
Dachang, China (dä-chäŋ)	191b	31.18N	121.25E
Dachangshan Dao, i., China (dä-chäŋ-shän dou)	190	39.21N	122.31E
Dachau, Ger. (dä'κou)	154	48.16N	11.26E
Dacotah, Can. (dȧ-kō'tȧ)	83f	49.52N	97.38W
Dadar, neigh., India	240e	19.01N	72.50E
Dade City, Fl., U.S. (dād)	115a	28.22N	82.09W
Dadeville, Al., U.S. (dād'vĭl)	114	32.48N	85.44W
Dādra & Nagar Haveli, India	183	20.00N	73.00E
Dadu, r., China (dä-dōō)	193	29.20N	103.03E
Daet, mtn., Phil. (dä'ăt)	197a	14.07N	122.59E
Dafoe, r., Can.	89	55.50N	95.50W
Dafter, Mi., U.S. (dăf'tĕr)	107k	46.21N	84.26W
Dagana, Sen. (dä-gä'nä)	210	16.31N	15.30W
Dagana, reg., Chad	215	12.20N	15.15E
Dagang, China (dä-gäŋ)	191a	22.48N	113.24E
Dagda, Lat. (dȧg'dȧ)	153	56.04N	27.30E
Dagenham, Eng., U.K. (dăg'ĕn-ăm)	144b	51.32N	0.09E
Dagestan, state, Russia (dä-gĕs-tän')	167	43.40N	46.10E
Daggafontein, S. Afr.	244b	26.18S	28.28E
Daggett, Ca., U.S. (dăg'ĕt)	108	34.50N	116.52W
Dagu, China (dä-gōō)	192	39.00N	117.42E
Dagu, r., China	190	36.29N	120.06W
Dagupan, Phil. (dä-gōō'pän)	197a	16.02N	120.20E
Daheishan Dao, i., China (dä-hā-shän dou)	190	37.57N	120.37E
Dahīrpur, neigh., India	240d	28.43N	77.12E
Dahl, Ger. (däl)	157c	51.18N	7.33E
Dahlak Archipelago, is., Erit.	211	15.45N	40.30E
Dahlem, neigh., Ger.	238a	52.28N	13.17E
Dahlerau, Ger.	236	51.13N	7.19E
Dahlwitz, Ger.	238a	52.30N	13.38E
Dahomey see Benin, nation, Afr.	210	8.00N	2.00E
Dahra, Libya	184	29.34N	17.50E
Daibu, China (dī-bōō)	190	31.22N	119.29E
Daigo, Japan (dī-gō)	195b	34.57N	135.49E
Daimiel Manzanares, Spain (dī-myĕl'män-zä-nä'rĕs)	158	39.05N	3.36W
Dairen see Dalian, China	188	38.54N	121.35E
Dairy, r., Or., U.S. (dâr'ĭ)	106c	45.33N	123.04W
Dai-Sen, mtn., Japan (dī'sĕn')	195	35.22N	133.35E
Dai-Tenjo-dake, mtn., Japan (dī-tĕn'jō dä-κä)	195	36.21N	137.38E
Daiyun Shan, mtn., China (dī-yòn shän)	193	25.40N	118.08E
Dajabón, Dom. Rep. (dä-kä-bō'n)	123	19.35N	71.40W
Dajarra, Austl. (dȧ-jär'ȧ)	202	21.45S	139.30E
Dakar, Sen. (dȧ-kär')	210	14.40N	17.26W
Dakhla, W. Sah.	210	23.45N	16.04W
Dakouraoua, Niger	215	13.58N	6.15E
Dakovica, Yugo.	161	42.33N	20.28E
Dalälven, r., Swe.	142	60.26N	15.50E
Dalby, Austl. (dôl'bē)	203	27.10S	151.15E
Dalcour, La., U.S. (dăl-kour)	100d	29.49N	89.59W
Dale, Nor. (dä'lĕ)	152	60.35N	5.55E
Dale Hollow Lake, res., Tn., U.S. (dāl hŏl'ō)	97	36.33N	85.03W
Dalemead, Can. (dä'lĕ-mēd)	83e	50.53N	113.38W
Dalen, Nor. (dä'lĕn)	152	59.28N	8.01E
Daleside, S. Afr. (dāl'sīd)	218d	26.30S	28.03E
Dalesville, Can. (dālz'vĭl)	83a	45.42N	74.23W
Daley Waters, Austl. (dā lē)	202	16.15N	133.30E
Dalhart, Tx., U.S. (dăl härt)	110	36.04N	102.32W
Dalhousie, Can. (dăl-hōō'zē)	92	48.04N	66.23W
Dali, China	188	26.00N	100.08E
Dali, China	188	35.00N	109.38E
Dali, China (dä-lē)	191a	23.07N	113.06E
Dalian, China (lů-dä)	189	38.54N	121.35E
Dalian Wan, b., China (dä-lĭēn wän)	190	38.55N	121.50E
Dalías, Spain (dä-lē'ȧs)	158	36.49N	2.50W
Dall, i., Ak., U.S. (dăl)	95	54.50N	133.10W
Dallas, Or., U.S. (dăl'lȧs)	104	44.55N	123.20W
Dallas, S.D., U.S.	102	43.13N	99.34W
Dallas, Tx., U.S.	96	32.45N	96.48W
Dalles Dam, Or., U.S.	104	45.36N	121.08W
Dallgow, Ger.	238a	52.32N	13.05E
Dall Island, i., Ak., U.S.	86	54.50N	132.55W
Dalmacija, hist. reg., Yugo. (däl-mä'tsē-yä)	160	43.25N	16.37E
Dalnerechensk, Russia	165	46.07N	133.21E
Daloa, C. Iv.	214	6.53N	6.27W
Dalroy, Can. (dăl'roi)	83e	51.07N	113.39W
Dalrymple, Mount, mtn., Austl. (dăl'rĭm-p'l)	203	21.14S	148.46E
Dalton, S. Afr. (dôl'tŏn)	213c	29.21S	30.41E
Dalton, Eng., U.K.	237a	53.34N	2.46W
Dalton, Ga., U.S. (dôl'tŭn)	114	34.46N	84.58W
Daly, r., Austl. (dā'lĭ)	202	14.15S	131.15E
Daly City, Ca., U.S. (dā'lē)	106b	37.42N	122.27W
Damān, India	183	20.32N	72.53E
Damanhūr, Egypt (dä-män-hōōr')	211	30.59N	30.31E
Damar, Pulau, i., Indon.	197	7.15S	129.15E
Damara, Cen. Afr. Rep.	215	4.58N	18.42E
Damaraland, hist. reg., Nmb. (dă'nȧ-rȧ-lănd)	212	22.15S	16.15E
Damas Cays, is., Bah. (dä'mäs)	122	23.50N	79.50W
Damascus, Syria	182	33.30N	36.18E
Damāvand, Qolleh-ye, mtn., Iran	182	36.05N	52.05E
Damba, Ang. (däm'bä)	212	6.41S	15.08E
Dâmbovița, r., Rom.	161	44.43N	25.41E
Dame Marie, Cap, c., Haiti (dām mȧrē')	123	18.35N	74.50W
Dāmghān, Iran (dăm-gän')	182	35.50N	54.15E
Daming, China (dä-mĭŋ)	192	36.15N	115.09E
Dammartin-en-Goële, Fr. (däN-mär-tăN-äN-gō-ĕl')	157b	49.03N	2.40E
Dampier, Selat, strt., Indon. (däm'pēr)	197	0.40S	131.15E
Dampier Archipielago, is., Austl.	202	20.15S	116.25E
Dampier Land, reg., Austl.	202	17.30S	122.25E
Dan, r., N.C., U.S. (dăn)	115	36.26N	79.40W
Dana, Mount, mtn., Ca., U.S.	108	37.54N	119.13W
Da Nang, Viet.	196	16.08N	108.22E
Danbury, Eng., U.K.	144b	51.42N	0.34E
Danbury, Ct., U.S. (dăn'bĕr-ĭ)	100a	41.23N	73.27W
Danbury, Tx., U.S.	113a	29.14N	95.22W
Dandenong, Austl. (dăn'dē-nông)	204	37.59S	145.13E
Dandong, China (dän-dôŋ)	189	40.10N	124.30E
Dane, r., Eng., U.K. (dān)	144a	53.11N	2.14W
Danea, Gui.	214	11.27N	13.12W
Danforth, Me., U.S.	92	45.38N	67.53W
Dan Gora, Nig.	215	11.30N	8.09E
Dangtu, China (däŋ-tōō)	193	31.35N	118.28E
Dani, Burkina	210	13.43N	0.10W
Dania, Fl., U.S. (dă'nĭ-ȧ)	115a	26.01N	80.10W

ŋ-sing; ŋ-baŋk; N-nasalized n; nŏd; cŏmmit; ōld; ōbey; ôrder; oi-boil; fōōd; ȯ-as oo in foot; ou-out; s-soft; sh-dish; th-thin; pūre; ůnite; ûrn; stŭd; circŭs; ü-as in French tu; '-indeterminate vowel.

280 Daniels–Derbyshire

PLACE (Pronunciation)	PAGE	Lat. °′	Long. °′
Daniels, Md., U.S.	229c	39.26N	77.03W
Danilov, Russia (dä′nē-lôf)	166	58.12N	40.08E
Danissa Hills, hills, Kenya	217	3.20N	40.55E
Dänizkänarı, Azer.	168	40.13N	49.33E
Dankov, Russia (däŋ′kôf)	166	53.17N	39.09E
Dannemora, N.Y., U.S. (dăn-ê-mō′rȧ)	99	44.45N	73.45W
Dannhauser, S. Afr. (dän′hou-zẽr)	213c	28.07S	30.04E
Dansville, N.Y., U.S. (dănz′vĭl)	99	42.30N	77.40W
Danube, r., Eur.	142	43.00N	24.00E
Danube, Mouths of the, mth., Rom. (dăn′ūb)	163	45.13N	29.37E
Danvers, Ma., U.S. (dăn′vẽrz)	93a	42.34N	70.57W
Danville, Ca., U.S. (dăn′vĭl)	106b	37.49N	122.00W
Danville, Il., U.S.	98	40.10N	87.35W
Danville, In., U.S.	98	39.45N	86.30W
Danville, Ky., U.S.	98	37.35N	84.50W
Danville, Pa., U.S.	99	41.00N	76.35W
Danville, Va., U.S.	97	36.35N	79.24W
Danxian, China (dän shyĕn)	193	19.30N	109.38E
Danyang, China (dän-yäŋ)	190	32.01N	119.32E
Danzig *see* Gdańsk, Pol.	142	54.20N	18.40E
Danzig, Gulf of, b., Eur. (dȧn′tsĭk)	146	54.41N	19.01E
Daoxian, China (dou shyĕn)	193	25.35N	111.27E
Dapango, Togo	214	10.52N	0.12E
Daphnae, hist., Egypt	181a	30.43N	32.12E
Daqin Dao, i., China (dä-chyĭn dou)	190	38.18N	120.50E
Darabani, Rom. (dă-ră-băn′ĭ)	155	48.13N	26.38E
Daraj, Libya	210	30.12N	10.14E
Dār as-Salām, Egypt	244a	29.59N	31.13E
Darāw, Egypt (dȧ-rä′o͞o)	218b	24.24N	32.56E
Darbhanga, India (dŭr-bŭŋ′gä)	183	26.03N	85.09E
Darby, Pa., U.S. (där′bĭ)	100f	39.55N	75.16W
Darby, i., Bah.	122	23.50N	76.20W
Dardanelles *see* Çanakkale Boğazi, strt., Tur.	149	40.05N	25.50E
Dar es Salaam, Tan. (där ĕs sȧ-läm′)	213	6.48S	39.17E
Dārfūr, hist. reg., Sudan (där-fo͞or′)	211	13.21N	23.46E
Dargai, Pak. (dŭr-gä′ê)	186	34.35N	72.00E
Darien, Col. (dā-rĭ-ĕn′)	130a	3.56N	76.30W
Darien, Ct., U.S. (dâ-rē-ĕn′)	100a	41.04N	73.28W
Darién, Cordillera de, mts., Nic.	120	13.00N	85.42W
Darien, Serranía del, mts.	121	8.13N	77.28W
Darjeeling, India (dŭr-jē′lĭng)	183	27.05N	88.16E
Darling, r., Austl.	203	31.50S	143.20E
Darling Downs, reg., Austl.	203	27.22S	150.00E
Darling Range, mts., Austl.	202	30.30S	115.45E
Darlington, Eng., U.K. (där′lĭng-tŭn)	150	54.32N	1.35W
Darlington, S.C., U.S.	115	34.15N	79.52W
Darlington, Wi., U.S.	103	42.41N	90.06W
Darłowo, Pol. (där-lô′vô)	154	54.26N	16.23E
Darmstadt, Ger. (därm′shtät)	147	49.53N	8.40E
Darnah, Libya	211	32.44N	22.41E
Darnley Bay, b., Ak., U.S. (därn′lē)	95	70.00N	124.00W
Daroca, Spain (dä-rō-kä)	158	41.08N	1.24W
Dartford, Eng., U.K.	144b	51.27N	0.14E
Dartmoor, for., Eng., U.K. (därt′mo͞or)	150	50.35N	4.05W
Dartmouth, Can. (därt′mŭth)	85	44.40N	63.34W
Dartmouth, Eng., U.K.	150	50.33N	3.28W
Daru, Pap. N. Gui. (dä′ro͞o)	197	9.04S	143.21E
Daruvar, Cro. (där′ro͞o-vär)	161	45.37N	17.16E
Darwen, Eng., U.K. (där′wĕn)	144a	53.42N	2.28W
Darwin, Austl. (där′wĭn)	202	12.25S	131.00E
Darwin, Cordillera, mts., Chile (kôr-dēl-yĕ′rä-där′wēn)	132	54.40S	69.30W
Dash Point, Wa., U.S. (dăsh)	106a	47.19N	122.25W
Dasht, r., Pak. (dŭsht)	182	25.30N	62.30E
Dasol Bay, b., Phil. (dä-sōl′)	197a	15.53N	119.40E
Datchet, Eng., U.K.	235	51.29N	0.34W
Datian Ding, mtn., China (dä-tĭĕn dĭŋ)	193	22.25N	111.20E
Datong, China (dä-tôŋ)	192	40.00N	113.30E
Dattapukur, India	186a	22.45N	88.32E
Datteln, Ger. (dät′tĕln)	157c	51.39N	7.20E
Datu, Tandjung, c., Asia	196	2.08N	110.15E
Datuan, China (dä-tůän)	191b	30.57N	121.43E
Daugava (Zapadnaya Dvina), r., Eur.	153	56.40N	24.40E
Daugavpils, Lat. (dä′ŏ-gäv-pēls)	166	55.52N	26.32E
Dauphin, Can. (dô′fĭn)	84	51.09N	100.00W
Dauphin Lake, l., Can.	89	51.17N	99.48W
Dāvangere, India	187	14.30N	75.55E
Davao, Phil. (dä′vä-ō)	197	7.05N	125.30E
Davao Gulf, b., Phil.	197	6.30N	125.45E
Davenport, Ia., U.S. (dăv′ĕn-pōrt)	97	41.34N	90.38W
Davenport, Wa., U.S.	104	47.39N	118.07W
Daveyton Location, S. Afr.	244b	26.09S	28.25E
David, Pan. (dȧ-vēdh′)	117	8.27N	82.27W
David City, Ne., U.S. (dā′vĭd)	102	41.15N	97.10W
David-Gorodok, Bela. (dä-vēt′ gô-rō′dôk)	167	52.02N	27.14E
Davis, Ok., U.S. (dā′vĭs)	111	34.34N	97.08W
Davis, W.V., U.S.	99	39.15N	79.25W
Davis Lake, l., Or., U.S.	104	43.38N	121.43W
Davis Mountains, mts., Tx., U.S.	112	30.45N	104.17W
Davis Strait, strt., N.A.	82	66.00N	60.00W
Davlekanovo, Russia	166	54.15N	55.05E
Davos, Switz. (dä′vōs)	154	46.47N	9.50E
Davyhulme, Eng., U.K.	237b	53.27N	2.22W
Dawa, r., Afr.	211	4.30N	40.30E
Dawāsir, Wādī ad, val., Sau. Ar.	182	20.48N	44.07E
Dawei, Myanmar	196	14.04N	98.19E
Dawen, r., China (dä-wŭn)	190	35.58N	116.53E
Dawley, Eng., U.K. (dô′lĭ)	144a	52.38N	2.28W
Dawna Range, mts., Myanmar (dô′nȧ)	196	17.02N	98.01E
Dawson, Can. (dô′sŭn)	84	64.04N	139.22W
Dawson, Ga., U.S.	114	31.45N	84.29W
Dawson, Mn., U.S.	102	44.54N	96.03W
Dawson, r., Austl.	203	24.20S	149.45E
Dawson Bay, b., Can.	89	52.55N	100.50W
Dawson Creek, Can.	84	55.46N	120.14W
Dawson Range, mts., Can.	95	62.15N	138.10W
Dawson Springs, Ky., U.S.	114	37.10N	87.40W
Dawu, China (dä-wo͞o)	190	31.33N	114.07E
Dawuji, China	240b	39.51N	116.30E
Dax, Fr. (dȧks)	147	43.42N	1.06W
Daxian, China (dä-shyĕn)	188	31.12N	107.30E
Daxing, China (dä-shyĭŋ)	192a	39.44N	116.19E
Dayiqiao, China (dä-yē-chyou)	190	31.43N	120.40E
Dayr az Zawr, Syria (dȧ-ērêz-zôr′)	182	35.15N	40.01E
Dayton, Ky., U.S. (dā′tŭn)	101f	39.07N	84.28W
Dayton, N.M., U.S.	110	32.44N	104.23W
Dayton, Oh., U.S.	97	39.54N	84.15W
Dayton, Tn., U.S.	114	35.30N	85.00W
Dayton, Tx., U.S.	113	30.03N	94.53W
Dayton, Wa., U.S.	104	46.18N	117.59W
Daytona Beach, Fl., U.S. (dā-tō′nȧ)	97	29.11N	81.02W
Dayu, China (dä-yo͞o)	193	25.20N	114.20E
Da Yunhe (Grand Canal), can., China (dä yòn-hŭ)	189	35.00N	117.00E
Dayville, Ct., U.S. (dā′vĭl)	99	41.50N	71.55W
De Aar, S. Afr. (dē-är′)	212	30.45S	24.05E
Dead, l., Mn., U.S. (dĕd)	102	46.28N	96.00W
Dead Sea, l., Asia	182	31.30N	35.30E
Deadwood, S.D., U.S. (dĕd′wŏd)	96	44.23N	103.43W
Deal Island, Md., U.S. (dēl-ī′lănd)	99	38.10N	75.55W
Dean, r., Can. (dēn)	86	52.45N	125.30W
Dean Channel, strt., Can.	86	52.33N	127.13W
Deán Funes, Arg. (dē-ȧ′n-fo͞o-nēs)	132	30.26S	64.12W
Dean Row, Eng., U.K.	237b	53.20N	2.11W
Dearborn, Mi., U.S. (dēr′bŭrn)	101b	42.18N	83.15W
Dearborn Heights, Mi., U.S.	230c	42.19N	83.14W
Dearg, Ben, mtn., Scot., U.K. (bĕn dŭrg)	150	57.48N	4.59W
Dease Strait, strt., Can. (dēz)	84	68.50N	108.20W
Death Valley, Ca., U.S.	108	36.18N	116.26W
Death Valley, val., Ca., U.S.	96	36.30N	117.00W
Death Valley National Monument, rec., Ca., U.S.	108	36.34N	117.00W
Debal′tseve, Ukr.	163	48.23N	38.29E
Debao, China (dŭ-bou)	188	23.18N	106.40E
Debar, Mac. (dĕ′bär) (dĕ′brä)	161	41.31N	20.32E
Dęblin, Pol. (däN′blĭn)	155	51.34N	21.49E
Dębno, Pol. (dĕb-nô′)	154	52.47N	13.43E
Debo, Lac, l., Mali	214	15.15N	4.40W
Debrecen, Hung. (dĕ′brĕ-tsĕn)	142	47.32N	21.40E
Debre Markos, Eth.	211	10.15N	37.45E
Debre Tabor, Eth.	211	11.57N	38.09E
Decatur, Al., U.S. (dē-kā′tŭr)	114	34.35N	87.00W
Decatur, Ga., U.S.	100c	33.47N	84.18W
Decatur, Il., U.S.	97	39.50N	88.59W
Decatur, In., U.S.	98	40.50N	84.55W
Decatur, Mi., U.S.	98	42.10N	86.00W
Decatur, Tx., U.S.	111	33.14N	97.33W
Decazeville, Fr. (dē-käz′vēl′)	147	44.33N	2.16E
Deccan, plat., India (dĕk′ăn)	183	19.05N	76.40E
Deception Lake, l., Can.	88	56.33N	104.15W
Deception Pass, p., Wa., U.S. (dē-sĕp′shŭn)	106a	48.24N	122.44W
Děčín, Czech Rep. (dyĕ′chēn)	154	50.47N	14.14E
Decorah, Ia., U.S. (dē-kō′rȧ)	103	43.18N	91.48W
Dedenevo, Russia (dyĕ-dyĕ′nyĕ-vô)	172b	56.14N	37.31E
Dedham, Ma., U.S. (dĕd′ăm)	93a	42.15N	71.11W
Dedo do Deus, mtn., Braz. (dĕ-dô-dô-dĕ′o͞os)	132b	22.30S	43.02W
Dédougou, Burkina (dā-dô-go͞o′)	210	12.38N	3.28W
Dee, r., U.K.	144a	53.15N	3.05E
Dee, r., Scot., U.K.	150	57.05N	2.25W
Deep, r., N.C., U.S. (dēp)	115	35.36N	79.32W
Deep Fork, r., Ok., U.S.	111	35.35N	96.42W
Deep River, Can.	91	46.06N	77.20W
Deepwater, Mo., U.S. (dep-wô-tẽr)	111	38.15N	93.46W
Deer, i., Me., U.S.	92	44.07N	68.38W
Deerfield, Il., U.S. (dēr′fēld)	101a	42.10N	87.51W
Deer Island, Or., U.S.	106c	45.56N	122.51W
Deer Lake, Can.	85a	49.10N	57.25W
Deer Lake, l., Can.	89	52.40N	94.30W
Deer Lodge, Mt., U.S. (dēr lŏj)	105	46.23N	112.42W
Deer Park, Oh., U.S.	101f	39.12N	84.24W
Deer Park, Wa., U.S.	104	47.58N	117.28W
Deer River, Mn., U.S.	103	47.20N	93.49W
Dee Why, Austl.	243a	33.45S	151.17E
Dee Why Head, c., Austl.	243a	33.46S	151.19E
Dee Why Lagoon, b., Austl.	243a	33.45S	151.18E
Defiance, Oh., U.S. (dē-fī′ăns)	98	41.15N	84.20W
DeFuniak Springs, Fl., U.S. (dē fū′nĭ-ăk)	114	30.42N	86.06W
Deganga, India	186a	22.41N	88.41E
Degeh Bur, Eth.	218a	8.10N	43.25E
Deggendorf, Ger. (dĕ′ghĕn-dôrf)	154	48.50N	12.59E
Degollado, Mex. (dā-gô-lyä′dō)	118	20.27N	102.11W
DeGrey, r., Austl. (dē grā′)	202	20.20S	119.25E
Degtyarsk, Russia (dĕg-ty′arsk)	172a	56.42N	60.05E
Dehiwala-Mount Lavinia, Sri L.	187	6.47N	79.55E
Dehra Dūn, India (dā′rū)	183	30.09N	78.07E
Dehua, China (dŭ-hwä)	193	25.30N	118.15E
Dej, Rom. (dāzh)	149	47.09N	23.53E
De Kalb, Il., U.S. (dē kălb′)	98	41.54N	88.46W
Dekese, Zaire	216	3.27S	21.24E
Delacour, Can. (dĕ-lä-ko͞or′)	83e	51.09N	113.45W
Delagua, Co., U.S. (dĕl-ä′gwä)	110	37.19N	104.42W
Delair, N.J., U.S.	229b	39.59N	75.03W
De Land, Fl., U.S. (dē lănd′)	115	29.00N	81.19W
Delano, Ca., U.S. (dĕl′ȧ-nō)	108	35.47N	119.15W
Delano Peak, mtn., Ut., U.S.	96	38.25N	112.25W
Delavan, Wi., U.S. (dĕl′ȧ-văn)	103	42.39N	88.38W
Delaware, Oh., U.S. (dĕl′ȧ-wâr)	98	40.15N	83.05W
Delaware, state, U.S.	97	38.40N	75.30W
Delaware, r., U.S.	99	41.50N	75.20W
Delaware, r., Ks., U.S.	111	39.45N	95.47W
Delaware Bay, b., U.S.	97	39.05N	75.10W
Delaware Reservoir, res., Oh., U.S.	99	40.30N	83.05E
Delémont, Switz. (dĕ-lā-môN′)	154	47.21N	7.18E
De Leon, Tx., U.S. (dē lē-ŏn′)	112	32.06N	98.33W
Delft, Neth. (dĕlft)	151	52.01N	4.20E
Delfzijl, Neth.	151	53.20N	6.50E
Delgada, Punta, c., Arg. (po͞o′n-tä-dĕl-gä′dä)	132	43.46S	63.46W
Delgado, Cabo, c., Moz. (kȧ′bô-dĕl-gä′dō)	213	10.40S	40.35E
Delhi, India	183	28.54N	77.13E
Delhi, Il., U.S. (dĕl′hī)	107e	39.03N	90.16W
Delhi, La., U.S.	113	32.26N	91.29W
Delhi, state, India	183	28.30N	76.50E
Delhi Cantonment, India	240d	28.36N	77.08E
Delitzsch, Ger. (dā′lĭch)	154	51.32N	12.18E
Dellansjöarna, l., Swe.	152	61.57N	16.25E
Delles, Alg. (dê′lēs′)	210	36.59N	3.40E
Dell Rapids, S.D., U.S. (dĕl)	102	43.50N	96.43W
Dellwig, neigh., Ger.	236	51.29N	6.56E
Dellwood, Mn., U.S. (dĕl′wŏd)	107g	45.05N	92.58W
Del Mar, Ca., U.S. (dĕl mär′)	108a	32.57N	117.16W
Delmas, S. Afr. (dĕl′mȧs)	218d	26.08S	28.43E
Delmenhorst, Ger. (dĕl′mĕn-hôrst)	154	53.03N	8.38E
Del Norte, Co., U.S. (dĕl nôrt′)	109	37.40N	106.25W
De-Longa, i., Russia	165	76.21N	148.56E
De Long Mountains, mts., Ak., U.S. (dē′lŏng)	95	68.38N	162.30W
Deloraine, Austl. (dĕ-lŭ-rān)	204	41.30S	146.40E
Delphi, In., U.S. (dĕl′fī)	98	40.35N	86.40W
Delphos, Oh., U.S. (dĕl′fŏs)	98	40.50N	84.20W
Delran, N.J., U.S.	229b	40.02N	74.58W
Delray Beach, Fl., U.S. (dĕl-rā′)	115a	26.27N	80.05W
Del Rio, Tx., U.S. (dĕl rē′ō)	96	29.21N	100.52W
Delson, Can. (dĕl′sŭn)	83a	45.24N	73.32W
Delta, Co., U.S.	109	38.45N	108.05W
Delta, Ut., U.S.	109	39.20N	112.35W
Delta Beach, Can.	83f	50.10N	98.20W
Delvine, Alb. (dĕl′vê-nȧ)	161	39.58N	20.10E
Del Viso, Arg.	233d	34.26S	58.46W
Dëma, r., Russia (dyĕm′ä)	166	53.40N	54.30E
Demarest, N.J., U.S.	228	40.57N	73.58W
Demba, Zaire	216	5.30S	22.16E
Dembi Dolo, Eth.	211	8.46N	34.46E
Demidov, Russia (dzyĕ′mê-dô′f)	162	55.16N	31.32E
Deming, N.M., U.S. (dĕm′ĭng)	96	32.15N	107.45W
Demmeltrath, neigh., Ger.	236	51.11N	7.03E
Demmin, Ger. (dĕm′mēn)	154	53.54N	13.04E
Demnat, Mor. (dĕm-nät)	210	31.58N	7.03W
Demopolis, Al., U.S. (dē-mŏp′ō-lĭs)	114	32.30N	87.50W
Demotte, In., U.S. (dē′mŏt)	101a	41.12N	87.13W
Dempo, Gunung, mtn., Indon. (dĕm′pō)	196	4.04S	103.11E
Dem′yanka, r., Russia (dyĕm-yän′kä)	170	59.07N	72.58E
Demyansk, Russia (dyĕm-yänsk′)	162	57.39N	32.26E
Denain, Fr. (dē-năN′)	156	50.23N	3.21E
Denakil Plain, pl., Eth.	211	12.45N	41.01E
Denali National Park, rec., Ak., U.S.	96a	63.48N	153.02W
Denbigh, Wales, U.K. (dĕn′bĭ)	150	53.15N	3.25W
Dendermonde, Bel.	145a	51.02N	4.04E
Dendron, Va., U.S. (dĕn′drŭn)	115	37.02N	76.53W
Denenchōfu, neigh., Japan	242a	35.35N	139.41E
Denezhkin Kamen, Gora, mtn., Russia (dzyĕ-ŋĕ′zhkĕn kämĭēŋ)	172a	60.26N	59.35E
Denham, Mount, mtn., Jam.	117	18.20N	77.30W
Den Helder, Neth. (dĕn hĕl′dẽr)	151	52.55N	5.45E
Denia, Spain (dā′nyä)	159	38.48N	0.06E
Deniliquin, Austl. (dĕ-nĭl′ĭ-kwĭn)	203	35.20S	144.52E
Denison, Ia., U.S. (dĕn′ĭ-sŭn)	102	42.01N	95.22W
Denison, Tx., U.S.	96	33.45N	97.02W
Denisovka, Kaz. (dĕ-nĕ′sof-kȧ)	169	52.26N	61.45E
Denizli, Tur. (dĕn-ĭz-lē′)	149	37.40N	29.10E
Denklingen, Ger. (dĕn′klĕn-gĕn)	157c	50.54N	7.40E
Denmark, S.C., U.S. (dĕn′märk)	115	33.18N	81.09W
Denmark, nation, Eur.	142	56.14N	8.30E
Denmark Strait, strt., Eur.	82	66.30N	27.00W
Dennilton, S. Afr. (dĕn-ĭl-tŭn)	218d	25.18S	29.13E
Dennison, Oh., U.S. (dĕn′ĭ-sŭn)	98	40.25N	81.20W
Denpasar, Indon.	196	8.35S	115.10E
Denshaw, Eng., U.K.	237b	53.35N	2.02W
Denton, Eng., U.K. (dĕn′tŭn)	144a	53.27N	2.07W
Denton, Md., U.S.	99	38.55N	75.50W
Denton, Tx., U.S.	111	33.12N	97.06W
D'Entrecasteaux, Point, c., Austl. (däN-tr′kȧs-tō′)	202	34.50S	114.45E
D'Entrecasteaux Islands, is., Pap. N. Gui. (däN-tr′-kȧs-tō′)	197	9.45S	152.00E
Denver, Co., U.S. (dĕn′vẽr)	96	39.44N	104.59W
Deoli, India	186	25.52N	75.23E
De Pere, Wi., U.S. (dē pēr′)	103	44.25N	88.04W
Depew, N.Y., U.S. (dē-pū′)	101c	42.55N	78.43W
Deping, China (dŭ-pĭŋ)	190	37.28N	116.57E
Deptford, neigh., Eng., U.K.	235	51.28N	0.02W
Depue, Il., U.S. (dē pū)	98	41.15N	89.55W
De Queen, Ar., U.S. (dē kwēn′)	111	34.02N	94.21W
De Quincy, La., U.S. (dē kwĭn′sĭ)	113	30.27N	93.27W
Dera, Lach, r., Afr. (lăk dā′rä)	218a	0.45N	41.26E
Dera, Lak, r., Afr.	211	0.45N	41.30E
Dera Ghāzi Khān, Pak. (dā′rū gä-zē′ kan′)	183	30.09N	70.39E
Dera Ismāīl Khān, Pak. (dā′rū ĭs-mä-ēl′ kän′)	186	31.55N	70.51E
Derbent, Russia (dĕr-bĕnt′)	167	42.00N	48.10E
Derby, Austl. (där′bē) (dûr′bē)	202	17.20S	123.40E
Derby, S. Afr. (där′bĭ)	218d	25.55S	27.02E
Derby, Eng., U.K. (där′bē)	147	52.55N	1.29W
Derby, Ct., U.S. (dûr′bē)	99	41.20N	73.05W
Derbyshire, co., Eng., U.K.	144a	53.11N	1.30W

ăt; finăl; rāte; senâte; ärm; ȧsk; sofȧ; fâre; ch-choose; dh-as th in other; bē; ēvent; bĕt; recĕnt; cratẽr; g-gō; gh-guttural g; bĭt; ĭ-short neutral; rīde; K-guttural k as ch in German ich;

PLACE (Pronunciation)	PAGE	Lat. °′	Long. °′
Derdepoort, S. Afr.	218d	24.39S	26.21E
Derendorf, neigh., Ger.	236	51.15N	6.48E
Derg, Lough, l., Ire. (lŏk dĕrg)	150	53.00N	8.09W
De Ridder, La., U.S. (dē rĭd'ẽr)	113	30.50N	93.18W
Dermott, Ar., U.S. (dûr'mŏt)	111	33.32N	91.24W
Derne, neigh., Ger.	236	51.34N	7.31E
Derry, N.H., U.S. (dâr'ĭ)	93a	42.53N	71.22W
Derventa, Bos. (dĕr'ven-tȧ)	161	44.58N	17.58E
Derwent, r., Austl. (dẽr'wĕnt)	204	42.21S	146.30E
Derwent, r., Eng., U.K.	144a	52.54N	1.24W
Desagüe, Gran Canal del, can., Mex.	233a	19.29N	99.05W
Des Arc, Ar., U.S. (dāz ärk')	111	34.59N	91.31W
Descalvado, Braz. (dĕs-käl-vȧ-dō)	129a	21.55S	47.37W
Descartes, Fr.	156	46.58N	0.42E
Deschambault Lake, l., Can.	88	54.40N	103.35W
Deschênes, Can.	83c	45.23N	75.47W
Deschenes, Lake, l., Can.	83c	45.25N	75.53W
Deschutes, r., Or., U.S. (dā-shōōt')	104	44.25N	121.21W
Desdemona, Tx., U.S. (dĕz-dē-mō'nȧ)	112	32.16N	98.33W
Dese, Eth.	211	11.00N	39.51E
Deseado, Río, r., Arg. (rē-ō-dā-sā-ä'dhō)	132	46.50S	67.45W
Desirade Island, i., Guad. (dā-zē-räs')	121b	16.21N	60.51W
De Smet, S.D., U.S. (dē smĕt')	102	44.23N	97.33W
Des Moines, Ia., U.S. (dē moin')	97	41.35N	93.37W
Des Moines, N.M., U.S.	110	36.42N	103.48W
Des Moines, Wa., U.S.	106a	46.24N	122.20W
Des Moines, r., U.S.	97	42.30N	94.20W
Desna, r., Eur. (dyĕs-nȧ')	167	51.55N	31.45E
Desolación, i., Chile (dĕ-sō-lä-syô'n)	132	53.05S	74.00W
De Soto, Mo., U.S. (dē sō'tō)	111	38.07N	90.32W
Des Peres, Mo., U.S. (dĕs pĕr'ĕs)	107e	38.36N	90.26W
Des Plaines, Il., U.S. (dĕs plānz')	101a	42.02N	87.54W
Des Plaines, r., U.S.	101a	41.39N	87.56W
Dessau, Ger. (dĕsou)	147	51.50N	12.15E
Detmold, Ger. (dĕt'mōld)	154	51.57N	8.55E
Detroit, Mi., U.S. (dē-troit')	97	42.22N	83.10W
Detroit, Tx., U.S.	111	33.41N	95.16W
Detroit, r., Mi., U.S.	230c	42.06N	83.08W
Detroit Lake, res., Or., U.S.	104	44.42N	122.10W
Detroit Lakes, Mn., U.S. (dē-troit'lăkz)	102	46.48N	95.51W
Detroit Metropolitan-Wayne County Airport, arpt., Mi., U.S.	230c	42.13N	83.22W
Detva, Slvk. (dyĕt'vȧ)	155	48.32N	19.21E
Deuil-la-Barre, Fr.	237c	48.59N	2.20E
Deurne, Bel.	145a	51.13N	4.27E
Deusen, neigh., Ger.	236	51.33N	7.26E
Deutsch Wagram, Aus.	145e	48.19N	16.34E
Deux-Montagnes, Can.	83a	45.33N	73.53W
Deux Montagnes, Lac des, l., Can.	83a	45.28N	74.00W
Deva, Rom. (dā'vä)	149	45.52N	22.52E
Dévaványa, Hung. (dā'vô-vän-yô)	155	47.01N	20.58E
Develi, Tur. (dĕ'vȧ-lē)	167	38.20N	35.10E
Deventer, Neth. (dĕv'ĕn-tẽr)	151	52.14N	6.07E
Devils, r., Tx., U.S.	112	29.55N	101.10W
Devils Island *see* Diable, Île du, i., Fr. Gu.	131	5.15N	52.40W
Devils Lake, N.D., U.S.	96	48.10N	98.55W
Devils Lake, l., N.D., U.S. (dĕv''lz)	102	47.57N	99.04W
Devils Lake Indian Reservation, I.R., N.D., U.S.	102	48.08N	99.40W
Devils Postpile National Monument, rec., Ca., U.S.	108	37.42N	119.12W
Devils Tower National Monument, rec., Wy., U.S.	105	44.38N	105.07W
Devoll, r., Alb.	161	40.55N	20.10E
Devon, Can.	83g	53.23N	113.43W
Devon, S. Afr. (dĕv'ŭn)	218d	26.23S	28.47E
Devonport, Austl. (dĕv'ŭn-pôrt)	203	41.20S	146.30E
Devonport, N.Z.	203a	36.50S	174.45E
Devore, Ca., U.S. (dē-vôr')	107a	34.13N	117.24W
Dewatto, Wa., U.S. (dē-wät'ō)	106a	47.27N	123.04W
Dewey, Ok., U.S. (dū'ĭ)	111	36.48N	95.55W
De Witt, Ar., U.S. (dē wĭt')	111	34.17N	91.22W
De Witt, Ia., U.S.	103	41.46N	90.34W
Dewsbury, Eng., U.K. (dūz'bẽr-ĭ)	144a	53.42N	1.39W
Dexter, Me., U.S. (dĕks'tẽr)	92	45.01N	69.19W
Dexter, Mo., U.S.	111	36.46N	89.56W
Dezfūl, Iran	182	32.14N	48.37E
Dezhnëva, Mys, c., Russia (dyĕzh'nyĭf)	180	68.00N	172.00W
Dezhou, China (dŭ-jō)	192	37.28N	116.17E
Dháfni, Grc.	239d	38.01N	23.39E
Dhahran *see* Az̧ Z̧ahrān, Sau. Ar.	182	26.13N	50.00E
Dhaka, Bngl. (dä'kä) (däk'ȧ)	183	23.45N	90.29E
Dharamtar Creek, r., India	187b	18.49N	72.54E
Dharmavaram, India	187	14.32N	77.43E
Dhawalāgiri, mtn., Nepal	183	28.42N	83.31E
Dhenoúsa, i., Grc.	161	37.09N	25.53E
Dhībān, Jord.	181a	31.30N	35.46E
Dhidhimótikhon, Grc.	161	41.20N	26.27E
Dhodhekánisos (Dodecanese), is., Grc.	161	38.00N	26.10E
Dhule, India	183	20.58N	74.43E
Día, i., Grc. (dē'ä)	160a	35.27N	25.17E
Diable, Île du, i., Fr. Gu.	131	5.15N	52.40W
Diablo, Mount, mtn., Ca., U.S. (dyä'blō)	106b	37.52N	121.55W
Diablo Heights, Pan. (dyȧ'blō)	116a	8.58N	79.34W
Diablo Range, mts., Ca., U.S.	106b	37.47N	121.50W
Diablotins, Morne, mtn., Dom.	121b	15.31N	61.24W
Diaca, Moz.	217	11.30S	39.59E
Diaka, r., Mali	215	14.40N	5.00E
Diamantina, Braz.	131	18.14S	43.32W
Diamantina, r., Austl. (dī'man-tē'nȧ)	202	25.38S	139.53E
Diamantino, Braz. (dē-ȧ-män-tē'nō)	131	14.22S	56.23W
Diamond Creek, Austl.	243b	37.41S	145.09E
Diamond Peak, mtn., Or., U.S.	104	43.32N	122.08W
Diana Bank, bk. (dī'ăn'ȧ)	123	22.30N	74.45W
Dianbai, China (dĭĕn-bī)	193	21.30N	111.20E
Dian Chi, l., China (dĭĕn chē)	188	24.58N	103.18E
Diancun, China	240b	39.55N	116.14E
Dickinson, N.D., U.S. (dĭk'ĭn-sŭn)	96	46.52N	102.49W
Dickinson, Tx., U.S. (dĭk'ĭn-sŭn)	113a	29.28N	95.02W
Dickinson Bayou, Tx., U.S.	113a	29.26N	95.08W
Dickson, Tn., U.S. (dĭk'sŭn)	114	36.03N	87.24W
Dickson City, Pa., U.S.	99	41.25N	75.40W
Didcot, Eng., U.K. (dĭd'cŏt)	144b	51.35N	1.15W
Didiéni, Mali	214	13.53N	8.06W
Didsbury, neigh., Eng., U.K.	237b	53.25N	2.14W
Die, Fr. (dē)	157	44.45N	5.22E
Diefenbaker, res., Can.	84	51.20N	108.10W
Diego de Ocampo, Pico, mtn., Dom. Rep. (pē'-kō-dyĕ'gô-dĕ-ō-kä'm-pō)	123	19.40N	70.45W
Diego Ramirez, Islas, is., Chile (dē ā'gō rä-mē'räz)	132	56.15S	70.15W
Diéma, Mali	214	14.32N	9.12W
Dien Bien Phu, Viet.	188	21.38N	102.49E
Diepensee, Ger.	238a	52.22N	13.31E
Dieppe, Can. (dē-ĕp')	92	46.06N	64.45W
Dieppe, Fr.	147	49.54N	1.05E
Dierks, Ar., U.S. (dērks)	111	34.06N	94.02W
Diessem, neigh., Ger.	236	51.20N	6.35E
Diessen, Ger. (dēs'sĕn)	145d	47.57N	11.06E
Diest, Bel.	145a	50.59N	5.05E
Digby, Can. (dĭg'bĭ)	85	44.37N	65.46W
Dighton, Ma., U.S. (dī-tŭn)	100b	41.49N	71.05W
Digmoor, Eng., U.K.	237a	53.32N	2.45W
Digne, Fr. (dēn'y')	157	44.07N	6.16E
Digoin, Fr. (dē-gwăn')	156	46.28N	4.06E
Digra, India	240a	22.50N	88.20E
Digul, r., Indon.	197	7.00S	140.27E
Dijohan Point, c., Phil. (dē-kō-än)	197a	16.24N	122.25E
Dijon, Fr. (dē-zhôn')	142	47.21N	5.02E
Dikson, Russia (dĭk'sŏn)	164	73.30N	80.35E
Dikwa, Nig. (dē'kwȧ)	211	12.06N	13.53E
Dili, Indon. (dĭl'ē)	197	8.35S	125.35E
Di Linosa Island, i., Italy (dē-lē-nō'sä)	148	36.01N	12.43E
Dilizhan, Arm.	167	40.45N	45.00E
Dillingham, Ak., U.S. (dĭl'ĭng-hăm)	96a	59.10N	158.38W
Dillon, Mt., U.S. (dĭl'ŭn)	105	45.12N	112.40W
Dillon, S.C., U.S.	115	34.24N	79.28W
Dillon Park, Md., U.S.	229d	38.52N	76.56W
Dillon Reservoir, res., Oh., U.S.	98	40.05N	82.05W
Dilolo, Zaire (dē-lō'lō)	212	10.19S	22.23E
Dimashq *see* Damascus, Syria	182	33.31N	36.18E
Dimbokro, C. Iv.	214	6.39N	4.42W
Dimitrovo *see* Pernik, Bul.	149	42.36N	23.04E
Dimlang, mtn., Nig.	215	8.24N	11.47E
Dimona, Isr.	181a	31.03N	35.01E
Dinagat Island, i., Phil.	197	10.15N	126.15E
Dinājpur, Bngl.	186	25.38N	87.39E
Dinan, Fr. (dē-nän')	156	48.27N	2.03W
Dinant, Bel. (dē-nän')	151	50.17N	4.50E
Dinara, mts., Yugo. (dē'nä-rä)	149	43.50N	16.15E
Dinard, Fr.	156	48.38N	2.04W
Dindigul, India	187	10.25N	78.03E
Dingalan Bay, b., Phil. (dĭŋ-gä'län)	197a	15.19N	121.33E
Dingle, Ire. (dĭng''l)	150	52.10N	10.13W
Dingle, neigh., Eng., U.K.	237a	53.23N	2.57W
Dingle Bay, b., Ire.	147	52.02N	10.15W
Dingo, Austl. (dĭŋ'gō)	203	23.45S	149.26E
Dinguiraye, Gui.	214	11.18N	10.43W
Dingwall, Scot., U.K. (dĭng'wôl)	150	57.37N	4.23W
Dingxian, China (dĭŋ shyĕn)	192	38.30N	115.00E
Dingxing, China (dĭŋ-shyĭŋ)	192	39.18N	115.50E
Dingyuan, China (dĭŋ-yůän)	190	32.32N	117.40E
Dingzi Wan, b., China	190	36.33N	121.06E
Dinosaur National Monument, rec., Co., U.S. (dī'nō-sôr)	105	40.45N	109.17W
Dinslaken, Ger. (dēns'lä-kĕn)	157c	51.33N	6.44E
Dinslakener Bruch, Ger.	236	51.35N	6.43E
Dinteloord, Neth.	145a	51.38N	4.21E
Dinuba, Ca., U.S. (dĭ-nū'bȧ)	108	36.33N	119.29W
Dinwiddie, S. Afr.	244b	26.16S	28.10E
Dios, Cayo de, i., Cuba (kä'yō-dĕ-dē-ōs')	122	22.05N	83.05W
Diourbel, Sen. (dē-ōōr-bĕl')	210	14.40N	16.15W
Diphu Pass, p., Asia (dĭ-pōō)	188	28.15N	96.45E
Diquis, r., C.R. (dē-kēs')	121	8.59N	83.24W
Dire Dawa, Eth.	211	9.40N	41.47E
Diriamba, Nic. (dēr-yäm'bä)	120	11.52N	86.15W
Dirk Hartog, i., Austl.	202	26.25S	113.15E
Dirksland, Neth.	145a	51.45N	4.04E
Dirranbandi, Austl. (dĭ-rȧ-băn'dē)	203	28.24S	148.29E
Dirty Devil, r., Ut., U.S. (dûr'tĭ dĕv''l)	109	38.20N	110.30W
Disappointment, l., Austl.	202	23.20S	123.00E
Disappointment, Cape, c., Wa., U.S. (dĭs'ȧ-point'ment)	106c	46.16N	124.11W
Discovery, S. Afr. (dĭs-kŭv'ẽr-ĭ)	213b	26.10S	27.53E
Discovery, is., Can. (dĭs-kŭv'ẽr-ē)	106a	48.25N	123.13W
Disko, i., Grnld. (dĭs'kō)	82	70.00N	54.00W
Disna, Bela. (dēs'nȧ)	166	55.34N	28.15E
Disneyland, pt. of i., Ca., U.S.	232	33.48N	117.55W
Dispur, India	186	26.00N	91.50E
Disraëli, Can. (dĭs-rā'lĭ)	91	45.53N	71.23W
Disteln, Ger.	236	51.36N	7.09E
District Heights, Md., U.S.	229d	38.51N	76.53W
District of Columbia, state, U.S.	97	38.50N	77.00W
Distrito Federal, dept., Braz. (dēs-trē'tô-fē-dē-rä'l)	131	15.49S	47.39W
Distrito Federal, dept., Mex.	118	19.14N	99.08W
Disūq, Egypt (dē-sōōk')	218b	31.07N	30.41E
Ditton, Eng., U.K.	235	51.18N	0.27E
Diu, India (dē'ōō)	183	20.48N	70.58E
Divilacan Bay, b., Phil. (dē-vē-lä'kän)	197a	17.26N	122.25E
Divinópolis, Braz. (dē-vē-nô'pō-lēs)	131	20.10S	44.53W
Divo, C. Iv.	214	5.50N	5.22W
Dixon, Il., U.S. (dĭks'ŭn)	103	41.50N	89.30W
Dixon Entrance, strt., N.A.	84	54.25N	132.00W
Diyarbakir, Tur. (dē-yär-bĕk'ĭr)	182	38.00N	40.10E
Dja, r., Afr.	211	2.30N	14.00E
Djakovo, neigh., Russia	239b	55.39N	37.40E
Djambala, Congo	216	2.33S	14.45E
Djanet, Alg.	210	24.29N	9.26E
Djebobo, mtn., Ghana	214	8.20N	0.37E
Djedi, Oued, r., Alg.	148	34.18N	4.39E
Djelo-Binza, Zaire	244c	4.23S	15.16E
Djember, Chad	215	10.25N	17.50E
Djerba, Île de, i., Tun.	148	33.53N	11.26E
Djerid, Chott, l., Tun. (jĕr'ĭd)	210	33.15N	8.29E
Djibasso, Burkina	214	13.07N	4.10W
Djibo, Burkina	214	14.06N	1.38W
Djibouti, Dji. (jē-bōō-tē')	218a	11.34N	43.00E
Djibouti, nation, Afr.	218a	11.35N	48.08E
Djokoumatombi, Congo	216	0.47N	15.22E
Djokupunda, Zaire	212	5.27S	20.58E
Djoua, r., Afr.	216	1.25N	13.40E
Djursholm, Swe. (djōōrs'hōlm)	152	59.26N	18.01E
Dmitriyev-L'govskiy, Russia (d'mē'trĭ-yĕf l'gôf'skĭ)	162	52.07N	35.05E
Dmitrov, Russia (d'mē'trôf)	162	56.21N	37.32E
Dmitrovsk, Russia (d'mē'trôfsk)	162	52.30N	35.10E
Dmytrivka, Ukr.	163	47.57N	38.56E
Dnepropetrovsk *see* Dnipropetrovs'k, Ukr.	164	48.15N	34.08E
Dnestrovskiy Liman, l., Ukr.	163	46.13N	29.50E
Dnieper (Dnipro), r., Eur.	167	46.45N	33.40E
Dniester, r., Eur.	167	48.21N	28.10E
Dniprodzerzhyns'k, Ukr.	167	48.32N	34.38E
Dniprodzerzhyns'ke vodoskhovyshche, res., Ukr.	164	49.00N	34.10E
Dnipropetrovs'k, Ukr.	164	48.15N	34.08E
Dnipropetrovs'k, prov., Ukr.	163	48.15N	34.10E
Dniprovs'kyy lyman, b., Ukr.	163	46.33N	31.45E
Dno, Russia (d'nô')	162	57.49N	29.59E
Do, Lac, l., Mali	214	15.50N	2.20W
Doba, Chad	215	8.39N	16.51E
Dobbs Ferry, N.Y., U.S. (dŏbz'fĕ'rē)	100a	41.01N	73.53W
Dobbyn, Austl. (dôb'ĭn)	202	19.45S	140.02E
Dobele, Lat. (dô'bĕ-lĕ)	153	56.37N	23.18E
Doberai, Jazirah, pen., Indon.	197	1.25S	133.15E
Döbling, neigh., Aus.	239e	48.15N	16.22E
Dobo, Indon.	197	6.00S	134.18E
Doboj, Bos. (dō'boi)	161	44.42N	18.04E
Dobrich, Bul.	149	43.33N	27.52E
Dobryanka, Russia (dôb-ryän'kȧ)	172a	58.27N	56.26E
Dobšina, Slvk. (dôp'shē-nä)	155	48.48N	20.25E
Doce, r., Braz. (dō'sȧ)	131	19.01S	42.14W
Doce, Canal Numero, can., Arg.	129c	36.47S	59.00W
Doce Leguas, Cayos de las, is., Cuba	122	20.55N	79.05W
Doctor Arroyo, Mex. (dōk-tōr' är-rō'yō)	118	23.41N	100.10W
Doddinghurst, Eng., U.K.	235	51.40N	0.18E
Doddington, Eng., U.K. (dŏd'dĭng-tŏn)	144b	51.17N	0.47E
Dodecanese *see* Dhodhekánisos, is., Grc.	161	38.00N	26.10E
Dodge City, Ks., U.S. (dŏj)	96	37.44N	100.01W
Dodgeville, Wi., U.S. (dŏj'vĭl)	103	42.58N	90.07W
Dodoma, Tan. (dō'dō-mȧ)	212	6.11S	35.45E
Dog, l., Can. (dŏg)	90	48.42N	89.24W
Dogger Bank, bk. (dŏg'gẽr)	151	55.07N	2.25E
Dogubayazit, Tur.	167	39.35N	44.00E
Doha *see* Ad Dawhah, Qatar	182	25.02N	51.28E
Dohad, India	186	22.52N	74.18E
Doiran, l., Grc.	161	41.10N	23.00E
Dokshitsy, Bela. (dôk-shētsē)	162	54.53N	27.49E
Dolbeau, Can.	85	48.52N	72.16W
Dole, Fr. (dōl)	147	47.07N	5.28E
Dolgaya, Kosa, c., Russia (kô'sȧ dôl-gä'yä)	163	46.42N	37.42E
Dolgeville, N.Y., U.S.	99	43.10N	74.45W
Dolgiy, i., Russia	166	69.20N	59.20E
Dolgoprudnyy, Russia	172b	55.57N	37.33E
Dolinsk, Russia (dá-lēnsk')	171	47.29N	142.31E
Dollard-des-Ormeaux, Can.	227b	45.29N	73.49W
Dollar Harbor, b., Bah.	122	25.30N	79.15W
Dolomite, Al., U.S. (dŏl'ō-mīt)	100h	33.28N	86.57W
Dolomiti, mts., Italy	160	46.16N	11.43E
Dolores, Arg. (dō-lō'rĕs)	132	36.20S	57.42W
Dolores, Col.	130a	3.33N	74.54W
Dolores, Tx., U.S. (dō-lō'rĕs)	112	27.42N	99.47W
Dolores, Ur.	129c	33.32S	58.15W
Dolores, r., Co., U.S.	109	38.35N	108.50W
Dolores Hidalgo, Mex. (dō-lô'rĕs-ē-däl'gō)	118	21.09N	100.56W
Dolphin and Union Strait, strt., Can. (dŏl'fĭn ūn'yŭn)	84	69.22N	117.10W
Dolton, Il., U.S.	231a	41.39N	87.37W
Dolyna, Ukr.	155	48.57N	24.01E
Domažlice, Czech Rep. (dō'mäzh-lē-tsĕ)	154	49.27N	12.55E
Dombasle-sur-Meurthe, Fr. (dôn-bäl')	157	48.38N	6.18E
Dombóvár, Hung. (dŏm'bō-vär)	155	46.22N	18.08E
Domeyko, Cordillera, mts., Chile (kôr-dēl-yĕ'rä-dō-mā'kō)	130	20.50S	69.02W
Dominguez, Ca., U.S.	232	33.50N	118.31W
Dominica, nation, N.A. (dō-mĭ-nē'kȧ)	117	15.30N	60.45W
Dominica Channel, strt., N.A.	121b	15.00N	61.30W
Dominican Republic, nation, N.A. (dō-mĭn'ĭ-kăn)	117	19.00N	70.45W
Dominion, Can. (dō-mĭn'yŭn)	93	46.13N	60.01W
Domiongo, Zaire	216	4.37S	21.15E
Domitilla, Catacombe di, pt. of i., Italy	239c	41.52N	12.31E
Domodedovo, Russia (dô-mô-dyĕ'do-vô)	172b	55.27N	37.45E
Dom Silvério, Braz. (dôn-sĕl-vĕ'ryō)	129a	20.09S	42.57W
Don, r., Can.	227c	43.39N	79.21W
Don, r., Russia	164	49.50N	41.30E

ng-sing; ŋ-baŋk; ɴ-nasalized n; nŏd; cŏmmit; ōld; ôbey; ôrder; oi-boil; fōōd; ŏŏ-as oo in foot; ou-out; s-soft; sh-dish; th-thin; pūre; ûnite; ûrn; stŭd; circŭs; ü-as in French tu; '-indeterminate vowel.

PLACE (Pronunciation)	PAGE	Lat. °′	Long. °′
Don, r., Eng., U.K.	144a	53.39N	0.58W
Don, r., Scot., U.K.	150	57.19N	2.39W
Donaldson, Mi., U.S. (dŏn'ăl-sŭn)	107k	46.19N	84.22W
Donaldsonville, La., U.S. (dŏn'ăld-sŭn-vĭl)	113	30.05N	90.58W
Donalsonville, Ga., U.S.	114	31.02N	84.50W
Donaufeld, neigh., Italy	239e	48.15N	16.25E
Donaustadt, neigh., Aus.	239e	48.13N	16.30E
Donauturm, pt. of i., Aus.	239e	48.14N	16.25E
Donawitz, Aus. (dō'nȧ-vĭts)	154	47.23N	15.05E
Don Benito, Spain (dōn'bȧ-nē'tō)	158	38.55N	5.52W
Dönberg, Ger.	236	51.18N	7.10E
Don Bosco, neigh., Arg.	233d	34.42S	58.19W
Doncaster, Austl. (doŋ'kăs-tẽr)	201a	37.47S	145.08E
Doncaster, Can.	227c	43.48N	79.25W
Doncaster, Eng., U.K. (doŋ'kăs-tẽr)	150	53.32N	1.07W
Doncaster East, Austl.	243b	37.47S	145.10E
Dondo, Ang. (dōn'dō)	212	9.38S	14.25E
Dondo, Moz.	212	19.33S	34.47E
Dondra Head, c., Sri L.	183b	5.52N	80.52E
Donegal, Ire. (dŏn-ē-gôl')	150	54.44N	8.05W
Donegal Bay, Ire. (dŏn-ē-gôl')	146	54.35N	8.36W
Donets Coal Basin, reg., Ukr. (dō-nyĕts')	163	48.15N	38.50E
Donets'k, Ukr.	164	48.00N	37.35E
Donets'k, prov., Ukr.	163	47.55N	37.40E
Dong, r., China (dôŋ)	189	24.13N	115.08E
Dongara, Austl. (dôn-gă'rȧ)	202	29.15S	115.00E
Dongba, China (dôŋ-bä)	190	31.40N	119.02E
Dongba, China	240b	39.58N	116.32E
Dongbahe, China	240b	39.58N	116.27E
Dong'e, China (dôŋ-ŭ)	190	36.21N	116.14E
Dong'ezhen, China	192	36.11N	116.16E
Dongfang, China (dôŋ-fäŋ)	193	19.08N	108.42E
Donggala, Indon. (dôn-gä'lä)	196	0.45S	119.32E
Dongguan, China (dôŋ-gůän)	191a	23.03N	113.46E
Dongguang, China (dôŋ-gůäŋ)	190	37.54N	116.33E
Donghai, China (dôŋ-hī)	192	34.35N	119.05E
Dong Hoi, Viet. (dông-hô-ē')	196	17.25N	106.42E
Dongila, Eth.	211	11.17N	37.00E
Dongming, China (dôŋ-mĭŋ)	190	35.16N	115.06E
Dongo, Ang. (dôŋ'gō)	212	14.45S	15.30E
Dongon Point, c., Phil. (dŏng-ōn')	197a	12.43N	120.35E
Dongou, Congo (dôŋ-gōō')	211	2.02N	18.04E
Dongping, China (dôŋ-pĭŋ)	192	35.50N	116.24E
Dongping Hu, l., China (dôŋ-pĭŋ hōō)	190	36.06N	116.24E
Dongshan, China (doŋ-shän)	190	31.05N	120.24E
Dongshi, China	240b	39.49N	116.34E
Dongtai, China	190	32.51N	120.20E
Dongting Hu, l., China (dôŋ-tĭŋ hōō)	189	29.10N	112.30E
Dongxiang, China (dôŋ-shyän)	193	28.18N	116.38E
Doniphan, Mo., U.S. (dŏn'ĭ-făn)	111	36.37N	90.50W
Donji Vakuf, Bos. (dōn'yĭ väk'ŏŏf)	161	44.08N	17.25E
Don Martin, Presa de, res., Mex. (prĕ'sä-dĕ-dôn-mär-tē'n)	112	27.35N	100.38W
Donnacona, Can.	91	46.40N	71.46W
Donnemarie-en-Montois, Fr. (dôn-mä-rē'ĕN-môN-twä')	157b	48.29N	3.09E
Donner und Blitzen, r., Or., U.S. (dŏn'ẽr ŏnt'blĭ'tsĕn)	104	42.45N	118.57W
Donnybrook, S. Afr. (dŏ-nĭ-brŏŏk)	213c	29.56S	29.54E
Donora, Pa., U.S. (dŏ-nō'rȧ)	101e	40.10N	79.51W
Don Torcuato, Arg.	233d	34.29S	58.37W
Doolow, Som.	218a	4.10N	42.05E
Doonerak, Mount, mtn., Ak., U.S. (dōō'nē-răk)	95	68.00N	150.34W
Doorn, Neth.	145a	52.02N	5.21E
Door Peninsula, pen., Wi., U.S. (dōr)	103	44.40N	87.36W
Dora Baltea, r., Italy (dō'rä bäl'tä-ä)	160	45.40N	7.34E
Doraville, Ga., U.S. (dō'rȧ-vĭl)	100c	33.54N	84.17W
Dorchester, Eng., U.K. (dôr'chĕs-tẽr)	150	50.45N	2.34W
Dorchester Heights National Historic Site, hist., Ma., U.S.	227a	42.20N	71.03W
Dordogne, r., Fr. (dôr-dôn'yĕ)	142	44.53N	0.16E
Dordrecht, Neth. (dôr'drĕĸt)	151	51.48N	4.39E
Dordrecht, S. Afr. (dô'drĕĸt)	213c	31.24S	27.06E
Doré Lake, l., Can.	88	54.31N	107.06W
Dorgali, Italy (dôr'gä-lē)	160	40.18N	9.37E
Dörgön Nuur, l., Mong.	188	47.47N	94.01E
Dorion-Vaudreuil, Can. (dôr-yō)	83a	45.23N	74.01W
Dorking, Eng., U.K. (dôr'kĭng)	144b	51.12N	0.20W
Dormont, Pa., U.S. (dôr'mŏnt)	101e	40.24N	80.02W
Dornap, Ger.	236	51.15N	7.04E
Dornbirn, Aus. (dôrn'bĕrn)	154	47.24N	9.45E
Dornoch, Scot., U.K. (dôr'nŏĸ)	146	57.55N	4.01W
Dornoch Firth, b., Scot., U.K. (dôr'nŏĸ fûrth)	150	57.55N	3.55W
Dorogobuzh, Russia (dôrôgô'-bōō'zh)	162	54.57N	33.18E
Dorohoi, Rom. (dō-rō-hoi')	155	47.57N	26.28E
Dorre Island, i., Austl. (dôr)	202	25.19S	113.10E
Dorseyville, Pa., U.S.	230b	40.35N	79.53W
Dorstfeld, neigh., Ger.	236	51.31N	7.25E
Dorstsen, Ger.	157c	51.40N	6.58E
Dortmund, Ger. (dôrt'mŏŏnt)	147	51.31N	7.28E
Dortmund-Ems-Kanal, can., Ger. (dōrt'mōōnd-ĕms'kä-näl')	157c	51.50N	7.25E
Dörtyol, Tur. (dûrt'yōl)	149	36.50N	36.20E
Dorval, Can. (dôr-vȧl')	83a	45.26N	73.44W
Dos Bahías, Cabo, c., Arg. (kȧ'bō-dōs-bä-ē'äs)	132	44.55S	65.35W
Dos Caminos, Ven. (dôs-kä-mē'nōs)	131b	9.38N	67.17W
Dosewallips, r., Wa., U.S. (dō'sē-wäl'lĭps)	106a	47.45N	123.04W
Dos Hermanas, Spain (dōsĕr-mä'näs)	158	37.17N	5.56W
Dosso, Niger (dŏs-sō')	210	13.03N	3.12E
Dothan, Al., U.S. (dō'thăn)	97	31.13N	85.23W
Douai, Fr. (dōō-ā')	147	50.23N	3.04E
Douala, Cam. (dōō-ä'lä)	210	4.03N	9.42E
Douarnenez, Fr. (dōō-ȧr nĕ-nĕs')	156	48.06N	4.18W
Double Bayou, Tx., U.S. (dŭb''l bī'yōō)	113a	29.40N	94.38W
Doubs, r., Eur.	157	46.15N	5.50E
Douentza, Mali	214	15.00N	2.57W
Douglas, I. of Man (dŭg'lăs)	150	54.10N	4.24W
Douglas, Ak., U.S. (dŭg'lăs)	95	58.18N	134.35W
Douglas, Az., U.S.	96	31.20N	109.30W
Douglas, Ga., U.S.	115	31.30N	82.53W
Douglas, Wy., U.S. (dŭg'lăs)	105	42.45N	105.21W
Douglas, r., Eng., U.K. (dŭg'lăs)	144a	53.38N	2.48W
Douglas Channel, strt., Can.	86	53.30N	129.12W
Douglas Lake, res., Tn., U.S. (dŭg'lăs)	114	36.00N	83.35W
Douglas Lake Indian Reserve, I.R., Can.	87	50.10N	120.49W
Douglasville, Ga., U.S. (dŭg'lăs-vĭl)	114	33.45N	84.47W
Dourada, Serra, mts., Braz. (sĕ'r-rä-dôōō-rȧ'dä)	131	15.11S	49.57W
Dourdan, Fr. (dōōr-däN')	157b	48.32N	2.01E
Douro, r., Eur. (dwĕ'rō)	142	41.30N	4.30W
Douro, r., Port. (dô'ō-rō)	158	41.03N	8.12W
Dove, r., Eng., U.K. (dŭv)	144a	52.53N	1.47W
Dover, S. Afr.	218d	27.05S	27.44E
Dover, Eng., U.K.	142	51.08N	1.19E
Dover, De., U.S. (dō vẽr)	97	39.10N	75.30W
Dover, N.H., U.S.	99	43.15N	71.00W
Dover, N.J., U.S.	100a	40.53N	74.33W
Dover, Oh., U.S.	98	40.35N	81.30W
Dover, Strait of, strt., Eur.	142	50.50N	1.15W
Dover-Foxcroft, Me., U.S. (dō'vẽr fôks'krôft)	92	45.10N	69.15W
Dover Heights, Austl.	243a	33.53S	151.17E
Doveton, Austl.	243b	38.00S	145.14E
Dovre Fjell, mts., Nor. (dŏv'rĕ fyĕl')	142	62.03N	8.36E
Dow, Il., U.S. (dou)	107e	39.01N	90.20W
Dowagiac, Mi., U.S. (dō-wô'jăk)	98	42.00N	86.05W
Dowlatābād, Iran	241h	35.37N	51.27E
Downers Grove, Il., U.S. (dou'nẽrz grōv)	101a	41.48N	88.00W
Downey, Ca., U.S. (dou'nĭ)	107a	33.56N	118.08W
Downieville, Ca., U.S. (dou'nĭ-nĭl)	108	39.35N	120.48W
Downs, Ks., U.S. (dounz)	110	39.29N	98.32W
Doylestown, Oh., U.S. (doilz'toun)	101d	40.58N	81.43W
Drâa, Cap, c., Mor. (drȧ)	210	28.39N	12.15W
Drâa, Oued, r., Afr.	210	28.00N	9.31W
Drabiv, Ukr.	163	49.57N	32.14E
Drac, r., Fr. (dräk)	157	44.50N	5.47E
Dracut, Ma., U.S. (drā'kŭt)	93a	42.40N	71.19W
Draganovo, Bul. (drä-gä-nō'vō)	161	43.13N	25.45E
Drăgăşani, Rom. (drä-gȧ-shän'ĭ)	161	44.39N	24.18E
Draguignan, Fr. (drä-gēn-yäN')	157	43.35N	6.28E
Drakensberg, mts., Afr. (drä'kĕnz-bĕrgh)	212	29.15S	29.07E
Drake Passage, strt. (drāk păs'ĭj)	128	57.00S	65.00W
Dráma, Grc. (drä'mä)	149	41.09N	24.10E
Drammen, Nor. (dräm'ĕn)	146	59.45N	10.15E
Drancy, Fr.	237c	48.56N	2.27E
Drau (Drava), r., Eur. (drou)	154	46.44N	13.45E
Drava, r., Eur. (drä'vä)	142	45.45N	17.30E
Draveil, Fr.	237c	48.41N	2.25E
Dravograd, Slvn. (drä'vō-gräd')	160	46.37N	15.01E
Dravosburg, Pa., U.S.	230b	40.21N	79.51W
Drawsko Pomorskie, Pol. (dräv'skō pō-mōr'skyĕ)	154	53.31N	15.50E
Drayton Harbor, b., Wa., U.S. (drā'tŭn)	106d	48.58N	122.40W
Drayton Plains, Mi., U.S.	101b	42.41N	83.23W
Drayton Valley, Can.	87	53.13N	114.59W
Drensteinfurt, Ger. (drĕn'shtīn-fōōrt)	157c	51.47N	7.44E
Dresden, Ger. (drās'dĕn)	142	51.05N	13.45E
Dreux, Fr. (drû)	156	48.44N	1.24E
Drewitz, neigh., Ger.	238a	52.22N	13.08E
Drexel Hill, Pa., U.S.	229b	39.57N	75.19W
Driefontein, S. Afr.	218d	25.53S	29.10E
Drin, r., Alb. (drēn)	161	42.13N	20.13E
Drina, r., Yugo. (drē'nä)	149	44.09N	19.30E
Drinit, Pellg i, b., Alb.	161	41.42N	19.17E
Dr. Ir. W. J. van Blommestein Meer, res., Sur.	131	4.45N	55.05W
Drissa, Bela. (drĭs'sä)	162	55.48N	27.59E
Drissa, r., Eur.	162	55.44N	28.58E
Driver, Va., U.S.	100g	36.50N	76.30W
Dröbak, Nor. (drû'bäk)	152	59.40N	10.35E
Drobeta-Turnu Severin, Rom. (sĕ-vĕ-rēn')	149	43.54N	24.49E
Drogheda, Ire. (drŏ'hē-dȧ)	146	53.43N	6.15W
Drogichin, Bela. (drō-gē'chĭn)	155	52.10N	25.11E
Drohobych, Ukr.	155	49.21N	23.31E
Drôme, r., Fr. (drōm)	156	44.42N	4.53E
Dronfield, Eng., U.K. (drŏn'fēld)	144a	53.18N	1.28W
Droylsden, Eng., U.K.	237b	53.29N	2.10W
Drumheller, Can. (drŭm-hĕl-ẽr)	84	51.28N	112.42W
Drummond, i., Mi., U.S. (drŭm'ŭnd)	98	46.00N	83.50W
Drummondville, Can. (drŭm'ŭnd-vĭl)	85	45.53N	72.33W
Drummoyne, Austl.	243a	33.51S	151.09E
Drumright, Ok., U.S. (drŭm'rīt)	111	35.59N	96.37W
Drunen, Neth.	145a	51.41N	5.10E
Drut', r., Bela. (drōōt)	162	53.40N	29.45E
Druya, Bela. (drŏ'yȧ)	162	55.45N	27.26E
Družba, Russia	239b	55.53N	37.45E
Drwęca, r., Pol. (d'r-văn'tsȧ)	155	53.06N	19.13E
Dryden, Can. (drī-dĕn)	85	49.47N	92.50W
Drysdale, Austl.	201a	38.11S	144.34E
Dry Tortugas, is., Fl., U.S. (tôr-tōō'gäz)	115a	24.37N	82.45W
Dschang, Cam. (dshäng)	210	5.34N	10.09E
Duabo, Lib.	214	5.40N	8.05W
Duagh, Can.	83g	53.43N	113.24W
Duarte, Ca., U.S.	232	34.08N	117.58W
Duarte, Pico, mtn., Dom. Rep. (dŭŭ'ärtĕh pēcō)	117	19.00N	71.00W
Duas Barras, Braz. (dōō'äs-bȧ'r-räs)	129a	22.03S	42.30W
Dubai see Dubayy, U.A.E.	182	25.18N	55.26E
Dubăsari, Mol.	163	47.16N	29.11E
Dubawnt, l., Can. (dōō-bônt')	84	63.27N	103.30W
Dubawnt, r., Can.	84	61.30N	103.49W
Dubayy, U.A.E.	182	25.18N	55.26E
Dubbo, Austl. (dŭb'ō)	203	32.20S	148.42E
Dubie, Zaire	217	8.33S	28.32E
Dublin, Ire.	142	53.20N	6.15W
Dublin, Ca., U.S. (dŭb'lĭn)	106b	37.42N	121.56W
Dublin, Ga., U.S.	115	32.33N	82.55W
Dublin, Tx., U.S.	112	32.05N	98.20W
Dubno, Ukr. (dōō'b-nô)	155	50.24N	25.44E
Du Bois, Pa., U.S. (dŏ-bois')	99	41.10N	78.45W
Dubovka, Russia (dŏ-bôf'kȧ)	167	49.00N	44.50E
Dubrovka, Russia (dōō-brôf'kȧ)	172c	59.51N	30.56E
Dubrovnik, Cro. (dŏ'brôv-nĕk) (rä-gōō'sä)	142	42.40N	18.10E
Dubrovno, Bela. (dōō-brôf'nō)	162	54.39N	30.54E
Dubuque, Ia., U.S. (dŏ-būk')	97	42.30N	90.43W
Duchesne, Ut., U.S. (dŏ-shān')	109	40.12N	110.23W
Duchesne, r., Ut., U.S.	109	40.20N	110.50W
Duchess, Austl. (dŭch'ĕs)	202	21.30S	139.55E
Ducie Island, i., Pit. (dū-sē')	2	25.30S	126.20W
Duck, r., Tn., U.S.	114	35.55N	87.40W
Duckabush, r., Wa., U.S. (dŭk'ȧ-bŏsh)	106a	47.41N	123.09W
Duck Lake, Can.	88	52.47N	106.13W
Duck Mountain, mtn., Can.	89	51.35N	101.00W
Ducktown, Tn., U.S. (dŭk'toun)	114	35.03N	84.20W
Duck Valley Indian Reservation, I.R., Id., U.S.	104	42.02N	115.49W
Duckwater Peak, mtn., Nv., U.S. (dŭk-wô-tẽr)	108	39.00N	115.31W
Duda, r., Col. (dōō'dä)	130a	3.25N	74.23W
Dudinka, Russia (dōō-dĭn'kȧ)	164	69.15N	85.42E
Dudley, Eng., U.K. (dŭd'lĭ)	147	52.28N	2.07E
Dufourspitze, mtn., Eur.	154	45.55N	7.52E
Dugger, In., U.S. (dŭg'ẽr)	98	39.00N	87.10W
Dugi Otok, i., Yugo. (dōō'gē o'tôk)	160	44.03N	14.40E
Dugny, Fr.	237c	48.57N	2.25E
Duisburg, Ger. (dōō'ĭs-bŏrgh)	147	51.26N	6.46E
Duissern, neigh., Ger.	236	51.26N	6.47E
Dukhān, Qatar	185	25.25N	50.48E
Dukhovshchina, Russia (dōō-ĸôfsh-'chēnȧ)	162	55.13N	32.26E
Dukinfield, Eng., U.K. (dŭk'ĭn-fēld)	144a	53.28N	2.05W
Dukla Pass, p., Eur. (dŏ'klä)	147	49.25N	21.44E
Dulce, Golfo, b., C.R. (gōl'fō dōōl'sā)	117	8.25N	83.13W
Dülken, Ger. (dül'kĕn)	157c	51.15N	6.21E
Dülmen, Ger. (dül'mĕn)	157c	51.50N	7.17E
Duluth, Mn., U.S. (dŏ-lōōth')	97	46.50N	92.07W
Dulwich, neigh., Eng., U.K.	235	51.26N	0.05W
Dumai, Indon.	181b	1.39N	101.30E
Dumali Point, c., Phil. (dōō-mä'lē)	197a	13.07N	121.42E
Dumas, Tx., U.S.	110	35.52N	101.58W
Dumbarton, Scot., U.K. (dŭm'băr-tŭn)	150	56.00N	4.35W
Dum-Dum, India	186a	22.37N	88.25E
Dumfries, Scot., U.K. (dŭm-frēs')	150	55.05N	3.40W
Dumjor, India	186a	22.37N	88.14E
Dumont, N.J., U.S. (dōō'mŏnt)	100a	40.56N	74.00W
Dümpten, neigh., Ger.	236	51.27N	6.54E
Dumyāt, Egypt	211	31.22N	31.50E
Dunaföldvár, Hung. (dŏ'nô-fûld'vär)	155	46.48N	18.55E
Dunajec, r., Pol. (dŏ-nä'yĕts)	155	49.52N	20.53E
Dunaújváros, Hung.	155	46.57N	18.55E
Dunay, Russia (dōō'nī)	172c	59.59N	30.57E
Dunayivtsi, Ukr.	163	48.52N	26.51E
Dunbar, W.V., U.S.	98	38.20N	81.45W
Duncan, Can. (dŭŋ'kăn)	84	48.47N	123.42W
Duncan, Ok., U.S.	111	34.29N	97.56W
Duncan, r., Can.	87	50.30N	116.45W
Duncan Dam, dam, Can.	87	50.15N	116.55W
Duncan Lake, l., Can.	87	50.20N	117.00W
Duncansby Head, c., Scot., U.K. (dŭn'kănz-bĭ)	150	58.40N	3.01W
Duncanville, Tx., U.S. (dŭn'kăn-vĭl)	107c	32.39N	96.55W
Dundalk, Ire. (dŭn'kôk)	146	54.00N	6.18W
Dundalk, Md., U.S.	100e	39.16N	76.31W
Dundalk Bay, b., Ire. (dŭn'dôk)	150	53.55N	6.15W
Dundas, Austl.	243a	33.48S	151.02E
Dundas, Can. (dŭn-dăs')	91	43.16N	79.58W
Dundas, l., Austl. (dŭn-dȧs)	202	32.15S	122.00E
Dundas Island, i., Can.	86	54.33N	130.55W
Dundas Strait, strt., Austl.	202	10.35S	131.15E
Dundedin, Fl., U.S. (dŭn-ē'dĭn)	115a	28.00N	82.43W
Dundee, S. Afr.	213c	28.14S	30.16E
Dundee, Scot., U.K.	142	56.30N	2.55W
Dundee, Il., U.S. (dŭn-dē)	101a	42.06N	88.17W
Dundrum Bay, b., N. Ire., U.K. (dŭn-drŭm')	150	54.13N	5.47W
Dunedin, N.Z.	203a	45.48S	170.32E
Dunellen, N.J., U.S. (dŭn-ĕl'l'n)	100a	40.36N	74.28W
Dunfermline, Scot., U.K. (dŭn-fẽrm'lĭn)	150	56.05N	3.30W
Dungarvan, Ire. (dŭn-gȧr'văn)	150	52.06N	7.50W
Dungeness, Wa., U.S. (dŭnj-nĕs')	106a	48.09N	123.07W
Dungeness, r., Wa., U.S.	106a	48.03N	123.10W
Dungeness Spit, Wa., U.S.	106a	48.11N	123.03W
Dunham Town, Eng., U.K.	237b	53.23N	2.24W
Dunheved, Austl.	243a	33.45S	150.47E
Dunhua, China (dŏn-hwä)	189	43.18N	128.10E
Dunkerque, Fr. (dŭN-kĕrk')	147	51.02N	2.37E
Dunkirk, In., U.S. (dŭn'kûrk)	98	40.20N	85.25W
Dunkwa, Ghana	214	5.22N	1.12W
Dun Laoghaire, Ire. (dŭn-lā'rē)	146	53.16N	6.09W
Dunlap, Ia., U.S. (dŭn'lăp)	102	41.53N	95.33W
Dunlap, Tn., U.S.	114	35.23N	85.23W
Dunmore, Pa., U.S. (dŭn'mōr)	99	41.25N	75.30W
Dunn, N.C., U.S. (dŭn)	115	35.18N	78.37W
Dunnellon, Fl., U.S. (dŭn-ĕl'ŏn)	115	29.02N	82.28W

ăt; finăl; rāte; senȧte; ärm; ȧsk; sofȧ; fâre; ch-choose; dh-as th in other; bē; ēvent; bĕt; recĕnt; cratẽr; g-gō; gh-guttural g; bĭt; ĭ-short neutral; rīde; ĸ-guttural k as ch in German ich;

PRONOUNCING INDEX

Dunn Loring-Edremit 283

PLACE (Pronunciation)	PAGE	Lat. °′	Long. °′
Dunn Loring, Va., U.S.	229d	38.53N	77.14W
Dunnville, Can. (dŭn'vĭl)	91	42.55N	79.40W
Dunqulah, Sudan	211	19.21N	30.19E
Dunsmuir, Ca., U.S. (dŭnz'mūr)	104	41.08N	122.17W
Dunton Green, Eng., U.K.	235	51.18N	0.11E
Dunton Wayletts, Eng., U.K.	235	51.35N	0.24E
Dunvegan, S. Afr.	244b	26.09S	28.09E
Dunwoody, Ga., U.S. (dŭn-wŏŏd'ĭ)	100c	33.57N	84.20W
Duolun, China (dwô-lo͞on)	189	42.12N	116.15E
Duomo, rel., Italy	238c	45.27N	9.11E
Du Page, r., Il., U.S. (do͞o pāj)	101a	41.41N	88.11W
Du Page, East Branch, r., Il., U.S.	101a	41.42N	88.09W
Du Page, West Branch, r., Il., U.S.	101a	41.42N	88.09W
Dupax, Phil. (do͞o'päks)	197a	16.16N	121.06E
Dupo, Il., U.S. (dū'pō)	107e	38.31N	90.12W
Duque de Caxias, Braz. (do͞o'kĕ-dĕ-kä'shyäs)	129a	22.46S	43.18W
Duquesne, Pa., U.S. (dŏŏ-kān')	101e	40.22N	79.51W
Du Quoin, Il., U.S. (dŏŏ-kwoin')	111	38.01N	89.14W
Durance, r., Fr. (dü-räɴs')	147	43.46N	5.52E
Durand, Mi., U.S. (dŭ-rănd')	98	42.50N	84.00W
Durand, Wi., U.S.	103	44.37N	91.58W
Durango, Mex. (do͞o-rä'n-gŏ)	116	24.02N	104.42W
Durango, Co., U.S. (dŏŏ-răŋ'gō)	109	37.15N	107.55W
Durango, state, Mex.	116	25.00N	106.00W
Durant, Ms., U.S. (dŭ-rănt')	114	33.05N	89.50W
Durant, Ok., U.S.	111	33.59N	96.23W
Duratón, r., Spain (do͞o-rä-tōn')	158	41.30N	3.55W
Durazno, Ur. (do͞o-räz'nō)	132	33.21S	56.31W
Durazno, dept., Ur.	129c	33.00S	56.35W
Durban, S. Afr. (dûr'băn)	212	29.48S	31.00E
Durbanville, S. Afr. (dûr-băn'vĭl)	212a	33.50S	18.39E
Durbe, Lat. (do͞or'bĕ)	153	56.36N	21.24E
Durchholz, Ger.	236	51.23N	7.17E
Đurđevac, Cro.	149	46.03N	17.03E
Düren, Ger. (dü'rĕn)	157c	50.48N	6.30E
Durham, Eng., U.K. (dûr'ăm)	150	54.47N	1.46W
Durham, N.C., U.S.	97	36.00N	78.55W
Durham Downs, Austl.	204	27.30S	141.55E
Durrës, Alb. (dŏŏr'ĕs)	142	41.19N	19.27E
Duryea, Pa., U.S. (do͞or-yā')	99	41.20N	75.50W
Dushan, China	190	31.38N	116.16E
Dushan, China (do͞o-shän)	193	25.50N	107.42E
Dushanbe, Taj.	169	38.30N	68.45E
Düssel, Ger.	236	51.16N	7.03E
Düsseldorf, Ger. (düs'ĕl-dôrf)	147	51.14N	6.47E
Dussen, Neth.	145a	51.43N	4.58E
Dutalan Ula, mts., Mong.	192	49.25N	112.40E
Dutch Harbor, Ak., U.S. (dŭch här'bēr)	96a	53.58N	166.30W
Duvall, Wa., U.S. (do͞o'vâl)	106a	47.44N	121.59W
Duwamish, r., Wa., U.S. (do͞o-wăm'ĭsh)	106a	47.24N	122.18W
Duyun, China (do͞o-yŏŏn)	188	26.18N	107.40E
Dvinskaya Guba, b., Russia	166	65.10N	38.40E
Dwārka, India	186	22.18N	68.59E
Dwight, Il., U.S. (dwīt)	98	41.00N	88.20W
Dworshak Res, Id., U.S.	104	46.45N	115.50W
Dyat'kovo, Russia (dyät'kō-vō)	162	53.36N	34.19E
Dyer, In., U.S. (dī'ēr)	101a	41.30N	87.31W
Dyersburg, Tn., U.S. (dī'ērz-bûrg)	114	36.02N	89.23W
Dyersville, Ia., U.S. (dī'ērz-vĭl)	103	42.28N	91.09W
Dyes Inlet, Wa., U.S. (dīz)	106a	47.37N	122.45W
Dykhtau, Gora, mtn., Russia	168	43.03N	43.08E
Dyment, Can. (dī'mĕnt)	89	49.37N	92.19W
Dzamïn Üüd, Mong.	189	44.38N	111.32E
Dzaoudzi, May. (dzou'dzĭ)	213	12.44S	45.15E
Dzavhan, r., Mong.	188	48.19N	94.08E
Dzerzhinsk, Bela.	162	53.41N	27.14E
Dzerzhinsk, Russia	166	56.20N	43.50E
Dzerzhyns'k, Ukr.	163	48.26N	37.50E
Dzeržinskij, Russia	239b	55.38N	37.50E
Dzhalal-Abad, Kyrg. (jȧ-läl'ȧ-bät')	169	40.56N	73.00E
Dzhambul *see* Zhambyl, Kaz.	158	42.51N	71.29E
Dzhankoy, Ukr. (dzhän'koi)	167	45.43N	34.22E
Dzhizak, Uzb. (dzhĕ'zäk)	169	40.13N	67.58E
Dzhugdzhur Khrebet, mts., Russia (jŏŏg-jo͞or')	165	56.15N	137.00E
Działoszyce, Pol. (jyä-wō-shē'tsĕ)	155	50.21N	20.22E
Dzibalchén, Mex. (zē-bäl-chĕ'n)	120a	19.25N	89.39W
Dzidzantún, Mex. (zēd-zän-to͞o'n)	120a	21.18N	89.00W
Dzierżoniów, Pol. (dzyĕr-zhôn'yŭf)	154	50.44N	16.38E
Dzilam González, Mex. (zē-lä'm-gôn-zä'lĕz)	120a	21.21N	88.53W
Dzitás, Mex. (zē-tá's)	120a	20.47N	88.32W
Dzungaria, reg., China (dzŏŏn-gä'rĭ-ȧ)	188	44.39N	86.13E
Dzungarian Gate, p., Asia	188	45.00N	88.00E

E

PLACE (Pronunciation)	PAGE	Lat. °′	Long. °′
Eagle, W.V., U.S.	98	38.10N	81.20W
Eagle, r., Co., U.S.	109	39.32N	106.28W
Eaglecliff, Wa., U.S. (ē'gl-klĭf)	106c	46.10N	123.13W
Eagle Creek, r., In., U.S.	101g	39.54N	86.17W
Eagle Grove, Ia., U.S.	103	42.39N	93.55W
Eagle Lake, Me., U.S.	92	47.03N	68.38W
Eagle Lake, Tx., U.S.	113	29.37N	96.20W
Eagle Lake, l., Ca., U.S.	104	40.45N	120.52W
Eagle Mountain, Ca., U.S.	108	33.49N	115.27W
Eagle Mountain L, Tx., U.S.	107c	32.56N	97.27W
Eagle Pass, Tx., U.S.	96	28.49N	100.30W
Eagle Pk, Ca., U.S.	104	41.18N	120.11W
Eagle Rock, neigh., Ca., U.S.	232	34.09N	118.12W
Ealing, Eng., U.K. (ē'lĭng)	144b	51.29N	0.19W
Earle, Ar., U.S. (ûrl)	111	35.14N	90.28W
Earlington, Ky., U.S. (ûr'lĭng-tŭn)	114	37.15N	87.31W
Easley, S.C., U.S. (ēz'lĭ)	115	34.48N	82.37W
East, r., N.Y., U.S.	228	40.48N	73.48W
East, Mount, mtn., Pan.	116a	9.09N	79.46W
East Alton, Il., U.S. (ôl'tŭn)	107e	38.53N	90.08W
East Angus, Can. (ăŋ'gŭs)	91	45.35N	71.40W
East Arlington, Ma., U.S.	227a	42.25N	71.08W
East Aurora, N.Y., U.S. (ô-rō'rȧ)	101c	42.46N	78.38W
East Barnet, neigh., Eng., U.K.	235	51.38N	0.09W
East Bay, b., Tx., U.S.	113a	29.30N	94.41W
East Bedfont, neigh., Eng., U.K.	235	51.27N	0.26W
East Bernstadt, Ky., U.S. (bûrn'stát)	114	37.09N	84.08W
Eastbourne, Eng., U.K. (ēst'bôrn)	151	50.48N	0.16E
East Braintree, Ma., U.S.	227a	42.13N	70.58W
East Burwood, Austl.	243b	37.51S	145.09E
Eastbury, Eng., U.K.	235	51.37N	0.25W
East Caicos, i., T./C. Is. (kī'kōs)	123	21.40N	71.35W
East Cape, c., N.Z.	203a	37.37S	178.33E
East Cape *see* Dezhnëva, Mys, c., Russia	180	68.00N	172.00W
East Carondelet, Il., U.S. (kȧ-rŏn'dĕ-lĕt)	107e	38.33N	90.14W
East Cherokee Indian Reservation, I.R., N.C., U.S.	114	35.33N	83.12W
Eastchester, N.Y., U.S.	228	40.57N	73.49W
East Chicago, In., U.S. (shĭ-kô'gō)	101a	41.39N	87.29W
East China Sea, sea, Asia	189	30.28N	125.52E
East Cleveland, Oh., U.S. (klēv'lănd)	101d	41.33N	81.35W
Eastcote, neigh., Eng., U.K.	235	51.35N	0.24W
East Cote Blanche Bay, b., La., U.S. (kōt bläɴsh')	113	29.30N	92.07W
East Des Moines, r., Ia., U.S. (dē moin')	103	42.57N	94.17W
East Detroit, Mi., U.S. (dē-troit')	101b	42.28N	82.57W
Easter Island *see* Pascua, Isla de, i., Chile	225	26.50S	109.00W
Eastern Ghāts, mts., India	183	13.50N	78.45E
Eastern Native, neigh., S. Afr.	244b	26.13S	28.05E
Eastern Turkestan, hist. reg., China (tòr-kĕ-stän')(tûr-kĕ-stăn')	188	39.40N	78.20E
East Falls, neigh., Pa., U.S.	229b	40.01N	75.11W
East Grand Forks, Mn., U.S. (grănd fôrks)	102	47.56N	97.02W
East Greenwich, R.I., U.S. (grĭn'ĭj)	100b	41.40N	71.27W
Eastham, Eng., U.K.	237a	53.19N	2.58W
East Ham, neigh., Eng., U.K.	235	51.32N	0.03E
Easthampton, Ma., U.S. (ēst-hămp'tŭn)	99	42.15N	72.45W
East Hartford, Ct., U.S. (härt'fērd)	99	41.45N	72.35W
East Helena, Mt., U.S. (hĕ-hē'nȧ)	105	46.31N	111.50W
East Hills, Austl.	243a	33.58S	150.59E
East Hills, N.Y., U.S.	228	40.47N	73.38W
East Ilsley, Eng., U.K. (ĭl'slē)	144b	51.30N	1.18W
East Jordan, Mi., U.S. (jôr'dăn)	98	45.05N	85.05W
East Kansas City, Mo., U.S. (kăn'zȧs)	107f	39.09N	94.30W
East Lamma Channel, strt., H.K.	241c	22.15N	114.07E
Eastland, Tx., U.S. (ēst'lănd)	112	32.24N	98.47W
East Lansdowne, Pa., U.S.	229b	39.56N	75.16W
East Lansing, Mi., U.S. (lăn'sĭng)	98	42.45N	84.30W
Eastlawn, Mi., U.S.	101b	42.15N	83.35W
East Leavenworth, Mo., U.S. (lĕv'ĕn-wûrth)	107f	39.18N	94.50W
East Liberty, neigh., Pa., U.S.	230b	40.27N	79.55W
East Lindfield, Austl.	243a	33.46S	151.11E
East Liverpool, Oh., U.S. (lĭv'ēr-po͞ol)	98	40.40N	80.35W
East London, S. Afr. (lŭn'dŭn)	212	33.02S	27.54E
East Los Angeles, Ca., U.S. (lōs ăŋ'hȧ-lās)	107a	34.01N	118.09W
Eastmain, r., Can. (ēst'mān)	85	52.12N	73.19W
East Malling, Eng., U.K.	235	51.17N	0.26E
Eastman, Ga., U.S. (ēst'măn)	114	32.10N	83.11W
East Meadow, N.Y., U.S.	228	40.43N	73.34W
East Millstone, N.J., U.S. (mĭl'stōn)	100a	40.30N	74.35W
East Molesey, Eng., U.K.	235	51.24N	0.21W
East Moline, Il., U.S. (mō-lēn')	103	41.31N	90.28W
East Newark, N.J., U.S.	228	40.45N	74.10W
East New York, neigh., N.Y., U.S.	228	40.40N	73.53W
East Nishnabotna, r., Ia., U.S. (nĭsh-nȧ-bŏt'nȧ)	102	40.53N	95.23W
East Norwich, N.Y., U.S.	228	40.50N	73.32W
Easton, Md., U.S. (ēs'tŭn)	99	38.45N	76.05W
Easton, Pa., U.S.	99	40.45N	75.15W
Easton L, Ct., U.S.	100a	41.18N	73.17W
East Orange, N.J., U.S. (ŏr'ĕnj)	100a	40.46N	74.12W
East Pakistan *see* Bangladesh, nation, Asia	183	24.15N	90.00E
East Palo Alto, Ca., U.S.	106b	37.27N	122.07W
East Peoria, Il., U.S. (pē-ō'rĭ-ȧ)	98	40.40N	89.30W
East Pittsburgh, Pa., U.S. (pĭts'bûrg)	101e	40.24N	79.50W
East Point, Ga., U.S.	100c	33.41N	84.27W
Eastport, Me., U.S. (ēst'pōrt)	92	44.53N	67.01W
East Providence, R.I., U.S. (prŏv'ĭ-dĕns)	100b	41.49N	71.22W
East Retford, Eng., U.K. (rĕt'fērd)	144a	53.19N	0.56W
East Richmond, Ca., U.S.	231b	37.57N	122.19W
East Rochester, N.Y., U.S. (rŏch'ĕs-tēr)	99	43.10N	77.30W
East Rockaway, N.Y., U.S.	228	40.39N	73.40W
East Saint Louis, Il., U.S.	97	38.38N	90.10W
East Siberian Sea, sea, Russia (sī-bĭr'y'n)	165	73.00N	153.28E
Eastsound, Wa., U.S. (ēst-sound)	106d	48.42N	122.42W
East Stroudsburg, Pa., U.S. (stroudz'bûrg)	99	41.00N	75.10W
East Syracuse, N.Y., U.S. (sĭr'ȧ-kūs)	99	43.05N	76.00W
East Tavaputs Plateau, plat., Ut., U.S. (tă-vă'-pŭts)	109	39.25N	109.45W
East Tawas, Mi., U.S. (tô'wȧs)	98	44.15N	83.30W
East Tilbury, Eng., U.K.	235	51.28N	0.26E
East Tustin, Ca., U.S.	232	33.46N	117.49W
East Walker, r., U.S. (wôk'ēr)	108	38.36N	119.02W
East Walpole, Ma., U.S.	227a	42.10N	71.13W
East Watertown, Ma., U.S.	227a	42.22N	71.10W
East Weymouth, Ma., U.S.	227a	42.13N	70.55W
Eastwick, neigh., Pa., U.S.	229b	39.55N	75.14W
East Wickham, neigh., Eng., U.K.	235	51.28N	0.07E
Eastwood, Austl.	243a	33.48S	151.05E
East York, Can.	83d	43.41S	79.20W
Eaton, Co., U.S. (ē'tŭn)	110	40.31N	104.42W
Eaton, Oh., U.S.	98	39.45N	84.40W
Eaton Estates, Oh., U.S.	101d	41.19N	82.01W
Eaton Rapids, Mi., U.S. (răp'ĭdz)	98	42.30N	84.40W
Eatonton, Ga., U.S. (ē'tŭn-tŭn)	114	33.20N	83.24W
Eatontown, N.J., U.S. (ē'tŭn-toun)	100a	40.18N	74.04W
Eaubonne, Fr.	237c	49.00N	2.17E
Eau Claire, Wi., U.S. (ō klâr')	97	44.47N	91.32W
Ebeltoft, Den. (ĕ'bĕl-tŭft)	152	56.11N	10.39E
Ebensburg, Pa., U.S.	99	40.29N	78.44W
Ebersberg, Ger. (ĕ'bĕrs-bĕrgh)	145d	48.05N	11.58E
Ebina, Japan	242a	35.26N	139.25E
Ebingen, Ger. (ā'bĭng-ĕn)	154	48.13N	9.04E
Eboli, Italy (ĕb'ō-lē)	160	40.38N	15.04E
Ebolowa, Cam.	210	2.54N	11.09E
Ebreichsdorf, Aus.	145e	47.58N	16.24E
Ebrié, Lagune, b., C. Iv.	214	5.20N	4.50W
Ebro, r., Spain (ā'brō)	142	42.00N	2.00W
Ebute-Ikorodu, Nig.	244d	6.37N	3.30E
Eccles, Eng., U.K. (ĕk''lz)	144a	53.29N	2.20W
Eccles, W.V., U.S.	98	37.45N	81.10W
Eccleshall, Eng., U.K.	144a	52.51N	2.15W
Eccleston, Eng., U.K.	237a	53.27N	2.47W
Eccleston, Md., U.S.	229c	39.24N	76.44W
Eceabat, Tur.	161	40.10N	26.21E
Echague, Phil. (ā-chä'gwä)	197a	16.43N	121.40E
Echandi, Cerro, mtn., N.A. (sĕ'r-rō-ĕ-chä'nd)	121	9.05N	82.51W
Ech Cheliff, Alg.	210	36.14N	1.32E
Echimamish, r., Can.	89	54.15N	97.30W
Echmiadzin, Arm.	168	40.10N	44.18E
Echo Bay, Can. (ĕk'ō)	107k	46.29N	84.04W
Echoing, r., Can. (ĕk'ō-ĭng)	89	55.15N	91.30W
Echternach, Lux. (ĕk'tēr-näk)	157	49.48N	6.25E
Echuca, Austl. (ē-chō'kȧ)	203	36.10S	144.47E
Écija, Spain (ā'thē-hä)	148	37.20N	5.07W
Eckernförde, Ger.	154	54.27N	9.51E
Eclipse, Va., U.S. (ē-klĭps')	100g	36.55N	76.29W
Ecorse, Mi., U.S. (ē-kôrs')	101b	42.15N	83.09W
Ecuador, nation, S.A. (ĕk'wȧ-dôr)	130	0.00N	78.30W
Ed, Erit.	211	13.57N	41.37E
Eda, neigh., Japan	242a	35.34N	139.34E
Eddyville, Ky., U.S. (ĕd'ĭ-vĭl)	114	37.03N	88.03W
Ede, Nig.	215	7.44N	4.27E
Edéa, Cam. (ĕ-dā'ä)	210	3.48N	10.08E
Éden, Braz.	234c	22.48S	43.24W
Eden, Tx., U.S.	112	31.13N	99.51W
Eden, Ut., U.S.	107b	41.18N	111.49W
Eden, r., Eng., U.K. (ē'dĕn)	150	54.40N	2.35W
Edenbridge, Eng., U.K. (ē'dĕn-brĭj)	144b	51.11N	0.05E
Edendale, S. Afr.	244b	26.09S	28.09E
Edenham, Eng., U.K. (ē'd'n-ȧm)	144a	52.46N	0.25W
Eden Prairie, Mn., U.S. (prâr'ĭ)	107g	44.51N	93.29W
Edenton, N.C., U.S. (ē'dĕn-tŭn)	115	36.02N	76.37W
Edenton, Oh., U.S.	101f	39.14N	84.02W
Edenvale, S. Afr. (ĕd'ĕn-vāl)	213b	26.09S	28.10E
Edenvale Location, S. Afr.	244b	26.08S	28.11E
Edenville, S. Afr. (ē'd'n-vĭl)	218d	27.33S	27.42E
Eder, r., Ger. (ā'dēr)	154	51.05N	8.52E
Edgefield, S.C., U.S. (ĕj'fēld)	115	33.52N	81.55W
Edge Hill, neigh., Eng., U.K.	237a	53.24N	2.57W
Edgeley, N.D., U.S. (ĕj'lĭ)	102	46.24N	98.43W
Edgemere, Md., U.S.	229c	39.14N	76.27W
Edgemont, S.D., U.S. (ĕj'mŏnt)	102	43.19N	103.50W
Edgerton, Wi., U.S. (ĕj'ēr-tŭn)	103	42.49N	89.06W
Edgewater, Al., U.S. (ĕj-wô-tēr)	100h	33.31N	86.52W
Edgewater, Md., U.S.	100e	38.58N	76.35W
Edgewater, N.J., U.S.	228	40.50N	73.58W
Edgewood, Can. (ĕj'wŏŏd)	87	49.47N	118.08W
Edgware, neigh., Eng., U.K.	235	51.37N	0.17W
Edgwater, N.Y., U.S.	230a	43.03N	78.55W
Edgworth, Eng., U.K.	237b	53.39N	2.24W
Édhessa, Grc.	149	40.48N	22.04E
Edina, Mn., U.S. (ē-dī'nȧ)	107g	44.55N	93.20W
Edina, Mo., U.S.	111	40.10N	92.11W
Edinburg, In., U.S. (ĕd''n-bûrg)	98	39.20N	85.55W
Edinburg, Tx., U.S.	112	26.18N	98.08W
Edinburgh, Scot., U.K. (ĕd''n-bŭr-ō)	142	55.57N	3.10W
Edirne, Tur.	161	41.41N	26.35E
Edison Park, neigh., Il., U.S.	231a	42.01N	87.49W
Edisto, r., S.C., U.S. (ĕd'ĭs-tō)	115	33.10N	80.50W
Edisto, North Fork, r., S.C., U.S.	115	33.42N	81.24W
Edisto, South Fork, r., S.C., U.S.	115	33.43N	81.35W
Edisto Island, S.C., U.S.	115	32.32N	80.20W
Edmond, Ok., U.S. (ĕd'mŭnd)	111	35.39N	97.29W
Edmonds, Wa., U.S. (ĕd'mŭndz)	106a	47.49N	122.23W
Edmonston, Md., U.S.	229d	38.57N	76.56W
Edmonton, Can.	84	53.33N	113.28W
Edmonton, neigh., Eng., U.K.	235	51.37N	0.04W
Edmundston, Can. (ĕd'mŭn-stŭn)	85	47.22N	68.20W
Edna, Tx., U.S. (ĕd'nȧ)	113	28.59N	96.39W
Edo, r., Japan	242a	35.41N	139.53E
Edogawa, neigh., Japan	242a	35.42N	139.52E
Edremit, Tur. (ĕd-rĕ-mēt')	149	39.35N	27.00E

PLACE (Pronunciation)	PAGE	Lat. °′	Long. °′
Edremit Körfezi, b., Tur.	161	39.28N	26.35E
Edson, Can. (ĕd'sŭn)	84	53.35N	116.26W
Edward, l., Can. (ĕd'wẽrd)	90	48.21N	88.29W
Edward, l., Afr.	212	0.25S	29.40E
Edwardsville, Il., U.S. (ĕd'wẽrdz-vĭl)	107e	38.49N	89.58W
Edwardsville, In., U.S.	101h	38.17N	85.53W
Edwardsville, Ks., U.S.	107f	39.04N	94.49W
Eel, r., Ca., U.S. (ēl)	104	40.39N	124.15W
Eel, r., In., U.S.	98	40.50N	85.55W
Efate, i., Vanuatu (ā-fä'tä)	203	18.02S	168.29E
Effigy Mounds National Monument, rec., Ia., U.S. (ĕf'ĭ-jŭ mounds)	103	43.04N	91.15W
Effingham, Il., U.S. (ĕf'ĭng-hăm)	98	39.05N	88.30W
Ega, r., Spain (ā'gä)	158	42.40N	2.20W
Egadi, Isole, is., Italy (ĕ'sō-lĕ-ĕ'gä-dē)	148	38.01N	12.00E
Egea de los Caballeros, Spain	158	42.07N	1.05W
Egegik, Ak., U.S. (ĕg'ĕ-jĭt)	95	58.10N	157.22W
Eger, Hung. (ĕ gĕr)	155	47.53N	20.24E
Egersund, Nor. (ĕ'ghĕr-sŏon')	146	58.29N	6.01E
Egg Harbor, N.J., U.S. (ĕg här'bẽr)	99	39.30N	74.35W
Egham, Eng., U.K. (ĕg'ŭm)	144b	51.24N	0.33W
Egiyn, r., Mong.	188	49.41N	100.40E
Egmont, Cape, c., N.Z. (ĕg'mŏnt)	203a	39.18S	173.49E
Egota, neigh., Japan	242a	35.43N	139.40E
Egypt, nation, Afr. (ē'jĭpt)	211	26.58N	27.01E
Eha-Amufu, Nig.	215	6.40N	7.46E
Ehingen, neigh., Ger.	236	51.22N	6.42E
Ehringhausen, Ger.	236	51.11N	7.33E
Ehringhausen, neigh., Ger.	236	51.09N	7.11E
Eibar, Spain (ā'ē-bär)	158	43.12N	2.20W
Eiche, Ger.	238a	52.34N	13.36E
Eichlinghofen, neigh., Ger.	236	51.29N	7.24E
Eichstätt, Ger. (īk'shtät)	154	48.54N	11.14E
Eichwalde, Ger. (īĸ'väl-dĕ)	145b	52.22N	13.37E
Eickerend, Ger.	236	51.13N	6.34E
Eidfjord, Nor. (ĕĭd'fyōr)	152	60.28N	7.04E
Eidsvoll, Nor. (ĭdhs'vôl)	146	60.19N	11.15E
Eifel, mts., Ger. (ī'fĕl)	154	50.08N	6.30E
Eiffel, Tour, pt. of i., Fr.	237c	48.51N	2.18E
Eigen, neigh., Ger.	236	51.33N	6.57E
Eighty Mile Beach, cst., Austl.	202	19.00S	121.00E
Eilenburg, Ger. (ī'lĕn-bŏrgh)	154	51.27N	12.38E
Einbeck, Ger. (īn'bĕk)	154	51.49N	9.52E
Eindhoven, Neth. (īnd'hō-vĕn)	151	51.29N	5.20E
Eisenach, Ger. (ī'zĕn-äĸ)	147	50.58N	10.18E
Eisenhüttenstadt, Ger.	154	52.08N	14.40E
Ejura, Ghana	214	7.23N	1.22W
Ejutla de Crespo, Mex. (ā-hōt'lä dā kräs'pō)	119	16.34N	96.44W
Ekanga, Zaire	216	2.23S	23.14E
Ekenäs, Fin. (ĕ'kĕ-nâs)	153	59.59N	23.25E
Ekeren, Bel.	145a	51.17N	4.27E
Ekoli, Zaire	216	0.23S	24.16E
Eksāra, India	240a	22.38N	88.17E
El Aaiún, W. Sah.	210	26.45N	13.15W
El Affroun, Alg. (ĕl áf-froun')	159	36.28N	2.38E
El Aguacate, Ven.	234a	10.28N	66.59W
Elands, r., S. Afr. (ĕlånds)	213c	31.48S	26.09E
Elands, r., S. Afr.	218d	25.11S	28.52E
Elandsfontein, S. Afr.	244b	26.10S	28.12E
El Arahal, Spain (ĕl ä-rä-äl')	158	37.17N	5.32W
El Arba, Alg.	159	36.35N	3.10E
Elat, Isr.	182	29.34N	34.57E
Elâziğ, Tur. (ĕl-ä'zĭz)	182	38.40N	39.00E
Elba, Al., U.S. (ĕl'bȧ)	114	31.25N	86.01W
Elba, Isola d', i., Italy (ē-sō lä-d-ĕl'bȧ)	148	42.42N	10.25E
El Banco, Col. (ĕl băn'cō)	130	8.58N	74.01W
Elbansan, Alb. (ĕl-bä-sän')	149	41.08N	20.05E
El Barco de Valdeorras, Spain (ĕl bär'kō)	158	42.26N	6.58W
Elbe (Labe), r., Eur. (ĕl'bĕ)(lä'bĕ)	142	52.30N	11.30E
Elberfeld, neigh., Ger.	236	51.16N	7.08E
Elbert, Mount, mtn., Co., U.S. (ĕl'bērt)	96	39.05N	106.25W
Elberton, Ga., U.S. (ĕl'bēr-tŭn)	115	34.05N	82.53W
Elbeuf, Fr. (ĕl-bûf')	147	49.16N	0.59E
El Beyadh, Alg.	148	33.42N	1.06E
Elbistan, Tur. (ĕl-bē-stän')	149	38.20N	37.10E
Elblag, Pol. (ĕl'blăng)	146	54.11N	19.25E
El Bonillo, Spain (ĕl bō-nēl'yō)	158	38.56N	2.31W
El Boulaïda, Alg.	210	36.33N	2.45E
Elbow, r., Can. (ĕl'bō)	83e	51.03N	114.24W
Elbow Cay, i., Bah.	122	26.25N	76.55W
Elbow Lake, Mn., U.S.	102	46.00N	95.59W
El'brus, Gora, mtn., Russia (ĕl'brŏs')	164	43.20N	42.25E
Elbrus, Mount see El'brus, Gora, mtn., Russia	164	43.20N	42.25E
El Burgo de Osma, Spain	158	41.35N	3.02W
Elburz Mountains, mts., Iran (ĕl'bŏrz')	182	36.30N	51.00E
El Cajon, Col. (ĕl-kä-kō'n)	130a	4.50N	76.35W
El Cajon, Ca., U.S.	108a	32.48N	116.58W
El Calvario, neigh., Cuba	233b	23.05N	82.20W
El Cambur, Ven. (käm-bōō'r')	131b	10.24N	68.06W
El Campamento, neigh., Spain	238b	40.24N	3.46W
El Campo, Tx., U.S. (kăm'pō)	113	29.13N	96.17W
El Caribe, Ven.	234a	10.37N	66.49W
El Carmen, Chile (kȧ'r-mĕn)	129b	34.14S	71.23W
El Carmen, Col. (kȧ'r-mĕn)	130	9.54N	75.12W
El Casco, Ca., U.S. (käs'kō)	107a	33.59N	117.08W
El Centro, Ca., U.S. (sĕn'trō)	108	32.47N	115.33W
El Cerrito, Ca., U.S. (sĕr-rē'tō)	106b	37.55N	122.19W
Elche, Spain (ĕl'chā)	159	38.15N	0.42W
El Cojo, Ven.	234a	10.37N	66.53W
El Corozo, Ven.	234a	10.35N	66.58W
El Cotorro, Cuba	233b	23.03N	82.16W
El Cuyo, Mex.	120a	21.30N	87.42W
Elda, Spain (ĕl'dä)	159	38.28N	0.44W
Elder Mills, Can.	227c	43.49N	79.38W

PLACE (Pronunciation)	PAGE	Lat. °′	Long. °′
El Djelfa, Alg.	210	34.40N	3.17E
El Djouf, des., Afr. (ĕl djōōf)	210	21.45N	7.05W
Eldon, Ia., U.S. (ĕl-dŭn)	103	40.55N	92.15W
Eldon, Mo., U.S.	111	38.21N	92.36W
Eldora, Ia., U.S. (ĕl-dō'rȧ)	103	42.21N	93.08W
El Dorado, Ar., U.S. (ĕl dō-rä'dō)	97	33.13N	92.39W
Eldorado, Il., U.S.	98	37.50N	88.30W
El Dorado, Ks., U.S.	111	37.49N	96.51W
Eldorado Springs, Mo., U.S. (sprĭngz)	111	37.51N	94.02W
Eldoret, Kenya (ĕl-dō-rĕt')	217	0.31N	35.17E
El Ebano, Mex. (ā-bä'nō)	118	22.13N	98.26W
Electra, Tx., U.S. (ē-lĕk'trȧ)	110	34.02N	98.54W
Electric Peak, mtn., Mt., U.S. (ē-lĕk'trĭk)	105	45.03N	110.52W
Elektrogorsk, Russia (ĕl-yĕk'trō-gôrsk)	172b	55.53N	38.48E
Elektrostal', Russia (ĕl-yĕk'trō-stál)	172b	55.47N	38.27E
Elektrougli, Russia	172b	55.43N	38.13E
El Encantado, Ven.	234a	10.27N	66.47W
Elephanta Island (Ghārāpuri), i., India	240e	18.57N	72.55E
Elephant Butte Reservoir, res., N.M., U.S. (ĕl'ē-fănt būt)	96	33.25N	107.10W
El Escorial, Spain (ĕl-ĕs-kō-ryä'l)	159a	40.38N	4.08W
El Espino, Nic. (ĕl-ĕs-pē'nō)	120	13.26N	86.48W
Eleuthera, i., Bah. (ē-lū'thēr-ȧ)	117	25.05N	76.10W
Eleuthera Point, c., Bah.	122	24.35N	76.05W
Eleven Point, r., Mo., U.S. (ē-lĕv'ĕn)	111	36.53N	91.39W
El Ferrol, Spain (fä-rōl')	142	43.30N	8.12W
Elgin, Scot., U.K.	150	57.40N	3.30W
Elgin, Il., U.S. (ĕl'jĭn)	101a	42.03N	88.16W
Elgin, Ne., U.S.	102	41.58N	98.04W
Elgin, Or., U.S.	104	45.34N	117.58W
Elgin, Tx., U.S.	113	30.21N	97.22W
Elgin, Wa., U.S.	106a	47.23N	122.42W
Elgon, Mount, mtn., Afr. (ĕl'gŏn)	211	1.00N	34.25E
El Granada, Ca., U.S.	231b	37.30N	122.28W
El Grara, Alg.	148	32.50N	4.26E
El Grullo, Mex. (grōōl-yō)	118	19.46N	104.10W
El Guapo, Ven. (gwá'pō)	131b	10.07N	66.00W
El Guarapo, Ven.	234a	10.36N	66.58W
El Hank, reg., Afr.	210	23.44N	6.45W
El Hatillo, Ven. (ä-tē'l-yō)	131b	10.08N	65.13W
Elie, Can. (ē'lē)	83f	49.55N	97.45W
Elila, r., Zaire (ē-lē'lȧ)	212	3.30S	28.00E
Elisa, i., Wa., U.S. (ē-lī'sȧ)	106d	48.43N	122.37W
Élisabethville see Lubumbashi, Zaire	212	11.40S	27.28E
Elisenvaara, Russia (ā-lē'sĕn-vä'rȧ)	153	61.25N	29.46E
Elizabeth, La., U.S. (ē-lĭz'ȧ-bĕth)	113	30.50N	92.47W
Elizabeth, N.J., U.S.	100a	40.40N	74.13W
Elizabeth, Pa., U.S.	101e	40.16N	79.53W
Elizabeth City, N.C., U.S.	115	36.15N	76.15W
Elizabethton, Tn., U.S. (ē-lĭz-ȧ-bĕth'tŭn)	115	36.19N	82.12W
Elizabethtown, Ky., U.S. (ē-lĭz'ȧ-bĕth-toun)	98	37.40N	85.55W
El Jadida, Mor.	210	33.14N	8.34W
Elk, Pol.	146	53.53N	22.23E
Elk, r., Can.	87	50.00N	115.00W
Elk, r., Tn., U.S.	114	35.05N	86.36W
Elk, r., W.V., U.S.	98	38.30N	81.05W
El Kairouan, Tun. (kĕr-ō-än)	210	35.46N	10.04E
Elk City, Ok., U.S. (ĕlk)	110	35.23N	99.23W
El Kef, Tun. (xĕf')	148	36.14N	8.42E
Elkhart, In., U.S. (ĕlk'härt)	98	41.40N	86.00W
Elkhart, Ks., U.S.	110	37.00N	101.54W
Elkhart, Tx., U.S.	113	31.38N	95.35W
Elkhorn, Wi., U.S. (ĕlk'hôrn)	103	42.39N	88.32W
Elkhorn, r., Ne., U.S.	102	42.06N	97.46W
Elkin, N.C., U.S. (ĕl'kĭn)	115	36.15N	80.50W
Elkins Park, Pa., U.S.	229b	40.05N	75.08W
Elk Island, i., Can.	89	50.45N	96.32W
Elk Island National Park, rec., Can. (ĕlk ī'lănd)	84	53.37N	112.45W
Elko, Nv., U.S. (ĕl'kō)	96	40.51N	115.46W
Elk Point, S.D., U.S.	102	42.41N	96.41W
Elk Rapids, Mi., U.S. (răp'ĭdz)	98	44.55N	85.25W
Elkridge, Md., U.S.	229c	39.13N	76.42W
Elk River, Id., U.S. (rĭv'ēr)	104	46.47N	116.11W
Elk River, Mn., U.S.	103	45.17N	93.33W
Elkton, Ky., U.S. (ĕlk'tŭn)	114	36.47N	87.08W
Elkton, Md., U.S.	99	39.35N	75.50W
Elkton, S.D., U.S.	102	44.15N	96.28W
Elland, Eng., U.K. (ĕl'ănd)	144a	53.41N	1.50W
Ellen, Mount, mtn., Ut., U.S. (ĕl'ĕn)	109	38.05N	110.50W
Ellendale, N.D., U.S. (ĕl'ĕn-dāl)	102	46.01N	98.33W
Ellensburg, Wa., U.S. (ĕl'ĕnz-bûrg)	104	47.00N	120.31W
Ellenville, N.Y., U.S. (ĕl'ĕn-vĭl)	99	41.40N	74.25W
Ellerslie, Can. (ĕl'ērz-lē)	83g	53.25N	113.30W
Ellesmere, Eng., U.K. (ĕlz'mĕr)	144a	52.55N	2.54W
Ellesmere Island, i., Can.	82	81.00N	80.00W
Ellesmere Park, Eng., U.K.	237b	53.29N	2.20W
Ellesmere Port, Eng., U.K.	144a	53.17N	2.54W
Ellice Islands see Tuvalu, nation, Oc.	3	5.20S	174.00E
Ellicott City, is., Md., U.S. (ĕl'ĭ-kŏt sĭ'tē)	100e	39.16N	76.48W
Ellicott Creek, r., N.Y., U.S.	101c	43.00N	78.46W
El Limoncito, Ven.	234a	10.29N	66.47W
Ellinghorst, neigh., Ger.	236	51.34N	6.57E
Elliot, S. Afr.	213c	31.19S	27.52E
Elliot, Wa., U.S. (ĕl'ĭ-ŭt)	106a	47.28N	122.08W
Elliotdale, S. Afr. (ĕl-ĭ-ŏt'dāl)	213c	31.58S	28.42E
Elliot Lake, Can.	90	46.23N	82.39W
Ellis, Ks., U.S. (ĕl'ĭs)	110	38.56N	99.34W
Ellisville, Ms., U.S. (ĕl'ĭs-vĭl)	114	31.37N	89.10W
Ellisville, Mo., U.S.	107e	38.35N	90.35W
Ellsworth, Ks., U.S. (ĕlz'wûrth)	110	38.43N	98.14W
Ellsworth, Me., U.S.	92	44.33N	68.26W
Ellsworth Mountains, mts., Ant.	219	77.00S	90.00W
Ellwangen, Ger. (ĕl'väng-gĕn)	154	48.47N	10.08E
Elm, Ger. (ĕlm)	145c	53.31N	9.13E
Elm, r., S.D., U.S.	102	45.47N	98.28W

PLACE (Pronunciation)	PAGE	Lat. °′	Long. °′
Elm, r., W.V., U.S.	98	38.30N	81.05W
Elma, Wa., U.S. (ĕl'mȧ)	104	47.02N	123.20W
El Mahdia, Tun. (mä-dēȧ)(mä'dē-ȧ)	148	35.30N	11.09E
Elmendorf, Tx., U.S. (ĕl'mĕn-dôrf)	107d	29.16N	98.20W
El Menia, Alg.	210	30.39N	2.52E
Elm Fork, Tx., U.S. (ĕlm fôrk)	107c	32.55N	96.56W
Elmhurst, Il., U.S. (ĕlm'hûrst)	101a	41.54N	87.56W
Elmhurst, neigh., N.Y., U.S.	228	40.44N	73.53W
El Miliyya, Alg. (mē'ä)	210	36.30N	6.16E
Elmira, N.Y., U.S. (ĕl-mī'rȧ)	99	42.05N	76.50W
Elmira Heights, N.Y., U.S.	99	42.10N	76.50W
El Modena, Ca., U.S. (mō-dē'nō)	107a	33.47N	117.48W
El Mohammadia, Alg.	159	35.35N	0.05E
El Molinito, Mex.	233a	19.27N	99.15W
Elmont, N.Y., U.S.	228	40.42N	73.42W
El Monte, Ca., U.S. (mŏn'tȧ)	107a	34.04N	118.02W
El Morro National Monument, rec., N.M., U.S.	109	35.05N	108.20W
Elmshorn, Ger. (ĕlms'hôrn)	154	53.45N	9.39E
Elmwood, neigh., Pa., U.S.	229b	39.56N	75.14W
Elmwood Park, Il., U.S.	231a	41.55N	87.49W
Elmwood Place, Oh., U.S. (ĕlm'wŏŏd plās)	101f	39.11N	84.30W
Elokomin, r., Wa., U.S. (ē-lō'kō-mĭn)	106c	46.16N	123.16W
El Oro, Mex. (ō-rō)	118	19.49N	100.04W
El Palmar, Ven.	234a	10.38N	66.52W
El Pao, Ven. (ĕl pá'ō)	130	8.08N	62.37W
El Paraíso, Hond. (pä-rä-ē'sō)	120	13.55N	86.35W
El Pardo, Spain (pä'r-dō)	159a	40.31N	3.47W
El Paso, Tx., U.S. (pas'ō)	96	31.47N	106.27W
El Pedregal, neigh., Ven.	234a	10.30N	66.51W
El Pilar, Ven. (pē-lä'r)	131b	9.56N	64.48W
El Plantío, neigh., Spain	238b	40.28N	3.49W
El Porvenir, Pan. (pôr-vä-nēr')	121	9.34N	78.55W
El Puerto de Santa María, Spain	158	36.36N	6.18W
El Qala, Alg.	148	36.52N	8.23E
El Qoll, Alg.	210	37.02N	6.29E
El Real, Pan. (rā-äl)	121	8.07N	77.43W
El Recreo, neigh., Ven.	234a	10.30N	66.53W
El Reloj, Mex.	233a	19.18N	99.08W
El Reno, Ok., U.S. (rē'nō)	111	35.31N	97.57W
El Rincón de la Florida, Chile	234b	33.33S	70.34W
Elroy, Wi., U.S. (ĕl'roi)	103	43.44N	90.17W
Elsa, Can.	95	63.55N	135.25W
Elsah, Il., U.S. (ĕl'zȧ)	107e	38.57N	90.22W
El Salto, Mex. (säl'tō)	118	23.48N	105.22W
El Salvador, nation, N.A.	116	14.00N	89.30W
El Sauce, Nic. (ĕl-sá'ō-sē)	120	13.00N	86.40W
Elsberry, Mo., U.S. (ĕlz'bĕr-ĭ)	111	39.09N	90.44W
Elsburg, S. Afr.	244b	26.15S	28.12E
Elsdorf, Ger. (ĕls'dōrf)	157c	50.56N	6.35E
El Segundo, Ca., U.S. (sĕgŭn'dō)	107a	33.55N	118.24W
Elsinore, Ca., U.S. (ĕl'sĭ-nôr)	107a	33.40N	117.19W
Elsinore Lake, l., Ca., U.S.	107a	33.38N	117.21W
Elstorf, Ger. (ĕls'tōrf)	145c	53.25N	9.48E
Elstree, Eng., U.K.	235	51.39N	0.16W
Eltham, Austl. (ĕl'thăm)	201a	37.43S	145.08E
Eltham, neigh., Eng., U.K.	235	51.27N	0.04E
El Tigre, Ven. (tē'grē)	130	8.49N	64.15W
Elton, Eng., U.K.	237a	53.16N	2.49W
El'ton, l., Russia	167	49.10N	47.00E
El Toreo, pt. of i., Mex.	233a	19.27N	99.13W
El Toro, Ca., U.S. (tō'rō)	107a	33.37N	117.42W
El Triunfo, El Sal.	120	13.17N	88.32W
El Triunfo, Hond. (ĕl-trē-ōō'n-fō)	120	13.06N	87.00W
Elūru, India	183	16.44N	80.09E
El Vado Res, N.M., U.S.	109	36.37N	106.30W
El Valle, neigh., Ven.	234a	10.27N	66.55W
Elvas, Port. (ĕl'väzh)	148	38.53N	7.11W
Elverum, Nor. (ĕl'vĕ-rŏŏm)	152	60.53N	11.33E
El Viejo, Nic. (ĕl-vyĕ'ĸō)	120	12.10N	87.10W
El Viejo, vol., Nic.	120	12.44N	87.03W
Elvins, Mo., U.S. (ĕl'vĭnz)	111	37.49N	90.31W
El Wad, Alg.	210	33.23N	6.49E
El Wak, Kenya (wäk')	211	3.00N	41.00E
Elwell, Lake, res., Mt., U.S.	105	48.22N	111.17W
Elwood, Il., U.S. (ĕ'wŏŏd)	101a	41.24N	88.07W
Elwood, In., U.S.	98	40.15N	85.50W
Ely, Eng., U.K. (ē'lĭ)	151	52.25N	0.17E
Ely, Mn., U.S.	103	47.54N	91.53W
Ely, Nv., U.S.	96	39.16N	114.53W
Elyria, Oh., U.S. (ē-lĭr'ĭ-ȧ)	101d	41.22N	82.07W
El Zamural, Ven.	234a	10.27N	67.00W
El Zig-Zag, Ven.	234a	10.33N	66.58W
Ema, r., Est. (å'mȧ)	153	58.25N	27.00E
Emāmshahr, Iran	182	36.25N	55.01E
Emån, r., Swe.	152	57.15N	15.46E
Embarrass, r., Il., U.S. (ĕm-băr'ăs)	98	39.15N	88.05W
Embrun, Can. (ĕm'brŭn)	83c	45.16N	75.17W
Embrun, Fr. (äɴ-brûɴ')	157	44.35N	6.32E
Embu, Braz.	234d	23.39S	46.51W
Embu, Kenya	217	0.32S	37.27E
Emden, Ger. (ĕm'dĕn)	154	53.21N	7.15E
Émerainville, Fr.	237c	48.49N	2.37E
Emerson, Can. (ĕm'ēr-sŭn)	84	49.00N	97.12W
Emerson, N.J., U.S.	228	40.58N	74.02W
Emeryville, Ca., U.S. (ĕm'ēr-ĭ-vĭl)	106b	37.50N	122.17W
Emi Koussi, mtn., Chad (ā'mē kōō-sē')	211	19.50N	18.30E
Emiliano Zapata, Mex. (ĕ-mē-lyä'nō-zä-pá'tä)	119	17.45N	91.46W
Emilia-Romagna, hist. reg., Italy (ē-mēl'yä rô-má'n-yä)	160	44.35N	10.48E
Eminence, Ky., U.S. (ĕm'ĭ-nĕns)	98	38.25N	85.15W
Emira Island, i., Pap. N. Gui. (ā-mē-rä')	197	1.40S	150.28E
Emmen, Neth. (ĕm'ĕn)	151	52.48N	6.55E
Emmerich, Ger. (ĕm'ēr-ĭk)	157c	51.51N	6.16E
Emmetsburg, Ia., U.S. (ĕm'ĕts-bûrg)	103	43.07N	94.41W

PRONOUNCING INDEX

Emmett-Everard Ranges 285

PLACE (Pronunciation)	PAGE	Lat. °'	Long. °'
Emmett, Id., U.S. (ĕm'ĕt)	104	43.53N	116.30W
Emmons, Mount, mtn., Ut., U.S. (ĕm'ŭnz)	96	40.43N	110.20W
Emory Peak, mtn., Tx., U.S. (ĕ'mō-rē pēk)	112	29.13N	103.20W
Empoli, Italy (ām'pô-lē)	160	43.43N	10.55E
Emporia, Ks., U.S. (ĕm-pō'rĭ-ȧ)	96	38.24N	96.11W
Emporia, Va., U.S.	115	37.40N	77.34W
Emporium, Pa., U.S. (ĕm-pō'rĭ-ŭm)	99	41.30N	78.15W
Empty Quarter see Ar Rub'al Khālī, des., Asia	182	20.00N	51.00E
Ems, r., Ger. (ĕms)	154	52.52N	7.16E
Emst, neigh., Ger.	236	51.21N	7.30E
Ems-Weser Kanal, can., Ger.	154	52.23N	8.11E
Emsworth, Pa., U.S.	230b	40.30N	80.04W
Enånger, Swe. (ĕn-ôŋ'gĕr)	152	61.36N	16.55E
Encantada, Cerro de la, mtn., Mex. (sĕ'r-rô-dĕ-lä-ĕn-kän-tä'dä)	116	31.58N	115.15W
Encanto, Cape, c., Phil. (ĕn-kän'tō)	197a	15.44N	121.46E
Encarnação, neigh., Port.	238d	38.47N	9.06W
Encarnación, Para. (ĕn-kär-nä-syōn')	132	27.26S	55.52W
Encarnación de Díaz, Mex. (ĕn-kär-nä-syōn dā dē'áz)	118	21.34N	102.15W
Encinal, Tx., U.S. (ĕn'sĭ-nôl)	112	28.02N	99.22W
Encino, neigh., Ca., U.S.	232	34.09N	118.30W
Encontrados, Ven. (ĕn-kōn-trä'dōs)	130	9.01N	72.10W
Encounter Bay, b., Austl. (ĕn-koun'tẽr)	202	35.50S	138.45E
Endako, r., Can.	86	54.05N	125.30W
Endau, r., Malay.	181b	2.29N	103.40E
Enderbury, i., Kir. (ĕn'dẽr-bûrĭ)	224	2.00S	171.00W
Enderby Land, reg., Ant. (ĕn'dẽr bĭĭ)	219	72.00S	52.00E
Enderlin, N.D., U.S. (ĕn'dẽr-lĭn)	102	46.38N	97.37W
Endicott, N.Y., U.S. (ĕn'dĭ-kŏt)	99	42.05N	76.00W
Endicott Mountains, mts., Ak., U.S.	95	67.30N	153.45W
Enez, Tur.	161	40.42N	26.05E
Enfer, Pointe d', c., Mart.	121b	14.21N	60.48W
Enfield, Austl.	243a	33.53S	151.06E
Enfield, Eng., U.K.	144b	51.38N	0.06W
Enfield, Ct., U.S. (ĕn'fēld)	99	41.55N	72.35W
Enfield, N.C., U.S.	115	36.10N	77.41W
Engaño, Cabo, c., Dom. Rep. (ká'-bô- ĕn-gä-nô)	117	18.40N	68.30W
Engcobo, S. Afr. (ĕŋg-cô-bô)	213c	31.41S	27.59E
Engel's, Russia (ĕn'gĕls)	167	51.20N	45.40E
Engelskirchen, Ger. (ĕn'gĕls-kĕr'ĸĕn)	157c	50.59N	7.25E
Engenho de Dentro, neigh., Braz.	234c	22.54S	43.18W
Engenho do Mato, Braz.	234c	22.57S	43.01W
Engenho Nofrvo, neigh., Braz.	234c	22.55S	43.17W
Enggano, Pulau, i., Indon. (ĕng-gä'nō)	196	5.22S	102.18E
Enghien-les-Bains, Fr.	237c	48.58N	2.19E
England, Ar., U.S. (ĭŋ'glȧnd)	111	34.33N	91.58W
England, , U.K. (ĭŋ'glȧnd)	142	51.35N	1.40W
Englefield Green, Eng., U.K.	235	51.26N	0.35W
Englewood, Co., U.S. (ĕn'g'l-wŏod)	110	39.39N	105.00W
Englewood, N.J., U.S.	100a	40.54N	73.59W
Englewood, neigh., Il., U.S.	231a	41.47N	87.39W
Englewood Cliffs, N.J., U.S.	228	40.53N	73.57W
English, In., U.S. (ĭn'glĭsh)	98	38.15N	86.25W
English, r., Can.	85	50.31N	94.12W
English Channel, strt., Eur.	142	49.45N	3.06W
Enguera, Spain (ān'gārā)	159	38.58N	0.42W
Enid, Ok., U.S. (ē'nĭd)	96	36.25N	97.52W
Enid Lake, res., Ms., U.S.	114	34.13N	89.47W
Enkeldoring, S. Afr. (ĕŋ'k'l-dôr-ĭng)	218d	25.24S	28.43E
Enköping, Swe. (ĕn'kû-pĭng)	152	59.39N	17.05E
Ennedi, mts., Chad (ĕn-nĕd'ē)	211	16.45N	22.45E
Ennepetal, Ger.	236	51.18N	7.22E
Ennis, Ire. (ĕn'ĭs)	150	52.54N	9.05W
Ennis, Tx., U.S.	113	32.20N	96.38W
Enniscorthy, Ire. (ĕn-ĭs-kôr'thĭ)	150	52.33N	6.27W
Enniskillen, N. Ire., U.K. (ĕn-ĭs-kĭl'ĕn)	150	54.20N	7.25W
Ennis Lake, res., Mt., U.S.	105	45.15N	111.30W
Enns, r., Aus. (ĕns)	147	47.37N	14.35E
Enoree, S.C., U.S. (ē-nō'rē)	115	34.43N	81.58W
Enoree, r., S.C., U.S.	115	34.35N	81.55W
Enriquillo, Dom. Rep. (ĕn-rē-kē'l-yô)	123	17.55N	71.15W
Enriquillo, Lago, l., Dom. Rep. (lä'gô-ĕn-rē-kē'l-yô)	123	18.35N	71.35W
Enschede, Neth. (ĕns'ĸā-dĕ)	147	52.10N	6.50E
Enseñada, Arg.	129c	34.50S	57.55W
Ensenada, Mex. (ĕn-sĕ-nä'dä)	116	32.00N	116.30W
Enshi, China (ŭn-shr)	188	30.18N	109.25E
Enshū-Nada, b., Japan (ĕn'shōō nä-dä)	195	34.25N	137.14E
Entebbe, Ug.	211	0.04N	32.28E
Enterprise, Al., U.S. (ĕn'tẽr-prīz)	114	31.20N	85.50W
Enterprise, Or., U.S.	104	45.25N	117.16W
Entiat, L, Wa., U.S.	104	45.43N	120.11W
Entraygues, Fr. (ĕɴ-trĕg')	156	44.39N	2.33E
Entre Rios, prov., Arg.	132	31.30S	59.00W
Enugu, Nig. (ĕ-nōō'gōō)	210	6.27N	7.27E
Enumclaw, Wa., U.S. (ĕn'ŭm-klô)	106a	47.12N	121.59W
Envigado, Col. (ĕn-vē-gá'dô)	130a	6.10N	75.34W
Eolie, Isole, is., Italy (ĕ'ŏ-lē-ē-ô'lyĕ)	148	38.43N	14.43E
Epe, Nig.	215	6.37N	3.59E
Épernay, Fr. (ā-pĕr-nĕ')	147	49.02N	3.54E
Épernon, Fr. (ā-pĕr-nôɴ')	157b	48.36N	1.41E
Ephraim, Ut., U.S. (ē'frā-ĭm)	109	39.20N	111.40W
Ephrata, Wa., U.S. (ēfrā'tȧ)	104	47.18N	119.35W
Epi, Vanuatu (ā'pē)	203	16.59S	168.29E
Épila, Spain (ā'pē-lä)	158	41.38N	1.15W
Épinal, Fr. (ā-pē-näl')	147	48.11N	6.27E
Épinay-sous-Sénart, Fr.	237c	48.42N	2.31E
Épinay-sur-Seine, Fr.	237c	48.57N	2.19E
Episkopi, Cyp.	181a	34.38N	32.55E
Eppendorf, neigh., Ger.	236	51.27N	7.11E
Eppenhausen, neigh., Ger.	236	51.21N	7.31E
Epping, Austl.	243a	33.46S	151.05E

PLACE (Pronunciation)	PAGE	Lat. °'	Long. °'
Epping, Eng., U.K. (ĕp'ĭng)	144b	51.41N	0.06E
Epping Green, Eng., U.K.	235	51.44N	0.05E
Epping Upland, Eng., U.K.	235	51.43N	0.06E
Epsom, Eng., U.K.	144b	51.20N	0.16W
Epupa Falls, wtfl., Afr.	216	17.00S	13.05E
Epworth, Eng., U.K. (ĕp'wûrth)	144a	53.31N	0.50W
Equatorial Guinea, nation, Afr.	210	2.00N	7.15E
Équilles, Fr.	156a	43.34N	5.21E
Eramosa, r., Can. (ĕr-ȧ-mō'sȧ)	83d	43.39N	80.08W
Erba, Jabal, mtn., Sudan (ĕr-bȧ)	211	20.53N	36.45E
Erciyeş Daği, mtn., Tur.	149	38.30N	35.36E
Erding, Ger. (ĕr'dēng)	145d	48.19N	11.54E
Erechim, Braz. (ĕ-rĕ-shē'ɴ)	132	27.43S	52.11W
Ereğli, Tur. (ĕ-rā'ĭ-le)	149	37.40N	34.00E
Ereğli, Tur.	149	41.15N	31.25E
Erenköy, neigh., Tur.	239f	40.58N	29.04E
Erfurt, Ger. (ĕr'fŏort)	147	50.59N	11.04E
Ergene, r., Tur. (ĕr'gĕ-nĕ)	161	41.17N	26.50E
Erges, r., Eur. (ĕr'-zhĕs)	158	39.45N	7.01W
Ērgli, Lat.	153	56.54N	25.38E
Ergste, Ger.	236	51.25N	7.34E
Eria, r., Spain (ā-rē'ä)	158	42.10N	6.08W
Erick, Ok., U.S. (âr'ĭk)	110	35.14N	99.51W
Erie, Ks., U.S. (ē'rĭ)	111	37.35N	95.17W
Erie, Pa., U.S.	97	42.05N	80.05W
Erie, Lake, l., N.A.	97	42.15N	81.25W
Erimo Saki, c., Japan (ā'rē-mō sä-kē)	189	41.53N	143.20E
Erin, Can. (ĕ'rĭn)	83d	43.46N	80.04W
Erith, neigh., Eng., U.K.	235	51.29N	0.10E
Eritrea, nation, Afr. (ā-rē-trā'ȧ)	211	16.15N	38.30E
Erkrath, Ger.	236	51.13N	6.55E
Erlangen, Ger. (ĕr'läng-ĕn)	154	49.36N	11.03E
Erlanger, Ky., U.S. (ĕr'läng-ẽr)	101f	39.01N	84.36W
Erle, neigh., Ger.	236	51.33N	7.05E
Ermont, Fr.	237c	48.59N	2.16E
Ermoúpolis, Grc.	161	37.30N	24.56E
Ernākulam, India	183	9.58N	76.23E
Erne, Lower Lough, l., N. Ire., U.K.	150	54.30N	7.40W
Erne, Upper Lough, l., N. Ire., U.K. (lŏk ûrn)	150	54.20N	7.24W
Erode, India	187	11.20N	77.45E
Eromanga, i., Vanuatu	203	18.58S	169.18E
Eros, La., U.S. (ē'rōs)	113	32.23N	92.22W
Errego, Moz.	217	16.02S	37.14E
Errigal, mtn., Ire. (ĕr-ĭ-gôl')	150	55.02N	8.07W
Errol Heights, Or., U.S.	106c	45.29N	122.38W
Erskine Park, Austl.	243a	33.49S	150.47E
Erstein, Fr. (ĕr'shtīn)	157	48.27N	7.40E
Erwin, N.C., U.S. (ûr'wĭn)	115	35.16N	78.40W
Erwin, Tn., U.S.	115	36.07N	82.25W
Erzgebirge, mts., Eur. (ĕrts'gĕ-bē'gĕ)	142	50.29N	12.40E
Erzincan, Tur. (ĕr-zĭn-jän')	182	39.50N	39.30E
Erzurum, Tur. (ĕrz'rōōm')	182	39.55N	41.10E
Esambo, Zaire	216	3.40S	23.24E
Esashi, Japan (ĕs'ä-shē)	189	41.50N	140.10E
Esbjerg, Den. (ĕs'byĕrgh)	146	55.29N	8.25E
Esborn, Ger.	236	51.23N	7.20E
Escalante, Ut., U.S. (ĕs-kȧ-län'tē)	109	37.50N	111.40W
Escalante, r., Ut., U.S.	109	37.40N	111.20W
Escalón, Mex.	112	26.45N	104.20W
Escambia, r., Fl., U.S. (ĕs-kăm'bĭ-ȧ)	114	30.38N	87.20W
Escanaba, Mi., U.S. (ĕs-kȧ-nô'bȧ)	97	45.44N	87.05W
Escanaba, r., Mi., U.S.	103	46.10N	87.22W
Escarpada Point, Phil.	196	18.40N	122.45E
Esch-sur-Alzette, Lux.	157	49.32N	6.21E
Eschwege, Ger. (ĕsh'vā-gĕ)	154	51.11N	10.02E
Eschweiler, Ger. (ĕsh'vī-lẽr)	157c	50.49N	6.15E
Escondido, Ca., U.S. (ĕs-kŏn-dē'dō)	108	33.07N	117.00W
Escondido, r., Nic.	121	12.04N	84.09W
Escondido, Río, r., Mex. (rē'ō-ĕs-kōn-dē'dô)	112	28.30N	100.45W
Escuadrón 201, Mex.	233a	19.22N	99.06W
Escudo de Veraguas, i., Pan. (ĕs-kōō'dä dā vā-rä'gwäs)	121	9.07N	81.25W
Escuinapa, Mex. (ĕs-kwē-nä'pä)	116	22.49N	105.44W
Escuintla, Guat. (ĕs-kwēn'tlä)	120	14.16N	90.47W
Ese, Cayos de, i., Col.	121	12.24N	81.07W
Eşfahān, Iran	182	32.38N	51.30E
Esgueva, r., Spain (ĕs-gĕ'vä)	158	41.48N	4.10W
Esher, Eng., U.K.	144b	51.23N	0.22W
Eshowe, S. Afr. (ĕsh'ô-wē)	213c	28.54S	31.28E
Esiama, Ghana	214	4.56N	2.21W
Eskdale, W.V., U.S. (ĕsk'dāl)	98	38.05N	81.25W
Eskifjördur, Ice. (ĕs'kē-fyŭr'dōōr)	142	65.04N	14.01W
Eskilstuna, Swe. (å'shĕl-stü-na)	146	59.23N	16.28E
Eskimo Lakes, l., Can. (ĕs'kĭ-mō)	84	69.40N	130.10W
Eskişehir, Tur. (ĕs-kē-shĕ'h'r)	182	39.40N	30.20E
Esko, Mn., U.S. (ĕs'kô)	107h	46.27N	92.22W
Esla, r., Spain (ĕs-lä)	158	41.50N	5.48W
Eslöv, Swe. (ĕs'lûv)	152	55.50N	13.17E
Esmeraldas, Ec. (ĕs-mā-räl'däs)	130	0.58N	79.45W
Espanola, Can. (ĕs-pȧ-nō'lȧ)	85	46.11N	81.59W
Esparta, C.R. (ĕs-pär'tä)	121	9.59N	84.40W
Esperance, Austl. (ĕs'pē-rȧns)	202	33.45S	122.07E
Esperanza, Cuba (ĕs-pĕ-rä'n-zä)	122	22.30N	80.10W
Espichel, Cabo, c., Port. (ká'bō-ĕs-pē-shĕl')	158	38.25N	9.13W
Espinal, Col. (ĕs-pē-näl')	130	4.10N	74.53W
Espinhaço, Serra do, mts., Braz. (sĕ'r-rä-dô-ĕs-pē-ná-sô)	131	16.00S	44.00W
Espinillo, Punta, c., Ur. (pōō'n-tä-ĕs-pē-nē'l-yô)	129c	34.49S	56.27W
Espírito Santo, Braz. (ĕs-pē'rē-tô-sän'tô)	131	20.27S	40.18W
Espírito Santo, state, Braz.	131	19.57S	40.58W
Espiritu Santo, i., Vanuatu (ĕs-pē'rē-tōō sän'tō)	203	15.45S	166.50E
Espíritu Santo, Bahía del, b., Mex.	120a	19.25N	87.28W

PLACE (Pronunciation)	PAGE	Lat. °'	Long. °'
Espita, Mex. (ĕs-pē'tä)	120a	20.57N	88.22W
Esplugas, Spain	238e	41.23N	2.06E
Espoo, Fin.	153	60.13N	24.41E
Esposende, Port. (ĕs-pō-zĕn'dā)	158	41.33N	8.45W
Esquel, Arg. (ĕs-kĕ'l)	132	42.47S	71.22W
Esquimalt, Can. (ĕs-kwī'mŏlt)	86	48.26N	123.24W
Essaouira, Mor.	210	31.34N	9.44W
Essel, neigh., Ger.	236	51.37N	7.15E
Essen, Bel.	145a	51.28N	4.27E
Essen, Ger. (ĕs'sĕn)	142	51.26N	6.59E
Essenberg, Ger.	236	51.26N	6.42E
Essendon, Austl.	201a	37.46S	144.55E
Essequibo, r., Guy. (ĕs-ā-kē'bō)	131	4.26N	58.17W
Essex, Il., U.S.	101a	41.11N	88.11W
Essex, Md., U.S.	100e	39.19N	76.29W
Essex, Ma., U.S.	93a	42.38N	70.47W
Essex, Vt., U.S.	99	44.30N	73.05W
Essex Fells, N.J., U.S. (ĕs'ĕks fĕlz)	100a	40.50N	74.16W
Essexville, Mi., U.S. (ĕs'ĕks-vĭl)	98	43.35N	83.50W
Essington, Pa., U.S.	229b	39.52N	75.18W
Essling, neigh., Aus.	239e	48.13N	16.32E
Esslingen, Ger. (ĕs'slēn-gĕn)	154	48.45N	9.19E
Estacado, Llano, pl., U.S. (yá-nō ĕs-tȧcȧ-dō')	96	33.50N	103.20W
Estância, Braz. (ĕs-tän'sĭ-ä)	131	11.17S	37.18W
Estarreja, Port. (ĕ-tär-rā'zhä)	158	40.44N	8.39W
Estats, Pique d', mtn., Eur.	159	42.43N	1.30E
Estcourt, S. Afr. (ĕst-coort)	213c	29.04S	29.53E
Este, Italy (ĕs'tā)	160	45.13N	11.40E
Estella, Spain (ĕs-täl'yä)	158	42.40N	2.01W
Estepa, Spain (ĕs-tā'pä)	158	37.18N	4.54W
Estepona, Spain (ĕs-tā-pō'nä)	158	36.26N	5.08W
Esterhazy, Can. (ĕs'tẽr-hä-zē)	89	50.40N	102.08W
Estero Bay, b., Ca., U.S. (ĕs-tā'rōs)	108	35.22N	121.04W
Estevan, Can. (ĕ-stē'vȧn)	84	49.07N	103.05W
Estevan Group, is., Can.	86	53.05N	129.40W
Estherville, Ia., U.S. (ĕs'tẽr-vĭl)	103	43.24N	94.49W
Estill, S.C., U.S. (ĕs'tĭl)	115	32.46N	81.15W
Eston, Can.	88	51.10N	108.45W
Estonia, nation, Eur.	164	59.10N	25.00E
Estoril, Port. (ĕs-tô-rēl')	159b	38.45N	9.24W
Estrêla, mtn., Port. (mäl-you'ɴ-dä-ĕs-trĕ'lä)	158	40.20N	7.38W
Estrêla, r., Braz. (ĕs-trĕ'lȧ)	132b	22.39S	43.16W
Estrêla, Serra da, mts., Port. (sĕr'rȧ dä ĕs-trā'lȧ)	158	40.25N	7.45W
Estrella, Cerro de la, mtn., Mex.	233a	19.21N	99.05W
Estremadura, hist. reg., Port. (ĕs-trä-mä-dōō'rȧ)	158	39.00N	8.36W
Estremoz, Port. (ĕs-trā-mōzh')	158	38.50N	7.35W
Estrondo, Serra do, mts., Braz. (sĕr'-rȧ dô ĕs-trôn'-dô)	131	9.52S	48.56W
Esumba, Île, i., Zaire	216	2.00N	21.12E
Esztergom, Hung. (ĕs'tẽr-gōm)	155	47.46N	18.45E
Etah, Grnld. (ē'tȧ)	82	78.20N	72.42W
Étampes, Fr. (ā-täɴp')	156	48.26N	2.09E
Étaples, Fr. (ā-täp'l')	156	50.32N	1.38E
Etchemin, r., Can. (ĕch'ĕ-mĭn)	83b	46.39N	71.03W
Ethiopia, nation, Afr. (ē-thē-ō'pē-ȧ)	211	7.53N	37.55E
Eticoga, Gui.-B.	214	11.09N	16.08W
Etiwanda, Ca., U.S. (ĕ-tĭ-wän'dȧ)	107a	34.07N	117.31W
Etna, Pa., U.S. (ĕt'nȧ)	101e	40.30N	79.55W
Etna, Mount, vol., Italy	142	37.48N	15.00E
Etobicoke, Can.	91	43.39N	79.34W
Etobicoke Creek, r., Can.	83d	43.44N	79.48W
Etolin Strait, strt., Ak., U.S. (ĕt ō lĭn)	95	60.35S	165.40W
Eton, Eng., U.K.	235	51.31N	0.37W
Eton College, educ., Eng., U.K.	235	51.30N	0.36W
Etoshapan, pl., Nmb. (ĕtō'shä)	212	19.07S	15.30E
Etowah, Tn., U.S. (ĕt'ô-wä)	114	35.18N	84.31W
Etowah, r., Ga., U.S.	114	34.23N	84.19W
Étréchy, Fr. (ā-trā-shē')	157b	48.29N	2.12E
Etten-Leur, Neth.	145a	51.34N	4.38E
Etterbeek, Bel. (ĕt'ẽr-bāk)	145a	50.51N	4.24E
Etzatlán, Mex. (ĕt-zä-tlän')	118	20.44N	104.04W
Eucla, Austl. (ū'klȧ)	202	31.45S	128.50E
Euclid, Oh., U.S. (ū'klĭd)	101d	41.34N	81.32W
Eudora, Ar., U.S. (u-dō'rȧ)	111	33.07N	91.16W
Eufaula, Al., U.S. (ů-fô'lȧ)	114	31.53N	85.09W
Eufaula, Ok., U.S.	111	35.16N	95.35W
Eufaula Reservoir, res., Ok., U.S.	111	35.00N	94.45W
Eugene, Or., U.S. (ů-jēn')	96	44.02N	123.06W
Euless, Tx., U.S. (ū'lĕs)	107c	32.50N	97.05W
Eunice, La., U.S. (ū'nĭs)	113	30.30N	92.25W
Eupen, Bel. (oi'pĕn)	151	50.39N	6.05E
Euphrates, r., Asia (ů-frā'tēz)	182	36.00N	40.00E
Eure, r., Fr. (ûr)	156	49.03N	1.22E
Eureka, Ca., U.S. (ů-rē'kȧ)	96	40.45N	124.10W
Eureka, Ks., U.S.	111	37.48N	96.17W
Eureka, Mt., U.S.	104	48.53N	115.07W
Eureka, Nv., U.S.	108	39.33N	115.58W
Eureka, S.D., U.S.	102	45.46N	99.38W
Eureka, Ut., U.S.	109	39.55N	112.10W
Eureka Springs, Ar., U.S.	111	36.24N	93.43W
Europe, cont. (ū'rŭp)	142	50.00N	15.00E
Eustis, Fl., U.S. (ūs'tĭs)	115	28.50N	81.41W
Eutaw, Al., U.S. (ū-tȧ)	114	32.48N	87.50W
Eutsuk Lake, l., Can. (ōōt'sŭk)	86	53.20N	126.44W
Evanston, Il., U.S. (ĕv'ăn-stŭn)	97	42.03N	87.41W
Evanston, Wy., U.S.	105	41.17N	111.02W
Evansville, In., U.S. (ĕv'ănz-vĭl)	97	38.00N	87.30W
Evansville, Wi., U.S.	103	42.46N	89.19W
Evart, Mi., U.S. (ĕv'ẽrt)	98	43.55N	85.10W
Evaton, S. Afr. (ĕv'ȧ-tŏn)	218d	26.32S	27.53E
Eveleth, Mn., U.S. (ĕv'ē-lĕth)	103	47.27N	92.35W
Everard, l., Austl. (ĕv'ẽr-ård)	202	31.20S	134.10E
Everard Ranges, mts., Austl.	202	27.15S	132.00E

ng-sing; ŋ-baŋk; ɴ-nasalized n; nŏd; cŏmmit; ōld; ôbey; ôrder; oi-boil; fōōd; ŏo-as oo in foot; ou-out; s-soft; sh-dish; th-thin; pūre; ůnite; ûrn; stŭd; circŭs; ü-as in French tu; '-indeterminate vowel.

286 Everest-Fertile

PLACE (Pronunciation)	PAGE	Lat. °′	Long. °′
Everest, Mount, mtn., Asia (ĕv′ẽr-ĕst)	183	28.00N	86.57E
Everett, Ma., U.S. (ĕv′ẽr-ĕt)	93a	42.24N	71.03W
Everett, Wa., U.S. (ĕv′ẽr-ĕt)	96	47.59N	122.11W
Everett Mountains, mts., Can.	85	62.34N	68.00W
Everglades, The, sw., Fl., U.S.	115a	25.35N	80.55W
Everglades City, Fl., U.S. (ĕv′ẽr-glădz)	115a	25.50N	81.25W
Everglades National Park, rec., Fl., U.S.	97	25.39N	80.57W
Evergreen, Al., U.S. (ĕv′ẽr-grēn)	114	31.25N	87.56W
Evergreen Park, Il., U.S.	101a	41.44N	87.42W
Everman, Tx., U.S. (ĕv′ẽr-măn)	107c	32.38N	97.17W
Everson, Wa., U.S. (ĕv′ẽr-sŭn)	106d	48.55N	122.21W
Everton, neigh., Eng., U.K.	237a	53.25N	2.58W
Eving, neigh., Ger.	236	51.33N	7.29E
Évora, Port. (ĕv′ô-rä)	148	38.35N	7.54W
Évreux, Fr. (ā-vrû′)	147	49.02N	1.11E
Evrótas, r., Grc. (ĕv-rō′täs)	161	37.15N	22.17E
Évvoia, i., Grc.	149	38.38N	23.45E
Ewa Beach, Hi., U.S. (ē′wä)	94a	21.17N	158.03E
Ewaso Ng'iro, r., Kenya	211	0.59N	37.47E
Ewell, Eng., U.K.	235	51.21N	0.15W
Ewu, Nig.	244d	6.33N	3.19E
Excelsior, Mn., U.S. (ĕk-sel′sĭ-ŏr)	107g	44.54N	93.35W
Excelsior Springs, Mo., U.S.	111	39.20N	94.13W
Exe, r., Eng., U.K. (ĕks)	150	50.57N	3.37W
Exeter, Eng., U.K.	147	50.45N	3.33W
Exeter, Ca., U.S. (ĕk′sė-tẽr)	108	36.18N	119.09W
Exeter, N.H., U.S.	99	43.00N	71.00W
Exmoor, for., Eng., U.K. (ĕks′mŏr)	150	51.10N	3.55W
Exmouth, Eng., U.K. (ĕks′mŭth)	150	50.40N	3.20W
Exmouth Gulf, b., Austl.	202	21.45S	114.30E
Exploits, r., Can. (ĕks-ploits′)	93	48.50N	56.15W
Extórrax, r., Mex. (ĕx-tó′räx)	118	21.04N	99.39W
Extrema, Braz. (ĕsh-trĕ′mä)	129a	22.52S	46.19W
Extremadura, hist. reg., Spain (ĕks-trā-mä-doo′rä)	158	38.43N	6.30W
Exuma Sound, strt., Bah. (ĕk-sōō′mä)	122	24.20N	76.20W
Eyasi, Lake, l., Tan. (å-yä′sė)	212	3.25S	34.55E
Eyjafjördur, b., Ice.	146	66.21N	18.20W
Eyl, Som.	218a	7.53N	49.45E
Eynsford, Eng., U.K.	235	51.22N	0.13E
Eyrarbakki, Ice.	146	63.51N	20.52W
Eyre, Austl. (âr)	202	32.15S	126.20E
Eyre, l., Austl.	202	28.43S	137.50E
Eyre Peninsula, pen., Austl.	202	33.30S	136.00E
Eyüp, neigh., Tur.	239f	41.03N	28.55E
Ezbekīyah, neigh., Egypt	244a	30.03N	31.15E
Ezeiza, Arg. (ĕ-zā′zä)	132a	34.52S	58.31W
Ezine, Tur. (å′zĭ-nå)	161	39.47N	26.18E

F

PLACE (Pronunciation)	PAGE	Lat. °′	Long. °′
Fabens, Tx., U.S. (fā′bĕnz)	112	31.30N	106.07W
Fåborg, Den. (fô′bŏrg)	152	55.06N	10.19E
Fabreville, neigh., Can.	227b	45.34N	73.50W
Fabriano, Italy (fä-brē-ä′nō)	160	43.20N	12.55E
Fada, Chad (fä′dä)	211	17.06N	21.18E
Fada Ngourma, Burkina (fä′dä′n gōōr′mä)	210	12.04N	0.21E
Faddeya, i., Russia (fåd-yä′)	165	76.12N	145.00E
Faenza, Italy (fä-ĕnd′zä)	160	44.16N	11.53E
Faeroe Islands, is., Eur. (fā′rō)	142	62.00N	5.45W
Fafe, Port. (fä′fă)	158	41.30N	8.10W
Fafen, r., Eth.	218a	8.15N	42.40E
Făgăras, Rom. (fâ-gä′räsh)	161	45.50N	24.55E
Fagerness, Nor. (fä′ghĕr-nĕs)	146	61.00N	9.10E
Fagnano, l., S.A. (fäk-nä′nō)	132	54.35S	68.20W
Faguibine, Lac, l., Mali	214	16.50N	4.20W
Fahrland, Ger.	238a	52.28N	13.01E
Faial, i., Port. (fä-yä′l)	210a	38.40N	29.19W
Fā'id, Egypt (fä-yēd′)	218c	30.19N	32.18E
Failsworth, Eng., U.K.	237b	53.31N	2.09W
Fairbanks, Ak., U.S. (fâr′bănks)	96a	64.50N	147.48W
Fairbury, Il., U.S. (fâr′bĕr-ĭ)	98	40.45N	88.25W
Fairbury, Ne., U.S.	111	40.09N	97.11W
Fairchild Creek, r., Can. (fâr′chīld)	83d	43.18N	80.10W
Fairfax, Mn., U.S. (fâr′făks)	103	44.29N	94.44W
Fairfax, S.C., U.S.	115	32.29N	81.13W
Fairfax, Va., U.S.	100e	38.51N	77.20W
Fairfield, Austl.	201b	33.52S	150.57E
Fairfield, Al., U.S. (fâr′fēld)	100h	33.30N	86.50W
Fairfield, Ct., U.S.	100a	41.08N	73.22W
Fairfield, Il., U.S.	98	38.25N	88.20W
Fairfield, Ia., U.S.	103	41.00N	91.59W
Fairfield, Me., U.S.	92	44.35N	69.38W
Fairfield, N.J., U.S.	228	40.53N	74.17W
Fairhaven, Md., U.S.	229d	38.47N	77.05W
Fairhaven, Ma., U.S. (fâr-hā′vĕn)	99	41.35N	70.55W
Fair Haven, Vt., U.S.	99	43.35N	73.15W
Fair Island, i., Scot., U.K. (fâr)	150a	59.34N	1.41W
Fair Lawn, N.J., U.S.	228	40.56N	74.07W
Fairlee, Md., U.S.	229d	38.52N	77.16W
Fairmont, Mn., U.S. (fâr′mŏnt)	103	43.39N	94.26W
Fairmont, W.V., U.S.	98	39.30N	80.10W
Fairmont City, Il., U.S.	107e	38.39N	90.05W
Fairmount, In., U.S.	98	40.25N	85.45W
Fairmount, Ks., U.S.	107f	39.12N	95.55W
Fairmount Heights, Md., U.S.	229d	38.54N	76.55W
Fair Oaks, Ga., U.S. (fâr ōks)	100c	33.56N	84.33W
Fairport, N.Y., U.S. (fâr′pōrt)	99	43.05N	77.30W
Fairport Harbor, Oh., U.S.	98	41.45N	81.15W
Fairseat, Eng., U.K.	235	51.20N	0.20E
Fairview, N.J., U.S.	228	40.49N	74.00W
Fairview, Ok., U.S. (fâr′vū)	110	36.16N	98.28W
Fairview, Or., U.S.	106c	45.32N	112.26W
Fairview, Ut., U.S.	109	39.35N	111.30W
Fairview Park, Oh., U.S.	101d	41.27N	81.52W
Fairweather, Mount, mtn., N.A. (fâr-wĕdh′ẽr)	95	59.12N	137.22W
Faisalabad, Pak.	183	31.29N	73.06E
Faith, S.D., U.S. (fāth)	102	45.02N	120.02W
Faizābād, India	183	26.50N	82.17E
Fajardo, P.R.	117b	18.20N	65.40W
Fakfak, Indon.	197	2.56S	132.25E
Faku, China (fä-kōō)	192	42.28N	123.20E
Falcón, dept., Ven. (fäl-kô′n)	131b	11.00N	68.28W
Falconer, N.Y., U.S. (fô′k′n-ẽr)	99	42.10N	79.10W
Falcon Heights, Mn., U.S. (fô′k′n)	107g	44.59N	93.10W
Falcon Reservoir, res., N.A. (fôk′n)	112	26.47N	99.03W
Fălești, Mol.	163	47.33N	27.46E
Falfurrias, Tx., U.S. (fäl′fōō-rē′äs)	112	27.15N	98.08W
Falher, Can. (fäl′ẽr)	87	55.44N	117.12W
Falkenberg, Swe. (fäl′kĕn-bĕrgh)	152	56.54N	12.25E
Falkensee, Ger. (fäl′kĕn-zā)	145b	52.34N	13.05E
Falkenthal, Ger. (fäl′kĕn-täl)	145b	52.54N	13.18E
Falkirk, Scot., U.K. (fôl′kûrk)	150	55.59N	3.55W
Falkland Islands, dep., S.A. (fôk′lănd)	132	50.45S	61.00W
Falköping, Swe. (fäl′chûp-ĭng)	152	58.09N	13.30E
Fall City, Wa., U.S.	106a	47.34N	121.53W
Fall Creek, r., In., U.S. (fôl)	101g	39.52N	86.04W
Fallon, Nv., U.S. (făl′ŭn)	108	39.30N	118.48W
Fall River, Ma., U.S.	97	41.42N	71.07W
Falls Church, Va., U.S. (fälz chûrch)	100e	38.53N	77.10W
Falls City, Ne., U.S.	111	40.04N	95.37W
Fallston, Md., U.S. (fâls′ton)	100e	39.32N	76.26W
Falmouth, Jam.	122	18.30N	77.40W
Falmouth, Eng., U.K. (făl′mŭth)	150	50.08N	5.04W
Falmouth, Ky., U.S.	98	38.40N	84.20W
False Divi Point, c., India	187	15.45N	80.50E
Falster, i., Den. (fäls′tẽr)	152	54.48N	11.58E
Fălticeni, Rom. (fŭl-tė-chån′y′)	155	47.27N	26.17E
Falun, Swe. (fä-lōōn′)	146	60.38N	15.35E
Famadas, Spain	238e	41.21N	2.05E
Famagusta, N. Cyp. (fä-mä-gōōs′tä)	149	35.08N	33.59E
Famatina, Sierra de, mts., Arg.	132	29.00S	67.50W
Fangxian, China (fäŋ-shyĕn)	192	32.05N	110.45E
Fanning, i., Can.	83f	49.45N	97.46W
Fano, Italy (fä′nō)	160	43.49N	13.01E
Fanø, i., Den. (fän′û)	152	55.24N	8.10E
Fan Si Pan, mtn., Viet.	193	22.25N	103.50E
Farafangana, Madag. (fä-rä-fäŋ-gä′nä)	213	23.18S	47.59E
Farāh, Afg. (fä-rä′)	182	32.15N	62.13E
Farallón, Punta, c., Mex. (pö′n-tä-fä-rä-lōn)	118	19.21N	105.03W
Faranah, Gui. (fä-rä′nä)	210	10.02N	10.44W
Farasān, Jaza'ir, is., Sau. Ar.	182	16.45N	41.08E
Faregh, Wadi al, r., Libya (wädē ĕl fä-rēg′)	149	30.10N	19.34E
Farewell, Cape, c., N.Z. (fâr-wĕl′)	203a	40.37S	172.40E
Fargo, N.D., U.S. (fär′gō)	96	46.53N	96.48W
Far Hills, N.J., U.S. (fär hĭlz)	100a	40.41N	74.38W
Faribault, Mn., U.S. (fâ′rĭ-bō)	103	44.19N	93.16W
Farilhões, is., Port. (fä-rė-lyôɴzh′)	158	39.28N	9.32W
Faringdon, Eng., U.K. (fă′rĭng-dŏn)	144b	51.38N	1.35W
Fāriskūr, Egypt (fä-rės-kōōr′)	218b	31.19N	31.46E
Farit, Amba, mtn., Eth.	211	10.51N	37.52E
Farley, Mo., U.S. (fär′lē)	107f	39.16N	94.49W
Farmers Branch, Tx., U.S.	107c	32.56N	96.53W
Farmersburg, In., U.S. (fär′mẽrz-bûrg)	98	39.15N	87.25W
Farmersville, Tx., U.S. (fär′mẽrz-vĭl)	111	33.11N	96.22W
Farmingdale, N.J., U.S. (färm′ĕng-dāl)	100a	40.11N	74.10W
Farmingdale, N.Y., U.S.	100a	40.44N	73.26W
Farmingham, Ma., U.S. (färm-ĭng-hăm)	93a	42.17N	71.25W
Farmington, Il., U.S. (färm-ĭng-tŭn)	111	40.42N	90.01W
Farmington, Me., U.S.	92	44.40N	70.10W
Farmington, Mi., U.S.	101b	42.28N	83.23W
Farmington, Mo., U.S.	111	37.46N	90.26W
Farmington, N.M., U.S.	109	36.40N	108.10W
Farmington, Ut., U.S.	107b	40.59N	111.53W
Farmington Hills, Mi., U.S.	230c	42.28N	83.23W
Farmville, N.C., U.S. (färm-vĭl)	115	35.35N	77.35W
Farmville, Va., U.S.	115	37.15N	78.23W
Farnborough, Eng., U.K. (färn′bŭr-ô)	144b	51.15N	0.45W
Farnborough, neigh., Eng., U.K.	235	51.21N	0.04E
Farne Islands, is., Eng., U.K. (färn)	150	55.40N	1.32W
Farnham, Can. (fär′năm)	99	45.15N	72.55W
Farningham, Eng., U.K. (fär′nĭng-ŭm)	144b	51.22N	0.14E
Farnworth, Eng., U.K. (färn′wŭrth)	144a	53.34N	2.24W
Faro, Braz. (fä′rö)	131	2.05S	56.32W
Faro, Port.	148	37.01N	7.57W
Farodofay, Madag.	213	24.59S	46.58E
Fårön, i., Swe.	153	57.57N	19.10E
Farquhar, Cape, c., Austl. (fär′kwår)	202	23.50S	112.55E
Farrell, Pa., U.S. (făr′ĕl)	98	41.10N	80.30W
Far Rockaway, neigh., N.Y., U.S.	228	40.36N	73.45W
Farrukhābād, India (fŭ-rök-hä-bäd′)	183	27.29N	79.35E
Fársala, Grc.	161	39.18N	22.25E
Farsund, Nor. (fär′sŏn)	152	58.05N	6.47E
Fartak, Ra's, c., Yemen	182	15.43N	52.17E
Fartura, Serra da, mts., Braz. (sĕ′r-rä-då-fär-tōō′rä)	132	26.40S	53.15W
Farvel, Kap, c., Grnld.	82	60.00N	44.00W
Farwell, Tx., U.S. (fär′wĕl)	110	34.24N	103.03W
Fasano, Italy (fä-zä′nō)	161	40.50N	17.22E
Fastiv, Ukr.	163	50.04N	29.57E
Fatëzh, Russia	162	52.06N	35.51E
Fatima, Port.	159	39.36N	9.36E
Fatsa, Tur. (fät′sä)	149	40.50N	37.30E
Faucilles, Monts, mts., Fr. (môɴ′ fō-sēl′)	157	48.07N	6.13E
Fauske, Nor.	146	67.15N	15.24E
Faust, Can. (foust)	87	55.19N	115.38W
Faustovo, Russia	172b	55.27N	38.29E
Faversham, Eng., U.K. (fă′vẽr-sh′m)	144b	51.19N	0.54E
Favoriten, neigh., Aus.	239e	48.11N	16.23E
Fawkham Green, Eng., U.K.	235	51.22N	0.17E
Fawkner, Austl.	243b	37.43S	144.58E
Fawsett Farms, Md., U.S.	229d	38.59N	77.14W
Faxaflói, b., Ice.	146	64.33N	22.40W
Fayette, Al., U.S. (få-yĕt′)	114	33.40N	87.54W
Fayette, Ia., U.S.	103	42.49N	91.49W
Fayette, Ms., U.S.	114	31.43N	91.00W
Fayette, Mo., U.S.	111	39.09N	92.41W
Fayetteville, Ar., U.S. (få-yĕt′vĭl)	111	36.03N	94.08W
Fayetteville, N.C., U.S.	115	35.02N	78.54W
Fayetteville, Tn., U.S.	114	35.10N	86.33W
Fazao, Forêt Classée du, for., Togo	214	8.50N	0.40E
Fazilka, India	186	30.30N	74.02E
Fazzān (Fezzan), hist. reg., Libya	211	26.45N	13.01E
Fdérik, Maur.	210	22.45N	12.38W
Fear, Cape, c., N.C., U.S. (fēr)	115	33.52N	77.48W
Feather, r., Ca., U.S. (fĕth′ẽr)	108	38.56N	121.41W
Feather, Middle Fork of, r., Ca., U.S.	108	39.49N	121.10W
Feather, North Fork of, r., Ca., U.S.	108	40.00N	121.20W
Featherstone, Eng., U.K. (fĕdh′ẽr stŭn)	144a	53.39N	1.21W
Fécamp, Fr. (fā-käɴ′)	147	49.45N	0.20E
Federal, Distrito, dept., Ven. (dės-trē′tô-fĕ-dĕ-rä′l)	131b	10.34N	66.55W
Federal Way, Wa., U.S.	106a	47.20N	122.20W
Fëdorovka, Russia (fyô′dō-rôf-kå)	172b	56.15N	37.14E
Fehmarn, i., Ger. (fā′märn)	154	54.28N	11.15E
Fehrbellin, Ger. (fĕr′bĕl-lēn)	145b	52.49N	12.46E
Feia, Logoa, l., Braz. (lô-gôä-fĕ′yä)	129a	21.54S	41.15W
Feicheng, China (fā-chŭŋ)	190	36.18N	116.45E
Feidong, China (fā-dôŋ)	190	31.53N	117.28E
Feira de Santana, Braz. (fĕ′ē-rä dä sänt-än′ä)	131	12.16S	38.46W
Feixian, China (fā-shyĕn)	190	35.17N	117.59E
Felanitx, Spain (fā-lä-nēch′)	148	39.29N	3.09E
Feldkirch, Aus. (fĕlt′kĭrk)	154	47.15N	9.36E
Feldkirchen, Ger. (fĕld′kēr-ĸĕn)	145d	48.09N	11.44E
Felipe Carrillo Puerto, Mex.	120a	19.36N	88.04W
Feltre, Italy (fĕl′trā)	160	46.02N	11.56E
Femunden, l., Nor.	146	62.17N	11.40E
Fengcheng, China	191b	30.55N	121.38E
Fengcheng, China (fŭŋ-chŭŋ)	192	40.28N	124.03E
Fengdu, China (fŭŋ-dōō)	188	29.58N	107.50E
Fengjie, China (fŭŋ-jyĕ)	188	31.02N	109.30E
Fengming Dao, i., China (fŭŋ-mĭŋ dou)	190	39.19N	121.15E
Fengrun, China (fŭŋ-rōn)	190	39.51N	118.06E
Fengtai, China (fŭŋ-tī)	192a	39.51N	116.19E
Fengxian, China	190	34.41N	116.36E
Fengxian, China (fŭŋ-shyĕn)	191b	30.55N	121.26E
Fengxiang, China (fŭŋ-shyäŋ)	188	34.25N	107.20E
Fengyang, China (fŭng′yäng′)	192	32.55N	117.32E
Fengzhen, China (fŭŋ-jŭn)	189	40.28N	113.20E
Fennimore Pass, strt., Ak., U.S. (fĕn-ĭ-mōr)	95a	51.40N	175.38W
Fenoarivo Atsinanana, Madag.	213	17.30S	49.31E
Fenton, Mi., U.S. (fĕn-tŭn)	98	42.50N	83.40W
Fenton, Mo., U.S.	107e	38.31N	90.27W
Fenyang, China	189	37.20N	111.48E
Feodosiya, Ukr.	167	45.02N	35.21E
Ferbitz, Ger.	238a	52.30N	13.01E
Ferdows, Iran	182	34.00N	58.13E
Ferencváros, neigh., Hung.	239g	47.28N	19.06E
Ferentino, Italy (fā-rĕn-tē′nō)	160	41.42N	13.18E
Fergana, Uzb.	169	40.23N	71.46E
Fergus Falls, Mn., U.S. (fûr′gŭs)	96	46.17N	96.03W
Ferguson, Mo., U.S. (fûr-gŭ-sŭn)	107e	38.45N	90.18W
Ferkéssédougou, C. Iv.	214	9.36N	5.12W
Fermo, Italy (fĕr′mō)	160	43.10N	13.43E
Fermoselle, Spain (fĕr-mō-säl′yå)	158	41.20N	6.23W
Fermoy, Ire. (fûr-moi′)	150	52.05N	8.06W
Fernandina Beach, Fl., U.S. (fûr-năn-dē′nă)	115	30.38N	81.29W
Fernando de Noronha, , Braz.	131	3.51S	32.25W
Fernando Póo see Bioko, i., Eq. Gui.	210	3.35N	7.45E
Fernán-Núñez, Spain (fĕr-nän′nōōn′yåth)	158	37.42N	4.43W
Fernâo Veloso, Baia de, b., Moz.	217	14.20S	40.55E
Ferndale, Ca., U.S. (fûrn′dāl)	104	40.34N	124.18W
Ferndale, Md., U.S.	229c	39.11N	76.38W
Ferndale, Mi., U.S.	101b	42.27N	83.08W
Ferndale, Mi., U.S.	230c	42.28N	83.08W
Ferndale, Wa., U.S.	106d	48.51N	122.36W
Fernie, Can. (fûr′nĭ)	84	49.30N	115.03W
Fern Prairie, Wa., U.S. (fûrn prâr′ĭ)	106c	45.38N	122.25W
Ferny Creek, Austl.	243b	37.53S	145.21E
Ferrara, Italy (fĕr-rä′rä)	148	44.50N	11.37E
Ferrat, Cap, c., Alg. (käp fĕr-rät)	159	35.49N	0.29W
Ferraz de Vasconcelos, Braz.	234d	23.32S	46.22W
Ferreira do Alentejo, Port.	158	38.03N	8.06W
Ferreira do Zezere, Port. (fĕr-rĕ′ē-rä dō zā-zā′rĕ)	158	39.49N	8.17W
Ferrelview, Mo., U.S. (fĕr′rĕl-vū)	107f	39.18N	94.40W
Ferreñafe, Peru (fĕr-rĕn-yä′fĕ)	130	6.38S	79.48W
Ferriday, La., U.S. (fĕr′ĭ-dā)	113	31.38N	91.33W
Ferrieres, Fr.	237c	48.49N	2.42E
Ferry Village, N.Y., U.S.	230a	43.58N	78.57W
Fershampenuaz, Russia (fĕr-shäm′pĕn-wäz)	172a	53.32N	59.50E
Fertile, Mn., U.S. (fur′tĭl)	102	47.33N	96.18W

ăt; finăl; rāte; senåte; ärm; åsk; sofȧ; fâre; ch-choose; dh-as th in other; bē; ėvent; bĕt; recĕnt; cratẽr; g-gō; gh-guttural g; bĭt; ĭ-short neutral; rīde; ĸ-guttural k as ch in German ich;

PLACE (Pronunciation)	PAGE	Lat. °′	Long. °′
Fès, Mor. (fĕs)	210	34.08N	5.00W
Fessenden, N.D., U.S. (fĕs'ĕn-dĕn)	102	47.39N	99.40W
Festus, Mo., U.S. (fĕst'ŭs)	111	38.12N	90.22W
Fetcham, Eng., U.K.	235	51.17N	0.22W
Fethiye, Tur. (fĕt-hē'yĕ)	149	36.40N	29.05E
Feuilles, Rivière aux, r., Can.	85	58.30N	70.50W
Ffestiniog, Wales, U.K.	150	52.59N	3.58W
Fianarantsoa, Madag. (fyȧ-nä'rȧn-tsō'ȧ)	213	21.21S	47.15E
Fichtenau, Ger.	238a	52.27N	13.42E
Ficksburg, S. Afr. (fĭks'bûrg)	218d	28.53S	27.53E
Fidalgo Island, i., Wa., U.S. (fĭ-dăl'gō)	106a	48.28N	122.39W
Fiddlers Hamlet, Eng., U.K.	235	51.41N	0.08E
Fieldbrook, Ca., U.S. (fēld'brŏok)	104	40.59N	124.02W
Fier, Alb. (fyĕr)	161	40.43N	19.34E
Fife Ness, c., Scot., U.K. (fīf'nes')	150	56.15N	2.19W
Fifth Cataract, wtfl., Sudan	211	18.27N	33.38E
Figeac, Fr. (fē-zhȧk')	156	44.37N	2.02E
Figeholm, Swe. (fē-ghĕ-hōlm)	152	57.24N	16.33E
Figueira da Foz, Port. (fē-gwĕy-rä-dȧ-fô'z)	158	40.10N	8.50W
Figuig, Mor.	210	32.20N	1.30W
Fiji, nation, Oc. (fē'jē)	3	18.40S	175.00E
Filadelfia, C.R. (fĭl-ȧ-dĕl'fĭ-ȧ)	120	10.26N	85.37W
Filatovskoye, Russia (fĭ-lä'tôf-skô-yĕ)	172a	56.49N	62.20E
Filchner Ice Shelf, ice., Ant. (fĭlk'nĕr)	219	80.00S	35.00W
Fili, neigh., Russia	239b	55.45N	37.31E
Filicudi, i., Italy (fē'le-kōō'dē)	160	38.34N	14.39E
Filippovskoye, Russia (fĭ-lĭ-pôf'skô-yĕ)	172b	56.06N	38.38E
Filipstad, Swe. (fĭl'ĭps-städh)	152	59.44N	14.09E
Fillmore, Ut., U.S. (fĭl'môr)	109	39.00N	112.20W
Filsa, Nor.	152	60.35N	12.03E
Fimi, r., Zaire	212	2.43S	17.50E
Finaalspan, S. Afr.	244b	26.17S	28.15E
Finch, Can. (fĭnch)	83c	45.09N	75.06W
Finchley, neigh., Eng., U.K.	235	51.36N	0.10W
Findlay, Oh., U.S. (fĭnd'lȧ)	98	41.05N	83.40W
Fingoe, Moz.	217	15.12S	31.50E
Finisterre, Cabo de, c., Spain (kȧ'bô-dĕ-fĭn-ĭs-târ')	142	42.52N	9.48W
Finke, r., Austl. (fĭŋ'kĕ)	202	25.25S	134.30E
Finkenkrug, Ger.	238a	52.34N	13.03E
Finland, nation, Eur. (fĭn'lănd)	142	62.45N	26.13E
Finland, Gulf of, b., Eur. (fĭn'lănd)	142	59.35N	23.35E
Finlandia, Col. (fēn-lä'n-dēä)	130a	4.38N	75.39W
Finlay, r., Can. (fĭn'lā)	84	57.45N	125.30W
Finow, Ger. (fē'nōv)	145b	52.50N	13.44E
Finowfurt, Ger. (fē'nō-fōōrt)	145b	52.50N	13.41E
Fircrest, Wa., U.S. (fûr'krĕst)	106a	47.14N	122.31W
Firenze see Florence, Italy	142	43.47N	11.15E
Firenzuola, Italy (fē-rĕnt-swō'lä)	160	44.08N	11.21E
Firgrove, Eng., U.K.	237b	53.37N	2.08W
Firozpur, India	183	30.58N	74.39E
Fischa, r., Aus.	145e	48.04N	16.33E
Fischamend Markt, Aus.	145e	48.07N	16.37E
Fischeln, neigh., Ger.	236	51.18N	6.35E
Fish, r., Nmb. (fĭsh)	212	28.00S	17.30E
Fish Cay, i., Bah.	123	22.30N	74.20W
Fish Creek, r., Can. (fĭsh)	83e	50.52N	114.21W
Fisher, La., U.S. (fĭsh'ĕr)	113	31.28N	93.30W
Fisher Bay, b., Can.	89	51.30N	97.16W
Fisher Channel, strt., Can.	86	52.10N	127.42W
Fisherman's Wharf, pt. of i., Ca., U.S.	231b	37.48N	122.25W
Fisher Strait, strt., Can.	85	62.43N	84.28W
Fisherville, Can.	227c	43.47N	79.28W
Fishpool, Eng., U.K.	237b	53.35N	2.17W
Fitchburg, Ma., U.S. (fĭch'bûrg)	99	42.35N	71.48W
Fitri, Lac, l., Chad	215	12.50N	17.28E
Fitzgerald, Ga., U.S. (fĭts-jĕr'ăld)	114	31.42N	83.17W
Fitz Hugh Sound, strt., Can. (fĭts hū)	86	51.40N	127.57W
Fitzroy, Austl.	243b	37.48S	144.59E
Fitzroy, r., Austl. (fĭts-roi')	202	18.00S	124.05E
Fitzroy, r., Austl.	203	23.45S	150.02E
Fitzroy, Monte (Cerro Chaltel), mtn., S.A.	132	48.10S	73.18W
Fitzroy Crossing, Austl.	202	18.08S	126.00E
Fitzwilliam, i., Can. (fĭts-wĭl'yŭm)	90	45.30N	81.45W
Fiume see Rijeka, Cro.	148	45.22N	14.24E
Fiumicino, Italy (fyōō-mē-chē'nō)	159d	41.47N	12.19E
Five Dock, Austl.	243a	33.52S	151.08E
Fjällbacka, Swe. (fyĕl'bĕk-ȧ)	152	58.37N	11.17E
Flagstaff, S. Afr. (flăg'stäf)	213c	31.06S	29.31E
Flagstaff, Az., U.S. (flăg-stáf)	96	35.15N	111.40W
Flagstaff, l., Me., U.S. (flăg-stáf)	99	45.05N	70.30W
Flåm, Nor. (flôm)	152	60.50N	7.00E
Flambeau, r., Wi., U.S. (flăm-bō')	103	45.32N	91.05W
Flaming Gorge Reservoir, res., U.S.	96	41.13N	109.30W
Flamingo, Fl., U.S. (flȧ-mĭŋ'gō)	115	25.10N	80.55W
Flamingo Cay, i., Bah. (flȧ-mĭŋ'gō)	123	22.50N	75.50W
Flamingo Point, c., V.I.U.S.	117c	18.19N	65.00W
Flanders, hist. reg., Fr. (flăn'dērz)	151	50.53N	2.29E
Flandreau, S.D., U.S. (flăn'drō)	102	44.02N	96.35W
Flatbush, neigh., N.Y., U.S.	228	40.39N	73.56W
Flathead, r., N.A.	87	49.30N	114.30W
Flathead, Middle Fork, r., Mt., U.S.	105	48.30N	113.47W
Flathead, North Fork, r., N.A.	105	48.45N	114.20W
Flathead, South Fork, r., Mt., U.S.	105	48.05N	113.45W
Flathead Indian Reservation, I.R., Mt., U.S.	105	47.30N	114.25W
Flathead Lake, l., Mt., U.S. (flăt'hĕd)	96	47.57N	114.20W
Flatow, Ger.	145b	52.44N	12.58E
Flat Rock, Mi., U.S. (flăt rŏk)	101b	42.06N	83.17W
Flattery, Cape, c., Wa., U.S. (flăt'ēr-ĭ)	104	48.22N	124.45W
Flatwillow Creek, r., Mt., U.S. (flat wĭl'ō)	105	46.45N	108.47W
Flaunden, Eng., U.K.	235	51.42N	0.32W
Flehe, neigh., Ger.	236	51.12N	6.47E
Flekkefjord, Nor. (flăk'kĕ-fyôr)	152	58.19N	6.38E
Flemingsburg, Ky., U.S. (flĕm'ĭngz-bûrg)	98	38.25N	83.45W
Flensburg, Ger. (flĕns'bŏorgh)	146	54.48N	9.27E
Flers, Fr. (flĕr)	147	48.43N	0.37W
Fletcher, N.C., U.S.	115	35.26N	82.30W
Fley, neigh., Ger.	236	51.23N	7.30E
Flinders, i., Austl.	203	39.35S	148.10E
Flinders, r., Austl.	203	18.48S	141.07E
Flinders, reg., Austl. (flĭn'dērz)	202	32.15S	138.45E
Flinders Reefs, rf., Austl.	203	17.30S	149.02E
Flin Flon, Can. (flĭn flŏn)	84	54.46N	101.53W
Flingern, neigh., Ger.	236	51.14N	6.49E
Flint, Wales, U.K.	144a	53.15N	3.07W
Flint, Mi., U.S.	97	43.00N	83.45W
Flint, r., Ga., U.S. (flĭnt)	97	31.25N	84.15W
Flora, Il., U.S. (flō'rȧ)	98	38.40N	88.25W
Flora, In., U.S.	98	40.25N	86.30W
Florala, Al., U.S. (flŏr-ăl'ȧ)	114	31.01N	86.19W
Floral Park, N.Y., U.S. (flôr'ăl pärk)	100a	40.42N	73.42W
Florence, Italy	142	43.47N	11.15E
Florence, Al., U.S. (flŏr'ĕns)	97	34.46N	87.40W
Florence, Az., U.S.	109	33.00N	111.25W
Florence, Ca., U.S.	232	33.58N	118.15W
Florence, Co., U.S.	110	38.23N	105.08W
Florence, Ks., U.S.	111	38.14N	96.56W
Florence, S.C., U.S.	115	34.10N	79.45W
Florence, Wa., U.S.	106a	48.13N	122.21W
Florencia, Col. (flō-rĕn'sē-ȧ)	130	1.31N	75.13W
Florencio Sánchez, Ur. (flō-rĕn-sēō-sá'n-chĕz)	129c	33.52S	57.24W
Florencio Varela, Arg. (flō-rĕn'sē-o vä-rā'lä)	132a	34.50S	58.16W
Florentia, S. Afr.	244b	26.16S	28.08E
Flores, Braz. (flō'rĕzh)	131	7.57S	37.48W
Flores, Guat.	120a	16.53N	89.54W
Flores, dept., Ur.	129c	33.33S	57.00W
Flores, neigh., Arg.	233d	34.38S	58.28W
Flores, i., Indon.	196	8.14S	121.08E
Flores, r., Arg.	129c	36.13S	60.28W
Flores, Laut (Flores Sea), sea, Indon.	196	7.09S	120.30E
Floresta, neigh., Arg.	233d	34.38S	58.29W
Floresville, Tx., U.S. (flō'rĕs-vĭl)	112	29.10N	98.08W
Floriano, Braz. (flō-rȧ-ä'nō)	131	6.17S	42.58W
Florianópolis, Braz. (flō-rē-ä-nō'pō-lēs)	132	27.30S	48.30W
Florida, Col. (flō-rē'dä)	130a	3.20N	76.12W
Florida, Cuba	122	22.10N	79.50W
Florida, S. Afr.	213b	26.11S	27.56E
Florida, N.Y., U.S. (flŏr'ĭ-dȧ)	100a	41.20N	74.21W
Florida, Ur. (flō-rē-dhä)	132	34.06S	56.14W
Florida, dept., Ur. (flō-rē'dhä)	129c	33.48S	56.15W
Florida, state, U.S. (flŏr'ĭ-dȧ)	97	30.30N	84.40W
Florida, i., Sol.Is.	203	8.56S	159.45E
Florida, Straits of, strt., N.A.	117	24.10N	81.00W
Florida Bay, b., Fl., U.S. (flŏr'ĭ-dȧ)	115a	24.55N	80.55W
Florida Keys, is., Fl., U.S.	97	24.33N	81.20W
Florida Mountains, mts., N.M., U.S.	109	32.10N	107.35W
Florido, Río, r., Mex. (flō-rē'dō)	112	27.21N	104.48W
Floridsdorf, Aus. (flō'rĭds-dôrf)	145e	48.16N	16.25E
Florina, Grc. (flō-rē'nä)	149	40.48N	21.24E
Florissant, Mo., U.S. (flŏr'ĭ-sănt)	107e	38.47N	90.20W
Flotantes, Jardines, rec., Mex.	233a	19.16N	99.06W
Flourtown, Pa., U.S.	229b	40.07N	75.13W
Flower Hill, N.Y., U.S.	228	40.49N	73.41W
Floyd, r., Ia., U.S. (floid)	102	42.38N	96.15W
Floydada, Tx., U.S. (floi-dā'dȧ)	110	33.59N	101.19W
Floyds Fork, r., Ky., U.S. (floi-dz)	101h	38.08N	85.30W
Flumendosa, r., Italy	160	39.45N	9.18E
Flushing, Mi., U.S. (flûsh'ĭng)	98	43.05N	83.50W
Flushing, neigh., N.Y., U.S.	228	40.45N	73.49W
Fly, r. (flī)	197	8.00S	141.45E
Foča, Bos. (fō'chä)	161	43.29N	18.48E
Fochville, S. Afr. (fŏk'vĭl)	218d	26.29S	27.29E
Focşani, Rom. (fōk-shä'nē)	155	45.41N	27.17E
Fogang, China (fwo-gäŋ)	193	23.50N	113.35E
Foggia, Italy (fŏd'jä)	149	41.30N	15.34E
Fogo, Can. (fō'gō)	93	49.43N	54.17W
Fogo, i., Can.	91	49.40N	54.13W
Fogo, i., C.V.	210b	14.46N	24.51W
Fohnsdorf, Aus. (fōns'dôrf)	154	47.13N	14.40E
Föhr, i., Ger. (fûr)	154	54.47N	8.30E
Foix, Fr. (fwä)	156	42.58N	1.34E
Fokku, Nig.	215	11.40N	4.31E
Folcroft, Pa., U.S.	229b	39.54N	75.17W
Folgares, Ang.	216	14.54S	15.08E
Foligno, Italy (fō-lēn'yō)	160	42.58N	12.41E
Folkeston, Eng., U.K.	151	51.05N	1.18E
Folkingham, Eng., U.K. (fō'kĭng-ăm)	144a	52.53N	0.24W
Folkston, Ga., U.S.	115	30.50N	82.01W
Folsom, Ca., U.S.	108	38.40N	121.10W
Folsom, N.M., U.S. (fōl'sŭm)	110	36.47N	103.56W
Folsom, Pa., U.S.	229b	39.54N	75.19W
Fomento, Cuba (fō-mĕ'n-tō)	122	21.35N	78.20W
Fómeque, Col. (fō'mē-kĕ)	130a	4.29N	73.52W
Fonda, Ia., U.S. (fŏn'dȧ)	103	42.33N	94.51W
Fond du Lac, Wi., U.S. (fŏn dū lăk')	97	43.47N	88.29W
Fond du Lac Indian Reservation, I.R., Mn., U.S.	103	46.44N	93.04W
Fondi, Italy (fōn'dē)	160	41.23N	13.25E
Fonsagrada, Spain (fŏn-sä-grä'dhä)	158	43.08N	7.07W
Fonseca, Golfo de, b., N.A. (gôl-fô-dĕ-fŏn-sä'kä)	116	13.09N	87.55W
Fontainebleau, Fr. (fôN-tĕn-blō')	147	48.24N	2.42E
Fontainebleau, S. Afr.	244b	26.07S	27.59E
Fontana, Ca., U.S. (fŏn-tă'nȧ)	107a	34.06N	117.27W
Fonte Boa, Braz. (fōn'tȧ bō'ȧ)	130	2.32S	66.05W
Fontenay-aux-Roses, Fr.	237c	48.47N	2.17E
Fontenay-le-Comte, Fr. (fôNt-nĕ'lĕ-kôNt')	156	46.28N	0.53W
Fontenay-le-Fleury, Fr.	237c	48.49N	2.03E
Fontenay-sous-Bois, Fr.	237c	48.51N	2.29E
Fontenay-Trésigny, Fr. (fôN-te-nā' tra-sēn-yē')	157b	48.43N	2.53E
Fontenelle Reservoir, res., Wy., U.S.	105	42.05N	110.05W
Fontera, Punta, c., Mex. (pōō'n-tä-fōn-tē'rä)	119	18.36N	92.43W
Fontibón, Col. (fōn-tē-bôn')	130a	4.42N	74.09W
Fontur, c., Ice.	142	66.21N	14.02W
Foothills, S. Afr. (fŏt-hĭls)	213b	25.55S	27.36E
Footscray, Austl.	201a	37.48S	144.54E
Fora, Ponta de, c., Braz.	234c	22.57S	43.07W
Foraker, Mount, mtn., Ak., U.S. (fŏr'ȧ-kēr)	95	62.40N	152.40W
Forbach, Fr. (fōr'bäk)	157	49.12N	6.54E
Forbes, Austl. (fôrbz)	203	33.24S	148.05E
Forbes, Mount, mtn., Can.	87	51.52N	116.56W
Forbidden City, bldg., China	240b	39.55N	116.23E
Forchheim, Ger. (fôrk'hīm)	154	49.43N	11.05E
Fordham University, pt. of i., N.Y., U.S.	228	40.51N	73.53W
Fords, N.J., U.S.	228	40.32N	74.19W
Fordsburg, neigh., S. Afr.	244b	26.13S	28.02E
Fordyce, Ar., U.S. (fôr'dīs)	111	33.48N	92.24W
Forécariah, Gui. (fōr-kȧ-rē'ä')	210	9.26N	13.06W
Forel, Mont, mtn., Grnld.	82	65.50N	37.41W
Forest, Ms., U.S. (fŏr'ĕst)	114	32.22N	89.29W
Forest, r., N.D., U.S.	102	48.08N	97.45W
Forest City, Ia., U.S.	103	43.14N	93.40W
Forest City, N.C., U.S.	115	35.20N	81.52W
Forest City, Pa., U.S.	99	41.35N	75.30W
Forest Gate, neigh., Eng., U.K.	235	51.33N	0.02E
Forest Grove, Or., U.S. (grōv)	106c	45.31N	123.07W
Forest Heights, Md., U.S.	229d	38.49N	77.00W
Forest Hill, Austl.	243b	37.50S	145.11E
Forest Hill, Md., U.S.	100e	39.35N	76.26W
Forest Hill, Tx., U.S.	107c	32.40N	97.16W
Forest Hill, neigh., Can.	227c	43.42N	79.24W
Forest Hills, Pa., U.S.	230b	40.26N	79.52W
Forest Hills, neigh., N.Y., U.S.	228	40.42N	73.51W
Forest Park, Il., U.S.	231a	41.53N	87.50W
Forest Park, neigh., Md., U.S.	229c	39.19N	76.41W
Forestville, Austl.	243a	33.46S	151.13E
Forestville, Can. (fŏr'ĕst-vĭl)	92	48.45N	69.06W
Forestville, Md., U.S.	100e	38.51N	76.55W
Forez, Monts du, mts., Fr. (môN dü fō-rā')	156	44.55N	3.43E
Forfar, Scot., U.K. (fôr'fȧr)	150	57.10N	2.55W
Forillon, Parc National, rec., Can.	92	48.50N	64.05W
Forio, mtn., Italy (fô'ryō)	159c	40.29N	13.55E
Forked Creek, r., Il., U.S. (fôrk'd)	101a	41.16N	88.01W
Forked Deer, r., Tn., U.S.	114	35.53N	89.29W
Forli, Italy (fōr-lē')	148	44.13N	12.03E
Formby, Eng., U.K. (fôrm'bē)	144a	53.34N	3.04W
Formby Point, c., Eng., U.K.	144a	53.33N	3.06W
Formentera, Isla de, i., Spain (ē's-lä-dĕ-fōr-mĕn-tä'rä)	148	38.43N	1.25E
Formiga, Braz. (fōr-mē'gȧ)	131	20.27S	45.25W
Formigas Bank, bk. (fōr-mē'gȧs)	123	18.30N	75.40W
Formosa, Arg. (fōr-mō'sä)	132	27.25S	58.12W
Formosa, Braz.	131	15.32S	47.10W
Formosa, prov., Arg.	132	24.30S	60.45W
Formosa, Serra, mts., Braz. (sĕ'r-rä)	131	12.59S	55.11W
Formosa Bay, b., Kenya	217	2.45S	40.30E
Formosa Strait see Taiwan Strait, strt., Asia	189	24.30N	120.00E
Fornosovo, Russia (fōr-nō'sô vô)	172c	59.35N	30.34E
Forrest City, Ar., U.S. (for'ĕst sĭ'tĭ)	111	35.00N	90.46W
Forsayth, Austl. (fôr-sīth')	203	18.33S	143.42E
Forshaga, Swe. (fōrs'hä'gä)	152	59.34N	13.25E
Forst, Ger. (fôrst)	147	51.45N	14.38E
Forsyth, Ga., U.S. (fôr-sīth')	114	33.02N	83.56W
Forsyth, Mt., U.S.	105	46.15N	106.41W
Fort, neigh., India	240e	18.56N	72.50E
Fort Albany, Can. (fôrt ôl'bȧ nĭ)	85	52.20N	81.30W
Fort Alexander Indian Reserve, I.R., Can.	89	50.27N	96.15W
Fortaleza, Braz. (fôr'tä-lā'zȧ)	131	3.35S	38.31W
Fort Atkinson, Wi., U.S. (ăt'kĭn-sŭn)	103	42.55N	88.46W
Fort Beaufort, S. Afr. (bō'fôrt)	213c	32.47S	26.39E
Fort Belknap Indian Reservation, I.R., Mt., U.S.	105	48.16N	108.38W
Fort Bellefontaine, Mo., U.S. (bĕl-fōn-tān')	107f	38.50N	90.15W
Fort Benton, Mt., U.S. (bĕn'tŭn)	105	47.51N	110.40W
Fort Berthold Indian Reservation, I.R., N.D., U.S. (bĕrth'ôld)	102	47.47N	103.28W
Fort Bragg, Ca., U.S.	108	39.26N	123.48W
Fort Branch, In., U.S. (brănch)	98	38.15N	87.35W
Fort Chipewyan, Can.	84	58.46N	111.15W
Fort Cobb Reservoir, res., Ok., U.S.	110	35.12N	98.28W
Fort Collins, Co., U.S. (kŏl'ĭns)	96	40.36N	105.04W
Fort Crampel, Cen. Afr. Rep. (krám-pĕl')	211	6.59N	19.11E
Fort-de-France, Mart. (dē fräNs)	117	14.37N	61.06W
Fort Deposit, Al., U.S. (dē-pŏz'ĭt)	114	31.58N	86.35W
Fort-de-Possel, Cen. Afr. Rep. (dē pō-sĕl')	211	5.03N	19.11E
Fort Dodge, Ia., U.S. (dŏj)	97	42.31N	94.10W
Fort Edward, N.Y., U.S. (wērd)	99	43.15N	73.30W
Fort Erie, Can. (ē'rĭ)	101c	42.55N	78.56W
Fortescue, r., Austl. (fôr'tĕs-kū)	202	21.25S	116.50E
Fort Fairfield, Me., U.S. (fâr'fēld)	92	46.46N	67.53W
Fort Fitzgerald, Can. (fĭts-jĕr'ăld)	84	59.48N	111.50W
Fort Frances, Can. (frăn'sĕs)	85	48.36N	93.24W
Fort Frederica National Monument, rec., Ga., U.S. (frĕd'ē-rĭ-kȧ)	114	31.13N	85.25W
Fort Gaines, Ga., U.S. (gānz)	114	31.35N	85.03W
Fort Gibson, Ok., U.S. (gĭb'sŭn)	111	35.50N	95.13W
Fort Good Hope, Can. (gŏŏd hōp)	84	66.19N	128.52W

ng-sing; ŋ-baŋk; N-nasalized n; nŏd; cŏmmit; ōld; ôbey; ôrder; oi-boil; fōōd; ŏ-as oo in foot; ou-out; s-soft; sh-dish; th-thin; pūre; ûnite; ûrn; stŭd; circŭs; ü-as in French tu; '-indeterminate vowel.

288 Forth–Frydlant

PLACE (Pronunciation)	PAGE	Lat. °'	Long. °'
Forth, Firth of, b., Scot., U.K. (fûrth ôv fôrth)	142	56.04N	3.03W
Fort Hall, Kenya (hôl)	213	0.47S	37.13E
Fort Hall Indian Reservation, I.R., Id., U.S.	105	43.02N	112.21W
Fort Howard, Md., U.S.	229c	39.12N	76.27W
Fort Huachuca, Az., U.S. (wä-chōō'kä)	109	31.30N	110.25W
Fortier, Can. (fôr'tyā')	83f	49.56N	97.55W
Fort Jefferson National Monument, rec., Fl., U.S. (jĕf'ēr-sŭn)	115a	24.42N	83.02W
Fort Kent, Me., U.S. (kĕnt)	92	47.14N	68.37W
Fort Langley, Can. (lăng'lĭ)	106d	49.10N	122.35W
Fort Lauderdale, Fl., U.S. (lô'dēr-dāl)	115a	26.07N	80.09W
Fort Lee, N.J., U.S.	100a	40.50N	73.58W
Fort Liard, Can.	84	60.16N	123.34W
Fort Loudoun Lake, res., Tn., U.S. (fôrt lou'dĕn)	114	35.52N	84.10W
Fort Lupton, Co., U.S. (lŭp'tŭn)	110	40.04N	104.54W
Fort Macleod, Can. (mȧ-kloud')	84	49.43N	113.25W
Fort Madison, Ia., U.S. (măd'ĭ-sŭn)	103	40.40N	91.17W
Fort Matanzas, Fl., U.S. (mä-tän'zäs)	115	29.39N	81.17W
Fort McDermitt Indian Reservation, I.R., Or., U.S. (mȧk dēr'mĭt)	104	42.04N	118.07W
Fort McHenry National Monument, pt. of i., Md., U.S.	229c	39.16N	76.35W
Fort McMurray, Can. (mȧk-mŭr'ĭ)	84	56.44N	111.23W
Fort McPherson, Can. (mȧk-fŭr's'n)	84	67.37N	134.59W
Fort Meade, Fl., U.S. (mēd)	115a	27.45N	81.48W
Fort Mill, S.C., U.S. (mĭl)	115	35.03N	80.57W
Fort Mojave Indian Reservation, I.R., Ca., U.S. (mō-hä'vâ)	108	34.59N	115.02W
Fort Morgan, Co., U.S. (môr'gȧn)	110	40.14N	103.49W
Fort Myers, Fl., U.S. (mī'ērz)	115a	26.36N	81.45W
Fort Nelson, Can. (nĕl'sŭn)	84	58.57N	122.30W
Fort Nelson, r., Can. (nĕl'sŭn)	84	58.44N	122.20W
Fort Payne, Al., U.S. (pān)	114	34.26N	85.41W
Fort Peck, Mt., U.S. (pĕk)	105	47.58N	106.30W
Fort Peck Indian Reservation, I.R., Mt., U.S.	102	48.22N	105.40W
Fort Peck Lake, res., Mt., U.S.	96	47.52N	106.59W
Fort Pierce, Fl., U.S. (pērs)	115a	27.25N	80.20W
Fort Portal, Ug. (pōr'tâl)	211	0.40N	30.16E
Fort Providence, Can. (prŏv'ĭ-dĕns)	84	61.27N	117.59W
Fort Pulaski National Monument, rec., Ga., U.S. (pu-lăs'kĭ)	115	31.59N	80.56W
Fort Qu'Appelle, Can.	88	50.46N	103.55W
Fort Randall Dam, dam, S.D., U.S.	102	42.48N	98.35W
Fort Resolution, Can. (rĕz'ō-lū'shŭn)	84	61.08N	113.42W
Fort Riley, Ks., U.S. (rī'lĭ)	111	39.05N	96.46W
Fort Saint James, Can. (fôrt sānt jāmz)	84	54.26N	124.15W
Fort Saint John, Can. (sānt jŏn)	84	56.15N	120.51W
Fort Sandeman, Pak. (săn'da-mȧn)	183	31.28N	69.29E
Fort Saskatchewan, Can. (săs-kăt'chōō-ån)	83g	53.43N	113.13W
Fort Scott, Ks., U.S. (skŏt)	97	37.50N	94.43W
Fort Severn, Can. (sĕv'ērn)	85	55.58N	87.50W
Fort Shevchenko, Kaz. (shĕv-chĕn'kô)	170	44.30N	50.18E
Fort Sibut, Cen. Afr. Rep. (fôr sē-bü')	211	5.44N	19.05E
Fort Sill, Ok., U.S. (fôrt sĭl)	110	34.41N	98.25W
Fort Simpson, Can. (sĭmp'sŭn)	84	61.52N	121.48W
Fort Smith, Can.	84	60.09N	112.08W
Fort Smith, Ar., U.S. (smĭth)	97	35.23N	94.24W
Fort Stockton, Tx., U.S. (stŏk'tŭn)	112	30.54N	102.51W
Fort Sumner, N.M., U.S. (sŭm'nēr)	110	34.30N	104.17W
Fort Sumter National Monument, rec., S.C., U.S. (sŭm'tēr)	115	32.43N	79.54W
Fort Thomas, Ky., U.S. (tŏm'ăs)	101f	39.05N	84.27W
Fortuna, Ca., U.S. (fôr-tū'nȧ)	104	40.36N	124.10W
Fortune, Can. (fôr'tŭn)	93	47.04N	55.51W
Fortune, i., Bah.	123	22.35N	74.20W
Fortune Bay, b., Can.	85a	47.25N	55.25W
Fort Union National Monument, rec., N.M., U.S. (ūn'yŭn)	110	35.51N	104.57W
Fort Valley, Ga., U.S. (văl'ĭ)	114	32.33N	83.53W
Fort Vermilion, Can. (vēr-mĭl'yŭn)	84	58.23N	115.50W
Fort Victoria *see* Masvingo, Zimb.	212	20.07S	30.47E
Fort Wayne, In., U.S. (wān)	97	41.00N	85.10W
Fort Wayne Military Museum, pt. of i., Mi., U.S.	230c	42.18N	83.06W
Fort William, Scot., U.K. (wĭl'yŭm)	150	56.50N	3.00W
Fort William, hist., India	240a	22.33N	88.20E
Fort William, Mount, mtn., Austl. (wĭ'ĭ-ăm)	204	24.45S	151.15E
Fort Worth, Tx., U.S. (wûrth)	96	32.45N	97.20W
Fort Yukon, Ak., U.S. (yōō'kŏn)	96a	66.30N	145.00W
Fort Yuma Indian Reservation, I.R., Ca., U.S. (yōō'mä)	109	32.54N	114.47W
Foshan, China	189	23.02N	113.07E
Fossano, Italy (fôs-sä'nō)	160	44.34N	7.42E
Fossil Creek, r., Tx., U.S. (fŏs-ĭl)	107c	32.53N	97.19W
Fossombrone, Italy (fôs-sôm-brō'nā)	160	43.41N	12.48E
Foss Res, Ok., U.S.	110	35.38N	99.11W
Fosston, Mn., U.S. (fôs'tŭn)	102	47.34N	95.44W
Fosterburg, Il., U.S. (fŏs'tēr-bûrg)	107e	38.58N	90.04W
Foster City, Ca., U.S.	231b	37.34N	122.16W
Fostoria, Oh., U.S. (fŏs-tō'rĭ-ȧ)	98	41.10N	83.20W
Fougéres, Fr. (fōō-zhâr')	147	48.23N	1.14W
Foula, i., Scot., U.K. (fou'lȧ)	150a	60.08N	2.04W
Foulwind, Cape, c., N.Z. (foul'wĭnd)	203a	41.45S	171.00E
Foumban, Cam. (fōōm-bän')	210	5.43N	10.55E
Fountain Creek, r., Co., U.S. (foun'tĭn)	110	38.36N	104.37W
Fountain Valley, Ca., U.S.	107a	33.42N	117.57W
Fourche la Fave, r., Ar., U.S. (fōōrsh lä fäv')	111	34.46N	93.45W
Fouriesburg, S. Afr. (fō'rēz-bûrg)	218d	28.38S	28.13E
Fourmies, Fr. (fōōr-mē')	156	50.01N	4.01E
Four Mountains, Islands of the, is., Ak., U.S.	95a	52.58N	170.40W
Fourqueux, Fr.	237c	48.53N	2.04E
Fourth Cataract, wtfl., Sudan	211	18.52N	32.07E
Fouta Djallon, mts., Gui. (fōō'tä jä-lôN)	210	11.37N	12.29W
Foveaux Strait, strt., N.Z. (fō-vō')	203a	46.30S	167.43E
Fowler, Co., U.S. (foul'ēr)	110	38.04N	104.02W
Fowler, In., U.S.	98	40.35N	87.20W
Fowler, Point, c., Austl.	202	32.05S	132.30E
Fowlerton, Tx., U.S. (foul'ēr-tŭn)	112	28.26N	98.48W
Fox, i., Wa., U.S. (fŏks)	106a	47.15N	122.08W
Fox, r., Il., U.S.	103	41.35N	88.43W
Fox, r., Wi., U.S.	103	44.18N	88.23W
Foxboro, Ma., U.S. (fŏks'bŭrō)	93a	42.04N	71.15W
Fox Chapel, Pa., U.S.	230b	40.30N	79.55W
Foxe Basin, b., Can. (fŏks)	85	67.35N	79.21W
Foxe Channel, strt., Can.	85	64.30N	79.23W
Foxe Peninsula, pen., Can.	85	64.57N	77.26W
Fox Islands, is., Ak., U.S. (fŏks)	95a	53.04N	167.30W
Fox Lake, Il., U.S. (lăk)	101a	42.24N	88.11W
Fox Lake, l., Il., U.S.	101a	42.24N	88.07W
Fox Point, Wi., U.S.	101a	43.10N	87.54W
Fox Valley, Austl.	243a	33.45S	151.06E
Foyle, Lough, b., Eur. (lŏk foil')	150	55.07N	7.08W
Foz do Cunene, Ang.	216	17.16S	11.50E
Fraga, Spain (frä'gä)	159	41.31N	0.20E
Fragoso, Cayo, i., Cuba (kä'yō-frä-gō'sō)	122	22.45N	79.30W
Framnes Mountains, mts., Ant.	219	67.50S	62.35E
Franca, Braz. (frä'n-kä)	131	20.28S	47.20W
Francavilla, Italy (fräŋ-kä-vēl'lä)	161	40.32N	17.37E
France, nation, Eur. (fråns)	142	46.39N	0.47E
Frances, l., Can. (frăn'sĭs)	84	61.27N	128.28W
Frances, Cabo, c., Cuba (kä'bō-frän-sĕ's)	122	21.55N	84.05W
Frances, Punta, c., Cuba (pōō'n-tä-frän-sĕ's)	122	21.45N	83.10W
Francés Viejo, Cabo, c., Dom. Rep. (kä'bō-frän'sås vyä'hō)	123	19.40N	69.35W
Franceville, Gabon (fräNs-vēl')	212	1.38S	13.35E
Francis Case, Lake, res., S.D., U.S. (frăn'sĭs)	96	43.15N	99.00W
Francisco Sales, Braz. (frän-sē's-kô-sá'lĕs)	129a	21.42S	44.26W
Francistown, Bots. (frăn'sĭs-toun)	212	21.17S	27.28E
Franconville, Fr.	237c	48.59N	2.14E
Frank, Pa., U.S.	230b	40.16N	79.48W
Frankby, Eng., U.K.	237a	53.22N	3.08W
Frankford, neigh., Pa., U.S.	229b	40.01N	75.05W
Frankfort, S. Afr. (frănk'fŏrt)	213c	32.43S	27.28E
Frankfort, S. Afr.	218d	27.17S	28.30E
Frankfort, Il., U.S. (fräŋk'fŭrt)	101a	41.30N	87.51W
Frankfort, In., U.S.	98	40.15N	86.30W
Frankfort, Ks., U.S.	111	39.42N	96.27W
Frankfort, Ky., U.S.	97	38.10N	84.55W
Frankfort, Mi., U.S.	98	44.40N	86.15W
Frankfort, N.Y., U.S.	99	43.05N	75.05W
Frankfurt am Main, Ger.	142	50.07N	8.40E
Frankfurt an der Oder, Ger.	147	52.20N	14.31E
Franklin, S. Afr.	213c	30.19S	29.28E
Franklin, In., U.S. (frănk'lĭn)	98	39.25N	86.00W
Franklin, Ky., U.S.	114	36.42N	86.34W
Franklin, La., U.S.	113	29.47N	91.31W
Franklin, Ma., U.S.	93a	42.05N	71.24W
Franklin, Mi., U.S.	230c	42.31N	83.18W
Franklin, Ne., U.S.	110	40.06N	99.01W
Franklin, N.H., U.S.	99	43.25N	71.40W
Franklin, N.J., U.S.	100a	41.08N	74.35W
Franklin, Oh., U.S.	98	39.30N	84.20W
Franklin, Pa., U.S.	99	41.25N	79.50W
Franklin, Tn., U.S.	114	35.54N	86.54W
Franklin, Va., U.S.	115	36.41N	76.57W
Franklin, l., Nv., U.S.	108	40.23N	115.10W
Franklin D. Roosevelt Lake, res., Wa., U.S.	104	48.12N	118.43W
Franklin Mountains, mts., Can.	84	65.36N	125.55W
Franklin Park, Il., U.S.	101a	41.56N	87.53W
Franklin Park, Pa., U.S.	230b	40.35N	80.06W
Franklin Park, Va., U.S.	229d	38.55N	77.09W
Franklin Roosevelt Park, neigh., S. Afr.	244b	26.09S	27.59E
Franklin Square, N.Y., U.S.	100a	40.43N	73.40W
Franklinton, La., U.S. (fräŋk'lĭn-tŭn)	113	30.49N	90.09W
Frankston, Austl.	201a	38.09S	145.08E
Franksville, Wi., U.S. (frănkz'vĭl)	101a	42.46N	87.55W
Fransta, Swe.	152	62.30N	16.04E
Franz Josef Land *see* Zemlya Frantsa-Iosifa, is., Russia	164	81.32N	40.00E
Frascati, Italy (fräs-kä'tē)	160	41.49N	12.45E
Fraser, Mi., U.S. (frā'zēr)	101b	42.32N	82.57W
Fraser, i., Austl.	203	25.12S	153.00E
Fraser, r., Can.	84	51.30N	122.00W
Fraserburgh, Scot., U.K. (frā'zēr-bûrg)	150	57.40N	2.01W
Fraser Plateau, plat., Can.	87	51.30N	122.00W
Frattamaggiore, Italy (frät-tä-mäg-zhyō'rē)	159c	40.41N	14.16E
Fray Bentos, Ur. (frī bĕn'tōs)	132	33.10S	58.19W
Frazee, Mn., U.S. (frā-zē')	102	46.42N	95.43W
Fraziers Hog Cay, i., Bah.	122	25.25N	77.55W
Frechen, Ger. (frĕ'kĕn)	157c	50.54N	6.49E
Fredericia, Den. (frĕdh-ĕ-rē'tsē-å)	152	55.35N	9.45E
Frederick, Md., U.S. (frĕd'ēr-ĭk)	97	39.25N	77.25W
Frederick, Ok., U.S.	110	34.23N	99.01W
Frederick House, r., Can.	90	49.05N	81.20W
Fredericksburg, Tx., U.S. (frĕd'ēr-ĭkz-bûrg)	112	30.16N	98.52W
Fredericksburg, Va., U.S.	99	38.20N	77.30W
Fredericktown, Mo., U.S. (frĕd'ēr-ĭk-toun)	111	37.32N	90.16W
Fredericton, Can. (frĕd'-ēr-ĭk-tŭn)	85	45.48N	66.39W
Frederikshavn, Den. (frĕdh'ĕ-rēks-houn)	146	57.27N	10.31E
Frederikssund, Den. (frĕdh'ĕ-rēks-sŏn)	152	55.51N	12.04E
Fredersdorf bei Berlin, Ger.	238a	52.31N	13.44E
Fredonia, Col. (frē-dō'nyå)	130a	5.55N	75.40W
Fredonia, Ks., U.S. (frē-dō'nĭ-ȧ)	111	36.31N	95.50W
Fredonia, N.Y., U.S.	99	42.25N	79.20W
Fredrikstad, Nor. (frådh'rēks-ståd)	146	59.14N	10.58E
Freeburg, Il., U.S. (frē'bûrg)	107e	38.26N	89.59W
Freehold, N.J., U.S. (frē'hōld)	100a	40.15N	74.16W
Freeland, Pa., U.S. (frē'lȧnd)	99	41.00N	75.50W
Freeland, Wa., U.S.	106a	48.01N	122.32W
Freels, Cape, c., Can. (frēlz)	93	46.37N	53.45W
Freelton, Can. (frēl'tŭn)	83d	43.24N	80.02W
Freeport, Bah.	122	26.30N	78.45W
Freeport, Il., U.S. (frē'pōrt)	97	42.19N	89.30W
Freeport, N.Y., U.S.	100a	40.39N	73.35W
Freeport, Tx., U.S.	113	28.56N	95.21W
Freetown, S.L. (frē'toun)	210	8.30N	13.15W
Fregenal de la Sierra, Spain (frä-hå-näl' dā lä syĕr'rä)	158	38.09N	6.40W
Fregene, Italy (frĕ-zhĕ'-nĕ)	159d	41.52N	12.12E
Freiberg, Ger. (frī'bĕrgh)	147	50.54N	13.18E
Freiburg, Ger.	147	48.00N	7.50E
Freienried, Ger. (frī'ĕn-rēd)	145d	48.20N	11.08E
Freirina, Chile (frå-ĭ-rē'nä)	132	28.35S	71.26W
Freisenbruch, neigh., Ger.	236	51.27N	7.06E
Freising, Ger. (frī'zĭng)	154	48.25N	11.45E
Fréjus, Fr. (frā-zhüs')	157	43.28N	6.46E
Fremantle, Austl. (frē'măn-t'l)	202	32.03S	116.05E
Fremont, Ca., U.S. (frē-mŏnt')	106b	37.33N	122.00W
Fremont, Mi., U.S.	98	43.25N	85.55W
Fremont, Ne., U.S.	102	41.26N	96.30W
Fremont, Oh., U.S.	98	41.20N	83.05W
Fremont, r., Ut., U.S.	109	38.20N	111.30W
Fremont Peak, mtn., Wy., U.S.	105	43.05N	109.35W
French Broad, r., Tn., U.S. (frĕnch brôd)	114	35.59N	83.01W
French Frigate Shoals, Hi., U.S.	94b	23.30N	167.10W
French Guiana, dep., S.A. (gē-ä'nä)	131	4.20N	53.00W
French Lick, In., U.S. (frĕnch lĭk)	98	38.35N	86.35W
Frenchman, r., N.A.	88	49.25N	108.30W
Frenchman Creek, r., Mt., U.S. (frĕnch-mȧn)	105	48.51N	107.20W
Frenchman Creek, r., Ne., U.S.	110	40.24N	101.50W
Frenchman Flat, Nv., U.S.	108	36.55N	116.11W
French Polynesia, dep., Oc.	2	15.00S	140.00W
French River, Mn., U.S.	107h	46.54N	91.54W
French's Forest, Austl.	243a	33.45S	151.14E
Freshfield, Eng., U.K.	237a	53.34N	3.04W
Freshfield, Mount, mtn., Can. (frĕsh'fēld)	87	51.44N	116.57W
Fresh Meadows, neigh., N.Y., U.S.	228	40.44N	73.48W
Fresnes, Fr.	237c	48.45N	2.19E
Fresnillo, Mex. (frås-nēl'yō)	116	23.10N	102.52W
Fresno, Col. (frĕs'nō)	130a	5.10N	75.01W
Fresno, Ca., U.S.	96	36.44N	119.46W
Fresno, r., Ca., U.S. (frĕz'nō)	108	37.00N	120.24W
Fresno Slough, Ca., U.S.	108	36.39N	120.12W
Freudenstadt, Ger. (froi'den-shtät)	154	48.28N	8.26E
Freycinet Peninsula, pen., Austl. (frå-sē-nĕ')	204	42.13S	148.56E
Fria, Gui.	214	10.05N	13.32W
Fria, r., Az., U.S. (frē-ä)	109	34.03N	112.12W
Fria, Cape, c., Nmb. (frīȧ)	212	18.15S	12.10E
Friant-Kern Canal, can., Ca., U.S. (kûrn)	108	36.57N	119.37W
Frias, Arg. (frē-äs)	132	28.43S	65.03W
Fribourg, Switz. (frē-bōōr')	147	46.48N	7.07E
Fridley, Mn., U.S. (frĭd'lĭ)	107g	45.05N	93.16W
Friedberg, Ger. (frēd'bĕrgh)	145d	48.22N	11.00E
Friedenau, neigh., Ger.	238a	52.28N	13.20E
Friedland, Ger. (frēt'länt)	154	53.39N	13.34E
Friedrichsfeld, Ger.	236	51.38N	6.39E
Friedrichsfelde, neigh., Ger.	238a	52.31N	13.31E
Friedrichshafen, Ger. (frē-drēks-häf'ĕn)	154	47.39N	9.28E
Friedrichshagen, neigh., Ger.	238a	52.27N	13.38E
Friedrichshain, neigh., Ger.	238a	52.31N	13.27E
Friemersheim, Ger.	236	51.23N	6.42E
Friend, Ne., U.S. (frĕnd)	111	40.40N	97.16W
Friends Colony, neigh., India	240d	28.34N	77.16E
Friendship International Airport, arpt., Md., U.S.	229c	39.11N	76.40W
Friendswood, Tx., U.S. (frĕnds'wŏod)	113a	29.31N	95.11W
Friern Barnet, neigh., Eng., U.K.	235	51.37N	0.10W
Fries, Va., U.S. (frēz)	115	36.42N	80.59W
Friesack, Ger. (frē'säk)	145b	52.44N	12.35E
Frillendorf, neigh., Ger.	236	51.28N	7.05E
Frio, Cabo, c., Braz. (kä'bō-frē'ō)	131	22.58S	42.08W
Frio R, Tx., U.S.	112	29.00N	99.15W
Frisian Islands, is., Neth. (frē'zhȧn)	146	53.30N	5.20E
Friuli-Venezia Giulia, hist. reg., Italy	160	46.20N	13.20E
Frobisher Bay, b., Can.	85	62.49N	66.41W
Frobisher Lake, l., Can. (frŏb'ĭsh'ēr)	84	56.25N	108.20W
Frodsham, Eng., U.K. (frŏdz'ăm)	144a	53.18N	2.48W
Frohavet, b., Nor.	146	63.49N	9.12E
Frohnau, neigh., Ger.	238a	52.38N	13.18E
Frohnhausen, neigh., Ger.	236	51.27N	6.58E
Frome, Lake, l., Austl. (frōōm)	202	30.40S	140.13E
Frontenac, Ks., U.S. (frŏn'tē-năk)	111	37.27N	94.41W
Frontera, Mex. (frôn-tā'rä)	119	18.34N	92.38W
Front Range, mts., Co., U.S. (frŭnt)	110	40.59N	105.29W
Front Royal, Va., U.S. (frŭnt)	99	38.55N	78.10W
Frosinone, Italy (frō-zē-nō'nå)	160	41.38N	13.22E
Frostburg, Md., U.S. (frôst'bûrg)	99	39.40N	78.55W
Fruita, Co., U.S. (frōōt-ȧ)	109	39.10N	108.45W
Frunze *see* Bishkek, Kyrg.	169	42.49N	74.42E
Fryanovo, Russia (f'ryä'nô-vô)	172b	56.08N	38.28E
Fryazino, Russia (f'ryä'zĭ-nô)	172b	55.58N	38.05E
Frydlant, Czech Rep. (frĕd'länt)	154	50.56N	15.05E

ăt; finȧl; rāte; senåte; ärm; åsk; sofȧ; fâre; ch-choose; dh-as th in other; bē; ėvent; bĕt; recĕnt; cratēr; g-gō; gh-guttural g; bĭt; ĭ-short neutral; rīde; K-guttural k as ch in German ich;

PLACE (Pronunciation)	PAGE	Lat. °′	Long. °′
Fryerning, Eng., U.K.	235	51.41N	0.22E
Fucheng, China (fo͞o-chŭŋ)	190	37.53N	116.08E
Fuchu, Japan (fo͞o′cho͞o)	195a	35.41N	139.29E
Fuchun, r., China (fo͞o-chȯn)	193	29.50N	120.00E
Fuego, vol., Guat. (fwā′gō)	120	14.29N	90.52W
Fuencarral, Spain (fuān-kär-räl′)	159a	40.29N	3.42W
Fuensalida, Spain (fwān-sä-lē′dä)	158	40.04N	4.15W
Fuente, Mex. (fwĕ′n-tĕ′)	112	28.39N	100.34W
Fuente de Cantos, Spain (fwĕn′tå dā kän′tōs)	158	38.15N	6.18W
Fuente el Saz, Spain (fwĕn′tå ĕl säth′)	159a	40.39N	3.30W
Fuenteobejuna, Spain	158	38.15N	5.30W
Fuentesaúco, Spain (fwĕn-tå-sä-o͞o′kō)	158	41.18N	5.25W
Fuerte, Río del, r., Mex. (rē′ō-dĕl-fo͞o-ĕ′r-tĕ)	116	26.15N	108.50W
Fuerte Olimpo, Para. (fwĕr′tå ō-lēm-pō)	132	21.10S	57.49W
Fuerteventura Island, i., Spain (fwĕr′tå-vĕn-to͞o′rä)	210	28.24N	13.21W
Fuhai, China	188	47.01N	87.07E
Fuhlenbrock, neigh., Ger.	236	51.32N	6.54E
Fuji, Japan (jo͞o′jė)	195	35.11N	138.44E
Fuji, r., Japan	195	35.20N	138.23E
Fujian, prov., China (fo͞o-jyĕn)	189	25.40N	117.30E
Fujidera, Japan	195b	34.34N	135.37E
Fujiidera, Japan	242b	34.34N	135.36E
Fujin, China (fo͞o-jyĭn)	189	47.13N	132.11E
Fuji San, mtn., Japan (fo͞o′jė sän)	189	35.23N	138.44E
Fujisawa, Japan (fo͞o′jė-sä′wa)	195a	35.20N	139.29E
Fujiyama *see* Fuji San, mtn., Japan	189	35.23N	138.44E
Fukagawa, neigh., Japan	242a	35.40N	139.48E
Fukiai, neigh., Japan	242b	34.42N	135.12E
Fukuchiyama, Japan (fȯ′kȯ-chė-yä′ma)	195	35.18N	135.07E
Fukue, i., Japan (fȯ-ko͞o′ā)	194	32.40N	129.02E
Fukui, Japan (fo͞o′ko͞o-ė)	189	36.05N	136.14E
Fukuoka, Japan (fo͞o′kȯ-ō′kȧ)	189	33.35N	130.23E
Fukuoka, Japan	195a	35.52N	139.31E
Fukushima, Japan (fo͞o′kȯ-shē′mȧ)	194	37.45N	140.29E
Fukushima, neigh., Japan	242b	34.42N	135.29E
Fukuyama, Japan (fo͞o′kȯ-yä′mȧ)	194	34.31N	133.21E
Fulda, Ger.	147	50.33N	9.41E
Fulda, r., Ger. (fȯl′dä)	154	51.05N	9.40E
Fulerum, neigh., Ger.	236	51.26N	6.57E
Fuling, China (fo͞o-lĭŋ)	188	29.40N	107.30E
Fullerton, Ca., U.S. (fȯl′ẽr-tŭn)	107a	33.53N	117.56W
Fullerton, La., U.S.	113	31.00N	93.00W
Fullerton, Ne., U.S.	102	41.21N	97.59W
Fulmer, Eng., U.K.	235	51.33N	0.34W
Fulton, Ky., U.S. (fŭl′tŭn)	114	36.30N	88.53W
Fulton, Mo., U.S.	111	38.51N	91.56W
Fulton, N.Y., U.S.	99	43.20N	76.25W
Fultondale, Al., U.S. (fŭl′tŭn-dāl)	100h	33.37N	86.48W
Funabashi, Japan (fo͞o′nȧ-bä′shē)	195	35.43N	139.59E
Funasaka, Japan	242b	34.49N	135.17E
Funaya, Japan (fo͞o-nä′yä)	195b	34.45N	135.52E
Funchal, Port. (fȯn-shäl′)	210	32.41N	16.15W
Fundación, Col. (fo͞on-dä-syō′n)	130	10.43N	74.13W
Fundão, Port. (fȯn-douɴ′)	158	40.08N	7.32W
Fundão, Ilha do, i., Braz.	234c	22.51S	43.14W
Funde, India	240e	18.54N	72.58E
Fundy, Bay of, b., Can. (fŭn′dĭ)	85	45.00N	66.00W
Fundy National Park, rec., Can.	85	45.38N	65.00W
Funing, China	190	39.55N	119.16E
Funing, China (fo͞o-nĭŋ)	192	33.55N	119.54E
Funing Wan, b., China	193	26.48N	120.35E
Funtua, Nig.	215	11.31N	7.17E
Furancungo, Moz.	217	14.55S	33.35E
Furbero, Mex. (fo͞or-bĕ′rô)	119	20.21N	97.32W
Furgun, mtn., Iran	182	28.47N	57.00E
Furmanov, Russia (fûr-mä′nȯf)	166	57.14N	41.11E
Furnas, Reprêsa de, res., Braz.	131	21.00S	46.00W
Furneaux Group, is., Austl. (fûr′nō)	203	40.15S	146.27E
Fürstenfeld, Aus. (für′stĕn-fĕlt)	154	47.02N	16.03E
Fürstenfeldbruck, Ger. (fur′stĕn-fĕld′bro͞ok)	145d	48.11N	11.16E
Fürstenwalde, Ger. (für′stĕn-väl-dĕ)	154	52.21N	14.04E
Fürth, Ger. (fürt)	147	49.28N	11.03E
Furuichi, Japan (fo͞o′rȯ-ē′chė)	195b	34.33N	135.37E
Fusa, Japan (fo͞o′sä)	195a	35.52N	140.08E
Fuse, Japan	195b	34.40N	135.33E
Fushimi, Japan (fo͞o′shē-mė)	195b	34.57N	135.47E
Fushun, China (fo͞o′sho͞on′)	189	41.50N	124.00E
Fusong, China (fo͞o-soŋ)	192	42.12N	127.12E
Futatsubashi, Japan	242a	35.29N	139.30E
Futtsu, Japan (fo͞o′tso͞o′)	195a	35.19N	139.49E
Futtsu Misaki, c., Japan (fo͞ot′tso͞o′ mė-sä′kē)	195a	35.19N	139.46E
Fuwah, Egypt (fo͞o′wȧ)	218b	31.13N	30.35E
Fuxian, China (fo͞o shyĕn)	190	39.36N	121.59E
Fuxin, China (fo͞o-shyĭn)	192	42.05N	121.40E
Fuyang, China (fo͞o-yäŋ)	189	32.53N	115.48E
Fuyang, China	193	30.10N	119.58E
Fuyang, r., China (fo͞o-yäŋ)	190	36.59N	114.48E
Fuyu, China (fo͞o-yo͞o)	189	45.20N	125.00E
Fuzhou, China (fo͞o-jō)	189	26.02N	119.18E
Fuzhou, r., China	190	39.38N	121.43E
Fuzhoucheng, China (fo͞o-jō-chŭŋ)	190	39.46N	121.44E
Fyfield, Eng., U.K.	235	51.45N	0.16E
Fyn, i., Den. (fü′′n)	152	55.24N	10.33E
Fyne, Loch, l., Scot., U.K. (fīn)	150	56.14N	5.10W
Fyresvatn, l., Nor.	152	59.04N	7.55E

G

PLACE (Pronunciation)	PAGE	Lat. °′	Long. °′
Gaalkacyo, Som.	218a	7.00N	47.30E
Gabela, Ang.	216	10.48S	14.20E
Gabès, Tun. (gä′bĕs)	210	33.51N	10.04E
Gabés, Golfe de, b., Tun.	210	32.22N	10.59E
Gabil, Chad	215	11.09N	18.12E
Gąbin, Pol. (gŏɴ′bėn)	155	52.23N	19.47E
Gabon, nation, Afr. (gȧ-bôɴ′)	212	0.30S	10.45E
Gaborone, Bots.	212	24.28S	25.59E
Gabriel, r., Tx., U.S. (gā′brĭ-ĕl)	113	30.38N	97.15W
Gabrovo, Bul. (gäb′rȯ-vō)	161	42.52N	25.19E
Gachsārān, Iran	185	30.12N	50.47E
Gacko, Bos. (gäts′kȯ)	161	43.10N	18.34E
Gadsden, Al., U.S. (gădz′dĕn)	97	34.00N	86.00W
Gadyach, Ukr. (gäd-yäch′)	167	50.22N	33.59E
Găești, Rom. (gä-yĕsh′tė)	161	44.43N	25.21E
Gaeta, Italy (gä-å′tä)	160	41.18N	13.34E
Gaffney, S.C., U.S. (găf′nĭ)	115	35.04N	81.47W
Gafsa, Tun. (gäf′sä)	210	34.16N	8.37E
Gagarin, Russia	162	55.32N	34.58E
Gagnoa, C. Iv.	214	6.08N	5.56W
Gagny, Fr.	237c	48.53N	2.32E
Gagra, Geor.	168	43.20N	40.15E
Gahmen, neigh., Ger.	236	51.36N	7.32E
Gaillac-sur-Tarn, Fr. (gȧ-yäk′sür-tärn′)	156	43.54N	1.52E
Gaillard Cut, reg., Pan. (gä-ėl-yä′rd)	116a	9.03N	79.42W
Gainesville, Fl., U.S. (gānz′vĭl)	97	29.40N	82.20W
Gainesville, Ga., U.S.	114	34.16N	83.48W
Gainesville, Tx., U.S.	111	33.38N	97.08W
Gainsborough, Eng., U.K. (gānz′bŭr-ȯ)	144a	53.23N	0.46W
Gairdner, Lake, l., Austl. (gård′nẽr)	202	32.20S	136.30E
Gaithersburg, Md., U.S. (gā′thẽrs′bûrg)	100e	39.08N	77.13W
Gaixian, China (gī-shyĕn)	192	40.25N	122.20E
Galana, r., Kenya	217	3.00S	39.30E
Galapagar, Spain (gä-lä-pä-gär′)	159a	40.36N	4.00W
Galapagos Islands *see* Colón, Archipiélago de, is., Ec.	130	0.10S	87.45W
Galaria, r., Italy	159d	41.58N	12.21E
Galashiels, Scot., U.K. (găl-ȧ-shēlz)	150	55.40N	2.57W
Galata, neigh., Tur.	239f	41.01N	28.58E
Galați, Rom.	142	45.25N	28.05E
Galatina, Italy (gä-lä-tē′nä)	161	40.10N	18.12E
Galátsion, Grc.	239d	38.01N	23.45E
Galaxídhion, Grc.	161	38.26N	22.22E
Galdhøpiggen, mtn., Nor.	152	61.37N	8.17E
Galeana, Mex. (gä-lå-ä′nä)	112	24.50N	100.04W
Galena, Il., U.S. (gȧ-lē′nȧ)	103	42.26N	90.27W
Galena, In., U.S.	101h	38.21N	85.55W
Galena Peak, mtn., Tx., U.S.	113a	29.44N	95.14W
Galera, Cerro, mtn., Pan. (sĕ′r-rȯ-gä-lĕ′rä)	116a	8.55N	79.38W
Galeras, vol., Col. (gä-lĕ′răs)	130	0.57N	77.27W
Gales, r., Or., U.S. (gālz)	106c	45.33N	123.11W
Galesburg, Il., U.S. (gālz′bûrg)	97	40.56N	90.21W
Galesville, Wi., U.S. (gālz′vĭl)	103	44.04N	91.22W
Galeton, Pa., U.S. (gāl′tŭn)	99	41.45N	77.40W
Galich, Russia (gȧl′ĭch)	166	58.20N	42.38E
Galicia, hist. reg., Pol. (gȧ-lĭsh′ĭ-ȧ)	155	49.48N	21.05E
Galicia, hist. reg., Spain (gä-lē′thyä)	158	43.35N	8.03W
Galilee, l., Austl. (găl′ĭ-lē)	203	22.23S	145.09E
Galilee, Sea of, l., Isr.	181a	32.53N	35.45E
Galina Point, c., Jam. (gä-lē′nä)	122	18.25N	76.50W
Galion, Oh., U.S. (găl′ĭ-ŭn)	98	40.45N	82.50W
Galisteo, N.M., U.S. (gä-lĭs-tå′ō)	110	35.20N	106.00W
Gallarate, Italy (gäl-lä-rä′tā)	160	45.37N	8.48E
Gallardon, Fr. (gä-lär-dôɴ′)	157b	48.31N	1.40E
Gallatin, Mo., U.S. (găl′ȧ-tĭn)	111	39.55N	93.58W
Gallatin, Tn., U.S.	114	36.23N	86.28W
Gallatin, r., Mt., U.S.	105	45.12N	111.10W
Galle, Sri L. (gäl)	183b	6.13N	80.10E
Gállego, r., Spain (gäl-yā′gō)	159	42.27N	0.37W
Gallinas, Punta de, c., Col. (gä-lyē′näs)	130	12.10N	72.10W
Gallipoli, Italy (gäl-lē′pȯ-lē)	161	40.03N	17.58E
Gallipoli *see* Gelibolu, Tur.	149	40.25N	26.40E
Gallipoli Peninsula, pen., Tur.	161	40.23N	25.10E
Gallipolis, Oh., U.S. (găl-ĭ-pȯ-lēs)	98	38.50N	82.10W
Gällivare, Swe. (yĕl-ĭ-vär′ĕ)	146	68.06N	20.29E
Gallo, r., Spain (gäl′yō)	158	40.43N	1.42W
Gallup, N.M., U.S. (găl′ŭp)	96	35.30N	108.45W
Galty Mountains, mts., Ire.	150	52.19N	8.20W
Galva, Il., U.S. (găl′vȧ)	111	41.11N	90.02W
Galveston, Tx., U.S. (găl′vĕs-tŭn)	97	29.18N	94.48W
Galveston Bay, b., Tx., U.S.	97	29.39N	94.45W
Galveston I, Tx., U.S.	113a	29.12N	94.53W
Galvin, Austl.	243b	37.51S	144.49E
Galway, Ire.	142	53.16N	9.05W
Galway Bay, b., Ire. (gôl′wā)	150	53.10N	9.47W
Gamba, China (gäm-bä)	186	28.23N	89.42E
Gambaga, Ghana (gäm-bä′gä)	210	10.32N	0.26W
Gambela, Eth. (găm-bā′lȧ)	211	8.15N	34.33E
Gambia, nation, Afr. (găm′bė-ȧ)	210	13.38N	19.38W
Gambia (Gambie), r., Afr.	214	13.20N	15.55W
Gambie, r., Afr.	210	12.30N	13.00W
Gamboma, Congo (gäm-bō′mä)	212	1.53S	15.51E
Gamleby, Swe. (gäm′lĕ-bü)	152	57.54N	16.20E
Gan, r., China (gän)	193	26.50N	115.00E
Gäncä, Azer.	166	40.40N	46.22E
Gandak, r., India	186	26.37N	84.22E
Gander, Can. (găn′dẽr)	85	48.57N	54.34W
Gander, r., Can.	93	49.10N	54.35W
Gander Lake, l., Can.	93	48.55N	55.40W
Gandhinagar, India	186	23.30N	72.47E
Gandi, Nig.	215	12.55N	5.49E
Gandía, Spain (gän-dē′ä)	159	38.56N	0.10W
Gangdisê Shan (Trans Himalayas), mts., China	188	30.25N	83.43E
Ganges, r., Asia (găn′jēz)	183	24.00N	89.30E
Ganges, Mouths of the, mth., Asia (găn′jēz)	183	21.18N	88.40E
Gangi, Italy (gän′jē)	160	37.48N	14.15E
Gangtok, India	183	27.15N	88.30E
Gannan, China (gän-nän)	192	47.50N	123.30E
Gannett Peak, mtn., Wy., U.S. (găn′ĕt)	96	43.10N	109.38W
Gano, Oh., U.S. (ğ′nȯ)	101f	39.18N	84.24W
Gänserndorf, Aus.	145e	48.21N	16.43E
Gansu, prov., China (gän-so͞o)	188	38.50N	101.10E
Ganwo, Nig.	215	11.13N	4.42E
Ganyu, China (gän-yo͞o)	190	34.52N	119.07E
Ganzhou, China (gän-jō)	189	25.50N	114.30E
Gao, Mali (gä′ō)	210	16.16N	0.03W
Gao'an, China (gou-än)	193	28.30N	115.02E
Gaobaita, China	240b	39.53N	116.30E
Gaobeidian, China	240b	39.54N	116.33E
Gaomi, China (gou-mē)	190	36.23N	119.46E
Gaoqiao, China (gou-chyou)	191b	31.21N	121.35E
Gaoshun, China (gou-shȯn)	190	31.22N	118.50E
Gaotang, China (gou-täŋ)	190	36.52N	116.12E
Gaoyao, China (gou-you)	193	23.08N	112.25E
Gaoyi, China (gou-yē)	190	37.37N	114.39E
Gaoyou, China (gou-yō)	192	32.46N	119.26E
Gaoyou Hu, l., China (kä′ō-yo͞o′ho͞o)	189	32.42N	118.40E
Gap, Fr. (gȧp)	147	44.34N	6.08E
Gapan, Phil. (gä-pän)	197a	15.18N	120.56E
Gar, China	188	31.11N	80.35E
Garanhuns, Braz. (gä-rän-yȯɴsh′)	131	8.49S	36.28W
Garbagnate Milanese, Italy	238c	45.35N	9.05E
Garbatella, neigh., Italy	239c	41.52N	12.29E
Garber, Ok., U.S. (gȧr′bēr)	111	36.28N	97.35W
Garches, Fr.	237c	48.51N	2.11E
Garching, Ger. (gär′ᴋēng)	145d	48.15N	11.39E
Garcia, Mex. (gär-sē′ä)	112	25.50N	100.37W
García de la Cadena, Mex.	118	21.14N	103.26W
Garda, Lago di, l., Italy (lä-gō-dē-gär′dä)	148	45.43N	10.26E
Gardanne, Fr. (gȧr-dȧn′)	156a	43.28N	5.29E
Gardelegen, Ger. (gär-dẽ-lå′ghĕn)	154	52.32N	11.22E
Garden, i., Mi., U.S. (gär′d′n)	98	45.50N	85.50W
Gardena, Ca., U.S. (gär-dē′nȧ)	107a	33.53N	118.19W
Garden City, Ks., U.S.	110	37.58N	100.52W
Garden City, Mi., U.S.	101b	42.20N	83.21W
Garden City, N.Y., U.S.	228	40.43N	73.37W
Garden City Park, N.Y., U.S.	228	40.44N	73.40W
Garden Grove, Ca., U.S. (gär′d′n grōv)	107a	33.47N	117.56W
Garden Reach, India	186a	22.33N	88.17E
Garden River, Can.	107k	46.33N	84.10W
Gardēz, Afg.	186	33.43N	69.09E
Gardiner, Me., U.S. (gärd′nẽr)	92	44.12N	69.46W
Gardiner, Mt., U.S.	105	45.03N	110.43W
Gardiner, Wa., U.S.	106a	48.03N	122.55W
Gardiner Dam, dam, Can.	88	51.17N	106.51W
Gardner, Ma., U.S.	99	42.35N	72.00W
Gardner Canal, strt., Can.	86	53.28N	128.15W
Gardner Pinnacles, Hi., U.S.	94b	25.10N	167.00W
Gareloi, i., Ak., U.S. (gär-lo͞o-ä′)	95a	51.40N	178.48W
Garenfeld, Ger.	236	51.24N	7.31E
Garfield, N.J., U.S. (gär′fēld)	100a	40.53N	74.06W
Garfield, N.J., U.S.	228	40.53N	74.07W
Garfield, Ut., U.S.	107b	40.45N	112.10W
Garfield Heights, Oh., U.S.	101d	41.25N	81.36W
Gargaliánoi, Grc. (gȧr-gä-lyä′nē)	161	37.07N	21.50E
Garges-lès-Gonesse, Fr.	237c	48.58N	2.25E
Gargždai, Lith. (gärgzh′dī)	153	55.43N	20.09E
Garibaldi, Mount, mtn., Can. (gâr-ĭ-băl′dė)	86	49.51N	123.01W
Garin, Arg. (gä-rē′n)	132a	34.25S	58.44W
Garissa, Kenya	217	0.28S	39.38E
Garland, Md., U.S.	229c	39.11N	76.39W
Garland, Tx., U.S. (gär′lănd)	107c	32.55N	96.39W
Garland, Ut., U.S.	105	41.45N	112.10W
Garm, Taj.	169	39.12N	70.28E
Garmisch-Partenkirchen, Ger. (gär′mēsh pär′tĕn-kēr′ᴋĕn)	154	47.38N	11.10E
Garnett, Ks., U.S. (gär′nĕt)	111	38.16N	95.15W
Garonne, r., Fr. (gȧ-rȯn)	142	44.00N	1.00E
Garoua, Cam. (gär′wä)	211	9.18N	13.24E
Garrett, In., U.S. (găr′ĕt)	98	41.20N	85.10W
Garrison, Md., U.S.	229c	39.24N	76.45W
Garrison, N.Y., U.S. (găr′ĭ-sŭn)	100a	41.23N	73.57W
Garrison, N.D., U.S.	102	47.38N	101.24W
Garrovillas, Spain (gä-rȯ-vēl′yäs)	158	39.42N	6.30W
Garry, l., Can. (găr′ĭ)	84	66.16N	99.23W
Garsen, Kenya	217	2.16S	40.07E
Garson, Can.	91	46.34N	80.52W
Garstedt, Ger. (gär′shtĕt)	145c	53.40N	9.58E
Garston, Eng., U.K.	235	51.41N	0.23W
Garston, neigh., Eng., U.K.	237a	53.21N	2.53W
Gartenstadt, neigh., Ger.	236	51.30N	7.26E
Garulia, India	186a	22.48N	88.23E
Garwolin, Pol. (gär-vō′lėn)	155	51.54N	21.40E
Garwood, N.J., U.S.	228	40.39N	74.19W
Gary, In., U.S. (gā′rĭ)	97	41.35N	87.21W
Gary, W.V., U.S. (fĭl′bĕrt)	115	37.21N	81.33W

ng-sing; ŋ-baŋk; ɴ-nasalized n; nŏd; cŏmmit; ōld; ȯbey; ôrder; oi-boil; fo͞od; ȯ-as oo in foot; ou-out; s-soft; sh-dish; th-thin; pūre; ůnite; ûrn; stŭd; circŭs; ü-as in French tu; ′-indeterminate vowel.

PLACE (Pronunciation)	PAGE	Lat. °'	Long. °'
Garzón, Col. (gär-thōn′)	130	2.13N	75.44W
Gasan, Phil. (gä-sän′)	197a	13.19N	121.52E
Gasan-Kuli, Turk.	170	37.25N	53.55E
Gas City, In., U.S. (găs)	98	40.30N	85.40W
Gascogne, reg., Fr. (gäs-kôn′yĕ)	156	43.45N	1.49W
Gasconade, r., Mo., U.S. (găs-kô-nād′)	111	37.46N	92.15W
Gascoyne, r., Austl. (găs-koin′)	202	25.15S	117.00E
Gashland, Mo., U.S. (găsh′-lănd)	107f	39.15N	94.35W
Gashua, Nig.	215	12.54N	11.00E
Gasny, Fr. (gäs-nē′)	157b	49.05N	1.36E
Gaspé, Can.	85	48.50N	64.29W
Gaspé, Péninsule de, pen., Can.	85	48.30N	65.00W
Gasper Hernández, Dom. Rep. (gäs-pär′ ĕr-nän′dāth)	123	19.40N	70.15W
Gassaway, W.V., U.S. (găs′á-wā)	98	38.40N	80.45W
Gaston, Or., U.S. (găs′tŭn)	106c	45.26N	123.08W
Gastonia, N.C., U.S. (găs-tô′nĭ-á)	115	35.15N	81.14W
Gastre, Arg. (gäs-trĕ)	132	42.12S	68.50W
Gata, Cabo de, c., Spain (ká′bô-dĕ-gä′tä)	148	36.42N	2.00W
Gata, Sierra de, mts., Spain (syĕr′rá dā gä′tä)	148	40.12N	6.39W
Gatchina, Russia (gä-chē′ná)	166	59.33N	30.08E
Gateacre, neigh., Eng., U.K.	237a	53.23N	2.51W
Gátes, Akrotírion, c., Cyp.	181a	34.30N	33.15E
Gateshead, Eng., U.K. (gāts′hĕd)	150	54.56N	1.38W
Gates of the Arctic National Park, rec., Ak., U.S.	95	67.45N	153.30W
Gatesville, Tx., U.S. (gāts′vĭl)	113	31.26N	97.34W
Gateway of India, hist., India	240e	18.55N	72.50E
Gâtine, Hauteurs de, hills, Fr.	156	46.40N	0.50W
Gatineau, Can. (gá′tē-nō)	83c	45.29N	75.38W
Gatineau, r., Can.	91	45.45N	75.50W
Gatineau, Parc de la, rec., Can.	91	45.32N	75.53W
Gatley, Eng., U.K.	237b	53.23N	2.14W
Gato Negro, Ven.	234a	10.33N	66.57W
Gattendorf, Aus.	145e	48.01N	17.00E
Gatun, Pan. (gä-tōōn′)	121	9.16N	79.25W
Gatun, r., Pan.	116a	9.21N	79.40W
Gatún, Lago, l., Pan.	121	9.13N	79.24W
Gatun Locks, trans., Pan.	116a	9.16N	79.57W
Gauhāti, India	183	26.09N	91.51E
Gauja, r., Lat. (gá′ŏ-yá)	153	57.10N	24.30E
Gaula, r., Nor.	152	62.55N	10.45E
Gāvanpāda, India	240e	18.57N	73.01E
Gávdhos, i., Grc. (gäv′dôs)	149	34.48N	24.08E
Gavins Point Dam, Ne., U.S. (gă′-vĭns)	102	42.47N	97.47W
Gāvkhūnī, Bātlāq-e, l., Iran	182	31.40N	52.48E
Gävle, Swe. (yĕv′lĕ)	142	60.40N	17.07E
Gävlebukten, b., Swe.	152	60.45N	17.30E
Gavrilov Posad, Russia (gá′vrê-lôf′ka po-sát)	162	56.34N	40.09E
Gavrilov-Yam, Russia (gá′vrê-lôf yäm′)	162	57.17N	39.49E
Gawler, Austl. (gô′lēr)	202	34.35S	138.47E
Gawler Ranges, mts., Austl.	204	32.35S	136.30E
Gaya, India (gŭ′yä)(gī′á)	183	24.53N	85.00E
Gaya, Nig. (gä′yä)	210	11.58N	9.05E
Gaylord, Mi., U.S. (gā′lôrd)	98	45.00N	84.35W
Gayndah, Austl. (gān′dăh)	204	25.43S	151.33E
Gayton, Eng., U.K.	237a	53.19N	3.06W
Gaza, Gaza	182	31.30N	34.29E
Gaziantep, Tur. (gä-zē-än′tĕp)	182	37.10N	37.30E
Gbarnga, Lib.	214	7.00N	9.29W
Gdańsk, Pol. (g′dänsk)	142	54.20N	18.40E
Gdov, Russia (g′dôf′)	166	58.44N	27.51E
Gdynia, Pol. (g′dēn′yä)	146	54.29N	18.30E
Geary, Ok., U.S. (gē′rĭ)	110	35.36N	98.19W
Géba, r., Gui.-B.	214	12.25N	14.35W
Gebo, Wy., U.S. (gĕb′ō)	105	43.49N	108.13W
Ged, La., U.S. (gĕd)	113	30.07N	93.36W
Gediz, r., Tur.	149	38.44N	28.45E
Gedney, i., Wa., U.S. (gĕd-nē)	106a	48.01N	122.18W
Gedser, Den.	152	54.35N	12.08E
Gee Cross, Eng., U.K.	237b	53.26N	2.04W
Geel, Bel.	145a	51.09N	5.01E
Geelong, Austl. (jē-lông′)	203	38.06S	144.13E
Gegu, China (gŭ-gōō)	190	39.00N	117.30E
Ge Hu, l., China (gŭ hōō)	190	31.37N	119.57E
Geidam, Nig.	210	12.57N	11.57E
Geikie Range, mts., Austl. (gē′kē)	202	17.35S	125.32E
Geislingen, Ger. (gis′lĭng-ĕn)	154	48.37N	9.52E
Geist Reservoir, res., In., U.S. (gēst)	101g	39.57N	85.59W
Geita, Tan.	217	2.52S	32.10E
Gejiu, China (gŭ-jĭo)	193	23.32N	102.50E
Geldermalsen, Neth.	145a	51.53N	5.18E
Geldern, Ger. (gĕl′dĕrn)	157c	51.31N	6.20E
Gelibolu, Tur. (gĕ-lĭb′ō-lō)	149	40.25N	26.40E
Gellep-Stratum, neigh., Ger.	236	51.20N	6.41E
Gellibrand, Point, c., Austl.	243b	37.52S	144.54E
Gelsenkirchen, Ger. (gĕl-zĕn-kĭrk-ĕn)	154	51.31N	7.05E
Gemas, Malay. (jĕm′ás)	181b	2.35N	102.37E
Gemena, Zaire	211	3.15N	19.46E
Gemlik, Tur. (gĕm′lĭk)	149	40.30N	29.10E
Genale (Jubba), r., Afr.	218a	5.15N	41.00E
General Alvear, Arg. (gĕ-nĕ-räl′äl-vĕ-á′r)	129c	36.04S	60.02W
General Arenales, Arg. (ä-rĕ-nä′lĕs)	129c	34.19S	61.16W
General Belgrano, Arg. (bĕl-grá′nô)	129c	35.45S	58.32W
General Cepeda, Mex. (sĕ-pĕ′dä)	112	25.24N	101.29W
General Conesa, Arg. (kô-nĕ′sä)	129c	36.30S	57.19W
General Guido, Arg. (gē′dô)	129c	36.41S	57.48W
General Lavalle, Arg. (lá-vá′l-yĕ)	129c	36.25S	56.55W
General Madariaga, Arg. (män-dá-rêá′gä)	132	36.59S	57.14W
General Pacheco, Arg.	233d	34.28S	58.37W
General Paz, Arg. (pá′z)	129c	35.30S	58.20W
General Pedro Antonio Santos, Mex.	118	21.37N	98.58W
General Pico, Arg. (pē′kô)	132	36.46S	63.44W
General Roca, Arg. (rô-kä)	132	39.01S	67.31W
General San Martín, Arg. (săn-már-tē′n)	132a	34.35S	58.32W
General Sarmiento (San Miguel), Arg.	132a	34.33S	58.43W
General Urquiza, neigh., Arg.	233d	34.34S	58.29W
General Viamonte, Arg. (vēä′môn-tē)	129c	35.01S	60.59W
General Zuazua, Mex. (zwä′zwä)	112	25.54N	100.07W
Genesee, r., N.Y., U.S. (jĕn-ē-sē′)	99	42.25N	78.10W
Geneseo, Il., U.S. (jē-nĕsēō)	98	41.28N	90.11W
Geneva (Genève), Switz.	142	46.14N	6.04E
Geneva, Al., U.S. (jē-nē′vá)	114	31.03N	85.50W
Geneva, Il., U.S.	101a	41.53N	88.18W
Geneva, Ne., U.S.	111	40.32N	97.37W
Geneva, N.Y., U.S.	99	42.50N	77.00W
Geneva, Oh., U.S.	98	41.45N	80.55W
Geneva, Lake, l., Switz.	147	46.28N	6.30E
Genève see Geneva, Switz.	142	46.14N	6.04E
Genil, r., Spain (hā-nēl′)	158	37.15N	4.05W
Gennebreck, Ger.	236	51.19N	7.12E
Gennevilliers, Fr.	237c	48.56N	2.18E
Genoa, Italy	142	44.23N	9.52E
Genoa, Ne., U.S. (jen′ô-á)	111	41.26N	97.43W
Genoa City, Wi., U.S.	101a	42.31N	88.19W
Genova, Golfo di, b., Italy (gôl-fô-dē-jĕn′ô-vä)	142	44.10N	8.45E
Genovesa, i., Ec. (ĕ′s-lä-gĕ-nō-vĕ-sä)	130	0.08N	90.15W
Gent, Bel.	147	51.05N	3.40E
Genthin, Ger. (gĕn-tēn′)	154	52.24N	12.10E
Gentilly, Fr.	237c	48.49N	2.21E
Genzano di Roma, Italy (gzhĕnt-zá′-nō-dē-rō′mä)	159d	41.43N	12.49E
Geographe Bay, b., Austl. (jē-ô-grăf′)	202	33.00S	114.00E
Geographe Channel, strt., Austl. (jēô′grä-fĭk)	202	24.15S	112.50E
George, l., N.Y., U.S. (jôrj)	99	43.40N	73.30W
George, Lake, l., N.A. (jôrg)	107k	46.26N	84.09W
George, Lake, l., Ug.	217	0.02N	30.25E
George, Lake, l., Fl., U.S. (jôr-ĭj)	115	29.10N	81.50W
George, Lake, l., In., U.S.	101a	41.31N	87.17W
Georges, r., Austl.	201b	33.57S	151.00E
Georges Hall, Austl.	243a	33.55S	150.59E
George Town, Bah.	123	23.30N	75.50W
Georgetown, Can. (jôrg-toun)	83d	43.39N	79.56W
Georgetown, Can. (jôr-ĭj-toun)	93	46.11N	62.32W
George Town, Cay. Is.	122	19.20N	81.20W
Georgetown, Guy. (jôrj′toun)	131	7.45N	58.04W
George Town, Malay.	196	5.21N	100.09E
Georgetown, Ct., U.S.	100a	41.15N	73.25W
Georgetown, De., U.S.	99	38.40N	75.20W
Georgetown, Il., U.S.	98	40.00N	87.40W
Georgetown, Ky., U.S.	98	38.10N	84.35W
Georgetown, Md., U.S.	99	39.25N	75.55W
Georgetown, Ma., U.S. (jôrg-toun)	93a	42.43N	71.00W
Georgetown, S.C., U.S. (jôr-ĭj-toun)	115	33.22N	79.17W
Georgetown, Tx., U.S. (jôrg-toun)	113	30.37N	97.40W
Georgetown, neigh., D.C., U.S.	229d	38.54N	77.03W
Georgetown University, pt. of i., D.C., U.S.	229d	38.54N	77.04W
George Washington Birthplace National Monument, rec., Va., U.S. (jôrj wŏsh′ĭng-tŭn)	99	38.10N	77.00W
George Washington Carver National Monument, rec., Mo., U.S. (jôrg wăsh-ĭng-tŭn kär′vēr)	111	36.58N	94.21W
George West, Tx., U.S.	112	28.20N	98.07W
Georgia, nation, Asia	164	42.17N	43.00E
Georgia, state, U.S. (jôr′ji-ă)	97	32.40N	83.50W
Georgia, Strait of, strt., N.A.	86	49.20N	124.00W
Georgiana, Al., U.S. (jôr-jē-ăn′á)	114	31.39N	86.44W
Georgian Bay, b., Can.	85	45.15N	80.50W
Georgian Bay Islands National Park, rec., Can.	90	45.20N	81.40W
Georgina, r., Austl. (jôr-jē′ná)	202	22.00S	138.15E
Georgiyevsk, Russia (gyôr-gyĕfsk′)	167	44.05N	43.30E
Gera, Ger. (gā′rä)	147	50.52N	12.06E
Geral, Serra, mts., Braz. (sĕr′rá zhá-räl′)	132	28.30S	51.00W
Geral de Goiás, Serra, mts., Braz. (zhá-räl′-dĕ-gô-yá′s)	131	14.22S	45.40W
Geraldton, Austl. (jĕr′ăld-tŭn)	202	28.40S	114.35E
Geraldton, Can.	85	49.43N	87.00W
Gerdview, S. Afr.	244b	26.10S	28.11E
Gérgal, Spain (gĕr′gäl)	158	37.08N	2.29W
Gering, Ne., U.S. (gē′rĭng)	102	41.49N	103.41W
Gerlachovský štít, mtn., Slvk.	155	49.12N	20.08E
Gerli, neigh., Arg.	233d	34.41S	58.23W
Germantown, Oh., U.S. (jûr′măn-toun)	98	39.35N	84.25W
Germantown, neigh., Pa., U.S.	229b	40.03N	75.11W
Germany, nation, Eur. (jûr′mà-nĭ)	142	51.00N	10.00E
Germiston, S. Afr. (jûr′mĭs-tŭn)	212	26.19S	28.11E
Gerona, Phil. (hā-rō′nä)	197a	15.36N	120.36E
Gerona, Spain (hĕ-rō′nä)	148	41.55N	2.48E
Gerrards Cross, Eng., U.K. (jĕrărds krŏs)	144b	51.34N	0.33W
Gers, r., Fr. (zhĕr)	159	43.25N	0.30E
Gersthofen, Ger. (gĕrst-hō′fĕn)	145d	48.26N	10.54E
Getafe, Spain (hā-tä′fā)	158	40.19N	3.44W
Gettysburg, Pa., U.S. (gĕt′ĭs-bûrg)	99	39.50N	77.15W
Gettysburg, S.D., U.S.	102	45.01N	99.59W
Getzville, N.Y., U.S.	230a	43.01N	78.46W
Gevelsberg, Ger. (gĕ-fĕls′bĕrgh)	157c	51.18N	7.20E
Geweke, neigh., Ger.	236	51.22N	7.25E
Ghāghra, r., India	183	26.00N	83.00E
Ghana, nation, Afr. (gän′ä)	210	8.00N	2.00W
Ghanzi, Bots. (gän′zē)	212	21.30S	22.00E
Ghārāpuri, India	240e	18.57N	72.56E
Ghardaïa, Alg. (gär-dä′ē-ä)	210	32.29N	3.38E
Gharo, Pak.	186	24.50N	68.35E
Ghāt, Libya	210	24.52N	10.16E
Ghātkopar, neigh., India	240e	19.05N	72.54E
Ghazāl, Bahr al-, r., Sudan	211	9.30N	30.00E
Ghazal, Bahr el, r., Chad (bär ĕl ghä-zäl′)	215	14.30N	17.00E
Ghāzipur, neigh., India	240d	28.38N	77.19E
Ghazzah see Gaza, Gaza	182	31.30N	34.29E
Gheorgheni, Rom.	149	46.48N	25.30E
Gherla, Rom. (gĕr′lä)	155	47.01N	23.55E
Ghilizane, Alg.	210	35.43N	0.43E
Ghonda, neigh., India	240d	28.41N	77.16E
Ghondi, neigh., India	240d	28.42N	77.16E
Ghost Lake, Can.	83e	51.15N	114.46W
Ghudāmis, Libya	210	30.07N	9.26E
Ghūrīān, Afg.	185	34.21N	61.30E
Ghushuri, India	240a	22.37N	88.22E
Gia-dinh, Viet.	241j	10.48N	106.42E
Giannutri, Isola di, i., Italy (jän-nōō′trē)	160	42.15N	11.06E
Gibara, Cuba (hē-bä′rä)	122	21.05N	76.10W
Gibbsboro, N.J., U.S.	229b	39.50N	74.58W
Gibeon, Nmb. (gĭb′ē-ŭn)	212	25.15S	17.30E
Gibraleón, Spain (hē-brä-lå-ōn′)	158	37.24N	7.00W
Gibraltar, dep., Eur. (gĭ-brăl-tă′r)	142	36.08N	5.22W
Gibraltar, Strait of, strt.	142	35.55N	5.45W
Gibraltar Point, c., Can.	227c	43.36N	79.23W
Gibson City, Il., U.S. (gĭb′sŭn)	98	40.25N	88.20W
Gibson Desert, des., Austl.	202	24.45S	123.15E
Gibson Island, Md., U.S.	100e	39.05N	76.26W
Gibson Reservoir, res., Ok., U.S.	111	36.07N	95.08W
Giddings, Tx., U.S. (gĭd′ĭngz)	113	30.11N	96.55W
Gidea Park, neigh., Eng., U.K.	235	51.35N	0.12E
Gideon, Mo., U.S. (gĭd′ē-ŭn)	111	36.27N	89.56W
Gien, Fr. (zhē-äN′)	147	47.43N	2.37E
Giessen, Ger. (gēs′sĕn)	154	50.35N	8.40E
Gif-sur-Yvette, Fr.	237c	48.42N	2.08E
Gifu, Japan (gē′fōō)	189	35.25N	136.45E
Gig Harbor, Wa., U.S. (gĭg)	106a	47.20N	122.36W
Giglio, Isola del, i., Italy (jēl′yō)	160	42.23N	10.55E
Gijón, Spain (hē-hōn′)	142	43.33N	5.37W
Gila, r., U.S. (hē′lá)	96	33.00N	110.00W
Gila Bend, Az., U.S.	109	32.59N	112.41W
Gila Cliff Dwellings National Monument, rec., N.M., U.S.	109	33.15N	108.20W
Gila River Indian Reservation, I.R., Az., U.S.	109	33.11N	112.38W
Gilbert, Mn., U.S. (gĭl′bērt)	103	47.27N	92.29W
Gilbert, r., Austl. (gĭl-bērt)	203	17.15S	142.09E
Gilbert, Mount, mtn., Can.	86	50.51N	124.20W
Gilbert Islands, is., Kir.	225	0.30S	174.00E
Gilboa, Mount, mtn., S. Afr. (gĭl-bôá)	213c	29.13S	30.17W
Gilford Island, i., Can. (gĭl′fērd)	86	50.45N	126.25W
Gilgit, Pak. (gĭl′gĭt)	183	35.58N	73.48E
Gil Island, i., Can. (gĭl)	86	53.13N	129.15W
Gillen, l., Austl. (jĭl′ĕn)	202	26.15S	125.15E
Gillett, Ar., U.S. (jĭ-lĕt′)	111	34.07N	91.22W
Gillette, Wy., U.S.	105	44.17N	105.30W
Gillingham, Eng., U.K. (gĭl′ĭng ăm)	151	51.23N	0.33E
Gilman, Il., U.S. (gĭl′măn)	98	40.45N	87.55W
Gilman Hot Springs, Ca., U.S.	107a	33.49N	116.57W
Gilmer, Tx., U.S. (gĭl′mēr)	113	32.43N	94.57W
Gilmore, Ga., U.S. (gĭl′môr)	100c	33.51N	84.29W
Gilo, r., Eth.	211	7.40N	34.17E
Gilroy, Ca., U.S. (gĭl-roi′)	108	37.00N	121.34W
Giluwe, Mount, mtn., Pap. N. Gui.	197	6.04S	144.00E
Gimli, Can. (gĭm′lē)	89	50.39N	97.00W
Gimone, r., Fr. (zhē-mōn′)	156	43.26N	0.36E
Ginir, Eth.	211	7.13N	40.44E
Ginosa, Italy (jē-nō′zä)	160	40.35N	16.48E
Ginza, neigh., Japan	242a	35.40N	139.47E
Ginzo, Spain (hēn-thō′)	158	42.03N	7.43W
Gioia del Colle, Italy (jô′yä dĕl kôl′lā)	160	40.48N	16.55E
Girard, Ks., U.S. (jĭ-rärd′)	111	37.30N	94.50W
Girardot, Col. (hē-rär-dōt′)	130	4.19N	74.47W
Giresun, Tur. (ghĕr′ĕ-sŏn′)	182	40.55N	38.20E
Girgaum, neigh., India	240e	18.57N	72.48E
Giridih, India (jē-rē-dē)	183	24.12N	86.18E
Gironde, r., Fr. (zhē-rôNd′)	142	45.31N	1.00W
Girvan, Scot., U.K. (gûr′văn)	150	55.15N	5.01W
Gisborne, N.Z. (gĭz′bŭrn)	203a	38.40S	178.08E
Gisenyi, Rw.	212	1.43S	29.15E
Gisors, Fr. (zhē-zôr′)	156	49.19N	1.47E
Gitambo, Zaire	216	4.21N	24.45E
Gitega, Bdi.	212	3.39S	30.05E
Giurgiu, Rom. (jôr′jō)	161	43.53N	25.58E
Givet, Fr. (zhē-vĕ′)	156	50.08N	4.47E
Givors, Fr. (zhē-vôr′)	156	45.35N	4.46E
Giza see Al Jīzah, Egypt	218b	30.01N	31.12E
Gizhiga, Russia (gē′zhi-gá)	165	61.59N	160.46E
Gizo, Sol.Is.	198e	8.06S	156.51E
Gizycko, Pol. (gĭ′zhĭ-ko)	146	54.03N	21.48E
Gjirokastër, Alb.	149	40.04N	20.10E
Gjøvik, Nor. (gyû′vĕk)	146	60.47N	10.36E
Glabeek-Zuurbemde, Bel.	145a	50.52N	4.59E
Glace Bay, Can. (glās bā)	93	46.12N	59.57W
Glacier Bay National Park, rec., Ak., U.S. (glā′shēr)	96a	58.40N	136.50W
Glacier National Park, rec., Can.	84	51.45N	117.35W
Glacier Peak, mtn., Wa., U.S.	104	48.07N	121.10W
Glacier Point, c., Can.	106a	48.24N	123.59W
Gladbeck, Ger. (glăd′bĕk)	154	51.35N	6.59E
Gladdeklipkop, S. Afr.	218d	24.17S	29.36E
Gladesville, Austl.	243a	33.50S	151.08E
Gladstone, Austl.	202	33.15S	138.20E
Gladstone, Austl. (glăd′stōn)	203	23.45S	152.00E
Gladstone, Mi., U.S.	103	45.50N	87.04W
Gladstone, N.J., U.S.	100a	40.43N	74.39W
Gladstone, Or., U.S.	106c	45.23N	122.36W
Gladwin, Mi., U.S. (glăd′wĭn)	98	44.00N	84.25W
Gladwyne, Pa., U.S.	229b	40.02N	75.17W
Glåma, r., Nor.	142	61.30N	10.30E

PRONOUNCING INDEX

Glarus - Grand Canal 291

PLACE (Pronunciation)	PAGE	Lat. °′	Long. °′
Glarus, Switz. (glä′rȯs)	154	47.02N	9.03E
Glasgow, Scot., U.K. (glȧs′gō)	142	55.54N	4.25W
Glasgow, Ky., U.S.	114	37.00N	85.55W
Glasgow, Mo., U.S.	111	39.14N	92.48W
Glasgow, Mt., U.S.	105	48.14N	106.39W
Glashütte, neigh., Ger.	236	51.13N	6.52E
Glassmanor, Md., U.S.	229d	38.49N	76.59W
Glassport, Pa., U.S. (glȧs′pōrt)	101e	40.19N	79.53W
Glassport, Pa., U.S.	230b	40.19N	79.54W
Glauchau, Ger. (glou′kou)	154	50.51N	12.28E
Glazov, Russia (glä′zôf)	164	58.05N	52.52E
Glehn, Ger.	236	51.10N	6.35E
Glen, r., Eng., U.K. (glĕn)	144a	52.44N	0.18W
Glénan, Îles de, is., Fr. (ĕl-dē-glā-näN′)	156	47.43N	4.42W
Glenarden, Md., U.S.	229d	38.56N	76.52W
Glen Burnie, Md., U.S. (bûr′nē)	100e	39.10N	76.38W
Glen Canyon, val., Ut., U.S.	109	37.10N	110.50W
Glen Canyon Dam, dam, Az., U.S. (glĕn kăn′yŭn)	96	36.57N	111.25W
Glen Canyon National Recreation Area, rec., U.S.	109	37.00N	111.20W
Glen Carbon, Il., U.S. (kär′bŏn)	107e	38.45N	89.59W
Glencoe, S. Afr. (glĕn-cō)	213c	28.14S	30.09E
Glencoe, Il., U.S.	101a	42.08N	87.45W
Glencoe, Mn., U.S. (glĕn′kō)	103	44.44N	94.07W
Glen Cove, N.Y., U.S. (kōv)	100a	40.51N	73.38W
Glendale, Az., U.S. (glĕn′dāl)	109	33.30N	112.15W
Glendale, Ca., U.S.	96	34.09N	118.15W
Glendale, Oh., U.S.	101f	31.16N	84.22W
Glendive, Mt., U.S. (glĕn′dīv)	96	47.08N	104.41W
Glendo, Wy., U.S.	105	42.32N	104.54W
Glendora, Ca., U.S. (glĕn-dō′rȧ)	107a	34.08N	117.52W
Glendora, N.J., U.S.	229b	39.50N	75.04W
Glen Echo, Md., U.S.	229d	38.58N	77.08W
Glenelg, r., Austl.	204	37.20S	141.30E
Glen Ellyn, Il., U.S. (glĕn ĕl′-lĕn)	101a	41.53N	88.04W
Glenfield, Austl.	243a	33.58S	150.54E
Glen Head, N.Y., U.S.	228	40.50N	73.37W
Glenhuntly, Austl.	243b	37.54S	145.03E
Glen Innes, Austl. (ĭn′ĕs)	203	29.45S	152.02E
Glenmore, Md., U.S.	229c	39.11N	76.36W
Glenns Ferry, Id., U.S. (fĕr′ĭ)	104	42.58N	115.21W
Glen Olden, Pa., U.S. (ōl′d′n)	100f	39.54N	75.17W
Glenomra, La., U.S. (glĕn-mō′rȧ)	113	30.58N	92.36W
Glen Ridge, N.J., U.S.	228	40.49N	74.13W
Glen Rock, N.J., U.S.	228	40.58N	74.08W
Glenrock, Wy., U.S. (glĕn′rŏk)	105	42.50N	105.53W
Glenroy, Austl.	243b	37.42S	144.55E
Glens Falls, N.Y., U.S. (glĕnz fôlz)	99	43.20N	73.40W
Glenshaw, Pa., U.S. (glĕn′shô)	101e	40.33N	79.57W
Glenside, Pa., U.S.	229b	40.06N	75.09W
Glen Valley, Can.	106d	49.09N	122.30W
Glenview, Il., U.S. (glĕn′vū)	101a	42.04N	87.48W
Glenville, Ga., U.S. (glĕn′vĭl)	115	31.55N	81.56W
Glen Waverley, Austl.	243b	37.53S	145.10E
Glenwood, Ia., U.S.	102	41.03N	95.44W
Glenwood, Mn., U.S.	102	45.39N	95.23W
Glenwood, N.M., U.S.	109	33.19N	108.52W
Glenwood Landing, N.Y., U.S.	228	40.50N	73.39W
Glenwood Springs, Co., U.S.	109	39.35N	107.20W
Glienicke, Ger. (glē′nē-kē)	145b	52.38N	13.19E
Glinde, Ger. (glĕn′dē)	145c	53.32N	10.13E
Gliwice, Pol. (gwĭ-wĭt′sĕ)	147	50.18N	18.40E
Globe, Az., U.S. (glōb)	96	33.20N	110.50W
Głogów, Pol. (gwō′go͞ov)	147	51.40N	16.04E
Glommen, r., Nor. (glôm′ĕn)	152	60.03N	11.15E
Glonn, Ger. (glônn)	145d	47.59N	11.52E
Glorieuses, Îles, is., Reu.	213	11.28S	47.50E
Glossop, Eng., U.K. (glŏs′ŭp)	144a	53.26N	1.57W
Gloster, Ms., U.S. (glŏs′tēr)	114	31.10N	91.00W
Gloucester, Eng., U.K. (glŏs′tēr)	147	51.54N	2.11W
Gloucester, Ma., U.S.	93a	42.37N	70.40W
Gloucester City, N.J., U.S.	100f	39.53N	75.08W
Glouster, Oh., U.S. (glŏs′tēr)	98	39.35N	82.05W
Glover Island, i., Can. (glŭv′ēr)	93	48.44N	57.45W
Gloversville, N.Y., U.S. (glŭv′ērz-vĭl)	99	43.05N	74.20W
Glovertown, Can. (glŭv′ēr-toun)	93	48.41N	54.02W
Glubokoye, Bela. (glo͞o-bô-kō′yĕ)	166	55.08N	27.44E
Glückstadt, Ger. (glük-shtät)	145c	53.47N	9.25E
Glushkovo, Russia (glōsh′kô-vō)	163	51.21N	34.43E
Gmünden, Aus. (g′mo̅n′dĕn)	154	47.57N	13.47E
Gniezno, Pol. (g′nyåz′nô)	147	52.32N	17.34E
Gnjilane, Yugo. (gnyē′lä-nĕ)	161	42.28N	21.27E
Goa, , India (gō′ȧ)	183	15.45N	74.00E
Goascorán, Hond. (gō-äs′kō-rän′)	120	13.37N	87.43W
Goba, Eth. (gō′bä)	211	7.17N	39.58E
Gobabis, Nmb. (gō-bä′bĭs)	212	22.25S	18.50E
Gobi, des., Asia (gō′be)	188	43.29N	103.15E
Goble, Or., U.S. (gō′b'l)	106c	46.01N	122.53W
Goch, Ger. (gōk)	157c	51.35N	6.10E
Godāvari, r., India (gō-dä′vŭ-rē)	183	19.00N	78.30E
Goddards Soak, sw., Austl. (gŏd′ȧrdz)	202	31.20S	123.30E
Goderich, Can. (gŏd′rĭch)	90	43.45N	81.45W
Godfrey, Il., U.S. (gŏd′frē)	107e	38.57N	90.12W
Godhavn, Grnld. (gōdh′hȧvn)	82	69.15N	53.30W
Gods, r., Can. (gŏdz)	89	55.17N	93.35W
Gods Lake, Can.	85	54.40N	94.09W
Godthåb, Grnld. (gŏt′hŏb)	82	64.10N	51.32W
Godwin Austen *see* K2, mtn., Asia	182	36.06N	76.38E
Goéland, Lac au, l., Can.	91	49.47N	76.41W
Goffs, Ca., U.S. (gôfs)	108	34.57N	115.06W
Goff's Oak, Eng., U.K.	235	51.43N	0.05W
Gogebic, l., Mi., U.S. (gō-gē′bĭk)	103	46.24N	89.25W
Gogebic Range, mts., Mi., U.S.	103	46.37N	89.48W
Göggingen, Ger. (gûg′gĕn-gĕn)	145d	48.21N	10.53E
Gogland, i., Russia	153	60.04N	26.55E
Gogonou, Benin	215	10.50N	2.50E
Gogorrón, Mex. (gō-gô-rōn′)	118	21.51N	100.54W
Goiânia, Braz. (gô-vȧ′nyä)	131	16.41S	48.57W
Goiás, Braz. (gô-yȧ′s)	131	15.57S	50.10W
Goiás, state, Braz.	131	16.00S	48.00W
Goirle, Neth.	145a	51.31N	5.06E
Gökçeada, i., Tur.	161	40.10N	25.27E
Göksu, r., Tur. (gûk′so͞o′)	167	36.40N	33.30E
Gol, Nor. (gûl)	152	60.58N	8.54E
Golabāri, India	240a	22.36N	88.20E
Golax, Va., U.S. (gō′lăks)	115	36.41N	80.56W
Golcar, Eng., U.K. (gŏl′kȧr)	144a	53.38N	1.52W
Golconda, Il., U.S. (gŏl-kŏn′dȧ)	111	37.21N	88.32W
Gołdap, Pol. (gôl′dăp)	155	54.17N	22.17E
Golden, Can.	87	51.18N	116.58W
Golden, Co., U.S.	110	39.44N	105.15W
Goldendale, Wa., U.S. (gōl′dĕn-dāl)	104	45.49N	120.48W
Golden Gate, strt., Ca., U.S. (gōl′dĕn gāt)	106b	37.48N	122.32W
Golden Hinde, mtn., Can. (hīnd)	86	49.40N	125.45W
Golden's Bridge, N.Y., U.S.	100a	41.17N	73.41W
Golden Valley, Mn., U.S.	107g	44.58N	93.23W
Golders Green, neigh., Eng., U.K.	235	51.35N	0.12W
Goldfield, Nv., U.S. (gōld′fēld)	108	37.42N	117.15W
Gold Hill, mtn., Pan.	116a	9.03N	79.08W
Gold Mountain, mtn., Wa., U.S. (gōld)	106a	47.33N	122.48W
Goldsboro, N.C., U.S. (gōldz-bûr′ō)	115	35.23N	77.59W
Goldthwaite, Tx., U.S. (gōld′thwāt)	112	31.27N	98.34W
Goleniów, Pol. (gô-lĕ-nyŭf′)	154	53.33N	14.51E
Golets-Purpula, Gora, mtn., Russia	165	59.08N	115.22E
Golf, Il., U.S.	231a	42.03N	87.48W
Golfito, C.R. (gôl-fē′tō)	121	8.40N	83.12W
Golf Park Terrace, Il., U.S.	231a	42.03N	87.51W
Goliad, Tx., U.S. (gō-lĭ-ăd′)	113	28.40N	97.12W
Golo, r., Fr.	160	42.28N	9.18E
Golo Island, i., Phil. (gō′lō)	197a	13.38N	120.17E
Golovchino, Russia (gō-lôf′chĕ-nō)	163	50.34N	35.52E
Golyamo Konare, Bul. (gō′lȧ-mō-kō′nä-rĕ)	161	42.16N	24.33E
Golzow, Ger. (gōl′tsōv)	145b	52.17N	12.36E
Gombe, Nig.	210	10.19N	11.02E
Gomel′, Bela. (go′mĕl′)	164	52.20N	31.03E
Gomel′, prov., Bela. (Oblast)	162	52.18N	29.00E
Gomera Island, i., Spain (gô-mä′rä)	210	28.00N	18.01W
Gomez Farias, Mex. (gō′măz fä-rē′ás)	112	24.59N	101.02W
Gómez Palacio, Mex. (pä-lä′syō)	116	25.35N	103.30W
Gonaïves, Haiti (gō-nȧ-ēv′)	117	19.25N	72.45W
Gonaïves, Golfe des, b., Haiti (gō-nȧ-ēv′)	123	19.20N	73.20W
Gonâve, Île de la, i., Haiti (gô-nȧv′)	117	18.50N	73.30W
Gonda, India	186	27.13N	82.00E
Gondal, India	186	22.02N	70.47E
Gonder, Eth.	211	12.39N	37.30E
Gonesse, Fr. (gô-nĕs′)	157b	48.59N	2.28E
Gongga Shan, mtn., China (gôŋ-gä shän)	188	29.16N	101.46E
Goniri, Nig.	215	11.30N	12.20E
Gonō, r., Japan (gō′nō)	195	35.00N	132.25E
Gonor, Can. (gō′nŏr)	83f	50.04N	96.57W
Gonubie, S. Afr. (gŏn′o͞o-bē)	213c	32.56S	28.02E
Gonzales, Mex. (gôn-zá′lĕs)	118	22.47N	98.26W
Gonzales, Tx., U.S. (gŏn-zä′lĕz)	113	29.31N	97.25W
González Catán, Arg. (gōn-zá′lĕz-kä-tá′n)	132a	34.47S	58.39W
Good Hope, Cape of, c., S. Afr. (kăp ov go͝od hōp)	212	34.21S	18.29E
Good Hope Mountain, mtn., Can.	86	51.09N	124.10W
Gooding, Id., U.S. (gȯd′ĭng)	105	42.55N	114.43W
Goodland, In., U.S. (gȯd′lănd)	98	40.50N	87.15W
Goodland, Ks., U.S.	110	39.19N	101.43W
Goodwood, S. Afr. (gȯd′wȯd)	212a	33.54S	18.33E
Goole, Eng., U.K. (go͞ol)	144a	53.42N	0.52W
Goose, r., N.D., U.S.	102	47.40N	97.41W
Gooseberry Creek, r., Wy., U.S. (go͞os-bĕr′ĭ)	105	44.04N	108.35W
Goose Creek, r., Id., U.S. (go͞os)	105	42.07N	113.53W
Goose Lake, l., Ca., U.S.	104	41.56N	120.35W
Gorakhpur, India (gō′rŭk-po͞or)	183	26.45N	82.39E
Gorda, Punta, c., Cuba (po͞o′n-tä-gôr-dä)	122	22.25N	82.10W
Gorda Cay, i., Bah. (gôr′dä)	122	26.05N	77.30W
Gordon, Can. (gôr′dŭn)	83f	50.00N	97.20W
Gordon, Ne., U.S.	102	42.47N	102.14W
Gordons Corner, Md., U.S.	229d	39.50N	76.57W
Gore, Eth. (gō′rĕ)	211	8.12N	35.34E
Gore Hill, Austl.	243a	33.49S	151.11E
Gorgān, Iran	182	36.44N	54.30E
Gorgona, Isola di, Italy (gôr-gō′nä)	148	43.27N	9.55E
Gori, Geor. (gō′rĕ)	167	42.00N	44.08E
Gorinchem, Neth. (gō′rĭn-kĕm)	145a	51.50N	4.59E
Goring, Eng., U.K. (gôr′ĭng)	144b	51.30N	1.08W
Gorizia, Italy (gō-rē′tsē-yä)	160	45.56N	13.40E
Gor′kiy *see* Nizhniy Novgorod, Russia	164	56.15N	44.05E
Gor′kovskoye, res., Russia	164	56.38N	43.40E
Gor′kovskoye, res., Russia	166	57.00N	43.55E
Gorlice, Pol. (gôr-lē′tsĕ)	155	49.38N	21.11E
Görlitz, Ger. (gûr′lĭts)	147	51.10N	15.01E
Gorman, Tx., U.S. (gôr′măn)	112	32.13N	98.40W
Gorna Oryakhovitsa, Bul. (gôr′nä-ôr-yĕk′ō-vē-tsȧ)	161	43.08N	25.40E
Gornji Milanovac, Yugo. (gôrn′yē-mē′la-nô-väts)	161	44.02N	20.29E
Gorno-Altay, state, Russia	170	51.00N	86.00E
Gorno-Altaysk, Russia (gôr′nŭ′ŭl-tīsk′)	164	51.58N	85.58E
Gorodishche, Russia (gō-rô′dĭsh-chĕ)	172a	57.57N	57.03E
Gorodok, Bela.	162	55.27N	29.58E
Gorodok, Russia	165	50.30N	103.58E
Gorontalo, Indon. (gō-rōn-tä′lo)	197	0.40N	123.04E
Gorton, neigh., Eng., U.K.	237b	53.27N	2.10W
Gorzów Wielkopolski, Pol. (gō-zho͞ov′vyĕl-ko-pōl′skĕ)	146	53.44N	15.15E
Gosely, Eng., U.K.	144a	52.33N	2.10W
Gosen, Ger.	238a	52.24N	13.43E
Goshen, In., U.S. (gō′shĕn)	98	41.35N	85.50W
Goshen, Ky., U.S.	101h	38.24N	85.34W
Goshen, N.Y., U.S.	100a	41.24N	74.19W
Goshen, Oh., U.S.	101f	39.14N	84.09W
Goshute Indian Reservation, I.R., Ut., U.S. (gō-sho͞ot′)	109	39.50N	114.00W
Goslar, Ger. (gôs′lär)	154	51.55N	10.25E
Gospa, r., Ven. (gôs-pä)	131b	9.43N	64.23W
Gostivar, Mac. (gos′tĕ-vär)	161	41.46N	20.58E
Gostynin, Pol. (gôs-tē′nĭn)	155	52.24N	19.30E
Göta, r., Swe. (gōĕtä)	152	58.11N	12.03E
Göta Kanal, can., Swe. (yû′tȧ)	152	58.35N	15.24E
Gotanno, neigh., Japan	242a	35.46N	139.49E
Göteborg, Swe. (yû′tĕ-bôrgh)	142	57.39N	11.56E
Gotel Mountains, mts., Afr.	215	7.05N	11.20E
Gotera, El Sal. (gō-tä′rä)	120	13.41N	88.06W
Gotha, Ger. (gō′tȧ)	147	50.47N	10.43E
Gothenburg *see* Göteborg, Swe.	142	57.39N	11.56E
Gothenburg, Ne., U.S. (gŏth′ĕn-bûrg)	110	40.57N	100.08W
Gotland, i., Swe.	142	57.35N	17.35E
Gotska Sandön, i., Swe.	153	58.24N	19.15E
Götterswickerhamm, Ger.	236	51.35N	6.40E
Göttingen, Ger. (gût′ĭng-ĕn)	154	51.32N	9.57E
Gouda, Neth. (gou′dä)	145a	52.00N	4.42E
Gough, i., St. Hel. (gŏf)	2	40.00S	10.00W
Gouin, Réservoir, res., Can.	85	48.15N	74.15W
Goukou, China (gō-kō)	189	48.45N	121.42E
Goulais, r., Can.	90	46.45N	84.10W
Goulburn, Austl. (gōl′bŭrn)	203	34.47S	149.40E
Goumbati, mtn., Sen.	214	13.08N	12.06W
Goumbou, Mali (go͞om-bo͞o′)	210	14.59N	7.27W
Gouna, Cam.	215	8.32N	13.34E
Goundam, Mali (go͞on-däN′)	210	16.29N	3.37W
Gournay-sur-Marne, Fr.	237c	48.52N	2.34E
Goussainville, Fr.	237c	49.01N	2.28E
Gouverneur, N.Y., U.S. (gŭv-ĕr-no͞or′)	99	44.20N	75.25W
Go-vap, Viet.	241j	10.49N	106.42E
Govenlock, Can. (gŭvĕn-lŏk)	84	49.15N	109.48W
Governador, Ilha do, i., Braz. (gô-vĕr-nä-dō-′r-ē-lä′dō)	132b	22.48S	43.13W
Governador Portela, Braz. (pōr-tĕ′lȧ)	132b	22.28S	43.30W
Governador Valadares, Braz. (vä-lä-dä′rĕs)	131	18.47S	41.45W
Governor's Harbour, Bah.	122	25.15N	76.15W
Gowanda, N.Y., U.S. (gô-wŏn′dȧ)	99	42.30N	78.55W
Goya, Arg. (gō′yä)	132	29.06S	59.12W
Göyçay, Azer. (gē-ōk′chī)	167	40.40N	47.40E
Goyt, r., Eng., U.K. (goit)	144a	53.19N	2.03W
Graaff-Reinet, S. Afr. (gräf′rī′nĕt)	212	32.10S	24.40E
Gračac, Cro. (grä′chäts)	160	44.16N	15.50E
Gračanica, Bos.	161	44.42N	18.18E
Graceville, Fl., U.S. (grās′vĭl)	114	30.57N	85.30W
Graceville, Mn., U.S.	102	45.33N	96.25W
Gracias, Hond. (grä′sē-äs)	120	14.35N	88.37W
Graciosa Island, i., Port. (grä-syō′sä)	210a	39.07N	27.30W
Gradačac, Bos. (gra-dä′chats)	149	44.50N	18.28E
Grado, Spain (grä′dō)	158	43.24N	6.04W
Gräfelfing, Ger. (grä′fĕl-fĕng)	145d	48.07N	11.27E
Grafenberg, neigh., Ger.	236	51.14N	6.50E
Grafing bei München, Ger. (grä′fĕng)	145d	48.03N	11.58E
Grafton, Austl. (graf′tŭn)	203	29.38S	153.05E
Grafton, Il., U.S.	107e	38.58N	90.26W
Grafton, Ma., U.S.	93a	42.13N	71.41W
Grafton, N.D., U.S.	102	48.24N	97.25W
Grafton, Oh., U.S.	101d	41.16N	82.04W
Grafton, W.V., U.S.	98	39.20N	80.00W
Gragnano, Italy (grän-yä′nō)	159c	40.27N	14.32E
Graham, N.C., U.S. (grā′ăm)	115	36.03N	79.23W
Graham, Tx., U.S.	110	33.07N	98.34W
Graham, Wa., U.S.	106a	47.03N	122.18W
Graham, i., Can.	84	53.50N	132.40W
Grahamstown, S. Afr. (grā′ăms′toun)	213c	33.19S	26.33E
Grajewo, Pol. (grä-yä′vo)	155	53.38N	22.28E
Grama, Serra de, mtn., Braz. (sĕ′r-rä-dĕ-grá′má)	129a	20.42S	42.28W
Gramada, Bul. (grä′mä-dä)	161	43.46N	22.41E
Gramatneusiedl, Aus.	145e	48.02N	16.29E
Grampian Mountains, mts., Scot., U.K. (grăm′pĭ-ăn)	142	56.30N	4.55W
Granada, Nic. (grä-nä′dhä)	116	11.55N	85.58W
Granada, Spain (grä-nä′dä)	148	37.13N	3.37W
Gran Bajo, reg., Arg. (grȧn′bä′kō)	132	47.35S	68.45W
Granbury, Tx., U.S. (grăn′bĕr-ĭ)	113	32.26N	97.45W
Granby, Can. (grăn′bĭ)	85	45.30N	72.40W
Granby, Mo., U.S.	111	36.54N	94.15W
Granby, l., Co., U.S.	110	40.07N	105.40W
Gran Canaria Island, i., Spain (grän′kä-nä′rē-ä)	210	27.39N	15.39W
Gran Chaco, reg., S.A. (grȧn′chȧ′kō)	132	25.30S	62.15W
Grand, i., Mi., U.S.	103	46.37N	86.38W
Grand, l., Can.	92	45.59N	66.15W
Grand, l., Me., U.S.	92	45.17N	67.42W
Grand, r., Can.	91	43.45N	80.20W
Grand, r., Mi., U.S.	98	42.58N	85.13W
Grand, r., Mo., U.S.	111	39.50N	93.52W
Grand, r., S.D., U.S.	102	45.40N	101.55W
Grand, North Fork, r., U.S.	102	45.52N	102.49W
Grand, South Fork, r., S.D., U.S.	102	45.38N	102.56W
Grand Bahama, i., Bah.	117	26.35N	78.30W
Grand Bank, Can. (grănd băngk)	85a	47.06N	55.47W
Grand Bassam, C. Iv. (grän bȧ-säN′)	210	5.12N	3.44W
Grand Bourg, Guad. (grän bo͞or′)	121b	15.54N	61.20W
Grand Caicos, i., T./C. Is. (grănd kä-ē′kōs)	123	21.45N	71.50W
Grand Canal *see* Da Yunhe, can., China	189	35.00N	117.00E

ng-sing; ŋ-baŋk; N-nasalized n; nŏd; cŏmmit; ōld; ôbey; ôrder; oi-boil; fo͞od; ŏ-as oo in foot; ou-out; s-soft; sh-dish; th-thin; pūre; ûnite; ûrn; stŭd; circŭs; ü-as in French tu; ′-indeterminate vowel.

292 Grand Canal-Grey Range

PLACE (Pronunciation)	PAGE	Lat. °′	Long. °′
Grand Canal, can., Ire.	150	53.21N	7.15W
Grand Canyon, Az., U.S.	109	36.05N	112.10W
Grand Canyon, val., Az., U.S.	96	35.50N	113.16W
Grand Canyon National Park, rec., Az., U.S.	96	36.15N	112.20W
Grand Cayman, i., Cay. Is. (kā'măn)	117	19.15N	81.15W
Grand Coulee Dam, dam, Wa., U.S. (ko͞o'lē)	96	47.58N	119.28W
Grande, r., Arg.	129b	35.25S	70.14W
Grande, r., Mex.	119	17.37N	96.41W
Grande, r., Nic. (grän'dĕ)	121	13.01N	84.21W
Grande, r., Ur.	129c	33.19S	57.15W
Grande, Arroyo, r., Mex. (är-rō'yō-grä'n-dĕ)	118	23.30N	98.45W
Grande, Bahía, b., Arg. (bä-ē'ä-grän'dĕ)	132	50.45S	68.00W
Grande, Boca, mth., Ven. (bō'kä-grä'n-dĕ)	131	8.46N	60.17W
Grande, Cuchilla, mts., Ur. (ko͞o-chē'l-yä)	132	33.00S	55.15W
Grande, Ilha, i., Braz. (grän'dĕ)	129a	23.11S	44.14W
Grande, Río, r., Bol.	130	16.49S	63.19W
Grande, Rio, r., Braz.	131	19.48S	49.54W
Grande, Rio, r., N.A. (grän'dā)	96	26.50N	99.10W
Grande, Salinas, l., Arg. (sä-lē'näs)	132	29.45S	65.00W
Grande, Salto, wtfl., Braz. (säl-tô)	131	16.18S	39.38W
Grande Cayemite, Île, i., Haiti	123	18.45N	73.45W
Grande de Otoro, r., Hond. (grä'dą dā ô-tô'rô)	120	14.42N	88.21W
Grande de Santiago, Río, r., Mex. (rē'ō-grä'n-dĕ-dĕ-sän-tyà'gô)	116	20.30N	104.00W
Grande Pointe, Can. (grănd point')	83f	49.47N	97.03W
Grande Prairie, Can. (prâr'ĭ)	84	55.10N	118.48W
Grand Erg Occidental, des., Alg.	210	30.00N	1.00E
Grand Erg Oriental, des., Alg.	210	30.00N	7.00E
Grande Rivière du Nord, Haiti (rē-vyâr' dü nôr')	123	19.35N	72.10W
Grande Ronde, r., Or., U.S. (rŏnd')	104	45.32N	117.52W
Gran Desierto, des., Mex. (grän-dĕ-syĕ'r-tô)	109	32.14N	114.28W
Grande Terre, i., Guad.	121b	16.28N	61.13W
Grande Vigie, Pointe de la, c., Guad. (grănd vē-gē')	121b	16.32N	61.25W
Grand Falls, Can. (fôlz)	85a	48.56N	55.40W
Grandfather Mountain, mtn., N.C., U.S. (grănd-fä-thẽr)	115	36.07N	81.48W
Grandfield, Ok., U.S. (grănd'fēld)	110	34.13N	98.39W
Grand Forks, Can. (fôrks)	84	49.02N	118.27W
Grand Forks, N.D., U.S.	96	47.55N	97.05W
Grand Haven, Mi., U.S. (hā'v'n)	98	43.05N	86.15W
Grand I, N.Y., U.S.	101c	43.03N	78.58W
Grand Island, Ne., U.S. (ī'lănd)	96	40.56N	98.20W
Grand Island, N.Y., U.S.	230a	42.49N	78.58W
Grand Junction, Co., U.S. (jŭngk'shŭn)	96	39.05N	108.35W
Grand Lake, l., Can. (lāk)	85a	49.00N	57.10W
Grand Lake, l., La., U.S.	113	29.57N	91.25W
Grand Lake, l., Mn., U.S.	107h	46.54N	92.26W
Grand Ledge, Mi., U.S. (lĕj)	98	42.45N	84.50W
Grand Lieu, Lac de, l., Fr. (grän'-lyû)	156	47.00N	1.45W
Grand Manan, i., Can. (mȧ-năn)	92	44.40N	66.50W
Grand Mère, Can. (grän mâr')	85	46.36N	72.43W
Grândola, Port. (grän'dô-lȧ)	158	38.10N	8.36W
Grand Portage Indian Reservation, I.R., Mn., U.S. (pōr'tĭj)	103	47.54N	89.34W
Grand Portage National Monument, rec., Mi., U.S.	103	47.59N	89.47W
Grand Prairie, Tx., U.S. (prĕ'rē)	107c	32.45N	97.00W
Grand Rapids, Can.	89	53.08N	99.20W
Grand Rapids, Mi., U.S. (răp'ĭdz)	97	43.00N	85.45W
Grand Rapids, Mn., U.S.	103	47.16N	93.33W
Grand-Riviere, Can.	92	48.26N	64.30W
Grand Teton, mtn., Wy., U.S.	96	43.46N	110.50W
Grand Teton National Park, Wy., U.S. (tē'tŏn)	105	43.54N	110.15W
Grand Traverse Bay, b., Mi., U.S. (trăv'ẽrs)	98	45.00N	85.30W
Grand Turk, T./C. Is. (tûrk)	123	21.30N	71.10W
Grand Turk, i., T./C. Is.	123	21.30N	71.10W
Grandview, Mo., U.S. (grănd'vyo͞o)	107f	38.53N	94.32W
Grandyle, N.Y., U.S.	230a	43.00N	78.57W
Grange Hill, Eng., U.K.	235	51.37N	0.05E
Granger, Wy., U.S. (grān'jẽr)	105	41.37N	109.58W
Grangeville, Id., U.S. (grānj'vĭl)	104	45.56N	116.08W
Granite, Md., U.S.	229c	39.21N	76.51W
Granite City, Il., U.S. (grăn'ĭt sĭt'ĭ)	107e	38.42N	90.09W
Granite Falls, Mn., U.S. (fôlz)	102	44.46N	95.34W
Granite Falls, N.C., U.S.	115	35.49N	81.25W
Granite Falls, Wa., U.S.	106a	48.05N	121.59W
Granite Lake, l., Can.	93	48.01N	57.00W
Granite Peak, mtn., Mt., U.S.	96	45.13N	109.48W
Graniteville, S.C., U.S. (grăn'ĭt-vĭl)	115	33.35ND1.50	W
Granito, Braz. (grä-nē'tō)	131	7.39S	39.34W
Granma, prov., Cuba	122	20.10N	76.50W
Gränna, Swe. (grĕn'à)	152	58.02N	14.38E
Granollers, Spain (grä-nôl-yĕrs')	159	41.36N	2.19E
Gran Pajonal, reg., Peru (grä'n-pä-ĸô-näl')	130	11.14S	71.45W
Gran Paradiso, mtn., Italy	160	45.32N	7.16E
Gran Piedra, mtn., Cuba (grän-pyĕ'drä)	123	20.00N	75.40W
Grantham, Eng., U.K. (grăn'tȧm)	150	52.54N	0.38W
Grant Park, Il., U.S. (grȧnt pärk)	101a	41.14N	87.39W
Grant Park, pt. of i., Il., U.S.	231a	41.52N	87.37W
Grants Pass, Or., U.S. (grȧnts pås)	104	42.26N	123.20W
Granville, Austl.	243a	33.50S	151.01E
Granville, Fr. (grän-vēl')	147	48.52N	1.35W
Granville, N.Y., U.S. (grăn'vĭl)	99	43.25N	73.15W
Granville, l., Can.	84	56.18N	100.30W
Grão Mogol, Braz. (groun' mô-gôl')	131	16.34S	42.35W
Grapevine, Tx., U.S. (grāp'vīn)	107c	32.56N	97.05W
Gräso, i., Swe.	152	60.30N	18.35E
Grass, r., N.Y., U.S.	99	44.45N	75.10W
Grass Cay, i., V.I.U.S.	117c	18.22N	64.50W
Grasse, Fr. (gräs)	157	43.39N	6.57E
Grassendale, neigh., Eng., U.K.	237a	53.21N	2.54W
Grass Mountain, mtn., Wa., U.S. (grås)	106a	47.13N	121.48W
Grates Point, c., Can. (grāts)	93	48.09N	52.57W
Gravelbourg, Can. (grăv'ĕl-bôrg)	84	49.53N	106.34W
Gravesend, Eng., U.K. (grāvz'ĕnd')	144b	51.26N	0.22E
Gravina, Italy (grä-vē'nä)	160	40.48N	16.27E
Gravois, Pointe à, c., Haiti (grȧ-vwä')	123	18.00N	74.20W
Gray, Fr. (grå)	157	47.26N	5.35E
Grayling, Mi., U.S. (grā'lĭng)	98	44.40N	84.40W
Grays, Eng., U.K.	235	51.29N	0.20E
Grays Harbor, b., Wa., U.S. (grās)	96	46.55N	124.23W
Grayslake, Il., U.S. (grāz'lāk)	101a	42.20N	88.20W
Grays Peak, mtn., Co., U.S. (grāz)	110	39.29N	105.52W
Grays Thurrock, Eng., U.K. (thŭ'rŏk)	144b	51.28N	0.19E
Grayvoron, Russia (grȧ-ē'vô-rôn)	163	50.28N	35.41E
Graz, Aus. (gräts)	142	47.05N	15.26E
Greasby, Eng., U.K.	237a	53.23N	3.07W
Great Abaco, i., Bah. (ă'bä-kō)	117	26.30N	77.05W
Great Altcar, Eng., U.K.	237a	53.33N	3.01W
Great Artesian Basin, basin, Austl. (är-tēzh-ȧn bā-sĭn)	203	23.16S	143.37E
Great Australian Bight, bt., Austl. (ôs-trā'lĭ-ăn bĭt)	202	33.30S	127.00E
Great Bahama Bank, bk. (bȧ-hā'mȧ)	122	25.00N	78.50W
Great Barrier, i., N.Z. (băr'ĭ-ẽr)	203a	36.10S	175.30E
Great Barrier Reef, rf., Austl. (bȧ-rĭ-ẽr rēf)	203	16.43S	146.34E
Great Basin, basin, U.S. (grāt bā's'n)	96	40.08N	117.10W
Great Bear Lake, l., Can. (bâr)	84	66.10N	119.53W
Great Bend, Ks., U.S. (bĕnd)	110	38.41N	98.46W
Great Bitter Lake, l., Egypt	218b	30.24N	32.27E
Great Blasket Island, i., Ire. (blăs'kĕt)	150	52.05N	10.55W
Great Bookham, Eng., U.K.	235	51.16N	0.22W
Great Burstead, Eng., U.K.	235	51.36N	0.25E
Great Corn Island, i., Nic.	121	12.10N	82.54W
Great Crosby, Eng., U.K.	237a	53.29N	3.01W
Great Dismal Swamp, sw., U.S. (dĭz'mȧl)	115	36.35N	76.34W
Great Divide Basin, basin, Wy., U.S. (dĭ-vīd' bā's'n)	105	42.10N	108.10W
Great Dividing Range, mts., Austl. (dĭ-vī-dĭng rānj)	203	35.16S	146.38E
Great Duck, i., Can. (dŭk)	90	45.40N	83.22W
Greater Antilles, is., N.A.	117	20.30N	79.15W
Greater Khingan Range, mts., China (dä hĭŋ-gän lĭŋ)	189	46.30N	120.00E
Greater Leech Indian Reservation, I.R., Mn., U.S. (grāt'ẽr lēch)	103	47.39N	94.27W
Greater Manchester, co., Eng., U.K.	144a	53.34N	2.41W
Greater Sunda Islands, is., Asia	196	4.00S	108.00E
Great Exuma, i., Bah. (ĕk-so͞o'mä)	122	23.35N	76.00W
Great Falls, Mt., U.S. (fôlz)	96	47.30N	111.15W
Great Falls, S.C., U.S.	115	34.32N	80.53W
Great Falls, Va., U.S.	229d	39.00N	77.17W
Great Guana Cay, i., Bah. (gwä'nä)	122	24.00N	76.20W
Great Harbor Cay, i., Bah. (kē)	122	25.45N	77.50W
Great Inagua, i., Bah. (ē-nä'gwä)	117	21.00N	73.15W
Great Indian Desert, des., Asia	183	27.35N	71.37E
Great Isaac, i., Bah. (ī'zȧk)	122	26.05N	79.05W
Great Karroo, plat., S. Afr. (grāt kȧ'ro͞o)	212	32.45S	22.00E
Great Kills, neigh., N.Y., U.S.	228	40.33N	74.10W
Great Namaland, hist. reg., Nmb.	212	25.45S	16.15E
Great Neck, N.Y., U.S. (nĕk)	100a	40.48N	73.44W
Great Nicobar Island, i., India (nĭk-ō-bär')	196	7.00N	94.18E
Great Oxney Green, Eng., U.K.	235	51.44N	0.25E
Great Parndon, Eng., U.K.	235	51.45N	0.05E
Great Pedro Bluff, c., Jam.	122	17.50N	78.05W
Great Pee Dee, r., S.C., U.S. (pē-dē')	97	34.01N	79.26W
Great Plains, pl., N.A. (plāns)	82	45.00N	104.00W
Great Ragged, i., Bah.	123	22.10N	75.45W
Great Ruaha, r., Tan.	212	7.30S	37.00E
Great Salt Lake, l., Ut., U.S. (sôlt lāk)	96	41.19N	112.48W
Great Salt Lake Desert, des., Ut., U.S.	96	41.00N	113.30W
Great Salt Plains Reservoir, res., Ok., U.S.	110	36.56N	98.14W
Great Sand Dunes National Monument, rec., Co., U.S.	110	37.56N	105.25W
Great Sand Hills, hills, Can. (sănd)	88	50.35N	109.05W
Great Sandy Desert, des., Austl. (săn'dē)	202	21.50S	123.10E
Great Sandy Desert, des., Or., U.S. (săn'dĭ)	104	43.43N	120.44W
Great Sitkin, i., Ak., U.S. (sĭt-kĭn)	95a	52.18N	176.22W
Great Slave Lake, l., Can. (slāv)	84	61.37N	114.58W
Great Smoky Mountains National Park, rec., U.S. (smōk-ē)	97	35.43N	83.20W
Great Stirrup Cay, i., Bah. (stĭr-ŭp)	122	25.50N	77.55W
Great Sutton, Eng., U.K.	237a	53.17N	2.56W
Great Victoria Desert, des., Austl. (vĭk-tō'rĭ-ȧ)	202	29.45S	124.30E
Great Wall, hist., China	188	38.00N	109.00E
Great Waltham, Eng., U.K. (wôl'thŭm)	144b	51.47N	0.27E
Great Warley, Eng., U.K.	235	51.35N	0.17E
Great Yarmouth, Eng., U.K. (yär-mŭth)	147	52.35N	1.45E
Grebbestad, Swe. (grĕb-bĕ-städh)	152	58.42N	11.15E
Gréboun, Mont, mtn., Niger	210	20.00N	8.35E
Greco, neigh., Italy	238c	45.30N	9.13E
Gredos, Sierra de, mts., Spain (syĕr'rä dā grā'dōs)	158	40.13N	5.30W
Greece, nation, Eur. (grēs)	142	39.00N	21.30E
Greeley, Co., U.S. (grē'lĭ)	96	40.25N	104.41W
Green, r., U.S.	96	38.30N	110.10W
Green, r., Ky., U.S. (grēn)	114	37.13N	86.30W
Green, r., N.D., U.S.	102	47.05N	103.05W
Green, r., Ut., U.S.	109	38.30N	110.05W
Green, r., Wa., U.S.	106a	47.17N	121.57W
Green, r., Wy., U.S.	105	41.08N	110.27W
Greenbank, Wa., U.S. (grēn'bănk)	106a	48.06N	122.35W
Green Bay, Wi., U.S.	97	44.30N	88.04W
Green Bay, b., U.S.	97	44.55N	87.40W
Green Bayou, Tx., U.S.	113a	29.53N	95.13W
Greenbelt, Md., U.S. (grēn'bĕlt)	100e	38.59N	76.53W
Greenbrae, Ca., U.S.	231b	37.57N	122.31W
Greencastle, In., U.S. (grēn-kȧs''l)	98	39.40N	86.50W
Green Cay, i., Bah.	122	24.05N	77.10W
Green Cove Springs, Fl., U.S. (kōv)	115	29.56N	81.42W
Greendale, Wi., U.S. (grēn'dāl)	101a	42.56N	87.59W
Greenfield, In., U.S. (grēn'fēld)	98	39.45N	85.40W
Greenfield, Ia., U.S.	103	41.16N	94.30W
Greenfield, Ma., U.S.	99	42.35N	72.35W
Greenfield, Mo., U.S.	111	37.23N	93.48W
Greenfield, Oh., U.S.	98	39.15N	83.25W
Greenfield, Tn., U.S.	114	36.08N	88.45W
Greenfield Park, Can.	83a	45.29N	73.29W
Greenhills, Oh., U.S. (grēn-hĭls)	101f	39.16N	84.31W
Greenhithe, Eng., U.K.	235	51.27N	0.17E
Greenland, dep., N.A. (grēn'lănd)	82	74.00N	40.00W
Greenland Sea, sea	220	77.00N	1.00W
Green Meadows, Md., U.S.	229d	38.58N	76.57W
Greenmount, Eng., U.K.	237b	53.37N	2.20W
Green Mountain, mtn., Or., U.S.	106c	45.52N	123.24W
Green Mountain Reservoir, res., Co., U.S.	109	39.50N	106.20W
Green Mountains, mts., N.A.	97	43.10N	73.05W
Greenock, Scot., U.K. (grēn'ŭk)	146	55.55N	4.45W
Green Peter Lake, res., Or., U.S.	104	44.28N	122.30W
Green Pond Mountain, mtn., N.J., U.S. (pŏnd)	100a	41.00N	74.32W
Greenport, N.Y., U.S.	99	41.06N	72.22W
Green River, Ut., U.S. (grēn rĭv'ẽr)	109	39.00N	110.05W
Green River, Wy., U.S.	105	41.32N	109.26W
Green River Lake, res., Ky., U.S.	114	37.15N	85.15W
Greensboro, Al., U.S. (grēnz'bŭro)	114	32.42N	87.36W
Greensboro, Ga., U.S. (grēns-bûr'ô)	114	33.34N	83.11W
Greensboro, N.C., U.S.	97	36.04N	79.45W
Greensborough, Austl.	243b	37.42S	145.06E
Greensburg, In., U.S. (grēnz'bûrg)	98	39.20N	85.30W
Greensburg, Ks., U.S. (grēns-bûrg)	110	37.36N	99.17W
Greensburg, Pa., U.S.	99	40.20N	79.30W
Greenside, neigh., S. Afr.	244b	26.09S	28.01E
Greenstead, Eng., U.K.	235	51.42N	0.14E
Green Street, Eng., U.K.	235	51.40N	0.16W
Green Street Green, neigh., Eng., U.K.	235	51.21N	0.04E
Greenvale, N.Y., U.S.	228	40.49N	73.38W
Greenville, Lib.	210	5.01N	9.03W
Greenville, Al., U.S. (grēn'vĭl)	114	31.49N	86.39W
Greenville, Il., U.S.	111	38.52N	89.22W
Greenville, Ky., U.S.	114	37.11N	87.11W
Greenville, Me., U.S.	92	45.26N	69.35W
Greenville, Mi., U.S.	98	43.10N	85.25W
Greenville, Ms., U.S.	97	33.25N	91.00W
Greenville, N.C., U.S.	115	35.35N	77.22W
Greenville, Oh., U.S.	98	40.05N	84.35W
Greenville, Pa., U.S.	98	41.20N	80.25W
Greenville, S.C., U.S.	97	34.50N	82.25W
Greenville, Tn., U.S.	115	36.08N	82.50W
Greenville, Tx., U.S.	113	33.09N	96.07W
Greenwich, Eng., U.K.	144b	51.28N	0.00
Greenwich, Ct., U.S.	100a	41.01N	73.37W
Greenwich Observatory, pt. of i., Eng., U.K.	235	51.28N	0.00
Greenwich Village, neigh., N.Y., U.S.	228	40.44N	74.00W
Greenwood, Ar., U.S. (grēn-wo͝od)	111	35.13N	94.15W
Greenwood, In., U.S.	101g	39.37N	86.07W
Greenwood, Ma., U.S.	227a	42.29N	71.04W
Greenwood, Ms., U.S.	114	33.30N	90.09W
Greenwood, S.C., U.S.	115	34.10N	82.10W
Greenwood, Lake, res., S.C., U.S.	115	34.17N	81.55W
Greenwood Lake, l., N.Y., U.S.	100a	41.13N	74.20W
Greer, S.C., U.S. (grēr)	115	34.55N	81.56W
Grefrath, Ger. (grĕf'rät)	157c	51.20N	6.21E
Gregory, S.D., U.S. (grĕg'ô-rĭ)	102	43.12N	99.27W
Gregory, Lake, l., Austl. (grĕg'ô-rē)	202	28.47S	139.15E
Gregory Range, mts., Austl.	203	19.23S	143.45E
Greifenberg, Ger. (grī'fĕn-bĕrgh)	145d	48.04N	11.06E
Greiffenburg, hist., Ger.	236	51.20N	6.38E
Greifswald, Ger. (grīfs'vält)	154	54.05N	13.24E
Greiz, Ger. (grīts)	154	50.39N	12.14E
Gremyachinsk, Russia (grâ'myȧ-chinsk)	172a	58.35N	57.53E
Grenada, Ms., U.S. (grē-nä'da)	114	33.45N	89.47W
Grenada, nation, N.A.	117	12.02N	61.15W
Grenada Lake, res., Ms., U.S.	114	33.52N	89.30W
Grenadines, The, is., N.A. (grĕn'ȧ-dēnz)	121b	12.37N	61.35W
Grenen, c., Den.	146	57.43N	10.31E
Grenoble, Fr. (grē-nô'bl')	147	45.14N	5.45E
Grenora, N.D., U.S. (grē-nō'rȧ)	102	48.38N	103.55W
Grenville, Can. (grĕn'vĭl)	99	45.40N	74.35W
Grenville, Gren.	121b	12.07N	61.38W
Gresham, Or., U.S. (grĕsh'ăm)	106c	45.30N	122.25W
Gretna, La., U.S. (grĕt'nȧ)	100d	29.56N	90.03W
Grevel, neigh., Ger.	236	51.34N	7.33E
Grevelingen Krammer, r., Neth.	145a	51.42N	4.03E
Grevenbroich, Ger. (grĕ'fĕn-broik)	157c	51.05N	6.36E
Grey, r., Can. (grā)	93	47.53N	57.00W
Grey, Point, c., Can.	106d	49.22N	123.16W
Greybull, Wy., U.S. (grā'bo͝ol)	105	44.28N	108.05W
Greybull, r., Wy., U.S.	105	44.13N	108.43W
Greylingstad, S. Afr. (grā-lĭng'shtät)	218d	26.40S	29.13E
Greymouth, N.Z. (grā'mouth)	203a	42.27S	171.17E
Grey Range, mts., Austl.	203	28.40S	142.05E

ăt; finȧl; rāte; senāte; ärm; åsk; sofȧ; fâre; ch-choose; dh-as th in other; bē; ēvent; bĕt; recĕnt; cratẽr; g-gō; gh-guttural g; bĭt; ĭ-short neutral; rīde; ĸ-guttural k as ch in German ich;

PRONOUNCING INDEX Greystanes–Guysborough 293

PLACE (Pronunciation)	PAGE	Lat. °′	Long. °′
Greystanes, Austl.	243a	33.49S	150.58E
Greytown, S. Afr. (grā'toun)	213c	29.07S	30.38E
Grey Wolf Peak, mtn., Wa., U.S. (grā wolf)	106a	48.53N	123.12W
Gridley, Ca., U.S. (grĭd'lĭ)	108	39.22N	121.43W
Griffin, Ga., U.S. (grĭf'ĭn)	114	33.15N	84.16W
Griffith, Austl. (grĭf-ĭth)	204	34.16S	146.10E
Griffith, In., U.S.	101a	41.31N	87.26W
Grigoriopol', Mol. (grĭ'gor-i-ô'pôl)	163	47.09N	29.18E
Grijalva, r., Mex. (grē-häl'vä)	119	17.25N	93.23W
Grim, Cape, c., Austl. (grĭm)	204	40.43S	144.30E
Grimma, Ger. (grĭm'à)	154	51.14N	12.43E
Grimsby, Can. (grĭmz'bĭ)	83d	43.11N	79.33W
Grimsby, Eng., U.K.	146	53.35N	0.05W
Grímsey, i., Ice. (grĭms'â)	146	66.30N	17.50W
Grimstad, Nor. (grĭm-städh)	146	58.21N	8.30E
Grindstone Island, Can.	93	47.25N	61.51W
Grinnel, Ia., U.S. (grĭ-nĕl')	103	41.44N	92.44W
Grinzing, neigh., Aus.	239e	48.15N	16.21E
Griswold, Ia., U.S. (grĭz'wŭld)	102	41.11N	95.05W
Groais Island, i., Can.	93	50.57N	55.35W
Grobina, Lat. (grō'bĭnĭa)	153	56.35N	21.10E
Groblersdal, S. Afr.	218d	25.11S	29.25E
Grodno, Bela. (grôd'nô)	166	53.40N	23.49E
Grodzisk, Pol. (grō'jēsk)	154	52.14N	16.22E
Grodzisk Masowiecki, Pol. (grō'jēsk mä-zō-vyĕts'ke)	155	52.06N	20.40E
Groesbeck, Tx., U.S. (grōs'bĕk)	113	31.32N	96.31W
Groix, Île de, i., Fr. (ēl dē grwä')	156	47.39N	3.28W
Grójec, Pol. (grò'yĕts)	155	51.53N	20.52E
Gronau, Ger. (grō'nou)	154	52.12N	7.05E
Groningen, Neth. (grō'nĭng-ĕn)	146	53.13N	6.30E
Groote Eylandt, i., Austl. (grō'tē ī'lănt)	202	13.50S	137.30E
Grootfontein, Nmb. (grōt'fōn-tān')	212	19.30S	18.15E
Groot-Kei, r., Afr. (kē)	213c	32.17S	27.30E
Grootkop, mtn., S. Afr.	212a	34.11S	18.23E
Groot Marico, S. Afr.	218d	25.36S	26.23E
Groot Marico, r., Afr.	218d	25.13S	26.20E
Groot-Vis, r., S. Afr.	213c	33.04S	26.08E
Groot Vloer, pl., S. Afr. (grōt' vlòr')	212	30.00S	21.00E
Gros-Mécatina, i., Can.	93	50.50N	58.33W
Gros Morne, mtn., Can. (grō môrn')	93	49.36N	57.48W
Gros Morne National Park, rec., Can.	85a	49.45N	59.15W
Gros Pate, mtn., Can.	93	50.16N	57.25W
Grossbeeren, Ger.	238a	52.21N	13.18E
Grosse Island, i., Mi., U.S. (grōs)	101b	42.08N	83.09W
Grosse Isle, Can. (ĭl')	83f	50.04N	97.27W
Grossenbaum, neigh., Ger.	236	51.22N	6.47E
Grossenhain, Ger. (grōs'ĕn-hīn)	154	51.17N	13.33E
Gross-Enzersdorf, Aus.	145e	48.13N	16.33E
Grosse Pointe, Mi., U.S. (point')	101b	42.23N	82.54W
Grosse Pointe Farms, Mi., U.S. (färm)	101b	42.25N	82.53W
Grosse Pointe Park, Mi., U.S. (pärk)	101b	42.23N	82.55W
Grosse Pointe Woods, Mi., U.S.	230c	42.27N	82.55W
Grosseto, Italy (grôs-sā'tō)	160	42.46N	11.09E
Grossglockner, mtn., Aus.	147	47.06N	12.45E
Gross Höbach, Ger. (hû'bäk)	145d	48.21N	11.36E
Grossjedlersdorf, neigh., Aus.	239e	48.17N	16.25E
Gross Kreutz, Ger. (kroitz)	145b	52.24N	12.47E
Gross Schönebeck, Ger. (shō'nē-bĕk)	145b	52.54N	13.32E
Gross Ziethen, Ger.	238a	52.24N	13.27E
Gros Ventre, r., Wy., U.S. (grōvĕn't'r)	105	43.38N	110.34W
Groton, Ct., U.S. (grŏt'ŭn)	99	41.20N	72.00W
Groton, Ma., U.S.	93a	42.37N	71.34W
Groton, S.D., U.S.	102	45.25N	98.04W
Grottaglie, Italy (grôt-täl'yā)	161	40.32N	17.26E
Grouard Mission, Can.	84	55.31N	116.09W
Groveland, Ma., U.S. (grōv'land)	93a	42.25N	71.02W
Groveton, N.H., U.S. (grōv'tŭn)	99	44.35N	71.30W
Groveton, Tx., U.S.	113	31.04N	95.07W
Groznyy, Russia (grôz'nĭ)	164	43.20N	45.40E
Grudziądz, Pol. (grò'jyônts)	146	53.30N	18.48E
Grues, Île aux, i., Can. (ō grü)	83b	47.05N	70.32W
Gruiten, Ger.	236	51.14N	7.01E
Grumme, neigh., Ger.	236	51.30N	7.14E
Grünau, neigh., Ger.	238a	52.25N	13.34E
Grundy Center, Ia., U.S. (grŭn'dĭ sĕn'tēr)	103	42.22N	92.45W
Grünewald, Ger.	236	51.13N	7.37E
Grunewald, neigh., Ger.	238a	52.30N	13.17E
Gruñidora, Mex. (grōō-nyē-dō'rō)	118	24.10N	101.49W
Grünwald, Ger. (grōōn'väld)	145d	48.04N	11.34E
Gryazi, Russia (gryä'zĭ)	162	52.31N	39.59E
Gryazovets, Russia (gryä'zô-vĕts)	166	58.52N	40.14E
Gryfice, Pol. (grĭ'fĭ-tsĕ)	154	53.55N	15.11E
Gryfino, Pol. (grĭ'fē-nô)	154	53.16N	14.30E
Guabito, Pan. (gwä-bē'tô)	121	9.30N	82.33W
Guacanayabo, Golfo de, b., Cuba (gôl-fô-dĕ-gwä-kä-nä-yä'bō)	122	20.30N	77.40W
Guacara, Ven. (gwá'kä-rä)	131b	10.16N	67.48W
Guadalajara, Mex. (gwä-dhä-lä-hä'rä)	116	20.41N	103.21W
Guadalajara, Spain (gwä-dä-lä-kä'rä)	148	40.37N	3.10W
Guadalcanal, Spain (gwä-dhäl-kä-näl')	158	38.05N	5.48W
Guadalcanal, i., Sol.Is.	203	9.48S	158.43E
Guadalcázar, Mex. (gwä-dhäl-kä'zär)	118	22.38N	100.24W
Guadalete, r., Spain (gwä-dhä-lā'tå)	158	36.53N	5.38W
Guadalhorce, r., Spain (gwä-dhäl-ôr'thā)	158	37.05N	4.50W
Guadalimar, r., Spain (gwä-dhä-lē-mär')	158	38.29N	2.53W
Guadalope, r., Spain (gwä-dä-lô-pē)	159	40.48N	0.10W
Guadalquivir, Río, r., Spain (rē'ō-gwä-dhäl-kē-vēr')	142	37.30N	5.00W
Guadalupe, Mex.	112	31.23N	106.06W
Guadalupe, i., Mex.	116	29.00N	118.45W
Guadalupe, r., Tx., U.S. (gwä-dhä-lōō'pä)	112	29.54N	99.03W
Guadalupe, Basílica de, rel., Mex.	233a	19.29N	99.07W
Guadalupe, Sierra de, mts., Spain (syĕr'rä dā gwä-dhä-lōō'pä)	148	39.30N	5.25W

PLACE (Pronunciation)	PAGE	Lat. °′	Long. °′
Guadalupe Mountains, mts., N.M., U.S.	112	32.00N	104.55W
Guadalupe Peak, mtn., Tx., U.S.	112	31.55N	104.55W
Guadarrama, r., Spain (gwä-dhär-rä'mä)	159a	40.34N	3.58W
Guadarrama, Sierra de, mts., Spain (gwä-dhär-rä'mä)	142	41.00N	3.40W
Guadatentin, r., Spain	158	37.43N	1.58W
Guadeloupe, dep., N.A. (gwä-dē-lōōp)	117	16.40N	61.10W
Guadeloupe Passage, strt., N.A.	121b	16.26N	62.00W
Guadiana, r., Eur. (gwä-dvä'nä)	142	39.00N	6.00W
Guadiana, Bahía de, b., Cuba (bä-ē'ä-dĕ-gwä-dhē-ä'nä)	122	22.10N	84.35W
Guadiana Alto, r., Spain (äl'tō)	158	39.02N	2.52W
Guadiana Menor, r., Spain (mä'nôr)	158	37.43N	2.45W
Guadiaro, r., Spain (gwä-dhē-ä rō)	158	36.38N	5.25W
Guadiela, r., Spain (gwä-dhē-ā'lä)	158	40.27N	2.05W
Guadix, Spain (gwä-dēsh')	158	37.18N	3.09W
Guaianazes, neigh., Braz.	234d	23.33S	46.25W
Guaira, Braz. (gwä-ē-rä)	131	24.03S	54.02W
Guaire, r., Ven. (gwī'rē)	131b	10.25N	66.43W
Guajaba, Cayo, i., Cuba (kä'yō-gwä-hä'bä)	122	21.50N	77.35W
Guajará Mirim, Braz. (gwä-zhä-rä'mē-rēɴ')	130	10.58S	65.12W
Guajira, Península de, pen., S.A.	130	12.35N	73.00W
Gualán, Guat. (gwä-län')	120	15.08N	89.21W
Gualeguay, Arg. (gwä-lĕ-gwä'y)	132	33.10S	59.20W
Gualeguay, r., Arg.	132	32.49S	59.05W
Gualicho, Salina, l., Arg. (sä-lē'nä-gwä-lē'chō)	132	40.20S	65.15W
Guam, i., Oc. (gwäm)	3	14.00N	143.20E
Guamo, Col. (gwá'mō)	130a	4.02N	74.58W
Gu'an, China (gōō-än)	192a	39.25N	116.18E
Guan, r., China (gůän)	190	31.56N	115.19E
Guanabacoa, Cuba (gwä-nä-bä-kō'ä)	117	23.08N	82.19W
Guanabara, Baía de, b., Braz.	129a	22.44S	43.09W
Guanacaste, Cordillera, mts., C.R.	120	10.54N	85.27W
Guanacevi, Mex. (gwä-nä-sĕ-vē')	116	25.30N	105.45W
Guanahacabibes, Península de, pen., Cuba	122	21.55N	84.35W
Guanajay, Cuba (gwäŋä-hī')	122	22.55N	82.40W
Guanajuato, Mex. (gwä-nä-hwä'tō)	116	21.01N	101.16W
Guanajuato, state, Mex.	116	21.00N	101.00W
Guanape, Ven. (gwä-nä'pē)	131b	9.55N	65.32W
Guanape, r., Ven.	131b	9.52N	65.20W
Guanare, Ven. (gwä-nä'rå)	130	8.57N	69.47W
Guanduçu, r., Braz. (gwä'n-dōō'sōō)	132b	22.50S	43.40W
Guane, Cuba (gwä'nå)	122	22.10N	84.05W
Guangchang, China (gůäŋ-chäŋ)	193	26.50N	116.18E
Guangde, China (gůäŋ-dŭ)	193	30.40N	119.20E
Guangdong, prov., China (gůäŋ-dôŋ)	189	23.45N	113.15E
Guanglu Dao, i., China (gůäŋ-lōō dou)	190	39.13N	122.21E
Guangping, China (gůäŋ-pĭŋ)	190	36.30N	114.57E
Guangrao, China (gůaŋ-rou)	190	37.04N	118.24E
Guangshan, China (gůäŋ-shän)	190	32.02N	114.53E
Guangxi Zhuangzu, prov., China (gůäŋ-shyē)	188	24.00N	108.30E
Guangzhou, China	188	23.07N	113.15W
Guanhu, China (gůän-hōō)	190	34.26N	117.59E
Guannan, China (gůän-nän)	190	34.17N	119.17E
Guanta, Ven. (gwän'tä)	131b	10.15N	64.35W
Guantánamo, Cuba (gwän-tä'nä-mô)	123	20.10N	75.10W
Guantánamo, prov., Cuba	123	20.10N	75.05W
Guantánamo, Bahía de, b., Cuba	123	19.35N	75.35W
Guantao, China (gůän-tou)	190	36.39N	115.25E
Guanxian, China (gůän-shyĕn)	190	36.30N	115.28E
Guanyao, China (gůän-you)	191a	23.13N	113.04E
Guanyintang, China	240b	39.52N	116.31E
Guanyun, China (gůän-yòn)	190	34.28N	119.16E
Guapiles, C.R. (gwä-pē-lĕs)	121	10.05N	83.54W
Guapimirim, Braz. (gwä-pē-mē-rē'ɴ)	132b	22.31S	42.59W
Guaporé, r., S.A. (gwä-pô-rā')	130	12.11S	63.47W
Guaqui, Bol. (gwä'kē)	130	16.42S	68.47W
Guara, Sierra de, mts., Spain (sē-ĕ'r-rä-dĕ-gwä'rä)	159	42.24N	0.15W
Guarabira, Braz. (gwä-rä-bē'rȧ)	131	6.49S	35.27W
Guaracarumbo, Ven.	234a	10.34N	66.59W
Guaranda, Ec. (gwä-rán'dä)	130	1.39S	78.57W
Guarapari, Braz. (gwä-rä-pä'rē)	131	20.34S	40.31W
Guarapiranga, Represa do, res., Braz.	129a	23.45S	46.44W
Guarapuava, Braz. (gwä-rä-pwä'vȧ)	132	25.29S	51.26W
Guarda, Port. (gwär'dä)	158	40.32N	7.17W
Guardiato, r., Spain	158	38.10N	5.05W
Guarena, Spain (gwä-rā'nyä)	158	38.52N	6.08W
Guaribe, r., Ven. (gwä-rē'bē)	131b	9.48N	65.17W
Guárico, dept., Ven.	131b	9.42N	67.25W
Guarulhos, Braz. (gwá-rö'l-yôs)	129a	23.28S	46.30W
Guarus, Braz. (gwá'rōōs)	129a	21.44S	41.19W
Guasca, Col. (gwäs'kä)	130a	4.52N	73.52W
Guasipati, Ven. (gwä-sē-pä'tē)	131	7.26N	61.57W
Guastalla, Italy (gwäs-täl'lä)	160	44.53N	10.39E
Guasti, Ca., U.S. (gwäs'tĭ)	107a	34.04N	117.35W
Guatemala, Guat. (guä-tå-mä'lä)	116	14.37N	90.32W
Guatemala, nation, N.A.	116	15.45N	91.45W
Guatire, Ven. (gwä-tē'rē)	131b	10.28N	66.34W
Guaviare, r., Col.	130	3.35N	69.28W
Guayabal, Cuba (gwä-yä-bä'l)	122	20.40N	77.40W
Guayalejo, r., Mex. (gwä-yä-lĕ'hô)	118	23.24N	99.09W
Guayama, P.R. (gwä-yä'mä)	117b	18.00N	66.08W
Guayamouc, r., Haiti	123	19.05N	72.00W
Guayaquil, Ec. (gwī-ä-kēl')	130	2.16S	79.53W
Guayaquil, Golfo de, b., Ec. (gôl-fô-dĕ)	130	3.03S	82.12W
Guaymas, Mex. (gwá'y-mäs)	116	27.49N	110.58W
Guayubin, Dom. Rep. (gwá-yōō-bē'n)	123	19.40N	71.25W
Guazacapán, Guat. (gwä-zä-kä-pän')	120	14.04N	90.26W
Gubakha, Russia (gōō-bä'kå)	164	58.53N	57.35E
Gubbio, Italy (gōōb'byô)	160	43.23N	12.36E
Guben, Ger.	154	51.57N	14.43E

PLACE (Pronunciation)	PAGE	Lat. °′	Long. °′
Gucheng, China (gōō-chŭŋ)	190	39.09N	115.43E
Gudar, Sierra de, mts., Spain (syĕr'rä dā gōō'dhär)	159	40.28N	0.47W
Gudena, r., Den.	152	56.20N	9.47E
Gudermes, Russia	168	43.20N	46.08E
Gudvangen, Nor. (gōōdh'väŋ-gĕn)	152	60.52N	6.45E
Guebwiller, Fr. (gĕb-vē-lâr')	157	47.53N	7.10E
Guédi, Mont, mtn., Chad	215	12.14N	18.58E
Guelma, Alg. (gwĕl'mä)	210	36.32N	7.17E
Guelph, Can. (gwĕlf)	91	43.33N	80.15W
Güere, r., Ven. (gwĕ'rĕ)	131b	9.39N	65.00W
Guéret, Fr. (gā-rĕ')	156	46.09N	1.52E
Guermantes, Fr.	237c	48.51N	2.42E
Guernsey, dep., Eur.	156	49.28N	2.35W
Guernsey, i., Guernsey (gûrn'zĭ)	147	49.27N	2.36W
Guerrero, Mex. (gĕr-rā'rō)	112	26.47N	99.20W
Guerrero, Mex.	112	28.20N	100.24W
Guerrero, state, Mex.	116	17.45N	100.15W
Gueydan, La., U.S. (gā'dăn)	113	30.01N	92.31W
Guia de Pacobaíba, Braz. (gwē'ä-dē-pä'kō-bī'bä)	132b	22.42S	43.10W
Guiana Highlands, mts., S.A.	128	3.20N	60.00W
Guichi, China (gwā-chr)	193	30.35N	117.28E
Guichicovi, Mex. (gwē-chē-kō'vē)	119	16.58N	95.10W
Guidonia, Italy (gwē-dō'nyȧ)	160	42.00N	12.45E
Guiglo, C. Iv.	214	6.33N	7.29W
Guignes-Rabutin, Fr. (gēɴ'yē)	157b	48.38N	2.48E
Güigüe, Ven. (gwē'gwē)	131b	10.05N	67.48W
Guija, Lago, l., N.A. (gē'hä)	120	14.16N	89.21W
Guildford, Austl.	243a	33.51S	150.59E
Guildford, Eng., U.K. (gĭl'fērd)	150	51.13N	0.34W
Guilford, In., U.S. (gĭl'fērd)	101f	39.10N	84.55W
Guilin, China (gwā-lĭn)	189	25.18N	110.22E
Guimarães, Port. (gē-mä-rāɴsh')	158	41.27N	8.22W
Guinea, nation, Afr. (gĭn'ē)	210	10.48N	12.28W
Guinea, Gulf of, b., Afr.	210	2.00N	1.00E
Guinea-Bissau, nation, Afr. (gĭn'ē)	210	12.00N	20.00W
Guingamp, Fr. (găɴ-gäɴ')	156	48.35N	3.10W
Guir, r., Mor.	148	31.55N	2.48W
Güira de Melena, Cuba (gwē'rä dā må-lā'nä)	122	22.45N	82.30W
Güiria, Ven. (gwē-rē'ä)	130	10.43N	62.16W
Guise, Fr. (guēz)	156	49.54N	3.37E
Guisisil, vol., Nic. (gē-sē-sēl')	120	12.40N	86.11W
Guiyang, China (gwā-yäŋ)	188	26.45N	107.00E
Guizhou, China (gwā-jō)	191a	22.46N	113.15E
Guizhou, prov., China	188	27.00N	106.10E
Gujānwāla, Pak. (gòj-rän'va-lȧ)	183	32.08N	74.14E
Gujarat, India	183	22.54N	72.00E
Gulbarga, India (gòl-bûr'gȧ)	183	17.25N	76.52E
Gulbene, Lat. (gòl-bă'nē)	153	57.09N	26.49E
Gulfport, Ms., U.S. (gŭlf'pōrt)	114	30.24N	89.05W
Gulja *see* Yining, China	188	43.58N	80.40E
Gull Lake, Can.	88	50.10N	108.25W
Gull Lake, l., Can.	87	52.35N	114.00W
Gulph Mills, Pa., U.S.	229b	40.04N	75.21W
Gulu, Ug.	217	2.47N	32.18E
Gumaca, Phil. (gōō-mä-kä')	197a	13.55N	122.06E
Gumbeyka, r., Russia (gòm-bĕy'kȧ)	172a	53.20N	59.42E
Gumel, Nig.	210	12.39N	9.22E
Gummersbach, Ger. (gòm'ērs-bäk)	154	51.02N	7.34E
Gummi, Nig.	215	12.09N	5.09E
Gumpoldskirchen, Aus.	145e	48.04N	16.15E
Guna, India	186	24.44N	77.17E
Gunisao, r., Can. (gŭn-ĭ-sā'ō)	89	53.40N	97.35W
Gunisao Lake, l., Can.	89	53.35N	96.10W
Gunnedah, Austl. (gŭ'nē-dä)	204	31.00S	150.10E
Gunnison, Co., U.S. (gŭn'ĭ-sŭn)	109	38.33N	106.56W
Gunnison, Ut., U.S.	109	39.10N	111.50W
Gunnison, r., Co., U.S.	109	38.45N	108.20W
Guntersville, Al., U.S. (gŭn'tērz-vĭl)	114	34.20N	86.19W
Guntersville Lake, res., Al., U.S.	114	34.30N	86.20W
Guntramsdorf, Aus.	145e	48.04N	16.19E
Guntūr, India (gòn'tōōr)	183	16.22N	80.29E
Guoyang, China (gwô-yäŋ)	190	33.32N	116.10E
Gurdon, Ar., U.S. (gûr'dŭn)	111	33.56N	93.10W
Gurgueia, r., Braz.	131	8.12S	43.49W
Guri, Embalse, res., Ven.	130	7.30N	63.00W
Gurnee, Il., U.S. (gûr'nē)	101a	42.22N	87.55W
Gurskøy, i., Nor. (gōōrskûê)	152	62.18N	5.20E
Gurupi, Serra do, mts., Braz. (sĕ'r-rä-dô-gōō-rōō-pē')	131	5.32S	47.02W
Guru Sikhar, mtn., India	186	29.42N	72.50E
Gur'yevsk, Russia (gōōr-yĭfsk')	164	54.17N	85.56E
Gusau, Nig. (gōō-zä'ōō)	210	12.12N	6.40E
Gusev, Russia (gōō'sĕf)	153	54.35N	22.15E
Gushi, China (gōō-shr)	190	32.11N	115.39E
Gushiago, Ghana	214	9.55N	0.12W
Gusinje, Yugo. (gōō-sĕn'yĕ)	161	42.34N	19.54E
Gus'-Khrustal'nyy, Russia (gōōs-κrōō-stäl'ny')	166	55.39N	40.41E
Gustavo A. Madero, Mex. (gōōs-tä'vô-ä-mä-dĕ'rô)	118	19.29N	99.07W
Güstrow, Ger. (güs'trō)	154	53.48N	12.12E
Gütersloh, Ger. (gü'tērs-lo)	154	51.54N	8.22E
Guthrie, Ok., U.S. (gŭth'rĭ)	111	35.52N	97.26W
Guthrie Center, Ia., U.S.	103	41.41N	94.33W
Gutiérrez Zamora, Mex. (gōō-tĭ-âr'räz zä-mō'rä)	119	20.27N	97.17W
Guttenberg, Ia., U.S. (gŭt'ĕn-bûrg)	103	42.48N	91.09W
Guttenberg, N.J., U.S.	228	40.48N	74.01W
Guyana, nation, S.A. (gŭy'ănä)	131	7.45N	59.00W
Guyancourt, Fr.	237c	48.46N	2.04E
Guyang, China (gōō-yäŋ)	190	34.56N	114.57E
Guye, China (gōō-yŭ)	190	39.46N	118.23E
Guymon, Ok., U.S. (gī'mŏn)	110	36.41N	101.29W
Guysborough, Can. (gīz'bŭr-ô)	93	45.23N	61.30W

ng-sing; ŋ-baŋk; ɴ-nasalized n; nŏd; cŏmmit; ōld; ôbey; ôrder; oi-boil; fōōd; ò-as oo in foot; ou-out; s-soft; sh-dish; th-thin; pūre; ûnite; ûrn; stŭd; circŭs; ü-as in French tu; '-indeterminate vowel.

PLACE (Pronunciation)	PAGE	Lat. °′	Long. °′
Guzhen, China (go͞o-jün)	192	33.20N	117.18E
Gvardeysk, Russia (gvȧr-dĕysk′)	153	54.39N	21.11E
Gwadabawa, Nig.	215	13.20N	5.15E
Gwādar, Pak. (gwä′dŭr)	182	25.15N	62.29E
Gwalior, India	183	26.13N	78.10E
Gwane, Zaire (gwän)	211	4.43N	25.50E
Gwardafuy, Gees, c., Som.	218a	11.55N	51.30E
Gwda, r., Pol.	154	53.27N	16.52E
Gwembe, Zam.	217	16.30S	27.35E
Gweru, Zimb.	212	19.15S	29.48E
Gwinn, Mi., U.S. (gwĭn)	103	46.15N	87.30W
Gyaring Co, l., China	186	30.37N	88.33E
Gydan, Khrebet (Kolymskiy), mts., Russia	165	61.45N	155.00E
Gydanskiy Poluostrov, pen., Russia	164	70.42N	76.03E
Gympie, Austl. (gĭm′pė)	203	26.20S	152.50E
Gyöngyös, Hung. (dyûn′dyûsh)	149	47.47N	19.55E
Győr, Hung. (dyûr)	149	47.40N	17.37E
Gyōtoku, Japan (gyō′tồ-ko͞o′)	195a	35.42N	139.56E
Gypsumville, Can. (jĭp′sŭm′vĭl)	84	51.45N	98.35W
Gyula, Hung. (dyŏŏ′lä)	155	46.38N	21.18E
Gyumri, Arm.	167	40.40N	43.50E

H

PLACE (Pronunciation)	PAGE	Lat. °′	Long. °′
Haan, Ger. (hän)	157c	51.12N	7.00E
Haapamäki, Fin. (häp′ȧ-mĕ-kĕ)	153	62.16N	24.20E
Haapsalu, Est. (häp′sä-lò)	153	58.56N	23.33E
Haar, Ger. (här)	145d	48.06N	11.44E
Haar, neigh., Ger.	236	51.26N	7.13E
Ha'Arava (Wādī al Jayb), val., Asia	181a	30.33N	35.10E
Haarlem, Neth. (här′lĕm)	151	52.22N	4.37E
Habana, prov., Cuba (hä-vä′nä)	122	22.45N	82.25W
Haberfield, Austl.	243a	33.53S	151.08E
Hābra, India	186a	22.49N	88.38E
Hachinohe, Japan (hä′chē-nō′hȧ)	194	40.29N	141.40E
Hachiōji, Japan (hä′chė-ō′jė)	194	35.39N	139.18E
Hacienda Heights, Ca., U.S.	232	33.58N	117.58W
Hackensack, N.J., U.S. (hăk′ĕn-săk)	100a	40.54N	74.03W
Hacketts, Eng., U.K.	235	51.45N	0.05W
Hackney, neigh., Eng., U.K.	235	51.33N	0.03W
Ḥadd, Ra's al, c., Oman	182	22.29N	59.46E
Haddonfield, N.J., U.S. (hăd′ŭn-fēld)	100f	39.53N	75.02W
Haddon Heights, N.J., U.S. (hăd′ŭn hīts)	100f	39.53N	75.03W
Hadejia, Nig. (hä-dä′jä)	210	12.30N	9.59E
Hadejia, r., Nig.	210	12.15N	10.00E
Ḥadera, Isr. (ĸȧ-dĕ′rȧ)	181a	32.26N	34.55E
Hadersdorf, neigh., Aus.	239e	48.13N	16.14E
Haderslev, Den. (hä′dhĕrs-lĕv)	152	55.17N	9.28E
Hadfield, Austl.	243b	37.42S	144.56E
Ḥadīdū, Yemen	182	12.40N	53.50E
Hadlock, Wa., U.S. (hăd′lŏk)	106a	48.02N	122.46W
Ḥaḍramawt, reg., Yemen	182	15.22N	48.40E
Hadūr Shu'ayb, mtn., Yemen	182	15.45N	43.45E
Haeju, N. Kor. (hä′ĕ-jŭ)	194	38.03N	125.42E
Hafnarfjörđur, Ice.	146	64.02N	21.32W
Haft Gel, Iran	185	31.27N	49.27E
Hafun, Ras, c., Som. (hä-fo͞on′)	218a	10.15N	51.35E
Hageland, Mt., U.S. (hăge′lȧnd)	105	48.53N	108.43W
Hagen, Ger. (hä′gĕn)	154	51.21N	7.29E
Hagerstown, In., U.S. (hā′gẽrz-toun)	98	39.55N	85.10W
Hagerstown, Md., U.S.	97	39.40N	77.45W
Hagi, Japan (hä′gĭ)	195	34.25N	131.25E
Hague, Cap de la, c., Fr. (dē lȧ ȧg′)	156	49.44N	1.55W
Haguenau, Fr. (ȧg′nō′)	157	48.47N	7.48E
Hahnenberg, Ger.	236	51.12N	7.24E
Hai'an, China (hī-än)	190	32.35N	120.25E
Haibara, Japan (hä′ė-bä′rä)	195	34.29N	135.57E
Haicheng, China (hī-chŭŋ)	192	40.58N	122.45E
Haidārpur, neigh., India	240d	28.43N	77.09E
Haidian, China (hī-dĭĕn)	190	39.59N	116.17E
Haifa, Isr. (hä′ē-fȧ)	182	32.48N	35.00E
Haifeng, China (hä′ė-fĕng′)	193	23.00N	115.20E
Haifuzhen, China (hī-fo͞o-jŭn)	190	31.57N	121.48E
Haijima, Japan	242a	35.42N	139.21E
Haikou, China	189	20.03N	110.19E
Haikou, China (hī-kō)	193	20.00N	110.20E
Ḥā'il, Sau. Ar.	182	27.30N	41.47E
Hailar, China	189	49.10N	118.40E
Hailey, Id., U.S. (hā′lĭ)	105	43.31N	114.19W
Haileybury, Can.	91	47.27N	79.38W
Haileyville, Ok., U.S. (hā′lĭ-vĭl)	111	34.51N	95.34W
Hailing Dao, i., China (hī-lĭŋ dou)	193	21.30N	112.15E
Hailong, China (hī-loŋ)	192	42.32N	125.52E
Hailun, China (hä′ė-lo͞on′)	189	47.18N	126.50E
Hainan, prov., China	188	19.00N	109.30E
Hainan Dao, i., China (hī-nän dou)	189	19.00N	111.10E
Hainault, neigh., Eng., U.K.	235	51.36N	0.06E
Hainburg, Aus.	154	48.09N	16.57E
Haines, Ak., U.S. (hānz)	95	59.10N	135.38W
Haines City, Fl., U.S.	115a	28.05N	81.38W
Hai Phong, Viet. (hī′fông′)(hä′ėp-hŏng)	196	20.52N	106.40E
Haiti, nation, N.A. (hā′tĭ)	117	19.00N	72.15W
Haizhou, China	190	34.34N	119.11E
Haizhou Wan, b., China	192	34.49N	120.35E
Hajdúböszormény, Hung. (hôl′dò-bû′sûr-mān′)	155	47.41N	21.30E
Hajdúhadház, Hung. (hô′ĭ-dò-hôd′häz)	155	47.32N	21.32E
Hajdúnánás, Hung. (hô′ĭ-dò-nä′näsh)	155	47.52N	21.27E
Hakodate, Japan (hä-kō-dä′t ȧ)	189	41.46N	140.42E
Haku-San, mtn., Japan (hä′ko͞o-sän′)	194	36.11N	136.45E
Halā'ib, Egypt (hä-lä′ēb)	211	22.10N	36.40E
Halbe, Ger. (häl′bē)	145b	52.07N	13.43E
Halberstadt, Ger. (häl′bĕr-shtät)	154	51.54N	11.07E
Halcon, Mount, mtn., Phil. (häl-kōn′)	197a	13.19N	120.55E
Halden, Nor. (häl′dĕn)	146	59.10N	11.21E
Halden, neigh., Ger.	236	51.23N	7.31E
Haldensleben, Ger.	154	52.18N	11.23E
Hale, Eng., U.K. (hāl)	144a	53.22N	2.20W
Haleakala Crater, Hi., U.S. (hä′lȧ-ä′kä-lä)	94a	20.44N	156.15W
Haleakala National Park, Hi., U.S.	94a	20.46N	156.00W
Halebarns, Eng., U.K.	237b	53.22N	2.19W
Haledon, N.J., U.S.	228	40.56N	74.11W
Hales Corners, Wi., U.S. (hālz kôr′nẽrz)	101a	42.56N	88.03W
Halesowen, Eng., U.K. (hālz′ō-wĕn)	144a	52.26N	2.03W
Halethorpe, Md., U.S. (hāl-thôrp)	100e	39.15N	76.40W
Halewood, Eng., U.K.	237a	53.22N	2.49W
Haleyville, Al., U.S. (hā′lĭ-vĭl)	114	34.11N	87.36W
Half Moon Bay, Ca., U.S. (hăf′mo͞on)	106b	37.28N	122.26W
Halfway House, S. Afr. (häf-wā hous)	213b	26.00S	28.08E
Halfweg, Neth.	145a	52.23N	4.45E
Halifax, Can. (hăl′ĭ-făks)	85	44.39N	63.36W
Halifax, Eng., U.K.	150	53.44N	1.52W
Halifax Bay, b., Austl. (hăl′ĭ-făx)	203	18.56S	147.07E
Halifax Harbour, b., Can.	92	44.35N	63.31W
Halkett, Cape, c., Ak., U.S.	95	70.50N	151.15W
Hallam, Austl.	243b	38.01S	145.16E
Hallam Peak, mtn., Can.	87	52.11N	118.46E
Halla San, mtn., S. Kor. (häl′lȧ-sän)	194	33.20N	126.37E
Halle, Bel. (häl′lĕ)	145a	50.45N	4.13E
Halle, Ger.	147	51.30N	11.59E
Hallettsville, Tx., U.S. (hăl′ĕts-vĭl)	113	29.26N	96.55W
Hallock, Mn., U.S. (hăl′ŭk)	102	48.46N	96.57W
Hall Peninsula, pen., Can. (hôl)	85	63.14N	65.40W
Halls Bayou, Tx., U.S.	113a	29.55N	95.23W
Hallsberg, Swe. (häls′bĕrgh)	152	59.04N	15.04E
Halls Creek, Austl. (hôlz)	202	18.15S	127.45E
Halmahera, i., Indon. (häl-mä-hä′rä)	197	0.45N	128.45E
Halmahera, Laut, Indon.	197	1.00S	129.00E
Halmstad, Swe. (hälm′städ)	146	56.40N	12.46E
Halsafjorden, fj., Nor. (häl′sĕ fyồrd)	152	63.03N	8.23E
Halstead, Eng., U.K.	235	51.20N	0.08E
Halstead, Ks., U.S. (hôl′stĕd)	111	38.02N	97.36W
Haltern, Ger. (häl′tĕrn)	157c	51.45N	7.10E
Haltom City, Tx., U.S. (hôl′tŏm)	107c	32.48N	97.13W
Halver, Ger.	157c	51.11N	7.30E
Ham, neigh., Eng., U.K.	235	51.26N	0.19W
Hamada, Japan	194	34.53N	132.05E
Hamadān, Iran (hŭ-mŭ-dän′)	182	34.45N	48.07E
Ḥamāh, Syria (hä′mä)	182	35.08N	36.53E
Hamamatsu, Japan (hä′mä-mät′sò)	194	34.41N	137.43E
Hamar, Nor. (hä′mär)	146	60.49N	11.05E
Hamasaka, Japan (hä′mȧ-sä′kȧ)	195	35.37N	134.27E
Hamberg, S. Afr.	244b	26.11S	27.53E
Hamborn, Ger. (häm′bōrn)	157c	51.30N	6.43E
Hamburg, Ger. (häm′bo͝orgh)	142	53.34N	10.02E
Hamburg, S. Afr. (häm′bûrg)	213c	33.18S	27.28E
Hamburg, Ar., U.S. (hăm′bûrg)	111	33.15N	91.49W
Hamburg, N.J., U.S.	100a	41.09N	74.35W
Hamburg, N.Y., U.S.	101c	42.44N	78.51W
Hamburg, state, Ger.	145c	53.35N	10.00E
Hamden, Ct., U.S. (hăm′dĕn)	99	41.20N	72.55W
Hämeenlinna, Fin. (hĕ′mån-lĭn-nȧ)	146	61.00N	24.29E
Hameln, Ger. (hä′mĕln)	154	52.06N	9.23E
Hamelwörden, Ger. (hä′mĕl-vûr-dĕn)	145c	53.47N	9.19E
Hamersley Range, mts., Austl. (hăm′ẽrz-lē)	202	22.15S	117.50E
Hamhŭng, N. Kor. (häm′hòng′)	189	39.57N	127.35E
Hamhŭng, N. Kor.	194	39.54N	127.32E
Hami, China (hä-mē)(kō-mo͞ol′)	188	42.58N	93.14E
Hamilton, Austl. (hăm′ĭl-tŭn)	203	37.50S	142.10E
Hamilton, Can.	85	43.15N	79.52W
Hamilton, N.Z.	203a	37.45S	175.28E
Hamilton, Al., U.S.	114	34.09N	88.01W
Hamilton, Ma., U.S.	93a	42.37N	70.52W
Hamilton, Mo., U.S.	111	39.43N	93.59W
Hamilton, Mt., U.S.	105	46.15N	114.09W
Hamilton, Oh., U.S.	97	39.22N	84.33W
Hamilton, Tx., U.S.	112	31.42N	98.07W
Hamilton, Lake, l., Ar., U.S.	111	34.25N	93.32W
Hamilton Harbour, b., Can.	83d	43.17N	79.50W
Hamilton Inlet, b., Can.	85	54.20N	56.57W
Hamina, Fin. (hȧ′mē-nȧ)	153	60.34N	27.15E
Hamlet, N.C., U.S. (hăm′lĕt)	115	35.52N	79.46W
Hamlin, Tx., U.S. (hăm′lĭn)	110	32.54N	100.08W
Hamm, Ger. (häm)	154	51.40N	7.48E
Hamm, neigh., Ger.	236	51.12N	6.44E
Hammanskraal, S. Afr. (hä-mȧns-kräl′)	218d	25.24S	28.17E
Hamme, Bel.	145a	51.06N	4.07E
Hamme-Oste Kanal, can., Ger. (hä′mĕ-ōs′tĕ kä-näl)	145c	53.20N	8.59E
Hammerfest, Nor. (hä′mĕr-fĕst)	142	70.38N	23.59E
Hammersmith, neigh., Eng., U.K.	235	51.30N	0.14W
Hammond, In., U.S. (hăm′ŭnd)	97	41.37N	87.31W
Hammond, La., U.S.	113	30.30N	90.28W
Hammond, Or., U.S.	106c	46.12N	123.57W
Hammondville, Austl.	243a	33.57S	150.57E
Hammonton, N.J., U.S. (hăm′ŭn-tŭn)	99	39.40N	74.45W
Hampden, Me., U.S. (hăm′dĕn)	92	44.44N	68.51W
Hampstead, Md., U.S.	100e	39.36N	76.54W
Hampstead, neigh., Eng., U.K.	235	51.33N	0.11W
Hampstead Heath, pt. of i., Eng., U.K.	235	51.34N	0.10W
Hampstead Norris, Eng., U.K. (hămp-stĕd nŏ′rĭs)	144b	51.27N	1.14W
Hampton, Austl.	243b	37.56S	145.00E
Hampton, Can. (hămp′tŭn)	92	45.32N	65.51W
Hampton, Ia., U.S.	103	42.43N	93.15W
Hampton, Va., U.S.	99	37.02N	76.21W
Hampton, neigh., Eng., U.K.	235	51.25N	0.22W
Hampton National Historic Site, pt. of i., Md., U.S.	229c	39.25N	76.35W
Hampton Roads, b., Va., U.S.	100g	36.56N	76.23W
Hams Fork, r., Wy., U.S.	105	41.55N	110.40W
Hamtramck, Mi., U.S. (hăm-trăm′ĭk)	101b	42.24N	83.03W
Han, r., China	189	31.40N	112.04E
Han, r., China (hän)	193	25.00N	116.35E
Han, r., S. Kor.	194	37.10N	127.40E
Hana, Hi., U.S. (hä′nä)	94a	20.43N	155.59W
Hanábana, r., Cuba (hä-nä-bä′nä)	122	22.30N	80.55W
Hanalei Bay, b., Hi., U.S. (hä-nä-lä′ė)	94a	22.15N	159.40W
Hanang, mtn., Tan.	217	4.26S	35.24E
Hanau, Ger. (hä′nou)	154	50.08N	8.56E
Hancock, Mi., U.S. (hăn′kŏk)	97	47.08N	88.37W
Handan, China (hän-dän)	190	36.37N	114.30E
Handforth, Eng., U.K.	237b	53.21N	2.13W
Haney, Can. (hā-nė)	87	49.13N	122.36W
Hanford, Ca., U.S. (hăn′fẽrd)	108	36.20N	119.38W
Hangayn Nuruu, mts., Mong.	188	48.03N	99.45E
Hang Hau Town, H.K.	241c	22.19N	114.16E
Hango, Fin. (häŋ′gû)	142	59.49N	22.56E
Hangzhou, China (hăng′chō′)	189	30.17N	120.12E
Hangzhou Wan, b., China (häŋ-jō wän)	193	30.20N	121.25E
Hankamer, Tx., U.S. (hăn′kȧ-mẽr)	113a	29.52N	94.42W
Hankinson, N.D., U.S. (hăŋ′kĭn-sŭn)	102	46.04N	96.54W
Hankou, China (hän-kō)	193	30.42N	114.22E
Hann, Mount, mtn., Austl. (hän)	202	16.05S	126.07E
Hanna, Can. (hăn′ȧ)	84	51.38N	111.54W
Hanna, Wy., U.S.	105	41.51N	106.34W
Hannah, N.D., U.S.	102	48.58N	98.42W
Hannibal, Mo., U.S. (hăn′ĭ bȧl)	97	39.42N	91.22W
Hannover, Ger. (hän-ō′vẽr)	142	52.22N	9.45E
Hanöbukten, b., Swe.	152	55.54N	14.55E
Hanoi, Viet. (hä-noi′)	196	21.04N	105.50E
Hanover, Can. (hăn′ô-vẽr)	90	44.10N	81.05W
Hanover, Md., U.S.	229c	39.11N	76.42W
Hanover, Ma., U.S.	93a	42.07N	70.49W
Hanover, N.H., U.S.	99	43.45N	72.15W
Hanover, Pa., U.S.	99	39.50N	77.00W
Hanover, i., Chile	132	51.00S	74.45W
Hanshan, China (hän′shän′)	190	31.43N	118.06E
Hans Lollick, i., V.I.U.S. (häns′lôl′ĭk)	117c	18.24N	64.55W
Hanson, Ma., U.S. (hăn′sŭn)	93a	42.04N	70.53W
Hansville, Wa., U.S. (hăns′-vĭl)	106a	47.55N	122.33W
Hantengri Feng, mtn., Asia (hän-tŭŋ-rē fŭŋ)	188	42.10N	80.20E
Hantsport, Can. (hănts′pōrt)	92	45.04N	64.11W
Hanworth, neigh., Eng., U.K.	235	51.26N	0.23W
Hanyang, China (han′yăng′)	189	30.30N	114.10E
Hanzhong, China (hän-jôŋ)	192	33.02N	107.00E
Haocheng, China (hou-chŭŋ)	190	33.19N	117.33E
Haparanda, Swe. (hä-pa-rän′dä)	146	65.54N	23.57E
Hapeville, Ga., U.S. (hăp′vĭl)	100c	33.39N	84.25W
Happy Camp, Ca., U.S.	104	41.47N	123.22W
Happy Valley-Goose Bay, Can.	85	53.19N	60.33W
Hapsford, Eng., U.K.	237a	53.16N	2.48W
Ḥaql, Sau. Ar.	181a	29.15N	34.57E
Ḥar, Laga, r., Kenya	217	2.15N	39.30E
Haramachida, Japan	242a	35.33N	139.27E
Harare, Zimb.	212	17.50S	31.03E
Harbin, China	189	45.40N	126.30E
Harbor Beach, Mi., U.S. (här′bẽr bēch)	98	43.50N	82.40W
Harbor City, neigh., Ca., U.S.	232	33.48N	118.17W
Harbord, Austl.	243a	33.47S	151.17E
Harbor Isle, N.Y., U.S.	228	40.36N	73.40W
Harbor Springs, Mi., U.S.	98	45.25N	85.05W
Harbour Breton, Can. (brĕt′ŭn) (brĕ-tôn′)	93	47.29N	55.48W
Harbour Grace, Can. (grās)	93	47.32N	53.13W
Harburg, Ger. (här-bòrgh)	145c	53.28N	9.58E
Hardangerfjorden, Nor. (här-däng′ẽr fyồrd)	146	59.58N	6.30E
Hardin, Mt., U.S. (här′dĭn)	105	45.44N	107.36W
Harding, S. Afr. (här′dĭng)	212	30.34S	29.54E
Harding, Lake, res., U.S.	114	32.43N	85.00W
Hardwār, India (hŭr′dvär)	183	29.56N	78.06E
Hardy, r., Mex. (här′dĭ)	108	32.04N	115.10W
Hare Bay, b., Can. (hâr)	93	51.18N	55.50W
Harefield, neigh., Eng., U.K.	235	51.36N	0.29W
Harer, Eth.	211	9.43N	42.10E
Hararge, hist. reg., Eth.	211	8.15N	41.00E
Hargeysa, Som. (här-gā′ė-sȧ)	218a	9.20N	43.57E
Harghita, Munţii, mts., Rom.	155	46.25N	25.40E
Harima-Nada, b., Japan (hä′rē-mä nä-dä)	195	34.34N	134.37E
Haringey, neigh., Eng., U.K.	235	51.35N	0.07W
Haringvliet, r., Neth.	145a	51.49N	4.03E
Hari Rud, r., Asia	182	34.29N	61.16E
Harker Village, N.J., U.S.	229b	39.51N	75.09W
Harlan, Ia., U.S. (här′lăn)	111	41.40N	95.10W
Harlan, Ky., U.S.	114	36.50N	83.19W
Harlan County Reservoir, res., Ne., U.S.	110	40.03N	99.51W
Harlem, Mt., U.S. (hár′lĕm)	105	48.33N	108.50W
Harlem, neigh., N.Y., U.S.	228	40.49N	73.56W
Harlesden, neigh., Eng., U.K.	235	51.32N	0.15W
Harlingen, Neth. (här′lĭng-ĕn)	151	53.10N	5.24E
Harlingen, Tx., U.S.	96	26.12N	97.42W
Harlington, neigh., Eng., U.K.	235	51.29N	0.26W
Harlow, Eng., U.K. (här′lō)	144b	51.46N	0.08E
Harlowton, Mt., U.S. (här′lō-tun)	105	46.26N	109.50W
Harmar Heights, Pa., U.S.	230b	40.33N	79.49W
Harmarville, Pa., U.S.	230b	40.32N	79.51W

ăt; finȧl; rāte; senåte; ärm; ȧsk; sofȧ; fâre; ch-choose; dh-as th in other; bē; ėvent; bĕt; recĕnt; cratẽr; g-gō; gh-guttural g; bĭt; ĭ-short neutral; rīde; ĸ-guttural k as ch in German ich;

PRONOUNCING INDEX

Harmony–Hengyang 295

PLACE (Pronunciation)	PAGE	Lat. °′	Long. °′
Harmony, In., U.S. (här′mō-nĭ)	98	39.35N	87.00W
Harney Basin, Or., U.S. (här′nĭ)	104	43.26N	120.19W
Harney Lake, l., Or., U.S.	104	43.11N	119.23W
Harney Peak, mtn., S.D., U.S.	96	43.52N	103.32W
Härnosand, Swe. (hĕr-nû-sänd)	146	62.37N	17.54E
Haro, Spain (ä′rō)	158	42.35N	2.49W
Harola, India	240d	28.36N	77.19E
Harold Hill, neigh., Eng., U.K.	235	51.36N	0.13E
Harold Wood, neigh., Eng., U.K.	235	51.36N	0.14E
Haro Strait, strt., N.A. (hă′rō)	106a	48.27N	123.11W
Harpen, neigh., Ger.	236	51.29N	7.16E
Harpenden, Eng., U.K. (här′pĕn-d′n)	144b	51.48N	0.22W
Harper, Lib.	210	4.25N	7.43W
Harper, Ks., U.S. (här′pẽr)	110	37.17N	98.02W
Harper, Wa., U.S.	106a	47.31N	122.32W
Harpers Ferry, W.V., U.S. (här′pẽrz)	99	39.20N	77.45W
Harper Woods, Mi., U.S.	230c	42.24N	82.55W
Harpurhey, neigh., Eng., U.K.	237b	53.31N	2.13W
Harricana, r., Can.	91	50.10N	78.50W
Harriman, Tn., U.S. (hă′ĭ-măn)	114	35.55N	84.34W
Harrington, De., U.S. (hăr′ĭng-tŭn)	99	38.55N	75.35W
Harris, i., Scot., U.K. (hăr′ĭs)	150	57.55N	6.40W
Harris, Lake, l., Fl., U.S.	115a	28.43N	81.40W
Harrisburg, Il., U.S. (hăr′ĭs-bûrg)	98	37.45N	88.35W
Harrisburg, Pa., U.S.	97	40.15N	76.50W
Harrismith, S. Afr. (hă-rĭs′mĭth)	218d	28.17S	29.08E
Harrison, Ar., U.S. (hăr′ĭ-sŭn)	111	36.13N	93.06W
Harrison, N.J., U.S.	228	40.45N	74.10W
Harrison, N.Y., U.S.	228	40.58N	73.43W
Harrison, Oh., U.S.	101f	39.16N	84.45W
Harrisonburg, Va., U.S. (hăr′ĭ-sŭn-bûrg)	99	38.30N	78.50W
Harrison Lake, l., Can.	87	49.31N	121.59W
Harrisonville, Md., U.S.	229c	39.23N	77.50W
Harrisonville, Mo., U.S. (hăr-ĭ-sŭn-vĭl)	111	38.39N	94.21W
Harris Park, Austl.	243a	33.49S	151.01E
Harrisville, Ut., U.S. (hăr′ĭs-vĭl)	107b	41.17N	112.00W
Harrisville, W.V., U.S.	98	39.10N	81.05W
Harrodsburg, Ky., U.S. (hăr′ŭdz-bûrg)	98	37.45N	84.50W
Harrods Creek, r., Ky., U.S. (hăr′ŭdz)	101h	38.24N	35.33W
Harrow, Eng., U.K. (hăr′ō)	144b	51.34N	0.21W
Harrow on the Hill, neigh., Eng., U.K.	235	51.34N	0.20W
Harsefeld, Ger. (här′zĕ-fĕld′)	145c	53.27N	9.30E
Harstad, Nor. (här′städh)	146	68.49N	16.10E
Hart, Mi., U.S. (härt)	98	43.40N	86.25W
Hartbeesfontein, S. Afr.	218d	26.46S	26.25E
Hartbeespoortdam, res., S. Afr.	213b	25.47S	27.43E
Hartford, Al., U.S. (härt′fẽrd)	114	31.05N	85.42W
Hartford, Ar., U.S.	111	35.01N	94.21W
Hartford, Ct., U.S.	97	41.45N	72.40W
Hartford, Il., U.S.	107e	38.50N	90.06W
Hartford, Ky., U.S.	114	37.25N	86.50W
Hartford, Mi., U.S.	98	42.15N	86.15W
Hartford, Wi., U.S.	103	43.19N	88.25W
Hartford City, In., U.S.	98	40.35N	85.25W
Hartington, Eng., U.K. (härt′ĭng-tŭn)	144a	53.08N	1.48W
Hartington, Ne., U.S.	102	42.37N	97.18W
Hartland Point, c., Eng., U.K.	150	51.03N	4.40W
Hartlepool, Eng., U.K. (här′t′l-po͞ol)	146	54.40N	1.12W
Hartley, Eng., U.K.	235	51.23N	0.19E
Hartley, Ia., U.S. (härt′lĭ)	102	43.12N	95.29W
Hartley Bay, Can.	86	53.25N	129.15W
Hart Mountain, mtn., Can. (härt)	89	52.25N	101.30W
Hartsbeespoort, S. Afr.	213b	25.44S	27.51E
Hartselle, Al., U.S. (härt′sĕl)	114	34.24N	86.55W
Hartshorne, Ok., U.S. (härts′hôrn)	111	34.49N	95.34W
Hartsville, S.C., U.S. (härts′vĭl)	115	34.20N	80.04W
Hartwell, Ga., U.S. (härt′wĕl)	115	34.21N	82.56W
Hartwell Lake, res., U.S.	97	34.30N	83.00W
Hārua, India	186a	22.36N	88.40E
Harvard, Il., U.S. (här′vȧrd)	103	42.25N	88.39W
Harvard, Ma., U.S.	93a	42.30N	71.35W
Harvard, Ne., U.S.	110	40.36N	98.08W
Harvard, Mount, mtn., Co., U.S.	109	38.55N	106.20W
Harvel, Eng., U.K.	235	51.21N	0.22E
Harvey, Can.	92	45.44N	64.46W
Harvey, Il., U.S.	101a	41.37N	87.39W
Harvey, La., U.S.	100d	29.54N	90.05W
Harvey, N.D., U.S.	102	47.46N	99.55W
Harwich, Eng., U.K. (här′wĭch)	151	51.53N	1.13E
Harwick, Pa., U.S.	230b	40.34N	79.48W
Harwood, Eng., U.K.	237b	53.35N	2.23W
Harwood, Md., U.S.	229c	38.52N	76.37W
Harwood Heights, Il., U.S.	231a	41.59N	87.48W
Harwood Park, Md., U.S.	229c	39.12N	76.44W
Haryana, state, India	183	29.00N	75.45E
Harz Mountains, mts., Ger. (härts)	154	51.42N	10.50E
Hasanābād, Iran	241h	35.44N	51.19E
Hasbrouck Heights, N.J., U.S.	228	40.52N	74.04W
Hashimoto, Japan (hä′shē-mō′tō)	195	34.19N	135.37E
Haskayne, Eng., U.K.	237a	53.34N	2.58W
Haskell, Ok., U.S. (hăs′kĕl)	111	35.49N	95.41W
Haskell, Tx., U.S.	110	33.09N	99.43W
Hasköy, neigh., Tur.	239f	41.02N	28.58E
Haslingden, Eng., U.K. (hăz′lĭng dĕn)	144a	53.43N	2.19W
Hasselbeck-Schwarzbach, Ger.	236	51.16N	6.53E
Hassels, neigh., Ger.	236	51.10N	6.53E
Hassi Messaoud, Alg.	210	31.17N	6.13E
Hässleholm, Swe. (hăs′lĕ-hōlm)	152	56.10N	13.44E
Hasslinghausen, Ger.	236	51.20N	7.17E
Hästen, neigh., Ger.	236	51.09N	7.06E
Hasten, neigh., Ger.	236	51.12N	7.09E
Hastings, N.Z.	203a	39.33S	176.53E
Hastings, Eng., U.K. (hās′tĭngz)	147	50.52N	0.28E
Hastings, Mi., U.S.	98	42.40N	85.20W
Hastings, Mn., U.S.	107g	44.44N	92.51W
Hastings, Ne., U.S.	96	40.34N	98.42W

PLACE (Pronunciation)	PAGE	Lat. °′	Long. °′
Hastings-on-Hudson, N.Y., U.S. (ōn-hŭd′sŭn)	100a	40.59N	75.53W
Hastingwood, Eng., U.K.	235	51.45N	0.09E
Hatay, Tur.	182	36.20N	36.10E
Hatchie, r., Tn., U.S. (hăch′ē)	114	35.28N	89.14W
Haţeg, Rom. (kät-säg′)	161	45.35N	22.57E
Hatfield Broad Oak, Eng., U.K. (hăt-fēld brôd ōk)	144b	51.50N	0.14E
Hatogaya, Japan (hä′tō-gä-yä)	195a	35.50N	139.45E
Hatsukaichi, Japan (hät′so͞o-kȧ′ē-chē)	195	34.22N	132.19E
Hatteras, Cape, c., N.C., U.S. (hăt′ẽr-ȧs)	97	35.15N	75.24W
Hattiesburg, Ms., U.S. (hăt′ĭz-bûrg)	97	31.20N	89.18W
Hattingen, Ger. (hä′tĕn-gĕn)	157c	51.24N	7.11E
Hatton, neigh., Eng., U.K.	235	51.28N	0.25W
Hattori, Japan	242b	34.46N	135.27E
Hatvan, Hung. (hôt′vôn)	155	47.39N	19.44E
Hatzfeld, neigh., Ger.	236	51.17N	7.11E
Haugesund, Nor. (hou′gē-soon′)	146	59.26N	5.20E
Haughton Green, Eng., U.K.	237b	53.27N	2.06W
Haukivesi, l., Fin. (hou′kē-vē′sē)	153	62.02N	29.02E
Haultain, r., Can.	88	56.15N	106.35W
Hauptsrus, S. Afr.	218d	26.35S	26.16E
Hauraki Gulf, b., N.Z. (hä-o͞o-rä′kē)	203a	36.30S	175.00E
Haut, Isle au, Me., U.S. (hō)	92	44.03N	68.13W
Haut Atlas, mts., Mor.	148	32.10N	5.49W
Hauterive, Can.	92	49.11N	68.16W
Hauula, Hi., U.S.	94a	21.37N	157.45W
Hauz Rāni, neigh., India	240d	28.32N	77.13E
Havana, Cuba	117	23.08N	82.23W
Havana, Il., U.S. (hȧ-vă′nȧ)	111	40.17N	90.02W
Havasu, Lake, res., U.S. (hăv′ȧ-so͞o)	109	34.26N	114.09W
Havel, r., Ger. (hä′fĕl)	154	53.09N	13.10E
Havel-Kanal, can., Ger.	145b	52.36N	13.12E
Haverford, Pa., U.S.	229b	40.01N	75.18W
Haverhill, Ma., U.S. (hā′vẽr-hĭl)	93a	42.46N	71.05W
Haverhill, N.H., U.S.	99	44.00N	72.05W
Havering, neigh., Eng., U.K.	235	51.34N	0.14E
Havering's Grove, Eng., U.K.	235	51.38N	0.23E
Haverstraw, N.Y., U.S. (hā′vẽr-strô)	100a	41.11N	73.58W
Havertown, Pa., U.S.	229b	39.59N	75.18W
Havlíckuv Brod, Czech Rep.	147	49.38N	15.34E
Havre, Mt., U.S. (hăv′ẽr)	96	48.34N	109.42W
Havre-Boucher, Can. (hăv′rȧ-bo͞o-shā′)	93	45.42N	61.30W
Havre de Grace, Md., U.S. (hăv′ẽr dē grās′)	99	39.35N	76.05W
Havre-Saint Pierre, Can.	92	50.15N	63.36W
Haw, r., N.C., U.S. (hô)	115	36.17N	79.46W
Hawaii, state, U.S.	96c	20.00N	157.40W
Hawaii, i., Hi., U.S. (hä wī′ē)	96c	19.50N	157.15W
Hawaiian Gardens, Ca., U.S.	232	33.50N	118.04W
Hawaiian Islands, is., Hi., U.S. (hä-wī′ȧn)	96c	22.00N	158.00W
Hawaii Volcanoes National Park, rec., Hi., U.S.	96c	19.30N	155.25W
Hawarden, Ia., U.S. (hā′wȧr-dĕn)	102	43.00N	96.28W
Hawf, Jabal, hills, Egypt	244a	29.55N	31.21E
Hawi, Hi., U.S. (hä′wē)	94a	20.16N	155.48W
Hawick, Scot., U.K. (hô′ĭk)	150	55.25N	2.55W
Hawke Bay, b., N.Z. (hôk)	203a	39.17S	177.20E
Hawker, Austl. (hô′kẽr)	204	31.58S	138.12E
Hawkesbury, Can. (hôks′bẽr-ĭ)	91	45.35N	74.35W
Hawkinsville, Ga., U.S. (hô′kĭnz-vĭl)	114	32.15N	83.30W
Hawks Nest Point, c., Bah.	123	24.05N	75.30W
Hawley, Eng., U.K.	235	51.25N	0.14E
Hawley, Mn., U.S. (hô′lĭ)	102	46.52N	96.18W
Haworth, Eng., U.K. (hā′wûrth)	144a	53.50N	1.57W
Haworth, N.J., U.S.	228	40.58N	73.59W
Hawthorn, Austl.	243b	37.49S	145.02E
Hawthorne, Ca., U.S. (hô′thôrn)	107a	33.55N	118.22W
Hawthorne, Nv., U.S.	108	38.33N	118.39W
Hawthorne, N.J., U.S.	228	40.57N	74.09W
Haxtun, Co., U.S. (hăks′tŭn)	110	40.39N	102.38W
Hay, r., Austl. (hā)	202	23.00S	136.45E
Hay, r., Can.	84	60.21N	117.14W
Hayama, Japan (hä-yä′mä)	195a	35.16N	139.35E
Hayashi, Japan (hä-yä′shē)	195a	35.13N	139.38E
Hayden, Az., U.S. (hā′dĕn)	109	33.00N	110.50W
Hayes, neigh., Eng., U.K.	235	51.23N	0.01E
Hayes, r., Can.	85	55.25N	93.55W
Hayes, Mount, mtn., Ak., U.S. (hāz)	95	63.32N	146.40W
Haynesville, La., U.S. (hānz′vĭl)	113	32.55N	93.08W
Hayrabolu, Tur.	161	41.14N	27.05E
Hay River, Can.	84	60.50N	115.53W
Hays, Ks., U.S. (hāz)	110	38.51N	99.20W
Haystack Mountain, mtn., Wa., U.S. (hā-stăk′)	106a	48.26N	122.07W
Haysyn, Ukr.	167	48.46N	29.22E
Hayward, Ca., U.S. (hā′wẽrd)	106b	37.40N	122.06W
Hayward, Wi., U.S.	103	46.01N	91.31W
Hazard, Ky., U.S. (hăz′ȧrd)	114	37.13N	83.10W
Hazel Grove, Eng., U.K.	237b	53.23N	2.08W
Hazelhurst, Ga., U.S. (hā′z′l-hûrst)	115	31.50N	82.36W
Hazelhurst, Ms., U.S.	114	31.52N	90.23W
Hazel Park, Mi., U.S.	101b	42.28N	83.06W
Hazelton, Can. (hā′z′l-tŭn)	84	55.15N	127.40W
Hazelton Mountains, mts., Can.	86	55.00N	128.00W
Hazleton, Pa., U.S.	99	41.00N	76.00W
Headland, Al., U.S. (hĕd′lănd)	114	31.22N	85.20W
Headley, Eng., U.K.	235	51.17N	0.16W
Heald Green, Eng., U.K.	237b	53.22N	2.14W
Healdsburg, Ca., U.S. (hēldz′bûrg)	108	38.37N	122.52W
Healdton, Ok., U.S. (hēld′tŭn)	111	34.13N	97.28W
Heanor, Eng., U.K. (hēn′ŏr)	144a	53.01N	1.22W
Heard Island, i., Austl. (hûrd)	3	53.10S	74.35E
Hearne, Tx., U.S. (hûrn)	113	30.53N	96.35W
Hearst, Can. (hûrst)	85	49.36N	83.40W
Heart, r., N.D., U.S. (härt)	102	46.46N	102.34W
Heart Lake Indian Reserve, I.R., Can.	87	55.02N	111.30W

PLACE (Pronunciation)	PAGE	Lat. °′	Long. °′
Heart's Content, Can. (härts kŏn′tĕnt)	93	47.52N	53.22W
Heathmont, Austl.	243b	37.49S	145.15E
Heaton Moor, Eng., U.K.	237b	53.25N	2.11W
Heavener, Ok., U.S. (hēv′nẽr)	111	34.52N	94.36W
Heaverham, Eng., U.K.	235	51.18N	0.15E
Heaviley, Eng., U.K.	237b	53.24N	2.09W
Hebbronville, Tx., U.S. (hē′brŭn-vĭl)	112	27.18N	98.40W
Hebbville, Md., U.S.	229c	39.20N	77.46W
Hebei, prov., China (hŭ-bā)	189	39.15N	115.40E
Heber City, Ut., U.S. (hē′bẽr)	109	40.30N	111.25W
Heber Springs, Ar., U.S.	111	35.28N	91.59W
Hebgen Lake, res., Mt., U.S. (hĕb′gĕn)	105	44.47N	111.38W
Hebrides, is., Scot., U.K.	142	57.00N	6.30W
Hebrides, Sea of the, sea, Scot., U.K.	150	57.00N	7.00W
Hebron, Can. (hēb′rŭn)	85	58.11N	62.56W
Hebron, In., U.S.	101a	41.19N	87.13W
Hebron, Ky., U.S.	101f	39.04N	84.43W
Hebron, Ne., U.S.	111	40.11N	97.36W
Hebron, N.D., U.S.	102	46.54N	102.04W
Hebron see Al Khalīl, W. Bank	181a	31.31N	35.07E
Heby, Swe. (hĭ′bü)	152	59.56N	16.48E
Hecate Strait, strt., Can. (hĕk′ȧ-tē)	84	53.00N	131.00W
Hecelchakán, Mex. (ā-sĕl-chä-kän′)	119	20.10N	90.09W
Hechi, China (hŭ-chr)	193	24.50N	108.18E
Hechuan, China (hŭ-chyuän)	188	30.00N	106.20E
Hecla Island, i., Can.	89	51.08N	96.45W
Hedemora, Swe. (hĭ-dĕ-mō′rä)	152	60.16N	15.55E
Hedon, Eng., U.K. (hĕ-dŭn)	144a	53.44N	0.12W
Heemstede, Neth.	145a	52.20N	4.36E
Heerdt, neigh., Ger.	236	51.13N	6.43E
Heerlen, Neth.	151	50.55N	5.58E
Hefei, China (hŭ-fā)	189	31.51N	117.15E
Heflin, Al., U.S. (hĕf′lĭn)	114	33.40N	85.33W
Heide, Ger. (hī′dē)	154	54.13N	9.06E
Heide, neigh., Ger.	236	51.31N	6.52E
Heidelberg, Austl. (hī′dĕl-bûrg)	201a	37.45S	145.04E
Heidelberg, Ger. (hīdĕl-bĕrgh)	147	49.24N	8.43E
Heidelberg, S. Afr.	218d	26.32S	28.22E
Heidelberg, Pa., U.S.	230b	40.23N	80.05W
Heidenheim, Ger. (hī′dĕn-hīm)	154	48.41N	10.09E
Heil, Ger.	236	51.38N	7.35E
Heilbron, S. Afr. (hĭl′brōn)	218d	27.17S	27.58E
Heilbronn, Ger. (hīl′brōn)	147	49.09N	9.16E
Heiligenhaus, Ger. (hī′lē-gĕn-houz)	157c	51.19N	6.58E
Heiligensee, neigh., Ger.	238a	52.36N	13.13E
Heiligenstadt, Ger. (hī′lē-gĕn-shtät)	154	51.21N	10.10E
Heilongjiang, prov., China (hā-lôŋ-jyäŋ)	189	46.36N	128.07E
Heinersdorf, Ger.	238a	52.23N	13.20E
Heinersdorf, neigh., Ger.	238a	52.34N	13.27E
Heinola, Fin. (hā-nō′lä)	153	61.13N	26.03E
Heinsberg, Ger. (hīnz′bĕrgh)	157c	51.04N	6.07E
Heisingen, neigh., Ger.	236	51.25N	7.04E
Heist-op-den-Berg, Bel.	145a	51.05N	4.14E
Hejaz see Al Ḩijāz, reg., Sau. Ar.	182	23.45N	39.08E
Hejian, China (hŭ-jyĕn)	192	38.28N	116.05E
Hekla, vol., Ice.	142	63.53N	19.37W
Hel, Pol. (hāl)	155	54.37N	18.53E
Helagsfjället, mtn., Swe.	146	62.54N	12.24E
Helan Shan, mts., China (hŭ-län shän)	188	38.02N	105.20E
Helena, Ar., U.S. (hē-lē′nȧ)	97	34.33N	90.35W
Helena, Mt., U.S. (hĕ-lĕ′nȧ)	96	46.35N	112.01W
Helensburgh, Austl. (hĕl′ĕnz-bŭr-ō)	201b	34.11S	150.59E
Helensburgh, Scot., U.K.	150	56.01N	4.53W
Helgoland, i., Ger. (hĕl′gō-länd)	154	54.13N	7.30E
Heliopolis, hist., Egypt	244a	30.08N	31.17E
Hellier, Ky., U.S. (hĕl′yẽr)	115	37.16N	82.27W
Hellín, Spain (ĕl-yĕn′)	148	38.30N	1.40W
Hells Canyon, val., U.S.	104	45.20N	116.45W
Helmand, r., Afg. (hĕl′mŭnd)	182	31.00N	63.48E
Helmond, Neth. (hĕl′mōnt) (ĕl′môN′)	151	51.35N	5.04E
Helmstedt, Ger. (hĕlm′shtĕt)	154	52.14N	11.03E
Hel′myaziv, Ukr.	163	49.49N	31.54E
Helotes, Tx., U.S. (hē′lōts)	107d	29.35N	98.41W
Helper, Ut., U.S. (hĕlp′ẽr)	109	39.40N	110.55W
Helsby, Eng., U.K.	237a	53.16N	2.46W
Helsingborg, Swe. (hĕl′sĭng-bôrgh)	146	56.04N	12.40E
Helsingfors see Helsinki, Fin.	142	60.10N	24.53E
Helsingør, Den. (hĕl-sĭng-ûr′)	146	56.03N	12.33E
Helsinki, Fin. (hĕl′sĕn-kē)	142	60.10N	24.53E
Hemel Hempstead, Eng., U.K. (hĕm′ĕl hĕmp′stĕd)	144b	51.43N	0.29W
Hemer, Ger.	157c	51.22N	7.46E
Hemet, Ca., U.S. (hĕm′ĕt)	107a	33.45N	116.57W
Hemingford, Ne., U.S. (hĕm′ĭng-fẽrd)	102	42.21N	103.30W
Hemphill, Tx., U.S. (hĕmp′hĭl)	113	31.20N	93.48W
Hempstead, N.Y., U.S. (hĕmp′stĕd)	100a	40.42N	73.37W
Hempstead, Tx., U.S.	113	30.07N	96.05W
Hemse, Swe. (hĕm′sĕ)	152	57.15N	18.25E
Hemsön, i., Swe.	152	62.43N	18.22E
Henan, prov., China (hŭ-nän)	189	33.58N	112.33E
Henares, r., Spain (å-nä′rås)	158	40.50N	2.55W
Henderson, Ky., U.S. (hĕn′dẽr-sŭn)	98	37.50N	87.30W
Henderson, Nv., U.S.	108	36.09N	115.04W
Henderson, N.C., U.S.	115	36.18N	78.24W
Henderson, Tn., U.S.	114	35.25N	88.40W
Henderson, Tx., U.S.	113	32.09N	94.48W
Hendersonville, N.C., U.S. (hĕn′dẽr-sŭn-vĭl)	115	35.17N	82.28W
Hendersonville, Tn., U.S.	114	36.18N	86.37W
Hendon, Eng., U.K. (hĕn′dŭn)	144b	51.34N	0.13W
Hendrina, S. Afr. (hĕn-drē′nȧ)	218d	26.10S	29.44E
Hengch'un, Tai. (hĕng′chŭn′)	193	22.00N	120.42E
Hengelo, Neth. (hĕngĕ-lō)	151	52.20N	6.45E
Hengshan, China (hĕng′shän′)	193	27.20N	112.40E
Hengshui, China (hĕng′sho͞o-ē′)	190	37.43N	115.42E
Hengxian, China (hŭŋ shyĕn)	193	22.40N	109.20E
Hengyang, China	189	26.58N	112.30E

296 Heniches'k – Holly

PLACE (Pronunciation)	PAGE	Lat. °′	Long. °′
Heniches'k, Ukr.	167	46.11N	34.47E
Henley on Thames, Eng., U.K. (hĕn'lē ŏn tĕmz)	144b	51.31N	0.54W
Henlopen, Cape, c., De., U.S. (hĕn-lō'pĕn)	99	38.45N	75.05W
Hennebont, Fr. (ĕn-bôN')	156	47.47N	3.16W
Hennenman, S. Afr.	218d	27.59S	27.03E
Hennessey, Ok., U.S. (hĕn'ĕ-sĭ)	111	36.04N	97.53W
Hennigsdorf, Ger. (hĕ'nĕngz-dōrf))	145b	52.39N	13.12E
Hennops, r., S. Afr. (hĕn'ŏps)	213b	25.51S	27.57E
Hennopsrivier, S. Afr.	213b	25.50S	27.59E
Henrietta, Ok., U.S. (hĕn-rĭ-ĕt'ȧ)	111	35.25N	95.58W
Henrietta, Tx., U.S. (hen-rĭ-ĕ'tȧ)	110	33.47N	98.11W
Henrietta Maria, Cape, c., Can. (hĕn-rĭ-ĕt'ȧ)	85	55.10N	82.20W
Henry Mountains, mts., Ut., U.S. (hĕn'rĭ)	96	37.55N	110.45W
Henrys Fork, r., Id., U.S.	105	43.52N	111.55W
Henteyn Nuruu, mtn., Russia	192	49.40N	111.00E
Hentiyn Nuruu, mts., Mong.	188	49.25N	107.51E
Henzada, Myanmar	183	17.38N	95.28E
Heppner, Or., U.S. (hĕp'nẽr)	104	45.21N	119.33W
Hepu, China (hŭ-po͞o)	193	21.28N	109.10E
Herāt, Afg. (hĕ-rät')	182	34.28N	62.13E
Herbede, Ger.	236	51.25N	7.16E
Hercules, Can.	83g	53.27N	113.20W
Herdecke, Ger. (hĕr'dĕ-kĕ)	157c	51.24N	7.26E
Heredia, C.R. (ā-rā'dhē-ä)	121	10.04N	84.06W
Hereford, Eng., U.K. (hĕrĕ'fẽrd)	150	52.05N	2.44W
Hereford, Md., U.S.	100e	39.35N	76.42W
Hereford, Tx., U.S. (hĕr'ĕ-fẽrd)	110	34.47N	102.25W
Hereford and Worcester, co., Eng., U.K.	144a	52.24N	2.15W
Herencia, Spain (å-rān'thē-ä)	158	39.23N	3.22W
Herentals, Bel.	145a	51.10N	4.51E
Herford, Ger. (hĕr'fôrt)	154	52.06N	8.42E
Herington, Ks., U.S. (hĕr'ĭng-tŭn)	111	38.41N	96.57W
Herisau, Switz. (hā'rē-zou)	154	47.23N	9.18E
Herk-de-Stad, Bel.	145a	50.56N	5.13E
Herkimer, N.Y., U.S. (hûr'kĭ-mẽr)	99	43.05N	75.00W
Hermannskogel, mtn., Aus.	239e	48.16N	16.18E
Hermansville, Mi., U.S. (hûr'mȧns-vĭl)	98	45.40N	87.35W
Hermantown, Mn., U.S. (hẽr'mȧn-toun)	107h	46.46N	92.12W
Hermanusdorings, S. Afr.	218d	24.08S	27.46E
Herminie, Pa., U.S. (hûr-mĭ'nē)	101e	40.16N	79.45W
Hermitage Bay, b., Can. (hûr'mĭ-tĕj)	93	47.35N	56.05W
Hermit Islands, is., Pap. N. Gui. (hûr'mĭt)	197	1.48S	144.55E
Hermosa Beach, Ca., U.S. (hẽr-mō'sȧ)	107a	33.51N	118.24W
Hermosillo, Mex. (ĕr-mô-sē'l-yō)	116	29.00N	110.57W
Hermsdorf, neigh., Ger.	238a	52.37N	13.18E
Hernals, neigh., Aus.	239e	48.13N	16.20E
Herndon, Va., U.S. (hĕrn'don)	100e	38.58N	77.22W
Herne, Ger. (hĕr'nĕ)	157c	51.32N	7.13E
Herning, Den. (hĕr'nĭng)	146	56.08N	8.55E
Hernwood Heights, Md., U.S.	229c	39.22N	77.50W
Héroes Chapultepec, Mex.	233a	19.28N	99.04W
Héroes de Churubusco, Mex.	233a	19.22N	99.06W
Heron, l., Mn., U.S. (hĕr'ŭn)	102	43.42N	95.23W
Herongate, Eng., U.K.	235	51.36N	0.21E
Heron Lake, Mn., U.S.	102	43.48N	95.20W
Heronsgate, Eng., U.K.	235	51.38N	0.31W
Herrero, Punta, Mex. (pö'n-tä-ĕr-rĕ'rô)	120a	19.18N	87.24W
Herrin, Il., U.S. (hĕr'ĭn)	98	37.50N	89.00W
Herschel, S. Afr. (hĕr'-shĕl)	213c	30.37S	27.12E
Herscher, Il., U.S. (hĕr'shẽr)	101a	41.03N	88.06W
Hersham, Eng., U.K.	235	51.22N	0.23W
Herstal, Bel. (hĕr'stäl)	151	50.42N	5.32E
Herten, Ger.	236	51.35N	7.07E
Hertford, Eng., U.K.	150	51.48N	0.05W
Hertford, N.C., U.S. (hûrt'fẽrd)	115	36.10N	76.30W
Hertfordshire, co., Eng., U.K.	144b	51.46N	0.05W
Hertzberg, Ger. (hĕrtz'bĕrgh)	145b	52.54N	12.58E
Hervás, Spain	158	40.16N	5.51W
Herzliyya, Isr.	181a	32.10N	34.49E
Hessen, hist. reg., Ger. (hĕs'ĕn)	154	50.42N	9.00E
Heswall, Eng., U.K.	237a	53.20N	3.06W
Hetch Hetchy Aqueduct, Ca., U.S. (hĕtch hĕt'chĭ ăk'wē-dŭkt)	108	37.27N	120.54W
Hettinger, N.D., U.S. (hĕt'ĭn-jẽr)	102	45.58N	102.36W
Hetzendorf, neigh., Aus.	239e	48.10N	16.18E
Heuningspruit, S. Afr.	218d	27.28S	27.26E
Heven, neigh., Ger.	236	51.26N	7.17E
Hewlett, N.Y., U.S.	228	40.38N	73.42W
Hewlett Harbor, N.Y., U.S.	228	40.38N	73.41W
Hexian, China	190	31.44N	118.20E
Hexian, China (hŭ shyĕn)	193	24.20N	111.28E
Hextable, Eng., U.K.	235	51.25N	0.11E
Heyang, China (hŭ-yäŋ)	192	35.18N	110.18E
Heystekrand, S. Afr.	218d	25.16S	27.14E
Heyuan, China (hŭ-yůän)	193	23.48N	114.45E
Heywood, Eng., U.K. (hā'wŏd)	144a	53.36N	2.12W
Heze, China (hŭ-dzŭ)	190	35.13N	115.28E
Hialeah, Fl., U.S. (hī-ȧ-lē'ăh)	115a	25.49N	80.18W
Hiawatha, Ks., U.S. (hī-ȧ-wô'thȧ)	111	39.50N	95.33W
Hiawatha, Ut., U.S.	109	39.25N	111.05W
Hibbing, Mn., U.S. (hĭb'ĭng)	97	47.26N	92.58W
Hickman, Ky., U.S. (hĭk'mȧn)	114	34.33N	89.10W
Hickory, N.C., U.S. (hĭk'ō-rĭ)	115	35.43N	81.21W
Hickory Hills, Il., U.S.	231a	41.43N	87.49W
Hicksville, N.Y., U.S.	98	41.15N	84.45W
Hicksville, N.Y., U.S. (hĭks'vĭl)	100a	40.47N	73.25W
Hico, Tx., U.S. (hī'kō)	112	32.00N	98.02W
Hidalgo, Mex.	112	27.49N	99.53W
Hidalgo, Mex. (ē-dhäl'gō)	118	24.14N	99.25W
Hidalgo, state, Mex.	116	20.45N	99.30W
Hidalgo del Parral, Mex. (ē-dä'l-gō-dĕl-pär-rá'l)	116	26.55N	105.40W

PLACE (Pronunciation)	PAGE	Lat. °′	Long. °′
Hidalgo Yalalag, Mex. (ē-dhäl'gō-yä-lä-läg)	119	17.12N	96.11W
Hiddinghausen, Ger.	236	51.22N	7.17E
Hierro Island, i., Spain (yĕ'r-rô)	210	27.37N	18.29W
Hiesfeld, Ger.	236	51.33N	6.46E
Hietzing, neigh., Aus.	239e	48.11N	16.18E
Higashi, neigh., Japan	242b	34.41N	135.31E
Higashimurayama, Japan	195a	35.46N	139.28E
Higashinada, neigh., Japan	242b	34.43N	135.16E
Higashinakano, Japan	242a	35.38N	139.25E
Higashinari, neigh., Japan	242b	34.40N	135.33E
Higashiōizumi, neigh., Japan	242a	35.45N	139.36E
Higashiōsaka, Japan	195b	34.40N	135.44E
Higashisumiyoshi, neigh., Japan	242b	34.37N	135.32E
Higashiyama, neigh., Japan	241e	35.00N	135.48E
Higashiyodogawa, neigh., Japan	242b	34.44N	135.29E
Higgins, l., Mi., U.S. (hĭg'ĭnz)	98	44.20N	84.45W
Higginsville, Mo., U.S. (hĭg'ĭnz-vĭl)	111	39.05N	93.44W
High, i., Mi., U.S.	98	45.45N	85.45W
Higham, Eng., U.K.	235	51.26N	0.28E
High Beach, Eng., U.K.	235	51.39N	0.02E
High Bluff, Can.	83f	50.01N	98.08W
Highborne Cay, i., Bah. (hībôrn kē)	122	24.45N	76.50W
Highcliff, Pa., U.S.	230b	40.32N	80.03W
Higher Broughton, neigh., Eng., U.K.	237b	53.30N	2.15W
Highgrove, Ca., U.S. (hī'grōv)	107a	34.01N	117.20W
High Island, Tx., U.S.	113a	29.34N	94.24W
Highland, Ca., U.S. (hī'lănd)	107a	34.08N	117.13W
Highland, Il., U.S.	111	38.44N	89.41W
Highland, In., U.S.	101a	41.33N	87.28W
Highland, Mi., U.S.	101b	42.38N	83.37W
Highland, Pa., U.S.	230b	40.33N	80.04W
Highland Park, Il., U.S.	101a	42.11N	87.47W
Highland Park, Md., U.S.	229d	38.54N	76.54W
Highland Park, Mi., U.S.	101b	42.24N	83.06W
Highland Park, N.J., U.S.	100a	40.30N	74.25W
Highland Park, Tx., U.S.	107c	32.49N	96.48W
Highlands, N.J., U.S. (hī-lăndz)	100a	40.24N	73.59W
Highlands, Tx., U.S.	113a	29.49N	95.01W
High Laver, Eng., U.K.	235	51.45N	0.13E
Highmore, S.D., U.S. (hī'mōr)	102	44.30N	99.26W
High Ongar, Eng., U.K. (on'gẽr)	144b	51.43N	0.15E
High Peak, mtn., Phil.	197a	15.38N	120.05E
High Point, N.C., U.S.	115	35.55N	80.00W
High Prairie, Can.	84	55.26N	116.29W
High Ridge, Mo., U.S.	107e	38.27N	90.32W
High River, Can.	84	50.35N	113.52W
High Rock Lake, res., N.C., U.S. (hī'-rŏk)	115	35.40N	80.15W
High Springs, Fl., U.S.	115	29.48N	82.38W
High Tatra Mountains, mts., Eur.	155	49.15N	19.40E
Hightown, Eng., U.K.	237a	53.32N	3.04W
Hightstown, N.J., U.S. (hīts-toun)	100a	40.16N	74.32W
High Wycombe, Eng., U.K. (wĭ-kŭm)	150	51.36N	0.45W
Higuero, Punta, c., P.R.	117b	18.21N	67.11W
Higuerote, Ven. (ē-gĕ-rô'tĕ)	131b	10.29N	66.06W
Higüey, Dom. Rep. (ē-gwĕ'y)	123	18.40N	68.45W
Hiiumaa, i., Est. (hē'ŏm-ô)	166	58.47N	22.05E
Hikone, Japan (hē'kô-nĕ)	195	35.15N	136.15E
Hildburghausen, Ger. (hĭld'bŏrg hou-zĕn)	154	50.26N	10.45E
Hilden, Ger. (hĕl'dĕn)	157c	51.10N	6.56E
Hildesheim, Ger. (hĭl'dĕs-hīm)	147	52.08N	9.56E
Hillaby, Mount, mtn., Barb. (hĭl'ȧ-bĭ)	121b	13.15N	59.35W
Hill City, Ks., U.S. (hĭl)	110	39.22N	99.54W
Hill City, Mn., U.S.	103	46.58N	93.38W
Hill Crest, Pa., U.S.	229b	40.05N	75.11W
Hillcrest Heights, Md., U.S.	229d	38.52N	76.57W
Hillegersberg, Neth.	145a	51.57N	4.29E
Hillen, neigh., Ger.	236	51.37N	7.13E
Hillerød, Den. (hē'lĕ-rûdh)	152	55.56N	12.17E
Hillingdon, neigh., Eng., U.K.	235	51.32N	0.27W
Hillsboro, Il., U.S. (hĭlz'bŭr-ō)	111	39.09N	89.28W
Hillsboro, Ks., U.S.	111	38.22N	97.11W
Hillsboro, N.H., U.S.	99	43.05N	71.55W
Hillsboro, N.D., U.S.	102	47.23N	97.05W
Hillsboro, Oh., U.S.	98	39.10N	83.40W
Hillsboro, Or., U.S.	106c	45.31N	122.59W
Hillsboro, Tx., U.S.	113	32.01N	97.06W
Hillsboro, Wi., U.S.	103	43.39N	90.20W
Hillsburgh, Can. (hĭlz'bûrg)	83d	43.48N	80.09W
Hills Creek Lake, res., Or., U.S.	104	43.41N	122.26W
Hillsdale, Mi., U.S. (hĭls-dāl)	109	41.55N	84.35W
Hillside, Md., U.S.	229d	38.52N	76.55W
Hillside, neigh., N.Y., U.S.	228	40.42N	73.47W
Hillwood, Va., U.S.	229d	38.52N	77.10W
Hilo, Hi., U.S. (hē'lō)	96c	19.44N	155.01W
Hiltrop, neigh., Ger.	236	51.30N	7.15E
Hilvarenbeek, Neth.	145a	51.29N	5.10E
Hilversum, Neth. (hĭl'vẽr-sŭm)	145a	52.13N	5.10E
Himachal Pradesh, India	183	32.00N	77.30E
Himalayas, mts., Asia	183	29.30N	85.02E
Himeji, Japan (hē'mȧ-jē)	194	34.50N	134.42E
Himmelgeist, neigh., Ger.	236	51.10N	6.49E
Himmelpforten, Ger. (hē'mĕl-pfôr-tĕn)	145c	53.37N	9.19E
Ḥimṣ, Syria	182	34.44N	36.43E
Hinche, Haiti (hēn'chȧ) (äNsh)	123	19.10N	72.05W
Hinchinbrook, i., Austl. (hĭn-chĭn-bro͝ok)	202	18.23S	146.57W
Hinckley, Eng., U.K. (hĭnk'lĭ)	144a	52.32N	1.21W
Hindley, Eng., U.K. (hĭnd'lĭ)	144a	53.32N	2.35W
Hindu Kush, mts., Asia (hĭn'do͞o ko͞osh')	183	35.15N	68.44E
Hindupur, India (hĭn'do͞o-po͞or)	187	13.52N	77.34E
Hingham, Ma., U.S. (hĭng'ăm)	93a	42.14N	70.53W
Hinkley, Oh., U.S. (hĭnk'-lĭ)	101d	41.14N	81.45W
Hino, Japan	242a	35.41N	139.24E
Hinojosa del Duque, Spain (ē-nô-kô'sä)	158	38.30N	5.09W
Hinsdale, Il., U.S. (hĭnz'dāl)	101a	41.48N	87.56W

PLACE (Pronunciation)	PAGE	Lat. °′	Long. °′
Hinsel, neigh., Ger.	236	51.26N	7.05E
Hinton, Can. (hĭn'tŭn)	87	53.25N	117.34W
Hinton, W.V., U.S. (hĭn'tŭn)	98	37.40N	80.55W
Hirado, i., Japan (hē'rä-dō)	194	33.19N	129.18E
Hirakata, Japan (hē'rä-kä'tä)	195b	34.49N	135.40E
Hirara, Japan	198d	24.48N	125.17E
Hiratsuka, Japan (hē-rät-so͞o'kȧ)	195	35.20N	139.19E
Hirosaki, Japan (hē'rô-sä'kē)	189	40.31N	140.38E
Hirose, Japan (hē'rô-sä)	195	35.20N	133.11E
Hiroshima, Japan (hē-rô-shē'mȧ)	189	34.22N	132.25E
Hirota, Japan	242b	34.45N	135.21E
Hirschstetten, neigh., Aus.	239e	48.14N	16.29E
Hirson, Fr. (ēr-sôN')	156	49.54N	4.00E
Hisar, India	186	29.15N	75.47E
Hispaniola, i., N.A. (hĭ'spăn-ĭ-ō-lȧ)	117	17.30N	73.15W
Hitachi, Japan (hē-tä'chē)	194	36.42N	140.47E
Hitchcock, Tx., U.S. (hĭch'kŏk)	113a	29.21N	95.01W
Hither Green, neigh., Eng., U.K.	235	51.27N	0.01W
Hitoyoshi, Japan (hē'tô-yō'shē)	195	32.13N	130.45E
Hitra, i., Nor. (hĭträ)	146	63.34N	7.37E
Hittefeld, Ger. (hē'tĕ-fĕld)	145c	53.23N	9.59E
Hiwasa, Japan (hē'wȧ-sä)	195	33.44N	134.31E
Hiwassee, r., Tn., U.S. (hī-wôs'sē)	114	35.10N	84.35W
Hjälmaren, l., Swe.	146	59.07N	16.05E
Hjo, Swe. (yō)	152	58.19N	14.11E
Hjørring, Den. (jûr'ĭng)	146	57.27N	9.59E
Hlobyne, Ukr.	163	49.22N	33.17E
Hlohovec, Slvk. (hlō'ho-vĕts)	155	48.24N	17.49E
Hlukhiv, Ukr.	167	51.42N	33.52E
Hobart, Austl. (hō'bȧrt)	203	43.00S	147.30E
Hobart, In., U.S.	101a	41.31N	87.15W
Hobart, Ok., U.S.	110	35.02N	99.06W
Hobart, Wa., U.S.	106a	47.25N	121.58W
Hobbs, N.M., U.S. (hŏbs)	110	32.41N	103.15W
Hoboken, Bel. (hō'bō-kĕn)	145a	51.11N	4.20E
Hoboken, N.J., U.S.	100a	40.43N	74.03W
Hobro, Den. (hô-brô')	152	56.38N	9.47E
Hobson, Va., U.S. (hŏb'sŭn)	100g	36.54N	76.31W
Hobson's Bay, b., Austl. (hŏb'sŭnz)	201a	37.54S	144.45E
Hobyo, Som.	218a	5.24N	48.28E
Hochdahl, Ger.	236	51.13N	6.56E
Hochheide, Ger.	236	51.27N	6.41E
Ho Chi Minh City, Viet.	196	10.46N	106.34E
Hochlar, neigh., Ger.	236	51.36N	7.10E
Höchsten, Ger.	236	51.27N	7.29E
Hockinson, Wa., U.S. (hŏk'ĭn-sŭn)	106c	45.44N	122.29W
Hoctún, Mex. (ŏk-to͞o'n)	120a	20.52N	89.10W
Hodgenville, Ky., U.S. (hŏj'ĕn-vĭl)	98	37.35N	85.45W
Hodges Hill, mtn., Can. (hŏj'ĕz)	93	49.04N	55.53W
Hodgkins, Il., U.S.	231a	41.46N	87.51W
Hódmezővásárhely, Hung. (hōd'mĕ-zû-vō'shôr-hĕl-y')	155	46.24N	20.21E
Hodna, Chott el, l., Alg.	148	35.20N	3.27E
Hodonin, Czech Rep. (hē'dô-nén)	155	48.50N	17.06E
Hoegaarden, Bel.	145a	50.46N	4.55E
Hoek van Holland, Neth.	145a	51.59N	4.05E
Hoeryŏng, N. Kor. (hwĕr'yŭng)	194	42.28N	129.39E
Hof, Ger. (hōf)	154	50.19N	11.55E
Hofburg, pt. of i., Aus.	239e	48.12N	16.22E
Hofsjökull, ice., Ice. (hôfs'yŭ'ko͞ol)	146	64.55N	18.40W
Hog, i., Mi., U.S.	98	45.50N	85.20W
Hogansville, Ga., U.S. (hō'gănz-vĭl)	114	33.10N	84.54W
Hogar y Redención, Mex.	233a	19.22N	99.13W
Hog Cay, i., Bah.	123	23.35N	75.30W
Hogsty Reef, rf., Bah.	123	21.45N	73.50W
Hohenbrunn, Ger. (hō'hĕn-bro͞on)	145d	48.03N	11.42E
Hohenlimburg, Ger. (hō'hĕn lĕm'bo͞org)	157c	51.20N	7.35E
Hohen Neuendorf, Ger. (hō'hĕn noi'ĕn-dōrf)	145b	52.40N	13.22E
Hohenschönhausen, neigh., Ger.	238a	52.33N	13.30E
Hohensyburg, hist., Ger.	236	51.25N	7.29E
Hohe Tauern, mts., Aus. (hō'ĕ tou'ĕrn)	154	47.11N	12.12E
Hohhot, China (hŭ-ho͞o-tŭ)	189	41.05N	111.50E
Hohoe, Ghana	214	7.09N	0.28E
Hohokus, N.J., U.S. (hō-hō-kŭs)	100a	41.01N	74.08W
Höhscheid, neigh., Ger.	236	51.09N	7.04E
Hoi An, Viet.	193	15.48N	108.30E
Hoisington, Ks., U.S. (hoi'zĭng-tŭn)	110	38.30N	98.46W
Hoisten, Ger.	236	51.08N	6.42E
Hojo, Japan (hō'jō)	195	33.58N	132.50E
Hokitika, N.Z. (hō-kĭ-tē'kä)	203a	42.43S	170.59E
Hokkaidō, i., Japan (hŏk'kĭ-dō)	194	43.30N	142.45E
Holbaek, Den. (hôl'bĕk)	152	55.42N	11.40E
Holborn, neigh., Eng., U.K.	235	51.31N	0.07W
Holbox, Mex. (ôl-bŏ'x)	120a	21.33N	87.19W
Holbox, Isla, i., Mex. (ē's-lä-ôl-bŏ'x)	120a	21.40N	87.21W
Holbrook, Az., U.S. (hōl'brŏk)	109	34.55N	110.15W
Holbrook, Ma., U.S.	93a	42.10N	71.01W
Holden, Ma., U.S. (hōl'dĕn)	93a	42.21N	71.51W
Holden, Mo., U.S.	111	38.42N	94.00W
Holden, W.V., U.S.	98	37.45N	82.05W
Holdenville, Ok., U.S. (hōl'dĕn-vĭl)	111	35.05N	96.25W
Holdrege, Ne., U.S. (hōl'drĕj)	110	40.25N	99.28W
Holguín, Cuba (ôl-gēn')	117	20.55N	76.15W
Holguín, prov., Cuba	122	20.40N	76.15W
Holidaysburg, Pa., U.S. (hŏl'ĭ-dāz-bûrg)	99	40.30N	78.30W
Hollabrunn, Aus.	154	48.33N	16.04E
Holland, Mi., U.S. (hŏl'ănd)	98	42.45N	86.10W
Hollands Diep, strt., Neth.	145a	51.43N	4.25E
Hollenstedt, Ger. (hō'lĕn-shtĕt)	145c	53.22N	9.43E
Hollins, Eng., U.K.	237b	53.34N	2.17W
Hollis, N.H., U.S. (hŏl'ĭs)	93a	42.30N	71.29W
Hollis, Ok., U.S.	110	34.39N	99.56W
Hollis, neigh., N.Y., U.S.	228	40.43N	73.46W
Hollister, Ca., U.S. (hŏl'ĭs-tẽr)	108	36.50N	121.25W
Holliston, Ma., U.S. (hōl'ĭs-tŭn)	93a	42.12N	71.25W
Holly, Mi., U.S. (hŏl'ĭ)	98	42.45N	83.30W

ăt; finăl; rāte; senāte; ärm; ȧsk; sofȧ; fâre; ch-choose; dh-as th in other; bē; ēvent; bĕt; recĕnt; cratẽr; g-gō; gh-guttural g; bĭt; ĭ-short neutral; rīde; K-guttural k as ch in German ich;

PLACE (Pronunciation)	PAGE	Lat. °′	Long. °′
Holly, Wa., U.S.	106a	47.34N	122.58W
Holly Springs, Ms., U.S. (hŏl'ĭ sprĭngz)	114	34.45N	89.28W
Hollywood, Ca., U.S. (hŏl'ē-wŏd)	107a	34.06N	118.20W
Hollywood, Fl., U.S.	115a	26.00N	80.11W
Hollywood Bowl, pt. of i., Ca., U.S.	232	34.07N	118.20W
Holmes, Pa., U.S.	229b	39.54N	75.19W
Holmes Reefs, rf., Austl. (hōmz)	203	16.33S	148.43E
Holmes Run Acres, Va., U.S.	229d	38.51N	77.13W
Holmestrand, Nor. (hôl'mĕ-strän)	152	59.29N	10.17E
Holmsbu, Nor. (hôlms'bo͞o)	152	59.36N	10.26E
Holmsjön, l., Swe.	152	62.23N	15.43E
Holroyd, Austl.	243a	33.50S	150.58E
Holstebro, Den. (hôl'stĕ-brô)	146	56.22N	8.39E
Holston, r., Tn., U.S. (hōl'stŭn)	114	36.02N	83.42W
Holt, Eng., U.K. (hōlt)	144a	53.05N	2.53W
Holten, neigh., Ger.	236	51.31N	6.48E
Holthausen, neigh., Ger.	236	51.34N	7.26E
Holton, Ks., U.S. (hōl'tŭn)	111	39.27N	95.43W
Holy Cross, Ak., U.S. (hō'lĭ krôs)	95	62.10N	159.40W
Holyhead, Wales, U.K. (hŏl'ē-hĕd)	150	53.18N	4.45W
Holy Island, i., Eng., U.K.	150	55.43N	1.48W
Holy Island, i., Wales, U.K. (hō'lĭ)	150	53.15N	4.45W
Holyoke, Co., U.S. (hōl'yōk)	110	40.36N	102.18W
Holyoke, Ma., U.S.	99	42.10N	72.40W
Holzen, Ger.	236	51.26N	7.31E
Holzheim, Ger.	236	51.09N	6.39E
Holzwickede, Ger.	236	51.30N	7.36E
Homano, Japan (hō-mä'nō)	195a	35.33N	140.08E
Homberg, Ger. (hōm'bĕrgh)	157c	51.27N	6.42E
Hombori, Mali	214	15.17N	1.42W
Home Gardens, Ca., U.S. (hōm gär'd'nz)	107a	33.53N	117.32W
Homeland, Ca., U.S. (hōm'lănd)	107a	33.44N	117.07W
Homer, Ak., U.S. (hō'mẽr)	95	59.42N	151.30W
Homer, La., U.S.	113	32.46N	93.05W
Homer Youngs Peak, mtn., Mt., U.S.	105	45.19N	113.41W
Homestead, Fl., U.S. (hōm'stĕd)	115a	25.27N	80.28W
Homestead, Mi., U.S.	107k	46.20N	84.07W
Homestead, Pa., U.S.	101e	40.29N	79.55W
Homestead National Monument of America, rec., Ne., U.S.	111	40.16N	96.51W
Hometown, Il., U.S.	231a	41.44N	87.44W
Homewood, Al., U.S. (hōm'wŏd)	100h	33.28N	86.48W
Homewood, Il., U.S.	101a	41.34N	87.40W
Homewood, neigh., Pa., U.S.	230b	40.27N	79.54W
Hominy, Ok., U.S. (hŏm'ĭ-nĭ)	111	36.25N	96.24W
Homochitto, r., Ms., U.S. (hō-mō-chĭt'ō)	114	31.23N	91.15W
Honda, Col. (hōn'dȧ)	130	5.13N	74.45W
Honda, Bahía, b., Cuba (bä-ē'ä-ō'n-dä)	122	23.10N	83.20W
Hondo, Tx., U.S.	112	29.20N	99.08W
Hondo, r., N.M., U.S.	110	33.22N	105.06W
Hondo, Río, r., N.A. (hon-dō')	120a	18.16N	88.32W
Honduras, nation, N.A. (hŏn-do͞o'rȧs)	116	14.30N	88.00W
Honduras, Gulf of, b., N.A.	116	16.30N	87.30W
Honea Path, S.C., U.S. (hŭn'ĭ păth)	115	34.25N	82.16W
Hønefoss, Nor. (hē'nĕ-fôs)	146	60.10N	10.15E
Honesdale, Pa., U.S. (hōnz'dāl)	99	41.30N	75.15W
Honey Grove, Tx., U.S. (hŭn'ĭ grōv)	111	33.35N	95.54W
Honey Lake, l., Ca., U.S. (hŭn'ĭ)	108	40.11N	120.34W
Honfleur, Can. (ôɴ-flûr')	83b	46.39N	70.53W
Honfleur, Fr. (ôɴ-flûr')	156	49.26N	0.13E
Hon Gay, Viet.	193	20.58N	107.10E
Hong Kong, dep., Asia (hŏng' kŏng')	189	21.45N	115.00E
Hongshui, r., China (hôŋ-shwā)	188	24.30N	105.00E
Honguedo, Détroit d', strt., Can.	92	49.08N	63.45W
Hongze Hu, l., China	189	33.17N	118.37E
Honiara, Sol.Is.	203	9.26S	159.57E
Honiton, Eng., U.K. (hŏn'ĭ-tŏn)	150	50.49N	3.10W
Honolulu, Hi., U.S. (hŏn-ō-lo͞o'lo͞o)	96c	21.18N	157.50W
Honomu, Hi., U.S. (hŏn'ō-mo͞o)	94a	19.50N	155.04W
Honshū, i., Japan	189	36.00N	138.00E
Höntrop, neigh., Ger.	236	51.27N	7.08E
Hood, Mount, mtn., Or., U.S.	96	45.20N	121.43W
Hood Canal, b., Wa., U.S. (hŏd)	106a	47.45N	122.45W
Hood River, Or., U.S.	96	45.42N	121.30W
Hoodsport, Wa., U.S. (hŏdz'pōrt)	106a	47.25N	123.09W
Hooghly-Chinsura, India	240a	22.54N	88.24E
Hoogly, r., India (ho͞og'lĭ)	183	21.35N	87.50E
Hoogstraten, Bel.	145a	51.24N	4.46E
Hooker, Ok., U.S. (hŏk'ẽr)	110	36.49N	101.13W
Hool, Mex. (o͞o'l)	120a	19.32N	90.22W
Hoonah, Ak., U.S. (ho͞o'nä)	95	58.05N	135.25W
Hoopa Valley Indian Reservation, I.R., Ca., U.S.	104	41.18N	123.35W
Hooper, Ne., U.S. (hŏp'ẽr)	111	41.37N	96.31W
Hooper, Ut., U.S.	107b	41.10N	112.08W
Hooper Bay, Ak., U.S.	95	61.32N	166.02W
Hoopeston, Il., U.S. (ho͞ops'tŭn)	98	40.35N	87.40W
Hoosick Falls, N.Y., U.S. (ho͞o'sĭk)	99	42.55N	73.15W
Hooton, Eng., U.K.	237a	53.18N	2.57W
Hoover Dam, Nv., U.S. (ho͞o'vẽr)	108	36.00N	115.06W
Hoover Dam, dam, U.S.	96	36.00N	114.27W
Hopatcong, Lake, l., N.J., U.S. (hō-păt'kong)	100a	40.57N	74.38W
Hope, Ak., U.S. (hōp)	95	60.54N	149.48W
Hope, Ar., U.S.	111	33.41N	93.35W
Hope, N.D., U.S.	102	47.17N	97.45W
Hope, Ben, mtn., Scot., U.K. (bĕn hōp)	150	58.25N	4.25W
Hopedale, Can. (hōp'dāl)	85	55.26N	60.11W
Hopedale, Ma., U.S. (hōp'dāl)	93a	42.08N	71.33W
Hopelchén, Mex. (o-pĕl-chĕ'n)	120a	19.47N	89.51W
Hopes Advance, Cap, c., Can. (hōps ăd-vans')	85	61.05N	69.35W
Hopetoun, Austl. (hōp'toun)	202	33.50S	120.15E
Hopetown, S. Afr. (hōp'toun)	212	29.35S	24.10E
Hopewell, Va., U.S. (hōp'wĕl)	115	37.14N	77.15W
Hopewell Culture National Historical Park, rec., Oh., U.S.	98	39.25N	83.00W
Hopi Indian Reservation, I.R., Az., U.S. (hō'pē)	109	36.20N	110.30W
Hopkins, Mn., U.S. (hŏp'kĭns)	107g	44.55N	93.24W
Hopkinsville, Ky., U.S. (hŏp'kĭns-vĭl)	97	36.50N	87.28W
Hopkinton, Ma., U.S. (hŏp'kĭn-tŭn)	93a	42.14N	71.31W
Hoppegarten, Ger.	238a	52.31N	13.40E
Hoquiam, Wa., U.S. (hō'kwĭ-ăm)	96	47.00N	123.53W
Horconcitos, Pan. (ŏr-kôn-sē'-tôs)	121	8.18N	82.11W
Hörde, neigh., Ger.	236	51.29N	7.30E
Horgen, Switz. (hôr'gĕn)	154	47.16N	8.35E
Horicon, Wi., U.S. (hŏr'ĭ-kŏn)	103	43.26N	88.40W
Horinouchi, neigh., Japan	242a	35.41N	139.40E
Horlivka, Ukr.	167	48.17N	38.03E
Hormuz, Strait of, strt., Asia (hôr'mŭz')	182	26.30N	56.30E
Horn, i., Austl. (hôrn)	203	10.30S	143.30E
Horn, Cape see Hornos, Cabo de, c., Chile	132	56.00S	67.00W
Hornavan, l., Swe.	146	65.54N	16.17E
Hornchurch, neigh., Eng., U.K.	235	51.34N	0.12E
Horndon on the Hill, Eng., U.K.	235	51.31N	0.25E
Horneburg, Ger. (hōr'nĕ-bōrgh)	145c	53.30N	9.35E
Horneburg, Ger.	236	51.38N	7.18E
Hornell, N.Y., U.S. (hôr-nĕl')	99	42.20N	77.40W
Horn Hill, Eng., U.K.	235	51.37N	0.32W
Hornos, Cabo de, c., Chile	132	56.00S	67.00W
Horn Plateau, plat., Can.	84	62.12N	120.29W
Hornsby, Austl. (hôrnz'bĭ)	201b	33.43S	151.06E
Hornsey, neigh., Eng., U.K.	235	51.35N	0.07W
Horodenka, Ukr.	155	48.40N	25.30E
Horodnya, Ukr.	163	51.54N	31.31E
Horodok, Ukr.	155	49.47N	23.39E
Horqueta, Para. (ŏr-kĕ'tä)	132	23.20S	57.00W
Horse Creek, r., Co., U.S. (hôrs)	110	38.49N	103.48W
Horse Creek, r., Wy., U.S.	102	41.33N	104.39W
Horse Islands, is., Can.	93	50.11N	55.45W
Horsell, Eng., U.K.	235	51.19N	0.34W
Horsens, Den. (hôrs'ĕns)	152	55.50N	9.49E
Horseshoe Bay, Can. (hôrs-sho͞o)	106d	49.23N	123.16W
Horsforth, Eng., U.K. (hôrs'fŭrth)	144a	53.50N	1.38W
Horsham, Austl. (hôr'shăm) (hôrs'ăm)	203	36.42S	142.17E
Horsley, Austl.	243a	33.51S	150.51E
Horst, Ger. (hôrst)	145c	53.49N	9.37E
Horst, neigh., Ger.	236	51.32N	7.02E
Horsthausen, neigh., Ger.	236	51.33N	7.13E
Horstmar, neigh., Ger.	236	51.36N	7.33E
Hortaleza, neigh., Spain	238b	40.28N	3.39W
Horten, Nor. (hôr'tĕn)	152	59.26N	10.27E
Horton, Ks., U.S. (hôr'tŭn)	111	39.38N	95.32W
Horton, r., Ak., U.S. (hôr'tŭn)	95	68.38N	122.00W
Horton Kirby, Eng., U.K.	235	51.23N	0.15E
Horwich, Eng., U.K. (hŏr'ĭch)	144a	53.36N	2.33W
Horyn, r., Eur.	155	50.55N	26.07E
Hösel, Ger.	236	51.19N	6.54E
Hososhima, Japan (hō'sō-shē'mä)	194	32.25N	131.40E
Hospitalet, Spain	238e	41.22N	2.08E
Hoste, i., Chile (ŏs'tä)	132	55.20S	70.45W
Hostotipaquillo, Mex. (ŏs-tō'tĭ-pä-kēl'yō)	118	21.09N	104.05W
Hota, Japan (hō'tä)	195a	35.08N	139.50E
Hotan, China (hwô-tän)	188	37.11N	79.50E
Hotan, r., China	188	39.09N	81.08E
Hoto Mayor, Dom. Rep. (ô-tô-mä-yō'r)	123	18.45N	69.10W
Hot Springs, Ak., U.S. (hŏt sprĭngs)	95	65.00N	150.20W
Hot Springs, Ar., U.S.	97	34.29N	93.02W
Hot Springs, S.D., U.S.	102	43.28N	103.32W
Hot Springs, Va., U.S.	99	38.00N	79.55W
Hot Springs National Park, rec., Ar., U.S.	97	34.30N	93.00W
Hotte, Massif de la, mts., Haiti	123	18.25N	74.00W
Hotville, Ca., U.S. (hŏt'vĭl)	108	32.50N	115.24W
Houdan, Fr. (o͞o-däɴ')	157b	48.47N	1.36E
Hough Green, Eng., U.K.	237a	53.23N	2.47W
Houghton, Mi., U.S. (hō'tŭn)	103	47.06N	88.36W
Houghton, l., Mi., U.S.	98	44.20N	84.45W
Houilles, Fr. (o͞o-yĕs')	157b	48.55N	2.11E
Houjie, China (hwô-jyĕ)	191a	22.58N	113.39E
Houlton, Me., U.S. (hōl'tŭn)	92	46.07N	67.50W
Houma, La., U.S. (ho͞o'mȧ)	113	29.36N	90.43W
Hounslow, neigh., Eng., U.K.	235	51.29N	0.22W
Housatonic, r., U.S. (ho͞o-sȧ-tŏn'ĭk)	99	41.50N	73.25W
House Springs, Mo., U.S. (hous sprĭngs)	107e	38.24N	90.34W
Houston, Ms., U.S. (hūs'tŭn)	114	33.53N	89.00W
Houston, Tx., U.S.	97	29.46N	95.21W
Houston Ship Channel, strt., Tx., U.S.	113a	29.38N	94.57W
Houtbaai, S. Afr.	212a	34.03S	18.22E
Houtman Rocks, is., Austl. (hout'män)	202	28.15S	112.45E
Houzhen, China (hwô-jŭn)	190	36.59N	118.59E
Hovd, Mong.	188	48.08N	91.40E
Hovd Gol, r., Mong.	188	49.06N	91.16E
Hove, Eng., U.K. (hōv)	150	50.50N	0.09W
Hövsgöl Nuur, l., Mong.	188	51.11N	99.11E
Howard, Ks., U.S. (hou'ărd)	111	37.27N	96.10W
Howard, S.D., U.S.	102	44.01N	97.31W
Howard Beach, neigh., N.Y., U.S.	228	40.40N	73.51W
Howden, Eng., U.K. (hou'dĕn)	144a	53.44N	0.52W
Howe, Cape, c., Austl. (hou)	203	37.30S	150.40E
Howell, Mi., U.S. (hou'ĕl)	98	42.40N	84.00W
Howe Sound, strt., Can.	86	49.22N	123.18W
Howick, Can. (hou'ĭk)	83a	45.11N	73.51W
Howick, S. Afr.	213c	29.29S	30.16E
Howland, i., Oc. (hou'lănd)	2	1.00N	176.00W
Howrah, India (hou'rä)	183	22.33N	88.20E
Howrah Bridge, trans., India	240a	22.35N	88.21E
Howse Peak, mtn., Can.	87	51.30N	116.40W
Howson Peak, mtn., Can.	86	54.25N	127.45W
Hoxie, Ar., U.S. (kŏh'sĭ)	111	36.03N	91.00W
Hoxton Park, Austl.	243a	33.55S	150.51E
Hoy, i., Scot., U.K. (hoi)	150a	58.53N	3.10W
Hōya, Japan	195a	35.45N	139.35E
Hoylake, Eng., U.K. (hoi-lāk')	144a	53.23N	3.11W
Hoyo, Sierra del, mts., Spain (sē-ĕ'r-rä-dĕl-ō'yō)	159a	40.39N	3.56W
Hradec Králové, Czech Rep.	147	50.12N	15.50E
Hradyz'k, Ukr.	163	49.12N	33.06E
Hranice, Czech Rep. (hrän'yĕ-tsĕ)	155	49.33N	17.45E
Hröby, Swe. (hûr'bü)	152	55.50N	13.41E
Hron, r., Slvk.	155	48.22N	18.42E
Hrubieszów, Pol. (hro͞o-byā'sho͞of)	155	50.48N	23.54E
Hsawnhsup, Myanmar	188	24.29N	94.45E
Hsinchu, Tai. (hsĭn'cho͞o')	193	24.48N	121.00E
Hsinchuang, Tai.	241d	25.02N	121.26E
Hsinkao Shan, mtn., Tai.	189	23.38N	121.05E
Huadian, China (hwä-dĭĕn)	192	42.38N	126.45E
Huai, r., China (hwī)	189	32.07N	114.38E
Huai'an, China (hwī-än)	192	33.31N	119.11E
Huailai, China	192	40.20N	115.45E
Huailin, China (hwī-lĭn)	190	31.27N	117.36E
Huainan, China	190	32.38N	117.02E
Huaiyang, China (ho͞oäi'yang)	192	33.45N	114.54E
Huaiyuan, China (hwī-yüän)	192	32.53N	117.13E
Huajicori, Mex. (wä-jē-kō'rē)	118	22.41N	105.24W
Huajuapan de León, Mex. (wäj-wä'päm dā lā-ón')	119	17.46N	97.45W
Hualapai Indian Reservation, I.R., Az., U.S. (wälåpī)	109	35.41N	113.38W
Hualapai Mountains, mts., Az., U.S.	109	34.53N	113.54W
Hualien, Tai. (hwä'lyĕn')	193	23.58N	121.58E
Huallaga, r., Peru (wäl-yä'gä)	130	8.12S	76.34W
Huamachuco, Peru (wä-mä-cho͞o'kō)	130	7.52S	78.11W
Huamantla, Mex. (wä-män'tlȧ)	119	19.18N	97.54W
Huambo, Ang.	212	12.44S	15.47E
Huamuxtitlán, Mex. (wä-mo͞os-tē-tlän')	118	17.49N	98.38W
Huancavelica, Peru (wän'kä-vä-lē'kä)	130	12.47S	75.02W
Huancayo, Peru (wän-kä'yō)	130	12.09S	75.04W
Huanchaca, Bol. (wän-chä'kä)	130	20.09S	66.40W
Huang (Yellow), r., China (hŭäŋ)	189	35.06N	113.39E
Huang, Old Beds of the, mth., China	188	40.28N	106.34E
Huang, Old Course of the, r., China	190	34.28N	116.59E
Huangchuan, China (hŭäŋ-chüän)	192	32.07N	115.01E
Huangcun, China	240b	39.56N	116.11E
Huanghua, China (hŭäŋ-hwä)	190	38.28N	117.18E
Huanghuadian, China (hŭäŋ-hwä-dĭĕn)	190	39.22N	116.53E
Huangli, China (ho͞oäɴg'lē)	190	31.39N	119.42E
Huangpu, China (hŭäŋ-po͞o)	191a	22.44N	113.20E
Huangpu, r., China	191b	30.56N	121.16E
Huangqiao, China (hŭän-chyou)	190	32.15N	120.13E
Huangxian, China (hŭäŋ shyĕn)	190	37.39N	120.32E
Huangyuan, China (hŭäŋ-yüän)	188	37.00N	101.01E
Huanren, China (hŭän-rŭn)	192	41.10N	125.30E
Huánuco, Peru (wä-no͞o'kō)	130	9.50S	76.17W
Huánuni, Bol. (wä-no͞o'nē)	130	18.11S	66.43W
Huaquechula, Mex. (wä-kē-cho͞o'lä)	118	18.44N	98.37W
Huaral, Peru (wä-rä'l)	130	11.28S	77.11W
Huarás, Peru (ŏä'rȧ's)	130	9.32S	77.29W
Huascarán, Nevados, mts., Peru (wäs-kä-rän')	130	9.05S	77.50W
Huasco, Chile (wäs'kō)	132	28.32S	71.16W
Huatla de Jiménez, Mex. (wä'tlä-dĕ-kē-mĕ'nĕz)	119	18.08N	96.49W
Huatlatlauch, Mex. (wä-tlä-tlä-o͞o'ch)	118	18.40N	98.04W
Huatusco, Mex. (wä-to͞os'kō)	119	19.09N	96.57W
Huauchinango, Mex. (wä-o͞o-chē-näŋ'gō)	118	20.09N	98.03W
Huaunta, Nic. (wä-ŏ'n-tä)	121	13.30N	83.32W
Huaunta, Laguna, l., Nic. (lä-gō'nä-wä-ŏ'n-tä)	121	13.35N	83.46W
Huautla, Mex. (wä-o͞o'tlä)	118	21.04N	98.13W
Huaxian, China (hwä shyĕn)	192	35.34N	114.32E
Huaynamota, Río de, r., Mex. (rē'ō-dĕ-wäy-nä-mō'tä)	118	22.10N	104.36W
Huazolotitlán, Mex. (wäzō-lō-tlē-tlän')	119	16.18N	97.55W
Hubbard, N.H., U.S. (hŭb'ẽrd)	93a	42.53N	71.12W
Hubbard, Tx., U.S.	113	31.53N	96.46W
Hubbard, l., Mi., U.S.	98	44.45N	83.30W
Hubbard Creek Reservoir, res., Tx., U.S.	112	32.50N	98.55W
Hubbelrath, Ger.	236	51.16N	6.55E
Hubei, prov., China (ho͞o-bā)	189	31.20N	111.58E
Hubli, India (hŏ'blē)	183	15.25N	75.09E
Hückeswagen, Ger. (hü'kĕs-vä'gĕn)	157c	51.09N	7.20E
Hucknall, Eng., U.K. (hŭk'năl)	144a	53.02N	1.12W
Huddersfield, Eng., U.K. (hŭd'ẽrz-fēld)	150	53.39N	1.47W
Hudiksvall, Swe. (ho͞o'dĭks-väl)	146	61.44N	17.05E
Hudson, Can. (hŭd'sŭn)	83a	45.26N	74.08W
Hudson, Ma., U.S.	93a	42.24N	71.34W
Hudson, Mi., U.S.	98	41.50N	84.15W
Hudson, N.Y., U.S.	99	42.15N	73.45W
Hudson, Oh., U.S.	101d	41.15N	81.27W
Hudson, Wi., U.S.	107g	44.59N	92.45W
Hudson, r., U.S.	97	42.30N	73.55W
Hudson Bay, Can.	89	52.52N	102.25W
Hudson Bay, b., Can.	85	60.15N	85.30W
Hudson Falls, N.Y., U.S.	99	43.20N	73.30W
Hudson Heights, Can.	83a	45.28N	74.09W
Hudson Strait, strt., Can.	85	63.25N	74.05W
Hue, Viet. (ü-ā')	196	16.28N	107.42E
Huebra, r., Spain (wĕ'brä)	158	40.44N	6.17W
Huehuetenango, Guat. (wā-wȧ-tȧ-näŋ'gō)	120	15.19N	91.26W
Huejotzingo, Mex. (wā-hō-tzĭŋ'gō)	118	19.09N	98.24W
Huejúcar, Mex. (wā-ho͞o'kär)	118	22.26N	103.12W
Huejuquilla el Alto, Mex. (wā-ho͞o-kēl'yä ĕl äl'tō)	118	22.42N	103.54W
Huejutla, Mex. (wā-ho͞o'tlä)	118	21.08N	98.26W

298 Huelma–Ilo

PLACE (Pronunciation)	PAGE	Lat. °′	Long. °′
Huelma, Spain (wĕl′mä)	158	37.39N	3.36W
Huelva, Spain (wĕl′vä)	148	37.16N	6.58W
Huércal-Overa, Spain (wĕr-käl′ ō-vā′rä)	158	37.12N	1.58W
Huerfano, r., Co., U.S. (wâr′fȧ-nō)	110	37.41N	105.13W
Huésca, Spain (wĕs-kä)	148	42.07N	0.25W
Huéscar, Spain (wās′kär)	158	37.50N	2.34W
Huetamo de Núñez, Mex.	118	18.34N	100.53W
Huete, Spain (wā′tå)	158	40.09N	2.42W
Hueycatenango, Mex. (wĕy-kȧ-tĕ-nă′n-gô)	118	17.31N	99.10W
Hueytlalpan, Mex. (wā′ĭ-tlăl′păn)	119	20.03N	97.41W
Hueytown, Al., U.S.	100h	33.28N	86.59W
Huffman, Al., U.S. (hŭf′mȧn)	100h	33.36N	86.42W
Hügel, Villa, pt. of i., Ger.	236	51.25N	7.01E
Hugh Butler, l., Ne., U.S.	110	40.21N	100.40W
Hughenden, Austl. (hū′ĕn-dĕn)	203	20.58S	144.13E
Hughes, Austl. (hūz)	202	30.45S	129.30E
Hughesville, Md., U.S.	100e	38.32N	76.48W
Hugo, Mn., U.S. (hū′gō)	107g	45.10N	93.00W
Hugo, Ok., U.S.	111	34.01N	95.32W
Hugoton, Ks., U.S. (hū′gō-tŭn)	110	37.10N	101.28W
Hugou, China (ho͞o-gō)	190	33.22N	117.07E
Huichapan, Mex. (wē-chä-pän′)	118	20.22N	99.39W
Huila, dept., Col. (wē′lä)	130a	3.10N	75.20W
Huila, Nevado de, mtn., Col. (nĕ-vä-dô-de-wē′lä)	130a	2.59N	76.01W
Huilai, China	193	23.02N	116.18E
Huili, China	188	26.48N	102.20E
Huimanguillo, Mex. (wē-män-gēl′yō)	119	17.50N	93.16W
Huimin, China (ho͞oĭ mīn)	189	37.29N	117.32E
Huipulco, Mex.	233a	19.17N	99.09W
Huitzilac, Mex. (ōē′t-zē-lä′k)	119a	19.01N	99.16W
Huitzitzilingo, Mex. (wē-tzē-tzē-lė′n-go)	118	21.11N	98.42W
Huitzuco, Mex. (wė-tzo͞o′kō)	118	18.16N	99.20W
Huixquilucan, Mex. (ōē′x-kē-lo͞o-kä′n)	119a	19.21N	99.22W
Huiyang, China	193	23.05N	114.25E
Hukou, China (ho͞o-kō)	189	29.58N	116.20E
Hulan, China (ho͞o′län′)	189	45.58N	126.32E
Hulan, r., China	192	47.20N	126.30E
Hulin, China (ho͞o′lĭn′)	194	45.45N	133.25E
Hull, Can. (hŭl)	85	45.26N	75.43W
Hull, Ma., U.S.	93a	42.18N	70.54W
Hull, r., Eng., U.K.	144a	53.47N	0.20W
Hülscheid, Ger.	236	51.16N	7.34E
Hulst, Neth. (hōlst)	145a	51.17N	4.01E
Huludao, China (ho͞o-lo͞o-dou)	189	40.40N	120.55E
Hulun Nur, l., China (ho͞o-lōn nōr)	189	48.50N	116.45E
Hulyaypole, Ukr.	163	47.39N	36.12E
Humacao, P.R. (o͞o-mä-kä′ō)	117b	18.09N	65.49W
Humansdorp, S. Afr. (ho͞o′mäns-dôrp)	212	33.57S	24.45E
Humbe, Ang. (hōm′bâ)	212	16.50S	14.55E
Humber, r., Can.	83d	43.53N	79.40W
Humber, r., Eng., U.K. (hŭm′bẽr)	146	53.30N	0.30E
Humbermouth, Can. (hŭm′bẽr-mŭth)	93	48.58N	57.55W
Humberside, co., Eng., U.K.	144a	53.47N	0.36W
Humble, Tx., U.S. (hŭm′b′l)	113	29.58N	95.15W
Humboldt, Can. (hŭm′bōlt)	84	52.12N	105.07W
Humboldt, Ia., U.S.	103	42.43N	94.11W
Humboldt, Ks., U.S.	111	37.48N	95.26W
Humboldt, Ne., U.S.	111	40.10N	95.57W
Humboldt, r., Nv., U.S.	96	40.30N	116.50W
Humboldt, East Fork, r., Nv., U.S.	104	40.59N	115.21W
Humboldt, North Fork, r., Nv., U.S.	104	41.25N	115.45W
Humboldt, Planetario, bldg., Ven.	234a	10.30N	66.50W
Humboldt Bay, b., Ca., U.S.	104	40.48N	124.25W
Humboldt Range, mts., Nv., U.S.	108	40.12N	118.16W
Humbolt, Tn., U.S.	114	35.47N	88.55W
Humbolt Salt Marsh, Nv., U.S.	108	39.49N	117.41W
Humbolt Sink, Nv., U.S.	108	39.58N	118.54W
Humen, China (ho͞o-mŭn)	191a	22.49N	113.39E
Humphreys Peak, mtn., Az., U.S. (hŭm′frĭs)	96	35.20N	111.40W
Humpolec, Czech Rep. (hōm′pō-lĕts)	154	49.33N	15.21E
Humuya, r., Hond. (o͞o-mo͞o′yä)	120	14.38N	87.36W
Hunaflói, b., Ice. (ho͞o′nä-flō′ĭ)	146	65.41N	20.44W
Hunan, prov., China (ho͞o′nän′)	189	28.08N	111.25E
Hunchun, China (hōn-chůn)	189	42.53N	130.34E
Hunedoara, Rom. (κo͞o′nĕd-wä′rȧ)	161	45.45N	22.54E
Hungary, nation, Eur. (hŭŋ′gȧ-rĭ)	142	46.44N	17.55E
Hungerford, Austl. (hŭn′gẽr-fẽrd)	203	28.50S	144.32E
Hungry Horse Reservoir, res., Mt., U.S. (hŭŋ′gȧ-rĭ hôrs)	105	48.11N	113.30W
Hunsrück, mts., Ger. (ho͞ons′rûk)	154	49.43N	7.12E
Hunte, r., Ger. (hōn′tẽ)	154	52.45N	8.26E
Hunter Islands, is., Austl. (hŭn-tẽr)	203	40.33S	143.36E
Hunters Hill, Austl.	243a	33.50S	151.09E
Huntingburg, In., U.S. (hŭnt′ĭng-bûrg)	98	38.15N	86.55W
Huntingdon, Can. (hŭnt′ĭng-dŭn)	91	45.10N	74.05W
Huntingdon, Can.	106d	49.00N	122.16W
Huntingdon, Tn., U.S.	114	36.00N	88.23W
Huntington, In., U.S.	98	40.55N	85.30W
Huntington, Pa., U.S.	99	40.30N	78.00W
Huntington, Va., U.S.	229d	38.48N	77.15W
Huntington, W.V., U.S.	97	38.25N	82.25W
Huntington Beach, Ca., U.S.	107a	33.39N	118.00W
Huntington Park, Ca., U.S.	107a	33.59N	118.14W
Huntington Station, N.Y., U.S.	100a	40.51N	73.25W
Huntington Woods, Mi., U.S.	230c	42.29N	83.10W
Huntley, Mt., U.S.	105	45.54N	108.01W
Hunt's Cross, neigh., Eng., U.K.	237a	53.21N	2.51W
Huntsville, Can.	85	45.20N	79.15W
Huntsville, Al., U.S. (hŭnts′vĭl)	114	34.44N	86.36W
Huntsville, Md., U.S.	229d	38.55N	76.54W
Huntsville, Mo., U.S.	111	39.24N	92.32W
Huntsville, Tx., U.S.	113	30.44N	95.34W
Huntsville, Ut., Ut., U.S.	107b	41.16N	111.46W
Huolu, China (hōŭ lo͞o)	190	38.05N	114.20E

PLACE (Pronunciation)	PAGE	Lat. °′	Long. °′
Huon Gulf, b., Pap. N. Gui.	197	7.15S	147.45E
Huoqiu, China (hwō-chyō)	190	32.19N	116.17E
Huoshan, China (hwō-shän)	193	31.30N	116.25E
Ḫuraydin, Wādī, r., Egypt	181a	30.55N	34.12E
Hurd, Cape, c., Can. (hûrd)	90	45.15N	81.45W
Hurdiyo, Som.	218a	10.43N	51.05E
Hurley, Wi., U.S. (hûr′lĭ)	103	46.26N	90.11W
Hurlingham, Arg. (o͞o′r-lēn-gäm)	132a	34.36S	58.38W
Huron, Oh., U.S. (hū′rŏn)	98	41.20N	82.35W
Huron, S.D., U.S.	96	44.22N	98.15W
Huron, r., Mi., U.S.	101b	42.12N	83.26W
Huron, Lake, l., N.A. (hū′rŏn)	97	45.15N	82.40W
Huron Mountains, mts., Mi., U.S. (hū′rŏn)	103	46.47N	87.52W
Hurricane, Ak., U.S. (hŭr′ĭ-kān)	95	63.00N	149.30W
Hurricane, Ut., U.S.	109	37.10N	113.20W
Hurricane Flats, bk. (hŭ-rĭ-kȧn flăts)	122	23.35N	78.30W
Hurst, Tx., U.S.	107c	32.48N	97.12W
Hurstville, Austl.	243a	33.58S	151.06E
Húsavik, Ice.	146	66.00N	17.10W
Husen, neigh., Ger.	236	51.33N	7.36E
Huşi, Rom. (kōsh′)	163	46.52N	28.04E
Huskvarna, Swe. (hōsk-vär′nȧ)	152	57.48N	14.16E
Husum, Ger. (ho͞o′zōm)	154	54.29N	9.04E
Hutchins, Tx., U.S. (hŭch′ĭnz)	107c	32.38N	96.43W
Hutchinson, Ks., U.S. (hŭch′ĭn-sŭn)	96	38.02N	97.56W
Hutchinson, Mn., U.S.	103	44.53N	94.23W
Hütteldorf, neigh., Aus.	239e	48.12N	16.16E
Hüttenheim, neigh., Ger.	236	51.22N	6.43E
Hutton, Eng., U.K.	235	51.38N	0.22E
Huttrop, neigh., Ger.	236	51.27N	7.03E
Hutuo, r., China	192	38.10N	114.00E
Huy, Bel. (û-ē′) (hû′ė)	151	50.33N	5.14E
Huyton, Eng., U.K.	237a	53.24N	2.50W
Hvannadalshnúkur, mtn., Ice.	146	64.09N	16.46W
Hvar, i., Yugo. (κhvär)	160	43.08N	16.28E
Hwange, Zimb.	212	18.22S	26.29E
Hwangju, N. Kor. (hwäng′jo͞o′)	194	38.39N	125.49E
Hyargas Nuur, l., Mong.	188	48.00N	92.32E
Hyattsville, Md., U.S. (hī′ăt′s-vil)	100e	38.57N	76.58W
Hyco Lake, res., N.C., U.S. (rŏks′ bŭr-ō)	115	36.22N	78.58W
Hydaburg, Ak., U.S. (hī-dă′bûrg)	95	55.12N	132.49W
Hyde, Eng., U.K. (hīd)	144a	53.27N	2.05W
Hyde Park, neigh., Il., U.S.	231a	41.48N	87.36W
Hyderabad, India	183	18.30N	76.50E
Hyderābād, India (hī-dẽr-å-băd′)	183	17.29N	78.28E
Hyderābād, Pak.	183	25.29N	68.28E
Hyéres, Fr. (ē-âr′)	147	43.09N	6.08E
Hyéres, Îles d′, is., Fr. (ēl′dyâr′)	147	42.57N	6.17E
Hyesanjin, N. Kor. (hyĕ′sän-jĭn′)	194	41.11N	128.12E
Hymera, In., U.S. (hī-mē′rȧ)	98	39.10N	87.20W
Hyndman Peak, mtn., Id., U.S. (hīnd′măn)	96	43.38N	114.04W
Hyōgo, dept., Japan (hĭyō′gō)	195b	34.54N	135.15E
Hyōgo, neigh., Japan	242b	34.47N	135.10E
Hythe End, Eng., U.K.	235	51.27N	0.32W

I

PLACE (Pronunciation)	PAGE	Lat. °′	Long. °′
Ia, r., Japan (ė′ä)	195b	34.54N	135.34E
Ialomiţa, r., Rom.	161	44.37N	26.42E
Iaşi, Rom. (yä′shė)	142	47.10N	27.40E
Iba, Phil. (ē′bä)	197a	15.20N	119.59E
Ibadan, Nig. (ė-bä′dän)	210	7.17N	3.30E
Ibagué, Col.	130	4.27N	75.14W
Ibar, r., Yugo. (ē′bär)	161	43.22N	20.35E
Ibaraki, Japan (ē-bä′rä-gē)	195b	34.49N	135.35E
Ibarra, Ec. (ė-bär′rä)	130	0.19N	78.08W
Ibb, Yemen	185	14.01N	44.10E
Íberoamericana, Universidad, educ., Mex.	233a	19.21N	99.08W
Iberville, Can. (ė-bår-vēl′) (ī′bẽr-vĭl)	91	45.14N	73.01W
Ibese, Nig.	244d	6.33N	3.29E
Ibi, Nig. (ē′bė)	210	8.12N	9.45E
Ibiapaba, Serra da, mts., Braz. (sĕ′r-rä-dä-ē-byä-pȧ′bä)	131	3.30S	40.55W
Ibirapuera, neigh., Braz.	234d	23.37S	46.40W
Ibiza, Spain (ė-bē′thä)	159	38.55N	1.24E
Ibiza (Iviza), i., Spain (ē-bė′zä)	142	39.07N	1.05E
Ibo, Moz. (ē′bō)	213	12.20S	40.35E
Ibrāhīm, Būr, b., Egypt	218c	29.57N	32.33E
Ibrahim, Jabal, mtn., Sau. Ar.	182	20.31N	41.17E
Ibwe Munyama, Zam.	217	16.09S	28.34E
Ica, Peru (ē′kȧ)	130	14.09S	75.42W
Icá (Putumayo), r., S.A.	130	3.00S	69.00W
Içana, Braz. (ē-sä′nä)	130	0.15N	67.19W
Ice Harbor Dam, Wa., U.S.	104	46.15N	118.54W
İçel, Tur.	182	37.00N	34.40E
Iceland, nation, Eur. (īs′lănd)	142	65.12N	19.45W
Ichāpur, India	240a	22.50N	88.24E
Ichibusayama, mtn., Japan (ē′chė-bo͞o′sȧ-yä′mä)	195	32.19N	131.08E
Ichihara, Japan	195a	35.31N	140.05E
Ichikawa, Japan (ē′chė-kä′wä)	195a	35.44N	139.54E
Ichinomiya, Japan (ē′chē-nō-mē′yȧ)	195	35.19N	136.49E
Ichinomoto, Japan (ē-chē′nō-mō-tō)	195b	34.37N	135.50E
Ichnya, Ukr. (ĭch′nyä)	167	50.47N	32.23E

PLACE (Pronunciation)	PAGE	Lat. °′	Long. °′
Ickenham, neigh., Eng., U.K.	235	51.34N	0.27W
Ickern, neigh., Ger.	236	51.36N	7.21E
Icy Cape, c., Ak., U.S. (ī′sĭ)	95	70.20N	161.40W
Idabel, Ok., U.S. (ī′dȧ-bĕl)	111	33.52N	94.47W
Idagrove, Ia., U.S. (ī′dȧ-grōv)	102	42.22N	95.29W
Idah, Nig. (ē′dä)	210	7.07N	6.43E
Idaho, state, U.S. (ī′dȧ-hō)	96	44.00N	115.10W
Idaho Falls, Id., U.S.	96	43.30N	112.01W
Idaho Springs, Co., U.S.	110	39.43N	105.32W
Idanha-a-Nova, Port. (ė-dän′yȧ-ä-nō′vȧ)	158	39.58N	7.13W
Iddo, neigh., Nig.	244d	6.28N	3.23E
Ider, r., Mong.	188	48.58N	98.38E
Idhra, i., Grc.	161	37.20N	23.30E
Idi, Indon. (ē′dė)	196	4.58N	97.47E
Idkū Lake, l., Egypt	218b	31.13N	30.22E
Idle, r., Eng., U.K. (īd′′l)	144a	53.22N	0.56W
Idlib, Syria	184	35.55N	36.38E
Idriaj, Slvn. (ē′drė-ȧ)	160	46.01N	14.01E
Idutywa, S. Afr. (ē-dō-tī′wȧ)	213c	32.06S	28.18E
Idylwood, Va., U.S.	229d	38.54N	77.12W
Ieper, Bel.	151	50.50N	2.53E
Ierápetra, Grc.	160a	35.01N	25.48E
Iesi, Italy (yā′sė)	160	43.37N	13.20E
Ife, Nig.	210	7.30N	4.30E
Iferouâne, Niger (ēf′ro͞o-än′)	210	19.04N	8.24E
Ifôghas, Adrar des, plat., Afr.	210	19.55N	2.00E
Igalula, Tan.	217	5.14S	33.00E
Iganmu, neigh., Nig.	244d	6.29N	3.22E
Igarka, Russia (ė-gär′kȧ)	164	67.22N	86.16E
Igbobi, Nig.	244d	6.32N	3.22E
Ightham, Eng., U.K.	235	51.17N	0.17E
Iglesias, Italy (ē-lĕ′syôs)	148	39.20N	8.34E
Igli, Alg. (ė-glē′)	210	30.32N	2.15W
Igloolik, Can.	85	69.33N	81.18W
Ignacio, Ca., U.S. (ĭg-nā′cĭ-ō)	106b	38.05N	122.32W
Iguaçu, r., Braz. (ē-gwä-so͞o′)	132b	22.42S	43.19W
Iguala, Mex. (ė-gwä′lä)	118	18.18N	99.34W
Igualada, Spain (ė-gwä-lä′dä)	159	41.35N	1.38E
Iguassu, r., S.A. (ė-gwä-so͞o′)	132	25.45S	52.30W
Iguassu Falls, wtfl., S.A.	131	25.40S	54.16W
Iguatama, Braz. (ē-gwä-tȧ′mä)	129a	20.13S	45.40W
Iguatu, Braz. (ė-gwä-to͞o′)	131	6.22S	39.17W
Iguidi, Erg, Afr.	210	26.22N	6.53W
Iguig, Phil. (ē-gēg′)	197a	17.46N	121.44E
Iharana, Madag.	213	13.35S	50.05E
Ihiala, Nig.	215	5.51N	6.51E
Iida, Japan (ē′ė-dȧ)	195	35.39N	137.53E
Iijoki, r., Fin. (ē′yō′kĭ)	166	65.28N	27.00E
Iizuka, Japan (ē′ė-zō-kȧ)	195	33.39N	130.39E
Ijebu-Ode, Nig. (ė-jĕ′bo͞o ōdå)	210	6.50N	3.56E
IJmuiden, Neth.	145a	52.27N	4.36E
IJsselmeer, l., Neth. (ī′sĕl-mār)	151	52.46N	5.14E
Ikaalinen, Fin. (ē′kä-lĭ-nĕn)	153	61.47N	22.55E
Ikaría, i., Grc. (ē-kä′ryȧ)	161	37.43N	26.07E
Ikeda, Japan (ē′kå-dä)	195b	34.49N	135.26E
Ikeja, Nig.	244d	6.36N	3.21E
Ikerre, Nig.	215	7.31N	5.14E
Ikhtiman, Bul. (ėk′tė-män)	161	42.26N	23.49E
Iki, i., Japan (ē′kė)	194	33.46N	129.44E
Ikoma, Japan	195b	34.41N	135.43E
Ikoma, Tan. (ė-kō′mä)	212	2.08S	34.47E
Ikorodu, Nig.	244d	6.37N	3.31E
Ikoyi, neigh., Nig.	244d	6.27N	3.26E
Ikoyi Island, i., Nig.	244d	6.27N	3.26E
Iksha, Russia (ĭk′shȧ)	172b	56.10N	37.30E
Ikuno, neigh., Japan	242b	34.39N	135.33E
Ila, Nig.	215	8.01N	4.55E
Ilagan, Phil.	197a	17.09N	121.52E
Ilan, Tai. (ē′län′)	193	24.50N	121.42E
Iława, Pol. (ė-lä′vȧ)	155	53.35N	19.36E
Ilchester, Md., U.S.	229c	39.15N	76.46W
Ïle, r., Asia	170	44.30N	76.45E
Île-á-la-Crosse, Can.	88	55.34N	108.00W
Ilebo, Zaire	212	4.19S	20.35E
Ilek, Russia (ē′lyĕk)	167	51.30N	53.10E
Île-Perrot, Can. (yl-pĕ-rōt′)	83a	45.21N	73.54W
Ilesha, Nig.	210	7.38N	4.45E
Ilford, Eng., U.K. (ĭl′fẽrd)	144b	51.33N	0.06E
Ilfracombe, Eng., U.K. (ĭl-frȧ-ko͞om′)	150	51.13N	4.08W
Ilhabela, Braz. (ē′lä-bĕ′lä)	129a	23.47S	45.21W
Ilha Grande, Baía de, b., Braz. (ēl′yȧ grän′dĕ)	129a	23.17S	44.25W
Ílhavo, Port. (ēl′yȧ-vō)	148	40.36N	8.41W
Ilhéus, Braz. (ē-lĕ′o͞os)	131	14.52S	39.00W
Iliamna, Ak., U.S. (ē-lė-ăm′nȧ)	95	59.45N	155.05W
Iliamna, Ak., U.S.	95	60.18N	153.25W
Iliamna, l., Ak., U.S.	95	59.25N	155.30W
Ilim, r., Russia (ė-lyėm′)	170	57.28N	103.00E
Ilimsk, Russia (ė-lyėmsk′)	165	56.47N	103.43E
Ilin Island, i., Phil. (ė-lyēn′)	197a	12.16N	120.57E
Ilion, N.Y., U.S. (ĭl′ĭ-ŭn)	99	43.00N	75.05W
Ilioúpolis, Grc.	239d	37.56N	23.45E
Ilkeston, Eng., U.K. (ĭl′kĕs-tŭn)	144a	52.58N	1.19W
Illampu, Nevado, mtn., Bol. (nĕ-vȧ′dō-ėl-yäm-po͞o′)	130	15.50S	68.15W
Illapel, Chile (ē-zhä-pĕ′l)	132	31.37S	71.10W
Iller, r., Ger. (ĭlėr)	154	47.52N	10.06E
Illimani, Nevado, mtn., Bol. (nĕ-vȧ′dō-ēl-yė-mä′nė)	130	16.50S	67.38W
Illinois, state, U.S. (ĭl-ĭ-noi′) (ĭl-ĭ-noiz′)	97	40.25N	90.40W
Illinois, r., Il., U.S.	97	39.00N	90.30W
Illintsi, Ukr.	163	49.07N	29.13E
Illizi, Alg.	210	26.35N	8.24E
Illovo, S. Afr.	244b	26.08S	28.03E
Il′men, l., Russia (ô′zĕ-rō el′′men′′) (ĭl′mĕn)	166	58.18N	32.00E
Ilo, Peru	130	17.46S	71.13W

ăt; finăl; rāte; senåte; ärm; åsk; sofȧ; fâre; ch-choose; dh-as th in other; bē; ėvent; bĕt; recĕnt; cratẽr; g-gō; gh-guttural g; bĭt; ĭ-short neutral; rīde; κ-guttural k as ch in German ich;

PRONOUNCING INDEX

Ilobasco–Istmina 299

PLACE (Pronunciation)	PAGE	Lat. °′	Long. °′
Ilobasco, El Sal. (ē-lỏ-bäs′kō)	120	13.57N	88.46W
Iloilo, Phil. (ē-lō-ē′lō)	196	10.49N	122.33E
Ilopango, Lago, I., El Sal. (ē-lỏ-päŋ′gō)	120	13.48N	88.50W
Ilorin, Nig. (ē-lỏ-rēn′)	210	8.30N	4.32E
Ilūkste, Lat.	153	55.59N	26.20E
Ilverich, Ger.	236	51.17N	6.42E
Ilwaco, Wa., U.S. (ĭl-wā′kō)	106c	46.19N	124.02W
Ilych, r., Russia (ē′l′ĭch)	166	62.30N	57.30E
Imabari, Japan (ē′mä-bä′rē)	194	34.05N	132.58E
Imai, Japan (ē-mī′)	195b	34.30N	135.47E
Iman, r., Russia (ē-män′)	194	45.40N	134.31E
Imandra, I., Russia (ē-män′drȧ)	166	67.40N	32.30E
Imbābah, Egypt (ēm-bä′bȧ)	218b	30.06N	31.09E
Imeni Morozova, Russia (ĭm-yĕ′nyĭ mô rô′zô vȧ)	172c	59.58N	31.02E
Imeni Moskvy, Kanal (Moscow Canal), can., Russia (kȧ-näl′ĭm-yă′nĭ mŏs-kvĭ)	162	56.33N	37.15E
Imeni Tsyurupy, Russia	172b	55.30N	38.39E
Imeni Vorovskogo, Russia	172b	55.43N	38.21E
Imlay City, Mi., U.S. (ĭm′lā)	98	43.00N	83.15W
Immenstadt, Ger. (ĭm′ĕn-shtät)	154	47.34N	10.12E
Immerpan, S. Afr. (ĭmĕr-pän)	218d	24.29S	29.14E
Imola, Italy (ē′mỏ-lä)	160	44.19N	11.43E
Imotski, Cro. (ē-môts′kē)	161	43.25N	17.15E
Impameri, Braz.	131	17.44S	48.03W
Impendle, S. Afr. (ĭm-pĕnd′lȧ)	213c	29.38S	29.54E
Imperia, Italy (ēm-pā′rē-ä)	148	43.52N	8.00E
Imperial, Pa., U.S. (ĭm-pē′rĭ-ăl)	101e	40.27N	80.15W
Imperial Beach, Ca., U.S.	108a	32.34N	117.08W
Imperial Valley, Ca., U.S.	108	33.00N	115.22W
Impfondo, Congo (ĭmp-fōn′dō)	211	1.37N	18.04E
Imphāl, India (ĭmp′hŭl)	183	24.42N	94.00E
Ina, r., Japan (ē-nä′)	195b	34.56N	135.21E
Inagi, Japan	242a	35.38N	139.30E
Inaja Indian Reservation, I.R., Ca., U.S. (ē-nä′hä)	108	32.56N	116.37W
Inari, I., Fin.	146	69.02N	26.22E
Inatsuke, neigh., Japan	242a	35.46N	139.43E
Inca, Spain (ēŋ′kä)	159	39.43N	2.53E
Ince, Eng., U.K.	237a	53.17N	2.49W
Ince Blundell, Eng., U.K.	237a	53.31N	3.02W
Ince Burun, c., Tur. (ĭn′jȧ)	149	42.00N	35.00E
Inch'ŏn, S. Kor. (ĭn′chŭn)	189	37.26N	126.46E
Incudine, Monte, mtn., Fr. (ēn-kōō-dē′nȧ) (äN-kü-dēn′)	160	41.53N	9.17E
Indalsälven, r., Swe.	146	62.50N	16.50E
Independence, Ks., U.S. (ĭn-dē-pĕn′dĕns)	111	37.14N	95.42W
Independence, Mo., U.S.	107f	39.06N	94.26W
Independence, Oh., U.S.	101d	41.23N	81.39W
Independence, Or., U.S.	104	44.49N	123.13W
Independence Mountains, mts., Nv., U.S.	104	41.15N	116.02W
Independence National Historical Park, rec., N.J., U.S.	229b	39.57N	75.09W
In der Bredde, Ger.	236	51.20N	7.23E
Inder kölī, I., Kaz.	170	48.20N	52.10E
India, nation, Asia (ĭn′dĭ-ȧ)	183	23.00N	77.30E
India Gate, hist., India	240d	28.37N	77.12E
Indian, I., Mi., U.S. (ĭn′dĭ-ăn)	103	46.04N	86.34W
Indian, r., N.Y., U.S.	99	44.05N	75.45W
Indiana, Pa., U.S. (ĭn-dĭ-ăn′ȧ)	99	40.40N	79.10W
Indiana, state, U.S.	97	39.50N	86.45W
Indianapolis, In., U.S. (ĭn-dĭ-ăn-ăp′ô-lĭs)	97	39.45N	86.08W
Indian Arm, b., Can. (ĭn′dĭ-ăn ärm)	106d	49.21N	122.55W
Indian Head, Can.	84	50.29N	103.44W
Indian Head Park, Il., U.S.	231a	41.47N	87.54W
Indian Lake, I., Can.	90	47.00N	82.00W
Indian Ocean, o.	5	10.00S	70.00E
Indianola, Ia., U.S. (ĭn-dĭ-ăn-ō′lȧ)	103	41.22N	93.33W
Indianola, Ms., U.S.	114	33.29N	90.35W
Indianola, Pa., U.S.	230b	40.34N	79.51W
Indianópolis, neigh., Braz.	234d	23.36S	46.38W
Indian Springs, Va., U.S.	229d	38.49N	77.10W
Indigirka, r., Russia (ēn-dē-gēr′kȧ)	171	67.45N	145.45E
Indio, r., Pan. (ē′n-dyô)	116a	9.13N	79.28W
Indochina, reg., Asia (ĭn-dō-chī′nȧ)	196	17.22N	105.18E
Indonesia, nation, Asia (ĭn′dỏ-nē-zhȧ)	196	4.38S	118.45E
Indonesian Culture, Museum of, bldg., Indon.	241i	6.11S	106.49E
Indore, India (ĭn-dōr′)	183	22.48N	76.51E
Indragiri, r., Indon. (ĭn-drȧ-jē′rē)	196	0.27S	102.05E
Indrāvati, r., India (ĭn-drŭ-vä′tē)	183	19.00N	82.00E
Indre, r., Fr. (ăN′dr′)	156	47.13N	0.29E
Indus, Can. (ĭn′dŭs)	83e	50.55N	113.45W
Indus, r., Asia	183	26.43N	67.41E
Industria, neigh., S. Afr.	244b	26.12S	27.59E
Indwe, S. Afr. (ĭnd′wȧ)	213c	31.30S	27.21E
Inebolu, Tur. (ē-nā-bō′lōō)	149	41.50N	33.40E
Inego, Tur. (ē′nȧ-gŭ)	167	40.05N	29.20E
Infanta, Phil. (ēn-fän′tä)	197a	14.44N	121.39E
Infanta, Phil.	197a	15.50N	119.53E
Inferror, Laguna, I., Mex. (lä-gō′nä-ēn-fĕr-rôr)	119	16.18N	94.40W
Infiernillo, Presa de, res., Mex.	118	18.50N	101.50W
Infiesto, Spain (ēn-fyĕ′s-tō)	158	43.21N	5.24W
I-n-Gall, Niger	215	16.47N	6.56E
Ingatestone, Eng., U.K.	235	51.41N	0.22E
Ingeniero Budge, neigh., Arg.	233d	34.43S	58.28W
Ingersoll, Can. (ĭn′gēr-sŏl)	90	43.05N	81.00W
Ingham, Austl. (ĭng′ăm)	203	18.45S	146.14E
Ingleburn, Austl.	243a	34.00S	150.52E
Ingles, Cayos, is., Cuba (kä-yōs-ē′n-glĕ′s)	122	21.55N	82.35W
Ingleside, neigh., Ca., U.S.	231b	37.43N	122.28W
Inglewood, Can.	83d	43.48N	79.56W
Inglewood, Ca., U.S. (ĭn′g′l-wŏŏd)	107a	33.57N	118.22W

PLACE (Pronunciation)	PAGE	Lat. °′	Long. °′
Ingoda, r., Russia (ēn-gō′dȧ)	171	51.29N	112.32E
Ingolstadt, Ger. (ĭŋ′gỏl-shtät)	154	48.46N	11.27E
Ingomar, Pa., U.S.	230b	40.35N	80.05W
Ingram, Pa., U.S.	230b	40.26N	80.04W
Ingrave, Eng., U.K.	235	51.36N	0.21E
Ingur, r., Geor. (ēn-gỏr′)	167	42.30N	42.00E
Inhambane, Moz. (ēn-äm-bä′-nē)	212	23.47S	35.28E
Inhambupe, Braz. (ēn-yäm-bōō′pä)	131	11.47S	38.13W
Inharrime, Moz. (ēn-yär-rē′mä)	212	24.17S	35.07E
Inhomirim, Braz. (ē-nô-mē-rē′N)	132b	22.34S	43.11W
Inhul, r., Ukr.	163	47.22N	32.52E
Inhulets', r., Ukr.	163	47.12N	33.12E
Inírida, r., Col. (ē-nē-rē′dä)	130	2.25N	70.38W
Injune, Austl. (ĭn′jōn)	204	25.52S	148.30E
Inkeroinem, Fin. (ĭn′kĕr-oi-nĕn)	153	60.42N	26.50E
Inkster, Mi., U.S. (ĭngk′stēr)	101b	42.18N	83.19W
Inn, r., Eur. (ĭn)	147	48.00N	12.00E
Innamincka, Austl. (ĭnn-ȧ′mĭn-kȧ)	204	27.50S	140.48E
Inner Brass, i., V.I.U.S. (bräs)	117c	18.23N	64.58W
Inner Hebrides, is., Scot., U.K.	150	57.20N	6.20W
Inner Mongolia *see* Nei Monggol, , China	188	40.15N	105.00E
Innisfail, Can.	84	52.02N	113.57W
Innsbruck, Aus. (ĭns′brŏŏk)	147	47.15N	11.25E
Ino, Japan (ē′nỏ)	195	33.34N	133.23E
Inongo, Zaire (ē-nôŋ′gō)	212	1.57S	18.16E
Inowrocław, Pol. (ē-nô-vrôts′läf)	155	52.48N	18.16E
In Salah, Alg.	210	27.13N	2.22E
Inscription House Ruin, Az., U.S. (ĭn′skrĭp-shŭn hous rōō′ĭn)	109	36.45N	110.47W
International Falls, Mn., U.S. (ĭn′tēr-năsh′ŭn-ăl fôlz)	97	48.34N	93.26W
Inuvik, Can.	84	68.40N	134.10W
Inuyama, Japan (ē′nōō-yä′mä)	195	35.24N	137.01E
Invercargil, N.Z. (ĭn-vēr-kär′gĭl)	205	46.25S	168.27E
Inverel, Austl. (ĭn-vēr-el′)	203	29.50S	151.32E
Invergrove Heights, Mn., U.S. (ĭn′vēr-grōv)	107g	44.51N	93.01W
Inverness, Can. (ĭn-vēr-nĕs′)	93	46.14N	61.18W
Inverness, Scot., U.K.	146	57.30N	4.07W
Inverness, Fl., U.S.	115	28.48N	82.22W
Investigator Strait, strt., Austl. (ĭn-vĕst′ĭ′gā-tôr)	204	35.33S	137.00E
Inwood, N.Y., U.S.	228	40.37N	73.45W
Inyangani, mtn., Zimb. (ēn-yän-gä′nē)	212	18.06S	32.37E
Inyokern, Ca., U.S.	108	35.39N	117.51W
Inyo Mountains, mts., Ca., U.S. (ĭn′yō)	96	36.55N	118.04W
Inzer, r., Russia (ĭn′zĕr)	172a	54.24N	57.17E
Inzersdorf, neigh., Aus.	239e	48.09N	16.21E
Inzia, r., Zaire	216	5.55S	17.50E
Ioánnina, Grc. (yō-ä′nē-nȧ)	149	39.39N	20.52E
Ioco, Can.	106d	49.18N	122.53W
Iola, Ks., U.S. (ī-ō′lȧ)	111	37.55N	95.23W
Iôna, Parque Nacional do, rec., Ang.	216	16.35S	12.00E
Ionia, Mi., U.S. (ī-ō′nĭ-ȧ)	98	43.00N	85.10W
Ionian Islands, is., Grc. (ī-ō′nĭ-ăn)	149	39.10N	20.05E
Ionian Sea, sea, Eur.	142	38.59N	18.48E
Iori, r., Asia	168	41.03N	46.17E
Íos, i., Grc. (ī′ŏs)	161	36.48N	25.25E
Iowa, state, U.S. (ī′ō-wȧ)	97	42.05N	94.20W
Iowa, r., Ia., U.S.	103	41.55N	92.20W
Iowa City, Ia., U.S.	97	41.39N	91.31W
Iowa Falls, Ia., U.S.	103	42.32N	93.16W
Iowa Park, Tx., U.S.	110	33.57N	98.39W
Ipala, Tan.	217	4.30S	32.53E
Ipanema, neigh., Braz.	234c	22.59S	43.12W
Ipeirus, hist. reg., Grc.	161	39.35N	20.45E
Ipel', r., Eur. (ē′pĕl)	155	48.08N	19.00E
Ipiales, Col. (ē-pē-ä′lås)	130	0.48N	77.45W
Ipoh, Malay.	196	4.45N	101.05E
Ipswich, Austl. (ĭps′wĭch)	203	27.40S	152.50E
Ipswich, Eng., U.K.	147	52.05N	1.05E
Ipswich, Ma., U.S.	93a	42.41N	70.50W
Ipswich, S.D., U.S.	102	45.26N	99.01W
Ipu, Braz. (ē-pōō)	131	4.11S	40.45W
Iput', r., Eur. (ē-pỏt′)	167	52.53N	31.57E
Iqaluit, Can.	85	63.48N	68.31W
Iquique, Chile (ē-kē′kē)	130	20.16S	70.07W
Iquitos, Peru (ē-kē′tōs)	130	3.39S	73.18W
Iráklion, Grc.	142	35.20N	25.10E
Iran, nation, Asia (ē-rän′)	182	31.15N	53.30E
Iran, Plateau of, plat., Iran	182	32.28N	58.00E
Iran Mountains, mts., Asia	196	2.30N	114.30E
Irapuato, Mex. (ē-rä-pwä′tō)	118	20.41N	101.24W
Iraq, nation, Asia (ē-räk′)	182	32.00N	42.30E
Irazú, vol., C.R. (ē-rä-zōō′)	121	9.58N	83.54W
Irbid, Jord. (ēr-bēd′)	184	32.33N	35.51E
Irbīl, Iraq	182	36.10N	44.00E
Irbit, Russia (ēr-bēt′)	164	57.40N	63.10E
Irby, Eng., U.K.	237a	53.21N	3.07W
Irébou, Zaire (ē-rā′bōō)	212	0.40S	17.48E
Ireland, nation, Eur. (īr-lănd)	142	53.33N	8.00W
Iremel', Gora, mtn., Russia (gȧ-rä′ĭ-rē′mĕl)	172a	54.32N	58.52E
Irene, S. Afr. (ĭ-rē-nē)	213b	25.53S	28.13E
Irîgui, reg., Mali	214	16.45N	5.35W
Iriklinskoye Vodokhranilishche, res., Russia	167	52.20N	58.50E
Iringa, Tan. (ē-rĭŋ′gä)	212	7.46S	35.42E
Iriomote Jima, i., Japan (ērē′-ō-mō-tä)	189	24.20N	123.30E
Iriona, Hond. (ē-rē-ō′nä)	120	15.53N	85.12W
Irish Sea, sea, Eur. (ī′rĭsh)	142	53.55N	5.25W
Irkutsk, Russia (ĭr-kỏtsk′)	165	52.16N	104.00E
Irlam, Eng., U.K. (ûr′lăm)	144a	53.26N	2.26W
Irois, Cap des, c., Haiti	123	18.25N	74.50W
Iron Bottom Sound, strt., Sol.Is.	198e	9.15S	160.00E
Iron Cove, b., Austl.	243a	33.52S	151.10E

PLACE (Pronunciation)	PAGE	Lat. °′	Long. °′
Irondale, Al., U.S. (ī′ērn-dăl)	100h	33.32N	86.43W
Iron Gate, val., Eur.	161	44.43N	22.32E
Iron Knob, Austl. (ī-ăn nŏb)	204	32.47S	137.10E
Iron Mountain, Mi., U.S. (ī′ērn)	103	45.49N	88.04W
Iron River, Mi., U.S.	103	46.09N	88.39W
Ironton, Oh., U.S. (ī′ērn-tŭn)	98	38.30N	82.45W
Ironwood, Mi., U.S. (ī′ērn-wŏŏd)	103	46.28N	90.10W
Iroquois, r., Il., U.S. (ĭr′ō-kwoi)	98	40.55N	87.20W
Iroquois Falls, Can.	85	48.41N	80.39W
Irō-Saki, c., Japan (ē′rō sä′kē)	194	34.35N	138.54E
Irpen', r., Ukr. (ĭr-pĕn′)	163	50.13N	29.55E
Irrawaddy, r., Myanmar (ĭr-ȧ-wăd′ē)	183	23.27N	96.25E
Irtysh, r., Asia (ĭr-tĭsh′)	164	59.00N	69.00E
Irumu, Zaire (ē-rō′mōō)	211	1.30N	29.52E
Irun, Spain (ē-rōōn′)	158	43.20N	1.47W
Irvine, Scot., U.K.	150	55.39N	4.40W
Irvine, Ca., U.S. (ûr′vĭn)	107a	33.40N	117.45W
Irvine, Ky., U.S.	98	37.40N	84.00W
Irving, Tx., U.S. (ûr′vēng)	107c	32.49N	96.57W
Irving Park, neigh., Il., U.S.	231a	41.57N	87.43W
Irvington, N.J., U.S. (ûr′vēng-tŭn)	100a	40.43N	74.15W
Irvington, neigh., Md., U.S.	229c	39.17N	76.41W
Irwin, Pa., U.S. (ûr′wĭn)	101e	40.19N	79.42W
Is, Russia (ēs)	172a	58.48N	59.44E
Isa, Nig.	215	13.14N	6.24E
Isaacs, Mount, mtn., Pan. (ē-sä-ä′ks)	116a	9.22N	79.31W
Isabela, i., Ec. (ē-sä-bä′lä)	130	0.47S	91.35W
Isabela, Cabo, c., Dom. Rep. (kȧ′bō-ē-sä-bĕ′lä)	123	20.00N	71.00W
Isabella, Cordillera, mts., Nic. (kôr-dēl-yĕ′rä-ē-sä-bĕlä)	120	13.20N	85.37W
Isabella Indian Reservation, I.R., Mi., U.S. (ĭs-ȧ-bĕl′-lȧ)	98	43.35N	84.55W
Isaccea, Rom. (ē-säk′chä)	163	45.16N	28.26E
Ísafjördur, Ice. (ēs′ȧ-fyr-dōr)	146	66.09N	22.39W
Isando, S. Afr.	244b	26.09S	28.12E
Isangi, Zaire (ē-säŋ′gē)	188	0.46N	24.15E
Isar, r., Ger. (ē′zär)	147	48.30N	12.30E
Isarco, r., Italy (ē-sär′kō)	160	46.37N	11.25E
Isarog, Mount, mtn., Phil. (ē-sä-rō-g)	197a	13.40N	123.23E
Ischia, Italy (ēs′kyä)	159c	40.29N	13.58E
Ischia, Isola d', i., Italy (dē′sh-kyä)	148	40.26N	13.55E
Ise, Japan (ĭs′hē) (ū′gē-yä′mä′dȧ)	194	34.30N	136.43E
Iselin, N.J., U.S.	228	40.34N	74.19W
Iseo, Lago d', I., Italy (lä-′gō-dē-ē-zĕ′ō)	160	45.50N	9.55E
Isére, r., Fr. (ē-zâr′)	147	45.15N	5.15E
Iserlohn, Ger. (ē′zĕr-lōn)	157c	51.22N	7.42E
Isernia, Italy (ē-zĕr′nyä)	160	41.35N	14.14E
Ise-Wan, b., Japan (ē′sē wän)	194	34.49N	136.44E
Iseyin, Nig.	210	7.58N	3.36E
Ishigaki, Japan	198d	24.20N	124.09E
Ishikari Wan, b., Japan (ē′shē-kä-rē wän)	194	43.30N	141.05E
Ishim, Russia (ĭsh-ēm′)	164	56.07N	69.13E
Ishim, r., Asia	164	53.17N	67.45E
Ishimbay, Russia (ē-shĕm-bī′)	172a	53.28N	56.02E
Ishinomaki, Japan (ĭsh-nō-mä′kē)	189	38.22N	141.22E
Ishinomaki Wan, b., Japan (ē-shē-nō-mä′kē wän)	194	38.10N	141.40E
Ishly, Russia (ĭsh′lĭ)	172a	54.13N	55.55E
Ishlya, Russia (ĭsh′lyȧ)	172a	53.54N	57.48E
Ishmant, Egypt	218b	29.17N	31.15E
Ishpeming, Mi., U.S. (ĭsh′pē-mĭng)	103	46.28N	87.42W
Isidro Casanova, Arg.	233d	34.42S	58.35W
Isipingo, S. Afr. (ĭs-ĭ-pĭŋ-gō)	213c	29.59S	30.58E
Isiro, Zaire	211	2.47N	27.37E
İskenderun, Tur. (ĭs-kĕn′dĕr-ōōn)	182	36.45N	36.15E
İskenderun Körfezi, b., Tur.	149	36.22N	35.25E
İskilip, Tur. (ĭs′kĭ-lēp′)	149	40.40N	34.30E
Iskūr, r., Bul. (ĭs′k′r)	161	43.05N	23.37E
Isla-Cristina, Spain (ī′lä-krē-stē′nä)	158	37.13N	7.20W
Islāmābād, Pak.	183	33.55N	73.05E
Isla Mujeres, Mex. (ē′s-lä-mōō-kĕ′rĕs)	120a	21.25N	86.53W
Island Lake, I., Can.	85	53.47N	94.25W
Island Park, N.Y., U.S.	228	40.36N	73.40W
Islands, Bay of, b., Can. (ī′lăndz)	93	49.10N	58.15W
Islay, i., Scot., U.K. (ī′lā)	146	55.55N	6.35W
Isle, r., Fr. (ēl)	156	45.02N	0.29E
Isle of Axholme, reg., Eng., U.K. (ăks′-hōm)	144a	53.33N	0.48W
Isle of Man, dep., Eur. (măn)	150	54.26N	4.21W
Isle Royale National Park, rec., Mi., U.S. (īl′roi-ăl′)	97	47.57N	88.37W
Isleta, N.M., U.S. (ēs-lä′tȧ) (ī-lē′tȧ)	109	34.55N	106.45W
Isleta Indian Reservation, I.R., N.M., U.S.	109	34.55N	106.45W
Isleworth, neigh., Eng., U.K.	235	51.28N	0.20W
Islington, neigh., Can.	227c	43.39N	79.32W
Islington, neigh., Eng., U.K.	235	51.34N	0.06W
Ismailia, Egypt (ēs-mä-ēl′ēȧ)	218b	30.35N	32.17E
Ismā'īlīyah, neigh., Egypt	244a	30.03N	31.14E
Ismā'īlīyah Canal, can., Egypt	218b	30.25N	31.45E
Ismaning, Ger. (ēz′mä-nēng)	145d	48.14N	11.41E
Isparta, Tur. (ē-spär′tȧ)	182	37.50N	30.40E
Israel, nation, Asia	182	32.40N	34.00E
Issaquah, Wa., U.S. (ĭz′sȧ-kwăh)	106a	47.32N	122.02W
Isselburg, Ger. (ē′sĕl-bōōrg)	157c	51.50N	6.28E
Issoire, Fr. (ē-swȧr′)	156	45.32N	3.13E
Issoudun, Fr. (ē-sōō-dăN′)	156	46.56N	2.00E
Issum, Ger. (ē′sōōm)	157c	51.32N	6.24E
Issyk-Kul, Ozero, I., Kyrg.	169	42.13N	76.12E
Issy-les-Moulineaux, Fr.	237c	48.49N	2.17E
Īstādeh-ye Moqor, Āb-e, I., Afg.	186	32.35N	68.00E
İstanbul, Tur. (ē-stän-bōōl′)	182	41.02N	29.00E
İstanbul Boğazi (Bosporus), strt., Tur.	182	41.10N	29.10E
Istead Rise, Eng., U.K.	235	51.24N	0.22E
Istiaía, Grc. (ĭs-tyī′yä)	161	38.58N	23.11E
Istmina, Col. (ēst-mē′nä)	130a	5.10N	76.40W

ng-sing; ŋ-baŋk; N-nasalized n; nŏd; cŏmmit; ōld; ôbey; ôrder; oi-boil; fōōd; ŏŏ-as oo in foot; ou-out; s-soft; sh-dish; th-thin; pūre; ûnite; ûrn; stŭd; circŭs; ü-as in French tu; ′-indeterminate vowel.

300 Istokpoga–Jelgava

PLACE (Pronunciation)	PAGE	Lat. °′	Long. °′
Istokpoga, Lake, l., Fl., U.S. (ĭs-tŏk-pō′gȧ)	115a	27.20N	81.33W
Istra, pen., Yugo. (ê-strä)	160	45.18N	13.48E
Istranca Dağlari, mts., Eur. (ĭ-strän′jȧ)	161	41.50N	27.25E
Istres, Fr. (ēs′tr′)	156a	43.30N	5.00E
Itabaiana, Braz. (ē-tä-bä-yȧ-nä)	131	10.42S	37.17W
Itabapoana, Braz. (ē-tä′-bä-pôä′nä)	129a	21.19S	40.58W
Itabapoana, r., Braz.	129a	21.11S	41.18W
Itabirito, Braz. (ē-tä-bê-rē′tô)	129a	20.15S	43.46W
Itabuna, Braz. (ē-tä-bōō′nȧ)	131	14.47S	39.17W
Itacoara, Braz. (ē-tä-kô′ä-rä)	129a	21.41S	42.04W
Itacoatiara, Braz. (ē-tȧ-kwȧ-tyä′rȧ)	131	3.03S	58.18W
Itagüí, Col. (ē-tä′gwê)	130a	6.11N	75.36W
Itagui, r., Braz.	132b	22.53S	43.43W
Itaipava, Braz. (ē-tī-pȧ′-vä)	132b	22.23S	43.09W
Itaipu, Braz. (ē-tī′pōō)	132b	22.58S	43.02W
Itaipu, Ponta de, c., Braz.	234c	22.59S	43.03W
Itaituba, Braz. (ê-tä′ī-tōō′bȧ)	131	4.12S	56.00W
Itajái, Braz. (ē-tä-zhī′)	132	26.52S	48.39W
Italy, Tx., U.S.	113	32.11N	96.51W
Italy, nation, Eur. (ĭt′ȧ-lê)	142	43.58N	11.14E
Itambi, Braz. (ē-tä′m-bê)	132b	22.44S	42.57W
Itami, Japan (ē′tä′mē′)	195b	34.47N	135.25E
Itapecerica, Braz. (ē-tä-pē-sē-rē′kȧ)	129a	20.29S	45.08W
Itapecuru-Mirim, Braz. (ê-tä-pĕ′kōō-rōō-mê-rēɴ′)	131	3.17S	44.15W
Itaperuna, Braz. (ē-tä′pȧ-rōō′nä)	131	21.12S	41.53W
Itapetininga, Braz. (ē-tä-pē-tê-nē′ɴ-gä)	131	23.37S	48.03W
Itapira, Braz.	129a	22.27S	46.47W
Itapira, Braz. (ē-tȧ-pē′rȧ)	131	20.42S	51.19W
Itaquaquecetuba, Braz.	234d	23.29S	46.21W
Itarsi, India	186	22.43N	77.45E
Itasca, Tx., U.S. (ĭ-tăs′kȧ)	113	32.09N	97.08W
Itasca, l., Mn., U.S.	102	47.13N	95.14W
Itatiaia, Pico da, mtn., Braz. (pē′-kô-dȧ-ē-tä-tyä′ēä)	131	22.18S	44.41W
Itatiba, Braz. (ē-tä-tē′bä)	129a	23.01S	46.48W
Itaúna, Braz. (ē-tä-ōō′nä)	129a	20.05S	44.35W
Ithaca, Mi., U.S. (ĭth′ȧ-kȧ)	98	43.20N	84.35W
Ithaca, N.Y., U.S.	97	42.25N	76.30W
Itháka, i., Grc. (ē′thä-kĕ)	161	38.27N	20.48E
Itigi, Tan.	217	5.42S	34.29E
Itimbiri, r., Zaire	216	2.40N	23.30E
Itire, Nig.	244d	6.31N	3.21E
Itoko, Zaire (ê-tō′kō)	212	1.13S	22.07E
Itu, Braz. (ê-tōō′)	129a	23.16S	47.16W
Ituango, Col. (ē-twäŋ′gō)	130	7.07N	75.44W
Ituiutaba, Braz. (ê-tōō-êōō-tä′bä)	131	18.56S	49.17W
Itumirim, Braz. (ē-tōō-mê-rē′ɴ)	129a	21.20S	44.51W
Itundujia Santa Cruz, Mex. (ê-tōōn-dōō-hē′ȧ sä′n-tä krōō′z)	119	16.50N	97.43W
Iturbide, Mex. (ē′tōōr-bē′dhä)	120a	19.38N	89.31W
Iturup, i., Russia (ē-tōō-rōōp′)	171	45.35N	147.15E
Ituzaingo, Arg. (ê-tōō-zä-ē′n-gô)	132a	34.40S	58.40W
Itzehoe, Ger. (ē′tzĕ-hō)	154	53.55N	9.31E
Iuka, Ms., U.S. (ī-ū′kȧ)	114	34.47N	88.10W
Iúna, Braz. (ē-ōō′-nä)	129a	20.22S	41.32W
Iupeba, Braz.	234d	23.41S	46.22W
Ivanhoe, Austl. (ĭv′ăn-hō)	204	32.53S	144.10E
Ivanhoe, Austl.	243b	37.46S	145.03E
Ivanivka, Ukr.	162	46.43N	34.33E
Ivano-Frankivs′k, Ukr.	167	48.53N	24.46E
Ivanopil′, Ukr.	163	49.51N	28.11E
Ivanovo, Russia (ê-vä′nô-vō)	164	57.02N	41.54E
Ivanovo, prov., Russia	162	56.55N	40.30E
Ivanteyevka, Russia (ê-vȧn-tyē′yĕf-kȧ)	172b	55.58N	37.56E
Ivdel′, Russia (ĭv′dyĕl)	172a	60.42N	60.27E
Iver, Eng., U.K.	235	51.31N	0.30W
Iver Heath, Eng., U.K.	235	51.32N	0.31W
Iviza *see* Ibiza, i., Spain	142	38.55N	1.24E
Ivohibé, Madag. (ê-vô-hê-bā′)	213	22.28S	46.59E
Ivory Coast *see* Cote d'Ivoire, nation, Afr.	210	7.43N	6.30W
Ivrea, Italy (ê-vrĕ′ä)	148	45.25N	7.54E
Ivry-sur-Seine, Fr.	157b	48.49N	2.23E
Ivujivik, Can.	85	62.17N	77.52W
Iwaki, Japan	194	37.03N	140.57E
Iwate Yama, mtn., Japan (ē-wä-tē-yä′mä)	194	39.50N	140.56E
Iwatsuki, Japan	195a	35.48N	139.43E
Iwaya, Japan (ē′wȧ-yȧ)	195b	34.35N	135.01E
Iwo, Nig.	210	7.38N	4.11E
Ixcateopán, Mex. (ēs-kä-tä-ō-pän′)	118	18.29N	99.49W
Ixelles, Bel.	145a	50.49N	4.23E
Ixhautlán, Mex. (ēs-wȧt-län′)	118	20.41N	98.01W
Ixhuatán, Mex. (ēs-hwä-tän′)	119	16.19N	94.30W
Ixmiquilpan, Mex. (ēs-mê-kēl′pän)	118	20.30N	99.12W
Ixopo, S. Afr.	213c	30.10S	30.04E
Ixtacalco, Mex. (ēs-tȧ-käl′kō)	119a	19.23N	99.07W
Ixtaltepec, Mex. (ēs-täl-tē-pĕk′)	119	16.33N	95.04W
Ixtapalapa, Mex. (ēs′tä-pä-lä′pä)	119a	19.21N	99.06W
Ixtapaluca, Mex. (ēs′tä-pä-lōō′kä)	119a	19.18N	98.53W
Ixtepec, Mex. (êks-tĕ′pĕk)	119	16.37N	95.09W
Ixtlahuaca, Mex. (ēs-tlä-wä′kä)	118	19.34N	99.46W
Ixtlán de Juárez, Mex. (ēs-tlän′ dä hwä′rāz)	119	17.20N	96.29W
Ixtlán del Río, Mex. (ēs-tlän′dĕl rē′ō)	118	21.05N	104.22W
Iya, r., Russia	170	53.45N	99.30E
Iyo-Nada, b., Japan (ē′yō nä-dä)	195	33.33N	132.07E
Izabal, Guat. (ē′zä-bäl′)	120	15.23N	89.10W
Izabal, Lago, l., Guat.	120	15.30N	89.04W
Izalco, El Sal. (ē-zäl′kō)	120	13.50N	89.40W
Izamal, Mex. (ē-zä-mä′l)	120a	20.55N	89.00W
Izberbash, Russia	168	42.33N	47.52E
Izhevsk, Russia (ê-zhyĕfsk′)	164	56.50N	53.15E
Izhma, Russia (ĭzh′mȧ)	166	65.00N	54.05E
Izhma, r., Russia	166	64.00N	53.00E
Izhora, r., Russia (ēz′hô-rȧ)	172c	59.36N	30.20E
Izmayil, Ukr.	167	45.00N	28.49E
İzmir, Tur. (ĭz-mēr′)	182	38.25N	27.05E
Izmit, Tur. (ĭz-mēt′)	149	40.45N	29.45E
Iznajar, Embalse de, res., Spain	158	37.15N	4.30W
Iztaccíhuatl, mtn., Mex.	118	19.10N	98.38W
Izuhara, Japan (ē′zōō-hä′rä)	195	34.11N	129.18E
Izumi-Ōtsu, Japan (ē′zōō-mōō ō′tsōō)	195b	34.30N	135.24E
Izumo, Japan (ē′zōō-mō)	195	35.22N	132.45E
Izu Shichitō, is., Japan	189	34.32N	139.25E

J

PLACE (Pronunciation)	PAGE	Lat. °′	Long. °′
Jabal, Bahr al, r., Sudan	211	7.30N	31.00E
Jabalpur, India	183	23.18N	79.59E
Jabavu, S. Afr.	244b	26.15S	27.53E
Jablonec nad Nisou, Czech Rep. (yäb′lô-nyĕts)	154	50.43N	15.12E
Jablunkov Pass, p., Eur. (yäb′lòn-kôf)	155	49.31N	18.35E
Jaboatão, Braz. (zhä-bô-ȧ-touɴ)	131	8.14S	35.08W
Jaca, Spain (hä′kä)	159	42.35N	0.30W
Jacala, Mex. (hä-kȧ′lä)	118	21.01N	99.11W
Jacaltenango, Guat. (hä-kȧl-tē-näŋ′gō)	120	15.39N	91.41W
Jacarézinho, Braz. (zhä-kä-rĕ′zê-nyô)	131	23.13S	49.58W
Jachymov, Czech Rep. (yä′chĭ-môf)	154	50.22N	12.51E
Jacinto City, Tx., U.S. (hä-sēn′tô) (jȧ-sĭn′tō)	113a	29.45N	95.14W
Jacksboro, Tx., U.S. (jăks′bŭr-ô)	110	33.13N	98.11W
Jackson, Al., U.S. (jăk′sŭn)	114	31.31N	87.52W
Jackson, Ca., U.S.	108	38.22N	120.47W
Jackson, Ga., U.S.	114	33.19N	83.55W
Jackson, Ky., U.S.	114	37.32N	83.17W
Jackson, La., U.S.	113	30.50N	91.13W
Jackson, Mi., U.S.	97	42.15N	84.25W
Jackson, Mn., U.S.	102	43.37N	95.00W
Jackson, Ms., U.S.	97	32.17N	90.10W
Jackson, Mo., U.S.	111	37.23N	89.40W
Jackson, Oh., U.S.	98	39.00N	82.40W
Jackson, Tn., U.S.	97	35.37N	88.49W
Jackson, Port, b., Austl.	201b	33.50S	151.18E
Jackson Heights, neigh., N.Y., U.S.	228	40.45N	73.53W
Jackson Lake, l., Wy., U.S.	105	43.57N	110.28W
Jacksonville, Al., U.S. (jăk′sŭn-vĭl)	114	33.52N	85.45W
Jacksonville, Fl., U.S.	97	30.20N	81.40W
Jacksonville, Il., U.S.	97	39.43N	90.12W
Jacksonville, Tx., U.S.	113	31.58N	95.18W
Jacksonville Beach, Fl., U.S.	115	31.18N	81.25W
Jacmel, Haiti (zhȧk-mĕl′)	123	18.15N	72.30W
Jaco, l., Mex. (hä′kō)	112	27.51N	103.50W
Jacobābād, Pak.	186	28.22N	68.30E
Jacobina, Braz. (zhä-kô-bē′nȧ)	131	11.13S	40.30W
Jacomino, Cuba	233b	23.06N	82.20W
Jacques-Cartier, r., Can.	83b	47.04N	71.28W
Jacques Cartier, Détroit de, strt., Can.	92	50.07S	63.58W
Jacques-Cartier, Mont, mtn., Can.	92	48.59N	66.00W
Jacquet River, Can. (zhȧ-kĕ′) (jăk′ĕt)	92	47.55N	66.00W
Jacutinga, Braz. (zhȧ-kōō-tēn′gä)	129a	22.17S	46.36W
Jade Buddha, Temple of the (Yufosi), rel., China	241a	31.14N	121.26E
Jadebusen, b., Ger.	154	53.28N	8.17E
Jadotville *see* Likasi, Zaire	212	10.59S	26.44E
Jaén, Peru (ĸä-ĕ′n)	130	5.38S	78.49W
Jaen, Spain	148	37.45N	3.48W
Jaffa, Cape, c., Austl. (jăf′ȧ)	202	36.58S	139.29E
Jaffna, Sri L. (jăf′nȧ)	183b	9.44N	80.09E
Jagüey Grande, Cuba (hä′gwā grän′dā)	122	22.35N	81.05W
Jahore Strait, strt., Asia	181b	1.22N	103.37E
Jahrom, Iran	182	28.30N	53.28E
Jaibo, r., Cuba (hä-ē′bō)	123	20.10N	75.20W
Jaipur, India	183	27.00N	75.50E
Jaisalmer, India	186	27.00N	70.54E
Jajce, Bos. (yī′tsĕ)	161	44.20N	17.19E
Jajpur, India	183	20.49N	86.37E
Jakarta, Indon. (yä-kär′tä)	196	6.17S	106.45E
Jakobstad, Fin. (yȧ′kôb-stȧdh)	146	63.33N	22.31E
Jalacingo, Mex. (hä-lä-sĭŋ′gō)	119	19.47N	97.16W
Jalālābād, Afg. (jŭ-lä-lȧ-bäd)	183a	34.25N	70.27E
Jalālah al Baḩrīyah, Jabal, mts., Egypt	218b	29.20N	32.00E
Jalapa, Guat. (hä-lä′pȧ)	120	14.38N	89.58W
Jalapa de Díaz, Mex.	119	18.06N	96.33W
Jalapa del Marqués, Mex. (dĕl mär-kās′)	119	16.30N	95.29W
Jaleswar, Nepal	186	26.50N	85.55E
Jalgaon, India	186	21.08N	75.33E
Jalisco, Mex. (hä-lēs′kō)	118	21.27N	104.54W
Jalisco, state, Mex.	116	20.07N	104.45W
Jalón, r., Spain (hä-lōn′)	158	41.22N	1.46W
Jalostotitlán, Mex. (hä-lōs-tē-tlȧn′)	118	21.09N	102.30W
Jalpa, Mex. (häl′pä)	118	21.40N	103.04W
Jalpa, Mex. (häl′pä)	119	18.12N	93.06W
Jalpan, Mex. (häl′pän)	118	21.13N	99.31W
Jaltepec, Mex. (häl-tȧ-pĕk′)	119	17.20N	95.15W
Jaltipan, Mex. (häl-tĭ-pän′)	119	17.59N	94.42W
Jaltocan, Mex. (häl-tō-kän′)	118	21.08N	98.32W
Jamaare, r., Nig.	215	11.50N	10.10E
Jamaica, nation, N.A.	117	17.45N	78.00W
Jamaica Bay, b., N.Y., U.S.	228	40.36N	73.51W
Jamaica Cay, i., Bah.	123	22.45N	75.55W
Jamālīyah, neigh., Egypt	244a	30.03N	31.16E
Jamālpur, Bngl.	186	24.56N	89.58E
Jamay, Mex. (hä-mī′)	118	20.16N	102.43W
Jambi, Indon. (mäm′bê)	196	1.45S	103.28E
James, r., U.S.	96	46.25N	98.55W
James, r., Mo., U.S.	111	36.51N	93.22W
James, r., Va., U.S.	97	37.35N	77.50W
James, Lake, res., N.C., U.S.	115	36.07N	81.48W
James Bay, b., Can. (jāmz)	85	53.53N	80.40W
Jamesburg, N.J., U.S. (jāmz′bûrg)	100a	40.21N	74.26W
Jameson Raid Memorial, hist., S. Afr.	244b	26.11S	27.49E
James Point, c., Bah.	122	25.20N	76.30W
James Range, mts., Austl.	202	24.15S	133.30E
James Ross, i., Ant.	128	64.20S	58.20W
Jamestown, S. Afr.	213c	31.07S	26.49E
Jamestown, N.Y., U.S. (jāmz′toun)	97	42.05N	79.15W
Jamestown, N.D., U.S.	96	46.54N	98.42W
Jamestown, R.I., U.S.	100b	41.30N	71.21W
Jamestown Reservoir, res., N.D., U.S.	102	47.16N	98.40W
Jamiltepec, Mex. (hä-mēl-tȧ-pĕk)	119	16.16N	97.54W
Jammerbugten, b., Den.	152	57.20N	9.28E
Jammu, India	183	32.50N	74.52E
Jammu and Kashmīr, hist. reg., Asia (kȧsh-mēr′)	183	39.10N	75.05E
Jāmnagar, India (jäm-nŭ′gŭr)	183	22.33N	70.03E
Jamshedpur, India (jäm′shĕd-pōōr)	183	22.52N	86.11E
Jándula, r., Spain (hän′dōō-lȧ)	158	38.28N	3.52W
Janesville, Wi., U.S. (jānz′vĭl)	103	42.41N	89.03W
Janin, W. Bank	181a	32.27N	35.19E
Jan Mayen, i., Nor. (yän mī′ĕn)	146	70.59N	8.05W
Jánoshalma, Hung. (yä′nôsh-hôl-mô)	155	46.17N	19.18E
Janów Lubelski, Pol. (yä′nōōf lŭ-bĕl′skĭ)	155	50.40N	22.25E
Januária, Braz. (zhä-nwä′rê-ä)	131	15.31S	44.17W
Japan, nation, Asia (jȧ-păn′)	189	36.30N	133.30E
Japan, Sea of, sea, Asia (jȧ-păn′)	189	40.08N	132.55E
Japeri, Braz. (zhȧ-pĕ′rê)	132b	22.38S	43.40W
Japurá (Caquetá), r., S.A.	130	2.00S	68.00W
Jarabacoa, Dom. Rep. (ĸä-rä-bä-kô′ä)	123	19.05N	70.40W
Jaral del Progreso, Mex. (hä-räl dĕl prô-grā′sō)	118	20.21N	101.05W
Jarama, r., Spain (hä-rä′mä)	158	40.33N	3.30W
Jarash, Jord.	181a	32.17N	35.53E
Jardim Paulista, neigh., Braz.	234d	23.35S	46.40W
Jardines, Banco, bk., Cuba (bä′n-kō-här-dē′nȧs)	122	21.45N	81.40W
Jargalant, Mong.	192	46.28N	115.10E
Jari, r., Braz. (zhä-rē)	131	0.28N	53.00W
Jarocin, Pol. (yä-rō′tsyēn)	155	51.58N	17.31E
Jarosław, Pol. (yȧ-rôs-wȧf)	147	50.01N	22.41E
Jarud Qi, China (jya-lōō-tŭ shyē)	189	44.35N	120.40E
Jasenevo, neigh., Russia	239b	55.36N	37.33E
Jasin, Malay.	181b	2.19N	102.26E
Jašiūnai, Lith. (dzȧ-shōō-nȧ′yê)	153	54.27N	25.25E
Jāsk, Iran (jäsk)	182	25.46N	57.48E
Jasło, Pol. (yäs′wō)	155	49.44N	21.28E
Jason Bay, b., Malay.	181b	1.53N	104.14E
Jasonville, In., U.S. (jā′sŭn-vĭl)	98	39.10N	87.15W
Jasper, Can.	84	52.53N	118.05W
Jasper, Al., U.S. (jăs′pēr)	114	33.50N	87.17W
Jasper, Fl., U.S.	115	30.30N	82.56W
Jasper, In., U.S.	98	38.20N	86.55W
Jasper, Mn., U.S.	102	43.51N	96.22W
Jasper, Tx., U.S.	113	30.55N	93.59W
Jasper National Park, rec., Can.	84	53.09N	117.45W
Jászapáti, Hung. (yäs′ô-pä-tê)	155	47.29N	20.10E
Jászberény, Hung.	155	47.30N	19.56E
Jatibonico, Cuba (hä-tê-bō-nē′kō)	122	22.00N	79.15W
Játiva, Spain (hä′tē-vä)	148	38.58N	0.31W
Jauja, Peru (ĸä-ōō′ĸ)	130	11.43S	75.32W
Jaumave, Mex. (hou-mä′vȧ)	118	23.23N	99.24W
Jaunjelgava, Lat. (youn′yĕl′gȧ-vȧ)	166	56.37N	25.06E
Java (Jawa), i., Indon.	196	8.35S	111.11E
Javari, r., S.A. (ĸȧ-vä-rē)	130	4.25S	72.07W
Java Trench, deep	196	9.45S	107.30E
Jávea, Spain (hȧ-vā′ä)	159	38.45N	0.07E
Jawa, Laut (Java Sea), sea, Indon.	196	5.10S	110.30E
Jawor, Pol. (yä′vôr)	154	51.04N	16.12E
Jaworzno, Pol. (yä-vôzh′nô)	155	50.11N	19.18E
Jaya, Puncak, mtn., Indon.	197	4.00S	137.00E
Jayapura, Indon.	196	2.30S	140.45W
Jayb, Wādī al (Ha'Arava), val., Asia	181a	30.33N	35.10E
Jazīrat Muhammad, Egypt	244a	30.07N	31.12E
Jazzīn, Leb.	181a	33.34N	35.37E
Jeanerette, La., U.S. (jĕn-ẽr-et′) (zhän-rĕt′)	113	29.54N	91.41W
Jebba, Nig. (jĕb′ȧ)	210	9.07N	4.46E
Jeddore Lake, l., Can.	93	48.07N	55.35W
Jedlesee, neigh., Aus.	239e	48.16N	16.23E
Jędrzejów, Pol. (yăɴ-dzhā′yòf)	155	50.38N	20.18E
Jefferson, Ga., U.S. (jĕf′ẽr-sŭn)	114	34.05N	83.35W
Jefferson, Ia., U.S.	103	42.10N	94.22W
Jefferson, La., U.S.	100d	29.57N	90.04W
Jefferson, Pa., U.S.	230b	39.56N	80.04W
Jefferson, Tx., U.S.	113	32.47N	94.21W
Jefferson, Wi., U.S.	103	42.59N	88.45W
Jefferson, r., Mt., U.S.	105	45.37N	112.22W
Jefferson, Mount, mtn., Or., U.S.	104	44.41N	121.50W
Jefferson City, Mo., U.S.	97	38.34N	92.10W
Jefferson Park, neigh., Il., U.S.	231a	41.59N	87.46W
Jeffersontown, Ky., U.S. (jĕf′ẽr-sŭn-toun)	101h	38.11N	85.34W
Jeffersonville, In., U.S. (jĕf′ẽr-sŭn-vĭl)	101h	38.17N	85.44W
Jega, Nig.	215	12.15N	4.23E
Jehol, hist. reg., China (jĕ-hŏl)	189	42.31N	118.12E
Jēkabpils, Lat. (yĕk′ȧb-pĭls)	166	56.29N	25.50E
Jelenia Góra, Pol. (yĕ-lĕn′yȧ gò′rȧ)	154	50.53N	15.43E
Jelgava, Lat.	153	56.39N	23.42E

ăt; finăl; rāte; senāte; ärm; ȧsk; sofȧ; fâre; ch-choose; dh-as th in other; bē; ēvent; bĕt; recĕnt; cratẽr; g-gō; gh-guttural g; bĭt; ĭ-short neutral; rīde; ĸ-guttural k as ch in German ich;

PRONOUNCING INDEX Jellico–Južna Morava 301

PLACE (Pronunciation)	PAGE	Lat. °′	Long. °′
Jellico, Tn., U.S. (jĕl′ĭ-kō)	114	36.34N	84.06W
Jemez Indian Reservation, I.R., N.M., U.S.	109	35.35N	106.45W
Jena, Ger. (yā′nä)	147	50.55N	11.37E
Jenkins, Ky., U.S. (jĕŋ′kĭnz)	115	37.09N	82.38W
Jenkintown, Pa., U.S. (jĕŋ′kĭn-toun)	100f	40.06N	75.08W
Jennings, La., U.S. (jĕn′ĭngz)	113	30.14N	92.40W
Jennings, Mi., U.S.	98	44.20N	85.20W
Jennings, Mo., U.S.	107e	38.43N	90.16W
Jequitinhonha, r., Braz. (zhĕ-kē-tēŋ-ō′n-yä)	131	16.47S	41.19W
Jérémie, Haiti (zhā-rā-mē′)	123	18.40N	74.10W
Jeremoabo, Braz. (zhĕ-rā-mō-á′bō)	131	10.03S	38.13W
Jerez, Punta, c., Mex. (pōō′n-tä-κĕ-räz′)	119	23.04N	97.44W
Jerez de la Frontera, Spain	148	36.42N	6.09W
Jerez de los Caballeros, Spain	158	38.20N	6.45W
Jericho, Austl. (jĕr′ĭ-kō)	203	23.38S	146.24E
Jericho, S. Afr. (jĕr-ĭkô)	218d	25.16N	27.47E
Jericho, N.Y., U.S.	228	40.48N	73.32W
Jericho see Arīḥā, W. Bank	181a	31.51N	35.28E
Jerome, Az., U.S. (jē-rōm′)	96	34.45N	112.10W
Jerome, Id., U.S.	105	42.44N	114.31W
Jersey, dep., Eur.	156	49.15N	2.10W
Jersey, i., Jersey (jûr′zĭ)	147	49.13N	2.07W
Jersey City, N.J., U.S.	97	40.43N	74.05W
Jersey Shore, Pa., U.S.	99	41.10N	77.15W
Jerseyville, Il., U.S. (jēr′zē-vĭl)	111	39.07N	90.18W
Jerusalem, Isr. (jē-rōō′sá-lĕm)	182	31.46N	35.14E
Jesup, Ga., U.S. (jĕs′ŭp)	115	31.36N	81.53W
Jésus, Île, i., Can.	227b	45.35N	73.45W
Jesús Carranza, Mex. (hē-sōō′s-kär-rá′n-zä)	119	17.26N	95.01W
Jesús del Monte, neigh., Cuba	233b	23.06N	82.22W
Jesús María, Peru	233c	12.04S	77.04W
Jewel, Or., U.S. (jū′ĕl)	106c	45.56N	123.30W
Jewel Cave National Monument, rec., S.D., U.S.	102	43.44N	103.52W
Jhālawār, India	183	24.30N	76.00E
Jhang Maghiāna, Pak.	186	31.21N	72.19E
Jhānsi, India (jän′sē)	183	25.29N	78.32E
Jhārsuguda, India	186	22.51N	84.13E
Jhelum, Pak.	183	32.59N	73.43E
Jhelum, r., Asia (jā′lŭm)	183	31.40N	71.51E
Jhenkāri, India	240a	22.46N	88.18E
Jhil Kuranga, neigh., India	240d	28.40N	77.17E
Jiading, China (jyä-dĭŋ)	190	31.23N	121.15E
Jialing, r., China (jyä-lĭŋ)	188	32.30N	105.30E
Jiamusi, China	194	46.50N	130.21E
Ji′an, China (jyē-än)	189	27.15N	115.10E
Ji′an, China	192	41.00N	126.04E
Jianchangying, China (jyĕn-chäŋ-yĭŋ)	190	40.09N	118.47E
Jiangcun, China (jyän-tsōn)	191a	23.16N	113.14E
Jiangling, China (jyäŋ-lĭŋ)	189	30.30N	112.10E
Jiangshanzhen, China (jyäŋ-shän-jŭn)	190	36.39N	120.31E
Jiangsu, prov., China (jyäŋ-sōō)	189	33.45N	120.30E
Jiangwan, China (jyäŋ-wän)	191b	31.18N	121.29E
Jiangxi, prov., China (jyäŋ-shyē)	189	28.15N	116.00E
Jiangyin, China (jyäŋ-yĭn)	193	31.54N	120.15E
Jianli, China (jyĕn-lē)	193	29.50N	112.50E
Jianning, China (jyĕn-nĭŋ)	193	26.50N	116.55E
Jian′ou, China (jyĕn-ō)	193	27.10N	118.18E
Jianshi, China (jyĕn-shr)	193	30.40N	109.45E
Jiaohe, China	190	38.03N	116.18E
Jiaohe, China (jyou-hŭ)	192	43.40N	127.20E
Jiaoxian, China (jyou shyĕn)	189	36.18N	120.01E
Jiaozuo, China (jyou-dzwô)	190	35.15N	113.18E
Jiashan, China (jyä-shän)	190	32.41N	118.00E
Jiaxing, China (jyä-shyĭŋ)	189	30.45N	120.50E
Jiayu, China (jyä-yōō)	193	30.00N	114.00E
Jiazhou Wan, b., China (jyä-jō wän)	189	36.10N	119.55E
Jicarilla Apache Indian Reservation, I.R., N.M., U.S. (κē-kà-rēl′yá)	109	36.45N	107.00W
Jicarón, Isla, i., Pan. (κē-kä-rōn′)	121	7.14N	81.41W
Jiddah, Sau. Ar.	182	21.30N	39.15E
Jieshou, China	190	33.17N	115.20E
Jieyang, China (jyĕ-yäŋ)	189	23.38N	116.20E
Jiggalong, Austl. (jĭg′ȧ-lông)	202	23.20S	120.45E
Jiguani, Cuba (κē-gwä-nē′)	122	20.20N	76.30W
Jigüey, Bahía, b., Cuba (bä-ē′ä-κĕ′gwā)	122	22.15N	78.10W
Jihlava, Czech Rep. (yē′hlá-vá)	147	49.23N	15.33E
Jijel, Alg.	147	36.49N	5.47E
Jijia, r., Rom.	155	47.35N	27.02E
Jijiashi, China (jyē-jyä-shr)	190	32.10N	120.17E
Jijiga, Eth.	218a	9.15N	42.48E
Jijona, Spain (κē-hō′nä)	159	38.31N	0.29W
Jilin, China (jyē-lĭn)	189	43.58N	126.40E
Jilin, prov., China	189	44.20N	124.50E
Jiloca, r., Spain (κē-lō′ká)	158	41.13N	1.30W
Jilotepeque, Guat. (κē-lō-tĕ-pĕ′kĕ)	120	14.39N	89.36W
Jima, Eth.	211	7.41N	36.52E
Jimbolia, Rom. (zhĭm-bô′lyä)	161	45.45N	20.44E
Jiménez, Mex.	112	27.09N	104.55W
Jiménez, Mex.	112	29.03N	100.42W
Jiménez, Mex. (κē-mā′nâz)	118	24.12N	98.29W
Jiménez del Téul, Mex. (tĕ-ōō′l)	118	21.28N	103.51W
Jimo, China (jyē-mwo)	192	36.22N	120.28E
Jim Thorpe, Pa., U.S. (jĭm′ thôrp′)	99	40.50N	75.45W
Jinan, China (jyē-nän)	189	36.40N	117.01E
Jincheng, China (jyĭn-chŭŋ)	192	35.30N	112.50E
Jindřichův Hradec, Czech Rep. (yēn′d′r-zhĭ-kōōf hrä′dĕts)	154	49.09N	15.02E
Jing, r., China (jyĭŋ)	192	34.40N	108.20E
Jing′anji, China (jyĭŋ-än-jē)	190	34.30N	116.55E
Jingdezhen, China (jyĭn-dŭ-jŭn)	193	29.18N	117.18E
Jingjiang, China (jyĭŋ-jyäŋ)	190	32.02N	120.15E
Jingning, China (jyĭŋ-nĭŋ)	192	35.28N	105.50E
Jingpo Hu, l., China (jyĭŋ-pwo hōō)	192	44.10N	129.00E
Jingxian, China	190	37.43N	116.17E
Jingxian, China (jyĭŋ shyĕn)	193	26.32N	109.45E
Jingxing, China (jyĭŋ-shyĭŋ)	192	47.00N	123.00E
Jingzhi, China (jyĭŋ-jr)	190	36.19N	119.23E
Jinhua, China (jyĭn-hwä)	189	29.10N	119.42E
Jining, China (jyē-nĭŋ)	189	35.26N	116.34E
Jining, China	192	41.00N	113.10E
Jinja, Ug. (jĭn′jä)	211	0.26N	33.12E
Jinotega, Nic. (κē-nō-tā′gä)	120	13.07N	86.00W
Jinotepe, Nic. (κē-nō-tā′pā)	120	11.52N	86.12W
Jinqiao, China (jyĭn-chyou)	190	31.46N	116.46E
Jinshan, China (jyĭn-shän)	191b	30.53N	121.09E
Jinta, China (jyĭn-tä)	188	40.11N	98.45E
Jintan, China (jyĭn-tän)	190	31.47N	119.34E
Jin Xian, China (jyĭn shyĕn)	192	39.04N	121.40E
Jinxiang, China (jyĭn-shyäŋ)	190	35.03N	116.20E
Jinyun, China (jyĭn-yōn)	193	28.40N	120.08E
Jinzhai, China (jyĭn-jī)	190	31.41N	115.51E
Jinzhou, China (jyĭn-jō)	189	41.00N	121.00E
Jinzhou Wan, b., China (jyĭn-jō wän)	190	39.07N	121.17E
Jinzū-Gawa, r., Japan (jĕn′zōō gä′wä)	195	36.26N	137.18E
Jipijapa, Ec. (κē-pē-hä′pä)	130	1.36S	80.52W
Jiquilisco, El Sal. (κē-kē-lē′s-kô)	120	13.18N	88.32W
Jiquilpan de Juárez, Mex. (κē-kēl′pän dā hwä′râz)	118	20.00N	102.43W
Jiquipilco, Mex. (hē-kē-pē′l-kô)	119a	19.32N	99.37W
Jitotol, Mex. (κē-tô-tōl′)	119	17.03N	92.54W
Jiu, r., Rom.	161	44.45N	23.17E
Jiugang, China	240b	39.49N	116.27E
Jiujiang, China	189	29.43N	116.00E
Jiujiang, China (jyō-jyän)	191a	22.50N	113.02E
Jiuquan, China (jyō-chyän)	188	39.46N	98.26E
Jiurongcheng, China (jyō-rôŋ-chŭŋ)	190	37.23N	122.31E
Jiushouzhang, China (jyō-shō-jäŋ)	190	35.59N	115.52E
Jiuwuqing, China (jyō-wōō-chyĭŋ)	192a	32.31N	116.51E
Jiuyongnian, China (jyō-yôŋ-nĭĕn)	190	36.41N	114.46E
Jixian, China (jyē shyĕn)	190	35.25N	114.03E
Jixian, China	190	37.37N	115.33E
Jixian, China	190	40.03N	117.25E
Jiyun, r., China (jyē-yōōm)	190	39.35N	117.34E
Joachimsthal, Ger.	145b	52.58N	13.45E
João Pessoa, Braz.	131	7.09S	34.45W
João Ribeiro, Braz. (zhô-uɴ-rē-bā′rō)	129a	20.42S	44.03W
Jobabo, r., Cuba (hō-bä′bä)	122	20.50N	77.15W
Jock, r., Can. (jŏk)	83c	45.08N	75.51W
Jocotepec, Mex. (jô-kô-tá-pĕk′)	118	20.17N	103.26W
Jodar, Spain (hō′där)	158	37.54N	3.20W
Jodhpur, India (hŏd′pōōr)	183	26.23N	73.00E
Joensuu, Fin. (yô-ĕn′sōō)	153	62.35N	29.46E
Joffre, Mount, mtn., Can. (jŏ′f′r)	87	50.32N	115.13W
Jõgeva, Est. (yû′gĕ-vá)	153	58.45N	26.23E
Joggins, Can. (jŏ′gĭnz)	92	45.42N	64.27W
Johannesburg, S. Afr. (yô-hän′ĕs-bôrgh)	212	26.08S	27.54E
Johannisthal, neigh., Ger.	238a	52.26N	13.30E
John Carroll University, pt. of i., Oh., U.S.	229a	41.29N	81.32W
John Day, r., Or., U.S. (jŏn′dā)	104	44.46N	120.15W
John Day, Middle Fork, r., Or., U.S.	104	44.53N	119.04W
John Day, North Fork, r., Or., U.S.	104	45.03N	118.50W
John Day Dam, Or., U.S.	104	45.40N	120.15W
John F. Kennedy International Airport, arpt., N.Y., U.S.	228	40.38N	73.47W
John H. Kerr Reservoir, res., U.S.	97	36.30N	78.38W
John Martin Reservoir, res., Co., U.S. (jŏn mär′tĭn)	110	37.57N	103.04W
Johns Hopkins University, pt. of i., Md., U.S.	229c	39.20N	76.37W
Johnson, r., Or., U.S. (jŏn′sŭn)	106c	45.27N	122.20W
Johnsonburg, Pa., U.S. (jŏn′sŭn-bûrg)	99	41.30N	78.40W
Johnson City, Il., U.S. (jŏn′sŭn)	98	37.50N	88.55W
Johnson City, N.Y., U.S.	99	42.10N	76.00W
Johnson City, Tn., U.S.	97	36.17N	82.23W
Johnston, i., Oc. (jŏn′stŭn)	2	17.00N	168.00W
Johnstone Strait, strt., Can.	86	50.25N	126.00W
Johnston Falls, wtfl., Afr.	217	10.35S	28.50E
Johnstown, N.Y., U.S. (jonz′toun)	99	43.00N	74.20W
Johnstown, Pa., U.S.	97	40.20N	78.50W
Johor, r., Malay. (jŭ-hōr′)	181b	1.39N	103.52E
Johor Baharu, Malay.	196	1.28N	103.46E
Jõhvi, Est. (yû′vĭ)	153	59.21N	27.21E
Joigny, Fr. (zhwán-yē′)	156	47.58N	3.26E
Joinville, Braz. (zhwăɴ-vēl′)	132	26.18S	48.47W
Joinville, Fr.	157	48.28N	5.05E
Joinville, i., Ant.	128	63.00S	53.30W
Joinville-le-Pont, Fr.	237c	48.49N	2.28E
Jojutla, Mex. (hō-hōō′tlá)	118	18.39N	99.11W
Jola, Mex. (κō′lä)	118	21.08N	104.26W
Joliet, Il., U.S. (jō-lĭ-ĕt′)	101a	41.32N	88.05W
Joliette, Can. (zhô-lyĕt′)	85	46.01N	73.30W
Jolo, Phil. (hō-lō)	196	5.59N	121.05E
Jolo Island, i., Phil.	196	5.55N	121.15E
Jomalig, i., Phil. (hô-mä′lēg)	197a	14.44N	122.34E
Jomulco, Mex. (hô-mōōl′kō)	118	21.08N	104.24W
Jonacatepec, Mex.	118	18.39N	98.46W
Jonava, Lith. (yō-nä′vá)	153	55.05N	24.15E
Jones, Phil. (jōnz)	197a	12.56N	122.05E
Jones, Phil.	197a	16.35N	121.39E
Jonesboro, Ar., U.S. (jōnz′bûro)	97	35.49N	90.42W
Jonesboro, La., U.S.	113	32.14N	92.43W
Jonesville, La., U.S. (jōnz′vĭl)	113	31.35N	91.50W
Jonesville, Mi., U.S.	98	42.00N	84.45W
Jong, r., S.L.	214	8.10N	12.10W
Joniškis, Lith. (yô′nĭsh-kĭs)	153	56.14N	23.36E
Jönköping, Swe. (yûn′chû-pĭng)	146	57.47N	14.10E
Jonquiere, Can. (zhôɴ-kyâr′)	85	48.25N	71.15W
Jonuta, Mex. (hô-nōō′tä)	119	18.07N	92.09W
Jonzac, Fr. (zhôɴ-zák′)	156	45.27N	0.27W
Joplin, Mo., U.S. (jŏp′lĭn)	97	37.05N	94.31W
Jordan, nation, Asia (jôr′dăn)	182	30.15N	38.00E
Jordan, r., Asia	181a	32.05N	35.35E
Jordan, r., Ut., U.S.	107b	40.42N	111.56W
Jorhāt, India (jôr-hät′)	183	26.43N	94.16E
Jorullo, Volcán de, vol., Mex. (vôl-ká′n-dĕ-hô-rōōl′yō)	118	18.54N	101.38W
José C. Paz, Arg.	132a	34.32S	58.44W
Joseph Bonaparte Gulf, b., Austl. (jō′sĕf bō′ná-pärt)	202	13.30S	128.40E
Josephburg, Can.	83g	53.45N	113.06W
Joseph Lake, l., Can. (jō′sĕf lăk)	83g	53.18N	113.06W
Joshua Tree National Monument, rec., Ca., U.S. (jō′shū-ȧ trē)	108	34.02N	115.53W
Jos Plateau, plat., Nig. (jôs)	215	9.53N	9.05E
Jostedalsbreen, ice., Nor. (yôstĕ-däls-brĕĕn)	146	61.40N	6.55E
Jotunheimen, mts., Nor.	146	61.44N	8.11E
Joulter′s Cays, is., Bah. (jōl′tērz)	122	25.20N	78.10W
Jouy-en-Josas, Fr.	237c	48.46N	2.10E
Jouy-le-Chatel, Fr. (zhwē-lĕ-shä-tĕl′)	157b	48.40N	3.07E
Jovellanos, Cuba (hō-vĕl-yä′nōs)	122	22.50N	81.10W
J. Percy Priest Lake, res., Tn., U.S.	114	36.00N	86.45W
Juan Aldama, Mex. (kòä′n-äl-dá′mä)	118	24.16N	103.21W
Juan Anchorena, neigh., Arg.	233d	34.29S	58.30W
Juan de Fuca, Strait of, strt., N.A. (hwän′ dā fōō′kä)	84	48.25N	124.37W
Juan de Nova, Île, i., Reu.	213	17.18S	43.07E
Juan Diaz, r., Pan. (κōōä′n-dē′äz)	116a	9.05N	79.30W
Juan Fernández, Islas de, is., Chile	128	33.30S	79.00W
Juan González Romero, Mex.	233a	19.30N	99.04W
Juan L. Lacaze, Ur. (hōōá′n-ĕ′lĕ-lä-kä′zē)	129c	34.25S	57.28W
Juan Luis, Cayos de, is., Cuba (ka-yōs-dĕ-hwän lōō-ēs′)	122	22.15N	82.00W
Juárez, Arg. (hōōá′rĕz)	132	37.42S	59.46W
Juázeiro, Braz. (zhōōá′zā′rō)	131	9.27S	40.28W
Juazeiro do Norte, Braz. (zhōōá′zā′rō-dō-nôr-tĕ)	131	7.16S	38.57W
Jubayl, Leb. (jōō-bĭl′)	181a	34.07N	35.38E
Jubba (Genale), r., Afr.	218a	1.30N	42.25E
Juby, Cap, c., Mor. (yōō′bē)	210	28.01N	13.21W
Júcar, r., Spain (hōō′kär)	148	39.10N	1.22W
Júcaro, Cuba (hōō′ká-rō)	122	21.40N	78.50W
Juchipila, Mex. (hōō-chē-pē′lä)	118	21.26N	103.09W
Juchitán, Mex. (hōō-chē-tän′)	116	16.15N	95.00W
Juchitlán, Mex. (hōō-chē-tlän)	118	20.05N	104.07W
Jucuapa, El Sal. (κōō-kwä′pä)	120	13.30N	88.24W
Judenburg, Aus. (jōō′dĕn-bûrg)	154	47.10N	14.40E
Judith, r., Mt., U.S. (jōō′dĭth)	105	47.20N	109.36W
Jugo-Zapad, neigh., Russia	239b	55.40N	37.32E
Juhua Dao, i., China (jyōō-hwä dou)	190	40.30N	120.47E
Juigalpa, Nic. (hwē-gäl′pä)	120	12.02N	85.24W
Juilly, Fr.	237c	49.01N	2.42E
Juiz de Fora, Braz. (zhò-ēzh′ dā fō′rä)	131	21.47S	43.20W
Jujuy, Arg. (hōō-hwē′)	132	24.14S	65.15W
Jujuy, prov., Arg. (hōō-hwē′)	132	23.00S	65.45W
Jukskei, r., S. Afr.	213b	25.58S	27.58E
Julesburg, Co., U.S. (jōōlz′bûrg)	110	40.59N	102.16W
Juliaca, Peru (hōō-lē-ä′kä)	130	15.26S	70.12W
Julian Alps, mts., Yugo.	148	46.05N	14.05E
Julianehåb, Grnld.	82	60.07N	46.20W
Jülich, Ger. (yü′lĕk)	157c	50.55N	6.22E
Jullundur, India	183	31.29N	75.39E
Julpaiguri, India	186	26.35N	88.48E
Jumento Cays, is., Bah. (hōō-mĕn′tō)	123	23.05N	75.40W
Jumilla, Spain (hōō-mēl′yä)	158	38.28N	1.20W
Jump, r., Wi., U.S. (jŭmp)	103	45.18N	90.53W
Jumpingpound Creek, r., Can. (jŭmp-ĭng-pound)	83e	51.01N	114.34W
Jumrah, Indon.	181b	1.48N	101.04E
Junagādh, India (jò-nä′gŭd)	183	21.33N	70.25E
Junayfah, Egypt	218c	30.11N	32.26E
Junaynah, Ra′s al, mtn., Egypt	181a	29.02N	33.58E
Junction, Tx., U.S. (jŭŋk′shŭn)	112	30.29N	99.48W
Junction City, Ks., U.S.	111	39.01N	96.49W
Jundiaí, Braz.	131	23.11S	46.52W
Juneau, Ak., U.S. (jōō′nō)	96a	58.25N	134.30W
Jungfrau, mtn., Switz. (yòng′frou)	154	46.30N	7.59E
Juniata, neigh., Pa., U.S.	229b	40.01N	75.07W
Junín, Arg. (hōō-nē′n)	132	34.35S	60.56W
Junín, Col.	130a	4.47N	73.39W
Juniyah, Leb. (jōō-nē′ĕ)	181a	33.59N	35.38E
Jupiter, r., Can.	92	49.40N	63.20W
Jupiter, Mount, mtn., Wa., U.S.	106a	47.42N	123.04W
Jur, r., Sudan (jòr)	211	6.38N	27.52E
Jura, mts., Eur. (zhü-rá′)	147	46.55N	6.49E
Jura, i., Scot., U.K. (jōō′rá)	150	56.09N	6.45W
Jura, Sound of, strt., Scot., U.K. (jōō′rȧ)	150	55.45N	5.55W
Jurbarkas, Lith. (yōōr-bär′käs)	153	55.06N	22.50E
Jūrmala, Lat.	153	56.57N	23.37E
Jurong, China (jyōō-roŋ)	190	31.58N	119.12E
Jurong, Sing.	240c	1.21N	103.42E
Juruá, r., S.A.	130	5.30S	67.30W
Juruena, r., Braz. (zhōō-rōōĕ′nä)	131	12.22S	58.34W
Justice, Il., U.S.	231a	41.45N	87.50W
Jutiapa, Guat. (hōō-tē-ä′pä)	120	14.16N	89.55W
Juticalpa, Hond. (hōō-tē-käl′pä)	116	14.35N	86.17W
Jutland see Jylland, reg., Den.	146	56.04N	9.00E
Juventino Rosas, Mex.	118	20.38N	101.02W
Juventud, Isla de la, i., Cuba	117	21.40N	82.45W
Juvisy-sur-Orge, Fr.	237c	48.41N	2.23E
Juxian, China (jyōō shyĕn)	192	35.35N	118.50E
Juxtlahuaca, Mex. (hōōs-tlá-hwä′kä)	118	17.20N	98.02W
Juye, China (jyōō-yŭ)	190	35.25N	116.05E
Južna Morava, r., Yugo. (ū′zhnä mô′rä-vä)	161	42.30N	22.00E

302 Jwālahari – Karabalā'

PLACE (Pronunciation)	PAGE	Lat. °′	Long. °′
Jwālahari, neigh., India	240d	28.40N	77.06E
Jylland, reg., Den.	146	56.04N	9.00E
K			
K2, mtn., Asia	183	36.06N	76.38E
Kaabong, Ug.	217	3.31N	34.08E
Kaalfontein, S. Afr. (kärl-fōn-tān)	213b	26.02S	28.16E
Kaappunt, c., S. Afr.	212a	34.21S	18.30E
Kaarst, Ger.	236	51.14N	6.37E
Kabaena, Pulau, i., Indon. (kä-bȧ-ā'nȧ)	196	5.35S	121.07E
Kabala, S.L. (kȧ-bä'lȧ)	210	9.43N	11.39W
Kabale, Ug.	217	1.15S	29.59E
Kabalega Falls, wtfl., Ug.	211	2.15N	31.41E
Kabalo, Zaire (kä-bä'lō)	212	6.03S	26.55E
Kabambare, Zaire (kä-bäm-bä'rȧ)	212	4.47S	27.45E
Kabardino-Balkaria, state, Russia	166	43.30N	43.30E
Kabba, Nig.	215	7.50N	6.03E
Kabe, Japan (kä'bā)	195	34.32N	132.30E
Kabel, neigh., Ger.	236	51.24N	7.29E
Kabinakagami, r., Can.	90	49.00N	84.15W
Kabinda, Zaire (kä-bĕn'dä)	212	6.08S	24.29E
Kabompo, r., Zam. (kȧ-bôm'pō)	212	14.00S	23.40E
Kabongo, Zaire (kȧ-bông'ō)	212	7.58S	25.10E
Kabot, Gui.	214	10.48N	14.57W
Kaboudia, Ra's, c., Tun.	148	35.17N	11.28E
Kābul, Afg. (kä'bōōl)	183	34.39N	69.14E
Kabul, r., Asia (kä'bōōl)	183	34.44N	69.43E
Kabunda, Zaire	217	12.25S	29.22E
Kabwe, Zam.	212	14.27S	28.27E
Kachuga, Russia (kȧ-chōō-gȧ)	165	54.09N	105.43E
Kadei, r., Afr.	215	4.00N	15.10E
Kadıköy, neigh., Tur.	239f	40.59N	29.01E
Kadnikov, Russia (käd'nė-kôf)	166	59.30N	40.10E
Kadoma, Japan	195b	34.43N	135.36E
Kadoma, Zimb.	212	18.21S	29.55E
Kaduna, Nig. (kä-dōō'nä)	210	10.33N	7.27E
Kaduna, r., Nig.	215	9.30N	6.00E
Kaédi, Maur. (kä-ā-dē')	210	16.09N	13.30W
Kaena Point, c., Hi., U.S. (kä'ā-nä)	96d	21.33N	158.19W
Kaesŏng, N. Kor. (kä'ĕ-sŭng) (kī'jō)	189	38.00N	126.35E
Kafanchan, Nig.	215	9.36N	8.17E
Kafia Kingi, Sudan (kä'fē-ȧ kĭŋ'gē)	211	9.17N	24.28E
Kafue, Zam. (kä'fōō)	212	15.45S	28.17E
Kafue, r., Zam.	212	15.45S	26.30E
Kafue Flats, sw., Zam.	217	16.15S	26.30E
Kafue National Park, rec., Zam.	217	15.00S	25.35E
Kafwira, Zaire	217	12.10S	27.33E
Kagal'nik, r., Russia (kä-gäl''nėk)	163	46.58N	39.25E
Kagera, r., Afr. (kä-gā'rȧ)	212	1.10S	31.10E
Kagoshima, Japan (kä'gō-shē'mȧ)	189	31.35N	130.31E
Kagoshima-Wan, b., Japan (kä'gō-shē'mä wän)	194	31.24N	130.39E
Kagran, neigh., Aus.	239e	48.15N	16.27E
Kahayan, r., Indon.	196	1.45S	113.40E
Kahemba, Zaire	216	7.17S	19.00E
Kahia, Zaire	217	6.21S	28.24E
Kahoka, Mo., U.S. (kȧ-hō'kȧ)	111	40.26N	91.42W
Kahoolawe, Hi., U.S. (kä-hōō-lä'wē)	94a	20.28N	156.48W
Kahramanmaraş, Tur.	182	37.40N	36.50W
Kahshahpiwi, r., Can.	103	48.24N	90.56W
Kahuku Point, c., Hi., U.S. (kä-hōō'kōō)	96d	21.50N	157.50W
Kahului, Hi., U.S.	96c	20.53N	156.28W
Kai, Kepulauan, is., Indon.	197	5.35S	132.45E
Kaiang, Malay.	181b	3.00N	101.47E
Kaiashk, r., Can.	90	49.40N	89.30W
Kaibab Indian Reservation, I.R., Az., U.S. (kä'ē-bàb)	109	36.55N	112.45W
Kaibab Plat, Az., U.S.	109	36.30N	112.10W
Kaidori, Japan	242a	35.37N	139.27E
Kaidu, r., China (kī-dōō)	188	42.35N	84.04E
Kaieteur Fall, wtfl., Guy. (kī-ĕ-tōōr')	131	4.48N	59.24W
Kaifeng, China (kī-fŭŋ)	189	34.48N	114.22E
Kai Kecil, i., Indon.	197	5.45S	132.40E
Kailua, Hi., U.S. (kä'ē-lōō'ä)	96c	21.18N	157.43W
Kailua Kona, Hi., U.S.	94a	19.49N	155.59W
Kaimana, Indon.	197	3.32S	133.47E
Kaimanawa Mountains, mts., N.Z.	205	39.10S	176.00E
Kainan, Japan (kä'ē-nän')	195	34.09N	135.14E
Kainji Lake, res., Nig.	210	10.25N	4.50E
Kaisermühlen, neigh., Aus.	239e	48.14N	16.26E
Kaiserslautern, Ger. (kī-zĕrs-lou'tĕrn)	147	49.26N	7.46E
Kaiserwerth, neigh., Ger.	236	51.18N	6.44E
Kaitaia, N.Z. (kä-ē-tä'ē-ȧ)	203a	35.30S	173.28E
Kaiwi Channel, strt., Hi., U.S. (kää-wē)	96c	21.10N	157.38W
Kaiyuan, China	192	42.30N	124.00E
Kaiyuan, China (kū-yuän)	193	23.42N	103.20E
Kaiyuh Mountains, mts., Ak., U.S. (kī-yōō')	95	64.25N	157.38W
Kajaani, Fin. (kä'yä-nė)	146	64.15N	27.16E
Kajang, Gunong, mtn., Malay.	181b	2.47N	104.05E
Kajiki, Japan (kä'jē-kė)	194	31.44N	130.41E
Kakhovka, Ukr. (kä-κôf'kȧ)	163	46.46N	33.32E
Kakhovs'ke vodoskhovyshche, res., Ukr.	164	47.21N	33.33E
Kākināda, India	183	16.58N	82.18E

PLACE (Pronunciation)	PAGE	Lat. °′	Long. °′
Kaktovik, Ak., U.S. (kăk-tō'vĭk)	95	70.08N	143.51W
Kakwa, r., Can. (kăk'wȧ)	87	54.00N	118.55W
Kalach, Russia (kȧ-lȧch')	167	50.15N	40.55E
Kaladan, r., Asia	188	21.07N	93.04E
Ka Lae, c., Hi., U.S.	94a	18.55N	155.41W
Kalahari Desert, des., Afr. (kä-lä-hä'rė)	212	23.00S	22.03E
Kalama, Wa., U.S. (kȧ-lăm'ȧ)	106c	46.01N	122.50W
Kalama, r., Wa., U.S.	106c	46.03N	122.47W
Kalámai, Grc. (kä-lä-mī')	142	37.04N	22.08E
Kalamákion, Grc.	239d	37.55N	23.43E
Kalamazoo, Mi., U.S. (kăl-ȧ-mȧ-zōō')	97	42.20N	85.40W
Kalamazoo, r., Mi., U.S.	98	42.35N	86.00W
Kalanchak, Ukr. (kä-län-chäk')	163	46.17N	33.14E
Kalandula, Ang. (dōō'kȧ dȧ brä-gäN'sä)	212	9.06S	15.57E
Kalaotoa, Pulau, i., Indon.	196	7.22S	122.30E
Kalapana, Hi., U.S. (kä-lä-pä'nä)	94a	19.25N	155.00W
Kalar, mtn., Iran	182	31.43N	51.41E
Kalāt, Pak. (kŭ-lät')	183	29.05N	66.36E
Kalemie, Zaire	212	5.56S	29.12E
Kalgan see Zhangjiakou, China	189	40.45N	114.58E
Kalgoorlie-Boulder, Austl. (kăl-gōōr'lė)	202	30.45S	121.35E
Kaliakra, Nos, c., Bul.	149	43.25N	28.42E
Kalima, Zaire	217	2.34S	26.37E
Kalina, neigh., Zaire	244c	4.18S	15.16E
Kaliningrad, Russia	164	54.42N	20.32E
Kaliningrad, Russia (kä-lē-nēn'grät)	172b	55.55N	37.49E
Kalinkovichi, Bela. (kä-lēn-ko-vē'chė)	162	52.07N	29.19E
Kalispel Indian Reservation, I.R., Wa., U.S. (kăl-ĭ-spĕl')	104	48.25N	117.30W
Kalispell, Mt., U.S. (kăl'ĭ-spĕl)	96	48.12N	114.18W
Kalisz, Pol. (kä'lēsh)	147	51.45N	18.05E
Kaliua, Tan.	217	5.04S	31.48E
Kalixälven, r., Swe.	146	67.12N	22.00E
Kālkāji, neigh., India	240d	28.33N	77.16E
Kalksburg, neigh., Aus.	239e	48.08N	16.15E
Kalkum, Ger.	236	51.18N	6.46E
Kallithéa, Grc.	239d	37.57N	23.42E
Kalmar, Swe. (käl'mär)	146	56.40N	16.19E
Kalmarsund, strt., Swe. (käl'mär)	152	56.30N	16.17E
Kal'mius, r., Ukr. (käl''myōōs)	163	47.15N	37.38E
Kalmykia, state, Russia	167	46.56N	46.00E
Kalocsa, Hung. (kä'lō-chä)	155	46.32N	19.00E
Kalohi Channel, strt., Hi., U.S. (kä-lō'hī)	94a	20.55N	157.15W
Kaloko, Zaire	217	6.47S	25.48E
Kalomo, Zam. (kä-lō'mō)	212	17.02S	26.30E
Kalsubai Mount, mtn., India	186	19.43N	73.47E
Kaltenkirchen, Ger. (käl'tĕn-kēr-κĕn)	145c	53.50N	9.57E
Kālu, r., India	187b	19.18N	73.14E
Kaluga, Russia (kȧ-lō'gä)	164	54.29N	36.12E
Kaluga, prov., Russia	162	54.10N	35.00E
Kalundborg, Den. (kȧ-lōn''bôr')	152	55.42N	11.07E
Kalush, Ukr. (kä'lōsh)	155	49.02N	24.24E
Kalvarija, Lith. (käl-vä-rē'yȧ)	153	54.24N	23.17E
Kalwa, India	187b	19.12N	72.59E
Kal'ya, Russia (käl'yȧ)	172a	60.17N	59.58E
Kalyān, India	186	19.16N	73.07E
Kalyazin, Russia (käl-yȧ'zēn)	162	57.13N	37.55E
Kama, r., Russia (kä'mä)	164	56.10N	53.50E
Kamaishi, Japan (kä'mä-ē'shė)	194	39.16N	142.03E
Kamakura, Japan (kä'mä-kōō'rä)	195	35.19N	139.33E
Kamarān, i., Yemen	182	15.19N	41.47E
Kāmārhāti, India	186a	22.41N	88.23E
Kamata, neigh., Japan	242a	35.33N	139.43E
Kambove, Zaire (käm-bō'vĕ)	212	10.58S	26.43E
Kamchatka, r., Russia	171	54.15N	158.38E
Kamchatka, Poluostrov, pen., Russia	171	55.19N	157.45E
Kāmdebpur, India	240a	22.54N	88.20E
Kameari, neigh., Japan	242a	35.46N	139.51E
Kameido, neigh., Japan	242a	35.42N	139.50E
Kamen, Ger. (kä'mĕn)	157c	51.35N	7.40E
Kamenjak, Rt, c., Cro. (κä'mĕ-nyäk)	160	44.45N	13.57E
Kamen'-na-Obi, Russia (kä-mĭny'nŭ ô'bē)	164	53.43N	81.28E
Kamensk-Shakhtinskiy, Russia (kä'mĕnsk shäk'tĭn-skĭ)	163	48.17N	40.16E
Kamensk-Ural'skiy, Russia (kä'mĕnsk ōō-räl'skĭ)	166	56.27N	61.55E
Kamenz, Ger. (kä'mĕnts)	154	51.16N	14.05E
Kameoka, Japan (kä'mä-ōkä)	195b	35.01N	135.35E
Kāmet, mtn., Asia	186	30.50N	79.42E
Kamiakatsuka, neigh., Japan	242a	35.46N	139.39E
Kamiasao, Japan	242a	35.35N	139.30E
Kamień Pomorski, Pol.	154	53.57N	14.48E
Kamiishihara, Japan	242a	35.39N	139.32E
Kamikitazawa, neigh., Japan	242a	35.40N	139.38E
Kamikoma, Japan (kä'mė-kō'mä)	195b	34.45N	135.50E
Kamina, Zaire	212	8.44S	25.00E
Kaministikwia, r., Can. (kȧ-mĭ-nĭ-stĭk'wĭ-ȧ)	103	48.40N	89.41W
Kamioyamada, Japan	242a	35.35N	139.24E
Kamitsuruma, Japan	242a	35.31N	139.25E
Kamituga, Zaire	217	3.04S	28.11E
Kamloops, Can. (kăm'lōōps)	84	50.40N	120.20W
Kamoshida, neigh., Japan	242a	35.34N	139.30E
Kamp, r., Aus. (kämp)	154	48.30N	15.45E
Kampala, Ug. (käm-pä'lä)	211	0.19N	32.25E
Kampar, r., Indon. (käm'pär)	196	0.30N	101.30E
Kampene, Zaire	217	3.36S	26.40E
Kampenhout, Bel.	145a	50.56N	4.33E
Kamp-Lintfort, Ger. (kämp-lĕnt'fōrt)	157c	51.30N	6.34E
Kampong Kranji, Sing.	240c	1.26N	103.46E
Kampong Loyang, Sing.	240c	1.22N	103.58E
Kâmpóng Saôm, Camb.	196	10.40N	103.50E
Kampong Tanjong Keling, Sing.	240c	1.18N	103.42E
Kâmpóng Thum, Camb. (kŏm'pŏng-tŏm)	196	12.41N	104.29E

PLACE (Pronunciation)	PAGE	Lat. °′	Long. °′
Kâmpôt, Camb. (käm'pōt)	196	10.41N	104.07E
Kampuchea see Cambodia, nation, Asia	196	12.15N	104.00E
Kamsack, Can. (kăm'săk)	84	51.34N	101.54W
Kamskoye, res., Russia	164	59.08N	56.30E
Kamudilo, Zaire	217	7.42S	27.18E
Kamuela, Hi., U.S.	94a	20.01N	155.40W
Kamui Misaki, c., Japan	194	43.25N	139.35E
Kámuk, Cerro, mtn., C.R. (sĕ'r-rô-kä-mōō'k)	121	9.18N	83.02W
Kam'yanets'-Podil's'kyy, Ukr.	167	48.41N	26.34E
Kam'yanka-Buz'ka, Ukr.	155	50.06N	24.20E
Kamyshevatskaya, Russia	163	46.24N	37.58E
Kamyshin, Russia (kä-mwĭsh'ĭn)	164	50.08N	45.20E
Kamyshlov, Russia (kä-mēsh'lôf)	164	56.50N	62.32E
Kan, r., Russia (kän)	170	56.30N	94.17E
Kanab, Ut., U.S. (kăn'ăb)	109	37.00N	112.30W
Kanabeki, Russia (kȧ-nä'byē-kĭ)	172a	57.48N	57.16E
Kanab Plateau, plat., Az., U.S.	109	36.31N	112.55W
Kanaga, i., Ak., U.S. (kä-nä'gä)	95a	52.02N	177.38W
Kanagawa, dept., Japan (kä'nä-gä'wä)	195a	35.29N	139.32E
Kanai, Japan	242a	35.35N	139.28E
Kanā'is, Ra's al, c., Egypt	149	31.14N	28.08E
Kanamachi, Japan (kä-nä-mä'chė)	195a	35.46N	139.52E
Kanamori, Japan	242a	35.32N	139.28E
Kananga, Zaire	212	6.14S	22.17E
Kananikol'skoye, Russia	172a	52.48N	57.29E
Kanasín, Mex. (kä-nä-sē'n)	120a	20.54N	89.31W
Kanatak, Ak., U.S. (kă-nă'tŏk)	95	57.35N	155.48W
Kanawha, r., W.V., U.S. (kȧ-nô'wȧ)	97	37.55N	81.50W
Kanaya, Japan (kä-nä'yä)	195a	35.10N	139.49E
Kanazawa, Japan (kä'nȧ-zä'wȧ)	189	36.34N	136.38E
Kānchenjunga, mtn., Asia (kĭn-chĭn-jòn'gä)	183	27.30N	88.18E
Kānchipuram, India	183	12.55N	79.43E
Kanda Kanda, Zaire (kän'dȧ kän'dȧ)	212	6.56S	23.36E
Kandalaksha, Russia (kȧn-dȧ-lȧk'shȧ)	164	67.10N	33.05E
Kandalakshskiy Zaliv, b., Russia	166	66.20N	35.00E
Kandava, Lat. (kän'dȧ-vȧ)	153	57.03N	22.45E
Kandi, Benin (käN-dē')	210	11.08N	2.56E
Kandiāro, Pak.	186	27.09N	68.12E
Kandla, India (kŭnd'lŭ)	186	23.00N	70.20E
Kandy, Sri L. (kän'dė)	183b	7.18N	80.42E
Kane, Pa., U.S. (kān)	99	41.40N	78.50W
Kaneohe, Hi., U.S. (kä-nä-ō'hä)	94a	21.25N	157.47W
Kaneohe Bay, b., Hi., U.S.	96d	21.32N	157.40W
Kanevskaya, Russia (kä-nyĕf'skȧ)	163	46.07N	38.58E
Kangaroo, i., Austl. (kăŋ-gȧ-rōō')	202	36.05S	137.05E
Kangaroo Ground, Austl.	243b	37.41S	145.13E
Kangāvar, Iran (kŭŋ'gā-vär)	182	34.37N	46.45E
Kangean, Kepulauan, is., Indon. (käŋ'gē-än)	196	6.50S	116.22E
Kanggye, N. Kor. (käng'gyĕ)	189	40.55N	126.40E
Kanghwa, i., S. Kor. (käng'hwä)	194	37.38N	126.00E
Kangnŭng, S. Kor. (käng'nò ng)	194	37.42N	128.50E
Kango, Gabon (käN-gō)	212	0.09N	10.08E
Kangowa, Zaire	216	9.55S	22.48E
Kanin, Poluostrov, pen., Russia	164	68.00N	45.00E
Kaningo, Kenya	217	0.49S	38.32E
Kanin Nos, Mys, c., Russia	166	68.40N	44.00E
Kaniv, Ukr.	163	49.46N	31.27E
Kanivs'ke vodoskhovyshche, res., Ukr.	164	50.10N	30.40E
Kanjiža, Yugo. (kä'nyē-zhä)	161	46.05N	20.02E
Kankakee, Il., U.S. (kăŋ-kȧ-kē')	98	41.07N	87.53W
Kankakee, r., Il., U.S.	98	41.15N	88.15W
Kankan, Gui. (käN-käN) (kän-kän')	210	10.23N	9.18W
Kannapolis, N.C., U.S. (kăn-ăp'ō-lĭs)	115	35.30N	80.38W
Kannoura, Japan (kä'nō-ōō'rä)	195	33.34N	134.18E
Kano, Nig. (kä'nō)	210	12.00N	8.30E
Kanonkop, mtn., S. Afr.	212a	33.49S	18.37E
Kanopolis Reservoir, res., Ks., U.S. (kăn-ŏp'ō-lĭs)	110	38.44N	98.01W
Kānpur, India (kän'pûr)	186	26.30N	80.10E
Kansas, state, U.S. (kăn'zȧs)	96	38.30N	99.40W
Kansas, r., Ks., U.S.	111	39.08N	95.52W
Kansas City, Ks., U.S.	97	39.06N	94.39W
Kansas City, Mo., U.S.	97	39.05N	94.35W
Kansk, Russia	165	56.14N	95.43E
Kansŏng, S. Kor.	194	38.09N	128.29E
Kantang, Thai. (kän'täng')	196	7.26N	99.28E
Kantchari, Burkina	214	12.29N	1.31E
Kanton, i., Kir.	224	3.50S	174.00W
Kantunilkin, Mex. (kän-tōō-nēl-kē'n)	120a	21.07N	87.30W
Kanzaki, r., Japan	242b	34.42N	135.25E
Kanzhakovskiy Kamen, Gora, mtn., Russia (kȧn-zhä'kôvs-kēē kämĭen)	172a	59.38N	59.12E
Kaohsiung, Tai. (kä-ō-syŏng')	189	22.35N	120.25E
Kaolack, Sen.	210	14.09N	16.04W
Kaouar, oasis, Niger	211	19.16N	13.09E
Kapaa, Hi., U.S.	94a	22.06N	159.20W
Kapanga, Zaire	216	8.21S	22.35E
Kapellen, Ger.	236	51.25N	6.35E
Kapfenberg, Aus. (käp'fĕn-bĕrgh)	154	47.27N	15.16E
Kapiri Mposhi, Zam.	217	13.58S	28.41E
Kapoeta, Sudan	211	4.45N	33.35E
Kaposvár, Hung. (kô'pôsh-vär)	155	46.21N	17.45E
Kapotn'a, neigh., Russia	239b	55.38N	37.48E
Kapsan, N. Kor. (käp'sän')	194	40.59N	128.22E
Kapuskasing, Can.	85	49.28N	82.22W
Kapuskasing, r., Can.	90	48.55N	82.55W
Kapustin Yar, Russia (kä'pòs-tėn yär')	167	48.30N	45.40E
Kaputar, Mount, mtn., Austl. (kă-pū-tár)	204	30.11S	150.11E
Kapuvár, Hung. (kô'pōō-vär)	155	47.35N	17.02E
Kara, Russia (kärȧ)	164	68.42N	65.30E
Kara, r., Russia	166	68.30N	65.20E
Karabalā', Iraq (kŭr'bȧ-lä)	182	32.31N	43.58E

PRONOUNCING INDEX

Karabanovo–Kentucky 303

PLACE (Pronunciation)	PAGE	Lat. °′	Long. °′
Karabanovo, Russia (kä′rȧ-bȧ-nō-vō̇)	162	56.19N	38.43E
Karabash, Russia (kó-rȧ-bäsh′)	172a	55.27N	60.14E
Kara-Bogaz-Gol, Zaliv, b., Turk. (kȧ-rä′ bŭ-gäs′)	169	41.30N	53.40E
Karachay-Cherkessia, state, Russia	168	44.00N	42.00E
Karachev, Russia (kȧ-rȧ-chôf′)	166	53.08N	34.54E
Karāchi, Pak.	183	24.59N	68.56E
Karaganda see Qaraghandy, Kaz.	169	49.42N	73.18E
Karaidel′, Russia (kä′rī-dĕl)	172a	55.52N	56.54E
Kara-Khobda, r., Kaz. (kä-rȧ ᴋôb′dȧ)	170	50.40N	55.00E
Karakoram Pass, p., Asia	183	35.35N	77.45E
Karakoram Range, mts., India (kä′rä kō′ro̤m)	183	35.24N	76.38E
Karakorum, hist., Mong.	188	47.25N	102.22E
Kara Kum Canal, can., Turk.	169	37.35N	61.50E
Karakumy, des., Turk. (kara-kum)	169	40.00N	57.00E
Karaman, Tur. (kä-rä-män′)	149	37.10N	33.00E
Karamay, China (kär-äm-ā)	188	45.37N	84.53E
Karamea Bight, bt., N.Z. (kȧ-rȧ-mē′ȧ bīt)	203a	41.20S	171.30E
Kara Sea see Karskoye More, sea, Russia	164	74.00N	68.00E
Karashahr (Yanqui), China (kä-rä-shä-är) (yän-chyē)	188	42.14N	86.28E
Karatsu, Japan (kä′rȧ-tso͞o)	195	33.28N	129.59E
Karaul, Russia (kä-rä-o̤l′)	170	70.13N	83.46E
Karave, India	240e	19.01N	73.01E
Karawanken, mts., Eur.	154	46.32N	14.07E
Karcag, Hung. (kär′tsäg)	155	47.18N	20.58E
Kardhítsa, Grc.	161	39.23N	21.57E
Kärdla, Est. (kĕrd′lȧ)	153	58.59N	22.44E
Karelia, state, Russia	170	62.30N	32.35E
Karema, Tan.	212	6.49S	30.26E
Kargat, Russia (kär-gät′)	164	55.17N	80.07E
Karghalik see Yecheng, China	188	37.54N	77.25E
Kargopol′, Russia (kär-gō-pōl′′)	164	61.30N	38.50E
Kariba, Lake, res., Afr.	212	17.15S	27.55E
Karibib, Nmb. (kȧr′ȧ-bĭb)	212	21.55S	15.50E
Kārikāl, India (kä-rē̇-käl′)	187	10.58N	79.49E
Karimata, Kepulauan, is., Indon. (kä-rē̇-mä′tȧ)	196	1.08S	108.10E
Karimata, Selat, strt., Indon.	196	1.00S	107.10E
Karimun Besar, i., Indon.	181b	1.10N	103.28E
Karimunjawa, Kepulauan, is., Indon. (kä′rē̇-mo͞on-yä′vä)	196	5.36S	110.15E
Karin, Som. (kȧr′ĭn)	218a	10.43N	45.50E
Karkar Dūmān, neigh., India	240d	28.39N	77.18E
Karkar Island, i., Pap. N. Gui. (kär′kär)	197	4.50S	146.45E
Karkheh, r., Iran	182	32.45N	47.50E
Karkinits′ka zatoka, b., Ukr.	163	45.50N	32.45E
Karlivka, Ukr.	163	49.26N	35.08E
Karlobag, Cro. (kär-lō-bäg′)	160	44.30N	15.03E
Karlovac, Cro. (kär′lō̇-vȧts)	149	45.29N	15.16E
Karlovo, Bul. (kär′lō̇-vō)	161	42.39N	24.48E
Karlovy Vary, Czech Rep. (kär′lō̇-vē̇ vä′rē̇)	147	50.13N	12.53E
Karlshamn, Swe. (kärls′häm)	152	56.11N	14.50E
Karlskrona, Swe. (kärls′krō̇-nä)	146	56.10N	15.33E
Karlsruhe, Ger. (kärls′ro͞o-ĕ)	147	49.00N	8.23E
Karlstad, Swe. (kärl′städ)	142	59.25N	13.28E
Karluk, Ak., U.S. (kär′lŭk)	95	57.30N	154.22W
Karmøy, i., Nor. (kärm-ûe)	152	59.14N	5.00E
Karnataka, state, India	183	14.55N	75.00E
Karnobat, Bul. (kär-nō̇′bät)	161	42.39N	26.59E
Kärnten (Carinthia), prov., Aus. (kĕrn′tĕn)	154	46.55N	13.42E
Karolinenhof, neigh., Ger.	238a	52.23N	13.38E
Karonga, Mwi. (kȧ-rōŋ′gȧ)	212	9.52S	33.57E
Kárpathos, i., Grc.	149	35.34N	27.26E
Karpinsk, Russia (kär′pĭnsk)	172a	59.46N	60.00E
Kars, Tur. (kärs)	182	40.35N	43.00E
Kārsava, Lat. (kär′sä-vä)	153	56.46N	27.39E
Karshi, Uzb. (kär′shē)	169	38.30N	66.08E
Karskiye Vorota, Proliv, strt., Russia	164	70.30N	58.07E
Karskoye More (Kara Sea), sea, Russia	164	74.00N	68.00E
Kartaly, Russia (kȧr′tá lē̇)	164	53.05N	60.40E
Karunagapalli, India	187	9.09N	76.34E
Karvina, Czech Rep.	155	49.50N	18.30E
Kasaan, Ak., U.S.	87	55.32N	132.24E
Kasai, neigh., Japan	242a	35.39N	139.53E
Kasai (Cassai), r., Afr.	212	3.45S	19.10E
Kasama, Zam. (kȧ-să′mȧ)	212	10.13S	31.12E
Kasanga, Tan. (kȧ-säŋ′gȧ)	212	8.28S	31.09E
Kasaoka, Japan (kä′sȧ-ō′kȧ)	195	34.33N	133.29E
Kasba-Tadla, Mor. (käs′bȧ-täd′lȧ)	210	32.37N	5.57W
Kasempa, Zam. (kȧ-sĕm′pȧ)	212	13.27S	25.50E
Kasenga, Zaire (kȧ-seŋ′gȧ)	212	10.22S	28.38E
Kasese, Ug.	217	0.10N	30.05E
Kasese, Zaire	217	1.38S	27.07E
Kāshān, Iran (kā-shān′)	182	33.52N	51.15E
Kashgar see Kashi, China	188	39.29N	76.00E
Kashi (Kashgar), China (kä-shr) (käsh-gär)	188	39.29N	76.00E
Kashihara, Japan (kä′shē̇-hä′rä)	195b	34.31N	135.48E
Kashiji Plain, pl., Zam.	216	13.25S	22.30E
Kashin, Russia (kä-shēn′)	162	57.20N	37.38E
Kashira, Russia (kä-shē′rȧ)	162	54.49N	38.11E
Kashiwa, Japan (kä′shē̇-wä)	195a	35.51N	139.58E
Kashiwara, Japan	195b	34.35N	135.38E
Kashiwazaki, Japan (kä′shē-wä-zä′kē̇)	194	37.06N	138.17E
Kāshmar, Iran	185	35.12N	58.27E
Kashmir see Jammu and Kashmir, hist. reg., Asia	183	39.10N	75.05E
Kashmor, Pak.	186	28.33N	69.34E
Kashtak, Russia (käsh′tȧk)	172a	55.18N	61.25E
Kasimov, Russia (kȧ-sē′môf)	166	54.56N	41.23E
Kaskanak, Ak., U.S. (kăs-kă′nāk)	95	60.00N	158.00W
Kaskaskia, r., Il., U.S. (kăs-kăs′kĭ-ȧ)	98	39.10N	88.50W
Kaskattama, r., Can. (kăs-kă-tä′mȧ)	89	56.28N	90.55W
Kaskö (Kaskinen), Fin. (käs′kû) (käs′kē-nĕn)	153	62.24N	21.18E
Kasli, Russia (käs′lĭ)	166	55.53N	60.46E
Kasongo, Zaire (kä-sō̇ŋ′gō)	212	4.31S	26.42E
Kásos, i., Grc.	149	35.20N	26.55E
Kaspiysk, Russia	168	42.52N	47.38E
Kassándras, Kólpos, b., Grc.	161	40.10N	23.35E
Kassel, Ger. (käs′ĕl)	147	51.19N	9.30E
Kasslerfeld, neigh., Ger.	236	51.26N	6.45E
Kasson, Mn., U.S. (kăs′ŭn)	103	44.01N	92.45W
Kastamonu, Tur. (kä-stȧ-mō′no͞o)	182	41.20N	33.50E
Kastoría, Grc. (kȧs-tō′rĭ-ȧ)	149	40.28N	21.17E
Kasūr, Pak.	186	31.10N	74.29E
Kataba, Zam.	217	16.05S	25.10E
Katahdin, Mount, mtn., Me., U.S. (kȧ-tä′dĭn)	92	45.56N	68.57W
Katanga, hist. reg., Zaire (kȧ-täŋ′gȧ)	212	8.30S	25.00E
Katanning, Austl. (kȧ-tăn′ĭng)	202	33.45S	117.45E
Katano, Japan	242b	34.48N	135.42E
Katav-Ivanovsk, Russia (kä′tăf ĭ-vä′nō̇fsk)	172a	54.46N	58.13E
Katayama, neigh., Japan	242a	35.46N	139.34E
Kateninskiy, Russia (kȧtyĕ′nĭs-kĭ)	172a	53.12N	61.05E
Kateríni, Grc.	161	40.18N	22.36E
Katernberg, neigh., Ger.	236	51.29N	7.04E
Katete, Zam.	217	14.05S	32.07E
Katherine, Austl. (kăth′ẽr-ĭn)	202	14.15S	132.20E
Kāthiāwār, pen., India (kä′tyȧ-wär′)	183	22.10N	70.20E
Kathmandu, Nepal (kāt-mān-do͞o′)	183	27.49N	85.21E
Kathryn, Can. (kăth′rĭn)	83e	51.13N	113.42W
Kathryn, Ca., U.S.	107a	33.42N	117.45W
Katihār, India	186	25.39N	87.39E
Katiola, C. Iv.	214	8.08N	5.06W
Katmai National Park, rec., Ak., U.S. (kăt′mī)	96a	58.38N	155.00W
Katompi, Zaire	217	6.11S	26.20E
Katopa, Zaire	217	2.45S	25.06E
Katowice, Pol.	142	50.15N	19.00E
Katrineholm, Swe. (kȧ-trē′nĕ-hōlm)	152	59.01N	16.10E
Katsbakhskiy, Russia (kȧts-bäk′skĭ)	172a	52.57N	59.37E
Katsina, Nig. (kät′sē̇-nȧ)	210	13.00N	7.32E
Katsina Ala, Nig.	210	7.10N	9.17E
Katsura, r., Japan (kä′tso̤-rä)	195b	34.55N	135.43E
Katsushika, neigh., Japan	242a	35.43N	139.51E
Katta-Kurgan, Uzb. (kȧ-tȧ-ko̤r-gän′)	169	39.45N	66.42E
Kattegat, strt., Eur. (kăt′ĕ-gät)	142	56.57N	11.25E
Katternberg, neigh., Ger.	236	51.09N	7.02E
Katumba, Zaire	217	7.45S	25.18E
Katun′, r., Russia (kȧ-to̤n′)	170	51.30N	86.18E
Katwijk aan Zee, Neth.	145a	52.12N	4.23E
Kauai, i., Hi., U.S.	96c	22.09N	159.15W
Kauai Channel, strt., Hi., U.S. (kä-o͞o-ä′ē̇)	96c	21.35N	158.52W
Kaufbeuren, Ger. (kouf′boi-rĕn)	154	47.52N	10.38E
Kaufman, Tx., U.S. (kôf′măn)	113	32.36N	96.18W
Kaukauna, Wi., U.S. (kô-kô′nȧ)	103	44.17N	88.15W
Kaulakahi Channel, strt., Hi., U.S. (kä′o͞o-lȧ-kä′hē̇)	94a	22.00N	159.55W
Kaulsdorf-Süd, neigh., Ger.	238a	52.29N	13.34E
Kaunakakai, Hi., U.S. (kä′o͞o-nȧ-kä′kī)	94a	21.06N	156.59W
Kaunas, Lith. (kou′nȧs) (kō̇v′nō̇)	164	54.42N	23.54E
Kaura Namoda, Nig.	210	12.35N	6.35E
Kavála, Grc. (kä-vä′lä)	149	40.55N	24.24E
Kavieng, Pap. N. Gui. (kä-vē̇-ĕng′)	197	2.44S	151.02E
Kavīr, Dasht-e, des., Iran (dŭsht-ē̇-ka-vēr′)	182	34.41N	53.30E
Kawagoe, Japan (kä-wă-gō′ȧ)	195	35.55N	139.29E
Kawaguchi, Japan (kä-wä-go͞o-chē)	195a	35.48N	139.44E
Kawaikini, mtn., Hi., U.S. (kä-wä′ē̇-kĭ-nĭ)	94a	22.05N	159.33W
Kawanishi, Japan (kä-wä′nē̇-shē)	195b	34.49N	135.26E
Kawasaki, Japan (kä-wä-sä′kē̇)	194	35.32N	139.43E
Kawashima, neigh., Japan	242a	35.28N	139.35E
Kaxgar, r., China	188	39.30N	75.00E
Kaya, Burkina (kä′yä)	210	13.05N	1.05W
Kayan, r., Indon.	196	1.45N	115.38E
Kaycee, Wy., U.S. (kā-sē′)	105	43.43N	106.38W
Kayes, Mali (kāz)	210	14.27N	11.26W
Kayseri, Tur. (kī′sĕ-rē)	182	38.45N	35.20E
Kazach′ye, Russia	165	70.46N	135.47E
Kazakhstan, nation, Asia	164	48.45N	59.00E
Kazan′, Russia (kȧ-zän′)	164	55.50N	49.18E
Kazanka, Ukr. (kȧ-zän′kȧ)	163	47.49N	32.50E
Kazanlŭk, Bul. (kȧ′zȧn-lē̇k)	161	42.47N	25.23E
Kazbek, Gora, mtn. (kȧz-bĕk′)	167	42.42N	44.31E
Kāzerūn, Iran	182	29.37N	51.44E
Kazincbarcika, Hung. (kô′zĭnts-bôr-tsĭ-ko)	155	48.15N	20.39E
Kazungula, Zam.	217	17.45S	25.20E
Kazusa Kameyama, Japan (kä-zo͞o-sä kä-mȧ′yä-mä)	195a	35.14N	140.06E
Kazym, r., Russia (kä-zēm′)	170	63.30N	67.41E
Kéa, i., Grc.	161	37.36N	24.13E
Kealaikahiki Channel, strt., Hi., U.S. (kā-ä′lä-ē-kä-hē′kē)	94a	20.38N	157.00W
Keansburg, N.J., U.S. (kēnz′bûrg)	100a	40.26N	74.08W
Kearney, Ne., U.S. (kär′nĭ)	102	40.42N	99.05W
Kearny, N.J., U.S.	100a	40.46N	74.09W
Kearsley, Eng., U.K.	237b	53.32N	2.23W
Keasey, Or., U.S. (kēz′ĭ)	106c	45.51N	123.20W
Kebayoram, neigh., Indon.	241i	6.14S	106.46E
Kebnekaise, mtn., Swe. (kĕp′nĕ-kȧ-ēs′ĕ)	142	67.53N	18.10E
Kecskemét, Hung. (kĕch′kĕ-māt)	149	46.52N	19.42E
Kedah, hist. reg., Malay. (kā′dä)	196	6.00N	100.31E
Kédainiai, Lith. (kē-dī′nĭ-ī)	153	55.16N	23.58E
Kedgwick, Can. (kĕdj′wĭk)	92	47.39N	67.21W
Keenbrook, Ca., U.S. (kēn′bro̤k)	107a	34.16N	117.29W
Keene, N.H., U.S. (kēn)	99	42.55N	72.15W
Keetmanshoop, Nmb. (kāt′mȧns-hōp)	212	26.30S	18.05E
Keet Seel Ruin, Az., U.S. (kēt sēl)	109	36.46N	110.32W
Keewatin, Mn., U.S. (kē-wä′tĭn)	103	47.24N	93.03W
Kefallinía, i., Grc.	149	38.08N	20.58E
Keffi, Nig. (kĕf′ē̇)	210	8.51N	7.52E
Ke Ga, Mui, c., Viet.	196	12.58N	109.50E
Kei, r., Afr. (kā)	213c	32.57S	26.50E
Keila, Est. (kā′lȧ)	153	59.19N	24.25E
Keilor, Austl.	201a	37.43S	144.50E
Kei Mouth, S. Afr.	213c	32.40S	28.23E
Keiskammahoek, S. Afr. (kās′kämä-ho͞ok′)	213c	32.42S	27.11E
Kéita, Bahr, r., Chad	215	9.30N	19.17E
Keitele, l., Fin. (kā′tĕ-lĕ)	153	62.50N	25.40E
Kekaha, Hi., U.S.	94a	21.57N	159.42W
Kelafo, Eth.	218a	5.40N	44.00E
Kelang, Malay.	196	3.20N	101.27E
Kelang, r., Malay.	181b	3.00N	101.40E
Kelenföld, neigh., Hung.	239g	47.28N	19.03E
Kelkit, r., Tur.	149	40.38N	37.03E
Keller, Tx., U.S. (kĕl′ẽr)	107c	32.56N	97.15W
Kellinghusen, Ger. (kĕ′lēng-ho͞o-zĕn)	145c	53.57N	9.43E
Kellogg, Id., U.S. (kĕl′ŏg)	104	47.32N	116.07W
Kellyville, Austl.	243a	33.43S	150.57E
Kelme′, Lith. (kĕl-mȧ)	153	55.36N	22.53E
Kélo, Chad	215	9.19N	15.48E
Kelowna, Can.	84	49.53N	119.29W
Kelsey Bay, Can. (kĕl′sē̇)	86	50.24N	125.57W
Kelso, Wa., U.S.	106c	46.09N	122.54W
Keluang, Malay.	181b	2.01N	103.19E
Kelvedon Hatch, Eng., U.K.	235	51.40N	0.16E
Kem′, Russia (kĕm)	164	65.00N	34.48E
Kemah, Tx., U.S. (kē′mȧ)	113a	29.32N	95.01W
Kemerovo, Russia	164	55.31N	86.05E
Kemi, Fin. (kā′mē̇)	146	65.48N	24.38E
Kemi, r., Fin.	146	67.02N	27.50E
Kemigawa, Japan (kĕ′mē̇-gä′wä)	195a	35.38N	140.07E
Kemijarvi, Fin. (kā′mē̇-yĕr-vē)	146	66.48N	27.21E
Kemi-joki, l., Fin.	146	66.37N	28.13E
Kemmerer, Wy., U.S. (kém′ẽr-ẽr)	105	41.48N	110.36W
Kemp, l., Tx., U.S. (kĕmp)	110	33.55N	99.22W
Kempen, Ger. (kĕm′pĕn)	157c	51.22N	6.25E
Kempsey, Austl. (kĕmp′sē̇)	203	30.59S	152.50E
Kempt, l., Can. (kĕmpt)	91	47.28N	74.00W
Kempten, Ger. (kĕmp′tĕn)	147	47.44N	10.17E
Kempton Park, S. Afr. (kĕmp′tŏn pärk)	218d	26.07S	28.29E
Kemsing, Eng., U.K.	235	51.18N	0.14E
Ken, r., India	186	25.00N	79.55E
Kenai, Ak., U.S. (kĕ-nī′)	95	60.38N	151.18W
Kenai Fjords National Park, rec., Ak., U.S.	95	59.45N	150.00W
Kenai Mountains, mts., Ak., U.S.	95	60.00N	150.00W
Kenai Pen, Ak., U.S.	95	64.40N	150.18W
Kenberma, Ma., U.S.	227a	42.17N	70.52W
Kendal, S. Afr.	218d	26.03S	28.58E
Kendal, Eng., U.K. (kĕn′dȧl)	150	54.20N	1.48W
Kendallville, In., U.S. (kĕn′dăl-vĭl)	98	41.25N	85.20W
Kenedy, Tx., U.S. (kĕn′ĕ-dĭ)	113	28.49N	97.50W
Kenema, S.L.	214	7.52N	11.12W
Kenilworth, Il., U.S.	231a	42.05N	87.43W
Kenilworth, N.J., U.S.	228	40.41N	74.18W
Kenitra, Mor. (kĕ-nē′trȧ)	148	34.21N	6.34W
Kenley, neigh., Eng., U.K.	235	51.19N	0.06W
Kenmare, N.D., U.S. (kĕn-mâr′)	102	48.41N	102.05W
Kenmore, N.Y., U.S. (kĕn′mōr)	101c	42.58N	78.53W
Kennebec, r., Me., U.S. (kĕn-ē̇-bĕk′)	92	44.23N	69.48W
Kennebunk, Me., U.S. (kĕn-ē̇-buŋk′)	92	43.24N	70.33W
Kennedale, Tx., U.S. (kĕn′-ē̇-dāl)	107c	32.38N	97.13W
Kennedy, Cape see Canaveral, Cape, c., Fl., U.S.	97	28.30N	80.23W
Kennedy, Mount, mtn., Can.	95	60.25N	138.50W
Kenner, La., U.S. (kĕn′ẽr)	113	29.58N	90.15W
Kennett, Mo., U.S. (kĕn′ĕt)	111	36.14N	90.01W
Kennewick, Wa., U.S. (kĕn′ē̇-wĭk)	104	46.12N	119.06W
Kenney Dam, dam, Can.	86	53.37N	124.58W
Kennydale, Wa., U.S. (kĕn-nē̇′dāl)	106a	47.31N	122.12W
Kénogami, Can. (kĕn-ō̇′gä-mē̇)	85	48.26N	71.14W
Kenogamissi Lake, l., Can.	90	48.15N	81.31W
Keno Hill, Can.	95	63.58N	135.18W
Kenora, Can. (kē̇-nō′rȧ)	85	49.47N	94.29W
Kenosha, Wi., U.S. (kĕ-nō′shȧ)	97	42.34N	87.50W
Kenova, W.V., U.S. (kē̇-nō′vȧ)	98	38.20N	82.35W
Kensico Reservoir, res., N.Y., U.S. (kĕn′sĭ-kō)	100a	41.08N	73.45W
Kensington, Austl.	243a	33.55S	151.14E
Kensington, Ca., U.S.	231b	37.54N	122.16W
Kensington, Md., U.S.	229d	39.02N	77.03W
Kensington, neigh., S. Afr.	244b	26.12S	28.06E
Kensington, neigh., N.Y., U.S.	228	40.39N	73.58W
Kensington, neigh., Pa., U.S.	229b	39.58N	75.08W
Kensington and Chelsea, neigh., Eng., U.K.	235	51.29N	0.11W
Kent, Oh., U.S. (kĕnt)	98	41.05N	81.20W
Kent, Wa., U.S.	106a	47.23N	122.14W
Kentani, S. Afr. (kĕnt-änĭ′)	213c	32.31S	28.19E
Kentland, In., U.S. (kĕnt′lȧnd)	98	40.50N	87.25W
Kentland, Md., U.S.	229d	38.55N	76.53W
Kenton, Oh., U.S. (kĕn′tŭn)	98	40.40N	83.35W
Kent Peninsula, pen., Can.	84	68.28N	108.10W
Kentucky, state, U.S. (kĕn-tŭk′ĭ)	97	37.30N	87.35W
Kentucky, res., U.S.	97	36.20N	88.50W

304 Kentucky – Kirchhörde

PLACE (Pronunciation)	PAGE	Lat. °′	Long. °′
Kentucky, r., Ky., U.S.	97	38.15N	85.01W
Kentwood, La., U.S. (kĕnt'wo͝od)	113	30.56N	90.31W
Kenya, nation, Afr. (kĕn'yȧ)	212	1.00N	36.53E
Kenya, Mount (Kirinyaga), mtn., Kenya	213	0.10S	37.20E
Kenyon, Mn., U.S. (kĕn'yŭn)	103	44.15N	92.58W
Keokuk, Ia., U.S. (kē'ō-kŭk)	97	40.24N	91.34W
Keoma, Can. (kē-ō'mȧ)	83e	51.13N	113.39W
Keon Park, Austl.	243b	37.42S	145.01E
Kepenkeck Lake, l., Can.	93	48.13N	54.45W
Kępno, Pol. (kăŋ'pnō)	155	51.17N	17.59E
Kerala, state, India	183	16.38N	76.00E
Kerang, Austl. (kē-răng')	203	35.32S	143.58E
Keratsinion, Grc.	239d	37.58N	23.37E
Kerch, Ukr. (kĕrch)	164	45.20N	36.26E
Kerchenskiy Proliv, strt., Eur. (kĕr-chĕn'skĭ prô'lĭf)	163	45.08N	36.35E
Kerempe Burun, c., Tur.	149	42.00N	33.20E
Keren, Erit.	211	15.46N	38.28E
Kerguélen, Îles, is., Afr. (kĕr'gā-lĕn)	3	49.50S	69.30E
Kericho, Kenya	217	0.22S	35.17E
Kerinci, Gunung, mtn., Indon.	196	1.45S	101.18E
Keriya *see* Yutian, China	188	36.55N	81.39E
Keriya, r., China (kē'rē-yä)	188	37.13N	81.59E
Kerkebet, Erit.	184	16.18N	37.24E
Kerkenna, Îles, i., Tun. (kĕr'kĕn-nä)	210	34.49N	11.37E
Kerki, Turk. (kĕr'kē)	170	37.52N	65.15E
Kérkira, Grc.	149	39.36N	19.56E
Kérkira, i., Grc.	142	39.33N	19.36E
Kermadec Islands, is., N.Z. (kēr-măd'ĕk)	3	30.30S	177.00E
Kermān, Iran (kĕr-män')	182	30.23N	57.08E
Kermānshāh *see* Bakhtarān, Iran	182	34.01N	47.00E
Kern, r., Ca., U.S.	108	35.31N	118.37W
Kern, South Fork, r., Ca., U.S.	108	35.40N	118.15W
Kerpen, Ger. (kĕr'pĕn)	157c	50.52N	6.42E
Kerrobert, Can.	88	51.53N	109.13W
Kerrville, Tx., U.S. (kûr'vĭl)	112	30.02N	99.07W
Kerulen, r., Asia (kĕr'o͞o-lĕn)	189	47.52N	113.22E
Kesagami Lake, l., Can.	91	50.23N	80.15W
Keşan, Tur. (kĕ'shan)	161	40.50N	26.37E
Keshan, China (kŭ-shän)	189	48.00N	126.30E
Kesour, Monts des, mts., Alg.	148	32.51N	0.30W
Kestell, S. Afr. (kĕs'tĕl)	218d	28.19N	28.43E
Keszthely, Hung. (kĕst'hĕl-lĭ)	155	46.46N	17.12E
Ket', r., Russia (kyĕt)	170	58.30N	84.15E
Keta, Ghana	210	6.00N	1.00E
Ketamputih, Indon.	181b	1.25N	102.19E
Ketapang, Indon. (kē-tȧ-päng')	196	2.00S	109.57E
Ketchikan, Ak., U.S. (kĕch-ĭ-kăn')	96a	55.21N	131.35W
Kętrzyn, Pol. (kăŋ't'r-zĭn)	155	54.04N	21.24E
Kettering, Eng., U.K. (kĕt'ēr-ĭng)	144a	52.23N	0.43W
Kettering, Oh., U.S.	98	39.40N	84.15W
Kettle, r., Can.	87	49.40N	119.00W
Kettle, r., Mn., U.S. (kĕt''l)	103	46.20N	92.57W
Kettwig, Ger. (kĕt'vēg)	157c	51.22N	6.56E
Kęty, Pol. (kăŋ tĭ)	155	49.54N	19.16E
Ketzin, Ger. (kĕ'tzēn)	145b	52.29N	12.51E
Keuka, l., N.Y., U.S. (kē-ū'kȧ)	99	42.30N	77.10W
Kevelaer, Ger. (kĕ'fĕ-lär)	157c	51.35N	6.15E
Kew, Austl.	201a	37.49S	145.02E
Kew, S. Afr.	244b	26.08S	28.06E
Kewanee, Il., U.S. (kē-wä'nē)	103	41.15N	89.55W
Kewaunee, Wi., U.S. (kē-wô'nē)	103	44.27N	87.33W
Keweenaw Bay, b., Mi., U.S. (kē'wē-nô)	103	46.59N	88.15W
Keweenaw Peninsula, pen., Mi., U.S.	103	47.28N	88.12W
Kew Gardens, pt. of i., Eng., U.K.	235	51.28N	0.18W
Keya Paha, r., S.D., U.S. (kē-yȧ pä'hä)	102	43.11N	100.10W
Key Largo, i., Fl., U.S.	115a	25.11N	80.15W
Keyport, N.J., U.S. (kē'pōrt)	100a	40.26N	74.12W
Keyport, Wa., U.S.	106a	47.42N	122.38W
Keyser, W.V., U.S. (kī'sēr)	99	39.25N	79.00W
Key West, Fl., U.S. (kē wĕst')	97	24.31N	81.47W
Kežmarok, Slvk. (kĕzh'mȧ-rôk)	155	49.10N	20.27E
Khabarovo, Russia (kŭ-bȧr-ôvŏ)	164	69.31N	60.41E
Khabarovsk, Russia (kä-bä'rôfsk)	165	48.35N	135.12E
Khaïdhárion, Grc.	239d	38.01N	23.39E
Khajuri, neigh., India	240d	28.43N	77.16E
Khakassia, state, Russia	170	52.32N	89.33E
Khalándrion, Grc.	239d	38.01N	23.48E
Khālāpur, India	187b	18.48N	73.17E
Khalkidhiki, pen., Grc.	161	40.30N	23.18E
Khalkís, Grc. (ĸäl'kĭs)	149	38.28N	23.38E
Khal'mer-Yu, Russia (kŭl-myĕr'-yo͞o')	164	67.52N	64.25E
Khalturin, Russia (ĸäl'to͞o-rēn)	166	58.28N	49.00E
Khambhāt, Gulf of, b., India	183	21.20N	72.27E
Khammam, India	187	17.09N	80.13E
Khānābād, Afg.	186	36.43N	69.11E
Khānaqīn, Iraq	185	34.21N	45.22E
Khandwa, India	186	21.53N	76.22E
Khaníon, Kólpos, b., Grc.	160a	35.35N	23.55E
Khanka, l., Asia (ĸän'kȧ)	165	45.09N	133.28E
Khānpur, Pak.	186	28.42N	70.42E
Khanty-Mansiysk, Russia (kŭn-tē'mŭn-sēsk')	164	61.02N	69.01E
Khān Yūnus, Gaza	181a	31.21N	34.19E
Kharagpur, India (kŭ-rŭg'po͝or)	183	22.26N	87.21E
Khardah, India	240a	22.44N	88.22E
Kharkiv, Ukr.	164	50.00N	36.10E
Kharkiv, prov., Ukr.	163	49.33N	35.55E
Kharkov *see* Kharkiv, Ukr.	164	50.00N	36.10E
Kharlovka, Russia	166	68.47N	37.20E
Kharmanli, Bul. (ĸȧr-män'lē)	161	41.54N	25.55E
Khartoum, Sudan	211	15.34N	32.36E
Khasavyurt, Russia	168	43.15N	46.37E
Khāsh, Iran	182	28.08N	61.08E
Khāsh, r., Afg.	182	32.30N	64.27E
Khasi Hills, hills, India	183	25.38N	91.55E
Khaskovo, Bul. (ĸäs'kô-vô)	149	41.56N	25.32E
Khatanga, Russia (kȧ-tän'gȧ)	165	71.48N	101.47E
Khatangskiy Zaliv, b., Russia (kä-tän'g-skē)	165	73.45N	108.30E
Khayāla, neigh., India	240d	28.40N	77.06E
Khaybār, Sau. Ar.	182	25.45N	39.28E
Kherson, Ukr. (ĸĕr-sôn')	167	46.38N	32.34E
Kherson, prov., Ukr.	163	46.32N	32.55E
Khichripur, neigh., India	240d	28.37N	77.19E
Khiitola, Russia (khē'tō-lȧ)	153	61.14N	29.40E
Khimki, Russia (ĸēm'kĭ)	172b	55.54N	37.27E
Khíos, Grc. (kē'ôs)	149	38.23N	26.09E
Khíos, i., Grc.	149	38.20N	25.45E
Khmel'nyts'kyy, Ukr.	167	49.29N	26.54E
Khmel'nyts'kyy, prov., Ukr.	163	49.27N	26.30E
Khmil'nyk, Ukr.	163	49.34N	27.58E
Kholargós, Grc.	239d	38.00N	23.48E
Kholm, Russia (ĸôlm)	162	57.09N	31.07E
Kholmsk, Russia (ĸŭlmsk)	165	47.09N	142.33E
Khomeynīshahr, Iran	185	32.41N	51.31E
Khon Kaen, Thai.	196	16.37N	102.41E
Khopër, r., Russia (ĸô'pēr)	167	52.00N	43.00E
Khor, Russia (ĸôr')	194	47.50N	134.52E
Khor, r., Russia	194	47.23N	135.20E
Khóra Sfakíon, Grc.	160a	35.12N	24.10E
Khorel, India	240a	22.42N	88.19E
Khorog, Taj.	169	37.30N	71.36E
Khorol, Ukr. (ĸô'rôl)	163	49.48N	33.17E
Khorol, r., Ukr.	163	49.50N	33.21E
Khorramābād, Iran	185	33.30N	48.20E
Khorramshahr, Iran (kô-ram'shär)	182	30.36N	48.15E
Khot'kovo, Russia	172b	56.15N	38.00E
Khotyn, Ukr.	167	48.29N	26.32E
Khoyniki, Bela.	163	51.54N	30.00E
Khudzhand, Taj.	169	40.17N	69.37E
Khulna, Bngl.	183	22.50N	89.38E
Khūryān Mūryān, is., Oman	182	17.27N	56.02E
Khust, Ukr. (ĸōst)	155	48.10N	23.18E
Khvalynsk, Russia (ĸvȧ-lĭnsk')	167	52.30N	48.00E
Khvoy, Iran	182	38.32N	45.01E
Khyber Pass, p., Asia (kī'bēr)	183	34.28N	71.18E
Kialwe, Zaire	217	9.22S	27.08E
Kiambi, Zaire (kyäm'bē)	212	7.20S	28.01E
Kiamichi, r., Ok., U.S. (kyȧ-mē'chē)	111	34.31N	95.34W
Kianta, l., Fin. (kyȧn'tȧ)	166	65.00N	28.15E
Kibenga, Zaire	216	7.55S	17.35E
Kibiti, Tan.	217	7.44S	38.57E
Kibombo, Zaire	217	3.54S	25.55E
Kibondo, Tan.	217	3.35S	30.42E
Kičevo, Mac. (kē'chĕ-vô)	161	41.30N	20.59E
Kichijōji, Japan	242a	35.42N	139.35E
Kickapoo, r., Wi., U.S. (kĭk'ȧ-po͞o)	103	43.20N	90.55W
Kicking Horse Pass, p., Can.	87	51.25N	116.10W
Kidal, Mali (kē-dȧl')	210	18.33N	1.00E
Kidderminster, Eng., U.K. (kĭd'ēr-mĭn-stēr)	144a	52.23N	2.14W
Kidderpore, neigh., India	240a	22.31N	88.19E
Kidd's Beach, S. Afr. (kĭdz)	213c	33.09S	27.43E
Kidsgrove, Eng., U.K. (kĭdz'grōv)	144a	53.05N	2.15W
Kiel, Ger. (kēl)	142	54.19N	10.08E
Kiel, Wi., U.S.	103	43.52N	88.04W
Kiel Bay, b., Ger.	154	54.33N	10.19E
Kiel Canal *see* Nord-Ostsee Kanal, can., Ger.	154	54.03N	9.23E
Kielce, Pol. (kyĕl'tsĕ)	155	50.50N	20.41E
Kieldrecht, Bel. (kēl'drĕĸt)	145a	51.17N	4.09E
Kierspe, Ger.	236	51.08N	7.35E
Kiev (Kyyiv), Ukr. (kē'yĕf)	164	50.27N	30.30E
Kiffa, Maur. (kēf'ȧ)	210	16.37N	11.24W
Kigali, Rw. (kē-gä'lē)	212	1.59S	30.05E
Kigoma, Tan. (kē-gō'mä)	212	4.57S	29.38E
Kii-Suido, strt., Japan (kē so͞o-ē'dō)	194	33.53N	134.55E
Kikaiga, i., Japan	194	28.25N	130.10E
Kikinda, Yugo. (kē'kēn-dä)	161	45.49N	20.30E
Kikládhes, is., Grc.	142	37.30N	24.45E
Kikwit, Zaire (kē'kwēt)	212	5.02S	18.49E
Kil, Swe. (kēl)	152	59.30N	13.15E
Kilauea, Hi., U.S. (kē-lä-o͞o-ā'ä)	94a	22.12N	159.25W
Kilauea Crater, Hi., U.S.	94a	19.28N	155.18W
Kilbuck Mountains, mts., Ak., U.S. (kĭl-bŭk)	95	60.05N	160.00W
Kilchu, N. Kor. (kĭl'chō)	194	40.59N	129.23E
Kildare, Ire. (kĭl-dār')	150	53.09N	7.05W
Kilembe, Zaire	216	5.42S	19.55E
Kilgore, Tx., U.S.	113	32.23N	94.53W
Kilifi, Kenya	217	3.38S	39.51E
Kilimanjaro, mtn., Tan. (kyl-ē-män-jä'rō)	213	3.09S	37.19E
Kilimatinde, Tan. (kĭl-ē-mä-tĭn'dȧ)	212	5.48S	34.58E
Kilindoni, Tan.	217	7.55S	39.39E
Kilingi-Nõmme, Est. (kē'lĭn-gē-nôm'mĕ)	153	58.08N	25.03E
Kilis, Tur. (kē'lēs)	149	36.50N	37.20E
Kiliya, Ukr. (kē'lyȧ)	163	45.28N	29.17E
Kilkenny, Ire. (kĭl-kĕn-ĭ)	147	52.40N	7.30W
Kilkis, Grc. (kĭl'kĭs)	161	40.59N	22.51E
Killala, Ire. (kĭ-lă'lȧ)	150	54.11N	9.10W
Killara, Austl.	243a	33.46S	151.09E
Killarney, Ire.	150	52.03N	9.05W
Killarney Heights, Austl.	243a	33.46S	151.13E
Killdeer, N.D., U.S. (kĭl'dēr)	102	47.22N	102.45W
Killiniq Island, i., Can.	85	60.32N	63.56W
Kilmarnock, Scot., U.K. (kĭl-mär'nŭk)	150	55.38N	4.25W
Kilrush, Ire. (kĭl'rŭsh)	150	52.40N	9.16W
Kilwa Kisiwani, Tan.	217	8.58S	39.30E
Kilwa Kivinje, Tan.	213	8.43S	39.18E
Kim, r., Cam.	215	5.40N	11.17E
Kimamba, Tan.	217	6.47S	37.08E
Kimba, Austl. (kĭm'bȧ)	204	33.08S	136.25E
Kimball, Ne., U.S. (kĭm-bȧl)	102	41.14N	103.41W
Kimball, S.D., U.S.	102	43.44N	98.58W
Kimberley, Can. (kĭm'bēr-lĭ)	84	49.41N	115.59W
Kimberley, S. Afr.	212	28.40S	24.50E
Kimi, Cam.	215	6.05N	11.30E
Kími, Grc.	161	38.38N	24.05E
Kímolos, i., Grc. (kē'mô-lôs)	161	36.52N	24.20E
Kimry, Russia (kĭm'rē)	166	56.53N	37.24E
Kimvula, Zaire	216	5.44S	15.58E
Kinabalu, Gunong, mtn., Malay.	196	5.45N	115.26E
Kincardine, Can. (kĭn-kär'dĭn)	85	44.10N	81.15W
Kinda, Zaire	217	9.18S	25.04E
Kindanba, Congo	216	3.44S	14.31E
Kinder, La., U.S. (kĭn'dēr)	113	30.30N	92.50W
Kindersley, Can. (kĭn'dērz-lē)	84	51.27N	109.10W
Kindia, Gui. (kĭn'dē-ȧ)	210	10.04N	12.51W
Kindu, Zaire	212	2.57S	25.56E
Kinel'-Cherkassy, Russia	166	53.32N	51.32E
Kineshma, Russia (kē-nĕsh'mȧ)	166	57.27N	41.02E
King, i., Austl. (kĭng)	203	39.35S	143.40E
Kingaroy, Austl. (kĭŋ'gȧ-roi)	204	26.37S	151.50E
King City, Can.	83d	43.56N	79.32W
King City, Ca., U.S. (kĭng sĭ'tĭ)	108	36.12N	121.08W
Kingcome Inlet, b., Can. (kĭng'kŭm)	86	50.50N	126.10W
Kingfisher, Ok., U.S. (kĭng'fĭsh-ēr)	111	35.51N	97.55W
King George Sound, strt., Austl. (jôrj)	202	35.17S	118.30E
King George's Reservoir, res., Eng., U.K.	235	51.39N	0.01W
Kingisepp, Russia (kĭŋ-gē-sep')	166	59.22N	28.38E
King Leopold Ranges, mts., Austl. (lē'ō-pōld)	202	16.25S	125.00E
Kingman, Az., U.S. (kĭng'măn)	109	35.10N	114.05W
Kingman, Ks., U.S. (kĭng'măn)	110	37.38N	98.07W
King of Prussia, Pa., U.S.	229b	40.05N	75.23W
Kings, r., Ca., U.S.	108	36.28N	119.43W
Kingsbury, neigh., Eng., U.K.	235	51.35N	0.17W
Kings Canyon National Park, rec., Ca., U.S. (kăn'yŭn)	96	36.52N	118.53W
Kingsclere, Eng., U.K. (kĭngs-clēr)	144b	51.18N	1.15W
Kingscote, Austl. (kĭngz'kŭt)	204	35.45S	137.32E
Kingsdown, Eng., U.K.	235	51.21N	0.17E
Kingsford, Austl.	243a	33.56S	151.14E
Kingsgrove, Austl.	243a	33.57S	151.06E
Kings Langley, Eng., U.K.	235	51.43N	0.28W
King's Lynn, Eng., U.K. (kĭngz lĭn')	151	52.45N	0.20E
Kings Mountain, N.C., U.S.	115	35.13N	81.30W
Kings Norton, Eng., U.K. (nôr'tŭn)	144a	52.25N	1.54W
King Sound, strt., Austl.	202	16.50S	123.35E
Kings Park, N.Y., U.S. (kĭngz pärk)	100a	40.53N	73.16W
Kings Park, Va., U.S.	229d	38.48N	77.15W
Kings Peak, mtn., Ut., U.S.	96	40.46N	110.20W
Kings Point, N.Y., U.S.	228	40.49N	73.45W
Kingsport, Tn., U.S. (kĭngz'pōrt)	115	36.33N	82.36W
Kingston, Austl. (kĭngz'tŭn)	202	37.52S	139.52E
Kingston, Can.	85	44.15N	76.30W
Kingston, Jam.	117	18.00N	76.45W
Kingston, N.Y., U.S.	97	42.00N	74.00W
Kingston, Pa., U.S.	99	41.15N	75.50W
Kingston, Wa., U.S.	106a	47.04N	122.29W
Kingston upon Hull, Eng., U.K.	142	53.45N	0.25W
Kingston upon Thames, neigh., Eng., U.K.	235	51.25N	0.19W
Kingstown, St. Vin. (kĭngz'toun)	117	13.10N	61.14W
Kingstree, S.C., U.S. (kĭngz'trē)	115	33.30N	79.50W
Kingsville, Tx., U.S. (kĭngz'vĭl)	113	27.32N	97.52W
King William Island, i., Can. (kĭng wĭl'yăm)	84	69.25N	97.00W
King William's Town, S. Afr. (kĭng-wĭl'-yŭmz-toun)	213c	32.53S	27.24E
Kinira, r., S. Afr.	213c	30.37S	28.52E
Kinloch, Mo., U.S. (kĭn-lŏk)	107e	38.44N	90.19W
Kinnaird, Can. (kĭn-ärd')	87	49.17N	117.39W
Kinnairds Head, c., Scot., U.K. (kĭn-ârds'hĕd)	146	57.42N	3.55W
Kinomoto, Japan (kē'nō-mō'tō)	195	33.53N	136.07E
Kinosaki, Japan (kē'nō-sä'kē)	195	35.38N	134.47E
Kinshasa, Zaire	212	4.18S	15.18E
Kinshasa-Est, neigh., Zaire	244c	4.18S	15.18E
Kinshasa-Ouest, neigh., Zaire	244c	4.20S	15.15E
Kinsley, Ks., U.S. (kĭnz'lĭ)	110	37.55N	99.24W
Kinston, N.C., U.S. (kĭnz'tŭn)	115	35.15N	77.35W
Kintamo, Rapides de, wtfl., Afr.	244c	4.19S	15.15E
Kintampo, Ghana (kĕn-täm'pō)	210	8.03N	1.43W
Kintsana, Congo	244c	4.19S	15.10E
Kintyre, pen., Scot., U.K.	150	55.50N	5.40W
Kiowa, Ks., U.S. (kī'ô-wȧ)	110	37.01N	98.30W
Kiowa, Ok., U.S.	111	34.42N	95.53W
Kiparissía, Grc.	149	37.17N	21.43E
Kiparissiakós Kólpos, b., Grc.	161	37.28N	21.15E
Kipawa, Lac, l., Can.	91	46.55N	79.00W
Kipembawe, Tan. (kē-pĕm-bä'wȧ)	212	7.39S	33.24E
Kipengere Range, mts., Tan.	217	9.10S	34.00E
Kipili, Tan.	217	7.26S	30.36E
Kipushi, Zaire	217	11.46S	27.14E
Kirakira, Sol.Is.	198e	10.27S	161.55E
Kirby, Tx., U.S. (kŭr'bĭ)	107d	29.29N	98.23W
Kirbyville, Tx., U.S. (kŭr'bĭ-vĭl)	113	30.39N	93.54W
Kirchderne, neigh., Ger.	236	51.33N	7.30E
Kirchende, Ger.	236	51.25N	7.26E
Kirchhellen, Ger.	236	51.36N	6.55E
Kirchheller Heide, for., Ger.	236	51.36N	6.53E
Kirchhörde, neigh., Ger.	236	51.27N	7.27E

PRONOUNCING INDEX

Kirchlinde-Konstanz 305

PLACE (Pronunciation)	PAGE	Lat. °′	Long. °′
Kirchlinde, neigh., Ger.	236	51.32N	7.22E
Kirdāsah, Egypt	244a	30.02N	31.07E
Kirenga, r., Russia (kê-rěŋ'gȧ)	171	56.30N	108.18E
Kirensk, Russia (kē-rěnsk')	165	57.47N	108.22E
Kirghiz Steppe, plat., Kyrg.	169	49.28N	57.07E
Kiri, Zaire	216	1.27S	19.00E
Kiribati, nation, Oc.	3	1.30S	173.00E
Kirin *see* Chilung, Tai.	189	25.02N	121.48E
Kiritimati, i., Kir.	2	2.20N	157.40W
Kirkby, Eng., U.K.	144a	53.29N	2.54W
Kirkby-in-Ashfield, Eng., U.K. (kûrk'bē-ĭn-ăsh'fēld)	144a	53.06N	1.16W
Kirkcaldy, Scot., U.K. (kẽr-kô'dĭ)	150	56.06N	3.15W
Kirkdale, neigh., Eng., U.K.	237a	53.26N	2.59W
Kirkenes, Nor.	146	69.40N	30.03E
Kirkham, Eng., U.K. (kûrk'ăm)	144a	53.47N	2.53W
Kirkland, Can.	227b	45.27N	73.52W
Kirkland, Wa., U.S. (kûrk'lănd)	106a	47.41N	122.12W
Kirklareli, Tur. (kėrk'lár-ĕ'lė)	149	41.44N	27.15E
Kirksville, Mo., U.S. (kûrks'vĭl)	97	40.12N	92.35W
Kirkūk, Iraq (kĭr-ko͞ok')	182	35.28N	44.22E
Kirkwall, Scot., U.K. (kûrk'wôl)	146	58.58N	2.59W
Kirkwood, S. Afr.	213c	33.26S	25.24E
Kirkwood, Md., U.S.	229d	38.57N	76.58W
Kirkwood, Mo., U.S. (kûrk'wŏod)	107e	38.35N	90.24W
Kirn, Ger. (kėrn)	154	49.47N	7.23E
Kirov, Russia	162	54.04N	34.19E
Kirov, Russia	164	58.35N	49.35E
Kirovakan, Arm.	168	40.48N	44.30E
Kirovgrad, Russia (kē'rŭ-vŭ-grad)	172a	57.26N	60.03E
Kirovohrad, Ukr.	167	48.33N	32.17E
Kirovohrad, prov., Ukr.	163	48.23N	31.10E
Kirovsk, Russia	164	67.40N	33.58E
Kirovsk, Russia (kė-rôfsk')	172c	59.52N	30.59E
Kirsanov, Russia (kėr-sá'nôf)	167	52.40N	42.40E
Kirşehir, Tur. (kėr-shĕ'hĕr)	182	39.10N	34.00E
Kirtachi Seybou, Niger	215	12.48N	2.29E
Kīrthar Range, mts., Pak. (kĭr-tŭr)	183	27.00N	67.10E
Kirton, Eng., U.K. (kûr'tŭn)	144a	53.29N	0.35W
Kiruna, Swe. (kē-ro͞o'nä)	146	67.49N	20.08E
Kirundu, Zaire	217	0.44S	25.32E
Kirwan Heights, Pa., U.S.	230b	40.22N	80.06W
Kirwin Reservoir, res., Ks., U.S. (kûr'wĭn)	110	39.34N	99.04W
Kiryū, Japan	194	36.24N	139.20E
Kirzhach, Russia (kėr-zhák')	162	56.08N	38.53E
Kisaki, Tan. (kē-sá'kē)	213	7.37S	37.43E
Kisangani, Zaire	211	0.30N	25.12E
Kisarazu, Japan (kē'sȧ-rä'zo͞o)	195a	35.23N	139.55E
Kiselëvsk, Russia (kē-sĭ-lyôfsk')	164	54.00N	86.39E
Kishinev *see* Chişinău, Mol.	164	47.02N	28.52E
Kishiwada, Japan (kē'shē-wä'dä)	194	34.25N	135.18E
Kishkino, Russia (kēsh'kĭ-nô)	172b	55.15N	38.04E
Kisiwani, Tan.	217	4.08S	37.57E
Kiska, i., Ak., U.S. (kĭs'kä)	96b	52.08N	177.10E
Kiskatinaw, r., Can.	87	55.10N	120.20W
Kiskittogisu Lake, l., Can.	89	54.05N	99.00W
Kiskitto Lake, l., Can. (kĭs-kĭ'tō)	89	54.16N	98.34W
Kiskunfélegyháza, Hung. (kĭsh'kòn-fā'lĕd-y'hä'zô)	155	46.42N	19.52E
Kiskunhalas, Hung. (kĭsh'kòn-hô'lôsh)	155	46.24N	19.26E
Kiskunmajsa, Hung. (kĭsh'kòn-mĭ'shô)	155	46.29N	19.42E
Kislovodsk, Russia	168	43.55N	42.44E
Kismaayo, Som.	213	0.18S	42.30E
Kiso, Japan	242a	35.34N	139.26E
Kiso-Gawa, r., Japan (kē'sō-gä'wä)	195	35.29N	137.12E
Kiso-Sammyaku, mts., Japan (kē'sō säm'myá-ko͞o)	195	35.47N	137.39E
Kissamos, Grc.	160a	35.13N	23.35E
Kissidougou, Gui. (kē'sė-do͞o'go͞o)	210	9.11N	10.06W
Kissimmee, Fl., U.S. (kĭ-sĭm'ė)	115a	28.17N	81.25W
Kissimmee, r., Fl., U.S.	115a	27.45N	81.07W
Kissimmee, Lake, l., Fl., U.S.	115a	27.58N	81.17W
Kistarcsa, Hung.	239g	47.33N	19.16E
Kisujszallás, Hung.	155	47.12N	20.47E
Kisumu, Kenya (kē'so͞o-mo͞o)	212	0.06S	34.45E
Kita, Mali (kē'tá)	210	13.03N	9.29W
Kita, neigh., Japan	242a	35.45N	139.44E
Kitakami Gawa, r., Japan	194	39.20N	141.10E
Kitakyūshū, Japan	189	33.53N	130.50E
Kitale, Kenya	217	1.01N	35.00E
Kitamachi, neigh., Japan	242a	35.46N	139.39E
Kitamba, neigh., Zaire	244c	4.19S	15.14E
Kitatawara, Japan	242b	34.44N	135.42E
Kit Carson, Co., U.S.	110	38.46N	102.48W
Kitchener, Can. (kĭch'ĕ-nẽr)	85	43.25N	80.35W
Kitenda, Zaire	216	6.53S	17.21E
Kitgum, Ug. (kĭt'gòm)	211	3.29N	33.04E
Kíthira, i., Grc.	149	36.15N	22.56E
Kíthnos, i., Grc.	161	37.24N	24.10E
Kitimat, Can. (kĭ'tĭ-măt)	84	54.03N	128.33W
Kitimat, r., Can.	86	53.50N	129.00W
Kitimat Ranges, mts., Can.	86	53.30N	128.50W
Kitlope, r., Can. (kĭt'lōp)	86	53.00N	128.00W
Kitsuki, Japan (kėt'sò-kė)	195	33.24N	131.35E
Kittanning, Pa., U.S. (kĭ-tăn'ĭng)	99	40.50N	79.30W
Kittatinny Mountains, mts., N.J., U.S. (kĭ-tŭ-tĭ'nė)	100a	41.16N	74.44W
Kittery, Me., U.S. (kĭt'ẽr-ĭ)	92	43.07N	70.45W
Kittsee, Aus.	145e	48.05N	17.05E
Kitty Hawk, N.C., U.S. (kĭt'tė hôk)	115	36.04N	75.42W
Kitunda, Tan.	217	6.48S	33.13E
Kitwe, Zam.	217	12.49S	28.13E
Kitzingen, Ger. (kĭt'zĭng-ĕn)	154	49.44N	10.08E
Kiunga, Kenya	217	1.45S	41.29E
Kivu, Lac, l., Afr.	212	1.45S	28.55E
Kiyev *see* Kiev, Ukr.	164	50.27N	30.30E
Kīyose, Japan	195a	35.47N	139.32E
Kizel, Russia (kē'zĕl)	166	59.05N	57.42E
Kızıl, r., Tur.	182	40.00N	34.00E
Kizil'skoye, Russia (kĭz'ĭl-skô-yĕ)	172a	52.43N	58.53E
Kizlyar, Russia (kĭz-lyär')	167	44.00N	46.50E
Kizlyarskiy Zaliv, b., Russia	168	44.33N	46.55E
Kizu, Japan (kē'zo͞o)	195	34.43N	135.49E
Kizuki, Japan	242a	35.34N	139.40E
Kizuri, Japan	242b	34.39N	135.34E
Kizyl-Arvat, Turk. (kē'zĭl-ŭr-vät')	169	38.55N	56.33E
Klaas Smits, r., S. Afr.	213c	31.45S	26.33E
Klaaswaal, Neth.	145a	51.46N	4.25E
Kladno, Czech Rep. (kläd'nō)	154	50.10N	14.05E
Klagenfurt, Aus. (klä'gĕn-fòrt)	147	46.38N	14.19E
Klaipėda, Lith. (klī'pȧ-dȧ)	166	55.43N	21.10E
Klamath, r., U.S.	104	41.40N	123.25W
Klamath Falls, Or., U.S.	96	42.13N	121.49W
Klamath Mountains, mts., Ca., U.S.	104	42.00N	123.25W
Klarälven, r., Swe.	146	60.40N	13.00E
Klaskanine, r., Or., U.S. (klăs'kȧ-nīn)	106c	46.02N	123.43W
Klatovy, Czech Rep. (klȧ'tô-vė)	147	49.23N	13.18E
Klawock, Ak., U.S. (klä'wăk)	95	55.32N	133.10W
Kleef, Ger.	236	51.11N	6.56E
Kleinebroich, Ger.	236	51.12N	6.35E
Kleinmachnow, Ger. (klīn-mäĸ'nō)	145b	52.22N	13.12E
Klein Ziethen, Ger.	238a	52.23N	13.27E
Klerksdorp, S. Afr. (klẽrks'dôrp)	218d	26.52S	26.40E
Klerksraal, S. Afr. (klẽrks'räl)	218d	26.15N	27.10E
Kletnya, Russia (klyĕt'nyȧ)	162	53.19N	33.14E
Kletsk, Bela. (klĕtsk)	162	53.04N	26.43E
Kleve, Ger. (klĕ'fĕ)	154	51.47N	6.09E
Kley, neigh., Ger.	236	51.30N	7.22E
Klickitat, r., Wa., U.S.	104	46.01N	121.07W
Klimovichi, Bela. (klē-mô-vē'chė)	162	53.37N	31.21E
Klimovsk, Russia (klĭ'môfsk)	172b	55.21N	37.32E
Klin, Russia (klėn)	162	56.18N	36.43E
Klintehamn, Swe. (klēn'tĕ-häm)	152	57.24N	18.14E
Klintsy, Russia (klĭn'tsĭ)	167	52.46N	32.14E
Klip, r., S. Afr. (klĭp)	218d	27.18N	29.25E
Klipgat, S. Afr.	218d	25.26S	27.57E
Klippan, Swe. (klyp'pȧn)	152	56.08N	13.09E
Klippoortje, S. Afr.	244b	26.17S	28.14E
Kliptown, S. Afr.	244b	26.17S	27.53E
Kłodzko, Pol. (klôd'skô)	154	50.26N	16.38E
Klondike Region, hist. reg., N.A. (klŏn'dĭk)	84	64.12N	142.38W
Klosterfelde, Ger. (klōs'tẽr-fĕl-dĕ)	145b	52.47N	13.29E
Klosterneuburg, Aus. (klōs-tẽr-noi'bo͝orgh)	145e	48.19N	16.20E
Kluane, l., Can.	84	61.15N	138.40W
Kluane National Park, rec., Can.	84	60.25N	137.53W
Kluczbork, Pol. (klo͞och'bòrk)	155	50.59N	18.15E
Klyaz'ma, r., Russia (klyäz'mȧ)	162	55.49N	39.19E
Klyuchevskaya, vol., Russia (klyo͞o-chĕfskä'yä)	165	56.13N	160.00E
Klyuchi, Russia (klyo͞o'chĭ)	172a	57.03N	57.20E
Knezha, Bul. (knyā'zhȧ)	149	43.27N	24.03E
Knife, r., N.D., U.S. (nīf)	102	47.06N	102.33W
Knight Inlet, b., Can. (nīt)	86	50.41N	125.40W
Knightstown, In., U.S. (nīts'toun)	98	39.45N	85.30W
Knin, Cro. (knēn)	160	44.02N	16.14E
Knittelfeld, Aus.	147	47.13N	14.50E
Knob Peak, mtn., Phil. (nŏb)	197a	12.30N	121.20E
Knockholt, Eng., U.K.	235	51.18N	0.06E
Knockholt Pound, Eng., U.K.	235	51.19N	0.08E
Knoppiesfontein, S. Afr.	244b	26.05S	28.25E
Knottingley, Eng., U.K. (nŏt'ĭng-lĭ)	144a	53.42N	1.14W
Knott's Berry Farm, pt. of i., Ca., U.S.	232	33.50N	118.00W
Knotty Ash, neigh., Eng., U.K.	237a	53.25N	2.54W
Knowsley, Eng., U.K.	237a	53.27N	2.51W
Knox, Austl.	243b	37.53S	145.18E
Knox, In., U.S. (nŏks)	98	41.15N	86.40W
Knox, Cape, c., Can.	86	54.12N	133.20W
Knoxville, Ia., U.S. (nŏks'vĭl)	103	41.19N	93.05W
Knoxville, Tn., U.S.	97	35.58N	83.55W
Knutsford, Eng., U.K. (nŭts'fẽrd)	144a	53.18N	2.22W
Knyszyn, Pol. (knĭ'shĭn)	155	53.16N	22.59E
Kobayashi, Japan (kō'bá-yä'shė)	195	31.58N	130.59E
Kōbe, Japan (kō'bĕ)	189	34.30N	135.10E
Kobelyaky, Ukr.	167	49.11N	34.12E
København *see* Copenhagen, Den.	142	55.43N	12.27E
Koblenz, Ger. (kō'blĕntz)	147	50.18N	7.36E
Kobozha, r., Russia (kô-bô'zhȧ)	162	58.55N	35.18E
Kobrin, Bela. (kō'brėn')	167	52.13N	24.23E
Kobrinskoye, Russia (kô-brĭn'skô-yĕ)	172c	59.25N	30.07E
Kobuk, r., Ak., U.S. (kō'bŭk)	95	66.58N	158.48W
Kobuk Valley National Park, rec., Ak., U.S.	95	67.20N	159.00W
Kobuleti, Geor. (kō-bò-lyā'tė)	167	41.50N	41.40E
Kočani, Mac. (kô'chä-nĕ)	161	41.54N	22.25E
Kočevje, Slvn. (kō'chāv-ye)	160	45.38N	14.51E
Kocher, r., Ger. (kôĸ'ẽr)	154	49.00N	9.52E
Kōchi, Japan (kō'chė)	189	33.35N	133.32E
Kodaira, Japan	195a	35.43N	139.29E
Kodiak, Ak., U.S. (kō'dyăk)	96a	57.50N	152.30W
Kodiak Island, i., Ak., U.S.	95	57.24N	153.32W
Kodok, Sudan (kō'dŏk)	211	9.57N	32.08E
Koforidua, Ghana (kō fō-rĭ-do͞o'ȧ)	210	6.03N	0.17W
Kōfu, Japan (kō'fo͞o')	194	35.41N	138.34E
Koga, Japan (kō'gȧ)	195	36.13N	139.40E
Kogan, r., Gui.	214	11.30N	14.05W
Kogane, Japan (kō'gȧ-nā)	195a	35.50N	139.56E
Koganei, Japan (kō'gä-nā)	195a	35.42N	139.31E
Kogarah, Austl.	243a	33.58S	151.08E
Køge, Den. (kû'gĕ)	152	55.27N	12.09E
Køge Bugt, b., Den.	152	55.30N	12.25E
Kogil'nik, r., Eur. (kô-gėl-nēk')	163	46.08N	29.10E
Kogoni, Mali	214	14.44N	6.02W
Kohīma, India (kô-ē'mȧ)	183	25.45N	94.41E
Koito, r., Japan (kô'ė-tō)	195a	35.19N	139.58E
Kōje, i., S. Kor. (kû'jĕ)	194	34.53N	129.00E
Kokand, Uzb. (kô-känt')	169	40.27N	71.07E
Kokemäenjoki, r., Fin.	153	61.23N	22.03E
Kokhma, Russia (kôĸ'mȧ)	162	56.57N	41.08E
Kokkola, Fin. (kô'kô-lȧ)	146	63.47N	22.58E
Kokomo, In., U.S. (kō'kô-mō)	98	40.30N	86.20W
Koko Nor (Qinghai Hu), l., China (kō'kô nor) (chyĭŋ-hī ho͞o)	188	37.26N	98.30E
Kokopo, Pap. N. Gui. (kô-kō'pō)	197	4.25S	152.27E
Kökshetau, Kaz.	169	53.15N	69.13E
Koksoak, r., Can. (kôk'sô-ăk)	85	57.42N	69.50W
Kokstad, S. Afr. (kôk'shtät)	213c	30.33S	29.27E
Kokubu, Japan (kō'ko͞o-bo͞o)	195	31.42N	130.46E
Kokubunji, Japan	242a	35.42N	139.29E
Kokuou, Japan (kô'ko͞o-ô'o͞o)	195b	34.34N	135.39E
Kola Peninsula *see* Kol'skiy Poluostrov, pen., Russia	164	67.15N	37.40E
Kolār (Kolār Gold Fields), India (kôl-är')	183	13.39N	78.33E
Kolárvo, Slvk. (kôl-árôvô)	155	47.54N	17.59E
Kolbio, Kenya	217	1.10S	41.15E
Kol'chugino, Russia (kôl-chô'gē-nô)	162	56.19N	39.29E
Kolda, Sen.	214	12.53N	14.57W
Kolding, Den. (kŭl'dĭng)	152	55.29N	9.24E
Kole, Zaire (kō'lȧ)	212	3.19S	22.46E
Kolguyev, i., Russia (kôl-gò'yĕf)	164	69.00N	49.00E
Kolhāpur, India	187	16.48N	74.15E
Kolín, Czech Rep. (kō'lēn)	154	50.01N	15.11E
Kolkasrags, c., Lat. (kôl-käs'rágz)	153	57.46N	22.39E
Köln *see* Cologne, Ger.	157c	50.56N	6.57E
Kolno, Pol. (kôw'nô)	155	53.23N	21.56E
Koło, Pol. (kô'wô)	155	52.11N	18.37E
Kołobrzeg, Pol. (kô-lôb'zhĕk)	146	54.10N	15.35E
Kolomenskoje, neigh., Russia	239b	55.40N	37.41E
Kolomna, Russia (kál-ôm'nȧ)	166	55.06N	38.47E
Kolomyya, Ukr. (kō'lô-mē'yȧ)	155	48.32N	25.04E
Kolonie Stolp, Ger.	238a	52.28N	13.46E
Kolp', r., Russia (kôlp)	162	59.18N	35.32E
Kolpashevo, Russia (kŭl pȧ shô'vȧ)	164	58.16N	82.43E
Kolpino, Russia (kôl'pē-nô)	166	59.45N	30.37E
Kolpny, Russia (kôlp'nyė)	162	52.14N	36.54E
Kol'skiy Poluostrov, pen., Russia	164	67.15N	37.40E
Kolva, r., Russia	166	61.00N	57.00E
Kolwezi, Zaire (kôl-wĕ'zē)	212	10.43S	25.28E
Kolyberovo, Russia (kô-lĭ-byā'rô-vô)	172b	55.16N	38.45E
Kolyma, r., Russia	165	66.30N	151.45E
Kolymskiy Mountains *see* Gydan, Khrebet, mts., Russia	165	61.45N	155.00E
Kom, r., Afr.	216	2.15N	12.05E
Komadugu Gana, r., Nig.	215	12.15N	11.10E
Komae, Japan	195a	35.37N	139.35E
Komagome, neigh., Japan	242a	35.44N	139.45E
Komandorskiye Ostrova, is., Russia	181	55.40N	167.13E
Komárno, Slvk. (kô'mär-nô)	155	47.46N	18.08E
Komarno, Ukr.	155	49.38N	23.42E
Komárom, Hung. (kô'mä-rôm)	155	47.45N	18.06E
Komatipoort, S. Afr. (kō-mä'tė-pōrt)	212	25.21S	32.00E
Komatsu, Japan (kō-mät'so͞o)	194	36.23N	136.26E
Komatsushima, Japan (kō-mät'so͞o-shē'mä)	195	34.04N	134.32E
Komeshia, Zaire	217	8.01S	27.07E
Komga, S. Afr. (kōm'gȧ)	213c	32.36S	27.54E
Komi, state, Russia (kô'mė)	170	63.00N	55.00E
Kommetjie, S. Afr.	212a	34.09S	18.19E
Kommunizma, Pik, mtn., Taj.	169	38.57N	72.01E
Komoé, r., C. Iv.	214	5.40N	3.40W
Komsomol, Kaz.	169	53.45N	62.04E
Komsomol's'ke, Ukr.	163	49.42N	28.44E
Komsomol'sk-na-Amure, Russia	165	50.46N	137.14E
Kona, Mali	214	14.57N	3.53W
Konda, r., Russia (kôn'dȧ)	166	60.50N	64.00E
Kondas, r., Russia (kôn'dȧs)	172a	59.30N	56.28E
Kondli, neigh., India	240d	28.37N	77.19E
Kondoa, Tan. (kôn-dō'ȧ)	212	4.52S	36.00E
Kondolole, Zaire	217	1.20N	25.58E
Koné, N. Cal.	198f	21.04S	164.52E
Kong, C. Iv. (kông)	210	9.05N	4.41W
Kongbo, Cen. Afr. Rep.	216	4.44N	21.23E
Kongolo, Zaire (kôŋ'gō'lō)	212	5.23S	27.00E
Kongsberg, Nor. (kŭngs'bĕrg)	152	59.40N	9.36E
Kongsvinger, Nor. (kŭngs'vĭŋ-gẽr)	152	60.12N	12.00E
Koni, Zaire (kō'nė)	212	10.32S	27.27E
Königsberg *see* Kaliningrad, Russia	164	54.42N	20.32E
Königsbrunn, Ger. (kû'nēgs-bro͞on)	145d	48.16N	10.53E
Königshardt, neigh., Ger.	236	51.33N	6.51E
Königs Wusterhausen, Ger. (kû'nēgs vo͞os'tẽr-hou-zĕn)	145b	52.18N	13.38E
Konin, Pol. (kô'nyēn)	147	52.11N	18.17E
Kónitsa, Grc. (kô'nyē'tsȧ)	161	40.03N	20.46E
Konjic, Bos. (kôn'yēts)	161	43.38N	17.59E
Konju, S. Kor.	194	36.21N	127.05E
Konnagar, India	186a	22.41N	88.22E
Konohana, neigh., Japan	242b	34.41N	135.26E
Kōnoike, Japan	242b	34.42N	135.37E
Konotop, Ukr. (kô-nô-tôp')	167	51.13N	33.14E
Konpienga, r., Burkina	214	11.15N	0.35E
Konqi, r., China (kôn-chyĕ)	188	41.09N	87.46E
Końskie, Pol. (koin''skyĕ)	155	51.12N	20.26E
Konstanz, Ger. (kôn'shtänts)	154	47.39N	9.10E

306 Kontagora–Kup'yans'k

PLACE (Pronunciation)	PAGE	Lat. °′	Long. °′
Kontagora, Nig. (kōn-tȧ-gō'rä)	210	10.24N	5.28E
Konya, Tur. (kōn'yȧ)	182	36.55N	32.25E
Koocanusa, Lake, res., N.A.	104	49.00N	115.10W
Kootenay (Kootenai), r., N.A.	87	49.45N	117.05W
Kootenay Lake, l., Can.	87	49.35N	116.50W
Kootenay National Park, Can. (ko͞o'tė-nȧ)	84	51.06N	117.02W
Kooyong, Austl.	243b	37.50S	145.02E
Kōō-zan, mtn., Japan (ko͞o'zän)	195b	34.53N	135.32E
Kopervik, Nor. (kô'pěr-vėk)	152	59.18N	5.20E
Kopeysk, Russia (kȯ-pāsk')	170	55.07N	61.37E
Köping, Swe. (chû'pĭng)	152	59.32N	15.58E
Kopparberg, Swe. (kŏp'pȧr-běrgh)	152	59.53N	15.00E
Koppeh Dāgh, mts., Asia	182	37.28N	58.29E
Koppies, S. Afr.	218d	27.15S	27.35E
Koprivnica, Cro. (kô'prēv-nė'tsȧ)	160	46.10N	16.48E
Kopychyntsi, Ukr.	155	49.06N	25.55E
Korčula, i., Yugo. (kȯr'cho͞o-lȧ)	161	42.50N	17.05E
Korea, North, nation, Asia	189	40.00N	127.00E
Korea, South, nation, Asia	189	36.30N	128.00E
Korea Bay, b., Asia	192	39.18N	123.50E
Korean Archipelago, is., S. Kor.	189	34.05N	125.35E
Korea Strait, strt., Asia	189	33.30N	128.30E
Korets', Ukr.	155	50.35N	27.13E
Korhogo, C. Iv. (kȯr-hō'gō)	210	9.27N	5.38W
Kōri, Japan	242b	34.47N	135.39E
Koridhallós, Grc.	239d	37.59N	23.39E
Korinthiakós Kólpos, b., Grc.	149	38.15N	22.33E
Kórinthos, Grc. (kȯ-rėn'thȯs) (kŏr'ĭnth)	142	37.56N	22.54E
Kōriyama, Japan (kō'rė-yä'mä)	194	37.18N	140.25E
Korkino, Russia (kôr'kē-nŭ)	172a	54.53N	61.25E
Korla, China (kōr-lä)	188	41.37N	86.03E
Körmend, Hung. (kûr'měnt)	154	47.02N	16.36E
Kornat, i., Yugo. (kȯr-nät')	160	43.46N	15.10E
Korneuburg, Aus. (kȯr'noi-bo̊rgh)	145e	48.22N	16.21E
Koro, Mali	214	14.04N	3.05W
Korocha, Russia (kȯ-rō'chȧ)	163	50.50N	37.13E
Korop, Ukr. (kō'rôp)	163	51.33N	32.54E
Koro Sea, sea, Fiji	198g	18.00S	179.50E
Korosten', Ukr. (kô'rȯs-těn)	167	50.51N	28.39E
Korostyshiv, Ukr.	163	50.19N	29.05E
Koro Toro, Chad	215	16.05N	18.30E
Korotoyak, Russia (kȯ'rȯ-tȯ-yák')	163	51.00N	39.06E
Korsakov, Russia (kôr'sȧ-kôf')	165	46.42N	143.16E
Korsnäs, Fin. (kôrs'něs)	153	62.51N	21.17E
Korsør, Den. (kôrs'ûr')	152	55.19N	11.08E
Kortrijk, Bel.	151	50.49N	3.10E
Koryakskiy Khrebet, mts., Russia	165	62.00N	168.45E
Koryukivka, Ukr. (kôr-yo͞o-kôf'kȧ)	163	51.44N	32.24E
Kosa Byryuchyy ostriv, i., Ukr.	163	46.07N	35.12E
Kościan, Pol. (kŭsh'tsyȧn)	154	52.05N	16.38E
Kościerzyna, Pol. (kŭsh-tsyě-zhē'nȧ)	155	54.08N	17.59E
Kosciusko, Ms., U.S. (kŏs-ĭ-ŭs'kō)	114	33.04N	89.35W
Kosciusko, Mount, mtn., Austl.	203	36.26S	148.20E
Kosha, Sudan	211	20.49N	30.27E
Koshigaya, Japan (kȯ'shė-gä'yä)	195a	35.53N	139.48E
Kòshïm, r., Kaz.	170	50.30N	50.40E
Kosi, r., India (kȯ'sē)	186	26.00N	86.20E
Košice, Slvk. (kō'shė-tsě')	147	48.43N	21.17E
Kosino, Russia	239b	55.43N	37.52E
Kosmos, S. Afr. (kŏz'mŏs)	213b	25.45S	27.51E
Kosmosa, Monument, hist., Russia	239b	55.49N	37.38E
Kosobrodskiy, Russia (kä-sô'brȯd-skĭ)	172a	54.14N	60.53E
Kosovo, hist. reg., Yugo.	161	42.35N	21.00E
Kosovska Mitrovica, Yugo. (kȯ'sȯv-skä' mė'trȯ-vė-tsä')	161	42.51N	20.50E
Kostajnica, Cro. (kôs'tä-ė-nē'tsȧ)	160	45.14N	16.32E
Koster, S. Afr.	218d	25.52S	26.52E
Kostino, Russia (kôs'tĭ-nô)	172b	55.54N	37.51E
Kostroma, Russia (kȯs-trȯ-mȧ')	164	57.46N	40.55E
Kostroma, prov., Russia	162	57.50N	41.10E
Kostrzyn, Pol. (kôst'chėn)	147	52.35N	14.38E
Kostyantynivka, Ukr.	163	48.33N	37.42E
Kos'va, r., Russia (kôs'vȧ)	172a	58.44N	57.08E
Koszalin, Pol. (kô-shä'lĭn)	146	54.12N	16.10E
Köszeg, Hung. (kû'sěg)	154	47.21N	16.32E
Kota, India	183	25.17N	75.49E
Kota Baharu, Malay. (kō'tä bä'ro͞o)	196	6.15N	102.23E
Kotabaru, Indon.	196	3.22S	116.15E
Kota Kinabalu, Malay.	196	5.55N	116.05E
Kota Tinggi, Malay.	181b	1.43N	103.54E
Kotel, Bul. (kō-těl')	161	42.54N	26.28E
Kotel'nich, Russia (kȯ-tyěl'nėch)	166	58.15N	48.20E
Kotel'nyy, i., Russia (kȯ-tyěl'nė)	165	74.51N	134.09E
Kotka, Fin. (kŏt'kȧ)	146	60.28N	26.56E
Kotlas, Russia (kôt'lȧs)	166	61.10N	46.50E
Kotlin, Ostrov, i., Russia (ȯs-trôf' kôt'lĭn)	172c	60.02N	29.49E
Kōtō, neigh., Japan	242a	35.41N	139.48E
Kotor, Yugo.	161	42.25N	18.46E
Kotorosl', r., Russia (kȯ-tô'rȯsl)	162	57.18N	39.08E
Kotovs'k, Ukr.	163	47.49N	29.31E
Kotte, Sri L.	187	6.50N	80.05E
Kotto, r., Cen. Afr. Rep.	211	5.17N	22.04E
Kotuy, r., Russia (kô-to͞o')	170	71.00N	103.15E
Kotzebue, Ak., U.S. (kȯt'sē-bo͞o)	96a	66.48N	162.42W
Kotzebue Sound, strt., Ak., U.S.	95	67.00N	164.28W
Kouchibouguac National Park, rec., Can.	92	46.53N	65.35W
Koudougou, Burkina (ko͞o-do͞o'go͞o)	210	12.15N	2.22W
Kouilou, r., Congo	212	4.30S	12.00E
Koula-Moutou, Gabon	216	1.08S	12.29E
Koulikoro, Mali (ko͞o-lė-kō'rȯ)	210	12.53N	7.33W
Koulouguidi, Mali	215	13.27N	17.33E
Koumac, N. Cal.	198f	20.33S	164.17E
Koumra, Chad	215	8.55N	17.33E
Koundara, Gui.	214	12.29N	13.18W
Kouroussa, Gui. (ko͞o-ro͞o'sä)	210	10.39N	9.53W
Koutiala, Mali (ko͞o-tė-ä'lä)	210	12.29N	5.29W
Kouvola, Fin. (kō'ȯ-vȯ-lä)	153	60.51N	26.40E
Kouzhen, China (kō-jŭn)	190	36.19N	117.37E
Kovda, l., Russia (kôv'dȧ)	166	66.45N	32.00E
Kovel', Ukr. (kō'věl)	167	51.13N	24.45E
Kovno *see* Kaunas, Lith.	164	54.42N	23.54E
Kovrov, Russia (kȯv-rôf')	166	56.23N	41.21E
Kowloon (Jiulong), H.K.	189	22.18N	114.10E
Kowloon City, H.K.	241c	22.19N	114.11E
Koyuk, Ak., U.S. (kȯ-yo͞ok')	95	65.00N	161.18W
Koyukuk, r., Ak., U.S. (kȯ-yo͞o'kȯk)	95	66.25N	153.50W
Kozáni, Grc.	149	40.16N	21.51E
Kozelets', Ukr. (kȯzě-lyěts)	163	50.53N	31.07E
Kozel'sk, Russia (kȯ-zělsk')	162	54.01N	35.49E
Kozienice, Pol. (kō-zyě-nē'tsě)	155	51.34N	21.35E
Koźle, Pol. (kôzh'lě)	155	50.19N	18.10E
Kozloduy, Bul. (kŭz'lȯ-dwē)	161	43.45N	23.42E
Kōzu, i., Japan (kō'zo͞o)	195	34.16N	139.03E
Kozyatyn, Ukr.	167	49.43N	28.50E
Kra, Isthmus of, isth., Asia	196	9.30S	99.45E
Kraai, r., S. Afr. (krā'ė)	213c	30.50S	27.03E
Krabbendijke, Neth.	145a	51.26N	4.05E
Krâchéh, Camb.	196	12.28N	106.06E
Kragujevac, Yugo. (krä'go͞o'yě-vȧts)	149	44.01N	20.55E
Krahenhöhe, neigh., Ger.	236	51.10N	7.06E
Kraków, Pol. (krä'kȯf)	142	50.05N	20.00E
Kraljevo, Yugo. (kräl'ye-vô)	149	43.39N	20.48E
Kramators'k, Ukr.	163	48.43N	37.32E
Kramfors, Swe. (kräm'fȯrs)	152	62.54N	17.49E
Krampnitz, Ger.	238a	52.28N	13.04E
Kranj, Slvn. (krän')	148	46.16N	14.23E
Kranskop, S. Afr. (kränz'kŏp)	213c	28.57S	30.54E
Krãslava, Lat. (kräs'lä-vä)	153	55.53N	27.12E
Kraslice, Czech Rep. (kräs'lė-tsě)	154	50.19N	12.30E
Krasnaya Gorka, Russia	172a	55.12N	56.40E
Krasnaya Sloboda, Russia	167	48.25N	44.35E
Kraśnik, Pol. (kräsh'nĭk)	155	50.53N	22.15E
Krasnoarmeysk, Russia (kräs'nȯ-ȧr-maśk')	172b	56.06N	38.09E
Krasnoarmiys'k, Ukr.	163	48.19N	37.04E
Krasnodar, Russia (kräs'nȯ-dȧr)	164	45.03N	38.55E
Krasnodarskiy, prov., Russia (krȧs-nȯ-där'skĭ ôb'lȧst)	163	45.25N	38.10E
Krasnogorsk, Russia	172b	55.49N	37.20E
Krasnogorskiy, Russia (kräs-nȯ-gôr'skĭ)	172a	54.36N	61.15E
Krasnogvardeyskiy, Russia (krȧ'sno-gvăr-dzyē ės-kēė)	172a	57.17N	62.05E
Krasnohrad, Ukr.	163	49.23N	35.26E
Krasnokamsk, Russia (kräs-nȯ-kämsk')	166	58.00N	55.45E
Krasnokuts'k, Ukr.	163	50.03N	35.05E
Krasnoslobodsk, Russia (kräs'nȯ-slȯbôtsk')	166	54.20N	43.50E
Krasnotur'insk, Russia (krŭs-nŭ-to͞o-rensk')	164	59.47N	60.15E
Krasnoufimsk, Russia (krŭs-nŭ-o͞o-fēmsk')	164	56.38N	57.46E
Krasnoural'sk, Russia (kräs'nȯ-o͞o-rälsk')	166	58.21N	60.05E
Krasnousol'skiy, Russia (kräs-nȯ-ȯ-sôl'skĭ)	172a	53.54N	56.27E
Krasnovishersk, Russia (kräs-nȯ-vėshersk')	166	60.22N	57.20E
Krasnovodsk, Turk.	169	40.00N	52.50E
Krasnoyarsk, Russia (kräs-nȯ-yȧrsk')	165	56.13N	93.12E
Krasnoye Selo, Russia (kräs'nŭ-yŭ sâ'lō)	172c	59.44N	30.06E
Krasnyj Stroitel', neigh., Russia	239b	55.35N	37.37E
Krasny Kholm, Russia (kräs'nė kōlm)	162	58.03N	37.11E
Krasnystaw, Pol. (kräs-nė-stäf')	155	50.59N	23.11E
Krasnyy Bor, Russia (kräs'nė bôr)	172c	59.41N	30.40E
Krasnyy Klyuch, Russia (kräs'nė'klyûch')	172a	55.24N	56.43E
Krasnyy Kut, Russia (krȧs-nė ko͞ot')	167	50.50N	47.00E
Kratovo, Mac. (krä'tȯ-vȯ)	161	42.04N	22.12E
Kratovo, Russia (krä'tô-vô)	172b	55.35N	38.10E
Kray, neigh., Ger.	236	51.28N	7.05E
Krefeld, Ger. (krā'fělt)	157c	51.20N	6.34E
Kremenchuk, Ukr.	167	49.04N	33.26E
Kremenchuk vodoskhovyshche, res., Ukr.	167	49.20N	32.45E
Kremenets', Ukr.	155	50.06N	25.43E
Kreml', bldg., Russia	239b	55.45N	37.37E
Kremmen, Ger. (krě'měn)	145b	52.45N	13.02E
Krempe, Ger. (krěm'pě)	145c	53.50N	9.29E
Krems, Aus. (krěms)	154	48.25N	15.36E
Krestovyy, Pereval, p., Geor.	168	42.32N	44.28E
Kresttsy, Russia (kråst'sė)	162	58.16N	32.25E
Kretinga, Lith. (krě-tĭŋ'gȧ)	153	55.55N	21.17E
Kreuzberg, Ger.	236	51.09N	7.27E
Kreuzberg, neigh., Ger.	238a	52.30N	13.23E
Kribi, Cam. (krē'bė)	210	2.57N	9.55E
Krichëv, Bela. (krē'chôf)	162	53.44N	31.39E
Krilon, Mys, c., Russia (mĭs krĭl'ȯn)	194	45.58N	142.00E
Krimpen aan de IJssel, Neth.	145a	51.55N	4.34E
Krishna, r., India	183	16.00N	79.00E
Krishnanagar, India	186	23.29N	88.33E
Krishnapur, India	240a	22.36N	88.26E
Kristiansand, Nor. (krĭs-tyȧn-sän'')	142	58.09N	7.59E
Kristianstad, Swe. (krĭs-tyȧn-städ')	146	56.02N	14.09E
Kristiansund, Nor. (krĭs-tyȧn-sȯn'')	146	63.07N	7.49E
Kristinehamn, Swe. (krės-tē'ně-häm')	146	59.20N	14.05E
Kristinestad, Fin. (krĭs-tē'ně-städh)	153	62.16N	21.28E
Kriva-Palanka, Mac. (krē-vȧ-pȧ-läŋ'kȧ)	161	42.12N	22.21E
Krivoy Rog *see* Kryvyy Rih, Ukr.	164	47.54N	33.22E
Križevci, Cro. (krē'zhěv-tsĭ)	160	46.02N	16.30E
Krk, i., Yugo. (k'rk)	160	45.06N	14.33E
Krnov, Czech Rep. (k'r'nôf)	155	50.05N	17.41E
Krokodil, r., S. Afr. (krŏ'kŏ-dī)	218d	24.25S	27.08E
Krolevets', Ukr.	167	51.33N	33.21E
Kromy, Russia (krȯ'mė)	162	52.44N	35.41E
Kronshtadt, Russia (krōn'shtät)	166	59.59N	29.47E
Kroonstad, S. Afr. (krōn'shtät)	212	27.40S	27.15E
Kropotkin, Russia (krȧ-pôt'kĭn)	167	45.25N	40.30E
Krosno, Pol. (krȯs'nȯ)	155	49.41N	21.46E
Krotoszyn, Pol. (krȯ-tō'shĭn)	155	51.41N	17.25E
Krško, Slvn. (k'rsh'kȯ)	160	45.58N	15.30E
Kruger National Park, rec., S. Afr. (kro͞o'gẽr) (krü'gěr)	212	23.22S	30.18E
Krugersdorp, S. Afr. (kro͞o'gěrz-dȯrp)	212	26.06S	27.46E
Krugersdorp West, S. Afr.	244b	26.06S	27.45E
Krummensee, Ger.	238a	52.36N	13.42E
Krung Thep *see* Bangkok, Thai.	196	13.50N	100.29E
Kruševac, Yugo. (krȯ'shě-vȧts)	161	43.34N	21.21E
Kruševo, Mac.	161	41.20N	21.15E
Krylatskoje, neigh., Russia	239b	55.45N	37.26E
Krylbo, Swe. (krŭl'bȯ)	152	60.07N	16.14E
Krym, Respublika, prov., Ukr.	163	45.08N	34.05E
Krymskaya, Russia (krĭm'skȧ-yȧ)	163	44.58N	38.01E
Kryms'kyy pivostriv (Crimean Peninsula), pen., Ukr.	167	45.18N	33.30E
Krynki, Pol. (krĭn'kė)	155	53.15N	23.47E
Kryve Ozero, Ukr.	163	47.57N	30.21E
Kryvyy Rih, Ukr.	164	47.54N	33.22E
Ksar Chellala, Alg.	159	35.12N	2.20E
Ksar-el-Kebir, Mor.	148	35.01N	5.48W
Ksar-es-Souk, Mor.	148	31.58N	4.25W
Kuai, r., China (ko͞o-ī)	190	33.30N	116.56E
Kuala Klawang, Malay.	181b	2.57N	102.04E
Kuala Lumpur, Malay. (kwä'lä lo̊m-po͞or')	196	3.08N	101.42E
Kuandian, China (kůän-dĭěn)	192	40.40N	124.50E
Kuban, r., Russia	167	45.20N	40.05E
Kubenskoye, l., Russia	166	59.40N	39.40E
Kuching, Malay. (ko͞o'chĭng)	196	1.30N	110.26E
Kuchinoerabo, i., Japan (ko͞o'chė nō ěr'ȧ-bō)	195	30.31N	129.53E
Kudamatsu, Japan (ko͞o'dȧ-mä'tso͞o)	195	34.00N	131.51E
Kudap, Indon.	181b	1.14N	102.30E
Kudat, Malay. (ko͞o-dät')	196	6.56N	116.48E
Kudbrooke, neigh., Eng., U.K.	235	51.28N	0.03E
Kudirkos Naumietis, Lith. (ko͞odĭr-kȯs nȧ'ȯ-mě'tĭs)	153	54.51N	23.00E
Kudymkar, Russia (ko͞o-dĭm-kär')	164	58.43N	54.52E
Kufstein, Aus. (ko͞of'shtīn)	154	47.34N	12.11E
Kuhstedt, Ger. (ko͞o'shtě)	145c	53.23N	8.58E
Kuibyshev *see* Kuybyshev, Russia	164	53.10N	50.05E
Kuilsrivier, S. Afr.	212a	33.56S	18.41E
Kuito, Ang.	212	12.22S	16.56E
Kuji, Japan	189	40.11N	141.46E
Kujū-san, mtn., Japan (ko͞o'jȯ-sän')	195	33.07N	131.14E
Kukës, Alb. (ko͞o'kěs)	161	42.03N	20.25E
Kula, Bul. (ko͞o'lȧ)	161	43.52N	23.13E
Kula, Tur.	149	38.32N	28.30E
Kula Kangri, mtn., Bhu.	183	33.11N	90.36E
Kular, Khrebet, mts., Russia (kȯ-lär')	171	69.00N	131.45E
Kuldīga, Lat. (kȯl'dė-gȧ)	153	56.59N	21.59E
Kulebaki, Russia (ko͞o-lě-bäk'ĭ)	166	55.22N	42.30E
Küllenhahn, neigh., Ger.	236	51.14N	7.08E
Kulmbach, Ger. (klȯlm'bäκ)	154	50.07N	11.28E
Kulunda, Russia (kȯ-lȯn'dȧ)	164	52.38N	79.00E
Kulundinskoye, l., Russia	170	52.45N	77.18E
Kum, r., S. Kor. (kȯm)	194	36.50N	127.30E
Kuma, r., Russia (ko͞o'mä)	167	44.50N	45.10E
Kumamoto, Japan (ko͞o'mä-mō'tȯ)	189	32.49N	130.40E
Kumano-Nada, b., Japan (ko͞o-mä'nō nä-dä)	195	34.03N	136.36E
Kumanovo, Mac. (kȯ-mä'nȯ-vȯ)	161	42.10N	21.41E
Kumasi, Ghana (ko͞o-mä'sė)	210	6.41N	1.35W
Kumba, Cam. (kȯm'bȧ)	210	4.38N	9.25E
Kumbakonam, India (kȯm'bŭ-kō'nŭm)	183	10.59N	79.25E
Kumkale, Tur.	161	39.59N	26.10E
Kumo, Nig.	215	10.03N	11.13E
Kumta, India	187	14.19N	75.28E
Kumul *see* Hami, China	188	42.58N	93.14E
Kunashak, Russia (kû-nä'shȧk)	172a	55.43N	61.35E
Kunashir (Kunashiri), i., Russia (ko͞o-nŭ-shēr')	189	44.00N	145.45E
Kunda, Est.	153	59.30N	26.28E
Kundravy, Russia (ko͞on'drȧ-vĭ)	172a	54.50N	60.14E
Kundur, i., Indon.	181b	0.49N	103.20E
Kunene (Cunene), r., Afr.	212	17.05S	12.35E
Kungälv, Swe. (kŭng'ělf)	152	57.53N	12.01E
Kungsbacka, Swe. (kŭngs'bä-kȧ)	152	57.31N	12.04E
Kungur, Russia (kȯn-go͞or')	164	57.27N	56.53E
Kunitachi, Japan	242a	35.41N	139.26E
Kunlun Shan, mts., China (ko͞on-lo͞on shän)	188	35.26N	83.09E
Kunming, China (ko͞on-mĭŋ)	188	25.10N	102.50E
Kunsan, S. Kor. (kȯn'sän')	189	35.54N	126.46E
Kunshan, China (ko͞onshän)	191b	31.23N	120.57E
Kuntsëvo, Russia (kȯn-tsyô'vȯ)	162	55.43N	37.27E
Kun'ya, Russia	172a	58.42N	56.47E
Kun'ya, r., Russia (kȯn'yȧ)	162	56.45N	30.53E
Kuopio, Fin. (kȯ-ô'pė-ŏ)	146	62.48N	28.30E
Kupa, r., Yugo.	160	45.32N	14.50E
Kupang, Indon.	197	10.14S	123.37E
Kupavna, Russia	172b	55.49N	38.11E
Kupferdreh, neigh., Ger.	236	51.23N	7.05E
Kupino, Russia (ko͞o-pĭ'nȯ)	164	54.00N	77.47E
Kupiškis, Lith. (kȯ-pĭsh'kĭs)	153	55.50N	24.55E
Kup'yans'k, Ukr.	167	49.44N	37.38E

ăt; finăl; rāte; senåte; ärm; ȧsk; sofȧ; fâre; ch-choose; dh-as th in other; bē; ėvent; bět; recěnt; cratẽr; g-gō; gh-guttural g; bĭt; ĭ-short neutral; rīde; κ-guttural k as ch in German ich;

PLACE (Pronunciation)	PAGE	Lat. °′	Long. °′
Kuqa, China (ko͞o-chyä)	188	41.34N	82.44E
Kür, r., Asia	167	41.10N	45.40E
Kurashiki, Japan (ko͞o'rä-shē'kė)	195	34.37N	133.44E
Kuraymah, Sudan	211	18.34N	31.49E
Kurayoshi, Japan (ko͞o'rá-yō'shė)	195	35.25N	133.49E
Kurdistan, hist. reg., Asia (kûrd'ĭ-stăn)	182	37.40N	43.30E
Kurdufān, hist. reg., Sudan (kôr-dỏ-făn')	211	14.08N	28.39E
Kŭrdzhali, Bul.	161	41.39N	25.21E
Kure, Japan (ko͞o'rĕ)	189	34.17N	132.35E
Kuressaare, Est. (kỏ'rĕ-sä'rĕ)	153	58.15N	22.26E
Kurgan, Russia (kỏr-găn')	164	55.28N	65.14E
Kurgan-Tyube, Taj. (kỏr-gän' tyỏ'bĕ)	169	38.00N	68.49E
Kurihama, Japan (ko͞o-rē-hä'mä)	195a	35.14N	139.42E
Kuril Islands, is., Russia (ko͞o'rĭl)	171	46.20N	149.30E
Ku-ring-gai, Austl.	243a	33.45S	151.08E
Kurisches Haff, b., Eur.	153	55.10N	21.08E
Kurl, neigh., Ger.	236	51.35N	7.35E
Kurla, neigh., India	187b	19.03N	72.53E
Kurmuk, Sudan (kỏr'mo͝ok)	211	10.40N	34.13E
Kurnell, Austl.	243a	34.01S	151.13E
Kurnool, India (kỏr-no͞ol')	183	16.00N	78.04E
Kurrajong, Austl.	201b	33.33S	150.40E
Kuršenai, Lith. (kỏr'shå-nī)	153	56.01N	22.56E
Kursk, Russia (kỏrsk)	164	51.44N	36.08E
Kuršumlija, Yugo. (kỏr'shỏm'lĭ-yȧ)	161	43.08N	21.18E
Kuruçeşme, neigh., Tur.	239f	41.03N	29.02E
Kuruman, S. Afr. (ko͞o-ro͞o-män')	212	27.25S	23.30E
Kurume, Japan (ko͞o'rỏ-mĕ)	189	33.10N	130.30E
Kurume, Japan	242a	35.45N	139.32E
Kururi, Japan (ko͞o'rỏ-rė)	195a	35.17N	140.05E
Kusa, Russia (ko͞o'sȧ)	172a	55.19N	59.27E
Kushchëvskaya, Russia	163	46.34N	39.40E
Kushikino, Japan (ko͞o'shĭ-kē'nō)	195	31.44N	130.19E
Kushimoto, Japan (ko͞o'shĭ-mō'tō)	195	33.29N	135.47E
Kushiro, Japan (ko͞o'shē-rō)	189	43.00N	144.22E
Kushva, Russia (ko͞osh'vȧ)	164	58.18N	59.51E
Kuskokwim, r., Ak., U.S.	95	61.32N	160.36W
Kuskokwim Bay, b., Ak., U.S. (kŭs'kỏ-kwĭm)	95	59.25N	163.14W
Kuskokwim Mountains, mts., Ak., U.S.	95	62.08N	158.00W
Kuskovak, Ak., U.S. (kŭs-kō'văk)	95	60.10N	162.50W
Kuskovo, neigh., Russia	239b	55.44N	37.49E
Kütahya, Tur. (kû-tä'hyȧ)	182	39.20N	29.50E
Kutaisi, Geor. (ko͞o-tŭ-ē'sē)	167	42.15N	42.40E
Kutch, Gulf of, b., India	183	22.45N	68.33E
Kutch, Rann of, sw., Asia	183	23.59N	69.13E
Kutenholz, Ger. (ko͞o'tĕn-hōlts)	145c	53.29N	9.20E
Kutim, Russia (ko͞o'tĭm)	172a	60.22N	58.51E
Kutina, Cro. (ko͞o'tė-nȧ)	160	45.29N	16.48E
Kutno, Pol. (kỏt'nô)	147	52.14N	19.22E
Kutno, l., Russia	166	65.15N	31.30E
Kutulik, Russia (kỏ to͞o'lyĭk)	165	53.12N	102.51E
Kuty, Ukr. (ko͞o'tė)	155	48.16N	25.12E
Kuujjuaq, Can.	85	58.06N	68.25W
Kuusamo, Fin. (ko͞o'sȧ-mỏ)	146	65.59N	29.10E
Kuvshinovo, Russia (kỏv-shē'nô-vỏ)	162	57.01N	34.09E
Kuwait see Al Kuwait, Kuw.	182	29.04N	47.59E
Kuwait, nation, Asia	182	29.00N	48.45E
Kuwana, Japan (ko͞o'wȧ-nȧ)	195	35.02N	136.40E
Kuybyshev see Samara, Russia	166	53.10N	50.05E
Kuybyshevskoye, res., Russia	164	53.40N	49.00E
Kuz'minki, neigh., Russia	239b	55.42N	37.48E
Kuzneckovo, Russia	172b	55.29N	38.22E
Kuznetsk, Russia (ko͞oz-nyĕtsk')	166	53.00N	46.30E
Kuznetsk Basin, basin, Russia	164	56.30N	86.15E
Kuznetsovka, Russia (kỏz-nyĕt'sôf-kȧ)	172a	54.41N	56.40E
Kuznetsovo, Russia (kỏz-nyĕt-sô'vỏ)	162	56.39N	36.55E
Kuznetsy, Russia	172b	55.50N	38.39E
Kvarner Zaliv, b., Yugo. (kvär'nĕr)	160	44.41N	14.05E
Kwa, r., Zaire	216	3.00S	16.45E
Kwahu Plateau, plat., Ghana	214	7.00N	1.35W
Kwando (Cuando), r., Afr.	216	16.50S	22.40E
Kwangju, S. Kor.	194	35.09N	126.54E
Kwango (Cuango), r., Afr. (kwäng'ō')	216	6.35S	16.50E
Kwangwazi, Tan.	217	7.47S	38.15E
Kwa-Thema, S. Afr.	244b	26.18S	28.23E
Kwekwe, Zimb.	212	18.49S	29.45E
Kwenge, r., Afr. (kwĕŋ'gē)	212	6.45S	18.23E
Kwilu, r., Afr. (kwē'lo͞o)	212	4.00S	18.00E
Kyakhta, Russia (kyäk'ta)	165	51.00N	107.30E
Kyaukpyu, Myanmar (chouk'pyoo')	183	19.19N	93.33E
Kybartai, Lith. (kē'bär-tī')	153	54.40N	22.46E
Kyn, Russia (kĭn')	172a	57.52N	58.42E
Kynuna, Austl. (kī-no͞o'nȧ)	203	21.30S	142.12E
Kyoga, Lake, l., Ug.	211	1.30N	32.45E
Kyōga-Saki, c., Japan (kyō'gȧ sa'kė)	195	35.46N	135.14E
Kyŏngju, S. Kor. (kyŭng'yo͞o)	189	35.48N	129.12E
Kyŏngju, S. Kor.	194	35.51N	129.14E
Kyōto, Japan (kyō'tō')	189	35.00N	135.46E
Kyōto, dept., Japan	195b	34.56N	135.42E
Kyren, Russia (kĭ-rĕn')	165	51.46N	102.13E
Kyrgyzstan, nation, Asia	164	41.45N	74.38E
Kyrönjoki, r., Fin.	153	63.03N	22.20E
Kyrya, Russia (kĕr'yȧ)	172a	59.18N	59.03E
Kyshtym, Russia (kĭsh-tĭm')	166	55.42N	60.34E
Kytlym, Russia (kĭt'lĭm)	172a	59.30N	59.15E
Kyūhōji, neigh., Japan	242b	34.38N	135.35E
Kyūshū, i., Japan	189	33.00N	131.00E
Kyustendil, Bul. (kyỏs-tĕn-dĭl')	149	42.16N	22.39E
Kyyiv, prov., Ukr.	163	50.05N	30.40E
Kyyivs'ke vodoskhovyshche, res., Ukr.	164	51.00N	30.20E
Kyzyl, Russia (kĭ zĭl)	165	51.37N	93.38E

L

PLACE (Pronunciation)	PAGE	Lat. °′	Long. °′
Laa, Aus.	154	48.42N	16.23E
Laab im Walde, Aus.	239e	48.09N	16.11E
La Almunia de Doña Godina, Spain	158	41.29N	1.22W
Laas Caanood, Som.	218a	8.24N	47.20E
La Asunción, Ven. (lä ä-so͞on-syōn')	130	11.02N	63.57W
La Baie, Can.	91	48.21N	70.53W
La Banda, Arg. (lä bän'dä)	132	27.48S	64.12W
La Bandera, Chile	234b	33.34S	70.39W
La Barca, Mex. (lä bär'kȧ)	118	20.17N	102.33W
Laberge, Lake, l., Can. (lȧ-bĕrzh')	84	61.08N	136.42W
Laberinto de las Doce Leguas, is., Cuba	122	20.40N	78.35W
Labinsk, Russia	167	44.30N	40.40E
Labis, Malay. (läb'ĭs)	181b	2.23N	103.01E
La Bisbal, Spain (lä bēs-bäl')	159	41.55N	3.00E
Labo, Phil. (lä'bỏ)	197a	14.11N	122.49E
Labo, Mount, mtn., Phil.	197a	14.00N	122.47E
Labouheyre, Fr. (lȧ-bo͞o-âr')	156	44.14N	0.58W
Laboulaye, Arg. (lä-bô'o͞o-lä-yĕ)	132	34.01S	63.10W
Labrador, reg., Can. (lăb'rȧ-dôr)	85	53.05N	63.30W
Labrador Sea, sea, Can.	93	50.38N	55.00W
Lábrea, Braz. (lä-brā'ä)	130	7.28S	64.39W
Labuan, Pulau, i., Malay. (lä-bỏ-än')	196	5.28N	115.11E
Labuha, Indon.	197	0.43S	127.35E
L'Acadie, Can. (lȧ-kȧ-dē')	83a	45.18N	73.22W
L'Acadie, r., Can.	83a	45.24N	73.21W
La Calera, Chile (lä-kä-lĕ-rä)	129b	32.47S	71.11W
La Calera, Col.	130a	4.43N	73.58W
Lac Allard, Can.	92	50.38N	63.28W
La Canada, Ca., U.S. (lä kän-yä'dä)	107a	34.13N	118.12W
La Candelaria, Mex.	233a	19.20N	99.09W
Lacantum, r., Mex. (lä-kän-to͞o'm)	119	16.13N	90.52W
La Carolina, Spain (lä kä-rỏ-lē'nä)	158	38.16N	3.48W
La Catedral, Cerro, mtn., Mex. (sĕ'r-rỏ-lä-kä-tĕ-drȧ'l)	119a	19.32N	99.31W
Lac-Beauport, Can. (läk-bō-pōr')	83b	46.58N	71.17W
Laccadive Islands see Lakshadweep, is., India	183	11.00N	73.02E
Laccadive Sea, sea, Asia	187	9.10N	75.17E
Lac Court Oreille Indian Reservation, I.R., Wi., U.S.	103	46.04N	91.18W
Lac du Flambeau Indian Reservation, I.R., Wi., U.S.	103	46.12N	89.50W
La Ceiba, Hond. (lȧ sĕbä)	116	15.45N	86.52W
La Ceja, Col. (lä-sĕ-kä)	130a	6.02N	75.25W
Lac-Frontière, Can.	85	46.42N	70.00W
Lacha, l., Russia (lá'chä)	166	61.15N	39.05E
La Chaux de Fonds, Switz. (lȧ shō dē-fôn')	154	47.07N	6.47E
L'Achigan, r., Can. (lä-shē-gän)	83a	45.49N	73.48W
Lachine, Can. (lȧ-shēn')	83a	45.26N	73.40W
Lachlan, r., Austl. (läk'lăn)	203	34.00S	145.00E
La Chorrera, Pan. (láchỏr-rā'rä)	121	8.54N	79.47W
Lachta, neigh., Russia	239a	60.00N	30.10E
Lachute, Can. (lȧ-sho͞ot')	91	45.39N	74.20W
La Ciotat, Fr. (lȧ syō-tȧ')	157	43.13N	5.35E
La Cisterna, Chile	234b	33.33S	70.41W
Lackawanna, N.Y., U.S. (lak-ȧ-wŏn'ȧ)	101c	42.49N	78.50W
Lac La Biche, Can.	84	54.46N	112.58W
Lacombe, Can.	84	52.28N	113.44W
Laconia, N.H., U.S. (lȧ-kō'nĭ-ȧ)	99	43.30N	71.30W
La Conner, Wa., U.S. (lä kŏn'ĕr)	106a	48.23N	122.30W
La Coruña, Spain (lä kỏ-ro͞on'yä)	142	43.20N	8.20W
La Courneuve, Fr.	237c	48.56N	2.23E
Lacreek, l., S.D., U.S. (lă'krēk)	102	43.04N	101.46W
La Crescenta, Ca., U.S. (lȧ krĕs'ĕnt-ȧ)	107a	34.14N	118.13W
La Cross, Ks., U.S. (lȧ-krôs')	110	38.30N	99.20W
La Crosse, Wi., U.S.	97	43.48N	91.14W
La Cruz, Col. (lȧ kro͞oz')	130	1.37N	77.00W
La Cruz, C.R. (lä-kro͞o'z)	120	11.05N	85.37W
Lacs, Riviere des, r., N.D., U.S. (rē-vyĕr' de läk)	102	48.30N	101.45W
La Cuesta, C.R. (lä-kwĕ's-tä)	121	8.32N	82.51W
La Cygne, Ks., U.S. (lȧ-sēn'y') (lȧ-sēn')	111	38.20N	94.45W
Ladd, Il., U.S. (lăd)	98	41.25N	89.25W
Ladíspoli, Italy (lä-dė's-pỏ-lē)	159d	41.57N	12.05E
Lādīz, Iran	185	28.56N	61.19E
Ladner, Can. (lăd'nĕr)	86	49.05N	123.05W
Lādnun, India (läd'nỏn)	186	27.45N	74.20E
Ladoga, Lake see Ladozhskoye Ozero, l., Russia	164	60.59N	31.30E
La Dolorita, Ven.	234a	10.29N	66.47W
La Dorado, Col. (lä dỏ-rä'dȧ)	130	5.28N	74.42W
Ladozhskoye Ozero, Russia (lȧ-dôsh'skō-yē ô'zĕ-rỏ)	164	60.59N	31.30E
La Durantaye, Can. (lä dü-rän-tä')	83b	46.51N	70.51W
Lady Frere, S. Afr. (lā-dē frâ'r')	213c	31.48S	27.16E
Lady Grey, S. Afr.	213c	30.44S	27.17E
Ladysmith, Can. (lā'dĭ-smĭth)	86	48.58N	123.49W
Ladysmith, S. Afr.	212	28.38S	29.48E
Ladysmith, Wi., U.S.	103	45.27N	91.07W
Lae, Pap. N. Gui. (lä'å)	197	6.15S	146.57E
Laerdalsøyri, Nor.	152	61.08N	7.26E
La Esperanza, Hond. (lä ĕs-pȧ-rän'zä)	120	14.20N	88.21W
La Estrada, Spain (lä ĕs-trä'dä)	158	42.42N	8.29W
Lafayette, Al., U.S.	114	32.52N	85.25W
Lafayette, Ca., U.S.	106b	37.53N	122.07W
Lafayette, Ga., U.S. (lä-fȧ-yĕt')	114	34.41N	85.19W
Lafayette, In., U.S.	97	40.25N	86.55W
Lafayette, La., U.S.	97	30.15N	92.02W
La Fayette, R.I., U.S.	100b	41.34N	71.29W
Lafayette Hill, Pa., U.S.	229b	40.05N	75.15W
Laferrere, Arg.	233d	34.45S	58.35W
La Ferté-Alais, Fr. (lä-fĕr-tā'ä-lā')	157b	48.29N	2.19E
La Ferté-sous-Jouarre, Fr. (lȧ fĕr-tā'so͞o-zho͞o-är')	157b	48.56N	3.07E
Lafia, Nig.	215	8.30N	8.30E
Lafiagi, Nig.	215	8.52N	5.25E
Laflèche, Can.	227b	45.30N	73.28W
La Flèche, Fr. (lȧ flāsh')	156	47.43N	0.03W
La Floresta, Spain	238e	41.27N	2.04E
La Florida, Chile	234b	33.32S	70.33W
La Follete, Tn., U.S. (lä-fŏl'ĕt)	114	36.23N	84.07W
Lafourche, Bayou, r., La., U.S. (bä-yo͞o'lȧ-fo͞orsh')	113	29.25N	90.15W
La Frette-sur-Seine, Fr.	237c	48.58N	2.11E
La Gaiba, Braz. (lä-gī'bä)	131	17.54S	57.32W
La Galite, i., Tun. (gä-lēt)	148	37.36N	8.03E
Lågan, r., Nor. (lô'ghĕn)	142	61.00N	10.00E
Lagan, r., Swe.	152	56.34N	13.25E
Lagan, r., N. Ire., U.K. (lă'găn)	150	54.30N	6.00W
La Garenne-Colombes, Fr.	237c	48.55N	2.15E
Lagarto, r., Pan. (lä-gä'r-tō)	116a	9.08N	80.05W
Lagartos, l., Mex. (lä-gä'r-tôs)	120a	21.32N	88.15W
Laghouat, Alg. (lä-gwät')	210	33.45N	2.49E
Lagny, Fr. (län-yē')	157b	48.53N	2.41E
Lagoa da Prata, Braz. (lȧ-gô'ä-dȧ-prä'tȧ)	129a	20.04S	45.33W
Lagoa Dourada, Braz. (lȧ-gô'ä-dỏ-rä'dä)	129a	20.55S	44.03W
Lagogne, Fr. (lan-gōn'y')	156	44.43N	3.50E
Lagonay, Phil.	197a	13.44N	123.31E
Lagos, Nig. (lä'gōs)	210	6.27N	3.24E
Lagos, Port. (lä'gōzh)	158	37.08N	8.43W
Lagos de Moreno, Mex. (lä'gōs dā mỏ-rā'nō)	116	21.21N	101.55W
La Grand' Combe, Fr. (lȧ grän kanb')	156	44.12N	4.03E
La Grande, Or., U.S. (lȧ grănd')	96	45.20N	118.06W
La Grande, r., Can.	85	53.55N	77.30W
La Grange, Austl. (lä grănj)	202	18.40S	122.00E
La Grange, Ga., U.S. (lȧ-grānj')	97	33.01N	85.00W
La Grange, Il., U.S.	101a	41.49N	87.53W
Lagrange, In., U.S.	98	41.40N	85.25W
La Grange, Ky., U.S.	98	38.20N	85.25W
La Grange, Mo., U.S.	111	40.04N	91.30W
Lagrange, Oh., U.S.	101d	41.14N	82.07W
Lagrange, Tx., U.S.	113	29.55N	96.50W
La Grange Highlands, Il., U.S.	231a	41.48N	87.53W
La Grange Park, Il., U.S.	231a	41.50N	87.52W
La Granja, Chile	234b	33.32S	70.39W
La Grita, Ven. (lä grē'tȧ)	130	8.02N	71.59W
La Guaira, Ven. (lä gwä'ē-rä)	130	10.36N	66.54W
La Guardia, Spain (lä gwär'dē-ä)	158	41.55N	8.48W
La Guardia Airport, arpt., N.Y., U.S.	228	40.46N	73.53W
Laguna, Braz. (lä-go͞o'nä)	132	28.19S	48.42W
Laguna, Cayos, is., Cuba (kä'yōs-lä-gỏ'nä)	122	22.15N	82.45W
Laguna Indian Reservation, I.R., N.M., U.S.	109	35.00N	107.30W
Lagunillas, Bol. (lä-go͞o-nēl'yäs)	130	19.42S	63.38W
Lagunillas, Mex. (lä-go͞o-nē'l-yäs)	118	21.34N	99.41W
La Habana see Havana, Cuba	117	23.08N	82.23W
La Habra, Ca., U.S. (lȧ hȧb'rȧ)	107a	34.56N	117.57W
La Habra Heights, Ca., U.S.	232	33.57N	117.57W
Lahaina, Hi., U.S. (lä-hä'ē-nä)	94a	20.52N	156.39W
La Häy-les-Roses, Fr.	237c	48.47N	2.21E
Lāhījān, Iran	185	37.12N	50.01E
Laholm, Swe. (lä'hỏlm)	152	56.30N	13.00E
La Honda, Ca., U.S. (lä hôn'dȧ)	106b	37.20N	122.16W
Lahore, Pak. (lä-hōr')	183	32.00N	74.18E
Lahr, Ger. (lär)	154	48.19N	7.52E
Lahti, Fin. (lä'tė)	146	60.59N	27.39E
Lai, Chad	211	9.29N	16.18E
Lai'an, China (lī-än)	190	32.27N	118.25E
Laibin, China (lī-bĭn)	193	23.42N	109.20E
L'Aigle, Fr. (lĕ'gl')	156	48.45N	0.37E
Lainate, Italy	238c	45.34N	9.02E
Lainz, neigh., Aus.	239e	48.11N	16.17E
Laisamis, Kenya	217	1.36N	37.48E
Laiyang, China (lăī'yäng)	192	36.59N	120.42E
Laizhou Wan, b., China (lī-jō wän)	189	37.22N	119.19E
Laja, Río de la, r., Mex. (rē'ō-dĕ-lä-lä'kä)	118	21.17N	100.57W
Lajas, Cuba (lä'häs)	122	22.25N	80.20W
Laje, Ponta da, c., Port.	238d	38.40N	9.19W
Lajeado, Braz. (lä-zhĕä'dō)	132	29.24S	51.46W
Lajeado Velho, neigh., Braz.	234d	23.32S	46.23W
Lajes, Braz. (lȧ'zhĕs)	132	27.47S	50.17W
Lajinha, Braz. (lä-zhē'nyä)	129a	20.08S	41.36W
La Jolla, Ca., U.S. (lȧ hoi'yȧ)	108a	32.51N	117.16W
La Jolla Indian Reservation, I.R., Ca., U.S.	108	33.19N	116.21W
La Junta, Co., U.S. (lȧ ho͞on'tȧ)	110	37.59N	103.35W
Lake Arrowhead, Ca., U.S.	232	33.52N	118.05W
Lake Arthur, La., U.S. (är'thŭr)	113	30.06N	92.40W
Lake Barcroft, Va., U.S.	229d	38.51N	77.09W
Lake Barkley, res., U.S.	114	36.45N	88.00W
Lake Benton, Mn., U.S. (bĕn'tŭn)	102	44.15N	96.17W
Lake Bluff, Il., U.S. (blŭf)	101a	42.17N	87.50W
Lake Brown, Austl. (broun)	202	31.03S	118.30E
Lake Charles, La., U.S. (chärlz')	97	30.15N	93.14W

308 Lake City–L'Assomption

PLACE (Pronunciation)	PAGE	Lat. °′	Long. °′
Lake City, Fl., U.S.	115	30.09N	82.40W
Lake City, Ia., U.S.	103	42.14N	94.43W
Lake City, Mn., U.S.	103	44.28N	92.19W
Lake City, S.C., U.S.	115	33.57N	79.45W
Lake Clark National Park, rec., Ak., U.S.	95	60.30N	153.15W
Lake Cowichan, Can. (kou'ĭ-chăn)	86	48.50N	124.03W
Lake Crystal, Mn., U.S. (krĭs'tăl)	103	44.05N	94.12W
Lake District, reg., Eng., U.K. (lāk)	150	54.25N	3.20W
Lake Elmo, Mn., U.S. (ĕlmō)	107g	45.00N	92.53W
Lake Forest, Il., U.S. (fŏr'ĕst)	101a	42.16N	87.50W
Lake Fork, r., Ut., U.S.	109	40.30N	110.25W
Lake Geneva, Wi., U.S. (jĕ-nē'vȧ)	103	42.36N	88.28W
Lake Harbour, Can. (här'bẽr)	85	62.43N	69.40W
Lake Havasu City, Az., U.S.	109	34.27N	114.22W
Lake June, Tx., U.S. (jo͞on)	107c	32.43N	96.45W
Lakeland, Fl., U.S. (lāk'lănd)	97	28.02N	81.58W
Lakeland, Ga., U.S.	114	31.02N	83.02W
Lakeland, Mn., U.S.	107g	44.57N	92.47W
Lake Linden, Mi., U.S. (lĭn'dĕn)	103	47.11N	88.26W
Lake Louise, Can. (lo͞o-ēz')	87	51.26N	116.11W
Lakemba, Austl.	243a	33.55S	151.05E
Lake Mead National Recreation Area, rec., U.S.	109	36.00N	114.30W
Lake Mills, Ia., U.S. (mĭlz')	103	43.25N	93.32W
Lakemore, Oh., U.S. (lāk-mōr)	101d	41.01N	81.24W
Lake Odessa, Mi., U.S.	98	42.50N	85.15W
Lake Oswego, Or., U.S. (ŏs-wē'go)	106c	45.25N	122.40W
Lake Placid, N.Y., U.S.	99	44.17N	73.59W
Lake Point, Ut., U.S.	107b	40.41N	112.16W
Lakeport, Ca., U.S. (lāk'pōrt)	108	39.03N	122.54W
Lake Preston, S.D., U.S. (prēs'tŭn)	102	44.21N	97.23W
Lake Providence, La., U.S. (prŏv'ĭ-dĕns)	113	32.48N	91.12W
Lake Red Rock, res., Ia., U.S.	103	41.30N	93.15W
Lake Sharpe, res., S.D., U.S.	102	44.30N	100.00W
Lakeside, S. Afr.	244b	26.06S	28.09E
Lakeside, Ca., U.S. (lāk'sīd)	108a	32.52N	116.55W
Lake Station, In., U.S.	101a	41.34N	87.15W
Lake Stevens, Wa., U.S.	106a	48.01N	122.04W
Lake Success, N.Y., U.S. (sŭk-sĕs')	100a	40.46N	73.43W
Lakeview, Or., U.S.	104	42.11N	120.21W
Lakeview, neigh., Il., U.S.	231a	41.57N	87.39W
Lake Village, Ar., U.S.	111	33.20N	91.17W
Lake Wales, Fl., U.S. (wālz')	115a	27.54N	81.35W
Lakewood, Ca., U.S. (lāk'wo͝od)	107a	33.50N	118.09W
Lakewood, Co., U.S.	110	39.44N	105.06W
Lakewood, Oh., U.S.	97	41.29N	81.48W
Lakewood, Pa., U.S.	99	40.05N	74.10W
Lakewood, Wa., U.S.	106a	48.09N	122.13W
Lakewood Center, Wa., U.S.	106a	47.10N	122.31W
Lake Worth, Fl., U.S. (wûrth')	115a	26.37N	80.04W
Lake Worth Village, Tx., U.S.	107c	32.49N	97.26W
Lake Zurich, Il., U.S. (tsü'rĭk)	101a	42.11N	88.05W
Lakhdenpokh'ya, Russia (l'ăk-dīe'npōkyȧ)	153	61.33N	30.10E
Lakhtinskiy, Russia (lȧk-tĭn'skĭ)	172c	59.59N	30.10E
Lakota, N.D., U.S. (lȧ-kō'tȧ)	102	48.04N	98.21W
Lakshadweep, state, India	183	10.10N	72.50E
Lakshadweep, is., India	183	11.00N	73.02E
Laleham, Eng., U.K.	235	51.25N	0.30W
La Libertad, El Sal.	120	13.29N	89.20W
La Libertad, Guat. (lä lē-bĕr-tädh')	120	15.31N	91.44W
La Libertad, Guat.	120a	16.46N	90.12W
La Ligua, Chile (lä lē'gwä)	129b	32.21S	71.13W
Lalín, Spain (lä-lē'n)	158	42.40N	8.05W
La Línea, Spain (lä lē'nȧ-ä)	148	36.11N	5.22W
La Lisa, Cuba	233b	23.04N	82.26W
Lalitpur, Nepal	183	27.23N	85.24E
La Louviere, Bel. (lȧ lo͞o-vyâr')	151	50.30N	4.10E
La Luz, Mex. (lä lo͞oz')	118	21.04N	101.19W
Lama-Kara, Togo	214	9.33N	1.12E
La Malbaie, Can. (lȧ mȧl-bâ')	85	47.39N	70.10W
La Mancha, reg., Spain (lä män'chä)	158	38.55N	4.20W
Lamar, Co., U.S. (lȧ-mär')	110	38.04N	102.44W
Lamar, Mo., U.S.	111	37.28N	94.15W
La Marmora, Punta, mtn., Italy (lä-mä'r-mô-rä)	148	40.00N	9.28E
La Marque, Tx., U.S. (lȧ-märk)	113a	29.23N	94.58W
Lamas, Peru (lä'mȧs)	130	6.24S	76.41W
Lamballe, Fr. (läɴ-bäl')	156	48.29N	2.36W
Lambari, Braz. (läm-bȧ'rē)	129a	21.58S	45.22W
Lambasa, Fiji	198g	16.26S	179.24E
Lambayeque, Peru (läm-bä-yā'kā)	130	6.41S	79.58W
Lambert, Ms., U.S. (lăm'bẽrt)	114	34.10N	90.16W
Lambertville, N.J., U.S. (lăm'bẽrt-vĭl)	99	40.20N	75.00W
Lambeth, neigh., Eng., U.K.	235	51.28N	0.07W
Lambourne End, Eng., U.K.	235	51.38N	0.08E
Lambrate, neigh., Italy	238c	45.29N	9.15E
Lambro, r., Italy	238c	45.26N	9.16E
Lambton, S. Afr.	244b	26.15S	28.10E
Lame Deer, Mt., U.S. (lăm dēr')	105	45.36N	106.40W
Lamego, Port. (lä-mā'gō)	158	41.07N	7.47W
La Mesa, Col.	130a	4.38N	74.27W
La Mesa, Ca., U.S. (lä mā'sä)	108a	32.46N	117.01W
Lamesa, Tx., U.S.	110	32.44N	101.54W
Lamía, Grc. (lȧ-mē'ȧ)	149	38.54N	22.25E
La Mirada, Ca., U.S.	232	33.54N	118.01W
Lamon Bay, b., Phil. (lä-mōn')	196	14.35N	121.52E
La Mora, Chile (lä-mō'rä)	129b	32.28S	70.56W
La Mott, Pa., U.S.	229b	40.04N	75.08W
La Moure, N.D., U.S. (lȧ mo͞or')	102	46.23N	98.17W
Lampa, r., Chile (lä'm-pä)	129b	33.15S	70.55W
Lampasas, Tx., U.S. (lăm-păs'ȧs)	112	31.06N	98.10W
Lampasas, r., Tx., U.S.	112	31.18N	98.08W
Lampazos, Mex. (läm-pä'zōs)	116	27.03N	100.30W
Lampedusa, i., Italy (läm-pȧ-do͞o'sä)	148	35.29N	12.58E

PLACE (Pronunciation)	PAGE	Lat. °′	Long. °′
Lamstedt, Ger. (läm'shtĕt)	145c	53.38N	9.06E
Lamu, Kenya (lä'mo͞o)	213	2.16S	40.54E
Lamu Island, i., Kenya	217	2.25S	40.50E
La Mure, Fr. (lȧ mür')	157	44.55N	5.50E
Lan', r., Bela. (lȧn')	162	52.38N	27.05E
Lanai, i., Hi., U.S. (lä-nä'ē)	96c	20.48N	157.06W
Lanai City, Hi., U.S.	94a	20.50N	156.56W
Lanak La, p., China	188	34.40N	79.50E
Lanark, Scot., U.K. (lăn'ȧrk)	150	55.40N	3.50W
Lancashire, co., Eng., U.K. (lăŋ'kȧ-shĭr)	144a	53.49N	2.42W
Lancaster, Eng., U.K.	146	54.04N	2.55W
Lancaster, Ky., U.S.	98	37.35N	84.30W
Lancaster, Ma., U.S.	93a	42.28N	71.40W
Lancaster, N.H., U.S.	99	44.25N	71.30W
Lancaster, N.Y., U.S.	101c	42.54N	78.42W
Lancaster, Oh., U.S.	98	39.40N	82.35W
Lancaster, Pa., U.S.	97	40.05N	76.20W
Lancaster, Tx., U.S.	107c	32.36N	96.45W
Lancaster, Wi., U.S.	103	42.51N	90.44W
Lândana, Ang. (län-dä'nä)	212	5.15S	12.07E
Landau, Ger. (län'dou)	154	49.13N	8.07E
Lander, Wy., U.S. (lăn'dẽr)	105	42.49N	108.24W
Landerneau, Fr. (läɴ-dĕr-nō')	156	48.28N	4.14W
Landes, reg., Fr. (läɴd)	156	44.22N	0.52W
Landover, Md., U.S.	229d	38.56N	76.54W
Landsberg, Ger. (länds'bo͝orgh)	154	48.03N	10.53E
Lands End, c., Eng., U.K.	142	50.03N	5.45W
Landshut, Ger. (länts'ho͞ot)	147	48.32N	12.09E
Landskrona, Swe. (lȧns-krō'nȧ)	152	55.51N	12.47E
Lane Cove, Austl.	243a	33.49S	151.10E
Lanett, Al., U.S. (lȧ-nĕt')	114	32.52N	85.13W
Langadhás, Grc.	161	40.44N	23.10E
Langat, r., Malay.	181b	2.46N	101.33E
Langdon, Can. (lăng'dŭn)	83e	50.58N	113.40W
Langdon, Mn., U.S.	107g	44.49N	92.56W
Langdon Hills, Eng., U.K.	235	51.34N	0.25E
L'Ange-Gardien, Can. (länzh gȧr-dyăɴ')	83b	46.55N	71.06W
Langeland, i., Den.	152	54.52N	10.46E
Langenberg, Ger.	236	51.21N	7.09E
Langenbochum, Ger.	236	51.37N	7.07E
Langendreer, neigh., Ger.	236	51.28N	7.19E
Langenhorst, Ger.	236	51.22N	7.02E
Langenzersdorf, Aus.	145e	48.30N	16.22E
Langesund, Nor. (läng'ĕ-so͝on')	152	58.59N	9.38E
Langfjorden, fj., Nor.	152	62.40N	7.45E
Langhorne, Pa., U.S. (lăng'hôrn)	100f	40.10N	74.55W
Langhorne Acres, Md., U.S.	229d	38.51N	77.16W
Langia Mountains, mts., Ug.	217	3.35N	33.35E
Langjökoll, ice., Ice. (läng-yû'ko͞ol)	146	64.40N	20.31W
Langla Co, l., China (läŋ-lä tswo)	186	30.42N	80.40E
Langley, Can. (lăng'lĭ)	87	49.06N	122.39W
Langley, Md., U.S.	229d	38.57N	77.10W
Langley, S.C., U.S.	115	33.32N	81.52W
Langley, Wa., U.S.	106a	48.02N	122.25W
Langley Indian Reserve, I.R., Can.	106d	49.12N	122.31W
Langley Park, Md., U.S.	229d	38.59N	76.59W
Langnau, Switz. (läng'nou)	154	46.56N	7.46E
Langon, Fr. (läɴ-gôɴ')	156	44.34N	0.16W
Langres, Fr. (läɴ'gr')	157	47.53N	5.20E
Langres, Plateau de, plat., Fr. (plä-tō' dĕ-läɴ'grĕ)	156	47.39N	5.00E
Langsa, Indon. (läng'sȧ)	196	4.33N	97.52E
Lang Son, Viet. (läng'sŏn')	196	21.52N	106.42E
Langst-Kierst, Ger.	236	51.18N	6.43E
L'Anguille, r., Ar., U.S. (läɴ-gē'y')	111	35.23N	90.52W
Langxi, China (läŋ-shyē)	190	31.10N	119.09E
Langzhong, China (läŋ-jôŋ)	188	31.40N	106.05E
Lanham, Md., U.S. (lăn'ăm)	100e	38.58N	76.54W
Lanigan, Can. (lăn'ĭ-găn)	84	51.52N	105.02W
Länkäran, Azer. (lĕn-kȯ-rän')	164	38.52N	48.58E
Lank-Latum, Ger.	236	51.18N	6.41E
Lankoviri, Nig.	215	9.00N	11.25E
Lankwitz, neigh., Ger.	238a	52.26N	13.21E
Lansdale, Pa., U.S. (lănz'dāl)	99	40.20N	75.15W
Lansdowne, Austl.	243a	33.54S	150.59E
Lansdowne, Md., U.S.	229c	39.15N	76.40W
Lansdowne, Pa., U.S.	100f	39.57N	75.17W
L'Anse, Mi., U.S. (lȧns)	103	46.43N	88.28W
L'Anse and Vieux Desert Indian Reservation, I.R., Mi., U.S.	103	46.41N	88.12W
Lansford, Pa., U.S. (lănz'fẽrd)	99	40.50N	75.50W
Lansing, Il., U.S.	101a	41.34N	87.33W
Lansing, Ia., U.S.	103	43.22N	91.16W
Lansing, Ks., U.S.	107f	39.15N	94.53W
Lansing, Mi., U.S.	97	42.45N	84.35W
Lansing, neigh., Can.	227c	43.45N	79.25W
Lantianchang, China	240b	39.58N	116.17E
Lanús, Arg. (lä-no͞os')	132a	34.42S	58.24W
Lanusei, Italy (lä-no͞o-sĕ'y)	160	39.51N	9.34E
Lanúvio, Italy (lä-no͞o'vyô)	159d	41.41N	12.42E
Lanzarote Island, i., Spain (län-zȧ-rō'tä)	210	29.04N	13.03W
Lanzhou, China (län-jō)	188	35.55N	103.55E
Laoag, Phil. (lä-wäg')	196	18.13N	120.38E
Laohumiao, China	240b	39.58N	116.20E
Laon, Fr. (läɴ)	156	49.36N	3.35E
La Oroya, Peru (lä-ō-rō'yä)	130	11.30S	76.00W
Laos, nation, Asia (lä-ōs) (lȧ-ōs')	196	20.15N	102.00E
Laoshan Wan, b., China (lou-shän wän)	190	36.21N	120.48E
Lapa, neigh., Braz.	234c	22.55S	43.11W
La Palma, Pan. (lä-päl'mä)	121	8.25N	78.07W
La Palma, Spain	158	37.24N	6.36W
La Palma Island, i., Spain	210	28.42N	19.03W
La Pampa, prov., Arg.	132	37.25S	67.00W
Lapa Rio Negro, Braz. (lä-pä-rē'ō-nĕ'grô)	132	26.12S	49.56W

PLACE (Pronunciation)	PAGE	Lat. °′	Long. °′
La Paternal, neigh., Arg.	233d	34.36S	58.28W
La Paz, Arg. (lä päz')	132	30.48S	59.47W
La Paz, Bol.	130	16.31S	68.03W
La Paz, Hond.	120	14.15N	87.40W
La Paz, Mex.	116	24.00N	110.15W
La Paz, Mex. (lä-pȧ'z)	118	23.39N	100.44W
Lapeer, Mi., U.S. (lȧ-pēr')	98	43.05N	83.15W
La-Penne-sur-Huveaune, Fr. (la-pĕn'sür-ü-vōn')	156a	43.18N	5.33E
La Perouse, Austl.	201b	33.59S	151.14E
La Piedad Cabadas, Mex. (lä pyā-dhädh' kä-bä'dhäs)	118	20.20N	102.04W
Lapland, hist. reg., Eur. (lăp'lănd)	142	68.20N	22.00E
La Plata, Arg. (lä plä'tä)	132	34.54S	57.57W
La Plata, Mo., U.S. (lȧ plā'tȧ)	111	40.03N	92.28W
La Plata Peak, mtn., Co., U.S.	109	39.00N	106.25W
La Playa, Cuba	233b	23.06N	82.27W
La Pocatière, Can. (lȧ pō-kȧ-tyâr')	91	47.24N	70.01W
La Poile Bay, b., Can. (lȧ pwäl')	93	47.38N	58.20W
La Porte, In., U.S. (lȧ pōrt')	98	41.35N	86.45W
Laporte, Oh., U.S.	101d	41.19N	82.05W
La Porte, Tx., U.S.	113a	29.40N	95.01W
La Porte City, Ia., U.S.	103	42.20N	92.10W
Lappeenranta, Fin. (lä'pēn-rän'tä)	153	61.04N	28.08E
La Prairie, Can. (lä-prâ-rē')	83a	45.24N	73.30W
Lâpseki, Tur. (läp'sȧ-kē)	161	40.20N	26.41E
Laptev Sea, sea, Russia (läp'tyĭf)	165	75.39N	120.00E
La Puebla, Spain (lä pwā'blä)	159	39.46N	3.02E
La Puebla de Montalbán, Spain	158	39.54N	4.21W
La Puente, Ca., U.S. (pwĕn'tē)	107a	34.01N	117.57W
La Punta, Peru	233c	12.05S	77.10W
Lapuşul, r., Rom. (lä'po͞o-sho͞ol)	155	47.29N	23.46E
La Queue-en-Brie, Fr.	237c	48.47N	2.35E
La Quiaca, Arg. (lä kē-ä'kä)	132	22.15S	65.44W
L'Aquila, Italy (lȧ'kē-lä)	148	42.22N	13.24E
Lār, Iran (lär)	182	27.31N	54.12E
Lara, Austl.	201a	38.02S	144.24E
Larache, Mor. (lä-räsh')	210	35.15N	6.09W
Laramie, Wy., U.S. (lăr'ȧ-mĭ)	96	41.20N	105.40W
Laramie, r., Co., U.S.	110	40.56N	105.55W
Laranjeiras, neigh., Braz.	234c	22.56S	43.11W
Larchmont, N.Y., U.S. (lärch'mŏnt)	100a	40.56N	73.46W
Larch Mountain, mtn., Or., U.S. (lärch)	106c	45.32N	122.06W
Laredo, Spain (lȧ-rā'dhō)	158	43.24N	3.24W
Laredo, Tx., U.S.	96	27.31N	99.29W
La Reina, Chile	234b	33.27S	70.33W
La Réole, Fr. (lȧ rȧ-ōl')	156	44.37N	0.03W
Largeau, Chad (lär-zhō')	211	17.55N	19.07E
Largo, Cayo, Cuba (kä'yō-lär'gō)	122	21.40N	81.30W
Larimore, N.D., U.S. (lăr'ĭ-môr)	102	47.53N	97.38W
Larino, Italy (lä-rē'nô)	160	41.48N	14.54E
La Rioja, Arg. (lä rē-ōhä)	132	29.18S	67.42W
La Rioja, prov., Arg. (lä-rē-ô'kä)	132	28.45S	68.00W
Lárisa, Grc. (lä'rē-sȧ)	149	39.38N	22.25E
Lārkāna, Pak.	186	27.40N	68.12E
Larkspur, Ca., U.S.	231b	37.56N	122.32W
Larnaca, Cyp.	149	34.55N	33.37E
Lárnakos, Kólpos, b., Cyp.	181a	36.50N	33.45E
Larned, Ks., U.S. (lär'nĕd)	110	38.09N	99.07W
La Robla, Spain (lä rōb'lä)	158	42.48N	5.36W
La Rochelle, Fr. (lȧ rō-shĕl')	142	46.10N	1.09W
La Roche-sur-Yon, Fr. (lȧ rōsh'sûr-yôɴ')	147	46.39N	1.27W
La Roda, Spain (lä rō'dä)	158	39.13N	2.08W
La Romona, Dom. Rep. (lä-rä-mô'nä)	123	18.25N	69.00W
Larrey Point, c., Austl. (lăr'ē)	202	19.15S	118.15E
Laruns, Fr. (lȧ-răɴs')	156	42.58N	0.28W
Larvik, Nor. (lär'vĕk)	146	59.06N	10.03E
La Sabana, Ven. (lä-sä-bȧ'nä)	131b	10.38N	66.24W
La Sabina, Cuba (lä-sä-bē'nä)	123a	22.51N	82.05W
La Sagra, mtn., Spain (lä sä'grä)	148	37.56N	2.35W
La Sal, Ut., U.S. (lȧ săl')	109	38.10N	109.20W
La Salle, Can.	83a	45.26N	73.39W
La Salle, Can.	83f	49.41N	97.16W
La Salle, Can. (lȧ săl')	101b	42.14N	83.06W
La Salle, Il., U.S.	98	41.20N	89.05W
Las Animas, Co., U.S. (lȧs ă'nĭ-mȧs)	110	38.03N	103.16W
La Sarre, Can.	85	48.43N	79.12W
Lascahobas, Haiti (läs-kä-ō'bȧs)	123	19.00N	71.55W
Las Cruces, Mex. (läs-kro͞o'sĕs)	119	16.37N	93.54W
Las Cruces, N.M., U.S.	96	32.20N	106.50W
La Selle, Massif de, mtn., Haiti (lä'sĕl')	123	18.25N	72.05W
La Serena, Chile (lä-sĕ-rē'nä)	132	29.55S	71.24W
La Seyne, Fr. (lä-sån')	147	43.07N	5.52E
Las Flores, Arg. (läs flo'rĕs)	132	36.01S	59.07W
Las Flores, Ven.	234a	10.34N	66.56W
Lashio, Myanmar (lăsh'ē-ō)	188	22.58N	98.03E
Las Juntas, C.R. (läs-ko͞o'n-täs)	120	10.15N	85.00W
Las Maismas, sw., Spain (läs-mī's-mäs)	158	37.05N	6.25W
Las Minas, Ven.	234a	10.27N	66.52W
La Solana, Spain (lä-sō-lä-nä)	158	38.56N	3.13W
Las Palmas, Pan.	121	8.08N	81.30W
Las Palmas de Gran Canaria, Spain (läs päl'mäs)	210	28.07N	15.28W
La Spezia, Italy (lä-spĕ'zyä)	142	44.07N	9.48E
Las Piedras, Ur. (läs-pyĕ'drȧs)	129c	34.42S	56.08W
Las Pilas, vol., Nic. (läs-pē'läs)	120	12.32N	86.43W
Las Rejas, Chile	234b	33.28S	70.44W
Las Rosas, Mex. (läs rō thäs)	119	16.24N	92.23W
Las Rozas de Madrid, Spain (läs rō'thas dā mä-dhrēd')	159a	40.29N	3.53W
Lassee, Aus.	145e	48.14N	16.50E
Lassen Peak, mtn., Ca., U.S. (lăs'ĕn)	96	40.30N	121.32W
Lassen Volcanic National Park, rec., Ca., U.S.	96	40.43N	121.35W
L'Assomption, Can. (lȧs-sôm-syôɴ)	83a	45.50N	73.25W

PRONOUNCING INDEX

Lass Qoray–Les Grésillons 309

PLACE (Pronunciation)	PAGE	Lat. °'	Long. °'
Lass Qoray, Som.	218a	11.13N	48.19E
Las Tablas, Pan. (läs tä'bläs)	121	7.48N	80.16W
Last Mountain, l., Can. (lȧst moun'tĭn)	84	51.05N	105.10W
Lastoursville, Gabon (lȧs-to͞or-vēl')	212	1.00S	12.49E
Las Tres Vírgenes, Volcán, vol., Mex. (vē'r-hĕ-nĕs)	116	26.00N	111.45W
Las Tunas, prov., Cuba	122	21.05N	77.00W
Las Vacas, Mex. (läs-vá'käs)	119	16.24N	95.48W
Las Vegas, Chile (läs-vĕ'gäs)	129b	32.50S	70.59W
Las Vegas, Nv., U.S. (läs vā'gäs)	96	36.12N	115.10W
Las Vegas, N.M., U.S.	96	35.36N	105.13W
Las Vegas, Ven. (läs-vĕ'gäs)	131b	10.26N	64.08W
Las Vigas, Mex.	119	19.38N	97.03W
Las Vizcachas, Meseta de, plat., Arg.	132	49.35S	71.00W
Latacunga, Ec. (lä-tä-kōŋ'gä)	130	1.02S	78.33W
Latakia see Al Lādhiqīyah, Syria	182	35.32N	35.51E
La Teste-de-Buch, Fr. (lä-tĕst-dĕ-büsh)	156	44.38N	1.11W
Lathrop, Mo., U.S. (lā'thrŭp)	111	39.32N	94.21W
Latimer, Eng., U.K.	235	51.41N	0.33W
La Tortuga, Isla, i., Ven. (ĕ's-lä-lä-tôr-to͞o'gä)	130	10.55N	65.18W
Latorytsya, r., Eur.	155	48.27N	22.30E
Latourell, Or., U.S. (lȧ-tou'rĕl)	106c	45.32N	122.13W
La Tremblade, Fr. (lä-trĕN-bläd')	156	45.45N	1.12W
Latrobe, Pa., U.S. (lȧ-trōb')	99	40.25N	79.15W
Lattingtown, N.Y., U.S.	228	40.54N	73.36W
La Tuque, Can. (lȧ'tük')	85	47.27N	72.49W
Lātūr, India (lä-to͞or')	186	18.20N	76.35E
Latvia, nation, Eur.	164	57.28N	24.29E
Lau Group, is., Fiji	198g	18.20S	178.30W
Launceston, Austl. (lôn'sĕs-tŭn)	203	41.35S	147.22E
Launceston, Eng., U.K. (lôrn'stŏn)	150	50.38N	4.26W
La Unión, Chile (lä-o͞o-nyô'n)	132	40.15S	73.04W
La Unión, El Sal.	120	13.18N	87.51W
La Unión, Mex. (lä o͞on-nyōn')	118	17.59N	101.48W
La Unión, Spain	148	37.38N	0.50W
Laupendahl, Ger.	236	51.21N	6.56E
Laura, Austl. (lôrȧ)	203	15.40S	144.45E
Laurel, De., U.S. (lô'rĕl)	99	38.30N	75.40W
Laurel, Md., U.S.	100e	39.06N	76.51W
Laurel, Ms., U.S.	97	31.42N	89.07W
Laurel, Mt., U.S.	105	45.41N	108.45W
Laurel, Wa., U.S.	106d	48.52N	122.29W
Laurel Gardens, Pa., U.S.	230b	40.31N	80.01W
Laurel Hollow, N.Y., U.S.	228	40.52N	73.28W
Laurelwood, Or., U.S. (lô'rĕl-wŏŏd)	106c	45.25N	123.05W
Laurens, S.C., U.S. (lô'rĕnz)	115	34.29N	82.03W
Laurentian Highlands, hills, Can. (lô'rĕn-tĭ-ȧn)	82	49.00N	74.50W
Laurentides, Can. (lô'rĕn-tīdz)	83a	45.51N	73.46W
Lauria, Italy (lou'rē-ä)	149	40.03N	15.02E
Laurinburg, N.C., U.S. (lô'rĭn-bûrg)	115	34.45N	79.27W
Laurium, Mi., U.S. (lô'rĭ-ŭm)	103	47.13N	88.28W
Lausanne, Switz. (lō-zȧn')	142	46.32N	6.35E
Laut, Pulau, i., Indon.	196	3.39S	116.07E
Lautaro, Chile (lou-tä'rō)	132	38.40S	72.24W
Laut Kecil, Kepulauan, is., Indon.	196	4.44S	115.43E
Lautoka, Fiji	198g	17.37S	177.27E
Lauzon, Can. (lō-zōN')	83b	46.50N	71.10W
Lava Beds National Monument, rec., Ca., U.S. (lä'vȧ bĕds)	104	41.38N	121.44W
Lavaca, r., Tx., U.S. (lȧ-vȧk'ȧ)	113	29.05N	96.50W
Lava Hot Springs, Id., U.S.	105	42.37N	111.58W
Laval, Can.	85	45.31N	73.44W
Laval, Fr. (lä-väl')	147	48.05N	0.47W
Laval-des-Rapides, neigh., Can.	227b	45.33N	73.42W
Laval-Ouest, neigh., Can.	227b	45.33N	73.52W
La Vecilla de Curueno, Spain	158	42.53N	5.18W
La Vega, Dom. Rep. (lä-vĕ'gä)	123	19.15N	70.35W
La Vega, neigh., Ven.	234a	10.28N	66.57W
Lavello, Italy (lä-vĕl'lō)	160	41.05N	15.50E
La Verne, Ca., U.S. (lȧ vûrn')	107a	34.06N	117.46W
Laverton, Austl. (lā'vĕr-tŭn)	202	28.45S	122.30E
La Victoria, Peru	233c	12.04S	77.02W
La Victoria, Ven. (lä vēk-tô'rē-ä)	130	10.14N	67.20W
Lavonia, Ga., U.S. (lȧ-vō'nĭ-ȧ)	114	34.26N	83.05W
Lavon Reservoir, res., Tx., U.S.	113	33.06N	96.20W
Lavras, Braz. (lä'vräzh)	129a	21.15S	44.59W
Lávrion, Grc. (läv'rĭ-ŏn)	161	37.44N	24.05E
Lavry, Russia (lou'rȧ)	162	57.35N	27.28E
Lawndale, Ca., U.S. (lôn'dāl)	107a	33.54N	118.22W
Lawndale, neigh., Il., U.S.	231a	41.51N	87.43W
Lawndale, neigh., Pa., U.S.	229b	40.03N	75.05W
Lawnside, N.J., U.S.	229b	39.52N	75.03W
Lawra, Ghana	214	10.39N	2.52W
Lawrence, In., U.S. (lô'rĕns)	101g	39.59N	86.01W
Lawrence, Ks., U.S.	97	38.57N	95.13W
Lawrence, Ma., U.S.	93a	42.42N	71.09W
Lawrence, Pa., U.S.	101e	40.18N	80.07W
Lawrenceburg, In., U.S. (lô'rĕns-bûrg)	101f	39.06N	84.47W
Lawrenceburg, Ky., U.S.	98	38.00N	85.00W
Lawrenceburg, Tn., U.S.	114	35.13N	87.20W
Lawrenceville, Ga., U.S. (lô-rĕns-vĭl)	114	33.56N	83.57W
Lawrenceville, Il., U.S.	98	38.45N	87.45W
Lawrenceville, N.J., U.S.	100a	40.17N	74.44W
Lawrenceville, Va., U.S.	115	36.43N	77.52W
Lawrenceville, neigh., Pa., U.S.	230b	40.28N	79.57W
Lawsonia, Md., U.S. (lô-sō'nĭ-ȧ)	99	38.00N	75.50W
Lawton, Ok., U.S. (lô'tŭn)	96	34.36N	98.25W
Lawz, Jabal al, mtn., Sau. Ar.	182	28.46N	35.37E
Layang Layang, Malay. (lä-yäng' lä-yäng')	181b	1.49N	103.28E
Laysan, i., Hi., U.S.	94b	26.00N	171.00W
Layton, Ut., U.S. (lā'tŭn)	107b	41.04N	111.58W
Lazdijai, Lith. (läzh'dē-yī')	153	54.12N	23.35E
Lazio (Latium), hist. reg., Italy	160	42.05N	12.25E
Lead, S.D., U.S. (lēd)	96	44.22N	103.47W
Leader, Can.	88	50.55N	109.32W
Leadville, Co., U.S. (lĕd'vĭl)	110	39.14N	106.18W
Leaf, r., Ms., U.S. (lēf)	114	31.43N	89.20W
League City, Tx., U.S. (lēg)	113a	29.31N	95.05W
Leamington, Can. (lĕm'ĭng-tŭn)	90	42.05N	82.35W
Leamington, Eng., U.K. (lĕ'mĭng-tŭn)	150	52.17N	1.25W
Leatherhead, Eng., U.K. (lĕdh'ĕr-hĕd')	144b	51.17N	0.20W
Leavenworth, Ks., U.S. (lĕv'ĕn-wûrth)	97	39.19N	94.54W
Leavenworth, Wa., U.S.	104	47.35N	120.39W
Leawood, Ks., U.S. (lē'wŏŏd)	107f	38.58N	94.37W
Łeba, Pol. (lā'bä)	155	54.45N	17.34E
Lebam, r., Malay.	181b	1.35N	104.09E
Lebango, Congo	216	0.22N	14.49E
Lebanon, Il., U.S. (lĕb'ȧ-nŭn)	107e	38.36N	89.49W
Lebanon, In., U.S.	98	40.00N	86.30W
Lebanon, Ky., U.S.	114	37.32N	85.15W
Lebanon, Mo., U.S.	111	37.40N	92.43W
Lebanon, N.H., U.S.	99	43.40N	72.15W
Lebanon, Oh., U.S.	98	39.25N	84.10W
Lebanon, Or., U.S.	104	44.31N	122.53W
Lebanon, Pa., U.S.	99	40.20N	76.20W
Lebanon, Tn., U.S.	114	36.10N	86.16W
Lebanon, nation, Asia	182	34.00N	34.00E
Lebedyan', Russia (lyĕ'bĕ-dyän')	166	53.03N	39.08E
Lebedyn, Ukr.	163	48.56N	31.35E
Lebedyn, Ukr.	167	50.34N	34.27E
Le Blanc, Fr. (lĕ-bläN')	156	46.38N	0.59E
Le Blanc-Mesnil, Fr.	237c	48.56N	2.28E
Leblon, neigh., Braz.	234c	22.59S	43.13W
Le Borgne, Haiti (lĕ bōrn'y')	123	19.50N	72.30W
Lębork, Pol. (lăN-bŏrk')	155	54.33N	17.46E
Le Bourget, Fr.	237c	48.56N	2.26E
Lebrija, Spain (lȧ-brē'hä)	158	36.55N	6.06W
Lecce, Italy (lĕt'chā)	149	40.22N	18.11E
Lecco, Italy (lĕk'kō)	160	45.52N	9.28E
Lech, r., Ger. (lĕk)	154	47.41N	10.52E
Le Châtelet-en-Brie, Fr. (lĕ-shä-tĕ-lā'ĕN-brē')	157b	48.29N	2.50E
Leche, Laguna de, l., Cuba (lä-gŏ'nä-dĕ-lĕ'chĕ)	122	22.10N	78.30W
Leche, Laguna de la, l., Mex.	112	27.16N	102.45W
Lecompte, La., U.S.	113	31.06N	92.25W
Le Creusot, Fr. (lĕkrû-zō)	147	46.48N	4.23E
Ledesma, Spain (lȧ-dĕs'mä)	158	41.05N	5.59W
Ledsham, Eng., U.K.	237a	53.16N	2.58W
Leduc, Can. (lĕ-do͞ok')	87	53.16N	113.33W
Leech, l., Mn., U.S. (lēch)	103	47.06N	94.16W
Leeds, Eng., U.K.	142	53.48N	1.33W
Leeds, Al., U.S. (lēdz)	100h	33.33N	86.33W
Leeds, N.D., U.S.	102	48.18N	99.24W
Leeds and Liverpool Canal, can., Eng., U.K. (lĭv'ĕr-po͞ol)	144a	53.36N	2.38W
Leegebruch, Ger. (lĕh'gĕn-bro͞oK)	145b	52.43N	13.12E
Leek, Eng., U.K. (lēk)	144a	53.06N	2.01W
Lee Manor, Va., U.S.	229d	38.52N	77.15W
Leer, Ger. (lār)	154	53.14N	7.27E
Lees, Eng., U.K.	237b	53.32N	2.04W
Leesburg, Fl., U.S. (lēz'bûrg)	115	28.49N	81.53W
Leesburg, Va., U.S.	99	39.10N	77.30W
Lees Summit, Mo., U.S.	107f	38.55N	94.23W
Lee Stocking, i., Bah.	122	23.45N	76.05W
Leesville, La., U.S. (lēz'vĭl)	113	31.09N	93.17W
Leetonia, Oh., U.S. (lē-tō'nĭ-ȧ)	98	40.50N	80.45W
Leeuwarden, Neth. (lā'wär-dĕn)	147	52.12N	5.50E
Leeuwin, Cape, c., Austl. (lo͞o'wĭn)	202	34.15S	114.30E
Leeward Islands, is., N.A. (lē'wẽrd)	113	17.00N	62.15W
Le François, Mart.	121b	14.37N	60.55W
Lefroy, l., Austl. (lĕ-froi')	202	31.30S	122.00E
Leganés, Spain (lȧ-gä'nȧs)	159a	40.20N	3.46W
Legazpi, Phil. (lä-gäs'pē)	197	13.09N	123.44E
Legge Peak, mtn., Austl. (lĕg)	204	41.33S	148.10E
Leggett, Ca., U.S.	108	39.51N	123.42W
Leghorn see Livorno, Italy	142	43.32N	11.18E
Legnano, Italy (lȧ-nyä'nō)	160	45.35N	8.53E
Legnica, Pol. (lĕk-nĭt'sȧ)	147	51.13N	16.10E
Leh, India (lā)	186	34.10N	77.40E
Le Havre, Fr. (lĕ ȧv'r')	142	49.31N	0.07E
Lehi, Ut., U.S. (lē'hī)	109	40.25N	111.55W
Lehman Caves National Monument, rec., Nv., U.S. (lē'mȧn)	109	38.54N	114.08W
Lehnin, Ger. (lĕh'nēn)	145b	52.19N	12.45E
Leião, Port.	238d	38.44N	9.18W
Leicester, Eng., U.K. (lĕs'tẽr)	142	52.37N	1.08W
Leicestershire, co., Eng., U.K.	144a	52.40N	1.12W
Leichhardt, Austl.	243a	33.53S	151.09E
Leichhardt, r., Austl. (līk'härt)	202	18.30S	139.45E
Leiden, Neth. (lī'dĕn)	151	52.09N	4.29E
Leigh Creek, Austl. (lē krēk)	204	30.33S	138.30E
Leikanger, Nor. (lī'käŋ'gẽr)	152	61.11N	6.51E
Leimuiden, Neth.	145a	52.13N	4.40E
Leine, r., Ger. (lī'nĕ)	154	51.58N	9.56E
Leinster, hist. reg., Ire. (lĕn-stẽr)	150	52.45N	7.19W
Leipsic, Oh., U.S. (līp'sĭk)	98	41.05N	84.00W
Leipzig, Ger. (līp'tsĭk)	142	51.20N	12.24E
Leiria, Port. (lā-rē'ä)	158	39.45N	8.50W
Leitchfield, Ky., U.S. (lēch'fēld)	114	37.28N	86.20W
Leitha, r., Aus.	145e	48.04N	16.57E
Leithe, neigh., Ger.	236	51.29N	7.06E
Leitrim, Can.	83c	45.20N	75.36W
Leizhou Bandao, pen., China (lä-jō bän-dou)	188	20.42N	109.10E
Le Kremlin-Bicêtre, Fr.	237c	48.49N	2.21E
Leksand, Swe. (lĕk'sänd)	152	60.45N	14.56E
Leland, Wa., U.S. (lē'lănd)	106a	47.54N	122.53W
Leliu, China (lŭ-lĭō)	191a	22.52N	113.09E
Le Locle, Switz. (lĕ lō'kl')	154	47.03N	6.43E
Le Maire, Estrecho de, strt., Arg. (ĕs-trĕ'chō-dĕ-lĕ-mī'rĕ)	132	55.15S	65.30W
Le Mans, Fr. (lĕ mäN')	147	48.01N	0.12E
Le Marin, Mart.	121b	14.28N	60.55W
Le Mars, Ia., U.S. (lē märz')	102	42.46N	96.09W
Lemay, Mo., U.S.	107e	38.32N	90.17W
Lemdiyya, Alg.	210	36.18N	2.40E
Leme, Morro do, mtn., Braz.	234c	22.58S	43.10W
Lemery, Phil. (lā-mā-rē')	197a	13.51S	120.55E
Le Mesnil-Amelot, Fr.	237c	49.01N	2.36E
Le Mesnil-le-Roi, Fr.	237c	48.56N	2.08E
Lemhi, r., Id., U.S.	105	44.40N	113.27W
Lemhi Range, mts., Id., U.S. (lĕm'hī)	105	44.35N	113.33W
Lemmon, S.D., U.S. (lĕm'ŭn)	102	45.55N	102.10W
Le Môle, Haiti (lĕ mōl')	123	19.50N	73.20W
Lemon Grove, Ca., U.S. (lĕm'ŭn-grōv)	108a	32.44N	117.02W
Lemon Heights, Ca., U.S.	232	33.46N	117.48W
Le Moule, Guad. (lĕ mo͞ol')	121b	16.19N	61.22W
LeMoyne, Can.	227b	45.31N	73.29W
Lempa, r., N.A. (lĕm'pä)	120	13.20N	88.46W
Lemvig, Den. (lĕm'vēgh)	152	56.33N	8.16E
Lena, r., Russia	165	68.00N	123.00E
Lençóes Paulista, Braz. (lĕN-sônS' pou-lēs'tȧ)	132	22.30S	48.45W
Lençóis, Braz. (lĕn-sóis)	131	12.38S	41.28W
Lenexa, Ks., U.S. (lē'nĕx-ȧ)	107f	38.58N	99.44W
Lengyandong, China (lŭŋ-yän-dôŋ)	191a	23.12N	113.21E
Lenik, r., Malay.	181b	1.59N	102.51E
Lenina, Gora, hill, Russia	239b	55.42N	37.31E
Leningrad see Saint Petersburg, Russia	164	59.57N	30.20E
Leningrad, prov., Russia	162	59.15N	30.30E
Leningradskaya, Russia (lyĕ-nĭn-gräd'skȧ-yȧ)	163	46.19N	39.23E
Lenino, Russia (lyĕ'nĭ-nô)	172b	55.37N	37.41E
Leninogor, Kaz.	169	50.29N	83.25E
Leninsk, Russia (lyĕ-nēnsk')	167	48.40N	45.10E
Leninsk-Kuznetski, Russia (lyĕ-nênsk'ko͞oz-nyĕt'skĭ)	164	54.28N	86.48E
Lennox, Ca., U.S.	232	33.56N	118.21W
Lennox, S.D., U.S. (lĕn'ŭks)	102	43.22N	96.53W
Lenoir, N.C., U.S. (lē-nōr')	115	35.54N	81.35W
Lenoir City, Tn., U.S.	114	35.47N	84.16W
Lenox, Ia., U.S.	103	40.51N	94.29W
Lenz, S. Afr.	244b	26.19S	27.49E
Léo, Burkina	214	11.06N	2.06W
Leoben, Aus. (lā-ō'bĕn)	154	47.22N	15.09E
Léogane, Haiti (lā-ō-gan')	123	18.30N	72.35W
Leola, S.D., U.S. (lē-ō'lȧ)	102	45.43N	99.55W
Leominster, Ma., U.S. (lĕm'ĭn-stẽr)	99	42.32N	71.45W
León, Mex. (lā-ōn')	116	21.08N	101.41W
León, Nic. (lĕ-ô'n)	116	12.28N	86.53W
León, Spain (lĕ-ô'n)	148	42.38N	5.33W
Leon, Ia., U.S. (lē'ŏn)	103	40.43N	93.44W
Leon, hist. reg., Spain (lĕ-ô'n)	158	41.18N	5.50W
Leon, r., Tx., U.S. (lē'rĕ)	112	31.54N	98.20W
Leonforte, Italy (lā-ôn-fôr'tä)	160	37.40N	14.27E
Leonia, N.J., U.S.	228	40.52N	73.59W
Léopold, Mont, Zaire	244c	4.19S	15.15E
Leopoldau, neigh., Aus.	239e	48.16N	16.27E
Leopold II, Lac see Mai-Ndombe, Lac, l., Zaire	212	2.16S	19.00E
Leopoldina, Braz. (lā-ô-pôl-dē'nä)	129a	21.32S	42.38W
Leopoldsburg, Bel.	145a	51.07N	5.18E
Leopoldsdorf im Marchfelde, Aus. (lā'ô-pôlts-dōrf')	145e	48.14N	16.42E
Leopoldstadt, neigh., Aus.	239e	48.13N	16.23E
Léopoldville see Kinshasa, Zaire	212	4.18S	15.18E
Leova, Mol.	163	46.30N	28.16E
Lepe, Spain (lā'pā)	158	37.15N	7.12W
Le Pecq, Fr.	237c	48.54N	2.07E
Lepel', Bela. (lyĕ-pĕl')	162	54.52N	28.41E
Le Perreux-sur-Marne, Fr.	237c	48.51N	2.30E
Leping, China (lŭ-pĭŋ)	193	29.02N	117.12E
L'Épiphanie, Can. (lā-pē-fä-nē')	83a	45.51N	73.29W
Le Plessis-Belleville, Fr. (lĕ-plĕ-sē'bĕl-vēl')	157b	49.05N	2.46E
Le Plessis-Bouchard, Fr.	237c	49.00N	2.14E
Le Plessis-Trévise, Fr.	237c	48.49N	2.34E
Le Port-Marly, Fr.	237c	48.53N	2.06E
Lepreau, Can. (lē-prō')	92	45.10N	66.28W
Le Pré-Saint-Gervais, Fr.	237c	48.53N	2.25E
Lepsinsk, Kaz.	169	45.32N	80.47E
Le Puy, Fr. (lĕ pwē')	147	45.02N	3.54E
Le Raincy, Fr.	237c	48.54N	2.31E
Lercara Friddi, Italy (lĕr-kä'rä)	160	37.47N	13.36E
Lerdo, Mex. (lĕr'dō)	116	25.31N	103.30W
Leribe, Leso.	213c	28.53S	28.02E
Lérida, Spain (lā'rē-dhä)	148	41.38N	0.37E
Lerma, Mex. (lĕr'mä)	119	19.49N	90.34W
Lerma, Mex.	119a	19.17N	99.30W
Lerma, Spain (lĕ'r-mä)	158	42.03N	3.45W
Lerma, r., Mex.	118	20.14N	101.50W
Le Roy, N.Y., U.S. (lē roi')	99	43.00N	78.00W
Lerwick, Scot., U.K. (lĕr'ĭk) (lûr'wĭk)	142	60.08N	1.27W
Léry, Can. (lā-rī')	83a	45.21N	73.49W
Lery, Lake, l., La., U.S. (lĕ'rē)	100d	29.48N	89.45W
Les Andelys, Fr. (lā-zäN-dē-lē')	157b	49.15N	1.25E
Lesbos see Lésvos, i., Grc.	142	39.15N	25.40E
Les Cayes, Haiti	123	18.15N	73.45W
Les Cèdres, Can. (lā-sĕdr'')	83a	45.18N	74.03W
Les Clayes-sous-Bois, Fr.	237c	48.49N	1.59E
Les Grésillons, Fr.	237c	48.56N	2.01E

ŋ-sing; ŋ-baŋk; N-nasalized n; nŏd; cŏmmit; ōld; ōbey; ôrder; oi-boil; fo͞od; ŏŏ-as oo in foot; ou-out; s-soft; sh-dish; th-thin; pūre; ůnite; ûrn; stŭd; circŭs; ü-as in French tu; '-indeterminate vowel.

PLACE (Pronunciation)	PAGE	Lat. °′	Long. °′
Lesh, Alb. (lĕshĕ) (ä-lä′sē-ō)	161	41.47N	19.40E
Leshan, China (lŭ-shän)	188	29.40N	103.40E
Lésigny, Fr.	237c	48.45N	2.37E
Lésina, Lago di, l., Italy (lā′gō dē lā′zē-nä)	160	41.48N	15.12E
Leskovac, Yugo. (lĕs′kō-váts)	149	43.00N	21.58E
Leslie, S. Afr.	218d	26.23S	28.57E
Leslie, Ar., U.S. (lĕz′lĭ)	111	35.49N	92.32W
Les Lilas, Fr.	237c	48.53N	2.25E
Les Loges-en-Josas, Fr.	237c	48.46N	2.09E
Lesnoj, neigh., Russia	239a	60.00N	30.20E
Lesnoy, Russia (lĕs′noi)	166	66.45N	34.45E
Lesogorsk, Russia (lyĕs′ō-gôrsk)	194	49.28N	141.59E
Lesotho, nation, Afr. (lĕsō′thō)	212	29.45S	28.07E
Lesozavodsk, Russia (lyĕ-sô-zá-vôdsk′)	194	45.21N	133.19E
Les Pavillons-sous-Bois, Fr.	237c	48.55N	2.30E
Les Sables-d'Olonne, Fr. (lā sá′bl′dō-lŭn′)	147	46.30N	1.47W
Les Saintes Islands, is., Guad. (lā-sănt′)	121b	15.50N	61.40W
Lesser Antilles, is.	117	12.15N	65.00W
Lesser Caucasus, mts., Asia	168	41.00N	44.35E
Lesser Khingan Range, mts., China	189	49.50N	129.26E
Lesser Slave, r., Can.	87	55.15N	114.30W
Lesser Slave Lake, l., Can. (lĕs′ēr slāv)	84	55.25N	115.30W
Lesser Sunda Islands, is., Indon.	196	9.00S	120.00E
L'Estaque, Fr. (lĕs-täl)	156a	43.22N	5.20E
Lester, Pa., U.S.	229b	39.52N	75.17W
Les Thilliers-en-Vexin, Fr. (lā-tē-yā′ĕn-vē-săn′)	157b	49.19N	1.36E
Le Sueur, Mn., U.S. (lē sōōr′)	103	44.27N	93.53W
Lésvos, i., Grc.	142	39.15N	25.40E
Leszno, Pol. (lĕsh′nō)	147	51.51N	16.35E
L'Étang-la-Ville, Fr.	237c	48.52N	2.05E
Letchmore Heath, Eng., U.K.	235	51.40N	0.20W
Le Teil, Fr. (lē tā′y′)	156	44.34N	4.39E
Lethbridge, Austl.	243a	33.44S	150.48E
Lethbridge, Can. (lĕth′brĭj)	84	49.42N	112.50W
Le Thillay, Fr.	237c	49.00N	2.28E
Leticia, Col. (lĕ-tē′syä)	130	4.04S	69.57W
Leting, China (lŭ-tĭŋ)	190	39.26N	118.53E
Le Tréport, Fr. (lē-trā′pôr′)	156	50.03N	1.21E
Letychiv, Ukr.	163	49.22N	27.29E
Leuven, Bel.	151	50.53N	4.42E
Levack, Can.	90	46.38N	81.23W
Levádhia, Grc.	161	38.25N	22.51E
Le Val-d'Albian, Fr.	237c	48.45N	2.11E
Levallois-Perret, Fr. (lē-vál-wä′pĕ-rē′)	157b	48.53N	2.17E
Levanger, Nor. (lĕ-väng′ĕr)	146	63.42N	11.01E
Levanna, mtn., Eur. (lā-vä′nä)	160	45.25N	7.14E
Levenshulme, neigh., Eng., U.K.	237b	53.27N	2.10W
Leveque, Cape, c., Austl. (lē-vĕk′)	202	16.26S	123.08E
Leverkusen, Ger. (lĕ′fĕr-kōō-zĕn)	157c	51.01N	6.59E
Le Vésinet, Fr.	237c	48.54N	2.08E
Levice, Slvk. (lā′vĕt-sĕ)	155	48.13N	18.37E
Levico, Italy (lā′vē-kō)	160	46.02N	11.20E
Le Vigan, Fr. (lē vē-gän′)	156	43.59N	3.36E
Lévis, Can. (lā-vē′) (lĕ′vĭs)	85	46.49N	71.11W
Levittown, N.Y., U.S.	228	40.41N	73.31W
Levittown, Pa., U.S. (lĕ′vĭt-toun)	100f	40.08N	74.50W
Levkás, Grc. (lyĕfkäs′)	161	38.49N	20.43E
Levkás, i., Grc.	149	38.42N	20.22E
Levoča, Slvk. (lā′vō-chä)	155	49.03N	20.38E
Levuka, Fiji	198g	17.41S	178.50E
Lewes, Eng., U.K.	151	50.51N	0.01E
Lewes, De., U.S. (lōō′ĭs)	99	38.45N	75.10W
Lewinsville, Va., U.S.	229d	38.54N	77.12W
Lewinsville Heights, Va., U.S.	229d	38.53N	77.12W
Lewis, r., Wa., U.S.	104	46.05N	122.09W
Lewis, East Fork, r., Wa., U.S.	106c	45.52N	122.40W
Lewis, Island of, i., Scot., U.K. (lōō′ĭs)	150	58.05N	6.07W
Lewisburg, Tn., U.S. (lū′ĭs-bûrg)	114	35.27N	86.47W
Lewisburg, W.V., U.S.	98	37.50N	80.20W
Lewisdale, Md., U.S.	229d	38.58N	76.58W
Lewisham, S. Afr.	244b	26.07S	27.49E
Lewisham, neigh., Eng., U.K.	235	51.27N	0.01E
Lewis Hills, hills, Can.	93	48.48N	58.30W
Lewisporte, Can. (lū′ĭs-pōrt)	93	49.15N	55.04W
Lewis Range, mts., Mt., U.S. (lū′ĭs)	105	48.15N	113.20W
Lewis Smith Lake, res., Al., U.S.	114	34.05N	87.07W
Lewiston, Id., U.S. (lū′ĭs-tŭn)	96	46.24N	116.59W
Lewiston, Me., U.S.	97	44.05N	70.14W
Lewiston, N.Y., U.S.	101c	43.11N	79.02W
Lewiston, Ut., U.S.	105	41.58N	111.51W
Lewistown, Il., U.S. (lū′ĭs-toun)	111	40.23N	90.06W
Lewistown, Mt., U.S.	96	47.05N	109.25W
Lewistown, Pa., U.S.	99	40.35N	77.30W
Lexington, Ky., U.S. (lĕk′sĭng-tŭn)	97	38.05N	84.30W
Lexington, Ma., U.S.	93a	42.27N	71.14W
Lexington, Ms., U.S.	114	33.08N	90.02W
Lexington, Mo., U.S.	111	39.11N	93.52W
Lexington, Ne., U.S.	110	40.46N	99.44W
Lexington, N.C., U.S.	115	35.47N	80.15W
Lexington, Tn., U.S.	114	35.37N	88.24W
Lexington, Va., U.S.	99	37.45N	79.20W
Leybourne, Eng., U.K.	235	51.18N	0.25E
Leyte, i., Phil. (lā′tā)	197	10.35N	125.35E
Leżajsk, Pol. (lĕ′zhä-ĭsk)	155	50.14N	22.25E
Lezha, r., Russia (lĕ-zhä′)	162	58.59N	40.27E
L'gov, Russia (lgôf)	163	51.42N	35.15E
Lhasa, China (läs′ä)	188	29.41N	91.12E
L'Hautil, Fr.	237c	49.00N	2.01E
Liangxiangzhen, China (lĭäŋ-shyäŋ-jŭn)	192a	39.43N	116.08E
Lianjiang, China (lĭĕn-jyäŋ)	193	21.38N	110.15E
Lianozovo, Russia (lĭ-a-nô′zô-vô)	172b	55.54N	37.36E
Lianshui, China (lĭĕn-shwā)	190	33.46N	119.15E
Lianyungang, China (lĭĕn-yòn-gäŋ)	189	34.35N	119.09E
Liao, r., China	189	43.37N	120.05E
Liaocheng, China (lĭou-chŭŋ)	192	36.27N	115.56E
Liaodong Bandao, pen., China (lĭou-dôŋ bän-dou)	189	39.45N	122.22E
Liaodong Wan, b., China (lĭou-dôŋ wäŋ)	192	40.25N	121.15E
Liaoning, prov., China	189	41.31N	122.11E
Liaoyang, China (lyä′ō-yäng′)	189	41.18N	123.10E
Liaoyuan, China (lĭou-yüän)	192	43.00N	124.59E
Liard, r., Can. (lē-är′)	84	59.43N	126.42W
Libano, Col. (lē′bá-nō)	130a	4.55N	75.05W
Libby, Mt., U.S. (lĭb′ē)	104	48.27N	115.35W
Libenge, Zaire (lē-bĕŋ′gā)	211	3.39N	18.40E
Liberal, Ks., U.S. (lĭb′ēr-ăl)	110	37.01N	100.56W
Liberdade, neigh., Braz.	234d	23.35S	46.37W
Liberec, Czech Rep. (lē′bĕr-ĕts)	147	50.45N	15.06E
Liberia, C.R.	120	10.38N	85.28W
Liberia, nation, Afr. (lī-bē′rĭ-ȧ)	210	6.30N	9.55W
Libertad, Arg.	132a	34.42S	58.42W
Libertad de Orituco, Ven. (lē-bĕr-tä′d-dĕ-ō-rē-tōō′kō)	131b	9.32N	66.24W
Liberty, In., U.S. (lĭb′ēr-tĭ)	98	39.35N	84.55W
Liberty, Mo., U.S.	107f	39.15N	94.25W
Liberty, Pa., U.S.	230b	40.20N	79.51W
Liberty, S.C., U.S.	115	34.47N	82.41W
Liberty, Tx., U.S.	113	30.03N	94.46W
Liberty, Ut., U.S.	107b	41.20N	111.52W
Liberty Bay, b., Wa., U.S.	106a	47.43N	122.41W
Liberty Lake, l., Md., U.S.	100e	39.25N	76.56W
Liberty Manor, Md., U.S.	229c	39.21N	76.47W
Libertyville, Il., U.S. (lĭb′ēr-tĭ-vĭl)	101a	42.17N	87.57W
Libode, S. Afr. (lĭ-bō′dē)	213c	31.33S	29.03E
Libón, r., N.A.	123	19.30N	71.45W
Libourne, Fr. (lē-bōōrn′)	147	44.55N	0.12W
Library, Pa., U.S.	230b	40.18N	80.02W
Libres, Mex. (lē′brās)	119	19.26N	97.41W
Libreville, Gabon (lē-br′vēl′)	212	0.23N	9.27E
Liburn, Ga., U.S. (lĭb′ûrn)	100c	33.53N	84.09W
Libya, nation, Afr. (lĭb′ē-ä)	211	27.38N	15.00E
Libyan Desert, des., Afr. (lĭb′ē-ăn)	211	28.23N	23.34E
Libyan Plateau, plat., Afr.	184	30.58N	26.20E
Licancábur, Cerro, mtn., S.A. (sĕ′r-rô-lē-kán-ká′bōōr)	132	22.45S	67.45W
Licanten, Chile (lē-kän-tĕ′n)	129b	34.58S	72.00W
Lichfield, Eng., U.K. (lĭch′fēld)	144a	52.41N	1.49W
Lichinga, Moz.	217	13.18S	35.14E
Lichtenberg, neigh., Ger.	238a	52.31N	13.29E
Lichtenburg, S. Afr. (lĭk′tĕn-bĕrgh)	218d	26.09S	26.10E
Lichtendorf, Ger.	236	51.28N	7.37E
Lichtenplatz, neigh., Ger.	236	51.15N	7.12E
Lichtenrade, neigh., Ger.	238a	52.23N	13.25E
Lichterfelde, neigh., Ger.	238a	52.26N	13.19E
Lick Creek, r., In., U.S. (lĭk)	101g	39.43N	86.06W
Licking, r., Ky., U.S. (lĭk′ĭng)	98	38.30N	84.10W
Lida, Bela. (lē′dá)	155	53.53N	25.19E
Lidcombe, Austl.	243a	33.52S	151.03E
Lidgerwood, N.D., U.S. (lĭj′ēr-wood)	102	46.04N	97.10W
Lidköping, Swe. (lĕt′chû-pĭng)	152	58.31N	13.06E
Lido Beach, N.Y., U.S.	228	40.35N	73.38W
Lido di Roma, Italy (lē′dō-dē-rō′mä)	159d	41.19N	12.17E
Lidzbark, Pol. (lĭts′bärk)	155	54.07N	20.36E
Liebenbergsvlei, r., S. Afr.	218d	27.35S	28.25E
Liebenwalde, Ger. (lē′bĕn-väl-dĕ)	145b	52.52N	13.24E
Liechtenstein, nation, Eur. (lēk′tĕn-shtīn)	147	47.10N	10.00E
Liège, Bel.	147	50.38N	5.34E
Lienz, Aus. (lē-ĕnts′)	154	46.49N	12.45E
Liepāja, Lat. (le′pä-yä′)	166	56.31N	20.59E
Lier, Bel.	145a	51.08N	4.34E
Lierenfeld, neigh., Ger.	236	51.13N	6.51E
Liesing, Aus. (lē′sĭng)	145e	48.09N	16.17E
Liestal, Switz. (lēs′täl)	154	47.28N	7.44E
Lifanga, Zaire	216	0.19N	21.57E
Lifou, i., N. Cal.	203	21.15S	167.32E
Ligao, Phil. (lē-gä′ō)	197a	13.14N	123.33E
Lightning Ridge, Austl.	204	29.23S	147.50E
Ligonha, r., Moz. (lē-gō′nyȧ)	213	16.14S	39.00E
Ligonier, In., U.S. (lĭg-ō-nēr)	98	41.30N	85.35W
Ligovo, Russia (lē′gô-vô)	172c	59.51N	30.13E
Liguria, hist. reg., Italy (lē-gōō-rē-ä)	160	44.24N	8.27E
Ligurian Sea, sea, Eur. (lĭ-gū′rĭ-ăn)	148	43.42N	8.32E
Lihou Reef, rf., Austl. (lē-hōō′)	203	17.23S	152.43E
Lihuang, China (lē′hōōäng)	190	31.32N	115.46E
Lihue, Hi., U.S. (lē-hōō′ä)	96c	21.59N	159.23W
Lihula, Est. (lē′hò-lá)	153	58.41N	23.50E
Liji, China (lē-jyē)	190	33.47N	117.47E
Lijiang, China (lē-jyäŋ)	188	27.00N	100.08E
Lijin, China (lē-jyĭn)	192	37.30N	118.15E
Likasi, Zaire	212	10.59S	26.44E
Likhoslavl', Russia (lyē-kôsläv″l)	162	57.07N	35.27E
Likhovka, Ukr. (lyē-kôf′ká)	163	48.52N	33.57E
Likouala, r., Congo	216	0.10S	16.30E
Lille, Fr. (lēl)	142	50.38N	3.01E
Lille Baelt, strt., Den.	152	55.09N	9.53E
Lillehammer, Nor. (lēl′ĕ-häm′mĕr)	146	61.07N	10.25E
Lillesand, Nor. (lēl′ĕ-sän′)	152	58.16N	8.19E
Lilleström, Nor. (lēl′ĕ-strûm)	152	59.56N	11.04E
Lilliwaup, Wa., U.S. (lĭl′ĭ-wŏp)	106a	47.28N	123.07W
Lillooet, Can. (lĭ′lōō-ĕt)	84	50.30N	121.55W
Lillooet, r., Can.	87	49.50N	122.10W
Lilongwe, Mwi. (lē-lō-än)	212	13.59S	33.44E
Liluāh, India	240a	22.37N	88.20E
Lilydale, Austl.	243b	37.45S	145.21E
Lilyfield, Austl.	243a	33.52S	151.10E
Lima, Peru (lē′mä)	130	12.06S	76.55W
Lima, Swe.	152	60.54N	13.24E
Lima, Oh., U.S. (lī′mȧ)	97	40.40N	84.05W
Lima, r., Eur.	158	41.45N	8.22W
Lima Duarte, Braz. (dwä′r-tĕ)	129a	21.52S	43.47W
Limão, neigh., Braz.	234d	23.30S	46.40W
Lima Reservoir, res., Mt., U.S.	105	44.45N	112.15W
Limassol, Cyp.	149	34.39N	33.02E
Limay, r., Arg. (lē-mä′ē)	132	39.50S	69.15W
Limbazi, Lat. (lēm′bä-zĭ)	153	57.32N	24.44E
Limbdi, India	186	22.37N	71.52E
Limbe, Cam.	210	4.01N	9.12E
Limburg an der Lahn, Ger. (lem-bòrg′)	154	50.22N	8.03E
Limefield, Eng., U.K.	237b	53.37N	2.18W
Limeira, Braz. (lē-mā′rä)	129a	22.34S	47.24W
Limerick, Ire. (lĭm′nák)	147	52.39N	8.35W
Limestone Bay, b., Can. (lĭm′stōn)	89	53.50N	98.50W
Limfjorden, Den.	146	56.55N	8.56E
Limmen Bight, bt., Austl. (lĭm′ĕn)	202	14.45S	136.00E
Limni, Grc. (lēm′nē)	161	38.47N	23.22E
Límnos, i., Grc.	149	39.58N	24.48E
Limoges, Can. (lē-môzh′)	83c	45.20N	75.15W
Limoges, Fr.	147	45.50N	1.15E
Limón, C.R. (lē-mōn′)	117	10.01N	83.02W
Limón, Hond. (lē-mō′n)	120	15.53N	85.34W
Limon, Co., U.S. (lī′mŏn)	110	39.15N	103.41W
Limon, r., Dom. Rep.	123	18.20N	71.40W
Limón, Bahía, b., Pan.	116a	9.21N	79.58W
Limours, Fr. (lē-mōōr′)	157b	48.39N	2.05E
Limousin, Plateaux du, plat., Fr. (plä-tō′ dü lē-mōō-zăn′)	156	45.44N	1.09E
Limoux, Fr. (lē-mōō′)	156	43.03N	2.14E
Limpopo, r., Afr. (lĭm-pō′pō)	212	23.15S	27.46E
Linares, Chile (lē-nä′rās)	132	35.51S	71.35W
Linares, Mex.	116	24.53N	99.34W
Linares, Spain (lē-nä′rĕs)	148	38.07N	3.38W
Linares, prov., Chile	129b	35.53S	71.30W
Linaro, Cape, c., Italy (lē-nä′rä)	160	42.02N	11.53E
Lince, Peru	233c	12.05S	77.03W
Linchuan, China (lĭn-chüän)	189	27.58N	116.18E
Lincoln, Arg. (lĭŋ′kŭn)	132	34.51S	61.29W
Lincoln, Can.	83d	43.10N	79.29W
Lincoln, Eng., U.K.	146	53.14N	0.33W
Lincoln, Ca., U.S.	108	38.51N	121.19W
Lincoln, Il., U.S.	111	40.09N	89.21W
Lincoln, Ks., U.S.	110	39.02N	98.08W
Lincoln, Me., U.S.	92	45.23N	68.31W
Lincoln, Ma., U.S.	93a	42.25N	71.19W
Lincoln, Ne., U.S.	96	40.49N	96.43W
Lincoln, Pa., U.S.	230b	40.18N	79.51W
Lincoln, Mount, mtn., Co., U.S.	110	39.20N	106.19W
Lincoln Center, pt. of i., N.Y., U.S.	228	40.46N	73.59W
Lincoln Heath, reg., Eng., U.K.	144a	53.23N	0.39W
Lincolnia Heights, Va., U.S.	229d	38.50N	77.09W
Lincoln Park, Mi., U.S.	101b	42.14N	83.11W
Lincoln Park, N.J., U.S.	100a	40.56N	74.18W
Lincoln Park, pt. of i., Il., U.S.	231a	41.56N	87.38W
Lincoln Place, neigh., Pa., U.S.	230b	40.22N	79.55W
Lincolnshire, co., Eng., U.K.	144a	53.12N	0.29W
Lincolnshire Wolds, Eng., U.K. (woldz′)	150	53.25N	0.23W
Lincolnton, N.C., U.S. (lĭŋ′kŭn-tŭn)	115	35.27N	81.15W
Lincolnwood, Il., U.S.	231a	42.00N	87.46W
Linda-a-Velha, Port.	238d	38.43N	9.14W
Lindale, Ga., U.S. (lĭn′dāl)	114	34.10N	85.10W
Lindau, Ger. (lĭn′dou)	154	47.33N	9.40E
Linden, Al., U.S. (lĭn′dĕn)	114	32.16N	87.47W
Linden, Ma., U.S.	227a	42.26N	71.02W
Linden, Mo., U.S.	107f	39.13N	94.35W
Linden, N.J., U.S.	100a	40.39N	74.14W
Linden, neigh., S. Afr.	244b	26.08S	28.00E
Lindenberg, Ger.	238a	52.36N	13.31E
Linden-Dahlhausen, neigh., Ger.	236	51.26N	7.09E
Lindenhorst, neigh., Ger.	236	51.33N	7.27E
Lindenhurst, N.Y., U.S. (lĭn′dĕn-hûrst)	100a	40.41N	73.23W
Lindenwold, N.J., U.S. (lĭn′dĕn-wôld)	100f	39.50N	75.00W
Linderhausen, Ger.	236	51.18N	7.17E
Lindesberg, Swe. (lĭn′dĕs-bĕrgh)	152	59.37N	15.14E
Lindesnes, c., Nor. (lĭn′ĕs-nĕs)	142	58.00N	7.05E
Lindfield, Austl.	243a	33.47S	151.10E
Lindi, Tan. (lĭn′dē)	213	10.00S	39.43E
Lindi, r., Zaire	211	1.00N	27.13E
Lindian, China (lĭn-dĭĕn)	192	47.08N	124.59E
Lindley, S. Afr. (lĭnd′lē)	218d	27.52S	27.55E
Lindow, Ger. (lēn′dōv)	145b	52.58N	12.59E
Lindsay, Can. (lĭn′zē)	91	44.20N	78.45W
Lindsay, Ok., U.S.	111	34.50N	97.38W
Lindsborg, Ks., U.S. (lĭnz′bôrg)	111	38.34N	97.42W
Lineville, Al., U.S. (līn′vĭl)	114	33.18N	85.45W
Linfen, China	189	36.00N	111.38E
Linga, Kepulauan, is., Indon.	196	0.35S	105.05E
Lingao, China (lĭn-gou)	193	19.58N	109.40E
Lingayen, Phil. (lĭŋ′gä-yān′)	196	16.01N	120.13E
Lingayen Gulf, b., Phil.	197a	16.18N	120.11E
Lingdianzhen, China	190	31.52N	121.28E
Lingen, Ger. (lĭŋ′gĕn)	154	52.32N	7.20E
Lingling, China (lĭŋ-lĭŋ)	193	26.10N	111.40E
Lingshou, China (lĭŋ-shō)	190	38.21N	114.41E
Linguère, Sen. (lĭŋ-gĕr′)	210	15.24N	15.07W
Lingwu, China	192	38.05N	106.18E
Lingyuan, China (lĭŋ-yüän)	192	41.12N	119.20E
Linhai, China	193	28.52N	121.08E
Linhe, China (lĭn-hŭ)	192	40.49N	107.45E
Linhuaiguan, China (lĭn-hwī-guän)	190	32.55N	117.38E
Linhuanji, China	190	33.42N	116.33E
Linjiang, China (lĭn-jyäŋ)	192	41.45N	127.00E
Linköping, Swe. (lĭn′chû-pĭng)	146	58.25N	15.35E
Linksfield, neigh., S. Afr.	244b	26.10S	28.06E

PRONOUNCING INDEX
Linmeyer–London 311

PLACE (Pronunciation)	PAGE	Lat. °′	Long. °′
Linmeyer, S. Afr.	244b	26.16S	28.04E
Linn, neigh., Ger.	236	51.20N	6.38E
Linnhe, Loch, b., Scot., U.K. (lĭn'ē)	150	56.35N	4.30W
Linqing, China (lĭn-chyĭŋ)	189	36.49N	115.42E
Linqu, China (lĭn-chyo͞o)	190	36.31N	118.33E
Lins, Braz. (lē'ɴs)	131	21.42S	49.41W
Linthicum Heights, Md., U.S. (lĭn'thĭ-kŭm)	100e	39.12N	76.39W
Linton, In., U.S. (lĭn'tŭn)	98	39.05N	87.15W
Linton, N.D., U.S.	102	46.16N	100.15W
Lintorf, Ger.	236	51.20N	6.49E
Linwu, China (lĭn'wo͞o')	193	25.20N	112.30E
Linxi, China (lĭn-shyē)	192	43.30N	118.02E
Linyi, China (lĭn-yē)	189	35.04N	118.21E
Linying, China (lĭn'yĭng')	190	33.48N	113.56E
Linz, Aus. (lĭnts)	147	48.18N	14.18E
Linzhang, China (lĭn-jäŋ)	190	36.19N	114.40E
Lion, Golfe du, b., Fin.	142	43.00N	4.00E
Lipa, Phil. (lē-pä')	196	13.55N	121.10E
Lipari, Italy (lē'pä-rē)	160	38.29N	15.00E
Lipari, i., Italy	160	38.32N	15.04E
Lipetsk, Russia (lyĕ'pĕtsk)	164	52.26N	39.34E
Lipetsk, prov., Russia	162	52.18N	38.30E
Liping, China (lē-pĭŋ)	188	26.18N	109.00E
Lipno, Pol. (lēp'nô)	155	52.50N	19.12E
Lippe, r., Ger. (lĭp'ē)	157b	51.36N	6.45E
Lippolthausen, neigh., Ger.	236	51.37N	7.29E
Lippstadt, Ger. (lĭp'shtät)	154	51.39N	8.20E
Lipscomb, Al., U.S. (lĭp'skŭm)	100h	33.26N	86.56W
Lipu, China (lē-po͞o)	193	24.38N	110.35E
Lira, Ug.	217	2.15N	32.54E
Liri, r., Italy (lē'rē)	160	41.49N	13.30E
Liria, Spain (lē'ryä)	159	39.35N	0.34W
Lisala, Zaire (lē-sä'lä)	211	2.09N	21.31E
Lisboa *see* Lisbon, Port.	142	38.42N	9.05W
Lisbon (Lisboa), Port.	142	38.42N	9.05W
Lisbon, N.D., U.S.	102	46.21N	97.43W
Lisbon, Oh., U.S.	98	40.45N	80.50W
Lisbon Falls, Me., U.S.	92	43.59N	70.03W
Lisburn, N. Ire., U.K. (lĭs'bŭrn)	150	54.35N	6.05W
Lisburne, Cape, c., Ak., U.S.	96a	68.20N	165.40W
Lishi, China (lē-shr)	192	37.32N	111.12E
Lishu, China	192	43.12N	124.18E
Lishui, China	189	28.28N	120.00E
Lishui, China (lĭ'shwĭ')	190	31.41N	119.01E
Lisianski Island, i., Hi., U.S.	94b	25.30N	174.00W
Lisieux, Fr. (lē-zyû')	156	49.10N	0.13E
Lisiy Nos, Russia (lĭ'sĭy-nôs)	172c	60.01N	30.00E
Liski, Russia (lyēs'kē)	163	50.56N	39.28E
Lisle, Il., U.S. (līl)	101a	41.48N	88.04W
L'Isle-Adam, Fr. (lēl-ädäɴ')	157b	49.05N	2.13E
Lismore, Austl. (lĭz'môr)	203	28.48S	153.18E
Litani, r., Leb.	181a	33.28N	35.42E
Litchfield, Il., U.S. (lĭch'fēld)	111	39.10N	89.38W
Litchfield, Mn., U.S.	103	45.08N	94.34W
Litchfield, Oh., U.S.	101d	41.10N	82.01W
Litherland, Eng., U.K.	237a	53.28N	2.59W
Lithgow, Austl. (lĭth'gō)	203	33.23S	149.31E
Lithinon, Akra, c., Grc.	160a	34.59N	24.35E
Lithonia, Ga., U.S. (lĭ-thō'nĭ-*à*)	100c	33.43N	84.07W
Lithuania, nation, Eur. (lĭth-ů-ā'nĭ-*à*)	164	55.42N	23.30E
Litókhoron, Grc. (lē'tō-ĸô-rôn)	161	40.05N	22.29E
Litoko, Zaire	216	1.13S	24.47E
Litoměřice, Czech Rep. (lē'tô-myĕr'zhĭ-tsĕ)	154	50.33N	14.10E
Litomyšl, Czech Rep. (lē'tô-mēsh'l)	154	49.52N	16.14E
Litoo, Tan.	217	9.45S	38.24E
Little, r., Austl.	201a	37.54S	144.27E
Little, r., Tn., U.S.	114	36.28N	89.39W
Little, r., Tx., U.S.	113	30.48N	96.50W
Little Abaco, i., Bah. (ä'bä-kō)	122	26.55N	77.45W
Little Abitibi, r., Can.	90	50.15N	81.30W
Little America, sci., Ant.	219	78.30S	161.30W
Little Andaman, i., India (ăn-d*à*-măn')	196	10.39N	93.08E
Little Bahama Bank, bk. (b*à*-hā'm*à*)	122	26.55N	78.40W
Little Belt Mountains, mts., Mt., U.S. (bĕlt)	96	47.00N	110.50W
Little Berkhamsted, Eng., U.K.	235	51.45N	0.08W
Little Bighorn, r., Mt., U.S. (bĭg-hôrn)	105	45.08N	107.30W
Little Bitter Lake, l., Egypt	218b	30.10N	32.36E
Little Bitterroot, r., Mt., U.S. (bĭt'ĕr-o͞ot)	105	47.45N	114.45W
Little Blue, r., Ia., U.S. (blo͞o)	107f	38.52N	94.25W
Little Blue, r., Ne., U.S.	110	40.15N	98.01W
Littleborough, Eng., U.K. (lĭt''l-bŭr-ô)	144a	53.39N	2.06W
Little Burstead, Eng., U.K.	235	51.36N	0.24E
Little Calumet, r., Il., U.S. (kăl-ů-mĕt')	101a	41.38N	87.38W
Little Cayman, i., Cay. Is. (kā'm*à*n)	122	19.40N	80.05W
Little Chalfont, Eng., U.K.	235	51.40N	0.34W
Little Colorado, r., Az., U.S. (kŏl-ô-rä'dō)	96	36.05N	111.35W
Little Compton, R.I., U.S. (kŏmp'tŏn)	100b	41.31N	71.07W
Little Corn Island, i., Nic.	121	12.19N	82.50W
Little End, Eng., U.K.	235	51.41N	0.14E
Little Exuma, i., Bah. (ĕk-so͞o'mä)	123	23.25N	75.40W
Little Falls, Mn., U.S. (fôlz)	103	45.58N	94.23W
Little Falls, N.J., U.S.	228	40.53N	74.14W
Little Falls, N.Y., U.S.	99	43.05N	74.55W
Little Ferry, N.J., U.S.	228	40.51N	74.03W
Littlefield, Tx., U.S. (lĭt''l-fēld)	110	33.55N	102.17W
Little Fork, r., Mn., U.S. (fôrk)	103	48.24N	93.30W
Little Goose Dam, dam, Wa., U.S.	104	46.35N	118.02W
Little Hans Lollick, i., V.I.U.S. (häns lôl'lĭk)	117c	18.25N	64.54W
Little Hulton, Eng., U.K.	237b	53.32N	2.25W
Little Humboldt, r., Nv., U.S. (hŭm'bōlt)	104	41.10N	117.40W
Little Inagua, i., Bah. (ē-nä'gwä)	123	21.30N	73.00W

PLACE (Pronunciation)	PAGE	Lat. °′	Long. °′
Little Isaac, i., Bah. (ī'z*à*k)	122	25.55N	79.00W
Little Kanawha, r., W.V., U.S. (k*à*-nô'w*à*)	98	39.05N	81.30W
Little Karroo, plat., S. Afr. (kä-ro͞o)	212	33.50S	21.02E
Little Lever, Eng., U.K.	237b	53.34N	2.22W
Little Mecatina, r., Can. (mĕ c*à* tĭ nå)	85	52.40N	62.21W
Little Miami, r., Oh., U.S. (mī-*ă*m'ĭ)	101f	39.19N	84.15W
Little Minch, strt., Scot., U.K.	150	57.35N	6.45W
Little Missouri, r., U.S.	96	46.00N	104.00W
Little Missouri, r., Ar., U.S. (mĭ-so͞o'rĭ)	111	34.15N	93.54W
Little Nahant, Ma., U.S.	227a	42.25N	70.56W
Little Neck, neigh., N.Y., U.S.	228	40.46N	73.44W
Little Pee Dee, r., S.C., U.S. (pē-dē')	115	34.35N	79.21W
Little Powder, r., Wy., U.S. (pou'dĕr)	105	44.51N	105.20W
Little Red, r., Ar., U.S. (rĕd)	111	35.25N	91.55W
Little Red, r., Ok., U.S.	111	33.53N	94.38W
Little Rock, Ar., U.S. (rôk)	97	34.42N	92.16W
Little Sachigo Lake, l., Can. (să'chĭ-gō)	89	54.09N	92.11W
Little Salt Lake, l., Ut., U.S.	109	37.55N	112.53W
Little San Salvador, i., Bah. (săn săl'vá-dôr)	123	24.35N	75.55W
Little Satilla, r., Ga., U.S. (sá-tĭl'*à*)	115	31.43N	82.47W
Little Sioux, r., Ia., U.S. (so͞o)	102	42.22N	95.47W
Little Smoky, r., Can. (smōk'ĭ)	87	55.10N	116.55W
Little Snake, r., Co., U.S. (snāk)	105	40.40N	108.21W
Little Stanney, Eng., U.K.	237a	53.15N	2.53W
Little Sutton, Eng., U.K.	237a	53.17N	2.57W
Little Tallapoosa, r., Al., U.S. (tăl-á-po͞o'sä)	114	32.25N	85.28W
Little Tennessee, r., Tn., U.S. (tĕn-*ĕ*-sē')	114	35.36N	84.05W
Little Thurrock, Eng., U.K.	235	51.28N	0.21E
Littleton, Eng., U.K.	235	51.24N	0.28W
Littleton, Co., U.S. (lĭt''l-tŭn)	110	39.34N	105.01W
Littleton, Ma., U.S.	93a	42.32N	71.29W
Littleton, N.H., U.S.	99	44.15N	71.45W
Little Wabash, r., Il., U.S. (wô'băsh)	98	38.50N	88.30W
Little Warley, Eng., U.K.	235	51.35N	0.19E
Little Wood, r., Id., U.S. (wŏod)	105	43.00N	114.08W
Lityn, Ukr.	163	49.16N	28.11E
Liuhe, China	192	42.10N	125.38E
Liuli, Tan.	217	11.05S	34.38E
Liulicun, China	240b	39.56N	116.28E
Liupan Shan, mts., China	192	36.20N	105.30E
Liuwa Plain, pl., Zam.	216	14.30S	22.40E
Liuyang, China (lyo͞o'yăng')	193	28.10N	113.35E
Liuyuan, China (liô-yůän)	190	36.09N	114.37E
Liuzhou, China (liō-jō)	188	24.25N	109.30E
Līvāni, Lat. (lē'vá-nē)	153	56.24N	26.12E
Lively, Can.	90	46.26N	81.09W
Livengood, Ak., U.S. (lĭv'ĕn-gŏd)	95	65.30N	148.35W
Live Oak, Fl., U.S. (lĭv'ōk)	114	30.15N	83.00W
Livermore, Ca., U.S. (lĭv'ĕr-mōr)	106b	37.41N	121.46W
Livermore, Ky., U.S.	98	37.30N	87.05W
Liverpool, Austl. (lĭv'ĕr-po͞ol)	201b	33.55S	150.56E
Liverpool, Can.	85	44.02N	64.41W
Liverpool, Eng., U.K.	142	53.25N	2.52W
Liverpool, Tx., U.S.	113a	29.18N	95.17W
Liverpool Bay, b., Can.	95	69.45N	130.00W
Liverpool Range, mts., Austl.	203	31.47S	151.00E
Livindo, r., Afr.	211	1.09N	13.30E
Livingston, Guat.	120	15.50N	88.45W
Livingston, Al., U.S. (lĭv'ĭng-stŭn)	114	32.35N	88.09W
Livingston, Il., U.S.	107e	38.58N	89.51W
Livingston, Mt., U.S.	96	45.40N	110.35W
Livingston, N.J., U.S.	100a	40.47N	74.20W
Livingston, Tn., U.S.	114	36.23N	85.20W
Livingstone, Zam. (lĭv-ĭng-stŏn)	212	17.50S	25.53E
Livingstone, Chutes de, wtfl., Afr.	216	4.50S	14.30E
Livingstonia, Mwi. (lĭv-ĭng-stō'nĭ-*à*)	212	10.36S	34.07E
Livno, Bos. (lēv'nô)	149	43.50N	17.03E
Livny, Russia (lĕv'nē)	167	52.28N	37.36E
Livonia, Mi., U.S. (lĭ-vō-nĭ-*à*)	101b	42.25N	83.23W
Livorno, Italy (lē-vôr'nō) (lĕg'hôrn)	142	43.32N	11.18E
Livramento, Braz. (lē-vrä-mĕ'n-tô)	132	30.46S	55.21W
Livry-Gargan, Fr.	237c	48.56N	2.33E
Lixian, China	190	38.30N	115.38E
Lixian, China (lē shyĕn)	193	29.42N	111.40E
Liyang, China (lē'yăng')	193	31.30N	119.29E
Lizard Point, c., Eng., U.K. (lĭz'*à*rd)	147	49.55N	5.09W
Lizy-sur-Ourcq, Fr. (lēk-sē'sür-o͞ork')	157b	49.01N	3.02E
Ljubljana, Slvn. (lyo͞o'blyä'na)	142	46.04N	14.29E
Ljubuški, Bos. (lyo͞o'bŏsh-kē)	161	43.11N	17.29E
Ljungan, r., Swe.	152	62.50N	13.45E
Ljungby, Swe. (lyŏng'bü)	152	56.49N	13.56E
Ljusdal, Swe. (lyo͞os'däl)	152	61.50N	16.11E
Ljusnan, r., Swe.	146	61.55N	15.33E
Llandudno, Wales, U.K. (lăn-düd'nō)	150	53.20N	3.46W
Llanelli, Wales, U.K. (lá-nĕl'ĭ)	147	51.44N	4.09W
Llanes, Spain (lyä'nås)	148	43.25N	4.41W
Llano, Tx., U.S. (lă'nō) (lyä'nō)	112	30.45N	98.41W
Llano, r., Tx., U.S.	112	30.38N	99.04W
Llanos, reg., S.A. (lyá'nōs)	130	4.00N	71.15W
Llera, Mex. (lyā'rä)	118	23.16N	99.03W
Llerena, Spain (lyā-rā'nä)	158	38.14N	6.02W
Llobregat, r., Spain (lyô-brĕ-gät')	159	41.55N	1.55E
Lloyd Lake, l., Can. (loid)	83e	50.52N	114.13W
Lloydminster, Can.	84	53.17N	110.00W
Lluchmayor, Spain (lyo͞och-mä-yôr')	159	39.28N	2.53E
Llullaillaco, Volcán, vol., S.A. (lyo͞o-lyī-lyä'kō)	132	24.50S	68.30W
Loange, r., Afr. (lô-äŋ'gä)	212	5.00S	20.15E
Lo Aranguiz, Chile	234b	33.23S	70.40W
Lobamba, Swaz.	212	26.27S	31.12E
Lobatse, Bots. (lō-bä'tsē)	212	25.13S	25.35E
Lobau, reg., Aus.	239e	48.10N	16.32E

PLACE (Pronunciation)	PAGE	Lat. °′	Long. °′
Lobería, Arg. (lô-bĕ'rē'ä)	132	38.13S	58.48W
Lobito, Ang. (lô-bē'tō)	212	12.30S	13.34E
Lobnya, Russia (lôb'nyá)	172b	56.01N	37.29E
Lobo, Phil.	197a	13.39N	121.14E
Lobos, Arg. (lō'bôs)	129c	35.10S	59.08W
Lobos, Cayo, i., Bah. (lō'bôs)	122	22.25N	77.40W
Lobos, Isla de, i., Mex. (ē's-lä-dĕ-lô'bōs)	119	21.24N	97.11W
Lobos de Tierra, i., Peru (lô'bō-dĕ-tyĕ'r-rä)	130	6.29S	80.55W
Lobva, Russia (lôb'vá)	172a	59.12N	60.28E
Lobva, r., Russia	172a	59.14N	60.17E
Locarno, Switz. (lô-kär'nō)	154	46.10N	8.43E
Lochearn, Md., U.S.	229c	39.21N	76.43W
Loches, Fr. (lôsh)	156	47.08N	0.56E
Loch Raven Reservoir, res., Md., U.S.	100e	39.28N	76.38W
Lockeport, Can.	92	43.42N	65.07W
Lockhart, S.C., U.S. (lŏk'hárt)	115	34.47N	81.30W
Lockhart, Tx., U.S.	113	29.54N	97.40W
Lock Haven, Pa., U.S. (lŏk'hā-vĕn)	99	41.05N	77.30W
Lockland, Oh., U.S. (lŏk'lănd)	101f	39.14N	84.27W
Lockport, Il., U.S.	101a	41.35N	88.04W
Lockport, N.Y., U.S.	99	43.11N	78.43W
Lockwillow, S. Afr.	244b	26.17S	27.50E
Loc Ninh, Viet. (lŏk'nĭng')	196	12.00N	106.30E
Locust Grove, N.Y., U.S.	228	40.48N	73.30W
Locust Valley, N.Y., U.S.	228	40.53N	73.36W
Lod, Isr. (lôd)	181a	31.57N	34.55E
Lodève, Fr. (lô-dĕv')	156	43.43N	3.18E
Lodeynoye Pole, Russia (lô-dĕy-nô'yĕ)	166	60.43N	33.24E
Lodge Creek, r., N.A. (lŏj)	105	49.20N	110.20W
Lodge Creek, r., Mt., U.S.	105	48.51N	109.30W
Lodgepole Creek, r., Wy., U.S. (lŏj'pōl)	102	41.22N	104.48W
Lodhran, Pak.	186	29.40N	71.39E
Lodi, Italy (lô'dē)	160	45.18N	9.30E
Lodi, Ca., U.S. (lō'dī)	108	38.07N	121.17W
Lodi, N.J., U.S.	228	40.53N	74.05W
Lodi, Oh., U.S. (lō'dī)	101d	41.02N	82.01W
Lodosa, Spain (lô-dô'sä)	158	42.27N	2.04W
Lodwar, Kenya	217	3.07N	35.36E
Łódź, Pol.	142	51.46N	19.30E
Loeches, Spain (lô-āch'ĕs)	159a	40.22N	3.25W
Loffa, r., Afr.	214	7.10N	10.35W
Lofoten, is., Nor. (lô'fō-tĕn)	142	68.26N	13.42E
Logan, Oh., U.S. (lō'g*à*n)	98	39.35N	82.25W
Logan, Ut., U.S.	96	41.46N	111.51W
Logan, W.V., U.S.	98	37.50N	82.00W
Logan, Mount, mtn., Can.	84	60.54N	140.33W
Logansport, In., U.S. (lō'g*ă*nz-pōrt)	97	40.45N	86.25W
Logan Square, neigh., Il., U.S.	231a	41.56N	87.42W
Lognes, Fr.	237c	48.50N	2.38E
Logone, r., Afr. (lō-gō'nä) (lô-gôn')	211	10.20N	15.30E
Logroño, Spain (lô-grō'nyō)	148	42.28N	2.25W
Logrosán, Spain (lô-grô-sän')	158	39.22N	5.29W
Løgstør, Den. (lügh-stûr')	152	56.56N	9.15E
Lohausen, neigh., Ger.	236	51.16N	6.44E
Lohberg, Ger.	236	51.35N	6.46E
Lo Hermida, Chile	234b	33.29S	70.33W
Lohheide, Ger.	236	51.30N	6.40E
Löhme, Ger.	238a	52.37N	13.40E
Lohmühle, Ger.	236	51.31N	6.40E
Löhnen, Ger.	236	51.36N	6.39E
Loir, r., Fr. (lwår)	156	47.40N	0.07E
Loire, r., Fr.	142	47.30N	2.00E
Loja, Ec. (lō'hä)	130	3.49S	79.13W
Loja, Spain (lô'-kä)	158	37.10N	4.11W
Loka, Zaire	216	0.20N	17.57E
Lokala Drift, Bots. (lô'kä-l*à* drĭft)	218d	24.00S	26.38E
Lokandu, Zaire	217	2.31S	25.47E
Lokhvytsya, Ukr.	167	50.21N	33.16E
Lokichar, Kenya	217	2.23N	35.39E
Lokitaung, Kenya	217	4.16N	35.45E
Lokofa-Bokolongo, Zaire	216	0.12N	19.22E
Lokoja, Nig. (lô-kō'yä)	210	7.47N	6.45E
Lokolama, Zaire	216	2.34S	19.53E
Lokosso, Burkina	214	10.19N	3.40W
Lol, r., Sudan (lōl)	211	9.06N	28.09E
Loliondo, Tan.	217	2.03S	35.37E
Lolland, i., Den. (lôl'än')	152	54.41N	11.00E
Lolo, Mt., U.S.	105	46.45N	114.05W
Lom, Bul. (lôm)	149	43.48N	23.15E
Loma Linda, Ca., U.S. (lō'm*à* lĭn'd*à*)	107a	34.04N	117.16W
Lomami, r., Zaire	212	0.50S	24.40E
Lomas Chapultepec, neigh., Mex.	233a	19.26N	99.13W
Lomas de Zamora, Arg. (lō'mäs dā zä-mō'rä)	129c	34.46S	58.24W
Lombard, Il., U.S. (lŏm-bärd)	101a	41.53N	88.01W
Lombardia, hist. reg., Italy (lôm-bär-dē'ä)	160	45.20N	9.30E
Lombardy, S. Afr.	244b	26.07S	28.08E
Lomblen, Pulau, i., Indon. (lŏm-blĕn')	197	8.08S	123.45E
Lombok, i., Indon. (lŏm-bŏk')	196	9.15S	116.15E
Lomé, Togo	210	6.08N	1.13E
Lomela, Zaire (lô-mā'lá)	212	2.19S	23.33E
Lomela, r., Zaire	212	0.35S	21.20E
Lometa, Tx., U.S. (lô-mē't*à*)	112	31.10N	98.25W
Lomié, Cam. (lô-mê-ā')	215	3.10N	13.37E
Lomita, Ca., U.S. (lō-mē't*à*)	107a	33.48N	118.20W
Lommel, Bel.	145a	51.14N	5.21E
Lommond, Loch, l., Scot., U.K. (lôk lō'm*ŭ*nd)	150	56.15N	4.40W
Lomonosov, Russia (lô-mô'nô-sof)	172c	59.54N	29.47E
Lompoc, Ca., U.S. (lŏm-pōk')	108	34.39N	120.30W
Łomża, Pol. (lôm'zhá)	155	53.11N	22.04E
Lonaconing, Md., U.S. (lō-n*ă*-kō'nĭng)	99	39.35N	78.55W
London, Can. (lŭn'd*ŭ*n)	85	43.00N	81.20W

ŋ-sing; ŋ-baŋk; ɴ-nasalized n; nŏd; cŏmmit; ōld; ôbey; ôrder; oi-boil; fo͞od; ŏ-as oo in foot; ou-out; s-soft; sh-dish; th-thin; pūre; ůnite; ûrn; stŭd; circŭs; ü-as in French tu; '-indeterminate vowel.

PLACE (Pronunciation)	PAGE	Lat. °′	Long. °′
London, Eng., U.K.	142	51.30N	0.07W
London, Ky., U.S.	114	37.07N	84.06W
London, Oh., U.S.	98	39.50N	83.30W
London (Heathrow) Airport, arpt., Eng., U.K.	235	51.27N	0.28W
London Colney, Eng., U.K.	235	51.43N	0.18W
Londonderry, Can. (lŭn′dŭn-dĕr-ĭ)	92	45.29N	63.36W
Londonderry, N. Ire., U.K.	146	55.00N	7.19W
Londonderry, Cape, c., Austl.	202	13.30S	127.00E
London Zoo, pt. of i., Eng., U.K.	235	51.32N	0.09W
Londrina, Braz. (lôn-drē′nä)	131	21.53S	51.17W
Lonely, i., Can. (lōn′lĭ)	85	45.35N	81.30W
Lone Pine, Ca., U.S.	108	36.36N	118.03W
Lone Star, Nic.	121	13.58N	84.25W
Long, i., Bah.	117	23.25N	75.10W
Long, i., Can.	92	44.21S	66.25W
Long, l., N.D., U.S.	102	46.47N	100.14W
Long, l., Wa., U.S.	106a	47.29N	122.36W
Longa, r., Ang. (lôŋ′gȧ)	212	10.20S	15.15E
Long Bay, b., S.C., U.S.	115	33.30N	78.54W
Long Beach, Ca., U.S. (lông bēch)	96	33.46N	118.12W
Long Beach, N.Y., U.S.	100a	40.35N	73.38W
Long Branch, N.J., U.S. (lông brȧnch)	100a	40.18N	73.59W
Long Ditton, Eng., U.K.	235	51.23N	0.20W
Longdon, N.D., U.S. (lông′-dŭn)	102	48.45N	98.23W
Long Eaton, Eng., U.K. (ē′tŭn)	144a	52.54N	1.16W
Longfield, Eng., U.K.	235	51.24N	0.18E
Longford, Ire. (lŏng′fĕrd)	150	53.43N	7.40W
Longgu, China (lôŋ-gōō)	190	34.52N	116.48E
Longhorn, Tx., U.S. (lông-hôrn)	107d	29.33N	98.23W
Longhua, China	241a	31.09N	121.26E
Longido, Tan.	217	2.44S	36.41E
Long Island, i., Pap. N. Gui.	197	5.10S	147.30E
Long Island, i., Ak., U.S.	86	54.54N	132.45W
Long Island, i., N.Y., U.S. (lông)	97	40.50N	72.50W
Long Island City, neigh., N.Y., U.S.	228	40.45N	73.56W
Long Island Sound, strt., U.S. (lông ī′lănd)	97	41.05N	72.45W
Longjumeau, Fr. (lôN-zhü-mō′)	157b	48.42N	2.17E
Longkou, China (lôŋ-kō)	190	37.39N	120.21E
Longlac, Can. (lông′lȧk)	85	49.41N	86.28W
Longlake, S.D., U.S. (lông-lāk)	102	45.52N	99.06W
Long Lake, l., Can.	90	49.10N	86.45W
Longmont, Co., U.S. (lông′mŏnt)	110	40.11N	105.07W
Longnor, Eng., U.K. (lông′nôr)	144a	53.11N	1.52W
Long Pine, Ne., U.S. (lông pīn)	102	42.31N	99.42W
Long Point, Austl.	243a	34.01S	150.54E
Long Point, c., Can.	89	53.02N	98.40W
Long Point, c., Can.	91	42.35N	80.05W
Long Point, c., Can.	93	48.48N	58.46W
Long Point Bay, b., Can.	91	42.40N	80.10W
Long Range Mountains, mts., Can.	85a	48.00N	58.30W
Longreach, Austl. (lông′rēch)	203	23.32S	144.17E
Long Reach, r., Can.	92	45.26N	66.05W
Long Reef, c., Austl.	201b	33.45S	151.22E
Longridge, Eng., U.K. (lông′rĭj)	144a	53.51N	2.37W
Longs Peak, mtn., Co., U.S. (lôngz)	96	40.17N	105.37W
Longtansi, China (lôŋ-tä-sz)	190	32.12N	115.53E
Longton, Eng., U.K. (lông′tŭn)	144a	52.59N	2.08W
Longueuil, Can. (lôN-gû′y′)	91	45.32N	73.30W
Longueville, Austl.	243a	33.50S	151.10E
Longview, Tx., U.S.	113	32.29N	94.44W
Longview, Wa., U.S. (lông-vū)	104	46.06N	123.02W
Longville, La., U.S. (lông′vĭl)	113	30.36N	93.14W
Longwy, Fr. (lôN-wē′)	157	49.32N	6.14E
Longxi, China (lôŋ-shyē)	188	35.00N	104.40E
Long Xuyen, Viet. (loung′ sōō′yĕn)	196	10.31N	105.28E
Longzhou, China (lôŋ-jō)	188	22.20N	107.02E
Lonoke, Ar., U.S. (lō′nōk)	111	34.48N	91.52W
Lons-le-Saunier, Fr. (lôN-lē-sō-nyā′)	157	46.40N	5.33E
Lontue, r., Chile (lōn-tōē′)	129b	35.20S	70.45W
Looc, Phil. (lō-ōk′)	197a	12.16N	121.59E
Loogootee, In., U.S.	98	38.40N	86.55W
Lookout, Cape, c., N.C., U.S. (lo͝ok′out)	115	34.34N	76.38W
Lookout Point Lake, res., Or., U.S.	104	43.51N	122.38W
Loolmalasin, mtn., Tan.	217	3.03S	35.46E
Looma, Can. (ō′mȧ)	83g	53.22N	113.15W
Loop, neigh., Il., U.S.	231a	41.53N	87.38W
Loop Head, c., Ire. (lo͞op)	150	52.32N	9.59W
Loosahatchie, r., Tn., U.S. (lōz-ȧ-hă′chē)	114	35.20N	89.45W
Loosdrechtsche Plassen, l., Neth.	145a	52.11N	5.09E
Lopatka, Mys, c., Russia (lō-pät′kȧ)	181	51.00N	156.52E
Lopez, Cap, c., Gabon	216	0.37N	8.43E
Lopez Bay, b., Phil. (lō′pāz)	197a	14.04N	122.00E
Lopez I, Wa., U.S.	106a	48.25N	122.53W
Lopori, r., Zaire (lō-pō′rē)	211	1.35N	20.43E
Lo Prado Arriba, Chile	234b	33.26S	70.45W
Lora, Spain (lō′rä)	158	37.40N	5.31W
Lorain, Oh., U.S. (lō-rān′)	101d	41.28N	82.10W
Loralai, Pak. (lō-rŭ-lī′)	183	30.31N	68.35E
Lorca, Spain (lôr′kä)	148	37.39N	1.40W
Lord Howe, i., Austl. (lôrd hou)	202	31.44S	157.56W
Lordsburg, N.M., U.S. (lôrdz′bûrg)	109	32.20N	108.45W
Lorena, Braz. (lō-rā′nȧ)	129a	22.45S	45.07W
Loreto, Braz. (lō-rā′tō)	131	7.09S	45.10W
Loretteville, Can. (lō-rĕt-vēl′)	83b	46.51N	71.21W
Lorica, Col. (lō-rē′kä)	130	9.14N	75.54W
Lorient, Fr. (lō-rē′äN′)	147	47.45N	3.22W
Lorn, Firth of, b., Scot., U.K. (fûrth ŏv lôrn′)	150	56.10N	6.09W
Lörrach, Ger. (lûr′äK)	154	47.36N	7.38E
Lorraine, hist. reg., Fr.	157	49.00N	6.00E
Los Alamitos, Ca., U.S. (lōs ăl-ȧ-mē′tōs)	107a	33.48N	118.04W
Los Alamos, N.M., U.S. (ăl-ȧ-mōs′)	109	35.53N	106.20W
Los Altos, Ca., U.S. (ăl-tōs′)	106b	37.23N	122.06W
Los Andes, Chile (ȧn′dēs)	129b	32.44S	70.36W
Los Angeles, Chile (äŋ′hā-lās)	132	37.27S	72.15W
Los Angeles, Ca., U.S.	108	34.03N	118.14W
Los Angeles, r., Ca., U.S.	107a	33.50N	118.13W
Los Angeles Aqueduct, Ca., U.S.	108	35.12N	118.02W
Los Angeles International Airport, arpt., Ca., U.S.	232	33.56N	118.24W
Los Bronces, Chile (lōs brō′n-sĕs)	129b	33.09S	70.18W
Loscha, r., Id., U.S. (lŏs′chă)	104	46.20N	115.11W
Los Cuatro Álamos, Chile	234b	33.32S	70.44W
Los Dos Caminos, Ven.	234a	10.31N	66.50W
Los Estados, Isla de, i., Arg. (ē′s-lä dē lōs ĕs-dōs)	132	54.45S	64.25W
Los Gatos, Ca., U.S. (gä′tōs)	108	37.13N	121.59W
Los Herreras, Mex. (ĕr-rā-räs)	112	25.55N	99.23W
Los llanos, Dom. Rep. (lōs ê-lä′nōs)	123	18.35N	69.30W
Los Indios, Cayos de, is., Cuba (kä′vōs dē lōs ē′n-dvō′s)	122	21.50N	83.10W
Lošinj, i., Yugo.	160	44.35N	14.34E
Losino Petrovskiy, Russia	172b	55.52N	38.12E
Los Nietos, Ca., U.S. (nyā′tōs)	107a	33.57N	118.05W
Los Palacios, Cuba	122	22.35N	83.15W
Los Pinos, r., Co., U.S. (pē′nōs)	109	36.58N	107.35W
Los Reyes, Mex.	116	19.35N	102.29W
Los Reyes, Mex.	119a	19.21N	98.58W
Los Santos, Pan. (sän′tōs)	121	7.57N	80.24W
Los Santos de Maimona, Spain (sän′tōs)	158	38.38N	6.30W
Lost, r., Or., U.S.	104	42.07N	121.30W
Los Teques, Ven. (tĕ′kĕs)	130	10.22N	67.04W
Lost River Range, mts., Id., U.S. (rĭ′vĕr)	105	44.23N	113.48W
Los Vilos, Chile (vē′lōs)	132	31.56S	71.29W
Lot, r., Fr. (lôt)	147	44.30N	1.30E
Lota, Chile (lō′tä)	132	37.11S	73.14W
Lothian, Md., U.S. (lōth′ĭăn)	100e	38.50N	76.38W
Lotikipi Plain, pl., Afr.	217	4.25N	34.55E
Lötschberg Tunnel, trans., Switz.	154	46.26N	7.54E
Louangphrabang, Laos (lo͞o-ang′prä-bäng′)	196	19.47N	102.15E
Loudon, Tn., U.S. (lou′dŭn)	114	35.43N	84.20W
Loudonville, Oh., U.S. (lou′dŭn-vĭl)	98	40.40N	82.15W
Loudun, Fr.	156	47.03N	0.00
Loughborough, Eng., U.K. (lŭf′bŭr-ō)	144a	52.46N	1.12W
Loughton, Eng., U.K.	235	51.39N	0.03E
Louisa, Ky., U.S. (lo͞o′ēz-ȧ)	98	38.05N	82.40W
Louisade Archipelago, is., Pap. N. Gui.	203	10.44S	153.58E
Louisberg, N.C., U.S. (lo͞o′ĭs-bûrg)	115	36.05N	79.19W
Louisburg, Can. (lo͞o′ĭs-bourg)	93	45.55N	59.58W
Louiseville, Can.	91	46.17N	72.58W
Louisiana, Mo., U.S. (lo͞o-ē-zē-ăn′ȧ)	111	39.24N	91.03W
Louisiana, state, U.S.	97	30.50N	92.50W
Louis Trichardt, S. Afr. (lo͞o′ĭs trĭchȧrt)	212	22.52S	29.53E
Louisville, Co., U.S. (lo͞o′ĭs-vĭl) (lo͞o′ē-vĭl)	110	39.58N	105.08W
Louisville, Ga., U.S.	115	33.00N	82.25W
Louisville, Ky., U.S.	97	38.15N	85.45W
Louisville, Ms., U.S.	114	33.07N	89.02W
Louis XIV, Pointe, c., Can.	85	54.35N	79.51W
Louny, Czech Rep. (lō′nē)	154	50.20N	13.47E
Loup, r., Ne., U.S. (lo͞op)	102	41.17N	97.58W
Loup City, Ne., U.S.	102	41.15N	98.59W
Lourdes, Fr. (lo͞ord)	147	43.06N	0.03W
Lourenço Marques see Maputo, Moz.	212	26.50S	32.30E
Loures, Port. (lō′rēzh)	159b	38.49N	9.10W
Lousa, Port. (lō′zȧ)	158	40.05N	8.12W
Louth, Eng., U.K. (louth)	150	53.27N	0.02W
Louvain see Leuven, Bel.	151	50.53N	4.42E
Louveciennes, Fr.	237c	48.52N	2.07E
Louviers, Fr. (lo͞o-vyā′)	156	49.13N	1.11E
Louvre, bldg., Fr.	237c	48.52N	2.20E
Lovech, Bul. (lō′vĕts)	161	43.10N	24.40E
Lovedale, Pa., U.S.	230b	40.17N	79.52W
Loveland, Co., U.S. (lŭv′lănd)	110	40.24N	105.04W
Loveland, Oh., U.S.	101f	39.16N	84.15W
Lovell, Wy., U.S. (lŭv′ĕl)	105	44.50N	108.23W
Lovelock, Nv., U.S. (lŭv′lŏk)	108	40.10N	118.37W
Loves Green, Eng., U.K.	235	51.43N	0.24E
Lovick, Al., U.S. (lŭ′vĭk)	100h	33.34N	86.38W
Loviisa, Fin. (lô′vē-sȧ)	153	60.28N	26.10E
Low, Cape, c., Can. (lō)	85	62.58N	86.50W
Lowa, r., Zaire (lō′wȧ)	212	1.30S	27.18E
Lowell, In., U.S.	101a	41.17N	87.26W
Lowell, Ma., U.S.	97	42.38N	71.18W
Lowell, Mi., U.S.	98	42.55N	85.20W
Löwenberg, Ger. (lû′vĕn-bĕrgh)	145b	52.53N	13.09E
Lower Broughton, neigh., Eng., U.K.	237b	53.29N	2.15W
Lower Brule Indian Reservation, I.R., S.D., U.S. (brü′lā)	102	44.15N	100.21W
Lower California see Baja California, pen., Mex.	82	28.00N	113.30W
Lower Granite Dam, dam, Wa., U.S.	104	46.40N	117.26W
Lower Higham, Eng., U.K.	235	51.26N	0.28E
Lower Hutt, N.Z. (hŭt)	203a	41.10S	174.55E
Lower Klamath Lake, l., Ca., U.S. (klăm′ăth)	104	41.55N	121.50W
Lower Lake, l., Ca., U.S.	104	41.21N	119.53W
Lower Marlboro, Md., U.S. (lō′ēr mărl′bōrō)	100e	38.40N	76.42W
Lower Monumental Dam, dam, Wa., U.S.	104	46.34N	118.32W
Lower Nazeing, Eng., U.K.	235	51.44N	0.01E
Lower New York Bay, b., N.Y., U.S.	228	40.33N	74.02W
Lower Otay Lake, res., Ca., U.S. (ō′tā)	108a	32.37N	116.46W
Lower Place, Eng., U.K.	237b	53.36N	2.09W
Lower Red Lake, l., Mn., U.S.	103	47.58N	94.31W
Lower Saxony see Niedersachsen, hist. reg., Ger.	154	52.52N	8.27E
Lowestoft, Eng., U.K. (lō′stŏf)	151	52.31N	1.45E
Łowicz, Pol. (lô′vĭch)	155	52.06N	19.57E
Lowville, N.Y., U.S. (lou′vĭl)	99	43.45N	75.30W
Loxicha, Mex.	119	16.03N	96.46W
Loxton, Austl. (lôks′tŭn)	204	34.25S	140.38E
Loyauté, Îles, is., N. Cal.	203	21.00S	167.00E
Loznica, Yugo. (lōz′nē-tsȧ)	149	44.31N	19.16E
Lozova, Ukr.	167	48.53N	36.23E
Luama, r., Zaire (lo͞o′ä-mȧ)	212	4.17S	27.45E
Lu'an, China (lo͞o-än)	193	31.45N	116.29E
Luan, r., China	189	41.25N	117.15E
Luanda, Ang. (lo͞o-än′dä)	212	8.48S	13.14E
Luanguinga, r., Afr. (lo͞o-ä-gĭŋ′gȧ)	212	14.00S	20.45E
Luanshya, Zam.	217	13.08S	28.24E
Luanxian, China (luän shyĕn)	190	39.47N	118.40E
Luao, Ang.	216	10.42S	22.12E
Luarca, Spain (lwä′kä)	148	43.33N	6.30W
Lubaczów, Pol. (lo͞o-bä′chôf)	155	50.08N	23.10E
Lubán, Pol. (lo͞o′bän′)	154	51.08N	15.17E
Lubānas Ezers, l., Lat. (lo͞o-bä′nȧs ā′zĕrs)	153	56.48N	26.30E
Lubang, Phil. (lo͞o-bäng′)	197a	13.49N	120.07E
Lubang Islands, is., Phil.	196	13.47N	119.56E
Lubango, Ang.	212	14.55S	13.30E
Lubartów, Pol. (lo͞o-bär′tôf)	155	51.27N	22.37E
Lubawa, Pol. (lo͞o-bä′vä)	155	53.31N	19.47E
Lübben, Ger. (lüb′ĕn)	154	51.56N	13.53E
Lubbock, Tx., U.S.	97	33.35N	101.50E
Lubec, Me., U.S. (lū′bĕk)	92	44.49N	67.01W
Lübeck, Ger. (lü′bĕk)	142	53.53N	10.42E
Lübecker Bucht, b., Ger. (lü′bĕ-kĕr bo͞oKt)	146	54.10N	11.20E
Lubilash, r., Zaire (lo͞o-bē-lȧsh′)	212	7.35S	23.55E
Lubin, Pol. (lyō′bĭn)	154	51.24N	16.14E
Lublin, Pol. (lyō′blēn′)	142	51.14N	22.33E
Lubny, Ukr. (lōb′nē)	167	50.01N	33.02E
Lubuagan, Phil. (lō-bwä-gä′n)	197a	17.24N	121.11E
Lubudi, Zaire	217	9.57S	25.58E
Lubudi, r., Zaire (lō-bō′dē)	212	10.00S	24.30E
Lubumbashi, Zaire	212	11.40S	27.28E
Lucano, Ang.	216	11.16S	21.38E
Lucca, Italy (lo͞ok′kä)	148	43.51N	10.29E
Lucea, Jam.	122	18.25N	78.10W
Luce Bay, b., Scot., U.K. (lūs)	150	54.45N	4.45W
Lucena, Phil. (lo͞o-sā′nä)	197a	13.55N	121.36E
Lucena, Spain (lo͞o-thā′nä)	148	37.25N	4.28W
Lucena del Cid, Spain	159	40.08N	0.18W
Lučenec, Slvk. (lo͞o′châ-nyĕts)	147	48.19N	19.41E
Lucera, Italy (lo͞o-châ′rä)	160	41.31N	15.22E
Luchi, China	193	28.18N	110.10E
Luchou, Tai.	241d	25.05N	121.28E
Lucin, Ut., U.S. (lů-sēn′)	105	41.23N	113.59W
Lucipara, Kepulauan, is., Indon.	197	5.45S	128.15E
Luckenwalde, Ger.	154	52.05N	13.10E
Lucknow, India (lŭk′nou)	183	26.54N	80.58E
Lucky Peak Lake, res., Id., U.S.	104	43.33N	116.00W
Luçon, Fr. (lü-sôN′)	156	46.27N	1.12W
Lucrecia, Cabo, c., Cuba	123	21.05N	75.30W
Luda Kamchiya, r., Bul.	161	42.46N	27.13E
Luddesdown, Eng., U.K.	235	51.22N	0.24E
Lüdenscheid, Ger. (lü′dĕn-shīt)	157c	51.13N	7.38E
Lüderitz, Nmb. (lü′dĕr-ĭts) (lü′dĕ-rĭts)	212	26.35S	15.15E
Lüderitz Bucht, b., Nmb.	212	26.35S	14.30E
Ludhiāna, India	183	31.00N	75.52E
Lüdinghausen, Ger.	157c	51.46N	7.27E
Ludington, Mi., U.S. (lŭd′ĭng-tŭn)	98	44.00N	86.25W
Ludlow, Eng., U.K. (lŭd′lō)	144a	52.22N	2.43W
Ludlow, Ky., U.S.	101f	39.05N	84.33W
Ludvika, Swe. (loodh-vē′kȧ)	152	60.10N	15.09E
Ludwigsburg, Ger.	154	48.53N	9.14E
Ludwigsfelde, Ger.	145b	52.18N	13.16E
Ludwigshafen, Ger.	154	49.29N	8.26E
Ludwigslust, Ger.	154	53.18N	11.31E
Ludza, Lat. (lo͞od′zȧ)	153	56.33N	27.45E
Luebo, Zaire (lo͞o-ā′bō)	212	5.15S	21.22E
Luena, Ang.	212	11.45S	19.55E
Luena, Zaire	217	9.27S	25.47E
Lufira, r., Zaire (lo͞o-fē′rȧ)	212	9.32S	27.15E
Lufkin, Tx., U.S. (lŭf′kĭn)	113	31.21N	94.43W
Luga, Russia (lo͞o′gȧ)	166	58.43N	29.52E
Luga, r., Russia	162	59.00N	29.25E
Lugano, Switz. (lo͞o-gä′nō)	154	46.01N	8.52E
Lugarno, Austl.	243a	33.59S	151.03E
Lugenda, r., Moz.	213	12.05S	38.15E
Lugo, Italy (lo͞o′gō)	160	44.28N	11.57E
Lugo, Spain (lo͞o′gō)	148	43.01N	7.32W
Lugoj, Rom.	149	45.51N	21.56E
Lugouqiao, China	240b	39.51N	116.13E
Luhans'k, Ukr.	164	48.34N	39.18E
Luhans'k, prov., Ukr.	163	49.30N	38.35E
Luhe, China (lo͞o-hŭ)	190	32.22N	118.50E
Luiana, Ang.	216	17.23S	23.03E
Luilaka, r., Zaire (lo͞o-ē-lä′kȧ)	212	2.18S	21.15E
Luis Moya, Mex. (lo͞oē′s-mô-yä)	118	22.26N	102.14W
Luján, Arg. (lo͞o′hän′)	129c	34.36S	59.07W
Luján, r., Arg.	129c	34.33S	58.59W
Lujia, China (lo͞o-jyä)	190	31.17N	120.54W
Lukanga Swamp, sw., Zam. (lo͞o-käŋ′gȧ)	212	14.30S	27.25E
Lukenie, r., Zaire (lo͞o-kā′ynȧ)	212	3.10S	19.05E
Lukolela, Zaire	212	1.03S	17.01E
Lukovit, Bul. (lo͞o′kō-vĕt′)	161	43.13N	24.07E
Łuków, Pol. (wō′kōf)	155	51.57N	22.25E
Lukuga, r., Zaire (lo͞o-ko͞o′gȧ)	212	5.50S	27.35E
Lüleburgaz, Tur. (lü′lē-bōr-gäs′)	161	41.25N	27.23E
Luling, Tx., U.S. (lū′lĭng)	113	29.41N	97.38W

PRONOUNCING INDEX Lulong–Magiscatzin 313

PLACE (Pronunciation)	PAGE	Lat. °′	Long. °′
Lulong, China (lo͞o-lôŋ)	189	39.54N	118.53E
Lulonga, r., Zaire	216	1.00N	18.37E
Luluabourg *see* Kananga, Zaire	212	6.14S	22.17E
Lulu Island, i., Can.	106d	49.09N	123.05W
Lulu Island, i., Ak., U.S.	84	55.28N	133.30W
Lumajangdong Co, l., China	186	34.00N	81.47E
Lumber, r., N.C., U.S. (lŭm'bẽr)	115	34.45N	79.10W
Lumberton, Ms., U.S. (lŭm'bẽr-tŭn)	114	31.00N	89.25W
Lumberton, N.C., U.S.	115	34.47N	79.00W
Luminárias, Braz. (lo͞o-mē-nä'ryäs)	129a	21.32S	44.53W
Lummi, i., Wa., U.S.	106d	48.42N	122.43W
Lummi Bay, b., Wa., U.S. (lŭm'ĭ)	106d	48.47N	122.44W
Lummi Island, Wa., U.S.	106d	48.44N	122.42W
Lumwana, Zam.	217	11.50S	25.10E
Lün, Mong.	188	47.58N	104.52E
Luna, Phil. (lo͞o'nȧ)	197a	16.51N	120.22E
Lund, Swe. (lŭnd)	146	55.42N	13.10E
Lundy, i., Eng., U.K. (lŭn'dē)	150	51.12N	4.50W
Lüneburg, Ger. (lü'nē-bōrgh)	154	53.16N	10.25E
Lunel, Fr. (lü-nĕl')	156	43.41N	4.07E
Lünen, Ger. (lü'nĕn)	157c	51.36N	7.30E
Lunenburg, Can. (lo͞o'nĕn-bûrg)	85	44.23N	64.19W
Lunenburg, Ma., U.S.	93a	42.36N	71.44W
Lunéville, Fr. (lü-nā-vel')	157	48.37N	6.29E
Lunga, Ang.	216	14.42S	18.32E
Lungué-Bungo, r., Afr.	212	13.00S	20.30E
Lunsar, S.L.	214	8.41N	12.32W
Lunt, Eng., U.K.	237a	53.31N	2.59W
Luodian, China (lwô-dĭĕn)	190	31.25N	121.20E
Luoding, China (lwô-dĭŋ)	193	23.42N	111.35E
Luohe, China (lwô-hŭ)	190	33.35N	114.02E
Luoyang, China (lwô-yäŋ)	189	34.45N	112.32E
Luozhen, China (lwô-jŭn)	190	37.45N	118.29E
Luque, Para. (loo'kā)	132	25.18S	57.17W
Luray, Va., U.S. (lū-rā')	99	38.40N	78.25W
Lurgan, N. Ire., U.K. (lûr'gǎn)	146	54.27N	6.28W
Lurigancho, Peru	233c	12.02S	77.01W
Lúrio, Moz. (lo͞o'rē-ō)	213	13.17S	40.29E
Lúrio, Moz.	213	14.00S	38.45E
Lurnea, Austl.	243a	33.56S	150.54E
Lusaka, Zaire	217	7.10S	29.27E
Lusaka, Zam. (lō-sä'kȧ)	212	15.25S	28.17E
Lusambo, Zaire (lo͞o-säm'bō)	212	4.58S	23.27E
Lusanga, Zaire	212	5.13S	18.43E
Lusangi, Zaire	217	4.37S	27.08E
Lushan, China	192	33.45N	113.00E
Lushiko, r., Afr.	216	6.35S	19.45E
Lushoto, Tan. (lo͞o-shō'tō)	213	4.47S	38.17E
Lüshun, China (lü-shŭn)	189	38.49N	121.15E
Lusikisiki, S. Afr. (lo͞o-sē-kē-sē'kē)	213c	31.22S	29.37E
Lusk, Wy., U.S. (lŭsk)	102	42.46N	104.27W
Lūt, Dasht-e, des., Iran (dă'sht-ē-lo͞ot)	182	31.47N	58.38E
Lutcher, La., U.S. (lŭch'ẽr)	113	30.03N	90.43W
Lütgendortmund, neigh., Ger.	236	51.30N	7.21E
Luton, Eng., U.K. (lū'tŭn)	150	51.55N	0.28W
Luts'k, Ukr.	167	50.45N	25.20E
Lüttringhausen, neigh., Ger.	236	51.13N	7.14E
Luuq, Som.	218a	3.38N	42.35E
Luverne, Al., U.S. (lū-vûn')	114	31.42N	86.15W
Luverne, Mn., U.S.	102	43.40N	96.13W
Luwingu, Zam.	217	10.15S	29.55E
Luxapallila Creek, r., U.S. (lŭk-sȧ-pôl'ĭ-lȧ)	114	33.36N	88.08W
Luxembourg, Lux.	142	49.38N	6.30E
Luxembourg, nation, Eur.	142	49.30N	6.22E
Luxeuil-les-Baines, Fr.	157	47.49N	6.19E
Luxomni, Ga., U.S. (lŭx'ŏm-nī)	100c	33.54N	84.07W
Luxor *see* Al Uqṣur, Egypt	211	25.38N	32.59E
Lu Xun Museum, bldg., China	241a	31.16N	121.28E
Luya Shan, mtn., China	192	38.50N	111.40E
Luyi, China (lo͞o-yē)	190	33.52N	115.32E
Luyuan, China	240b	39.54N	116.27E
Luz, Braz.	234c	22.48S	43.05W
Luz, neigh., Port.	238d	38.46N	9.10W
Luzern, Switz. (lō-tsĕrn)	147	47.03N	8.18E
Luzhou, China (lo͞o-jō)	188	28.58N	105.25E
Luziânia, Braz. (lo͞o-zyȧ'nēȧ)	131	16.17S	47.44W
Lužniki, neigh., Russia	239b	55.43N	37.33E
Luzon, i., Phil. (lo͞o-zŏn')	196	17.10N	119.45E
Luzon Strait, strt., Asia	193	20.40N	121.00E
L'viv, Ukr.	164	49.50N	24.00E
L'vov *see* L'viv, Ukr.	164	49.50N	24.00E
Lyalta, Can.	83e	51.07N	113.36W
Lyalya, r., Russia (lyä'lyȧ)	172a	58.58N	60.17E
Lyaskovets, Bul.	161	43.07N	25.41E
Lydenburg, S. Afr. (lī'dĕn-bûrg)	212	25.06S	30.21E
Lydiate, Eng., U.K.	237a	53.32N	2.57W
Lye Green, Eng., U.K.	235	51.43N	0.35W
Lyell, Mount, mtn., Ca., U.S. (lī'ĕl)	108	37.44N	119.22W
Lykens, Pa., U.S. (lī'kĕnz)	99	40.35N	76.45W
Lyna, r., Eur. (lĭn'ȧ)	155	53.56N	20.30E
Lynbrook, N.Y., U.S.	228	40.39N	73.41W
Lynch, Ky., U.S. (lĭnch)	115	36.56N	82.55W
Lynchburg, Va., U.S. (lĭnch'bûrg)	97	37.23N	79.08W
Lynch Cove, Wa., U.S. (lĭnch)	106a	47.26N	122.54W
Lynden, Can. (lĭn'dĕn)	83d	43.14N	80.08W
Lynden, Wa., U.S.	106d	48.56N	122.27W
Lyndhurst, Austl.	201a	38.03S	145.14E
Lyndhurst, N.J., U.S.	228	40.49N	74.07W
Lyndhurst, Oh., U.S.	229a	41.31N	81.30W
Lyndon, Ky., U.S. (lĭn'dŭn)	101h	38.15N	85.36W
Lyndonville, Vt., U.S. (lĭn'dŭn-vĭl)	99	44.35N	72.00W
Lyne, Eng., U.K.	235	51.23N	0.33W
Lynn, Ma., U.S. (lĭn)	97	42.28N	70.57W
Lynnewood Gardens, Pa., U.S.	229b	40.04N	75.09W
Lynnfield, Ma., U.S.	227a	42.32N	71.03W
Lynn Lake, Can. (lăk)	84	56.51N	101.05W
Lynwood, Ca., U.S. (lĭn'wŏŏd)	107a	33.56N	118.13W
Lyon, Fr. (lē-ôn')	142	45.44N	4.52E
Lyons, Ga., U.S. (lī'ŭnz)	115	32.08N	82.19W
Lyons, Il., U.S.	231a	41.49N	87.50W
Lyons, Ks., U.S.	110	38.20N	98.11W
Lyons, Ne., U.S.	102	41.57N	96.28W
Lyons, N.J., U.S.	100a	40.41N	74.33W
Lyons, N.Y., U.S.	99	43.05N	77.00W
Lyptsi, Ukr.	163	50.11N	36.25E
Lysefjorden, fj., Nor.	152	58.59N	6.35E
Lysekil, Swe. (lü'sĕ-kĕl)	152	58.17N	11.22E
Lysterfield, Austl.	243b	37.56S	145.18E
Lys'va, Russia (lĭs'vȧ)	166	58.07N	57.47E
Lytham, Eng., U.K. (lĭth'ǎm)	144a	53.44N	2.58W
Lytkarino, Russia	172b	55.35N	37.55E
Lyttelton, S. Afr. (lĭt'l'ton)	213b	25.51S	28.13E
Lyuban', Russia (lyo͞o'bȧn)	162	59.21N	31.15E
Lyubar, Ukr. (lyo͞o'bär)	163	49.56N	27.44E
Lyubertsy, Russia (lyo͞o'bĕr-tsē)	162	55.40N	37.55E
Lyubim, Russia (lyo͞o-bēm')	162	58.24N	40.39E
Lyublino, Russia (lyo͞ob'lĭ-nō)	172b	55.41N	37.45E
Lyudinovo, Russia (lū-dē'novō)	162	53.52N	34.28E

M

PLACE (Pronunciation)	PAGE	Lat. °′	Long. °′
Ma'ān, Jord. (mä-än')	182	30.12N	35.45E
Maartensdijk, Neth.	145a	52.09N	5.10E
Maas (Meuse), r., Eur.	151	51.50N	5.40E
Maastricht, Neth. (mäs'trĭkt)	151	50.51N	5.35E
Mabaia, Ang.	216	7.13S	14.03E
Mabana, Wa., U.S. (mä-bä-nä)	106a	48.06N	122.25W
Mabank, Tx., U.S. (mā'bănk)	113	32.21N	96.05W
Mabeskraal, S. Afr.	218d	25.12S	26.47E
Mableton, Ga., U.S. (mā'b'l-tŭn)	100c	33.49N	84.34W
Mabrouk, Mali	210	19.27N	1.16W
Mabula, S. Afr. (mä'bo͞o-la)	218d	24.49S	27.59E
Macalelon, Phil. (mä-kä-lā-lōn')	197a	13.46N	122.09E
Macao, dep., Asia	189	22.00N	113.00E
Macau, Braz. (mä-kà'ō)	131	5.12S	36.34W
Macaya, Pico de, mtn., Haiti	123	18.25N	74.00W
Macclesfield, Eng., U.K. (măk''lz-fēld)	144a	53.15N	2.07W
Macclesfield Canal, can., Eng., U.K. (măk''lz-fēld)	144a	53.14N	2.07W
Macdona, Tx., U.S. (măk-dō'nȧ)	107d	29.20N	98.42W
Macdonald, l., Austl. (mǎk-dŏn'ǎld)	202	23.40S	127.40E
Macdonnell Ranges, mts., Austl. (mǎk-dŏn'ĕl)	202	23.40S	131.30E
MacDowell Lake, l., Can. (mǎk-dou ĕl)	89	52.15N	92.45W
Macdui, Ben, mtn., Scot., U.K. (bĕn măk-do͞o'ē)	146	57.06N	3.45W
Macedonia, Oh., U.S. (măs-ē-dō'nĭ-ȧ)	101d	41.19N	81.30E
Macedonia, hist. reg., Eur. (măs-ē-dō'nĭ-ȧ)	149	41.05N	22.15E
Macedonia, nation, Eur.	161	41.50N	22.00E
Maceió, Braz.	131	9.40S	35.43W
Macerata, Italy (mä-chȧ-rä'tä)	160	43.18N	13.28E
Macfarlane, Lake, l., Austl. (mȧc'fär-lān)	204	32.10S	137.00E
Machache, mtn., Leso.	213c	29.22S	27.53E
Machado, Braz. (mä-shȧ-dō)	129a	21.42S	45.55W
Machakos, Kenya	217	1.31S	37.16E
Machala, Ec. (mä-chȧ'lä)	130	3.18S	78.54W
Machens, Mo., U.S. (măk'ĕns)	107e	38.54N	90.20W
Machias, Me., U.S. (mȧ-chī'ȧs)	92	44.22N	67.29W
Machida, Japan (mä-chē'dä)	195a	35.32N	139.28E
Machilīpatnam, India	183	16.22N	81.10E
Machu Picchu, Peru (mȧ'chō-pē'k-chō)	130	13.07S	72.34W
Măcin, Rom. (mȧ-chēn')	163	45.15N	28.09E
Macina, reg., Mali	214	14.50N	4.40W
Mackay, Austl. (mǎ-kī')	203	21.15S	149.08E
Mackay, Id., U.S. (mǎk-kā')	105	43.55N	113.38W
Mackay, l., Austl. (mǎ-kī')	202	22.30S	127.45E
MacKay, l., Can. (mǎk-kā')	84	64.10N	112.35W
Mackenzie, r., Can.	84	63.38N	124.23W
Mackenzie Bay, b., Can.	95	69.20N	137.10W
Mackenzie Mountains, mts., Can. (mȧ-kĕn'zĭ)	84	63.41N	129.27W
Mackinaw, r., Il., U.S.	98	40.35N	89.25W
Mackinaw City, Mi., U.S. (măk'ĭ-nô)	98	45.45N	84.45W
Mackinnon Road, Kenya	217	3.44S	39.03E
Macleantown, S. Afr. (mǎk-lǎn'toun)	213c	32.48S	27.48E
Maclear, S. Afr. (mȧ-klēr')	212	31.06S	28.23E
Macleod, Austl.	243b	37.43S	145.04E
Macomb, Il., U.S. (mȧ-ko͞om')	111	40.27N	90.40W
Mâcon, Fr. (mä-kôN)	147	46.19N	4.51E
Macon, Ga., U.S. (mā'kŏn)	97	32.49N	83.39W
Macon, Ms., U.S.	114	32.07N	88.31W
Macon, Mo., U.S.	111	39.42N	92.29W
Macquarie, r., Austl.	203	31.43S	148.04E
Macquarie Fields, Austl.	243a	33.59S	150.53E
Macquarie Islands, is., Austl. (mȧ-kwŏr'ē)	3	54.36S	158.45E
Macquarie University, educ., Austl.	243a	33.46S	151.06E
Macritchie Reservoir, res., Sing.	240c	1.21N	103.50E
Macuelizo, Hond. (mä-kwĕ-lē'zō)	120	15.22N	88.32W
Macuto, Ven.	234a	10.37N	66.53W
Mad, r., Ca., U.S. (măd)	104	40.38N	123.37W
Madagascar, nation, Afr. (măd-ȧ-găs'kȧr)	213	18.05S	43.12E
Madame, i., Can. (mȧ-dȧm')	93	45.33N	61.02W
Madanapalle, India	187	13.06N	78.09E
Madang, Pap. N. Gui. (mä-däng')	197	5.15S	145.45E
Madaoua, Niger (mȧ-dou'ȧ)	210	14.04N	6.03E
Madawaska, r., Can. (măd-ȧ-wôs'kȧ)	91	45.20N	77.25W
Madeira, r., S.A.	130	6.48S	62.43W
Madeira, Arquipélago da, is., Port.	209	33.26N	16.44W
Madeira, Ilha da, i., Port. (mä-dā'rä)	210	32.41N	16.15W
Madelia, Mn., U.S. (mȧ-dē'lĭ-ȧ)	103	44.03N	94.23W
Madeline, i., Wi., U.S. (măd'ĕ-lĭn)	103	46.47N	91.30W
Madera, Ca., U.S. (mȧ-dā'rȧ)	108	36.57N	120.04W
Madera, vol., Nic.	120	11.27N	85.30W
Madgaon, India	187	15.09N	73.58E
Madhya Pradesh, state, India (mŭd'vŭ prŭ-dāsh')	183	22.04N	77.48E
Madill, Ok., U.S. (mȧ-dĭl')	111	34.04N	96.45W
Madīnat ash Sha'b, Yemen	182	12.45N	44.00E
Madingo, Congo	216	4.07S	11.22E
Madingou, Congo	216	4.09S	13.34E
Madison, Fl., U.S. (măd'ĭ-sŭn)	114	30.28N	83.25W
Madison, Ga., U.S.	114	33.34N	83.29W
Madison, Il., U.S.	107e	38.40N	90.09W
Madison, In., U.S.	98	38.45N	85.25W
Madison, Ks., U.S.	111	38.08N	96.07W
Madison, Me., U.S.	92	44.47N	69.52W
Madison, Mn., U.S.	102	44.59N	96.13W
Madison, Ne., U.S.	102	41.49N	97.27W
Madison, N.J., U.S.	100a	40.46N	74.25W
Madison, N.C., U.S.	115	36.22N	79.59W
Madison, S.D., U.S.	102	44.01N	97.08W
Madison, Wi., U.S.	97	43.05N	89.23W
Madison Heights, Mi., U.S.	230c	42.30N	83.06W
Madison Res, Mt., U.S.	105	45.25N	111.28W
Madisonville, Ky., U.S. (măd'ĭ-sŭn-vĭl)	98	37.20N	87.30W
Madisonville, La., U.S.	113	30.22N	90.10W
Madisonville, Tx., U.S.	113	30.57N	95.55W
Madjori, Burkina	214	11.26N	1.15E
Mado Gashi, Kenya	217	0.44N	39.10E
Madona, Lat. (mȧ'dō'nȧ)	153	56.50N	26.14E
Madrakah, Ra's al, c., Oman	182	18.53N	57.48E
Madras, India (mȧ-drȧs') (mŭ-drŭs')	183	13.08N	80.15E
Madre, Laguna, l., Mex. (lä-go͞o'nä mä'drȧ)	113	25.08N	97.41W
Madre, Sierra, mts., N.A. (sē-ĕ'r-rä-mä'drē)	119	15.55N	92.40W
Madre, Sierra, mts., Phil.	197a	16.40N	122.10E
Madre de Dios, Archipiélago, is., Chile (mä'drä dā dē-ōs')	132	50.40S	76.30W
Madre de Dios, Río, r., S.A. (rē'ō-mä'drä dā dē-ōs')	130	12.07S	68.02W
Madre del Sur, Sierra, mts., Mex. (sē-ĕ'r-rä-mä'drā dĕlso͞or')	116	17.35N	100.35W
Madre Occidental, Sierra, mts., Mex.	116	29.30N	107.30W
Madre Oriental, Sierra, mts., Mex.	116	25.30N	100.45W
Madrid, Spain (mä-drē'd)	142	40.26N	3.42W
Madrid, Ia., U.S. (măd'rĭd)	103	41.51N	93.48W
Madridejos, Spain (mä-dhrē-dhā'hōs)	158	39.29N	3.32W
Madrillon, Va., U.S.	229d	38.55N	77.14W
Madura, i., Indon. (mȧ-do͞o'rä)	196	6.45S	113.30E
Madurai, India (mä-do͞o'rä)	183	9.57N	78.04E
Madureira, neigh., Braz.	234c	22.53S	43.21W
Madureira, Serra do, mtn., Braz. (sĕ'r-rä-dō-mä-do͞o-rā'rȧ)	132b	22.49S	43.30W
Maebashi, Japan (mä-ē-bä'shē)	189	36.26N	139.04E
Maeno, neigh., Japan	242a	35.46N	139.42E
Maestra, Sierra, mts., Cuba (sē-ĕ'r-rä-mä-ās'trä)	117	20.05N	77.05W
Maewo, i., Vanuatu	203	15.17S	168.16E
Mafeking, S. Afr. (mȧf'ĕ'kĭng)	212	25.46S	24.45E
Mafra, Braz. (mä'frä)	132	26.21N	49.59W
Mafra, Port. (mäf'rȧ)	159b	38.56N	9.20W
Magadan, Russia (mȧ-gȧ-dän')	165	59.39N	150.43E
Magadan Oblast, Russia	171	65.00N	160.00E
Magadi, Kenya	217	1.54S	36.17E
Magalhães Bastos, neigh., Braz.	234c	22.53S	43.23W
Magalies, r., S. Afr. (mä-gä'lyĕs)	213b	25.51S	27.42E
Magaliesberg, mts., S. Afr.	213b	25.45S	27.43E
Magaliesburg, S. Afr.	218d	26.01S	27.32E
Magallanes, Estrecho de, strt., S.A.	132	52.30S	68.45W
Magat, r., Phil. (mä-gät')	197a	16.45N	121.16E
Magdalena, Arg. (mäg-dä-lā'nä)	129c	35.05S	57.32W
Magdalena, Bol.	130	13.17S	63.57W
Magdalena, Mex.	96	30.34N	110.50W
Magdalena, N.M., U.S.	109	34.10N	107.45W
Magdalena, i., Chile	132	44.45S	73.15W
Magdalena, Bahía, b., Mex. (bä-ē'ä-mäg-dä-lā'nä)	116	24.30N	114.00W
Magdalena, Río, r., Col.	130	7.45N	74.04W
Magdalena del Mar, Peru	233c	12.06S	77.05W
Magdalen Laver, Eng., U.K.	235	51.45N	0.11E
Magdeburg, Ger. (mäg'dē-bōrgh)	142	52.07N	11.39E
Magellan, Strait of *see* Magallanes, Estrecho de, strt., S.A.	132	52.30S	68.45W
Magenta, Italy (mȧ-jĕn'tȧ)	160	45.26N	8.53E
Magerøya, i., Nor.	146	71.10N	24.11E
Maggiore, Lago, l., Italy	148	46.03N	8.25E
Maghāghah, Egypt	218b	28.38N	30.50W
Maghniyya, Alg.	148	34.52N	1.40W
Maghull, Eng., U.K.	237a	53.32N	2.57W
Maginu, Japan	242a	35.35N	139.36E
Magiscatzin, Mex. (mä-kēs-kät-zēn')	118	22.48N	98.42W

314 Maglaj–Manistique

PLACE (Pronunciation)	PAGE	Lat. °′	Long. °′
Maglaj, Bos. (må′glä-ė)	161	44.34N	18.12E
Magliana, neigh., Italy	239c	41.50N	12.25E
Maglie, Italy (mäl′yā)	161	40.06N	18.20E
Magna, Ut., U.S. (măg′nå)	107b	40.43N	112.06W
Magnitogorsk, Russia (måg-nyē′tỏ-gỏrsk)	164	53.26N	59.05E
Magnolia, Ar., U.S. (măg-nō′lĭ-ȧ)	111	33.16N	93.13W
Magnolia, Ms., U.S.	114	31.08N	90.27W
Magnolia, N.J., U.S.	229b	39.51N	75.02W
Magny-en-Vexin, Fr. (mä-nyē′ĕɴ-vĕ-săɴ′)	157b	49.09N	1.45E
Magny-les-Hameaux, Fr.	237c	48.44N	2.04E
Magog, Can. (mȧ-gŏg′)	91	45.15N	72.10W
Magome, neigh., Japan	242a	35.35N	139.43E
Magpie, r., Can.	90	48.13N	84.50W
Magpie, r., Can.	92	50.40N	64.30W
Magpie, Lac, l., Can.	92	50.55N	64.39W
Magrath, Can.	84	49.25N	112.52W
Maguanying, China	240b	39.52N	116.17E
Magude, Moz. (mä-gōō′då)	212	24.58S	32.39E
Magwe, Myanmar (mŭg-wā′)	183	20.19N	94.57E
Mahābād, Iran	185	36.55N	45.50E
Mahahi Port, Zaire (mä-hä′gė)	211	2.14N	31.12E
Mahajanga, Madag.	213	15.12S	46.26E
Mahakam, r., Indon.	196	0.30S	116.15E
Mahali Mountains, mts., Tan.	217	6.20S	30.00E
Mahaly, Madag. (må-hål-ē′)	213	24.09S	46.20E
Mahanoro, Madag. (må-hå-nỏ′rō)	213	19.57S	48.47E
Mahanoy City, Pa., U.S. (mä-hȧ-noi′)	99	40.50N	76.10W
Maḥaṭṭat al-Ḥilmīyah, neigh., Egypt	244a	30.07N	31.19E
Maḩaţţat al Qaţrānah, Jord.	181a	31.15N	36.04E
Maḩaţţat ʿAqabat al Ḩijāzīyah, Jord.	181a	29.45N	35.55E
Maḩaţţat ar Ramlah, Jord.	181a	29.31N	35.57E
Maḩaţţat Jurf ad Darāwīsh, Jord.	181a	30.41N	35.51E
Mahd adh-Dhahab, Sau. Ar.	185	23.30N	40.52E
Mahe, India (mä-ā′)	183	11.42N	75.39E
Mahenge, Tan. (mä-hĕŋ′gå)	212	7.38S	36.16E
Mahi, r., India	186	23.16N	73.20E
Māhīm, neigh., India	240e	19.03N	72.49E
Māhīm Bay, b., India	187b	19.03N	72.45E
Mahlabatini, S. Afr. (mä′lå-bå-tē′nė)	213c	28.15S	31.29E
Mahlow, Ger. (mä′lōv)	145b	52.23N	13.24E
Mahlsdorf, neigh., Ger.	238a	52.31N	13.37E
Mahlsdorf-Süd, neigh., Ger.	238a	52.29N	13.36E
Mahnomen, Mn., U.S. (mô-nō′mĕn)	102	47.18N	95.58W
Mahón, Spain (mä-ōn′)	148	39.52N	4.15E
Mahone Bay, Can. (mȧ-hōn′)	92	44.27N	64.23W
Mahone Bay, b., Can.	92	44.30N	64.15W
Mahopac, Lake, l., N.Y., U.S. (mā-hō′păk)	100a	41.24N	73.45W
Mahrauli, neigh., India	240d	28.31N	77.11E
Māhul, neigh., India	240e	19.01N	72.53E
Mahwah, N.J., U.S. (mȧ-wă′)	100a	41.05N	74.09W
Maidenhead, Eng., U.K. (mād′ĕn-hĕd)	144b	51.30N	0.44W
Maidstone, Austl.	243b	37.47S	144.52E
Maidstone, Eng., U.K.	151	51.17N	0.32E
Maiduguri, Nig. (mä′ē-då-gōō′rė)	211	11.51N	13.10E
Maigualida, Sierra, mts., Ven. (sē-ĕ′r-rå-mī-gwä′lē-dĕ)	130	6.30N	65.50W
Maijdi, Bngl.	186	22.59N	91.08E
Maikop *see* Maykop, Russia	164	44.35N	40.07E
Main, r., Ger. (mīn)	154	49.49N	9.20E
Main Barrier Range, mts., Austl. (băr′′ĕr)	203	31.25S	141.40E
Mai-Ndombe, Lac, l., Zaire	212	2.16S	19.00E
Maine, state, U.S. (mān)	97	45.25N	69.50W
Mainland, i., Scot., U.K. (mān-lănd)	146	60.19N	2.40W
Maintenon, Fr. (mäɴ-tĕ-nŏɴ′)	157b	48.35N	1.35E
Maintirano, Madag. (mä′ėn-tė-rä′nō)	213	18.05S	44.08E
Mainz, Ger. (mīnts)	142	49.59N	8.16E
Maio, i., C.V. (mä′yo)	210b	15.15N	22.50W
Maipo, S.A.	132	34.08S	69.51W
Maipo, r., Chile (mī′pỏ)	129b	33.45S	71.08W
Maiquetía, Ven. (mī-kĕ-tė′ä)	130	10.37N	66.56W
Maison-Rouge, Fr. (må-zŏɴ-rōōzh′)	157b	48.34N	3.09E
Maisons-Alfort, Fr.	237c	48.48N	2.26E
Maisons-Laffitte, Fr.	157b	48.57N	2.09E
Maitani, Japan	242b	34.49N	135.22E
Maitland, Austl. (māt′lănd)	203	32.45S	151.40E
Maizuru, Japan (mä-ĭ′zōō-rōō)	195	35.26N	135.15E
Majene, Indon.	196	3.34S	119.00E
Maji, Eth.	211	6.14N	35.34E
Majorca *see* Mallorca, i., Spain	142	39.18N	2.22E
Makah Indian Reservation, I.R., Wa., U.S.	104	48.17N	124.52W
Makala, Zaire	244c	4.25S	15.15E
Makanya, Tan. (mä-kän′yä)	213	4.15S	37.49E
Makanza, Zaire	211	1.42N	19.08E
Makarakomburu, Mount, mtn., Sol.Is.	198e	9.43S	160.02E
Makarska, Cro. (må′kär-skå)	161	43.17N	17.05E
Makar′yev, Russia	166	57.50N	43.48E
Makasar *see* Ujung Pandang, Indon.	196	5.08S	119.28E
Makasar, Selat (Makassar Strait), strt., Indon.	196	2.00S	118.07E
Makati, Phil.	241g	14.34N	121.01E
Makaw, Zaire	216	3.29S	18.19E
Make, i., Japan (mä′kå)	195	30.43N	130.49E
Makeni, S.L.	210	8.53N	12.03W
Makgadikgadi Pans, pl., Bots.	212	20.38S	21.31E
Makhachkala, Russia (mäκ′äch-kä′lä)	167	43.00N	47.40E
Makhaleng, r., Leso.	213c	29.53S	27.33E
Makindu, Kenya	217	2.17S	37.49E
M′akino, Russia	239b	55.48N	37.22E
Makiyivka, Ukr.	167	48.03N	38.00E
Makkah *see* Mecca, Sau. Ar.	182	21.27N	39.45E
Makkovik, Can.	85	55.01N	59.10W
Makokou, Gabon (må-kỏ-kōō′)	210	0.34N	12.52E

PLACE (Pronunciation)	PAGE	Lat. °′	Long. °′
Maków Mazowiecki, Pol. (mä′kōov mä-zō-vyĕts′kē)	155	52.51N	21.07E
Makuhari, Japan (mä-kōō-hä′rē)	195a	35.39N	140.04E
Makurazaki, Japan (mä′kỏ-rä-zä′kė)	195	31.16N	130.18E
Makurdi, Nig.	210	7.45N	8.32E
Makushin, Ak., U.S. (må-kỏ′shĭn)	95	53.57N	166.28W
Makushino, Russia (må-kỏ-shėn′ỏ)	164	55.03N	67.43E
Mala, Punta, c., Pan. (pỏ′n-tä-mä′lä)	121	7.32N	79.44W
Malabar Coast, cst., India (măl′å-bär)	187	11.19N	75.33E
Malabar Point, c., India	187b	18.57N	72.47E
Malabo, Eq. Gui.	210	3.45N	8.47E
Malabon, Phil.	197a	14.39N	120.57E
Malacca, Strait of, strt., Asia (mȧ-lăk′ȧ)	196	4.15N	99.44E
Malad City, Id., U.S. (mȧ-läd′)	105	42.11N	112.15W
Málaga, Col. (må′lä-gå)	130	6.41N	72.46W
Málaga, Spain	142	36.45N	4.25W
Malagón, Spain (mä-lä-gōn′)	158	39.12N	3.52W
Malaita, i., Sol.Is. (mȧ-lä′ė-tȧ)	203	8.38S	161.15E
Malakāl, Sudan (må-lå-käl′)	211	9.46N	31.54E
Malakhovka, Russia (må-läk′ôf-kå)	172b	55.38N	38.01E
Malakoff, Fr.	237c	48.49N	2.19E
Malakpur, neigh., India	240d	28.42N	77.12E
Malang, Indon.	196	8.06S	112.50E
Malanje, Ang. (mä-läŋ-gå)	212	9.32S	16.20E
Malanville, Benin	210	12.04N	3.09E
Mälaren, l., Swe.	146	59.38N	16.55E
Malartic, Can.	85	48.07N	78.11W
Malatya, Tur. (må-lä′tyå)	182	38.30N	38.15E
Malawi, nation, Afr.	212	11.15S	33.45E
Malawi, Lake *see* Nyasa, Lake, l., Afr.	212	10.45S	34.30E
Malaya Vishera, Russia (vė-shā′rä)	164	58.51N	32.13E
Malay Peninsula, pen., Asia (mȧ-lā′) (mā′lā)	196	6.00N	101.00E
Malaysia, nation, Asia (må-lā′zhå)	196	4.10N	101.22E
Malbon, Austl. (măl′bŭn)	202	21.15S	140.30E
Malbork, Pol. (mäl′börk)	146	54.02N	19.04E
Malcabran, r., Port. (mäl-kä-brän′)	159b	38.47N	8.46W
Malden, Ma., U.S. (môl′dĕn)	93a	42.26N	71.04W
Malden, Mo., U.S.	111	36.32N	89.56W
Malden, i., Kir.	2	4.20S	154.30W
Maldives, nation, Asia	180	4.30N	71.30E
Maldon, Eng., U.K. (môrl′dŏn)	144b	51.44N	0.39E
Maldonado, Ur. (mäl-dŏ-nå′dỏ)	132	34.54S	54.57W
Maldonado, Punta, c., Mex. (pōō′n-tä)	118	16.18N	98.34W
Maléa, Ákra, c., Grc.	149	36.31N	23.13E
Mālegaon, India	186	20.35N	74.30E
Malé Karpaty, mts., Slvk.	155	48.31N	17.15E
Malekula, i., Vanuatu (mä-lā-kōō′lä)	203	16.44S	167.45E
Malema, Moz.	217	14.57S	37.20E
Malheur, r., Or., U.S. (må-lōōr′)	104	43.45N	117.41W
Malheur Lake, l., Or., U.S. (må-lōōr′)	104	43.16N	118.37W
Mali, nation, Afr.	210	15.45N	0.15W
Malibu, Ca., U.S. (mă′lĭ-bōō)	107a	34.03N	118.38W
Malik, Wādī al, r., Sudan	211	16.48N	29.30E
Malimba, Monts, mts., Zaire	217	7.45S	29.15E
Malinalco, Mex. (mä-lė-näl′kō)	118	18.54N	99.31W
Malinaltepec, Mex. (mä-lė-näl-tå-pĕk′)	118	17.01N	98.41W
Malindi, Kenya (mä-lēn′dė)	213	3.14S	40.04E
Malin Head, c., Ire.	146	55.23N	7.24W
Malino, Russia (mä′lĭ-nô)	172b	55.07N	38.12E
Malkara, Tur. (mäl′κå-rå)	161	40.51N	26.52E
Malko Tŭrnovo, Bul. (mäl′kō-t′r′nỏ-vå)	161	41.59N	27.28E
Mallaig, Scot., U.K.	150	56.59N	5.55W
Mallet Creek, Oh., U.S. (măl′ĕt)	101d	41.10N	81.55W
Mallorca, i., Spain	142	39.30N	3.00E
Mallorquinas, Spain	238e	41.28N	2.16E
Mallow, Ire. (măl′ō)	150	52.07N	9.04W
Malmédy, Bel. (mål-mā-dē′)	151	50.25N	6.01E
Malmesbury, S. Afr. (mämz′bēr-ĭ)	212	33.30S	18.35E
Malmköping, Swe. (mälm′chû′pĭng)	152	59.09N	16.39E
Malmö, Swe.	142	55.36N	13.00E
Malmyzh, Russia (mål-mėzh′)	165	49.58N	137.07E
Malmyzh, Russia	166	56.30N	50.48E
Malnoue, Fr.	237c	48.50N	2.36E
Maloarkhangelsk, Russia (mä′lỏ-år-κäŋ′gĕlsk)	162	52.26N	36.29E
Malolos, Phil. (mä-lỏ′lỏs)	197a	14.51N	120.49E
Malomal′sk, Russia (må-lỏ-mälsk′′)	172a	58.47N	59.55E
Malone, N.Y., U.S. (mȧ-lōn′)	99	44.50N	74.20W
Malonga, Zaire	216	10.24S	23.10E
Maloti Mountains, mts., Leso.	213c	29.00S	28.29E
Maloyaroslavets, Russia (mä′lỏ-yä-rỏ-slä-vyĕts)	162	55.01N	36.25E
Malozemel′skaya Tundra, reg., Russia	166	67.30N	50.00E
Malpas, Eng., U.K. (măl′pȧz)	144a	53.01N	2.46W
Malpelo, Isla de, i., Col. (mäl-pā′lō)	130	3.55N	81.30W
Malpeque Bay, b., Can. (môl-pĕk′)	92	46.30N	63.47W
Malta, Mt., U.S. (môl′tȧ)	105	48.20N	107.50W
Malta, nation, Eur.	142	35.52N	13.30E
Maltahöhe, Nmb. (mäl′tä-hō′ĕ)	212	24.45S	16.45E
Maltrata, Mex. (mäl-trä′tä)	119	18.48N	97.16W
Maluku (Moluccas), is., Indon.	197	2.22S	128.25E
Maluku, Laut (Molucca Sea), sea, Indon.	197	0.15N	125.41E
Malūţ, Sudan	211	10.30N	32.17E
Mālvan, India	187	16.08N	73.32E
Malvern, Austl.	243b	37.52S	145.02E
Malvern, Ar., U.S. (măl′vērn)	111	34.21N	92.47W
Malvern, neigh., S. Afr.	244b	26.12S	28.06E
Malverne, N.Y., U.S.	228	40.40N	73.40W
Malvern East, S. Afr.	244b	26.12S	28.08E
Malyn, Ukr.	163	50.44N	29.15E
Malynivka, Ukr.	163	49.50N	36.43E
Malyy Anyuy, r., Russia	171	67.52N	164.30E
Malyy Tamir, i., Russia	171	78.10N	107.30E
Mamantel, Mex. (mä-mån-tĕl′)	119	18.36N	91.06W

PLACE (Pronunciation)	PAGE	Lat. °′	Long. °′
Mamaroneck, N.Y., U.S. (măm′å-rō-nĕk)	100a	40.57N	73.44W
Mambasa, Zaire	217	1.21N	29.03E
Mamburao, Phil. (mäm-bōō′rä-ō)	197a	13.14N	120.35E
Mamera, Ven.	234a	10.27N	66.59W
Mamfe, Cam. (mäm′fĕ)	210	5.46N	9.17E
Mamihara, Japan (mä′mė-hä-rä)	195	32.41N	131.12E
Mammoth Cave, Ky., U.S. (măm′ŏth)	114	37.10N	86.04W
Mammoth Cave National Park, rec., Ky., U.S.	97	37.20N	86.21W
Mammoth Hot Springs, Wy., U.S. (măm′ŭth hôt sprĭngz)	105	44.55N	110.50W
Mamnoli, India	187b	19.17N	73.15E
Mamoré, r., S.A.	130	13.00S	65.20W
Mamou, Gui.	210	10.26N	12.07W
Mampong, Ghana	214	7.04N	1.24W
Mamry, Jezioro, l., Pol. (mäm′rĭ)	155	54.10N	21.28E
Man, C. Iv.	214	7.24N	7.33W
Manacor, Spain (mä-nä-kỏr′)	159	39.35N	3.15E
Manado, Indon.	197	1.29N	124.50E
Managua, Cuba (mä-nä′gwä)	123a	22.58N	82.17W
Managua, Nic.	116	12.10N	86.16W
Managua, Lago de, l., Nic. (lå′gô-dĕ)	120	12.28N	86.10W
Manakara, Madag. (mä-nä-kä′rŭ)	213	22.17S	48.06E
Manama *see* Al Manāmah, Bahr.	182	26.01N	50.33E
Mananara, r., Madag. (mä-nä-nä′rŭ)	213	23.15S	48.15E
Mananjary, Madag. (mä-nän-zhä′rė)	213	20.16S	48.13E
Manas, China	188	44.30N	86.00E
Manassas, Va., U.S. (mȧ-năs′ȧs)	99	38.45N	77.30W
Manaus, Braz. (mä-nä′ōōzh)	131	3.01S	60.00W
Manayunk, neigh., Pa., U.S.	229b	40.01N	75.13W
Mancelona, Mi., U.S. (măn-sė-lō′nå)	98	44.50N	85.05W
Mancha Real, Spain (män′chä rā-äl′)	158	37.48N	3.37W
Manchazh, Russia (män′chåsh)	172a	56.30N	58.10E
Manchester, Eng., U.K.	142	53.28N	2.14W
Manchester, Ct., U.S. (măn′chĕs-tẽr)	99	41.45N	72.30W
Manchester, Ga., U.S.	114	32.50N	84.37W
Manchester, Ia., U.S.	103	42.30N	91.30W
Manchester, Ma., U.S.	93a	42.35N	70.47W
Manchester, Mo., U.S.	107e	38.36N	90.31W
Manchester, N.H., U.S.	97	43.00N	71.30W
Manchester, Oh., U.S.	98	38.40N	83.35W
Manchester Docks, pt. of i., Eng., U.K.	237b	53.28N	2.17W
Manchester Ship Canal, Eng., U.K.	144a	53.20N	2.40W
Manchuria, hist. reg., China (măn-chōō′rē-å)	189	48.00N	124.58E
Mandal, Nor. (män′däl)	152	58.03N	7.28E
Mandalay, Myanmar (măn′dȧ-lā)	183	22.00N	96.08E
Mandalselva, r., Nor.	152	58.25N	7.30E
Mandaluyong, Phil.	241g	14.35N	121.02E
Mandan, N.D., U.S. (măn′dăn)	96	46.49N	100.54W
Mandāoli, neigh., India	240d	28.38N	77.18E
Mandara Mountains, mts., Afr. (män-dä′rä)	211	10.15N	13.23E
Mandau Siak, r., Indon.	181b	1.03N	101.25E
Mandeb, Bab-el-, strt. (bäb′ĕl män-dĕb′)	182	13.17N	42.49E
Mandimba, Moz.	217	14.21S	35.39E
Mandinga, Pan. (män-dĭŋ′gä)	121	9.32N	79.04W
Mandla, India	186	22.43N	80.23E
Mándra, Grc. (män′drä)	161	38.06N	23.32E
Mandres-les-Roses, Fr.	237c	48.42N	2.33E
Mandritsara, Madag. (mån-drēt-sä′rå)	213	15.49S	48.47E
Manduria, Italy (män-dōō′rė-ä)	161	40.23N	17.41E
Mandve, India	187b	18.47N	72.52E
Māndvi, India (mŭnd′vē)	183	22.54N	69.23E
Māndvi, India (mŭnd′vē)	187b	19.29N	72.53E
Mandvi, neigh., India	240e	18.57N	72.50E
Mandya, India	187	12.40N	77.00E
Manfredonia, Italy (män-frå-dô′nyä)	160	41.39N	15.55E
Manfredónia, Golfo di, b., Italy (gỏl-fỏ-dē)	160	41.34N	16.05E
Mangabeiras, Chapada das, pl., Braz.	131	8.05S	47.32W
Mangalore, India (mŭŋ-gŭ-lōr′)	183	12.53N	74.52E
Manganji, Japan	242a	35.40N	139.26E
Mangaratiba, Braz. (män-gä-rä-tē′bȧ)	129a	22.56S	44.03W
Mangatarem, Phil. (män′gȧ-tä′rĕm)	197a	15.48N	120.18E
Mange, Zaire	216	0.54N	20.30E
Mangkalihat, Tanjung, c., Indon.	196	1.25N	119.55E
Mangles, Islas de, Cuba (ė′s-läs-dĕ-mäŋ′glās) (măn′g′lz)	122	22.05N	82.50W
Mangoche, Mwi.	212	14.16S	35.14E
Mangoky, r., Madag. (män-gō′kē)	213	22.02S	44.11E
Mangole, Pulau, i., Indon.	197	1.35S	126.22E
Mangualde, Port. (män-gwäl′dĕ)	158	40.38N	7.44W
Mangueira, Lagoa da, l., Braz.	132	33.15S	52.45W
Mangum, Ok., U.S. (măŋ′gŭm)	110	34.52N	99.31W
Mangzhangdian, China (mäŋ-jäŋ-dĭĕn)	190	32.07N	114.44E
Manhasset, N.Y., U.S.	228	40.48N	73.42W
Manhattan, Il., U.S.	101a	41.25N	87.29W
Manhattan, Ks., U.S. (măn-hăt′ăn)	96	39.11N	96.34W
Manhattan Beach, Ca., U.S.	107a	33.53N	118.24W
Manhuaçu, Braz. (män-ỏå′sōō)	129a	20.17S	42.01W
Manhumirim, Braz. (män-ōō-mė-rē′ɴ)	129a	22.30S	41.57W
Manicouagane, r., Can.	85	50.00N	68.35W
Manicouagane, Lac, res., Can.	85	51.30N	68.19W
Manicuare, Ven. (mä-nē-kwä′rĕ)	131b	10.35N	64.10W
Manihiki Islands, is., Cook Is. (mä′nē-hē′kė)	225	9.40S	158.00W
Manila, Phil.	196	14.37N	121.00E
Manila Bay, b., Phil. (mȧ-nĭl′ȧ)	197a	14.38N	120.46E
Manique de Baixo, Port.	238d	38.44N	9.22W
Manisa, Tur. (mä′nė-så)	149	38.40N	27.30E
Manistee, Mi., U.S. (măn-ĭs-tē′)	98	44.15N	86.20W
Manistee, r., Mi., U.S.	98	44.25N	85.45W
Manistique, Mi., U.S. (măn-ĭs-tēk′)	103	45.58N	86.16W
Manistique, l., Mi., U.S.	103	46.14N	85.30W

ăt; finăl; rāte; senåte; ärm; åsk; sofȧ; fâre; ch-choose; dh-as th in other; bē; ėvent; bĕt; recĕnt; cratẽr; g-gō; gh-guttural g; bĭt; ĭ-short neutral; rīde; ĸ-guttural k as ch in German ich;

PRONOUNCING INDEX

Manistique–Marquette 315

PLACE (Pronunciation)	PAGE	Lat. °′	Long. °′
Manistique, r., Mi., U.S.	103	46.05N	86.09W
Manitoba, prov., Can. (măn-ĭ-tō′bȧ)	84	55.12N	97.29W
Manitoba, Lake, l., Can.	84	51.00N	98.45W
Manito Lake, l., Can. (măn′ĭ-tō)	88	52.45N	109.45W
Manitou, i., Mi., U.S. (măn′ĭ-to͞o)	103	47.21N	87.33W
Manitou, l., Can.	103	49.21N	93.01W
Manitou Islands, is., Mi., U.S.	98	45.05N	86.00W
Manitoulin Island, i., Can. (măn-ĭ-to͞o′lĭn)	85	45.45N	81.30W
Manitou Springs, Co., U.S.	110	38.51N	104.58W
Manitowoc, Wi., U.S. (măn-ĭ-tỏ-wŏk′)	103	44.05N	87.42W
Manitqueira, Serra da, mts., Braz.	129a	22.40S	45.12W
Maniwaki, Can.	91	46.23N	76.00W
Manizales, Col. (mä-nė-zä′lås)	130	5.05N	75.31W
Manjacaze, Moz. (man′yä-kä′zĕ)	212	24.37S	33.49E
Mankato, Ks., U.S. (măn-kā′tō)	110	39.45N	98.12W
Mankato, Mn., U.S.	97	44.10N	93.59W
Mankim, Cam.	215	5.01N	12.00E
Manlléu, Spain (män-lyā′o͞o)	159	42.00N	2.16E
Manly, Austl.	243a	33.48S	151.17E
Mannar, Sri L. (mȧ-när′)	183b	9.48N	80.03E
Mannar, Gulf of, b., Asia	183	8.47N	78.33E
Mannheim, Ger. (män′hīm)	147	49.30N	8.31E
Manning, Ia., U.S. (măn′ĭng)	102	41.53N	95.04W
Manning, S.C., U.S.	115	33.41N	80.12W
Mannington, W.V., U.S. (măn′ĭng-tŭn)	98	39.30N	80.55W
Mannswörth, neigh., Aus.	239e	48.09N	16.31E
Mano, r., Afr.	214	7.00N	11.25W
Man of War Bay, b., Bah.	123	21.05N	74.05W
Man of War Channel, strt., Bah.	122	22.45N	76.10W
Manokwari, Indon. (mȧ-nŏk-wä′rė)	197	0.56S	134.10E
Manono, Zaire	217	7.18S	27.25E
Manor, Can. (măn′ẽr)	89	49.36N	102.05W
Manor, Wa., U.S.	106c	45.45N	122.36W
Manorhaven, N.Y., U.S.	228	40.50N	73.42W
Manori, neigh., India	187b	19.13N	72.43E
Manosque, Fr. (mȧ-nȯsh′)	157	43.51N	5.48E
Manotick, Can.	83c	45.13N	75.41W
Manouane, r., Can.	91	50.15N	70.30W
Manouane, Lac, l., Can. (mä-no͞o′ȧn)	92	50.36N	70.50W
Manresa, Spain (män-rā′sä)	148	41.44N	1.52E
Mansa, Zam.	212	11.12S	28.53E
Mansel, i., Can. (măn′sĕl)	85	61.56N	81.10W
Manseriche, Pongo de, reg., Peru (pŏ′n-gỏ-dĕ-män-sĕ-rė′chĕ)	130	4.15S	77.45W
Mansfield, Eng., U.K. (mănz′fēld)	144a	53.08N	1.12W
Mansfield, La., U.S.	113	32.02N	93.43W
Mansfield, Oh., U.S.	98	40.45N	82.30W
Mansfield, Wa., U.S.	104	47.48N	119.39W
Mansfield, Mount, mtn., Vt., U.S.	99	44.30N	72.45W
Mansfield Woodhouse, Eng., U.K. (wȯd-hous)	144a	53.08N	1.12W
Manta, Ec. (män′tä)	130	1.03S	80.16W
Manteno, Il., U.S. (măn-tē-nō)	101a	41.15N	87.50W
Manteo, N.C., U.S.	115	35.55N	75.40W
Mantes-la-Jolie, Fr. (mäɴt-ĕ-lä-zhŏ-lē′)	156	48.59N	1.42E
Manti, Ut., U.S. (măn′tī)	109	39.15N	11.40W
Mantilla, neigh., Cuba	233b	23.04N	82.20W
Mantova, Italy (män′tỏ-vä) (măn′tů-ȧ)	148	45.09N	10.47E
Mantua, Cuba (män-to͞o′ȧ)	122	22.20N	84.15W
Mantua *see* Mantova, Italy	148	45.09N	10.47E
Mantua, Md., U.S.	229d	38.51N	77.15W
Mantua, Ut., U.S. (măn′tů-ȧ)	107b	41.30N	111.57W
Manua Islands, is., Am. Sam.	198a	14.13S	169.35W
Manui, Pulau, i., Indon. (mä-no͞o′ē)	197	3.35S	123.38E
Manus Island, i., Pap. N. Gui. (mä′no͞os)	197	2.22S	146.22E
Manvel, Tx., U.S. (măn′vel)	113a	29.28N	95.22W
Manville, N.J., U.S. (măn′vĭl)	100a	40.33N	74.36W
Manville, R.I., U.S.	100b	41.57N	71.27W
Manyal Shīhah, Egypt	244a	29.57N	31.14E
Manzala Lake, l., Egypt	218b	31.14N	32.04E
Manzanares, Col. (män-sä-nä′rĕs)	130a	5.15N	75.09W
Manzanares, r., Spain (mänz-nä′rĕs)	159a	40.36N	3.48W
Manzanares, Canal del, Spain (kä-nä′l-dĕl-män-thä-nä′rĕs)	159a	40.20N	3.38W
Manzanillo, Cuba (män′zä-nēl′yō)	117	20.20N	77.05W
Manzanillo, Mex.	116	19.02N	104.21W
Manzanillo, Bahía de, b., Mex. (bä-ē′ä-dĕ-män-zä-nė′l-yō)	118	19.00N	104.38W
Manzanillo, Bahía de, b., N.A.	123	19.55N	71.50W
Manzanillo, Punta, c., Pan.	121	9.40N	79.33W
Manzhouli, China (män-jō-lē)	189	49.25N	117.15E
Manzovka, Russia (mȧn-zhỏ′f-kȧ)	194	44.16N	132.13E
Mao, Chad (mä′ỏ)	211	14.07N	15.19E
Mao, Dom. Rep.	123	19.35N	71.10W
Maoke, Pegunungan, mts., Indon.	197	4.00S	138.00E
Maoming, China	189	21.55N	110.40E
Maoniu Shan, mtn., China (mou-nĭỏ shän)	192	32.45N	104.09E
Mapastepec, Mex. (ma-päs-tȧ-pĕk′)	119	15.24N	92.52W
Mapia, Kepulauan, i., Indon.	197	0.57N	134.22E
Mapimí, Mex. (mä-pė-mē′)	112	25.50N	103.50W
Mapimí, Bolsón de, des., Mex. (bôl-sŏ′n-dĕ-mä-pē′mē)	112	27.27N	103.20W
Maple Creek, Can. (mā′p'l) (crēk)	84	49.55N	109.27W
Maple Cross, Eng., U.K.	235	51.37N	0.30W
Maple Grove, Can. (grōv)	83a	45.19N	73.51W
Maple Heights, Oh., U.S.	101d	41.25N	81.34W
Maple Leaf Gardens, rec., Can.	227c	43.40N	79.23W
Maple Shade, N.J., U.S. (shād)	100f	39.57N	75.01W
Maple Valley, Wa., U.S. (văl′ė)	106a	47.24N	122.02W
Maplewood, Mn., U.S. (wȯd)	107g	45.00N	93.03W
Maplewood, Mo., U.S.	107e	38.37N	90.20W
Maplewood, N.J., U.S.	228	40.44N	74.17W
Mapocho, r., Chile	234b	33.25S	70.47W
Mapumulo, S. Afr. (mä-pä-mo͞o′lō)	213c	29.12S	31.05E
Maputo, Moz.	212	26.50S	32.30E
Maquela do Zombo, Ang. (mȧ-kā′lȧ dỏ zỏm′bỏ)	212	6.08S	15.15E
Maquoketa, Ia., U.S. (mȧ-kō-kė-tȧ)	103	42.04N	90.42W
Maquoketa, r., Ia., U.S.	103	42.08N	90.40W
Mar, Serra do, mts., Braz. (sĕr′rȧ dỏ mär′)	132	26.30S	49.15W
Maracaibo, Ven. (mä-rä-kī′bō)	130	10.38N	71.45W
Maracaibo, Lago de, l., Ven. (lä′gô-dĕ-mä-rä-kī′bō)	130	9.55N	72.13W
Maracay, Ven. (mä-rä-käy′)	130	10.15N	67.35W
Marādah, Libya	211	29.10N	19.07E
Maradi, Niger (mȧ-rȧ-dē′)	210	13.29N	7.06E
Marāgheh, Iran	185	37.20N	46.10E
Maraisburg, S. Afr.	213b	26.12S	27.57E
Marais des Cygnes, r., Ks., U.S.	111	38.30N	95.30W
Marajó, Ilha de, i., Braz.	131	1.00S	49.30W
Maralal, Kenya	217	1.06N	36.42E
Marali, Cen. Afr. Rep.	215	6.01N	18.24E
Marand, Iran	185	38.26N	45.46E
Maranguape, Braz. (mä-rȧŋ-gwä′pĕ)	131	3.48S	38.38W
Maranhão, state, Braz. (mä-rän-youɴ)	131	5.15S	45.52W
Maranoa, r., Austl. (mä-rä-nō′ä)	203	27.01S	148.03E
Marano di Napoli, Italy (mä-rä′nỏ-dē-nȧ′pô-lē)	159c	40.39N	14.12E
Marañón, Río, r., Peru (rė′ō-mä-rä-nyōn′)	130	4.26S	75.08W
Maraoli, neigh., India	240e	19.03N	72.54E
Marapanim, Braz. (mä-rä-pä-nė′ɴ)	131	0.45S	47.42W
Marathon, Can.	85	48.50N	86.10W
Marathon, Fl., U.S. (măr′ȧ-thŏn)	115a	24.41N	81.06W
Marathon, Oh., U.S.	101f	39.09N	83.59W
Maravatio, Mex. (mä-rȧ-vä′tė-ō)	118	19.54N	100.25W
Marawi, Sudan	211	18.07N	31.57E
Marayong, Austl.	243a	33.45S	150.54E
Marble Bar, Austl. (märb′'l bär)	202	21.15S	119.15E
Marble Canal, can., Az., U.S. (mär′b'l)	109	36.21N	111.48W
Marblehead, Ma., U.S. (mär′b'l-hĕd)	93a	42.30N	70.51W
Marburg an der Lahn, Ger.	154	50.49N	8.46E
Marca, Ponta da, c., Ang.	216	16.31S	11.42E
Marcala, Hond. (mär-kä-lä)	120	14.08N	88.01W
Marceline, Mo., U.S. (mär-sė-lēn′)	111	39.42N	92.56W
Marche, hist. reg., Italy (mär′kā)	160	43.35N	12.33E
Marchegg, Aus.	145e	48.18N	16.55E
Marchena, Spain (mär-chā′nä)	148	37.20N	5.25W
Marchena, i., Ec. (ė′s-lä-mär-chĕ′nä)	130	0.29N	90.31W
Marchfeld, reg., Aus.	145e	48.14N	16.37E
Mar Chiquíta, Laguna, l., Arg. (lä-go͞o′nä-mȧr-chė-kē′tä)	129c	34.25S	61.10W
Marco Polo Bridge, trans., China	240b	39.52N	116.12E
Marcos Paz, Arg. (mär-kōs′ päz)	129c	34.49S	58.51W
Marcus, i., Japan (mär′kŭs)	225	24.00N	155.00E
Marcus Hook, Pa., U.S. (mär′kŭs hȯk)	100f	39.49N	75.25W
Marcy, Mount, mtn., N.Y., U.S. (mär′sė)	99	44.10N	73.55W
Mar de Espanha, Braz. (mär-dĕ-ĕs-pȧ′nyȧ)	129a	21.53S	43.00W
Mar del Plata, Arg. (mär dĕl- plä′ta)	132	37.59S	57.35W
Mardin, Tur. (mär-dēn′)	182	37.25N	40.40E
Maré, i., N. Cal. (mȧ-rā′)	203	21.53S	168.30E
Maree, Loch, b., Scot., U.K. (mä-rē′)	150	57.40N	5.44W
Mareil-Marly, Fr.	237c	48.53N	2.05E
Marengo, Ia., U.S. (mȧ-rĕŋ′gō)	103	41.47N	92.04W
Marennes, Fr. (mȧ-rĕn′)	156	45.49N	1.08W
Marfa, Tx., U.S. (mär′fȧ)	112	30.19N	104.01W
Margarethenhöhe, neigh., Ger.	236	51.26N	6.58E
Margaretting, Eng., U.K.	235	51.41N	0.25E
Margarita, Pan. (mär-go͞o-rē′tä)	116a	9.20N	79.55W
Margarita, Isla de, i., Ven. (mä-gȧ-rē′tȧ)	130	11.00N	64.15W
Margate, S. Afr. (mä-gāt′)	213c	30.52S	30.21E
Margate, Eng., U.K. (mär′gāt)	151	51.21N	1.17E
Margherita Peak, mtn., Afr.	211	0.22N	29.51E
Marguerite, r., Can.	92	50.39N	66.42W
Marhanets', Ukr.	163	47.41N	34.33E
Maria, Can. (mȧ-rē′ȧ)	92	48.10N	66.04W
Mariager, Den. (mä-rė-ägh′ẽr)	152	56.38N	10.00E
Mariana, Braz. (mä-ryȧ′nä)	129a	20.23S	43.24W
Mariana Islands, is., Oc.	5	16.00N	145.30E
Marianao, Cuba (mä-rė-ä-nä′ō)	117	23.05N	82.26W
Mariana Trench, deep	225	12.00N	144.00E
Marianna, Ar., U.S. (mā-rĭ-ăn′ȧ)	111	34.45N	90.45W
Marianna, Fl., U.S.	114	30.46N	85.14W
Marianna, Pa., U.S.	101e	40.01N	80.05W
Mariano Acosta, Arg. (mä-rėä′nỏ-ȧ-kōs′tä)	132a	34.28S	58.48W
Mariano J. Haedo, Arg.	233d	34.39S	58.36W
Mariánské Lázně, Czech Rep. (mär′yȧn-skĕ′läz′nyĕ)	154	49.58N	12.42E
Maria Paula, Braz.	234c	22.54S	43.02W
Marias, r., Mt., U.S. (mȧ-rī′ȧz)	105	48.15N	110.50W
Marias, Islas, is., Mex. (mä-rē′äs)	116	21.30N	106.40W
Mariato, Punta, c., Pan.	121	7.17N	81.09W
Maribo, Den. (mä′rė-bỏ)	152	54.46N	11.29E
Maribor, Slvn. (mä′re-bỏr)	142	46.33N	15.37E
Maribyrnong, Austl.	243b	37.46S	144.54E
Maricaban, i., Phil. (mä-rė-kä-bän′)	197a	13.40N	120.44E
Mariefred, Swe. (mä-rē′ĕ-frĭd)	152	59.17N	17.09E
Marie Galante, i., Guad. (mȧ-rē′ gȧ-läɴt′)	121b	15.58N	61.05W
Mariehamn, Fin. (mȧ-rē′ê-hām′'n)	153	60.07N	19.57E
Mari El, state, Russia	166	56.30N	48.00E
Mariendorf, neigh., Ger.	238a	52.26N	13.23E
Marienfelde, neigh., Ger.	238a	52.25N	13.22E
Mariestad, Swe. (mä-rē′ĕ-städ′)	152	58.43N	13.45E
Marietta, Ga., U.S. (mā-rĭ′-ĕt′ȧ)	100c	33.57N	84.33W
Marietta, Oh., U.S.	98	39.25N	81.30W
Marietta, Ok., U.S.	111	33.53N	97.07W
Marietta, Wa., U.S.	106d	48.48N	122.35W
Mariinsk, Russia (mȧ-re′ĭnsk)	170	56.15N	87.28E
Marijampole, Lith. (mä-rė-yäm-pô′lĕ)	153	54.33N	23.26E
Marikana, S. Afr. (mă′-rĭ-kä-nă)	218d	25.40S	27.28E
Marikina, Phil.	241g	14.37N	121.06E
Marília, Braz. (mä-rē′lyȧ)	131	22.02S	49.48W
Marimba, Ang.	216	8.28S	17.08E
Marín, Spain	158	42.24N	8.40W
Marina del Rey, Ca., U.S.	232	33.59N	118.28W
Marina del Rey, b., Ca., U.S.	232	33.58N	118.27W
Marin City, Ca., U.S.	231b	37.52N	122.21W
Marinduque Island, i., Phil. (mä-rėn-do͞o′kā)	197a	13.14N	121.45E
Marine, Il., U.S. (mȧ-rēn′)	107e	38.48N	89.47W
Marine City, Mi., U.S.	98	42.45N	82.30W
Marine Lake, l., Mn., U.S.	107g	45.13N	92.55W
Marineland of the Pacific, pt. of i., Ca., U.S.	232	33.44N	118.24W
Marine on Saint Croix, Mn., U.S.	107g	45.11N	92.47W
Marinette, Wi., U.S. (măr-ĭ-nĕt′)	97	45.04N	87.40W
Maringa, r., Zaire (mă-riŋ′gä)	211	0.30N	21.00E
Marinha Grande, Port. (mä-rēn′yȧ grän′dĕ)	158	39.49N	8.53W
Marion, Al., U.S. (măr′ĭ-ŭn)	114	32.36N	87.19W
Marion, Il., U.S.	98	37.40N	88.55W
Marion, In., U.S.	97	40.35N	85.45W
Marion, Ia., U.S.	103	42.01N	91.39W
Marion, Ks., U.S.	111	38.21N	97.02W
Marion, Ky., U.S.	114	37.19N	88.05W
Marion, N.C., U.S.	115	35.40N	82.00W
Marion, N.D., U.S.	102	46.37N	98.20W
Marion, Oh., U.S.	98	40.35N	83.10W
Marion, S.C., U.S.	115	34.08N	79.23W
Marion, Va., U.S.	115	36.48N	81.33W
Marion, Lake, res., S.C., U.S.	115	33.25N	80.35W
Marion Reef, rf., Austl.	203	18.57S	151.31E
Mariposa, Chile (mä-rė-pỏ′sä)	129b	35.33S	71.21W
Mariposa Creek, r., Ca., U.S.	108	37.14N	120.30W
Mariquita, Col. (mä-rē-kė′tä)	130a	5.13N	74.52W
Mariscal Estigarribia, Para.	132	22.03S	60.28W
Marisco, Ponta do, c., Braz. (pô′n-tä-dỏ-mä-rė′s-kö)	132b	23.01S	43.17W
Maritime Alps, mts., Eur. (mȧ′rĭ-tīm ălps)	147	44.20N	7.02E
Mariupol', Ukr.	164	47.07N	37.32E
Mariveles, Phil.	197a	14.27N	120.29E
Marj Uyan, Leb.	181a	33.21N	35.36E
Marka, Som.	218a	1.45N	44.47E
Markaryd, Swe. (mär′kä-rüd)	152	56.30N	13.34E
Marked Tree, Ar., U.S. (märkt trē)	111	35.31N	90.26W
Marken, i., Neth.	145a	52.26N	5.08E
Market Bosworth, Eng., U.K. (bŏz′wûrth)	144a	52.37N	1.23W
Market Deeping, Eng., U.K. (dēp′ĭng)	144a	52.40N	0.19W
Market Drayton, Eng., U.K. (drā′tŭn)	144a	52.54N	2.29W
Market Harborough, Eng., U.K. (här′bŭr-ỏ)	144a	52.28N	0.55W
Market Rasen, Eng., U.K. (rā′zĕn)	144a	53.23N	0.21W
Markham, Can. (märk′ȧm)	91	43.53N	79.15W
Markham, Mount, mtn., Ant.	219	82.59S	159.30E
Markivka, Ukr.	163	49.32N	39.34E
Markovo, Russia (mär′kô-vỏ)	165	64.46N	170.48E
Markrāna, India	186	27.08N	74.43E
Marks, Russia	167	51.42N	46.46E
Marksville, La., U.S. (märks′vĭl)	113	31.09N	92.05W
Markt Indersdorf, Ger. (märkt ēn′dĕrs-dōrf)	145d	48.22N	11.23E
Marktredwitz, Ger. (märk-rĕd′vēts)	154	50.02N	12.05E
Markt Schwaben, Ger. (märkt shvä′bĕn)	145d	48.12N	11.52E
Marl, Ger. (märl)	157c	51.40N	7.05E
Marlboro, N.J., U.S.	100a	40.18N	74.15W
Marlborough, Ma., U.S.	93a	42.21N	71.33W
Marlette, Mi., U.S. (mär-lĕt′)	98	43.25N	83.05W
Marlin, Tx., U.S. (mär′lĭn)	113	31.18N	96.52W
Marlinton, W.V., U.S. (mär′lĭn-tŭn)	98	38.15N	80.10W
Marlow, Eng., U.K. (mär′lō)	144b	51.33N	0.46W
Marlow, Ok., U.S.	111	34.38N	97.56W
Marls, The, b., Bah. (märls)	122	26.30N	77.15W
Marly-le-Roi, Fr.	237c	48.52N	2.05E
Marmande, Fr. (mȧr-mäɴd′)	156	44.30N	0.10E
Marmara Denizi, sea, Tur.	182	40.40N	28.00E
Marmarth, N.D., U.S. (mär′mȧrth)	102	46.19N	103.57W
Mar Muerto, l., Mex. (mär-mỏĕ′r-tô)	119	16.13N	94.22W
Marne, Ger. (mär′nĕ)	145c	53.57N	9.01E
Marne, r., Fr. (märn)	147	49.00N	4.30E
Maroa, Ven. (mä-rō′ä)	130	2.43N	67.37W
Maroantsetra, Madag. (mȧ-rō-äŋ-tsā′trȧ)	213	15.18S	49.48E
Maro Jarapeto, mtn., Col. (mä-rỏ-hä-rä-pĕ′tỏ)	130a	6.29N	76.39W
Marolles-en-Brie, Fr.	237c	48.44N	2.33E
Maromokotro, mtn., Madag.	213	14.00S	49.11E
Marondera, Zimb.	212	18.10S	31.36E
Maroni, r., S.A. (mȧ-rō′nė)	131	3.02N	53.54W
Maro Reef, rf., Hi., U.S.	94b	25.15N	170.00W
Maroua, Cam. (mär′wä)	211	10.36N	14.20E
Maroubra, Austl.	243a	33.57S	151.16E
Marple, Eng., U.K. (mär′p'l)	144a	53.24N	2.04W
Marquard, S. Afr.	218d	28.41S	27.26E
Marquesas Islands, is., Fr. Poly. (mär-kĕ′säs)	2	8.50S	141.00W
Marquesas Keys, is., Fl., U.S. (mȧr-kē′zȧs)	115a	24.37N	82.15W
Marquês de Valença, Braz. (mȧr-kĕ′s-dĕ-vä-lĕ′n-sȧ)	129a	22.16S	43.42W
Marquette, Can. (mȧr-kĕt′)	83f	50.04N	97.43W

ng-sing; ŋ-baŋk; ɴ-nasalized n; nŏd; cŏmmit; ōld; ôbey; ôrder; oi-boil; fo͞od; ȯ-as oo in foot; ou-out; s-soft; sh-dish; th-thin; pūre; ůnite; ûrn; stŭd; circŭs; ü-as in French tu; '-indeterminate vowel.

316 Marquette-McCormick Place

PLACE (Pronunciation)	PAGE	Lat. °′	Long. °′
Marquette, Mi., U.S.	97	46.32N	87.25W
Marquez, Tx., U.S. (mär-kāz′)	113	31.14N	96.15W
Marra, Jabal, mtn., Sudan (jĕb′ĕl mär′ä)	211	13.00N	23.47E
Marrakech, Mor. (mȧr-rä′kĕsh)	210	31.38N	8.00W
Marree, Austl. (măr′rē)	202	29.38S	137.55E
Marrero, La., U.S.	100d	29.55N	90.06W
Marrickville, Austl.	243a	33.55S	151.09E
Marrupa, Moz.	217	13.08S	37.30E
Mars, Pa., U.S. (märz)	101e	40.42N	80.01W
Marsabit, Kenya	217	2.20N	37.59E
Marsala, Italy (mär-sä′lä)	148	37.48N	12.28E
Marscheid, neigh., Ger.	236	51.14N	7.14E
Marsden, Eng., U.K. (märz′dĕn)	144a	53.36N	1.55W
Marseille, Fr. (mȧr-sâ′y′)	142	43.18N	5.25E
Marseilles, Il., U.S. (mär-sĕlz′)	98	41.20N	88.40W
Marsfield, Austl.	243a	33.47S	151.07E
Marshall, Il., U.S. (mär′shăl)	98	39.20N	87.40W
Marshall, Mi., U.S.	98	42.20N	84.55W
Marshall, Mn., U.S.	102	44.28N	95.49W
Marshall, Mo., U.S.	111	39.07N	93.12W
Marshall, Tx., U.S.	97	32.33N	94.22W
Marshall Islands, nation, Oc.	3	10.00N	165.00E
Marshalltown, Ia., U.S. (mär′shăl-toun)	103	42.02N	92.55W
Marshallville, Ga., U.S. (mär′shăl-vĭl)	114	32.29N	83.55W
Marshfield, Ma., U.S. (märsh′fēld)	93a	42.06N	70.43W
Marshfield, Mo., U.S.	111	37.20N	92.53W
Marshfield, Wi., U.S.	103	44.40N	90.10W
Marsh Harbour, Bah.	122	26.30N	77.00W
Mars Hill, In., U.S. (märz′hĭl′)	101g	39.43N	86.15W
Mars Hill, Me., U.S.	92	46.34N	67.54W
Marstrand, Swe. (mär′stränd)	152	57.54N	11.33E
Marsyaty, Russia (märs′yȧ-tĭ)	172a	60.03N	60.28E
Mart, Tx., U.S. (märt)	113	31.32N	96.49W
Martaban, Gulf of, b., Myanmar (mär-tŭ-bän′)	196	16.34N	96.58E
Martapura, Indon.	196	3.19S	114.45E
Marten, neigh., Ger.	236	51.31N	7.23E
Martha's Vineyard, i., Ma., U.S. (mär′thȧz vĭn′yȧrd)	99	41.25N	70.35W
Martigny, Switz. (mȧr-tē-nyē′)	154	46.06N	7.00E
Martigues, Fr.	157	43.24N	5.05E
Martin, Tn., U.S. (mär′tĭn)	114	36.20N	88.45W
Martina Franca, Italy (mär-tē′nä frăŋ′kä)	161	40.43N	17.21E
Martinez, Ca., U.S. (mär-tē′nĕz)	106b	38.01N	122.08W
Martinez, Tx., U.S.	107d	29.25N	98.20W
Martínez, neigh., Arg.	233d	34.29S	58.30W
Martinique, dep., N.A. (mȧr-tē-nēk′)	117	14.50N	60.40W
Martin Lake, res., Al., U.S.	114	32.40N	86.05W
Martin Point, c., Ak., U.S.	95	70.10N	142.00W
Martinsburg, W.V., U.S. (mär′tĭnz-bûrg)	99	39.30N	78.00W
Martins Ferry, Oh., U.S. (mär′tĭnz)	98	40.05N	80.45W
Martinsville, In., U.S. (mär′tĭnz-vĭl)	98	39.25N	86.25W
Martinsville, Va., U.S.	115	36.40N	79.53W
Martos, Spain (mär′tōs)	158	37.43N	3.58W
Martre, Lac la, l., Can. (läk la märtr)	84	63.24N	119.58W
Marugame, Japan (mä′ro͞o-gä′mä)	195	34.19N	133.48E
Marungu, mts., Zaire	217	7.50S	29.50E
Marve, neigh., India	187b	19.12N	72.43E
Marwitz, Ger.	238a	52.41N	13.09E
Mary, Turk. (mä′rē)	169	37.45N	61.47E
Mar'yanskaya, Russia (mȧr-yän′skȧ-yȧ)	163	45.04N	38.39E
Maryborough, Austl. (mâ′rĭ-bŭr-ō)	203	25.35S	152.40E
Maryborough, Austl.	203	37.00S	143.50E
Maryland, state, U.S. (mĕr′ĭ-lănd)	97	39.10N	76.25W
Maryland Park, Md., U.S.	229d	38.53N	76.54W
Marys, r., Nv., U.S. (mā′rĭz)	104	41.25N	115.10W
Marystown, Can. (mâr′ĭz-toun)	93	47.11N	55.10W
Marysville, Can.	92	45.59N	66.35W
Marysville, Ca., U.S.	108	39.09N	121.37W
Marysville, Oh., U.S.	98	40.15N	83.25W
Marysville, Wa., U.S.	106a	48.03N	122.11W
Maryville, Il., U.S. (mā′rĭ-vĭl)	107e	38.44N	89.57W
Maryville, Mo., U.S.	111	40.21N	94.51W
Maryville, Tn., U.S.	114	35.44N	83.59W
Marzahn, neigh., Ger.	238a	52.33N	13.33E
Mārzuq, Libya	211	26.00N	14.09E
Marzūq, Idehan, des., Libya	210	24.30N	13.00E
Masai Steppe, plat., Tan.	217	4.30S	36.40E
Masaka, Ug.	217	0.20S	31.44E
Masalasef, Chad	215	11.43N	17.08E
Masalembo-Besar, i., Indon.	196	5.40S	114.28E
Masan, S. Kor. (mä-sän′)	189	35.10N	128.31E
Masangwe, Tan.	217	5.28S	30.05E
Masasi, Tan. (mä-sä′sē)	213	10.43S	38.48E
Masatepe, Nic. (mä-sä-tĕ′pĕ)	120	11.57N	86.10W
Masaya, Nic. (mä-sä′yä)	120	11.58N	86.05W
Masbate, Phil. (mäs-bä′tä)	197a	12.21N	123.38E
Masbate, i., Phil.	197	12.19N	123.03E
Mascarene Islands, is., Afr.	5	20.20S	56.40E
Mascot, Austl.	243a	33.56S	151.12E
Mascot, Tn., U.S. (măs′kŏt)	114	36.04N	83.45W
Mascota, Mex. (mäs-kō′tä)	118	20.33N	104.45W
Mascota, r., Mex.	118	20.33N	104.52W
Mascouche, Can. (mȧs-ko͞osh′)	83a	45.45N	73.36W
Mascouche, r., Can.	83a	45.44N	73.45W
Mascoutah, Il., U.S. (măs-kū′tä)	107e	38.29N	89.48W
Maseru, Leso. (măz′ēr-o͞o)	212	29.09S	27.11E
Mashhad, Iran	182	36.17N	59.30E
Māshkel, Hāmūn-i-, l., Asia (hä-mo͞on′ē māsh-kĕl′)	182	28.28N	64.13E
Mashra'ar Raqq, Sudan	211	8.28N	29.15E
Masi-Manimba, Zaire	216	4.46S	17.55E
Masindi, Ug. (mä-sēn′dē)	211	1.44N	31.43E
Masjed Soleymān, Iran	182	31.45N	49.17E
Mask, Lough, b., Ire. (lŏk mȧsk)	150	53.35N	9.23W
Maslovo, Russia (mäs′lô-vô)	172a	60.08N	60.28E
Mason, Mi., U.S. (mā′sŭn)	98	42.35N	84.25W
Mason, Oh., U.S.	101f	39.22N	84.18W
Mason, Tx., U.S.	112	30.46N	99.14W
Mason City, Ia., U.S.	97	43.08N	93.14W
Masonville, Va., U.S.	229d	38.51N	77.12W
Maspeth, neigh., N.Y., U.S.	228	40.43N	73.55W
Massa, Italy (mäs′sä)	160	44.02N	10.08E
Massachusetts, state, U.S. (măs-ȧ-cho͞o′sĕts)	97	42.20N	72.30W
Massachusetts Bay, b., Ma., U.S.	92	42.26N	70.20W
Massafra, Italy (mäs-sä′frä)	161	40.35N	17.05E
Massa Marittima, Italy	160	43.03N	10.55E
Massapequa, N.Y., U.S.	100a	40.41N	73.28W
Massaua *see* Mitsiwa, Erit.	211	15.40N	39.19E
Massena, N.Y., U.S. (mă-sē′nȧ)	99	44.55N	74.55W
Masset, Can. (măs′ĕt)	84	54.02N	132.09W
Masset Inlet, b., Can.	87	53.42N	132.20E
Massif Central, Fr. (mȧ-sēf′ säɴ-trȧl′)	142	45.12N	3.02E
Massillon, Oh., U.S. (măs′ĭ-lŏn)	98	40.50N	81.35W
Massinga, Moz. (mä-sĭn′gä)	212	23.18S	35.18E
Massive, Mount, mtn., Co., U.S. (măs′ĭv)	96	39.05N	106.30W
Masson, Can. (mă-sŭn)	83c	45.33N	75.25W
Massy, Fr.	237c	48.44N	2.17E
Masuda, Japan (mä-so͞o′dȧ)	195	34.42N	131.53E
Masuria, reg., Pol.	155	53.40N	21.10E
Masvingo, Zimb.	212	20.07S	30.47E
Matadi, Zaire (mȧ-tä′dē)	212	5.49S	13.27E
Matagalpa, Nic. (mä-tä-gäl′pä)	116	12.52N	85.57W
Matagami, l., Can. (mȧ-tä-gä′mē)	85	50.10N	78.28W
Matagorda Bay, b., Tx., U.S. (măt-ȧ-gôr′dȧ)	113	28.32N	96.13W
Matagorda Island, i., Tx., U.S.	113	28.13N	96.27W
Matam, Sen. (mä-täm′)	210	15.40N	13.15W
Matamoros, Mex. (mä-tä-mō′rôs)	112	25.32N	103.13W
Matamoros, Mex.	116	25.52N	97.30W
Matane, Can. (mȧ-tȧn′)	85	48.51N	67.32W
Matanzas, Cuba (mä-tän′zäs)	117	23.05N	81.35W
Matanzas, prov., Cuba	122	22.45N	81.20W
Matanzas, Bahía, b., Cuba (bä-ē′ä)	122	23.10N	81.30W
Matapalo, Cabo, c., C.R. (kä′bô-mä-tä-pä′lō)	121	8.22N	83.25W
Matapédia, Can. (mă-tȧ-pā′dē-ȧ)	92	47.58N	66.56W
Matapédia, l., Can.	92	48.33N	67.32W
Matapédia, r., Can.	92	48.10N	67.10W
Mataquito, r., Chile (mä-tä-kē′tô)	129b	35.08S	71.35W
Matara, Sri L. (mä-tä′rä)	183b	5.59N	80.35E
Mataram, Indon.	196	8.45S	116.15E
Matatiele, S. Afr. (mä-tä-tyā′lä)	213c	30.21S	28.49E
Matawan, N.J., U.S.	100a	40.24N	74.13W
Matehuala, Mex. (mä-tȧ-wä′lä)	116	23.38N	100.39W
Matera, Italy (mä-tā′rä)	160	40.42N	16.37E
Mateur, Tun. (mȧ-tûr′)	148	37.09N	9.43E
Mātherān, India	187b	18.58N	73.16E
Matheson, Can.	91	48.35N	80.33W
Mathews, Lake, l., Ca., U.S. (măth ūz)	107a	33.50N	117.24W
Mathura, India (mu-tö′rü)	183	27.39N	77.39E
Matias Barbosa, Braz. (mä-tē′äs-bär-bô-sä)	129a	21.53S	43.19W
Matillas, Laguna, l., Mex. (lä-go͞o′nä-mä-tē′l-yäs)	119	18.02N	92.36W
Matina, C.R. (mä-tē′nä)	121	10.06N	83.20W
Matiši, Lat. (mä′tē-sē)	153	57.43N	25.09E
Matlalcueyetl, Cerro, mtn., Mex. (sĕ′r-rä-mä-tläl-kwĕ′yĕtl)	118	19.13N	98.02W
Matlock, Eng., U.K. (măt′lŏk)	144a	53.08N	1.33W
Matochkin Shar, Russia (mä′tŏch-kĭn)	164	73.57N	56.16E
Mato Grosso, Braz. (mät′ō grōs′ō)	131	15.04S	59.58W
Mato Grosso, state, Braz.	131	14.38S	55.36W
Mato Grosso, Chapada de, hills, Braz. (shä-pä′dä-dē)	131	13.39S	55.42W
Mato Grosso do Sul, state, Braz.	131	20.00S	56.00W
Matosinhos, Port.	158	41.10N	8.48W
Maṭraḥ, Oman (mȧ-trä′)	182	23.36N	58.27E
Matsubara, Japan	195b	34.34N	135.34E
Matsudo, Japan (mät′sō-dō)	195a	35.48N	139.55E
Matsue, Japan (mät′sō-ĕ)	189	35.29N	133.04E
Matsumoto, Japan (mät′sō-mō′tō)	194	36.15N	137.59E
Matsuyama, Japan (mät′sō-yä′mä)	189	33.48N	132.45E
Matsuzaka, Japan (mät′sō-zä′kä)	195	34.35N	136.34E
Mattamuskeet, Lake, l., N.C., U.S. (măt-tȧ-mŭs′kēt)	115	35.34N	76.03W
Mattaponi, r., Va., U.S. (măt′ȧ-poni′)	99	37.45N	77.00W
Mattawa, Can. (măt′ȧ-wȧ)	85	46.15N	78.49W
Matterhorn, mtn., Eur. (mät′ēr-hôrn)	154	45.57N	7.36E
Matteson, Il., U.S. (mătt′ē-sŭn)	101a	41.30N	87.42W
Matthew Town, Bah. (măth′ū toun)	123	21.00N	73.40W
Mattoon, Il., U.S. (mă-to͞on′)	97	39.30N	88.20W
Maturín, Ven. (mä-to͞o-rēn′)	130	9.48N	63.16W
Mátyásföld, neigh., Hung.	239g	47.31N	19.13E
Mátyas-Templom, rel., Hung.	239g	47.30N	19.02E
Maúa, Moz.	217	13.51S	37.10E
Mauban, Phil. (mä′o͞o-bän′)	197a	14.11N	121.44E
Maubeuge, Fr. (mō-bûzh′)	156	50.18N	3.57E
Maud, Oh., U.S. (môd)	101f	39.21N	84.23W
Mauer, Aus. (mou′ēr)	145e	48.09N	16.16E
Maués, Braz. (mȧ-wĕ′s)	131	3.34S	57.30W
Mau Escarpment, cliff, Kenya	217	0.45S	35.50E
Maui, i., Hi., U.S. (mä′o͞o-ē)	96c	20.52N	156.02W
Maule, r., Chile (mä′ō-lĕ)	129b	35.45S	70.50W
Maumee, Oh., U.S. (mô-mē′)	98	41.30N	83.40W
Maumee, r., In., U.S.	98	41.10N	84.50W
Maumee Bay, b., Oh., U.S.	98	41.50N	83.20W
Maun, Bots. (mä-ōn′)	212	19.52S	23.40E
Mauna Kea, mtn., Hi., U.S. (mä′ō-nä-kā′ä)	96c	19.52N	155.30W
Mauna Loa, mtn., Hi., U.S. (mä′ō-nälō′ä)	96c	19.28N	155.38W
Maurecourt, Fr.	237c	49.00N	2.04E
Maurepas Lake, l., La., U.S. (mō-rē-pä′)	113	30.18N	90.40W
Mauricie, Parc National de la, rec., Can.	91	46.46N	73.00W
Mauritania, nation, Afr. (mô-rē-tā′nĭ-ȧ)	210	19.38N	13.30W
Mauritius, nation, Afr. (mô-rĭsh′ĭ-ŭs)	3	20.18S	57.36E
Maury, Wa., U.S. (mô′rĭ)	106a	47.22N	122.23W
Mauston, Wi., U.S. (môs′tŭn)	103	43.46N	90.05W
Maverick, r., Az., U.S. (mă-vûr′ĭk)	109	33.40N	109.30W
Mavinga, Ang.	216	15.50S	20.21E
Mawlamyine, Myanmar	196	16.30N	97.39E
Maxville, Can. (măks′vĭl)	83c	45.17N	74.52W
Maxville, Mo., U.S.	107e	38.26N	90.24W
Maya, r., Russia (mä′yä)	171	58.00N	135.45E
Mayaguana, i., Bah.	123	22.25N	73.00W
Mayaguana Passage, strt., Bah.	123	22.20N	73.25W
Mayagüez, P.R. (mä-yä-gwāz′)	117	18.12N	67.10W
Mayari, r., Cuba	123	20.25N	75.35W
Mayas, Montañas, mts., N.A. (môn-tăŋ′äs mä′äs)	120a	16.43N	89.00W
Mayd, i., Som.	218a	11.24N	46.38E
Mayen, Ger. (mī′ĕn)	154	50.19N	7.14E
Mayenne, r., Fr. (mȧ-yĕn)	156	48.14N	0.45W
Mayfair, neigh., S. Afr.	244b	26.12S	28.01E
Mayfair, neigh., Pa., U.S.	229b	40.02N	75.03W
Mayfield, Ky., U.S. (mā′fēld)	114	36.44N	88.19W
Mayfield Creek, r., Ky., U.S.	114	36.54N	88.47W
Mayfield Heights, Oh., U.S.	101d	41.31N	81.26W
Mayfield Lake, res., Wa., U.S.	104	46.31N	122.34W
Maykop, Russia	164	44.35N	40.07E
Maykor, Russia (mī-kôr′)	172a	59.01N	55.52E
Maymyo, Myanmar (mī′myō)	188	22.14N	96.32E
Maynard, Ma., U.S. (mā′nȧrd)	93a	42.25N	71.27W
Mayne, Can. (mān)	106d	48.51N	123.18W
Mayne, i., Can.	106d	48.52N	123.14W
Mayo, Can. (mä-yō′)	84	63.40N	135.51W
Mayo, Fl., U.S.	114	30.02N	83.08W
Mayo, Md., U.S.	100e	38.54N	76.31W
Mayodan, N.C., U.S. (mā-yō′dăn)	115	36.25N	79.59W
Mayon Volcano, vol., Phil. (mä-yōn′)	197a	13.21N	123.43E
Mayotte, dep., Afr. (mȧ-yŏt′)	213	13.07S	45.32E
May Pen, Jam.	122	18.00N	77.25W
Mayraira Point, c., Phil.	193	18.40N	120.45E
Mayran, Laguna de, l., Mex. (lä-ō′nä-dē-mī-rän′)	116	25.40N	102.35W
Mayskiy, Russia	168	43.38N	44.04E
Maysville, Ky., U.S. (māz′vĭl)	98	38.35N	83.45W
Mayumba, Gabon	212	3.25S	10.39E
Mayville, N.Y., U.S. (mā′vĭl)	99	42.15N	79.30W
Mayville, N.D., U.S.	102	47.30N	97.20W
Mayville, Wi., U.S.	103	43.30N	88.45W
Maywood, Ca., U.S. (mā′wo͝od)	107a	33.59N	118.11W
Maywood, Il., U.S.	101a	41.53N	87.51W
Maywood, N.J., U.S.	228	40.56N	74.04W
Mazabuka, Zam. (mä-zä-bo͞o′kä)	212	15.51S	27.46E
Mazagão, Braz. (mä-zä-gou′ɴ)	131	0.05S	51.27W
Mazapil, Mex. (mä-zä-pēl′)	112	24.40N	101.30W
Mazara del Vallo, Italy (mät-sä′rä dĕl väl′lō)	160	37.40N	12.37E
Mazār-i-Sharīf, Afg. (mȧ-zär′-ē-shȧ-rēf′)	183	36.48N	67.12E
Mazarrón, Spain (mä-zär-rô′n)	158	37.37N	1.29W
Mazatenango, Guat. (mä-zä-tȧ-näŋ′gō)	116	14.30N	91.30W
Mazatla, Mex.	119a	19.30N	99.24W
Mazatlán, Mex.	116	23.14N	106.27W
Mazatlán (San Juan), Mex. (mä-zä-tlän′) (sañ hwän′)	119	17.05N	95.26W
Mažeikiai, Lith. (mä-zhā′kē-ī)	153	56.19N	22.24E
Mazhafah, Jabal, mtn., Sau. Ar.	181a	28.56N	35.05E
Mazilovo, neigh., Russia	239b	55.44N	37.26E
Mazorra, Cuba	233b	23.01N	82.24W
Mbabane, Swaz. (m′bä-bä′nē)	212	26.18S	31.14E
Mbaiki, Cen. Afr. Rep. (m′bȧ-ē′kē)	211	3.53N	18.00E
Mbakana, Montagne de, mts., Cam.	215	7.55N	14.40E
Mbakaou, Barrage de, dam, Cam.	215	6.10N	12.55E
Mbala, Zam.	212	8.50S	31.22E
Mbale, Ug.	217	1.05N	34.10E
Mbamba Bay, Tan.	217	11.17S	34.46E
Mbandaka, Zaire	212	0.04N	18.16E
M'banza Congo, Ang.	212	6.30S	14.10E
Mbanza-Ngungu, Zaire	212	5.20S	10.55E
Mbarara, Ug.	217	0.37S	30.39E
Mbasay, Chad	215	7.39N	15.40E
Mbigou, Gabon (m-bē-go͞o′)	212	2.07S	11.30E
Mbinda, Congo	216	2.00S	12.55E
Mbogo, Tan.	217	7.26S	33.26E
Mbomou (Bomu), r., Afr. (m′bō′mo͞o)	211	4.50N	24.00E
Mbout, Maur. (m′bo͞o′)	210	16.03N	12.31W
Mbuji-Mayi, Zaire	216	6.09S	23.38E
McAdam, Can. (măk-ăd′ăm)	92	45.36N	67.20W
McAfee, N.J., U.S. (măk-ȧ′fē)	100a	41.10N	74.32W
McAlester, Ok., U.S. (măk ăl′ĕs-tēr)	97	34.55N	95.45W
McAllen, Tx., U.S. (măk-ăl′ĕn)	112	26.12N	98.14W
McBride, Can. (măk-brīd′)	84	53.18N	120.10W
McCalla, Al., U.S. (măk-kăl′lȧ)	100h	33.20N	87.00W
McCamey, Tx., U.S. (mȧ-kā′mĭ)	112	31.08N	102.13W
McColl, S.C., U.S. (mȧ-kōl′)	115	34.40N	79.34W
McComb, Ms., U.S. (mȧ-kōm′)	114	31.14N	90.27W
McConaughy, Lake, l., Ne., U.S. (măk kŏ′nō ĭ′)	102	41.24N	101.40W
McCook, Il., U.S.	231a	41.48N	87.50W
McCook, Ne., U.S. (mȧ-ko͝ok′)	110	40.13N	100.37W
McCormick, S.C., U.S. (mȧ-kôr′mĭk)	115	33.56N	82.20W
McCormick Place, pt. of i., Il., U.S.	231a	41.51N	87.37W

ăt; finăl; rāte; senāte; ärm; ȧsk; sofȧ; fâre; ch-choose; dh-as th in other; bē; ēvent; bĕt; recĕnt; cratēr; g-gō; gh-guttural g; bĭt; ĭ-short neutral; rīde; ᴋ-guttural k as ch in German ich;

PRONOUNCING INDEX McDonald – Merrimack 317

PLACE (Pronunciation)	PAGE	Lat. °′	Long. °′
McDonald, Pa., U.S. (măk-dŏn'ăld)	101e	40.22N	80.13W
McDonald Island, i., Austl.	219	53.00S	72.45E
McDonald Lake, l., Can. (măk-dŏn-ăld)	83e	51.12N	113.53W
McGehee, Ar., U.S. (mȧ-gē')	111	33.39N	91.22W
McGill, Nv., U.S. (mȧ-gĭl')	109	39.25N	114.47W
McGill University, educ., Can.	227b	45.30N	73.35W
McGowan, Wa., U.S. (măk-gou'ăn)	106c	46.15N	123.55W
McGrath, Ak., U.S. (măk'grăth)	96a	62.58N	155.20W
McGregor, Can. (măk-grĕg'ẽr)	101b	42.08N	82.58W
McGregor, Ia., U.S.	103	42.58N	91.12W
McGregor, Tx., U.S.	113	31.26N	97.23W
McGregor, r., Can.	87	54.10N	121.00W
McGregor Lake, l., Can. (măk-grĕg'ẽr)	83c	45.38N	75.44W
McHenry, Il., U.S. (măk-hĕn'rĭ)	101a	42.21N	88.16W
Mchinji, Mwi.	212	13.42S	32.50E
McIntosh, S.D., U.S. (măk'ĭn-tŏsh)	102	45.54N	101.22W
McKay, r., Or., U.S.	106c	45.43N	123.00W
McKeesport, Pa., U.S. (mȧ-kez'pōrt)	101e	40.21N	79.51W
McKees Rocks, Pa., U.S. (mȧ-kēz' rŏks)	101e	40.29N	80.05W
McKenzie, Tn., U.S. (mȧ-kĕn'zĭ)	114	36.07N	88.30W
McKenzie, r., Or., U.S.	104	44.07N	122.20W
McKinley, Mount, mtn., Ak., U.S. (mȧ-kĭn'lĭ)	96a	63.00N	151.02W
McKinney, Tx., U.S. (mȧ-kĭn'ĭ)	111	33.12N	96.35W
McKnight Village, Pa., U.S.	230b	40.31N	80.00W
McLaughlin, S.D., U.S. (mȧk-lŏf'lĭn)	102	45.48N	100.45W
McLean, Va., U.S. (măc'lān)	100e	38.56N	77.11W
McLeansboro, Il., U.S. (mȧ-klānz'bŭr-ō)	98	38.10N	88.35W
McLennan, Can. (măk-lĕn'năn)	84	55.42N	116.54W
McLeod, r., Can.	87	53.45N	115.55W
McLeod Lake, Can.	86	54.59N	123.02W
McLoughlin, Mount, mtn., Or., U.S. (măk-lŏk'lĭn)	104	42.27N	122.20W
McMillan Lake, l., Tx., U.S. (măk-mĭl'ăn)	112	32.40N	104.09W
McMillin, Wa., U.S. (mȧk-mĭl'ĭn)	106a	47.08N	122.14W
McMinnville, Or., U.S. (măk-mĭn'vĭl)	104	45.13N	123.13W
McMinnville, Tn., U.S.	114	35.41N	85.47W
McMurray, Pa., U.S.	230b	40.17N	80.05W
McMurray, Wa., U.S. (mȧk-mŭr'ĭ)	106a	48.19N	122.15W
McNary, Az., U.S. (mȧk-nâr'ē)	109	34.10N	109.55W
McNary, La., U.S.	113	30.58N	92.32W
McNary Dam, Or., U.S.	104	45.57N	119.15W
McPherson, Ks., U.S. (mȧk-fŭr's'n)	111	38.21N	97.41W
McRae, Ga., U.S. (mȧk-rā')	115	32.02N	82.55W
McRoberts, Ky., U.S. (mȧk-rŏb'ẽrts)	115	37.12N	82.40W
Mead, Ks., U.S. (mēd)	110	37.17N	100.21W
Mead, Lake, l., U.S.	96	36.20N	114.14W
Meade Peak, mtn., Id., U.S.	105	42.19N	111.16W
Meadow Lake, Can. (mĕd'ō lāk)	84	54.08N	108.26W
Meadowlands, S. Afr.	244b	26.13S	27.54E
Meadows, Can. (mĕd'ōz)	83f	50.02N	97.35W
Meadville, Pa., U.S. (mēd'vĭl)	98	41.40N	80.10W
Meaford, Can. (mē'fẽrd)	91	44.35N	80.40W
Mealy Mountains, mts., Can. (mē'lē)	85	53.32N	57.58W
Meandarra, Austl. (mē-ăn-dă'rȧ)	204	27.47S	149.40E
Meaux, Fr. (mō)	156	48.58N	2.53E
Mecapalapa, Mex. (mā-kä-pä-lä'pä)	119	20.32N	97.52W
Mecatina, r., Can. (mā-kȧ-tē'nȧ)	93	50.50N	59.45W
Mecca (Makkah), Sau. Ar. (mĕk'ȧ)	182	21.27N	39.45E
Mechanic Falls, Me., U.S. (mē-kăn'ĭk)	92	44.05N	70.23W
Mechanicsburg, Pa., U.S. (mē-kăn'ĭks-bûrg)	99	40.15N	77.00W
Mechanicsville, Md., U.S. (mē-kăn'ĭks-vĭl)	100e	38.27N	76.45W
Mechanicville, N.Y., U.S. (mē-kăn'ĭk-vĭl)	99	42.55N	73.45W
Mechelen, Bel.	151	51.01N	4.28E
Mechriyya, Alg.	148	33.30N	0.13W
Mecicine Bow Range, mts., Co., U.S. (mĕd'ĭ-sĭn bō)	110	40.55N	106.02W
Meckinghoven, Ger.	236	51.37N	7.19E
Mecklenburg, hist. reg., Ger.	154	53.30N	13.00E
Medan, Indon. (mā-dän')	196	3.35N	98.35E
Medanosa, Punta, c., Arg. (pōō'n-tä-mē-dä-nô'sä)	132	47.50S	65.53W
Medden, r., Eng., U.K. (mĕd'ĕn)	144a	53.14N	1.05W
Medellín, Col. (mā-dhĕl-yēn')	130	6.15N	75.34W
Medellín, Mex. (mĕ-dĕl-yē'n)	119	19.03N	96.08W
Medenine, Tun. (mā-dē-nēn')	148	33.22N	10.33E
Medfeld, Ma., U.S. (mĕd'fēld)	93a	42.11N	71.19W
Medford, Ma., U.S. (mĕd'fẽrd)	93a	42.25N	71.07W
Medford, N.J., U.S.	100f	39.54N	74.50W
Medford, Ok., U.S.	111	36.47N	97.44W
Medford, Or., U.S.	96	42.19N	122.52W
Medford, Wi., U.S.	103	45.09N	90.22W
Medford Hillside, Ma., U.S.	227a	42.24N	71.07W
Media, Pa., U.S. (mē'dĭ-ȧ)	100f	39.55N	75.24W
Mediaş, Rom. (mĕd-yäsh')	155	46.09N	24.21E
Medical Lake, Wa., U.S. (mĕd'ĭ-kăl)	104	47.34N	117.40W
Medicine Bow, r., Wy., U.S.	105	41.58N	106.30W
Medicine Hat, Can. (mĕd'ĭ-sĭn hăt)	84	50.03N	110.40W
Medicine Lake, l., Mt., U.S. (mĕd'ĭ-sĭn)	105	48.24N	104.15W
Medicine Lodge, Ks., U.S.	110	37.17N	98.37W
Medicine Lodge, r., Ks., U.S.	110	37.20N	98.57W
Medina *see* Al Madīnah, Sau. Ar.	182	24.26N	39.42E
Medina, N.Y., U.S. (mē-dī'nȧ)	99	43.15N	78.20W
Medina, Oh., U.S.	101d	41.08N	81.52W
Medina, r., Tx., U.S.	112	29.45N	99.13W
Medina del Campo, Spain (mä-dē'nä dĕl käm'pō)	148	41.18N	4.54W
Medina de Ríoseco, Spain (mȧ-dē'nä dä rē-ō-sā'kō)	158	41.53N	5.05W
Medina Lake, l., Tx., U.S.	112	29.36N	98.47W
Medina Sidonia, Spain	158	36.28N	5.58W

PLACE (Pronunciation)	PAGE	Lat. °′	Long. °′
Mediterranean Sea, sea (mĕd-ĭ-tẽr-ā'nē-ăn)	148	36.22N	13.25E
Medjerda, Oued, r., Afr.	148	36.43N	9.54E
Mednogorsk, Russia	164	51.27N	57.22E
Medveditsa, r., Russia (mĕd-vyĕ'dē tsȧ)	167	50.10N	43.40E
Medvedkovo, neigh., Russia	239b	55.53N	37.38E
Medvezhegorsk, Russia (mĕd-vyĕzh'yĕ-gôrsk')	166	63.00N	34.20E
Medway, Ma., U.S. (mĕd'wā)	93a	42.08N	71.23W
Medyn', Russia (mĕ-dēn')	162	54.58N	35.53E
Medzhybizh, Ukr.	163	49.23N	27.29E
Meekatharra, Austl. (mē-kȧ-thăr'ȧ)	202	26.30S	118.38E
Meeker, Co., U.S. (mēk'ẽr)	109	40.00N	107.55W
Meelpaeg Lake, l., Can. (mēl'pȧ-ĕg)	93	48.22N	56.52W
Meerane, Ger. (mā-rä'nē)	154	50.51N	12.27E
Meerbusch, Ger.	157c	51.15N	6.41E
Meerut, India (mē'rŏŏt)	183	28.59N	77.43E
Megalópolis, Grc. (mĕg-ȧ lŏ'pō-lĭs)	161	37.22N	22.08E
Meganom, Mys, c., Ukr.	163	44.48N	35.17E
Mégara, Grc. (mĕg'ȧ-rȧ)	161	37.59N	23.21E
Megget, S.C., U.S. (mĕg'ĕt)	115	32.44N	80.15W
Megler, Wa., U.S. (mĕg'lẽr)	106c	46.15N	123.52W
Meguro, neigh., Japan	242a	35.38N	139.42E
Meherrin, r., Va., U.S. (mē-hĕr'ĭn)	115	36.40N	77.49W
Mehlville, Mo., U.S.	107e	38.30N	90.19W
Mehpālpur, neigh., India	240d	28.33N	77.08E
Mehrābād, Iran	241h	35.40N	51.20E
Mehram Nagar, neigh., India	240d	28.34N	77.07E
Mehrow, Ger.	238a	52.34N	13.37E
Mehrum, Ger.	236	51.35N	6.37E
Mehsāna, India	186	23.42N	72.23E
Mehun-sur-Yévre, Fr. (mē-ŭN-sür-yĕvr')	156	47.11N	2.14E
Meide, Ger.	236	51.11N	6.55E
Meiderich, neigh., Ger.	236	51.28N	6.46E
Meidling, neigh., Aus.	239e	48.11N	16.20E
Meiersberg, Ger.	236	51.17N	6.57E
Meiji Shrine, rel., Japan	242a	35.41N	139.42E
Meiling Pass, p., China (mā'lĭng')	189	25.22N	115.00E
Meinerzhagen, Ger. (mī'nĕrts-hä-gĕn)	157c	51.06N	7.39E
Meiningen, Ger. (mī'nĭng-ĕn)	154	50.35N	10.25E
Meiringen, Switz.	154	46.45N	8.11E
Meissen, Ger.	154	51.11N	13.28E
Meizhu, China (mā-jōō)	190	31.17N	119.12E
Mejillones, Chile (mā-kē-lyō'nås)	132	23.07S	70.31W
Mekambo, Gabon	216	1.01N	13.56E
Mekele, Eth.	211	13.31N	39.19E
Meknés, Mor. (mĕk'nĕs) (mĕk-nĕs')	210	33.56N	5.44W
Mekong, r., Asia	196	18.00N	104.30E
Melaka, Malay.	196	2.11N	102.15E
Melaka, state, Malay.	181b	2.19N	102.09E
Melanesia, is., Oc.	224	13.00S	164.00E
Melbourne, Austl. (mĕl'bŭrn)	203	37.52S	145.08E
Melbourne, Eng., U.K.	144a	52.49N	1.26W
Melbourne, Fl., U.S.	115a	28.05N	80.37W
Melbourne, Ky., U.S.	101f	39.02N	84.22W
Melcher, Ia., U.S. (mĕl'chẽr)	103	41.13N	93.11W
Melekess, Russia (mĕl-yĕk-ĕs)	166	54.14N	49.39E
Melenki, Russia (mĕ-lyĕŋ'kē)	166	55.25N	41.34E
Melfort, Can. (mĕl'fôrt)	84	52.52N	104.36W
Melghir, Chott, l., Alg.	210	33.52N	5.22E
Melilla, Sp. N. Afr. (mā-lēl'yä)	210	35.24N	3.30W
Melipilla, Chile (mā-lē-pē'lyä)	132	33.40S	71.12W
Melita, Can.	89	49.11N	101.09W
Melitopol', Ukr. (mā-lē-tô'pôl-y')	167	46.49N	35.19E
Melívoia, Grc.	161	39.42N	22.47E
Melkrivier, S. Afr.	218d	24.01S	28.23E
Mellen, Wi., U.S. (mĕl'ĕn)	103	46.20N	90.40W
Mellerud, Swe. (mål'ē-rōōdh)	152	58.43N	12.25E
Melling, Eng., U.K.	237a	53.30N	2.56W
Melmoth, S. Afr.	213c	28.38S	31.26E
Melo, Ur. (mā'lō)	132	32.18S	54.07W
Melocheville, Can. (mĕ-lôsh-vĕl')	83a	45.24N	73.56W
Melozha, r., Russia (myĕ'lō-zhȧ)	172b	56.06N	38.34E
Melrose, Ma., U.S. (mĕl'rōz)	93a	42.29N	71.06W
Melrose, Mn., U.S.	103	45.39N	94.49W
Melrose Highlands, Ma., U.S.	227a	42.28N	71.04W
Melrose Park, Il., U.S.	101a	41.54N	87.52W
Meltham, Eng., U.K. (mĕl'thăm)	144a	53.35N	1.51W
Melton, Austl. (mĕl'tŭn)	201a	37.41S	144.35E
Melton Mowbray, Eng., U.K. (mō'brâ)	144a	52.45N	0.52W
Melúli, r., Moz.	217	16.10S	39.30E
Melun, Fr. (mē-lŭN')	147	48.32N	2.40E
Melunga, Ang.	216	17.16S	16.24E
Melville, Can. (mĕl'vĭl)	84	50.55N	102.48W
Melville, La., U.S.	113	30.39N	91.45W
Melville, i., Austl.	202	11.30S	131.12E
Melville, l., Can.	85	53.46N	59.31W
Melville, Cape, c., Austl.	203	14.15S	145.50E
Melville Hills, hills, Can.	84	69.18N	124.57W
Melville Peninsula, pen., Can.	85	67.44N	84.09W
Melvindale, Mi., U.S. (mĕl'vĭn-dāl)	101b	42.17N	83.11W
Melyana, Alg.	147	36.19N	1.56E
Mélykút, Hung. (mā'l'kōōt)	155	46.14N	19.21E
Memba, Moz. (mĕm'bȧ)	213	14.12N	40.35E
Memel *see* Klaipėda, Lith.	166	55.43N	21.10E
Memel, S. Afr. (mĕ'měl)	218d	27.42S	29.35E
Memmingen, Ger. (mĕm'ĭng-ĕn)	154	47.59N	10.10E
Memo, r., Ven. (mĕ'mō)	131b	9.32N	66.30W
Memphis, Mo., U.S. (mĕm'fĭs)	111	40.27N	92.11W
Memphis, Tn., U.S. (mĕm'fĭs)	97	35.07N	90.03W
Memphis, Tx., U.S.	110	34.42N	100.33W
Memphis, hist., Egypt	218b	29.50N	31.12E
Mena, Ukr. (mē-nȧ')	163	51.31N	32.14E
Mena, Ar., U.S. (mē'nȧ)	111	34.35N	94.09W
Menangle, Austl.	201b	34.08S	150.48E

PLACE (Pronunciation)	PAGE	Lat. °′	Long. °′
Menard, Tx., U.S. (mē-närd')	112	30.56N	99.48W
Menasha, Wi., U.S. (mē-năsh'ȧ)	103	44.12N	88.29W
Mende, Fr. (mäNd)	156	44.31N	3.30E
Menden, Ger. (mĕn'dĕn)	157c	51.26N	7.47E
Menden, neigh., Ger.	236	51.24N	6.54E
Mendes, Braz. (mĕ'n-dĕs)	132b	22.32S	43.44W
Mendocino, Ca., U.S.	108	39.18N	123.47W
Mendocino, Cape, c., Ca., U.S. (mĕn'dō-sē'nō)	97	40.25N	12.42W
Mendota, Il., U.S. (mĕn-dō'tȧ)	103	41.34N	89.06W
Mendota, l., Wi., U.S.	103	43.09N	89.41W
Mendoza, Arg. (mĕn-dō'sä)	132	32.48S	68.45W
Mendoza, prov., Arg.	132	35.10S	69.00W
Mengcheng, China (mŭŋ-chŭŋ)	190	33.15N	116.34E
Mengede, neigh., Ger.	236	51.34N	7.23E
Menglinghausen, neigh., Ger.	236	51.28N	7.25E
Meng Shan, mts., China (mŭŋ shän)	190	35.47N	117.23E
Mengzi, China	188	23.22N	103.20E
Menindee, Austl. (mĕ-nĭn-dē)	204	32.23S	142.30E
Menlo Park, Ca., U.S. (mĕn'lō pärk)	106b	37.27N	122.11W
Menlo Park Terrace, N.J., U.S.	228	40.32N	74.20W
Menno, S.D., U.S. (mĕn'ō)	102	43.14N	97.34W
Menominee, Mi., U.S. (mē-nŏm'ĭ-nē)	103	45.08N	87.40W
Menominee, r., Mi., U.S.	103	45.37N	87.54W
Menominee Falls, Wi., U.S. (fôls)	101a	43.11N	88.06W
Menominee Ra, Mi., U.S.	103	46.07N	88.53W
Menomonee, r., Wi., U.S.	101a	43.09N	88.06W
Menomonie, Wi., U.S.	103	44.53N	91.55W
Menongue, Ang.	216	14.36S	17.48E
Menorca (Minorca), i., Spain (mē-nō'r-kä)	142	40.05N	3.58E
Mentana, Italy (mĕn-tȧ'nä)	159d	42.02N	12.40E
Mentawai, Kepulauan, is., Indon. (mĕn-tä-vī')	196	1.08S	98.10E
Menton, Fr. (mäN-tôN')	157	43.46N	7.37E
Mentone, Austl.	243b	37.59S	145.05E
Mentone, Ca., U.S. (mĕn'tōne)	107a	34.05N	117.08W
Mentz, l., S. Afr. (mĕnts)	213c	33.13S	25.15E
Menzel Bourguiba, Tun.	148	37.12N	9.51E
Menzelinsk, Russia (mĕn'zyĕ-lĕnsk')	166	55.40N	53.15E
Menzies, Austl. (mĕn'zēz)	202	29.45S	122.15E
Meogui, Mex. (må-ō'gē)	112	28.17N	105.28W
Meopham, Eng., U.K.	235	51.22N	0.22E
Meopham Station, Eng., U.K.	235	51.23N	0.21E
Meppel, Neth. (mĕp'ĕl)	151	52.41N	6.08E
Meppen, Ger. (mĕp'ĕn)	154	52.40N	7.18E
Merabéllou, Kólpos, b., Grc.	160a	35.16N	25.55E
Meramec, r., Mo., U.S. (mĕr'ȧ-mĕk)	111	38.06N	91.06W
Merano, Italy (må-rä'nō)	148	46.39N	11.10E
Merasheen, i., Can. (mē'rȧ-shēn)	93	47.30N	54.15W
Merauke, Indon. (må-rou'kä)	197	8.32S	140.17E
Meraux, La., U.S. (mē-ro')	100d	29.56N	89.56W
Mercader y Millás, Spain	238e	41.21N	2.05E
Mercato San Severino, Italy	159c	40.34N	14.38E
Merced, Ca., U.S. (mẽr-sĕd')	108	37.17N	120.30W
Merced, Ca., U.S.	108	37.25N	120.31W
Mercedario, Cerro, mtn., Arg. (mĕr-sȧ-dhä'rē-ō)	132	31.58S	70.07W
Mercedes, Arg.	129c	34.41S	59.26W
Mercedes, Arg. (mĕr-sā'dhās)	132	29.04S	58.01W
Mercedes, Tx., U.S.	113	26.09N	97.55W
Mercedes, Ur.	132	33.17S	58.04W
Mercedita, Chile (mĕr-sē-dē'tä)	129b	33.51S	71.10W
Mercer Island, Wa., U.S. (mûr'sẽr)	106a	47.35N	122.15W
Mercês, Braz. (mĕ-sĕ's)	129a	21.13S	43.20W
Mercês, Port.	238d	38.47N	9.19W
Merchtem, Bel.	145a	50.57N	4.13E
Mercier, Can.	83a	45.19N	73.45W
Mercy, Cape, c., Can.	85	64.48N	63.22W
Merdeka Palace, bldg., Indon.	241i	6.10S	106.49E
Mere, Eng., U.K.	237b	53.20N	2.25W
Meredale, S. Afr.	244b	26.17S	27.59E
Meredith, N.H., U.S. (mĕr'ē-dĭth)	99	43.35N	71.35W
Merefa, Ukr. (må-rĕf'ȧ)	163	49.49N	36.04E
Merendón, Serranía de, mts., Hond.	120	15.01N	89.05W
Mereworth, Eng., U.K. (mĕ-rē wûrth)	144b	51.15N	0.23E
Mergui, Myanmar (mẽr-gē')	196	12.29N	98.39E
Mergui Archipelago, is., Myanmar	196	12.04N	97.02E
Meric (Maritsa), r., Eur.	153	40.43N	26.19E
Mérida, Mex.	116	20.58N	89.37W
Mérida, Ven.	130	8.30N	71.15W
Mérida, Cordillera de, mts., Ven. (mĕ'rē-dhä)	130	8.30N	70.45W
Meriden, Ct., U.S. (mĕr'ĭ-dĕn)	99	41.30N	72.50W
Meridian, Ms., U.S. (mē-rĭd-ĭ-ăn)	97	32.21N	88.41W
Meridian, Tx., U.S.	113	31.56N	97.37W
Mérignac, Fr.	156	44.50N	0.40W
Merikarvia, Fin. (mā'rē-kár'vē-ä)	153	61.51N	21.30E
Mering, Ger. (mē'rĕng)	145d	48.16N	11.00E
Merion Station, Pa., U.S.	229b	40.00N	75.15W
Merkel, Tx., U.S. (mûr'kĕl)	112	32.26N	100.02W
Merkinė, Lith.	153	54.10N	24.10E
Merksem, Bel.	145a	51.15N	4.27E
Merkys, r., Lith. (mär'kĭs)	155	54.23N	25.00E
Merlo, Arg. (mĕr-lō)	132a	34.40S	58.44W
Merlynston, Austl.	243b	37.43S	144.58E
Meron, Hare, mtn., Isr.	181a	32.58N	35.25E
Merriam, Ks., U.S. (mĕr-rĭ-yăm)	107f	39.01N	94.42W
Merriam, Mn., U.S.	107g	44.44N	93.36W
Merrick, N.Y., U.S. (mĕr'ĭk)	100a	40.40N	73.33W
Merri Creek, r., Austl.	243b	37.48S	144.59E
Merrifield, Va., U.S. (mĕr'ĭ-fēld)	100e	38.50N	77.12W
Merrill, Wi., U.S. (mĕr'ĭl)	103	45.11N	89.42W
Merrimac, Ma., U.S. (mĕr'ĭ-măk)	93a	45.20N	71.00W
Merrimack, N.H., U.S.	93a	42.51N	71.25W

ng-sing; ŋ-baŋk; N-nasalized n; nŏd; cŏmmit; ōld; ôbey; ôrder; oi-boil; fōōd; ŏŏ-as oo in foot; ou-out; s-soft; sh-dish; th-thin; pūre; ůnite; ûrn; stŭd; circŭs; ü-as in French tu; '-indeterminate vowel.

318 Merrimack-Minato

PLACE (Pronunciation)	PAGE	Lat. °′	Long. °′
Merrimack, r., Ma., U.S. (měr'ĭ-măk)	99	43.10N	71.30W
Merrionette Park, Il., U.S.	231a	41.41N	87.42W
Merritt, Can. (měr'ĭt)	84	50.07N	120.47W
Merrylands, Austl.	243a	33.50S	150.59E
Merryville, La., U.S. (měr'ĭ-vĭl)	113	30.46N	93.34W
Mersa Fatma, Erit.	211	14.54N	40.14E
Merscheid, neigh., Ger.	236	51.10N	7.01E
Merseburg, Ger. (měr'zě-bo͞orgh)	154	51.21N	11.59E
Mersey, r., Eng., U.K. (mûr'zē)	144a	53.20N	2.55W
Merseyside, co., Eng., U.K.	144a	53.29N	2.59W
Mersing, Malay.	181b	2.25N	103.51E
Merta Road, India (mär'tŭ rōd)	186	26.50N	73.54E
Merthyr Tydfil, Wales, U.K. (mûr'thẽr tĭd'vĭl)	150	51.46N	3.30W
Mértola Almodóvar, Port. (měr-tô-lȧ-äl-mô-dô'vär)	158	37.39N	8.04W
Merton, neigh., Eng., U.K.	235	51.25N	0.12W
Méru, Fr. (mā-rü')	156	49.14N	2.08E
Meru, Kenya (mā'ro͞o)	211	0.01N	37.45E
Meru, Mount, mtn., Tan.	217	3.15S	36.43E
Merume Mountains, mts., Guy. (měr-ü'mě)	131	5.45N	60.15W
Merwede Kanaal, can., Neth.	145a	52.15N	5.01E
Merwin, l., Wa., U.S. (měr'wĭn)	106c	45.58N	122.27W
Merzifon, Tur. (měr'ze-fōn)	182	40.50N	35.30E
Mesa, Az., U.S. (mā'sȧ)	109	33.25N	111.50W
Mesabi Range, mts., Mn., U.S. (mā-sŏb'bē)	103	47.17N	93.04W
Mesagne, Italy (mā-sän'yå)	161	40.34N	17.51E
Mesa Verde National Park, rec., Co., U.S. (vẽr'dē)	96	37.22N	108.27W
Mescalero Apache Indian Reservation, I.R., N.M., U.S. (měs-kä-lā'rō)	109	33.10N	105.45W
Meščerskij, Russia	239b	55.40N	37.25E
Meshchovsk, Russia (myěsh'chěfsk)	162	54.17N	35.19E
Mesilla, N.M., U.S. (må-sē'yä)	109	32.15N	106.45W
Meskine, Chad	215	11.25N	15.21E
Mesolóngion, Grc. (mě-sô-lôŋ'gê-ôn)	161	38.23N	21.28E
Mesopotamia, hist. reg., Asia	185	34.00N	44.00E
Mesquita, Braz.	132b	22.48S	43.26W
Messina, Italy (mě-sē'nȧ)	142	38.11N	15.34E
Messina, S. Afr.	212	22.17S	30.13E
Messina, Stretto di, strt., Italy (stě't-tô dē)	149	38.10N	15.34E
Messini, Grc.	161	37.05N	22.00E
Messy, Fr.	237c	48.58N	2.42E
Mestaganem, Alg.	210	36.04N	0.11E
Mestre, Italy (měs'trā)	160	45.29N	12.15E
Meta, dept., Col. (mě'tä)	130a	3.28N	74.07W
Meta, r., S.A.	130	4.33N	72.09W
Métabetchouane, r., Can. (mě-tá-bět-cho͞o-än')	91	47.45N	72.00W
Metairie, La., U.S.	113	30.00N	90.11W
Metán, Arg. (mě-tà'n)	132	25.32S	64.51W
Metangula, Moz.	212	12.42S	34.48E
Metapán, El Sal. (må-täpän')	120	14.21N	89.26W
Metcalfe, Can. (mět-käf)	83c	45.14N	75.27W
Metchosin, Can.	106a	48.22N	123.33W
Metepec, Mex. (må-tě-pěk')	118	18.56N	98.31W
Metepec, Mex.	118	19.15N	99.36W
Methow, r., Wa., U.S. (mět'hou) (mět hou')	104	48.26N	120.15W
Methuen, Ma., U.S. (mê-thū'ĕn)	93a	42.44N	71.11W
Metković, Cro. (mět'kô-vĭch)	161	43.02N	17.40E
Metlakatla, Ak., U.S. (mět-lȧ-kăt'lȧ)	95	55.08N	131.35W
Metropolis, Il., U.S. (mê-trŏp'ô-lĭs)	111	37.09N	88.46W
Metropolitan Museum of Art, pt. of i., N.Y., U.S.	228	40.47N	73.58W
Metter, Ga., U.S. (mět'ẽr)	115	32.21N	82.05W
Mettmann, Ger. (mět'män)	157c	51.15N	6.58E
Metuchen, N.J., U.S. (mě-tŭ'chěn)	100a	40.32N	74.21W
Metz, Fr. (mětz)	147	49.08N	6.10E
Metztitlán, Mex. (mětz-têt-län)	118	20.36N	98.45W
Meuban, Cam.	215	2.27N	12.41E
Meudon, Fr.	237c	48.48N	2.14E
Meuse (Maas), r., Eur. (mûz) (müz)	151	50.32N	5.22E
Mexborough, Eng., U.K. (měks'bŭr-ô)	144a	53.30N	1.17W
Mexia, Tx., U.S. (må-hē'ä)	113	31.32N	96.29W
Mexian, China	189	24.20N	116.10E
Mexicalcingo, Mex. (mě-kē-käl-sēn'go)	119a	19.13N	99.34W
Mexicali, Mex. (måk-sê-kä'lē)	116	32.28N	115.29W
Mexicana, Altiplanicie, plat., Mex.	118	22.38N	102.33W
Mexican Hat, Ut., U.S. (měk'sĭ-kǎn hăt)	109	37.10N	109.55W
Mexico, Me., U.S. (měk'sĭ-kō)	92	44.34N	70.33W
Mexico, Mo., U.S.	111	39.09N	91.51W
Mexico, nation, N.A.	116	23.45N	104.00W
Mexico, Gulf of, b., N.A.	116	25.15N	93.45W
Mexico City, Mex. (měk'sĭ-kō)	116	19.28N	99.09W
Mexticacán, Mex. (měs'tê-kä-kän')	118	21.12N	102.43W
Meyers Chuck, Ak., U.S.	86	55.44N	132.15W
Meyersdale, Pa., U.S. (mī'ẽrz-dāl)	99	39.55N	79.00W
Meyerton, S. Afr. (mī'ẽr-tǔn)	218d	26.35S	28.01E
Meymaneh, Afg.	182	35.53N	64.38E
Mezen', Russia	164	65.50N	44.05E
Mezen', r., Russia	166	65.20N	44.45E
Mézenc, Mont, mtn., Fr. (mōn-mā-zěn')	156	44.55N	4.12E
Mezha, r., Eur. (myā'zhá)	162	55.53N	31.44E
Mézieres-sur-Seine, Fr. (mā-zyâr'sür-sån')	157b	48.58N	1.49E
Mezőkövesd, Hung. (mě'zû-kû'věsht)	155	47.49N	20.36E
Mezőtur, Hung. (mě'zû-to͞or)	155	47.00N	20.36E
Mezquital, Mex. (måz-kê-täl')	118	23.30N	104.20W
Mezquitic, Mex. (måz-kê-tēk')	118	22.25N	103.43W
Mezquitic, r., Mex.	118	22.25N	103.45W
Mfangano Island, i., Kenya	217	0.28S	33.35E

PLACE (Pronunciation)	PAGE	Lat. °′	Long. °′
Mga, Russia (m'gȧ)	172c	59.45N	31.04E
Mglin, Russia (m'glēn')	162	53.03N	32.52W
Mia, Oued, r., Alg.	148	29.26N	3.15E
Miacatlán, Mex. (mê'ä-kä-tlän')	118	18.42N	99.17W
Mia-dong, neigh., S. Kor.	241b	37.37N	127.01E
Miahuatlán, Mex. (mê'ä-wä-tlän')	119	16.20N	96.38W
Miajadas, Spain (mê-ä-hä'däs)	158	39.10N	5.53W
Miami, Az., U.S.	96	33.20N	110.55W
Miami, Fl., U.S.	97	25.45N	80.11W
Miami, Ok., U.S.	111	36.51N	94.51W
Miami, Tx., U.S.	110	35.41N	100.39W
Miami Beach, Fl., U.S.	115a	25.47N	80.07W
Miamisburg, Oh., U.S. (mī-ăm'iz-bûrg)	98	39.40N	84.20W
Miamitown, Oh., U.S. (mī-ăm'ĭ-toun)	101f	39.13N	84.43W
Mīāneh, Iran	182	37.15N	47.13E
Miangas, Pulau, i., Indon.	197	5.30N	127.00E
Miaoli, Tai. (mê-ou'lĭ)	193	24.30N	120.48E
Miaozhen, China (miou-jŭn)	190	31.44N	121.28E
Miass, Russia (mī-äs')	170	54.59N	60.06E
Miastko, Pol. (myäst'kô)	154	54.01N	17.00E
Miccosukee Indian Reservation, I.R., Fl., U.S.	115a	26.10N	80.50W
Michajlovskoje, Russia	239b	55.35N	37.35E
Michalovce, Slvk. (mē'ĸä-lôf'tsě)	155	48.44N	21.56E
Michel Peak, mtn., Can.	86	53.35N	126.25W
Michelson, Mount, mtn., Ak., U.S. (mĭch'ĕl-sŭn)	95	69.11N	144.12W
Michendorf, Ger. (mē'ĸĕn-dōrf)	145b	52.19N	13.02E
Miches, Dom. Rep. (mē'chěs)	123	19.00N	69.05W
Michigan, state, U.S. (mĭsh-'ĭ-gǎn)	97	45.55N	87.00W
Michigan, Lake, l., U.S.	97	43.20N	87.10W
Michigan City, In., U.S.	98	41.40N	86.55W
Michillinda, Ca., U.S.	232	34.07N	118.05W
Michipicoten, r., Can.	103	47.56N	84.42W
Michipicoten Harbour, Can.	103	47.58N	84.58W
Michurinsk, Russia (mĭ-cho͞o-rĭnsk')	167	52.53N	40.32E
Mico, Punta, c., Nic. (po͞o'n-tä-mē'kô)	121	11.38N	83.24W
Micronesia, is., Oc.	224	11.00N	159.00E
Micronesia, Federated States of, nation, Oc.	3	5.00N	152.00E
Midas, Nv., U.S. (mī'dȧs)	104	41.15N	116.50W
Middelfart, Den. (mēd''l-färt)	152	55.30N	9.45E
Middle, r., Can.	86	55.00N	125.50W
Middle Andaman, i., India (ăn-dȧ-măn')	196	12.44N	93.21E
Middle Bayou, Tx., U.S.	113a	29.38N	95.06W
Middleburg, S. Afr. (mĭd'ĕl-bûrg)	212	31.30S	25.00E
Middleburg, S. Afr.	218d	25.47S	29.30E
Middleburgh Heights, Oh., U.S.	229a	41.22N	81.48W
Middlebury, Vt., U.S. (mĭd''l-bĕr-ĭ)	99	44.00N	73.10W
Middle Concho, Tx., U.S. (kōn'chō)	112	31.21N	100.50W
Middle River, Md., U.S.	100e	39.20N	76.27W
Middlesboro, Ky., U.S. (mĭd''lz-bŭr-ô)	114	36.36N	83.42W
Middlesbrough, Eng., U.K. (mĭd''lz-brŭ)	146	54.35N	1.18W
Middlesex, N.J., U.S. (mĭd''l-sěks)	100a	40.34N	74.30W
Middleton, Can. (mĭd''l-tŭn)	92	44.57N	65.04W
Middleton, Eng., U.K.	144a	53.34N	2.12W
Middletown, Ct., U.S.	99	41.35N	72.40W
Middletown, De., U.S.	99	39.30N	75.40W
Middletown, Ma., U.S.	93a	42.35N	71.01W
Middletown, N.Y., U.S.	99	41.26N	74.25W
Middletown, Oh., U.S.	98	39.30N	84.25W
Middlewich, Eng., U.K. (mĭd''l-wĭch)	144a	53.11N	2.27W
Middlewit, S. Afr. (mĭd'l-wĭt)	218d	24.50S	27.00E
Midfield, Al., U.S.	100h	33.28N	86.54W
Midi, Canal du, Fr. (kä-näl-dü-mê-dē')	147	43.22N	1.35E
Mid Illovo, S. Afr. (mĭd ĭl'ô-vō)	213c	29.59S	30.32E
Midland, Can. (mĭd'lǎnd)	85	44.45N	79.50W
Midland, Mi., U.S.	98	43.40N	84.20W
Midland, Tx., U.S.	112	32.05N	102.05W
Midland Beach, neigh., N.Y., U.S.	228	40.34N	74.05W
Midlothian, Il., U.S.	231a	41.38N	87.42W
Midvale, Ut., U.S. (mĭd'vāl)	107b	40.37N	111.54W
Midway, S. Afr.	244b	26.18S	27.51E
Midway, Al., U.S. (mĭd'wā)	114	32.03N	85.30W
Midway City, Ca., U.S.	232	33.45N	118.00W
Midway Islands, is., Oc.	2	28.00N	179.00W
Midwest, Wy., U.S. (mĭd-wěst')	105	43.25N	106.15W
Midye, Tur. (mēd'yě)	167	41.35N	28.10E
Międzyrzecz, Pol. (myăn-dzû'zhěch)	154	52.26N	15.35E
Mielec, Pol. (myě'lěts)	155	50.17N	21.27E
Mier, Mex. (myâr)	112	26.26N	99.08W
Mieres, Spain (myā'räs)	158	43.14N	5.45W
Mier y Noriega, Mex. (myâr'ê nô-rê-ā'gä)	118	23.28N	100.08W
Miguel Auza, Mex.	118	24.17N	103.27W
Miguel Pereira, Braz.	132b	22.27S	43.28W
Mijares, r., Spain	159	39.55N	0.01W
Mikage, Japan (mē'kȧ-gå)	195b	34.42N	135.15E
Mikawa-Wan, b., Japan (mē'kä-wä wän)	195	34.43N	137.09E
Mikhaylov, Russia (mē-ĸäy'lôf)	166	54.14N	39.03E
Mikhaylovka, Russia	167	50.05N	43.10E
Mikhaylovka, Russia	172a	55.35N	57.57E
Mikhaylovka, Russia	172c	59.20N	30.21E
Mikhnëvo, Russia (mĭk-nyô'vô)	172b	55.08N	37.57E
Miki, Japan (mē'kê)	195b	34.47N	134.59E
Mikindani, Tan. (mê-kên-dä'nê)	213	10.17S	40.07E
Mikkeli, Fin. (měk'ě-lĭ)	146	61.42N	27.14E
Míkonos, i., Grc.	161	37.26N	25.30E
Mikulov, Czech Rep. (mĭ'ko͞o-lôf)	154	48.47N	16.39E
Mikumi, Tan.	217	7.24S	36.59E
Mikuni, Japan (mē'ko͞o-nê)	195	36.09N	136.14E
Mikuni-Sammyaku, mts., Japan (säm'myä-ko͞o)	195	36.51N	138.38E
Mikura, i., Japan (mē'ko͞o-rȧ)	195	33.53N	139.26E
Milaca, Milaca, Mn., U.S. (mê-lăk'ȧ)	103	45.45N	93.41W
Milan (Milano), Italy (mê-lä'nō)	160	45.29N	9.12E

PLACE (Pronunciation)	PAGE	Lat. °′	Long. °′
Milan, Mi., U.S. (mĭ'lăn)	98	42.05N	83.40W
Milan, Mo., U.S.	111	40.13N	93.07W
Milan, Tn., U.S.	114	35.54N	88.47W
Milâs, Tur. (mê'läs)	149	37.10N	27.25E
Milazzo, Italy	160	38.13N	15.17E
Milbank, S.D., U.S. (mĭl'băŋĸ)	102	45.13N	96.38W
Mildura, Austl. (mĭl-dū'rȧ)	203	34.10S	142.18E
Miles City, Mt., U.S. (mīlz)	96	46.24N	105.50W
Milford, Ct., U.S. (mĭl'fẽrd)	99	41.15N	73.05W
Milford, De., U.S.	99	38.55N	75.25W
Milford, Md., U.S.	229c	39.21N	76.44W
Milford, Ma., U.S.	93a	42.09N	71.31W
Milford, Mi., U.S.	101b	42.35N	83.36W
Milford, N.H., U.S.	99	42.50N	71.40W
Milford, Oh., U.S.	101f	39.11N	84.18W
Milford, Ut., U.S.	109	38.20N	113.05W
Milford Sound, strt., N.Z.	205	44.35S	167.47E
Miling, Austl. (mĭl''ng)	202	30.30S	116.25E
Milipitas, Ca., U.S. (mĭl-ĭ-pĭ'tăs)	106b	37.26N	121.54W
Milk, r., N.A.	96	48.30N	107.00W
Millau, Fr. (mē-yō')	147	44.06N	3.04E
Millbourne, Pa., U.S.	229b	39.58N	75.15W
Millbrae, Ca., U.S. (mĭl'brā)	106b	37.36N	122.23W
Millburn, N.J., U.S.	228	40.44N	74.20W
Millbury, Ma., U.S. (mĭl'bĕr-ĭ)	93a	42.12N	71.46W
Mill Creek, r., Can. (mĭl)	83g	53.28N	113.25W
Mill Creek, r., Ca., U.S.	108	40.07N	121.55W
Milledgeville, Ga., U.S. (mĭl'ĕj-vĭl)	114	33.05N	83.15W
Mille Îles, Rivière des, r., Can. (rê-vyâr' dā mĭl'ĭl')	83a	45.41N	73.40W
Mille Lac Indian Reservation, I.R., Mn., U.S. (mĭl lăk')	103	46.14N	94.13W
Mille Lacs, l., Mn., U.S.	103	46.25N	93.22W
Mille Lacs, Lac des, l., Can. (läk dě mēl läks)	90	48.52N	90.53W
Millen, Ga., U.S. (mĭl'ĕn)	115	32.47N	81.55W
Miller, S.D., U.S. (mĭl'ẽr)	102	44.31N	99.00W
Millerovo, Russia (mĭl'ĕ-rô-vô)	167	48.58N	40.27E
Millersburg, Ky., U.S. (mĭl'ẽrz-bûrg)	98	38.15N	84.10W
Millersburg, Oh., U.S.	98	40.35N	81.55W
Millersburg, Pa., U.S.	99	40.35N	76.55W
Millerton, Can. (mĭl'ẽr-tǔn)	92	46.56N	65.40W
Millertown, Can. (mĭl'ẽr-toun)	93	48.49N	56.32W
Mill Green, Eng., U.K.	235	51.41N	0.22E
Mill Hill, neigh., Eng., U.K.	235	51.37N	0.13W
Millicent, Austl. (mĭl-ĭ-sěnt)	204	37.30S	140.20E
Millinocket, Me., U.S. (mĭl-ĭ-nŏk'ĕt)	92	45.40N	68.44W
Millis, Ma., U.S. (mĭl-ĭs)	93a	42.10N	71.22W
Mill Neck, N.Y., U.S.	228	40.52N	73.34W
Millstadt, Il., U.S. (mĭl'stăt)	107e	38.27N	90.06W
Millstone, r., N.J., U.S. (mĭl'stōn)	100a	40.27N	74.38W
Millstream, Austl. (mĭl'strēm)	202	21.45S	117.10E
Milltown, Can. (mĭl'toun)	92	45.13N	67.19W
Millvale, Pa., U.S.	230b	40.29N	79.58W
Mill Valley, Ca., U.S. (mĭl)	106b	37.54N	122.32W
Millwood Reservoir, res., Ar., U.S.	111	33.00N	94.00W
Milly-la-Forêt, Fr. (mē-yē'-la-fŏ-rě')	157b	48.24N	2.28E
Milmont Park, Pa., U.S.	229b	39.53N	75.20W
Milnerton, S. Afr. (mĭl'nẽr-tǔn)	212a	33.52S	18.30E
Milnor, N.D., U.S. (mĭl'nẽr)	102	46.17N	97.29W
Milnrow, Eng., U.K.	237b	53.37N	2.06W
Milo, Me., U.S.	92	44.16N	69.01W
Milon-la-Chapelle, Fr.	237c	48.44N	2.03E
Milos, i., Grc. (mē'lŏs)	149	36.45N	24.35E
Milpa Alta, Mex. (mē'l-pä-á'l-tä)	119a	19.11N	99.01W
Milspe, Ger.	236	51.18N	7.21E
Milton, Can.	83d	43.31N	79.53W
Milton, Fl., U.S. (mĭl'tǔn)	114	30.37N	87.02W
Milton, Pa., U.S.	99	41.00N	76.50W
Milton, Ut., U.S.	107b	41.04N	111.44W
Milton, Wa., U.S.	106a	47.15N	122.20W
Milton, Wi., U.S.	103	42.45N	89.00W
Milton-Freewater, Or., U.S.	104	45.57N	118.25W
Milvale, Pa., U.S. (mĭl'vāl)	101e	40.29N	79.58W
Milville, N.J., U.S. (mĭl'vĭl)	99	39.25N	75.00W
Milwaukee, Wi., U.S.	97	43.03N	87.55W
Milwaukee, r., Wi., U.S.	101a	43.10N	87.56W
Milwaukie, Or., U.S. (mĭl-wô'kê)	104	45.27N	122.38W
Mimiapan, Mex. (mē-myä-pàn')	119a	19.26N	99.28W
Mimoso do Sul, Braz. (mē-mô'sŏ-dô-so͞o'l)	129a	21.03S	41.21W
Min, r., China (mēn)	189	26.03N	118.30E
Min, r., China	193	29.30N	104.00E
Mina, r., Alg. (mē'nà)	159	35.24N	0.51E
Minago, r., Can. (mĭ-nä'gō)	89	54.25N	98.45W
Minakuchi, Japan (mē'nà-ko͞o'chê)	195	34.59N	136.06E
Minami, neigh., Japan	241e	34.58N	135.45E
Minamisenju, neigh., Japan	242a	35.44N	139.48E
Minas, Cuba (mē'näs)	122	21.30N	77.35W
Minas, Indon.	181b	0.52N	101.29E
Minas, Ur. (mē'näs)	132	34.18S	55.12W
Minas, Sierra de las, mts., Guat. (syĕr'rä dā läs mē'näs)	120	15.08N	90.25W
Minas Basin, b., Can. (mĭ'nȧs)	92	45.20N	64.00W
Minas Channel, strt., Can.	92	45.15N	64.45W
Minas de Oro, Hond. (mē'näs-dě-ŏ-rô)	120	14.52N	87.19W
Minas de Riotinto, Spain (mě'näs dä rē-ô-tēn'tō)	158	37.43N	6.35W
Minas Novas, Braz. (mē'năzh nō'vàzh)	131	17.20S	42.19W
Minatare, l., Ne., U.S. (mĭn'á-târ)	102	41.56N	103.07W
Minatitlán, Mex. (mê-nä-tê-tlän')	116	17.59N	94.33W
Minatitlán, Mex.	118	19.21N	104.02W
Minato, Japan (mē'nà-tô)	195	35.13N	139.52E
Minato, neigh., Japan	242a	35.39N	139.45E

PLACE (Pronunciation)	PAGE	Lat. °′	Long. °′
Minato, neigh., Japan	242b	34.39N	135.26E
Minch, The, strt., Scot., U.K.	142	58.04N	6.04W
Mindanao, i., Phil.	197	8.00N	125.00E
Mindanao Sea, sea, Phil.	197	8.55N	124.00E
Minden, Ger. (mĭn′dĕn)	154	52.17N	8.58E
Minden, La., U.S.	113	32.36N	93.19W
Minden, Ne., U.S.	110	40.30N	98.54W
Mindoro, i., Phil.	196	12.50N	121.05E
Mindoro Strait, strt., Phil.	197a	12.28N	120.33E
Mindyak, Russia (mēn′dyák)	172a	54.01N	58.48E
Mineola, N.Y., U.S. (mĭn-ē-ō′lȧ)	100a	40.43N	73.38W
Mineola, Tx., U.S.	113	32.39N	95.31W
Mineral del Chico, Mex. (mē-nä-räl′dĕl chē′kō)	118	20.13N	98.46W
Mineral del Monte, Mex. (mē-nä-räl dĕl mōn′tå)	118	20.18N	98.39W
Mineral'nyye Vody, Russia	167	44.10N	43.15E
Mineral Point, Wi., U.S. (mĭn′ẽr-ăl)	103	42.50N	90.10W
Mineral Wells, Tx., U.S. (mĭn′ẽr-ăl wĕlz)	112	32.48N	98.06W
Minerva, Oh., U.S. (mĭ-nur′vȧ)	98	40.45N	81.10W
Minervino, Italy (mē-nĕr-vē′nō)	160	41.07N	16.05E
Mineyama, Japan (mē-nē-yä′mä)	195	35.38N	135.05E
Mingäçevir, Azer.	168	40.45N	47.03E
Mingäçevir su anbarı, res., Azer.	168	40.50N	46.50E
Mingan, Can.	85	50.18N	64.02W
Mingenew, Austl. (mĭn′gĕ-nů)	202	29.15S	115.45E
Mingo Junction, Oh., U.S. (mĭŋ′gō)	98	40.15N	80.40W
Minho, hist. reg., Port. (mēn yō)	158	41.32N	8.13W
Minho (Miño), r., Eur. (mē′n-yō)	158	41.28N	9.05W
Ministik Lake, l., Can. (mĭ-nĭs′tĭk)	83g	53.23N	113.05W
Minna, Nig. (mĭn′ȧ)	210	9.37N	6.33E
Minneapolis, Ks., U.S. (mĭn-ē-ăp′ō-lĭs)	111	39.07N	97.41W
Minneapolis, Mn., U.S.	97	44.58N	93.15W
Minnedosa, Can. (mĭn-ē-dō′sȧ)	84	50.14N	99.51W
Minneota, Mn., U.S. (mĭn-ē-ō′tȧ)	102	44.34N	95.59W
Minnesota, state, U.S. (mĭn-ē-sō′tȧ)	97	46.10N	90.20W
Minnesota, r., Mn., U.S.	97	44.30N	95.00W
Minnetonka, l., Mn., U.S. (mĭn-ē-tôŋ′kȧ)	103	44.52N	93.34W
Minnitaki Lake, l., Can. (mĭ′nĭ-tä′kē)	89	49.58N	92.00W
Mino, r., Japan	195b	34.56N	135.06E
Minonk, Il., U.S. (mĭ′nŏnk)	98	40.55N	89.00W
Minooka, Il., U.S. (mĭ-nōō′kȧ)	101a	41.27N	88.15W
Minot, N.D., U.S.	96	48.13N	101.17W
Minsk, Bela. (mênsk)	164	53.54N	27.35E
Minsk, prov., Bela.	162	53.50N	27.43E
Mińsk Mazowiecki, Pol. (mēn′sk mä-zō-vyĕt′skĭ)	155	52.10N	21.35E
Minsterley, Eng., U.K. (mĭnstẽr-lē)	144a	52.38N	2.55W
Mintard, Ger.	236	51.22N	6.54E
Minto, Austl.	243a	34.01S	150.51E
Minto, Can.	92	46.05N	66.05W
Minto, l., Can.	85	57.18N	75.50W
Minturno, Italy (mēn-tōōr′nō)	160	41.17N	13.44E
Minūf, Egypt (mē-nōōf′)	218b	30.26N	30.55E
Minusinsk, Russia (mē-nō-sēnsk′)	165	53.47N	91.45E
Min'yar, Russia	172a	55.06N	57.33E
Miquelon Lake, l., Can. (mĭ′kē-lôn)	83g	53.16N	112.55W
Miquihuana, Mex. (mē-kē-wä′nä)	118	23.36N	99.45W
Miquon, Pa., U.S.	229b	40.04N	75.16W
Mir, Bela. (mēr)	155	53.27N	26.25E
Miracema, Braz. (mē-rä-sē′mä)	129a	21.24S	42.10W
Miracema do Tocantins, Braz.	131	9.34S	48.24W
Mirador, Braz. (mē-rá-dōr′)	131	6.19S	44.12W
Miraflores, Col. (mē-rä-flō′räs)	130	5.10N	73.13W
Miraflores, Peru	130	16.19S	71.20W
Miraflores, Peru	233c	12.08S	77.03W
Miraflores Locks, trans., Pan.	116a	9.00N	79.35W
Miragoâne, Haiti (mē-rá-gwän′)	123	18.25N	73.05W
Mira Loma, Ca., U.S. (mĭ′rȧ lō′mȧ)	107a	34.01N	117.32W
Miramar, Ca., U.S. (mĭr′ă-mär)	108a	32.53N	117.08W
Miramar, neigh., Cuba	233b	23.07N	82.25W
Miramas, Fr.	156	43.35N	5.00E
Miramichi Bay, b., Can. (mĭr′ȧ-mē-shē′)	92	47.08N	65.08W
Miranda, Austl.	243a	34.02S	151.06E
Miranda, Col. (mē-rä′n-dä)	130a	3.14N	76.11W
Miranda, Ca., U.S.	108	40.14N	123.49W
Miranda, Ven.	131b	10.09N	68.24W
Miranda, dept., Ven.	131b	10.17N	66.41W
Miranda de Ebro, Spain (mē-rá′n-dä-dē-ĕ′brō)	158	42.42N	2.59W
Miranda do Douro, Port. (mē-rän′dä dō-dwĕ′rō)	158	41.30N	6.17W
Mirandela, Port. (mē-rän-dā′lȧ)	158	41.28N	7.10W
Mirando City, Tx., U.S. (mĭr-ȧn′dō)	112	27.25N	99.03W
Mira Por Vos Islets, is., Bah. (mē′rä pôr vōs)	123	22.05N	74.30W
Mira Por Vos Pass, strt., Bah.	123	22.10N	74.35W
Mirbāṭ, Oman	182	16.58N	54.42E
Mirebalais, Haiti (mēr-bá-lĕ′)	123	18.50N	72.05W
Mirecourt, Fr. (mēr-kōōr′)	157	48.20N	6.08E
Mirfield, Eng., U.K. (mûr′fēld)	144a	53.41N	1.42W
Miri, Malay. (mē′rē)	196	4.13N	113.56E
Mirim, Lagoa, l., S.A. (mē-rēN′)	132	33.00S	53.15W
Mírina, Grc.	161	39.52N	25.01E
Miropol'ye, Ukr. (mē-rō-pôl′yĕ)	163	51.02N	35.13E
Mīrpur Khās, Pak. (mēr′pōōr κäs)	186	25.36N	69.10E
Mirzāpur, India (mĕr′zä-pōōr)	183	25.12N	82.38E
Mirzāpur, India	240a	22.50N	88.24E
Misailovo, Russia	239b	55.34N	37.49E
Misantla, Mex. (mē-sän′tlä)	119	19.55N	96.49W
Miscou, i., Can. (mĭs′kō)	92	47.58N	64.35W
Miscou Point, c., Can.	92	48.04N	64.32W
Miseno, Cape, c., Italy (mē-zĕ′nō)	159c	40.33N	14.12E
Misery, Mount, mtn., St. K./N. (mĭz′rē-ĭ)	121b	17.28N	62.47W
Mishan, China (mĭ′shäN)	194	45.32N	132.19E
Mishawaka, In., U.S. (mĭsh-ȧ-wôk′ȧ)	98	41.45N	86.15W
Mishina, Japan (mē′shē-mä)	195	35.09N	138.56E
Misiones, prov., Arg. (mē-syō′nās)	132	27.00S	54.30W
Miskito, Cayos, is., Nic.	121	14.34N	82.30W
Miskolc, Hung. (mĭsh′kôlts)	142	48.07N	20.50E
Misool, Pulau, i., Indon. (mē-sōl′)	197	2.00S	130.05E
Misquah Hills, Mn., U.S. (mĭs-kwä′ hĭlz)	103	47.50N	90.30W
Miṣr al Jadīdah, Egypt	218b	30.06N	31.35E
Miṣr al-Qadīmah (Old Cairo), neigh., Egypt	244a	30.00N	31.14E
Misrātah, Libya	211	32.23N	14.58E
Missinaibi, r., Can. (mĭs′ĭn-ă′ē-bē)	85	50.27N	83.01W
Missinaibi Lake, l., Can.	90	48.23N	83.40W
Mission, Ks., U.S. (mĭsh′ŭn)	107f	39.02N	94.39W
Mission, Tx., U.S.	112	26.14N	98.19W
Mission City, Can. (sĭ′tĭ)	87	49.08N	112.18W
Mississagi, r., Can.	90	46.35N	83.30W
Mississauga, Can.	91	43.34N	79.37W
Mississippi, state, U.S. (mĭs-ĭ-sĭp′ē)	97	32.30N	89.45W
Mississippi, l., Can.	91	45.05N	76.15W
Mississippi, r., U.S.	97	32.00N	91.30W
Mississippi Sound, strt., Ms., U.S.	114	34.16N	89.10W
Missoula, Mt., U.S. (mĭ-zōō′lȧ)	96	46.55N	114.00W
Missouri, state, U.S. (mĭ-sōō′rē)	97	38.00N	93.40W
Missouri, r., U.S.	96	40.40N	96.00W
Missouri City, Tx., U.S.	113a	29.37N	95.32W
Missouri Coteau, hills, U.S.	96	47.30N	101.00W
Missouri Valley, Ia., U.S.	102	41.35N	95.53W
Mist, Or., U.S. (mĭst)	106c	46.00N	123.15W
Mistassini, Can. (mĭs-tȧ-sĭ′nē)	91	48.56N	71.55W
Mistassini, l., Can. (mĭs-tȧ-sĭ′nē)	85	50.48N	73.30W
Mistelbach, Aus. (mĭs′tĕl-bäk)	154	48.34N	16.33E
Misteriosa, Lago, l., Mex. (mēs-tē-ryō′sä)	120a	18.05N	90.15W
Misti, Volcán, vol., Peru	130	16.04S	71.20W
Mistretta, Italy (mē-strĕt′tä)	160	37.54N	14.22E
Misty Fjords National Monument, rec., Ak., U.S.	95	51.00N	131.00W
Mita, Punta de, c., Mex. (pōō′n-tä-dē-mē′tä)	118	20.44N	105.34W
Mitaka, Japan (mē′tä-kä)	195a	35.42N	139.34E
Mitcham, Austl.	243b	37.49S	145.12E
Mitcham, neigh., Eng., U.K.	235	51.24N	0.10W
Mitchell, Il., U.S. (mĭch′ĕl)	107e	38.46N	90.05W
Mitchell, In., U.S.	98	38.45N	86.25W
Mitchell, Ne., U.S.	102	41.56N	103.49W
Mitchell, S.D., U.S.	96	43.42N	98.01W
Mitchell, Mount, mtn., N.C., U.S.	97	35.47N	82.15W
Mīt Ghamr, Egypt	218b	30.43N	31.20E
Mitilíni, Grc.	149	39.09N	26.35E
Mitla Pass, p., Egypt	181a	30.03N	32.40E
Mito, Japan (mē′tō)	194	36.20N	140.23E
Mitry-Mory, Fr.	237c	48.59N	2.37E
Mitsiwa, Erit.	211	15.40N	39.19E
Mitsu, Japan (mēt′sō)	195	34.21N	132.49E
Mitte, neigh., Ger.	238a	52.31N	13.24E
Mittelland Kanal, can., Ger. (mĭt′ĕl-länd)	154	52.18N	10.42E
Mittenwalde, Ger. (mē′tĕn-väl-dĕ)	145b	52.16N	13.33E
Mittweida, Ger. (mĭt-vī′dä)	154	50.59N	12.58E
Mitumba, Monts, mts., Zaire	217	10.50S	27.00E
Mityayevo, Russia (mĭt-yä′yĕ-vô)	172a	60.17N	61.02E
Miura, Japan	195a	35.08N	139.37E
Miwa, Japan (mē′wä)	195b	34.32N	135.51E
Mixcoac, neigh., Mex.	233a	19.23N	99.12W
Mixico, Guat. (mēs′kō)	120	14.37N	90.37W
Mixquiahuala, Mex. (mēs-kē-wä′lä)	118	20.12N	99.13W
Mixteco, r., Mex. (mēs-tā′kō)	118	17.45N	98.10W
Miyake, Japan (mē′yä-kå)	195b	34.35N	135.34E
Miyake, i., Japan (mē′yä-kå)	195	34.06N	139.21E
Miyakojima, neigh., Japan	242b	34.43N	135.33E
Miyakonojō, Japan	194	31.44N	131.04E
Miyazaki, Japan (mē′yä-zä′kē)	194	31.55N	131.27E
Miyoshi, Japan (mē-yō′shē′)	194	34.48N	132.49E
Mizdah, Libya (mēz′dä)	184	31.29N	13.09E
Mizil, Rom. (mē′zēl)	161	45.01N	26.30E
Mizonuma, Japan	242a	35.48N	139.36E
Mizoram, state, India	183	23.25N	92.45E
Mizue, neigh., Japan	242a	35.41N	139.54E
Mizuho, Japan	242a	35.46N	139.21E
Mjölby, Swe. (myûl′bü)	152	58.20N	15.09E
Mjörn, l., Swe.	152	57.55N	12.22E
Mjösa, l., Nor. (myûsä)	146	60.41N	11.25E
Mkalama, Tan.	212	4.07S	34.38E
Mkushi, Zam.	217	13.40S	29.20E
Mkwaja, Tan.	217	5.47S	38.51E
Mladá Boleslav, Czech Rep. (mlä′dä bô′lĕ-sláf)	154	50.26N	14.52E
Mlala Hills, hills, Tan.	217	6.47S	31.45E
Mlanje Mountains, mts., Mwi.	217	15.55S	35.30E
Mława, Pol. (mwä′vá)	146	53.07N	20.25E
Mmabatho, S. Afr.	212	25.42S	25.43E
Mnevniki, neigh., Russia	239b	55.45N	37.28E
Moa, r., Afr.	214	7.40N	11.15W
Moa, Pulau, i., Indon.	197	8.30S	128.30E
Moab, Ut., U.S. (mō′ăb)	109	38.35N	109.35W
Moanda, Gabon	212	1.37S	13.09E
Moar Lake, l., Can. (môr)	89	52.00N	95.09W
Moba, Nig.	244d	6.27N	3.28E
Moba, Zaire	212	7.12S	29.39E
Mobaye, Cen. Afr. Rep. (mō-bä′y′)	211	4.19N	21.11E
Mobayi-Mbongo, Zaire	211	4.14N	21.11E
Moberly, Mo., U.S. (mō′bẽr-lĭ)	97	39.24N	92.25W
Mobile, Al., U.S. (mō-bēl′)	97	30.42N	88.03W
Mobile, r., Al., U.S.	114	31.15N	88.00W
Mobile Bay, b., Al., U.S.	97	30.26N	87.56W
Mobridge, S.D., U.S. (mō′brĭj)	102	45.32N	100.26W
Moca, Dom. Rep. (mô′kä)	123	19.25N	70.35W
Moçambique, Moz. (mō-säN-bē′kĕ)	217	15.03S	40.42E
Moçâmedes, Ang. (mō-zá-mĕ-dĕs)	212	15.10S	12.09E
Moçâmedes, hist. reg., Ang.	212	16.00S	12.15E
Mochitlán, Mex. (mō-chē-tlän′)	118	17.10N	99.19W
Mochudi, Bots. (mō-chōō′dē)	212	24.13S	26.07E
Mocímboa da Praia, Moz. (mô-sē′ēm-bō-ȧ prä′ēä)	213	11.20S	40.21E
Moclips, Wa., U.S.	104	47.14N	124.13W
Môco, Serra do, mtn., Ang.	216	12.25S	15.10E
Mococa, Braz. (mô-kô′kȧ)	129a	21.29S	46.58W
Moctezuma, Mex. (mōk′tā-zōō′mä)	118	22.44N	101.06W
Mocuba, Moz.	217	16.50S	36.59E
Modderbee, S. Afr.	244b	26.10S	28.24E
Modderfontein, S. Afr.	213b	26.06S	28.10E
Modena, Italy (mô′dĕ-nä)	148	44.38N	10.54E
Modesto, Ca., U.S. (mô-dĕs′tō)	108	37.39N	121.00W
Modjeska, Ca., U.S.	232	33.43N	117.37W
Mödling, Aus. (mûd′lĭng)	145e	48.06N	16.17E
Moelv, Nor.	152	60.55N	10.40E
Moengo, Sur.	131	5.43N	54.19W
Moenkopi, Az., U.S.	109	36.07N	111.13W
Moers, Ger. (mûrs)	157c	51.27N	6.38E
Moffat Tunnel, trans., Co., U.S. (môf′ăt)	110	39.52N	106.20W
Mofolo, S. Afr.	244b	26.14S	27.53E
Mogadishu (Muqdisho), Som.	218a	2.08N	45.22E
Mogadore, Oh., U.S. (mŏg-ȧ-dōr′)	101d	41.04N	81.23E
Mogaung, Myanmar (mō-gä′ông)	183	25.30N	96.52E
Mogi das Cruzes, Braz. (mô-gê-däs-krōō′sēs)	131	23.33S	46.10W
Mogi-Guaçu, r., Braz. (mô-gê-gwá′sōō)	129a	22.06S	47.12W
Mogilëv, Bela. (mô-gē-lyôf′)	164	53.53N	30.22E
Mogilëv, prov., Bela. (mô-gē-lyôf′)	162	53.28N	30.15E
Mogilno, Pol. (mô-gēl′nō)	154	52.38N	17.58W
Mogi-Mirim, Braz. (mô-gê-mē-rē′N)	129a	22.26S	46.57W
Mogok, Myanmar (mô-gōk′)	183	23.14N	96.38E
Mogol, r., S. Afr. (mô-gōl)	218d	24.12S	27.55E
Mogollon Plateau, plat., Az., U.S.	96	34.15N	110.45W
Mogollon Rim, cliff, Az., U.S. (mō-gō-yōn′)	109	34.26N	111.17W
Moguer, Spain (mō-gĕr′)	158	37.15N	6.50W
Mohács, Hung. (mô′häch)	155	45.59N	18.38E
Mohale's Hoek, Leso.	213c	30.09S	27.28E
Mohall, N.D., U.S. (mō′hôl)	102	48.46N	101.29W
Mohave, l., Nv., U.S. (mô-hä′vä)	109	35.23N	114.40W
Mohe, China (mwo-hŭ)	189	53.33N	122.30E
Mohenjo-Dero, hist., Pak.	183	27.20N	68.10E
Mohili, neigh., India	240e	19.06N	72.53E
Mohyliv-Podil's'kyy, Ukr.	167	48.27N	27.51E
Mõisaküla, Est. (mẽē′sȧ-kü′lä)	153	58.07N	25.12E
Moissac, Fr. (mwä-sák′)	156	44.07N	1.05E
Moita, Port. (mō-ē′tȧ)	159b	38.39N	9.00W
Mojave, Ca., U.S.	108	35.06N	118.09W
Mojave, r., Ca., U.S. (mô-hä′vä)	108	34.46N	117.24W
Mojave Desert, Ca., U.S.	108	35.05N	117.30W
Mojave Desert, des., Ca., U.S.	96	35.00N	117.00W
Mokhotlong, Leso.	213c	29.18S	29.06E
Mokp'o, S. Kor. (mŏk′pō′)	189	34.50N	126.30E
Mol, Bel.	145a	51.21N	5.09E
Moldavia, hist. reg., Rom.	155	47.20N	27.12E
Moldavia see Moldova, nation, Eur.	164	48.00N	28.00E
Molde, Nor. (môl′dĕ)	146	62.44N	7.15E
Moldova, nation, Eur.	164	48.00N	28.00E
Moldova, r., Rom.	155	47.17N	26.27E
Moldoveanu, Vârful, mtn., Rom.	161	45.33N	24.38E
Molepolole, Bots. (mō-lā-pō-lō′lå)	212	24.15S	25.33W
Molfetta, Italy (mōl-fĕt′tä)	149	41.11N	16.38E
Molina, Chile (mŏ-lē′nä)	129b	35.07S	71.17W
Molina de Aragón, Spain (mô-lē′nä dĕ ä-rä-gô′n)	158	40.40N	1.54W
Molína de Segura, Spain (mô-lē′nä dĕ sĕ-gōō′rä)	158	38.03N	1.07W
Moline, Il., U.S. (mô-lēn′)	111	41.31N	90.34W
Molino de Rosas, Mex.	233a	19.22N	99.13W
Molíns de Rey, Spain	238e	41.25N	2.01E
Moliro, Zaire	212	8.13S	30.34E
Moliterno, Italy (mōl-ē-tĕr′nō)	160	40.13N	15.54W
Möllen, Ger.	236	51.35N	6.42E
Mollendo, Peru (mō-lyĕn′dō)	130	17.02S	71.59W
Moller, Port, Ak., U.S. (pōrt mōl′ẽr)	95	56.18N	161.30W
Mölndal, Swe. (mûln′däl)	152	57.39N	12.01E
Molochna, r., Ukr.	163	47.05N	35.22E
Molochnyy lyman, l., Ukr.	163	46.35N	35.32E
Molodechno, Bela. (mô-lô-dĕch′nō)	166	54.18N	26.57E
Molody Tud, Russia (mō-lō-dô′ē tōō′d)	172b	55.17N	37.31E
Molokai, i., Hi., U.S. (mō-lō kä′ē)	96c	21.15N	157.05E
Molokcha, r., Russia (mô′lôk-chä)	172b	56.15N	38.29E
Molopo, r., Afr. (mō-lō-pō)	212	27.45S	20.45E
Molson Lake, l., Can. (mōl′sŭn)	89	54.12N	96.45W
Molteno, S. Afr. (mŏl-tā′nō)	213c	31.24S	26.23E
Moluccas see Maluku, is., Indon.	197	2.22S	128.25E
Moma, Moz.	217	16.44S	39.14E
Mombasa, Kenya (mōm-bä′sä)	213	4.03S	39.40E
Mombetsu, Japan (mōm′bĕt-sōō′)	194	44.21N	142.48E
Momence, Il., U.S. (mô-mĕns′)	101a	41.09N	87.40W
Momostenango, Guat. (mô-môs-tā-näŋ′gō)	120	15.02N	91.25W
Momotombo, Nic.	120	12.25N	86.43W
Mompog Pass, strt., Phil. (mŏm-pŏg′)	197a	13.35N	122.09E
Mompos, Col. (mōm-pōs′)	130	9.05N	74.30W
Møn, i., Den. (mûn)	152	54.54N	12.30E
Monaca, Pa., U.S. (mō-nȧ′kō)	101e	40.41N	80.17W
Monaco, nation, Eur. (mŏn′ȧ-kō)	142	43.43N	7.47E
Monaghan, Ire. (mō′ȧ-găn)	150	54.16N	7.20W
Mona Passage, strt., N.A. (mō′nä)	117	18.00N	68.10W

ng-sing; ŋ-baŋk; N-nasalized n; nŏd; cŏmmit; ōld; ôbey; ôrder; oi-boil; fōōd; ŏŏ-as oo in foot; ou-out; s-soft; sh-dish; th-thin; pūre; ûnite; ûrn; stŭd; circŭs; ü-as in French tu; ′-indeterminate vowel.

PLACE (Pronunciation)	PAGE	Lat. °′	Long. °′
Monarch Mountain, mtn., Can. (mŏn′ërk)	86	51.41N	125.53W
Monashee Mountains, mts., Can. (mŏ-nă′shē)	87	50.30N	118.30W
Monastir see Bitola, Mac.	160	41.02N	21.22E
Monastir, Tun. (mŏn-ȧs-tēr′)	148	35.49N	10.56E
Monastyrshchina, Russia (mô-nȧs-tērsh′chĭ-nȧ)	162	54.19N	31.49E
Monastyryshche, Ukr.	163	48.57N	29.53E
Moncada, Spain	238e	41.29N	2.11E
Monção, Braz. (mon-souN′)	131	3.39S	45.23W
Moncayo, mtn., Spain (mŏn-kä′yō)	158	41.44N	1.48W
Monchegorsk, Russia (mōn′chĕ-gôrsk)	166	69.00N	33.35E
Mönchengladbach, Ger. (mûn′kĕn glät′bäκ)	154	51.12N	6.28E
Moncique, Serra de, mts., Port. (sĕr′rä dā mōn-chē′kĕ)	158	37.22N	8.37W
Monclova, Mex. (mōn-klō′vä)	116	26.53N	101.25W
Moncton, Can. (mŭŋk′tŭn)	85	46.06N	64.47W
Mondêgo, r., Port. (mōn-dĕ′gō)	158	40.10N	8.36W
Mondego, Cabo, c., Port. (kȧ′bō mōn-dā′gō)	158	40.12N	8.55W
Mondeor, S. Afr.	244b	26.17S	28.00E
Mondombe, Zaire (mōn-dôm′bā)	212	0.45S	23.06E
Mondoñedo, Spain (mōn-dō-nyā′dō)	158	43.35N	7.18W
Mondovi, Wi., U.S. (mŏn-dō′vĭ)	103	44.35N	91.42W
Monee, Il., U.S. (mŏ-nī)	101a	41.25N	87.45W
Monessen, Pa., U.S. (mŏ-nĕs′sĕn)	101e	40.09N	79.53W
Monett, Mo., U.S. (mō-nĕt′)	111	36.55N	93.55W
Monfalcone, Italy	160	45.49N	13.30E
Monforte de Lemos, Spain (mōn-fôr′tä dĕ lĕ′mōs)	158	42.30N	7.30W
Mongala, r., Zaire (mŏŋ-gäl′ȧ)	211	3.20N	21.30E
Mongalla, Sudan	211	5.11N	31.46E
Mongat, Spain	238e	41.28N	2.17E
Monghyr, India (mŏn-gēr′)	183	25.23N	86.34E
Mongo, r., Afr.	214	9.50N	11.50W
Mongolia, nation, Asia (mŏŋ-gō′lĭ-ȧ)	188	46.00N	100.00E
Mongos, Chaîne des, mts., Cen. Afr. Rep.	211	8.04N	21.59E
Mongoumba, Cen. Afr. Rep. (mŏŋ-gōōm′bȧ)	211	3.38N	18.36E
Mongu, Zam. (mŏŋ-gōō′)	212	15.15S	23.09E
Monken Hadley, neigh., Eng., U.K.	235	51.40N	0.11W
Monkey Bay, Mwi.	217	14.05S	34.55E
Monkey River, Belize (mŭŋ′kĭ)	120a	16.22N	88.33W
Monkland, Can. (mŭngk-lănd)	83c	45.12N	74.52W
Monkoto, Zaire (mōn-kō′tō)	212	1.38S	20.39E
Monmouth, Il., U.S. (mŏn′mŭth)(mŏn′mouth)	111	40.54N	90.38W
Monmouth Junction, N.J., U.S. (mŏn′mouth jŭngk′shŭn)	100a	40.23N	74.33W
Monmouth Mountain, mtn., Can. (mŏn′mŭth)	86	51.00N	123.47W
Mono, r., Afr.	214	7.20N	1.25E
Mono Lake, l., Ca., U.S. (mō′nō)	108	38.04N	119.00W
Monon, In., U.S. (mō′nŏn)	98	40.55N	86.55W
Monongah, W.V., U.S. (mō-nŏŋ′gȧ)	98	39.25N	80.10W
Monongahela, Pa., U.S. (mō-nŏn-gȧ-hē′lȧ)	101a	40.11N	79.55W
Monongahela, r., W.V., U.S.	98	39.30N	80.10W
Monopoli, Italy (mō-nô′pō-lē)	161	40.55N	17.17E
Monóvar, Spain (mō-nō′vär)	159	38.26N	0.50W
Monreale, Italy (mōn-rā-ä′lä)	160	38.04N	13.15E
Monroe, Ga., U.S. (mŭn-rō′)	114	33.47N	83.43W
Monroe, La., U.S.	97	32.30N	92.06W
Monroe, Mi., U.S.	98	41.55N	83.25W
Monroe, N.Y., U.S.	100a	41.19N	74.11W
Monroe, N.C., U.S.	115	34.58N	80.34W
Monroe, Ut., U.S.	109	38.35N	112.10W
Monroe, Wa., U.S.	106a	47.52N	121.58W
Monroe, Wi., U.S.	103	42.35N	89.40W
Monroe, Lake, l., Fl., U.S.	115	28.50N	81.15W
Monroe City, Mo., U.S.	111	39.38N	91.41W
Monroeville, Al., U.S. (mŭn-rō′vĭl)	114	31.33N	87.19W
Monrovia, Lib.	210	6.18N	10.47W
Monrovia, Ca., U.S. (mŏn-rō′vĭ-ȧ)	107a	34.09N	118.00W
Mons, Bel. (môN′)	147	50.29N	3.55E
Monson, Me., U.S. (mŏn′sŭn)	92	45.17N	69.28W
Mönsterås, Swe. (mŭn′stĕr-ōs)	152	57.04N	16.24E
Montagne Tremblant Provincial Park, rec., Can.	97	46.30N	75.51W
Montague, Can. (mŏn′tȧ-gū)	93	46.10N	62.39W
Montague, Mi., U.S.	98	43.30N	86.25W
Montague, i., Ak., U.S.	95	60.10N	147.00W
Montalbán, Ven. (mōnt-äl-bän)	131b	10.14N	68.19W
Montalbancito, Ven.	234a	10.28N	66.59W
Montalegre, Port. (mōn-tä-lă′grĕ)	158	41.49N	7.48W
Montana, state, U.S. (mŏn-tăn′ȧ)	96	47.10N	111.50W
Montánchez, Spain (mōn-tän′chāth)	158	39.18N	6.09W
Montara, Ca., U.S.	231b	37.33N	122.31W
Montargis, Fr. (môN-tȧr-zhē′)	147	47.59N	2.42E
Montataire, Fr. (môN-tȧ-târ)	157b	49.15N	2.26E
Montauban, Fr. (môN-tō-bäN′)	147	44.01N	1.22E
Montauk, N.Y., U.S.	99	41.03N	71.57W
Montauk Point, c., N.Y., U.S. (mŏn-tôk′)	99	41.05N	71.55W
Montbanch, Spain (mōnt-bän′ch)	159	41.20N	1.08E
Montbard, Fr. (môN-bȧr′)	156	47.40N	4.19E
Montbéliard, Fr. (môN-bā-lyȧr′)	157	47.32N	6.45E
Mont Belvieu, Tx., U.S. (mŏnt bĕl′vū)	113a	29.51N	94.53W
Montbrison, Fr. (môN-brē-zôN′)	156	45.38N	4.06E
Montceau, Fr. (môN-sō′)	156	46.39N	4.22E
Montclair, Ca., U.S.	232	34.06N	117.41W
Montclair, N.J., U.S. (mŏnt-klâr′)	100a	40.49N	74.13W
Mont-de-Marsan, Fr. (môN-dē-mȧr-säN′)	147	43.54N	0.32W
Montdidier, Fr. (môN-dē-dyā′)	156	49.42N	2.33E
Monte, Arg. (mō′n-tĕ)	129c	35.25S	58.49W
Monteagudo, Bol. (mōn′tȧ-ä-gōō′dhō)	130	19.49S	63.48W
Montebello, Can.	83c	45.40N	74.56W
Montebello, Ca., U.S. (mŏn-tē-bĕl′ō)	107a	34.01N	118.06W
Monte Bello Islands, is., Austl.	202	20.30S	114.10E
Monte Caseros, Arg. (mō′n-tĕ-kä-sĕ′rōs)	132	30.16S	57.39W
Monte Chingolo, neigh., Arg.	233d	34.45S	58.20W
Montecillos, Cordillera de, mts., Hond.	120	14.19N	87.52W
Monte Cristi, Dom. Rep. (mō′n-tĕ-krē′s-tē)	123	19.50N	71.40W
Montecristo, Isola di, i., Italy (mōn′tȧ-krēs′tō)	160	42.20N	10.19E
Monte Escobedo, Mex. (mōn′tā ĕs-kō-bā′dhō)	118	22.18N	103.34W
Monteforte Irpino, Italy (mōn-tĕ-fô′r-tĕ ē′r-pē′nō)	159c	40.39N	14.42E
Montefrío, Spain (mōn-tȧ-frē′ō)	158	37.20N	4.02W
Montego Bay, Jam. (mŏn-tē′gō)	117	18.30N	77.55W
Montelavar, Port. (mōn-tĕ-lȧ-vär′)	159b	38.51N	9.20W
Montélimar, Fr. (môN-tā-lē-mär′)	147	44.33N	4.47E
Montellano, Spain (mōn-tȧ-lyä′nō)	158	37.00N	5.34W
Montello, Wi., U.S. (mŏn-tĕl′ō)	103	43.47N	89.20W
Montemorelos, Mex. (mōn′tȧ-mō-rā′lōs)	116	25.14N	99.50W
Montemor-o-Novo, Port. (mōN-tĕ-môr′ō-nō′vō)	158	38.39N	8.11W
Montenegro see Crna Gora, state, Yugo.	161	42.55N	18.52E
Montenegro, reg., Moz.	217	13.07S	39.00E
Montepulciano, Italy (mōn′tȧ-pōōl-chä′nō)	160	43.05N	11.48E
Montereau-faut-Yonne, Fr. (môN-t′rō′fō-yōn′)	156	48.24N	2.57E
Monterey, Ca., U.S. (mŏn-tĕ-rā′)	96	36.36N	121.53W
Monterey, Tn., U.S.	114	36.06N	85.15W
Monterey Bay, b., Ca., U.S.	96	36.48N	122.01W
Monterey Park, Ca., U.S.	107a	34.04N	118.08W
Montería, Col. (mōn-tā-rā′ä)	130	8.47N	75.57W
Monteros, Arg. (mōn-tĕ′rōs)	132	27.14S	65.29W
Monterotondo, Italy (mōn-tĕ-rō-tô′n-dō)	159d	42.03N	12.39E
Monterrey, Mex. (mōn-tĕr-rā′)	116	25.43N	100.19W
Montesano, Wa., U.S. (mŏn-tē-sä′nō)	104	46.59N	123.35W
Monte Sant'Angelo, Italy (mô′n-tĕ sän ä′n-gzhĕ-lō)	149	41.43N	15.59E
Montes Claros, Braz. (mōn-tēs-klä′rōs)	131	16.44S	43.41W
Montespaccato, neigh., Italy	239c	41.54N	12.23E
Montevallo, Al., U.S. (mōn-tē-väl′ō)	114	33.05N	86.49W
Montevarchi, Italy (mōn-tȧ-vär′kē)	160	43.30N	11.45E
Monteverde Nuovo, neigh., Italy	239c	41.51N	12.27E
Montevideo, Mn., U.S. (mŏn′tȧ-vē-dhā′ō)	102	44.56N	95.42W
Montevideo, Ur. (mōn′tȧ-vē-dhā′ō)	132	34.50S	56.10W
Monte Vista, Co., U.S. (mŏn′tē vĭs′tȧ)	109	37.35N	106.10W
Montezuma, Ga., U.S. (mŏn-tē-zōō′mȧ)	114	32.17N	84.00W
Montezuma Castle National Monument, rec., Az., U.S.	109	34.38N	111.50W
Montfermeil, Fr.	237c	48.54N	2.34E
Montflorit, Spain	238e	41.29N	2.08E
Montfoort, Neth.	145a	52.02N	4.56E
Montfor-l'Amaury, Fr. (môN-fôr′lä-mō-rē′)	157b	48.47N	1.49E
Montfort, Fr. (môn-fôr)	156	48.09N	1.58W
Montgeron, Fr.	237c	48.42N	2.27E
Montgomery, Al., U.S. (mŏnt-gŭm′ēr-ĭ)	97	32.23N	86.17W
Montgomery, W.V., U.S.	98	38.10N	81.25W
Montgomery City, Mo., U.S.	111	38.58N	91.29W
Montgomery Knolls, Md., U.S.	229c	39.14N	76.48W
Monticello, Ar., U.S. (mŏn-tĭ-sĕl′ō)	111	33.38N	91.47W
Monticello, Fl., U.S.	114	30.32N	83.53W
Monticello, Ga., U.S.	114	33.00N	83.11W
Monticello, Il., U.S.	98	40.05N	88.35W
Monticello, In., U.S.	98	40.40N	86.50W
Monticello, Ia., U.S.	103	42.14N	91.13W
Monticello, Ky., U.S.	114	36.47N	84.50W
Monticello, Me., U.S.	92	46.19N	67.53W
Monticello, Mn., U.S.	103	45.18N	93.48W
Monticello, N.Y., U.S.	99	41.35N	74.40W
Monticello, Ut., U.S.	109	37.55N	109.25W
Montigny-le-Bretonneux, Fr.	237c	48.46N	2.02E
Montigny-lés-Cormeilles, Fr.	237c	48.59N	2.12E
Montijo, Port. (mōn-tē′zhō)	159b	38.42N	8.58W
Montijo, Spain (mōn-tē′hō)	158	38.55N	6.35W
Montijo, Bahía, b., Pan. (bä-ē′ä mōn-tē′hō)	117	7.36N	81.11W
Mont-Joli, Can. (môN zhō-lē′)	85	48.35N	68.11W
Montjuich, Castillo de, hist., Spain	238e	41.22N	2.10E
Montluçon, Fr. (môN-lü-sôN′)	147	46.20N	2.35E
Montmagny, Can. (môN-mȧn-yē′)	91	46.59N	70.33W
Montmagny, Fr.	237c	48.58N	2.21E
Montmartre, neigh., Fr.	237c	48.53N	2.21E
Montmorency, Austl.	243b	37.43S	145.07E
Montmorency, Fr. (môN′mō-räN-sē′)	157b	48.59N	2.19E
Montmorency, r., Can. (mŏnt-mō-rĕn′sĭ)	83b	47.03N	71.10W
Montmorillon, Fr. (môN′mō-rē-yôN′)	156	46.26N	0.50E
Montone, r., Italy (mōn-tō′nĕ)	160	44.03N	11.45E
Montoro, Spain (mōn-tō′rō)	158	38.01N	4.22W
Montpelier, Id., U.S.	105	42.19N	111.19W
Montpelier, In., U.S. (mŏnt-pēl′yēr)	98	40.35N	85.20W
Montpelier, Oh., U.S.	98	41.35N	84.35W
Montpelier, Vt., U.S.	97	44.20N	72.35W
Montpellier, Fr. (môN-pĕ-lyā′)	147	43.38N	3.53E
Montréal, Can. (mŏn-trē-ôl′)	85	45.30N	73.35W
Montreal, r., Can.	90	47.15N	84.20W
Montreal, r., Can.	91	47.50N	80.30W
Montreal Lake, l., Can.	88	54.20N	105.40W
Montréal-Nord, Can.	83a	45.36N	73.38W
Montréal-Ouest, Can.	227b	45.27N	73.39W
Montreuil, Fr.	157b	48.52N	2.27E
Montreux, Switz. (môN-trû′)	154	46.26N	6.52E
Montrose, Austl.	243b	37.49S	145.21E
Montrose, Scot., U.K.	150	56.45N	2.25W
Montrose, Ca., U.S. (mŏnt-rōz)	107a	34.13N	118.13W
Montrose, Co., U.S. (mŏn-trōz′)	109	38.30N	107.55W
Montrose, Oh., U.S.	101d	41.08N	81.38W
Montrose, Pa., U.S. (mŏnt-rōz′)	99	41.50N	75.50W
Montrose Hill, Pa., U.S.	230b	40.30N	79.51W
Montrouge, Fr.	157b	48.49N	2.19E
Mont-Royal, Can.	83a	47.31N	73.39W
Monts, Pointe des, c., Can. (pwănt′ dā môN′)	92	49.19N	67.22W
Mont Saint Martin, Fr. (môN săN mär-tăN′)	157	49.34N	6.13E
Montserrat, dep., N.A. (mŏnt-sĕ-răt′)	117	16.48N	63.15W
Montvale, N.J., U.S. (mŏnt-văl′)	100a	41.02N	74.01W
Monywa, Myanmar (mŏn′yōō-wȧ)	183	22.02N	95.16E
Monza, Italy (mōn′tsä)	160	45.34N	9.17E
Monzón, Spain (mōn-thōn′)	159	41.54N	0.09E
Moóca, neigh., Braz.	234d	23.33S	46.35W
Moody, Tx., U.S. (mōō′dĭ)	113	31.18N	97.20W
Mooi, r., S. Afr.	213c	29.00S	30.15E
Mooi, r., S. Afr. (mōō′ĭ)	218d	26.34S	27.03E
Mooirivier, S. Afr.	213c	29.14S	29.59E
Moolap, Austl.	201a	38.11S	144.26E
Moonachie, N.J., U.S.	228	40.50N	74.03W
Moonta, Austl. (mōōn′tȧ)	202	34.05S	137.42E
Moora, Austl. (môr′ȧ)	202	30.35S	116.12E
Moorabbin, Austl.	201a	37.56S	145.02E
Moore, l., Austl. (mōr)	202	29.50S	118.12E
Moorebank, Austl.	243a	33.56S	150.56E
Moorenweis, Ger. (mō′rĕn-vīz)	145d	48.10N	11.05E
Moore Reservoir, res., Vt., U.S.	99	44.20N	72.10W
Moorestown, N.J., U.S. (mōrz′toun)	100f	39.58N	74.56W
Mooresville, In., U.S. (mōrz′vĭl)	101g	39.37N	86.22W
Mooresville, N.C., U.S.	115	35.34N	80.48W
Moorhead, Mn., U.S. (mōr′hĕd)	102	46.52N	96.44W
Moorhead, Ms., U.S.	114	33.25N	90.30W
Mooroolbark, Austl.	243b	37.47S	145.19E
Moorside, Eng., U.K.	237b	53.34N	2.04W
Moose, r., Can.	85	51.01N	80.42W
Moose Creek, Can.	83c	45.16N	74.58W
Moosehead, Me., U.S. (mōōs′hĕd)	92	45.37N	69.15W
Moose Island, i., Can.	89	51.50N	97.09W
Moose Jaw, Can. (mōōs jô)	84	50.23N	105.32W
Moose Jaw, r., Can.	88	50.34N	105.17W
Moose Lake, Can.	89	53.40N	100.28W
Moose Mountain, mtn., Can.	89	49.45N	102.37W
Moose Mountain Creek, r., Can.	89	49.12N	102.10W
Moosilauke, mtn., N.H., U.S. (mōō-sĭ-lȧ′kē)	99	44.00N	71.50W
Moosinning, Ger. (mō′zē-nĕng)	145d	48.17N	11.51E
Moosomin, Can. (mōō′sō-mĭn)	89	50.07N	101.40W
Moosonee, Can. (mōō′sō-nē)	85	51.20N	80.44W
Mopti, Mali (mŏp′tē)	210	14.30N	4.12W
Moquegua, Peru (mō-kā′gwä)	130	17.15S	70.54W
Mór, Hung. (mōr)	155	47.25N	18.14E
Mora, India	187b	18.54N	72.56E
Mora, Spain (mō-rä)	158	39.42N	3.45W
Mora, Swe. (mō′rä)	152	61.00N	14.29E
Mora, Mn., U.S. (mō′rȧ)	103	45.52N	93.18W
Mora, N.M., U.S.	110	35.58N	105.17W
Morādābād, India (mō-rä-dä-bäd′)	183	28.57N	78.48E
Morales, Guat. (mō-rä′lĕs)	120	15.29N	88.46W
Moramanga, Madag. (mō-rä-mäŋ′gä)	213	18.48S	48.09E
Morangis, Fr.	237c	48.42N	2.20E
Morant Point, c., Jam. (mō-rănt′)	122	17.55N	76.10W
Morata de Tajuña, Spain (mō-rä′tä dā tä-hōō′nyä)	159a	40.14N	3.27W
Moratuwa, Sri L.	187	6.35N	79.59E
Morava (Moravia), hist. reg., Czech Rep.	154	49.21N	16.57E
Morava, r., Eur.	147	49.00N	17.30E
Moravia see Morava, hist. reg., Czech Rep.	154	49.21N	16.57E
Morawhanna, Guy. (mō-rȧ-hwä′nȧ)	131	8.12N	59.33W
Moray Firth, b., Scot., U.K. (mŭr′ā)	142	57.41N	3.55W
Mörbylånga, Swe. (mûr′bü-lôŋ′gȧ)	152	56.32N	16.23E
Morden, Can. (môr′dĕn)	84	49.11N	98.05W
Mordialloc, Austl. (môr-dĭ-ăl′ŏk)	201a	38.00S	145.05E
Mordvinia, state, Russia	166	54.18N	43.50E
More, Ben, mtn., Scot., U.K. (bĕn môr)	150	58.09N	5.01W
Moreau, r., S.D., U.S. (mō-rō′)	102	45.13N	102.22W
Moree, Austl. (mō′rē)	203	29.20S	149.50E
Morehead, Ky., U.S.	98	38.10N	83.25W
Morehead City, N.C., U.S. (mōr′hĕd)	115	34.43N	76.43W
Morehouse, Mo., U.S. (mōr′hous)	111	36.49N	89.41W
Morelia, Mex. (mō-rā′lyä)	116	19.43N	101.12W
Morella, Spain (mō-rāl′yä)	159	40.38N	0.07W
Morelos, Mex.	112	28.24N	100.51W
Morelos, Mex. (mō-rā′lōs)	118	22.46N	102.36W
Morelos, Mex.	119a	19.41N	99.29W
Morelos, neigh., Mex.	233a	19.27N	99.07W
Morelos, r., Mex.	112	25.27N	99.35W
Morena, Sierra, mtn., Ca., U.S. (syĕr′rä mō-rā′nä)	106b	37.24N	122.19W
Morena, Sierra, mts., Spain (syĕr′rä mō-rā′nä)	142	38.15N	5.45W
Morenci, Az., U.S. (mō-rĕn′sĭ)	109	33.05N	109.25W
Morenci, Mi., U.S.	98	41.50N	84.50W
Moreno, Arg. (mō-rĕ′nō)	132a	34.39S	58.47W
Moreno, Ca., U.S.	107a	33.55N	117.09W
Mores, i., Bah. (mōrz)	122	26.20N	77.35W

ăt; finăl; rāte; senāte; ärm; åsk; sofȧ; fâre; ch-choose; dh-as th in other; bē; ēvent; bĕt; recĕnt; cratēr; g-gō; gh-guttural g; bĭt; ĭ-short neutral; rīde; κ-guttural k as ch in German ich;

PRONOUNCING INDEX

Moresby–Mullins 321

PLACE (Pronunciation)	PAGE	Lat. °′	Long. °′
Moresby, i., Can. (mōrz′bĭ)	106d	48.43N	123.15W
Moresby Island, i., Can.	84	52.50N	131.55W
Moreton, Eng., U.K.	237a	53.24N	3.07W
Moreton, i., Austl. (môr′tŭn)	204	26.53S	152.42E
Moreton Bay, b., Austl. (môr′tŭn)	204	27.12S	153.10E
Morewood, Can. (mōr′wo̅o̅d)	83c	45.11N	75.17W
Morgan, Mt., U.S. (môr′găn)	105	48.55N	107.56W
Morgan, Ut., U.S.	105	41.04N	111.42W
Morgan City, La., U.S.	113	29.41N	91.11W
Morganfield, Ky., U.S. (môr′găn-fēld)	98	37.40N	87.55W
Morgan's Bay, S. Afr.	213c	32.42S	28.19E
Morganton, N.C., U.S. (môr′găn-tŭn)	115	35.44N	81.42W
Morgantown, W.V., U.S. (môr′găn-toun)	99	39.40N	79.55W
Morga Range, mts., Afg.	183a	34.02N	70.38E
Morgenzon, S. Afr. (môr′gănt-sŏn)	218d	26.44S	29.39E
Moriac, Austl.	201a	38.15S	144.20E
Morice Lake, l., Can.	86	54.00N	127.37W
Moriguchi, Japan (mō′rė-go͞o′chė)	195b	34.44N	135.34E
Morinville, Can. (mō′rĭn-vĭl)	83g	53.48N	113.39W
Morioka, Japan (mō′rė-ō′kȧ)	189	39.40N	141.21E
Morivione, neigh., Italy	238c	45.26N	9.12E
Morkoka, r., Russia (mȯr-kô′kȧ)	171	65.35N	111.00E
Morlaix, Fr. (mŏr-lĕ′)	147	48.36N	3.48W
Morley, Can. (mŏr′lė)	83e	51.10N	114.51W
Morley Green, Eng., U.K.	237b	53.20N	2.16W
Mormant, Fr.	157b	48.35N	2.54E
Morne Gimie, St. Luc. (mȯrn′ zhė-mē′)	121b	13.53N	61.03W
Morningside, Md., U.S.	229d	38.50N	76.53W
Mornington, Austl.	201a	38.13S	145.02E
Morobe, Pap. N. Gui.	197	8.03S	147.45E
Morocco, nation, Afr. (mȯ-rŏk′ō)	210	32.00N	7.00W
Morogoro, Tan. (mō-rȯ-gō′rō)	213	6.49S	37.40E
Moroleón, Mex. (mȯ-rō-lā-ōn′)	118	20.07N	101.15W
Morombe, Madag. (mo͞o-ro͞om′bā)	213	21.39S	43.34E
Morón, Arg. (mo-rŏ′n)	129c	34.39S	58.37W
Morón, Cuba (mȯ-rōn′)	122	22.05N	78.35W
Morón, Ven. (mȯ-rŏ′n)	131b	10.29N	68.11W
Morondava, Madag. (mȯ-rōn-dȧ′vȧ)	213	20.17S	44.18E
Morón de la Frontera, Spain (mȯ-rōn′dā läf rȯn-tā′rä)	158	37.08N	5.20W
Morongo Indian Reservation, I.R., Ca., U.S. (mō-rôŋ′gō)	108	33.54N	116.47W
Moroni, Com.	213	11.41S	43.16E
Moroni, Ut., U.S. (mȯ-rō′nĭ)	109	39.30N	111.40W
Morotai, i., Indon. (mō-rȯ-tä′ė)	197	2.12N	128.30E
Moroto, Ug.	217	2.32N	34.39E
Morozovsk, Russia	167	48.20N	41.50E
Morrill, Ne., U.S. (mŏr′ĭl)	102	41.59N	103.54W
Morrilton, Ar., U.S. (mŏr′ĭl-tŭn)	111	35.09N	92.42W
Morrinhos, Braz. (mȯ-rēn′yōzh)	131	17.45S	48.56W
Morris, Can. (mŏr′ĭs)	84	49.21N	97.22W
Morris, Il., U.S.	98	41.20N	88.25W
Morris, Mn., U.S.	102	45.35N	95.53W
Morris, r., Can.	89	49.30N	97.30W
Morrison, Il., U.S. (mŏr′ĭ-sŭn)	103	41.48N	89.58W
Morris Reservoir, res., Ca., U.S.	107a	34.11N	117.49W
Morristown, N.J., U.S. (mŏr′rĭs-toun)	100a	40.48N	74.29W
Morristown, Tn., U.S.	114	36.10N	83.18W
Morrisville, Pa., U.S. (mŏr′ĭs-vĭl)	100f	40.12N	74.46W
Morro, Castillo del, hist., Cuba	233b	23.09N	82.21W
Morro do Chapéu, Braz. (mȯr-ō dȯ-shä-pĕ′o͞o)	131	11.34S	41.03W
Morrow, Oh., U.S. (mŏr′ō)	101f	39.21N	84.07W
Mors, i., Den.	152	56.46N	8.38E
Mörsenbroich, neigh., Ger.	236	51.15N	6.48E
Morshansk, Russia (môr-shȧnsk′)	166	53.25N	41.35E
Mortara, Italy (mȯr-tä′rä)	160	45.13N	8.47E
Morteros, Arg. (mȯr-tĕ′tȯs)	132	30.47S	62.00W
Mortes, Rio das, r., Braz. (rēȯ-däs-mô′r-tĕs)	129a	21.04S	44.29W
Mortlake, Austl.	243a	33.51S	151.07E
Mortlake, neigh., Eng., U.K.	235	51.28N	0.16W
Morton, Pa., U.S.	229b	39.55N	75.20W
Morton Grove, Il., U.S.	231a	42.02N	87.47W
Morton Indian Reservation, I.R., Mn., U.S. (mŏr′tŭn)	103	44.35N	94.48W
Mortsel, Bel. (mȯr-sĕl′)	145a	51.10N	4.28E
Morvan, mts., Fr. (mōr-väN′)	156	47.11N	4.10E
Morzhovets, i., Russia (mȯr′zhô-vyĕts′)	166	66.40N	42.30E
Mosal'sk, Russia (mō-zȧlsk′)	162	54.27N	34.57E
Moscavide, Port.	159b	38.47N	9.06W
Moscow (Moskva), Russia	164	55.45N	37.37E
Moscow, Id., U.S. (mŏs′kō)	96	46.44N	116.57W
Mosel (Moselle), r., Eur. (mō′sĕl) (mȯ-zĕl)	154	49.49N	7.00E
Moses, r., S. Afr.	218d	25.17S	29.04E
Moses Lake, Wa., U.S.	104	47.08N	119.15W
Moses Lake, l., Wa., U.S. (mō′zĕz)	104	47.09N	119.30W
Moshchnyy, is., Russia (môsh′chnĭ)	153	59.56N	28.07E
Moshi, Tan. (mō′shė)	213	3.21S	37.20E
Mosjøen, Nor.	146	65.50N	13.10E
Moskháton, Grc.	239d	37.57N	23.41E
Moskva *see* Moscow, Russia	164	55.45N	37.37E
Moskva, prov., Russia	162	55.38N	36.48E
Moskva, r., Russia	166	55.30N	37.05E
Mosman, Austl.	243a	33.49S	151.14E
Mosonmagyaróvár, Hung.	155	47.51N	17.16E
Mosquitos, Costa de, cst., Nic. (kȯs-tä-dĕ-mŏs-kē′tō)	121	12.05N	83.49W
Mosquitos, Gulfo de los, b., Pan. (go͞o′l-fô-dĕ-lȯs-mŏs-kē′tōs)	117	9.17N	80.59W
Moss, Nor. (môs)	146	59.29N	10.39E
Moss Bank, Eng., U.K.	237a	53.29N	2.44W
Moss Beach, Ca., U.S. (môs bēch)	106b	37.32N	122.31W
Moss Crest, mtn., Va., U.S.	229d	38.55N	77.15W
Mosselbaai, S. Afr. (mô′sul bā)	212	34.06S	22.23E
Mossendjo, Congo	216	2.57S	12.44E
Mossley, Eng., U.K. (môs′lĭ)	144a	53.31N	2.02W
Mossley Hill, neigh., Eng., U.K.	237a	53.23N	2.55W
Moss Point, Ms., U.S. (môs)	114	30.25N	88.32W
Most, Czech Rep. (mȯst)	154	50.32N	13.37E
Mostar, Bos. (môs′tär)	149	43.20N	17.51E
Móstoles, Spain (mȯs-tō′lās)	159a	40.19N	3.52W
Mostoos Hills, hills, Can. (mŏs′to͞os)	88	54.50N	108.45W
Mosvatnet, l., Nor.	152	59.55N	7.50E
Motagua, r., N.A. (mȯ-tä′gwä)	120	15.29N	88.39W
Motala, Swe. (mȯ-tô′lä)	152	58.34N	15.00E
Motherwell, Scot., U.K. (mŭdh′ẽr-wĕl)	146	55.45N	4.05W
Motril, Spain (mȯ-trēl′)	148	36.44N	3.32W
Mottingham, neigh., Eng., U.K.	235	51.26N	0.03E
Motul, Mex. (mō-to͞o′l)	120a	21.07N	89.14W
Mouaskar, Alg.	210	35.25N	0.08E
Mouchoir Bank, bk. (mo͞o-shwȧr′)	123	21.35N	70.40W
Mouchoir Passage, strt., T./C. Is.	123	21.05N	71.05W
Moudjéria, Maur.	214	17.53N	12.20W
Mouila, Gabon	216	1.52S	11.01E
Mouille Point, c., S. Afr.	212a	33.54S	18.19E
Moulins, Fr. (mo͞o-lăN′)	147	46.34N	3.19E
Moulouya, Oued, r., Mor. (mo͞o-lo͞o′yȧ)	210	34.00N	4.00W
Moultrie, Ga., U.S. (mōl′trĭ)	114	31.10N	83.48W
Moultrie, Lake, l., S.C., U.S.	115	33.12N	80.00W
Mound City, Il., U.S.	111	37.06N	89.13W
Mound City, Mo., U.S.	111	40.08N	95.13W
Moundou, Chad	215	8.34N	16.05E
Moundsville, W.V., U.S. (moundz′vĭl)	98	39.50N	80.50W
Mount, Cape, c., Lib.	214	6.47N	11.20W
Mountain Brook, Al., U.S. (moun′tĭn brȯȯk)	100h	33.30N	86.45W
Mountain Creek Lake, l., Tx., U.S.	107c	32.43N	97.03W
Mountain Grove, Mo., U.S. (grōv)	111	37.07N	92.16W
Mountain Home, Id., U.S. (hōm)	104	43.08N	115.43W
Mountain Park, Can. (pärk)	84	52.55N	117.14W
Mountain View, Ca., U.S. (moun′tĭn vū)	106b	37.25N	122.07W
Mountain View, Mo., U.S.	111	36.59N	91.46W
Mount Airy, N.C., U.S. (âr′ĭ)	115	36.28N	80.37W
Mount Ayliff, S. Afr. (ā′lĭf)	213c	30.48S	29.24E
Mount Ayr, Ia., U.S. (âr)	103	40.43N	94.06W
Mount Baldy, Ca., U.S.	232	34.14N	117.40W
Mount Carmel, Il., U.S. (kär′mĕl)	98	38.25N	87.45W
Mount Carmel, Pa., U.S.	99	40.50N	76.25W
Mount Carooll, Il., U.S.	103	42.05N	89.55W
Mount Clemens, Mi., U.S. (klĕm′ĕnz)	101b	42.36N	82.52W
Mount Dennis, neigh., Can.	227c	43.42N	79.30W
Mount Desert, i., Me., U.S. (dė-zûrt′)	92	44.15N	68.08W
Mount Dora, Fl., U.S. (dō′rȧ)	115a	28.45N	81.38W
Mount Druitt, Austl.	243a	33.46S	150.49E
Mount Duneed, Austl.	201a	38.15S	144.20E
Mount Eliza, Austl.	201a	38.11S	145.05E
Mount Ephraim, N.J., U.S.	229b	39.53N	75.06W
Mount Fletcher, S. Afr. (flĕ′chẽr)	213c	30.42S	28.32E
Mount Forest, Can. (fŏr′ĕst)	91	44.00N	80.45W
Mount Frere, S. Afr. (frâr′)	213c	30.54S	29.02E
Mount Gambier, Austl. (găm′bēr)	202	37.30S	140.53E
Mount Gilead, Oh., U.S. (gĭl′ėăd)	98	40.30N	82.50W
Mount Greenwood, neigh., Il., U.S.	231a	41.42N	87.43W
Mount Healthy, Oh., U.S. (hĕlth′ė)	101f	39.14N	84.32W
Mount Hebron, Md., U.S.	229c	39.18N	76.50W
Mount Holly, N.J., U.S. (hŏl′ĭ)	100f	39.59N	74.47W
Mount Hope, Can.	83d	43.09N	79.55W
Mount Hope, N.J., U.S. (hōp)	100a	40.55N	74.32W
Mount Hope, W.V., U.S.	98	37.55N	81.10W
Mount Isa, Austl. (ī′zȧ)	202	21.00S	139.45E
Mount Kisco, N.Y., U.S. (kĭs′ko)	100a	41.12N	73.44W
Mountlake Terrace, Wa., U.S. (mount lāk tĕr′ĭs)	106a	47.48N	122.19W
Mount Lebanon, Pa., U.S. (lĕb′ȧ-nŭn)	101e	40.22N	80.03W
Mount Magnet, Austl. (măg-nĕt)	202	28.00S	118.00E
Mount Martha, Austl.	201a	38.17S	145.01E
Mount Morgan, Austl. (môr-găn)	203	23.42S	150.45E
Mount Moriac, Austl.	201a	38.13S	144.12E
Mount Morris, Mi., U.S. (mĭr′ĭs)	98	43.10N	83.45W
Mount Morris, N.Y., U.S.	99	42.45N	77.50W
Mountnessing, Eng., U.K.	235	51.39N	0.21E
Mount Nimba National Park, rec., C. Iv.	214	7.35N	8.10W
Mount Olive, N.C., U.S. (ŏl′ĭv)	115	35.11N	78.05W
Mount Oliver, Pa., U.S.	230b	40.28N	79.59W
Mount Peale, Ut., U.S.	109	38.26N	109.16W
Mount Pleasant, Ia., U.S. (plĕz′ănnt)	103	40.59N	91.34W
Mount Pleasant, Mi., U.S.	98	43.35N	84.45W
Mount Pleasant, S.C., U.S.	115	32.46N	79.51W
Mount Pleasant, Tn., U.S.	114	35.31N	87.12W
Mount Pleasant, Tx., U.S.	113	33.10N	94.56W
Mount Pleasant, Ut., U.S.	109	39.35N	111.20W
Mount Pritchard, Austl.	243a	33.54S	150.54E
Mount Prospect, Il., U.S. (prŏs′pĕkt)	101a	42.03N	87.56W
Mount Rainier, Md., U.S.	229d	38.56N	76.58W
Mount Rainier National Park, rec., Wa., U.S. (rȧ-nēr′)	96	46.47N	121.17W
Mount Revelstoke National Park, Can. (rĕv′ĕl-stōk)	84	51.22N	120.15W
Mount Savage, Md., U.S. (săv′ȧj)	99	39.45N	78.55W
Mount Shasta, Ca., U.S. (shăs′tȧ)	104	41.18N	122.17W
Mount Sterling, Il., U.S. (stûr′lĭng)	111	39.59N	90.44W
Mount Sterling, Ky., U.S.	98	38.05N	84.00W
Mount Stewart, Can. (stū′ărt)	93	46.22N	62.52W
Mount Union, Pa., U.S. (ūn′yŭn)	99	40.25N	77.50W
Mount Vernon, Il., U.S. (vûr′nŭn)	98	38.20N	88.50W
Mount Vernon, In., U.S.	98	37.55N	87.50W
Mount Vernon, Mo., U.S.	111	37.09N	93.48W
Mount Vernon, N.Y., U.S.	100a	40.55N	73.51W
Mount Vernon, Oh., U.S.	98	40.25N	82.30W
Mount Vernon, Pa., U.S.	230b	40.17N	79.48W
Mount Vernon, Va., U.S.	100e	38.43N	77.06W
Mount Vernon, Wa., U.S.	104	48.25N	122.20W
Mount Washington, neigh., Md., U.S.	229c	39.22N	76.40W
Mount Washington Summit, Md., U.S.	229c	39.23N	76.40W
Mount Waverley, Austl.	243b	37.53S	145.08E
Moura, Braz. (mō′rȧ)	131	1.33S	61.38W
Moura, Port.	158	38.08N	7.28W
Mourne Mountains, mts., N. Ire., U.K. (mȯrn)	150	54.10N	6.09W
Moussoro, Chad	215	13.39N	16.29E
Moûtiers, Fr. (mo͞o-tyâr′)	157	45.31N	6.34E
Mowbullan, Mount, mtn., Austl.	204	26.50S	151.34E
Moyahua, Mex. (mȯ-yä′wä)	118	21.16N	103.10W
Moyale, Kenya (mȯ-yä′lä)	211	3.28N	39.04E
Moyamba, S.L. (mȯ-yäm′bä)	210	8.10N	12.26W
Moyen Atlas, mts., Mor.	148	32.49N	5.28W
Moyeuvre-Grande, Fr.	157	49.15N	6.26E
Moyie, r., Id., U.S. (moi′yė)	104	38.50N	116.10W
Moylan, Pa., U.S.	229b	39.54N	75.23W
Moyobamba, Peru (mō-yȯ-bäm′bä)	130	6.12S	76.56W
Moyuta, Guat. (mȯ-ē-o͞o′tä)	120	14.01N	90.05W
Moyyero, r., Russia	170	67.15N	104.10E
Moyynqūm, des., Kaz.	169	44.30N	70.00E
Mozambique, nation, Afr. (mō-zăm-bēk′)	212	20.15S	33.53E
Mozambique Channel, strt., Afr. (mō-zăm-bek′)	213	24.00S	38.00E
Mozdok, Russia (mȯz-dôk′)	167	43.45N	44.35E
Mozhaysk, Russia (mȯ-zhäysk′)	162	55.31N	36.02E
Mozhayskiy, Russia (mȯ-zhȧy′skĭ)	172c	59.42N	30.08E
Mozyr', Bela. (mȯ-zür′)	167	52.03N	29.14E
Mpanda, Tan.	217	6.22S	31.02E
Mpika, Zam.	217	11.54S	31.26E
Mpimbe, Mwi.	217	15.18S	35.04E
Mporokoso, Zam. ('m-pō-rȯ-kō′sō)	212	9.23S	30.05E
Mpwapwa, Tan. ('m-pwä′pwä)	212	6.21S	36.29E
Mqanduli, S. Afr. ('m-kän′do͞o-lė)	213c	31.50S	28.42E
Mrągowo, Pol. (mräŋ′gô-vȯ)	155	53.52N	21.18E
M'Sila, Alg. (m'sē′lȧ)	210	35.47N	4.34E
Msta, r., Russia (m'stȧ′)	166	58.30N	33.00E
Mstislavl', Bela. (m'stē-slävl′)	162	54.01N	31.42E
Mtakataka, Mwi.	217	14.12S	34.32E
Mtamvuna, r., Afr.	213c	30.43S	29.53E
Mtata, r., S. Afr.	213c	31.48S	29.03E
Mtsensk, Russia (m'tsĕnsk)	166	53.17N	36.33E
Mtwara, Tan.	217	10.16S	40.11E
Muar, r., Malay.	181b	2.18N	102.43E
Mubende, Ug.	217	0.35N	31.23E
Mubi, Nig.	215	10.18N	13.20E
Mucacata, Moz.	217	13.20S	39.59E
Much, Ger. (mo͞oK)	157c	50.54N	7.24E
Muchinga Mountains, mts., Zam.	217	12.40S	30.50E
Much Wenlock, Eng., U.K. (mŭch wĕn′lŏk)	144a	52.35N	2.33W
Muckalee Creek, r., Ga., U.S. (mŭk′ă lē)	114	31.55N	84.10W
Mucking, Eng., U.K.	235	51.30N	0.26E
Muckleshoot Indian Reservation, I.R., Wa., U.S. (mŭck′'l-sho͞ot)	106a	47.21N	122.04W
Mucubela, Moz.	217	16.55S	37.52E
Mud, l., Mi., U.S. (mŭd)	103	46.12N	84.32W
Mudan, r., China (mo͞o-dän)	192	45.30N	129.40E
Mudanjiang, China (mo͞o-dän-jyäŋ)	192	44.28N	129.38E
Muddy, r., Nv., U.S. (mŭd′ĭ)	109	36.56N	114.42W
Muddy Boggy Creek, r., Ok., U.S. (mud′ĭ bôg′ĭ)	111	34.42N	96.11W
Muddy Creek, r., Ut., U.S. (mŭd′ĭ)	109	38.45N	111.10W
Mudgee, Austl. (mŭ-jē)	204	32.47S	149.10E
Mudjatik, r., Can.	88	56.23N	107.40W
Mufulira, Zam.	217	12.33S	28.14E
Muğla, Tur. (mo͞og′lä)	182	37.10N	28.20E
Mühileiten, Aus.	239e	48.10N	16.34E
Mühldorf, Ger. (mül-dôrf)	154	48.15N	12.33E
Mühlenbeck, Ger.	238a	52.40N	13.22E
Mühlhausen, Ger. (mül′hou-zĕn)	154	51.13N	10.25E
Muhu, i., Est. (mo͞o′ho͞o)	153	58.41N	22.55E
Muir Woods National Monument, rec., Ca., U.S. (mūr)	108	37.54N	123.22W
Muizenberg, S. Afr. (mwĭz-ĕn-bûrg′)	212a	34.07S	18.28E
Mujāhidpur, neigh., India	240d	28.34N	77.13E
Mukacheve, Ukr.	155	48.25N	22.43E
Mukden *see* Shenyang, China	188	41.45N	123.22E
Mukhtuya, Russia (mȯk-to͞o′yȧ)	165	61.00N	113.00E
Mukilteo, Wa., U.S. (mū-kĭl-tā′ō)	106a	47.57N	122.18W
Muko, Japan (mo͞o′kȯ)	195b	34.57N	135.43E
Muko, r., Japan (mo͞o′kȯ)	195b	34.52N	135.17E
Mukutawa, r., Can.	89	53.10N	97.28W
Mukwonago, Wi., U.S. (mū-kwō-nȧ′gō)	101a	42.52N	88.19W
Mula, Spain (mo͞o′lä)	158	38.05N	1.12W
Mula, Al., U.S. (mŭl′gȧ)	100h	33.33N	86.59W
Mulde, r., Ger. (mȯl′dĕ)	154	50.30N	12.30E
Muleros, Mex. (mo͞o-lā′rōs)	118	23.44N	104.00W
Muleshoe, Tx., U.S.	110	34.13N	102.43W
Mulgrave, Can. (mŭl′grāv)	93	45.37N	61.23W
Mulhacén, mtn., Spain	148	37.04N	3.18W
Mülheim, Ger. (mül′hīm)	157c	51.25N	6.53E
Mulhouse, Fr. (mü-lo͞oz′)	147	47.46N	7.20E
Muling, China (mo͞o-lĭŋ)	192	44.32N	130.18E
Muling, r., China	192	44.40N	130.30E
Mull, Island of, i., Scot., U.K. (mŭl)	150	56.40N	6.19W
Mullan, Id., U.S. (mŭl′ăn)	104	47.26N	115.50W
Müller, Pegunungan, mts., Indon. (mül′ẽr)	196	0.22N	113.05E
Mullingar, Ire. (mŭl-ĭn-gär)	150	53.31N	7.26W
Mullins, S.C., U.S. (mŭl′ĭnz)	115	34.11N	79.13W

ng-sing; ŋ-baŋk; N-nasalized n; nŏd; cŏmmit; ōld; ȯbey; ôrder; oi-boil; fo͞od; ȯ-as oo in foot; ou-out; s-soft; sh-dish; th-thin; pūre; u̇nite; ûrn; stŭd; circŭs; ü-as in French tu; '-indeterminate vowel.

322 Mullins River – Nanga Parbat

PLACE (Pronunciation)	PAGE	Lat. °′	Long. °′
Mullins River, Belize	120a	17.08N	88.18W
Multān, Pak. (mo̍-tän′)	183	30.17N	71.13E
Multnomah Channel, strt., Or., U.S. (mŭl nō mȧ)	106c	45.41N	122.53W
Mulumbe, Monts, mts., Zaire	217	8.47S	27.20E
Mulvane, Ks., U.S. (mŭl-vān′)	111	37.30N	97.13W
Mumbwa, Zam. (mo̍m′bwä)	212	14.59S	27.04E
Mumias, Kenya	217	0.20N	34.29E
Muna, Mex. (mo͞o′nå)	120a	20.28N	89.42W
Münchehofe, Ger.	238a	52.30N	13.40E
München *see* Munich, Ger.	142	48.08N	11.35E
Muncie, In., U.S. (mŭn′sĭ)	97	40.10N	85.30W
Mundelein, Il., U.S. (mŭn-dė-lĭn′)	101a	42.16N	88.00W
Mündelheim, neigh., Ger.	236	51.21N	6.41E
Mundonueva, Pico de, mtn., Col. (pē′kǒ-dě-mo͞o′n-dǒ-nwě′vä)	130a	4.18N	74.12W
Muneco, Cerro, mtn., Mex. (sě′r-rǒ-mo͞o-ně′kō)	119a	19.13N	99.20W
Mungana, Austl. (mŭn-găn′ȧ)	203	17.15S	144.18E
Mungbere, Zaire	217	2.38N	28.30E
Munger, Mn., U.S. (mŭn′gẽr)	107h	46.48N	92.20W
Mungindi, Austl. (mŭn-gĭn′dė)	203	29.00S	148.45E
Munhall, Pa., U.S. (mŭn′hôl)	101e	40.24N	79.53W
Munhango, Ang. (mo̍n-häŋ′gȧ)	212	12.15S	18.55E
Munich, Ger.	142	48.08N	11.35E
Munirka, neigh., India	240d	28.34N	77.10E
Munising, Mi., U.S. (mū′nĭ-sĭng)	103	46.24N	86.41W
Muniz Freire, Braz.	129a	20.29S	41.25W
Munku Sardyk, mtn., Asia (mo̍n′ko̍ sär-dĭk′)	165	51.45N	100.30E
Muñoz, Phil. (mo͞on-nyōth′)	197a	15.44N	120.53E
Munro, neigh., Arg.	233d	34.32S	58.31W
Münster, Ger. (mün′stěr)	147	51.57N	7.38E
Munster, In., U.S. (mŭn′stẽr)	101a	41.34N	87.31W
Munster, hist. reg., Ire. (mŭn-stẽr)	150	52.30N	9.24W
Muntok, Indon. (mo̍n-tŏk′)	196	2.05S	105.11E
Muong Sing, Laos (mo͞o′ông-sĭng′)	196	21.06N	101.17E
Muping, China (mo͞o-pĭŋ)	190	37.23N	121.36E
Muqui, Braz. (mo͞o-ko̍ė)	129a	20.56S	41.20W
Mur, r., Eur. (mo͞or)	147	47.00N	15.00E
Muradiye, Tur. (mo͞o-rä′dė-yě)	167	39.00N	43.40E
Murat, Fr. (mü-rä′)	156	45.05N	2.56E
Murat, r., Tur. (mo͞o-rȧt′)	182	39.00N	42.00E
Murayama, Japan	242a	35.45N	139.23E
Murchison, r., Austl. (mûr′chĭ-sŭn)	202	26.45S	116.15E
Murcia, Spain (mo͞or′thyä)	142	38.00N	1.10W
Murcia, hist. reg., Spain	158	38.35N	1.51W
Murdo, S.D., U.S. (mûr′dǒ)	102	43.53N	100.42W
Mureş, r., Rom. (mo͞o′rěsh)	149	46.02N	21.50E
Muret, Fr. (mü-rě′)	156	43.28N	1.17E
Murfreesboro, Tn., U.S. (mûr′frėz-bŭr-ǒ)	114	35.50N	86.19W
Murgab, Taj.	169	38.10N	73.59E
Murgab, r., Asia (mo͞or-gäb′)	182	37.07N	62.32E
Muriaé, r., Braz.	129a	21.20S	41.40W
Murino, Russia (mo͞o′rĭ-nǒ)	172c	60.03N	30.28E
Müritz, l., Ger. (mür′its)	154	53.20N	12.33E
Murmansk, Russia (mo͞or-mänsk′)	164	69.00N	33.20E
Murom, Russia (mo͞o′rǒm)	164	55.30N	42.00W
Muroran, Japan (mo͞o′rǒ-rȧn)	189	42.21N	141.05E
Muros, Spain (mo͞o′rōs)	158	42.48N	9.00W
Muroto-Zaki, c., Japan (mo͞o′rǒ-tō zä′kė)	194	33.14N	134.12E
Murphy, Mo., U.S. (mŭr′fĭ)	107e	38.29N	90.29W
Murphy, N.C., U.S.	114	35.05N	84.00W
Murphysboro, Il., U.S. (mŭr′fĭz-bŭr-ǒ)	111	37.46N	89.21W
Murray, Ky., U.S. (mŭr′ĭ)	114	36.39N	88.17W
Murray, Ut., U.S.	107b	40.40N	111.53W
Murray, r., Austl.	202	34.20S	140.00E
Murray, r., Can.	87	55.00N	121.00W
Murray, Lake, res., S.C., U.S. (mŭr′í)	115	34.07N	81.18W
Murray Bridge, Austl.	202	35.10S	139.35E
Murray Harbour, Can.	93	46.00N	62.31W
Murray Region, reg., Austl. (mŭ′rē)	203	33.20S	142.30E
Murrumbidgee, r., Austl. (mŭr-ŭm-bĭd′jė)	203	34.30S	145.20E
Murrupula, Moz.	217	15.27S	38.47E
Murshidābād, India (mo̍r′shė-dä-bäd′)	186	24.08N	88.11E
Murska Sobota, Slvn. (mo͞or′skä sǒ′bǒ-tä)	160	46.40N	16.14E
Murtal, Port.	238d	38.42N	9.22W
Muruasigar, mtn., Kenya	217	3.08N	35.02E
Murwāra, India	183	23.54N	80.23E
Murwillumbah, Austl. (mŭr-wĭl′lŭm-bŭ)	204	28.15S	153.30E
Mürz, r., Aus. (mürts)	154	47.30N	15.21E
Mürzzuschlag, Aus. (mürts′tso͞o-shlägh)	154	47.37N	15.41E
Mus, Tur. (mo͞osh)	167	38.55N	41.30E
Musala, mtn., Bul.	161	42.05N	23.24E
Musan, N. Kor. (mo̍′sän)	189	41.11N	129.10E
Musashino, Japan (mo͞o-sä′shē-nō)	195a	35.43N	139.35E
Muscat, Oman (mŭs-kăt′)	182	23.23N	58.30E
Muscat and Oman *see* Oman, nation, Asia	182	20.00N	57.45E
Muscatine, Ia., U.S. (mŭs-kȧ-tēn)	103	41.26N	91.00W
Muscle Shoals, Al., U.S. (mŭs′′l shōlz)	114	34.44N	87.38W
Musgrave Ranges, mts., Austl. (mŭs′grāv)	202	26.15S	131.15E
Mushie, Zaire (mŭsh′ė)	212	3.04S	16.50E
Mushin, Nig.	215	6.32N	3.22E
Musi, r., Indon. (mo͞o′sė)	196	2.40S	103.42E
Musinga, Alto, mtn., Col. (ä′l-tǒ-mo͞o-sė′n-gä)	130a	6.40N	76.13W
Muskego Lake, l., Wi., U.S. (mŭs-kē′gō)	101a	42.53N	88.10W
Muskegon, Mi., U.S. (mŭs-kē′gŭn)	97	43.15N	86.20W
Muskegon, r., Mi., U.S.	98	43.20N	85.55W
Muskegon Heights, Mi., U.S.	98	43.10N	86.20W
Muskingum, r., Oh., U.S. (mŭs-kĭŋ′gŭm)	98	39.45N	81.55W
Muskogee, Ok., U.S. (mŭs-kō′gė)	97	35.44N	95.21W
Muskoka, l., Can. (mŭs-kō′kȧ)	91	45.00N	79.30W
Musoma, Tan.	217	1.30S	33.48E
Mussau Island, i., Pap. N. Gui. (mo͞o-sä′o͞o)	197	1.30S	149.32E
Musselshell, r., Mt., U.S. (mŭs′′l-shěl)	105	46.25N	108.20W
Mussende, Ang.	216	10.32S	16.05E
Mussuma, Ang.	216	14.14S	21.59E
Mustafakemalpaşa, Tur.	149	40.05N	28.30E
Mustang Bayou, Tx., U.S.	113a	29.22N	95.12W
Mustang Creek, r., Tx., U.S. (mŭs′tăng)	110	36.22N	102.46W
Mustang Island, i., Tx., U.S.	113	27.43N	97.00W
Mustique, i., St. Vin. (müs-tēk′)	121b	12.53N	61.03W
Musturud, Egypt	244a	30.08N	31.17E
Mustvee, Est. (mo͞ost′vě-ě)	153	58.50N	26.54E
Musu Dan, c., N. Kor. (mo̍′so̍ dȧn)	189	40.51N	130.00E
Muswellbrook, Austl. (mŭs′wŭnl-bro̍k)	204	32.15S	150.50E
Mutare, Zimb.	212	18.49S	32.39E
Mutombo Mukulu, Zaire (mo͞o-tôm′bō mo͞o-ko͞o′lo͞o)	212	8.12S	23.56E
Mutsu Wan, b., Japan (mo͞ot′so͞o wän)	194	41.20N	140.55E
Mutton Bay, Can. (mŭt′′n)	93	50.48N	59.02W
Mutum, Braz. (mo͞o-to͞o′m)	129a	19.48S	41.24W
Muzaffargarh, Pak.	186	30.09N	71.15E
Muzaffarpur, India	186	26.13N	85.20E
Muzon, Cape, c., Ak., U.S.	86	54.41N	132.44W
Muzquiz, Mex. (mo͞oz′kēz)	112	27.53N	101.31W
Muztagata, mtn., China	188	38.20N	75.28E
Mvomero, Tan.	217	6.20S	37.25E
Mvoti, r., S. Afr.	213c	29.18S	30.52E
Mwali, i., Com.	213	12.15S	43.45E
Mwanza, Tan. (mwän′zä)	212	2.31S	32.54E
Mwaya, Tan. (mwä′yä)	212	9.19S	33.51E
Mwenga, Zaire	217	3.02S	28.26E
Mweru, l., Afr.	212	8.50S	28.50E
Mwingi, Kenya	217	0.56S	38.04E
Myanmar (Burma), nation, Asia	180	21.00N	95.15E
Myingyan, Myanmar (myĭng-yŭn′)	183	21.37N	95.26E
Myitkyina, Myanmar (myĭ′chē-nȧ)	183	25.33N	97.25E
Myjava, Slvk. (mûė′yȧ-vä)	155	48.45N	17.33E
Mykhaylivka, Ukr.	163	47.16N	35.12E
Mykolayiv, Ukr.	164	46.58N	32.02E
Mykolayiv, prov., Ukr.	163	47.27N	31.25E
Mymensingh, Bngl.	183	24.48N	90.28E
Mynämäki, Fin.	153	60.41N	21.58E
Myohyang San, mtn., N. Kor. (myō′hyang)	194	40.00N	126.12E
Mýrdalsjökull, ice., Ice. (mür′däls-yû′ko̍l)	146	63.34N	18.04W
Myrhorod, Ukr.	167	49.56N	33.36E
Myrtle Beach, S.C., U.S. (mûr′t′l)	115	33.42N	78.53W
Myrtle Point, Or., U.S.	104	43.04N	124.08W
Mysen, Nor.	152	59.32N	11.16E
Myshikino, Russia (mėsh′kė-nǒ)	162	57.48N	38.21E
Mysore, India (mī-sōr′)	183	12.31N	76.42E
Mysovka, Russia (mė′ sǒf-kȧ)	153	55.11N	21.17E
Mystic, Ia., U.S. (mĭs′tĭk)	103	40.47N	92.54W
Mytishchi, Russia (mė-tēsh′chi)	172b	55.55N	37.46E
Mziha, Tan.	217	5.54S	37.47E
Mzimba, Mwi. (′m-zĭm′bä)	212	11.52S	33.34E
Mzimkulu, r., Afr.	213c	30.12S	29.57E
Mzimvubu, r., S. Afr.	213c	31.22S	29.20E
Mzuzu, Mwi.	217	11.30S	34.10E

N

PLACE (Pronunciation)	PAGE	Lat. °′	Long. °′
Naab, r., Ger. (näp)	154	49.38N	12.15E
Naaldwijk, Neth.	145a	52.00N	4.11E
Naalehu, Hi., U.S.	94a	19.00N	155.35W
Naantali, Fin. (nän′tȧ-lė)	153	60.29N	22.03E
Nabberu, l., Austl. (năb′ēr-o͞o)	202	26.05S	120.35E
Naberezhnyye Chelny, Russia	164	55.42N	52.19E
Nabeul, Tun. (nā-bûl′)	210	36.34N	10.45E
Nabiswera, Ug.	217	1.28N	32.16E
Naboomspruit, S. Afr.	218d	24.32S	28.43E
Nābulus, W. Bank	181a	32.13N	35.16E
Nacala, Moz. (nă-kȧ′lȧ)	213	14.34S	40.41E
Nacaome, Hond. (nä-kä-ō′må)	120	13.32N	87.28W
Na Cham, Viet. (nä chäm′)	193	22.02N	106.30E
Naches, r., Wa., U.S. (năch′ĕz)	104	46.51N	121.03W
Náchod, Czech Rep. (näk′ǒt)	154	50.25N	16.08E
Nächstebreck, neigh., Ger.	236	51.18N	7.14E
Nacimiento, Lake, res., Ca., U.S. (nȧ-sĭ-myěn′tǒ)	108	35.50N	121.00W
Nacogdoches, Tx., U.S. (năk′ǒ-dō′chěz)	113	31.36N	94.40W
Nadadores, Mex. (nä-dä-dō′rās)	112	27.04N	101.36W
Nadiād, India	186	22.45N	72.51E
Nadir, V.I.U.S.	117c	18.19N	64.53W
Nădlac, Rom.	161	46.09N	20.52E
Nadvirna, Ukr.	155	48.37N	24.35E
Nadym, r., Russia (nȧ′dĭm)	170	64.30N	72.48E
Naestved, Den. (něst′vĭdh)	146	55.14N	11.46E
Nafada, Nig.	215	11.08N	11.20E
Nafishah, Egypt	218c	30.34N	32.15E
Nafūd ad Dahy, des., Sau. Ar.	182	22.15N	44.15E
Nag, Co, l., China	186	31.38N	91.18E
Naga, Phil. (nä′gä)	197	13.37N	123.12E
Naga, i., Japan	195	32.09N	130.16E
Nagahama, Japan (nä′gä-hä′mä)	195	33.32N	132.29E
Nagahama, Japan	195	35.23N	136.16E
Nagaland, India	183	25.47N	94.15E
Nagano, Japan (nä′gä-nǒ)	189	36.42N	138.12E
Nagao, Japan	242b	34.50N	135.43E
Nagaoka, Japan (nä′gȧ-ō′kȧ)	189	37.22N	138.49E
Nagaoka, Japan	195b	34.54N	135.42E
Nāgappattinam, India	183	10.48N	79.51E
Nagarote, Nic. (nä-gä-rô′tě)	120	12.17N	86.35W
Nagasaki, Japan (nä′gȧ-sä′kė)	189	32.48N	129.53E
Nagata, neigh., Japan	242b	34.40N	135.09E
Nagatino, neigh., Russia	239b	55.41N	37.41E
Nagatsuta, neigh., Japan	242a	35.32N	139.30E
Nāgaur, India	186	27.19N	73.41E
Nagaybakskiy, Russia (nȧ-gȧy-bäk′skĭ)	172a	53.33N	59.33E
Nagcarlan, Phil. (näg-kär-län′)	197a	14.07N	121.24E
Nāgercoil, India	187	8.15N	77.29E
Nagorno Karabakh, hist. reg., Azer. (nu-gôr′nŭ-kŭ-rŭ-bäk′)	167	40.10N	46.50E
Nagoya, Japan	189	35.09N	136.53E
Nāgpur, India (näg′po͞or)	183	21.12N	79.09E
Nagua, Dom. Rep. (nȧ′gwä)	123	19.20N	69.40W
Nagykanizsa, Hung. (nôd′y′kô′nė-shô)	149	46.27N	17.00E
Nagykōrōs, Hung. (nôd′y′kŭ-rŭsh)	155	47.02N	19.46E
Nagytarcsa, Hung.	239g	47.32N	19.17E
Naha, Japan (nä′hä)	189	26.02N	127.43E
Nahanni National Park, rec., Can.	84	62.10N	125.15W
Nahant, Ma., U.S. (nȧ-hănt)	93a	42.26N	70.55W
Nahant Bay, b., Ma., U.S.	227a	42.27N	70.55W
Nahariyya, Isr.	181a	33.01N	35.06E
Nahaut, Ma., U.S.	227a	42.25N	70.55W
Nahmer, Ger.	236	51.20N	7.35E
Nahuel Huapi, l., Arg. (nä′ẇl wä′pė)	132	41.00S	71.30W
Nahuizalco, El Sal. (nä-wė-zäl′kō)	120	13.50N	89.43W
Naic, Phil. (nä-ēk)	197a	14.20N	120.46E
Naica, Mex. (nä-ē′kä)	112	27.53N	105.30W
Naiguata, Pico, mtn., Ven. (pē′kǒ)	131b	10.32N	66.44W
Naihāti, India	240a	22.54N	88.25E
Nain, Can. (nīn)	85	56.29N	61.52W
Nā′īn, Iran	185	32.52N	53.05E
Nairn, Scot., U.K. (nârn)	150	57.35N	3.54W
Nairobi, Kenya (nī-rō′bė)	212	1.17S	36.49E
Naivasha, Kenya (nī-vä′shȧ)	212	0.47S	36.29E
Najd, hist. reg., Sau. Ar.	182	25.18N	42.38E
Najin, N. Kor. (nä′jĭn)	189	42.04N	130.35E
Najran, des., Sau. Ar. (nŭj-rän′)	182	17.29N	45.30E
Naju, S. Kor. (nä′jo͞o′)	194	35.02N	126.42E
Najusa, r., Cuba (nä-ho͞o′sä)	122	20.55N	77.55W
Naka, r., Japan	242a	35.39N	139.51E
Nakajima, Japan	242a	35.26N	139.56E
Nakanobu, neigh., Japan	242a	35.36N	139.43E
Nakatsu, Japan (nä′käts-o͞o)	194	33.34N	131.10E
Nakhodka, Russia (nŭ-ᴋôt′kŭ)	165	43.03N	133.08E
Nakhon Ratchasima, Thai.	196	14.56N	102.14E
Nakhon Sawan, Thai.	196	15.42N	100.06E
Nakhon Si Thammarat, Thai.	196	8.27N	99.58E
Nakło nad Notecia, Pol.	155	53.10N	17.35E
Nakskov, Den. (näk′skou)	146	54.51N	11.06E
Naktong, r., S. Kor. (näk′tŭng)	194	36.10N	128.30E
Nal′chik, Russia (nȧl-chēk′)	167	43.30N	43.35E
Nalón, r., Spain (nä-lōn′)	158	43.15N	5.38W
Nālūt, Libya (nä-lo͞ot′)	210	31.51N	10.49E
Namak, Daryacheh-ye, l., Iran	182	34.58N	51.33E
Namakan, l., Mn., U.S. (nă′mȧ-kȧn)	103	48.20N	92.43W
Namamugi, neigh., Japan	242a	35.29N	139.41E
Namangan, Uzb. (nȧ-mȧn-gän′)	169	41.08N	71.59E
Namao, Can.	83g	53.43N	113.30W
Namatanai, Pap. N. Gui. (nä′mä-tȧ-nä′ė)	197	3.43S	152.26E
Nambour, Austl. (năm′bo̍r)	204	26.48S	153.00E
Nam Co, l., China (näm tswo)	188	30.30N	91.10E
Nam Dinh, Viet. (näm dēnᴋ′)	196	20.30N	106.10E
Nametil, Moz.	217	15.43S	39.21E
Namhae, i., S. Kor. (näm′hī′)	194	34.23N	128.05E
Namib Desert, des., Nmb. (nä-mēb′)	212	18.45S	12.45E
Namibia, nation, Afr.	212	19.30S	16.13E
Namoi, r., Austl. (nămǒi)	203	30.10S	148.43E
Namous, Oued en, r., Alg. (nȧ-mo͞os′)	148	31.48N	0.19W
Nampa, Id., U.S. (năm′pȧ)	96	43.35N	116.35W
Namp′o, N. Kor.	189	38.47N	125.28E
Nampuecha, Moz.	217	13.59S	40.18E
Nampula, Moz.	217	15.07S	39.15E
Namsos, Nor. (näm′sǒs)	146	64.28N	11.14E
Namu, Can.	86	51.53N	127.50W
Namuli, Serra, mts., Moz.	217	15.05S	37.05E
Namur, Bel. (nȧ-mür′)	147	50.29N	4.55E
Namutoni, Nmb. (nȧ-mo͞o-tō′nė)	212	18.45S	17.00E
Nan, r., Thai.	196	18.11N	100.29E
Nanacamilpa, Mex. (nä-nä-kä-mė′l-pä)	119a	19.30N	98.33W
Nanaimo, Can. (nȧ-nī′mō)	84	49.10N	123.56W
Nanam, N. Kor. (nä′nän′)	194	41.38N	129.37E
Nanao, Japan (nä′nä-ō)	194	37.03N	136.59E
Nan′ao Dao, i., China (nän-ou dou)	193	23.30N	117.30E
Nancefield, S. Afr.	244b	26.17S	27.53E
Nanchang, China (nän′chäng′)	189	28.38N	115.48E
Nanchangshan Dao, i., China (nän-chäŋ-shän dou)	190	37.56N	120.42E
Nancheng, China (nän-chäŋ)	189	26.50N	116.40E
Nanchong, China (nän-chǒŋ)	188	30.45N	106.05E
Nancy, Fr. (nänɴ-sē′)	147	48.42N	6.11E
Nancy Creek, r., Ga., U.S. (năn′cē)	100c	33.51N	84.25W
Nanda Devi, mtn., India (nän′dä dā′vē)	183	30.30N	80.25E
Nānded, India	186	19.13N	77.21E
Nandurbār, India	186	21.29N	74.13E
Nandyāl, India	187	15.54N	78.09E
Nanga Parbat, mtn., Pak.	186	35.20N	74.35E

ăt; finăl; rāte; senåte; ärm; ȧsk; sofȧ; fâre; ch-choose; dh-as th in other; bē; ėvent; bět; recĕnt; cratẽr; g-gō; gh-guttural g; bĭt; ĭ-short neutral; rīde; ᴋ-guttural k as ch in German ich;

PRONOUNCING INDEX

Nangi–Nerchinskiy Zavod 323

PLACE (Pronunciation)	PAGE	Lat. °′	Long. °′
Nangi, India	186a	22.30N	88.14E
Nangis, Fr. (näN-zhē′)	157b	48.33N	3.01E
Nangong, China (nän-gôŋ)	192	37.22N	115.22E
Nangweshi, Zam.	216	16.26S	23.17E
Nanhuangcheng Dao, i., China (nän-hûäŋ-chŭŋ dou)	190	38.22N	120.54E
Nanhui, China	190	31.03N	121.45E
Naniwa, neigh., Japan	242b	34.39N	135.30E
Nanjing, China (nän-jyĭŋ)	189	32.04N	118.46E
Nanjuma, r., China (nän-jyōō-mä)	190	39.37N	115.45E
Nanking see Nanjing, China	188	32.04N	118.46E
Nanle, China (nän-lŭ)	190	36.03N	115.13E
Nan Ling, mts., China	189	25.15N	111.40E
Nanliu, r., China (nän-lĭô)	193	22.00N	109.18E
Nannine, Austl. (nă-nēn′)	202	25.50S	118.30E
Nanning, China (nän′nĭng′)	188	22.56N	108.10E
Nānole, neigh., India	240e	19.01N	72.55E
Nanpan, r., China (nän-pän)	193	24.50N	105.30E
Nanping, China (nän-pĭŋ)	189	26.40N	118.05E
Nansei-shotō, is., Japan	189	27.30N	127.00E
Nansemond, Va., U.S. (năn′sē-mŭnd)	100g	36.46N	76.32W
Nantai Zan, mtn., Japan (nän-täē zän)	194	36.47N	139.28E
Nanterre, Fr.	237c	48.53N	2.12E
Nantes, Fr. (näNt′)	142	47.13N	1.37W
Nanteuil-le-Haudouin, Fr. (näN-tû-lĕ-ō-dwăN′)	157b	49.08N	2.49E
Nanticoke, Pa., U.S. (năn′tĭ-kōk)	99	41.10N	76.00W
Nantong, China (nän-tôŋ)	190	32.02N	120.51E
Nantong, China	190	32.08N	121.06E
Nantouillet, Fr.	237c	49.00N	2.42E
Nantucket, i., Ma., U.S. (năn-tŭk′ĕt)	97	41.15N	70.05W
Nantwich, Eng., U.K. (nănt′wĭch)	144a	53.04N	2.31W
Nanxiang, China (nän-shyäŋ)	190	31.17N	121.17E
Nanxiong, China (nän-shôŋ)	193	25.10N	114.20E
Nanyang, China	189	33.00N	112.42E
Nanyang Hu, l., China (nän-yäŋ hōō)	190	35.14N	116.24E
Nanyuan, China (nän-yûän)	192a	39.48N	116.24E
Nao, Cabo de la, c., Spain (kȧ′bô-dĕ-lä-nä′ō)	142	38.43N	0.14E
Naoābād, India	240a	22.28N	88.27E
Naolinco, Mex. (nä-o-lēŋ′kō)	119	19.39N	96.50W
Naopukuria, India	240a	22.55N	88.16E
Náousa, Grc. (nä′ōō-sȧ)	161	40.38N	22.05E
Naozhou Dao, i., China (nou-jō dou)	193	20.58N	110.58E
Napa, Ca., U.S. (năp′ȧ)	96	38.20N	122.17W
Napanee, Can. (năp′ȧ-nē)	91	44.15N	77.00W
Naperville, Il., U.S. (nā′pĕr-vĭl)	101a	41.46N	88.09W
Napier, N.Z. (nā′pĭ-ĕr)	203a	39.30S	177.00E
Napierville, Can. (nā′pĭ-ē-vĭl)	83a	45.11N	73.24W
Naples (Napoli), Italy	142	40.37N	14.12E
Naples, Fl., U.S. (nā′p′lz)	115a	26.07N	81.46W
Napo, r., S.A. (nä′pō)	130	1.49S	74.20W
Napoleon, Oh., U.S. (nȧ-pō′lē-ŭn)	98	41.20N	84.10W
Napoleonville, La., U.S. (nȧ-pō′lē-ŭn-vĭl)	113	29.56N	91.03W
Napoli see Naples, Italy	142	40.37N	14.12E
Napoli, Golfo di, b., Italy	148	40.29N	14.08E
Nappanee, In., U.S. (năp′ȧ-nē)	98	41.30N	86.00W
Nara, Japan (nä′rä)	189	34.41N	135.50E
Nara, Mali	210	15.09N	7.27W
Nara, dept., Japan	195b	34.36N	135.49E
Nara, r., Russia	162	55.05N	37.16E
Naracoorte, Austl. (nȧ-rȧ-kōōn′tē)	202	36.50S	140.50E
Narashino, Japan	195a	35.41N	140.01E
Naraspur, India	187	16.32N	81.43E
Nārāyanpāra, India	240a	22.54N	88.19E
Narberth, Pa., U.S. (när′bûrth)	100f	40.01N	75.17W
Narbonne, Fr. (nȧr-bôn′)	147	43.12N	3.00E
Nare, Col. (nä′rē)	130a	6.12N	74.37W
Narew, r., Pol. (när′ĕf)	155	52.43N	21.19E
Narmada, r., India	183	22.30N	75.30E
Naroch′, l., Bela. (nä′rôch)	162	54.51N	27.00E
Narodnaya, Gora, mtn., Russia (nȧ-rôd′nȧ-yȧ)	164	65.10N	60.10E
Naro-Fominsk, Russia (nä′rô-mēnsk′)	166	55.23N	36.43E
Narrabeen, Austl. (năr-ȧ-bĭn)	201b	33.44S	151.18E
Narragansett, R.I., U.S. (năr-ȧ-găn′sĕt)	100b	41.26N	71.27W
Narragansett Bay, b., R.I., U.S.	99	41.20N	71.15W
Narrandera, Austl. (nȧ-rȧn-dē′rȧ)	203	34.40S	146.40E
Narraweena, Austl.	243a	33.45S	151.16E
Narre Warren North, Austl.	243b	37.59S	145.19E
Narrogin, Austl. (năr′ô-gĭn)	202	33.00S	117.15E
Naruo, Japan	242b	34.43N	135.23E
Narva, Est. (nȧr′vȧ)	166	59.24N	28.12E
Narvacan, Phil. (när-vä-kän′)	197a	17.27N	120.29E
Narva Jõesuu, Est. (nȧr′vȧ ô-ô-ă′sōō-ô)	153	59.26N	28.02E
Narvik, Nor. (när′vĕk)	142	68.21N	17.18E
Narvskiy Zaliv, b., Eur. (nȧr′vskĭ zä′lĭf)	153	59.35N	27.25E
Narvskoye, res., Eur.	153	59.18N	28.14E
Nar′yan-Mar, Russia (när′yȧn mär′)	164	67.42N	53.30E
Narylico, Austl. (năr-ĭl′kō)	204	28.40S	141.50E
Narym, Russia (nä-rēm′)	164	58.47N	82.05E
Naryn, r., Asia (nŭ-rĭn′)	170	41.20N	76.00E
Naseby, Eng., U.K. (nāz′bĭ)	144a	52.23N	0.59W
Nashua, Mo., U.S. (năsh′ū-ȧ)	107f	39.18N	94.34W
Nashua, N.H., U.S.	97	42.47N	71.23W
Nashville, Ar., U.S. (năsh′vĭl)	111	33.56N	93.50W
Nashville, Ga., U.S.	114	31.12N	83.15W
Nashville, Il., U.S.	111	38.21N	89.42W
Nashville, Mi., U.S.	98	42.35N	85.50W
Nashville, Tn., U.S.	97	36.10N	86.48W
Nashwauk, Mn., U.S. (năsh′wôk)	103	47.21N	93.12W
Näsi, l., Fin.	146	61.42N	24.05E
Našice, Cro. (nä′shē-tsĕ)	149	45.29N	18.06E
Nasielsk, Pol. (nä′syĕlsk)	155	52.35N	20.50E
Nāsik, India (nä′sĭk)	183	20.02N	73.49E

PLACE (Pronunciation)	PAGE	Lat. °′	Long. °′
Nāşir, Sudan (nä-zēr′)	211	8.30N	33.06E
Nasirabād, India	186	26.13N	74.48E
Naskaupi, r., Can. (năs′kô-pĭ)	85	53.59N	61.10W
Nasondoye, Zaire	217	10.22S	25.06E
Nass, r., Can. (năs)	86	55.00N	129.30W
Nassau, Bah. (năs′ô)	117	25.05N	77.20W
Nassenheide, Ger. (nä′sĕn-hī-dĕ)	145b	52.49N	13.13E
Nasser, Lake, res., Egypt	211	23.50N	32.50E
Nasugbu, Phil. (nȧ-sòg-bōō′)	197a	14.05N	120.37E
Nasworthy Lake, l., Tx., U.S. (năz′wûr-thē)	112	31.17N	100.30W
Natagaima, Col. (nä-tä-gī′mä)	130a	3.38N	75.07W
Nātāgarh, India	240a	22.42N	88.25E
Natal, Braz. (nä-täl′)	131	6.00S	35.13W
Natalspruit, S. Afr.	244b	26.19S	28.09E
Natashquan, Can. (nä-tăsh′kwăn)	85	50.11N	61.49W
Natashquan, r., Can.	93	50.35N	61.35W
Natchez, Ms., U.S. (năch′ĕz)	97	31.35N	91.20W
Natchitoches, La., U.S. (năk′ĭ-tŏsh)(nȧch-ĭ-tŏsh′)	113	31.46N	93.06W
Natick, Ma., U.S. (nā′tĭk)	93a	42.17N	71.21W
National Bison Range, I.R., Mt., U.S. (năsh′ŭn-ăl bī′s′n)	105	47.18N	113.58W
National City, Ca., U.S.	108a	32.38N	117.01W
National Park, Pa., U.S.	229b	39.51N	75.12W
Natitingou, Benin	210	10.19N	1.22E
Natividade, Braz. (nä-tē-vē-dä′dē)	131	11.43S	47.34W
Natron, Lake, l., Tan. (nā′trŏn)	212	2.17S	36.10E
Natrona Heights, Pa., U.S. (nā′trō nā)	101e	40.38N	79.43W
Naṭrūn, Wādī an, val., Egypt	218b	30.33N	30.12E
Natuna Besar, i., Indon.	196	4.00N	106.50E
Natural Bridges National Monument, rec., Ut., U.S. (năt′ū-rȧl brĭj′ĕs)	109	37.20N	110.20W
Naturaliste, Cape, c., Austl. (năt-ū-rȧ-lĭst′)	202	33.30S	115.10E
Naucalpan de Juárez, Mex.	119a	19.28N	99.14W
Nauchampatepetl, mtn., Mex. (näōō-chäm-pä-tē′pĕtl)	119	19.32N	97.09W
Nauen, Ger. (nou′ĕn)	145b	52.36N	12.53E
Naugatuck, Ct., U.S. (nô′gȧ-tŭk)	99	41.25N	73.05W
Naujan, Phil. (nä-ō-hän′)	197a	13.19N	121.17E
Naumburg, Ger. (noum′bŏrgh)	154	51.10N	11.50E
Naupada, neigh., India	240e	19.04N	72.50E
Nauru, nation, Oc.	3	0.30S	167.00E
Nautla, Mex. (nä-ōōt′lä)	116	20.14N	96.44W
Nava, Mex. (nä′vä)	112	28.25N	100.44W
Nava del Rey, Spain (nä-vä dĕl rā′ē)	158	41.22N	5.04W
Navahermosa, Spain (nä-vä-ĕr-mō′sä)	158	39.39N	4.28W
Navajas, Cuba (nä-vä-häs′)	122	22.40N	81.20W
Navajo Hopi Joint Use Area, I.R., Az., U.S.	109	36.15N	110.30W
Navajo Indian Reservation, I.R., U.S. (năv′ȧ-hō)	109	36.31N	109.24W
Navajo National Monument, rec., Az., U.S.	109	36.43N	110.39W
Navajo Reservoir, res., N.M., U.S.	109	36.57N	107.26W
Navalcarnero, Spain (nä-väl′kär-nā′rō)	159a	40.17N	4.05W
Navalmoral de la Mata, Spain	158	39.53N	5.32W
Navan, Can. (nă′vȧn)	83c	45.25N	75.26W
Navarino, i., Chile (nä-vä-rē′nô)	132	55.30S	68.15W
Navarra, hist. reg., Spain (nä-vär′rä)	158	42.40N	1.35W
Navarro, Arg. (nä-vá′r-rō)	129c	35.00S	59.16W
Navasota, Tx., U.S. (năv-a-ȧ-sō′tȧ)	113	30.24N	96.05W
Navasota, r., Tx., U.S.	113	31.03N	96.11W
Navassa, i., N.A. (nȧ-văs′ȧ)	123	18.25N	75.15W
Navestock, Eng., U.K.	235	51.39N	0.13E
Navestock Side, Eng., U.K.	235	51.39N	0.16E
Navia, r., Spain (nä-vē′ä)	158	43.10N	6.45W
Navidad, Chile (nä-vē-dä′d)	129b	33.57S	71.51W
Navidad Bank, bk. (nä-vē-dädh′)	123	20.05N	69.00W
Navidade do Carangola, Braz. (nä-vē-dä′dô-kȧ-rän-gô′la)	129a	21.04S	41.58W
Navojoa, Mex. (nä-vô-kô′ä)	116	27.00N	109.40W
Navotas, Phil.	241g	14.40N	120.57E
Návplion, Grc.	161	37.33N	22.46E
Nawābshāh, Pak. (nȧ-wäb′shä)	186	26.20N	68.30E
Naxçıvan, Azer.	167	39.10N	45.30E
Naxçıvan Muxtar, state, Azer.	168	39.20N	45.30E
Náxos, i., Grc. (nák′sôs)	149	37.15N	25.20E
Nayābās, India	240d	28.35N	77.19E
Nayarit, state, Mex. (nä-yä-rēt′)	116	22.00N	105.15W
Nayarit, Sierra de, mts., Mex. (sē-ĕ′r-rä-dē)	118	23.20N	105.07W
Naye, Sen.	214	14.25N	12.12W
Naylor, Md., U.S. (nā′lōr)	100e	38.43N	76.46W
Nazaré da Mata, Braz. (dä-mä-tä)	131	7.46S	35.13W
Nazas, Mex. (nä′zäs)	112	25.14N	104.08W
Nazas, r., Mex.	116	25.30N	104.40W
Naẕerat, Isr.	181a	32.43N	35.19E
Nazilli, Tur. (nȧ-zĭ-lē′)	167	37.40N	28.10E
Naziya, r., Russia (nȧ-zē′yȧ)	172c	59.48N	31.18E
Nazko, r., Can.	86	52.35N	123.10W
Nazlat as-Sammān, Egypt	244a	29.59N	31.08E
Nazlat Khalīfah, Egypt	244a	30.01N	31.10E
N′dalatando, Ang.	216	9.18S	14.54E
Ndali, Benin	215	9.51N	2.43E
Ndikiniméki, Cam.	215	4.46N	10.50E
N′Djamena, Chad	211	12.07N	15.03E
Ndjili, neigh., Zaire	244c	4.21S	15.19E
Ndola, Zam. (n′dō′lä)	212	12.58S	28.38E
Ndoto Mountains, mts., Kenya	217	1.55N	37.05E
Ndrhamcha, Sebkha de, l., Maur.	214	18.50N	15.15W
Nduye, Zaire	217	1.50N	29.01E
Neagh, Lough, l., N. Ire., U.K. (lŏk nā)	146	54.40N	6.47W
Néa Ionía, Grc.	239d	38.02N	23.45E

PLACE (Pronunciation)	PAGE	Lat. °′	Long. °′
Néa Liósia, Grc.	239d	38.02N	23.42E
Néa Páfos, Cyp.	181a	34.46N	32.27E
Neapean, r., Austl.	201b	33.40S	150.39E
Neápolis, Grc.	160a	35.17N	25.37E
Neápolis, Grc. (nā-ŏp′ ō-lĭs)	161	36.35N	23.08E
Near Islands, is., Ak., U.S. (nēr)	95a	52.20N	172.40E
Near North Side, neigh., Il., U.S.	231a	41.54N	87.38W
Néa Smírni, Grc.	239d	37.57N	23.43E
Neath, Wales, U.K. (nēth)	150	51.41N	3.50W
Nebine Creek, r., Austl. (nĕ-bēne′)	204	27.50S	147.00E
Nebit-Dag, Turk. (nyĕ-bēt′däg′)	170	39.30N	54.20E
Nebraska, state, U.S. (nē-brăs′kȧ)	96	41.45N	101.30W
Nebraska City, Ne., U.S.	111	40.40N	95.50W
Nechako, r., Can.	86	53.45N	124.55W
Nechako Plateau, plat., Can. (nĭ-chă′kō)	86	54.00N	124.30W
Nechako Range, mts., Can.	86	53.20N	124.30W
Nechako Reservoir, res., Can.	86	53.25N	125.10W
Neches, r., Tx., U.S. (nĕch′ĕz)	113	31.03N	94.40W
Neckar, r., Ger. (nĕk′är)	154	49.16N	9.06E
Necker Island, i., Hi., U.S.	94b	24.00N	164.00W
Necochea, Arg. (nā-kô-chā′ä)	132	38.30S	58.45W
Nedlitz, neigh., Ger.	238a	52.26N	13.03E
Nedryhayliv, Ukr.	163	50.49N	33.52E
Needham, Ma., U.S. (nēd′ăm)	93a	42.17N	71.14W
Needham Heights, Ma., U.S.	227a	41.28N	71.14W
Needles, Ca., U.S. (nē′d′lz)	109	34.51N	114.39W
Neenah, Wi., U.S. (nē′nȧ)	103	44.10N	88.30W
Neepawa, Can.	84	50.13N	99.29W
Nee Reservoir, res., Co., U.S. (nee)	110	38.26N	102.56W
Nee Soon, Sing.	240c	1.24N	103.49E
Negareyama, Japan (nā′gä-rȧ-yä′mä)	195a	35.52N	139.54E
Negaunee, Mi., U.S. (nē-gô′nē)	103	46.30N	87.37W
Negeri Sembilan, state, Malay. (nā′grē-sĕm-bē-län′)	181b	2.46N	101.54E
Negev, des., Isr. (nē′gĕv)	181a	30.34N	34.43E
Negombo, Sri L.	187	7.39N	79.49E
Negotin, Yugo. (nĕ′gô-tēn)	161	44.13N	22.33E
Negro, r., Arg.	132	39.50S	65.00W
Negro, r., N.A.	120	13.01N	87.10W
Negro, r., S.A.	129c	33.17S	58.18W
Negro, Cerro, mtn., Pan. (sĕ′-rrô-nā′grô)	121	8.44N	80.37W
Negro, Rio, r., S.A. (rē′ō nā′grō)	130	0.18S	63.21W
Negros, i., Phil. (nā′grōs)	196	9.50N	121.45E
Nehalem, r., Or., U.S. (nē-hăl′ĕm)	104	45.52N	123.37W
Nehaus an der Oste, Ger. (noi′houz)(ōz′tē)	145c	53.48N	9.02E
Nehbandān, Iran	185	31.32N	60.02E
Nehe, China (nŭ-hŭ)	192	48.23N	124.58E
Neheim-Hüsten, Ger. (nĕ′hīm)	157c	51.28N	7.58E
Neiba, Dom. Rep. (nā-ē′bä)	123	18.30N	71.20W
Neiba, Bahía de, b., Dom. Rep.	123	18.10N	71.00W
Neiba, Sierra de, mts., Dom. Rep. (sē-ĕr′rä-dē)	123	18.40N	71.40W
Neihart, Mt., U.S. (nī′hărt)	105	46.54N	110.39W
Neijiang, China (nā-jyäŋ)	193	29.38N	105.01E
Neillsville, Wi., U.S. (nēlz′vĭl)	103	44.35N	90.37W
Neiqiu, China (nā-chyō)	190	37.17N	114.32E
Neira, Col. (nā′rä)	130a	5.10N	75.32W
Neisse, r., Eur. (nēs)	154	51.30N	15.00E
Neiva, Col. (nȧ-ē′vä)(nā′vä)	130	2.55N	75.16W
Neixiang, China (nā-shyäŋ)	192	33.00N	111.38E
Nekemte, Eth.	211	9.09N	36.29E
Nekoosa, Wi., U.S. (nē-kōō′sȧ)	103	44.19N	89.54W
Neligh, Ne., U.S. (nē′-lē)	102	42.06N	98.02W
Nel′kan, Russia (nĕl-kän′)	165	57.45N	136.36E
Nellore, India (nĕl-lōr′)	183	14.28N	79.59E
Nel′ma, Russia (nĕl-mä′)	194	47.34N	139.05E
Nelson, Can. (nĕl′sŭn)	84	49.29N	117.17W
Nelson, N.Z.	203a	41.15S	173.22E
Nelson, Eng., U.K.	144a	53.50N	2.13W
Nelson, i., Ak., U.S.	95	60.38N	164.42W
Nelson, r., Can.	89	56.50N	93.40W
Nelson, Cape, c., Austl.	204	38.29S	141.20E
Nelsonville, Oh., U.S. (nĕl′sŭn-vĭl)	98	39.30N	82.15W
Néma, Maur. (nā′mä)	210	16.37N	7.15W
Nemadji, r., Wi., U.S. (nē-măd′jē)	107h	46.33N	92.16W
Neman, Russia (ŋĕ′-mȧn)	153	55.02N	22.01E
Neman, r., Eur.	166	53.28N	24.45E
Nematābād, Iran	241h	35.38N	51.21E
Nembe, Nig.	215	4.35N	6.26E
Nemčinovka, Russia	239b	55.43N	37.23E
Nemeiben Lake, l., Can. (nĕ-mē′bȧn)	88	55.20N	105.20W
Nemours, Fr.	156	48.16N	2.41E
Nemuro, Japan (nā′mô-rō)	189	43.13N	145.10E
Nemuro Strait, strt., Asia	194	43.07N	145.10E
Nemyriv, Ukr.	163	48.56N	28.51E
Nen, r., China (nŭn)	189	47.07N	123.28E
Nen, r., Eng., U.K. (nĕn)	144a	52.32N	0.19W
Nenagh, Ire. (nē′nȧ)	150	52.50N	8.05W
Nenana, Ak., U.S. (nȧ-nä′nȧ)	95	64.28N	149.18W
Nenets, state, Russia	166	67.30N	54.00E
Nenikyul′, Russia (nĕ-nyĕ′kyûl)	172c	59.26N	30.40E
Nenjiang, China (nŭn-jyäŋ)	189	49.02N	125.15E
Neodesha, Ks., U.S. (nē-ô-dĕ-shô′)	111	37.24N	95.41W
Neosho, Mo., U.S.	111	36.51N	94.22W
Neosho, r., Ks., U.S. (nē-ō′shō)	111	38.07N	95.40W
Nepal, nation, Asia (nĕ-pôl′)	183	28.45N	83.00E
Nephi, Ut., U.S. (nē′fī)	109	39.40N	111.50W
Nepomuceno, Braz. (nĕ-pô-mōō-sĕ′no)	129a	21.15S	45.13W
Nera, r., Italy (nā′rä)	160	42.45N	12.54E
Nérac, Fr. (nā-rák′)	156	44.08N	0.19E
Nerchinsk, Russia (nyĕr′chĕnsk)	165	51.47N	116.17E
Nerchinskiy Khrebet, mts., Russia	165	50.30N	118.30E
Nerchinskiy Zavod, Russia (nyĕr′chĕn-skĭzá-vôt′)	165	51.35N	119.46E

ng-sing; ŋ-baŋk; N-nasalized n; nŏd; cŏmmit; ōld; ôbey; ôrder; oi-boil; fōōd; ŏŏ-as oo in foot; ou-out; s-soft; sh-dish; th-thin; pūre; ûnite; ûrn; stŭd; circŭs; ü-as in French tu; ′-indeterminate vowel.

PLACE (Pronunciation)	PAGE	Lat. °′	Long. °′
Nerekhta, Russia (nyĕ-rĕκ'tȧ)	162	57.29N	40.34E
Neretva, r., Yugo. (nĕ'rĕt-vȧ)	161	43.08N	17.50E
Nerja, Spain (nĕr'hä)	158	36.45N	3.53W
Nerl', r., Russia (nyĕrl)	162	56.59N	37.57E
Nerskaya, r., Russia (nyĕr'skȧ-yȧ)	172b	55.31N	38.46E
Nerussa, r., Russia (nyå-rōō'sȧ)	162	52.24N	34.20E
Ness, Eng., U.K.	237a	53.17N	3.03W
Ness, Loch, l., Scot., U.K. (lŏκ nĕs)	150	57.23N	4.20W
Ness City, Ks., U.S. (nĕs)	110	38.27N	99.55W
Nesterov, Russia (nyĕs-tâ'rôf)	153	54.39N	22.38E
Neston, Eng., U.K.	237a	53.18N	3.04W
Néstos (Mesta), r., Eur. (nās'tōs)	161	41.25N	24.12E
Nesvizh, Bela. (nyĕs'vēsh)	162	53.13N	26.44E
Netanya, Isr.	181a	32.19N	34.52E
Netcong, N.J., U.S. (nĕt'cŏnj)	100a	40.54N	74.42W
Netherlands, nation, Eur. (nĕdh'ĕr-lăndz)	142	53.01N	3.57E
Netherlands Guiana see Suriname, nation, S.A.	131	4.00N	56.00W
Netherton, Eng., U.K.	237a	53.30N	2.58W
Nette, neigh., Ger.	236	51.33N	7.25E
Nettilling, l., Can.	85	66.30N	70.40W
Nett Lake Indian Reservation, I.R., Mn., U.S. (nĕt lāk)	103	48.23N	93.19W
Nettuno, Italy (nĕt-tōō'nô)	159d	41.28N	12.40E
Neubeckum, Ger. (noi'bĕ-kōōm)	157c	51.48N	8.01E
Neubrandenburg, Ger. (noi-brän'dĕn-bòrgh)	154	53.33N	13.16E
Neuburg, Ger. (noi'bòrgh)	154	48.43N	11.12E
Neuchâtel, Switz. (nû-shȧ-tĕl')	147	47.00N	6.52E
Neuchâtel, Lac de, l., Switz.	154	46.48N	6.53E
Neudorf, neigh., Ger.	236	51.25N	6.47E
Neuenhagen, Ger. (noi'ĕn-hä-gĕn)	145b	52.31N	13.41E
Neuenhof, neigh., Ger.	236	51.10N	7.13E
Neuenkamp, neigh., Ger.	236	51.26N	6.44E
Neuenrade, Ger. (noi'ĕn-rä-dĕ)	157c	51.17N	7.47E
Neu-Erlaa, neigh., Aus.	239e	48.08N	16.19E
Neu Fahrland, Ger.	238a	52.26N	13.03E
Neufchâtel-en-Bray, Fr. (nû-shä-tĕl'ĕɴ-brā')	156	49.43N	1.25E
Neuilly-sur-Marne, Fr.	237c	48.51N	2.32E
Neuilly-sur-Seine, Fr.	237c	48.53N	2.16E
Neukirchen, Ger.	236	51.27N	6.33E
Neulengbach, Aus.	145e	48.13N	15.55E
Neumarkt, Ger. (noi'märkt)	154	49.17N	11.30E
Neumünster, Ger. (noi'mùn'stĕr)	146	54.04N	10.00E
Neunkirchen, Aus. (noin'kĭrκ-ĕn)	154	47.43N	16.05E
Neuquén, Arg. (nĕ-ò-kān')	132	38.52S	68.12W
Neuquén, prov., Arg.	132	39.40S	70.45W
Neuquén, r., Arg.	132	38.45S	69.00W
Neuruppin, Ger. (noi'rōō-pēn)	154	52.55N	12.48E
Neuse, r., N.C., U.S. (nūz)	115	36.12N	78.50W
Neusiedler See, l., Eur. (noi-zēd'lēr)	154	47.54N	16.31E
Neuss, Ger. (nois)	157c	51.12N	6.41E
Neusserweyhe, neigh., Ger.	236	51.13N	6.39E
Neustadt, Ger. (noi'shtät)	154	49.21N	8.08E
Neustadt bei Coburg, Ger. (bī kō'bōōrgh)	154	50.20N	11.09E
Neustadt in Holstein, Ger.	154	54.06N	10.50E
Neustift am Walde, neigh., Aus.	239e	48.15N	16.18E
Neustrelitz, Ger. (noi-strā'lĭts)	154	53.21N	13.05E
Neutral Hills, hills, Can. (nū'trăl)	88	52.10N	110.50W
Neu Ulm, Ger. (noi ò lm')	154	48.23N	10.01E
Neuva Pompeya, neigh., Arg.	233d	34.39S	58.25W
Neuville, Can. (nū'vĭl)	83b	46.39N	71.35W
Neuville-sur-Oise, Fr.	237c	49.01N	2.04E
Neuwaldegg, neigh., Aus.	239e	48.14N	16.17E
Neuwied, Ger. (noi'vēdt)	154	50.26N	7.28E
Neva, r., Russia (nyĕ-vä')	162	59.49N	30.54E
Nevada, Ia., U.S. (nē-vä'dȧ)	103	42.01N	93.27W
Nevada, Mo., U.S.	111	37.49N	94.21W
Nevada, state, U.S. (nĕ vȧ'dȧ)	96	39.30N	117.00W
Nevada, Sierra, mts., Spain (syĕr'rä nä-vä'dhä)	142	37.01N	3.28W
Nevada, Sierra, mts., U.S. (sē-ĕ'r-rä nē-vä'dȧ)	96	39.20N	120.05W
Nevado, Cerro el, mtn., Col. (sĕ'r-rô-ĕl-nē-vä'dô)	130a	4.02N	74.08W
Neva Stantsiya, Russia (nyĕ-vä' stän'tsĭ-yȧ)	172c	59.53N	30.30E
Neve, Serra da, mts., Ang.	216	13.40S	13.20E
Nevel', Russia (nyĕ'vĕl)	166	56.03N	29.57E
Neveri, r., Ven. (nĕ-vĕ-rē)	131b	10.13N	64.18W
Nevers, Fr. (nē-vâr')	147	46.59N	3.10E
Neves, Braz.	132b	22.51S	43.06W
Nevesinje, Bos. (nĕ-vĕ'sēn-yĕ)	161	43.15N	18.08E
Neviges, Ger.	236	51.19N	7.05E
Neville Island, i., Pa., U.S.	230b	40.31N	80.08W
Nevinnomyssk, Russia	168	44.38N	41.56E
Nevis, i., St. K./N. (nē'vĭs)	117	17.05N	62.38W
Nevis, Ben, mtn., Scot., U.K. (bĕn)	146	56.47N	5.00W
Nevis Peak, mtn., St. K./N.	121b	17.11N	62.33W
Nevşehir, Tur. (nĕv-shĕ'hēr)	149	38.40N	34.35E
Nev'yansk, Russia (nĕv-yänsk')	164	57.29N	60.14E
New, r., Va., U.S. (nū)	115	37.20N	80.35W
Newabāgam, India	240a	22.48N	88.24E
New Addington, neigh., Eng., U.K.	235	51.21N	0.01W
Newala, Tan.	217	10.56S	39.18E
New Albany, In., U.S. (nû ôl'bȧ-nĭ)	101h	38.17N	85.49W
New Albany, Ms., U.S.	115	34.28N	39.00W
New Amsterdam, Guy. (ăm'stĕr-dăm)	131	6.14N	57.30W
Newark, Eng., U.K. (nū'ĕrk)	144a	53.04N	0.49W
Newark, Ca., U.S. (nū'ĕrk)	106b	37.32N	122.02W
Newark, De., U.S. (nōō'ärk)	99	39.40N	75.45W
Newark, N.J., U.S. (nōō'ûrk)	97	40.44N	74.10W
Newark, N.Y., U.S. (nū'ĕrk)	99	43.05N	77.10W
Newark, Oh., U.S.	98	40.05N	82.25W
Newaygo, Mi., U.S. (nū'wā-go)	98	43.25N	85.50W
New Bedford, Ma., U.S. (bĕd'fĕrd)	97	41.35N	70.55W
Newberg, Or., U.S. (nū'bûrg)	98	45.17N	122.58W
New Bern, N.C., U.S. (bûrn)	97	35.05N	77.05W
Newbern, Tn., U.S.	114	36.05N	89.12W
Newberry, Mi., U.S. (nū'bĕr-ĭ)	103	46.22N	85.31W
Newberry, S.C., U.S.	115	34.15N	81.40W
New Boston, Mi., U.S. (bôs'tŭn)	101b	42.10N	83.24W
New Boston, Oh., U.S.	98	38.45N	82.55W
New Braunfels, Tx., U.S. (nū broun'fĕls)	112	29.43N	98.07W
New Brighton, Eng., U.K.	237a	53.26N	3.03W
New Brighton, Mn., U.S. (brī'tŭn)	107g	45.04N	93.12W
New Brighton, Pa., U.S.	101e	40.34N	80.18W
New Brighton, neigh., N.Y., U.S.	228	40.38N	74.06W
New Britain, Ct., U.S. (brĭt''n)	99	41.40N	72.45W
New Britain, i., Pap. N. Gui.	197	6.45S	149.38E
New Brunswick, N.J., U.S. (brŭnz'wĭk)	100a	40.29N	74.27W
New Brunswick, prov., Can.	85	47.14N	66.30W
Newburg, In., U.S.	98	38.00N	87.25W
Newburg, Mo., U.S.	111	37.54N	91.53W
Newburgh, N.Y., U.S.	99	41.30N	74.00W
Newburgh Heights, Oh., U.S.	101d	41.27N	81.40W
Newbury, Eng., U.K. (nū'bĕr-ĭ)	150	51.24N	1.26W
Newbury, Ma., U.S.	93a	42.48N	70.52W
Newburyport, Ma., U.S. (nū'bĕr-ĭ-pōrt)	93a	42.48N	70.53W
New Caledonia, dep., Oc.	203	21.28S	164.40E
New Canaan, Ct., U.S. (kā-năn)	100a	41.06N	73.30W
New Carlisle, Can. (kär-līl')	85	48.01N	65.20W
New Carrollton, Md., U.S.	229d	35.58N	76.53W
Newcastle, Austl. (nū-kȧs''l)	204	33.00S	151.55E
Newcastle, Can.	85	47.00N	65.34W
New Castle, De., U.S.	99	39.40N	75.35W
New Castle, In., U.S.	98	39.55N	85.25W
New Castle, Oh., U.S.	98	40.20N	82.10W
New Castle, Pa., U.S.	98	41.00N	80.25W
Newcastle, Tx., U.S.	110	33.13N	98.44W
Newcastle, Wy., U.S.	102	43.51N	104.11W
Newcastle under Lyme, Eng., U.K. (nū-kȧs''l) (nū-kȧs''l)	144a	53.01N	2.14W
Newcastle upon Tyne, Eng., U.K.	142	55.00N	1.45W
Newcastle Waters, Austl. (wô'tĕrz)	202	17.10S	133.25E
Newclare, neigh., S. Afr.	244b	26.11S	27.58E
Newcomerstown, Oh., U.S. (nū'kŭm-ĕrz-toun)	98	40.15N	81.40W
New Croton Reservoir, res., N.Y., U.S. (krō'tôn)	100a	41.15N	73.47W
New Delhi, India (dĕl'hī)	183	28.43N	77.18E
Newell, S.D., U.S. (nū'ĕl)	102	44.43N	103.26W
New Eltham, neigh., Eng., U.K.	235	51.26N	0.04E
New England Range, mts., Austl. (nû ĭŋ'glănd)	203	29.32S	152.30E
Newenham, Cape, c., Ak., U.S. (nū-ĕn-hăm)	95	58.40N	162.32W
Newfane, N.Y., U.S. (nū-fān)	101c	43.17N	78.44W
New Ferry, Eng., U.K.	237a	53.22N	2.59W
Newfoundland, prov., Can.	85a	48.15N	56.53W
Newgate, Can. (nû'gāt)	87	49.01N	115.10W
Newgate Street, Eng., U.K.	235	51.44N	0.07W
New Georgia, i., Sol.Is. (jôr'jĭ-ȧ)	203	8.08S	158.00E
New Georgia Group, is., Sol.Is.	198e	8.30S	157.20E
New Georgia Sound, strt., Sol.Is.	198e	8.00S	158.10E
New Glasgow, Can. (glȧs'gō)	85	45.35N	62.36W
New Guinea, i. (gĭne)	197	5.45S	140.00E
Newhalem, Wa., U.S. (nū hā'lŭm)	104	48.44N	121.11W
Newham, neigh., Eng., U.K.	235	51.32N	0.03E
New Hampshire, state, U.S. (hămp'shĭr)	97	43.55N	71.40W
New Hampton, Ia., U.S. (hămp'tŭn)	103	43.03N	92.20W
New Hanover, S. Afr. (hăn'ôvĕr)	213c	29.23S	30.32E
New Hanover, i., Pap. N. Gui.	197	2.37S	150.15E
New Harmony, In., U.S. (nū här'mō-nĭ)	98	38.10N	87.55W
New Haven, Ct., U.S. (hā'vĕn)	97	41.20N	72.55W
New Haven, In., U.S. (nū hāv''n)	98	41.05N	85.00W
New Hebrides, is., Vanuatu	203	16.00S	167.00E
New Hey, Eng., U.K.	237b	53.36N	2.06W
New Holland, Eng., U.K. (hŏl'ănd)	144a	53.42N	0.21W
New Holland, N.C., U.S.	115	35.27N	76.14W
New Hope Mountain, mtn., Al., U.S. (hōp)	100h	33.23N	86.45W
New Hudson, Mi., U.S. (hŭd'sŭn)	101b	42.30N	83.36W
New Hyde Park, N.Y., U.S.	228	40.44N	73.41W
New Hythe, Eng., U.K.	235	51.19N	0.27E
New Iberia, La., U.S. (ī-bē'rĭ-ȧ)	113	30.00N	91.50W
Newington, Can. (nū'ēng-tŏn)	83c	45.07N	75.00W
New Ireland, i., Pap. N. Gui. (īr'lănd)	197	3.15S	152.30E
New Jersey, state, U.S. (jûr'zĭ)	97	40.30N	74.50W
New Kensington, Pa., U.S. (kĕn'zĭng-tŭn)	101e	40.34N	79.35W
Newkirk, Ok., U.S. (nū'kûrk)	111	36.52N	97.03W
New Kowloon (Xinjiulong), H.K.	241c	22.20N	114.10E
New Lagos, neigh., Nig.	244d	6.30N	3.22E
New Lenox, Il., U.S. (lĕn'ŭk)	101a	41.31N	87.58W
New Lexington, Oh., U.S. (lĕk'sĭng-tŭn)	98	39.40N	82.10W
New Lisbon, Wi., U.S. (lĭz'bŭn)	103	43.52N	90.11W
New Liskeard, Can.	91	47.30N	79.40W
New London, Ct., U.S. (lŭn'dŭn)	99	41.20N	72.05W
New London, Wi., U.S.	103	44.24N	88.45W
New Madrid, Mo., U.S. (măd'rĭd)	111	36.34N	89.31W
Newman's Grove, Ne., U.S. (nū'măn grōv)	102	41.46N	97.44W
Newmarket, Can. (nū'mär-kĕt)	91	44.00N	79.30W
Newmarket, S. Afr.	244b	26.17S	28.08E
New Martinsville, W.V., U.S. (mär'tĭnz-vĭl)	98	39.35N	80.50W
New Meadows, Id., U.S.	104	44.58N	116.20W
New Mexico, state, U.S. (mĕk'sĭ-kō)	96	34.30N	107.10W
New Milford, N.J., U.S.	228	40.56N	74.01W
New Mills, Eng., U.K. (mĭlz)	144a	53.22N	2.00W
New Munster, Wi., U.S. (mŭn'stĕr)	101a	42.35N	88.13W
Newnan, Ga., U.S. (nū'năn)	114	33.22N	84.47W
New Norfolk, Austl. (nôr'fŏk)	203	42.50S	147.17E
New Orleans, La., U.S. (ôr'lē-ănz)	97	30.00N	90.05W
New Philadelphia, Oh., U.S. (fĭl-ȧ-dĕl'fĭ-ȧ)	98	40.30N	81.30W
New Plymouth, N.Z. (plĭm'ūth)	203a	39.04S	174.13E
Newport, Austl.	201b	33.39S	151.19E
Newport, Austl.	243b	37.51S	144.53E
Newport, Eng., U.K.	144a	52.46N	2.22W
Newport, Eng., U.K. (nū-pôrt)	150	50.41N	1.25W
Newport, Wales, U.K.	147	51.36N	3.05W
Newport, Ar., U.S. (nū'pōrt)	111	35.35N	91.16W
Newport, Ky., U.S.	97	39.05N	84.30W
Newport, Me., U.S.	92	44.49N	69.20W
Newport, Mn., U.S.	107g	44.52N	92.59W
Newport, N.H., U.S.	99	43.20N	72.10W
Newport, Or., U.S.	104	44.39N	124.02W
Newport, R.I., U.S.	99	41.29N	71.16W
Newport, Tn., U.S.	114	35.55N	83.12W
Newport, Vt., U.S.	99	44.55N	72.15W
Newport, Wa., U.S.	104	48.12N	117.01W
Newport Beach, Ca., U.S. (bēch)	107a	33.36N	117.55W
Newport News, Va., U.S.	97	36.59N	76.24W
New Prague, Mn., U.S. (nū prāg)	103	44.33N	93.35W
New Providence, i., Bah. (prŏv'ĭ-dĕns)	122	25.00N	77.25W
New Redruth, S. Afr.	244b	26.16S	28.07E
New Richmond, Oh., U.S. (rĭch'mŭnd)	98	38.55N	84.15W
New Richmond, Wi., U.S.	103	45.07N	92.34W
New Roads, La., U.S. (rōds)	113	30.42N	91.26W
New Rochelle, N.Y., U.S. (rū-shĕl')	100a	40.55N	73.47W
New Rockford, N.D., U.S. (rŏk'fōrd)	102	47.40N	99.08W
New Ross, Ire. (rôs)	150	52.25N	6.55W
New Sarepta, Can.	83g	53.17N	113.09W
New Siberian Islands see Novosibirskiye Ostrova, is., Russia	165	74.00N	140.30E
New Smyrna Beach, Fl., U.S. (smûr'nȧ)	115	29.00N	80.57W
New South Wales, state, Austl. (wālz)	203	32.45S	146.14E
Newton, Can. (nū'tŭn)	83f	49.56N	98.04W
Newton, Eng., U.K.	144a	53.27N	2.37W
Newton, Il., U.S.	98	39.00N	88.10W
Newton, Ia., U.S.	103	41.42N	93.04W
Newton, Ks., U.S.	111	38.03N	97.22W
Newton, Ma., U.S.	93a	42.21N	71.13W
Newton, Ms., U.S.	114	32.18N	89.10W
Newton, N.J., U.S.	100a	41.03N	74.45W
Newton, N.C., U.S.	115	35.40N	81.19W
Newton, Tx., U.S.	113	30.47N	93.45W
Newton Brook, neigh., Can.	227c	43.48N	79.24W
Newton Highlands, Ma., U.S.	227a	41.19N	71.13W
Newton Lower Falls, Ma., U.S.	227a	42.19N	71.23W
Newtonsville, Oh., U.S. (nū'tŭnz-vĭl)	101f	39.11N	84.04W
Newton Upper Falls, Ma., U.S.	227a	42.19N	71.13W
Newtonville, Ma., U.S.	227a	42.21N	71.13W
Newtown, N.D., U.S. (nū'toun)	102	47.57N	102.25W
Newtown, Oh., U.S.	101f	39.08N	84.22W
Newtown, Pa., U.S.	100f	40.13N	74.56W
Newtown, neigh., Austl.	243a	33.54S	151.11E
Newtownards, N. Ire., U.K. (nu-t'n-ardz')	150	54.35N	5.39W
New Ulm, Mn., U.S. (ŭlm)	103	44.18N	94.27W
New Utrecht, neigh., N.Y., U.S.	228	40.36N	73.59W
New Waterford, Can. (wô'tēr-fērd)	85	46.15N	60.05W
New Westminster, Can. (wĕst'mĭn-stĕr)	87	49.12N	122.55W
New York, N.Y., U.S. (yôrk)	97	40.40N	73.58W
New York, state, U.S.	97	42.45N	78.05W
New Zealand, nation, Oc. (zē'lănd)	203a	42.00S	175.00E
Nexapa, r., Mex. (nĕks-ä'pä)	118	18.32N	98.29W
Neya-gawa, Japan (nā'yä gä'wä)	195b	34.47N	135.38E
Neyshābūr, Iran	182	36.06N	58.45E
Neyva, r., Russia (nĕy'vȧ)	172a	57.39N	60.37E
Nezahualcóyotl, Mex.	119a	19.27N	99.03W
Nez Perce, Id., U.S. (nĕz' pûrs')	104	46.16N	116.15W
Nez Perce Indian Reservation, I.R., Id., U.S.	104	46.20N	116.30W
Ngami, l., Bots. (n'gä'mē)	212	20.56S	22.31E
Ngamouéri, Congo	244c	4.14S	15.14E
Ngangerabeli Plain, pl., Kenya	217	1.20S	40.10E
Ngangla Ringco, l., China (ŋäŋ-lä rĭŋ-tswo)	186	31.42N	82.53E
Ngarimbi, Tan.	217	8.28S	38.36E
Ngoko, r., Afr.	216	1.55N	15.53E
Ngol-Kedju Hill, mtn., Cam.	215	6.20N	9.45E
Ngombe, Zaire	244c	4.24S	15.11E
Ngong, Kenya ('n-gông)	212	1.27S	36.39E
Ngounié, r., Gabon	216	1.15S	10.43E
Ngoywa, Tan.	217	5.56S	32.48E
Ngqeleni, S. Afr. ('ng-kĕ-lā'nē)	213c	31.41S	29.04E
Nguigmi, Niger ('n-gēg'mē)	211	14.15N	13.07E
Ngurore, Nig.	215	9.18N	12.14E
Nguru, Nig. ('n-gōō'rōō)	210	12.53N	10.26E
Nguru Mountains, mts., Tan.	217	6.10S	37.35E
Nha Trang, Viet. (nyä-träng')	196	12.08N	108.56E
Niafounke, Mali	210	16.03N	4.17W
Niagara, Wi., U.S. (nī-ăg'ȧ-rȧ)	103	45.45N	88.05W
Niagara, r., N.A.	101c	43.12N	79.03W
Niagara Falls, Can.	101c	43.05N	79.05W
Niagara Falls, N.Y., U.S.	97	43.06N	79.02W
Niagara-on-the-Lake, Can.	83d	43.16N	79.05W
Niakaramandougou, C. Iv.	214	8.40N	5.17W
Niamey, Niger (nē-ä-mā')	210	13.31N	2.07E
Niamtougou, Togo	214	9.46N	1.06E
Niangara, Zaire (nē-äŋ-gȧ'rȧ)	211	3.42N	27.52E

ăt; finăl; rāte; senâte; ärm; åsk; sofȧ; fâre; ch-choose; dh-as th in other; bē; ēvent; bĕt; recĕnt; cratēr; g-gō; gh-guttural g; bĭt; ĭ-short neutral; rīde; κ-guttural k as ch in German ich;

PRONOUNCING INDEX Niangua–North Borneo 325

PLACE (Pronunciation)	PAGE	Lat. °′	Long. °′
Niangua, r., Mo., U.S. (nī-ăŋ'gwȧ)	111	37.30N	93.05W
Nias, Pulau, i., Indon. (nē'äs')	196	0.58N	97.43E
Nibe, Den. (nē'bĕ)	152	56.57N	9.36E
Nicaragua, nation, N.A. (nĭk-ȧ-rä'gwȧ)	116	12.45N	86.15W
Nicaragua, Lago de, l., Nic. (lä'gô dĕ)	116	11.45N	85.28W
Nicastro, Italy (nē-käs'trō)	149	38.39N	16.15E
Nicchehabin, Punta, c., Mex. (pōō'n-tä-nĕk-chĕ-ä-bē'n)	120a	19.50N	87.20W
Nice, Fr. (nēs)	142	43.42N	7.21E
Nicheng, China (nē-chŭŋ)	191b	30.54N	121.48E
Nichicun, l., Can. (nĭch'ĭ-kŭn)	85	53.07N	72.10W
Nicholas Channel, strt., N.A. (nĭk'ô-lȧs)	122	23.30N	80.20W
Nicholasville, Ky., U.S. (nĭk'ô-lȧs-vĭl)	98	37.55N	84.35W
Nicobar Islands, is., India (nĭk-ô-bär')	196	8.28N	94.04E
Nicolai Mountain, mtn., Or., U.S. (nē-cō lī')	106c	46.05N	123.27W
Nicolás Romero, Mex. (nē-kô-lä's rō-mĕ'rô)	119a	19.38N	99.20W
Nicolet, Lake, l., Mi., U.S. (nĭ'kŏ-lĕt)	107k	46.22N	84.14W
Nicolls Town, Bah.	122	25.10N	78.00W
Nicols, Mn., U.S. (nĭk'ĕls)	107g	44.50N	93.12W
Nicomeki, r., Can.	106d	49.04N	122.47W
Nicosia, Cyp. (nē-kô-sē'ȧ)	182	35.10N	33.22E
Nicoya, C.R. (nē-kō'yä)	120	10.08N	85.27W
Nicoya, Golfo de, b., C.R. (gôl-fô-dĕ)	120	10.03N	85.04W
Nicoya, Península de, pen., C.R.	120	10.05N	86.00W
Nidzica, Pol. (nē-jēt'sȧ)	155	53.21N	20.30E
Niederaden, neigh., Ger.	236	51.36N	7.34E
Niederbonsfeld, Ger.	236	51.23N	7.08E
Niederdonk, Ger.	236	51.14N	6.41E
Niederelfringhausen, Ger.	236	51.21N	7.10E
Niedere Tauern, mts., Aus.	154	47.15N	13.41E
Niederkrüchten, Ger. (nē'dĕr-krük-tĕn)	157c	51.12N	6.14E
Nieder-Neuendorf, Ger.	238a	52.37N	13.12E
Niederösterreich, prov., Aus.	145e	48.24N	16.20E
Niedersachsen (Lower Saxony), hist. reg., Ger. (nē'dĕr-zäk-sĕn)	154	52.52N	8.27E
Niederschöneweide, neigh., Ger.	238a	52.27N	13.31E
Niederschönhausen, neigh., Ger.	238a	52.35N	13.23E
Niellim, Chad	215	9.42N	17.49E
Niemeyer, neigh., Braz.	234c	23.00S	43.15W
Nienburg, Ger. (nē'ĕn-bŏorgh)	154	52.40N	9.15E
Nierst, Ger.	236	51.19N	6.43E
Nietverdiend, S. Afr.	218d	25.02S	26.10E
Nieuw Nickerie, Sur. (nē-nē'kĕ-rē')	131	5.51N	57.00W
Nieves, Mex. (nyā'vås)	118	24.00N	102.57W
Niğde, Tur. (nĭg'dĕ)	149	37.55N	34.40E
Nigel, S. Afr. (nī'jĕl)	218d	26.26S	28.27E
Niger, nation, Afr. (nī'jẽr)	210	18.02N	8.30E
Niger, r., Afr.	210	8.00N	6.00E
Niger Delta, d., Nig.	215	4.45N	5.20E
Nigeria, nation, Afr. (nī-jē'rĭ-ȧ)	210	8.57N	6.30E
Nihoa, i., Hi., U.S.	94b	23.15N	161.30W
Nihonbashi, neigh., Japan	242a	35.41N	139.47E
Nii, i., Japan (nē)	195	34.26N	139.23E
Niigata, Japan (nē'ē-gä'tȧ)	189	37.47N	139.04E
Niihau, i., Hi., U.S. (nē'ē-ha'ōō)	96c	21.50N	160.05W
Niimi, Japan (nē'mē)	195	34.59N	133.28E
Niiza, Japan	195a	35.48N	139.34E
Nijmegen, Neth. (nī'mä-gĕn)	151	51.50N	5.52E
Nikaia, Grc.	239d	37.58N	23.39E
Nikitinka, Russia (nē-kĭ'tĭn-kȧ)	162	55.33N	33.19E
Nikolayevka, Russia (nē-kô-lä'yĕf-kȧ)	172c	59.29N	29.48E
Nikolayevka, Russia	194	48.37N	134.09E
Nikolayevskiy, Russia	167	50.00N	45.30E
Nikolayevsk-na-Amure, Russia	165	53.18N	140.49E
Nikolo-Chovanskoje, Russia	239b	55.36N	37.27E
Nikol'sk, Russia (nē-kôlsk')	164	59.30N	45.40E
Nikol'skoye, Russia (nē-kôl'skô-yĕ)	172c	59.27N	30.00E
Nikopol, Bul. (nē'kô-pōl')	149	43.41N	24.52E
Nikopol', Ukr.	167	47.36N	34.24E
Nilahue, r., Chile (nē-lȧ'wĕ)	129b	34.36S	71.50W
Nile, r., Afr. (nīl)	211	27.30N	31.00E
Niles, Il., U.S.	231a	42.01N	87.49W
Niles, Mi., U.S. (nīlz)	98	41.50N	86.15W
Niles, Oh., U.S.	98	41.15N	80.45W
Nileshwar, India	187	12.08N	74.14E
Nilgani, India	240a	22.46N	88.26E
Nilgiri Hills, hills, India	187	12.05N	76.22E
Nilópolis, Braz. (nē-lô'pō-lēs)	129a	22.48S	43.25W
Nīmach, India	186	24.32N	74.51E
Nimba, Mont, mtn., Afr. (nĭm'bȧ)	210	7.40N	8.33W
Nimba Mountains, mts., Afr.	214	7.30N	8.35W
Nîmes, Fr. (nēm)	142	43.49N	4.22E
Nimrod Reservoir, res., Ar., U.S. (nĭm'rŏd)	111	34.58N	93.46W
Nimule, Sudan (nē-mōō'lȧ)	211	3.38N	32.12E
Ninda, Ang.	216	14.47S	21.24E
Nine Ashes, Eng., U.K.	235	51.42N	0.18E
Nine Mile Creek, r., Ut., U.S. (mīn'īmôd')	109	39.50N	110.30W
Ninety Mile Beach, cst., Austl.	203	38.20S	147.30E
Nineveh, Iraq (nĭn'ē-vȧ)	182	36.30N	43.10E
Ning'an, China (nĭŋ-än)	189	44.20N	129.20E
Ningbo, China (nĭŋ-bwo)	189	29.56N	121.30E
Ningde, China (nĭŋ-dŭ)	189	26.38N	119.33E
Ninghai, China (nĭng'hī')	193	29.20N	121.20E
Ninghe, China (nĭŋ-hŭ)	190	39.20N	117.50E
Ningjin, China (nĭŋ-jyĭn)	190	37.39N	116.47E
Ningjin, China	190	37.37N	114.55E
Ningming, China	193	22.22N	107.06E
Ningwu, China (nĭng'wōō')	189	39.00N	112.12E
Ningxia Huizu, prov., China (nĭŋ-shyä)	188	37.10N	106.00E
Ningyang, China (nĭng'yäng')	190	35.46N	116.48E
Ninh Binh, Viet. (nēn bĕnk')	196	20.22N	106.00E

PLACE (Pronunciation)	PAGE	Lat. °′	Long. °′
Ninigo Group, is., Pap. N. Gui.	197	1.15S	143.30E
Ninnescah, r., Ks., U.S. (nĭn'ĕs-kä)	110	37.37N	98.31W
Nioaque, Braz. (nēō-ä'-kĕ)	131	21.14S	55.41W
Niobrara, r., U.S. (nī-ô-brâr'ȧ)	96	42.46N	98.46W
Niokolo Koba, Parc National du, rec., Sen.	214	13.05N	13.00W
Nioro du Sahel, Mali (nē-ō'rō)	210	15.15N	9.35W
Nipawin, Can.	84	53.22N	104.00W
Nipe, Bahía de, b., Cuba (bä-ē'ä-dĕ-nē'pā)	123	20.50N	75.30W
Nipe, Sierra de, mts., Cuba (sē-ĕ'r-rȧ-dĕ)	123	20.20N	75.50W
Nipigon, Can. (nĭp'ĭ-gŏn)	85	48.58N	88.17W
Nipigon, l., Can.	85	49.37N	89.55W
Nipigon Bay, b., Can.	90	48.56N	88.00W
Nipisiguit, r., Can. (nĭ-pĭ'sĭ-kwĭt)	92	47.26N	66.15W
Nipissing, l., Can. (nĭp'ĭ-sĭng)	85	45.59N	80.19W
Niquero, Cuba (nē-kā'rō)	122	20.00N	77.35W
Nirmali, India	186	26.30N	86.43E
Niš, Yugo.	142	43.19N	21.54E
Nisa, Port. (nē'sȧ)	158	39.32N	7.41W
Nišava, r., Eur. (nē'shȧ-vȧ)	161	43.17N	22.17E
Nishi, Japan	242b	34.41N	135.30E
Nishinari, neigh., Japan	242b	34.38N	135.28E
Nishino, i., Japan (nēsh'ē-nô)	195	36.06N	132.49E
Nishinomiya, Japan (nēsh'ē-nô-mē'yȧ)	195b	34.44N	135.21E
Nishio, Japan (nēsh'ē-ô)	195	34.50N	137.01E
Nishiyodogawa, neigh., Japan	242b	34.42N	135.27E
Niska Lake, l., Can. (nĭs'kȧ)	88	55.35N	108.38W
Nisko, Pol. (nēs'kô)	155	50.30N	22.07E
Nisku, Can. (nĭs-kū')	83g	53.21N	113.33W
Nisqually, r., Wa., U.S. (nĭs-kwôl'ĭ)	104	46.51N	122.33W
Nissan, r., Swe.	152	57.06N	13.22E
Nisser, l., Nor. (nĭs'ẽr)	152	59.14N	8.35E
Nissum Fjord, fj., Den.	152	56.24N	7.35E
Niterói, Braz. (nē-tĕ-rô'ĭ)	131	22.53S	43.07W
Nith, r., Scot., U.K. (nĭth)	150	55.13N	3.55W
Nitra, Slvk. (nē'trȧ)	155	48.18N	18.04E
Nitra, r., Slvk.	155	48.13N	18.14E
Nitro, W.V., U.S. (nī'trō)	98	38.25N	81.50W
Niue, dep., Oc. (nĭ'ô)	225	19.50S	167.00W
Nivelles, Bel. (nē-vĕl')	151	50.33N	4.17E
Nixon, Tx., U.S. (nĭk'sŭn)	113	29.16N	97.48W
Nizāmābād, India	183	18.48N	78.07E
Nizhne-Angarsk, Russia (nyĕzh'nyĭ-ŭngärsk')	165	55.49N	108.46E
Nizhne-Chirskaya, Russia	167	48.20N	42.50E
Nizhne-Kolymsk, Russia (kô-lēmsk')	165	68.32N	160.56E
Nizhneudinsk, Russia (nĕzh'nyĭ-ōōdēnsk')	165	54.58N	99.15E
Nizhniye Sergi, Russia (nyĕzh' nyĕ sĕr'gĕ)	166	56.41N	59.19E
Nizhniy Novgorod (Gor'kiy), Russia	164	56.15N	44.05E
Nizhniy Tagil, Russia (tŭgĕl')	164	57.54N	59.59E
Nizhnyaya Kur'ya, Russia (nyĕ'zhnyȧ-yȧ koor'yȧ)	172a	58.01N	56.00E
Nizhnyaya Salda, Russia (nyĕ'zhnya'ya säl'da')	172a	58.05N	60.43E
Nizhnyaya Taymyra, r., Russia	170	72.30N	95.18E
Nizhnyaya Tunguska, r., Russia	165	64.13N	91.30E
Nizhnyaya Tura, Russia (tōō'rȧ)	172a	58.38N	59.50E
Nizhnyaya Us'va, Russia (ôs'vȧ)	172a	59.05N	58.53E
Nizhyn, Ukr.	167	51.03N	31.52E
Nízke Tatry, mts., Slvk.	155	48.57N	19.18E
Njazidja, i., Com.	213	11.44S	42.38E
Njombe, Tan.	217	9.20S	34.46E
Njurunda, Swe. (nyōō-rôn'dȧ)	152	62.15N	17.24E
Nkala Mission, Zam.	217	15.55S	26.00E
Nkandla, S. Afr. ('n-känd'lä)	213c	28.40S	31.06E
Nkawkaw, Ghana	214	6.33N	0.47W
Nkhota, Mwi. (kō-tȧ kō-tȧ)	212	12.52S	34.16E
Noākhāli, Bngl.	183	22.52N	91.08E
Noatak, Ak., U.S. (nô-ȧ'tȧk)	95	67.22N	163.28W
Noatak, r., Ak., U.S.	95	67.58N	162.15W
Nobeoka, Japan (nō-bȧ-ō'kȧ)	194	32.36N	131.41E
Noblesville, In., U.S. (nō'bl'z-vĭl)	98	40.00N	86.00W
Nobleton, Can. (nō'bl'tŭn)	83d	43.54N	79.39W
Noborito, Japan	242a	35.37N	139.34E
Nocera Inferiore, Italy (ĕn-fĕ-ryō'rĕ)	159c	40.30N	14.38E
Nochistlán, Mex. (nô-chēs-tlän')	118	21.23N	102.52W
Nochixtlón, Mex. (ä-sôn-syōn')	119	17.28N	97.12W
Nogales, Mex.	116	31.15N	111.00W
Nogales, Mex. (nō-gä'lĕs)	119	18.49N	97.09W
Nogales, Az., U.S. (nô-gä'lĕs)	96	31.20N	110.55W
Nogal Valley, val., Som. (nô'gȧl)	218a	8.30N	47.50E
Nogent-le-Roi, Fr. (nŏ-zhŏn-lĕ-rwä')	157b	48.39N	1.32E
Nogent-le-Rotrou, Fr. (rō-trōō')	156	48.22N	0.47E
Nogent-sur-Marne, Fr.	237c	48.50N	2.29E
Noginsk, Russia (nô-gēnsk')	166	55.52N	38.28E
Noguera Pallares, r., Spain	159	42.18N	1.03E
Noirmoutier, Île de, i., Fr. (nwȧr-mōō-tyā')	147	47.03N	3.08W
Noisy-le-Grand, Fr.	237c	48.51N	2.33E
Noisy-le-Roi, Fr.	237c	48.51N	2.04E
Noisy-le-Sec, Fr.	237c	48.53N	2.28E
Nojima-Zaki, c., Japan (nō'jē-mä zä-kē)	195	34.54N	139.48E
Nokomis, Il., U.S. (nô-kō'mĭs)	98	39.15N	89.10W
Nola, Italy (nô'lä)	160	40.41N	14.32E
Nolinsk, Russia (nô-lēnsk')	166	57.32N	49.50E
Noma Misaki, c., Japan (nô'mä mē'sä-kē)	195	31.25N	130.09E
Nombre de Dios, Mex. (nôm-brĕ-dĕ-dyō's)	118	23.50N	104.14W
Nombre de Dios, Pan. (nô'm-brĕ)	121	9.34N	79.28W
Nome, Ak., U.S. (nōm)	96a	64.30N	165.20W
Nonacho, l., Can.	84	61.48N	111.20W

PLACE (Pronunciation)	PAGE	Lat. °′	Long. °′
Nonantum, Ma., U.S.	227a	42.20N	71.12W
Nong'an, China (nôŋ-än)	192	44.25N	125.10E
Nongoma, S. Afr. (nŏn-gō'mȧ)	212	27.48S	31.45E
Nooksack, Wa., U.S. (nŏŏk'săk)	106d	48.55N	122.19W
Nooksack, r., Wa., U.S.	106d	48.54N	122.31W
Noordwijk aan Zee, Neth.	145a	52.14N	4.25E
Noordzee Kanaal, can., Neth.	145a	52.27N	4.42E
Nootka, i., Can. (nōōt'kȧ)	84	49.32N	126.42W
Nootka Sound, strt., Can.	86	49.33N	126.38W
Nóqui, Ang. (nô-kē')	212	5.51S	13.25E
Nor, r., China (nou')	194	46.55N	132.45E
Nora, Swe.	152	59.32N	14.56E
Nora, In., U.S. (nō'rä)	101g	39.54N	86.08W
Noranda, Can.	91	48.15N	79.01W
Norbeck, Md., U.S. (nōr'bĕk)	100e	39.06N	77.05W
Norborne, Mo., U.S. (nôr'bôrn)	111	39.17N	93.39W
Norco, Ca., U.S. (nôr'kô)	107a	33.57N	117.33W
Norcross, Ga., U.S. (nôr'krôs)	100c	33.56N	84.13W
Nord, Riviere du, Can. (rēv-yĕr' dü nōr)	83a	45.45N	74.02W
Nordegg, Can. (nûr'dĕg)	87	52.28N	116.04W
Norden, Ger. (nôr'dĕn)	154	53.35N	7.14E
Norden, Eng., U.K.	237b	53.38N	2.13W
Norderney, i., Ger. (nōr'dĕr-nĕy)	154	53.45N	6.58E
Nordfjord, fj., Nor. (nô'fyôr)	152	61.50N	5.35E
Nordhausen, Ger. (nôrt'hau-zĕn)	147	51.30N	10.48E
Nordhorn, Ger. (nôrt'hôrn)	154	52.26N	7.05E
Nord Kapp, c., Nor.	166	71.11N	25.48E
Nordland, Wa., U.S. (nôrd'lȧnd)	106a	48.03N	122.41W
Nördlingen, Ger. (nûrt'lĭng-ĕn)	154	48.51N	10.30E
Nord-Ostsee Kanal (Kiel Canal), can., Ger. (nōrd-ōzt-zā) (kēl)	154	54.03N	9.23E
Nordrhein-Westfalen (North Rhine-Westphalia), hist. reg., Ger. (nōrd'hīn-vĕst-fä-lĕn)	154	50.50N	6.53E
Nordvik, Russia (nôrd'vĕk)	165	73.57N	111.15E
Nore, r., Ire. (nōr)	150	52.34N	7.15W
Norf, Ger.	236	51.09N	6.43E
Norfolk, Ma., U.S. (nôr'fŏk)	93a	42.07N	71.19W
Norfolk, Ne., U.S.	96	42.10N	97.25W
Norfolk, Va., U.S.	97	36.55N	76.15W
Norfolk, i., Oc.	225	27.10S	166.50E
Norfork, Lake, l., Ar., U.S.	111	36.25N	92.09W
Noril'sk, Russia (nô rēlsk')	164	69.00N	87.11E
Normal, Il., U.S. (nôr'mȧl)	98	40.35N	89.00W
Norman, r., Austl.	203	18.27S	141.29E
Norman, Lake, res., N.C., U.S.	97	35.30N	80.53W
Normandie, hist. reg., Fr. (nŏr-mäN-dē')	156	49.02N	0.17E
Normandie, Collines de, hills, Fr. (kō-lēn'dĕ-nôr-män-dē')	156	48.46N	0.50W
Normandy see Normandie, hist. reg., Fr.	156	49.02N	0.17E
Normandy Heights, Md., U.S.	229c	39.17N	76.48W
Normanhurst, Austl.	243a	33.43S	151.06E
Normanton, Austl. (nôr'mȧn-tŭn)	203	17.45S	141.10E
Normanton, Eng., U.K.	144a	53.40N	1.21W
Norman Wells, Can.	84	65.26N	127.00W
Nornalup, Austl. (nôr-näl'ŭp)	202	35.00S	117.00E
Nørresundby, Den. (nû-rĕ-sôn'bü)	152	57.04N	9.55E
Norridge, Il., U.S.	231a	41.57N	87.49W
Norris, Tn., U.S. (nŏr'ĭs)	114	36.09N	84.05W
Norris Lake, res., Tn., U.S.	97	36.17N	84.10W
Norristown, Pa., U.S. (nŏr'ĭs-town)	100f	40.07N	75.21W
Norrköping, Swe. (nôr'chûp'ĭng)	142	58.37N	16.10E
Norrtälje, Swe. (nôr-tĕl'yĕ)	146	59.47N	18.39E
Norseman, Austl. (nôrs'mȧn)	202	32.15S	122.00E
Norte, Punta, c., Arg. (pōō'n-tä-nŏr'tĕ)	129c	36.17S	56.46W
Norte, Serra do, mts., Braz. (sĕ'r-rä-dô-nôr'te)	131	12.04S	59.08W
North, Cape, c., Can.	93	47.02N	60.25W
North Abington, Ma., U.S.	227a	42.08N	70.57W
North Adams, Ma., U.S. (ăd'ămz)	99	42.40N	73.05W
Northam, Austl. (nôr-dhăm)	202	31.50S	116.45E
Northam, S. Afr. (nôr'thăm)	218d	24.52S	27.16E
North America, cont.	82	45.00N	100.00W
North American Basin, deep (ȧ-mĕr'ĭ-kȧn)	4	23.45N	62.45W
Northampton, Austl. (nôr-thămp'tŭn)	202	28.22S	114.45E
Northampton, Eng., U.K. (nôrth-ămp'tŭn)	147	52.14N	0.56W
Northampton, Ma., U.S.	99	42.20N	72.45W
Northampton, Pa., U.S.	99	40.45N	75.30W
Northamptonshire, co., Eng., U.K.	144a	52.25N	0.47W
North Andaman Island, i., India (ăn-dȧ-măn')	196	13.15N	93.30E
North Andover, Ma., U.S. (ăn'dô-vẽr)	93a	42.42N	71.07W
North Arlington, N.J., U.S.	228	40.47N	74.08W
North Arm, mth., Can. (ärm)	106d	49.13N	123.01W
North Atlanta, Ga., U.S. (ăt-lăn'tȧ)	100c	33.52N	84.20W
North Attleboro, Ma., U.S. (ăt''l-bŭr-ô)	100b	41.59N	71.18W
North Auburn, Austl.	243a	33.50S	151.02E
North Baltimore, Oh., U.S. (bôl'tĭ-môr)	98	41.10N	83.40W
North Balwyn, Austl.	243b	37.48S	145.05E
North Barnaby, Md., U.S.	229d	38.49N	76.57W
North Barrackpore, India	240a	22.46N	88.22E
North Basque, Tx., U.S. (băsk)	112	31.56N	98.01W
North Battleford, Can. (băt''l-fẽrd)	84	52.47N	108.17W
North Bay, Can.	85	46.13N	79.26W
North Beach, neigh., Ca., U.S.	231b	37.48N	122.25W
North Bellmore, N.Y., U.S.	228	40.41N	73.32W
North Bend, Or., U.S. (bĕnd)	104	43.23N	124.13W
North Bergen, N.J., U.S.	228	40.48N	74.01W
North Berwick, Me., U.S. (bûr'wĭk)	92	43.18N	70.46W
North Bight, bt., Bah. (bĭt)	122	24.30N	77.40W
North Bimini, i., Bah. (bĭ'mĭ-nē)	122	25.45N	79.20W
North Borneo see Sabah, hist. reg., Malay.	196	5.10N	116.25E

326 Northborough – Nubah

PLACE (Pronunciation)	PAGE	Lat. °'	Long. °'
Northborough, Ma., U.S.	93a	42.19N	71.39W
North Box Hill, Austl.	243b	37.48S	145.07E
North Braddock, Pa., U.S.	230b	40.24N	79.52W
Northbridge, Austl.	243a	33.49S	151.13E
Northbridge, Ma., U.S. (nôrth'brĭj)	93a	42.09N	71.39W
North Caicos, i., T./C. Is. (kī'kōs)	123	21.55N	72.00W
North Caldwell, N.J., U.S.	228	40.52N	74.16W
North Cape, c., N.Z.	203a	34.31S	173.02E
North Carolina, state, U.S. (kăr-ō-lī'nȧ)	97	35.40N	81.30W
North Cascades National Park, rec., Wa., U.S.	87	48.50N	120.50W
North Cat Cay, i., Bah.	122	25.35N	79.20W
North Channel, strt., Can.	90	46.10N	83.20W
North Channel, strt., U.K.	142	55.15N	7.56W
North Charleston, S.C., U.S. (chärlz'tŭn)	115	32.49N	79.57W
North Chicago, Il., U.S. (shĭ-kô'gō)	101a	42.19N	87.51W
Northcliff, neigh., S. Afr.	244b	26.09S	27.58E
North College Hill, Oh., U.S. (kŏl'ĕj hĭl)	101f	39.13N	84.33W
North Concho, Tx., U.S. (kŏn'chō)	112	31.40N	100.48W
North Cooking Lake, Can. (kŏŏk'ĭng lāk)	83g	53.28N	112.57W
Northcote, Austl.	243b	37.46S	145.00E
North Cyprus, nation, Asia	182	35.15N	33.40E
North Dakota, state, U.S. (dȧ-kō'tȧ)	96	47.20N	101.55W
North Downs, Eng., U.K. (dounz)	150	51.11N	0.01W
North Dum-Dum, India	186a	22.38N	88.23E
Northeast Cape, c., Ak., U.S. (nôrth-ēst)	95	63.15N	169.04W
Northeast Point, c., Bah.	123	22.45N	73.50W
Northeast Point, c., Bah.	123	21.25N	73.00W
Northeast Providence Channel, strt., Bah. (prŏv'ĭ-dĕns)	122	25.45N	77.00W
Northeim, Ger. (nôrt'hīm)	154	51.42N	9.59E
North Elbow Cays, is., Bah.	122	23.55N	80.30W
North Englewood, Md., U.S.	229d	38.55N	76.55W
Northern Cheyenne Indian Reservation, I.R., Mt., U.S.	105	45.32N	106.43W
Northern Dvina *see* Severnaya Dvina, r., Russia	164	63.00N	42.40E
Northern Ireland, , U.K. (īr'lănd)	142	54.48N	7.00W
Northern Land *see* Severnaya Zemlya, is., Russia	165	79.33N	101.15E
Northern Mariana Islands, dep., Oc. (mä-rē-ä'nȧ)	3	17.20N	145.00E
Northern Territory, , Austl.	202	18.15S	133.00E
Northern Yukon National Park, rec., Can.	95	69.00N	140.00W
North Essendon, Austl.	243b	37.45S	144.54E
Northfield, Il., U.S.	231a	42.06N	87.46W
Northfield, Mn., U.S. (nôrth'fēld)	103	44.28N	93.11W
North Fitzroy, Austl.	243b	37.47S	144.59E
Northfleet, Eng., U.K.	235	51.27N	0.21E
North Flinders Ranges, mts., Austl. (flĭn'dẽrz)	204	31.55S	138.45E
North Foreland, Eng., U.K. (nôrth-fōr'lănd)	151	51.20N	1.30E
North Franklin Mountain, mtn., Tx., U.S. (frăŋ'klĭn)	112	31.55N	106.30W
North Frisian Islands, is., Eur.	146	55.16N	8.15E
North Gamboa, Pan. (gäm-bô'ä)	121	9.07N	79.40W
North Germiston, S. Afr.	244b	26.14S	28.09E
North Gower, Can. (gŏw'ẽr)	83c	45.08N	75.43W
North Haledon, N.J., U.S.	228	40.58N	74.11W
North Hanover, Ma., U.S.	227a	42.09N	70.52W
North Hills, N.Y., U.S.	228	40.47N	73.41W
North Hollywood, Ca., U.S. (hŏl'ē-wŏŏd)	107a	34.10N	118.23W
North Island, i., N.Z.	203a	37.20S	173.30E
North Island, i., Ca., U.S.	108a	32.39N	117.14W
North Judson, In., U.S. (jŭd'sŭn)	98	41.15N	86.50W
North Kansas City, Mo., U.S. (kăn'zȧs)	107f	39.08N	94.34W
North Kingstown, R.I., U.S.	100b	41.34N	71.26W
Northlake, Il., U.S.	231a	41.55N	87.54W
North Little Rock, Ar., U.S. (lĭt''l rŏk)	111	34.46N	92.13W
North Loup, r., Ne., U.S. (lōōp)	102	42.05N	100.10W
North Magnetic Pole, pt. of i.	220	77.19N	101.49W
North Manchester, In., U.S. (măn'chĕs-tẽr)	98	41.00N	85.45W
North Manly, Austl.	243a	33.46S	151.16E
Northmead, Austl.	243a	33.47S	151.00E
Northmead, S. Afr.	244b	26.10S	28.20E
North Merrick, N.Y., U.S.	228	40.41N	73.34W
Northmoor, Mo., U.S. (nôth'mōōr)	107f	39.10N	94.37W
North Moose Lake, l., Can.	89	54.09N	100.20W
North Mount Lofty Ranges, mts., Austl.	204	33.50S	138.30E
North Ockendon, neigh., Eng., U.K.	235	51.32N	0.18E
North Ogden, Ut., U.S. (ŏg'dĕn)	107b	41.18N	111.58W
North Ogden Peak, mtn., Ut., U.S.	107b	41.23N	111.59W
North Olmsted, Oh., U.S. (ōlm-stĕd)	101d	41.25N	81.55W
North Ossetia, state, Russia	166	43.00N	44.15E
North Parramatta, Austl.	243a	33.48S	151.00E
North Pease, r., Tx., U.S. (pēz)	110	34.19N	100.58W
North Pender, i., Can. (pĕn'dẽr)	106d	48.48N	123.16W
North Philadelphia, neigh., Pa., U.S.	229b	39.58N	75.09W
North Plains, Or., U.S. (plānz)	106c	45.36N	123.00W
North Platte, Ne., U.S. (plăt)	96	41.08N	100.45W
North Platte, r., U.S.	96	41.20N	102.40W
North Point, H.K.	241c	22.17N	114.12E
North Point, c., Barb.	121b	13.22N	59.36W
North Point, c., Mi., U.S.	98	45.00N	83.20W
North Pole, pt. of i.	220	90.00N	0.00
Northport, Al., U.S. (nôrth'pōrt)	114	33.12N	87.35W
Northport, N.Y., U.S.	100a	40.53N	73.20W
Northport, Wa., U.S.	104	48.53N	117.47W
North Quincy, Ma., U.S.	227a	42.17N	71.01W
North Randolph, Ma., U.S.	227a	42.12N	71.04W
North Reading, Ma., U.S. (rĕd'ĭng)	93a	42.34N	71.04W
North Richland Hills, Tx., U.S.	107c	32.50N	97.13W

PLACE (Pronunciation)	PAGE	Lat. °'	Long. °'
North Richmond, Ca., U.S.	231b	37.57N	122.22W
Northridge, Ca., U.S. (nôrth'rĭdj)	107a	34.14N	118.32W
North Ridgeville, Oh., U.S. (rĭj-vĭl)	101d	41.23N	82.01W
North Riverside, Il., U.S.	231a	41.51N	87.49W
North Ronaldsay, i., Scot., U.K.	150a	59.21N	2.23W
North Royalton, Oh., U.S. (roi'ăl-tŭn)	101d	41.19N	81.44W
North Ryde, Austl.	243a	33.48S	151.07E
North Saint Paul, Mn., U.S. (sånt pôl')	103	45.01N	92.59W
North Santiam, r., Or., U.S. (săn'tyăm)	104	44.42N	122.50W
North Saskatchewan, r., Can. (săn-kăch'ē-wän)	84	54.00N	111.30W
North Sea, Eur.	142	56.09N	3.16E
North Side, neigh., Pa., U.S.	230b	40.28N	80.01W
North Skunk, r., Ia., U.S. (skŭnk)	103	41.39N	92.46W
North Springfield, Va., U.S.	229d	38.48N	77.13W
North Stradbroke Island, i., Austl. (străd'brōk)	203	27.45S	154.18E
North Sydney, Austl.	243a	33.50S	151.13E
North Sydney, Can. (sĭd'nē)	93	46.13N	60.15W
North Taranaki Bight, N.Z. (tä-rä-nä'kĭ bīt)	203a	38.40S	174.00E
North Tarrytown, N.Y., U.S. (tăr'ĭ-toun)	100a	41.05N	73.52W
North Thompson, r., Can.	87	50.50N	120.10W
North Tonawanda, N.Y., U.S. (tŏn-ȧ-wŏn'dȧ)	101c	43.02N	78.53W
North Truchas Peaks, mtn., N.M., U.S. (trōō'chäs)	96	35.58N	105.40W
North Twillingate, i., Can. (twĭl'ĭn-gāt)	92	35.58N	105.37W
North Uist, i., Scot., U.K. (û'ĭst)	150	57.37N	7.22W
Northumberland, N.H., U.S.	99	44.30N	71.30W
Northumberland Islands, is., Austl.	203	21.42S	151.30E
Northumberland Strait, strt., Can. (nôr thŭm'bẽr-lȧnd)	92	46.25N	64.20W
North Umpqua, r., Or., U.S. (ŭmp'kwȧ)	104	43.20N	122.50W
North Valley Stream, N.Y., U.S.	228	40.41N	73.41W
North Vancouver, Can. (văn-kōō'vẽr)	84	49.19N	123.04W
North Vernon, In., U.S. (vûr'nŭn)	98	39.05N	85.45W
North Versailles, Pa., U.S.	230b	40.22N	79.48W
Northville, Mi., U.S. (nôrth-vĭl)	101b	42.26N	83.28W
North Wales, Pa., U.S. (wālz)	100f	40.12N	75.16W
North Weald Bassett, Eng., U.K.	235	51.43N	0.10E
North West Cape, c., Austl. (nôrth'wĕst)	202	21.50S	112.25E
Northwest Cape Fear, r., N.C., U.S. (căp fēr)	115	34.34N	79.46W
Northwestern University, pt. of i., Il., U.S.	231a	42.04N	87.40W
North West Gander, r., Can. (găn'dẽr)	93	48.40N	55.15W
Northwest Harbor, b., Md., U.S.	229c	39.16N	76.35W
Northwest Providence Channel, strt., Bah. (prŏv'ĭ-dĕns)	122	26.15N	78.45W
Northwest Territories, , Can. (tĕr'ĭ-tō'rĭs)	84	64.42N	119.09W
North Weymouth, Ma., U.S.	227a	42.15N	70.57W
Northwich, Eng., U.K. (nôrth'wĭch)	144a	53.15N	2.31W
North Wilkesboro, N.C., U.S. (wĭlks'bûrō)	115	36.08N	81.10W
North Wilmington, Ma., U.S.	227a	42.34N	71.10W
Northwood, Ia., U.S. (nôrth'wŏŏd)	103	43.26N	93.13W
Northwood, N.D., U.S.	102	47.44N	97.36W
Northwood, neigh., Eng., U.K.	235	51.37N	0.25W
North Yamhill, r., Or., U.S. (yăm' hĭl)	106c	45.22N	123.21W
North York, Can.	91	43.47N	79.25W
North York Moors, for., Eng., U.K. (yôrk mŏŏrz')	150	54.20N	0.40W
North Yorkshire, co., Eng., U.K.	144a	53.50N	1.10W
Norton, Ks., U.S. (nôr'tŭn)	110	39.40N	99.54W
Norton, Ma., U.S.	100b	41.58N	71.08W
Norton, Va., U.S.	115	36.54N	82.36W
Norton Bay, b., Ak., U.S.	95	64.22N	162.18W
Norton Heath, Eng., U.K.	235	51.43N	0.19E
Norton Reservoir, res., Ma., U.S.	100b	42.01N	71.07W
Norton Sound, strt., Ak., U.S.	95	63.48N	164.50W
Norval, Can. (nôr'vål)	83d	43.39N	79.52W
Norwalk, Ca., U.S. (nôr'wôk)	107a	33.54N	118.05W
Norwalk, Ct., U.S.	100a	41.06N	73.25W
Norwalk, Oh., U.S.	98	41.15N	82.35W
Norway, Me., U.S.	92	44.11N	70.35W
Norway, Mi., U.S.	103	45.47N	87.55W
Norway, nation, Eur. (nôr'wā)	142	63.48N	11.17E
Norway House, Can.	84	53.59N	97.50W
Norwegian Sea, sea, Eur. (nôr-wē'jăn)	146	66.54N	1.43E
Norwell, Ma., U.S. (nôr'wĕl)	93a	42.10N	70.47W
Norwich, Eng., U.K.	147	52.40N	1.15E
Norwich, Ct., U.S. (nôr'wĭch)	99	41.20N	72.00W
Norwich, N.Y., U.S.	99	42.35N	75.30W
Norwood, Ma., U.S. (nôr'wŏŏd)	93a	42.11N	71.13W
Norwood, N.C., U.S.	115	35.15N	80.08W
Norwood, Oh., U.S.	101f	39.10N	84.27W
Norwood, Pa., U.S.	229b	39.53N	75.18W
Norwood Park, neigh., Il., U.S.	231a	41.59N	87.48W
Nose, neigh., Japan	242b	34.49N	135.09E
Nose Creek, r., Can. (nōz)	83e	51.09N	114.02W
Noshiro, Japan (nō'shē-rō)	194	40.09N	140.02E
Nosivka, Ukr. (nō'sĭf-kȧ)	163	50.54N	31.35E
Nossob, r., Afr. (nŏ'sŏb)	212	24.15S	19.10E
Noteć, r., Pol. (nō'tĕcn)	154	52.50N	16.19E
Notodden, Nor. (nōt'ôd'n)	152	59.35N	9.15E
Notre-Dame, rel., Fr.	237c	48.51N	2.21E
Notre Dame, Monts, mts., Can.	92	46.35N	70.35W
Notre Dame Bay, b., Can. (nō't'r dām')	85a	49.45N	55.15W
Notre-Dame-des-Victoires, neigh., Can.	227b	45.35N	73.34W
Notre-Dame-du-Lac, Can.	92	47.37N	68.51W
Nottawasaga Bay, b., Can. (nŏt'ȧ-wȧ-sä'gȧ)	91	44.45N	80.35W
Nottaway, r., Can. (nôt'ȧ-wā)	85	50.58N	78.02W
Nottingham, Eng., U.K. (nŏt'ĭng-ăm)	147	52.58N	1.09W

PLACE (Pronunciation)	PAGE	Lat. °'	Long. °'
Nottingham, Pa., U.S.	229b	40.07N	74.58W
Nottingham Island, i., Can.	85	62.58N	78.53W
Nottingham Park, Il., U.S.	231a	41.46N	87.48W
Nottinghamshire, co., Eng., U.K.	144a	53.03N	1.05W
Notting Hill, Austl.	243b	37.54S	145.08E
Nottoway, r., Va., U.S. (nôt'ȧ-wā)	115	36.53N	77.47W
Notukeu Creek, r., Can.	88	49.55N	106.30W
Nouadhibou, Maur.	210	21.02N	17.09W
Nouakchott, Maur.	210	18.06N	15.57W
Nouamrhar, Maur.	210	19.22N	16.31W
Nouméa, N. Cal. (nōō-mā'ä)	203	22.16S	166.27E
Nouvelle, Can. (nōō-vĕl')	92	48.09N	66.22W
Nouvelle-France, Cap de, c., Can.	85	62.03N	74.00W
Nouzonville, Fr. (nōō-zôn-vēl')	156	49.51N	4.43E
Nova Cachoeirinha, neigh., Braz.	234d	23.28S	46.40W
Nova Cruz, Braz. (nō'vȧ-krōō'z)	131	6.22S	35.20W
Nova Friburgo, Braz. (frē-bōōr'gō)	131	22.18S	42.31W
Nova Iguaçu, Braz. (nō'vä-ē-gwä-sōō')	131	22.45S	43.27W
Nova Lima, Braz. (lē'mä)	129a	19.59S	43.51W
Nova Lisboa *see* Huambo, Ang.	212	12.44S	15.47E
Nova Mambone, Moz. (nō'vȧ-mȧm-bō'nĕ)	212	21.04S	35.13E
Nova Odesa, Ukr.	163	47.18N	31.48E
Nova Praha, Ukr.	163	48.34N	32.54E
Novara, Italy (nô-vä'rä)	148	45.24N	8.38E
Nova Resende, Braz.	129a	21.12S	46.25W
Nova Scotia, prov., Can. (skō'shȧ)	85	44.28N	65.00W
Novate Milanese, Italy	238c	45.32N	9.08E
Nova Vodolaha, Ukr.	163	49.43N	35.51E
Novaya Ladoga, Russia (nô'vȧ-ya lȧ-dô-gȧ)	153	60.06N	32.16E
Novaya Lyalya, Russia (lyȧ'lyȧ)	172a	59.03N	60.36E
Novaya Sibir, i., Russia (sē-bēr')	165	75.00N	149.00E
Novaya Zemlya, i., Russia (zĕm-lyȧ')	164	72.00N	54.46E
Nova Zagora, Bul. (zä'gō-rȧ)	161	42.30N	26.01E
Novelda, Spain (nō-vĕl'dȧ)	159	38.22N	0.46W
Nové Mesto nad Váhom, Slvk. (nō'vě myĕs'tō)	155	48.44N	17.47E
Nové Zámky, Slvk. (zȧm'kĕ)	147	47.58N	18.10E
Novgorod, Russia (nôv'gō-rŏt)	166	58.32N	31.16E
Novgorod, prov., Russia	162	58.27N	31.55E
Novhorod-Sivers'kyy, Ukr.	167	52.01N	33.14E
Novi, Mi., U.S. (nō'vĭ)	101b	42.29N	83.28W
Novigrad, Cro. (nō'vĭ grȧd)	160	44.09N	15.34E
Novi Ligure, Italy (nô'vē)	160	44.43N	8.48E
Novinger, Mo., U.S. (nŏv'ĭn-jẽr)	111	40.14N	92.43W
Novi Pazar, Bul. (pä-zär')	161	43.22N	27.26E
Novi Pazar, Yugo. (pȧ-zär')	149	43.08N	20.30E
Novi Sad, Yugo. (säd')	142	45.15N	19.53E
Novoarchangel'skoje, Russia	239b	55.55N	37.33E
Novoasbest, Russia (nô-vô-äs-bĕst')	172a	57.43N	60.14E
Novoaydar, Ukr. (nō'vô-ī-där')	163	48.57N	39.01E
Novocherkassk, Russia (nô'vô-chĕr-kȧsk')	167	47.25N	40.04E
Novochovrino, neigh., Russia	239b	55.52N	37.30E
Novogirejevo, neigh., Russia	239b	55.45N	37.49E
Novokuznetsk, Russia (nô'vô-kô'z-nyĕ'tsk) (stä'lĕnsk)	164	53.43N	86.59E
Novo-Ladozhskiy Kanal, can., Russia (nô-vô-lä'dôzh-skĭ kȧ-näl')	153	59.54N	31.19E
Novo Mesto, Slvn. (nôvô mäs'tô)	160	45.48N	15.13E
Novomoskovsk, Russia (nô'vô-môs-kôfsk')	164	54.06N	38.08E
Novomoskovs'k, Ukr.	167	48.37N	35.12E
Novomyrhorod, Ukr.	163	48.46N	31.44E
Novonikol'skiy, Russia (nô'vô-nyĭ-kôl'skĭ)	172a	52.28N	57.12E
Novorossiysk, Russia (nô'vô-rô-sēsk')	164	44.43N	37.48E
Novorzhev, Russia (nô'vô-rzhêv')	162	57.01N	29.17E
Novo-Selo, Bul. (nô'vô-sĕ'lô)	161	44.09N	22.46E
Novosibirsk, Russia (nô'vô-sē-bērsk')	164	55.09N	82.58E
Novosibirskiye Ostrova (New Siberian Islands), is., Russia	165	74.00N	140.30E
Novosil', Russia (nô'vô-sĭl)	162	52.58N	37.03E
Novosokol'niki, Russia (nô'vô-sô-kôl'nē-kē)	162	56.18N	30.07E
Novotatishchevskiy, Russia (nô'vô-tȧ-tyĭsh'chĕv-skĭ)	172a	53.22N	60.24E
Novoukrayinka, Ukr.	167	48.18N	31.33E
Novouzensk, Russia (nô-vô-ŏŏ-zĕnsk')	167	50.40N	48.08E
Novozybkov, Russia (nô'vô-zĕp'kôf)	167	52.31N	31.54E
Nový Jičín, Czech Rep. (nô'vē yē'chēn)	155	49.36N	18.02E
Novyy Buh, Ukr.	163	47.43N	32.33E
Novyy Oskol, Russia (ôs-kôl')	163	50.46N	37.53E
Novyy Port, Russia (nô'vē)	164	67.19N	72.28E
Nowa Sól, Pol. (nô'vȧ sŭl')	154	51.49N	15.41E
Nowata, Ok., U.S. (nō-wä'tȧ)	111	36.42N	95.38W
Nowood Creek, r., Wy., U.S.	105	44.02N	107.37W
Nowra, Austl. (nou'rȧ)	204	34.55S	150.45E
Nowy Dwór Mazowiecki, Pol. (nô'vĭ dvōōr mä-zo-vyĕts'ke)	155	52.26N	20.46E
Nowy Sącz, Pol. (nô'vē sônch')	155	49.36N	20.42E
Nowy Targ, Pol. (tärk')	155	49.29N	20.02E
Noxon Reservoir, res., Mt., U.S.	104	47.50N	115.40W
Noxubee, r., Ms., U.S. (nŏks'ū-bē)	114	33.20N	88.55W
Noya, Spain (no'yä)	158	42.46N	8.50W
Noyes Island, i., Ak., U.S. (noiz)	86	55.30N	133.40W
Nozaki, Japan (nō'zä-kē)	195b	34.43N	135.39E
Nozuta, Japan	242a	35.35N	139.27E
Nqamakwe, S. Afr. ('n-gä-mä'kwā)	213c	32.13S	27.57E
Nqutu, S. Afr. ('n-kōō'tōō)	213c	28.17S	30.41E
Nsawam, Ghana	214	5.50N	0.20W
Ntshoni, mtn., S. Afr.	213c	29.34S	30.03E
Ntwetwe Pan, pl., Bots.	212	20.00S	24.18E
Nubah, Jibāl an, mts., Sudan	211	12.22N	30.39E

ăt; finăl; rāte; senāte; ärm; åsk; sofȧ; fâre; ch-choose; dh-as th in other; bē; ēvent; bĕt; recĕnt; cratẽr; g-gō; gh-guttural g; bĭt; ĭ-short neutral; rīde; ĸ-guttural k as ch in German ich;

PRONOUNCING INDEX

Nubian Desert–Ogoyo 327

PLACE (Pronunciation)	PAGE	Lat. °′	Long. °′
Nubian Desert, des., Sudan (nōō'bĭ-ăn)	211	21.13N	33.09E
Nudo Coropuna, mtn., Peru (nōō'dô kō-rō-pōō'nä)	130	15.53S	72.04W
Nudo de Pasco, mtn., Peru (dĕ päs'kô)	130	10.34S	76.12W
Nueces, r., Tx., U.S. (nů-ā'sås)	96	28.20N	98.08W
Nueltin, l., Can. (nwĕl'tin)	84	60.14N	101.00W
Nueva Armenia, Hond. (nwā'vä är-mā'nē-å)	120	15.47N	86.32W
Nueva Atzacoalco, Mex.	233a	19.29N	99.05W
Nueva Chicago, neigh., Arg.	233d	34.40S	58.30W
Nueva Coronela, Cuba	233b	23.04N	82.28W
Nueva Esparta, dept., Ven. (nwĕ'vä ĕs-pä'r-tä)	131b	10.50N	64.35W
Nueva Gerona, Cuba (ĸĕ-rô'nä)	122	21.55N	82.45W
Nueva Palmira, Ur. (päl-mē'rä)	129c	33.53S	58.23W
Nueva Rosita, Mex. (nòĕ'vä rô-sĕ'tä)	96	27.55N	101.10W
Nueva San Salvador, El Sal.	120	13.41N	89.16W
Nueve, Canal Numero, can., Arg.	129c	36.22S	58.19W
Nueve de Julio, Arg. (nwā'vå dā hōō'lyô)	132	35.26S	60.51W
Nuevitas, Cuba (nwā-vē'täs)	117	21.35N	77.15W
Nuevitas, Bahía de, b., Cuba (bä-ē'ä dĕ nwā-vē'täs)	122	21.30N	77.05W
Nuevo, Ca., U.S. (nwā'vō)	107a	33.48N	117.09W
Nuevo Laredo, Mex. (lä-rā'dhō)	116	27.29N	99.30W
Nuevo Leon, state, Mex. (lå-ōn')	116	26.00N	100.00W
Nuevo San Juan, Pan. (nwĕ'vô sän ĸōō-ä'n)	116a	9.14N	79.43W
Nugumanovo, Russia (nû-gû-mä'nô-vô)	172a	55.28N	61.50E
Nulato, Ak., U.S. (nōō-lä'tō)	95	64.40N	158.18W
Nullagine, Austl. (nŭ-lă'jēn)	202	22.00S	120.07E
Nullarbor Plain, pl., Austl. (nŭ-lär'bôr)	202	31.45S	126.30E
Numabin Bay, b., Can. (nōō-mä'bĭn)	88	56.30N	103.08W
Numansdorp, Neth.	145a	51.43N	4.25E
Numazu, Japan (nōō'mä-zōō)	194	35.06N	138.55E
Numfoor, Pulau, i., Indon.	197	1.20S	134.48E
Nun, r., Nig.	215	5.05N	6.10E
Nunawading, Austl.	201a	37.49S	145.10E
Nuneaton, Eng., U.K. (nŭn'ē-tŭn)	150	52.31N	1.28W
Nunivak, i., Ak., U.S. (nōō'nĭ-văk)	96a	60.25N	167.42W
Ñuñoa, Chile	234b	33.28S	70.36W
Nunyama, Russia (nûn-yä'må)	95	65.49N	170.32W
Nuoro, Italy (nwô'rō)	160	40.29N	9.20E
Nūra, r., Kaz.	169	49.48N	73.54E
Nurata, Uzb. (nōōr'ät'å)	169	40.33N	65.28E
Nuremberg *see* Nürnberg, Ger.	142	49.28N	11.07E
Nürnberg, Ger. (nürn'bĕrgh)	142	49.28N	11.07E
Nurse Cay, i., Bah.	123	22.30N	75.50W
Nusabyin, Tur. (nōō'sĭ-bĕn)	167	37.05N	41.10E
Nushagak, r., Ak., U.S. (nū-shä-găk')	95	59.28N	157.40W
Nushan Hu, l., China	190	32.50N	117.59E
Nushki, Pak. (nŭsh'kē)	183	29.30N	66.02E
Nussdorf, neigh., Aus.	239e	48.15N	16.22E
Nuthe, r., Ger. (nōō'tĕ)	145b	52.15N	13.11E
Nutley, N.J., U.S. (nŭt'lē)	100a	40.49N	74.09W
Nutter Fort, W.V., U.S. (nŭt'ĕr fôrt)	98	39.15N	80.15W
Nutwood, Il., U.S. (nŭt'wòd)	107e	39.05N	90.34W
Nuwaybi 'al Muzayyinah, Egypt	181a	28.59N	34.40E
Nuweland, S. Afr.	212a	33.58S	18.28E
Nyack, N.Y., U.S. (nī'ăk)	100a	41.05N	73.55W
Nyainqêntanglha Shan, mts., China (nyä-ĭn-chyŭn-tāŋ-lä shän)	188	29.55N	88.08E
Nyakanazi, Tan.	217	3.00S	31.15E
Nyala, Sudan	211	12.00N	24.52E
Nyanga, r., Gabon	216	2.45S	10.30E
Nyanza, Rw.	217	2.21S	29.45E
Nyasa, Lake, l., Afr. (nyä'sä)	212	10.45S	34.30E
Nyazepetrovsk, Russia (nyä'zĕ-pĕ-trôvsk')	172a	56.04N	59.38E
Nyborg, Den. (nü'bôr'')	152	55.20N	10.45E
Nybro, Swe. (nü'brō)	152	56.44N	15.56E
Nyeri, Kenya	217	0.25S	36.57E
Nyika Plateau, plat., Mwi.	217	10.30S	35.50E
Nyíregyháza, Hung. (nyē'rĕd-y'hä'zä)	149	47.58N	21.45E
Nykøbing, Den. (nü'kû-bĭng)	146	56.46N	8.47E
Nykøbing, Den.	152	54.45N	11.54E
Nykøbing Sjaelland, Den.	152	55.55N	11.37E
Nyköping, Swe. (nü'chû-pĭng)	146	58.46N	16.58E
Nylstroom, S. Afr. (nĭl'strōm)	212	24.42S	28.25E
Nymagee, Austl. (nī-mă-gē')	203	32.17S	146.18E
Nymburk, Czech Rep. (nĕm'bòrk)	147	50.12N	15.03E
Nynäshamn, Swe. (nü-nĕs-häm'n)	152	58.53N	17.55E
Nyngan, Austl. (nĭŋ'găn)	203	31.31S	147.25E
Nyong, r., Cam. (nyông)	210	4.00N	12.00E
Nyou, Burkina	214	12.46N	1.56W
Nýřany, Czech Rep. (nĕr-zhä'nĕ)	154	49.43N	13.13E
Nysa, Pol. (nē'så)	155	50.29N	17.20E
Nytva, Russia	166	58.00N	55.10E
Nyungwe, Mwi.	217	10.16S	34.07E
Nyunzu, Zaire	217	5.57S	28.01E
Nyuya, r., Russia (nyōō'yå)	171	60.30N	111.45E
Nyzhni Sirohozy, Ukr.	163	46.51N	34.25E
Nzega, Tan.	217	4.13S	33.11E
N'zeto, Ang.	212	7.14S	12.52E
Nzi, r., C. Iv.	214	7.00N	4.27W
Nzwani, i., Com. (äɴ-zhwäɴ)	213	12.14S	44.47E

O

PLACE (Pronunciation)	PAGE	Lat. °′	Long. °′
Oahe, Lake, res., U.S.	96	45.20N	100.00W
Oahu, i., Hi., U.S. (ō-ä'hōō) (ō-ä'hü)	96c	21.38N	157.48W
Oak Bay, Can.	86	48.27N	123.18W
Oak Bluff, Can. (ōk blŭf)	83f	49.47N	97.21W
Oak Creek, Co., U.S. (ōk krēk')	105	40.20N	106.50W
Oakdale, Ca., U.S. (ōk'dāl)	108	37.45N	120.52W
Oakdale, Ky., U.S.	98	38.15N	85.50W
Oakdale, La., U.S.	113	30.49N	92.40W
Oakdale, Pa., U.S.	101e	40.24N	80.11W
Oakengates, Eng., U.K. (ōk'ĕn-gāts)	144a	52.41N	2.27W
Oakes, N.D., U.S. (ōks)	102	46.10N	98.50W
Oakfield, Me., U.S. (ōk'fēld)	92	46.08N	68.10W
Oakford, Pa., U.S. (ōk'fōrd)	100f	40.08N	74.58W
Oak Forest, Il., U.S.	231a	41.36N	87.45W
Oak Grove, Or., U.S. (grōv)	106c	45.25N	122.38W
Oakham, Eng., U.K. (ōk'ăm)	144a	52.40N	0.38W
Oak Harbor, Oh., U.S. (ōk'här'bĕr)	98	41.30N	83.05W
Oak Harbor, Wa., U.S.	106a	48.18N	122.39W
Oakland, Ca., U.S. (ōk'lănd)	96	37.48N	122.16W
Oakland, Md., U.S.	229d	38.52N	76.55W
Oakland, Ne., U.S.	102	41.50N	96.28W
Oakland, neigh., Pa., U.S.	230b	40.26N	79.58W
Oakland City, In., U.S.	98	38.20N	87.20W
Oakland Gardens, neigh., N.Y., U.S.	228	40.45N	73.45W
Oaklawn, Il., U.S. (ōk'lôn)	101a	41.43N	87.45W
Oakleigh, Austl. (ōk'lå)	201a	37.54S	145.05E
Oakleigh South, Austl.	243b	37.56S	145.05E
Oakley, Id., U.S. (ōk'lĭ)	104	42.15N	135.53W
Oakley, Ks., U.S.	110	39.08N	100.49W
Oakman, Al., U.S. (ōk'măn)	114	33.42N	87.20W
Oakmont, Pa., U.S. (ōk'mōnt)	101e	40.31N	79.50W
Oak Mountain, mtn., Al., U.S.	100h	33.22N	86.42W
Oak Park, Il., U.S. (pärk)	101a	41.53N	87.48W
Oak Park, Mi., U.S.	230c	42.28N	83.11W
Oak Point, Wa., U.S.	106c	46.11N	123.11W
Oak Ridge, Tn., U.S. (rĭj)	114	36.01N	84.15W
Oak View, Md., U.S.	229d	39.01N	76.59W
Oakview, N.J., U.S.	229b	39.51N	75.09W
Oakville, Can.	83f	49.56N	97.58W
Oakville, Can. (ōk'vĭl)	91	43.27N	79.40W
Oakville, Mo., U.S.	107e	38.27N	90.18W
Oakville Creek, r., Can.	83d	43.34N	79.54W
Oakwood, Oh., U.S.	229a	41.06N	84.23W
Oakwood, Tx., U.S. (ōk'wòd)	113	31.36N	95.48W
Oatley, Austl.	243a	33.59S	151.05E
Oatman, Az., U.S. (ōt'măn)	109	34.00N	114.25W
Oaxaca, Mex.	116	17.03N	96.42W
Oaxaca, state, Mex. (wä-hä'kä)	116	16.45N	97.00W
Oaxaca, Sierra de, mts., Mex. (sē-ĕ'r-rä dĕ)	119	16.15N	97.25W
Ob', r., Russia	164	62.15N	67.00E
Oba, Can. (ō'bå)	85	48.58N	84.09W
Obama, Japan (ō'bà-mä)	195	35.29N	135.44E
Oban, Scot., U.K. (ō'băn)	150	56.25N	5.35W
Oban Hills, hills, Nig.	215	5.35N	8.30E
O'Bannon, Ky., U.S. (ō-băn'nŏn)	101h	38.17N	85.30W
Obatogamau, l., Can. (ō-bå-tō'găm-ô)	91	49.38N	74.10W
Oberbauer, Ger.	236	51.17N	7.26E
Oberbonsfeld, Ger.	236	51.22N	7.08E
Oberelfringhausen, Ger.	236	51.20N	7.11E
Oberhaan, Ger.	236	51.13N	7.02E
Oberhausen, Ger. (ō'bĕr-hou'zĕn)	157c	51.27N	6.51E
Oberkassel, neigh., Ger.	236	51.14N	6.46E
Ober-kirchbach, Aus.	239e	48.17N	16.12E
Oberlaa, neigh., Aus.	239e	48.08N	16.24E
Oberlin, Ks., U.S. (o'bĕr-lĭn)	110	39.49N	100.30W
Oberlin, Oh., U.S.	98	41.15N	82.15W
Oberösterreich, prov., Aus.	154	48.05N	13.15E
Oberroth, Ger. (ō'bĕr-rōt)	145d	48.19N	11.20E
Ober Sankt Veit, neigh., Aus.	239e	48.11N	16.16E
Oberschöneweide, neigh., Ger.	238a	52.28N	13.31E
Oberwengern, Ger.	236	51.23N	7.22E
Obgruiten, Ger.	236	51.13N	7.01E
Obi, Kepulauan, is., Indon. (ō'bē)	197	1.25S	128.15E
Obi, Pulau, i., Indon.	197	1.30S	127.45E
Óbidos, Braz. (ō'bē-dòzh)	131	1.57S	55.32W
Obihiro, Japan (ō'bē-hē'rō)	194	42.55N	142.50E
Obion, r., Tn., U.S.	114	36.10N	89.25W
Obion, North Fork, r., Tn., U.S. (ō-bī'ŏn)	114	35.49N	89.06W
Obitsu, r., Japan (ō'bēt'sōō)	195a	35.19N	140.03E
Obock, Dji. (ō-bŏk')	218a	11.55N	43.15E
Obol', r., Bela. (ô-bŏl')	162	55.24N	29.24E
Oboyan', Russia (ô-bô-yän')	167	51.14N	36.16E
Obskaya Guba, b., Russia	164	67.13N	73.45E
Obu, neigh., Japan	242b	34.44N	135.09E
Obuasi, Ghana	214	6.14N	1.39W
Óbuda, neigh., Hung.	239g	47.33N	19.02E
Obukhiv, Ukr.	163	50.07N	30.36E
Obukhovo, Russia	172b	55.50N	38.17E
Obytichna kosa, spit, Ukr.	163	46.32N	36.07E
Očakovo, neigh., Russia	239b	55.41N	37.27E
Ocala, Fl., U.S. (ô-kä'lă)	115	29.11N	82.09W
Ocampo, Mex. (ô-käm'pō)	118	22.49N	99.23W
Ocaña, Col. (ô-kän'yä)	130	8.15N	73.37W
Ocaña, Spain (ô-kä'n-yä)	158	39.58N	3.31W
Occidental, Cordillera, mts., Col.	130a	5.05N	76.04W
Occidental, Cordillera, mts., Peru	130	10.12S	76.58W
Ocean Beach, Ca., U.S. (ō'shăn bēch)	108a	32.44N	117.14W
Ocean Bight, bt., Bah.	123	21.15N	73.15W
Ocean City, Md., U.S.	99	38.20N	75.10W
Ocean City, N.J., U.S.	99	39.15N	74.35W
Ocean Falls, Can. (Fôls)	84	52.21N	127.40W
Ocean Grove, Austl.	201a	38.16S	144.32E
Ocean Grove, N.J., U.S. (grōv)	99	40.10N	74.00W
Oceanside, Ca., U.S. (ō'shăn-sīd)	108	33.11N	117.22W
Oceanside, N.Y., U.S.	100a	40.38N	73.39W
Ocean Springs, Ms., U.S. (sprĭngs)	114	30.25N	88.49W
Ochakiv, Ukr.	163	46.38N	31.33E
Ochamchira, Geor.	168	42.44N	41.28E
Ochiai, neigh., Japan	242a	35.43N	139.42E
Ochlockonee, r., Fl., U.S. (ŏk-lô-kō'nē)	114	30.10N	84.38W
Ocilla, Ga., U.S. (ô-sĭl'ă)	114	31.36N	83.15W
Ockelbo, Swe. (ôk'ĕl-bō)	152	60.54N	16.35E
Ockham, Eng., U.K.	235	51.18N	0.27W
Ocklawaha, Lake, res., Fl., U.S.	115	29.30N	81.50W
Ocmulgee, r., Ga., U.S.	114	32.25N	83.30W
Ocmulgee National Monument, rec., Ga., U.S. (ôk-mŭl'gē)	114	32.45N	83.28W
Ocoa, Bahía de, b., Dom. Rep.	123	18.20N	70.40W
Ococingo, Mex. (ô-kô-sē'n-gô)	119	17.03N	92.18W
Ocom, Lago, l., Mex. (ô-kô'm)	120a	19.26N	88.18W
Oconee, r., Ga., U.S. (ô-kō'nē)	97	32.45N	83.00W
Oconee, Lake, res., Ga., U.S.	114	33.30N	83.15W
Oconomowoc, Wi., U.S. (ô-kŏn'ô-mô-wŏk')	103	43.06N	88.24W
Oconto, Wi., U.S. (ô-kŏn'tō)	103	44.54N	87.55W
Oconto, r., Wi., U.S.	103	45.08N	88.24W
Oconto Falls, Wi., U.S.	103	44.53N	88.11W
Ocós, Guat. (ô-kōs')	120	14.31N	92.12W
Ocotal, Nic. (ō-kô-täl')	120	13.36N	86.31W
Ocotepeque, Hond. (ō-kō-tå-pā'kå)	120	14.25N	89.13W
Ocotlán, Mex. (ō-kô-tlän')	118	20.19N	102.44W
Ocotlán de Morelos, Mex. (dā mô-rā'lōs)	119	16.46N	96.41W
Ocozocoautla, Mex. (ô-kō'zô-kwä-ōō'tlä)	119	16.44N	93.22W
Ocumare del Tuy, Ven. (ô-kōō-mä'ra del twē')	130	10.07N	66.47W
Oda, Ghana	214	5.55N	0.59W
Odawara, Japan (ō'dà-wä'rä)	195	35.15N	139.10E
Odda, Nor. (ôdh-å)	152	60.04N	6.30E
Odebolt, Ia., U.S. (ō'dē-bōlt)	102	42.20N	95.14W
Odemira, Port. (ō-dâ-mē'rå)	158	37.35N	8.40W
Ödemiş, Tur. (û'dĕ-mēsh)	149	38.12N	28.00E
Odendaalsrus, S. Afr. (ō'dĕn-däls-rûs')	218d	27.52S	26.41E
Odense, Den. (ō'dhĕn-sĕ)	146	55.24N	10.20E
Odenton, Md., U.S. (ō'dĕn-tŭn)	100e	39.05N	76.43W
Odenwald, for., Ger. (ō'dĕn-väld)	154	49.39N	8.55E
Oder, r., Eur. (ō'dĕr)	142	52.40N	14.19E
Oderhaff, l., Eur.	154	53.47N	14.02E
Odesa, Ukr.	164	46.28N	30.44E
Odesa, prov., Ukr.	163	46.05N	29.48E
Odessa, Tx., U.S. (ô-dĕs'á)	112	31.52N	102.21W
Odessa, Wa., U.S.	104	47.20N	118.42W
Odiel, r., Spain (ō-dē-ĕl')	158	37.47N	6.42W
Odiham, Eng., U.K. (ŏd'ē-ăm)	144b	51.14N	0.56W
Odintsovo, Russia (ô-dēn'tsô-vô)	172b	55.40N	37.16E
Odiongan, Phil. (ō-dē-ôŋ'gän)	197a	12.24N	121.59E
Odivelas, Port. (ō-dē-vä'lyäs)	159b	38.47N	9.11W
Odobeşti, Rom. (ō-dô-bĕsh't')	155	45.46N	27.08E
O'Donnell, Tx., U.S. (ō-dŏn'ĕl)	110	32.59N	101.51W
Odorhei, Rom. (ō-dôr-hā')	155	46.18N	25.17E
Odra *see* Oder, r., Eur. (ô'drà)	142	52.40N	14.19E
Oeiras, Braz. (wå-ē-räzh')	131	7.05S	42.01W
Oeirás, Port. (ô-ē'y-rà's)	159b	38.42N	9.18W
Oella, Md., U.S.	229c	39.16N	76.47W
Oelwein, Ia., U.S. (ōl'wīn)	103	42.40N	91.56W
Oespel, neigh., Ger.	236	51.30N	7.23E
Oestrich, Ger.	236	51.22N	7.38E
Oestrich, neigh., Ger.	236	51.34N	7.22E
Oestrum, Ger.	236	51.25N	6.40E
O'Fallon, Il., U.S. (ō-făl'ŭn)	107e	38.36N	89.55W
O'Fallon Creek, r., Mt., U.S.	105	46.25N	104.47W
Ofanto, r., Italy (ô-făn'tō)	160	41.08N	15.33E
Offa, Nig.	215	8.09N	4.44E
Offenbach, Ger. (ôf'ĕn-băk)	154	50.06N	8.50E
Offenburg, Ger. (ôf'ĕn-bòrgh)	154	48.28N	7.57E
Ofin, Nig.	244d	6.33N	3.30E
Ofomori, neigh., Japan	242a	35.34N	139.44E
Ofuna, Japan (ō'fōō-nä)	195a	35.21N	139.32E
Ogaden Plateau, plat., Eth.	218a	6.45N	44.53E
Ogaki, Japan	194	35.21N	136.36E
Ogallala, Ne., U.S. (ō-gä-lä'lä)	102	41.08N	101.44W
Ogawa, Japan	242a	35.44N	139.28E
Ogbomosho, Nig. (ŏg-bô-mō'shō)	210	8.08N	4.15E
Ogden, Ia., U.S. (ŏg'dĕn)	103	42.10N	94.20W
Ogden, Ut., U.S.	96	41.14N	111.58W
Ogden, r., Ut., U.S.	107b	41.16N	111.54W
Ogden Peak, mtn., Ut., U.S.	107b	41.11N	111.51W
Ogdensburg, N.J., U.S. (ŏg'dĕnz-bûrg)	100a	41.05N	74.36W
Ogdensburg, N.Y., U.S.	97	44.40N	75.30W
Ogeechee, r., Ga., U.S. (ô-gē'chē)	115	32.35N	81.50W
Ogies, S. Afr.	218d	26.03S	29.04E
Ogilvie Mountains, mts., Can. (ō'g'l-vĭ)	84	64.45N	138.10W
Oglesby, Il., U.S. (ō'g'lz-bĭ)	98	41.20N	89.00W
Oglio, r., Italy (ôl'yō)	160	45.15N	10.19E
Ōgo, Japan (ō'gô)	195b	34.49N	135.06E
Ogou, r., Togo	214	8.05N	1.30E
Ogoyo, Nig.	244d	6.26N	3.29E

PLACE (Pronunciation)	PAGE	Lat. °′	Long. °′
Ogudnëvo, Russia (ôg-ôd-nyô'vô)	172b	56.04N	38.17E
Ogudu, Nig.	244d	6.34N	3.24E
Ogulin, Cro. (ō-go͞o-lēn')	160	45.17N	15.11E
Ogwashi-Uku, Nig.	215	6.10N	6.31E
O'Higgins, prov., Chile (ô-kē'gēns)	129b	34.17S	70.52W
Ohio, state, U.S. (ô'hī'ō)	97	40.30N	83.15W
Ohio, r., U.S.	97	37.25N	88.05W
Ohoopee, r., Ga., U.S. (ô-ho͞o'pe-mc)	115	32.32N	82.38W
Ohře, r., Eur. (ōr'zhě)	154	50.08N	12.45E
Ohrid, Mac. (ō'ĸrēd)	161	41.08N	20.46E
Ohrid, Lake, l., Eur.	161	40.58N	20.35E
Ōi, Japan (oi')	195a	35.51N	139.31E
Oi-Gawa, r., Japan (ō'ē-gä'wȧ)	195	35.09N	138.05E
Oil City, Pa., U.S. (oil sĭ'tĭ)	99	41.25N	79.40W
Oirschot, Neth.	145a	51.30N	5.20E
Oise, r., Fr. (wäz)	147	49.30N	2.56E
Oisterwijk, Neth.	145a	51.34N	5.13E
Oita, Japan (ō'ē-tä)	194	33.14N	131.38E
Oji, Japan (ō'jē)	195b	35.45N	135.43E
Ojinaga, Mex. (ō-κē-nä'gä)	116	29.34N	104.26W
Ojitlán, Mex. (ōkē-tlän') (sän-lo͞o'käs)	119	18.04N	96.23W
Ojo Caliente, Mex. (ōκō käl-yĕn'tȧ)	118	21.50N	100.43W
Ojocaliente, Mex. (ô-κô-kä-lyĕ'n-tĕ)	118	22.39N	102.15W
Ojo del Toro, Pico, mtn., Cuba (pē'kô-ô-κō-dĕl-tô'rô)	122	19.55N	77.25W
Oka, Can. (ō-kä)	83a	45.28N	74.05W
Oka, r., Russia (ô-kȧ')	166	55.10N	42.10E
Oka, r., Russia (ô-kä')	167	52.10N	35.20E
Oka, r., Russia (ō-kä')	170	53.28N	101.09E
Okahandja, Nmb.	212	21.50S	16.45E
Okanagan (Okanogan), r., N.A. (ō'kȧ-näg'ȧn)	87	49.06N	119.43W
Okanagan Lake, l., Can.	84	50.00N	119.28W
Okano, r., Gabon (ō'kä'nō)	210	0.15N	11.08E
Okanogan, Wa., U.S.	104	48.20N	119.34W
Okanogan, r., Wa., U.S.	104	48.36N	119.33W
Okatibbee, r., Ms., U.S. (ō'kä-tĭb'ē)	114	32.37N	88.54W
Okatoma Creek, r., Ms., U.S. (ô-kȧ-tō'mă)	114	31.43N	89.34W
Okavango (Cubango), r., Afr.	212	18.00S	20.00E
Okavango Swamp, sw., Bots.	212	19.30S	23.02E
Okaya, Japan (ō'kȧ-yȧ)	195	36.04N	138.01E
Okayama, Japan (ō'kȧ-yä'mȧ)	189	34.39N	133.54E
Okazaki, Japan (ō'kȧ-zä'kē)	194	34.58N	137.09E
Okeechobee, Fl., U.S. (ō-kē-chō'bē)	115	27.15N	80.50W
Okeechobee, Lake, l., Fl., U.S.	97	27.00N	80.49W
O'Keefe Centre, bldg., Can.	227c	43.37N	79.22W
Okeene, Ok., U.S. (ô-kēn')	110	36.06N	98.19W
Okefenokee Swamp, sw., U.S. (ō'kē-fē-nō'kē)	115	30.54N	82.20W
Okemah, Ok., U.S. (ô-kē'mä)	111	35.26N	96.18W
Okene, Nig.	215	7.33N	6.15E
Oke Ogbe, Nig.	244d	6.24N	3.23E
Okha, Russia (ŭ-κä')	165	53.44N	143.12E
Okhotino, Russia (ô-κô'tĭ-nô)	172b	56.14N	38.24E
Okhotsk, Russia (ô-κôtsk')	165	59.28N	143.32E
Okhotsk, Sea of, sea, Asia (ô-kôtsk')	165	56.45N	146.00E
Okhtyrka, Ukr.	167	50.18N	34.53E
Okinawa, i., Japan	189	26.30N	128.00E
Okino, i., Japan (ō'kē-nō)	195	36.22N	133.27E
Ōkino Erabu, i., Japan (ō-kē'nô-å-rä'bo͞o)	194	27.18N	129.00E
Oklahoma, state, U.S. (ô-klȧ-hō'mȧ)	96	36.00N	98.20W
Oklahoma City, Ok., U.S.	96	35.27N	97.32W
Oklawaha, r., Fl., U.S. (ŏk-lȧ-wô'hô)	115	29.13N	82.00W
Okmulgee, Ok., U.S. (ôk-mŭl'gē)	111	35.37N	95.58W
Okolona, Ky., U.S. (ō-kô-lō'nȧ)	101h	38.08N	85.41W
Okolona, Ms., U.S.	114	33.59N	88.43W
Oktemberyan, Arm.	168	40.09N	44.02E
Okushiri, i., Japan (ō'koo-shē'rē)	194	42.12N	139.30E
Okuta, Nig.	215	9.14N	3.15E
Olalla, Wa., U.S. (ō-lä'lȧ)	106a	47.26N	122.33W
Olanchito, Hond. (ō'län-chē'tô)	120	15.28N	86.35W
Öland, i., Swe. (û-länd')	142	57.03N	17.15E
Olathe, Ks., U.S. (ô-lā'thē)	107f	38.53N	94.49W
Olavarría, Arg. (ō-lä-vär-rē'ä)	132	36.49N	60.15W
Oława, Pol. (ô-lä'vȧ)	155	50.57N	17.18E
Olazoago, Arg. (ô-läz-kôä'gô)	129c	35.14S	60.37W
Olbia, Italy (ô'l-byä)	160	40.55N	9.28E
Olching, Ger. (ōl'κēng)	145d	48.13N	11.21E
Old Bahama Channel, strt., N.A. (bȧ-hā'mȧ)	122	22.45N	78.30W
Old Bight, Bah.	123	24.15N	75.20W
Old Bridge, N.J., U.S. (brĭj)	100a	40.24N	74.22W
Old Brookville, N.Y., U.S.	228	40.49N	73.36W
Old Crow, Can. (crō)	84	67.51N	139.58W
Oldenburg, Ger. (ôl'dĕn-bôrgh)	146	53.09N	8.13E
Old Forge, Pa., U.S. (fôrj)	99	41.20N	75.50W
Oldham, Eng., U.K. (ōld'ȧm)	150	53.32N	2.07W
Oldham Pond, l., Ma., U.S.	227a	42.03N	70.51W
Old Harbor, Ak., U.S. (här'bẽr)	95	57.18N	153.20W
Old Head of Kinsale, c., Ire. (ōld hĕd ŏv kĭn-săl)	150	51.35N	8.35W
Old Malden, neigh., Eng., U.K.	235	51.23N	0.15W
Old North Church, pt. of i., Ma., U.S.	227a	42.22N	71.03W
Old R, Tx., U.S.	113a	29.54N	94.52W
Olds, Can. (ōldz)	84	51.47N	114.06W
Old Tate, Bots.	212	21.18S	27.43E
Old Town, Me., U.S. (toun)	92	44.55N	68.42W
Old Westbury, N.Y., U.S.	228	40.47N	73.37W
Old Windsor, Eng., U.K.	235	51.28N	0.35W
Old Wives Lake, l., Can. (wīvz)	88	50.05N	106.00W
Olean, N.Y., U.S. (ō-lē-ăn')	97	42.05N	78.25W
Olecko, Pol. (ô-lĕt'skô)	155	54.02N	22.29E
Olekma, r., Russia (ô-lyĕk-mȧ')	171	55.41N	120.33E
Olëkminsk, Russia (ô-lyĕk-mĕnsk')	165	60.39N	120.40E

PLACE (Pronunciation)	PAGE	Lat. °′	Long. °′
Oleksandriya, Ukr.	162	48.40N	33.07E
Olenëk, r., Russia (ô-lyĕ-nyôk')	165	68.00N	113.00E
Oléron Île, d', i., Fr. (ēl' dō lā-rôɴ')	147	45.52N	1.58W
Oleśnica, Pol. (ô-lĕsh-nĭ'tsȧ)	147	51.13N	17.24E
Olfen, Ger. (ōl'fĕn)	157c	51.43N	7.22E
Ol'ga, Russia (ôl'gȧ)	165	43.48N	135.44E
Ol'gi, Zaliv, b., Russia (zä'lĭf ôl'gĭ)	194	43.43N	135.25E
Olhão, Port. (ôl-youɴ')	148	37.02N	7.54W
Ol'hopil', Ukr.	163	48.11N	29.28E
Olievenhoutpoort, S. Afr.	213b	25.58S	27.55E
Ólimbos, Grc.	149	40.03N	22.22E
Ólimbos, mtn., Cyp.	181a	34.56N	32.52E
Olinda, Austl.	243b	37.51S	145.22E
Olinda, Braz. (ô-lē'n-dä)	131	8.00S	34.58W
Olinda, Braz.	132b	22.49S	43.25W
Oliva, Spain (ô-lē'vä)	159	38.54N	0.07W
Oliva de la Frontera, Spain (ô-lē'vä dā)	158	38.33N	6.55W
Olivais, neigh., Port.	238d	34.46N	9.06W
Olive Hill, Ky., U.S. (ŏl'ĭv)	98	38.15N	83.10W
Oliveira, Braz. (ō-lē-vā'rä)	129a	20.42S	44.49W
Olive Mount, neigh., Eng., U.K.	237a	53.24N	2.55W
Olivenza, Spain (ō-lē-vēn'thä)	158	38.42N	7.06W
Oliver, Can.	83g	53.38N	113.21W
Oliver, Can. (ŏ'lĭ-vẽr)	84	49.11N	119.33W
Oliver, Wi., U.S. (ŏ'lĭvẽr)	107h	46.39N	92.12W
Oliver Lake, l., Can.	83g	53.19N	113.00W
Olivia, Mn., U.S. (ō-lĭv'ē-ȧ)	102	44.46N	95.00W
Olivos, Arg. (ōlē'vōs)	132a	34.30S	58.29W
Ollagüe, Chile (ô-lyä'gȧ)	130	21.17S	68.17W
Ollerton, Eng., U.K. (ôl'ẽr-tŭn)	144a	53.12N	1.02W
Olmos Park, Tx., U.S. (ōl'mŭs pärk')	107d	29.27N	98.32W
Olmsted, Oh., U.S.	229a	41.24N	81.44W
Olmsted Falls, Oh., U.S.	229a	41.22N	81.55W
Olney, Il., U.S. (ŏl'nĭ)	98	38.45N	88.05W
Olney, Or., U.S. (ŏl'nē)	106c	46.06N	123.45W
Olney, Tx., U.S.	110	33.24N	98.43W
Olney, neigh., Pa., U.S.	229b	40.02N	75.08W
Olomane, r., Can. (ō'lō mȧ'nĕ)	93	51.05N	60.50W
Olomouc, Czech Rep. (ō'lō-mōts)	147	49.37N	17.15E
Olonets, Russia (ô-lô'nĕts)	153	60.58N	32.54E
Olongapo, Phil.	196	14.49S	120.17E
Oloron, Gave d', r., Fr. (gäv-dō-lō-rôɴ')	156	43.21N	0.44W
Oloron-Sainte Marie, Fr. (ō-lō-rôɴt'săɴt mȧ-rē')	156	43.11N	1.37W
Olot, Spain (ō-lōt')	148	42.09N	2.30E
Olpe, Ger. (ōl'pĕ)	157c	51.02N	7.51E
Olsnitz, Ger. (ōlz'nētz)	154	50.25N	12.11E
Olsztyn, Pol. (ôl'shtĭn)	146	53.47N	20.28E
Olt, r., Rom.	149	44.09N	24.40E
Olten, Switz. (ôl'tĕn)	154	47.20N	7.53E
Oltenița, Rom. (ôl-tā'nĭ-tsȧ)	161	44.05N	26.39E
Olvera, Spain (ôl-vĕ'rä)	158	36.55N	5.16W
Olympia, Wa., U.S. (ô-lĭm'pĭ-ȧ)	96	47.02N	122.52W
Olympic Mountains, mts., Wa., U.S.	104	47.54N	123.58W
Olympic National Park, rec., Wa., U.S. (ô-lĭm'pĭk)	96	47.54N	123.00W
Olympieion, pt. of i., Grc.	239d	37.58N	23.44E
Olympus, Mount, mtn., Wa., U.S. (ô-lĭm'pŭs)	104	47.43N	123.30W
Olyphant, Pa., U.S. (ŏl'ĭ-fănt)	99	41.30N	75.40W
Olyutorskiy, Mys, c., Russia (ŭl-yo͞o'tŏr-skē)	165	59.49N	167.16E
Omae-Zaki, c., Japan (ō'mä-å zä'kē)	195	34.37N	138.15E
Omagh, N. Ire., U.K. (ō'mä)	150	54.35N	7.25W
Omaha, Ne., U.S. (ō'mȧ-hä)	97	41.18N	95.57W
Omaha Indian Reservation, I.R., Ne., U.S.	102	42.09N	96.08W
Oman, nation, Asia	182	20.00N	57.45E
Oman, Gulf of, b., Asia	182	24.24N	58.58E
Omaruru, Nmb. (ō-mä-ro͞o'ro͞o)	212	21.25S	16.50E
Ombrone, r., Italy (ôm-brō'nā)	160	42.48N	11.18E
Omdurman, Sudan	211	15.45N	32.30E
Omealca, Mex. (ōmā-äl'kō)	119	18.44N	96.45W
Ometepec, Mex. (ō-mā-tȧ-pĕk')	118	16.41N	98.27W
Om Hajer, Eth.	211	14.06N	36.46E
Omineca, r., Can. (ō-mĭ-nĕk'ȧ)	86	55.50N	125.45W
Omineca Mountains, mts., Can.	86	56.00N	125.00W
Ōmiya, Japan (ō'mē-yȧ)	195	35.54S	139.38E
Omo, r., Eth. (ō'mō)	211	5.54N	36.09E
Omoa, Hond. (ô-mō'rä)	120	15.43N	88.03W
Omoko, Nig.	215	5.20N	6.39E
Omolon, r., Russia (ō'mō)	171	67.43N	159.15E
Ōmori, Japan (ō'mô-rē)	195a	35.50N	140.09E
Omotepe, Isla de, i., Nic. (ē's-lä-dĕ-ō-mô-tā'pȧ)	120	11.32N	85.30W
Omro, Wi., U.S. (ŏm'rō)	103	44.01N	89.46W
Omsk, Russia (ômsk)	164	55.12N	73.19E
Ōmura, Japan (ō'mo͞o-rȧ)	195	32.56N	129.57E
Ōmuta, Japan (ō-mô-tȧ)	195	33.02N	130.28E
Omutninsk, Russia (ō'mo͞o-tnēnsk)	166	58.38N	52.10E
Onawa, Ia., U.S. (ŏn-ȧ-wȧ)	102	42.02N	96.05W
Onaway, Mi., U.S.	98	45.25N	84.10W
Once, neigh., Arg.	233d	34.36S	58.24W
Oncócua, Ang.	216	16.34S	13.28E
Onda, Spain (ōn'dä)	159	39.58N	0.13W
Ondava, r., Slvk. (ōn'dȧ-vȧ)	155	48.51N	21.40E
Ondo, Nig.	215	7.04N	4.47E
Öndörhaan, Mong.	189	47.20N	110.40E
Onega, Russia (ô-nyĕ'gȧ)	164	63.50N	38.08E
Onega, r., Russia	166	63.20N	39.20E
Onega, Lake *see* Onezhskoye Ozero, l., Russia	166	62.02N	34.35E
Oneida, N.Y., U.S. (ō-nī'dȧ)	99	43.05N	75.40W
Oneida, l., N.Y., U.S.	99	43.10N	76.00W
O'Neill, Ne., U.S. (ō-nēl')	102	42.28N	98.38W

PLACE (Pronunciation)	PAGE	Lat. °′	Long. °′
Oneonta, N.Y., U.S. (ō-nē-ŏn'tȧ)	99	42.25N	75.05W
Onezhskaja Guba, b., Russia	166	64.30N	36.00E
Onezhskiy, Poluostrov, pen., Russia	166	64.30N	37.40E
Onezhskoye Ozero, Russia (ô-nāsh'skô-yē ô'zē-rô)	166	62.02N	34.35E
Ongiin Hiid, Mong.	188	46.00N	102.46E
Ongole, India	187	15.36N	80.03E
Onilahy, r., Madag.	213	23.41S	45.00E
Onitsha, Nig. (ô-nĭt'shȧ)	210	6.09N	6.47W
Onomichi, Japan (ō'nô-mē'chē)	194	34.27N	133.12E
Onon, r., Asia (ô'nôn)	165	49.00N	112.00E
Onoto, Ven. (ô-nō'tô)	131b	9.38N	65.03W
Onslow, Austl. (ŏnz'lō)	202	21.53S	115.00E
Onslow B, N.C., U.S. (ônz'lō)	115	34.22N	77.35W
Ontake San, mtn., Japan (ôn'tä-kȧ sän)	194	35.55N	137.29E
Ontario, Ca., U.S. (ŏn-tā'rĭ-ō)	107a	34.04N	117.39E
Ontario, Or., U.S.	104	44.02N	116.57W
Ontario, prov., Can.	85	50.47N	88.50W
Ontario, Lake, l., N.A.	97	43.35N	79.05W
Ontario Science Centre, bldg., Can.	227c	43.43N	79.21W
Onteniente, Spain (ōn-tȧ-nyĕn'tā)	159	38.48N	0.35W
Ontonagon, Mi., U.S. (ŏn-tô-näg'ŏn)	103	46.50N	89.20W
Ōnuki, Japan (ō'no͞o-kē)	195a	35.17N	139.51E
Oodnadatta, Austl. (o͞od'nȧ-dȧ'tȧ)	202	27.38S	135.40E
Ooldea Station, Austl. (o͞ol-dā'ä)	202	30.35S	132.08E
Oologah Reservoir, res., Ok., U.S.	97	36.43N	95.32W
Ooltgensplaat, Neth.	145a	51.41N	4.19E
Oostanaula, r., Ga., U.S. (o͞o-stȧ-nô'lȧ)	114	34.25N	85.10W
Oostende, Bel. (ōst-ĕn'dē)	147	51.14N	2.55E
Oosterhout, Neth.	145a	51.38N	4.52E
Ooster Schelde, r., Neth.	145a	51.40N	3.40E
Ootsa Lake, l., Can.	86	53.49N	126.18W
Opalaca, Sierra de, mts., Hond. (sē-sĕ'r-rä-dĕ-ō-pä-lä'kä)	120	14.30N	88.29W
Opasquia, Can. (ō-päs'kwē-ȧ)	89	53.16N	93.53W
Opatów, Pol. (ô-pä'tōf)	155	50.47N	21.25E
Opava, Czech Rep. (ō'pä-vä)	155	49.56N	17.52E
Opelika, Al., U.S. (ŏp-ē-lī'kȧ)	114	32.39N	85.23W
Opelousas, La., U.S. (ŏp-ē-lo͞o'sȧs)	113	30.33N	92.04W
Opeongo, l., Can. (ŏp-ē-ôŋ'gō)	91	45.40N	78.20W
Opheim, Mt., U.S. (ō-fīm')	105	48.51N	106.19W
Ophir, Ak., U.S. (ō'fẽr)	95	63.10N	156.28W
Ophir, Mount, mtn., Malay.	181b	2.22N	102.37E
Ophirton, neigh., S. Afr.	244b	26.14S	28.01E
Opico, El Sal. (ô-pē'kô)	120	13.50N	89.23W
Opinaca, r., Can. (ŏp-ĭ-nä'kȧ)	85	52.28N	77.40W
Opishnya, Ukr.	163	49.57N	34.34E
Opladen, Ger. (ŏp'lä-dĕn)	157c	51.04N	7.00E
Opobo, Nig.	215	4.34N	7.27E
Opochka, Russia (ō-pôch'kȧ)	166	56.43N	28.39E
Opoczno, Pol. (ô-pôch'nô)	155	51.22N	20.18E
Opole, Pol. (ô-pôl'ā)	147	50.42N	17.55E
Opole Lubelskie, Pol. (ō-pō'lā lo͞o-bĕl'skyĕ)	155	51.09N	21.58E
Opp, Al., U.S. (ŏp)	114	31.18N	86.15W
Oppdal, Nor. (ôp'däl)	152	62.37N	9.41E
Opportunity, Wa., U.S. (ŏp-ŏr tū'nĭ tĭ)	104	47.37N	117.20W
Oppum, neigh., Ger.	236	51.19N	6.37E
Oquirrh Mountains, mts., Ut., U.S. (ō'kwēr)	107b	40.38N	112.11W
Oradea, Rom. (ô-räd'yä)	142	47.02N	21.55E
Oradell, N.J., U.S.	228	40.57N	74.02W
Oral, Kaz.	169	51.14N	51.22E
Oran, Alg. (ō-rän)(ô-räɴ')	210	35.46N	0.45W
Orán, Arg. (ô-rȧ'n)	132	23.13S	64.17W
Oran, Mo., U.S. (ôr'ȧn)	111	37.05N	89.39W
Oran, Sebkha d', l., Alg.	159	35.28N	0.28W
Orange, Austl. (ŏr'ĕnj)	203	33.15S	149.08E
Orange, Fr. (ô-raɴzh')	147	44.08N	4.48E
Orange, Ca., U.S.	107a	33.48N	117.51W
Orange, Ct., U.S.	99	41.15N	73.00W
Orange, N.J., U.S.	100a	40.46N	74.14W
Orange, Tx., U.S.	111	30.07N	93.44W
Orange, r., Afr.	212	29.15S	17.30E
Orange, Cabo, c., Braz. (kȧ-bô-rȧ'n-zhĕ)	131	4.25N	51.30W
Orangeburg, S.C., U.S. (ŏr'ĕnj-bûrg)	115	33.30N	80.50W
Orange Cay, i., Bah. (ŏr-ĕnj kē)	122	24.55N	79.05W
Orange City, Ia., U.S.	102	43.01N	96.06W
Orange Grove, neigh., S. Afr.	244b	26.10S	28.05E
Orange Lake, l., Fl., U.S.	115	29.30N	82.12W
Orangeville, Can. (ŏr'ĕnj-vĭl)	91	43.55N	80.06W
Orangeville, S. Afr.	218d	27.05S	28.13E
Orange Walk, Belize (wôl''k)	120a	18.09N	88.32W
Orani, Phil. (ō-rä'nē)	197a	14.47N	120.32E
Oranienburg, Ger. (ō-rä'nē-ĕn-bôrgh)	154	52.45N	13.14E
Oranjemund, Nmb.	212	28.33S	16.20E
Orăştie, Rom. (ô-rûsh'tyȧ)	161	45.50N	23.14E
Orbetello, Italy (ôr-bȧ-tĕl'lō)	160	42.27N	11.15E
Orbigo, r., Spain (ôr-bē'gō)	158	42.30N	5.55W
Orbost, Austl. (ôr'bŭst)	204	37.43S	148.20E
Orcas, i., Wa., U.S. (ôr'kȧs)	106d	48.43N	122.52W
Orchard Farm, Mo., U.S. (ôr'chẽrd färm)	107e	38.53N	90.27W
Orchard Park, N.Y., U.S.	101c	42.46N	78.46W
Orchards, Wa., U.S. (ôr'chẽdz)	106c	45.40N	122.33W
Orchila, Isla, i., Ven.	130	11.47N	66.34W
Ord, Ne., U.S. (ôrd)	102	41.35N	98.57W
Ord, r., Austl.	202	17.30S	128.40E
Ord, Mount, mtn., Az., U.S.	109	33.55N	109.40W
Orda, Russia (ôr'dȧ)	172a	57.10N	57.12E
Órdenes, Spain (ôr'dȧ-nās)	158	43.00N	8.24W
Ordos Desert, des., China	188	39.12N	108.10E
Ordu, Tur. (ôr'dô)	149	41.00N	37.50E
Ordway, Co., U.S. (ôrd'wā)	110	38.11N	103.46W
Örebro, Swe. (û'rē-brō)	146	59.16N	15.11E
Oredezh, r., Russia (ô'rē-dĕzh)	172c	59.23N	30.21E

ăt; finăl; rāte; senāte; ärm; åsk; sofȧ; fâre; ch-choose; dh-as th in other; bē; ēvent; bĕt; recĕnt; cratẽr; g-gō; gh-guttural g; bĭt; ĭ-short neutral; rīde; κ-guttural k as ch in German ich;

PLACE (Pronunciation)	PAGE	Lat. °′	Long. °′
Oregon, Il., U.S.	103	42.01N	89.21W
Oregon, state, U.S.	96	43.40N	121.50W
Oregon Caves National Monument, rec., Or., U.S. (căvz)	104	42.05N	123.13W
Oregon City, Or., U.S.	106c	45.21N	122.36W
Öregrund, Swe. (û-rĕ-grónd)	152	60.20N	18.26E
Orekhovo, Bul.	161	43.43N	23.59E
Orekhovo-Zuyevo, Russia (ôr-yĕ'κô-vô zò'yĕ-vô)	164	55.46N	39.00E
Orël, Russia (ôr-yôl')	164	52.59N	36.05E
Orël, prov., Russia	162	52.35N	36.08E
Orel', r., Ukr.	163	49.08N	34.55E
Oreland, Pa., U.S.	229b	40.07N	75.11W
Orem, Ut., U.S. (ŏ'rĕm)	109	40.15N	111.50W
Ore Mountains see Erzgebirge, mts., Eur.	142	50.29N	12.40E
Orenburg, Russia (ô'rĕn-bo͞org)	164	51.50N	55.05E
Orense, Spain (ô-rĕn'sā)	158	42.20N	7.52W
Øresund, strt., Eur.	152	55.50N	12.40E
Órganos, Sierra de los, mts., Cuba (sē-ĕ'r-rä-dĕ-lôs-ŏ'r-gä-nôs)	122	22.20N	84.10W
Organ Pipe Cactus National Monument, rec., Az., U.S. (ôr'găn pīp kăk'tŭs)	109	32.14N	113.05W
Orgãos, Serra das, mtn., Braz. (sĕ'r-rä-däs-ôr-gouɴ's)	129a	22.30S	43.01W
Orhei, Mol.	167	47.27N	28.49E
Orhon, r., Mong.	188	48.33N	103.07E
Oriental, Cordillera, mts., Col. (kôr-dēl-yĕ'rä)	130a	3.30N	74.27W
Oriental, Cordillera, mts., Dom. Rep. (kôr-dēl-yĕ'rä-ô-ryĕ'n-täl)	123	18.55N	69.40W
Oriental, Cordillera, mts., S.A. (kôr-dēl-yĕ'rä ō-rē-ĕn-täl')	130	14.00S	68.33W
Orihuela, Spain (ō'rē-wā'lä)	159	38.04N	0.55W
Orikhiv, Ukr.	163	47.34N	35.51E
Orillia, Can. (ô-rĭl'ĭ-ȧ)	85	44.35N	79.25W
Orin, Wy., U.S.	105	42.40N	105.10W
Orinda, Ca., U.S.	106b	37.53N	122.11W
Orinoco, Río, r., Ven. (rē'ō-ō-rĭ-nō'kō)	130	8.32N	63.13W
Orion, Phil. (ō-rē-ōn')	197a	14.37N	120.34E
Orissa, state, India (ō-rĭs'ȧ)	183	25.09N	83.50E
Oristano, Italy (ō-rēs-tä'nō)	148	39.53N	8.38E
Oristano, Golfo di, b., Italy (gôl-fô-dē-ō-rēs-tä'nō)	160	39.53N	8.12E
Orituco, r., Ven. (ō-rē-to͞o'kō)	131b	9.37N	66.25W
Oriuco, r., Ven. (ō-rēo͞o'kō)	131b	9.36N	66.25W
Orivesi, l., Fin.	153	62.15N	29.55E
Orizaba, Mex. (ō-rē-zä'bä)	117	18.52N	97.05W
Orizaba, Pico de, vol., Mex.	116	19.04N	97.14W
Orkanger, Nor.	152	63.19N	9.54W
Orkla, r., Nor. (ôr'klȧ)	152	62.55N	9.50E
Orkney, S. Afr. (ôrk'nĭ)	218d	26.58S	26.39E
Orkney Islands, is., Scot., U.K.	142	59.01N	2.08W
Orlando, S. Afr. (ôr-lăn-dō)	213b	26.15S	27.56E
Orlando, Fl., U.S. (ôr-lăn'dō)	97	28.32N	81.22W
Orlando West Extension, S. Afr.	244b	26.15S	27.54E
Orland Park, Il., U.S. (ôr-lănd')	101a	41.38N	87.52W
Orleans, Can. (ôr-lā-äɴ')	83c	45.28N	75.31W
Orléans, Fr. (ôr-lā-äɴ')	142	47.55N	1.56E
Orleans, In., U.S. (ôr-lēnz')	98	38.40N	86.25W
Orléans, Île d', i., Can.	91	46.56N	70.57W
Orly, Fr.	157b	48.45N	2.24E
Ormond, Austl.	243b	37.54S	145.03E
Ormond Beach, Fl., U.S. (ôr'mŏnd)	115	29.15N	81.05W
Ormskirk, Eng., U.K. (ôrms'kĕrk)	144a	53.34N	2.53W
Ormstown, Can. (ôrms'toun)	83a	45.07N	74.00W
Orneta, Pol. (ôr-nyĕ'tä)	155	54.07N	20.10E
Örnsköldsvik, Swe. (ûrn'skôlts-vĕk)	146	63.10N	18.32E
Oro, Río del, r., Mex.	109	26.04N	105.40W
Oro, Río del, r., Mex. (rē'ō dĕl ō'rō)	118	18.04N	100.59W
Orobie, Alpi, mts., Italy (äl'pē-ô-rō'byĕ)	160	46.05N	9.47E
Oron, Nig.	215	4.48N	8.14E
Orosei, Golfo di, b., Italy (gôl-fô-dē-ō-rô-sā'ē)	160	40.12N	9.45E
Orosháza, Hung. (ô-rôsh-hä'sô)	155	46.33N	20.31E
Orosi, vol., C.R. (ō-rō'sē)	120	11.00N	85.30W
Oroville, Ca., U.S. (ōr'ô-vĭl)	108	39.29N	121.34W
Oroville, Wa., U.S.	104	48.55N	119.25W
Oroville, Lake, res., Ca., U.S.	108	39.32N	121.25W
Orpington, neigh., Eng., U.K.	235	51.23N	0.06E
Orrville, Oh., U.S. (ôr'vĭl)	98	40.45N	81.50W
Orsa, Swe. (ōr'sä)	152	61.08N	14.35E
Orsay, Fr.	237c	48.42N	2.11E
Orsett, Eng., U.K.	235	51.31N	0.22E
Orsha, Bela. (ôr'shȧ)	166	54.29N	30.28E
Orsk, Russia (ôrsk)	164	51.15N	58.50E
Orşova, Rom. (ôr'shô-vä)	161	44.43N	22.26E
Orsoy, Ger.	236	51.31N	6.41E
Ortega, Col. (ôr-tĕ'gä)	130a	3.56N	75.12W
Ortegal, Cabo, c., Spain (kȧ'bô-ôr-tā-gäl')	148	43.46N	8.15W
Orth, Aus.	145e	48.09N	16.42E
Orthez, Fr. (ôr-tĕz')	157	43.29N	0.43W
Ortigueira, Spain (ôr-tē-gā'ē-rä)	148	43.40N	7.50W
Orting, Wa., U.S. (ôrt'ĭng)	106a	47.06N	122.12W
Ortona, Italy (ôr-tō'nä)	160	42.22N	14.22E
Ortonville, Mn., U.S. (ôr-tŭn-vĭl)	102	45.18N	96.26W
Oruba, Nig.	244d	6.35N	3.25E
Orūmīyeh, Iran	182	37.30N	45.15E
Orūmīyeh, Daryacheh-ye, l., Iran	182	38.01N	45.17E
Oruro, Bol. (ō-ro͞o'rō)	130	17.57S	66.59W
Orvieto, Italy (ôr-vyå'tō)	160	42.43N	12.08E
Oryu-dong, neigh., S. Kor.	241b	37.29N	126.51E
Osa, Russia (ō'sȧ)	166	57.18N	55.25E
Osa, Península de, pen., C.R. (ō'sä)	121	8.30N	83.25W

PLACE (Pronunciation)	PAGE	Lat. °′	Long. °′
Osage, Ia., U.S. (ō'sāj)	103	43.16N	92.49W
Osage, N.J., U.S.	229b	39.51N	75.01W
Osage, r., Mo., U.S.	111	38.10N	93.12W
Osage City, Ks., U.S. (ō'sāj sĭ'tĭ)	111	38.28N	95.53W
Ōsaka, Japan (ō'sä-kä)	189	34.40N	135.27E
Ōsaka, dept., Japan	195b	34.45N	135.36E
Osaka Castle, hist., Japan	242b	34.41N	135.32E
Ōsaka-Wan, b., Japan (wän)	194	34.34N	135.16E
Osakis, Mn., U.S. (ô-sā'kĭs)	102	45.51N	95.09W
Osakis, l., Mn., U.S.	103	45.55N	94.55W
Osasco, Braz.	234d	23.32S	46.46W
Osawatomie, Ks., U.S. (ŏs-ȧ-wăt'ō-mē)	111	38.29N	94.57W
Osborne, Ks., U.S. (ŏz'bŭrn)	110	39.25N	98.42W
Osceola, Ar., U.S. (ŏs-ē-ō'lȧ)	111	35.42N	89.58W
Osceola, Ia., U.S.	103	41.04N	93.45W
Osceola, Mo., U.S.	111	38.02N	93.41W
Osceola, Ne., U.S.	102	41.11N	97.34W
Oscoda, Mi., U.S. (ŏs-kō'dȧ)	98	44.25N	83.20W
Osëtr, r., Russia (ô'sĕt'r)	162	54.27N	38.15E
Osgood, In., U.S. (ŏz'go͝od)	98	39.10N	85.20W
Osgoode, Can.	83c	45.09N	75.37W
Osh, Kyrg. (ôsh)	169	40.33N	72.48E
Oshawa, Can. (ŏsh'ȧ-wȧ)	85	43.50N	78.50W
Ōshima, i., Japan (ō'shē'mä)	195	34.47N	139.35E
Oshkosh, Ne., U.S. (ŏsh'kŏsh)	102	41.24N	102.22W
Oshkosh, Wi., U.S.	97	44.01N	88.35W
Oshmyany, Bela. (ôsh-myä'nĭ)	153	54.27N	25.55E
Oshodi, Nig.	244d	6.34N	3.21E
Oshogbo, Nig.	210	7.47N	4.34E
Osijek, Cro. (ôs'ĭ-yĕk)	149	45.33N	18.48E
Osinniki, Russia (ŭ-sē'nyĭ-kē)	170	53.37N	87.21E
Oskaloosa, Ia., U.S. (ŏs-kȧ-lo͞o'sȧ)	103	41.16N	92.40W
Oskarshamn, Swe. (ôs'kärs-häm'n)	152	57.16N	16.24E
Oskarström, Swe. (ôs'kärs-strûm)	152	56.48N	12.55E
Oskemen, Kaz.	169	49.58N	82.38E
Oskol, r., Eur. (ôs-kôl')	167	51.00N	37.41E
Oslo, Nor. (ôs'lō)	142	59.56N	10.41E
Oslofjorden, fj., Nor.	152	59.03N	10.35E
Osmaniye, Tur.	149	37.10N	36.30E
Osnabrück, Ger. (ôs-nä-brük')	154	52.16N	8.05E
Osorno, Chile (ō-sō'r-nō)	132	40.42S	73.13W
Osorun, Nig.	244d	6.33N	3.29E
Osøyra, Nor.	152	60.24N	5.22E
Osprey Reef, rf., Austl. (ŏs'prā)	203	14.00S	146.45E
Ossa, Mount, mtn., Austl. (ŏsȧ)	203	41.45S	146.05E
Ossenberg, Ger.	236	51.34N	6.35E
Osseo, Mn., U.S. (ŏs'sē-ō)	107g	45.07N	93.24W
Ossining, N.Y., U.S. (ŏs'ĭ-nĭng)	100a	41.09N	73.51W
Ossipee, N.H., U.S. (ŏs'ĭ-pē)	92	43.42N	71.08W
Ossjøen, l., Nor. (ôs-syûĕn)	152	61.20N	12.00E
Ossum-Bösinghoven, Ger.	236	51.18N	6.39E
Ostankino, neigh., Russia	239b	55.49N	37.37E
Ostashkov, Russia (ôs-tăsh'kôf)	166	57.07N	33.04E
Oster, Ukr. (ōs'tĕr)	163	50.55N	30.52E
Osterdalälven, r., Swe.	146	61.40N	13.00E
Osterfeld, neigh., Ger.	236	51.30N	6.53E
Osterfjord, fj., Nor. (ûs'tĕr fyôr')	152	60.40N	5.25E
Östersund, Swe. (ûs'tĕr-so͞ond)	146	63.09N	14.49E
Östhammar, Swe. (ûst'häm'är)	152	60.16N	18.21E
Ostrava, Czech Rep.	142	49.51N	18.18E
Ostróda, Pol. (ôs'trŏt-ȧ)	155	53.41N	19.58E
Ostrogozhsk, Russia (ôs-tr-gôzhk')	167	50.53N	39.03E
Ostroh, Ukr.	167	50.21N	26.40E
Ostrołęka, Pol. (ôs-trô-woɴ'kȧ)	155	53.04N	21.35E
Ostrov, Russia (ôs-trôf')	166	57.21N	28.22E
Ostrov, Russia	239b	55.35N	37.51E
Ostrowiec Świętokrzyski, Pol. (ôs-trō'vyĕts shvyĕɴ-tō-kzhĭ'ske)	147	50.55N	21.24E
Ostrów Lubelski, Pol. (ôs'trôf lo͞o'bĕl-skĭ)	155	51.32N	22.49E
Ostrów Mazowiecka, Pol. (mä-zô-vyĕt'skä)	147	52.47N	21.54E
Ostrów Wielkopolski, Pol. (ôs'tro͞of vyĕl-kō-pōl'skē)	147	51.38N	17.49E
Ostrzeszów, Pol. (ôs-tzhā'shôf)	155	51.26N	17.56E
Ostuni, Italy (ôs-to͞o'nē)	161	40.44N	17.35E
Osum, r., Alb. (ō'sŏm)	161	40.37N	20.00E
Osuna, Spain (ō-so͞o'nä)	158	37.18N	5.05W
Osveya, Bela. (ôs'vĕ-yȧ)	162	56.00N	28.08E
Oswaldtwistle, Eng., U.K. (ŏz-wȧld-twĭs''l)	144a	53.44N	2.23W
Oswegatchie, r., N.Y., U.S. (ŏs-wē-găch'ĭ)	99	44.15N	75.20W
Oswego, Ks., U.S. (ŏs-wē'gō)	111	37.10N	95.08W
Oswego, N.Y., U.S.	97	43.25N	76.30W
Oświęcim, Pol. (ôsh-vyăɴ'tsyĭm)	155	50.02N	19.17E
Otaru, Japan (ō'tȧ-rò)	189	43.07N	141.00E
Otavalo, Ec. (ōtä-vä'lō)	130	0.14N	78.16W
Otavi, Nmb. (ô-tä'vē)	212	19.35S	17.20E
Otay, Ca., U.S. (ō'tā)	108a	32.36N	117.04W
Otepää, Est.	153	58.03N	26.30E
Otford, Eng., U.K.	235	51.19N	0.12E
Óthris, Óros, mtn., Grc.	161	39.00N	22.15E
Oti, r., Afr.	214	9.00N	0.10E
Otish, Monts, mts., Can. (ô-tĭsh')	85	52.15N	70.20W
Otjiwarongo, Nmb. (ŏt-jē-wȧ-rôn'gō)	212	20.20S	16.25E
Otočac, Cro. (ō'tō-chȧts)	160	44.53N	15.15E
Otra, r., Nor.	152	59.13N	7.20E
Otra, r., Russia (ôt'rȧ)	172b	55.22N	38.20E
Otradnoye, Russia (ô-trȧ'd-nôyĕ)	172c	59.46N	30.50E
Otranto, Italy (ô'trän-tô) (ô-trän'tō)	161	40.07N	18.30E
Otranto, Strait of, strt., Eur.	142	40.30N	18.45E
Otsego, Mi., U.S. (ŏt-sē'gō)	98	42.25N	85.45W
Otsu, Japan (ō'tsò)	194	35.00N	135.54E
Otta, l., Nor. (ôt'tȧ)	152	61.53N	8.40E

PLACE (Pronunciation)	PAGE	Lat. °′	Long. °′
Ottakring, neigh., Aus.	239e	48.12N	16.19E
Ottavia, neigh., Italy	239c	41.58N	12.24E
Ottawa, Can. (ŏt'ȧ-wȧ)	85	45.25N	75.43W
Ottawa, Il., U.S.	98	41.20N	88.50W
Ottawa, Ks., U.S.	111	38.37N	95.16W
Ottawa, Oh., U.S.	98	41.00N	84.00W
Ottawa, r., Can.	85	46.05N	77.20W
Otter Creek, r., Ut., U.S. (ŏt'ēr)	109	38.20N	111.55W
Otter Creek, r., Vt., U.S.	99	44.05N	73.15W
Otter Point, c., Can.	106a	48.21N	123.50W
Ottershaw, Eng., U.K.	235	51.22N	0.32W
Otter Tail, l., Mn., U.S.	102	46.21N	95.52W
Otterville, Il., U.S. (ôt'ēr-vĭl)	107e	39.03N	90.24W
Ottery, S. Afr. (ŏt'ĕr-ĭ)	212a	34.02S	18.31E
Ottumwa, Ia., U.S. (ô-tŭm'wȧ)	97	41.00N	92.26W
Otukpa, Nig.	215	7.09N	7.41E
Otumba, Mex. (ō-tŭm'bä)	118	19.41N	98.46W
Otway, Cape, c., Austl. (ŏt'wā)	203	38.55S	153.40E
Otway, Seno, b., Chile (sĕ'nō-ō't-wä'y)	132	53.00S	73.00W
Otwock, Pol. (ôt'vôtsk)	155	52.05N	21.18E
Ouachita, r., U.S.	97	33.25N	92.30W
Ouachita Mountains, mts., U.S. (wŏsh'ĭ-tô)	97	34.29N	95.01W
Ouagadougou, Burkina (wä'gȧ-do͞o'go͞o)	210	12.22N	1.31W
Ouahigouya, Burkina (wä-ē-go͞o'yä)	210	13.35N	2.25W
Oualâta, Maur. (wä-lä'tä)	210	17.11N	6.50W
Ouallene, Alg. (wäl-lân')	210	24.43N	1.15E
Ouanaminthe, Haiti	123	19.35N	71.45W
Ouarane, reg., Maur.	210	20.44N	10.27W
Ouarkoye, Burkina	214	12.05N	3.40W
Ouassel, r., Alg.	159	35.30N	1.55E
Oubangui (Ubangi), r., Afr. (o͞o-bäŋ'gē)	216	4.30N	20.35E
Oude Rijn, r., Neth.	145a	52.09N	4.33E
Oudewater, Neth.	145a	52.01N	4.52E
Oud-Gastel, Neth.	145a	51.35N	4.27E
Oudtshoorn, S. Afr. (outs'hōrn)	212	33.33S	23.36E
Oued Rhiou, Alg.	159	35.55N	0.57E
Oued Tlelat, Alg.	159	35.33N	0.28W
Oued-Zem, Mor. (wĕd-zĕm')	210	33.05N	5.49W
Ouessant, Island d', i., Fr. (ĕl-dwĕ-säɴ')	147	48.28N	5.00W
Ouesso, Congo	211	1.37N	16.04E
Ouest, Point, c., Haiti	123	19.00N	73.25W
Ouezzane, Mor. (wĕ-zan')	210	34.48N	5.40W
Ouham, r., Afr.	215	8.30N	17.50E
Ouidah, Benin (wē-dä')	210	6.25N	2.05E
Oujda, Mor.	210	34.41N	1.45W
Oulins, Fr. (o͞o-lăɴ')	157b	48.52N	1.27E
Oullins, Fr. (o͞o-lăɴ')	156	45.44N	4.46E
Oulu, Fin. (ō'lò)	142	64.58N	25.43E
Oulujärvi, l., Fin.	146	64.20N	25.48E
Oum Chalouba, Chad (o͞om shä-lo͞o'bä)	211	15.48N	20.30E
Oum Hadjer, Chad	215	13.18N	19.41E
Ounas, r., Fin. (ō'nȧs)	146	67.46N	24.40E
Oundle, Eng., U.K. (ōn'd'l)	144a	52.28N	0.28W
Ounianga Kébir, Chad (o͞o-nē-äŋ'gȧ kē-bēr')	211	19.04N	20.22E
Ouray, Co., U.S. (o͞o-rā')	110	38.00N	107.40W
Ourinhos, Braz. (ôö-rē'nyôs)	131	23.04S	49.45W
Ourique, Port. (ō-rē'kĕ)	158	37.39N	8.10W
Ouro Fino, Braz. (ōŭ-rô-fē'nō)	129a	22.18S	46.21W
Ouro Prêto, Braz. (ō'rò prā'tò)	132	20.24S	43.30W
Outardes, Rivière aux, r., Can.	85	50.53N	68.50W
Outer, i., Wi., U.S. (out'ēr)	103	47.03N	90.20W
Outer Brass, i., V.I.U.S. (bräs)	117c	18.24N	64.58W
Outer Hebrides, is., Scot., U.K.	150	57.20N	7.50W
Outjo, Nmb. (ōt'yō)	212	20.05S	17.10E
Outlook, Can.	88	51.31N	107.05W
Outremont, Can. (o͞o-trē-môɴ')	83a	45.31N	73.36W
Ouvéa, i., N. Cal.	203	20.43S	166.48E
Ouyen, Austl. (o͞o-ĕn)	204	35.05S	142.10E
Ovalle, Chile (ō-väl'yā)	132	30.43S	71.16W
Ovando, Bahía de, b., Cuba (bä-ē'ä-dĕ-ō-vä'n-dō)	123	20.10N	74.05W
Ovar, Port. (ô-vär')	158	40.52N	8.38W
Overbrook, neigh., Pa., U.S.	229b	39.58N	75.16W
Overbrook, neigh., Pa., U.S.	230b	40.24N	79.59W
Overijse, Bel.	145a	50.46N	4.32E
Overland, Mo., U.S. (ō-vēr-lănd)	107e	38.42N	90.22W
Overland Park, Ks., U.S.	107f	38.59N	94.40W
Overlea, Md., U.S. (ō'vēr-lā)(ō'vēr-lē)	100e	39.21N	76.31W
Övertornea, Swe.	146	66.19N	23.31E
Ovidiopol', Ukr.	163	46.15N	30.28E
Oviedo, Dom. Rep. (ô-vyĕ'dō)	123	17.50N	71.25W
Oviedo, Spain (ō-vē-ā'dhō)	142	43.22N	5.50W
Ovruch, Ukr.	163	51.19N	28.51E
Owada, Japan (ō'wä-dȧ)	195a	35.49N	139.33E
Owambo, hist. reg., Nmb.	212	18.10S	15.00E
Owando, Congo	212	0.29S	15.55E
Owasco, l., N.Y., U.S. (ō-wăsk'kō)	99	42.50N	76.30W
Owase, Japan (ō'wä-shē)	195	34.03N	136.12E
Owego, N.Y., U.S. (ō-wē'gō)	99	42.05N	76.15W
Owen, Wi., U.S. (ō'ĕn)	103	44.56N	90.35W
Owensboro, Ky., U.S. (ō'ĕnz-bŭr-ō)	97	37.45N	87.05W
Owens Lake, l., Ca., U.S.	108	37.13N	118.20W
Owen Sound, Can. (ō'ĕn)	85	44.30N	80.55W
Owen Stanley Range, mts., Pap. N. Gui. (stăn'lē)	197	9.00S	147.30E
Owensville, In., U.S. (ō'ĕnz-vĭl)	98	38.15N	87.40W
Owensville, Mo., U.S.	111	38.20N	91.29W
Owensville, Oh., U.S.	101f	39.08N	84.07W
Owenton, Ky., U.S. (ō'ĕn-tŭn)	98	38.35N	84.55W
Owerri, Nig. (ô-wĕr'ē)	210	5.26N	7.04E
Owings Mill, Md., U.S. (ōwĭngz mĭl)	100e	39.25N	76.50W
Owl Creek, r., Wy., U.S. (oul)	105	43.45N	108.46W
Owo, Nig.	215	7.15N	5.37E

330 Oworonsoki – Paracel Islands

PLACE (Pronunciation)	PAGE	Lat. °′	Long. °′
Oworonsoki, Nig.	244d	6.33N	3.24E
Owosso, Mi., U.S. (ô-wŏs'ō)	98	43.00N	84.15W
Owyhee, r., U.S.	96	43.04N	117.45W
Owyhee, Lake, res., Or., U.S.	96	43.27N	117.30W
Owyhee, South Fork, r., Id., U.S.	104	42.07N	116.43W
Owyhee Mountains, mts., Id., U.S. (ô-wī'hē)	96	43.15N	116.48W
Oxbow, Can.	89	49.12N	102.11W
Oxchuc, Mex. (ôs-chōōk')	119	16.47N	92.24W
Oxford, Can. (ŏks'fẽrd)	92	45.44N	63.52W
Oxford, Eng., U.K.	147	51.43N	1.16W
Oxford, Al., U.S. (ŏks'fẽrd)	115	33.38N	80.46W
Oxford, Ma., U.S.	93a	42.07N	71.52W
Oxford, Mi., U.S.	98	42.50N	83.15W
Oxford, Ms., U.S.	114	34.22N	89.30W
Oxford, N.C., U.S.	115	36.17N	78.35W
Oxford, Oh., U.S.	98	39.30N	84.45W
Oxford Falls, Austl.	243a	33.44S	151.15E
Oxford Lake, l., Can.	89	54.51N	95.37W
Oxfordshire, co., Eng., U.K.	144b	51.36N	1.30W
Oxkutzcab, Mex. (ôx-kōō'tz-käb)	120a	20.18N	89.22W
Oxmoor, Al., U.S. (ŏks'mōr)	100h	33.25N	86.52W
Oxnard, Ca., U.S. (ŏks'närd)	108	34.08N	119.12W
Oxon Hill, Md., U.S. (ōks'ōn hĭl)	100e	38.48N	77.00W
Oxshott, Eng., U.K.	235	51.20N	0.21W
Oyama, Japan	242a	35.36N	139.22E
Oyapock, r., S.A. (ō-yà-pŏk')	131	2.45N	52.15W
Oyem, Gabon	210	1.37N	11.35E
Øyeren, l., Nor. (ûĭẽrĕn)	152	59.50N	11.25E
Oymyakon, Russia (oi-myŭ-kôn')	165	63.14N	142.58E
Oyo, Nig. (ō'yō)	210	7.51N	3.56E
Oyodo, neigh., Japan	242b	34.43N	135.30E
Oyonnax, Fr. (ō-yō-náks')	157	46.16N	5.40E
Oyster Bay, N.Y., U.S.	100a	40.52N	73.32W
Oyster Bay Cove, N.Y., U.S.	228	40.52N	73.31W
Oyster Bayou, Tx., U.S.	113a	29.41N	94.33W
Oyster Creek, r., Tx., U.S. (ois'tẽr)	113a	29.13N	95.29W
Oyyl, r., Kaz.	170	49.30N	55.10E
Ozama, r., Dom. Rep. (ô-zä'mä)	123	18.45N	69.55W
Ozamiz, Phil. (ô-zä'mēz)	197	8.06N	123.43E
Ozark, Al., U.S. (ō'zärk)	114	31.28N	85.28W
Ozark, Ar., U.S.	111	35.29N	93.49W
Ozark Plateau, plat., U.S.	97	36.37N	93.56W
Ozarks, Lake of the, l., Mo., U.S. (ō'zärksz)	97	38.06N	93.26W
Ozëry, Russia (ô-zyô'rê)	162	54.53N	38.31E
Ozieri, Italy	148	40.38N	8.53E
Ozoir-la-Ferrière, Fr.	237c	48.46N	2.40E
Ozone Park, neigh., N.Y., U.S.	228	40.40N	73.51W
Ozorków, Pol. (ô-zôr'kôf)	155	51.58N	19.20E
Ozuluama, Mex.	119	21.34N	97.52W
Ozumba, Mex.	119a	19.02N	98.48W
Ozurgeti, Geor.	168	41.56N	42.00E

P

PLACE (Pronunciation)	PAGE	Lat. °′	Long. °′
Paarl, S. Afr. (pärl)	212	33.45S	18.55E
Paarlshoop, neigh., S. Afr.	244b	26.13S	27.59E
Paauilo, Hi., U.S. (pä-ä-ōō'ē-lō)	94a	20.03N	155.25W
Pabianice, Pol. (pä-byà-nē'tsĕ)	155	51.40N	19.29E
Pacaás Novos, Massiço de, mts., Braz.	130	11.03S	64.02W
Pacaraima, Serra, mts., S.A. (sĕr'rȧ pä-kä-rä-ē'mä)	130	3.45N	62.30W
Pacasmayo, Peru (pä-käs-mä'yō)	130	7.24S	79.30W
Pachuca, Mex. (pä-chōō'kä)	116	20.07N	98.43W
Pacific, Wa., U.S. (pȧ-sĭf'ĭk)	106a	47.16N	122.15W
Pacifica, Ca., U.S. (pȧ-sĭf'ĭ-kä)	106b	37.38N	122.29W
Pacific Beach, Ca., U.S.	108a	32.47N	117.22W
Pacific Grove, Ca., U.S.	108	36.37N	121.54W
Pacific Ocean, o.	2	0.00	170.00W
Pacific Palisades, neigh., Ca., U.S.	232	34.03N	118.32W
Pacific Ranges, mts., Can.	86	51.00N	125.30W
Pacific Rim National Park, rec., Can.	86	49.00N	126.00W
Paço de Arcos, Port.	238d	38.42N	9.17W
Pacolet, r., S.C., U.S. (pă'cō-lĕt)	115	34.55N	81.49W
Pacy-sur-Eure, Fr. (pä-sē-sür-ûr')	157b	49.01N	1.24E
Padang, Indon. (pä-däng')	196	1.01S	100.28E
Padang, i., Indon.	181b	1.12N	102.21E
Padang Endau, Malay.	181b	2.39N	103.38E
Paddington, neigh., Eng., U.K.	235	51.31N	0.10W
Paden City, W.V., U.S. (pā'dĕn)	98	39.30N	80.55W
Paderborn, Ger. (pä-dẽr-bôrn')	154	51.43N	8.46E
Paderno Dugnano, Italy	238c	45.34N	9.10E
Padibe, Ug.	217	3.28N	32.50E
Padiham, Eng., U.K. (păd'ĭ-hăm)	144a	53.48N	2.19W
Padilla, Mex. (pä-dēl'yä)	118	24.00N	98.45W
Padilla Bay, b., Wa., U.S. (pä-dēl'lȧ)	106a	48.31N	122.34W
Padova, Italy (pä'dō-vä)(păd'ū-ȧ)	148	45.24N	11.53E
Padre Island, i., Tx., U.S. (pä'drā)	113	27.09N	97.15W
Padre Miguel, neigh., Braz.	234c	22.53S	43.26W
Padua *see* Padova, Italy	148	45.24N	11.53E
Paducah, Ky., U.S.	97	37.05N	88.36W
Paducah, Tx., U.S.	110	34.01N	100.18W
Paektu-san, mtn., Asia (pâk'tōō-sän')	194	42.00N	128.03E
Pag, i., Yugo. (päg)	160	44.30N	14.48E
Pagai Selatan, Pulau, i., Indon.	196	2.48S	100.22E
Pagai Utara, Pulau, i., Indon.	196	2.45S	100.02E
Pagasitikós Kólpos, b., Grc.	161	39.15N	23.00E
Page, Az., U.S.	109	36.57N	111.27W
Pago Pago, Am. Sam.	198a	14.16S	170.42W
Pagosa Springs, Co., U.S. (pȧ-gō'sȧ)	110	37.15N	107.05W
Pagote, India	240e	18.54N	72.59E
Pahala, Hi., U.S. (pä-hä'lä)	94a	19.11N	155.28W
Pahang, state, Malay.	181b	3.02N	102.57E
Pahang, r., Malay.	196	3.39N	102.41E
Pahokee, Fl., U.S. (pȧ-hō'kē)	115a	26.45N	80.40W
Paide, Est. (pī'dĕ)	153	58.54N	25.30E
Päijänne, l., Fin. (pĕ'ē-yĕn-nĕ)	146	61.38N	25.05E
Pailolo Channel, strt., Hi., U.S. (pä-ē-lō'lō)	94a	21.05N	156.41W
Paine, Chile (pī'nĕ)	129b	33.49S	70.44W
Painesville, Oh., U.S. (pānz'vĭl)	98	41.40N	81.15W
Painted Desert, des., Az., U.S. (pānt'ĕd)	110	36.15N	111.35W
Painted Rock Reservoir, res., Az., U.S.	109	33.00N	113.05W
Paintsville, Ky., U.S. (pānts'vĭl)	98	37.50N	82.50W
Paisley, Austl.	243b	37.51S	144.51E
Paisley, Scot., U.K. (pāz'lĭ)	146	55.50N	4.30W
Paita, Peru (pä-ē'tä)	130	5.11S	81.12W
Pai T'ou Shan, mts., N. Kor.	189	40.30N	127.20E
Paiute Indian Reservation, I.R., Ut., U.S.	109	38.17N	113.50W
Pajápan, Mex. (pä-hä'pän)	119	18.16N	94.41W
Pakanbaru, Indon.	196	0.43N	101.15E
Pakhra, r., Russia (päк'rá)	172b	55.29N	37.51E
Pakistan, nation, Asia	183	28.00N	67.30E
Pakokku, Myanmar (pá-kŏk'kò)	188	21.29N	95.00E
Paks, Hung. (pôksh)	155	46.38N	18.53E
Pala, Chad	215	9.22N	14.54E
Palacios, Tx., U.S. (pä-lä'syōs)	113	28.42N	96.12W
Palagruža, Otoci, is., Cro.	160	42.20N	16.23E
Palaión Fáliron, Grc.	239d	37.55N	23.41E
Palaiseau, Fr. (pá-lĕ-zō')	157b	48.44N	2.16E
Palana, Russia	165	59.07N	159.58E
Palanan Bay, b., Phil. (pä-lä'nän)	197a	17.14N	122.35E
Palanan Point, c., Phil.	197a	17.12N	122.40E
Pālanpur, India (pä'lŭn-pōōr)	183	24.08N	73.29E
Palapye, Bots. (pá-läp'yĕ)	212	22.34S	27.28E
Palatine, Il., U.S. (păl'ȧ-tīn)	101a	42.07N	88.03W
Palatka, Fl., U.S. (pȧ-lăt'kȧ)	115	29.39N	81.40W
Palau (Belau), dep., Oc. (pä-lä'ò)	3	7.15N	134.30E
Palauig, Phil. (pá-lou'ĕg)	197a	15.27N	119.54E
Palawan, i., Phil. (pä-lä'wan)	196	9.50N	117.38E
Pālayankottai, India	187	8.50N	77.50E
Paldiski, Est. (päl'dĭ-skĭ)	153	59.22N	24.04E
Palembang, Indon. (pä-lĕm-bäng')	196	2.57S	104.40E
Palencia, Guat. (pä-lĕn'sē-á)	120	14.40N	90.22W
Palencia, Spain (pä-lĕ'n-syä)	148	42.02N	4.32W
Palenque, Mex. (pä-lĕŋ'kå)	119	17.34N	91.58W
Palenque, Punta, c., Dom. Rep. (pōō'n-tä)	123	18.10N	70.10W
Palermo, Col. (pä-lĕr'mô)	130a	2.53N	75.26W
Palermo, Italy	142	38.08N	13.24E
Palermo, neigh., Arg.	233d	34.35S	58.25W
Palestine, Tx., U.S.	97	31.46N	95.38W
Palestine, hist. reg., Asia (păl'ĕs-tīn)	181a	31.33N	35.00E
Paletwa, Myanmar (pŭ-lĕt'wä)	183	21.19N	92.52E
Palghāt, India	187	10.49N	76.40E
Pāli, India	186	25.53N	73.18E
Palín, Guat. (pä-lēn')	120	14.42N	90.42W
Palisades Park, N.J., U.S.	228	40.51N	74.00W
Palizada, Mex. (pä-lē-zä'dä)	119	18.17N	92.04W
Palk Strait, strt., Asia (pôk)	183	10.00N	79.23E
Palma, Braz. (päl'mä)	129a	21.23S	42.18W
Palma, Spain	142	39.35N	2.38E
Palma, Bahía de, b., Spain	159	39.24N	2.37E
Palma del Río, Spain	158	37.43N	5.19W
Palmar de Cariaco, Ven.	234a	10.34N	66.55W
Palmares, Braz. (päl-má'rĕs)	131	8.46S	35.28W
Palmas, Braz.	131	10.08S	48.18W
Palmas, Braz. (päl'mäs)	132	26.20S	51.56W
Palmas, Cape, c., Lib.	210	4.22N	7.44W
Palma Soriano, Cuba (sō-rē-ä'nō)	122	20.15N	76.00W
Palm Beach, Fl., U.S. (päm bēch')	115a	26.43N	80.03W
Palmeira dos Índios, Braz. (pä-mā'rä-dôs-ē'n-dyôs)	131	9.26S	36.33W
Palmeirinhas, Ponta das, c., Ang.	216	9.05S	13.00E
Palmela, Port. (päl-mā'lä)	158	38.34N	8.54W
Palmer, Ak., U.S. (päm'ẽr)	95	61.38N	149.15W
Palmer, Wa., U.S.	106a	47.19N	121.53W
Palmer Park, Md., U.S.	229d	38.55N	76.52W
Palmerston North, N.Z. (päm'ẽr-stŭn)	203a	40.20S	175.35E
Palmerville, Austl. (päm'ẽr-vĭl)	203	16.08S	144.15E
Palmetto, Fl., U.S. (pál-mĕt'ō)	115a	27.32N	82.34W
Palmetto Point, c., Bah.	123	21.15N	73.25W
Palmi, Italy (päl'mē)	160	38.21N	15.54E
Palmira, Col. (päl-mē'rä)	130	3.33N	76.17W
Palmira, Cuba	122	22.15N	80.25W
Palmyra, Mo., U.S. (păl-mī'rȧ)	111	39.45N	91.32W
Palmyra, N.J., U.S.	100f	40.01N	75.00W
Palmyra, i., Oc.	2	6.00N	162.20W
Palmyra, hist., Syria	182	34.25N	38.28E
Palmyras Point, c., India	186	20.42N	87.45E
Palo Alto, Ca., U.S. (pä'lō äl'tō)	106b	37.27N	122.09W
Paloduro Creek, r., Tx., U.S. (pä-lō-dōō'rō)	110	36.16N	101.12W
Paloh, Malay.	181b	2.11N	103.12E
Paloma, l., Mex. (pä-lō'mä)	112	26.53N	104.02W
Palomar Park, Ca., U.S.	231b	37.29N	122.16W
Palomo, Cerro el, mtn., Chile (sĕ'r-rō-ĕl-pä-lō'mō)	129b	34.36S	70.20W
Palos, Cabo de, c., Spain (ká'bō-dĕ-pä'lōs)	148	39.38N	0.43W
Palos Heights, Il., U.S.	231a	41.40N	87.48W
Palos Hills, Il., U.S.	231a	41.41N	87.49W
Palos Park, Il., U.S.	231a	41.40N	87.50W
Palos Verdes Estates, Ca., U.S. (pä'lŭs vûr'dĭs)	107a	33.48N	118.24W
Palouse, Wa., U.S. (pȧ-lōōz')	104	46.54N	117.04W
Palouse, r., Wa., U.S.	104	47.02N	117.35W
Palu, Tur. (pä-loo')	167	38.55N	40.10E
Paluan, Phil. (pä-lōō'än)	197a	13.25N	120.29E
Pamiers, Fr. (pá-myā')	147	43.07N	1.34E
Pamirs, mts., Asia	183	38.14N	72.27E
Pamlico, r., N.C., U.S. (păm'lĭ-kō)	115	35.25N	76.59W
Pamlico Sound, strt., N.C., U.S.	97	35.10N	76.10W
Pampa, Tx., U.S. (păm'pȧ)	96	35.32N	100.56W
Pampa de Castillo, pl., Arg. (pá'm-pä-dĕ-käs-tē'l-yō)	132	45.30S	67.30W
Pampana, r., S.L.	214	8.35N	11.55W
Pampanga, r., Phil. (päm-päŋ'gä)	197a	15.20N	120.48E
Pampas, reg., Arg. (päm'päs)	132	37.00S	64.30W
Pampilhosa do Botão, Port. (päm-pē-lyō'sȧ-dô-bō-toùn)	158	40.21N	8.32W
Pamplona, Col. (päm-plō'nä)	130	7.19N	72.41W
Pamplona, Spain (päm-plō'nä)	148	42.49N	1.39W
Pamunkey, r., Va., U.S. (pá-mŭŋ'kĭ)	99	37.40N	77.20W
Pana, Il., U.S. (pā'nȧ)	98	39.25N	89.05W
Panagyurishte, Bul. (pá-ná-gyōō'rēsh-tĕ)	161	42.30N	24.11E
Panaji (Panjim), India	183	15.33N	73.52E
Panamá, Pan.	117	8.58N	79.32W
Panama, nation, N.A.	117	9.00N	80.00W
Panamá, Istmo de, isth., Pan.	117	9.00N	80.00W
Panama Canal, can., Pan.	116a	9.20N	79.55W
Panama City, Fl., U.S. (păn-ȧ mä' sĭ'tĭ)	114	30.08N	85.39W
Panamint Range, mts., Ca., U.S. (păn-à-mĭnt')	108	36.40N	117.30W
Panarea, i., Italy (pä-nä'rē-a)	160	38.37N	15.05E
Panaro, r., Italy (pä-nä'rō)	160	44.47N	11.06E
Panay, i., Phil. (pä-nī')	196	11.15N	121.38E
Pančevo, Yugo. (pán'chĕ-vô)	149	44.52N	20.42E
Pānchghara, India	240a	22.44N	88.16E
Panch'iao, Tai.	241d	25.01N	121.27E
Panchor, Malay.	181b	2.11N	102.43E
Pānchur, India	186a	22.31N	88.17E
Panda, Zaire (pän'dä')	212	10.59S	27.24E
Pan de Guajaibon, mtn., Cuba (pän dä gwä-jà-bōn')	122	22.50N	83.20W
Panevėžys, Lith. (pä'nyē-vāzh'ēs)	166	55.44N	24.21E
Panfilov, Kaz. (pŭn-fē'lôf)	169	44.12N	79.58E
Panga, Zaire (päŋ'gä)	211	1.51N	26.25E
Pangani, Tan. (pän-gä'nē)	213	5.28S	38.58E
Pangani, r., Tan.	217	4.40S	37.45E
Pangkalpinang, Indon. (päng-käl'pē-näng')	196	2.11S	106.04E
Pangnirtung, Can.	85	66.08N	65.26W
Panguitch, Ut., U.S. (pän'gwĭch)	109	37.50N	112.30W
Panié, Mont, mtn., N. Cal.	198f	20.36S	164.46E
Pānihāti, India	186a	22.42N	88.23E
Panimávida, Chile (pä-nē-má'vē-dä)	129b	35.44S	71.26W
Panje, India	240e	18.54N	72.57E
Pankow, neigh., Ger.	238a	52.34N	13.24E
Panshi, China (pän-shē)	192	42.50N	126.48E
Pantar, Pulau, i., Indon. (pän'tär)	197	8.40N	123.45E
Pantelleria, i., Italy (pän-tĕl-lā-rē'ä)	148	36.43N	11.59E
Pantepec, Mex. (pän-tä-pĕk')	119	17.11N	93.04W
Pantheon, hist., Italy	239c	41.55N	12.29E
Pantin, Fr.	237c	48.54N	2.24E
Pantitlán, Mex.	233a	19.25N	99.05W
Panuco, Mex. (pä'nōō-kō)	118	22.04N	98.11W
Pánuco, Mex. (pä'nōō-kō)	118	23.25N	105.55W
Panuco, r., Mex.	116	21.59N	98.20W
Pánuco de Coronado, Mex. (pä'nōō-kô dā kō-rô-nä'dhō)	112	24.33N	104.20W
Panvel, India	187b	18.59N	73.06E
Panyu, China (pä-yōō)	191a	22.56N	113.22E
Panzós, Guat. (pä-zós')	120	15.26N	89.40W
Pao, r., Ven. (pá'ō)	131b	9.52N	67.57W
Paola, Ks., U.S. (pā-ō'lȧ)	111	38.34N	94.51W
Paoli, In., U.S. (pā-ō'lī)	98	38.35N	86.30W
Paoli, Pa., U.S.	100f	40.03N	75.29W
Paonia, Co., U.S. (pā-ō'nyȧ)	109	38.50N	107.40W
Pápa, Hung. (pä'pô)	149	47.18N	17.27E
Papagayo, r., Mex. (pä-pä-gä'yō)	118	16.52N	99.41W
Papagayo, Golfo del, b., C.R. (gôl-fô-dĕl-pä-pä-gá'yō)	120	10.44N	85.56W
Papagayo, Laguna, l., Mex. (lä-ò-nä)	118	16.44N	99.44W
Papago Indian Reservation, I.R., Az., U.S. (pä'pá'gō)	109	32.33N	112.12W
Papantla de Olarte, Mex. (pä-pän'tlä dā-ô-lä'r-tĕ)	116	20.30N	97.15W
Papatoapan, r., Mex. (pä-pä-tô-ä-pá'n)	119	18.00N	96.22W
Papelón, Ven.	234a	10.27N	66.47W
Papenburg, Ger. (päp'ĕn-bòrgh)	154	53.05N	7.23E
Papinas, Arg. (pä-pē'näs)	129c	35.30S	57.19W
Papineauville, Can. (pä-pē-nō'vĕl)	83c	45.38N	75.01W
Papua, Gulf of, b., Pap. N. Gui. (păp-ōō-ȧ)	197	8.20S	144.45E
Papua New Guinea, nation, Oc. (păp-ōō-ȧ)(gĭne)	197	7.00S	142.15E
Papudo, Chile (pä-pōō'dô)	129b	32.30S	71.25W
Paquequer Pequeno, Braz. (pä-kĕ-kĕ'r-pĕ-kĕ'nō)	132b	22.19S	43.02W
Para, r., Russia	162	53.45N	40.58E
Paracale, Phil. (pä-rä-kä'lå)	197a	14.17N	122.47E
Paracambi, Braz.	132b	22.36S	43.43W
Paracatu, Braz. (pä-rä-kä-tōō')	131	17.17S	46.43W
Paracel Islands, is., Asia	196	16.40N	113.00E

ăt; finȧl; rāte; senāte; ärm; ȧsk; sofȧ; fâre; ch-choose; dh-as th in other; bē; ēvent; bĕt; recĕnt; cratẽr; g-gō; gh-guttural g; bĭt; ĭ-short neutral; rīde; ĸ-guttural k as ch in German ich;

PRONOUNCING INDEX Paraćin–Peebles 331

PLACE (Pronunciation)	PAGE	Lat. °'	Long. °'
Paraćin, Yugo. (pá'rä-chēn)	149	43.51N	21.26E
Para de Minas, Braz. (pä-rä-dĕ-mē'näs)	131	19.52S	44.37W
Paradise, i., Bah.	122	25.05N	77.20W
Paradise Valley, Nv., U.S. (păr'á-dīs)	104	41.28N	117.32W
Parados, Cerro de los, mtn., Col. (sĕ'r-rô-dĕ-lôs-pä-rä'dōs)	130a	5.44N	75.13W
Paragould, Ar., U.S. (păr'ȧ-gōōld)	111	36.03N	90.29W
Paraguaçu, r., Braz. (pä-rä-gwä-zōō')	131	12.25S	39.46W
Paraguay, nation, S.A. (păr'ȧ-gwā)	132	24.00S	57.00W
Paraguay, Río, r., S.A. (rē'ō-pä-rä-gwä'y)	132	21.12S	57.31W
Paraíba, state, Braz. (pä-rä-ē'bä)	131	7.11S	37.05W
Paraíba, r., Braz.	129a	23.02S	45.43W
Paraíba do Sul, Braz. (dô-sōō'l)	129a	22.10S	43.18W
Paraibuna, Braz. (pä-räē-bōō'nä)	129a	23.23S	45.38W
Paraíso, C.R.	121	9.50N	83.53W
Paraíso, Mex.	119	18.24N	93.11W
Paraiso, Pan. (pä-rä-ē'sō)	116a	9.02N	79.38W
Paraisópolis, Braz. (pä-räē-sô'pō-lēs)	129a	22.35S	45.45W
Paraitinga, r., Braz. (pä-rä-ē-tē'n-gä)	129a	23.15S	45.24W
Parakou, Benin (pá-rá-kōō')	210	9.21N	2.37E
Paramaribo, Sur. (pá-rá-má'rē-bō)	131	5.50N	55.15W
Paramatta, Austl. (păr-ȧ-măt'ȧ)	201b	33.49S	150.59E
Paramillo, mtn., Col. (pä-rä-mē'l-yō)	130a	7.06N	75.55W
Paramount, Ca., U.S.	232	33.53N	118.09W
Paramus, N.J., U.S.	100a	40.56N	74.04W
Paran, r., Asia	181a	30.05N	34.50E
Paraná, Arg.	132	31.44S	60.32W
Paraná, Río, r., S.A.	132	24.00S	54.00W
Paranaíba, Braz. (pä-rä-ná-ē'bȧ)	131	19.43S	51.13W
Paranaíba, r., Braz.	131	18.58S	50.44W
Paraná Ibicuy, r., Arg.	129c	33.27S	59.26W
Paranam, Sur.	131	5.39N	55.13W
Paránápanema, r., Braz. (pä-rä-ná'pä-nĕ-mä)	131	22.28S	52.15W
Parañaque, Phil.	241g	14.30N	120.59E
Paraopeda, r., Braz. (pä-rä-o-pĕ'dä)	129a	20.09S	44.14W
Parapara, Ven. (pä-rä-pä-rä)	131b	9.44N	67.17W
Parati, Braz. (pä-rätē)	129a	23.14S	44.43W
Paray-le-Monial, Fr. (pá-rĕ'lē-mô-nyäl')	156	46.27N	4.14E
Pārbati, r., India	186	24.50N	76.44E
Parchim, Ger. (par'kĭm)	154	53.25N	11.52E
Parczew, Pol. (pär'chĕf)	155	51.38N	22.53E
Pardo, r., Braz.	129a	21.32S	46.40W
Pardo, r., Braz. (pär'dō)	131	15.25S	39.40W
Pardubice, Czech Rep. (pär'dŏ-bĭt-sĕ)	154	50.02N	15.47E
Parecis, Serra dos, mts., Braz. (sĕr'rä dōs pä-rå-sēzh')	131	13.45S	59.28W
Paredes de Nava, Spain (pä-rä'dås dä nä'vä)	158	42.10N	4.41W
Paredón, Mex.	112	25.56N	100.58W
Parent, Can.	85	47.59N	74.30W
Parent, Lac, l., Can.	91	48.40N	77.00W
Parepare, Indon.	196	4.01S	119.38E
Pargolovo, Russia (pár-gô'lô vô)	172c	60.04N	30.18E
Pari, neigh., Braz.	234d	23.32S	46.37W
Paria, r., Az., U.S.	109	37.07N	111.51W
Paria, Golfo de, b. (gôl-fô-dĕ-br-pä-rē-ä)	130	10.33N	62.14W
Paricutín, Volcán, vol., Mex.	118	19.27N	102.14W
Parida, Río de la, r., Mex. (rē'ō-dĕ-lä-pä-rē'dä)	112	26.23N	104.40W
Parima, Serra, mts., S.A. (sĕr'rȧ pä-rē'má)	130	3.45N	64.00W
Pariñas, Punta, c., Peru (pōō'n-tä-pä-rē'n-yäs)	130	4.30S	81.23W
Parintins, Braz. (pä-rĭn-tĭnzh')	131	2.34S	56.30W
Paris, Can.	91	43.15N	80.23W
Paris, Fr. (pá-rē')	142	48.51N	2.20E
Paris, Ar., U.S. (păr'ĭs)	111	35.17N	93.43W
Paris, Il., U.S.	98	39.35N	87.40W
Paris, Ky., U.S.	98	38.15N	84.15W
Paris, Mo., U.S.	111	39.27N	91.59W
Paris, Tn., U.S.	114	36.16N	88.20W
Paris, Tx., U.S.	97	33.39N	95.33W
Paris-le-Bourget, Aéroport de, arpt., Fr.	237c	48.57N	2.25E
Paris-Orly, Aéroport de, arpt., Fr.	237c	48.45N	2.25E
Parita, Golfo de, b., Pan. (gôl-fô-dĕ-pä-rē'tä)	121	8.06N	80.10W
Park City, Ut., U.S.	105	40.39N	111.33W
Parkdene, S. Afr.	244b	26.14S	28.16E
Parker, S.D., U.S. (pär'kēr)	102	43.24N	97.10W
Parker Dam, dam, U.S.	96	34.20N	114.00W
Parkersburg, W.V., U.S. (pär'kērz-bûrg)	97	39.15N	81.35W
Parkes, Austl. (pärks)	204	33.10S	148.10E
Park Falls, Wi., U.S. (pärk)	103	45.55N	90.29W
Park Forest, Il., U.S.	101a	41.29N	87.41W
Parkgate, Eng., U.K.	237a	53.18N	3.05W
Parkhill Gardens, S. Afr.	244b	26.14S	28.11E
Parkland, Wa., U.S. (pärk'lănd)	106a	47.09N	122.26W
Parklawn, Va., U.S.	229d	38.50N	77.09W
Parklea, Austl.	243a	33.44S	150.57E
Park Orchards, Austl.	243b	37.46S	145.13E
Park Range, mts., Co., U.S.	105	40.54N	106.40W
Park Rapids, Mn., U.S.	102	46.53N	95.05W
Park Ridge, Il., U.S.	101a	42.00N	87.50W
Park Ridge Manor, Il., U.S.	231a	42.02N	87.50W
Park River, N.D., U.S.	102	48.22N	97.43W
Parkrose, Or., U.S. (pärk'rōz)	106c	45.33N	122.33W
Park Rynie, S. Afr.	213c	30.22S	30.43E
Parkston, S.D., U.S. (pärks'tŭn)	102	43.22N	97.59W
Park Town, neigh., S. Afr.	244b	26.11S	28.03E
Parktown North, neigh., S. Afr.	244b	26.09S	28.02E
Parkview, Pa., U.S.	230b	40.30N	79.56W
Parkville, Md., U.S.	100e	39.22N	76.32W
Parkville, Mo., U.S.	107f	39.12N	94.41W
Parkwood, Md., U.S.	229d	39.01N	77.05W
Parla, Spain (pär'lä)	159a	40.14N	3.46W
Parliament, Houses of, pt. of i., Eng., U.K.	235	51.30N	0.07W
Parma, Italy (pär'mä)	148	44.48N	10.20E
Parma, Oh., U.S.	101d	41.23N	81.44W
Parma Heights, Oh., U.S.	101d	41.23N	81.36W
Parnaíba, Braz. (pär-nä-ē'bä)	131	3.00S	41.42W
Parnaiba, r., Braz.	131	3.57S	42.30W
Parnassós, mtn., Grc.	161	38.36N	22.35E
Parndorf, Aus.	145e	48.00N	16.52E
Pärnu, Est. (pĕr'nōō)	166	58.24N	24.29E
Pärnu, r., Est.	153	58.40N	25.05E
Pärnu Laht, b., Est. (läкt)	153	58.15N	24.17E
Paro, Bhu. (pä'rô)	186	27.30N	89.30E
Paroo, r., Austl. (pä'rōō)	203	30.00S	144.00E
Paropamisus, mts., Afg.	182	34.45N	63.58E
Páros, Grc. (pä'rôs) (pä'rŏs)	161	37.05N	25.14E
Páros, i., Grc.	149	37.11N	25.00E
Parow, S. Afr. (pă'rô)	212a	33.54S	18.36E
Parowan, Ut., U.S. (păr'ô-wăn)	109	37.50N	112.50W
Parral, Chile (pär-rä'l)	132	36.07S	71.47W
Parral, r., Mex.	112	27.25N	105.08W
Parramatta, r., Austl. (păr-ȧ-măt'ȧ)	201b	33.42S	150.58E
Parras, Mex. (pär-räs')	112	25.28N	102.08W
Parrita, C.R. (pär-rē'tä)	121	9.32N	84.17W
Parrsboro, Can. (pärz'bŭr-ô)	92	45.24N	64.20W
Parry, i., Can. (păr'ĭ)	91	45.15N	80.00W
Parry, Mount, mtn., Can.	86	52.53N	128.45W
Parry Islands, is., Can.	82	75.30N	110.00W
Parry Sound, Can.	85	45.20N	80.00W
Parsnip, r., Can. (pärs'nĭp)	87	54.45N	122.20W
Parsons, Ks., U.S. (pär's'nz)	97	37.20N	95.16W
Parsons, W.V., U.S.	99	39.05N	79.40W
Parthenay, Fr. (pár-t'nĕ')	156	46.39N	0.16W
Partington, Eng., U.K.	237b	53.25N	2.26W
Partinico, Italy (pär-tē'nê-kô)	160	38.02N	13.11E
Partizansk, Russia	165	43.15N	133.19E
Parys, S. Afr. (pá-rīs')	218d	26.53S	27.28E
Pasadena, Ca., U.S. (păs-á-dē'nȧ)	96	34.09N	118.09W
Pasadena, Md., U.S.	100e	39.06N	76.35W
Pasadena, Tx., U.S.	113a	29.43N	95.13W
Pasay, Phil.	241g	14.33N	121.00E
Pascagoula, Ms., U.S. (păs-kȧ-gōō'lȧ)	114	30.22N	88.33W
Pascagoula, r., Ms., U.S.	114	30.52N	88.48W
Paşcani, Rom. (päsh-kän')	155	47.46N	26.42E
Pasco, Wa., U.S. (păs'kō)	104	46.13N	119.04W
Pascoe Vale, Austl.	243b	37.44S	144.56E
Pascua, Isla de (Easter Island), i., Chile	225	26.50S	109.00W
Pasewalk, Ger. (pä'zĕ-välk)	154	53.31N	14.01E
Pashiya, Russia (pä'shĭ-yá)	172a	58.27N	58.17E
Pashkovo, Russia (pásh-kô'vô)	194	48.52N	131.09E
Pashkovskaya, Russia (pásh-kôf'ská-yá)	163	45.00N	39.04E
Pasig, Phil.	197a	14.34N	121.05E
Pasión, Río de la, r., Guat. (rē'ō-dĕ-lä-pä-syōn')	120a	16.31N	90.11W
Pasir Gudang, Malay.	240c	1.27N	103.53E
Pasir Panjang, Sing.	240c	1.17N	103.47E
Pasir Puteh, Malay.	240c	1.26N	103.56E
Paso de los Libres, Arg. (pä-sô-dĕ-lôs-lē'brĕs)	132	29.33S	57.05W
Paso de los Toros, Ur. (tō'rôs)	129c	32.43S	56.33W
Paso del Rey, Arg.	233d	34.39S	58.45W
Paso Robles, Ca., U.S. (pă'sō rō'blĕs)	108	35.38N	120.44W
Pasquia Hills, hills, Can. (păs'kwê-ȧ)	89	53.13N	102.37W
Passaic, N.J., U.S. (pă-sā'ĭk)	100a	40.52N	74.08W
Passaic, r., N.J., U.S.	100a	40.42N	74.26W
Passamaquoddy Bay, b., N.A. (păs'ȧ-mȧ-kwŏd'ĭ)	92	45.06N	66.59W
Passa Tempo, Braz. (pä's-sä-tĕ'm-pô)	129a	20.40S	44.29W
Passau, Ger. (päsou)	147	48.34N	13.27E
Pass Christian, Ms., U.S. (pás krĭs'tyĕn)	114	30.20N	89.15W
Passero, Cape, c., Italy (päs-sĕ'rô)	142	36.34N	15.13E
Passo Fundo, Braz. (pä'sō fōn'dô)	132	28.16S	52.13W
Passos, Braz. (pä's-sōs)	131	20.45S	46.37W
Pastaza, r., S.A. (päs-tä'zä)	130	3.05S	76.18W
Pasto, Col. (päs'tô)	130	1.15N	77.19W
Pastora, Mex. (päs-tō-rä)	118	22.08N	100.04W
Pasuruan, Indon.	196	7.45S	112.50E
Pasvalys, Lith. (päs-vä-lēs')	153	56.04N	24.23E
Patagonia, reg., Arg. (păt-á-gō'nĭ-ȧ)	132	46.45S	69.30W
Pātālganga, r., India	187b	18.52N	73.08E
Patapsco, r., Md., U.S. (pȧ-tăps'kō)	100e	39.12N	76.30W
Pateros, Lake, res., Wa., U.S.	104	48.05N	119.45W
Paterson, N.J., U.S. (păt'ēr-sŭn)	100a	40.55N	74.10W
Pathein, Myanmar	183	16.46N	94.47E
Pathfinder Reservoir, res., Wy., U.S. (păth'fīn-dēr)	105	42.22N	107.10W
Patiāla, India (pŭt-ê-ä'lŭ)	183	30.25N	76.28E
Pati do Alferes, Braz. (pä-tē-dô-ál-fĕ'rĕs)	132b	22.25S	43.25W
Patna, India (pŭt'nŭ)	183	25.33N	85.18E
Patnanongan, i., Phil. (pät-nä-nôn'gän)	197a	14.50N	122.25E
Patoka, r., In., U.S. (pȧ-tō'kȧ)	98	38.25N	87.25W
Patom Plateau, plat., Russia	165	59.30N	115.00E
Patos, Braz. (pä'tōzh)	131	7.03S	37.14W
Patos, Wa., U.S. (pä'tōs)	106d	48.47N	122.57W
Patos, Lagoa dos, l., Braz. (lä'gō-á dozh pä'tōzh)	132	31.15S	51.30W
Patos de Minas, Braz. (dĕ-mē'näzh)	131	18.39S	46.31W
Pátrai, Grc. (pä-trī') (pä-träs')	149	38.15N	21.48E
Patraïkós Kólpos, b., Grc.	161	38.16N	21.19E
Patras *see* Pátrai, Grc.	149	38.15N	21.48E
Patrocínio, Braz. (pä-trō-sē'nê-ò)	131	18.48S	46.47W
Pattani, Thai. (pät'á-nê)	196	6.56N	101.13E
Patten, Me., U.S. (păt''n)	92	45.59N	68.27W
Patterson, La., U.S. (păt'ēr-sŭn)	113	29.41N	91.20W
Patterson, i., Can.	90	48.38N	87.14W
Patton, Pa., U.S.	99	40.40N	78.45W
Patuca, r., Hond.	121	15.22N	84.31W
Patuca, Punta, c., Hond. (pōō'n-tä-pä-tōō'kä)	121	15.55N	84.05W
Patuxent, r., Md., U.S. (pȧ-tŭk'sĕnt)	99	39.10N	77.10W
Pátzcuaro, Mex. (päts'kwä-rô)	118	19.30N	101.36W
Pátzcuaro, Lago de, l., Mex. (lä'gô-dĕ)	118	19.36N	101.38W
Patzicia, Guat. (pät-zē'syä)	120	14.36N	90.57W
Patzún, Guat. (pät-zōōn')	120	14.40N	91.00W
Pau, Fr. (pō)	147	43.18N	0.23W
Pau, Gave de, r., Fr. (gäv-dĕ)	156	43.33N	0.51W
Paulding, Oh., U.S. (pôl'dĭng)	98	41.05N	84.35W
Paulinenaue, Ger. (pou'lē-nĕ-nou-ĕ)	145b	52.40N	12.43E
Paulistano, Braz. (pá'ò-lēs-tá-nä)	131	8.13S	41.06W
Paulo Afonso, Salto, wtfl., Braz. (säl-tô-pou'lô äf-fôn'sô)	131	9.33S	38.32W
Paul Roux, S. Afr. (pôrl rōō)	218d	28.18S	27.57E
Paulsboro, N.J., U.S. (pôlz'bē-rô)	100f	39.50N	75.16W
Pauls Valley, Ok., U.S. (pôlz văl'ê)	111	34.43N	97.13W
Pavarandocito, Col. (pä-vä-rän-dô-sē'tô)	130a	7.18N	76.32W
Pavda, Russia (päv'da)	172a	59.16N	59.32E
Pavia, Italy (pä-vē'ä)	148	45.12N	9.11E
Pavlodar, Kaz. (páv-lô-dár')	169	52.17N	77.23E
Pavlof Bay, b., Ak., U.S. (păv-lŏf)	95	55.20N	161.20W
Pavlohrad, Ukr.	167	48.32N	35.52E
Pavlovsk, Russia (páv-lôfsk')	163	50.28N	40.05E
Pavlovsk, Russia	172c	59.41N	30.27E
Pavlovskiy Posad, Russia (páv-lôf'skĭ pô-sát')	166	55.47N	38.39E
Pavuna, Braz. (pä-vōō'nȧ)	132b	22.48S	43.21W
Päwesin, Ger. (pă'vĕ-zēn)	145b	52.31N	12.44E
Pawhuska, Ok., U.S. (pô-hŭs'kȧ)	111	36.41N	96.20W
Pawnee, Ok., U.S. (pô-nē')	111	36.20N	96.47W
Pawnee, r., Ks., U.S.	110	38.18N	99.42W
Pawnee City, Ne., U.S.	111	40.08N	96.09W
Paw Paw, Mi., U.S. (pô'pô)	98	42.15N	85.55W
Paw Paw, r., Mi., U.S.	103	42.14N	86.21W
Pawtucket, R.I., U.S. (pô-tŭk'ĕt)	99	41.53N	71.23W
Paxoi, i., Grc.	161	39.14N	20.15E
Paxton, Il., U.S. (păks'tŭn)	98	40.35N	88.00W
Paya Lebar, Sing.	240c	1.22N	103.53E
Payette, Id., U.S. (pá-ĕt')	104	44.05N	116.55W
Payette, r., Id., U.S.	104	43.57N	116.26W
Payette, North Fork, r., Id., U.S.	104	44.10N	116.10W
Payette, South Fork, r., Id., U.S.	104	44.07N	115.43W
Pay-Khoy, Khrebet, mts., Russia	166	68.08N	63.04E
Payne, l., Can. (pān)	85	59.22N	73.16W
Paynesville, S. Afr.	244b	26.14S	28.28E
Paynesville, Mn., U.S. (pānz'vĭl)	103	45.23N	94.43W
Paysandú, Ur. (pī-sän-dōō')	132	32.16S	57.55W
Payson, Ut., U.S. (pā's'n)	109	40.05N	111.45W
Pazardzhik, Bul. (pä-zár-dzhek')	149	42.10N	24.22E
Pazin, Cro. (pä'zēn)	160	45.14N	13.57E
Peabody, Ks., U.S. (pē'bŏd-ĭ)	111	38.09N	97.09W
Peabody, Ma., U.S.	93a	42.32N	70.56W
Peabody Institute, pt. of i., Md., U.S.	229c	39.18N	76.37W
Peace, r., Can.	84	57.30N	117.30W
Peace Creek, r., Fl., U.S. (pēs)	115a	27.16N	81.53W
Peace Dale, R.I., U.S. (dāl)	100b	41.27N	71.30W
Peace River, Can. (rĭv'ēr)	84	56.14N	117.17W
Peacock Hills, hills, Can. (pē-kŏk' hĭlz)	84	66.08N	109.55W
Peak Hill, Austl.	202	25.38S	118.50E
Peakhurst, Austl.	243a	33.58S	151.04E
Pearl, r., U.S. (pûrl)	97	30.30N	89.45W
Pearland, Tx., U.S. (pûrl'ănd)	113a	29.34N	95.17W
Pearl Harbor, Hi., U.S.	94a	21.20N	157.53W
Pearl Harbor, b., Hi., U.S.	96d	21.22N	157.58W
Pearsall, Tx., U.S. (pēr'sôl)	112	28.53N	99.06W
Pearse Island, i., Can. (pērs)	86	54.51N	130.21W
Pearston, S. Afr. (pē'ērstŏn)	213c	32.36S	25.09E
Peary Land, reg., Grnld. (pēr'ĭ)	220	82.00N	40.00W
Pease, r., Tx., U.S. (pēz)	110	34.07N	99.53W
Peason, La., U.S. (pēz''n)	113	31.25N	93.19W
Pebane, Moz. (pĕ-bá'nē)	213	17.10S	38.08E
Pecan Bay, Tx., U.S. (pê-kăn')	112	32.04N	99.15W
Peçanha, Braz. (pā-kän'yȧ)	131	18.37S	42.26W
Pecatonica, r., Il., U.S. (pĕk-ȧ-tŏn-ĭ-kȧ)	103	42.21N	89.28W
Pechenga, Russia (pyĕ'chĕŋ-gá)	166	69.30N	31.10E
Pechincha, neigh., Braz.	234c	22.56S	43.21W
Pechora, r., Russia	164	66.00N	54.00E
Pechora Basin, Russia (pyĕ-chô'rá)	164	67.55N	58.37E
Pechori, Russia (pĕt'sĕ-rē)	162	57.48N	27.33E
Pecos, N.M., U.S. (pā'kôs)	109	35.29N	105.41W
Pecos, Tx., U.S.	112	31.26N	103.30W
Pecos, r., U.S.	96	31.10N	103.10W
Pécs, Hung. (pāch)	149	46.04N	18.15E
Peddie, S. Afr.	213c	33.13S	27.09E
Pedley, Ca., U.S. (pĕd'lē)	107a	33.59N	117.29W
Pedra Azul, Braz. (pä'drä-zōō'l)	131	16.03S	41.13W
Pedreiras, Braz. (pĕ-drā'räs)	131	4.30S	44.31W
Pedro, Point, c., Sri L. (pē'drô)	187	9.50N	80.14E
Pedro Antonio Santos, Mex.	120a	18.55N	88.13W
Pedro Betancourt, Cuba (bā-täŋ-kōrt')	122	22.40N	81.15W
Pedro de Valdivia, Chile (pĕ'drô-dĕ-väl-dē'vē-ä)	132	22.32S	69.55W
Pedro do Rio, Braz. (dô-rē'rô)	132b	22.20S	43.09W
Pedro II, Braz. (pä'drō sā-gōn'dô)	131	4.20S	41.27W
Pedro Juan Caballero, Para. (hóä'n-kä-bäl-yĕ'rō)	132	22.40S	55.42W
Pedro Miguel, Pan. (mê-gāl')	116a	9.01N	79.36W
Pedro Miguel Locks, trans., Pan. (mê-gāl')	116a	9.01N	79.36W
Peebinga, Austl. (pē-bĭng'á)	202	34.43S	140.55E
Peebles, Scot., U.K. (pē'b'lz)	150	55.40N	3.15W

PLACE (Pronunciation)	PAGE	Lat. °′	Long. °′
Peekskill, N.Y., U.S. (pēks'kĭl)	100a	41.17N	73.55W
Pegasus Bay, b., N.Z. (pĕg'ȧ-sŭs)	203a	43.18S	173.25E
Pegnitz, r., Ger. (pĕgh-nēts)	154	49.38N	11.40E
Pego, Spain (pā'gō)	159	38.50N	0.09W
Peguis Indian Reserve, I.R., Can.	89	51.20N	97.35W
Pegu Yoma, mts., Myanmar (pĕ-go͞o'yō'mä)	183	19.16N	95.59E
Pehčevo, Mac. (pĕκ'chĕ-vō)	161	41.42N	22.57E
Pehladpur, neigh., India	240d	28.35N	77.06E
Peigan Indian Reserve, I.R., Can.	87	49.35N	113.40W
Peipus, Lake see Chudskoye Ozero, l., Eur.	166	58.43N	26.45E
Peit'ou, Tai.	241d	25.08N	121.29E
Pekin, Il., U.S. (pē'kĭn)	98	40.35N	89.30W
Peking see Beijing, China	189	39.55N	116.23E
Pelagie, Isole, is., Italy	148	35.46N	12.32E
Pélagos, i., Grc.	161	39.17N	24.05E
Pelahatchie, Ms., U.S. (pĕl-á-hăch'ē)	114	32.17N	89.48W
Pelat, Mont, mtn., Fr. (pĕ-lá')	147	44.16N	6.43E
Peleduy, Russia (pyĕl-yĭ-do͞o'ē)	165	59.50N	112.47E
Pelée, Mont, mtn., Mart. (pē-lā')	121b	14.49N	61.10W
Pelee, Point, c., Can.	90	41.55N	82.30W
Pelee Island, i., Can. (pē'lē)	90	41.45N	82.30W
Pelequén, Chile (pĕ-lĕ-kĕ'n)	129b	34.26S	71.52W
Pelham, Ga., U.S. (pĕl'hăm)	114	31.07N	84.10W
Pelham, N.H., U.S.	93a	42.43N	71.22W
Pelham, N.Y., U.S.	228	40.55N	73.49W
Pelham Manor, N.Y., U.S.	228	40.54N	73.48W
Pelican, l., Mn., U.S.	103	46.36N	94.00W
Pelican Bay, b., Can.	89	52.45N	100.20W
Pelican Harbor, b., Bah. (pĕl'ĭ-kăn)	122	26.20N	76.45W
Pelican Rapids, Mn., U.S. (pĕl'ĭ-kăn)	102	46.34N	96.05W
Pella, Ia., U.S. (pĕl'ȧ)	103	41.25N	92.50W
Pellworm, i., Ger. (pĕl'vȯrm)	154	54.33N	8.25E
Pelly, l., Can.	84	66.08N	102.57W
Pelly, r., Can.	84	62.20N	133.00W
Pelly Bay, b., Can. (pĕl'ĭ)	85	68.57N	91.05W
Pelly Crossing, Can.	95	62.50N	136.50W
Pelly Mountains, mts., Can.	84	61.50N	133.05W
Peloncillo Mountains, mts., Az., U.S. (pĕl-ôn-sĭl'lō)	109	32.40N	109.20W
Peloponnisos, pen., Grc.	161	37.28N	22.14E
Pelotas, Braz. (på-lō'tăzh)	132	31.45S	52.18W
Pelton, Can. (pĕl'tŭn)	101b	42.15N	82.57W
Pelym, r., Russia	166	60.20N	63.05E
Pelzer, S.C., U.S. (pĕl'zĕr)	115	34.38N	82.30W
Pemanggil, i., Malay.	181b	2.37N	104.41E
Pematangsiantar, Indon.	196	2.58N	99.03E
Pemba, Moz. (pĕm'bá)	213	12.58S	40.30E
Pemba, Zam.	212	15.29S	27.22E
Pemba Channel, strt., Afr.	217	5.10S	39.30E
Pemba Island, i., Tan.	217	5.20S	39.57E
Pembina, N.D., U.S. (pĕm'bĭ-nȧ)	102	48.58N	97.15W
Pembina, r., Can.	87	53.05N	114.30W
Pembina, r., N.A.	89	49.08N	98.20W
Pembroke, Can. (pĕm' brōk)	85	45.50N	77.00W
Pembroke, Wales, U.K.	150	51.40N	5.00W
Pembroke, Ma., U.S. (pĕm'brōk)	93a	42.05N	70.49W
Pen, India	187b	18.44N	73.06E
Penafiel, Port. (pā-ná-fyĕl')	158	41.12N	8.19W
Peñafiel, Spain (pā-nyá-fyĕl')	158	41.38N	4.08W
Peña Grande, neigh., Spain	238b	40.23N	3.44W
Peñalara, mtn., Spain (pā-nyä-lä'rä)	148	40.52N	3.57W
Pena Nevada, Cerro, Mex.	118	23.47N	99.52W
Peñaranda de Bracamonte, Spain	158	40.54N	5.11W
Peñarroya-Pueblonuevo, Spain (pĕn-yär-rō'yä-pwĕ'blô-nwĕ'vô)	158	38.18N	5.18W
Peñas, Cabo de, c., Spain (ká'bô-dĕ-pā'nyäs)	158	43.42N	6.12W
Penas, Golfo de, b., Chile (gôl-fô-dĕ-pĕ'n-äs)	132	47.15S	77.30W
Penasco, r., Tx., U.S. (pä-nás'kō)	112	32.50N	104.45W
Pendembu, S.L. (pĕn-dĕm'bo͞o)	210	8.06N	10.42W
Pender, Ne., U.S. (pĕn'dĕr)	102	42.08N	96.43W
Penderisco, r., Col. (pĕn-dĕ-rē's-kō)	130a	6.30N	76.21W
Pendjari, Parc National de la, rec., Benin	214	11.25N	1.30E
Pendlebury, Eng., U.K.	237b	53.31N	2.20W
Pendleton, Or., U.S. (pĕn'd'l-tŭn)	96	45.41N	118.47W
Pend Oreille, r., Wa., U.S.	104	48.44N	117.20W
Pend Oreille, Lake, l., Id., U.S. (pŏn-dô-rā') (pĕn-dô-rĕl')	96	48.09N	116.38W
Penedo, Braz. (pā-nā'dô)	131	10.17S	36.28W
Penetanguishene, Can. (pĕn'ē-tăŋ-gĭ-shēn')	91	44.45N	79.55W
Pengcheng, China (pŭŋ-chŭŋ)	190	36.24N	114.11E
Penglai, China (pŭŋ-lī)	192	37.49N	120.45E
Penha, neigh., Braz.	234c	22.49S	43.17W
Penha de França, neigh., Braz.	234d	23.32S	46.32W
Peniche, Port. (pĕ-nē'chå)	158	39.22N	9.24W
Peninsula, Oh., U.S. (pĕn-ĭn'sŭ-lȧ)	101d	41.14N	81.32W
Penistone, Eng., U.K. (pĕn'ĭ-stŭn)	144a	53.31N	1.38W
Penjamillo, Mex. (pĕn-hä-mēl'yō)	118	20.06N	101.56W
Pénjamo, Mex. (pān'hä-mō)	118	20.27N	101.43W
Penk, r., Eng., U.K. (pĕnk)	144a	52.41N	2.10W
Penkridge, Eng., U.K. (pĕnk'rĭj)	144a	52.43N	2.07W
Pennant Hills, Austl.	243a	33.44S	151.04E
Penne, Italy (pĕn'nā)	160	42.28N	13.57E
Penner, r., India (pĕn'ĕr)	183	14.43N	79.09E
Penn Hills, Pa., U.S.	230b	40.28N	79.53W
Pennines, hills, Eng., U.K. (pĕn-īn')	150	54.30N	2.10W
Pennines, Alpes, mts., Eur.	154	46.02N	7.07E
Pennsauken, N.J., U.S.	229b	39.58N	75.04W
Pennsboro, W.V., U.S. (pĕnz'bŭr-ô)	98	39.10N	81.00W
Penns Grove, N.J., U.S. (pĕnz grōv)	100f	39.44N	75.28W

PLACE (Pronunciation)	PAGE	Lat. °′	Long. °′
Pennsylvania, state, U.S. (pĕn-sĭl-vā'nĭ-ȧ)	97	41.00N	78.10W
Penn Valley, Pa., U.S.	229b	40.01N	75.16W
Penn Wynne, Pa., U.S.	229b	39.59N	75.16W
Penn Yan, N.Y., U.S. (pĕn yăn')	99	42.40N	77.00W
Pennycutaway, r., Can.	89	56.10N	93.25W
Peno, l., Russia (pā'nō)	162	56.55N	32.28E
Penobscot, r., Me., U.S.	97	45.00N	68.36W
Penobscot Bay, b., Me., U.S. (pē-nŏb'skŏt)	92	44.20N	69.00W
Penong, Austl. (pē-nông')	202	32.00S	133.00E
Penrith, Austl.	201b	33.45S	150.42E
Pensacola, Fl., U.S. (pĕn-sȧ-kō'lȧ)	97	30.25N	87.13W
Pensacola Dam, Ok., U.S.	111	36.27N	95.02W
Pensby, Eng., U.K.	237a	53.21N	3.06W
Pensilvania, Col. (pĕn-sēl-vá'nyä)	130a	5.31N	75.05W
Pentagon, pt. of i., Va., U.S.	229d	38.52N	77.03W
Pentecost, i., Vanuatu (pĕn'tē-kŏst)	203	16.05S	168.28E
Penticton, Can.	84	49.30N	119.35W
Pentland Firth, strt., Scot., U.K. (pĕnt'lănd)	150	58.44N	3.25W
Penza, Russia (pĕn'zá)	164	53.10N	45.00E
Penzance, Eng., U.K. (pĕn-zăns')	150	50.07N	5.40W
Penzberg, Ger. (pĕnts'bĕrgh)	154	47.43N	11.21E
Penzhina, r., Russia (pyĭn-zē-nŭ)	171	62.15N	166.30E
Penzhino, Russia	165	63.42N	168.00E
Penzhinskaya Guba, b., Russia	171	60.30N	161.30E
Penzing, neigh., Aus.	239e	48.12N	16.18E
Peoria, Il., U.S. (pē-ō'rĭ-ȧ)	97	40.45N	89.35W
Peotillos, Mex. (på-ō-tel'yōs)	118	22.30N	100.39W
Peotone, Il., U.S. (pē'ō-tōn)	101a	41.20N	87.47W
Pepacton Reservoir, res., N.Y., U.S. (pĕp-ăc'tŭn)	99	42.05N	74.40W
Pepe, Cabo, c., Cuba (kä'bō-pĕ'pĕ)	122	21.30N	83.10W
Pepperell, Ma., U.S. (pĕp'ĕr-ĕl)	93a	42.40N	71.36W
Peqin, Alb. (pĕ-kēn')	161	41.03N	19.48E
Pequannock, N.J., U.S.	228	40.57N	74.18W
Perales, r., Spain (pā-rä'läs)	159a	40.24N	4.07W
Perales de Tajuña, Spain (dā tä-ho͞o'nyä)	159a	40.14N	3.22W
Perche, Collines du, hills, Fr.	156	48.25N	0.40E
Perchtoldsdorf, Aus. (pĕrk'tōlts-dôrf)	145e	48.07N	16.17E
Perdekop, S. Afr.	218d	27.11S	29.38E
Perdido, r., Al., U.S. (pĕr-dī'dō)	114	30.45N	87.38W
Perdido, Monte, mtn., Spain (pĕr-dē'dō)	159	42.40N	0.00
Perdões, Braz. (pĕr-dô'ĕs)	129a	21.05S	45.05W
Pereira, Col. (pā-rā'rä)	130	4.49N	75.42W
Pere Marquette, Mi., U.S.	98	43.55N	86.10W
Pereshchepyne, Ukr.	163	49.02N	35.19E
Pereslavl'-Zalesskiy, Russia (på-rå-slàv'l zá-lyĕs'kĭ)	166	56.43N	38.52E
Pereyaslav-Khmel'nyts'kyy, Ukr.	167	50.05N	31.25E
Pergamino, Arg. (pĕr-gä-mē'nō)	132	33.53S	60.36W
Perham, Mn., U.S. (pĕr'hăm)	102	46.37N	95.35W
Peribonca, r., Can. (pĕr-ĭ-bŏŋ'kȧ)	85	50.30N	71.00W
Périgueux, Fr. (pā-rē-gû')	147	45.12N	0.43E
Perija, Sierra de, mts., Col. (sē-ĕ'r-rá-dĕ-pĕ-rē'κä)	130	9.25N	73.30W
Peristérion, Grc.	239d	38.01N	23.42E
Perivale, neigh., Eng., U.K.	235	51.32N	0.19W
Perkam, Tanjung, c., Indon.	197	1.20S	138.45E
Perkins, Can. (pĕr'kĕns)	83c	45.37N	75.37W
Perlas, Archipiélago de las, is., Pan.	121	8.29N	79.15W
Perlas, Laguna las, l., Nic. (lä-gō'nä-dĕ-läs)	121	12.34N	83.19W
Perleberg, Ger. (pĕr'lĕ-bĕrg)	154	53.06N	11.51E
Perm', Russia (pĕrm)	164	58.00N	56.15E
Pernambuco see Recife, Braz.	131	8.09S	34.59W
Pernambuco, state, Braz. (pĕr-näm-bo͞o'kō)	131	8.08S	38.54W
Pernik, Bul. (pĕr-nēk')	149	42.36N	23.04E
Péronne, Fr. (pā-rôn')	156	49.57N	2.49E
Perote, Mex. (pĕ-rô'tē)	119	19.33N	97.13W
Perovo, Russia (pâ'rô-vô)	172b	55.43N	37.47E
Perpignan, Fr. (pĕr-pē-nyäN')	147	42.42N	2.48E
Perris, Ca., U.S. (pĕr'ĭs)	107a	33.46N	117.14W
Perros, Bahía de, b., Cuba (bä-ē'ä-pā'rōs)	122	22.25N	78.35W
Perrot, Île, i., Can.	83a	45.23N	73.57W
Perry, Fl., U.S. (pĕr'ĭ)	114	30.06N	83.35W
Perry, Ga., U.S.	114	32.27N	83.44W
Perry, Ia., U.S.	103	41.49N	94.40W
Perry, N.Y., U.S.	99	42.45N	78.00W
Perry, Ok., U.S.	111	36.17N	97.18W
Perry, Ut., U.S.	107b	41.27N	112.02W
Perry Hall, Md., U.S.	100e	39.24N	76.29W
Perrymont, Pa., U.S.	230b	40.33N	80.02W
Perryopolis, Pa., U.S. (pĕ-rē-ŏ'pō-lĭs)	101e	40.05N	79.45W
Perrysburg, Oh., U.S. (pĕr ĭz-bûrg)	98	41.35N	83.35W
Perryton, Tx., U.S. (pĕr'ĭ-tŭn)	110	36.23N	100.48W
Perryville, Ak., U.S. (pĕr-ĭ-vĭl)	95	55.58N	159.28W
Perryville, Mo., U.S.	111	37.41N	89.52W
Persan, Fr. (pĕr-säN')	157b	49.09N	2.15E
Persepolis, hist., Iran (pĕr-sĕpō-lĭs)	182	30.15N	53.08E
Persian Gulf, b., Asia (pûr'zhăn)	182	27.38N	50.30E
Perth, Austl. (pûrth)	202	31.50S	116.10E
Perth, Can.	91	44.40N	76.15W
Perth, Scot., U.K.	146	56.24N	3.25W
Perth Amboy, N.J., U.S. (ăm'boi)	100a	40.31N	74.16W
Pertuis, Fr. (pĕr-tüē')	157	43.43N	5.29E
Peru, Il., U.S. (pē-ro͞o')	98	41.20N	89.10W
Peru, In., U.S.	98	40.45N	86.00W
Peru, nation, S.A.	130	10.00S	75.00W
Perugia, Italy (pā-ro͞o'jä)	148	43.08N	12.24E
Peruque, Mo., U.S. (pē rō'kē)	107e	38.52N	90.36W
Pervomays'k, Ukr.	167	48.04N	30.52E

PLACE (Pronunciation)	PAGE	Lat. °′	Long. °′
Pervoural'sk, Russia (pĕr-vô-ô-rálsk')	172a	56.54N	59.58E
Perwenitz, Ger.	238a	52.40N	13.01E
Pesaro, Italy (pā'zä-rō)	148	43.54N	12.55E
Pescado, r., Ven. (pĕs-kä'dō)	131b	9.33N	65.32W
Pescara, Italy (pās-kä'rä)	160	42.26N	14.15E
Pescara, r., Italy	160	42.18N	13.22E
Peschanyy mŭĭs, c., Kaz.	170	43.10N	51.20E
Pescia, Italy (pā'shä)	160	43.53N	11.42E
Peshāwar, Pak. (pĕ-shä'wŭr)	183	34.01N	71.34E
Peshtera, Bul.	161	42.03N	24.19E
Peshtigo, Wi., U.S. (pĕsh'tē-gō)	103	45.03N	87.46W
Peshtigo, r., Wi., U.S.	103	45.15N	88.14W
Peski, Russia (pyâs'kĭ)	172b	55.13N	38.48E
Pêso da Régua, Port. (pā-sō-dä-rā'gwä)	158	41.09N	7.47W
Pespire, Hond. (pås-pē'rå)	120	13.35N	87.20W
Pesqueria, r., Mex. (pås-kå-rē'ȧ)	112	25.55N	100.25W
Pessac, Fr.	156	44.48N	0.38W
Pesterzsébet, neigh., Hung.	239g	47.26N	19.07E
Pestlorinc, neigh., Hung.	239g	47.26N	19.12E
Pestújhely, neigh., Hung.	239g	47.32N	19.07E
Petacalco, Bahía de, b., Mex. (bä-ē'ä-dĕ-pĕ-tä-käl'kō)	118	17.55N	102.00W
Petah Tiqwa, Isr.	181a	32.05N	34.53E
Petaluma, Ca., U.S. (pĕt-ȧ-lō'mȧ)	108	38.15N	122.38W
Petare, Ven. (pĕ-tä'rĕ)	131b	10.28N	66.48W
Petatlán, Mex. (pā-tä-tlän')	118	17.31N	101.17W
Petawawa, Can.	91	45.54N	77.17W
Petén, Laguna de, l., Guat. (lä-gō'nä-dĕ-på-tān')	120a	17.05N	89.54W
Petenwell Reservoir, res., Wi., U.S.	103	44.10N	89.55W
Peterborough, Austl.	202	32.53S	138.58E
Peterborough, Can. (pē'tĕr-bŭr-ô)	85	44.20N	78.20W
Peterborough, Eng., U.K.	150	52.35N	0.14W
Peterhead, Scot., U.K. (pē-tĕr-hĕd')	150	57.36N	3.47W
Peter Pond Lake, l., Can. (pŏnd)	84	55.55N	108.44W
Petersburg, Ak., U.S. (pē'tĕrz-bûrg)	95	56.52N	133.10W
Petersburg, Il., U.S.	111	40.01N	89.51W
Petersburg, In., U.S.	98	38.30N	87.15W
Petersburg, Ky., U.S.	101f	39.04N	84.52W
Petersburg, Va., U.S.	97	37.12N	77.30W
Peters Creek, r., Pa., U.S.	230b	40.18N	79.52W
Petershagen, Ger. (pē'tĕrs-hä-gĕn)	145b	52.32N	13.46E
Petersham, Austl.	243a	33.54S	151.09E
Petershausen, Ger. (pĕ'tĕrs-hou-zĕn)	145d	48.25N	11.29E
Pétionville, Haiti	123	18.30N	72.20W
Petit, S. Afr.	244b	26.06S	28.22E
Petitcodiac, Can. (pē-tē-kō-dyăk')	92	45.56N	65.10W
Petite Terre, i., Guad. (pē-tēt'târ')	121b	16.12N	61.00W
Petit Goâve, Haiti (pē-tē' gō-áv')	123	18.25N	72.50W
Petit Jean Creek, r., Ar., U.S. (pē-tē'zhäN')	111	35.05N	93.55W
Petit Loango, Gabon	216	2.16S	9.35E
Petlalcingo, Mex. (pĕ-tläl-sĕŋ'gō)	119	18.05N	97.53W
Peto, Mex. (pĕ'tô)	120a	20.07N	88.49W
Petorca, Chile (pā-tōr'kȧ)	129b	32.14S	70.55W
Petoskey, Mi., U.S. (pē-tŏs-kĭ)	98	45.25N	84.55W
Petra, hist., Jord.	181a	30.21N	35.25E
Petra Velikogo, Zaliv, b., Russia	194	42.40N	131.50E
Petre, Point, c., Can.	91	43.50N	77.00W
Petrich, Bul. (pā'trĭch)	149	41.24N	23.13E
Petrified Forest National Park, rec., Az., U.S. (pĕt'rĭ-fīd fŏr'ĕst)	109	34.58N	109.35W
Petrikov, Bela. (pyĕ'trē-kô-v)	162	52.09N	28.30E
Petrinja, Cro. (pā'trĕn-yȧ)	160	45.25N	16.17E
Petrodvorets, Russia (pyĕ-trô-dvô-ryĕts')	172c	59.53N	29.55E
Petrokrepost', Russia (pyĕ'trô-krĕ-pôst)	166	59.56N	31.03E
Petrolia, Can. (pē-trō'lĭ-ȧ)	90	42.50N	82.10W
Petrolina, Braz. (pĕ-trō-lē'nȧ)	131	9.18S	40.28W
Petronell, Aus.	145e	48.07N	16.52E
Petropavl, Kaz.	169	54.44N	69.07E
Petropavlivka, Ukr.	163	48.24N	36.23E
Petropavlovka, Russia	172a	54.10N	59.50E
Petropavlovsk-Kamchatskiy, Russia (kăm-chăt'skĭ)	165	53.13N	158.56E
Petrópolis, Braz. (på-trō-pô-lēzh')	131	22.31S	43.10W
Petroşani, Rom.	161	45.24N	23.24E
Petrovsk, Russia (pyĕ-trôfsk')	167	52.20N	45.15E
Petrovskaya, Russia (pyĕ-trôf'ská-yȧ)	163	45.25N	37.50E
Petrovsko-Razumovskoje, neigh., Russia	239b	55.50N	37.34E
Petrovskoye, Russia	167	45.20N	43.00E
Petrovsk-Zabaykal'skiy, Russia (pyĕ-trôfskzä-bī-käl'skĭ)	165	51.13N	109.08E
Petrozavodsk, Russia (pyā'trô-zá-vôtsk')	164	61.46N	34.25E
Petrus Steyn, S. Afr.	218d	27.40S	28.09E
Petrykivka, Ukr.	163	48.43N	34.29E
Pewaukee, Wi., U.S. (pĭ-wô'kē)	101a	43.05N	88.15W
Pewaukee Lake, l., Wi., U.S.	101a	43.03N	88.18W
Pewee Valley, Ky., U.S. (pe wē)	101h	38.19N	85.29W
Peza, r., Russia (pyâ'zá)	166	65.35N	46.50E
Pézenas, Fr. (pā-zē-nä')	156	43.26N	3.24E
Pforzheim, Ger. (pfôrts'hīm)	147	48.52N	8.43E
Phalodi, India	186	27.13N	72.22E
Phan Thiet, Viet. (p'hän')	196	11.30N	108.43E
Phelps Corner, Md., U.S.	229d	38.48N	76.58W
Phelps Lake, l., N.C., U.S.	115	35.46N	76.27W
Phenix City, Al., U.S. (fē'nĭks)	114	32.29N	85.00W
Philadelphia, Ms., U.S. (fĭl-ȧ-dĕl'phĭ-ȧ)	114	32.45N	89.07W
Philadelphia, Pa., U.S.	97	40.00N	75.13W
Philip, S.D., U.S. (fĭl'ĭp)	102	44.03N	101.35W
Philippeville see Skikda, Alg.	210	36.58N	6.51E
Philippines, nation, Asia (fĭl'ĭ-pēnz)	197	14.25N	125.00E
Philippine Sea, sea (fĭl'ĭ-pēn)	225	16.00N	133.00E
Philippine Trench, deep	197	10.30N	127.15E
Philipsburg, Pa., U.S. (fĭl'lĭps-bĕrg)	99	40.55N	78.10W

PRONOUNCING INDEX Philipsburg–Playas Lake 333

PLACE (Pronunciation)	PAGE	Lat. °'	Long. °'
Philipsburg, Wy., U.S.	105	46.19N	113.19W
Phillip, i., Austl. (fĭl'ĭp)	204	38.32S	145.10E
Phillip Channel, strt., Indon.	181b	1.04N	103.40E
Phillipi, W.V., U.S. (fĭ-lĭp'ĭ)	98	39.10N	80.00W
Phillips, Wi., U.S. (fĭl'ĭps)	103	45.41N	90.24W
Phillipsburg, Ks., U.S. (fĭl'lĭps-bērg)	110	39.44N	99.19W
Phillipsburg, N.J., U.S.	99	40.45N	75.10W
Phinga, India	240a	22.41N	88.25E
Phitsanulok, Thai.	196	16.51N	100.15E
Phnom Penh see Phnum Pénh, Camb.	196	11.39N	104.53E
Phnum Pénh, Camb. (nŏm'pĕn')	196	11.39N	104.53E
Phoenix, Az., U.S. (fē'nĭks)	96	33.30N	112.00W
Phoenix, Md., U.S.	100e	39.31N	76.40W
Phoenix Islands, is., Kir.	2	4.00S	174.00W
Phoenixville, Pa., U.S. (fē'nĭks-vĭl)	100f	40.08N	75.31W
Phou Bia, mtn., Laos	196	19.36N	103.00E
Phra Nakhon Si Ayutthaya, Thai.	196	14.16N	100.37E
Phuket, Thai.	196	7.57N	98.19E
Phu Quoc, Dao, i., Viet.	196	10.13N	104.00E
Phu-tho-hoa, Viet.	241j	10.46N	106.39E
Pi, r., China (bē)	190	32.06N	116.31E
Piacenza, Italy (pyä-chĕnt'sä)	148	45.02N	9.42E
Pianosa, i., Italy (pyä-nō'sä)	160	42.13N	15.45E
Piave, r., Italy (pyä'vā)	160	45.45N	12.15E
Piazza Armerina, Italy (pyät'sä är-mä-rē'nä)	160	37.23N	14.26E
Pibor, r., Sudan (pē'bôr)	211	7.21N	32.54E
Pic, r., Can. (pēk)	90	48.48N	86.28W
Picara Point, c., V.I.U.S. (pē-kä'rä)	117c	18.23N	64.57W
Picayune, Ms., U.S. (pĭk'á yōōn)	114	30.32N	89.41W
Picher, Ok., U.S. (pĭch'ēr)	111	36.58N	94.49W
Pichilemu, Chile (pē-chē-lĕ'mōō)	129b	34.22S	72.01W
Pichucalco, Mex. (pē-chōō-käl'kō)	119	17.34N	93.06W
Pickerel, l., Can. (pĭk'ēr-ĕl)	90	48.35N	91.10W
Pickwick Lake, res., U.S. (pĭk'wĭck)	114	35.04N	88.05W
Pico, Ca., U.S. (pē'kō)	107a	34.01N	118.05W
Pico Island, i., Port. (pē'kō)	210a	38.16N	28.49W
Pico Rivera, Ca., U.S.	107a	34.01N	118.05W
Picos, Braz. (pē'kōzh)	131	7.13S	41.23W
Picton, Austl. (pĭk'tŭn)	201b	34.11S	150.37E
Picton, Can.	91	44.00N	77.15W
Pictou, Can. (pĭk-tōō')	93	45.41N	62.43W
Pidálion, Akrotírion, c., Cyp.	181a	34.50N	34.05E
Pidurutalagala, mtn., Sri L. (pē'dō-rō-tä'lá-gä'lá)	183	7.00N	80.46E
Pidvolochys'k, Ukr.	163	49.32N	26.16E
Pie, i., Can. (pī)	90	48.10N	89.07W
Piedade, Braz. (pyā-dä'dĕ)	129a	23.42S	47.25W
Piedade do Baruel, Braz.	234d	23.37S	46.18W
Piedmont, Al., U.S. (pēd'mŏnt)	114	33.54N	85.36W
Piedmont, Ca., U.S.	106b	37.50N	122.14W
Piedmont, Mo., U.S.	111	37.09N	90.42W
Piedmont, S.C., U.S.	115	34.40N	82.27W
Piedmont, W.V., U.S.	99	39.30N	79.05W
Piedrabuena, Spain (pyā-drä-bwā'nä)	158	39.01N	4.10W
Piedras, Punta, c., Arg. (pōō'n-tä-pyĕ'dräs)	129c	35.25S	57.10W
Piedras Negras, Mex. (pyā'dräs nā'gräs)	116	28.41N	100.33W
Pieksämäki, Fin. (pyĕk'sĕ-mĕ-kē)	153	62.18N	27.14E
Piemonte, hist. reg., Italy (pyĕ-mô'n-tĕ)	160	44.30N	7.42E
Pienaars, r., S. Afr.	218d	25.13S	28.05E
Pienaarsrivier, S. Afr.	218d	25.12S	28.18E
Pierce, Ne., U.S. (pērs)	102	42.11N	97.33W
Pierce, W.V., U.S.	99	39.15N	79.30W
Piermont, N.Y., U.S. (pēr'mŏnt)	100a	41.03N	73.55W
Pierre, S.D., U.S. (pēr)	96	44.22N	100.20W
Pierrefitte-sur-Seine, Fr.	237c	48.58N	2.22E
Pierrefonds, Can.	83a	45.29N	73.52W
Piešt'any, Slvk.	155	48.36N	17.48E
Pietermaritzburg, S. Afr. (pē-tēr-mä-rĭts-bûrg)	212	29.36S	30.23E
Pietersburg, S. Afr. (pē'tērz-bûrg)	212	23.56S	29.30E
Pietersfield, S. Afr.	244b	26.14S	28.26E
Piet Retief, S. Afr. (pēt rĕ-tēf')	212	27.00S	30.58E
Pietrosu, Vârful, mtn., Rom.	155	47.35N	24.49E
Pieve di Cadore, Italy (pyā'vā dē kä-dō'rā)	148	46.26N	12.22E
Pigeon, r., N.A. (pĭj'ŭn)	103	48.05N	90.13W
Pigeon Lake, Can.	83f	49.57N	97.36W
Pigeon Lake, l., Can.	87	53.00N	114.00W
Piggott, Ar., U.S. (pĭg-ŭt)	111	36.22N	90.10W
Pijijiapan, Mex. (pēĸē-kē-ä'pän)	119	15.40N	93.12W
Pijnacker, Neth.	145a	52.01N	4.25E
Pikes Peak, mtn., Co., U.S. (pīks)	96	38.49N	105.03W
Pikesville, Md., U.S.	229c	39.23N	76.44W
Pikeville, Ky., U.S. (pīk'vĭl)	98	37.28N	82.31W
Pikou, China (pē-kō)	192	39.25N	122.19E
Pikwitonei, Can. (pĭk'wĭ-tōn)	89	55.35N	97.09W
Piła, Pol. (pē'lá)	154	53.09N	16.44E
Pilansberg, mtn., S. Afr. (pē'ăns'bûrg)	218d	25.08S	26.55E
Pilar, Arg. (pē'lär)	129c	34.27S	58.55W
Pilar, Para.	132	27.00S	58.15W
Pilar de Goiás, Braz. (dĕ-gô'yá's)	131	14.47S	49.33W
Pilchuck, r., Wa., U.S.	106a	48.03N	121.58W
Pilchuck Creek, r., Wa., U.S. (pĭl'chŭck)	106a	48.19N	122.11W
Pilchuck Mountain, mtn., Wa., U.S.	106a	48.03N	121.48W
Pilcomayo, r., S.A. (pēl-cō-mī'ō)	132	24.45S	59.15W
Pilgrim Gardens, N.J., U.S.	229b	39.57N	75.19W
Pilgrims Hatch, Eng., U.K.	235	51.38N	0.17E
Pili, Phil. (pē'lē)	197a	13.34N	123.17E
Pilica, r., Pol. (pē-lēt'sä)	155	51.00N	19.48E
Pillar Point, c., Wa., U.S. (pĭl'ár)	106a	48.14N	124.06W
Pillar Rocks, Wa., U.S.	106c	46.16N	123.35W
Pilón, r., Mex. (pē-lōn')	118	24.13N	99.03W
Pilot Point, Tx., U.S. (pī'lŭt)	111	33.24N	97.00W
Pilsen see Plzeň, Czech Rep.	142	49.46N	13.25E
Piltene, Lat. (pĭl'tĕ-nĕ)	153	57.17N	21.40E
Pimal, Cerra, mtn., Mex. (sĕ'r-rä-pē-mäl')	118	22.58N	104.19W
Pimba, Austl. (pĭm'bá)	202	31.15S	137.50E
Pimville, neigh., S. Afr. (pĭm'vĭl)	213b	26.17S	27.54E
Pinacate, Cerro, mtn., Mex. (sĕ'r-rō-pē-nä-kä'tĕ)	116	31.45N	113.30W
Pinamalayan, Phil. (pē-nä-mä-lä'yän)	197a	13.04N	121.31E
Pinang see George Town, Malay.	196	5.21N	100.09E
Pinarbaşi, Tur. (pē'när-bä'shĭ)	149	38.50N	36.10E
Pinar del Río, Cuba (pē-när' dĕl rē'ō)	117	22.25N	83.35W
Pinar del Río, prov., Cuba	122	22.45N	83.25W
Pinatubo, mtn., Phil. (pē-nä-tōō'bō)	197a	15.09N	120.19E
Pincher Creek, Can. (pĭn'chēr krēk)	87	49.29N	113.57W
Pinckneyville, Il., U.S. (pĭnk'nĭ-vĭl)	111	38.06N	89.22W
Pińczów, Pol. (pēn''chōf)	155	50.32N	20.33E
Pindamonhangaba, Braz. (pē'n-dä-mōnyä'n-gä-bä)	129a	22.56S	45.26W
Pinder Point, c., Bah.	122	26.35N	78.35W
Píndhos Oros, mts., Grc.	142	39.48N	21.19E
Pindiga, Nig.	215	9.59N	10.54E
Pine, r., Can. (pīn)	87	55.30N	122.20W
Pine, r., Wi., U.S.	103	45.50N	88.37W
Pine Bluff, Ar., U.S. (pīn blŭf)	97	34.13N	92.01W
Pine Brook, N.J., U.S.	228	40.52N	74.20W
Pine City, Mn., U.S. (pīn)	103	45.50N	93.01W
Pine Creek, Austl.	202	13.45S	132.00E
Pine Creek, r., Nv., U.S.	108	40.15N	116.17W
Pinecrest, Va., U.S.	229d	38.50N	77.09W
Pine Falls, Can.	89	50.35N	96.15W
Pine Flat Lake, res., Ca., U.S.	108	36.52N	119.18W
Pine Forest Range, mts., Nv., U.S.	104	41.35N	118.45W
Pinega, Russia (pē-nyĕ'gá)	164	64.40N	43.30E
Pinega, r., Russia	166	64.10N	42.30E
Pine Grove, Can.	227c	43.48N	79.35W
Pine Hill, N.J., U.S. (pīn hĭl)	100f	39.47N	74.59W
Pinehurst, Ma., U.S.	227a	42.32N	71.14W
Pine Island Sound, strt., Fl., U.S.	115a	26.32N	82.30W
Pine Lake Estates, Ga., U.S. (lāk ĕs-tāts')	100c	33.47N	84.13W
Pinelands, S. Afr. (pīn'lănds)	212a	33.57S	18.30E
Pine Lawn, Mo., U.S. (lôn)	107e	38.42N	90.17W
Pine Pass, p., Can.	87	55.22N	122.40W
Pine Ridge, Va., U.S.	229d	38.52N	77.14W
Pinerolo, Italy (pē-nâ-rô'lō)	160	44.47N	7.18E
Pines, Lake o' the, Tx., U.S.	113	32.50N	94.40W
Pinetown, S. Afr. (pīn'toun)	213c	29.47S	30.52E
Pine View Reservoir, res., Ut., U.S. (vū)	107b	41.17N	111.54W
Pineville, Ky., U.S. (pīn'vĭl)	114	36.48N	83.43W
Pineville, La., U.S.	113	31.20N	92.25W
Ping, r., Thai.	196	17.54N	98.29E
Pingding, China (pĭŋ-dĭŋ)	192	37.50N	113.30E
Pingdu, China (pĭŋ-dōō)	192	36.46N	119.57E
Pingfang, China	240b	39.56N	116.33E
Pinggir, Indon.	181b	1.05N	101.12E
Pinghe, China (pĭŋ-hŭ)	193	24.30N	117.02E
Pingle, China (pĭŋ-lŭ)	193	24.30N	110.22E
Pingliang, China (pĭng'lyäng')	188	35.12N	106.50E
Pingquan, China (pĭŋ-chyüän)	192	40.58N	118.40E
Pingtan, China (pĭŋ-tän)	193	25.30N	119.45E
Pingtan Dao, i., China (pĭŋ-tän dou)	193	25.40N	119.45E
P'ingtung, Tai.	193	22.40N	120.35E
Pingwu, China (pĭŋ-wōō)	192	32.20N	104.40E
Pingxiang, China (pĭŋ-shyäŋ)	193	27.40N	113.50E
Pingyi, China (pĭŋ-yē)	190	35.30N	117.38E
Pingyuan, China (pĭŋ-yüän)	190	37.11N	116.26E
Pingzhou, China (pĭŋ-jō)	191a	23.01N	113.11E
Pinhal, Braz. (pē-nyá'l)	129a	22.11S	46.43W
Pinhal Novo, Port. (nō vō)	159b	38.38N	8.54W
Pinheiros, r., Braz.	234d	23.38S	46.43W
Pinhel, Port.	158	40.46N	7.04W
Pinhel, Port. (pēn-yĕl')	158	40.45N	7.03W
Pini, Pulau, i., Indon.	196	0.07S	98.38E
Piniós, r., Grc.	161	39.30N	21.40E
Pinnacles National Monument, rec., Ca., U.S. (pĭn'á-k'lz)	108	36.30N	121.00W
Pinneberg, Ger. (pĭn'ĕ-bĕrg)	145c	53.40N	9.48E
Pinner, neigh., Eng., U.K.	235	51.36N	0.23W
Pinole, Ca., U.S. (pĭ-nō'lē)	106b	38.01N	122.17W
Pinos-Puente, Spain (pwān'tá)	158	37.15N	3.43W
Pinotepa Nacional, Mex. (pē-nō-tä'pä nä-syō-näl')	118	16.21N	98.04W
Pins, Île des, i., N. Cal.	203	22.44S	167.44E
Pinsk, Bela. (pēn'sk)	164	52.07N	26.05E
Pinta, i., Ec.	130	0.41N	90.47W
Pintendre, Can. (pĕɴ-tăɴdr')	83b	46.45N	71.07W
Pinto, Spain (pēn'tō)	159a	40.14N	3.42W
Pinto Butte, Can. (pĭn'tō)	88	49.22N	107.25W
Pioche, Nv., U.S. (pī-ō'chē)	109	37.56N	114.28W
Piombino, Italy (pyôm-bē'nō)	148	42.56N	10.33E
Pioneer Mountains, mts., Mt., U.S. (pī'ō-nēr')	105	45.23N	112.51W
Piotrków Trybunalski, Pol. (pyōtr'kōōv trĭ-bōō-nal'skē)	147	51.23N	19.44E
Piper, Al., U.S. (pī'pēr)	114	33.04N	87.00W
Piper, Ks., U.S.	107f	39.09N	94.51W
Pipéri, i., Grc. (pē'per-ē)	161	39.19N	24.20E
Pipe Spring National Monument, rec., Az., U.S. (pīp sprĭng)	109	36.50N	112.45W
Pipestone, Mn., U.S. (pīp'stōn)	102	44.00N	96.19W
Pipestone National Monument, rec., Mn., U.S.	102	44.03N	96.24W
Pipmuacan, Réservoir, res., Can. (pĭp-mä-kän')	91	49.45N	70.00W
Piqua, Oh., U.S. (pĭk'wá)	98	40.10N	84.15W
Piracaia, Braz. (pē-rä-ká'yä)	129a	23.04S	46.20W
Piracicaba, Braz. (pē-rä-sē-kä'bä)	131	22.43S	47.39W
Piraíba, r., Braz. (pä-rä-ē'bá)	129a	21.38S	41.29W
Piraiévs, Grc.	149	37.57N	23.38E
Piramida, mtn., Russia	165	54.00N	96.00E
Pirámide de Cuicuilco, hist., Mex.	233a	19.18N	99.11W
Piran, Slvn. (pē-rá'n)	160	45.31N	13.34E
Piranga, Braz. (pē-rä'n-gä)	129a	20.41S	43.17W
Pirapetinga, Braz. (pē-rä-pē-tē'n-gä)	129a	21.40S	42.20W
Pirapora, Braz. (pē-rá-pō'rá)	131	17.39S	44.54W
Pirassununga, Braz. (pē-rä-sōō-nōō'n-gä)	129a	22.00S	47.24W
Pirenópolis, Braz. (pē-rē-nō'pō-lēs)	131	15.56S	48.49W
Pírgos, Grc.	149	37.51N	21.28E
Piritu, Laguna de, l., Ven. (lä-gō'nä-dĕ-pē-rē'tōō)	131b	10.00N	64.57W
Pirmasens, Ger. (pĭr-mä-zĕns')	154	49.12N	7.34E
Pirna, Ger. (pĭr'nä)	154	50.57N	13.56E
Pirot, Yugo. (pē'rōt)	149	43.09N	22.35E
Pirtleville, Az., U.S. (pûr't'l-vĭl)	109	31.25N	109.35W
Piru, Indon. (pē-rōō')	197	3.15S	128.25E
Pisa, Italy (pē'sä)	148	43.52N	10.24E
Pisagua, Chile (pē-sä'gwä)	130	19.43S	70.12W
Piscataway, Md., U.S. (pĭs-kă-tă-wā)	100e	38.42N	76.59W
Piscataway, N.J., U.S.	100a	40.35N	74.27W
Pisco, Peru (pēs'kō)	130	13.43S	76.07W
Pisco, Bahía de, b., Peru	130	13.43S	77.48W
Piseco, l., N.Y., U.S. (pĭ-sā'kō)	99	43.25N	74.35W
Pisek, Czech Rep. (pē'sĕk)	147	49.18N	14.08E
Pisticci, Italy (pēs-tē'chē)	160	40.24N	16.34E
Pistoia, Italy (pēs-tô'yä)	148	43.57N	11.54E
Pisuerga, r., Spain (pē-swĕr'gä)	158	41.48N	4.28W
Pit, r., Ca., U.S. (pĭt)	104	40.58N	121.42W
Pitalito, Col. (pē-tä-lē'tō)	130	1.45N	75.09W
Pitampura Kālan, neigh., India	240d	28.42N	77.08E
Pitcairn, Pa., U.S. (pĭt'kârn)	101e	40.29N	79.47W
Pitcairn, dep., Oc.	2	25.04S	130.05W
Piteälven, r., Swe.	146	66.08N	18.51E
Piteşti, Rom. (pē-tĕsht'')	161	44.51N	24.51E
Pithara, Austl. (pĭt'ără)	202	30.27S	116.45E
Pithiviers, Fr. (pē-tē-vyā')	156	48.12N	2.14E
Pitman, N.J., U.S. (pĭt'mán)	100f	39.44N	75.08W
Pitseng, Leso.	213c	29.03S	28.13E
Pitt, r., Can.	106d	49.19N	122.39W
Pitt Island, i., Can.	86	53.35N	129.45W
Pittsburg, Ca., U.S. (pĭts'bûrg)	106b	38.01N	121.52W
Pittsburg, Ks., U.S.	97	37.25N	94.43W
Pittsburg, Tx., U.S.	111	32.00N	94.57W
Pittsburgh, Pa., U.S.	97	40.26N	80.01W
Pittsfield, Il., U.S. (pĭts'fēld)	111	39.37N	90.47W
Pittsfield, Me., U.S.	92	44.45N	69.44W
Pittsfield, Ma., U.S.	99	42.25N	73.15W
Pittston, Pa., U.S. (pĭts'tŭn)	99	41.20N	75.50W
Piũi, Braz. (pē-ōō'ē)	129a	20.27S	45.57W
Piura, Peru (pē-ōō'rä)	130	5.13S	80.46W
Pivdennyy Buh, r., Ukr.	167	48.12N	30.13E
Piya, Russia (pē'yá)	172a	58.34N	61.12E
Placentia, Can.	93	47.15N	53.58W
Placentia, Ca., U.S. (plă-sĕn'shĭ-á)	107a	33.52N	117.50W
Placentia Bay, b., Can.	85a	47.14N	54.30W
Placerville, Ca., U.S. (plăs'ēr-vĭl)	108	38.43N	120.47W
Placetas, Cuba (plä-thā'täs)	122	22.10N	79.40W
Placid, l., N.Y., U.S. (plăs'ĭd)	99	44.20N	74.00W
Plain City, Ut., U.S. (plān)	107b	41.18N	112.06W
Plainfield, Il., U.S. (plān'fēld)	101a	41.37N	88.12W
Plainfield, In., U.S.	101g	39.42N	86.23W
Plainfield, N.J., U.S.	100a	40.38N	74.25W
Plainview, Ar., U.S. (plān'vū)	111	34.59N	93.15W
Plainview, Mn., U.S.	103	44.09N	93.12W
Plainview, Ne., U.S.	102	42.20N	97.47W
Plainview, Tx., U.S.	110	34.11N	101.42W
Plainwell, Mi., U.S. (plān'wĕl)	98	42.25N	85.40W
Plaisance, Can. (plĕ-zäɴs')	83c	45.37N	75.07W
Plana or Flat Cays, is., Bah. (plä'nä)	123	22.35N	73.35W
Plandome Manor, N.Y., U.S.	228	40.49N	73.42W
Planegg, Ger. (plä'nĕg)	145d	48.06N	11.27E
Plano, Tx., U.S. (plā'nō)	111	33.01N	96.42W
Plantagenet, Can. (plăɴ-tàzh-nĕ')	83c	45.33N	75.00W
Plant City, Fl., U.S. (plănt sĭ'tĭ)	115a	28.00N	82.07W
Plaquemine, La., U.S. (plăk'mēn')	113	30.17N	91.14W
Plasencia, Spain (plä-sĕn'thē-ä)	158	40.02N	6.07W
Plast, Russia (plást)	166	54.22N	60.48E
Plaster Rock, Can. (plás'tēr rŏk)	92	46.54N	67.24W
Plastun, Russia (plás-tōōn')	194	44.41N	136.08E
Plata, Río de la, est., S.A. (dālä plä'tä)	132	34.35S	58.15W
Platani, r., Italy (plä-tä'nē)	160	37.26N	13.28E
Plateforme, Pointe, c., Haiti	123	19.35N	73.50W
Platinum, Ak., U.S. (plăt'ĭ-nŭm)	95	59.00N	161.27W
Plato, Col. (plä'tō)	130	9.49N	74.48W
Platón Sánchez, Mex. (plä-tōn' sän'chĕz)	118	21.14N	98.20W
Platt, Eng., U.K.	235	51.17N	0.20E
Platte, S.D., U.S. (plăt)	102	43.22N	98.51W
Platte, r., Mo., U.S.	111	40.09N	94.40W
Platte, r., Ne., U.S.	96	40.50N	100.40W
Platteville, Wi., U.S. (plăt'vĭl)	103	42.44N	90.31W
Plattsburg, Mo., U.S. (plăts'bûrg)	111	39.33N	94.26W
Plattsburg, N.Y., U.S.	99	44.40N	73.30W
Plattsmouth, Ne., U.S. (plăts'mŭth)	102	41.00N	95.53W
Plauen, Ger. (plou'ĕn)	147	50.30N	12.08E
Playa de Guanabo, Cuba (plä-yä-dĕ-gwä-nä'bō)	123a	23.10N	82.07W
Playa del Rey, neigh., Ca., U.S.	232	33.58N	118.26W
Playa de Santa Fé, Cuba	123a	23.05N	82.31W
Playas Lake, l., N.M., U.S. (plä'yás)	109	31.50N	108.30W

ŋ-sing; ŋ-baŋk; ɴ-nasalized n; nŏd; cŏmmit; ōld; ōbey; ôrder; oi-boil; fōōd; ō-as oo in foot; ou-out; s-soft; sh-dish; th-thin; pūre; ûnite; ûrn; stŭd; circŭs; ü-as in French tu; '-indeterminate vowel.

334 Playa Vicente-Porto Mendes

PLACE (Pronunciation)	PAGE	Lat. °′	Long. °′
Playa Vicente, Mex. (vē-sĕn′tá)	119	17.49N	95.49W
Playa Vicente, r., Mex.	119	17.36N	96.13W
Playgreen Lake, l., Can. (plā′grēn)	89	54.00N	98.10W
Plaza de Toros Monumental, rec., Spain	238e	41.24N	2.11E
Pleasant, l., N.Y., U.S. (plĕz′ănt)	99	43.25N	74.25W
Pleasant Grove, Al., U.S.	100h	33.29N	86.57W
Pleasant Hill, Ca., U.S.	106b	37.57N	122.04W
Pleasant Hill, Mo., U.S.	111	38.46N	94.18W
Pleasant Hills, Pa., U.S.	230b	40.20N	79.58W
Pleasanton, Ca., U.S. (plĕz′ăn-tŭn)	106b	37.40N	121.53W
Pleasanton, Ks., U.S.	111	38.10N	94.41W
Pleasanton, Tx., U.S.	112	28.58N	98.30W
Pleasant Plain, Oh., U.S. (plĕz′ănt)	101f	39.17N	84.06W
Pleasant Ridge, Mi., U.S.	101b	42.28N	83.09W
Pleasant View, Ut., U.S. (plĕz′ănt vū)	107b	41.20N	112.02W
Pleasantville, Md., U.S.	229c	39.11N	76.38W
Pleasantville, N.Y., U.S. (plĕz′ănt-vĭl)	100a	41.08N	73.47W
Pleasure Ridge Park, Ky., U.S. (plĕzh′ẽr rĭj)	101h	38.09N	85.49W
Plenty, Bay of, b., N.Z. (plĕn′tė)	203a	37.30S	177.10E
Plentywood, Mt., U.S. (plĕn′tė-wo͝od)	105	48.47N	104.38W
Ples, Russia (plyĕs)	162	57.26N	41.29E
Pleshcheyevo, l., Russia (plĕsh-chā′yĕ-vô)	162	56.50N	38.22E
Plessisville, Can. (plĕ-sē′vēl′)	91	46.12N	71.47W
Pleszew, Pol. (plĕ′zhĕf)	155	51.54N	17.48E
Plettenberg, Ger. (plĕ′tĕn-bĕrgh)	157c	51.13N	7.53E
Pleven, Bul. (plĕ′vĕn)	149	43.24N	24.26E
Pljevlja, Yugo. (plĕv′lyä)	149	43.20N	19.21E
Płock, Pol. (pwôtsk)	147	52.32N	19.44E
Ploërmel, Fr. (plô-ĕr-mĕl′)	156	47.56N	2.25W
Ploieşti, Rom. (plô-yĕsht′′)	142	44.56N	26.01E
Plomárion, Grc. (plô-mä′rĭ-ŏn)	161	38.51N	26.24E
Plomb du Cantal, mtn., Fr. (plôɴ′dükäɴ-tál′)	147	45.30N	2.49E
Plonge, Lac la, l., Can. (plōɴzh)	88	55.08N	107.25W
Plovdiv, Bul. (plôv′dĭf) (fĭl-ĭp-ŏp′ô-lĭs)	142	42.09N	24.43E
Pluma Hidalgo, Mex. (plo͞o′mä ē-däl′gō)	119	15.54N	96.23W
Plumpton, Austl.	243a	33.45S	150.50E
Plunge, Lith. (plŏn′gä)	153	55.56N	21.45E
Plymouth, Monts.	121b	16.43N	62.12W
Plymouth, Eng., U.K. (plĭm′ŭth)	147	50.25N	4.14W
Plymouth, In., U.S.	98	41.20N	86.20W
Plymouth, Ma., U.S.	99	42.00N	70.45W
Plymouth, Mi., U.S.	101b	42.23N	83.27W
Plymouth, N.H., U.S.	99	43.50N	71.40W
Plymouth, N.C., U.S.	115	35.50N	76.44W
Plymouth, Pa., U.S.	99	41.15N	75.55W
Plymouth, Wi., U.S.	103	43.45N	87.59W
Plyussa, r., Russia (plyo͞o′sȧ)	162	58.33N	28.30E
Plzeň, Czech Rep.	142	49.45N	13.23E
Po, r., Italy	142	45.10N	11.00E
Pocahontas, Ar., U.S. (pō-kȧ-hŏn′tȧs)	111	36.15N	91.01W
Pocahontas, Ia., U.S.	103	42.43N	94.41W
Pocatello, Id., U.S. (pō-kȧ-tĕl′ō)	96	42.54N	112.30W
Pochëp, Russia (pô-chĕp′)	167	52.56N	33.27E
Pochinok, Russia (pô-chē′nôk)	162	54.14N	32.27E
Pochinski, Russia	166	54.40N	44.50E
Pochotitán, Mex. (pô-chô-tē-tá′n)	118	21.37N	104.33W
Pochutla, Mex.	119	15.46N	96.28W
Pocomoke City, Md., U.S. (pō-kō-mōk′)	99	38.05N	75.35W
Pocono Mountains, mts., Pa., U.S. (pō-cō′nō)	99	41.10N	75.30W
Poços de Caldas, Braz. (pō-sôs-dĕ-käl′dás)	131	21.48S	46.34W
Poder, Sen. (pô-dôr′)	210	16.35N	15.04W
Podgorica, Yugo.	161	42.25N	19.15E
Podkamennaya Tunguska, r., Russia	165	61.43N	93.45E
Podol′sk, Russia (pô-dôl′sk)	166	55.26N	37.33E
Poggibonsi, Italy (pôd-jē-bôn′sē)	160	43.27N	11.12E
Pogodino, Bela. (pô-gô′dē-nô)	166	54.17N	31.00E
P′ohangdong, S. Kor.	194	35.57N	129.23E
Point Cook, Austl.	243b	37.56S	144.45E
Pointe-à-Pitre, Guad. (pwăɴt′ á pē-tr′)	117	16.15N	61.32W
Pointe-aux-Trembles, Can. (po͞o-äɴt′ ō-trāɴbl)	83a	45.39N	73.30W
Pointe Claire, Can. (po͞o-äɴt′ klĕr)	83a	45.27N	73.48W
Pointe-des-Cascades, Can. (käs-kädz′)	83a	45.19N	73.58W
Pointe Fortune, Can. (fôr′tūn)	83a	45.34N	74.23W
Pointe-Gatineau, Can. (po͞o-äɴt′gä-tē-nō′)	83c	45.28N	75.42W
Pointe Noire, Congo	212	4.48S	11.51E
Point Hope, Ak., U.S. (hōp)	95	68.18N	166.38W
Point Pleasant, Md., U.S.	229c	39.11N	76.35W
Point Pleasant, W.V., U.S. (plĕz′ănt)	98	38.50N	82.10W
Point Roberts, Wa., U.S. (rŏb′ẽrts)	106d	48.59N	123.04W
Poissy, Fr. (pwá-sē′)	157b	48.55N	2.02E
Poitiers, Fr. (pwá-tyā′)	147	46.35N	0.18E
Pokaran, India (pō′kŭr-ŭn)	186	27.00N	72.05E
Pokrov, Russia (pô-krôf)	162	55.56N	39.09E
Pokrovsko-Strešnevo, neigh., Russia	239b	55.49N	37.29E
Pokrovskoye, Russia (pô-krôf′skô-yĕ)	163	47.27N	38.54E
Pola, r., Russia (pō′lä)	162	57.44N	31.53E
Pola de Laviana, Spain (dĕ-lä-vyä′nä)	158	43.15N	5.29W
Pola de Siero, Spain	158	43.24N	5.39W
Poland, nation, Eur. (pō′lănd)	142	52.37N	17.01E
Polangui, Phil. (pô-läŋ′gē)	197a	13.18N	123.29E
Polazna, Russia (pô′láz-ná)	172a	58.18N	56.25E
Polessk, Russia (pô′lĕsk)	153	54.50N	21.14E
Poles′ye (Pripyat Marshes), sw., Eur.	167	52.10N	27.30E
Polevskoy, Russia (pô-lĕ′vs-kô′ĕ)	172a	56.28N	60.14E
Polgár, Hung. (pôl′gär)	155	47.54N	21.10E
Policastro, Golfo di, b., Italy	160	40.00N	13.23E
Poligny, Fr. (pō-lē-nyē′)	157	46.48N	5.42E
Polikhnitos, Grc.	161	39.05N	26.11E
Polillo, Phil. (pô-lēl′yō)	197a	14.42N	121.56W
Polillo Islands, is., Phil.	183	15.05N	122.15E
Polillo Strait, strt., Phil.	197a	15.02N	121.40E
Polist′, r., Russia (pô′lĭst)	162	57.42N	31.02E
Polistena, Italy (pō-lēs-tā′nä)	160	38.25N	16.05E
Políyiros, Grc.	161	40.23N	23.27E
Polkan, Gora, mtn., Russia	165	60.18N	92.08E
Pollensa, Spain (pōl-yĕn′sä)	159	39.50N	3.00E
Polochic, r., Guat. (pō-lō-chēk′)	120	15.19N	89.45W
Polonne, Ukr.	163	50.07N	27.31E
Polotsk, Bela. (pô′lôtsk)	166	55.30N	28.48E
Polpaico, Chile (pôl-pá′y-kô)	129b	33.10S	70.53W
Polson, Mt., U.S. (pōl′sŭn)	105	47.40N	114.10W
Polsum, Ger.	236	51.37N	7.03E
Poltava, Ukr. (pôl-tä′vä)	164	49.35N	34.33E
Poltava, prov., Ukr.	163	49.53N	32.58E
Põltsamaa, Est. (pölt′sá-mä)	153	58.39N	26.00E
Polunochnoye, Russia (pô-lo͞o-nô′ch-nô′yĕ)	172a	60.52N	60.27E
Poluy, r., Russia (pôl′wē)	170	65.45N	68.15E
Polyakovka, Russia (pŭl-yä′kôv-kȧ)	172a	54.38N	59.42E
Polyarnyy, Russia (pŭl-yär′nē)	164	69.10N	33.30E
Polynesia, is., Oc.	224	4.00S	156.00W
Pomba, r., Braz. (pô′m-bȧ)	129a	21.28S	42.28W
Pomerania, hist. reg., Pol. (pŏm-ē-rā′nĭ-ȧ)	154	53.50N	15.20E
Pomeroy, S. Afr. (pŏm′ẽr-roi)	213c	28.36S	30.26E
Pomeroy, Wa., U.S. (pŏm′ẽr-oi)	104	46.28N	117.35W
Pomezia, Italy (pô-mĕ′t-zyä)	159d	41.41N	12.31E
Pomigliano d′Arco, Italy (pô-mē-lyä′nô-d-ä′r-kô)	159c	40.39N	14.23E
Pomme de Terre, Mn., U.S. (pŏm dē tĕr′)	102	45.22N	95.52W
Pomona, Ca., U.S. (pō-mō′nȧ)	96	34.04N	117.45W
Pomona Estates, S. Afr.	244b	26.06S	28.15E
Pomorie, Bul.	149	42.24N	27.41E
Pompano Beach, Fl., U.S. (pŏm′pȧ-nô)	115a	26.12N	80.07W
Pompeii Ruins, hist., Italy	159c	40.31N	14.29E
Pomponne, Fr.	237c	48.53N	2.41E
Pompton Lakes, N.J., U.S. (pŏmp′tŏn)	100a	41.01N	74.16W
Pompton Plains, N.J., U.S.	228	40.58N	74.18W
Pomuch, Mex. (pô-mo͞o′ch)	120a	20.12N	90.10W
Ponca, Ne., U.S. (pŏn′kȧ)	102	42.34N	96.43W
Ponca City, Ok., U.S.	111	36.42N	97.07W
Ponce, P.R. (pōn′sā)	117	18.01N	66.43W
Ponders End, neigh., Eng., U.K.	235	51.39N	0.03W
Pondicherry, India	183	11.58N	79.48E
Pondicherry, state, India	183	11.50N	74.50E
Ponferrada, Spain (pôn-fĕr-rä′dhä)	148	42.33N	6.38W
Ponoka, Can. (pŏ-nō′kȧ)	84	52.42N	113.35W
Ponoy, Russia	166	66.58N	41.00E
Ponoy, r., Russia	166	67.00N	39.00E
Ponta Delgada, Port. (pôn′tȧ dĕl-gä′dȧ)	210a	37.40N	25.45W
Ponta Grossa, Braz. (grō′sȧ)	131	25.09S	50.05W
Pont-à-Mousson, Fr. (pôɴ′tȧ-mo͞osôɴ′)	157	48.55N	6.02E
Pontarlier, Fr. (pôɴ′tȧr-lyā′)	157	46.53N	6.22E
Pont-Audemer, Fr. (pôɴ′tōd′mâr′)	156	49.23N	0.28E
Pontault-Combault, Fr.	237c	48.47N	2.36E
Pontchartrain Lake, l., La., U.S. (pôɴ-shȧr-trăn′)	113	30.10N	90.10W
Pontedera, Italy (pōn-tȧ-dā′rä)	160	43.37N	10.37E
Ponte de Sor, Port.	158	39.14N	8.03W
Pontefract, Eng., U.K. (pŏn′tē-frăkt)	144a	53.41N	1.18W
Ponte Nova, Braz. (pô′n-tē-nô′vȧ)	131	20.26S	42.52W
Pontevedra, Arg.	233d	34.46S	58.43W
Pontevedra, Spain (pôn-tĕ-vĕ-drä)	148	42.28N	8.38W
Ponthierville *see* Ubundi, Zaire	212	0.21S	25.29E
Pontiac, Il., U.S. (pŏn′tĭ-ăk)	98	40.55N	88.35W
Pontiac, Mi., U.S.	97	42.37N	83.17W
Pontianak, Indon. (pôn-tē-ä′nák)	196	0.04S	109.20E
Pontian Kechil, Malay.	181b	1.29N	103.24E
Pontic Mountains, mts., Tur.	167	41.20N	34.30E
Pontinha, neigh., Port.	238d	38.46N	9.11W
Pontivy, Fr. (pôɴ-tē-vē′)	156	48.05N	2.57W
Pontoise, Fr. (pôɴ-twȧz′)	156	49.03N	2.05E
Pontonnyy, Russia (pôn′tôn-nyĭ)	172c	59.47N	30.39E
Pontotoc, Ms., U.S. (pŏn-tô-tŏk′)	114	34.11N	88.59W
Pontremoli, Italy (pôn-trĕm′ô-lē)	160	44.21N	9.50E
Ponziane, Isole, i., Italy (ē′sō-lĕ)	148	40.55N	12.58E
Poole, Eng., U.K. (po͞ol)	150	50.43N	2.00W
Poolesville, Md., U.S. (poolēs-vĭl)	100e	39.08N	77.26W
Pooley Island, i., Can. (po͞o′lē)	86	52.44N	128.16W
Poopó, Lago de, l., Bol.	130	18.45S	67.07W
Popayán, Col. (pō-pä-yän′)	130	2.21N	76.43W
Popivka, Ukr.	163	50.03N	33.41E
Popivka, Ukr.	163	51.13N	33.08E
Poplar, Mt., U.S. (pŏp′lẽr)	105	48.08N	105.10W
Poplar, neigh., Eng., U.K.	235	51.31N	0.01W
Poplar, r., Mt., U.S.	105	48.34N	105.20W
Poplar, West Fork, r., Mt., U.S.	105	48.59N	106.06W
Poplar Bluff, Mo., U.S. (blŭf)	111	36.43N	90.22W
Poplar Heights, Va., U.S.	229d	38.53N	77.12W
Poplar Plains, Ky., U.S. (plāns)	98	38.20N	83.40W
Poplar Point, Can.	83f	50.04N	97.57W
Poplarville, Ms., U.S. (pŏp′lẽr-vĭl)	114	30.50N	89.33W
Popocatépetl Volcán, Mex. (pô-pô-kä-tā′pĕ′t′l)	116	19.01N	98.38W
Popokabaka, Zaire (pō′pō-kȧ-bä′kȧ)	212	5.42S	16.35E
Popovo, Bul. (pô′pô-vō)	161	43.23N	26.17E
Porbandar, India (pōr-bŭn′dŭr)	183	21.44N	69.40E
Porce, r., Col. (pôr-sē)	130a	7.11N	74.55W
Porcher Island, i., Can. (pôr′kẽr)	86	53.57N	130.30W
Porcuna, Spain (pôr-ko͞o′nä)	158	37.54N	4.10W
Porcupine, r., N.A.	95	67.38N	140.07W
Porcupine Creek, r., Mt., U.S.	105	48.27N	106.24W
Porcupine Hills, hills, Can.	89	52.30N	101.45W
Pordenone, Italy (pōr-dā-nō′nā)	160	45.58N	12.38E
Pori, Fin. (pô′rē)	146	61.29N	21.45E
Poriúncula, Braz.	129a	20.58S	42.02W
Porkhov, Russia (pôr′kôf)	166	57.46N	29.33E
Porlamar, Ven. (pôr-lä-mär′)	130	11.00N	63.55W
Pornic, Fr. (pōr-nēk′)	156	47.08N	2.07W
Poronaysk, Russia (pô′rô-nīsk)	165	49.21N	143.23E
Porrentruy, Switz. (pô-räɴ-trüē′)	154	47.25N	7.02E
Porsgrunn, Nor. (pôrs′grôn′)	152	59.09N	9.36E
Portachuelo, Bol. (pôrt-ä-chwā′lō)	130	17.20S	63.12W
Portage, Pa., U.S. (pôr′tāj)	99	40.25N	78.35W
Portage, Wi., U.S.	103	43.33N	89.29W
Portage Des Sioux, Mo., U.S. (dē so͞o)	107e	38.56N	90.21W
Portage la Prairie, Can. (lä-prā′rĭ)	84	49.57N	98.25W
Port Alberni, Can. (pōr äl-bĕr-nē′)	84	49.14N	124.48W
Portalegre, Port. (pôr-tä-lā′grĕ)	148	39.18N	7.26W
Portales, N.M., U.S. (pôr-tä′lĕs)	110	34.10N	103.11W
Port Alfred, S. Afr.	212	33.36S	26.55E
Port Alice, Can. (ăl′ĭs)	84	50.23N	127.27W
Port Allegany, Pa., U.S. (ăl-ē-gā′nĭ)	99	41.50N	78.10W
Port Angeles, Wa., U.S. (ăn′jē-lĕs)	96	48.07N	123.26W
Port Antonio, Jam.	117	18.10N	76.25W
Portarlington, Austl.	201a	38.07S	144.39E
Port Arthur, Tx., U.S.	97	29.52N	93.59W
Port Augusta, Austl. (ô-gŭs′tȧ)	204	32.28S	137.50E
Port au Port Bay, b., Can. (pôr′tō pōr′)	93	48.41N	58.45W
Port-au-Prince, Haiti (prăɴs′)	117	18.35N	72.20W
Port Austin, Mi., U.S. (ôs′tĭn)	98	44.00N	83.00W
Port Blair, India (blâr)	196	12.07N	92.45E
Port Bolivar, Tx., U.S. (bŏl′ĭ-vȧr)	113a	29.22N	94.46W
Port Borden, Can. (bôr′dĕn)	92	46.15N	63.42W
Port-Bouët, C. Iv.	210	5.24N	3.56W
Port-Cartier, Can.	92	50.01N	66.53W
Port Chester, N.Y., U.S. (chĕs′tẽr)	100a	40.59N	73.40W
Port Chicago, Ca., U.S. (shĭ-kô′gō)	106b	38.03N	122.01W
Port Clinton, Oh., U.S. (klĭn′tŭn)	98	41.30N	83.00W
Port Colborne, Can.	91	42.53N	79.13W
Port Coquitlam, Can. (kô-kwĭt′lȧm)	87	49.16N	122.46W
Port Credit, Can. (krĕd′ĭt)	83d	43.33N	79.35W
Port-de-Bouc, Fr. (pôr-dē-bo͞ok′)	156a	43.24N	5.00E
Port de Paix, Haiti (pē)	123	19.55N	72.50W
Port Dickson, Malay. (dĭk′sŭn)	181b	2.33N	101.49E
Port Discovery, b., Wa., U.S. (dĭs-kŭv′ẽr-ĭ)	106a	48.05N	122.55W
Port Edward, S. Afr. (ĕd′wẽrd)	213c	31.04S	30.14E
Port Elgin, Can. (ĕl′jĭn)	92	46.03N	64.05W
Port Elizabeth, S. Afr. (ē-lĭz′ȧ-bĕth)	212	33.57S	25.37E
Porterdale, Ga., U.S. (pōr′tẽr-dāl)	114	33.34N	83.53W
Porterville, Ca., U.S. (pōr′tẽr-vĭl)	108	36.03N	119.05W
Port Francqui *see* Ilebo, Zaire	212	4.19S	20.35E
Port Gamble, Wa., U.S. (găm′bŭl)	106a	47.52N	122.36W
Port Gamble Indian Reservation, I.R., Wa., U.S.	106a	47.54N	122.33W
Port-Gentil, Gabon (zhäɴ-tē′)	212	0.43S	8.47E
Port Gibson, Ms., U.S.	114	31.56N	90.57W
Port Harcourt, Nig. (här′kŭrt)	210	4.43N	7.05E
Port Hardy, Can. (här′dĭ)	86	50.43N	127.29W
Port Hawkesbury, Can.	93	45.37N	61.21W
Port Hedland, Austl. (hĕd′lănd)	202	20.30S	118.30E
Porthill, Id., U.S.	104	49.00N	116.30W
Port Hood, Can. (ho͝od)	93	46.01N	61.32W
Port Hope, Can. (hōp)	91	43.55N	78.10W
Port Huron, Mi., U.S. (hū′rŏn)	97	43.00N	82.30W
Portici, Italy (pôr′tē-chē)	159c	40.34N	14.20E
Portillo, Chile (pôr-tē′l-yô)	129b	32.51S	70.09W
Portimão, Port. (pôr-tē-mouɴ)	158	37.09N	8.34W
Port Jervis, N.Y., U.S. (jûr′vĭs)	100a	41.22N	74.41W
Portland, Austl. (pōrt′lănd)	203	38.20S	142.40E
Portland, In., U.S.	98	40.25N	85.00W
Portland, Me., U.S.	97	43.40N	70.16W
Portland, Mi., U.S.	98	42.50N	85.00W
Portland, Or., U.S.	96	45.31N	122.41W
Portland, Tx., U.S.	113	27.53N	97.20W
Portland Bight, bt., Jam.	122	17.45N	77.05W
Portland Canal, can., Ak., U.S.	86	55.10N	130.08W
Portland Inlet, b., Can.	86	54.50N	130.15W
Portland Point, c., Jam.	122	17.40N	77.20W
Port Lavaca, Tx., U.S. (lȧ-vä′kȧ)	113	28.36N	96.38W
Port Lincoln, Austl. (lĭŋ-kŭn)	202	34.39S	135.50E
Port Ludlow, Wa., U.S. (lŭd′lō)	106a	47.26N	122.41W
Port Macquarie, Austl. (mȧ-kwŏ′rĭ)	203	31.25S	152.45E
Port Madison Indian Reservation, I.R., Wa., U.S. (măd′ĭ-sŭn)	106a	47.46N	122.38W
Port Maria, Jam. (mȧ-rī′ȧ)	122	18.20N	76.55W
Port Melbourne, Austl.	243b	37.51S	144.56E
Port Moody, Can. (mo͞od′ĭ)	87	49.17N	122.51W
Port Moresby, Pap. N. Gui. (mōrz′bē)	197	9.34S	147.20E
Port Neches, Tx., U.S. (nĕch′ĕz)	113	29.59N	93.57W
Port Nelson, Can. (nĕl′sŭn)	89	57.03N	92.36W
Portneuf-Sur-Mer, Can. (pôr-nûf′sür mĕr)	92	48.36N	69.06W
Port Nolloth, S. Afr. (nŏl′ŏth)	212	29.10S	17.00E
Porto (Oporto), Port. (pōr′tō)	142	41.10N	8.38W
Porto Acre, Braz. (ä′krĕ)	130	9.38S	67.34W
Porto Alegre, Braz. (ä-lā′grĕ)	132	29.58S	51.11W
Porto Amboim, Ang.	212	11.01S	13.45E
Portobelo, Pan. (pôr′tô-bā′lô)	117	9.32N	79.40W
Pôrto de Pedras, Braz. (pā′drăzh)	131	9.09S	35.20W
Pôrto Feliz, Braz. (fē-lē′s)	129a	23.12S	47.30W
Portoferraio, Italy (pōr′tō-fĕr-rä′yō)	160	42.47N	10.20E
Port of Spain, Trin. (spān)	131	10.44N	61.24W
Portogruaro, Italy (pōr′tō-grō-ä′rō)	160	45.48N	12.49E
Portola, Ca., U.S. (pôr′tō-lá)	108	39.47N	120.29W
Porto Mendes, Braz. (mĕ′n-dĕs)	131	24.41S	54.13W

ăt; finăl; rāte; senāte; ärm; åsk; sofȧ; fâre; ch-choose; dh-as th in other; bē; ėvent; bĕt; recĕnt; cratẽr; g-gō; gh-guttural g; bĭt; ĭ-short neutral; rīde; ᴋ-guttural k as ch in German ich;

PLACE (Pronunciation)	PAGE	Lat. °'	Long. °'
Porto Murtinho, Braz. (mòr-tēn'yò)	131	21.43S	57.43W
Porto Nacional, Braz. (nä-syô-näl')	131	10.43S	48.14W
Porto Novo, Benin (pōr'tô-nō'vō)	210	6.29N	2.37E
Port Orchard, Wa., U.S. (ôr'chẽrd)	106a	47.32N	122.38W
Port Orchard, b., Wa., U.S.	106a	47.40N	122.39W
Porto Salvo, Port.	238d	38.43N	9.18W
Porto Santo, Ilha de, i., Port. (säɴ'tò)	210	32.41N	16.15W
Porto Seguro, Braz. (sā-gōō'rò)	131	16.26S	38.59W
Porto Torres, Italy (tôr'rĕs)	160	40.49N	8.25E
Porto-Vecchio, Fr. (vĕk'ê-ô)	160	41.36N	9.17E
Porto Velho, Braz. (väl'yò)	130	8.45S	63.43W
Portoviejo, Ec. (pôr-tō-vyā'hō)	130	1.11S	80.28W
Port Phillip Bay, b., Austl. (fĭl'ĭp)	203	37.57S	144.50E
Port Pirie, Austl. (pĭ'rê)	202	33.10S	138.00E
Port Reading, N.J., U.S.	228	40.34N	74.16W
Port Royal, b., Jam. (roi'ăl)	122	17.50N	76.45W
Port Said, Egypt	218c	31.15N	32.19E
Port Saint Johns, S. Afr. (sânt jŏnz)	212	31.37S	29.32E
Port Shepstone, S. Afr. (shĕps'tŭn)	212	30.45S	30.23E
Portsmouth, Dom.	121b	15.33N	61.28W
Portsmouth, Eng., U.K. (pôrts'mŭth)	142	50.45N	1.03W
Portsmouth, N.H., U.S.	97	43.05N	70.50W
Portsmouth, Oh., U.S.	97	38.45N	83.00W
Portsmouth, Va., U.S.	97	36.50N	76.19W
Port Sulphur, La., U.S. (sŭl'fẽr)	114	29.28N	89.41W
Port Sunlight, Eng., U.K.	237a	53.21N	2.59W
Port Susan, b., Wa., U.S. (sū-zȧn')	106a	48.11N	122.25W
Port Townsend, Wa., U.S. (tounz'ĕnd)	106a	48.07N	122.46W
Port Townsend, b., Wa., U.S.	106a	48.05N	122.47W
Portugal, nation, Eur. (pōr'tu-găl)	142	38.15N	8.08W
Portugalete, Spain (pōr-tōō-gä-lā'tā)	158	43.18N	3.05W
Portuguese West Africa *see* Angola, nation, Ang.	212	14.15S	16.00E
Port Vendres, Fr.	156	42.32N	3.07E
Port Vila, Vanuatu	203	17.44S	168.19E
Port Vue, Pa., U.S.	230b	40.20N	79.52W
Port Wakefield, Austl. (wāk'fēld)	202	34.12S	138.10E
Port Washington, N.Y., U.S. (wôsh'ĭng-tŭn)	100a	40.49N	73.42W
Port Washington, Wi., U.S.	103	43.24N	87.52W
Posadas, Arg. (pō-sä'dhäs)	132	27.32S	55.56W
Posadas, Spain (pò-sä-däs)	158	37.48N	5.09W
Poshekhon'ye Volodarsk, Russia (pô-shyĕ'kôn-yĕ vôl'ô-dársk)	162	58.31N	39.07E
Poso, Danau, l., Indon. (pō'sō)	196	2.00S	119.40E
Pospelokova, Russia (pôs-pyĕl'kô-vá)	172a	59.25N	60.50E
Possession Sound, strt., Wa., U.S. (pŏ-zĕsh-ŭn)	106a	47.59N	122.17W
Possum Kingdom Reservoir, res., Tx., U.S. (pŏs'ŭm kĭng'dŭm)	112	32.58N	98.12W
Post, Tx., U.S. (pōst)	110	33.12N	101.21W
Postojna, Slvn. (pōs-tōyná)	160	45.45N	14.13E
Pos'yet, Russia (pos-yĕt')	194	42.27N	130.47E
Potawatomi Indian Reservation, I.R., Ks., U.S. (pŏt-å-wä'tō mē)	111	39.30N	96.11W
Potchefstroom, S. Afr. (pŏch'ĕf-strōm)	212	26.42S	27.06E
Poteau, Ok., U.S. (pò-tō')	111	35.03N	94.37W
Poteet, Tx., U.S. (pò-tēt)	112	29.05N	98.35W
Potenza, Italy (pò-tĕnt'sä)	149	40.39N	15.49E
Potenza, r., Italy	160	43.09N	13.00E
Potgietersrus, S. Afr. (pôt-ĸē'tẽrs-rûs)	212	24.09S	29.04E
Potholes Reservoir, res., Wa., U.S.	104	47.00N	119.20W
Poti, Geor. (pô'tê)	167	42.10N	41.40E
Potiskum, Nig.	210	11.43N	11.05E
Potomac, Md., U.S. (pò-tō'măk)	100e	39.01N	77.13W
Potomac, r., U.S. (pò-tō'măk)	97	38.15N	76.55W
Poto Poto, neigh., Congo	244c	4.15S	15.18E
Potosí, Bol.	130	19.35S	65.45W
Potosi, Mo., U.S. (pŏ-tō'sĭ)	111	37.56N	90.46W
Potosí, r., Mex. (pō-tô-sē')	112	25.04N	99.36W
Potrerillos, Hond. (pō-trå-rēl'yôs)	120	15.13N	87.58W
Potsdam, Ger. (pôts'däm)	147	52.24N	13.04E
Potsdam, N.Y., U.S. (pŏts'dăm)	99	44.40N	75.00W
Pottenstein, Aus.	145e	47.58N	16.06E
Potters Bar, Eng., U.K. (pŏt'ẽz bär)	144b	51.41N	0.12W
Potter Street, Eng., U.K.	235	51.46N	0.08E
Pottstown, Pa., U.S. (pŏts'toun)	99	40.15N	75.40W
Pottsville, Pa., U.S. (pôts'vĭl)	99	40.40N	76.15W
Poughkeepsie, N.Y., U.S. (pŏ-kĭp'sê)	97	41.45N	73.55W
Poulsbo, Wa., U.S. (pōlz'bò)	106a	47.44N	122.38W
Poulton-le-Fylde, Eng., U.K. (pōl'tŭn-lē-fīld')	144a	53.52N	2.59W
Pouso Alegre, Braz. (pō'zò ä-lā'grĕ)	131	22.13S	45.56W
Póvoa de Varzim, Port. (pō-vō'á dā vär'zēɴ)	148	41.23N	8.44W
Powder, r., U.S. (pou'dẽr)	96	45.18N	105.37W
Powder, r., Or., U.S.	104	44.55N	117.35W
Powder, South Fork, r., Wy., U.S.	105	43.13N	106.54W
Powder River, Wy., U.S.	105	43.06N	106.55W
Powell, Wy., U.S. (pou'ĕl)	105	44.44N	108.44W
Powell, Lake, res., U.S.	96	37.26N	110.25W
Powell Lake, l., Can.	86	50.10N	124.13W
Powell Point, c., Bah.	122	24.50N	76.20W
Powell Reservoir, res., Ky., U.S.	114	36.30N	83.35W
Powell River, Can.	84	49.52N	124.33W
Poyang Hu, l., China	189	29.20N	116.28E
Poygan, r., Wi., U.S. (poi'gán)	103	44.10N	89.05W
Poyle, Eng., U.K.	235	51.28N	0.31W
Poynton, Eng., U.K.	237b	53.21N	2.07W
Požarevac, Yugo. (pô'zhá'rĕ-váts)	161	44.38N	21.12E
Poza Rica, Mex. (pô-zô-rē'kä)	119	20.32N	97.25W
Poznań, Pol.	142	52.25N	16.55E
Pozoblanco, Spain (pò-thō-blăŋ'kō)	158	38.23N	4.50W
Pozos, Mex. (pô'zōs)	118	22.05N	100.50W
Pozuelo de Alarcón, Spain (pò-thwā'lō dā ä-lär-kōn')	159a	40.27N	3.49W
Pozzuoli, Italy (pôt-swô'lē)	160	40.34N	14.08E
Pra, r., Ghana (prá)	214	5.45N	1.35W
Pra, r., Russia	162	55.00N	40.13E
Prachin Buri, Thai. (prä'chĕn)	196	13.59N	101.15E
Pradera, Col. (prä-dĕ'rä)	130a	3.24N	76.13W
Prades, Fr. (prád)	156	42.37N	2.23E
Prado, Col. (prädō)	130a	3.44N	74.55W
Prado, Museo del, bldg., Spain	238b	40.25N	3.41W
Prado Churubusco, Mex.	233a	19.21N	99.07W
Prado Reservoir, res., Ca., U.S. (prā'dō)	107a	33.45N	117.40W
Prados, Braz. (prá'dôs)	129a	21.05S	44.04W
Prague, Czech Rep.	154	50.05N	14.26E
Praha *see* Prague, Czech Rep.	142	50.05N	14.26E
Prahran, Austl.	243b	37.51S	144.59E
Praia, C.V. (prä'yá)	210b	15.00N	23.30W
Praia Funda, Ponta da, c., Braz. (pôn'tä-dá-prä'yá-fōō'n-dä)	132b	23.04S	43.34W
Prairie du Chien, Wi., U.S. (prā'rĭ dò shēn')	103	43.02N	91.10W
Prairie Grove, Can. (prā'rĭ grōv)	83f	49.48N	96.57W
Prairie Island Indian Reservation, I.R., Mn., U.S.	103	44.42N	92.32W
Prairies, Rivière des, r., Can. (rē-vyâr' dā prâ-rē')	83a	45.40N	73.34W
Pratas Island, i., Asia	193	20.40N	116.30E
Prat del Llobregat, Spain	238e	41.20N	2.06E
Prato, Italy (prä'tō)	160	43.53N	11.03E
Pratt, Ks., U.S. (prăt)	110	37.37N	98.43W
Pratt's Bottom, neigh., Eng., U.K.	235	51.20N	0.07E
Prattville, Al., U.S. (prăt'vĭl)	114	32.28N	86.27W
Pravdinsk, Russia	153	54.26N	21.00E
Pravdinskiy, Russia (práv-dĕn'skĭ)	172b	56.03N	37.52E
Pravia, Spain (prä'vē-ä)	158	43.30N	6.08W
Pregolya, r., Russia (prĕ-gô'lă)	153	54.37N	20.50E
Premont, Tx., U.S. (prē-mŏnt')	112	27.20N	98.07W
Prenton, Eng., U.K.	237a	53.22N	3.03W
Prenzlau, Ger. (prĕnts'lou)	154	53.19N	13.52E
Prenzlauer Berg, neigh., Ger.	238a	52.32N	13.26E
Přerov, Czech Rep. (przhĕ'rôf)	147	49.28N	17.28E
Prescot, Eng., U.K. (prĕs'kŭt)	144a	53.25N	2.48W
Prescott, Can. (prĕs'kŭt)	99	44.45N	75.35W
Prescott, Az., U.S. (prĕs'kŏt)	96	34.30N	112.30W
Prescott, Ar., U.S.	111	33.47N	93.23W
Prescott, Wi., U.S. (prĕs'kŏt)	107g	44.45N	92.48W
Presho, S.D., U.S. (prĕsh'ō)	102	43.56N	100.04W
Presidencia Rogue Sáenz Peña, Arg.	132	26.52S	60.15W
Presidente Epitácio, Braz. (prā-sê-dĕn'tĕ å-pê-tä'syò)	131	21.56S	52.01W
Presidente Roosevelt, Estação, trans., Braz.	234d	23.33S	46.36W
Presidio, Tx., U.S. (prĕ-sĭ'dĭ-ō)	112	29.33N	104.23W
Presidio, Río del, r., Mex. (rē'ō-dĕl-prĕ-sē'dyô)	118	23.54N	105.44W
Presidio of San Francisco, pt. of i., Ca., U.S.	231b	37.48N	122.28W
Prešov, Slvk. (prĕ'shôf)	147	49.00N	21.18E
Prespa, Lake, l., Eur. (prĕs'pä)	161	40.49N	20.50E
Prespuntal, r., Ven.	131b	9.55N	64.32W
Presque Isle, Me., U.S. (prĕsk'ēl')	92	46.41N	68.03W
Pressbaum, Aus.	145e	48.12N	16.06E
Prestea, Ghana	214	5.27N	2.08W
Preston, Austl.	201a	37.45S	145.01E
Preston, Eng., U.K. (prĕs'tŭn)	150	53.46N	2.42W
Preston, Id., U.S. (pres'tŭn)	105	42.05N	111.54W
Preston, Mn., U.S. (prĕs'tŭn)	103	43.42N	92.06W
Preston, Wa., U.S.	106a	47.31N	121.56W
Prestonburg, Ky., U.S. (prĕs'tŭn-bûrg)	98	37.35N	82.50W
Prestwich, Eng., U.K. (prĕst'wĭch)	144a	53.32N	2.17W
Pretoria, S. Afr. (prê-tō'rĭ-á)	212	25.43S	28.16E
Pretoria North, S. Afr. (prĕ-tô'rĭ-á nōōrd)	218d	25.41S	28.11E
Préveza, Grc. (prĕ'vå-zä)	161	38.58N	20.44E
Pribilof Islands, is., Ak., U.S. (prĭ'bĭ-lof)	95	57.00N	169.20W
Priboj, Yugo. (prē'boi)	161	43.33N	19.33E
Price, Ut., U.S. (prīs)	109	39.35N	110.50W
Price, r., Ut., U.S.	109	39.21N	110.35W
Prichard, Al., U.S. (prĭt'chârd)	114	30.44N	88.04W
Priddis, Can. (prĭd'dĭs)	83e	50.53N	114.20W
Priddis Creek, r., Can.	83e	50.56N	114.32W
Priego, Spain (prê-ā'gō)	158	37.27N	4.13W
Prienai, Lith. (prê-ĕn'ī)	153	54.38N	23.56E
Prieska, S. Afr. (prê-ĕs'ká)	212	29.40S	22.50E
Priest Lake, l., Id., U.S. (prēst)	104	48.30N	116.43W
Priest Rapids Dam, Wa., U.S.	104	46.39N	119.55W
Priest Rapids Lake, res., Wa., U.S.	104	46.42N	119.58W
Priiskovaya, Russia (prĭ-ēs'kô-vá-yá)	172a	60.50N	58.55E
Prijedor, Bos. (prē'yĕ-dōr)	160	44.58N	16.43E
Prijepolje, Yugo. (prē'yĕ-pô'lyĕ)	161	43.22N	19.41E
Prilep, Mac. (prē'lĕp)	149	41.20N	21.35E
Primorsk, Russia (prē-môrsk')	153	60.24N	28.35E
Primorsko-Akhtarskaya, Russia (prē-môr'skô äk-tär'skĭ-ê)	167	46.03N	38.09E
Primos, Pa., U.S.	229b	39.55N	75.18W
Primrose, S. Afr.	213b	26.11S	28.11E
Primrose Lake, l., Can.	88	54.55N	109.45W
Prince Albert, Can. (prĭns ăl'bẽrt)	84	53.12N	105.46W
Prince Albert National Park, rec., Can.	84	54.10N	105.25W
Prince Albert Sound, strt., Can.	84	70.23N	116.57W
Prince Charles Island, i., Can. (chärlz)	85	67.41N	74.10W
Prince Edward Island, prov., Can.	85	46.45N	63.10W
Prince Edward Islands, is., S. Afr.	219	46.36S	37.57E
Prince Edward National Park, rec., Can. (ĕd'wẽrd)	85	46.33N	63.35W
Prince Edward Peninsula, pen., Can.	99	44.00N	77.15W
Prince Frederick, Md., U.S. (prĭnce frĕdĕrĭk)	100e	38.33N	76.35W
Prince George, Can. (jôrj)	84	53.51N	122.57W
Prince of Wales, i., Austl.	203	10.47S	142.15E
Prince of Wales, i., Ak., U.S.	95	55.47N	132.50W
Prince of Wales, Cape, c., Ak., U.S. (wālz)	95	65.48N	169.08W
Prince Rupert, Can. (roo'pẽrt)	84	54.19N	130.19W
Princes Risborough, Eng., U.K. (prĭns'ĕz rĭz'brŭ)	144b	51.41N	0.51W
Princess Charlotte Bay, b., Austl. (shär'lŏt)	203	13.45S	144.15E
Princess Royal Channel, strt., Can. (roi'ăl)	86	53.10N	128.37W
Princess Royal Island, i., Can.	86	52.57N	128.49W
Princeton, Can. (prĭns'tŭn)	84	49.27N	120.31W
Princeton, Il., U.S.	98	41.20N	89.25W
Princeton, In., U.S.	98	38.20N	87.35W
Princeton, Ky., U.S.	114	37.07N	87.52W
Princeton, Mi., U.S.	103	46.16N	87.33W
Princeton, Mn., U.S.	103	45.34N	93.36W
Princeton, Mo., U.S.	111	40.23N	93.34W
Princeton, N.J., U.S.	99	40.21N	74.40W
Princeton, W.V., U.S.	115	37.21N	81.05W
Princeton, Wi., U.S.	103	43.50N	89.09W
Prince William Sound, strt., Ak., U.S. (wĭl'yăm)	95	60.40N	147.10W
Príncipe, i., S. Tom./P. (prēn'sē-pĕ)	210	1.37N	7.25E
Principe Channel, strt., Can. (prĭn'sĭ-pē)	86	53.28N	129.45W
Prineville, Or., U.S. (prīn'vĭl)	104	44.17N	120.48W
Prineville Reservoir, res., Or., U.S.	104	44.07N	120.45W
Prinzapolca, Nic. (prēn-zä-pōl'kä)	121	13.18N	83.35W
Prinzapolca, r., Nic.	121	13.23N	84.23W
Prior Lake, Mn., U.S. (prī'ẽr)	107g	44.43N	93.26W
Priozërsk, Russia (prĭ-ô'zĕrsk)	153	61.03N	30.08E
Pripet, r., Eur.	167	51.50N	29.45E
Pripyat Marshes *see* Poles'ye, sw., Eur.	167	52.10N	27.30E
Priština, Yugo. (prēsh'tĭ-nä)	149	42.39N	21.12E
Pritzwalk, Ger. (prēts'välk)	154	53.09N	12.12E
Privas, Fr. (prē-väs')	156	44.44N	4.37E
Prizren, Yugo. (prē'zrĕn)	149	42.11N	20.45E
Procida, Italy (prô'chê-dă)	159c	40.31N	14.02E
Procida, Isola di, i., Italy	159c	40.32N	13.57E
Proctor, Mn., U.S. (prŏk'tẽr)	107h	46.45N	92.14W
Proctor, Vt., U.S.	99	43.40N	73.00W
Proebstel, Wa., U.S. (prōb'stĕl)	106c	45.40N	122.29W
Proenca-a-Nova, Port. (prô-ĕn'sá-ä-nō'vá)	158	39.44N	7.55W
Progreso, Hond. (prô-grĕ'sò)	120	15.28N	87.49W
Progreso, Mex.	112	27.29N	101.05W
Progreso, Mex. (prô-grā'sō)	116	21.14N	89.39W
Prokhladnyy, Russia	168	43.46N	44.00E
Prokop'yevsk, Russia	170	53.53N	86.45E
Prokuplje, Yugo. (prô'kòp'l-yĕ)	161	43.16N	21.40E
Prome, Myanmar	196	18.46N	95.15E
Pronya, r., Bela. (prô'nyä)	162	54.08N	30.58E
Pronya, r., Russia	162	54.08N	39.30E
Prospect, Austl.	243a	33.48S	150.56E
Prospect, Ky., U.S. (prŏs'pĕkt)	101h	38.21N	85.36W
Prospect Heights, Il., U.S.	231a	42.06N	87.56W
Prospect Park, N.J., U.S.	228	40.56N	74.10W
Prospect Park, Pa., U.S. (prŏs'pĕkt pärk)	100f	39.53N	75.18W
Prosser, Wa., U.S. (prŏs'ẽr)	104	46.10N	119.46W
Prostějov, Czech Rep. (prŏs'tyĕ-yôf)	155	49.28N	17.08E
Protea, S. Afr.	244b	26.17S	27.51E
Protection, i., Wa., U.S. (prò-tĕk'shŭn)	106a	48.07N	122.56W
Protoka, r., Russia (prôt'ô-kȧ)	162	55.00N	36.42E
Provadiya, Bul. (prō-väd'ê-yȧ)	161	43.13N	27.28E
Providence, Ky., U.S. (prŏv'ĭ-dĕns)	98	37.25N	87.45W
Providence, R.I., U.S.	97	41.50N	71.23W
Providence, Ut., U.S.	105	41.42N	111.50W
Providencia, Chile	234b	33.26S	70.37W
Providencia, Isla de, i., Col.	121	13.21N	80.55W
Providenciales, i., T./C. Is.	123	21.50N	72.15W
Provideniya, Russia (prô-vĭ-dă'nĭ-yȧ)	95	64.30N	172.54W
Provincetown, Ma., U.S.	99	42.03N	70.11W
Provo, Ut., U.S. (prō'vō)	96	40.15N	111.40W
Prozor, Bos. (prô'zôr)	161	43.48N	17.59E
Prudence Island, i., R.I., U.S. (prōō'dĕns)	100b	41.38N	71.20W
Prudhoe Bay, b., Ak., U.S.	95	70.40N	147.25W
Prudnik, Pol. (prŏd'nĭk)	155	50.19N	17.34E
Prussia, hist. reg., Eur. (prŭsh'á)	154	50.43N	8.35E
Pruszków, Pol. (prŏsh'kŏf)	155	52.09N	20.50E
Prut, r., Eur. (prōōt)	142	48.05N	27.07E
Pryluky, Ukr.	167	50.36N	32.21E
Prymors'k, Ukr.	163	46.43N	36.21E
Pryor, Ok., U.S. (prī'ẽr)	111	36.16N	95.19W
Pryvil'ne, Ukr.	163	47.30N	32.21E
Przedbórz, Pol.	155	51.05N	19.53E
Przemyśl, Pol. (pzhĕ'mĭsh'l)	142	49.47N	22.45E
Przheval'sk, Kyrg. (p'r-zhĭ-välsk')	169	42.29N	78.24E
Psikhikón, Grc.	239d	38.00N	23.47E
Pskov, Russia (pskôf)	164	57.48N	28.19E
Pskov, prov., Russia	162	57.33N	29.05E
Pskovskoye Ozero, l., Eur. (p'skôv'skô'yĕ ôzê-rô)	166	58.05N	28.15E
Ps'ol, r., Eur.	167	49.45N	33.42E
Ptich', r., Bela. (p'têch)	166	53.17N	28.16E
Ptuj, Slvn. (ptōō'ê)	160	46.24N	15.54E
Pucheng, China (pōō-chŭŋ)	190	35.43N	115.22E
Pucheng, China (pōō'chĕng')	193	28.02N	118.25E
Puck, Pol. (pòtsk)	155	54.43N	18.23E

g-sing; ŋ-baŋk; ɴ-nasalized n; nŏd; cŏmmit; ōld; ôbey; ôrder; oi-boil; fōōd; ò-as oo in foot; ou-out; s-soft; sh-dish; th-thin; pūre; ûnite; ûrn; stŭd; circŭs; ü-as in French tu; '-indeterminate vowel.

336 Puddington – Querenburg

PLACE (Pronunciation)	PAGE	Lat. °′	Long. °′
Puddington, Eng., U.K.	237a	53.15N	3.00W
Pudozh, Russia (po͞o′dôzh)	166	61.50N	36.50E
Puebla, Mex. (pwā′blä)	116	19.02N	98.11W
Puebla, state, Mex.	119	19.00N	97.45W
Puebla de Don Fadrique, Spain	158	37.55N	2.55W
Pueblo, Co., U.S. (pwā′blō)	96	38.15N	104.36W
Pueblo Libre, Peru	233c	12.05S	77.05W
Pueblo Nuevo, Mex. (nwā′vô)	118	23.23N	105.21W
Pueblo Nuevo, neigh., Spain	238b	40.26N	3.39W
Pueblo Viejo, Mex. (vyā′hô)	119	17.23N	93.46W
Puente Alto, Chile (pwĕ′n-tĕ ál′tô)	129b	33.36S	70.34W
Puenteareas, Spain (pwĕn-tä-ä-rä′äs)	158	42.09N	8.23W
Puentedeume, Spain (pwĕn-tå-dhå-o͞o′må)	158	43.28N	8.09W
Puente-Genil, Spain (pwĕn′tå-hå-nēl′)	158	37.25N	4.18W
Puerco, Rio, r., N.M., U.S. (pwĕr′kō)	109	35.15N	107.05W
Puerto Aisén, Chile (pwĕ′r-tô ä′y-sĕ′n)	132	45.28S	72.44W
Puerto Angel, Mex. (pwĕ′r-tô äŋ′hál)	119	15.42N	96.32W
Puerto Armuelles, Pan. (pwe′r-tô är-mo͞o-ā′lyās)	121	8.18N	82.52W
Puerto Barrios, Guat. (pwĕ′r-tô bär′rê-ôs)	116	15.43N	88.36W
Puerto Bermúdez, Peru (pwĕ′r-tō bĕr-mo͞o′dāz)	130	10.17S	74.57W
Puerto Berrío, Col. (pwĕ′r-tō bĕr-rē′ō)	130	6.29N	74.27W
Puerto Cabello, Ven. (pwĕ′r-tō kä-bĕl′yō)	130	10.28N	68.01W
Puerto Cabezas, Nic. (pwĕ′r-tô kä-bā′zäs)	121	14.01N	83.26W
Puerto Casado, Para. (pwĕ′r-tō kä-sä′dō)	132	22.16S	57.57W
Puerto Castilla, Hond. (pwĕ′r-tō käs-tēl′yō)	120	16.01N	86.01W
Puerto Chicama, Peru (pwĕ′r-tō chē-kä′mä)	130	7.46S	79.18W
Puerto Colombia, Col. (pwĕr′tô kô-lôm′bê-ä)	130	11.08N	75.09W
Puerto Cortés, C.R. (pwĕ′r-tô kôr-tās′)	121	9.00N	83.37W
Puerto Cortés, Hond. (pwĕ′r-tô kôr-tās′)	116	15.48N	87.57W
Puerto Cumarebo, Ven. (pwĕ′r-tō ko͞o-mä-rĕ′bô)	130	11.25N	69.17W
Puerto de Luna, N.M., U.S. (pwĕr′tô då lo͞o′nä)	110	34.49N	104.36W
Puerto de Nutrias, Ven. (pwĕ′r-tō dĕ no͞o-trê-äs′)	130	8.02N	69.19W
Puerto Deseado, Arg. (pwĕ′r-tō dā-sâ-ä′dhō)	132	47.38S	66.00W
Puerto de Somport, p., Eur.	159	42.51N	0.25W
Puerto Eten, Peru (pwĕ′r-tō ĕ-tĕ′n)	130	6.59S	79.51W
Puerto Jiménez, C.R. (pwĕ′r-tô ĸê-mĕ′nĕz)	121	8.35N	83.23W
Puerto La Cruz, Ven. (pwĕ′r-tō lä kro͞o′z)	130	10.14N	64.38W
Puertollano, Spain (pwĕ-tôl-yä′nō)	148	38.41N	4.05W
Puerto Madryn, Arg. (pwĕ′r-tō mä-drĕn′)	132	42.45S	65.01W
Puerto Maldonado, Peru (pwĕ′r-tō mäl-dō-nä′dô)	130	12.43S	69.01W
Puerto Miniso, Mex. (pwĕ′r-tō mē-nē′sô)	118	16.06N	98.02W
Puerto Montt, Chile (pwĕ′r-tō mô′nt)	132	41.29S	73.00W
Puerto Natales, Chile (pwĕ′r-tō nä-tä′lēs)	132	51.48S	72.01W
Puerto Niño, Col. (pwĕ′r-tō nê′n-yô)	130a	5.57N	74.36W
Puerto Padre, Cuba (pwĕ′r-tō pä′drā)	122	21.10N	76.40W
Puerto Peñasco, Mex. (pwĕ′r-tô pĕn-yä′s-kô)	116	31.39N	113.15W
Puerto Pinasco, Para. (pwĕ′r-tō pē-nä′s-kô)	132	22.31S	57.50W
Puerto Píritu, Ven. (pwĕ′r-tō pē′rē-to͞o)	131b	10.05N	65.04W
Puerto Plata, Dom. Rep. (pwĕ′r-tô plä′tä)	117	19.50N	70.40W
Puerto Princesa, Phil. (pwĕr-tô prên-sä′sä)	196	9.45N	118.41E
Puerto Rico, dep., N.A. (pwĕr′tô rē′kō)	117	18.16N	66.50W
Puerto Rico Trench, deep	117	19.45N	66.30W
Puerto Salgar, Col. (pwĕ′r-tō säl-gär′)	130a	5.30N	74.39W
Puerto Santa Cruz, Arg. (pwĕ′r-tō sän′tä kro͞oz′)	132	50.04S	68.32W
Puerto Suárez, Bol. (pwĕ′r-tō swä′râz)	131	18.55S	57.39W
Puerto Tejada, Col. (pwĕ′r-tō tĕ-kä′dä)	130	3.13N	76.23W
Puerto Vallarta, Mex. (pwĕ′r-tō väl-yär′tä)	118	20.36N	105.13W
Puerto Varas, Chile (pwĕ′r-tō vä′räs)	132	41.16S	73.03W
Puerto Wilches, Col. (pwĕ′r-tō vĕl′c-hĕs)	130	7.19N	73.54W
Pugachëv, Russia (po͞o′gá-chyôf)	167	52.00N	48.40E
Puget, Wa., U.S. (pū′jĕt)	106c	46.10N	123.23W
Puget Sound, strt., Wa., U.S.	104	47.49N	122.26W
Puglia (Apulia), hist. reg., Italy (po͞o′lyä) (ä-po͞o′lyä)	160	41.13N	16.10E
Pukaskwa National Park, rec., Can.	85	48.22N	85.55W
Pukeashun Mountain, mtn., Can.	87	51.12N	119.14W
Pukin, r., Malay.	181b	2.53N	102.54E
Pula, Cro. (po͞o′lä)	148	44.52N	13.55E
Pulacayo, Bol. (po͞o-lä-kä′yō)	130	20.12N	66.33W
Pulaski, Tn., U.S. (pů-lăs′kĭ)	114	35.11N	87.03W
Pulaski, Va., U.S.	115	37.00N	81.45W
Puławy, Pol. (pò-wä′vê)	155	51.24N	21.59E
Pulicat, r., India	187	13.58N	79.52E
Pullman, Wa., U.S. (pòl′măn)	104	46.44N	117.10W
Pullman, neigh., Il., U.S.	231a	41.43N	87.36W
Pulog, Mount, mtn., Phil. (po͞o′lòg)	197a	16.38N	120.53E
Puma Yumco, l., China (po͞o-mä yo͞om-tswo)	186	28.30N	90.10E
Pumphrey, Md., U.S.	229c	39.13N	76.38W
Pumpkin Creek, r., Mt., U.S. (pŭmp′kĭn)	105	45.47N	105.35W
Punakha, Bhu. (po͞o-nŭk′ŭ)	183	27.45N	89.59E
Punata, Bol. (po͞o-nä′tä)	130	17.43S	65.43W
Punchbowl, Austl.	243a	33.56S	151.03E
Pune, India	183	18.38N	73.53E
Punggol, Sing.	240c	1.25N	103.55E
Punjab, state, India (pŭn′jäb′)	183	31.00N	75.30E
Puno, Peru (po͞o′nō)	130	15.58S	70.02W
Punta Arenas, Chile (po͞o′n-tä-rĕ′näs)	132	53.09S	70.48W
Punta Brava, Cuba	233b	23.01N	82.30W
Punta de Piedras, Ven. (po͞o′n-tä dĕ pyĕ′dräs)	131b	10.54N	64.06W
Punta Gorda, Belize (pōn′tä gôr′dä)	120	16.07N	88.50W
Punta Gorda, Fl., U.S. (pŭn′tȧ gôr′dȧ)	115a	26.55N	82.02W
Punta Gorda, Río, r., Nic. (po͞o′n-tä gô′r-dä)	121	11.34N	84.13W
Punta Indio, Canal, strt., Arg. (po͞o′n-tä- ē′n-dyô)	129c	34.56S	57.20W
Puntarenas, C.R. (pònt-ä-rä′näs)	117	9.59N	84.49W
Punto Fijo, Ven. (po͞o′n-tô fē′ĸô)	130	11.48N	70.14W
Punxsutawney, Pa., U.S. (pŭnk-sŭ-tô′nê)	99	40.55N	79.00W
Puquio, Peru (po͞o′kyô)	130	14.43S	74.02W
Pur, r., Russia	170	65.30N	77.30E
Purcell, Ok., U.S. (pûr-sĕl′)	111	35.01N	97.22W
Purcell Mountains, mts., N.A. (pûr-sĕl′)	87	50.00N	116.30W
Purdy, Wa., U.S. (pûr′dē)	106a	47.23N	122.37W
Purépero, Mex. (po͞o-rā′pá-rō)	118	19.56N	102.02W
Purfleet, Eng., U.K.	235	51.29N	0.15E
Purgatoire, r., Co., U.S. (pûr-gá-twär′)	110	37.25N	103.53W
Puri, India (pò′rê)	183	19.52N	85.51E
Purial, Sierra de, mts., Cuba (sē-ĕ′r-rá-dĕ-po͞o-rē-äl′)	123	20.15N	74.40W
Purificación, Col. (po͞o-rē-fê-kä-syōn′)	130	3.52N	74.54W
Purificación, Mex. (po͞o-rē-fê-kä-syô′n)	118	19.44N	104.38W
Purificación, r., Mex.	118	19.30N	104.54W
Purkersdorf, Aus.	145e	48.13N	16.11E
Purley, neigh., Eng., U.K.	235	51.20N	0.07W
Puruandiro, Mex. (pò-ro͞o-än′dê-rō)	118	20.04N	101.33W
Purús, r., S.A. (po͞o-ro͞o′s)	130	6.45S	64.34W
Pusan, S. Kor.	189	35.08N	129.05E
Pushkin, Russia (pòsh′kĭn)	166	59.43N	30.25E
Pushkino, Russia (po͞osh′kê-nô)	162	56.01N	37.51E
Pustoshka, Russia (pûs-tôsh′ká)	162	56.20N	29.33E
Pustunich, Mex. (po͞os-to͞o′nêch)	119	19.10N	90.29W
Putaendo, Chile (po͞o-tä-ĕn-dô)	129b	32.37S	70.42W
Puteaux, Fr. (pü-tō′)	157b	48.52N	2.12E
Putfontein, S. Afr. (pòt′fŏn-tān)	213b	26.08S	28.24E
Puth Kalān, neigh., India	240d	28.43N	77.05E
Putian, China (po͞o-tĭĕn)	193	25.40N	119.02E
Putilkovo, Russia	239b	55.52N	37.23E
Putla de Guerrero, Mex. (po͞o′tlä-dĕ-gĕr-rĕ′rō)	119	17.03N	97.55W
Putnam, Ct., U.S. (pŭt′năm)	99	41.55N	71.55W
Putney, neigh., Eng., U.K.	235	51.28N	0.13W
Putorana, Gory, mts., Russia	165	68.45N	93.15E
Pütt, Ger.	236	51.11N	6.59E
Puttalam, Sri L.	183b	8.02N	79.44E
Putumayo, r., S.A. (po͞o-to͞o-mä′yō)	130	1.02S	73.50W
Putung, Tanjung, c., Indon.	196	3.35S	111.50E
Putyvl′, Ukr.	163	51.21N	33.52E
Puulavesi, l., Fin.	153	61.49N	27.10E
Puyallup, Wa., U.S. (pū-ăl′ŭp)	106a	47.12N	122.18W
Puyang, China (po͞o-yäŋ)	192	35.42N	114.58E
Pweto, Zaire (pwä′tō)	212	8.29S	28.58E
Pyasina, r., Russia (pyä-sē′nȧ)	170	72.45N	87.37E
Pyatigorsk, Russia (pyȧ-tē-gôrsk′)	167	44.00N	43.00E
Pyhäjärvi, l., Fin.	153	60.57N	21.50E
Pyinmana, Myanmar (pyĕn-mä′nȧ)	183	19.47N	96.15E
Pymatuning Reservoir, res., Pa., U.S. (pī-mȧ-tŭn′ĭng)	98	41.40N	80.30W
Pymble, Austl.	243a	33.45S	151.09E
Pyŏnggang, N. Kor. (pyŭng′găng′)	194	38.21N	127.18E
P′yŏngyang, N. Kor.	189	39.03N	125.48E
Pyramid, l., Nv., U.S. (pĭ′rȧ-mĭd)	108	40.02N	119.50W
Pyramid Lake Indian Reservation, I.R., Nv., U.S.	108	40.17N	119.52W
Pyramids, hist., Egypt	218b	29.53N	31.10E
Pyrenees, mts., Eur. (pĭr-e-nēz′)	142	43.00N	0.05E
Pyrford, Eng., U.K.	235	51.19N	0.30W
Pyryatyn, Ukr.	167	50.13N	32.31E
Pyrzyce, Pol. (pĕzhĭ′tsĕ)	154	53.09N	14.53E

Q

PLACE (Pronunciation)	PAGE	Lat. °′	Long. °′
Qal′at Bīshah, Sau. Ar.	182	20.01N	42.30E
Qamdo, China (chyäm-dwō)	188	31.06N	96.30E
Qandahār, Afg.	183	31.43N	65.58E
Qandala, Som.	185	11.28N	49.52E
Qapal, Kaz.	169	45.13N	79.08E
Qaraghandy, Kaz.	169	49.42N	73.18E
Qarqan see Qiemo, China	188	38.02N	85.16E
Qarqan, r., China	188	38.55N	87.15E
Qarqaraly, Kaz.	169	49.18N	75.28E
Qārūn, Birket, l., Egypt	211	29.34N	30.34E
Qaṣr al Burayqah, Libya	211	30.25N	19.20E
Qasr al-Farāfirah, Egypt	211	27.04N	28.13E
Qaṣr Banī Walīd, Libya	211	31.45N	14.04E
Qasr-e Fīrūzeh, Iran	241h	35.40N	51.32E
Qasr el Boukhari, Alg.	148	35.50N	2.48E
Qatar, nation, Asia (kä′tȧr)	182	25.00N	52.45E
Qaṭārah, Munkhafaḍ al, depr., Egypt	211	30.07N	27.30E
Qāyen, Iran	182	33.45N	59.08E
Qazvīn, Iran	182	36.10N	49.59E
Qeshm, Iran	182	26.51N	56.10E
Qeshm, i., Iran	182	26.52N	56.15E
Qezel Owzan, r., Iran	182	36.30N	49.00E
Qezi′ot, Isr.	181a	30.53N	34.28E
Qianwei, China (chyĕn-wā)	190	40.11N	120.05E
Qi′anzhen, China (chyē-än-jŭn)	190	32.16N	120.59E
Qibao, China (chyē-bou)	191b	31.06N	121.16E
Qiblīyah, Jabal al Jalālat al, mts., Egypt	181a	28.49N	32.21E
Qieshikou, China	240b	39.59N	116.24E
Qijiang, China (chyē-jyäŋ)	193	29.05N	106.40E
Qikou, China (chyē-kō)	190	38.37N	117.33E
Qilian Shan, mts., China (chyē-lĭĕn shän)	188	38.43N	98.00E
Qiliping, China (chyē-lē-pĭŋ)	190	31.28N	114.41E
Qindao, China (chyĭn-dou)	189	36.05N	120.10E
Qing′an, China (chyĭŋ-än)	192	46.50N	127.30E
Qingcheng, China (chyĭŋ-chŭŋ)	190	37.12N	117.43E
Qingfeng, China (chyĭŋ-fŭŋ)	190	35.52N	115.05E
Qinghai, prov., China (chyĭŋ-hī)	188	36.14N	95.30E
Qinghai Hu see Koko Nor, l., China	188	37.26N	98.30E
Qinghe, China (chyĭŋ-hŭ)	192a	40.08N	116.16E
Qinghuayuan, China	240b	40.00N	116.19E
Qingjiang, China	190	33.34N	118.58E
Qingjiang, China (chyĭŋ-jyäŋ)	193	28.00N	115.30E
Qingliu, China (chyĭŋ-lĭō)	193	26.15N	116.50E
Qingningsi, China (chyĭŋ-nĭŋ-sz)	191b	31.16N	121.33E
Qingping, China (chyĭŋ-pĭŋ)	190	36.46N	116.03E
Qingpu, China (chyĭŋ-po͞o)	193	31.08N	121.06E
Qingxian, China (chyĭŋ shyĕn)	190	38.37N	116.48E
Qingyang, China (chyĭŋ-yäŋ)	188	36.02N	107.42E
Qingyuan, China	192	42.05N	125.00E
Qingyuan, China (chyĭŋ-yŏän)	193	23.43N	113.10E
Qingyun, China (chyĭŋ-yòn)	190	37.52N	117.26E
Qingyundian, China (chĭŋ-yòn-dĭĕn)	192a	39.41N	116.31E
Qinhuangdao, China (chyĭn-huaŋ-dou)	189	39.57N	119.34E
Qin Ling, mts., China (chyĭn lĭŋ)	188	33.25N	108.58E
Qinyang, China (chyĭn-yäŋ)	192	35.00N	112.55E
Qinzhou, China (chyĭn-jō)	193	22.00N	108.35E
Qionghai, China (chyôŋ-hī)	193	19.10N	110.28E
Qiqian, China (chyē-chyĕn)	189	52.23N	121.04E
Qiqihar, China	189	47.18N	124.00E
Qiryat Gat, Isr.	181a	31.38N	34.36E
Qiryat Shemona, Isr.	181a	33.12N	35.34E
Qitai, China (chyē-tī)	188	44.07N	89.04E
Qiuxian, China (chyô shyĕn)	190	36.43N	115.13E
Qixian, China (chyē-shyĕn)	190	34.33N	114.47E
Qixian, China	192	35.36N	114.13E
Qiyang, China (chyē-yäŋ)	193	26.40N	112.00E
Qom, Iran	182	34.28N	50.53E
Qostanay, Kaz.	169	53.10N	63.39E
Quabbin Reservoir, res., Ma., U.S. (kwā′bĭn)	99	42.20N	72.10W
Quachita, Lake, l., Ar., U.S. (kwä shĭ′tô)	111	34.47N	93.37W
Quadra Island, i., Can.	86	50.08N	125.16W
Quadraro, neigh., Italy	239c	41.51N	12.33E
Quakers Hill, Austl.	243a	33.43S	150.53E
Quakertown, Pa., U.S. (kwā′kĕr-toun)	99	40.30N	75.20W
Quanah, Tx., U.S. (kwä′nȧ)	110	34.19N	99.43W
Quang Ngai, Viet. (kwäng n′gä′ê)	196	15.05N	108.58E
Quang Ngai, mtn., Viet.	193	15.10N	108.20E
Quanjiao, China (chyuän-jyou)	190	32.06N	118.17E
Quanzhou, China (chyuän-jō)	189	24.58N	118.40E
Quanzhou, China	193	25.58N	111.02E
Qu′Appelle, r., Can.	84	50.30N	104.00W
Qu′Appelle Dam, dam, Can.	88	51.00N	106.25W
Quartu Sant′Elena, Italy (kwär-to͞o′ sänt a′lå-nä)	160	39.16N	9.12E
Quartzsite, Az., U.S.	109	33.40N	114.13W
Quatsino Sound, strt., Can. (kwŏt-sē′nō)	86	50.25N	128.10W
Quba, Azer. (ko͞o′bä)	167	41.05N	48.30E
Qūchān, Iran	185	37.06N	58.30E
Qudi, China	190	37.06N	117.15E
Québec, Can. (kwê-bĕk′) (kå-bĕk′)	83b	46.49N	71.13W
Quebec, prov., Can.	85	51.07N	70.25W
Quedlinburg, Ger. (kvĕd′lĕn-bo͞orgh)	154	51.45N	11.10E
Queen Bess, Can.	86	51.16N	124.34W
Queen Charlotte Islands, is., Can. (kwēn shär′lŏt)	84	53.30N	132.25W
Queen Charlotte Ranges, mts., Can.	86	53.00N	132.00W
Queen Charlotte Sound, strt., Can.	86	51.30N	129.30W
Queen Charlotte Strait, strt., Can. (strāt)	84	50.40N	127.25W
Queen Elizabeth Islands, is., Can. (ê-lĭz′á-bĕth)	82	78.20N	110.00W
Queen Maud Gulf, b., Can. (mäd)	84	68.27N	102.55W
Queen Maud Land, reg., Ant.	219	75.00S	10.00E
Queen Maud Mountains, mts., Ant.	219	85.00S	179.00W
Queens Channel, strt., Austl. (kwēnz)	202	14.25S	129.10E
Queenscliff, Austl.	201a	38.16S	144.39E
Queensland, state, Austl. (kwēnz′lănd)	203	22.45S	141.01E
Queenstown, Austl. (kwēnz′toun)	204	42.00S	145.40E
Queenstown, S. Afr.	213c	31.54S	26.53E
Queimados, Braz. (kā-mȧ′dôs)	132b	22.42S	43.34W
Quela, Ang.	216	9.16S	17.02E
Quelimane, Moz. (kā-lê-mä′nĕ)	213	17.48S	37.05E
Queluz, Port.	159b	38.45N	9.15W
Quemado de Güines, Cuba (kä-mä′dhä-dĕ-gwē′nĕs)	122	22.45N	80.20W
Quemoy, Tai.	193	24.30N	118.20E
Quemoy, i., Tai.	193	24.27N	118.23E
Quepos, C.R. (kā′pôs)	121	9.26N	84.10W
Quepos, Punta, c., C.R. (po͞o′n-tä)	121	9.23N	84.20W
Querenburg, neigh., Ger.	236	51.27N	7.16E

ăt; finăl; rāte; senāte; ärm; ȧsk; sofȧ; fâre; ch-choose; dh-as th in other; bē; ēvent; bĕt; recĕnt; cratĕr; g-gō; gh-guttural g; bĭt; ĭ-short neutral; rīde; ĸ-guttural k as ch in German ich;

PRONOUNCING INDEX Querétaro–Razorback Mountain 337

PLACE (Pronunciation)	PAGE	Lat. °′	Long. °′
Querétaro, Mex. (kå-rā'tä-rō)	116	20.37N	100.25W
Querétaro, state, Mex.	118	21.00N	100.00W
Quesada, Spain (kå-sä'dhä)	158	37.51N	3.04W
Quesnel, Can. (kā-nĕl')	84	52.59N	122.30W
Quesnel, r., Can.	87	52.15N	122.00W
Quesnel Lake, l., Can.	84	52.32N	121.05W
Quetame, Col. (kĕ-tä'mĕ)	130a	4.20N	73.50W
Quetta, Pak. (kwĕt'ä)	183	30.19N	67.01E
Quezaltenango, Guat. (kå-zäl'tå-näŋ'gō)	116	14.50N	91.30W
Quezaltepeque, El Sal. (kĕ-zäl'tĕ'pĕ-kĕ)	120	13.50N	89.17W
Quezaltepeque, Guat. (kå-zäl'tå-pā'kå)	120	14.39N	89.26W
Quezon City, Phil. (kā-zōn)	196	14.40N	121.02E
Qufu, China (chyōō-fōō)	190	35.37N	116.54E
Quibdo, Col. (kēb'dō)	130	5.42N	76.41W
Quiberon, Fr. (kē-bē-rôN')	156	47.29N	3.08W
Quiçama, Parque Nacional de, rec., Ang.	216	10.00S	13.25E
Quicksborn, Ger. (kvēks'bōrn)	145c	53.44N	9.54E
Quilcene, Wa., U.S. (kwĭl-sēn')	106a	47.50N	122.53W
Quilimari, Chile (kē-lē-mä'rē)	129b	32.06S	71.28W
Quillan, Fr. (kē-yäN')	156	42.53N	2.13E
Quillota, Chile (kēl-yō'tä)	132	32.52S	71.14W
Quilmes, Arg. (kēl'mās)	129c	34.43S	58.16W
Quilon, India (kwē-lōn')	183b	8.58N	76.16E
Quilpie, Austl. (kwĭl'pē)	203	26.34S	149.20E
Quimbaya, Col. (kēm-bä'yä)	130a	4.38N	75.46W
Quimbele, Ang.	216	6.28S	16.13E
Quimbonge, Ang.	216	8.36S	18.30E
Quimper, Fr. (kăN-pĕr')	147	47.59N	4.04W
Quinalt, r., Wa., U.S.	104	47.23N	124.10W
Quinault Indian Reservation, I.R., Wa., U.S.	104	47.27N	124.34W
Quincy, Fl., U.S. (kwĭn'sē)	114	30.35N	84.35W
Quincy, Il., U.S.	97	39.55N	91.23W
Quincy, Ma., U.S.	93a	42.15N	71.00W
Quincy, Mi., U.S.	98	42.00N	84.50W
Quincy, Or., U.S.	106c	46.08N	123.10W
Quincy Bay, b., Ma., U.S.	227a	42.17N	70.58W
Qui Nhon, Viet. (kwĭnyôn)	196	13.51N	109.03E
Quinn, r., Nv., U.S. (kwĭn)	104	41.42N	117.45W
Quintanar de la Orden, Spain (kēn-tä-när')	158	39.36N	3.02W
Quintana Roo, state, Mex. (rô'ô)	116	19.30N	88.30W
Quinta Normal, Chile	234b	33.27S	70.42W
Quintero, Chile (kēn-tĕ'rō)	129b	32.48S	71.30W
Quinto Romano, neigh., Italy	238c	45.29N	9.05E
Quionga, Moz.	217	10.37S	40.30E
Quiroga, Mex. (kē-rō'gä)	118	19.39N	101.30W
Quiroga, Spain (kē-rō'gä)	158	42.28N	7.18W
Quitaúna, Braz.	234d	23.31S	46.47W
Quitman, Ga., U.S. (kwĭt'măn)	114	30.46N	83.35W
Quitman, Ms., U.S.	114	33.02N	88.43W
Quito, Ec. (kē'tō)	130	0.17S	78.32W
Qumbu, S. Afr. (kŏŏm'bōō)	213c	31.10S	28.48E
Quorn, Austl. (kwôrn)	204	32.20S	138.00E
Qurayyah, Wādī, r., Egypt	181a	30.08N	34.27E
Qūsmūryn Kölī, l., Kaz.	169	52.30N	64.15E
Qutang, China (chyōō-täŋ)	190	32.33N	120.07E
Quthing, Leso.	213c	30.35S	27.42E
Quxian, China (chyōō-shyĕn)	189	28.58N	118.58E
Quxian, China	193	30.40N	106.48E
Quzhou, China (chyoŏ-jō)	190	36.47N	114.58E
Qyrghyz zhot, mts., Asia	168	37.58N	72.23E
Qyzylorda, Kaz.	169	44.58N	65.45E

R

PLACE (Pronunciation)	PAGE	Lat. °′	Long. °′
Raab (Raba), r., Eur. (räp)	154	46.55N	15.55E
Raadt, neigh., Ger.	236	51.24N	6.56E
Raahe, Fin. (rä'ĕ)	146	64.39N	24.22E
Raasdorf, Aus.	239e	48.15N	16.34E
Rab, i., Yugo. (räb)	160	44.45N	14.40E
Raba, Indon.	196	8.32S	118.49E
Raba (Raab), r., Eur.	155	47.28N	17.12E
Rabat, Mor. (rá-bät')	210	33.59N	6.47W
Rabaul, Pap. N. Gui. (rä'boul)	197	4.15S	152.19E
Rābigh, Sau. Ar.	185	22.48N	39.01E
Raby, Eng., U.K.	237a	53.19N	3.02W
Raccoon, r., Ia., U.S. (ră-kōōn')	103	42.07N	94.45W
Raccoon Cay, i., Bah.	123	22.25N	75.50W
Race, Cape, c., Can. (rās)	93	46.40N	53.10W
Raceview, S. Afr.	244b	26.17S	28.08E
Rachado, Cape, c., Malay.	181b	2.26N	101.29E
Racibórz, Pol. (rä-chē'bōōzh)	155	50.06N	18.14E
Racine, Wi., U.S. (rá-sēn')	97	42.43N	87.49W
Raco, Mi., U.S. (rá cō)	107k	46.22N	84.43W
Rădăuţi, Rom.	149	47.53N	25.55E
Radcliffe, Eng., U.K. (răd'klĭf)	144a	53.34N	2.20W
Radevormwald, Ger. (rä'dĕ-fōrm-väld)	157c	51.12N	7.22E
Radford, Va., U.S. (răd'fērd)	115	37.06N	81.33W
Rādhanpur, India	186	23.57N	71.38E
Radium, S. Afr. (rā'dĭ-ŭm)	218d	25.06S	28.18E
Radlett, Eng., U.K.	235	51.42N	0.20W
Radnor, Pa., U.S.	229b	40.02N	75.21W
Radom, Pol. (rä'dôm)	147	51.24N	21.11E
Radomir, Bul. (rä'dō-mēr)	161	42.33N	22.58E
Radomsko, Pol. (rä-dôm'skô)	147	51.04N	19.27E
Radomyshl, Ukr. (rä-dô-mēsh''l)	167	50.30N	29.13E
Radul', Ukr. (rá'dōōl)	163	51.52N	30.46E
Radviliškis, Lith. (räd'vē-lēsh'kēs)	153	55.49N	23.31E
Radwah, Jabal, mtn., Sau. Ar.	182	24.44N	38.14E
Radzyń Podlaski, Pol. (räd'zēn-y' pŭd-lä'skĭ)	155	51.49N	22.40E
Raeford, N.C., U.S. (rā'fērd)	115	34.57N	79.15W
Raesfeld, Ger. (răz'fĕld)	157c	51.46N	6.50E
Raeside, l., Austl. (rā'sīd)	202	29.20S	122.30E
Rae Strait, strt., Can. (rā)	84	68.40N	95.03W
Rafaela, Arg. (rä-fä-å'lä)	132	31.15S	61.21W
Rafael Castillo, Arg.	233d	34.42S	58.37W
Rafah, Pak. (rä'fä)	181a	31.14N	34.12E
Rafsanjān, Iran	182	30.45N	56.30E
Raft, r., Id., U.S. (răft)	105	42.20N	113.17W
Ragay, Phil. (rä-gī')	197a	13.49N	122.45E
Ragay Gulf, b., Phil.	197a	13.44N	122.38E
Ragunda, Swe. (rä-gŏn'dä)	152	63.07N	16.24E
Ragusa, Italy (rä-gōō'sä)	148	36.58N	14.41E
Rahm, neigh., Ger.	236	51.21N	6.47E
Rahnsdorf, neigh., Ger.	238a	52.26N	13.42E
Rahway, N.J., U.S. (rô'wā)	100a	40.37N	74.16W
Rāichūr, India (rä'ē-chōōr')	183	16.23N	77.18E
Raigarh, India (rī'gŭr)	183	21.57N	83.32E
Rainbow Bridge National Monument, rec., Ut., U.S. (rān'bō)	109	37.05N	111.00W
Rainbow City, Pan.	116a	9.20N	79.53W
Rainford, Eng., U.K.	237a	53.30N	2.48W
Rainhill, Eng., U.K.	237a	53.26N	2.46W
Rainhill Stoops, Eng., U.K.	237a	53.24N	2.45W
Rainier, Or., U.S.	106c	46.05N	122.56W
Rainier, Mount, mtn., Wa., U.S. (rā-nēr')	96	46.52N	121.46W
Rainy, r., N.A.	97	48.50N	94.41W
Rainy Lake, l., N.A. (rān'ē)	85	48.43N	94.29W
Rainy River, Can.	85	48.43N	94.29W
Raipur, India (rä'jŭ-bōō-rē')	186	21.25N	81.37E
Raisin, r., Mi., U.S. (rā'zĭn)	98	42.00N	83.35W
Raitan, N.J., U.S. (rā-tăn)	100a	40.34N	74.40W
Rājahmundry, India (räj-ŭ-mŭn'drē)	183	17.03N	81.51E
Rajang, r., Malay.	196	2.10N	113.30E
Rājapālaiyam, India	187	9.30N	77.33E
Rājasthān, state, India (rä'jŭs-tän)	183	26.00N	72.00E
Rājkot, India (räj'kŏt)	183	22.20N	70.48E
Rājpur, India	186a	22.24N	88.25E
Rājpur, neigh., India	240d	28.41N	77.12E
Rājshāhi, Bngl.	183	24.26S	88.39E
Rakhiv, Ukr.	155	48.02N	24.13E
Rakh'oya, Russia (räk'yå)	172c	60.06N	30.50E
Rakitnoye, Russia (rå-kēt'nŏ-yĕ)	167	50.51N	35.53E
Rákoscsaba, neigh., Hung.	239g	47.29N	19.17E
Rákoshegy, neigh., Hung.	239g	47.28N	19.14E
Rákoskeresztúr, neigh., Hung.	239g	47.29N	19.15E
Rákosliget, neigh., Hung.	239g	47.30N	19.16E
Rákospalota, neigh., Hung.	239g	47.34N	19.08E
Rákosszentmihály, neigh., Hung.	239g	47.32N	19.11E
Rakovník, Czech Rep.	154	50.07N	13.45E
Rakvere, Est. (råk'vĕ-rĕ)	166	59.22N	26.14E
Raleigh, N.C., U.S.	97	35.45N	78.39W
Ram, r., Can.	87	52.10N	115.05W
Rama, Nic. (rä'mä)	121	12.11N	84.14W
Ramallo, Arg. (rä-mä'l-yō)	129c	33.28S	60.02W
Ramanāthapuram, India	187	9.13N	78.52E
Rambouillet, Fr. (räN-bōō-yĕ')	156	48.39N	1.49E
Rame Head, c., S. Afr.	213c	31.48S	29.22E
Ramenka, neigh., Russia	239b	55.41N	37.30E
Ramenskoye, Russia (rå'mĕn-skŏ-yĕ)	162	55.34N	38.15E
Ramlat as Sab'atayn, reg., Asia	182	16.08N	45.15E
Ramm, Jabal, mtn., Jord.	181a	29.37N	35.32E
Râmnicu Sărat, Rom.	149	45.24N	27.06E
Râmnicu Vâlcea, Rom.	161	45.07N	24.22E
Ramos, Mex. (rä'mōs)	118	22.46N	101.52W
Ramos, r., Nig.	215	5.10N	5.40E
Ramos Arizpe, Mex. (ä-rēz'pā)	112	25.33N	100.57W
Rampart, Ak., U.S. (răm'pärt)	95	65.28N	150.18W
Rampo Mountains, mts., N.J., U.S. (răm'pō)	100a	41.06N	72.12W
Rāmpur, India (räm'pōōr)	183	28.53N	79.03E
Ramree Island, i., Myanmar (räm'rē')	196	19.01N	93.23E
Ramsayville, Can. (răm'zē vĭl)	83c	45.23N	75.34W
Ramsbottom, Eng., U.K. (rămz'bŏt-ŭm)	144a	53.39N	2.20W
Ramsden Heath, Eng., U.K.	235	51.38N	0.28E
Ramsey, I. of Man (răm'zē)	150	54.20N	4.25W
Ramsey, N.J., U.S.	100a	41.03N	74.09W
Ramsey Lake, l., Can.	90	47.15N	82.16W
Ramsgate, Austl.	243a	33.59S	151.08E
Ramsgate, Eng., U.K. (rămz''gāt)	151	51.19N	1.20E
Ramu, r., Pap. N. Gui. (rä'mōō)	197	5.35S	145.16E
Rancagua, Chile (rän-kä'gwä)	132	34.10S	70.43W
Rance, r., Fr. (räNs)	156	48.17N	2.30W
Rānchī, India	183	23.21N	85.20E
Ranchleigh, Md., U.S.	229c	39.22N	76.40W
Rancho Boyeros, Cuba (rä'n-chô-bô-yĕ'rôs)	123a	23.00N	82.23W
Rancho Palos Verdes, Ca., U.S.	232	33.45N	118.24W
Randallstown, Md., U.S. (răn'dălz-toun)	100e	39.22N	76.48W
Randburg, S. Afr.	244b	26.06S	27.59E
Randers, Den. (rän'ĕrs)	146	56.28N	10.03E
Randfontein, S. Afr. (ränt'fŏn-tān)	213b	26.10S	27.42E
Randleman, N.C., U.S. (răn'd'l-măn)	115	35.49N	79.50W
Randolph, Ma., U.S. (răn'dôlf)	93a	42.10N	71.03W
Randolph, Ne., U.S.	102	42.22N	97.22W
Randolph, Vt., U.S.	99	43.55N	72.40W
Random Island, i., Can. (răn'dŭm)	93	48.12N	53.25W
Randsfjorden, Nor.	152	60.35N	10.10E
Randwick, Austl.	201b	33.55S	151.15E
Ranérou, Sen.	214	15.18N	13.58W
Rangeley, Me., U.S. (rānj'lē)	92	44.56N	70.38W
Rangeley, l., Me., U.S.	92	45.00N	70.25W
Ranger, Tx., U.S. (rān'jēr)	96	32.26N	98.41W
Rangia, India	186	26.32N	91.39E
Rangoon (Yangon), Myanmar (răŋ-gōōn')	183	16.46N	96.09E
Rangpur, Bngl. (rŭng'pōōr)	183	25.48N	89.19E
Rangsang, i., Indon. (räng'säng')	181b	0.53N	103.05E
Rangsdorf, Ger. (rängs'dōrf)	145b	52.17N	13.25E
Ranholas, Port.	238d	38.47N	9.22W
Rānīganj, India (rä-nē-gŭnj')	186	23.40N	87.08E
Rankin, Pa., U.S.	230b	40.25N	79.53W
Rankin Inlet, b., Can. (răŋ'kĕn)	85	62.45N	94.27W
Ranova, r., Russia (rä'nô-vå)	162	53.55N	40.03E
Rantau, Malay.	181b	2.35N	101.58E
Rantekombola, Bulu, mtn., Indon.	196	3.22S	119.50E
Rantoul, Il., U.S. (răn-tōōl')	98	40.25N	88.05W
Raoyang, China (rou-yäŋ)	190	38.16N	115.45E
Rapallo, Italy (rä-päl'lō)	160	44.21N	9.14E
Rapel, r., Chile (rä-pål')	129b	34.05S	71.30W
Rapid, r., Mn., U.S. (răp'ĭd)	103	48.21N	94.50W
Rapid City, S.D., U.S.	96	44.06N	103.14W
Rapla, Est. (räp'lå)	153	59.02N	24.46E
Rappahannock, r., Va., U.S. (răp'å-hăn'ŭk)	99	38.20N	75.25W
Raquette, l., N.Y., U.S. (răk'ĕt)	99	43.50N	74.35W
Raritan, r., N.J., U.S. (răr'ĭ-tăn)	100a	40.32N	74.27W
Rarotonga, Cook Is. (rä'rô-tôŋ'gå)	2	20.40S	163.00W
Ra's an Naqb, Jord.	181a	30.00N	35.29E
Raşcov, Mol.	163	47.55N	28.51E
Ras Dashen Terara, mtn., Eth. (räs dä-shän')	211	12.49N	38.14E
Raseiniai, Lith. (rä-syā'nyĭ)	153	55.23N	23.04E
Rashayya, Leb.	181a	33.30N	35.50E
Rashīd, Egypt (rå-shēd') (rô-zĕt'å)	184	31.22N	30.25E
Rashīd, Masabb, mth., Egypt	218b	31.30N	29.58E
Rashkina, Russia (råsh'kĭ-nå)	172a	59.57N	61.30E
Rasht, Iran	182	37.13N	49.45E
Raška, Yugo. (räsh'kå)	161	43.16N	20.40E
Rasskazovo, Russia (räs-kä'sô-vô)	167	52.40N	41.40E
Rastatt, Ger. (rä-shtät)	154	48.51N	8.12E
Rastes, Russia (rås'tĕs)	172a	59.24N	58.49E
Rastunovo, Russia (rås-tōō'nô-vô)	172b	55.15N	37.50E
Ratangarh, India (rŭ-tŭn'gŭr)	186	28.10N	74.30E
Ratcliff, Tx., U.S. (răt'klĭf)	113	31.22N	95.09W
Rath, neigh., Ger.	236	51.17N	6.49E
Rathenow, Ger. (rä'tĕ-nō)	154	52.36N	12.20E
Rathlin Island, i., N. Ire., U.K. (răth-lĭn)	150	55.18N	6.13W
Rathmecke, Ger.	236	51.15N	7.38E
Ratingen, Ger. (rä'tēn-gĕn)	157c	51.18N	6.51E
Rat Islands, is., Ak., U.S. (răt)	95a	51.35N	176.48E
Ratlām, India	186	23.19N	75.05E
Ratnāgiri, India	187	17.04N	73.24E
Raton, N.M., U.S. (rå-tōn')	96	36.52N	104.26W
Rattlesnake Creek, r., Or., U.S. (răt''l snāk)	104	42.38N	117.39W
Rättvik, Swe. (rĕt'vēk)	152	60.54N	15.07E
Rauch, Arg. (rå'ŏŏch)	132	36.47S	59.05W
Raufoss, Nor. (rou'fôs)	152	60.44N	10.30E
Raúl Soares, Braz. (rä-ōō'l-sôä'rĕs)	129a	20.05S	42.28W
Rauma, Fin. (rä'ŏ-må)	146	61.07N	21.31E
Rauna, Lat. (rä'ŏŏ-nå)	153	57.21N	25.31E
Raurkela, India	183	22.15N	84.53E
Rautalampi, Fin. (rä'ōō-tē-läm'pō)	153	62.39N	26.25E
Rava-Rus'ka, Ukr.	155	50.14N	23.40E
Ravenna, Italy (rä-vĕn'nä)	148	44.27N	12.13E
Ravenna, Ne., U.S. (rå-vĕn'å)	102	41.20N	98.50W
Ravenna, Oh., U.S.	98	41.10N	81.20W
Ravensburg, Ger. (rä'vĕns-bōōrgh)	154	47.48N	9.35E
Ravensdale, Wa., U.S. (rā'vĕnz-dāl)	106a	47.22N	121.58W
Ravensthorpe, Austl. (rā'vĕns-thôrp)	202	33.30S	120.20E
Ravenswood, S. Afr.	244b	26.11S	28.15E
Ravenswood, W.V., U.S. (rā'vĕnz-wŏŏd)	98	38.55N	81.50W
Ravensworth, Va., U.S.	229d	38.48N	77.13W
Ravenwood, Va., U.S.	229d	38.52N	77.09W
Rāwalpindi, Pak. (rä-wŭl-pēn'dē)	183	33.40N	73.10E
Rawa Mazowiecka, Pol.	155	51.46N	20.17E
Rawāndūz, Iraq	182	36.37N	44.30E
Rawicz, Pol. (rä'vĕch)	154	51.36N	16.51E
Rawlina, Austl. (rôr-lēnå)	202	31.13S	125.45E
Rawlins, Wy., U.S. (rô'lĭnz)	96	41.46N	107.15W
Rawson, Arg.	129c	34.36S	60.03W
Rawson, Arg. (rô'sŭn)	132	43.16S	65.09W
Rawtenstall, Eng., U.K. (rô'tĕn-stôl)	144a	53.42N	2.17W
Ray, Cape, c., Can. (rā)	85a	47.40N	59.18W
Raya, Bukit, mtn., Indon.	196	0.45S	112.11E
Raychikinsk, Russia (rī'chĭ-kēnsk)	171	49.52N	129.17E
Rayleigh, Eng., U.K. (rā'lē)	144b	51.35N	0.36E
Raymond, Can. (rā'mŭnd)	87	49.27N	112.39W
Raymond, Wa., U.S.	104	46.41N	123.42W
Raymondville, Tx., U.S. (rā'mŭnd-vĭl)	111	26.30N	97.46W
Ray Mountains, mts., Ak., U.S.	95a	65.40N	151.45W
Rayne, La., U.S. (rān)	113	30.12N	92.15W
Rayón, Mex. (rä-yōn')	118	21.49N	99.39W
Rayton, S. Afr. (rā'tŭn)	213b	25.45S	28.33E
Raytown, Mo., U.S. (rā'toun)	107f	39.01N	94.48W
Rayville, La., U.S. (rā-vĭl)	113	32.28N	91.46W
Raz, Pointe du, c., Fr. (pwänt dü rä)	147	48.02N	4.43W
Razdan, Arm.	168	40.30N	44.46E
Razdol'noye, Russia (räz-dôl'nô-yĕ)	194	43.38N	131.58E
Razgrad, Bul.	149	43.32N	26.32E
Razlog, Bul. (räz'lôk)	161	41.54N	23.32E
Razorback Mountain, mtn., Can. (rā'zēr-băk)	86	51.35N	124.42W

PLACE (Pronunciation)	PAGE	Lat. °'	Long. °'
Rea, r., Eng., U.K. (rē)	144a	52.25N	2.31W
Reaburn, Can. (rā'bûrn)	83f	50.06N	97.53W
Reading, Eng., U.K. (rĕd'ĭng)	147	51.25N	0.58W
Reading, Ma., U.S.	93a	42.32N	71.07W
Reading, Mi., U.S.	98	41.45N	84.45W
Reading, Oh., U.S.	101f	39.14N	84.26W
Reading, Pa., U.S.	97	40.20N	75.55W
Readville, neigh., Ma., U.S.	227a	42.14N	71.08W
Realengo, Braz. (rĕ-ä-län-gô)	129a	23.50S	43.25W
Real Felipe, Castillo, hist., Peru	233c	12.04S	77.09W
Rebel Hill, Pa., U.S.	229b	40.04N	75.20W
Rebiana, Libya	211	24.10N	22.03E
Rebun, i., Japan (rē'bo͞on)	194	45.25N	140.54E
Recanati, Italy (rā-kä-nä'tē)	160	43.25N	13.35E
Recherche, Archipelago of the, is., Austl. (rē-shârsh')	202	34.17S	122.30E
Rechitsa, Bela. (ryĕ'chêt-så)	167	52.22N	30.24E
Recife, Braz. (rå-sē'fĕ)	131	8.09S	34.59W
Recife, Kapp, c., S. Afr. (rå-sē'fĕ)	213c	34.03S	25.43E
Recklinghausen, Ger. (rĕk'lĭng-hou-zĕn)	157c	51.36N	7.13E
Recklinghausen Süd, neigh., Ger.	236	51.34N	7.13E
Reconquista, Arg. (rā-kôn-kēs'tä)	132	29.01S	59.41W
Reconquista, r., Arg.	233d	34.39S	58.45W
Rector, Ar., U.S. (rĕk'tẽr)	111	36.16N	90.21W
Red, r., Asia	196	21.00N	103.00E
Red, r., N.A. (rĕd)	96	48.00N	97.00W
Red, r., U.S.	97	31.40N	92.55W
Red, r., Tn., U.S.	114	36.35N	86.55W
Red, North Fork, r., U.S.	110	35.20N	100.08W
Red, Prairie Dog Town Fork, r., U.S. (prā'rĭ)	110	34.54N	101.31W
Red, Salt Fork, r., U.S.	110	35.04N	100.31W
Redan, Ga., U.S. (rê-dăn') (rĕd'ăn)	100c	33.44N	84.09W
Red Bank, N.J., U.S. (băngk)	100a	40.21N	74.06W
Red Bank National Park, N.J., U.S.	229b	39.52N	75.10W
Red Bluff Reservoir, res., Tx., U.S.	112	32.03N	103.52W
Redbridge, neigh., Eng., U.K.	235	51.34N	0.05E
Redby, Mn., Mn., U.S. (rĕd'bē)	103	47.52N	94.55W
Red Cedar, r., Wi., U.S. (sē'dẽr)	103	45.03N	91.48W
Redcliff, Can. (rĕd'clĭf)	84	50.05N	110.47W
Redcliffe, Austl. (rĕd'clĭf)	204	27.20S	153.12E
Red Cliff Indian Reservation, I.R., Wi., U.S.	103	46.48N	91.22W
Red Cloud, Ne., U.S. (kloud)	110	40.06N	98.32W
Red Deer, Can. (dēr)	84	52.16N	113.48W
Red Deer, r., Can.	84	51.00N	111.00W
Red Deer, r., Can.	89	52.55N	102.10W
Red Deer Lake, l., Can.	89	52.58N	101.28W
Reddick, Il., U.S. (rĕd'dĭk)	101a	41.06N	88.16W
Redding, Ca., U.S. (rĕd'ĭng)	104	40.36N	122.25W
Reddish, Eng., U.K.	237b	53.26N	2.09W
Redenção da Serra, Braz. (rĕ-dĕn-souN-dä-sĕ'r-rä)	129a	23.17S	45.31W
Redfield, S.D., U.S. (rĕd'fēld)	102	44.53N	98.30W
Red Fish Bar, Tx., U.S.	113a	29.29N	94.53W
Redford, neigh., Mi., U.S.	230c	42.25N	83.16W
Redford Township, Mi., U.S.	230c	42.25N	83.16W
Red Hill, Ca., U.S.	232	33.45N	117.48W
Red Indian Lake, l., Can. (ĭn'dĭ-ăn)	85a	48.40N	56.50W
Red Lake, Can. (lāk)	85	51.02N	93.49W
Red Lake, r., Mn., U.S.	102	48.02N	96.04W
Red Lake Falls, Mn., U.S. (lāk fôls)	102	47.52N	96.17W
Red Lake Indian Reservation, I.R., Mn., U.S.	102	48.09N	95.55W
Redlands, Ca., U.S. (rĕd'lăndz)	107a	34.04N	117.11W
Red Lion, Pa., U.S. (lī'ŭn)	99	39.55N	76.30W
Red Lodge, Mt., U.S.	105	45.13N	107.16W
Redmond, Wa., U.S. (rĕd'mŭnd)	106a	47.40N	122.07W
Rednitz, r., Ger. (rĕd'nētz)	154	49.10N	11.00E
Red Oak, Ia., U.S. (ōk)	102	41.00N	95.12W
Redon, Fr. (rē-dôN')	156	47.42N	2.03W
Redonda, Isla, i., Braz. (ē's-lä-rĕ-dô'n-dä)	132b	23.05S	43.11W
Redonda Island, i., Antig. (rĕ-dŏn'dȧ)	121b	16.55N	62.28W
Redondela, Spain (rā-dhôn-dā'lä)	158	42.16N	8.34W
Redondo, Port. (rå-dôn'dò)	158	38.40N	7.32W
Redondo, Wa., U.S. (rē-dŏn'dō)	106a	47.21N	122.19W
Redondo Beach, Ca., U.S.	107a	33.50N	118.23W
Red Pass, Can. (pȧs)	87	52.59N	118.59W
Red Rock, r., Mt., U.S.	105	44.54N	112.44W
Red Sea, sea	182	23.15N	37.00E
Redstone, Can. (rĕd'stōn)	86	52.08N	123.42W
Red Sucker Lake, l., Can. (sŭk'ẽr)	89	54.09N	93.40W
Redwater, r., Mt., U.S.	105	47.37N	105.25W
Red Willow Creek, r., Ne., U.S.	110	40.34N	100.48W
Red Wing, Mn., U.S.	103	44.34N	92.35W
Redwood City, Ca., U.S. (rĕd' wo͝od)	106b	37.29N	122.13W
Redwood Falls, Mn., U.S.	102	44.32N	95.06W
Redwood Valley, Ca., U.S.	108	39.15N	123.12W
Ree, Lough, l., Ire. (lŏK'rē')	146	53.30N	7.45W
Reed City, Mi., U.S. (rēd)	98	43.50N	85.35W
Reed Lake, l., Can.	89	54.37N	100.30W
Reedley, Ca., U.S. (rēd'lê)	108	36.37N	119.27W
Reedsburg, Wi., U.S. (rēdz'bûrg)	103	43.32N	90.01W
Reedsport, Or., U.S. (rēdz'pôrt)	104	43.42N	124.08W
Reelfoot Lake, res., Tn., U.S. (rēl'fo͝ot)	114	36.18N	89.20W
Rees, Ger. (rĕz)	157c	51.46N	6.25E
Reeves, Mount, mtn., Austl. (rēv's)	204	33.50S	149.56E
Reform, Al., U.S. (rē-fôrm')	114	33.23N	88.00W
Refugio, Tx., U.S. (rå-fo͞o'hyô) (rĕ-fū'jō)	113	28.18N	97.15W
Rega, r., Pol. (rĕ-gä)	154	53.48N	15.30E
Regen, r., Ger. (rā'ghĕn)	154	49.09N	12.21E
Regensburg, Ger. (rā'ghĕns-bòrgh)	147	49.02N	12.06E
Regents Park, Austl.	243a	33.53S	151.02E
Regent's Park, pt. of i., Eng., U.K.	235	51.32N	0.09W

PLACE (Pronunciation)	PAGE	Lat. °'	Long. °'
Reggio, La., U.S. (rĕg'jĭ-ō)	100d	29.50N	89.46W
Reggio di Calabria, Italy (rĕ'jô dē kä-lä'brê-ä)	149	38.07N	15.42E
Reggio nell' Emilia, Italy	148	44.43N	10.34E
Reghin, Rom. (rå-gēn')	155	46.47N	24.44E
Regina, Can. (rê-jī'nȧ)	88	50.25N	104.39W
Regla, Cuba (răg'lä)	122	23.08N	82.20W
Regnitz, r., Ger. (rĕg'nētz)	154	49.50N	10.55E
Rego Park, neigh., N.Y., U.S.	228	40.44N	73.52W
Reguengos de Monsaraz, Port.	158	38.26N	7.30W
Rehoboth, Nmb.	212	23.10S	17.15E
Reḥovot, Isr.	181a	31.53N	34.49E
Reichenbach, Ger. (rī'kĕn-bäk)	154	50.36N	12.18E
Reidsville, N.C., U.S. (rēdz'vĭl)	115	36.20N	79.37W
Reigate, Eng., U.K. (rī'gāt)	150	51.12N	0.12W
Reims, Fr. (răNs)	142	49.16N	4.00E
Reina Adelaida, Archipiélago, is., Chile	132	52.00S	74.15W
Reinbeck, Ia., U.S. (rīn'bĕk)	103	42.22N	92.34W
Reindeer, l., Can. (rān'dēr)	84	57.36N	101.23W
Reindeer, r., Can.	88	55.45N	103.30W
Reindeer Island, i., Can.	89	52.25N	98.00W
Reinosa, Spain (rå-ê-nō'sä)	158	43.01N	4.08W
Reisholz, neigh., Ger.	236	51.11N	6.52E
Reistertown, Md., U.S. (rēs'tẽr-toun)	100e	39.28N	76.50W
Reitz, S. Afr.	218d	27.48S	28.25E
Rema, Jabal, mtn., Yemen	182	14.13N	44.38E
Rembau, Malay.	181b	2.36N	102.06E
Remedios, Col. (rĕ-mĕ'dyōs)	130a	7.03N	74.42W
Remedios, Cuba (rā-mā'dhē-ōs)	122	22.30N	79.35W
Remedios, Pan. (rĕ-mĕ'dyōs)	121	8.14N	81.46W
Remedios de Escalada, neigh., Arg.	233d	34.43S	58.23W
Remiremont, Fr. (rẽ-mēr-môN')	157	48.01N	6.35E
Rempang, i., Indon.	181b	0.51N	104.04E
Remscheid, Ger. (rĕm'shīt)	157c	51.10N	7.11E
Rena, Nor.	152	61.08N	11.17E
Renca, Chile	234b	33.24S	70.44W
Renca, Cerro, mtn., Chile	234b	33.23S	70.43W
Rendova, i., Sol.Is. (rĕn'dô-vȧ)	203	8.38S	156.26E
Rendsburg, Ger. (rĕnts'bòrgh)	154	54.19N	9.39E
Renfrew, Can. (rĕn'fro͞o)	85	45.30N	76.30W
Rengam, Malay. (rĕn'gäm')	181b	1.53N	103.24E
Rengo, Chile (rĕn'gō)	129b	34.22S	70.50W
Reni, Ukr. (ran')	163	45.26N	28.18E
Renmark, Austl. (rĕn'märk)	202	34.10S	140.50E
Rennel, i., Sol.Is. (rĕn-nĕl')	203	11.50S	160.38E
Rennes, Fr. (rĕn)	142	48.07N	1.02W
Reno, Nv., U.S. (rē'nō)	96	39.32N	119.49W
Reno, r., Italy (rā'nô)	160	44.10N	10.55E
Renovo, Pa., U.S. (rê-nō'vō)	99	41.20N	77.50W
Renqiu, China (rŭn-chyō)	190	38.44N	116.05E
Rensselaer, In., U.S. (rĕn'sē-lâr)	98	41.00N	87.10W
Rensselaer, N.Y., U.S. (rĕn'sē-lâr)	99	42.40N	73.45W
Rentchler, Il., U.S. (rĕnt'chlẽr)	107e	38.30N	89.52W
Renton, Wa., U.S. (rĕn'tŭn)	106a	47.29N	122.13W
Repentigny, Can.	83a	45.47N	73.26W
Republic, Al., U.S. (rê-pŭb'lĭk)	100h	33.37N	86.54W
Republic, Wa., U.S.	104	48.38N	118.44W
Republican, r., U.S.	96	40.15N	100.00W
Republican, South Fork, r., Co., U.S. (rê-pŭb'lĭ-kăn)	110	39.35N	102.28W
Repulse Bay, b., Austl. (rê-pŭls')	203	20.56S	149.22E
Requena, Spain (rå-kā'nä)	148	39.29N	1.03W
Reseda, neigh., Ca., U.S.	232	34.12N	118.31W
Resende, Braz. (rĕ-sĕ'n-dĕ)	129a	22.30S	44.26W
Resende Costa, Braz. (kôs-tä)	129a	20.55S	44.12W
Reservoir, Austl.	243b	37.43S	145.00E
Reshetylivka, Ukr.	163	49.34N	34.04E
Resistencia, Arg. (rā-sês-tĕn'syä)	132	27.24S	58.54W
Reşiţa, Rom. (rå'shê-tȧ)	161	45.18N	21.56E
Resolute, Can. (rĕz-ô-lūt')	82	74.41N	95.00W
Resolution, i., Can. (rĕz-ô-lū'shŭn)	85	61.30N	63.58W
Resolution Island, i., N.Z. (rĕz-ŏl-ûshûn)	203a	45.43S	166.20E
Resse, neigh., Ger.	236	51.34N	7.07E
Restigouche, r., Can.	92	47.35N	67.35W
Restrepo, Col. (rĕs-trĕ'pô)	130a	3.49N	76.31W
Restrepo, Col.	130a	4.16N	73.32W
Retalhuleu, Guat. (rā-täl-o͞o-lān')	120	14.31N	91.41W
Rethel, Fr. (r-tĕl')	156	49.34N	4.20E
Réthimnon, Grc.	160a	35.21N	24.30E
Retie, Bel.	145a	51.16N	5.08E
Retiro, Parque del, rec., Spain	238b	40.25N	3.41W
Retsil, Wa., U.S. (rĕt'sĭl)	106a	47.33N	122.37W
Reunion, dep., Afr. (rā-ü-nyôn')	3	21.06S	55.36E
Reus, Spain (rā'o͞os)	148	41.08N	1.05E
Reutlingen, Ger. (roit'lĭng-ĕn)	154	48.29N	9.14E
Reutov, Russia (rĕ-o͞o'ôf)	172b	55.45N	37.52E
Revda, Russia (ryâv'dȧ)	172a	56.48N	59.57E
Revelstoke, Can. (rĕv'ĕl-stōk)	84	51.00N	118.12W
Reventazón, Río, r., C.R. (rå-vĕn-tä-zōn')	121	10.10N	83.30W
Revere, Ma., U.S. (rê-vēr')	93a	42.24N	71.01W
Revesby, Austl.	243a	33.57S	151.01E
Revillagigedo, Islas, is., Mex. (ē's-läs-rĕ-vēl-yä-hĕ'gĕ-dô)	116	18.45N	111.00W
Revillagigedo Chan, Ak., U.S. (rĕ-vĭl'ȧ-gĭ-gē'dō)	86	55.10N	131.13W
Revillagigedo Island, i., Ak., U.S.	86	55.35N	131.23W
Revin, Fr. (rĕ-văN)	156	49.56N	4.34E
Rewa, India (rā'wä)	183	24.41N	81.11E
Rewāri, India	186	28.19N	76.39E
Rexburg, Id., U.S. (rĕks'bûrg)	105	43.50N	111.48W
Rey, Iran	185	35.35N	51.25E
Rey, l., Mex. (rā)	112	27.00N	103.33W
Rey, Isla del, i., Pan. (ē's-lä-dĕl-rā'ē)	121	8.20N	78.40W
Reyes, Bol. (rā'yĕs)	130	14.19S	67.16W

PLACE (Pronunciation)	PAGE	Lat. °'	Long. °'
Reyes, Point, c., Ca., U.S.	108	38.00N	123.00W
Reykjanes, c., Ice. (rā'kyȧ-nĕs)	142	63.37N	24.33W
Reykjavík, Ice. (rā'kyȧ-vĕk)	142	64.09N	21.39W
Reynosa, Mex. (rā-ê-nō'sä)	112	26.05N	98.21W
Rēzekne, Lat. (rā'zĕk-nĕ)	166	56.31N	27.19E
Rezh, Russia (rĕzh')	172a	57.22N	61.23E
Rezina, Mol. (ryĕzh'ĕ-nĭ)	163	47.44N	28.56E
Rhaetian Alps, mts., Eur.	154	46.30N	10.00E
Rhaetien Alps, mts., Eur.	160	46.22N	10.33E
Rheinberg, Ger. (rīn'bĕrgh)	157c	51.33N	6.37E
Rheine, Ger. (rī'nĕ)	154	52.16N	7.26E
Rheinen, Ger.	236	51.27N	7.38E
Rheinhausen, Ger.	236	51.24N	6.44E
Rhein-Herne-Kanal, can., Ger.	236	51.27N	6.47E
Rheinkamp, Ger.	157c	51.30N	6.37E
Rheinland-Pfalz (Rhineland-Palatinate), hist. reg., Ger.	154	50.05N	6.40E
Rheydt, Ger. (rĕ'yt)	157c	51.10N	6.28E
Rhin, r., Ger. (rēn)	145b	52.52N	12.49E
Rhine, r., Eur.	142	50.34N	7.21E
Rhinelander, Wi., U.S. (rīn'lăn-dẽr)	103	45.39N	89.25W
Rhin Kanal, can., Ger. (rēn kä-näl')	145b	52.47N	12.40E
Rhiou, r., Alg.	159	35.45N	1.18E
Rho, Italy	238c	45.32N	9.02E
Rhode Island, state, U.S. (rōd ī'lănd)	97	41.35N	71.40W
Rhode Island, i., R.I., U.S.	100b	41.31N	71.14W
Rhodes, Austl.	243a	33.50S	151.05E
Rhodes, S. Afr. (rōdz)	213c	30.48S	27.56E
Rhodes, Eng., U.K.	237b	53.33N	2.14W
Rhodes *see* Ródhos, i., Grc.	142	36.00N	28.29E
Rhodesia *see* Zimbabwe, nation, Afr.	212	17.50S	29.30E
Rhodon, Fr.	237c	48.43N	2.04E
Rhodope Mountains, mts., Eur. (rô'dô-pĕ)	142	42.00N	24.08E
Rhondda, Wales, U.K. (rŏn'dhȧ)	150	51.40N	3.40W
Rhône, r., Fr. (rōn)	142	44.30N	4.45E
Rhoon, Neth.	145a	51.52N	4.24E
Rhum, i., Scot., U.K. (rŭm)	150	57.00N	6.20W
Riachão, Braz. (rē-ä-chouN')	131	7.15S	46.30W
Rialto, Ca., U.S. (rê-äl'tō)	107a	34.06N	117.23W
Riau, prov., Indon.	181b	0.56N	101.25E
Riau, Kepulauan, i., Indon.	196	0.30N	104.55E
Riau, Selat, strt., Indon.	181b	0.40N	104.27E
Riaza, r., Spain (rê-ä'thä)	158	41.25N	3.25W
Ribadavia, Spain (rē-bä-dhā'vê-ä)	158	42.18N	8.06W
Ribadeo, Spain (rē-bä-dhā'ō)	158	43.32N	7.05W
Ribadesella, Spain (rē'bä-dā-säl'yä)	158	43.30N	5.02W
Ribe, Den. (rē'bĕ)	152	55.20N	8.45E
Ribeirão Prêto, Braz. (rê-bā-rouN-prĕ'tô)	131	21.11S	47.47W
Ribera, N.M., U.S. (rē-bĕ'rä)	110	35.23N	105.27W
Riberalta, Bol. (rē-bå-räl'tä)	130	11.06S	66.02W
Rib Lake, Wi., U.S. (rĭb lāk)	103	45.20N	90.11W
Rîbniţa, Mol.	163	47.45N	29.02E
Rice, l., Can.	91	44.05N	78.10W
Rice Lake, Wi., U.S.	103	45.30N	91.44W
Rice Lake, l., Mn., U.S.	107g	45.10N	93.09W
Richards Island, i., Can. (rĭch'ẽrds)	95	69.45N	135.30W
Richards Landing, Can. (lănd'ĭng)	107k	46.18N	84.02W
Richardson, Tx., U.S. (rĭch'ẽrd-sŭn)	107c	32.56N	96.44W
Richardson, Wa., U.S.	106a	48.27N	122.54W
Richardson Mountains, mts., Can.	84	66.58N	136.19W
Richardson Mountains, mts., N.Z.	205	44.50S	168.30E
Richardson Park, De., U.S. (pärk)	99	39.45N	75.35W
Richelieu, r., Can. (rēsh'lyû')	91	45.05N	73.25W
Richfield, Mn., U.S.	107g	44.53N	93.17W
Richfield, Oh., U.S.	101d	41.14N	81.38W
Richfield, Ut., U.S.	109	38.45N	112.05W
Richford, Vt., U.S. (rĭch'fẽrd)	99	45.00N	72.35W
Rich Hill, Mo., U.S. (rĭch hĭl)	111	38.05N	94.21W
Richibucto, Can. (rĭ-chĭ-bŭk'tō)	85	46.41N	64.52W
Richland, Ga., U.S. (rĭch'lănd)	114	32.05N	84.40W
Richland, Wa., U.S.	104	46.17N	119.19W
Richland Center, Wi., U.S. (sĕn'tẽr)	103	43.20N	90.25W
Richmond, Austl.	201b	33.36S	150.45E
Richmond, Austl. (rĭch'mŭnd)	203	20.47S	143.14E
Richmond, Austl.	243b	37.49S	145.00E
Richmond, Can.	83c	45.12N	75.49W
Richmond, Can.	91	45.40N	72.07W
Richmond, S. Afr.	213c	29.52S	30.17E
Richmond, Il., U.S.	101a	42.29N	88.18W
Richmond, In., U.S.	98	39.50N	85.00W
Richmond, Ky., U.S.	98	37.45N	84.20W
Richmond, Mo., U.S.	111	39.16N	93.58W
Richmond, Tx., U.S.	113	29.35N	95.45W
Richmond, Ut., U.S.	105	41.55N	111.50W
Richmond, Va., U.S.	97	37.35N	77.30W
Richmond, neigh., Eng., U.K.	235	51.28N	0.18W
Richmond, neigh., N.J., U.S.	229b	39.59N	75.06W
Richmond Beach, Wa., U.S.	106a	47.47N	122.23W
Richmond Heights, Mo., U.S.	107e	38.38N	90.20W
Richmond Heights, Oh., U.S.	229a	41.33N	81.29W
Richmond Highlands, Wa., U.S.	106a	47.46N	122.22W
Richmond Hill, Can. (hĭl)	91	43.53N	79.26W
Richmondtown Restoration, pt. of i., N.Y., U.S.	228	40.34N	74.09W
Richmond Valley, neigh., N.Y., U.S.	228	40.31N	74.13W
Richton, Ms., U.S. (rĭch'tŭn)	114	31.20N	89.54W
Richwood, W.V., U.S. (rĭch'wo͝od)	98	38.10N	80.30W
Ricketts Point, c., Austl.	243b	38.00S	145.02E
Rickmansworth, Eng., U.K.	235	51.39N	0.29W
Ridderkerk, Neth.	145a	51.52N	4.35E
Rideau, r., Can.	83c	45.17N	75.41W
Rideau Lake, l., Can. (rê-dō')	91	44.40N	76.20W
Ridge, Eng., U.K.	235	51.41N	0.15W
Ridgefield, Ct., U.S. (rĭj'fēld)	100a	41.16N	73.30W

ăt; finăl; rāte; senåte; ärm; åsk; sofȧ; fâre; ch-choose; dh-as th in other; bē; êvent; bĕt; recĕnt; cratẽr; g-gō; gh-guttural g; bĭt; ĭ-short neutral; rīde; K-guttural k as ch in German ich;

PRONOUNCING INDEX

Ridgefield-Rohrbeck 339

PLACE (Pronunciation)	PAGE	Lat. °'	Long. °'
Ridgefield, N.J., U.S.	228	40.50N	74.00W
Ridgefield, Wa., U.S.	106c	45.49N	122.40W
Ridgefield Park, N.J., U.S.	228	40.51N	74.01W
Ridgeway, Can. (rĭj′wā)	101c	42.53N	79.02W
Ridgewood, N.J., U.S. (ridj′wood)	100a	40.59N	74.08W
Ridgewood, neigh., N.Y., U.S.	228	40.42N	73.53W
Ridgway, Pa., U.S.	99	41.25N	78.40W
Riding Mountain, mtn., Can. (rīd′ĭng)	89	50.37N	99.37W
Riding Mountain National Park, rec., Can. (rīd′ĭng)	84	50.59N	99.19W
Riding Rocks, is., Bah.	122	25.20N	79.10W
Ridley Park, Pa., U.S.	229b	39.53N	75.19W
Riebeek-Oos, S. Afr.	213c	33.14S	26.09E
Ried, Aus. (rēd)	154	48.13N	13.30E
Riemke, neigh., Ger.	236	51.30N	7.13E
Riesa, Ger. (rē′zȧ)	154	51.17N	13.17E
Rieti, Italy (rê-ā′tē)	148	42.25N	12.51E
Rietvlei, S. Afr.	244b	26.18S	28.03E
Rievleidam, res., S. Afr.	213b	25.52S	28.18E
Riffe Lake, res., Wa., U.S.	104	46.20N	122.10W
Rifle, Co., U.S. (rī′f′l)	109	39.35N	107.50W
Rīga, Lat. (rē′gȧ)	164	56.55N	24.05E
Riga, Gulf of, b., Eur.	166	57.56N	23.05E
Rīgān, Iran	182	28.45N	58.55E
Rigaud, Can. (rê-gō′)	83a	45.29N	74.18W
Rigby, Id., U.S. (rĭg′bê)	105	43.40N	111.55W
Rigeley, W.V., U.S. (rĭj′lê)	99	39.40N	78.45W
Rīgestān, des., Afg.	182	30.53N	64.42E
Rigolet, Can. (rĭg-ō-lā′)	85	54.10N	58.40W
Riihimäki, Fin.	153	60.44N	24.44E
Rijeka, Cro. (rĭ-yĕ′kä)	148	45.22N	14.24E
Rijkevorsel, Bel.	145a	51.21N	4.46E
Rijswijk, Neth.	145a	52.03N	4.19E
Rika, r., Ukr. (rē′kȧ)	155	48.21N	23.37E
Rima, r., Nig.	215	13.30N	5.50E
Rímac, Peru	233c	12.02S	77.03W
Rímac, r., Peru	233c	12.02S	77.09W
Rimavska Sobota, Slvk. (rē′måf-skȧ sô′bô-tȧ)	155	48.25N	20.01E
Rimbo, Swe. (rēm′bô)	152	59.45N	18.22E
Rimini, Italy (rē′mê-nē)	148	44.03N	12.33E
Rimouski, Can. (rê-mōōs′kê)	85	48.27N	68.32W
Rincón de Romos, Mex. (rēn-kōn dā rō-mōs′)	118	22.13N	102.21W
Ringkøbing, Den. (rĭng′kûb-ĭng)	146	56.06N	8.14E
Ringkøbing Fjord, fj., Den.	152	55.55N	8.04E
Ringsted, Den. (rĭng′stĕdh)	152	55.27N	11.49E
Ringvassøya, i., Nor. (rĭng′väs-ûê)	146	69.58N	16.43E
Ringwood, Austl.	201a	37.49S	145.14E
Ringwood North, Austl.	243b	37.48S	145.14E
Rinjani, Gunung, mtn., Indon.	196	8.39S	116.22E
Río Abajo, Pan. (rē′ō-ä-bä′kô)	116a	9.01N	78.30W
Río Balsas, Mex. (rē′ō-bäl-säs)	118	17.59N	99.45W
Riobamba, Ec. (rē′ō-bäm-bä)	130	1.45S	78.37W
Rio Bonito, Braz. (rē′ô bō-nē′tô)	129a	22.44S	42.38W
Rio Branco, Braz. (rē′ô bräŋ′kô)	130	9.57S	67.50W
Río Branco, Ur. (rĭô brănċô)	132	32.33S	53.29W
Rio Casca, Braz. (rē′ō-kȧ′s-kä)	129a	20.15S	42.39W
Río Chico, Ven. (rê′ō chê′kŏ)	131b	10.20N	65.58W
Rio Claro, Braz. (rē′ô klä′rô)	131	22.25S	47.33W
Rio Comprido, neigh., Braz.	234c	22.55S	43.12W
Río Cuarto, Arg. (rē′ō kwär′tō)	132	33.05S	64.15W
Rio das Flores, Braz. (rē′ō-däs-flô-rēs)	129a	22.10S	43.35W
Rio de Janeiro, Braz. (rē′ô dā zhä-nâ′ê-rô)	132b	22.50S	43.20W
Rio de Janeiro, state, Braz.	131	22.27S	42.43W
Río de Jesús, Pan.	121	7.54N	80.59W
Rio de Mouro, Port.	238d	38.46N	9.20W
Río Frío, Mex. (rē′ō-frē′ō)	119a	19.21N	98.40W
Río Gallegos, Arg. (rē′ō gä-lā′gōs)	132	51.43S	69.15W
Rio Grande, Braz. (rē′ō grän′dĕ)	132	31.04S	52.14W
Río Grande, Mex. (rē′ō grän′dā)	118	23.51N	102.59W
Riogrande, Tx., U.S. (rē′ō grăn-dā)	112	26.23N	98.48W
Río Grande, Ven.	234a	10.35N	66.57W
Rio Grande do Norte, state, Braz.	131	5.26S	37.20W
Rio Grande do Sul, state, Braz. (rē′ō grän′dĕ-dô-sōō′l)	132	29.00S	54.00W
Ríohacha, Col. (rē′ō-ä′chä)	130	11.30N	72.54W
Río Hato, Pan. (rê′ō-ä′tô)	121	8.19N	80.11W
Riom, Fr. (rê-ôN′)	156	45.54N	3.08E
Rio Muni, hist. reg., Eq. Gui. (rē′ō mōō′nê)	210	1.47N	8.33E
Ríonegro, Col. (rê′ō-nĕ′grō)	130a	6.09N	75.22W
Río Negro, prov., Arg. (rē′ō nā′grō)	132	40.15S	68.15W
Río Negro, dept., Ur. (rê′ō-nĕ′grō)	129c	32.48S	57.45W
Río Negro, Embalse del, res., Ur.	132	32.45S	55.50W
Rionero, Italy (rē-ō-nâ′rô)	160	40.55N	15.42E
Rioni, r., Geor.	168	42.08N	41.39E
Rio Novo, Braz. (rē′ō-nô′vô)	129a	21.30S	43.08W
Rio Pardo de Minas, Braz. (rē′ō pär′dō-dĕ-mē′näs)	131	15.43S	42.24W
Rio Pombo, Braz. (rē′ō pôm′bä)	129a	21.17S	43.09W
Rio Sorocaba, Represa do, res., Braz.	129a	23.37S	47.19W
Ríosucio, Col. (rē′ō-sōō′syô)	130a	5.25N	75.41W
Río Tercero, Arg. (rê′ō dĕr-sĕ′rô)	132	32.12S	63.59W
Rio Verde, Braz. (vĕr′dĕ)	131	17.47S	50.49W
Rioverde, Mex. (rē′ō-vĕr′dā)	116	21.54N	99.59W
Ripley, Eng., U.K. (rĭp′lê)	144a	53.03N	1.24W
Ripley, Eng., U.K.	235	51.18N	0.29W
Ripley, Ms., U.S.	114	34.44N	88.55W
Ripley, Tn., U.S.	114	35.44N	89.34W
Ripoll, Spain (rê-pōl′′)	159	42.10N	2.10E
Ripon, Wi., U.S. (rĭp′ŏn)	103	43.49N	88.50W
Ripon, i., Austl.	202	20.05S	118.10E
Ripon Falls, wtfl., Ug.	212	0.38N	33.02E

PLACE (Pronunciation)	PAGE	Lat. °'	Long. °'
Risaralda, dept., Col.	130a	5.15N	76.00W
Risdon, Austl. (rĭz′dŭn)	203	42.37S	147.32E
Rishiri, i., Japan (rē-shē′rē)	194	45.10N	141.08E
Rishon le Ziyyon, Isr.	181a	31.57N	34.48E
Rishra, India	186a	22.42N	88.22E
Rising Sun, In., U.S. (rīz′ĭng sŭn)	98	38.55N	84.55W
Risor, Nor. (rēs′ûr)	146	58.44N	9.10E
Ritacuva, Alto, mtn., Col. (ä′l-tô-rē-tä-kōō′vä)	130	6.22N	72.13W
Ritchie, Va., U.S.	229d	38.52N	76.52W
Rithāla, neigh., India	240d	28.43N	77.06E
Rittman, Oh., U.S. (rĭt′năn)	101d	40.58N	81.47W
Ritzville, Wa., U.S. (rĭts′vĭl)	104	47.08N	118.23W
Riva, Dom. Rep. (rē′vä)	123	19.10N	69.55W
Riva, Italy (rē′vä)	160	45.54N	10.49E
Riva, Md., U.S. (rī′vă)	100e	38.57N	76.36W
Rivas, Nic. (rē′väs)	120	11.25N	85.51W
Rive-de-Gier, Fr. (rēv-dē-zhê-ā′)	156	45.32N	4.37E
Rivera, Ur. (rê-vā′rä)	132	30.52S	55.32W
River Cess, Lib. (rĭv′ẽr sĕs)	210	5.46N	9.52W
Riverdale, Il., U.S. (rĭv′ẽr dāl)	101a	41.38N	87.36W
Riverdale, Md., U.S.	229d	38.58N	76.55W
Riverdale, Ut., U.S.	107b	41.11N	112.00W
Riverdale, neigh., N.Y., U.S.	228	40.54N	73.54W
River Edge, N.J., U.S.	228	40.56N	74.02W
River Falls, Al., U.S.	114	31.20N	86.25W
River Falls, Wi., U.S.	103	44.48N	92.38W
River Forest, Il., U.S.	231a	41.53N	87.49W
River Grove, Il., U.S.	231a	41.56N	87.50W
Riverhead, Eng., U.K.	235	51.17N	0.10E
Riverhead, N.Y., U.S. (rĭv′ẽr hĕd)	99	40.55N	72.40W
Riverina, reg., Austl. (rĭv-ẽr-ē′nä)	203	34.55S	144.30E
River Jordan, Can. (jôr′dăn)	106a	48.25N	124.03W
River Oaks, Tx., U.S. (ōkz)	107c	32.47N	97.24W
River Rouge, Mi., U.S. (rōōzh)	101b	42.16N	83.09W
Rivers, Can.	89	50.01N	100.15W
Riverside, Ca., U.S. (rĭv′ẽr-sīd)	96	33.59N	117.21W
Riverside, Il., U.S.	231a	41.50N	87.49W
Riverside, N.J., U.S.	100f	40.02N	74.58W
Rivers Inlet, Can.	86	51.45N	127.15W
Riverstone, Austl.	201b	33.41S	150.52E
Riverton, Va., U.S.	99	39.00N	78.15W
Riverton, Wy., U.S.	105	43.02N	108.24W
Rivesaltes, Fr. (rēv′zält′)	156	42.48N	2.48E
Riviera Beach, Fl., U.S. (rĭv-ĭ-ĕr′ȧ bēch)	115a	26.46N	80.04W
Riviera Beach, Md., U.S.	100e	39.10N	76.32W
Rivière-Beaudette, Can.	83a	45.14N	74.20W
Rivière-du-Loup, Can. (rê-vyâr′ dü lōō′)	85	47.50N	69.32W
Rivière Qui Barre, Can. (rēv-yĕr′ kē-băr)	83g	53.47N	113.51W
Rivière-Trois-Pistoles, Can. (trwä′pês-tôl′)	92	48.07N	69.10W
Rivne, Ukr.	163	48.11N	31.46E
Rivne, Ukr.	167	50.37N	26.17E
Rivne, prov., Ukr.	163	50.55N	27.00E
Riyadh, Sau. Ar.	182	24.31N	46.47E
Rize, Tur. (rē′zĕ)	149	41.00N	40.30E
Rizhao, China (rē-jou)	192	35.27N	119.28E
Rizzuto, Cape, c., Italy (rēt-sōō′tô)	161	38.53N	17.05E
Rjukan, Nor. (ryōō′kän)	146	59.53N	8.30E
Roanne, Fr. (rō-än′)	147	46.02N	4.04E
Roanoke, Al., U.S. (rō′ȧ-nōk)	114	33.08N	85.21W
Roanoke, Va., U.S.	97	37.16N	79.55W
Roanoke, r., U.S.	97	36.17N	77.22W
Roanoke Rapids, N.C., U.S.	115	36.25N	77.40W
Roanoke Rapids Lake, res., N.C., U.S.	115	36.28N	77.37W
Roan Plateau, plat., Co., U.S. (rōn)	109	39.25N	110.00W
Roatan, Hond. (rō-ä-tän′)	120	16.18N	86.33W
Roatán, i., Hond.	120	16.19N	86.46W
Robbeneiland, i., S. Afr.	212a	33.48S	18.22E
Robbins, Il., U.S. (rŏb′ĭnz)	101a	41.39N	87.42W
Robbinsdale, Mn., U.S. (rŏb′ĭnz-dāl)	107g	45.03N	93.22W
Robe, Wa., U.S. (rōb)	106a	48.06N	121.50W
Roberts, Mount, mtn., Austl. (rŏb′ẽrts)	203	28.05S	152.30E
Roberts, Point, c., Wa., U.S. (rŏb′ẽrts)	106d	48.58N	123.05W
Robertsham, neigh., S. Afr.	244b	26.15S	28.00E
Robertson, Lac, l., Can.	93	51.00N	59.10W
Robertsport, Lib. (rŏb′ẽrts-pōrt)	210	6.45N	11.22W
Roberval, Can. (rŏb′ẽr-văl) (rô-bĕr-vȧl′)	85	48.32N	72.15W
Robinson, Can.	93	48.16N	58.50W
Robinson, S. Afr.	244b	26.09S	27.43E
Robinson, Il., U.S. (rŏb′ĭn-sŭn)	98	39.00N	87.45W
Robinvale, Austl. (rŏb-ĭn′vāl)	204	34.45S	142.45E
Roblin, Can.	89	51.15N	101.25W
Robson, Mount, mtn., Can. (rŏb′sŭn)	87	53.07N	119.09W
Robstown, Tx., U.S. (rŏbz′toun)	113	27.46N	97.41W
Roby, Eng., U.K.	237a	53.25N	2.51W
Roca, Cabo da, c., Port. (kȧ′bō-dä-rô′kä)	158	38.47N	9.30W
Rocas, Atol das, atoll, Braz. (ä-tôl-däs-rô′kȧs)	131	3.50S	33.46W
Rocha, Ur. (rō′chȧs)	132	34.26S	54.14W
Rocha Miranda, neigh., Braz.	234c	22.52S	43.22W
Rocha Sobrinho, Braz.	234c	22.47S	43.25W
Rochdale, Eng., U.K. (rŏch′dāl)	150	53.37N	2.09W
Roche à Bateau, Haiti (rôsh á bȧ-tō′)	123	18.10N	74.00W
Rochefort, Fr. (rôsh-fŏr′)	147	45.55N	0.57W
Rochelle, Il., U.S. (rô-shĕl′)	103	41.53N	89.06W
Rochelle Park, N.J., U.S.	228	40.55N	74.04W
Rochester, Eng., U.K.	144a	51.24N	0.30E
Rochester, In., U.S. (rŏch′ĕs-tẽr)	98	41.05N	86.20W
Rochester, Mi., U.S.	101b	42.41N	83.09W
Rochester, Mn., U.S.	97	44.01N	92.30W
Rochester, N.H., U.S.	99	43.20N	71.00W
Rochester, N.Y., U.S.	97	43.15N	77.35W
Rochester, Pa., U.S.	101e	40.42N	80.16W

PLACE (Pronunciation)	PAGE	Lat. °'	Long. °'
Rock, r., U.S.	97	41.40N	90.00W
Rock, r., Ia., U.S.	102	43.17N	96.13W
Rock, r., Or., U.S.	106c	45.34N	122.52W
Rock, r., Or., U.S.	106c	45.52N	123.14W
Rockaway, N.J., U.S. (rŏck′ȧ-wā)	100a	40.54N	74.30W
Rockaway Park, neigh., N.Y., U.S.	228	40.35N	73.50W
Rockaway Point, neigh., N.Y., U.S.	228	40.33N	73.55W
Rockbank, Austl.	201a	37.44S	144.40E
Rockcliffe Park, Can. (rok′klĭf pärk)	83c	45.27N	75.40W
Rock Creek, r., Can. (rŏk)	105	49.01N	107.00W
Rock Creek, r., Il., U.S.	101a	41.16N	87.54W
Rock Creek, r., Mt., U.S.	105	46.25N	113.40W
Rock Creek, r., Or., U.S.	104	45.30N	120.06W
Rock Creek, r., Wa., U.S.	104	47.09N	117.50W
Rock Creek Park, pt. of i., D.C., U.S.	229d	38.58N	77.03W
Rockdale, Austl.	201b	33.57S	151.08E
Rockdale, Md., U.S.	100e	39.22N	76.49W
Rockdale, Tx., U.S. (rŏk′dāl)	113	30.39N	97.00W
Rockefeller Center, pt. of i., N.Y., U.S.	228	40.45N	74.00W
Rock Falls, Il., U.S. (rŏk fôlz)	103	41.45N	89.42W
Rock Ferry, Eng., U.K.	237a	53.22N	3.00W
Rockford, Il., U.S. (rŏk′fẽrd)	97	42.16N	89.07W
Rockhampton, Austl. (rŏk-hămp′tŭn)	203	23.26S	150.29E
Rock Hill, S.C., U.S. (rŏk′hĭl)	97	34.55N	81.01W
Rockingham, N.C., U.S. (rŏk′ĭng-hăm)	115	34.54N	79.45W
Rockingham Forest, for., Eng., U.K. (rok′ĭng-hăm)	144a	52.29N	0.43W
Rock Island, Il., U.S.	97	41.31N	90.37W
Rock Island Dam, Wa., U.S. (ī lănd)	104	47.17N	120.33W
Rockland, Can. (rŏk′lănd)	83c	45.33N	75.17W
Rockland, Me., U.S.	92	44.06N	69.09W
Rockland, Ma., U.S.	93a	42.07N	70.55W
Rockland Reservoir, res., Austl.	204	36.55S	142.20E
Rockledge, Pa., U.S.	229b	40.03N	75.05W
Rockmart, Ga., U.S. (rŏk′märt)	114	33.58N	85.00W
Rockmont, Wi., U.S. (rŏk′mŏnt)	107h	46.34N	91.54W
Rockport, In., U.S. (rŏk′pōrt)	98	38.20N	87.00W
Rockport, Ma., U.S.	93a	42.39N	70.37W
Rockport, Mo., U.S.	111	40.25N	95.30W
Rockport, Tx., U.S.	113	28.03N	97.03W
Rock Rapids, Ia., U.S. (răp′ĭdz)	102	43.26N	96.10W
Rock Sound, strt., Bah.	122	24.50N	76.05W
Rocksprings, Tx., U.S. (rŏk sprĭngs)	112	30.02N	100.12W
Rock Springs, Wy., U.S.	96	41.35N	109.13W
Rockstone, Guy. (rŏk′stôn)	131	5.55N	57.27W
Rock Valley, Ia., U.S. (văl′ĭ)	102	43.13N	96.17W
Rockville, In., U.S. (rŏk′vĭl)	98	39.45N	87.15W
Rockville, Md., U.S.	100e	39.05N	77.11W
Rockville Centre, N.Y., U.S. (sĕn′tẽr)	100a	40.39N	73.39W
Rockwall, Tx., U.S. (rŏk′wôl)	111	32.55N	96.23W
Rockwell City, Ia., U.S. (rŏk′wĕl)	103	42.22N	94.37W
Rockwood, Can. (rŏk-wood)	83d	43.37N	80.08W
Rockwood, Me., U.S.	92	45.39N	69.45W
Rockwood, Tn., U.S.	114	35.51N	84.41W
Rocky, r., Oh., U.S.	229a	41.30N	81.49W
Rocky, East Branch, r., Oh., U.S.	101d	41.13N	81.43W
Rocky, West Branch, r., Oh., U.S.	101d	41.17N	81.54W
Rocky Boys Indian Reservation, I.R., Mt., U.S.	105	48.08N	109.34W
Rocky Ford, Co., U.S.	110	38.02N	103.43W
Rocky Hill, N.J., U.S. (hĭl)	100a	40.24N	74.38W
Rocky Island Lake, l., Can.	90	46.56N	83.04W
Rocky Mount, N.C., U.S.	115	35.55N	77.47W
Rocky Mountain House, Can.	87	52.22N	114.55W
Rocky Mountain National Park, rec., Co., U.S.	96	40.29N	106.06W
Rocky Mountains, mts., N.A.	82	50.00N	114.00W
Rocky River, Oh., U.S.	101d	41.29N	81.51W
Rocky River, Oh., U.S.	229a	41.30N	81.40W
Rocquencourt, Fr.	237c	48.50N	2.07E
Rodas, Cuba (rō′dhȧs)	122	22.20N	80.35W
Roden, r., Eng., U.K. (rō′dĕn)	144a	52.49N	2.38W
Rodeo, Mex. (rô-dā′ō)	112	25.12N	104.34W
Rodeo, Ca., U.S. (rō′dêō)	106b	38.02N	122.16W
Roderick Island, i., Can. (rŏd′ẽ-rĭk)	86	52.40N	128.22W
Rodez, Fr. (rô-dĕz′)	147	44.22N	2.34E
Rōdhos, Grc.	149	36.24N	28.15E
Ródhos, i., Grc.	142	36.00N	28.29E
Rodnei, Munții, mts., Rom.	155	47.41N	24.05E
Rodniki, Russia (rôd′nê-kê)	166	57.08N	41.48E
Rodonit, Kep I, c., Alb.	161	41.38N	19.01E
Roebling, N.J., U.S. (rōb′lĭng)	100f	40.07N	74.48W
Roebourne, Austl. (rō′bŭrn)	202	20.50S	117.15E
Roebuck Bay, b., Austl. (rō′bŭck)	202	18.15S	121.10E
Roedtan, S. Afr.	218d	24.37S	29.08E
Roehampton, neigh., Eng., U.K.	235	51.27N	0.14W
Roeselare, Bel.	151	50.55N	3.05E
Roesiger, l., Wa., U.S. (rŏz′ĭ-gẽr)	106a	47.59N	121.56W
Roes Welcome Sound, strt., Can. (rōz)	85	64.10N	87.23W
Rogachëv, Bela. (rŏg′á-chyôf)	166	53.07N	30.04E
Rogans Hill, Austl.	243a	33.44S	151.01E
Rogatica, Bos. (rô-gä′tê-tsä)	161	43.46N	19.00E
Rogers, Ar., U.S. (rŏj-ẽrz)	111	36.19N	94.07W
Rogers City, Mi., U.S.	98	45.30N	83.50W
Rogers Park, neigh., Il., U.S.	231a	42.01N	87.40W
Rogersville, Tn., U.S.	114	36.21N	83.00W
Rognac, Fr. (rôn-yäk′)	156a	43.29N	5.15E
Rogoaguado, l., Bol. (rô′gō-ä-gwä-dō)	130	12.42S	66.46W
Rogovskaya, Russia (rô-gôf′skȧ-yȧ)	163	45.43N	38.42E
Rogózno, Pol. (rô′gôzh-nô)	154	52.44N	16.53E
Rogue, r., Or., U.S. (rōg)	104	42.32N	124.13W
Rohatyn, Ukr.	155	49.22N	24.37E
Rohdenhaus, Ger.	236	51.18N	7.01E
Röhlinghausen, neigh., Ger.	236	51.31N	7.08E
Rohrbeck, Ger.	238a	52.32N	13.02E

ŋ-sing; ŋ-baŋk; N-nasalized n; nŏd; cŏmmit; ōld; ôbey; ôrder; oi-boil; fōōd; o͝o-as oo in foot; ou-out; s-soft; sh-dish; th-thin; pūre; ûnite; ûrn; stŭd; circŭs; ü-as in French tu; ′-indeterminate vowel.

340 Roissy–Ruse

PLACE (Pronunciation)	PAGE	Lat. °′	Long. °′
Roissy, Fr.	237c	48.47N	2.39E
Roissy-en-France, Fr.	237c	49.00N	2.31E
Rojas, Arg. (rō'häs)	129c	34.11S	60.42W
Rojo, Cabo, c., Mex. (rō'hō)	119	21.35N	97.16W
Rojo, Cabo, c., P.R. (rō'hō)	117b	17.55N	67.14W
Rokel, r., S.L.	214	9.00N	11.55W
Rokkō-Zan, mtn., Japan (rôk'kō zän)	195b	34.46N	135.16E
Roksana, S. Afr.	244b	26.07S	28.24E
Rokycany, Czech Rep. (rô'kĭ'tsà-nĭ)	154	49.44N	13.37E
Roldanillo, Col. (rôl-dä-nē'l-yō)	130a	4.24N	76.09W
Rolla, Mo., U.S.	111	37.56N	91.45W
Rolla, N.D., U.S.	102	48.52N	99.32W
Rolleville, Bah.	122	23.40N	76.00W
Rolling Acres, Md., U.S.	229c	39.17N	76.52W
Röllinghausen, neigh., Ger.	236	51.36N	7.14E
Rolling Hills, Ca., U.S.	232	33.46N	118.21W
Roma, Austl. (rō'mà)	203	26.30S	148.48E
Roma *see* Rome, Italy	142	41.52N	12.37E
Roma, Leso.	213c	29.28S	27.43E
Romaine, r., Can. (rô-mĕn')	85	51.22N	63.23W
Romainville, Fr.	237c	48.53N	2.26E
Roman, Rom. (rō'män)	155	46.56N	26.57E
Romania, nation, Eur. (rō-mā'nē-à)	142	46.18N	22.53E
Romano, Cape, c., Fl., U.S. (rō-mä'nō)	115a	25.48N	82.00W
Romano, Cayo, i., Cuba (kä'yō-rô-mà'nô)	122	22.15N	78.00W
Romanovo, Russia (rô-mä'nô-vô)	172a	59.09N	61.24E
Romans, Fr. (rô-mäN')	156	45.04N	4.49E
Romblon, Phil. (rōm-blōn')	197a	12.34N	122.16E
Romblon Island, i., Phil.	197a	12.33N	122.17E
Rome (Roma), Italy	142	41.52N	12.37E
Rome, Ga., U.S. (rōm)	97	34.14N	85.10W
Rome, N.Y., U.S.	99	43.15N	75.25W
Romeo, Mi., U.S. (rō'mē-ō)	98	42.50N	83.00W
Romford, Eng., U.K. (rŭm'fērd)	144b	51.35N	0.11E
Romiley, Eng., U.K.	237b	53.25N	2.05W
Romilly-sur-Seine, Fr. (rô-mē-yē'sür-sān')	156	48.32N	3.41E
Romita, Mex. (rō-mē'tä)	118	20.53N	101.32W
Romny, Ukr. (rôm'nĭ)	167	50.46N	33.31E
Rømø, i., Den. (rûm'û)	152	55.08N	8.17E
Romoland, Ca., U.S. (rō'mō'lănd)	107a	33.44N	117.11W
Romorantin-Lanthenay, Fr. (rô-mô-räN-täN')	156	47.24N	1.46E
Rompin, Malay.	181b	2.42N	102.30E
Rompin, r., Malay.	181b	2.54N	103.10E
Romsdalsfjorden, Nor.	152	62.40N	7.05W
Romulus, Mi., U.S. (rom'ū lŭs)	101b	42.14N	83.24W
Ron, Mui, c., Viet.	193	18.05N	106.45E
Ronan, Mt., U.S. (rō'năn)	105	47.28N	114.03W
Roncador, Serra do, mts., Braz. (sĕr'rá dō rôn-kä-dôr')	131	12.44S	52.19W
Roncesvalles, Spain (rôn-sĕs-vä'l-yĕs)	158	43.00N	1.17W
Ronceverte, W.V., U.S. (rŏn'sē-vûrt)	98	37.45N	80.30W
Ronda, Spain (rōn'dä)	167	36.45N	5.10W
Ronda, Sierra de, mts., Spain	158	36.35N	5.03W
Rondebult, S. Afr.	244b	26.18S	28.14E
Rondônia, , Braz.	130	10.15S	63.07W
Ronge, Lac la, l., Can. (rōnzh)	84	55.10N	105.00W
Rongjiang, China (rôŋ-jyäŋ)	193	25.52N	108.45E
Rongxian, China	193	22.50N	110.32E
Rønne, Den. (rûn'ĕ)	146	55.08N	14.46E
Ronneby, Swe. (rōn'ĕ-bü)	152	56.13N	15.17E
Ronne Ice Shelf, ice., Ant.	219	77.30S	38.00W
Ronsdorf, neigh., Ger.	236	51.14N	7.12E
Roodepoort, S. Afr. (rō'dĕ-pōrt)	213b	26.10S	27.52E
Roodhouse, Il., U.S. (rōōd'hous)	111	39.29N	90.21W
Rooiberg, S. Afr.	218d	24.46S	27.42E
Roosendaal, Neth. (rō'zĕn-däl)	145a	51.32N	4.27E
Roosevelt, N.Y., U.S.	228	40.41N	73.36W
Roosevelt, Ut., U.S. (rōz''vĕlt)	109	40.20N	110.00W
Roosevelt, r., Braz. (rô'sĕ-vĕlt)	131	9.22S	60.28W
Roosevelt Island, i., Ant.	219	79.30S	168.00W
Root, r., Wi., U.S.	101a	42.49N	87.54W
Rooty Hill, Austl.	243a	33.46S	150.50E
Roper, r., Austl. (rōp'ēr)	202	14.50S	134.00E
Ropsha, Russia (rôp'shà)	172c	59.44N	29.53E
Roque Pérez, Arg. (rô'kĕ-pĕ'rĕz)	129c	35.23S	59.22W
Roques, Islas los, is., Ven.	130	12.25N	67.40W
Roraima, , Braz. (rô'rīy-mă)	130	2.00N	62.15W
Roraima, Mount, mtn., S.A. (rō-rä-ē'mä)	131	5.12N	60.52W
Røros, Nor. (rûr'ôs)	146	62.36N	11.25E
Ros', r., Ukr. (rôs)	163	49.40N	30.22E
Rosa, Monte, mtn., Italy (mōn'tä rō'zä)	148	45.56N	7.51E
Rosales, Mex. (rō-zä'läs)	112	28.15N	100.43W
Rosales, Phil. (rō-sä'lĕs)	197a	15.54N	120.38E
Rosamorada, Mex. (rō'zä-mō-rä'dhä)	118	22.06N	105.16W
Rosanna, Austl.	243b	37.45S	145.04E
Rosaria, Laguna, l., Mex. (lä-gō'nä-rō-sà'ryä)	119	17.50N	93.51W
Rosario, Arg. (rō-zä'rē-ō)	132	32.58S	60.42W
Rosario, Braz. (rō-zä'rē-ō)	131	2.49S	44.15W
Rosario, Mex.	112	26.31N	105.40W
Rosario, Mex.	118	22.58N	105.54W
Rosario, Phil.	197a	13.49N	121.13W
Rosario, Ur.	129c	34.19S	57.24E
Rosario, Cayo, i., Cuba (kä'yō-rō-sä'ryō)	122	21.40N	81.55W
Rosário do Sul, Braz. (rō-zä'rē-ō-dō-sōō'l)	132	30.17S	54.52W
Rosário Oeste, Braz. (ō'ĕst'ĕ)	131	14.47S	56.20W
Rosario Strait, strt., Wa., U.S.	106a	48.27N	122.45W
Rosas, Golfo de, b., Spain (gôl-fô-dĕ-rō'zäs)	159	42.10N	3.20E
Rosbach, Ger. (rōz'bäK)	157c	50.47N	7.38E
Roscoe, Tx., U.S. (rôs'kō)	112	32.26N	100.38W
Roseau, Dom.	121b	15.17N	61.23W
Roseau, Mn., U.S. (rō-zō')	102	48.52N	95.47W
Roseau, r., Mn., U.S.	102	48.52N	96.11W
Rosebank, neigh., S. Afr.	244b	26.09S	28.02E
Roseberg, Or., U.S. (rōz'bûrg)	96	43.13N	123.30W
Rosebery, neigh., Austl.	243a	33.55S	151.12E
Rosebud, r., Can. (rōz'bŭd)	87	51.20N	112.20W
Rosebud Creek, r., Mt., U.S.	105	45.48N	106.34W
Rosebud Indian Reservation, I.R., S.D., U.S.	102	43.13N	100.42W
Rosedale, Ms., U.S.	114	33.49N	90.56W
Rosedale, Wa., U.S.	106a	47.20N	122.39W
Rosedale, neigh., Can.	227c	43.41N	79.22W
Rosedale, neigh., N.Y., U.S.	228	40.39N	73.45W
Roseires Reservoir, res., Sudan	211	11.15N	34.45E
Roseland, neigh., Il., U.S.	231a	41.42N	87.38W
Roselle, Il., U.S. (rō-zĕl')	101a	41.59N	88.05W
Roselle, N.J., U.S.	228	40.40N	74.16W
Rosemead, Ca., U.S.	232	34.04N	118.03W
Rosemère, Can. (rōz'mĕr)	83a	45.38N	73.48W
Rosemont, Il., U.S.	231a	41.59N	87.52W
Rosemont, Pa., U.S.	229b	40.01N	75.19W
Rosemount, Mn., U.S. (rōz'mount)	107g	44.44N	93.08W
Rosendal, S. Afr. (rô-sĕn'täl)	218d	28.32S	27.56E
Roseneath, S. Afr.	244b	26.17S	28.11E
Rosenheim, Ger. (rō'zĕn-hīm)	147	47.52N	12.06E
Rosenthal, neigh., Ger.	238a	52.36N	13.23E
Rosetown, Can. (rōz'toun)	84	51.33N	108.00W
Rose Tree, Pa., U.S.	229b	39.56N	75.23W
Rosetta *see* Rashīd, Egypt	184	31.22N	30.25E
Rosettenville, neigh., S. Afr.	213b	26.15S	28.04E
Roseville, Austl.	243a	33.47S	151.11E
Roseville, Ca., U.S. (rōz'vĭl)	108	38.44N	121.19W
Roseville, Mi., U.S.	101b	42.30N	82.55W
Roseville, Mn., U.S.	107g	45.01N	93.10W
Rosiclare, Il., U.S. (rōz'y-klâr)	98	37.30N	88.15W
Rosignol, Guy. (rôs-ĭg-nōl)	131	6.16N	57.37W
Roșiori de Vede, Rom. (rō-shôr'ē dĕ vĕ-dĕ)	161	44.06N	25.00E
Roskilde, Den. (rôs'kēl-dĕ)	152	55.39N	12.04E
Roslavl', Russia (rôs'läv'l)	166	53.56N	32.52E
Roslyn, N.Y., U.S.	228	40.48N	73.39W
Roslyn, Wa., U.S. (rŏz'lĭn)	104	47.14N	121.00W
Roslyn Estates, N.Y., U.S.	228	40.47N	73.40W
Roslyn Heights, N.Y., U.S.	228	40.47N	73.39W
Rosny-sous-Bois, Fr.	237c	48.53N	2.29E
Rösrath, Ger. (rûz'rät)	157c	50.53N	7.11E
Ross, Oh., U.S. (rôs)	101f	39.19N	84.39W
Rossano, Italy (rô-sä'nō)	149	39.34N	16.38E
Rossan Point, c., Ire.	150	54.45N	8.30W
Ross Creek, r., Can.	83g	53.40N	113.08W
Rosseau, l., Can. (rôs-sō')	91	45.15N	79.30W
Rossel, i., Pap. N. Gui. (rô-sĕl')	203	11.31S	154.00E
Rosser, Can. (rôs'sēr)	83f	49.59N	97.27W
Ross Ice Shelf, ice., Ant.	219	81.30S	175.00W
Rossignol, Lake, l., Can.	92	44.10N	65.10W
Ross Island, i., Can.	89	54.14N	97.45W
Ross Lake, res., Wa., U.S.	104	48.40N	121.07W
Rossland, Can. (rôs'lănd)	84	49.05N	118.48W
Rossmore, Austl.	243a	33.57S	150.46E
Rossosh', Russia (rôs'sŭsh)	167	50.12N	39.32E
Rossouw, S. Afr.	213c	31.12S	27.18E
Ross Sea, sea, Ant.	219	76.00S	178.00W
Rossvatnet, l., Nor.	146	65.36N	13.08E
Rossville, Ga., U.S. (rôs'vĭl)	114	34.57N	85.22W
Rossville, Md., U.S.	229c	39.20N	76.29W
Rosthern, Can.	88	52.41N	106.25W
Rostherne, Eng., U.K.	237b	53.21N	2.23W
Rostock, Ger. (rôs'tŭk)	146	54.04N	12.06E
Rostov, Russia	166	57.13N	39.23E
Rostov, prov., Russia	163	47.38N	39.15E
Rostov-na-Donu, Russia (rôstôv-nà-dô-nōō)	164	47.16N	39.47E
Roswell, Ga., U.S. (rôz'wĕl)	114	34.02N	84.21W
Roswell, N.M., U.S.	96	33.23N	104.32W
Rosyln, Pa., U.S.	229b	40.07N	75.08W
Rotan, Tx., U.S. (rō-tăn')	110	32.51N	100.27W
Rothenburg, Ger.	154	49.20N	10.10E
Rotherham, Eng., U.K. (rŏdh'ēr-ăm)	144a	53.26N	1.21W
Rothesay, Can. (rôth'sà)	92	45.23N	66.00W
Rothesay, Scot., U.K.	150	55.50N	3.14W
Rothneusiedl, neigh., Aus.	239e	48.08N	16.23E
Rothwell, Eng., U.K.	144a	53.44N	1.30W
Roti, Pulau, i., Indon. (rō'tē)	196	10.30S	122.52E
Roto, Austl. (rō'tō)	204	33.07S	145.30E
Rotorua, N.Z.	205	38.07S	176.17E
Rotterdam, Neth. (rôt'ēr-däm')	142	51.55N	4.27E
Rottweil, Ger. (rōt'vīl)	154	48.10N	8.36E
Roubaix, Fr. (rōō-bĕ')	156	50.42N	3.10E
Rouen, Fr. (rōō-äN')	142	49.25N	1.05E
Rouge, r., Can. (rōōzh)	83d	43.53N	79.21W
Rouge, r., Can.	91	46.40N	74.50W
Rouge, r., Mi., U.S.	101b	42.30N	83.15W
Rough River Reservoir, res., Ky., U.S.	98	37.45N	86.10W
Round Lake, Il., U.S.	101a	42.21N	88.05W
Round Pond, l., Can.	93	48.15N	55.57W
Round Rock, Tx., U.S.	113	30.31N	97.41W
Round Top, mtn., Or., U.S. (tŏp)	106c	45.41N	123.22W
Roundup, Mt., U.S. (round'ŭp)	105	46.25N	108.35W
Rousay, i., Scot., U.K. (rōō'zà)	150a	59.10N	3.04W
Rouyn, Can. (rōōn)	85	48.22N	79.03W
Rovaniemi, Fin. (rô'vá-nyĕ'mĭ)	146	66.29N	25.45E
Rovato, Italy (rō-vä'tō)	160	45.33N	10.00E
Roven'ki, Russia	163	49.54N	38.54E
Roven'ky, Ukr.	163	48.06N	39.44E
Rovereto, Italy (rō-vå-rā'tō)	160	45.53N	11.05E
Rovigo, Italy (rô-vē'gô)	160	45.05N	11.48E
Rovinj, Cro. (rō'ēn')	160	45.05N	13.40E
Rovira, Col. (rô-vē'rä)	130a	4.14N	75.13W
Rovuma (Ruvuma), r., Afr.	217	10.50S	39.50E
Rowland Heights, Ca., U.S.	232	33.59N	117.54W
Rowley, Ma., U.S. (rou'lē)	93a	42.43N	70.53W
Rowville, Austl.	243b	37.56S	145.14E
Roxana, Il., U.S. (rŏks'ăn-nà)	107e	38.51N	90.05W
Roxas, Phil. (rô-xäs)	196	11.30N	122.47E
Roxboro, Can.	227b	45.31N	73.48W
Roxborough, neigh., Pa., U.S.	229b	40.02N	75.13W
Roxbury, neigh., N.Y., U.S.	228	40.34N	73.54W
Roxo, Cap, c., Sen.	214	12.20N	16.43W
Roy, N.M., U.S. (roi)	110	35.54N	104.09W
Roy, Ut., U.S.	107b	41.10N	112.02W
Royal, i., Bah.	122	25.30N	76.50W
Royal Albert Hall, pt. of i., Eng., U.K.	235	51.30N	0.11W
Royal Canal, can., Ire. (roi-ăl)	150	53.28N	6.45W
Royal Natal National Park, rec., S. Afr.	213c	28.35S	28.54E
Royal Naval College, pt. of i., Eng., U.K.	235	51.29N	0.01W
Royal Oak, Can. (roi'ăl ōk)	106a	48.30N	123.24W
Royal Oak, Mi., U.S.	101b	42.29N	83.09W
Royal Oak Township, Mi., U.S.	230c	42.27N	83.10W
Royal Ontario Museum, bldg., Can.	227c	43.40N	79.24W
Royalton, Mi., U.S. (roi'ăl-tŭn)	98	42.00N	86.25W
Royan, Fr. (rwä-yäN')	156	45.40N	1.02W
Roye, Fr. (rwä)	156	49.43N	2.40E
Royersford, Pa., U.S. (rô' yērz-fērd)	100f	40.11N	75.32W
Royston, Ga., U.S. (roiz'tŭn)	114	34.15N	83.06W
Royton, Eng., U.K. (roi'tŭn)	144a	53.34N	2.07W
Rozay-en-Brie, Fr. (rô-zā-ĕN-brē')	157b	48.41N	2.57E
Rozdil'na, Ukr.	163	46.47N	30.08E
Rozelle, Austl.	243a	33.52S	151.10E
Rozhaya, r., Russia (rô'zhà-yà)	172b	55.20N	37.37E
Rozivka, Ukr.	163	47.14N	36.35E
Rožňava, Slvk. (rôzh'nyà-và)	155	48.39N	20.32E
Rtishchevo, Russia ('r-tĭsh'chĕ-vô)	167	52.15N	43.40E
Ru, r., China (rōō)	190	33.07N	114.18E
Ruacana Falls, wtfl., Afr.	212	17.15S	14.45E
Ruaha National Park, rec., Tan.	217	7.15S	34.50E
Ruapehu, vol., N.Z. (rò-à-pā'hōō)	203a	39.15S	175.37E
Rub' al Khali *see* Ar Rub' al Khālī, des., Asia	182	20.00N	51.00E
Rubeho Mountains, mts., Tan.	217	6.45S	36.15E
Rubidoux, Ca., U.S.	107a	33.59N	117.24W
Rubondo Island, i., Tan.	217	2.10S	31.55E
Rubtsovsk, Russia	164	51.31N	81.17E
Ruby, Ak., U.S. (rōō'bē)	96a	64.38N	155.22W
Ruby, l., Nv., U.S.	108	40.11N	115.20W
Ruby, r., Mt., U.S.	105	45.06N	112.10W
Ruby Mountains, mts., Nv., U.S.	108	40.11N	115.36W
Rüdersdorf, Ger.	238a	52.29N	13.47E
Rudge Ramos, Braz.	234d	23.41S	46.34W
Rüdinghausen, neigh., Ger.	236	51.27N	7.25E
Rudkøbing, Den. (rōōdh'kûb-ĭng)	152	54.56N	10.44E
Rüdnitz, Ger. (rüd'nētz)	145b	52.44N	13.38E
Rudolf, Lake, l., Afr. (rōō'dôlf)	211	3.30N	36.05E
Rudow, neigh., Ger.	238a	52.25N	13.30E
Rueil-Malmaison, Fr.	237c	48.53N	2.11E
Rufā'ah, Sudan (rōō-fä'ä)	211	14.52N	33.30E
Ruffec, Fr. (rü-fĕk')	156	46.03N	0.11E
Rufiji, r., Tan. (rò-fē'jē)	213	8.00S	38.00E
Rufisque, Sen. (rü-fēsk')	210	14.43N	17.17W
Rufunsa, Zam.	217	15.05S	29.40E
Rufus Woods, Wa., U.S.	104	48.02N	119.33W
Rugao, China (rōō-gou)	192	32.24N	120.33E
Rugby, Eng., U.K. (rŭg'bē)	144a	52.22N	1.15W
Rugby, N.D., U.S.	102	48.22N	100.00W
Rugeley, Eng., U.K. (rōōj'lē)	144a	52.46N	1.56W
Rügen, i., Ger. (rü'ghĕn)	142	54.28N	13.47E
Rüggeberg, Ger.	236	51.16N	7.22E
Ruhlsdorf, Ger.	238a	52.23N	13.16E
Ruhnu-Saar, i., Est. (rōōnò-sà'âr)	153	57.46N	23.15E
Ruhr, r., Ger. (ròr)	154	51.18N	8.17E
Ruhrort, neigh., Ger.	236	51.26N	6.45E
Rui'an, China (rwā-än)	193	27.48N	120.40E
Ruislip, neigh., Eng., U.K.	235	51.34N	0.25W
Ruiz, Mex. (rōē'z)	118	21.55N	105.09W
Ruiz, Nevado del, vol., Col. (nĕ-vá'dô-dĕl-rōōē'z)	130a	4.52N	75.20W
Rūjiena, Lat. (rò'yĭ-ă-nà)	153	57.54N	25.19E
Ruki, r., Zaire	216	0.05S	18.55E
Rukwa, Lake, l., Tan. (rōōk-wä')	212	8.00S	32.25E
Rum, r., Mn., U.S. (rŭm)	103	45.52N	93.45W
Ruma, Yugo. (rōō'mà)	161	45.00N	19.53E
Rum'ancevo, Russia	239b	55.38N	37.26E
Rumbek, Sudan (rŭm'bĕk)	211	6.52N	29.43E
Rum Cay, i., Bah.	123	23.40N	74.50W
Rumelihisari, neigh., Tur.	239f	41.05N	29.03E
Rumford, Me., U.S. (rŭm'fērd)	92	44.32N	70.35W
Rummah, Wādī ar, val., Sau. Ar.	182	26.17N	41.45E
Rummānah, Egypt	181a	31.01N	32.39E
Rummelsburg, neigh., Ger.	238a	52.30N	13.29E
Rummenohl, Ger.	236	51.17N	7.32E
Runan, China (rōō-nän)	192	32.59N	114.22E
Runcorn, Eng., U.K. (rŭŋ'kôrn)	144a	53.20N	2.44W
Runnemede, N.J., U.S.	229b	39.51N	75.04W
Runnymede, pt. of i., Eng., U.K.	235	51.26N	0.34W
Ruo, r., China (rwô)	188	41.15N	100.46E
Rupat, i., Indon. (rōō'pät)	181b	1.55N	101.35E
Rupat, Selat, strt., Indon.	181b	1.55N	101.17E
Rupert, Id., U.S. (rōō'pērt)	105	42.36N	113.41W
Rupert, Rivière de, r., Can.	85	51.35N	76.30W
Rural Ridge, Pa., U.S.	230b	40.35N	79.50W
Ruse, Bul. (rōō'sĕ) (rò'sĕ)	142	43.50N	25.59

ăt; finăl; rāte; senåte; ärm; åsk; sofă; fâre; ch-choose; dh-as th in other; bē; ėvent; bĕt; recĕnt; cratēr; g-gō; gh-guttural g; bĭt; ĭ-short neutral; rīde; K-guttural k as ch in German ich;

PRONOUNCING INDEX

Rushan–Saint François de Boundji 341

PLACE (Pronunciation)	PAGE	Lat. °′	Long. °′
Rushan, China (ro͞o-shän)	190	36.54N	121.31E
Rush City, Mn., U.S.	103	45.40N	92.59W
Rusholme, neigh., Eng., U.K.	237b	53.27N	2.12W
Rushville, Il., U.S. (rŭsh'vĭl)	111	40.08N	90.34W
Rushville, In., U.S.	98	39.35N	85.30W
Rushville, Ne., U.S.	102	42.43N	102.27W
Rusizi, r., Afr.	217	3.00S	29.05E
Rusk, Tx., U.S. (rŭsk)	113	31.49N	95.09W
Ruskin, Can. (rŭs'kĭn)	106d	49.10N	122.25W
Russ, r., Aus.	145e	48.12N	16.55E
Russas, Braz. (ro͞o's-säs)	131	4.48S	37.50W
Russell, Can.	83c	45.15N	75.22W
Russell, Can. (rŭs'ĕl)	84	50.47N	101.15W
Russell, Ca., U.S.	106b	37.39N	122.08W
Russell, Ks., U.S.	110	38.51N	98.51W
Russell, Ky., U.S.	98	38.30N	82.45W
Russel Lake, l., Can.	89	56.15N	101.30W
Russell Gardens, N.Y., U.S.	228	40.47N	73.43W
Russell Islands, is., Sol.Is.	203	9.16S	158.30E
Russellville, Al., U.S. (rŭs'ĕl-vĭl)	114	34.29N	87.44W
Russellville, Ar., U.S.	111	35.16N	93.08W
Russelville, Ky., U.S.	114	36.48N	86.51W
Russia, nation, Russia	164	61.00N	60.00E
Russian, r., Ca., U.S. (rŭsh'ăn)	108	38.59N	123.10W
Rustavi, Geor.	168	41.33N	45.02E
Rustenburg, S. Afr. (rŭs'tĕn-bûrg)	218d	25.40S	27.15E
Ruston, La., U.S. (rŭs'tŭn)	113	32.32N	92.39W
Ruston, Wa., U.S.	106a	47.18N	122.30W
Rusville, S. Afr.	244b	26.10S	28.18E
Rute, Spain (ro͞o'tā)	158	38.20N	4.34W
Ruth, Nv., U.S. (ro͞oth)	108	39.17N	115.00W
Ruthenia, hist. reg., Ukr.	155	48.25N	23.00E
Rutherford, N.J., U.S.	228	40.49N	74.07W
Rutherfordton, N.C., U.S. (rŭdh'ẽr-fẽrd-tŭn)	115	35.23N	81.58W
Rutland, Vt., U.S.	99	43.35N	72.55W
Rutledge, Md., U.S. (rût'lĕdj)	100e	39.34N	76.33W
Rutledge, Pa., U.S.	229b	39.54N	75.20W
Rutog, China	188	33.29N	79.26E
Rutshuru, Zaire (ro͞ot-sho͞o'ro͞o)	212	1.11S	29.27E
Rüttenscheid, neigh., Ger.	236	51.26N	7.00E
Ruvo, Italy (ro͞o'vô)	160	41.07N	16.32E
Ruvuma, r., Afr.	212	11.30S	37.00E
Ruza, Russia (ro͞o'zȧ)	162	55.42N	36.12E
Ruzhany, Bela. (rö-zhän'ĭ)	155	52.49N	24.54E
Rwanda, nation, Afr.	212	2.10S	29.37E
Ryabovo, Russia (ryä'bô-vô)	172c	59.24N	31.08E
Ryarsh, Eng., U.K.	235	51.19N	0.24E
Ryazan', Russia (ryä-zän'')	164	54.37N	39.43E
Ryazan', prov., Russia	162	54.10N	39.37E
Ryazhsk, Russia (ryäzh'sk')	166	53.43N	40.04E
Rybachiy, Poluostrov, pen., Russia	166	69.50N	33.20E
Rybatskoye, Russia	172c	59.50N	30.31E
Rybinsk, Russia	164	58.02N	38.52E
Rybinskoye, res., Russia	164	58.23N	38.15E
Rybnik, Pol. (rĭb'nĕk)	155	50.06N	18.37E
Rydal, Pa., U.S.	229b	40.06N	75.06W
Rydalmere, Austl.	243a	33.49S	151.02E
Ryde, Austl.	243a	33.49S	151.06E
Ryde, Eng., U.K. (rīd)	150	50.43N	1.16W
Rye, N.Y., U.S. (rī)	100a	40.58N	73.42W
Ryl'sk, Russia (rêl''sk)	167	51.33N	34.42E
Rynfield, S. Afr.	244b	26.09S	28.20E
Ryōtsu, Japan (ryōt'so͞o)	194	38.02N	138.23E
Rypin, Pol. (rĭ'pĕn)	155	53.04N	19.25E
Rysy, mtn., Eur.	155	49.12N	20.04E
Ryukyu Islands see Nansei-shotō, is., Japan	189	27.30N	127.00E
Rzeszów, Pol. (zhä-shôf)	147	50.02N	22.00E
Rzhev, Russia ('r-zhĕf)	164	56.16N	34.17E
Rzhyshchiv, Ukr.	163	49.58N	31.05E

S

PLACE (Pronunciation)	PAGE	Lat. °′	Long. °′
Saale, r., Ger. (sä-lĕ)	154	51.14N	11.52E
Saalfeld, Ger. (säl'fĕlt)	154	50.38N	11.20E
Saarbrücken, Ger. (zähr'brü-kĕn)	147	49.15N	7.01E
Saaremaa, i., Est.	166	58.25N	22.30E
Saarland, state, Ger.	154	49.25N	6.50E
Saarn, neigh., Ger.	236	51.24N	6.53E
Saarnberg, neigh., Ger.	236	51.25N	6.53E
Saavedra, Arg. (sä-ä-vä'drä)	132	37.45S	62.23W
Saba, i., Neth. Ant. (sä'bä)	121b	17.39N	63.20W
Šabac, Yugo. (shä'bats)	149	44.45N	19.49E
Sabadell, Spain (sä-bä-dhål')	148	41.32N	2.07E
Sabah, hist. reg., Malay.	196	5.10N	116.25E
Sabana, Archipiélago de, is., Cuba	122	23.05N	80.00W
Sabana, Río, r., Pan. (sä-bä'nä)	121	8.40N	78.02W
Sabana de la Mar, Dom. Rep. (sä-bä'nä dā lä mär')	123	19.05N	69.30W
Sabana de Uchire, Ven. (sä-bà'nä dĕ o͞o-chē'rĕ)	131b	10.02N	65.32W
Sabanagrande, Hond. (sä-bä'nä-grä'n-dĕ)	120	13.47N	87.16W
Sabanalarga, Col. (sä-bä'nä-lär'gä)	130	10.38N	75.02W

PLACE (Pronunciation)	PAGE	Lat. °′	Long. °′
Sabanas Páramo, mtn., Col. (sä-bá'näs pá'rä-mô)	130a	6.28N	76.08W
Sabancuy, Mex. (sä-bäŋ-kwē')	119	18.58N	91.09W
Sabang, Indon. (sä'bäng)	196	5.52N	95.26E
Sabaudia, Italy (sȧ-bou'dē-ä)	160	41.19N	13.00E
Sabetha, Ks., U.S. (sȧ-bĕth'ȧ)	111	39.54N	95.49W
Sabi (Rio Save), r., Afr. (sä'bē)	212	20.18S	32.07E
Sabile, Lat. (sà'bē-lĕ)	153	57.03N	22.34E
Sabinal, Tx., U.S. (sȧ-bī'nȧl)	112	29.19N	99.27W
Sabinal, Cayo, i., Cuba (kä'yō sä-bē-näl')	122	21.40N	77.20W
Sabinas, Mex.	116	28.05N	101.30W
Sabinas, r., Mex. (sä-bē'näs)	112	26.37N	99.52W
Sabinas, Río, r., Mex. (rē'ō sä-bē'näs)	112	27.25N	100.33W
Sabinas Hidalgo, Mex. (ē-däl'gō)	112	26.30N	100.10W
Sabine, Tx., U.S. (sȧ-bēn')	113	29.44N	93.54W
Sabine, r., U.S.	97	32.00N	94.30W
Sabine, Mount, mtn., Ant.	219	72.05S	169.10E
Sabine Lake, l., La., U.S.	113	29.53N	93.41W
Sablayan, Phil. (säb-lä-yän')	197a	12.49N	120.47E
Sable, Cape, c., Can. (sā'b'l)	85	43.25N	65.24W
Sable, Cape, c., Fl., U.S.	97	25.12N	81.10W
Sables, Rivière aux, r., Can.	91	49.00N	70.20W
Sablé-sur-Sarthe, Fr. (säb-lā-sür-särt')	156	47.50N	0.17W
Sablya, Gora, mtn., Russia	166	64.50N	59.00E
Sâbor, r., Port. (sä-bōr')	158	41.18N	6.54W
Sabunchu, Azer.	168	40.26N	49.56E
Saburovo, neigh., Russia	239b	55.38N	37.42E
Sabzevār, Iran	185	36.13N	57.42E
Sac, r., Mo., U.S. (sôk)	111	38.11N	93.45W
Sacandaga Reservoir, res., N.Y., U.S. (să-kăn-dâ'gȧ)	99	43.10N	74.15W
Sacavém, Port. (sä-kä-vĕɴ')	159b	38.47N	9.06W
Sacavém, r., Port.	159b	38.52N	9.06W
Sac City, Ia., U.S. (sôk)	102	42.25N	95.00W
Sachigo Lake, l., Can. (săch'ĭ-gō)	89	53.49N	92.08W
Sachsen, hist. reg., Ger. (zäĸ'sĕn)	154	50.45N	12.17E
Sacketts Harbor, N.Y., U.S. (săk'ĕts)	99	43.55N	76.05W
Sackville, Can. (săk'vĭl)	92	45.54N	64.22W
Saco, Me., U.S. (sô'kō)	92	43.30N	70.28W
Saco, r., Braz. (sä'kō)	132b	22.20S	43.26W
Saco, r., Me., U.S.	92	43.53N	70.46W
Sacramento, Mex.	112	25.45N	103.22W
Sacramento, Mex.	112	27.05N	101.45W
Sacramento, Ca., U.S. (săk-rȧ-mĕn'tō)	96	38.35N	121.30W
Sacramento, r., Ca., U.S.	108	40.20N	122.07W
Sacrow, neigh., Ger.	238a	52.26N	13.06E
Şa'dah, Yemen	182	16.50N	43.45E
Saddle Brook, N.J., U.S.	228	40.54N	74.06W
Saddle Lake Indian Reserve, I.R., Can.	87	54.00N	111.40W
Saddle Mountain, mtn., Or., U.S. (săd''l)	106c	45.58N	123.40W
Saddle Rock, N.Y., U.S.	228	40.48N	73.45W
Sadiya, India (sü-dē'yä)	183	27.53N	95.35E
Sado, i., Japan (sä'dō)	189	38.05N	138.26E
Sado, r., Port. (sä'dō)	158	38.15N	8.20W
Saeby, Den. (sĕ'bü)	152	57.21N	10.29E
Saeki, Japan (sä'ā-kē)	194	32.56N	131.51E
Safdar Jang's Tomb, rel., India	240d	28.36N	77.13E
Säffle, Swe.	152	59.10N	12.55E
Safford, Az., U.S. (săf'fẽrd)	109	32.50N	109.45W
Safi, Mor. (sä'fē) (ăs'fē)	210	32.24N	9.09W
Saga, Japan (sä'gä)	195	33.15N	130.18E
Sagamihara, Japan	242a	35.34N	139.23E
Sagami-Nada, b., Japan (sä'gä'mē nä-dä)	195	35.06N	139.24E
Sagamore Hills, Oh., U.S. (săg'ȧ-môr hĭlz)	101d	41.19N	81.34W
Saganaga, l., N.A. (să-gȧ-nä'gȧ)	103	48.13N	91.17W
Sāgar, India	183	23.55N	78.45E
Saghyz, r., Kaz.	170	48.30N	56.10E
Saginaw, Mi., U.S. (săg'ĭ-nô)	97	43.25N	84.00W
Saginaw, Mn., U.S.	107h	46.51N	92.26W
Saginaw, Tx., U.S.	107c	32.52N	97.22W
Saginaw Bay, b., Mi., U.S.	97	43.50N	83.40W
Saguache, Co., U.S. (sȧ-wăch') (sȧ-gwä'chē)	109	38.05N	106.10W
Saguache Creek, r., Co., U.S.	98	38.05N	106.40W
Sagua de Tánamo, Cuba (sä-gwä dĕ tá'nä-mō)	123	20.40N	75.15W
Sagua la Grande, Cuba (sä-gwä lä grä'n-dĕ)	122	22.45N	80.05W
Saguaro National Monument, rec., Az., U.S. (säg-wä'rō)	109	32.12N	110.40W
Saguenay, r., Can. (săg-ē-nā')	85	48.20N	70.15W
Sagunto, Spain (sä-gōn'tō)	148	39.40N	0.17W
Sahara, des., Afr. (sȧ-hä'rȧ)	210	23.44N	1.40W
Saharan Atlas, mts., Afr.	148	32.51N	1.02W
Sahāranpur, India (sŭ-hä'rŭn-po͞or')	183	29.58N	77.41E
Sahara Village, Ut., U.S. (sȧ-hä'rȧ)	107b	41.06N	111.58W
Sahel see Sudan, reg., Afr.	210	15.00N	7.00E
Sāhīwāl, Pak.	186	30.43N	73.04E
Sahuayo de Dias, Mex.	118	20.03N	102.43W
Saigon see Ho Chi Minh City, Viet.	196	10.46N	106.34E
Saijō, Japan (sä'ē-jō)	195	33.55N	133.13E
Saimaa, l., Fin. (sä'ĭ-mä)	146	61.24N	28.45E
Sain Alto, Mex. (sä-ēn' äl'tō)	118	23.35N	103.13W
Saint Adolphe, Can. (sånt a'dŏlf) (sănt' tȧ-dŏlf')	83f	49.40N	97.07W
Saint Afrique, Fr. (săɴ' tȧ-frēk')	156	43.58N	2.52E
Saint Albans, Austl. (sånt ôl'bănz)	201a	37.44S	144.47E
Saint Albans, Eng., U.K.	150	51.44N	0.20W
Saint Albans, Vt., U.S.	99	44.50N	73.05W
Saint Albans, W.V., U.S.	98	38.20N	81.50W
Saint Albans, neigh., N.Y., U.S.	228	40.42N	73.46W
Saint Albans Cathedral, pt. of i., Eng., U.K.	235	51.45N	0.20W

PLACE (Pronunciation)	PAGE	Lat. °′	Long. °′
Saint Albert, Can. (sånt ăl'bẽrt)	87	53.38N	113.38W
Saint Amand-Mont Rond, Fr. (săɴ't ȧ-mäɴ' môɴ-rôɴ')	156	46.44N	2.28E
Saint André-Est, Can.	83a	45.33N	74.19W
Saint Andrews, Can.	85	45.05N	67.03W
Saint Andrews, Scot., U.K.	150	56.20N	2.40W
Saint Andrew's Channel, strt., Can.	93	46.06N	60.28W
Saint Anicet, Can. (sĕɴt ȧ-nē-sĕ')	83a	45.07N	74.23W
Saint Ann, Mo., U.S. (sånt ăn')	107e	38.44N	90.23W
Sainte Anne, Guad.	121b	16.15N	61.23W
Saint Anne, Il., U.S.	101a	41.01N	87.44W
Sainte-Anne, r., Can.	83b	47.07N	70.50W
Sainte Anne, r., Can. (săɴt ȧn') (sånt ăn')	91	46.55N	71.46W
Sainte Anne-des-Plaines, Can. (dā plĕɴ)	83a	45.46N	73.49W
Saint Anne of the Congo, rel., Congo	244c	4.16S	15.17E
Saint Ann's Bay, Jam.	122	18.25N	77.15W
Saint Anns Bay, b., Can. (ănz)	93	46.20N	60.30W
Saint Anselme, Can. (săɴ' täɴ-sĕlm')	83b	46.37N	70.58W
Saint Anthony, Can. (săɴ ăn'thō-nē)	85	51.24N	55.35W
Saint Anthony, Id., U.S. (sånt ăn'thō-nē)	105	43.59N	111.42W
Saint Antoine-de-Tilly, Can.	83b	46.40N	71.31W
Saint Apollinaire, Can. (săɴ' tȧ-pŏl-ē-nâr')	83b	46.36N	71.30W
Saint Arnoult-en-Yvelines, Fr. (sȧɴ-tär-no͞o'ĕɴ-nēv-lēn')	157b	48.33N	1.55E
Saint Augustin-de-Québec, Can. (sĕn tō-gūs-tēn')	83b	46.45N	71.27W
Saint Augustin-Deux-Montagnes, Can.	83a	45.38N	73.59W
Saint Augustine, Fl., U.S. (sånt ô'gŭs-tēn)	97	29.53N	81.21W
Sainte Barbe, Can. (sånt bärb')	83a	45.14N	74.12W
Saint Barthélemy, i., Guad.	121b	17.55N	62.32W
Saint Bees Head, c., Eng., U.K. (sånt bēz' hĕd)	150	54.30N	3.40W
Saint Benoit, Can. (sĕɴ bē-no͞o-ä')	83a	45.34N	74.05W
Saint Bernard, La., U.S. (bẽr-närd')	100d	29.52N	89.52W
Saint Bernard, Oh., U.S.	101f	39.10N	84.30W
Saint Bride, Mount, mtn., Can. (sånt brīd)	87	51.30N	115.57W
Saint Brieuc, Fr. (săɴ' brēs')	147	48.32N	2.47W
Saint Bruno, Can. (brū'nō)	83a	45.31N	73.20W
Saint Canut, Can. (săɴ' kȧ-nü')	83a	45.43N	74.04W
Saint Casimir, Can. (kȧ-zē-mēr')	91	46.45N	72.34W
Saint Catharines, Can. (kăth'ȧ-rĭnz)	85	43.10N	79.14W
Saint Catherine, Mount, mtn., Gren.	121b	12.10N	61.42W
Saint Chamas, Fr. (sȧɴ-shä-mä')	156a	43.32N	5.03E
Saint Chamond, Fr. (săɴ' shȧ-môɴ')	147	45.30N	4.17E
Saint Charles, Can. (săɴ' shärlz')	83b	46.47N	70.57W
Saint Charles, Il., U.S. (sånt chärlz')	101a	41.55N	88.19W
Saint Charles, Mi., U.S.	98	43.20N	84.10W
Saint Charles, Mn., U.S.	103	43.56N	92.05W
Saint Charles, Mo., U.S.	107e	38.47N	90.29W
Saint Charles, Lac, l., Can.	83b	46.56N	71.21W
Saint Christopher-Nevis see Saint Kitts and Nevis, nation, N.A.	116	17.24N	63.30W
Saint Clair, Mi., U.S. (sånt klâr)	98	42.55N	82.30W
Saint Clair, l., Can.	97	42.25N	82.30W
Saint Clair, r., Can.	90	42.45N	82.25W
Sainte Claire, Can.	83b	46.36N	70.52W
Saint Clair Shores, Mi., U.S.	101b	42.30N	82.54W
Saint Claude, Fr. (săɴ' klōd')	157	46.24N	5.53E
Saint Clet, Can. (săɴt' klā')	83a	45.22N	74.21W
Saint-Cloud, Fr.	237c	48.51N	2.13E
Saint Cloud, Fl., U.S. (sånt kloud')	115a	28.13N	81.17W
Saint Cloud, Mn., U.S.	97	45.33N	94.08W
Saint Constant, Can. (kŏn'stănt)	83a	45.23N	73.34W
Saint Croix, i., V.I.U.S. (sånt kroi')	117	17.40N	64.43W
Saint Croix, r., N.A. (kroi')	92	45.28N	67.32W
Saint Croix, r., U.S. (sånt kroi')	97	45.45N	93.00W
Saint Croix Indian Reservation, I.R., Wi., U.S.	103	45.40N	92.21W
Saint Croix Island, i., S. Afr. (săɴ krwä)	213c	33.48S	25.45E
Saint-Cyr-l'Ecole, Fr.	237c	48.48N	2.04E
Saint Damien-de-Buckland, Can. (sånt dä'mē-ĕn)	83b	46.37N	70.39W
Saint David, Can. (dā'vĭd)	83b	46.47N	71.11W
Saint Davids, Pa., U.S.	229b	40.02N	75.22W
Saint David's Head, c., Wales, U.K.	150	51.54N	5.25W
Saint-Denis, Fr. (săɴ'dē-nē')	147	48.26N	2.22E
Saint Dizier, Fr. (dē-zyā')	147	48.49N	4.55E
Saint Dominique, Can. (sĕɴ dō-mē-nēk')	83a	45.19N	74.09W
Sainte-Dorothée, neigh., Can.	227b	45.32N	73.49W
Saint Edouard-de-Napierville, Can. (sĕɴ-tĕ-do͞o-är')	83a	45.14N	73.31W
Saint Elias, Mount, mtn., N.A. (sånt ē-lī'ăs)	84	60.25N	141.00W
Saint Étienne, Fr.	147	45.26N	4.22E
Saint Etienne-de-Lauzon, Can. (săɴ' tā-tyĕn')	83b	46.39N	71.19W
Sainte Euphémie, Can. (sĕɴt û-fē-mē')	83b	46.47N	70.27W
Saint Eustache, Can. (săɴ' tû-stásh')	83a	45.34N	73.54W
Saint Eustache, Can.	83f	49.58N	97.47W
Sainte Famille, Can. (săɴ't fȧ-mē'y')	83b	46.58N	70.58W
Saint Félicien, Can. (săɴ fā-lē-syăɴ')	85	48.39N	72.28W
Sainte Felicite, Can.	92	48.54N	67.20W
Saint Féréol, Can. (fa-rā-ōl')	83b	47.07N	70.52W
Saint Florent-sur-Cher, Fr. (săɴ' flō-räɴ'sür-shâr')	156	46.58N	2.15E
Saint Flour, Fr. (săɴ flo͞or')	156	45.02N	3.09E
Sainte Foy, Can. (săɴt fwä)	91	46.47N	71.18W
Saint Francis, r., Ar., U.S.	111	35.56N	90.27W
Saint Francis Lake, l., Can. (săɴ frăn'sĭs)	91	45.00N	74.20W
Saint François, Can. (săɴ'frăɴ-swä')	83b	47.01N	70.49W
Saint François de Boundji, Congo	216	1.03S	15.22E

g-sing; ŋ-baŋk; ɴ-nasalized n; nŏd; cŏmmit; ōld; ōbey; ôrder; oi-boil; fo͞od; ö-as oo in foot; ou-out; s-soft; sh-dish; th-thin; pūre; ůnite; ûrn; stŭd; circŭs; ü-as in French tu; '-indeterminate vowel.

342 Saint Francois Xavier–Sale

PLACE (Pronunciation)	PAGE	Lat. °′	Long. °′
Saint Francois Xavier, Can.	83f	49.55N	97.32W
Saint Gaudens, Fr. (gō-dăNs′)	156	43.07N	0.43E
Sainte-Geneviève, Can.	227b	45.29N	73.52W
Sainte Genevieve, Mo., U.S. (sånt jĕn′ĕ-vēv)	111	37.58N	90.02W
Saint George, Austl. (sånt jôrj′)	203	28.02S	148.40E
Saint George, Can. (săN′zhôrzh′)	83d	43.14N	80.15W
Saint George, Can. (săN jôrj′)	85	45.08N	66.49W
Saint George, S.C., U.S. (sånt jôrj′)	115	33.11N	80.35W
Saint George, Ut., U.S.	109	37.05N	113.40W
Saint George, neigh., N.Y., U.S.	228	40.39N	74.05W
Saint George, i., Ak., U.S.	95	56.30N	169.40W
Saint George, Cape, c., Can.	85a	48.28N	59.15W
Saint George, Cape, c., Fl., U.S.	114	29.30N	85.20W
Saint George's, Can. (jôrj′ĕs)	85	48.26N	58.29W
Saint Georges, Fr. Gu.	131	3.48N	51.47W
Saint George's, Gren.	121b	12.02N	61.57W
Saint George's Bay, b., Can.	85a	48.20N	59.00W
Saint Georges Bay, b., Can.	93	45.49N	61.45W
Saint George's Channel, strt., Eur. (jôr-jĕz)	142	51.45N	6.30W
Saint Germain-en-Laye, Fr. (săN′ zhĕr-măN-ăN-lā′)	156	48.53N	2.05E
Saint Gervais, Can. (zhĕr-vĕ′)	83b	46.43N	70.53W
Saint Girons, Fr. (zhē-rôN′)	156	42.58N	1.08E
Saint Gotthard Pass, p., Switz.	154	46.33N	8.34E
Saint-Gratien, Fr.	237c	48.58N	2.17E
Saint Gregory, Mount, mtn., Can. (sånt grĕg′ēr-ē)	93	49.19N	58.13W
Saint Helena, i., St. Hel.	209	16.01S	5.16W
Saint Helenabaai, b., S. Afr.	212	32.25S	17.15E
Sainte-Hélène, Île, i., Can.	227b	45.31N	73.32W
Saint Helens, Eng., U.K. (sånt hĕl′ĕnz)	144a	53.27N	2.44W
Saint Helens, Or., U.S. (hĕl′ĕnz)	106c	45.52N	122.49W
Saint Helens, Mount, vol., Wa., U.S.	104	46.13N	122.10W
Saint Helier, Jersey (hyĕl′yĕr)	156	49.12N	2.06W
Saint Henri, Can. (săN′ hĕn′rē)	83b	46.41N	71.04W
Saint Hubert, Can.	83a	45.29N	73.24W
Saint Hyacinthe, Can.	85	45.35N	72.55W
Saint Ignace, Mi., U.S. (sånt ĭg′nås)	103	45.51N	84.39W
Saint Ignace, i., Can. (săN′ ĭg′nås)	90	48.47N	88.14W
Saint Irenee, Can. (săN′ tē-rå-nā′)	91	47.34N	70.15W
Saint Isidore-de-Laprairie, Can.	83a	45.18N	73.41W
Saint Isidore-de-Prescott, Can. (săN′ ĭz′ĭ-dôr-prĕs-kŏt)	83c	45.23N	74.54W
Saint Isidore-Dorchester, Can. (dŏr-chĕs′tĕr)	83b	46.35N	71.05W
Saint Ives, Austl.	243a	33.44S	151.10E
Saint Jacob, Il., U.S. (jā-kŏb)	107e	38.43N	89.46W
Saint James, Mn., U.S. (sånt jāmz′)	103	43.58N	94.37W
Saint James, Mo., U.S.	111	37.59N	91.37W
Saint James, Cape, c., Can.	86	51.58N	131.00W
Saint Janvier, Can. (săN′ zhän-vyā′)	83a	45.43N	73.56W
Saint Jean, Can.	83b	46.55N	70.54W
Saint Jean, Can. (săN′ zhäN′)	85	45.20N	73.15W
Saint Jean, Lac, l., Can.	85	48.35N	72.00W
Saint Jean-Chrysostome, Can. (krĭ-zōs-tōm′)	83b	46.43N	71.12W
Saint Jean-d'Angely, Fr. (däN-zhå-lē′)	156	45.56N	0.33W
Saint Jean-de-Luz, Fr. (dē lüz′)	156	43.23N	1.40W
Saint Jérôme, Can. (sånt jĕ-rōm′) (săN zhā-rōm′)	83a	45.47N	74.00W
Saint Joachim-de-Montmorency, Can. (sånt jō′á-kĭm)	83b	47.04N	70.51W
Saint John, Can. (sånt jŏn)	85	45.16N	66.03W
Saint John, In., U.S.	101a	41.27N	87.29W
Saint John, Ks., U.S.	110	37.59N	98.44W
Saint John, N.D., U.S.	102	48.57N	99.42W
Saint John, i., V.I.U.S.	117b	18.16N	64.48W
Saint John, r., N.A.	85	47.00N	68.00W
Saint John, Cape, c., Can.	93	50.00N	55.32W
Saint Johns, Antig.	121b	17.07N	61.50W
Saint John's, Can. (jŏns)	85a	47.34N	52.43W
Saint Johns, Az., U.S. (jŏnz)	109	34.30N	109.25W
Saint Johns, Mi., U.S.	98	43.05N	84.35W
Saint Johns, r., Fl., U.S.	97	29.54N	81.32W
Saint Johnsburg, N.Y., U.S.	230a	43.05N	78.53W
Saint Johnsbury, Vt., U.S. (jŏnz′bĕr-ē)	99	44.25N	72.00W
Saint John's University, pt. of i., N.Y., U.S.	228	40.43N	73.48W
Saint Joseph, Dom.	121b	15.25N	61.26W
Saint Joseph, Mi., U.S.	98	42.05N	86.30W
Saint Joseph, Mo., U.S. (sånt jō-sĕf)	97	39.44N	94.49W
Saint Joseph, i., Can.	98	46.15N	83.55W
Saint Joseph, l., Can. (jō′zhûf)	85	51.31N	90.40W
Saint Joseph, r., Mi., U.S. (sånt jō′sĕf)	98	41.45N	85.50W
Saint Joseph Bay, b., Fl., U.S. (jō′zhûf)	114	29.48N	85.26W
Saint Joseph-de-Beauce, Can. (sĕN zhō-zĕf′ dĕ bōs)	91	46.18N	70.52W
Saint Joseph-du-Lac, Can. (sĕN zhō-zĕf′ dü läk)	83a	45.32N	74.00W
Saint Joseph Island, i., Tx., U.S. (sånt jō-sĕf)	113	27.58N	96.50W
Saint Junien, Fr. (săN′zhü-nyăN′)	156	45.53N	0.54E
Sainte Justine-de-Newton, Can. (sånt jŭs-tēn′)	83a	45.22N	74.22W
Saint Kilda, Austl.	201a	37.52S	144.59E
Saint Kilda, i., Scot., U.K. (kĭl′dá)	150	57.50N	8.32W
Saint Kitts, i., St. K./N. (sānt kĭtts)	117	17.24N	63.30W
Saint Kitts and Nevis, nation, N.A.	117	17.24N	63.30W
Saint Lambert, Can.	99	45.29N	73.29W
Saint Lambert-de-Lévis, Can.	83b	46.35N	71.12W
Saint Laurent, Can. (săN′lō-rän)	83a	45.31N	73.41W
Saint Laurent, Fr. Gu.	131	5.27N	53.56W
Saint Laurent-d'Orleans, Can.	83b	46.52N	71.00W
Saint Lawrence, Can. (sānt lô′rĕns)	93	46.55N	55.23W
Saint Lawrence, i., Ak., U.S. (sånt lô′rĕns)	96a	63.10N	172.12W
Saint Lawrence, r., N.A.	85	48.24N	69.30W
Saint Lawrence, Gulf of, b., Can.	85	48.00N	62.00W
Saint Lazare, Can. (săN′lå-zár′)	83b	46.39N	70.48W
Saint Lazare-de-Vaudreuil, Can.	83a	45.24N	74.08W
Saint Léger-en-Yvelines, Fr. (săN-lā-zhĕ′ĕN-nēv-lēn′)	157b	48.43N	1.45E
Saint Léonard, Can.	83a	45.36N	73.35W
Saint Leonard, Can. (sånt lĕn′árd)	92	47.10N	67.56W
Saint Leonard, Md., U.S.	100e	38.29N	76.31W
Saint Lô, Fr.	147	49.07N	1.05W
Saint-Louis, Sen.	210	16.02N	16.30W
Saint Louis, Mi., U.S. (sånt lo͞o′ĭs)	98	43.25N	84.35W
Saint Louis, Mo., U.S. (sånt lo͞o′ĭs) (lo͞o′ē)	97	38.39N	90.15W
Saint Louis, r., Mn., U.S. (sånt lo͞o′ĭs)	103	46.57N	92.58W
Saint Louis, Lac, l., Can. (săN′ lo͞o-ē′)	83a	45.24N	73.51W
Saint Louis-de-Gonzague, Can. (săN′ lo͞o ē′)	83a	45.13N	74.00W
Saint Louis Park, Mn., U.S.	107g	44.56N	93.21W
Saint Lucia, nation, N.A.	117	13.54N	60.40W
Saint Lucia Channel, strt., N.A. (lū′shĭ-á)	121b	14.15N	61.00W
Saint Lucie Canal, can., Fl., U.S. (lū′sē)	115a	26.57N	80.25W
Saint Magnus Bay, b., Scot., U.K. (măg′nŭs)	150a	60.25N	2.09W
Saint Malo, Fr. (săN′ må-lō′)	147	48.40N	2.02W
Saint Malo, Golfe de, b., Fr. (gôlf-dĕ-săN-mä-lō′)	147	48.50N	2.49W
Saint Marc, Haiti (săN′ mårk′)	123	19.10N	72.40W
Saint-Marc, Canal de, strt., Haiti	123	19.05N	73.15W
Saint Marcellin, Fr. (mär-sĕ-lăN′)	157	45.08N	5.15E
Saint Margarets, Md., U.S.	100e	39.02N	76.30W
Sainte Marie, Cap, c., Madag.	213	25.31S	45.00E
Sainte-Marie-aux-Mines, Fr. (săN′tĕ-mä-rē′ō-mēn′)	157	48.14N	7.08E
Sainte Marie-Beauce, Can. (săNt′må-rē′)	91	46.27N	71.03W
Saint Maries, Id., U.S. (sånt mā′rēs)	104	47.18N	116.34W
Saint Martin, i., N.A. (mär′tĭn)	121b	18.06N	62.54W
Sainte Martine, Can.	83a	45.14N	73.37W
Saint Martins, Can. (mär′tĭnz)	92	45.21N	65.32W
Saint Martinville, La., U.S. (mär′tĭn-vĭl)	113	30.08N	91.50W
Saint Mary, r., Can. (mā′rē)	87	49.25N	113.00W
Saint Mary, Cape, c., Gam.	214	13.28N	16.40W
Saint Mary Cray, neigh., Eng., U.K.	235	51.23N	0.07E
Saint Marylebone, neigh., Eng., U.K.	235	51.31N	0.10W
Saint Mary Reservoir, res., Can.	87	49.30N	113.00W
Saint Marys, Austl. (mā′rēz)	204	41.40S	148.10E
Saint Marys, Austl.	243a	33.47S	150.47E
Saint Marys, Can.	90	43.15N	81.10W
Saint Marys, Ga., U.S.	115	30.43N	81.35W
Saint Mary's, Ks., U.S.	111	39.12N	96.03W
Saint Mary's, Oh., U.S.	98	40.30N	84.25W
Saint Marys, Pa., U.S.	99	41.25N	78.30W
Saint Marys, W.V., U.S.	98	39.20N	81.15W
Saint Marys, r., N.A.	107k	46.27N	84.33W
Saint Marys, r., U.S.	115	30.37N	82.05W
Saint Mary's Bay, b., Can.	92	44.20N	66.10W
Saint Mary's Bay, b., Can.	93	46.50N	53.47W
Saint Mathew, S.C., U.S. (măth′ū)	115	33.40N	80.46W
Saint Matthew, i., Ak., U.S.	95	60.25N	172.10W
Saint Matthews, Ky., U.S. (măth′ūz)	101h	38.15N	85.39W
Saint Maur-des-Fossés, Fr.	157b	48.48N	2.29E
Saint-Maurice, Fr.	237c	48.49N	2.25E
Saint Maurice, r., Can. (săN′ mō-rēs′) (sånt mô′rĭs)	85	47.20N	72.55W
Saint-Mesmes, Fr.	237c	48.59N	2.42E
Saint Michael, Ak., U.S. (sånt mī′kĕl)	95	63.22N	162.20W
Saint Michel, Can. (săN′ mē-shĕl′)	83b	46.52N	70.54W
Saint-Michel, neigh., Can.	227b	45.35N	73.35W
Saint Michel, Bras, r., Can.	83b	46.47N	70.51W
Saint Michel-de-l'Atalaye, Haiti	123	19.25N	72.20W
Saint Michel-de-Napierville, Can.	83a	45.14N	73.34W
Saint Mihiel, Fr. (săN′ mē-yĕl′)	157	48.53N	5.30E
Saint Nazaire, Fr. (săN′ná-zâr′)	142	47.18N	2.13W
Saint Nérée, Can. (nā-rā′)	83b	46.43N	70.43W
Saint Nicolas, Can. (ne-kô-lā′)	83b	46.42N	71.22W
Saint Nicolas, Cap, c., Haiti	123	19.45N	73.35W
Saint Omer, Fr. (săN′tō-mâr′)	156	50.44N	2.16E
Saint-Ouen, Fr.	237c	48.54N	2.20E
Saint Pancras, neigh., Eng., U.K.	235	51.32N	0.07W
Saint Pascal, Can. (sĕN pä-skäl′)	92	47.32N	69.48W
Saint Paul, Can. (sånt pôl′)	84	53.59N	111.17W
Saint Paul, Mn., U.S.	97	44.57N	93.05W
Saint Paul, Ne., U.S.	102	41.13N	98.28W
Saint Paul, i., Can.	93	47.15N	60.10W
Saint Paul, i., Ak., U.S.	95	57.10N	170.20W
Saint Paul, r., Lib.	214	7.10N	10.00W
Saint Paul, Île, i., Afr.	3	38.43S	77.31E
Saint Paul Park, Mn., U.S. (pärk)	107g	44.51N	93.00W
Saint Pauls, N.C., U.S. (pôls)	115	34.47N	78.57W
Saint Paul's Cathedral, pt. of i., Eng., U.K.	235	51.31N	0.06W
Saint Paul's Cray, neigh., Eng., U.K.	235	51.24N	0.07E
Saint Peter, Mn., U.S. (pē tĕr)	103	44.20N	93.56W
Saint Peter Port, Guernsey	156	49.27N	2.35W
Saint Petersburg (Sankt-Peterburg) (Leningrad), Russia	164	59.57N	30.20E
Saint Petersburg, Fl., U.S. (pē′tĕrz-bûrg)	97	27.47N	82.38W
Sainte Pétronille, Can. (sĕNt pĕt-rō-nēl′)	83b	46.51N	71.08W
Saint Philémon, Can. (sĕN fĕl-mōN′)	83b	46.41N	70.28W
Saint Philippe-d'Argenteuil, Can. (săN′fe-lēp′)	83a	45.38N	74.25W
Saint Philippe-de-Lapairie, Can.	83a	45.20N	73.28W
Saint-Pierre, Can.	227b	45.27N	73.39W
Saint Pierre, Mart. (săN′pyâr′)	121b	14.45N	61.12W
Saint Pierre, St. P./M.	93	46.47N	56.11W
Saint Pierre, i., St. P./M.	93	46.47N	56.11W
Saint Pierre, Lac, l., Can.	91	46.07N	72.45W
Saint Pierre and Miquelon, dep., N.A.	85a	46.53N	56.40W
Saint Pierre-d'Orléans, Can.	83b	46.53N	71.04W
Saint Pierre-Montmagny, Can.	83b	46.55N	70.37W
Saint Placide, Can. (plăs′ĭd)	83a	45.32N	74.11W
Saint Pol-de-Léon, Fr. (săN-pô′dĕ-lā-ôN′)	156	48.41N	4.00W
Saint-Prix, Fr.	237c	49.01N	2.16E
Saint Quentin, Fr. (săN′kăN-tăN′)	147	49.52N	3.16E
Saint Raphaël, Can. (rä-fâ-ĕl′)	83b	46.48N	70.46W
Saint Raymond, Can.	91	46.50N	71.51W
Saint Rédempteur, Can. (săN rā-däNp-tûr′)	83b	46.42N	71.18W
Saint Rémi, Can. (sĕN rĕ-mē′)	83a	45.15N	73.36W
Saint-Rémy-lès-Chevreuse, Fr.	237c	48.42N	2.04E
Saint Romuald-d'Etchemin, Can. (sĕN rō′mo͞o-äl)	91	46.45N	71.14W
Sainte Rose, Guad.	121b	16.19N	61.45W
Sainte-Rose, neigh., Can.	227b	45.36N	73.47W
Saintes, Fr.	156	45.44N	0.41W
Sainte Scholastique, Can. (skô-lås-tēk′)	83a	45.39N	74.05W
Saint Siméon, Can.	91	47.51N	69.55W
Saint Stanislas-de-Kostka, Can.	83a	45.11N	74.08W
Saint Stephen, Can. (stē′vĕn)	85	45.12N	66.17W
Saint Sulpice, Can.	83a	45.50N	73.21W
Saint Thérèse-de-Blainville, Can. (tĕ-rĕz′ dĕ blĕN-vēl′)	91	45.38N	73.51W
Saint-Thibault-des-Vignes, Fr.	237c	48.52N	2.41E
Saint Thomas, Can. (tŏm′ás)	85	42.45N	81.15W
Saint Thomas, i., V.I.U.S.	117	18.22N	64.57W
Saint Thomas Harbor, b., V.I.U.S. (tŏm′ás)	117c	18.19N	64.56W
Saint Timothée, Can. (tē-mô-tā′)	83a	45.17N	74.03W
Saint Tropez, Fr. (trô-pĕ′)	157	43.15N	6.42E
Saint Valentin, Can. (vål-ĕn-tīn)	83a	45.07N	73.19W
Saint Valéry-sur-Somme, Fr. (vá-lā-rē′)	156	50.10N	1.39E
Saint Vallier, Can. (väl-yā′)	83b	46.54N	70.49W
Saint Victor, Can. (vĭk′tĕr)	91	46.09N	70.56W
Saint Vincent, Gulf, b., Austl. (vĭn′sĕnt)	204	34.55S	138.00E
Saint Vincent and the Grenadines, nation, N.A.	117	13.20N	60.50W
Saint-Vincent-de-Paul, neigh., Can.	227b	45.37N	73.39W
Saint Vincent Passage, strt., N.A.	121b	13.35N	61.10W
Saint Walburg, Can.	84	53.39N	109.12W
Saint Yrieix-la-Perche, Fr. (ē-rē-ĕ)	156	45.30N	1.08E
Saitama, dept., Japan (sī′tä-mä)	195a	35.52N	139.40E
Saitbaba, Russia (sá-ĕt′bá-bá)	172a	54.06N	56.42E
Sajama, Nevada, mtn., Bol. (nĕ-vá′dä-sä-hä′mä)	130	18.13S	68.53W
Sakai, Japan (sä′kä-ē)	194	34.34N	135.28E
Sakaiminato, Japan	195	35.33N	133.15E
Sakākah, Sau. Ar.	182	29.58N	40.03E
Sakakawea, Lake, res., N.D., U.S.	96	47.49N	101.58W
Sakania, Zaire (sá-kä′nĭ-á)	212	12.45S	28.34E
Sakarya, r., Tur. (sá-kär′yá)	182	40.10N	31.00E
Sakata, Japan (sä′kä-tä)	189	38.56N	139.57E
Sakchu, N. Kor. (säk′chò)	194	40.29N	125.09E
Sakha (Yakutia), state, Russia	171	65.21N	117.13E
Sakhalin, i., Russia (sá-kä-lēn′)	165	52.00N	143.00E
Šakiai, Lith. (shä′kĭ-ī)	153	54.59N	23.05E
Sakishima-guntō, is., Japan (sä′kē-shē′ma gòn′tō′)	189	24.25N	125.00E
Sakmara, r., Russia	167	52.00N	56.10E
Sakomet, r., R.I., U.S. (sä-kō′mĕt)	100b	41.32N	71.11W
Sakurai, Japan	195b	34.31N	135.51E
Sakwaso Lake, l., Can. (sá-kwá′sō)	89	53.01N	91.55W
Sal, i., C.V. (säal)	210b	16.45N	22.39W
Sal, r., Russia (sál)	167	47.30N	43.00E
Sal, Cay, i., Bah. (kē säl)	122	23.45N	80.25W
Sala, Swe. (sô′lä)	152	59.56N	16.34E
Sala Consilina, Italy (sä′lä kôn-sē-lē′nä)	160	40.24N	15.38E
Salada, Laguna, l., Mex. (lä-gò′nä-sä-lä′dä)	108	32.34N	115.45W
Saladillo, Arg. (sä-lä-dēl′yō)	132	35.38S	59.48W
Salado, Hond. (sä-lä′dhō)	120	15.44N	87.03W
Salado, r., Arg.	129c	35.53S	58.12W
Salado, r., Arg. (sä-lä′dô)	132	26.05S	63.35W
Salado, r., Arg.	132	37.00S	67.00W
Salado, r., Mex.	116	28.00N	102.00W
Salado, r., Mex. (sä-lä′dô)	119	18.30N	97.29W
Salado Creek, r., Tx., U.S.	107d	29.23N	98.25W
Salado de los Nadadores, Río, r., Mex. (dĕ-lôs-nä-dä-dô′rĕs)	112	27.26N	101.35W
Salal, Chad	215	14.51N	17.13E
Salamanca, Chile (sä-lä-mä′n-kä)	129b	31.48S	70.57W
Salamanca, Mex.	116	20.36N	101.10W
Salamanca, Spain (sä-lä-mä′n-kå)	142	40.54N	5.42W
Salamanca, N.Y., U.S. (sál-á-măŋ′kå)	99	42.10N	78.45W
Salamat, Bahr, r., Chad (bär sä-lä-mät′)	211	10.06N	19.16E
Salamina, Col. (sä-lä-mē′-nä)	130a	5.25N	75.29W
Salamis, Grc. (săl′á-mĭs)	161	37.58N	23.30E
Salat-la-Canada, Fr.	156	44.52N	1.13E
Salaverry, Peru (sä-lä-vā′rē)	130	8.16S	78.54W
Salawati, i., Indon. (sä-lä-wä′tē)	197	1.07S	130.52E
Salawe, Tan.	217	3.19S	32.52E
Sala y Gómez, Isla, i., Chile	225	26.50S	105.50W
Salcedo, Dom. Rep. (säl-sā′dō)	123	19.25N	70.30W
Saldaña, r., Col. (säl-dá′n-yä)	130a	3.42N	75.16W
Saldanha, S. Afr.	212	32.55S	18.05E
Saldus, Lat. (säl′dòs)	153	56.39N	22.30E
Sale, Austl. (sāl)	204	38.10S	147.07E
Sale, Eng., U.K.	144a	53.24N	2.20W

ăt; finăl; rāte; senāte; ärm; åsk; sofá; fâre; ch-choose; dh-as th in other; bē; ēvent; bĕt; recĕnt; cratĕr; g-gō; gh-guttural g; bĭt; ĭ-short neutral; rīde; K-guttural k as ch in German ich;

PLACE (Pronunciation)	PAGE	Lat. °′	Long. °′
Sale, r., Can. (sål'rê-vyâr')	83f	49.44N	97.11W
Salekhard, Russia (sŭ-lyĭ-kärt)	166	66.35N	66.50E
Salem, India	183	11.39N	78.11E
Salem, S. Afr.	213c	33.29S	26.30E
Salem, Il., U.S. (sā'lĕm)	98	38.40N	89.00W
Salem, In., U.S.	98	38.35N	86.00W
Salem, Ma., U.S.	93a	42.31N	70.54W
Salem, Mo., U.S.	111	37.36N	91.33W
Salem, N.H., U.S.	93a	42.46N	71.16W
Salem, N.J., U.S.	99	39.35N	75.30W
Salem, Oh., U.S.	98	40.55N	80.50W
Salem, Or., U.S.	96	44.55N	123.03W
Salem, S.D., U.S.	102	43.43N	97.23W
Salem, Va., U.S.	115	37.16N	80.05W
Salem, W.V., U.S.	98	39.15N	80.35W
Salemi, Italy (sä-lå'mē)	160	37.49N	12.48E
Salerno, Italy (sä-lĕr'nô)	148	40.27N	14.46E
Salerno, Golfo di, b., Italy (gôl-fô-dē)	148	40.30N	14.40E
Salford, Eng., U.K. (săl'fẽrd)	150	53.26N	2.19W
Salgótarján, Hung. (shôl'gô-tôr-yän)	155	48.06N	19.50E
Salhyr, r., Ukr.	163	45.25N	34.22E
Salida, Co., U.S. (sȧ-lī'dȧ)	110	38.31N	106.01W
Salies-de-Béan, Fr.	156	43.27N	0.58W
Salima, Mwi.	217	13.47S	34.26E
Salina, Ks., U.S. (sȧ-lī'nȧ)	96	38.50N	97.37W
Salina, Ut., U.S.	109	39.00N	111.55W
Salina, i., Italy (sä-lē'nä)	160	38.35N	14.48E
Salina Cruz, Mex. (sä-lē'nä kro͞oz')	116	16.10N	95.12W
Salina Point, c., Bah.	123	22.10N	74.20W
Salinas, Mex.	116	22.38N	101.42W
Salinas, P.R.	117b	17.58N	66.16W
Salinas, Ca., U.S. (sȧ-lē'nȧs)	108	36.41N	121.40W
Salinas, r., Mex. (sä-lē'näs)	119	16.15N	90.31W
Salinas, r., Ca., U.S.	108	36.33N	121.29W
Salinas, Bahía de, b., N.A. (bä-ē'ä-dĕ-sȧ-lē'nȧs)	120	11.05N	85.55W
Salinas, Cape, c., Spain (sä-lēnäs)	159	39.14N	1.02E
Salinas National Monument, rec., N.M., U.S.	109	34.10N	106.05W
Salinas Victoria, Mex. (sä-lē'näs vēk-tō'rē-ä)	112	25.59N	100.19W
Saline, r., Ar., U.S. (sȧ-lēn')	111	34.06N	92.30W
Saline, r., Ks., U.S.	110	39.05N	99.43W
Salins-les-Bains, Fr. (sȧ-lăɴ'-lā-băɴ')	157	46.55N	5.54E
Salisbury, Can.	92	46.03N	65.05W
Salisbury, Eng., U.K. (sôlz'bē-rē)	147	50.35N	1.51W
Salisbury, Md., U.S.	99	38.20N	75.40W
Salisbury, Mo., U.S.	111	39.24N	92.47W
Salisbury, N.C., U.S.	115	35.40N	80.29W
Salisbury *see* Harare, Zimb.	212	17.50S	31.03E
Salisbury Island, i., Can.	85	63.36N	76.20W
Salisbury Plain, pl., Eng., U.K.	150	51.15N	1.52W
Salkehatchie, r., S.C., U.S. (sô-kê-hăch'ê)	115	33.09N	81.10W
Salkhia, India	240a	22.35N	88.21E
Sallisaw, Ok., U.S. (săl'ĭ-sô)	111	35.27N	94.48W
Salmon, Id., U.S. (săm'ŭn)	105	45.11N	113.54W
Salmon, r., Can.	86	54.00N	123.50W
Salmon, r., Can.	92	46.19N	65.36W
Salmon, r., Id., U.S.	96	45.30N	115.45W
Salmon, r., Id., U.S.	104	44.51N	115.47W
Salmon, r., Id., U.S.	105	44.54N	114.50W
Salmon, r., N.Y., U.S.	99	44.35N	74.15W
Salmon, r., Wa., U.S.	106c	45.44N	122.36W
Salmon Arm, Can.	87	50.42N	119.16W
Salmon Falls Creek, r., Id., U.S.	105	42.22N	114.53W
Salmon Gums, Austl. (gŭmz)	202	33.00S	122.00E
Salmon River Mountains, mts., Id., U.S.	96	44.15N	115.44W
Salon-de-Provence, Fr. (sȧ-lôɴ-dĕ-prô-văɴs')	157	43.48N	5.09E
Salonika *see* Thessaloníki, Grc.	142	40.38N	22.59E
Salonta, Rom. (sä-lôn'tä)	155	46.46N	21.38E
Salop, co., Eng., U.K.	144a	52.36N	2.45W
Saloum, r., Sen.	214	14.10N	15.45W
Salsette Island, i., India	187b	19.12N	72.52E
Sal'sk, Russia (sälsk)	167	46.30N	41.20E
Salt, r., Az., U.S. (sôlt)	96	33.28N	111.35W
Salt, r., Mo., U.S.	111	39.54N	92.11W
Salta, Arg. (säl'tä)	132	24.50S	65.16W
Salta, prov., Arg.	132	25.15S	65.00W
Saltair, Ut., U.S. (sôlt'âr)	107b	40.46N	112.09W
Salt Cay, i., T./C. Is.	123	21.20N	71.15W
Salt Creek, r., Il., U.S. (sôlt)	101a	42.01N	88.01W
Saltillo, Mex. (säl-tēl'yō)	116	25.24N	100.59W
Salt Lake City, Ut., U.S. (sôlt lāk sĭ'tĭ)	96	40.45N	111.52W
Salto, Arg. (säl'tō)	129c	34.17S	60.15W
Salto, Ur.	132	31.18S	57.45W
Salto, r., Mex.	118	22.16N	99.18W
Salto, Serra do, mtn., Braz. (sĕ'r-rä-dô)	129a	20.26S	43.28W
Salto Grande, Braz. (grän'dă)	131	22.57S	49.58W
Salton Sea, Ca., U.S. (sôlt'ŭn)	108	33.28N	115.43W
Salton Sea, l., Ca., U.S.	96	33.19N	115.50W
Saltpond, Ghana	210	5.16N	1.07W
Salt River Indian Reservation, I.R., Az., U.S. (sôlt rĭv'ẽr)	109	33.40N	112.01W
Saltsjöbaden, Swe. (sält'shû-bäd'ĕn)	152	59.15N	18.20E
Saltspring Island, i., Can. (sält'sprĭng)	86	48.47N	123.30W
Saltville, Va., U.S. (sôlt'vĭl)	115	36.50N	81.45W
Saltykovka, Russia (sál-tē'kôf-kȧ)	172b	55.45N	37.56E
Salud, Mount, mtn., Pan. (sä-lo͞o'th)	116a	9.14N	79.42W
Saluda, S.C., U.S. (sȧ-lo͞o'dȧ)	115	34.02N	81.46W
Saluda, r., S.C., U.S.	115	34.07N	81.48W
Saluzzo, Italy (sä-lo͞ot'sō)	160	44.39N	7.31E
Salvador, Braz. (säl-vä-dōr') (bä-ē'ä)	131	12.59S	38.27W
Salvador Lake, l., La., U.S.	113	29.45N	90.20W
Salvador Point, c., Bah.	122	24.30N	77.45W
Salvatierra, Mex. (säl-vä-tyĕr'rä)	118	20.13N	100.52W
Salween, r., Asia	180	21.00N	98.00E
Salyan, Azer.	167	39.40N	49.10E
Salzburg, Aus. (sälts'bōorgh)	147	47.48N	13.04E
Salzburg, state, Aus.	154	47.30N	13.18E
Salzwedel, Ger. (sälts-vä'dĕl)	154	52.51N	11.10E
Samāika, neigh., India	240d	28.32N	77.05E
Samālūt, Egypt (sä-mä-lo͞ot')	184	28.17N	30.43E
Samana, Cabo, c., Dom. Rep.	117	19.20N	69.00W
Samana or Atwood Cay, i., Bah.	123	23.05N	73.45W
Samar, i., Phil. (sä'mär)	197	11.30N	126.07E
Samara (Kuybyshev), Russia	166	53.10N	50.05E
Samara, r., Russia	167	52.50N	50.35E
Samara, r., Ukr. (sȧ-mä'rȧ)	163	48.47N	35.30E
Samarai, Pap. N. Gui. (sä-mä-rä'ē)	197	10.45S	150.49E
Samarinda, Indon.	196	0.30S	117.10E
Samarkand, Uzb. (sȧ-mȧr-känt')	169	39.42N	67.00E
Şamaxı, Azer.	167	40.35N	48.40E
Šamba, Zaire	217	4.38S	26.22E
Sambalpur, India (sŭm'bŭl-pōr)	183	21.30N	84.05E
Sāmbhar, r., India	186	27.00N	74.58E
Sambir, Ukr.	155	49.31N	23.12E
Samborombón, r., Arg.	129c	35.20S	57.52W
Samborombón, Bahía, b., Arg. (bä-ē'ä-säm-bô-rôm-bô'n)	129c	35.57S	57.05W
Sambre, r., Eur. (säɴ'br')	151	50.20N	4.15E
Sambungo, Ang.	216	8.39S	20.43E
Sammamish, r., Wa., U.S.	106a	47.43N	122.08W
Sammamish, Lake, l., Wa., U.S. (sȧ-măm'ĭsh)	106a	47.35N	122.02W
Samoa Islands, is., Oc.	198a	14.00S	171.00W
Samokov, Bul. (sä'mô-kôf)	161	42.20N	23.33E
Samora Correia, Port. (sä-mō'rä-kôr-rē'yä)	159b	38.55N	8.52W
Samorovo, Russia (sȧ-mȧ-rô'vô)	170	60.47N	69.13E
Sámos, i., Grc. (sä'mŏs)	149	37.53N	26.35E
Samothráki, i., Grc.	149	40.23N	25.10E
Sampaloc Point, c., Phil. (säm-pä'lŏk)	197a	14.43N	119.56E
Sam Rayburn Reservoir, res., Tx., U.S.	113	31.10N	94.15W
Samson, Al., U.S. (săm'sŭn)	114	31.06N	86.02W
Samsu, N. Kor. (säm'so͞o')	194	41.12N	128.00E
Samsun, Tur. (sȧm'so͞on')	182	41.20N	36.05E
Samtredia, Geor. (sȧm'trĕ-dē)	167	42.18N	42.25E
Samuel, i., Can. (săm'ū-ĕl)	106d	48.50N	123.10W
Samur, r. (sä-mo͞or')	167	41.40N	47.20E
San, Mali (sän)	210	13.18N	4.54W
San, r., Eur.	147	50.33N	22.12E
Şan'ā', Yemen (sän'ä)	182	15.17N	44.05E
Sanaga, r., Cam. (sä-nä'gä)	210	4.30N	12.00E
San Ambrosio, Isla, i., Chile (ē's-lä-dĕ-sän äm-brō'zē-ō)	128	26.40S	80.00W
Sanana, Pulau, i., Indon.	197	2.15S	126.38E
Sanandaj, Iran	182	36.44N	46.43E
San Andreas, Ca., U.S. (săn ăn'drē-ăs)	108	38.10N	120.42W
San Andreas, l., Ca., U.S.	106b	37.36N	122.26W
San Andrés, Col. (sän-än-drĕ's)	130a	6.57N	75.41W
San Andrés, Mex. (sän än-drās')	119a	19.15N	99.10W
San Andrés, i., Col.	121	12.32N	81.34W
San Andres, Laguna de, l., Mex.	119	22.40N	97.50W
San Andres Mountains, mts., N.M., U.S. (săn ăn'drē-ăs)	96	33.00N	106.40W
San Andrés Tuxtla, Mex. (sän-än-drā's-to͞os'tlä)	116	18.27N	95.12W
San Angelo, Tx., U.S. (săn ăn-jĕ-lō)	96	31.28N	100.22W
San Antioco, Isola di, i., Italy (ē'sō-lä-dē-sän-än-tyŏ'kô)	160	39.00N	8.25E
San Antonio, Chile (sän-ån-tô'nyō)	132	33.34S	71.36W
San Antonio, Col.	130a	2.57N	75.06W
San Antonio, Col.	130a	3.55N	75.28W
San Antonio, Phil.	197a	14.57N	120.05E
San Antonio, Tx., U.S. (săn ăn-tō'nē-ô)	96	29.25N	98.30W
San Antonio, r., Tx., U.S.	113	29.00N	97.58W
San Antonio, Cabo, c., Cuba (kȧ'bô-sän-än-tō'nyô)	117	21.55N	84.55W
San Antonio, Lake, res., Ca., U.S.	108	36.00N	121.13W
San Antonio Abad, Spain (sän än-tō'nyō ä-bädh')	159	38.59N	1.17E
San Antonio Bay, b., Tx., U.S.	113	28.20N	97.08W
San Antonio de Areco, Arg. (dā ä-rä'kô)	129c	34.16S	59.30W
San Antonio de Galipán, Ven.	234a	10.33N	66.53W
San Antonio de las Vegas, Cuba	123a	22.51N	82.23W
San Antonio de los Baños, Cuba (dā lōs bän'yōs)	122	22.54N	82.30W
San Antonio de los Cobres, Arg. (dā lōs kō'brås)	132	24.15S	66.29W
San Antonio de Pádua, Braz. (dĕ-pȧ'dwä)	129a	21.32S	42.09W
San Antonio de Tamanaco, Ven.	131b	9.42N	66.03W
San Antonio Heights, Ca., U.S.	232	34.10N	117.40W
San Antonio Oeste, Arg. (sän-nä-tō'nyō ō-ĕs'tå)	132	40.49S	64.56W
San Antonio Peak, mtn., Ca., U.S. (săn ăn-tō'nĭ-ô)	107a	34.17N	117.39W
Sanarate, Guat. (sä-nä-rä'tĕ)	120	14.47N	90.12W
San Augustine, Tx., U.S. (săn ô'gŭs-tēn)	113	31.33N	94.08W
San Bartolo, Mex.	112	24.43N	103.12W
San Bartolo, Mex. (sän bär-tō'lô)	119a	19.36N	99.43W
San Bartolomé de la Cuadra, Spain	238e	41.26N	2.02E
San Bartolomeo, Italy (bär-tô-lô-mā'ô)	160	41.25N	15.04E
San Baudilio de Llobregat, Spain	238e	41.21N	2.03E
San Benedetto del Tronto, Italy (bā'nȧ-dĕt'tô dĕl trōn'tô)	160	42.58N	13.54E
San Benito, Tx., U.S. (săn bĕ-nē'tô)	113	26.07N	97.37W
San Benito, r., Ca., U.S.	108	36.40N	121.20W
San Bernardino, Ca., U.S. (bûr-när-dē'nô)	96	34.07N	117.19W
San Bernardino Mountains, mts., Ca., U.S.	108	34.05N	116.23W
San Bernardo, Chile (sän bĕr-när'dô)	129b	33.35S	70.42W
San Blas, Mex. (sän bläs')	116	21.33N	105.19W
San Blas, Cape, c., Fl., U.S.	97	29.38N	85.38W
San Blas, Cordillera de, mts., Pan.	121	9.17N	78.20W
San Blas, Golfo de, b., Pan.	121	9.33N	78.42W
San Blas, Punta, c., Pan.	121	9.35N	78.55W
San Bruno, Ca., U.S. (săn brū-nô)	106b	37.38N	122.25W
San Buenaventura, Mex. (bwā'nȧ-vĕn-to͞o'rȧ)	112	27.07N	101.30W
San Carlos, Chile (sän-kȧ'r-lŏs)	132	36.23S	71.58W
San Carlos, Col.	130a	6.11N	74.58W
San Carlos, Eq. Gui.	216	3.27N	8.33E
San Carlos, Mex.	112	24.36N	98.52W
San Carlos, Mex. (sän kär'lōs)	119	17.49N	92.33W
San Carlos, Nic. (sän-kä'r-lôs)	121	11.08N	84.48W
San Carlos, Phil.	197a	15.56N	120.20E
San Carlos, Ca., U.S. (săn kär'lōs)	106b	37.30N	122.15W
San Carlos, Ven.	130	9.36N	68.35W
San Carlos, r., C.R.	121	10.36N	84.18W
San Carlos de Bariloche, Arg.	132	41.15S	71.26W
San Carlos Indian Reservation, I.R., Az., U.S. (săn kär'lōs)	109	33.27N	110.15W
San Carlos Lake, res., Az., U.S.	109	33.05N	110.29W
San Casimiro, Ven. (kä-sē-mē'rô)	131b	10.01N	67.02W
San Cataldo, Italy (kä-täl'dō)	160	37.30N	13.59E
Sánchez, Dom. Rep. (sän'chĕz)	117	19.15N	69.40W
Sanchez, Río de los, r., Mex. (rē'ō-dĕ-lôs)	118	20.31N	102.29W
Sánchez Román, Mex. (rô-mȧ'n)	118	21.48N	103.20W
Sanchung, Tai.	241d	25.04N	121.29E
San Clemente, Spain (sän klå-mĕn'tå)	158	39.25N	2.24W
San Clemente de Llobregat, Spain	238e	41.20N	2.00E
San Clemente Island, i., Ca., U.S.	96	32.54N	118.29W
San Cristóbal, Dom. Rep. (krēs-tô'bäl)	123	18.25N	70.05W
San Cristóbal, Guat.	120	15.22N	90.26W
San Cristóbal, Ven.	130	7.43N	72.15W
San Cristóbal, i., Sol.Is.	203	10.47S	162.17E
San Cristóbal de las Casas, Mex.	116	16.44N	92.39W
Sancti Spíritus, Cuba (säŋk'tē spē'rē-to͞os)	117	21.55N	79.25W
Sancti Spiritus, prov., Cuba	122	22.05N	79.20W
San Cugat del Vallés, Spain	238e	41.28N	2.05E
Sancy, Puy de, mtn., Fr. (pwē-dĕ-säɴ-sē')	147	45.30N	2.53E
Sand, i., Or., U.S. (sănd)	106c	46.16N	124.01W
Sand, i., Wi., U.S.	103	46.03N	91.09W
Sand, r., S. Afr.	213c	28.30S	29.30E
Sand, r., S. Afr.	218d	28.09S	26.46E
Sanda, Japan (sän'dä)	195	34.53N	135.14E
Sandakan, Malay. (sȧn-dä'kȧn)	196	5.51N	118.03E
Sanday, i., Scot., U.K. (sănd'ā)	150a	59.17N	2.25W
Sandbach, Eng., U.K. (sănd'băch)	144a	53.08N	2.22W
Sandefjord, Nor. (sän'dĕ-fyôr')	152	59.09N	10.14E
San de Fuca, Wa., U.S. (de-fo͞o-cä)	106a	48.14N	122.44W
Sanders, Az., U.S.	109	35.13N	109.20W
Sanderson, Tx., U.S. (săn'dẽr-sŭn)	112	30.09N	102.24W
Sanderstead, neigh., Eng., U.K.	235	51.20N	0.05W
Sandersville, Ga., U.S. (săn'dẽrz-vĭl)	115	32.57N	82.50W
Sandhammaren, c., Swe. (sänt'häm-mår)	146	55.24N	14.37E
Sand Hills, reg., Ne., U.S. (sănd)	102	41.57N	101.29W
Sand Hook, N.J., U.S. (sănd hŏok)	100a	40.29N	74.05W
Sandhurst, Eng., U.K. (sănd'hûrst)	144b	51.20N	0.48W
Sandia Indian Reservation, I.R., N.M., U.S.	109	35.15N	106.30W
San Diego, Ca., U.S. (săn dē-ā'gô)	96	32.43N	117.10W
San Diego, Tx., U.S.	110	27.47N	98.13W
San Diego, r., Ca., U.S.	108	32.53N	116.57W
San Diego de la Unión, Mex. (sän dĕ-å-gô dā lä o͞o-nyōn')	118	21.27N	100.52W
Sandies Creek, r., Tx., U.S. (sănd'ēz)	113	29.13N	97.34W
San Dimas, Mex. (dē-mäs')	118	24.08N	105.57W
San Dimas, Ca., U.S. (săn dē-mȧs)	107a	34.07N	117.49W
Sandnes, Nor. (sänd'nĕs)	152	58.52N	5.44E
Sandoa, Zaire (sän-dō'ȧ)	212	9.39S	23.00E
Sandomierz, Pol. (sȧn-dô'myĕzh)	155	50.39N	21.45E
San Doná di Piave, Italy (sän dô nȧ' dē pyä'vĕ)	160	45.38N	12.34E
Sandoway, Myanmar (sän-dô-wī')	183	18.24N	94.28E
Sandpoint, Id., U.S. (sănd point)	104	48.17N	116.34W
Sandringham, Austl. (săn'drĭng-ăm)	201a	37.57S	145.01E
Sandringham, neigh., S. Afr.	244b	26.09S	28.07E
Sandrio, Italy (sä'n-dryô)	160	46.11N	9.53E
Sands Point, N.Y., U.S.	228	40.51N	73.43W
Sand Springs, Ok., U.S. (sănd sprĭnz)	111	36.08N	96.06W
Sandstone, Austl. (sănd'stōn)	202	28.00S	119.25E
Sandstone, Mn., U.S.	103	46.08N	92.53W
Sanduo, China (sän-dwô)	190	32.49N	119.39E
Sandusky, Al., U.S. (săn-dŭs'kē)	100h	33.32N	86.50W
Sandusky, Mi., U.S.	98	43.25N	82.50W
Sandusky, Oh., U.S.	97	41.25N	82.45W
Sandusky, r., Oh., U.S.	98	41.10N	83.20W
Sandwich, Il., U.S. (sănd'wĭch)	98	42.35N	88.53W
Sandy, Or., U.S. (sănd'ē)	106c	45.24N	122.16W
Sandy, Ut., U.S.	107b	40.36N	111.53W
Sandy, r., Or., U.S.	106c	45.28N	122.17W
Sandy Cape, c., Austl.	203	24.25S	153.10E
Sandy Hook, Ct., U.S. (hŏok)	100a	41.25N	73.17W
Sandy Lake, l., Can.	83g	53.46N	113.58W
Sandy Lake, l., Can.	89	53.00N	93.07W
Sandy Lake, l., Can.	93	49.16N	57.00W

344 Sandy Point-San Rafael

PLACE (Pronunciation)	PAGE	Lat. °′	Long. °′
Sandy Point, Tx., U.S.	113a	29.22N	95.27W
Sandy Point, c., Wa., U.S.	106d	48.48N	122.42W
Sandy Springs, Ga., U.S. (springz)	100c	33.55N	84.23W
San Estanislao, Para. (ĕs-tä-nĕs-lá'ō)	132	24.38S	56.20W
San Esteban, Hond. (ĕs-tĕ'bän)	120	15.13N	85.53W
San Fabian, Phil. (fä-byä'n)	197a	16.14N	120.28E
San Felipe, Chile (fâ-lē'pâ)	132	32.45S	70.43W
San Felipe, Mex. (fĕ-lē'pĕ)	118	21.29N	101.13W
San Felipe, Mex.	118	22.21N	105.26W
San Felipe, Ven. (fĕ-lē'pĕ)	130	10.13N	68.45W
San Felipe, Cayos de, is., Cuba (kä'yōs-dĕ-sän-fĕ-lē'pĕ)	122	22.00N	83.30W
San Felipe Creek, r., Ca., U.S. (săn fĕ-lēp'ă)	108	33.10N	116.03W
San Felipe Indian Reservation, I.R., N.M., U.S.	109	35.26N	106.26W
San Felíu de Guixols, Spain (sän fâ-lē'ŏ dâ gē-hôls)	159	41.45N	3.01E
San Félix, Isla, i., Chile (ē's-lä-dĕ-sän fā-lēks')	128	26.20S	80.10W
San Fernanda, Spain (fĕr-nä'n-dä)	158	36.28N	6.13W
San Fernando, Arg. (fĕr-ná'n-dô)	132a	34.26S	58.34W
San Fernando, Chile	129b	35.36S	70.58W
San Fernando, Mex. (fĕr-nän'dô)	112	24.52N	98.10W
San Fernando, Phil. (sän fĕr-nä'n-dô)	196	16.38N	120.19E
San Fernando, Ca., U.S. (fĕr-nän'dô)	107a	34.17N	118.27W
San Fernando, r., Mex. (sän fĕr-nän'dô)	112	25.07N	98.25W
San Fernando de Apure, Ven. (sän-fĕr-nä'n-dō-dĕ-ä-pōō'râ)	130	7.46N	67.29W
San Fernando de Atabapo, Ven. (dĕ-ä-tä-bä'pô)	130	3.58N	67.41W
San Fernando de Henares, Spain (dĕ-ā-nä'rås)	159a	40.23N	3.31W
Sånfjället, mtn., Swe.	146	62.19N	13.30E
Sanford, Can. (săn'fērd)	83f	49.41N	97.27W
Sanford, Fl., U.S. (săn'fôrd)	97	28.46N	81.18W
Sanford, Me., U.S. (săn'fērd)	92	43.26N	70.47W
Sanford, N.C., U.S.	115	35.26N	79.10W
San Francisco, Arg. (sän frän'sĭs'kô)	132	31.23S	62.09W
San Francisco, El Sal.	120	13.48N	88.11W
San Francisco, Ca., U.S.	96	37.45N	122.26W
San Francisco, r., N.M., U.S.	109	33.35N	108.55W
San Francisco Bay, b., Ca., U.S. (săn frăn'sĭs'kô)	108	37.45N	122.21W
San Francisco Culhuacán, Mex.	233a	19.20N	99.06W
San Francisco del Oro, Mex. (dĕl ō'rō)	116	27.00N	106.37W
San Francisco del Rincón, Mex. (dĕl rēn-kōn')	118	21.01N	101.51W
San Francisco de Macaira, Ven. (dĕ-mä-kī'rä)	131b	9.58N	66.17W
San Francisco de Macoris, Dom. Rep. (dā-mä-kō'rēs)	123	19.20N	70.15W
San Francisco de Paula, Cuba (dā pou'lä)	123a	23.04N	82.18W
San Francisco el Grande, Iglesia de, rel., Spain	238b	40.25N	3.43W
San Gabriel, Ca., U.S. (săn gä-brē-ĕl') (gā'brē-ĕl)	107a	34.06N	118.06W
San Gabriel, r., Ca., U.S.	107a	33.47N	118.06W
San Gabriel Chilac, Mex. (sän-gä-brē-ĕl-chē-läk')	119	18.19N	97.22W
San Gabriel Mts, Ca., U.S.	107a	34.17N	118.03W
San Gabriel Reservoir, res., Ca., U.S.	107a	34.14N	117.48W
Sangamon, r., Il., U.S. (săn'gȧ-msion)	111	40.08N	90.08W
Sangenjaya, neigh., Japan	242a	35.38N	139.40E
Sanger, Ca., U.S. (săng'ẽr)	108	36.42N	119.33W
Sangerhausen, Ger. (säng'ẽr-hou-zĕn)	154	51.28N	11.17E
Sangha, r., Afr.	211	2.40N	16.10E
Sangihe, Pulau, i., Indon.	197	3.30N	125.30E
San Gil, Col. (sän-кē'l)	130	6.32N	73.13W
San Giovanni in Fiore, Italy (sän jô-vän'nē ēn fyō'rā)	160	39.15N	16.40E
San Giuseppe Vesuviano, Italy	159c	40.36N	14.31E
Sangju, S. Kor. (säng'jōō')	194	36.20N	128.07E
Sāngli, India	183	16.56N	74.38E
Sangmélima, Cam.	215	2.56N	11.59E
San Gorgonio Mountain, mtn., Ca., U.S. (săn gôr-gō'nĭ-ō)	107a	34.06N	116.50W
Sangre de Cristo Mountains, mts., U.S.	96	37.45N	105.50W
San Gregoria, Ca., U.S. (săn grē-gôr'ā)	106b	37.20N	122.23W
San Gregorio Atlapulco, Mex.	233a	19.15N	99.03W
Sangro, r., Italy (säŋ'grô)	160	41.38N	13.56E
Sangüesa, Spain (sän-gwĕ'sä)	158	42.36N	1.15W
Sanhe, China (sän-hŭ)	190	39.59N	117.06E
Sanibel Island, i., Fl., U.S. (săn'ĭ-bĕl)	115a	26.26N	82.15W
San Ignacio, Belize	120a	17.11N	89.04W
San Ildefonso, Cape, c., Phil. (sän-ēl-dĕ-fôn-sô)	197a	16.03N	122.10E
San Ildefonso o la Granja, Spain (ō lä grän'khä)	158	40.54N	4.02W
San Isidro, Arg. (ē-sē'drô)	129c	34.28S	58.31W
San Isidro, C.R.	121	9.24N	83.43W
San Isidro, Peru	233c	12.07S	77.03W
San Jacinto, Phil. (sän hä-sēn'tô)	197a	12.33N	123.43E
San Jacinto, Ca., U.S. (săn jȧ-sĭn'tô)	107a	33.47N	116.57W
San Jacinto, r., Ca., U.S. (săn jȧ-sĭn'tô)	107a	33.44N	117.14W
San Jacinto, r., Tx., U.S.	113	30.25N	95.05W
San Jacinto, West Fork, r., Tx., U.S.	113	30.35N	95.37W
San Javier, Chile (sän-hä-vē'ĕr)	129b	35.35S	71.43W
San Jerónimo, Mex.	119a	19.31N	98.46W
San Jerónimo de Juárez, Mex. (hâ-rō'nē-mô dā hwä'râz)	118	17.08N	100.30W
San Jerónimo Lídice, Mex.	233a	19.20N	99.13W
San Joaquin, Ven.	131b	10.16N	67.47W
San Joaquin, r., Ca., U.S. (săn hwä-kēn')	108	37.10N	120.51W
San Joaquin Valley, Ca., U.S.	108	36.45N	120.30W
San Jorge, Golfo, b., Arg. (gôl-fô-sän-кô'r-кĕ)	132	46.15S	66.45W
San José, C.R. (sän hô-sā')	117	9.57N	84.05W
San Jose, Phil.	197a	12.22N	121.04E
San Jose, Phil.	197a	15.49N	120.57E
San Jose, Ca., U.S. (săn hô-zā')	96	37.20N	121.54W
San José, i., Mex. (кô-sĕ')	116	25.00N	110.35W
San José, Isla de, i., Pan. (ē's-lä-dĕ-sän hô-sā')	121	8.17N	79.20W
San Jose, Rio, r., N.M., U.S. (săn hô-zā')	109	35.15N	108.10W
San José de Feliciano, Arg. (dā lä ĕs-kē'nà)	132	30.26S	58.44W
San José de Galipán, Ven.	234a	10.35N	66.54W
San José de Gauribe, Ven. (sän-hô-sĕ'dĕ-gáōō-rē'bĕ)	131b	9.51N	65.49W
San José de las Lajas, Cuba (sän-кô-sĕ'dĕ-läs-lä'käs)	123a	22.58N	82.10W
San José Iturbide, Mex. (ē-tōōr-bē'dĕ)	118	21.00N	100.24W
San Juan, Arg. (hwän')	132	31.36S	68.29W
San Juan, Col. (hòá'n)	130a	3.23N	73.48W
San Juan, Dom. Rep. (sän hwän')	123	18.50N	71.15W
San Juan, Phil.	197a	16.41N	120.20E
San Juan, P.R. (sän hwän')	117	18.30N	66.10W
San Juan, prov., Arg.	132	31.00S	69.30W
San Juan, r., Mex. (sän-hōō-än')	119	18.10N	95.23W
San Juan, r., N.A.	117	10.58N	84.18W
San Juan, r., U.S.	96	36.30N	109.00W
San Juan, Cabezas de, c., P.R.	117b	18.29N	65.30W
San Juan, Cabo, c., Eq. Gui.	216	1.08N	9.23E
San Juan, Pico, mtn., Cuba (pē'kô-sän-kòá'n)	122	21.55N	80.00W
San Juan, Río, r., Mex. (rē'ō-sän-hwän)	112	25.35N	99.15W
San Juan Bautista, Para. (sän hwän' bou-tēs'tä)	132	26.48S	57.09W
San Juan Capistrano, Mex. (sän-hōō-än' kä-pēs-trä'nô)	118	22.41N	104.07W
San Juan Creek, r., Ca., U.S. (săn hwän')	108	35.24N	120.12W
San Juan de Aragón, Mex.	233a	19.28N	99.05W
San Juan de Aragón, Bosque, rec., Mex.	233a	19.28N	99.04W
San Juan de Aragón, Zoológico de, rec., Mex.	233a	19.28N	99.05W
San Juan de Dios, Ven.	234a	10.35N	66.57W
San Juan de Guadalupe, Mex. (sän hwan dâ gwä-dhä-lōō'pâ)	112	24.37N	102.43W
San Juan del Monte, Phil.	241g	14.36N	121.02E
San Juan del Norte, Nic.	121	10.55N	83.44W
San Juan del Norte, Bahía de, b., Nic.	121	11.12N	83.40W
San Juan de los Lagos, Mex. (sän-hōō-än'dâ lōs lä'gôs)	118	21.15N	102.18W
San Juan de los Lagos, r., Mex. (dâ lōs lä'gôs)	118	21.13N	102.12W
San Juan de los Morros, Ven. (dĕ-lôs-mô'r-rôs)	131b	9.54N	67.22W
San Juan del Río, Mex. (sän hwän del rē'ô)	112	24.47N	104.29W
San Juan del Río, Mex.	118	20.21N	99.59W
San Juan del Sur, Nic. (dĕl sōōr)	116	11.15N	85.53W
San Juan Evangelista, Mex. (sän-hōō-ä'n-å-väŋ-kå-lēs'ta')	119	17.57N	95.08W
San Juan Island, i., Wa., U.S.	106a	48.28N	123.08W
San Juan Islands, is., Can. (săn hwän)	86	48.49N	123.14W
San Juan Islands, is., Wa., U.S.	172a	48.36N	122.50W
San Juan Ixtenco, Mex. (ēx-tĕ'n-kō)	119	19.14N	97.52W
San Juan Martínez, Cuba	122	22.15N	83.50W
San Juan Mountains, mts., Co., U.S. (san hwán')	96	37.50N	107.30W
San Julián, Arg. (sän hōō-lyá'n)	132	49.17S	68.02W
San Justo, Arg. (hōōs'tô)	132a	34.40S	58.33W
San Justo Desvern, Spain	238e	41.23N	2.05E
Sankanbiriwa, mtn., S.L.	214	8.56N	10.48W
Sankarani, r., Afr. (sän'kä-rä'nē)	210	11.10N	8.35W
Sankt Gallen, Switz.	147	47.25N	9.22E
Sankt Moritz, Switz. (sånt mō'rĭts) (zäŋkt mō'rēts)	154	46.31N	9.50E
Sankt Pölten, Aus. (zäŋkt-pûl'tĕn)	154	48.12N	15.38E
Sankt Veit, Aus. (zäŋkt vīt')	154	46.46N	14.20E
Sankuru, r., Zaire (sän-kōō'rōō)	212	4.00S	22.35E
San Lázaro, Cabo, c., Mex. (sän-lá'zä-rō)	116	24.58N	113.30W
San Leandro, Ca., U.S. (săn lē-ăn'drô)	106b	37.43N	122.10W
Şanlıurfa, Tur.	182	37.20N	38.45E
San Lorenzo, Arg. (sän lô-rĕn'zô)	132	32.46S	60.44W
San Lorenzo, Hond. (sän lô-rĕn'zô)	120	13.24N	87.24W
San Lorenzo, Ca., U.S. (săn lô-rĕn'zô)	106b	37.41N	122.08W
San Lorenzo de El Escorial, Spain	158	40.36N	4.09W
San Lorenzo Tezonco, Mex.	233a	19.18N	99.04W
Sanlúcar de Barrameda, Spain (sän-lōō'kär)	148	36.46N	6.21W
San Lucas, Bol. (lōō'kås)	130	20.12S	65.06W
San Lucas, Cabo, c., Mex.	116	22.45N	109.45W
San Luis, Arg. (lô-ēs')	132	33.16S	66.15W
San Luis, Col. (lòē's)	130a	6.03N	74.57W
San Luis, Cuba	123	20.15N	75.50W
San Luis, Guat.	120	14.38N	89.42W
San Luis, prov., Arg.	132	32.45S	66.00W
San Luis, neigh., Cuba	233b	23.05N	82.20W
San Luis de la Paz, Mex. (dā lä päz')	118	21.17N	100.32W
San Luis del Cordero, Mex. (dĕl kôr-dā'rô)	112	25.25N	104.20W
San Luis Obispo, Ca., U.S. (ô-bĭs'pō)	96	35.18N	120.40W
San Luis Obispo Bay, b., Ca., U.S.	108	35.07N	121.05W
San Luis Potosí, Mex.	116	22.08N	100.58W
San Luis Potosí, state, Mex.	116	22.45N	101.45W
San Luis Rey, r., Ca., U.S. (rā'ē)	108	33.22N	117.06W
San Luis Tlaxialtemalco, Mex.	233a	19.15N	99.03W
San Manuel, Az., U.S. (săn măn'ū-ĕl)	109	32.30N	110.45W
San Marcial, N.M., U.S. (săn mår-shäl')	109	33.40N	107.00W
San Marco, Italy (sän mär'kô)	160	41.53N	15.50E
San Marcos, Guat. (mär'kôs)	120	14.57N	91.49W
San Marcos, Mex.	118	16.46N	99.23W
San Marcos, Tx., U.S. (săn mär'kôs)	113	29.53N	97.56W
San Marcos, r., Tx., U.S.	112	30.08N	98.15W
San Marcos, Universidad de, educ., Peru	233c	12.03S	77.05W
San Marcos de Colón, Hond. (sän-má'r-kōs-dĕ-kô-lô'n)	120	13.17N	86.50W
San Maria di Léuca, Cape, c., Italy (dē-lĕ'ōō-kä)	149	39.47N	18.20E
San Marino, S. Mar. (sän mä-rē'nô)	160	44.55N	12.26E
San Marino, Ca., U.S. (săn mẽr-ē'nô)	107a	34.07N	118.06W
San Marino, nation, Eur.	142	43.40N	13.00E
San Martín, Col. (sän mär-tē'n)	130a	3.42N	73.44W
San Martín, vol., Mex. (mär-tē'n)	119	18.36N	95.11W
San Martín, l., S.A.	132	48.15S	72.30W
San Martín Chalchicuautla, Mex.	118	21.22N	98.39W
San Martin de la Vega, Spain (sän mär ten' dā lä vā'gä)	159a	40.12N	3.34W
San Martín Hidalgo, Mex. (sän mär-tē'n-ē-däl'gô)	118	20.27N	103.55W
San Mateo, Mex.	119	16.59N	97.04W
San Mateo, Spain (sän mä-tā'ō)	159	40.26N	0.09E
San Mateo, Ca., U.S. (săn mä-tā'ô)	106b	37.34N	122.20W
San Mateo, Ven. (sän må-tĕ'ô)	131b	9.45N	64.34W
San Matías, Golfo, b., Arg. (sän mä-tē'äs)	132	41.30S	63.45W
Sanmen Wan, b., China	193	29.00N	122.15E
San Miguel, Chile	234b	33.30S	70.40W
San Miguel, El Sal. (sän mē-gāl')	116	13.28N	88.11W
San Miguel, Mex. (sän mē-gāl')	119	18.18N	97.09W
San Miguel, Pan.	121	8.26N	78.55W
San Miguel, Peru	233c	12.06S	77.06W
San Miguel, Phil. (sän mē-gĕ'l)	197a	15.09N	120.56E
San Miguel, Ven. (sän mē-gĕ'l)	131b	9.56N	64.58W
San Miguel, vol., El Sal.	120	13.27N	88.17W
San Miguel, i., Ca., U.S.	108	34.03N	120.23W
San Miguel, r., Bol. (sän-mē-gĕl')	130	13.34S	63.58W
San Miguel, r., N.A. (sän mē-gāl')	119	15.27N	92.00W
San Miguel, r., Co., U.S. (săn mē-gĕl')	109	38.15N	108.40W
San Miguel, Bahía, b., Pan. (bä-ē'ä-sän mē-gāl')	121	8.17N	78.26W
San Miguel Bay, b., Phil.	197a	13.55N	123.12E
San Miguel de Allende, Mex. (dā ä-lyĕn'dā)	118	20.54N	100.44W
San Miguel del Padrón, Cuba	233b	23.05N	82.19W
San Miguel el Alto, Mex. (ĕl äl'tô)	118	21.03N	102.26W
Sannār, Sudan	211	14.25N	33.30E
San Narcisco, Phil. (sän när-sē'sô)	197a	15.01N	120.05E
San Narcisco, Phil.	197a	13.34N	122.33E
San Nicolás, Arg. (sän nē-kô-lá's)	132	33.20S	60.14W
San Nicolas, Phil. (nē-kô-läs')	197a	16.05N	120.45E
San Nicolas, i., Ca., U.S. (săn nĭ'kô-là)	108	33.14N	119.10W
San Nicolás, r., Mex.	118	19.40N	105.08W
Sanniquellie, Lib.	214	7.22N	8.43W
Sannois, Fr.	237c	48.58N	2.15E
Sannūr, Wādī, Egypt	218b	28.48N	31.12E
Sanok, Pol. (sä'nôk)	155	49.31N	22.13E
San Pablo, Phil. (sän-pä-blô)	197a	14.05N	121.20E
San Pablo, Ca., U.S. (săn păb'lô)	106b	37.58N	122.21W
San Pablo, Ven. (sän-pá'blô)	131b	9.46N	65.04W
San Pablo, r., Pan. (sän päb'lô)	121	8.12N	81.12W
San Pablo Bay, b., Ca., U.S. (săn păb'lô)	106b	38.04N	122.25W
San Pablo Res, Ca., U.S.	106b	37.55N	122.12W
San Pascual, Phil. (päs-kwäl')	197a	13.08N	122.59E
San Pedro, Arg.	129c	33.41S	59.42W
San Pedro, Arg. (sän pā'drô)	132	24.15S	64.15W
San Pedro, Chile (sän pĕ'drô)	129b	33.54S	71.27W
San Pedro, El Sal. (sän pā'drô)	120	13.49N	88.58W
San Pedro, Mex. (sän pā'drô)	119	18.38N	92.25W
San Pedro, Para. (sän-pĕ'drô)	132	24.13S	57.00W
San Pedro, Ca., U.S. (săn pē'drô)	107a	33.44N	118.17W
San Pedro, r., Cuba (sän-pĕ'drô)	122	21.05N	78.15W
San Pedro, r., Mex.	112	27.56N	105.50W
San Pedro, r., Mex. (sän pā'drô)	118	22.08N	104.59W
San Pedro, r., Az., U.S.	109	32.48N	110.37W
San Pedro, Río de, r., Mex.	118	21.51N	102.24W
San Pedro, Río de, r., N.A.	119	18.23N	92.13W
San Pedro Bay, b., Ca., U.S. (săn pē'drô)	107a	33.42N	118.12W
San Pedro de las Colonias, Mex. (dĕ-läs-kô-lô'nyäs)	112	25.47N	102.58W
San Pedro de Macorís, Dom. Rep. (sän-pĕ'drō-dĕ-mä-kô-rēs')	123	18.30N	69.30W
San Pedro Lagunillas, Mex. (sän pā'drô lä-gōō-nēl'yäs)	118	21.12N	104.47W
San Pedro Sula, Hond. (sän pā'drô sōō'lä)	120	15.29N	88.01W
San Pedro Xalostoc, Mex.	233a	19.32N	99.05W
San Pedro Zacatenco, Mex.	233a	19.31N	99.08W
San Pietro, Isola di, i., Italy (ē'sō-lä-dē-sän pyā'trô)	160	39.09N	8.15E
San Pietro in Vaticano, rel., Vat.	239c	41.54N	12.28E
San Quentin, Ca., U.S. (săn kwĕn-tēn')	106b	37.57N	122.29W
San Quintin, Phil. (kēn-tēn')	197a	15.59N	120.47E
San Rafael, Arg. (sän rä-fä-ĕl')	132	34.30S	68.13W
San Rafael, Col. (sän-rä-fä-ĕ'l)	130a	6.18N	75.02W

ăt; finăl; rāte; senåte; ärm; åsk; sofȧ; fâre; ch-choose; dh-as th in other; bē; ėvent; bĕt; recĕnt; cratẽr; g-gō; gh-guttural g; bĭt; ĭ-short neutral; rīde; κ-guttural k as ch in German ich;

PRONOUNCING INDEX

San Rafael-São Pedro e São Paulo 345

PLACE (Pronunciation)	PAGE	Lat. °′	Long. °′
San Rafael, Ca., U.S. (săn rȧ-fĕl)	106b	37.58N	122.31W
San Rafael, r., Ut., U.S. (săn rȧ-fĕl′)	109	39.05N	110.50W
San Rafael, Cabo, c., Dom. Rep. (kȧ′bô)	123	19.00N	68.50W
San Ramón, C.R.	121	10.07N	84.30W
San Ramon, Ca., U.S. (săn rȧ-mōn′)	106b	37.47N	122.59W
San Remo, Italy (săn rā′mô)	160	43.48N	7.46E
San Roque, Col. (săn-rô′kĕ)	130a	6.29N	75.00W
San Roque, Spain	158	36.13N	5.23W
San Saba, Tx., U.S. (săn să′bȧ)	112	31.12N	98.43W
San Saba, r., Tx., U.S.	112	30.58N	99.12W
San Salvador, El Sal. (săn săl-vä-dōr′)	116	13.45N	89.11W
San Salvador (Watling), i., Bah. (săn săl′vȧ-dôr)	123	24.05N	74.30W
San Salvador, i., Ec.	130	0.14S	90.50W
San Salvador, r., Ur. (sän-säl-vä-dô′r)	129c	33.42S	58.04W
Sansanné-Mango, Togo (săn-sȧ-nā′ mäN′gô)	210	10.21N	0.28E
San Sebastián, Spain	142	43.19N	1.59W
San Sebastian, Spain (săn sȧ-bȧs-tyän′)	210	28.09N	17.11W
San Sebastián, Ven. (sän-sĕ-bäs-tyá′n)	131b	9.58N	67.11W
San Sebastiàn de los Reyes, Spain	159a	40.33N	3.38W
San Severo, Italy (săn sĕ-vâ′rō)	149	41.43N	15.24E
Sanshui, China (sän-shwā)	189	23.14N	112.51E
San Simon Creek, r., Az., U.S. (sȧn sī-mōn′)	109	32.45N	109.30W
San Siro, neigh., Italy	238c	45.29S	9.07E
Sanssouci, Schloss, hist., Ger.	238a	52.24N	13.02E
Santa Ana, El Sal.	116	14.02N	89.35W
Santa Ana, Mex. (sän′tä ä′nä)	118	19.18N	98.10W
Santa Ana, Ca., U.S. (săn′tȧ ăn′ȧ)	96	33.45N	117.52W
Santa Ana, r., Ca., U.S.	107a	33.41N	117.57W
Santa Ana Mountains, mts., Ca., U.S.	107a	33.44N	117.36W
Santa Anna, Tx., U.S.	112	31.44N	99.18W
Santa Antão, i., C.V. (sä-tä-ă′n-zhĕ-lô)	210b	17.20N	26.05W
Santa Bárbara, Braz. (sän-tä-bä′r-bä-rä)	131	19.57S	43.25W
Santa Bárbara, Hond.	120	14.52N	88.20W
Santa Barbara, Mex.	112	26.48N	105.50W
Santa Barbara, Ca., U.S.	96	34.26N	119.43W
Santa Barbara, i., Ca., U.S.	108	33.30N	118.44W
Santa Barbara Channel, strt., Ca., U.S.	108	34.15N	120.00W
Santa Branca, Braz. (sän-tä-brä′N-kä)	129a	23.25S	45.52W
Santa Catalina, i., Ca., U.S.	96	33.29N	118.37W
Santa Catalina, Cerro de, mtn., Pan.	121	8.39N	81.36W
Santa Catalina, Gulf of, b., Ca., U.S. (săn′tȧ kă-tȧ-lē′nȧ)	108	33.00N	117.58W
Santa Catarina, Mex. (sän′tȧ kä-tä-rē′nä)	112	25.41N	100.27W
Santa Catarina, state, Braz. (sän-tä-kä-tä-rē′nȧ)	132	27.15S	50.30W
Santa Catarina, r., Mex.	118	16.31N	98.39W
Santa Clara, Cuba (sän′t klä′rá)	117	22.25N	80.00W
Santa Clara, Mex.	112	24.29N	103.22W
Santa Clara, Ca., U.S. (săn′tȧ klărȧ)	104	37.21N	121.56W
Santa Clara, Ur.	132	32.46S	54.51W
Santa Clara, vol., Nic.	120	12.44N	87.00W
Santa Clara, r., Ca., U.S. (săn′tȧ klă′rȧ)	108	34.22N	118.53W
Santa Clara, Bahía de, b., Cuba (bä-ē′ä-dĕ-sän-tä-klä-rä)	122	23.05N	80.50W
Santa Clara, Sierra, mts., Mex. (sē-ĕ′r-rä-săn′tȧ klȧ′rȧ)	116	27.30N	113.50W
Santa Clara Indian Reservation, I.R., N.M., U.S.	109	35.59N	106.10W
Santa Coloma de Gramanet, Spain	238e	41.27N	2.13E
Santa Cruz, Bol. (săn′tȧ krōōz′)	130	17.45S	63.03W
Santa Cruz, Braz. (sän-tä-krōō′s)	132	29.43S	52.15W
Santa Cruz, Braz.	132b	22.55S	43.41W
Santa Cruz, Chile	129b	34.38S	71.21W
Santa Cruz, C.R.	120	10.16N	85.37W
Santa Cruz, Mex.	112	25.50N	105.25W
Santa Cruz, Phil.	197a	13.28N	122.02E
Santa Cruz, Phil.	197a	14.17N	121.25E
Santa Cruz, Phil.	197a	15.46N	119.53E
Santa Cruz, Ca., U.S.	96	36.59N	122.02W
Santa Cruz, prov., Arg.	132	48.00S	70.00W
Santa Cruz, i., Ec. (sän-tä-krōō′z)	130	0.38S	90.20W
Santa Cruz, r., Arg. (sän′tȧ krōōz′)	132	50.05S	71.00W
Santa Cruz, r., Az., U.S. (săn′tȧ krōōz′)	109	32.30N	111.30W
Santa Cruz Barillas, Guat. (sän-tä-krōō′z-bä-rē′l-yäs)	120	15.47N	91.22W
Santa Cruz del Sur, Cuba (sän-tä-krōō′s-dĕl-sōō′r)	122	20.45N	78.00W
Santa Cruz de Tenerife, Spain (sän′tä krōōz dȧ tā-nā-rē′fā)	209	28.07N	15.27W
Santa Cruz Islands, is., Sol.Is.	203	10.58S	166.47E
Santa Cruz Meyehualco, Mex.	233a	19.20N	99.03W
Santa Cruz Mountains, mts., Ca., U.S. (săn′tȧ krōōz′)	106b	37.30N	122.19W
Santa Domingo, Cay, i., Bah.	123	21.50N	75.45W
Santa Eduviges, Chile	234b	33.33S	70.39W
Santa Elena del Gomero, Chile	234b	33.29S	70.46W
Santa Eugenia de Ribeira, Spain	158	42.34N	8.55W
Santa Eulalia del Río, Spain	159	38.58N	1.29E
Santa Fe, Arg. (sän′tä fā′)	132	31.33S	60.45W
Santa Fé, Cuba (sän-tä-fĕ′)	122	21.45N	82.40W
Santa Fe, Mex.	233a	19.23N	99.14W
Santa Fe, Spain (sän′tä-fā′)	158	37.12N	3.43W
Santa Fe, N.M., U.S. (săn′tȧ fā′)	96	35.40N	106.00W
Santa Fe, prov., Arg. (sän′tä fā′)	132	32.00S	61.15W
Santa Fe de Bogotá, Col.	130	4.36N	74.05W
Santa Filomena, Braz. (sän-tä-fē-lô-mĕ′nä)	131	9.09S	44.45W
Santa Genoveva, mtn., Mex. (sän-tä-hĕ-nō-vĕ′vä)	116	23.30N	110.00W
Santai, China (san-tī)	188	31.02N	105.02E
Santa Inés, Ven. (sän′tä ē-nĕ′s)	131b	9.54N	64.21W
Santa Inés, i., Chile (sän′tä ê-nās′)	132	53.45S	74.15W

PLACE (Pronunciation)	PAGE	Lat. °′	Long. °′
Santa Isabel, i., Sol.Is.	203	7.57S	159.28E
Santa Isabel, Pico de, mtn., Eq. Gui.	215	3.35N	8.46E
Santa Lucia, Cuba (sän′tȧ lōō-sē′ȧ)	122	21.15N	77.30W
Santa Lucia, Ur. (sän-tä-lōō-sē′ä)	132	34.27S	56.23W
Santa Lucia, Ven.	131b	10.18N	66.40W
Santa Lucia, r., Ur.	129c	34.19S	56.13W
Santa Lucia Bay, b., Cuba (sän′tȧ lōō-sē′ȧ)	122	22.55N	84.20W
Santa Margarita, i., Mex. (săn′tȧ mär-gȧ-rē′tȧ)	116	24.15N	112.00W
Santa Maria, Braz. (sän-tȧ mä-rē′ȧ)	132	29.40S	54.00W
Santa Maria, Italy (sän-tä mä-rē′ä)	160	41.05N	14.15E
Santa Maria, Phil. (sän-tä-mä-rē′ä)	197a	14.48N	120.57E
Santa Maria, Ca., U.S. (săn-tȧ mȧ-rē′ȧ)	108	34.57N	120.28W
Santa María, vol., Guat.	120	14.45N	91.33W
Santa Maria, r., Mex. (sän′tȧ mä-rē′ȧ)	118	21.33N	100.17W
Santa Maria, Cabo de, c., Port. (kȧ′bō-dĕ-sän-tä-mä-rē′ä)	158	36.58N	7.54W
Santa Maria, Cape, c., Bah.	123	23.45N	75.30W
Santa Maria, Cayo, i., Cuba	122	22.40N	79.00W
Santa María del Oro, Mex. (sän′tä-mä-rē′ä-dĕl-ô-rô)	118	21.21N	104.35W
Santa Maria de los Angeles, Mex. (dĕ-lôs-ȧ′n-hĕ-lĕs)	118	22.10N	103.34W
Santa María del Río, Mex.	118	21.46N	100.43W
Santa María del Rosario, Cuba	233b	23.04N	82.15W
Santa María de Ocotán, Mex.	118	22.56N	104.30W
Santa Maria Island, i., Port. (sän-tä-mä-rē′ȧ)	210a	37.09N	26.02W
Santa Maria Madalena, Braz.	129a	22.00S	42.00W
Santa Marta, Col. (sän′tȧ mär′tȧ)	130	11.15N	74.13W
Santa Marta, Peru	233c	12.02S	76.56W
Santa Marta, Cabo de, c., Ang.	216	13.52S	12.25E
Santa Martha Acatitla, Mex.	233a	19.22N	99.01W
Santa Monica, Ca., U.S. (săn′tȧ mōn′ĭ-kȧ)	96	34.01N	118.29W
Santa Mónica, neigh., Ven.	234a	10.29N	66.53W
Santa Monica Bay, b., Ca., U.S.	232	33.54N	118.25W
Santa Monica Mountains, mts., Ca., U.S.	107a	34.08N	118.38W
Santana, r., Braz. (sän-tä′nä)	132b	22.33S	43.37W
Santander, Col. (sän-tän-dĕr′)	130a	3.00N	76.25W
Santander, Spain (sän-tän-dâr′)	142	43.27N	3.50W
Santa Paula, Ca., U.S. (săn′tȧ pô′lȧ)	108	34.24N	119.05W
Santarém, Braz. (sän-tä-rĕN′)	131	2.28S	54.37W
Santarém, Port.	158	39.18N	8.48W
Santaren Channel, strt., Bah. (săn-tȧ-rĕn′)	122	24.15N	79.30W
Santa Rita do Sapucai, Braz. (sä-pō-kȧ′ē)	129a	22.15S	45.41W
Santa Rosa, Arg. (sän-tä-rô-sä)	132	36.45S	64.10W
Santa Rosa, Col. (sän-tä-rô-sä)	130a	6.38N	75.26W
Santa Rosa, Ec.	130	3.29S	79.55W
Santa Rosa, Guat. (sän′tȧ rō′sȧ)	120	14.21N	90.16W
Santa Rosa, Hond.	120	14.45N	88.51W
Santa Rosa, Ca., U.S. (săn′tȧ rō′zȧ)	96	38.27N	122.42W
Santa Rosa, N.M., U.S. (săn′tȧ rō′sȧ)	110	34.55N	104.41W
Santa Rosa, Ven. (sän-tä-rô-sä)	131b	9.37N	64.10W
Santa Rosa de Cabal, Col. (sän-tä-rô-sä-dĕ-kä-bä′l)	130a	4.53N	75.38W
Santa Rosa de Huechuraba, Chile	234b	33.21S	70.41W
Santa Rosa de Viterbo, Braz. (sän-tä-rô-sä-dĕ-vē-tĕr′-bô)	129a	21.30S	47.21W
Santa Rosa Indian Reservation, I.R., Ca., U.S. (săn′tȧ rō′zȧ′)	108	33.28N	116.50W
Santa Rosalía, Mex. (sän′tȧ rô-zä′lē-ȧ)	116	27.13N	112.15W
Santa Rosa Range, mts., Nv., U.S. (săn′tȧ rō′zȧ)	104	41.33N	117.50W
Santa Susana, Ca., U.S. (săn′tȧ sōō-zä′nȧ)	107a	34.16N	118.42W
Santa Teresa, Arg. (sän-tä-tĕ-rĕ′sä)	129c	33.27S	60.47W
Santa Teresa, Ven.	131b	10.14N	66.40W
Santa Teresa de lo Ovalle, Chile	234b	33.23S	70.47W
Santa Úrsula Coapa, Mex.	233a	19.17N	99.11W
Santa Vitória do Palmar, Braz. (sän-tä-vē-tō′ryä-dô-päl-mär)	132	33.30S	53.16W
Santa Ynez, r., Ca., U.S. (săn′tȧ ē-nĕz′)	108	34.40N	120.20W
Santa Ysabel Indian Reservation, I.R., Ca., U.S. (sän-tȧ ĭ-zȧ-bĕl′)	108	33.05N	116.46W
Santee, Ca., U.S. (săn tē′)	108a	32.50N	116.58W
Santee, r., S.C., U.S.	97	33.00N	79.45W
Santeny, Fr.	237c	48.43N	2.34E
Sant' Eufemia, Golfo di, b., Italy (gôl-fô-dē-sän-tĕ′ô-fĕ′myä)	160	38.53N	15.53E
Santiago, Braz. (sän-tyä′gô)	132	29.05S	54.46W
Santiago, Chile (sän-tē-ä′gô)	132	33.26S	70.40W
Santiago, Pan.	117	8.07N	80.58W
Santiago, Phil. (sän-tyä′gô)	197a	16.42N	121.33E
Santiago, prov., Chile (sän-tyȧ′gō)	129b	33.28S	70.55W
Santiago, i., Phil.	197a	16.29N	120.03E
Santiago de Compostela, Spain	148	42.52N	8.32W
Santiago de Cuba, Cuba (sän-tyȧ′gô-dā kōō′bȧ)	117	20.00N	75.50W
Santiago de Cuba, prov., Cuba	122	20.20N	76.05W
Santiago de las Vegas, Cuba (sän-tyȧ′gô-dĕ-läs-vĕ′gäs)	123a	22.58N	82.23W
Santiago del Estero, Arg.	132	27.50S	64.14W
Santiago del Estero, prov., Arg. (sän-tē-ä′gō-dĕl ĕs-tä-rō)	132	27.15S	63.30W
Santiago de los Cabelleros, Dom. Rep.	117	19.30N	70.45W
Santiago Mountains, mts., Tx., U.S. (sän-tē-ä′gō)	96	30.00N	103.30W
Santiago Reservoir, res., Ca., U.S.	107a	33.47N	117.42W
Santiago Rodriguez, Dom. Rep. (sän-tyȧ′gô-rō-drē′gĕz)	123	19.30N	71.25W

PLACE (Pronunciation)	PAGE	Lat. °′	Long. °′
Santiago Tepalcatlalpan, Mex.	233a	19.15N	99.08W
Santiago Tuxtla, Mex. (sän-tyȧ′gô-tōō′x-tlä)	119	18.28N	95.18W
Santiaguillo, Laguna de, l., Mex. (lä-ōō′nä-dĕ-sän-tē-a-gēl′yō)	112	24.51N	104.43W
Santissimo, neigh., Braz.	234c	22.53S	43.31W
Santisteban del Puerto, Spain (sän′tē stȧ-bän′dĕl pwĕr′tō)	158	38.15N	3.12W
Santo Amaro, Braz. (sän′tô ä-mä′rô)	131	12.32S	38.33W
Santo Amaro, neigh., Braz.	234d	23.39S	46.42W
Santo Amaro de Campos, Braz.	129a	22.01S	41.05W
Santo André, Braz.	129a	23.40S	46.31W
Santo Angelo, Braz. (sän-tô-ȧ′n-zhĕ-lô)	132	28.16S	53.59W
Santo Antônio do Monte, Braz. (sän-tô-än-tô′nyô-dô-môn′tĕ)	129a	20.06S	45.18W
Santo Domingo, Cuba (sän′tô-dōmĭŋ′gô)	122	22.35N	80.20W
Santo Domingo, Dom. Rep. (sän′tô dô-mĭn′gô)	117	18.30N	69.55W
Santo Domingo, Nic. (sän-tô-dô-mē′n-gō)	121	12.15N	84.56W
Santo Domingo de la Caizada, Spain (dā lä käl-thä′dä)	158	42.27N	2.55W
Santoña, Spain (sän-tō′nyä)	158	43.25N	3.27W
Sant' Onofrio, neigh., Italy	239c	41.56N	12.25E
Santos, Braz. (sän′tozh)	131	23.58S	46.20W
Santos Dumont, Braz. (sän′tôs-dô-mô′nt)	131	21.28S	43.33W
Sanuki, Japan (sä′nōō-kē)	195a	35.16N	139.53E
San Urbano, Arg. (sän-ōr-bä′nô)	129c	33.39S	61.28W
San Valentin, Monte, mtn., Chile (sän-vä-lĕn-tē′n)	132	46.41S	73.30W
San Vicente, Arg. (sän-vē-sĕn′tĕ)	129c	35.00S	58.26W
San Vicente, Chile	129b	34.25S	71.06W
San Vicente, El Sal. (sän vē-sĕn′tȧ)	120	13.41N	88.43W
San Vicente de Alcántara, Spain	158	39.24N	7.08W
San Vicente dels Horts, Spain	238e	41.24N	2.01E
San Vito al Tagliamento, Italy (san vē′tô)	160	45.53N	12.52E
San Xavier Indian Reservation, I.R., Az., U.S. (x-ā′vĭēr)	109	32.07N	111.12W
San Ysidro, Ca., U.S. (sän ysĭ-drō′)	108a	32.33N	117.02W
Sanyuanli, China (sän-yūän-lē)	191a	23.11N	113.16E
São Bernardo do Campo, Braz. (souN-bĕr-när′dô-dô-kä′m-pô)	129a	23.44S	46.33W
São Borja, Braz. (souN-bôr-zhä)	132	28.44S	55.59W
São Caetano do Sul, Braz.	234d	23.37S	46.34W
São Carlos, Braz. (souN kär′lōzh)	131	22.02S	47.54W
São Cristovão, Braz. (souN-krĕs-tō-vouN)	131	11.04S	37.11W
São Cristóvão, neigh., Braz.	234c	22.54S	43.14W
São Fidélis, Braz. (souN-fē-dĕ′lĕs)	129a	21.41S	41.45W
São Francisco, Braz. (souN frăN-sĕsh′kô)	131	15.59S	44.42W
São Francisco, Rio, r., Braz. (rē′ō-sän-frän-sĕ′s-kō)	131	8.56S	40.20W
São Francisco do Sul, Braz. (souN frăN-sĕsh′kô-dô-sōō′l)	132	26.15S	48.42W
São Gabriel, Braz. (souN′gä-brē-ĕl′)	132	30.28S	54.11W
São Geraldo, Braz. (souN-zhĕ-rä′l-dô)	129a	21.01S	42.49W
São Gonçalo, Braz. (souN′gōŋ-sä′lô)	129a	22.55S	43.04W
Sao Hill, Tan.	217	8.20S	35.12E
São João, Gui.-B.	214	11.32N	15.26W
São João da Barra, Braz. (souN-zhôuN-dä-bȧ′rä)	129a	21.40S	41.03W
São João da Boa Vista, Braz. (souN-zhôuN-dä-bôä-vē′s-tä)	129a	21.58S	46.45W
São João del Rei, Braz. (souN zhô-ouN′dĕl-rā)	132	21.08S	44.14W
São João de Meriti, Braz. (souN-zhôuN-dĕ-mĕ-rē-tē)	132b	22.47S	43.22W
São João do Araguaia, Braz. (souN zhô-ouN′dô-ä-rä-gwä′yä)	131	5.29S	48.44W
São João dos Lampas, Port. (souN′ zhô-ouN′ dōzh län-päzh′)	159b	38.52N	9.24W
São João Nepomuceno, Braz. (souN-zhôuN-nĕ-pô-mōō-sĕ-nō)	129a	21.33S	43.00W
São Jorge Island, i., Port. (souN zhôr′zhĕ)	210a	38.28N	27.34W
São José do Rio Pardo, Braz. (souN-zhô-sĕ′dô-rē′ō-pä′r-dō)	129a	21.36S	46.50W
São José do Rio Prêto, Braz. (souN zhô-zĕ′dô-rē′ō-prĕ-tō)	131	20.57S	49.12W
São José dos Campos, Braz. (souN zhô-zā′dōzh kăN pōzh′)	129a	23.12S	45.53W
São Julião da Barra, Port.	238d	38.40N	9.21W
São Leopoldo, Braz. (souN-lĕ-ô-pôl′dô)	132	29.46S	51.09W
São Luis, Braz.	131	2.31S	43.14W
São Luis do Paraitinga, Braz. (souN-lōōē′s-dô-pä-rä-ē-tē′n-gä)	129a	23.15S	45.18W
São Manuel, r., Braz.	131	8.28S	57.07E
São Mateus, Braz. (souN mä-tā′ōzh)	131	18.44S	39.45W
São Mateus, Braz.	132b	22.49S	43.23W
São Miguel Arcanjo, Braz. (souN-mē-gĕ′l-ár-kän-zhō)	129a	23.54S	47.59W
São Miguel Island, i., Port.	210a	37.59N	26.38W
Saona, i., Dom. Rep. (sä-ō′nä)	123	18.10N	68.55W
Saône, r., Fr. (sōn)	142	47.00N	5.30E
São Nicolau, i., C.V. (souN′ nē-kô-louN′)	210b	16.19N	25.19W
São Paulo, Braz. (souN′ pou′lô)	131	23.34S	46.38W
São Paulo, state, Braz. (souN pou′lô)	131	21.45S	50.47W
São Paulo de Olivença, Braz. (souN′pou′lôdȧ ô-lē-vĕn′sȧ)	130	3.32S	68.46W
São Pedro, Braz. (souN-pĕ′drô)	129a	22.34S	47.54W
São Pedro de Aldeia, Braz. (souN-pĕ′drô-dĕ-äl-dĕ′yä)	129a	22.50S	42.04W
São Pedro e São Paulo, Rocedos, rocks, Braz.	128	1.50N	30.00W

346 São Raimundo Nonato-Seal

PLACE (Pronunciation)	PAGE	Lat. °′	Long. °′
São Raimundo Nonato, Braz. (soun′ rī-mô′n-do nô-nä′tô)	131	9.09S	42.32W
São Roque, Braz. (soun′ rō′kĕ)	129a	23.32S	47.08W
São Roque, Cabo de, c., Braz. (kä′bo-dĕ-soun′ rō′kĕ)	131	5.06S	35.11W
São Sebastião, Braz. (soun så-bäs-tê-oun′)	129a	23.48S	45.25W
São Sebastião, Ilha de, i., Braz.	129a	23.52S	45.22W
São Sebastião do Paraíso, Braz.	129a	20.54S	46.58W
São Simão, Braz. (soun-sē-moun)	129a	21.30S	47.33W
São Tiago, i., C.V. (soun tê-ä′gô)	210b	15.09N	24.45W
São Tomé, S. Tom./P.	210	0.20N	6.44E
Sao Tome and Principe, nation, Afr. (prēn′sē-pĕ)	210	1.00N	6.00E
Saoura, Oued, r., Alg.	210	29.39N	1.42W
São Vicente, Braz. (soun ve-se′n-tĕ)	131	23.57S	46.25W
São Vicente, i., C.V. (soun vê-sĕn′tå)	210b	16.51N	24.35W
São Vicente, Cabo de, c., Port. (kå′bō-dĕ-sän-vê-sĕ′n-tĕ)	142	37.03N	9.31W
Sapele, Nig. (sä-pā′lā)	210	5.54N	5.41E
Sapitwa, mtn., Mwi.	217	15.58S	35.38E
Sapozhok, Russia (sä-pô-zhôk′)	162	53.58N	40.44E
Sapporo, Japan (säp-pô′rô)	189	43.02N	141.29E
Sapronovo, Russia (såp-rô′nô-vô)	172b	55.13N	38.25E
Sapucaí, r., Braz. (sä-pōō-kå-ē′)	129a	22.20S	45.53W
Sapucaia, Braz. (sä-pōō-kä′yå)	129a	22.01S	42.54W
Sapucaí Mirim, r., Braz. (sä-pōō-kå-ē′mē-rēn)	129a	21.06S	47.03W
Sapulpa, Ok., U.S. (så-pŭl′på)	111	36.01N	96.05W
Saqqez, Iran	185	36.14N	46.16E
Saquarema, Braz. (sä-kwä-rĕ-mä)	129a	22.56S	42.32W
Sara, Wa., U.S. (sä′rä)	106c	45.45N	122.42W
Sara, Bahr, r., Chad (bär)	211	8.19N	17.44E
Sarajevo, Bos. (sä-rå-yĕv′ô) (så-rä′ya-vô)	142	43.50N	18.26E
Sarakhs, Iran	185	36.32N	61.11E
Sarana, Russia (så-rä′nå)	172a	56.31N	57.44E
Saranac Lake, N.Y., U.S.	99	44.20N	74.05W
Saranac Lake, l., N.Y., U.S. (săr′å-năk)	99	44.15N	74.20W
Sarandi, Arg. (sä-rän′dê)	132a	34.41S	58.21W
Sarandi Grande, Ur. (sä-rän′dē-grän′dĕ)	129c	33.42S	56.21W
Saranley, Som.	218a	2.28N	42.15E
Saransk, Russia (så-ränsk′)	164	54.10N	45.10E
Sarany, Russia (så-rå′nĭ)	172a	58.33N	58.48E
Sara Peak, mtn., Nig.	215	9.37N	9.25E
Sarapul, Russia (sä-räpôl′)	166	56.28N	53.50E
Sarasota, Fl., U.S. (săr-å-sōtå)	115a	27.27N	82.30W
Saratoga, Tx., U.S. (săr-å-tō′gå)	113	30.17N	94.31W
Saratoga, Wa., U.S.	106a	48.04N	122.29W
Saratoga Pass, Wa., U.S.	106a	48.09N	122.33W
Saratoga Springs, N.Y., U.S. (sprĭngz)	99	43.05N	74.50W
Saratov, Russia (så rä′tôf)	164	51.30N	45.30E
Saravane, Laos	193	15.48N	106.40E
Sarawak, hist. reg., Malay. (så-rä′wäk)	196	2.30N	112.45E
Sárbogárd, Hung. (shär′bô-gärd)	155	46.53N	18.38E
Sarcee Indian Reserve, I.R., Can. (sär′sê)	83e	50.58N	114.23W
Sarcelles, Fr.	157b	49.00N	2.23E
Sardalas, Libya	210	25.59N	10.33E
Sardinia, i., Italy (sär-dĭn′ĭå)	142	40.08N	9.05E
Sardis, Ms., U.S. (sär′dĭs)	114	34.26N	89.55W
Sardis Lake, res., Ms., U.S.	114	34.27N	89.43W
Sargent, Ne., U.S. (sär′jĕnt)	102	41.40N	99.38W
Sarh, Chad (är-chan-bō′)	211	9.09N	18.23E
Sarikamis, Tur.	167	40.30N	42.40E
Sariñena, Spain (sä-rēn-yĕ′nä)	159	41.46N	0.11W
Sark, i., Guernsey (särk)	156	49.28N	2.22W
Şarköy, Tur. (shär′kû-ê)	161	40.39N	27.07E
Sarmiento, Monte, mtn., Chile (mô′n-tĕ-sär-myĕn′tō)	132	54.28S	70.40W
Sarnia, Can. (sär′nē-å)	85	43.00N	82.25W
Sarno, Italy (sä′r-nô)	159c	40.35N	14.38E
Sarny, Ukr. (sär′nê)	167	51.17N	26.39E
Saronikós Kólpos, b., Grc.	161	37.51N	23.30E
Saros Körfezi, b., Tur. (sä′rôs)	161	40.30N	26.20E
Sárospatak, Hung. (shä′rôsh-pô′tôk)	155	48.19N	21.35E
Šar Planina, mts., Yugo. (shär plä′nê-na)	161	42.07N	21.54E
Sarpsborg, Nor. (särps′bôrg)	152	59.17N	11.07E
Sarratt, Eng., U.K.	235	51.41N	0.29W
Sarrebourg, Fr. (sär-bōōr′)	157	48.44N	7.02E
Sarreguemines, Fr. (sär-gē-mēn′)	147	49.06N	7.05E
Sarria, Spain (sär′ê-ä)	148	42.14N	7.17W
Sarstun, r., N.A. (särs-tōō′n)	120	15.50N	89.26W
Sartène, Fr. (sär-tĕn′)	160	41.36N	8.59E
Sarthe, r., Fr. (särt)	147	47.44N	0.32W
Sartrouville, Fr.	237c	48.57N	2.10E
Şärur, Azer.	168	39.33N	44.58E
Sárvár, Hung. (shär′vär)	154	47.14N	16.55E
Sarych, Mys, c., Ukr. (mĭs så-rēch′)	167	44.25N	33.00E
Sary-Ishikotrau, Peski, des., Kyrg. (sä′rē ē′ shĕk-ō′trou)	169	46.12N	75.30E
Sarysu, r., Kaz. (sä′rē-sōō)	169	47.47N	69.14E
Sasarām, India (sŭs-ŭ-räm′)	183	25.00N	84.00E
Sasayama, Japan (sä′sä-yä′mä)	195	35.05N	135.14E
Sasebo, Japan (sä′så-bô)	189	33.12N	129.43E
Sashalom, neigh., Hung.	239g	47.31N	19.11E
Saskatchewan, prov., Can.	84	54.46N	107.40W
Saskatchewan, r., Can. (săs-kăch′ê-wän)	84	53.45N	103.20W
Saskatoon, Can. (săs-kå-tōōn′)	84	52.07N	106.38W
Sasolburg, S. Afr.	218d	26.52S	27.47E
Sasovo, Russia (sás′ō-vô)	166	54.20N	42.00E
Saspamco, Tx., U.S. (săs-păm′cō)	107d	29.13N	98.18W
Sassafras, Austl.	243b	37.52S	145.21E
Sassandra, C. Iv.	214	4.58N	6.05W
Sassandra, r., C. Iv. (sås-sän′drå)	210	5.35N	6.25W
Sassari, Italy (säs′sä-rê)	148	40.44N	8.33E
Sassnitz, Ger. (säs′nĕts)	154	54.31N	13.37E

PLACE (Pronunciation)	PAGE	Lat. °′	Long. °′
Satadougou, Mali (sä-tå-dōō-gōō′)	214	12.21N	12.07W
Säter, Swe. (sĕ′tĕr)	152	60.21N	15.50E
Sātghara, India	240a	22.44N	88.21E
Satilla, r., Ga., U.S. (så-tĭl′å)	115	31.15N	82.13W
Satka, Russia (sät′kå)	166	55.03N	59.02E
Sátoraljaujhely, Hung. (shä′tô-rô-lyô-ōō′yĕl′)	155	48.24N	21.40E
Satu Mare, Rom. (så′tōō-må′rĕ)	149	47.50N	22.53E
Saturna, Can. (să-tûr′nå)	106d	48.48N	123.12W
Saturna, i., Can.	106d	48.47N	123.03W
Sauda, Nor.	146	59.40N	6.21E
Saudárkrókur, Ice.	142	65.41N	19.38W
Saudi Arabia, nation, Asia (så-ô′dĭ å-rā′bĭ-å)	182	22.40N	46.00E
Sauerlach, Ger. (zou′ĕr-läk)	145d	47.58N	11.39E
Saugatuck, Mi., U.S. (sô′gå-tŭk)	98	42.40N	86.10W
Saugeen, r., Can.	90	44.20N	81.20W
Saugerties, N.Y., U.S. (sô′gēr-tēz)	99	42.05N	73.55W
Saugus, Ma., U.S. (sô′gŭs)	93a	42.28N	71.01W
Sauk, r., Mn., U.S. (sôk)	103	45.30N	94.45W
Sauk Centre, Mn., U.S.	103	45.43N	94.58W
Sauk City, Wi., U.S.	103	43.16N	89.45W
Sauk Rapids, Mn., U.S. (răp′ĭd)	103	45.35N	94.08W
Sault Sainte Marie, Can.	85	46.31N	84.20W
Sault Sainte Marie, Mi., U.S. (sōō sānt må-rē′)	97	46.29N	84.21W
Saumatre, Étang, l., Haiti	123	18.40N	72.10W
Saunders Lake, l., Can. (sän′dĕrs)	83g	53.18N	113.25W
Saurimo, Ang.	212	9.39S	20.24E
Sausalito, Ca., U.S. (sô-så-lē′tô)	106b	37.51N	122.29W
Sausset-les-Pins, Fr. (sō-sĕ′lā-păn′)	156a	43.20N	5.08E
Saútar, Ang.	216	11.06S	18.27E
Sauvie Island, i., Or., U.S. (sô′vē)	106c	45.43N	123.49W
Sava, r., Yugo. (sä′vä)	142	44.50N	18.30E
Savage, Md., U.S. (săv′ĕj)	100e	39.07N	76.49W
Savage, Mn., U.S.	107g	44.47N	93.20W
Savai′i, i., W. Sam.	198a	13.35S	172.25W
Savalen, l., Nor.	152	62.19N	10.15E
Savalou, Benin	210	7.56N	1.58E
Savanna, Il., U.S. (så-văn′å)	103	42.05N	90.09W
Savannah, Ga., U.S. (så-văn′å)	97	32.04N	81.07W
Savannah, Mo., U.S.	111	39.58N	94.49W
Savannah, Tn., U.S.	114	35.13N	88.14W
Savannah, r., U.S.	97	33.11N	81.51W
Savannakhét, Laos	196	16.33N	104.45E
Savanna la Mar, Jam. (så-văn′å lå mär′)	122	18.10N	78.10W
Save, r., Fr.	156	43.32N	0.50E
Save, Rio (Sabi), r., Afr. (rē′ō-sä′vĕ)	212	21.28S	34.14E
Sāveh, Iran	185	35.01N	50.20E
Saverne, Fr. (så-vĕrn′)	157	48.40N	7.22E
Savigliano, Italy (sä-vēl-yä′nô)	160	44.38N	7.42E
Savigny-sur-Orge, Fr.	157b	48.41N	2.22E
Savona, Italy (sä-nō′nä)	148	44.19N	8.28E
Savonlinna, Fin. (så′vôn-lēn′nå)	153	61.53N	28.49E
Savran′, Ukr. (säv-rän′)	163	48.07N	30.09E
Sawahlunto, Indon.	196	0.37S	100.50E
Sawākin, Sudan	211	19.02N	37.19E
Sawda, Jabal as, mts., Libya	211	28.14N	13.46E
Sawhāj, Egypt	211	26.34N	31.40E
Sawknah, Libya	211	29.04N	15.53E
Sawu, Laut (Savu Sea), sea, Indon.	196	9.15S	122.15E
Sawyer, l., Wa., U.S. (sô′yĕr)	106a	47.20N	122.02W
Saxony see Sachsen, hist. reg., Ger.	154	50.45N	12.17E
Say, Niger (sä′ê)	210	13.09N	2.16E
Sayan Khrebet, mts., Russia (sŭ-yän′)	165	51.30N	90.00E
Sayḩūt, Yemen	182	15.23N	51.28E
Sayre, Ok., U.S. (sâ′ĕr)	110	35.19N	99.40W
Sayre, Pa., U.S.	99	41.55N	76.30W
Sayreton, Al., U.S. (sâ′ĕr-tŭn)	100h	33.34N	86.51W
Sayreville, N.J., U.S. (sâr′vĭl)	100a	40.28N	74.21W
Sayr Usa, Mong.	188	44.15N	107.00E
Sayula, Mex.	118	19.50N	103.33W
Sayula, Mex. (sä-yōō′lä)	119	17.51N	94.56W
Sayula, Luguna de, l., Mex. (lä-gô′nä-dĕ)	118	20.00N	103.33W
Say′un, Yemen	182	16.00N	48.59E
Sayville, N.Y., U.S. (sā′vĭl)	99	40.45N	73.10W
Sazanit, i., Alb.	149	40.30N	19.17E
Sázava, r., Czech Rep.	154	49.36N	15.24E
Sazhino, Russia (sáz-hē′nô)	172a	56.20N	58.15E
Scala, Teatro alla, bldg., Italy	238c	45.28N	9.11E
Scandinavian Peninsula, pen., Eur.	180	62.00N	14.00E
Scanlon, Mn., U.S. (skăn′lôn)	107h	46.27N	92.26W
Scappoose, Or., U.S. (skă-pōōs′)	106c	45.46N	122.53W
Scappoose, r., Or., U.S.	106c	45.47N	122.57W
Scarborough, Can. (skär′bēr-ô)	91	43.45N	79.12W
Scarborough, Eng., U.K. (skär′bŭr-ô)	150	54.16N	0.19W
Scarsdale, N.Y., U.S. (skärz′dāl)	100a	41.01N	73.47W
Scarth Hill, Eng., U.K.	237a	53.33N	2.52W
Scatari I, Can. (skăt′å-rē)	93	46.00N	59.44W
Sceaux, Fr.	237c	48.47N	2.17E
Schaerbeek, Bel. (skär′bāk)	145a	50.50N	4.23E
Schaffhausen, Switz. (shäf′hou-zĕn)	147	47.42N	8.38E
Schalksmühle, Ger.	236	51.14N	7.31E
Schapenrust, S. Afr.	244b	26.16S	28.22E
Scharnhorst, neigh., Ger.	236	51.32N	7.32E
Schefferville, Can.	85	54.52N	67.01W
Scheiblingstein, Aus.	239e	48.16N	16.13E
Schelde,, r., Eur.	151	51.04N	3.55E
Schenectady, N.Y., U.S. (skĕ-nĕk′tå-dē)	97	42.50N	73.55W
Scheveningen, Neth.	145a	52.06N	4.15E
Schiedam, Neth.	145a	51.55N	4.23E
Schildow, Ger.	238a	52.38N	13.23E
Schiller Park, Il., U.S.	231a	41.58N	87.52W
Schiltigheim, Fr. (shēl′tegh-hīm)	157	48.48N	7.47E
Schio, Italy (skē′ô)	160	45.43N	11.23E

PLACE (Pronunciation)	PAGE	Lat. °′	Long. °′
Schleswig, Ger. (shĕls′vēgh)	146	54.32N	9.32E
Schleswig-Holstein, hist. reg., Ger. (shlĕs′vēgh-hōl′shtīn)	154	54.40N	9.10E
Schmalkalden, Ger. (shmäl′käl-dĕn)	154	50.41N	10.25E
Schneider, In., U.S. (schnīd′ēr)	101a	41.12N	87.26W
Schofield, Wi., U.S. (skō′fēld)	103	44.52N	89.37W
Schöller, Ger.	236	51.14N	7.01E
Scholven, neigh., Ger.	236	51.36N	7.01E
Schönbrunn, Schloss, pt. of i., Aus.	239e	48.11N	16.19E
Schönebeck, Ger. (shû′nĕ-bergh)	154	52.01N	11.44E
Schönebeck, neigh., Ger.	236	51.28N	6.56E
Schöneberg, neigh., Ger.	238a	52.29N	13.21E
Schönefeld, Ger.	238a	52.23N	13.30E
Schöneiche, Ger.	238a	52.28N	13.41E
Schönerlinde, Ger.	238a	52.39N	13.27E
Schonnebeck, neigh., Ger.	236	51.29N	7.04E
Schönow, Ger.	238a	52.40N	13.32E
Schönwalde, Ger.	238a	52.37N	13.07E
Schoonhoven, Neth.	145a	51.56N	4.51E
Schramberg, Ger. (shräm′bĕrgh)	154	48.14N	8.24E
Schreiber, Can.	90	48.50N	87.10W
Schroon, l., N.Y., U.S. (skrōōn)	99	43.50N	73.50W
Schultzendorf, Ger. (shōōl′tzĕn-dōrf)	145b	52.21N	13.55E
Schumacher, Can.	90	48.30N	81.30W
Schüren, neigh., Ger.	236	51.30N	7.32E
Schuyler, Ne., U.S. (slī′ler)	102	41.28N	97.05W
Schuylkill, r., Pa., U.S. (skōōl′kĭl)	100f	40.10N	75.31W
Schuylkill-Haven, Pa., U.S. (skōōl′kĭl hā-vĕn)	99	40.35N	76.10W
Schwabach, Ger. (shvä′bäk)	154	49.19N	11.02E
Schwäbische Alb, mts., Ger. (shvă′bē-shĕ ălb)	154	48.11N	9.09E
Schwäbisch Gmünd, Ger. (shvă′bēsh gmünd)	154	48.47N	9.49E
Schwäbisch Hall, Ger. (häl)	154	49.08N	9.44E
Schwafheim, Ger.	236	51.25N	6.39E
Schwandorf, Ger. (shvän′dôrf)	154	49.19N	12.08E
Schwanebeck, Ger.	238a	52.37N	13.32E
Schwanenwerder, neigh., Ger.	238a	52.27N	13.10E
Schwaner, Pegunungan, mts., Indon. (skvän′ĕr)	196	1.05S	112.30E
Schwarzenberg, Ger.	236	51.24N	6.42E
Schwarzwald, for., Ger. (shvärts′väld)	154	47.54N	7.57E
Schwaz, Aus.	154	47.20N	11.45E
Schwechat, Aus. (shvĕk′ät)	154	48.09N	16.29E
Schwedt, Ger. (shvĕt)	154	53.04N	14.17E
Schweflinghausen, Ger.	236	51.16N	7.25E
Schweinfurt, Ger. (shvīn′fōrt)	154	50.03N	10.14E
Schwelm, Ger. (shvĕlm)	157c	51.17N	7.18E
Schwenke, Ger.	236	51.11N	7.26E
Schwerin, Ger. (shvĕ-rēn′)	154	53.36N	11.25E
Schwerin, neigh., Ger.	236	51.33N	7.20E
Schweriner See, l., Ger. (shvĕ′rē-nĕr zā)	154	53.40N	11.06E
Schwerte, Ger. (shvĕr′tĕ)	157c	51.26N	7.34E
Schwielowsee, l., Ger. (shvē′lōv zā)	145b	52.20N	12.52E
Schwyz, Switz. (schēts)	154	47.01N	8.38E
Sciacca, Italy (shê-äk′kä)	160	37.30N	13.09E
Science and Industry, Museum of, pt. of i., Il., U.S.	231a	41.47N	87.35W
Scilly, Isles of, is., Eng., U.K. (sĭl′ê)	142	49.56N	6.50W
Scioto, r., Oh., U.S. (sī-ō′tō)	97	39.10N	82.55W
Scituate, Ma., U.S. (sĭt′ū-āt)	93a	42.12N	70.45W
Scobey, Mt., U.S. (skō′bê)	105	48.48N	105.29W
Scoggin, Or., U.S. (skō′gĭn)	106c	45.28N	123.14W
Scoresby, Austl.	243b	37.54S	145.14E
Scotch, r., Can. (skŏch)	83c	45.21N	74.56W
Scotia, Ca., U.S. (skō′shå)	104	40.29N	124.06W
Scotland, S.D., U.S.	102	43.08N	97.43W
Scotland, , U.K. (skŏt′lånd)	142	57.05N	5.10W
Scotland Neck, N.C., U.S. (nĕk)	115	36.06N	77.25W
Scotstown, Can. (skŏts′toun)	99	45.35N	71.15W
Scott, r., Ca., U.S.	104	41.20N	122.55W
Scott, Cape, c., Can. (skŏt)	84	50.47N	128.26W
Scott, Mount, mtn., Or., U.S.	104	42.55N	122.00W
Scott, Mount, mtn., Or., U.S.	106c	45.27N	122.33W
Scott Air Force Base, Il., U.S.	107e	38.33N	89.52W
Scottburgh, S. Afr. (skŏt′bŭr-ō)	212	30.18S	30.42E
Scott City, Ks., U.S.	110	38.28N	100.54W
Scottdale, Ga., U.S. (skŏt′dāl)	100c	33.47N	84.16W
Scott Islands, is., Ant.	219	67.00S	178.00E
Scottsbluff, Ne., U.S. (skŏts′blŭf)	102	41.52N	103.40W
Scottsboro, Al., U.S. (skŏts′bŭro)	114	34.40N	86.03W
Scottsburg, In., U.S. (skŏts′bûrg)	98	38.40N	85.50W
Scottsdale, Austl. (skŏts′dāl)	204	41.12S	147.37E
Scottsville, Ky., U.S. (skŏts′vĭl)	114	36.45N	86.10W
Scott Township, Pa., U.S.	230b	40.24N	80.06W
Scottville, Mi., U.S.	98	44.00N	86.20W
Scranton, Pa., U.S. (skrăn′tŭn)	97	41.15N	75.45W
Scugog, l., Can. (skū′gôg)	91	44.05N	78.55W
Scunthorpe, Eng., U.K. (skŭn′thôrp)	144a	53.36N	0.38W
Scutari see Shkodër, Alb.	142	42.04N	19.30E
Scutari, Lake, l., Eur. (skōō′tä-rē)	149	42.14N	19.33E
Seabeck, Wa., U.S. (sē′bĕck)	106a	47.38N	122.50W
Sea Bright, N.J., U.S. (sē brīt)	100a	40.22N	73.58W
Seabrook, Md., U.S.	229d	38.58N	76.51W
Seabrook, Tx., U.S. (sē′brŏk)	113	29.34N	95.01W
Sea Cliff, N.Y., U.S.	228	40.51N	73.38W
Seacombe, Eng., U.K.	237a	53.25N	3.01W
Seaford, De., U.S. (sē′fērd)	99	38.35N	75.40W
Seaford, N.Y., U.S.	228	40.40N	73.30W
Seaforth, Austl.	243a	33.48S	151.15E
Seaforth, Eng., U.K.	237a	53.28N	3.01W
Seagraves, Tx., U.S. (sē′grāvs)	110	32.51N	102.38W
Sea Islands, is., Ga., U.S. (sē)	115	31.21N	81.05W
Seal, Eng., U.K.	235	51.17N	0.14E

ăt; finăl; rāte; senāte; ärm; åsk; sofå; fâre; ch-choose; dh-as th in other; bē; êvent; bĕt; recĕnt; cratẽr; g-gō; gh-guttural g; bĭt; ĭ-short neutral; rīde; ĸ-guttural k as ch in German ich;

PLACE (Pronunciation)	PAGE	Lat. °′	Long. °′
Seal, r., Can.	84	59.08N	96.37W
Seal Beach, Ca., U.S.	107a	33.44N	118.06W
Seal Cays, is., Bah.	123	22.40N	75.55W
Seal Cays, is., T./C. Is.	123	21.10N	71.45W
Seal Island, i., S. Afr. (sēl)	212a	34.07S	18.36E
Seal Rocks, Ca., U.S.	231b	37.47N	122.31W
Sealy, Tx., U.S. (sē'lė)	113	29.46N	96.10W
Searcy, Ar., U.S. (sûr'sė)	111	35.13N	91.43W
Searles, l., Ca., U.S. (sûrl's)	108	35.44N	117.22W
Searsport, Me., U.S. (sērz'pōrt)	92	44.28N	68.55W
Seaside, Or., U.S. (sē'sīd)	104	45.59N	123.55W
Seat Pleasant, Md., U.S.	229d	38.53N	76.52W
Seattle, Wa., U.S. (sė-ăt''l)	96	47.36N	122.20W
Sebaco, Nic. (sē-bä'kō)	120	12.50N	86.03W
Sebago, Me., U.S. (sė-bā'gō)	92	43.52N	70.20W
Sebastián Vizcaíno, Bahía, b., Mex.	116	28.45N	115.15W
Sebastopol, Ca., U.S. (sė-băs'tō-pōl)	108	38.27N	122.50W
Sebderat, Erit.	211	15.30N	36.45E
Sebewaing, Mi., U.S. (se'bė-wăng)	98	43.45N	83.25W
Sebezh, Russia (syĕ'bĕzh)	162	56.16N	28.29E
Sebinkarahisar, Tur.	149	40.15N	38.10E
Sebnitz, Ger. (zĕb'nēts)	154	51.01N	14.16E
Sebou, Oued, r., Mor.	210	34.23N	5.18W
Sebree, Ky., U.S. (sė-brē')	98	37.35N	87.30W
Sebring, Fl., U.S. (sē'brĭng)	115a	27.30N	81.26W
Sebring, Oh., U.S.	98	40.55N	81.05W
Secane, Pa., U.S.	229b	39.55N	75.18W
Secaucus, N.J., U.S.	228	40.47N	74.04W
Secchia, r., Italy (sĕ'kyä)	160	44.25N	10.25E
Seco, r., Mex. (sĕ'kō)	119	18.11N	93.18W
Sedalia, Mo., U.S.	97	38.42N	93.12W
Sedan, Fr. (sē-däN)	147	49.49N	4.55E
Sedan, Ks., U.S. (sė-dăn')	111	37.07N	96.08W
Sedom, Isr.	181a	31.04N	35.24E
Sedro Woolley, Wa., U.S. (sē'drō-wōōl'ė)	106a	48.30N	122.14W
Šeduva, Lith. (shē'dō-vȧ)	153	55.46N	23.45E
Seeberg, Ger.	238a	52.33N	13.41E
Seeburg, Ger.	238a	52.31N	13.07E
Seefeld, Ger.	238a	52.37N	13.40E
Seer Green, Eng., U.K.	235	51.37N	0.36W
Seestall, Ger. (zā'shtäl)	145d	47.58N	10.52E
Sefrou, Mor. (sē-frōō')	148	33.49N	4.46W
Sefton, Eng., U.K.	237a	53.30N	2.58W
Seg, l., Russia (syĕgh)	166	63.20N	33.30E
Segamat, Malay. (sā'gȧ-mát)	181b	2.30N	102.49E
Segang, China (sŭ-gäŋ)	190	31.59N	114.13E
Segbana, Benin	215	10.56N	3.42E
Segorbe, Spain (sĕ-gôr-bĕ)	159	39.50N	0.30W
Ségou, Mali (sā-gōō')	210	13.27N	6.16W
Segovia, Col. (sĕ-gō'vēä)	130a	7.08N	74.42W
Segovia, Spain (så-gō'vē-ä)	148	40.58N	4.05W
Segre, r., Spain (sā'grä)	159	41.54N	1.10E
Seguam, i., Ak., U.S. (sē'gwăm)	95a	52.16N	172.10W
Seguam Passage, strt., Ak., U.S.	95a	52.20N	173.00W
Séguédine, Niger	215	20.12N	12.59E
Séguéla, C. Iv. (sā-gā-lä')	210	7.57N	6.40W
Seguin, Tx., U.S. (sĕ-gēn')	113	29.35N	97.58W
Segula, i., Ak., U.S. (sē-gū'lȧ)	95a	52.08N	178.35E
Segura, r., Spain	148	38.24N	2.12W
Segura, Sierra de, mts., Spain (sē-ē'r-rä-dĕ)	158	38.05N	2.45W
Sehwān, Pak.	186	26.33N	67.51E
Seibeeshiden, Japan	242a	35.34N	139.22E
Seibo, Dom. Rep. (sĕ'y-bō)	123	18.45N	69.05W
Seiling, Ok., U.S.	110	36.09N	98.56W
Seinäjoki, Fin. (sā'ē-nĕ-yō'kė)	153	62.47N	22.50E
Seine, r., Can. (sån)	83f	49.48N	97.03W
Seine, r., Can. (sån)	90	49.04N	91.00W
Seine, r., Fr.	142	48.00N	4.30E
Seine, Baie de la, b., Fr. (bī dĕ lä sån)	156	49.37N	0.53W
Seio do Venus, mtn., Braz. (sĕ-yō-dō-vĕ'nōōs)	132b	22.28S	43.12W
Seixal, Port. (så-ē-shäl')	159b	38.38N	9.06W
Sekenke, Tan.	217	4.16S	34.10E
Şeki, Azer.	168	41.12N	47.12E
Sekondi-Takoradi, Ghana (sĕ-kōn'dē tä-kō-rä'dė)	210	4.59N	1.43W
Sekota, Eth.	211	12.47N	38.59E
Selangor, state, Malay. (så-län'gōr)	181b	2.53N	101.29E
Selanovtsi, Bul. (sĕl'á-nôv-tsĭ)	161	43.42N	24.05E
Selaru, Pulau, i., Indon.	197	8.30S	130.30E
Selatan, Tanjung, c., Indon. (så-lä'tän)	196	4.09S	114.40E
Selawik, Ak., U.S. (sē-lȧ-wĭk)	95	66.30N	160.09W
Selayar, Pulau, i., Indon.	196	6.15S	121.15E
Selbecke, neigh., Ger.	236	51.20N	7.28E
Selbusjøen, l., Nor. (sĕl'bōō)	152	63.18N	11.55E
Selby, Eng., U.K. (sĕl'bė)	144a	53.47N	1.03W
Selby, neigh., S. Afr.	244b	26.13S	28.02E
Seldovia, Ak., U.S. (sĕl-dō'vē-ȧ)	95	59.26N	151.42W
Selection Park, S. Afr.	244b	26.18S	28.27E
Selemdzha, r., Russia (sâ-lĕmt-zhä')	171	52.28N	131.50E
Selenga (Selenge), r., Asia (sĕ lĕŋ gä')	165	49.00N	102.00E
Selenge, r., Asia	188	49.04N	102.23E
Selennyakh, r., Russia (sĕl-yĭn-yäk)	171	67.42N	141.45E
Sélestat, Fr. (sĕ-lĕ-stä')	157	48.16N	7.27E
Seletar, Sing.	240c	1.25N	103.53E
Sélibaby, Maur. (så-lė-bȧ-bē')	210	15.21N	12.11W
Seliger, l., Russia (sĕl'lĕ-gĕr)	166	57.14N	33.18E
Selizharovo, Russia (sâ'lē-zhä'rō-vō)	162	56.51N	33.28E
Selkirk, Can. (sĕl'kûrk)	84	50.09N	96.52W
Selkirk Mountains, mts., Can.	84	51.00N	117.40W
Selleck, Wa., U.S. (sĕl'ĕck)	106a	47.22N	121.52W
Sellersburg, In., U.S. (sĕl'ērs-bûrg)	101h	38.25N	85.45W
Sellya Khskaya, Guba, b., Russia (sĕl-yäk'sKȧ-yȧ)	171	72.30N	136.00E
Selma, Al., U.S. (sĕl'mȧ)	97	32.25N	87.00W
Selma, Ca., U.S.	108	36.34N	119.37W
Selma, N.C., U.S.	115	35.33N	78.16W
Selma, Tx., U.S.	107d	29.33N	98.19W
Selmer, Tn., U.S.	114	35.11N	88.36W
Selsingen, Ger. (zĕl'zēn-gĕn)	145c	53.22N	9.13E
Selway, r., Id., U.S. (sĕl'wā)	104	46.07N	115.12W
Selwyn, l., Can. (sĕl'wĭn)	84	59.41N	104.30W
Seman, r., Alb.	161	40.48N	19.53E
Semarang, Indon. (sĕ-mä'räng)	196	7.03S	110.27E
Sembawang, Sing.	240c	1.27N	103.50E
Semenivka, Ukr.	167	52.10N	32.34E
Semeru, Gunung, mtn., Indon.	196	8.06S	112.55E
Semey (Semipalatinsk), Kaz.	169	50.28N	80.29E
Semiahmoo Indian Reserve, I.R., Can.	106d	49.01N	122.43W
Semiahmoo Spit, Wa., U.S. (sĕm'ĭ-â-mōō)	106d	48.59N	122.52W
Semichi Islands, is., Ak., U.S. (sē-mē'chī)	95a	52.40N	174.50E
Seminoe Reservoir, res., Wy., U.S. (sĕm'ĭ nō)	105	42.08N	107.10W
Seminole, Ok., U.S. (sĕm'ĭ-nōl)	111	35.13N	96.41W
Seminole, Tx., U.S.	112	32.43N	102.39W
Seminole, Lake, res., U.S.	114	30.57N	84.46W
Semisopochnoi, i., Ak., U.S. (sĕ-mē-sȧ-pōsh' noi)	95a	51.45N	179.25E
Semliki, r., Afr. (sĕm'lė-kē)	211	0.45N	29.36E
Semmering Pass, p., Aus. (sĕm'ĕr-ĭng)	154	47.39N	15.50E
Senador Pompeu, Braz. (sĕ-nä-dōr-pôm-pĕ'ō)	131	5.34S	39.18W
Senaki, Geor.	168	42.17N	42.04E
Senatobia, Ms., U.S. (sĕ-nȧ-tō'bē-ȧ)	114	34.36N	89.56W
Send, Eng., U.K.	235	51.17N	0.31W
Sendai, Japan (sĕn-dī')	189	38.18N	141.02E
Seneca, Ks., U.S. (sĕn'ĕ-kȧ)	111	39.49N	96.03W
Seneca, Md., U.S.	100e	39.04N	77.20W
Seneca, S.C., U.S.	115	34.40N	82.58W
Seneca, l., N.Y., U.S.	99	42.30N	76.55W
Seneca Falls, N.Y., U.S.	99	42.55N	76.55W
Senegal, nation, Afr. (sĕn-ĕ-gôl')	210	14.53N	14.58W
Sénégal, r., Afr.	210	16.00N	14.00W
Senekal, S. Afr. (sĕn'ĕ-kȧl)	218d	28.20S	27.37E
Senftenberg, Ger. (zĕnf'tĕn-bĕrgh)	154	51.32N	14.00E
Sengunyane, r., Leso.	213c	29.35S	28.08E
Senhor do Bonfim, Braz. (sĕn-yōr dō bôN-fē'N)	131	10.21S	40.09W
Senigallia, Italy (så-nė-gäl'lyä)	160	43.42N	13.16E
Senj, Cro. (sĕn')	160	44.58N	14.55E
Senja, i., Nor. (sĕnyä)	146	69.28N	16.10E
Senlis, Fr. (sän-lēs')	157b	49.13N	2.35E
Sennar Dam, dam, Sudan	211	13.38N	33.38E
Senneterre, Can.	85	48.20N	77.22W
Senno, Bela. (syĕ'nō)	162	54.48N	29.43E
Senriyama, Japan	242b	34.47N	135.30E
Sens, Fr. (säNs)	156	48.05N	3.18E
Sensuntepeque, El Sal. (sĕn-sōōn-tȧ-pā'kȧ)	120	13.53N	88.34W
Senta, Yugo. (sĕn'tä)	149	45.54N	20.05E
Sentosa, i., Sing.	240c	1.15N	103.50E
Senzaki, Japan (sĕn'zä-kē)	195	34.22N	131.09E
Seoul (Sŏul), S. Kor.	189	37.35N	127.03E
Sepang, Malay.	181b	2.43N	101.45E
Sepetiba, Baia de, b., Braz. (bäē'ä dĕ sā-pȧ-tē'bȧ)	132b	23.01S	43.42W
Sepik, r. (sĕp-ĕk')	197	4.07S	142.40E
Septentrional, Cordillera, mts., Dom. Rep.	123	19.50N	71.15W
Septeuil, Fr. (sĕ-tû')	157b	48.53N	1.40E
Sept-Îles, Can. (sĕ-tēl')	92	50.12N	66.23W
Sequatchie, r., Tn., U.S. (sė-kwăch'ė)	114	35.33N	85.14W
Sequim, Wa., U.S. (sē'kwĭm)	106a	48.05N	123.07W
Sequim Bay, b., Wa., U.S.	106a	48.04N	122.58W
Sequoia National Park, rec., Ca., U.S. (sė-kwoi'ȧ)	96	36.34N	118.37W
Seraing, Bel. (sē-răN')	151	50.38N	5.28E
Serāmpore, India	186a	22.44N	88.21E
Serang, Indon. (så-räng')	196	6.13S	106.10E
Seranggung, Indon.	181b	0.49N	104.11E
Serangoon, Sing.	240c	1.22N	103.54E
Serangoon Harbour, b., Sing.	240c	1.23N	103.57E
Serbia *see* Srbija, hist. reg., Yugo.	161	44.05N	20.35E
Serdobsk, Russia (sĕr-dôpsk')	167	52.30N	44.20E
Serebr'anyj Bor, neigh., Russia	239b	55.47N	37.25E
Sered', Slvk.	155	48.17N	17.43E
Seredyna-Buda, Ukr.	162	52.11N	34.03E
Seremban, Malay. (sĕr-ĕm-bän')	181b	2.44N	101.57E
Serengeti National Park, rec., Tan.	217	2.20S	34.50E
Serengeti Plain, pl., Tan.	217	2.40S	34.55E
Serenje, Zam. (sē-rĕn'yė)	212	13.12S	30.49E
Seret, r., Ukr. (sĕr'ĕt)	155	49.45N	25.30E
Sergeya Kirova, i., Russia (sĕr-gyē'yȧ kė'rō-vȧ)	170	77.30N	86.10E
Sergipe, state, Braz. (sĕr-zhē'pĕ)	131	10.27S	37.04W
Sergiyev Posad, Russia	172b	56.18N	38.08E
Sergiyevsk, Russia	166	53.58N	51.00E
Sérifos, Grc.	161	37.10N	24.32E
Sérifos, i., Grc.	161	37.42N	24.17E
Serodino, Arg. (sĕ-rō-dĕ'nō)	129c	32.36S	60.56W
Seropédica, Braz. (sĕ-rō-pĕ'dē-kä)	132b	22.44S	43.43W
Serov, Russia (syĕ-rôf')	170	59.36N	60.30E
Serowe, Bots. (sĕ-rō'wĕ)	212	22.18S	26.39E
Serpa, Port. (sĕr-pä)	158	37.56N	7.38W
Serpukhov, Russia (syĕr'pō-Kôf)	164	54.53N	37.27E
Sérrai, Grc. (sĕr'rĕ) (sĕr'ĕs)	149	41.06N	23.36E
Serrinha, Braz. (sĕr-rēn'yȧ)	131	11.43S	38.49W
Serta, Port. (sĕr'tȧ)	158	39.48N	8.01W
Sertânia, Braz. (sĕr-tȧ'nyä)	131	8.28S	37.13W
Sertãozinho, Braz. (sĕr-touN-zē'n-yō)	129a	21.10S	47.58W
Serting, r., Malay.	181b	3.01N	102.32E
Servon, Fr.	237c	48.43N	2.35E
Sese Islands, is., Ug.	217	0.30S	32.30E
Sesia, r., Italy (sâz'yä)	160	45.33N	8.25E
Sesimbra, Port. (sĕ-sē'm-brä)	159b	38.27N	9.06W
Sesmyl, r., S. Afr.	213b	25.51S	28.06E
Sesto San Giovanni, Italy	238c	45.32N	9.14E
Sestri Levante, Italy (sĕs'trē lȧ-vän'tȧ)	160	44.15N	9.24E
Sestroretsk, Russia (sĕs-trō-rĕtsk)	166	60.06N	29.58E
Sestroretskiy Razliv, Ozero, l., Russia	172c	60.05N	30.07E
Seta, Japan (sĕ'tä)	195b	34.58N	135.56W
Setagaya, neigh., Japan	242a	35.39N	139.40E
Séte, Fr. (sĕt)	147	43.24N	3.42E
Sete Lagoas, Braz. (sĕ-tĕ lä-gô'äs)	131	19.23S	43.58W
Sete Pontes, Braz.	132b	22.51S	43.05W
Seto, Japan (sĕ'tō)	195	35.11N	137.07E
Seto-Naikai, sea, Japan (sĕ'tō nī'kī)	195	33.50N	132.25E
Seton Hall University, pt. of i., N.Y., U.S.	228	40.45N	74.15W
Settat, Mor. (sĕt-ät') (sĕ-tȧ')	210	33.02N	7.30W
Sette-Cama, Gabon (sĕ-tĕ-kä-mä')	212	2.29S	9.40E
Settecamini, neigh., Italy	239c	41.56N	12.37E
Settimo Milanese, Italy	238c	45.29N	9.03E
Settlement Point, c., Bah. (sĕt'l-mĕnt)	122	26.40N	79.00W
Settlers, S. Afr. (sĕt'lērs)	218d	24.57S	28.33E
Settsu, Japan	195b	34.46N	135.33E
Setúbal, Port. (så-tōō'bäl)	148	30.32N	8.54W
Setúbal, Baía de, b., Port.	158	38.27N	9.08W
Seul, Lac, l., Can. (làk sûl)	85	50.20N	92.30W
Sevan, l., Arm. (syĭ-vän')	167	40.10N	45.20E
Sevastopol', Ukr. (syĕ-väs-tô'pôl'')	164	44.34N	33.34E
Seven Hills, Austl.	243a	33.46S	150.57E
Seven Hills, Oh., U.S.	229a	41.22N	81.41W
Seven Kings, neigh., Eng., U.K.	235	51.34N	0.05E
Sevenoaks, Eng., U.K. (sĕ-vĕn-ôks')	144b	51.16N	0.12E
Severka, r., Russia (sâ'vĕr-kȧ)	172b	55.11N	38.41E
Severn, r., Can. (sĕv'ērn)	85	55.21N	88.42W
Severn, r., U.K.	150	51.50N	2.25W
Severna Park, Md., U.S. (sĕv'ērn-ȧ)	100e	39.04N	76.33W
Severnaya Dvina, r., Russia	164	63.00N	42.40E
Severnaya Zemlya (Northern Land), is., Russia (sĕ-vyĭr-nīŭ zĭ-m'lyä')	165	79.33N	101.15E
Severoural'sk, Russia (sĕ-vyĭ-rŭ-ōō-rälsk')	170	60.08N	59.53E
Sevier, r., Ut., U.S.	96	39.25N	112.20W
Sevier, East Fork, r., Ut., U.S.	109	37.45N	112.10W
Sevier Lake, l., Ut., U.S. (sė-vēr')	109	38.55N	113.10W
Sevilla, Col. (sĕ-vē'l-yä)	130a	4.16N	75.56W
Sevilla, Spain (så-vēl'yä)	142	37.29N	5.58W
Seville, Oh., U.S. (sĕ'vĭl)	101d	41.01N	81.45W
Sevlievo, Bul. (sĕv'lyĕ-vō)	149	43.02N	25.05E
Sevran, Fr.	237c	48.56N	2.32E
Sèvres, Fr.	237c	48.49N	2.12E
Sevsk, Russia (syĕfsk)	162	52.08N	34.28E
Seward, Ak., U.S. (sū'ărd)	96a	60.18N	149.28W
Seward, Ne., U.S.	111	40.55N	97.06W
Seward Peninsula, pen., Ak., U.S.	95	65.40N	164.00W
Sewell, Chile (sĕ'ō-ĕl)	132	34.01S	70.18W
Sewickley, Pa., U.S. (sė-wĭk'lė)	101e	40.33N	80.11W
Seybaplaya, Mex. (sā-ē-bä-plä'yä)	119	19.38N	90.40W
Seychelles, nation, Afr. (sā-shĕl')	3	5.20S	55.10E
Seydisfjördur, Ice. (sā'dės-fyûr-dòr)	146	65.21N	14.08W
Seyhan, r., Tur.	149	37.28N	35.40E
Seylac, Som.	218a	11.19N	43.20E
Seym, r., Eur. (sĕym)	167	51.23N	33.22E
Seymour, S. Afr. (sē'môr)	213c	32.33S	26.48E
Seymour, In., U.S. (sē'mōr)	98	38.55N	85.55W
Seymour, Ia., U.S.	103	40.41N	93.03W
Seymour, Tx., U.S.	110	33.35N	99.16W
Sezela, S. Afr.	213c	30.33S	30.37W
Sezze, Italy (sĕt'sȧ)	160	41.32N	13.00E
Sfântu Gheorghe, Rom.	149	45.53N	25.49E
Sfax, Tun. (sfăks)	210	34.51N	10.45E
's-Gravenhage *see* The Hague, Neth. ('s KRä'vĕn-hä'Kĕ) (hāg)	142	52.05N	4.16E
Sha, r., China (shä)	189	33.33N	114.30E
Shaanxi, prov., China (shän-shyē)	188	35.30N	109.10E
Shabeelle (Shebele), r., Afr.	218a	1.38N	43.50E
Shache, China (shä-chŭ)	188	38.15N	77.15E
Shackleton Ice Shelf, ice., Ant. (shăk''l-tŭn)	219	65.00S	100.00E
Shades Creek, r., Al., U.S. (shādz)	100h	33.20N	86.55W
Shades Mountain, mtn., Al., U.S.	100h	33.22N	86.51W
Shagamu, Nig.	215	6.51N	3.39E
Shāhdād, Namakzār-e, l., Iran (nū-mŭk-zär')	182	31.00N	58.30E
Shāhdara, neigh., India	240d	28.40N	77.18E
Shāhjahānpur, India (shä-jŭ-hän'pōōr)	183	27.58N	79.58E
Shah Mosque, rel., Iran	241h	35.40N	51.25E
Shajing, China (shä-jyĭŋ)	191a	22.44N	113.48E
Shakarpur Khās, neigh., India	240d	28.38N	77.17E
Shaker Heights, Oh., U.S. (shā'kēr)	101d	41.28N	81.34W
Shakhty, Russia (shäK'tė)	164	47.41N	40.11E
Shaki, Nig.	215	8.39N	3.25E
Shakopee, Mn., U.S. (shăk'ō-pe)	107g	44.48N	93.31W
Shakūrpur, neigh., India	240d	28.41N	77.09E
Shala Lake, l., Eth. (shä'lȧ)	211	7.34N	39.00E
Shalqar, Kaz.	169	47.52N	59.41E
Shalqar köli, l., Kaz.	170	50.30N	51.30E
Shām, Jabal ash, mtn., Oman	182	23.01N	57.45E
Shambe, Sudan (shäm'bȧ)	211	7.08N	30.46E
Shammar, Jabal, mts., Sau. Ar. (jĕb'ĕl shŭm'ȧr)	182	27.13N	40.16E

ng-sing; ŋ-baŋk; N-nasalized n; nŏd; cŏmmit; ōld; ôbey; ôrder; oi-boil; fōōd; ō-as oo in foot; ou-out; s-soft; sh-dish; th-thin; pūre; ûnite; ûrn; stŭd; circŭs; ü-as in French tu; '-indeterminate vowel.

348 Shamokin – Sidi bel Abbès

PLACE (Pronunciation)	PAGE	Lat. °′	Long. °′
Shamokin, Pa., U.S. (shȧ-mō′kĭn)	99	40.45N	76.30W
Shamrock, Tx., U.S. (shăm′rŏk)	110	35.14N	100.12W
Shamva, Zimb. (shäm′vȧ)	212	17.18S	31.35E
Shandon, Oh., U.S. (shăn-dŭn)	101f	39.20N	84.13W
Shandong, prov., China (shän-dôŋ)	189	36.08N	117.09E
Shandong Bandao, pen., China (shän-dôŋ bän-dou)	189	37.00N	120.10E
Shangcai, China (shäŋ-tsī)	190	33.16N	114.16E
Shangcheng, China (shäŋ-chŭŋ)	190	31.47N	115.22E
Shangdu, China (shäŋ-dōō)	192	41.38N	113.22E
Shanghai, China (shäng′hī′)	189	31.14N	121.27E
Shanghai-Shi, prov., China (shäŋ-hī shr)	189	31.30N	121.45E
Shanghe, China (shäŋ-hŭ)	190	37.18N	117.10E
Shanglin, China (shäŋ-lĭn)	190	38.20N	116.05E
Shangqiu, China (shäŋ-chyō)	192	34.24N	115.39E
Shangrao, China (shäŋ-rou)	193	28.25N	117.58E
Shangzhi, China (shäŋ-jr)	192	45.18N	127.52E
Shanhaiguan, China	192	40.01N	119.45E
Shannon, Al., U.S. (shăn′ŭn)	100h	33.23N	86.52W
Shannon, r., Ire. (shăn′ŏn)	147	52.30N	10.15W
Shanshan, China (shän′shän′)	188	42.51N	89.53E
Shantar, i., Russia (shän′tär)	171	55.13N	138.42E
Shantou, China (shän-tō)	189	23.20N	116.40E
Shanxi, prov., China (shän-shyē)	189	37.30N	112.00E
Shan Xian, China (shän shyĕn)	190	34.47N	116.04E
Shaobo, China (shou-bwo)	192	32.33N	119.30E
Shaobo Hu, l., China (shou-bwo hōō)	190	32.47N	119.13E
Shaoguan, China (shou-gŭän)	189	24.58N	113.42E
Shaoxing, China (shou-shyĭŋ)	189	30.00N	120.40E
Shaoyang, China	189	27.15N	111.28E
Shapki, Russia (shäp′kĭ)	172c	59.36N	31.11E
Shark Bay, b., Austl. (shärk)	202	25.30S	113.00E
Sharon, Ma., U.S. (shăr′ŏn)	93a	42.07N	71.11W
Sharon, Pa., U.S.	98	41.15N	80.30W
Sharon Hill, Pa., U.S.	229b	39.55N	75.16W
Sharon Springs, Ks., U.S.	110	38.51N	101.45W
Sharonville, Oh., U.S. (shăr′ŏn vĭl)	101f	39.16N	84.24W
Sharpsburg, Pa., U.S. (shärps′bûrg)	101e	40.30N	79.54W
Sharps Hill, Pa., U.S.	230b	40.30N	79.56W
Sharr, Jabal, mtn., Sau. Ar.	182	28.00N	36.07E
Shashi, China (shä-shē)	189	30.20N	112.18E
Shasta, Mount, mtn., Ca., U.S.	96	41.35N	122.12W
Shasta Lake, res., Ca., U.S. (shăs′tȧ)	96	40.51N	122.32W
Shatsk, Russia (shätsk)	166	54.00N	41.40E
Shattuck, Ok., U.S. (shăt′ŭk)	110	36.16N	99.53W
Shaunavon, Can.	84	49.40N	108.25W
Shaw, Eng., U.K.	237b	53.35N	2.06W
Shaw, Ms., U.S. (shô)	114	33.36N	90.44W
Shawano, Wi., U.S. (shȧ-wô′nō)	103	44.41N	88.13W
Shawinigan, Can.	85	46.32N	72.46W
Shawnee, Ks., U.S. (shô-nē′)	107f	39.01N	94.43W
Shawnee, Ok., U.S.	96	35.20N	96.54W
Shawneetown, Il., U.S. (shô′nē-toun)	98	37.40N	88.05W
Shayang, China	193	31.00N	112.38E
Shchara, r., Bela. (sh-chä′rä)	155	53.17N	25.12E
Shchëlkovo, Russia (shchĕl′kô-vô)	162	55.55N	38.00E
Shchigry, Russia (shchē′grē)	163	51.52N	36.54E
Shchors, Ukr. (shchôrs)	163	51.38N	31.58E
Shchuch′ye Ozero, Russia (shchōōch′yē ô′zĕ-rō)	172a	56.31N	56.35E
Sheakhala, India	186a	22.47N	88.10E
Shebele (Shabeelle), r., Afr. (shā′bå-lē)	218a	6.07N	43.10E
Sheboygan, Wi., U.S. (shē-boi′gǎn)	97	43.45N	87.44W
Sheboygan Falls, Wi., U.S.	103	43.43N	87.51W
Shechem, hist., W. Bank	181a	32.15N	35.22E
Shedandoah, Pa., U.S.	99	40.50N	76.15W
Shediac, Can. (shĕ′dē-ăk)	92	46.13N	64.32W
Shedin Peak, mtn., Can. (shĕd′ĭn)	86	55.55N	127.32W
Sheepshead Bay, neigh., N.Y., U.S.	228	40.35N	73.56W
Sheerness, Eng., U.K. (shēr′nĕs)	144b	51.26N	0.46E
Sheffield, Can.	83d	43.20N	80.13W
Sheffield, Eng., U.K.	146	53.23N	1.28W
Sheffield, Al., U.S. (shĕf′fēld)	114	35.42N	87.42W
Sheffield, Oh., U.S.	101d	41.26N	82.05W
Sheffield Lake, Oh., U.S.	101d	41.30N	82.03W
Sheksna, r., Russia (shĕks′nȧ)	166	59.50N	38.40E
Shelagskiy, Mys, c., Russia (shĭ-läg′skē)	165	70.08N	170.52E
Shelbina, Ar., U.S. (shĕl-bī′nȧ)	111	39.41N	92.03W
Shelburn, In., U.S. (shĕl′bŭrn)	98	39.10N	87.30W
Shelburne, Can.	85	43.46N	65.19W
Shelburne, Can.	91	44.04N	80.12W
Shelby, In., U.S. (shĕl′bē)	101a	41.12N	87.21W
Shelby, Mi., U.S.	98	43.35N	86.20W
Shelby, Ms., U.S.	114	33.56N	90.44W
Shelby, Mt., U.S.	105	48.35N	111.55W
Shelby, N.C., U.S.	115	35.16N	81.35W
Shelby, Oh., U.S.	98	40.50N	82.40W
Shelbyville, Il., U.S. (shĕl′bē-vĭl)	98	39.20N	88.45W
Shelbyville, In., U.S.	98	39.30N	85.45W
Shelbyville, Ky., U.S.	98	38.10N	85.15W
Shelbyville, Tn., U.S.	114	35.30N	86.28W
Shelbyville Reservoir, res., Il., U.S.	98	39.30N	88.45W
Sheldon, Ia., U.S. (shĕl′dŭn)	102	43.10N	95.50W
Sheldon, Tx., U.S.	113a	29.52N	95.07W
Shelekhova, Zaliv, b., Russia	165	60.00N	156.00E
Shelikof Strait, strt., Ak., U.S. (shĕ′lē-kôf)	95	57.56N	154.20W
Shellbrook, Can.	88	53.15N	106.22W
Shelley, Id., U.S. (shĕl′lē)	105	43.24N	112.06W
Shellow Bowells, Eng., U.K.	235	51.45N	0.20E
Shellrock, r., Ia., U.S. (shĕl′rŏk)	103	43.25N	93.19W
Shelon′, r., Russia (shå′lôn)	162	57.50N	29.40E
Shelter, Port, b., H.K.	241c	22.21N	114.17E
Shelton, Ct., U.S. (shĕl′tŭn)	99	41.15N	73.05W
Shelton, Ne., U.S.	110	40.46N	98.41W
Shelton, Wa., U.S.	104	47.14N	123.05W
Shemakha, Russia (shĕ-mȧ-kä′)	172a	56.16N	59.19E
Shenandoah, Ia., U.S. (shĕn-ǎn-dō′ȧ)	111	40.46N	95.23W
Shenandoah, Va., U.S.	99	38.30N	78.30W
Shenandoah, r., Va., U.S.	99	38.55N	78.05W
Shenandoah National Park, rec., Va., U.S.	97	38.35N	78.25W
Shendam, Nig.	215	8.53N	9.32E
Shenfield, Eng., U.K.	235	51.38N	0.19E
Shengfang, China (shengfäng)	190	39.05N	116.40E
Shenkursk, Russia (shĕn-kōōrsk′)	164	62.10N	43.08E
Shenmu, China	192	38.55N	110.35E
Shenqiu, China	192	33.11N	115.06E
Shenxian, China (shŭn shyän)	190	38.02N	115.33E
Shenxian, China (shŭn shyĕn)	190	36.14N	115.38E
Shenyang, China (shŭn-yäŋ)	189	41.45N	123.22E
Shenze, China (shŭn-dzŭ)	190	38.12N	115.12E
Shenzhen, China	193	22.32N	114.08E
Sheopur, India	183	25.37N	77.10E
Shepard, Can. (shĕ′pärd)	83e	50.57N	113.55W
Shepetivka, Ukr.	167	50.10N	27.01E
Shepparton, Austl. (shĕp′ȧr-tŭn)	204	36.15S	145.25E
Shepperton, Eng., U.K.	235	51.24N	0.27W
Sherborn, Ma., U.S. (shûr′bŭrn)	93a	42.15N	71.22W
Sherbrooke, Can.	85	45.24N	71.54W
Sherburn, Eng., U.K. (shûr′bŭrn)	144a	53.47N	1.15W
Shereshevo, Bela. (shĕ-rĕ-shĕ-vô)	155	52.31N	24.08E
Sheridan, Ar., U.S. (shĕr′ĭ-dǎn)	111	34.19N	92.21W
Sheridan, Or., U.S.	104	45.06N	123.22W
Sheridan, Wy., U.S.	96	44.48N	106.56W
Sherman, Tx., U.S. (shĕr′măn)	96	33.39N	96.37W
Sherman Oaks, neigh., Ca., U.S.	232	34.09N	118.26W
Sherna, r., Russia (shĕr′nȧ)	172b	56.08N	38.45E
Sherridon, Can.	89	55.10N	101.10W
′s Hertogenbosch, Neth. (sĕr-tō′ghĕn-bôs)	151	51.41N	5.19E
Sherwood, Or., U.S.	106c	45.21N	122.50W
Sherwood Forest, for., Eng., U.K.	144a	53.11N	1.07W
Sherwood Park, Can.	87	53.31N	113.19W
Shetland Islands, is., Scot., U.K. (shĕt′lǎnd)	142	60.35N	2.10W
Sheva, India	240e	18.56N	72.57E
Shewa Gimira, Eth.	211	7.13N	35.49E
Shexian, China (shŭ shyĕn)	190	36.34N	113.42E
Sheyang, r., China (she-yäŋ)	190	33.42N	119.40E
Sheyenne, r., N.D., U.S. (shī-ĕn′)	102	46.42N	97.52W
Shi, r., China (shr)	190	31.58N	115.50E
Shi, r., China	190	32.09N	114.11E
Shiawassee, r., Mi., U.S. (shī-ȧ-wôs′ē)	98	43.15N	84.05W
Shibām, Yemen (shē′băm)	182	16.02N	48.40E
Shibīn al Kawn, Egypt (shē-bēn′ĕl kōm′)	218b	30.31N	31.01E
Shibīn al Qanāṭir, Egypt (kȧ-nä′tēr)	218b	30.18N	31.21E
Shibuya, neigh., Japan	242a	35.40N	139.42E
Shicun, China (shr-tsōn)	190	33.47N	117.18E
Shields, r., Mt., U.S. (shēldz)	105	45.54N	110.40W
Shifnal, Eng., U.K. (shĭf′nǎl)	144a	52.40N	2.22W
Shihlin, Tai.	241d	25.05N	121.31E
Shijian, China (shr-jyĕn)	190	31.27N	117.51E
Shijiazhuang, China (shr-jyä-jûäŋ)	189	38.04N	114.31E
Shijiu Hu, l., China (shr-jyō hōō)	190	31.29N	119.07E
Shijōnawate, Japan	242b	34.45N	135.39E
Shikārpur, Pak.	183	27.51N	68.52E
Shiki, Japan (shē′kē)	195a	35.50N	139.35E
Shikoku, i., Japan (shē′kō′kōō)	189	33.43N	133.33E
Shilibao, China	240b	39.55N	116.29E
Shilka, r., Russia (shĭl′kȧ)	171	53.00N	118.45E
Shilla, mtn., India	186	32.18N	78.17E
Shillong, India (shĕl-lông′)	183	25.39N	91.58E
Shiloh, Il., U.S. (shī′lō)	107e	38.34N	89.54W
Shilong, China (shr-lôŋ)	193	23.05N	113.58E
Shilou, China	191a	22.58N	113.29E
Shimabara, Japan (shē′mä-bä′rä)	195	32.46N	130.22E
Shimada, Japan (shē′mä-dä)	195	34.49N	138.13E
Shimbiris, mtn., Som.	218a	10.40N	47.23E
Shimizu, Japan (shē′mē-zōō)	194	35.00N	138.29E
Shimminato, Japan (shēm′mē′nä-tō)	195	36.47N	137.05E
Shimoda, Japan (shē′mō-dȧ)	195	34.41N	138.58E
Shimoga, India	187	13.59N	75.38E
Shimohōya, Japan	242a	35.45N	139.34E
Shimoigusa, neigh., Japan	242a	35.43N	139.37E
Shimomizo, Japan	242a	35.31N	139.23E
Shimoni, Kenya	217	4.39S	39.23E
Shimonoseki, Japan	189	33.58N	130.55E
Shimo-Saga, Japan (shē′mō sä′gä)	195b	35.01N	135.41E
Shimo-shakujii, neigh., Japan	242a	35.45N	139.37E
Shimotsuruma, Japan	242a	35.29N	139.28E
Shimoyugi, Japan	242a	35.38N	139.23E
Shin, Loch, l., Scot., U.K. (lŏk shĭn)	150	58.08N	4.02W
Shinagawa-Wan, b., Japan (shē′nä-gä′wä wän)	195a	35.37N	139.49E
Shinano-Gawa, r., Japan (shē-nä′nō gä′wä)	195	36.43N	138.22E
Shīndand, Afg.	185	33.18N	62.08E
Shinji, l., Japan (shĭn′jē)	195	35.23N	133.05E
Shinjuku, neigh., Japan	242a	35.41N	139.42E
Shinkolobwe, Zaire	217	11.02S	26.35E
Shinyanga, Tan. (shĭn-yäŋ′gä)	212	3.40S	33.26E
Shiono Misaki, c., Japan (shē-ō′nō mē′sä-kē)	194	33.20N	136.10E
Shipai, China (shr-pī)	191a	23.07N	113.23E
Ship Channel Cay, i., Bah. (shĭp chă-nĕl kē)	122	24.50N	76.50W
Shipley, Eng., U.K. (shĭp′lē)	144a	53.50N	1.47W
Shippegan, Can. (shĭ′pē-găn)	92	47.45N	64.42W
Shippegan Island, i., Can.	92	47.50N	64.38W
Shippenburg, Pa., U.S. (shĭp′ĕn bûrg)	99	40.00N	77.30W
Shipshaw, r., Can. (shĭp′shô)	91	48.50N	71.03W
Shiqma, r., Isr.	181a	31.31N	34.40E
Shirane-san, mtn., Japan (shē′rä′nȧ-sän′)	195	35.44N	138.14E
Shirati, Tan. (shē-rä′tē)	212	1.15S	34.02E
Shīrāz, Iran (shē-räz′)	182	29.32N	52.27E
Shire, r., Afr. (shē′rȧ)	212	15.00S	35.00E
Shiriya Saki, c., Japan (shē′rē sä′kē)	194	41.25N	142.10E
Shirley, Ma., U.S. (shûr′lē)	93a	42.33N	71.39W
Shishaldin Volcano, vol., Ak., U.S. (shī-shăl′dĭn)	95a	54.48N	164.00W
Shively, Ky., U.S. (shīv′lē)	101h	38.11N	85.47W
Shivpuri, India	183	25.31N	77.46E
Shivta, Horvot, hist., Isr.	181a	30.54N	34.36E
Shivwits Plateau, plat., Az., U.S.	109	36.13N	113.42W
Shiwan, China (shr-wän)	191a	23.01N	113.04E
Shiwan Dashan, mts., China (shr-wän dä-shän)	193	22.10N	107.30E
Shizuki, Japan (shē′zōō-kē)	195	34.29N	134.51E
Shizuoka, Japan (shē′zōō′ōkȧ)	194	34.58N	138.24E
Shklov, Bela. (shklôf)	162	54.11N	30.23E
Shkodër, Alb. (shkô′dûr) (skōō′tärē)	142	42.04N	19.30E
Shkotovo, Russia (shkô′tô-vô)	194	43.15N	132.21E
Shoal Creek, r., Il., U.S. (shōl)	111	38.37N	89.25W
Shoal Lake, l., Can.	89	49.32N	95.00W
Shoals, In., U.S. (shōlz)	98	38.40N	86.45W
Shōdai, Japan	242b	34.51N	135.42E
Shōdo, i., Japan (shō′dō)	195	34.27N	134.27E
Shogunle, Nig.	244d	6.35N	3.21E
Sholāpur, India (shō′lä-pōōr)	183	17.42N	75.51E
Shomolu, Nig.	244d	6.32N	3.23E
Shoreham, Eng., U.K.	235	51.20N	0.11E
Shorewood, Wi., U.S. (shōr′wŏŏd)	101a	43.05N	87.54W
Shoshone, Id., U.S. (shō-shōn′tē)	105	42.56N	114.24W
Shoshone, r., Wy., U.S.	105	44.35N	108.50W
Shoshone Lake, l., Wy., U.S.	105	44.17N	110.50W
Shoshoni, Wy., U.S.	105	43.14N	108.05W
Shostka, Ukr. (shôst′kȧ)	163	51.51N	33.31E
Shouguang, China (shō-gŭäŋ)	190	36.53N	118.45E
Shouxian, China (shō shyĕn)	190	32.36N	116.45E
Shpola, Ukr. (shpô′lȧ)	167	49.01N	31.36E
Shreveport, La., U.S. (shrēv′pōrt)	97	32.30N	93.46W
Shrewsbury, Eng., U.K. (shrōōz′bēr-ĭ)	150	52.43N	2.44W
Shrewsbury, Ma., U.S.	93a	42.18N	71.43W
Shroud Cay, i., Bah.	122	24.20N	76.40W
Shuangcheng, China (shůäŋ-chŭŋ)	192	45.18N	126.18E
Shuanghe, China (shůäŋ-hŭ)	190	31.33N	116.48E
Shuangliao, China	189	43.37N	123.30E
Shuangyang, China	192	43.28N	125.45E
Shubrā al-Khaymah, Egypt	244a	30.06N	31.15E
Shuhedun, China (shōō-hŭ-dōn)	190	31.33N	117.01E
Shuiye, China (shwā-yŭ)	190	36.08N	114.07E
Shule, r., China (shōō-lŭ)	188	40.53N	94.55E
Shullsburg, Wi., U.S. (shŭlz′bûrg)	103	42.35N	90.16W
Shumagin, is., Ak., U.S. (shōō′mȧ-gĕn)	95	55.22N	159.20W
Shumen, Bul.	149	43.15N	26.54E
Shunde, China (shōn-dŭ)	191a	22.50N	113.15E
Shungnak, Ak., U.S. (shŭng′nȧk)	95	66.55N	157.20W
Shunut, Gora, mtn., Russia (gȧ-rä shōō′nōt)	172a	56.33N	59.45E
Shunyi, China (shōn-yē)	190	40.09N	116.38E
Shuqrah, Yemen	182	13.32N	46.02E
Shūrāb, r., Iran (shōō räb)	182	31.08N	55.30E
Shuri, Japan (shōō′rē)	194	26.10N	127.48E
Shurugwi, Zimb.	212	19.34S	30.03E
Shūshtar, Iran (shōōsh′tŭr)	182	31.50N	48.46E
Shuswap Lake, l., Can. (shōōs′wŏp)	87	50.57N	119.15W
Shuya, Russia (shōō′yȧ)	164	56.52N	41.23E
Shuyang, China (shōō yäng)	190	34.09N	118.47E
Shweba, Myanmar	183	22.23N	96.13E
Shyghys Qongyrat, Kaz.	169	47.25N	75.10E
Shymkent, Kaz.	169	42.17N	69.42E
Shyroke, Ukr.	163	47.40N	33.18E
Siak Kecil, r., Indon.	181b	1.01N	101.45E
Siaksriinderapura, Indon. (sē-äks′rĭ ĕn′drȧ-pōō′rä)	181b	0.48N	102.05E
Siālkot, Pak. (sē-äl′kōt)	183	32.39N	74.30E
Siátista, Grc. (syä′tĭs-ta)	161	40.15N	21.32E
Şiau, Pulau, i., Indon.	197	2.40N	126.00E
Šiauliai, Lith. (shē-ou′lē-ī)	166	55.57N	23.19E
Şibay, Russia (sē′báy)	172a	52.41N	58.40E
Šibenik, Cro. (shē-bä′nĕk)	149	43.44N	15.55E
Siberia, reg., Russia	180	57.00N	97.00E
Siberut, Pulau, i., Indon. (sē′bȧ-rōōt)	196	1.22S	99.45E
Sibiti, Congo (sē-bē-tē′)	212	3.41S	13.21E
Sibiu, Rom. (sē-bĭ-ōō′)	149	45.47N	24.09E
Sibley, Ia., U.S. (sĭb′lē)	102	43.24N	95.33W
Sibolga, Indon. (sē-bō′gä)	196	1.45N	98.45E
Sibpur, India	240a	22.34N	88.19E
Sibsāgar, India (sēb-sŭ′gŭr)	183	26.47N	94.45E
Sibutu Island, i., Phil.	196	4.40N	119.30E
Sibuyan, i., Phil. (sē-bōō-yän′)	197a	12.19N	122.25E
Sibuyan Sea, sea, Phil.	196	12.43N	122.38E
Sichuan, prov., China (sz-chůän)	188	31.20N	103.00E
Sicily, i., Italy (sĭs′ĭ-lē)	142	37.38N	13.30E
Sico, r., Hond. (sē-kō)	120	15.32N	85.42W
Sidamo, hist. reg., Eth. (sē-dä′mō)	211	5.08N	37.45E
Sidao, China	240b	39.51N	116.26E
Sidcup, neigh., Eng., U.K.	235	51.25N	0.06E
Siderno Marina, Italy (sē-dĕr′nô mä-rē′nä)	160	38.18N	16.19E
Sídheros, Ákra, c., Grc.	160a	35.19N	26.20E
Sidhirókastron, Grc.	161	41.13N	23.27E
Sidi Aïssa, Alg.	159	35.53N	3.44E
Sidi bel Abbès, Alg. (sē′dē-bĕl ȧ-bĕs′)	210	35.15N	0.43W

ăt; finǎl; rāte; senåte; ärm; åsk; sofȧ; fâre; ch-choose; dh-as th in other; bē; ēvent; bĕt; recĕnt; cratẽr; g-gō; gh-guttural g; bĭt; ĭ-short neutral; rīde; κ-guttural k as ch in German ich;

PRONOUNCING INDEX Sidi Ifni–Slobodka 349

PLACE (Pronunciation)	PAGE	Lat. °′	Long. °′
Sidi Ifni, Mor. (ēf'nē)	210	29.22N	10.15W
Sidley, Mount, mtn., Ant. (sĭd'lē)	219	77.25S	129.00W
Sidney, Can.	86	48.39N	123.24W
Sidney, Mt., U.S. (sĭd'nē)	105	47.43N	104.07W
Sidney, Ne., U.S.	102	41.10N	103.00W
Sidney, Oh., U.S.	98	40.20N	84.10W
Sidney Lanier, Lake, res., Ga., U.S. (lăn'yẽr)	97	34.27N	83.56W
Sido, Mali	214	11.40N	7.36W
Sidon see Saydā, Leb.	182	33.34N	35.23E
Sidr, Wādī, r., Egypt	181a	29.43N	32.58E
Sidra, Gulf of see Surt, Khalīj, b., Libya	211	31.30N	18.28E
Siedlce, Pol. (syĕd''l-tsĕ)	155	52.09N	22.20E
Siegburg, Ger. (zēg'bo͞orgh)	154	50.48N	7.13E
Siegen, Ger. (zē'ghĕn)	154	50.52N	8.01E
Sieghartskirchen, Aus.	145e	48.16N	16.00E
Siemensstadt, neigh., Ger.	238a	52.32N	13.17E
Siemiatycze, Pol. (syĕm'yä'tē-chĕ)	155	52.26N	22.52E
Siemionówka, Pol. (sĕĕ-mēō'nôf-kä)	155	52.53N	23.50E
Siem Reap, Camb. (syĕm'rā'äp)	196	13.32N	103.54E
Siena, Italy (sē-ĕn'ä)	148	43.19N	11.21E
Sieradz, Pol. (syĕ'rädz)	155	51.35N	18.45E
Sierpc, Pol. (syĕrpts)	155	52.51N	19.42E
Sierra Blanca, Tx., U.S. (sē-ĕ'rȧ blaŋ-kä)	112	31.10N	105.20W
Sierra Blanca Peak, mtn., N.M., U.S. (blăn'kȧ)	96	33.25N	105.50W
Sierra Leone, nation, Afr. (sē-ĕr'rä lā-ō'nā)	210	8.48N	12.30W
Sierra Madre, Ca., U.S. (mä'drē)	107a	34.10N	118.03W
Sierra Mojada, Mex. (sē-ĕ'r-rä-mô-κä'dä)	112	27.22N	103.42W
Sífnos, i., Grc.	161	36.58N	24.30E
Sigean, Fr. (sē-zhôɴ')	156	43.02N	2.56E
Sigeurney, Ia., U.S. (sē-gûr-nĭ)	103	41.16N	92.10W
Sighetu Marmaţiei, Rom.	155	47.57N	23.55E
Sighişoara, Rom. (sē-gē-shwä'rȧ)	155	46.11N	24.48E
Siglufjördur, Ice.	146	66.06N	18.45W
Signakhi, Geor.	167	41.45N	45.50E
Signal Hill, Ca., U.S. (sĭg'nȧl hĭl)	107a	33.48N	118.11W
Sigsig, Ec. (sēg-sēg')	130	3.04S	78.44W
Sigtuna, Swe. (sēgh-to͞o'nȧ)	152	59.40N	17.39E
Siguanea, Ensenada de la, b., Cuba	122	21.45N	83.15W
Siguatepeque, Hond. (sē-gwä'tē-pĕ-kĕ)	120	14.33N	87.51W
Sigüenza, Spain (sē-gwĕ'n-zä)	148	41.03N	2.38W
Siguiri, Gui. (sē-gē-rē')	210	11.25N	9.10W
Sihong, China (sz-hôŋ)	190	33.25N	118.13E
Siirt, Tur. (sĭ-ērt')	167	38.00N	42.00E
Sikalongo, Zam.	217	16.46S	27.07E
Sikasso, Mali (sē-käs'sō)	210	11.19N	5.40W
Sikeston, Mo., U.S. (sĭks'tŭn)	111	36.50N	89.35W
Sikhote Alin', Khrebet, mts., Russia (se-κô'ta a-lēn')	165	45.00N	135.45E
Sikinos, i., Grc. (sĭ'kĭ-nōs)	161	36.45N	24.55E
Sikkim, state, India	183	27.42N	88.25E
Siklós, Hung. (sĭ'klōsh)	155	45.51N	18.18E
Sil, r., Spain (sē'l)	158	42.20N	7.13W
Silāmpur, neigh., India	240d	28.40N	77.16E
Silang, Phil. (sē-läng')	197a	14.14N	120.58E
Silao, Mex. (sē-lä'ō)	118	20.56N	101.25W
Silchar, India (sĭl-chär')	183	24.52N	92.50E
Silent Valley, S. Afr. (sī'lĕnt vă'lē)	218d	24.32S	26.40E
Siler City, N.C., U.S. (sī'lẽr)	115	35.45N	79.29W
Silesia, hist. reg., Pol. (sĭ-lē'shȧ)	154	50.58N	16.53E
Silifke, Tur.	149	36.20N	34.00E
Siling Co, l., China	188	32.05N	89.10E
Silistra, Bul. (sē-lēs'trȧ)	149	44.01N	27.13E
Siljan, l., Swe. (sēl'yän)	146	60.48N	14.28E
Silkeborg, Den. (sĭl'kĕ-bôr')	152	56.10N	9.33E
Sillery, Can. (sēl'-re')	83b	46.46N	71.15W
Siloam Springs, Ar., U.S. (sī-lōm)	111	36.10N	94.32W
Siloana Plains, pl., Zam.	216	16.55S	23.10E
Silocayoápan, Mex. (sē-lô-kä-yô-ä'păn)	118	17.29N	98.09W
Silsbee, Tx., U.S. (sĭlz' bē)	113	30.19N	94.09W
Şilschede, Ger.	236	51.21N	7.19E
Šilutė, Lith.	153	55.21N	21.29E
Silva Jardim, Braz. (sē'l-vä-zhär-dēɴ)	129a	22.40N	42.24W
Silvana, Wa., U.S. (sĭl-văn' ȧ)	106a	48.12N	122.16W
Silvânia, Braz. (sēl-vá'nyä)	131	16.43S	48.33W
Silvassa, India	186	20.10N	73.00E
Silver, l., Mo., U.S.	111	39.38N	93.12W
Silverado, Ca., U.S. (sĭl-vẽr-ä'dō)	107a	33.45N	117.40W
Silver Bank, bk.	123	20.40N	69.40W
Silver Bank Passage, strt., N.A.	123	20.40N	70.20W
Silver Bay, Mn., U.S.	103	47.24N	91.07W
Silver City, Pan.	121	9.20N	79.54W
Silver City, N.M., U.S. (sĭl'vẽr sĭ'tĭ)	109	32.45N	108.20W
Silver Creek, N.Y., U.S. (crēk)	99	42.35N	79.10W
Silver Creek, r., Az., U.S.	109	34.30N	110.05W
Silver Creek, r., In., U.S.	101h	38.20N	85.45W
Silver Creek, Muddy Fork, r., In., U.S.	101h	38.26N	85.52W
Silverdale, Wa., U.S. (sĭl'vẽr-dāl)	106a	49.39N	122.42W
Silver Hill, Md., U.S.	229d	38.51N	76.57W
Silver Lake, Ma., U.S.	227a	42.00N	70.48W
Silver Lake, Wi., U.S. (lāk)	101a	42.33N	88.10W
Silver Lake, l., Wi., U.S.	101a	42.35N	88.08W
Silver Spring, Md., U.S. (sprĭng)	100e	39.00N	77.00W
Silver Star Mountain, mtn., Wa., U.S.	106c	45.45N	122.15W
Silverthrone Mountain, mtn., Can. (sĭl'vẽr-thrōn)	86	51.31N	126.06W
Silverton, S. Afr.	218d	25.45S	28.13E
Silverton, Co., U.S. (sĭl'vẽr-tŭn)	109	37.50N	107.40W
Silverton, Oh., U.S.	101f	39.12N	84.24W
Silverton, Or., U.S.	104	45.02N	122.46W
Silves, Port. (sēl'vĕzh)	148	37.15N	8.24W
Silvies, r., Or., U.S. (sĭl'vēz)	104	43.44N	119.15W
Sim, Russia (sĭm)	172a	55.00N	57.42E

PLACE (Pronunciation)	PAGE	Lat. °′	Long. °′
Sim, r., Russia	172a	54.50N	56.50E
Simao, China (sz-mou)	188	22.56N	101.07E
Simard, Lac, l., Can.	91	47.38N	78.40W
Simba, Zaire	216	0.36N	22.55E
Simcoe, Can. (sĭm'kō)	150	42.50N	80.20W
Simcoe, l., Can.	85	44.30N	79.20W
Simeulue, Pulau, i., Indon.	196	2.27N	95.30E
Simferopol', Ukr.	164	44.58N	34.04E
Simi, i., Grc.	149	36.27N	27.41E
Similk Beach, Wa., U.S. (sē'mĭlk)	106a	48.27N	122.35W
Simla, India (sĭm'lȧ)	183	31.09N	77.15E
Simla, neigh., India	240a	22.35N	88.22E
Şimleu Silvaniei, Rom.	149	47.14N	22.46E
Simms Point, c., Bah.	122	25.00N	77.40W
Simojovel, Mex. (sē-mō-hō-vĕl')	119	17.12N	92.43W
Simonésia, Braz. (sē-mô-nĕ'syä)	129a	20.04S	41.53W
Simonette, r., Can. (sī-mŏn-ĕt')	87	54.15N	118.00W
Simonstad, S. Afr.	212a	34.11S	18.25E
Simood Sound, Can.	86	50.45N	126.25W
Simplon Pass, p., Switz. (sĭm'plŏn) (săɴ-plôɴ')	154	46.13N	7.53E
Simpson, i., Can.	103	48.43N	87.44W
Simpson Desert, des., Austl. (sĭmp-sŭn)	202	24.40S	136.40E
Simrishamn, Swe. (sēm'rēs-häm'n)	152	55.35N	14.19E
Sims Bayou, Tx., U.S. (sĭmz bī-yo͞o')	113a	29.37N	95.23W
Simushir, i., Russia (sē-mo͞o'shēr)	189	47.15N	150.47E
Sinaia, Rom. (sĭ-nä'yȧ)	161	45.20N	25.30E
Sinai Peninsula, pen., Egypt (sī'nī)	211	29.24N	33.29E
Sinaloa, state, Mex. (sē-nä-lô-ä)	116	25.15N	107.45W
Sinan, China (sz-nän)	188	27.50N	108.30E
Sinanju, N. Kor. (sĭ'năn-jŏ')	194	39.39N	125.41E
Sincelejo, Col. (sēn-sȧ-lā'hō)	130	9.12N	75.30W
Sinclair Inlet, Wa., U.S. (sĭn-klâr')	106a	47.31N	122.41W
Sinclair Mills, Can.	87	54.02N	121.41W
Sindi, Est. (sēn'dē)	153	58.20N	24.40E
Sines, Port. (sē'nâzh)	158	37.57N	8.50W
Singapore, Sing. (sĭn'gȧ-pōr')	196	1.18N	103.52E
Singapore, nation, Asia	196	1.22N	103.45E
Singapore Strait, strt., Asia	181b	1.14N	104.20E
Singlewell or Ifield, Eng., U.K.	235	51.25N	0.23E
Singu, Myanmar (sĭn'gŭ)	188	22.37N	96.04E
Siniye Lipyagi, Russia (sēn'ē lēp'yä-gē)	163	51.24N	38.29E
Sinj, Cro. (sēn')	160	43.42N	16.39E
Sinjah, Sudan	211	13.09N	33.52E
Sinkāt, Sudan	184	18.50N	36.50E
Sinkiang see Xinjiang Uygur, , China	188	40.15N	82.15E
Sin'kovo, Russia (sĭn-kô'vô)	172b	56.23N	37.19E
Sinnamary, Fr. Gu.	131	5.15N	52.52W
Sinni, r., Italy (sēn'nē)	160	40.05N	16.15E
Sinnūris, Egypt	218b	29.25N	30.52E
Sino, Pedra de, mtn., Braz. (pĕ'drä-dô-sē'nô)	132b	22.27S	43.02W
Sinop, Tur.	182	42.00N	35.05E
Sint Eustatius, i., Neth. Ant.	121b	17.32N	62.45W
Sint Niklaas, Bel.	145a	51.10N	4.07E
Sinton, Tx., U.S. (sĭn'tŭn)	113	28.03N	97.30W
Sintra, Port. (sēn'trȧ)	158	38.48N	9.23W
Sint Truiden, Bel.	145a	50.49N	5.14E
Sinŭiju, N. Kor. (sĭ'nōī-jo͞o)	189	40.04N	124.33E
Sinyavino, Russia (sĭn-yä'vĭ-nô)	172c	59.50N	31.07E
Sinyaya, r., Eur. (sēn'yȧ-yȧ)	162	56.40N	28.20E
Sinyukha, r., Ukr. (sē'nyō-κȧ)	163	48.34N	30.49E
Sion, Switz. (sē'ôɴ')	154	46.15N	7.17E
Sioux City, Ia., U.S. (so͞o sĭ'tĭ)	96	42.30N	96.25W
Sioux Falls, S.D., U.S. (fôlz)	96	43.33N	96.43W
Sioux Lookout, Can.	85	50.06N	91.55W
Siping, China (sz-pĭŋ)	189	43.05N	124.24E
Sipiwesk, Can.	84	55.27N	97.24W
Sipsey, r., Al., U.S. (sĭp'sē)	114	33.26N	87.42W
Sipura, Pulau, i., Indon.	196	2.15S	99.33E
Siqueros, Mex. (sē-kä'rōs)	118	23.19N	106.14W
Siquia, Río, r., Nic. (sē-kē'ä)	121	12.23N	84.36W
Siracusa, Italy (sē-rä-koo'sä)	149	37.02N	15.19E
Sirājganj, Bngl. (sĭ-räj'gŭnj)	183	24.23N	89.43E
Sirama, El Sal. (Sē-rä-mä)	120	13.23N	87.55W
Sir Douglas, Mount, mtn., Can. (sûr dŭg'lăs)	87	50.44N	115.20W
Sir Edward Pellew Group, is., Austl. (pĕl'ū)	202	15.15S	137.15E
Siret, Rom.	155	47.58N	26.01E
Siret, r., Eur.	149	47.00N	27.00E
Sirhān, Wadi, depr., Sau. Ar.	182	31.02N	37.16E
Síros, i., Grc.	149	37.23N	24.55E
Sirsa, India	186	29.39N	75.02E
Sir Sandford, Mount, mtn., Can. (sûr sănd'fẽrd)	87	51.40N	117.52W
Sirvintos, Lith. (shēr'vĭn-tōs)	153	55.02N	24.59E
Sir Wilfrid Laurier, Mount, mtn., Can. (sûr wĭl'frĭd lôr'yẽr)	87	52.47N	119.45W
Sisak, Cro. (sē'sȧk)	149	45.29N	16.20E
Sisal, Mex. (sē-säl')	116	21.09N	90.03W
Sishui, China (sz-shwā)	190	35.40N	117.17E
Sisquoc, r., Ca., U.S. (sĭs'kwŏk)	108	34.47N	120.13W
Sisseton, S.D., U.S. (sĭs'tŭn)	102	45.39N	97.04W
Sistān, Daryacheh-ye, l., Asia	182	31.45N	61.15E
Sisteron, Fr. (sēst'rôɴ')	157	44.10N	5.55E
Sisterville, W.V., U.S. (sĭs'tẽr-vĭl)	98	39.30N	81.00W
Sitía, Grc. (sē'tĭ-ȧ)	160a	35.09N	26.10E
Sitka, Ak., U.S. (sĭt'kȧ)	96a	57.08N	135.18W
Sittingbourne, Eng., U.K. (sĭt-ĭng-bôrn)	144b	51.20N	0.44E
Sittwe, Myanmar	183	20.09N	92.54E
Sivas, Tur. (sē'väs)	182	39.50N	36.50E
Siverek, Tur. (sē'vĕ-rĕk)	182	37.50N	39.20E
Siverskaya, Russia (sē'vĕr-skȧ-yȧ)	153	59.17N	30.03E
Sivers'kyy Donec', r., Eur.	163	48.48N	38.42E

PLACE (Pronunciation)	PAGE	Lat. °′	Long. °′
Sīwah, Egypt	184	29.12N	25.31E
Siwah, oasis, Egypt (sē'wä)	211	29.33N	25.11E
Sixaola, r., C.R.	121	9.31N	83.07W
Sixian, China (sz shyĕn)	190	33.37N	117.51E
Sixth Cataract, wtfl., Sudan	211	16.26N	32.44E
Siyang, China (sz-yäŋ)	190	33.43N	118.42E
Sjaelland, i., Den. (shĕl'lȧn')	152	55.34N	11.35E
Sjenica, Yugo. (syĕ'nē-tsȧ)	161	43.15N	20.02E
Skadovs'k, Ukr.	163	46.08N	32.54E
Skagen, Den. (skä'ghĕn)	152	57.43N	10.32E
Skagerrak, strt., Eur. (skä-ghĕ-räk')	142	57.43N	8.28E
Skagit, r., Wa., U.S.	104	48.29N	121.52W
Skagit Bay, b., Wa., U.S. (skăg'ĭt)	106a	48.20N	122.32W
Skagway, Ak., U.S. (skăg-wā)	96a	59.30N	135.28W
Skälderviken, b., Swe.	152	56.20N	12.25E
Skalistyy, Golets, mtn., Russia	165	57.28N	119.48E
Skalistyy Khrebet, mts., Russia	168	43.15N	43.00E
Skamania, Wa., U.S. (skȧ-mā'nĭ-ȧ)	106c	45.37N	112.03W
Skamokawa, Wa., U.S.	106c	46.16N	123.27W
Skanderborg, Den. (skän-ĕr-bôr')	152	56.04N	9.55E
Skaneateles, N.Y., U.S. (skăn-ĕ-ăt'lĕs)	99	42.55N	76.25W
Skaneateles, l., N.Y., U.S.	99	42.50N	76.20W
Skänninge, Swe. (shĕn'ĭng-ĕ)	152	58.24N	15.02E
Skanör-Falseterbo, Swe. (skän'ûr)	152	55.24N	12.49E
Skara, Swe. (skä'rȧ)	152	58.25N	13.24E
Skeena, r., Can. (skē'nȧ)	84	54.30N	129.00W
Skeena Mountains, mts., Can.	86	56.00N	128.00W
Skeerpoort, S. Afr.	213b	25.49S	27.45E
Skeerpoort, r., S. Afr.	213b	25.58S	27.41E
Skeldon, Guy. (skĕl'dŭn)	131	5.49N	57.15W
Skellefteå, Swe. (shĕl'ĕf-tē-a')	146	64.47N	20.48E
Skellefteälven, r., Swe.	146	65.15N	19.30E
Skelmersdale, Eng., U.K.	237a	53.33N	2.48W
Skhodnya, Russia (skôd'nyȧ)	172b	55.57N	37.21E
Skhodnya, r., Russia	172b	55.55N	37.16E
Skíathos, i., Grc. (skē'ȧ-thôs)	161	39.15N	23.25E
Skibbereen, Ire. (skĭb'ẽr-ēn)	150	51.32N	9.25W
Skidegate, b., Can. (skĭ'-dē-gāt')	86	53.15N	132.00W
Skidmore, Tx., U.S. (skĭd'mōr)	113	28.16N	97.40W
Skien, Nor. (skē'ĕn)	146	59.13N	9.35E
Skierniewice, Pol. (skyĕr-nyē-vēt'sĕ)	155	51.58N	20.13E
Skihist Mountain, mtn., Can.	87	50.11N	121.54W
Skikda, Alg.	210	36.58N	6.51E
Skilpadfontein, S. Afr.	218d	25.02S	28.50E
Skíros, Grc.	161	38.53N	24.32E
Skiros, i., Grc.	149	38.50N	24.43E
Skive, Den. (skē'vĕ)	152	56.34N	8.56E
Skjálfandafljót, r., Ice. (skyäl'fänd-ô)	146	65.24N	16.40W
Şkjerstad, Nor. (skyĕr-städ)	146	67.12N	15.37E
Škofja Loka, Slvn. (shkôf'yȧ lō'kȧ)	160	46.10N	14.20E
Skokie, Il., U.S. (skō'kē)	101a	42.02N	87.45W
Skokomish Indian Reservation, I.R., Wa., U.S. (Skŏ-kō'mĭsh)	106a	47.22N	123.07W
Skole, Ukr. (skô'lĕ)	155	49.03N	23.32E
Skópelos, i., Grc. (skô'pā-lôs)	161	39.04N	23.31E
Skopin, Russia (skô'pēn)	166	53.49N	39.35E
Skopje, Mac. (skôp'yĕ)	160	42.02N	21.26E
Skövde, Swe. (shûv'dĕ)	146	58.25N	13.48E
Skovorodino, Russia (skô'vô-rô'dĭ-nô)	165	53.53N	123.56E
Skowhegan, Me., U.S. (skou-hē'gǎn)	92	44.45N	69.27W
Skradin, Cro. (skrä'dēn)	161	43.49N	17.58E
Skreia, Nor. (skrā'ȧ)	152	60.40N	10.55E
Skudeneshavn, Nor. (sko͞o'dĕ-nes-houn')	152	59.10N	5.19E
Skuilte, S. Afr.	244b	26.07S	28.19E
Skull Valley Indian Reservation, I.R., Ut., U.S. (skŭl)	109	40.25N	112.50W
Skuna, r., Ms., U.S. (skû'nȧ)	114	33.57N	89.36W
Skunk, r., Ia., U.S. (skŭnk)	103	41.12N	92.14W
Skuodas, Lith. (skwô'dȧs)	153	56.16N	21.32E
Skurup, Swe. (skû'rŏp)	152	55.29N	13.27E
Skvyra, Ukr.	167	49.43N	29.41E
Skwierzyna, Pol. (skvē-ĕr'zhĭ-nȧ)	154	52.35N	15.30E
Skye, Island of, i., Scot., U.K. (skī)	146	57.25N	6.17W
Skykomish, r., Wa., U.S. (skī'kō-mĭsh)	106a	47.50N	121.55W
Skyring, Seno de, b., Chile (sĕ'nô-s-krē'ng)	132	52.35S	72.30W
Slade Green, neigh., Eng., U.K.	235	51.28N	0.12E
Slagese, Den.	152	55.25N	11.19E
Slamet, Gunung, mtn., Indon. (slä'mĕt)	196	7.15S	109.15E
Slănic, Rom. (slŭ'nēk)	161	45.13N	25.56E
Slater, Mo., U.S. (slāt'ẽr)	111	39.13N	93.03W
Slatina, Rom. (slä'tē-nä)	161	44.26N	24.21E
Slaton, Tx., U.S. (slā'tŭn)	110	33.26N	101.38W
Slattocks, Eng., U.K.	237b	53.35N	2.10W
Slave, r., Can. (slāv)	84	59.40N	111.21W
Slavgorod, Russia (slȧf'gô-rôt)	164	52.58N	78.43E
Slavonija, hist. reg., Yugo. (slä-vô'nē-yä)	161	45.29N	17.31E
Slavonska Požega, Cro. (slä-vôn'skä pô'zhĕ-gä)	161	45.18N	17.42E
Slavonski Brod, Cro. (skä-vôn'skē brôd)	149	45.10N	18.01E
Slavuta, Ukr. (slȧ-vo͞o'tȧ)	163	50.18N	27.01E
Slavyanskaya, Russia (slȧv-yȧn'skȧ-yȧ)	163	45.14N	38.09E
Sławno, Pol. (swav'nō)	154	54.21N	16.38E
Slayton, Mn., U.S. (slā'tŭn)	102	44.00N	95.44W
Sleaford, Eng., U.K. (slē'fẽrd)	144a	53.00N	0.25W
Sleepy Eye, Mn., U.S. (slēp'ĭ ī)	103	44.17N	94.44W
Sleepy Hollow, Ca., U.S.	232	33.57N	117.47W
Slidell, La., U.S. (slī-dĕl')	113	30.17N	89.47W
Sliedrecht, Neth.	145a	51.49N	4.46E
Sligo, Ire. (slī'gō)	146	54.17N	8.19W
Slite, Swe. (slē'tĕ)	152	57.41N	18.47E
Sliven, Bul. (slē'vĕn)	149	42.41N	26.20E
Sloan, N.Y., U.S.	230a	42.54N	78.47W
Sloatsburg, N.Y., U.S. (slōts'bŭrg)	100a	41.09N	74.11W
Slobodka, Bela. (slô'bôd-kȧ)	153	54.34N	26.12E

ng-sing; ŋ-baŋk; ɴ-nasalized n; nŏd; cŏmmit; ōld; ôbey; ôrder; oi-boil; fo͞od; ŏ-as oo in foot; ou-out; s-soft; sh-dish; th-thin; pūre; ûnite; ûrn; stŭd; circŭs; ü-as in French tu; '-indeterminate vowel.

350 Slonim – South Green

PLACE (Pronunciation)	PAGE	Lat. °′	Long. °′
Slonim, Bela. (swŏ'nêm)	155	53.05N	25.19E
Slough, Eng., U.K. (slou)	144b	51.29N	0.36W
Slovakia, nation, Eur.	155	48.50N	20.00E
Slovenia, nation, Eur.	160	45.58N	14.43E
Slov'yans'k, Ukr.	167	48.52N	37.34E
Sluch, r., Ukr.	167	50.56N	26.48E
Slunj, Cro. (slòn')	160	45.08N	15.46E
Słupsk, Pol. (swópsk)	146	54.28N	17.02E
Slutsk, Bela. (slòtsk)	166	53.02N	27.34E
Slyne Head, c., Ire. (slīn)	146	53.25N	10.05W
Smackover, Ar., U.S. (smăk'ô-vẽr)	111	33.22N	92.42W
Smederevo, Yugo.	161	44.39N	20.54E
Smederevska Palanka, Yugo. (smĕ-dĕ-rĕv'skä pä-län'kä)	161	44.21N	21.00E
Smedjebacken, Swe. (smĭ'tyĕ-bä-kĕn)	152	60.09N	15.19E
Smethport, Pa., U.S. (smĕth'pōrt)	99	41.50N	78.25W
Smethwick, Eng., U.K.	150	52.31N	2.04W
Smila, Ukr.	167	49.14N	31.52E
Smile, Ukr.	163	50.55N	33.36E
Smiltene, Lat. (smēl'tĕ-nĕ)	153	57.26N	25.57E
Smith, Can. (smĭth)	84	55.10N	114.02W
Smith, i., Wa., U.S.	106a	48.20N	122.53W
Smith, r., Mt., U.S.	105	47.00N	111.20W
Smith Center, Ks., U.S. (sĕn'tẽr)	110	39.45N	98.46W
Smithers, Can. (smĭth'ẽrs)	84	54.47N	127.10W
Smithfield, Austl.	243a	33.51S	150.57E
Smithfield, N.C., U.S. (smĭth'fēld)	115	35.30N	78.21W
Smithfield, Ut., U.S.	105	41.50N	111.49W
Smithland, Ky., U.S. (smĭth'lănd)	98	37.10N	88.25W
Smith Mountain Lake, res., Va., U.S.	115	37.00N	79.45W
Smith Point, Tx., U.S.	113a	29.32N	94.45W
Smiths Falls, Can. (smĭths)	85	44.55N	76.05W
Smithton, Austl. (smĭth'tŭn)	204	40.55S	145.12E
Smithton, Il., U.S.	107e	38.24N	89.59W
Smithville, Tx., U.S. (smĭth'vĭl)	113	30.00N	97.08W
Smitswinkelvlakte, pl., S. Afr.	212a	34.16S	18.25E
Smoke Creek Desert, des., Nv., U.S. (smōk crēk)	108	40.28N	119.40W
Smoky, r., Can. (smōk'ĭ)	87	55.30N	117.30W
Smoky Hill, r., U.S. (smōk'ĭ hĭl)	96	38.40N	100.00W
Smøla, i., Nor. (smûlä)	146	63.16N	7.40E
Smolensk, Russia (smô-lyĕnsk')	164	54.46N	32.03E
Smolensk, prov., Russia	162	55.00N	32.18E
Smyadovo, Bul.	161	43.04N	27.00E
Smyrna *see* İzmir, Tur.	182	38.25N	27.05E
Smyrna, De., U.S. (smûr'nȧ)	99	39.20N	75.35W
Smyrna, Ga., U.S.	100c	33.53N	84.31W
Snag, Can. (snăg)	95	62.18N	140.30W
Snake, r., U.S.	96	45.30N	117.00W
Snake, r., Mn., U.S. (snāk)	103	45.58N	93.20W
Snake Range, mts., Nv., U.S.	109	39.20N	114.15W
Snake River Plain, pl., Id., U.S.	105	43.08N	114.46W
Snap Point, c., Bah.	122	23.45N	77.30W
Sneffels, Mount, mtn., Co., U.S. (snĕf'ĕlz)	109	38.00N	107.50W
Snelgrove, Can. (snĕl'grōv)	83d	43.44N	79.50W
Śniardwy, Jezioro, l., Pol. (snyärt'vĭ)	155	53.46N	21.59E
Snodland, Eng., U.K.	235	51.20N	0.27E
Snöhetta, mtn., Nor. (snû-hĕttä)	146	62.18N	9.12E
Snohomish, Wa., U.S. (snô-hō'mĭsh)	106a	47.55N	122.05W
Snohomish, r., Wa., U.S.	106a	47.53N	122.04W
Snoqualmie, Wa., U.S. (snō qwäl'mē)	106a	47.32N	121.50W
Snoqualmie, r., Wa., U.S.	104	47.32N	121.53W
Snov, r., Eur. (snôf)	163	51.38N	31.38E
Snowden, Pa., U.S.	230b	40.16N	79.58W
Snowdon, mtn., Wales, U.K.	150	53.05N	4.04W
Snow Hill, Md., U.S. (hĭl)	99	38.15N	75.20W
Snow Lake, Can.	89	54.50N	100.10W
Snowy Mountains, mts., Austl. (snō'ē)	203	36.17S	148.30E
Snyder, Ok., U.S. (snī'dẽr)	110	34.40N	98.57W
Snyder, Tx., U.S.	112	32.48N	100.53W
Soar, r., Eng., U.K. (sōr)	144a	52.44N	1.09W
Sobat, r., Sudan (sō'bȧt)	211	9.04N	32.02E
Sobinka, Russia (sô-bĭŋ'kȧ)	162	55.59N	40.02E
Sobo Zan, mtn., Japan (sô'bô zän)	194	32.47N	131.27E
Sobral, Braz. (sô-brä'l)	131	3.39S	40.16W
Sochaczew, Pol. (sô-ĸä'chĕf)	155	52.14N	20.18E
Sochi, Russia (sôch'ĭ)	164	43.35N	39.50E
Society Islands, is., Fr. Poly. (sô-sī'ĕ-tē)	225	15.00S	157.30W
Socoltenango, Mex. (sô-kôl-tĕ-näŋ'gō)	119	16.17N	92.20W
Socorro, Braz. (sô-kô'r-rō)	129a	22.35S	46.32W
Socorro, Col. (sô-kôr'rō)	130	6.23N	73.19W
Socorro, N.M., U.S.	109	34.05N	106.55W
Socúellamos, Spain (sô-kōō-äl'yä-mōs)	158	39.18N	2.48W
Soda, l., Ca., U.S. (sō'dȧ)	108	35.12N	116.25W
Soda Peak, mtn., Wa., U.S.	106c	45.53N	122.04W
Soda Springs, Id., U.S. (sprĭngz)	105	42.39N	111.37W
Söderhamn, Swe. (sû-dẽr-häm''n)	146	61.20N	17.00E
Söderköping, Swe.	152	58.30N	16.14E
Södertälje, Swe. (sû-dẽr-tĕl'yĕ)	146	59.12N	17.35E
Sodingen, neigh., Ger.	236	51.32N	7.15E
Sodo, Eth.	211	7.03N	37.46E
Sodpur, India	240a	22.42N	88.23E
Soest, Ger. (zōst)	154	51.35N	8.05E
Soeurs, Île des, i., Can.	227b	45.28N	73.33W
Sofia (Sofiya), Bul. (sō'fē-yȧ) (sô'fē-ȧ)	142	42.43N	23.20E
Sofiya *see* Sofia, Bul.	142	42.43N	23.20E
Sofiyivka, Ukr.	163	48.03N	33.53E
Soga, Japan (sō'gä)	195a	35.35N	140.08E
Sogamoso, Col. (sô-gä-mô'sō)	130	5.42N	72.51W
Sognafjorden, fj., Nor.	142	61.09N	5.30E
Sogozha, r., Russia (sô'gô-zhȧ)	162	58.35N	39.08E
Sohano, Pap. N. Gui.	198e	5.27S	154.40E
Soissons, Fr. (swä-sôɴ')	156	49.23N	3.17E
Soisy-sous-Montmorency, Fr.	237c	48.59N	2.18E
Sōka, Japan (sō'kä)	195a	35.50N	139.49E
Sokal', Ukr. (sô'käl')	155	50.28N	24.20E
Söke, Tur. (sû'kĕ)	149	37.40N	27.10E
Sokółka, Pol. (sô-kōl'kȧ)	155	53.23N	23.30E
Sokol'niki, neigh., Russia	239b	55.48N	37.41E
Sokolo, Mali (sô-kô-lō')	210	14.51N	6.09W
Sokołów Podlaski, Pol. (sô-kô-wōf' pŭd-lä'skĭ)	155	52.24N	22.15E
Sokone, Sen.	214	13.53N	16.22W
Sokoto, Nig. (sō'kô-tō)	210	13.04N	5.16E
Sola de Vega, Mex.	119	16.31N	96.58W
Solander, Cape, c., Austl.	201b	34.03S	151.16E
Solano, Phil. (sō-lä'nō)	197a	16.31N	121.11E
Sölderholz, neigh., Ger.	236	51.29N	7.35E
Soledad, Col. (sŏ-lĕ-dä'd)	130	10.47N	75.00W
Soledad Díez Gutiérrez, Mex.	118	22.19N	100.54W
Soleduck, r., Wa., U.S. (sōl'dŭk)	104	47.59N	124.28W
Solentiname, Islas de, is., Nic. (ē's-läs-dĕ-sô-lĕn-tē-nä'mȧ)	120	11.15N	85.16W
Solheim, S. Afr.	244b	26.11S	28.10E
Solihull, Eng., U.K. (sō'lĭ-hŭl)	144a	52.25N	1.46W
Solikamsk, Russia (sô-lē-kȧmsk')	166	59.38N	56.48E
Sol'-Iletsk, Russia	164	51.10N	55.05E
Solimões, Rio, r., Braz. (rē'ō-sô-lē-mô'ĕs)	130	2.45S	67.44W
Solingen, Ger. (zō'lĭng-ĕn)	154	51.10N	7.05E
Sóller, Spain (sō'lyĕr)	159	39.45N	2.40E
Solncevo, Russia	239b	55.39N	37.24E
Sologne, reg., Fr. (sō-lōn'yĕ)	156	47.36N	1.53E
Sololá, Guat. (sō-lō'lä)	120	14.45N	91.12W
Solomon, r., Ks., U.S.	110	39.24N	98.19W
Solomon, North Fork, r., Ks., U.S.	110	39.34N	99.52W
Solomon, South Fork, r., Ks., U.S.	110	39.19N	99.52W
Solomon Islands, nation, Oc. (sŏl'ō-mŭn)	3	7.00S	160.00E
Solon, China (swo-lōōn)	189	46.32N	121.18E
Solon, Oh., U.S. (sō'lŭn)	101d	41.23N	81.26W
Solothurn, Switz. (zō'lō-thōōrn)	154	47.13N	7.30E
Solovetskiye Ostrova, is., Russia	166	65.10N	35.40E
Šolta, i., Yugo. (shôl'tä)	160	43.20N	16.15E
Soltau, Ger. (sôl'tou)	154	53.00N	9.50E
Sol'tsy, Russia (sôl'tsē)	162	58.04N	30.13E
Solvay, N.Y., U.S. (sŏl'vā)	99	43.05N	76.10W
Sölvesborg, Swe. (sûl'vĕs-bôrg)	152	56.04N	14.35E
Sol'vychegodsk, Russia (sôl'vē-chĕ-gôtsk')	166	61.18N	46.58E
Solway Firth, b., U.K. (sŏl'wā fûrth')	146	54.42N	3.55W
Solwezi, Zam.	217	12.11S	26.25E
Somalia, nation, Afr. (sō-mä'lē-ȧ)	218a	3.28N	44.47E
Somanga, Tan.	217	8.24S	39.17E
Sombor, Yugo. (sôm'bôr)	149	45.45N	19.10E
Sombrerete, Mex. (sōm-brā-rā'tā)	118	23.38N	103.37W
Sombrero, Cayo, i., Ven. (kä-yō-sôm-brĕ'rô)	131b	10.52N	68.12W
Somerdale, N.J., U.S.	229b	39.51N	75.01W
Somerset, Ky., U.S. (sŭm'ẽr-sĕt)	114	37.05N	84.35W
Somerset, Md., U.S.	229d	38.58N	77.05W
Somerset, Ma., U.S.	100b	41.46N	71.05W
Somerset, Pa., U.S.	99	40.00N	79.05W
Somerset, Tx., U.S.	107d	29.13N	98.39W
Somerset East, S. Afr.	213c	32.44S	25.36E
Somersworth, N.H., U.S. (sŭm'ẽrz-wûrth)	92	43.16N	70.53W
Somerton, Az., U.S. (sŭm'ẽr-tŭn)	109	32.36N	114.43W
Somerton, neigh., Pa., U.S.	229b	40.06N	75.01W
Somerville, Ma., U.S. (sŭm'ẽr-vĭl)	93a	42.23N	71.06W
Somerville, N.J., U.S.	100a	40.34N	74.37W
Somerville, Tn., U.S.	114	35.14N	89.21W
Somerville, Tx., U.S.	113	30.21N	96.31W
Someș, r., Eur.	155	47.43N	23.09E
Somma Vesuviana, Italy (sôm'mä vā-zōō-vē-ä'nä)	159c	40.38N	14.27E
Somme, r., Fr. (sôm)	156	50.02N	2.04E
Sommerberg, Ger.	236	51.27N	7.32E
Sommerfeld, Ger. (zō'mĕr-fĕld)	145b	52.48N	13.02E
Sommerville, Austl.	201a	38.14S	145.10E
Somoto, Nic. (sô-mō'tō)	120	13.28N	86.37W
Son, r., India (sōn)	183	24.40N	82.35E
Sonari, India	240e	18.52N	72.59E
Sŏnchŏn, N. Kor. (sŭn'shŭn)	194	39.49N	124.56E
Sondags, r., S. Afr.	213c	33.17S	25.14E
Sønderborg, Den. (sûn''ẽr-bôrgh)	146	54.55N	9.47E
Sondershausen, Ger. (zōn'dẽrz-hou'zĕn)	154	51.17N	10.45E
Song Ca, r., Viet.	193	19.15N	105.00E
Songea, Tan. (sôn-gä'ȧ)	212	10.41S	35.39E
Songjiang, China	189	31.01N	121.14E
Sŏngjin, N. Kor. (sŭng'jĭn')	194	40.38N	129.10E
Songkhla, Thai. (sông'ĸlä')	196	7.09N	100.34E
Songwe, Zaire	217	12.25S	29.40E
Sonneberg, Ger. (sôn'ĕ-bĕrgh)	154	50.20N	11.14E
Sonora, Ca., U.S. (sô-nō'rȧ)	108	37.58N	120.22W
Sonora, Tx., U.S.	112	30.33N	100.38W
Sonora, state, Mex.	116	29.45N	111.15W
Sonora, r., Mex.	116	28.45N	111.35W
Sonora Peak, mtn., Ca., U.S.	96	38.22N	119.39W
Sonseca, Spain (sôn-sā'kä)	158	39.41N	3.56W
Sonsón, Col. (sôn-sôn')	130	5.42N	75.28W
Sonsonate, El Sal. (sōn-sô-nä'tȧ)	120	13.46N	89.43W
Sonsorol Islands, is., Palau (sŏn-sô-rōl')	197	5.03N	132.33E
Sooke Basin, b., Can. (sòk)	106a	48.21N	123.47W
Soo Locks, trans., Mi., U.S. (sōō lŏks)	107a	46.30N	84.30W
Sopetrán, Col. (sô-pĕ-trä'n)	130a	6.30N	75.44W
Sopot, Pol. (sô'pôt)	155	54.26N	18.25E
Sopron, Hung. (shŏp'rôn)	149	47.41N	16.36E
Sora, Italy (sō'rä)	160	41.43N	13.37E
Sorbas, Spain (sôr'bäs)	158	37.05N	2.07W
Sorbonne, educ., Fr.	237c	48.51N	2.21E
Sordo, r., Mex. (sô'r-dō)	119	16.39N	97.33W
Sorel, Can. (sô-rĕl')	85	46.01N	73.07W
Sorell, Cape, c., Austl.	204	42.10S	144.50E
Soresina, Italy (sō-rā-zē'nä)	160	45.17N	9.51E
Soria, Spain (sō'rē-ä)	148	41.46N	2.28W
Soriano, dept., Ur. (sō-rēä'nō)	129c	33.25S	58.00W
Soroca, Mol.	167	48.09N	28.17E
Sorocaba, Braz. (sô-rô-kä'bȧ)	131	23.29S	47.27W
Sorong, Indon. (sō-rông')	197	1.00S	131.20E
Sorot', r., Russia (sō-rō'tzh)	162	57.08N	29.23E
Soroti, Ug. (sō-rō'tē)	211	1.43N	33.37E
Sørøya, i., Nor.	146	70.37N	20.58E
Sorraia, r., Port. (sôr-rī'ȧ)	158	38.55N	8.42W
Sorrento, Italy (sôr-rĕn'tō)	160	40.23N	14.23E
Sorsogon, Phil. (sôr-sôgōn')	197	12.51N	124.02E
Sortavala, Russia (sôr'tä-vä-lä)	164	61.43N	30.40E
Sosenki, Russia	239b	55.34N	37.26E
Sosna, r., Russia (sôs'nȧ)	163	50.33N	38.15E
Sosnogorsk, Russia	164	63.13N	54.09E
Sosnowiec, Pol. (sôs-nô'vyĕts)	155	50.17N	19.10E
Sosnytsya, Ukr. (sôs-nē'tsȧ)	163	51.30N	32.29E
Sosunova, Mys, c., Russia (mĭs sô'sô-nôf'ȧ)	194	46.28N	138.06E
Sos'va, r., Russia (sôs'vȧ)	166	63.10N	63.30E
Sos'va, r., Russia (sôs'vȧ)	172a	59.55N	60.40E
Sota, r., Benin	215	11.10N	3.20E
Sota la Marina, Mex. (sô-tä-lä-mä-rē'nä)	118	23.45N	98.11W
Soteapan, Mex. (sō-tā-ä'pän)	119	18.14N	94.51W
Soto la Marina, Río, r., Mex. (rē'ō-so'tō lä mä-rē'nä)	118	23.55N	98.30W
Sotuta, Mex. (sô-tōō'tä)	120a	20.35N	89.00W
Soublette, Ven. (sō-ōō-blĕ'tĕ)	131b	9.55N	66.06W
Souflíon, Grc.	161	41.12N	26.17E
Soufrière, St. Luc. (sōō-frē-âr')	121b	13.50N	61.03W
Soufrière, mtn., St. Vin.	121b	13.19N	61.12W
Soufrière, vol., Guad. (sōō-frē-âr')	121b	16.06N	61.42W
Sŏul *see* Seoul, S. Kor.	189	37.35N	127.03E
Sounding Creek, r., Can. (soun'dĭng)	88	51.35N	111.00W
Souq Ahras, Alg.	147	36.23N	8.00E
Sources, Mount aux, mtn., Afr. (môɴ'tō sôrs')	212	28.47S	29.04E
Soure, Port. (sōr-ĕ)	158	40.04N	8.37W
Souris, Can.	84	49.38N	100.15W
Souris, Can. (sōō'rē')	93	46.20N	62.17W
Souris, r., N.A.	84	48.30N	101.30W
Sourlake, Tx., U.S. (sour'lāk)	113	30.09N	94.24W
Sousse, Tun. (sōōs)	210	36.00N	10.39E
South, r., Ga., U.S.	100c	33.40N	84.15W
South, r., N.C., U.S.	115	34.49N	78.33W
South Africa, nation, Afr.	212	28.00S	24.50E
Southall, neigh., Eng., U.K.	235	51.31N	0.23W
South Amboy, N.J., U.S. (south'ăm'boi)	100a	40.28N	74.17W
South America, cont.	128	15.00S	60.00W
Southampton, Eng., U.K. (south-ămp'tŭn)	142	50.54N	1.30W
Southampton, N.Y., U.S.	99	40.53N	72.24W
Southampton Island, i., Can.	85	64.38N	84.00W
South Andaman Island, i., India (ăn-dȧ-măn')	196	11.57N	93.24E
South Australia, state, Austl. (ôs-trā'lĭ-ȧ)	202	29.45S	132.00E
South Bay, b., Bah.	123	20.55N	73.35W
South Bend, In., U.S. (bĕnd)	97	41.40N	86.20W
South Bend, Wa., U.S. (bĕnd)	104	46.39N	123.48W
South Bight, bt., Bah.	122	24.20N	77.35W
South Bimini, i., Bah. (bē'mē-nē)	122	25.40N	79.20W
Southborough, Ma., U.S. (south'bŭr-ō)	93a	42.18N	71.33W
South Boston, Va., U.S. (bôs'tŭn)	115	36.41N	78.55W
South Boston, neigh., Ma., U.S.	227a	42.20N	71.03W
Southbridge, Ma., U.S. (south'brĭj)	99	42.05N	72.00W
South Brooklyn, neigh., N.Y., U.S.	228	40.41N	73.59W
South Caicos, i., T./C. Is. (kī'kōs)	123	21.30N	71.35W
South Carolina, state, U.S. (kăr-ô-lī'nȧ)	97	34.15N	81.10W
South Cave, Eng., U.K. (cāv)	144a	53.45N	0.35W
South Charleston, W.V., U.S.	98	38.20N	81.40W
South Chicago, neigh., Il., U.S.	231a	41.44N	87.33W
South China Sea, sea, Asia (chī'nȧ)	196	15.23N	114.12E
South Creek, r., Austl.	201b	33.43S	150.50E
Southcrest, S. Afr.	244b	26.15S	28.07E
South Dakota, state, U.S. (dȧ-kō'tȧ)	96	44.20N	101.55W
South Darenth, Eng., U.K.	235	51.24N	0.15E
South Downs, Eng., U.K. (dounz)	150	50.55N	1.13W
South Dum-Dum, India	186a	22.36N	88.25E
South East Cape, c., Austl.	203	43.47S	146.03E
Southend-on-Sea, Eng., U.K. (south-ĕnd')	151	51.33N	0.41E
Southern Alps, mts., N.Z. (sŭ-thûrn ălps)	203a	43.35S	170.00E
Southern California, University of, pt. of i., Ca., U.S.	232	34.02N	118.17W
Southern Cross, Austl.	202	31.13S	119.30E
Southern Indian, l., Can. (sŭth'ẽrn ĭn'dĭ-ăn)	84	56.46N	98.57W
Southern Pines, N.C., U.S. (sŭth'ẽrn pīnz)	115	35.10N	79.23W
Southern Ute Indian Reservation, I.R., Co., U.S. (ūt)	109	37.05N	108.23W
South Euclid, Oh., U.S. (ū'klĭd)	101d	41.30N	81.34W
Southfield, Mi., U.S.	230c	42.29N	83.17W
Southfleet, Eng., U.K.	235	51.25N	0.19E
South Fox, i., Mi., U.S. (fŏks)	98	45.25N	85.55W
South Gate, Ca., U.S. (gāt)	107a	33.57N	118.13W
Southgate, neigh., Eng., U.K.	235	51.38N	0.08W
South Georgia, i., S. Geor. (jôr'jȧ)	128	54.00S	37.00W
South Germiston, S. Afr.	244b	26.15S	28.10E
South Green, Eng., U.K.	235	51.37N	0.26E

ăt; finăl; rāte; senāte; ärm; ȧsk; sofȧ; fâre; ch-choose; dh-as th in other; bē; ēvent; bĕt; recĕnt; cratẽr; g-gō; gh-guttural g; bĭt; ĭ-short neutral; rīde; ĸ-guttural k as ch in German ich;

PRONOUNCING INDEX

South Haven–Start Point 351

PLACE (Pronunciation)	PAGE	Lat. °′	Long. °′
South Haven, Mi., U.S. (hāv'’n)	98	42.25N	86.15W
South Head, c., Austl.	243a	33.50S	151.17E
South Hempstead, N.Y., U.S.	228	40.41N	73.37W
South Hill, Va., U.S.	115	36.44N	78.08W
South Hills, neigh., S. Afr.	244b	26.15S	28.05E
South Holston Lake, res., U.S.	115	36.35N	82.00W
South Indian Lake, Can.	89	56.50N	99.00W
Southington, Ct., U.S. (sŭdh'ĭng-tŭn)	99	41.35N	72.55W
South Island, i., N.Z.	203a	42.40S	169.00E
South Loup, r., Ne., U.S. (lo͞op)	102	41.21N	100.08W
South Lynnfield, Ma., U.S.	227a	42.31N	71.00W
South Magnetic Pole, pt. of i.	219	65.18S	139.30E
South Media, Pa., U.S.	229b	39.54N	75.23W
South Melbourne, Austl.	243b	37.50S	144.57E
South Merrimack, N.H., U.S. (mĕr'ĭ-măk)	93a	42.47N	71.36W
South Milwaukee, Wi., U.S. (mĭl-wô'kē)	101a	42.55N	87.52W
South Mimms, Eng., U.K.	235	51.42N	0.14W
South Moose Lake, l., Can.	89	53.51N	100.20W
South Nation, r., Can.	91	45.00N	75.25W
South Negril Point, c., Jam. (nå-grēl')	122	18.15N	78.25W
South Ockendon, Eng., U.K.	235	51.32N	0.18E
South Ogden, Ut., U.S. (ŏg'dĕn)	107b	41.12N	111.58W
South Orange, N.J., U.S.	228	40.45N	74.15W
South Orkney Islands, is., Ant.	128	57.00S	45.00W
South Ossetia, hist. reg., Geor.	168	42.20N	44.00E
South Oxhey, Eng., U.K.	235	51.38N	0.23W
South Paris, Me., U.S. (păr'ĭs)	92	44.13N	70.32W
South Park, Ky., U.S. (pärk)	101h	38.06N	85.43W
South Pasadena, Ca., U.S. (păs-å-dē'nå)	107a	34.06N	118.08W
South Pease, r., Tx., U.S. (pēz)	110	33.54N	100.45W
South Pender, i., Can. (pĕn'dẽr)	106d	48.45N	123.09W
South Philadelphia, neigh., Pa., U.S.	229b	39.56N	75.10W
South Pittsburg, Tn., U.S. (pĭs'bûrg)	114	35.00N	85.42W
South Platte, r., U.S. (plăt)	96	40.40N	102.40W
South Point, c., Barb.	121b	13.00N	59.43W
South Point, c., Mi., U.S.	98	44.50N	83.20W
South Pole, pt. of i., Ant.	219	90.00S	0.00
South Porcupine, Can.	90	48.28N	81.13W
Southport, Austl. (south'pōrt)	203	27.57S	153.27E
Southport, Eng., U.K. (south'pôrt)	150	53.38N	3.00W
Southport, In., U.S.	101g	39.40N	86.07W
Southport, N.C., U.S.	115	35.55N	78.02W
South Portland, Me., U.S. (pōrt-länd)	92	43.37N	70.15W
South Prairie, Wa., U.S. (prâ'rĭ)	106a	47.08N	122.06W
South Range, Wi., U.S. (rānj)	107h	46.37N	91.59W
South River, N.J., U.S. (rĭv'ẽr)	100a	40.27N	74.23W
South Ronaldsay, i., Scot., U.K. (rŏn'ăld-s'ā)	150a	58.48N	2.55W
South Saint Paul, Mn., U.S.	107g	44.54N	93.02W
South Salt Lake, Ut., U.S. (sôlt lāk)	107b	40.44N	111.53W
South Sandwich Islands, is., S. Geor. (sănd'wĭch)	128	58.00S	27.00W
South Sandwich Trench, deep	128	55.00S	27.00W
South San Francisco, Ca., U.S. (săn frăn-sĭs'kô)	106b	37.39N	122.24W
South San Jose Hills, Ca., U.S.	232	34.01N	117.55W
South Saskatchewan, r., Can. (săs-kach'ē-wän)	84	50.30N	110.30W
South Shetland Islands, is., Ant.	128	62.00S	70.00W
South Shields, Eng., U.K. (shēldz)	146	55.00N	1.22W
South Shore, neigh., Il., U.S.	231a	41.46N	87.35W
South Side, neigh., Pa., U.S.	230b	40.26N	79.58W
South Sioux City, Ne., U.S. (so͞o sĭt'ē)	102	42.48N	96.26W
South Taranaki Bight, bt., N.Z. (tä-rä-nä'kē)	203a	39.35S	173.50E
South Thompson, r., Can. (tŏmp'sŭn)	87	50.41N	120.21W
Southton, Tx., U.S. (south'tŭn)	107d	29.18N	98.26W
South Uist, i., Scot., U.K. (ū'ĭst)	150	57.15N	7.24W
South Umpqua, r., Or., U.S. (ŭmp'kwå)	104	43.00N	122.54W
South Walpole, Ma., U.S.	227a	42.06N	71.16W
South Waltham, Ma., U.S.	227a	42.22N	71.15W
Southwark, neigh., Eng., U.K.	235	51.30N	0.06W
South Weald, Eng., U.K.	235	51.37N	0.16E
Southwell, Eng., U.K. (south'wĕl)	144a	53.04N	0.56W
South West Africa see Namibia, nation, Afr.	212	19.30S	16.13E
South Westbury, N.Y., U.S.	228	40.45N	73.35W
Southwest Miramichi, r., Can. (mĭr å-mē'shē)	92	46.35N	66.17W
Southwest Point, c., Bah.	122	25.50N	77.10W
Southwest Point, c., Bah.	123	23.55N	74.30W
South Weymouth, Ma., U.S.	227a	42.10N	70.57W
South Whittier, Ca., U.S.	232	33.56N	118.03W
South Yorkshire, co., Eng., U.K.	144a	53.29N	1.35W
Sovetsk, Russia (sô-vyĕtsk')	166	55.04N	21.54E
Sovetskaya Gavan', Russia (sŭ-vyĕt'skĭ-u gä'vŭn')	165	48.59N	140.14E
Sow, r., Eng., U.K. (sou)	144a	52.45N	2.12W
Soweto, neigh., S. Afr.	244b	26.14S	27.54E
Soya Kaikyō, strt., Asia	194	45.45N	141.38E
Sōya Misaki, c., Japan (sō'yå mē'sä-kē)	194	45.35N	141.25E
Soyo, Ang.	212	6.10S	12.25E
Sozh, r., Eur. (sôzh)	167	52.50N	31.00E
Sozopol, Bul. (sôz'ō-pôl')	161	42.18N	27.50E
Spa, Bel. (spä)	151	50.30N	5.50E
Spain, nation, Eur. (spān)	142	40.15N	4.30W
Spalding, Ne., U.S. (spôl'dĭng)	102	41.43N	98.23W
Spanaway, Wa., U.S. (spăn'å-wā)	106a	47.06N	122.26W
Spandau, neigh., Ger.	238a	52.32N	13.12E
Spangler, Pa., U.S. (spăng'lẽr)	99	40.40N	78.50W
Spanish Fork, Ut., U.S. (spăn'ĭsh fôrk)	109	40.10N	111.40W
Spanish Town, Jam.	117	18.00N	76.55W
Sparks, Nv., U.S. (spärks)	108	39.34N	119.45W
Sparrows Point, Md., U.S. (spăr'ōz)	100e	39.13N	76.29W
Sparta see Spárti, Grc.	149	37.07N	22.28E
Sparta, Ga., U.S. (spär'tå)	115	33.16N	82.59W
Sparta, Il., U.S.	111	38.07N	89.42W
Sparta, Mi., U.S.	98	43.10N	85.45W
Sparta, Tn., U.S.	114	35.54N	85.26W
Sparta, Wi., U.S.	103	43.56N	90.50W
Sparta Mountains, mts., N.J., U.S.	100a	41.00N	74.38W
Spartanburg, S.C., U.S. (spär'tăn-bûrg)	97	34.57N	82.13W
Spartel, Cap, c., Mor. (spär-tĕl')	158	35.48N	5.50W
Spárti (Sparta), Grc.	149	37.07N	22.28E
Spartivento, Cape, c., Italy	142	38.54N	8.52E
Spartivento, Cape, c., Italy (spär-tē-vĕn'tô)	160	37.55N	16.09E
Spas-Demensk, Russia (spås dyĕ-mĕnsk')	162	54.24N	34.02E
Spas-Klepiki, Russia (spås klĕp'ē-kē)	162	55.09N	40.11E
Spassik-Ryazanskiy, Russia (ryä-zän'skĭ)	162	54.24N	40.21E
Spassk-Dal'niy, Russia (spŭsk'däl'nyē)	165	44.30N	133.00E
Spátha, Ákra, c., Grc.	160a	35.42N	23.45E
Spaulding, Al., U.S. (spôl'dĭng)	100h	33.27N	86.50W
Spear, Cape, c., Can. (spēr)	93	47.32N	52.32W
Spearfish, S.D., U.S. (spēr'fĭsh)	102	44.28N	103.52W
Speed, In., U.S. (spēd)	101h	38.25N	85.45W
Speedway, In., U.S. (spēd'wā)	101g	39.47N	86.14W
Speichersee, l., Ger.	145d	48.12N	11.47E
Speke, neigh., Eng., U.K.	237a	53.21N	2.51W
Speldorf, neigh., Ger.	236	51.25N	6.52E
Spellen, Ger.	236	51.37N	6.37E
Spencer, In., U.S. (spĕn'sẽr)	98	39.15N	86.45W
Spencer, Ia., U.S.	102	43.09N	95.08W
Spencer, N.C., U.S.	115	35.43N	80.25W
Spencer, W.V., U.S.	98	38.55N	81.20W
Spencer Gulf, b., Austl. (spĕn'sẽr)	202	34.20S	136.55E
Sperenberg, Ger. (shpĕ'rĕn-bĕrgh)	145b	52.09N	13.22E
Sperkhiós, r., Grc.	161	38.54N	22.02E
Spey, l., Scot., U.K. (spā)	150	57.25N	3.29W
Speyer, Ger. (shpī'ẽr)	154	49.18N	8.26E
Sphinx, hist., Egypt (sfĭnks)	218b	29.57N	31.08E
Spijkenisse, Neth.	145a	51.51N	4.18E
Spinazzola, Italy (spē-nät'zō-lä)	160	40.58N	16.05E
Spirit Lake, Id., U.S. (spĭr'ĭt)	104	47.58N	116.51W
Spirit Lake, Ia., U.S. (lāk)	102	43.25N	95.08W
Spišská Nová Ves, Slvk. (spĕsh'skä nō'vä vĕs)	147	48.56N	20.35E
Spitsbergen see Svalbard, dep., Nor.	164	77.00N	20.00E
Split, Cro. (splēt)	142	43.30N	16.28E
Split Lake, l., Can.	89	56.08N	96.15W
Spokane, Wa., U.S. (spōkăn')	96	47.39N	117.25W
Spokane, r., Wa., U.S.	104	47.47N	118.00W
Spokane Indian Reservation, I.R., Wa., U.S.	104	47.55N	118.00W
Spoleto, Italy (spô-lā'tō)	160	42.44N	12.44E
Spoon, r., Il., U.S. (spo͞on)	111	40.36N	90.22W
Spooner, Wi., U.S. (spo͞on'ẽr)	103	45.50N	91.53W
Sportswood, Austl.	243b	37.50S	144.53E
Spotswood, N.J., U.S. (spŏtz'wo͝od)	100a	40.23N	74.22W
Sprague, r., Or., U.S. (sprāg)	104	42.30N	121.42W
Spratly, i., Asia (sprăt'lē)	196	8.38N	111.54E
Spray, N.C., U.S. (sprā)	115	36.30N	79.44W
Spree, r., Ger. (shprā)	154	51.53N	14.08E
Spremberg, Ger. (shprĕm'bĕrgh)	154	51.35N	14.23E
Spring, r., Ar., U.S.	111	36.25N	91.35W
Springbok, S. Afr. (sprĭng'bŏk)	212	29.35S	17.55E
Spring Creek, r., Nv., U.S. (sprĭng)	108	40.18N	117.45W
Spring Creek, r., Tx., U.S.	112	31.08N	100.50W
Spring Creek, r., Tx., U.S.	113	30.03N	95.43W
Springdale, Can.	93	49.30N	56.05W
Springdale, Ar., U.S. (sprĭng'dāl)	111	36.10N	94.07W
Springdale, Pa., U.S.	101e	40.33N	79.46W
Springer, N.M., U.S. (sprĭng'ẽr)	110	36.21N	104.37W
Springerville, Az., U.S.	109	34.08N	109.17W
Springfield, Co., U.S. (sprĭng'fēld)	110	37.24N	102.04W
Springfield, Il., U.S.	97	39.46N	89.37W
Springfield, Ky., U.S.	98	37.35N	85.10W
Springfield, Ma., U.S.	97	42.05N	72.35W
Springfield, Mn., U.S.	103	44.14N	94.59W
Springfield, Mo., U.S.	97	37.13N	93.17W
Springfield, Oh., U.S.	97	39.55N	83.50W
Springfield, Or., U.S.	104	44.01N	123.02W
Springfield, Pa., U.S.	229b	39.55N	75.24W
Springfield, Tn., U.S.	114	36.30N	86.53W
Springfield, Vt., U.S.	99	43.20N	72.35W
Springfield, Va., U.S.	229d	38.45N	77.13W
Springfontein, S. Afr. (sprĭng'fōn-tīn)	212	30.16S	25.45E
Springhill, Can. (sprĭng-hĭl')	85	45.39N	64.03W
Spring Mill, Pa., U.S.	229b	40.04N	75.17W
Spring Mountains, mts., Nv., U.S.	108	36.18N	115.49W
Springs, S. Afr. (sprĭngs)	218d	26.16S	28.27E
Springstein, Can. (sprĭng'stīn)	83f	49.49N	97.29W
Springton Reservoir, res., Pa., U.S. (sprĭng-tŭn)	100f	39.57N	75.26W
Springvale, Austl.	201a	37.57N	145.09E
Springvale South, Austl.	243b	37.58S	145.09E
Spring Valley, Ca., U.S.	108a	32.46N	117.01W
Springvalley, Il., U.S. (sprĭng-văl'ĭ)	98	41.20N	89.15W
Spring Valley, Mn., U.S.	103	43.41N	92.26W
Spring Valley, N.Y., U.S.	100a	41.07N	74.03W
Springville, Ut., U.S. (sprĭng-vĭl)	109	40.10N	111.40W
Springwood, Austl.	201b	33.42S	150.34E
Sprockhövel, Ger.	236	51.22N	7.15E
Spruce Grove, Can. (spro͞os grōv)	83g	53.32N	113.55W
Spur, Tx., U.S. (spûr)	110	33.29N	100.51W
Squam, l., N.H., U.S. (skwôm)	99	43.45N	71.30W
Squamish, Can. (skwŏ'mĭsh)	86	49.42N	123.09W
Squamish, r., Can.	86	50.10N	123.30W
Squillace, Golfo di, b., Italy (go͞ol'-fô-dē skwē-lä'chå)	160	38.44N	16.47E
Squirrel Hill, neigh., Pa., U.S.	230b	40.26N	79.55W
Squirrel's Heath, neigh., Eng., U.K.	235	51.35N	0.13E
Srbija (Serbia), hist. reg., Yugo. (sr bē-yä) (sẽr'bē-ä)	161	44.05N	20.35E
Srbobran, Yugo. (s'r'bô-brän')	161	45.32N	19.50E
Sredne-Kolymsk, Russia (s'rĕd'nyē kô-lēmsk')	165	67.49N	154.55E
Sredne Rogatka, Russia (s'red'nå-ya) (rô gär'tkå)	172c	59.49N	30.20E
Sredniy Ik, r., Russia (srĕd'nĭ ĭk)	172a	55.46N	58.50E
Sredniy Ural, mts., Russia (ô'räl)	172a	57.47N	59.00E
Śrem, Pol. (shrĕm)	155	52.06N	17.01E
Sremska Karlovci, Yugo. (srĕm'skē kär'lov-tsē)	161	45.10N	19.57E
Sremska Mitrovica, Yugo. (srĕm'skä mē'trô-vē-tsä')	161	44.59N	19.39E
Sretensk, Russia (s'rĕ'tĕnsk)	165	52.13N	117.39E
Sri Lanka, nation, Asia	183b	8.45N	82.30E
Srīnagar, India (srē-nŭg'ŭr)	183	34.11N	74.49E
Środa, Pol. (shrŏ'då)	155	52.14N	17.17E
Staaken, neigh., Ger.	238a	52.32N	13.08E
Stabroek, Bel.	145a	51.20N	4.21E
Stade, Ger. (shtä'dē)	154	53.36N	9.28E
Städjan, mtn., Swe. (stĕd'yän)	152	61.53N	12.50E
Stadlau, neigh., Aus.	239e	48.14N	16.28E
Stafford, Eng., U.K. (stăf'fẽrd)	150	52.48N	2.06W
Stafford, Ks., U.S.	110	37.58N	98.37W
Staffordshire, co., Eng., U.K.	144a	52.45N	2.00W
Stahnsdorf, Ger. (shtäns'dôrf)	145b	52.22N	13.10E
Staines, Eng., U.K.	144b	51.26N	0.13W
Stains, Fr.	237c	48.57N	2.23E
Stakhanov, Ukr.	167	48.34N	38.37E
Stalingrad see Volgograd, Russia	164	48.40N	42.20E
Stalybridge, Eng., U.K.	144a	53.29N	2.03W
Stambaugh, Mi., U.S. (stăm'bô)	103	46.03N	88.38W
Stamford, Eng., U.K.	144a	52.39N	0.28W
Stamford, Ct., U.S. (stăm'fẽrd)	100a	41.03N	73.32W
Stamford, Tx., U.S.	110	32.57N	99.48W
Stammersdorf, Aus. (shtäm'ĕrs-dôrf)	145e	48.19N	16.25E
Stamps, Ar., U.S. (stămps)	111	33.22N	93.31W
Stanberry, Mo., U.S. (stan'bĕr-ē)	111	40.12N	94.34W
Standerton, S. Afr. (stăn'dẽr-tŭn)	212	26.57S	29.17E
Standing Rock Indian Reservation, I.R., N.D., U.S. (stănd'ĭng rŏk)	102	47.07N	101.05W
Standish, Eng., U.K. (stăn'dĭsh)	144a	53.36N	2.39W
Stanford, Ky., U.S. (stăn'fẽrd)	114	37.29N	84.40W
Stanford le Hope, Eng., U.K.	235	51.31N	0.26E
Stanford Rivers, Eng., U.K.	235	51.41N	0.13E
Stanger, S. Afr. (stăŋ-ger)	213c	29.22S	31.18E
Staniard Creek, Bah.	122	24.50N	77.55W
Stanislaus, r., Ca., U.S. (stăn'ĭs-lô)	108	38.10N	120.16W
Stanley, Can. (stăn'lē)	92	46.17N	66.44W
Stanley, Falk. Is.	132	51.46S	57.59W
Stanley, H.K.	241c	22.13N	114.12E
Stanley, N.D., U.S.	102	48.20N	102.25W
Stanley, Wi., U.S.	103	44.56N	90.56W
Stanley Mound, hill, H.K.	241c	22.14N	114.12E
Stanley Pool, l., Afr.	212	4.07S	15.40E
Stanley Reservoir, res., India (stăn'lē)	187	12.07N	77.27E
Stanleyville see Kisangani, Zaire	211	0.30S	25.12E
Stanlow, Eng., U.K.	237a	53.17N	2.52W
Stanmore, neigh., Eng., U.K.	235	51.37N	0.19W
Stann Creek, Belize (stăn krēk)	120a	17.01N	88.14W
Stanovoy Khrebet, mts., Russia (stŭn-å-voi')	165	56.12N	127.12E
Stansted, Eng., U.K.	235	51.20N	0.18E
Stanton, Ca., U.S. (stăn'tŭn)	107a	33.48N	118.00W
Stanton, Ne., U.S.	102	41.57N	97.15W
Stanton, Tx., U.S.	112	32.08N	101.46W
Stanwell, Eng., U.K.	235	51.27N	0.29W
Stanwell Moor, Eng., U.K.	235	51.28N	0.30W
Stanwood, Wa., U.S. (stăn'wo͝od)	106a	48.14N	122.23W
Stapleford Abbots, Eng., U.K.	235	51.38N	0.10E
Stapleford Tawney, Eng., U.K.	235	51.40N	0.11E
Staples, Mn., U.S. (stā'p'lz)	103	46.21N	94.48W
Stapleton, Al., U.S.	114	30.45N	87.48W
Stara Planina, mts., Bul.	142	42.50N	24.45E
Staraya Kupavna, Russia (stä'rå-yå kû-päf'nå)	172b	55.48N	38.10E
Staraya Russa, Russia (stä'rå-yå ro͞os'så)	166	57.58N	31.21E
Stara Zagora, Bul. (zä'gô-rå)	149	42.26N	25.37E
Starbuck, Can. (stär'bŭk)	83f	49.46N	97.36W
Stargard Szczeciński, Pol. (shtär'gärt shchĕ-chyn'skē)	146	53.19N	15.03E
Staritsa, Russia (stä'rē-tså)	162	56.29N	34.58E
Starke, Fl., U.S. (stärk)	115	29.55N	82.07W
Starkville, Co., U.S. (stärk'vĭl)	110	37.06N	104.34W
Starkville, Ms., U.S.	114	33.27N	88.47W
Starnberg, Ger. (shtärn-bĕrgh)	145d	47.59N	11.20E
Starnberger See, l., Ger.	154	47.58N	11.30E
Starobil's'k, Ukr.	167	49.19N	38.57E
Starodub, Russia (stä-rô-drŏp')	162	52.25N	32.49E
Starogard Gdański, Pol. (stä'rō-grad gdĕn'skē)	146	53.58N	18.33E
Starokostyantyniv, Ukr.	167	49.45N	27.12E
Staro-Minskaya, Russia (stä'rô mĭn'skå-yå)	167	46.19N	38.51E
Staro-Shcherbinovskaya, Russia	163	46.38N	38.38E
Staro-Subkhangulovo, Russia (stäro-so͞ob-kan-go͞o'lôvō)	172a	53.08N	57.24E
Staroutkinsk, Russia (stå-rô-o͞ot'kĭnsk)	172a	57.14N	59.21E
Starovirivka, Ukr.	163	49.31N	35.48E
Start Point, c., Eng., U.K. (stärt)	147	50.14N	3.34W

ng-sing; ŋ-baŋk; N-nasalized n; nŏd; cŏmmit; ōld; ôbey; ôrder; oi-boil; fo͞od; o͝o-as oo in foot; ou-out; s-soft; sh-dish; th-thin; pūre; ůnite; ûrn; stŭd; circŭs; ü-as in French tu; '-indeterminate vowel.

352 Stary Sącz–Sullana

PLACE (Pronunciation)	PAGE	Lat. °'	Long. °'
Stary Sącz, Pol. (stä-rė sônch')	155	49.32N	20.36E
Staryy Oskol, Russia (stä'rė ôs-kôl')	167	51.18N	37.51E
Staryy Ostropil', Ukr.	163	49.48N	27.32E
Stassfurt, Ger. (shtäs'fo͞ort)	154	51.52N	11.35E
Staszów, Pol. (stä'shòf)	155	50.32N	21.13E
State College, Pa., U.S. (stāt kŏl'ĕj)	99	40.50N	77.55W
State Line, Mn., U.S. (līn)	107h	46.36N	92.18W
Staten Island, i., N.Y., U.S. (stăt'ĕn)	100a	40.35N	74.10W
Statesboro, Ga., U.S. (stāts'bŭr-ò)	115	32.26N	81.47W
Statesville, N.C., U.S. (stās'vĭl)	115	34.45N	80.54W
Statue of Liberty National Monument, rec., N.Y., U.S.	228	40.41N	74.03W
Staunton, Il., U.S. (stôn'tŭn)	107e	39.01N	89.47W
Staunton, Va., U.S.	99	38.10N	79.05W
Stavanger, Nor. (stä'väng'ĕr)	142	58.59N	5.44E
Stave, r., Can. (stāv)	106d	49.12N	122.24W
Staveley, Eng., U.K. (stāv'lē)	144a	53.17N	1.21W
Stavenisse, Neth.	145a	51.35N	3.59E
Stavropol', Russia	164	45.05N	41.50E
Steamboat Springs, Co., U.S. (stēm'bōt')	110	40.30N	106.48W
Stebliv, Ukr.	163	49.23N	31.03E
Steel, r., Can. (stēl)	90	49.08N	86.55W
Steelton, Pa., U.S. (stēl'tŭn)	99	40.15N	76.45W
Steenbergen, Neth.	145a	51.35N	4.18E
Steens Mountain, mts., Or., U.S. (stēnz)	104	42.15N	118.52W
Steep Point, c., Austl. (stēp)	202	26.15N	112.05E
Stefanie, Lake *see* Chew Bahir, l., Afr.	211	4.46N	37.31E
Steglitz, neigh., Ger.	238a	52.28N	13.19E
Steiermark (Styria), prov., Aus. (shtī'ĕr-märk)	154	47.22N	14.40E
Steinbach, Can.	84	49.32N	96.41W
Steinkjer, Nor. (stĕĭn-kyĕr)	146	64.00N	11.19E
Steinstücken, neigh., Ger.	238a	52.23N	13.08E
Stella, Wa., U.S. (stĕl'*à*)	106c	46.11N	123.12W
Stellarton, Can. (stĕl'*ár*-tŭn)	85	45.34N	62.40W
Stendal, Ger. (shtĕn'däl)	154	52.37N	11.51E
Stepanakert *see* Xankändi, Azer.	166	39.50N	46.40E
Stephens, Port, b., Austl. (stē'fĕns)	204	32.43N	152.55E
Stephenville, Can. (stē'vĕn-vĭl)	85a	48.33N	58.35W
Stepn'ak, Kaz.	169	52.50N	70.50E
Stepney, neigh., Eng., U.K.	235	51.31N	0.02W
Sterkrade, Ger. (shtĕr'krädē)	157c	51.31N	6.51E
Sterkstroom, S. Afr.	213c	31.33S	26.36E
Sterling, Co., U.S. (stûr'lĭng)	96	40.38N	103.14W
Sterling, Il., U.S.	98	41.48N	89.42W
Sterling, Ks., U.S.	110	38.11N	98.11W
Sterling, Ma., U.S.	93a	42.26N	71.41W
Sterling, Tx., U.S.	112	31.53N	100.58W
Sterling Park, Ca., U.S.	231b	37.41N	122.26W
Sterlitamak, Russia (styĕr'lē-ta-mäk')	164	53.38N	55.56E
Šternberk, Czech Rep. (shtĕrn'bĕrk)	155	49.44N	17.18E
Stettin *see* Szczecin, Pol.	142	53.25N	14.35E
Stettler, Can.	84	52.19N	112.43W
Steubenville, Oh., U.S. (stū'bĕn-vĭl)	98	40.20N	80.40W
Stevens, l., Wa., U.S. (stē'vĕnz)	106a	47.59N	122.06W
Stevens Point, Wi., U.S.	103	44.30N	89.35W
Stevensville, Mt., U.S. (stē'vĕnz-vĭl)	105	46.31N	114.03E
Stewart, r., Can. (stū'ērt)	84	63.27N	138.48W
Stewart Island, i., N.Z.	203a	46.56S	167.40E
Stewart Manor, N.Y., U.S.	228	40.43N	73.41W
Stewiacke, Can. (stū'wē-ăk)	92	45.08N	63.21W
Steynsrus, S. Afr. (stīns'ro͞os)	218d	27.58S	27.33E
Steyr, Aus. (shtīr)	147	48.03N	14.24E
Stickney, Il., U.S.	231a	41.49N	87.47W
Stiepel, neigh., Ger.	236	51.25N	7.15E
Stif, Alg.	210	36.18N	5.21E
Stikine, r., Can. (stĭ-kēn')	84	58.17N	130.10W
Stikine Ranges, Can.	84	59.05N	130.00W
Stillaguamish, r., Wa., U.S.	106a	48.11N	122.18W
Stillaguamish, South Fork, r., Wa., U.S. (stĭl-*à*-gwä'mĭsh)	106a	48.05N	121.59W
Stillwater, Mn., U.S. (stĭl'wô-tĕr)	107g	45.04N	92.48W
Stillwater, Mt., U.S.	105	45.23N	109.45W
Stillwater, Ok., U.S.	111	36.06N	97.03W
Stillwater, r., Mt., U.S.	105	48.47N	114.40W
Stillwater Range, mts., Nv., U.S.	108	39.43N	118.11W
Stintonville, S. Afr.	244b	26.14S	28.13E
Štip, Mac. (shtĭp)	161	41.43N	22.07E
Stirling, Scot., U.K. (stûr'lĭng)	150	56.05N	3.59W
Stittsville, Can. (stĭts'vĭl)	83c	45.15N	75.54W
Stizef, Alg. (mĕr-syā' lá-kônb)	159	35.18N	0.11W
Stjördalshalsen, Nor. (styûr-däls-hälsĕn)	152	63.26N	11.00E
Stockbridge Munsee Indian Reservation, I.R., Wi., U.S. (stŏk'brĭdj mŭn-sē)	103	44.49N	89.00W
Stockerau, Aus. (shtô'kĕ-rou)	154	48.24N	16.13E
Stockholm, Swe. (stôk'hôlm)	142	59.23N	18.00E
Stockholm, Me., U.S. (stŏk'hōlm)	92	47.05N	68.08W
Stockport, Eng., U.K. (stŏk'pôrt)	150	53.24N	2.09W
Stockton, Eng., U.K.	150	54.35N	1.25W
Stockton, Ca., U.S. (stŏk'tŭn)	96	37.56N	121.16W
Stockton, Ks., U.S.	110	39.26N	99.16W
Stockton, i., Wi., U.S.	103	46.56N	90.25W
Stockton Plateau, plat., Tx., U.S.	96	30.34N	102.35W
Stockton Reservoir, res., Mo., U.S.	111	37.40N	93.45W
Stockum, neigh., Ger.	236	51.28N	7.22E
Stöde, Swe. (stû'dĕ)	152	62.26N	16.35E
Stoeng Trêng, Camb. (stông'trĕng')	196	13.36N	106.00E
Stoke d'Abernon, Eng., U.K.	235	51.19N	0.23W
Stoke Newington, neigh., Eng., U.K.	235	51.34N	0.05W
Stoke-on-Trent, Eng., U.K. (stōk-ŏn-trĕnt)	146	53.01N	2.12W
Stoke Poges, Eng., U.K.	235	51.33N	0.35W
Stokhid, r., Ukr.	155	51.24N	25.20E
Stolac, Bos. (stô'láts)	161	43.03N	17.59E
Stolbovoy, is., Russia (stôl-bò-voi')	171	74.05N	136.00E
Stolin, Bela. (stô'lēn)	155	51.54N	26.52E
Stolpe, Ger.	238a	52.40N	13.16E
Stömstad, Swe.	152	58.58N	11.09E
Stondon Massey, Eng., U.K.	235	51.41N	0.18E
Stone, Eng., U.K.	144a	52.54N	2.09W
Stone, Eng., U.K.	235	51.27N	0.16E
Stoneham, Can. (stōn'*ă*m)	83b	46.59N	71.22W
Stoneham, Ma., U.S.	93a	42.30N	71.05W
Stonehaven, Scot., U.K. (stōn'hā-v'n)	150	56.57N	2.09W
Stone Mountain, Ga., U.S. (stōn)	100c	33.49N	84.10W
Stone Park, Il., U.S.	231a	41.45N	87.53W
Stonewall, Can. (stōn'wôl)	83f	50.09N	97.21W
Stonewall, Ms., U.S.	114	32.08N	88.44W
Stoney Creek, Can. (stō'nē)	83d	43.13N	79.45W
Stonington, Ct., U.S. (stōn'ĭng-tŭn)	99	41.20N	71.55W
Stony Indian Reserve, I.R., Can.	83e	51.10N	114.45W
Stony Mountain, Can.	83f	50.05N	97.13W
Stony Plain, Can. (stō'nē plān)	83g	53.32N	114.00W
Stony Plain Indian Reserve, I.R., Can.	83g	53.29N	113.48W
Stony Point, N.Y., U.S.	100a	41.13N	73.58W
Stony Run, Md., U.S.	229c	39.11N	76.42W
Stora Sotra, i., Nor.	152	60.24N	4.35E
Stord, i., Nor. (stôrd)	152	59.54N	5.15E
Store Baelt, strt., Den.	152	55.25N	10.50E
Storeton, Eng., U.K.	237a	53.21N	3.03W
Storfjorden, fj., Nor.	152	62.17N	6.19E
Stormberg, mts., S. Afr. (stôrm'bûrg)	213c	31.28S	26.35E
Storm Lake, Ia., U.S.	102	42.39N	95.12W
Stormy Point, c., V.I.U.S. (stôr'mē)	117c	18.22N	65.01W
Stornoway, Scot., U.K. (stôr'nò-wā)	146	58.13N	6.21W
Storozhynets', Ukr.	155	48.10N	25.44E
Störsjo, Swe. (stòr'shû)	152	62.49N	13.08E
Störsjoen, l., Nor. (stòr-syûĕn)	152	61.32N	11.30E
Störsjon, l., Swe.	146	63.06N	14.00E
Storvik, Swe.	152	60.37N	16.31E
Stoughton, Wi., U.S.	103	42.54N	89.15W
Stour, r., Eng., U.K. (stour)	151	52.09N	0.29E
Stourbridge, Eng., U.K. (stour'brĭj)	144a	52.27N	2.08W
Stow, Ma., U.S. (stō)	93a	42.56N	71.31W
Stow, Oh., U.S.	101d	41.09N	81.26W
Stowe Township, Pa., U.S.	230b	40.29N	80.04W
Straatsdrif, S. Afr.	218d	25.19S	26.22E
Strabane, N. Ire., U.K. (stră-băn')	150	54.59N	7.27W
Straelen, Ger. (shtrā'lĕn)	157c	51.26N	6.16E
Strahan, Austl. (strā'*ă*n)	203	42.08S	145.28E
Strakonice, Czech Rep. (strä'kò-nyē-tsĕ)	154	49.18N	13.52E
Straldzha, Bul. (strāl'dzhá)	161	42.37N	26.44E
Stralsund, Ger. (shräl'sònt)	146	54.18N	13.04E
Strangford Lough, l., N. Ire., U.K.	150	54.30N	5.34W
Strängnäs, Swe. (strĕng'nĕs)	152	59.23N	16.59E
Stranraer, Scot., U.K. (străn-rär')	150	54.55N	5.05W
Strasbourg, Fr. (strás-bo͞or')	142	48.36N	7.49E
Stratford, Can. (străt'fērd)	90	43.20N	81.05W
Stratford, Ct., U.S.	99	41.10N	73.05W
Stratford, Wi., U.S.	103	44.16N	90.02W
Stratford-upon-Avon, Eng., U.K.	150	52.13N	1.41W
Strathfield, Austl.	243a	33.52S	151.06E
Strathmoor, neigh., Mi., U.S.	230c	42.23N	83.11W
Straubing, Ger. (strou'bĭng)	154	48.52N	12.36E
Strauch, Ger.	236	51.09N	6.56E
Strausberg, Ger. (strous'bĕrgh)	154	52.35N	13.50E
Strawberry, r., Ut., U.S.	109	40.05N	110.55W
Strawberry Point, Ca., U.S.	231b	37.54N	122.31W
Strawn, Tx., U.S. (strôn)	112	32.38N	98.28W
Streatham, neigh., Eng., U.K.	235	51.26N	0.08W
Streator, Il., U.S. (strē'tēr)	98	41.05N	88.50W
Streeter, N.D., U.S.	102	46.40N	99.22W
Streetsville, Can. (strētz'vĭl)	83d	43.34N	79.43W
Strehaia, Rom. (strĕ-κa'yá)	161	44.37N	23.13E
Strel'na, Russia (strĕl'ná)	172c	59.52N	30.01E
Stretford, Eng., U.K. (strĕt'fērd)	144a	53.25N	2.19W
Strickland, r., Pap. N. Gui. (strĭk'l*ă*nd)	197	6.15S	142.00E
Strijen, Neth.	145a	51.44N	4.32E
Stromboli, Italy (stròm'bò-lē)	149	38.46N	15.16E
Stromyn, Russia (strô'mĭn)	172b	56.02N	38.29E
Strong, r., Ms., U.S. (strông)	114	32.03N	89.42W
Strongsville, Oh., U.S. (strôngz'vĭl)	101d	41.19N	81.50W
Stronsay, i., Scot., U.K. (strŏn'sā)	150a	59.09N	2.35W
Stroudsburg, Pa., U.S. (stroudz'bûrg)	99	41.00N	75.15W
Strubenvale, S. Afr.	244b	26.16S	28.28E
Struer, Den.	152	56.29N	8.34E
Strugi Krasnyye, Russia (stro͞o'gĭ krä's-ny'yĕ)	162	58.14N	29.10E
Struisbelt, S. Afr.	244b	26.19S	28.29E
Struma, r., Eur. (stro͞o'má)	161	41.55N	23.05E
Strumica, Mac. (stro͞o'mĭ-tsá)	161	41.26N	22.38E
Strümp, Ger.	236	51.17N	6.40E
Strunino, Russia	172b	56.23N	38.34E
Struthers, Oh., U.S. (strŭdh'ērz)	98	41.00N	80.35W
Struvenhütten, Ger. (shtro͞o'vĕn-hü-tĕn)	145c	53.52N	10.04E
Strydpoortberge, mts., S. Afr.	218d	24.08N	29.18E
Stryy, Ukr. (strē')	155	49.16N	23.51E
Strzelce Opolskie, Pol. (stzhĕl'tsĕ o-pŏl'skyĕ)	155	50.31N	18.20E
Strzelin, Pol. (stzhĕ-lĭn)	155	50.48N	17.06E
Strzelno, Pol. (stzhäl'nò)	155	52.37N	18.10E
Stuart, Fl., U.S. (stū'ērt)	115a	27.10N	80.14W
Stuart, Ia., U.S.	103	41.31N	94.20W
Stuart, i., Ak., U.S.	95	63.25N	162.45W
Stuart, i., Wa., U.S.	106d	48.42N	123.10W
Stuart Lake, l., Can.	86	54.32N	124.35W
Stuart Range, mts., Austl.	202	29.00S	134.30E
Sturgeon, r., Can.	83g	53.41N	113.46W
Sturgeon, r., Mi., U.S.	103	46.43N	88.43W
Sturgeon Bay, Wi., U.S.	103	44.50N	87.22W
Sturgeon Bay, b., Can.	89	52.00N	98.00W
Sturgeon Falls, Can.	85	46.19N	79.49W
Sturgis, Ky., U.S.	98	37.35N	88.00W
Sturgis, Mi., U.S.	98	41.45N	85.25W
Sturgis, S.D., U.S.	102	44.25N	103.31W
Sturt Creek, r., Austl.	202	19.40S	127.40E
Sturtevant, Wi., U.S. (stûr'tē-vănt)	101a	42.42N	87.54W
Stutterheim, S. Afr. (stŭrt'ĕr-hīm)	213c	32.34S	27.27E
Stuttgart, Ger. (shto͞ot'gärt)	142	48.48N	9.15E
Stuttgart, Ar., U.S. (stŭt'gärt)	111	34.30N	91.33W
Styal, Eng., U.K.	237b	53.21N	2.15W
Stykkishólmur, Ice.	146	65.00N	21.48W
Styr', r., Eur. (stêr)	155	51.44N	26.07E
Styria *see* Steiermark, prov., Aus.	154	47.22N	14.40E
Styrum, neigh., Ger.	236	51.27N	6.51E
Suao, Tai. (so͞oôu)	193	24.35N	121.45E
Subarnarekha, r., India	186	22.38N	86.26E
Subata, Lat. (sò'bá-tá)	153	56.02N	25.54E
Subic, Phil. (so͞o'bĭk)	197a	14.52N	120.15E
Subic Bay, b., Phil.	197a	14.41N	120.11E
Subotica, Yugo. (so͞o'bô'tē-tsá)	142	46.06N	19.41E
Subugo, mtn., Kenya	217	1.40S	35.49E
Succasunna, N.J., U.S. (sŭk'k*à*-sŭn'n*à*)	100a	40.52N	74.37W
Suceava, Rom. (so͞o-chá-ä'vá)	155	47.39N	26.17E
Suceava, r., Rom.	155	47.45N	26.10E
Sucha, Pol. (so͞o'κá)	155	49.44N	19.40E
Suchiapa, Mex. (so͞o-chē-ä'pä)	119	16.38N	93.08W
Suchiapa, r., Mex.	119	16.27N	93.26W
Suchitoto, El Sal. (so͞o-chē-tō'tō)	120	13.58N	89.03W
Sucio, r., Col. (so͞o'syô)	130a	6.55N	76.15W
Suck, r., Ire. (sŭk)	150	53.34N	8.16W
Sucre, Bol. (so͞o'krā)	130	19.06S	65.16W
Sucre, dept., Ven. (so͞o'krē)	131b	10.18N	64.12W
Sucy-en-Brie, Fr.	237c	48.46N	2.32E
Sud, Canal du, strt., Haiti	123	18.40N	73.15W
Sud, Rivière du, r., Can. (rē-vyâr'dü süd')	83b	46.56N	70.35W
Suda, Russia (sò'dá)	172a	56.58N	56.45E
Suda, r., Russia (sò'dá)	162	59.24N	36.40E
Sudair, Sau. Ar. (sŭ-dä'ĕr)	182	25.48N	46.28E
Sudalsvatnet, l., Nor.	152	59.35N	6.59E
Sudan, nation, Afr.	211	14.00N	28.00E
Sudan, reg., Afr. (so͞o-dän')	210	15.00N	7.00E
Sudberg, neigh., Ger.	236	51.11N	7.08E
Sudbury, Can. (sŭd'bĕr-ē)	85	46.28N	81.00W
Sudbury, Ma., U.S.	93a	42.23N	71.25W
Suderwich, neigh., Ger.	236	51.37N	7.15E
Sudetes, mts., Eur.	142	50.41N	15.37E
Sudogda, Russia (sò'dôk-dá)	162	55.57N	40.29E
Sudost', r., Eur. (sò-dôst')	162	52.43N	33.13E
Sudzha, Russia (sòd'zhá)	163	51.14N	35.11E
Sueca, Spain (swā'kä)	159	39.12N	0.18W
Suez, Egypt	211	29.58N	32.34E
Suez, Gulf of, b., Egypt (so͞o-ĕz')	211	29.53N	32.33E
Suez Canal, can., Egypt	211	30.53N	32.21E
Suffern, N.Y., U.S. (sŭf'fērn)	100a	41.07N	74.09W
Suffolk, Va., U.S. (sŭf'*ŭ*k)	100g	36.43N	76.35W
Sugandha, India	240a	22.54N	88.20E
Sugar City, Co., U.S.	110	38.12N	103.42W
Sugar Creek, Mo., U.S.	107f	39.07N	94.27W
Sugar Creek, r., Il., U.S. (shòg'ēr)	111	40.14N	89.28W
Sugar Creek, r., In., U.S.	98	39.55N	87.10W
Sugar Island, i., Mi., U.S.	107k	46.31N	84.12W
Sugarloaf Point, c., Austl. (sòg̈ēr'lōf)	204	32.19S	153.04E
Suggi Lake, l., Can.	89	54.22N	102.47W
Suginami, neigh., Japan	242a	35.42N	139.38E
Sühbaatar, Mong.	188	50.18N	106.31E
Suhl, Ger. (zo͞ol)	154	50.37N	10.41E
Suichuan, mtn., China	193	26.25N	114.10E
Suide, China (swā-dü)	192	37.32N	110.12E
Suifenhe, China (swā-fŭn-hŭ)	189	44.47N	131.13E
Suihua, China	189	46.38N	126.50E
Suining, China (so͞o'ē-nĭng')	190	33.54N	117.57E
Suipacha, Arg. (swē-pä'chä)	129c	34.45S	59.43W
Suiping, China (swā-pĭŋ)	190	33.09N	113.58E
Suir, r., Ire. (sūr)	150	52.20N	7.32W
Suisun Bay, b., Ca., U.S. (so͞oē-so͞on')	106b	38.07N	122.02W
Suita, Japan (sò'ē-tä)	195b	34.45N	135.32E
Suitland, Md., U.S. (sōt'lănd)	100e	38.51N	76.57W
Suixian, China (swā shyĕn)	193	31.42N	113.20E
Suiyüan, hist. reg., China (swā-yůĕn)	188	41.31N	107.04E
Suizhong, China (swā-jôŋ)	192	40.22N	120.20E
Sukabumi, Indon.	196	6.52S	106.56E
Sukadana, Indon.	196	1.15S	110.30E
Sukagawa, Japan (so͞o'kä-gä'wä)	195	37.08N	140.07E
Sukhinichi, Russia (so͞o'kē'nē-chē)	166	54.07N	35.18E
Sukhona, r., Russia (sò-kô'ná)	166	59.30N	42.20E
Sukhoy Log, Russia (so͞o'kôy lôg)	172a	56.55N	62.03E
Sukhumi, Geor. (sò-kòm')	167	43.00N	41.00E
Sukkur, Pak. (sŭk'ŭr)	183	27.49N	68.50E
Sukkwan Island, i., Ak., U.S.	86	55.05N	132.45W
Suksun, Russia (sòk'sòn)	172a	57.08N	57.22E
Sukumo, Japan (so͞o'kò-mò)	195	32.58N	132.45E
Sukunka, r., Can.	87	55.00N	121.50W
Sula, r., Ukr. (so͞o-lá')	163	50.36N	33.13E
Sula, Kepulauan, is., Indon.	197	2.20S	125.20E
Sulaco, r., Hond. (so͞o-lä'kō)	120	14.55N	87.31W
Sulaimān Range, mts., Pak. (sò-lä-ē-män')	183	29.47N	69.10E
Sulak, r., Russia (so͞o-lák')	167	43.30N	47.00E
Sulfeld, Ger. (zo͞o'fĕld)	145c	53.48N	10.13E
Sulina, Rom. (so͞o-lē'ná)	149	45.08N	29.38E
Sulitelma, mtn., Eur. (so͞o-lē-tyĕl'má)	146	67.03N	16.35E
Sullana, Peru (so͞o-lyä'nä)	130	4.57S	80.47W

ăt; fin*ă*l; rāte; senāte; ärm; ȧsk; sof*à*; fâre; ch-choose; dh-as th in other; bē; ėvent; bĕt; recĕnt; cratẽr; g-gō; gh-guttural g; bĭt; ĭ-short neutral; rīde; κ-guttural k as ch in German ich;

PRONOUNCING INDEX

Sulligent–Taboão da Serra 353

PLACE (Pronunciation)	PAGE	Lat. °′	Long. °′
Sulligent, Al., U.S. (sŭl'ĭ-jĕnt)	114	33.52N	88.06W
Sullivan, Il., U.S. (sŭl'ĭ-văn)	98	41.35N	88.35W
Sullivan, In., U.S.	98	39.05N	87.20W
Sullivan, Mo., U.S.	111	38.13N	91.09W
Sulmona, Italy (so͞ol-mō'nä)	160	42.02N	13.58E
Sulphur, Ok., U.S. (sŭl'fŭr)	111	34.31N	96.58W
Sulphur, r., Tx., U.S.	111	33.26N	95.06W
Sulphur Springs, Tx., U.S. (sprĭngz)	111	33.09N	95.36W
Sultan, Wa., U.S. (sŭl'tăn)	106a	47.52N	121.49W
Sultan, r., Wa., U.S.	106a	47.55N	121.49W
Sultepec, Mex. (so͞ol-tå-pĕk')	118	18.50N	99.51W
Sulu Archipelago, is., Phil. (so͞o'lo͞o)	196	5.52N	122.00E
Suluntah, Libya	149	32.39N	21.49E
Sulūq, Libya	211	31.39N	20.15E
Sulu Sea, sea, Asia	196	8.25N	119.00E
Suma, Japan (so͞o'mä)	195b	34.39N	135.08E
Sumas, Wa., U.S. (sū'mȧs)	106d	49.00N	122.16W
Sumatera, i., Indon. (sö-mä-trȧ)	196	2.06N	99.40E
Sumatra *see* Sumatera, i., Indon.	196	2.06N	99.40E
Sumba, i., Indon. (sŭm'bȧ)	196	9.52S	119.00E
Sumba, Île, i., Zaire	216	1.44N	19.32E
Sumbawa, i., Indon. (söm-bä'wä)	196	9.00S	118.18E
Sumbawa-Besar, Indon.	196	8.32S	117.20E
Sumbawanga, Tan.	217	7.58S	31.37E
Sumbe, Ang.	212	11.13S	13.50E
Sümeg, Hung. (shü'mĕg)	155	46.59N	17.19E
Sumida, r., Japan (so͞o'mē-dä)	195	36.01N	139.24E
Sumidouro, Braz. (so͞o-mē-dō'rö)	129a	22.04S	42.41W
Sumiyoshi, Japan (so͞o'mē-yō'shē)	195b	34.43N	135.16E
Sumiyoshi, neigh., Japan	242b	34.36N	135.31E
Summer Lake, l., Or., U.S. (sŭm'ẽr)	104	42.50N	120.35W
Summerland, Can. (sŭ'mẽr-lănd)	87	49.39N	119.40W
Summerseat, Eng., U.K.	237b	53.38N	2.19W
Summerside, Can. (sŭm'ẽr-sīd)	85	46.25N	63.47W
Summerton, S.C., U.S. (sŭm'ẽr-tŭn)	115	33.37N	80.22W
Summerville, S.C., U.S. (sŭm'ẽr-vĭl)	115	33.00N	80.10W
Summit, Il., U.S. (sŭm'mĭt)	101a	41.47N	87.48W
Summit, N.J., U.S.	100a	40.43N	74.21W
Summit Lake Indian Reservation, I.R., Nv., U.S.	104	41.35N	119.30W
Summit Park, Md., U.S.	229c	39.23N	76.41W
Summit Peak, mtn., Co., U.S.	109	37.20N	106.40W
Sumner, Wa., U.S. (sŭm'nẽr)	106a	47.12N	122.14W
Šumperk, Czech Rep. (shöm'pĕrk)	155	49.57N	17.02E
Sumqayıt, Azer.	168	40.36N	49.38E
Sumrall, Ms., U.S. (sŭm'rôl)	114	31.25N	89.34W
Sumter, S.C., U.S. (sŭm'tẽr)	115	33.55N	80.21W
Sumy, Ukr. (so͞o'mĭ)	164	50.54N	34.47E
Sumy, prov., Ukr.	163	51.02N	34.05E
Sun, r., Mt., U.S. (sŭn)	105	47.34N	111.53W
Sunburst, Mt., U.S.	105	48.53N	111.55W
Sunbury, Eng., U.K.	235	51.25N	0.26W
Sunda, Selat, strt., Indon.	196	5.45S	106.15E
Sundance, Wy., U.S. (sŭn'dăns)	105	44.24N	104.27W
Sundarbans, sw., Asia (sön'dẽr-bŭns)	183	21.50N	89.00E
Sunday Strait, strt., Austl. (sŭn'dā)	202	15.50S	122.45E
Sundbyberg, Swe. (sön'bü-bĕrgh)	152	59.24N	17.56E
Sunderland, Eng., U.K. (sŭn'dẽr-lănd)	146	54.55N	1.25W
Sunderland, Md., U.S.	100e	38.41N	76.36W
Sundridge, Eng., U.K.	235	51.17N	0.08E
Sundsvall, Swe. (sönds'väl)	142	62.24N	19.19E
Sungari (Songhua), r., China	189	46.09N	127.53E
Sungari Reservoir, res., China	192	42.55N	127.50E
Sungurlu, Tur. (so͞on'gör-lö')	149	40.08N	34.20E
Sun Kosi, r., Nepal	186	27.13N	85.52E
Sunland, Ca., U.S. (sŭn-lănd)	107a	34.16N	118.18W
Sunne, Swe. (so͞on'ĕ)	152	59.51N	13.07E
Sunninghill, Eng., U.K. (sŭnĭng'hĭl)	144b	51.23N	0.40W
Sunnymead, Ca., U.S. (sŭn'ĭ-mēd)	107a	33.56N	117.15W
Sunnyside, Ut., U.S.	109	39.35N	110.20W
Sunnyside, Wa., U.S.	104	46.19N	120.00W
Sunnyvale, Ca., U.S. (sŭn-nē-vāl)	106b	37.23N	122.02W
Sunol, Ca., U.S. (so͞o'nŭl)	106b	37.36N	122.53W
Sunset, Ut., U.S. (sŭn-sĕt)	107b	41.08N	112.02W
Sunset Beach, Ca., U.S.	232	33.43N	118.04W
Sunset Crater National Monument, rec., Az., U.S. (krā'tẽr)	109	35.20N	111.30W
Sunshine, Austl.	201a	37.47S	144.50E
Suntar, Russia (sön-tär')	165	62.14N	117.49E
Sunyani, Ghana	214	7.20N	2.20W
Suoyarvi, Russia (so͞o'ō-yĕr'vē)	166	62.12N	32.29E
Superior, Az., U.S. (su-pē'rĭ-ẽr)	109	33.15N	111.10W
Superior, Ne., U.S.	110	40.04N	98.05W
Superior, Wi., U.S.	97	46.44N	92.06W
Superior, Wy., U.S.	105	41.45N	108.57W
Superior, Laguna, l., Mex. (lä-go͞o'nȧ so͞o-pā-rē-ōr')	119	16.20N	94.55W
Superior, Lake, l., N.A.	97	47.38N	89.20W
Superior Village, Wi., U.S.	107h	46.38N	92.07W
Sup'ung Reservoir, res., Asia (so͞o'po͝ong)	194	40.35N	126.00E
Suqian, China (so͞o-chyĕn)	190	33.57N	118.17E
Suquamish, Wa., U.S. (so͞o-gwä'mĭsh)	106a	47.44N	122.34W
Suquṭrā (Socotra), i., Yemen (sö-kō'trȧ)	182	13.00N	52.30E
Şūr, Leb. (so͞or) (tīr)	181a	33.16N	35.13E
Şūr, Oman	182	22.23N	59.28E
Şura, neigh., India	240a	22.33N	88.25E
Surabaya, Indon.	196	7.23S	112.45E
Surakarta, Indon.	196	7.35S	110.45E
Šurany, Slvk. (sho͞o'rȧ-nû')	155	48.05N	18.11E
Surat, Austl. (sū-răt)	204	27.18S	149.00E
Surat, India (sö'rŭt)	183	21.08N	73.22E
Surat Thani, Thai.	196	8.59N	99.14E
Surazh, Bela.	162	55.24N	30.46E
Surazh, Russia (so͞o-rȧzh')	162	53.02N	32.27E

PLACE (Pronunciation)	PAGE	Lat. °′	Long. °′
Surbiton, neigh., Eng., U.K.	235	51.24N	0.18W
Surco, Peru	233c	12.09S	77.01W
Suresnes, Fr.	237c	48.52N	2.14E
Surgères, Fr. (sür-zhâr')	156	46.06N	0.51W
Surgut, Russia (sör-göt')	164	61.18N	73.38E
Suriname, nation, S.A. (so͞o-rē-näm')	131	4.00N	56.00W
Sūrmaq, Iran	185	31.03N	52.48E
Surquillo, Peru	233c	12.07S	77.02W
Surt, Libya	211	31.14N	16.37E
Surt, Khalīj, b., Libya	211	31.30N	18.28E
Suruga-Wan, b., Japan (so͞o'ro͞o-gä wän)	194	34.52N	138.36E
Suru-Lere, neigh., Nig.	244d	6.31N	3.22E
Susa, Japan	195	34.40N	131.39E
Sušak, i., Yugo.	160	42.45N	16.30E
Susak, Otok, i., Yugo.	160	44.31N	14.15E
Susaki, Japan (so͞o'sä-kē)	195	33.23N	133.16E
Sušice, Czech Rep.	154	49.14N	13.31E
Susitna, Ak., U.S. (so͞o-sĭt'nȧ)	95	61.28N	150.28W
Susitna, r., Ak., U.S.	95	62.00N	150.28W
Susong, China (so͞o-sôŋ)	193	30.18N	116.08E
Susquehanna, Pa., U.S. (sŭs'kwē-hăn'ȧ)	99	41.55N	73.55W
Susquehanna, r., U.S.	99	39.50N	76.20W
Sussex, Can. (sŭs'ĕks)	85	45.43N	65.31W
Sussex, N.J., U.S.	100a	41.12N	74.36W
Sussex, Wi., U.S.	101a	43.08N	88.12W
Sutherland, Austl. (sŭdh'ẽr-lănd)	201b	34.02S	151.04E
Sutherland, S. Afr. (sŭ'thẽr-lănd)	212	32.25S	20.40E
Sutlej, r., Asia (sŭt'lĕj)	183	30.15N	73.00E
Sutton, Eng., U.K. (sut''n)	144b	51.21N	0.12W
Sutton, Ma., U.S.	93a	42.09N	71.46W
Sutton-at-Hone, Eng., U.K.	235	51.25N	0.14E
Sutton Coldfield, Eng., U.K. (kōld'fēld)	144a	52.34N	1.49W
Sutton-in-Ashfield, Eng., U.K. (ĭn-ăsh'fēld)	144a	53.07N	1.15W
Suurbekom, S. Afr.	244b	26.19S	27.44E
Suurberge, mts., S. Afr.	213c	33.15S	25.32E
Suva, Fiji	198g	18.08S	178.25E
Suwa, Japan (so͞o'wä)	195	36.03N	138.08E
Suwałki, Pol. (sö-vou'kē)	155	54.05N	22.58E
Suwanee Lake, l., Can.	89	56.08N	100.10W
Suwannee, r., U.S. (sö-wô'nē)	97	29.42N	83.00W
Suways al Ḩulwah, Tur' at as, can., Egypt	218c	30.15N	32.20E
Suxian, China (so͞o shyĕn)	192	33.29N	117.51E
Suzdal', Russia (so͞oz'dȧl)	162	56.26N	40.29E
Suzhou, China (so͞o-jō)	189	31.19N	120.37E
Suzuki-shinden, Japan	242a	35.43N	139.31E
Suzu Misaki, c., Japan (so͞o'zo͞o mē'sä-kē)	194	37.30N	137.35E
Svalbard (Spitsbergen), dep., Nor. (sväl'bärt) (spĭts'bûr-gĕn)	164	77.00N	20.00E
Svaneke, Den. (svä'nĕ-kĕ)	152	55.08N	15.07E
Svatove, Ukr.	167	49.23N	38.10E
Svedala, Swe. (svĕ'dä-lä)	152	55.29N	13.11E
Sveg, Swe.	152	62.03N	14.22E
Svelvik, Nor. (svĕl'vĕk)	152	59.37N	10.18E
Svenčionys, Lith.	153	55.09N	26.09E
Svendborg, Den. (svĕn-bôrgh)	152	55.05N	10.35E
Svensen, Or., U.S. (svĕn'sĕn)	106c	46.10N	123.39W
Sverdlovsk *see* Yekaterinburg, Russia	164	56.51N	60.36E
Svetlaya, Russia (svyĕt'lȧ-yȧ)	194	46.09N	137.53E
Svicha, r., Ukr.	155	49.09N	24.10E
Svilajnac, Yugo. (svē'lȧ-ē-nȧts)	161	44.12N	21.14E
Svilengrad, Bul. (svĕl'ĕn-grȧt)	161	41.44N	26.11E
Svir', r., Russia	166	60.55N	33.40E
Svir Kanal, can., Russia (kȧ-näl')	153	60.10N	32.40E
Svishtov, Bul. (svēsh'tôf)	149	43.36N	25.21E
Svisloch', r., Bela. (svēs'lôk)	162	53.38N	28.10E
Svitavy, Czech Rep.	154	49.46N	16.28E
Svobodnyy, Russia (svö-bôd'nĭ)	165	51.28N	128.28E
Svolvaer, Nor. (svôl'vĕr)	146	68.15N	14.29E
Svyatoy Nos, Mys, c., Russia (svyŭ'toi nôs)	165	72.18N	139.28E
Swadlincote, Eng., U.K. (swŏd'lĭn-kōt)	144a	52.46N	1.33W
Swain Reefs, rf., Austl. (swän)	203	22.12S	152.08E
Swainsboro, Ga., U.S. (swänz'bŭr-ō)	115	32.37N	82.21W
Swakopmund, Nmb. (svä'kôp-mönt) (swȧ'kôp-mŏnd)	212	22.40S	14.30E
Swallowfield, Eng., U.K. (swŏl'ō-fēld)	144b	51.21N	0.58W
Swampscott, Ma., U.S. (swômp'skŏt)	93a	42.28N	70.55W
Swan, r., Austl.	202	31.30S	116.30E
Swan, r., Can.	89	51.58N	101.45W
Swan, r., Mt., U.S.	105	47.50N	113.40W
Swan Acres, Pa., U.S.	230b	40.33N	80.02W
Swan Hill, Austl.	203	35.20S	143.30E
Swan Hills, Can. (hĭlz)	84	54.52N	115.45W
Swan Island, i., Austl. (swŏn)	201a	38.15S	144.41E
Swan Lake, l., Can.	89	52.30N	100.45W
Swanland, reg., Austl. (swŏn'lănd)	202	31.45S	119.15E
Swanley, Eng., U.K.	235	51.24N	0.12E
Swan Range, mts., Mt., U.S.	105	47.50N	113.40W
Swan River, Can. (swŏn rĭv'ẽr)	84	52.06N	101.16W
Swanscombe, Eng., U.K.	235	51.26N	0.18E
Swansea, Wales, U.K.	147	51.37N	3.59W
Swansea, Il., U.S. (swŏn'sē)	107e	38.32N	89.59W
Swansea, Ma., U.S.	100b	41.45N	71.09W
Swansea, neigh., Can.	227c	43.38N	79.28W
Swanson Reservoir, res., Ne., U.S. (swŏn'sŭn)	110	40.13N	101.30W
Swartberg, mtn., Afr.	213c	30.08S	29.34E
Swarthmore, Pa., U.S.	229b	39.54N	75.21W
Swartkop, mtn., S. Afr.	212a	34.13S	18.27E
Swartruggens, S. Afr.	218d	25.40S	26.40E
Swartspruit, S. Afr.	213b	25.44S	28.01E
Swatow *see* Shantou, China	189	23.20N	116.40E

PLACE (Pronunciation)	PAGE	Lat. °′	Long. °′
Swaziland, nation, Afr. (swä'zē-lănd)	212	26.45S	31.30E
Sweden, nation, Eur. (swē'dĕn)	142	60.10N	14.10E
Swedesboro, N.J., U.S. (swēdz'bē-rō)	100f	39.45N	75.22W
Sweetwater, Tn., U.S. (swēt'wô-tẽr)	114	35.36N	84.29W
Sweetwater, Tx., U.S.	96	32.28N	100.25W
Sweetwater, l., N.D., U.S.	102	48.15N	98.35W
Sweetwater, r., Wy., U.S.	105	42.19N	108.35W
Sweetwater Reservoir, res., Ca., U.S.	108a	32.42N	116.54W
Świdnica, Pol. (shvĭd-nē'tsä)	154	50.50N	16.30E
Świdwin, Pol. (shvĭd'vĭn)	154	53.46N	15.48E
Świebodzice, Pol.	154	50.51N	16.17E
Świebodzin, Pol. (shvyĕn-bo'jĕts)	154	52.16N	15.36E
Świecie, Pol. (shvyăn'tsyĕ)	155	53.23N	18.26E
Świętokrzyskie, Góry, mts., Pol. (shvyĕn-tō-kzhĭ'skyĕ go͞o'rĭ)	155	50.57N	21.02E
Swift, r., Eng., U.K.	144a	52.26N	1.08W
Swift, r., Me., U.S. (swĭft)	93	44.42N	70.40E
Swift Creek Reservoir, res., Wa., U.S.	104	46.03N	122.10W
Swift Current, Can. (swĭft kûr'ĕnt)	84	50.17N	107.50W
Swindle Island, i., Can.	86	52.32N	128.35W
Swindon, Eng., U.K. (swĭn'dŭn)	150	51.35N	1.55W
Swinomish Indian Reservation, I.R., Wa., U.S. (swĭ-nō'mĭsh)	106a	48.25N	122.27W
Świnoujście, Pol. (shvĭ-nĭ-ô-wĕsh'chyĕ)	154	53.56N	14.14E
Swinton, Eng., U.K. (swĭn'tŭn)	144a	53.30N	1.19W
Swinton, Eng., U.K.	237b	53.31N	2.20W
Swissvale, Pa., U.S. (swĭs'vāl)	101e	40.25N	79.53W
Switzerland, nation, Eur. (swĭt'zẽr-lănd)	142	46.30N	7.43E
Syas', r., Russia (syäs)	162	59.28N	33.24E
Sycamore, Il., U.S. (sĭk'ȧ-mōr)	103	42.00N	88.42W
Sycan, r., Or., U.S.	104	42.45N	121.00W
Sychëvka, Russia (sē-chôf'kȧ)	162	55.52N	34.18E
Sydenham, Austl.	243b	37.42S	144.46E
Sydenham, neigh., S. Afr.	244b	26.09S	28.06E
Sydenham, neigh., Eng., U.K.	235	51.26N	0.03W
Sydney, Austl. (sĭd'nē)	203	33.55S	151.17E
Sydney, Can.	85	46.09N	60.11W
Sydney Mines, Can.	85	46.14N	60.14W
Syktyvkar, Russia (sük-tüf'kär)	164	61.35N	50.40E
Sylacauga, Al., U.S. (sĭl-ȧ-kô'gȧ)	114	33.10N	86.15W
Sylarna, mtn., Eur.	152	63.00N	12.10E
Sylt, i., Ger. (sĭlt)	154	54.55N	8.30E
Sylvania, Austl.	243a	34.01S	151.07E
Sylvania, Ga., U.S. (sĭl-vā'nĭ-ȧ)	115	32.44N	81.40W
Sylvania Heights, Austl.	243a	34.02S	151.06E
Sylvester, Ga., U.S. (sĭl-vĕs'tẽr)	114	31.32N	83.50W
Syndal, Austl.	243b	37.53S	145.09E
Synel'nykove, Ukr.	167	48.19N	35.33E
Syosset, N.Y., U.S.	228	40.50N	73.30W
Syracuse, Ks., U.S. (sĭr'ȧ-kūs)	110	37.59N	101.44W
Syracuse, N.Y., U.S.	97	43.05N	76.10W
Syracuse, Ut., U.S.	107b	41.06N	112.04W
Syr Darya, r., Asia	164	44.15N	65.45E
Syria, nation, Asia (sĭr'ĭ-ȧ)	182	35.00N	37.15E
Syrian Desert, des., Asia	182	32.00N	40.00E
Sysert', Russia (sĕ'sĕrt)	172a	56.30N	60.48E
Sysola, r., Russia	166	60.50N	50.40E
Syukunosho, Japan	242b	34.50N	135.32E
Syvash, zatoka, b., Ukr.	163	45.55N	34.42E
Syzran', Russia (sĕz-rän')	164	53.09N	48.27E
Szamotuły, Pol. (shȧ-mō-to͞o'wē)	154	52.36N	16.34E
Szarvas, Hung. (sôr'vôsh)	155	46.51N	20.36E
Szczebrzeszyn, Pol. (shchĕ-bzhä'shĕn)	155	50.41N	22.58E
Szczecin, Pol. (shchĕ'tsĭn)	142	53.25N	14.35E
Szczecinek, Pol. (shchĕ'tsĭ-nĕk)	146	53.41N	16.42E
Szczuczyn, Pol. (shcho͞o'chĕn)	155	53.32N	22.17E
Szczytno, Pol. (shchĭt'nö)	155	53.33N	21.00E
Szechwan Basin, basin, China	188	30.45N	104.40E
Szeged, Hung. (sĕ'gĕd)	142	46.15N	20.12E
Székesfehérvár, Hung. (sā'kĕsh-fĕ'hār-vär)	149	47.12N	18.26E
Szekszárd, Hung. (sĕk'särd)	149	46.19N	18.42E
Szentendre, Hung. (sĕnt'ĕn-drĕ)	155	47.40N	19.07E
Szentes, Hung. (sĕn'tĕsh)	155	46.38N	20.18E
Szigetvar, Hung. (sĕ'gĕt-vär)	155	46.05N	17.50E
Szolnok, Hung.	155	47.11N	20.12E
Szombathely, Hung. (sŏm'bôt-hĕl')	149	47.13N	16.35E
Szprotawa, Pol. (shprō-tä'vä)	154	51.34N	15.29E
Szydłowiec, Pol. (shid-wô'vyets)	155	51.13N	20.53E

T

PLACE (Pronunciation)	PAGE	Lat. °′	Long. °′
Taal, l., Phil. (tä-äl')	197a	13.58N	121.06E
Tabaco, Phil. (tä-bä'kō)	197a	13.27N	123.40E
Tabankulu, S. Afr. (tä-bän-ko͞o'la)	213c	30.56S	29.19E
Tabasará, Serranía de, mts., Pan.	121	8.29N	81.22W
Tabasco, Mex. (tä-bäs'kō)	118	21.47N	103.04W
Tabasco, state, Mex.	116	18.10N	93.00W
Taber, Can.	84	49.47N	112.08W
Tablas, i., Phil. (tä'bläs)	197a	12.26N	122.00E
Tablas Strait, strt., Phil.	197a	12.17N	121.41E
Table Bay, b., S. Afr. (tā'b'l)	212a	33.41S	18.27E
Table Mountain, mtn., S. Afr.	212a	33.58S	18.26E
Table Rock Lake, Mo., U.S.	111	36.37N	93.29W
Tabligbo, Togo	214	6.35N	1.30E
Taboão da Serra, Braz.	234d	23.38S	46.46W

PLACE (Pronunciation)	PAGE	Lat. °′	Long. °′
Taboga, i., Pan. (tä-bō′gä)	116a	8.48N	79.35W
Taboguilla, i., Pan. (tä-bȯ-gė′l-yä)	116a	8.48N	79.31W
Tábor, Czech Rep. (tä′bȯr)	154	49.25N	14.40E
Tabora, Tan. (tä-bō′rä)	212	5.01S	32.48E
Tabou, C. Iv. (tȧ-bo͞o′)	210	4.25N	7.21W
Tabrīz, Iran (tȧ-brēz′)	182	38.00N	46.13E
Tabuaeran, i., Kir.	2	3.52N	159.20W
Tabwémasana, Mont, mtn., Vanuatu	198f	15.20S	166.44E
Tacámbaro, r., Mex. (tä-käm′bä-rō)	118	18.55N	101.25W
Tacámbaro de Codallos, Mex.	118	19.12N	101.28W
Tacarigua, Laguna de la, l., Ven.	131b	10.18N	65.43W
Tacheng, China (tä-chŭŋ)	188	46.50N	83.24E
Tachie, r., Can.	86	54.30N	125.00W
Tachikawa, Japan	242a	35.42N	139.25E
Tacloban, Phil. (tä-klō′bän)	197	11.06N	124.58E
Tacna, Peru (täk′nä)	130	18.34S	70.16W
Tacoma, Wa., U.S. (tȧ-kō′mȧ)	96	47.14N	122.27W
Taconic Range, mts., N.Y., U.S. (tȧ-kŏn′ĭk)	99	41.55N	73.40W
Tacony, neigh., Pa., U.S.	229b	40.02N	75.03W
Tacotalpa, Mex. (tä-kȯ-täl′pä)	119	17.37N	92.51W
Tacotalpa, r., Mex.	119	17.24N	92.38W
Tacuba, neigh., Mex.	233a	19.28N	99.12W
Tacubaya, neigh., Mex.	233a	19.25N	99.12W
Tademaït, Plateau du, plat., Alg. (tä-dė-mä′ėt)	210	28.00N	2.15E
Tadio, Lagune, b., C. Iv.	214	5.20N	5.25W
Tadjoura, Dji. (tȧd-zho͞o′rȧ)	218a	11.48N	42.54E
Tadley, Eng., U.K. (tăd′lė)	144b	51.19N	1.08W
Tadotsu, Japan (tä′dȯ-tsȯ)	195	34.14N	133.43E
Tadoussac, Can. (tȧ-do͞o-sȧk′)	91	48.09N	69.43W
Tadworth, Eng., U.K.	235	51.17N	0.14W
Tadzhikistan *see* Tajikistan, nation, Asia	164	39.22N	69.30E
Taebaek Sanmaek, mts., Asia (tī-bīk′ sän-mīk′)	194	37.20N	128.50E
Taedong, r., N. Kor. (tī-dŏng)	194	38.38N	124.32E
Taegu, S. Kor. (tī′go͞o′)	189	35.49N	128.41E
Taejŏn, S. Kor.	194	36.20N	127.26E
Tafalla, Spain (tä-fäl′yä)	158	42.30N	1.42W
Tafna, r., Alg. (täf′nä)	158	35.28N	1.00W
Taft, Ca., U.S. (tȧft)	108	35.09N	119.27W
Tagama, reg., Niger	215	15.50N	6.30E
Taganrog, Russia (tȧ-gȧn-rôk′)	167	47.12N	38.56E
Taganrogskiy Zaliv, b., Eur. (tȧ-gȧn-rôk′skĭ zä′lĭf)	167	46.55N	38.17E
Tagula, i., Pap. N. Gui. (tä′go͞o-lȧ)	203	11.45S	153.46E
Tagus (Tajo), r., Eur. (tā′gŭs)	142	39.40N	5.07W
Tahan, Gunong, mtn., Malay.	196	4.33N	101.52E
Tahat, mtn., Alg. (tä-hät′)	210	23.22N	5.21E
Tahiti, i., Fr. Poly. (tä-hē′tė) (tä′ė-tė′)	2	17.30S	149.30W
Tahkuna Nina, c., Est. (tȧh-ko͞o′nȧ nē′nȧ)	153	59.08N	22.03E
Tahlequah, Ok., U.S. (tă-lĕ-kwä′)	111	35.54N	94.58W
Tahoe, l., U.S. (tä′hō)	96	39.09N	120.18W
Tahoua, Niger (tä′o͞o-ä)	210	14.54N	5.16E
Tahtsa Lake, l., Can.	86	53.33N	127.47W
Tahuya, Wa., U.S. (tȧ-hū-yā′)	106a	47.23N	123.03W
Tahuya, r., Wa., U.S.	106a	47.28N	122.55W
Tai'an, China (tī-än)	192	36.13N	117.08E
Taibai Shan, mtn., China (tī-bī shän)	192	33.42N	107.25E
Taibus Qi, China (tī-bo͞o-sz chyē)	192	41.52N	115.25E
Taicang, China (tī-tsäŋ)	190	31.26N	121.06E
T'aichung, Tai. (tī′chȯng)	189	24.10N	120.42E
Tai'erzhuang, China (tī-är-jůäŋ)	190	34.34N	117.44E
Taigu, China (tī-go͞o)	192	37.25N	112.35E
Taihang Shan, mts., China (tī-häŋ shän)	192	35.45N	112.00E
Taihe, China (tī-hŭ)	190	33.10N	115.38E
Tai Hu, l., China (tī ho͞o)	189	31.13N	120.00E
Tailagoin, reg., Mong. (tī′lȧ-gān′ kä′rä)	188	43.39N	105.54E
Tailai, China (tī-lī)	192	46.20N	123.10E
Tailem Bend, Austl. (tā-lĕm)	204	35.15S	139.30E
T'ainan, Tai. (tī′nan′)	189	23.08N	120.18E
Taínaron, Ákra, c., Grc.	142	37.45N	22.00E
Taining, China (tī′nĭng′)	193	26.58N	117.15E
T'aipei, Tai. (tī′pā′)	189	25.02N	121.38E
Taipei Institute of Technology, educ., Tai.	241d	25.02N	121.32E
Taiping, pt. of i., Malay.	196	4.56N	100.39E
Taiping Ling, mtn., China	192	47.03N	120.30E
Tai Po Tsai, H.K.	241c	22.21N	114.15E
Taisha, Japan (tī′shä)	195	35.23N	132.40E
Taishan, China (tī-shän)	193	22.15N	112.50E
Tai Shan, mts., China (tī shän)	192	36.16N	117.05E
Taitao, Península de, pen., Chile	132	46.20S	77.15W
Taitō, neigh., Japan	242a	35.43N	139.47E
T'aitung, Tai. (tī′to͞ong′)	193	22.45N	121.02E
Taiwan, nation, Asia (tī-wän) (fŏr-mō′sȧ)	189	23.30N	122.20E
Taiwan Normal University, educ., Tai.	241d	25.02N	121.31E
Taiwan Strait, strt., Asia	189	24.30N	120.00E
Tai Wan Tau, H.K.	241c	22.18N	114.17E
Tai Wan Tsun, H.K.	241c	22.19N	114.12E
Taixian, China (tī shyĕn)	190	32.31N	119.54E
Taixing, China (tī-shyĭŋ)	190	32.12N	119.58E
Taiyanggong, China	240b	39.58N	116.25E
Taiyuan, China (tī-yůän)	189	37.32N	112.38E
Taizhou, China (tī-jō)	190	32.23N	119.41E
Ta'Izz, Yemen	185	13.38N	44.04E
Tajano de Morais, Braz. (tĕ-zhä′nȯ-dĕ-mô-rä′ēs)	129a	22.05S	42.04W
Tajikistan, nation, Asia	164	39.22N	69.30E
Tajninka, Russia	239b	55.54N	37.45E
Tajumulco, vol., Guat. (tä-ho͞o-mo͞ol′kȯ)	120	15.03N	91.53W
Tajuña, r., Spain (tä-ko͞o′n-yä)	158	40.23N	2.36W
Tājūrā', Libya	148	32.56N	13.24W
Tak, Thai.	196	16.57N	99.12E

PLACE (Pronunciation)	PAGE	Lat. °′	Long. °′
Taka, i., Japan (tä′kä)	195	30.47N	130.23E
Takada, Japan (tä′kȧ-dä)	194	37.08N	138.30E
Takahashi, Japan (tä′kä′hä-shĭ)	195	34.47N	133.35E
Takaishi, Japan	195b	34.32N	135.27E
Takamatsu, Japan (tä′kä′mä-tso͞o′)	189	34.20N	134.02E
Takamori, Japan (tä′kä′mȯ-rē′)	195	32.50N	131.08E
Takaoka, Japan (ta′kä′ȯ-kä′)	194	36.45N	136.59E
Takapuna, N.Z.	205	36.48S	174.47E
Takarazuka, Japan (tä′kä-rä-zo͞o′kä)	195b	34.48N	135.22E
Takasaki, Japan (tä′kät′so͞o-kē′)	194	36.20N	139.00E
Takatsu, Japan (tä-kät′so͞o) (mė′zō-nȯ-kȯ′chė)	195a	35.36N	139.37E
Takatsuki, Japan (tä′kät′so͞o-kē′)	195b	34.51N	135.38E
Takayama, Japan (tä′kä′yä′mä)	195	36.11N	137.16E
Takefu, Japan (tä′kĕ-fo͞o)	194	35.57N	136.09E
Takenotsuka, neigh., Japan	242a	35.48N	139.48E
Takla Lake, l., Can.	84	55.25N	125.53W
Takla Makan, des., China (mä-kȧn′)	188	39.22N	82.34E
Takoma Park, Md., U.S. (tă′kōmă pärk)	100e	38.59N	77.00W
Takum, Nig.	215	7.17N	9.59E
Tala, Mex. (tä′lä)	118	20.39N	103.42W
Talagante, Chile (tä-lä-gȧ′n-tĕ)	129b	33.39S	70.54W
Talamanca, Cordillera de, mts., C.R.	121	9.37N	83.55W
Talanga, Hond. (tä-lä′n-gä)	120	14.21N	87.09W
Talara, Peru (tä-lä′rä)	130	4.32S	81.17W
Talasea, Pap. N. Gui. (tä-lä-sā′ä)	197	5.20S	150.00E
Talata Mafara, Nig.	215	12.35N	6.04E
Talaud, Kepulauan, is., Indon. (tä-lout′)	197	4.17N	127.30E
Talavera de la Reina, Spain	148	39.58N	4.51W
Talca, Chile (täl′kä)	132	35.25S	71.39W
Talca, prov., Chile	129b	35.23S	71.15W
Talca, Punta, c., Chile (po͞o′n-tä-täl′kä)	129b	33.25S	71.42W
Talcahuano, Chile (täl-kä-wä′nō)	132	36.41S	73.05W
Taldom, Russia (täl-dȯm)	162	56.44N	37.33E
Taldyqorghan, Kaz.	169	45.03N	77.18E
Talea de Castro, Mex. (tä′lå-ä dā käs′trō)	119	17.22N	96.14W
Talibu, Pulau, i., Indon.	197	1.30S	125.00E
Talim, i., Phil. (tä-lēm′)	197a	14.21N	121.14E
Talisay, Phil. (tä-lē′sī)	197a	14.08N	122.56E
Talkeetna, Ak., U.S. (tȧl-kēt′nȧ)	95	62.18N	150.02W
Talladega, Al., U.S. (tăl-ȧ-dē′gȧ)	114	33.25N	86.06W
Tallahassee, Fl., U.S. (tăl-ȧ-hăs′ė)	97	30.25N	84.17W
Tallahatchie, r., Ms., U.S. (tal-ȧ hăch′ė)	114	34.21N	90.03W
Tallapoosa, Ga., U.S. (tăl-ȧ-po͞o′sȧ)	114	33.44N	85.15W
Tallapoosa, r., Al., U.S.	114	32.22N	86.08W
Tallassee, Al., U.S. (tăl′ȧ-sė)	114	32.30N	85.54W
Tallinn, Est. (tȧl′lėn) (rā′väl)	164	59.26N	24.44E
Tallmadge, Oh., U.S. (tăl′mĭj)	101d	41.06N	81.26W
Tallulah, La., U.S. (tă-lo͞o′lȧ)	113	32.25N	91.13W
Tally Ho, Austl.	243b	37.52S	145.09E
Tal'ne, Ukr.	163	48.52N	30.43E
Talo, mtn., Eth.	211	10.45N	37.55E
Taloje Budrukh, India	187b	19.05N	73.05E
Talpa de Allende, Mex. (täl′pä dā äl-yĕn′dȧ)	118	20.25N	104.48W
Talquin, Lake, res., Fl., U.S.	114	30.26N	84.33W
Talsi, Lat. (tal′sĭ)	153	57.16N	22.35E
Taltal, Chile (täl-täl′)	132	25.26S	70.32W
Taly, Russia (täl′ĭ)	163	49.51N	40.07E
Tama, Ia., U.S. (tā′mä)	103	41.57N	92.36W
Tama, r., Japan	195a	35.38N	139.35E
Tamagawa, neigh., Japan	242a	35.37N	139.39E
Tama-kyūryō, mts., Japan	242a	35.35N	139.30E
Tamale, Ghana (tä-mä′lå)	210	9.25N	0.50W
Taman', Russia (tȧ-män″)	163	45.13N	36.46E
Tamanaco, r., Ven. (tä-mä-nä′kō)	131b	9.32N	66.00W
Tamaqua, Pa., U.S. (tȧ-mô′kwă)	99	40.45N	75.50W
Tamar, r., Eng., U.K. (tā′mär)	150	50.35N	4.15W
Tamarite de Litera, Spain (tä-mä-rē′tā)	159	41.52N	0.24E
Tamaulipas, state, Mex. (tä-mä-o͞o-lē′päs′)	116	23.45N	98.30W
Tamazula de Gordiano, Mex.	118	19.44N	103.09W
Tamazulapan del Progreso, Mex.	119	17.41N	97.34W
Tamazunchale, Mex. (tä-mä-zȯn-chä′lå)	118	21.16N	98.46W
Tambacounda, Sen. (täm-bä-ko͞on′dä)	210	13.47N	13.40W
Tambador, Serra do, mts., Braz. (sĕ′r-rä-dȯ-täm′bä-dōr)	131	10.33S	41.16W
Tambelan, Kepulauan, is., Indon. (täm-bå-län′)	196	0.38N	107.38E
Tambo, Austl. (tăm′bō)	203	24.50S	146.15E
Tambov, Russia (tȧm-bôf′)	164	52.45N	41.10E
Tambov, prov., Russia	162	52.50N	40.42E
Tambre, r., Spain (täm′brā)	158	42.59N	8.33W
Tambura, Sudan (täm-bo͞o′rä)	211	5.34N	27.30E
Tame, r., Eng., U.K. (tām)	144a	52.41N	1.42W
Tâmega, r., Port. (tȧ-mā′gȧ)	158	41.30N	7.45W
Tamenghest, Alg.	210	22.34N	5.34E
Tamenghest, Oued, r., Alg.	210	22.15N	2.51E
Tamgak, Monts, mtn., Niger (tam-gäk′)	210	18.40N	8.40E
Tamgué, Massif du, mtn., Gui.	210	12.15N	12.35W
Tamiahua, Mex. (tä-myä-wä)	119	21.17N	97.26W
Tamiahua, Laguna, l., Mex. (lä-gȯ′nä-tä-myä-wä)	119	21.38N	97.33W
Tamiami Canal, can., Fl., U.S. (tă-mī-ăm′ĭ)	115a	25.52N	80.08W
Tamil Nadu, state, India	183	11.30N	78.00E
Tampa, Fl., U.S. (tăm′pȧ)	97	27.57N	82.25W
Tampa Bay, b., Fl., U.S.	97	27.35N	82.38W
Tampere, Fin. (tȧm′pĕ-rĕ)	146	61.21N	23.39E
Tampico, Mex. (täm-pē′kō)	116	22.14N	97.51W
Tampico Alto, Mex. (täm-pē′kō äl′tō)	119	22.07N	97.48W
Tampin, Malay.	181b	2.28N	102.15E
Tam Quan, Viet.	193	14.20N	109.10E
Tamuín, Mex. (tä-mo͞o-ė′n)	118	22.04N	98.47W

PLACE (Pronunciation)	PAGE	Lat. °′	Long. °′
Tamworth, Austl. (tăm′wûrth)	203	31.01S	151.00E
Tamworth, Eng., U.K.	144a	52.38N	1.41W
Tana, i., Vanuatu	203	19.32S	169.27E
Tana, r., Kenya (tä′nä)	213	0.30S	39.30E
Tanabe, Japan (tä-nä′bā)	194	33.45N	135.21E
Tanabe, Japan	195b	34.49N	135.46E
Tanacross, Ak., U.S. (tă′nȧ-crōs)	95	63.20N	143.30W
Tanaga, i., Ak., U.S. (tä-nä′gä)	95a	51.28N	178.10W
Tanahbala, Pulau, i., Indon. (tȧ-nä-bä′lä)	196	0.30S	98.22E
Tanahmasa, Pulau, i., Indon. (tȧ-nä-mä′sä)	196	0.03S	97.30E
Tanakpur, India (tăn′ăk-pȯr)	186	29.10N	80.07E
Tana Lake, l., Eth.	211	12.09N	36.41E
Tanami, Austl. (tȧ-nā′mė)	202	19.45S	129.50E
Tanana, Ak., U.S. (tă′nȧ-nô)	95	65.18N	152.20W
Tanana, r., Ak., U.S.	95	64.26N	148.40W
Tanaro, r., Italy (tä-nä′rô)	160	44.45N	8.02E
Tanashi, Japan	195a	35.44N	139.34E
Tan-binh, Viet.	241j	10.48N	106.40E
Tanbu, China (tän-bo͞o)	191a	23.20N	113.06E
Tancheng, China (tän-chŭŋ)	192	34.37N	118.22E
Tanchŏn, N. Kor. (tän′chŭn)	194	40.29N	128.50E
Tancítaro, Mex. (tän-sē′tä-rō)	118	19.16N	102.24W
Tancítaro, Cerro de, mtn., Mex. (sĕ′r-rȯ-dĕ)	118	19.24N	102.19W
Tancoco, Mex. (tän-kō′kō)	119	21.16N	97.45W
Tandil, Arg. (tän-dēl′)	132	36.16S	59.01W
Tandil, Sierra del, mts., Arg.	132	38.40S	59.40W
Tanega, i., Japan (tä′nȧ-gä′)	189	30.36N	131.11E
Tanezrouft, reg., Alg. (tä′nĕz-rȯft)	210	24.17N	0.30W
Tang, r., China (täŋ)	190	33.38N	117.29E
Tang, r., China	190	39.13N	114.45E
Tanga, Tan. (tăŋ′gȧ)	213	5.04S	39.06E
Tangancícuaro, Mex. (täŋ-gän-sē′kwa-rȯ)	118	19.52N	102.13W
Tanganyika, Lake, l., Afr.	212	5.15S	29.40E
Tanger, Mor. (tăn-jēr′)	210	35.52N	5.55W
Tangermünde, Ger. (täŋ′ĕr-mün′de)	154	52.33N	11.58E
Tanggu, China (täŋ-go͞o)	190	39.04N	117.41E
Tanggula Shan, mts., China (täŋ-go͞o-lä shän)	188	33.15N	89.07E
Tanghe, China	192	32.40N	112.50E
Tangier *see* Tanger, Mor.	210	35.52N	5.55W
Tangipahoa, r., La., U.S. (tăn′jė-pȧ-hō′ȧ)	113	30.48N	90.28W
Tangra Yumco, l., China (täŋ-rä yo͞om-tswo)	186	30.50N	85.40E
T'angshan, China	192	39.38N	118.11E
Tangxian, China (täŋ shyĕn)	190	38.49N	115.00E
Tangzha, China (täŋ-jä)	190	32.06N	120.48E
Tanimbar, Kepulauan, is., Indon.	197	8.00S	132.00E
Tanjong Piai, c., Malay.	181b	1.16N	103.11E
Tanjong Ramunia, c., Malay.	181b	1.27N	104.44E
Tanjungbalai, Indon. (tän′jông-bä′lå)	181b	1.00N	103.26E
Tanjungkarang-Telukbetung, Indon.	196	5.16S	105.06E
Tanjungpandan, Indon.	196	2.47S	107.51E
Tanjungpinang, Indon. (tän′jŏng-pē′näng)	181b	0.55N	104.29E
Tanjungpriok, neigh., Indon.	241i	6.06S	106.53E
Tannu-Ola, mts., Asia	165	51.00N	94.00E
Tannūrah, Ra's at, c., Sau. Ar.	182	26.45N	49.59E
Tano, r., Afr.	214	5.40N	2.30W
Tan-qui-dong, Viet.	241j	10.44N	106.43E
Tanquijo, Arrecife, i., Mex. (är-rĕ-sē′fĕ-tän-kė′kô)	119	21.07N	97.16W
Tanshui Ho, r., Tai.	241d	25.08N	121.27E
Tan Son Nhut Airport, arpt., Viet.	241j	10.49N	106.40E
Ţanţā, Egypt	211	30.47N	31.00E
Tan-thuan-dong, Viet.	241j	10.45N	106.44E
Tantoyuca, Mex. (tän-tō-yo͞o′kä)	118	21.22N	98.13W
Tanyang, S. Kor.	194	36.53N	128.20E
Tanzania, nation, Afr.	212	6.48S	33.58E
Tao, r., China (tou)	192	35.30N	103.40E
Tao'an, China (tou-än)	189	45.15N	122.45E
Tao'er, r., China (tou-är)	189	45.40N	122.00E
Taormina, Italy (tä-ôr-mē′nä)	160	37.53N	15.18E
Taos, N.M., U.S. (tä′ȯs)	109	36.25N	105.35W
Taoudenni, Mali (tä′o͞o-dĕ-nė′)	210	22.57N	3.37W
Taoussa, Mali	214	16.55N	0.35W
Taoyuan, China (tou-yůän)	193	29.00N	111.15E
Tapa, Est. (tȧ′pȧ)	153	59.16N	25.56E
Tapachula, Mex.	120	14.55N	92.20W
Tapajós, r., Braz. (tä-pä-zhô′s)	131	3.27S	55.33W
Tapalque, Arg. (tä-päl-kĕ′)	129c	36.22S	60.05W
Tapanatepec, Mex. (tä-pä-nä-tĕ-pĕk)	119	16.22N	94.19W
Tāpi, r., India	183	21.00N	76.30E
Tapiales, Arg.	233d	34.42S	58.30W
Tappi Saki, c., Japan (täp′pė sä′kė)	194	41.05N	139.40E
Tapps, l., Wa., U.S. (tăpz)	106a	47.20N	122.12W
Taquara, neigh., Braz.	234c	22.55S	43.21W
Taquara, Serra de, mts., Braz. (sĕ′r-rä-dĕ-tä-kwä′rä)	131	15.28S	54.33W
Taquari, r., Braz. (tä-kwä′rĭ)	131	18.35S	56.50W
Tar, r., N.C., U.S. (tär)	115	35.58N	78.06W
Tara, Russia (tä′rȧ)	164	56.58N	74.13E
Tara, i., Phil. (tä′rä)	197a	12.18N	120.28E
Tara, r., Russia (tä′rȧ)	170	56.32N	76.13E
Ţarābulus, Leb. (tȧ-rä′bȯ-lo͞os)	182	34.25N	35.50E
Ţarābulus (Tripolitania), hist. reg., Libya	210	31.00N	12.26E
Tarakan, Indon.	196	3.17N	118.04E
Taranaki, Mount, vol., N.Z.	205	39.18S	174.04E
Tarancón, Spain (tä-rän-kōn′)	158	40.01N	3.00W
Taranto, Italy (tä′rän-tô)	149	40.30N	17.15E
Taranto, Golfo di, b., Italy (gȯl-fȯ-dē tä′rän-tô)	142	40.03N	17.10E
Tarapoto, Peru (tä-rä-pȯ′tō)	130	6.29S	76.26W
Tarare, Fr. (tȧ-rär′)	156	45.55N	4.23E

ăt; finăl; rāte; senåte; ärm; ȧsk; sofȧ; fâre; ch-choose; dh-as th in other; bē; ėvent; bĕt; recĕnt; cratẽr; g-gō; gh-guttural g; bĭt; ĭ-short neutral; rīde; κ-guttural k as ch in German ich;

PRONOUNCING INDEX

Tarascon–Términos 355

PLACE (Pronunciation)	PAGE	Lat. °'	Long. °'
Tarascon, Fr. (tȧ-rȧs-kôN′)	156	42.53N	1.35E
Tarascon, Fr. (tä-räs-kôN)	156	43.47N	4.41E
Tarashcha, Ukr. (tä′rȧsh-chȧ)	163	49.34N	30.52E
Tarasht, Iran	241h	35.42N	51.21E
Tarata, Bol. (tä-rä′tä)	130	17.43S	66.00W
Taravo, r., Fr.	160	41.54N	8.58E
Tarazit, Massif de, mts., Niger	215	20.05N	7.35E
Tarazona, Spain (tä-rä-thō′nä)	158	41.54N	1.45W
Tarazona de la Mancha, Spain (tä-rä-zō′nä-dĕ-lä-mä′n-chä)	158	39.13N	1.50W
Tarbes, Fr. (tȧrb)	147	43.04N	0.05E
Tarbock Green, Eng., U.K.	237a	53.23N	2.49W
Tarboro, N.C., U.S. (tär′bŭr-ō)	115	35.53N	77.34W
Taredo, neigh., India	240e	19.58N	72.49E
Taree, Austl. (tă-rē′)	204	31.52S	152.21E
Tarentum, Pa., U.S. (tȧ-rĕn′tŭm)	101e	40.36N	79.44W
Tarfa, Wādī at, val., Egypt	218b	28.14N	31.00E
Târgovişte, Rom.	149	44.54N	25.29E
Târgu Jiu, Rom.	149	45.02N	23.17E
Târgu Mureş, Rom.	149	46.33N	24.33E
Târgu Neamţ, Rom.	155	47.14N	26.23E
Târgu Ocna, Rom.	155	46.18N	26.38E
Târgu Secuiesc, Rom.	155	46.04N	26.06E
Tarhūnah, Libya	184	32.26N	13.38E
Tarija, Bol. (tär-rē′hä)	130	21.42S	64.52W
Tarīm, Yemen (tȧ-rīm′)	182	16.13N	49.08E
Tarim, r., China (tȧ-rīm′)	188	40.45N	85.39E
Tarim Basin, basin, China (tȧ-rīm′)	188	39.52N	82.34E
Tarka, r., S. Afr. (tä′kȧ)	213c	32.15S	26.00E
Tarkastad, S. Afr.	213c	32.01S	26.18E
Tarkhankut, Mys, c., Ukr. (mĭs tȧr-кän′kȯt)	167	45.21N	32.30E
Tarkio, Mo., U.S. (tär′kĭ-ō)	111	40.27N	95.22W
Tarkwa, Ghana (tärk′wä)	210	5.19N	1.59W
Tarlac, Phil. (tär′läk)	196	15.29N	120.36E
Tarlton, S. Afr. (tärl′tŭn)	213b	26.05S	27.38E
Tarma, Peru (tär′mä)	130	11.26S	75.40W
Tarn, r., Fr. (tärn)	147	43.45N	2.00E
Târnăveni, Rom.	155	46.19N	24.18E
Tarnów, Pol. (tär′nòf)	147	50.02N	21.00E
Taro, r., Italy (tä′rō)	160	44.41N	10.03E
Taroudant, Mor. (tȧ-roo-dänt′)	210	30.39N	8.52W
Tarpon Springs, Fl., U.S. (tär′pŏn)	115a	28.07N	82.44W
Tarporley, Eng., U.K. (tär′pẽr-lė)	144a	53.09N	2.40W
Tarpum Bay, b., Bah. (tär′pŭm)	122	25.05N	76.20W
Tarquinia, Italy (tär-kwē′nė-ä)	160	42.16N	11.46E
Tarragona, Spain (tär-rä-gō′nä)	142	41.05N	1.15E
Tarrant, Al., U.S. (tăr′ănt)	100h	33.35N	86.46W
Tarrasa, Spain (tär-rä′sä)	159	41.34N	2.01E
Tárrega, Spain (tä rå-gä)	159	41.40N	1.09E
Tarrejón de Ardoz, Spain (tär-rĕ-кō′n-dĕ-är-dôz)	159a	40.28N	3.29W
Tarrytown, N.Y., U.S. (tăr′ĭ-toun)	100a	41.04N	73.52W
Tarsus, Tur. (tȧr′sòs) (tär′sŭs)	182	37.00N	34.50E
Tartagal, Arg. (tär-tä-gá′l)	132	23.31S	63.47W
Tartu, Est. (tär′too) (dôr′pät)	164	58.23N	26.44E
Ţarţūs, Syria	184	34.54N	35.59E
Tarumi, Japan (tä′roo-mė)	195b	34.38N	135.04E
Tarusa, Russia (tä-roos′à)	162	54.43N	37.11E
Tarzana, Ca., U.S. (tär-ză′ă)	107a	34.10N	118.32W
Tashauz, Turk. (tŭ-shŭ-oos′)	169	41.50N	59.45E
Tashkent, Uzb. (tȧsh′kĕnt)	169	41.23N	69.04E
Tasman Bay, b., N.Z. (tăz′măn)	203a	40.50S	173.20E
Tasmania, state, Austl.	203	41.28S	142.30E
Tasman Peninsula, pen., Austl.	204	43.00S	148.30E
Tasman Sea, sea, Oc.	225	29.30S	155.00E
Tasquillo, Mex. (täs-kē′lyō)	118	20.34N	99.21W
Tatarsk, Russia (tȧ-tärsk′)	164	55.13N	75.58E
Tatarstan, state, Russia	166	55.00N	51.00E
Tatar Strait, strt., Russia	165	51.00N	141.45E
Tate Gallery, pt. of i., Eng., U.K.	235	51.29N	0.08W
Tater Hill, mtn., Or., U.S. (tāt′ẽr hĭl)	106c	45.47N	123.02W
Tateyama, Japan (tä′tė-yä′mä)	195	35.04N	139.52E
Tathong Channel, strt., H.K.	241c	22.15N	114.15E
Tatlow, Mount, mtn., Can.	86	51.23N	123.52W
Tatsfield, Eng., U.K.	235	51.18N	0.02E
Tau, Nor.	152	59.05N	5.59E
Tauern Tunnel, trans., Aus.	154	47.12N	13.17E
Taung, S. Afr. (tä′ông)	212	27.25S	24.47E
Taunton, Ma., U.S. (tän′tŭn)	99	41.54N	71.03W
Taunton, r., R.I., U.S.	100b	41.50N	71.02W
Taupo, Lake, l., N.Z. (tä′oo-pō)	203a	38.42S	175.55E
Taurage, Lith. (tou′rȧ-gä)	153	55.15N	22.18E
Taurus Mountains see Toros Dağlari, mts., Tur.	182	37.00N	32.40E
Tauste, Spain (tä-oos′tå)	158	41.55N	1.15W
Tavda, Russia (tȧv-dȧ′)	164	58.00N	64.44E
Tavda, r., Russia	170	58.30N	64.15E
Taverny, Fr. (tȧ-vẽr-nē′)	157b	49.02N	2.13E
Taviche, Mex. (tä-vē′chĕ)	119	16.43N	96.35W
Tavira, Port. (tä-vē′rȧ)	158	37.09N	7.42W
Tavistock, N.J., U.S.	229b	39.53N	75.02W
Tavşanlı, Tur. (tȧv′shän-lĭ)	167	39.30N	29.30E
Tawakoni, l., Tx., U.S.	113	32.51N	95.59W
Tawaramoto, Japan (tä′wä-rä-mô-tô)	195b	34.33N	135.48E
Tawas City, Mi., U.S.	98	44.15N	83.30W
Tawas Point, c., Mi., U.S. (tô′wȧs)	98	44.15N	83.25W
Tawitawi Group, is., Phil. (tä′wė-tä′wė)	196	4.52N	120.35E
Tawkar, Sudan	211	18.28N	37.46E
Taxco de Alarcón, Mex. (täs′kō dĕ ä-lär-kō′n)	118	18.34N	99.37W
Tay, r., Scot., U.K.	150	56.35N	3.37W
Tay, Loch, l., Scot., U.K.	150	56.25N	4.07W
Tayabas Bay, b., Phil. (tä-yä′bäs)	197a	13.44N	121.40E
Tayga, Russia (tī′gä)	170	56.12N	85.47E
Taygonos, Mys, c., Russia	165	60.37N	160.17E
Taylor, Mi., U.S.	230c	42.13N	83.16W
Taylor, Tx., U.S.	113	30.35N	97.25W
Taylor, Mount, mtn., N.M., U.S.	96	35.20N	107.40W
Taylorville, Il., U.S. (tā′lẽr-vĭl)	98	39.30N	89.20W
Taymyr, l., Russia (tī-mĭr′)	165	74.13N	100.45E
Taymyr, Poluostrov, pen., Russia	165	75.15N	95.00E
Táyros, Grc.	239d	37.58N	23.42E
Tayshet, Russia (tī-shĕt′)	165	56.09N	97.49E
Taytay, Phil.	241g	14.34N	121.08E
Tayug, Phil.	197a	16.01N	120.45E
Taz, r., Russia (táz)	170	67.15N	80.45E
Taza, Mor. (tä′zä)	210	34.08N	4.00W
Tazovskoye, Russia	164	66.58N	78.28E
Tbessa, Alg.	210	35.27N	8.13E
Tbilisi, Geor. (′tbĭl-yē′sē)	167	41.40N	44.45E
Tchentlo Lake, l., Can.	86	55.11N	125.00W
Tchibanga, Gabon (chė-băŋ′gä)	212	2.51S	11.02E
Tchien, Lib.	214	6.04N	8.08W
Tchigai, Plateau du, plat., Afr.	215	21.20N	14.50E
Tczew, Pol. (t′chĕf′)	146	54.06N	18.48E
Teabo, Mex. (tĕ-ä′bô)	120a	20.25N	89.14W
Teague, Tx., U.S. (tēg)	113	31.39N	96.16W
Teaneck, N.J., U.S.	228	40.53N	74.01W
Teapa, Mex. (tā-ä′pä)	119	17.35N	92.56W
Tebing Tinggi, i., Indon. (teb′ĭng-tĭng′gä)	181b	0.54N	102.39E
Tecalitlán, Mex. (tā-kä-lė-tlän′)	118	19.28N	103.17W
Techiman, Ghana	214	7.35N	1.56W
Tecoanapa, Mex. (tāk-wä-nä-pä′)	118	16.33N	98.46W
Tecoh, Mex. (tĕ-kô)	120a	20.46N	89.27W
Tecolotlán, Mex. (tā-kô-lô-tlän′)	118	20.13N	103.57W
Tecolutla, Mex. (tā-kô-loo′tlä)	119	20.33N	97.00W
Tecolutla, r., Mex.	119	20.16N	97.14W
Tecomán, Mex. (tā-kô-män′)	118	18.53N	103.53W
Tecómitl, Mex. (tĕ-kŏ′mētl)	119a	19.13N	98.59W
Tecozautla, Mex. (tā′kô-zä-oo′tlä)	118	20.33N	99.38W
Tecpan de Galeana, Mex. (tĕk-pän′ dā gä-lā-ä′nä)	118	17.13N	100.41W
Tecpatán, Mex. (tĕk-pä-tá′n)	119	17.08N	93.18W
Tecuala, Mex. (tĕ-kwä-lä)	118	22.24N	105.29W
Tecuci, Rom. (ta-kòch′)	149	45.51N	27.30E
Tecumseh, Can. (tė-kŭm′sė)	101b	42.19N	82.53W
Tecumseh, Mi., U.S.	98	42.00N	84.00W
Tecumseh, Ne., U.S.	111	40.21N	96.09W
Tecumseh, Ok., U.S.	111	35.18N	96.55W
Teddington, neigh., Eng., U.K.	235	51.25N	0.20W
Tees, r., Eng., U.K. (tēz)	150	54.40N	2.10W
Teganuna, l., Japan (tā′gä-noo′nä)	195a	35.50N	140.02E
Tegel, neigh., Ger.	238a	52.35N	13.17E
Tegeler See, l., Ger.	238a	52.35N	13.15E
Tegucigalpa, Hond. (tå-goo-sė-gäl′pä)	116	14.08N	87.15W
Tehachapi Mountains, mts., Ca., U.S. (tē-hă-shă′pĭ)	108	34.50N	118.55W
Tehar, neigh., India	240d	28.38N	77.07E
Tehrān, Iran (tĕ-hrän′)	182	35.45N	51.30E
Tehuacan, Mex. (tā-wä-kän′)	116	18.27N	97.23W
Tehuantepec, Mex.	116	16.20N	95.14W
Tehuantepec, r., Mex.	119	16.30N	95.23W
Tehuantepec, Golfo de, b., Mex. (gôl-fô dĕ)	116	15.45N	95.00W
Tehuantepec, Istmo de, isth., Mex. (ē′st-mô dĕ)	119	17.55N	94.35W
Tehuehuetla, Arroyo, r., Mex. (tĕ-wĕ-wĕ′tlä är-rō-yô)	118	17.54N	100.26W
Tehuitzingo, Mex. (tā-wė-tzĭŋ′gō)	118	18.21N	98.16W
Tejeda, Sierra de, mts., Spain (sē-ĕ′r-rä dĕ tĕ-kĕ′dä)	158	36.55N	4.00W
Tejúpan, Mex. (tĕ-koo-pä′n) (sän-tyä′gô)	119	17.39N	97.34W
Tejúpan, Punta, c., Mex.	118	18.19N	103.30W
Tejupilco de Hidalgo, Mex. (tå-hoo-pēl′kô dā ė-dhäl′gō)	118	18.52N	100.07W
Tekamah, Ne., U.S. (tē-kā′mȧ)	102	41.46N	96.13W
Tekax de Alvaro Obregon, Mex.	120a	20.12N	89.11W
Tekeze, r., Afr.	211	13.38N	38.00E
Tekit, Mex. (tĕ-kē′t)	120a	20.35N	89.18W
Tekoa, Wa., U.S. (tē-kō′ȧ)	104	47.15N	117.03W
Tekstil′ščiki, neigh., Russia	239b	55.42N	37.44E
Tela, Hond. (tā′lä)	116	15.45N	87.25W
Tela, India	240d	28.44N	77.20E
Tela, Bahía de, b., Hond.	120	15.53N	87.29W
Telapa Burok, Gunong, mtn., Malay.	181b	2.51N	102.04E
Telavi, Geor.	167	42.00N	45.20E
Tel Aviv-Yafo, Isr. (tĕl-ä-vēv′já′já′fȧ)	182	32.03N	34.46E
Telegraph Creek, Can. (tĕl′ē-grȧf)	84	57.59N	131.22W
Teleneşti, Mol.	163	47.31N	28.22E
Telescope Peak, mtn., Ca., U.S. (tĕl′ē skōp)	96	36.12N	117.05W
Telesung, Indon.	181b	1.07N	102.53E
Telica, vol., Nic. (tå-lē′kä)	120	12.38N	86.52W
Tell City, In., U.S. (tĕl)	98	38.00N	86.45W
Teller, Ak., U.S. (tĕl′ẽr)	95	65.17N	166.28W
Tello, Col. (tĕ′l-yō)	130a	3.05N	75.08W
Telluride, Co., U.S. (tĕl′ū-rīd)	109	37.55N	107.50W
Telok Datok, Malay.	181b	2.51N	101.33E
Teloloapan, Mex. (tā′lô-lô-ä′pän)	118	18.19N	99.54W
Tel′pos-Iz, Gora, mtn., Russia (tyĕl′pôs-ēz′)	164	63.50N	59.20E
Telšiai, Lith. (tĕl′sha′ė)	153	55.59N	22.17E
Teltow, Ger. (tĕl′tō)	145b	52.24N	13.12E
Teltower Hochfläche, reg., Ger.	238a	52.22N	13.20E
Teluklecak, Indon.	181b	1.53N	101.45E
Tema, Ghana	214	5.38N	0.01E
Temascalcingo, Mex. (tā′mäs-käl-sĭŋ′gō)	118	19.55N	100.00W
Temascaltepec, Mex. (tā′mäs-käl-tå pĕk)	118	19.00N	100.03W
Temax, Mex. (tĕ′mäx)	116	21.10N	88.51W
Temir, Kaz.	169	49.10N	57.15E
Temirtau, Kaz.	169	50.08N	73.13E
Temiscouata, l., Can. (tĕ′mĭs-kō-ä′tä)	92	47.40N	68.50W
Témiskaming, Can. (tė-mĭs′kȧ-mĭng)	85	46.41N	79.01W
Temoaya, Mex. (tĕ-mô-a-um-yä)	119a	19.28N	99.36W
Tempe, Az., U.S.	109	33.24N	111.54W
Tempelhof, neigh., Ger.	238a	52.28N	13.23E
Temperley, Arg. (tĕ′m-pĕr-lā)	132a	34.47S	58.24W
Tempio Pausania, Italy (tĕm′pė-ō pou-sä′nė-ä)	160	40.55N	9.05E
Temple, Tx., U.S. (tĕm′p′l)	113	31.06N	97.20W
Temple City, Ca., U.S.	107a	34.07N	118.02W
Temple Hills, Md., U.S.	229d	38.49N	76.57W
Temple of Heaven, rel., China	240b	39.53N	116.25E
Templestowe, Austl.	243b	37.45S	145.07E
Templeton, Can. (tĕm′p′l-tŭn)	83c	45.29N	75.37W
Temple University, pt. of i., Pa., U.S.	229b	39.59N	75.09W
Templin, Ger. (tĕm-plēn′)	154	53.08N	13.30E
Tempoal, r., Mex. (tĕm-pô-ä′l)	118	21.38N	98.23W
Temryuk, Russia (tyĕm-ryòk′)	167	45.17N	37.21E
Temuco, Chile (tå-moo′kō)	132	38.46S	72.38W
Temyasovo, Russia (tĕm-yä′sô-vô)	172a	53.00N	58.06E
Tenafly, N.J., U.S.	228	40.56N	73.58W
Tenāli, India	187	16.10N	80.32E
Tenamaxtlán, Mex. (tā′nä-mäs-tlän′)	118	20.13N	104.06W
Tenancingo, Mex. (tå-nän-sēŋ′gō)	118	18.54N	99.36W
Tenango, Mex. (tå-näŋ′gō)	119a	19.09N	98.51W
Tenasserim, Myanmar (tĕn-ăs′ẽr-ĭm)	196	12.09N	99.01E
Tendrivs′ka Kosa, ostriv, i., Ukr.	163	46.12N	31.17E
Tenerife Island, i., Spain (tå-nå-rē′fā) (tĕn-ẽr-ĭf′)	210	28.41N	17.02W
Tènés, Alg. (tā-nĕs′)	147	36.28N	1.22E
Tengiz kölí, l., Kaz.	169	50.45N	68.39E
Tengxian, China (tŭŋ shyĕn)	192	35.07N	117.08E
Tenjin, Japan (tĕn′jĕn)	195b	34.54N	135.04E
Tenke, Zaire (tĕŋ′kȧ)	212	11.26S	26.45E
Tenkiller Ferry Reservoir, res., Ok., U.S. (tĕn-kĭl′ẽr)	111	35.42N	94.47W
Tenkodogo, Burkina (tĕŋ-kô-dō′gô)	210	11.47N	0.22W
Tenmile, r., Wa., U.S. (tĕn mīl)	106d	48.52N	122.32W
Tennant Creek, Austl. (tĕn′ănt)	202	19.45S	134.00E
Tennessee, state, U.S. (tĕn-ĕ-sē′)	97	35.50N	88.00W
Tennessee, r., U.S.	97	35.35N	88.20W
Tennille, Ga., U.S. (tĕn′ĭl)	114	32.55N	86.50W
Tennōji, neigh., Japan	242b	34.39N	135.31E
Teno, r., Chile (tĕ′nô)	129b	34.55S	71.00W
Tenora, Austl. (tĕn-ôrȧ)	204	34.23S	147.33E
Tenosique, Mex. (tā-nô-sē′kȧ)	119	17.27N	91.25W
Tenri, Japan	195b	34.36N	135.50E
Tenryū-Gawa, r., Japan (tĕn′ryoo′gä′wä)	195	35.16N	137.54E
Tensas, r., La., U.S. (tĕn′sô)	113	31.54N	91.30W
Tensaw, r., Al., U.S. (tĕn′sô)	114	30.45N	87.52W
Tenterfield, Austl. (tĕn′tẽr-fēld)	203	29.00S	152.06E
Ten Thousand, Islands, is., Fl., U.S. (tĕn thou′zănd)	115a	25.45N	81.35W
Teocaltiche, Mex. (tā′ô-käl-tē′chȧ)	118	21.27N	102.38W
Teocelo, Mex. (tā-ô-sā′lō)	119	19.22N	96.57W
Teocuitatlán de Corona, Mex.	118	20.06N	103.22W
Teófilo Otoni, Braz. (tĕ-ô′fē-lō-tô′nė)	131	17.49S	41.18W
Teoloyucan, Mex. (tā′ô-lô-yoo′kän)	118	19.43N	99.12W
Teopisca, Mex. (tā-ô-pēs′kä)	119	16.30N	92.33W
Teotihuacán, Mex. (tĕ-ô-tē-wá-ká′n)	119a	19.40N	98.52W
Teotitlán del Camino, Mex. (tā-ô-tē-tlän′ dĕl kä-mē′nô)	119	18.07N	97.04W
Tepalcatepec, Mex. (tā′päl-kä-tä′pĕk)	118	19.11N	102.51W
Tepalcatepec, r., Mex.	118	18.54N	102.25W
Tepalcates, Mex.	233a	19.23N	99.04W
Tepalcingo, Mex. (tā-päl-sēŋ′gô)	118	18.34N	98.49W
Tepatitlán de Morelos, Mex. (tā-pä-tė-tlän′ dā mô-rā′los)	116	20.55N	102.47W
Tepeaca, Mex. (tā-pā-ä′kä)	119	18.57N	97.54W
Tepecoacuilco de Trujano, Mex.	118	18.15N	99.29W
Tepeji del Río, Mex. (tā-pā-кe′ dĕl rē′ō)	118	19.55N	99.22W
Tepelmeme, Mex. (tā′pĕl-mā′må)	119	17.51N	97.23W
Tepepan, Mex.	233a	19.16N	99.08W
Tepetlaoxtoc, Mex. (tā′pā-tlä′ós-tōk′)	118	19.34N	98.49W
Tepezala, Mex. (tā-pā-zä-lä′)	118	22.12N	102.12W
Tepic, Mex. (tā-pēk′)	116	21.32N	104.53W
Tëplaya Gora, Russia (tyôp′lá-yá gô-rà)	172a	58.32N	59.08E
Teplice, Czech Rep.	147	50.39N	13.50E
Teposcolula, Mex.	119	17.33N	97.29W
Tequendama, Salto de, wtfl., Col. (säl′-tô dĕ tĕ-kĕn-dä′mä)	130	4.34N	74.18W
Tequila, Mex. (tå-kē′lä)	118	20.53N	103.48W
Tequisistlán, r., Mex. (tĕ-kē-sės-tlá′n)	119	16.20N	95.40W
Tequisquiapan, Mex. (tå-kēs-kė-ä′pän)	118	20.33N	99.57W
Ter, r., Spain (tĕr)	159	42.04N	2.52E
Téra, Niger	214	14.01N	0.45E
Tera, r., Spain (tā′rä)	158	42.05N	6.24W
Teramo, Italy (tā′rä-mô)	160	42.40N	13.41E
Terborg, Neth. (tĕr-bōrg)	157c	51.55N	6.23E
Tercan, Tur. (tĕr′jän)	167	39.40N	40.12E
Terceira Island, i., Port. (tĕr-sā′rä)	210a	38.49N	26.36W
Terebovlya, Ukr. (tĕ-rä′bôv-lyȧ)	155	49.18N	25.43E
Terek, r., Russia	167	43.30N	45.10E
Terenkul′, Russia (tĕ-rĕn′kól)	172a	55.38N	62.18E
Teresina, Braz. (tĕr-å-sē′nȧ)	131	5.04S	42.42W
Teresópolis, Braz. (tĕr-ā-sô′pō-lēzh)	129a	22.25S	42.59W
Teriberka, Russia (tyĕr-ė-byôr′kȧ)	166	69.00N	35.15E
Terme, Tur. (tĕr′mĕ)	167	41.05N	37.00E
Termez, Uzb. (tyĕr′mĕz)	170	37.19N	67.20E
Terminal, Ca., U.S.	232	33.45N	118.15W
Termini, Italy (tĕr′mė-nė)	160	37.58N	13.39E
Términos, Laguna de, l., Mex. (lä-gō′nä dĕ ĕ′r-mē-nôs)	116	18.37N	91.32W

ng-sing; ŋ-baŋk; N-nasalized n; nŏd; cŏmmit; ōld; ôbey; ôrder; oi-boil; fōōd; ȯ-as oo in foot; ou-out; s-soft; sh-dish; th-thin; pūre; ûnite; ûrn; stŭd; circŭs; ü-as in French tu; ′-indeterminate vowel.

356 Termoli–Tinguiririca

PLACE (Pronunciation)	PAGE	Lat. °′	Long. °′
Termoli, Italy (tĕr′mô-lē)	160	42.00N	15.01E
Tern, r., Eng., U.K. (tûrn)	144a	52.49N	2.31W
Ternate, Indon. (tĕr-nä′tä)	197	0.52N	127.25E
Terni, Italy (tĕr′nē)	148	42.38N	12.41E
Ternopil', Ukr.	167	49.32N	25.36E
Terpeniya, Mys, c., Russia	165	48.44N	144.42E
Terpeniya, Zaliv, b., Russia (zä′lĭf tĕr-pă′nĭ-yá)	194	49.10N	143.05E
Terrace, Can. (tĕr′ĭs)	84	54.31N	128.35W
Terracina, Italy (tĕr-rä-chē′nä)	148	41.18N	13.14E
Terra Nova National Park, rec., Can.	85a	48.37N	54.15W
Terrebonne, Can. (tĕr-bŏn′)	99	45.42N	73.38W
Terrebonne Bay, b., La., U.S.	113	28.55N	90.30W
Terre Haute, In., U.S. (tĕr-ē hōt′)	97	39.25N	87.25W
Terrell, Tx., U.S. (tĕr′ĕl)	113	32.44N	96.15W
Terrell, Wa., U.S.	106d	48.53N	122.44W
Terrell Hills, Tx., U.S. (tĕr′ĕl hĭlz)	107d	29.28N	98.27W
Terschelling, i., Neth. (tĕr-skĕl′ĭng)	151	53.25N	5.12E
Teruel, Spain (tå-ro͞o-ĕl′)	148	40.20N	1.05W
Tešanj, Bos. (tĕ′shän′)	161	44.36N	17.59E
Teschendorf, Ger. (tĕ′shĕn-dōrf)	145b	52.51N	13.10E
Tesecheacan, Mex. (tĕ-sĕ-chĕ-ä-kà′n)	119	18.10N	95.41W
Teshekpuk, l., Ak., U.S. (tē-shĕk′pŭk)	95	70.18N	152.36W
Teshio Dake, mtn., Japan (tĕsh′ē-ō-dä′kä)	194	44.00N	142.50E
Teshio Gawa, r., Japan (tĕsh′ē-ō gä′wä)	194	44.53N	144.55E
Tesiyn, r., Asia	188	49.45N	96.00E
Teslin, Can. (tĕs-lĭn)	95	60.10N	132.30W
Teslin, l., Can.	84	60.12N	132.08W
Teslin, r., Can.	84	61.18N	134.14W
Tessaoua, Niger (tĕs-sä′ö-ä)	210	13.53N	7.53E
Tessenderlo, Bel.	145a	51.04N	5.08E
Test, r., Eng., U.K. (tĕst)	150	51.10N	1.30W
Testa del Gargano, c., Italy (tās′tä dĕl gär-gä′nō)	160	41.48N	16.13E
Tetachuck Lake, l., Can.	86	53.20N	125.50W
Tete, Moz. (tā′tĕ)	212	16.13S	33.35E
Tête Jaune Cache, Can. (tĕt′zhōn-kăsh)	87	52.57N	119.26W
Teterboro, N.J., U.S.	228	40.52N	74.03W
Teteriv, r., Ukr.	167	51.05N	29.30E
Teterow, Ger. (tā′tĕ-rō)	154	53.46N	12.33E
Teteven, Bul. (tĕt′ĕ-ven′)	161	42.57N	24.15E
Teton, r., Mt., U.S. (tē′tŏn)	105	47.54N	111.37W
Tétouan, Mor.	210	35.42N	5.34W
Tetovo, Mac. (tä′tŏ-vŏ)	161	42.01N	21.00E
Tetyukhe-Pristan, Russia (tĕt-yo͞o′kĕ prī-stän′)	194	44.21N	135.44E
Tetyushi, Russia (tÿt-yŏ′shĭ)	166	54.57N	48.50E
Teupitz, Ger. (toi′pĕtz)	145b	42.08N	13.37E
Tevere, r., Italy	148	42.30N	12.14E
Teverya, Isr.	181a	32.48N	35.32E
Tewksbury, Ma., U.S. (tūks′bĕr-ĭ)	93a	42.37N	71.14W
Texada Island, i., Can.	86	49.40N	124.24W
Texarkana, Ar., U.S. (tĕk-sär-kăn′ȧ)	97	33.26N	94.02W
Texarkana, Tx., U.S.	97	33.26N	94.04W
Texas, state, U.S.	96	31.00N	101.00W
Texas City, Tx., U.S.	113	29.23N	94.54W
Texcaltitlán, Mex. (tās-käl′tē-tlän′)	118	18.54N	99.51W
Texcoco, Mex. (tās-kō′kō)	118	19.31N	98.53W
Texcoco, Lago de, l., Mex.	119a	19.30N	99.00W
Texel, i., Neth. (tĕk′sĕl)	151	53.10N	4.45E
Texistepec, Mex. (tĕk-sēs-tă-pĕk′)	119	17.51N	94.46W
Texmelucan, Mex.	118	19.17N	98.26W
Texoma, Lake, res., U.S. (tĕk′ō-mă)	96	34.03N	96.28W
Texontepec, Mex. (tå-zōn-tå-pĕk′)	118	19.52N	98.48W
Texontepec de Aldama, Mex. (dā äl-dä′mä)	118	20.19N	99.19W
Teyateyaneng, Leso.	213c	29.11S	27.43E
Teykovo, Russia (tĕy-kô-vŏ)	166	56.52N	40.34E
Teziutlán, Mex. (tå-zē-o͞o-tlän′)	119	19.48N	97.21W
Tezpur, India	186	26.42N	92.52E
Tha-anne, r., Can.	84	60.50N	96.56W
Thabana Ntlenyana, mtn., Leso.	213c	29.28S	29.17E
Thabazimbi, S. Afr.	218d	24.36S	27.22E
Thailand, nation, Asia	196	16.30N	101.00E
Thailand, Gulf of, b., Asia	196	11.37N	100.46E
Thākurpukur, India	240a	22.28N	88.19E
Thale Luang, l., Thai.	196	7.51N	99.39E
Thame, Eng., U.K. (tām)	144b	51.43N	0.59W
Thames, r., Can. (tĕmz)	90	42.40N	81.45W
Thames, r., Eng., U.K.	142	51.30N	1.30W
Thames Ditton, Eng., U.K.	235	51.23N	0.21W
Thāmit, Wadi, r., Libya	149	30.39N	16.23E
Thāna, India (thä′nŭ)	186	19.13N	72.58E
Thāna Creek, r., India	187b	19.03N	72.58E
Thanh Hoa, Viet. (tän′hō′ȧ)	196	19.46N	105.42E
Thanjāvūr, India	183	10.51N	79.11E
Thann, Fr. (tän)	157	47.49N	7.05E
Thaon-les-Vosges, Fr. (tä-ôn-lā-vōzh′)	157	48.16N	6.24E
Thargomindah, Austl. (thár′gō-mĭn′dȧ)	203	27.58S	143.57E
Thásos, i., Grc. (thă′sŏs)	149	40.41N	24.53E
Thatch Cay, i., V.I.U.S. (thăch)	117c	18.22N	64.53W
Thatto Heath, Eng., U.K.	237a	53.26N	2.45W
Thaya, r., Eur. (tä′yȧ)	154	48.48N	15.40E
Thayer, Mo., U.S. (thâ′ẽr)	111	36.30N	91.34W
The Basin, Austl.	243b	37.51S	145.19E
Thebes *see* Thívai, Grc.	149	38.20N	23.18E
Thebes, hist., Egypt (thēbz)	211	25.47N	32.39E
The Brothers, mtn., Wa., U.S.	106a	47.39N	123.08W
The Capital, pt. of i., D.C., U.S.	229d	38.53N	77.00W
The Coorong, l., Austl. (kŏ′rŏng)	204	36.07S	139.45E
The Coteau, hills, Can.	88	51.10N	107.30W
The Dalles, Or., U.S. (dălz)	96	45.36N	121.10W
The Father, mtn., Pap. N. Gui.	197	5.05S	151.30E
The Hague ('s-Gravenhage), Neth.	142	52.05N	4.16E

PLACE (Pronunciation)	PAGE	Lat. °′	Long. °′
The Narrows, strt., N.Y., U.S.	228	40.37N	74.03W
The Oaks, Austl.	201b	34.04S	150.36E
Theodore, Austl. (thē′ō′dôr)	204	24.51S	150.09E
Theodore Roosevelt Dam, dam, Az., U.S. (thē-ô-dōr ro͞o-sȧ-vĕlt)	109	33.46N	111.25W
Theodore Roosevelt Lake, res., Az., U.S.	109	33.45N	111.00W
Theodore Roosevelt National Park, N.D., U.S.	102	47.20N	103.42W
Theológos, Grc.	161	40.37N	24.41E
The Oval, pt. of i., Eng., U.K.	235	51.29N	0.07W
The Pas, Can. (pä)	84	53.50N	101.15W
Thermopolis, Wy., U.S. (thẽr-mŏp′ō-lĭs)	105	43.38N	108.11W
The Round Mountain, mtn., Austl.	204	30.17S	152.19E
The Sound, strt., Austl.	243a	33.49S	151.17E
Thessalía, hist. reg., Grc.	161	39.50N	22.09E
Thessalon, Can.	85	46.11N	83.37W
Thessaloníki, Grc. (thĕs-sȧ-lô-nē′kē)	142	40.38N	22.59E
Thetford Mines, Can. (thĕt′fẽrd mīns)	91	46.05N	71.20W
The Twins, mtn., Afr. (twĭnz)	213c	30.09S	28.29E
Theunissen, S. Afr.	218d	28.25S	26.44E
Theydon Bois, Eng., U.K.	235	51.40N	0.06E
Thiais, Fr.	237c	48.46N	2.23E
Thibaudeau, Can. (tĭ′bō-dō′)	89	57.05N	94.08W
Thibodaux, La., U.S. (tē-bō-dō′)	113	29.48N	90.48W
Thief, l., Mn., U.S. (thēf)	102	48.32N	95.46W
Thief, r., Mn., U.S.	103	48.18N	96.07E
Thief River Falls, Mn., U.S. (thēf rĭv′ẽr fôlz)	102	48.07N	96.11W
Thiers, Fr. (tyâr)	156	45.51N	3.32E
Thiès, Sen. (tē-ĕs′)	210	14.48N	16.56W
Thika, Kenya	217	1.03S	37.05E
Thimphu, Bhu.	183	27.33N	89.42E
Thingvallavatn, l., Ice.	146	64.12N	20.22W
Thio, N. Cal.	198f	21.37S	166.14E
Thionville, Fr. (tyôN-vēl′)	147	49.23N	6.31E
Third Cataract, wtfl., Sudan	211	19.53N	30.11E
Thisted, Den. (tēs′tĕdh)	152	56.57N	8.38E
Thistilfjördur, b., Ice.	146	66.29N	14.59W
Thistle, i., Austl. (thĭs′′l)	204	34.55S	136.11E
Thistletown, neigh., Can.	227c	43.44N	79.33W
Thjórsá, r., Ice. (tyûr′sá)	146	64.23N	19.18W
Thohoyandou, S. Afr.	212	23.00S	30.29E
Tholen, Neth.	145a	51.32N	4.11E
Thomas, Ok., U.S. (tŏm′ăs)	110	35.44N	98.43W
Thomas, W.V., U.S.	99	39.15N	79.30W
Thomaston, Ga., U.S. (tŏm′ăs-tŭn)	114	32.51N	84.17W
Thomaston, N.Y., U.S.	228	40.47N	73.43W
Thomastown, Austl.	243b	37.41S	145.01E
Thomasville, Al., U.S. (tŏm′ăs-vĭl)	114	31.55N	87.43W
Thomasville, N.C., U.S.	115	35.52N	80.05W
Thomlinson, Mount, mtn., Can.	86	55.33N	127.29W
Thompson, Can.	84	55.48N	97.59W
Thompson, r., Can.	87	50.15N	121.20W
Thompson, r., Mo., U.S.	111	40.32N	93.49W
Thompson Falls, Mt., U.S.	104	47.35N	115.20W
Thomson, r., Austl. (tŏm-sŏn)	203	24.30S	143.07E
Thomson's Falls, Kenya	217	0.02N	36.22E
Thon Buri, neigh., Thai.	241f	13.43N	100.29E
Thong, Eng., U.K.	235	51.24N	0.24E
Thong Hoe, Sing.	240c	1.25N	103.42E
Thong-tay-hoi, Viet.	241j	10.50N	106.39E
Thonon-les-Bains, Fr. (tô-nôN′lȧ-băN′)	157	46.22N	6.27E
Thorigny-sur-Marne, Fr.	237c	48.53N	2.42E
Thornbury, Austl.	243b	37.45S	145.00E
Thorne, Eng., U.K. (thôrn)	144a	53.37N	0.58W
Thornhill, S. Afr.	244b	26.07S	28.09E
Thornleigh, Austl.	243a	33.44S	151.05E
Thornton, Eng., U.K.	237a	53.30N	3.00W
Thornton Hough, Eng., U.K.	237a	53.19N	3.03W
Thornton-le-Moors, Eng., U.K.	237a	53.16N	2.50W
Thorntown, In., U.S. (thôrn′tŭn)	98	40.05N	86.35W
Thornwood Common, Eng., U.K.	235	51.43N	0.08E
Thorold, Can. (thō′rōld)	91	43.13N	79.12W
Thouars, Fr. (to͞o-är′)	156	47.00N	0.17W
Thousand Islands, is., N.Y., U.S. (thou′zănd)	99	44.15N	76.10W
Thrace, hist. reg. (thrās)	161	41.20N	26.07E
Thrapston, Eng., U.K. (thrăp′stŭn)	144a	52.23N	0.32W
Three Forks, Mt., U.S. (thrē fôrks)	105	45.56N	111.35W
Three Oaks, Mi., U.S. (thrē ōks)	98	41.50N	86.40W
Three Points, Cape, c., Ghana	210	4.45N	2.06W
Three Rivers, Mi., U.S.	98	42.00N	83.40W
Thule, Grnld.	82	76.34N	68.47W
Thun, Switz. (to͞on)	154	46.46N	7.34E
Thunder Bay, Can.	90	48.28N	89.12W
Thunder Bay, b., Can. (thŭn′dẽr)	90	48.29N	88.52W
Thunder Hills, hills, Can.	88	54.30N	106.00W
Thunersee, l., Switz.	154	46.40N	7.30E
Thurber, Tx., U.S. (thûr′bẽr)	112	32.30N	98.23W
Thüringen (Thuringia), hist. reg., Ger. (tü′rĭng-ĕn)	154	51.07N	10.45E
Thurles, Ire. (thûrlz)	150	52.44N	7.45W
Thursday, i., Austl. (thûrz-dā)	203	10.17S	142.23E
Thurso, Can. (thŭn′sō)	83c	45.36N	75.15W
Thurso, Scot., U.K.	150	58.35N	3.40W
Thurston Island, i., Ant. (thûrs′tŭn)	219	71.20S	98.00W
Tiananmen, hist., China	240b	39.55N	116.23E
Tiandong, China (tĭĕn-dôŋ)	193	23.32N	107.10E
Tianjin, China	189	39.08N	117.14E
Tianjin Shi, China (tĭĕn-jyĭn shr)	192	39.30N	117.13E
Tianmen, China (tĭĕn-mŭn)	193	30.40N	113.10E
Tianshui, China (tĭĕn-shwā)	192	34.25N	105.40E
Tibagi, Braz. (tē′bȧ-zhē)	131	24.40S	50.35W
Tibasti, Sarir, des., Libya	211	24.00N	16.30E

PLACE (Pronunciation)	PAGE	Lat. °′	Long. °′
Tibati, Cam.	215	6.27N	12.38E
Tiber *see* Tevere, r., Italy	148	42.30N	12.14E
Tibesti, mts., Chad	211	20.40N	17.48E
Tibet *see* Xizang, prov., China (tĭ-bĕt′)	188	32.22N	83.30E
Tibnīn, Leb.	181a	33.12N	35.23E
Tiburon, Haiti	123	18.35N	74.25W
Tiburon, Ca., U.S. (tē-bo͞o-rōn′)	106b	37.53N	122.27W
Tiburon, Ca., U.S.	231b	36.04N	119.19W
Tiburón, i., Mex.	116	28.45N	113.10W
Tiburón, Cabo, c. (ká′bô)	121	8.42N	77.19W
Tiburon Island, i., Ca., U.S.	106b	37.52N	122.26W
Ticao Island, i., Phil. (tē-kä′ō)	197a	12.40N	123.30E
Tickhill, Eng., U.K. (tĭk′ĭl)	144a	53.26N	1.06W
Ticonderoga, N.Y., U.S. (tī-kŏn-dẽr-ō′gȧ)	99	43.50N	73.30W
Ticul, Mex. (tē-ko͞o′l)	120a	20.22N	89.32W
Tidaholm, Swe. (tē′dȧ-hōlm)	152	58.11N	13.53E
Tideswell, Eng., U.K. (tīdz′wĕl)	144a	53.17N	1.47W
Tidikelt, reg., Alg. (tē-dē-kĕlt′)	210	25.53N	2.11E
Tidjikdja, Maur. (tē-jĭk′jä)	210	18.33N	11.25W
Tidra, Île, i., Maur.	214	19.50N	16.45W
Tiefenbroich, Ger.	236	51.18N	6.49E
Tieling, China (tĭĕ-lĭŋ)	189	42.18N	123.50E
Tielmes, Spain (tyâl-màs′)	159a	40.15N	3.20W
Tienen, Bel.	145a	50.49N	4.58E
Tien Shan, mts., Asia	188	42.00N	78.46E
Tientsin *see* Tianjin, China	189	39.08N	117.14E
Tiergarten, neigh., Ger.	238a	52.31N	13.21E
Tierp, Swe. (tyĕrp)	152	60.21N	17.28E
Tierpoort, S. Afr.	213b	25.53N	28.26E
Tierra Blanca, Mex. (tyĕ′r-rä-blă′n-kä)	119	18.28N	96.19W
Tierra del Fuego, i., S.A. (tyĕr′rä dĕl fwā′gō)	132	53.50S	68.45W
Tiétar, r., Spain (tē-ā′tär)	158	39.56N	5.44W
Tiffin, Oh., U.S. (tĭf′ĭn)	98	41.10N	83.15W
Tifton, Ga., U.S. (tĭf′tŭn)	114	31.25N	83.34W
Tigard, Or., U.S. (tī′gärd)	106c	45.25N	122.46W
Tighina, Mol.	167	46.49N	29.29E
Tignish, Can. (tĭg′nĭsh)	92	46.57N	64.02W
Tigoda, r., Russia (tē′gô-dȧ)	172c	59.29N	31.15E
Tigre, r., Peru	130	2.20S	75.41W
Tigres, Península dos, pen., Ang. (pĕ-nē′ŋ-so͞o-lä-dōs-tē′grĕs)	212	16.30S	11.45E
Tigris, r., Asia	182	34.45N	44.10E
Tīh, Jabal at, mts., Egypt	181a	29.23N	34.05E
Tihert, Alg.	210	35.28N	1.15E
Tihuatlán, Mex. (tē-wä-tlän′)	119	20.43N	97.34W
Tijuana, Mex. (tē-hwä′nä)	116	32.32N	117.02W
Tijuca, Pico da, mtn., Braz. (pē′kō-dä-tē-zho͞o′kȧ)	132b	22.56S	43.17W
Tikal, hist., Guat. (tē-käl′)	120a	17.16N	89.49W
Tikhoretsk, Russia (tē-kôr-yĕtsk′)	167	45.55N	40.05E
Tikhvin, Russia (tēk-vēn′)	164	59.36N	33.38E
Tikrīt, Iraq	182	34.36N	43.31E
Tiksi, Russia (tēk-sē′)	165	71.42N	128.32E
Tilburg, Neth. (tĭl′bŭrg)	147	51.33N	5.05E
Tilbury, Eng., U.K.	144b	51.28N	0.23E
Tilemsi, Vallée du, val., Mali	214	17.50N	0.25E
Tilichiki, Russia (tyĭ-le-chĭ-kē)	165	60.49N	166.14E
Tilimsen, Alg.	210	34.53N	1.21W
Tillabéry, Niger (tē-yȧ-bā-rē′)	210	14.14N	1.30E
Tillamook, Or., U.S. (tĭl′ȧ-mo̤k)	104	45.27N	123.50W
Tillamook Bay, b., Or., U.S.	104	45.32N	124.26W
Tillberga, Swe. (tĕl-bĕr′ghȧ)	152	59.40N	16.34E
Tillsonburg, Can. (tĭl′sŭn-bûrg)	91	42.50N	80.50W
Tim, Russia (têm)	163	51.39N	37.07E
Timaru, N.Z. (tĭm′á-ro͞o)	203a	44.26S	171.17E
Timashevskaya, Russia (tēmä-shĕfs-kă′yä)	167	45.47N	38.57E
Timbalier Bay, b., La., U.S. (tĭm′bȧ-lēr)	113	28.55N	90.14W
Timber, Or., U.S. (tĭm′bẽr)	106c	45.43N	123.17W
Timberview, Md., U.S.	229c	39.13N	76.45W
Timbo, Gui. (tĭm′bō)	210	10.41N	11.51W
Timbuktu *see* Tombouctou, Mali	210	16.46N	3.01W
Times Square, pt. of i., N.Y., U.S.	228	40.45N874.00	W
Timétrine Monts, mts., Mali	214	19.50N	0.30W
Timimoun, Alg. (tē-mē-mo͞on′)	210	29.14N	0.22E
Timiris, Cap, c., Maur.	210	19.23N	16.32W
Timiş, r., Eur.	161	45.28N	21.06E
Timişoara, Rom.	149	45.44N	21.21E
Timmins, Can. (tĭm′ĭnz)	85	48.25N	81.22W
Timmonsville, S.C., U.S. (tĭm′ŭnz-vĭl)	115	34.09N	79.55W
Timok, r., Eur.	161	43.35N	22.13E
Timor, i., Indon. (tē-mōr′)	197	10.08S	125.00E
Timor Sea, sea	202	12.40S	125.00E
Timpanogos Cave National Monument, rec., Ut., U.S. (tĭ-măn′ō-gōz)	109	40.25N	111.45W
Timperley, Eng., U.K.	237b	53.24N	2.19W
Timpson, Tx., U.S. (tĭmp′sŭn)	113	31.55N	94.24W
Timsāh, l., Egypt (tĭm′sä)	218b	30.34N	32.22E
Tina, r., S. Afr. (tē′nȧ)	213c	30.50S	28.44E
Tina, Monte, mtn., Dom. Rep. (mô′n-tĕ-tē′nȧ)	123	18.50N	70.40W
Tinaguillo, Ven. (tē-nä-gē′l-yō)	131b	9.55N	68.18W
Tīnah, Khalīj at, b., Egypt	181a	31.06N	32.42E
Tindouf, Alg. (tĕn-do͞of′)	210	27.43N	7.44W
Tinggi, i., Malay.	181b	2.16N	104.16E
Tinghert, Plateau du, plat., Alg.	210	27.30N	7.30E
Tingi Mountains, mts., S.L.	214	9.00N	10.50W
Ting Kau, H.K.	241c	22.23N	114.04E
Tinglin, China	191b	30.53N	121.18E
Tingo María, Peru (tē′ngô-mä-rē′ä)	130	9.15S	76.04W
Tingréla, C. Iv.	214	10.29N	6.24W
Tingsryd, Swe. (tĭngs′rüd)	152	56.32N	14.58E
Tinguindio, Mex.	118	19.38N	102.02W
Tinguiririca, r., Chile (tē′n-gē-rē-rē′kä)	129b	34.48S	70.45W

ăt; finăl; rāte; senāte; ärm; åsk; sofȧ; fâre; ch-choose; dh-as th in other; bē; ēvent; bĕt; recĕnt; cratẽr; g-gō; gh-guttural g; bĭt; ĭ-short neutral; rīde; κ-guttural k as ch in German ich;

PLACE (Pronunciation)	PAGE	Lat. °′	Long. °′
Tosya, Tur. (tôz'yà)	149	41.00N	34.00E
Totana, Spain (tō-tä-nä)	158	37.45N	1.28W
Tot'ma, Russia (tôt'mà)	166	60.00N	42.20E
Totness, Sur.	131	5.51N	56.17W
Totonicapán, Guat. (tōtō-nē-kä'pän)	116	14.55N	91.20W
Totoras, Arg. (tō-tō'räs)	129c	32.33S	61.13W
Totowa, N.J., U.S.	228	40.54N	74.13W
Totsuka, Japan (tōt'sōō-kä)	195a	35.24N	139.32E
Tottenham, Eng., U.K. (tŏt'ĕn-ăm)	144b	51.35N	0.06W
Tottenville, neigh., N.Y., U.S.	228	40.31N	74.15W
Totteridge, neigh., Eng., U.K.	235	51.38N	0.12W
Tottington, Eng., U.K.	237b	53.37N	2.20W
Tottori, Japan (tô'tô-rē)	189	35.30N	134.15E
Touba, C. Iv.	214	8.17N	7.41W
Touba, Sen.	214	14.51N	15.53W
Toubkal, Jebel, mtn., Mor.	210	31.15N	7.46W
Tougan, Burkina	214	13.04N	3.04W
Touggourt, Alg. (tò-gōōrt') (tōō-gōōr')	210	33.09N	6.07E
Touil, Oued, r., Alg. (tōō-ēl')	148	34.42N	2.16E
Toul, Fr. (tōōl)	147	48.39N	5.51E
Toulon, Fr. (tōō-lôn')	142	43.09N	5.54E
Toulouse, Fr. (tōō-lōōz')	142	43.37N	1.27E
Toungoo, Myanmar (tō-ŏŋ-gōō')	196	19.00N	96.29E
Tourcoing, Fr. (tòr-kwăn')	147	50.44N	3.06E
Tournan-en-Brie, Fr. (tōōr-nän-ĕn-brē')	157b	48.45N	2.47E
Tours, Fr. (tōōr)	142	47.23N	0.39E
Touside, Pic, mtn., Chad (tōō-sē-dā')	211	21.10N	16.30E
Toussus-le-Noble, Fr.	237c	48.45N	2.07E
Tovdalselva, r., Nor. (tôv-däls-ĕlvà)	152	58.23N	8.16E
Towaco, N.J., U.S.	228	40.56N	74.21W
Towanda, Pa., U.S. (tō-wän'dà)	99	41.45N	76.30W
Tower Hamlets, neigh., Eng., U.K.	235	51.32N	0.03W
Tower of London, pt. of i., Eng., U.K.	235	51.30N	0.05W
Towers of Silence, rel., India	240e	18.58N	72.48E
Town Bluff Lake, l., Tx., U.S.	113	30.52N	94.30W
Towner, N.D., U.S. (tou'nēr)	102	48.21N	100.24W
Town Reach, strt., Asia	240c	1.28N	103.44E
Townsend, Ma., U.S. (toun'zĕnd)	93a	42.41N	71.42W
Townsend, Mt., U.S.	105	46.19N	111.35W
Townsend, Mount, mtn., Wa., U.S.	106a	47.52N	123.03W
Townsville, Austl. (tounz'vĭl)	203	19.18S	146.50E
Towson, Md., U.S. (tou'sŭn)	100e	39.24N	76.36W
Towuti, Danau, l., Indon. (tō-wōō'tē)	196	3.00S	121.45E
Toxkan, r., China	188	40.34N	77.15E
Toyah, Tx., U.S. (tô'yà)	112	31.19N	103.46W
Toyama, Japan (tō'yä-mä)	189	36.42N	137.14E
Toyama-Wan, b., Japan	195	36.58N	137.16E
Toyoda, Japan	242a	35.39N	139.23E
Toyohashi, Japan (tō'yō-hä'shē)	194	34.44N	137.21E
Toyonaka, Japan (tō'yō-nä'kà)	195b	34.47N	135.28E
Tozeur, Tun. (tō-zûr')	148	33.59N	8.11E
Traar, neigh., Ger.	236	51.23N	6.36E
Trabzon, Tur. (tràb'zòn)	182	41.00N	39.45E
Tracy, Can.	91	46.00N	73.13W
Tracy, Ca., U.S. (trā'sē)	108	37.45N	121.27W
Tracy, Mn., U.S.	102	44.13N	95.37W
Tracy City, Tn., U.S.	114	35.15N	85.44W
Trafalgar, Cabo, c., Spain (kà'bô-trä-fäl-gä'r)	158	36.10N	6.02W
Trafaria, Port.	238d	38.40N	9.14W
Trafford Park, Eng., U.K.	237b	53.28N	2.20W
Trafonomby, mtn., Madag.	213	24.32S	46.35E
Trail, Can. (trāl)	84	49.06N	117.42W
Traisen, r., Aus.	145e	48.15N	15.55E
Traiskirchen, Aus.	145e	48.01N	16.18E
Trakai, Lith. (trá-káy)	153	54.38N	24.59E
Trakiszki, Pol. (trá-kē'-sh-kē)	155	54.16N	23.07E
Tralee, Ire. (trà-lē')	147	52.16N	9.20W
Tranås, Swe. (trän'ôs)	152	58.03N	14.56E
Trancoso, Port. (träŋ-kō'sò)	158	40.46N	7.23W
Trangan, Pulau, i., Indon. (träŋ'gän)	197	6.52S	133.30E
Trani, Italy (trä'nē)	160	41.15N	16.25E
Tranmere, Eng., U.K.	237a	53.23N	3.01W
Transylvania, hist. reg., Rom. (trăn-sĭl-vā'nĭ-à)	155	46.30N	22.35E
Trapani, Italy	148	38.01N	12.31E
Trappes, Fr. (tràp)	157b	48.47N	2.01E
Traralgon, Austl. (trä'răl-gŏn)	204	38.15S	146.33E
Trarza, reg., Maur.	214	17.35N	15.15W
Trasimeno, Lago, l., Italy (lä'gō trä-sē-mā'nō)	160	43.00N	12.12E
Trás-os-Montes, hist. reg., Port. (träzh'ōzh môn'tāzh)	148	41.33N	7.13W
Traun, r., Aus. (troun)	154	48.10N	14.15E
Traunstein, Ger. (troun'stīn)	154	47.52N	12.38E
Traverse, Lake, l., Mn., U.S. (trăv'ērs)	102	45.46N	96.53W
Traverse City, Mi., U.S.	98	44.45N	85.40W
Travnik, Bos. (träv'nēk)	161	44.13N	17.43E
Treasure Island, i., Ca., U.S. (trĕzh'ēr)	106b	37.49N	122.22W
Trebbin, Ger. (trĕ'bēn)	145b	52.13N	13.13E
Trebinje, Bos. (trå'bēn-yĕ)	161	42.43N	18.21E
Trebišov, Slvk. (trĕ'bē-shôf)	155	48.36N	21.32E
Tregrosse Islands, is., Austl. (trē-grōs')	203	18.08S	150.53E
Treinta y Tres, Ur. (trå-ēn'tä ē träs')	132	33.14S	54.17W
Trelew, Arg. (trē'lū)	132	43.15S	65.25W
Trelleborg, Swe.	152	55.24N	13.07E
Tremblay-lès-Gonnesse, Fr.	237c	48.59N	2.34E
Tremiti, Isole, is., Italy (ē'sō-lĕ trā-mē'tē)	160	42.07N	16.33E
Tremont, neigh., N.Y., U.S.	228	40.51N	73.55W
Trenčín, Czech Rep. (trĕn'chēn)	147	48.52N	18.02E
Trenque Lauquén, Arg. (trĕn'kĕ-lâ'ō-kĕ'n)	132	35.50S	62.44W
Trent, r., Can. (trĕnt)	91	44.15N	77.55W
Trent, r., Eng., U.K.	144a	53.25N	0.45W
Trent and Mersey Canal, can., Eng., U.K. (trĕnt) (mûr zē)	144a	53.11N	2.24W
Trentino-Alto Adige, hist. reg., Italy	160	46.16N	10.47E
Trento, Italy (trĕn'tô)	148	46.04N	11.07E
Trenton, Can. (trĕn'tŭn)	85	44.05N	77.35W
Trenton, Can.	93	45.37N	62.38W
Trenton, Mi., U.S.	101b	42.08N	83.12W
Trenton, Mo., U.S.	111	40.05N	93.36W
Trenton, N.J., U.S.	97	40.13N	74.46W
Trenton, Tn., U.S.	114	35.57N	88.55W
Trepassey, Can. (trē-păs'ē)	93	46.44N	53.22W
Trepassey Bay, b., Can.	93	46.40N	53.20W
Treptow, neigh., Ger.	238a	52.29N	13.29E
Tres Arroyos, Arg. (träs'är-rō'yōs)	132	38.18S	60.16W
Três Corações, Braz. (trĕ's kō-rä-zô'ĕs)	129a	21.41S	45.14W
Tres Cumbres, Mex. (trĕ's kōō'm-brĕs)	119a	19.03N	99.14W
Três Lagoas, Braz. (trĕ's lä-gô'ás)	131	20.48S	51.42W
Três Marias, Reprêsa, res., Braz.	131	18.15S	45.30W
Tres Morros, Alto de, mtn., Col. (á'l-tō dĕ trĕ's mô'r-rôs)	130a	7.08N	76.10W
Três Pontas, Braz. (trĕ'pô'n-täs)	129a	21.22S	45.30W
Três Pontas, Cabo das, c., Ang.	216	10.23S	13.32E
Três Rios, Braz. (trĕ's rē'ōs)	129a	22.07S	43.13W
Très-Saint Rédempteur, Can. (săn rā-dänp-tûr')	83a	45.26N	74.23W
Tressancourt, Fr.	237c	48.55N	2.00E
Treuenbrietzen, Ger. (troi'ĕn-brē-tzĕn)	145b	52.06N	12.52E
Treviglio, Italy (trā-vē'lyô)	160	45.30N	9.34E
Treviso, Italy (trĕ-vē'sō)	148	45.39N	12.15E
Trichardt, S. Afr. (trĭ-κärt')	218d	26.32N	29.16E
Triel-sur-Seine, Fr.	237c	48.59N	2.00E
Trier, Ger.	147	49.45N	6.38E
Trieste, Italy (trē-ĕs'tä)	142	45.39N	13.48E
Triglav, mtn., Slvn.	160	46.23N	13.50E
Trigueros, Spain (trē-gā'rōs)	158	37.23N	6.50W
Tríkala, Grc.	149	39.33N	21.49E
Trikora, Puncak, mtn., Indon.	197	4.15S	138.45E
Trim Creek, r., Il., U.S. (trĭm)	101a	41.19N	87.39W
Trincomalee, Sri L. (trĭŋ-kō-mà-lē')	183b	8.39N	81.12E
Tring, Eng., U.K. (trĭng)	144b	51.46N	0.40W
Trinidad, Bol. (trē-nē-dhädh')	130	14.48S	64.43W
Trinidad, Cuba (trē-nē-dhädh')	117	21.50N	80.00W
Trinidad, Co., U.S. (trĭn'ĭdăd)	96	37.11N	104.31W
Trinidad, Ur.	132	33.29S	56.55W
Trinidad, i., Trin. (trĭn'ĭ-dăd)	131	10.00N	61.00W
Trinidad, r., Pan.	116a	8.55N	80.01W
Trinidad, Sierra de, mts., Cuba (sē-ĕ'r-rà dĕ trē-nē-dä'd)	122	21.50N	79.55W
Trinidad and Tobago, nation, N.A. (trĭn'ĭ-dăd) (tô-bā'gō)	117	11.00N	61.00W
Trinitaria, Mex. (trē-nē-tä'ryä)	119	16.09N	92.04W
Trinity, Can. (trĭn'ĭ-tē)	93	48.59N	53.55W
Trinity, Tx., U.S.	113	30.52N	95.27W
Trinity, is., Ak., U.S.	95	56.25N	153.15W
Trinity, r., Ca., U.S.	104	40.50N	123.20W
Trinity, r., Tx., U.S.	97	30.50N	95.09W
Trinity, East Fork, r., Tx., U.S.	111	33.24N	96.42W
Trinity, West Fork, r., Tx., U.S.	110	33.22N	98.26W
Trinity Bay, b., Can.	85	48.00N	53.40W
Trino, Italy (trē'nô)	160	45.11N	8.16E
Trion, Ga., U.S. (trī'ŏn)	114	34.32N	85.18W
Tripoli (Tarābulus), Libya	211	32.50N	13.13E
Trípolis, Grc. (trĭ'pô-lĭs)	149	37.32N	22.32E
Tripolitania see Tarābulus, hist. reg., Libya	210	31.00N	12.26E
Tripura, state, India	183	24.00N	92.00E
Tristan da Cunha Islands, is., St. Hel. (três-tän'dä kōōn'yà)	2	35.30S	12.15W
Triste, Golfo, b., Ven. (gôl-fô trē's-tē)	131b	10.40N	68.05W
Triticus Reservoir, res., N.Y., U.S. (trī tĭ-cŭs)	100a	41.20N	73.36W
Trivandrum, India (trē-vŭn'drŭm)	183b	8.34N	76.58E
Trnava, Slvk. (t'r'nà-vá)	155	48.22N	17.34E
Trobriand Islands, is., Pap. N. Gui. (trō-brē-ănd')	197	8.25S	151.45E
Trogir, Cro. (trô'gēr)	160	43.32N	16.17E
Troice-Lykovo, neigh., Russia	239b	55.47N	37.24E
Trois Fourches, Cap des, c., Mor.	158	35.28N	2.58W
Trois-Rivières, Can. (trwä'rē-vyâ')	85	46.21N	72.35W
Troitsk, Russia (trô'ĭtsk)	170	54.06N	61.35E
Troitsko-Pechorsk, Russia (trô'ĭtsk-ô-pyĕ-chôrsk')	164	62.18N	56.07E
Trollhättan, Swe. (trôl'hĕt-ĕn)	146	58.17N	12.17E
Trollheimen, mts., Nor. (trôll-hĕĭm)	152	62.48N	9.05E
Trombay, neigh., India	240e	19.02N	72.57E
Trona, Ca., U.S. (trō'nà)	108	35.49N	117.20W
Tronador, Cerro, mtn., S.A. (sĕ'r-rô trō-nä'dôr)	132	41.17S	71.56W
Troncoso, Mex. (trôn-kō'sō)	118	22.43N	102.22W
Trondheim, Nor. (trôn'hâm)	142	63.25N	11.35E
Tropar'ovo, neigh., Russia	239b	55.39N	37.29E
Trosa, Swe. (trô'sä)	152	58.54N	17.25E
Trottiscliffe, Eng., U.K.	235	51.19N	0.21E
Trout, l., Can.	84	61.10N	121.30W
Trout, l., Can.	85	51.16N	92.46W
Trout Creek, r., Or., U.S.	104	42.18N	118.31W
Troutdale, Or., U.S. (trout'dāl)	106c	45.32N	122.23W
Trout Lake, Mi., U.S.	103	46.20N	85.02W
Trouville, Fr. (trōō-vēl')	156	49.23N	0.05E
Troy, Al., U.S. (troi)	114	31.47N	85.46W
Troy, Il., U.S.	107e	38.44N	89.53W
Troy, Ks., U.S.	111	39.46N	95.07W
Troy, Mo., U.S.	110	38.56N	99.57W
Troy, Mt., U.S.	104	48.28N	115.56W
Troy, N.Y., U.S.	97	42.45N	73.45W
Troy, N.C., U.S.	115	35.21N	79.58W
Troy, Oh., U.S.	98	40.00N	84.10W
Troy, hist., Tur.	182	39.59N	26.14E
Troyes, Fr. (trwä)	147	48.18N	4.03E
Troyits'ke, Ukr.	163	47.39N	30.16E
Trstenik, Yugo. (t'r'stĕ-nēk)	149	43.36N	21.00E
Trubchëvsk, Russia (tròp'chĕfsk)	167	52.36N	33.46E
Trucial States see United Arab Emirates, nation, Asia	182	24.00N	54.00E
Truckee, Ca., U.S. (trŭk'ē)	108	39.20N	120.12W
Truckee, r., Ca., U.S.	108	39.25N	120.07W
Truganina, Austl.	201a	37.49N	144.44E
Trujillo, Col. (trò-κē'l-yō)	130a	4.10N	76.20W
Trujillo, Peru	130	8.08S	79.00W
Trujillo, Spain (trōō-κē'l-yô)	148	39.27N	5.50W
Trujillo, Ven.	130	9.15N	70.28W
Trujillo, r., Mex.	118	23.12N	103.10W
Trujin, Lago, l., Dom. Rep. (trōō-κēn')	123	17.45N	71.25W
Truk Islands, is., Micron.	198c	7.25N	151.47E
Trumann, Ar., U.S. (trōō'măn)	111	35.41N	90.31W
Trŭn, Bul. (trŭn)	161	42.49N	22.39E
Truro, Can. (trōō'rō)	85	45.22N	63.16W
Truro, Eng., U.K.	150	50.17N	5.05W
Trussville, Al., U.S. (trŭs'vĭl)	100h	33.37N	86.37W
Truth or Consequences, N.M., U.S. (trōōth ŏr kŏn'sē-kwĕn-sĭs)	109	33.10N	107.20W
Trutnov, Czech Rep. (tròt'nôf)	154	50.36N	15.36E
Trzcianka, Pol. (tchyän'kà)	154	53.02N	16.27E
Trzebiatów, Pol. (tchĕ-byä'tò-v)	154	54.03N	15.16E
Tsaidam Basin, basin, China (tsī-däm)	188	37.19N	94.08E
Tsala Apopka Lake, r., Fl., U.S. (tsä'lá ă-pŏp'ká)	115	28.57N	82.11W
Tsast Bogd, mtn., Mong.	188	46.44N	92.34E
Tsavo National Park, rec., Kenya	217	2.35S	38.45E
Tsawwassen Indian Reserve, I.R., Can.	106d	49.03N	123.11W
Tsentral'nyy-Kospashskiy, Russia (tsĕn-träl'nyĭ-kôs-pàsh'skĭ)	172a	59.03N	57.48E
Tshela, Zaire (tshā'là)	212	4.59S	12.56E
Tshikapa, Zaire (tshē-kä'pä)	212	6.25S	20.48E
Tshofa, Zaire	217	5.14S	25.15E
Tshuapa, r., Zaire	212	0.30S	22.00E
Tsiafajovona, mtn., Madag.	213	19.17S	47.27E
Tsing Island, i., H.K.	241c	22.21N	114.05E
Tsin Shui Wan, b., H.K.	241c	22.13N	114.10E
Tsiribihina, r., Madag. (tsē'rē-bē-hē-nä')	213	19.45S	43.30E
Tsitsa, r., S. Afr. (tsē'tsà)	213c	31.28S	28.53E
Tskhinvali, Geor.	168	42.13N	43.56E
Tsolo, S. Afr. (tsō'lō)	213c	31.19S	28.47E
Tsomo, S. Afr.	213c	32.03S	27.49E
Tsomo, r., S. Afr.	213c	31.53S	27.48E
Tsu, Japan (tsōō)	194	34.42N	136.31E
Tsuchiura, Japan (tsōō'chē-ōō-rä)	195	36.04N	140.09E
Tsuda, Japan (tsōō'dä)	195b	34.48N	135.43E
Tsugaru Kaikyō, strt., Japan	189	41.25N	140.20E
Tsukumono, neigh., Japan	242b	34.50N	135.11E
Tsumeb, Nmb. (tsōō'mĕb)	212	19.10S	17.45E
Tsunashima, Japan (tsōō'nä-shē'mä)	195a	35.32N	139.37E
Tsuruga, Japan (tsōō'rò-gä)	194	35.39N	136.04E
Tsurugi San, mtn., Japan (tsōō'rò-gē sän)	194	33.52N	134.07E
Tsurumi, r., Japan	242a	35.29N	139.41E
Tsuruoka, Japan (tsōō'rò-ō'kä)	194	38.43N	139.51E
Tsurusaki, Japan (tsōō'rò-sä'kē)	195	33.15N	131.42E
Tsu Shima, is., Japan (tsōō shē'mä)	189	34.28N	129.30E
Tsushima Strait, strt., Asia	189	34.00N	129.00E
Tsu Wan (Quanwan), H.K.	241c	22.22N	114.07E
Tsuwano, Japan (tsōō'wà-nō')	195	34.28N	131.47E
Tsuyama, Japan (tsōō'yä-mä')	194	35.05N	134.00E
Tua, r., Port. (tōō'ä)	158	41.23N	7.18W
Tualatin, r., Or., U.S. (tōō'á-lā-tĭn)	106c	45.25N	122.54W
Tuamoto, Îles, Fr. Poly. (tōō-ä-mō'tōō)	225	19.00S	141.20W
Tuapse, Russia (tò'áp-sē)	167	44.00N	39.10E
Tuareg, hist. reg., Alg.	210	21.26N	2.51E
Tubarão, Braz. (tōō-bä-rouN')	132	28.23N	48.56W
Tübingen, Ger. (tü'bĭng-ĕn)	154	48.33N	9.05E
Tubinskiy, Russia (tû bĭn'skĭ)	172a	52.53N	58.15E
Tubruq, Libya	211	32.03N	24.04E
Tucacas, Ven. (tōō-kä'käs)	130	10.48N	68.20W
Tuckahoe, N.Y., U.S.	228	40.57N	73.50W
Tucker, Ga., U.S. (tŭk'ēr)	100c	33.51N	84.13W
Tucson, Az., U.S. (tōō-sŏn')	96	32.15N	111.00W
Tucumán, Arg. (tōō-kōō-män')	132	26.52S	65.08W
Tucumán, prov., Arg.	132	26.30S	65.30W
Tucumcari, N.M., U.S. (tò'kŭm-kâr-ē)	110	35.11N	103.43W
Tucupita, Ven. (tōō-kōō-pē'tä)	130	9.00N	62.09W
Tudela, Spain (tōō-dhā'lä)	148	42.03N	1.37W
Tugaloo, r., Ga., U.S. (tŭg'à-lōō)	114	34.35N	83.05W
Tugela, r., S. Afr. (tōō-gel'à)	213c	28.50S	30.52E
Tugela Ferry, S. Afr.	213c	28.44S	30.27E
Tug Fork, r., U.S. (tŭg)	98	37.50N	82.30W
Tuguegarao, Phil. (tōō-gā-gà-rä'ō)	196	17.37N	121.44E
Tuhai, r., China (tōō-hī)	190	37.05N	116.56E
Tuinplaas, S. Afr.	218d	24.54S	28.46E
Tujunga, Ca., U.S. (tōō-jŭŋ'gà)	107a	34.15N	118.16W
Tukan, Russia (tōō'kàn)	172a	53.52N	57.25E
Tukangbesi, Kepulauan, is., Indon.	197	6.00S	124.15E
Tūkrah, Libya	211	32.34N	20.47E
Tuktoyaktuk, Can.	84	69.32N	132.37W
Tukums, Lat. (tò'kòms)	166	56.57N	23.09E
Tukuyu, Tan. (tōō-kōō'yä)	212	9.13S	33.43E
Tukwila, Wa., U.S. (tŭk'wĭ-là)	106a	47.28N	122.16W
Tula, Mex. (tōō'lä)	118	20.04N	99.22W
Tula, Russia (tōō'là)	166	54.12N	37.37E
Tula, prov., Russia	162	53.45N	37.19E
Tula, r., Mex.	118	20.40N	99.27W

PRONOUNCING INDEX

Tulagai–Uman' 359

PLACE (Pronunciation)	PAGE	Lat. °'	Long. °'
Tulagai, i., Sol.Is. (to͞o-lä'gē)	203	9.15S	160.17E
Tulaghi, Sol.Is.	198e	9.06S	160.09E
Tulalip, Wa., U.S. (tū-lā'lĭp)	106a	48.04N	122.18W
Tulalip Indian Reservation, I.R., Wa., U.S.	106a	48.06N	122.16W
Tulancingo, Mex. (to͞o-län-sĭŋ'gō)	116	20.04N	98.24W
Tulangbawang, r., Indon.	196	4.17S	105.00E
Tulare, Ca., U.S. (to͞o-lä'rȧ) (tul-âr')	108	36.12N	119.22W
Tulare Lake Bed, l., Ca., U.S.	108	35.57N	120.18W
Tularosa, N.M., U.S. (to͞o-lȧ-rō'zȧ)	109	33.05N	106.05W
Tulcán, Ec. (to͞ol-kän')	130	0.44N	77.52W
Tulcea, Rom. (tòl'chȧ)	149	45.10N	28.47E
Tul'chyn, Ukr.	167	48.42N	28.53E
Tulcingo, Mex. (to͞ol-sĭŋ'gō)	118	18.03N	98.27W
Tule, r., Ca., U.S. (to͞ol'lȧ)	108	36.08N	118.50W
Tule River Indian Reservation, I.R., Ca., U.S. (to͞o'lȧ)	108	36.05N	118.35W
Tuli, Zimb. (to͞o'lė)	212	20.58S	29.12E
Tulia, Tx., U.S. (to͞o'lĭ-ȧ)	110	34.32N	101.46W
Tulik Volcano, vol., Ak., U.S. (tò'lĭk)	95a	53.28N	168.10W
Tūlkarm, W. Bank (to͞ol kärm)	181a	32.19N	35.02E
Tullahoma, Tn., U.S. (tŭl-ȧ-hō'mȧ)	114	35.21N	86.12W
Tullamarine, Austl.	243b	37.41S	144.52E
Tullamore, Ire. (tŭl-ȧ-mōr')	150	53.15N	7.29W
Tulle, Fr. (tül)	156	45.15N	1.45E
Tulln, Aus. (tòln)	154	48.21N	16.04E
Tullner Feld, reg., Aus.	145e	48.20N	15.59E
Tulpetlac, Mex. (to͞ol-pȧ-tlȧk')	119a	19.33N	99.04W
Tulsa, Ok., U.S. (tŭl'sȧ)	97	36.08N	95.58W
Tulum, Mex. (to͞o-lò'm)	120a	20.17N	87.26W
Tulun, Russia (tò-lo͞on')	165	54.29N	100.43E
Tuma, r., Nic. (to͞o'mä)	120	13.07N	85.32W
Tumba, Lac, l., Zaire (tòm'bä)	212	0.50S	17.45E
Tumbes, Peru (to͞o'm-bĕs)	130	3.39S	80.27W
Tumbiscatío, Mex. (to͞om-bė-skȧ-tē'ō)	118	18.32N	102.23W
Tumbo, i., Can.	106d	48.49N	123.04W
Tumen, China (to͞o-mŭn)	192	43.00N	129.50E
Tumen, r., Asia	194	42.08N	128.40E
Tumeremo, Ven. (to͞o-må-rā'mō)	131	7.15N	61.28W
Tumkūr, India	187	13.22N	77.05E
Tumuacacori National Monument, rec., Az., U.S. (to͞o-mä-kä'kå-rē)	109	31.36N	110.20W
Tumuc-Humac Mountains, mts., S.A. (to͞o-mòk'o͞o-mäk')	131	2.15N	54.50W
Tunas de Zaza, Cuba (to͞o'näs dā zä'zä)	122	21.40N	79.35W
Tunbridge Wells, Eng., U.K. (tŭn'brĭj welz')	151	51.05N	0.09E
Tunduru, Tan.	217	11.07S	37.21E
Tungabhadra Reservoir, res., India	187	15.26N	75.57E
Tuni, India	187	17.29N	82.38E
Tunica, Ms., U.S. (tū'nĭ-kȧ)	114	34.41N	90.23W
Tunis, Tun. (tū'nĭs)	210	36.59N	10.06E
Tunis, Golfe de, b., Tun.	148	37.06N	10.43E
Tunisia, nation, Afr. (tu-nĭzh'ė-ȧ)	210	35.00N	10.11E
Tunja, Col. (to͞o'n-hȧ)	130	5.32N	73.19W
Tunkhannock, Pa., U.S. (tŭnk-hăn'ŭk)	99	41.35N	75.55W
Tunnel, r., Wa., U.S. (tŭn'ĕl)	106a	47.48N	123.04W
Tuoji Dao, i., China (twô-jyē dou)	190	38.11N	120.45E
Tuolumne, r., Ca., U.S. (twô-lŭm'nė)	108	37.35N	120.37W
Tuostakh, r., Russia	171	67.09N	137.30E
Tupelo, Ms., U.S. (tū'pė-lō)	114	34.14N	88.43W
Tupinambaranas, Ilha, i., Braz.	131	3.04S	58.09W
Tupiza, Bol. (to͞o-pē'zä)	130	21.26S	65.43W
Tupper Lake, N.Y., U.S. (tŭp'ẽr)	99	44.15N	74.25W
Tüpqaraghan tübek, pen., Kaz.	170	44.30N	50.40E
Tupungato, Cerro, vol., S.A.	132	33.30S	69.52W
Tuquerres, Col. (to͞o-kĕ'r-rĕs)	130	1.12N	77.44W
Tura, Russia (tòr'ȧ)	165	64.08N	99.58E
Turbio, r., Mex. (to͞or-byȯ)	118	20.28N	101.40W
Turbo, Col. (to͞o'bō)	130	8.02N	76.43W
Turda, Rom. (tòr'dȧ)	155	46.35N	23.47E
Turfan Depression, depr., China	188	42.16N	90.00E
Turffontein, neigh., S. Afr.	213b	26.15S	28.02E
Tŭrgovishte, Bul.	161	43.14N	26.36E
Turgutlu, Tur.	167	38.30N	27.20E
Türi, Est. (tü'rĭ)	153	58.49N	25.29E
Turia, r., Spain (to͞o'ryä)	158	40.12N	1.18W
Turicato, Mex. (to͞o-rė-kä'tō)	118	19.03N	101.24W
Turiguano, i., Cuba (to͞o-rė-gwä'nō)	122	22.20N	78.35W
Turin, Italy	142	45.05N	7.44E
Turiya, r., Ukr.	155	51.18N	24.55E
Turka, Ukr. (tòr'kȧ)	155	49.10N	23.02E
Turkey, nation, Asia	143	38.45N	32.00E
Turkey, r., Ia., U.S. (tûrk'ė)	103	43.20N	92.16W
Türkistan, Kaz.	169	44.00N	68.00E
Turkmenistan, nation, Asia	164	40.46N	56.01E
Turks, is., T./C. Is. (tûrks)	117	21.40N	71.45W
Turks Island Passage, strt., T./C. Is.	123	21.15N	71.25W
Turku, Fin. (tòrgokò)	142	60.28N	22.12E
Turlock, Ca., U.S. (tûr'lŏk)	108	37.30N	120.51W
Turneffe, i., Belize	116	17.25N	87.43W
Turner, Ks., U.S. (tûr'nẽr)	107f	39.05N	94.42W
Turner Sound, strt., Bah.	122	24.20N	78.05W
Turners Peninsula, pen., S.L.	214	7.20N	12.40W
Turnhout, Bel. (tŭrn-hout')	151	51.19N	4.58E
Turnov, Czech Rep. (tòr'nôf)	154	50.36N	15.12E
Turnu Măgurele, Rom.	149	43.54N	24.49E
Turpan, China (to͞o-är-pän)	188	43.06N	88.41E
Turquino, Pico, mtn., Cuba (pē'kō dā to͞or-kē'nō)	122	20.00N	76.50W
Turramurra, Austl.	243a	33.44S	151.08E
Turrialba, C.R. (to͞or-ryä'l-bä)	121	9.54N	83.41W
Turtkul', Uzb. (tòrt-kòl')	169	41.28N	61.02E
Turtle, r., Can.	89	49.20N	92.30W
Turtle Bay, b., Tx., U.S.	113a	29.48N	94.38W
Turtle Creek, Pa., U.S.	230b	40.25N	79.49W
Turtle Creek, r., S.D., U.S.	102	44.40N	98.53W
Turtle Mountain Indian Reservation, I.R., N.D., U.S.	102	48.45N	99.57W
Turtle Mountains, mts., N.D., U.S.	102	48.57N	100.11W
Turukhansk, Russia (to͞o-ro͞o-ĸänsk')	164	66.03N	88.39E
Tuscaloosa, Al., U.S. (tŭs-kȧ-lo͞o'sȧ)	97	33.10N	87.35W
Tuscarora, Nv., U.S. (tŭs-kȧ-rō'rȧ)	104	41.18N	116.15W
Tuscarora Indian Reservation, I.R., N.Y., U.S.	101c	43.10N	78.51W
Tuscola, Il., U.S. (tŭs-kō-lȧ)	98	39.50N	88.20W
Tuscumbia, Al., U.S. (tŭs-kŭm'bĭ-ȧ)	114	34.41N	87.42W
Tushino, Russia (to͞o'shĭ-nô)	172b	55.51N	37.24E
Tuskegee, Al., U.S. (tŭs-kē'gė)	114	32.25N	85.40W
Tustin, Ca., U.S. (tŭs'tĭn)	107a	33.44N	117.49W
Tutayev, Russia (to͞o-tȧ-yĕf')	166	57.53N	39.34E
Tutbury, Eng., U.K. (tŭt'bẽr-ė)	144a	52.52N	1.51W
Tuticorin, India (to͞o-tė-kò-rĭn')	183b	8.51N	78.09E
Tutitlan, Mex. (to͞o-tē-tlä'n)	119a	19.38N	99.10W
Tutóia, Braz. (to͞o-tō'yȧ)	131	2.42S	42.21W
Tutrakan, Bul.	149	44.02N	26.36E
Tuttle Creek Reservoir, res., Ks., U.S.	111	39.30N	96.38W
Tuttlingen, Ger. (tòt'lĭng-ĕn)	154	47.58N	8.50E
Tutuila, i., Am. Sam.	198a	14.18S	170.42W
Tutwiler, Ms., U.S. (tŭt'wĭ-lẽr)	114	34.01N	90.25W
Tuva, state, Russia	170	51.15N	90.45E
Tuvalu, nation, Oc.	3	5.20S	174.00E
Tuwayq, Jabal, mts., Sau. Ar.	182	20.45N	46.30E
Tuxedo, Md., U.S.	229d	38.55N	76.55W
Tuxedo Park, N.Y., U.S. (tŭk-sē'dō pärk)	100a	41.11N	74.11W
Tuxford, Eng., U.K. (tŭks'fẽrd)	144a	53.14N	0.54W
Túxpan, Mex.	116	20.57N	97.26W
Tuxpan, Mex. (to͞os'pän)	118	19.34N	103.22W
Túxpan, r., Mex. (to͞os'pän)	119	20.55N	97.52W
Túxpan, Arrecife, i., Mex. (är-rĕ-sė'fĕ-to͞o'x-pä'n)	119	21.01N	97.12W
Tuxtepec, Mex. (tòs-tå-pĕk')	119	18.06N	96.09W
Tuxtla Gutiérrez, Mex. (tòs'tlä go͞o-tyår'rĕs)	116	16.44N	93.08W
Tuy, r., Ven. (to͞o'ė)	131b	10.15N	66.03W
Tuyra, r., Pan. (to͞o-ē'rȧ)	121	7.55N	77.37W
Tuz Gölü, l., Tur.	166	38.45N	33.25E
Tuzigoot National Monument, rec., Az., U.S.	109	34.40N	111.52W
Tuzla, Bos. (tòz'lȧ)	149	44.33N	18.46E
Tvedestrand, Nor. (tvĭ'dhĕ-stränd)	152	58.39N	8.54E
Tveitsund, Nor. (tvåt'sònd)	152	59.03N	8.29E
Tver', Russia	164	56.52N	35.57E
Tver', prov., Russia	162	56.50N	33.08E
Tvertsa, r., Russia (tvĕr'tsȧ)	162	56.58N	35.22E
Tweed, r., U.K. (twēd)	150	55.32N	2.35W
Tweeling, S. Afr. (twē'lĭng)	218d	27.34S	28.31E
Twenty Mile Creek, r., Can. (twĕn'tĭ mīl)	83d	43.09N	79.49W
Twickenham, Eng., U.K. (twĭk''n-ăm)	144b	51.26N	0.20W
Twillingate, Can. (twĭl'ĭn-gāt)	85a	49.39N	54.46W
Twin Bridges, Mt., U.S. (twĭn brĭ-jėz)	105	45.34N	112.17W
Twin Falls, Id., U.S. (fôls)	96	42.33N	114.29W
Twinsburg, Oh., U.S. (twĭnz'bŭrg)	101d	41.19N	81.26W
Twitchell Reservoir, res., Ca., U.S.	108	34.50N	120.10W
Two Butte Creek, r., Co., U.S. (to͞o būt)	110	37.39N	102.45W
Two Harbors, Mn., U.S.	103	47.00N	91.42W
Two Prairie Bay, Ar., U.S. (prā'rĭ bī o͞o')	111	34.48N	92.07W
Two Rivers, Wi., U.S. (rĭv'ẽrz)	103	44.09N	87.36W
Tyabb, Austl.	201a	38.16S	145.11E
Tyachiv, Ukr.	155	48.01N	23.42E
Tyasmin, r., Ukr. (tyȧs-mĭn')	163	49.14N	32.23E
Tylden, S. Afr. (tĭl-dĕn)	213c	32.08S	27.06E
Tyldesley, Eng., U.K. (tĭldz'lė)	144a	53.32N	2.28W
Tyler, Mn., U.S. (tī'lẽr)	102	44.18N	96.08W
Tyler, Tx., U.S.	97	32.21N	95.19W
Tyler Park, Va., U.S.	229d	38.52N	77.12W
Tylertown, Ms., U.S. (tī'lẽr-toun)	114	31.08N	90.06W
Tylihul, r., Ukr.	163	47.25N	30.27E
Tyndall, S.D., U.S. (tĭn'dȧl)	102	42.58N	97.52W
Tyndinskiy, Russia	165	55.22N	124.45E
Tyne, r., Eng., U.K. (tīn)	150	54.59N	1.56W
Tynemouth, Eng., U.K. (tīn'mŭth)	146	55.04N	1.39W
Tyngsboro, Ma., U.S. (tĭnj-bûr'ȯ)	93a	42.40N	71.27W
Tynset, Nor. (tün'sĕt)	146	62.17N	10.45E
Tyre *see* Şūr, Leb.	181a	33.16N	35.13E
Tyrifjorden, l., Nor.	152	60.03N	10.25E
Tyrone, Pa., U.S.	99	40.40N	78.15W
Tyrrell, Lake, l., Austl. (tir'ĕll)	204	35.12S	143.00E
Tyrrhenian Sea, sea, Italy (tĭr-rē'nĭ-ȧn)	142	40.10N	12.15E
Tysons Corner, Va., U.S.	229d	38.55N	77.14W
Tyukalinsk, Russia (tyò-kȧ-lĭnsk')	164	56.03N	71.43E
Tyukyan, r., Russia (tyȯk'yȧn)	171	65.42N	116.09E
Tyuleniy, i., Russia	167	44.30N	48.00E
Tyumen', Russia (tyo͞o-mĕn')	164	57.02N	65.28E
Tzucacab, Mex. (tzo͞o-kä-kä'b)	120a	20.06N	89.03W

U

PLACE (Pronunciation)	PAGE	Lat. °'	Long. °'
Uaupés, Braz. (wä-o͞o'pās)	130	0.02S	67.03W
Ubangi, r., Afr. (o͞o-bäŋ'gė)	211	3.00N	18.00E
Ubatuba, Braz. (o͞o-bå-to͞o'bȧ)	129a	23.25S	45.06W
Ubeda, Spain (o͞o'bå-dä)	158	38.01N	3.23W
Uberaba, Braz. (o͞o-bå-rä'bȧ)	131	19.47S	47.47W
Uberlândia, Braz. (o͞o-bĕr-lȧ'n-dyä)	131	18.54S	48.11W
Ubombo, S. Afr. (o͞o-bôm'bȯ)	212	27.33S	32.13E
Ubon Ratchathani, Thai. (o͞o'bŭn rä'chätá-nē)	196	15.15N	104.52E
Ubort', r., Eur. (o͞o-bôrt')	163	51.18N	27.43E
Ubrique, Spain (o͞o-brē'kȧ)	158	36.43N	5.36W
Ubundu, Zaire	212	0.21S	25.29E
Ucayali, r., Peru (o͞o'kä-yä'lē)	130	8.58S	74.13W
Uccle, Bel. (ū'kl')	145a	50.48N	4.17E
Uchaly, Russia (û-chä'lĭ)	172a	54.22N	59.28E
Uchiko, Japan (o͞o'chė-kō)	195	33.30N	132.39E
Uchinoura, Japan (o͞o'chė-nȯ-o͞o'rȧ)	195	31.16N	131.03E
Uchinskoye Vodokhranilishche, res., Russia	172b	56.08N	37.44E
Uchiura-Wan, b., Japan (o͞o'chė-o͞o'rä wän)	194	42.20N	140.44E
Uchur, r., Russia (ò-chòr')	171	57.25N	130.35E
Ückendorf, neigh., Ger.	236	51.30N	7.07E
Uda, r., Russia (ò'dȧ)	171	52.28N	110.51E
Uda, r., Russia	171	53.54N	131.29E
Udaipur, India (ò-dŭ'ė-po͞or)	186	24.41N	73.41E
Uday, r., Ukr. (ò-dī')	163	50.45N	32.13E
Uddevalla, Swe. (o͞od'dĕ-väl-ȧ)	146	58.21N	11.55E
Udine, Italy (o͞o'dė-nȧ)	148	46.05N	13.14E
Udmurtia, state, Russia	166	57.00N	53.00E
Udon Thani, Thai.	196	17.31N	102.51E
Udskaya Guba, b., Russia	165	55.00N	136.30E
Ueckermünde, Ger.	154	53.43N	14.01E
Ueda, Japan (wā'dä)	194	36.26N	138.16E
Uedesheim, neigh., Ger.	236	51.10N	6.48E
Uele, r., Zaire (wā'lå)	211	3.55N	23.30E
Uelzen, Ger. (ült'sĕn)	154	52.58N	10.34E
Uerdingen, neigh., Ger.	236	51.21N	6.39E
Ufa, Russia (ò'fa)	164	54.45N	55.57E
Ufa, r., Russia	166	56.00N	57.05E
Ugab, r., Nmb. (o͞o'gäb)	212	21.10S	14.00E
Ugalla, r., Tan. (o͞o-gä'lä)	212	6.15S	32.30E
Uganda, nation, Afr. (o͞o-gän'dä) (û-găn'dȧ)	211	2.00N	32.28E
Ugashik Lake, l., Ak., U.S. (o͞o'gȧ-shėk)	95	57.36N	157.10W
Ugie, S. Afr. (ò'jē)	213c	31.13S	28.14E
Uglegorsk, Russia (o͞o-glĕ-gôrsk)	165	49.00N	142.31E
Ugleural'sk, Russia (òg-lĕ-ò-rálsk')	172a	58.58N	57.35E
Uglich, Russia (o͞og-lėch')	162	57.33N	38.19E
Uglitskiy, Russia (òg-lĭt'skĭ)	172a	53.50N	60.18E
Uglovka, Russia (o͞og-lôf'kȧ)	162	58.14N	33.24E
Ugra, r., Russia (o͞og'rȧ)	166	54.43N	34.20E
Ugŭrchin, Bul.	161	43.06N	24.23E
Uhrichsville, Oh., U.S. (ū'rĭks-vĭl)	98	40.25N	81.20W
Uíge, Ang.	212	7.37S	15.03E
Uiju, N. Kor. (ò'ėjo͞o)	189	40.09N	124.33E
Uinkaret Plateau, plat., Az., U.S. (ů-ĭn'kâr-ĕt)	109	36.43N	113.15W
Uinskoye, Russia (ò-ĭn'skô-yĕ)	172a	56.53N	56.25E
Uinta, r., Ut., U.S. (ů-ĭn'tȧ)	109	40.25N	109.55W
Uintah and Ouray Indian Reservation, I.R., Ut., U.S.	109	40.20N	110.20W
Uinta Mountains, mts., Ut., U.S.	96	40.35N	111.00W
Uitenhage, S. Afr.	212	33.46S	25.26E
Uithoorn, Neth.	145a	52.13N	4.49E
Uji, Japan (o͞o'jē)	195b	34.53N	135.49E
Ujiji, Tan. (o͞o-jē'jė)	212	4.55S	29.41E
Ujjain, India (o͞o-jŭėn)	183	23.18N	75.37E
Ujungpandang, Indon.	196	5.08S	119.28E
Ukerewe Island, i., Tan.	217	2.00S	32.40E
Ukhta, Russia (o͞ok'tȧ)	166	65.22N	31.30E
Ukhta, Russia	166	63.08N	53.42E
Ukiah, Ca., U.S. (ū-kī'ȧ)	108	39.09N	122.12W
Ukita, neigh., Japan	242a	35.40N	139.52E
Ukmerge, Lith. (òk'mĕr-ghå)	166	55.16N	24.45E
Ukraine, nation, Eur.	164	49.15N	30.15E
Uku, i., Japan (o͞ok'o͞o)	195	33.18N	129.02E
Ulaangom, Mong.	188	50.23N	92.14E
Ulan Bator (Ulaanbaatar), Mong.	188	47.56N	107.00E
Ulan-Ude, Russia (o͞o'län o͞o'då)	165	51.59N	107.41E
Ulchin, S. Kor. (o͞ol'chĕn')	194	36.57N	129.26E
Ulcinj, Yugo. (o͞ol'tsĕn')	149	41.56N	19.15E
Ulhās, r., India	187b	19.13N	73.03E
Ulhāsnagar, India	186	19.10N	73.07E
Uliastay, Mong.	188	47.49N	97.00E
Ulindi, r., Zaire (o͞o-lĭn'dė)	212	1.55S	26.17E
Ülkenözen, r.	167	49.50N	49.35E
Ulla, Bela. (òl'ȧ)	162	55.14N	29.15E
Ulla, r., Bela.	162	54.58N	29.03E
Ulla, r., Spain (o͞o'lä)	158	42.45N	8.33W
Ullŭng, i., S. Kor. (o͞ol'lòng')	194	37.29N	130.50E
Ulm, Ger. (òlm)	147	48.24N	9.59E
Ulmer, Mount, mtn., Ant. (ŭl'mûr')	219	77.30S	86.00W
Ulricehamn, Swe. (òl-rē'sĕ-häm)	152	57.49N	13.23E
Ulsan, S. Kor. (o͞ol'sän')	194	35.35N	129.22E
Ulster, hist. reg., Eur. (ŭl'stẽr)	150	54.41N	7.10W
Ulua, r., Hond. (o͞o-lo͞o'ȧ)	120	15.49N	87.45W
Ulubāria, India	186a	22.27N	88.09E
Ulukişla, Tur. (o͞o-lo͞o-kēsh'lȧ)	149	36.40N	34.30E
Ulunga, Russia (ò-lo͞on'gȧ)	194	46.16N	136.29E
Ulungur, r., China (o͞o-lo͞on-gůr)	188	46.31N	88.00E
Ulu-Telyak, Russia (o͞o lò'tĕlyăk)	172a	54.54N	57.01E
Ulverstone, Austl. (ŭl'vẽr-stŭn)	203	41.20S	146.22E
Ul'yanovka, Russia	172c	59.38N	30.47E
Ul'yanovsk, Russia (o͞o-lyä'nôfsk)	164	54.20N	48.24E
Ulysses, Ks., U.S. (ū-lĭs'ēz)	110	37.34N	101.25W
Umán, Mex. (o͞o-män')	120a	20.52N	89.44W
Uman', Ukr. (ò-mȧn')	167	48.44N	30.13E

360 Umatilla Indian Reservation–Valldoreix

PLACE (Pronunciation)	PAGE	Lat. °′	Long. °′
Umatilla Indian Reservation, I.R., Or., U.S. (ū-mȧ-tĭl'ȧ)	104	45.38N	118.35W
Umberpāda, India	187b	19.28N	73.04E
Umbria, hist. reg., Italy (ŭm'brĭ-ȧ)	160	42.53N	12.22E
Umeålven, r., Swe.	142	64.57N	18.51E
Umhlatuzi, r., S. Afr. (ȯm'hlȧ-tōō'zĭ)	213c	28.47S	31.17E
Umiat, Ak., U.S. (ōō'mĭ-ăt)	96a	69.20N	152.28W
Umkomaas, S. Afr. (ȯm-kō'mäs)	213c	30.12S	30.48E
Umnak, i., Ak., U.S. (ōōm'nȧk)	96b	53.10N	169.08W
Umnak Pass, Ak., U.S.	95a	53.10N	168.04W
Umniati, r., Zimb.	212	17.08S	29.11E
Umpqua, r., Or., U.S. (ŭmp'kwȧ)	104	43.42N	123.50W
Umtata, S. Afr. (ȯm-tä'tä)	212	31.36S	28.47E
Umtentweni, S. Afr.	213c	30.41S	30.29E
Umzimkulu, S. Afr. (ȯm-zēm-kōō'lōō)	213c	30.12S	29.53E
Umzinto, S. Afr. (ȯm-zĭn'tȯ)	213c	30.19S	30.41E
Una, r., Yugo. (ōō'nȧ)	160	44.38N	16.10E
Unalakleet, Ak., U.S. (ū-nȧ-lăk'lēt)	95	63.50N	160.42W
Unalaska, Ak., U.S. (ū-nȧ-lȧs'kȧ)	95a	53.30N	166.20W
Unare, r., Ven.	131b	9.45N	65.12W
Unare, Laguna de, l., Ven. (lä-gȯ'nä-de-ōō-nȧ'rĕ)	131b	10.07N	65.23W
Unayzah, Sau. Ar.	182	25.50N	44.02E
Uncas, Can. (ŭŋ'kȧs)	83g	53.30N	113.02W
Uncia, Bol. (ōōn'sē-ä)	130	18.28S	66.32W
Uncompahgre, r., Co., U.S.	109	38.20N	107.45W
Uncompahgre Peak, mtn., Co., U.S. (ŭn-kŭm-pä'grē)	109	38.00N	107.30W
Uncompahgre Plateau, plat., Co., U.S.	109	38.40N	108.40W
Underberg, S. Afr. (ŭn'dēr-bûrg)	213c	29.51S	29.32E
Unecha, Russia (ȯ-nĕ'chȧ)	162	52.51N	32.44E
Ungava, Péninsule d', pen., Can.	85	59.55N	74.00W
Ungava Bay, b., Can. (ŭŋ-gä'vȧ)	85	59.46N	67.18W
União da Vitória, Braz. (ōō-nē-ouN' dä vē-tô'ryä)	132	26.17S	51.13W
Unidad Sante Fe, Mex.	233a	19.23N	99.15W
Unije, i., Yugo. (ōō'nē-yĕ)	160	44.39N	14.10E
Unimak, i., Ak., U.S. (ōō-nē-mȧk')	95	54.30N	163.35W
Unimak Pass, Ak., U.S.	95a	54.22N	165.22W
Union, Ms., U.S. (ūn'yŭn)	114	32.35N	89.07W
Union, Mo., U.S.	111	38.28N	90.59W
Union, N.J., U.S.	228	40.42N	74.16W
Union, N.C., U.S.	115	34.42N	81.40W
Union, Or., U.S.	104	45.13N	117.52W
Union City, Ca., U.S.	106b	37.36N	122.01W
Union City, In., U.S.	98	40.10N	85.00W
Union City, Mi., U.S.	98	42.00N	85.10W
Union City, N.J., U.S.	228	40.46N	74.02W
Union City, Pa., U.S.	99	41.50N	79.50W
Union City, Tn., U.S.	114	36.25N	89.04W
Uniondale, N.Y., U.S.	228	40.43N	73.36W
Unión de Reyes, Cuba	122	22.45N	81.30W
Unión de San Antonio, Mex.	118	21.07N	101.56W
Unión de Tula, Mex.	118	19.57N	104.14W
Union Grove, Wi., U.S. (ūn-yŭn grōv)	101a	42.41N	88.03W
Unión Hidalgo, Mex. (ē-dä'lgȯ)	119	16.29N	94.51W
Union Point, Ga., U.S.	114	33.37N	83.08W
Union Springs, Al., U.S. (sprĭngz)	114	32.08N	85.43W
Uniontown, Al., U.S. (ūn'yŭn-toun)	114	32.26N	87.30W
Uniontown, Oh., U.S.	101d	40.58N	81.25W
Uniontown, Pa., U.S.	99	39.55N	79.45W
Unionville, Mo., U.S. (ūn'yŭn-vĭl)	111	40.28N	92.58W
Unisan, Phil. (ōō-nē'sän)	197a	13.50N	121.59E
United Arab Emirates, nation, Asia	182	24.00N	54.00E
United Kingdom, nation, Eur.	142	56.30N	1.40W
United Nations Headquarters, pt. of i., N.Y., U.S.	228	40.45N	73.58W
United States, nation, N.A.	96	38.00N	110.00W
Unity, Can.	88	52.27N	109.10W
Universal, In., U.S. (ū-nĭ-vûr'sȧl)	98	39.35N	87.30W
University City, Mo., U.S. (ū'nĭ-vûr'sĭ-tĭ)	107e	38.40N	90.19W
University Heights, Oh., U.S.	229a	41.30N	81.32W
University Park, Md., U.S.	229d	38.58N	76.57W
University Park, Tx., U.S.	107c	32.51N	96.48W
Unna, Ger. (ōō'nä)	157c	51.32N	7.41E
Uno, Canal Numero, can., Arg.	129c	36.43S	58.14W
Unterhaching, Ger. (ōōn'tĕr-hä-kĕng)	145d	48.03N	11.38E
Untermauerbach, Aus.	239e	48.14N	16.12E
Ünye, Tur. (ün'yĕ)	149	41.00N	37.10E
Unzha, r., Russia (ȯn'zhȧ)	166	57.45N	44.10E
Upa, r., Russia (ȯ'pȧ)	162	53.54N	36.48E
Upata, Ven. (ōō-pä'tä)	130	7.58N	62.27W
Upemba, Parc National de l', rec., Zaire	217	9.10S	26.15E
Up Holland, Eng., U.K.	237a	53.33N	2.44W
Upington, S. Afr. (ŭp'ĭng-tŭn)	212	28.25S	21.15E
Upland, Ca., U.S. (ŭp'lănd)	107a	34.06N	117.38W
Upland, Pa., U.S.	229b	39.51N	75.23W
Upolu, i., W. Sam.	198a	13.55S	171.45W
Upolu Point, c., Hi., U.S. (ōō-pô'lōō)	94a	20.15N	155.48W
Upper Arrow Lake, l., Can. (ăr'ō)	87	50.30N	117.55W
Upper Brookville, N.Y., U.S.	228	40.51N	73.34W
Upper Darby, Pa., U.S. (där'bĭ)	100f	39.58N	75.16W
Upper des Lacs, l., N.A. (dē läk)	102	48.58N	101.55W
Upper Ferntree Gully, Austl.	243b	37.54S	145.19E
Upper Kapuas Mountains, mts., Asia	196	1.45N	112.06E
Upper Klamath Lake, l., Or., U.S.	104	42.23N	122.55W
Upper Lake, l., Nv., U.S. (ŭp'ēr)	104	41.42N	119.59W
Upper Marlboro, Md., U.S. (ûpēr mărl'bōrȯ)	100e	38.49N	76.46W
Upper Mill, Wa., U.S. (mĭl)	106a	47.11N	121.55W
Upper New York Bay, b., N.Y., U.S.	228	40.41N	74.03W
Upper Red Lake, l., Mn., U.S. (rĕd)	103	48.14N	94.53W
Upper Saint Clair, Pa., U.S.	230b	40.21N	80.05W
Upper Sandusky, Oh., U.S. (săn-dŭs'kē)	98	40.50N	83.20W
Upper San Leandro Reservoir, res., Ca., U.S. (ŭp'ēr săn lē-ăn'drȯ)	106b	37.47N	122.04W
Upper Tooting, neigh., Eng., U.K.	235	51.26N	0.10W
Upper Volta see Burkina Faso, nation, Afr.	210	13.00N	2.00W
Uppingham, Eng., U.K. (ŭp'ĭng-ăm)	144a	52.35N	0.43W
Uppsala, Swe. (ōōp'sȧ-lä)	142	59.53N	17.39E
Upton, Eng., U.K.	235	51.30N	0.35W
Uptown, Ma., U.S. (ŭp'toun)	93a	42.10N	71.36W
Uptown, neigh., Il., U.S.	231a	41.58N	87.40W
Upwey, Austl.	243b	37.54S	145.20E
Uraga, Japan (ōō'rȧ-gȧ')	195a	35.15N	139.43E
Ural, r. (ȯ-räl'') (ū-rôl)	164	48.00N	51.00E
Urals, mts., Russia	164	56.28N	58.13E
Uran, India (ōō-rän')	187b	18.53N	72.46E
Uranium City, Can.	84	59.34N	108.59W
Urawa, Japan (ōō'rä-wä')	194	35.52N	139.39E
Urayasu, Japan (ōō'rä-yä'sōō)	195a	35.40N	139.54W
Urazovo, Russia (ȯ-rá'zô-vô)	163	50.08N	38.03E
Urbana, Il., U.S. (ûr-băn'ȧ)	98	40.10N	88.15W
Urbana, Oh., U.S.	98	40.05N	83.50W
Urbino, Italy (ōōr-bē'nȯ)	160	43.43N	12.37E
Urda, Kaz. (ȯr'dȧ)	170	48.50N	47.30E
Urdaneta, Phil. (ōōr-dä-nä'tä)	197a	15.59N	120.34E
Urdinarrain, Arg. (ōōr-dē-när-rȧē'n)	129c	32.43S	58.53W
Uritsk, Russia (ōō'rĭtsk)	172c	59.50N	30.11E
Urla, Tur. (ȯr'lȧ)	161	38.20N	26.44E
Urman, Russia (ȯr'mȧn)	172a	54.53N	56.52E
Urmi, r., Russia (ȯr'mē)	194	48.50N	134.00E
Urmston, Eng., U.K.	237b	53.27N	2.21W
Uromi, Nig.	215	6.44N	6.18E
Urrao, Col. (ōōr-rȧ'ō)	130	6.19N	76.11W
Urshel'skiy, Russia (ōōr-shĕl'skĕĕ)	162	55.50N	40.11E
Ursus, Pol.	155	52.12N	20.53E
Urubamba, r., Peru (ōō-rōō-bäm'bä)	130	11.48S	72.34W
Uruguaiana, Braz.	132	29.45S	57.00W
Uruguay, nation, S.A. (ōō-rōō-gwī') (ū'rōō-gwā)	132	32.45S	56.00W
Uruguay, Río, r., S.A. (rē'ō-ȯ-rōō-gwī)	132	27.05S	55.15W
Ürümqi, China (ů-rům-chyē)	188	43.49N	87.43E
Urup, i., Russia (ȯ'rȯp')	189	46.00N	150.00E
Uryupinsk, Russia (ȯr'yȯ-pēn-sk')	167	50.50N	42.00E
Ürzhar, Kaz.	169	47.28N	82.00E
Urziceni, Rom. (ȯ-zē-chĕn'')	161	44.45N	26.42E
Usa, Japan	194	33.31N	131.22E
Usa, r., Russia (ȯ'sȧ)	166	66.00N	58.20E
Uşak, Tur. (ōō'shȧk)	149	38.45N	29.15E
Usakos, Nmb. (ōō-sä'kōs)	212	22.00S	15.40E
Usambara Mountains, mts., Tan.	217	4.40S	38.25E
Usangu Flats, sw., Tan.	217	8.10S	34.00E
Ushaki, Russia (ōō'shȧ-kĭ)	172c	59.28N	31.00E
Ushakovskoye, Russia (ȯ-shȧ-kôv'skô-yĕ)	172a	56.18N	62.23E
Usharal, Kaz.	169	46.14N	80.58E
Ushashi, Tan.	217	2.00S	33.57E
Ushiku, Japan (ōō'shē-kōō)	195a	35.24N	140.09E
Ushimado, Japan (ōō'shē-mä'dȯ)	195	34.37N	134.09E
Ushuaia, Arg. (ōō-shōō-ī'ä)	132	54.46S	68.24W
Usman', Russia (ōōs-mȧn')	167	52.03N	39.40E
Usmānpur, neigh., India	240d	28.41N	77.15E
Usol'ye, Russia (ȯ-sô'lyĕ)	172a	59.24N	56.40E
Usol'ye-Sibirskoye, Russia (ȯ-sô'lyĕsĭ' bēr'skô-yĕ)	170	52.44N	103.46E
Uspallata Pass, p., S.A. (ōōs-pä-lyä'tä)	132	32.47S	70.08W
Uspanapa, r., Mex. (ōōs-pä-nä'pä)	119	17.43N	94.14W
Ussel, Fr. (üs'ĕl)	156	45.33N	2.17E
Ussuri, r., Asia (ōō-sōō'rē)	171	47.30N	134.00E
Ussuriysk, Russia	165	43.48N	132.09E
Ust'-Bol'sheretsk, Russia	165	52.41N	157.00E
Ustica, Isola di, i., Italy	160	38.43N	12.11E
Ústí nad Labem, Czech Rep.	154	50.40N	14.02E
Ust'-Izhora, Russia (ȯst-ēz'hô-rȧ)	172c	59.49N	30.35E
Ustka, Pol. (ōōst'kȧ)	154	54.34N	16.52E
Ust'-Kamchatsk, Russia	165	56.13N	162.18E
Ust'-Katav, Russia (ȯst kȧ'tȧf)	172a	54.55N	58.12E
Ust'-Kishert', Russia (ȯst kē'shĕrt)	172a	57.21N	57.13E
Ust'-Kulom, Russia (kȯ'lŭm)	164	61.38N	54.00E
Ust'-Maya, Russia (mȧ'yȧ)	165	60.33N	134.43E
Ust' Olenëk, Russia	165	72.52N	120.15E
Ust-Ordynskiy, Russia (ȯst-ôr-dyĕnsk'ĭ)	170	52.47N	104.39E
Ust' Penzhino, Russia	171	63.00N	165.10E
Ust' Port, Russia (ȯst'pôrt')	164	69.20N	83.41E
Ust'-Tsil'ma, Russia (tsĭl'mȧ)	164	65.25N	52.10E
Ust'-Tyrma, Russia (tur'mȧ)	165	50.27N	131.17E
Ust' Uls, Russia	172a	60.35N	58.32E
Ust'-Urt, Plato, plat., Asia	164	44.03N	54.58E
Ustynivka, Ukr.	163	47.59N	32.31E
Ustyuzhna, Russia (yōōzh'nȧ)	166	58.49N	36.19E
Usu, China (ů-sōō)	188	44.28N	84.07E
Usuki, Japan (ōō'sōō-kē')	195	33.06N	131.47E
Usulutan, El Sal. (ōō-sōō-lä-tän')	120	13.22N	88.25W
Usumacinta, r., N.A. (ōō'sōō-mä-sēn'tō)	119	18.24N	92.30W
Us'va, Russia (ōōs'vȧ)	172a	58.41N	57.38E
Utah, state, U.S. (ū'tô)	96	39.25N	112.40W
Utah Lake, l., Ut., U.S.	109	40.10N	111.55W
Utan, India	187b	19.17N	72.43E
Ute Mountain Indian Reservation, I.R., N.M., U.S.	109	36.57N	108.34W
Utena, Lith. (ōō'tā-nä)	153	55.32N	25.40E
Utete, Tan. (ōō-tā'tȧ)	213	8.05S	38.47E
Utfort, Ger.	236	51.28N	6.38E
Utica, In., U.S. (ū'tĭ-kȧ)	101h	38.20N	85.39W
Utica, N.Y., U.S.	97	43.05N	75.10W
Utiel, Spain (ōō-tyȧl')	158	39.34N	1.13W
Utika, Mi., U.S. (ū'tĭ-kȧ)	101b	42.37N	83.02W
Utik Lake, l., Can.	89	55.16N	96.00W
Utikuma Lake, l., Can.	87	55.50N	115.25W
Utila, i., Hond. (ōō-tē'lä)	120	16.07N	87.05W
Utinga, Braz.	234d	23.38S	46.32W
Uto, Japan (ōō'tō')	194	32.43N	130.39E
Utrecht, Neth. (ü'trĕkt) (ū'trĕkt)	147	52.05N	5.06E
Utrera, Spain (ōō-trā'rä)	148	37.12N	5.48W
Utsunomiya, Japan (ōōt'sȯ-nȯ-mē-yȧ')	189	36.35N	139.52E
Uttaradit, Thai.	196	17.47N	100.10E
Uttarpara-Kotrung, India	186a	22.40N	88.21E
Uttar Pradesh, state, India (ȯt-tär-prä-dĕsh)	183	27.00N	80.00E
Uttoxeter, Eng., U.K. (ŭt-tôk'sē-tēr)	144a	52.54N	1.52W
Utuado, P.R. (ōō-tōō-ä'dhō)	117b	18.16N	66.40W
Uusikaupunki, Fin.	153	60.48N	21.24E
Uvalde, Tx., U.S. (ū-văl'dē)	112	29.14N	99.47W
Uvel'skiy, Russia (ȯ-vyĕl'skĭ)	172a	54.27N	61.22E
Uvinza, Tan.	217	5.06S	30.22E
Uvira, Zaire (ōō-vē'rä)	212	3.28S	29.03E
Uvod', r., Russia (ȯ-vôd')	162	56.40N	41.10E
Uvongo Beach, S. Afr.	213c	30.49S	30.23E
Uvs Nuur, l., Asia	188	50.29N	93.32E
Uwajima, Japan (ōō-wä'jē-mä)	194	33.12N	132.35E
Uxbridge, Ma., U.S. (ŭks'brĭj)	93a	42.05N	71.38W
Uxbridge, neigh., Eng., U.K.	235	51.33N	0.29W
Uxmal, hist., Mex. (ōō'x-mä'l)	120a	20.22N	89.44W
Uy, r., Russia (ōōy)	172a	54.05N	62.11E
Uyama, Japan	242b	34.50N	135.41E
Uyskoye, Russia (ûy'skô-yĕ)	172a	54.22N	60.01E
Uyuni, Bol. (ōō-yōō'nē)	130	20.28S	66.45W
Uyuni, Salar de, pl., Bol. (sä-lär-dĕ)	130	20.58S	67.09W
Uzbekistan, nation, Asia	164	42.42N	60.00E
Uzh, r., Ukr. (ȯzh)	163	51.07N	29.05E
Uzhhorod, Ukr.	155	48.38N	22.18E
Užice, Yugo. ōō'zhĕ-tsĕ	161	43.51N	19.53E
Uzunköprü, Tur.	161	41.17N	26.42E

V

PLACE (Pronunciation)	PAGE	Lat. °′	Long. °′
Vaal, r., S. Afr. (väl)	212	28.15S	24.30E
Vaaldam, res., S. Afr.	218d	26.58S	28.37E
Vaalplaas, S. Afr.	218d	25.39S	28.56E
Vaalwater, S. Afr.	218d	24.17S	28.08E
Vaasa, Fin. (vä'sȧ)	142	63.06N	21.39E
Vác, Hung. (väts)	155	47.46N	19.10E
Vache, Île à, i., Haiti	123	18.05N	73.40W
Vadstena, Swe. (väd'stĭ'nȧ)	152	58.27N	14.53E
Vaduz, Liech. (vä'dȯts)	154	47.10N	9.32E
Vaga, r., Russia (va'gȧ)	166	61.55N	42.30E
Vah, r., Slvk. (väk)	147	48.07N	17.52E
Vaigai, r., India	187	10.20N	78.13E
Vaires-sur-Marne, Fr.	237c	48.52N	2.39E
Vakh, r., Russia (vák)	170	61.30N	81.33E
Valachia, hist. reg., Rom.	161	44.45N	24.17E
Valcanuta, neigh., Italy	239c	41.53N	12.25E
Valcartier-Village, Can. (väl-kärt-yĕ'vē-läzh')	83b	46.56N	71.28W
Valdai Hills, hills, Russia (vȧl-dī' gô'rĭ)	166	57.50N	32.35E
Valday, Russia (vȧl-dī')	166	57.58N	33.13E
Valdecañas, Embalse de, res., Spain	158	39.45N	5.30W
Valdemārpils, Lat.	153	57.22N	22.34E
Valdemorillo, Spain (väl-dȧ-mȯ-rēl'yō)	159a	40.30N	4.04W
Valdepeñas, Spain (väl-dȧ-pān'yäs)	148	38.46N	3.22W
Valderaduey, r., Spain (väl-dĕ-rä-dwĕ'y)	158	41.39N	5.35W
Valdés, Península, pen., Arg. (väl-dĕ's)	132	42.15S	63.15W
Valdez, Ak., U.S. (văl'dĕz)	95	61.10N	146.18W
Valdilecha, Spain (väl-dē-lā'chä)	159a	40.17N	3.19W
Valdivia, Chile (väl-dē'vä)	132	39.47S	73.13W
Valdivia, Col. (väl-dē'vēä)	130a	7.10N	75.26W
Val-d'Or, Can.	85	48.03N	77.50W
Valdosta, Ga., U.S. (văl-dŏs'tȧ)	97	30.50N	83.18W
Valdoviño, Spain (väl-dȯ-vē'nō)	158	43.36N	8.05W
Vale, Or., U.S. (vāl)	104	43.59N	117.14W
Valença, Braz. (vä-lĕn'sȧ)	131	13.43S	38.58W
Valença, Port.	158	42.03N	8.36W
Valence, Fr. (vä-lĕnns)	147	44.56N	4.54E
Valencia, Spain (vä-lĕn'thē-ä)	142	39.26N	0.23W
Valencia, Ven. (vä-lĕn'syä)	130	10.11N	68.00W
Valencia, hist. reg., Spain (vä-lĕn'thē-ä)	159	39.08N	0.43W
Valencia, Golfo de, b., Spain	159	39.50N	0.30E
Valencia, Lago de, l., Ven.	131b	10.11N	67.45W
Valencia de Alcántara, Spain	158	39.34N	7.13W
Valenciennes, Fr. (vȧ-läN-syĕn')	156	50.24N	3.36E
Valentín Alsina, neigh., Arg.	233d	34.40S	58.25W
Valentine, Ne., U.S. (vȧ läN-tē-nyĕ')	96	42.52N	100.34W
Valera, Ven. (vä-lĕ'rä)	130	9.12N	70.45W
Valerianovsk, Russia (vȧ-lĕ-rĭ-ä'nôvsk)	172a	58.47N	59.34E
Valérien, Mont, hill, Fr.	237c	48.53N	2.13E
Valga, Est. (väl'gȧ)	166	57.47N	26.03E
Valhalla, S. Afr. (vál-häl-ȧ)	213b	25.49S	28.09E
Valier, Mt., U.S. (vă-lēr')	105	48.17N	112.14W
Valjevo, Yugo. (väl'yȧ-vô)	161	44.17N	19.57E
Valky, Ukr.	163	49.49N	35.40E
Valladolid, Mex. (väl-yä-dhô-lēdh')	116	20.39N	88.13W
Valladolid, Spain (väl-yä-dhô-lēdh')	142	41.41N	4.41W
Valldoreix, Spain	238e	41.28N	2.04E

PLACE (Pronunciation)	PAGE	Lat. °′	Long. °′
Valle, Arroyo del, Ca., U.S. (ä-rō′yō dĕl väl′yȧ)	108	37.36N	121.43W
Vallecas, Spain (väl-yā′käs)	159a	40.23N	3.37W
Valle de Allende, Mex. (väl′yā dā äl-yĕn′dȧ)	112	26.55N	105.25W
Valle de Bravo, Mex. (brä′vȯ)	118	19.12N	100.07W
Valle de Guanape, Ven. (vä′l-yĕ-dĕ-gwä-nä′pĕ)	131b	9.54N	65.41W
Valle de la Pascua, Ven. (lä-pä′s-ko͞oä)	130	9.12N	65.08W
Valle del Cauca, dept., Col. (vä′l-yĕ del kou′kä)	130a	4.03N	76.13W
Valle de Santiago, Mex. (sän-tė-ä′gȯ)	118	20.23N	101.11W
Valledupar, Col. (do͞o-pär′)	130	10.13N	73.39W
Valle Grande, Bol. (grän′dā)	130	18.27S	64.03W
Vallejo, Ca., U.S. (vä-yā′hō) (vă-lā′hō)	96	38.06N	122.15W
Vallejo, Sierra de, mts., Mex. (sē-ĕ′r-rä-dĕ-väl-yĕ′kȯ)	118	21.00N	105.10W
Vallenar, Chile (väl-yȧ-när′)	132	28.39S	70.52W
Valles, Mex.	116	21.59N	99.02W
Valletta, Malta (väl-lĕt′ä)	148	35.50N	14.29E
Valle Vista, Ca., U.S. (văl′yā vĭs′tȧ)	107a	33.45N	116.53W
Valley City, N.D., U.S.	96	46.55N	97.59W
Valley City, Oh., U.S. (văl′ĭ)	101d	41.14N	81.56W
Valleydale, Ca., U.S.	232	34.06N	117.56W
Valley Falls, Ks., U.S.	111	39.25N	95.26W
Valleyfield, Can. (văl′ė-fēld)	85	45.16N	74.09W
Valley Mede, Md., U.S.	229c	39.17N	76.50W
Valley Park, Mo., U.S. (văl′ė pärk)	107e	38.33N	90.30W
Valley Stream, N.Y., U.S. (văl′ĭ strēm)	100a	40.39N	73.42W
Valli di Comácchio, I., Italy (vä′lē-dē-kô-mȧ′chyȯ)	160	44.38N	12.15E
Vallière, Haiti (väl-yâr′)	123	19.30N	71.55W
Vallimanca, r., Arg. (väl-yē-mä′n-kä)	129c	36.21S	60.55W
Valls, Spain (väls)	148	41.15N	1.15E
Valmiera, Lat. (vȧl′myĕ-rȧ)	166	57.34N	25.54E
Valognes, Fr. (vȧ-lȯn′y′)	156	49.32N	1.30W
Valona *see* Vlorë, Alb.	149	40.28N	19.31E
Valparaíso, Chile (väl′pä-rä-ē′sȯ)	132	33.02S	71.32W
Valparaíso, Mex.	118	22.49N	103.33W
Valparaiso, In., U.S. (văl-pȧ-rā′zȯ)	98	41.25N	87.05W
Valpariso, prov., Chile	129b	32.58S	71.23W
Valréas, Fr. (vȧl-rȧ-ä′)	156	44.25N	4.56E
Vals, r., S. Afr.	218d	27.32S	26.51E
Vals, Tanjung, c., Indon.	197	8.30S	137.15E
Valsbaai, b., S. Afr.	212a	34.14S	18.35E
Valuyevo, Russia (vȧ-lo͞o′yĕ-vô)	172b	55.34N	37.21E
Valuyki, Russia (vȧ-lȯ-ē′kė)	167	50.14N	38.04E
Valverde del Camino, Spain (väl-vĕr-dĕ-dĕl-kä-mė′nō)	158	37.34N	6.44W
Vammala, Fin.	153	61.19N	22.51E
Van, Tur. (vȧn)	182	38.04N	43.10E
Van Buren, Ar., U.S. (văn bū′rĕn)	111	35.26N	94.20W
Van Buren, Me., U.S.	92	47.09N	67.58W
Vanceburg, Ky., U.S. (văns′bûrg)	98	38.35N	83.20W
Vancouver, Can. (văn-ko͞o′vẽr)	84	49.16N	123.06W
Vancouver, Wa., U.S.	96	45.37N	122.40W
Vancouver Island, i., Can.	84	49.50N	125.05W
Vancouver Island Ranges, mts., Can.	86	49.25N	125.25W
Vandalia, Il., U.S. (văn-dā′lĭ-ȧ)	98	39.00N	89.00W
Vandalia, Mo., U.S.	111	39.19N	91.30W
Vanderbijlpark, S. Afr.	218d	26.43S	27.50E
Vanderhoof, Can.	84	54.01N	124.01W
Van Diemen, Cape, c., Austl. (văndē′mĕn)	202	11.05S	130.15E
Van Diemen Gulf, b., Austl.	202	11.50S	131.30E
Vanegas, Mex. (vä-nĕ′gäs)	116	23.54N	100.54W
Vänern, l., Swe.	142	58.52N	13.17E
Vänersborg, Swe. (vĕ′nẽrs-bôr′)	146	58.24N	12.15E
Vanga, Kenya (väŋ′gä)	213	4.38S	39.10E
Vangani, India	187b	19.07N	73.15E
Van Gölü, l., Tur.	166	38.33N	42.46E
Van Horn, Tx., U.S.	112	31.03N	104.50W
Vanier, Can.	83c	45.27N	75.39W
Vaniköy, neigh., Tur.	239f	41.04N	29.04E
Van Lear, Ky., U.S. (văn lēr′)	98	37.45N	82.50W
Vannes, Fr. (vȧn)	147	47.42N	2.46W
Van Nuys, Ca., U.S. (văn nīz′)	107a	34.11N	118.27W
Van Rees, Pegunungan, mts., Indon.	197	2.30S	138.45E
Vantaan, r., Fin.	153	60.25N	24.43E
Vanua Levu, i., Fiji	198g	16.33S	179.15E
Vanuatu, nation, Oc.	203	16.02S	169.15E
Vanves, Fr.	237c	48.50N	2.18E
Van Wert, Oh., U.S. (văn wûrt′)	98	40.50N	84.35W
Vanzago, Italy	238c	45.32N	9.00E
Vara, Swe. (vä′rä)	152	58.17N	12.55E
Varaklāni, Lat.	153	56.38N	26.46E
Varallo, Italy (vä-räl′lô)	160	45.44N	8.14E
Vārānasi (Benares), India	183	25.25N	83.00E
Varangerfjorden, b., Nor.	143	70.05N	30.20E
Varano, Lago di, l., Italy (lä′gō-dē-vä-rä′nȯ)	160	41.52N	15.55E
Varaždin, Cro. (vä′räzh′dėn)	149	46.17N	16.20E
Varazze, Italy (vä-rät′sā)	160	44.23N	8.34E
Varberg, Swe. (vär′bĕrg)	152	57.06N	12.16E
Vardar, r., Yugo. (vär′där)	161	41.40N	21.50E
Varėna, Lith. (vä-rä′nȧ)	153	54.16N	24.35E
Varennes, Can. (vȧ-rĕn′)	83a	45.41N	73.27W
Vareš, Bos. (vä′rĕsh)	161	44.10N	18.20E
Varese, Italy (vä-rā′sȧ)	160	45.45N	8.49E
Vargem Grande, neigh., Braz.	234c	22.59S	43.29W
Varginha, Braz. (vär-zhė′n-yä)	131	21.33S	45.25W
Varkaus, Fin. (vär′kous)	153	62.19N	27.51E
Varlamovo, Russia (vár-lȧ′mô-vô)	172a	54.37N	60.41E
Varna, Bul. (vär′nȧ)	142	43.14N	27.58E
Varna, Russia	172a	53.22N	60.59E
Värnamo, Swe. (vĕr′nȧ-mȯ)	152	57.11N	13.45E
Varnsdorf, Czech Rep. (värns′dôrf)	154	50.54N	14.36E
Varnville, S.C., U.S. (värn′vĭl)	115	32.49N	81.05W
Várpalota, pt. of i., Hung.	239g	47.30N	19.02E
Vasa, India	187b	19.20N	72.47E
Vascongadas, hist. reg., Spain (väs-kȯn-gä′däs)	158	43.00N	2.46W
Vashka, r., Russia	166	64.00N	48.00E
Vashon, Wa., U.S. (văsh′ŭn)	106a	47.27N	122.28W
Vashon Heights, Wa., U.S. (hītz)	106a	47.30N	122.28W
Vashon Island, i., Wa., U.S.	106a	47.27N	122.27W
Vasiljevskij, Ostrov, i., Russia	239a	59.56N	30.15E
Vaslui, Rom. (vȧs-lo͞o′ė)	155	46.39N	27.49E
Vassar, Mi., U.S. (văs′ẽr)	98	43.25N	83.35W
Vassouras, Braz. (väs-sō′räzh)	129a	22.25S	43.40W
Västerås, Swe. (vĕs′tĕr-ȯs)	146	59.39N	16.30E
Västerdalälven, r., Swe.	146	61.06N	13.10E
Västervik, Swe. (vĕs′tĕr-vēk)	146	57.45N	16.35E
Vasto, Italy (väs′tô)	148	42.06N	12.42E
Vasyl′kiv, Ukr.	167	50.10N	30.22E
Vasyugan, r., Russia (vȧs-yo͞o-gȧn′)	170	58.52N	77.30E
Vatican City, nation, Eur.	160	41.54N	12.22E
Vaticano, Cape, c., Italy (vä-tė-kä′nô)	160	38.38N	15.52E
Vatnajökull, ice., Ice. (vät′nȧ-yû-kȯl)	146	64.34N	16.41W
Vatomandry, Madag.	213	18.53S	48.13E
Vatra Dornei, Rom. (vät′rȧ dôr′nȧ′)	155	47.22N	25.20E
Vättern, l., Swe.	142	58.15N	14.24E
Vattholma, Swe.	152	60.01N	17.40E
Vaucluse, Austl.	243a	33.51S	151.17E
Vaudreuil, Can. (vȯ-drû′y′)	83a	45.24N	74.02W
Vaugh, Wa., U.S. (vôn)	106a	47.21N	122.47W
Vaughan, Can.	83d	43.47N	79.36W
Vaughn, N.M., U.S.	110	34.37N	105.13W
Vauhallan, Fr.	237c	48.44N	2.12E
Vaujours, Fr.	237c	48.56N	2.35E
Vaupés, r., S.A. (vȧ′o͞o-pĕ′s)	130	1.18N	71.14W
Vaxholm, Swe. (väks′hȯlm)	152	59.26N	18.19E
Växjo, Swe. (vĕks′shû)	146	56.53N	14.46E
Vaygach, i., Russia (vī-gȧch′)	164	70.00N	59.00E
Veadeiros, Chapadas dos, hills, Braz. (shä-pä′däs-dȯs-vĕ-ȧ-dā′rōs)	131	14.00S	47.00W
Vedea, r., Rom. (vȧ′dyȧ)	161	44.25N	24.45E
Vedia, Arg. (vĕ′dyä)	129c	34.29S	61.30W
Veedersburg, In., U.S. (vē′dẽrz-bûrg)	98	40.05N	87.15W
Vega, i., Nor.	146	65.38N	10.51E
Vega de Alatorre, Mex. (vā′gä dā ä-lä-tōr′rȧ)	119	20.02N	96.39W
Vega Real, reg., Dom. Rep. (vĕ′gä-rĕ-ä′l)	123	19.30N	71.05W
Vegreville, Can.	84	53.30N	112.03W
Vehār Lake, l., India	187b	19.11N	72.52E
Veinticinco de Mayo, Arg.	129c	35.26S	60.09W
Vejer de la Frontera, Spain	158	36.15N	5.58W
Vejle, Den. (vī′lĕ)	146	55.41N	9.29E
Velbert, Ger. (fĕl′bĕrt)	157c	51.20N	7.03E
Velebit, mts., Yugo. (vā′lĕ-bėt)	149	44.25N	15.23E
Velen, Ger. (fĕ′lĕn)	157c	51.54N	7.00E
Vélez-Málaga, Spain (vā′lāth-mä′lä-gä)	158	36.48N	4.05W
Vélez-Rubio, Spain (ro͞o′bė-ȯ)	158	37.38N	2.05W
Velika Kapela, mts., Yugo. (vĕ′lė-kä kä-pĕ′lä)	149	45.03N	15.20E
Velika Morava, r., Yugo. (mȯ′rä-vä)	149	44.00N	21.30E
Velikaya, r., Russia (vȧ-lē′kȧ-yȧ)	162	57.25N	28.07E
Velikiye Luki, Russia (vyē-lē′-kyė lo͞o′ke)	164	56.19N	30.32E
Velikiy Ustyug, Russia (vȧ-lē′kĭ o͞os-tyȯg′)	164	60.45N	46.38E
Veliko Tŭrnovo, Bul.	149	43.06N	25.38E
Velikoye, Russia (vȧ-lē′kȯ-yĕ)	162	57.21N	39.45E
Velikoye, l., Russia	162	57.00N	36.53E
Veli Lošinj, Cro. (lȯ′shėn′)	160	44.30N	14.29E
Velizh, Russia (vȧ′lėzh)	166	55.37N	31.11E
Vella Lavella, i., Sol.Is.	203	8.00S	156.42E
Velletri, Italy (vĕl-lā′trē)	160	41.42N	12.48E
Vellore, India (vĕl-lōr′)	183	12.57N	79.09E
Vels, Russia (vĕls)	172a	60.35N	58.47E
Vel′sk, Russia (vĕlsk)	164	61.00N	42.18E
Velten, Ger. (fel′tĕn)	145b	52.41N	13.11E
Velya, r., Russia (vĕl′yȧ)	172b	56.23N	37.54E
Velyka Lepetykha, Ukr.	163	47.11N	33.58E
Velyka Vradyyivka, Ukr.	163	47.51N	30.38E
Velykyy Bychkiv, Ukr.	155	47.59N	24.01E
Venadillo, Col. (vĕ-nä-dē′l-yō)	130a	4.43N	74.55W
Venado, Mex. (vȧ-mä′dō)	118	22.54N	101.07W
Venado Tuerto, Arg. (vĕ-nä′dô-to͞oĕ′r-tô)	132	33.28S	61.47W
Vendôme, Fr. (väN-dōm′)	156	47.46N	1.05E
Veneto, hist. reg., Italy (vĕ-nĕ′tȯ)	160	45.58N	11.24E
Venëv, Russia (vĕn-ĕf′)	166	54.19N	38.14E
Venezia *see* Venice, Italy	142	45.25N	12.18E
Venezuela, nation, S.A. (vĕn-ė-zwē′lȧ)	130	8.00N	65.00W
Venezuela, Golfo de, b., S.A. (gȯl-fô-dĕ)	130	11.34N	71.02W
Veniaminof, Mount, mtn., Ak., U.S.	95	56.12N	159.20W
Venice, Italy	142	45.25N	12.18E
Venice, Ca., U.S. (vĕn′ĭs)	107a	33.59N	118.28W
Venice, Il., U.S.	107e	38.40N	90.10W
Venice, neigh., Ca., U.S.	232	34.00N	118.29W
Venice, Gulf of, b., Italy	148	45.23N	13.00E
Venlo, Neth.	157c	51.22N	6.11E
Vennhausen, neigh., Ger.	236	51.13N	6.51E
Venta, r., Eur. (vĕn′tȧ)	153	57.05N	21.45E
Ventana, Sierra de la, mts., Arg. (sē-ĕ-rȧ-dĕ-lä-vĕn-tȧ′nä)	132	38.00S	63.00W
Ventersburg, S. Afr. (vĕn-tẽrs′bûrg)	218d	28.06S	27.10E
Ventersdorp, S. Afr. (vĕn-tẽrs′dôrp)	218d	26.20S	26.48E
Ventimiglia, Italy (vĕn-tė-mēl′yä)	160	43.46N	7.37E
Ventnor, N.J., U.S. (vĕnt′nẽr)	99	39.20N	74.25W
Ventspils, Lat. (vĕnt′spėls)	166	57.24N	21.41E
Ventuari, r., Ven. (vĕn-to͞oȧ′rē)	130	4.47N	65.56W
Ventura, Ca., U.S. (vĕn-to͞o′rȧ)	108	34.18N	119.18W
Venukovsky, Russia (vĕ-no͞o′kôv-skĭ)	172b	55.10N	37.26E
Venustiano Carranza, Mex. (vĕ-no͞os-tyä′nō-kär-rä′n-zä)	118	19.44N	103.48W
Venustiano Carranzo, Mex. (kär-rä′n-zȯ)	119	16.21N	92.36W
Vera, Arg. (vĕ-rä)	132	29.22S	60.09W
Vera, Spain (vā′rä)	158	37.18N	1.53W
Veracruz, Mex.	116	19.13N	96.07W
Vera Cruz, state, Mex. (vā-rä-kro͞oz′)	116	20.30N	97.15W
Verāval, India (vĕr′vŭ-väl)	183	20.59N	70.49E
Verberg, neigh., Ger.	236	51.22N	6.36E
Vercelli, Italy (vĕr-chĕl′lė)	160	45.18N	8.27E
Verchères, Can. (vĕr-shâr′)	83a	45.46N	73.21W
Verde, i., Phil. (vĕr′dȧ)	197a	13.34N	121.11E
Verde, r., Mex.	118	21.48N	99.50W
Verde, r., Mex.	118	20.50N	103.00W
Verde, r., Mex.	119	16.05N	97.44W
Verde, r., Az., U.S. (vûrd)	109	34.04N	111.40W
Verde, Cap, c., Bah.	123	22.50N	75.00W
Verde, Cay, i., Bah.	123	22.00N	75.05W
Verde Island Passage, strt., Phil. (vĕr′dē)	197a	13.36N	120.39E
Verdemont, Ca., U.S. (vûr′dė-mŏnt)	107a	34.12N	117.22W
Verden, Ger. (fĕr′dĕn)	154	52.55N	9.15E
Verdigris, r., Ok., U.S. (vûr′dė-grēs)	111	36.50N	95.29W
Verdun, Can. (vĕr′dŭN′)	91	45.27N	73.34W
Verdun, Fr. (vâr-dûN′)	147	49.09N	5.21E
Verdun, Fr.	157	43.48N	1.10E
Vereeniging, S. Afr. (vĕ-rā′nĭ-gĭng)	218d	26.40S	27.56E
Verena, S. Afr. (vĕr-ėn ȧ)	218d	25.30S	29.02E
Vereya, Russia (vĕ-rȧ′yȧ)	162	55.21N	36.08E
Verga, N.J., U.S.	229b	39.52N	75.10W
Vergara, Spain (vĕr-gä′rä)	158	43.08N	2.23W
Verín, Spain (vȧ-rēn′)	158	41.56N	7.26W
Verkhne-Kamchatsk, Russia (vyĕrk′nyĕ kȧm-chatsk′)	165	54.42N	158.41E
Verkhne Neyvinskiy, Russia (nā-vĭn′skĭ)	172a	57.17N	60.10E
Verkhne Ural′sk, Russia (ȯ-ralsk′)	164	53.53N	59.13E
Verkhniy Avzyan, Russia (vyĕrk′nyĕ ȧv-zyȧn′)	172a	53.32N	57.30E
Verkhniye Kigi, Russia (vyĕrk′nĭ-yĕ kĭ′gĭ)	172a	55.23N	58.37E
Verkhniy Ufaley, Russia (ȯ-fȧ′lā)	172a	56.04N	60.15E
Verkhnyaya Pyshma, Russia (vyĕrk′nyä-yä po͞osh′mȧ)	172a	56.57N	60.37E
Verkhnyaya Salda, Russia (säl′dȧ)	172a	58.03N	60.33E
Verkhnyaya Tunguska (Angara), r., Russia (tȯn-gȯs′kȧ)	170	58.13N	97.00E
Verkhnyaya Tura, Russia (tȯ′rȧ)	172a	58.22N	59.51E
Verkhnyaya Yayva, Russia (yäy′vȧ)	172a	59.28N	57.38E
Verkhnye, Ukr.	163	48.53N	38.29E
Verkhotur′ye, Russia (vyĕr-kô-to͞or′yĕ)	172a	58.52N	60.47E
Verkhoyansk, Russia (vyĕr-kȯ-yänsk′)	165	67.43N	133.33E
Verkhoyanskiy Khrebet, mts., Russia (vyĕr-kȯ-yänskĭ)	165	67.45N	128.00E
Vermilion, Can. (vẽr-mĭl′yŭn)	84	53.22N	110.51W
Vermilion, l., Mn., U.S.	103	47.49N	92.35W
Vermilion, r., Can.	88	53.30N	111.00W
Vermilion, r., Can.	91	47.30N	73.15W
Vermilion, r., Il., U.S.	98	41.05N	89.00W
Vermilion, r., Mn., U.S.	103	48.09N	92.31W
Vermilion Hills, hills, Can.	88	50.43N	106.50W
Vermilion Range, mts., Mn., U.S.	103	47.55N	91.59W
Vermillion, S.D., U.S.	102	42.46N	96.56W
Vermillion, r., S.D., U.S.	102	43.54N	97.14W
Vermillion Bay, b., La., U.S.	113	29.47N	92.00W
Vermont, Austl.	243b	37.50S	145.12E
Vermont, state, U.S. (vẽr-mŏnt′)	97	43.50N	72.50W
Vernal, Ut., U.S. (vûr′nȧl)	105	40.29N	109.40W
Verneuk Pan, pl., S. Afr. (vĕr-nŭk′)	212	30.10S	21.46E
Vernon, Can.	83c	45.10N	75.27W
Vernon, Can. (vĕr-nôN′)	84	50.18N	119.15W
Vernon, Ca., U.S. (vŭr′nŭn)	107a	34.01N	118.12W
Vernon, In., U.S. (vûr′nŭn)	98	39.00N	85.40W
Vernon, N.J., U.S.	100a	39.00N	85.40W
Vernon, Tx., U.S.	110	34.09N	99.16W
Vernonia, Or., U.S. (vûr-nō′nyȧ)	106c	45.52N	123.12W
Vero Beach, Fl., U.S. (vē′rȯ)	115a	27.36N	80.25W
Véroia, Grc.	161	40.30N	22.13E
Verona, Italy (vā-rō′nä)	148	45.28N	11.02E
Verona, N.J., U.S.	228	40.50N	74.12W
Verona, Pa., U.S.	230b	40.30N	79.50W
Verrières-le-Buisson, Fr.	237c	48.45N	2.16E
Versailles, Fr. (vĕr-sī′y′)	147	48.48N	2.07E
Versailles, Ky., U.S. (vēr-sālz′)	98	38.05N	84.45W
Versailles, Mo., U.S.	111	38.27N	92.52W
Versailles, Pa., U.S.	230b	40.21N	79.51W
Versailles, neigh., Arg.	233d	34.38S	58.31W
Versailles, Château de, hist., Fr.	237c	48.48N	2.07E
Vert, Cap, c., Sen.	210	14.43N	17.30W
Verulam, S. Afr. (vĕ-ro͞o-lăm)	213c	29.39S	31.08E
Verulamium, pt. of i., Eng., U.K.	235	51.45N	0.22W
Verviers, Bel. (vĕr-vyā′)	151	50.35N	5.57E
Vesijärvi, l., Fin.	153	61.09N	25.10E
Vesle, Ukr.	163	46.59N	34.56E
Vešn′aki, neigh., Russia	239b	55.44N	37.49E
Vesoul, Fr. (vē-so͞ol′)	157	47.38N	6.11E
Vestavia Hills, Al., U.S.	100h	33.26N	86.46W
Vesterålen, is., Nor. (vĕs′tẽr ȯ′lĕn)	146	68.54N	14.03E
Vestfjord, fj., Nor.	142	67.33N	12.59E
Vestmannaeyjar, Ice. (vĕst′män-ä-ā′yär)	146	63.12N	20.17W
Vesuvio, vol., Italy (vĕ-so͞o′vyä)	142	40.35N	14.26E
Ves′yegonsk, Russia (vĕ-syĕ-gônsk′)	162	58.42N	37.09E
Veszprem, Hung. (vĕs′prām)	155	47.05N	17.53E
Vészto, Hung. (vĕs′tû)	155	46.55N	21.18E
Vet, r., S. Afr. (vĕt)	218d	28.25S	26.37E

ng-sing; ŋ-baŋk; N-nasalized n; nŏd; cŏmmit; ōld; ôbey; ôrder; oi-boil; fo͞od; ȯ-as oo in foot; ou-out; s-soft; sh-dish; th-thin; pūre; ůnite; ûrn; stŭd; circŭs; ü-as in French tu; ′-indeterminate vowel.

PLACE (Pronunciation)	PAGE	Lat. °′	Long. °′
Vetka, Bela. (vyĕt'kȧ)	162	52.36N	31.05E
Vetlanda, Swe. (vĕt-län'dä)	152	57.26N	15.05E
Vetluga, Russia (vyĕt-lo͞o'gȧ)	166	57.50N	45.42E
Vetluga, r., Russia	166	56.50N	45.50E
Vetovo, Bul. (vā'tô-vô)	161	43.42N	26.18E
Vetren, Bul. (vĕt'rĕn')	161	42.16N	24.04E
Vevay, In., U.S. (vē'vā)	98	38.45N	85.05W
Veynes, Fr. (vān'')	157	44.31N	5.47E
Vézère, r., Fr. (vā-zer')	156	45.01N	1.00E
Viacha, Bol. (vēá'chȧ)	130	16.43S	68.16W
Viadana, Italy (vē-ä-dä'nä)	160	44.55N	10.30E
Vian, Ok., U.S. (vī'ăn)	111	35.30N	95.00W
Viana, Braz. (vē-ä'nä)	131	3.09S	44.44W
Viana del Bollo, Spain (vē-ä'nä dĕl bôl'yō)	158	42.10N	7.07W
Viana do Alentejo, Port. (vē-ä'nȧ dò ä-lĕn-tā'hò)	158	38.20N	8.02W
Viana do Castelo, Port. (dò käs-tā'lò)	148	41.41N	8.45W
Viangchan, Laos	196	18.07N	102.33E
Viar, r., Spain (vē-ä'rä)	158	38.15N	6.08W
Viareggio, Italy (vē-ä-rĕd'jō)	160	43.52N	10.14E
Viborg, Den. (vē'bôr)	152	56.27N	9.22E
Vibo Valentia, Italy (vē'bô-vä-lĕ'n-tyä)	160	38.47N	16.06E
Vicálvaro, Spain	159a	40.25N	3.37W
Vicente López, Arg. (vē-sĕ'n-tĕ-lŏ'pĕz)	132a	34.31S	58.29W
Vicenza, Italy (vē-chĕnt'sä)	148	45.33N	11.33E
Vich, Spain (vēch)	159	41.55N	2.14E
Vichuga, Russia (vē-cho͞o'gȧ)	166	57.13N	41.58E
Vichy, Fr. (vē-shē')	147	46.06N	3.28E
Vickersund, Nor.	152	60.00N	9.59E
Vicksburg, Mi., U.S. (vĭks'bûrg)	98	42.10N	85.30W
Vicksburg, Ms., U.S.	97	32.20N	90.50W
Viçosa, Braz. (vē-sô'sä)	129a	20.46S	42.51W
Victoria, Arg. (vēk-tô'rēä)	132	32.36S	60.09W
Victoria, Can. (vĭk-tō'rĭ-ȧ)	84	48.26N	123.23W
Victoria, Chile (vēk-tô-rēä)	132	38.15S	72.16W
Victoria, Col. (vēk-tô'rēä)	130a	5.19N	74.54W
Victoria, H.K.	241c	22.17N	114.08E
Victoria, Phil. (vēk-tô-ryä)	197a	15.34N	120.41E
Victoria, Tx., U.S. (vĭk-tō'rĭ-ȧ)	113	28.48N	97.00W
Victoria, Va., U.S.	115	36.57N	78.13W
Victoria, state, Austl.	203	36.46S	143.15E
Victoria, neigh., Arg.	233d	34.28S	58.31W
Victoria, l., Afr.	212	0.50S	32.50E
Victoria, r., Austl.	202	17.25S	130.50E
Victoria, Mount, mtn., Myanmar	183	21.26N	93.59E
Victoria, Mount, mtn., Pap. N. Gui.	197	9.35S	147.45E
Victoria de las Tunas, Cuba (vēk-tō'rē-ä dā läs to͞o'näs)	122	20.55N	77.05W
Victoria Falls, wtfl., Afr.	212	17.55S	25.51E
Victoria Island, i., Can.	82	70.13N	107.45W
Victoria Island, i., Nig.	244d	6.26N	3.26E
Victoria Lake, l., Can.	93	48.20N	57.40W
Victoria Land, reg., Ant.	219	75.00S	160.00E
Victoria Nile, r., Ug.	217	2.20N	31.35E
Victoria Peak, mtn., Belize (vēk-tōrĭ'ȧ)	120a	16.47N	88.40W
Victoria Peak, mtn., Can.	86	50.03N	126.06W
Victoria Peak, mtn., H.K.	241c	22.17N	114.08E
Victoria River Downs, Austl. (vĭc-tôr'ĭȧ)	202	16.30S	131.10E
Victoria Station, pt. of i., Eng., U.K.	237b	53.29N	2.15W
Victoria Strait, strt., Can. (vĭk-tō'rĭ-ȧ)	84	69.10N	100.58W
Victoriaville, Can. (vĭk-tō'rĭ-ȧ-vĭl)	85	46.04N	71.59W
Victoria West, S. Afr. (wĕst)	212	31.25S	23.10E
Vidalia, Ga., U.S. (vĭ-dā'lĭ-ȧ)	115	32.10N	82.26W
Vidalia, La., U.S.	113	31.33N	91.28W
Vidin, Bul. (vĭ'dĭn)	149	44.00N	22.53E
Vidnoye, Russia	172b	55.33N	37.41E
Vidzy, Bela. (vē'dzĭ)	162	55.23N	26.46E
Viedma, Arg. (vyād'mä)	132	40.55S	63.03W
Viedma, l., Arg.	132	49.40S	72.35W
Viejo, r., Nic. (vyā'hō)	120	12.45N	86.19W
Vienna (Wien), Aus.	142	48.13N	16.22E
Vienna, Ga., U.S. (vē-ĕn'ȧ)	114	32.03N	83.50W
Vienna, Il., U.S.	111	37.24N	88.50W
Vienna, Va., U.S.	100e	38.54N	77.16W
Vienne, Fr. (vyĕn')	147	45.31N	4.54E
Vienne, r., Fr.	156	47.06N	0.20E
Vientiane *see* Viangchan, Laos	196	18.07N	102.33E
Vieques, P.R. (vyā'kās)	117b	18.09N	65.27W
Vieques, i., P.R. (vyā'kās)	117b	18.05N	65.28W
Vierfontein, S. Afr. (vēr'fōn-tān)	218d	27.06S	26.45E
Vieringhausen, neigh., Ger.	236	51.11N	7.10E
Viersen, Ger. (fēr'zĕn)	157c	51.15N	6.24E
Vierwaldstätter See, l., Switz.	154	46.54N	8.36E
Vierzon, Fr. (vyâr-zôN')	147	47.14N	2.04E
Viesca, Mex. (vē-ās'kä)	112	25.21N	102.47W
Viesca, Laguna de, l., Mex. (lä-ō'nä-dĕ)	112	25.30N	102.40W
Vieste, Italy (vyĕs'tå)	160	41.52N	16.10E
Vietnam, nation, Asia (vyĕt'näm')	186	18.00N	107.00E
View Park, Ca., U.S.	232	34.00N	118.21W
Vigan, Phil. (vēgän)	196	17.36N	120.22E
Vigentino, neigh., Italy	238c	45.25N	9.11E
Vigevano, Italy (vē-jā-vä'nô)	160	45.18N	8.52E
Vigny, Fr. (vēn-y'ē')	157b	49.05N	1.54E
Vigo, Spain (vē'gō)	142	42.18N	8.42W
Vihti, Fin. (vē'tĭ)	153	60.27N	24.18E
Vijayawāda, India	183	16.31N	80.37E
Viksøyri, Nor.	152	61.06N	6.35E
Vila Augusta, Braz.	234d	23.28S	46.32W
Vila Boacaya, neigh., Braz.	234d	23.29S	46.44W
Vila Caldas Xavier, Moz.	217	15.59S	34.12E
Vila de Manica, Moz. (vē'lä dä mä-nē'kȧ)	212	18.48S	32.49E
Vila de Rei, Port. (vē'lȧ dā rā'ĭ)	158	39.42N	8.03W
Vila do Conde, Port. (vē'lä dò kôn'dĕ)	158	41.21N	8.44W
Vilafranca de Xira, Port. (frän'kȧ dā shē'rȧ)	158	38.58N	8.59W
Vila Guilherme, neigh., Braz.	234d	23.30S	46.36W
Vilaine, r., Fr. (vē-lân')	156	47.34N	2.15W
Vila Isabel, neigh., Braz.	234c	22.55S	43.15W
Vila Jaguára, neigh., Braz.	234d	23.31S	46.45W
Vila Madalena, neigh., Braz.	234d	23.33S	46.42W
Vila Mariana, neigh., Braz.	234d	23.35S	46.38W
Vilanculos, Moz. (vē-län-ko͞o'lôs)	212	22.03S	35.13E
Vilāni, Lat. (vē'lá-nĭ)	153	56.31N	27.00E
Vila Nova de Foz Côa, Port. (nō'vȧ dā fôz-kō'ȧ)	158	41.08N	7.11W
Vila Nova de Gaia, Port. (vē'lȧ nō'vȧ dā gä'yä)	158	41.08N	8.40W
Vila Nova de Milfontes, Port. (nō'vȧ dā mēl-fôn'tāzh)	158	37.44N	8.48W
Vila Progresso, Braz.	234c	22.55S	43.03W
Vila Prudente, neigh., Braz.	234d	23.35S	46.33W
Vila Real, Port. (rā-äl')	148	41.18N	7.48W
Vila Real de Santo Antonio, Port.	158	37.14N	7.25W
Vila Viçosa, Port. (vē-sō'zȧ)	158	38.47N	7.24W
Vileyka, Bela. (vē-lā'ē-kȧ)	162	54.19N	26.58E
Vilhelmina, Swe.	146	64.37N	16.30E
Viljandi, Est. (vēl'yän-dē)	166	58.24N	25.34E
Viljoenskroon, S. Afr.	218d	27.13S	26.58E
Vilkaviškis, Lith. (vēl-kȧ-vēsh'kēs)	153	54.40N	23.08E
Vil'kitskogo, i., Russia (vyl-kēts-kōgō)	170	73.25N	76.00E
Villa Acuña, Mex. (vêl'yä-ko͞o'n-yä)	112	29.20N	100.56W
Villa Adelina, neigh., Arg.	233d	34.31S	58.32W
Villa Ahumada, Mex. (ä-o͞o-mä'dä)	112	30.43N	106.30W
Villa Alta, Mex. (äl'tä)(sän ĕl-dȧ-fōn'sō)	119	17.20N	96.08W
Villa Angela, Arg. (vē'l-yä å'n-κĕ-lä)	132	27.31S	60.42W
Villa Ballester, Arg. (vē'l-yä-bál-yĕs-tĕr)	132a	34.33S	58.33W
Villa Bella, Bol. (bĕ'l-yä)	130	10.25S	65.22W
Villablino, Spain (vēl-yä-blē'nō)	158	42.58N	6.18W
Villa Borghese, pt. of i., Italy	239c	41.55N	12.29E
Villa Bosch, neigh., Arg.	233d	34.36S	58.34W
Villacañas, Spain (vēl-yä-kän'yäs)	158	39.39N	3.20W
Villacarrillo, Spain (vēl-yä-kä-rēl'yô)	158	38.09N	3.07W
Villach, Aus. (fē'läk)	147	46.38N	13.50E
Villacidro, Italy (vē-lä-chē'drô)	160	39.28N	8.41E
Villa Ciudadela, neigh., Arg.	233d	34.38S	58.34W
Villa Clara, prov., Cuba	122	22.40N	80.10W
Villa Constitución, Arg. (kōn-stē-to͞o-syōn')	129c	33.15S	60.19W
Villa Coronado, Mex. (kō-rō-nä'dhō)	112	26.45N	105.10W
Villa Cuauhtémoc, Mex. (vēl'yä-ko͞o-äò-tĕ'môk)	119	22.11N	97.50W
Villa de Allende, Mex. (vēl'yä'dä äl-yĕn'dȧ)	112	25.18N	100.01W
Villa de Alvarez, Mex. (vēl'yä-dĕ-ä'l-vä-rĕz)	118	19.17N	103.44W
Villa de Cura, Ven. (dē-ko͞o'rä)	131b	10.03N	67.29W
Villa de Guadalupe, Mex. (dĕ-gwä-dhä-lo͞o'pȧ)	118	23.22N	100.44W
Villa de Mayo, Arg.	132a	34.31S	58.41W
Villa Devoto, neigh., Arg.	233d	34.36S	58.31W
Villa Diamante, neigh., Arg.	233d	34.41S	58.26W
Villa Dolores, Arg. (vēl'yä dō-lō'rās)	132	31.50S	65.05W
Villa Domínico, neigh., Arg.	233d	34.41S	58.20W
Villa Escalante, Mex. (vēl'yä-ĕs-kä-lán'tĕ)	118	19.24N	101.36W
Villa Flores, Mex. (vēl'yä-flō'rās)	119	16.13N	93.17W
Villafranca, Italy (vēl-lä-frän'kä)	160	45.22N	10.53E
Villafranca del Bierzo, Spain	158	42.37N	6.49W
Villafranca de los Barros, Spain	158	38.34N	6.22W
Villafranca del Panadés, Spain	159	41.20N	1.40E
Villafranche-de-Rouergue, Fr. (dē-ro͞o-ĕrg')	156	44.21N	2.02E
Villa García, Mex. (gär-sē'ä)	118	22.07N	101.55W
Villagarcia, Spain (vēl'yä-gär-thē'ä)	158	42.38N	8.43W
Villagrán, Mex.	112	24.28N	99.30W
Villa Grove, Il., U.S. (vĭl'ȧ grōv')	98	39.55N	88.15W
Villaguay, Arg. (vē'l-yä-gwī)	132	31.47S	58.53W
Villa Hayes, Para. (vēl'yä äyås)(hāz)	132	25.07S	57.31W
Villahermosa, Mex. (vēl'yä-ĕr-mō'sä)	116	17.59N	92.56W
Villa Hidalgo, Mex. (vēl'yäē-dăl'gō)	118	21.39N	102.41W
Villa José L. Suárez, neigh., Arg.	233d	34.32S	58.34W
Villajoyosa, Spain (vēl'yä-hō-yō'sä)	159	38.30N	0.14W
Villalba, Spain	158	43.18N	7.43W
Villaldama, Mex. (vēl-yäl-dä'mä)	116	26.30N	100.26W
Villa Lopez, Mex. (vēl'yä lō'pĕz)	112	27.00N	105.02W
Villalpando, Spain (vēl-yäl-pän'dō)	158	41.54N	5.24W
Villa Lugano, neigh., Arg.	233d	34.41S	58.28W
Villa Lynch, neigh., Arg.	233d	34.36S	58.32W
Villa Madero, Arg.	233d	34.41S	58.30W
Villa María, Arg. (vē'l-yä-mä-rē'ä)	132	32.17S	63.08W
Villamatín, Spain (vēl-yä-mä-tē'n)	158	36.50N	5.38W
Villa Mercedes, Arg. (mĕr-sā'dås)	132	33.38S	65.16W
Villa Montes, Bol. (vē'l-yä-mô'n-tĕs)	130	21.13S	63.26W
Villa Morelos, Mex. (mō-rĕ'lomcs)	118	20.01N	101.24W
Villa Nova, Md., U.S.	229c	39.21N	76.44W
Villanova, Pa., U.S.	229b	40.02N	75.21W
Villanueva, Col. (vē'l-yä-nòĕ'vä)	130	10.44N	73.08W
Villanueva, Hond. (vēl'yä-nwä'vä)	120	15.19N	88.02W
Villanueva, Mex. (vēl'yä-nòĕ'vä)	118	22.25N	102.53W
Villanueva de Córdoba, Spain (vēl-yä-nwĕ'vä-dä kôr'dô-bä)	158	38.18N	4.38W
Villanueva de la Serena, Spain (lä sā-rā'nä)	158	38.59N	5.56W
Villa Obregón, Mex. (vē'l-yä-ô-brĕ-gô'n)	119a	19.21N	99.11W
Villa Ocampo, Mex. (ô-käm'pō)	112	26.26N	105.30W
Villa Pedro Montoya, Mex. (vēl'yä-pĕ'drô-môn-tô'yá)	118	21.38N	99.51W
Villard-Bonnot, Fr. (vēl-yär'bôn-nō')	157	45.15N	5.53E
Villa Real, neigh., Arg.	233d	34.37S	58.31W
Villarreal, Spain (vēl-yär-rē-äl)	159	39.55N	0.07W
Villarrica, Para. (vēl-yä-rē'kä)	132	25.55S	56.23W
Villarrobledo, Spain (vēl-yär-rô-blā'dhō)	148	39.15N	2.37W
Villa Sáenz Peña, neigh., Arg.	233d	34.36S	58.31W
Villa San Andrés, neigh., Arg.	233d	34.33S	58.32W
Villa Santos Lugares, neigh., Arg.	233d	34.36S	58.32W
Villa Unión, Mex. (vēl'yä-o͞o-nyōn')	118	23.10N	106.14W
Villaverde, neigh., Spain	238b	40.21N	3.42W
Villavicencio, Col. (vē'l-yä-vē-sĕ'n-syō)	130	4.09N	73.38W
Villaviciosa de Odón, Spain	159a	40.22N	3.38W
Villavieja, Col. (vē'l-yä-vē-ĕ'κä)	130a	3.13N	75.13W
Villazón, Bol. (vē'l-yä-zô'n)	130	22.02S	65.42W
Villecresnes, Fr.	237c	48.43N	2.32E
Ville-d'Avray, Fr.	237c	48.50N	2.11E
Villefranche, Fr.	147	45.59N	4.43E
Villejuif, Fr. (vēl'zhüst')	157b	48.48N	2.22E
Ville-Marie, Can.	85	47.18N	79.22W
Villemomble, Fr.	237c	48.53N	2.31E
Villena, Spain (vē-lyā'nȧ)	148	38.37N	0.52W
Villenbon-sur-Yvette, Fr.	237c	48.42N	2.15E
Villeneuve, Can. (vēl'nûv')	83g	53.40N	113.49W
Villeneuve-le-Roi, Fr.	237c	48.44N	2.25E
Villeneuve-Saint Georges, Fr. (săN-zhôrzh')	157b	48.43N	2.27E
Villeneuve-sur-Lot, Fr. (sür-lō')	156	44.25N	0.41E
Villeparisis, Fr.	237c	48.56N	2.37E
Ville Platte, La., U.S. (vēl plát')	113	30.41N	92.17W
Villers Cotterêts, Fr. (vē-ār'kô-trā')	157b	49.15N	3.05E
Villers-sur-Marne, Fr.	237c	48.50N	2.33E
Villerupt, Fr. (vēl'rüp')	157	49.28N	6.16E
Ville-Saint Georges, Can. (vĭl-sĕN-zhôrzh')	91	46.07N	70.40W
Villeta, Col. (vē'l-yĕ'tȧ)	130a	5.02N	74.29W
Villeurbanne, Fr. (vēl-ûr-bän')	147	45.43N	4.55E
Villiers, S. Afr. (vĭl'ĭ-ĕrs)	218d	27.03S	28.38E
Villiers-le-Bâcle, Fr.	237c	48.44N	2.08E
Villiers-le-Bel, Fr.	237c	49.00N	2.23E
Villingen-Schwenningen, Ger.	154	48.04N	8.33E
Villisca, Ia., U.S. (vĭ'lĭs'kȧ)	103	40.56N	94.56W
Villupuram, India	187	11.59N	79.33E
Vilnius, Lith. (vĭl'nē-ôs)	164	54.40N	25.26E
Vilppula, Fin. (vĭl'pŭ-lȧ)	153	62.01N	24.24E
Vil'shanka, Ukr.	163	48.14N	30.52E
Vil'shany, Ukr.	163	50.02N	35.54E
Vilvoorde, Bel.	145a	50.56N	4.25E
Vilyuy, r., Russia (vēl'yĭ)	165	63.00N	121.00E
Vilyuysk, Russia (vē-lyo͞o'ĭsk')	165	63.41N	121.47E
Vimmerby, Swe. (vĭm'ĕr-bü)	152	57.41N	15.51E
Vimperk, Czech Rep. (vĭm-pĕrk')	154	49.04N	13.41E
Viña del Mar, Chile (vē'nyä dĕl mär')	132	33.00S	71.33W
Vinalhaven, Me., U.S. (vī-năl-hā'vĕn)	92	44.03N	68.49W
Vinaroz, Spain (vē-nä'rōth)	159	40.29N	0.27E
Vincennes, Fr. (văN-sĕn')	157b	48.51N	2.27E
Vincennes, In., U.S. (vĭn-zĕnz')	97	38.40N	87.30W
Vincennes, Château de, hist., Fr.	237c	48.51N	2.26E
Vincent, Al., U.S. (vĭn'sĕnt)	114	33.21N	86.25W
Vindelälven, r., Swe.	146	65.02N	18.30E
Vindeln, Swe. (vĭn'dĕln)	146	64.10N	19.52E
Vindhya Range, mts., India (vĭnd'yä)	183	22.30N	75.50E
Vineland, N.J., U.S. (vīn'lănd)	99	39.30N	75.00W
Vinh, Viet. (vēn'y')	196	18.38N	105.42E
Vinhais, Port. (vēn-yä'ēzh)	158	41.51N	7.00W
Vinings, Ga., U.S. (vī'nĭngz)	100c	33.52N	84.28W
Vinita, Ok., U.S. (vĭ-nē'tȧ)	111	36.38N	95.09W
Vinkovci, Cro. (vēn'kôv-tsē)	161	45.17N	18.47E
Vinnytsya, Ukr.	164	49.13N	28.31E
Vinnytsya, prov., Ukr.	163	48.45N	28.01E
Vinogradovo, Russia (vĭ-nô-grä'do-vô)	172b	55.25N	38.33E
Vinson Massif, mtn., Ant.	219	77.40S	87.00W
Vinton, Ia., U.S. (vĭn'tŭn)	103	42.08N	92.01W
Vinton, La., U.S.	113	30.12N	93.35W
Violet, La., U.S. (vī'ô-lĕt)	100d	29.54N	89.54W
Virac, Phil. (vē-räk')	193	13.38N	124.20E
Virbalis, Lith. (vēr'bá-lēs)	153	54.38N	22.55E
Virden, Can. (vûr'dĕn)	84	49.51N	101.55W
Virden, Il., U.S.	111	39.28N	89.46W
Vírgen del San Cristóbal, rel., Chile	234b	33.26S	70.39W
Virgin, r., U.S.	109	36.51N	113.50W
Virginia, S. Afr.	218d	28.07S	26.54E
Virginia, Mn., U.S. (vĕr-jĭn'yȧ)	97	47.32N	92.36W
Virginia, state, U.S.	97	37.00N	80.45W
Virginia Beach, Va., U.S.	99	36.50N	75.58W
Virginia City, Nv., U.S.	108	39.18N	119.40W
Virginia Hills, Va., U.S.	229d	38.47N	77.06W
Virginia Water, Eng., U.K.	235	51.24N	0.34W
Virgin Islands, is., N.A. (vûr'jĭn)	117	18.15N	64.00W
Viroflay, Fr.	237c	48.48N	2.10E
Víron, Grc.	239d	37.57N	23.45E
Viroqua, Wi., U.S. (vĭ-rō'kwȧ)	103	43.33N	90.54W
Virovitica, Cro. (vē-rô-vē'tē-tsä)	161	45.50N	17.24E
Virpazar, Yugo. (vĕr'pä-zär')	161	42.16N	19.06E
Virrat, Fin. (vĭr'ät)	153	62.15N	23.45E
Virserum, Swe. (vĭr'sĕ-rom)	152	57.22N	15.35E
Vis, Cro. (vēs)	160	43.03N	16.11E
Vis, i., Yugo.	149	43.00N	16.10E
Visalia, Ca., U.S. (vĭ-sā'lĭ-ȧ)	108	36.20N	119.18W
Visby, Swe. (vĭs'bü)	142	57.39N	18.19E
Viscount Melville Sound, strt., Can.	82	74.00N	110.00W
Višegrad, Bos. (vē'shĕ-gräd)	161	43.48N	19.17E
Vishākhapatnam, India	183	17.48N	83.21E
Vishera, r., Russia (vĭ'shĕ-rȧ)	172a	60.40N	58.46E
Vishnyakovo, Russia	172b	55.44N	38.10E
Vishoek, S. Afr.	212a	34.13S	18.26E
Visim, Russia (vē'sĭm)	172a	57.38N	59.32E
Viskan, r., Swe.	152	57.20N	12.25E

ăt; finăl; rāte; senåte; ärm; åsk; sofȧ; fâre; ch-choose; dh-as th in other; bē; ėvent; bĕt; recĕnt; cratĕr; g-gō; gh-guttural g; bĭt; ĭ-short neutral; rīde; κ-guttural k as ch in German ich;

PLACE (Pronunciation)	PAGE	Lat. °′	Long. °′
Viški, Lat. (vēs'kĭ)	153	56.02N	26.47E
Visoko, Bos. (vē'sô-kô)	161	43.59N	18.10E
Vistula see Wisła, r., Pol.	142	52.30N	20.00E
Vitarte, Peru	233c	12.02S	76.54W
Vitebsk, Bela. (vē'tyĕpsk)	164	55.12N	30.16E
Vitebsk, prov., Bela.	162	55.05N	29.18E
Viterbo, Italy (vē-tĕr'bō)	148	42.24N	12.08E
Viti Levu, i., Fiji	198g	18.00S	178.00E
Vitim, Russia (vē'tēm)	165	59.22N	112.43E
Vitim, r., Russia (vē'tēm)	165	54.00N	115.00E
Vitino, Russia (vē'tĭ-nô)	172c	59.40N	29.51E
Vitória, Braz. (vē-tō'rē-ä)	131	20.09S	40.17W
Vitoria, Spain (vē-tô-ryä)	148	42.43N	2.43W
Vitória de Conquista, Braz. (vē-tō'rē-ä-dä-kōn-kwē's-tä)	131	14.51S	40.44W
Vitry-le-François, Fr. (vē-trē'lĕ-fräN-swà')	156	48.44N	4.34E
Vitry-sur-Seine, Fr.	237c	48.48N	2.24E
Vittorio, Italy (vē-tô'rē-ô)	160	45.59N	12.17E
Vivero, Spain (vē-vä'rō)	158	43.39N	7.37W
Vivian, La., U.S. (vĭv'ĭ-ăn)	113	32.51N	93.59W
Vizianagaram, India	183	18.10N	83.29E
Vlaardingen, Neth. (vlär'dĭng-ĕn)	151	51.54N	4.20E
Vladikavkaz, Russia	167	43.05N	44.35E
Vladimir, Russia (vlá-dyē'mēr)	164	56.08N	40.24E
Vladimir, prov., Russia (vlä-dyē'mēr)	162	56.08N	39.53E
Vladimiro-Aleksandrovskoye, Russia	194	42.50N	133.00E
Vladivostok, Russia (vlá-dē-vôs-tŏk')	165	43.06N	131.47E
Vladykino, neigh., Russia	239b	55.52N	37.36E
Vlasenica, Bos. (vlä'sĕ-nēt'sá)	161	44.11N	18.58E
Vlasotince, Yugo. (vlä'sô-tēn-tsĕ)	161	42.58N	22.08E
Vlieland, i., Neth. (vlē'länt)	151	53.19N	4.55E
Vlissingen, Neth. (vlĭs'sĭng-ĕn)	151	51.30N	3.34E
Vlorë, Alb.	149	40.27N	19.30E
Vltava, r., Czech Rep.	154	49.24N	14.18E
Vodl, l., Russia (vôd''l)	166	62.20N	37.20E
Voerde, Ger.	157c	51.35N	6.41E
Vogelheim, neigh., Ger.	236	51.29N	6.59E
Voghera, Italy (vô-gā'rä)	160	44.58N	9.02E
Vohwinkel, neigh., Ger.	236	51.14N	7.09E
Voight, r., Wa., U.S.	106a	47.03N	122.08W
Voinjama, Lib.	214	8.25N	9.45W
Voiron, Fr. (vwà-rôN')	157	45.23N	5.48E
Voisin, Lac, l., Can. (vwŏ'-zĭn)	88	54.13N	107.15W
Volchansk, Ukr. (vôl-chänsk')	167	50.18N	36.56E
Volchonka-Zil, neigh., Russia	239b	55.40N	37.37E
Volga, r., Russia (vôl'gä)	164	47.30N	46.20E
Volga, Mouths of the, mth.	167	46.00N	49.10E
Volgograd, Russia (vŏl-gō-grä't)	164	48.40N	42.20E
Volgogradskoye, res., Russia (vôl-gô-grad'skô-yĕ)	164	51.10N	45.10E
Volkhov, Russia (vôl'kôf)	153	59.54N	32.21E
Volkhov, r., Russia	166	58.45N	31.40E
Volkovysk, Bela. (vôl-kô-vēsk')	155	53.11N	24.29E
Vollme, Ger.	236	51.10N	7.36E
Volmarstein, Ger.	236	51.22N	7.23E
Volmerswerth, neigh., Ger.	236	51.11N	6.46E
Volodarskiy, Russia (vô-lô-där'skĭ)	172c	59.49N	30.06E
Volodymyr-Volyns'kyy, Ukr.	155	50.50N	24.20E
Vologda, Russia (vô'lôg-dá)	164	59.12N	39.52E
Vologda, prov., Russia	162	59.00N	37.26E
Volokolamsk, Russia (vô-lô-kô-lámsk)	162	56.02N	35.58E
Volokonovka, Russia (vô-lô-kô'nôf-ká)	163	50.28N	37.52E
Volozhin, Bela. (vô'lô-shēn)	162	54.04N	26.38E
Vol'sk, Russia (vôl'sk)	167	52.02N	47.23E
Volta, r., Ghana	214	6.05N	0.30E
Volta, Lake, res., Ghana (vôl'tá)	210	7.10N	0.30W
Volta Blanche (White Volta), r., Afr.	214	11.30N	0.40W
Volta Noire see Black Volta, r., Afr.	210	11.30N	4.00W
Volta Redonda, Braz. (vōl'tä-rā-dôn'dä)	131	22.32S	44.05W
Volterra, Italy (vôl-tĕr'rä)	160	43.22N	10.51E
Voltri, Italy (vōl'trē)	160	44.25N	8.45E
Volturno, r., Italy (vôl-tōōr'nô)	160	41.12N	14.20E
Vólvi, Límni, l., Grc.	161	40.41N	23.23E
Volzhskoye, l., Russia (vôl'sh-skô-yĕ)	162	56.43N	36.18E
Von Ormy, Tx., U.S. (vŏn ôr'mē)	107d	29.18N	98.36W
Vōōpsu, Est. (vōōp'sò)	153	58.06N	27.30E
Voorburg, Neth.	145a	52.04N	4.21E
Voortrekkerhoogte, S. Afr.	213b	25.48S	28.10E
Vop', r., Russia (vôp)	162	55.20N	32.55E
Vopnafjördur, Ice.	146	65.43N	14.58W
Vorarlberg, prov., Aus.	154	47.20N	9.55E
Vordingborg, Den. (vôr'dĭng-bôr)	152	55.10N	11.55E
Vorhalle, neigh., Ger.	236	51.23N	7.28E
Voríai Sporádhes, is., Grc.	161	38.55N	24.05E
Vorkuta, Russia (vôr-kōō'tá)	164	67.28N	63.40E
Vormholz, Ger.	236	51.24N	7.18E
Vormsi, i., Est. (vôrm'sĭ)	153	59.06N	23.05E
Vórois Evvoïkós Kólpos, b., Grc.	161	38.48N	23.02E
Vorona, r., Russia (vô-rô'na)	167	51.50N	42.00E
Voronezh, Russia (vô-rô'nyĕzh)	164	51.39N	39.11E
Voronezh, prov., Russia	163	51.10N	39.13E
Voronezh, r., Russia	167	52.17N	39.32E
Voronovo, Bela. (vô'rô-nô-vô)	155	54.07N	25.16E
Vorontsovka, Russia (vô-rônt'sôv-ká)	172a	59.40N	60.14E
Voron'ya, r., Russia (vô-rônyá)	166	68.20N	35.20E
Võrts-Järv, l., Est. (vôrts yärv)	153	58.15N	26.12E
Võru, Est. (vô'rû)	166	57.50N	26.58E
Vorya, r., Russia (vôr'yá)	172b	55.55N	38.15E
Vosges, mts., Fr. (vōzh)	147	48.09N	6.57E
Voskresensk, Russia (vôs-krĕ-sĕnsk')	172b	55.20N	38.42E
Voss, Nor. (vôs)	146	60.40N	6.24E
Vostryakovo, Russia	172b	55.23N	37.49E
Votkinsk, Russia (vôt-kēnsk')	166	57.00N	54.00E
Votkinskoye Vodokhranilishche, res., Russia	166	57.30N	55.00E
Vouga, r., Port. (vō'gá)	158	40.43N	7.51W
Vouziers, Fr. (vōō-zyā')	156	49.25N	4.40E
Voxnan, r., Swe.	152	61.30N	15.24E
Voyageurs National Park, Mn., U.S.	103	48.30N	92.40W
Vozhe, l., Russia (vôzh'yĕ)	166	60.40N	39.00E
Voznesens'k, Ukr.	167	47.34N	31.22E
Vrangelya (Wrangel), i., Russia	164	71.25N	178.30W
Vranje, Yugo. (vrän'yĕ)	161	42.33N	21.55E
Vratsa, Bul. (vrät'tsá)	149	43.12N	23.31E
Vrbas, Yugo. (v'r'bäs)	161	45.34N	19.43E
Vrbas, r., Yugo.	161	44.25N	17.17E
Vrchlabí, Czech Rep. (v'r'chlä-bē)	154	50.32N	15.51E
Vrede, S. Afr. (vrĭ'dĕ)(vrĕd)	218d	27.25S	29.11E
Vredefort, S. Afr. (vrĭ'dĕ-fōrt)(vrĕd'fōrt)	218d	27.00S	27.21E
Vreeswijk, Neth.	145a	52.00N	5.06E
Vršac, Yugo. (v'r'shàts)	149	45.08N	21.18E
Vrutky, Slvk. (vrōōt'kē)	155	49.09N	18.55E
Vryburg, S. Afr. (vrī'bûrg)	212	26.55S	24.45E
Vryheid, S. Afr. (vrī'hīt)	212	27.43S	30.58E
Vsetín, Czech Rep. (fsĕt'yēn)	155	49.21N	18.01E
Vsevolozhskiy, Russia (vsyĕ'vôlô'zh-skēē)	172c	60.01N	30.41E
Vuelta Abajo, reg., Cuba (vwĕl'tä ä-bä'hō)	122	22.20N	83.45W
Vught, Neth.	145a	51.38N	5.18E
Vukovar, Cro. (vŏ'kô-vär)	161	45.20N	19.00E
Vulcan, Mi., U.S. (vŭl'kăn)	98	45.45N	87.50W
Vulcano, i., Italy (vōōl-kä'nô)	160	38.23N	15.00E
Vûlchedrŭma, Bul.	161	43.43N	23.29E
Vyartsilya, Russia (vyár-tsē'lyá)	153	62.10N	30.40E
Vyatka, r., Russia (vyát'ká)	166	59.20N	51.25E
Vyazemskiy, Russia (vyá-zĕm'skĭ)	194	47.29N	134.39E
Vyaz'ma, Russia (vyáz'má)	166	55.12N	34.17E
Vyazniki, Russia (vyáz'nē-kē)	166	56.10N	42.10E
Vyborg, Russia (vwē'bôrk)	164	60.43N	28.46E
Vychegda, r., Russia (vē'chĕg-dá)	166	61.40N	48.00E
Vylkove, Ukr.	167	45.24N	29.36E
Vym, r., Russia (vwēm)	166	63.15N	51.20E
Vyritsa, Russia (vē'rĭ-tsá)	172c	59.24N	30.20E
Vyshnevolotskoye, l., Russia (vŭy'sh-ŋĕ'vôlôt's-kô'yĕ)	162	57.30N	34.27E
Vyshniy Volochëk, Russia (vēsh'nyĭ vôl-ô-chĕk')	164	57.34N	34.35E
Vyškov, Czech Rep. (vēsh'kôf)	154	49.17N	16.58E
Vysoké Mýto, Czech Rep. (vû'sô-kä mû'tô)	154	49.58N	16.07E
Vysokovsk, Russia (vĭ-sô'kôfsk)	162	56.16N	36.32E
Vytegra, Russia (vû'tĕg-rá)	164	61.00N	36.20E

W

PLACE (Pronunciation)	PAGE	Lat. °′	Long. °′
W, Parcs Nationaux du, rec., Niger	215	12.20N	2.40E
Waal, r., Neth. (väl)	151	51.46N	5.00E
Waalwijk, Neth.	145a	51.41N	5.05E
Wabamun, Grc.	149	39.23N	22.56E
Wabamuno, Can. (wŏ'bă-mŭn)	87	53.33N	114.28W
Wabasca, Can. (wŏ-bás'kă)	87	56.00N	113.53W
Wabash, In., U.S. (wô'băsh)	98	40.45N	85.50W
Wabash, r., U.S.	97	38.00N	88.00W
Wabasha, Mn., U.S. (wä'bá-shô)	103	44.24N	92.04W
Wabe Gestro, r., Eth.	211	6.25N	41.21E
Wabowden, Can. (wă-bō'd'n)	89	54.55N	98.38W
Wąbrzeźno, Pol. (vôŋ-bzĕzh'nō)	155	53.17N	18.59E
Wabu Hu, l., China (wä-bōō hōō)	190	32.25N	116.35E
W. A. C. Bennett Dam, dam, Can.	87	56.01N	122.10W
Waccamaw, r., S.C., U.S. (wăk'ă-mô)	115	33.47N	78.55W
Waccasassa Bay, b., Fl., U.S. (wă-kă-să'să)	114	29.02N	83.10W
Wachow, Ger. (vä'kōv)	145b	53.32N	12.46E
Waco, Tx., U.S. (wā'kō)	96	31.35N	97.06W
Waconda Lake, res., Ks., U.S.	110	39.45N	98.15W
Wadayama, Japan (wä'dä'yä-mä)	195	35.19N	134.49E
Waddenzee, sea, Neth.	151	53.00N	4.50E
Waddington, Mount, mtn., Can. (wŏd'dĭng-tŭn)	84	51.23N	125.15W
Wadena, Can.	88	51.57N	103.50W
Wadena, Mn., U.S. (wŏ-dē'nă)	102	46.26N	95.09W
Wadesboro, N.C., U.S. (wādz'bŭr-ō)	115	34.57N	80.05W
Wadeville, S. Afr.	244b	26.16S	28.11E
Wadley, Ga., U.S. (wŭd'lē)	115	32.54N	82.25W
Wad Madani, Sudan (wäd mē-dä'nē)	211	14.27N	33.31E
Wadowice, Pol. (vá-dô'vēt-sĕ)	155	49.53N	19.31E
Wadsworth, Oh., U.S. (wŏdz'wûrth)	101d	41.01N	81.44W
Wager Bay, b., Can. (wā'jĕr)	85	65.48N	88.19W
Wagga Wagga, Austl. (wŏg'ă wŏg'ă)	203	35.10S	147.30E
Wagoner, Ok., U.S. (wăg'ŭn-ĕr)	111	35.58N	95.22W
Wagon Mound, N.M., U.S. (wăg'ŭn mound)	110	35.59N	104.45W
Wągrowiec, Pol. (vôŋ-grô'vyĕts)	155	52.47N	17.14E
Waha, Libya	184	28.16N	19.54E
Wahiawa, Hi., U.S.	96d	21.30N	158.03W
Wahoo, Ne., U.S. (wä-hōō')	102	41.14N	96.39W
Wahpeton, N.D., U.S. (wô'pē-tŭn)	102	46.17N	96.38W
Währing, neigh., Aus.	239e	48.14N	16.21E
Wahroonga, Austl.	243a	33.43S	150.07E
Waialua, Hi., U.S. (wä'ē-ä-lōō'ä)	94a	21.33N	158.08W
Waianae, Hi., U.S. (wä'ē-á-nä'ä)	94a	21.25N	158.11W
Waidhofen, Aus. (vīd'hôf-ĕn)	154	47.58N	14.46E
Waidmannslust, neigh., Ger.	238a	52.36N	13.20E
Waigeo, Pulau, i., Indon. (wä-ē-gā'ô)	197	0.07N	131.00E
Waikato, r., N.Z. (wä'ē-kä'to)	203a	38.10S	175.35E
Waikerie, Austl. (wā'kēr-ē)	204	34.15S	140.00E
Wailuku, Hi., U.S. (wä'ē-lōō'kōō)	96c	20.55N	156.30W
Waimanalo, Hi., U.S. (wä-ē-mä'nä-lo)	94a	21.19N	157.53W
Waimea, Hi., U.S. (wä-ē-mā'ä)	94a	21.56N	159.38W
Wainganga, r., India (wä-ēn-gŭŋ'gä)	183	20.30N	80.15E
Waingapu, Indon.	196	9.32S	120.00E
Wainwright, Can.	84	52.49N	110.52W
Wainwright, Ak., U.S. (wān-rīt)	95	74.40N	159.00W
Waipahu, Hi., U.S. (wä'ē-pä'hōō)	96d	21.20N	158.02W
Waiska, r., Mi., U.S. (wă-ĭz-kă)	107k	46.20N	84.38W
Waitara, Austl.	243a	33.43S	150.06E
Waitsburg, Wa., U.S. (wāts'bûrg)	104	46.17N	118.08W
Wajima, Japan (wä'jē-má)	195	37.23N	136.56E
Wajir, Kenya	217	1.45N	40.04E
Wakami, r., Can.	90	47.43N	82.22W
Wakasa-Wan, b., Japan (wä'kä-sä wän)	194	35.43N	135.39E
Wakatipu, l., N.Z. (wä-kä-tē'pōō)	203a	45.04S	168.30E
Wakayama, Japan (wä-kä'yä-mä)	189	34.14N	135.11E
Wake, i., Oc. (wāk)	3	19.25N	167.00E
Wa Keeney, Ks., U.S. (wô-kē'nē)	110	39.01N	99.53W
Wakefield, Can. (wāk-fēld)	83c	45.39N	75.55W
Wakefield, Eng., U.K.	150	53.41N	1.25W
Wakefield, Ma., U.S.	93a	42.31N	71.05W
Wakefield, Mi., U.S.	103	46.28N	89.55W
Wakefield, Ne., U.S.	102	42.15N	96.52W
Wakefield, R.I., U.S.	100b	41.26N	71.30W
Wake Forest, N.C., U.S. (wāk fŏr'ĕst)	115	35.58N	78.31W
Waki, Japan (wä'kē)	195	34.05N	134.10E
Wakkanai, Japan (wä'kä-nä'ē)	189	45.19N	141.43E
Wakkerstroom, S. Afr. (vák'ĕr-strōm)(wăk'ĕr-strōōm)	212	27.19S	30.04E
Wakonassin, r., Can.	90	46.35N	82.10W
Waku Kundo, Ang.	212	11.25S	15.07E
Wałbrzych, Pol. (väl'bzhûk)	154	50.46N	16.16E
Walcott, Lake, res., Id., U.S.	105	42.40N	113.23W
Wałcz, Pol. (välch)	154	53.11N	16.30E
Waldbauer, neigh., Ger.	236	51.18N	7.28E
Waldoboro, Me., U.S. (wôl'dô-bŭr-ô)	92	44.06N	69.22W
Waldo Lake, l., Or., U.S. (wôl'dō)	104	43.46N	122.10W
Waldorf, Md., U.S. (wăl'dôrf)	100e	38.37N	76.57W
Waldron, Mo., U.S.	107f	39.14N	94.47W
Waldron, i., Wa., U.S.	106d	48.42N	123.02W
Wales, Ak., U.S. (wālz)	95	65.35N	168.14W
Wales, , U.K.	142	52.12N	3.40W
Walewale, Ghana	214	10.21N	0.48W
Walgett, Austl. (wôl'gĕt)	203	30.00S	148.10E
Walhalla, S.C., U.S. (wŭl-hăl'ă)	114	34.45N	83.04W
Walikale, Zaire	217	1.25S	28.03E
Walkden, Eng., U.K.	144a	53.32N	2.24W
Walker, Mn., U.S. (wôk'ĕr)	103	47.06N	94.37W
Walker, r., Nv., U.S.	108	39.07N	119.10W
Walker, Mount, mtn., Wa., U.S.	106a	47.47N	122.54W
Walker Lake, l., Can.	89	54.42N	96.57W
Walker Lake, l., Nv., U.S.	108	38.46N	118.30W
Walker River Indian Reservation, I.R., Nv., U.S.	108	39.06N	118.20W
Walkerville, Mt., U.S. (wôk'ĕr-vĭl)	105	46.20N	112.32W
Wallace, Id., U.S. (wŏl'ās)	104	47.27N	115.55W
Wallaceburg, Can.	90	42.39N	82.25W
Wallach, Ger.	236	51.35N	6.34E
Wallacia, Austl.	201b	33.52S	150.40E
Wallaroo, Austl. (wŏl-ă-rōō)	202	33.52S	137.45E
Wallasey, Eng., U.K. (wŏl'ă-sē)	144a	53.25N	3.03W
Walla Walla, Wa., U.S. (wŏl'á wŏl'á)	96	46.03N	118.20W
Walled Lake, Mi., U.S. (wôl'd lāk)	101b	42.32N	83.29W
Wallel, Tulu, mtn., Eth.	211	9.00N	34.52E
Wallgrove, Austl.	243a	33.47S	150.51E
Wallingford, Eng., U.K. (wŏl'ĭng-fērd)	144b	51.34N	1.08W
Wallingford, Pa., U.S.	229b	39.54N	75.22W
Wallingford, Vt., U.S.	99	43.30N	72.55W
Wallington, N.J., U.S.	228	40.51N	74.07W
Wallington, neigh., Eng., U.K.	235	51.21N	0.09W
Wallis and Futuna Islands, dep., Oc.	225	13.00S	176.10E
Wallisville, Tx., U.S. (wŏl'ĭs-vĭl)	113a	29.50N	94.44W
Wallowa, Or., U.S. (wôl'ô-wă)	104	45.34N	117.32W
Wallowa, r., Or., U.S.	104	45.28N	117.28W
Wallowa Mountains, mts., Or., U.S.	104	45.10N	117.22W
Wallula, Wa., U.S.	104	46.08N	118.55W
Walmersley, Eng., U.K.	237b	53.37N	2.18W
Walnut, Ca., U.S. (wôl'nŭt)	107a	34.00N	117.51W
Walnut, r., Ks., U.S.	111	37.28N	97.06W
Walnut Canyon National Mon, rec., Az., U.S.	109	35.10N	111.30W
Walnut Creek, Ca., U.S.	106b	37.54N	122.04W
Walnut Creek, r., Tx., U.S.	107c	32.37N	97.03W
Walnut Ridge, Ar., U.S. (rĭj)	111	36.04N	90.56W
Walpole, Ma., U.S. (wôl'pōl)	93a	42.09N	71.15W
Walpole, N.H., U.S.	99	43.05N	72.25W
Walsall, Eng., U.K. (wôl-sôl)	150	52.35N	1.58W
Walsenburg, Co., U.S. (wôl'sĕn-bûrg)	110	37.38N	104.46W
Walsum, Ger.	157c	51.32N	6.41E
Walter F. George Reservoir, res., U.S.	114	32.00N	85.00W
Walter Reed Army Medical Center, pt. of i., D.C., U.S.	229d	38.58N	77.02W
Walters, Ok., U.S. (wôl'tērz)	110	34.21N	98.19W
Waltersdorf, Ger.	238a	52.22N	13.35E
Waltham, Ma., U.S. (wôl'thăm)	93a	42.22N	71.14W
Waltham Forest, neigh., Eng., U.K.	235	51.35N	0.01W
Walthamstow, Eng., U.K. (wôl'tăm-stō)	144b	51.34N	0.01W
Walton, Eng., U.K.	235	51.24N	0.25W

364 Walton–Weleetka

PLACE (Pronunciation)	PAGE	Lat. °′	Long. °′
Walton, N.Y., U.S.	99	42.10N	75.05W
Walton-le-Dale, Eng., U.K. (lē-dāl′)	144a	53.44N	2.40W
Walton on the Hill, Eng., U.K.	235	51.17N	0.15W
Waltrop, Ger.	236	51.37N	7.23E
Walt Whitman Homes, N.J., U.S.	229b	39.52N	75.11W
Walvis Bay, Nmb. (wôl′vĭs)	212	22.50S	14.30E
Walworth, Wi., U.S. (wôl′wŭrth)	103	42.33N	88.39W
Walze, Ger.	236	51.16N	7.31E
Wama, Ang.	216	12.14S	15.33E
Wamba, r., Zaire	212	7.00S	18.00E
Wambel, neigh., Ger.	236	51.32N	7.32E
Wamego, Ks., U.S. (wŏ-mē′gō)	111	39.13N	96.17W
Wami, r., Tan. (wä′mē)	213	6.31S	37.17E
Wanapitei Lake, l., Can.	91	46.45N	80.45W
Wanaque, N.J., U.S. (wŏn′ȧ-kū)	100a	41.03N	74.16W
Wanaque Reservoir, res., N.J., U.S.	100a	41.06N	74.20W
Wanda Shan, mts., China (wän-dä shän)	189	45.54N	131.45E
Wandhofen, Ger.	236	51.26N	7.33E
Wandoan, Austl.	204	26.09S	149.51E
Wandsbek, Ger. (vänds′bĕk)	145c	53.34N	10.07E
Wandsworth, Eng., U.K. (wôndz′wûrth)	144b	51.26N	0.12W
Wanganui, N.Z. (wôŋ′gȧ-nōō′ē)	203a	39.53N	175.01E
Wangaratta, Austl. (wŏŋ′gȧ-răt′ȧ)	204	36.23N	146.18E
Wangeroog, i., Ger. (vän′gĕ-rōg)	154	53.49N	7.57E
Wangqingtuo, China (wäŋ-chyĭŋ-twō)	190	39.14N	116.56E
Wangsi, China (wäŋ-sē)	190	37.59N	116.57E
Wangsim-ni, neigh., S. Kor.	241b	37.36N	127.03E
Wanheimerort, neigh., Ger.	236	51.24N	6.46E
Wanne-Eickel, Ger.	236	51.32N	7.09E
Wannsee, neigh., Ger.	238a	52.25N	13.09E
Wansdorf, Ger.	238a	52.38N	13.05E
Wanstead, neigh., Eng., U.K.	235	51.34N	0.02E
Wantage, Eng., U.K. (wŏn′tȧj)	144b	51.33N	1.26W
Wantagh, N.Y., U.S.	100a	40.41N	73.30W
Wantirna, Austl.	243b	37.51S	145.14E
Wantirna South, Austl.	243b	37.52S	145.14E
Wanxian, China (wän-shyĕn)	188	30.48N	108.22E
Wanxian, China (wän shyĕn)	190	38.51N	115.10E
Wanzai, China (wän-dzī)	193	28.05N	114.25E
Wanzhi, China (wän-jr)	190	31.11N	118.31E
Wapakoneta, Oh., U.S. (wä′pȧ-kō-nĕt′ȧ)	98	40.35N	84.10W
Wapawekka Hills, hills, Can. (wŏ′pă-wĕ′kă-hĭlz)	88	54.45N	104.20W
Wapawekka Lake, l., Can.	88	54.55N	104.40W
Wapello, Ia., U.S. (wŏ-pĕl′ō)	103	41.10N	91.11W
Wappapello Reservoir, res., Mo., U.S. (wă′pȧ-pĕl-lō)	97	37.07N	90.10W
Wappingers Falls, N.Y., U.S. (wŏp′ĭn-jẽrz)	99	41.35N	73.55W
Wapsipinicon, r., Ia., U.S. (wŏp′sĭ-pĭn′ĭ-kŏn)	103	42.16N	91.35W
Warabi, Japan (wä′rä-bē)	195a	35.50N	139.41E
Warangal, India (wŭ′raŋ-gȧl)	183	18.03N	79.45E
Warburton, The, r., Austl. (wŏr′bûr-tŭn)	202	27.30S	138.45E
Wardān, Wādī, r., Egypt	181a	29.22N	33.00E
Ward Cove, Ak., U.S.	86	55.24N	131.43W
Warden, S. Afr. (wôr′dĕn)	218d	27.52S	28.59E
Wardha, India (wŭr′dä)	183	20.46N	78.42E
Wardle, Eng., U.K.	237b	53.39N	2.08W
War Eagle, W.V., U.S. (wôr ē′g′l)	98	37.30N	81.50W
Waren, Ger. (vä′rĕn)	154	53.32N	12.43E
Warendorf, Ger. (vä′rĕn-dōrf)	157c	51.57N	7.59E
Wargla, Alg.	210	32.00N	5.18E
Warialda, Austl.	204	29.32S	150.34E
Warlingham, Eng., U.K.	235	51.19N	0.04W
Warmbad, Nmb. (värm′bäd) (wôrm′băd)	212	28.25S	18.45E
Warmbad, S. Afr.	218d	24.52S	28.18E
Warm Beach, Wa., U.S. (wôrm)	106a	48.10N	122.22W
War Memorial Stadium, pt. of i., N.Y., U.S.	230a	42.54N	78.52W
Warm Springs Indian Reservation, I.R., Or., U.S. (wôrm sprĭnz)	104	44.55N	121.30W
Warm Springs Reservoir, res., Or., U.S.	104	43.42N	118.40W
Warner Mountains, mts., Ca., U.S.	96	41.30N	120.17W
Warner Robins, Ga., U.S.	114	32.37N	83.36W
Warnow, r., Ger. (vär′nō)	154	53.51N	11.55E
Warracknabeal, Austl.	204	36.20S	142.28E
Warragamba Reservoir, res., Austl.	204	33.40S	150.00E
Warrandyte, Austl.	243b	37.45S	145.13E
Warrandyte South, Austl.	243b	37.46S	145.14E
Warrāq al-'Arab, Egypt	244a	30.06N	31.12E
Warrāq al-Hadar, Egypt	244a	30.06N	31.13E
Warrawee, Austl.	243a	33.44S	151.07E
Warrego, r., Austl. (wôr′ē-gō)	203	27.13S	145.58E
Warren, Can.	83f	50.08N	97.32W
Warren, Ar., U.S. (wŏr′ĕn)	111	33.37N	92.03W
Warren, In., U.S.	98	40.40N	85.25W
Warren, Mi., U.S.	101b	42.33N	83.03W
Warren, Mn., U.S.	102	48.11N	96.44W
Warren, Oh., U.S.	98	41.15N	80.50W
Warren, Or., U.S.	106c	45.49N	122.51W
Warren, Pa., U.S.	99	41.50N	79.10W
Warren, R.I., U.S.	100b	41.44N	71.14W
Warrendale, Pa., U.S. (wŏr′ĕn-dāl)	101e	40.39N	80.04W
Warrensburg, Mo., U.S. (wŏr′ĕnz-bûrg)	111	38.45N	93.42W
Warrensville Heights, Oh., U.S.	229a	41.26N	81.29W
Warrenton, Ga., U.S. (wŏr′ĕn-tŭn)	115	33.26N	82.37W
Warrenton, Or., U.S.	106c	46.10N	123.56W
Warrenton, Va., U.S.	99	38.45N	77.50W
Warri, Nig. (wär′ē)	210	5.33N	5.43E
Warrington, Eng., U.K.	144a	53.22N	2.30W
Warrington, Fl., U.S. (wŏ′ĭng-tŭn)	114	30.21N	87.15W
Warrnambool, Austl. (wôr′năm-bōōl)	203	38.20S	142.28E
Warroad, Mn., U.S. (wôr′rōd)	102	48.55N	95.20W
Warrumbungle Range, mts., Austl. (wôr′ŭm-bŭŋ-g'l)	203	31.18S	150.00E
Warsaw, Pol.	142	52.15N	21.05E
Warsaw, Il., U.S. (wôr′sô)	111	40.21N	91.26W
Warsaw, In., U.S.	98	41.15N	85.50W
Warsaw, N.Y., U.S.	99	42.45N	78.10W
Warsaw, NC, N.C., U.S.	115	35.00N	78.07W
Warsop, Eng., U.K. (wôr′sŭp)	144a	53.13N	1.05W
Warszawa see Warsaw, Pol.	142	52.15N	21.05E
Warta, r., Pol. (vär′tȧ)	147	52.30N	16.00E
Wartburg, S. Afr.	213c	29.26S	30.39E
Wartenberg, neigh., Ger.	238a	52.34N	13.31E
Warwick, Austl. (wŏr′ĭk)	203	28.05S	152.10E
Warwick, Can.	91	45.58N	71.57W
Warwick, Eng., U.K.	150	52.19N	1.46W
Warwick, N.Y., U.S.	100a	41.15N	74.22W
Warwick, R.I., U.S.	99	41.42N	71.27W
Warwickshire, co., Eng., U.K.	144a	52.30N	1.35W
Wasatch Mountains, mts., Ut., U.S. (wô′săch)	107b	40.45N	111.46W
Wasatch Plateau, plat., Ut., U.S.	109	38.55N	111.40W
Wasatch Range, mts., U.S.	96	39.10N	111.30W
Wasbank, S. Afr.	213c	28.27S	30.09E
Wasco, Or., U.S. (wăs′kō)	104	45.36N	120.42W
Waseca, Mn., U.S. (wô-sē′kȧ)	103	44.04N	93.31W
Waseda University, educ., Japan	242a	35.42N	139.43E
Wash, The, Eng., U.K. (wŏsh)	146	53.00N	0.20E
Washburn, Me., U.S. (wŏsh′bŭrn)	92	46.46N	68.10W
Washburn, Wi., U.S.	103	46.41N	90.55W
Washburn, Mount, mtn., Wy., U.S.	105	44.55N	110.10W
Washington, D.C., U.S. (wŏsh′ĭng-tŭn)	97	38.50N	77.00W
Washington, Ga., U.S.	115	33.43N	82.46W
Washington, In., U.S.	98	38.40N	87.10W
Washington, Ia., U.S.	103	41.17N	91.42W
Washington, Ks., U.S.	111	39.48N	97.04W
Washington, Mo., U.S.	111	38.33N	91.00W
Washington, N.C., U.S.	115	35.32N	77.01W
Washington, Pa., U.S.	98	40.10N	80.14W
Washington, state, U.S.	96	47.30N	121.10W
Washington, i., Wi., U.S.	103	45.18N	86.42W
Washington, Lake, l., Wa., U.S.	106a	47.34N	122.12W
Washington, Mount, mtn., N.H., U.S.	97	44.15N	71.15W
Washington Court House, Oh., U.S.	98	39.30N	83.25W
Washington Monument, pt. of i., D.C., U.S.	229d	38.53N	77.03W
Washington National Airport, arpt., Va., U.S.	229d	38.51N	77.02W
Washington Park, Il., U.S.	107e	38.38N	90.06W
Washita, r., Ok., U.S. (wŏsh′ĭ-tô)	110	35.33N	99.16W
Washougal, Wa., U.S. (wŏ-shōō′gȧl)	106c	45.35N	122.21W
Washougal, r., Wa., U.S.	106c	45.38N	122.17W
Wasilków, Pol. (vȧ-sēl′kôf)	155	53.12N	23.13E
Waskaiowaka Lake, l., Can. (wŏ′skă-yŏ′wŏ-kă)	89	56.30N	96.20W
Wassenberg, Ger. (vä′sĕn-bĕrgh)	157c	51.06N	6.07E
Wassmannsdorf, Ger.	238a	52.22N	13.28E
Wassuk Range, mts., Nv., U.S. (wȧs′sŭk)	108	38.58N	119.00W
Waswanipi, Lac, l., Can.	91	49.35N	76.15W
Water, i., V.I.U.S. (wô′tẽr)	117c	18.20N	64.57W
Waterberge, mts., S. Afr. (wôrtẽr′bûrg)	218d	24.25S	27.53E
Waterboro, S.C., U.S. (wô′tẽr-bûr-ō)	115	32.50N	80.40W
Waterbury, Ct., U.S. (wô′tẽr-bĕr-ē)	99	41.30N	73.00W
Water Cay, i., Bah.	123	22.55N	75.50W
Waterdown, Can. (wô′tẽr-doun)	83d	43.20N	79.54W
Wateree Lake, res., S.C., U.S. (wô′tẽr-ē)	115	34.40N	80.48W
Waterford, Ire. (wô′tẽr-fẽrd)	147	52.20N	7.03W
Waterford, Wi., U.S.	101a	42.46N	88.13W
Waterloo, Bel.	145a	50.44N	4.24E
Waterloo, Can. (wô-tẽr-lōō′)	91	43.30N	80.40W
Waterloo, Can.	91	45.25N	72.30W
Waterloo, Eng., U.K.	237a	53.28N	3.02W
Waterloo, Il., U.S.	111	38.19N	90.08W
Waterloo, Ia., U.S.	97	42.30N	92.22W
Waterloo, Md., U.S.	100e	39.11N	76.50W
Waterloo, N.Y., U.S.	99	42.55N	76.50W
Waterton-Glacier International Peace Park, rec., N.A. (wô′ter-tŭn-glā′shûr)	96	48.55N	114.10W
Waterton Lakes National Park, rec., Can.	87	49.05N	113.50W
Watertown, Ma., U.S. (wô′tẽr-toun)	93a	42.22N	71.11W
Watertown, N.Y., U.S.	97	44.00N	75.55W
Watertown, S.D., U.S.	96	44.53N	97.07W
Watertown, Wi., U.S.	103	43.13N	88.40W
Water Valley, Ms., U.S. (văl′ē)	114	34.08N	89.38W
Waterville, Me., U.S.	92	44.34N	69.37W
Waterville, Mn., U.S.	103	44.10N	93.35W
Waterville, Wa., U.S.	104	47.38N	120.04W
Watervliet, N.Y., U.S. (wô′tẽr-vlēt′)	99	42.45N	73.54W
Watford, Eng., U.K. (wŏt′fŏrd)	150	51.38N	0.24W
Wathaman Lake, l., Can.	88	56.55N	103.43W
Watlington, Eng., U.K.	144b	51.37N	1.01W
Watonga, Ok., U.S. (wŏ-tôŋ′gȧ)	111	35.50N	98.26W
Watsa, Zaire (wät′sä)	211	3.03N	29.32E
Watseka, Il., U.S. (wŏt-sē′kȧ)	98	40.45N	87.45W
Watson, In., U.S. (wŏt′sŭn)	101h	38.21N	85.42W
Watsonia, Austl.	243b	37.43S	145.05E
Watson Lake, Can.	84	60.18N	128.50W
Watsons Bay, Austl.	243a	33.51S	151.17E
Watsonville, Ca., U.S. (wŏt′sŭn-vĭl)	108	36.55N	121.46W
Wattenscheid, Ger. (vä′tĕn-shīd)	157c	51.30N	7.07E
Watts, Ca., U.S. (wŏts)	107a	33.56N	118.15W
Watts Bar Lake, res., Tn., U.S. (bär)	114	35.45N	84.49W
Wattville, S. Afr.	244b	26.13S	28.18E
Waubay, S.D., U.S. (wô′bā)	102	45.19N	97.18W
Wauchula, Fl., U.S. (wô-chōō′lȧ)	115a	27.32N	81.48W
Wauconda, Il., U.S. (wô-kŏn′dȧ)	101a	42.15N	88.08W
Waukegan, Il., U.S. (wŏ-kē′gȧn)	97	42.22N	87.51W
Waukesha, Wi., U.S. (wô′kĕ-shô)	101a	43.01N	88.13W
Waukon, Ia., U.S. (wô kŏn)	103	43.15N	91.30W
Waupaca, Wi., U.S. (wô-păk′ȧ)	103	44.22N	89.06W
Waupun, Wi., U.S. (wô-pŭn′)	103	43.37N	88.45W
Waurika, Ok., U.S. (wô-rē′kȧ)	111	34.09N	97.59W
Wausau, Wi., U.S. (wô′sô)	97	44.58N	89.40W
Wausaukee, Wi., U.S. (wô-sô′kē)	103	45.22N	87.58W
Wauseon, Oh., U.S. (wô′sē-ŏn)	98	41.30N	84.10W
Wautoma, Wi., U.S. (wô-tō′mȧ)	103	44.04N	89.11W
Wauwatosa, Wi., U.S. (wô-wȧ-t′ō′sȧ)	101a	43.03N	88.00W
Waveland, Ma., U.S.	227a	42.17N	70.53W
Waveney, r., Eng., U.K. (wāv′nē)	151	52.27N	1.17E
Waverley, Austl.	243a	33.54S	151.16E
Waverly, S. Afr.	213c	31.54S	26.29E
Waverly, Ia., U.S. (wā′vẽr-lē)	103	42.43N	92.29W
Waverly, Ma., U.S.	227a	42.23N	71.11W
Waverly, Tn., U.S.	114	36.04N	87.46W
Wāw, Sudan	211	7.41N	28.00E
Wawa, Can.	90	47.59N	84.47W
Wāw al-Kabir, Libya	211	25.23N	16.52E
Wawanesa, Can. (wŏ′wŏ-nē′sȧ)	89	49.36N	99.41W
Wawasee, l., In., U.S. (wô-wô-sē′)	98	41.25N	85.45W
Waxahachie, Tx., U.S. (wăk-sȧ-hăch′ē)	113	32.23N	96.50W
Wayland, Ky., U.S. (wā′lănd)	115	37.25N	82.47W
Wayland, Ma., U.S.	93a	42.23N	71.22W
Wayne, Mi., U.S.	101b	42.17N	83.23W
Wayne, Ne., U.S.	102	42.13N	97.03W
Wayne, N.J., U.S.	100a	40.56N	74.16W
Wayne, Pa., U.S.	100f	40.03N	75.22W
Waynesboro, Ga., U.S. (wānz′bŭr-ō)	115	33.05N	82.02W
Waynesboro, Pa., U.S.	99	39.45N	77.35W
Waynesboro, Va., U.S.	99	38.05N	78.50W
Waynesburg, Pa., U.S. (wānz′bûrg)	98	39.55N	80.10W
Waynesville, N.C., U.S. (wānz′vĭl)	115	35.28N	82.58W
Waynoka, Ok., U.S. (wā-nō′kȧ)	110	36.34N	98.52W
Wayzata, Mn., U.S. (wā-zä-tȧ)	107g	44.58N	93.31W
Wazīrābād, neigh., India	240d	28.43N	77.14E
Wazīrbad, Pak.	186	32.39N	74.11E
Wāzīrpur, neigh., India	240d	28.41N	77.10E
Weagamow Lake, l., Can. (wē′ăg-ă-mou)	89	52.53N	91.22W
Weald, The, reg., Eng., U.K. (wēld)	150	50.58N	0.15W
Wealdstone, neigh., Eng., U.K.	235	51.36N	0.20W
Weatherford, Ok., U.S. (wĕ-dhẽr-fẽrd)	110	35.32N	98.41W
Weatherford, Tx., U.S.	113	32.45N	97.46W
Weaver, r., Eng., U.K. (wē′vẽr)	144a	53.09N	2.31W
Weaverville, Ca., U.S. (wē′vẽr-vĭl)	104	40.44N	122.55W
Webb City, Mo., U.S.	111	37.10N	94.26W
Weber, r., Ut., U.S.	107b	41.13N	112.07W
Webster, Ma., U.S.	93a	42.04N	71.52W
Webster, S.D., U.S.	102	45.19N	97.30W
Webster City, Ia., U.S.	103	42.28N	93.49W
Webster Groves, Mo., U.S. (grōvz)	107e	38.36N	90.22W
Webster Springs, W.V., U.S. (sprĭngz)	98	38.30N	80.20W
Wedau, neigh., Ger.	236	51.24N	6.48E
Weddell Sea, sea, Ant. (wĕd′ĕl)	219	73.00S	45.00W
Wedding, neigh., Ger.	238a	52.33N	13.22E
Weddinghofen, Ger.	236	51.36N	7.37E
Wedel, Ger. (vā′dĕl)	145c	53.35N	9.42E
Wedge Mountain, mtn., Can. (wĕj)	87	50.10N	122.50W
Wedgeport, Can. (wĕj′pōrt)	92	43.44N	65.59W
Wednesfield, Eng., U.K. (wĕd′'nz-fēld)	144a	52.36N	2.04W
Weed, Ca., U.S. (wēd)	104	41.35N	122.21W
Weehawken, N.J., U.S.	228	40.46N	74.01W
Weenen, S. Afr. (vā′nĕn)	213c	28.52S	30.05E
Weert, Neth.	151	51.16N	5.39E
Weesow, Ger.	238a	52.39N	13.43E
Weesp, Neth.	145a	52.18N	5.01E
Wegendorf, Ger.	238a	52.36N	13.45E
Węgorzewo, Pol. (vôŋ-gô′zhĕ-vô)	155	54.14N	21.46E
Węgrow, Pol. (vôŋ′grôf)	155	52.23N	22.02E
Wehofen, neigh., Ger.	236	51.32N	6.46E
Wehringhausen, neigh., Ger.	236	51.21N	7.27E
Wei, r., China (wā)	188	34.00N	108.10E
Wei, r., China (wā)	190	35.47N	114.27E
Weichang, China (wā-chäŋ)	189	41.50N	118.00E
Weiden, Ger.	154	49.41N	12.09E
Weidling, Aus.	239e	48.17N	16.19E
Weidlingau, neigh., Aus.	239e	48.13N	16.13E
Weidlingbach, Aus.	239e	48.16N	16.15E
Weifang, China	189	36.43N	119.08E
Weihai, China (wā′hăī′)	189	37.30N	122.05E
Weilheim, Ger. (vīl′hīm′)	154	47.50N	11.06E
Weimar, Ger. (vī′mȧr)	147	50.59N	11.20E
Weinan, China	192	34.32N	109.40E
Weipa, Austl.	203	12.25S	141.54E
Weir, r., Can. (wēr-rĭv-ẽr)	89	56.49N	94.04W
Weirton, W.V., U.S.	98	40.25N	80.35W
Weiser, Id., U.S. (wē′zẽr)	104	44.15N	116.58W
Weiser, r., Id., U.S.	104	44.26N	116.40W
Weishi, China (wā-shr)	192	34.23N	114.12E
Weissenburg, Ger.	154	49.04N	11.20E
Weissenfels, Ger. (vī′sĕn-fĕlz)	154	51.13N	11.58E
Weiss Lake, res., Al., U.S.	114	34.15N	85.35W
Weitmar, neigh., Ger.	236	51.27N	7.12E
Weixi, China (wā-shyē)	188	27.27N	99.30E
Weixian, China (wā shyĕn)	190	36.59N	115.17E
Wejherowo, Pol. (vā-hĕ-rŏ′vô)	155	54.36N	18.15E
Welch, W.V., U.S. (wĕlch)	115	37.24N	81.28W
Welcome Monument, hist., Indon.	241i	6.11S	106.49E
Weldon, N.C., U.S. (wĕl′dŭn)	115	36.24N	77.36W
Weldon, r., Mo., U.S.	111	40.22N	93.39W
Weleetka, Ok., U.S. (wē-lēt′kȧ)	111	35.19N	96.08W

ăt; finăl; rāte; senȧte; ärm; ȧsk; sofȧ; fâre; ch-choose; dh-as th in other; bē; ēvent; bĕt; recĕnt; cratẽr; g-gō; gh-guttural g; bĭt; ĭ-short neutral; rīde; κ-guttural k as ch in German ich;

PLACE (Pronunciation)	PAGE	Lat. °′	Long. °′
Welford, Austl. (wĕl′fẽrd)	204	25.08S	144.43E
Welhamgreen, Eng., U.K.	235	51.44N	0.13W
Welheim, neigh., Ger.	236	51.32N	6.59E
Welkom, S. Afr. (wĕl′kŏm)	212	27.57S	26.45E
Welland, Can. (wĕl′ănd)	91	42.59N	79.13W
Wellesley, Ma., U.S. (wĕlz′lė)	93a	42.18N	71.17W
Wellesley Hills, Ma., U.S.	227a	42.19N	71.17W
Wellesley Islands, is., Austl.	202	16.15S	139.25E
Well Hill, Eng., U.K.	235	51.21N	0.09E
Wellinghofen, neigh., Ger.	236	51.28N	7.29E
Wellington, Austl. (wĕl′lĭng-tŭn)	204	32.40S	148.50E
Wellington, N.Z.	203a	41.15S	174.45E
Wellington, Eng., U.K.	144a	52.42N	2.30W
Wellington, Ks., U.S.	111	37.16N	97.24W
Wellington, Oh., U.S.	98	41.10N	82.10W
Wellington, Tx., U.S.	110	34.51N	100.12W
Wellington, i., Chile (ȯĕ′lēng-tŏn)	132	49.30S	76.30W
Wells, Can.	84	53.06N	121.34W
Wells, Mi., U.S.	98	45.50N	87.00W
Wells, Mn., U.S.	103	43.44N	93.43W
Wells, Nv., U.S.	104	41.07N	115.04W
Wells, l., Austl. (wĕlz)	202	26.35S	123.40E
Wellsboro, Pa., U.S. (wĕlz′bŭ-rȯ)	99	41.45N	77.15W
Wellsburg, W.V., U.S. (wĕlz′bûrg)	98	40.10N	80.40W
Wells Dam, dam, Wa., U.S.	104	48.00N	119.39W
Wellston, Oh., U.S. (wĕlz′tŭn)	98	39.05N	82.30W
Wellsville, Mo., U.S. (wĕlz′vĭl)	111	39.04N	91.33W
Wellsville, N.Y., U.S.	99	42.10N	78.00W
Wellsville, Oh., U.S.	98	40.35N	80.40W
Wellsville, Ut., U.S.	105	41.38N	111.57W
Welper, Ger.	236	51.25N	7.12E
Wels, Aus. (vĕls)	147	48.10N	14.01E
Welshpool, Wales, U.K. (wĕlsh′po͞ol)	150	52.44N	3.10W
Welverdiend, S. Afr. (vĕl-vẽr-dēnd′)	218d	26.23S	27.16E
Welwyn Garden City, Eng., U.K. (wĕlĭn)	144b	51.46N	0.17W
Wem, Eng., U.K. (wĕm)	144a	52.51N	2.44W
Wembere, r., Tan.	217	4.35S	33.55E
Wembley, neigh., Eng., U.K.	235	51.33N	0.18W
Wen, r., China (wŭn)	190	36.24N	119.00E
Wenan Wa, sw., China (wĕn′än′ wä)	190	38.56N	116.29E
Wenatchee, Wa., U.S. (wė-năch′ė)	104	47.24N	120.18W
Wenatchee Mountains, mts., Wa., U.S.	104	47.28N	121.10W
Wenchang, China (wŭn-chäŋ)	193	19.32N	110.42E
Wenchi, Ghana	214	7.42N	2.07W
Wendelville, N.Y., U.S.	230a	43.04N	78.47W
Wendeng, China (wŭn-dŭŋ)	190	37.14N	122.03E
Wendo, Eth.	211	6.37N	38.29E
Wendorer, Ut., U.S.	105	40.47N	114.01W
Wendover, Can. (wĕn-dōv′ẽr)	83c	45.34N	75.07W
Wendover, Eng., U.K.	144b	51.44N	0.45W
Wengern, Ger.	236	51.24N	7.21E
Wenham, Ma., U.S. (wĕn′ăm)	93a	42.36N	70.53W
Wennington, neigh., Eng., U.K.	235	51.30N	0.13E
Wenquan, China (wŭn-chyůän)	189	47.10N	120.00E
Wenshan, China	188	23.20N	104.15E
Wenshang, China (wĕn′shäng)	190	35.43N	116.31E
Wensu, China (wĕn-sȯ)	188	41.45N	80.30E
Wentworth, Austl. (wĕnt′wûrth)	203	34.03S	141.53E
Wentworthville, Austl.	243a	33.49S	150.58E
Wenzhou, China (wŭn-jō)	189	28.00N	120.40E
Wepener, S. Afr. (wē′pĕn-ẽr) (vā′pĕn-ĕr)	212	29.43S	27.04E
Werden, neigh., Ger.	236	51.23N	7.00E
Werder, Ger. (vĕr′dĕr)	145b	52.23N	12.56E
Were Ilu, Eth.	211	10.39N	39.21E
Werl, Ger. (vĕrl)	157c	51.33N	7.55E
Wermelskirchen, Ger.	157c	51.08N	7.13E
Werne, neigh., Ger.	236	51.29N	7.18E
Werneuchen, Ger. (vĕr′hoi-ĸĕn)	145b	52.38N	13.44E
Wernsdorf, Ger.	238a	52.22N	13.43E
Werra, r., Ger. (vĕr′ä)	154	51.16N	9.54E
Werribee, Austl.	201a	37.54S	144.40E
Werribee, r., Austl.	201a	37.40S	144.37E
Wersten, neigh., Ger.	236	51.11N	6.49E
Wertach, r., Ger. (vĕr′täk)	154	48.12N	10.40E
Weseke, Ger. (vĕ′zĕ-kĕ)	157c	51.54N	6.51E
Wesel, Ger. (vā′zĕl)	157c	51.39N	6.37E
Weser, r., Ger. (vā′zĕr)	142	51.00N	10.30E
Weslaco, Tx., U.S. (wĕs-lā′kō)	113	26.10N	97.59W
Weslemkoon, l., Can.	91	45.02N	77.25W
Wesleyville, Can. (wĕs′lē-vĭl)	93	49.09N	53.34W
Wessel Islands, is., Austl. (wĕs′ĕl)	202	11.45S	136.25E
Wesselsbron, S. Afr. (wĕs′ĕl-brŏn)	218d	27.51S	26.22E
Wessington Springs, S.D., U.S. (wĕs′ĭng-tŭn)	102	44.06N	98.35W
West, Mount, mtn., Pan.	116a	9.10N	79.52W
West Abington, Ma., U.S.	227a	42.08N	70.59W
West Allis, Wi., U.S. (wĕst-ăl′ĭs)	101a	43.01N	88.01W
West Alton, Mo., U.S. (ôl′tŭn)	107e	38.52N	90.13W
West Athens, Ca., U.S.	232	33.55N	118.18W
West Bay, b., Fl., U.S.	114	30.20N	85.45W
West Bay, b., Tx., U.S.	113a	29.11N	95.03W
West Bend, Wi., U.S. (wĕst bĕnd)	103	43.25N	88.13W
West Bengal, state, India (bĕn-gôl′)	183	23.30N	87.30E
West Blocton, Al., U.S. (blŏk′tŭn)	114	33.05N	87.05W
Westborough, Ma., U.S. (wĕst′bŭr-ȯ)	93a	42.17N	71.37W
West Boylston, Ma., U.S. (boil′stŭn)	93a	42.22N	71.46W
West Branch, Mi., U.S. (wĕst brȧnch)	98	44.15N	84.10W
West Bridgford, Eng., U.K. (brĭj′fẽrd)	144a	52.55N	1.08W
West Bromwich, Eng., U.K. (wĕst brŭm′ĭj)	144a	52.32N	1.59W
Westbrook, Me., U.S. (wĕst′bro̍ok)	92	43.41N	70.23W
Westbury, N.Y., U.S.	228	40.45N	73.35W
Westby, Wi., U.S. (wĕst′bė)	103	43.40N	90.52W
West Caicos, i., T./C. Is. (käē′kō) (kī′kōs)	123	21.40N	72.30W
West Caldwell, N.J., U.S.	228	40.51N	74.17W
West Cape Howe, c., Austl.	202	35.15S	117.30E
West Carson, Ca., U.S.	232	33.50N	118.18W
Westchester, Il., U.S.	231a	41.51N	87.53W
West Chester, Oh., U.S. (chĕs′tẽr)	101f	39.20N	84.24W
West Chester, Pa., U.S.	100f	39.57N	75.36W
Westchester, neigh., Ca., U.S.	232	33.55N	118.25W
Westchester, neigh., N.Y., U.S.	228	40.51N	73.52W
West Chicago, Il., U.S. (chĭ-kȧ′gō)	101a	41.53N	88.12W
West Collingswood, N.J., U.S.	229b	39.54N	75.06W
West Columbia, S.C., U.S. (cŏl′ŭm-bē-ȧ)	115	33.58N	81.05W
West Columbia, Tx., U.S.	113	29.08N	95.39W
West Conshohocken, N.J., U.S.	229b	40.04N	75.19W
West Cote Blanche Bay, b., La., U.S.	113	29.30N	92.17W
West Covina, Ca., U.S. (wĕst kȯ-vē′nȧ)	107a	34.04N	117.55W
Westdale, Il., U.S.	231a	41.56N	87.55W
West Derby, neigh., Eng., U.K.	237a	53.26N	2.54W
West Des Moines, Ia., U.S. (dē moin′)	103	41.35N	93.42W
West Des Moines, r., Ia., U.S.	103	42.52N	94.32W
West Drayton, neigh., Eng., U.K.	235	51.30N	0.29W
West Elizabeth, Pa., U.S.	230b	40.17N	79.54W
West End, Bah.	122	26.40N	78.55W
West End, Eng., U.K.	235	51.44N	0.04W
West End, neigh., Eng., U.K.	235	51.32N	0.24W
West End, neigh., Pa., U.S.	230b	40.27N	80.02W
Westende, Ger.	236	51.25N	7.24E
Westenfeld, neigh., Ger.	236	51.28N	7.09E
Westerbauer, neigh., Ger.	236	51.20N	7.23E
Westerham, Eng., U.K. (wĕ′stẽr′ŭm)	144b	51.15N	0.05E
Westerholt, Ger.	236	51.36N	7.05E
Westerhörn, Ger. (vĕs′tĕr-hōrn)	145c	53.52N	9.41E
Westerlo, Bel.	145a	51.05N	4.57E
Westerly, R.I., U.S. (wĕs′tẽr-lė)	99	41.25N	71.50W
Western Australia, state, Austl. (ôs-trā′lĭ-ȧ)	202	24.15S	121.30E
Western Dvina *see* Zapadnaya Dvina, r., Eur.	153	55.30N	28.27E
Western Ghāts, mts., India	183	17.35N	74.00E
Western Port, Md., U.S. (wĕs′tẽrn pōrt)	99	39.30N	79.00W
Western Sahara, dep., Afr. (sȧ-hä′rȧ)	210	23.05N	15.33W
Western Samoa, nation, Oc.	2	14.30S	172.00W
Western Siberian Lowland, depr., Russia	164	63.37N	72.45E
Western Springs, Il., U.S.	231a	41.47N	87.53W
Westerville, Oh., U.S. (wĕs′tẽr-vĭl)	98	40.10N	83.00W
Westerwald, for., Ger. (vĕs′tĕr-väld)	154	50.35N	7.45E
Westfalenhalle, pt. of i., Ger.	236	51.30N	7.27E
Westfield, Ma., U.S. (wĕst′fēld)	99	42.05N	72.45W
Westfield, N.J., U.S.	100a	40.39N	74.21W
Westfield, N.Y., U.S. (wĕst′fēld)	100a	42.20N	79.40W
Westford, Ma., U.S. (wĕst′fẽrd)	93a	42.35N	71.26W
West Frankfort, Il., U.S. (frăŋk′fŭrt)	98	37.55N	88.55W
West Ham, Eng., U.K.	144b	51.30N	0.00W
West Hanover, Ma., U.S.	227a	42.07N	70.53W
West Hartford, Ct., U.S. (härt′fẽrd)	99	41.45N	72.45W
Westhead, Eng., U.K.	237a	53.34N	2.51W
West Heidelberg, Austl.	243b	37.45S	145.02E
West Helena, Ar., U.S. (hĕl′ĕn-ȧ)	111	34.32N	90.39W
West Hempstead, N.Y., U.S.	228	40.42N	73.39W
Westhofen, Ger.	236	51.25N	7.31E
West Hollywood, Ca., U.S.	232	34.05N	118.24W
West Homestead, Pa., U.S.	230b	40.24N	79.55W
West Horndon, Eng., U.K.	235	51.34N	0.21E
West Hoxton, Austl.	243a	33.55S	150.50E
West Hyde, Eng., U.K.	235	51.37N	0.30W
Westick, Ger.	236	51.35N	7.38E
West Indies, is. (ĭn′dēz)	117	19.00N	78.30W
West Jordon, Ut., U.S. (jôr′dăn)	107b	40.37N	111.56W
West Kirby, Eng., U.K. (kûr′bė)	144a	53.22N	3.11W
West Lafayette, In., U.S. (lä-fȧ-yĕt′)	98	40.25N	86.55W
Westlake, Oh., U.S.	101d	41.27N	81.55W
Westland, Mi., U.S.	230c	42.19N	83.23W
West Lawn, Va., U.S.	229d	38.52N	77.11W
Westleigh, S. Afr. (wĕst-lē)	218d	27.39S	27.18E
West Liberty, Ia., U.S. (wĕst lĭb′ẽr-tĭ)	103	41.34N	91.15W
West Liberty, neigh., Pa., U.S.	230b	40.24N	80.01W
West Linn, Or., U.S. (lĭn)	106c	45.22N	122.37W
Westlock, Can. (wĕst′lŏk)	87	54.09N	113.52W
West Los Angeles, neigh., Ca., U.S.	232	34.03N	118.28W
West Malling, Eng., U.K.	235	51.18N	0.25E
West Manayunk, Pa., U.S.	229b	40.01N	75.14W
West Memphis, Ar., U.S.	111	35.08N	90.11W
West Midlands, co., Eng., U.K.	144a	52.26N	1.50W
West Mifflin, Pa., U.S.	230b	40.22N	79.52W
Westminster, Ca., U.S. (wĕst′min-stẽr)	107a	33.45N	117.59W
Westminster, Md., U.S.	99	39.40N	76.55W
Westminster, S.C., U.S.	114	34.38N	83.10W
Westminster Abbey, pt. of i., Eng., U.K.	235	51.30N	0.07W
Westmont, Ca., U.S.	232	33.56N	118.18W
Westmount, Can. (wĕst′mount)	83a	45.29N	73.36W
West Newbury, Ma., U.S. (nū′bẽr-ė)	93a	42.47N	70.57W
West Newton, Ma., U.S.	227a	42.21N	71.14W
West Newton, Pa., U.S. (nū′tŭn)	101e	40.12N	79.45W
West New York, N.J., U.S. (nů yŏrk)	100a	40.47N	74.01W
West Nishnabotna, r., Ia., U.S. (nĭsh-nȧ-bŏt′nȧ)	102	40.56N	95.37W
West Norwood, neigh., Eng., U.K.	235	51.26N	0.06W
Weston, Ma., U.S. (wĕs′tŭn)	93a	42.22N	71.18W
Weston, W.V., U.S.	98	39.00N	80.30W
Westonaria, S. Afr.	218d	26.19S	27.38E
Weston-super-Mare, Eng., U.K. (wĕs′tŭn sū′pẽr-mā′rė)	150	51.23N	3.00W
West Orange, N.J., U.S. (wĕst ŏr′ĕnj)	100a	40.46N	74.14W
West Palm Beach, Fl., U.S. (päm bēch)	97	26.44N	80.04W
West Peabody, Ma., U.S.	227a	42.30N	70.57W
West Pensacola, Fl., U.S. (pĕn-sȧ-kō′lȧ)	114	30.24N	87.18W
West Pittsburg, Ca., U.S. (pĭts′bûrg)	106b	38.02N	121.56W
Westplains, Mo., U.S. (wĕst-plānz′)	111	36.42N	91.51W
West Point, Ga., U.S.	114	32.52N	85.10W
West Point, Ms., U.S.	114	33.36N	88.39W
Westpoint, Ne., U.S.	102	41.50N	96.00W
West Point, N.Y., U.S.	100a	41.23N	73.58W
West Point, Ut., U.S.	107b	41.07N	112.05W
West Point, Va., U.S.	99	37.25N	76.50W
West Point Lake, res., U.S.	114	33.00N	85.10W
Westport, Ire.	150	53.44N	9.36W
Westport, Ct., U.S. (wĕst′pōrt)	100a	41.07N	73.22W
Westport, Or., U.S. (wĕst′pôrt)	106c	46.08N	123.22W
West Puente Valley, Ca., U.S.	232	34.04N	117.59W
West Pymble, Austl.	243a	33.46S	151.08E
Westray, i., Scot., U.K. (wĕs′trȧ)	150a	59.19N	3.05W
West Road, r., Can. (rōd)	86	53.00N	124.00W
West Ryde, Austl.	243a	33.48S	151.05E
West Saint Paul, Mn., U.S. (sȧnt pôl′)	107g	44.55N	93.05W
West Sand Spit, i., T./C. Is.	123	21.25N	72.10W
West Seneca, N.Y., U.S.	230a	42.50N	78.45W
West Slope, Or., U.S.	106c	45.30N	122.46W
West Somerville, Ma., U.S.	227a	42.24N	71.07W
West Tavaputs Plateau, plat., Ut., U.S. (wĕst tăv′á-pȯts)	109	39.45N	110.35W
West Terre Haute, In., U.S. (tĕr-ė hōt′)	98	39.30N	87.30W
West Thurrock, Eng., U.K.	235	51.29N	0.16E
West Tilbury, Eng., U.K.	235	51.29N	0.24E
West Turffontein, neigh., S. Afr.	244b	26.16S	28.02E
West Union, Ia., U.S. (ūn′yŭn)	103	42.58N	91.48W
West University Place, Tx., U.S.	113a	29.43N	95.26W
Westview, Oh., U.S. (wĕst′vů)	101d	41.21N	81.54W
West View, Pa., U.S.	101e	40.31N	80.02W
Westville, Can. (wĕst′vĭl)	93	45.35N	62.43W
Westville, Il., U.S.	98	40.00N	87.40W
Westville, N.J., U.S.	229b	39.52N	75.08W
Westville Grove, N.J., U.S.	229b	39.51N	75.07W
West Virginia, state, U.S. (wĕst vẽr-jĭn′ĭ-ȧ)	97	39.00N	80.50W
West Walker, r., Ca., U.S. (wôk′ẽr)	108	38.25N	119.25W
West Warwick, R.I., U.S. (wŏr′ĭk)	100b	41.42N	71.31W
Westwego, La., U.S. (wĕst-wē′gō)	100d	29.55N	90.09W
West Whittier, Ca., U.S.	232	33.59N	118.04W
West Wickham, neigh., Eng., U.K.	235	51.22N	0.01W
Westwood, Ca., U.S. (wĕst′wȯd)	108	40.18N	121.00W
Westwood, Ks., U.S.	107f	39.03N	94.37W
Westwood, Ma., U.S.	93a	42.13N	71.14W
Westwood, N.J., U.S.	100a	40.59N	74.02W
Westwood, neigh., Ca., U.S.	232	34.04N	118.27W
West Wyalong, Austl. (wīȧlông)	203	34.00S	147.20E
West Yorkshire, co., Eng., U.K.	144a	53.37N	1.48W
Wetar, Pulau, i., Indon. (wĕt′ȧr)	197	7.34S	126.00E
Wetaskiwin, Can. (wĕ-tăs′kė-wŏn)	84	52.58N	113.22W
Wetherill Park, Austl.	243a	33.51S	150.54E
Wethmar, Ger.	236	51.37N	7.33E
Wetmore, Tx., U.S. (wĕt′mōr)	107d	29.34N	98.25W
Wetter, Ger.	157c	51.23N	7.23E
Wetumpka, Al., U.S. (wė-tŭmp′kȧ)	114	32.33N	86.12W
Wetzlar, Ger. (vets′lär)	154	50.35N	8.30E
Wewak, Pap. N. Gui. (wȧ-wäk′)	197	3.19S	143.30E
Wewoka, Ok., U.S. (wė-wō′kȧ)	111	35.09N	96.30W
Wexford, Ire. (wĕks′fẽrd)	147	52.20N	6.30W
Weybridge, Eng., U.K. (wā′brĭj)	144b	51.20N	0.26W
Weyburn, Can. (wā′bûrn)	84	49.41N	103.52W
Weyer, neigh., Ger.	236	51.10N	7.01E
Weymouth, Eng., U.K. (wā′mŭth)	150	50.37N	2.34W
Weymouth, Ma., U.S.	93a	42.44N	70.57W
Weymouth, Oh., U.S.	101d	41.11N	81.48W
Whalan, Austl.	243a	33.45S	150.49E
Whale Cay, i., Bah.	122	25.20N	77.45W
Whale Cay Channels, strt., Bah.	122	26.45N	77.10W
Wharton, N.J., U.S. (hwôr′tŭn)	100a	40.54N	74.35W
Wharton, Tx., U.S.	113	29.19N	96.06W
What Cheer, Ia., U.S. (hwŏt chēr)	103	41.23N	92.24W
Whatcom, Lake, l., Wa., U.S. (hwät′kŭm)	106c	48.44N	123.34W
Whatshan Lake, l., Can. (wŏt′shăn)	87	50.00N	118.03W
Wheatland, Wy., U.S. (hwēt′lănd)	105	42.04N	104.52W
Wheatland Reservoir Number 2, res., Wy., U.S.	105	41.52N	105.36W
Wheaton, Il., U.S. (hwē′tŭn)	101a	41.52N	88.06W
Wheaton, Md., U.S.	100e	39.05N	77.05W
Wheaton, Mn., U.S.	102	45.48N	96.29W
Wheeler Peak, mtn., Nv., U.S.	96	38.58N	114.15W
Wheeler Peak, mtn., N.M., U.S.	110	36.34N	105.25W
Wheeling, Il., U.S. (hwēl′ĭng)	101a	42.08N	87.54W
Wheeling, W.V., U.S.	98	40.05N	80.45W
Wheelwright, Arg. (ȯė′l-rē′gt)	129c	33.46S	61.14W
Whelpleyhill, Eng., U.K.	235	51.44N	0.33W
Whidbey Island, i., Wa., U.S. (hwĭd′bė)	106a	48.13N	122.50W
Whippany, N.J., U.S. (hwĭp′á-nē)	100a	40.49N	74.25W
Whiston, Eng., U.K.	237a	53.25N	2.50W
Whitaker, Pa., U.S.	230b	40.24N	79.53W
Whitby, Can. (hwĭt′bė)	85	43.50N	79.00W
Whitby, Eng., U.K.	237a	53.17N	2.54W
Whitchurch, Eng., U.K. (hwĭt′chûrch)	144a	52.58N	2.49W
White, l., Can.	90	48.47N	85.50W
White, l., Can.	91	45.15N	76.35W
White, r., Can.	90	48.34N	85.46W
White, r., U.S.	97	35.30N	92.00W
White, r., U.S.	102	43.41N	99.48W
White, r., U.S.	109	40.10N	108.55W
White, r., In., U.S.	98	39.15N	86.45W
White, r., S.D., U.S.	102	43.13N	101.04W
White, r., Tx., U.S.	110	36.25N	102.20W

ŋg-sing; ŋ-baŋk; ɴ-nasalized n; nŏd; cŏmmit; ōld; ȯbey; ôrder; oi-boil; fo͞od; ȯ-as oo in foot; ou-out; s-soft; sh-dish; th-thin; pūre; ůnite; ûrn; stŭd; circŭs; ü-as in French tu; ′-indeterminate vowel.

ăt; fīnāl; rāte; senáte; ärm; ásk; sofá; fâre;　ch-choose;　dh-as th in other;　bē; ěvent; bět; recěnt; cratēr;　g-gō; gh-guttural g;　bĭt; ī-short neutral; rīde;　κ-guttural k as ch in German ich;

PRONOUNCING INDEX Winter Haven-Xinhuai 367

PLACE (Pronunciation)	PAGE	Lat. °′	Long. °′
Winter Haven, Fl., U.S. (hā'vĕn)	115a	28.01N	81.38W
Winter Park, Fl., U.S. (pärk)	115a	28.35N	81.21W
Winters, Tx., U.S. (wĭn'tẽrz)	112	31.59N	99.58W
Winterset, Ia., U.S. (wĭn'tẽr-sĕt)	103	41.19N	94.03W
Winterswijk, Neth.	157c	51.58N	6.44E
Winterthur, Switz. (vĭn'tĕr-tōōr)	154	47.30N	8.32E
Winterton, S. Afr.	213c	28.51S	29.33E
Winthrop, Me., U.S. (wĭn'thrŭp)	92	44.19N	70.00W
Winthrop, Ma., U.S.	93a	42.23N	70.59W
Winthrop, Mn., U.S.	103	44.31N	94.20W
Winton, Austl. (wĭn-tŭn)	203	22.17S	143.08E
Winz, Ger.	236	51.23N	7.09E
Wipperfürth, Ger. (vē'pĕr-fürt)	157c	51.07N	7.23E
Wirksworth, Eng., U.K. (wûrks'wûrth)	144a	53.05N	1.35W
Wisconsin, state, U.S. (wĭs-kŏn'sĭn)	97	44.30N	91.00W
Wisconsin, r., Wi., U.S.	97	43.14N	90.34W
Wisconsin Dells, Wi., U.S.	103	43.38N	89.46W
Wisconsin Rapids, Wi., U.S.	103	44.24N	89.50W
Wishek, N.D., U.S. (wĭsh'ĕk)	102	46.15N	99.34W
Wisła, r., Pol. (vēs'wȧ)	142	52.30N	20.00E
Wisłoka, r., Pol. (vēs-wō'kȧ)	155	49.55N	21.26E
Wismar, Ger. (vĭs'mär)	146	53.53N	11.28E
Wismar, Guy. (wĭs'mȧr)	131	5.58N	58.15W
Wisner, Ne., U.S. (wĭz'nẽr)	102	42.00N	96.55W
Wissembourg, Fr. (vē-säN-bōōr')	157	49.03N	7.58E
Wissinoming, neigh., Pa., U.S.	229b	40.01N	75.04W
Wissous, Fr.	237c	48.44N	2.20E
Wister, Lake, l., Ok., U.S. (vĭs'tẽr)	111	35.02N	94.52W
Witbank, S. Afr. (wĭt-băŋk)	218d	25.53S	29.14E
Witberg, mtn., Afr.	213c	30.32S	27.18E
Witfield, S. Afr.	244b	26.11S	28.12E
Witham, Eng., U.K. (wĭdh'ăm)	144b	51.48N	0.37E
Witham, r., Eng., U.K.	144a	53.11N	0.20W
Withamsville, Oh., U.S. (wĭdh'ămz-vĭl)	101f	39.04N	84.16W
Withington, neigh., Eng., U.K.	237b	53.26N	2.14W
Withlacoochee, r., Fl., U.S. (wĭth-lȧ-kōō'chē)	115a	28.58N	82.30W
Withlacoochee, r., Ga., U.S.	114	31.15N	83.30W
Withrow, Mn., U.S. (wĭdh'rō)	107g	45.08N	92.54W
Witney, Eng., U.K. (wĭt'nē)	144b	51.45N	1.30W
Witpoortje, S. Afr.	244b	26.08S	27.50E
Witt, Il., U.S. (vĭt)	98	39.10N	89.15W
Witten, Ger. (vē'tĕn)	157c	51.26N	7.19E
Wittenau, neigh., Ger.	238a	52.35N	13.20E
Wittenberg, Ger. (vē'tĕn-bĕrgh)	154	51.53N	12.40E
Wittenberge, Ger. (vĭt-ĕn-bĕr'gē)	154	52.59N	11.45E
Wittlaer, Ger.	236	51.19N	6.44E
Wittlich, Ger. (vĭt'lĭk)	154	49.58N	6.54E
Witu, Kenya (wē'tōō)	213	2.18S	40.28E
Witu Islands, is., Pap. N. Gui.	197	4.45S	149.50E
Witwatersberg, mts., S. Afr. (wĭt-wôr-tẽrz-bûrg)	213b	25.58S	27.53E
Witwatersrand, mtn., S. Afr. (wĭt-wôr'tẽrs-rănd)	218d	25.55S	26.27E
Witwatersrand, University of, educ., S. Afr.	244b	26.12S	28.02E
Witwatersrand Gold Mines, quarry, S. Afr.	244b	26.12S	28.10E
Wkra, r., Pol. (f'krȧ)	155	52.40N	20.35E
Włocławek, Pol. (vwô-tswä'vĕk)	155	52.38N	19.08E
Włodawa, Pol. (vwô-dä'vä)	155	51.33N	23.33E
Włoszczowa, Pol. (vwôsh-chô'vä)	155	50.51N	19.58E
Woburn, Ma., U.S. (wō'bŭrn) (wō'bŭrn)	93a	42.29N	71.10W
Woburn, neigh., Can.	227c	43.46N	79.13W
Woerden, Neth.	145a	52.05N	4.52E
Woking, Eng., U.K.	144b	51.18N	0.33W
Wokingham, Eng., U.K. (wō'kĭng-hăm)	144b	51.23N	0.50W
Wolcott, Ks., U.S. (wȯl'kŏt)	107f	39.12N	94.47W
Woldingham, Eng., U.K.	235	51.17N	0.02W
Wolf, i., Can. (wȯlf)	91	44.10N	76.25W
Wolf, r., Ms., U.S.	114	30.45N	89.36W
Wolf, r., Wi., U.S.	103	45.14N	88.45W
Wolfenbüttel, Ger. (vôl'fĕn-büt-ĕl)	154	52.10N	10.32E
Wolf Lake, l., Il., U.S.	101a	41.39N	87.33W
Wolf Point, Mt., U.S. (wȯlf point)	105	48.07N	105.40W
Wolfratshausen, Ger. (vōlf'räts-hou-zĕn)	145d	47.55N	11.25E
Wolfsburg, Ger. (vôlfs'bōōrgh)	154	52.30N	10.37E
Wolfville, Can. (wȯlf'vĭl)	92	45.05N	64.22W
Wolgast, Ger. (vôl'gäst)	154	54.04N	13.46E
Wolhuterskop, S. Afr.	213b	25.41S	27.40E
Wolkersdorf, Aus.	145e	48.24N	16.31E
Wollaston, Ma., U.S.	227a	42.16N	71.01W
Wollaston, l., Can. (wȯl'ăs-tŭn)	84	58.15N	103.20W
Wollaston Peninsula, pen., Can.	84	70.00N	115.00W
Wollongong, Austl. (wȯl'ŭn-gŏng)	203	34.26S	151.05E
Wołomin, Pol. (vō-wō'mēn)	155	52.19N	21.17E
Wolseley, Can.	88	50.25N	103.15W
Woltersdorf, Ger. (vōl'tĕs-dōrf)	145b	52.07N	13.13E
Woltersdorf, Ger.	238a	52.26N	13.45E
Wolverhampton, Eng., U.K. (wȯl'vẽr-hămp-tŭn)	147	52.35N	2.07W
Wolverine, Mi., U.S.	230c	42.33N	83.29W
Wolwehoek, S. Afr.	218d	26.55S	27.50E
Wonga Park, Austl.	243b	37.44S	145.16E
Wŏnsan, N. Kor. (wŭn'sän')	189	39.08N	127.24E
Wonthaggi, Austl. (wȯnt-hăg'ē)	203	38.45S	145.42E
Wood, S.D., U.S. (wȯd)	102	43.26N	100.25W
Woodbine, Ia., U.S. (wȯd'bīn)	102	41.44N	95.42W
Woodbridge, N.J., U.S. (wȯd'brĭj')	100a	40.33N	74.18W
Woodbrook, Md., U.S.	229c	39.23N	76.37W
Wood Buffalo National Park, rec., Can.	84	59.50N	118.53W
Woodburn, Il., U.S. (wȯd'bûrn)	107e	39.03N	90.01W
Woodburn, Or., U.S.	104	45.10N	122.51W
Woodbury, N.J., U.S. (wȯd'bĕr-ē)	100f	39.50N	75.14W
Woodbury, N.Y., U.S.	228	40.49N	73.28W
Woodbury Terrace, N.J., U.S.	229b	39.51N	75.08W
Woodcrest, Ca., U.S. (wȯd'krĕst)	107a	33.53N	117.18W
Woodford, Eng., U.K.	237b	53.21N	2.10W
Woodford Bridge, neigh., Eng., U.K.	235	51.36N	0.04E
Wood Green, neigh., Eng., U.K.	235	51.36N	0.07W
Woodhaven, neigh., N.Y., U.S.	228	40.41N	73.51W
Woodinville, Wa., U.S. (wȯd'ĭn-vĭl)	106a	47.46N	122.09W
Woodland, Ca., U.S. (wȯd'lănd)	108	38.41N	121.47W
Woodland, Wa., U.S.	106c	45.54N	122.45W
Woodland Hills, Ca., U.S.	107a	34.10N	118.36W
Woodlands, Sing.	240c	1.27N	103.46E
Woodlark Island, i., Pap. N. Gui. (wȯd'lärk)	197	9.07S	152.00E
Woodlawn, Md., U.S.	229c	39.19N	76.43W
Woodlawn, Md., U.S.	229d	38.57N	76.53W
Woodlawn, neigh., Il., U.S.	231a	41.47N	87.36W
Woodlawn Beach, N.Y., U.S. (wȯd'lôn bēch)	101c	42.48N	78.51W
Woodlawn Heights, Md., U.S.	229c	39.11N	76.39W
Woodlyn, Pa., U.S.	229b	39.52N	75.21W
Woodlynne, N.J., U.S.	229b	39.55N	75.05W
Woodmansterne, Eng., U.K.	235	51.19N	0.10W
Woodmere, N.Y., U.S.	228	40.38N	73.43W
Woodmoor, Md., U.S.	229c	39.20N	76.44W
Wood Mountain, mtn., Can.	88	49.14N	106.20W
Wood Ridge, N.J., U.S.	228	40.51N	74.05W
Wood River, Il., U.S.	107e	38.52N	90.06W
Woodroffe, Mount, mtn., Austl. (wȯd'rŭf)	202	26.05S	132.00E
Woodruff, S.C., U.S. (wȯd'rŭf)	115	34.43N	82.03W
Woods, l., Austl. (wȯdz)	202	18.00S	133.18E
Woods, Lake of the, l., N.A.	85	49.25N	93.25W
Woodsburgh, N.Y., U.S.	228	40.37N	73.42W
Woods Cross, Ut., U.S. (krôs)	107b	40.53N	111.54W
Woodsfield, Oh., U.S. (wȯdz-fēld)	98	39.45N	81.10W
Woodside, neigh., N.Y., U.S.	228	40.45N	73.55W
Woodson, Or., U.S. (wȯdsŭn)	106c	46.07N	123.20W
Woodstock, Can.	85	46.09N	67.34W
Woodstock, Can. (wȯd'stŏk)	91	43.10N	80.50W
Woodstock, Eng., U.K.	144b	51.48N	1.22W
Woodstock, Il., U.S.	103	42.20N	88.29W
Woodstock, Va., U.S.	99	38.55N	78.25W
Woodsville, N.H., U.S. (wȯdz'vĭl)	99	44.10N	72.00W
Woodville, Ms., U.S. (wȯd'vĭl)	114	31.06N	91.11W
Woodville, Tx., U.S.	113	30.48N	94.25W
Woodward, Ok., U.S. (wȯd'wôrd)	110	36.25N	99.24W
Woollahra, Austl.	243a	33.53S	151.15E
Woolton, neigh., Eng., U.K.	237a	53.23N	2.52W
Woolwich, Eng., U.K. (wȯl'ĭj)	144b	51.28N	0.05E
Woomera, Austl. (wōōm'ẽrȧ)	202	31.15S	136.43E
Woonsocket, R.I., U.S. (wōōn-sŏk'ĕt)	100b	42.00N	71.30W
Woonsocket, S.D., U.S.	102	44.03N	98.17W
Wooster, Oh., U.S. (wȯs'tẽr)	98	40.50N	81.55W
Worcester, S. Afr. (wōōs'tẽr)	212	33.35S	19.31E
Worcester, Eng., U.K. (wȯ'stẽr)	147	52.09N	2.14W
Worcester, Ma., U.S. (wȯs'tẽr)	97	42.16N	71.49W
Worden, Il., U.S. (wôr'dĕn)	107e	38.56N	89.50W
Workington, Eng., U.K. (wûr'kĭng-tŭn)	150	54.40N	3.30W
Worksop, Eng., U.K. (wûrk'sŏp) (wûr'sŭp)	144a	53.18N	1.07W
Worland, Wy., U.S. (wûr'lănd)	105	44.02N	107.56W
Wormley, Eng., U.K.	235	51.44N	0.01W
Worms, Ger. (vōrms)	147	49.37N	8.22E
Worona Reservoir, res., Austl.	201b	34.12S	150.55E
Woronora, Austl.	243a	34.01S	151.03E
Worsley, Eng., U.K.	237b	53.30N	2.23W
Worth, Il., U.S. (wûrth)	101a	41.42N	87.47W
Wortham, Tx., U.S. (wûr'dhăm)	113	31.46N	96.22W
Worthing, Eng., U.K. (wûr'dhĭng)	150	50.48N	0.29W
Worthington, In., U.S. (wûr'dhĭng-tŭn)	98	39.05N	87.00W
Worthington, Md., U.S.	229c	39.14N	76.47W
Worthington, Mn., U.S.	102	43.38N	95.36W
Worth Lake, l., Tx., U.S.	107c	32.48N	97.32W
Wowoni, Pulau, i., Indon. (wō-wō'nē)	197	4.05S	123.45E
Wragby, Eng., U.K. (răg'bē)	144a	53.17N	0.19W
Wrangell, Ak., U.S. (răn'gĕl)	96a	56.28N	132.25W
Wrangell, Mount, mtn., Ak., U.S.	95	61.58N	143.50W
Wrangell Mountains, mts., Ak., U.S.	95	62.28N	142.40W
Wrangell-Saint Elias National Park, rec., Ak., U.S.	95	61.00N	142.00W
Wrath, Cape, c., Scot., U.K. (răth)	150	58.34N	5.01W
Wray, Co., U.S. (rā)	110	40.06N	102.14W
Wraysbury, Eng., U.K.	235	51.27N	0.33W
Wreak, r., Eng., U.K. (rēk)	144a	52.45N	0.59W
Wreck Reefs, rf., Austl. (rĕk)	203	22.00S	155.52E
Wrekin, The, mtn., Eng., U.K. (rĕk'ĭn)	144a	52.40N	2.33W
Wrens, Ga., U.S. (rĕnz)	115	33.15N	82.25W
Wrentham, Ma., U.S.	93a	42.04N	71.20W
Wrexham, Wales, U.K. (rĕk'săm)	150	53.03N	3.00W
Wrights Corners, N.Y., U.S. (rīts kôr'nẽrz)	101c	43.14N	78.42W
Wrightsville, Ga., U.S. (rīts'vĭl)	115	32.44N	82.44W
Writtle, Eng., U.K.	235	51.44N	0.26E
Wrocław, Pol. (vrôtsläv) (brĕs'lou)	155	51.07N	17.10E
Wrotham, Eng., U.K. (rōōt'ŭm)	144b	51.18N	0.19E
Wrotham Heath, Eng., U.K.	235	51.18N	0.21E
Września, Pol. (vzhăsh'nyȧ)	155	52.19N	17.33E
Wu, r., China (wōō')	188	27.30N	107.00E
Wuchang, China (wōō-chäŋ)	189	30.32N	114.25E
Wuchang, China	192	44.59N	127.00E
Wucheng, China (wōō-chŭŋ)	190	37.14N	116.03E
Wuhan, China	189	30.30N	114.15E
Wuhu, China (wōō'hōō)	193	31.22N	118.22E
Wuji, China (wōō-jyē)	190	38.12N	114.57E
Wujiang, China (wōō-jyäŋ)	190	31.10N	120.38E
Wuleidao Wan, b., China (wōō-lā-dou wän)	190	36.55N	122.00E
Wülfrath, Ger.	236	51.17N	7.02E
Wulidian, China (wōō-lē-diĕn)	190	32.09N	114.17E
Wünsdorf, Ger. (vüns'dorf)	145b	52.10N	13.29E
Wupatki National Monument, rec., Az., U.S.	109	35.35N	111.45W
Wuping, China (wōō-pĭŋ)	193	25.05N	116.01E
Wupper, r., Ger.	236	51.14N	7.06E
Wuppertal, Ger. (vȯp'ẽr-täl)	147	51.16N	7.14E
Wuqiao, China (wōō-chyou)	190	37.37N	116.29E
Würm, r., Ger. (vürm)	145d	48.07N	11.20E
Würselen, Ger. (vür'zĕ-lĕn)	157c	50.49N	6.09E
Würzburg, Ger. (vürts'bȯrgh)	147	49.48N	9.57E
Wurzen, Ger. (vȯrt'sĕn)	147	51.22N	12.45E
Wushi, China (wōō-shr)	188	41.13N	79.08E
Wusong, China (wōō-sôŋ)	190	31.23N	121.29E
Wustermark, Ger. (vōōs'tẽr-märk)	145b	52.33N	12.57E
Wustrau, Ger. (vōost'rou)	145b	52.40N	12.51E
Wuustwezel, Bel.	145a	51.23N	4.36E
Wuwei, China (wōō'wā')	193	31.19N	117.53E
Wuxi, China (wōō-shyē)	189	31.36N	120.17E
Wuxing, China (wōō-shyĭŋ)	189	30.38N	120.10E
Wuyi Shan, mts., China (wōō-yē shän)	193	26.38N	116.35E
Wuyou, China (wōō-yō)	190	33.18N	120.15E
Wuzhi Shan, mtn., China (wōō-jr shän)	193	18.48N	109.30E
Wuzhou, China (wōō-jō)	189	23.32N	111.25E
Wyandotte, Mi., U.S. (wī'ăn-dŏt)	101b	42.12N	83.10W
Wye, Eng., U.K. (wī)	144b	51.12N	0.57E
Wye, r., Eng., U.K.	144a	53.14N	1.46W
Wylie, Lake, res., S.C., U.S.	115	35.02N	81.21W
Wymore, Ne., U.S. (wī'mōr)	111	40.09N	96.41W
Wynberg, S. Afr. (wĭn'bĕrg)	212a	34.00S	18.28E
Wyncote, Pa., U.S.	229b	40.05N	75.09W
Wyndham, Austl. (wĭnd'ăm)	202	15.30S	128.15E
Wyndmoor, Pa., U.S.	229b	40.05N	75.12W
Wynne, Ar., U.S. (wĭn)	111	35.12N	90.46W
Wynnewood, Ok., U.S. (wĭn'wȯd)	111	34.39N	97.10W
Wynnewood, Pa., U.S.	229b	40.01N	75.17W
Wynona, Ok., U.S. (wī-nō'nȧ)	111	36.33N	96.19W
Wynyard, Can. (wĭn'yẽrd)	84	51.47N	104.10W
Wyoming, Oh., U.S. (wī-ō'mĭng)	101f	39.14N	84.28W
Wyoming, state, U.S.	96	42.50N	108.30W
Wyoming Range, mts., Wy., U.S.	96	42.43N	110.35W
Wyre Forest, for., Eng., U.K. (wīr)	144a	52.24N	2.24W
Wysokie Mazowieckie, Pol. (vē-sô'kyĕ mä-zô-vyĕts'kyĕ)	155	52.55N	22.42E
Wyszków, Pol. (vēsh'kȯf)	155	52.35N	21.29E
Wythenshawe, neigh., Eng., U.K.	237b	53.24N	2.17W
Wytheville, Va., U.S. (wĭth'vĭl)	115	36.55N	81.06W

X

PLACE (Pronunciation)	PAGE	Lat. °′	Long. °′
Xabregas, neigh., Port.	238d	38.44N	9.07W
Xagua, Banco, bk., Cuba (bä'n-kō-sä'gwä)	122	21.35N	80.50W
Xai Xai, Moz.	212	25.00S	33.45E
Xalapa, Mex.	116	19.32N	96.53W
Xangongo, Ang.	212	16.50S	15.05E
Xankändi (Stepanakert), Azer. (styĕ'pän-ȧ-kĕrt)	167	39.50N	46.40E
Xanten, Ger. (ksän'tĕn)	157c	51.40N	6.28E
Xánthi, Grc.	149	41.08N	24.53E
Xau, Lake, l., Bots.	212	21.15S	24.38E
Xcalak, Mex. (sä-lä'k)	120a	18.15N	87.50W
Xenia, Oh., U.S. (zē'nĭ-ȧ)	98	39.40N	83.55W
Xi, r., China (shyē)	193	23.15N	112.10E
Xiajin, China (shyä-jyĭn)	192	36.58N	115.59E
Xiamen, China	189	24.30N	118.10E
Xiamen, i., Tai. (shyä-mŭn)	193	24.28N	118.20E
Xi'an, China (shyē-än)	188	34.20N	109.00E
Xiang, r., China (shyäŋ)	189	27.30N	112.30E
Xianghe, China (shyäŋ-hŭ)	190	39.46N	116.59E
Xiangtan, China (shyäŋ-tän)	189	27.55N	112.45E
Xianyang, China (shyĕn-yäŋ)	192	34.20N	108.40E
Xiaoxingkai Hu, l., China (shyou-shyĭŋ-kī hōō)	194	42.25N	132.45E
Xiaoxintian, China	240b	39.58N	116.22E
Xiapu, China (shyä-pōō)	189	27.00N	120.00E
Xiayi, China (shyä-yē)	190	34.15N	116.07E
Xicotencatl, Mex. (sē-kō-tĕn-kät'l)	118	23.00N	98.58W
Xifeng, China (shyē-fŭŋ)	192	42.40N	124.40E
Xiheying, China (shyē-hŭ-yĭŋ)	190	39.58N	114.50E
Xiliao, r., China (shyē-lĭou)	192	41.40N	122.40E
Xiliao, r., China	192	43.23N	121.40E
Xilitla, Mex. (sē-lē'tlä)	118	21.24N	98.59W
Xinchang, China (shyĭn-chäŋ)	191b	31.02N	121.38E
Xing'an, China (shyĭŋ-än)	193	25.44N	110.32E
Xingcheng, China (shyĭŋ-chŭŋ)	190	40.38N	120.41E
Xinghua, China (shyĭŋ-hwä)	190	32.58N	119.48E
Xingjiawan, China (shyĭŋ-jyä-wän)	190	37.16N	114.54E
Xingtai, China (shyĭŋ-tī)	192	37.04N	114.33E
Xingu, r., Braz. (zhĕŋ-gō')	131	6.20S	52.34W
Xinhai, China (shyĭn-hī)	190	36.59N	117.33E
Xinhua, China (shyĭn-hwä)	193	27.45N	111.20E
Xinhuai, r., China (shyĭn-hwī)	190	33.48N	119.39E

ng-sing; ŋ-baŋk; N-nasalized n; nŏd; cŏmmit; ōld; ōbey; ôrder; oi-boil; fōōd; ȯ-as oo in foot; ou-out; s-soft; sh-dish; th-thin; pūre; ůnite; ûrn; stŭd; circŭs; ü-as in French tu; '-indeterminate vowel.

368 Xinhui – York

PLACE (Pronunciation)	PAGE	Lat. °′	Long. °′
Xinhui, China (shyn-hwä)	193	22.40N	113.08E
Xining, China (shyē-niŋ)	188	36.52N	101.36E
Xinjiang Uygur (Sinkiang), prov., China (shyĭn-jyäŋ)	188	40.15N	82.15E
Xinjin, China (shyĭn-jyĭn)	192	39.23N	121.57E
Xinmin, China (shyĭn-mĭn)	192	42.00N	122.42E
Xintai, China (shyĭn-tī)	190	35.55N	117.44E
Xintang, China (shyĭn-täŋ)	191a	23.08N	113.36E
Xinxian, China (shyĭn shyĕn)	190	31.47N	114.50E
Xinxian, China	192	38.20N	112.45E
Xinxiang, China (shyĭn-shyäŋ)	192	35.17N	113.49E
Xinyang, China (shyĭn-yäŋ)	189	32.08N	114.04E
Xinye, China (shyĭn-yŭ)	192	32.40N	112.20E
Xinzao, China (shyĭn-dzou)	191a	23.01N	113.25E
Xinzheng, China (shyĭn-jŭŋ)	190	34.24N	113.43E
Xinzhuang, China	240b	39.56N	116.31E
Xiongyuecheng, China (shyôŋ-yůě-chŭŋ)	190	40.10N	122.08E
Xiping, China (shyē-pĭŋ)	190	33.21N	114.01E
Xishui, China (shyē-shwā)	193	30.30N	115.10E
Xixian, China (shyē shyĕn)	190	32.20N	114.42E
Xiyang, China (shyē-yäŋ)	190	37.37N	113.42E
Xiyou, China (shyē-yō)	190	37.21N	119.59E
Xizang (Tibet), prov., China (shyē-dzäŋ)	188	31.15N	87.30E
Xizhong Dao, i., China (shyē-jôŋ dou)	190	39.27N	121.06E
Xochihuehuetlán, Mex. (sô-chē-wĕ-wĕ-tlá'n)	119	17.53N	98.29E
Xochimilco, Mex. (sō-chė-mēl'kô)	119a	19.15N	99.06W
Xochimilco, Lago de, l., Mex.	233a	19.16N	99.06W
Xuancheng, China (shyůän-chŭŋ)	193	30.52N	118.48E
Xuanhua, China (shyůän-hwä)	192	40.35N	115.05E
Xuanhuadian, China (shyůän-hwä-dĭĕn)	190	31.42N	114.29E
Xuchang, China (shyōō-chäŋ)	192	34.02N	113.49E
Xudat, Azer.	168	41.38N	48.42E
Xuddur, Som.	218a	3.55N	43.45E
Xun, r., China (shyòn)	193	23.28N	110.30E
Xuzhou, China	189	34.17N	117.10E

Y

PLACE (Pronunciation)	PAGE	Lat. °′	Long. °′
Ya'an, China (yä-än)	188	30.00N	103.20E
Yablonovyy Khrebet, mts., Russia (yȧ-blô-nô-vė')	165	51.15N	111.30E
Yablunivs'kyy, Pereval, p., Ukr.	155	48.20N	24.25E
Yacheng, China (yä-chŭŋ)	193	18.20N	109.10E
Yachiyo, Japan	195a	35.43N	140.07E
Yacolt, Wa., U.S. (yă'kôlt)	106c	45.52N	122.24W
Yacolt Mountain, mtn., Wa., U.S.	106c	45.52N	122.27W
Yacona, r., Ms., U.S. (yá'cō nă)	114	34.13N	89.30W
Yacuiba, Bol. (yá-kōō-ē'bá)	130	22.02S	63.44W
Yadkin, r., N.C., U.S. (yăd'kĭn)	115	36.12N	80.40W
Yafran, Libya	210	31.57N	12.04E
Yaguajay, Cuba (yä-guä-hä'ė)	122	22.20N	79.20W
Yahagi-Gawa, r., Japan (yä'hä-gė gä'wä)	195	35.16N	137.22E
Yaho, Japan	242a	35.41N	139.27E
Yahongqiao, China (yä-hôŋ-chyou)	190	39.45N	117.52E
Yahotyn, Ukr.	163	50.18N	31.46E
Yahualica, Mex. (yä-wä-lē'kä)	118	21.08N	102.53W
Yajalón, Mex. (yä-hä-lōn')	119	17.16N	92.20W
Yakhroma, Russia (yäl'rô-ma)	172b	56.17N	37.30E
Yakhroma, r., Russia	172b	56.15N	37.38E
Yakima, Wa., U.S. (yăk'ĭmȧ)	96	46.35N	120.30W
Yakima, r., Wa., U.S. (yăk'ĭ-mȧ)	104	46.48N	120.22W
Yakima Indian Reservation, I.R., Wa., U.S.	104	46.16N	121.03W
Yakō, neigh., Japan	242a	35.32N	139.41E
Yakoma, Zaire	216	4.05N	22.27E
Yaku, i., Japan (yä'kōō)	189	30.15N	130.41E
Yakutat, Ak., U.S. (yăk'ò-tăt)	95	59.32N	139.35W
Yakutsk, Russia (yá-kòtsk')	165	62.13N	129.49E
Yale, Mi., U.S.	98	43.05N	82.45W
Yale, Ok., U.S.	111	36.07N	96.42W
Yale Lake, res., Wa., U.S.	104	46.00N	122.20W
Yalinga, Cen. Afr. Rep. (yá-lĭŋ'gá)	211	6.56N	23.22E
Yalobusha, r., Ms., U.S. (yá-lô-bòsh'ȧ)	114	33.48N	90.02W
Yalong, r., China (yä-lòŋ)	188	32.29N	98.41E
Yalta, Ukr. (yäl'tà)	167	44.29N	34.12E
Yalu, r., Asia	189	41.20N	126.35E
Yalutorovsk, Russia (yä-lōō-tô'rôfsk)	164	56.42N	66.32E
Yamada, Japan (yä'má-dá)	195	33.37N	133.39E
Yamagata, Japan (yä-mä'gä-tä)	189	38.12N	140.24E
Yamaguchi, Japan (yä-má'gōō-chė)	194	34.10N	131.30E
Yamaguchi, Japan	242b	34.50N	135.15E
Yamal, Poluostrov, pen., Russia (yä-mäl')	164	71.15N	70.00E
Yamal-Nenets, state, Russia	170	67.00N	75.00E
Yamantau, Gora, mtn., Russia (gá-rä' yä'man-tâw)	172a	54.16N	58.08E
Yamasaki, Japan (yä'má'sä-kė)	195	35.01N	134.33E
Yamasaki, Japan	195b	34.53N	135.41E
Yamashina, Japan (yä'mä-shė'nä)	195b	34.59N	135.50E
Yamashita, Japan (yä'mä-shė'tä)	195b	34.53N	135.25E
Yamato, Japan	195a	35.28N	139.28E
Yamato, Japan	242a	35.44N	139.26E
Yamato, Japan	242a	35.47N	139.37E
Yamato, r., Japan	242b	34.36N	135.26E
Yamato-Kōriyama, Japan	195b	34.39N	135.48E
Yamato-takada, Japan (yä'mä-tô tä'kä-dä)	195b	34.31N	135.45E
Yambi, Mesa de, mtn., Col. (mě'sä-dě-yá'm-bē)	130	1.55N	71.45W
Yambol, Bul. (yàm'bôl)	149	42.28N	26.31E
Yamdena, i., Indon.	197	7.23S	130.30E
Yamenkou, China	240b	39.53N	116.12E
Yamethin, Myanmar (yŭ-mē'thèn)	183	20.14N	96.27E
Yamhill, Or., U.S. (yăm'hĭl)	106c	45.20N	123.11W
Yamkino, Russia (yäm'kĭ-nô)	172b	55.56N	38.25E
Yamma Yamma, Lake, l., Austl. (yăm'á yăm'á)	203	26.15S	141.30E
Yamoussoukro, C. Iv.	210	6.49N	5.17W
Yamsk, Russia (yämsk)	165	59.41N	154.09E
Yamuna, r., India	183	25.30N	80.30E
Yamzho Yumco, l., China (yäm-jwo yōōm-tswo)	188	29.11N	91.26E
Yana, r., Russia (yä'ná)	165	71.00N	136.00E
Yanac, Austl. (yăn'ăk)	203	36.10S	141.30E
Yanagawa, Japan (yä-nä'gä-wä)	195	33.11N	130.24E
Yanam, India (yŭnŭm')	183	16.48N	82.15E
Yan'an, China (yän-än)	188	36.46N	109.15E
Yanbu', Sau. Ar.	182	23.57N	38.02E
Yancheng, China (yän-chŭŋ)	192	33.23N	120.11E
Yancheng, China	192	33.38N	113.59E
Yandongi, Zaire	216	2.51N	22.16E
Yangcheng Hu, l., China (yäŋ-chŭŋ hōō)	190	31.30N	120.31E
Yangchun, China (yäŋ-chòn)	193	22.08N	111.48E
Yang'erzhuang, China (yäŋ-är-jůäŋ)	190	38.18N	117.31E
Yanggezhuang, China (yäŋ-gŭ-jůäŋ)	192a	40.10N	116.48E
Yanggu, China (yäŋ-gōō)	190	36.06N	115.46E
Yanghe, China (yäŋ-hŭ)	190	33.48N	118.23E
Yangjiang, China (yäŋ-jyäŋ)	193	21.52N	111.58E
Yangjiaogou, China (yäŋ-jyou-gō)	190	37.17N	118.53E
Yangon *see* Rangoon, Myanmar	183	16.46N	96.09E
Yangquan, China (yäŋ-chyůän)	190	37.52N	113.36E
Yangtze (Chang), r., China (yăng'tse) (chäŋ)	189	30.30N	117.25E
Yangxin, China (yäŋ-shyĭn)	190	37.39N	117.34E
Yangyang, S. Kor. (yäng'yäng')	194	38.02N	128.38E
Yangzhou, China (yäŋ-jō)	189	32.24N	119.24E
Yanji, China (yän-jyē)	189	42.55N	129.35E
Yanjiahe, China (yän-jyä-hŭ)	190	31.55N	114.47E
Yanjin, China (yän-jyĭn)	190	35.09N	114.13E
Yankton, S.D., U.S. (yănk'tŭn)	96	42.51N	97.24W
Yanling, China (yän-lĭŋ)	190	34.07N	114.12E
Yanshan, China (yän-shän)	192	38.05N	117.15E
Yanshou, China (yän-shō)	192	45.25N	128.43E
Yantai, China	189	37.32N	121.22E
Yanychi, Russia (yä'nĭ-chĭ)	172a	57.42N	56.24E
Yanzhou, China (yäŋ-jō)	189	35.35N	116.50E
Yanzhuang, China (yän-jůäŋ)	190	36.08N	117.47E
Yao, Chad (yä'ō)	202	13.00N	17.38E
Yao, Japan	195b	34.37N	135.37E
Yaoundé, Cam.	210	3.52N	11.31E
Yap, i., Micron. (yăp)	3	11.00N	138.00E
Yapen, Pulau, i., Indon.	197	1.30S	136.15E
Yaque del Norte, r., Dom. Rep. (yä'kå děl nôr'tå)	117	19.40N	71.25W
Yaque del Sur, r., Dom. Rep. (yä-kě-děl-sōō'r)	123	18.35N	71.05W
Yaqui, r., Mex. (yä'kē)	116	28.15N	109.40W
Yaracuy, dept., Ven. (yä-rä-kōō'ē)	131b	10.10N	68.31W
Yaraka, Austl. (yȧ-răk'ȧ)	203	24.50S	144.08E
Yaransk, Russia (yä-ränsk')	164	57.18N	48.05E
Yarda, oasis, Chad (yär'dȧ)	211	18.29N	19.13E
Yare, r., Eng., U.K.	151	52.40N	1.32E
Yarkand *see* Shache, China (yär'mŭth)	188	38.15N	77.15E
Yarkand *see* Shache, China	188	38.15N	77.15E
Yaroslavka, Russia (yȧ-rô-släv'kȧ)	172a	55.52N	57.59E
Yaroslavl', Russia (yȧ-rô-släv''l)	164	57.37N	39.54E
Yaroslavl', prov., Russia	162	58.05N	38.05E
Yarra, r., Austl.	201a	37.51S	144.54E
Yarra Canal, can., Austl.	243b	37.49S	144.55E
Yarraville, Austl.	243b	37.49S	144.53E
Yarro-to, l., Russia (yȧ'rô-tô')	166	67.55N	71.35E
Yartsevo, Russia	165	60.13N	89.52E
Yartsevo, Russia (yär'tsyě-vô)	166	55.04N	32.38E
Yarumal, Col. (yä-rōō-mäl')	130	6.57N	75.24W
Yasawa Group, is., Fiji	198g	17.00S	177.23E
Yasel'da, r., Bela. (yä-syŭl'dá)	155	52.13N	25.53E
Yasinya, Ukr.	155	48.17N	24.21E
Yateras, Cuba (yä-tā'räs)	123	20.00N	75.00W
Yates Center, Ks., U.S. (yāts)	111	37.53N	95.44W
Yathkyed, l., Can. (yáth-kī-ĕd')	84	62.41N	98.00W
Yatsuga-take, mtn., Japan (yät'sōō-gä dä'kä)	195	36.01N	138.21W
Yatsushiro, Japan (yät'sōō'shė-rô)	195	32.30N	130.35E
Yatta Plateau, plat., Kenya	217	1.55S	38.10E
Yautepec, Mex. (yä-ōō-tå-pěk')	118	18.53N	99.04W
Yavoriv, Ukr.	155	49.56N	23.24E
Yawata, Japan (yä'wä-tä)	195	34.52N	135.43E
Yawatahama, Japan (yä'wä'tä'hä-mä)	195	33.24N	132.25E
Yaxian, China (yä shyěn)	193	18.10N	109.32E
Yayama, Zaire	216	1.16S	23.07E
Yayao, China (yä-you)	191a	23.10N	113.40E
Yazd, Iran	182	31.59N	54.03E
Yazoo, r., Ms., U.S. (yă'zōō)	97	32.32N	90.40W
Yazoo City, Ms., U.S.	114	32.50N	90.18W
Ye, Myanmar (yā)	196	15.13N	97.52E
Yeading, neigh., Eng., U.K.	235	51.32N	0.24W
Yeadon, Pa., U.S. (yē'dŭn)	100f	39.56N	75.16W
Yecla, Spain (yā'klä)	158	38.35N	1.09W
Yedikule, neigh., Tur.	239f	40.59N	28.55E
Yefremov, Russia (yě-frá'môf)	162	53.08N	38.04E
Yegor'yevsk, Russia (yě-gôr'yěfsk)	166	55.23N	38.59E
Yeji, China (yŭ-jyē)	190	31.52N	115.57E
Yekaterinburg, Russia	164	56.51N	60.36E
Yelabuga, Russia (yě-lä'bò-gá)	166	55.50N	52.18E
Yelan, Russia	167	50.50N	44.00E
Yelek, r.	167	51.20N	53.10E
Yelets, Russia (yě-lyěts')	164	52.35N	38.28E
Yelizavetpol'skiy, Russia (yě'lĭ-za-vět-pôl-skĭ)	172a	52.51N	60.38E
Yelizavety, Mys, c., Russia (yě-lyě-sȧ-vyě'tĭ)	165	54.28N	142.59E
Yell, i., Scot., U.K. (yěl)	150a	60.35N	1.27W
Yellow *see* Huang, r., China	189	35.06N	113.39E
Yellow, r., Fl., U.S. (yěl'ō)	114	30.33N	86.53W
Yellowhead Pass, p., Can. (yěl'ō-hěd)	87	52.52N	118.35W
Yellowknife, Can. (yěl'ō-nīf)	84	62.29N	114.38W
Yellow Sea, sea, Asia	189	35.20N	122.15E
Yellowstone, r., U.S.	96	46.00N	108.00W
Yellowstone, Clarks Fork, r., U.S.	105	44.55N	109.05W
Yellowstone Lake, l., Wy., U.S.	96	44.27N	110.03W
Yellowstone National Park, rec., U.S. (yěl'ō-stōn)	96	44.45N	110.35W
Yel'nya, Russia (yěl'nyȧ)	162	54.34N	33.12E
Yemanzhelinsk, Russia (yě-mȧn-zhâ'lĭnsk)	172a	54.47N	61.24E
Yemen, nation, Asia (yěm'ěn)	182	15.00N	47.00E
Yemetsk, Russia	166	63.28N	41.28E
Yenakiyeve, Ukr.	163	48.14N	38.12E
Yenangyaung, Myanmar (yā'năn-d oung)	183	20.27N	94.59E
Yencheng, China	188	37.30N	79.26E
Yendi, Ghana (yěn'dė)	210	9.26N	0.01W
Yengisar, China (yŭn-gē-sär)	188	39.01N	75.29E
Yenice, r., Tur.	167	41.10N	33.00E
Yenikapi, neigh., Tur.	239f	41.00N	28.57E
Yenisey, r., Russia (yě-nė-sě'ė)	164	71.00N	82.00E
Yeniseysk, Russia (yě-nĭěsä'ĭsk)	165	58.27N	90.28E
Yeo, l., Austl. (yō)	202	28.15S	124.00E
Yerevan, Arm. (yě-rě-vän')	167	40.10N	44.30E
Yerington, Nv., U.S. (yě'rĭng-tŭn)	108	38.59N	119.10W
Yermak, i., Russia	166	66.45N	71.30E
Yeste, Spain (yěs'tå)	158	38.23N	2.19W
Yeu, Île d', i., Fr. (ēl dyû)	147	46.43N	2.45W
Yevlax, Azer.	168	40.36N	47.09E
Yevpatoriya, Ukr. (yěf-pä'tô-rĭ-yȧ)	167	45.13N	33.22E
Yexian, China (yŭ-shyěn)	190	37.09N	119.57E
Yeya, r., Russia (yä'yȧ)	163	46.25N	39.17E
Yeysk, Russia (yěysk)	167	46.41N	38.13E
Yi, r., China	190	34.38N	118.07E
Yiannitsá, Grc.	161	40.47N	22.26E
Yiaros, i., Grc.	161	37.52N	24.42E
Yibin, China (yē-bĭn)	188	28.50N	104.40E
Yichang, China (yē-chäŋ)	189	30.38N	111.22E
Yidu, China (yē-dōō)	192	36.42N	118.30E
Yiewsley, neigh., Eng., U.K.	235	51.31N	0.28W
Yilan, China (yē-län)	189	46.10N	129.40E
Yinchuan, China (yĭn-chůän)	188	38.22N	106.22E
Yingkou, China (yĭŋ-kō)	189	40.35N	122.10E
Yining, China (yē-nĭŋ)	188	43.58N	80.40E
Yin Shan, mts., China (yĭng'shän')	192	40.50N	110.30E
Yio Chu Kang, Sing.	240c	1.23N	103.51E
Yishan, China (yē-shän)	188	24.32N	108.42E
Yishui, China (yē-shwā)	190	35.49N	118.40E
Yíthion, Grc.	161	36.50N	22.37E
Yitong, China (yē-tôŋ)	189	43.15N	125.10E
Yixian, China (yē shyěn)	192	41.30N	121.15E
Yixing, China	190	31.26N	119.57E
Yiyang, China (yē-yäŋ)	193	28.52N	112.12E
Yoakum, Tx., U.S. (yō'kŭm)	113	29.18N	97.09W
Yockanookany, r., Ms., U.S. (yŏk'á-nōō-kă-nĭ)	114	32.47N	89.38W
Yodo-Gawa, strt., Japan (yō'dō'gä-wä)	195b	34.46N	135.35E
Yog Point, c., Phil. (yōg)	193	14.00N	124.30E
Yogyakarta, Indon. (yŏg-yȧ-kär'tȧ)	196	7.50S	110.20E
Yoho National Park, Can. (yō'hō)	84	51.26N	116.30W
Yojoa, Lago de, l., Hond. (lä'gô dě yô-hō'ä)	120	14.49N	87.53W
Yokkaichi, Japan (yô'kä'ė-chė)	194	34.58N	136.35E
Yokohama, Japan (yō'kō-hä'mą)	189	35.37N	139.40E
Yokosuka, Japan (yô-kō'sò-kä)	194	35.17N	139.40E
Yokota, Japan (yō-kō'tä)	195a	35.23N	140.02E
Yola, Nig. (yō'lä)	210	9.13N	12.27E
Yolaina, Cordillera de, mts., Nic.	121	11.34N	84.34W
Yomou, Gui.	214	7.34N	9.16W
Yonago, Japan (yō'nä-gō)	194	35.27N	133.19E
Yŏnch'on, neigh., S. Kor.	241b	37.38N	127.04E
Yonezawa, Japan (yō'nĕ'zȧ-wä)	194	37.50N	140.07E
Yong'an, China (yôŋ-än)	193	26.00N	117.22E
Yongding, r., China (yôŋ-dĭŋ)	192	40.25N	115.00E
Yŏngdŏk, S. Kor. (yŭng'dŭk')	194	36.28N	129.25E
Yongdŭngp'o, neigh., S. Kor.	241b	37.32N	126.54E
Yŏnghŭng, N. Kor. (yŭng'hòng')	194	39.31N	127.11E
Yonghŭng Man, b., N. Kor.	194	39.10N	128.00E
Yongnian, China (yôŋ-nĭěn)	192	36.47N	114.32E
Yongqing, China (yôŋ-chyĭŋ)	192a	39.18N	116.27E
Yongshun, China (yôŋ-shòn)	188	29.05N	109.58E
Yonkers, N.Y., U.S. (yŏŋ'kẽrz)	100a	40.57N	73.54W
Yonne, r., Fr. (yòn)	156	48.18N	3.15E
Yono, Japan (yō'nō)	195a	35.53N	139.36E
Yorba Linda, Ca., U.S. (yôr'bȧ lĭn'dȧ)	107a	33.55N	117.51W
York, Austl.	202	32.00S	117.00E
York, Can.	83d	43.41N	79.29W
York, Eng., U.K.	146	53.58N	1.10W
York, Al., U.S. (yôrk)	114	32.33N	88.16W
York, Ne., U.S.	111	40.52N	97.36W
York, Pa., U.S.	97	40.00N	76.40W

ăt; finăl; rāte; senåte; ärm; åsk; sofȧ; fâre; ch-choose; dh-as th in other; bē; ėvent; bět; recĕnt; cratẽr; g-gō; gh-guttural g; bĭt; ĭ-short neutral; rīde; ᴋ-guttural k as ch in German ich;

PLACE (Pronunciation)	PAGE	Lat. °'	Long. °'
York, S.C., U.S.	115	34.59N	81.14W
York, Cape, c., Austl.	203	10.45S	142.35E
York, Kap, c., Grnld.	82	75.30N	73.00W
Yorke Peninsula, pen., Austl.	204	34.24S	137.20E
Yorketown, Austl.	204	35.00S	137.28E
York Factory, Can.	89	57.05N	92.18W
Yorkfield, Il., U.S.	231a	41.52N	87.56W
Yorkshire Wolds, Eng., U.K. (yôrk'shĭr)	150	54.00N	0.35W
Yorkton, Can. (yôrk'tŭn)	84	51.13N	102.28W
Yorktown, Tx., U.S. (yôrk'toun)	113	28.57N	97.30W
Yorktown, Va., U.S.	115	37.12N	76.31W
Yorkville, neigh., Can.	227c	43.40N	79.24W
Yoro, Hond. (yō'rô)	120	15.09N	87.05W
Yoron, i., Japan	194	26.48N	128.40E
Yosemite National Park, rec., Ca., U.S. (yô-sĕm'ĭ-tê)	96	38.03N	119.36W
Yoshida, Japan (yō'shê-dȧ)	195	34.39N	132.41E
Yoshikawa, Japan (yō-shê'kä'wä')	195a	35.53N	139.51E
Yoshino, r., Japan (yō'shē-nō)	195	34.04N	133.57E
Yoshkar-Ola, Russia (yôsh-kär'ô-lä')	166	56.35N	48.05E
Yos Sudarsa, Pulau, i., Indon.	197	7.20S	138.30E
Yŏsu, S. Kor. (yŭ'sōō')	194	34.42N	127.42W
You, r., China (yō)	193	23.55N	106.50E
Youghal, Ire. (yōō'ôl) (yôl)	151	51.58N	7.57E
Youghal Bay, b., Ire.	150	51.52N	7.46W
Young, Austl. (yŭng)	204	34.15S	148.18E
Young, Ur. (yô-ōō'ng)	129c	32.42S	57.38W
Youngs, l., Wa., U.S. (yŭngz)	106a	47.25N	122.08W
Youngstown, N.Y., U.S.	101c	43.15N	79.02W
Youngstown, Oh., U.S.	98	41.05N	80.40W
Yozgat, Tur. (yôz'gȧd)	182	39.50N	34.50E
Ypsilanti, Mi., U.S. (ĭp-sĭ-lăn'tĭ)	101b	42.15N	83.37W
Yreka, Ca., U.S. (wī-rē'kȧ)	104	41.43N	122.36W
Yrghyz, Kaz.	169	48.30N	61.17E
Yrghyz, r., Kaz.	169	49.30N	60.32E
Ysleta, Tx., U.S. (ēz-lĕ'tȧ)	112	31.42N	106.18W
Yssingeaux, Fr. (ē-săN-zhō)	156	45.09N	4.08E
Ystad, Swe.	146	55.25N	13.49E
Yu'alliq, Jabal, mts., Egypt	181a	30.12N	33.42E
Yuan, r., China (yüän)	189	28.50N	110.50E
Yuan'an, China (yüän-än)	193	31.08N	111.28E
Yuan Huan, pt. of i., Tai.	241d	25.03N	121.31E
Yuanling, China (yüän-lĭŋ)	193	28.30N	110.18E
Yuanshi, China (yüän-shr)	192	37.45N	114.32E
Yuasa, Japan	195	34.02N	135.10E
Yuba City, Ca., U.S. (yōō'bȧ)	108	39.08N	121.38W
Yucaipa, Ca., Ca., U.S. (yŭ-kȧ-ē'pȧ)	107a	34.02N	117.02W
Yucatán, state, Mex. (yōō-kä-tän')	116	20.45N	89.00W
Yucatan Channel, strt., N.A.	116	22.30N	87.00W
Yucatan Peninsula, pen., N.A.	120	19.30N	89.00W
Yucheng, China (yōō-chŭŋ)	190	34.31N	115.54E
Yucheng, China	192	36.55N	116.39E
Yuci, China (yōō-tsz)	192	37.32N	112.40E
Yudoma, r., Russia (yōō-dō'mȧ)	171	59.13N	137.00E
Yueqing, China (yüĕ-chyĭn)	193	28.02N	120.40E
Yueyang, China (yüĕ-yäŋ)	189	29.25N	113.05E
Yuezhuang, China (yüĕ-jüäŋ)	190	36.13N	118.17E
Yug, r., Russia (yôg)	166	59.50N	45.55E
Yugoslavia, nation, Eur. (yōō-gô-slä-vĭ-ȧ)	142	44.00N	21.00E
Yukhnov, Russia (yôk'nof)	162	54.44N	35.15E
Yukon, , Can. (yōō'kŏn)	84	63.16N	135.30W
Yukon, r., N.A.	96a	64.00N	159.30W
Yukutat Bay, b., Ak., U.S. (yōō-kŭ tăt')	95	59.34N	140.50W
Yuldybayevo, Russia (yôld'bä'yĕ-vô)	172a	52.20N	57.52E
Yulin, China	188	38.18N	109.45E
Yulin, China (yōō-lĭn)	193	22.38N	110.10E
Yuma, Az., U.S. (yōō'mä)	96	32.40N	114.40W
Yuma, Co., U.S.	110	40.08N	102.50W
Yuma, r., Dom. Rep.	123	19.05N	70.05W
Yumbi, Zaire	217	1.14S	26.14E
Yumen, China (yōō-mŭn)	188	40.14N	96.56E
Yuncheng, China (yôn-chŭŋ)	192	35.00N	110.40E
Yungho, Tai.	241d	25.01N	121.31E
Yung Shu Wan, H.K.	241c	22.14N	114.06E
Yunnan, prov., China (yun'nän')	188	24.23N	101.03E
Yunnan Plat, plat., China (yô-nän)	188	26.03N	101.26E
Yunxian, China (yôn shyĕn)	189	32.50N	110.55E
Yunxiao, China (yôn-shyou)	193	24.00N	117.20E
Yura, Japan (yōō'rä)	195	34.18N	134.54E
Yurécuaro, Mex. (yōō-rā'kwä-rô)	118	20.21N	102.16W
Yurimaguas, Peru (yōō-rê-mä'gwäs)	130	5.59S	76.12W
Yuriria, Mex. (yōō'rē-rē'ä)	118	20.11N	101.08W
Yurovo, Russia	172b	55.30N	38.24E
Yur'yevets, Russia	166	57.15N	43.08E
Yuscarán, Hond. (yōōs-kä-rän')	120	13.57N	86.48W
Yushan, China (yōō-shän)	193	28.42N	118.20E
Yushu, China (yōō-shōō)	192	44.58N	126.32E
Yutian, China (yōō-tĭĕn) (kŭ-r-yä)	188	36.55N	81.39E
Yutian, China (yōō-tĭĕn)	192	39.54N	117.45E
Yuty, Para. (yōō-tē')	132	26.45S	56.13W
Yuwangcheng, China (yü'wäng'chĕng)	190	31.32N	114.26E
Yuxian, China (yōō shyĕn)	192	39.40N	114.38E
Yuzha, Russia (yōō'zhȧ)	166	56.38N	42.20E
Yuzhno-Sakhalinsk, Russia (yōōzh'nô-sä-kä-lĭnsk')	165	47.11N	143.04E
Yuzhnoural'skiy, Russia (yōōzh-nô-ô-räl'skĭ)	172a	54.26N	61.17E
Yuzhnyy Ural, mts., Russia (yōō'zhnĭ ô-räl')	172a	52.51N	57.48E
Yverdon, Switz. (ē-vĕr-dôn)	154	46.46N	6.35E
Yvetot, Fr. (ēv-tō')	156	49.39N	0.45E

Z

PLACE (Pronunciation)	PAGE	Lat. °'	Long. °'
Za, r., Mor.	148	34.19N	2.23W
Zaachila, Mex. (sä-ä-chē'lä)	119	16.56N	96.45W
Zaandam, Neth. (zän'dȧm)	151	52.25N	4.49E
Ząbkowice Śląskie, Pol.	154	50.35N	16.48E
Zabrze, Pol. (zäb'zhĕ)	147	50.18N	18.48E
Zacapa, Guat. (sä-kä'pä)	120	14.56N	89.30W
Zacapoaxtla, Mex. (sä-kä-pō-äs'tlä)	119	19.51N	97.34W
Zacatecas, Mex. (sä-kä-tā'käs)	116	22.44N	102.32W
Zacatecas, state, Mex.	116	24.00N	102.45W
Zacatecoluca, El Sal. (sä-kä-tå-kô-lōō'kä)	120	13.31N	88.50W
Zacatelco, Mex.	118	19.12N	98.12W
Zacatepec, Mex. (sä-kä-tå-pĕk') (sän-tē-ä'gô)	119	17.10N	95.53W
Zacatlán, Mex. (sä-kä-tlän')	119	19.55N	97.57W
Zacoalco de Torres, Mex. (sä-kô-äl'kō dä tōr'rĕs)	118	20.12N	103.33W
Zacualpan, Mex. (sä-kô-äl-pän')	118	18.43N	99.46W
Zacualtipan, Mex. (sä-kô-äl-tē-pän')	118	20.38N	98.39W
Zadar, Cro. (zä'där)	142	44.08N	15.16E
Zadonsk, Russia (zä-dônsk')	162	52.22N	38.55E
Žagare, Lat. (zhȧgȧrĕ)	153	56.21N	23.14E
Zagarolo, Italy (tzä-gä-rô'lô)	159d	41.51N	12.53E
Zaghouan, Tun. (zȧ-gwäN')	210	36.30N	10.04E
Zagreb, Cro. (zä'grĕb)	142	45.50N	15.58E
Zagros Mountains, mts., Iran	182	33.30N	46.30E
Zāhedān, Iran (zä'hȧ-dän)	182	29.37N	60.31E
Zahlah, Leb. (zä'lä')	181a	33.50N	35.54E
Zaire, nation, Afr.	212	1.00S	22.15E
Zaječar, Yugo. (zä'yĕ-chär')	161	43.54N	22.16E
Zakhidnyy Buh (Bug), r., Eur.	154	52.29N	21.20E
Zákinthos, Grc.	161	37.48N	20.55E
Zákinthos, i., Grc.	149	37.45N	20.32E
Zakopane, Pol. (zȧ-kô-pä'nĕ)	155	49.18N	19.57E
Zakouma, Parc National de, rec., Chad	215	10.50N	19.20E
Zalaegerszeg, Hung. (zŏ'lô-ĕ'gĕr-sĕg)	154	46.50N	16.50E
Zalău, Rom. (zȧ-lŭ'ô)	155	47.11N	23.06E
Zalṭan, Libya	211	28.20N	19.40E
Zaltbommel, Neth.	145a	51.48N	5.15E
Zama, Japan	242a	35.29N	139.24E
Zambezi, r., Afr. (zȧm-bā'zē)	212	16.00S	29.45E
Zambia, nation, Afr. (zăm'bē-ȧ)	212	14.23S	24.15E
Zamboanga, Phil. (säm-bô-äŋ'gä)	196	6.58N	122.02E
Zambrów, Pol. (zäm'brôf)	155	52.29N	22.17E
Zamora, Mex. (sä-mō'rä)	116	19.59N	102.16W
Zamora, Spain (thä-mō'rä)	148	41.32N	5.43W
Zanatepec, Mex.	119	16.30N	94.22W
Zandvoort, Neth.	145a	52.22N	4.30E
Zanesville, Oh., U.S. (zānz'vĭl)	98	39.55N	82.00W
Zangasso, Mali	214	12.09N	5.37W
Zanjān, Iran	182	36.26N	48.24E
Zanzibar, Tan. (zăn'zĭ-bär)	213	6.10S	39.11E
Zanzibar, i., Tan.	213	6.20S	39.37E
Zanzibar Channel, strt., Tan.	217	6.05S	39.00E
Zaozhuang, China (dzou-jüäŋ)	190	34.51N	117.34E
Zapadnaya Dvina, r., Eur. (zä'pȧd-nȧ-yȧ dvē'nȧ)	153	55.30N	28.27E
Zapala, Arg. (zä-pä'lä)	132	38.53S	70.02W
Zapata, Tx., U.S. (sä-pä'tä)	112	26.52N	99.18W
Zapata, Ciénaga de, sw., Cuba (syĕ'nä-gä-dĕ-zä-pȧ'tä)	122	22.30N	81.20W
Zapata, Península de, pen., Cuba (pĕ-nē'n-sōō-lä-dĕ-zä-pȧ'tä)	122	22.20N	81.30W
Zapatera, Isla, i., Nic. (ē's-lä-sä-pä-tā'rō)	120	11.45N	85.45W
Zapopan, Mex. (sä-pō'pän)	118	20.42N	103.23W
Zaporizhzhya, Ukr.	164	47.50N	35.10E
Zaporizhzhya, prov., Ukr.	163	47.20N	35.05E
Zaporoshskoye, Russia (zȧ-pô-rôsh'skô-yĕ)	153	60.36N	30.31E
Zapotiltic, Mex. (sä-pô-tēl-tēk')	118	19.37N	103.25W
Zapotitlán, Mex. (sä-pô-tē-tlän')	118	17.13N	98.58W
Zapotitlán, Mex.	233a	19.18N	99.02W
Zapotitlán, Punta, c., Mex.	119	18.34N	94.48W
Zapotlanejo, Mex. (sä-pô-tlä-nā'hô)	118	20.38N	103.05W
Zaragoza, Mex. (sä-rä-gō'sä)	118	23.59N	99.45W
Zaragoza, Mex.	118	22.02N	100.45W
Zaragoza, Spain (thä-rä-gō'thä)	142	41.39N	0.53W
Zarand, Munţii, mts., Rom.	155	46.07N	22.21E
Zaranda Hill, mtn., Nig.	215	10.15N	9.35E
Zaranj, Afg.	185	31.06N	61.53E
Zarasai, Lith. (zä-rä-sī')	153	55.45N	26.18E
Zárate, Arg. (zä-rä'tä)	132	34.05S	59.05W
Zaraysk, Russia (zä-rä'ēsk)	166	54.46N	38.53E
Zarečje, Russia	239b	55.41N	37.23E
Zaria, Nig. (zä'rē-ä)	210	11.07N	7.44E
Zarqā', r., Jord.	181a	32.13N	35.43E
Zarzal, Col. (zär-zä'l)	130a	4.23N	76.04W
Zashiversk, Russia (zá'shĭ-vĕrsk')	165	67.08N	144.02E
Zastavna, Ukr. (zȧs-täf'nȧ)	155	48.32N	25.50E
Zastron, S. Afr. (zȧs'trŭn)	213c	30.19S	27.07E
Žatec, Czech Rep. (zhä'tĕts)	154	50.19N	13.32E
Zavitinsk, Russia	171	50.12N	129.44E
Zawiercie, Pol. (zȧ-vyĕr'tsyĕ)	155	50.28N	19.25E
Zāwiyat al-Baydā', Libya	211	32.49N	21.46E
Zāwiyat Nābit, Egypt	244a	30.07N	31.09E
Zāyandeh, r., Iran	182	32.15N	51.00E
Zaysan, Kaz. (zī'sȧn)	169	47.43N	84.44E
Zaysan, l., Kaz.	169	48.16N	84.05E
Zaza, r., Cuba (zá'zȧ)	122	21.40N	79.25W
Zbarazh, Ukr. (zbä-räzh')	155	49.39N	25.48E
Zbruch, r., Ukr. (zbrôch)	155	48.56N	26.18E
Zdolbuniv, Ukr.	155	50.31N	26.17E
Zduńska Wola, Pol. (zdōōn''skä vō'lä)	155	51.36N	18.27E
Zebediela, S. Afr.	218d	24.19S	29.21E
Zeeland, Mi., U.S. (zē'lănd)	98	42.50N	86.00W
Zefat, Isr.	181a	32.58N	35.30E
Zehdenick, Ger. (tsā'dē-nĕk)	154	52.59N	13.20E
Zehlendorf, Ger. (tsā'lĕn-dôrf)	145b	52.47N	13.23E
Zehlendorf, neigh., Ger.	238a	52.26N	13.15E
Zeist, Neth.	145a	52.05N	5.14E
Zelenogorsk, Russia (zĕ-lă'nô-gôrsk)	153	60.13N	29.39E
Zella-Mehlis, Ger. (tsĕl'á-mā'lēs)	154	50.40N	10.38E
Zémio, Cen. Afr. Rep. (za-myō')	211	5.03N	25.11E
Zemlya Frantsa-Iosifa (Franz Josef Land), is., Russia	164	81.32N	40.00E
Zempoala, Punta, c., Mex. (pōō'n-tä-sĕm-pô-ä'lä)	119	19.30N	96.18W
Zempoatlépetl, mtn., Mex. (sĕm-pô-ä-tlā'pĕt'l)	119	17.13N	95.59W
Zemun, Yugo. (zĕ'mōōn) (sĕm'lĭn)	149	44.50N	20.25E
Zengcheng, China (dzŭŋ-chŭŋ)	191a	23.18N	113.49E
Zenica, Bos. (zĕ'nêt-sä)	161	44.10N	17.54E
Zeni-Su, is., Japan (zĕ'nē sōō)	195	33.55N	138.55E
Žepče, Bos. (zhĕp'chĕ)	163	44.26N	18.01E
Zepernick, Ger. (tsĕ'pĕr-nĕk)	145b	52.39N	13.32E
Zerbst, Ger. (tsĕrbst)	154	51.58N	12.03E
Zerpenschleuse, Ger. (tsĕr'pĕn-shloi-zĕ)	145b	52.51N	13.30E
Zeuthen, Ger. (tsoi'tĕn)	145b	52.21N	13.38E
Zevenaar, Neth.	157c	51.56N	6.06E
Zevenbergen, Neth.	145a	51.38N	4.36E
Zeya, Russia (zâ'yȧ)	165	53.43N	127.29E
Zeya, r., Russia	171	52.31N	128.30E
Zeytinburnu, neigh., Tur.	239f	40.59N	28.54E
Zeytun, Tur. (zā-tōōn')	167	38.00N	36.40E
Zezere, r., Port. (zĕ'zȧ-rĕ)	158	39.54N	8.12W
Zgierz, Pol. (zgyĕzh)	155	51.51N	19.26E
Zhambyl, Kaz.	169	42.51N	71.29E
Zhangaqazaly, Kaz.	169	45.47N	62.00E
Zhangbei, China (jäŋ-bā)	189	41.12N	114.50E
Zhanggezhuang, China (jäŋ-gŭ-jüäŋ)	190	40.09N	116.56E
Zhangguangcai Ling, mts., China (jäŋ-güäŋ-tsī lĭŋ)	192	43.50N	127.55E
Zhangjiakou, China	189	40.45N	114.58E
Zhangqiu, China (jäŋ-chyō)	190	36.50N	117.29E
Zhangye, China (jäŋ-yu)	188	38.46N	101.00E
Zhangzhou, China (jäŋ-jō)	189	24.35N	117.45E
Zhangzi Dao, i., China (jäŋ-dz dou)	190	39.02N	122.44E
Zhanhua, China (jän-hwä)	190	37.42N	117.49E
Zhanjiang, China (jän-jyäŋ)	189	21.20N	110.28E
Zhanyu, China (jän-yōō)	192	44.30N	122.30E
Zhao'an, China (jou-än)	193	23.48N	117.10E
Zhaodong, China (jou-dôŋ)	192	45.58N	126.00E
Zhaotong, China (jou-tôŋ)	188	27.18N	103.50E
Zhaoxian, China (jou shyĕn)	190	37.46N	114.48E
Zhaoyuan, China (jou-yuän)	190	37.22N	120.23E
Zhecheng, China (jŭ-chŭŋ)	192	34.05N	115.19E
Zhegao, China (jŭ-gou)	190	31.47N	117.44E
Zhejiang, prov., China (jŭ-jyäŋ)	189	29.30N	120.00E
Zhelaniya, Mys, c., Russia (zhĕ'lä-nĭ-yȧ)	164	75.43N	69.10E
Zhem, r., Kaz.	170	46.50N	54.10E
Zhengding, China (jŭŋ-dĭŋ)	192	38.10N	114.35E
Zhen'guosi, China	240b	39.51N	116.21E
Zhengyang, China (jŭŋ-yäŋ)	190	32.34N	114.22E
Zhengzhou, China (jŭŋ-jō)	189	34.46N	113.42E
Zhenjiang, China (jŭn-jyäŋ)	189	32.13N	119.24E
Zhenru, China	241a	31.15N	121.24E
Zhenyuan, China (jŭn-yüän)	193	27.08N	108.30E
Zhetiqara, Kaz.	169	52.12N	61.18E
Zhigalovo, Russia (zhē-gä'lô-vô)	165	54.52N	105.05E
Zhigansk, Russia (zhē-gänsk')	165	66.45N	123.20E
Zhijiang, China (jr-jyäŋ)	193	27.25N	109.45E
Zhizdra, Russia (zhēz'drȧ)	162	53.47N	34.41E
Zhizhitskoye, l., Russia (zhē-zhēt'skô-yĕ)	162	56.08N	31.34E
Zhmerynka, Ukr.	167	49.02N	28.09E
Zhongshan Park, rec., China	241a	31.13N	121.25E
Zhongwei, China (jôŋ-wā)	188	37.32N	105.10E
Zhongxian, China (jôŋ shyĕn)	188	30.20N	108.00E
Zhongxin, China (jôŋ-shyĭn)	191a	23.16N	113.38E
Zhoucun, China (jō-tsōōn)	192	36.49N	117.52E
Zhoukouzhen, China (jō-kō-jŭn)	190	33.39N	114.40E
Zhoupu, China (jō-pōō)	190	31.07N	121.33E
Zhoushan Qundao, is., China (jō-shän-chyôn-dou)	189	30.00N	123.00E
Zhouxian, China (jō shyĕn)	192	39.30N	115.59E
Zhovkva, Ukr.	155	50.03N	23.58E
Zhu, r., China (jōō)	191a	22.48N	113.36E
Zhuanghe, China (jüäŋ-hŭ)	192	39.40N	123.00E
Zhuanqiao, China (jüäŋ-chyou)	191b	31.02N	121.24E
Zhucheng, China (jōō-chŭŋ)	192	36.01N	119.24E
Zhuji, China (jōō-jyĕ)	193	29.58N	120.10E
Zhujiang Kou, b., Asia (jōō-jyäŋ kō)	193	22.00N	114.00E
Zhukovskiy, Russia (zhô-kôf'skĭ)	172b	55.33N	38.09E
Zhurivka, Ukr.	163	50.31N	31.43E
Zhytomyr, Ukr.	164	50.15N	28.40E
Zhytomyr, prov., Ukr.	163	50.40N	28.07E
Zi, r., China (dzē)	193	26.50N	111.00E
Zia Indian Reservation, I.R., N.M., U.S.	109	35.30N	106.43W
Zibo, China (dzē-bwo)	190	36.48N	118.04E

PLACE (Pronunciation)	PAGE	Lat. ˚′	Long. ˚′
Ziel, Mount, mtn., Austl. (zēl)	202	23.15S	132.45E
Zielona Góra, Pol. (zhyĕ-lô′nä gōō′rä)	154	51.56N	15.30E
Zigazinskiy, Russia (zĭ-gazinskĕĕ)	172a	53.50N	57.18E
Ziguinchor, Sen.	210	12.35N	16.16W
Zile, Tur. (zĕ-lĕ′)	149	40.20N	35.50E
Žilina, Slvk. (zhĕ′lĭ-nä)	147	49.14N	18.45E
Zillah, Libya	211	28.26N	17.52E
Zima, Russia (zē′mä)	170	53.58N	102.08E
Zimapan, Mex. (sē-mä′pän)	118	20.43N	99.23W
Zimatlán de Alvarez, Mex.	119	16.52N	96.47W
Zimba, Zam.	217	17.19S	26.13E
Zimbabwe, nation, Afr. (rŏ-dĕ′zhĭ-á)	212	17.50S	29.30E
Zimnicea, Rom. (zĕm-nĕ′chä)	161	43.39N	25.22E
Zin, r., Isr.	181a	30.50N	35.12E
Zinacatepec, Mex. (zē-nä-kä-tĕ′pĕk)	119	18.19N	97.15W
Zinapécuaro, Mex. (sē-nä-pä′kwä-rŏ)	118	19.50N	100.49W
Zinder, Niger (zĭn′dĕr)	210	13.48N	8.59E
Zin′kiv, Ukr.	163	50.13N	34.23E
Zion, Il., U.S. (zī′ŭn)	101a	42.27N	87.50W
Zion National Park, rec., Ut., U.S.	96	37.20N	113.00W
Zionsville, In., U.S. (zīŭnz-vĭl)	101g	39.57N	86.15W
Zirandaro, Mex. (sē-rän-dä′rŏ)	118	18.28N	101.02W
Zitacuaro, Mex. (sē-tá-kwä′rŏ)	118	19.25N	100.22W
Zitlala, Mex. (sē-tlä′lä)	118	17.38N	99.09W
Zittau, Ger. (tsē′tou)	154	50.55N	14.48E
Ziway, l., Eth.	211	8.08N	39.11E
Ziya, r., China (dzē-yä)	190	38.38N	116.31E
Zlatograd, Bul.	161	41.24N	25.05E
Zlatoust, Russia (zlá-tô-ôst′)	164	55.13N	59.39E
Zlītan, Libya	211	32.27N	14.33E
Złoczew, Pol. (zwô′chĕf)	155	51.23N	18.34E
Zlynka, Russia (zlĕŋ′ká)	162	52.28N	31.39E
Znamensk, Russia (znä′mĕnsk)	153	54.37N	21.13E
Znam'yanka, Ukr.	163	48.43N	32.35E
Znojmo, Czech Rep. (znoi′mô)	147	48.52N	16.03E
Zoetermeer, Neth.	145a	52.08N	4.29E
Zoeterwoude, Neth.	145a	52.08N	4.29E
Zográfos, Grc.	239d	37.59N	23.46E
Zolochiv, Ukr.	155	49.48N	24.55E
Zolotonosha, Ukr. (zŏ′lô-tŏ-nŏ′shá)	167	49.41N	32.03E
Zolotoy, Mys, c., Russia (mĭs zŏ-lô-tôy′)	194	47.24N	139.10E
Zomba, Mwi. (zŏm′bá)	212	15.23S	35.18E
Zongo, Zaire (zŏŋ′gŏ)	211	4.19N	18.36E
Zonguldak, Tur. (zŏn′gōōl′dák)	182	41.25N	31.50E
Zonhoven, Bel.	145a	50.59N	5.24E
Zoquitlán, Mex. (sŏ-kĕt-län′)	119	18.09N	97.02W
Zorita, Spain (thŏ-rē′tä)	158	39.18N	5.41W
Zossen, Ger. (tsŏ′sĕn)	145b	52.13N	13.27E
Zouar, Chad	215	20.27N	16.32E
Zouxian, China (dzŏ shyĕn)	192	35.24N	116.54E
Zubtsov, Russia (zóp-tsôf′)	162	56.13N	34.34E
Zuera, Spain (thwä′rä)	159	41.40N	0.48W
Zugdidi, Geor.	168	42.30N	41.53E
Zuger See, l., Switz. (tsōōg)	154	47.10N	8.40E
Zugspitze, mtn., Eur.	154	47.25N	11.00E
Zuidelijk Flevoland, reg., Neth.	145a	52.22N	5.20E
Zújar, r., Spain (zōō′kär)	158	38.55N	5.05W
Zújar, Embalse del, res., Spain	158	38.50N	5.20W
Zulueta, Cuba (zōō-lŏ-ĕ′tä)	122	22.20N	79.35W
Zumbo, Moz. (zōōm′bó)	212	15.36S	30.25E
Zumbro, r., Mn., U.S. (zŭm′brŏ)	103	44.18N	92.14W
Zumbrota, Mn., U.S. (zŭm-brŏ′tá)	103	44.16N	92.39W
Zumpango, Mex. (sŏm-päŋ-gŏ)	118	19.48N	99.06W
Zundert, Neth.	145a	51.28N	4.39E
Zungeru, Nig. (zŏŋ-gä′rōō)	210	9.48N	6.09E
Zunhua, China (dzŏn-hwä)	192	40.12N	117.55E
Zuni, r., Az., U.S.	109	34.40N	109.30W
Zuni Indian Reservation, I.R., N.M., U.S. (zōō′nĕ)	109	35.10N	108.40W
Zuni Mountains, mts., N.M., U.S.	109	35.10N	108.10W
Zunyi, China	188	27.58N	106.40E
Zürich, Switz. (tsü′rĭk)	142	47.22N	8.32E
Zürichsee, l., Switz.	154	47.18N	8.47E
Zushi, Japan (zōō′shĕ)	195a	35.17N	139.35E
Zuurbekom, S. Afr.	244b	26.19S	27.49E
Zuwārah, Libya	210	32.58N	12.07E
Zuwayzā, Jord.	181a	31.42N	35.55E
Zvenigorod, Russia (zvä-nĕ′gŏ-rôt)	162	55.46N	36.54E
Zvenyhorodka, Ukr.	167	49.07N	30.59E
Zvishavane, Zimb.	212	20.15S	30.28E
Zvolen, Slvk. (zvô′lĕn)	155	48.35N	19.10E
Zvornik, Bos. (zvôr′nĕk)	161	44.24N	19.08E
Zweckel, neigh., Ger.	236	51.36N	6.59E
Zweibrücken, Ger. (tsvī-brük′ĕn)	154	49.16N	7.20E
Zwickau, Ger. (tsvīkŏu)	147	50.43N	12.30E
Zwolle, Neth. (zvôl′ĕ)	147	52.33N	6.05E
Żyradów, Pol. (zhĕ-rär′dóf)	155	52.04N	20.28E
Zyryan, Kaz.	169	49.43N	84.20E
Zyryanka, Russia (zĕ-ryän′ká)	165	65.45N	151.15E

Listed below are major topics covered by the thematic maps, graphs and/or statistics.
Page citations are for world, continent and country maps and for world tables.

SOURCES

The sources listed below have been consulted during the process of creating and updating the thematic maps and statistics for the 18th edition.

AAMA Motor Vehicle Facts and Figures, American Automobile Manufacturers Association

Agricultural Atlas of the United States, U.S. Dept. of Commerce, Bureau of the Census

Agricultural Statistics, U.S. Dept. of Agriculture

Air Carrier Traffic and Canadian Airports, Statistics Canada, Minister of Industry, Science and Technology

Annual Report series (various titles), U.S. Dept. of the Interior, Bureau of Mines

Anuario Estatistico do Brasil, Fundacao Instituto Brasileiro de Geografia e Estatistica

Atlas of African Agriculture, United Nations, Food and Agriculture Organization

Atlas of Economic Mineral Deposits, Cornell University Press

Atlas of India, TT Maps and Publications\Government of India

Atlas of the Middle East, U.S. Central Intelligence Agency

Canada Year Book, Statistics Canada, Minister of Industry, Science and Technology

Catalog of Significant Earthquakes, National Oceanic and Atmospheric Administration, National Geophysical Data Center

Census of Agriculture, Dept. of Commerce, Bureau of the Census

Census of Population Characteristics: United States, U.S. Dept. of Commerce, Economics and Statistics Administration

China Statistical Yearbook, State Statistical Bureau of the People's Republic of China

City and County Data Book, U.S. Dept of Commerce, Bureau of the Census

Coal Fields of the United States, U.S. Dept. of the Interior, Geological Survey

Coal Production U.S., U.S. Dept. of Energy, Energy Information Administration

Commercial Nuclear Power Plants Around the World, Nuclear News

Commercial Nuclear Power Plants in the United States, Nuclear News

Compendium of Social Statistics and Indicators, United Nations, Department of International Economic and Social Affairs

The Copper Industry of the U.S.S.R., U.S. Dept. of the Interior, Bureau of Mines

Demographic Yearbook, United Nations, Dept. of Economic and Social Development

Earthquakes and Volcanoes, U.S. Dept. of the Interior, U.S. Geological Survey

Eastern Europe Coal Infrastructure, U.S. Central Intelligence Agency

Ecoregions of the Continents, U.S. Dept. of Agriculture, Forest Service

Energy in the Newly Independent States of Eurasia, U.S. Central Intelligence Agency

Energy Map of Central Asia, Petroleum Economist

Energy Map of the World, Petroleum Economist

Energy Statistics Yearbook, United Nations, Dept. of Economic and Social Information and Policy Analysis

FAA Statistical Handbook of Aviation, U.S. Dept. of Transportation, Federal Aviation Administration

FAO Atlas of the Living Resources of the Seas, United Nations, Food and Agriculture Organization

FAO Fertilizer Yearbook, United Nations, Food and Agriculture Organization

FAO Production Yearbook, United Nations, Food and Agriculture Organization

FAO Trade Yearbook, United Nations, Food and Agriculture Organization

FAO Yearbook of Fishery Statistics, United Nations, Food and Agriculture Organization

FAO Yearbook of Forest Products, United Nations, Food and Agriculture Organization

Fiber Organon, Fiber Economics Bureau, Inc.

Geothermal Energy in the Western United States and Hawaii, U.S. Dept. of Energy/Energy Information Administration

Geothermal Resources Council, unpublished data

A Guide to Your National Forests, U.S. Dept. of Agriculture, Forest Service

Handbook of International Economic Statistics, U.S. Central Intelligence Agency

Handbook of International Trade and Development Statistics, United Nations, Conference on Trade and Development

International Data Base, U.S. Bureau of the Census, Center for International Research

International Energy Annual, U.S. Dept. of Energy, Energy Information Administration

International Energy Outlook, Dept. of Energy, Energy Information Administration

International Petroleum Encyclopedia, PennWell Publishing Co.

International Trade Statistics Yearbook, United Nations, Dept. of Economic and Social Development

International Water Power and Dam Construction Yearbook, Reed Business Publishing

Largest U.S. Oil and Gas Fields, U.S. Dept. of Energy, Energy Information Administration

Major Coalfields of the World, International Energy Agency Coal Research

Maritime Transport, Organization for Economic Co-operation and Development

Merchant Fleets of the World, U.S. Dept. of Transportation, Maritime Administration

Mineral Industries of Africa, U.S. Dept. of the Interior, Bureau of Mines

Mineral Industries of Asia and the Pacific, U.S. Dept. of the Interior, Bureau of Mines

Mineral Industries of Europe and Central Eurasia, U.S. Dept. of the Interior, Bureau of Mines

Mineral Industries of Latin America and Canada, U.S. Dept. of the Interior, Bureau of Mines

Mineral Industries of the Middle East, U.S. Dept. of the Interior, Bureau of Mines

Minerals Yearbook, U.S. Dept. of the Interior, Bureau of Mines

Monthly Bulletin of Statistics, United Nations, Dept. of Economic and Social Development

National Atlas - Canada, Dept. of Energy, Mines, and Resources

National Atlas - Chile, Instituto Geografico Militar

National Atlas - China, Cartographic Publishing House

National Atlas - Japan, Geographical Survey Institute

National Atlas - United States, U.S. Dept. of the Interior, Geological Survey

National Atlas - U.S.S.R., Central Administration of Geodesy and Cartography

National Priorities List, U.S. Environmental Protection Agency

Natural Gas Annual, U.S. Dept. of Energy, Energy Information Administration

Non-Ferrous Metal Data, American Bureau of Metal Statistics

Nuclear Power Reactors in the World, International Atomic Energy Agency

Oxford Economic Atlas of the World, Oxford University Press

The People's Republic of China - A New Industrial Power, U.S. Dept. of the Interior, Bureau of Mines

Petroleum Supply Annual, U.S. Dept. of Energy, Energy Information Administration

Population and Dwelling Counts: A National Overview, Minister of Industry, Science and Technology, Statistics Canada

Population and Vital Statistics Reports, United Nations, Dept. for Economic and social Information and Policy Analysis

Post-Soviet Geography, V.H. Winston and Son, Inc.

Primary Aluminum Plants Worldwide, U.S. Dept. of the Interior, Bureau of Mines

Public Land Surveys, U.S. Dept. of the Interior, Geological Survey

Rail in Canada, Statistics Canada, Transportation Section

Rand McNally Road Atlas, Rand McNally

Refugees, United Nations High Commissioner for Refugees

Refugee Survey Quarterly, United Nations, Centre for Documentation on Refugees

The State of the World's Refugees, United Nations High Commissioner for Refugees

The States of the Former Soviet Union: An Updated Overview, U.S. Central Intelligence Agency, Directorate of Intelligence

Statistical Abstract of India, Central Statistical Organisation

Statistical Abstract of the United States, U.S. Dept. of Commerce, Bureau of the Census

Statistical Pocket-Book of Yugoslavia, Federal Statistical Office

Statistical Yearbook, United National Educational, Scientific and Cultural Organization (UNESCO)

Sugar Yearbook, International Sugar Organization

Survey of Energy Resources, World Energy Council

This Dynamic Planet: World Map of Volcanoes, Earthquakes and Plate Tectonics, Smithsonian Institution/U.S. Geological Survey

Tin Ore Resources of Asia and Australia, United Nations, Economic Commission for Asia and the Far East

Uranium Resources, Production and Demand, Organization for Economic Co-operation and Development/International Atomic Energy Agency

U.S.S.R. Energy Atlas, U.S. Central Intelligence Agency

World Atlas of Agriculture, Isituto Geografico De Agostini

World Atlas of Geology and Mineral Deposits, Mining Journal Books, Ltd.

World Coal Resources and Major Trade Routes, Miller Freeman Publications, Inc.

World Development Report, The World Bank

The World Factbook, U.S. Central Intelligence Agency

World Gas Map, Petroleum Economist

World Mineral Statistics, British Geological Survey

World Mining Porphyry Copper, Miller Freeman Publications, Inc.

World Oil, Gulf Publishing Company

World Population Prospects, United Nations, Dept. for Economic and Social Information and Policy Analysis

World Refugee Report, U.S. Dept. of Stats, Bureau for Refugee Programs

World Transport Data, International Road Transport Union

World Urbanization Prospects, United Nations, Dept. of Economic and Social Information and Policy Analysis

Year Book Australia, Australian Bureau of Statistics

Year Book of Labour Statistics, International Labour Organization